GAINSB...
STALLION...

CW00663052

IN ENGLAND

CADEAUX GENEREUX
£20,000 October 1st SLF

FANTASTIC LIGHT
£30,000 October 1st SLF

GREEN DESERT
£60,000 October 1st SLF

ROYAL APPLAUSE
£10,000 October 1st

ZILZAL
£5,000 October 1st

IN IRELAND

DILSHAAN
€6,000 October 1st

KEY OF LUCK
€12,500 October 1st

ASCOT KNIGHT
$6,500 (Canadian) Live Foal

IN USA

at Gainsborough Farm
ELUSIVE QUALITY
$30,000 October 1st Live Foal

LABEEB
$7,500 October 1st Live Foal

QUIET AMERICAN
$35,000 October 1st Live Foal

SHADEED
$2,500 October 1st Live Foal

at Three Chimneys Farm
RAHY
$80,000 September 1st Live Foal

Enquiries to:
M.H. Goodbody,
Gainsborough Stud,
Woolton Hill,
Newbury, RG20 9TE
Tel: (01635) 253273
Fax: (01635) 254690
Email:
office@gainsborough-stud.com
Website:
www.gainsborough-equine.com

or
Allen Kershaw,
Gainsborough Farm,
7200 Steele Road,
Versailles,Ky 40383, USA
Tel: (859) 873 8918
Fax: (859) 873 2462
Email:
info@gainsboroughfarm.com
Website:
www.gainsboroughfarm.com

AGE, WEIGHT & DISTANCE TABLE

Timeform's scale of weight-for-age for the flat

Dist	Age	Jan 1-16	Jan 17-31	Feb 1-16	Feb 17-28	Mar 1-16	Mar 17-31	Apr 1-16	Apr 17-30	May 1-16	May 17-31	June 1-16	June 17-30
5f	4	10-0	10-0	10-0	10-0	10-0	10-0	10-0	10-0	10-0	10-0	10-0	10-0
	3	9—5	9—5	9—6	9—7	9—7	9—8	9—8	9—9	9—9	9-10	9-10	9-11
	2						8—0	8—1	8—3	8—4	8—5	8—6	8—7
6f	4	10-0	10-0	10-0	10-0	10-0	10-0	10-0	10-0	10-0	10-0	10-0	10-0
	3	9—2	9—3	9—4	9—5	9—5	9—6	9—7	9—7	9—8	9—8	9—9	9—9
	2									8—0	8—2	8—3	8—4
7f	4	9-13	9-13	10-0	10-0	10-0	10-0	10-0	10-0	10-0	10-0	10-0	10-0
	3	9—0	9—1	9—2	9—3	9—4	9—4	9—5	9—6	9—6	9—7	9—8	9—8
	2											7-13	8—1
1m	4	9-13	9-13	9-13	9-13	10-0	10-0	10-0	10-0	10-0	10-0	10-0	10-0
	3	8-12	8-13	9—0	9—1	9—2	9—2	9—3	9—4	9—5	9—5	9—6	9—7
	2												
9f	4	9-12	9-12	9-12	9-13	9-13	9-13	9-13	10-0	10-0	10-0	10-0	10-0
	3	8-10	8-11	8-12	8-13	9—0	9—1	9—2	9—2	9—3	9—4	9—5	9—5
	2												
1¼m	4	9-11	9-12	9-12	9-12	9-13	9-13	9-13	9-13	9-13	10-0	10-0	10-0
	3	8—8	8—9	8-10	8-11	8-12	8-13	9—0	9—1	9—2	9—2	9—3	9—4
	2												
11f	4	9-10	9-11	9-11	9-12	9-12	9-12	9-13	9-13	9-13	9-13	9-13	10-0
	3	8—6	8—7	8—8	8—9	8-10	8-11	8-12	8-13	9—0	9—1	9—2	9—2
1½m	4	9-10	9-10	9-10	9-11	9-11	9-12	9-12	9-12	9-13	9-13	9-13	9-13
	3	8—4	8—5	8—6	8—7	8—8	8—9	8-10	8-11	8-12	8-13	9—0	9—1
13f	4	9—9	9—9	9-10	9-10	9-11	9-11	9-11	9-12	9-12	9-12	9-13	9-13
	3	8—2	8—3	8—4	8—5	8—7	8—8	8—9	8-10	8-11	8-12	8-13	9—0
1¾m	4	9—8	9—8	9—9	9—9	9-10	9-10	9-11	9-11	9-12	9-12	9-12	9-13
	3	8—0	8—2	8—3	8—4	8—5	8—6	8—7	8—8	8—9	8-10	8-11	8-12
15f	4	9—7	9—8	9—8	9—9	9—9	9-10	9-10	9-11	9-11	9-11	9-12	9-12
	3	7-13	8—0	8—1	8—2	8—4	8—5	8—6	8—7	8—8	8—9	8-10	8-11
2m	4	9—6	9—7	9—7	9—8	9—9	9—9	9-10	9-10	9-11	9-11	9-11	9-12
	3	7-11	7-12	7-13	8—1	8—2	8—3	8—4	8—5	8—6	8—7	8—8	8—9
2¼m	4	9—5	9—5	9—6	9—7	9—7	9—8	9—9	9—9	9-10	9-10	9-10	9-11
	3	7—8	7—9	7-11	7-12	7-13	8—0	8—2	8—3	8—4	8—5	8—6	8—7
2½m	4	9—3	9—4	9—5	9—6	9—6	9—7	9—7	9—8	9—9	9—9	9-10	9-10
	3	7—5	7—7	7—8	7—9	7-11	7-12	7-13	8—1	8—2	8—3	8—4	8—5

For 5-y-o's and older, use 10-0 in all cases
Race distances in the above tables are shown only at 1 furlong intervals.
For races over odd distances, the nearest distance shown in the table should be used:
thus for races of 1m to 1m 109 yards, use the table weights for 1m;
for 1m 110 yards to 1m 219 yards use the 9f table

**The age, weight and distance table covering July to December
appears on the end paper at the back of the book**

RACEHORSES
OF 2002

Price £70.00

A TIMEFORM PUBLICATION

CONTENTS

The age, weight and distance tables, for use in applying the ratings in races involving horses of different ages, appear on the end papers at the front and back of the book

Compiled and produced by

G. Greetham (Director), C. S. Williams (Managing Editor & Handicapper), P. Morrell (Essays & Editor), S. D. Rowlands (Handicapper & Editor), J. Ingles (Essays & Editor for pedigrees & 'Top Horses Abroad'), G. J. North, S. Molyneux (Handicappers), R. J. C. Austen, J. Early, G. J. McGibbon, M. S. Rigg, E. K. Wilkinson (Essays), S. Boow, M. J. Dwyer, R. J. O'Brien, J. A. Todd (Short Commentaries), G. Crowther, M. Hall, D. Holdsworth, G. Johnstone, W. Muncaster, A-M. Stevens, R. Todd, C. Wright (Production)

© **Portway Press Limited 2003**   ISBN 1 901570 35 5

Racehorses of 2002

Introduction

One obituary of Lord [Denis] Howell, who died in 1998, recalled the anecdote that sport was divided between 'those who think that Denis Howell was the best Minister of Sport we ever had, and those who think he still has the job.' Howell had two stints in charge of sport and is credited, among other things, with persuading the Government to put £500,000 towards the 1966 World Cup, and with setting up the Sports Council and the forerunner of the Football Trust. Howell's influence on racing wasn't as long-lasting as on other sports and he failed in one of his main aims—to replace the anachronistic Jockey Club with a Racing Board. Howell believed in the total abolition of the power of the Jockey Club and, decades later, if the latest Minister for Sport Richard Caborn is true to his word, Howell's vision should at last be fulfilled. Under the astute senior stewardship of Lord Hartington from 1989 to 1994, the Jockey Club co-operated in the transfer of its administrative role to the more widely-based British Horseracing Board (which nonetheless still included Jockey Club nominees), but the Club was left with complete authority over regulatory and disciplinary matters. In the aftermath and ramifications of two television documentaries in 2002 alleging corruption in racing, the Minister for Sport signalled the end of the Jockey Club's role, with its likely replacement by an independent regulator for racing. 'In the twenty-first century, people want transparency and accountability and the Club is what it is—a club. I think they acknowledge that.'

The chairman of the BHB Peter Savill also called for a new structure to oversee security, one possibility being the transfer of the Jockey Club's remaining powers to an independent authority under the umbrella of the BHB.

Denis Howell tried to abolish the power of the Jockey Club during his two stints as Minister of Sport

The present minister Richard Caborn has signalled the end of the Jockey Club's historic role

3

Savill described the television documentaries, including one with 3.9m viewers by the BBC's flagship current affairs programme *Panorama*, as 'embarrassing for racing and in particular for the Jockey Club'. The *Panorama* documentary, screened in October, relied heavily on presentation, rather than content, and was neither fair nor balanced in its portrayal of racing. The main informants were discredited or disreputable and the programme relied mostly on innuendo and suspicion, but it did cost the job of the Jockey Club's head of security who was caught on camera and made to look ridiculous. Objective reporting, even on programmes like *Panorama* it seems, can no longer be taken for granted, and any organisation under attack has to fight back using modern methods. The Jockey Club had months to work behind the scenes or make a pre-emptive response to the well-trailed programme but it seemed complacent. It failed to protect racing's image or even to limit the damage to the sport's reputation, which was undoubtedly tarnished in the eyes of the general public. In short, the whole affair was a shambles, with the Jockey Club made the scapegoat for allowing alleged skulduggery to go unchecked. Most of the allegations stemmed from racing activities masterminded by fugitive from justice Brian Wright, whose involvement with jockeys, trainers and stable employees had

been known about for some time by the Jockey Club, and became public knowledge when reporting restrictions were lifted, after a two-year embargo, on a series of trials held following a major Customs & Excise investigation into drug trafficking and money-laundering. The Jockey Club announced its intention, immediately after the lifting of restrictions, to bring disciplinary proceedings against some of those implicated, but it was mid-November before it started hearing the cases. Eight individuals, including Wright in his absence, were eventually 'warned off', among them banned ex-jump jockey and trainer Dermot Browne—a key *Panorama* witness—who received another twenty years after admitting doping, and jump jockey turned bloodstock agent Graham Bradley who is in the process of appealing against an eight-year ban. At the end of January 2003, the Jockey Club announced the introduction of a range of measures aimed at tightening security. These included restricting the use of mobile phones on racecourses by jockeys, improved CCTV for racecourse stables, and the Jockey Club becoming responsible for weighing room security.

Christopher Spence, senior steward of the 250-year-old Jockey Club which was made the scapegoat for a spate of scandals and corruption in 2002

The Jockey Club celebrated its two hundred and fiftieth anniversary in 2002—a milestone marked with a maiden race which opened the Newmarket Craven meeting—and it also introduced a new slogan for the twenty-first century. 'Working to promote public confidence in British racing' was the ironic heading to a statement outlining the Club's 'principles and priorities'. These included more transparent regulation, enhanced safety and welfare, improved security, and commercial development of the thirteen racecourses owned by Racecourse Holdings Trust and the acres of training grounds at Newmarket of which the Jockey Club is guardian. The Jockey Club has done much to bring itself up to date—there are some first-rate people among its present members and staff—but, constitutionally, no private club, whatever its traditions, history or background, should play any part in the control of racing. Judged by the initial stance of senior steward Sir Christopher Spence—'We are a highly professional organisation which is very good for racing'—the Jockey Club looked as if it intended to hold on to its remaining powers for as long as it could. It held out in the 'seventies—until a general election saw the end of Denis Howell—by giving various associations representation on an advisory body, chaired by the Jockey Club's senior steward. The Horseracing Advisory Council was developed from this original advisory body and Timeform's founder Phil Bull became its first chairman in 1980, a position from which he resigned, after less than six months, describing it as a cosmetic charade. Bull felt that 'neither the Jockey Club nor the Levy Board had any intention of accepting, or paying attention, to the HAC's advice on any matters of real moment, if they themselves didn't agree with it.' The Jockey Club maintained its autonomous position for a further thirteen years, until the setting up of the BHB in 1993. In a surprise move in mid-February 2003, the Club published its own plans to delegate responsibility for regulating racing to 'a new independent board' in 2004. The outline proposal, said to be supported by the Minister for Sport, is for a board in which independent members would be in the majority (there would still be two Jockey Club nominees) with the present regulatory staff and racecourse officials transferred across from the Jockey Club. The board would have an independent chairman. Who would own and fund the new company, who would appoint the 'independent' directors and to whom would they be accountable, were among points not immediately clear. Will the creation of the new board really mean the end of Jockey Club control and influence?

Against the background of an on-going Office of Fair Trading investigation, which could have very serious consequences for the structure of racing, the BHB and the Racecourse Association spent much of the year at loggerheads after the collapse of an industry-wide agreement on plans for the future funding of racing. The plans involved the tracks putting 40% of income from media rights and other new deals into prize-money. In a hard-hitting Gimcrack speech, delivered on Sheikh Mohammed's behalf in December, it was claimed that, according to BHB figures, racecourses had earned an extra £46m in 2002, but only £5m of that had found its way into prize-money. Sheikh Mohammed warned that the Maktoum family might boycott those courses which refused to pass on an 'appropriate' portion of new funds. The racecourses in general, which, somewhat incongruously, currently benefit from interest-free loans of over £30m from the Levy Board, might claim that they are simply adopting a commercial approach to running their tracks, though this does not apply to some, including the Racecourse Holdings Trust courses and others, which have never been run for shareholder profit. Most of racing's extra income, created in the climate of tax-free betting introduced by the Government the previous year, came from deals over media rights. A commercial agreement for the use

5

of pre-race data (runners and riders etc) was announced in the spring between the big bookmakers and the BHB, potentially worth a total of around £600m over the next five years. Payments were to be channelled for the time being through the Levy Board—due to be abolished soon—and were offset against payments made under the existing levy scheme. Agreement between the racecourses and bookmakers on live pictures for Britain's betting shops was reached just in time to avoid a blackout of British racing in May, though the BHB chairman slammed the annual £23m deal—the previous ten-year deal with SIS had been worth £12m a year—as 'a betrayal of racing's interests'. The terms of the deal exempted betting shops from paying for races screened by terrestrial television, a concession which mostly affected the biggest tracks.

The BHB's own attempts later in the year to hike charges to national newspapers for printing race cards led only to a humiliating climbdown. Acting without consultation with other constituent bodies in racing—including sponsors who found their names temporarily dropped by some newspapers—the BHB succeeded only in provoking an unnecessary row with one of the sport's biggest allies. The benefits for betting turnover of newspaper coverage of racing programmes, for which the current licensing charges have now been extended to 2007, are immeasurable; the benefits for newspapers of devoting acres of space to a minority sport are not so easy to quantify (some overseas racing authorities actually pay newspapers for printing cards). This was an episode that racing, already plagued with tiresome confrontations and public relations disasters, could well have done without. The BHB may well consider that, in addition to its announcement in June that it is holding a root-and-branch review of British racing, it might also incorporate another review of its own function (which may be needed anyway when the Office of Fair Trading reports). The BHB probably needs to constitute itself more democratically and, with funding battles now won, should, to use the words of its chairman, 'do its best to ensure that all sectors are treated fairly', if it is to avoid ongoing rumblings of discontent. Bookmakers, racecourses, the Levy Board, the publicly-owned Tote and now sponsors and newspapers are groups that have been at loggerheads at some time or other with the BHB during the tenancy of the present chairman, whose robustness has, nevertheless, helped to bring about the prospect of a much brighter financial future for the sport.

One of BHB chairman Peter Savill's greatest achievements, in a period which has seen the amount received from bookmakers and media companies almost doubled, was the renegotiation in 2001 of the rights deal with Go Racing, which subsequently changed its trade name to attheraces. Racing is due to receive £307m over the next ten years from the interactive television channel jointly owned by BSkyB, Channel 4 and the racecourse group Arena. The channel started broadcasting in May but encountered teething problems with some of its ground-breaking technology for interactive betting. It was said to be generating only around £250,000 a week in betting by the end of the year, at which time its average daily viewing figure reportedly stood at 33,000. It may be early days, but attheraces says it needs betting turnover of more than £2 billion by 2011 just to break even, worrying figures for racing as well as for attheraces.

The traditional methods of placing a bet—filling in a slip at a betting shop, picking up a phone or face to face with an on-course bookie—have also been joined in recent times by clicking a mouse. The major bookmaking chains, one of which reported in the spring a 40% increase in turnover since betting tax was abolished, faced a threat from the rise during the year of internet, person-to-person betting exchanges, the largest of which, Betfair, was said to be matching around £50m-worth of bets each week by the end of the year.

Bookmakers in general faced a new commercial threat from person-to-person betting exchanges, while racecourse bookmakers face much increased BHB charges from April

Perceived by some as a threat to racing's integrity, by enabling clients to profit directly from a horse losing, the on-line betting exchanges also had to face the prospect of a legal challenge when Hills called on the Government to enforce the 1963 Betting & Gaming Act which, it claimed, is being breached by layers on the exchanges acting without a legal permit; regular layers on the exchanges pay no gross profits tax, unlike licensed bookmakers. The exchanges survived adverse publicity when two of their number ceased trading in July, and there was comment about a small number of races with unusual betting patterns, involving beaten horses noticeably easy to back on the exchanges. Betfair continued to thrive, though, and, with the legal argument seemingly cutting little ice with the Government, responsibly-managed betting exchanges, co-operating with the turf authorities (it seems likely that trainers will be banned from laying horses on the exchanges), would seem to have a bright future. Even the major bookmakers acknowledge that punters are readily able to get better odds on the exchanges, with percentages much more favourable than in the betting shops. The moneyspinning multiple bets which contribute greatly to the big bookmakers' profits and are the lifeblood of the betting shops are not traded on the betting exchanges, but it will still be interesting to see whether the big bookmakers eventually enter the market themselves. They did so temporarily with spread betting which, in the event, turned out to be less of a threat to their businesses than they thought. The advent of betting exchanges provides some degree of protection for punters against a possible worsening of starting price margins. This looks likely if the BHB goes ahead in April with plans to impose the extra cost of a 10% gross profits charge on racecourse bookmakers for supplying runners. Punters' interests have traditionally come way down the priorities of the racing authorities and were overridden when the new arrangements for the wider funding of racing linked bookmakers' payments to their profits. Both the off-course bookmakers (from which the BHB derives the bulk of its income) and the sport's governing body now have a vested interest in maximising bookmakers' profits, a situation which could work to the clear detriment of punters.

The first race on which trading on Betfair topped the £1m mark was the Breeders' Cup Mile at Arlington at the end of October. Over £850,000 of the

*Hawk Wing may have been setting the gallops alight
but he couldn't catch stable-companion High Chaparral in the Derby;
TV viewers were estimated at a somewhat disappointing 2.7 million, a figure probably affected
by football's World Cup, possibly also responsible for a dip in betting on the Derby which slipped a place
into third behind the Grand National and, for the first time, also behind the Cheltenham Gold Cup*

total was traded on the hot favourite, Europe's Horse of the Year **Rock of Gibraltar**, and the layers came out on top. Rock of Gibraltar's controversial defeat by French-trained **Domedriver** ended a splendid run of seven successive victories in Group 1 company, including, in 2002, the Two Thousand Guineas at both Newmarket and the Curragh, the St James's Palace Stakes, the Sussex Stakes and the Prix du Moulin. Coupled with the exploits of **High Chaparral**, who added the Breeders' Cup Turf at Arlington—earning him the prestigious Eclipse award as America's leading male turf horse—to wins in the Derby at Epsom and the Curragh, it was another splendid year for Irish-based trainer Aidan O'Brien who, for the second year in a row, topped the trainers' table in Britain (he was also champion for the sixth successive year in Ireland). O'Brien had only ten winners in Britain, half the number of the previous year and the smallest number by a champion trainer since Vincent O'Brien took the title with eight in 1966. Seven of Aidan O'Brien's victories came in Group 1 races, the much-vaunted **Hawk Wing** (Eclipse Stakes), **Sophisticat** (Coronation Stakes) and **Brian Boru** (Racing Post Trophy) supplementing those of the stable's 'big two'. The stable had nineteen Group/Grade 1 victories worldwide. Brian Boru galloped to 2003 Derby favouritism but it was far from plain sailing with the Ballydoyle two-year-olds in general, the stable being affected by a coughing outbreak in August. Though Ballydoyle did not dominate the two-year-old scene as in the previous year—its achievements are dealt with in Brian Boru's essay—there is every likelihood that the stable will still have a big say in the 2003 classics. **Tomahawk**, **Hold That Tiger**, **Chevalier**, **Powerscourt**, **Alberto Giacometti** and, last but no means least, **Statue of Liberty**—not seen out after Royal Ascot—are probably its other leading contenders, along with the filly **Yesterday**, a sister to the same stable's **Quarter Moon** who was runner-up in three classics in the latest season.

With High Chaparral and Hawk Wing both staying in training, racing's other 'superpower' Godolphin faces a stiff challenge in the top open-aged races. Godolphin's ambitions are on a global scale and it won sixteen Group/Grade 1 races worldwide in 2002, a total bettered only once before in its nine-year existence. **Street Cry** gave Godolphin its third win in four years in the world's richest race, the Dubai World Cup, and the essay on him outlines the stable's achievements. One Thousand Guineas and Oaks winner **Kazzia** and Prince of Wales's Stakes winner **Grandera** supplied Godolphin's only British Group 1 victories, Grandera also following in the footsteps of Daylami and

8

Fantastic Light (twice) in winning the World Series, which is framed around the existing structure of the world's top middle-distance races. The Maktoum family remains the dominant force in British racing and Hamdan Al Maktoum became leading owner for the fourth time, finishing in the top three in the table for the fifteenth consecutive year. Godolphin finished second, with Maktoum Al Maktoum fifth.

The Loder stable, which trains the pick of the Maktoum family's two-year-olds, had a disappointing season, as outlined in the essay on Maktoum Al Maktoum's Gimcrack winner **Country Reel**. With the Godolphin 'nursery' looking less fruitful as a source of future winners, and mindful of the powerful hand held by Ballydoyle, Godolphin moved to strengthen its team for 2003 by purchasing its usual crop of classic hopefuls from other stables, among them the very promising **Lateen Sails** and **Echoes In Eternity**—in whose essays the development of sectional time analysis is discussed—and Godolphin also acquired the latest Prix du Jockey Club winner **Sulamani**, whose purchase was probably the most surprising of any so far. Perhaps the Godolphin team shared the general feeling that their **Marienbard** was a shade fortunate in the Prix de l'Arc de Triomphe to beat Sulamani, who might have won with a different ride, and High Chaparral, who might have won with a smoother preparation. Lateen Sails was purchased from Khalid Abdulla (third in the owners' table) who had the season's top two-year-old, Middle Park winner **Oasis Dream**, and also has other leading classic prospects in **Trade Fair** and French-trained fillies **Etoile Montante** and **Intercontinental**. **Banks Hill**, **Burning Sun** (whose essay records another relatively poor year for the Cecil stable), **Tillerman** and Zenda (of whom more later) were others to carry the Abdulla colours with distinction.

The Maktoum family just failed in Britain's most important all-aged middle-distance prize, the King George VI and Queen Elizabeth Stakes, Hamdan Al Maktoum's **Nayef** beaten a head in a rousing finish with **Golan**. The absence of the previous year's Arc winner **Sakhee**, a defector on the morning of the race because the going was deemed too firm, and of any representative of the classic generation (for the first time since 1969) led to some talk of a decline in the race's relevance, an argument examined in the essay on the winner. Nayef took his revenge on Golan in the Juddmonte International—which also lacked any significant three-year-old challenge—but Golan's trainer Sir Michael Stoute (second in the table to O'Brien) celebrated York victories both remarkable in their own way, with **Islington** (Yorkshire Oaks) and **Russian Rhythm** (Lowther). Russian Rhythm looks very much a Guineas filly, though she will face a tough task if the leading French two-year-old of her sex **Six Perfections** is sent to Newmarket.

Racecourse attendances for the year topped five and a half million, the highest for many a day, despite the summer of 2002 being a wash-out, with higher than normal rainfall, and also being the gloomiest since 1988, with an average of 5.53 hours of sunshine a day in June, July and August. If the big-race supremacy of the Maktoum family and of Coolmore's racing arm Ballydoyle was in danger of becoming as monotonous as the weather, a series of Group 1 victories for small owners in the autumn provided some welcome relief. The best British-trained three-year-old **Bollin Eric** won the St Leger for long-standing owner-breeders Sir Neil and Lady Westbrook, while his stable-companion the two-year-old **Somnus** won two very valuable races outside the pattern for a trio of Yorkshire owners. It was a notable year for syndicates with **Tout Seul**, owned by a partnership of friends of trainer Fulke Johnson Houghton, winning the Dewhurst and **Soviet Song**, owned by thousands of Elite Racing Club members, taking the Fillies' Mile and vying for winter

*Bollin Eric—only the second winner of an English classic
in a quarter of a century to be trained in the North*

favouritism for the One Thousand Guineas. The Henry Candy-trained **Kyllachy**, the season's top sprinter, was also owned by a syndicate, and the same stable won the Cheveley Park with **Airwave**, who raced for a partnership. Trainer Terry Mills realised his ambition of Group 1 success with Queen Elizabeth II Stakes winner **Where Or When**, while the training career of David Nicholls reached new heights when the five-year-old gelding **Continent** won the July Cup and the Prix de l'Abbaye (the first gelding to win since they became eligible to run in 2001). Asked whether he felt increased pressure Nicholls replied in typical style: 'Pressure is living in a caravan eight years ago with my wife, looking after half a dozen moderate horses and wondering where the wages for the two stable girls was going to come from.' Nicholls' fellow Yorkshire-based trainer Mark Johnston started his career in a similarly small way and continues to go from strength to strength. He finished third in the trainers' prize-money tables in 2002, behind O'Brien and Stoute, and saddled most winners for the second year running, reaching a century for the ninth successive season, something no other trainer has achieved in that period. Johnston's attributes and achievements are covered in essays on a number of his winners, including the stable's best horse **Zindabad** and those progressive performers **Scott's View** and **Systematic**.

Johnston also sent out **Royal Rebel** to win the Gold Cup at Royal Ascot for the second year, though the win created plenty of controversy and drew attention once again to the unfortunate consequences for racing's image of having whip guidelines that are too rigid. Royal Rebel denied the favourite, Irish-trained **Vinnie Roe**, whose trainer Dermot Weld added another remarkable chapter to his story when winning his second Melbourne Cup with **Media Puzzle**, whose entry recounts some of the highlights of Weld's career. Weld has a strong classic candidate for 2003 in **Refuse To Bend** and also enjoyed a

Grade 1 victory in America with the Sun Chariot winner **Dress To Thrill**. Like another of the top three-year-old fillies, the Poule d'Essai des Pouliches winner **Zenda**, she will be racing in America as a four-year-old (the lack of good opportunities for older fillies in Europe is touched on in the essays on Kazzia, Zenda and Sophisticat).

Figures compiled by the International Racing Bureau show that racing continues to become more international—the number of horses sent from leading racing countries to compete on foreign soil in 2002 was just short of 900, a new record—but overseas earnings by British trainers of £8,443,479 were below the totals of the two previous years and well behind the record £11,295,984 earned in 1996. France, Ireland, Italy and Germany were, as usual, the countries most frequently targeted by British stables. It wasn't all one way traffic, though, with nine of Britain's twenty-eight Group 1 races going to overseas-trained horses. As well as the seven victories for Ballydoyle, France's top older miler **Keltos** won the Lockinge and **Boreal** became the first German-trained winner of a British Group 1 for twenty-seven years when he took the Coronation Cup. Germany's top horses are campaigned more widely than they used to be and the latest German Derby winner **Next Desert** is one to look out for on the international stage in 2003. Similar remarks apply to the Italian champion **Falbrav**, who won the Japan Cup and is to be trained in Britain by Luca Cumani. One of the most memorable victories achieved by a British-trained horse in Germany was that of **Yavana's Pace** who, at ten, became the oldest horse to win a Group 1 race in Europe when successful at Cologne in August. Another ten-year-old **Tedburrow** became the oldest horse to win a Flat pattern race in Britain, while ever-popular **Persian Punch** also helped to keep the flag flying for the veterans.

One of Persian Punch's old rivals **Rainbow High**, now at stud, came a creditable second under 9-13 when attempting a third Chester Cup victory (an apparently exceptional weight-carrying effort examined critically in his essay). Talking of the big handicaps, generalised preconceptions about the strength of the gallop in such races are challenged in the entry on Cambridgeshire winner **Beauchamp Pilot**. The best performance of the season in a handicap was recorded by **Ulundi** in the Wolferton Rated Stakes at Royal Ascot, one of a number of races devised or modified when the meeting was extended to five days—Saturday's card replacing the traditional Heath fixture—in the Queen's Golden Jubilee year. The extra day pushed the Royal Ascot attendance to over 300,000, though the news that the meeting is again to be five days in 2003 may not be greeted with universal approval. Punters experienced a series of results which made investing on the crashing stock market look appealing by comparison. **Malhub**, who had twice undergone operations to help his breathing, sprang a 16/1 surprise in the new Golden Jubilee Stakes (replacing the Cork And Orrery), now the first Group 1 race of the season in which three-year-olds can take on their elders. The Golden Jubilee turned out to be the final race for the previous season's top two-year-old **Johannesburg** after he had made an unsuccessful challenge for the Kentucky Derby. The previous season's top two-year-old filly **Queen's Logic** also had a short-lived three-year-old career, plagued by injury and illness after making a satisfactory reappearance. The latest renewal of the Queen Mary Stakes, a race won by Queen's Logic, was won by **Romantic Liason** (another 16/1-shot) who provided Pat Eddery with his 4,493rd winner in Britain, equalling Lester Piggott's total and leaving him behind only Sir Gordon Richards.

Trainer John Dunlop, for whom Pat Eddery came close to another classic success with the filly **Snowfire**, also celebrated a milestone in the latest season, saddling his 3,000th winner worldwide. Dunlop's fortunes and those of his

11

*Four jockeys who made the headlines—clockwise, Pat Eddery equalled Lester Piggott's
career total of domestic winners on Romantic Liason in the Queen Mary Stakes;
Oscar Urbina (Soviet Song), Chris Rutter (Airwave) and Steve Carson (Tout Seul)
all rode their first Group 1 winners in a notable year for syndicates and small owners*

stable are covered in the essays on Haydock Sprint Cup winner **Invincible
Spirit** and classic prospect **Muqbil**. Invincible Spirit provided jockey John
Carroll with the first Group 1 winner of his long career, a feat mirrored by
now-retired Chris Rutter (Airwave), Oscar Urbina (Soviet Song) and Steve
Carson (Tout Seul). The year was notable also for the fact that no fewer than
ten jockeys reached the hundred-winner mark (eleven-times champion Eddery
finished on ninety-nine in search of his twenty-ninth century). Richard Hughes
and Seb Sanders were Kieren Fallon's closest pursuers, Fallon's one hundred
and forty-nine winners being the lowest total by a champion since Steve

Trainer Ian Balding and jockey Michael Roberts both announced their retirement

Cauthen in 1984 (Eddery and George Duffield are the only two in that year's top twelve still riding).

The most notable retirement from the ranks of the jockeys in the latest season was the leading rider of 1992 Michael Roberts, also eleven times champion in South Africa, who decided to call it a day after making a slow recovery from a serious fall at Wolverhampton the previous season. The champion apprentice of 2000 Lee Newman, who rode eighty-seven winners that year, quit at the age of twenty after losing a battle with the scales. Paul Hanagan was the leading apprentice in 2002 with eighty-four winners. Among the trainers, Ian Balding, forever linked with the great Mill Reef, handed over at Park House to his son Andrew and top dual-purpose trainer Denys Smith announced his retirement after a forty-five-year career. The deaths of owner-breeders Lord Weinstock (whose achievements are covered in the essay on Islington) and Gerald Leigh (dealt with under **Gossamer**), and of the head of the Thoroughbred Corporation Prince Ahmed Salman (reported in the essay on **Elusive City**), were a great loss to racing. Prince Ahmed suffered a heart attack at the age of forty-three, just twelve months after the sudden death of his brother Prince Fahd.

Prince Ahmed's Kentucky Derby and Preakness winner War Emblem is among those reviewed in the increasingly relevant Timeform 'Top Horses Abroad' section at the back of this Annual. It covers Ireland, France, Germany, Italy, Scandinavia, the UAE, North America, Japan, Hong Kong and Australia/ New Zealand, and includes Timeform ratings for all the top horses. The list of ratings in the Irish section has been extended to cover more horses than previously (the full Timeform Irish Handicap now appears in the *Timeform Statistical Review*). As usual, the horses highlighted in bold in this introduction are among those which have essays or extended entries. The essays set out to entertain and inform in equal measure and, along with the extensive photographic coverage, help to fulfil the long-standing aim of the *Racehorses* series in providing an accurate, authoritative and permanent record of the racing year, as well as a wealth of facts, analysis and informed opinion of practical value to the punter.

February 2003

2002 STATISTICS

The following tables show the leading owners, trainers, jockeys, sires of winners and horses on the Flat in Britain during 2002 (Jan 1–Dec 31). The prize-money statistics, compiled by *Timeform*, relate to first-three prize money and win-money. Win money was traditionally used to decide the trainers' championship until, in 1994, the BHB and the National Trainers' Federation established a championship decided by total prize-money as determined by *Racing Post*. The jockeys' championship has traditionally been decided by the number of winners ridden during the year, though since 1997 the Jockeys' Association has recognised a championship that runs for the turf season (Mar–Nov).

	OWNERS (1,2,3 earnings)	Horses	Indiv'l Wnrs	Races Won	Runs	%	Stakes £
1	Mr Hamdan Al Maktoum	156	72	97	495	19.5	2,160,974
2	Godolphin	41	19	21	88	23.8	1,548,044
3	Mr K. Abdulla	111	60	76	358	21.2	1,209,656
4	Mr M. Tabor & Mrs John Magnier	15	4	4	27	14.8	1,048,776
5	Maktoum Al Maktoum	71	24	36	211	17.0	865,949
6	Mrs John Magnier	9	3	3	13	23.0	834,229
7	Exors of the late Lord Weinstock	13	4	5	27	18.5	801,490
8	Cheveley Park Stud	53	31	46	191	24.0	587,955
9	Lucayan Stud	28	14	19	181	10.4	505,428
10	Sir Alex Ferguson & Mrs John Magnier	1	1	3	3	100.0	495,900
11	Mr Abdulla Buhaleeba	16	6	9	52	17.3	353,086
12	Sir Neil Westbrook	4	3	3	19	15.7	341,566

	OWNERS (win-money, £½m+)	Horses	Indiv'l Wnrs	Races Won	Runs	%	Stakes £
1	Mr Hamdan Al Maktoum	156	72	97	495	19.5	1,458,150
2	Mr M. Tabor & Mrs John Magnier	15	4	4	27	14.8	983,700
3	Godolphin	41	19	21	88	23.8	895,270
4	Maktoum Al Maktoum	71	24	36	211	17.0	684,654
5	Mr K. Abdulla	111	60	76	358	21.2	679,207
6	Exors of the late Lord Weinstock	13	4	5	27	18.5	668,525

	TRAINERS (1,2,3 earnings)	Horses	Indiv'l Wnrs	Races Won	Runs	%	Stakes £
1	A. P. O'Brien, Ireland	48	8	10	83	12.0	2,718,114
2	Sir Michael Stoute	151	81	105	484	21.6	2,263,315
3	M. Johnston	159	79	134	748	17.9	2,183,185
4	R. Hannon	187	81	121	1099	11.0	1,627,722
5	B. W. Hills	163	65	91	746	12.2	1,586,838
6	Saeed bin Suroor	41	19	21	88	23.8	1,548,044
7	T. D. Easterby	133	49	81	826	9.8	1,413,223
8	M. R. Channon	149	77	123	1008	12.2	1,402,044
9	J. L. Dunlop	149	56	79	573	13.7	1,365,216
10	J. H. M. Gosden	132	65	85	375	22.6	1,265,993
11	M. P. Tregoning	61	25	32	155	20.6	1,032,807
12	D. Nicholls	92	39	65	696	9.3	971,711

TRAINERS (win-money, £1m+)	Horses	Indiv'l Wnrs	Races Won	Runs	%	Stakes £
1 A. P. O'Brien, Ireland	48	8	10	83	12.0	1,833,234
2 M. Johnston	159	79	134	748	17.9	1,638,996
3 Sir Michael Stoute	151	81	105	484	21.6	1,549,117
4 T. D. Easterby	133	49	81	826	9.8	1,034,256
5 B. W. Hills	163	65	91	746	12.2	1,027,753

TRAINERS (with 100+ winners)	Horses	Indiv'l Wnrs	Races Won	2nd	3rd	Runs	%
1 M. Johnston	159	79	134	100	95	748	17.9
2 M. R. Channon	149	77	123	128	133	1008	12.2
3 R. Hannon	187	81	121	146	131	1099	11.0
4 Sir Michael Stoute	151	81	105	72	69	484	21.6

JOCKEYS (by winners)	1st	2nd	3rd	Unpl	Total Mts	%
1 K. Fallon	149	86	88	487	810	18.4
2 R. Hughes	126	137	92	451	806	15.6
3 S. Sanders	123	97	87	525	832	14.8
4 D. Holland	113	117	98	520	848	13.3
5 K. Darley	113	108	81	497	799	14.1
6 Martin Dwyer	104	104	104	646	958	10.8
7 T. Quinn	104	99	100	462	765	13.5
8 S. Drowne	104	85	106	682	977	10.6
9 J. Quinn	101	95	91	820	1107	9.1
10 F. Lynch	100	77	89	490	756	13.2
11 Pat Eddery	99	88	77	502	766	12.9
12 J. Fortune	92	88	78	484	742	12.3

Note: K. Fallon was leading jockey in the turf season with 144 winners

JOCKEYS (1,2,3 earnings)	Races Won	Rides	%	Stakes £
1 K. Fallon	149	810	18.4	2,750,926
2 K. Darley	113	799	14.1	2,535,869
3 R. Hills	82	445	18.4	1,899,330
4 R. Hughes	126	806	15.6	1,885,139
5 L. Dettori	69	353	19.5	1,811,975
6 J. P. Spencer	86	657	13.0	1,797,477
7 D. Holland	113	848	13.3	1,727,328
8 M. J. Kinane	15	125	12.0	1,704,825
9 J. Murtagh	15	127	11.8	1,575,119
10 Pat Eddery	99	766	12.9	1,429,836
11 T. Quinn	104	765	13.5	1,384,178
12 Martin Dwyer	104	958	10.8	1,265,916

JOCKEYS (win-money, £1m+)	Races Won	Rides	%	Stakes £
1 K. Fallon	149	810	18.4	2,104,524
2 K. Darley	113	799	14.1	1,882,509
3 J. Murtagh	15	127	11.8	1,342,124
4 R. Hills	82	445	18.4	1,292,552
5 L. Dettori	69	353	19.5	1,255,146
6 D. Holland	113	848	13.3	1,136,300
7 R. Hughes	126	806	15.6	1,035,184

APPRENTICES (by winners)	1st	2nd	3rd	Unpl	Total Mts	%
1 P. Hanagan	84	67	57	521	729	11.5
2 L. Enstone	44	48	39	317	448	9.8
3 D. Corby......................................	42	39	49	280	410	10.2
4 R. L. Moore	39	47	43	257	386	10.1

SIRES OF WINNERS (1,2,3 earnings)	Races Won	Runs	%	Stakes £
1 Sadler's Wells (by Northern Dancer)	52	368	14.1	1,870,900
2 Danehill (by Danzig)	57	498	11.4	1,479,807
3 Selkirk (by Sharpen Up)	57	444	12.8	1,023,718
4 Pivotal (by Polar Falcon)	40	322	12.4	836,959
5 Green Desert (by Danzig)	54	353	15.2	796,489
6 Spectrum (by Rainbow Quest)	31	345	8.9	793,146
7 Woodman (by Mr Prospector)	18	209	8.6	788,838
8 Machiavellian (by Mr Prospector)	27	289	9.3	758,826
9 Grand Lodge (by Chief's Crown)	62	453	13.6	752,266
10 Cadeaux Genereux (by Young Generation)	53	481	11.0	748,150
11 Indian Ridge (by Ahonoora)	48	502	9.5	691,755
12 Kingmambo (by Mr Prospector)	29	142	20.4	682,257

SIRES OF WINNERS (win-money)	Horses	Indiv'l Wnrs	Races Won	Stakes £
1 Sadler's Wells (by Northern Dancer)	118	38	52	1,466,273
2 Danehill (by Danzig)	112	42	57	981,134
3 Pivotal (by Polar Falcon)	52	24	40	721,258
4 Spectrum (by Rainbow Quest)	67	21	31	631,367
5 Grand Lodge (by Chief's Crown)	99	39	62	605,822
6 Green Desert (by Danzig)	61	32	54	600,584
7 Selkirk (by Sharpen Up)	79	33	57	566,682
8 Cadeaux Genereux (by Young Generation)	82	33	53	521,150
9 Polar Falcon (by Nureyev)	80	40	65	491,263
10 Machiavellian (by Mr Prospector)	54	17	27	483,676
11 Danehill Dancer (by Danehill)	48	27	48	483,239
12 Night Shift (by Northern Dancer)	96	46	76	472,848

LEADING HORSES (1,2,3 earnings)	Races Won	Runs	Stakes £
1 High Chaparral 3 b.c. Sadler's Wells – Kasora	1	1	800,400
2 Hawk Wing 3 b.c. Woodman – La Lorgnette	1	4	624,100
3 Golan 4 b.c. Spectrum – Highland Gift	1	2	534,000
4 Rock of Gibraltar 3 b.c. Danehill – Offshore Boom	3	3	495,900
5 Nayef 4 b.c. Gulch – Height of Fashion	1	3	426,000
6 Kazzia 3 b.f. Zinaad – Khoruna	2	3	377,000
7 Storming Home 4 b.c. Machiavellian – Try To Catch Me	2	7	367,600
8 Moon Ballad 3 ch.c. Singspiel – Velvet Moon	2	5	355,310
9 Bollin Eric 3 b.c. Shaamit – Bollin Zola	1	6	324,029
10 Zindabad 6 b.h. Shirley Heights – Miznah	3	6	298,930
11 Malhub 4 b.c. Kingmambo – Arjuzah	2	6	269,702
12 Islington 3 b.f. Sadler's Wells – Hellenic	4	5	258,445

HORSE OF THE YEAR
BEST THREE-YEAR-OLD COLT
BEST MILER
RATED AT 133

ROCK OF GIBRALTAR

BEST TWO-YEAR-OLD FILLY RATED AT 120p
SIX PERFECTIONS

BEST TWO-YEAR-OLD COLT RATED AT 122
OASIS DREAM

BEST THREE-YEAR-OLD FILLY RATED AT 124
BRIGHT SKY

BEST OLDER FEMALE RATED AT 126
BANKS HILL

BEST OLDER MALE RATED AT 132
KELTOS

BEST SPRINTER RATED AT 129
KYLLACHY

BEST MIDDLE-DISTANCE HORSES RATED AT 130
HIGH CHAPARRAL
SULAMANI

BEST STAYER RATED AT 126
VINNIE ROE

BEST PERFORMANCE IN A HANDICAP IN BRITAIN
ULUNDI
ran to 122
when winning Wolferton Rated Stakes at Ascot

BEST PERFORMANCE ON ALL-WEATHER IN BRITAIN
DIAMOND MAX
ran to 114
when second in Littlewoods Bet Direct Lincoln Trial Stakes
(Handicap) at Wolverhampton

THE TIMEFORM 'TOP HUNDRED'

Here are listed the 'Top 100' two-year-olds, three-year-olds and older horses in the annual. Fillies and mares are denoted by (f).

2 YEAR OLDS

122	Oasis Dream
121	Tout Seul
120p	Six Perfections (f)
118	Tomahawk
117p	Brian Boru
117p	Hold That Tiger
117	Elusive City
117	Somnus
116p	Dalakhani
115p	Chevalier
115p	Etoile Montante (f)
115p	Soviet Song (f)
114p	Airwave (f)
114p	Trade Fair
113p	Russian Rhythm (f)
112p	Alamshar
112p	Makhlab
112p	Powerscourt
111p	Alberto Giacometti
111p	Almushahar
111p	Saturn
111	Illustrator
111	Loving Kindness (f)
111	Rimrod
111	Zafeen
110p	Big Bad Bob
110p	Refuse To Bend
110	Le Vie dei Colori
110	Luvah Girl (f)
110	Summerland
109p	Statue of Liberty
109	Al Jadeed
109	Bahamian Dancer
109	Country Reel
109	Mister Links
109	Monsieur Bond
108p	Eagle Rise
108p	Romantic Liason (f)
108	Pakhoes
108	Rainwashed Gold
108	Steelaninch
108	Surbiton
108	Van Nistelrooy
107	Baron's Pit
107	Casual Look (f)
107	Deportivo
107	Dublin
107	Ego (f)
107	Fiepes Shuffle
107	Great Pyramid
107	Hanabad
107	Maghanim
107	Marshall
107	Never A Doubt (f)
107	Ontario

107	Songlark
107	Spartacus
107	Wunders Dream (f)
107	Zinziberine (f)
106P	Lateen Sails
106P	Muqbil
106p	Forest Magic
106p	Geminiani (f)
106p	Yesterday (f)
106	Danaskaya (f)
106	Marino Marini
106	Sir Albert
106	The Bonus King
106	Zaide
105p	Captain Saif
105p	Graikos
105p	Intercontinental (f)
105p	Peace Offering
105p	Splendid Era
105p	Striking Ambition
105p	Walayef (f)
105	Foss Way
105	Greek Revival
105	High Praise (f)
105	Irrawaddy
105	Polar Force
105	Summitville (f)
105	Sweet Return
105	Tacitus
105	The Great Gatsby
104p	Avonbridge
104p	Battle Chant
104p	Bourbonnais
104p	Desert Star
104p	New South Wales
104p	Some Kind of Tiger
104p	St Pancras
104p	Vallee Enchantee (f)
104	Governor Brown
104	The Lord
104	Wizard of Noz
103p	Reach For The Moon (f)
103+	Dhabyan
103	Cassis (f)
103	Cumbrian Venture
103	Dolmur
103	Luminata (f)
103	Mail The Desert (f)
103	Membership
103	Presto Vento (f)
103	Revenue
103	Sarayat
103	Spinola (f)

3 YEAR OLDS

133	Rock of Gibraltar
130	High Chaparral
130	Sulamani
127	Hawk Wing
125	Bollin Eric
125	Landseer
124	Act One
124	Bright Sky (f)
124	Moon Ballad
124	Where Or When
123	Ballingarry
123	Bandari
123	Dress To Thrill (f)
123	Highest
123	Islington (f)
122	Captain Rio
122	Next Desert
121	Balakheri
121	Kazzia (f)
121	Pearly Shells (f)
121	Scott's View
121	Sholokhov
121	Systematic
120	Margarula (f)
120	Quarter Moon (f)
119	Burning Sun
119	Dubai Destination
119	Feet So Fast
119	Funfair Wane
119	Highdown
119	Medecis
119	Nysaean
119	Zipping
118	Ana Marie (f)
118	Essence of Dubai
118	Firebreak
118	Ghannam
118	Gossamer (f)
118	Mamool
118	Rakti
118	Tashawak (f)
117p	Massigann
117	Black Sam Bellamy
117	Bowman
117	Century City
117	Fraulein (f)
117	Kaieteur
117	Khalkevi
117	Mr Dinos
117	Naheef
117	Rawyaan
117	Rouvres
117	Sophisticat (f)
117	Tau Ceti
116p	Gamut

EXPLANATORY NOTES

'Racehorses of 2002' deals individually, in alphabetical sequence, with every horse that ran on the Flat in Britain in 2002, plus numerous overseas-trained horses not seen in Britain. For each of these horses is given (1) its age, colour and sex, (2) its breeding, and, where this information has not been given in a previous Racehorses Annual, a family outline, (3) a form summary giving its Timeform rating at the end of the previous year, followed by the details of all its performances during the past year, (4) a Timeform rating, or ratings, of its merit in 2002 (which appears in the margin), (5) a Timeform commentary on its racing or general characteristics as a racehorse, with some suggestions, perhaps, regarding its prospects for 2003, and (6) the name of the trainer in whose charge it was on the last occasion it ran. For each two-year-old the foaling date is also given.

TIMEFORM RATINGS

The Timeform Rating of a horse is simply the merit of the horse expressed in pounds and is arrived at by careful examination of its running against other horses using a scale of weight for distance beaten which, without going into the complexities, ranges from around 3 lb a length at five furlongs and 2 lb a length at a mile and a quarter to 1 lb at two miles. Timeform maintains a 'running' handicap of all horses in training throughout the season.

THE LEVEL OF THE RATINGS

The attention of buyers of British bloodstock and others who may be concerned with Timeform ratings as a measure of absolute racing merit is drawn to the fact that at the close of each season the ratings of all the horses that have raced are re-examined. If necessary, the general level of the handicap is adjusted so that all the ratings are kept at the same standard level from year to year. Some of the ratings may, therefore, be different from those in the final issue of the 2002 Timeform Black Book series.

RATINGS AND WEIGHT-FOR-AGE

The reader has, in the ratings in this book, a universal handicap embracing all the horses in training it is possible to weigh up, ranging from tip-top performers, with ratings from 130 to 145, through categories such as high-class, very smart, smart, useful, fairly useful, fair and modest, down to the poorest, rated around the 20 mark. All the ratings are at weight-for-age, so that equal ratings mean horses of equal merit: perhaps it would be clearer if we said that the universal rating handicap is really not a single handicap, but four handicaps side by side: one for two-year-olds, one for three-year-olds, one for four-year-olds and one for older horses. Thus, a three-year-old rated, for argument's sake, at 117 is deemed to be identical in point of 'merit' with a four-year-old also rated at 117: but for them to have equal chances in, say, a mile race in May, the three-year-old would need to be receiving 9 lb from the four-year-old, which is the weight difference specified by the Age, Weight and Distance Tables on the end papers at the front and back of the book.

USING THE RATINGS

A. Horses of the Same Age

If the horses all carry the same weight there are no adjustments to be made, and the horses with the highest ratings have the best chances. If the horses carry different weights, jot down their ratings, and to the rating of each horse add one point for every pound the horse is set to carry less than 10 st, or subtract one point for every pound it has to carry more than 10 st.

B. Horses of Different Ages

Consult the Age, Weight and Distance Tables printed on the end papers at the front and back of the book. Treat each horse separately, and compare the weight it has to carry with the weight prescribed for it in the tables, according to the age of the horse, the distance of the race and the time of the year. Then, add one point to the rating for each pound the horse has to carry less than the weight given in the tables: or, subtract one point from the rating for every pound it has to carry more than the weight prescribed by the tables.

Example (1½ miles on June 30th)

(Table Weights: 5-y-o+ 10-0; 4-y-o 9-13; 3-y-o 9-1)

6 Bay Pearl (10-2)	....	Rating 115	....	subtract 2	113
4 Elshabeeba (9-9)	....	Rating 114	....	add 4	118
5 Regal Charge (9-5)	....	Rating 115	....	add 9	124
3 Inclination (9-2)	....	Rating 120	....	subtract 1	119

Regal Charge (124) has the best chance at the weights,
with 5 lb in hand of Inclination

TURF AND ARTIFICIAL-SURFACE RATINGS

When a horse has raced on turf and on an artificial surface and its form on one is significantly different from the other, the two ratings are given, the one for artificial surfaces set out below the turf preceded by 'a'. Where there is only one rating, that is to be used for races on both turf and artificial surfaces.

NOTE ON RIDERS' ALLOWANCES

For the purposes of rating calculations it should, in general, be assumed that the allowance a rider is able to claim is nullified by his or her inexperience. Therefore, the weight adjustments to the ratings should be calculated on the weight allotted by the handicapper, or determined by the race conditions.

WEIGHING UP A RACE

The ratings tell you which horses in a race are most favoured by the weights; but complete analysis demands that the racing character of each horse, as set out in its commentary, is also studied carefully to see if there is any reason why the horse might be expected not to run up to its rating or indeed, with a lightly raced or inexperienced horse, might improve on it. It counts for little that a horse is thrown in at the weights if it has no pretensions to staying the distance, is unable to act on the prevailing going, or to accommodate itself to the conformation of the track.

There are other factors to consider too. For example, the matter of pace versus stamina: as between two stayers of equal merit, racing over a distance suitable to both. Firm going, or a small field with the prospect of a slowly-run race, would favour the one with the better pace and acceleration, whereas good to soft or softer going, or a big field with the prospect of a strong gallop, would favour the sounder stayer. There is also the matter of the horse's temperament; nobody should be in a hurry to take a short price about a horse which might not put its best foot forward. The quality of jockeyship is also an important factor when deciding between horses with similar chances.

Incidentally, in setting out the various characteristics, requirements and peculiarities of each horse in its commentary, we have expressed ourselves in as critical a manner as possible, endeavouring to say just as much, and no more, than the facts seem to warrant. Where there are clear indications, and conclusions can be drawn with fair certainty, we have drawn them; if it is a matter of probability or possibility we have put it that way, being careful not to say the one when we mean the other; and where real conclusions are not to be drawn, we have been content to state the facts. Furthermore, when we say that a horse *may* not be suited by firm going, we do not expect it to be treated as though we had said the horse *is not* suited by firm going. In short, both in our thinking and in the setting out of our views we have aimed at precision.

THE FORM SUMMARIES

The form summary enclosed in the brackets lists each horse's performances on the Flat during the past year in chronological sequence, showing, for each race, the distance, the state of the going and the horse's placing at the finish.

The distance of each race is given in furlongs, fractional distances being expressed in the decimal notation to the nearest tenth of a furlong. The prefix 'a' signifies a race on an artificial surface (except for 'f' for fibresand at Southwell and Wolverhampton, and 'p' for polytrack at Lingfield).

The going is symbolised as follows: f=firm (turf) or fast (artificial surface); m=good to firm; g=good (turf) or standard (artificial surface); d=good to soft/dead; s=soft (turf) or slow, sloppy, muddy or wet (artificial surface); v=heavy.

Placings are indicated, up to sixth place, by the use of superior figures, an asterisk being used to denote a win.

Thus [2002 81: 10s* 12f³ 11.7g f11g² Sep 7] signifies that the horse was rated 81 the previous year (if there is no rating it indicates that the horse did not appear in 'Racehorses' for that year). In 2002 it ran four times, winning over 10 furlongs on soft going first time out, then finishing third over 12 furlongs on firm going, then out of the first six over 11.7 furlongs on good going, then second over 11 furlongs on standard going on a fibresand track. The date of its last run was September 7.

Included in the pedigree details are the highest Timeform Annual ratings during their racing careers of the sires, dams and sires of dams of all horses, where the information is available.

Where sale prices are considered relevant F denotes the price as a foal, Y the price as a yearling, 2-y-o as a two-year-old, and so on. These are given in guineas unless prefixed by IR (Irish guineas), $ (American dollars), € (euros) or accompanied by francs (French francs). Other currencies are converted approximately into guineas or pounds sterling at the prevailing exchange rate. Sales mentioned towards the end of the commentaries refer to those after the horse's final outing.

THE RATING SYMBOLS

The following may be attached to, or appear instead of, a rating:-

p   likely to improve.

P   capable of *much* better form.

+   the horse may be better than we have rated it.

d   the horse appears to have deteriorated, and might no longer be capable of running to the rating given.

§   unreliable (for temperamental or other reasons).

§§   so temperamentally unsatisfactory as not to be worth a rating.

?   the horse's rating is suspect. If used without a rating the symbol implies that the horse can't be assessed with confidence, or, if used in the in-season Timeform publications, that the horse is out of form.

RACEHORSES OF 2002

Horse	Commentary	Rating

AAHGOWANGOWAN (IRE) 3 b.f. Tagula (IRE) 116 – Cabcharge Princess (IRE) 64 (Rambo Dancer (CAN) 107) [2002 75: 7f⁵ 8g 6s 5m⁶ 5m⁵ 5f⁴ 6m⁴ 5g⁴ 6d 6m² 6m 6f 5d⁶ Oct 14] sturdy filly: poor mover: fair performer: effective at 5f to easy 7f: acts on any turf going, not discredited on fibresand: visored eighth/ninth starts (found little second occasion). *Denys Smith* **73**

AA-YOUKNOWNOTHING 6 b.g. Superpower 113 – Bad Payer 72 (Tanfirion 110) [2002 63: f5s⁶ p5g⁵ f5g* f5g⁵ f5g 5.1d² 5m 5.1d⁵ 5s f5g³ 5d³ 5m f5s 5f 5d³ f5g⁴ f5f³ f5g Dec 13] tall, angular gelding: modest handicapper: left Miss J. Craze prior to winning at Wolverhampton in February: best at 5f: acts on good to firm ground, soft and fibresand (some promise on polytrack): usually blinkered, occasionally visored: tongue tied: races up with pace: sometimes drifts left/looks none too keen. *M. A. Buckley* **63 a59**

ABAJANY 8 b.g. Akarad (FR) 130 – Miss Ivory Coast (USA) (Sir Ivor 135) [2002 75: p10g p10g⁵ p10g 10m⁶ 8.1d⁴ 10m 8.1g 8f⁴ 8m Sep 5] sturdy gelding: fair handicapper on turf, modest on all-weather: left M. Channon after third start: effective at 1m/1¼m: acts on polytrack, firm and soft going: tried visored (best form when not): tends to wander in front and usually held up. *R. J. Baker* **70 a62**

ABANINETOES (IRE) 2 b.f. (Feb 19) General Monash (USA) 107 – Gilly-G (IRE) (Tenby 125) [2002 5m 7m 5g 5s p6g Dec 28] IR 3,000F: first foal: dam unraced: modest maiden: best effort at 7f: left P. Mooney, Ireland before final start. *P. D. Evans* **59**

ABBAJABBA 6 b.g. Barrys Gamble 102 – Bo' Babbity 75 (Strong Gale 116) [2002 104+: 6g 6m 6f 6m 6m 6g³ 6f 6s² 6v Nov 9] quite good topped gelding: has a round action: useful handicapper: creditable efforts in 2002 only when 1½ lengths third to Funfair Wane in Ayr Gold Cup in September and length second to Smokin Beau at Newbury (despite being hampered final 1f) in October, ridden more prominently than usual both times: best at 5f/6f: has done all winning on good ground or softer: usually waited with. *C. W. Fairhurst* **103**

ABBALEVA 3 b.f. Shaddad (USA) 75 – Bo' Babbity 75 (Strong Gale 116) [2002 f6g³ 8g² 10m⁵ 7m* 8g 7f 7.9g 8.1m 7f f6g f7g⁶ f7g p7g Dec 30] leggy filly: half-sister to several winners, including useful sprinter Blue Iris (by Petong) and 6-y-o Abbajabba: dam, 2-y-o 5f winner, half-sister to high-class sprinter Anita's Prince: modest handicapper on turf: won at Newcastle in May: best form at 7f: acts on firm going, poor form on fibresand/polytrack. *C. W. Fairhurst* **60 a48**

ABBEY HILL 5 b.m. Then Again 126 – Galley Bay 55 (Welsh Saint 126) [2002 10d p12g⁴ 10m f12f Nov 11] fourth foal: half-sister to 1½m winner Artic Bay (by Arctic Lord): dam, Irish 1¾m winner, also won over hurdles: best effort (modest form) in maiden at Lingfield second start. *W. S. Kittow* **60**

ABBEY PARK (USA) 3 b. or br.f. Known Fact (USA) 135 – Taylor Park (USA) (Sir Gaylord) [2002 71: p7g 6g Sep 9] fair maiden at 2 yrs: tailed off both starts in 2002, leaving J. Hills in between. *J. G. Given* **–**

ABBIEJO (IRE) 5 b.m. Blues Traveller (IRE) 119 – Chesham Lady (IRE) (Fayruz 116) [2002 6.1g⁶ 7.6f⁶ 5g Sep 18] 1,700 3-y-o: fourth foal: half-sister to winner abroad by Petardia: dam Irish 2-y-o 5f winner: well held in maidens. *G. Fierro* **–**

ABCO BOY (IRE) 5 b.g. Full Extent (USA) 113 – Double Stitch 74 (Wolver Hollow 126) [2002 11.1g May 17] disappointing maiden: tried blinkered. *R. A. Fahey* **–**

A BEETOO (IRE) 2 b.f. (Mar 3) Bahhare (USA) 122 – Sonya's Pearl (IRE) (Conquering Hero (USA) 116) [2002 p6g f5g p6g Nov 19] IR 6,000F, IR 3,000Y, 19,000 2-y-o: fourth foal: half-sister to a winner up to 7f in Italy by Great Commotion: dam unraced: modest form in maidens: slowly away first 2 starts (markedly so on debut). *J. R. Best* **58**

ABERCORN (IRE) 3 b.g. Woodborough (USA) 112 – Ravensdale Rose (IRE) (Henbit (USA) 130) [2002 –: f7s⁴ f6s* f6g² f5g⁵ f6g* f7g* 6g f6g 5.1d 5s⁶ 7f 7g f6g⁵ 7m f7f f6s Sep 5] smallish, well-made gelding: fair handicapper on all-weather, modest on turf: won at Southwell in January and Wolverhampton (twice) in February: best form at 6f/easy 7f: **57 a68**

acts on fibresand and soft going: usually blinkered: tried tongue tied: usually races up with pace: sold 2,000 gns. *S. R. Bowring*

ABERKEEN 7 ch.g. Keen 116 – Miss Aboyne 64 (Lochnager 132) [2002 53: f7s⁴ f8s⁴ **66** f8s* f8g* f8g² f8g⁴ f11g⁶ f8g³ 10.3s* 10s f8.5g⁵ 9.2s 8.3s⁴ 10s⁴ f8s f8g⁴ f11g f11g Dec 17] workmanlike gelding: fair performer: won apprentice claimer and handicap at Southwell in January and ladies handicap at Doncaster in March: stays 1¼m: acts on firm going, soft and fibresand: visored once: sometimes slowly away: has found little: held up: usually claimer ridden nowadays. *Jedd O'Keeffe*

ABERTHATCH (FR) 3 b.f. Thatching 131 – Academy Angel (FR) (Royal Academy **58** (USA) 130) [2002 68: 8f 10d 12d 10s 10m 11.5s 10d² Oct 28] lengthy filly: modest maiden: stays 1¼m: acts on heavy going: wandered final start. *M. J. Ryan*

ABILITY 3 b.g. Alflora (IRE) 120 – Beatle Song 70 (Song 132) [2002 8.1m³ 8.1f⁵ 7s³ **68** f9.4s Dec 17] well-made gelding: fourth foal: half-brother to 5-y-o Adriana and winner in Italy by Silver Kite: dam 5.7f to 1m winner: fair maiden: should stay at least 1¼m: slowly away on debut: saddle slipped second/final starts. *C. E. Brittain*

ABLE BAKER CHARLIE (IRE) 3 b.g. Sri Pekan (USA) 117 – Lavezzola (IRE) **88** (Salmon Leap (USA) 131) [2002 73p: 10s 10m⁴ 10m⁴ p10g³ 10g* 10d² 8m² 8.1g⁶ Oct 5] useful-looking gelding: fairly useful performer: landed odds in maiden at Leicester in July: good efforts in handicaps after, including when short-headed at Leicester and Newmarket: stays 1¼m: acts on good to firm going, good to soft and polytrack: has worn crossed noseband: sometimes edges right. *J. R. Fanshawe*

ABLE MILLENIUM (IRE) 6 ch.g. Be My Guest (USA) 126 – Miami Life (Miami **51** Springs 121) [2002 57d: f11g⁴ f11g⁵ 8.3g³ 10m 10.1m May 29] lengthy, sparely-made gelding: modest performer: effective at 1m to easy 11f: acts on fibresand and soft going: tried blinkered, usually visored nowadays: none too consistent. *Mrs Lydia Pearce*

ABLE MIND 2 b.g. (Feb 18) Mind Games 121 – Chlo-Jo 65 (Belmez (USA) 131) **71** [2002 5g 6.1m² 7m² f7g³ Oct 22] 5,500Y: rather leggy, lengthy gelding: first foal: dam, 1¼m winner, out of sister to Pebbles: fair maiden: best effort when beaten ¾ length by Temeritas at Newcastle penultimate start: should stay 1m. *W. J. Haggas*

ABOUSTAR 2 b.c. (Apr 8) Abou Zouz (USA) 109 – Three Star Rated (IRE) 79 (Pips – Pride 117) [2002 6f⁶ Oct 11] 3,500Y: tall, leggy colt: first foal: dam 2-y-o 5f winner: 33/1, tailed off in maiden at York. *M. Brittain*

ABOU ZULU 2 ch.g. (Jan 23) Abou Zouz (USA) 109 – Mary From Dunlow 49 **58 d** (Nicholas Bill 125) [2002 6m⁶ 6f 7g 5.9g⁵ 7.1d⁶ 8d 7.5g 7m f8g Oct 17] 700Y: good-topped gelding: seventh foal: half-brother to 8-y-o Smokey From Caplaw and a winner in Scandinavia by Clantime: dam 2-y-o 5f winner: disappointing maiden: stays 7.5f: acts on good to firm going: blinkered last 3 starts. *H. A. McWilliams*

ABOVE BOARD 7 b.g. Night Shift (USA) – Bundled Up (USA) (Sharpen Up 127) [2002 –, a43: f5s⁵ f6s⁵ f6g f6g* f6g⁴ f6g⁶ f6g f6g 5g 6d f6g f5g⁶ f5g Dec 27] smallish, **a53** robust gelding: modest performer: won seller at Southwell in February: barely stays 7f: acts on fibresand, no recent form on turf: tried blinkered/tongue tied. *R. F. Marvin*

ABOVE THE CUT (USA) 10 ch.g. Topsider (USA) – Placer Queen (Habitat 134) – [2002 –: p12g Jan 12] of no account nowadays. *C. P. Morlock*

ABRACADABJAR 4 b.g. Royal Abjar (USA) 121 – Celt Song (IRE) (Unfuwain – (USA) 131) [2002 51, a59: 10.9f 10m p13g p10g Dec 30] of no account nowadays. *Miss Z. C. Davison*

ABRAXAS 4 b.c. Emperor Jones (USA) 119 – Snipe Hall 93 (Crofthall 110) [2002 56, **48** a63: p6g 7g 6d 5g 5d⁵ 5d 5m Aug 30] modest maiden handicapper: stays 6f: acts on **a58** polytrack and good to firm going: blinkered (well held) sixth start. *J. Akehurst*

ABSENT FRIENDS 5 b.g. Rock City 120 – Green Supreme (Primo Dominie 121) **96** [2002 82: f5g 5g⁶ 5d⁴ 5g⁴ 5m² 5g⁶ 5f 5.1m⁵ 5.2m⁶ 5g² 5m³ 5.2m* 5m* 5f⁴ Oct 4] strong, lengthy gelding: usually impresses in appearance: useful performer: progressed well in the autumn, winning handicap at Yarmouth and minor event at Beverley (beat Henry Hall by short head): good fourth to Proud Boast in listed event at Newmarket final start: best at 5f: best form on ground firmer than good: sometimes slowly away/hangs left: saddle slipped ninth start: usually races prominently. *J. Balding*

ABSINTHER 5 b.g. Presidium 124 – Heavenly Queen (Scottish Reel 123) [2002 66: **66** 11.8s 10m⁵ 11.9g³ 11.6s 11.8m³ 12m 10.2d 11.6m⁴ 10m² 12m* 10g⁴ Sep 10] good-bodied gelding: fair handicapper: won at Folkestone (for second year running) in August:

effective at 1¼m to 1½m: acts on fibresand, firm and soft ground: visored once: has run well when sweating: waited with. *M. R. Bosley*

ABSOLUTE CHARMER (IRE) 3 ch.f. Entrepreneur 123 – Diavolina (USA) (Lear **86** Fan (USA) 130) [2002 77: 9f⁴ 9m⁶ 10m* 10m² Aug 4] fairly useful performer: won maiden at Nottingham in July: very good second in handicap at Newbury final start: races freely but stays 1¼m: raced only on ground firmer than good: sent to USA. *R. Charlton*

ABSOLUTE FANTASY 6 b.m. Beveled (USA) – Sharp Venita 84 (Sharp Edge 123) **87** [2002 80: p5g⁵ f5s⁶ p6g* p6g² p6g² 5f 5m² 5g* May 10] lengthy mare: fairly useful performer: won minor event at Lingfield in February and handicap there in May: was best at 5f/easy 6f: acted on firm and soft going, and on all-weather: was blinkered: sometimes started slowly/edged left/found little: was usually waited with: dead. *E. A. Wheeler*

ABSOLUTELYMARVELOS 3 b.g. Royal Applause 124 – Snipe Hall 93 (Crofthall **–** 110) [2002 –: f7s f6g f8.5g 7.1g 5m⁶ 5g May 10] little form: blinkered last 2 starts. *N. Tinkler*

ABSOLUTE MAJORITY 7 ch.g. Absalom 128 – Shall We Run 59 (Hotfoot 126) **–** [2002 11.8g Jul 18] modest performer at 5 yrs: well held only Flat run in 2002. *H. S. Howe*

ABSOLUTE UTOPIA (USA) 9 b.g. Mr Prospector (USA) – Magic Gleam (USA) **58** 122 (Danzig (USA)) [2002 67: p10g² p10g⁴ p10g⁶ p10g⁴ 10.9f 11.9g 12m 10.9m p12g **a66** p10g Nov 27] tall gelding: hobdayed/had soft palate operation early in career: fair handicapper: left N. Berry after fourth start, E. Wheeler after seventh: best at 1¼m/1½m: acts on polytrack, firm and good to soft ground (well held both starts on soft): tried blinkered: held up. *J. L. Spearing*

ABSTRACT (IRE) 6 b.m. Perugino (USA) 84 – Kalapa (FR) (Mouktar 129) [2002 **–** 10.1m f12f f11g Dec 4] of little account nowadays. *J. Parkes*

ABUELOS 3 b.g. Sabrehill (USA) 120 – Miss Oasis 54 (Green Desert (USA) 127) **68** [2002 56: p6g⁶ p7g* 7d² 8.3m p7g⁵ 7g 8m Jul 26] smallish, well-made gelding: fair performer: won minor event at Lingfield in May: reportedly lost action final start: stays 7f: acts on polytrack and any turf going: held up. *S. Dow*

ABUNDANT 2 b.f. (Feb 25) Zafonic (USA) 130 – Glorious (Nashwan (USA) 135) **96** [2002 7s* 8s⁵ Nov 2] lengthy, useful-looking filly: has scope: second foal: dam unraced half-sister to smart miler Killer Instinct (by Zafonic) from family of Opera House and Kayf Tara: useful form when winning minor event at Yarmouth in October by 8 lengths from Ransom O'War, travelling strongly after slow start and pulling clear from over 1f out despite edging left: disappointing fifth of 7 in listed race at Newmarket, hanging markedly left: bred to stay 1m. *J. R. Fanshawe*

ACADEMIC ACCURACY 4 b.f. Environment Friend 128 – Branitska (Mummy's **–** Pet 125) [2002 66d: f9.4g⁶ Jan 18] leggy, lengthy filly: fair performer at 2/3 yrs: tailed off only run in 2002. *P. S. McEntee*

ACADEMIC GOLD (IRE) 4 ch.g. Royal Academy (USA) 130 – Penultimate (USA) **–** (Roberto (USA) 131) [2002 73: 9m p10g Jun 22] big, rangy gelding: fair maiden at best: well held since 3-y-o reappearance: tried tongue tied. *T. D. Barron*

ACADEMY BRIEF (IRE) 2 b.g. (Feb 17) Brief Truce (USA) 126 – Stylish **68** Academy (IRE) (Royal Academy (USA) 130) [2002 7g⁵ 6g 7d 8g 7s⁴ 8m² 8f² 7.5s 7v f8.5g⁵ Dec 14] IR 7,000Y, resold IR 2,000Y, IR 3,200 2-y-o: first foal: dam ran 4 times in Ireland: fair maiden: second in nurseries at Gowran and Listowel in September: well held last 3 starts, leaving P. Mullins in Ireland before final one: stays 1m: acts on firm going. *J. W. Mullins*

ACADEMY (IRE) 7 ch.g. Archway (IRE) 115 – Dream Academy (Town And Country **71** 124) [2002 f9.4g⁴ f12g³ f14.8g⁶ 16.2g⁴ 13.8m* 17.1m³ 19.1m* 13.8m* 17.1m* 16m⁴ **a45 +** 15.8f* 13.8g³ Oct 19] close-coupled gelding: fair handicapper on turf, poor on all-weather: won at Catterick (3), Warwick and Pontefract between May and October: effective at 13.8f to 19f: acts on firm going and fibresand. *Andrew Turnell*

ACCELERATION (IRE) 2 b.g. (Feb 16) Groom Dancer (USA) 128 – Overdrive 99 **– p** (Shirley Heights 130) [2002 f6g⁴ p7g f7g Oct 22] 25,000Y: sixth foal: half-brother to 3 winners, including 1½m and 2m winner Endorsement (by Warning) and 6f (at 2 yrs)/7f winner who stayed 1½m Zugudi (by Night Shift), both useful: dam, thorough stayer, from good middle-distance family: showed promise in maidens first 2 starts: gelded after final one: will be well suited by 1¼m+: almost certainly capable of better. *Sir Mark Prescott*

ACCENTOR (IRE) 2 ch.f. (Feb 15) Bluebird (USA) 125 – Law Review (IRE) 63 **57** (Case Law 113) [2002 6f⁴ p8g Nov 27] workmanlike filly: first foal: dam, ran 3 times (best run at 1m), half-sister to top-class sprinter Lake Coniston (by Bluebird): modest form, soon off bridle, in maidens at Redcar and Lingfield. *J. Noseda*

ACCEPTING   5 b.g. Mtoto 134 – D'Azy 91 (Persian Bold 123) [2002 89: 16g 15f 16m 17.2d⁶ 16.2m Jul 26] close-coupled gelding: fairly useful handicapper at 4 yrs: well held in 2002. *J. Mackie*   –

ACCLAMATION   3 b.c. Royal Applause 124 – Princess Athena 119 (Ahonoora 122) [2002 107: 6m³ 6g³ Oct 18] lengthy, attractive colt: smart performer: won £200000 St Leger Yearling Stakes at Doncaster at 2 yrs: off over 12 months, ran really well when 2½ lengths third to Crystal Castle in Diadem Stakes at Ascot (edged left) and when length third to Needwood Blade in listed event at Newmarket following month: should prove best at 5f/6f: acts on good to firm ground, shaped well on soft. *L. G. Cottrell*   **114**

ACCYSTAN   7 ch.g. Efisio 120 – Amia (CAN) (Nijinsky (CAN) 138) [2002 –: f12s f12g Mar 23] of little account. *A. Crook*   –

ACE IN THE HOLE   2 br.f. (Feb 2) So Factual (USA) 120 – Timely Raise (USA) (Raise A Man (USA)) [2002 6d⁶ 7g³ 7.1m f7g p8g Nov 23] half-sister to several winners, including 9f/1¼m winner Double Bluff (by Sharrood) and 3f (at 2 yrs)/6f winner Poker Chip (by Bluebird), both useful: dam, miler in North America, sister to smart middle-distance stayer Primitive Rising: modest maiden: left J. Eustace after third in seller at Folkestone: stays 7f: free-going sort. *F. Jordan*   **55 a–**

ACE-MA-VAHRA   4 b.f. Savahra Sound 111 – Asmarina 50 (Ascendant 96) [2002 52: f6s 7f 8.2m³ Oct 1] leggy filly: poor maiden: stays 1m: acts on fibresand and good to firm ground. *S. R. Bowring*   **44**

ACE OF HEARTS   3 b.g. Magic Ring (IRE) 115 – Lonely Heart 101 (Midyan (USA) 124) [2002 p7g⁴ f7g⁸ 8m³ 8.1d² 8m* 7m⁴ 8.1m 8g Oct 18] 34,000Y: first foal: dam 1¼m winner: fairly useful performer: won maiden at Wolverhampton in April and handicap at Newbury in July: stays 1m: acts on good to firm going, good to soft and fibresand: tends to hang: consistent. *C. F. Wall*   **88**

ACE OF TRUMPS   6 ch.g. First Trump 118 – Elle Reef (Shareef Dancer (USA) 135) [2002 66, a–: 8v 8m 9.2s* 8.3g 11.1g³ 10g 9.2v 9.1v* 9.2s⁵ 9.2s⁶ 9.2g 9.1d³ 9.2v⁵ 8.3s 10s² 9m 9.1g 8.3m 10s⁵ Oct 14] small, sturdy gelding: modest performer: won claimer at Hamilton in May and handicap at Ayr in June: effective at 9f to 11f: acts on any turf going: blinkered/visored earlier in career: usually tongue tied: races up with pace: unreliable. *Miss L. A. Perratt*   **63 § a– §**

ACHILLES RAINBOW   3 ch.g. Deploy 131 – Naughty Pistol (USA) 69 (Big Pistol (USA)) [2002 10g 10f⁵ 12.3m 11.6m⁴ 10m 8s⁴ 8.1m Sep 6] IR 15,000Y: angular gelding: first foal: dam, 6f winner (also sprint winner in USA), half-sister to smart performer up to 9f Lower Egypt: modest maiden at best: seems to stay 1¼m: raced freely fifth start. *K. R. Burke*   **63 d**

ACHILLES SPIRIT (IRE)   4 b.g. Deploy 131 – Scenic Spirit (IRE) (Scenic 128) [2002 84: p12g p12g f12g³ f16g⁵ f16.2g⁶ 11.7g 12m 10m f12g² 12m 12d⁵ 12.6m Jul 20] fair performer at best: on downgrade in 2002: barely stays 2m: acts on fibresand (probably on polytrack), firm and good to soft ground: blinkered last 6 starts. *J. A. Osborne*   **68 d a76 d**

ACHILLES SUN   4 b.g. Deploy 131 – Tsungani 64 (Cure The Blues (USA)) [2002 59: p13g p16g 10.9f 12.4m² 11.9s* 11.9s³ 13v 12d 11.6m³ 11.6m 12.4g³ p12g⁶ f12g² Sep 21] close-coupled gelding: modest performer: trained by T. McCarthy first 2 starts: won claimer at Carlisle in May: stays 1½m: acts on soft going, good to firm and all-weather: reportedly bled from nose second start: sometimes looks none too keen: sold 5,600 gns. *K. R. Burke*   **56**

ACHILLES THUNDER   3 b.g. Deploy 131 – Aegean Sound 71 (Distant Relative 128) [2002 10m 10g 10s 8.1d 7.1s 12m p13g Dec 28] 3,800Y: good-topped gelding: first foal: dam 2-y-o 6f winner: well held in maidens/handicaps: unruly stall and withdrawn on intended debut at 2 yrs: slowly away third outing. *K. R. Burke*   –

ACID TEST   7 ch.g. Sharpo 132 – Clunk Click 72 (Star Appeal 133) [2002 –, a59: f6g Dec 10] good-bodied gelding: modest handicapper in 2001: well held only 7-y-o start: tried visored/blinkered. *M. A. Buckley*   –

ACOMB   2 b.g. (Feb 29) Shaamit (IRE) 127 – Aurora Bay (IRE) (Night Shift (USA)) [2002 5f 5d 5g⁶ Jul 20] good-bodied gelding: second foal: dam, no form, out of useful half-sister to high-class 1¼m performer Shady Heights: well held in maidens: should be suited by 1m+: probably capable of better. *M. W. Easterby*   **– p**

ACT

ACONITE 3 b.f. Primo Dominie 121 – Laugharne (Known Fact (USA) 135) [2002 52: –
7m 6m 6d 5.5f 8f 7f Jul 29] sparely-made filly: disappointing maiden. *C. N. Allen*

ACORAZADO (IRE) 3 b.g. Petorius 117 – Jaldi (IRE) 75 (Nordico (USA)) [2002 **79**
79p: f7g⁵ p7g f6s Dec 26] quite good-topped gelding: fair performer, lightly raced: best
effort at 3 yrs on reappearance: stays 7f: acts on soft going and fibresand. *W. J. Haggas*

ACORN CATCHER 4 b.f. Emarati (USA) 74 – Anytime Baby 56 (Bairn (USA) 126) –
[2002 –, a52: f5g² Feb 15] poor performer: best at 5f/easy 6f: acts on good to firm ground **a47**
and fibresand: visored once: sometimes gives trouble stalls: not one to trust implicitly.
M. Wigham

ACQUAINTANCE 3 b.g. Selkirk (USA) 129 – Introducing 78 (Mtoto 134) [2002 **70**
10m 11.7g⁶ Oct 16] first foal: dam, 1¼m winner in France, sister to very smart performer
up to 13.3f (also third in Derby) Presenting: better effort in maidens when never-
dangerous sixth to Nirvana at Bath: slowly away on debut. *I. A. Balding*

ACQUITAINE (USA) 3 b.f. Colonial Affair (USA) 126 – Arctic Eclipse (USA) **58**
(Northern Dancer) [2002 7g 10.2d⁵ 7g⁶ Jul 20] 20,000 2-y-o: tall, good-bodied filly: has
scope: half-sister to several winners, including useful 7f (at 2 yrs) and 1¼m winner Icy
South (by Alleged) and fairly useful 1¼m winner Arctiid (by Trempolino): dam, French
7f winner, half-sister to St Leger fourth Nemain: modest form in maidens: sold 3,000 gns
in December. *A. G. Newcombe*

ACQUITTAL (IRE) 10 b.g. Danehill (USA) 126 – Perfect Alibi (Law Society (USA) **32 §**
130) [2002 45§: 12g 10.5s⁵ 14.1g 10m 14.1m 12m 12.3m Aug 30] poor handicapper:
stays 1¾m: acts on any turf going and fibresand: blinkered once, usually visored:
ungenuine. *P. L. Clinton*

ACTIVE ACCOUNT (USA) 5 b. or br.g. Unaccounted For (USA) 124 – Ameritop **75**
(USA) (Topsider (USA)) [2002 8.2m⁶ p8g³ 8.3d p7g⁶ f8.5s* f8.5g³ Dec 26] $35,000Y,
resold IR 110,000Y: second foal: dam unraced half-sister to smart US horse up to 9f
American Chance: fair performer: has reportedly had a wind operation: won handicap at
Wolverhampton (wandered) in December: stays 8.5f: acts on all-weather: has started
slowly. *Mrs H. Dalton*

ACTIVIST 4 ch.g. Diesis 133 – Shicklah (USA) 106 (The Minstrel (CAN) 135) [2002 **81**
75: 16.1m² 16d² 14.1f* 18f 16.5g³ 12m⁴ 16g 14m 17.5g Sep 20] leggy, lengthy gelding:
fairly useful performer: won 4-runner maiden at Redcar in June: mostly below form in
handicaps after: stays 2m: acts on firm and good to soft going: won over hurdles in
September. *G. M. Moore*

ACT ONE 3 gr.c. In The Wings 128 – Summer Sonnet (Baillamont (USA) 124) **124**
[2002 116p: 10.5g* 10.5g* 12m² Jun 2]
     The closing stages of the Prix du Jockey Club at Chantilly turned out to be a
pivotal moment in the latest French season. The colt who had looked the best of his
generation in France through the spring, the then-unbeaten Act One, quickened into
what briefly seemed a race-winning lead before Sulamani cut him down and, in the
process, took over Act One's mantle as France's top three-year-old. Act One never
had the opportunity to regain his position and, given that Act One's length and a
half defeat at Chantilly represented the best effort of his short career, it was very
probable that he still had improvement in him at the time; the second half of the
year was certainly the poorer without him.
     Although he had Englishmen as both his owner-breeder and his trainer, the
Epsom Derby had never figured in plans for Act One. 'In no circumstances will he
run at Epsom,' Gerald Leigh had stated as early as January. Instead, Act One was
directed to Chantilly, taking in two of the well-established French Derby trials at
Longchamp on the way, the Prix Greffulhe in April and the Prix Lupin in May. Act
One had looked a potential classic contender when winning all three of his starts as
a two-year-old, his breeding virtually guaranteeing him staying a mile and a half.
His final win at two had come in the inaugural Criterium International at Saint-
Cloud where his defeat of the subsequent Poule d'Essai des Poulains winner
Landseer had prevented a clean sweep of that year's ten Group 1 races for two-year-
old colts by Aidan O'Brien-trained horses.
     Act One did not need to improve on his two-year-old form to make a
successful reappearance against four rivals in the Prix Greffulhe and he won in
authoritative style by two and a half lengths from Caesarion. The Group 1 Prix
Lupin four weeks later was a sterner test, though Act One again did not have to be

27

*Prix Lupin, Longchamp—Act One settles matters early in the straight
and extends his unbeaten record to five; Secret Singer is second*

asked any serious questions to extend his unbeaten record. Racing with plenty of zest, he settled matters early in the straight and ran out a two-length winner from the outsider Secret Singer. Caesarion was only fifth this time, while Ballingarry, much the best horse in the field barring the winner, gave the impression that something was amiss in finishing a well-beaten sixth. Act One had earned his place as favourite for the Prix du Jockey Club, though whether he was entitled to start odds on was another matter. He was not the only improving colt in the line-up, that was for sure, and he lost little caste in defeat in going down to an even more progressive rival in Sulamani, one who went on to prove himself top class by the autumn. Later in June, Act One was being prepared for the Irish Derby and a clash with High Chaparral when he suffered a hairline fracture to a hind cannon bone, bringing an abrupt end to his career. The injury was sustained just days after the death of his owner-breeder Gerald Leigh.

		Sadler's Wells	Northern Dancer
	In The Wings	(b 1981)	Fairy Bridge
	(b 1986)	High Hawk	Shirley Heights
Act One		(b 1980)	Sunbittern
(gr.c. 1999)		Baillamont	Blushing Groom
	Summer Sonnet	(b 1982)	Lodeve
	(gr 1991)	Noesis	Persepolis
		(gr 1986)	Proskona

Leigh had forthright views on the bloodstock industry and he had stipulated a number of conditions relating to Act One's future stallion career, principally that Act One should stand in England and not be employed on a dual-hemisphere basis. It was also Leigh's wish to restrict the number of mares in Act One's books to eighty-five in his first season and one hundred in subsequent years (there is more about Act One's owner-breeder in the essay on Gossamer). Act One has been retired to Sheikh Hamdan Al Maktoum's Nunnery Stud in Norfolk at a fee of £10,000 (October 1st), with Leigh's Eydon Hall Farm retaining shares in his syndication. Act One's pedigree was dealt with in *Racehorses of 2001*. To recap briefly, his two elder half-sisters (both by Caerleon) showed useful form, Summer Solstice winning a listed race at Deauville over an extended mile and a half and Summer Symphony finishing second in the Fillies' Mile. Further back, Act One's great grandam Proskona was a high-class six/seven-furlong performer and a half-sister to the dam of classic winners Bosra Sham, Hector Protector and Shanghai. Act One's unraced two-year-old half-brother Main Event (by Machiavellian) is in training with Luca Cumani and there is a yearling close relative by Sadler's Wells, a filly named Summer Serenade. The tall, quite good-topped Act One was not the best of movers but he raced with plenty of zest. He stayed a mile and a half and acted on soft and good to firm going, the firmest he raced on. *J. E. Pease, France*

ADALEEL   3 b.c. Polar Falcon (USA) 126 – Ameerat Jumaira (USA) 64 (Alydar   **71**
(USA)) [2002 –p: 7.9g* 9.2g* 10m⁶ 7.9g⁶ 10m* 9.7m* 10.1m⁵ Sep 6] big, lengthy colt:

fair handicapper: won at Carlisle and Hamilton in May, Brighton in July and Folkestone (tended to carry head high/flash tail) in August: stays 1¼m: acts on good to firm ground, well beaten both starts on softer than good: sometimes races freely/finds little: sent to UAE. *A. C. Stewart*

ADALPOUR (IRE)   4 b.g. Kahyasi 130 – Adalya (IRE) (Darshaan 133) [2002 68: p12g³ p12g⁴ p10g 11g 10d⁴ 10g f12s 10.9m⁶ Sep 16] modest maiden: stays 1½m: acts on polytrack, raced mainly on good ground or softer on turf: has worn tongue strap: sometimes slowly away. *Miss J. Feilden*   **59**

ADAMANT JAMES (IRE)   3 b.g. Sri Pekan (USA) 117 – Classic Romance 79 (Cadeaux Genereux 131) [2002 8m 7g⁶ 8.3m 6d⁴ 8d 8.3g 6g Oct 28] 2,000Y: first foal: dam, 2-y-o 7f winner, should have stayed beyond 1¼m: poor maiden: seems to stay 7f: free-going sort: failed to handle home turn at Southwell second start, looked wayward fifth outing: gelded after final appearance. *T. D. McCarthy*   **48**

ADAMAS (IRE)   5 b.m. Fairy King (USA) – Corynida (USA) (Alleged (USA) 138) [2002 64d: 6f 7g 7m 7m 7f 8.3m* p10g f8.5s Dec 26] good-quartered mare: modest handicapper: won at Hamilton in September: effective at 1m to 1½m: best on good going or firmer: withdrawn after being unruly in stall intended fifth outing. *Andrew Turnell*   **50**

ADAMS ALE   3 b.f. Mistertopogigo (IRE) 118 – Knayton Lass 94 (Presidium 124) [2002 –: 8.5d Aug 14] leggy filly: well held in maidens/claimer: dead. *J. M. Jefferson*   **–**

ADANTINO   3 b.g. Glory of Dancer 121 – Sweet Whisper 63 (Petong 126) [2002 60: 8.2d³ 7.1f² 6d⁴ 7.1s 6.1d 7d⁴ 6m³ 7m³ 7d 6m Sep 23] smallish, compact gelding: fair maiden handicapper: barely stays 7f: acts on firm and good to soft going. *B. R. Millman*   **71**

ADDEYLL   3 ch.c. Efisio 120 – Rohita (IRE) 94 (Waajib 121) [2002 88: 7s 7.5m 9m 8g³ 8d Jun 15] small, sturdy colt: fairly useful handicapper: stayed 1m: was probably best on good ground or firmer: raced up with pace: dead. *M. R. Channon*   **80**

ADDITION   6 b.m. Dilum (USA) 115 – Cedar Lady (Telsmoss 91) [2002 49: 8.5d⁴ p10g³ Jul 20] modest performer: stayed easy 1¼m: acted on firm going, good to soft and polytrack: dead. *B. G. Powell*   **51**

ADEKSHAN (IRE)   2 ch.c. (Mar 23) Mark of Esteem (IRE) 137 – Adaiyka (IRE) 110 (Doyoun 124) [2002 7m* 8m⁶ Oct 12] third foal: half-brother to smart 7f (at 2 yrs) to 1¼m winner Adilabad (by Gulch): dam French 9f (including at 2 yrs)/1¼m winner: fairly useful form when winning 5-runner maiden at Yarmouth in September by 1¾ lengths from Franklins Gardens, leading over 1f out: again well backed, tailed-off last of 6 in listed race at Ascot: will stay at least 1m: worth another chance to show himself capable of better. *Sir Michael Stoute*   **88 p**

ADELPHI BOY (IRE)   6 ch.g. Ballad Rock 122 – Toda 53 (Absalom 128) [2002 67, a96d: f8s⁵ f11s p8g 13.8d⁶ 16m 10m 10m⁵ May 10] workmanlike gelding: poor mover: fair handicapper on all-weather, modest on turf: effective at 1m, seemingly at easy 2m: acts on all-weather, soft and good to firm going: sometimes slowly away: none too consistent. *M. C. Chapman*   **54 a65**

ADELPHI KNIGHT (IRE)   3 b.g. Desert Style (IRE) 121 – Sceal Siog (IRE) (Fairy King (USA)) [2002 f5g f12g Mar 21] IR 13,000F, IR 11,000Y, 5,500 2-y-o: first foal: dam, placed over jumps in Ireland, half-sister to smart Irish sprinter Fundraiser: always behind in maidens. *M. C. Chapman*   **–**

ADELPHI THEATRE (USA)   5 b.g. Sadler's Wells (USA) 132 – Truly Bound (USA) (In Reality) [2002 93: 14.1m⁵ 14d 10d Oct 14] good-topped gelding: fairly useful performer: stays 1¾m: acts on good to firm going, possibly not on softer than good: blinkered once. *R. Rowe*   **86**

ADEPT   3 b.f. Efisio 120 – Prancing 98 (Prince Sabo 123) [2002 71: 6.1f 7d f7f f5g⁶ f6g Dec 27] quite good-topped filly: fair maiden at 2 yrs: just modest in 2002 (left J. Hetherton after reappearance): should stay 7f: best effort on heavy ground. *C. W. Fairhurst*   **58**

ADHAABA (USA)   2 b. or br.f. (Feb 17) Dayjur (USA) 137 – Girchoop (USA) (Storm Cat (USA)) [2002 6s⁴ Oct 25] smallish filly: first foal: dam unraced sister to useful sprinter Elrafa Ah, herself dam of Dewhurst winner Mujahid: 8/1, 7 lengths fourth of 15 to Gilded Edge in maiden at Newbury, shuffled back early, switched widest of all and keeping on well: sure to improve. *M. P. Tregoning*   **76 p**

ADHATO   2 b.c. (May 22) Bandmaster (USA) 97 – Time To Move (IRE) (Cyrano de Bergerac 120) [2002 6.1d 5m 6g f7g 8.2v Oct 29] second foal: dam unraced half-sister to useful sprinter Miss Stamper: poor maiden. *W. G. M. Turner*   **40 a48**

Littlewoods Bet Direct On 0800 329393 Winter Derby, Lingfield—
Adiemus (nearest camera) justifies favouritism, nosing ahead near the line;
the grey Laissezaller and I Cried For You also help to provide a good finish

ADIEMUS 4 b.g. Green Desert (USA) 127 – Anodyne 100 (Dominion 123) [2002 87: **96 +**
p10g³ p10g* p10g* p10g* p10g* 8s² Mar 23] useful-looking gelding: useful performer: **a108**
much improved early in year, winning 2 handicaps, minor event and listed race (by short
head from Laissezaller), all at Lingfield: 5/2 favourite, strong-finishing head second to
Zucchero in Lincoln Handicap at Doncaster final start (subsequently gelded): reportedly
suffered setback in May: stays 1¼m: acts on polytrack and probably any turf going:
sometimes wanders/idles. *J. Noseda*

ADIOS AMIGO 3 ch.g. Efisio 120 – Los Alamos 73 (Keen 116) [2002 7.5g 7.1s 7.1m **45**
7.9s 8s⁶ 8.3v 10g 16.1m Oct 2] lengthy, workmanlike gelding: second foal: dam 1¾m/15f
winner: poor maiden: tongue tied final start.

ADIRIKA (IRE) 3 b.f. Miswaki (USA) 124 – Adaiyka (IRE) 110 (Doyoun 124) [2002 **81**
7g 9.9m³ 11.9g² 11.7g Oct 16] strong, lengthy, good sort: second foal: closely related to
smart 7f (at 2 yrs) to 1¼m winner Adilabad (by Gulch): dam French 9f (including at 2
yrs)/1¼m winner: fairly useful form in maidens, head second to Extremist at Brighton:
not certain to stay beyond 1½m: visored (raced freely/folded tamely) final start. *Sir
Michael Stoute*

ADJAWAR (IRE) 4 b.g. Ashkalani (IRE) 128 – Adjriyna 82 (Top Ville 129) [2002 **87**
99: p12g 10g 12m 11.9d* 10m² 10m³ 11.9g² 12m* 11.9m³ 13.3f⁶ Sep 21] good-topped
gelding: fairly useful performer: left C. Dwyer after third start: won minor event at
Brighton (hung left down camber) in July and 4-runner handicap at Epsom (made all) in
August: stays 1½m: acts on firm and good to soft going: looked none too resolute in visor
last 2 outings at 3 yrs: tried tongue tied: reportedly had breathing problem second start.
H. Morrison

ADJIRAM (IRE) 6 b.g. Be My Guest (USA) 126 – Adjriyna 82 (Top Ville 129) [2002 **36 +**
–: 12m⁴ 12m⁶ Jun 28] well-made gelding: fair winner in France in 1999: poor nowadays:
stays 1½m. *D. C. O'Brien*

ADJUDICATOR (IRE) 4 br.g. Barathea (IRE) 127 – Mnaafa (IRE) 70 (Darshaan **43**
133) [2002 67d: f7s f6g p7g⁵ p7g⁶ f12g 7m 8f May 13] poor maiden: stays 7f: acts on
all-weather, raced only on ground firmer than good on turf: tried visored: reportedly had
breathing problem fourth start. *Mrs K. Walton*

ADMIRAL COLLINS (IRE)   2 b.g. (Mar 16) Sadler's Wells (USA) 132 – Kanmary   **83**
(FR) 117 (Kenmare (FR) 125) [2002 7.2s⁴ 8s⁴ 8s⁴ Nov 6] good-topped gelding: brother to
very smart 1998 Racing Post Trophy winner Commander Collins (later stayed 1½m) and
closely related to several winners, notably Breeders' Cup Sprint winner Lit de Justice and
Derby third Colonel Collins (both by El Gran Senor): dam, won 5f Prix du Bois at 2 yrs,
stayed 9f: best effort in maidens (fairly useful form) when 2½ lengths fourth to Midas
Way at Newbury second start: bred to be suited by further than 1m, but will need to
become more tractable: very slowly away on debut: carries head awkwardly: gelded after
final outing. *J. H. M. Gosden*

ADMIRAL FITZROY (USA)   2 ch.c. (Apr 10) Hennessy (USA) 122 – Dorothy   **63**
Dear (USA) (Foolish Pleasure (USA)) [2002 7g⁶ 6g 7.1g Sep 12] $5,500Y, resold
35,000Y: half-brother to several winners in USA, including stakes-placed winner up to 6f
(including at 2 yrs) Not Now Bert (by Wild Again): dam unraced half-sister to Breeders'
Cup Turf second Sunshine Forever: modest maiden: should stay 1m. *E. A. L. Dunlop*

ADMIRALS PLACE (IRE)   6 ch.g. Perugino (USA) 84 – Royal Daughter (High
Top 131) [2002 83, a81: p12g p10g Mar 2] close-coupled gelding: fairly useful handicapper at best: well held both 6-y-o starts. *H. J. Collingridge*

ADOBE   7 b.g. Green Desert (USA) 127 – Shamshir 116 (Kris 135) [2002 90, a?: f7g⁶   **84 d**
f8.5g² f8.5g³ 8d 8d³ 8g 8m³ 7.9m³ 8g⁴ 8f⁴ 8d³ 8.5g³ 8f⁵ 8g 7.6f 8m³ 8m 8m p7g   **a70 d**
f8.5g f8.5s Dec 7] small, stocky gelding: fairly useful performer: on downgrade in 2002:
effective at 7f to easy 9f: acts on fibresand, firm and good to soft going, not on softer: used
to wear tongue strap: sometimes races too freely: usually waited with. *W. M. Brisbourne*

ADOPTED HERO (IRE)   2 b.c. (Apr 16) Sadler's Wells (USA) 132 – Lady Liberty   **–**
(NZ) (Noble Bijou (USA)) [2002 8.2v Oct 29] brother to 3-y-o Majority Rule and half-
brother to 3 winners, including smart 1996 2-y-o 7f/1m winner Equal Rights (by Royal
Academy): dam Australian Group 1 1½m winner: 5/1, very slowly away and always well
behind in Nottingham maiden. *J. H. M. Gosden*

ADRIANA   5 b.m. Tragic Role (USA) – Beatle Song 70 (Song 132) [2002 43+: f8s 8d   **38**
10.1f⁴ 10.9m Aug 26] poor performer: stays 11.5f: acts on firm ground and polytrack:
blinkered last 5 starts: has wandered. *C. E. Brittain*

ADRIANS PRIDE   3 ch.f. Keen 116 – Pride's Desire 41 (Grey Desire 115) [2002 7.5g   **–**
6m Jun 19] workmanlike filly: second foal: dam seemed of little account: tailed off in
maidens. *N. Wilson*

ADSTONE BLAZE   3 ch.f. Selkirk (USA) 129 – Galine 91 (Most Welcome 131)   **54**
[2002 55: 8.2d³ 7.5m 8g f8s Sep 5] tall, lengthy filly: modest maiden handicapper: should
stay 1¼m: acts on fibresand and good to soft going: sold 4,200 gns, sent to Saudi Arabia.
B. Smart

ADUKA (IRE)   6 b.g. Pursuit of Love 124 – Nsx 74 (Roi Danzig (USA)) [2002 6.9d   **–**
8m 7g Aug 23] first foal: dam 2-y-o 5f winner: no form. *A. C. Whillans*

ADVENTURIST   2 ch.g. (May 15) Entrepreneur 123 – Alik (FR) 113 (Targowice   **75 p**
(USA) 130) [2002 6s f8s³ Oct 8] closely related to a winner in Greece by Sadler's Wells
and half-brother to numerous winners, notably smart French 7f to 1¼m performer
Goofalik (by Lyphard): dam French 1m winner from family of Irish River: still green,
much better effort in maidens (fair form) when third to Eva Peron at Southwell, off bridle
before halfway: gelded after: will stay 1¼m: should improve further. *J. R. Fanshawe*

ADWEB   4 b.f. Muhtarram (USA) 125 – What A Present (Pharly (FR) 130) [2002 81:   **88 +**
6g 8d 6.1f³ 6.1d² 6m 6d* 6d³ 6g³ 6.1s Oct 29] tall, angular filly: poor mover: fairly useful
handicapper: won at Kempton in July: best effort when third to John O'Groats in Silver
Cup at Ayr penultimate start: best at 5f/6f: acts on soft and good to firm going, probably
on firm: sometimes slowly away (was markedly so at Ayr): best held up. *J. Cullinan*

AEGEAN DAISY   3 ch.f. Bal Harbour 13 – Dizzydaisy 57 (Sharpo 132) [2002 68d: **44 §**
p10g⁵ p10g⁴ p10g 10f 11.9g May 2] poor maiden: stays easy 1¼m: acts on good to firm
going and polytrack: sometimes blinkered: sometimes starts slowly/runs in snatches/
hangs left/flashes tail: not one to trust. *R. M. Flower*

AEGEAN LINE   2 b.f. (Apr 29) Bijou d'Inde 127 – Load Line (High Line 125) [2002   **72**
6d³ 6m⁶ 6s² 7g⁴ 7s⁶ 7.1g* Sep 23] half-sister to 2 winners, including German winner up
to 11f Amykos (by Emperor Jones): dam unraced sister to Park Hill Stakes winner Quay
Line: fair performer: won maiden at Chepstow by ½ length from Nuzzle, leading 2f out:
free-going sort, not sure to stay beyond 7f: acts on soft going. *R. Hannon*

AEGEAN MAGIC   2 b.f. (Feb 10) Wolfhound (USA) 126 – Sayulita 67 (Habitat 134)   **69**
[2002 6m⁶ 6f 5g² 6f² 6s² 6v⁶ p6g f6s⁶ p6g² p7g Dec 28] lengthy filly: eighth foal:
half-sister to Italian winner up to 13f Mr Goshawk (by Rambo Dancer) and French 1½m
winner Sayel (by Elmaamul): dam, maiden, stayed 1½m: fair maiden: bred to stay 1m:
acts on all-weather, firm and soft going. *R. Hannon*

AEGEAN MIST   2 ch.f. (Mar 17) Prince Sabo 123 – Dizzydaisy 57 (Sharpo 132)   **63**
[2002 6.1g 5m³ 5m⁴ 6d f6s f7g Dec 17] 6,200Y: fourth foal: half-sister to fairly useful   **a–**
1998 2-y-o 5f winner Aegean Flame (by Anshan) and 1½m winner Aegean Sunrise (by
Deploy): dam maiden who stayed 6f: modest maiden: left T. Easterby after fourth start:
should stay 6f: acts on good to firm going. *P. Howling*

AEGEAN SPIRIT   2 b.f. (Jan 16) Royal Applause 124 – Aegean Blue (Warning 136)   **–**
[2002 6m Jul 22] 12,000Y: first foal: dam unraced: 25/1, always behind in maiden at
Windsor. *B. J. Meehan*

AEGEAN THUNDER   2 b.g. (May 2) Amfortas (IRE) 115 – Sound Check 62   **–**
(Formidable (USA) 125) [2002 6g 7d f8.5g Nov 18] 500Y: third foal: half-brother to
3-y-o Piccolezza: dam 7f (at 2 yrs)/1m winner: well beaten in maidens. *J. White*

AFAAN (IRE)   9 ch.h. Cadeaux Genereux 131 – Rawaabe (USA) 87 (Nureyev (USA)   **74**
131) [2002 109?, a90: 6m 5m f5g f5g f5g Dec 10] big horse: poor mover: nothing like the
force of old in 2002: often blinkered/visored. *R. F. Marvin*

AFADAN (IRE)   4 br.g. Royal Academy (USA) 130 – Afasara (IRE) (Shardari 134)   **93**
[2002 79: p12g* 14.4s⁴ 12s 12d* 12d⁴ 11.9g⁵ 12g 12g Oct 17] rangy gelding: fifth foal:
half-brother to 3 winners in Ireland, including useful 1¼m/11f winner Afarad (by Slip
Anchor) and fairly useful 1½m winner Afarka (by Kahyasi): dam Irish 1¼m winner:
fairly useful performer: trained by J. Oxx in Ireland at 3 yrs: won maiden at Lingfield in
June and handicap at Newmarket in August: best effort when fifth to Spectrometer in
handicap at York in August: probably stays 1¾m: acts on polytrack, raced mainly on
good ground or softer on turf: sometimes tongue tied: sometimes slowly away/finds little.
J. R. Jenkins

AFEEF (USA)   3 br.c. Dayjur (USA) 137 – Jah (USA) (Relaunch (USA)) [2002 68:   **68**
10g⁵ 7.9g² May 10] good-topped colt: fair maiden: stays 1m: tongue tied: sold 12,000 gns
in July. *E. A. L. Dunlop*

AFFAIRE D'AMOUR   3 ch.f. Hernando (FR) 127 – Entente Cordiale (USA)   **100**
(Affirmed (USA)) [2002 50p: 12d² f14.8g* f16.2f* 16.4g* 16m 16.1m⁵ 16s* 15.5v f16g²
Dec 4] leggy, quite good-topped filly: useful performer: won handicaps at Wolverhampton (2) and Folkestone (idled) in August and Musselburgh (quite valuable event) in
November, 2 of them apprentice events: best effort when 7 lengths seventh to Al Nowhere
in listed race at Saint-Cloud penultimate start: stays 2m: acts on fibresand and heavy
going (found little both starts on good to firm). *Sir Mark Prescott*

AFFAIRE ROYALE (IRE)   4 b.f. Royal Academy (USA) 130 – Fleet Amour (USA)   **94**
(Afleet (CAN)) [2002 95: 9g⁶ 7m 6m² 7.1m⁵ 6d² 6m³ 6m² 6m Sep 18] tall, lengthy,
useful-looking filly: fairly useful performer: 4¾ lengths third of 4 to Three Points in listed
race at Newmarket sixth start: raced mainly at 6f/7f: acted on good to firm going, possibly
not on good to soft: tongue tied after second outing: often looked less than keen: stud.
J. R. Fanshawe

AFFRAY (USA)   3 b.c. Affirmed (USA) – Wee Miss Bee (USA) (Shelter Half (USA))   **85 §**
[2002 83: 10m 11.8m⁵ 10d³ 11.7d* 11.9g³ 14m³ 13v³ 12g 16.4g 14.4g⁶ 12d f12s² f12g⁴
Oct 17] angular colt: fairly useful performer: won minor event at Bath in June: probably
stays 2m: acts on fibresand, heavy and good to firm going: blinkered ninth to twelfth
starts: sometimes runs in snatches/finds little: ungenuine: sold 16,000 gns. *M. Johnston*

AFRICA (IRE)   5 b.m. Namaqualand (USA) – Tannerrun (IRE) 65 (Runnett 125)   **–**
[2002 –, a51: f14.8g Apr 8] sturdy mare: well held only Flat start in 2002: blinkered once.
A. Streeter

AFRICAN SAHARA (USA)   3 br.c. El Gran Senor (USA) 136 – Able Money   **82**
(USA) (Distinctive (USA)) [2002 78: 10m 8m³ 9.7m² 10m⁴ 12f⁶ 10f⁴ 9g⁶ 8g³ 7s Nov 2]
useful-looking colt: fairly useful maiden: left E. Dunlop 3,200 gns after reappearance and
Mrs D. Haine after fourth start: effective at 1m/1¼m: raced mainly on good going or
firmer: tongue tied: sometimes slowly away. *G. C. H. Chung*

AFRICAN SPUR (IRE)   2 b.c. (Mar 4) Flying Spur (AUS) – African Bloom (African   **73**
Sky 124) [2002 5d 5g* 6s⁵ 5m* 6d 6m³ f5s⁴ Sep 17] IR 5,000F, 4,200Y, 7,200 2-y-o:
deep-girthed colt: half-brother to 2 winners, including 5f (at 2 yrs) to 1¼m winner
Falcons Dawn (by Exhibitioner): dam Irish 7f winner: fair performer: won seller at

Leicester (hung right) in July and nursery at Musselburgh in August: effective at 5f/6f:
acts on fibresand, soft and good to firm going: pulled up (reportedly lost shoe/pulled
muscles in back) on debut. *R. Wilman*

AFTERJACKO (IRE)   6 ch.g. Seattle Dancer (USA) 119 – Shilka (Soviet Star   –
(USA) 128) [2002 –: 16m Apr 20] big, lengthy gelding: useful handicapper at 4 yrs:
soundly beaten both outings since. *D. R. C. Elsworth*

AGILIS (IRE)   2 b.g. (Apr 11) Titus Livius (FR) 115 – Green Life 63 (Green Desert   **89**
(USA) 127) [2002 5g 6m p6g⁴ p7g* p8g* p7g² p7g² Dec 28] fifth foal: half-brother to
3-y-o Tappit and a winning sprinter in Italy by College Chapel: dam, fourth at 7f in
Ireland at 2 yrs, half-sister to Molecomb winner Classic Ruler: fairly useful performer:
trained by K. McAuliffe on debut: won claimer (then left J. Hills) and nursery at Lingfield
in November/December: excellent second in nurseries there last 2 outings: effective at 7f/
1m: acts on polytrack, last both runs on turf. *Jamie Poulton*

AGINCOURT WARRIOR   3 b.c. Distant Relative 128 – Careful (IRE) 59 (Distinctly   –
North (USA) 115) [2002 70p: 6.1f Apr 10] good-topped colt: won maiden at Lingfield
only 2-y-o start: lost action sole outing at 3 yrs. *J. M. P. Eustace*

AGNETHA (GER)   3 ch.f. Big Shuffle (USA) 122 – Aerleona (IRE) (Caerleon   **113**
(USA) 132) [2002 98: 5s⁴ 5g³ 5d² 5g* 5g⁴ 6m⁵ 5.2f³ 5g⁵ 5m Dec 15] approx. 74,000Y in
Germany: lengthy, good-quartered filly: fifth foal: sister to smart German sprinter Areion
and half-sister to 3 winners in Germany, including useful sprinter Atalante (by Alkalde):
dam German 2-y-o 6f winner: smart performer: won King George 200th Anniversary
Stakes at Goodwood in August by short head from Rudi's Pet: creditable efforts last 2
starts in Europe when ¾-length third to Lady Dominatrix in Dubai International Airport
World Trophy at Newbury and close fifth to Continent in Prix de l'Abbaye de Longchamp: below form in Hong Kong Sprint at Sha Tin final outing: effective at 5f/6f: acts
on firm and soft going: consistent. *D. K. Weld, Ireland*

Mrs C. L. Weld's "Agnetha"

AGOODERN 2 b.c. (Mar 14) Young Ern 120 – Milly Molly Mango (Mango Express —
106) [2002 5m 6g 7g Jul 3] second foal: dam Norwegian 1m winner: tailed off in
maidens: blinkered final start. *M. A. Buckley*

AGOSTINI 3 b.g. Octagonal (NZ) 126 – Majestic Image 86 (Niniski (USA) 125) **62**
[2002 62: 11.9g⁴ 12m⁵ 14.1f 12.1g 16.2d⁵ Jul 22] smallish, sparely-made gelding: modest
maiden handicapper: stays 1½m: acts on good to firm going, possibly not on softer than
good. *T. D. Easterby*

AGRIPPINA 5 b.m. Timeless Times (USA) 99 – Boadicea's Chariot (Commanche **99**
Run 133) [2002 83: 6.1d³ 6s³ 7g 6m⁶ Jul 12] smallish, good-topped mare: unimpressive
mover: useful performer, lightly raced: best effort in 2002 when 1¼ lengths third to
Marika in listed race at Haydock second start: stays 7f: best form on good to soft/soft
ground: sometimes races freely. *W. J. Haggas*

AGUILA LOCO (IRE) 3 ch.g. Eagle Eyed (USA) 111 – Go Likecrazy 51 (Dowsing **64**
(USA) 124) [2002 60: 5d³ 5m 7m 5s f5g⁶ 5g⁵ 5m* 5f³ 5d* 5g⁵ 6.1m 6g 5f 5d Oct
14] smallish, good-topped gelding: modest handicapper: won at Redcar in July and
Doncaster in August: best at 5f: acts on firm going, good to soft and fibresand: blinkered
(raced freely) once: edgy sort (has been on toes/swished tail in preliminaries): sometimes
slowly away: usually races prominently. *E. J. Alston*

AILINCALA (IRE) 4 b.f. Pursuit of Love 124 – Diabaig 76 (Precocious 126) [2002 **71**
66: p8g² 8m⁵ 8.1m³ 8.2d* 8m 8.3m⁶ 8.1g⁵ 7.9m² 8.5d⁵ Sep 11] lengthy filly: fair
handicapper: won at Nottingham (apprentices) in May: best around 1m: acts on firm
going, good to soft and polytrack: sometimes slowly away: held up. *C. F. Wall*

AIMEE'S DELIGHT 2 b.f. (Feb 28) Robellino (USA) 127 – Lloc 79 (Absalom 128) **76**
[2002 f5s² 5g 5m* 5.2f 6g⁵ 6g⁴ 6m⁶ 6.5g⁴ 7s Oct 25] 12,000Y: strong filly: third foal:
dam, 5f winner (including at 2 yrs), half-sister to July Cup winner Compton Place: fair
performer: won maiden at Ripon in July: creditable fourth of 25 to Sharplaw Venture in
sales race at Ascot penultimate start: should stay 7f: acts on fibresand and good to firm
ground, well beaten on soft. *J. G. Given*

AIMING 2 br.f. (May 9) Highest Honor (FR) 124 – Sweeping 104 (Indian King (USA) **73**
128) [2002 6m⁴ 6m 7m³ Aug 12] half-sister to several winners, including 5-y-o Watching
and fairly useful 1½m to 2½m winner Puteri Wentworth (by Sadler's Wells): dam, 2-y-o
6f winner who stayed 9f, from very good family: fair maiden: should stay at least 1m.
R. Hannon

AINTNECESSARILYSO 4 ch.g. So Factual (USA) 120 – Ovideo 58 (Domynsky **58**
110) [2002 78: 5.1d 6m 5g 5s p5g 5g 5.1g 5m² 5m 5.1g Sep 12] workmanlike gelding:
has quick action: modest handicapper nowadays: best at 5f/6f: yet to race on heavy
ground, acts on any other turf: ran poorly in blinkers once at 2 yrs: has looked ill at ease at
Epsom/Goodwood. *J. M. Bradley*

AIR ADAIR (USA) 2 ch.f. (Jun 2) Storm Cat (USA) – Beyrouth (USA) (Alleged **93**
(USA) 138) [2002 6m⁶ 7m* 8g Sep 28] leggy, useful-looking filly: second foal: half-
sister to 3-y-o Golden Dixie: dam, useful French 1m winner and Grade 2 9f winner in
USA, half-sister to smart 1¼m performer Flame Valley: fairly useful form: won maiden
at Salisbury in September by 1¾ lengths from Tease: stiff task, 7½ lengths seventh of
10 to Soviet Song in Fillies' Mile at Ascot, racing freely: not sure to stay beyond 1m.
J. H. M. Gosden

AIR MAIL 5 b.g. Night Shift (USA) – Wizardry 83 (Shirley Heights 130) [2002 73, **56**
a100: f5s f6g⁴ f7s f5s⁵ f6g f6g³ f7g³ f6g⁶ f7g* f7g*⁷ 7g 7m 6m 5.7d⁴ 6d f5g p7g f6g⁶ f5g⁶ **a100**
f6g⁵ Dec 31] leggy gelding: useful on all-weather, modest on turf nowadays: won minor
event at Wolverhampton and handicap at Southwell, both in March: effective at 5f to 8.5f:
acts on any turf going and fibresand, tried blinkered/visored: tried blinkered/visored in
2000: occasionally wears cheekpieces. *Mrs N. Macauley*

AIR OF ESTEEM 6 b.g. Forzando 122 – Shadow Bird 70 (Martinmas 128) [2002 **52**
71d: f11s 8m f9.4s³ May 13] smallish gelding: modest handicapper nowadays: barely
stays 1¼m: acts on fibresand, good to soft and good to firm going: tried visored:
reportedly had breathing problem on reappearance: sometimes slowly away: often held
up: none too consistent: joined D. Nicholls. *P. C. Haslam*

AIR THULE (JPN) 5 gr.m. Tony Bin 134 – Ski Paradise (USA) 122 (Lyphard (USA) **113**
132) [2002 8d⁴ 6f 6g³ 6.5s² 6m 8f³ 8f Dec 15] Japanese-bred mare: dam French 7f/1m
performer: smart performer: won last 3 starts at 4 yrs, notably Grade 2 event at Hanshin:
ran well (able to dictate) on European debut when ¾-length second to May Ball in Prix

Maurice de Gheest at Deauville fourth start: well held in Sprint Cup at Haydock following month: effective at 6.5f, stays 1m: acts on firm and soft ground: has been blinkered. *Hideyuki Mori, Japan*

AIRWAVE   2 b.f. (Feb 12) Air Express (IRE) 125 – Kangra Valley 56 (Indian   **114 p**
Ridge 123) [2002 6m² 6s* 6m⁴ 6g* 6f* Oct 4]
        As a rule, Cheveley Park Stakes winners can be written up with varying degrees of enthusiasm for the classics, but not Airwave. There is every reason to feel enthusiastic about the filly, yet her prospects of being raced beyond six furlongs are virtually non-existent given her temperamental make-up, her speed and her trainer's expressed opinion that she is not even worth trying in any of the One Thousand Guineas trials over seven furlongs. Since the *Racehorses* series was founded, Sixpence in 1953 is the only other Cheveley Park winner written up as a pure sprinter, although a number of others reverted to sprint distances after being aimed at the classics, notably Marwell in 1981, Dead Certain in 1990 and Pas de Reponse in 1996.
        Airwave's performance in the Cheveley Park, sponsored by Betfair at Newmarket in October, shouldn't be underestimated since it was her first outing in pattern company, and she was up against the unbeaten Lowther Stakes winner Russian Rhythm who started at 13/8-on. Airwave was at 11/2 with the remainder of the smallest field since 1995 consisting of Lowther runner-up Danaskaya, Newmarket and Doncaster winner Ego, listed-placed Wimple and Bella Tusa, successful in two listed events. The early pace was not strong and when the tempo increased at halfway Airwave was still last. Producing a splendid turn of foot, she came through to lead approaching the final furlong and soon had the race sewn up, defeating Russian Rhythm by a length and a half with Danaskaya half a length away third. An impressive victory, though Russian Rhythm, subsequently found to have been in season, did not run up to her best. It was also the first, and last, Group 1 success for jockey Chris Rutter, whose career spanned twenty years; he retired the next day to become a stewards' secretary.
        The rest of Airwave's season was all about promise. Reportedly she was so immature in the first part of the year that she could not even be persuaded to go near

Betfair Cheveley Park Stakes, Newmarket—
Airwave (left) provides jockey Chris Rutter with a first Group 1 winner on the eve of his retirement;
odds-on Russian Rhythm is only second, blinkered Danaskaya third and Ego (right) fourth

starting stalls, and she did not make her debut until mid-July, when an unlucky second to Soviet Song when favourite in a maiden at Kempton, not getting a run and showing her inexperience. An easy victory in a Leicester maiden preceded another unfortunate run in the St Leger Yearling Stakes at Doncaster, where Airwave was beaten only a length behind Somnus after travelling really strongly and being denied a run against the stand rail on more than one occasion, eventually getting through inside the final furlong when it was too late. She made amends in the listed, and snappily-titled, Faucets First For Faucets Firth of Clyde Stakes at Ayr. Held up as usual, Airwave produced her hallmark acceleration to settle the issue in a matter of strides and beat Irresistible by a length and a half with plenty in hand.

Henry Candy reported quite a lot of interest in Airwave after the Cheveley Park but was adamant that she was not for sale. The trainer has reason to be delighted that another top sprint prospect should have turned up in his stable so soon after Kyllachy. So what are Airwave's prospects of emulating him, or Marwell, who became sprint champion with a string of majestic performances? Airwave needs to progress—Marwell was rated 124 at two—but improvement is likely and she looks a filly to follow. With luck, she will do much better than Sixpence, who was sold to the States after her juvenile season and won only three of her twenty-one starts there, none of them a stakes race. One cause for concern is that there are not many feasible options for a Group 1 winner racing over sprint distances early on as a three-year-old and none specifically for fillies—under-

Henry Candy & Partners' "Airwave"

standably, since any such race would inevitably be uncompetitive. In 2002 there were nine pattern races run over five and six furlongs in Europe up until early June and all were open to the classic crop, but most were Group 3 and penalties were the norm in all of them, for instance 9 lb for a Group 1 winner in the Prix de Saint Georges, 8 lb in the Palace House Stakes and Duke of York Stakes and 7 lb in the two Group 2s, the Temple Stakes and Prix du Gros-Chene. That makes it difficult; the lack of opportunities was one reason why Dominica, who would not have been penalised so stringently as a Group 3 winner, did not reappear until the King's Stand Stakes. The latter race involved only a 3 lb penalty for Group 1 winners while the Golden Jubilee Stakes at the same meeting had none. Either of these would be a good target for Airwave, who has raced exclusively at six furlongs but will prove at least as effective at five.

Airwave (b.f. Feb 12, 2000)	Air Express (IRE) (b 1994)	Salse (b 1985)	Topsider
			Carnival Princess
		Ibtisamm (ch 1981)	Caucasus
			Lorgnette
	Kangra Valley (ch 1991)	Indian Ridge (ch 1985)	Ahonoora
			Hillbrow
		Thorner Lane (b 1985)	Tina's Pet
			Spinner

Air Express, Airwave's sire, was not a sprinter. He showed his best form at a mile as a three-year-old when landing the Premio Parioli, the Mehl-Mulhens-Rennen and, most notably, the Queen Elizabeth II Stakes. Airwave, along with National Stakes and Weatherbys Super Sprint winner Presto Vento, come from his first crop of only twenty-three foals. His second crop of nine came from just fourteen mares and he died in October 2000, a loss to the National Stud. The 12,000 guineas paid for Airwave at Doncaster made her the fourth-most expensive of the fourteen Air Express yearlings sold that year. Speed dominates in the lower half of the pedigree. Airwave's dam Kangra Valley, a daughter of a sprinter, was an inconsistent five-furlong performer successful in a maiden race at Thirsk at two. She was named broodmare of the year by the Thoroughbred Breeders' Association after having four individual winners in 2002. The three others—Beverley Macca (by Piccolo), Kangarilla Road (by Magic Ring) and Danakim (by Emarati)—have done their winning in minor company over five and six furlongs. The well-made Airwave put up her best effort on firm going but has also won on soft. *H. Candy*

AISLE 5 b.g. Arazi (USA) 135 – Chancel (USA) 60 (Al Nasr (FR) 126) [2002 52: f8s f7s f11s f8s² f7g⁴ f8g² f8g f8g Mar 21] small gelding: poor performer: effective at 6f to 8.5f: acts on soft ground and fibresand: often blinkered: sometimes tongue tied: tends to carry head awkwardly/edge left. *S. R. Bowring* — **42**

AISLING'S DREAM (IRE) 3 ch.f. Desert King (IRE) 129 – Daftiyna (IRE) 74 (Darshaan 133) [2002 50: f6g⁶ f9.4g⁶ p8g Feb 23] little form. *S. Kirk* — **–**

AJEEL (IRE) 3 b.g. Green Desert (USA) 127 – Samheh (USA) 62 (Private Account (USA)) [2002 67p: 7s² 8g* 8m⁵ 8s⁵ 8m* 8g² a9f Dec 19] big, strong, rangy gelding: fluent mover: fairly useful performer: won handicaps at Newcastle (edged left) in May and Yarmouth (idled a bit) in July: good second to Macaw in similar event at Newmarket, then left J. Dunlop: stays 1m (well held at 9f): acts on soft and good to firm going: blinkered penultimate start. *P. L. Rudkin, UAE* — **93**

AJNAD (IRE) 8 b.g. Efisio 120 – Lotte Lenta (Gorytus (USA) 132) [2002 –: 5m Jul 28] deep-bodied gelding: one-time fairly useful handicapper on all-weather: well held both starts since 2000: was sometimes blinkered/visored: dead. *R. F. Marvin* — **–**

AJWAA (IRE) 4 ch.g. Mujtahid (USA) 118 – Nouvelle Star (AUS) (Luskin Star (AUS)) [2002 78: 6m 6m 6g⁵ 7m³ 7d 7.1g 8d 7m f8s⁶ Sep 17] smallish, sturdy gelding: modest handicapper: stays 7f: acts on soft and good to firm going: often blinkered/visored: sometimes slowly away/refuses to settle: sometimes looks none too keen: one to treat with caution: sold 3,200 gns. *J. A. Osborne* — **60 §**

AKALIM 9 b.g. Petong 126 – Tiszta Sharok 81 (Song 132) [2002 51: 7d⁴ 7.1s 7.1v Jun 14] good-topped gelding: modest handicapper, lightly raced: best at 6f//t: acts on fibresand and probably any turf going: tried blinkered/visored. *L. G. Cottrell* — **54**

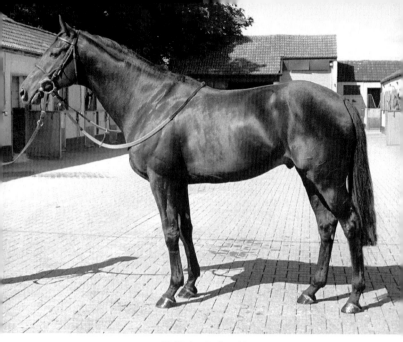

Mr Markus Graff's "Akbar"

AKBAR (IRE) 6 b. or br.h. Doyoun 124 – Akishka (Nishapour (FR) 125) [2002 118: **118**
12.3m² 13.9f⁵ 16.4m* Jun 3] sturdy horse: smart performer: 16/1, as good as ever when
winning Bonusprint Henry II Stakes at Sandown in June by ½ length from Invermark,
pair 5 lengths clear, held up, leading 1f out and holding on bravely: should stay 2½m: acts
on good to firm going, has won on soft: genuine: withdrawn from Ascot Gold Cup
(sustained suspensory ligament strain). *M. Johnston*

AKEBONO (IRE) 6 ch.g. Case Law 113 – Elanmatina (IRE) 77 (Burslem 123) [2002 **53**
52: 8.1m 9s p10g³ 8.1g p10g Sep 10] modest performer: stays 1¼m: acts on polytrack,
heavy and good to firm going: sometimes blinkered earlier in career: sometimes finds
little. *P. Burgoyne*

AKEESHA 3 b.f. Mukaddamah (USA) 125 – Butterwick Belle (IRE) 64 (Distinctly **63**
North (USA) 115) [2002 57: 7.5m* 8.2d 8g May 20] rather sparely-made filly: has
reportedly had trouble with joints: modest handicapper: won at Beverley in April: should
stay 1m: best efforts on good to firm going. *R. A. Fahey*

AKER WOOD 4 b.f. Bin Ajwaad (IRE) 119 – Wannaplantatree 72 (Niniski (USA) **86**
125) [2002 77, a65: p10g³ 10.9g p10g 12.3f* 12m² 13.3v⁴ 12g 16.1g p10g³ 12.3g³ 12m² **a70**
Aug 16] leggy, plain filly: fairly useful handicapper on turf, fair on all-weather: won
at Chester in May: effective at 1¼m/1½m: acts on firm going, soft and polytrack:
sometimes races freely: usually held up nowadays. *A. P. Jarvis*

AKRMINA 2 ch.f. (Jan 24) Zafonic (USA) 130 – Pastorale 91 (Nureyev (USA) 131) **75 p**
[2002 7.5m⁵ 6.1m³ Oct 1] good-topped filly: sister to useful 1998 2-y-o 7f winner
Kareymah and half-sister to 3 winners, including useful 1m winner Jathaabeh (by
Nashwan): dam, 7f winner from 3 starts, half-sister to high-class miler Cape Cross and
closely related to dam of Diktat: wearing crossed noseband, better effort in maidens
(modest form) when 1¾ lengths third of 12 to Bandit Queen at Nottingham, best work
late on: will stay at least 1m: should improve further. *M. A. Jarvis*

AKSHAR (IRE) 3 b.c. Danehill (USA) 126 – Akilara (IRE) 87 (Kahyasi 130) [2002 **95 p**
8m⁴ 9m* 10.5f* Sep 27] good-bodied colt: first living foal: dam, 9.6f winner from 2 starts
in Ireland, granddaughter of Arc winner Akiyda: progressive form: won maiden at
Redcar and handicap at Haydock in September, latter by 2½ lengths from Far Pavilions,
taking strong hold early, cruising into contention and not hard ridden to assert final 1f:
stays 10.5f: useful already, and likely to improve further. *Sir Michael Stoute*

AL AALI 4 b.c. Lahib (USA) 129 – Maraatib (IRE) 93 (Green Desert (USA) 127) **92**
[2002 92p: 7d 7g 6v Nov 20] good-bodied, quite attractive colt: fairly useful form, lightly
raced: ran as if something amiss on reappearance: off 5 months, creditable eighth of 30
to Lord Protector in handicap at Newmarket next time, not knocked about: sold from
J. Dunlop 34,000 gns before well held in listed race at Maisons-Laffitte final start: should
stay 1m: yet to race on ground firmer than good. *A. G. Newcombe*

ALABANG 11 ch.g. Valiyar 129 – Seleter (Hotfoot 126) [2002 77: p16g Jan 23] plain, **–**
quite good-topped gelding: fair handicapper at best: well held only run in 2002. *C. G. Cox*

ALAFZAR (IRE) 4 b.g. Green Desert (USA) 127 – Alasana (IRE) (Darshaan 133) **84**
[2002 71: f9.4g p10g 8.3g⁴ 8d 7m p8g* p7g 8.3m 7f² 7m* 6m 7m* 7.6f⁵ 7m⁶ 7f⁴ 7f Oct
5] lengthy gelding: fairly useful handicapper: won at Lingfield in May and Yarmouth/
Chester in August: best form at 7f/1m: acts on firm going, good to soft and polytrack:
tongue tied: sent to UAE. *P. D. Evans*

ALAMSHAR (IRE) 2 b.c. (Apr 18) Key of Luck (USA) 126 – Alaiyda (USA) 84 **112 p**
(Shahrastani (USA) 135) [2002 8f* 8d* Oct 13]
    The same owner/breeder (the Aga Khan), trainer (John Oxx) and jockey
(Johnny Murtagh) is not all that the promising Alamshar has in common with the
top three-year-old of 2000 Sinndar. Alamshar, like Sinndar, had just two outings in
his first season, both of them over a mile; and he too made a successful debut
in a maiden and followed up by winning a pattern race at the Curragh by a head.
For Alamshar to go on and match Sinndar's achievements at three would surely
be too much to expect, but it isn't beyond the bounds of possibility. The form of
Alamshar's win in the Group 3 Juddmonte Beresford Stakes is better, in our
opinion, than that of Sinndar's in the Group 1 National Stakes and, as with the latter
at the same stage, Alamshar looks open to a good deal of improvement.

*Juddmonte Beresford Stakes, the Curragh—Alamshar edges out Brian Boru (far side),
ending Aidan O'Brien's six-year stranglehold on the race*

Murtagh took the mount on Alamshar in a maiden at Listowel in September only after the withdrawal of former stable-companion New South Wales, now with Godolphin, who was also due to make his debut in that event. Easy in the market, Alamshar came from off the pace to take command in the final furlong and win by two lengths. He left that form well behind in the Beresford, thanks in no small part to the more testing ground which placed the emphasis very much on stamina. Preferred by Murtagh to a more exposed maiden winner, Adalar, also owned by the Aga Khan and trained by Oxx, Alamshar faced nine rivals at the Curragh, four of them attempting to give trainer Aidan O'Brien a seventh consecutive victory in the event. The O'Brien team included Brian Boru, winner of a maiden at the Curragh on his only previous start, and he was sent off favourite at 2/1, with Alamshar a 7/1-shot. Brian Boru looked the likely winner when taking up the running going into the final furlong, but Alamshar, niggled along towards the rear for much of the way, was starting to warm to his task and, staying on very strongly, he collared Brian Boru in the last strides, the pair finishing two lengths clear. What looked a good performance at the time by Alamshar looked even better in the light of Brian Boru's victory in the Racing Post Trophy, and it is no surprise that Alamshar figures prominently in the betting for the Derby, a race his owner has won with Shergar, Shahrastani, Kahyasi and Sinndar.

Alamshar (IRE) (b.c. Apr 18, 2000)	Key of Luck (USA) (b 1991)	Chief's Crown (b 1982)	Danzig Six Crowns
		Balbonella (b or br 1984)	Gay Mecene Bamieres
	Alaiyda (USA) (ch 1991)	Shahrastani (ch 1983)	Nijinsky Shademah
		Aliysa (b 1986)	Darshaan Alannya

Alamshar's dam Alaiyda ran five times and showed fairly useful form at three for Oxx, winning a mile and a quarter maiden at Roscommon and finishing a good third in the Leopardstown November Handicap run over two miles. Alaiyda was one of four foals produced by Aliysa, who died in 1994, and all are winners, the best of them the smart Desert Story who won the Horris Hill Stakes and the Craven Stakes and is now at stud. Aliysa herself won two races including the Oaks Trial at Lingfield, but she is best known for her 'victory' in the Oaks itself which was overturned nearly eighteen months after the event, a routine test revealing traces of camphor in her system. The next dam Alannya won twice over a mile in France where she was also placed in Group 3 company over an extended mile and a quarter. Alamshar is the fifth foal of Alaiyda and her second winner, his half-sister Alaya (by Ela-Mana-Mou) having shown fairly useful form when successful in an apprentice race over a mile and a half at the Curragh on the second of her two starts. Alamshar's sire Key of Luck, closely related to Anabaa and a useful sprinter/miler when trained in France, proved a revelation upped in trip and raced on dirt in Dubai as a five-year-old. On the day that Cigar won the Dubai World Cup, Key of Luck, also racing over a mile and a quarter, posted a faster time in taking the Dubai Duty Free by twenty lengths, making all. A step up to a mile and a quarter will suit Alamshar well, and he is likely to prove even better at a mile and a half. With that in mind, he has to be one for the Derby shortlist. *J. Oxx, Ireland*

ALAM (USA) 3 b.g. Silver Hawk (USA) 123 – Ghashtah (USA) (Nijinsky (CAN) 138) [2002 77P: 10.5d 12.1d³ 10d⁴ 9.2s⁶ Aug 20] fair maiden: left E. Dunlop 10,000 gns after second start: will probably stay 1½m: raced only on good to soft/soft going. *P. Monteith* — **75**

ALAN'S PRINCE (IRE) 4 b.g. Anita's Prince 126 – Fandangerina (USA) (Grey Dawn II 132) [2002 –: 7d p7g Jul 17] seems of little account. *B. Palling* — **–**

ALASHAAN 3 b.f. Darshaan 133 – Alessia 91 (Caerleon (USA) 132) [2002 8f⁶ 9.9m³ 12s³ 12.3m² 12.1g⁵ 10s⁴ Oct 26] smallish filly: second foal: half-sister to 4-y-o Patavellian: dam, 2-y-o 7f winner who stayed 1¼m, sister to Park Hill winner Casey: fair maiden: stays 1½m: acts on firm and soft going: twice fractious in stall: consistent. *B. W. Hills* — **73**

ALASHA (IRE) 3 ch.f. Barathea (IRE) 127 – Alasana (IRE) (Darshaan 133) [2002 89p: 7m⁴ 8m³ 8s 8f* 10d² Sep 29] well-made filly: has scope: fluent mover: smart — **115**

H.H. Aga Khan's "Alasha"

performer: landed odds in 6-runner listed race at Bath in August impressively by 6 lengths from Mamounia: also in frame in 2002 in Nell Gwyn Stakes and 1000 Guineas (hung fire briefly when beaten 2 necks by Kazzia), both at Newmarket, and very slowly-run E. P. Taylor Stakes at Woodbine (best effort, went down by a length to Fraulein despite carrying head high): stays 1¼m: acts on firm and good to soft going, possibly unsuited by soft. *Sir Michael Stoute*

ALASIL (USA) 2 b.c. (Feb 15) Swain (IRE) 134 – Asl (USA) 114 (Caro 133) [2002 **89** 8m² 8m² 8f* 10g⁴ Oct 14] good-topped colt: fifth living foal: half-brother to useful 1½m winner Labibeh (by Lyphard) and fairly useful 7f winner Zihaam (by Dayjur): dam, 7f (at 2 yrs) and 11f winner (also second in Oaks d'Italia), sister to Prix Saint-Alary winner Smuggly: fairly useful performer: landed odds in 4-runner maiden at Pontefract in September: well-backed favourite, creditable fourth to Summerland in minor event at Leicester, though unable to sustain effort after racing freely: bred to stay 1½m: raced only on good going or firmer. *J. L. Dunlop*

ALASSIO (USA) 4 b. or br.f. Gulch (USA) – Royal Ballerina (IRE) 117 (Sadler's **90 ?** Wells (USA) 132) [2002 87: 10s 10.4f May 15] $500,000Y: good-topped filly: second foal: dam, winner up to 1½m and second in Oaks/Irish Oaks, closely related to high-class winner up to 1½m Free Guest: seemingly fairly useful performer: won maiden at Ballinrobe at 3 yrs: possibly flattered when seventh to Rebelline in listed event at the Curragh on reappearance: blinkered, raced freely when last in similar event at York next time: stays 1¼m: acts on good to firm ground, probably on heavy. *M. J. Grassick, Ireland*

ALASTAIR SMELLIE 6 ch.g. Sabrehill (USA) 120 – Reel Foyle (USA) 77 (Irish **63 §** River (FR) 131) [2002 67§: f6g f5g 5s* f5g 5m 6s⁶ 5g⁶ 6g 5d p7g 5d p7g⁵ p7g Dec 18] **a50 §** good-topped gelding: has a quick action: modest handicapper: won at Newcastle in April: left D. Nicholls after ninth start: effective at 5f to 7f: acts on firm and soft going, probably

41

on polytrack: usually visored nowadays: sometimes slowly away (refused to race once): flashes tail: has refused to go in stall: unreliable. *S. L. Keightley*

AL AWWAM   3 b.g. Machiavellian (USA) 123 – Just A Mirage 76 (Green Desert (USA) 127) [2002 9d 9.2m⁵ 10s Oct 15] big, useful-looking gelding: has scope: fifth foal: brother to 7f performers Kahal (very smart) and Doomna (useful), and half-brother to 1m/9f winner Sawwaah (by Marju): dam maiden who stayed 1m: well held in maidens: reportedly had breathing problem on debut, and subsequently sold from E. Dunlop 4,500 gns. *W. M. Brisbourne*   –

AL AZHAR   8 b.g. Alzao (USA) 117 – Upend 120 (Main Reef 126) [2002 79: p13g 12.3g* 12.4g³ 11.9g* 12g² 12g* 11.9g⁵ 12s Oct 26] well-made gelding: has reportedly had knee trouble: fair performer: won handicap at Ripon in April, minor event at Carlisle in May and handicap at Thirsk in June: stays 1½m: acts on fibresand, heavy and good to firm going: sometimes starts slowly: usually patiently ridden. *M. Dods*   **79 a63**

ALBANIA   3 ch.g. Selkirk (USA) 129 – Elaine's Honor (USA) (Chief's Crown (USA)) [2002 75: 8f 6g* p7g 6g p7g⁴ 6m Aug 16] good-topped gelding: fairly useful handi-capper: won at Hamilton in May: well below form after: stays 6f: acts on firm and good to soft ground (well held 2 starts on polytrack): visored final 2-y-o start: sent to UAE. *M. R. Channon*   **84**

ALBANOVA   3 gr.f. Alzao (USA) 117 – Alouette 105 (Darshaan 133) [2002 75P: 10d* 10.2g* 12m⁵ Sep 15] rather leggy, close-coupled filly: smart form: won first 3 starts, namely maiden at Haydock at 2 yrs, and minor event at Pontefract and listed race at Chepstow (by ½ length from Salim Toto, racing freely after slow start then finishing strongly) both impressively in July: shade edgy, creditable 5 lengths fifth to Pearly Shells in Prix Vermeille at Longchamp final start: stays 1½m: yet to race on firm going, probably acts on any other. *Sir Mark Prescott*   **113**

Miss K. Rausing's "Albanova"

ALBANOV (IRE) 2 b.c. (Feb 6) Sadler's Wells (USA) 132 – Love For Ever (IRE) **83**
(Darshaan 133) [2002 7m 8m³ 8s³ 8v² Nov 8] 150,000Y: quite good-topped colt: first
foal: dam, French 1m and 9.5f winner, out of smart performer up to 1½m Fleur
d'Oranger: fairly useful maiden: best efforts when third at Goodwood (behind Itemise)
and Leicester (10 lengths behind Allergy): will be suited by 1½m+. *J. L. Dunlop*

ALBANY (IRE) 2 ch.g. (Apr 17) Alhaarth (IRE) 126 – Tochar Ban (USA) 83 (Assert **76**
134) [2002 6g 6d⁴ 6d³ 7m⁶ 6f 7s² 7v Nov 9] strong gelding: has scope: fifth foal:
half-brother to French 1999 2-y-o 1m winner Uncharted Haven (by Turtle Island), later
US Grade 2 1m winner: fair maiden: best effort when length second to
Star Vega in nursery at Doncaster in October: will stay at least 1m: acts on soft going:
gelded after final outing. *Mrs J. R. Ramsden*

ALBARAN (GER) 9 b.h. Sure Blade (USA) 130 – Araqueen (GER) (Konigsstuhl **105**
(GER)) [2002 112: 8g³ 9.8m³ 12s⁴ 11v⁶ 12g⁴ 9m 12g⁴ 12g⁵ Sep 29] tall, quite attractive
horse: second foal: dam, 1m and 1½m winner in Germany, third in Group 3 event: smart
performer at best, still useful in 2002: several creditable efforts in listed/pattern company,
including fourth in Scandinavian Open Championship at Copenhagen and Stockholm
Cup International at Taby fifth/seventh stars (had won both races in 1999): tongue tied,
last of 5 in Cumberland Lodge Stakes at Ascot final outing: stays 1¾m: acts on any
ground. *Ms C. Erichsen, Norway*

ALBAREQ (USA) 2 b.c. (Jan 23) Kingmambo (USA) 125 – Northern Hilite (CAN) **92 p**
(Vice Regent (CAN)) [2002 7m³ 7d⁴ 8m* 8.1g⁴ Oct 5] $1,200,000Y: robust, attractive
colt: second foal: closely related to a winner in USA by Carson City: dam Canadian 6f
and 8.5f winner, including minor stakes at 2 yrs: fairly useful performer: landed odds in
maiden at Kempton (by 2 lengths from Doc Watson) in September: creditable fourth in
minor event at Sandown final start: will stay 1¼m: tongue tied last 2 starts: sent to UAE:
looks type to make a better 3-y-o. *M. P. Tregoning*

ALBASHOOSH 4 b.g. Cadeaux Genereux 131 – Annona (USA) 72 (Diesis 133) **95**
[2002 84: 8s 6f⁶ 6g⁴ 7g 7m* 7m 7g² 6g 6g 8g⁵ Oct 18] quite good-topped gelding: useful
handicapper: better than ever when winning 22-runner event at York (beat Hurricane
Floyd 1¼ lengths) in July: unlucky second to Stormville at Newcastle in August: needs
further than 6f and stays 1m: acts on soft and good to firm going: blinkered/visored 3
times, racing freely on each occasion. *J. S. Goldie*

ALBA STELLA 2 b. or gr.f. (Feb 27) Nashwan (USA) 135 – Alouette 105 (Darshaan **70 p**
133) [2002 7m⁶ 7g 8s Oct 25] leggy, unfurnished filly: fifth foal: half-sister to very smart
7f (at 2 yrs) and 1¼m (dual Champion Stakes winner) Alborada and 3-y-o Albanova
(both by Alzao), and to fairly useful 11.6f winner Alakananda (by Hernando): dam, Irish
1m (at 2 yrs) and 1½m winner, half-sister to very smart 1¼m filly Last Second and smart
stayer Alleluia: never dangerous or knocked about in maidens: fair form when eighth of
22 to Richemaur at Doncaster final start: will be suited by 1¼m+: sure to do better. *Sir
Mark Prescott*

ALBAVILLA 2 b.f. (May 6) Spectrum (IRE) 126 – Lydia Maria 70 (Dancing Brave **69 p**
(USA) 140) [2002 7s³ Oct 25] well-made filly: half-sister to 3 winners, including useful
6f (at 2 yrs) and 10.4f winner Premier Bay (by Primo Dominie): dam, maiden who stayed
1¼m, sister to dam of smart sprinter Primo Valentino: 6/1, backward and green, 3½
lengths third of 12 to Kris Kin in maiden at Doncaster, keeping on despite wandering:
sure to improve. *P. W. Harris*

ALBERICH (IRE) 7 b.g. Night Shift (USA) – Tetradonna (IRE) 102 (Teenoso (USA) **93**
135) [2002 75+: p12g f12g² f12g* f12g³ f12g² f12g³ 12m 18.7f⁶ 13.9g 16.1g 12.3f³ 12m²
21g⁴ 11.7f* 12.1m* 13.9m³ 12g⁴ 18m f16g* f12s⁴ Dec 9] sturdy gelding: carries plenty
of condition: good mover: has reportedly had knee problem: fairly useful performer: won
claimer at Southwell, quite valuable ladies handicap at Bath, 3-runner minor event at
Beverley and handicap at Southwell in 2002: effective at 1½m, barely at 2¼f: acts on
fibresand and probably any turf going: sometimes hangs: usually races up with pace:
tough. *A. G. Newcombe*

ALBERKINNIE 7 b.m. Ron's Victory (USA) 129 – Trojan Desert 97 (Troy 137) **56 §**
[2002 46§, a23§: 10d 10m 10.1m 11.8m⁴ 10s* 12.1s 10s 10g 10s 12d Nov 1] sturdy mare: **a– §**
modest handicapper: won at Newmarket in August by 7 lengths: stays 1½m: acts on
heavy going, good to firm and fibresand: held up: not one to trust. *John A. Harris*

ALBERO (IRE) 3 b.g. Priolo (USA) 127 – Woody's Colours (USA) (Caro 133) [2002 **–**
49: p8g 10.9f⁶ 8.1g Jul 5] leggy gelding: disappointing maiden: blinkered/visored last 6
outings. *P. R. Chamings*

43

Criterium de Saint-Cloud—Alberto Giacometti (No.6) challenges wide and edges ahead of Summerland close home

ALBERTO GIACOMETTI (IRE)   2 b.c. (Apr 29) Sadler's Wells (USA) 132 –   **111 p**
Sweeten Up 76 (Shirley Heights 130) [2002 7g* 10v* Nov 9]
    Smart juveniles trained by Aidan O'Brien are not a rarity in themselves, but not many of them manage to achieve such a lofty level of form on only their second outing. The fact that Alberto Giacometti did just that when winning the Criterium de Saint-Cloud in November bodes well for his prospects as a three-year-old. Reportedly one of the most highly regarded two-year-olds at Ballydoyle, Alberto Giacometti looks certain to improve and win more good races. The ten-runner contest at Saint-Cloud was not run at a strong pace, but a mile and a quarter on heavy ground still made for a good test of stamina which clearly suited the stoutly-bred Alberto Giacometti. Held up in rear for much of the way, he was taken wide into the straight before delivering his challenge inside the final furlong and edging ahead near the finish, always looking as if he would get the better of British-trained Summerland whom he beat by a head. French-trained Marshall was two lengths back in third, with Alberto Giacometti's stable-companions The Great Gatsby and Delacroix a length and a half and two lengths further away in fourth and fifth respectively; the fourth O'Brien runner Cougar was tailed off.
    Alberto Giacometti had already shown useful form when justifying favouritism in a twenty-four-runner newcomers race at the Curragh in October nine days earlier. As at Saint-Cloud, Michael Kinane took the ride, having the pick of three O'Brien runners, the others being Mingun and Wordsworth, half-brothers to King-mambo (out of Miesque) and Giant's Causeway respectively. Alberto Giacometti won only narrowly but, as at Saint-Cloud, he looked value for a bit extra after giving the runner-up Mingun at least three lengths start from over a furlong out after being waited with in mid-division. The pair finished three lengths clear of third-placed Prominent Feature with Wordsworth fourth.
    Alberto Giacometti became the fifty-fifth individual Group/Grade 1 winner by Sadler's Wells. Judged on pedigree, the influence of Sadler's Wells alone would be enough to suggest that Alberto Giacometti will do better as a three-year-old, but his dam Sweeten Up is from a very good family whose members also usually come into their own at middle distances and beyond. Sweeten Up ran only twice, placed

44

Mrs John Magnier's "Alberto Giacometti"

Alberto Giacometti (IRE) (b.c. Apr 29, 2000)	Sadler's Wells (USA) (b 1981)	Northern Dancer (b 1961)	Nearctic
			Natalma
		Fairy Bridge (b 1975)	Bold Reason
			Special
	Sweeten Up (b 1994)	Shirley Heights (b 1975)	Mill Reef
			Hardiemma
		Honeybeta (b 1980)	Habitat
			Attica Meli

in maidens as a two-year-old, but she is a sister to the smart performer Sharan. He bucked the family trend by winning in Germany over a mile at two and nine furlongs at three, before being exported to the States where he won over a mile and finished third in Grade 1 company. Sweeten Up is also a sister to the fairly useful staying chaser Honey Mount, a former winner of the Kim Muir. Their dam Honeybeta was a useful winner at up to a mile and a half, finishing third in the Princess Royal Stakes, and is out of the high-class Attica Meli. Attica Meli won the Yorkshire Oaks and Park Hill Stakes and was a half-sister to another Park Hill winner Royal Hive, also second in the Yorkshire Oaks, Prix Vermeille and Gold Cup. Alberto Giacometti is a half-brother to the German mile-and-a-quarter winner Marco Andre (by Zilzal), and a brother to an unnamed filly foaled in 2001. Sweeten Up was barren to Raise A Grand in 2002 but is due again to Sadler's Wells in 2003. Alberto Giacometti will stay at least a mile and a half and, at the time of writing, is available at 25/1 for the Derby, around three times the odds of stable-companion Brian Boru who won the Racing Post Trophy. Incidentally, Alberto Giacometti is named after the existential artist famed for his sculptures in the immediate post-war period of thin, solitary human forms. Is it any more than coincidence that the colt should be trained by the softly-spoken, willowy Aidan O'Brien? *A. P. O'Brien, Ireland*

ALBUNDY (IRE) 3 b.g. Alzao (USA) 117 – Grove Daffodil (IRE) 83 (Salt Dome (USA)) [2002 –: 13d⁴ 16g 14.1d Oct 30] strong gelding: modest maiden: stays 2m: blinkered (looked reluctant) final 2-y-o start. *M. H. Tompkins*   **52**

ALBURACK 4 b.g. Rock City 120 – Suzannah's Song (Song 132) [2002 42: 6m⁶ 6m⁵ 6m Aug 28] leggy gelding: poor maiden: stays 6f: appears to act on good to firm and good to soft going: tried blinkered. *G. G. Margarson*   **42**

ALBURY HEATH 2 b.g. (Apr 10) Mistertopogigo (IRE) 118 – Walsham Witch 61 (Music Maestro 119) [2002 p6g p6g Dec 28] 800Y: fifth foal: brother to 4-y-o Mishka and half-brother to 7f winner who probably stayed 1½m Bunnies Own (by Flockton's Own) and 1999 2-y-o 5f winner Chiko (by Afif): dam 2-y-o 6f winner who probably stayed 2m: only a little sign of ability at Lingfield in seller (slowly into stride) and maiden. *T. M. Jones*   **57 ?**

ALCAYDE 7 ch.g. Alhijaz 122 – Lucky Flinders 77 (Free State 125) [2002 65: 17.2d 16.2f⁶ 17.1m p16g⁶ 16f Sep 8] good-bodied gelding: no form in 2002. *J. Akehurst*   **–**

ALCHEMIST MASTER 3 b.g. Machiavellian (USA) 123 – Gussy Marlowe 118 (Final Straw 127) [2002 7.1m⁵ 8m 8.?v p8g⁷ p8g Dec 3] leggy, quite-good topped gelding: fifth foal: brother to fairly useful 7f winner Sloane: dam won Musidora and Falmouth Stakes: fair performer: left E. Dunlop after second start (when reportedly choked): first past post in handicap at Lingfield (idled, edged right and disqualified) in December: may prove best around 1m: acts on polytrack. *R. M. Whitaker*   **53 i** **a79**

ALCHEMYSTIC (IRE) 2 b.c. (May 6) In The Wings 128 – Kama Tashoof 72 (Mtoto 134) [2002 8s⁴ Oct 26] 16,000Y: good-topped colt: has scope: third foal: half-brother to 5-y-o Judicious: dam, maiden who stayed 1½m, from family of Derby Italiano winner Central Park and Prix Royal-Oak winner Braashee: 33/1, well held (edged right and placed last) in maiden at Newbury: will be suited by 1½m+: should improve. *Mrs A. J. Perrett*   **– p**

ALCONLEIGH 7 ch.g. Pursuit of Love 124 – Serotina (IRE) 73 (Mtoto 134) [2002 41: f8g⁶ f7g⁴ 6f Apr 13] strong, lengthy gelding: poor handicapper: stays 1m: acts on firm going, soft and fibresand: tried blinkered/tongue tied: has reportedly bled from nose. *B. Ellison*   **39**

ALDAFRA 3 b.f. Spectrum (IRE) 126 – Abeyr 106 (Unfuwain (USA) 131) [2002 91: 8s⁴ 6m 6d* 6.1d² 7d⁵ 7.1d³ p7g 7d⁶ Aug 11] strong filly: fairly useful performer: won handicap at Haydock in May: best form at 6f: acted on good to firm and good to soft ground: visits Indian Ridge. *M. R. Channon*   **88**

ALDER PARK 2 b.c. (Feb 8) Alderbrook 120 – Melody Park 104 (Music Boy 124) [2002 7m 7s³ 7.5g 7m⁶ Oct 2] 9,000F, 15,000Y: workmanlike colt: half-brother to several winners, including 5f (at 2 yrs) to 7f winner Creche (by Bairn) and 6f (including at 2 yrs) winner Melanzana (by Alzao), both fairly useful: dam sprinter: fair maiden: should stay at least 1m: acts on good to soft ground. *T. D. Easterby*   **68**

ALDORA 3 ch.f. Magic Ring (IRE) 115 – Sharp Top 62 (Sharpo 132) [2002 83: 8.1d⁴ 7.1m* 7d* 7s³ 8m 7d² 7d 7g 8.2v⁵ 8s Nov 2] leggy, quite good-topped filly: useful performer: won minor event at Warwick and handicap at Goodwood in May: best effort when neck second to Reefs Sis in handicap at Newmarket in July: best at 7f/1m: has won six and acts on firm going, possibly ideally suited by good or softer (acts on heavy). *M. J. Ryan*   **99**

ALDWYCH ARROW (IRE) 7 ch.g. Rainbows For Life (CAN) – Shygate (Shy Groom (USA)) [2002 41, a55: f12g 12.3m 12g 12m³ Aug 16] smallish, sturdy gelding: poor handicapper: effective at 1½m to 2m: acts on fibresand and good to firm going (though all turf wins on good or softer): blinkered once at 4 yrs: successful over hurdles in October. *M. A. Buckley*   **38 a–**

ALERON (IRE) 4 b.c. Sadler's Wells (USA) 132 – High Hawk 124 (Shirley Heights 130) [2002 7.5g⁴ 10g² a8f a9f 7.5g* 11g² 10s 8.5g 10m⁶ 14.1d⁶ 13.8d* Nov 5] brother to several winners, notably high-class 1½m performer In The Wings, closely related to fairly useful 1m winner Eaglesham (by Barathea) and half-brother to 2 winners: dam, Ribblesdale and Park Hill Stakes winner, half-sister to dam of High-Rise: fair handicapper: won at Nad Al Sheba in April (left E. Charpy 52,000 gns after next start) and Catterick in November: stays 1¾m: acts on dirt, good to firm and good to soft ground: usually visored (not last 4 starts): has had tongue tied: has carried head awkwardly. *J. J. Quinn*   **68 a–**

ALESSANDRO SEVERO 3 gr.g. Brief Truce (USA) 126 – Altaia (FR) 90 (Sicyos (USA) 126) [2002 79: f7g² 8m 7g³ f8.5g* f12g* 11.9m⁵ 10.3s p10g⁴ f11g p10g⁵ p12g²   **71 a84**

f14.8g Dec 31] leggy, unfurnished gelding: fairly useful on all-weather, fair on turf: won maiden and handicap (hung left/seemed to idle) at Wolverhampton in June/July: stays 1½m: acts on all-weather and good to soft going (well below form on good to firm): blinkered last 3 starts: no easy ride. *N. P. Littmoden*

ALEXA (IRE) 2 b.f. (Jan 28) Danetime (IRE) 121 – Moonlight Path (IRE) (Fairy **53** King (USA)) [2002 5g⁵ 6s p5g 6m Jul 16] IR 12,000Y: first foal: dam unraced: modest maiden: ran badly in seller final start: sold only £600 in October. *R. Hannon*

ALEXANDER ACADEMY (USA) 3 b. or br.f. Royal Academy (USA) 130 – **69** Fantastic Bid (USA) (Auction Ring (USA) 123) [2002 70: 6m⁵ 5.3d⁵ 6d 6s Jun 6] tall, strong filly: fair maiden: should stay 7f: acts on good to firm and good to soft going: sometimes slowly away. *R. Hannon*

ALEXANDER PRINCE (IRE) 2 b.g. (Jan 31) Desert Prince (IRE) 130 – National **73** Ballet (Shareef Dancer (USA) 135) [2002 6m p7g⁶ Oct 16] 72,000Y: strong, compact gelding: sixth foal: half-brother to 3 winners, including useful 2-y-o 7f winners Name of Love (in 1997, including Rockfel Stakes, by Petardia) and Annapurna (in 1998, by Brief Truce), latter stayed 1¼m: dam unraced close relative of useful middle-distance stayer Saxon Maid: much better effort in maidens (fair form) when sixth of 15 to Machinist at Lingfield, stumbling leaving stall and wandering under pressure: will stay at least 1m: sold 16,000 gns, joined Lady Herries and gelded. *J. Noseda*

ALEXANDER RIDGE (IRE) 2 b.f. (May 12) Indian Ridge 123 – Dark Hyacinth **77** (IRE) 65 (Darshaan 133) [2002 7s 6m 7.2s³ p7g² f6f³ Nov 11] IR 30,000Y: leggy filly: sixth foal: sister to an Italian winner up to 9f and half-sister to 7f and 11f winner Melledgan (by Catrail): dam, placed at 1½m/13f in Ireland, from family of Arc winner Tony Bin: fair maiden: should stay 1¼m: acts on soft ground, probably on polytrack. *B. W. Hills*

ALEXANDER STAR (IRE) 4 b. or br.f. Inzar (USA) 112 – Business Centre (IRE) **–** 58 (Digamist (USA) 110) [2002 68: p7g p8g 6f 6.1d 7f 6m May 20] smallish, workman-like filly: fair maiden at best: little form in 2002: visored/tongue tied penultimate start, blinkered final one. *Miss D. A. McHale*

ALEXANDER THREE D (IRE) 3 b.f. Pennekamp (USA) 130 – Loon (FR) (Kal- **108** doun (FR) 122) [2002 101p: 10.4m³ 12s 12m⁵ 11.9m* 14.6m* Sep 11] strong, lengthy filly: unimpressive mover: useful performer: won Galtres Stakes at York (by 2½ lengths from Rosa Parks) in August and Rothmans Royals Park Hill Stakes at Doncaster (by 1½ lengths from Treble Heights) in September: had previously run creditably in Musidora Stakes at York (third to Islington), Oaks at Epsom (seventh to Kazzia) and Ribblesdale Stakes at Royal Ascot (fifth to Irresistible Jewel): will stay 2m: acts on soft and good to firm going: sometimes races freely: has edged left. *B. W. Hills*

ALFANO (IRE) 4 b.g. Priolo (USA) 127 – Sartigila 67 (Efisio 120) [2002 70+: p8g³ **70** p10g³ 8.1m⁵ 8d³ 10m³ 10s³ 9s⁵ 9m 12g 10.9m 11.7g³ 9s p12g⁴ p10g⁵ Nov 27] quite good-topped gelding: fair handicapper: effective at 1m to 1½m: acts on polytrack, soft and good to firm ground: occasionally visored/tongue tied in 2001. *P. Mitchell*

Rothmans Royals Park Hill Stakes, Doncaster—
Alexander Three D has no problems with the step up in trip,
justifying favouritism from Treble Heights and Bright And Clear (rail)

ALFELMA (IRE) 2 ch.f. (Mar 9) Case Law 113 – Billie Grey 72 (Chilibang 120) – [2002 5g Jul 30] 500Y: fifth foal: half-sister to a winner in Austria by Aragon: dam, 2-y-o 7f winner, half-sister to smart 7f performer Tumbleweed Ridge: 50/1, tailed off in maiden at Beverley. *P. R. Wood*

ALFIE LEE (IRE) 5 ch.g. Case Law 113 – Nordic Living (IRE) 53 (Nordico (USA)) **46 +** [2002 75d: 5m 6s 5g 5g 5m 7.2d 5m 5m⁶ 5g Sep 19] compact, well-made gelding: unimpressive mover: poor nowadays: raced mainly at 5f/6f: acts on good to firm going and fibresand: blinkered once: tongue tied nowadays. *D. A. Nolan*

ALFRED SISLEY 2 b.g. (Feb 12) Royal Applause 124 – Dalu (IRE) 72 (Dancing **65 p** Brave (USA) 140) [2002 p7g 7v f5g⁶ Dec 2] 56,000Y: third foal: half-brother to 5-y-o Hambleden: dam, 1m winner, half-sister to useful Cornwallis Stakes winner Mubhij: fair form in maidens: late headway having not faced kickback when sixth at Wolverhampton (gelded after): should be suited by 7f+: open to progress. *P. F. I. Cole*

AL GHABRAA 5 ch.m. Pursuit of Love 124 – Tenderetta (Tender King 123) [2002 **– §** 62§, a68§: f6g f7g p7g⁴ Apr 10] modest handicapper on all-weather: effective at 6f to **a64 §** 9.4f: often blinkered/visored: proved most troublesome in preliminaries final intended outing Apr 19 (subsequently banned from racing). *D. Shaw*

ALGUNAS VECES 3 b.g. Timeless Times (USA) 99 – Nuthatch (IRE) 36 (Thatching **62** 131) [2002 69: f8s* f8g⁶ p7g f9.4g 8g 8.2m⁶ Jul 13] lengthy gelding: modest performer: won claimer at Southwell in January: effective at 5f to 1m: acts on fibresand and good to firm going: blinkered once: sometimes hangs right: reportedly bled from nose second start: sold 1,800 gns, sent to Kuwait. *R. Wilman*

ALHESN (USA) 7 b. or br.g. Woodman (USA) 126 – Deceit Princess (CAN) (Vice **32** Regent (CAN)) [2002 39, a64: p16g⁶ f16.2g p16g f16.2g 14.1m⁵ 16f³ 14.1m f16g⁴ f16g **a44** f16g⁴ Dec 17] angular gelding: poor handicapper: will stay beyond 2m: acts on fibresand and firm going, possibly not on softer than good: tried visored/tongue tied: sometimes slowly away: usually soon off bridle in rear. *C. N. Allen*

ALHUWBILL 7 b.g. Full Extent (USA) 113 – Hale Lane 59 (Comedy Star (USA) – 121) [2002 35: p16g p12g p7g p7g p10g 7m 10m Jun 25] of little account nowadays. *J. J. Bridger*

ALIABAD (IRE) 7 b. or br.g. Doyoun 124 – Alannya (FR) (Relko 136) [2002 43, – a53: f12g f16.2g f14.8g Apr 8] modest performer at 6 yrs: well held in 2002: tried visored/ blinkered. *J. G. M. O'Shea*

ALI CAN (IRE) 3 b.g. Ali-Royal (IRE) 127 – Desert Native 42 (Formidable (USA) **65** 125) [2002 51: p7g⁶ f8.5g⁴ 10d⁶ f9.4g f8g³ f8.5g* 10.1m⁵ 8m⁶ 8.2g f9.4g* 8g f8g p10g Dec 14] fair performer: won seller in May and claimer in July, both at Wolverhampton: barely stays 1¼m: acts on all-weather and good to firm going: effective visored or not. *A. P. Jarvis*

ALICE 5 b.m. Rambo Dancer (CAN) 107 – Cold Line 74 (Exdirectory 129) [2002 10m – Jul 8] half-sister to bumpers/hurdles winner Give Best (by Dunbeath): dam 1½m winner, half-sister to high-class 2m hurdler Past Glories: modest form in bumpers: well beaten in Ripon seller. *J. Hetherton*

ALIGATOU 3 b.g. Distant Relative 128 – Follow The Stars 86 (Sparkler 130) [2002 – 78d: p10g f12g 7m f8g f8.5s Dec 26] disappointing maiden: tried blinkered/in cheek-pieces. *Mrs L. Stubbs*

ALI GEE GEE (IRE) 3 b.g. Desert Style (IRE) 121 – Molvina (ITY) (Final Straw – 127) [2002 37: 7g May 6] well held in seller/claimer. *J. L. Eyre*

Hackney Empire Royal Lodge Stakes, Ascot—the progressive Al Jadeed (rail) thwarts Bahamian Dancer; Irish-trained Van Nistelrooy takes third with Norse Dancer fourth

AL IHTITHAR (IRE) 2 b.f. (Apr 25) Barathea (IRE) 127 – Azyaa 101 (Kris 135) **98 p**
[2002 7m² 7s* 7s³ Oct 26] good-topped filly: closely related to smart 11f to 15f winner
Samsaam (by Sadler's Wells) and half-sister to several winners, including useful 7f/1m
performer Ihtiraz (by Soviet Star): dam 7.5f winner from good middle-distance family:
useful form: won maiden at Lingfield in September: very good third, beaten head and
neck, to Crystal Star in listed event at Newbury, staying on well: will be suited by 1¼m+:
acts on soft ground, shaped well on good to firm: swished tail in paddock on debut: open
to progress. *B. W. Hills*

ALI PASHA 3 b.g. Ali-Royal (IRE) 127 – Edge of Darkness 62 (Vaigly Great 127) **53**
[2002 49: p12g⁶ 10.2g f12g f12g Dec 2] modest maiden: should be suited by further than
1½m. *D. W. P. Arbuthnot*

ALI ROSE 4 b.f. Cigar 68 – Hurricane Rose (Windjammer (USA)) [2002 47: f8s f8g⁶ **45**
Jan 31] poor maiden: stays 1m: acts on fibresand: blinkered final start. *H. Morrison*

ALI'S IMAGES 4 b.f. Mind Games 121 – Question Ali 83 (Petoski 135) [2002 f7g **–**
f7g f7g Feb 19] of little account nowadays. *A. Berry*

ALIZARIN (IRE) 3 b.f. Tagula (IRE) 116 – Persian Empress (IRE) 51 (Persian Bold **–**
123) [2002 62: f7g 11m 7f 5m 6d 5m 9m Aug 22] disappointing maiden: sold from
J. L. Eyre 850 gns after reappearance: blinkered (raced freely) once. *R. E. Barr*

ALJAARIF 8 ch.g. Rainbow Quest (USA) 134 – Jasoorah (IRE) 98 (Sadler's Wells **104**
(USA) 132) [2002 a9.5g⁶ a9.5g² p10g⁵ 9.5s⁵ 10d³ 11s⁵ 11g a9.5g* p10g Nov 23] useful
performer: won minor event at Neuss in October by 15 lengths: creditable fifth to
Adiemus in listed race at Lingfield third start: effective at 9f, probably at 14.8f: acts on
soft going and sand/all-weather. *M. Hofer, Germany*

AL JADEED (USA) 2 b.c. (Mar 28) Coronado's Quest (USA) 130 – Aljawza (USA) **109**
86 (Riverman (USA) 131) [2002 7m⁴ 7m³ 7f* 7.1m* 8g* 7m Oct 19] close-coupled, quite
attractive colt: has a quick action: fifth foal: half-brother to fairly useful 6f (at 2 yrs) to (in

Mr Hamdan Al Maktoum's "Al Jadeed"

France/UAE) 1m winner Ishtihar (by Woodman), 1m winner Elsundas (by Gone West) and 3-y-o Mezya: dam, Irish 2-y-o 6f winner, half-sister to smart Queen Mary/Cheveley Park winner Gay Gallanta and to very smart Irish performer up to 1¼m Sportsworld, an outstanding family: useful performer: won maiden at Newbury in August and minor event at Sandown (by 3 lengths from Statement) and Hackney Empire Royal Lodge Stakes at Ascot (beat Bahamian Dancer by a head in 9-runner race, leading under 2f out), both in September: only tenth in Dewhurst Stakes at Newmarket: stays 1m: raced only on good going or firmer: has worn crossed noseband: game. *J. H. M. Gosden*

ALJARD (USA) 4 ch.g. Gilded Time (USA) – Diaspora (USA) (Vice Regent (CAN)) **59** [2002 59: f8s² f8g² f7g* f7g³ 7d 7m 8f 9.9g 8.1m² 9.9g Jul 30] lengthy gelding: fair **a69** handicapper on all-weather, modest on turf: left D. Barker prior to winning at Wolverhampton in February: best at 7f/1m: acts on fibresand, probably on firm going: reportedly had breathing problem final start: none too consistent. *Mrs S. J. Smith*

ALJAZ 12 b.g. Al Nasr (FR) 126 – Santa Linda (USA) (Sir Ivor 135) [2002 –, a52: f6g – Jan 29] probably of little account nowadays. *Mrs N. Macauley*

ALJAZEERA (USA) 2 b.f. (Apr 29) Swain (IRE) 134 – Matiya (IRE) 116 (Alzao **84** (USA) 117) [2002 7m⁴ 7m⁴ 7d* Nov 2] close-coupled filly: third foal: dam, 7f (at 2 yrs) and 1m (Irish 1000 Guineas) winner, probably stayed 10.5f: fairly useful form: bandaged off-hind, won maiden at Newmarket by ½ length from Elegant Shadow, travelling well just off pace and leading 1f out: will stay at least 1m. *B. Hanbury*

ALJOMAR 3 b.g. College Chapel 122 – Running For You (FR) (Pampabird 124) **45** [2002 55: 7m⁶ 6d 9.3s⁵ 8m 8.5d⁴ 8m 6d Aug 3] leggy gelding: poor maiden: stays 8.5f: acts on fibresand, best turf effort on good ground. *R. E. Barr*

ALKAASED (USA) 2 b.c. (Feb 19) Kingmambo (USA) 125 – Chesa Plana (Niniski **87 p** (USA) 125) [2002 7m⁴ 8g⁴ Oct 18] $325,000Y: big, strong, good-bodied colt: unimpressive mover: fourth foal: half-brother to French 2000 2-y-o 1m winner Vielle Senlis (by Cryptoclearance): dam, useful German filly up to 1¾m, sister to very smart stayer San Sebastian: green and edgy, shaped well and showed fairly useful form when fourth of 6 to Maghanim in minor event at Doncaster: favourite, no improvement when fourth of 16 to Persian Majesty in maiden at Newmarket following month: will be suited by 1¼m+: looks type to make a better 3-y-o. *Sir Michael Stoute*

ALKADEM (USA) 2 ch.c. (Feb 8) Diesis 133 – Alshoowg (USA) (Riverman (USA) **66** 131) [2002 7f 7.5d Aug 14] small, strong colt: shows knee action: first foal: dam unraced out of close relative to 2000 Guineas winner Lomond and half-sister to Seattle Slew: fair form when seventh in maiden at Newbury: upset in stall and raced too freely when well beaten in similar event at Beverley only subsequent start: sold 11,000 gns. *M. P. Tregoning*

ALKIFAF (USA) 3 b.f. Mtoto 134 – Ajab Alzamaan (Rainbow Quest (USA) 134) **?** [2002 f12g⁵ 13.9m⁴ 16m a11.5g* a8.8g⁵ 12s⁴ Sep 22] 2,000 3-y-o: lengthy filly: third foal: half-sister to 5-y-o Shuwaib: dam unraced: well beaten first 3 starts, then sold from A. Newcombe 1,500 gns: won maiden at Ovrevoll in August: stays 11.5f: acts on dirt. *A. Lund, Norway*

ALLA CAPPELLA (IRE) 2 ch.f. (Mar 20) College Chapel 122 – Keiko 76 (Gene- **64** rous (IRE) 139) [2002 p5g⁴ 5.2f Jul 20] IR 17,500Y: close-coupled, unfurnished filly: second living foal: dam, Irish 5f winner who stayed 9f, half-sister to useful 1999 2-y-o sprinter Halland Park Girl: modest form in maiden at Lingfield (slowly away) and sales race at Newbury. *C. F. Wall*

ALL BUSINESS 3 b.f. Entrepreneur 123 – Belle Esprit (Warning 136) [2002 79p: **92** p10g³ p10g³ p12g* 14.8m² 12g² 14.1f⁵ Sep 27] leggy, angular filly: fairly useful performer, lightly raced: won maiden at Lingfield in July: very good short-head second in handicap at Thirsk penultimate start: stays 14.8f: acts on polytrack and good to firm going, showed promise on soft: wandered/carried head awkwardly fourth start/hung final one. *J. Noseda*

ALLEGEDLY RED 3 ch.f. Sabrehill (USA) 120 – Tendency 77 (Ballad Rock 122) **–** [2002 –: f12g 16.2g Aug 15] sturdy filly: no form, including in sellers. *Mrs A. Duffield*

ALLEGRINA (IRE) 2 b.f. (May 24) Barathea (IRE) 127 – Pianola (USA) 76 (Diesis **70 p** 133) [2002 6g² 7.5m⁴ 8g⁴ Sep 7] IR 40,000Y: lengthy, unfurnished filly: third foal: dam, won at 10.4f only outing, out of half-sister to Washington D C International winner Vanlandingham and to dam of Distant Music: fair form, not knocked about, in maidens: will stay 1¼m: wore crossed noseband last 2 starts: probably capable of better. *T. D. Easterby*

ALLENBY 3 b.c. Inchinor 119 – Lady Lydia 66 (Ela-Mana-Mou 132) [2002 89p: 8g **86**
10g⁶ 12m 9.9d⁵ 8m 8d⁶ 8.1g Oct 5] lengthy colt: fairly useful performer: only respectable
efforts at best in 2002: stays 1¼m: acts on heavy going: tried blinkered: sent to Italy.
R. Hannon

ALLENWOOD 2 b.c. (Jan 18) Inchinor 119 – Bumpkin 108 (Free State 125) [2002 **60 §**
6m p6g⁵ f6g Nov 22] 3,000Y: half-brother to several winners, including fairly useful Irish
6f winner Castleross (by Selkirk) and4-y-o Cosi Fan Tutte: dam sprinter: modest form at
best in sellers (looked ungenuine in blinkers/visor last 2 starts). *D. J. S. Cosgrove*

ALLERGY 2 b.f. (Apr 1) Alzao (USA) 117 – Rash Gift 78 (Cadeaux Genereux 131) **99**
[2002 7m⁵ 8m² 8m* 10s² Nov 2] smallish, close-coupled filly: third foal: dam, maiden
(probably stayed 1¼m), out of useful 2-y-o 6f/7f winner who appeared to stay 1½m
Nettle: useful performer: made most when beating Illustrator by short head in maiden at
Leicester in October: length second of 10 to Forest Magic in listed race at Newmarket
final start, pair clear: should stay 1½m: best efforts on soft ground. *R. Charlton*

ALLERTON BOY 3 ch.g. Beveled (USA) – Darakah 78 (Doulab (USA) 115) [2002 **61**
67: 6g 5d 5.3m⁶ 5m 6.1d⁶ 5f Jul 15] modest maiden handicapper: likely to prove best at
5f: acts on firm ground. *R. J. Hodges*

ALLEZ MOUSSON 4 b.g. Hernando (FR) 127 – Rynechra 102 (Blakeney 126) **76**
[2002 85: f16.2g 12s 18s 17.1f⁶ 16.1m 17.1m 17.2d* 16.5g 15.9f⁶ 10.9g 17.5g 15.9f⁶
18m 16s Oct 25] tall, leggy gelding: fair handicapper: won at Bath in June: below form
after: best at 2m+: acts on soft and good to firm going: tried blinkered: often soon off
bridle. *A. Bailey*

ALL I ASK 4 b.g. Spectrum (IRE) 126 – Christine Daae 74 (Sadler's Wells (USA) **74 d**
132) [2002 70: 8.2d 8.2m⁴ 8.3g 11.9d⁵ 8.5d 8f⁶ 9d Oct 18] big, strong gelding: fair maiden
at best: on downgrade: stays 1m: yet to race on soft/heavy ground, probably acts on any
other: sold 1,200 gns. *P. W. Harris*

ALL IN ALL 3 ch.f. Halling (USA) 133 – Alligram (USA) 61 (Alysheba (USA)) **76**
[2002 74: 9.9m 8d² 8.1m² 8m Aug 6] leggy, unfurnished filly: fair maiden: stays 1m: yet
to race on extremes of ground. *L. M. Cumani*

ALLINJIM (IRE) 3 b.g. Turtle Island (IRE) 123 – Bounayya (USA) (Al Nasr (FR) **93**
126) [2002 69: 8.2d 9.2s³ 12.1g* 12.3d⁴ 14.1m* 14m⁶ 15g* 14f² Oct 5] big, good-bodied
gelding: fairly useful handicapper: won at Beverley in May, Nottingham (wandered) in
August and Ayr in September: very good second at Newmarket final start: stays 15f: acts
on any turf going: has worn crossed noseband: front runner: reliable. *J. A. Glover*

ALL NIGHT THING (IRE) 2 b.f. (Mar 8) General Monash (USA) 107 – Rose 'n **65**
Reason (IRE) (Reasonable (FR) 119) [2002 7d 6.5v 7g⁵ 6.5s³ 6g⁶ 6f 7g f7g⁶ f7g f6f* f6s **a56**
f8.5g⁶ f6g Dec 16] IR 5,000F, IR 3,500Y: fifth foal: half-sister to a winner up to 7f in Italy
by Mukaddamah: dam maiden: modest performer: won maiden at Wolverhampton in
November: should stay 1m: acts on fibresand and soft ground, probably on firm: tried
blinkered: often slowly away: tends to be taken wide: swished tail final run, and possibly
temperamental. *John A. Quinn, Ireland*

ALL NINES 2 b.c. (Mar 4) Royal Applause 124 – Jugendliebe (IRE) (Persian Bold **100**
123) [2002 5.2s³ 6g³ 6g* 6m* 6d² 6g 6m Sep 11] 20,000F, 48,000Y: good-bodied colt:
fourth foal: dam German 1¼m winner at 4 yrs: useful performer: won maiden and minor
event at Doncaster in July: good seventh of 21 to Somnus in sales race there final start:
likely to prove best at 5f/6f: acts on good to firm and good to soft ground. *B. W. Hills*

ALL ON MY OWN (USA) 7 ch.g. Unbridled (USA) 128 – Some For All (USA) **50**
(One For All (USA)) [2002 16m 14g⁶ 13.8g⁴ 10.5s⁴ 11.1v 9.2g⁶ 12m 9.2v² 9.9m³ 9.9m
Sep 24] close-coupled, workmanlike gelding: modest maiden: effective at 9f given test
and stays 2m: acts on heavy and good to firm going: tried visored. *I. W. McInnes*

ALLOVER (USA) 3 b.c. Spinning World (USA) 130 – Gossamer (USA) (Seattle **–**
Slew (USA)) [2002 10.9m Jul 7] IR 540,000Y: third live foal: half-brother to 4-y-o
Translucid: dam, winner up to 9f in USA at 4 yrs, from excellent family: 7/2, left
impression something amiss when tailed-off last in maiden at Warwick: sent to USA.
H. R. A. Cecil

ALL POINTS NORTH (IRE) 3 b.g. Distinctly North (USA) 115 – Winscarlet **–**
North (Garland Knight 92) [2002 54: 7.9g 10.1m 8.3s Aug 20] angular, unfurnished
gelding: modest maiden at 2 yrs: well held in 2002: tried blinkered: sent to Holland.
M. W. Easterby

ALL SMILES 4 ch.f. Halling (USA) 133 – Fairy Flax (IRE) 97 (Dancing Brave **41**
(USA) 140) [2002 41: f8.5g^d f8g^5 f7g^3 f8g^4 7m^6 7g 7f May 13] poor maiden: stays 7f:
acts on fibresand and firm ground. *Mrs J. R. Ramsden*

ALL'S NOT LOST 3 b.f. Binary Star (USA) – Flo's Choice (IRE) 35 (Dancing
Dissident (USA) 119) [2002 6d Oct 18] first foal: dam sprint maiden: 33/1, slowly away
when eighth to Formeric in maiden at Redcar, nearest finish. *Don Enrico Incisa*

ALL THE BEST 2 b.f. (Feb 15) Desert Story (IRE) 115 – Alioli (Nishapour (FR) 125) **60**
[2002 5.1m^5 5m^6 7m^3 p6g 5.9d^5 5.2d^5 p6g f5g Dec 4] small filly: third foal: half-sister to
a winner in Greece by Zilzal: dam (no form) out of half-sister to Last Second and to dams
of Alborada and Quarter Moon: modest maiden: stays 7f: acts on polytrack, good to firm
and good to soft going. *P. W. D'Arcy*

ALL TRUMPS 3 b.g. First Trump 118 – So Bold (Never So Bold 135) [2002 64: p10g **60**
p10g^5 10g^5 7m May 16] modest maiden: stays 1¼m: acts on polytrack and soft going:
blinkered (below form) final start: sometimes slowly away. *G. L. Moore*

ALLY MAKBUL 2 b.f. (Jan 17) Makbul 104 – Clarice Orsini (Common Grounds **53**
118) [2002 p5g^7 p5g^6 f3g 6m Sep 23] 3,000Y: first foal: dam third at 1m in France:
modest maiden: off 5 months, well beaten final start: should stay 6f: acts on polytrack.
J. R. Best

ALLY MCBEAL (IRE) 3 b.f. Ali-Royal (IRE) 127 – Vian (USA) (Far Out East **40**
(USA)) [2002 6g^5 8.1m Sep 16] 9,000Y: leggy filly: half-sister to several winners,
including useful 1994 2-y-o 5f winner Wavian (by Warning) and 1996 2-y-o 1m winner
Hindsight (by Don't Forget Me): dam unraced half-sister to smart 1¼m filly Optimistic
Lass, herself dam of high-class Golden Opinion: seemed green and only poor form in
maidens at Thirsk and Warwick, soon pushed along both times. *J. G. Given*

AL MAALI (IRE) 3 b.c. Polar Falcon (USA) 126 – Amwag (USA) 106 (El Gran **104**
Senor (USA) 136) [2002 82: 6.1m^* 6s^* 7m 6m 7.1g^* 6g^5 8f^3 a8f^3 a7.5f^2 Dec 26] rather
leggy, useful-looking colt: has a short action: useful performer: won maiden at Nottingham in May and handicaps at Newcastle in June and Sandown in August: beat Qazween by 1¾
lengths) in August: left A. Stewart, respectable efforts at Nad Al Sheba last 3 starts:
stays 1m: acts on soft going, good to firm and dirt: edgy type (sometimes sweats).
K. P. McLaughlin, UAE

AL MABROOK (IRE) 7 b.g. Rainbows For Life (CAN) – Sky Lover (Ela-Mana- **–**
Mou 132) [2002 –, a49: f16s^3 f16.2g^3 f16g f16g^6 f14.8s May 13] leggy gelding: poor **a45**
handicapper: stays 2m: acts on fibresand: sometimes blinkered. *K. A. Ryan*

AL MANSINGH (IRE) 3 b. or br.g. Alhaarth (IRE) 126 – Jacaranda City (IRE) 88 **–**
(In The Wings 128) [2002 10.2d Jul 8] 15,000Y: first foal: dam, ran once in Ireland,
closely related to useful winner up to 13.4f Nassma: 25/1, slowly away when last in
maiden at Bath. *S. Kirk*

ALMARA 2 b.f. (Feb 20) Wolfhound (USA) 126 – Alacrity 62 (Alzao (USA) 117) **59**
[2002 6g 5g^6 6d Oct 14] 5,000F: fifth foal: half-sister to French 7f and (including at 2 yrs)
1m winner Fast Trick (by First Trump): dam 11f winner out of sister to smart 1¼m
performer Perpendicular: modest maiden: should stay 7f. *M. Blanshard*

ALMASHROUK (IRE) 5 b.g. Common Grounds 118 – Red Note (Rusticaro (FR) **–**
124) [2002 59: 8.2d 6d 8m 8.1g Jul 5] smallish, good-topped gelding: modest maiden at 4
yrs: no form in 2002: tried blinkered. *M. R. Channon*

ALMAVIVA (IRE) 2 b.f. (Feb 8) Grand Lodge (USA) 125 – Kafayef (USA) 46 **90 p**
(Secreto (USA) 128) [2002 7m^* Aug 17] 180,000F: fourth foal: half-sister to 4-y-o
Gardrum and Italian winner up to 10.5f Persian Filly (by Persian Bold): dam ran 3 times:
12/1, fairly useful form when winning 15-runner maiden at Newmarket by 1¾ lengths
from Weqaar, staying on strongly to lead final 1f: will stay at least 1m: looked sure to
improve. *J. Noseda*

ALMAYDAN 4 b.g. Marju (IRE) 127 – Cunning 118 (Bustino 136) [2002 78: 15f^* **94**
14.1d^* 20m^6 16.2m2 Jul 26] strong, good-bodied gelding: fairly useful handicapper: made
all at Warwick in April and Nottingham in May: at least respectable efforts after: barely
stays 2½m: acts on firm and good to soft going: carries head awkwardly: often makes
running. *R. Lee*

ALMNADIA (IRE) 3 b.f. Alhaarth (IRE) 126 – Mnaafa (IRE) 70 (Darshaan 133) **62**
[2002 –: 14.1f p12g^* 12m^* 12m^5 12.1g 15.9f 13.8g^5 Oct 19] well-made filly: modest
performer: won seller at Lingfield in June and selling handicap at Pontefract in July: left

G. Butler 8,000 gns after fourth start: stays 1½m: acts on polytrack and good to firm going: held up: won juvenile hurdles in October/December. *S. Gollings*

AL MOHALLAB (FR) 3 b.g. Marju (IRE) 127 – Deyaajeer (USA) 64 (Dayjur (USA) 137) [2002 97p: 10d³ 8.1m⁶ 9m 7f³ 7g Oct 18] lengthy, attractive gelding: has scope: fluent mover: useful performer: best effort when third to Demonstrate in handicap at Newmarket penultimate start: effective at 7f/1m: acts on firm going, probably on good to soft: free-going sort: sent to UAE. *B. W. Hills* **106**

ALMOND BEACH 2 ch.g. (Apr 17) Hector Protector (USA) 124 – Dancing Spirit (IRE) 72 (Ahonoora 122) [2002 7m 7f³ 7m³ 7.1m Aug 31] 30,000Y: lengthy gelding: half-brother to several winners, including 3-y-o Pastel and fairly useful 6f (including at 2 yrs) and 1m (in Spain) winner Beware (by Warning): dam, 6f winner, sister to smart filly up to 1¼m Feminine Wiles: fair maiden: likely to prove best up to 1m. *B. J. Meehan* **78**

ALMOST FREE 5 b.g. Darshaan 133 – Light Fresh Air (USA) (Rahy (USA) 115) [2002 11.8s Oct 28] strong, good-bodied gelding: fairly useful form in 2 starts at 3 yrs, winning maiden at Newcastle: tailed off only Flat outing since. *B. S. Rothwell* **–**

ALMOST TWILIGHT (USA) 3 b.f. Silver Hawk (USA) 123 – Worood (USA) (Vaguely Noble 140) [2002 10d⁴ 12.3m³ 10g² 12.1d* 11.9g⁵ 16.2d⁴ Aug 14] lengthy, good-bodied filly: half-sister to several winners, including fairly useful 1m winner Wishing Stone (by Dayjur) and French 15f winner Sixty And Steel (by Theatrical): dam French 1m to 1½m winner: fair performer: won maiden at Beverley in July: stays 2m: yet to encounter extremes of going: races prominently. *M. Johnston* **77**

ALMOTAWAG 2 ch.g. (May 7) Abou Zouz (USA) 109 – As Mustard (Keen 116) [2002 5g⁵ 5m⁵ Sep 16] 800F: lengthy, good-bodied gelding: third foal: dam unraced: modest form in maidens: should stay at least 6f: capable of better. *Mrs L. Stubbs* **60 p**

AL MOUGHAZEL (USA) 3 b.c. Royal Academy (USA) 130 – Wild Vintage (USA) (Alysheba (USA)) [2002 100: 8m² 8m⁴ 10m 8.1d³ 8g² Aug 18] tall, good sort: useful performer: creditable efforts in 2002 in minor events at Doncaster and Deauville (blinkered, second to Massigann) on first and final starts and listed race at Kempton (fourth of 6 to Hero's Journey) on second one: should stay 1¼m: yet to race on extremes of going: sent to Hong Kong, where renamed Bullish Luck. *J. W. Payne* **104**

AL MOULATHAM 3 b.c. Rainbow Quest (USA) 134 – High Standard 83 (Kris 135) [2002 12m* 10g² Jun 1] rather leggy, attractive colt: third foal: half-brother to fairly useful 7f (at 2 yrs) to 1½m winner Summer Song (by Green Desert): dam, 2-y-o 1m winner who stayed 1½m, out of close relative to Nureyev and half-sister to dam of Sadler's Wells: smart form: won minor event at Newmarket in May by 8 lengths from Dusky Warbler: tongue tied and again favourite, good short-head second to Bustan in listed event on same course, rallying having again forced pace (unseated after post): stays 1½m: looked open to further progress, but sustained minor injury. *Saeed bin Suroor* **112**

AL MUALLIM (USA) 8 b.g. Theatrical 128 – Gerri N Jo Go (USA) (Top Command (USA)) [2002 89: 5m⁵ 6m⁶ 6g* 6d 7d⁴ 6.9d⁵ 6d³ 6d 6m 5m² 6m⁵ 7m* 6m 5m⁴ 5f⁵ 5g p7g p7g³ p7g⁵ Dec 18] compact gelding: fair on turf nowadays, modest on all-weather: won claimer at Catterick in May and seller at Brighton (sold from D. Nicholls 7,000 gns) in September: best at 6f/7f: acts on firm and soft going, probably on polytrack: tongue tied: sometimes slowly away/edges right: free-going sort: best held up. *Andrew Reid* **74 a57**

ALMUSHAHAR (USA) 2 b.c. (Apr 7) Silver Hawk (USA) 123 – Sayyedati 122 (Shadeed (USA) 135) [2002 7m* 7m* Sep 13] **111 p**
  A striking victory by Almushahar in the Rothmans Royals Champagne Stakes at Doncaster earned a comparison with Dubai Millennium, the joint-highest rated horse (along with Shergar and Dancing Brave) featured in these pages over the past thirty years. Trainer David Loder said afterwards 'Almushahar has always been very special at home—you look forward to work mornings when he is due out—and he looks as good as Dubai Millennium did at this stage.' Ironically, Almushahar injured a leg in a routine canter on Newmarket Heath shortly afterwards, causing him to miss the rest of the season. In that respect, a closer and possibly more relevant comparison could be made with another ex-graduate of the trainer's Godolphin 'academy', the 2001 Champagne winner Dubai Destination. Dubai Destination looked every inch a potential Guineas winner, giving a tremendous display in beating Rock of Gibraltar at Doncaster before, like Almushahar, succumbing to injury just as the stage looked set for him to tackle the season's most prestigious two-year-old race the Dewhurst.

Rothmans Royals Champagne Stakes, Doncaster—Almushahar temporarily leaps to the head of the Guineas betting with a striking success from St Pancras (checked cap) and Wizard of Noz (right)

The exact nature of Almushahar's injury was not revealed—he was described at the time as having 'banged a leg' and his soundness was still worrying Godolphin over the winter—but it is to be hoped that he enjoys a smoother run as a three-year-old than Dubai Destination who was seen out only once and had to be shipped back to Dubai before the end of the latest season. The form of Almushahar's Champagne Stakes victory didn't match that of Dubai Destination's in the race, but Almushahar put up a performance which marked him down as a very promising colt and cemented his place at the head of the ante-post betting on the Two Thousand Guineas (he was 12/1 co-favourite with the Tote even before the Champagne and was clear favourite with all the leading firms afterwards, as short as 7/1). The Champagne, for which he was a supplementary entry, was only Almushahar's second race. He had been all the rage when making his debut towards the end of August in a Newmarket maiden featuring plenty of well-bred types from prominent stables. Almushahar knuckled down really well to win from two other debutants, Maghanim and Trade Fair (the first three finishing clear). Maghanim franked the form when winning on the St Leger meeting's opening day and Almushahar started at 11/8-on for the Champagne in a field distinguished more by quantity—the eleven-runner line-up was larger than usual—than by quality. Only five of the eleven had previously contested a pattern race (Checkit recording the only such victory when awarded a Group 2 at Baden-Baden). Roughly four lengths covered the first nine home—partly attributable to the muddling pace at which the race was run—but the patiently-ridden Almushahar quickened in good style after looking as if he might be denied a clear run, Dettori manoeuvring him through a tight gap between the leaders over a furlong out. Once in the clear, Almushahar was soon on top and kept on under firm riding towards the finish to win by a length and a quarter from the Solario fourth St Pancras, with the once-raced maiden winner Wizard of Noz third and the Acomb runner-up Salcombe fourth.

		Roberto	Hail To Reason
	Silver Hawk (USA)	(b 1969)	Bramalea
	(b 1979)	Gris Vitesse	Amerigo
Almushahar (USA)		(gr 1966)	Matchiche II
(b.c. Apr 7, 2000)		Shadeed	Nijinsky
	Sayyedati	(b 1982)	Continual
	(b 1990)	Dubian	High Line
		(b 1982)	Melodina

Attractive but only medium-sized, Almushahar was outshone in terms of build by a number of his rivals before the Champagne Stakes. Judged on physique alone, he hardly appeals as the type to train on into a significantly better three-year-old. Looks aren't everything, though, Almushahar's sire, for example, having been represented by a number of good-class performers who wouldn't have won prizes in the show-ring. American-based Silver Hawk is well established as a sire of pattern-class performers and as a fairly strong influence for stamina. Derby winner Benny The Dip, St Leger winner Mutafaweq and Prix de Diane winner Lady In Silver are among his best-known offspring. Almushahar, a 425,000-dollar yearling, is the fourth foal of Sayyedati, winner of five Group 1 races including the Cheveley Park, the One Thousand Guineas and—still in training as a five-year-old—the Sussex Stakes. Sayyedati was never raced beyond a mile, somewhat surprisingly on her breeding at least, since her dam the Oaks third Dubian stayed a mile and a half well, as did the grandam and great grandam, Melodina and Rose of Medina, both racemares of similar ability to Dubian; Sayyedati is also a half-sister to the high-class mile-and-a-quarter to mile-and-a-half performer Golden Snake. Sayyedati's two winning offspring before Almushahar, both fillies, were successful at around a mile as three-year-olds, Djebel Amour (by Mt Livermore) in the States and Cunas (by Irish River) in a maiden at Windsor in the latest season. Sayyedati's fifth foal, a yearling full brother to Almushahar, went through the sale-ring at Keeneland two days before the Champagne Stakes and made only 12,000 dollars (reportedly resold privately afterwards for 62,000 dollars to Japanese interests). Almushahar, taken out of the Guineas betting after his setback, will certainly get a mile and may well stay further. He wore a crossed noseband on both his starts. *D. R. Loder*

ALMUTAN STAR   7 b.m. Almutanabbi – Salt of The Earth 85 (Sterling Bay (SWE))   – [2002 8.2d f8.5g Apr 20] plain mare: no form. *J. Neville*

ALMUTASADER   2 b.c. (Feb 25) Sadler's Wells (USA) 132 – Dreamawhile 85   **61** (Known Fact (USA) 135) [2002 7f 8m⁴ 8.2v Oct 29] 525,000Y: big, good-topped colt: fifth foal: closely related to 6f (including at 2 yrs) winner Vision of Night and 5f winner Struggler (both smart, by Night Shift), and half-brother to smart German 11f/1½m winner Baroon and useful 1½m winner Dream Quest (both by Rainbow Quest): dam, 7f winner, half-sister to Derby Italiano winner My Top: modest maiden: finished tired under testing conditions final start: likely to stay 1¼m. *J. L. Dunlop*

ALNAHDA   3 b.f. Mark of Esteem (IRE) 137 – Albertville (USA) 108 (Polish   **76** Precedent (USA) 131) [2002 9.9d³ 10s* Oct 23] third foal: dam, French listed 1¼m winner, out of Breeders' Cup Turf second Sierra Roberta: confirmed promise of debut when winning maiden at Nottingham 2 months later by ½ length from Ravenglass, leading 3f out and responding well: stayed 1¼m: raced only on going softer than good: visits Mtoto. *M. P. Tregoning*

ALNAJASHEE   6 b.g. Generous (IRE) 139 – Tahdid 91 (Mtoto 134) [2002 p12g 11.6g   – § 13.1f f14s Sep 5] temperamental handicapper nowadays. *M. R. Bosley*

ALPEN WOLF (IRE)   7 ch.g. Wolfhound (USA) 126 – Oatfield 69 (Great Nephew   **82** 126) [2002 85, a73: p6g² p6g p6g³ f7g² f7g² f6g* f6g⁴ f6g⁴ p6g⁴ 6g* 6.1f² 7g⁶ 6m⁴ 5.7g   **a76** 6f 6m⁴ 6m⁵ 6m² 6f 6m Sep 14] sturdy, rather dipped-backed gelding: fairly useful handicapper on turf, fair on all-weather: won at Wolverhampton in March and Brighton in May: best at 6f/7f: acts on all-weather, best on good going or firmer on turf: tried visored/blinkered: usually races prominently: tough and consistent. *W. R. Muir*

ALPHA ECHO (USA)   3 b. or br.c. Spinning World (USA) 130 – Add (USA) (Spec-   **81** tacular Bid (USA)) [2002 6m⁵ Apr 18] quite good-topped colt: half-brother to 3 winners in USA, including minor stakes-winning sprinter Inflate (by Forty Niner): dam, 6.5f to 8.3f winner in USA, half-sister to Grand Criterium winner Jade Robbery from family of Nureyev and Sadler's Wells: odds on, 6¾ lengths fifth of 7 to Indian Country in Newmarket maiden, very slowly away, picking up before halfway but tending to edge right late on: looked likely to do better. *A. P. O'Brien, Ireland*

ALPHA HEIGHTS (IRE)   5 b.m. Namaqualand (USA) – Mnaafa (IRE) 70 (Dar-   – shaan 133) [2002 41: f12s f16s f12g⁶ f12g f11g Mar 12] of little account nowadays. *Miss V. Haigh*

ALPHA OMEGA (IRE)   2 b.f. (Apr 9) Bahhare (USA) 122 – Trojan River (USA) 96   **67** (Riverman (USA)) [2002 6m⁶ 8.1m 7d³ 7f 8s⁵ Oct 22] IR 10,000F: close-coupled filly: sixth foal: half-sister to 3 winners in Italy, including 9f/1¼m winner Turwieser (by Lion Cavern): dam, 1¼m and 1¾m winner, half-sister to St Leger runner-up Air

Marshall: fair maiden: effective at 7f/1m: best efforts on ground softer than good: sold 7,000 gns. *B. J. Meehan*

ALPHA ROSE 5 ch.m. Inchinor 119 – Philgwyn 66 (Milford 119) [2002 78: p10g p12g⁶ p16g 11.9g³ 11.1g² 13.1g 12m 11.6m* 12g⁴ 12.6m⁴ 11.9g⁶ 11.9g* 11.9m⁶ 12g² 12d⁵ Nov 1] lengthy mare: modest performer: won handicap at Windsor in July and claimer at Brighton in August: best at 1½m/1¾m: acts on firm and soft going: usually held up. *M. L. W. Bell* — **64**

ALPINE HIDEAWAY (IRE) 9 b.g. Tirol 127 – Arbour (USA) 76 (Graustark) [2002 55: 8m 9.9g 8m⁴ 10g⁵ 10m⁴ 9.9d 8m 8.5d 8.9m Sep 8] poor nowadays: effective at 1m/1¼m: acts on any turf going and fibresand: tried blinkered/visored. *J. S. Wainwright* — **46**

ALPINE RACER (IRE) 3 b.g. Lake Coniston (IRE) 131 – Cut No Ice 97 (Great Nephew 126) [2002 64: 10f⁴ 10.1m⁵ 10f⁵ 10m⁶ 11m 11m 7.5m 12g Oct 19] leggy, lengthy gelding: modest maiden at best: stays 1¼m: acts on firm and soft going: tried blinkered (looked less than keen)/visored. *R. E. Barr* — **64 d**

ALQABAS (IRE) 4 b.g. Nashwan (USA) 135 – Harayir (USA) 119 (Gulch (USA)) [2002 71d: p12g f16.2g p12g p16g 1m 9] smallish gelding: disappointing maiden: tried blinkered: seems difficult ride. *M. R. Ewer-Hoad* — **–**

ALQHUTUB 3 b.g. Bering 136 – Yakin (USA) 86 (Nureyev (USA) 131) [2002 8f² 7m 8g⁴ 7f² 8m* 8f Sep 21] fifth foal: closely related to 1m/9f winner Kafezah (by Pennekamp): dam, 2-y-o 5f winner, sister to useful French 7f/1m performer Special Discount: fairly useful performer: won maiden at Salisbury in August: stays 1m: raced only on good going or firmer: blinkered fourth outing, tongue tied third/fourth: has shown signs of temperament: sent to UAE. *B. Hanbury* — **81**

ALRAFID (IRE) 3 ch.c. Halling (USA) 133 – Ginger Tree (USA) 86 (Dayjur (USA) 137) [2002 78: 8m* Apr 18] rather unfurnished colt: has a round action: fairly useful performer: won maiden at Ripon only 3-y-o start by 1¼ lengths from Golden Chalice: reportedly returned home lame: not sure to stay beyond 1m: acts on soft and good to firm going: sold 17,000 gns in October. *A. C. Stewart* — **82**

ALRAJI (USA) 3 b.f. Silver Hawk (USA) 123 – Ken de Saron (USA) (Kenmare (FR) 125) [2002 11.8d May 27] $42,000Y: sparely-made filly: third foal: half-sister to 2 winners by Theatrical, including useful 1½m winner Theatriken: dam, won Grade 3 8.5f event at 2 yrs in USA, out of sister to smart French filly around 1¼m Luth de Saron: slowly away, tailed off in maiden at Leicester: visits Bertolini. *C. E. Brittain* — **–**

ALRAYIHAH (IRE) 3 ch.f. Nashwan (USA) 135 – Irish Valley (USA) (Irish River (FR) 131) [2002 8m⁶ 9.9f* Sep 26] lengthy filly: sister to 4-y-o Morahib, closely related to high-class 7f (when champion 2-y-o) to 9.8f winner Alhaarth (by Unfuwain) and half-sister to 3 winners, including useful French 1990 2-y-o 7f (Prix du Calvados) winner Green Pola (by Nijinsky): dam maiden half-sister to Green Dancer: confirmed debut promise when winning maiden at Goodwood by ¾ length from Code Sign, niggled along at halfway and leading close home (still looked green): stayed 1¼m: to visit Danzig. *M. P. Tregoning* — **76**

ALRIDA (IRE) 3 b.g. Ali-Royal (IRE) 127 – Ride Bold (USA) (J O Tobin (USA) 130) [2002 78: 7.5m⁴ 10m² 11.5f³ 14.1f* 15.8f* 14m⁶ 16.1d³ 14.1m³ 16d² 16m³ 16.2g Sep 28] leggy gelding: fairly useful performer: won maiden at Yarmouth in June and handicap at Catterick (hung left) in July: better around 2m than 1¾m: acts on any going: held up: reliable. *W. Jarvis* — **93**

ALSAFI (USA) 3 b.c. Red Ransom (USA) – Altair (USA) (Alydar (USA)) [2002 8.3m* 8.3g⁶ Aug 12] third foal: half-brother to winner in USA by Seattle Slew: dam unraced out of half-sister to Kentucky Derby winner Cannonade: won maiden at Windsor in July by 1¾ lengths from Hardrada, carrying head shade high: favourite, pulled too hard (bit reportedly slipped, ran very wide bend, virtually pulled up) in minor event at same course following month. *J. Noseda* — **91**

ALSAHIB (USA) 9 b.g. Slew O' Gold (USA) – Khwlah (USA) 99 (Best Turn (USA)) [2002 –, a74d: p16g f16s² f14.8g³ f16g⁵ p12g³ p12g⁵ f14s f14.8g f16g³ f16g⁵ Dec 17] big gelding: modest performer: effective at 1½m to 2m: acts on firm going, soft and all-weather: tried blinkered/visored/tongue tied in cheekpieces: not one to trust. *W. R. Muir* — **a53 §**

AL'S ALIBI 9 b.g. Alzao (USA) 117 – Lady Kris (IRE) (Kris 135) [2002 52: f12g³ f12g* f12g³ p13g³ f12g³ f14g* f12g* f14.8g⁴ f16.2g⁶ f14.8g f14.8g² f12g⁴ f12g⁶ 11.6m² 11.6g f14s 11.8s⁴ Oct 15] smallish, sturdy gelding: shows knee action: modest performer: won selling handicap at Wolverhampton in January and claimer/seller at Southwell in — **58**

March: stays easy 1¾m: acts on good to firm going, soft and fibresand: waited with. *W. R. Muir*

ALSANUTTER 3 b.f. Royal Applause 124 – Andbell (Trojan Fen 118) [2002 –: 5m⁶ 6.1m 5g f5g Dec 31] of little account. *Mrs C. A. Dunnett* –

ALSCOT FOXY LADY (IRE) 5 b.m. Foxhound (USA) 103 – Arena 86 (Sallust 134) [2002 10m 8.1m 12g⁴ May 31] IR 6,500 3-y-o: strong, close-coupled mare: half-sister to several winners, including 1m/9.7f winner Wakil (by Tate Gallery): dam lightly-raced half-sister to dam of Vintage Crop: little sign of ability. *R. Dickin* –

AL'S FELLA (IRE) 7 br.g. Alzao (USA) 117 – Crystal Cross (USA) 88 (Roberto (USA) 131) [2002 –: p12g 14.1d 11.9f Apr 11] lightly raced and well beaten since 1999: sometimes blinkered. *D. J. S. ffrench Davis* –

AL'S ME TRAINER 4 b.g. Emarati (USA) 74 – Ray of Hope 53 (Rainbow Quest (USA) 134) [2002 70: f6g f6g a6g May 12] quite good-topped gelding: fair performer at best: well held in 2002, leaving A. Dickman for Spain after second start: visored last 6 starts in Britain. *C. Tinkler, Spain* –

ALSTEMERIA (IRE) 3 b.f. Danehill (USA) 126 – Teslemi (USA) 73 (Ogygian (USA)) [2002 75p: 6s* 8s⁴ 8m 8d⁴ 8.5d⁴ a6f Dec 7] good-topped filly: fifth foal: sister to smart Irish/Hong Kong performer up to 1¼m Johan Cruyff, 7f/1m winner at 2 yrs: dam 1m winner from good American family: useful performer: won maiden at Cork in March: ran well when 6½ lengths fourth to Gossamer in Irish 1000 Guineas at the Curragh 2 months later, making running: below form after in Coronation Stakes at Royal Ascot, listed race at Leopardstown (final outing for A. O'Brien, off nearly 4 months after) and allowance races at Aqueduct: should stay 1¼m: acts on soft going. *W. I. Mott, USA* **103**

ALSYATI 4 ch.g. Salse (USA) 128 – Rubbiyati 56 (Cadeaux Genereux 131) [2002 70: f12s⁴ p10g p7g f7g 8f³ 9f⁶ 10g⁶ 8m⁵ 8s* 9m 10s 9.7g* 8.5d 10.2g 10.2g Oct 16] quite attractive gelding: modest handicapper: won at Pontefract in July and Folkestone in September: effective at 1m to 11.5f: acts on soft going, firm and polytrack: effective blinkered or not. *C. E. Brittain* **62**

ALTAY 5 b.g. Erins Isle 121 – Aliuska (IRE) 70 (Fijar Tango (FR) 127) [2002 68: f11s p10g³ 9.9m* 10.1g⁴ 10g² 10m⁵ 9m 10.3f 10m 10s* 10.1s⁶ Oct 22] tall gelding: has a round action: fairly useful handicapper: won at Beverley in April and Ayr in October: best around 1¼m: acts on polytrack, firm and soft going: often races prominently. *R. A. Fahey* **83**

ALTER EGO 2 b.f. (Mar 26) Alzao (USA) 117 – Kirsten 77 (Kris 135) [2002 7g* 7m⁵ 7.9f Oct 10] small, close-coupled filly: seventh foal: half-sister to 4-y-o Marakabei and useful 1m (at 2 yrs) and 13f winner Kattegat (by Slip Anchor): dam, 1½m winner, half-sister to Petoski: fairly useful form: won maiden at Folkestone in August: better effort after when fifth of 7 in minor event at Newbury, dictating pace: should be suited by 1¼m+. *Sir Mark Prescott* **84**

ALTIERI 4 ch.c. Selkirk (USA) 129 – Minya (USA) (Blushing Groom (FR) 131) [2002 107: 10s* 10m⁴ 8m² 8s* 8g 8s* 8s⁴ 8d* Nov 17] half-brother to several winners, including smart French performer up to 10.5f Minydoun (by Kaldoun): dam French 1m winner out of high-class French performer up to 1½m Riverqueen: smart performer: won 4 times at 3 yrs, including listed races at Rome and Milan: improved in 2002, winning minor event at Milan in April, Prix Messidor at Deauville (rec 4 lb but still best effort when holding on well to beat Domedriver a neck) in July, another minor event at Milan in September and Premio Ribot at Rome (by ½ length from Salselon) in November: has form at 1½m, better at 1m/1¼m: acts on heavy and good to firm ground. *V. Caruso, Italy* **117**

ALTITUDE DANCER (IRE) 2 b.g. (Apr 8) Sadler's Wells (USA) 132 – Height of Passion (Shirley Heights 130) [2002 8f³ 10g 8v⁵ Nov 8] 40,000Y: closely related to fairly useful 1999 Irish 2-y-o 1m winner Albuquerque (by Barathea) and half-brother to several winners, including 6f (at 2 yrs) and 1¼m winner Precede (by Polish Precedent) and 1½m to 2m winner Warm Feeling (by Kalaglow), both smart: dam ran 3 times: seemed to show fair form when 10 lengths third of 4 to Alasil in maiden at Pontefract: well held in minor events after: likely to need 1½m+: blinkered final start (gelded after). *M. Johnston* **67 ?**

ALTOS 2 br.f. (Apr 13) Petong 126 – Gymcrak Lovebird 84 (Taufan (USA) 119) [2002 5d 7m Aug 16] half-sister to 2 winning sprinters, including Dominelle (by Domynsky): dam 5f (at 2 yrs) to 1¼m winner: well held in claimer/seller: gave trouble at stall both starts. *T. D. Easterby* –

AL TURF (IRE) 2 ch.c. (Feb 20) Alhaarth (IRE) 126 – Petomi 75 (Presidium 124) [2002 6s* 6g⁵ 6m⁶ Sep 20] 47,000F, 190,000Y: rather leggy, useful-looking colt: third foal: half-brother to winners in Italy by Prince of Birds (around 6f) and Sri Pekan (up to **101**

7.5f): dam, 6f/7f winner (latter at 2 yrs), sister to smart performer up to 7f Andreyev: useful form: won maiden at Newbury in June: best effort when 4 lengths fifth of 6 to Elusive City in Prix Morny at Deauville: sixth of 8 to Zafeen in Mill Reef Stakes at Newbury: should stay at least 7f. *R. Hannon*

ALUMNI NEWS (USA)   2 b.c. (Mar 18) Belong To Me (USA) – Private Status (USA) (Alydar (USA)) [2002 p10g² Dec 3] fourth foal: half-brother to very smart US Grade 1 9f winner Secret Status (by A P Indy): dam won around 1m in USA (including minor stakes) and third in 8.5f Grade 1 event: 5/1, 7 lengths second to Shield in maiden at Lingfield, keeping on for hands and heels: sure to improve. *J. H. M. Gosden*   **77 p**

ALUMNUS   2 ch.g. (Feb 18) Primo Dominie 121 – Katyushka (IRE) 73 (Soviet Star (USA) 128) [2002 6m⁶ 6m p7g Oct 31] first foal: dam, 7f winner, out of smart 5f performer Welsh Note: modest maiden: free-going sort, likely to prove best up to 7f. *C. A. Horgan*   **60**

ALUNISSAGE (USA)   4 b.c. Rainbow Quest (USA) 134 – Moonshell (IRE) 117 (Sadler's Wells (USA) 132) [2002 112: 12m³ Jun 29] attractive colt: smart performer at best, lightly raced: only useful form when third of 4 to Xtra in listed event at Newmarket only 4-y-o start: sustained minor injury after: stays 1¾m: raced only on good/good to firm going: visored last 4 starts: hung left first 2 outings at 3 yrs. *Saeed bin Suroor*   **106**

ALVARO (IRE)   5 ch.g. Priolo (USA) 127 – Gezalle (Shareef Dancer (USA) 135) [2002 ?: 10.3m⁶ 10m 15.8m 16.2g³ Aug 15] strong gelding: poor maiden: stays 2m: acts on good to firm and good to soft going: blinkered once. *M. C. Chapman*   **34**

ALWAYS   3 b.g. Dynaformer (USA) – Love And Affection (USA) (Exclusive Era (USA)) [2002 82: 12.3m² 12f* May 4] tall gelding: fairly useful performer: won maiden at Thirsk in May: will prove at least as effective at 1¼m as 1½m: acts on firm and good to soft ground: flashed tail/found little second 2-y-o start: sold 35,000 gns in July, joined N. Meade in Ireland. *J. L. Dunlop*   **84**

ALWAYS BELIEVE (USA)   6 b.h. Carr de Naskra (USA) – Wonder Mar (USA) (Fire Dancer (USA)) [2002 6.1f Sep 25] $11,000Y resold $37,000Y: half-brother to several winners, including 1½m winner Northern Kingdom (by Graustark): dam won up to 8.5f in USA: useful performer at best (has run only 8 times): won maiden at Del Mar at 2 yrs (for D. Hofmans) and allowance race at Churchill Downs at 3 yrs: left Saeed bin Suroor after reappearance in 2001: sold from J. Sadler 8,000 gns before tailed off (reportedly bled from nose) in minor event on British debut: effective at 6f/7f: raced only on dirt until final outing: blinkered penultimate 5-y-o start. *M. R. Bosley*   **–**

ALWAYS DARING   3 b.f. Atraf 116 – Steamy Windows § (Dominion 123) [2002 64: 7m 6g 7m 7g 7f Jun 7] rather unfurnished filly: modest maiden at 2 yrs: well below form in 2002: blinkered once. *K. R. Burke*   **–**

ALWAYS RAINBOWS (IRE)   4 b. or br.g. Rainbows For Life (CAN) – Maura's Guest (IRE) (Be My Guest (USA) 126) [2002 93: 8s⁴ 12s³ 10s 11s 12v Nov 9] sixth foal: brother to fairly useful 6f and (at 2 yrs) 7f winner Ray of Sunshine and half-brother to 2 winners: dam unraced: fairly useful handicapper: won maiden at Tipperary and nursery at Gowran at 2 yrs, and handicap at Cork at 3 yrs: creditable efforts in 2002 only on first 2 starts: left K. Prendergast, Ireland, 14,000 gns after fourth one: stays 1½m: acts on heavy ground: blinkered third start. *B. S. Rothwell*   **94**

ALZOLA (IRE)   5 b.m. Alzao (USA) 117 – Polistatic 53 (Free State 125) [2002 57: p10g⁶ p10g 11.6g⁴ p12g Jul 10] small, compact mare: modest maiden: stays 1¼m: acts on polytrack: has been very slowly away/refused to race: pulled up lame final outing: untrustworthy. *C. A. Horgan*   **54 §**

AMACITA   4 b.f. Shareef Dancer (USA) 135 – Kina (USA) (Bering 136) [2002 69d: 11.9g² 10d p12g 11.6m⁶ 11.7f⁴ Aug 23] neat filly: modest maiden: probably best around 1½m: acts on firm ground: visored nowadays: has hung left. *Miss E. C. Lavelle*   **52**

AMALIANBURG   2 b.f. (May 1) Hector Protector (USA) 124 – Ayodhya (IRE) (Astronef 116) [2002 8s Oct 25] strong, well-made filly: sixth foal: half-sister to 3 winners, including 7-y-o Ambitious and useful performer up to 1m Acrobatic (by Warning), 6f winner at 2 yrs: dam French 2-y-o 6f/7f winner: 5/1, backward and green, well beaten in maiden at Doncaster: likely to do better. *H. R. A. Cecil*   **– p**

AMANDA LOUISE (IRE)   2 ch.f. (Feb 22) Peruggio (USA) 84 – Duly Elected (Persian Bold 123) [2002 5s⁶ 5.3f³ 5f² 5f⁴ p5g* a8.5f a6.5f⁶ 7.5f* Dec 16] IR 2,500Y: rather plain filly: half-sister to several winners, including fairly useful 7-y-o 6f winner Kangaroo Island (by Turtle Island, later successful in USA) and 5-y-o Ladywell Blaise: dam, fourth at 1m/9f in Ireland, sister to Phoenix Stakes winner King Persian: **60**

modest performer: won seller at Lingfield in May (left W. Turner after) and, having left P. Aguirre, USA 2 starts later, claimer at Turf Paradise in December: stays 7.5f: acts on polytrack/dirt and firm going: blinkered penultimate outing: front runner in Britain. *D. L. McFarlane, USA*

AMANDA'S LAD (IRE) 2 b.c. (Apr 18) Danetime (IRE) 121 – Art Duo 86 (Artaius (USA) 129) [2002 7g 7.5d 6.1m 5g² f5s 5m⁵ 5.2d⁶ 6d⁵ f6g f5g f7g Dec 17] IR 10,000Y, 3,000 2-y-o: sturdy, close-coupled colt: half-brother to several winners, including useful 6f (at 2 yrs) to 10.4f winner Amyas (by Waajib): dam, fourth in 7f 2-y-o listed event, failed to train on: modest maiden: best at 5f: acts on good to firm and good to soft going, little form on fibresand: rearing leaving stall/wandered penultimate start: races prominently. *M. C. Chapman* **61 a–**

AMANDOLO (IRE) 3 ch.g. Grand Lodge (USA) 125 – Marquererie (USA) (Well Decorated (USA)) [2002 –: f7g* f5g⁶ f7g⁵ 7m f7s May 13] poor performer: won handicap at Wolverhampton in January: stays 7f: acts on fibresand: sent to Germany. *A. Bailey* **– a46**

AMANDUS (USA) 2 b.c. (Mar 17) Danehill (USA) 126 – Affection Affirmed (USA) (Affirmed (USA)) [2002 6f⁴ 7m² 7g⁴ Aug 20] $375,000Y: good-topped colt: has scope: half-brother to several winners, including smart but untrustworthy 6.5f to 8.5f winner in Britain/US River Deep (by Riverman) and useful performer up to 1½m in Britain/US Dreamer (by Zilzal): dam, US 1m/9f winner, half-sister to dam of very smart performer up to 1¼m Zoman: useful form: in frame in maidens at Doncaster and Ascot (took strong hold and again carried head awkwardly) prior to close fourth of 6 to Bourbonnais in listed race at York: should stay 1m: visored last 2 starts. *D. R. Loder* **95**

AMARAKU 3 b.g. Kylian (USA) – Shernborne (Kalaglow 132) [2002 p12g p10g⁵ p10g p12g 12m f16g Nov 20] 8,000Y: sixth foal: dam, lightly raced in France, from family of Morston and Blakeney: modest maiden: should prove suited by 1½m+: acts on polytrack: unseated/bolted at start and withdrawn intended sixth outing: sold £1,300. *P. D. Cundell* **58**

AMARANTH (IRE) 6 b.g. Mujadil (USA) 119 – Zoes Delight (IRE) (Hatim (USA) 121) [2002 96, a99: f8.5g 6m 7g 7.1d 7m 6m 7m* 7.2s⁴ 7.1m⁵ 7m 7.1m 7m² 8.9f f8.5f p7g Dec 28] tall, quite good-topped gelding: fairly useful handicapper nowadays: left J. L. Eyre after fifth start: won at Yarmouth in August: effective at 6f to easy 8.5f: successful on soft going, best efforts on good or firmer/all-weather: tongue tied: has sweated. *D. Carroll* **87**

AMARETTO EXPRESS (IRE) 3 b.g. Blues Traveller (IRE) 119 – Cappuchino (IRE) 59 (Roi Danzig (USA)) [2002 53: f7s⁵ 7m 5m 7f Jul 10] useful-looking gelding: temperamental maiden: left B. Meehan after reappearance: tried blinkered. *R. E. Barr* **– §**

AMARONE 4 b.g. Young Ern 120 – Tendresse (IRE) 60 (Tender King 123) [2002 27, a41: f16.2g⁶ f16g f12g⁵ Dec 4] workmanlike gelding: poor maiden on Flat: stays 2m: acts on fibresand: often blinkered/visored before 2002. *M. J. Ryan* **– a40**

AMBASSADOR LADY (IRE) 4 b.f. General Monash (USA) 107 – La Fandango (IRE) 51 (Taufan (USA) 119) [2002 43: 7g 10d May 24] probably of little account nowadays. *A. G. Newcombe* **–**

AMBER BROWN 6 b.m. Thowra (FR) – High Velocity 53 (Frimley Park 109) [2002 65: p7g⁶ f6g³ p6g p8g³ p7g Feb 27] workmanlike mare: modest handicapper: stays 7f: acts on all-weather, heavy and good to firm ground: usually blinkered: sometimes slowly away. *D. K. Ivory* **56**

AMBER FORT 9 gr.g. Indian Ridge 123 – Lammastide 93 (Martinmas 128) [2002 76, a–: 7d 7v 7g* 7m³ 7f⁵ 7g 7.1g⁴ 7d 7d⁶ 7.1s⁵ 7.1v⁵ 7d⁵ 7m Jul 13] tall gelding: fair handicapper: won at Leicester in April: best at 7f/1m: acts on any going (though all wins on good going or softer): blinkered/visored: flashes tail/tends to wander: best waited with: none too reliable. *J. M. Bradley* **75 a–**

AMBER GO GO 5 ch.m. Rudimentary (USA) 118 – Plaything 69 (High Top 131) [2002 12m 16d Jul 1] winning hurdler: of no account on Flat. *K. W. Hogg, Isle of Man* **–**

AMBER NECTAR TWO 2 b.g. (May 28) Bluegrass Prince (IRE) 110 – Another Batchworth 72 (Beveled (USA)) [2002 5f 6g 6m Aug 29] second foal: dam, untrustworthy 5f/6f winner, sister to 8-y-o Dancing Mystery: only a little sign of ability in maidens. *E. A. Wheeler* **–**

AMBER'S BLUFF 3 b.f. Mind Games 121 – Amber Mill 96 (Doulab (USA) 115) [2002 80p: 6s 5g⁵ p6g³ 6g³ 6m* 5m 5f Oct 13] tall filly: has scope: fairly useful performer: won handicap at Yarmouth in August: pulled up lame next time: raced only at 5f/6f: acts **80**

on polytrack and good to firm going, possibly not on soft: blinkered last 3 starts: reluctant to post fourth outing: sometimes slowly away: sold 6,000 gns. *A. C. Stewart*

AMBERSONG   4 ch.g. Hernando (FR) 127 – Stygian (USA) 73 (Irish River (FR) 131)   **60**
[2002 74d: 8.3g 8.2d 10m² f9.4g⁵ 9d 10.1g 10.1m⁴ f9.4f³ f9.4g⁶ f12g⁴ p10g Nov 27] strong, angular gelding: modest maiden: left J. Hills after third start, Mrs N. Macauley after eighth one: stays 1½m: acts on good to firm ground and fibresand: tried visored. *Ian Williams*

AMBITIOUS   7 b.m. Ardkinglass 114 – Ayodhya (IRE) (Astronef 116) [2002 98, a?:   **78**
5m⁶ 5d 5m Jul 24] lengthy mare: useful handicapper at best: only fair form in 2002:   **a?**
effective at 5f/sharp 6f: acts on fibresand and probably any turf going: visored/blinkered early in 1999: sometimes early to post/slowly away: reportedly in foal. *D. K. Ivory*

AMBITIOUS ANNIE   3 b.f. Most Welcome 131 – Pasja (IRE) (Posen (USA)) [2002   **49**
8.1s⁴ 10.9m⁶ 10g⁶ 10m 9.9m f8.5g f12g⁴ Oct 19] 1,500Y: big filly: second foal: dam, winning hurdler (at 21f), half-sister to grandam of Halling: poor maiden: should be suited by 1¾m+: acts on fibresand, soft and good to firm ground. *R. Hollinshead*

AMBONNAY   2 gh.f. (Feb 8) Ashkalani (IRE) 128 – Babycham Sparkle 80 (So   **83 p**
Blessed 130) [2002 6m* 6f⁶ Sep 8] sturdy filly: half-sister to several winning sprinters, notably useful winner around 5f (including at 2 yrs) Deep Finesse (by Reprimand), and to dam of 7-y-o Halmahera: dam 2-y-o 5f/6f winner: fairly useful form: won maiden at Newbury in August by head from Garmoucheh: stiff task, under 5 lengths sixth of 8 to Sir Edwin Landseer in listed event at Kempton, under pressure at halfway: should stay at least 7f: remains capable of better. *Mrs A. J. Perrett*

AMBROSINE   2 ch.f. (Feb 25) Nashwan (USA) 135 – Tularosa (In The Wings 128)   **67**
[2002 8g⁵ 8s Oct 25] rather sparely-made, plain filly: first living foal: dam, French 11f winner, half-sister to top-class 1m to 1½m performer Most Welcome out of very smart performer up to 1¼m Topsy, herself half-sister to Teenoso: fair form in maidens at Salisbury and Doncaster (edgy): will be suited by 1¼m+. *Mrs A. J. Perrett*

AMBRY   5 b.g. Machiavellian (USA) 123 – Alkaffeyeh (IRE) (Sadler's Wells (USA)   **61 §**
132) [2002 74§: p16g⁶ f16g⁶ 18d 11.9m⁵ 21g Jul 31] modest maiden handicapper on Flat: stays 2m: acts on all-weather and heavy going, probably on good to firm: blinkered/visored nowadays: ungenuine. *G. L. Moore*

AMBUSHED (IRE)   6 b.g. Indian Ridge 123 – Surprise Move (IRE) (Simply Great   **76**
(FR) 122) [2002 68: 8m² 8.3s* 8.3g² 8m 9g³ 9.2g³ 10d² 9.2v⁴ 10.1d 12s Nov 6] fair handicapper: won NH jockeys race at Hamilton in May: stays 1¼m: acts on fibresand and any turf going: tried blinkered earlier in career. *P. Monteith*

AMELIA (IRE)   4 b.f. General Monash (USA) 107 – Rose Tint (IRE) (Salse (USA)   **54**
128) [2002 77d: p6g p6g p7g⁶ p7g⁶ 9d 8.1m 5.7g⁵ f7g⁴ 6g* 6g 6g⁵ 6m f6g⁵ p6g* Dec 30] neat filly: has a short action: modest nowadays: won handicap at Leicester (made most) in June and claimer at Lingfield in December: best up to easy 7f: acts on all-weather, good to firm and good to soft going, probably on soft: edgy sort: sometimes hangs. *J. Cullinan*

AMERAS (IRE)   4 b.f. Hamas (IRE) 125§ – Amerindian 84 (Commanche Run 133)   **– §**
[2002 81§: 8.1g⁶ 7.1g f7g 7d 7g Oct 19] IR 20,000Y: sixth foal: sister to fairly useful Irish 1998 2-y-o 5f winner Royal Tern, later 1m winner in USA, and half-sister to French 1994 2-y-o 5f winner Amri (by Jalmood): dam 1¼m winner who stayed 1½m: fairly useful maiden for W. Mullins in Ireland in 2001: no form at 4 yrs: stays 1m: acts on firm and soft ground: tongue tied final 3-y-o start, visored last 2: unreliable. *D. Shaw*

AMERICAN COUSIN   7 b.g. Distant Relative 128 – Zelda (USA) (Sharpen Up 127)   **77**
[2002 77, a?: 5s 5m 6m 5f 5g 5s 6f 5m 6m⁴ 5g 5g* 5m 5m* 5m³ 5d⁶ 5m 5f 5f Oct 11]   **a?**
sturdy gelding: fair handicapper on turf: won at Beverley and Doncaster (apprentices) in July: barely stays 6f: acts on heavy and good to firm going: blinkered twice earlier in career: sometimes slowly away: often held up: none too consistent. *D. Nicholls*

AMERICAN EMBASSY (USA)   2 b.c. (Mar 22) Quiet American (USA) – Foreign   **–**
Courier (USA) (Sir Ivor 135) [2002 6m 6m 6d Oct 14] good-bodied colt: half-brother to several winners, notably high-class sprinter/miler Green Desert (by Danzig) and useful French 1m (at 2 yrs) and 1½m winner Latarmiss (by Sadler's Wells): dam unraced half-sister to top-class US filly Althea: well held in maidens. *E. A. L. Dunlop*

AMIABLA (IRE)   3 gr.f. Dr Devious (IRE) 127 – Safkana (IRE) 78 (Doyoun 124)   **–**
[2002 60: 7m 11.5f p7g 10m 10m 7f 8.2m Oct 1] leggy, rather unfurnished filly: disappointing maiden: tried blinkered. *C. E. Brittain*

AMIE 2 b.f. (Apr 14) Northern Amethyst 99 – Break Point (Reference Point 139) [2002 –
p8g p8g Dec 14] second foal: half-sister to fairly useful 1¼m winner Play Time (by
Unfuwain): dam, ran once, out of smart 1¼m winner Cut Loose, herself sister to St Leger
winner Cut Above and half-sister to Irish 2000 Guineas winner Sharp Edge: well held
in 2 maidens at Lingfield, though not knocked about: bred to be suited by 1¼m+.
Mrs A. J. Perrett

AMIGO (IRE) 4 b.c. Spectrum (IRE) 126 – Eleanor Antoinette (IRE) (Double **89**
Schwartz 128) [2002 54: p13g* p12g* p12g* p12g² p12g* 10m⁶ 12m 14m 12s* 12m
p12g³ Dec 18] tall, close-coupled colt: fairly useful handicapper: won at Lingfield (4
times) and Kempton in first half of year: off 5 months, ran well at Lingfield final outing:
effective at 1¼m/1½m, barely at 1¾m: acts on polytrack (some promise only start on
fibresand), soft and good to firm going: blinkered (raced freely) once. *P. Mitchell*

AMINDA 2 b.f. (Apr 11) Zamindar (USA) 116 – Illana Bay (USA) (Manila (USA)) –
[2002 7d 7g f7g Sep 21] 6,000Y: third foal: dam unraced: well held in sellers.
S. L. Keightley

AMIR ZAMAN 4 ch.g. Salse (USA) 128 – Colorvista (Shirley Heights 130) [2002 **73**
73: 12m⁴ 11.5m 14d⁵ 14.1m 14d² 16.1d 14m⁴ 14f³ p12g Oct 9] big, strong, lengthy
gelding: fair handicapper: probably stays 2m: acts on firm and good to soft going: has
found little/edged right: none too consistent: sold 26,000 gns. *J. W. Payne*

AMJAD 5 ch.g. Cadeaux Genereux 131 – Babita 107 (Habitat 134) [2002 75d: f8s⁵ –
f11s² f16g³ f12g³ 9d Aug 23] lengthy, useful-looking gelding: fair handicapper on **a68**
all-weather: left P. Haslam after fourth start: stays 11f: acts on fibresand: sometimes
blinkered/visored. *Miss Kate Milligan*

AMNESTY 3 ch.g. Salse (USA) 128 – Amaranthus (Shirley Heights 130) [2002 63: **68**
8m 10.2g 11f Sep 25] lengthy gelding: fair maiden: unlikely to stay beyond 1¼m.
H. Candy

AMONG FRIENDS (IRE) 2 b.g. (Apr 25) Among Men (USA) 124 – Anita's **75**
Contessa (IRE) 68 (Anita's Prince 126) [2002 5m* 6m⁶ 5m⁴ p6g p5g p6g Nov 27] leggy,
good-topped gelding: second foal: half-brother to 3-y-o A One: dam, 6f/7f winner,
sister to useful sprinter Carranita: fair performer: won maiden at Kempton in May: ran
creditably third and fifth starts: should stay 6f: raced only on polytrack/good to firm
ground. *B. Palling*

AMONG WOMEN 4 b.f. Common Grounds 118 – Key West (FR) (Highest Honor –
(FR) 124) [2002 67, a62: p8g f8g⁶ Jan 29] leggy, workmanlike filly: fair performer at 3
yrs: no form in 2002. *K. R. Burke*

AMORAS (IRE) 5 b.m. Hamas (IRE) 125§ – Red Lory 87 (Bay Express 132) [2002 **81**
78: p8g p10g⁴ 8.5g³ 8m* 8m* 8m⁴ 8.3m 8.3m 8g 7f 8g Oct 17] good-bodied mare: fairly
useful handicapper: won at Brighton in May and Leicester in June: effective at 1m/1¼m:
acts on any turf going and polytrack: usually held up. *J. W. Hills*

AMOROUS PURSUITS 2 b.f. (Mar 1) Pursuit of Love 124 – Rivers Rhapsody 104 –
(Dominion 123) [2002 5s Jun 5] 11,000Y: sixth foal: sister to smart 5f (at 2 yrs) to 1m
winner For Your Eyes Only, and half-sister to 2 winners, including useful 5f (including at
2 yrs) winner See You Later (by Emarati): dam sprinter: 25/1, tailed off in maiden at
Kempton. *D. K. Ivory*

AMOUNT 2 b.f. (May 9) Salse (USA) 128 – Quota 102 (Rainbow Quest (USA) 134) **80 p**
[2002 7g³ 7d* 7f⁶ Oct 5] small, leggy filly: third foal: half-sister to 3-y-o Protectress:
dam, lightly-raced 1¼m winner, sister to Racing Post Trophy winner and St Leger second
Armiger: fairly useful form: won maiden at Epsom in September by 2 lengths from Henri
Martin, soon niggled along: never-nearer sixth of 9 to Khulood in listed event at
Newmarket: should stay at least 1¼m: away to debut, blanketed for stall entry at
Newmarket: sold 25,000 gns, sent to France: remains capable of better. *Mrs A. J. Perrett*

AMOUR SANS FIN (FR) 3 b.c. Kendor (FR) 122 – Nuit Sans Fin (FR) (Lead On –
Time (USA) 123) [2002 91: 8g 8m 6s a6.5f⁶ 7f Sep 22] sturdy colt: fairly useful at 2 yrs:
well held in 2002: left B. Meehan after third start: often blinkered. *A. McKeever, USA*

AMPOULE 3 b.g. Zamindar (USA) 116 – Diamond Park (IRE) 91 (Alzao (USA) 117) **53**
[2002 f8g p10g Dec 30] 22,000Y: fourth foal: half-brother to 2-y-o 5f winners Key (in
1998, by Midyan) and Pop Shop (in 1999, by Owington): dam, disappointing maiden
who stayed 1¼m, from good family: modest form in maidens at Southwell (slowly away)
and Lingfield (forced to check when staying on). *C. E. Brittain*

AMRITSAR 5 ch.g. Indian Ridge 123 – Trying For Gold (USA) 103 (Northern Baby –
(CAN) 127) [2002 64: 8m 10m 11.5m 8s 11.6m Jul 29] angular gelding: modest maiden
at 4 yrs: no form in 2002. *P. Howling*

AMUNDSEN (USA) 2 b.c. (Apr 19) Gone West (USA) – Aunt Anne (USA) (Deputy **84 p**
Minister (CAN)) [2002 7.2g 9f* 10s⁶ Nov 2] $50,000Y: tall, lengthy colt: on the weak
side at 2 yrs: first foal: dam, US 2-y-o 6f and 1m winner and third in Grade 1 7f event at 2
yrs, sister/half-sister to smart US 9f performers Atelier and Aldiza: fairly useful form:
won 3-runner maiden at Redcar in September by ½ length from Condoleezza, off bridle
some way out: well-held sixth of 10 behind Forest Magic in listed race at Newmarket:
should stay 1¼m: acts on firm ground: type to do better. *M. Johnston*

AMUSED 3 ch.f. Prince Sabo 123 – Indigo 86 (Primo Dominie 121) [2002 63p: 5g⁶ **73**
6m⁶ 5g³ 5m² 7f* 6d 6s 6f³ 7g 7d² Oct 18] short-backed filly: fair performer: won maiden
at Catterick in July: stays 7f: acts on firm and good to soft going: sometimes slowly
away: reportedly lost action sixth start, found little seventh one: none too consistent.
Mrs J. R. Ramsden

AMWELL STAR (USA) 4 gr.f. Silver Buck (USA) – Markham Fair (CAN) (Wood- **46**
man (USA) 126) [2002 46: f16s³ f16g 14.1d 13.9f 14.1d 16.2f⁵ 12.1d⁶ 13.8m³ 14m Aug
31] poor maiden handicapper: will stay beyond 2m: acts on fibresand and soft ground:
has reared leaving stall (unseated once). *J. R. Jenkins*

ANABAA BLUE 4 b.c. Anabaa (USA) 130 – Allez Les Trois (USA) 114 (Riverman **122**
(USA) 131) [2002 120: 10.5g⁵ 12m* 12m⁵ 12m² 12g Oct 6] big, good-topped colt: very
smart performer: reportedly suffering from lung infection on reappearance but back to
form to win Grand Prix de Chantilly in June by 1½ lengths from dead-heaters St Expedit
and Ange Gabriel, leading under 1f out: always rear in Grand Prix de Saint-Cloud next
time but creditable efforts at Longchamp last 2 starts, length second to Aquarelliste in
Prix Foy then seventh to Marienbard in Prix de l'Arc de Triomphe: best around 1½m:
acted on heavy and good to firm going: has worn crossed noseband: genuine: to stand at
Haras d'Etreham, France, fee €8,000, Oct 1st. *C. Lerner, France*

ANAK PEKAN 2 ch.c. (Jan 26) In The Wings 128 – Trefoil (FR) (Blakeney 126) **– p**
[2002 8g Oct 18] 70,000F, 120,000Y: stocky colt: half-brother to several winners,
including useful 1½m winner Firecrest (by Darshaan): dam, French 10.5f to 1½m winner,
half-sister to dam of Melbourne Cup winner Jeune: 33/1: burly and green: well held in
maiden at Newmarket: likely to do better. *M. A. Jarvis*

ANALYZE (FR) 4 b.g. Anabaa (USA) 130 – Bramosia (Forzando 122) [2002 73: **79**
9.7m³ 8m 10m* 10.3m³ 10f⁵ 10m³ 10.1d 10.1m³ 10.1m³ 10m 10m 10m⁶ 10m² 9g 10.2g³ᵈ
p10g p10g³ p10g* p10g² Dec 28] smallish, workmanlike gelding: fair handicapper: won
at Leicester in April and claimer at Lingfield in December: best around 1¼m: acts on firm
going, good to soft and polytrack: has hung left: often held up. *M. R. Channon*

ANA MARIE (FR) 3 b.f. Anabaa (USA) 130 – Marie de Ken (FR) 110 (Kendor (FR) **118**
122) [2002 103: 9m⁴ 9.3g* 10m⁴ 10.5m³ 12m² 12m² 12g Oct 6] close-coupled,
useful-looking filly: second foal: closely related to French 1m winner Desert Melody (by
Green Desert): dam French 7f (at 2 yrs) to 10.5f (Prix Fille de l'Air) winner: smart
performer: got off mark in Prix Vanteaux at Longchamp in April by short head from
Bright Sky: best efforts when promoted to third behind Bright Sky in Prix de Diane at
Chantilly in June and when 1½ lengths second to Pearly Shells in Prix Vermeille at
Longchamp penultimate start: towards rear in Prix de l'Arc de Triomphe at Longchamp
final outing: stays 1½m: acts on good to firm ground, best effort at 2 yrs on heavy.
P. H. Demercastel, France

ANANI (USA) 2 b.c. (Apr 14) Miswaki (USA) 124 – Mystery Rays (USA) 122 **85 p**
(Nijinsky (CAN) 138) [2002 7d⁴ 8s² Oct 26] 100,000Y: lengthy colt: closely related to
useful French 1995 2-y-o 1m winner Metaphor (by Woodman) and half-brother to
several winners, including 3-y-o King of Happiness: dam, 1m (at 2 yrs) to 1½m (Prix
Minerve) winner, closely related to smart 6f to 1m performer Robin des Pins: off 2½
months, better effort in maidens (fairly useful form) when length second of 16 to Zeis at
Newbury, carrying head awkwardly: will probably stay 1¼m: should improve further.
E. A. L. Dunlop

ANASTASIA'S SHADOW 6 b.m. Theatrical Charmer 114 – Lamloum (IRE) –
(Vacarme (USA) 121) [2002 –: f9.4g Jan 18] no longer of any account. *T. T. Clement*

ANASTASIA VENTURE 5 b.m. Lion Cavern (USA) 117 – Our Shirley 84 (Shirley –
Heights 130) [2002 48: f9.4g⁵ p7g p6g 7m Apr 23] no longer of any account. *J. Akehurst*

ANCESTOR (IRE)   3 ch.c. Polish Precedent (USA) 131 – Anna of Saxony 111   **113**
(Ela-Mana-Mou 132) [2002 92p: 10s* 16.2m³ 14g Aug 30] big, lengthy colt: fourth foal:
half-brother to French 2-y-o 1m winners Anna Palariva (Prix d'Aumale in 1997, by
Caerleon) and Anshaam (in 1999, by Alzao), both useful: dam, 11.5f to 14.6f (Park Hill
Stakes) winner, half-sister to very smart performer up to 1½m Annaba: smart performer:
won maiden at the Curragh in May: excellent 1½ lengths third to Mamool in Queen's
Vase at Royal Ascot, staying on from unpromising position: pulled up (reportedly
suffered leg injury) in handicap at Tralee final start: stays 2m: acts on soft and good to
firm ground. *J. Oxx, Ireland*

ANDAAD   2 b.f. (May 5) Alzao (USA) 117 – Ghazwat (USA) (Riverman (USA) 131)   **–**
[2002 7.1m Sep 21] third foal: half-sister to 7f winner Istihsaan (by Barathea), later
successful in Spain: dam, unraced, out of close relative to Lomond and half-sister to
Seattle Slew: 25/1, last of 9 in maiden at Warwick. *N. A. Graham*

AND BEYOND (IRE)   4 b.c. Darshaan 133 – Al Najah (USA) 96 (Topsider (USA))   **113**
[2002 111: 16.4m 15d* 16m⁴ 14.6v⁴ Nov 8] rangy, good-topped colt: good walker/mover:
smart performer: won 4 races, including Queen's Vase at Royal Ascot at 3 yrs and listed
race at Chantilly (beat Clety gamely by neck) in June: creditable 7 lengths fourth to
Jardines Lookout in Goodwood Cup in August: folded tamely final start: would have
stayed beyond 2m: untried on firm going, acted on any other: tended to run in snatches on
reappearance: usually raced prominently: was genuine: to stand at Scarrow Hill Stud,
Carlisle, fee £800. *M. Johnston*

ANDILISA   3 b.f. Danehill (USA) 126 – Chloe Nicole (USA) 67 (Personal Flag   **78 ?**
(USA)) [2002 8g⁴ 7g 6g³ p6g Oct 9] 70,000F, 110,000Y: leggy, angular filly: first foal:
dam maiden from family of Zieten and Blue Duster: fairly useful maiden in France: left
D. Smaga after second start: just fair form in Britain subsequently: stays 1m: raced only
on good going or softer (acts on soft) on turf: pulled hard/carried head awkwardly
penultimate start. *J. R. Fanshawe*

ANDREW DOBLE   3 ch.g. Sabrehill (USA) 120 – Verchinina 99 (Star Appeal 133)   **82**
[2002 64p: 7g⁶ 10g² 10m p8g* May 29] strong, well-made gelding: fairly useful performer: won maiden at Lingfield in May: acts on polytrack, but stays 1½m: acts only on
good/good to firm going on turf: sold 16,000 gns. joined Miss V. Williams. *M. A. Jarvis*

ANDREYEV (IRE)   8 ch.g. Presidium 124 – Missish (Mummy's Pet 125) [2002 99:   **–**
5s 6g 7m 6m 6g 7.2v 8g 8v Nov 8] tall gelding: one-time smart winner: very much on
downgrade: blinkered/visored. *J. S. Goldie*

ANDROMACHE   3 ch.f. Hector Protector (USA) 124 – South Sea Bubble (IRE) 75   **66**
(Bustino 136) [2002 66p: 10.2g 8.2g⁵ 8m 10d² 10.2f² 12d 9d p8g Nov 23] rather leggy,
lengthy filly: has scope: fair maiden handicapper: stays 1¼m: acts on firm and good to
soft going: sold 6,000 gns. *L. M. Cumani*

ANDROMEDA (IRE)   3 b.f. Barathea (IRE) 127 – Royal York 75 (Bustino 136)   **–**
[2002 68p: 8.1g Aug 14] leggy, unfurnished filly: better effort in maidens only 2-y-o start:
bred to be well suited by 1m+: joined M. Todhunter. *J. Noseda*

AND TOTO TOO   2 br.f. (Mar 27) Averti (IRE) 117 – Divina Mia 66 (Dowsing (USA)   **69**
124) [2002 6m³ 5.9s² 6m³ 7m⁴ 7g⁶ f8.5g³ p7g Dec 28] 4,800F, 7,000Y: fourth foal:
half-sister to 2000 2-y-o 5f winner So Divine (by So Factual) and 3-y-o Mine Host: dam,
2-y-o 6f winner who stayed 11f, out of useful half-sister to Shirley Heights: fair maiden:
left M. Bell before penultimate start: ran as though amiss final one: stays 8.5f: acts on
fibresand, soft and good to firm going: slowly away first 2 outings. *P. D. Evans*

ANDY'S ELECTIVE   5 b.g. Democratic (USA) 101 – English Mint 66 (Jalmood   **56 §**
(USA) 126) [2002 68: p7g 8.3g f7g 8m 7m 7g⁵ 7m 6m Sep 19] modest handicapper
nowadays: stays 1m: acts on firm and soft ground: often visored: often races prominently:
unreliable. *J. R. Jenkins*

ANEMOS (IRE)   7 ch.g. Be My Guest (USA) 126 – Frendly Persuasion (General   **56**
Assembly (USA)) [2002 75: p10g p12g p10g 10.9f 8.3g* 8.1m⁴ 7g 8.3m 8.3g 9.7m 8.5m²
8.5d 8.1m³ Sep 21] tall gelding: modest performer: won seller at Windsor in April:
effective at 1m/1¼m: acts on soft and good to firm going (probably on fibresand): sometimes
blinkered (also often hooded nowadays): none too reliable. *T. D. McCarthy*

ANGE GABRIEL (FR)   4 b.c. Kaldounevees (FR) 118 – Mount Gable (Head For   **124**
Heights 125) [2002 108: 12d* 12g² 12g³ 12m² 12m* 12d* 12m* Dec 15]
Despite winning two Group 1 races in the most recent season, Ange Gabriel
has yet to show for certain that he has what it takes to go close in Europe's most
prestigious middle-distance events. Ange Gabriel's successes in the Grand Prix de

Grand Prix de Saint-Cloud—Ange Gabriel causes something of an upset;
Polish Summer holds off Aquarelliste for second, then come Califet and Anabaa Blue
as the pacemaker Virginian (partly hidden near rail) weakens

Saint-Cloud and the Hong Kong Vase were most praiseworthy efforts, but the form of those races does not put him among the very best mile-and-a-half performers in Europe. For the second year running the Grand Prix de Saint-Cloud had a substandard look to it and Ange Gabriel cannot compare with such luminaries as Carnegie, Helissio and Montjeu, all winners of the race over the last decade. The Hong Kong Vase, despite its value, is usually won with no better performance than Ange Gabriel produced and he will need to improve further if he is to be successful in what is said to be his main target as a five-year-old, the King George VI and Queen Elizabeth Diamond Stakes at Ascot. It should be said, however, in Ange Gabriel's favour, that he is reliable—he has won nine of his fifteen starts—and has progressed steadily with racing.

Third in a maiden at Angers on his only two-year-old outing, Ange Gabriel showed useful form when completing a five-timer at three in a maiden at Argentan, minor events at Angers, Nantes and Saint-Cloud and a listed race at Deauville. After a break of over two months, he wasn't the same horse on his last two outings as a three-year-old but got his career back on track on his reappearance in the latest season. He made much of the running and held on gamely to beat Califet by a head in a listed event at Longchamp in March. Ange Gabriel finished behind Califet on his next two starts, in the Prix d'Hedouville at the same course in April, beaten three lengths into second, and in the five-runner Prix Jean de Chaudenay at Saint-Cloud in May, finishing five lengths behind in third. A good effort in the Grand Prix de Chantilly in June, when dead-heating for second with St Expedit behind Anabaa Blue (Califet filling fourth half a length behind) preceded Ange Gabriel's success in the Grand Prix de Saint-Cloud. He turned the tables on Anabaa Blue and beat Califet again, as well as the previous season's Arc runner-up Aquarelliste who had made a winning reappearance in the Prix Ganay. Ange Gabriel started the rank outsider of six, returned at 16.3/1 on the pari-mutuel. After tracking Aquarelliste's pacemaker Virginian, who set a good pace, Ange Gabriel was left clear early in the straight when that horse capitulated and held on as the rest closed late. At the line Ange Gabriel had a two-length advantage over the lightly-raced Polish Summer, with Aquarelliste a short head back in third; Califet and Anabaa Blue were below form in fourth and fifth. Though Ange Gabriel could be said to have enjoyed the run of the race, it was still a very smart performance. He wasn't seen out again for nearly four months after his success, missing the Arc because of a 'minor health scare', and returned to carry a Group 1 penalty to victory in the Prix du Conseil de Paris over the Prix de l'Arc course and distance in late-October, dictating a steady gallop and holding off Thompson Rouge by half a length.

Hong Kong Vase, Sha Tin—a 1,2 for France as Ange Gabriel beats Aquarelliste (rail)

After a further two months off Ange Gabriel ran in the fourteen-runner Hong Kong Vase at Sha Tin, where he was the only European-trained winner at the valuable International meeting, beating Aquarelliste by three quarters of a length after tracking the leaders and edging ahead well inside the final furlong. The American horse Falcon Flight, third in the Breeders' Cup Turf, occupied the same position beaten a further neck, with the previous year's runner-up, Godolphin challenger Ekraar, a further three quarters of a length away in fourth. Ange Gabriel's away-day certainly proved lucrative for his connections; at around £650,000 to the winner the Hong Kong Vase is worth in the region of £75,000 more than the Arc, Europe's most valuable and most prestigious all-aged mile and a half race.

Ange Gabriel (FR) (b.c. 1998)			
	Kaldounevees (FR) (gr 1991)	Kaldoun (gr 1975)	Caro
			Katana
		Safaroa (b 1978)	Satingo
			Traverse Afar
	Mount Gable (b 1986)	Head For Heights (b 1981)	Shirley Heights
			Vivante
		Cupids Hill (b 1977)	Sallust
			Sweet J

Ange Gabriel is by Kaldounevees, a smart French performer who raced only as a three- and four-year-old. Like Ange Gabriel, he was reliable and improved with age, winning twice at a mile in Group 3 events at four before finishing in the frame in the Bayerisches Zuchtrennen in Germany, then in the States in the Arlington Million and the Man o'War Stakes. Kaldounevees' only other Group 1 winner is Ange Gabriel's stable-companion Terre A Terre, successful in the 2001 Prix de l'Opera and in the latest renewal of the Dubai Duty Free as a five-year-old. Ange Gabriel is the fourth foal out of Mount Gable; his year-older half-brother Dubayotte (by Turgeon) won at twelve and a half furlongs in France in the latest season. Mount Gable was unraced as a two-year-old but ran twenty-six times in France up to the age of five, winning twice at around a mile and three furlongs and proving effective at up to a mile and seven. Mount Gable is not from a particularly distinguished family, though she is out of a half-sister to the very smart miler in the 'seventies Ardoon, another horse who improved with age—he was at his best as a six-year-old. As a point of interest, Ange Gabriel's pedigree is free of any Northern Dancer influence, an increasingly rare occurrence for a Group 1 winner nowadays. He has shown his best form at around a mile and a half and has yet to race on firm ground, though he acts on any other. Incidentally, should Ange Gabriel prove up to winning the King George he will be the second winner of the race for the family of owner-breeders Henri and Antonia Devin, the proprietors of the Haras du Mesnil in France; Right Royal V beat three rivals in 1961 for Henri Devin's grandmother, Mme Elisabeth Couturie. That would be some feat, but perhaps no more remarkable than the one Ange Gabriel's breeders accomplished at the Hong Kong International meeting. As well as the Vase winner, they also bred the Hong Kong Cup winner Precision. *E. Libaud, France*

ANGEL ANNIE 2 b.f. (Jan 22) Alzao (USA) 117 – Pure (Slip Anchor 136) [2002 7d³ **80** 8g p7g³ f8.5g Dec 20] second foal: dam unraced sister to Oaks and St Leger winner User Friendly: fairly useful maiden: best effort on debut: bred to be suited by 1m+, but seems headstrong: has worn crossed noseband. *B. W. Hills*

ANGEL HILL 7 ch.m. King's Signet (USA) 110 – Tawny 81 (Grey Ghost 98) [2002 **61 d** 67: 6f³ 5m⁶ 5g 7f 6m 6.1m 7f a8g Dec 1] strong mare: modest handicapper: on the downgrade: left T. Etherington after seventh start: effective at 5f (given a test) to 7.5f: acts on firm going, soft and fibresand: tried blinkered/visored, not since 2000: sometimes slowly away/races freely: tends to hang right. *C. Tinkler, Spain*

ANGELICA GARNETT 2 ch.f. (Apr 9) Desert Story (IRE) 115 – Vanessa Bell **64** (IRE) (Lahib (USA) 129) [2002 7g 7d f8.5f⁶ Nov 29] 21,000Y: rather leggy filly: fluent mover: second foal: dam, 6f winner in Italy at 2 yrs, out of half-sister to disqualified Oaks winner Aliysa, herself dam of Desert Story: modest form in mid-field in maidens: should stay 1m: raced freely on debut: sweating next time. *R. Charlton*

ANGEL ISA (IRE) 2 b.f. (Mar 19) Fayruz 116 – Isa (Dance In Time (CAN)) [2002 **53** 5m⁶ 6g 5f³ f5g⁴ f6s⁶ Nov 30] IR 5,000Y: quite attractive filly: sister to 4 winners and **a59** half-sister to 3 winners, including fairly useful sprinter Time To Go Home (by Day Is

Done): dam unraced: modest maiden: seems to stay 6f: acts on firm going and fibresand. *R. A. Fahey*

ANGELS VENTURE 6 ch.g. Unfuwain (USA) 131 – City of Angels (Woodman (USA) 126) [2002 78, a75: p13g p16g 11.5m May 29] close-coupled gelding: fair handicapper: stays 1½m: acts on soft going, good to firm and polytrack: tried visored: often tongue tied: has hung left. *J. R. Jenkins* — **68**

ANGELUS DOMINI (IRE) 3 b.f. Blues Traveller (IRE) 119 – Lyphards Goddess (IRE) (Lyphard's Special (USA) 122) [2002 62: 6m⁶ 6s f6g⁶ 6.9d 8s³ 9.9m f12s⁶ 10g³ f7g Oct 22] leggy, unfurnished filly: modest maiden: barely stays 1½m: acts on fibresand and good to firm going, probably on soft: swerved violently left leaving stall/unseated second 2-y-o start: sometimes races freely. *B. A. McMahon* — **54**

ANGELUS SUNSET (USA) 3 b.g. Numerous (USA) – Angelic Note (USA) 90 (The Minstrel (CAN) 135) [2002 101: 8g² 10m⁶ 7d Dec 21] good-topped gelding: useful performer: creditable efforts in listed races at Kempton (2 lengths second to Flat Spin) and Royal Ascot (had plenty to do when 4½ lengths sixth to Burning Sun) 3 months later: left B. Meehan, renamed Top Prize and off another 6 months before final outing: stays 1¼m: yet to race on firm going, acts on any other. *P. F. Yiu, Hong Kong* — **106**

ANGEL WATCH 2 b.c. (Mar 10) Octagonal (NZ) 126 – Angel Chimes 77 (Most Welcome 131) [2002 5.1m⁵ 6d 7.1m 7.5g Sep 18] second foal: dam, 5f (at 2 yrs) and 7f winner, half-sister to useful performers Prince Babar (up to 1m) and Warning Order (up to 11.5f): poor maiden: blinkered final start. *T. D. Easterby* — **42**

ANGIE'S DOUBLE 2 ch.f. (Mar 2) Double Trigger (IRE) 123 – Arch Angel (IRE) 55 (Archway (IRE) 115) [2002 7m 7f 8g Oct 16] unfurnished filly: first foal: dam 2-y-o 6f/7f winner: signs of ability though well held in maidens: failed to handle turn at Bath final start. *D. J. S. ffrench Davis* — **–**

ANGIES QUEST 5 b.m. Inchinor 119 – Chanson d'Avril 54 (Chief Singer 131) [2002 47: f11g Feb 5] poor maiden at best: well beaten only start in 2002: tried tongue tied. *P. W. D'Arcy* — **–**

ANGUS-G 10 br.g. Chief Singer 131 – Horton Line 89 (High Line 125) [2002 82: p10g 83 p12g Feb 9] big, useful-looking gelding: impresses in appearance: good mover: fairly useful handicapper: effective at 1¼m/1½m: acts on polytrack, firm and good to soft going: held up, and tends to idle in front. *Mrs M. Reveley* — **83**

ANIKITOS 4 ch.c. Nashwan (USA) 135 – Tamassos 67 (Dance In Time (CAN)) [2002 90: 13.3v³ 12g 14.4d 13.3f 11.5m 11.7g Oct 16] heavy-bodied colt: fairly useful performer at best: on downgrade: stays 1½m: has wandered: sold 7,000 gns. *Mrs A. J. Perrett* — **86 d**

ANIMAL CRACKER 4 gr.f. Primo Dominie 121 – Child Star (FR) 58 (Bellypha 130) [2002 58: f7g⁶ f7g f5g⁵ f6g f7g 8.1d f12g 6.1m f6g 6g 7m Aug 29] close-coupled, workmanlike filly: modest performer: on the downgrade: left J. Unett after ninth start: best efforts at 5f/6f: acts on soft going, good to firm and fibresand: tried blinkered/tongue tied. *R. Curtis* — **52 d**

ANIMAL MAGIC 2 b.f. (Feb 28) Shareef Dancer (USA) 135 – Blessed Lass (HOL) 48 (Good Times (ITY)) [2002 5f 5g⁴ 5m 7g5 7.5g 8g Sep 10] 4,000Y: unfurnished filly: second living foal: dam lightly raced in Holland: poor maiden: should stay 1m: raced only on good going or firmer: blinkered (slowly away) twice. *M. W. Easterby* — **48**

ANKARA'S LADY 4 ch.f. King's Signet (USA) 110 – Ankara's Princess (USA) 81 (Ankara (USA) 106) [2002 f6g f6g f5g Apr 26] fifth live foal: half-sister to fairly useful Nominator Lad (7f to 10.5f winner by Nomination): dam 2-y-o 5f winner who stayed 6f: no form. *R. Hollinshead* — **–**

ANNABELLE 4 ch.f. Most Welcome 131 – Saluti Tutti 77 (Trojan Fen 118) [2002 72: p8g* p8g⁴ 10d³ 10m⁴ 9s⁶ 8g⁶ p8g Sep 4] strong filly: fair performer: won maiden at Lingfield in February: stays 1¼m: acts on polytrack, soft and good to firm going: sent to Saudi Arabia. *C. F. Wall* — **70**

ANNADAWI 7 b.g. Sadler's Wells (USA) 132 – Prayers'n Promises (USA) (Foolish 73 Pleasure (USA)) [2002 83d, a–: 12s⁶ 10s² 9.3g* May 18] quite good-topped gelding: fair a– handicapper: won at Carlisle in May: stayed 1½m: acted on heavy going, good to firm going and fibresand: tried blinkered/visored/tongue tied: dead. *M. E. Sowersby* — **73 a–**

ANNADUFF (IRE) 4 b.f. Indian Ridge 123 – Bazaar Promise 58 (Native Bazaar 122) [2002 7s p8g 8.3d f9.4g f12g Dec 21] IR 48,000Y: seventh foal (all by Indian Ridge): sister to 4 winners, including useful sprinter Cheyenne Spirit and 8.5f and 1¼m winner Indian Express: dam temperamental sister to smart sprinter Crofthall: no form. *J. A. Osborne* — **–**

66

ANNA ELISE (IRE)   6 b.m. Nucleon (USA) 94 – Tormented (USA) (Alleged (USA)   **93 ?**
138) [2002 103: 6d 5g 5d 5g Jul 27] lengthy mare: useful performer at best: won listed
race at Cork in 2001, when also third to Invincible Spirit in Boland Stakes at the Curragh:
difficult to assess in 2002: last in King's Stand Stakes at Royal Ascot second start: has
won at 1m but best efforts at 6f: acts on firm and soft going. *J. A. Flynn, Ireland*

ANNA KAREENA (IRE)   3 b. or br.f. Charnwood Forest (IRE) 125 – Anna Comnena   **97**
(IRE) 71 (Shareef Dancer (USA) 135) [2002 10m 11.1s* 10.3g* 9.9d⁵ p10g² 12g 10.3m*
Aug 30] IR 25,000Y: workmanlike filly: half-sister to several winners, including smart
Irish 1¼m/1½m winner Sadlers Wings (by In The Wings) and useful 1¼m winner who
stayed 12.5f Abyaan (by Ela-Mana-Mou): dam, maiden who should have stayed 1½m,
half-sister to dams of very smart performers Annus Mirabilis (9f to 1½m) and Annaba
(around 1½m): useful performer: won maiden at Hamilton and minor event and handicap
(comfortably by 2 lengths from Tertullian) at Chester between May and August: should
stay 1½m: acts on soft going, good to firm and polytrack. *J. Noseda*

ANNAMBO   2 ch.c. (Feb 18) In The Wings 128 – Anna Matrushka (Mill Reef (USA)   **82 p**
141) [2002 8.2m³ Sep 20] useful-looking colt: brother to very smart 1¼m/1½m performer
Annaba, closely related to useful Irish 1½m and 2m winner Ancelin (by Sadler's Wells),
and half-brother to several winners, including smart middle-distance stayers Anna of
Saxony (by Ela-Mana-Mou) and Pozarica (by Rainbow Quest): dam unraced close
relative to dam of Annus Mirabilis: 7/2 and green, 3 lengths last of 3 to Ballerina Suprema
in maiden at Nottingham, setting steady pace and not knocked about when unable to
quicken: will stay at least 1½m: should improve. *D. R. Loder*

ANNA WALHAAN (IRE)   3 b.g. Green Desert (USA) 127 – Queen's Music (USA)   **95**
66 (Dixieland Band (USA)) [2002 103: 8g⁵ 8g 9.9g 8g² 8g* 8m 7d 8m³ 8f³ 7m⁴ Oct 2]
deep-bodied, close-coupled gelding: useful performer: won 3-runner minor event at Ayr
(rallied to beat Pentecost a neck) in May: stays 1m: acts on firm going, possibly not on
good to soft: visored 6 of last 7 starts: looked difficult ride ninth outing: none too
consistent: sold 16,000 gns, and gelded. *M. R. Channon*

ANNEKA   2 b.f. (Apr 21) Among Men (USA) 124 – Treasure Hunt (Hadeer 118) [2002   **43**
6g⁶ 7m Jul 7] lengthy filly: second foal: dam unraced: poor form in seller/maiden.
Miss S. E. Hall

ANNE-LISE   4 ch.f. Inchinor 119 – Red Gloves 83 (Red God 128§) [2002 53: 10v³ 7s*   **63**
10d⁵ 7d² 8s² 7g 8m 10s 8g f7g Nov 30] lengthy filly: modest handicapper: won at the
Curragh in May: left P. Mooney, Ireland, before final start: effective at 7f, probably at
1¼m: unraced on firm going, probably acts on any other turf: blinkered sixth start.
P. Mooney, Ireland

ANNE NUTTER   3 ch.f. Kasakov – Bairn Glen (Bairn (USA) 126) [2002 8m 9.9m   **–**
10.1m 7f Sep 27] smallish filly: second foal: dam no sign of ability: well beaten in
maidens/seller (reared badly and toppled over before start second outing). *I. W. McInnes*

ANNE TUDOR (IRE)   3 b.f. Anabaa (USA) 130 – Alikhlas 81 (Lahib (USA) 129)   **79**
[2002 77: 7.1s* 8g 7s 7s Nov 2] good-topped filly: fair performer, lightly raced: won
maiden at Haydock in June: off over 4 months, just respectable efforts at best in handicaps after: may prove best up to 7f: acts on soft going (yet to race on firmer than good).
B. W. Hills

ANNIE APPLE (IRE)   6 ch.m. Petardia 113 – Art Duo 86 (Artaius (USA) 129) [2002   **37**
45, a49: f8.5g³ f9.4g f8g f8g 7f⁶ 7d p7g⁴ 8d 8f Jul 17] leggy, quite good-topped   **a40**
mare: poor performer: stays 1m: acts on firm going, soft and all-weather: tried visored.
J. R. Boyle

ANNIE DALY (IRE)   3 b.f. Spinning World (USA) 130 – Alleged Devotion (USA)   **–**
(Alleged (USA) 138) [2002 94: 8.3m 9.9m May 16] closely related to useful 1999 2-y-o
7f winner Thady Quill (by Nureyev) and half-sister to several winners, including US
Grade 3 8.5f winner Humble Eight (by Seattle Battle): dam unraced half-sister to Oaks/
Irish Derby winner Balanchine: maiden: blinkered, form (fairly useful) only when fourth
in listed race at Leopardstown final 2-y-o outing (left A. O'Brien in Ireland after): last
both starts in Britain: stays 9f: acts on soft going: sent to Australia. *J. W. Hills*

ANNIE RUAN   4 b.f. So Factual (USA) 120 – Sans Diablo (IRE) (Mac's Imp (USA)   **–**
116) [2002 65, a61: f6g p5g 5.1g Apr 30] fair maiden at best: no form in 2002: tried
visored. *D. Haydn Jones*

ANNIJAZ   5 b.m. Alhijaz 122 – Figment 75 (Posse (USA) 130) [2002 67, a56: f7g⁶   **57**
p7g 8f 8g 8g 7m⁴ 8m³ 8f³ 7.1g⁶ 8m 7.9m 8g 7m⁵ Sep 18] sparely-made mare: **a49**
modest performer: probably best at 7f/1m: acts on fibresand and any turf going: held up.
J. M. Bradley

ANNIVERSARY GUEST (IRE)   3 b. or br.f. Desert King (IRE) 129 – Polynesian   **54**
Goddess (IRE) (Salmon Leap (USA) 131) [2002 –: 11.9m 10m 10m 12m 16f 16m⁶ 14.1g
15.8f³ Oct 8] close-coupled filly: modest handicapper: stays 2m: acts on firm going. *Mrs
Lucinda Featherstone*

ANN'S FLYER   2 b.f. (Apr 9) Cool Jazz 116 – Spice And Sugar 65 (Chilibang 120)   **57 §**
[2002 5f⁶ f5s⁴ 6m² 5m³ 6g f5g⁶ 6f 6g² Aug 7] third foal: dam 6f (at 2 yrs) and 1½m
winner: modest maiden: best effort when second in selling nursery at Leicester final start:
should stay 7f: acts on good to firm going: usually blinkered prior to Leicester: often
slowly away: unreliable: sold 800 gns. *R. Wilman*

ANN'S MILL   5 b.m. Pelder (IRE) 125 – Honey Mill 67 (Milford 119) [2002 –: p6g   **–**
p6g⁶ 8.5g 8d p7g⁶ 6m⁴ 7m Jul 22] of little account nowadays. *N. I. M. Rossiter*

ANOOF   3 b.f. Marju (IRE) 127 – Waqood (USA) 75 (Riverman (USA) 131) [2002 75:   **75**
7m² 8f* 8m Aug 15] good-bodied filly: fair performer: made all in maiden at Ascot
in July: raced freely (reportedly coughed) final start: stays 1m: acts on any ground: sent
to South Africa. *M. P. Tregoning*

ANOTHER ASPECT (IRE)   3 b.g. Inzar (USA) 112 – The Aspecto Girl (IRE) 53   **–**
(Alzao (USA) 117) [2002 67: f8.5g⁶ f8.5g f12g Apr 15] modest performer at best: well
below form in 2002. *J. Cullinan*

ANOTHER DIAMOND (IRE)   4 b.f. First Trump 118 – Rockin' Rosie 59 (Song   **61**
132) [2002 60: f11s p13g 8m³ 10.2g* f12g³ f12g* f12g⁴ Dec 14] modest handicapper:
left P. Howling after second start: won at Chepstow in September and Wolverhampton
in December: seems to stay 1¾m: acts on fibresand, raced mainly on good/good to firm
going on turf. *L. G. Cottrell*

ANOTHER FRANK   2 b.g. (Mar 5) Wizard King 122 – Join The Clan 95 (Clantime   **–**
101) [2002 5f May 11] 2,500Y: fourth foal: dam multiple 5f/6f winner: 14/1, always
behind in claimer at Thirsk. *M. W. Easterby*

ANOTHER GLIMPSE   4 b.g. Rudimentary (USA) 118 – Running Glimpse (IRE) 84   **80**
(Runnett 125) [2002 –: p10g³ 7g* p8g 7m⁵ 7m* p6g* p7g⁵ Dec 28] strong, close-coupled
gelding: fairly useful performer: won maiden (made all)/minor event at Lingfield and
handicap at Kempton in 2002: effective at 6f to 1¼m: acts on good to firm going and
polytrack: swished tail continuously in paddock second outing: sometimes races freely.
Miss B. Sanders

ANOTHER SECRET   4 b.f. Efisio 120 – Secrets of Honour (Belmez (USA) 131)   **86**
[2002 87: 10m 8.1d³ 8.3m³ 9g² 10g 9m⁴ 10f⁶ 8g Oct 17] sturdy filly: fairly useful
handicapper: good placed efforts at Windsor and Goodwood third and fourth starts: best
form around 1m/9f: acts on soft and good to firm going. *R. Hannon*

ANOTHER TIME   10 ch.g. Clantime 101 – Another Move 69 (Farm Walk 111) [2002   **63**
83: 7g 10s 8m 8.3m 11.9m² 9.7m⁵ 12g³ 10m 12d 8m⁶ 10m 10.4f Oct 10] neat gelding:
carries condition: poor mover: modest nowadays: best at 1¼m/easy 1½m: acts on any turf
going except heavy, well beaten only run on fibresand: held up. *R. Guest*

ANOTHER VICTIM   8 ch.g. Beveled (USA) – Ragtime Rose (Ragstone 128) [2002   **65**
58+: 5.1d 5f f5g⁶ 5.7g 5d⁴ 5s* 5g* 5.1d 5.1g 5g Oct 28] leggy gelding: fair handicapper:
won at Windsor (for second year running, hung left/flashed tail) and Ayr in May: best at
5f/6f: has form on good to firm ground, but all wins on good or softer (acts on heavy):
none too consistent. *M. R. Bosley*

ANSWERED PROMISE (FR)   3 gr.g. Highest Honor (FR) 124 – Answered Prayer   **75**
(Green Desert (USA) 127) [2002 70p: 8s⁶ 10.2g 8.1d* 10m³ 8s 9m* 8.3m⁴ f8s f9.4g²ᵈ
f8.5g² f7s f9.4s f8.5g⁶ Dec 14] strong, short-backed gelding: has a quick action: fair
performer: left E. Dunlop 1,000 gns after second start: won claimer at Haydock (hung
left) in August and handicap at Musselburgh (made all) in September: well below form
last 3 starts: best around 1m/9f: acts on soft going, good to firm and fibresand. *I. Semple*

ANTHONY MON AMOUR (USA)   7 b.g. Nicholas (USA) 111 – Reine de La Ciel   **45**
(USA) (Conquistador Cielo (USA)) [2002 68: 5f 5g 6f 5d 5s⁶ 5.9d 5g⁶ Jul 3] big, strong
gelding: poor handicapper nowadays: best at 5f/6f: acts on fibresand, firm and soft going:
tongue tied: sometimes slowly away. *D. Nicholls*

ANTHONY ROYLE   4 ch.g. King's Signet (USA) 110 – La Thuile 46 (Statoblest   **48**
120) [2002 37, a49: f6s⁴ f7g⁶ p6g f6s³ f6g f6g f6g 7d f5g³ 7f² 5m f6g 5g⁵ 6g Jul 20]
sparely-made gelding: poor maiden: stays 7f: acts on fibresand, firm and good to soft
going: tried blinkered. *A. Berry*

ANTICIPATING 2 b.c. (Jun 9) Polish Precedent (USA) 131 – D'Azy 91 (Persian **68 p**
Bold 123) [2002 8s⁶ Oct 26] rather lengthy, good-topped colt: half-brother to several
winners, notably very smart 1m (at 2 yrs) to 13f winner Presenting (by Mtoto): dam, 2-y-o
7f winner, half-sister to smart middle-distance performer Sirk: 20/1, 10 lengths sixth of
15 to Midas Way in maiden at Newbury, keeping on under considerate handling: will stay
at least 1¼m: should improve. *I. A. Balding*

ANTIGONE'S FIRE 3 b.f. Lycius (USA) 124 – Buzzbomb 98 (Bustino 136) [2002 –
12d⁶ 12m⁶ 11.7g Oct 16] 3,500Y: seventh foal: half-sister to 3 winners, including useful
1½m to 2m winner Silent Warning (by Ela-Mana-Mou) and 7f winner Fizzygig (by
Efisio): dam 1¼m/1½m winner: tailed-off last in maidens. *I. A. Wood*

ANTON DE LOOKA (IRE) 2 b.g. (Mar 21) Sesaro (USA) 81 – Regal Fanfare –
(IRE) 94 (Taufan (USA) 119) [2002 5v 5d⁶ 8d Aug 23] IR 7,000F, IR 5,000Y: third foal:
dam 2-y-o 6f winner out of half-sister to Cherry Hinton winner Torgau: well held all starts
(slowly away first 2), seeming not to stay 1m final one. *R. F. Fisher*

ANTONIO CANOVA 6 ch.g. Komaite (USA) – Joan's Venture (Beldale Flutter **89**
(USA) 130) [2002 99: 6d 6m 7g Oct 18] stocky gelding: useful handicapper at 5 yrs: not
discredited first start in 2002, but well beaten subsequently: best at 5f/6f: acts on firm and
good to soft going. *Bob Jones*

ANTONY EBENEEZER 3 ch.c. Hurricane Sky (AUS) – Captivating (IRE) 63 (Wolf- **50**
hound (USA) 126) [2002 51: 6.1f 6m 10f 6d 12.1g f9.4g³ 12m³ 10d f12g p12g 11.5m⁶ **a42**
Sep 17] leggy colt: modest maiden on turf, poor on all-weather: stays 1½m: acts on good
to firm going and fibresand: none too consistent. *C. R. Dore*

ANY CAMP 2 b.f. (Apr 5) Hector Protector (USA) 124 – Honeyspike (IRE) 79 (Chief's **82**
Crown (USA)) [2002 7m² 7f* 8m⁵ 7m³ 7d⁴ Oct 15] sturdy filly: fifth foal: half-sister to 3
winners, including useful 2001 2-y-o 7f winner Dulcet Spear (by Vettori) and fairly useful
1999 2-y-o 7.5f winner Via Camp (by Kris): dam, second at 1m in Ireland, half-sister to
smart 1¼m winner Casey Tibbs: fairly useful performer: landed odds in minor event at
Catterick in July despite being slowly away/racing freely: creditable efforts in nursery/
minor event last 2 starts: effective at 7f/1m: acts on firm and good to soft going: sold
21,000 gns. *E. A. L. Dunlop*

ANYHOW (IRE) 5 b.m. Distant Relative 128 – Fast Chick 93 (Henbit (USA) 130) **75**
[2002 68, a54: p10g³ p7g p10g p10g⁴ p8g* p10g³ 8f⁴ 8.3g p10g² p10g* 9s³ p10g² 9m²
8m³ 9m⁴ p10g⁴ 9g 8.9m* 9.1g⁵ p8g p10g p10g² p10g⁴ Dec 28] angular mare: fair performer: won handicaps at Lingfield in April/May and claimer at York in September:
effective at 1m/easy 1¼m: acts on all-weather, firm and soft going: usually held up:
sometimes wanders: tough and consistent. *Andrew Reid*

AOIFE'S DREAM (IRE) 4 ch.f. Catrail (USA) 123 – Ardnamurchan (Ardross 134) –
[2002 50: p12g 8s 8m 6s May 26] fourth foal: half-sister to 1½m and 2m winner Murchan
Tyne (by Good Thyne) and Irish 6f winner Patricia's Dream (by Indian Ridge): dam ran 3
times on Flat, later second over hurdles in Ireland: modest maiden at best: well held in
2002. *Edward Butler, Ireland*

A ONE (IRE) 3 b.g. Alzao (USA) 117 – Anita's Contessa (IRE) 68 (Anita's Prince **65**
126) [2002 72: 6.1f 6g 7.1m 6d⁴ 7.1v* 6.1m⁵ 7d 7m 8.1g² p8g 7d* f7g Oct 22] rather **a–**
leggy gelding: fair performer: made all in claimer at Chepstow in June and selling
handicap at Leicester in October: stays 1m: acts on any turf going (below form in 2 starts
on all-weather): sometimes early to post. *B. Palling*

AONINCH 2 ch.f. (Feb 7) Inchinor 119 – Willowbank 66 (Gay Fandango (USA) 132) **61**
[2002 7d 7m 7f⁶ Sep 17] IR 4,200Y: seventh foal: half-sister to 1¼m winner Kimberley
(by Shareef Dancer) and 1½m winner Assured Gamble (by Rock Hopper), both fairly
useful: dam 1½m winner who stayed 17f: easily best effort in maidens (modest form)
when sixth of 13 at Salisbury, racing freely: bred to stay at least 1m. *Mrs P. N. Dutfield*

APACHE POINT (IRE) 5 ch.g. Indian Ridge 123 – Ausherra (USA) 106 (Diesis **68**
133) [2002 62: 7v³ 8.2m 8m⁴ 8d³ 8g⁴ f8g 6.9d⁴ 8.1m⁴ 7.9m 9.9d⁶ 9.1d* 8.1v² 9d* 7.9m
8m 9d Oct 18] rather leggy gelding: fair handicapper: won at Ayr and Newcastle in
August: stays 9f: has form on firm going, best 5-y-o efforts on softer than good: sometimes races freely: often held up. *N. Tinkler*

APACHE TIMES 2 ro.f. (May 6) Timeless Times (USA) 99 – Misty Rocket 75 (Roan –
Rocket 128) [2002 5m f6s Oct 8] half-sister to a winning chaser: dam, 1¼m/1½m
seller winner, also successful over hurdles: soundly beaten in maiden (slowly away) and
claimer (gave trouble at start). *I. W. McInnes*

APADI (USA) 6 ch.g. Diesis 133 – Ixtapa (USA) (Chief's Crown (USA)) [2002 53: – 8.3g Jul 8] probably of little account nowadays. *M. C. Chapman*

APEX STAR (USA) 2 ch.c. (Feb 18) Diesis 133 – Imroz (USA) 99 (Nureyev (USA) **95 p** 131) [2002 7d* 7m* Aug 29] first foal: dam, 6f (at 2 yrs)/7f winner, out of Prix du Moulin/Musidora Stakes winner and Oaks runner-up All At Sea: won maiden at Leicester (by length from Dalaram) and minor event at Lingfield (by 2 lengths from Western Fling) in August, making most each time: will probably stay 1m: already useful, and open to further improvement. *H. R. A. Cecil*

APHRA BENN (IRE) 3 b.f. In The Wings 128 – Aigue 96 (High Top 131) [2002 **67** 8.2m 7s² f7f⁶ Nov 11] rangy filly: half-sister to 3 winners, including 7f (at 2 yrs) and 1¼m winner Mezzogiorno (also third in Oaks, by Unfuwain) and winner around 1¼m Rainbow Top (by Rainbow Quest), both useful: dam, 1m winner, sister to smart 1½m/13f performer Torchon: best effort in maidens when 1¼ lengths second to Fig Leaf at Yarmouth: should be suited by 1m+: slowly away all starts: carries head awkwardly: temperament under suspicion. *G. Wragg*

APOLLONIUS (IRE) 5 ch.h. Nucleon (USA) 94 – Warthill Whispers 59 (Grey **53** Desire 115) [2002 67d: 5s 5m 5g f6g Nov 20] first foal: dam, sprint maiden, one to treat with caution: fair performer at best: modest form in 2002: left J. Flynn, Ireland, after third start: best efforts at 5f: acts on good to firm going: tongue tied before 2002. *G. M. Moore*

APOLLO PRINCE 2 b.c. (May 12) Prince Sabo 123 – Sweet Apollo (Common **57** Grounds 118) [2002 f6g⁵ f6f⁴ 6m 7s Oct 28] first foal: dam, ran 3 times, out of half-sister to smart middle-distance stayer Lemhill: modest maiden: should stay 7f: acts on good to firm ground and fibresand: sold 3,700 gns, sent to Kuwait. *M. G. Quinlan*

APPLEACRE 3 b.f. Polar Falcon (USA) 126 – Absaloute Service 96 (Absalom 128) **86** [2002 51: 7s* 7m 9m⁴ 10g⁴ 10g² f12g* 12d Nov 1] strong, useful-looking filly: fairly useful performer: won maiden at Leicester in March and handicap at Wolverhampton in October: effective at 1¼m/1½m: acts on fibresand, soft and good to firm going: races prominently: sold 19,000 gns, joined H. Cyzer. *J. M. P. Eustace*

APPLEHAYES 3 b.f. Night Shift (USA) – La Masse (High Top 131) [2002 8g Jun 16] – closely related to 1¾m winner Heracles (by Unfuwain) and half-sister to several winners abroad, including useful German middle-distance performers Flying Anshan (by Pennine Walk) and Turbo Drive (by Be My Chief): dam French middle-distance winner: broke leg in maiden at Salisbury, only outing: dead. *H. Morrison*

APPLEJACK (IRE) 2 ch.f. (Apr 24) Entrepreneur 123 – Strident Note 89 (The – Minstrel (CAN) 135) [2002 f6g f8.5s Nov 2] IR 4,500Y: half-sister to 3 winners, including 1991 2-y-o 1¼m winner Castillet (by Rousillon) and Irish 2000 2-y-o 5f winner Some Style (by Fayruz): dam, maiden best at 2 yrs, half-sister to Topsy and Teenoso: last in maidens. *J. D. Czerpak*

APPLE ZED 4 b.f. Catrail (USA) 123 – Mrs Croesus (USA) (Key To The Mint **46 +** (USA)) [2002 50: f7s² f7s p7g⁶ 7v⁵ 6.5s* 5d³ 7g⁴ 6g* 7d⁶ Oct 3] poor performer: sold from G. Bravery after third start: won maiden at Bad Doberan in August and handicap at Halle in September: best around 6f: acts on soft and good to firm ground and on all-weather. *W. Giedt, Germany*

APPROACH 2 gr.f. (Feb 18) Darshaan 133 – Last Second (IRE) 121 (Alzao (USA) **101 p** 117) [2002 7.5d² 7.5m* 8m² 8g⁶ Sep 28] well-made filly: second foal: dam, 6f (at 2 yrs) to 1¼m (Nassau/Sun Chariot) winner, half-sister to smart stayer Alleluia and to dams of Alborada and Quarter Moon: useful form: won maiden at Beverley in August: best efforts when 1½ lengths second of 9 to Summitville in May Hill Stakes at Doncaster (raced freely) and 4 lengths sixth of 10 to Soviet Song in Fillies' Mile at Ascot (reportedly finished lame): should be suited by 1¼m+: edgy in preliminaries (constantly bucking) second start, had 2 handlers on third: should be capable of better still. *Sir Mark Prescott*

APPROACHING STORM (IRE) 3 ch.f. Entrepreneur 123 – Fashion Front (Habitat **88** 134) [2002 80: 7g² 8.3m* 10d² 10v* 12m 10g⁶ 10m Aug 4] unfurnished filly: half-sister to several winners, including 8-y-o Peartree House and to dam of very smart sprinter Mind Games: dam unraced daughter of Irish 1000 Guineas winner Front Row: fairly useful performer: trained by T. Taaffe in Ireland at 2 yrs: won maiden at Windsor in April and handicap at Newbury in June: reportedly finished lame final start: stays 1¼m: has won on good to firm going, best form on softer than good: blinkered final 2-y-o start. *L. M. Cumani*

APPROVAL   3 b.c. Royal Applause 124 – Gentle Persuasion 95 (Bustino 136) [2002 **105**
95: 7m² 6d² 7m 6d² Jul 6] tall, lengthy colt: useful performer: second in European Free
Handicap at Newmarket (beaten 2½ lengths by Twilight Blues) in April, listed race at
Ascot (beaten short head by Lady Dominatrix) in May and minor contest at Haydock
(beaten 3½ lengths by Suggestive) in July: barely stays 7f: acts on good to firm and good
to soft going: blinkered (bit below form, pulled hard) penultimate start: carries head high.
R. Hannon

APRIL LEE   4 b.f. Superpower 113 – Petitesse 55 (Petong 126) [2002 68: f8g p10g **49**
p8g⁴ p8g³ p7g 7s Mar 28] fair performer at best: poor nowadays: best around 7f: acts on
all-weather and firm going, probably on soft: often blinkered/visored: not an easy ride.
K. McAuliffe

APRIL LOUISE   6 b.m. Meqdaam (USA) – California Dreamin (Slip Anchor 136)   **–**
[2002 –: 22.2m p13g 17.1m 15.9f⁵ Aug 31] little form on Flat. *T. Wall*

APRIL STOCK   7 ch.m. Beveled (USA) – Stockline (Capricorn Line 111) [2002 95: **95**
p12g⁴ p12g⁴ 10g³ 10.5m 10s 10.3v⁴ Nov 8] leggy mare: useful handicapper: mostly
respectable efforts at least in 2002, including third to Imperial Dancer in Rosebery Stakes
at Kempton in April: best at 1¼m/1½m: acts on polytrack, best on good ground or softer
on turf (acts on heavy): sometimes tongue tied: usually held up (wasn't when well below
form final start). *G. A. Butler*

APRIL VIEW (USA)   3 b.f. Distant View (USA) 126 – April Hot Stuff (USA) (Peter-   **–**
hof (USA) 116) [2002 7g 7g May 10] approx. 26,000Y in Italy: strong, lengthy filly: third
foal: half-sister to a winner in Italy by Mr Greeley: dam unraced half-sister to US Grade 2
8.5f winner April Axe: well held in newcomers race/maiden (raced freely). *J. L. Dunlop*

AQABA   3 b.f. Lake Coniston (IRE) 131 – Sahara Breeze 85 (Ela-Mana-Mou 132)   **62**
[2002 65: 5.1d⁶ 7m⁵ 8g f9.4s Nov 2] leggy filly: modest maiden: should stay 1m. *S. Kirk*

Mr Faisal Salman's "Approach"

AQRIBAA (IRE) 4 b. or br.g. Pennekamp (USA) 130 – Karayb (IRE) 93 (Last — Tycoon 131) [2002 74: 9.9g 8.5d Aug 14] second foal: half-brother to useful French 1¼m winner Ghyraan (by Cadeaux Genereux): dam 6f (at 2 yrs)/7f winner: third in newcomers race at Deauville for J. Hammond in France only start at 2 yrs: fair form for D. Hanley in Ireland at 3 yrs: well held both 4-y-o starts: stays 1m: raced only on good/good to soft going: blinkered final 3-y-o start. *A. J. Lockwood*

AQUAE SULIS 3 ch.f. Greensmith 121 – Stealthy 73 (Kind of Hush 118) [2002 –: — 5.9d 6f 7.5m f6g⁶ 5.9g 7.1d Aug 8] good-bodied filly: no form. *R. Ford*

AQUA PURA (GER) 3 b.c. Acatenango (GER) 127 – Actraphane (Shareef Dancer ? (USA) 135) [2002 10.5g⁴ 11s³ 11m⁴ 11.8g² 12s* 11.9g³ 14g 16v Oct 29] 11,000F, 300,000 francs Y: sixth foal: half-brother to 1998 2-y-o winner Ashbourne Pat (later 1¼m/1½m winner in France) and 1m winner Besweetome (both by Mtoto): dam French 1½m winner: fair performer: won maiden at Hamburg in June: left A. Trybuhl in Germany before well held final start: stays 1½m: acts on soft going: has run well in blinkers. *B. J. Curley*

AQUARELLISTE (FR) 4 b.f. Danehill (USA) 126 – Agathe (USA) 114 **121** (Manila (USA)) [2002 123: 10.5g* 12m³ 12m⁴ 12m* 12g⁶ 12m² Dec 15]

The decision to keep Aquarelliste in training was rewarded with further success but she fell well short of fulfilling her owner's optimistic prediction that she was another Allez France. Winner of the Prix de Diane and Prix Vermeille and second in the Prix de l'Arc de Triomphe as a three-year-old, Aquarelliste added to her Group 1 haul at the earliest opportunity in the latest season—in the Prix Ganay in April. Reportedly not fully wound up, Aquarelliste was still sent off at odds on in a field of seven at Longchamp, her task made easier when Rebelline missed the race due to being in season and also by Sagacity's refusal to race. Kept close to the steady pace set by Anabaa Blue, Aquarelliste was pushed along to lead under two furlongs out and held on well, runner-up Execute finishing best of all on the outside but only able to get within half a length. The previous season's Prix du Jockey Club winner Anabaa Blue weakened to finish fifth and Aquarelliste confirmed the form with him in three subsequent meetings, including when the pair filled the first two places in the Prix Foy back at Longchamp in September. Aquarelliste hadn't needed to be at her very best in the Ganay, but her success in the Prix Foy confirmed that she was just about as good as ever. Again odds on, Aquarelliste moved through steadily to lead halfway up the straight and kept on gamely to hold off the strong-finishing Anabaa Blue by a length, with Falbrav a short head away in third.

Aquarelliste ran two fair races in between her two successes, finishing third in the Grand Prix de Saint-Cloud and fourth in the King George VI and Queen Elizabeth Stakes at Ascot. Despite the assistance of a pacemaker in the former, she

Prix Ganay, Longchamp—only three lengths covers the field at the finish as Aquarelliste lands the odds; Execute (No.1) is second, ahead of Sensible (partly hidden), Idaho Quest (centre), Anabaa Blue (rail) and the blinkered Jomana

was beaten two lengths and a short head by Ange Gabriel and Polish Summer. Of the excuses offered by connections for this defeat, Aquarelliste's being in season was a more plausible one than the suggestion that she had not taken to racing left-handed for the first time. She played up in the paddock and before the start but appeared to handle the turns well. Aquarelliste's pre-race demeanour didn't totally satisfy at Ascot either where, after reportedly proving difficult in the pre-paddock, she went freely to post before being beaten about five and half lengths behind Golan. Aquarelliste couldn't improve on her second in Sakhee's Arc when returned to Longchamp for the latest renewal, though she still ran creditably to come sixth, finishing closer to the winner on this occasion, beaten around two and a half lengths by Marienbard. Aquarelliste rounded off the year with her first race outside Europe, producing yet another creditable effort when second, beaten three quarters of a length by Ange Gabriel, in the Hong Kong Vase at Sha Tin in December.

	Danehill (USA) (b 1986)	Danzig (b 1977)	Northern Dancer
			Pas de Nom
Aquarelliste (FR) (b.f. 1998)		Razyana (b 1981)	His Majesty
			Spring Adieu
	Agathe (USA) (ch 1991)	Manila (b 1983)	Lyphard
			Dona Ysidra
		Albertine (b 1981)	Irish River
			Almyre

The pedigree of Aquarelliste was covered in *Racehorses of 2001*. The only addition of note is that her year-younger half-sister Arme Ancienne (by Sillery) made a winning debut over a mile and a quarter at Longchamp, on the same day Aquarelliste won the Ganay, before going on to show useful form in a couple of

Ecurie Wildenstein's "Aquarelliste"

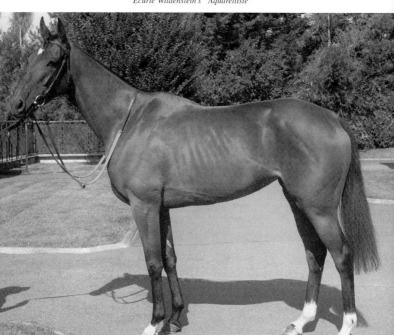

listed races over the same distance. The big, strong Aquarelliste is rather plain in appearance but is a good walker. Apart from the Ganay (run over ten and a half furlongs) she raced exclusively at a mile and a half in the latest season. Aquarelliste has yet to encounter extremes of going but acts on both soft and good to firm ground. She has yet to run a poor race in eleven career starts, the latest Arc being the only occasion she has failed to make the frame. Aquarelliste could reportedly have one final race before being retired to the paddocks, in either the Dubai World Cup or the Sheema Classic on the same card in March. *E. Lellouche, France*

AQUARIUS (IRE)   4 b.g. Royal Academy (USA) 130 – Rafha 123 (Kris 135) [2002   **107 d**
110: 14.1m⁴ 12d⁶ 10.4m 12.3m⁶ 13.1g 12f⁶ Oct 3] smallish gelding: smart performer at 3 yrs: useful effort in 2002 only when fourth to Hannibal Lad in minor event at Nottingham on reappearance (left J. Dunlop 12,500 gns after next start): best form at 1¾m/2m: acts on soft and good to firm ground: below form all 3 starts in visor: usually held up: has joined M. Pipe. *D. Nicholls*

AQUA TIGER   2 b.g. (Apr 6) Unfuwain (USA) 131 – Bassmaat (USA) 81 (Cadeaux Genereux 131) [2002 6g 7m Aug 14] fourth foal: brother to fairly useful Irish 2000 2-y-o 1m winner El-Libaab: dam, 7f winner, out of smart French performer up to 1½m Mangayah: last in maiden/claimer. *B. J. Meehan*

AQUILINE   4 ch.g. Sanglamore (USA) 126 – Fantasy Flyer (USA) (Lear Fan (USA) 130) [2002 –: 12.3m⁵ Apr 27] well held in maiden/minor event. *John A. Harris*   –

ARAB GOLD   7 b.g. Presidium 124 – Parklands Belle 73 (Stanford 121§) [2002 –: p12g f7g 10.9g Apr 1] no form since 2000: often blinkered/visored. *J. S. Moore*   –

ARABIAN GOGGLES   3 ch.f. Cosmonaut – Jarrettelle (All Systems Go 119) [2002 –: 7m 7d Jul 11] no form. *H. S. Howe*   –

Sheikh Ahmed Al Maktoum's "Aramram"

ARABIAN KNIGHT (IRE) 2 ch.g. (Mar 28) Fayruz 116 – Cheerful Knight (IRE) **69** (Mac's Imp (USA) 116) [2002 5.1m 5m 5m² 5m⁵ 6d 5m³ 5m³ 5m⁶ 5g 5f 5.1s⁶ 5s⁶ f5g **a61** f5g³ f5g² Dec 16] IR 3,000F, 5,800Y: close-coupled gelding: second living foal: dam Irish maiden: fair maiden on turf, modest on all-weather: raced mainly at 5f: acts on soft going, good to firm and fibresand: blinkered/visored 4 of last 6 starts: often races prominently: sometimes looks difficult ride. *A. Berry*

ARABIAN MOON (IRE) 6 ch.h. Barathea (IRE) 127 – Excellent Alibi (USA) **91** (Exceller (USA) 129) [2002 92, a84: p12g² 12m⁶ 12g⁶ 12m 13.3f³ 21g⁵ 13.9m 12m³ 13.3f 12g⁴ Sep 27] leggy, quite good-topped horse: easy mover: fairly useful handicapper: hasn't won on Flat since 2000: effective at 1½m to 21f: acts on polytrack, best turf efforts on good going or firmer: held up: often finds little: consistent. *S. Dow*

ARABIE 4 b.c. Polish Precedent (USA) 131 – Always Friendly 111 (High Line 125) **112** [2002 103: 10s² 10.1d⁴ 10m² 8.9m⁶ 10.3m³ Sep 13] lengthy, angular colt: smart performer: at least respectable efforts in 2002 when placed, including head second to Ulundi in valuable handicap at Royal Ascot on third start and third to Beekeeper in minor event at Doncaster on final one: possibly something amiss (after 10-week break) penultimate outing: seems best around 1¼m: yet to race on heavy going, acts on any other: free-going sort: sold 46,000 gns, joined Venetia Williams. *H. R. A. Cecil*

ARABIN 3 b.g. Bin Ajwaad (IRE) 119 – Just Julia (Natroun (FR) 128) [2002 58: 6s 6g⁵ **52** 5.3m Jun 25] leggy, quite good-topped gelding: modest maiden: may prove best at 6f: tends to give trouble at stall/start slowly: hung both 2-y-o starts. *A. Charlton*

ARACHINE 3 ch.g. Indian Ridge 123 – Hill Hopper (IRE) 106 (Danehill (USA) 126) **85** [2002 –p: 8m f8.5g* f8.5g* f9.4g³ Oct 21] fairly useful handicapper: won at Wolverhampton in September and October: ran creditably (carried head high, seemingly due to kickback) final start: stays 9.4f: acts on fibresand: sold 30,000 gns, to join P. Hughes in Ireland. *Sir Mark Prescott*

ARAF 3 b.g. Millkom 124 – Euphyllia 70 (Superpower 113) [2002 –: p8g f9.4g 8g⁶ **54** 10m* f12s³ Sep 7] modest performer: won seller at Brighton (carried head awkwardly) in August: stays 1½m: acts on good to firm going and fibresand: sold 6,400 gns. *A. G. Newcombe*

ARAGLIN 3 b.g. Sadler's Wells (USA) 132 – River Cara (USA) 86 (Irish River (FR) **– §** 131) [2002 79: 10g f12s⁶ Nov 30] useful-looking gelding: fair performer at 2 yrs: looked temperamental in 2002: tried blinkered. *Miss S. J. Wilton*

ARAKAN (USA) 2 br.c. (Feb 11) Nureyev (USA) 131 – Far Across (Common Grounds **91 p** 118) [2002 6g² 6g³ Oct 2] first foal: dam unraced half-sister to French 7f/1m performer Donkey Engine and to French/US 1m/1¼m performer Petit Poucet, both smart: green, shaped well in maiden at Newcastle and minor event at Salisbury (third of 6 to Marching Band): should stay 1m: useful performer in the making. *Sir Michael Stoute*

ARAMRAM (USA) 3 b.c. Danzig (USA) – Felawnah (USA) 111 (Mr Prospector **116 §** (USA)) [2002 8s⁵ p8g² 8f* 8m⁶ 9m 8g³ 10d 10f⁴ Jul 20] strong, attractive colt: fourth foal: half-brother to 3 winners, including Felona (9f/1¼m, by Caerleon) and Follow Lammtarra (1¾m, by Lammtarra), both fairly useful: dam 1¼m winner and fourth in 1000 Guineas, out of US Grade 1 1m winner Ambassador of Luck: smart performer: won listed race at Thirsk in April by length from Sohaib, tending to hang but getting on top late on: creditable efforts behind Rock of Gibraltar in 2000 Guineas at Newmarket (5 lengths sixth) and St James's Palace Stakes at Royal Ascot (5¾ lengths third) next 2 completed starts: should prove as effective at 7f as 1m: acts on firm going and polytrack: sometimes slowly away (has looked most reluctant to race): ducked sharply and unseated in France (has been banned from racing there) fifth and seventh outings: not to be trusted: sent to UAE. *M. R. Channon*

ARANA 7 b.m. Noble Patriarch 115 – Pod's Daughter (IRE) 43 (Tender King 123) **–** [2002 –: 11.9m 19.1m 16.5g Jul 11] of no account. *W. de Best-Turner*

ARAWAK PRINCE (IRE) 6 ch.g. College Chapel 122 – Alpine Symphony **–** (Northern Dancer) [2002 59: 10.1f 16f⁶ Jul 29] probably of little account nowadays. *G. Prodromou*

ARBIE (CAN) 3 b.g. Mountain Cat (USA) – Empress of Love (USA) (Czaravich **–** (USA)) [2002 59p: p10g Feb 20] strong gelding: modest form in maidens at 2 yrs: well held only 3-y-o start. *C. F. Wall*

ARCALIS 2 gr.g. (Mar 7) Lear Fan (USA) 130 – Aristocratique 71 (Cadeaux Genereux **72** 131) [2002 6d⁵ 6d⁵ 5g 6f⁶ 8d* Oct 21] 32,000F: tall, quite good-topped gelding: second foal: half-brother to 3-y-o Noble Academy: dam, Irish sprint maiden, half-sister to useful

6f/7f winner Royal Loft: fair performer: won 20-runner nursery at Pontefract in October, leading final 1f: should stay 1¼m: acts on good to soft ground, possibly not firm. *Mrs J. R. Ramsden*

ARC EL CIEL (ARG)   4 b.c. Fitzcarraldo (ARG) – Ardoise (USA) (Diamond Pros- **65** pect (USA) 126) [2002 65: f8.5g³ p10g⁶ 10d 8.1d f6g* f6g³ f8.5g⁴ f8.5s⁴ p7g Dec 30] fair handicapper: trained fifth to eighth starts by W. Jarvis, winning at Wolverhampton in September: returned to former trainer before final outing: effective at 6f (given test), probably at easy 1¼m: acts on good to firm going and all-weather. *B. R. Millman*

ARC EN CIEL   4 b.g. Rainbow Quest (USA) 134 – Nadia Nerina (CAN) 82 (Northern **–** Dancer) [2002 80: 12m 12s Jun 12] useful-looking gelding: fairly useful handicapper at best: well handled with 4-y-o starts (tongue tied final one): visored once. *Mrs L. Richards*

ARCHDUKE FERDINAND (FR)   4 ch.g. Dernier Empereur (USA) 125 – Lady **111 d** Norcliffe (USA) (Norcliffe (CAN)) [2002 111: 14.1m⁶ 18.7f 22.2m⁶ 16.1g 18m² 18m 16d 16.5v Nov 9] strong, close-coupled gelding: smart performer at best: some respectable efforts in 2002, including when runner-up in Queen Alexandra Stakes at Royal Ascot (beaten neck by Cover Up) and minor event at Pontefract (beaten ½ length by Tattrail): ran poorly last 3 starts: yet to race on heavy going, acts on any other: has worn crossed/dropped noseband: often races freely. *P. F. I. Cole*

ARCHER FOR FOUR (USA)   3 b. or br.g. Royal Academy (USA) 130 – Depelchin **–** (USA) (Star de Naskra (USA)) [2002 –: 5g 8g 8d May 29] strong gelding: little form. *N. Tinkler*

ARCHIE BABE (IRE)   6 ch.g. Archway (IRE) 115 – Frensham Manor (Le Johnston **62 §** 123) [2002 71§: 10d f12g⁵ Dec 27] workmanlike gelding: modest handicapper nowa- days: off 14 months before reappearance: effective at 1¼m/1½m: below form on firm going, acts on any other turf: unreliable. *J. J. Quinn*

ARCHIRONDEL   4 b.g. Bin Ajwaad (IRE) 119 – Penang Rose (NZ) (Kingdom Bay **76** (NZ)) [2002 60: 8.2m² 10g 10f⁴ 8.5g* 8m 8.5d 10g² 10m⁶ 9m 10.3f Sep 25] smallish gelding: fair handicapper: won at Beverley in June: best at 1m/1¼m: acts on firm ground, probably not on softer than good. *John Berry*

ARCHON (IRE)   5 ch.g. Archway (IRE) 115 – Lindas Delight 54 (Batshoof 122) **51** [2002 63: p13g f12g⁴ f9.4g³ f8.5g⁵ 8.3g² 9m⁴ p7g* 8.1m⁶ 8.1g⁶ f7g⁴ f9.4s⁴ Dec 9] strong **a60** gelding: modest performer: won claimer at Lingfield in May: effective at 7f to 1½m: acts on all-weather and good to firm ground: tried tongue tied: has looked less than keen: often comes from behind. *Mrs P. N. Dutfield*

ARC (IRE)   8 b.g. Archway (IRE) 115 – Columbian Sand (IRE) (Salmon Leap (USA) **86** 131) [2002 81: f8g 8v* 10.5m⁵ 8.5g⁴ 8.1d 8d 8.5g⁵ Jun 5] tall, good-topped gelding: fairly **a77** useful handicapper: won at Newcastle in April: best form around 1m/9f: acted on heavy going, good to firm and fibresand: tried blinkered: dead. *G. M. Moore*

ARCTIC BLUE   2 b.g. (Apr 17) Polar Prince (IRE) 117 – Miss Sarajane 74 (Skyliner **67** 117) [2002 6s⁶ p7g⁶ 7d 6s f8.5g Nov 18] 2,100Y, resold 2,600Y: fourth foal: dam won **a–** at 1m/9f: fair maiden: off 3½ months, best effort when seventh of 21 in sales race at Doncaster fourth start: should stay at least 1m: raced only on ground softer than good on turf. *J. S. Moore*

ARCTIC BURST (USA)   2 b.c. (Apr 8) Royal Academy (USA) 130 – Polar Bird 111 **95** (Thatching 131) [2002 7m⁴ 6g² 6m⁴ Sep 13] strong, lengthy colt: has scope: has a quick, fluent action: sixth foal: half-brother to 1996 2-y-o 5.5f (Prix Robert Papin)/6f winner Ocean Ridge (by Storm Bird), later smart at 1m, and fairly useful 5f winner Alpine Twist (by Seattle Dancer): dam sprinter: useful form in maidens at Goodwood and York (short-headed by Court Masterpiece) first 2 starts: odds on, only fourth of 12 behind Tarjman in similar event at Goodwood following month: effective at 6f/7f. *B. W. Hills*

ARCTIC DESERT   2 b.c. (Feb 9) Desert Prince (IRE) 130 – Thamud (IRE) (Lahib **77 p** (USA) 129) [2002 6d³ 6s⁶ Oct 25] 22,000Y: big, good-topped colt: has plenty of scope: first foal: dam, unraced, out of sister to top-class 1½m performer Celestial Storm and half-sister to Ribblesdale winner Thawakib, latter dam of Sakhee: fair form in maidens at Windsor (better effort, third of 21 to Turn Around) and Newbury (tired after travelling strongly) in October: bred to stay at least 1m, but races freely and not sure to do so: remains capable of better. *I. A. Balding*

ARCTIC FALCON (IRE)   3 b.f. Polar Falcon (USA) 126 – Chandni (IRE) (Ahonoora **64** 122) [2002 73: 5.1m 6.1d 6.1d⁵ 6m⁴ 6d 5.1g f6g³ Nov 15] rather angular filly: modest handicapper: left R. Hannon 800 gns before final start: will stay 7f: acts on good to firm going and fibresand. *S. L. Keightley*

ARCTIC FLIGHT 4 ch.f. Polar Falcon (USA) 126 – Laugharne (Known Fact (USA) **56**
135) [2002 71: 8d 7g⁵ 7m 7m 7m 7m Aug 25] modest handicapper nowadays: stays 7f:
acts on good to firm going: hung left penultimate start: sold 2,500 gns. *P. W. Harris*

ARCTIC HIGH 5 b.m. Polar Falcon (USA) 126 – Oublier L'Ennui (FR) 79 (Bellman **–**
(FR) 123) [2002 –, a60: f9.4f⁶ Aug 16] probably of little account nowadays. *I. A. Wood*

ARCTIC LAGOON (IRE) 3 ch.g. Bering 136 – Lake Pleasant (IRE) 90 (Elegant
Air 119) [2002 8m 10m p12g Jun 9] rangy, angular gelding: fifth foal: half-brother to
useful 7f (at 2 yrs) to 1½m winner Serpentine (by Grand Lodge) and a winner in Norway
by Salse: dam, 2-y-o 6f winner, from family of Bireme and Buoy: signs of a little ability
in maidens: sold £4,000 in October. *J. R. Fanshawe*

ARCTIC OWL 8 b.g. Most Welcome 131 – Short Rations (Lorenzaccio 130) [2002 **114**
13.3m³ 11.6m* Aug 24] rangy, raw-boned gelding: showed pronounced knee action:
very smart performer at best, successful in 10 races, including Irish St Leger at the
Curragh in 2000: much better effort in 2002 when beating Gamut by 1¼ lengths in
4-runner minor event at Windsor (after 3-month break) in August: was effective at 11.6f
to 2m: acted on heavy and good to firm going: had carried head awkwardly, and sometimes found little: retired after reportedly having recurrence of tendon problem after
Windsor. *J. R. Fanshawe*

ARDANZA (IRE) 5 b.m. Hernando (FR) 127 – Arrastra 79 (Bustino 136) [2002 –: **–**
9.1d 9.2v⁵ 12.1s Aug 20] probably of little account nowadays. *P. Monteith*

ARDARA (IRE) 3 b.f. Sadler's Wells (USA) 132 – Eilanden (IRE) (Akarad (FR) 130) **58**
[2002 81: 11.1s 9.2g 9.1g⁵ 11.9m f12g Nov 22] angular filly: first foal: dam unraced
half-sister to smart Irish performer up to 1½m Ebaziya, herself dam of Gold Cup winner
Enzeli and Irish Oaks/Prix Royal-Oak winner Ebadiyla (by Sadler's Wells): fairly useful
maiden at 2 yrs for A. O'Brien in Ireland: just modest form at best in 2002, leaving
J. Quinn after fourth start: should stay at least 1¼m: acts on soft ground: tried blinkered/
visored: sold 27,000 gns. *Mrs G. S. Rees*

ARDENT 8 b.g. Aragon 118 – Forest of Arden (Tap On Wood 130) [2002 39: p12g **36 §**
p10g Jan 30] well-made gelding: poor handicapper: best at 1m/1¼m: acts on firm and
good to soft going, probably on polytrack: blinkered once as 4-y-o: usually wears hood:
untrustworthy. *Miss B. Sanders*

ARDENT LADY 2 b.f. (Apr 10) Alhaarth (IRE) 126 – Arvika (FR) (Baillamont (USA) **67**
124) [2002 7m 7g Oct 14] 140,000 francs F, IR 60,000Y: unfurnished, quite attractive
filly: fourth foal: half-sister to 3 winners in France, including useful 1¼m winner
Premiere Chance (by Linamix): dam, French 1¼m winner, out of half-sister to dam of
high-class Japanese 1m/1¼m performer Agnes Digital: fair form in maidens: will stay
1¼m. *E. A. L. Dunlop*

AREEB (IRE) 2 b.f. (Apr 2) Emarati (USA) 74 – Racing Brenda 72 (Faustus (USA) **42**
118) [2002 5m 5m⁶ 6s 5.1g f5g³ Oct 5] IR 2,400F: lengthy filly: third foal: dam 7f/1m
winner: poor maiden: likely to prove best at 5f: acts on fibresand and good to firm ground:
races prominently. *J. D. Czerpak*

ARFABEAT 2 ch.f. (Mar 12) Abou Zouz (USA) 109 – Sans Egale (FR) (Lashkari 128) **40**
[2002 6g 6d p6g p8g⁵ f8.5g Dec 31] first foal: dam, maiden who stayed 1½m, half-sister
to smart 1¼m performer Maidment: poor maiden: should stay at least 1m. *J. S. Moore*

ARGAMIA (GER) 6 b.m. Orfano (GER) – Arkona (GER) 108 (Aspros (GER)) [2002 **59**
63: f16s³ f16g 12s³ 14.4f 14.1m⁵ f16.2f³ Aug 16] tall, angular mare: modest handicapper:
effective at 1½m (given test) to 2m: acts on fibresand, heavy and good to firm going:
blinkered last 3 starts at 4 yrs: usually held up. *M. G. Quinlan*

ARGOSTOLI 3 b.f. Marju (IRE) 127 – Barque Bleue (USA) (Steinlen 127) [2002 –: **–**
11.1v⁶ 11m⁶ Jul 27] smallish filly: no form. *P. C. Haslam*

ARIES (GER) 2 ch.f. (Feb 18) Big Shuffle (USA) 122 – Auenlust (GER) (Surumu **79**
(GER)) [2002 5m³ 6s² 7d* 7m 6g³ 7m² 8m 7f⁴ 7f² 7f 6g Oct 17] 95,000Y: lengthy, workmanlike filly: sister to several German winners, including 1997 5f/6f winner Auenflair
and 7f and 9f winner Auenlied, and half-sister to a winner there by Dashing Blade: dam,
German 1m winner, half-sister to dam of smart 5f/6f winner Auenklang (by Big Shuffle):
fair performer: won maiden at Folkestone in July: mostly good efforts in nurseries after
until last 2 starts: stays 7f: acts on soft and firm going: tough. *M. R. Channon*

ARIZONA LADY 5 ch.m. Lion Cavern (USA) 117 – Unfuwaanah 74 (Unfuwain **46**
(USA) 131) [2002 65: f9.1g³ f8.5g⁶ f9.4g⁴ Feb 15] sturdy mare: poor handicapper
nowadays: probably best at 1m/1¼m: acts on firm going, good to soft and fibresand: tried
blinkered: none too consistent. *J. D. Czerpak*

ARJAY   4 b.g. Shaamit (IRE) 127 – Jenny's Call (Petong 126) [2002 87: 8.1d 7d* 7.2v⁵   **86**
7m 7m 7f 7.1m 7.2g³ 8m⁴ 10s Oct 14] tall, rather leggy gelding: fairly useful performer:
made all in minor event at Thirsk in May: effective at 7f to 9f: acts on heavy and good to
firm going: blinkered last 3 starts: none too reliable. *Andrew Turnell*

ARJAYPEAR (IRE)   3 b.g. Petardia 113 – Lila Pedigo (IRE) 62 (Classic Secret (USA)   **–**
91) [2002 45: f9.4g⁵ 14.1f f7g Oct 22] angular gelding: no form at 3 yrs. *John R. Upson*

ARK ADMIRAL   3 b.g. Inchinor 119 – Kelimutu 58 (Top Ville 129) [2002 8m 12m⁵   **89**
10m² 8m 10d* 10.1s Oct 22] good-bodied gelding: fourth living foal: half-brother to
useful 1m (at 2 yrs) and 1¼m winner Whitefoot and 4-y-o Tenderfoot (both by Be My
Chief): dam, 1¼m/1½m winner, half-sister to useful dam of Compton Admiral and 5-y-o
Summoner: fairly useful performer: made all in handicap at Windsor in August: below
form final start (gelded after): may prove best at 1m/1¼m: acts on good to firm and good
to soft going: free-going type. *B. J. Meehan*

ARKATME   4 b.g. Then Again 126 – Watheeqah (USA) 60 (Topsider (USA)) [2002   **–**
62: f6s f6g f6g 9m May 2] good-topped gelding: modest maiden at 3 yrs: no form in 2002:
tried blinkered. *D. W. Chapman*

ARMADA GROVE   2 ch.f. (Jan 29) Fleetwood (IRE) 107 – Wannaplantatree 72   **75**
(Niniski (USA) 125) [2002 7m p7g* 7g⁶ 7m⁵ 6.5m 7f³ 7f⁵ p7g Dec 14] leggy, unfurnished
filly: second foal: half-sister to 4-y-o Aker Wood: dam 1¾m/2m winner: fair performer:
jinked and unseated rider on debut: won maiden at Lingfield in July: should stay 1m: acts
on polytrack, raced only on good going or firmer on turf. *A. P. Jarvis*

ARMAGNAC   4 b.g. Young Ern 120 – Arianna Aldini (Habitat 134) [2002 96: 6g 6m   **96**
7.6f 6f⁵ 6g³ 6g³ 6m* 7d 6m³ 6g 6m 6g⁴ 6g p7g Nov 23] tall, good-topped gelding:
unimpressive mover: useful handicapper: won at Haydock in July: several respectable
efforts otherwise in 2002, including when third to Budelli at Ascot and fourth to Cubism
at York later in season: stays 6f: yet to race on heavy going, acts on any other (unsuitable
trip on all-weather debut final start): occasionally slowly away/pulls hard. *M. A. Buckley*

ARMS ACROSSTHESEA   3 b.g. Namaqualand (USA) – Zolica 60 (Beveled (USA))   **70**
[2002 63: f8g⁶ 8m⁴ 7.9g² 8g* 8m 8.1s 9m³ 8g⁶ 11.9g Aug 5] leggy gelding: fair handicapper: won at Musselburgh in May: should stay 1¼m: acts on fibresand and good to firm
going, below form on soft: visored (below form) twice. *F. P. Murtagh*

ARNBI DANCER   3 b.g. Presidium 124 – Travel Myth 66§ (Bairn (USA) 126) [2002   **63**
51: f6s³ f8g² f6g* f6g³ f6g⁶ 5m f6g³ Dec 10] good-topped gelding: has scope: modest
handicapper: won at Wolverhampton in March: ran well final outing: likely to prove best
at 6f/7f: acts on fibresand and good to firm going: sometimes wanders/looks less than
keen. *P. C. Haslam*

AROGANT PRINCE   5 ch.g. Aragon 118 – Versaillesprincess (Legend of France   **72**
(USA) 124) [2002 59: f6g* f5g* f5g³ f7g* f7g 5g* f7g 5g⁶ 5s* 5.9s 7.2v³ 5g⁶ 6g⁴ 5g⁶ 6v*   **a86**
6d⁶ f6s f6g² f5g* f5f² f5g Dec 17] smallish gelding: fairly useful on all-weather,
fair on turf: won handicaps at Wolverhampton (3) and Musselburgh, and claimers at
Newcastle and Haydock between January/August and claimer at Wolverhampton in
November: effective at 5f to easy 7f: acts on any turf going and fibresand: blinkered (well
held) once: tough. *I. Semple*

AROUSHA (USA)   2 ch.c. (Apr 14) King of Kings (IRE) 125 – Hushi (USA) (River-   **71**
man (USA) 131) [2002 6m² Jul 3] $55,000F, $130,000Y: seventh living foal: half-brother
to winners abroad by Woodman and Java Gold: dam, sprinter in US, successful in minor
stakes (including at 2 yrs): 12/1 and green, 2 lengths equal-second of 6 to Indian Haven in
maiden at Yarmouth. *E. A. L. Dunlop*

ARPEGGIO   7 b.g. Polar Falcon (USA) 126 – Hilly 96 (Town Crier 119) [2002 86,   **80**
a81: p8g f8g 8s⁵ 7d 7.1m⁶ 8f⁶ 8.5g 9s 10f* 7.9d³ 8m* 8d⁶ 7m 8m 8s² 7.1m 7.2g Sep 21]   **a?**
good-topped gelding: has a quick action: fairly useful performer: won claimers at Redcar
in June and Yarmouth in July: winner at 1¼m, best form at 7f/1m: acts on soft going, firm
and fibresand: blinkered (below form) once: sometimes slowly away/wanders/looks less
than keen. *D. Nicholls*

ARRAN MIST   4 b.f. Alhijaz 122 – Saraswati 55 (Mansingh (USA) 120) [2002 48: 5s⁴   **38**
6f 5m f5g³ 5m 5g May 30] angular filly: poor maiden: effective at 5f/6f: acts on soft
going, good to firm and fibresand. *D. W. Barker*

ARRAN PILOT   2 b.c. (Apr 18) Wolfhound (USA) 126 – Al Raja 79 (Kings Lake   **90**
(USA) 133) [2002 5g³ 5m² 5m² 5.1d* 5s³ 5m² 5m 5d³ 5g 5g Sep 19] 11,000Y: sturdy colt:
ninth foal: dam, 1½m winner, out of smart performer up to 1m Rare Roberta: fairly useful
performer: won minor event at Nottingham in April: best efforts when placed in listed

races at Sandown on fifth and seventh starts (length second to Presto Vento on first occasion, 4¼ lengths third to Bella Tusa on second): should stay at least 6f: acts on good to firm and good to soft going, probably on soft. *Mrs L. Stubbs*

ARRIBILO (GER) 8 b.g. Top Ville 129 – Arborea (GER) (Priamos (GER) 123) [2002 74d: p10g Jan 12] winner in Germany: disappointing handicapper in Britain: tried blinkered. *G. M. McCourt* —

ARROW 3 b.g. Pivotal 124 – Cremets 94 (Mummy's Pet 125) [2002 7m⁴ 8m 7f 7d⁶ Oct 18] 28,000Y, 8,000 2-y-o: big gelding: half-brother to 3 winners, including smart Italian performer up to 15f My Irish (by Assert) and 1m winner Sejaal (by Persian Heights): dam, 6f (at 2 yrs) and 7f winner, sister to high-class sprinter Runnett: modest maiden: should stay 1m: remains capable of better. *R. A. Fahey* — 57 p

ARRY DASH 2 b.g. (Apr 13) Fraam 114 – Miletrian Cares (IRE) 67 (Hamas (IRE) 125§) [2002 7f 6g 7d² Nov 5] 12,000Y: small gelding: first foal: dam, ran 3 times at 2 yrs, may have proved best at 5f/6f: best effort when ½-length second to Bigalothegigalo in maiden at Catterick, finishing well: will stay 1m. *M. R. Channon* — 79

ARTE ET LABORE (IRE) 2 b.f. (Apr 16) Raphane (USA) 102 – Bouffant (High Top 131) [2002 6d 5g 6s 5m 6f⁴ f5g 7d³ f8.5g⁴ p8g⁶ Nov 23] IR 10,000F, 7,500Y: half-sister to several winners, including 1¼m winner Sahil (by Taufan) and 1¼m/1½m winner High Tatra (by Polish Patriot), both fairly useful: dam Irish middle-distance maiden: modest maiden on turf, poor on all-weather: may prove best at 6f/7f: acts on firm and good to soft ground, and on fibresand: visored when unseating rider leaving paddock/withdrawn third intended outing: edgy sort: sometimes slowly away/flashes tail. *K. A. Ryan* — 58 a48

ART EXPERT (FR) 4 b.g. Pursuit of Love 124 – Celtic Wing (Midyan (USA) 124) [2002 62: f11s³ f16.2g f16.2g f12g⁴ 21.6m f14.8g⁶ f12g f16.2g f16g Dec 17] sturdy gelding: modest maiden handicapper at best: stays 2¼m: acts on fibresand and any turf going: sometimes blinkered/visored: on downgrade. *Mrs N. Macauley* — 50 d

ARTHUR PENDRAGON 2 b.g. (May 7) Botanic (USA) – Blue Room 70 (Gorytus (USA) 132) [2002 p6g⁵ Dec 28] sixth foal: half-brother to useful 1m (at 2 yrs) to 1½m winner Prince of My Heart (by Prince Daniel): dam 7f winner who stayed 1m: fair form when 5½ lengths fifth of 12 to Dunhill Star in maiden at Lingfield, bit free early on: should improve. *B. W. Hills* — 65 p

ARTHURS KINGDOM (IRE) 6 b.g. Roi Danzig (USA) – Merrie Moment (IRE) (Taufan (USA) 119) [2002 –: 14.1m⁶ Jul 27] tall, angular gelding: poor maiden handicapper: stays 1¾m: acts on good to firm ground, good to soft and fibresand: sometimes visored. *Miss Kate Milligan* — 40

ARTIE 3 b.g. Whittingham (IRE) 104 – Calamanco 71 (Clantime 101) [2002 83p: 5d 6s³ 6g* 6d 6m³ 5.6m 6g 6f² 5g² 5s² Oct 26] big, good-topped gelding: useful handicapper: won William Hill Trophy at York in June by short head from Impressive Flight: good — 99

William Hill Trophy (Handicap), York—Artie (far side) just gets the better of Impressive Flight with Fire Up The Band (checks) and Just James (No.8) next home; the race was the principal event on the 32nd Timeform Charity Day, which raised £176,239, the third highest total in its history

efforts after when placed at Ripon (third to Deceitful in Great St Wilfrid), York (1½ lengths second to The Tatling), Newmarket (1¾ lengths second to Repertory) and Doncaster (dead-heated for second, 2 lengths behind Bond Boy): raced only at 5f/6f: probably acts on any going: usually leads: game. *T. D. Easterby*

ARTIFACT 4 b.f. So Factual (USA) 120 – Ancient Secret (Warrshan (USA) 117) – [2002 –, a72: f8s⁶ f8s⁵ f7g* f8g² f8g² f7g³ f9.4g f7g f8.5s 10m 10.9m 7m 7g f7g f8g f8.5g **a73 d** Dec 20] tall, lengthy filly: fair handicapper at best on all-weather: won at Wolverhampton in January: probably best at 7f to 8.5f: acts on fibresand: held up: on downgrade. *J. A. Pickering*

ARTISIA (IRE) 2 ch.f. (May 9) Peintre Celebre (USA) 137 – Almaaseh (IRE) 63 – (Dancing Brave (USA) 140) [2002 6f⁴ Sep 26] IR 145,000Y: closely related to smart 5f performer Almaty (by Dancing Dissident) and half-sister to useful 1¼m and (in France) 11f winner Salee (by Caerleon) and 3-y-o Impeller: dam twice-raced daughter of Irish 1000 Guineas winner Al Bahathri: 50/1, 10 lengths last of 4 in minor event at Goodwood. *W. R. Muir*

ARTISTIC LAD 2 ch.c. (Mar 28) Peintre Celebre (USA) 137 – Maid For The Hills **87 p** 101 (Indian Ridge 123) [2002 7d* Oct 15] 200,000Y: lengthy, unfurnished colt: third foal: half-brother to 2000 2-y-o 6f winner Green Tambourine (by Green Desert) and 3-y-o Maid To Perfection, both fairly useful: dam 2-y-o 6f winner: 8/1, overcame greenness to win 13-runner maiden at Leicester by 2 lengths from Fabulous Jet, nudged along at various stages before quickening to lead approaching final 1f: will probably stay 1¼m: useful prospect at least. *Sir Michael Stoute*

Mr W. J. P. Jackson's "Ashdown Express"

ARTISTRY   2 b.f. (Jan 23) Night Shift (USA) – Arriving 105 (Most Welcome 131)   **54**
[2002 6m 7s p7g⁴ 7g⁶ f7g f8.5g p7g Dec 28] first foal: dam 1¼m to 11.4f winner: modest   **a64**
maiden: best effort on first start: left J. Hills after next outing: stays 7f: acts on polytrack.
P. Howling

ARTISTS RETREAT   3 ch.f. Halling (USA) 133 – Jumairah Sunset 67 (Be My Guest   **–**
(USA) 126) [2002 63: 7.1f 7m 5.1d 10g 7m Aug 29] tall, leggy filly: modest maiden at 2
yrs: well beaten in 2002. *D. J. S. ffrench Davis*

ARZILLO   6 b.g. Forzando 122 – Titania's Dance (IRE) 61 (Fairy King (USA)) [2002   **–**
–, a44: f8s p7g p7g³ f7g p8g p7g Feb 20] small gelding: poor maiden: stays 7f: acts on   **a42**
firm going and all-weather, well beaten on softer than good: sometimes blinkered, including last 4 starts: has been slowly away/tended to hang. *J. M. Bradley*

ARZOO (IRE)   2 b.c. (Feb 23) Bahhare (USA) 122 – Ishtiyak 80 (Green Desert (USA)   **83**
127) [2002 6g⁴ 6g² 6m³ 5m* Sep 16] good-topped colt: fifth foal: half-brother to a winner
in Greece by Persian Bold: dam 5f (at 2 yrs)/6f winner: fairly useful form: won nursery at
Musselburgh in September by ¾ length from The Wizard Mul, overcoming unfavourable
draw and leading close home: effective at 5f/6f: raced only on good/good to firm going:
upset in stall on debut, slowly away next time. *L. M. Cumani*

ARZO (USA)   2 gr.f. (Apr 13) Nureyev (USA) 131 – Arctic Swing (USA) (Swing Till   **63**
Dawn (USA)) [2002 6d p7g⁶ Oct 31] sister to a winner in Japan and half-sister to several
winners, including Grade 2-placed winner in USA by Capote: dam US sprint winner:
better effort in maidens (modest form) when sixth of 13 at Lingfield, never a threat:
should stay 1m. *J. H. M. Gosden*

ASBO   2 b.f. (Apr 2) Abou Zouz (USA) 109 – Star 83 (Most Welcome 131) [2002 6f 6g   **66**
Oct 18] 2,000Y: leggy, workmanlike filly: second foal: dam, 5f winner, ran only at 2 yrs:
fair form: very green on debut: tenth of 30 in sales race at Newmarket next time: slowly
away both starts. *Dr J. D. Scargill*

ASCARI   6 br.g. Presidium 124 – Ping Pong 65 (Petong 126) [2002 60: p10g* p10g   **71**
p10g⁶ p12g² p12g⁶ p12g⁴ 10m² 10f³ 10.1m* 10m 10g 10.1m² 10.4m 10.9m Sep 16]   **a64**
strong gelding: fair performer: won minor event at Lingfield in January and handicap at
Yarmouth (apprentices) in May: effective at 1¼m/easy 1½m: acts on firm going, good to
soft and polytrack (some promise on fibresand): tried visored/blinkered earlier in career:
free-going sort: usually patiently ridden: sold 4,500 gns. *W. Jarvis*

ASEELAH   3 b.f. Nashwan (USA) 135 – Mawhiba (USA) 63 (Dayjur (USA) 137)   **–**
[2002 72p: 9.9m 10.2f Sep 30] fair form final 2-y-o start: well held in 2002: sold 3,000
gns. *J. L. Dunlop*

ASHANTIANA   3 ch.f. Ashkalani (IRE) 128 – Fast Chick 93 (Henbit (USA) 130)   **64**
[2002 55: f7g 10g² 10m⁶ 10m⁴ 10g³ 10g 8m² 8m 8f 8g⁶ 10g f7g Nov 22] modest maiden   **a–**
handicapper: left T. Mills after sixth start: stays 1¼m: acts on good to firm going: visored
final start. *R. Ingram*

ASHBOURNE LADY (IRE)   2 ch.f. (Apr 25) General Monash (USA) 107 – La   **65**
Fandango (IRE) 51 (Taufan (USA) 119) [2002 6d* 6m 7m³ p6g⁴ 6g⁴ Jul 18] strong,
lengthy filly: third foal: dam maiden who stayed 1m: fair performer: won seller at Thirsk
in May, edging left: creditable fourth in nurseries last 2 starts: will probably stay 1m: acts
on polytrack, good to firm and good to soft ground. *J. S. Moore*

ASHCOMBE   5 b.g. Polish Precedent (USA) 131 – Bonash 110 (Rainbow Quest (USA)   **72 d**
134) [2002 68: 9g³ 12d 12v 12g⁵ 11m 12s Oct 17] 3,000 3-y-o: second foal: half-brother
to 1998 2-y-o 7f winner Bionic (by Zafonic): dam French 1m (Prix d'Aumale at 2 yrs) to
1½m (Prix de Malleret) winner: fair maiden at best: trained by J. Harley in Ireland at 4
yrs: below form after reappearance, leaving S. Keightley before third outing: stays 1½m:
acts on good to soft ground. *Hugh O'Driscoll, Ireland*

ASHDOWN EXPRESS (IRE)   3 ch.g. Ashkalani (IRE) 128 – Indian Express 61   **112**
(Indian Ridge 123) [2002 100: 7m³ 8m 6g³ 6g³ 6f* 7m⁶ 6d² 6d Aug 27] sturdy, lengthy
gelding: smart performer: won listed race at Newbury in July by neck from Mugharreb,
leading close home: best efforts otherwise when length third to Tedburrow in Chipchase
Stakes at Newcastle on fourth outing and 3 lengths second to Feet So Fast in valuable
conditions event at Ascot on penultimate: has won at 1m, best at 6f: acts on firm and
good to soft going: blinkered final start (gelded after): has worn crossed noseband/been
early to post: tends to race freely/wander. *C. F. Wall*

ASHGAR SAYYAD (USA)   3 b.c. Kingmambo (USA) 125 – Quelle Affaire (USA)   **89**
(Riverman (USA) 131) [2002 89: 10m 9.2g⁴ 8g* 8d 8.2m² 8.1g² 8.5m⁴ 7m* Sep 3] rather
leggy, close-coupled colt: fairly useful performer: won maiden at Newcastle in June and

minor event at Yarmouth (made all) in September: stays 8.5f: yet to race on heavy going, seems to act on any other: visored (hung right) second start: sent to Hong Kong, where renamed Lucky Twins. *M. R. Channon*

ASHKALANI STAR (IRE) 3 ch.g. Ashkalani (IRE) 128 – Atacama (Green Desert (USA) 127) [2002 75: 9.2s 7.5m⁶ 8g 8f f8.5g Oct 5] strong gelding: fair at 2 yrs: well held in 2002: sold 2,500 gns, sent to Italy. *M. Johnston* —

ASHKELON 3 ch.c. Ashkalani (IRE) 128 – Subtle Blush 60 (Nashwan (USA) 135) [2002 86p: 8d² 10g 10f⁵ 10m 8m* 8.1g Oct 5] sturdy colt: fairly useful performer: won minor event at Pontefract in September: probably best around 1m: acts on good to firm and good to soft going, possibly not on soft: sold 30,000 gns. *Mrs A. J. Perrett* **90**

ASH LADDIE (IRE) 2 ch.g. (Apr 11) Ashkalani (IRE) 128 – Lady Ellen 67 (Horage 124) [2002 7s Oct 25] useful-looking gelding: half-brother to several winners, including 8-y-o Ellens Lad and 7-y-o Ellens Academy: dam, second at 5f at 2 yrs, half-sister to Indian Ridge: 50/1 and backward, 12 lengths tenth of 12 to Kris Kin in maiden at Doncaster. *E. J. Alston* **56**

ASHLEIGH BAKER (IRE) 7 b. or br.m. Don't Forget Me 127 – Gayla Orchestra (Lord Gayle (USA) 124) [2002 61: 10.9f 9.9m 12.3f³ 12g 11.8d⁴ 12.3g 10m 10.9g⁶ 10g 10.3f 10s⁴ 12s f12g f12g Dec 4] leggy, angular mare: modest handicapper: effective at 1¼m (given good test) to easy 2m: acts on any turf going, well held on fibresand: twice blinkered in 1998: usually waited with: none too consistent. *A. Bailey* **59 a–**

ASHLINN (IRE) 4 ch.f. Ashkalani (IRE) 128 – Always Far (USA) (Alydar (USA)) [2002 86: 6g 8f 7g 5m 5g 6d⁴ 7m 7.6s Sep 10] sturdy, lengthy filly: has a quick action: reportedly in foal to Inchinor: fair handicapper: effective at 6f (given a test) to 1m: acts on firm and soft going: usually blinkered/visored in 2001: usually races prominently. *S. Dow* **76**

ASH MOON (IRE) 4 ch.f. General Monash (USA) 107 – Jarmar Moon (Unfuwain (USA) 131) [2002 91: p12g³ p12g p12g p12g p10g⁵ 10g³ 10s⁴ 10g⁶ 10.4g⁵ 10m⁵ p8g³ f9.4g⁵ f8g p10g⁵ p10g Dec 28] lengthy, leggy filly: fairly useful performer at best: deteriorated in 2002: probably best at 1¼m/easy 1½m: acts on soft going, good to firm and polytrack: blinkered (ran creditably) once: sometimes slowly away/races freely/wanders. *K. R. Burke* **90 d**

ASHNAYA (FR) 4 b.f. Ashkalani (IRE) 128 – Upend 120 (Main Reef 126) [2002 79: 16.1m May 23] lengthy filly: fair handicapper at 3 yrs: well held only 4-y-o start on Flat: blinkered nowadays. *W. Storey* —

ASHTARA (FR) 3 b.c. Ashkalani (IRE) 128 – Green Light (FR) (Green Dancer (USA) 132) [2002 8m 10.1m Sep 18] big, lengthy colt: half-brother to several winners, notably smart French 1½m (Prix de Malleret) winner Another Dancer (by Groom Dancer), 1¼m winner at 2 yrs: dam French 1¼m/10.5f winner out of Sun Chariot winner Ranimer: well held in maiden/seller. *N. A. Callaghan* —

ASHTON VALE 3 ch.c. Ashkalani (IRE) 128 – My Valentina 84 (Royal Academy (USA) 130) [2002 65p: p8g f7g³ p7g⁵ f7g² f9.4g 8.2g⁴ 10.2m³ 10d⁶ 8d 9.9m⁴ Aug 14] fair maiden handicapper: stays 1¼m: acts on all-weather and good to firm going: joined P. Nicholls, won over hurdles in September/October. *R. Hannon* **65**

ASHTORETH (IRE) 3 ch.f. Ashkalani (IRE) 128 – Sally Chase 101 (Sallust 134) [2002 53: p8g 7s 8.2m³ 8.1d⁶ Jul 4] good-bodied filly: modest maiden: left Mrs A. Perrett after reappearance: stays 1m: acts on good to firm going and polytrack: sold 1,100 gns. *G. A. Butler* **52**

ASHTREE BELLE 3 b.f. Up And At 'em 109 – Paris Babe 94 (Teenoso (USA) 135) [2002 70: f6g² 6m 7s 6g 6g² 7g* 7m⁵ f7g³ f6g⁶ f7s⁵ f7g³ Nov 15] fair performer: won claimer at Leicester in August: unlikely to stay beyond 7f: acts on good to firm going, good to soft and all-weather: sometimes slowly away. *D. Haydn Jones* **75**

ASHVILLE LAD 5 b.h. Bigstone (IRE) 126 – Hooray Lady 92 (Ahonoora 122) [2002 60: f9.4g⁵ 8.2d 7.5g⁴ f8g⁵ Jun 20] strong horse: modest maiden: stays 1¼m: acts on fibresand and firm going: usually blinkered/visored and tongue tied. *B. A. McMahon* **51**

ASIAN HEIGHTS 4 b.c. Hernando (FR) 127 – Miss Rinjani 83 (Shirley Heights 130) [2002 119: 11.6s* 12m* 12g Oct 6] quite attractive colt: has a quick action: smart form (has won 4 of his 6 races): reportedly split pastern (and had 2 screws inserted) shortly after winning listed race at Goodwood in 2001: won similar contest at Windsor (by ¾ length from Potemkin, reportedly suffered infected hock after) in May and Milcars September Stakes at Kempton (poorly positioned when race began in earnest, strong run to lead near finish and beat Leadership a neck) in September: slowly away and always **116**

trailing in Prix de l' Arc de Triomphe at Longchamp final start: will stay 1¾m: acts on soft and good to firm going: has awkward head carriage but seems genuine: held up: stays in training. *G. Wragg*

ASIAN PERSUASION (IRE) 3 gr.g. Danehill Dancer (IRE) 117 – Kaitlin (IRE) **56** (Salmon Leap (USA) 131) [2002 65: 6m⁶ f7g⁵ 6m 7g 8.1f p10g p10g Dec 30] rather leggy, workmanlike gelding: modest maiden: sold from E. James 5,500 gns before final outing (wore cheekpieces): seems to stay easy 1¼m: acts on good to firm going and all-weather. *B. A. Pearce*

ASKARIYAH (USA) 2 b.f. (Feb 7) Kris S (USA) – Awaamir 102 (Green Desert – (USA) 127) [2002 8g 8s⁶ Oct 15] sturdy filly: second foal: dam, 7f (at 2 yrs)/1m winner who stayed 9f, granddaughter of US Grade 1 1¼m winner Castilla: green, well held in maidens: sold 3,000 gns. *J. H. M. Gosden*

ASKHAM (USA) 4 b.c. El Gran Senor (USA) 136 – Konvincha (USA) (Cormorant **112** (USA)) [2002 112: 9m⁵ Apr 17] good-topped colt: smart performer: successful twice in 2001: creditable 3 lengths fifth to Indian Creek in Earl of Sefton Stakes at Newmarket only 4-y-o start: stays 1¼m: acts on good to firm going: has taken good hold/worn crossed noseband. *L. M. Cumani*

ASSAYER (IRE) 3 b.g. Goldmark (USA) 113 – Romanovna (Mummy's Pet 125) – [2002 p7g⁶ p8g⁶ f8.5g³ 10d 7.9g 8.5g f9.4g⁴ f9.4f⁶ Aug 16] IR 10,500F, IR 17,000Y: **a46** half-brother to 2 winners by Mujadil, notably 5-y-o Cotton House: dam poor maiden out of half-sister to Eclipse winner Connaught: poor maiden: should stay 1¼m: acts on polytrack: sometimes slowly away. *N. P. Littmoden*

ASSIGNATION 2 b.c. (Feb 2) Compton Place 125 – Hug Me 96 (Shareef Dancer **82 ?** (USA) 135) [2002 5.1d 6d³ 6s 7d Jul 5] 7,200F, 15,000Y: strong, well-made colt: half-brother to several winners, including 1997 2-y-o 6f winner Generous Embrace (by Cadeaux Genereux) and fairly useful 1½m/1¾m winner Embracing (by Reference Point): dam 7f (at 2 yrs) and 1½m winner: seemingly fair form when third to Sarayat in maiden at Leicester: well held otherwise, including in nursery (visored): should stay 7f: raced only on going softer than good. *B. R. Millman*

ASSRAAR 2 b.f. (May 16) Cadeaux Genereux 131 – Possessive Dancer 118 (Shareef **86 p** Dancer (USA) 135) [2002 6m 7m⁴ 7.1g* Sep 12] seventh foal: half-sister to smart but temperamental 7f (at 2 yrs) to 1½m winner (stayed 2½m) Maylane (by Mtoto) and UAE 6f/7f winner Morshid (by Gulch): dam won Italian and Irish Oaks: progressive form: won maiden at Chepstow in September readily by 2½ lengths from Princess Magdalena, travelling strongly, quickening clear: will probably stay 1m: probably a useful performer in the making. *A. C. Stewart*

ASSUAGE 2 b.f. (Apr 17) Wolfhound (USA) 126 – Francfurter 89 (Legend of France – (USA) 124) [2002 5m 6m 5g 7.1d 6s 5m 8g Sep 19] 700Y, resold 6,500Y: small filly: fourth foal: half-sister to 3-y-o Fraulein and winners in Germany by Lion Cavern and Mtoto: dam, 1¼m winner, from good family: little sign of ability: blinkered last 2 starts, looking wayward on final one. *C. B. B. Booth*

ASSURED PHYSIQUE 5 b.g. Salse (USA) 128 – Metaphysique (FR) (Law Society **56** (USA) 130) [2002 –: p10g⁵ p10g f8.5g⁵ p13g Mar 2] tall gelding: modest maiden: stays 11.5f: acts on good to firm and good to soft going, probably on all-weather: sometimes blinkered/visored/tongue tied. *R. J. Baker*

ASTAFORT (FR) 3 ch.g. Kendor (FR) 122 – Tres Chic (USA) (Northern Fashion – (USA) 114) [2002 –: 6.9d 8m 12.1s 12.1m Sep 2] close-coupled gelding: no form. *A. C. Whillans*

ASTER FIELDS (IRE) 4 b.f. Common Grounds 118 – North Telstar 104 (Sallust **42** 134) [2002 –: f5g f5g⁵ 5m⁵ 6f f5g* f5g⁵ p5g f5g f5g Jul 11] sturdy filly: modest on **a50** all-weather, poor on turf: won maiden claimer at Wolverhampton in April: should stay at least 6f: acts on fibresand, soft and good to firm ground. *D. Shaw*

ASTER (IRE) 3 b.f. Danehill (USA) 126 – Abashed (Fairy King (USA)) [2002 7g 6m – 5g 7.1d Jul 31] 6,000F: big, good-topped filly: first foal: dam unraced close relation to very smart 6f/7f performer Diffident: well held in maidens/handicap: has been slowly away. *E. J. O'Neill*

AS TIME GOES BY 4 ch.g. Timeless Times (USA) 99 – Parfait Amour 73 (Clantime – 101) [2002 34: f7g Jan 7] of little account. *B. S. Rothwell*

ASTI F (IRE) 4 ch.g. Spectrum (IRE) 126 – Very Sophisticated (USA) (Affirmed – (USA)) [2002 –, a85d: f6s f7s⁶ f7s³ f6g f6g f7g⁶ f11g f14.8s⁶ f12g f8.5g Jul 26] big **a66 d**

AST

gelding: fairly useful performer at 3 yrs: very much on the downgrade: possibly best at 7f to 8.5f: acts on fibresand: blinkered first 6 starts. *Mrs N. Macauley*

ASTON MARA 5 b.g. Bering 136 – Coigach 110 (Niniski (USA) 125) [2002 50: 15g⁶ 15.8f 14.1m Jul 27] of little account nowadays. *M. A. Buckley* –

ASTORIA 3 ch.f. Primo Dominie 121 – Ciboure 74 (Norwick (USA) 125) [2002 56: 10g 7m Sep 17] big, good-topped filly: modest maiden at 2 yrs: well beaten both 3-y-o starts. *N. Tinkler* –

ASTORMYDAYISCOMING 4 b.g. Alhaatmi – Valentine Song 63 (Pas de Seul 133) [2002 –: 16m 14g 17.1m 17.2d⁶ Jun 26] lengthy gelding: poor form. *W. M. Brisbourne* 37

ASTRAC (IRE) 11 b.g. Nordico (USA) – Shirleen (Daring Display (USA) 129) [2002 57, a60: f6g f6g 7m* 7.5g 7m 7d⁶ 7m 5.9v⁶ f7s* f7g Oct 5] sturdy gelding: modest performer: won amateur handicap at Yarmouth in May and claimer at Wolverhampton in September: stays easy 7f: acts on firm going, soft and fibresand: tried blinkered: none too consistent. *Mrs A. L. M. King* 62

ASTRAL 3 b.f. Alhaarth (IRE) 126 – Carina Clare (Slip Anchor 136) [2002 8.2d p8g 8m⁶ Jun 23] 6,000Y: lengthy, unfurnished filly: second foal: dam unraced close relative of useful stayer Clare Heights: well held in maidens. *C. E. Brittain* –

ASTRAL PRINCE 4 ch.g. Efisio 120 – Val d'Erica 119 (Ashmore (FR) 125) [2002 70§, a79§: 10g 10m⁴ 12d³ 10.1m 12d 10f Sep 27] strong gelding: modest handicapper: stays 1¼m: acts on fibresand and good to firm going: usually blinkered at 3 yrs and on final start: has taken good hold: not one to trust. *A. Crook* 64 §

ASTROCHARM (IRE) 3 b.f. Charnwood Forest (IRE) 125 – Charm The Stars (Roi Danzig (USA)) [2002 77: 7.9f 10v 8f* 7m² 8m 9m⁵ 8g* 8.1m⁵ Sep 15] leggy, unfurnished filly: has a round action: useful handicapper: won at Pontefract in June and Thirsk in September (beat Puppet Play by 2 lengths): stays easy 9f: acts on firm and good to soft ground. *M. H. Tompkins* 99

ASTROMANCER (USA) 2 b. or br.f. (Mar 27) Silver Hawk (USA) 123 – Colour Dance (Rainbow Quest (USA) 134) [2002 8m⁵ 7d Nov 2] first foal: dam, ran twice in France, out of sister to Dancing Brave and Jolypha: 66/1, better effort in maidens (modest form) when mid-field at Newmarket second start: likely to do better at 1¼m+. *M. H. Tompkins* 62 p

ASTYANAX (IRE) 2 b.c. (Feb 22) Hector Protector (USA) 124 – Craigmill 85 (Slip Anchor 136) [2002 6.1m 6f 7m Oct 3] 12,000Y: lengthy colt: fourth foal: half-brother to fairly useful 10.5f winner Heather Mix (by Linamix) and a winner in Germany by Unfuwain: dam, 2-y-o 7f winner, half-sister to Park Hill winner Coigach and smart performer up to 1¾m Applecross (latter dam of Craigsteel and Invermark): signs of ability in maidens (slowly away final start): should do better at 1m+. *Sir Mark Prescott* – p

ASWAN (IRE) 4 ch.g. Ashkalani (IRE) 128 – Ghariba 112 (Final Straw 127) [2002 90: 7f 8m 8.2v p7g² p8g² p7g⁴ Dec 11] fairly useful performer: stays 1m: acts on good to firm going and polytrack. *T. J. Etherington* 81

ATAHUELPA 2 b.c. (Apr 27) Hernando (FR) 127 – Certain Story (Known Fact (USA) 135) [2002 6g⁴ 8.1g* f8.5g² 8s⁵ Oct 25] half-brother to several winners, including useful 8.5f to 1½m winner Pharly Story (by Pharly): dam unraced half-sister to dam of Shaamit: fairly useful performer: won maiden at Chepstow in September: creditable fifth in nursery at Doncaster final start: bred to stay at least 1¼m. *P. F. I. Cole* 89

ATALL'S FLYER 4 b.f. Atall Atall 112 – Branston Kristy 55 (Hallgate 127) [2002 –: 5m Jul 24] no form. *M. A. Barnes* –

ATARAMA (IRE) 3 b.f. Sadler's Wells (USA) 132 – Regal Portrait (IRE) 57 (Royal Academy (USA) 130) [2002 93p: 10f³ 12m 11v⁶ 8.5f* 8f⁶ Oct 14] rather leggy filly: useful performer: good efforts in 2002 in listed race at Newbury (6¼ lengths third to Monturani) and Ribblesdale Stakes at Royal Ascot (4¼ lengths eighth to Irresistible Jewel, weakened break): left J. Dunlop after won allowance race at Del Mar in August: respectable sixth in non-graded event at Santa Anita final outing: seems effective at 8.5f to 1½m: acts on firm going, possibly not on heavy: has wandered/carried head awkwardly. *K. Mulhall, USA* 102

ATAVUS 5 b.h. Distant Relative 128 – Elysian 94 (Northfields (USA)) [2002 109: 7m³ 8m 8g 7m* 7m 7m⁵ 7f 7m* 7m 7f⁵ 7m Oct 13] sturdy horse: poor mover: useful performer: won Antec International Criterion Stakes at Newmarket (beat King of Happiness by short head) in June and listed event at Epsom (beat Royal Quarters a head) 107

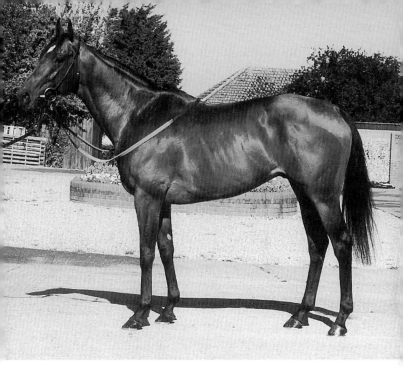

Stableside Racing Partnership II's "Atavus"

in September: mostly creditable efforts otherwise: best at 7f/1m on good going or firmer: sometimes slowly away: has edged right: best when able to lead. *G. G. Margarson*

A TEEN 4 ch.c. Presidium 124 – Very Good (Noalto 120) [2002 56, a61: f5g⁴ f6g⁵ p6g⁶ p6g p6g² f6g⁵ f5g f5g* f5g p6g 6m 5m 5m f5s p7g⁶ p7g Dec 18] modest performer: won claimer at Wolverhampton in April: barely stays 7f: acts on all-weather: tried blinkered: unreliable. *P. Howling* — §
a57 §

AT'EM DONUT (IRE) 5 ch.g. Up And At 'em 109 – Florentink (USA) (The Minstrel (CAN) 135) [2002 50: f5s f5g⁶ f5g⁶ f5g f5g 5g Aug 7] workmanlike gelding: poor maiden: reportedly broke down final start: probably best at 5f: acted on soft going and fibresand: tried visored/blinkered: was unreliable: dead. *C. N. Kellett* 44 §

ATEMME 4 b.f. Up And At 'em 109 – Petersford Girl (IRE) 84 (Taufan (USA) 119) [2002 p12g p7g 5m Sep 15] thoroughly temperamental maiden: tried blinkered: has refused to race. *Miss Jacqueline S. Doyle* §§

ATHEER (USA) 2 b.f. (Feb 5) Lear Fan (USA) 130 – Rhumba Rage (USA) (Nureyev (USA) 131) [2002 6m³ 6d² 7m³ 7g⁵ 6m Sep 23] $35,000Y: fourth foal: half-sister to useful 8.5f (in USA) and 1¼m winner (former in USA) Tough Men (by Woodman) and a winner in Japan by Rubiano: dam, lightly raced in France, sister to smart French 1986 2-y-o Fotitieng: fair maiden: below form last 2 starts: should stay at least 1m. *E. A. L. Dunlop* 72

ATHENA'S PROFILE 6 b.m. Sir Harry Lewis (USA) 127 – Caoimhe (Pollerton 115) [2002 f12g f7g Mar 18] third living foal: dam modest maiden hurdler: tailed off on Flat. *Miss K. M. George* —

ATHENIAN   3 b.g. Distant Relative 128 – Confection (Formidable (USA) 125) [2002   **84**
68: 9g f9.4g* 8.3s* p10g² 10m 8m⁵ f8.5g⁴ 8m⁵ 8g* 8f* 10.3s Oct 25] leggy gelding:
fairly useful handicapper: won at Wolverhampton in April, Windsor (edged right) in May,
Ascot in September and Pontefract in October: stays 1¼m: acts on all-weather, firm and
soft going: tough and game. *D. Morris*

ATLANTIC ACE   5 b.g. First Trump 118 – Risalah (Marju (IRE) 127) [2002 95: 8s   **101**
7.5m* 7d 7.6g³ 8m 8m² 7.9m 9m* 9f Oct 5] good-topped gelding: useful performer:
better than ever in 2002: won minor event at Beverley in April and handicap at Goodwood (beat Thaqib by ¾ length, tended to idle) in September: most unlucky head second
to Smirk in William Hill Mile (Handicap) on latter course sixth outing: effective at 7f to
9f: best form on good ground or firmer: usually held up. *B. Smart*

ATLANTIC QUEST (USA)   3 b. or br.g. Woodman (USA) 126 – Pleasant Pat (USA)   **89**
(Pleasant Colony (USA)) [2002 p8g* p10g² 8m 8m* 7.9f 8.1d⁵ May 25] $50,000Y: rather
unfurnished gelding: fourth foal: half-brother to winners in USA by Salem Drive and
Southern Sultan: dam unraced from very good US family: fairly useful performer: won
maiden at Lingfield in January and handicap at Newmarket (beat Far Lane by neck) in
May: creditable fifth to Common World in quite valuable handicap at Haydock final start
(gelded after): stays easy 1¼m: acts on polytrack, good to firm and good to soft going:
tends to wander/carry head high. *M. Johnston*

ATLANTIC VIKING (IRE)   7 b.g. Danehill (USA) 126 – Hi Bettina 96 (Henbit   **101**
(USA) 130) [2002 90: 5f 6m² 5f⁶ 6g 5m 5d⁶ 5f² 6s 5m* 5m 6f Oct 12] well-made gelding:
useful handicapper: career-best performance when winning at Epsom in August readily
by 1½ lengths from Elvington Boy: well held both runs after: best at 5f/easy 6f: below
form on heavy going, acts on any other: sometimes blinkered: often races prominently:
sometimes wanders. *D. Nicholls*

ATLANTIS PRINCE   4 ch.c. Tagula (IRE) 116 – Zoom Lens (IRE) 65 (Caerleon   **116**
(USA) 132) [2002 109: 8g⁶ a10f² 10g 8m* 8g Oct 26] lengthy, useful-looking colt: smart
performer: 9 lengths second to Sakhee in minor event at Nad Al Sheba in February:
improved form when winning listed race at Goodwood in June by 1¼ lengths from Priors
Lodge, leading 2f out and eased close home: well held in Group 2 handicap at Moonee
Valley 4 months later: probably better at 1m than 1¼m: acts on soft going, good to firm
and on dirt: has had tongue tied: usually races prominently. *Saeed bin Suroor*

ATOMIC FLAIR (IRE)   3 ch.g. Up And At 'em 109 – Gold Flair 93 (Tap On Wood   **62**
130) [2002 70: p8g⁵ 8m 8.1f 10.9g Jul 5] short-backed gelding: modest maiden: stays
8.5f: acts on all-weather and firm going, well held on soft: raced freely/hung right second
outing: sold 2,000 gns, sent to Kuwait. *P. R. Chamings*

ATTACHE   4 ch.g. Wolfhound (USA) 126 – Royal Passion 78 (Ahonoora 122) [2002   **105**
103: f8.5g 8s 8g 7.6f⁵ 8.1d 7f⁵ 7g 6g* 6v² 7m² 6m* 6g⁴ 7f³ Oct 10] lengthy gelding:
useful performer: left Mrs J. Ramsden after seventh start: won minor events at Haydock
in July and September: creditable efforts in Ayr Gold Cup (fourth to Funfair Wane) and
handicap at York (third to Surprise Encounter, again not clear run) last 2 starts: effective
at 6f/7f: acts on any going: blinkered (raced too freely) once: held up. *M. A. Jarvis*

ATTACK   6 gr.g. Sabrehill (USA) 120 – Butsova 93 (Formidable (USA) 125) [2002   **73**
14g 10d³ 11.9f 11g³ 9.5m 10g⁴ p10g Dec 11] fair maiden: left Mrs J. Harrington, Ireland,
8,500 gns prior to well held in Lingfield handicap on British debut final start: stays 11f:
acts on good to soft going: blinkered third start: often tongue tied. *Mrs A. L. M. King*

ATTILA THE HUN   3 b.g. Piccolo 121 – Katya (IRE) 93 (Dancing Dissident (USA)   **–**
119) [2002 5.1d 6f 8g May 20] second foal: brother to a 7f winner in Jersey: dam 5f (at 2
yrs) and 6f winner: last in maidens. *M. R. Channon*

ATTLEE (USA)   3 br. or b.g. Atticus (USA) 121 – No Rego (USA) (Riverman (USA)   **77**
131) [2002 75: p7g² p7g² f8.5g² f8.5g² 8m² a10f⁵ Dec 13] rather leggy gelding: shows
knee action: fair maiden: runner-up all starts in Britain in 2002: left E. Dunlop and off
7½ months before final outing: stays 8.5f: acts on good to firm going and all-weather:
sometimes slowly away/takes good hold. *M. Al Kurdi, UAE*

ATTORNEY   4 ch.g. Wolfhound (USA) 126 – Princess Sadie 86 (Shavian 125) [2002   **74 d**
81, a72: f7g⁵ f6g² f6g f5g f6g² f5g* f6g⁵ 5s² 5g 5.1d 5d 5d 5g f6g f6g f5f f6g f5g f6s⁶   **a71 d**
Dec 26] tall, quite good-topped gelding: fair handicapper at best: left M. Jarvis after
second start: won at Southwell in March: best at 5f/easy 6f: acts on soft going, good to
firm and fibresand: tried blinkered, visored after fourth start: has been on edge/sweating:
on downgrade. *D. Shaw*

ATTORNEY GENERAL (IRE) 3 b.g. Sadler's Wells (USA) 132 – Her Ladyship **93**
119 (Polish Precedent (USA) 131) [2002 10.9m* 12d* 12.3m⁶ 11.8g Oct 14] angular
gelding: has scope: fourth foal: half-brother to useful performer up to 11f Dignify (by
Rainbow Quest), 7f/1m winner at 2 yrs: dam, French 10.5f winner (second in Prix de
Diane), half-sister to smart performer up to 1¼m Lord of Men: fairly useful form: won
maiden at Warwick in July and 3-runner minor event at Thirsk (again showed good
attitude to beat Balladeer by head) in August: well below form in handicaps last 2 starts,
sweating profusely beforehand on penultimate: will be suited by 1¾m+: sold 75,000 gns,
joined J. Old and gelded. *Sir Michael Stoute*

A TWO (IRE) 3 b.f. Ali-Royal (IRE) 127 – Rainelle (Rainbow Quest (USA) 134) **56**
[2002 –: 10m* 10g⁴ 10.2g Oct 16] modest performer: won seller at Leicester in June:
stays 1¼m: raced only on good/good to firm going. *B. Palling*

AUBRIETA (USA) 6 b.m. Dayjur (USA) 137 – Fennel 97 (Slew O' Gold (USA)) –
[2002 55, a63: p6g⁶ f7g f7g Nov 20] tall mare: modest performer at 5 yrs: well beaten in
2001, leaving A. Reid after reappearance: usually blinkered/visored. *J. W. Unett*

AUBURN 2 ch.f. (Feb 6) Danzig Connection (USA) – Youdontsay 85 (Most Welcome –
131) [2002 6m 6d 6f Sep 8] first foal: dam 5f/6f winner: well held in maidens: tongue tied
final start. *J. R. Jenkins*

AU CONTRAIRE 2 b.f. (May 4) Groom Dancer (USA) 128 – Sarabah (IRE) 83 (Ela- – §
Mana-Mou 132) [2002 6.1m 7d 7m f8g Nov 25] 26,000Y: close-coupled filly: half-sister
to several winners, including 6f (including at 2 yrs)/7f winner Cryhavoc, unreliable 7f
(at 2 yrs) to 9f winner Ice (both by Polar Falcon) and 4-y-o Saratov, all useful: dam,
1¼m winner, half-sister to smart performer up to 7f/1m performer Gothenberg: temperamental maiden:
unseated rider on debut: again swerved left leaving stall when pulled up third outing:
blinkered final one. *M. A. Buckley*

AUDACIOUS PRINCE (IRE) 2 b.c. (Mar 3) Desert Prince (IRE) 130 – Sheer **91 p**
Audacity (Troy 137) [2002 7m³ 7g* Aug 15] half-brother to several winners, notably
Derby winner Oath (by Fairy King) and 1m to 1¼m performer Pelder (by Be My Guest),
both high class, and smart 1m to 1¾m winner Sheer Danzig (by Roi Danzig): dam, Italian
maiden, half-sister to Ribblesdale Stakes winner Miss Petard: better effort in maidens
when winning 4-runner event at Epsom by 2½ lengths from Regent's Secret, readily
making all: should stay at least 1¼m: useful prospect. *Sir Mark Prescott*

AUDIENCE 2 b.c. (Apr 2) Zilzal (USA) 137 – Only Yours 113 (Aragon 118) [2002 **85 p**
7g* 7g* Oct 18] 82,000Y: big, good-topped colt: fourth foal: half-brother to 3-y-o
Groovy: dam, 6f (at 2 yrs) to 1m winner, half-sister to smart 6f/7f performer Osario: won
maiden at Salisbury by 1¼ lengths from Khabir despite seeming green and racing freely:
landed odds in 4-runner minor event at Newmarket later in October by ½ length from
Wake, dictating pace and idling: will prove best up to 1m: useful performer in the making.
W. J. Haggas

AUDREY'S DILEMMA 3 b.f. Piccolo 121 – Yesterday's Song (Shirley Heights **63**
130) [2002 58: p7g 9.9m 8m 8.2g* May 31] modest performer: won apprentice selling
handicap at Nottingham in May: stays 1m: acts on soft going. *S. Dow*

AUNT DORIS 5 b.m. Distant Relative 128 – Nevis 61 (Connaught 130) [2002 48, **44**
a39: f6g⁴ f6g f5g⁵ f6g 5m Oct 5] poor handicapper: left M. Polglase after fourth start: has
won at 5f, probably best at 6f: acts on good to firm going and fibresand: often visored
nowadays. *Paul Johnson*

AUNT HILDA 3 b.f. Distant Relative 128 – Aloha Jane (USA) 57 (Hawaii) [2002 65: **69**
10g 10g⁵ 11.5f 11.7d⁶ 12d⁵ 11.9f p12g Dec 18] small filly: fair maiden handicapper: left
J. Dunlop 6,000 gns after fifth start: stays 11.7f: acts on firm and good to soft going:
free-going sort. *M. F. Harris*

AUNTIE DOT COM 3 ch.f. Tagula (IRE) 116 – Jadebelle 66 (Beldale Flutter (USA) **62 d**
130) [2002 70: 6d p5g 6m³ 6m Sep 3] small, lengthy filly: fair performer: below form in
2002: stays 7f: acts on firm and soft going: has been edgy/hung markedly right: usually
races prominently. *W. G. M. Turner*

AUNT RITA (IRE) 2 ch.f. (Mar 25) Grand Lodge (USA) 125 – Dance Alone (USA) **78**
(Monteverdi 129) [2002 6m* 6d Jul 9] IR 40,000Y: rather leggy, useful-looking filly:
sixth foal: half-sister to 3 winners, including useful Irish 7f (at 2 yrs) to 9f winner Balla
Sola (by Simply Great) and Irish 9f winner Celibate (by Shy Groom), both better known
as good jumpers: dam, Irish 6f/7f winner, half-sister to dam of dual Breeders' Cup Classic
winner Tiznow: fair form when winning minor event at York in May: wearing crossed

noseband, last of 9 in Cherry Hinton Stakes at Newmarket, always behind after another slow start: should stay 1m. *M. L. W. Bell*

AUNTY MARY   3 b.f. Common Grounds 118 – Flirtation (Pursuit of Love 124) [2002 –
82: 6m 5g 6g 5g Jul 30] useful-looking filly: fairly useful performer at 2 yrs: no form in 2002. *T. D. Easterby*

AURAMINE (IRE)   7 ch.g. Rainbows For Life (CAN) – Les Saintes (Kris 135) [2002   **48 d**
9m³ 9f 8m 8m 8.3s Aug 20] workmanlike gelding: fair maiden at best: very much on downgrade. *W. M. Brisbourne*

AUTUMNAL (IRE)   4 b.f. Indian Ridge 123 – Please Believe Me 93 (Try My Best   **99**
(USA) 130) [2002 104: 5.1g⁴ 5.1f⁴ 5m² 5m⁵ 5.2f 5f³ 5g⁵ Oct 17] good-topped filly: useful performer: mostly creditable efforts in 2002, including in listed races at Bath (fourth to Swiss Lake), Chester (fourth to Bishops Court) and Newmarket (third to Proud Boast): best at 5f/6f: unraced on heavy going, acts on any other: often blinkered: tongue tied final start: has been bandaged: tends to be on toes. *B. J. Meehan*

AUTUMN FANTASY (USA)   3 b. or br.c. Lear Fan (USA) 130 – Autumn Glory   **87**
(USA) (Graustark) [2002 67p: 10.5d⁵ 11s⁴ 11.9m² 13.9m 12.1g³ 16m* Oct 1] quite good-topped colt: fairly useful handicapper: won at Nottingham in October: effective at 1½m to 2m: acts on good to firm and good to soft going: has hung under pressure: sold 35,000 gns, joined B. Ellison. *J. H. M. Gosden*

AUTUMN RAIN (USA)   5 br.g. Dynaformer (USA) – Edda (USA) (Ogygian (USA))   **90**
[2002 78: p12g³ 9.7m* p10g 10.1g 10s 12g⁵ 10s* 10m³ 10.1g³ 10.1d* 10m Jul 25] big, strong gelding: fairly useful handicapper: won at Folkestone in April, Newbury (amateurs) in June and Epsom (final run for N. Callaghan) in July: shaped as though something amiss final outing: seems ideally suited by testing 1¼m: acts on good to firm going, soft and polytrack: blinkered (below form) fifth start: sometimes slowly away: usually waited with. *D. L. Williams*

AVARIS   2 b.f. (Apr 5) Savahra Sound 111 – Lucky Candy 61 (Lucky Wednesday 124)   –
[2002 10f Oct 7] 700Y: leggy filly: half-sister to several winners, including 11f winner Noble Canonire (by Gunner B) and 5f winner (including at 2 yrs) Lunar Music (by Komaite): dam maiden who should have stayed 1¼m: 100/1, tailed off in maiden at Pontefract. *Ronald Thompson*

AVEBURY   6 b.g. Fairy King (USA) – Circle of Chalk (FR) 74 (Kris 135) [2002 66,   –
a73+: f8s f8.5g f9.4g³ f8.5g Feb 25] tall, leggy gelding: fair performer: left S. Kettlewell   **a70**
before final start: stays 9.4f: acts on firm going and fibresand: tried tongue tied: held up: has found little. *G. M. Moore*

AVEIRO (IRE)   6 b.g. Darshaan 133 – Avila 76 (Ajdal (USA) 130) [2002 54+, a72+:   **63 d**
f16s p16g² f14.8g⁵ f16.2g⁴ f16.2g⁴ p13g f12g⁴ 11.9g* 12m⁵ 11.5m 12.6f⁴ 12d 17.2g⁶ f16.2f   **a66 d**
f14g⁴ f16.2g Dec 7] big gelding: fair handicapper at best: won at Brighton in May: on downgrade after: effective at 11.5f to easy 2m: acts on all-weather, firm and soft ground: blinkered: usually races prominently. *C. P. Morlock*

A VENDRE (FR)   3 b.g. Kendor (FR) 122 – Waaria (Shareef Dancer (USA) 135)   **67**
[2002 10d 8.1m³ 8m⁶ 7m⁵ 8g⁵ 9m³ f8s 7m³ 10m³ 10s⁴ 8d Nov 1] 350,000 francs Y: leggy gelding: half-brother to winners in USA by Irish River and Arctic Tern: dam unraced sister to very smart middle-distance stayer Rock Hopper: fair maiden: claimed from C. Brittain £6,000 eighth start: barely stays 1¼m: acts on good to firm going: tried blinkered (pulled hard first occasion). *M. C. Pipe*

AVENING   2 br.c. (Mar 14) Averti (IRE) 117 – Dependable (Formidable (USA) 125)   **95**
[2002 5.2d 5m* 6.1v³ 5.1d³ 5.1f² 5g* 5g 6f 6m³ 6g² 6m 6s Oct 26] useful-looking colt: eighth foal: half-brother to 3 winners, including 6f (at 2 yrs) to 15f winner Certain Magic and 7f to 1¼m winner Elba Magic (both by Faustus): dam unraced: useful performer: won maiden at Leicester in June and nursery at Goodwood in August: best efforts when placed in minor event at Doncaster and listed race at Saint-Cloud (¾-length second to Castor Troy) in September: ran badly final start: effective at 5f/6f: acts on firm going: has worn crossed noseband: went right leaving stall (tongue tied) fourth start. *R. Hannon*

AVENTURA (IRE)   2 b.c. (Feb 29) Sri Pekan (USA) 117 – La Belle Katherine (USA)   **83**
(Lyphard (USA) 132) [2002 p6g⁵ p5g* p5g³ Dec 11] 15,000F, 9,000Y: third foal: half-brother to 6f winner Criss Cross (by Lahib): dam ran twice in France: fairly useful form when winning maiden at Lingfield in November by neck from Calbrae, responding well to get on top close home: below form in minor event there final start: likely to prove best at 5f/6f: raced only on polytrack. *M. A. Jarvis*

AVERSHAM 2 b.c. (Apr 14) Averti (IRE) 117 – Vavona 60 (Ballad Rock 122) [2002 **90** 5.7f* 6d³ 5g³ 5.5g⁵ 7m* 6s² Oct 22] second foal: half-brother to a 10.5f winner in Italy by Dolphin Street: dam, maiden who should have been well suited by 7f+, half-sister to smart 6f/7f performer Savahra Sound: fairly useful performer: won maiden at Bath in July and minor event at Leicester (match) in September: creditable 5 lengths second to Fiddlers Reach in minor event at Yarmouth: may prove best at 5f/6f: acts on firm and soft going. *R. Hannon*

AVERTED VIEW (USA) 5 ch.m. Distant View (USA) 126 – Averti (USA) 97 **105** (Known Fact (USA) 135) [2002 85: 10.3m² 10m* 12g 10f* 10.2g 10f² 9.9m³ 10m* 9.9m⁶ Sep 14] good-topped mare: useful performer: much improved at 5 yrs: won handicap at Kempton and minor event at Pontefract in June, and listed rated stakes at Brighton (beat Mubkera by 2 lengths) in August: better at 1¼m than further: acts on any going: won in blinkers in France at 3 yrs: usually makes running (didn't when below form final start): sold 110,000 gns in December. *R. T. Phillips*

AVERTINA 2 b.f. (Mar 26) Averti (IRE) 117 – Two And Sixpence (USA) 74 (Chief's **45** Crown (USA)) [2002 6g f7g Oct 21] sixth foal: closely related to 7f winner Sarah's Song (by Warning) and half-sister to winners abroad by Faustus and Reprimand: dam 17f winner: poor form in maiden/seller: sold 2,200 gns. *J. G. Given*

A VERY GOOD YEAR (IRE) 2 b.c. (Jan 21) Indian Ridge 123 – Ma N'Ieme Biche **77 p** (USA) (Key To The Kingdom (USA)) [2002 7s⁶ 7d⁵ Nov 2] 75,000Y: big, strong colt: has plenty of scope: third foal: dam, French maiden, sister to Cheveley Park and 1000 Guineas winner Ma Biche: shaped very well (fair form) when sixth to Mustaneer in maiden at Leicester: favourite, raced much too freely when fifth to Blazing Thunder in similar event at Newmarket: will need to settle better to stay 1m: remains capable of better. *T. G. Mills*

AVESA 2 b.f. (Feb 2) Averti (IRE) 117 – Andalish 82 (Polish Precedent (USA) 131) **59** [2002 5.1f⁵ 5g⁴ 6s 6m 7g 7s Oct 28] smallish filly: first foal: dam, 10.5f winner, out of half-sister to Cheveley Park winner Prophecy: modest maiden: well held in nurseries last 3 starts, blinkered final one: should stay 7f: sold 1,200 gns, joined D. Nolan. *R. Hannon*

A VIEW INDEED (USA) 3 b.f. Distant View (USA) 126 – A Shadeed Indeed (USA) **77** (Shadeed (USA) 135) [2002 7g² 7f⁴ 7.1m⁵ a6.5f² a7f* Nov 23] $32,000F, IR 72,000Y: medium-sized, quite attractive filly: has a short action: second foal: dam unraced daughter of smart French 1¼m performer Vidor: second in newcomers race at Newbury in April: folded tamely third start, then left B. Hills: won maiden claimer at Woodbine in November: should stay 1m: acts on dirt. *J. Cardella, Canada*

AVOIDANCE (USA) 2 b.f. (Mar 3) Cryptoclearance (USA) – Averti (USA) 97 **96** (Known Fact (USA) 135) [2002 7m⁵ 7m* 7.9f* 8s² Nov 2] tall, leggy filly: fourth foal: half-sister to 2 winners, including 5-y-o Averted View: dam, 6f and (at 2 yrs) 7f winner, half-sister to very smart performer up to 11f Defensive Play: useful performer: won maiden at Epsom (raced freely) in September and nursery at York (by 2 lengths from Linby Lad) in October: good 2½ lengths second of 7 to Hanami in listed race at Newmarket final start, making running: should stay 1¼m: acts on firm and soft going. *B. W. Hills*

AVONBRIDGE 2 b.c. (Mar 18) Averti (IRE) 117 – Alessia 91 (Caerleon (USA) 132) **104 p** [2002 6g 6m* 6m* 6f* Oct 12] 29,000F: angular, quite attractive colt: third foal: half-brother to 4-y-o Patavellian: dam, 2-y-o 7f winner who stayed 1¼m, sister to Park Hill winner Casey: progressive form: won maiden at Lingfield in August, nursery at Goodwood in September and 7-runner listed event at York in October: beat Cumbrian Venture ½ length in last-named, leading final 100 yds having been outpaced early: should stay 7f: raced only on good going or firmer: smart performer in the making. *R. Charlton*

AVONDALE LAD (IRE) 2 ch.g. (Mar 30) Titus Livius (FR) 115 – Skinity (Rarity **68** 129) [2002 6d⁵ 5g³ f6f⁶ f6s* 7g 6d⁴ f6g³ Nov 20] 12,000Y, 12,000 2-y-o: half-brother to several winners, including 6-y-o Tianyi and 2001 2-y-o 5f winner Double Play (both by Mujadil): dam won 6 times in Belgium, including at 2 yrs: fair performer: won claimer at Southwell in October: stays 6f, possibly not 7f: acts on fibresand, raced only on good/good to soft going on turf. *K. A. Ryan*

AWAKE 5 ch.g. First Trump 118 – Pluvial 90 (Habat 127) [2002 87: 6s 5g³ 6d⁶ 6d 5m² **93** 5m 5s² 5d² 5d* 6m 6g 6g Sep 20] strong, smallish gelding: fairly useful handicapper: won Ladbroke Rockingham Handicap at the Curragh in July by head from Osterhase: effective at 5f/6f: acts on good to firm and heavy going: sometimes early to post. *D. Nicholls*

AWARDING 2 ch.c. (Feb 8) Mark of Esteem (IRE) 137 – Monaiya (Shareef Dancer **82 p** (USA) 135) [2002 6d 6s p5g* Nov 13] IR 45,000Y: good-topped colt: half-brother to several winners, including useful 7f (at 2 yrs) and 1¼m winner Musetta (by Cadeaux Genereux) and fairly useful 6f winner Fiametta (by Primo Dominie): dam French winner around 1m: best effort in maidens when winning at Lingfield by 1½ lengths from Tripti, leading final 1f: should stay 6f: tongue tied last 2 starts: open to further progress. *R. F. Johnson Houghton*

AWAY WIN   4 b.f. Common Grounds 118 – Cafe Glace (Beldale Flutter (USA) 130) **42** [2002 –: f6g p7g p6g p6g p6g 5.7d⁴ 5.7m 5m⁵ f6g Nov 25] poor maiden: probably stays 7f: acts on polytrack, yet to race on extremes of going on turf: blinkered fifth to seventh starts. *B. Palling*

A WOMAN IN LOVE   3 gr.f. Muhtarram (USA) 125 – Ma Lumiere (FR) (Niniski **69** (USA) 125) [2002 7g f8.5g⁵ 8g⁵ 8m⁵ 8g 8g* 7.9m 8m 7f 8m³ 8g⁴ p8g⁶ p10g p7g* Dec 30] angular filly: third foal: half-sister to French 12.5f winner Lune de Miel (by Zieten) and 4-y-o Te Quiero: dam German 7f winner out of half-sister to Grand Prix de Paris winner Soleil Noir: fair performer: won minor event at Brighton in August and, having left J. Hills 12,000 gns after eleventh start, handicap at Lingfield in December: effective at 7f/1m: acts on polytrack (well beaten only outing on fibresand), raced only on good going or firmer on turf: free-going sort. *Miss B. Sanders*

AWWAL MARRA (USA)   2 ch.f. (Apr 17) King of Kings (IRE) 125   Secretariat **71 p** Lass (USA) (Secretariat (USA)) [2002 7g² Aug 4] $40,000Y: half-sister to several winners in USA: dam, US 2-y-o 1m winner, half-sister to US Grade 2 2-y-o 6.5f winner Bright Launch: 11/2 and very green, staying-on 2½ lengths second of 9 to Late Claim in maiden at Chester: should improve. *M. Johnston*

AXFORD LORD   2 gr.g. (Apr 18) Petong 126 – Bellyphax (Bellypha 130) [2002 5m **64 §** 5g³ 5f² 5s² 5.1f 5m⁴ 6d⁵ 6m f7g 7d² f7g 5s⁴ Nov 6] 4,500Y: leggy, quite good-topped gelding: brother to 3 winners, including 1994 2-y-o 6f winner Belle Vue, and half-brother to 2 winners, including 3-y-o Beluga Bay: dam unraced half-sister to very smart sprinter/US Grade 1 1m winner Forzando: modest performer: won seller at Ripon in August: left K. Ryan after eleventh start: stays 7f: acts on firm and soft going: visored after debut: ungenuine. *A. C. Whillans*

AYIDA (IRE)   6 b.m. Shernazar 131 – Flower Dell 72 (Wolver Hollow 126) [2002 9g   – Jun 21] no form. *N. I. M. Rossiter*

AYUN (USA)   2 ch.f. (May 4) Swain (IRE) 134 – Oumaldaaya (USA) 111 (Nureyev **83** (USA) 131) [2002 7d⁵ 7.5m³ 7.1m² 7g Oct 14] close-coupled, unfurnished filly: fluent mover: seventh foal: closely related to smart 7f (at 2 yrs) to 9f winner Haami and to useful 1996 2-y-o 1m winner Asas (both by Nashwan): dam, 7f (at 2 yrs) and 1¼m (Italian Group 2 event) winner, half-sister to Derby winner Erhaab: fairly useful maiden: well below form final outing: bred to be suited by 1m+, but sometimes races freely. *J. L. Dunlop*

AZERI (USA)   4 ch.f. Jade Hunter (USA) – Zodiac Miss (AUS) (Ahonoora 122) [2002 **133** a8f* a9f² a9f* a8.5f* a8.5f* a9f* a8.5f* a8.5f* a9g* Oct 26] $110,000Y: second living foal: dam Australian Group 3 6f winner: top-class filly: successful in 10 of her 11 career starts: authoritative winner in 2002 of optional claimer and Santa Margarita Handicap at Santa Anita, Apple Blossom Handicap at Oaklawn (started slowly and wandered markedly in straight), Milady Breeders' Cup Handicap and Vanity Handicap (by easy 3 lengths from Affluent), both at Hollywood, Grade 2 handicaps at Del Mar and Santa Anita and Breeders' Cup Distaff at Arlington: put up a magnificent performance when beating Farda Amiga and Imperial Gesture by 5 lengths for last success: suffered only defeat when length second to Summer Colony in Grade 2 event at Santa Anita on second outing: stays 9f: yet to face sloppy/muddy conditions: effective tracking pace, but made all last 5 outings: stays in training in 2003. *L. De Seroux, USA*

AZREME   2 ch.c. (Mar 5) Unfuwain (USA) 131 – Mariette 35 (Blushing Scribe (USA) **71** 107) [2002 7.1d² p7g⁵ Jul 20] well-made colt: third foal: dam ran 3 times: fair form in minor event at Sandown (1½ lengths second of 4 to Puma) and maiden at Lingfield: should stay at least 1¼m. *P. W. D'Arcy*

AZUR (IRE)   5 b.m. Brief Truce (USA) 126 – Bayadere (USA) 61 (Green Dancer **70** (USA) 132) [2002 65: 8.1m 10m⁵ 8.5g 10m² 9d³ 10g* 10m 10s⁶ 9.9m 10m⁴ 10.1m⁶ 10.5f⁴ 12f* 12d* 12d Nov 1] quite good-topped mare: fair handicapper: won at Ascot in July and Pontefract in October: best at 1¼m/1½m: acts on firm and good to soft going, below form both starts on soft: tried visored, blinkered last 5 starts: sometimes slowly away: usually held up: genuine. *Mrs A. L. M. King*

AZZURRI (IRE)   3 ch.g. Ashkalani (IRE) 128 – Tiller Girl (IRE) (Mujtahid (USA) **45** 118) [2002 f7g³ f8.5g f8.5g 7m 9.9g p10g 7g Jun 17] 20,000F, 20,000Y: small, good-topped gelding: first foal: dam, ran twice at 2 yrs, out of half-sister to champion 1976 2-y-o J O Tobin and 1000 Guineas/Oaks winner Mysterious: poor maiden: has started slowly/raced freely. *J. A. Osborne*

B

BABA AU RHUM (IRE)   10 b.g. Baba Karam 117 – Spring About (Hard Fought 125) [2002 64: 9s Jun 7] tall gelding: one-time modest handicapper, lightly raced on Flat nowadays. *Ian Williams* —

BABA MIA   2 b.f. (Apr 14) Gothenberg (IRE) 117 – Kagram Queen 64 (Prince Ragusa 96) [2002 5m 5g 5d⁵ f5g⁶ 5m 6g 8m Sep 29] 7,200Y: leggy, unfurnished filly: fourth foal: half-sister to 3-y-o Gruff: dam 7f (at 2 yrs) to 11f winner: little form, including in nursery: left D. Barker after second start. *I. W. McInnes* —

BABODANA   2 ch.c. (Apr 23) Bahamian Bounty 116 – Daanat Nawal (Machiavellian (USA) 123) [2002 6v* 6d² 7.2g² 7s⁵ Oct 25] 3,000F, IR 17,000Y: good-topped colt: has scope: third foal: half-brother to a winner in Spain by Petong: dam, unraced, out of half-sister to Breeders' Cup Sprint winner Smile: useful performer: won maiden at Hamilton in June: runner-up in minor events at Windsor and Ayr (beaten short head by Go Tech) and under 7 lengths fifth of 10 to Makhlab in Horris Hill Stakes at Newbury after: barely stays testing 7f: raced on good going or softer. *M. H. Tompkins*   97

BABY BARRY   5 b.g. Komaite (USA) – Malcesine (IRE) 46 (Auction Ring (USA) 123) [2002 83: 5f 6m 5s 6f⁵ 6m² 6m 6m 6m* 6m⁴ 6m⁵ 6f⁴ 6f Oct 11] good-topped gelding: fairly useful handicapper: won at Pontefract in July: effective at 6f/easy 7f: acts on fibresand and firm going, possibly not on softer than good: tried blinkered, usually visored: mulish in preliminaries penultimate start: sometimes hangs/looks awkward ride: none too reliable. *Mrs G. S. Rees*   82

BABY BUNTING   5 b.f. Wolfhound (USA) 126 – Flitteriss Park 62§ (Beldale Flutter (USA) 130) [2002 61: 6g 6m Jul 3] good-quartered filly: poor mover: reportedly in foal to Royal Applause: modest maiden at best: well held in 2002. *M. L. W. Bell* —

BACCHANALIA (IRE)   3 b.f. Blues Traveller (IRE) 119 – Daffodil Dale (IRE) 78 (Cyrano de Bergerac 120) [2002 8g⁴ 8s⁴ 10.1m⁶ f9.4f 7.5m 7m 7m Sep 17] strong filly: poor performer: left J. Given after reappearance: stays 1m: acts on good to soft ground: went left from stall fifth start/visored last 2. *C. R. Dore*   46

BACHELORS PAD   8 b.g. Pursuit of Love 124 – Note Book 94 (Mummy's Pet 125) [2002 60, a64: 12.3m Aug 30] leggy gelding: has plenty of knee action: modest performer at best: showed little only run in 2002: tried blinkered. *Miss S. J. Wilton* —

BACH (IRE)   5 b.h. Caerleon (USA) 132 – Producer (USA) 130 (Nashua) [2002 121: 8m* 10.5s² 10m 10g⁵ 8v Nov 2] strong, good-quartered horse: not best of movers in slower paces: very smart performer: reportedly broke pelvis after final 3-y-o outing: third in Eclipse Stakes at Sandown, Irish Champion Stakes at Leopardstown and Breeders' Cup Mile at Belmont at 4 yrs: odds on, made all in listed race at Leopardstown in May: good 2 lengths second to Rebelline in Tattersalls Gold Cup at the Curragh later in month: well below best afterwards: stayed 10.5f: acted on firm and soft going: raced prominently: to stand at Beeches Stud, Ireland, fee €2,250. *A. P. O'Brien, Ireland*   121

BACK IN ACTION   2 b.c. (Feb 18) Hector Protector (USA) 124 – Lucca (Sure Blade (USA) 130) [2002 8g⁵ 7d³ Nov 2] 30,000Y, 92,000 2-y-o: leggy colt: fourth foal: half-brother to a winner in Japan by Keen: dam, behind in bumper, sister to smart 1m to 1½m performer Needle Gun, and half-sister to smart/very smart performers up to 1½m Cloud Castle and Luso: 20/1, much better effort in maidens (fairly useful form) when 3 lengths third of 22 to Blazing Thunder at Newmarket, staying on strongly having been outpaced: will stay at least 1¼m: tongue tied both starts: joined M. Magnusson: should improve further. *D. W. P. Arbuthnot*   85 p

BACK IN SPIRIT   2 ch.c. (Apr 29) Primo Dominie 121 – Pusey Street Girl 87 (Gildoran 123) [2002 5.1d f6g* 6.1v 7.1f⁶ 7g f8.5s⁴ 6.1s Oct 23] 5,200Y: well-grown colt: second foal: half-brother to 3-y-o Mornin Reserves: dam 7f winner: form only when making all in maiden at Wolverhampton in May: likely to prove best at 5f/6f: acts on fibresand. *B. A. McMahon*   76 d

BACK PASS (USA)   4 b. or br.f. Quest For Fame 127 – Skiable (IRE) (Niniski (USA) 125) [2002 65: p12g* p12g Jan 19] leggy, quite good-topped filly: fair performer: left   65

B. Hills (30,000 gns) before winning maiden at Lingfield (drifted right) in January: barely stays 1¾m: yet to race on ground softer than good: twice slowly away at 3 yrs: sent to Australia. *I. A. Balding*

BACKWELL (USA) 2 b.g. (Mar 7) Allied Forces (USA) 123 – Shehazahome (USA) **89** (Known Fact (USA) 135) [2002 7d³ 8f⁴ 7v⁴ Nov 8] $9,500F, 42,000Y: first foal: dam winning sprinter in USA: best effort in maidens (fairly useful form) when third to Tycoon Hall at Newmarket, keeping on from rear: pulled too hard next time: gelded after final outing: may prove best up to 7f. *M. A. Jarvis*

BACKWOODS 9 ch.g. In The Wings 128 – Kates Cabin 96 (Habitat 134) [2002 55: **–** 16g 18f⁶ Jun 24] heavy-topped gelding: has reportedly had leg trouble: modest performer in 2001: well held in 2002. *W. M. Brisbourne*

BAD INTENTIONS (IRE) 2 b.f. (Apr 6) Victory Note (USA) 120 – Fallacy (Selkirk **76** (USA) 129) [2002 7s 6f* 6s⁴ Oct 22] leggy filly: first foal: dam, unraced, out of half-sister to Lancashire Oaks winner Andaleeb: fair form: left Mrs D. Haine after debut: won maiden at Redcar in September, making all (wandered): improved again when fourth of 5 to Fiddlers Reach in minor event at Yarmouth: races freely, and may prove best at 6f/7f: acts on firm and soft ground. *G. C. H. Chung*

BADOU 2 b.c. (Feb 23) Averti (IRE) 117 – Bint Albadou (IRE) 91 (Green Desert (USA) **59** 127) [2002 5.7f 5.1g 6m 7s 7s³ f6g Dec 20] good-topped colt: fourth foal: half-brother to French 1½m winner Pibale (by Mujtahid): dam Irish 2-y-o 6f winner out of very smart filly up to 1¼m Cistus: modest maiden: will stay at least 1m: acts on soft ground: visored last 2 starts. *G. A. Butler*

BADRINATH (IRE) 8 b.g. Imperial Frontier (USA) 112 – Badedra (Kings Lake **54** (USA) 133) [2002 61: p10g p10g² p10g p10g³ 10.9f 9.7m 10d⁶ 10.1m³ p12g⁴ a10.5g **a58** a10.5g a9g a10.5g³ a10.5g⁶ Dec 15] quite good-topped gelding: modest performer: left H. Collingridge after ninth start and C. Tinkler in Spain after eleventh one: effective at 1m to 11.5f: acts on firm going, good to soft and all-weather/sand: finds little, and best held up as long as possible. *J. Bidgood, Spain*

BAGAN (FR) 3 b.c. Rainbow Quest (USA) 134 – Maid of Erin (USA) (Irish River **77** (FR) 131) [2002 12.1d³ 12m⁴ 12s⁵ Aug 10] good-topped, attractive colt: half-brother to several winners, notably smart 7.5f (at 2 yrs) and 1m winner Erin Bird (by Bluebird): dam, ran once in France, sister to smart dam of Spectrum (by Rainbow Quest) from excellent family: fair form in maidens: will stay beyond 1½m. *H. R. A. Cecil*

BAHAMIAN BELLE 2 b.f. (Jan 31) Bahamian Bounty 116 – Marjorie's Memory **62** (IRE) 76 (Fairy King (USA)) [2002 5m⁶ 5g⁵ 6f⁶ 5.1g 5g³ 5.1f⁶ 5m 5f Sep 27] 23,000Y: good-topped filly: fourth foal: half-sister to 3 winners by Petong, including fairly useful 2001 2-y-o 5f winner Keep The Silver and 4-y-o Pay The Silver: dam 5f winner, including at 2 yrs: modest maiden: well held in nurseries last 2 starts: best form at 5f: raced only on good ground or firmer: races freely. *J. Balding*

BAHAMIAN DANCER (IRE) 2 b.c. (May 9) Bering 136 – Fantastic Flame (IRE) **109** 79 (Generous (IRE) 139) [2002 6m² 7m⁵ 7d⁴ 8.5d* 8g² 8s⁵ Oct 26] 23,000F, 90,000Y: useful-looking colt: second foal: half-brother to 3-y-o Flaming Salsa: dam, 1¼m winner, sister to smart 1¼m/1½m performer Germano: useful performer: won maiden at Epsom in September: good head second of 9 to Al Jadeed in Royal Lodge Stakes at Ascot, settling better than previously and keeping on well: only fifth of 9 to Brian Boru in Racing Post Trophy at Doncaster final start, fading: bred to stay further than 8.5f: edgy/short to post when below form third start: sent to Hong Kong. *J. Noseda*

BAHAMIAN HEIR (IRE) 3 b.c. Lake Coniston (IRE) 131 – Bally Souza (IRE) 87 **50** (Alzao (USA) 117) [2002 45: 9m⁴ 10m⁶ Sep 5] lengthy colt: fluent mover: modest maiden, lightly raced: stays 1¼m. *D. Nicholls*

BAHAMIAN MINSTREL 3 b.g. Bahamian Bounty 116 – Penny Ghent (Dominion **–** 123) [2002 75: f5s* p5g 5.1d⁵ May 31] neat gelding: fairly useful performer: won **a83** handicap at Southwell (again drifted left) in January: should be at least as effective at 6f as 5f: acts on fibresand, probably on polytrack, best turf effort on good going: sold 1,000 gns. *Mrs L. Stubbs*

BAHAMIAN PIRATE (USA) 7 ch.g. Housebuster (USA) – Shining Through **120** (USA) (Deputy Minister (CAN)) [2002 120: 6s⁵ 5m³ 6f 5m 5g 6d² 6s² 5m 6m 6m⁵ 5g⁴ 6g⁵ Oct 18] sturdy gelding: very smart performer: without a win in 2002 but narrowly beaten in several top sprints: third to Kyllachy (beaten 2 short heads) in Palace House Stakes at Newmarket in May, ½-length second to stable-companion Continent in July Cup there on sixth outing, beaten short head by One Won One in Phoenix Sprint Stakes at the Curragh in August and very close fourth to Continent again in Prix de l'Abbaye at Longchamp penultimate start: best at 5f/6f: best recent form on ground no firmer than good to firm, and acts on soft (has won on fibresand): sometimes slowly away: usually held up. *D. Nicholls*

BAHAMIAN SUN 3 b.g. Bahamian Bounty 116 – Dear Person (Rainbow Quest (USA) 134) [2002 10m 8f 8.2g 10.2v⁶ 11.7d⁵ 16.2g f16g Dec 17] 1,800Y: sturdy gelding: half-brother to 1997 2-y-o 6f seller winner Figawin (by Rudimentary): dam twice-raced half-sister to Galtres Stakes winner Startino: modest performer: reportedly broke down on all-weather debut final start: stays 1½m (well beaten over 2m). *F. Jordan* **59**

BAHIA 3 ch.f. Grand Lodge (USA) 125 – Helens Dreamgirl 95 (Caerleon (USA) 132) [2002 59: 7g p7g Oct 31] sturdy filly: modest maiden at 2 yrs: no form in 2002. *S. L. Keightley* **–**

B A HIGHFLYER 2 b.g. (Mar 14) Compton Place 125 – Primulette 82 (Mummy's Pet 125) [2002 6s³ 6.1s³ 6f² p7g⁵ 5.1d³ 5.9g* 6m 6.1m³ 6m* 6.1m⁴ 6m* 6f² 6g³ 6s³ Oct 26] 16,000Y: good-bodied gelding: has a quick action: half-brother to numerous winners, including fairly useful 1996 2-y-o 6f winner Makhbar (by Rudimentary) and 7f (at 2 yrs) and 1½m winner Boogy Woogy (by Rock Hopper): dam 5f (at 2 yrs) and 1m winner: fairly useful performer: won maiden at Hamilton in July and nurseries at Epsom and Hamilton in September: gelded after final outing: best form around 6f: acts on firm going, soft and polytrack: tough and game. *M. R. Channon* **85**

Lucayan Stud's "Bahamian Dancer"

BAHITA (IRE)   2 b.f. (Jan 24) Bahhare (USA) 122 – Bolshoi Star 65§ (Soviet Star   **64**
(USA) 128) [2002 5.1f⁴ 5g 6f³ 6.3g 5.1f⁴ 5.9d⁴ 6.1g⁵ 7m 5f Sep 27] IR 10,000Y: lengthy
filly: first foal: dam, temperamental maiden, half-sister to useful performer up to 10.4f
Dahik: modest maiden: stays 6f: acts on firm going, probably on good to soft: sometimes
carries head awkwardly: none too consistent. *E. J. Alston*

BAHLINO (IRE)   2 gr.c. (Apr 17) Bahhare (USA) 122 – Azulino (IRE) (Bluebird   **56**
(USA) 125) [2002 7f 7d Oct 30] 30,000F, IR 60,000Y: first foal: dam maiden daughter of
useful 1m winner Page Blanche: better effort in maidens (modest form) when seventh at
Yarmouth on second start, slowly away and never nearer: will stay 1m. *W. Jarvis*

BAHRAIN (IRE)   6 ch.g. Lahib (USA) 129 – Twin Island (IRE) (Standaan (FR) 118   **47 §**
[2002 63, a47: 8f 7g 7m⁵ 8g⁶ 8.1g⁵ 7m⁴ 8m 8.1g 8.1m Sep 21] stocky gelding: poor   **a– §**
handicapper: effective at 7f to 8.5f: acts on fibresand, firm and soft going: tried tongue
tied: unreliable. *J. M. Bradley*

BAHRQUEEN (USA)   3 b.f. Bahri (USA) 125 – April In Kentucky (USA) (Palace   **78**
Music (USA) 129) [2002 86p: 8m² 8.1f² 8m² 8.3d³ Oct 14] quite attractive filly: has a
quick action: fair maiden: will be suited by 1¼m: acts on firm and good to soft going.
D. R. C. Elsworth

BAILIEBOROUGH (IRE)   3 b.g. Charnwood Forest (IRE) 125 – Sherannda (USA)   **80**
(Trempolino (USA) 135) [2002 80p: 8m 8.1d 10.2d⁵ 8m⁶ 7.1d² 7m 7d³ 8g 8.2s⁴ Oct 23]
quite good-topped gelding: fairly useful handicapper: placed at Haydock and Epsom
(handled turn poorly): effective at 7f, probably 1m: acts on good to soft going: visored
(ran respectably) final start: sold 18,000 gns. *E. A. L. Dunlop*

BAINESSE   3 b.f. Hernando (FR) 127 – Aeolina (FR) 60 (Kaldoun (FR) 122) [2002   **–**
8.2m May 10] good-topped filly: first foal: dam 11f winner from family of In The Wings
and High-Rise: 66/1, never threatened when tenth of 12 in maiden at Nottingham.
C. W. Thornton

BAJAN BROKER (IRE)   5 br.m. Turtle Island (IRE) 123 – Foxrock (Ribero 126)   **–**
[2002 45: f12g 8g Jun 17] probably of little account nowadays. *A. J. Lidderdale*

BAJAN DESERT   3 ch.g. Zamindar (USA) 116 – Bajan Rose 89 (Dashing Blade 117)   **51**
[2002 6s 6d⁴ p6g f8g⁵ f7g Dec 17] first foal: dam, 5f/6f winner (including at 2 yrs), half-
sister to smart sprinter Rambling Bear: modest maiden: may prove best at 6f/7f: tongue
tied on debut. *M. Blanshard*

BAKEWELL TART (IRE)   2 b.f. (Mar 25) Tagula (IRE) 116 – Almond Flower (IRE)   **92**
(Alzao (USA) 117) [2002 5.1d⁴ 7m* 6m⁵ 7m² f7f* 7m² 7g* 7.5s* 8s Oct 13] 40,000Y:
sixth foal: sister to useful 7f winner Macaroon and closely related/half-sister to 3 winners
abroad, including German 1m winner Almujita (by Mujtahid): dam, Irish 5f winner, ran
only at 2 yrs: fairly useful performer: won maiden at Folkestone in June, nursery at
Wolverhampton in August and nursery at Folkestone and listed race at Milan (by 2½
lengths from Inboden) in September: ran poorly in Premio Dormello at Milan final start:
should stay 1m: acts on fibresand, soft and good to firm going: sold 95,000 gns, sent to
USA. *M. L. W. Bell*

BAKIRI (IRE)   4 b.g. Doyoun 124 – Bakiya (USA) 94 (Trempolino (USA) 135) [2002   **–**
93: 11.6g 11.8g⁶ 10d Aug 11] leggy gelding: fairly useful performer in 2001 for Sir
Michael Stoute: well held in 2002. *R. T. Phillips*

BALADEUR (IRE)   4 b.g. Doyoun 124 – Singing Filly (Relkino 131) [2002 73d: f8g   **?**
f8g 8g⁴ 8d³ 9.5g* Aug 15] strong gelding: fair form at best in Britain: sold from
T. D. Barron 3,000 gns after well held in handicaps first 2 starts: won minor event at
Saarbrücken in August: stays 9.5f: acts on heavy ground. *C. Von Der Recke, Germany*

BALAKHERI (IRE)   3 b.c. Theatrical 128 – Balanka (IRE) 116 (Alzao (USA)   **121**
117) [2002 96p: 10m* 10.4f³ 12m* 12d⁵ 14.6m⁶ Sep 14]
    The shortest priced of the three Sir Michael Stoute representatives in the
St Leger failed by a long way to do himself justice. While one of his stable-companions Highest made a bold bid to provide Stoute with a first Leger victory, finishing
runner-up to Bollin Eric, Balakheri came home a well-beaten sixth, carrying his
head awkwardly under pressure in the straight. An uneasy second favourite on what
was his first start for almost three months, Balakheri seemed none too enthusiastic,
looking a shadow of the horse who had beaten Bollin Eric so comprehensively in
the King Edward VII Stakes at Royal Ascot. Perhaps his hard race on firmish going

*King Edward VII Stakes, Royal Ascot—Balakheri reverses Dante Stakes form with Bollin Eric;
First Charter (spots on cap) stays on for third*

that day, followed by a tough assignment in the Irish Derby just nine days later, had
left its mark.

Balakheri had done nothing but improve prior to the Irish Derby, in which
he finished fifth to High Chaparral. The winner of a maiden at Nottingham on the
last of his three starts at two, he won a handicap at Newmarket off a BHB mark of
86 on his reappearance and followed that with a smart performance when third
behind Moon Ballad and Bollin Eric in the Dante Stakes at York. The step up to a
mile and a half in the King Edward VII Stakes showed Balakheri in an even better
light. The race lacked a Derby runner, but it still brought together the form of
several Derby trials and also a runner from the Prix du Jockey Club, Diaghilev
having finished seventh to Sulamani at Chantilly. Balakheri was sent off favourite
despite his rider putting up 2 lb overweight, though as things turned out Johnny
Murtagh could have had a substantial lunch and the outcome would have been just
the same. Murtagh didn't exactly have an armchair ride, with his mount taking a
while to warm to his task, but Balakheri came with a good run on the outside
halfway up the straight and drew clear to win by three and a half lengths from Bollin
Eric. At this stage it looked as though Balakheri might develop into a high-class
performer, but, in view of his two subsequent efforts, there has to be some doubt as
to whether he will even recapture the very smart form he showed at Royal Ascot.
The hope must be that his enthusiasm will be restored by a winter's rest.

Balakheri (IRE) (b.c. 1999)	Theatrical (b 1982)	Nureyev (b 1977)	Northern Dancer
			Special
		Tree of Knowledge (b 1977)	Sassafras
			Sensibility
	Balanka (IRE) (b 1992)	Alzao (b 1980)	Lyphard
			Lady Rebecca
		Banana Peel (b 1981)	Green Dancer
			Barbra

Balakheri, bred by his owner the Aga Khan, is the third foal of Balanka, a
smart performer who won at a mile and a quarter in France and also
finished in the frame in the Prix de Diane and Prix de l'Opera as well as in the
Matriarch Stakes at Hollywood Park. Balanka, a half-sister to several winners, is a
daughter of Banana Peel, a winner in the States and half-sister to the dam of Bering.
Balakheri, a good-bodied, quite attractive colt, has yet to race on heavy going but
acts on any other. *Sir Michael Stoute*

BALAKIREF   3 b.g. Royal Applause 124 – Pluck 80 (Never So Bold 135) [2002 76:
7.6f 7s² 7f² 7d³ 7d² 6m* 6m² 6f 7f⁵ [6g Oct 17] quite attractive gelding: fairly useful
performer: won minor event at Doncaster in July: good placed efforts in handicaps most
other starts in 2002: best at 6f/7f: acts on firm going, soft and fibresand: slowly away final
outing: sold 28,000 gns, joined M. Dods and gelded. *W. Jarvis*   **82**

BALDOUR (IRE)   3 b.g. Green Desert (USA) 127 – Baldemara (FR) (Sanglamore
(USA) 126) [2002 87p: 7m* 7.6f³ 6f 6g 7.1f⁶ 7s Nov 2] good-topped gelding: reportedly
pin fired at 2 yrs: fairly useful performer: won maiden at Folkestone in April: well below
form after good effort next time: effective at 6f/7.5f: acts on firm going: visored fourth
outing: gelded after final appearance. *E. A. L. Dunlop*   **92 d**

95

BALERNO 3 b.g. Machiavellian (USA) 123 – Balabina (USA) 110 (Nijinsky (CAN) **68**
138) [2002 10f 8m⁶ 8.3m³ 8.2m³ 9.9d 8.2s f9.4g⁵ f8.5s² Dec 26] close-coupled gelding:
half-brother to numerous winners, including 7f (at 2 yrs) and 1¼m winner Bal Harbour
(by Shirley Heights) and 1½m winner Bequeath (by Rainbow Quest), both smart: dam,
1½m winner, from very good family: fair maiden: left R. Charlton 12,000 gns before
penultimate outing: worth a try at 7f: acts on good to firm going, good to soft and
fibresand: blinkered (pulled too hard) sixth start: often makes running (seemed to idle
final outing). *S. C. Williams*

BALIN'S SWORD (IRE) 2 b.c. (Mar 6) Spectrum (IRE) 126 – Green Delight (IRE) **93**
(Green Desert (USA) 127) [2002 7d⁴ 8.1g* 8d⁵ Oct 26] 2,800,000 francs Y: first foal:
dam unraced daughter of smart performer up to 11f Capo di Monte, herself half-sister to
smart middle-distance filly Wind In Her Hair: fairly useful form: impressive winner of
maiden at Chepstow in August: well held in Prix des Chenes at Longchamp and
Racing Post Trophy at Doncaster after: stays 1m: raced only on good ground or softer.
B. J. Meehan

BALI ROYAL 4 b.f. King's Signet (USA) 110 – Baligay 84 (Balidar 133) [2002 97: **104**
5f² 5.1f 5f³ 5d* 5m* 5m 5m 5.7g³ 5f 6g 5.1m³ 5m³ 5m Sep 29] strong, good-quartered
filly: useful handicapper: won at Haydock in May and Musselburgh in June: some
respectable efforts after: probably best at 5f: acts on any turf going and fibresand: has
been unruly stall/withdrawn earlier in career: sometimes carries head awkwardly: usually
races prominently. *J. M. Bradley*

BALI-STAR 7 b.g. Alnasr Alwasheek 117 – Baligay 84 (Balidar 133) [2002 52=: 6g **60**
p6g² p6g 5f⁵ 5d* f5g 5m 5.1g² 5f Sep 25] modest handicapper: left M. Weeden after third
start: gained first success at Windsor in August: effective at 5f/6f: acts on all-weather,
good to firm and good to soft going: often races handily. *R. J. Hodges*

BALKAN KNIGHT 2 b.c. (Feb 26) Selkirk (USA) 129 – Crown of Light 112 (Mtoto **79**
134) [2002 7d 7.5d* Jul 22] fair sort: first foal: dam, 7f (at 2 yrs) and 11.5f winner, also
third in Oaks: visored, much better effort (fair form) when winning 4-runner minor event
at Beverley by 5 lengths from Dr Sharp, making most despite handling home turn none
too well: should stay at least 1¼m: wore crossed noseband both starts. *D. R. Loder*

BALLADEER (IRE) 4 b.g. King's Theatre (IRE) 128 – Carousel Music 56 (On Your **93**
Mark 125) [2002 91: p12g6 13g⁵ 14s³ 20m 16f² 12d² 16.2d³ 13.9m⁶ 15.9f⁴ 18m Oct 19]
workmanlike gelding: fairly useful performer: largely creditable efforts in 2002: stays
2m: acts on any turf going/all-weather: often makes running: joined Miss H. Knight.
J. W. Hills

BALLARD CONNECTION 3 ch.f. Danzig Connection (USA) – Ballard Lady **–**
(IRE) 53 (Ballad Rock 122) [2002 –: 8.5m 6.9d 8m 9.9m 7m Sep 23] big filly: no form.
J. S. Wainwright

BALLARE (IRE) 3 b.g. Barathea (IRE) 127 – Raindancing (IRE) 94 (Tirol 127) [2002 **56**
7m 8.1s⁵ 7g 7g 8m 8.1g² 8d⁵ Nov 1] 42,000Y: good-topped gelding: second foal:
half-brother to fairly useful 2000 2-y-o 5f winner Jack Spratt (by So Factual): dam, 6f
winner at 2 yrs (stayed 1m) who became untrustworthy, out of sister to high-class 1m/
1¼m performer Bold Arrangement: modest maiden handicapper: stays 1m: best effort on
good going. *Bob Jones*

BALLERINA SUPREMA (IRE) 2 b.f. (Mar 27) Sadler's Wells (USA) 132 – **84 p**
Gravieres (FR) (Saint Estephe (FR) 123) [2002 8g³ 8.2m* Sep 20] 330,000Y: quite
good-topped filly: sixth foal: sister to 3 winners, including 9f winner Coliseum and Irish
1999 2-y-o 1m winner Homer, both useful: dam, 2-y-o 5.5f and 7f winner in France,
later Grade 1 9f winner in USA: fairly useful form: landed odds in 3-runner maiden at
Nottingham by 1¼ lengths from Constantine, still green but in control final 2f: will stay
at least 1¼m: well regarded (was entered in Fillies' Mile), and remains open to improvement. *M. L. W. Bell*

BALLERINE (IRE) 4 b.f. Sadler's Wells (USA) 132 – Lisana 97 (Alleged (USA) **66**
138) [2002 81: p8g³ p10g⁴ p8g³ 11.7g Apr 30] IR 140,000Y: half-sister to several winners
in France, including smart 10.5f and 1½m winner Linnga (by Shardari): dam, 1½m
winner, out of half-sister to top-class French 1½m performers Acamas, Akarad and
Akiyda: fairly useful maiden at 3 yrs for D. Weld in Ireland: fair form in Britain only
last 2 starts: stays 12.5f: acts on soft going, good to firm and polytrack: tried blinkered:
sometimes races freely: sold (in foal to Dansili) 26,000 gns in December. *G. A. Butler*

BALLET DANCER 2 b.f. (Feb 27) Victory Note (USA) 120 – Actress 73 (Known **55**
Fact (USA) 135) [2002 6g⁴ f6g³ f6g⁵ f6s⁶ Nov 2] 4,000Y: angular filly: sixth foal:

half-sister to 3 winners, including 5f (at 2 yrs) to 7f winner La Dolce Vita (by Mazilier): dam 7f winner: modest maiden: below form (helped set strong pace) final start: raced only at 6f: acts on fibresand. *Mrs A. Duffield*

BALLET FAME (USA) 3 br.f. Quest For Fame 127 – Bold Ballerina (Sadler's Wells –
(USA) 132) [2002 79p: 10m⁴ May 5] leggy, quite good-topped filly: fair form when winning maiden at Newmarket at 2 yrs: pulled hard when tailed-off last of 4 in listed race on same course only other outing: bred to stay 1¼m: sold 20,000 gns in July. *B. W. Hills*

BALLET GIRL (USA) 3 b.f. Theatrical 128 – Atelier (Warning 136) [2002 70p: **80**
11.7d³ 11.7g Oct 16] angular filly: fairly useful form in maidens: third at Bath on belated reappearance: dropped away quickly having travelled strongly for long way at same course following month (reportedly finished distressed): stays 1½m: raced only on good/good to soft going: sold 5,000 gns. *B. W. Hills*

BALLET MASTER (USA) 6 ch.h. Kingmambo (USA) 125 – Danse Royale (IRE) –
112 (Caerleon (USA) 132) [2002 83, a90: f7g⁶ Jan 18] strong horse: fairly useful handicapper at 5 yrs: well held only start in 2002: sometimes blinkered. *J. D. Czerpak*

BALLET SCORE (IRE) 3 b.f. Sadler's Wells (USA) 132 – Puzzled Look (USA) **90**
(Gulch (USA)) [2002 80p: 10f⁵ 10s⁶ 13.3f Jul 20] big, rangy filly: fairly useful performer: won maiden at Doncaster at 2 yrs: not discredited in listed events/handicap in 2002: should stay 1¼m: visored second start: has been bandaged behind: sent to Australia. *J. H. M. Gosden*

BALLETS RUSSES (IRE) 5 b.m. Marju (IRE) 127 – Elminya (IRE) (Sure Blade **40**
(USA) 130) [2002 42, a?: f16s f11s⁴ f12g² f12g⁶ Feb 11] poor maiden: stays 15.8f: acts on fibresand, good to firm and good to soft going: tried visored: has given trouble start: often slowly away: not an easy ride. *John Berry*

BALL GAMES 4 b.g. Mind Games 121 – Deb's Ball 70 (Glenstal (USA) 118) [2002 **58**
64: 8g⁵ 8f 8.3s² 8.3v⁵ 6.9d Jul 19] rather leggy, close-coupled gelding: modest maiden: seems to stay 9f: acts on heavy and good to firm going: visored last 3 starts: sold 1,200 gns. *D. Moffatt*

BALLINGARRY (IRE) 3 b.c. Sadler's Wells (USA) 132 – Flamenco Wave **123**
(USA) 103 (Desert Wine (USA)) [2002 114p: 11m* 10.5g⁶ 12m² 12d³ 14m³ 12d* 12d Oct 26]

Ballingarry was purchased privately out of Aidan O'Brien's stable, reportedly for a seven-figure sum (US dollars), after his success in the Canadian International at Woodbine in September. Judged on the improved form Ballingarry showed to win that race, the money could turn out to be well spent. In an eight-runner contest, Ballingarry was only fourth best in the local betting, which was headed by the American-trained Falcon Flight, an unlucky fifth to Beat Hollow in the Arlington Million on his previous outing. In an international field, Zindabad, the subsequently-demoted third in the 2001 renewal, started second favourite with German raider Paolini next. Zindabad's stablemate Yavana's Pace was the rank outsider and Ballingarry tracked him before depriving him of the lead a couple of furlongs out. Quickening well, Ballingarry was ridden out to win by two and a quarter lengths from Falcon Flight, with Yavana's Pace four lengths further back in third; Zindabad and Paolini finished fifth and sixth, behind Perfect Soul who fared best of the home team in fourth. Though to some extent Ballingarry enjoyed the run

Canadian International Stakes, Woodbine—Ballingarry puts up his best effort and captures his second Group/Grade 1 success

of the race, he nonetheless put up a very smart performance, looking a good prospect for 2003 in a relatively weak division—particularly with Beat Hollow now retired—for the turf events in North America from a mile and a quarter to a mile and a half. Furthermore, Ballingarry appears to have gone from one good trainer to another if the 2002 statistics for Laura De Seroux are anything to go by. Fifty-year-old de Seroux, completing only her third full season as a trainer, had eight Grade 1 successes in 2002, five of those with the top-class Breeders' Cup Distaff winner Azeri.

Ballingarry won a maiden at Leopardstown and the Criterium de Saint-Cloud from four outings at two and he had five races as a three-year-old prior to the Canadian International. He reappeared in the six-runner Prix Noailles at Longchamp in April, winning as his form entitled him to by three lengths from Great Pretender, but he then ran well below form, looking rather light in condition and clearly something amiss, in the Prix Lupin back at Longchamp the following month. Ballingarry's campaign got back on track in the Derby Italiano at Rome later in May with a good length-and-a-half second of sixteen to Rakti, after which he came third in the nine-runner Irish Derby, beaten five lengths by stable-companion High Chaparral, and in the Irish St Leger, two and a half lengths behind Vinnie Roe, before his success in Canada. Ballingarry's final outing of the year was in the Breeders' Cup Turf, before which he was required to be returned to Europe to complete quarantine procedures (with John Hammond in France) after his trip to Woodbine. The additional travelling may have contributed to a below-par seventh of eight at Arlington to High Chaparral, beaten eight and a half lengths after travelling well for much of the way.

		Northern Dancer (b 1961)	Nearctic
			Natalma
	Sadler's Wells (USA) (b 1981)		
		Fairy Bridge (b 1975)	Bold Reason
			Special
Ballingarry (IRE) (b.c. 1999)			
		Desert Wine (b 1980)	Damascus
			Anne Campbell
	Flamenco Wave (USA) (ch 1986)		
		Armada Way (ch 1976)	Sadair
			Hurry Call

The sturdy Ballingarry had his pedigree fully outlined in *Racehorses of 2001*, and there is nothing new to add. While Ballingarry showed he stays a mile and three quarters in the Irish St Leger, opportunities at that trip are few and far between in the States so he will almost certainly be campaigned at up to a mile and a half. If there is anything that might temper enthusiasm for Ballingarry's prospects it would be concern over prevailing ground conditions. The going tends to be on the firm side in American turf races and, though Ballingarry showed he is effective on good to firm going when winning on his reappearance, he may be ideally suited by softer conditions; he won the Criterium de Saint-Cloud on heavy and the Canadian International on good to soft. *L. De Seroux, USA*

BALLINGER RIDGE 3 b.g. Sabrehill (USA) 120 – Branston Ridge (Indian Ridge **77** 123) [2002 –: 10g 10m 8g² 9d 10g² 9m³ 7g³ 8f Sep 16] good-topped gelding: fair maiden: below form last 2 starts: stays easy 1¼m: acts on good to firm going: takes good hold and usually makes running. *B. Hanbury*

BALL KING (IRE) 4 ch.c. Ball Park (NZ) – Firey Encounter (IRE) (Kris 135) [2002 **74** 83: p8g f7g p8g p7g⁴ p8g⁴ Dec 14] rather sparely-made colt: fair handicapper, lightly raced: stays 1m: acts on soft going, good to firm and polytrack: often tongue tied. *P. J. Makin*

BALLYBUNION (IRE) 3 ch.g. Entrepreneur 123 – Clarentia 111 (Ballad Rock 122) **68** [2002 87p: 7m 6g 6f 9d 6m 7f 5m³ f6g Oct 17] strong gelding: fairly useful winner at 2 yrs: only fair at best in 2002: stays 6f: acts on good to firm going, probably on polytrack: reluctant to race/very slowly away third start: sometimes races freely: sold 10,000 gns, and gelded: needs treating with some caution. *P. F. I. Cole*

BALLYGRIFFIN KID 2 gr.g. (Apr 6) Komaite (USA) – Ballygriffin Belle (Another **65** Realm 118) [2002 5f⁴ 6g⁴ 5m 6g Oct 28] third foal: dam ran 3 times: fair maiden: below form last 2 starts: will probably stay 7f. *T. P. McGovern*

BALLY HALL (IRE) 2 b.c. (May 9) Saddlers' Hall (IRE) 126 – Sally Rose 92 **– p** (Sallust 134) [2002 8m p7g 6g 6s Oct 28] IR 22,000Y: close-coupled colt: half-brother to several winners, including useful middle-distance performer Trojan Miss (by Troy), 7f winner at 2 yrs, and 1¾m winner Mountain Bloom (by Shirley Heights): dam 1m to 1¼m winner: well held in maidens: has scope to do better at 3 yrs. *G. A. Butler*

BALLYHURRY (USA)   5 b.g. Rubiano (USA) – Balakhna (FR) (Tyrant (USA))   **60**
[2002 –: 8m 8m 8f 9f⁵ 9g² 10.1g⁴ 9.2g² 10.1g³ 9.2v 10s³ 10.1d³ 9m³ 8.3m⁵ 8.9f 9d³ Oct 18]
modest handicapper: won at Ayr in July: stays 1¼m: acts on firm and soft going: effective
blinkered or not (untried in 2002): reliable. *J. S. Goldie*

BALLYKISSANN   7 ch.g. Ballacashtal (CAN) – Mybella Ann (Anfield 117) [2002 –:   **–**
17.2d 10.2f 10.9m Aug 26] probably of little account nowadays. *J. C. Tuck*

BALMACARA   3 b.f. Lake Coniston (IRE) 131 – Diabaig 76 (Precocious 126) [2002   **53**
43: 5.1m³ 6g p6g² 6.1m p6g 6m⁴ 7.6m 6.1m⁵ 6f⁵ 7d f7g Dec 14] lengthy, angular filly:
modest maiden handicapper: stays 6f: acts on polytrack, raced mainly on good going or
firmer on turf: tried blinkered. *Miss K. B. Boutflower*

BALMY   3 b.f. Zafonic (USA) 130 – Balleta (USA) 87 (Lyphard (USA) 132) [2002   **89**
8.3d² 8.1m* Aug 31] seventh foal: sister to winner in Greece and half-sister to smart
French/US performer up to 1m Barricade (by Riverman) and useful 1¾m winner who
stayed 2m War Cabinet (by Rainbow Quest): dam, 1m to 1¼m winner, sister to Dancing
Brave and Jolypha: shaped well on debut, and justified favouritism in maiden at Sandown
later in August by 6 lengths from Sinamatella, driven clear from 2f out: stayed 1m: stud.
H. R. A. Cecil

BALTIC BREEZE (USA)   2 b.f. (Feb 16) Labeeb 124 – Blue Grass Baby (USA)   **70**
(Iceecapade (USA)) [2002 6g⁶ 5m² 6m³ 6m f8s Sep 17] 30,000Y: smallish filly: closely
related to 2 winners by Lear Fan, including 7f winner Aeroking who stayed 1¼m, and
half-sister to several winners in USA: dam unraced half-sister to dam of Royal Lodge
Stakes winner Robellino: fair maiden: ran poorly after first 2 starts: should stay at least
7f. *R. Hannon*

BALTIC KING   2 b.c. (Jan 10) Danetime (IRE) 121 – Lindfield Belle (IRE) 78 (Fairy   **87**
King (USA)) [2002 6g⁴ 6m² 6s⁴ 5g* Oct 4] 29,000F, IR 40,000Y: sixth foal: half-brother
to 3 winners, including 7f winner Red Amazon (by Magic Ring) and 9-y-o
Distant King: dam 2-y-o 5f winner: fairly useful form: unlucky second start: landed odds
in maiden at Lingfield (tongue tied) by 2½ lengths from Aegean Magic, leading final 1f:
effective at 5f/6f: acts on good to firm ground, probably on soft: raced freely third outing.
H. Morrison

BAMFORD CASTLE (IRE)   7 b.g. Scenic 128 – Allorette 100 (Ballymore 123)   **–**
[2002 89: 14.6s Oct 25] ex-Irish gelding: useful handicapper in 2000: lightly raced since:
left P. Mullins 8,000 gns after final outing at 6 yrs, and well held only run in 2002: stays
1¾m well: acts on firm and soft ground. *R. Ford*

BANCO   3 b.g. Efisio 120 – Peace Dance (Bikala 134) [2002 –: f7g f7g Jan 29] well   **–**
held in maidens: slowly away debut. *M. W. Easterby*

BANDANNA   5 gr.m. Bandmaster (USA) 97 – Gratclo 65 (Belfort (FR) 89) [2002 90:   **98**
6g³ 6m 5.1g* 6m 5.7d* 5g 5d* 5.7g* 6d⁶ 5m 5.6m 5m⁴ 6f 5m Oct 12] big, close-coupled
mare: useful performer: won minor events at Bath (2) and handicaps at Sandown and
Bath between May and July: good fourth to Peruvian Chief in handicap at Ascot in
September: effective at 5f/6f: acts on any turf going: lost chance with slow start fourth
outing: usually waited with: tough. *R. J. Hodges*

BANDARI (IRE)   3 b.c. Alhaarth (IRE) 126 – Miss Audimar (USA) (Mr Leader   **123**
(USA)) [2002 113p: 11.5g* 12d 12m* 11.9g* 14.6m³ Sep 14]
    Have you ever splashed out on a car, only to have it splutter to a halt during
its first spin on the motorway? If so, Sheikh Hamdan knows the feeling. Having
searched out a supposedly top-of-the-range product, admittedly from a limited
range, he unveiled his new pride and joy on a pleasant Saturday afternoon in June
but, metaphorically speaking, soon found himself twiddling his thumbs, at a
standstill on the hard shoulder. Sheikh Hamdan's purchase was Bandari, bought it
seemed specifically to win the Derby, but that first outing in the new ownership
saw the colt ridden along and virtually beaten before halfway. Bandari ended up
fifty-one lengths adrift of the winner, a long way removed from the performance
expected of the 9/2 third favourite. His purchase price was reputed to be
£2,000,000.
    Sheikh Hamdan's money wasn't wasted; this particular purchase could be
fixed. Bandari ran in three other pattern races at around a mile and a half, one before
the Derby and two after Sheikh Hamdan took over ownership, and he won them all.
In the attheraces Sky Channel 418 Derby Trial at Lingfield in May, he did so by
thirteen lengths, the longest winning distance in a British pattern race for many a

attheraces Sky Channel 418 Derby Trial Stakes, Lingfield—Bandari has thirteen lengths to spare over his five rivals

season. 'Sheikh Hamdan has a keen eye for a horse,' his racing manager later reported. 'Obviously he saw something he liked, and he's seldom wrong.' The Lingfield romp followed a nine-length success in a listed race at Pontefract on Bandari's final two-year-old start—a poor show in the Solario Stakes was his only defeat in four outings as a juvenile —so it is fair to say that he looked highly promising. In terms of form, Bandari's demolition job at Lingfield in a six-runner field that included smart colts Mamool and First Charter was also one of the best seen in a Derby trial in recent times. Excepting the various Guineas, Erhaab's 1994 Dante Stakes had previously been easily the best, but the latest Lingfield Derby Trial ran that close. The only problem was that Bandari had not been entered in the Derby. He was not the only one. Also from Johnston's yard, the Chester Vase winner Fight Your Corner was in the same boat, while another stablemate Simeon, winner of the Classic Trial at Sandown, lacked a Derby entry and was being aimed at the Prix du Jockey Club. However, one of Johnston's charges had been supplemented for the Derby at the £9,000 entry stage in April, and that was Sir George Turner who went on to be beaten in his two trials, the Dee Stakes (by a short head) and the Dante. For the connections of Bandari and Fight Your Corner there remained the option of buying into the Derby at the final supplementary stage a week before the race at a cost of £90,000.

For trainer Mark Johnston this situation was now truly an embarrassment of riches. Johnston's opposition to the current Derby entry system—with the prize-money fund heavily reliant on an initial yearling entry, and the second stage coming just before the three-year-old trials—was already well known. What came to pass in the spring of 2002 will not have made him any fonder of it and when the Epsom executive announced some tinkerings to the system in November—reducing the yearling fee from £310 to £295 and the final supplementary charge to £75,000, payable two days later than in 2002—Johnston restated his opinion that 'I will never endorse an entry system where the owners put up forty per cent of the prize-money. I will be making it clear to my owners what the situation is and the choice of whether or not to enter will be down to them'. Interestingly, the Johnston stable entered thirty-five yearlings for the 2004 Derby at the entry stage in December. Johnston's refusal to play the game with Fight Your Corner and Bandari for the 2002 Derby may have caused him some discomfort when they won their Derby trials, but it did not cost their owners anything, both Greenland Park Ltd and Mr Abdullah al-Rostamani soon counting more than their blessings when Sheikh Mohammed and Sheikh Hamdan stepped in to take over any soul-searching over the £90,000 supplementary fee. When Fight Your Corner was beaten twenty lengths in the Derby and Bandari out of sight, it seemed as if Johnston had not got it so wrong after all when he decided not to enter them in the first place.

Both Bandari and Fight Your Corner were a lot better than they showed at Epsom, though Fight Your Corner (a present from Sheikh Mohammed to one of his sons) fractured a cannon bone during the race and had to be retired for the season. Bandari, however, lived to fight another day and proved capable of quite a battle. The Derby proved a mere hiccup, albeit an expensive one, and when he next appeared at the end of July he ran away with the Peugeot Gordon Stakes at Goodwood. There were only three opponents and Bandari was able to dictate up front, but there was no mistaking his overwhelming superiority as he passed the post seven lengths in front of First Charter, who was receiving 3 lb. Sheikh Hamdan's first jockey Richard Hills was the only one connected with the horse who had reason to be disappointed. Having ridden him at Epsom he this time preferred to partner third-placed Izdiham, who was also preferred narrowly to Bandari in the betting.

Both Hills and the punters were happy enough when Bandari went on to land odds of 5/4-on in the Great Voltigeur Stakes at York. For the first time, though, Bandari was neither impressive in victory nor abject in defeat, having been one or the other in all his previous races. He was meeting a higher class of opponent than in any of his previous victories but with Highest, Bollin Eric, Bustan and Systematic all snapping at his heels at the finish, Bandari's performance isn't rated so highly as those at Lingfield or Goodwood. What he did show, however, was an admirable fighting spirit—Highest headed him for a few yards approaching the final furlong—and it seemed possible that Bandari would have prevailed in more decisive fashion had Hills set more than just a fair pace on him and kicked on sooner. The stiffer test of stamina in the St Leger looked to be all in his favour. With One Thousand Guineas and Oaks winner Kazzia on the sidelines, Bandari was made 13/8 favourite to register a classic success, albeit not the one he was bought for, but while Mamool and First Charter again finished among those behind, Bandari had to settle for third place, beaten three and a quarter lengths by the winner, as Great Voltigeur victims Bollin Eric and Highest turned the tables on him. Going to the front half a mile out, Bandari had every chance but could stay ahead for only a couple of furlongs.

The good far outweighs the bad, but Bandari has a mixed record. The thought has crossed his trainer's mind that the colt has temperamental short-comings. Reflecting on some 'rough and tumble' in the Solario Stakes and on Bandari's having to be pushed along after a slow start in the Derby, Johnston stated: 'He's a nervous, big horse and I don't think he liked it. He's a bit soft at the moment and I won't give him too many more runs.' In his post-mortem on the St Leger, Johnston observed that the sweating and edgy Bandari was upset in the parade ring and went on to criticise the presence of a funfair near the stalls. So at season's end that nervousness had not been eradicated. Although at its worst before the St Leger—when his performance over the longer trip by no means discredited him—it manifested itself on other occasions in the parade ring and Bandari also got upset in the stalls before his slow start in the Derby. What augurs well for Bandari's prospects in coming seasons is his genuine attitude—when he's on his game—and his trainer's superb record with high-class older horses. Bandari should win more good races and his connections can be relied on to leave no stone unturned in searching for them.

A medium-sized, angular colt, Bandari probably stays an extended mile and three quarters but his best efforts have been when ridden at or near the front over a

Great Voltigeur Stakes, York—tougher opposition this time for Bandari,
who holds off Highest (armlets), Bollin Eric (left), Bustan and Systematic (rail)

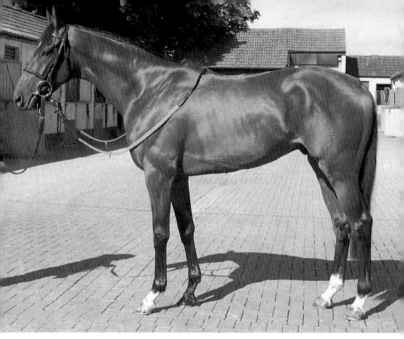

Mr Hamdan Al Maktoum's "Bandari"

	Alhaarth (IRE) (b 1993)	Unfuwain (b 1985)	Northern Dancer
Bandari (IRE) (b.c. 1999)			Height of Fashion
		Irish Valley (ch 1982)	Irish River
			Green Valley
	Miss Audimar (USA) (b 1981)	Mr Leader (b 1966)	Hail To Reason
			Jolie Deja
		Quick Selection (ch 1972)	Viceregal
			Lachine

mile and a half and he will almost certainly be campaigned over the shorter distance as a four-year-old. He acts on all types of going that he has encountered so far, ranging from soft to good to firm. Bandari's sire Alhaarth was top of his class as a two-year-old, some way off it at three and four—fourth in the Guineas and fifth in the Derby—but still capable of very smart form as he showed when winning three pattern races at around a mile and a mile and a quarter. Bandari is from his first crop, which also included King's Stand winner Dominica and Nell Gwyn winner Misterah. Bandari's dam Miss Audimar has had a long career at stud, with three offspring of at least useful ability in Bandari, middle-distance stayer Diaghilef (by Royal Academy) and two-year-old sprinter Noora Park (by Ahonoora). The 2002 four-year-old Gold Standard (by Goldmark), however, was disappointing in the latest season having been fairly useful at three. *M. Johnston*

BANDBOX (IRE) 7 ch.g. Imperial Frontier (USA) 112 – Dublah (USA) (Private **63** Account (USA)) [2002 74: f6g 7.1m 5.1g⁵ 6d 5.7d 6g 5.7g 7.1g Jul 26] small, strong gelding: modest handicapper: effective at 5f to 7f: acts on fibresand, firm and soft going: tried visored/blinkered/tongue tied: none too consistent. *M. Salaman*

BANDIT QUEEN 2 b.f. (Apr 13) Desert Prince (IRE) 130 Wildwood Flower 107 **90** (Distant Relative 128) [2002 5.2d⁵ 5.1d⁵ 6.1m* 6d* 6s Oct 26] 45,000Y: leggy filly:

second foal: dam 6f winner (including at 2 yrs), including Ayr Gold Cup: fairly useful performer: ran as if something amiss second start (off nearly 4 months after): won maiden at Nottingham and nursery at Ayr (well-backed favourite, clearly best effort, making all and idling) in October: ran poorly in listed race at Doncaster final start: likely to prove best at 5f/6f: acts on good to firm and good to soft ground: races prominently. *J. H. M. Gosden*

BANDLER CHING (IRE) 5 b.g. Sri Pekan (USA) 117 – Stanerra's Wish (IRE) **80** (Caerleon (USA) 132) [2002 70: 9.7m* 9.7g⁵ 10m* 10.3m² 10.1m⁵ 10f⁵ Oct 2] angular gelding: tubed: fairly useful handicapper: won at Folkestone in July and Kempton in September: ran very well next time: best around 1¼m: acts on good to firm going: tends to hang. *J. W. Payne*

BAND OF LOVE 3 b.f. Pursuit of Love 124 – Dixie Favor (USA) 82 (Dixieland Band **67 d** (USA)) [2002 8.5m³ 9.9g⁵ 7.5g² 7g⁵ 7.5m⁶ 8.1d f9.4g Dec 16] quite good-topped filly: fourth foal: half-sister to 5f winner Stately Favour (by Statoblest) and 9.4f to 1½m winner Favorisio (by Efisio): dam Irish 6f (at 2 yrs) to 1m winner: fair maiden: well below form last 4 starts: should prove better at 1¼m than shorter: yet to race on extremes of going. *Miss J. A. Camacho*

BANDOLINA 2 b.f. (May 12) Most Welcome 131 – Choral Sundown 81 (Night Shift **–** (USA)) [2002 6d 6s 6v Nov 9] sister to 3 winners, including useful 1m to 1½m winner Celestial Welcome, and half-sister to smart 2000 2-y-o 7f/1m winner who stayed 1½m Snowstorm (by Environment Friend): dam effective from 1m to 1½m: well beaten in maidens. *B. S. Rothwell*

BANDOS 2 ch.g. (Jun 2) Cayman Kai (IRE) 114 – Lekuti (Le Coq d'Or 101) [2002 7g **57** 8.3m 7.2s⁵ 7s⁴ f6f Nov 11] half-brother to 1½m/2m winner Kilernan (by K-Battery): dam unraced: modest maiden: will need to settle to stay beyond 7f: acts on soft ground: found little last 2 starts: gelded after. *I. Semple*

BANGALORE 6 ch.g. Sanglamore (USA) 126 – Ajuga (USA) 102 (The Minstrel **112** (CAN) 135) [2002 14.1m² 16m* 16.1g* 15.9g⁴ 15.5g² 20g Oct 6] big, lengthy gelding: poor mover: smart performer: sidelined with tendon trouble in 2001: better than ever on return, winning handicaps at Kempton and Newcastle (beat Mr Dinos by head in Foster's Lager Northumberland Plate) in June: good 1½ lengths fourth to Boreas in Lonsdale Stakes at York next time: not disgraced at Longchamp last 2 starts, in Prix Gladiateur (2 lengths second to Miraculous) and Prix du Cadran (seemed to find stamina stretched): very best form around 2m: acts on any going: sometimes bandaged in front: races prominently: game. *Mrs A. J. Perrett*

BANG IN TUNE 2 b.f. (Mar 27) Victory Note (USA) 120 – Canlubang (Mujtahid **53** (USA) 118) [2002 5d⁶ 6g² 6m 5.1d³ 6m 7.2g⁵ 6g⁵ 5m⁴ f5s⁵ 6g 5s f5g f5g⁴ Dec 4] unfurnished filly: third foal: half-sister to Swedish winner up to 1¼m Clear Ambition (by Definite Article): dam ran 3 times at 2 yrs: modest maiden: effective at 5f/6f: acts on fibresand, best turf efforts on good/good to soft ground: blinkered (carried head high) final start. *A. Bailey*

Foster's Lager Northumberland Plate (Handicap), Newcastle—six-year-old Bangalore narrowly beats favourite Mr Dinos (far side); Zibeline stays on really well for third

BANJAXED 3 b.f. Prince Sabo 123 – Classic Fan (USA) (Lear Fan (USA) 130) [2002 –
p6g⁶ p8g p6g p6g Dec 18] 4,200F: first foal: dam, maiden, out of Ribblesdale winner
Miss Boniface: little form: left D. ffrench Davis and off 8 months before final outing.
Mrs S. A. Liddiard

BANJO BAY (IRE) 4 b.c. Common Grounds 118 – Thirlmere (Cadeaux Genereux **100**
131) [2002 98: 8s 7m² 7d 6f⁴ 6m 6d³ 7.6g 6m Aug 17] close-coupled colt: useful
performer: creditable efforts in 2002 when in frame in handicaps at Newmarket (1½
lengths second to Sea Star) in April and York (under a length fourth to Chookie Heiton)
in May and minor event at Haydock (5½ lengths third to Suggestive) in July: at least as
effective at 6f/7f as easy 1m: acts on firm and soft going: sometimes slowly away earlier
in career: runs the occasional poor race. *B. A. McMahon*

BANK ON HIM 7 b.g. Elmaamul (USA) 125 – Feather Flower 74 (Relkino 131) **53**
[2002 53, a72: p10g* p10g* f8.5g² p10g² p10g* p10g p8g⁴ 10d⁴ p8g 9d p10g* p10g⁴ **a81**
p10g⁶ p10g* Dec 30] fairly useful on all-weather, modest on turf: won 2 claimers in
January, handicap in February and sellers (sold from G. L. Moore) in July and December,
all at Lingfield: seems best around 1¼m: acts on good to firm going, good to soft and
all-weather: sometimes hangs left/races freely: usually held up. *Andrew Reid*

BANKS HILL 4 b.f. Danehill (USA) 126 – Hasili (IRE) (Kahyasi 130) [2002 **126**
128: 9.3m³ 10m³ 8g* 8g² 10f³ 10d² 9f⁴ Dec 1]
  For the second year running, Banks Hill was the best racehorse of her sex in
Europe. However, those hoping for a regular view of her in the sort of form she
showed in the 2001 Breeders' Cup Filly & Mare Turf at Belmont Park were
disappointed. Going into 2002, Banks Hill's assignment was to prove herself
against the colts. As a three-year-old she had two starts against them, in the Jacques
le Marois and the Moulin, and was runner-up in both (promoted in the Jacques le
Marois). In 2002, the Prix du Haras de Fresnay-le-Buffard Jacques le Marois
provided her only victory. Four three-year-olds in the Deauville line-up included
the Poule d'Essai des Poulains second and third, Medecis and Bowman, and the
Falmouth Stakes winner Tashawak. The four older horses were Banks Hill, who
started favourite at 17/10, Prix d'Ispahan winner Best of The Bests and the Prix
Messidor first and second Altieri and Domedriver. Showing what turned out to be
easily her best form of the season, Banks Hill collared pacesetter Best of The Bests
inside the final furlong, went three lengths clear of him and also held off Domedriver's challenge by a length and a half. Domedriver won both of his subsequent
starts, famously claiming the scalp of an unlucky Rock of Gibraltar in the Breeders'
Cup Mile. When Banks Hill met Rock of Gibraltar, however, in the Moulin, the
Irish colt produced a well-timed run and Banks Hill was put firmly in her place. The
distance between them at the death, in a bunched finish, may have been only half a
length, but the confidently-ridden favourite's superiority was worth more than that.
Banks Hill did not run anywhere near her best that day, and it was the same story
with a variety of other circumstances in the remainder of her season.
  In the d'Ispahan at Longchamp in May, Banks Hill was beaten by both Best
of The Bests and Poussin in a four-runner race, reportedly short of peak fitness.
More disappointing was her failure in the Prince of Wales's Stakes at Royal Ascot.

*Prix du Haras de Fresnay-Le-Buffard Jacques le Marois, Deauville—Banks Hill crowns a magnificent
weekend for owner Khalid Abdulla, following successes in two Grade 1s for his horses at Arlington
the previous day; Domedriver (left) and Best of The Bests (third left) fill the places*

She might have put her head in front for a stride or two a furlong and a half out, but Banks Hill was no match for Grandera thereafter and finished behind Indian Creek as well. Andre Fabre, then trainer of Banks Hill, later observed that 'it was obvious she didn't last the longer distance'. Ascot's mile and a quarter is a lot more testing than that at Belmont Park, but by the end of the season Banks Hill had had two more races over a mile and a quarter, both in the United States, and those performances fell well short of her best as well. Withdrawn from the Flower Bowl Handicap at the end of September when the ground turned soft (as she had been from the Prix d'Astarte at Deauville in August), she finished only third the following week when evens favourite for the Yellow Ribbon Stakes at Santa Anita. Finding no way through behind four of her five rivals on the home turn was a major impediment, but she failed to make any significant inroads when in the clear. The winner Golden Apples was made favourite to beat her again in the Breeders' Cup Filly & Mare Turf at Arlington. Banks Hill, with Bobby Frankel now listed as her trainer, was made second favourite and she reversed the placings but, after most of the field had held a chance entering the straight, it was her new stablemate Starine who made the decisive move a furlong out; Banks Hill kept on to finish best of the rest, beaten a length and a half. The ground for her was softer than ideal, but firm going brought no better than fourth of six behind Dress To Thrill and Golden Apples when favourite for the nine-furlong Matriarch Stakes at Hollywood Park in December. Prior to that, she had run in a dozen pattern or graded races, eleven of them Group/ Grade 1, and had never been out of the first three. Her retirement was announced soon after the Matriarch.

	Danehill (USA) (b 1986)	Danzig (b 1977)	Northern Dancer
			Pas de Nom
		Razyana (b 1981)	His Majesty
Banks Hill (b.f. 1998)			Spring Adieu
	Hasili (IRE) (b 1991)	Kahyasi (b 1985)	Ile de Bourbon
			Kadissya
		Kerali (ch 1984)	High Line
			Sookera

Mr K. Abdulla's "Banks Hill"

Speaking on the day of Banks Hill's triumph in the Jacques le Marois, which followed Grade 1 victories the previous evening for his Beat Hollow and Chiselling in the United States, owner Khalid Abdulla reportedly said that he had just had the best twenty-four hours of his life. Another part in that pleasure was a winning debut for Intercontinental, a sister to Banks Hill, in the opening race on the Jacques le Marois card. Intercontinental went on to finish a close third when favourite for the Grand Criterium, and while it may be asking a lot of Intercontinental to emerge in the same class as her sister, Banks Hill herself completed a similar feat because the dam's first foal was the high-class miler Dansili, another by Danehill. Unsurprisingly, that clearly excellent broodmare Hasili visited Danehill again in 2000 and 2002; she was barren to him after a 2001 covering. Further information on this pedigree can be found in last year's essay on Banks Hill and in this year's on Intercontinental. A strong, lengthy filly who carried plenty of condition, Banks Hill was effective at a mile and, with the emphasis on speed, at a mile and a quarter. She won on heavy ground but her two best efforts were on good or firmer. A genuine sort, Banks Hill was held up to make best use of her good turn of foot. *R. J. Frankel, USA*

BANNING   3 b.g. Anabaa (USA) 130 – Sea Wedding 72 (Groom Dancer (USA) 128)   **65**
[2002 9m⁶ p12g⁵ Sep 4] 26,000Y: second foal: half-brother to 1m and (at 2 yrs) 9.4f winner Shakakhan (by Night Shift): dam, ran twice, closely related to St Leger second High And Low and smart stayer Corradini: better effort in maidens (fair form) when 10½ lengths sixth to Pagan Dance at Newbury on debut: sold 6,000 gns, sent to Kuwait. *R. F. Johnson Houghton*

BANNINGHAM BLAZE   2 b.f. (Mar 29) Averti (IRE) 117 – Ma Pavlova (USA)   **48**
102 (Irish River (FR) 131) [2002 f5s 6g 6d f5g 5g⁵ 7m³ 7.5g 8d⁴ Aug 23] 1,200Y: close-coupled, good-topped filly: half-sister to several winners, including smart Irish 9f and 1½m winner L'Opera (by Old Vic) and fairly useful 1997 2-y-o 7f winner (later won up to 13f in Sweden) Pure Nobility (by Darshaan): dam, French 2-y-o 6.5f winner, half-sister to dam of Breeders' Cup Turf winner Kotashaan: poor maiden: likely to stay 1¼m: yet to race on extremes of going: tried visored. *D. Shaw*

BANNINGHAM BLIZ   4 ch.f. Inchinor 119 – Mary From Dunlow 49 (Nicholas Bill   **–**
125) [2002 50: f6g f7g f8.5g 6f Apr 13] leggy filly: modest maiden at 3 yrs: well beaten in 2002: visored/blinkered. *D. Shaw*

BANNISTER   4 ch.g. Inchinor 119 – Shall We Run 59 (Hotfoot 126) [2002 96: 5s 5f   **–**
6g 6g 7f⁶ 9.2s Jul 2] useful-looking gelding: has a quick action: useful performer at best (won Gimcrack Stakes at York in 2000): left R. Hannon after 3 yrs, and well held in 2002: best at 6f/7f: acts on good to firm going: blinkered final 3-y-o start and penultimate one (hung left) at 4 yrs: tried tongue tied: sold 1,700 gns in October, gelded and joined D. Nicholls. *J. S. Goldie*

BANTAM   2 b.c. (Mar 28) Atraf 116 – Fran Godfrey 70 (Taufan (USA) 119) [2002 7d   **–**
Aug 23] 12,500Y, resold 8,000Y: third foal: dam, maiden, sister to smart middle-distance performer Captain Horatius: 25/1, well beaten in seller at Thirsk: dead. *M. W. Easterby*

BAPTISMAL ROCK (IRE)   8 ch.g. Ballad Rock 122 – Flower From Heaven   **45**
(Baptism 119) [2002 51: f5g 5.1f⁴ 6d Aug 3] good-bodied gelding: poor mover: poor handicapper: best at 5f/6f: acts on fibresand, firm and good to soft going: has found little/carried head awkwardly: usually races prominently. *A. G. Newcombe*

BARABASCHI   6 b.g. Elmaamul (USA) 125 – Hills' Presidium (Presidium 124)   **49**
[2002 58: 8.3g 8g 6.9d 5m Aug 6] angular gelding: poor nowadays: off P. Chamings after second start: stays 1m: acts on any going: blinkered once as 3-y-o: sometimes flashes tail/hangs. *D. Nicholls*

BARAKANA (IRE)   4 b.g. Barathea (IRE) 127 – Safkana (IRE) 78 (Doyoun 124)   **?**
[2002 10.1m a6g⁵ a9g³ a8g³ a10.5g⁶ a10.5g* a10.5g* a10.5g⁶ a10.5g Dec 1] good-topped gelding: well held for G. A. Swinbank on reappearance (only run in Britain since fair 2-y-o for B. Meehan): won twice at Mijas at 3 yrs (trained by P. Haley) and handicaps there in August/September: stays 10.5f: probably acts on any turf going, and on sand: tried blinkered. *J. H. Brown, Spain*

BARALINKA (IRE)   3 b.f. Barathea (IRE) 127 – Kalinka (IRE) 88 (Soviet Star (USA)   **93**
128) [2002 72+: 6.1f* f6g* 6f⁴ 6g 6m 5.2g² 6.1m* 6g 6f 5s² Oct 26] well-made filly: fairly useful performer: won minor event at Warwick in April and handicaps at Southwell

in May and Chester in August: ran well final start: best at 5f/6f: acts on fibresand, and firm and soft going: consistent. *P. F. I. Cole*

BARALOTI (IRE)   2 b.f. (Feb 7) Barathea (IRE) 127 – Charlotte Corday 105 (Kris **58 p** 135) [2002 p8g Nov 27] second foal: half-sister to 2001 2-y-o 7f winner Sainte Just (by Polish Precedent): dam, 1m winner, sister to 1¼m/1½m performer Gai Bulga and half-sister to smart 1½m performer Rockerlong: 9/4, seemed in need of experience (slowly away) when ninth of 12 in maiden at Lingfield: capable of better. *J. H. M. Gosden*

BARATHEA BLAZER   3 b.c. Barathea (IRE) 127 – Empty Purse (Pennine Walk **109** 120) [2002 86p: 10.5m² 9.9g⁴ 12m* 12m 11.9d² 13.9m³ Aug 21] sturdy colt: useful handicapper: landed gamble at Newbury in May: good efforts when second to Sun Bird in Old Newton Cup at Haydock and length third to Hugs Dancer in Ebor at York last 2 starts: better at 1½m+ than shorter, and should stay 2m: acts on soft and good to firm ground. *P. W. Harris*

BARATHIKI   4 gr.f. Barathea (IRE) 127 – Tagiki (IRE) (Doyoun 124) [2002 70: 5.1d **–** 6.1d 5.7g May 7] tall, useful-looking filly: formerly fair 6f/7f handicapper: well held in 2002: blinkered once at 2 yrs: sold 13,000 gns. *C. G. Cox*

BARBASON   10 ch.g. Polish Precedent (USA) 131 – Barada (USA) (Damascus **48** (USA)) [2002 58, a–: p8g p10g⁵ p10g² 10.2d 10m 11.9g⁴ 10m Aug 28] compact gelding: **a63** modest on all-weather, poor on turf: stays 1½m: acts on polytrack, firm and soft ground (below form on fibresand): has won in blinkers (not tried since 1999): sometimes pulls hard/finds little: usually held up. *G. L. Moore*

BARBERA   3 b.f. Barathea (IRE) 127 – Premiere Cuvee 109 (Formidable (USA) 125) **54** [2002 10g 9.9m 9d⁶ 11.9d Jun 13] closely related to useful Italian miler She Bat (by Batshoof) and half-sister to several winners, including useful 7f/1m winner Cask (by Be My Chief): dam sprinter: modest form when sixth in maiden at Goodwood: well held otherwise, probably failing to stay on handicap debut final start. *Mrs A. J. Perrett*

BARCELONA   5 b.g. Barathea (IRE) 127 – Pipitina 91 (Bustino 136) [2002 84d: **70** 16m⁵ Jun 1] sturdy gelding: fair form only Flat outing in 2002: stays 2m: acts on soft and good to firm going: tongue tied: has hung. *G. L. Moore*

BAREFOOTED FLYER (USA)   4 ch.f. Fly So Free (USA) 122 – Carmelita (USA) **60** (Mogambo (USA)) [2002 67: p6g⁵ p7g 7.1s 7g 7d⁴ 7m f7s f7g³ p8g⁴ p7g⁶ f8.5g⁶ f7g⁴ f6g⁴ Nov 25] big, leggy filly: modest performer: stays 1m: acts on good to firm going, good to soft and all-weather: wore cheekpieces/blinkers last 3 starts: sometimes slowly away/ rears leaving stall. *J. M. Bradley*

BARELLA (IRE)   3 b.c. Barathea (IRE) 127 – Daniella Drive (USA) (Shelter Half **57 d** (USA)) [2002 10.5d 10m⁶ 10m 10d 12s Nov 1] IR 35,000Y: tall, rather leggy colt: half-brother to 3 winners by Indian Ridge, including 4-y-o Dani Ridge and useful 7f to 8.5f winner Blomberg: dam won 12 races up to 6f in USA: modest form in maidens first 2 starts: well held subsequently, leaving P. Harris after third outing. *K. F. O'Brien, Ireland*

BARINGO (USA)   3 b.c. Miswaki (USA) 124 – Galega (Sure Blade (USA) 130) **87** [2002 66: 8s 8.1f³ 10d⁴ 11.7d 10g* 10.1m² 12f⁵ 11f Sep 25] strong, good-bodied colt: fairly useful performer: won handicap at Brighton in August: ran creditably next 2 outings: best form at 1¼m: acts on firm going: blinkered (too free) final start: races prominently: sold 45,000 gns. *R. Charlton*

BARITONE   8 b.g. Midyan (USA) 124 – Zinzi (Song 132) [2002 38+, a69: f6s f6g² **–** f6g f6g³ f6g Dec 14] close-coupled gelding: modest handicapper on all-weather: has form **a63** at 1m, raced mainly at 5f/6f nowadays: acts on fibresand: tried blinkered/visored: none too consistent. *I. Balding*

BARKBY (IRE)   3 b.g. Lahib (USA) 129 – Portree 82 (Slip Anchor 136) [2002 50: **66** 8.3v 12m 14.1m³ f16.2g* f16g⁵ f14g² f14.8s f14.8g Dec 31] tall, rather leggy gelding: fair handicapper: won at Wolverhampton in November by 13 lengths: clipped rival's heels and fell fatally final start: stayed 2m: acted on good to firm going and fibresand. *M. H. Tompkins*

BARKING MAD (USA)   4 b. or br.g. Dayjur (USA) 137 – Avian Assembly (USA) **96** (General Assembly (USA)) [2002 95: 7m 6m⁶ 6s⁵ 7m p8g² 7d² 7f⁶ 8g⁶ 7f² 7g 7s Nov 2] sturdy, lengthy gelding: useful performer: second in handicaps at Newmarket on sixth/ ninth starts, beaten 3 lengths by Demonstrate in latter: stays 1m: acts on firm and good to soft going: edgy sort: has run well when sweating: sometimes races freely/makes running: none too consistent. *M. L. W. Bell*

BARMAN (USA) 3 ch.g. Atticus (USA) 121 – Blue Tip (FR) 117 (Tip Moss (FR)) **93**
[2002 88p: 7g³ 8.1f* 9.9g 10.4m 11.6m³ 10.3s p12g³ p12g⁶ Nov 23] big, quite good-
topped gelding: fairly useful performer: made all in maiden at Warwick in April: ran well
after when third: stays easy 1½m: acts on firm going, soft and polytrack: free-going sort:
has edged right: carries head shade awkwardly: gelded after final outing. *P. F. I. Cole*

BARN DANCER (IRE) 7 b.m. Cataldi 123 – Dancing Gale (Strong Gale 116) [2002 **–**
7m Jul 27] third foal: dam bumper winner: tailed off only run on Flat. *G. P. Kelly*

BARNEY MCALL (IRE) 2 b.c. (May 12) Grand Lodge (USA) 125 – Persian Song **84 +**
45 (Persian Bold 123) [2002 7.1m³ 7.1v* 7.1m 8s Oct 20] 72,000Y: leggy, quite attractive
colt: half-brother to several winners, including smart 7f (at 2 yrs) to 1¼m winner
Mountain Song and fairly useful 1996 2-y-o 6f winner Raindancing (both by Tirol): dam,
ran 3 times at 2 yrs, sister to high-class performer up to 1¼m Bold Arrangement: fairly
useful form: won maiden at Haydock in August: well held after in Solario Stakes at
Sandown and Gran Criterium at Milan, though better than bare result both times: should
stay at least 1m: acts on good to firm and heavy ground. *Mrs A. J. Perrett*

BARNIE RUBBLE 6 ch.g. Pharly (FR) 130 – Sharp Fairy (Sharpo 132) [2002 75: p7g³ **72**
8m p8g May 29] smallish, sturdy gelding: fair handicapper: off 4 months, below form last
2 starts: stays easy 1m: acts on soft going, good to firm and polytrack. *P. W. D'Arcy*

BAR OF SILVER (IRE) 2 ch.c. (Apr 10) Bahhare (USA) 122 – Shaping Up (USA) **58 p**
89 (Storm Bird (CAN) 134) [2002 f6g⁴ Nov 18] sixth foal: half-brother to 3 winners,
including fairly useful 1m winner Thaman (by Sri Pekan) and Irish 9f winner Islamorada
(by Persian Bold), both later successful abroad: dam 2-y-o 5.7f winner: 11 lengths fourth
to Bond Royale in maiden at Wolverhampton, racing wide and keeping on: should
improve. *J. A. Osborne*

BAROLO 3 b.g. Danehill (USA) 126 – Lydia Maria 70 (Dancing Brave (USA) 140) **84 p**
[2002 77p: 8.1f³ 8.3d² Oct 14] strong, close-coupled gelding: half-brother to 3 winners,
including useful 6f (at 2 yrs) and 10.4f winner Premier Bay (by Primo Dominie): dam,
maiden who stayed 1¼m, out of very smart middle-distance performer Connaught
Bridge: fairly useful maiden: off 13 months, shaped encouragingly on reappearance then
best effort when ½-length second of 16 to Silken Brief at Windsor, going on strongly at
finish: will be suited by 1¼m: capable of better still. *P. W. Harris*

BARON CROCODILE 4 b.g. Puissance 110 – Glow Again 78 (The Brianstan 128) **52**
[2002 65: 5g 7m 6g 6f⁵ 5.9s 6d Oct 15] close-coupled gelding: modest performer: left
Mrs D. Sayer after penultimate start: best at 5f/6f: acts on any turf going: tried blinkered/
visored, tried tongue tied: sometimes slowly away: carries head high. *M. Todhunter*

BARON DE PICHON (IRE) 6 b.g. Perugino (USA) 84 – Ariadne 79 (Bustino 136) **–**
[2002 –, a78: f12g⁴ f12g² f12g⁶ f14.8g⁶ f12s Oct 8] workmanlike gelding: fair performer: **a69**
below form after 6-month break last 2 starts: probably best around 1½m nowadays: acts
on fibresand, little form on turf: visored once as 2-y-o. *Miss S. J. Wilton*

BARONESS SNOUCKART (USA) 4 b.f. Quest For Fame 127 – Balastra (USA) **56**
(Fappiano (USA)) [2002 10m⁶ 10m 10m 11.6m Jul 1] leggy filly: half-sister to several
winners, including fairly useful 8.5f and 1¼m winner Hakika (by Elmaamul): dam,
lightly raced in USA, half-sister to US Grade 1 1¼m winner and Belmont Stakes runner-
up Pine Circle: modest form in maidens/handicap: stays 1¼m. *R. M. Beckett*

BARON'S PIT 2 b.c. (Apr 9) Night Shift (USA) – Incendio (Siberian Express (USA) **107**
125) [2002 5m² 5m* 5m* 6m⁶ 6m Sep 20] big, well-made colt: has plenty of scope: type
to carry condition: fourth foal: half-brother to winner abroad by Be My Chief: dam
winning sprinter in Italy: useful performer: won minor event at Windsor (by 2 lengths
from Folio, making all) in May and Norfolk Stakes at Royal Ascot (by head from The
Bonus King, leading over 1f out) in June: well held after in Richmond Stakes at
Goodwood and Mill Reef Stakes at Newbury: should stay 6f: raced only on good to firm
going. *R. Hannon*

BARRANTES 5 b.m. Distant Relative 128 – Try The Duchess 99 (Try My Best (USA) **73**
130) [2002 68: p6g 7m⁶ 8.3g 7g* 7m 6g² 6g³ 7m 5d⁵ 6m² 6g* 5m² 6m 5f⁶ 6d Oct 14] fair
performer: won ladies handicap at Lingfield in May and minor event at Folkestone in
August: best at 5f to easy 7f: acts on firm and good to soft ground: edged left penultimate
start: often races prominently. *Miss S. West*

BARRISSIMO (IRE) 2 b.c. (May 28) Night Shift (USA) – Belle de Cadix (IRE) 82 **94 p**
(Law Society 130) [2002 6m 7s* Oct 25] 32,000Y: good-bodied colt: has a quick
action: fourth foal: half-brother to 3 winners abroad, including useful French performer
up to 1m Zeiting (by Zieten), 6f/6.5f winner at 2 yrs and later winner in USA: dam Irish

13f winner: shaped well when twelfth of 18 to Somnus in Two-Year-Old Trophy at Redcar: justified favouritism in maiden at Doncaster later in October by 10 lengths from Tyneham, making most: has plenty of speed, and likely to prove best up to 1m: acts on soft and good to firm ground: already bordering on useful, and sure to improve further. *P. W. Harris*

BARROSA 3 b.f. Sabrehill (USA) 120 – Shehana (USA) 86 (The Minstrel (CAN) 135) – [2002 51: 7.1g 7f f12g 8.1d 8.3m Jul 22] leggy, rather unfurnished filly: maiden: little form in 2002: left A. Berry after second outing. *Miss K. M. George*

BARRY ISLAND 3 b.g. Turtle Island (IRE) 123 – Pine Ridge 80 (High Top 131) **89** [2002 78p: p10g* p10g 9g⁴ 10m³ 9.9g⁶ 11m May 18] good-topped gelding: fairly useful performer: won handicap at Lingfield in February: creditable efforts after: will stay at least 1½m: acts on polytrack and good to firm going: comes from behind. *D. R. C. Elsworth*

BARRYS DOUBLE 5 br.g. Barrys Gamble 102 – Pennine Star (IRE) 68 (Pennine **35** Walk 120) [2002 40, a47: f14.8g⁴ 11.9f Apr 11] close-coupled gelding: poor maiden: best at 7f/1m: acts on fibresand, good to firm and good to soft going: tried visored/blinkered/tongue tied. *Jean-Rene Auvray*

BARSAYA 4 b.f. Wolfhound (USA) 126 – Zeffirella 88 (Known Fact (USA) 135) **49** [2002 59: p8g f8g³ f8g⁴ f8g 7s 10.2g 7d⁶ 6.1g⁴ 6m Jul 22] poor maiden: stays 1m: acts on good to firm going and fibresand: blinkered/visored: difficult ride. *P. R. Chamings*

BARTON BEAU (IRE) 3 b.g. Kylian (USA) – Hetty Green (Bay Express 132) [2002 – 10.5d 14s⁶ 12.3m Jun 19] IR 6,200F, IR 30,000Y: workmanlike gelding: seventh foal: half-brother to 3 winners, including 5-y-o Barton Sands and Irish 1¼m winner Sesame Heights (by High Estate): dam Irish 1½m and hurdles winner: tailed off in 3 maidens, blinkered last 2. *T. D. Easterby*

BARTON FLYER (IRE) 3 b.g. Eagle Eyed (USA) 111 – Boristova (IRE) 79 (Royal – Academy (USA) 130) [2002 p8g p10g f8.5g⁶ 12f Oct 8] IR 5,000Y, 14,000 2-y-o: third foal: half-brother to 4-y-o Lady Bear: dam, Irish 2-y-o 9f winner, half-sister to useful Irish middle-distance stayer Judicial Field: well held in 3 maidens for John Berry, and handicap (off 7 months, tongue tied, attracted support) final start. *Niall Moran, Ireland*

BARTON SANDS (IRE) 5 b.g. Tenby 125 – Hetty Green (Bay Express 132) [2002 **72 ?** 86+: 10f 8.3s 10.2s⁴ 8m 16.2m 10.4m 10m⁴ 10.3d 8.9m² Sep 8] neat gelding: formerly useful: fair at best in 2002: stays 1¼m: acts on firm and good to soft ground, well beaten on soft/heavy: joined M. Pipe. *R. Brotherton*

BARZAH (IRE) 3 b.f. Darshaan 133 – Lepikha (USA) 72 (El Gran Senor (USA) 136) **98** [2002 93: 11.5g² 12m 10m Aug 28] small, quite attractive filly: useful form when ½-length second to Birdie in listed race at Lingfield on reappearance: well held in Ribblesdale Stakes at Royal Ascot next time: off 2 months and stiff task, far from discredited when seventh to Averted View in listed rated stakes at Brighton final start: stayed 11.5f: raced only on good going or firmer: to visit Gulch. *Sir Michael Stoute*

BARZAK (IRE) 2 b.c. (Jan 30) Barathea (IRE) 127 – Zakuska 96 (Zafonic (USA) **80 p** 130) [2002 7d* Aug 11] first foal: dam, 1¼m winner from 3 starts, closely related to US Grade 1 9f winner Link River: 11/1 from 16/1, won 12-runner maiden at Leicester by ½ length from Khabir, well ridden close to pace and leading over 2f out: should improve. *S. R. Bowring*

BASBOUSATE NADIA 3 b.f. Wolfhound (USA) 126 – Sarabah (IRE) 83 (Ela-Mana-**68** Mou 132) [2002 92: 6m 5.1f⁴ 7m Sep 20] tall, good-topped filly: fairly useful performer at 2 yrs: just fair in 2002: will need to settle to stay further than 6f: raced only on good going or firmer. *W. R. Muir*

BASE LINE 4 b.g. Rudimentary (USA) 118 – Hemline 77 (Sharpo 132) [2002 40, a54: – p10g f8s³ f8g⁶ f9.4g⁵ p7g May 28] leggy gelding: poor handicapper: stays easy 1¼m: acts **a49** on fibresand, best turf run on good going: blinkered last 4 starts: sometimes goes too freely. *R. M. Flower*

BASFORD BOY 3 b.g. Tragic Role (USA) – Legatee 77 (Risk Me (FR) 127) [2002 – 10g 12.3g Aug 26] first foal: dam 5f (at 2 yrs) and 7f winner who stayed 8.5f: well beaten in maidens: dead. *A. Streeter*

BASHEERA 2 b.f. (Feb 26) Bahhare (USA) 122 – Samheh (USA) 62 (Private Account **46** (USA)) [2002 5m⁶ 6m 5d May 24] IR 12,000Y: strong, compact filly: fourth foal: half-sister to fairly useful 1999 2-y-o 7f winner Marah (by Machiavellian): dam, maiden who stayed 1¼m, out of US Grade 1 7f (at 2 yrs) and 9f winner Lucky Lucky Lucky: poor maiden. *E. J. Alston*

BASINET 4 b.g. Alzao (USA) 117 – Valiancy 87 (Grundy 137) [2002 63, a73: f8s 7.5m⁴   **72** 8s³ 8.5g³ 6.9g* 7.5m 9m* 8.3m² 9d⁵ Oct 18] strong, close-coupled, quite attractive gelding: fair performer: won minor event at Carlisle in August and handicap at Musselburgh in September: effective at 7f to 9f: acts on firm ground, soft and fibresand: sometimes slowly away: has taken strong hold/carried head high. *J. J. Quinn*

BASSERELLO (FR) 2 b.c. (Feb 17) Anabaa (USA) 130 – Passerella (FR) (Brustolon   **82 ?** 117) [2002 5s 5g* 5d⁶ 5.5g⁶ 6m³ 7g 7g Aug 20] 520,000 francs Y: close-coupled colt: has a fluent, round action: closely related to useful French 7f winner Past The Hill (by Danehill) and French 1m/10.5f winner Princess Ella (by Emperor Jones) and half-brother to winner in France by Exit To Nowhere: dam ran once: fairly useful performer: won minor event at Chantilly in April: left M. Channon after fourth start: below form last 2 outings: likely to prove best at 5f/6f: sold 13,000 gns, sent to Sweden. *R. Pritchard-Gordon, France*

BASSET 4 b.c. Salse (USA) 128 – Bempton 57 (Blakeney 126) [2002 54: p12g Jan 3]   **–** modest form at best in maidens at 3 yrs: well held only run in 2002: should stay at least 1½m. *J. A. Osborne*

BASTILLE 2 gr.f. (Jun 12) Medaaly 114 – Legal Drama (USA) 60 (Turkoman (USA))   **–** [2002 8.3d p10g Dec 3] second foal: dam, maiden, stayed 1m: last in maidens. *R. Curtis*

BATAILLEY 2 ch.f. (Feb 10) First Trump 118 – Phantom Ring 62 (Magic Ring (IRE)   **64** 115) [2002 5d 6m 7.1m⁵ 6d⁵ 5.1s² f6g Dec 20] first foal: dam 5f winner: modest maiden: effective at 5f/6f: acts on soft ground, probably on good to firm. *Mrs H. Dalton*

BATCHWORTH BREEZE 4 ch.f. Beveled (USA) – Batchworth Dancer 67 (Balla-   **–** cashtal (CAN)) [2002 –: 5.1d⁶ f8.5g Jul 12] of little account. *E. A. Wheeler*

BATCHWORTH LOCK 4 b.g. Beveled (USA) – Treasurebound 63 (Beldale   **–** Flutter (USA) 130) [2002 46: 6g 6g 6.1m 8.3d Oct 14] of little account. *E. A. Wheeler*

BATHWICK BRUCE (IRE) 4 b.g. College Chapel 122 – Naivity (IRE) 72 (Auction   **84** Ring (USA) 123) [2002 77: 7.1s⁴ 7.1v 8.2m* 7.1g 7.6s* p8g* 8.2v 8v Nov 8] fairly useful performer: won minor event at Nottingham in July, and handicaps at Lingfield in September and October: stays 1m: acts on soft going, good to firm and polytrack. *B. R. Millman*

BATOOL (USA) 3 b.f. Bahri (USA) 125 – Mrs Paddy (USA) (Woodman (USA) 126)   **69** [2002 73: 7m⁵ 8.1m² 7d⁵ 10.9m 7s⁴ Oct 22] $20,000F, IR 160,000Y: small, useful-looking filly: first foal: dam unraced daughter of Our Little Margie, placed in US Grade 1 events at 6f (at 2 yrs) and 8.5f: fair maiden: trained at 2 yrs by D. Hanley in Ireland: headstrong, but stays 1m: acts on good to firm and good to soft going: sold 5,500 gns. *N. A. Graham*

BATOUTOFTHEBLUE 9 br.g. Batshoof 122 – Action Belle (Auction Ring (USA)   **42** 123) [2002 –, a71: 16m³ 16g 17.1m Aug 18] big gelding: poor performer nowadays: stays   **a–** 2¼m: acts on fibresand: blinkered twice earlier in career: carries head awkwardly/often gets behind. *G. A. Swinbank*

BATTLE CHANT (USA) 2 b.c. (Feb 23) Coronado's Quest (USA) 130 – Appointed   **104 p** One (USA) (Danzig (USA)) [2002 6m³ 6m⁴ 7.1g* 8d* Oct 21] rangy, useful-looking colt: third foal: half-brother to fairly useful 7f winner Matoaka (by A P Indy) and 4-y-o Constitute: dam, minor 1m stakes winner in USA, sister to smart miler Emperor Jones and closely related to top-class 1985 2-y-o Bakharoff: ran as though amiss second start: impressive winner of maiden at Chepstow in September and 5-runner listed race at Pontefract (by 6 lengths from Inchberry, dictating pace and pulling readily clear in straight) in October: stays 1m: yet to race on extremes of going: should make a smart performer. *E. A. L. Dunlop*

BATTLE LINE 3 b.g. Brief Truce (USA) 126 – Forest Heights 81 (Slip Anchor 136)   **55 §** [2002 56: p8g² f8.5g⁵ f7g³ p6g⁴ f7g⁶ p8g³ f7g 10d³ 12g⁵ 14m 12g Oct 7] modest maiden handicapper: left K. McAuliffe after eighth start: stays 1½m: acts on all-weather and good to soft going: usually blinkered/visored: often slowly away: unreliable. *E. McNamara, Ireland*

BATTLE WARNING 7 b.g. Warning 136 – Royal Ballet (IRE) (Sadler's Wells (USA)   **75** 132) [2002 73: f16s⁴ f16g⁶ 18s* 18f² 15g² 15.9f⁴ 17.2g² Jul 14] well-made gelding: fair handicapper: banned under non-triers rule on reappearance: left A. Crook after second start: won at Chepstow in June: effective at 1¾m to 2¼m: acts on soft going, firm and fibresand. *P. Bowen*

BATTO 2 b.g. (May 1) Slip Anchor 136 – Frog 84 (Akarad (FR) 130) [2002 f7g f8.5s – Dec 9] third foal: half-brother to 3-y-o Froglet and 2000 2-y-o 7f seller winner Sel (by Salse): dam 1¼m/1½m winner: well held in maidens. *W. J. Haggas*

BAWSIAN 7 b.g. Persian Bold 123 – Bawaeth (USA) 72 (Blushing Groom (FR) 131) **89** [2002 94, a88: p12g 12s⁴ 11.9m⁵ 12m² 16f May 11] small, close-coupled gelding: fairly **a–** useful handicapper: creditable ½-length second of 23 to Solo Flight at Newmarket penultimate outing: well held final start: stays 1¾m: acts on all-weather, good to firm and heavy going: tongue tied: reportedly had breathing problem third start: sometimes gets behind: sent to Spain. *J. L. Eyre*

BAXTER THE GUVNER 6 ch.g. Wolfhound (USA) 126 – Current Raiser 108 – (Filiberto (USA) 123) [2002 6.1m 10.2g Aug 8] 5,500Y, 22,000 2-y-o, 1,200 3-y-o: half-brother to 6f winner Barren Lands (by Green Desert) and stayer Doyce (by Formidable): dam won Lupe Stakes: well held in 2 sellers. *W. Clay*

BAY OF DREAMS 3 ch.g. Salse (USA) 128 – Cantico 58 (Green Dancer (USA) 132) **46** [2002 –: 7m³ 11.6s May 13] poor maiden: should be suited by at least 1¼m: visored second start. *I. A. Balding*

BAY OF ISLANDS 10 b.g. Jupiter Island 126 – Lawyer's Wave (USA) (Advocator) **96** [2002 104: 16m 18.7f⁵ May 8] strong gelding: fluent mover: useful performer: reportedly missed second half of 2001 due to suspensory trouble: better effort in 2002 when fifth to Fantasy Hill in Chester Cup final start: stays 2¼m: acts on firm and good to soft going: usually visored. *D. Morris*

BAYONET 6 b.m. Then Again 126 – Lambay 88 (Lorenzaccio 130) [2002 62: 5.7g 6m – 6m 7m Jul 4] deep-girthed mare: modest handicapper at 5 yrs: no form in 2002: blinkered twice at 3 yrs. *Jane Southcombe*

BAYTOWN FLYER 2 ch.f. (Apr 29) Whittingham (IRE) 104 – The Fernhill Flyer **66** (IRE) 71 (Red Sunset 120) [2002 5s p5g⁶ 5.1d 5s⁶ p5g⁵ 7f* 6m* 6.1d² p6g³ 6g² 6g f5s 6m⁵ 6g* f6g⁶ Oct 19] 500Y: smallish filly: fourth foal: dam 2-y-o 5f/6f winner: fair performer: won sellers at Yarmouth and Windsor (left P. McEntee) in June and claimer at Lingfield in October: best at 6f/7f: acts on firm going, good to soft and polytrack (well below form on fibresand): blinkered (below form) once. *W. J. Haggas*

BAYTOWN GRACE 3 b.f. Presidium 124 – Thalya (Crofthall 110) [2002 42: p7g – p6g 8d Nov 1] maiden: little form in 2002. *P. S. McEntee*

BAYTOWN SUMMERCAT 2 b.f. (Apr 30) Young Ern 120 – Pitcairn Princess **39** (Capricorn Line 111) [2002 5s f5g² p5g 5.3f⁶ f5s 7f³ 5.2f⁶ 7g 6m Aug 9] 750Y: small filly: fourth foal: half-sister to a winner up to 10.5f in Italy by Tragic Role: dam tailed off in maidens at 2 yrs: poor maiden: stays 7f: acts on firm going and all-weather: tried blinkered. *P. S. McEntee*

B BEAUTIFUL (IRE) 3 ch.f. Be My Guest (USA) 126 – Lady Donna 92 (Dominion **57** 123) [2002 51: 8.2d* 10m 8g 8.1s⁴ 8.1d⁶ 8g³ f8.5g Dec 20] unfurnished filly: modest handicapper: won at Nottingham in April: appears to stay easy 1¼m: acts on soft and good to firm going. *M. L. W. Bell*

BEACON OF LIGHT (IRE) 4 b.f. Lake Coniston (IRE) 131 – Deydarika (IRE) – (Kahyasi 130) [2002 12.4g 12g Oct 19] quite good-topped filly: little form. *Ferdy Murphy*

BEACON WOOD (IRE) 3 b.c. Woodman (USA) 126 – Catch The Blues (IRE) 115 – (Bluebird (USA) 125) [2002 f7g* 8g 7d f8.5g³ f12s⁵ Dec 7] IR 60,000Y: first foal: dam **a81** Irish 5f (including Ballyogan Stakes) and 7f winner: fairly useful performer: reportedly broke a leg in March 2001: won maiden at Wolverhampton in March: left impression something amiss (after absence) next 2 starts: stays 8.5f: acts on fibresand: tongue tied last 2 outings: tends to carry head awkwardly. *M. Johnston*

BEADY (IRE) 3 b.g. Eagle Eyed (USA) 111 – Tales of Wisdom 70 (Rousillon (USA) **72** 133) [2002 73: f8.5g³ 8s⁴ 9.9m⁵ 9.2g⁴ 10m⁶ 10g⁴ f12s⁴ f12g⁵ f14g³ f9.4g⁴ Dec 20] good-topped gelding: fair maiden: barely stays 1¾m: acts on fibresand, soft and good to firm going: races freely: consistent. *B. Smart*

BEAMISH PRINCE 3 ch.c. Bijou d'Inde 127 – Unconditional Love (IRE) 104 (Polish **71** Patriot (USA) 128) [2002 9.2g* 7f⁶ 10m⁶ 9m 8g⁴ 8.3m⁶ 7.9m⁶ a12f⁴ Dec 26] close-coupled colt: first foal: dam 5f (at 2 yrs) and 1¼m winner: fair performer: won maiden at Hamilton in May: likely to prove better at 1¼m than 1m (ran respectably at 1½m): raced only on good going or firmer on turf. *M. Johnston*

BEANBOY 4 ch.g. Clantime 101 – Lady Blues Singer (Chief Singer 131) [2002 46, **44** a35: f8s f7g⁵ f9.4g³ f8g⁶ f8.5g f8g 10.3s 11g f6g 10m 10f³ 10g⁵ 10d 8m 7f 10s 10m 10f **a34** Sep 26] leggy gelding: poor maiden: stays 1¼m: acts on fibresand, firm and good to soft going: tried visored: usually front runner. *Mrs S. Lamyman*

BEASLEY 3 b.g. First Trump 118 – Le Shuttle 49 (Presidium 124) [2002 48§: 7m⁵ **45 §** p10g Apr 10] poor maiden: stays 7f: blinkered final 2-y-o start: ungenuine. *M. Pitman*

BEAT THE HEAT (IRE) 4 b.g. Salse (USA) 128 – Summer Trysting (USA) 83 **89** (Alleged (USA) 138) [2002 95: 10.1m² 12s⁴ 10m² 11.9m 10f⁴ Sep 26] lengthy ex-Irish gelding: second foal: half-brother to fairly useful Irish 8.5f winner Romantic Venture (by Indian Ridge) and 3-y-o Sights On Gold: dam, Irish maiden who stayed 1½m, half-sister to smart winner up to 1¼m Smooth Performance: useful performer at 3 yrs for D. Weld: fairly useful form first 4 starts in Britain: stays 1½m: probably acts on any ground: blinkered last 4 starts in 2001. *Jedd O'Keeffe*

BEAT TIME 3 ro.f. Lion Cavern (USA) 117 – Brilliant Timing (USA) (The Minstrel **78 §** (CAN) 135) [2002 6f* 7g³ p7g⁴ 6f³ 6.1m Jul 20] lengthy, angular filly: eighth foal: half-sister to several winners, including fairly useful 1994 2-y-o 6f/7.5f winner (stayed 10.4f) Watch The Clock (by Mtoto) and 1996 2 y o 5f/6f winner Perpetual (by Prince Sabo): dam once-raced half-sister to US Grade 1 winners Timely Writer and Timely Assertion: fair performer: won maiden at Pontefract in April: found little last 2 starts: stays 7f: races freely: tail flasher: ungenuine: sold 2,800 gns in December. *W. J. Haggas*

BEAUANARROW (IRE) 7 b.g. Beau Sher 119 – Ardnasagh Rose (Crash Course 128) [2002 f12g⁶ Feb 25] second foal: dam ran twice in Irish bumpers: fairly useful form in bumpers (won 2 of 4 starts): well held on Flat debut. *N. M. Babbage*

BEAU ARTISTE 2 ch.c. (Mar 23) Peintre Celebre (USA) 137 – Belle Esprit (Warning **81** 136) [2002 6m² 7g² 7.2g³ 8s² Nov 6] leggy, sparely-made colt: second foal: half-brother to 3-y-o All Business: dam, unraced half-sister to smart performer up to 1¼m Torch Rouge, from family of Opera House and Kayf Tara: fairly useful maiden: placed all starts, wandering/looking less than keen when beaten 1¼ lengths by Louis Napoleon at Mussel-burgh on final one: should be suited by 1¼m+: acts on soft and good to firm ground. *Jedd O'Keeffe*

BEAUCETTE (USA) 2 br.f. (Apr 26) Mr Prospector (USA) – Mackie (USA) **73 p** (Summer Squall (USA)) [2002 7m 6f Sep 8] third foal: dam, US Grade 3 8.5f winner, half-sister to Kentucky Derby winner Sea Hero: fair form, not knocked about, in maidens at Newmarket and Kempton: should stay at least 1m: probably capable of better. *Sir Michael Stoute*

BEAUCHAMP MAGIC 7 b.g. Northern Park (USA) 107 – Beauchamp Buzz 85 **57** (High Top 131) [2002 57: f16.2g⁴ f12g f14.8g² f14.8g⁴ f16.2f p13g Dec 28] good-bodied gelding: modest handicapper: left M. Usher before final start: stays 2m: acts on fibresand and firm ground: tried blinkered/visored/tongue tied, not since 1999: usually held up. *K. R. Burke*

BEAUCHAMP NYX 6 b.m. Northern Park (USA) 107 – Beauchamp Image 79 **–** (Midyan (USA) 124) [2002 –: 16.2g⁶ f14.8g 16.2g 16m f14.8g Dec 16] of little account. *P. A. Pritchard*

BEAUCHAMP PILOT 4 ch.g. Inchinor 119 – Beauchamp Image 79 (Midyan **118** (USA) 124) [2002 96p: 8.1d* 8m³ 10.4m⁴ 10f* 8d⁴ 9f* 9m³ 8s³ p10g* Nov 23] 'Roll up: it's the annual cavalry charge, a race in which they'll take no prisoners: they'll go a million miles an hour, and whatever wins will have to stay every yard!' Don't believe a word of some of the hackneyed previews which are trotted out for some of Britain's long-established handicaps. Despite the large fields they normally attract, the likes of the Royal Hunt Cup and the Cambridgeshire can often still have an element of cat and mouse about them; or at least of cats and mice! The reputation of these races for no-holds-barred contests is in itself an invitation for owners/trainers to warn their riders to go steadily early on and, if the majority of the riders in the field are receiving such instructions, then the ingredients are already in place for the reverse to prove true. Add to this, many modern-day riders' pre-occupation with so-called 'ground bias', and the result is tactical uncertainty early on. Then there is the widely-held belief that many horses by nature need to come late. It should hardly be surprising, therefore, that the big handicaps often produce something less frenetic than a cavalry charge. The last three runnings of the Cambridgeshire have illustrated the point to varying degrees. In none of them

was the early gallop anything to write home about and the three winners, Katy
Nowaitee, I Cried For You and Beauchamp Pilot respectively, all recorded timefigures a long way short of what they should have been capable of in a truly-run
race. In relative terms, each of them quickened well at Newmarket at the end of a
race which effectively didn't test stamina quite so much as it should have done.

Beauchamp Pilot proved well equipped to cope with the run of the race in
the Tote Cambridgeshire. In a field of thirty, he was soon going well close up in the
main group in the centre of the course and merely had to be nursed to the front as he
headed Goblet of Fire in the Dip, given a couple of cracks as he idled and pricked
his ears with the race won, scoring by a length and a half. Far Lane ran on very
strongly in the pack nearer the stand side to be second, while his fellow three-year-
olds Goblet of Fire and Waverley hung on for third and fourth respectively. Significantly, the first four were always prominent. The 4/1 favourite Zonergem finished
thirteenth, never on terms. Beauchamp Pilot, who went off third best at 9/1, had

been joint favourite for the race with Albanova at 14/1 when rival bookmakers Coral took the innovative step of issuing ante-post prices in July, well before the entries and the weights were even known. At the time Beauchamp Pilot had already reached the frame in the Royal Hunt Cup and the John Smith's Cup at York. He did particularly well at Royal Ascot, where he was beaten only a length behind Norton after unseating his rider beforehand and running loose to the start. Beauchamp Pilot's wins apart from the Cambridgeshire came in a handicap over a mile at Haydock on his reappearance in May, a minor event over ten furlongs at Ascot in July and the listed Churchill Stakes on polytrack at Lingfield in November. He beat a smart field at Lingfield, going three lengths clear entering the last furlong before idling and being eased a bit prematurely, holding Kirovski by only a short head. In between Lingfield and the Cambridgeshire, he was an unlucky third behind Golden Silca in a listed race over the same course and distance as the Newmarket race.

Beauchamp Pilot, a big, rather leggy gelding, has progressed steadily in the course of his sixteen races to date, winning seven of them. He carried 9-5 in the Cambridgeshire, putting up one of the handicap performances of the season, and he should hold his own in pattern races as a five-year-old. He is probably best at a mile and a mile and a quarter, and acts on firm and good to soft ground as well as polytrack. He was well below par on soft on his final turf run in 2002. Waited with as a rule, he carries his head somewhat awkwardly, but is reliable. He has been bandaged in front. *G. A. Butler*

BEAUCHAMP QUIZ   3 b. or gr.f. Inchinor 119 – Beauchamp Jade 105 (Kalaglow   **65**
132) [2002 54p: 10m⁴ 12m⁶ 11.9m* 12d 12.1g p10g p10g⁵ Dec 21] smallish, rather leggy filly: fair handicapper: won at Brighton in September by 7 lengths: stays 1½m: acts on polytrack and good to firm going: refused to enter stall twice in July: raced freely/dropped away tamely fifth start. *G. A. Butler*

BEAUCHAMP RIBBON   2 b.f. (Apr 20) Vettori (IRE) 119 – Beauchamp Kate 61   **– p**
(Petoski 135) [2002 6s 6d p5g⁶ Nov 13] smallish, sturdy filly: third foal: dam, disappointing maiden, half-sister to useful middle-distance stayer Beauchamp Jade out of half-sister to very smart 1½m winner Beauchamp Hero: signs of ability in maidens: should stay at least 1¼m: very slowly away second start: capable of better yet. *G. A. Butler*

BEAUCHAMP ROSE   2 ch.f. (Feb 19) Pharly (FR) 130 – Beauchamp Cactus 86   **– p**
(Niniski (USA) 125) [2002 6s f6s p5g⁶ Nov 13] seventh foal: half-sister to a 1m winner in Italy by Northern Park: dam, 17.6f winner at 4 yrs, half-sister to very smart 1½m winner Beauchamp Hero: clear signs of ability when mid-division in maidens, not at all knocked about each time (Swedish rider referred to Portman Square after admitting losing her nerve and being unable to ride to the best of her ability second start, when filly also played up in stall/slowly away): likely to be suited by 1¼m+: remains capable of better. *G. A. Butler*

BEAUDACIOUS (IRE)   3 b.g. Indian Ridge 123 – Marwell 133 (Habitat 134) [2002   **–**
58: 7.9g 12.1g May 21] leggy, quite good-topped gelding: modest maiden at 2 yrs: well held in handicaps in 2002. *N. Tinkler*

BEAU ROBERTO   8 b.g. Robellino (USA) 127 – Night Jar 102 (Night Shift (USA))   **30 +**
[2002 –: 14g 12.1d 12.1m 16.1d 16m 12s Nov 6] small, strong gelding: shows knee action: poor handicapper nowadays: tried blinkered earlier in career. *J. S. Goldie*

BEAU SAUVAGE   4 b.g. Wolfhound (USA) 126 – Maestrale (Top Ville 129) [2002   **54**
58: 8f⁶ 8m 8f⁵ 8d 7g 7.1d² 8m 7.5d 9.9g⁵ 8.5g⁵ 8m* f8g⁴ Nov 25] lengthy gelding: modest handicapper: won selling event at Pontefract in September: stays 1m: acts on firm going, good to soft and fibresand: sometimes blinkered: sometimes slowly away: often races prominently: none too reliable. *M. W. Easterby*

BEAUSEJOUR (USA)   4 ch.f. Diesis 133 – Libeccio (NZ) (Danzatore (CAN) 120)   **42**
[2002 54, a58: p8g 11.6g⁵ 11.7g 11.9m 10d 11.6s 8.5d⁵ 9.7d² 10.2f 8.1g 8.5m³ f9.4g Dec 16] rather sparely-made filly: has a fluent, round action: poor maiden: stays 11.6f: acts on fibresand, good to firm and good to soft going: tried visored/tongue tied. *B. G. Powell*

BEAUTEOUS (IRE)   3 ch.g. Tagula (IRE) 116 – Beauty Appeal (USA) (Shadeed   **66 d**
(USA) 135) [2002 72: 6f 6g 7f⁵ 7.9g³ 8.5g⁴ 9m 7m 6.9g f7g f7g Dec 17] tall, quite good-topped gelding: fair handicapper: well below form last 4 starts: stays 1m: acts on firm ground: often makes running. *A. Berry*

BEAUTIFULBALLERINA (USA)   2 b.f. (Jan 14) Nureyev (USA) 131 – Khulasah   **64 p**
(USA) (Affirmed (USA)) [2002 6f³ Sep 26] IR 500,000Y: first foal: dam, US 9f winner,

from family of high-class US Grade 1 9f/9.5f winner Flawlessly and 6-y-o Zindabad: 11/10 on but very green, 5 lengths third of 4 to Sharpbill in minor event at Goodwood, soon recovering from slow start but no extra from over 1f out: almost certainly capable of fair bit better. *J. Noseda*

BEAUTIFULTOMMORROW   3 ch.f. Pursuit of Love 124 – Bella Domani (Cadeaux Genereux 131) [2002 52: 8m 10m Aug 31] small, strong, angular filly: well beaten both starts in 2002 (reportedly had breathing problem on reappearance): tried visored. *K. R. Burke* —

BEAU TUDOR (IRE)   8 b.g. Aragon 118 – Sunley Silks 80 (Formidable (USA) 125) [2002 –: 6d Oct 18] workmanlike gelding: little form. *Miss L. C. Siddall* —

BEAUTY (IRE)   4 b.f. Alzao (USA) 117 – Kaguyahime (Distant Relative 128) [2002 74?: f12g³ f12g³ Feb 25] 72,000Y: second foal: sister to fairly useful 2-y-o 5f winner Marcus Aurelius: dam, French 9f winner, half-sister to high-class 1m/1¼m performer Bijou d'Inde: unraced at 2 yrs: fairly useful form for C. O'Brien in Ireland at 3 yrs: poor form both starts in 2002: stays 1¼m: blinkered (below form) final 3-y-o outing. *C. G. Cox* 47

BEAUVRAI   2 b.g. (Jan 31) Bahamian Bounty 116 – Lets Be Fair 94 (Efisio 120) [2002 6m f5g* p5g* Dec 11] 27,000Y: first foal: dam 2-y-o 5f winner: trained by R. Beckett on debut (off over 5 months after), then fairly useful form when easy winner of maiden at Wolverhampton and minor event at Lingfield (beat Dusty Dazzler by ½ length, quickened to front over 1f out and not extended), both in December: will prove best at 5f/easy 6f: acts on all-weather: open to further progress. *J. J. Quinn* 93 p

BE BUSY   2 b.f. (Apr 2) Rudimentary (USA) 118 – Heights of Love 51 (Persian Heights 129) [2002 5d p5g⁶ 6m Aug 9] 2,500Y: third foal: dam, headstrong maiden, best effort at 5f at 2 yrs: modest form when sixth of 9 in maiden at Lingfield: should stay at least 6f: acts on polytrack, well held on turf: slowly away first 2 outings. *Miss B. Sanders* 53

BECKON   6 ch.m. Beveled (USA) – Carolynchristensen 58 (Sweet Revenge 129) [2002 50: p10g² p10g* p10g p10g 11.9g 8g³ 9.7m p10g* 11.9m⁴ p10g 10m 10m p10g⁵ f8g f14.8g Dec 2] leggy, lengthy mare: modest handicapper on all-weather, poor on turf: won at Lingfield in January: left B. Johnson 2,200 gns after thirteenth start: stays easy 1½m: acts on polytrack, best turf form on going firmer than good: tried visored: sometimes slowly away/carries head high/hangs right. *R. Wilman* 44 a60

BEDAZZLED   2 b.f. (Mar 3) Wolfhound (USA) 126 – Glowing Jade 75 (Kalaglow 132) [2002 6m² 6.1m⁴ 5m⁴ 6.1m Sep 20] second foal: dam, 7f/1m winner, half-sister to smart performers Just A Flutter (in Britain/Germany at 1m) and Slicious (in Italy, up to 1½m): modest maiden: should stay 7f: raced only on good to firm ground. *A. G. Glover* 61

BED OF SILK (IRE)   2 b.f. (Feb 25) Marju (IRE) 127 – Hebony 75 (Sabrehill (USA) 120) [2002 7.5g⁵ 6m⁶ Oct 2] small, workmanlike filly: first foal: dam, 7f winner, half-sister to useful performers Helicon (2-y-o 1m winner) and Darrouzett (Irish 9f/1¼m winner) out of half-sister to top-class US middle-distance performer Creme Fraiche: better effort in maidens (modest form) when fifth at Beverley, fading: should stay 1m. *J. J. Quinn* 57

BEECHES STAR (IRE)   2 b.f. (Mar 22) Lake Coniston (IRE) 131 – Eleonora d'Arborea 78 (Prince Sabo 123) [2002 6m 6.1m² 6.1m p7g f6s p6g Dec 28] 1,000Y: lengthy filly: second foal: half-sister to 3-y-o Leonora Truce: dam 6f winner, ran only at 2 yrs: modest maiden: stays 6f: well held on all-weather: blinkered final start. *R. Brotherton* 60 a–

BEECHY BANK (IRE)   4 b.f. Shareef Dancer (USA) 135 – Neptunalia 70 (Slip Anchor 136) [2002 38: f9.4g 12.6m* Sep 21] modest performer: left R. Phillips, off 8 months and 200/1, won falsely-run minor event at Warwick in September, getting first run: stays 12.6f: tried blinkered. *Mrs Mary Hambro* 57

BEE HEALTH BOY   9 b.g. Superpower 113 – Rekindle 70 (Relkino 131) [2002 8.5m² 7g⁸ 8d 6v² 5.9d 8m² 9.2g⁴ 8g² 7.2d⁴ 8g 8.5d³ 8g Aug 26] good-topped gelding: modest performer: missed 2000 and 2001: won apprentice claimer at Newcastle in May: stays 8.5f: ideally suited by good ground or softer (acts on heavy): effective blinkered or not: has run well when sweating: usually races prominently. *R. A. Fahey* 55

BEE J GEE   4 b.g. Dilum (USA) 115 – Sound Check 62 (Formidable (USA) 125) [2002 –: f9.4g 10f May 17] maiden handicapper: no form since 2 yrs. *Mrs Lydia Pearce* —

BEEKEEPER   4 b.c. Rainbow Quest (USA) 134 – Chief Bee 89 (Chief's Crown (USA)) [2002 116: 16.4m 10.3m* 12g⁶ 16f³ Nov 5] tall, close-coupled, attractive colt: fluent mover: smart performer: folded tamely on reappearance, then off over 3 months: won minor event at Doncaster in September by 4 lengths from Vintage Premium: creditable efforts in Australia last 2 outings, 1¾ lengths sixth to Northerly in Caulfield 117

Cup at Caulfield and 2¼ lengths third to Media Puzzle in Melbourne Cup at Flemington: stays 2m: acts on firm going: has been tongue tied. *Saeed bin Suroor*

BEENABOUTABIT 4 b.f. Komaite (USA) – Tassagh Bridge (IRE) (Double Schwartz 128) [2002 61: 6m³ 6m 8.5d 7d Oct 15] angular filly: modest maiden handicapper: stays 6f: acts on good to firm ground: tried visored: sometimes tongue tied. *R. Ingram*   **51**

BEE ONE (IRE) 4 b.f. Catrail (USA) 123 – Ruwy 77 (Soviet Star (USA) 128) [2002 5g 6m² 6d⁵ 6m⁴ 8.1g 7m³ 7s p6g Nov 14] strong, useful-looking filly: fairly useful maiden: below form after second start: best form at 6f: raced mainly on good/good to firm ground on turf: often slowly away (refused to race fifth/final starts): one to avoid. *D. R. C. Elsworth*   **81 §**

BEER AND DONUTS (USA) 3 b.g. Carson City (USA) – Danzig's Bride (USA) (Danzig (USA)) [2002 5m Jun 1] $60,000Y: seventh foal: closely related to a winner in USA by Crafty Prospector and half-brother to 2 winners there: dam, winner in USA, half-sister to US Grade 3 9f winner Arctic Honeymoon: weak 7/1, slowly away and soon tailed off in maiden at Musselburgh: sold 1,000 gns. *M. Johnston*   **–**

BEERSHEBA 2 b.f. (May 4) Thowra (FR) – Hymn Book (IRE) 65 (Darshaan 133) [2002 6d p8g Dec 14] fourth living foal: half-sister to 2 winners, including 3-y-o Litany: dam maiden who should have stayed 15f: well held in minor event at Windsor and maiden at Lingfield 7 months apart. *B. R. Johnson*   **–**

BEETLE BUG 2 br.f. (Feb 11) Robellino (USA) 127 – Special Beat 65 (Bustino 136) [2002 8.3d Oct 28] 12,000Y: second foal: half-sister to 3-y-o Samba Beat: dam, 17f winner (also successful over hurdles), half-sister to useful 7f winner Cragganmore: 33/1, seventh of 12 in maiden at Windsor, fading: should do better. *J. G. Portman*   **– p**

BEFRIEND (USA) 2 ch.f. (Feb 20) Allied Forces (USA) 123 – Approcheer (USA) (With Approval (CAN)) [2002 6g* 6f³ Jul 15] $3,700F, $23,000Y resold, 46,000Y: second foal: dam unraced half-sister to 2 stakes winners in Canada: won maiden at Catterick in July by short head: better effort (fair form) when third of 4 to Elidore in minor event at Windsor, not knocked about once fading: will need to settle better to stay beyond 6f: sent to UAE. *M. R. Channon*   **76**

BEGLI STRUMENTI 3 ch.g. Piccolo 121 – Bella Helena (Balidar 133) [2002 8.1m Jul 25] 8,000Y: fourth foal: half-brother to fairly useful 5f (including at 2 yrs) winner Bevelena (by Beveled): dam, Italian sprint winner (tailed off only start in Britain), out of half-sister to useful 5f performer Up And At 'em: too green to do himself justice when eighth of 9 in maiden at Sandown. *J. R. Best*   **–**

BEHAN 3 ch.g. Rainbows For Life (CAN) – With Finesse (Be My Guest (USA) 126) [2002 58: f7s* f7g⁴ f8g f7g 7d² 7m⁴ 8g² 8d⁴ 7f² 7f⁴ 8m⁴ 7.9g⁴ 7f⁶ 8.5m³ 7m³ 6.9g⁶ 7m 8.1m Sep 6] smallish, sturdy gelding: modest performer: won seller at Southwell (left D. Cosgrove) in January: trained by D. Barker next 2 starts: stays 8.5f: acts on fibresand, firm and good to soft ground: blinkered. *G. M. Moore*   **59**

BEHRA (IRE) 3 b.f. Grand Lodge (USA) 125 – Behera 129 (Mill Reef (USA) 141) [2002 10d³ 12f² 10s* 10.5v³ Nov 26] strong, lengthy filly: half-sister to French 1½m and 13.5f winner Beharistan (by Rainbow Quest) and useful French stayer Bayrika (by Kahyasi): dam, won Prix Saint-Alary and second in Prix de l'Arc de Triomphe, would have stayed beyond 1½m: useful form: won maiden at Newbury in October by 2½ lengths from Saint Alebe: plenty of improvement when keeping-on 3 lengths third to Place Rouge in listed race at Saint-Cloud month later: bred to stay at least 1½m: acts on heavy going. *Sir Michael Stoute*   **101**

BEL 4 b.f. Darshaan 133 – Jezebel Monroe (USA) 98 (Lyphard (USA) 132) [2002 83p: 11.9m 11.7g 14.4m⁶ May 6] fairly useful handicapper, lightly raced: stays 1½m: yet to race on extremes of going: tended to hang on reappearance. *R. Charlton*   **80**

B'ELANNA TORRES 3 b.f. Entrepreneur 123 – Miss Kemble (Warning 136) [2002 66: 8.3m 8.1m p12g 11.9m Sep 3] sturdy, angular filly: no form in 2002: pulled up and dismounted penultimate start: should be suited by 1m+. *W. R. Muir*   **–**

BELIEVE 2 b.f. (Mar 17) Winged Love (IRE) 121 – Bright Future (FR) (Akarad (FR) 130) [2002 6.1g 6s Oct 28] second foal: half-sister to 4-y-o Blue Baloo: dam once-raced half-sister to useful French 1m and 10.5f winner Blue Sky: last in maidens. *J. Neville*   **–**

BELINDA 5 ch.m. Mizoram (USA) 105 – Mountain Dew (Pharly (FR) 130) [2002 53, a63: f14.8g³ f12g⁶ f12g⁶ f12g⁶ p10g⁶ f14.8g⁴ 11.8d f12²g³ Jun 19] modest handicapper at best: below form last 2 starts: stays 14.8f: acts on firm going and fibresand, probably on polytrack: tends to carry head awkwardly (reportedly blind in one eye). *K. Bell*   **a58 d**

BELIZE IT OR NOT 2 b.f. (Feb 29) Abou Zouz (USA) 109 – Rehaab 72 (Mtoto   –
134) [2002 5g Jul 18] 2,400Y, 1,600 2-y-o: first foal: dam 1¼m/1½m winner: 50/1, tailed
off in seller at Leicester. *A. G. Juckes*

BELLA BEGUINE 3 b.f. Komaite (USA) – On The Record 72 (Record Token 128)   **67**
[2002 –: 7f⁶ 7.1s³ 6.9s 7d² 7.1m⁵ 6g² 6m³ 6d³ f7f f6g* f7g² f6g⁶ Dec 16] workmanlike   **a71**
filly: fair performer: won maiden at Southwell in November: effective at 6f/7f: acts on
soft going, good to firm and fibresand: sometimes races freely. *A. Bailey*

BELLA BIANCA (IRE) 2 b.f. (Jan 18) Barathea (IRE) 127 – Alarme Belle 105   **78**
(Warning 136) [2002 6d⁵ 6f* 6d³ 6d⁶ Aug 3] lengthy, useful-looking filly: has a quick
action: first foal: dam, Irish 6f winner, half-sister to useful performer up to 1¼m Bound
For Pleasure (by Barathea): fair performer: won maiden at Pontefract in June: hung
markedly right when creditable third in minor event at Haydock: should stay 7f: acts on
firm and good to soft ground. *R. Hannon*

BELLA CASTANA 2 ch.f. (Apr 29) Efisio 120 – Simple Logic 73 (Aragon 118) [2002   –
6m 6f Sep 8] tall, leggy filly: second foal: dam 2-y-o 6f winner: slowly away and well
held in maidens. *A. Charlton*

BELLA CHICA (IRE) 3 b.f. Bigstone (IRE) 126 – Just Like Annie (IRE) 65 (Mujadil   **95 d**
(USA) 119) [2002 94: 8m 6m 6d 6m³ 6m 6.1m³ 5m 6.1f² 5f 6f² f6g p7g f6g Dec 16]
leggy, plain filly: good mover: useful performer at best: left J. Glover after tenth start:
best at 5f/6f: acts on firm going: tried in blinkers/cheekpieces (well below form) on
all-weather: seemed unsuited by track at Epsom once at 2 yrs: often races freely/has
looked none too keen: on downgrade. *I. Semple*

BELLA FREGATA 3 ch.f. Dancing Spree (USA) – Bella Bambola (IRE) 42 (Tate   –
Gallery (USA) 117) [2002 49: 9.9m Apr 25] quite good-topped filly: poor maiden.
J. S. Wainwright

BELLA PAVLINA 4 ch.f. Sure Blade (USA) 130 – Pab's Choice 61 (Telsmoss 91)   **48**
[2002 47: f9.4g⁶ f8.5g 11.6g 10d 11.9g 8g 9.7m⁵ 9.7d⁵ 10.2f⁴ 12.1g 10.1m³ 9.9g⁴ 11.8s⁵
Oct 15] poor maiden: claimed £8,000 final start: stays 1½m: acts on fibresand, soft and
firm going. *M. Blanshard*

BELLA PUPA 6 ch.m. Theatrical Charmer 114 – Louisa Anne 73 (Mummy's Pet 125)   –
[2002 –: 9.9g May 11] workmanlike mare: of no account. *N. M. Babbage*

BELLAS GATE BOY 10 b.g. Doulab (USA) 115 – Celestial Air 96 (Rheingold 137)   **– §**
[2002 –§: p12g Aug 29] leggy gelding: temperamental handicapper. *Mrs Lydia Pearce*

BELLA TUSA (IRE) 2 b.f. (Mar 31) Sri Pekan (USA) 117 – Coolrain Lady (IRE) 74   **101 +**
(Common Grounds 118) [2002 5d⁵ 5s² 6g* 5d* 5g* 6f⁶ 6s³ Oct 28] IR 20,000F, 31,000Y:
good-bodied filly: half-sister to 3 winners, including smart sprinter (1998 2-y-o
5f winner) Light The Rocket (by Pips Pride) and useful 2000 2-y-o 1m winner La Vita E
Bella (by Definite Article): dam placed at 1m/1¼m in Ireland: useful performer: won
maiden at Goodwood in June and listed events at Sandown in July and Ayr (beat
Membership by 1½ lengths) in September: respectable third of 5 to Zinziberine in
Criterium de Maisons-Laffitte: will prove best at 5f/6f: acts on soft going, looked ill at
ease on firm in Cheveley Park Stakes at Newmarket penultimate start: edgy and had 2
handlers at Sandown: sold 200,000 gns. *C. F. Wall*

BELL BOTTOM BLUES 2 b.f. (Apr 29) Whittingham (IRE) 104 – Bella Coola 50   **59**
(Northern State (USA) 91) [2002 6g⁵ f6g Nov 18] third foal: half-sister to 4-y-o Cosmocrat: dam, maiden sprinter, half-sister to smart sprinter Emma Peel: better effort when
close fifth to Baytown Flyer in claimer at Lingfield, showing good speed: left impression
something amiss 6 weeks later. *C. G. Cox*

BELLE BLEU 2 b.f. (Mar 22) Bluegrass Prince (IRE) 110 – Hello Lady (Wolverlife   –
115) [2002 6s Oct 28] leggy filly: third foal: dam maiden hurdler: 100/1, well beaten in
maiden at Leicester. *M. R. Bosley*

BELLE D'ANJOU (FR) 5 b.m. Saint Cyrien (FR) 128 – Epsibelle (IRE) (Darshaan   –
133) [2002 82: 12g Sep 27] small, leggy mare: fairly useful handicapper at best: well held
only 5-y-o Flat start. *P. J. Hobbs*

BELLE DE HAARTH 2 b.f. Alhaarth (IRE) 126 – Belle Ile (USA) 67 (Diesis 133)   **60**
[2002 8m 8.3m 8d 8.1m 10m Oct 1] IR 12,000Y, 8,500 2-y-o: smallish filly: fourth foal:
half-sister to French 10.5f winner Enchanted Isle (by Mujtahid): dam, 1m winner, out of
smart performer up to 1¾m Bonne Ile: modest maiden: should be suited by 1¼m/1½m.
R. Charlton

BELLE OF THE MANOR (IRE) 4 b.f. Bluebird (USA) 125 – Pharsala (FR) **77**
(Hello Gorgeous (USA) 128) [2002 73, a65: p12g⁶ p12g⁵ p7g* p10g* p12g⁵ Feb 6] quite
attractive filly: fair handicapper: won at Lingfield in January/February: probably best at
7f to 1¼m: acts on polytrack, good to firm and good to soft ground: tried blinkered,
visored last 3 starts: sold 41,000 gns later in February. *G. A. Butler*

BELLE ROUGE 4 b.f. Celtic Swing 138 – Gunner's Belle 69 (Gunner B 126) [2002 **64**
56: f16.2g* 13.3s² 14.1d⁵ f12g* 12d⁴ 11.6m f16.2f⁵ 16g⁶ f14s⁶ f14.8g p16g² 16v² Oct 29] **a71**
workmanlike filly: fair handicapper: won at Wolverhampton in May and Southwell in
June: suited by good test at 1½m and stays 2m: acts on good to firm going, heavy and
all-weather: waited in front. *M. Blanshard*

BELLESOEUR 2 ch.f. (Apr 16) Whittingham (IRE) 104 – Trina's Pet 65 (Efisio 120) **–**
[2002 f5g Apr 15] 2,000Y: first foal: dam 2-y-o 5f winner: 25/1, last in maiden at Southwell. *J. Balding*

BELLINO EMPRESARIO (IRE) 4 b.g. Robellino (USA) 127 – The Last Empress **57**
(IRE) 73 (Last Tycoon 131) [2002 29, a49: f11s f11s³ f12g³ 11.9g 10d 10d* 10m 10m*
Aug 28] modest handicapper: won seller in June and amateur handicap in August, both
at Brighton: stays 11f: acts on fibresand, good to firm and good to soft going: tried
blinkered/visored/tongue tied: often races prominently: sold 4,800 gns. *I. A. Wood*

BELL ROCK 4 ch.g. Charmer 123 – Sule Skerry 78 (Scottish Rifle 127) [2002 8.2d **–**
Mar 27] quite good-topped gelding: half-brother to several winners, including around
1¼m Zidac (by Statoblest): dam 1½m winner: well held in maiden at Nottingham, pulling
hard early. *Miss E. C. Lavelle*

BELLS BEACH (IRE) 4 ch.f. General Monash (USA) 107 – Clifton Beach (Auction **60**
Ring (USA) 123) [2002 60: f6g 5.7g⁵ f6g 5m² 5m 5.7g 5.1m² 5d⁶ 5m⁴ 5m 5.7f⁶ f7g Sep **a–**
30] strong, close-coupled filly: modest handicapper: raced mainly at 5f/6f: acts on good
to firm going, good to soft and fibresand: sometimes slowly away. *A. G. Newcombe*

BELLS BOY'S 3 b.g. Mind Games 121 – Millie's Lady (IRE) (Common Grounds **56**
118) [2002 56: f5g 5m³ 5d 5f² 6g² 5m 5m 5g f5g f5g Dec 27] workmanlike gelding:
modest maiden: barely stays 6f: acts on firm ground: often races prominently. *A. Dickman*

BELTANE 4 b.c. Magic Ring (IRE) 115 – Sally's Trust (IRE) 51 (Classic Secret (USA) **–**
91) [2002 42: 8m Oct 5] probably of little account nowadays. *W. de Best-Turner*

BELUGA BAY 3 b.g. Millkom 124 – Bellyphax (Bellypha 130) [2002 69p: 8.2d⁴ 7d* **86**
Jun 14] sturdy gelding: unimpressive mover: fair form: has won 2 of his 3 starts,
including minor event at Goodwood in June: suffered minor fracture after: should stay
1m: raced only on good to soft/soft going. *J. R. Fanshawe*

BE MY BUDDY 3 b.g. Be My Chief (USA) 122 – Trull (Lomond (USA) 128) [2002 **–**
53: 11.6s⁶ 14d 16.2g⁶ 11.5m Sep 17] useful-looking gelding: maiden: little form in 2002:
blinkered last 3 starts. *Lady Herries*

BE MY TINKER 4 ch.f. Be My Chief (USA) 122 – Tinkerbird 76 (Music Boy 124) **75**
[2002 54d: 5.5f* 5g² 5m² 5m² p5g² 5m* 5.1m* 6m 6m⁴ 6.1m² 5m⁵ f6g* Nov 25] lengthy
filly: fair handicapper: won at Warwick, Folkestone, Bath and Southwell in 2002: best at
5f/6f: acts on all-weather and firm going: blinkered once as 3-y-o: usually races
prominently. *M. A. Buckley*

BENBYAS 5 b.g. Rambo Dancer (CAN) 107 – Light The Way 72 (Nicholas Bill 125) **–**
[2002 78, a–: 10.3m May 6] sturdy, lengthy gelding: fair performer at best: well held only
5-y-o start on Flat: sometimes visored/blinkered: useful hurdler. *J. L. Eyre*

BEN EAGLE (IRE) 3 ch.g. Eagle Eyed (USA) 111 – Checkers (Habat 127) [2002 56: **–**
7m 5g 8g 9f 7f Sep 26] modest maiden at 2 yrs: no form in 2002, leaving B. R. Millman
after reappearance. *P. J. Flynn, Ireland*

BENEFACTOR (IRE) 2 b.c. (Apr 15) Hector Protector (USA) 124 – Beneficiary 69 **–**
(Jalmood (USA) 126) [2002 p7g Oct 9] 12,500F: fifth foal: half-brother to a winner
abroad by Lahib: dam, 6f and (including at 2 yrs) 7f winner, half-sister to very smart 7f/
1m performer Decorated Hero: 25/1, slowly away and always behind in maiden at
Lingfield: sold 7,000 gns. *R. F. Johnson Houghton*

BENEKING 2 b. or br.g. (Apr 4) Wizard King 122 – Gagajulu 75 (Al Hareb (USA) **73**
123) [2002 6g 6g² 6g f6g⁵ 6.1g² 7m³ 7.1g³ 7.1g³ 8.3d Oct 14] rather leggy gelding: third
foal: dam 2-y-o 5f winner: fair maiden: placed 5 times, including in 2 nurseries: stays 7f:
acts on good to firm going. *J. Gallagher*

BEN EWAR 8 b.g. Old Vic 136 – Sunset Reef (Mill Reef (USA) 141) [2002 108d: – p12g 12d⁵ Aug 3] useful performer at best: ran as if something amiss both 8-y-o starts: often breaks blood vessels. *K. O. Cunningham-Brown*

BEN HUR 3 b.g. Zafonic (USA) 130 – Gayane 125 (Nureyev (USA) 131) [2002 10.5d **65** 8.1s³ 7.2d⁴ 10.3f⁴ 8.5m³ 10g 8.1m⁴ Sep 6] 4,000 2-y-o: lengthy gelding: half-brother to 3 winners, including useful 1m winner Maramba (by Rainbow Quest) and fairly useful 6f winner Duel At Dawn (by Nashwan): dam, 6f/7f winner, half-sister to Sun Chariot winner Ristna from family of Oh So Sharp: fair maiden: free-going type, likely to prove best at 7f/1m: acts on soft going, probably on firm: has been early to post: troublesome at stall last 2 starts (slowly away final one). *W. M. Brisbourne*

BENJAMBO 4 b.g. Primo Dominie 121 – Young Lady (Young Generation 129) [2002 – –: p12g p10g Nov 19] workmanlike gelding: well held in 3 maidens. *R. M. Flower*

BENJAMIN (IRE) 4 b.g. Night Shift (USA) – Best Academy (USA) (Roberto (USA) – 131) [2002 p10g 8.3g 10d 8.1g Jul 5] little form. *P. Mitchell*

BEN KENOBI 4 ch.g. Accondy (IRE) 79 – Nour El Sahar (USA) (Sagace (FR) 135) – [2002 –: 8.1d 12.6m⁵ 10.9m 10.2g 12m Sep 13] well-made gelding: little form. *Mrs P. Ford*

BEN LOMAND 2 ch.c. (Mar 23) Inchinor 119 – Benjarong 50 (Sharpo 132) [2002 6s **82** 6d² Nov 1] 12,500Y, 12,000 2-y-o: good-bodied colt: second foal: dam 5f (at 2 yrs) and 1m winner: 50/1, much better effort in maidens (fairly useful form) when 3½ lengths second of 17 to Tante Rose at Newmarket, staying on: should stay 1m. *B. W. Duke*

BENNY THE VICE (USA) 3 ch.g. Benny The Dip (USA) 127 – Vice On Ice (USA) **71 d** (Vice Regent (CAN)) [2002 72: f9.4g² f9.4g² f8g² f12g* f11g f8.5g Dec 14] tall, rangy gelding: fair performer: won maiden at Wolverhampton (raced freely, final start for M. Johnston) in February: off over 9 months after: may prove best at 1¼m/1½m: acts on fibresand and heavy going, probably on good to firm: blinkered/visored last 3 starts: tends to carry head high. *Mrs A. Duffield*

BERGAMO 6 b.g. Robellino (USA) 127 – Pretty Thing 83 (Star Appeal 133) [2002 **41** 60, a–: 12.3m 12g 15.8f 12m 15.8f Sep 21] small, compact gelding: fluent mover: poor **a–** handicapper nowadays: stays easy 2m: acts on firm and soft going: usually blinkered/ visored: sometimes looks less than keen. *B. Ellison*

BERGEN (IRE) 7 b.g. Ballad Rock 122 – Local Custom (IRE) (Be My Native (USA) **44** 122) [2002 62: f6s p6g f6g 7d 6g 5.9d 6f Jul 17] quite good-topped gelding: poor nowadays: barely stays 8.5f: acts on fibresand, firm and good to soft going: tried visored: usually tongue tied. *D. Nicholls*

BERGERAC (IRE) 3 b.g. Lake Coniston (IRE) 131 – Regina St Cyr (IRE) (Doulab – (USA) 115) [2002 5.7g 6s p10g Jun 29] IR 1,800F, IR 1,300Y, 5,500 2-y-o, resold 2,600 2-y-o: sixth foal: half-brother to 3 winners, including fairly useful 8.5f to 2m winner Cyrian (by Persian Bold) and 1¼m winner Jalons Star (by Eagle Eyed): dam, Irish 9f winner, half-sister to very smart sprinter Cyrano de Bergerac: no show in claimer/ maidens. *S. Dow*

BERGERAC PIE 3 b.f. Cyrano de Bergerac 120 – Foxtrot Pie 77 (Shernazar 131) **67** [2002 9.9g 8m² 10m⁴ 10g 8.2s Oct 23] smallish filly: third foal: half-sister to 1999 2-y-o 6f/7f winner Dispol Jazz and 4-y-o Dispol Foxtrot (both by Alhijaz): dam, maiden, should have been suited by 1½m+: fair maiden: seems to stay 1¼m: acts on good to firm ground. *R. Hollinshead*

BERKELEY HALL 5 b.m. Saddlers' Hall (IRE) 126 – Serious Affair (Valiyar 129) **59** [2002 56, a–: 6m 5.7g³ 5.7g⁴ 6.1m⁵ 6d³ 6g 6m⁶ 6.1m Sep 20] stocky mare: modest **a–** handicapper: barely stays 7f: acts on firm and good to soft going: usually blinkered. *B. Palling*

BERKELEY HEIGHTS 2 b.f. (Feb 14) Hector Protector (USA) 124 – Dancing **73** Heights (IRE) 80 (High Estate 127) [2002 8g 8.3d⁴ 8v Nov 8] 15,000F, 20,000Y: fourth foal: half-sister to 3 winners, including useful 7f (at 2 yrs) to 9f winner (including in UAE) Bathwick (by Midyan) and 5-y-o Last Symphony: dam, 1¼m winner, sister to smart 1½m performer High Baroque: form in maidens only when 2½ lengths fourth to Desert View at Windsor: will stay at least 1¼m: very slowly away on debut, soon off bridle both starts after. *B. Smart*

BERNICE 2 b.f. (Apr 29) Young Ern 120 – Kalao Tua (IRE) 66 (Shaadi (USA) 126) **42** [2002 5g 5g 5m 5f f5g Apr 29] 2,000Y: lengthy filly: poor mover: first foal: dam, second at 6f at 2 yrs: poor maiden. *M. W. Easterby*

BERNINI (IRE)   2 b.c. (Mar 20) Grand Lodge (USA) 125 – Alsahah (IRE) (Unfuwain   –
(USA) 131) [2002 8.2v Oct 29] IR 52,000Y: second foal: half-brother to 4-y-o Esher
Common: dam once-raced close relative to smart 1¼m to 13f winner Burooj: 14/1, well
beaten in maiden at Nottingham. *M. L. W. Bell*

BERTIE BUCKS   2 br.g. (Apr 17) Charmer 123 – Dolly Mixture (Midyan (USA) 124)   –
[2002 8d Oct 18] first foal: dam unraced: 50/1, slowly away when 5 lengths eighth of 13
to Sir Haydn in maiden at Redcar. *J. Hetherton*

BESTAM   3 b.c. Selkirk (USA) 129 – Showery 76 (Rainbow Quest (USA) 134) [2002   **105**
103p: 8g* 8d² 8g 9s Oct 26] rather leggy, unfurnished colt: useful performer, lightly
raced: won 4-runner minor event at Thirsk (beat Anna Walhaan by length) in May: good
3 lengths second to Seihali in similar race at Salisbury next start: off 3½ months, well
held in handicaps last 2: stays 1m: acts on good to soft going: sent to UAE. *J. L. Dunlop*

BEST BOND   5 ch.g. Cadeaux Genereux 131 – My Darlingdaughter (Night Shift   **52 +**
(USA)) [2002 58: p7g p6g p6g⁵ p6g 6.1m p6g³ p6g 6m⁶ 7m⁵ 5.9s³ Jul 31] lengthy
gelding: modest performer: best at 6f/7f: acts on all-weather, soft and good to firm going:
blinkered once, usually visored (not last 2 starts): sometimes slowly away: doesn't look
easy ride. *N. P. Littmoden*

BEST EVER   5 ch.g. Rock City 120 – Better Still (IRE) (Glenstal (USA) 118) [2002   **49**
52, a–: f8.5g⁵ f11s⁴ f9.4g Jan 25] compact, workmanlike gelding: poor maiden handicapper: stays 11f: acts on firm, good to soft going and fibresand. *M. W. Easterby*

BEST LEAD   3 b.g. Distant Relative 128 – Bestemor 60 (Selkirk (USA) 129) [2002 89:   –
f5g Nov 20] leggy gelding: fairly useful at 2 yrs: well held only 3-y-o start. *Ian Emmerson*

BEST OF THE BESTS (IRE)   5 ch.h. Machiavellian (USA) 123 – Sueboog (IRE)   **122**
109 (Darshaan 133) [2002 122: a9f* a10f 9.3m* 8g 8g³ 10m³ 8g⁵ Sep 28]
He might never have been the 'best of the bests', nor at any stage of his
career shown a level of form worthy of earning the tag 'top class'. However, in four
years on the racecourse the usually reliable Best of The Bests often proved a good
yardstick to the form of some of the best races. The now-retired Best of The Bests
gained his first Group 1 success in the Prix d'Ispahan in May. In seven previous
attempts at the highest level he had managed no better than third but connections
found a good opportunity for him at Longchamp. The Prix d'Ispahan attracted only
four runners, though Best of The Bests still had to overcome the previous season's
top three-year-old filly Banks Hill. He caught her at the best time—short of peak
fitness on her reappearance. Starting third favourite behind the odds-on Banks Hill
and Prix d'Harcourt winner Execute, Best of The Bests was able to dictate matters
and responded well when pressed in the straight to win by half a length, the outsider
Poussin coming closest to denying him. Banks Hill was a length back in third, not
given too hard a race once unable to make any impression. This was Best of The
Bests' fourth pattern-race win, following those in the Solario Stakes at Sandown as
a two-year-old, the Prix Guillaume d'Ornano at Deauville the following year and,
on his reappearance in the latest season, the Sheikh Maktoum Bin Rashid Al
Maktoum Challenge (Round II) at Nad Al Sheba (raised to Group 3 status since his
victory in the same race the previous year).
A second consecutive disappointing run in the Dubai World Cup preceded
Longchamp, and Best of The Bests failed to enhance further Godolphin's excellent
record in the Queen Anne Stakes at Royal Ascot, his Group 1 penalty leaving him
with plenty on conceding weight all round. Best of The Bests found Banks Hill a
different proposition when they met in the Prix Jacques le Marois at Deauville in
August, running to form in finishing three lengths third to the filly, again dictating
the pace. In what was his busiest season to date, Best of The Bests had another two
attempts in Group 1 company, finishing third, beaten a short head and a neck by
Grandera and Hawk Wing, on the first of them in the Irish Champion Stakes, a race
in which he had filled the same place behind Giant's Causeway in the 2000 renewal.
Best of The Bests' racing career ended on a disappointing note when he folded
tamely to finish last of five in the Queen Elizabeth II Stakes at Ascot.
Best of The Bests' pedigree has been covered in two previous editions of
Racehorses. He remains by far the best foal of his dam Sueboog, a year-younger
half-sister Barateastar (by Barathea) had shown promise on both two-year-old
starts but was just a fair handicapper the following year, barely effective at a mile.

Prix d'Ispahan, Longchamp—Best of The Bests is able to dictate matters against his three opponents;
Poussin (rail) beats Banks Hill for second

Sueboog's fourth foal Sept Etoiles, a brother to Best of The Bests, made the racecourse only once in Britain, finishing well beaten in a two-year-old maiden at York for David Loder before being sent to the UAE. Sueboog's fifth foal the two-year-old Dunhill Star (by Danehill) made a winning debut at Lingfield in December. Best of The Bests will begin his career as a stallion at Dalham Hall Stud in Newmarket at a fee of £5,000 (Oct 1st special live foal).

Best of The Bests (IRE) (ch.h. 1997)	Machiavellian (USA) (b 1987)	Mr Prospector (b 1970)	Raise A Native
			Gold Digger
		Coup de Folie (b 1982)	Halo
			Raise The Standard
	Sueboog (IRE) (b 1990)	Darshaan (br 1981)	Shirley Heights
			Delsy
		Nordica (ch 1983)	Northfields
			Princess Arabella

The big, rangy Best of The Bests stayed a mile and a quarter. He never raced on heavy going but acted on any other turf going and on dirt. Bandaged behind as a three-year-old, he was usually tongue tied towards the end of his career and was inclined to get on edge and take a good hold. He was effective held up but often made the running. *Saeed bin Suroor*

BEST PORT (IRE) 6 b.g. Be My Guest (USA) 126 – Portree 82 (Slip Anchor 136) [2002 64: 16m³ 16m⁴ 16f³ 16d 16m⁴ 14.1m⁶ 16m* 14.1m⁶ 14.1d* 16s f14g Nov 25] lightly-made gelding: fair handicapper: won at Nottingham (carried head awkwardly) in September and Redcar (tended to idle) in October: best at 1¾m/2m: acts on firm going, good to soft and fibresand: usually held up: looked wayward earlier in career. *J. Parkes* **68**

BE SWIFT 3 ch.g. Millkom 124 – Conwy (Rock City 120) [2002 53: p8g 10m 12d 12m 16.4g⁴ f12g Dec 7] smallish, deep-girthed gelding: modest maiden: should stay at least 1m: looked far from keen from keen fourth start. *S. Dow* **50**

BETHANIA 4 gr.f. Mark of Esteem (IRE) 137 – Anneli Rose 56 (Superlative 118) [2002 70d: p12g p7g³ f6g Feb 19] sturdy, close-coupled filly: fluent mover: modest maiden: best efforts at 7f: acts on good to firm ground and polytrack: sold 30,000 gns: reportedly in foal to Bertolini. *Mrs A. J. Perrett* **58**

BETTER GAMBLE 3 b.g. Bluegrass Prince (IRE) 110 – Come To Good (Swing Easy (USA) 126) [2002 7m 6g 10g p8g 8m⁴ 10d f9.4f p10g Dec 30] 1,500Y: third foal: dam seemed of little account: maiden: form (modest) only on fifth start: blinkered 3 of last 4 outings: unreliable. *R. M. Flower* **50 §**
a– §

BETTER MOMENT (IRE) 5 b.g. Turtle Island (IRE) 123 – Snoozeandyoulose (IRE) 73 (Scenic 128) [2002 47: 10.2g Aug 26] small gelding: poor maiden on Flat: winning hurdler. *M. C. Pipe* **–**

BETTER OFF 4 ch.g. Bettergeton 97 – Miami Pride 48 (Miami Springs 121) [2002 –, a77: f6s f6s f6g f6g* f7g⁵ f6g³ f6g⁵ f7g² f6g³ f7g⁵ f6g⁶ f7g f7g⁶ f6g² f7g² f8g f7f² f6s⁵ f8g³ f6g⁴ f7s³ f7g² f8g² f7g f8g⁴ Dec 27] strong gelding: poor mover: fair handicapper: won at Southwell in February: best at 6f/7f: acts on fibresand (well held both starts on turf): sometimes slowly away/takes time to warm up: tough and consistent. *Mrs N. Macauley* **–**
a75

BETTER PAL   3 ch.g. Prince Sabo 123 – Rattle Along 80 (Tap On Wood 130) [2002   **78**
65: 6s⁴ 8.1d⁴ 10m⁵ 8m⁴ 9.7m 9.2m 7.5m 8.2s⁶ Oct 23] good-bodied gelding: fair maiden:
stays 1m, probably not 1¼m: acts on soft and good to firm going, reportedly lost action
on fibresand: blinkered once: sometimes slowly away/wanders: sold 4,000 gns. *W. Jarvis*

BETTY'S PRIDE   3 b.f. Lion Cavern (USA) 117 – Final Verdict (IRE) (Law Society   **89**
(USA) 130) [2002 80: 5g 5m² 5g⁴ 6f² 5m* 6d⁶ 5.1f² 5g³ 5g* 5g⁶ 6.1m 5.1f⁶ 5m² 5m³ 5f
Sep 28] leggy, quite good-topped filly: fairly useful performer: won maiden at Musselburgh in June and handicap at Thirsk in August: good second at Haydock in September:
best at 5f: acts on firm ground: sometimes takes good hold/carries head awkwardly: tough
and consistent. *A. Berry*

BETTYS VALENTINE   2 b.f. (Mar 16) My Best Valentine 122 – Fairy Ballerina   **–**
(Fairy King (USA)) [2002 7g f6s f7g Nov 26] 2,200Y: seventh foal: half-sister to 1¼m to
1¾m winner Aspirant Dancer (by Marju): dam Irish 2-y-o 7f winner: well held in
maidens. *J. R. Weymes*

BEVEL BLUE   4 b.g. Beveled (USA) – Blue Angel (Lord Gayle (USA) 124) [2002   **–**
48: 6g 7m 10.2f⁶ Jul 25] maiden: no form at 4 yrs. *G. B. Balding*

BEVELLER   3 ch.g. Beveled (USA) – Klairover 50 (Smackover 107) [2002 10.5d⁶   **–**
10m 10m 8g 7g 5.9v 8m Sep 19] 8,500Y: rangy, rather unfurnished gelding: has scope:
fifth foal: half-brother to 6f/7f winner General Klaire (by Presidium) and winner in
Scandinavia by King's Signet: dam, 5f/6f winner, half-sister to smart sprinter Bunty Boo:
little form: sometimes slowly away: sold 4,500 gns. *P. W. Harris*

BEVERLEY MACCA   4 ch.f. Piccolo 121 – Kangra Valley 56 (Indian Ridge 123)   **70**
[2002 68, a73: f5s p5g⁴ f5g f5g f5g⁵ 5f⁵ 5m* 5g f5f f5g³ f5g³ Dec 31] small, compact   **a66**
filly: unimpressive mover: fair performer: won minor event at Redcar in October: best
at 5f: acts on all-weather, firm and good to soft going, possibly not on soft/heavy: sometimes edges right: usually races prominently: none too reliable. *A. Berry*

BEVIER   8 b.g. Nashwan (USA) 135 – Bevel (USA) (Mr Prospector (USA)) [2002 12d   **–**
9.9m Jun 25] leggy gelding: modest handicapper in 1999: well held both starts since:
blinkered once. *T. Wall*

BE WARNED   11 b.g. Warning 136 – Sagar 74 (Habitat 134) [2002 –, a63: f8.5g⁴ f12g⁶   **–**
f9.4g³ f8.5g f12g⁵ f12g⁵ f12f f12f⁴ f12g Dec 26] good-topped gelding: unimpressive   **a53**
mover: modest performer: effective at 8.5f to easy 1½m: acts on fibresand: visored, used
to be blinkered: often gets behind. *R. Brotherton*

BEYOND CALCULATION (USA)   8 ch.g. Geiger Counter (USA) – Placer Queen   **81**
(Habitat 134) [2002 83, a64: 6m 5g 5g 5.3g 5.1d⁴ 5m 5.7m² 5m* 6.1m* 6f⁵ p6g⁵ 5g   **a70**
5m⁶ 5.3m⁶ 5m* 5m 5.1f Sep 25] sturdy gelding: fairly useful on turf, fair on all-weather:
won handicaps at Newcastle and Salisbury (apprentices), and minor event at Warwick
between June and September: effective at 5f/6f: acts on all-weather, firm and good to soft
going: often races up with pace. *J. M. Bradley*

BEYOND THE CLOUDS (IRE)   6 b.g. Midhish 109 – Tongabezi (IRE) 75 (Sher-   **90**
nazar 131) [2002 90: 5f⁵ 5g⁴ 5f⁵ 6d³ 6g² 6f 5g² 5m⁶ 5.2m 5d 5m* 5m 5m* 5g 6g 5d Oct
21] big gelding: fairly useful handicapper: won at Beverley in August and Doncaster in
September: stays 6f: acts on any going except soft/heavy: tried visored (not since 2000):
races prominently: consistent. *J. S. Wainwright*

BEZANT (IRE)   2 ch.f. (Mar 6) Zamindar (USA) 116 – Foresta Verde (USA) 46 (Green   **–**
Forest (USA) 134) [2002 8d 7v⁶ Nov 8] fifth foal: dam sprint maiden: little form in
maidens at Redcar and Doncaster. *C. B. B. Booth*

BEZWELL PRINCE   3 ch.g. Bluegrass Prince (IRE) 110 – Money Supply (Brigadier   **–**
Gerard 144) [2002 62: 12g⁵ Mar 28] strong gelding: modest maiden in 2001: well held
only 3-y-o start: should stay 1¼m. *N. Tinkler*

BEZWELL'S GUEST (IRE)   3 ch.g. Be My Guest (USA) 126 – Fine Project (IRE)   **57**
92 (Project Manager 111) [2002 55: 7m⁶ 8m 8.1s 7.5d⁶ 7m 11m* 11.7m⁶ 12m⁴ 14.1m⁴
Sep 3] tall gelding: modest performer: reportedly fractured a pastern after final 2-y-o
start: won maiden seller at Redcar in July: barely stayed 1¾m: acted on firm going:
visored once: dead. *R. M. Beckett*

BHANOYI (IRE)   3 ch.g. Perugino (USA) 84 – Bourgeonette 81 (Mummy's Pet 125)   **–**
[2002 f9.4g⁵ p10g⁶ 10g 10.2g 8.2f 7f p10g Dec 30] IR 10,000F: half-brother to several
winners, including useful 5f and 7f winner Wantage Park (by Pas de Seul) and 11f to 1¾m
winner The Where Withal (by Glint of Gold): dam 1m/1¼m winner: signs of only a little
ability: tried visored. *Mrs C. A. Dunnett*

BHUTAN (IRE)   7 b.g. Polish Patriot (USA) 128 – Bustinetta 89 (Bustino 136) [2002   **58**
74: 16m 14.1d 16.2g 13g 16m 14.1f² 12.6f² 12d⁶ 12m Aug 6] lengthy gelding: modest
handicapper: effective at 1½m to 17.5f: acts on any going: visored (below form) once:
usually held up: tends to find little: sold 6,200 gns after winning selling hurdle in
November. *Mrs M. Reveley*

BIBLE BOX (IRE)   4 b.f. Bin Ajwaad (IRE) 119 – Addie Pray (IRE) 68 (Great   **86**
Commotion (USA) 123) [2002 76: 8.3g 9m* 8.3m² 9.9m⁵ 10m Aug 28] fairly useful
performer: won handicap at Kempton in June: flattered in listed race at Salisbury
penultimate start: stays 9f: best efforts on good to firm going. *Mrs Lydia Pearce*

BIDDY   3 b.f. Rock Hopper 124 – Wanda 74 (Taufan (USA) 119) [2002 50: 8.5m Apr   **–**
25] small, compact filly: modest form at best in maidens at 2 yrs (rider suspended under
non-triers rule final start): well held only outing in 2002. *M. W. Easterby*

BID FOR FAME (USA)   5 b. or br.g. Quest For Fame 127 – Shroud (USA) (Vaguely   **91**
Noble 140) [2002 89: p12g f14g² p16g 14.4f* 14.4m³ 13.9f 14.1m³ 14.8g² 14m⁵ 13.1f²
14m⁴ 14.4m* 16m* Sep 20] leggy, lengthy, quite attractive gelding: has a quick, rather
round action: fairly useful handicapper: won at Kempton in April and at same course
and Newbury in September: stays 2m: acts on fibresand, best turf efforts on good going
or firmer: blinkered (ran poorly) final 4-y-o start: has won when sweating: races
prominently: consistent: sold 52,000 gns, joined N. Henderson. *T. G. Mills*

BID ME WELCOME   6 b.g. Alzao (USA) 117 – Blushing Barada (USA) 53 (Blush-   **45**
ing Groom (FR) 131) [2002 –: 10g 10d 12.4g⁴ 14.1g Oct 2] angular gelding: fluent
mover: one-time fairly useful handicapper, poor nowadays: left Mrs J. Ramsden before
final start: stays 2m: yet to race on heavy going, acts on any other: has raced freely/edged
left. *Miss D. A. McHale*

BID SPOTTER (IRE)   3 b.g. Eagle Eyed (USA) 111 – Bebe Auction (IRE) (Auction   **57**
Ring (USA) 123) [2002 62d: f7s⁵ f8g⁶ f8g³ f8g 10g⁶ f12g* 12m⁴ f12g⁵ 12.1g⁵ 14.1f f12g⁴
f12g⁵ f14.8g 12m f14g⁶ f12g² f16g f12g⁴ Dec 27] modest handicapper: won at Southwell
in April: left M. Chapman after eighth start: stays 1½m: acts on good to firm ground and
fibresand: visored (raced too freely) fourteenth outing: often makes running: none too
reliable. *Mrs Lucinda Featherstone*

BIEN TRANQUILLE (FR)   3 b.f. Reste Tranquille (FR) – Rainbow Brite (BEL)   **59**
(Captain's Treasure) [2002 a7.5g⁴ a6.5g⁶ 6d³ 8m⁵ 6g⁶ 7.6s 8v³ a7.5g⁵ Dec 21] half-sister
to Irish winners Carnabrae (at 7f, by Superlative) and Claude Greengrass (at 9f, by
Shalford): dam winner in Belgium: poor form fourth start, only outing in Britain for
J. Osborne: left B. Moretti after fifth start, and J. Bourdoncle after next one: stays 1m:
acts on heavy ground: has been blinkered. *J-L. Pelletan, France*

BIFF-EM (IRE)   8 ch.g. Durgam (USA) – Flash The Gold (Ahonoora 122) [2002 35d: **29**
7g 5g 6v 6s 5.9d 7.2d Aug 2] rather leggy gelding: poor performer: stays 7f: acts on any
going: has run well for amateur/when sweating. *Miss L. A. Perratt*

BIGALOTHEGIGALO (IRE)   2 b.g. (Apr 23) Desert Story (IRE) 115 – Noble   **81 p**
Clare (IRE) (The Noble Player (USA) 126) [2002 6d 7d* Nov 5] 5,000Y: fourth foal:
half-brother to a 1¼m and 11.5f winner in Italy by Balla Cove: dam unraced: slowly away
on debut, then confirmed that promise when winning maiden at Catterick by ½ length
from Arry Dash, leading under 2f out and responding well: will be suited by 1m+: open
to further improvement. *J. J. Quinn*

BIG BAD BOB (IRE)   2 br.c. (Mar 30) Bob Back (USA) 124 – Fantasy Girl (IRE)   **110 p**
55 (Marju (IRE) 127) [2002 7m 7m² 7m* 7.6m* 7.6f* 8m* Oct 12]
    Whilst enjoying a good deal of success over the years with the horses they
have had in training with John Dunlop, Windflower Overseas Holdings Inc has, as
yet, been unable to come up with one able to make its mark in the major pattern
races. Its sole pattern-race win was provided by Lucky Guest, and that came in a
Group 2 event in Turkey in 1991. Lucky Guest and other smart performers such
as Dawning Street, Pairumani Star and Son of Sharp Shot were among the best
to carry the red and yellow halved silks until the latest season; and now there is
Big Bad Bob. After only one season and six races his rating is up there with any
achieved by previous Windflower representatives, and with further improvement
very much on the cards Big Bad Bob will surely go on to surpass their achievements
easily. Big Bad Bob does not yet hold a Derby entry, but the Derby Italiano, a race
in which his sire Bob Back finished second in 1984 and which Dunlop won in 1986
with Tommy Way, looks a highly suitable alternative for a colt who, despite being

Tom McGee Autumn Stakes, Ascot—Big Bad Bob lands a four-timer in clear-cut style from Rainwashed Gold, Choir Master (partly hidden) and St Andrews (rail)

quite a free-going sort, should prove suited by a mile and a half at three, judged on pedigree.

Big Bad Bob won the last four of his six starts, and it would almost certainly have been the last five had he not drifted badly left under pressure when second in a maiden at Folkestone in July. Big Bad Bob kept a straight course in his remaining races and made amends easily in a similar event at Newcastle before coping well with the very different demands of Chester's sharp circuit when landing the odds in a couple of minor events there. Impressive in making all on the second occasion at Chester, Big Bad Bob gave a similar display when stepped up a little both in trip and in class at Ascot on his final start in the Tom McGee Autumn Stakes, a one-mile listed event won in the two previous seasons by Fight Your Corner and Nayef. Although not quite so impressive on the bare result as that pair had been, Big Bad Bob put up a fairly impressive performance all the same, responding well to pressure when challenged early in the straight and pulling clear to win by three and a half lengths from Rainwashed Gold.

		Roberto	Hail To Reason
Big Bad Bob (IRE)	Bob Back (USA)	(b 1969)	Bramalea
(br.c. Mar 30, 2000)	(br 1981)	Toter Back	Carry Back
		(ch 1967)	Romantic Miss
		Marju	Last Tycoon
	Fantasy Girl (IRE)	(br 1988)	Flame of Tara
	(br 1994)	Persian Fantasy	Persian Bold
		(br 1989)	Gay Fantasy

Big Bad Bob, a medium-sized, rather leggy colt bred by his owners, is the second foal of Fantasy Girl, a modest maiden who stayed a mile and a half, the longest distance at which she raced. Her first foal Demosthenes (by Lycius) is a lightly-raced maiden now trained in Ireland after starting out with Big Bad Bob's connections. Both Fantasy Girl and her half-sister, the useful stayer Height of Fantasy, raced for Windflower and Dunlop, as did their dam Persian Fantasy who showed fairly useful form up to two miles. Persian Fantasy is a half-sister to the aforementioned Lucky Guest and Son of Sharp Shot, whilst great grandam Gay Fantasy is a sister to the dam of Derby winner Oath. So far, Big Bad Bob has raced only on going firmer than good, and it was firm when he gained his second Chester win. *J. L. Dunlop*

BIG BERTHA 4 ch.f. Dancing Spree (USA) – Bertrade 75 (Homeboy 114) [2002 59?: **77**
7g³ 9.3g* Jun 27] unraced at 2 yrs: fair form: won handicap at Carlisle in June: will stay 1¼m: very slowly away second 3-y-o outing: lightly raced, and looked likely to improve further. *John Berry*

BIG BOPPER (IRE) 3 b.c. Danehill Dancer (IRE) 117 – Apocalypse (Auction Ring **80**
(USA) 123) [2002 69: 7m³ 8f* 7g⁶ 7.1m⁴ 7d³ p7g 6d³ 8.1m⁶ 7g 7m³ 7.1g⁶ Sep 23] tall, close-coupled colt: fairly useful performer: won minor event at Brighton in April: effective at 6f to 1m: yet to race on heavy going, acts on any other turf (below form only start on polytrack): blinkered seventh/eighth starts: sold 16,000 gns, sent to Italy. *R. Hannon*

BIG GENERAL (GER) 3 b.g. General Assembly (USA) – Broderie (USA) (Storm **78** Bird (CAN) 134) [2002 9g² 9v⁵ 9g⁴ 8.5g* 9.3d a9g² 10s⁴ a9.8g* a9.5g⁶ f12g⁶ Dec 27] fifth foal: dam, German 11f winner, closely related to smart Irish performer up to 1½m Magesterial: fair performer: won maiden at Krefeld in September and handicap at Dortmund in November (last start for A. Kleinkorres): left C. Von Der Recke in Germany, then ran too freely in front in handicap at Southwell on final start: stays 9.8f: acts on sand, best turf efforts on good going. *R. Wilman*

BIG LUCIANO (USA) 2 b.c. (Feb 8) Pleasant Colony (USA) – Fast Tipper (USA) **81 p** (Exceller (USA) 129) [2002 10s f9.4g³ p10g⁵ f8.5g* Dec 14] $10,000Y: half-brother to several winners in USA, notably Grade 3 9f winner Excellent Tipper (by Vice Regent): dam unraced half-sister to very smart French 1¼m performer Motley and to US Grade 1 9f winner Pattern Step: fairly useful form: won minor event at Wolverhampton in December by 1½ lengths from Blue Trojan: will probably stay 1½m: races up with pace: likely to do better still. *M. Johnston*

BIG MOMENT 4 ch.g. Be My Guest (USA) 126 – Petralona (USA) (Alleged (USA) **104** 138) [2002 104p: 12m 14d 16.1d² 14m 13.9m 12s Oct 26] leggy, quite attractive gelding: has a short, round action: useful handicapper: creditable efforts in 2002 only on second/third outings, second to Dancing Bay at Newmarket on latter: stays 2¼m: acts on firm and good to soft going: sweating profusely fourth start: sold 28,000 gns. *B. W. Hills*

BIG PEE TEE 2 gr.g. (Feb 18) Petong 126 – Duchess of Ferrara (IRE) 52 (Fairy King **45** (USA)) [2002 5m 5m 5f⁵ 6g⁵ 5m⁴ Jun 24] 18,000F, 19,000Y: first foal: dam, maiden, out of useful Irish 8.5f to 1¼m winner Tryarra: poor maiden: should stay 6f: visored (looked none too keen) penultimate start. *K. A. Ryan*

BIG SMOKE (IRE) 2 gr.g. (Apr 25) Perugino (USA) 84 – Lightning Bug (Prince **81** Bee 128) [2002 6s 6d* 7f⁴ 7m 7m Aug 26] 13,000F, 35,000Y: rather leggy gelding: fourth foal: brother to fairly useful 1999 2-y-o 6f winner Perugia and half-brother to 2 winners, including Irish 9f and 11f winner Queen of Fibres (by Scenic): dam, Irish 1½m and 2m winner, from family of Barathea and Gossamer: fairly useful form: won maiden at Salisbury in July: good fourth of 5 to Dublin in minor event at Newbury: well held in nurseries last 2 starts, including in blinkers: should stay at least 1m: found little penultimate outing, started slowly final one: gelded after. *B. J. Meehan*

BIGWIG (IRE) 9 ch.g. Thatching 131 – Sabaah (USA) 65 (Nureyev (USA) 131) [2002 **–** 50: p16g Jan 5] modest handicapper in 2001: off a year before only 9-y-o start (successful over hurdles in March/April): blinkered. *G. L. Moore*

BIJAN (IRE) 4 b.f. Mukaddamah (USA) 125 – Alkariyh (USA) 79 (Alydar (USA)) **60 d** [2002 68: f6s f5g f6g 6m 6m f6s 7m 6.1m⁶ f6g f6g⁶ Nov 25] leggy filly: modest handicapper: on downgrade: stays easy 7f: acts on fibresand, good to firm and good to soft going: tried visored: reportedly broke blood vessel fourth start. *R. Hollinshead*

BIJOU BELLE 3 b.f. Bijou d'Inde 127 – Primitive Gift 38 (Primitive Rising (USA) **–** 113) [2002 –: f6g Jun 22] tall filly: no sign of ability: dead. *Mrs A. Duffield*

BIJOU DANCER 2 ch.c. (May 20) Bijou d'Inde 127 – Dancing Diana 82 (Raga Navarro (ITY) 119) [2002 6s Jun 10] half-brother to several winners, including useful but unreliable 5f/6f performer Dancethenightaway (by Efisio), later winner in USA, and 7f winner who stayed 8.5f Silver Harrow (by Belmez): dam 5f (at 2 yrs) to 1m winner: 20/1, well held in maiden at Windsor. *R. Hannon*

BIJOU ROCK 2 ch.c. (Apr 12) Bijou d'Inde 127 – Heavy Rock (IRE) 31 (Ballad **44** Rock 122) [2002 5g 5m⁶ 6g⁶ 6m³ 7.2g⁶ 8d 8g Sep 10] 4,500Y (twice): workmanlike colt: third foal: dam, 9f winner at 4 yrs, half-sister to very smart French winner up to 10.5f Pitasia: poor maiden: should stay 1m. *G. M. Moore*

BIJOUX (USA) 2 ch.f. (Jan 19) King of Kings (IRE) 125 – Golden Wreath (USA) **84** (Majestic Light (USA)) [2002 7m³ 6g² 7g 7m⁴ Sep 20] 550,000 francs Y: leggy, quite good-topped filly: fifth foal: half-sister to winners in USA by Is It True and Brocco: dam, US maiden, half-sister to Canadian Grade 1 1½m winner Golden Act: fairly useful maiden: placed at Goodwood and Ascot: best effort when fourth to L'Ancresse in minor event at Newbury: should stay 1¼m. *R. Hannon*

BILLIE H 4 ch.f. Cool Jazz 116 – Rachels Eden (Ring Bidder 88) [2002 60§: f8.5g⁴ **53 §** f7s⁵ f7g³ f8g f7g⁶ 7m f7s⁶ f8.5g May 24] strong, sturdy filly: modest performer: effective at 7f/1m: acts on firm going and fibresand: visored once, usually blinkered (not last 2 starts): has started slowly: tends to look less than keen: unreliable. *P. D. Evans*

BILL MIDDLETON (USA) 2 b. or br.g. (Mar 9) K O Punch (USA) – Coin (USA) **70** (Lemhi Gold (USA) 123) [2002 p8g⁶ Dec 14] $14,000Y: eighth foal: half-brother to 3 winners in USA: dam won up to 1m in USA: 20/1, 3¾ lengths sixth to Nawow in maiden at Lingfield. *D. Shaw*

BILLY BATHWICK (IRE)   5 ch.g. Fayruz 116 – Cut It Fine (USA) (Big Spruce   **60**
(USA)) [2002 70: 10d³ 10f 10m⁵ 12s⁴ 10.2v³ 9.9m f8.5g⁵ Dec 20] smallish, close-coupled gelding: modest handicapper: barely stays 1½m: acts on soft and good to firm ground: tried blinkered. *Dr J. R. J. Naylor*

BILLY BIRD (IRE)   2 b.g. (Feb 29) Bluebird (USA) 125 – Classic Dilemma (Sand-   **–**
hurst Prince 128) [2002 f9.4g Nov 16] IR 55,000F, IR 50,000Y: half-brother to Italian 7f (at 2 yrs) and 7.5f winner by Soviet Lad and 1m to 1¼m winner in Hong Kong by Good Thyne: dam Irish 2-y-o 6f winner: green when well held in maiden at Wolverhampton. *J. A. Osborne*

BILLY BONNIE (IRE)   5 ch.g. Anshan 119 – Sinology (Rainbow Quest (USA) 134)   **99**
[2002 16s* 16d² 16s* 20m⁵ 16d² 16d⁵ Oct 13] useful handicapper: lightly raced on Flat (missed 2001): progressed well in 2002, winning at Wexford in May and Limerick in June: under 2 lengths fifth to Riyadh in Ascot Stakes at Royal Ascot (slightly checked when switched then finished very strongly) and ½-length second to Discerning Air at the Curragh on fourth/fifth starts: below form final one: stays 2½m: acts on soft and good to firm ground: winning hurdler. *N. Meade, Ireland*

BILLYJO (IRE)   4 b.g. Idris (IRE) 118 – Village Countess (IRE) (Reasonable (FR) 119)   **–**
[2002 33: 7f Jun 7] probably of little account nowadays. *Miss A. Stokell*

BILLY TWO RIVERS (IRE)   3 ch.g. Woodborough (USA) 112 – Good Visibility   **–**
(IRE) (Electric 126) [2002 10d 12f⁵ 13.8f⁵ f12g 16m Sep 16] IR 11,500Y: stocky gelding: first foal: dam poor maiden in Irish bumpers: well held in maidens/handicaps. *R. F. Fisher*

BINANTI   2 b.g. (Mar 3) Bin Ajwaad (IRE) 119 – Princess Rosananti (IRE) (Shareef   **100**
Dancer (USA) 135) [2002 6m p6g⁶ 7.1m⁴ f8s* 7.1m³ 7f* 7m³ Oct 12] 9,000Y: smallish, useful-looking gelding: half-brother to several winners, including 4-y-o Dilly and 1½m winner Indira (by Indian Ridge): dam unraced: useful performer: won maiden at Southwell and minor event at Goodwood (beat Naahy 7 lengths) in September: gave impression something amiss when tailed-off last of 3 in minor event at Ascot final start: stays 1m: acts on fibresand, raced only on going firmer than good on turf. *P. R. Chamings*

BINARY FILE (USA)   4 b.c. Nureyev (USA) 131 – Binary 109 (Rainbow Quest   **115**
(USA) 134) [2002 110: 8m 7f⁶ 8.9m* 7m⁴ 9.8g² Oct 5] deep-girthed colt: has a round action: smart performer, lightly raced: won listed event at York in September by ¾ length from Bourgainville, finishing well from rear: good 2½ lengths second to Dano-Mast in Prix Dollar at Longchamp final start, having to wait for run: needs further than 7f and stays 1¼m: raced only on good ground or firmer: has worn crossed noseband: settled better than usual last 3 starts. *J. H. M. Gosden*

BINCHE (USA)   3 ch.f. Woodman (USA) 126 – Binary 109 (Rainbow Quest (USA)   **51**
134) [2002 7s⁴ p10g⁶ Nov 19] second foal: half-sister to 4-y-o Binary File: dam, 9f/1¼m winner in France/USA, sister to smart 1½m performer Bequeath from very good family: better effort in maidens when 6 lengths sixth to Scent of Victory at Lingfield, off bridle long way out and never nearer: slowly away on debut: stud. *J. H. M. Gosden*

BINT ALHAARTH (IRE)   2 b.f. (Feb 20) Alhaarth (IRE) 126 – Idle Fancy 79 (Muj-   **74**
tahid (USA) 118) [2002 7d 7.1m² 7d⁵ 7f⁶ 8g⁶ Oct 18] 48,000Y: leggy filly: second foal: half-sister to 4-y-o Idle Power: dam, Irish 1m winner, half-sister to dam of smart 1½m performer Ela Athena: fair maiden: stays 1m: acts on firm ground, probably on good to soft. *B. W. Hills*

BINTANG TIMOR (USA)   8 ch.g. Mt Livermore (USA) – Frisky Kitten (USA)   **53**
(Isopach (USA)) [2002 75, a62: 6m 7m 7.5g⁶ 7m 6g⁴ Jul 18] close-coupled gelding: unimpressive mover: modest handicapper: hasn't won since 2000: effective at 6f to easy 1m: acts on any turf going/all-weather: sometimes slowly away: held up. *W. J. Musson*

BINT HABIBI   5 b.m. Bin Ajwaad (IRE) 119 – High Stepping (IRE) (Taufan (USA)   **–**
119) [2002 71: f9.4g f9.4g f9.4g Mar 2] angular mare: fair handicapper at best: no form in 2002: tried visored. *Mrs Lydia Pearce*

BINT ROYAL (IRE)   4 ch.f. Royal Abjar (USA) 121 – Living Legend (USA) (Sep-   **67**
tieme Ciel (USA) 123) [2002 54: p6g f6s² f5s⁴ p7g f7g² f8g f7g⁴ f6g⁵ f7g p6g f6g f7g³ 8m   **a78**
f7g* f7g* f6g* 7m² 6g* 6d 6g⁴ f6g* 7m 6g³ 6m 7f² 6m 8g³ f8g f7g p7g f6g Nov 25]
close-coupled, workmanlike filly: fair handicapper: won at Wolverhampton (4 times, including amateur event) and Pontefract between May and July: effective at 6f to 1m: acts on firm, good to soft ground and all-weather: visored once, effective blinkered or not: trained by B. Ellison fourteenth to twenty-fifth starts: tough. *Miss V. Haigh*

BI POLAR 2 b.c. (May 8) Polar Falcon (USA) 126 – Doctor Bid (USA) (Spectacular **80** Bid (USA)) [2002 6s⁶ 6m³ Jun 27] 31,000Y: useful-looking colt: closely related to 3-y-o Remedy and half-brother to 3 winners, including useful 1¾m/2m winner On Call (by Alleged) and fairly useful 5f (at 2 yrs)/6f winner Doctor's Glory (by Elmaamul): dam unraced from family of very smart sprinters Cassandra Go and Do The Honours: still green, better effort (fairly useful form) when third of 7 to Cosmo in minor event at Salisbury: should stay 7f. *D. R. C. Elsworth*

BIRAS CREEK (IRE) 3 ch.f. Most Welcome 131 – Orange Hill 75 (High Top 131) **–** [2002 10m Sep 15] half-sister to 3 winners, including 7f (at 2 yrs) and 1¼m winner Jackson Hill (by Priolo) and middle-distance stayer Old Provence (by Rainbow Quest), both useful: dam won Cesarewitch: always behind in Sandown maiden. *T. G. Mills*

BIRCHWOOD SUN 12 b.g. Bluebird (USA) 125 – Shapely Test (USA) (Elocu- **48** tionist (USA)) [2002 50: 7s 6f 7m 7g⁴ 6v⁵ 5.9d 7m² 5.9s⁴ Jul 31] compact gelding: poor mover: poor performer: effective at 6f (given test) to 1m: acts on any going: blinkered/visored: comes from behind. *M. Dods*

BIRDIE 3 b.f. Alhaarth (IRE) 126 – Fade (Persepolis (FR) 127) [2002 82: 8v* 11.5g* **99** 12g 11.9d⁵ 10.2g⁶ 8d⁶ Sep 29] good-topped filly: useful performer: won maiden at Newcastle in April and listed race at Lingfield (by ½ length from Barzah, racing freely) in May: at least respectable efforts in Lancashire Oaks at Haydock (fifth to Mellow Park) and listed races at Chepstow (sixth to Albanova) and Milan (sixth to Juvena) last 3 starts: stays 1½m: acts on heavy going: visored second/third/fifth outings: tail flasher at 2 yrs. *M. L. W. Bell*

BIRDWATCHING 3 b.g. Primo Dominie 121 – Area Girl 76 (Jareer (USA) 115) **58 §** [2002 –: f5g 5g⁴ 6.1d² 5d* 5f⁶ 5.9g 5d⁶ 5d³ 6m 5f 5d³ f5g Oct 17] quite good-topped **a– §** gelding: modest handicapper: won at Kempton in July: best at 5f/6f: acts on good to soft going, probably on firm (below form on fibresand): blinkered last 3 starts: has pulled hard/been slowly away/edged left: carries head high: not to be trusted: sold 4,500 gns, sent to Saudi Arabia. *S. C. Williams*

BIRJAND 3 b.f. Green Desert (USA) 127 – Belle Genius (USA) 111 (Beau Genius **99** (CAN)) [2002 7g⁴ 7m² 7f* 7m³ 6g* 6m 7m* 6f² 7s⁵ Oct 26] good-topped filly: second foal: half-sister to Irish 1½m winner Battish (by Pennekamp): dam, won Moyglare Stud Stakes, out of half-sister to smart performers Irish Shoal (French sprinter) and Hibernian Gold (at 1¼m): useful performer: won maiden at Yarmouth and handicaps at Newmarket and Doncaster (beat Deceitful by ½ length) between June and September: very good ½-length second to Lochridge in handicap at Newmarket in October: effective at 6f/7f: raced only on good going or firmer prior to final start (below form): free-going sort: visits Alhaarth. *M. A. Jarvis*

BIRTH OF THE BLUES 6 ch.g. Efisio 120 – Great Steps 88 (Vaigly Great 127) **52** [2002 52: 7m 10d³ 12g 12d 12d 12g⁴ 14.1m⁵ 11.9g⁴ 12g² 10.2g 12d Sep 11] lengthy, angular gelding: modest handicapper: stays 1½m: acts on any turf going: tried visored/blinkered at 4 yrs. *A. Charlton*

BISHOPS COURT 8 ch.g. Clantime 101 – Indigo 86 (Primo Dominie 121) [2002 **116** 117: 5g³ 5m⁵ 5d⁵ 5s² 5d³ 5.1f* 6.1g 5m 5m³ 5m* 5.2f Sep 21] big, good-quartered gelding: usually looks really well: smart performer: reportedly found to have sustained hairline fracture of pelvis final 7-y-o start: won listed events at Chester (by ½ length from Dragon Flyer) in July and Doncaster (confidently ridden to beat Olivia Grace ½ length) in September: generally respectable efforts at least otherwise: very speedy, and best at 5f: acts on any going: tongue tied in 2000: usually bandaged nowadays: has edged left/idled: usually held up. *Mrs J. R. Ramsden*

Scarbrough Stakes, Doncaster—Bishops Court gives weight away to his younger rivals and breaks the course record in the process; Olivia Grace (rail) is second and Saddad (striped cap, centre) third

BISHOPS FINGER 2 b.c. (Mar 5) Bishop of Cashel 122 – Bit of A Tart (Distant – Relative 128) [2002 6m⁴ 6m⁶ 6d 7m 6m p8g* f8.5g² p7g⁶ Dec 28] first foal: dam unraced: **a61** modest performer: won seller at Lingfield in November: should stay 1¼m: acts on all-weather: blinkered (ran creditably but looked bit wayward last 2 starts). *Jamie Poulton*

BISHOP'S LAKE 2 b.f. (Feb 29) Lake Coniston (IRE) 131 – Clincher Club 77 (Polish **87 d** Patriot (USA) 128) [2002 5m⁶ 6.1g* 6m² 6d* 5.2f⁶ 6.1m⁴ 6.5g 6g Oct 17] angular filly: second foal: half-sister to 3-y-o Spritzeria: dam 5f (at 2 yrs) and 7.5f winner: fairly useful performer: won minor events at Nottingham in May and Salisbury (made all) in July: 1¾ lengths second to Miss Mirasol in listed race at Newmarket: ran poorly last 2 starts: should prove best at 5f/6f: acts on good to firm and good to soft going. *M. G. Quinlan*

BISHOP'S SECRET 4 b.g. Bishop of Cashel 122 – Secret Rapture (USA) (Woodman – § (USA) 126) [2002 –§, a61d: f11g Jun 20] tall gelding: temperamental maiden: usually blinkered/visored. *P. T. Dalton*

BISHOPSTONE MAN 5 b.g. Piccolo 121 – Auntie Gladys 49 (Great Nephew 126) **75** [2002 69, a65: 7f³ 7g* 7m⁴ 6m⁵ 7m⁵ 7m³ 7.1g 7.5m⁵ 8m Sep 13] well-made gelding: fair **a–** handicapper: won at Brighton in May: effective at 6f to 8.5f: acts on firm going, soft and fibresand: effective visored or not: sometimes pulls hard: races prominently: consistent. *H. Candy*

BISHOP'S WING'S 4 br.f. Bishop of Cashel 122 – Butterfly Rose (USA) (Iron Ruler – (USA)) [2002 –: f6g Jan 29] little form. *P. R. Chamings*

BISHR 3 b.c. Royal Applause 124 – Hawayah (IRE) 68 (Shareef Dancer (USA) 135) **103 p** [2002 84: 6g³ 7.5g² 7m* 8f* Aug 18] leggy colt: useful performer: reportedly underwent wind operation prior to reappearance: won maiden at Thirsk in July and handicap at Bath (beat Dayglow Dancer by 1½ lengths) in August: stays 1m: raced only on good going or firmer: tongue tied final 2-y-o start: progressive, and probably capable of better still. *M. P. Tregoning*

BITHNAH 3 b.f. Halling (USA) 133 – Najmat Alshemaal (IRE) 98 (Dancing Brave **48** (USA) 140) [2002 7d⁴ 7m 10.1m Sep 18] third foal: half-sister to 1¼m/1½m winner Emteyaz (by Mark of Esteem): dam 1¼m winner who stayed 14.6f: form only in Salisbury maiden on debut (raced freely): left M. Channon 4,000 gns, and off 3 months before final start: should be suited by 1¼m+. *G. Prodromou*

BIT OF LUCK 3 ch.g. First Trump 118 – Elle Reef (Shareef Dancer (USA) 135) **99 d** [2002 93: p8g 8g* 10g⁴ 10.4f⁶ 8m 10m⁴ p8g³ 8m 8g Sep 21] strong gelding: useful performer: won handicap at Newbury in April by short head from Impeller: below form after: should stay 1¼m: acts on soft and good to firm going: visored final start: has had 2 handlers/been bit edgy: sometimes races freely: sold 25,000 gns, sent to USA. *M. H. Tompkins*

BITTER SWEET 6 gr.m. Deploy 131 – Julia Flyte 91 (Drone (USA)) [2002 58: 9s³ **59** 9g⁵ 9.7m* 9d⁵ 9.7d⁶ 9.7m⁴ 8.1g⁴ 8.5g 8.5d Sep 11] modest handicapper: won at Folkestone in June: probably best around 1¼m nowadays: acts on firm and soft going: sometimes visored in 2000: held up. *J. L. Spearing*

BLACK BELT SHOPPER (IRE) 2 b.f. (Mar 17) Desert Prince (IRE) 130 – Kou- **82** miss (Unfuwain (USA) 131) [2002 5.2g² 5.1g 6m* 6m⁶ 7g⁴ 7.1m 7.1m⁴ 7m⁶ 8d³ 10s Nov 2] IR 14,000Y: well-made filly: good walker: second foal: dam, French maiden who stayed 10.5f, half-sister to smart stayer Arden and useful French sprinter Kerulen: fairly useful performer: won maiden at Pontefract in June: creditable third of 5 to Battle Chant in listed race there: stays 1m: acts on good to firm and good to soft ground, tailed off on soft: tried blinkered: edgy and swished tail in paddock fifth start: none too consistent: temperament under suspicion. *B. W. Hills*

BLACK BOOTY (IRE) 2 b.g. (Apr 29) General Monash (USA) 107 – Northern **51** Amber (Shack (USA) 118) [2002 f5g⁶ f5g⁶ 5f f5g⁶ f6g⁵ May 20] IR 3,400Y: small, strong gelding: half-brother to 5f winner (including at 2 yrs) Minizen Music (by Anita's Prince) and 6f winner Karseam (by Mon Tresor): dam lightly raced: modest maiden: probably best at 5f: acts on fibresand: visored/blinkered last 3 starts: sometimes slowly away: none too genuine. *W. G. M. Turner*

BLACKHEATH (IRE) 6 ch.g. Common Grounds 118 – Queen Caroline (USA) 67 **72** (Chief's Crown (USA)) [2002 90d: 6s 7m 6m* 6g⁵ 6m 5m⁴ 6m 7m⁴ 5m* 5g 5m 6g⁴ 6s 6g 6f 6f Oct 12] barrel-shaped gelding: type to carry condition: fluent mover: fair nowadays: won apprentice minor event at Catterick in June and handicap at Pontefract in July: below form last 4 starts: effective at 5f to easy 7f: best on going firmer than good: tried blinkered/tongue tied: sometimes reluctant stall/slowly away. *D. Nicholls*

BLACK LEDGER (NZ)   6 b. or br.g. British Banker (CAN) – Chambertine (NZ)   **102**
(Markella (FR)) [2002 a9f⁵ 10g³ a10f³ a9.7f* a10f⁴ a10f⁵ 9.9d 7m⁴ 10d⁵ a9f Dec 19]
good-topped gelding: useful performer: won 4 races in Australasia prior to 2002: trained
by A. Smith/Paul Smith first 9 starts, winning handicap at Jebel Ali in February: below
form in listed races/minor event in Britain seventh to ninth outings in 2002: stays 1¼m:
acts on dirt. *D. J. Selvaratnam, UAE*

BLACKMAIL (USA)   4 b.g. Twining (USA) 120 – Black Penny (USA) (Private   **90**
Account (USA)) [2002 93+: p12g p10g⁶ p10g p8g 8d 8.3s 10.1m⁵ p7g p7g p10g p7g Dec
28] sturdy gelding: fairly useful performer: left B. Johnson after fourth start, N. Hamilton
after seventh: stays 1¼m: acts on polytrack: visored (ran creditably) second start: has
wandered. *Miss B. Sanders*

BLACK PAGODA (IRE)   3 b.g. Spectrum (IRE) 126 – Melodrama 102 (Busted 134)   **–**
[2002 67: 8.3d 8d⁵ 6.9g 8.3s 8g 10.9s Oct 14] 72,000Y: ex-Irish gelding: half-brother to
numerous winners, notably 5f (at 2 yrs) to 1m winner Lemon Souffle (by Salse) and 1m/
1¼m winner Caramba (by Belmez), both smart: dam 6f/1m winner: fair form in maidens
at 2 yrs for A. O'Brien: well held in 2002, including in selling handicap: should stay 1m:
sometimes slowly away. *P. Monteith*

BLACK PEPPER   2 b.f. (Mar 5) Salse (USA) 128 – Saint Ann (USA) 66 (Geiger
Counter (USA)) [2002 6m May 15] first foal: dam, ran 4 times at 2 yrs (looked rather
temperamental), out of half-sister to very smart sprinter Primo Dominie: 3/1, well-held
tenth of 12 in maiden at Newcastle, hanging badly left from halfway. *M. Johnston*

BLACKPOOL BEAU   2 b.c. (May 6) Danetime (IRE) 121 – Blackpool Belle 70 (The   **76**
Brianstan 128) [2002 5d² 6m⁴ f6s Nov 2] 10,000Y: close-coupled, quite good-topped
colt: half-brother to several winners, notably smart sprinter Croft Pool (by Crofthall):
dam sprinter: clearly best effort (fair form) when length second of 13 to Brantwood in
maiden at Haydock: off over 3 months before final outing: may prove best at 5f.
K. A. Ryan

BLACK SAM BELLAMY (IRE)   3 b.c. Sadler's Wells (USA) 132 – Urban Sea   **117**
(USA) 126 (Miswaki (USA) 124) [2002 111: 10s* 12g² 12m⁵ 16.2m⁵ 12g 12s* Oct 20]
big, strong, close-coupled colt: has a round, choppy action: smart performer: landed odds
in maiden at the Curragh in April and won Gran Premio del Jockey Club e Coppa d'Oro
at Milan in October, making most in latter and rallying to beat Guadalupe a short neck:
creditable third (promoted to second) to Khalkevi in Prix Hocquart at Longchamp and
fifth to Sulamani in Prix du Jockey Club at Chantilly second/third starts: acted as
pacemaker when good tenth in Prix de l'Arc de Triomphe at Longchamp penultimate

*Gran Premio del Jockey Club e Coppa d'Oro, Milan—Black Sam Bellamy (left) lands this Group 1 prize
from Oaks d'Italia winner Guadalupe and the visored Ekraar*

outing: will stay beyond 1½m (below form in Queen's Vase at 2m): acts on heavy and good to firm ground, though may not take repeated racing on latter: wears crossed noseband. *A. P. O'Brien, Ireland*

BLACKS GIRL   2 b.f. (Jan 19) Atraf 116 – Zaima (IRE) 92 (Green Desert (USA) 127)   **68 d** [2002 5m 5.1f² 5g⁴ 5m 5d⁶ 5d 5m Aug 22] 8,500Y: sturdy, good-bodied filly: second foal: dam, 7f winner at 2 yrs, out of half-sister to very smart miler Alhijaz: fair maiden at best: well below form last 3 starts: will prove best at bare 5f: acts on firm ground: weak finisher. *J. J. Quinn*

BLACK SWAN (IRE)   2 b.g. (Jan 28) Nashwan (USA) 135 – Sea Spray (IRE) 101   **– p** (Royal Academy (USA) 130) [2002 7m Aug 2] rangy, unfurnished gelding: has scope: second foal: dam, 7f (at 2 yrs)/1m winner who probably stayed 1¼m, out of smart performer up to 1½m Sailor's Mate, a good family: 9/1 and green, weakened from 2f out when well held in maiden at Goodwood: type to do better. *M. P. Tregoning*

BLACKTHORN   3 ch.g. Deploy 131 – Balliasta (USA) (Lyphard (USA) 132) [2002   **85 d** 82: 10.5m⁵ 12.3f 10.5d⁵ 12.3f⁴ 10m 10s 13.8d⁶ Nov 5] strong, compact gelding: has a fluent, round action: fairly useful performer at best: stays 1½m, at least when conditions aren't testing: acts on firm and soft going: sometimes on toes/races freely. *R. A. Fahey*

BLACKWATER ANGEL (USA)   2 b.f. (Feb 5) Kingmambo (USA) 125 – Zephyr   **79** (CAN) (His Majesty (USA)) [2002 7m³ 7m⁵ 8.1f* 8s Nov 2] $150,000Y: tall, leggy, angular filly: first foal: dam 8.5f to 1¼m winner in USA, also third in Grade 2 8.5f event: fair form: won maiden at Haydock in September: well beaten in listed race at Newmarket final start: will probably stay 1¼m: acts on firm going. *J. L. Dunlop*

BLACKWATER FEVER (USA)   2 b.c. (Mar 13) Irish River (FR) 131 – Crafty   **69 p** Buzz (USA) (Crafty Prospector (USA)) [2002 8m² Oct 2] good-topped colt: has scope: third foal: half-brother to a winner in USA by St Jovite: dam US 2-y-o 5.5f/6f (minor stakes) winner: 10/1, 6 lengths second of 9 to Rocket Force in maiden at Newcastle, late headway after running green in rear: sure to improve. *M. Johnston*

BLACK WEASEL (IRE)   7 br.g. Lahib (USA) 129 – Glowlamp (IRE) 93 (Glow   **–** (USA)) [2002 39, a44: f16g Jan 29] poor handicapper: stayed 17.5f: acted on soft going, good to firm and fibresand: tried blinkered/visored/tongue tied: dead. *A. Bailey*

BLADE'S DANCER   2 b.c. (Mar 13) Komaite (USA) – Banningham Blade 94 (Sure   **63** Blade (USA) 130) [2002 7.5g⁶ 7s f6g³ f7s Dec 9] 15,500Y: plain colt: first foal: dam best at 2 yrs when 5f winner: modest maiden: third at Wolverhampton: stays 7f. *Mrs A. Duffield*

BLAGOVEST   3 b.g. Singspiel (IRE) 133 – Tass (Soviet Star (USA) 128) [2002 81:   **103** 10m 9.9g² 12m* 12f* Oct 2] lengthy, good sort: useful performer: won maiden at Kempton (by 5 lengths, despite hanging markedly left) in September and handicap at Newmarket (much improved to beat Robandela by 6 lengths) in October: will stay 1¾m: acts firm going, probably on good to soft: sent to Australia. *R. Charlton*

BLAIR (IRE)   5 b.g. Persian Bold 123 – Zara's Birthday (IRE) 71 (Waajib 121) [2002   **68** 42: 16m 14g⁴ 13.8g* 12f⁵ 14.1f* 14d* 16m* 15.9f 14.1m Sep 5] sparely-made gelding: fair performer: won seller at Catterick in May, and handicaps at Redcar in June and Musselburgh/Redcar in July: well held last 2 starts: barely stays 2m: acts on firm and good to soft going, probably on soft: held up: sold 8,000 gns. *G. A. Swinbank*

BLAISE CASTLE (USA)   2 b.f. (Apr 10) Irish River (FR) 131 – Castellina (USA)   **94 p** (Danzig Connection (USA)) [2002 p7g³ 8d* Nov 1] quite attractive filly: third foal: sister to 3-y-o Castle River: dam, US 8.5f winner, half-sister to smart US Grade 1 1¼m winner Chelsey Flower: promising third in maiden at Lingfield: fairly useful form when winning 3-runner minor event at Newmarket following month by 5 lengths from Howle Hill, dictating pace: will stay 1¼m: should improve again. *G. A. Butler*

BLAKESEVEN   2 b.c. (May 19) Forzando 122 – Up And Going (FR) (Never So Bold   **73** 135) [2002 5m⁴ 5m⁴ 6d⁶ p7g p7g Dec 28] seventh foal: brother to smart 5f/6f winner (including at 2 yrs) Easycall and half-brother to 2 winners abroad: dam unraced half-sister to useful sprinter Up And At 'em: fair maiden: best effort when fourth to Peace Offering at Sandown second start: left W. Haggas 12,000 gns after third one: likely to prove best at 5f/6f. *W. J. Musson*

BLAKESHALL BOY   4 b.g. Piccolo 121 – Giggleswick Girl 67 (Full Extent (USA)   **82** 113) [2002 88: 5f 5f 6m 5g 5d 5.7d* 5f 5m² 5g⁶ 6m 6m Jun 30] rather leggy, quite attractive gelding: fairly useful handicapper: won at Bath in May: best up to 5.7f: acts on firm and soft going: reportedly had breathing problem once at 3 yrs: usually held up: has run respectably visored. *M. R. Channon*

BLAKESHALL QUEST   2 b.f. (Apr 11) Piccolo 121 – Corniche Quest (IRE) 74 **38**
(Salt Dome (USA)) [2002 5.3m⁶ 5f p6g f8.5g⁶ Dec 31] second foal: sister to 2001
2-y-o 5f seller winner Blakeshall: dam 5f to 1m winner: poor form in sellers/maiden.
M. R. Channon

BLANDYS (IRE)   2 b.f. (Feb 9) Dolphin Street (FR) 125 – Bodfaridistinction (IRE) **50**
77 (Distinctly North (USA) 115) [2002 6d⁵ 6d f5g³ f5g⁴ 5g⁴ p7g⁶ 8.2v⁵ f7g³ f9.4g⁵ Dec 7]
3,800Y: workmanlike filly: first foal: dam 2-y-o 5f winner: modest maiden: races freely,
but seems to stay 1m: acts on all-weather, raced on good ground or softer on turf: effective
blinkered or not: usually races up with pace. *J. White*

BLATANT   3 ch.c. Machiavellian (USA) 123 – Negligent 118 (Ahonoora 122) [2002 **114**
7s² 8d* 8g* 8m² Sep 15] closely related to 7f/1m winners Asad and Nabonassar (both by
Lion Cavern) and half-brother to 1995 2-y-o 7f winner Shawanni (by Shareef Dancer), all
useful: dam, won Rockfel Stakes and third in 1000 Guineas, half-sister to smart stayer
Ala Hounak: smart form: won maiden at Naas and listed race at Tralee in August,
impressive when beating Maumee 4 lengths in latter: good short-head second to Umistim
in listed race at the Curragh final start: stays 1m: tongue tied all starts: joined Godolphin.
J. Oxx, Ireland

BLAZEAWAY (USA)   2 b. or br.g. (Apr 17) Hansel (USA) – Alessia's Song (USA) **75**
(Air Forbes Won (USA)) [2002 7m 8.1m² 8f³ 8s a8g² Dec 12] $10,000Y, 33,000 2-y-o:
rather leggy, lengthy gelding: third foal: half-brother to 3 minor winners in USA: dam 5f
(at 2 yrs) to 1m winner in North America: fair maiden: placed at Haydock, Bath (below
form, seemed ill at ease on firm ground) and Nad Al Sheba: should stay 1¼m.
M. Johnston

BLAZING MOMENT   2 ch.c. (Mar 29) Timeless Times (USA) 99 – Kabella (Kabour **–**
80) [2002 5g 6m 6d Oct 21] 1,800Y: strong colt: sixth foal: brother to 1997 2-y-o 5f
winner Tempus Fugit: dam well beaten: well held in maidens. *R. Bastiman*

BLAZING SADDLES (IRE)   3 b.g. Sadler's Wells (USA) 132 – Dalawara (IRE) **–**
(Top Ville 129) [2002 68p: 10.2d⁶ 10.1g⁶ 16f 18d Oct 21] rather leggy, workmanlike
gelding: has a round action: disappointing maiden: should stay at least 1½m: sold 4,500
gns. *I. A. Balding*

BLAZING THUNDER   2 b.c. (Feb 26) Zafonic (USA) 130 – Bright Spells (USA) **94 p**
(Alleged (USA) 138) [2002 7f 7d* Nov 2] leggy, good-topped colt: third foal: brother to
smart 7f (including at 2 yrs) winner Clearing: dam, fairly useful French 1½m winner,
sister to smart performer up to 15.5f Non Partisan from good family: stepped up markedly
on debut form to win 22-runner maiden at Newmarket by 1¼ lengths from Private
Charter, taking time to hit full stride but storming through to lead final 1f: will stay 1m:
useful performer in the making at least, sure to win more races. *J. H. M. Gosden*

BLAZONRY (USA)   2 b.c. (Feb 19) Hennessy (USA) 122 – Altair (USA) (Alydar **89**
(USA)) [2002 6s⁵ 7m⁶ 6g² 5.2g* 6d⁶ Aug 26] $100,000Y: good-topped colt: fourth foal:
half-brother to 3-y-o Alsafi and a winner in USA by Seattle Slew: dam unraced out of
half-sister to Kentucky Derby winner Cannonade: fairly useful performer: landed odds in
maiden at Yarmouth in July: creditable sixth of 7 in listed race at Ripon final start:
effective at 5f/6f: acts on good to soft going: returned to USA. *J. Noseda*

BLENHEIM TERRACE   9 b.g. Rambo Dancer (CAN) 107 – Boulevard Girl 80 **51**
(Nicholas Bill 125) [2002 45: 14m⁴ 16m³ 16f⁵ 12.1m² 15.8f² 16d⁵ 12m* 15.8f 14.1m⁵
12g⁶ Oct 19] sturdy gelding: modest performer: won amateur handicap at Catterick in
August: stays 2m: acts on firm and good to soft ground: reportedly had breathing problem
sixth start. *W. H. Tinning*

BLESSED PLACE   2 ch.c. (Apr 23) Compton Place 125 – Cathedra (So Blessed 130) **47**
[2002 7.1g 6m 6g Oct 18] 2,500Y resold 3,000Y: half-brother to several winners,
including useful 1988 Irish 2-y-o 6f/7f winner Tantum Ergo (by Tanfirion): dam, maiden,
out of Park Hill winner Collyria: poor form in maidens/minor event. *Jean-Rene Auvray*

BLESS HER   2 b.f. (Apr 6) Piccolo 121 – Bliss (IRE) 75 (Statoblest 120) [2002 5g 6s **55**
5.7f² p5g Oct 31] 4,600Y: first foal: dam, 2-y-o 5f winner, half-sister to useful 1998
2-y-o 6f/7f winner Smittenby: modest maiden: stays 6f: acts on firm and soft ground.
Mrs P. N. Dutfield

BLESSINGINDISGUISE   9 b.g. Kala Shikari 125 – Blowing Bubbles 72 (Native **67 d**
Admiral (USA)) [2002 75: 5m 6f 5d² 5g* 5g 5d 5m 5m 5f 5m Oct 2] strong gelding: fair
handicapper: won at Catterick in May: well held after: barely stays 6f: possibly unsuited
by soft/heavy going, acts on any other turf: blinkered: often gives trouble at stall (lost
chance at start fifth outing). *M. W. Easterby*

BLONDE EN BLONDE (IRE) 2 ch.f. (Apr 20) Hamas (IRE) 125§ – Hulm (IRE) **54**
79 (Mujtahid (USA) 118) [2002 5.2g⁵ 5s³ 5m⁵ 6m³ 6f Oct 7] good-bodied filly: third foal:
dam 7f winner: modest maiden: third of 18 in nursery at Leicester fourth start: should stay
7f: acts on soft and good to firm ground: tail flasher. *N. P. Littmoden*

BLONDE STREAK (USA) 2 ch.f. (Mar 26) Dumaani (USA) 115 – Katiba (USA) **76**
99 (Gulch (USA)) [2002 7g³ 7m³ 7m² 8m⁶ Sep 12] $8,000Y: tall filly: fifth foal: half-
sister to 3 useful winners, including 1999 2-y-o 7f winner Meadaaar (by Diesis) and 1m/
1¼m winner Badaayer (by Silver Hawk): dam 6f (at 2 yrs) and 7f winner who stayed
1¼m: fair maiden: 4 lengths second to Big Bad Bob at Newcastle: probably stays 1m:
raced only on good/good to firm going. *T. D. Barron*

BLOOMING AMAZING 8 b.g. Mazilier (USA) 107 – Cornflower Blue (Tyrnavos **–**
129) [2002 f7g 7s 11.9f f9.4s 8d May 27] fair performer at best: well held in 2002: stayed
1½m: acted on good to firm going, good to soft and fibresand: tried visored/blinkered:
dead. *D. Burchell*

BLOOMING LUCKY (IRE) 3 b.f. Lucky Guest 109 – Persian Flower (Persian **40**
Heights 129) [2002 –: p7g* 10m f9.4g Jun 22] poor form: won handicap at Lingfield in
January: seems to stay easy 1¼m: acts on polytrack (well held on fibresand) and good to
firm going. *J. A. Osborne*

BLOSSOM WHISPERS 5 b.m. Ezzoud (IRE) 126 – Springs Welcome 86 (Blakeney **46**
126) [2002 60: p16g⁵ p13g⁶ p13g f16.2g 11.9g⁶ 16.2m⁵ 18d³ 17.2g⁵ 15.8m² Aug 6]
good-bodied mare: poor maiden nowadays: stays 2¼m: acts on good to firm going, good
to soft and fibresand: tried blinkered: joined Mrs M. Reveley £6,000 after final start.
C. A. Cyzer

BLOT 8 b.g. Warning 136 – Rattle Along 80 (Tap On Wood 130) [2002 10.9f 10d May **–**
7] possibly of little account nowadays. *A. J. Lidderdale*

BLOWING AWAY (IRE) 8 b. or br.m. Last Tycoon 131 – Taken By Force (Persian **36**
Bold 123) [2002 –, a29: 14.1m* f12f³ 15.8f⁶ 14.1d⁶ Oct 30] leggy mare: poor performer: **a–**
won selling handicap at Nottingham in July: stays 2m: probably acts on any turf going/
fibresand: has been visored: sometimes slowly away. *Julian Poulton*

BLUE A FUSE (IRE) 2 b.f. (Feb 19) Bluebird (USA) 125 – Gleaming Heather **–**
(USA) 61 (Irish River (FR) 131) [2002 7v Nov 8] IR 3,400, 5,200 2-y-o: second foal:
dam, Irish 2m winner, half-sister to very smart 1m to 1¼m winner Lear Spear: tailed off
in maiden at Doncaster. *M. Brittain*

BLUE BALOO 4 b.c. Turtle Island (IRE) 123 – Bright Future (FR) (Akarad (FR) 130) **91**
[2002 106: 10m⁶ 10s 10.5d² 10g³ 9.5g⁴ 10d 9.3d Sep 22] quite good-topped colt: first
foal: dam once-raced half-sister to useful French 1m and 10.5f winner Blue Sky: useful
performer at best: won 3 races prior to 2002, notably Group 3 event at Frankfurt at 3 yrs,
final start for A. Schutz: well beaten in minor event at Newmarket on reappearance but in
frame in similar contests afterwards at Dusseldorf and Dresden (2): stays 10.5f: acts on
heavy ground: blinkered penultimate start: sold €20,000 in October. *C. Von Der Recke,
Germany*

BLUEBERRY RHYME 3 b.g. Alhijaz 122 – Irenic 64 (Mummy's Pet 125) [2002 **69 §**
74: f6g³ 5d⁵ 5d f6g⁶ f5g² f5f f5g Dec 14] good-topped gelding: fair maiden: likely to
prove best at 5f/easy 6f: acts on soft ground and fibresand: often visored: looks a difficult
ride: sometimes finds little: can't be trusted. *P. J. Makin*

BLUEBIRD SPIRIT 2 ch.f. (Feb 10) Bluebird (USA) 125 – My Lewicia (IRE) 100 **60**
(Taufan (USA) 119) [2002 7d 7d Jul 31] second foal: dam, 1m winner who stayed 1¼m,
half-sister to smart sprinter To The Roof: modest form, never dangerous, in maidens at
Kempton: should stay 1m. *P. W. Harris*

BLUE BOUNTY (IRE) 2 b.f. (Apr 12) Blues Traveller (IRE) 119 – Cwm Deri (IRE) **55**
(Alzao (USA) 117) [2002 5.7m 6d⁶ 7d 7g Oct 24] IR 3,000Y: half-sister to several
winners, including 1995 2-y-o 6f winner Kossolian (by Emarati) and 1½m winner
Chocstaw (by Mtoto): dam unraced: modest maiden: off 3 months before below form
final start: should stay 1m. *J. Akehurst*

BLUE CASCADE (IRE) 3 b.g. Royal Academy (USA) 130 – Blaine (USA) (Lyp- **–**
hard's Wish (FR) 124) [2002 –: p8g⁶ a8g a10g⁴ p10g 10f 8.2f May 17] rather leggy **a58**
gelding: modest maiden: ran badly in handicaps last 3 starts (reportedly had breathing
problem final one): probably stays 1¼m: acts on all-weather: sometimes tongue tied/
slowly away: sold £1,400 in June. *S. Dow*

BLUE CIRCLE 2 b.c. (Jan 24) Whittingham (IRE) 104 – Reshift 94 (Night Shift –
(USA)) [2002 6m 5g 5.7f Sep 16] fifth foal: half-brother to 7-y-o Inchalong and
4-y-o Prince of Blues: dam 6f (including at 2 yrs)/7f winner: well held in maidens.
N. P. Littmoden

BLUEFLY (IRE) 3 b.c. Blues Traveller (IRE) 119 – Muckross Park 41 (Nomination –
125) [2002 7m May 2] 8,000Y, 13,500 2-y-o: third foal: half-brother to winners abroad
by Mac's Imp and Petardia: dam, sprint maiden, sister to useful performer up to 1m
Nominator: 16/1, tailed off in maiden at Redcar. *Mrs A. Duffield*

BLUEGRASS 3 ch.g. Bluegrass Prince (IRE) 110 – Seymour Ann (Krayyan 117) –
[2002 –: 7m 10m Jul 22] well held in maidens/claimer. *M. Madgwick*

BLUEGRASS BEAU 2 ch.c. (Mar 25) Bluegrass Prince (IRE) 110 – Blushing Belle **79**
74 (Local Suitor (USA) 128) [2002 5.3g^2 6m^6 7d^2 7.1m* 7f^4 7.5g^3 7.1m^2 8f^6 8f^3 8.3d Oct
14] rather leggy, workmanlike colt: fourth foal: half-brother to 3-y-o Rebelle: dam, 10.6f
seller winner at 2 yrs, also won over hurdles: fair performer: won maiden at Warwick in
July: creditable efforts in nurseries seventh to ninth starts: will stay at least 1¼m: acts on
firm and good to soft going: reliable. *I. A. Wood*

BLUEGRASS BOY 2 b.g. (Apr 17) Bluegrass Prince (IRE) 110 – Honey Mill 67 **80**
(Milford 119) [2002 7.1g^4 7g 7s Oct 25] 5,200Y: sixth foal: half-brother to 2 winners,
including 5f and 7f winner Erinvale (by Mon Tresor): dam maiden who should have
stayed 1m: fairly useful form when fourth to Assraar in maiden at Chepstow in
September: well held both starts after: should stay 1m. *G. B. Balding*

BLUE HAWK (IRE) 5 ch.g. Prince of Birds (USA) 121 – Classic Queen (IRE) **48**
(Classic Secret (USA) 91) [2002 55: 16.2m 16g^4 f16.2g^6 13.8m^3 Aug 6] neat gelding:
poor handicapper: stays 2m: acts on firm ground and fibresand: often makes running.
R. Hollinshead

BLUE JANNESSA 2 ch.f. (Apr 23) Blue Ocean (USA) 87 – Kakisa 81 (Forlorn River **69**
124) [2002 5.1m^6 6m* 5m^2 6.1m 5.3m* 6g^4 7g^3 Oct 19] 1,200Y, 3,000 2-y-o: deep-
girthed filly: half-sister to several winning sprinters, including fairly useful 5f performer
Lake Mistassiu (by Tina's Pet): dam 5f/6f winner: fair performer: won maiden in August
and seller in October, both at Brighton: creditable efforts in nurseries last 2 starts: barely
stays 7f: raced only on good/good to firm ground: tail flasher: sold 5,000 gns. *R. Wilman*

BLUE JESS 2 b.f. (Apr 19) Whittingham (IRE) 104 – Blush 57 (Gildoran 123) [2002 **35**
f6g^6 6m^3 5.1d^6 Jul 8] small, sturdy filly: second foal: dam, 11.6f winner, likely to have
stayed long distances: poor form in sellers: effective at 5f/6f. *B. R. Millman*

BLUE KNIGHT (IRE) 3 ch.g. Bluebird (USA) 125 – Fer de Lance (IRE) (Diesis **89**
133) [2002 72p: f7g* 7g^3 6g^2 7.1m^5 p7g 7.1m 7s^6 7d^4 7g 6.1m^5 6g^4 6m^2 5m 6m Sep
23] big, lengthy gelding: fairly useful performer: won maiden at Wolverhampton in
March and handicap at Brighton in August: effective at 5f/7f: acts on all-weather and
good to firm ground, probably on soft. *A. P. Jarvis*

BLUE LEADER (IRE) 3 b.c. Cadeaux Genereux 131 – Blue Duster (USA) 118 **86**
(Danzig (USA)) [2002 10.5d^4 8m^5 9.9m* 11.8g^6 10.1s Oct 22] rangy colt: has scope: first
foal: dam, 5f (at 2 yrs) to 7f winner, suited by 6f (also won Cheveley Park Stakes), sister
to smart performer up to 1m Zieten: fairly useful form: won maiden at Goodwood in
September: below form in handicaps last 2 starts: better at 1¼m than 1m: acts on good to
firm and good to soft going: carries head awkwardly: one to treat with caution: sold
14,000 gns, joined G. Brown. *E. A. L. Dunlop*

BLUE MANTLE (IRE) 3 ch.f. Barathea (IRE) 127 – Blue Wedding (USA) (Irish **79**
River (FR) 131) [2002 –p: 10g 9m* 8.3g* 9.3d^5 12g^3 12s* 10s Nov 1] big, strong filly:
fair performer: won handicap at Musselburgh and minor event at Hamilton in July then
(after being sold from Sir Mark Prescott 35,000 gns following fourth start) handicap at
Punchestown in October: stays 1½m: acts on soft and good to firm going. *P. Hughes,
Ireland*

BLUE MARINER 2 b.c. (Mar 23) Marju (IRE) 127 – Mazarine Blue 65 (Bellypha **81 p**
130) [2002 7g^2 Jul 24] 17,000Y: sixth foal: brother to smart 1997 2-y-o 6f winner who
later won in USA (including Grade 2 9f event) Sapphire Ring, and half-brother to 3
winners, including 4-y-o Putra Pekan: dam, 5f winner, half-sister to smart sprinter Rich
Charlie: favourite, promising 1¾ lengths second of 12 to Convent Girl in maiden at
Leicester, slowly away, challenging 1f out and keeping on: looked sure to improve.
P. W. Harris

BLUE MOMMA (IRE) 3 b.f. Petardia 113 – Heads We Called (IRE) (Bluebird –
(USA) 125) [2002 10g 10s May 13] 3,000Y: fifth foal: half-sister to 6f winner Seeking

Destiny (by Two Timing) and French 1m (at 2 yrs) and 1½m winner Riofrio (by Thatching): dam unraced sister to Derby third Blues Traveller: well held in maidens at Windsor. *P. R. Webber*

BLUE MUEMONIC 2 b.g. (Mar 7) Bluegrass Prince (IRE) 110 – Forget To Remind- **45**
me 51 (Forzando 122) [2002 p5g³ 5v⁵ 6m 5.1d² 6m⁶ 5g 6g⁵ 7m⁵ 5m 6g 8.3d f6g f9.4g⁴ f8.5g Dec 31] 5,400Y: second foal: dam 7f winner: poor maiden: seems to stay 9.4f: acts on good to soft going, good to firm and all-weather: has worn cheekpieces. *J. S. Moore*

BLUE MYST 2 b.f. (Mar 6) Blue Ocean (USA) 87 – Broom Isle 74 (Damister (USA) **–**
123) [2002 f8s Oct 8] 3,400Y: second foal: half-sister to 4-y-o Bolshoi Ballet: dam, 7f (at 2 yrs) to 15f winner, also won over hurdles: 25/1, last in maiden at Southwell. *E. J. Alston*

BLUE MYSTIQUE 3 b.f. Whittingham (IRE) 104 – Gold And Blue (IRE) (Bluebird **65**
(USA) 125) [2002 f6g⁴ f7g* f8.5g⁵ 6g³ 5.9d 7g 8g⁶ 6m³ 7m f7g² f7g f8.5s* f8.5s Dec 26] 6,500 2-y-o: sister to 4-y-o Blue Reigns and 6-y-o Blue Star and half-sister to 2 winners, including 5-y-o Jodeeka: dam lightly-raced Irish maiden: fair performer: won maiden in February and handicap in December, both at Wolverhampton: stays 8.5f: acts on fibresand and good to firm going: sometimes races freely. *N. P. Littmoden*

BLUE PATRICK 2 gr.c. (Mar 17) Wizard King 122 – Great Intent (Aragon 118) [2002 **87**
6m* 6m 7f⁵ Sep 25] 13,000Y: rather leggy colt: fluent mover: fourth foal: half-brother to a winner in Greece by Mind Games: dam once-raced sister to smart sprinter Argentum: fairly useful performer: won maiden at Yarmouth (beat Four Jays 2 lengths) in August: good ninth of 21 to Somnus in sales race at Doncaster next time: below form in minor event at Goodwood final start: stays 6f. *J. M. P. Eustace*

BLUE PLANET (IRE) 4 b.g. Bluebird (USA) 125 – Millie Musique (Miller's Mate **88**
116) [2002 88: p12g⁵ p12g⁴ 14.4m 12m 14.4s⁶ Jun 12] big, good-topped gelding: fairly useful handicapper: well held last 3 starts: stays easy 1½m: yet to race on heavy ground, acts on any other turf and polytrack: sometimes slowly away. *P. G. Murphy*

BLUE REIGNS 4 b.g. Whittingham (IRE) 104 – Gold And Blue (IRE) (Bluebird **65**
(USA) 125) [2002 93: 6m 8d 6m f6g⁴ f6s Nov 2] tall, useful-looking gelding: has a quick action: fairly useful handicapper at best, seems only fair nowadays: best at 5f/6f: acts on good to firm going, good to soft and fibresand: blinkered third outing: slowly away and early reminders final start. *N. P. Littmoden*

BLUE RIBBON (IRE) 6 b.g. Bluebird (USA) 125 – Sweet Justice (Law Society **–**
(USA) 130) [2002 f9.4g⁵ f9.4g 9g Mar 28] fair form in bumpers: little form on Flat: said to have bled from nose final start. *G. M. Moore*

BLUE RONDO (IRE) 2 b.c. (Feb 7) Hernando (FR) 127 – Blueberry Walk (Green **–**
Desert (USA) 127) [2002 p8g p7g Dec 21] IR 80,000Y: fifth foal: half-brother to 3 fairly useful winners, including French 1m (at 2 yrs) and 1¼m winner Jungle Rumbler (by Charnwood Forest) and 9.4f winner Joondey (by Pursuit of Love): dam unraced sister to useful stayer Hawait Al Barr: slowly away and well held in maiden and minor event at Lingfield: ran loose before both starts. *R. Charlton*

BLUE SAFARI (IRE) 3 b. or br.f. Blues Traveller (IRE) 119 – Lady Montekin (Mont- **51**
ekin 125) [2002 53: 7d 6m³ 6m 7m 7g⁴ 6m 7m Sep 3] tall, leggy filly: modest maiden handicapper: stays 7f: acts on good to firm ground: inconsistent. *J. Akehurst*

BLUE SAVANNA 2 ch.g. (Feb 24) Bluegrass Prince (IRE) 110 – Dusk In Daytona 64 **65**
(Beveled (USA)) [2002 8g p8g f7g⁵ Nov 26] 6,500Y: second foal: dam 7f winner (later successful in Jersey): best effort in maidens when 5 lengths seventh to Little Good Bay at Lingfield second start: slowly away on debut. *J. G. Portman*

BLUE SKY THINKING (IRE) 3 b.g. Danehill Dancer (IRE) 117 – Lauretta Blue **102 p**
(IRE) (Bluebird (USA) 125) [2002 8g³ 8m* 8d² 8m* Aug 29] IR 11,000F, IR 18,500Y: tall, rather leggy gelding: fifth foal: half-brother to 3 winners, including 1998 2-y-o 6f winner Paddock Inspection (by Archway) and 4-y-o Top Nolans: dam third at 1½m in Ireland: useful form: won maiden at Ascot in July and minor event at Salisbury (beat Passing Glance by neck despite wandering) in August: will be suited by 1¼m: yet to race on extremes of going: progressive. *K. R. Burke*

BLUE SONG 4 b.f. Shaamit (IRE) 127 – November Song (Scorpio (FR) 127) [2002 –: **–**
f9.4g f16.2g f12g 11.9g 13.1d Jun 21] of little account. *M. Mullineaux*

BLUES PRINCESS 2 b.f. (Feb 13) Bluebird (USA) 125 – Queen Shirley (IRE) **70**
(Fairy King (USA)) [2002 5g 5.1d 5m⁵ 5.1m 5.1d* 6m 5.1g 5g⁴ Oct 5] 14,000Y: smallish, sturdy filly: second foal: dam unraced out of half-sister to Cherry Hinton winner Crime of Passion: fair performer: won maiden at Bath in September: blinkered, creditable

fourth in nursery at Sandown: will prove best at 5f/6f: yet to race on extremes of going: none too consistent: sold 6,200 gns. *C. G. Cox*

BLUE STAR 6 b.g. Whittingham (IRE) 104 – Gold And Blue (IRE) (Bluebird (USA) 125) [2002 6g a6.5f* a7f² a7f² a7.5f* a6f⁶ 7.6f 6m 7.6g 6m 7m⁶ 7.1m² 7g⁴ 8.1m² 10.3f³ 8.9f* 7s² f8.5f Nov 11] rangy gelding: fairly useful handicapper on all-weather, fair on turf: won at Nad Al Sheba in January and February (left J. Sadler in UAE after sixth outing) and York (despite drifting right) in October: effective at 7f (given test) to 9f: acts on fibresand/dirt, firm and soft going: usually visored/blinkered: tends to be fractious stall/slowly away: often held up: tough. *M. Mullineaux* **79 a93**

BLUESTONE 3 ch.c. Bluebird (USA) 125 – Romoosh 69 (Formidable (USA) 125) [2002 8.2d 8.1f Apr 10] 190,000Y: medium-sized, lengthy colt: second foal: half-brother to 1m winner Ramzain (by Alzao): dam, 1¼m winner, half-sister to smart 6f/7f performer Unblest: well held in 2 maidens. *G. Wragg* **–**

BLUE STREAK (IRE) 5 ch.g. Bluebird (USA) 125 – Fleet Amour (USA) (Afleet (CAN)) [2002 61, a52+: p10g p12g⁶ p10g 8m 10.2f 10m³ 10m* 10m⁵ Aug 28] tall, rangy gelding: modest performer on Flat: won claimer at Brighton (claimed from K. Bell £3,000) in August: probably best at 1¼m/easy 1½m: acts on firm going, good to soft and polytrack: tried visored: blinkered (raced freely) sixth start: tried tongue tied: has edged left: successful over hurdles in October/November. *G. L. Moore* **58**

BLUE STYLE (IRE) 6 ch.g. Bluebird (USA) 125 – Style For Life (IRE) (Law Society (USA) 130) [2002 60: 11.9g 10d 14.1d 16.2m 18d 16.4d Jul 11] lengthy gelding: has a round action: only poor in 2002: should stay at least 1¾m: acts on heavy going, probably on good to firm: tried blinkered/visored/tongue tied. *P. Burgoyne* **47**

BLUE SYMPHONY 2 b.f. (Mar 23) Darshaan 133 – Blue Duster (USA) 118 (Danzig (USA)) [2002 7d 7m 7g 8m 10m Oct 1] smallish, quite good-topped filly: second foal: half-sister to 3-y-o Blue Leader: dam, 5f (at 2 yrs) to 7f winner but best at 6f (won Cheveley Park Stakes), sister to smart performer up to 1m Zieten: modest maiden: stays 1¼m: yet to race on extremes of going. *E. A. L. Dunlop* **57**

BLUE TROJAN (IRE) 2 b.g. (May 7) Inzar (USA) 112 – Roman Heights (IRE) (Head For Heights 125) [2002 7.1m f7g³ f7g² f7s* f8.5g² f8g³ Dec 27] IR 3,000F, 5,200 2-y-o: fifth foal: dam unraced: fairly useful performer: won maiden at Wolverhampton in December by 3 lengths from Zak Facta: ran creditably after: stays 8.5f: acts on fibresand: game. *S. Kirk* **80**

BLUE VELVET 5 gr.m. Formidable (USA) 125 – Sweet Whisper 63 (Petong 126) [2002 99d: 5f f5g² 6m³ 5.1g³ 6d⁴ f5g* 5m 5d⁵ 5m 6d⁵ 6g⁵ 5f⁴ 6f 6m 5g* 6g² 6f 5g³ 5s Oct 26] well-made mare: poor mover: useful handicapper: won at Southwell in June and Ayr in September: good second of 27 to John O'Groats in Silver Cup at Ayr day after latter win: effective at 5f/6f: acts on any turf going and fibresand: often bandaged: waited with. *D. K. Ivory* **92 + a100**

BLUE VENTURE (IRE) 2 ch.g. (Apr 26) Alhaarth (IRE) 126 – September Tide (IRE) 58 (Thatching 131) [2002 5g⁶ 6f³ f6g² Oct 17] IR 13,000F: good-bodied gelding: fourth foal: dam, third at 5f in Ireland, granddaughter of Irish 1000 Guineas winner Lady Capulet: fair maiden: placed at York and Southwell: not sure to stay beyond 6f: acts on firm going and fibresand. *P. C. Haslam* **74**

BLUE WATER 2 b.f. (Feb 12) Shaamit (IRE) 127 – November Song (Scorpio (FR) 127) [2002 6m 7g 7f f8.5g⁵ Sep 21] third foal: dam unraced: poor maiden. *M. Mullineaux* **42**

BLUNDELL LANE (IRE) 7 ch.g. Shalford (IRE) 124§ – Rathbawn Realm (Doulab (USA) 115) [2002 72, a58: p6g p7g⁵ p7g p8g 6m² 6.1f 6f 6g 6m* f6g 6m Aug 2] fair on turf, modest on all-weather: won claimer at Folkestone in June: best at 5f/6f: acts on firm going, good to soft and fibresand: sometimes visored/blinkered earlier in career: usually races prominently: unreliable. *A. P. Jarvis* **76 § a50 §**

BLUNHAM 2 b.g. (Apr 10) Danzig Connection (USA) – Relatively Sharp 86 (Sharpen Up 127) [2002 7m⁵ 8g³ 6d Oct 21] 9,000Y: tall, rather leggy gelding: half-brother to several winners, including fairly useful 7f/1m winner Wolf Venture (by Wolfhound): dam, 5f winner, half-sister to 2000 Guineas winner Tirol: fair form: third in minor event at Newcastle: soundly beaten final start: gelded after: stays 1m. *C. W. Fairhurst* **67**

BLUSHING GRENADIER (IRE) 10 ch.g. Salt Dome (USA) – La Duse 66 (Junius (USA) 124) [2002 51, a54: f6g⁵ f6s² f6g⁵ f6g⁴ f6g⁶ f6g f6g² f6g 6v³ 6v* 6d 5g f6s⁴ f5g Oct 17] leggy gelding: modest handicapper: won amateur event at Hamilton in June: stays 7f: acts on good to firm ground, heavy and fibresand: usually blinkered, tried visored: usually races prominently. *S. R. Bowring* **53**

BLUSHING PRINCE (IRE) 4 b.g. Priolo (USA) 127 – Eliade (IRE) 82 (Flash of –
Steel 120) [2002 ?, a81: f9.4g⁴ p10g f9.4g² f9.4g f9.4g⁴ f9.4g⁴ 11.6d f9.4g* 10.4m f9.4g* **a80**
p10g f9.4g f9.4g² f9.4g⁴ Dec 26] fairly useful performer: won seller in July and handicap
in October, both at Wolverhampton: stays 1¼m: acts on fibresand, well held on turf/
polytrack: usually tongue tied: none too consistent. *Mrs L. Stubbs*

BLUSHING SPUR 4 b.g. Flying Spur (AUS) – Bogus John (CAN) (Blushing John **76**
(USA) 120) [2002 60, a83: f6g² 6.1g³ f6g⁶ 6d* 6m² 6m 5g 6g f6g f6g f7g Dec 2] tall **a81**
gelding: fairly useful handicapper on all-weather, fair on turf: won at Goodwood in May:
below best last 6 starts: effective at 6f/7f: acts on fibresand, good to firm and heavy going:
visored/wears cheekpieces nowadays: sometimes slowly away/looks none too hearty.
D. Shaw

BLYTHE KNIGHT (IRE) 2 ch.c. (Feb 3) Selkirk (USA) 129 – Blushing Barada **82 p**
(USA) 53 (Blushing Groom (FR) 131) [2002 7m 8f² Aug 18] fourth foal: half-brother to
3 fairly useful winners, including 6-y-o Bid Me Welcome and winner around 2m High
Topper (by Wolfhound): dam maiden half-sister to Irish St Leger winner Authaal: still
green, better effort in maidens when 6 lengths second to Dhabyan at Kempton, taking
while to settle: should stay at least 1¼m: open to further improvement. *E. A. L. Dunlop*

BLYTHE SPIRIT 3 b.g. Bahamian Bounty 116 – Lithe Spirit (IRE) 74 (Dancing **89**
Dissident (USA) 119) [2002 68: 7f 7.9g* 8s² 7f* 8.1m 6d² 7.2g Sep 21] lengthy,
unfurnished gelding: fairly useful handicapper: won at Carlisle in May and Redcar in
June: effective at 6f to 1m: acts on any going: blinkered last 2 starts (weakened tamely
final one): temperament under suspicion. *R. A. Fahey*

B MAJOR (IRE) 3 b.g. Key of Luck (USA) 126 – Lingering Melody (IRE) 59 (Nor- **79**
dico (USA)) [2002 78p: p7g f8.5g* Feb 8] robust gelding: fair performer: won handicap
at Wolverhampton in February, edging right: stays easy 8.5f: acts on all-weather, some
promise on turf: sent to UAE. *M. A. Jarvis*

BO 2 b.f. (May 4) Shambo 113 – Abuzz 101 (Absalom 128) [2002 5m 5d⁴ 6m⁴ 8.3d 5.2d **70**
f7g⁴ f5g³ p6g³ p6g Dec 30] well-made filly: has a fluent, round action: sister to 3-y-o **a61**
Shiny and 4-y-o Shush and half-sister to several winners, including useful 5f/6f winner
(including at 2 yrs) World Premier (by Shareef Dancer): dam, 5f (at 2 yrs) and 7f winner,
half-sister to dam of very smart miler Revoque: fair maiden on turf, modest on all-
weather: reportedly struck into final start: stays 6f: acts on all-weather, good to firm and
good to soft going: sometimes wears cheekpieces/blinkers. *C. E. Brittain*

BOANERGES (IRE) 5 br.g. Caerleon (USA) 132 – Sea Siren 68 (Slip Anchor 136) **94**
[2002 89: 5f* 5f* 5f² 5m⁶ 5m 5f 6g 6m 6g 5m Oct 12] smallish, strong gelding: fairly
useful handicapper: won at Kempton and Thirsk in April: below form last 5 outings:
effective at 5f/sharp 6f: acts on firm and good to soft going: visored once at 2 yrs:
sometimes early to post (bolted and withdrawn once): usually held up: sold 13,000 gns.
R. Guest

BOATER 8 b.g. Batshoof 122 – Velvet Beret (IRE) (Dominion 123) [2002 61§: 12.6f⁵ **58 §**
Jun 26] well-made gelding: modest handicapper: stays 12.6f: acts on firm and soft
ground: tried blinkered: ungenuine. *R. J. Baker*

BOAVISTA (IRE) 2 b.f. (Apr 14) Fayruz 116 – Florissa (FR) (Persepolis (FR) 127) **65**
[2002 5f³ 5.1g⁴ Jun 15] IR 3,000F, 23,000Y: smallish, quite attractive filly: ninth foal:
sister to useful 1999 2-y-o 5f winner Tara's Girl and to 5f (at 2 yrs) to 7f winner Santa
Faye, and half-sister to 3 winners, including fairly useful 2001 2-y-o 6f and 7.5f winner
Florhill (by Danehill Dancer): dam Belgian 2-y-o 7f winner: fair form in frame in minor
event at Thirsk and maiden at Nottingham 2 months apart, edging left each time: will stay
6f. *T. D. Easterby*

BOBANVI 4 b.f. Timeless Times (USA) 99 – Bobanlyn (IRE) 76 (Dance of Life (USA)) –
[2002 –: 14.1d Apr 1] probably of little account nowadays. *J. S. Wainwright*

BOBBY KENNARD 3 b.g. Bobinski 115 – Midnight Break 78 (Night Shift (USA)) **76**
[2002 p8g² 9.3s⁴ 10g⁵ f14.8g² f14.8g² f16.2f² f16.2g² f16.2g* f14.8s⁴ Dec 13] second foal:
dam 5f/6f winner: fair handicapper: won at Wolverhampton in December: stays 2m: acts
on all-weather: carries head awkwardly: not one to trust implicitly. *J. A. Osborne*

BOB'S BUZZ 2 ch.g. (May 10) Zilzal (USA) 137 – Aethra (USA) 89 (Trempolino –
(USA) 135) [2002 6m Oct 7] 10,000Y: third foal: half-brother to 8.5f (at 2 yrs) and 1¼m
winner Alphaeus (by Sillery) and French 6f (at 2 yrs) and 1m winner Kane Ore (by Green
Desert), both useful: dam, maiden who should have stayed at least 1¼m, out of half-sister
to Prix de Diane winner Lacovia, herself dam of Tobougg: 33/1, last in maiden at
Windsor. *S. C. Williams*

BOBSLEIGH 3 b.g. Robellino (USA) 127 – Do Run Run 75 (Commanche Run 133) **87**
[2002 53: 11.6m⁵ 14.1m³ 14d³ 16.2d 14.1g* 14.1m² 14.1m² 14.1m* 14m 14.1g* Oct 2]
leggy, useful-looking gelding: fairly useful handicapper: won at Yarmouth in July and
September (made virtually all) and at Salisbury in October: should stay 2m: acts on good
to firm and good to soft going: carried head awkwardly and appeared to bite winner sixth
start. *Mrs A. J. Perrett*

BOB'S SHERIE 3 b.f. Bob's Return (IRE) 123 – Sheraton Girl 49 (Mon Tresor 113) **–**
[2002 f9.4g⁶ f9.4g Feb 2] first foal: dam 7f winner: well held in maidens at Wolverhampton. *W. M. Brisbourne*

BOCACCIO (IRE) 4 b.g. Brief Truce (USA) 126 – Idara 109 (Top Ville 129) [2002 **88**
86: 10s 8m⁵ 8d* 9g* 9d 8g 9.5g⁴ 9d p10g p8g Dec 30] half-brother to several winners,
including smart Irish 7f to 1¼m winner Idris (by Ahonoora) and useful 6f/7f winner
Sweet Mazarine (by Dancing Dissident): dam French 11f/1½m winner: fairly useful
performer: won maiden at Roscommon at 3 yrs: successful in handicaps at Limerick and
Leopardstown in June: left M. Grassick, Ireland, 16,000 gns after eighth start: stays 9f:
acts on good ground, some promise on polytrack: blinkered 6 of last 7 starts. *R. Ingram*

BODFARI KOMAITE 6 b.g. Komaite (USA) – Gypsy's Barn Rat 55 (Balliol 125) **88**
[2002 83: 5f 6m 5f⁶ 5g² 5f 5.1f³ 5m* 5.5m 5.1f 5m 5f 5v Nov 8] big, workmanlike
gelding: fairly useful handicapper: won at Haydock in July: was best at 5f: acted on firm
and good to soft going, probably on soft: blinkered: usually raced up with pace: tended to
wander: was none too reliable: dead. *M. W. Easterby*

BODFARI PRIDE (IRE) 7 b.g. Pips Pride 117 – Renata's Ring (IRE) (Auction Ring **82 d**
(USA) 123) [2002 87: 7.6f 7m³ 7f 5.1d³ 5g 5.1f 5.9d* 7.2d* 7m* 7.2d² 7.6g 7.6f 7m 5g
7.2g 6f 7g p7g Nov 14] strong, lengthy gelding: poor mover: fairly useful performer: on
downgrade in 2002, though won sellers at Hamilton/Ayr and ladies claimer at Newcastle
in July: reportedly finished lame final outing: effective at 5f to easy 7.6f: acts on soft
going, good to firm and fibresand: blinkered (well held) sixth outing. *A. Bailey*

BODFARI ROSE 3 ch.f. Indian Ridge 123 – Royale Rose (FR) 75 (Bering 136) [2002 **62**
p10g⁴ 11.5m³ 9.2m³ 13.8g f16.2f Nov 11] 44,000F: first foal: dam, 1m winner, sister to
useful French miler Rouen: modest maiden: trained first 2 starts by W. Haggas: pulled up
last 2 outings (reportedly struck into final one): stays 1¼m: sold 600 gns. *A. Bailey*

BODFARI SIGNET 6 ch.g. King's Signet (USA) 110 – Darakah 78 (Doulab (USA) **48**
115) [2002 56?: 12g⁴ 13v⁵ 16d² 16m 15.8f Oct 8] leggy, lengthy gelding: poor performer:
stays 2m: acts on soft and firm going: tried blinkered/visored/tongue tied: tends to find
little. *Mrs S. C. Bradburne*

BODIAM (IRE) 2 b.f. (Jan 31) Mukaddamah (USA) 125 – Partenza (USA) (Red **–**
Ransom (USA)) [2002 5g 5.1s f7s Dec 13] first foal: dam unraced out of half-sister to
smart French/US filly around 1¼m Aube Indienne: well beaten in minor event/maidens.
J. M. Bradley

BOGUS BALLET 3 ch.f. Halling (USA) 133 – Classic Ballet (FR) 75 (Fabulous **53 d**
Dancer (USA) 124) [2002 –: f12g 8.1f 8.2d 7g³ 7.1v 8.2m 8f 7g p10g p6g Dec 30] small,
workmanlike filly: modest performer: sold cheaply from M. Bell after sixth start: no form
after: should stay 1m+: acts on firm and good to soft ground: reportedly gave trouble in
preliminaries penultimate start. *J. J. Bridger*

BOHILL LAD (IRE) 8 b.g. Contract Law (USA) 108 – La Sass (Sassafras (FR) 135) **–**
[2002 11.7m⁵ Jun 26] fair hurdler/fairly useful chaser: showed nothing in maiden at Bath
on Flat debut. *J. D. Frost*

BOING BOING (IRE) 2 b.g. (Mar 26) King's Theatre (IRE) 128 – Limerick Princess **69 ?**
(IRE) 68 (Polish Patriot (USA) 128) [2002 p8g⁶ f8.5s Dec 9] 11,000Y: third foal: dam, 5f
(at 2 yrs) and 6f winner, closely related to useful 1994 2-y-o sprinter Limerick Belle:
better effort in maidens when sixth at Eloquent Silence at Lingfield: reportedly lost action
next time. *J. W. Hills*

BOISDALE (IRE) 4 b.g. Common Grounds 118 – Alstomeria 61 (Petoski 135) [2002 **60**
77: 7d 7d⁶ 6m⁴ 6d 6m Sep 19] workmanlike gelding: modest handicapper nowadays:
effective at 6f/7f: acts on soft ground, probably on good to firm: tongue tied final 3-y-o
start: sold 1,100 gns. *J. A. R. Toller*

BOJANGLES (IRE) 3 b.c. Danehill (USA) 126 – Itching (IRE) (Thatching 131) [2002 **89**
10f⁵ 10d² Jul 9] deep-girthed colt, type to carry plenty of condition: brother to very smart
1m to 1¼m winner Great Dane and half-brother to 2 winners, including fairly useful 1996
2-y-o 6f winner (later stayed 1m) Witching Hour (by Alzao): dam unraced half-sister to
Croco Rouge and to dam of Ali-Royal, Sleepytime and Taipan: short to post, better effort

in maidens (fairly useful form) when 1¼ lengths second to Spinnette at Newmarket, keeping on strongly having been held up: sold only 1,000 gns in October. *H. R. A. Cecil*

BOLD AMUSEMENT   12 ch.g. Never So Bold 135 – Hysterical 68 (High Top 131)   **59**
[2002 67: 12.4m⁶ 11.9s² 10.9d 9.2g² 9.2d² 9.2v⁶ 10.9g Sep 19] strong gelding: modest performer: effective at 9f to 1½m: acts on firm and good to soft going, probably not on softer nowadays: tried blinkered earlier in career: sometimes races freely/wanders. *W. S. Cunningham*

BOLD DANCE   3 b.f. Marju (IRE) 127 – Tropical Dance (USA) 93 (Thorn Dance   **35**
(USA) 107) [2002 58?: f8g⁶ f8g⁵ f7g⁶ 10f Apr 11] smallish filly: poor maiden: probably stays 1m: acts on fibresand, best turf effort on good going: tried blinkered. *K. McAuliffe*

BOLD DOLL (IRE)   3 b.f. Dolphin Street (FR) 125 – Bold Miss (Bold Lad (IRE)   **60**
133) [2002 69: p8g 10d 12m⁶ 14.1f 7d Oct 15] IR 16,000Y: half-sister to several winners, including useful 8.5f (at 2 yrs) to 1¼m winner Atlantic Desire and useful 1993 2-y-o 7f winner Lomas (both by Ela-Mana-Mou) and Irish 1¾m winner Tellyrand (by Cut Above): dam unraced: modest maiden: left K. Prendergast in Ireland after 2 yrs: stays 7f: blinkered once at 2 yrs. *Mrs P. N. Dutfield*

BOLD EFFORT (FR)   10 b.g. Bold Arrangement 127 – Malham Tarn (Riverman   **– §**
(USA) 131) [2002 85§, a69§: p7g p6g 5.7d 5.7d f6g Jun 28] good-quartered, dipped-backed gelding: poor mover: still fairly useful in 2001, well held in 2002: blinkered nowadays, has been visored. *K. O. Cunningham-Brown*

BOLD EWAR (IRE)   5 ch.g. Persian Bold 123 – Hot Curry (USA) (Sharpen Up 127)   **71**
[2002 82: p7g p10g⁶ p10g p8g p10g f8g p12g⁵ 8.5g 12m 16m 14.1d² 22.2m 15g 10m³ 10.1m³ p10g* 7.5m 9m 8m⁶ f14.8g* 15.9f³ 17.1f⁵ p16g* p12g f16.2g p16g⁴ p13g⁵ Dec 28] leggy, close-coupled gelding: easy mover: fair performer: won handicaps at Lingfield in August/October and minor event at Wolverhampton in September: best recent form at 1¼m to 2m: acts on all-weather, firm and good to soft going: usually blinkered: tongue tied (ran creditably) first 2 starts: sometimes carries head awkwardly/runs in snatches. *C. E. Brittain*

BOLD JOGGER (IRE)   5 b.g. Persian Bold 123 – Mouette (FR) (Fabulous Dancer   **–**
(USA) 124) [2002 9g 8.2m Oct 1] maiden when raced in Hong Kong and known as Eye's Magic: showed nothing on British debut. *N. A. Graham*

BOLD KING   7 br.g. Anshan 119 – Spanish Heart 86 (King of Spain 121) [2002 99d: **79**
7d 7d 8d⁴ 8d⁵ 7.6s f8g Oct 17] rangy gelding: fair performer at best nowadays: stays   **a–**
1m: acts on fibresand, best on going softer than good on turf: visored penultimate start. *J. W. Hills*

BOLD PRECEDENT   5 b.g. Polish Precedent (USA) 131 – Shining Water (USA)   **54 d**
(Riverman (USA) 131) [2002 63: p13g⁴ p12g⁶ p13g 10.1d 11.9g Aug 8] angular gelding: modest handicapper: left R. Stronge after third start and well held after: probably stays 13f: acts on all-weather and good to firm going, seemingly not on softer than good: sometimes visored. *R. J. White*

BOLD RAIDER   5 b.g. Rudimentary (USA) 118 – Spanish Heart 86 (King of Spain   **96**
121) [2002 87: 8.3g⁶ 10g* 10m³ 8.3s³ 10.1d 9s² 10m Sep 7] tall, leggy gelding: useful performer: won minor event at Windsor in April: very good second to Eastern Breeze in handicap at Kempton penultimate start: effective at 1m/1¼m: very best form on good ground or softer: sometimes found little earlier in career. *I. A. Balding*

BOLEYN CASTLE (USA)   5 ch.g. River Special (USA) – Dance Skirt (CAN)   **119**
(Caucasus (USA) 127) [2002 98?: 5s⁵ 5d² 5f⁵ 5.2f Sep 21]
Trainer Terry Mills' record at Ascot was highlighted by the big-race successes of Where Or When, Norton, Peace Offering and Olivia Grace in 2002. The much improved Boleyn Castle also played his part in July when putting up a fine weight-carrying effort in the Hong Kong Jockey Club Sprint. Boleyn Castle began the season as a useful performer, with just thirteen outings under his belt in three seasons, his best effort seemingly when winning a controversial handicap at Epsom in 2001 in which the stalls of several of his rivals were late opening. Boleyn Castle's improvement coincided with his having a new rider, apprentice Robert Miles. Ignoring the 7-lb claim, 20/1-shot Boleyn Castle defied a BHB mark of 108 when making all at Ascot, conceding upwards of 9 lb to all bar one (the veteran and top weight Tedburrow) of his eighteen rivals. This was a performance verging on very smart, as he gave runner-up Atlantic Viking 24 lb and a length and a quarter beating, with Proud Boast, who received 13 lb, a neck back in third.

Hong Kong Jockey Club Sprint (Handicap), Ascot—
a smart performance from Boleyn Castle, who makes all to beat Atlantic Viking

Boleyn Castle had shown himself an improved performer on his reappearance in a minor event at Sandown in June when, despite being slowly into his stride, he pulled off a 33/1-surprise to beat Bishops Court by a length. Boleyn Castle's next outing was also at Sandown, where he had to be mounted on the track and taken early to post before finishing two and a half lengths second to Palace Affair in a listed event. Boleyn Castle was seen out only once more after his Ascot win, in the Group 3 Dubai International Airport World Trophy at Newbury two months later. Unfortunately, he couldn't dominate and turned in a rather tame effort, the performance shedding little light on whether Boleyn Castle would, as his Ascot form entitles him to, prove capable of making his mark in pattern company. Boleyn Castle will get further opportunities in the next season to confirm his Ascot run, the King's Stand Stakes over the same course being a possible target, though it should be noted that Miles cannot claim his allowance in listed or pattern races. The strong, compact Boleyn Castle is best at five furlongs. Well held on his only outing on heavy going, he acts on any other turf going and has shown reluctance at the stalls. *T. G. Mills*

BOLHAM LADY   4 b.f. Timeless Times (USA) 99 – Stratford Lady 48 (Touching   –
Wood (USA) 127) [2002 –, a53: f5g f5g Feb 1] compact filly: modest performer at 3 yrs: well beaten in 2002: usually blinkered. *J. Balding*

BOLINGBROKE CASTLE (IRE)   4 ch.g. Goldmark (USA) 113 – Ruby River   –
(Red God 128§) [2002 –: 7.5g 6.9d Jun 26] lengthy, workmanlike gelding: disappointing maiden: tried visored/blinkered/tongue tied. *Miss J. A. Camacho*

BOLLIN EDWARD   3 b.c. Timeless Times (USA) 99 – Bollin Harriet (Lochnager   **75**
132) [2002 79: 6s 6m² 5g⁴ 5g³ 6m* 6d⁵ 5g Aug 7] good-bodied colt: fair performer: won maiden at Ripon in June, making all: will prove best at 5f/6f: acts on good to firm going: visored last 4 starts: pulled hard sixth outing. *T. D. Easterby*

BOLLIN ELLEN   3 b.f. Bin Ajwaad (IRE) 119 – Bollin Magdalene 55 (Teenoso   –
(USA) 135) [2002 10f 12.1m⁵ 12f⁶ Jun 24] lengthy filly: fourth foal: half-sister to 5-y-o Bollin Nellie and 4-y-o Bollin Thomas: dam, staying maiden on Flat, fairly useful winner over hurdles: well held in 3 maidens: should stay at least 1½m. *T. D. Easterby*

BOLLIN ERIC   3 b.c. Shaamit (IRE) 127 – Bollin Zola 90 (Alzao (USA) 117)   **125**
[2002 95p: 9m³ 10.4f² 12m² 11.9m³ 11.9g³ 14.6m* Sep 14]
'What's in a name?' According to Shakespearean coinage, that which we call a rose by any other name would smell as sweet. But not always, surely. Would Tiger Woods, for example, have been quite so charismatic a figure in golf had he

gone through life as an Eldrick, or John Wayne been such a huge movie star under the moniker of Marion Montgomery? The naming of thoroughbreds is something over which most owners are assiduous, in spite of the fact that they must realise no amount of time and research spent on such deliberations can enhance a thoroughbred's prospects. Good names are a joy, of course, but a racehorse does not have to be given a name with classical or refined undertones to take high rank. Among those who adopt a more straightforward approach to naming are a few who follow the practice of using a prefix or suffix. They include the small-scale owner-breeders Sir Neil and Lady Westbrook whose horses carry the prefix 'Bollin', after the river which runs through their farm in Cheshire. The horses usually take their second name from members of the family, those named after male members running in the red, white sleeves, black and yellow quartered cap of Sir Neil, and those with female names in the claret, white sleeves, black and yellow quartered cap of Lady Westbrook. While the naming policy readily identifies the owners, however, it does leave plenty of scope for confusing the horses—Edward, Ellen, Janet, Jeannie, Nellie and Thomas all running in the latest season, along with the most notable racehorse to carry the prefix, Bollin Eric (believed to be named after a cousin).

Bollin Eric won twice as a two-year-old—a maiden at Beverley and a nursery at Doncaster, both over a mile—and impressed as a staying type who would win a good prize at three. That said, few outside his connections, who regarded him highly, could have envisaged Bollin Eric's going on to classic success. When he won the St Leger—whose sponsorship by Rothmans is set to be ended by a ban on tobacco advertising—he became only the second winner of an English classic in a quarter of a century to be trained in the North, and the first sent out by his long-established stable, with which Bollin Eric's owners have been associated for around forty years. The licence at Habton Grange has been held since 1996 by Tim Easterby, who faced the daunting prospect of stepping into the shoes of a legendary father. Peter Easterby is the only trainer to have reached the one-thousand-winner milestone both on the Flat and over jumps. The list of good-class jumpers over the sticks saddled by him was a long one—he won three trainers' championships over jumps—but he won only two pattern events on the Flat (the King's Stand with Goldhill and the Gimcrack with Sonnen Gold) and never had a runner in a classic. Habton Grange's profile on the Flat has certainly been raised since Tim Easterby took over. The stable was one of only five in the latest season to top the million-pound mark in win prize-money in Britain. Tim has followed Peter ('No expensive horse ever did me any good') in the knack of purchasing good horses fairly cheaply. The second biggest contributor to the stable's earnings in the latest season was the two-year-old Somnus, a 13,500-guinea yearling successful in two of the biggest races outside the pattern, the St Leger Yearling Stakes and the Two-Year-Old Trophy at Redcar, his four victories in the season yielding £254,576. Bollin Eric earned £240,000 for winning the St Leger, and five other placed efforts took his total earnings for the campaign to £324,029.

The first important entry made for Bollin Eric as a three-year-old was in the Dante Stakes at York's May meeting. He was warmed up in the Feilden Stakes at Newmarket, justifying his Dante entry with a good third behind Playapart before demonstrating further improvement at York, where he showed smart form when a length-and-a-quarter second to Moon Ballad. But that was only half the story. Caught a little flat-footed early in the straight before staying on really strongly, Bollin Eric shaped very much as though he would benefit from a step up to a mile and a half plus, impressing even at this early stage as a likely St Leger contender. Bollin Eric had not been entered in the Derby and talk of his running next in the Prix du Jockey Club came to nothing. Bollin Eric had a hard race at York, where his jockey received a four-day suspension for excessive use of the whip, and he wasn't seen out again until the Ascot 'Derby', the King Edward VII Stakes. Bollin Eric's running again earned his rider—Kevin Darley on board for the first time in the season—a trip to the stewards' room, the stewards considering whether runner-up Bollin Eric, who came off a true line under pressure, interfered with the third and fifth in the final furlong. The placings were allowed to stand but, in going down by three and a half lengths to the Dante third Balakheri, Bollin Eric failed to improve as expected for the step up in trip. His rider reported that Bollin Eric had been feeling the firmish ground, but the theory that the round-actioned Bollin Eric might prove more effective on a more yielding surface, which he had never encountered, was not put to the test. The going was also good or firmer for his three remaining races, starting with the July Trophy at Haydock, in which he had another hard race on firmish going when beaten at odds on behind the Derby fourth Jelani. Bollin Eric had his last outing before Doncaster in the Great Voltigeur at York. A length covered the first five at the end of a relatively slowly-run affair in which Bollin Eric ran at least as well as ever to be beaten a head and a neck, again taking time to find his stride when the pace quickened and putting in all his best work in the closing stages, gradually hauling back the odds-on Bandari and Highest. The galloping Doncaster track and the extra two and a half furlongs or so in the St Leger looked as if it would suit Bollin Eric down to the ground.

Much interest in the latest St Leger focussed on the prospects of the One Thousand Guineas and Oaks winner Kazzia's becoming the first to land the fillies' triple crown since Oh So Sharp. Her enforced defection with a foot abscess and the late withdrawal of two of the final list of declared runners left a field of eight. As with Bollin Eric, the 13/8-favourite Bandari was from a family more noted for speed than stamina, but he too had given the strong impression that the St Leger trip would bring out the best of him. Balakheri, one of three representing the Stoute stable seeking a long-awaited first win in the St Leger, was second favourite at 7/2, with Bollin Eric and the Aidan O'Brien-selected Sholokhov next at 7/1. It would, incidentally, be something of a surprise nowadays if the Derby winner turned out for the St Leger (Reference Point was the last to do so fifteen years ago) and, when the race closed in July, High Chaparral was not even among the eight entries from Ballydoyle. Though there were criticisms about the quality of the St Leger field—trainer Barry Hills called it 'a stinking bad race'—there was certainly no shortage of enthusiasm for the winner from the Yorkshire crowd, cheering home the first winner of the oldest classic to be trained in the county since the outsider Peleid twenty-nine years earlier. Bollin Eric looked trained to the minute and was on his toes beforehand, having to be led by two handlers. Bandari, above himself in the paddock, troublesome at the start and sweating profusely by the time the race got underway, took over from the front-running Mr Dinos early in the straight but he couldn't assert himself and the patiently-ridden Bollin Eric quickened past him two furlongs out. Keeping on strongly, Bollin Eric held off the last-furlong challenge of Highest by a length and a quarter, with Bandari a further two lengths away third, the first three finishing in reverse order to the Great Voltigeur. Mamool and Mr Dinos, first and second in the Queen's Vase at Royal Ascot, came fourth and fifth, with Balakheri only sixth and Sholokhov last. As well as providing his trainer with his first classic success (his only previous classic runner was French Fellow in the millennium Two Thousand Guineas), Bollin Eric was also the first British classic winner for Kevin Darley. Darley was on board Bollin Eric for the first time since Royal Ascot, Kieren Fallon—suspended for the St Leger—having ridden Bollin Eric in the Voltigeur.

Rothmans Royals St Leger Stakes, Doncaster—Bollin Eric provides the North with a very rare modern-day classic; he relishes the step up in trip to beat Highest and Bandari

Sir Neil Westbrook's "Bollin Eric"

Bollin Eric (b.c. 1999)	Shaamit (IRE) (b 1993)	Mtoto (b 1983)	Busted
			Amazer
		Shomoose (b 1985)	Habitat
			Epithet
	Bollin Zola (b 1986)	Alzao (b 1980)	Lyphard
			Lady Rebecca
		Sauntry (br 1982)	Ballad Rock
			Crestia

The big, strong Bollin Eric, a good walker, is by the now-deceased Derby winner Shaamit, who began his stud career at the National Stud before being sent to Northern Ireland as a jumping stallion after completing only three seasons, in the course of which he was sent fewer than a hundred mares, covering only twenty-one in his final season at Newmarket. Bollin Eric's dam Bollin Zola visited Shaamit in each of his three seasons in England but was barren to him either side of the visit that yielded Bollin Eric. Bought as a yearling on behalf of Bollin Eric's owner-breeders for only IR 6,500 guineas, Bollin Zola proved a fairly useful handicapper, successful at up to seven and a half furlongs. She bred three winners before Bollin Eric, the smart sprinter Bollin Joanne (by Damister), the fairly useful miler Bollin Terry (by Terimon) and the fair sprint handicapper Bollin Ann (by Anshan). An initial examination shows Bollin Eric's pedigree dominated by speed on the dam's side—his unraced grandam Sauntry was by the sprinter Ballad Rock out of a Prince Tenderfoot mare—but there is stamina further back in the family. Bollin Eric's great grandam Crestia, a two-year-old six-furlong winner, was a half-sister to the dual Prix du Cadran winner El Badr. El Badr, incidentally, was by Weavers' Hall, a son of Shaamit's grandsire Busted, while one of the best offspring of Shaamit's sire Mtoto is the Gold Cup winner Celeric. If Bollin Eric is aimed at the Cup races as a four-year-old—it's a fair bet he'll run in the Yorkshire Cup at least—he should do very well. He showed improved form for the stiffer test of stamina at Doncaster and there is every prospect of his progressing again at longer distances with another year under his belt. The St Leger provided him with his only victory at three and the chances are that he will continue to find one or two too good for him again over middle distances. The game and genuine Bollin Eric has never finished out of the first three in ten races and is a credit to his connections. *T. D. Easterby*

BOLLIN JANET   2 b.f. (Mar 20) Sheikh Albadou 128 – Bollin Emily 82 (Lochnager 132) [2002 5g³ 6m⁴ 5g* Sep 18] strong, well-made filly: ninth foal: half-sister to winner around 1m Bollin Frank (by Rambo Dancer) and 7f to 8.5f winner Bollin Roberta (by Bob's Return): dam sprinter: fair form: in frame in maidens before readily winning similar event at Beverley by 1¾ lengths from Cayman Breeze: will prove best at 5f/6f: type to do fair bit better as 3-y-o, and could well prove useful. *T. D. Easterby*   **78 p**

BOLLIN JEANNIE   2 b.f. (Mar 6) Royal Applause 124 – Bollin Joanne 118 (Damister (USA) 123) [2002 6d⁴ 5g² 5d* 6m Sep 8] smallish, compact filly: has a quick action: first foal: dam, sprinter, half-sister to St Leger winner Bollin Eric: fair form: won maiden at Thirsk in August, edging right: disappointing in nursery at York only subsequent outing: should stay 6f. *T. D. Easterby*   **74**

BOLLIN NELLIE   5 ch.m. Rock Hopper 124 – Bollin Magdalene 55 (Teenoso (USA) 135) [2002 81: 11.9m 12m² 10.3m⁵ 12d* 11.9d* 11.9d 12d³ 13.9m 12g⁵ 12g 11.9f⁵ 12v² Nov 9] sparely-made, plain mare: useful handicapper: improved again in 2002: won at Thirsk in May and York (Queen Mother's Cup by 5 lengths from Court of Appeal) in June: gambled on, good head second to Red Wine in November Handicap at Doncaster final start, pair well clear: stays 1½m: has won on good to firm going, best form on softer than good: usually held up: tough, game and reliable. *T. D. Easterby*   **98**

Queen Mother's Cup (Ladies) Handicap, York—Bollin Nellie (partnered by Annie Elsey) is better than ever at the age of five; there's a healthy margin to spare over Court of Appeal (second right), Party Ploy, Gralmano (left) and Inver Gold (rail)

BOLLIN THOMAS 4 b.g. Alhijaz 122 – Bollin Magdalene 55 (Teenoso (USA) 135) **88**
[2002 77: 12.3g⁵ 14d² 14s* 15.9f² 14v² Aug 9] close-coupled, workmanlike gelding:
fairly useful handicapper: improved in 2002, winning at Haydock in June: effective from
1½m to 2m: acts on any ground: consistent. *T. D. Easterby*

BOLSHOI BALLET 4 b.g. Dancing Spree (USA) – Broom Isle 74 (Damister (USA) **71**
123) [2002 63: f11s* f11s² f12s* f11s⁶ 14.1d³ f14.8s* f16.2g⁴ May 20] quite good-
topped gelding: fair performer: won maiden (apprentices) and handicap at Southwell in
January and, having left T. D. Barron after fourth start, handicap at Wolverhampton (by
12 lengths) in May: probably stays 2m: acts on heavy going, good to firm and fibresand.
J. Mackie

BOLT FROM THE BLUE 6 b.g. Grand Lodge (USA) 125 – Lightning Legacy –
(USA) 78 (Super Concorde (USA) 128) [2002 –, a30: f16s f12s f11g f11g Mar 12] modest
maiden at best: dead. *Don Enrico Incisa*

BOLTOUTOFTHEBLUE 3 ch.g. Bluegrass Prince (IRE) 110 – Forget To Remind- –
me 51 (Forzando 122) [2002 52: 8.1d 10m 11.7f⁶ Aug 23] modest maiden at 2 yrs: well
held in 2002. *J. S. Moore*

BOLULA 3 b.f. Tagula (IRE) 116 – Bollin Dorothy 73 (Rambo Dancer (CAN) 107) **55**
[2002 61: 8g 6f 5g⁵ 5m⁵ 5g 6g 5.9d⁴ 5.9d³ 5.9g⁴ 5m³ Aug 17] strong, workmanlike filly:
modest maiden: stays 6f: acts on soft and good to firm going: blinkered last 7 starts: sold
800 gns. *T. D. Easterby*

BONAGUIL (USA) 5 b.g. Septieme Ciel (USA) 123 – Chateaubrook (USA) (Alleged **98**
(USA) 138) [2002 100: p10g⁵ 10g⁶ 12m 10.5m² 10d³ 10m 10.1m 10d Oct 14]
sparely-made gelding: useful handicapper: creditable efforts in 2002 only when placed
at Haydock and Newmarket (third to Invitation): stays 1½m: acts on any turf going
and polytrack: often held up: tends to wander/find little: sold 25,000 gns, sent to
USA. *C. F. Wall*

BON AMI (IRE) 6 b.g. Paris House 123 – Felin Special (Lyphard's Special (USA) **84**
122) [2002 92d: 7f 6m⁴ 8d 7.1m³ 10s⁵ 8.3s⁶ 7s 6m⁵ 7m³ 6m⁴ 6d⁴ 7f³ 6m 7m² 7g² 6g⁴
7g* 6m 7m* 7m 7.1m⁴ 7m 8m Sep 29] rather leggy gelding: fluent mover: fairly useful
performer: won handicap at Epsom (first success for 4 years) and minor event at Folkestone in August: better recent form at 7f than 6f: acts on any going: effective blinkered/
visored or not: sometimes edges left/carries head high: usually held up of late: tough: sold
20,000 gns. *D. K. Ivory*

BOND BECKS (IRE) 2 ch.c. (Mar 10) Tagula (IRE) 116 – At Amal (IRE) (Astronef **101**
116) [2002 5d 5m* 5g³ 5m⁴ 5g⁶ 5g* Oct 19] IR 4,000F, 7,000Y, 34,000 2-y-o: lengthy,
rather unfurnished colt: has scope: third foal: half-brother to a winner in Holland by
Rainbows For Life: dam unraced: useful performer: won maiden at Beverley in July and
minor event at Catterick in October: best efforts when in frame in listed race at York and
Flying Childers Stakes at Doncaster (close fourth of 14 to Wunders Dream): likely to
prove best at 5f/6f: unraced on extremes of going: has worn crossed noseband. *B. Smart*

BOND BOY 5 b.g. Piccolo 121 – Arabellajill 97 (Aragon 118) [2002 87: 5g 5.1g² 5m **103**
6g* 6m² 6m 6g* 6g 6g 5s* 6v Nov 9] useful handicapper: much improved in 2002: won
at York in June, Goodwood (Vodafone Stewards' Cup by length from Halmahera, edging
left) in August and Doncaster (beat dead-heaters Artie and Baralinka by 2 lengths) in
October: best at 5f/6f: yet to race on firm going, acts on any other. *B. Smart*

Vodafone Stewards' Cup (Handicap), Goodwood—
Bond Boy gives trainer Bryan Smart his biggest win of the year; Halmahera finishes second in the race
for the third time, ahead of Undeterred (hidden against far rail)

BOND DIAMOND   5 gr.g. Prince Sabo 123 – Alsiba 68 (Northfields (USA)) [2002   **83**
66+: p8g⁵ p10g* 8.2m* 8m* 8g* 8.5g 8f 8m² 8m* 8.9f Oct 12] strong, lengthy gelding:
fairly useful performer: won handicaps at Lingfield, Nottingham, Bath and Yarmouth and
minor event at Pontefract between February/September (left B. Smart after sixth start):
stays easy 1¼m: acts on firm going, good to soft and all-weather: sometimes wears
crossed noseband/carries head awkwardly. *P. R. Webber*

BOND DOMINGO   3 b.g. Mind Games 121 – Antonia's Folly 64 (Music Boy 124)   **76 d**
[2002 82§: f6s f5s⁴ 6m 5.7g 5d 5m 5g 5d⁴ f6g f6g Dec 7] strong, weak gelding: fair
handicapper: off 5½ months, below form after second outing: best at 5f: acts on fibresand
and heavy going: usually blinkered: sometimes hangs left. *B. Smart*

BONDI (FR)   2 b.f. (Apr 19) Sillery (USA) 122 – Biscay 67 (Unfuwain (USA) 131)   **–**
[2002 8g 7d Nov 2] leggy filly: third foal: dam, maiden, might have proved best short of
1m: well held in maidens. *I. A. Balding*

BOND JOVI (IRE)   3 b.g. Danehill Dancer (IRE) 117 – Vieux Carre (Pas de Seul 133)   **–**
[2002 72: 6.1f 6.1f 6g 5.1d 8.5m f6g f8.5s⁶ f7g Dec 17] smallish gelding: fair performer at
2 yrs: little form in 2002: blinkered final outing. *B. Smart*

BOND MAY DAY   2 b.f. (Apr 13) Among Men (USA) 124 – State Romance 67 (Free   **68**
State 125) [2002 6.1g 5g³ 5m 5.7f² 7m² 7m 6f Oct 7] 11,000Y: angular filly: half-sister to
several winners, including 7-y-o Mantles Pride and 5f (at 2 yrs) to 1m (in Sweden) winner
What Fun (both by Petong): dam 7f/1m winner: fair maiden: runner-up in minor event at
Bath and nursery at Chester, both in August: well below form last 2 starts (reportedly
finished lame on first of them): stays 7f: raced only on good going or firmer. *B. Smart*

BOND MIDNIGHT (IRE)   2 b.f. (Jan 7) Petardia 113 – Faypool (IRE) (Fayruz 116)   **64**
[2002 5m⁵ 6m³ 6m* Jul 16] 6,500Y: rather leggy filly: second foal: half-sister to 3-y-o
Mr Blue Sky: dam, maiden in Switzerland, half-sister to smart sprinter Croft Pool:
modest performer: won seller at Brighton in July by 5 lengths from Resilience: stays 6f:
raced only on good to firm going: sent to USA. *B. Smart*

BOND MILLENNIUM   4 ch.g. Piccolo 121 – Farmer's Pet 90 (Sharrood (USA)   **79**
124) [2002 76, a93: p10g 7.5m 8m⁵ 8.5d⁴ 8.5g* 8g 11.7f⁶ 8.9m 8m 10.2g Oct 16] sturdy   **a81 +**
gelding: fairly useful handicapper: won at Beverley in July: below form after: effective at
1m/1¼m: acts on firm going, soft and all-weather: waited with. *B. Smart*

BOND MIRAGE   4 b.g. Primo Dominie 121 – Arabellajill 97 (Aragon 118) [2002 42:   **–**
f8s 8m f8g* Dec 4] modest performer, lightly raced: off over 4 months before landing   **a56**
gamble in maiden at Southwell in December: unlikely to stay beyond 1m: acts on fibresand. *B. Smart*

BOND PLAYBOY   2 b.g. (Apr 8) Piccolo 121 – Highest Ever (FR) (Highest Honor   **87**
(FR) 124) [2002 5.1d 5.1g⁴ 6.1f⁵ 5m⁴ 6m f6g* 6g² 6d* p7g Dec 14] 31,000Y: good-
bodied gelding: third living foal: half-brother to fairly useful 1998 2-y-o 7f winner Dandy
Dancer (by Shareef Dancer): dam unraced: fairly useful performer: won maiden at
Southwell (by 4 lengths) in October and nursery at Catterick (by length from Dispol Peto)
in November: stays 6f: acts on fibresand (ran as if something amiss on polytrack), good
to firm and good to soft going: below form only try in blinkers. *B. Smart*

BOND ROYALE   2 ch.f. (Feb 19) Piccolo 121 – Passiflora 75 (Night Shift (USA))   **73**
[2002 6s 7f 7m⁴ 6.5g 7g 7g f6f² f6g* f6s² f6s* Dec 13] 25,000Y: close-coupled filly: first   **a89**
foal: dam, 2-y-o 6f winner who didn't progress, half-sister to very smart 6f/7f performer
Harmonic Way out of half-sister to In The Groove: fairly useful on all-weather, fair on
turf: won maiden (by 6 lengths) and nursery (beat Ronnie From Donny by 3½ lengths) at
Wolverhampton in November/December: stays 6f: acts on fibresand. *B. Smart*

BONDS GULLY (IRE)   6 b.h. Pips Pride 117 – Classic Ring (IRE) 50 (Auction Ring   **–**
(USA) 123) [2002 50: p10g p10g⁴ f9.4g⁵ p12g 10.3s⁴ 10m 10f 10.1m p12g⁶ 10.1f Jul 17]   **a44**
lengthy horse: poor maiden: stays easy 1½m: acts on firm going, soft and all-weather:
tried blinkered/visored: often tongue tied on all-weather. *Mrs Lydia Pearce*

BOND SOLITAIRE   2 ch.f. (Feb 26) Atraf 116 – Laena 72 (Roman Warrior 132)   **66 p**
[2002 6m Aug 24] 12,000Y: sixth foal: closely related to useful 5f/6f winner (including at
2 yrs) Cape Merino and 5f winner Calamanco (both by Clantime): dam third at 7f at 2 yrs:
16/1 and green, never going pace when seventh of 8 to Crimson Silk in minor event at
Windsor: should improve. *B. Smart*

BOND STASIA (IRE)   2 b.f. (Apr 25) Mukaddamah (USA) 125 – Idrak 68 (Young   **54**
Generation 129) [2002 5.1m³ 6g³ May 17] 7,500Y: sister to 2 winning sprinters, including
2001 2-y-o 5f winner Risalpur, and half-sister to 3 winners, including 7f winner Margue-

rite Bay (by Darshaan): dam 2-y-o 5f winner: modest form when third in minor event at Nottingham and maiden at Hamilton. *B. Smart*

BONECRUSHER   3 b.c. Revoque (IRE) 122 – Eurolink Mischief 84 (Be My Chief **110** (USA) 122) [2002 88: 8g⁵ 9.9g* 10.5d³ 8m⁵ 10g* Jul 10] strong colt: smart handicapper: won at Salisbury in May and Newmarket in July, latter quite valuable contest under 9-6 by ½ length from Salute: respectable efforts at Haydock (bit too free) and Royal Ascot in between: stays 10.5f: acts on soft and good to firm going: tends to get bit on edge in preliminaries: joined Godolphin. *J. L. Dunlop*

BONELLA (IRE)   4 gr.f. Eagle Eyed (USA) 111 – Mettlesome (Lomond (USA) 128) **55** [2002 56: 10m 10.1m 10m 12m² 12g⁶ 12g 11.9m² 10m Sep 3] tall filly: modest handicapper: stays 1½m: acts on soft and good to firm going: sometimes races freely. *Mrs Lydia Pearce*

BONITA JOANA (IRE)   4 gr.f. Sri Pekan (USA) 117 – Thistle Hill (IRE) 58 (Dane- hill (USA) 126) [2002 10.1f 7d 7m⁶ f8.5s Sep 7] IR 28,000Y, 800 3-y-o: first foal: dam Irish 1¼m winner out of half-sister to Ardross: little form. *P. S. McEntee*

BONITO   4 ch.g. Pivotal 124 – Bonita 57 (Primo Dominie 121) [2002 8.1d 7f 6v² 7f³ **69** 5.9v 6s³ f8g⁵ f6g⁶ Dec 10] 8,000F, 23,000Y: third foal: half-brother to fairly useful 6f **a62** winner (including at 2 yrs) Clunie (by Inchinor) and fairly useful 1999 2-y-o 6f winner (stays 7f) Indeedyedo (by Efisio): dam 6f/7f winner: fairly useful form when trained by A. Trybuhl in Germany at 3 yrs, winning maiden at Munich and handicap at Krefeld: fair form in Britain: effective at 6f (given a test) to 1m: acts on any turf going, probably on fibresand: has worn cheekpieces. *P. C. Haslam*

BONKERS   2 ch.f. (Feb 8) Efisio 120 – Flourishing (IRE) 85 (Trojan Fen 118) [2002 **63** 5m 6m f5g* f5s Sep 17] 3,500Y: good-bodied filly: half-sister to several winners, including 4-y-o Rampant and 1988 2-y-o 5f winner Kastaway (by Distant Relative), both fairly useful: dam, 2-y-o 7f winner, stayed 1m: easily best effort (modest form) when winning maiden at Southwell in June: should stay 6f: acts on fibresand. *T. D. Easterby*

BON MARCHE   3 ch.f. Definite Article 121 – Sabre Penny (IRE) (Sabrehill (USA) **85** 120) [2002 75: p7g² f7g² 7m p7g² 8m 7g* 7m 7m 8f³ 8.1m⁴ 8g 7s p8g p7g f8g Dec 27] **a89** lengthy, rather sparely-made filly: fairly useful handicapper: won at Newmarket in July: left A. Jarvis after tenth start: stays 1m: acts on firm going, good to soft and all-weather: races prominently: has worn cheekpieces. *I. A. Wood*

BONNIE FLORA   6 b.m. Then Again 126 – My Minnie 67 (Kind of Hush 118) [2002 **41** 52: 11.9g⁵ 11.9m⁶ 10.2d⁶ p12g⁵ 10.2f Jul 25] big, heavy-topped mare: only poor in 2002: effective at 1¼m/1½m: acts on firm going and polytrack: has hung right. *K. Bishop*

BONNIE LAD (IRE)   3 b.g. Tagula (IRE) 116 – Sabonis (USA) 68 (The Minstrel **56** (CAN) 135) [2002 73: 5.1d 7.1m 5m⁴ 6m⁵ 5g³ 6f² 6d Oct 18] rather leggy, useful- looking gelding: fair maiden at 2 yrs: only modest in 2002: best at 5f/easy 6f: acts on firm ground, probably not on softer than good: blinkered (raced too freely) once at 2 yrs: often slowly away. *A. Berry*

BONNY RUAN   3 b.f. So Factual (USA) 120 – Sans Diablo (IRE) (Mac's Imp (USA) **81** 116) [2002 84: 5m 5g 5.1f³ 5.1f 5.7f⁵ Sep 16] tall, leggy filly: fairly useful performer: below form after reappearance: may well prove best at 5f: acts on good to firm ground. *D. Haydn Jones*

BONTADINI   3 b.g. Emarati (USA) 74 – Kintail 76 (Kris 135) [2002 –: 8m 7g f9.4g* **–** f8s³ f9.4g Oct 21] 800Y: sixth foal: half-brother to 6f winner Invergordon (by Efisio), **a70** later winner in USA, and 5-y-o Ulshaw: dam runner-up on debut at 1¼m: fair form: won maiden at Wolverhampton in August: stays 9.4f: acts on fibresand. *D. Morris*

BONUS (IRE)   2 b.c. (Feb 20) Cadeaux Genereux 131 – Khamseh 85 (Thatching 131) **78** [2002 6d 6d² 6s⁵ Oct 25] 78,000F, 80,000Y: strong, angular colt: second foal: dam, 7f winner, half-sister to high-class performer up to 1½m Predappio: favourite, best effort in maidens when 3 lengths second to Turn Around in 21-runner event at Windsor, no chance with winner who raced alone on far rail: not sure to stay much beyond 6f. *R. Hannon*

BOOBALA (IRE)   3 b.f. General Monash (USA) 107 – Best Swinger (IRE) (Ela- **–** Mana-Mou 132) [2002 78: 6g 5m 7f 7s⁵ p7g Nov 19] leggy filly: fair at 2 yrs: on downgrade in 2002. *D. R. C. Elsworth*

BOO B PRIZE (USA)   3 b.g. Prized (USA) – Sugar Hollow (USA) (Val de L'Orne **74** (FR) 133) [2002 59: 7f* 8g 7m² Sep 5] tall gelding: fair performer: won handicap at Redcar in June: best form at 7f: acted on firm going: dead. *T. D. Barron*

BOOGARBAROO (IRE)   4 gr.g. Turtle Island (IRE) 123 – Lingdale Lass 60 (Petong **–** 126) [2002 60?: 7g 10.9m Jul 7] little form. *Julian Poulton*

BOOM OR BUST (IRE) 3 ch.g. Entrepreneur 123 – Classic Affair (USA) 66 (Trem- **58**
polino (USA) 135) [2002 61: 7f f8g 8.2f 10.9g* 12.3d 9f 10g² 9.2v⁶ 10d⁴ 10.9d⁵ 9.2v³
9m⁶ 12m⁴ 16.1d 13.8f⁶ Sep 21] unfurnished gelding: modest performer: won handicap at
Ayr in May: seems to stay 1¾m: probably acts on any turf going: usually visored/
blinkered (not last 5 starts): found little tenth outing: has looked none too keen. *A. Berry*

BO'ORTCHOU (FR) 3 ch.c. Valanour (IRE) 125 – Catania (USA) (Aloma's Ruler **72**
(USA)) [2002 a8f⁴ 7.9d a8f* a8g a8f Dec 27] 240,000 francs Y: good-bodied colt: second
foal: half-brother to fairly useful French 10.5f/11f winner St Barth (by Sillery): dam
unraced: fair performer: trained by A. Smith/P. Smith first 2 starts, eighth in maiden at
York on second occasion: won similar event at Nad Al Sheba in October: should stay
1¼m: acts on dirt: visored final start. *D. J. Selvaratnam, UAE*

BOOZY DOUZ 2 ch.f. (Feb 3) Abou Zouz (USA) 109 – Ackcontent (USA) (Key To **–**
Content (USA)) [2002 7m p10g Dec 3] 1,500Y: half-sister to several winners, including
winners up to 7f Eager To Please (by Keen) and No Sympathy (by Ron's Victory), both
also successful at 2 yrs: dam ran once in USA: well held in minor event/maiden.
H. S. Howe

BOPPYS LOVEBIRD 2 ch.f. (May 3) Clan of Roses – Joara (FR) (Radetzky 123) **–**
[2002 7.5d 7m 6g Aug 7] 500Y twice: fourth reported foal: dam, lightly raced on Flat but
winning hurdler, sister to useful but ungenuine stayer Petrizzo: well held in maidens.
J. S. Wainwright

BORDER ALLIANCE 2 ch.c. (Apr 27) Selkirk (USA) 129 – Regal Peace 94 (Known **80 p**
Fact (USA) 135) [2002 7f⁴ Sep 21] 100,000Y: well-made colt: half-brother to several
winners, including useful 2000 2-y-o 6f winner Earl Grey (by Twining), later 1m winner
in Hong Kong: dam, Irish sprinter, later won in USA: 16/1 and backward, encouraging
8¾ lengths fourth of 12 to Trade Fair in maiden at Newbury, keeping on from mid-field:
sure to do better. *D. W. P. Arbuthnot*

BORDER ARROW 7 ch.g. Selkirk (USA) 129 – Nibbs Point (IRE) 107 (Sure Blade **116 §**
(USA) 130) [2002 118: 10g* 9m 10d² 9.9d³ 11m³ 11.8g⁴ 10d⁴ 10g³ 12s⁶ 12v⁴ Nov 9] big,
lengthy gelding: has a markedly round action: has reportedly had leg problems: smart
performer: won listed race at Kempton for second year running in April by neck from
Chianti: some creditable placed efforts after, including 1½ lengths second to Chancellor
in Gordon Richards Stakes at Sandown, 3 lengths third to Imperial Dancer in listed
race at Goodwood and 3 lengths third to Simoun in Grosser Mercedes-Benz-Preis at
Baden-Baden third to fifth starts: effective at 1¼m/1½m: acts on heavy and good to firm
going, well below form on polytrack: sometimes visored: played up in preliminaries
when tongue tied first 2 starts: tends to sweat: sometimes slowly away/soon off bridle:
not one to trust nowadays. *I. A. Balding*

BORDER ARTIST 3 ch.g. Selkirk (USA) 129 – Aunt Tate (Tate Gallery (USA) 117) **69**
[2002 69: 6.1f⁶ 7g 6f 5.3d⁶ 5.1s p8g 8.1d⁴ 8m 8.1g⁵ 7.6m³ 6m 7.1g p7g 7s Oct 26] **a61**
well-made gelding: fair handicapper: barely stays 1m: acts on polytrack, firm going and
good to soft: blinkered (slowly away) fifth start: sold 2,200 gns, joined D. Nicholls.
M. Blanshard

BORDER EDGE 4 b.g. Beveled (USA) – Seymour Ann (Krayyan 117) [2002 59, **63**
a69: p7g⁵ p8g f9.4g f8.5g 10m² 8.1g 9.7g³ 7f³ 8m³ p10g f9.4s p8g p7g⁵ Dec 30] modest **a61**
handicapper: left K. McAuliffe after fifth start: effective at 7f to 1¼m: acts on all-weather,
best turf efforts on good going or firmer (acts on firm): sometimes visored/blinkered.
J. J. Bridger

BORDER GLEN 6 b.g. Selkirk (USA) 129 – Sulitelma (USA) 63 (The Minstrel **–**
(CAN) 135) [2002 50, a66: p6g³ p5g p6g p6g 6g 6m 5s 9m Jun 30] big gelding: poor **a61 d**
mover: modest handicapper on all-weather: below form after reappearance: effective at
5f to easy 1m: acts on soft going, good to firm and all-weather: usually blinkered/visored:
often races prominently: has found little: unreliable: sold cheaply, joined P. Wegmann.
J. J. Bridger

BORDER MARAUDER (IRE) 3 b.g. Priolo (USA) 127 – Irrestible Lady (IRE) 77 **–**
(Mtoto 134) [2002 72: f9.4g Jan 21] quite good-topped gelding: fair maiden at 2 yrs:
blinkered/tongue tied (well held) only run in 2002. *J. A. Osborne*

BORDERS 6 b.g. Selkirk (USA) 129 – Pretty Poppy 67 (Song 132) [2002 106: 5g² 5m **106**
5s 5m Jul 24] big, well-made gelding: useful performer: has reportedly suffered from
stress fractures in quarters/problem with hind joint: only creditable run in 2002 when 3
lengths second to Kier Park in minor event at Beverley: best at 5f: acts on soft and good to
firm going: has worn dropped noseband: blinkered final start: front runner. *Mrs L. Stubbs*

BORDERS BELLE (IRE)   4 b.f. Pursuit of Love 124 – Sheryl Lynn (Miller's Mate   **96** 116) [2002 86: 8f 9g⁴ 10.4f 8.5s³ 10.1g 11.9d⁶ Jul 6] sturdy filly: useful performer: often highly tried in 2002, in frame in listed events at Newmarket and Epsom (third to Kootenay): stays 1½m: acts on firm and soft going: often held up: sold 32,000 gns. *Jedd O'Keeffe*

BORDER SUBJECT   5 b.g. Selkirk (USA) 129 – Topicality (USA) (Topsider (USA))   **117** [2002 106: 6g 7.5m² 6g* 6m* 6m² 6g 7m 6m Sep 4] big, strong gelding: reportedly suffers from breathing problem: smart performer: won minor event at Windsor in April and handicap at Newmarket (beat Chookie Heiton 3 lengths) in May: very good 1¼ lengths second to Capricho in Wokingham Handicap at Royal Ascot: ran poorly last 3 starts: has won at 1m, but free-going sort and best form at 6f: yet to race on extremes of going: sometimes tongue tied before 2002: has won when edgy: usually front runner. *R. Charlton*

BORDER TALE   2 b.c. (Jan 8) Selkirk (USA) 129 – Likely Story (IRE) 94 (Night   **61** Shift (USA)) [2002 6f 6s 6s⁴ 7d³ 7.1m f8.5g³ 8s⁴ 7s Oct 25] 30,000Y: strong colt: first foal: dam, 6f winner (including at 2 yrs), out of half-sister to Phoenix Stakes winner Aviance, herself dam of very smart pair Chimes of Freedom (miler) and Denon (up to 1½m): modest maiden. In frame 4 times, including in 2 nurseries: should stay 1¼m: acts on soft ground and fibresand: visored last 3 starts, tongue tied last 4: sold 15,000 gns. *M. L. W. Bell*

BOREAL (GER)   4 ch.c. Java Gold (USA) – Britannia (GER) (Tarim) [2002 121:   **126** 12g³ 12s* 12m 12g⁶ 12g Oct 6]

Small fields may be the norm for the Coronation Cup but it is seldom that the race fails to attract interest from abroad. French-trained horses have enjoyed a good record, particularly in the period 1986-1996 when they won no fewer than seven Coronation Cups. Saint Estephe's win in 1986 preceded Triptych's back-to-back wins, and Andre Fabre supplied the four other successes with In The Wings, Apple Tree, Sunshack and Swain all successful in the 'nineties. In contrast, Germany's record in the race in the same period is in danger of being forgotten completely. Three German-trained horses took their chance at Epsom, Acatenango finishing a good third to Triptych in 1987, while three years later Mondrian was virtually pulled up and four years after that Monsun finished a below-form sixth behind Apple Tree.

There was no French challenger for the latest Coronation Cup, but Germany was represented for the first time in eight years by Boreal, who had run well on his reappearance when a staying-on third to Nayef in the Dubai Sheema Classic at Nad Al Sheba in March. At the time, Nayef's absence, and Sakhee's too, from the Coronation Cup seemed to detract from the quality of the race, though from an end-of-season viewpoint, the participation of future Arc winner Marienbard, Champion Stakes winner Storming Home and Hardwicke winner Zindabad in a field of six hardly made it short of big names. Derby week had begun with the prospect of good to firm ground at Epsom but deluges on the Wednesday and Thursday turned the going soft, producing conditions very much in Boreal's favour. With the rail dolled out from Tattenham Corner and the prospect of better ground wider in the straight, there was the unusual sight of the Coronation Cup field coming up the stand rail. Soon handily placed in just a steadily-run race, Boreal was the first across to the rail off the turn and ran on strongly all the way to the line, seeing off the challenge of Storming Home and being well on top at the finish, winning by three and a half lengths. Pacesetter Zindabad was beaten another six lengths back in third, ahead of a disappointing Marienbard, outsider Pawn Broker

Vodafone Coronation Cup, Epsom—Boreal acts well on the soft ground to account for Storming Home, Zindabad and the visored Marienbard

and an even more disappointing Kutub, who had started favourite. Boreal had been third choice in the betting at 4/1. Boreal's win was the first by a German-trained horse in a British Group 1 race since Star Appeal's win in the Eclipse twenty-seven years earlier.

The remainder of Boreal's campaign was a distinct anti-climax. The rain stayed away for the King George at Ascot and Boreal ran poorly racing on ground firmer than good for the first time, moving short to post before managing to beat only the two pacemakers. Back on home turf, Boreal was made the 18/10 favourite to confirm Epsom form with Marienbard in the Grosser Preis von Baden but finished only sixth of the eight runners before having an even more distant view of Marienbard on his final outing in the Prix de l'Arc de Triomphe. With less partisan support at Longchamp (he started at 105/1 on the pari-mutuel, with only Califet at longer odds), Boreal trailed home fifteenth of the sixteen runners.

The Arc was noteworthy for being the only time Boreal has been partnered by a German jockey (Andreas Suborics) in his pattern races. Kieren Fallon was in the saddle for his other races in the latest season except when Olivier Peslier took over at Ascot, where Fallon rode the winner Golan. As a three-year-old, Boreal's regular rider had been John Reid. They had won the Deutsches Derby and finished a good second in the Grosser Preis von Baden before taking a heavy fall in the Preis von Europa at Cologne. For Boreal, who suffered concussion and a lost tooth, it meant missing out on that year's Arc, while for Reid it prompted his retirement from the saddle.

Boreal (GER) (ch.c. 1998)	Java Gold (USA) (b 1984)	Key To The Mint (b 1969)	Graustark
			Key Bridge
		Javamine (b 1973)	Nijinsky
			Dusky Evening
	Britannia (GER) (b 1985)	Tarim (br 1969)	Tudor Melody
			Tamerella
		Bonna (b 1978)	Salvo
			Birgit

Gestut Ammerland's "Boreal"

Fallon and Peslier had struck up a successful relationship in the late-'nineties with Boreal's half-sister Borgia (by Acatenango), who wasn't far behind Boreal in terms of ability. She too won the German Derby, went one better than Boreal by winning the Grosser Preis von Baden as a three-year-old, and ended that season with excellent placed efforts in both the Arc and Breeders' Cup Turf. Injury restricted her four-year-old campaign, but as a five-year-old (by which time she had moved from Peter Schiergen to Andre Fabre) she did plenty of travelling, taking in the Coronation Cup (a respectable fifth to Daylami) among several big races before signing off with a win in the Hong Kong Vase. The only other foal of Britannia to have raced is Borgia's sister Bougainvillea, an eleven-furlong maiden winner in Germany. Much will be expected of Britannia's two-year-old, a Sadler's Wells colt named Borges in training with Andre Fabre. Britannia was reportedly in foal to Galileo in 2002. Further details of Boreal's family can be found in Borgia's essay in *Racehorses of 1997*. Suffice to say here that their dam Britannia won the German St Leger and, like her two best offspring, contested the Arc, finishing quite a close ninth (under Richard Quinn) behind Carroll House in 1989. Boreal, a stocky colt, reportedly stays in training in 2003. He stays a mile and a half well and, given the way his season went after Epsom, needs to redeem himself somewhat; from what we know of him, his best chance of doing so will be when the mud is flying.
P. Schiergen, Germany

BOREAS   7 b.g. In The Wings 128 – Reamur 68 (Top Ville 129) [2002 119: 12m⁴   **119**
13.9f² 14g² 14g⁵ 15.9g* 18m* 16m² Oct 19]
If the step up to two miles and more in the latest season didn't bring about any improvement in the form shown by Boreas over a mile and a half in the previous two—remarkably, he achieved an end-of-season rating of 119 for the third year in succession, a testament to his consistency—it did enable him to gain a first pattern-race success, which was quickly followed by a second. The Group 3 Weatherbys Insurance Lonsdale Stakes, run at York in August over a distance just short of two miles, and the GNER Doncaster Cup, also a Group 3 and run over two and a quarter miles in September, were the races won by Boreas in 2002. Despite the Goodwood Cup winner Jardines Lookout having a pacemaker, the Lonsdale Stakes was nothing like so strongly-run as might have been expected and Boreas was the one best equipped for the sprint up the straight, moving easily into contention, quickening under pressure to lead well over a furlong out and holding Cover Up's late challenge by a length and a quarter. Cover Up, Jardines Lookout and Darasim, who finished third, renewed rivalry with Boreas at Doncaster, where, with Persian Punch also in the line-up, there was never much likelihood of a falsely-run race. Indeed, the front-running Persian Punch made it such a good test that, in beating him by a length and a quarter, Boreas broke the track record by almost two seconds. Under a confident ride from his usual partner Jamie Spencer, Boreas travelled strongly as he crept closer in the straight and quickened well under pressure when asked for his effort to get on top inside the final furlong, his jockey found to have used his whip with excessive force and above shoulder height. The first two, who pulled five lengths clear of third-placed Darasim, met again in the Jockey Club Cup at Newmarket and, although Boreas was unable to confirm the placings on terms 3 lb worse, he ran as well as ever in finishing second, beaten three quarters of a length.

GNER Doncaster Cup—Boreas takes his second pattern race in a row, breaking the course record;
Persian Punch (rail) keeps on well as Darasim finishes third and Jardines Lookout fourth

Having established himself as one of the best stayers around, Boreas will continue to be a force to reckon with in the Cup races in the next season, even though he'll be in his eighth year. Not seen out at two, and off the course throughout 1999 due to a serious leg injury, Boreas has been relatively lightly raced—the Jockey Club Cup was his twenty-first appearance—and there seems no reason why he should not hold his form for some time yet. The two-years-older Persian Punch, for one, has shown that reaching the veteran stage is no barrier to continued success in the top staying races. The Yorkshire Cup, in which he finished second to Zinda-bad on his second outing in the latest season, seems a likely first target for Boreas, though the Gold Cup at Royal Ascot is reported to be the main race on the agenda in 2003, and that race will test his stamina still further. Whether his turn of foot will be as potent at the end of two and a half miles at Ascot is by no means certain.

Boreas (b.g. 1995)	In The Wings (b 1986)	Sadler's Wells (b 1981)	Northern Dancer
			Fairy Bridge
		High Hawk (b 1980)	Shirley Heights
			Sunbittern
	Reamur (b or br 1987)	Top Ville (b 1976)	High Top
			Sega Ville
		Brilliant Reay (ch 1972)	Ribero
			Brilliant Stone

The leggy Boreas doesn't catch the eye in the paddock but he certainly does on the way to post, being a good mover with a long stride. He is the third foal of Reamur, a maiden who stayed a mile and a half, and her second winner, her filly by Doyoun named Redeem having been successful at six furlongs to nine furlongs in France at two. Boreas, who acts on any going, is nearly always held up, his one disappointing effort in the latest season coming when asked to make the running in the Prix Maurice de Nieuil at Maisons-Laffitte and finishing last of five. *L. M. Cumani*

BORN SPECIAL 3 b.g. Bluebird (USA) 125 – Dixie Eyes Blazing (USA) 56 (Gone West (USA)) [2002 54: 8f f12g Dec 2] has a round action: modest maiden at 2 yrs: well held in 2002. *P. C. Haslam*   –

BORORA 3 gr.g. Shareef Dancer (USA) 135 – Bustling Nelly 94 (Bustino 136) [2002 61p: p10g⁴ p10g 10g⁶ 12.4m³ 12m 11.9m f12g Dec 14] fair maiden handicapper: left I. Balding 9,000 gns before final outing: stays 12.4f: raced only on polytrack and good/good to firm going. *D. E. Cantillon*   **65**

BOROUGHSET BOY (IRE) 2 b. or br.c. (Apr 20) Woodborough (USA) 112 – Alpine Sunset (Auction Ring (USA) 123) [2002 5m 5g⁴ 6g⁶ 5g 7m f5s f6g⁵ Oct 22] IR 11,500F, 7,500Y: good-bodied, useful-looking colt: ninth foal: brother to 3-y-o Woodland Blaze and half-brother to fairly useful 1991 2-y-o 5f/6f winner Afif (by Midyan) and 5f to 1m winner Alpine Johnny (by Salse): dam unraced half-sister to very smart sprinter Cyrano de Bergerac: modest maiden: best effort at Southwell (carried head awkwardly) final start: stays 6f: acts on fibresand, raced only on good/good to firm going on turf. *J. R. Weymes*   **61 a64**

BORU BORU (IRE) 3 b.g. Bluebird (USA) 125 – Tudor Loom (Sallust 134) [2002 6.9d* 7g⁵ 8g 7d Oct 18] IR 30,000Y: sixth foal: brother to smart Irish/US performer up to 9f Rainbow Blues (5f/6f winner at 2 yrs) and a winner in Greece, and half-brother to 2 winners, including useful 1999 2-y-o 6f winner Kashra (by Polish Precedent): dam third at 7f in Ireland: won maiden at Carlisle in July: well below that form after: should be suited by 1m+: sometimes slowly away: sold 2,000 gns. *M. Johnston*   **69**

BOSHAM MILL 4 ch.g. Nashwan (USA) 135 – Mill On The Floss 117 (Mill Reef (USA) 141) [2002 116: 14.1m² 16.4m 20m 16m 18m 16m Oct 19] tall, close-coupled gelding: fluent mover: smart performer: creditable neck second to Hannibal Lad in minor event at Nottingham on reappearance: behind in pattern company after: stays 2¼m: acts on soft and good to firm going: usually sweating/on edge: sometimes flashes tail/goes in snatches: untrustworthy: sold 25,000 gns. *G. Wragg*   **115 §**

BOSRA BADGER 4 ch.g. Emarati (USA) 74 – Mrs McBadger 67 (Weldnaas (USA) 112) [2002 53: f6s p7g p7g⁵ p6g⁴ p6g p6g² p6g 6f⁶ May 11] modest maiden: barely stays 6f: acts on polytrack, raced mainly on good going or firmer on turf: often visored: sometimes early to post/slowly away: not to be trusted. *Mrs L. C. Jewell*   **51 §**

BOSSCAT 5 b.g. Presidium 124 – Belltina 41 (Belfort (FR) 89) [2002 –: f6g f7g Feb 1] headstrong maiden: tried blinkered. *R. G. Frost*   –

BOSS MAN (IRE) 2 b.g. (Apr 10) Entrepreneur 123 – Triste Oeil (USA) 103 (Raise **– p**
A Cup (USA)) [2002 7g 5.9d 7.5d 7m Jul 27] 4,000Y: good-bodied gelding: half-brother
to several winners, including 7f (at 2 yrs) to 9f winner Right Tune (by Green Desert) and
Irish 7f (at 2 yrs) and 11f winner Desert Wish (by Shirley Heights), both fairly useful:
dam 7f (at 2 yrs) and 1¼m winner: well held in maidens, but shaped with some promise
at Newcastle final start, short of room and not knocked about: should stay at least 1m: has
worn crossed noseband: type to do better in handicaps. *T. D. Easterby*

BOSTON LODGE 2 ch.c. (Jan 17) Grand Lodge (USA) 125 – Ffestiniog (IRE) 96 **91**
(Efisio 120) [2002 6g 7.2v³ 5g³ 7m* 7m 7.5g⁴ 7m* p7g⁵ p8g* p7g⁶ Dec 14] well-made,
close-coupled colt: first foal: dam 6f (at 2 yrs) to 1m winner: fairly useful performer: won
nurseries at Catterick in July, Epsom (beat Bakewell Tart by neck) in August and
Lingfield (beat Looking Down by neck) in November: stays 1m: acts on polytrack and
good to firm going, showed promise on heavy: usually races close up: game. *P. F. I. Cole*

BOSWORTH DIXIE (IRE) 2 b.f. (May 17) Turtle Island (IRE) 123 – Alice En **–**
Ballade (Tap On Wood 130) [2002 8.1f⁵ 7g f8.5s Dec 9] 3,500Y: lengthy filly: has a
quick action: seventh foal: half-sister to 3 winners, including 1½m winners Glass Note
(in Ireland, by Spectrum) and I Am The Chief (in France, by Chief's Crown): dam,
French 1m winner, half-sister to dam of 1000 Guineas winner Las Meninas: only a little
sign of ability in maidens. *R. Hollinshead*

BOUCHRA (IRE) 4 ch.f. Inchinor 119 – My Darlingdaughter (Night Shift (USA)) **65 §**
[2002 75: f6s f7g² f6g* p6g p6g f7g Mar 12] fair performer: won handicap at Wolverhampton in February (left I. Semple): probably best at 6f/7f: acts on soft going, good to
firm going and fibresand, probably on polytrack: usually visored/blinkered: has rejoined
I. Semple. *J. D. Czerpak*

BOUDICA (IRE) 3 b.f. Alhaarth (IRE) 126 – Supportive (IRE) (Nashamaa 113) [2002 **–**
8.1m 7d 6g 6.1m 8g Oct 16] IR 62,000Y: lengthy filly: fifth foal: half-sister to several
winners, including useful/fairly useful sprinters Galloway Boy, Grand Lad (both by
Mujtahid) and 4-y-o La Stellina (by Marju): dam fairly useful Irish 5f performer: well
held all starts: has wandered markedly. *D. W. P. Arbuthnot*

BOUNCING BOWDLER 4 b.g. Mujadil (USA) 119 – Prima Volta 80 (Primo **109**
Dominie 121) [2002 106: 7m 7d 6d 7.1d² 7m 7.1d* 6.1d 8.5s⁶ 8m⁵ 8d* 7m 8m⁵ 7m 8v
a7.5f Dec 26] rather leggy, quite good-topped gelding: has a quick action: useful handicapper: won at Haydock in July and Ascot (again able to dictate when beating Dumaran
by short head) in August: below form on dirt at Nad Al Sheba final start: stays 1m: acts
on firm and soft going: usually races up with pace: none too consistent. *M. Johnston*

BOUNDLESS PROSPECT (USA) 3 b.c. Boundary (USA) 117 – Cape (USA) (Mr **95**
Prospector (USA)) [2002 62p: p6g 6.1d* 7m 7g* 7.6f² 8g 7m³ 7m⁵ Sep 14] good-bodied
colt: useful performer: won maiden at Nottingham in April and handicap at Leicester in
June: stays 7.6f: acts on firm and good to soft going: races freely. *J. W. Hills*

BOUND TO PLEASE 7 b.g. Warrshan (USA) 117 – Hong Kong Girl 94 (Petong **–**
126) [2002 50, a75: f7s² p7g f7g* f7g 7d⁵ f7g 6v⁵ f8s f8.5g⁴ Nov 18] neat gelding: fair on **a68 d**
all-weather at best: on downgrade after winning claimer at Southwell in February: stays
1m: acts on heavy going, good to firm and fibresand, below form both starts on polytrack:
usually visored: sold 600 gns. *P. J. Makin*

BOURBONNAIS (IRE) 2 b.c. (Mar 24) Singspiel (IRE) 133 – Rose Bourbon (USA) **104 p**
(Woodman (USA) 126) [2002 7m* 7g² 7g* Aug 20] 25,000Y: angular, good-bodied colt:
third foal: dam, useful French maiden who should have stayed 1m, half-sister to Poule
d'Essai des Pouliches winner Baiser Vole, very smart sprinter Tenue de Soiree and very
smart 1m/1¼m performer Squill: useful form: won maiden in July and listed race in
August, both at York: beat Salcombe by ¾ length in 6-runner race in latter, rallying to
lead again close home: slightly reluctant at stall, good 1¼ lengths second to Dublin in
Vintage Stakes at Goodwood in between: will probably stay 1¼m: joined Godolphin:
remains capable of better. *M. Johnston*

BOURGAINVILLE 4 b.g. Pivotal 124 – Petonica (IRE) 77 (Petoski 135) [2002 104: **110**
8d* 8.3s² 8.5d 8m 8m⁴ 9.9m 8m² 8.9m² 10m 9f Oct 5] tall, close-coupled gelding: usually
looks well: has a long, rather round stride: smart performer: won minor event at Ascot in
May: creditable efforts when after in frame in listed races at Windsor, Ascot, Salisbury
and York (¾-length second to Binary File): stays 9f, probably 1¼m: acts on heavy
going, acts on any other: sometimes races freely: gelded after final outing. *I. A. Balding*

BOURGEOIS 5 ch.g. Sanglamore (USA) 126 – Bourbon Girl 116 (Ile de Bourbon **103**
(USA) 133) [2002 –: 12s 12d 13.9g 10m³ 11.9m* 13.9m 12g 12s Oct 26] strong, deep-

girthed gelding: useful handicapper: won at York in July by 1¼ lengths from Dancing Phantom: effective at 1¼m to 15f: acts on good to firm and good to soft going, no form in Britain on soft: blinkered (ran creditably) final 3-y-o start: reportedly distressed on reappearance. *T. D. Easterby*

BOWFELL   4 b.f. Alflora (IRE) 120 – April City 56 (Lidhame 109) [2002 –: f7s Jan 2] – modest 5f winner at 2 yrs: little sign of ability since: tried blinkered/visored. *C. Smith*

BOWING   2 b.c. (Mar 13) Desert Prince (IRE) 130 – Introducing 78 (Mtoto 134) [2002 **82 p** 8f⁴ 8.1g³ 10s² Oct 23] second foal: dam, 1¼m winner in France, sister to very smart performer up to 13f (also third in Derby) Presenting: fairly useful maiden: in frame all starts, 6 lengths second to Forest Magic at Nottingham final one: will stay at least 1½m: acts on firm and soft ground: open to improvement. *J. H. M. Gosden*

BOWLAND PRINCE (USA)   4 gr.g. Rubiano (USA) – Lake Champlain 108 (Kings – Lake (USA) 133) [2002 46: f9.4g f12g 8.5m⁵ 12.4m 10.1m Aug 16] maiden: no form in 2002: tried visored/blinkered. *E. J. Alston*

BOWLERS BOY   9 ch.g. Risk Me (FR) 127 – Snow Wonder (Music Boy 124) [2002 **55** 68: 5g⁵ 6g 5s⁵ Jun 5] workmanlike gelding: modest performer: effective at 5f (on stiff track) to 7f: acts on heavy and good to firm ground: tried blinkered: comes from off pace: carries head high. *J. J. Quinn*

BOWMAN (USA)   3 b.c. Irish River (FR) 131 – Cherokee Rose (IRE) 122 (Dancing **117** Brave (USA) 140) [2002 8g* 8g* 8g³ 8g⁶ 8g⁶ 8g⁶ 8g⁵ Oct 5] quite good-topped colt: third foal: half-brother to French 9f winner Moyesii (by Diesis): dam 6f (Haydock Park Sprint Cup)/7f winner: smart performer: won minor event at Fontainebleau and Prix de Fontainebleau at Longchamp (by neck from Medecis) in April: good 1¾ lengths third to Landseer in Poule d'Essai des Poulains at Longchamp (finished well having missed break and been switched) in May: ran at least respectably afterwards, though never landed a blow, when sixth in St James's Palace Stakes at Royal Ascot (didn't take eye beforehand),

Sheikh Mohammed's "Bowman"

Prix Jacques le Marois at Deauville and Prix du Moulin de Longchamp and when close fifth to Domedriver in Prix Daniel Wildenstein at Longchamp: stays 1m: raced mostly on good going: held up: joined Godolphin. *A. Fabre, France*

BOWMORE (IRE) 3 b.c. Desert King (IRE) 129 – Eurobird 118 (Ela-Mana-Mou 132) [2002 10s⁵ 12d* 14d³ 12g³ 12s* Sep 10] half-brother to several winners, most useful, including middle-distance stayers Garden Society (by Caerleon) and Tamiami Trail (by Indian Ridge): dam, won Irish St Leger, half-sister to Prix du Jockey Club winners Bikala and Assert: smart performer: won maiden at Leopardstown in June and listed race at Galway (beat Mutakarrim 2 lengths) in September: creditable third in listed races at Leopardstown behind Queens Wharf and Vinnie Roe in between: stays 1¾m: yet to race on ground firmer than good: blinkered last 2 starts. *J. Oxx, Ireland* **112**

BOX BUILDER 5 ch.g. Fraam 114 – Ena Olley (Le Moss 135) [2002 86: 14.1d 17.2g p16g⁶ Dec 3] close-coupled, good-topped gelding: has reportedly had wind operation: only fair form at best on Flat in 2002: should stay beyond 2m: acts on soft and good to firm going: blinkered once: tongue tied in 2002. *B. G. Powell* **67**

BOX CAR (IRE) 5 b.g. Blues Traveller (IRE) 119 – Racey Naskra (USA) 75 (Star de Naskra (USA)) [2002 48: f11s⁴ f8.5g³ f12s⁵ f12s⁴ f9.4g Feb 8] poor maiden: effective at 8.3f to 11.6f: acts on fibresand and soft going. *R. Wilman* **48**

BOXER'S DOUBLE 5 b.g. Petoski 135 – Grayrose Double (Celtic Cone 116) [2002 16.2g Jul 26] tailed off in Chepstow claimer on Flat debut. *G. A. Ham* **–**

BRADY BOYS (USA) 5 b.g. Cozzene (USA) – Elvia (USA) (Roberto (USA) 131) [2002 54: f12s⁶ f9.4g 10.9f 11.1s⁵ May 5] strong, lengthy gelding: modest maiden: stays 11f: form only on heavy/soft going: tried blinkered/visored. *J. G. M. O'Shea* **54**

BRAGADINO 3 b.c. Zilzal (USA) 137 – Graecia Magna (USA) 109 (Private Account (USA)) [2002 104p: 7m 8m 9f⁴ Sep 21] close-coupled, quite good-topped colt: useful at 2 yrs: below form in 2002, off 5 months before final start: will probably stay 1¼m: acts on good to firm going, possibly not on soft. *Sir Michael Stoute* **94**

BRAIN BOX (IRE) 2 ch.g. (Apr 4) Entrepreneur 123 – Alcaidia (IRE) 91 (Thatching 131) [2002 6m 6f⁶ 7g⁵ 7g⁵ 8.5m⁴ 10m 8d Oct 21] well-made gelding: first foal: dam Irish 7f winner out of unraced close relative to US Grade 2 11f winner Sword Dance: fair maiden: soundly beaten in nurseries last 2 starts: should stay 1¼m: acts on firm going: gelded after final outing. *T. D. Easterby* **67**

BRAIN TEASER 2 b.f. (Feb 24) Mind Games 121 – Salacious (Sallust 134) [2002 6m 6.1m Oct 1] 18,000Y: smallish filly: sister to 2000 2-y-o 5f winner Quizzical Lady (later winner up to 1m in Spain) and half-sister to several winners, including 2-y-o winners King Foley (5f in 1998, by Petong) and Highland Spirit (6f/7f in 1990, by Scottish Reel): dam Irish 7f (at 2 yrs) and 9f winner: last in maidens. *B. J. Meehan* **–**

BRAMANTINO (IRE) 2 b.g. (Mar 27) Perugino (USA) 84 – Headrest (Habitat 134) [2002 5m⁶ 5g⁴ 5.1g 6d 5d 7m 7m³ Sep 14] IR 28,000Y: strong, lengthy gelding: has scope: closely related to useful Irish 7f (including at 2 yrs) and 1¼m winner Polaire (by Polish Patriot) and 1¼m winner Lurdi (by Lure) and half-brother to a winner in Hong Kong by Kalaglow: dam lightly-raced sister to Princess Royal winner One Way Street: modest maiden: blinkered, creditable third in nursery at Doncaster: will be suited by at least 1m: acts on good to firm going. *R. A. Fahey* **61**

BRAMBLE 4 ch.g. Polar Falcon (USA) 126 – Sharpthorne (USA) 91 (Sharpen Up 127) [2002 65: 5g f5g⁴ f5g 5m May 3] well-made gelding: modest performer: was best at 5f: acted on firm going and fibresand: tried tongue tied: was sometimes slowly away: dead. *Mrs L. Stubbs* **60**

BRAMLEY DANCER 3 b.c. Suave Dancer (USA) 136 – Hailgaf 61 (Raja Baba (USA)) [2002 –: f9.4g⁵ p12g f11g⁴ 7m⁵ 10d 10.1g 12m Aug 12] modest maiden: left J. Noseda after third start: not certain to stay beyond 11f (laboured effort and reportedly had respiratory problem over 1½m): tried visored/blinkered/tongue tied: sometimes starts slowly. *Miss B. Sanders* **52**

BRAND NEW DAY (IRE) 4 b.g. Robellino (USA) 127 – Nawaji (USA) 45 (Trempolino (USA) 135) [2002 –: f12g Jan 25] probably of little account. *D. W. P. Arbuthnot* **–**

BRANDY COVE 5 b.g. Lugana Beach 116 – Tender Moment (IRE) 78 (Caerleon (USA) 132) [2002 –, a74: 10.2d f9.4s⁶ Dec 9] tall, quite attractive gelding: fair performer: shaped as though retaining ability second 5-y-o start: best efforts at 1m: acts on fibresand. *B. Smart* **a65**

BRANDYWINE BAY (IRE) 2 b.f. (Feb 5) Mujadil (USA) 119 – Ned's Contessa (IRE) 48 (Persian Heights 129) [2002 f7g Dec 17] 16,000Y: second foal: sister to 2001

2-y-o 6f winner Simply The Guest: dam, 7f winner, half-sister to useful 5f winners Connemara and Presentation (both by Mujadil): 16/1 and blinkered, eighth of 16 in seller at Southwell, slowly away. *W. R. Muir*

BRANSTON FIZZ   5 b.m. Efisio 120 – Tuxford Hideaway 102 (Cawston's Clown **78** 113) [2002 7f⁶ 7m² 7g² Jun 5] small, sparely-made mare: fair handicapper: better at 7f than 6f: acts on firm ground, soft and fibresand. *J. G. Given*

BRANSTON NELL   3 b.f. Classic Cliche (IRE) 128 – Indefinite Article (IRE) **63** (Indian Ridge 123) [2002 7d³ 8m⁵ 9.9m⁵ 13.8f* 14.1g f12g p16g Nov 27] smallish filly: second foal: half-sister to 5-y-o Branston Pickle: dam unraced sister to very smart Irish performer up to 1½m Definite Article and half-sister to Dante winner Salford Express: modest performer: won seller at Catterick (sold from G. A. Swinbank 5,500 gns) in September: should stay 2m: acts on firm going. *I. A. Wood*

BRANSTON PICKLE   5 ch.g. Piccolo 121 – Indefinite Article (IRE) (Indian Ridge   **–** 123) [2002 50, a77: f6s⁴ f5g² f6g³ f6g* f5g³ f5g* f6g² f5g* f5g³ p6g⁶ f5g² 6d f5g 5s   **a72** f6g Jun 20] smallish gelding: fair performer on all-weather: won claimer and seller at Wolverhampton in February for P. D. Evans and seller there (only run for A. Reid) in March: claimed from R. White after eleventh start, and below form after: effective at 5f/easy 6f: acts on fibresand and probably on polytrack: tried blinkered, usually visored: tried tongue tied: usually races prominently: sent to Spain. *J. L. Eyre*

BRANSTON TIGER   3 b.c. Mark of Esteem (IRE) 137 – Tuxford Hideaway 102 **80** (Cawston's Clown 113) [2002 76: 7.1m³ 7.9f 7g² f7g³ 6s* 6m⁴ p6g⁵ Oct 9] rangy colt: fairly useful performer: won maiden at Newmarket in August: effective at 6f/7f: acts on all-weather, firm and soft going: consistent. *J. G. Given*

BRANTINGHAM (USA)   2 b.c. (Jan 26) Gulch (USA) – Flying Lauren (USA) **49** (Storm Bird (CAN) 134) [2002 6v⁴ 6g f8.5g² Sep 21] $15,000Y: first foal: dam, US 6f (at 2 yrs) to 1m winner, half-sister to smart US Grade 1 1¼m winner Pompeii: poor maiden: tongue tied, best effort final start: should stay 1¼m: acts on fibresand: sold 7,000 gns, sent to Kuwait. *M. Johnston*

BRANTWOOD (IRE)   2 b.c. (Apr 13) Lake Coniston (IRE) 131 – Angelic Sounds **87** (IRE) (The Noble Player (USA) 126) [2002 5d* 6g 5g 6m 5g² Oct 19] IR 44,000Y: lengthy, well-made colt: fifth foal: brother to useful Irish 5f winner Alegranza and half-brother to 2 winners by Pips Pride, including useful 1999 2-y-o 5f winner Seraphina: dam, Irish 2-y-o 5f winner, half-sister to 5-y-o Mount Abu: fairly useful performer: won maiden at Haydock in May: behind in pattern company next 2 starts: best efforts when ninth in Two-Year-Old Trophy at Redcar and second (to Bond Becks) in minor event at Catterick last 2: effective at 5f/6f: yet to race on extremes of going: sold 25,000 gns. *B. A. McMahon*

BRASSIKA   3 ch.f. Whittingham (IRE) 104 – Tough Nell (IRE) 61 (Archway (IRE) **59** 115) [2002 64: p6g 5m⁴ 5.3m 5m⁴ p5g² 6g² 5.3m p5g⁵ 5m⁶ f5f p5g Dec 21] smallish, good-topped filly: modest maiden handicapper: left S. Dow after ninth start: stays 6f: acts on polytrack, soft and good to firm going. *J. Akehurst*

BRAVE BURT (IRE)   5 ch.g. Pips Pride 117 – Friendly Song 48 (Song 132) [2002 **93** 95: 6g 5f 5d 5g 5g 5d* 5m* 5g⁴ 6g Sep 20] good-topped gelding: fairly useful handicapper: won at Newmarket and Ascot within 4 days in July: best at 5f: acts on firm and good to soft going: often bandaged: usually leads: game. *D. Nicholls*

BRAVE CALL (USA)   2 ch.c. (Feb 5) Theatrical 128 – Darya (USA) (Gulch (USA)) **82 p** [2002 6s² p6g* Nov 19] strong colt: first foal: dam unraced half-sister to US Grade 1 1¼m winner Stuka: 1¾ lengths second to Zabaglione in maiden at Newbury, then won similar event at Lingfield by ¾ length from Quiet Storm, making all: should be suited by at least 1m: capable of better. *J. W. Hills*

BRAVE DANE (IRE)   4 b.g. Danehill (USA) 126 – Nuriva (USA) 100 (Woodman **62** (USA) 126) [2002 10m⁶ 8.3m 11.6m 11.6d⁶ 10m Sep 3] lengthy, angular gelding: second foal: dam, 2-y-o 6f winner and third in Cork And Orrery Stakes, sister to smart 1990 2-y-o Mujtahid: fairly useful performer at best: won maiden at Dieppe in 2001 when trained by Mme C. Head-Maarek: modest form in Britain, leaving G. McCourt prior to final start (neither subject to challenge nor knocked about, subsequently banned for 40 days under non-triers rule, jockey suspended and trainer fined): probably stays 1¼m: best form on good going or softer, shaped well on good to firm: tried blinkered. *J. L. Spearing*

BRAVE DOMINIE   2 b.f. (Feb 23) Primo Dominie 121 – Red Embers 64 (Saddlers' **46** Hall (IRE) 126) [2002 5.7g 6m 6f 5.1g 6g f5g⁵ f7s⁴ Dec 9] 800Y: second foal: half-sister to 3-y-o Thesaurus: dam 2-y-o 6f winner who should have stayed beyond 8.5f: poor maiden: should stay 1m: acts on fibresand. *I. A. Wood*

BRAVE EMIR 3 b.g. Emarati (USA) 74 – Hearten (Hittite Glory 125) [2002 63: p5g³ **60 d** f6g 5.3m 6d Oct 14] modest maiden at best: left J. Hills and off 5 months after third start: likely to prove best at 5f/6f: acts on polytrack, probably on good to firm going: tongue tied final 2-y-o outing: looked headstrong at 2 yrs: reportedly finished distressed penultimate appearance. *I. A. Balding*

BRAVE GIRAFFE 3 b.c. Distant Relative 128 – Prinia (Priolo (USA) 127) [2002 –: **–** p8g Jan 19] leggy, quite attractive colt: well held in maidens: visored only 3-y-o start. *Miss D. A. McHale*

BRAVE KNIGHT 5 b.g. Presidium 124 – Agnes Jane (Sweet Monday 122) [2002 43: **48** 9.9m 12.1d⁶ 16.2m 9.9d³ 12.1g 9.9m Aug 24] big, lengthy gelding: poor maiden handicapper: stays 1¼m: acts on good to firm and good to soft ground: has looked temperamental. *N. Bycroft*

BRAVE VISION 6 b.g. Clantime 101 – Kinlet Vision (IRE) 56 (Vision (USA)) [2002 **51** 14m³ 16m May 3] modest maiden: stays 1¾m: acts on soft and good to firm going: tried blinkered. *A. C. Whillans*

BRAVO DANCER 2 ch.f. (Jan 18) Acatenango (GER) 127 – Nijoodh (Selkirk (USA) **83** 129) [2002 5.7d² 7m 7f⁴ Oct 5] rangy, rather unfurnished filly: has scope: first living foal: dam, German 1m/9f winner, closely related to useful German 1m/1¼m winner Speedster: off nearly 4 months, best effort (fairly useful form) when 7 lengths fourth to Khulood in listed event at Newmarket: free-going sort, but bred to stay at least 1¼m: acts on firm and good to soft ground. *M. R. Channon*

BRAVO RAGASSO (IRE) 2 gr.c. (Mar 9) Primo Dominie 121 – Sacristy 54 **82** (Godswalk (USA) 130) [2002 5g⁸ 5m⁵ 5.1g⁴ 6.1v⁵ 5.1f⁹ 6f⁴ a6f⁶ a6f a6s⁶ a8.3f Dec 22] **a–** IR 40,000Y: smallish colt: half-brother to several winners, including fairly useful 1999 2-y-o 7f winner Sanguine (by Sanglamore) and useful 7f (at 2 yrs) and 9f winner Holtye (by Danehill): dam lightly-raced half-sister to Desirable, Park Appeal and Alydaress: fairly useful performer: won maiden at Kempton in March and minor event at Chester in June: sold from M. Channon 20,000 gns, then creditable fourth in listed race at Newbury (only outing for R. Cowell): well held in claimers on dirt all 4 starts in US (first 2 for M. Puhich): effective at 5f/6f: acts on firm going, probably on heavy: folded tamely third/fourth outings. *R. Mosco, USA*

BRAVURA 4 ch.g. Never So Bold 135 – Sylvan Song (Song 132) [2002 54, a62: p8g² **a69** p10g* p10g p10g* f8g 10d May 7] fair handicapper: won twice at Lingfield in February: stays easy 1¼m: acts on polytrack, little form on turf and fibresand: effective blinkered or not. *G. L. Moore*

BRAZEN 3 b.c. Singspiel (IRE) 133 – Bulaxie 110 (Bustino 136) [2002 p10g* Mar 2] **80** fourth foal: half-brother to smart 1m (including at 2 yrs)/1¼m winner Claxon (by Caerleon): dam, won Fred Darling and Lupe Stakes (also 7f winner at 2 yrs), half-sister to smart/very smart middle-distance performers Dust Dancer and Zimzalabim: won maiden at Lingfield on debut in good style by 3 lengths from System, slowly away: reported in May to have died after injuring himself on gallops. *Mrs A. J. Perrett*

BRAZILIAN TERRACE 2 ch.f. (Feb 13) Zilzal (USA) 137 – Elaine's Honor (USA) **77** (Chief's Crown (USA)) [2002 7d⁵ 7d⁵ 6m⁴ 8m* Sep 19] 22,000Y: fifth foal: half-sister to several winners, including useful 1999 2-y-o 5f winner Areydha (by Cadeaux Genereux) and 5f (at 2 yrs)/6f winner Albania (by Selkirk): dam, French winner around 8.5f, half-sister to useful 1987 French 2-y-o Savannah's Honor, later winner up to 1½m in US: fair performer: best effort when winning 18-runner nursery at Yarmouth by 2½ lengths from Langford, leading final 100 yds: should stay 1¼m: acts on good to firm and good to soft ground. *M. L. W. Bell*

BREAK DANCER (IRE) 3 b.g. Danehill Dancer (IRE) 117 – Peep of Day (USA) **–** (Lypheor 118) [2002 p10g Nov 19] IR 6,000F, 5,500Y: third foal: half-brother to 1992 2-y-o 5f winner Aberlady (by Sizzling Melody): dam French 9f winner: slowly away (restless stall) when tailed off in maiden at Lingfield. *M. J. Roberts*

BREATHTAKING VIEW (USA) 6 b.h. Country Pine (USA) – Lituya Bay (USA) **–** (Empery (USA) 128) [2002 10.1d 12f Oct 2] smart performer for Saeed bin Suroor in UAE early in 2000: best effort in 2001 (useful form, trained by E. Charpy) when winning handicap at Jebel Ali: well held both starts in Britain: stays 1½m: acts on firm going and dirt: tried visored. *G. Prodromou*

BRECONGILL LAD 10 b.g. Clantime 101 – Chikala 81 (Pitskelly 122) [2002 82d: **64** 6f 7m³ 6g² 7g⁴ 5m 5g 7f 6f³ 5m² 5m³ 6m 5f⁵ Sep 26] tall, good-topped gelding: modest nowadays: effective at 5f to 7f: acts on firm and soft going: tried blinkered/visored earlier in career: has hung/carried head high/idled: usually held up. *Mrs M. Reveley*

BREEZER   2 b.g. (Mar 21) Forzando 122 – Lady Lacey 66 (Kampala 120) [2002 6d –
Oct 14] 5,000 2-y-o: third foal: dam 7f to 1¼m winner: 33/1, outpaced throughout in maiden at Windsor: unseated rider and ran loose to post. *G. B. Balding*

BRENDA'S DELIGHT (IRE)   4 b.f. Blues Traveller (IRE) 119 – Tara's Delight 67 –
(Dunbeath (USA) 127) [2002 10.2d May 31] seems of little account. *P. Butler*

BRESSBEE (USA)   4 ch.g. Twining (USA) 120 – Bressay (USA) (Nureyev (USA) **65**
131) [2002 79: f9.4g⁶ f9.4g f9.4g f9.4g 10.3s 9p* f8.5g² 9.2s 9s⁵ 10d⁵ 8m f7g⁴ 9.9d⁵ 8.1v* 9m **a81**
10.4m⁴ 8.5d 10.3f 12f 10s⁶ 9.1s² p8g⁴ f8.5g* f9.4s⁵ f9.4g* Dec 26] close-coupled gelding: fairly useful on all-weather, fair on turf: won seller at Musselburgh in March and (having left K. Burke after ninth start) handicaps at Haydock in August and Wolverhampton in November/December: barely stays 1¼m: acts on fibresand and any turf going: usually visored/blinkered: often races up with pace: none too reliable. *J. W. Unett*

BREST (IRE)   3 b.f. General Monash (USA) 107 – Armadillo (IRE) (Dominion 123) **68 d**
[2002 76: 7g 7m 7g⁶ 8s 8g 6.1m f7g p8g Oct 9] angular filly: fair handicapper: generally well held in 2002: stays 7f: best efforts on good going: visored/blinkered last 6 starts. *G. C. Bravery*

BREUDDWYD LYN   4 br.g. Awesome 73 – Royal Resort 57 (King of Spain 121) **42**
[2002 f7g f8.5s⁶ Dec 26] fourth foal: dam, 7f selling winner, stayed 1¼m: well held in bumper and novice hurdle: seemingly better effort in Wolverhampton maidens when sixth to Gallant Boy, never dangerous. *D. Burchell*

BREVITY   7 b.g. Tenby 125 – Rive (USA) (Riverman (USA) 131) [2002 108: 6f⁴ 6f⁵ **106**
6d 6m³ 6m 6f 6g 6g Aug 12] big, strong gelding: useful handicapper: won 8 times in 2001: some creditable efforts in 2002, including at York on second/fourth outings: below form last 4 starts: effective at stiff 5f to easy 7f: acts on fibresand, best turf efforts on good going or firmer: has worn crossed noseband/tongue tie and been early to post: sometimes carries head awkwardly. *J. M. Bradley*

BRIAN BORU   2 b.c. (Mar 16) Sadler's Wells (USA) 132 – Eva Luna (USA) 114 **117 p**
(Alleged (USA) 138) [2002 7g* 8d² 8s* Oct 26]
The dominance of Ballydoyle's juvenile colts, who won nine of the ten two-year-old European Group 1s open to them in 2001, wasn't repeated in the latest season. They had to settle for five out of ten, Spartacus, Hold That Tiger, Spartacus again, Brian Boru and Alberto Giacometti emulating the victories the previous year of Johannesburg, Rock of Gibraltar, Sholokhov, High Chaparral and Ballingarry in the Phoenix Stakes, the Grand Criterium, the Gran Criterium, the Racing Post Trophy and the Criterium de Saint-Cloud respectively. The Racing Post Trophy was one of only three races in Britain won by Ballydoyle's two-year-olds from thirty runners and, until Racing Post Trophy day, when Miguel Cervantes also won, Statue of Liberty's Coventry Stakes win was the only one recorded by twenty-six Ballydoyle two-year-olds sent to Britain. Thanks to the three-year-olds, however, Ballydoyle's overall performance was almost on a par with the previous year, with nineteen Group 1 or Grade 1 victories worldwide, only four short of the world record set by the stable in 2001. That was notwithstanding an outbreak of coughing in the yard in early-August which severely restricted the number of runners. Spartacus provided Ballydoyle with a Group 1 victory in the Phoenix Stakes in August but that compared to four in the same month the previous year. 'Normal service' was virtually resumed from September onwards, though the stable still ended up faring less well with its two-year-olds, having six rated 110 or higher in this Annual, compared to eleven the previous year.
Arguably the most promising potential classic colt among the latest crop of Ballydoyle two-year-olds is the Racing Post Trophy winner Brian Boru. Similarities are readily found with High Chaparral, whose exploits as a three-year-old, including the Derby double at Epsom and the Curragh and a victory in the Breeders' Cup Turf, contributed greatly to Ballydoyle's year. As well as being a son of Sadler's Wells—not exactly a rarity at Ballydoyle—Brian Boru won at Doncaster in a style not dissimilar to High Chaparral, displaying signs of his inexperience but putting a seal on matters inside the final furlong and winning going away from another Ballydoyle raider. While High Chaparral upset the odds laid on his stable-companion Castle Gandolfo, Brian Boru was the 11/8 favourite when beating

Racing Post Trophy, Doncaster—a fourth win in the race in the last six years for Aidan O'Brien as Brian Boru quickens well to beat stable-companion Powerscourt (right); Illustrator is third

6/1-shot Powerscourt, the first two ridden, incidentally, as in 2001, by Kevin Darley and George Duffield. Trainer Aidan O'Brien and stable-jockey Michael Kinane were both in America for the Breeders' Cup.

Like High Chaparral, Brian Boru had two outings before Doncaster, winning one and finishing second on the other. While High Chaparral's appearances were both in maiden company, Brian Boru won a maiden at the first time of asking. That was at the Curragh at the end of June and, after a fifteen-week absence, he returned to action over the same course in the Beresford Stakes a fortnight before the Racing Post Trophy. Several from Ballydoyle have used the Beresford as preparation for Doncaster, among them Castle Gandolfo and two other recent Beresford winners who have gone on to acquit themselves well, the 1999 Racing Post runner-up Lermontov and the 1997 Racing Post winner Saratoga Springs. Brian Boru looked the likely winner at the Curragh when forging a couple of lengths clear inside the final furlong, only to be caught by Alamshar in the final strides, possibly undone by his lack of a recent run. Of the nine Racing Post Trophy runners—the Beresford sixth The Great Gatsby completed a threesome for Ballydoyle—only 9/2 second favourite Bahamian Dancer, beaten a head in the Royal Lodge, boasted form at least as good as that shown by Brian Boru, though there was also money for the maiden Illustrator (10/1 to 8/1) from the Stoute stable. For the second year running, the race was run over Doncaster's straight mile but, on this occasion, it was by design. Atrocious ground and problems with the starting stalls had caused a late switch from the round course in 2001 and it was surprising not to see the race reverting to its traditional format. When it was inaugurated as the Timeform Gold Cup in 1961, carrying the fifth-biggest stake run for in Britain that year, the round course was chosen both for the convenience of spectators and because it provided a better education for prospective stayers. Doncaster justified its decision to keep to the straight course on the grounds that it made it more likely that the race would be run on 'a consistent surface'.

A steady pace led to the Racing Post Trophy turning into something of a muddling affair, with the eventual third and fourth, Illustrator and The Great

Gatsby, both meeting trouble after the race began in earnest from halfway. Brian Boru did not enjoy the smoothest of runs either, hemmed in on the rail by Powerscourt for a time. Once Darley managed to extricate him, Brian Boru responded in good style, despite carrying his head a little high (a trait of some Sadler's Wells offspring), to win by a length and a quarter, finishing with plenty of running left in him. The stewards held an inquiry into interference involving Brian Boru, who, just inside the two-furlong marker, crossed the fading, front-running outsider Balin's Sword; the stewards decided that the eventual fifth Bahamian Dancer, on Brian Boru's outside, had contributed by interfering with Brian Boru. Both incidents were deemed accidental and the placings were allowed to stand. The form of the Racing Post Trophy was probably around average for recent runnings, but, like High Chaparral, Brian Boru looked far from the finished article and seemed to possess the scope to shape up into a leading candidate for top middle-distance and staying honours as a three-year-old. He went into the New Year a worthy ante-post favourite—as short as 8/1—for the Derby.

Brian Boru (b.c. Mar 16, 2000)	Sadler's Wells (USA) (b 1981)	Northern Dancer (b 1961)	Nearctic
			Natalma
		Fairy Bridge (b 1975)	Bold Reason
			Special
	Eva Luna (USA) (b 1992)	Alleged (b 1974)	Hoist The Flag
			Princess Pout
		Media Luna (b 1981)	Star Appeal
			Sounion

Mrs John Magnier's "Brian Boru"

The Racing Post Trophy result was a triumph for the champion sire Sadler's Wells, whose four runners filled the first four places, and for Khalid Abdulla's Juddmonte Farms which bred the first three. Brian Boru, Powerscourt and Illustrator (the last-named carrying the Abdulla colours) were among the first produce of a new arrangement between Juddmonte Farms and Coolmore, by which Juddmonte send a batch of mares to Sadler's Wells and the offspring are shared between the two organisations. Brian Boru's dam Eva Luna (USA)—not to be confused with a sprinting contemporary of the same name (but with an IRE suffix) who won the Phoenix Stakes—was a stayer who didn't see a racecourse until she was four. Reportedly plagued by physical problems in her early days, Eva Luna made up for lost time by winning her first three races in the Abdulla colours, culminating in the Park Hill Stakes at Doncaster. She was kept in training at five and finished third in the Henry II Stakes, before showing that she didn't need long distances to bring out the best in her when running away with a listed event over a mile and a half at Leicester. A serious tendon injury, sustained at exercise, ended her racing career. Brian Boru is Eva Luna's second foal, her first being the late developing, progressive French filly Moon Search (by Rainbow Quest), a winner three times in the latest season at up to twelve and a half furlongs, over which distance she won a listed event at Maisons-Laffitte in November. Eva Luna was bred for stamina, by Alleged out of the Oaks runner-up Media Luna, an unreliable racemare who went on to produce a number of winners that stayed well, including the useful pair Petralona, a sister to Eva Luna successful in France, and Ebor runner-up Media Star, as well as the fair two-mile winner Medicosma. Another of Media Luna's daughters was the graded stakes-placed Blushing Groom mare Rougeur, a winner at up to a mile and a half before joining the Juddmonte broodmare band and becoming the dam of Kentucky Oaks and Alabama Stakes winner Flute. There are no stamina doubts about Brian Boru so far as the Derby distance is concerned, and he will stay the St Leger trip if returned to Doncaster in September. So far as his going requirements are concerned, he acts on soft going and has yet to encounter good to firm or firmer. It was little short of remarkable, given his stamina-packed pedigree, that the good-topped Brian Boru was able to show so much as a two-year-old, and he is sure to improve again at three. He has plenty to live up to, taking his name from one of Ireland's national heroes, an early-medieval warrior king known as the progenitor of the clan O'Brien. *A. P. O'Brien, Ireland*

BRIANS BAY 4 b.g. River Falls 113 – Petrina Bay 67 (Clantime 101) [2002 –: f6s Jan 22] of little account. *J. Gallagher* —

BRIANZA (USA) 3 b.f. Thunder Gulch (USA) 129 – Las Meninas (IRE) 115 (Glenstal (USA) 118) [2002 p8g⁴ 8g³ 10d Jul 10] IR 100,000Y: fourth foal: half-sister to 1¼m winner Swinging Trio (by Woodman): dam won 1000 Guineas: best effort in maidens (modest form) when third at Salisbury, tending to wander under pressure: dropped out tamely final start: stud. *J. H. M. Gosden* 61

BRIAREUS 2 ch.g. (Apr 21) Halling (USA) 133 – Lower The Tone (IRE) 74 (Phone Trick (USA)) [2002 8g Oct 18] big, rather leggy gelding: third foal: half-brother to 4-y-o More Sirens: dam, Irish 1m winner, half-sister to useful 1m/1¼m performer Pantar: 33/1 and backward, never-dangerous eighth of 16 to Calibre in maiden at Newmarket: type to do better at 3 yrs. *I. A. Balding* 77 p

BRICKS AND PORTER (IRE) 2 b.c. (Mar 13) College Chapel 122 – Camassina (IRE) 62 (Taufan (USA) 119) [2002 6d 6m 7d 6g 7s* 6g⁴ 8d 6.1s Oct 23] IR 6,500F, IR 5,000Y: second foal: half-brother to 3-y-o Mujasina: dam, Irish maiden, stayed 9f: fair performer: won nursery at Galway in September: well held in minor event at Nottingham on final start: stays 7f: acts on soft going: blinkered 3 of last 4 outings, twice also tongue tied (including for win): none too consistent. *John A. Quinn, Ireland* 75

BRIDEWELL (USA) 3 b.g. Woodman (USA) 126 – La Alleged (USA) (Alleged (USA) 138) [2002 84: 10f² 11m 10g 12f Sep 21] neat gelding: has a round action: fair maiden handicapper: well held after reappearance: visored (refused to settle) final start: stays 1¼m: acts on any ground. *F. Watson* 66

BRIDGE PAL 2 ch.f. (Apr 27) First Trump 118 – White Domino 67 (Sharpen Up 127) [2002 p6g⁵ Dec 28] half-sister to 3 winners, including 1993 2-y-o 6f winner Pinkerton's Pal (by Dominion) and sprinter Macrobian (by Bay Express), both useful: dam 1m 70 p winner: 33/1, 5½ lengths fifth of 11 to Wages in maiden at Lingfield, slowly away and green before good late headway: sure to do better. *W. Jarvis*

BRIDGE STREET LAD   4 b.g. Puissance 110 – Bridge Street Lady 93 (Decoy Boy   **43**
129) [2002 –: 5m 6g 5d 5s³ 5d 6.1m Jul 13] poor maiden: stays 6f. *M. R. Bosley*

BRIDGE THE GAP (IRE)   2 b.g. (Feb 23) Revoque (IRE) 122 – Madame Curie   **52**
(Polish Precedent (USA) 131) [2002 5m 5d 6.1d f7g⁴ Oct 21]   IR 30,000Y: lengthy
gelding: first foal: dam once-raced half-sister to useful Irish performer up to 1¼m
Apparatchik: modest maiden: carried head high when fourth in seller at Wolverhampton:
should stay 1m: acts on fibresand and good to soft ground: has worn crossed noseband:
sold 3,700 gns, sent to Kuwait. *B. W. Hills*

BRIDIE'S PRIDE   11 b.g. Alleging (USA) 120 – Miss Monte Carlo 75 (Reform 132)   **61**
[2002 –: 14.1d 18s² 17.2d⁴ f16g Nov 20] modest handicapper nowadays: stays 2¼m: **a–**
raced mainly on good or softer going, little form on fibresand: front runner. *G. A. Ham*

BRIEF GOODBYE   2 b.g. (Apr 29) Slip Anchor 136 – Queen of Silk (IRE) 93 (Brief   **72**
Truce (USA) 126) [2002 5m⁵ 6d⁵ Oct 21]   10,000Y: first foal: dam, Irish 2-y-o 1m winner,
half-sister to smart Irish 7f/1m performer Tarry Flynn: reluctant to enter stalls, better
effort in maidens (fair form) when fifth to Miss Assertive at Pontefract second start: will
be suited by 1m+. *John Berry*

BRIERY MEC   7 b.g. Ron's Victory (USA) 129 – Briery Fille 81 (Sayyaf 121) [2002   **53**
65: p12g⁵ 9.9g 10m 10d 10m⁴ 10s² 10m 10.4m p10g p12g Dec 18] tall gelding: modest   **a57**
handicapper: effective at 1¼m/easy 1½m: acts on soft going, good to firm and polytrack:
held up: has raced freely/wandered. *H. J. Collingridge*

BRIGADORE   3 b.g. Magic Ring (IRE) 115 – Music Mistress (IRE) 55 (Classic Music   **86**
(USA)) [2002 92: 5g 5g⁵ May 18] small, good-quartered gelding: fairly useful performer:
gelded after final outing: likely to prove best at 5f: acts on good to firm and good to soft
going: races prominently. *J. R. Weymes*

BRIGHT AND CLEAR   3 b.f. Danehill (USA) 126 – Shining Water 111 (Kalaglow   **106**
132) [2002 102: 11.4f² 11m² 12m 12m³ 14.6m³ 12g⁴ 12m² Oct 12] good-topped filly:
useful performer: mostly creditable efforts in 2002, including when placed in Oaks
d'Italia at Milan (length second to Guadalupe), Park Hill Stakes at Doncaster (1¾ lengths
third behind Alexander Three D) and Princess Royal Stakes at Ascot (settled better in
front than usual when 1¼ lengths second of 4 to Love Everlasting) on second, fifth and
final outings: stayed 1¾m, at least with emphasis on speed: acted on firm going, possibly
not on good to soft: had been early to post/given trouble/been mounted on track:
free-going sort: consistent, but was hard to win with: stud. *B. W. Hills*

BRIGHT EDGE   3 ch.f. Danehill Dancer (IRE) 117 – Beveled Edge 60 (Beveled   **102**
(USA)) [2002 87: 6m² 6.1d* 6s⁵ 6f³ 6.1d* 6d³ 6m⁶ 6g 6v² Nov 9] tall, lengthy, rather
unfurnished filly: useful performer: won listed race at Nottingham in May and minor
event at Chepstow in July: mostly creditable efforts otherwise, including when third to
Goldeva in handicap at Ascot and second to Tom Tun in listed race at Doncaster on sixth/
final starts: best efforts at 6f: acts on firm and soft going: consistent. *B. Palling*

BRIGHTER FUTURE   3 b.f. Night Shift (USA) – Welsh Mist 102 (Damister (USA)   **58**
123) [2002 56: p6g⁵ f7g⁴* 8.1m 7m 7s f7s* f7g⁴ f8.5s* Nov 30] close-coupled filly: useful   **a96**
on all-weather, modest on turf: successful in handicaps in April and September (best
effort when beating J M W Turner by 3 lengths), and in minor event in November, all at
Wolverhampton: stays 8.5f: easily best efforts on fibresand: sold 32,000 gns. *B. W. Hills*

BRIGHT GREEN   3 b.g. Green Desert (USA) 127 – Shining High 90 (Shirley   **85**
Heights 130) [2002 8m² 10m³ 10f 12m 8m* 8f⁵ 10s Oct 14] workmanlike gelding: second
foal: dam, 2m winner, half-sister to useful miler Polar Boy: fairly useful form: won
maiden at Pontefract in August: stays 1¼m: raced mainly on going firmer than good (well
below form on soft): has worn crossed noseband: sold 26,000 gns. *E. A. L. Dunlop*

BRIGHT MIST   3 b.f. Anita's Prince 126 – Out On Her Own (Superlative 118) [2002   **47**
–: f7g³ f7g³ 5.1d 6d p6g f6g Jun 19] rather leggy, quite good-topped filly: modest maiden   **a52**
on all-weather, poor on turf: barely stays 7f: visored (well beaten) fourth start. *B. Palling*

BRIGHT SKY (IRE)   3 ch.f. Wolfhound (USA) 126 – Bright Moon (USA) 123   **124**
(Alysheba (USA)) [2002 9m² 9.3g² 10m² 10.5m* 12m³ 10g* 11f Nov 24]
Bright Sky's facile success in the Prix de l'Opera on Arc day led some to
question why she had not been in the feature race itself, even though that race was
over two furlongs further. Bright Sky could hardly have been more impressive at
Longchamp. After travelling strongly halfway down the eleven-runner field, she

Prix de Diane Hermes, Chantilly—in the largest field for the race since 1988
Bright Sky wins fairly comfortably; Dance Routine (rail), Turtle Bow and Ana Marie follow her home

needed riding only with hands and heels to draw clear from early in the straight, beating Irresistible Jewel by four lengths, Bright Sky's rider able to start some showy celebrations fully a hundred yards from the finish. Allowing for some of her opponents being substandard for a race of Group 1 status, Bright Sky's performance in the mile-and-a-quarter Prix de l'Opera was, by our reckoning, the best by any three-year-old filly in Europe in 2002, and she would not have looked out of place in the Arc line-up. Bright Sky's connections had opted to run the year-older Aquarelliste instead in the Arc and, judged strictly on what the pair achieved in their respective races, the form of Bright Sky's Prix de l'Opera win surpassed that of her stable-companion's creditable sixth, just under three lengths behind the winner, in the main event. On a strict interpretation of her form, Bright Sky might just about have made the frame in the Arc, taking it as read that she would have proven just as effective at a mile and a half. The latest Arc wasn't one of the strongest renewals and, whether or not Bright Sky eventually proves up to winning a race of that quality—she stays in training at four with the Arc as her principal target—she created a most favourable impression in the Prix de l'Opera and is sure to win more good races.

Bright Sky's other win as a three-year-old came in the Prix de Diane Hermes at Chantilly in June. She had won three of her seven outings up to then and had finished second at Longchamp on each of her three prior to Chantilly. Bright Sky had won a maiden at Clairefontaine on her debut as a two-year-old—her only outing for Dominique Sepulchre—and, after coming unplaced in a minor event at Chantilly, she showed fairly useful form to win similar contests at Longchamp and Maisons-Laffitte. Stepped up in class in a listed event in April on her reappearance, Bright Sky showed much improved form to finish three quarters of a length behind Turtle Bow, and followed that with narrowly-beaten similar efforts behind Ana Marie in the Prix Vanteaux later in the month—going down only by a short head—and behind Marotta in the Prix Saint-Alary in May, beaten a neck in what is traditionally one of the weaker French Group 1 races. That effort was, however, good enough to give Bright Sky a leading chance in the fifteen-runner Prix de Diane and, starting joint-favourite with her pacemaker, she won fairly comfortably by two lengths from Dance Routine, the slightly longer trip and the good gallop set by Blue Lightning clearly suiting Bright Sky who showed her best form at up to that point. A little troublesome at the stalls, Bright Sky was held up before coming with a strong run down the outside in the home straight, leading with less than a furlong to

Prix de l'Opera - Casino Barriere d'Enghien-Les-Bains, Longchamp—
Bright Sky proves far too good for the Irish-trained Irresistible Jewel and Marotta (No.12)

go and providing a second consecutive winner of the race for the Wildenstein family, trainer Elie Lellouche and her regular rider Dominique Boeuf, following the success of Aquarelliste a year earlier. Back in third, fourth and fifth were Bright Sky's previous conquerors, Turtle Bow, Ana Marie and Marotta, though the positions of the third and fourth were reversed after some minor interference. The British raiders Music Club, Monturani and Fragrant View finished down the field. Bright Sky was off the course for three months after the Prix de Diane, returning for the Prix Vermeille in September. Tried at a mile and a half for the first time, she was not discredited, only able to stay on at one pace when three and a half lengths third of eleven to Pearly Shells. Bright Sky ran once after the Prix de l'Opera, off a further seven weeks before running her only poor race of the year in the Japan Cup at Nakayama in November, beaten too far out to blame the trip for her performance.

Bright Sky (IRE) (ch.f. 1999)	Wolfhound (USA) (ch 1989)	Nureyev (b 1977)	Northern Dancer Special
		Lassie Dear (b 1974)	Buckpasser Gay Missile
	Bright Moon (USA) (ch 1990)	Alysheba (b 1984)	Alydar Bel Sheba
		Bonshamile (b 1983)	Ile de Bourbon Narration

Bright Sky, a medium-sized, unfurnished filly with a quick action, really impressed with her well-being on Arc day, looking in great shape. She is by Wolfhound, winner of the Haydock Park Sprint Cup as a four-year-old. On the face

Ecurie Wildenstein's "Bright Sky"

of it, the sprinter Wolfhound was perhaps an odd choice of sire for the middle-distance stayer Bright Moon, especially as Wolfhound has proven singularly disappointing at stud. Bright Sky is his only pattern winner from six crops to race and he was exported in 2001 to South Africa where his half-brother Al Mufti has made a mark at stud. Bright Moon was a very smart performer who, like Wolfhound, proved better than ever at four. She finished fifth in the Prix de Diane on only her third start but showed better form over further, her wins including the Prix de Pomone (run over thirteen and a half furlongs) twice and her best effort coming on her final outing when fifth (beaten less than a length) to Carnegie in the 1994 Arc. Bright Moon is easily the best runner out of Bonshamile, a middle-distance performer who was useful when trained in Britain at two and three before going on to win the Group 3 Prix Corrida in France and a Grade 2 event in the USA at four. Bright Moon had three earlier foals. They all reached the racecourse but only one has won, the French nine-furlong/mile-and-a-quarter winner Bright Stone (by Bigstone) who was useful as a three-year-old. Bright Moon's two-year-old filly, a close relation to Bright Sky by Peintre Celebre called Blue Icon, did not race, and Bright Moon also has a yearling filly by Rainbow Quest named Boukhara. Bright Sky has shown her best form at around a mile and a quarter, and did tend to pull a little hard in the Prix Vermeille, but she has fair prospects of proving fully effective at a mile and a half as a four-year-old, the patient way she is ridden likely to help. Bright Sky won on heavy going as a two-year-old but did not encounter softish conditions as a three-year-old; she acts well on good going or firmer, ground conditions that tend to favour horses like Bright Sky whose most potent weapon is a good turn of foot. *E. Lellouche, France*

BRIGHT SPANGLE (IRE) 3 ch.f. General Monash (USA) 107 – No Shame 56 **55** (Formidable (USA) 125) [2002 67: f7g³ 8.1m 10.2g 7.1v² f8.5g 8.1d 7.1g p10g f12g⁵ 10g **a61** 10g⁴ p12g² f14.8s Dec 13] sturdy filly: modest performer: stays easy 1½m: acts on heavy going, good to firm and all-weather: tried visored: none too consistent. *B. Palling*

BRIGHT SPARK (IRE) 5 b.g. Sri Pekan (USA) 117 – Exciting (Mill Reef (USA) **58** 141) [2002 84: 8s 6m 8d 8f 7f 6m p7g f8.5s p7g p7g Dec 30] tall gelding: fairly useful at 4 yrs: modest form in 2002, leaving D. Nicholls after fifth start: stays 1m: acts on heavy and good to firm going: visored (early to post) fourth outing: usually slowly away (sometimes markedly so). *S. Dow*

BRILLANO (FR) 3 b.f. Desert King (IRE) 129 – Voliere (USA) (Artic Tern) [2002 – 75p: 10.5m 12m 9.2g 7f 7m Sep 15] sturdy filly: fair performer at 2 yrs: soundly beaten in 2002, leaving C. Thornton after fourth start: will need to settle to stay 1¼m: best effort on heavy going. *L. T. Reilly, Ireland*

BRILLIANT BASIL (USA) 3 b.g. Hazaam (USA) 113 – Speed Shift (USA) (Foyt – (USA)) [2002 80: f6g* 6g f7g* 6d p7g f7s Sep 7] fairly useful performer: won maiden in **a82** March and handicap in April, both at Southwell: well held in handicaps after: likely to prove best at 6f/7f: form only on fibresand: sold 11,000 gns, sent to Kuwait. *Mrs L. Stubbs*

BRILLIANT DIAMOND (USA) 2 b. or br.c. (Feb 3) Weather Break 84 – Ali's – Diamond (USA) (Caracolero (USA) 131) [2002 p7g Dec 11] fifth foal: half-brother to 3 winners in USA: dam lightly-raced winning US sprinter: never dangerous in maiden at Lingfield. *H. Candy*

BRILLIANT RED 9 b.g. Royal Academy (USA) 130 – Red Comes Up (USA) (Blush- **103** ing Groom (FR) 131) [2002 103: p12g p10g 9.9m 8f p12g³ p10g* p10g* p10g⁶ Dec 21] tall, lengthy gelding: has a long stride: useful performer: left Mrs L. Richards after fourth start: won handicap (by length from Kepler) and minor event (by length from Linning Wine) at Lingfield in December: effective at 1m to easy 1½m: acts on firm going, soft and polytrack: sometimes visored: often tongue tied: has started slowly: tends to carry head awkwardly. *Jamie Poulton*

BRILLIANTRIO 4 ch.f. Selkirk (USA) 129 – Loucoum (FR) 93 (Iron Duke (FR) **71** 122) [2002 71+: 10g 8.3g⁵ 8.3g⁴ 8.3m 9.3g³ 10.3f* 10.2d² 10g 12m⁵ Jul 26] big, work-manlike filly: fair performer: won claimer at Chester in June: stays 1¼m: acts on firm and good to soft going: visored/blinkered fifth to eighth starts: has run creditably when sweating: has been early/led to post: sometimes races freely/finds little. *J. G. M. O'Shea*

BRIMSTONE (IRE) 7 ch.g. Ballad Rock 122 – Blazing Glory (IRE) (Glow (USA)) – [2002 51: 7m 6f 7m 5m 6m 7m 6m Sep 19] tall, good-topped gelding: little form in 2002: usually visored, blinkered final start. *Mrs D. Haine*

BRIOS BOY 2 ch.c. (Apr 18) My Best Valentine 122 – Rose Elegance 83 (Bairn – (USA) 126) [2002 5g 5g Sep 18] 6,500Y: good-topped colt: fourth foal: half-brother to 2000 2-y-o 6f winner Myhat (by Factual): dam 1m/1¼m winner: showed little in maidens. *R. Bastiman*

BRIOSO (IRE) 2 b.c. (Mar 24) Victory Note (USA) 120 – Presently 48 (Cadeaux – Genereux 131) [2002 5g Oct 4] 15,000Y: fourth foal: half-brother to Italian 1m to 11.5f winner Breakthru (by Ezzoud): dam, 5f winner, half-sister to smart sprinter Sizzling Melody: 16/1, tailed off in maiden at Lingfield. *J. M. P. Eustace*

BRISSCOLA 2 ch.f. (Mar 12) First Trump 118 – Princess Dancer (Alzao (USA) 117) **52** [2002 5.1d² 5m⁶ 6g⁴ 6.1m 8g⁴ 10f 8.2v⁶ Oct 29] 3,000Y: smallish filly: eighth foal: half-sister to fairly useful 7f (at 2 yrs) and 9f winner who probably stayed 1½m Northern Sun (by Charmer): dam ran once at 2 yrs: modest maiden: likely to prove best up to 1m: acts on good to firm and heavy ground. *C. B. B. Booth*

BRITANNIA HOUSE (USA) 3 ch.f. Diesis 133 – Refill 88 (Mill Reef (USA) 141) **71** [2002 11.9d⁴ May 24] sturdy filly: sister to a winner in Japan and half-sister to several winners, including 1995 2-y-o 7f winner Winter Gardens and 1994 2-y-o 6f winner Jumilla (both by El Gran Senor and useful): dam, placed at 6f in Britain, later won up to 11f in USA: 20/1, 11¼ lengths fourth to Tawoos in maiden at Haydock, patiently ridden, then not knocked about when no extra from 2f out: sold 25,000 gns in December. *M. A. Jarvis*

BRITISH BLUE (USA) 2 ch.c. (Jan 26) Storm Cat (USA) – Memories of Silver **79** (USA) 123 (Silver Hawk (USA) 123) [2002 7d⁴ 7m⁴ Aug 29] $2,400,000Y: smallish, well-made colt: good walker: first foal: dam, US Grade 1 9f/9.5f winner, half-sister to dam of high-class 6f/7f performer Russian Revival: fourth in maiden at Doncaster and minor event at Lingfield, much better effort (fair form) in former: will probably stay 1m: wears crossed noseband. *D. R. Loder*

BROADWAY BANKER (FR) 3 b.g. Broadway Flyer (USA) 121 – Hariti (IRE) 45 – (Flash of Steel 120) [2002 58?: f8.5g* 11.6g⁶ 10g Aug 7] good-topped gelding: fair form, **a78** lightly raced: easily best effort when winning maiden at Wolverhampton in April: reportedly returned lame next time: gelded after final outing: should be suited by 1¼m+: acts on fibresand. *J. W. Hills*

BROADWAY BLUES 2 b.f. (Apr 20) Broadway Flyer (USA) 121 – Nashville Blues – (IRE) 94 (Try My Best (USA) 130) [2002 p7g Oct 31] sixth foal: half-sister to 3 winners, including 3-y-o Rhythm of Life: dam, 7f/1m winner, not one to trust implicitly: 50/1, well beaten in Lingfield maiden. *J. W. Hills*

BROADWAY SCORE (USA) 4 b.c. Theatrical 128 – Brocaro (USA) (Mr Prospector **108** (USA)) [2002 80p: 10.5m* 10m 8.1m² 8m 10d 8.3m* 10m 8m⁶ 8v p10g⁵ Dec 11] good-bodied colt: shows plenty of knee action: useful performer: won minor event at Haydock in April and handicap at Windsor (beat Colisay by a head despite carrying head awkwardly) in August: below form after: effective at 1m to 10.5f: acts on good to firm going: has shown reluctance at stall: reportedly lost action second start: often forces pace: goes well fresh. *J. W. Hills*

BROCKETEER 3 b.g. Prince Sabo 123 – Mistral's Dancer (Shareef Dancer (USA) **48** 135) [2002 –: p8g* f8.5g⁵ f9.4g p10g Feb 20] poor performer: won handicap at Lingfield in January: stays 1m: acts on polytrack. *J. A. Osborne*

BROCKHALL LAD 4 b.g. Primo Dominie 121 – Cremets 94 (Mummy's Pet 125) – [2002 f8g 5m Apr 18] seems of little account. *D. Eddy*

BROCTUNE LINE 8 ch.g. Safawan 118 – Ra Ra (Lord Gayle (USA) 124) [2002 – f14.8g Jun 7] close-coupled gelding: one-time modest performer: well held both starts since 1999: sometimes blinkered. *Mrs P. Ford*

BROKEN ARROW (IRE) 5 b.g. Sri Pekan (USA) 117 – Domniga (IRE) (Be My – Guest (USA) 126) [2002 p12g Aug 29] 31,000Y: first foal: dam, won up to 1m in France, half-sister to smart French middle-distance performers Tot Ou Tard and Execute: bumper winner: well held on Flat debut in Lingfield seller. *A. J. Lidderdale*

BROKEN BARRICADES (IRE) 3 gr.c. Common Grounds 118 – Gratclo 65 – (Belfort (FR) 89) [2002 88d: 6m⁵ 6.1f 7.1m f7g⁶ 7g f7s³ f8s* 8g f9.4g⁴ a10g⁴ Dec 1] **a77** medium-sized, close-coupled colt: fair handicapper nowadays: won at Southwell in September: sold from B. Hills 13,000 gns before final start: stays 1m: acts on fibresand and good to firm going, below form on good to soft: none too consistent. *J. Calderon, Spain*

BRONX BOMBER 4 ch.g. Prince Sabo 123 – Super Yankee (IRE) (Superlative 118) –
[2002 47: f7g Jun 20] poor maiden at best: tried tongue tied. *Dr J. D. Scargill*

BROS (IRE) 2 b.c. (Jan 24) Night Shift (USA) – Le Ciel (IRE) 92 (Law Society (USA) **69**
130) [2002 6g³ 6m Sep 13] 16,000F, 5,000Y: lengthy colt: first foal: dam Irish 1¼m to
13f winner: around 2 lengths third of 7 in maiden at Baden-Baden: wearing crossed
noseband, well beaten in sales race at Doncaster. *Bruce Hellier, Germany*

BROTHER JOE (NZ) 8 ch.g. Hula Town (NZ) – Olivia Rose (NZ) (Travolta (FR)) **106**
[2002 111+: 18.7f May 8] angular gelding: smart performer in 2001: visored, never-
dangerous ninth in Chester Cup only Flat outing in 2002: stays 2m: acts on firm and soft
going: has his quirks: smart hurdler. *P. J. Hobbs*

BROTHER KIT 2 b.g. (Mar 3) Bishop of Cashel 122 – Fabulous Night (FR) (Fabulous –
Dancer (USA) 124) [2002 p6g Nov 19] second foal: dam, third at 12.5f in France, out of
half-sister to Prix Jacques le Marois winner Miss Satamixa: twelfth in maiden at
Lingfield, taking good hold and running green. *Dr J. D. Scargill*

BROUGHTONS FLUSH 4 b.g. First Trump 118 – Glowing Reference (Reference **58**
Point 139) [2002 48: f16s f16.2g⁶ f16.2g³ f16g³ f16.2g² p16g* f16g* f16.2g⁵ 16.2g
May 11] modest handicapper: won at Lingfield (apprentice) and Southwell (twice, latter
on turf) in March/April: stays 2m: acts on all-weather: visored nowadays: usually held
up: reportedly struck into penultimate start. *W. J. Musson*

BROUGHTONS MILL 7 gr.g. Ron's Victory (USA) 129 – Sandra's Desire (Grey **47**
Desire 115) [2002 –: 9g 9.2s³ 12.4s⁴ 13v⁶ Jun 13] poor maiden: seems to stay 12.5f: acts
on soft going. *Mrs A. M. Naughton*

BROUGHTONS MOTTO 4 b.f. Mtoto 134 – Ice Chocolate (USA) 77 (Icecapade –
(USA)) [2002 –, a69: f8s p10g³ p10g f9.4g* f8.5g⁵ 10s⁶ p10g* p10g⁵ May 10] good- **a75**
topped filly: fair handicapper on all-weather: won at Wolverhampton in February and
Lingfield (apprentice event, hanging fire briefly) in April: should stay beyond 1¼m:
raced only on good going or softer on turf. *W. J. Musson*

BROUGHTON SPIRIT 2 b.f. (Apr 21) Bishop of Cashel 122 – Rainy Day Song 61 **41**
(Persian Bold 123) [2002 5f 7g p6g Nov 14] 800Y: third foal: half-sister to a winner
abroad by Colonel Collins: dam, lightly-raced maiden, half-sister to dam of smart miler
Princess Ellen: poor form in maiden/sellers. *W. J. Musson*

BROUGHTON ZEST 3 b.f. Colonel Collins (USA) 122 – Broughtons Relish (Nom- **69 §**
ination 125) [2002 –: f8g⁵ f8g⁶ 10.9g⁵ 16m* 12.1g* 10f² 14.1f 10d* f12g 11m⁵ 12g 9.7m
12m 11.9g² 12d p10g* Dec 18] smallish filly: fair performer: won claimer at Yarmouth
(left W. Musson after) in May, and handicaps at Beverley and Sandown in June, and
Lingfield in December: successful at 2m, best form at 1¼m/1½m: acts on polytrack, firm
and good to soft going: reluctant to go to start and unseated leaving stall thirteenth outing:
usually held up: one to treat with caution. *J. R. Best*

BROWN HOLLY 4 br.g. So Factual (USA) 120 – Scarlett Holly 81 (Red Sunset 120) **51**
[2002 –: f6g⁴ f6g⁶ f7g 8.3d f9.4g⁶ f9.4g³ Dec 20] modest maiden: will prove best short of
9.4f: acts on fibresand. *H. E. Haynes*

BROWNING 7 b.g. Warrshan (USA) 117 – Mossy Rose 78 (King of Spain 121) [2002 **86**
85: 14m 14m 13.3m⁴ 14f* 13.9f⁵ Oct 12] well-made gelding: fairly useful handicapper:
won at Haydock in September: barely stays 2m: acts on firm going and fibresand:
blinkered once at 5 yrs: takes good hold (has worn crossed noseband). *M. P. Tregoning*

BROWN MADDER (IRE) 3 ch.g. Perugino (USA) 84 – El Pina (Be My Guest –
(USA) 126) [2002 57: 10f Jun 11] big, close-coupled gelding: modest maiden at 2 yrs: no
show only outing in 2002. *T. D. Easterby*

BROWNS DELIGHT 5 b.m. Runnett 125 – Fearless Princess (Tyrnavos 129) [2002 –
–: f12g 12.6m Jul 20] of little account nowadays. *Mrs A. C. Tate*

BRYANO DE BERGERAC 3 b.c. Cyrano de Bergerac 120 – Cow Pastures (Homing **80**
130) [2002 82: 5m 5d 5g 5m 5.1d⁴ 5m 5m² 5d⁴ 5g 5m 5m² 5m⁴ 6m Sep 23] big colt: fairly
useful handicapper: best at 5f: acts on firm and good to soft going: has hung left: sold
11,000 gns. *M. D. I. Usher*

BUALADHBOS (IRE) 3 b.g. Royal Applause 124 – Goodnight Girl (IRE) (Alzao **61**
(USA) 117) [2002 61: 7.1f 10.2g⁵ 8.3s⁶ 10m⁵ 10.9d 11.6d Oct 28] good-topped gelding:
modest maiden handicapper: best around 1¼m: acts on good to firm going, probably on
soft. *F. Jordan*

BUBBLE UP (IRE) 3 b.f. Nicolotte 118 – Mousseux (IRE) (Jareer (USA) 115) [2002 **75**
7g⁶ 8.2d³ 8g⁴ 7g² 7g³ 7g³ 7d 7d 7f 7d Oct 30] 5,800Y: sturdy filly: fifth foal: half-sister to
3 winners, including 4-y-o Looking For Love: dam unraced half-sister to smart French
performer up to 11f Schwepperusschian: fair maiden handicapper: not sure to stay much
beyond 1m: raced mainly on good/good to soft going: has worn crossed noseband.
J. G. Portman

BUCKENHAM JEM 4 b.f. Wing Park 104 – Walk That Walk 61 (Hadeer 118) [2002 **–**
–: 7s f8.5g f12f Nov 29] well held in claimers/sellers. *Mrs Lydia Pearce*

BUCKS 5 b.g. Slip Anchor 136 – Alligram (USA) 61 (Alysheba (USA)) [2002 86: **79 d**
14.4s⁵ 14.1f² 18d 12.1g 11.6d 14.1m p12g Oct 4] quite good-topped gelding: fair maiden:
below form after second start, leaving Mrs A. Perrett after next outing: stays 1¾m: acts
on firm and soft ground: sometimes carries head awkwardly. *Ian Williams*

BUDE 3 gr.g. Environment Friend 128 – Gay Da Cheen (IRE) (Tenby 125) [2002 63: **–**
f9.4g 8.2d 10d 12.3m 12m 14.1m 14s Jun 7] small gelding: disappointing maiden:
blinkered last 3 starts. *S. A. Brookshaw*

BUDELLI (IRE) 5 b.g. Elbio 125 – Eves Temptation (IRE) (Glenstal (USA) 118) **100**
[2002 90: 6m 6g 6f 6d⁵ 6m² 6m* 5d⁵ 5g* 6m* 6s* 6m² 6g 5m 6g 5m² 6f⁴ 5g Oct 17]
strong gelding: useful handicapper: had an excellent summer, winning at Goodwood,
Pontefract, Ascot and Ripon: good efforts also when second to Deceitful in Great St
Wilfrid at Ripon in August and fourth to The Tatling in valuable race at York in October:
effective at 5f (given a test)/6f: acts on any going: visored (below form) once: sometimes edges left: usually ridden by apprentice D. Corby: most tough and consistent.
M. R. Channon

BUDOOR (IRE) 3 b.f. Darshaan 133 – Haddeyah (USA) 68 (Dayjur (USA) 137) **85**
[2002 80p: 10g⁵ 11.6g³ 14s Jun 7] rather lengthy filly: fairly useful performer: folded
tamely at 1¾m: acted on heavy going: visits Muhtarram. *J. L. Dunlop*

BUD THE WISER 2 ch.g. (May 26) Forzando 122 – Short And Sharp 88 (Sharpen **–**
Up 127) [2002 6s f7g Sep 21] 2,400 2-y-o: brother to useful 6f (at 2 yrs) to 7.5f winner
Golden Fortune and half-brother to several winners: dam, placed at 6f/7f, ran only at 2
yrs: well held, including in seller: left Mrs D. Haine after debut. *G. C. H. Chung*

BUENO VIDA (IRE) 3 b.g. Petardia 113 – Pat Said No (IRE) 59 (Last Tycoon 131) **57 d**
[2002 60: f7s* f7g³ f7g⁴ 8m f7g f7g Oct 22] small gelding: modest performer: won seller
at Southwell in January: trained fourth/fifth starts by H. Collingridge, then returned to
former trainer: may prove best at 6f/7f: acts on fibresand: sometimes blinkered/visored:
has looked none too resolute. *D. J. S. Cosgrove*

BUGATTI ROYALE (USA) 2 b.c. (Feb 10) Dynaformer (USA) – Cin Isa Luv (USA) **86**
(Private Account (USA)) [2002 7m⁴ 7.6m³ 10g³ 8.2v* Oct 29] $15,000Y: well-made colt:
second foal: dam, US 1m winner, half-sister to US Grade 1 2-y-o 8.5f winner Script Ohio:
fairly useful form: justified favouritism in maiden at Nottingham by 3½ lengths from
Melograno, leading over 2f out: stays 1¼m: acts on good to firm and heavy ground.
P. F. I. Cole

BULAWAYO 5 b.g. Prince Sabo 123 – Ra Ra Girl 77 (Shack (USA) 118) [2002 56, **a78 §**
a67: 5.7g f7g* 7.5m f8.5g f7f⁶ f7s⁵ f7g² f7s⁶ f7g⁴ f6g f6g⁴ Dec 14] strong, good-topped
gelding: fair handicapper on all-weather: won at Wolverhampton in June: probably best
around 7f: acts on fibresand: usually races prominently: unreliable. *B. A. McMahon*

BULGARIA MOON 2 ch.g. (Mar 6) Groom Dancer (USA) 128 – Gai Bulga 110 **–**
(Kris 135) [2002 6g 8g⁶ 8v Nov 8] 5,500Y: strong gelding: half-brother to fairly useful
1m winner Sword Arm (by Be My Guest), later successful in USA, and 3-y-o Chivalry:
dam, best at 1¼m/1½m, out of Nassau Stakes winner Dancing Rocks: little sign of ability
in maidens/minor event: tongue tied on debut. *C. Grant*

BULLFIGHTER 3 b.g. Makbul 104 – Bollin Victoria 51 (Jalmood (USA) 126) [2002 **62**
74, a63: p5g² p6g⁵ p5g* f5g p5g⁶ f5g p5g⁶ f5g² f5g² 5m⁴ f6g⁴ 6.1f f5g f7g³ f5g f5g Dec
13] smallish, robust gelding: modest performer: won seller at Lingfield in January: stays
easy 6f: acts on soft going, good to firm and all-weather: tried blinkered/in cheekpieces:
sometimes slowly away: usually races prominently. *N. P. Littmoden*

BUMBLEFLY 2 b.g. (Apr 26) Petong 126 – Doppio 62 (Dublin Taxi) [2002 6m 6f **–**
p6g p7g Nov 19] 600Y: brother to 1990 2-y-o 5f winner Garth and 6f winner Wandering
Stranger and half-brother to 6f (including at 2 yrs)/7f winner Thordis (by Mazilier): dam
2-y-o 5f winner: well held in sellers/claimer: has hung left. *Jamie Poulton*

BUNDY 6 b.g. Ezzoud (IRE) 126 – Sanctuary Cove (Habitat 134) [2002 67: 7v 6d² 6m **72**
5.9s* 6s³ 6d 5.9d² 6m⁴ 7g⁶ 5.9v⁵ 7m 6g* 6d Oct 15] smallish, leggy gelding: fair
handicapper: won at Carlisle in June and Newcastle in September: best at 6f/7f: acts on
heavy and good to firm going, below form on fibresand: blinkered once at 3 yrs: often
races prominently. *M. Dods*

BUNKUM 4 b.g. Robellino (USA) 127 – Spinning Mouse 65 (Bustino 136) [2002 –, **–**
a59: f12s f14.8s² f14.8g May 24] quite good-topped gelding: modest handicapper: stays **a55**
14.8f: acts on fibresand: tried visored: flashed tail for win. *R. Lee*

BUNNY HUG BRIDE 2 b.f. (Mar 28) Groom Dancer (USA) 128 – Tender Moment **–**
(IRE) 78 (Caerleon (USA) 132) [2002 6s 7.1m⁶ Sep 16] 12,000Y: quite good-topped
filly: half-sister to several winners, including 3-y-o Marlo and fairly useful 1m winner
Spring Fever (by Indian Ridge): dam 7f winner: signs of ability in maidens. *J. G. Given*

BURCOT GIRL (IRE) 5 b.m. Petardia 113 – Phoenix Forli (USA) (Forli (ARG)) **–**
[2002 12.6m Jul 20] probably of little account nowadays. *Mrs A. C. Tate*

BURDEROP 2 b.f. (Feb 8) Sheikh Albadou 128 – Grace Browning 84 (Forzando 122) **55**
[2002 5.1f 5.7f 6.1g⁴ f6g Dec 20] first foal: dam, 2-y-o 6f winner, no form at 3 yrs: modest
maiden: not sure to stay beyond 6f. *R. M. Beckett*

BURGHMUIR (IRE) 2 ch.f. (Feb 2) Cadeaux Genereux 131 – Luana 101 (Shaadi **–**
(USA) 126) [2002 7.2s 8s 6v Nov 9] 30,000Y: fourth foal: half-sister to UAE 7.5f winner
Luzern (by Green Desert): dam, 6f winner, half-sister to Luso, Needle Gun and Cloud Castle:
well held in maidens. *Miss L. A. Perratt*

BURGUNDY 5 b.g. Lycius (USA) 124 – Decant 68 (Rousillon (USA) 133) [2002 90: **96 §**
p10g p8g² p10g* 8g 8g 8g 8s² 9m⁶ 10.3f³ 10m* 12m³ 10.1m² 10.1d⁴ 10.1m 10d p12g⁴ p10g **a98 §**
Dec 3] smallish gelding: useful handicapper: won at Lingfield in March and Sandown in
July: well below form last 4 starts: effective at 1m to 1½m: acts on polytrack, soft and
good to firm ground: usually visored nowadays: sometimes slowly away/looks far from
keen: not to be trusted. *S. Dow*

BURJ AL ARAB 3 b.c. Alderbrook 120 – Princess Moodyshoe 72 (Jalmood (USA) **–**
126) [2002 81: 10m Jun 24] fairly useful maiden at 2 yrs: well held only start in 2002.
M. C. Pipe

BURLEY FIREBRAND 2 b.c. (Apr 23) Bahamian Bounty 116 – Vallauris 94 **58**
(Faustus (USA) 118) [2002 7.2g 7s⁶ 6d Nov 1] 21,000Y: quite good-topped colt: sixth
living foal: half-brother to 7f/1m winner Mystic Ridge (by Mystiko) and a winner in
Germany by Indian Ridge: dam 1¼m winner: modest form in maidens: will probably stay
1m. *J. G. Given*

BURMESE PRINCESS (USA) 2 ch.f. (Mar 14) King of Kings (IRE) 125 – **64**
Rangoon Ruby 110 (Sallust 134) [2002 6d⁵ 6m² 6s 6.1m³ 7m⁶ 7m⁵ 7g Oct 19] $85,000Y:
compact filly: half-sister to several winners, including smart 6f (at 2 yrs) to 1m winner
Gneiss (by Diesis): dam Irish 6f (at 2 yrs) to 1m winner who was later successful in USA:
modest maiden: stays 6f: acts on good to firm ground, below form on softer than good:
blinkered (took good hold and found little) fifth start: sold 10,000 gns. *P. F. I. Cole*

BURN BABY BURN (IRE) 3 b.f. King's Theatre (IRE) 128 – Tropicaro (FR) 116 **–**
(Caro 133) [2002 –: 12f 12f May 4] well held in 3 maidens. *R. Hollinshead*

BURNING SUN (USA) 3 b.c. Danzig (USA) – Media Nox 98 (Lycius (USA) **119**
124) [2002 76p: 10m³ 10g² 10f² 10m* 10d* 10g³ 10m Oct 19]
Those hoping for an upturn in Henry Cecil's fortunes in 2002 ended the year
disappointed. Cecil's career endured even more of a torrid time in 2002 than the
previous year which had been his worst since his early training days—he first took

*Hampton Court Stakes, Royal Ascot—in a race moved from the Saturday Heath meeting,
Burning Sun provides Henry Cecil with another Royal Ascot winner;
Izdiham (No.11) and Common World are second and third*

Prix Eugene Adam, Maisons-Laffitte—Henry Cecil's only pattern-race success of the year comes courtesy of Burning Sun, who overcomes the determined Kaieteur (rail); Louveteau takes third off Tau Ceti (right)

out a licence at the end of 1968. Only thirty winners on the domestic front in the latest season was Cecil's lowest annual total since he trained twenty-four in 1973. The Warren Place string—there were a hundred and twenty-two horses in the stable at the beginning of the year according to *Horses In Training*—was almost certainly the smallest Cecil has had for over twenty years. The stable sent out only a single pattern winner, Burning Sun in the Prix Eugene Adam at Maisons-Laffitte in July, and the horse had to work hard to win that six-runner Group 2 contest by three quarters of a length from the front-running Kaieteur. Burning Sun matched the form he had shown when successful in a listed race at Royal Ascot on his previous outing, which came after placed efforts earlier in the season in maidens at Newmarket and Windsor in April, won by Royal Stamp and Nysaean respectively, and at Newbury in May, behind Izdiham, those runs following a promising fifth in a Doncaster maiden on his only outing at two. Burning Sun broke his duck in some style in the thirteen-runner contest at Royal Ascot, travelling strongly on the heels of the leader before taking the lead approaching the final furlong and turning the tables on second-placed Izdiham as he held on well to win by a length and a half. The win provided ten-times champion Cecil with one of the few bright spots in his domestic racing year, Burning Sun giving him his seventieth success as a trainer at Royal Ascot and ensuring that 1971, 1973 and 1996 remain the only years he has drawn a blank at the meeting. Burning Sun's two other starts saw him produce vastly different performances. Returned to France in August, Burning Sun went down narrowly, beaten a short head and a head, conceding 4 lb all round, when third of seven to Highdown in the Prix Guillaume d'Ornano at Deauville, with Shaanmer splitting the pair after Burning Sun had had to make the running in a slowly-run affair. Burning Sun ran no sort of race on his final outing two months later, in the Champion Stakes at Newmarket, where he became his stable's only runner in a Group 1 race during the season. Though clearly progressive, Burning Sun still had a bit to find on form with most of his Champion Stakes rivals, but, starting third favourite, he came back tailed-off last of eleven, something clearly amiss.

		Danzig (USA) (b 1977)	Northern Dancer (b 1961)	Nearctic Natalma
Burning Sun (USA) (b.c. 1999)			Pas de Nom (b or br 1968)	Admiral's Voyage Petitioner
		Media Nox (ch 1993)	Lycius (ch 1988)	Mr Prospector Lypatia
			Sky Love (b 1985)	Nijinsky Gangster of Love

The good-topped Burning Sun, owned by one of Cecil's biggest and most loyal patrons Khalid Abdulla, is the first foal out of Media Nox, a useful performer in France as a two- and three-year-old; she won twice at both ages, including in the five-furlong Prix du Bois as a two-year-old, before being transferred to the USA at four when she won a Grade 2 mile event. Media Nox is a half-sister to the smart but lightly-raced French performer Bonash, winner of five races, including the Group 2 Prix de Malleret, and fifth in the 1994 Oaks. The grandam Sky Love, a fairly useful mile-and-a-quarter winner, is a half-sister to another lightly-raced runner in the shape of Raft, a high-class mile-and-a-quarter/mile-and-a-half performer in the early-'eighties, as well as to the dam of the very smart miler Missed Flight. Sky Love had a two-year-old filly by Storm Cat, Nebraska Tornado, in training with Andre Fabre but she wasn't seen out; Sky Love also has a yearling brother to Burning Sun and a filly foal by Lear Fan, and was due to visit Maria's Mon in 2002. Burning Sun stays a mile and a quarter and acts on firm and good to soft going. Though he flashed his tail through the closing stages at Royal Ascot, Burning Sun showed no wayward tendencies in his races afterwards; he needed to be attended by an expert in stalls entry on his debut and was also coltish before his reappearance. *H. R. A. Cecil*

BURNING TRUTH (USA) 8 ch.g. Known Fact (USA) 135 – Galega (Sure Blade **52** (USA) 130) [2002 65, a78: f11g⁶ f9.4g⁴ f12g Jun 22] angular gelding: fluent mover: only modest in 2002: effective at 1m to easy 1½m: acts on firm going, soft and fibresand: usually held up: none too consistent: joined M. Sheppard 2,200 gns and successful over hurdles twice in October. *Mrs A. Duffield*

BURNT COPPER (IRE) 2 b.c. (Apr 30) College Chapel 122 – Try My Rosie 93 **67** (Try My Best (USA) 130) [2002 p5g³ 5m⁴ 5m⁶ 6m⁵ 7m⁵ 8f 7m 6f⁶ Oct 5] IR 10,000Y, 8,500 2-y-o: leggy, quite good-topped colt: half-brother to 2 winners, including fairly useful Irish 5f winner Zebra Stripes (by Tirol): dam, Irish 2-y-o 6f winner, best at 1m: fair maiden: well below form last 3 starts, slowly away final 2: will prove best at 6f/7f: acts on polytrack, raced only on going firmer than good on turf. *J. R. Best*

BURPO MARX 2 ch.c. (Apr 13) Alhaarth (IRE) 126 – Reach The Wind (USA) **58** (Relaunch (USA)) [2002 5d⁵ 5d⁵ 6m 7m 7s 8.3d Oct 14] 25,000Y, 19,000Y: seventh foal: half-brother to 3 winners, including 3-y-o Thundergod: dam, Irish 6f winner (including at 2 yrs), half-sister to useful sprinter Ozone Friendly: modest form in maidens first 3 starts: disappointing after, looked none too keen fourth outing: stays 6f: acts on good to firm and good to soft ground: has worn cheekpieces: sold 4,500 gns, sent to Kuwait. *J. W. Hills*

BURRY BRAVE 3 b.g. Presidium 124 – Keep Mum 63 (Mummy's Pet 125) [2002 51: **–** 10g 5d⁶ 6d 5.9d 8m Jul 8] small gelding: little solid form. *J. S. Goldie*

BUSH BABY 2 b.f. (Apr 25) Zamindar (USA) 116 – Bempton 57 (Blakeney 126) **– §** [2002 7.5d 8g Sep 7] rather angular filly: half-sister to numerous winners, notably very smart Princess Royal Stakes winner Banket (by Glint of Gold) and Ribblesdale Stakes winner Gull Nook (by Mill Reef), herself dam of Pentire: dam maiden half-sister to Shirley Heights: well held in maidens: troublesome at stall and virtually refused to race second start: sold 30,000 gns in December. *T. D. Easterby*

BUSH CAT (USA) 2 b.f. (Mar 2) Kingmambo (USA) 125 – Arbusha (USA) 103 **87** (Danzig (USA)) [2002 p6g⁴ 7m* 8m⁵ 7f⁵ Oct 5] $100,000Y: smallish, quite attractive filly: fifth foal: half-sister to a winner in Japan by Wild Again: dam, 1m winner, sister to smart 6f/7f performer Nicholas and to dam of very smart 1½m/1¾m performer Strategic Choice: fairly useful performer: won maiden at Folkestone in August: best effort when fifth in May Hill Stakes at Doncaster next time: should stay 1¼m: raced on going firmer than good on turf: slowly away (fell over backwards behind stall) on debut. *C. E. Brittain*

BUSINESS 3 br.c. Bluegrass Prince (IRE) 110 – Dancing Doll (USA) (Buckfinder **–** (USA)) [2002 10g⁶ 12g 8m 8f Sep 17] second reported foal: dam unraced half-sister to useful performer up to 7f Kuantan: well beaten in maidens/minor event: left I. Wood after second start. *G. A. Ham*

BUSINESS TRAVELLER (IRE) 2 ch.c. (Apr 14) Titus Livius (FR) 115 – Dancing **–** Venus 61 (Pursuit of Love 124) [2002 5m⁵ May 23] 19,000Y, 8,000 2-y-o: strong colt: first foal: dam, Irish maiden, later won over hurdles: 16/1, well held in minor event at Newcastle: gave trouble in preliminaries. *G. A. Swinbank*

BUSTAN (IRE) 3 b.c. Darshaan 133 – Dazzlingly Radiant 81 (Try My Best (USA) 130) **116** [2002 8m* 10g* 12m⁵ 11.9g⁴ 11f³ Sep 21] 125,000F: strong, compact colt: brother to useful 7f winner (including at 2 yrs) Bedazzling and half-brother to 3 winners, including useful 7f (at 2 yrs) to 1¼m winner Bound For Pleasure (by Barathea): dam 6f winner: reportedly had a chip removed from a joint at 2 yrs: smart form: won maiden at Kempton (hung left/carried head awkwardly) in May and 5-runner listed event at Newmarket (by short head from Al Moulatham) in June: good efforts after when length fourth of 6 to Bandari in Great Voltigeur Stakes at York and ¾-length third to Legal Approach in listed event at Newbury: stays 1½m: raced only on good ground or firmer. *M. P. Tregoning*

BUSTER BROWN (FR) 2 b.g. (Apr 4) Presidium 124 – Penniless (IRE) 74 (Common Grounds 118) [2002 f5g* 7f⁴ 6m⁴ f7g 5.9m f5g 7g Oct 17] 1,000Y: first foal: dam 5f winner (including at 2 yrs): modest performer: won seller at Southwell in April despite flicking tail/drifting left: well held last 4 outings: probably better at 6f than 7f: acts on fibresand and firm ground: withdrawn second intended outing (reared/unseated rider start): difficult ride, and probably ungenuine. *B. S. Rothwell* **63 d**

BUSTLING RIO (IRE) 6 b.g. Up And At 'em 109 – Une Venitienne (FR) (Green Dancer (USA) 132) [2002 81: p16g f16g⁵ f16.2g⁴ Dec 7] big, good-topped gelding: fair handicapper: stays 2¼m well: acts on fibresand, best turf efforts on good going or firmer: held up, and tends to idle/hang in front: fairly useful hurdler. *P. C. Haslam* **72**

BUSY BUSY BEE 5 gr.m. Batshoof 122 – Rectitude 99 (Runnymede 123) [2002 –, a53: f9.4g⁶ f9.4g Feb 15] modest handicapper at 4 yrs: no form in 2002: blinkered/visored nowadays. *N. P. Littmoden*

BUTHAINA (IRE) 2 b.f. (Apr 12) Bahhare (USA) 122 – Haddeyah (USA) 68 (Dayjur (USA) 137) [2002 6d⁵ Jun 14] third foal: half-sister to 3-y-o Budoor and fairly useful 2000 2-y-o 6f winner Makboola (by Mujtahid): dam, 6f winner only 2-y-o start, tailed off both outings at 3 yrs: 12/1, well-beaten last of 5 in maiden at Goodwood. *J. L. Dunlop* **–**

BUT OF COURSE (USA) 2 b.c. (Feb 8) Kingmambo (USA) 125 – Sun And Shade 93 (Ajdal (USA) 130) [2002 7d³ 7m³ 6.1m² Sep 20] $800,000Y: leggy, close-coupled colt: fifth foal: half-brother to smart 1997 2-y-o 6f/7f winner Daggers Drawn (by Diesis) and useful 1998 2-y-o 6f winner Enemy Action (by Forty Niner): dam, 6f (at 2 yrs) and 9f (in USA) winner, half-sister to very smart Park Hill Stakes winner Madame Dubois: fairly useful form in maidens: good 4 lengths second to Oasis Dream at Nottingham: effective at 6f/7f. *E. A. L. Dunlop* **83**

BUTRINTO 8 ch.g. Anshan 119 – Bay Bay 101 (Bay Express 132) [2002 66: f8.5g⁵ p8g⁴ 8.5g 9.7m 10m 7d³ 8.1m 8g⁵ 7m 7g⁵ 7m 8f 9g f8.5s³ p10g³ Dec 30] tall, strong gelding: good mover: modest performer: best at 7f to 9f: acts on any turf going/all-weather: tried blinkered/visored earlier in career: sometimes slowly away: often carries head high. *B. R. Johnson* **53 a59**

BUYING A DREAM (IRE) 5 ch.g. Prince of Birds (USA) 121 – Cartagena Lady (IRE) (Prince Rupert (FR) 121) [2002 55: 9.9g⁵ 10.1m 11.8m Jun 3] lengthy, quite good-topped gelding: poor handicapper: stays 1¼m, possibly not 11.8f: acts on good to firm and good to soft going: sometimes blinkered. *Andrew Turnell* **45**

BUY THE SPORT (USA) 2 b.f. (Apr 25) Devil's Bag (USA) – Final Accord (USA) (D'Accord (USA)) [2002 6m* 6m⁴ 7m⁴ 8m⁴ Sep 12] $82,000Y: heavy-topped filly: half-sister to minor winners in USA by Sir Harry Lewis and Distinctive Pro: dam US 8.5f winner: useful performer: won 3-runner minor event at Windsor in July: fourth in Princess Margaret Stakes at Ascot, Prestige Stakes at Goodwood and May Hill Stakes at Doncaster after: should stay 1¼m: raced only on good to firm going. *B. J. Meehan* **97**

BUZ KIRI (USA) 4 b.g. Gulch (USA) – White Corners (USA) (Caro 133) [2002 62, a–: 14.1g 16.2m 16f⁶ 17.1f Oct 7] smallish, sturdy gelding: poor maiden handicapper: better at 2m than shorter: acts on fibresand and firm going, below form on softer than good: blinkered once. *A. W. Carroll* **46**

BY ALL MEN (IRE) 2 b.c. (May 28) Among Men (USA) 124 – Bellinzona (North-fields (USA)) [2002 7f Oct 3] IR 8,500F, 40,000 2-y-o: good-topped colt: half-brother to several winners, including useful 7f (at 2 yrs) to 1½m winner Maralinga (by Simply Great): dam French 9.5f winner: 66/1 and burly, soundly beaten in maiden at Newmarket. *N. A. Graham*

BY DEFINITION (IRE) 4 gr. or b.f. Definite Article 121 – Miss Goodbody (Castle Keep 121) [2002 54: 8.1m 8f 8.3v 8g 10.2f 10.2g 10m 9.9g Oct 2] rather sparely-made filly: poor maiden: stays 1m: form only on going firmer than good. *J. M. Bradley* **34**

BY FAR (FR) 4 b.c. Machiavellian (USA) 123 – Makri 65 (Night Shift (USA)) [2002 8d⁴ 7d² 7m⁶ 9g Sep 4] leggy colt: second foal: dam, maiden who stayed 1¼m, closely related to useful 1½m winner Rain In Spain: useful performer: won handicap at Longchamp in May and minor event at Saint-Cloud (by 3 lengths from Molto Vivace) in September: ran well in between when ½-length second to Chercheuse in listed race at Le Lion d'Angers and not discredited when sixth of 28 to Crystal Castle in Tote International **103**

(Handicap) at Ascot next time: stays 1m: very best form on good going or softer: tongue tied at Ascot. *J. E. Hammond, France*

BY HEC   2 ch.g. (Mar 11) Hector Protector (USA) 124 – Dancing Wolf (IRE) 76 (Wolf-hound (USA) 126) [2002 5g 6g 7m 8g⁵ 8g³ Sep 19] 2,000Y: first foal: dam, maiden, effective at 7f/1m: modest maiden: creditable never-nearer third in seller at Ayr: will stay 1¼m. *M. Dods*   **57**

BYINCHKA   2 br.c. (Mar 16) Inchinor 119 – Bystrouska (Gorytus (USA) 132) [2002 p7g 6s 7v Nov 8] 6,500F, 16,000Y: seventh foal: half-brother to fairly useful 6f (including at 2 yrs)/7f winner Charlie Sillett (by Handsome Sailor) and a winner in Belgium by Green Ruby: dam ran once: well held in maidens. *S. L. Keightley*   **–**

BYO (IRE)   4 gr.c. Paris House 123 – Navan Royal (IRE) 61 (Dominion Royale 112) [2002 88d: 5s p6g p5g² 5m 5d³ 5m Aug 18] smallish, workmanlike colt: fair handicapper: best at 5f: acts on polytrack and probably on any turf going: none too consistent. *G. M. McCourt*   **67 a74**

C

CABALLE (USA)   5 ch.m. Opening Verse (USA) 126 – Attirance (FR) (Crowned Prince (USA) 128) [2002 79: 13.1g May 20] strong, good sort: good walker: fair performer at 4 yrs: well held only 5-y-o start. *N. J. Henderson*   **–**

CABALLO NOBILE (USA)   3 b.f. Kris S (USA) – Serene Nobility (USA) (His Majesty (USA)) [2002 –: p10g a8f⁵ Sep 13] maiden: well held all starts: left B. Meehan after reappearance. *F. L. Brothers, USA*   **–**

CABARET QUEST   6 ch.g. Pursuit of Love 124 – Cabaret Artiste (Shareef Dancer (USA) 135) [2002 50: 8g 8f May 13] strong gelding: modest handicapper at 5 yrs: well held both 6-y-o starts: blinkered last 6 starts. *J. M. Bradley*   **–**

CABEZA DE VACA   2 ch.g. (Apr 3) Machiavellian (USA) 129 – Norbella (Nordico (USA)) [2002 5.2d⁴ 7m² 7m² 7g² Oct 19] fourth foal: half-brother to useful 5f (at 2 yrs) to 1m winner Achilles Star (by Deploy) and 3-y-o Esligier: dam unraced: fairly useful maiden: trained by B. McMahon on debut (off over 3 months after): favourite when runner-up last 3 starts (gelded after): stays 7f: yet to race on extremes of going. *M. Johnston*   **80**

CABO SALINAS (IRE)   4 b.g. Hamas (IRE) 125§ – Easter Heroine (IRE) 72 (Exactly Sharp (USA) 121) [2002 68: f8s f8g 5.1d 10.9f 7s⁵ 7d³ 8.5g 9g 12g 7g Sep 3] modest maiden: left B. Curley before final outing: probably best at 7f to 1¼m: acts on soft and good to firm going: tried blinkered. *T. Stack, Ireland*   **50**

CADEAUX CHER   8 ch.g. Cadeaux Genereux 131 – Home Truth 98 (Known Fact (USA) 135) [2002 94: 6s 6g 6d⁶ 6f 6d 5.7d³ 6d 5.7g 6s⁶ f6s⁵ f6s Oct 8] lengthy gelding: unimpressive mover: fairly useful handicapper: on downgrade: best around 6f: acts on any turf going (no form on all-weather): tried blinkered in 1998: wears bandages: held up: sometimes hangs left. *B. W. Hills*   **80 d**

CADRAVEL   3 b.c. Cadeaux Genereux 131 – Space Travel (Dancing Dissident (USA) 119) [2002 7g 6g p6g p5g Dec 21] 9,000Y: fifth foal: half-brother to useful 1997 2-y-o sprinter Tippitt Boy (by Prince Sabo), later successful in Germany, and 6f/7f winner Reverie (by Bishop of Cashel): dam unraced daughter of smart 6f/7f winner Rocket Alert: poor form in maidens (slowly away second start)/handicap. *J. Gallagher*   **49**

CAERNOMORE   4 b.g. Caerleon (USA) 132 – Nuryana 107 (Nureyev (USA) 131) [2002 72: p12g p16g p10g f7g⁵ 7g 8g May 20] modest maiden: stays 1¼m: tried blinkered. *T. P. McGovern*   **– a51**

CAERPHILLY GAL   2 b.f. (Apr 28) Averti (IRE) 117 – Noble Lustre (USA) 71 (Lyphard's Wish (FR) 124) [2002 5m 6d f6s Nov 2] 1,000Y: seventh foal: half-sister to 3 winners, including 5-y-o Doctor Dennis and useful 7f and (in USA) 1m winner Royal Rebuke (by Reprimand): dam, 6f winner, stayed 1m: form in maidens (modest) only when seventh of 21 to Maltese Falcon at Windsor second start. *P. L. Gilligan*   **57**

CAESAREAN HUNTER (USA)   3 ch.g. Jade Hunter (USA) – Grey Fay (USA) (Grey Dawn II 132) [2002 –: 11.6s 10d 8m⁶ f9.4f f12g* p12g⁶ Dec 18] big gelding: fair performer: much improved to win maiden at Wolverhampton in December by 11 lengths: stays 1½m: acts on all-weather. *S. Kirk*   **75**

CAESAR'S PALACE (GER) 5 ch.g. Lomitas 129 – Caraveine (FR) (Nikos 124) – [2002 16m Sep 16] second foal: half-brother to French 15f winner Canadian River (by Always Fair): dam German 1¼m winner: fairly useful performer at 3 yrs for Mme M. Bollack-Badel in France: well held only 5-y-o start: stays 12.5f: raced mainly on good to soft/soft ground: usually blinkered/visored. *Miss Lucinda V. Russell*

CAFE AMERICANO 2 b.g. (May 6) Labeeb 124 – Coffee Ice 92 (Primo Dominie 72 121) [2002 7f 6m⁵ 7.1g² 7g Oct 4] 40,000Y: fifth foal: half-brother to a 6f winner in USA by Twining: dam, 2-y-o 5f winner, later sprint winner in US: fair maiden: 9 lengths second to Battle Chant at Chepstow: effective at 6f/7f: free-going sort: gelded after final start. *D. W. P. Arbuthnot*

CAFE CONCERTO (USA) 2 b.f. (May 28) Trempolino (USA) 135 – Charmie – Carmie (USA) (Lyphard (USA) 132) [2002 7d 7v Nov 8] half-sister to several winners, including South American Grade 1 winner Faaz (by Fappiano) and fairly useful 6f/7f winner (including at 2 yrs) Himmah (by Habitat): dam, placed in USA, from excellent family: well beaten in maidens. *M. L. W. Bell*

CAHAN (IRE) 3 b.f. Up And At 'em 109 – Global Princess (USA) (Transworld – (USA) 121) [2002 p8g 7s p6g f8g Dec 4] IR 3,200Y: half-sister to several winners abroad, including fairly useful Irish 8.5f winner Kates Choice (by Taufan): dam placed in USA: well held in maidens. *S. L. Keightley*

CAITLAND 3 b.f. Puissance 110 – Lorlanne (Bustino 136) [2002 51: 12g⁴ 12m 9.2g 45 8d³ 9.2v² 6.9g 9m Sep 16] unfurnished filly: poor maiden: stays 1m: acts on heavy and good to firm ground: has been free to post/slowly away. *R. Allan*

CAKE IT EASY (IRE) 2 ch.f. (Apr 9) Kendor (FR) 122 – Diese Memory (USA) 71 (Diesis 133) [2002 7.1f³ 8s³ f8.5s² f8.5g⁴ Dec 20] 150,000 francs F, 16,500Y: leggy, quite good-topped filly: second foal: dam, French 9f winner, out of a US Grade 3 8.5f winner: fair maiden: second at Wolverhampton: likely to stay 1¼m: wandered on debut. *M. Johnston*

CALA (FR) 2 b.f. (Mar 7) Desert Prince (IRE) 130 – Badawi (USA) 103 (Diesis 133) 58 [2002 6f⁶ 6.1m⁶ Jul 27] unfurnished filly: sixth foal: closely related to winner around 7f Balfour and 8-y-o Saguaro (both by Green Desert) and half-sister to 2 winners, including useful 1m winner Badagara (by Warning): dam 1m/9f winner: modest form in maidens: should stay 7f. *C. E. Brittain*

CALAMELLA (IRE) 3 ch.f. Brief Truce (USA) 126 – Kindness Itself (IRE) 89 (Aho- 93 noora 122) [2002 89: 7m* 7s⁵ 6s 7g⁶ 6d Oct 13] rather leggy, lengthy filly: third reported foal: half-sister to fairly useful 1m/1½m winner Pirro (by Persian Bold): dam 7f winner: fairly useful performer: won maiden at Leopardstown in April: ran well after when fifth to Rum Charger in listed race and sixth to Bella Bella in valuable handicap, both at the Curragh: never dangerous in listed event at Haydock in between: stays 7f: acts on soft and good to firm ground: tongue tied first 4 starts. *M. Halford, Ireland*

CALAMINT 3 gr.g. Kaldoun (FR) 122 – Coigach 110 (Niniski (USA) 125) [2002 78p: 73 10m 12.1d⁵ p12g 16.4g Aug 14] close-coupled, good-topped gelding: unimpressive mover: fair maiden: disappointing in 2002: bred to be suited by 1¼m+: best effort on soft going: visored penultimate start: often tongue tied: sold 8,000 gns. *J. R. Fanshawe*

CALAMINTHA 2 b.f. (Mar 17) Mtoto 134 – Calendula 75 (Be My Guest (USA) 126) – [2002 p7g Oct 31] second foal: dam, 1¼m and 1½m winner, daughter of smart middle-distance stayer Sesame, herself half-sister to Gold Cup winner Celeric (by Mtoto): 50/1 and very green, well held in maiden at Lingfield, tending to hang/carry head awkwardly. *R. M. Beckett*

CALANDA 4 b.f. Aragon 118 – Henceforth 58 (Full of Hope 125) [2002 –: 7d 10d 7m – Jul 22] little form. *H. Candy*

CALATAGAN (IRE) 3 ch.g. Danzig Connection (USA) – Calachuchi 74 (Martinmas 66 128) [2002 65: 10g⁴ 10m⁵ 9.9g 9.9d³ 12m² 11.9g² 12.4g³ 12s Nov 6] short-backed gelding: fair maiden: left Miss J. Camacho after seventh start: stays 1½m: acts on good to firm and good to soft going: free-going sort: won over hurdles in December. *J. M. Jefferson*

CALBRAE (IRE) 2 b.f. (Mar 24) Indian Ridge 123 – Willow Dale (IRE) 89 (Danehill 83 (USA) 126) [2002 6f³ 6d³ p5g² p5g² p6g⁵ Dec 30] IR 17,000Y: good-quartered filly: second foal: dam 5f/6f winner, including at 2 yrs: fairly useful performer: placed in maidens/nursery: likely to prove best at 5f/6f: acts on polytrack: sometimes hangs right. *D. R. C. Elsworth*

CALCAR (IRE) 2 b.c. (Apr 25) Flying Spur (AUS) – Poscimur (IRE) (Prince Rupert **58**
(FR) 121) [2002 8g 7d f7g⁵ Nov 16] IR 28,000Y: well-made colt: fifth foal: half-brother
to 3-y-o Dust To Dust: dam ran 3 times in Ireland: modest form in maidens (not knocked
about final start): will stay 1m: slowly away second appearance. *J. W. Hills*

CALCUTTA 6 b.h. Indian Ridge 123 – Echoing 93 (Formidable (USA) 125) [2002 **112**
103: 8g 7d 7.9f⁴ 8.1m⁵ 8m 8m* 8.1d 7.9m* 8f* 8m 8m⁵ 7.9m 8m⁴ 8m² 8f* 8f⁴ 7.9f⁵ 8g²
7.5g³ Dec 19] smallish, sturdy horse: carries condition: smart performer: better than
ever in 2002, winning handicaps at Salisbury, York (by short head from Muchea) and
Newbury (by ½ length from Smirk) in June/July and minor event at Bath (by ¾ length
from sole rival Wannabe Around) in September: left B. Hills prior to creditable efforts in
Dubai last 2 starts: best at 7f/1m: acts on firm and good to soft going: blinkered final
4-y-o outing: sometimes swishes tail/looks less than keen, and best produced as late as
possible. *P. L. Rudkin, UAE*

CALGARTH (IRE) 3 b.f. Efisio 120 – Waypoint 95 (Cadeaux Genereux 131) [2002 **49**
54p: 7.9g⁶ f7g 9.3s 7g Oct 5] rather leggy filly: poor maiden: left W. Haggas after third
start: may prove best at 5f/6f: acts on fibresand: has raced freely. *P. F. Cashman, Ireland*

CALIBAN (IRE) 4 ch g Rainbows For Life (CAN) Amour Toujours (IRE) (Law **49**
Society (USA) 130) [2002 53: f14.8g⁵ Oct 21] lengthy gelding: poor performer: stays
1½m: acts on fibresand and good to firm going: usually visored: has been slowly away/
raced freely. *Ian Williams*

CALIBRE (USA) 2 b.c. (Apr 30) Lear Fan (USA) 130 – Carya (USA) (Northern **95 p**
Dancer) [2002 8g* Oct 18] strong, well-made colt: sixth foal: brother to very smart 7f (at
2 yrs) to 1¼m (including US Grade 1s) winner Ryafan, and half-brother to 2 winners,
including 5-y-o Stage Direction: dam, ran 3 times in France, closely related to smart
French performer up to 15f Glorify from very good US family: well-backed favourite,
won 16-runner maiden at Newmarket by 1½ lengths from Lundy's Lane, leading 3f out
and rallying despite carrying head high: will stay 1¼m: sure to progress, and could well
prove smart. *J. H. M. Gosden*

CALIFET (FR) 4 b.c. Freedom Cry 132 – Sally's Room (FR) (Kendor (FR) 122) **126**
[2002 108: 12.5v* 12d² 12g* 12g* 12m⁴ 12m⁴ 12.5g² 12g² 12g⁴ Oct 6]

British-born astronaut Piers Sellers had to abandon the country of his
birth and become an American citizen to follow his dream and journey to the
International Space Station in October, swapping the Union Jack for the Stars
and Stripes of NASA. French-trained Califet has changed colours too. As well
as purchasing Arc runner-up Sulamani, Godolphin has also acquired the fourth
Califet, who will presumably now embark on a voyage of his own through several
legs of the 2003 version of the World Series, won in 2002 by another mid-career
purchase of Godolphin's, Grandera.

Califet has joined Saeed bin Suroor from trainer Guy Cherel, for whom
he was one of only a handful of Flat horses among a string of jumpers. The
four-year-old Califet spent his first two seasons mainly in the French Provinces,
winning five times in minor events before taking a listed race at Lyon-Parilly.
Califet took another minor event at Saint-Cloud on his reappearance in March
before stepping up to pattern company and showing smart form to win the Group 3
Prix d'Hedouville at Longchamp in April and the Group 2 Prix Jean de Chaudenay
at Saint-Cloud in May. He took both races in style by three lengths, reversing

Prix Jean de Chaudenay - Grand Prix du Printemps, Saint-Cloud—
Califet quickens clear of Sangreal (left), Ange Gabriel (rail), Sensible and Yavana's Pace (white face)

placings from his previous start with runner-up Ange Gabriel at Longchamp and finishing still further in front of that rival at Saint-Cloud, showing easily the best turn of foot in a small field to beat Sangreal comfortably, with Ange Gabriel third. Califet didn't win again afterwards, but ran very well when fourth behind Anabaa Blue, Ange Gabriel and St Expedit, giving them all 4 lb, in the Grand Prix de Chantilly on his next start. He was below form on two occasions in Group 1 events, in the Grand Prix de Saint-Cloud and the Grosser Preis von Baden, before his excellent Arc effort on his final outing. Somewhat unflatteringly, he started at 131/1 at Longchamp, the rank outsider in a field of sixteen. He certainly belied his odds, moving typically strongly close up on the inside and keeping on gamely after being slightly short of room halfway up the straight, beaten only a length and three quarters behind Marienbard, Sulamani and High Chaparral. On form, it appears Califet's best performance so far.

			Soviet Star	Nureyev
	Freedom Cry		(b 1984)	Veruschka
	(b 1991)		Falling Star	Mount Hagen
Califet (FR)			(ch 1980)	Free French
(b.c. 1998)			Kendor	Kenmare
	Sally's Room (FR)		(gr 1986)	Belle Mecene
	(b 1991)		Square Room	Dewan Keys
			(ch 1983)	Stormy Love

Califet is bred to be a late developer. His sire Freedom Cry was the best horse of any age trained in France as a four-year-old, when he won the Prix d'Harcourt and Grosser Preis der Wirtschaft at Baden-Baden, for Andre Fabre, and was also second in the Arc and the Breeders' Cup Turf. Califet's dam Sally's Room was much more limited but she won at seven furlongs to nine furlongs at four and five in France. Califet is her second foal. Her first Sally's Cry, a brother to Califet, was also a winner, at around a mile/nine furlongs. Grandam Square Room is a half-sister to the dam of the Prix de Diane winner Escaline. Califet did all his racing at four over a mile and a half, but he shapes as though a return to a mile and a quarter won't trouble him. The sparely-made Califet has yet to race on firm ground, but acts on any other, though it's worth pointing out that consecutive races on good to firm ground in the latest season saw him below par on the second occasion, after which he was given a two-month break. A genuine sort and a straightforward-looking ride, as a five-year-old, like Sellers, he should carry his new colours with distinction. *G. Cherel, France*

CALIFORNIAN   2 ch.c. (Mar 8) Zafonic (USA) 130 – Asterita 103 (Rainbow Quest (USA) 134) [2002 7.1d³ p7g 7m 8m⁴ 8g⁵ 10m⁵ 8s³ p7g Nov 13] tall, quite attractive colt: has plenty of scope: third foal: half-brother to 2000 2-y-o 7f winner Gulchie (by Thunder Gulch), later winner in USA: dam, 11.5f winner who stayed 2m, half-sister to dam of top-class French miler Keltos: fair maiden: third at Sandown and Yarmouth (nursery): should stay 1½m: acts on soft and good to firm going, below form on polytrack: visored (found little) fifth outing: sometimes has 2 handlers/slowly away. *G. A. Butler*   **77**

CALIPH (IRE)   2 b.c. (Apr 7) Fayruz 116 – Kuda Chantik (IRE) 53 (Lashkari 128) [2002 6s 5.3m Oct 3] IR 7,800Y, resold IR 8,700Y, 9,000 2-y-o: first foal: dam, Irish maiden, half-sister to smart performer up to 1½m Madiriya: well held in maiden/seller: sold £300. *E. L. James*   **–**

CALIWAG (IRE)   6 b.g. Lahib (USA) 129 – Mitsubishi Style (Try My Best (USA) 130) [2002 50§: p12g² p12g⁶ p12g⁶ p13g p10g² p10g² p10g 10d 9g p10g p10g Jul 10] fair maiden at best: on downgrade: stays easy 1½m: acts on polytrack and firm going: tried blinkered: has looked temperamental. *Jamie Poulton*   **63 d**

CALKO   5 ch.g. Timeless Times (USA) 99 – Jeethgaya (USA) 61 (Critique (USA) 126) [2002 –, a55d: f11s³ f12g f8.5g 10m 13.8m 11.8m 10.5s Jun 7] sturdy gelding: poor nowadays: stays 11f: acts on fibresand, little form on turf since 2 yrs: usually blinkered/visored: sometimes hangs left, including when leaving stall. *R. Wilman*   **–**
a46

CALLDAT SEVENTEEN   6 b.g. Komaite (USA) – Westminster Waltz (Dance In Time (CAN)) [2002 77: p13g p16g Feb 13] good-bodied gelding: one-time fair performer: tried visored: sometimes tongue tied/led to post: temperamental (has twice refused to race, including final start): sold 5,200 gns, sent to Germany., *P. W. D'Arcy*   **– §**

CALLIGRAPHY 2 ch.f. (Mar 31) Kris 135 – Ink Pot (USA) 73 (Green Dancer (USA) **73 p**
132) [2002 6m³ Sep 18] third foal: closely related to 2000 2-y-o 6f/7f winner Quink (by
Selkirk), later 1m winner in Hong Kong: dam maiden who would have stayed at least
1¼m: weak 8/1-shot and green, 2½ lengths third of 5 to Camlet in maiden at Yarmouth,
staying on: should stay at least 1m: should do better. *W. J. Haggas*

CALLING DOT COM (IRE) 4 ch.g. Halling (USA) 133 – Rawya (USA) 80 **78**
(Woodman (USA) 126) [2002 65+: p10g* p10g p10g* p10g 7.6f⁶ 8d⁴ 10.3g⁶ a6g⁴ a8.2f³ **a83**
Nov 13] good-topped gelding: fairly useful performer on all-weather, fair on turf: won 2
handicaps at Lingfield in January: left N. Littmoden after seventh start, and renamed
Olympic Gold: effective at 1m/1¼m: acts on polytrack/dirt, firm and good to soft going:
best in blinkers: often slowly away. *I. W. Allan, Hong Kong*

CALLING THE SHOTS 5 b.g. Democratic (USA) 101 – Two Shots (Dom Racine **50**
(FR) 121) [2002 62, a77: f8s f7s* f8.5g² a8f⁴ a7f⁵ a7.5f⁵ a8f a8f⁶ a6f⁴ 7g⁴ a6f⁵ a7.5g **a74 d**
a5.5f⁶ Dec 19] fair on all-weather at best, modest on turf: won claimer at Southwell in
January: left S. R. Bowring after next start: regressed in UAE subsequently: has won at
easy 1½m, probably best at 6f to 1m: acts on firm going and fibresand: usually visored/
blinkered/tongue tied: tends to look none too keen. *C, Wroe, UAE*

CALLISTO (IRE) 3 br.f. Darshaan 133 – Moon Parade 73 (Welsh Pageant 132) **91**
[2002 –p: 11.1g⁴ 12m³ 14.6m³ 14d⁶ 16.2m³ 16.4g⁵ 16.2m* 16f³ 17.5g* 18m Oct 19]
leggy, plain filly: fairly useful handicapper: won at Warwick in August and at Ayr (again
idled) in September: stays 17.5f: acts on firm going: blinkered last 3 starts. *J. L. Dunlop*

CALL ME SUNSHINE 2 b.f. (Jan 28) Robellino (USA) 127 – Kirana (Niniski **78**
(USA) 125) [2002 5m⁵ 6m³ 7g² 8d³ f8.5g⁵ p8g² Dec 11] 3,000Y: compact filly: second **a72**
foal: dam, out of half-sister to Danzig, won at 11f/1½m in Germany: fair maiden: should
stay 1¼m: second at Thirsk and Lingfield (nursery): acts on polytrack, yet to race on
extremes of going on turf. *P. C. Haslam*

CALL OF THE WILD 2 ch.g. (Apr 26) Wolfhound (USA) 126 – Biba (IRE) (Super- **66**
lative 118) [2002 6f⁵ 6d⁶ 5.9s⁵ 6m 6d Nov 5] 4,200Y: lengthy gelding: third foal: dam,
poor maiden, half-sister to useful sprinter Farhana: fair maiden: should stay at least 7f:
acts on firm and soft ground. *R. A. Fahey*

CALL THE MARK (IRE) 3 b.g. Goldmark (USA) 113 – Shalerina (USA) (Shalford **–**
(IRE) 124§) [2002 67: p7g 7.1m p7g³ p10g p7g³ 8.5g 7d 7m p7g Oct 16] smallish, sturdy **a64**
gelding: modest maiden handicapper: effective at 7f/1m: acts on polytrack: tried tongue
tied: none too consistent. *P. Mitchell*

CAL MAC 3 b.g. Botanic (USA) – Shifting Mist 76 (Night Shift (USA)) [2002 78: **94**
f8.5g* 8f² 8m 8d 8.3m 7g Oct 18] smallish, quite good-topped gelding: has a quick
action: fairly useful performer: won maiden at Wolverhampton in April: good second in
handicap at Newmarket next time: well below form last 3 starts: stays 8.5f: acts on
fibresand and firm going. *H. Morrison*

CALUSA LADY (IRE) 2 ch.f. (Apr 10) Titus Livius (FR) 115 – Solas Abu (IRE) 82 **65**
(Red Sunset 120) [2002 6d 6s³ 6v Nov 9] 12,500Y: smallish, lengthy filly: fourth foal:
half-sister to fairly useful 1999 2-y-o 6f winner Shannon Dore (by Turtle Island) and a
winner in Holland by Dolphin Street: dam, Irish 9f/1¼m winner, out of half-sister to
smart Irish performer up to 1¼m Noora Abu: fair maiden: best effort when third at
Leicester: should stay 7f: raced only on ground softer than good. *G. B. Balding*

CALVADOS (USA) 3 b.c. Seattle Slew (USA) – A Votre Sante (USA) 109 (Irish **66**
River (FR) 131) [2002 8.3d 8m³ p12g⁶ 8m] lengthy, attractive colt: second foal:
half-brother to French 1¼m winner Vole Vole Monamour (by Woodman): dam, French 7f
(at 2 yrs) and 1m winner, half-sister to very smart US performer up to 1¼m Unaccounted
For: fair maiden: trained by Mme C. Head-Maarek in France until after reappearance:
should stay 1¼m: found little final start: sold 11,000 gns. *J. H. M. Gosden*

CALYPSO DANCER 2 ch.g. (Mar 10) Dancing Spree (USA) – Caribbee Beach **58**
(IRE) (Magical Strike (USA) 114) [2002 5g 5.1g 7m⁶ 7m⁴ 8g f8g⁵ Oct 17] 3,200Y: sturdy
gelding: second foal: dam, maiden, out of useful Irish 2-y-o performer up to 1m Madam
John: modest maiden: should stay 1m: acts on good to firm going. *S. Kirk*

CAMADERRY (IRE) 4 ch.g. Dr Devious (IRE) 127 – Rathvindon 93 (Realm 129) **69**
[2002 75: 10m 8.3m 9m³ p10g Jul 20] IR 55,000F, IR 115,000Y: strong gelding:
half-brother to several winners, including useful 1m winner Lady Fairfax (by Sharrood)
and fairly useful 1¼m/1½m winner Andrath (by Commanche Run): dam 5f winner: fair
maiden: trained at 3 yrs by D. Weld in Ireland: stays 1¼m: acts on good to firm and good
to soft ground: tried blinkered/visored: very slowly away final start. *Noel T. Chance*

CAMARADE (IRE)   4 b.g. Common Grounds 118 – Nymphs Echo (IRE) (Mujtahid   **73**
(USA) 118) [2002 84: f7g 8s 6g 8.1s 6s 6s 6m 5.9d Jul 19] IR 30,000Y: lengthy gelding:
first foal: dam unraced sister to useful performer up to 1m Glen Rosie and half-sister to
useful Irish winner up to 1¼m Artema (by Common Grounds) and smart French winner
up to 9f Hello Soso: fairly useful winner for J. Burns in Ireland at 3 yrs: fair form at best
in 2002: should stay 1m: acts on heavy going, never travelling fluently on good to firm
(blinkered) seventh start: has been tongue tied. *I. Semple*

CAMARADERIE   6 b.g. Most Welcome 131 – Secret Valentine 71 (Wollow 132)   **58**
[2002 55: 9.3g³ 7.9s 7.9s⁴ 9.9m⁶ 9.9g 10.1m² 9d 8g 12.1m⁴ Sep 24] leggy, workmanlike
gelding: modest performer: effective at 1m, probably at 1½m: probably acts on any turf
going: effective blinkered or not: sometimes starts slowly. *Mrs M. Reveley*

CAMARET (IRE)   3 b.f. Danehill (USA) 126 – Armorique (IRE) (Top Ville 129)   **92**
[2002 79p: 7m* 8g 8f⁵ Aug 18] rather leggy, useful-looking filly: good walker: sister to
useful Irish 6f (at 2 yrs)/7f winner Darwin: dam, French 1½m winner, half-sister to
several good middle-distance performers: won maiden at Newmarket (last and quietly to
post) in April by 2 lengths from Monturani, dictating pace: subsequently well held in
Poule d'Essai des Pouliches at Longchamp and listed event at Bath, racing too freely in
blinkers in latter: may prove best at 6f/7f. *J. H. M. Gosden*

CAMBERLEY (IRE)   5 b.g. Sri Pekan (USA) 117 – Nsx 74 (Roi Danzig (USA))   **–**
[2002 98: 7f Apr 8] rangy gelding: good mover: useful performer at best: well held only
5-y-o start (subsequently gelded): stays 7f: acts on firm and good to soft going: blinkered
last 3 starts at 4 yrs: reportedly bled penultimate 3-y-o outing: has worn crossed noseband: free-going sort: best held up: none too resolute. *P. F. I. Cole*

CAMBIO (IRE)   4 b.g. Turtle Island (IRE) 123 – Motley (Rainbow Quest (USA) 134)   **64**
[2002 61: p8g p8g⁶ p8g p8g 19.1m³ Jun 22] angular, quite good-topped gelding: modest
maiden: stays 19f, at least when conditions aren't testing: acts on soft and good to firm
going: tried visored/blinkered: usually slowly away. *B. R. Johnson*

CAMELOT   3 br.g. Machiavellian (USA) 123 – Bombazine (IRE) 97 (Generous (IRE)   **91**
139) [2002 8g² 8f 9.3s² 10s³ 10.2g 8.1f* 8m* 8s Nov 2] well-made gelding: first foal:
dam, 1¼m winner who stayed 1½m, half-sister to Barathea and Gossamer: fairly useful
performer: improved form when successful in maiden at Haydock in September and
handicap at Redcar in October: well held final start (gelded after): best form at 1m on
going firmer than good. *L. M. Cumani*

CAMEO COOLER   3 ch.g. Inchinor 119 – Mystique Smile 78 (Music Boy 124)   **41**
[2002 –: 5d 6g 8d 6f 7.2g 5g 5d⁵ Oct 14] good-topped gelding: poor maiden: should stay
6f: blinkered last 4 starts. *Miss L. A. Perratt*

CAMEO ROLE (GER)   2 b.f. (Jan 14) Acatenango (GER) 127 – Coyaima (GER)   **78**
100 (Night Shift (USA)) [2002 7m⁶ 7.2s Oct 14] second foal: dam, German 7f (at 2 yrs)
and 1m (listed) winner, half-sister to smart German middle-distance performer Concep-
cion (by Acatenango): 33/1, caught the eye when sixth to Almaviva in maiden at
Newmarket, short of room repeatedly: off 2 months, well held in similar event at Ayr,
finding little: free-going sort, but should stay at least 1m. *C. F. Wall*

CAMILLE PISSARRO (USA)   2 b.g. (Feb 21) Red Ransom (USA) – Serenity 98   **78**
(Selkirk (USA) 129) [2002 6.1m⁶ 7.2g³ Jul 22] 40,000Y: first foal: dam 2-y-o 6f winner
who stayed 7f: much better effort in maidens (fair form) when third to Double Obsession
at Ayr, headed final 1f: gelded after: not sure to stay much beyond 7f. *P. F. I. Cole*

CAMLET   2 b.f. (Apr 4) Green Desert (USA) 127 – Brocade 121 (Habitat 134) [2002   **94 p**
6m* 7m Oct 19] strong, angular filly: half-sister to several winners, including high-class
miler Barathea, 3-y-o Gossamer (both by Sadler's Wells) and smart French 1m to 1¼m
winner Zabar (by Dancing Brave): dam 7f (Challenge Stakes/Prix de la Foret)/1m winner: reluctant stall and green, landed odds in 5-runner maiden at Yarmouth in September
by ¾ length from Frieda Kahlo: never able to challenge when eighth to Luvah Girl in
Rockfel Stakes at Newmarket: will stay at least 1m: remains type to do better, and will
probably prove useful. *L. M. Cumani*

CAMMAEUS   3 ch.f. Greensmith 121 – Pastelle 52 (Tate Gallery (USA) 117) [2002   **– §**
51§: p5g Jan 3] temperamental sprint maiden. *J. Akehurst*

CAMP COMMANDER (IRE)   3 b.c. Pennekamp (USA) 130 – Khalatara (IRE)   **92**
(Kalaglow 132) [2002 69, a81: p7g³ 8.1d 8m 9g⁴ 8m⁵ 8g 6d 7m 8m³ 7.1m* 8f⁴ 7.1m⁶
8m p7g Nov 23] rather leggy colt: fluent mover: fairly useful performer: won maiden at
Warwick in August: effective at 7f to 9f: acts on firm going, soft and polytrack: tongue
tied. *C. E. Brittain*

CAMZO (USA) 4 ch.g. Diesis 133 – Cary Grove (USA) (Theatrical 128) [2002 73: **80**
11m⁵ 12m 11.5m³ 14.1m* 14m 14.1m* 14.1m⁴ Aug 25] compact gelding: fairly useful
handicapper: better than ever in 2002, winning at Salisbury in June (hung right) and
Yarmouth (ladies) in August: reportedly suffering a pulled muscle after final start: better
at 1¾m than shorter: acts on good to firm going: no easy ride. *P. W. Harris*

CANATRICE (IRE) 2 gr.f. (Apr 2) Brief Truce (USA) 126 – Cantata (IRE) (Saddlers'
Hall (IRE) 126) [2002 p6g f7g⁶ 7d Aug 9] second foal: half-sister to a winner in Spain by
Danehill Dancer: dam ran twice in France: slowly away, well beaten in maiden/sellers.
W. J. Musson

CANCUN CARIBE (IRE) 5 ch.g. Port Lucaya 118 – Miss Tuko (Good Times (ITY)) **71 d**
[2002 74: f9.4g⁵ f8g⁵ f9.4g² 9.2s May 5] leggy gelding: reportedly fractured a pastern
after third 2000 start: fair performer at best: below form after reappearance at 4 yrs: stays
1¼m: acts on heavy going and fibresand: often blinkered. *K. McAuliffe*

CANDELABRA 2 br.f. (Mar 26) Grand Lodge (USA) 125 – Chatterberry 67 (Aragon **72**
118) [2002 7m 8s Oct 15] 80,000Y: fifth foal: half-sister to 2-y-o 5f winners Cloudberry
(in 1997, by Night Shift) and Inkberry (in 1998, by Cadeaux Genereux): dam, 2-y-o 5f
winner, sister to smart sprinter Argentum: slowly away, better effort (fair form) when
seventh in maiden at Kempton: should prove best up to 7f. *Sir Michael Stoute*

CANDID 3 ch.f. Lion Cavern (USA) 117 – Shady Deed (USA) 80 (Shadeed (USA) **64**
135) [2002 76: 7.1m⁴ 7.1m 10g 7s 8m⁶ Jun 28] strong, rangy filly: modest maiden: seems
to stay 1m: acts on firm and soft going: blinkered 3 of last 4 starts (also tongue tied final
one): sold 4,500 gns in July, sent to Belgium. *B. J. Meehan*

CANDOUR 3 b.f. So Factual (USA) 120 – Outward's Gal 78 (Ashmore (FR) 125) **–**
[2002 –: 8.2m 7g Oct 14] angular filly: well held in maidens. *Mrs D. Haine*

CANDY ANCHOR (FR) 3 b.f. Slip Anchor 136 – Kandavu 87 (Safawan 118) [2002 **50**
41: 9f 9.9d² 16.2d⁴ 12.1g³ 11.5m⁴ f12g 11.5s Oct 22] lengthy filly: modest maiden: left
J. Given after fifth start: stays 1¼m/1½m: acts on good to soft going (below form both
starts on fibresand): unruly in stall and withdrawn fifth intended outing. *Andrew Reid*

CANLIS 3 b.c. Halling (USA) 133 – Fajjoura (IRE) 84 (Fairy King (USA)) [2002 –: **55**
8g³ 8.1d f8.5g 8g⁵ Oct 16] unfurnished colt: has a quick action: modest maiden: left
B. Hills after third start: stays 1m: has edged left. *K. A. Ryan*

CANNON BRIDGE (IRE) 4 ch.g. Definite Article 121 – Hit For Six (Tap On Wood **–**
130) [2002 f8.5g 6m 11.1s May 5] eighth foal: half-brother to winners in Italy by Cyrano
de Bergerac and Soviet Lad: dam, Irish 2-y-o 5f winner, from family of smart 2-y-o 6f/7f
winner Balla Cove: well held in maidens. *D. Shaw*

CANOE COVE (IRE) 2 b.f. (Mar 13) Grand Lodge (USA) 125 – Whispered Melody **55**
68 (Primo Dominie 121) [2002 5s⁵ 6m 5m 6m 6g Oct 18] IR 60,000F, IR 50,000Y:
quite good-topped filly: second foal: half-sister to 3-y-o Prayers For Rain: dam, 1m
winner, half-sister to smart 9f/1¼m winner Supreme Sound and useful stayer Top Cees:
modest maiden: headstrong, and needs to settle to stay beyond 6f: acts on soft and good
to firm ground: tried blinkered: sold 8,500 gns. *R. F. Johnson Houghton*

CANOSA (IRE) 2 gr.f. (Feb 28) Catrail (USA) 123 – Abergwrle (Absalom 128) [2002 **53**
5s Mar 23] IR 6,000Y: leggy, useful-looking filly: sister to useful 1998 French 2-y-o 5.5f/
6f winner Felicita, and half-sister to several winners, including useful Irish performer up
to 1m Anemone Garden (by Dancing Dissident): dam, ran twice, out of 1000 Guineas
winner Caergwrle: 12/1 and green, 6 lengths eighth of 16 to Intellibet One in maiden at
Doncaster. *E. J. Alston*

CANOVAS KINGDOM 4 ch.g. Aragon 118 – Joan's Venture (Beldale Flutter (USA) **61**
130) [2002 61: 7f⁴ 7m² 8m 7m Jul 16] strong, lengthy gelding: has a round action: modest
maiden: stays 1m: acts on firm and good to soft going: edgy sort: has carried head
awkwardly: sold 1,600 gns. *Bob Jones*

CAN PAU 3 b.f. Tragic Role (USA) – Distant Isle (IRE) (Bluebird (USA) 125) [2002 **–**
40: f8.5g 14.1f Jun 4] well-grown, quite good-topped filly: little form. *K. A. Ryan*

CAN'T BUY ME LOVE 3 ch.f. Bijou d'Inde 127 – Addicted To Love 73 (Touching **67**
Wood (USA) 127) [2002 8.1m 8.5m⁴ 8.1m² p10g p8g⁵ f8.5s Dec 9] tall filly: third foal:
half-sister to 7f/1m winner Unchain My Heart (by Pursuit of Love): dam 1¼m to 1¾m
winner: fair maiden: stays 1m: acts on good to firm going and polytrack. *B. J. Meehan*

CANTERLOUPE (IRE) 4 b.f. Wolfhound (USA) 126 – Missed Again 84 (High Top **98**
131) [2002 94p: 5g⁶ 6d³ 5.7d⁶ 6g* 6g 5m 6v Nov 9] quite good-topped filly: keen walker:
useful handicapper: clearly best effort in 2002 when winning at Windsor in August by

2½ lengths from Ceepio: effective at 5f/6f: acts on good to firm and good to soft going: has worn crossed noseband: has gone last/steadily to post: sometimes slowly away. *P. J. Makin*

CANTGETYOURBREATH (IRE) 6 ch.g. College Chapel 122 – Cathy Garcia –
(IRE) (Be My Guest (USA) 126) [2002 –: 6s 7g⁶ 8.3s 6.9m 12.3m 10.5m Sep 6] no longer of much account. *B. P. J. Baugh*

CANTRIP 2 b.f. (Feb 5) Celtic Swing 138 – Circe 73 (Main Reef 126) [2002 7d Nov **60 p**
2] small filly: eighth foal: half-sister to 3 winners, including fairly useful 9f to 1½m winner My Learned Friend (by Broken Hearted): dam 1m winner: 50/1, 11¾ lengths ninth of 19 to Goodness Gracious in maiden at Newmarket: will be suited by 1¼m+: should do better. *R. M. Beckett*

CAPACOOSTIC 5 ch.m. Savahra Sound 111 – Cocked Hat Girl 47 (Ballacashtal **45**
(CAN)) [2002 44: f8g f7g f6g² f8g 7f f5g⁶ f8.5s⁵ 7f⁴ 6f² 8f⁶ 7m 5g f5g Jul 11] angular **a41**
mare: poor maiden handicapper: probably best at 6f/7f: acts on firm going, soft and fibresand: usually blinkered: often forces pace. *S. R. Bowring*

CAPAL GARMON (IRE) 4 b.g. Caerleon (USA) 132 – Elevate 98 (Ela-Mana-Mou **106 ?**
132) [2002 116: 12m 11.8g⁶ 12g⁴ Jul 19] lengthy gelding: smart performer at 3 yrs, winning Jockey Club Cup at Newmarket (needed oxygen afterwards): beat only one horse in 3 outings in 2002 (finished distressed first 2): needs further than 1½m and should stay beyond 2m: best form on good to soft/soft going: tongue tied last 2 starts: has worn crossed noseband: has been blanketed for stall entry. *J. H. M. Gosden*

CAPALLIN (IRE) 3 gr.f. Desert Style (IRE) 121 – Rustic Lawn (Rusticaro (FR) 124) **50**
[2002 62: p10g 8g f8s 10g⁶ Oct 24] modest performer: stays 1¼m: acts on fibresand. *M. H. Tompkins*

CAPE COAST (IRE) 5 b.g. Common Grounds 118 – Strike It Rich (FR) 88 (Rhein- **43**
gold 137) [2002 67, a54: p6g 6v 6m 6v³ Aug 9] poor nowadays: left N. Littmoden 5,000 gns after third start: stays 7f: has form on good to firm going/fibresand, probably best on good or softer: tried blinkered. *R. M. Beckett*

CAPER 2 b.c. (Feb 2) Salse (USA) 128 – Spinning Mouse 65 (Bustino 136) [2002 –
8.5m⁵ 8g 7m⁶ 10m Oct 1] smallish, good-topped colt: second foal: half-brother to 4-y-o Bunkum: dam, 1¾m winner, half-sister to smart sprinter/miler May Ball: little form in maidens/nursery. *M. L. W. Bell*

CAPE ROYAL 2 b.g. (Mar 8) Prince Sabo 123 – Indigo 86 (Primo Dominie 121) [2002 **55**
5.1g⁶ Jun 15] brother to 3-y-o Amused and half-brother to several winning sprinters, notably smart Astonished (by Weldnaas) and 8-y-o Bishops Court: dam 2-y-o 5f winner: 4/1, 6 lengths sixth of 14 to Topkamp in maiden at Nottingham: subsequently gelded. *Mrs J. R. Ramsden*

CAPE TOWN (IRE) 5 gr.h. Desert Style (IRE) 121 – Rossaldene 79 (Mummy's Pet **111 d**
125) [2002 119: 8.1d² 8m 8.5d⁴ 10m 10d³ 8m 8m 8g 7m⁶ Sep 20] leggy, quite good-topped horse: smart performer at best: on downgrade in 2002: in frame in attheraces Mile at Sandown (second to Swallow Flight), Diomed Stakes at Epsom (fourth to Nayyir) and listed contest at Sandown (third to Izdiham): barely stays 1¼m: yet to race on heavy going, acts on any other turf: blinkered fourth to sixth starts and final one: tends to edge left: sold 58,000 gns. *R. Hannon*

CAPE WIND (USA) 2 ch.c. (Mar 12) Woodman (USA) 126 – Company (USA) **70**
(Nureyev (USA) 131) [2002 5m⁴ 6g p7g⁶ 7f⁵ 8.3d 8d 7s⁴ Oct 28] 1,200,000 francs Y: sturdy colt: half-brother to several winners, including useful 6f (at 2 yrs) and 7f winner in France Contexte (by Septieme Ciel): dam, French 2-y-o 5f winner, sister to smart sprinter King's Signet out of top-class French sprinter Sigy: fair maiden: stays 7f: acts on firm and soft ground: has worn crossed noseband: sold 15,000 gns. *B. W. Hills*

CAP FERRAT 2 b.c. (Feb 17) Robellino (USA) 127 – Trick (IRE) 76 (Shirley Heights **88 +**
130) [2002 6m* 6m³ Jun 1] 130,000Y: quite attractive colt: third foal: half-brother to 3-y-o White Rabbit and 2000 2-y-o 6f winner Shinner (by Charnwood Forest): dam, 1¼m winner, out of half-sister to high-class Flying Childers/Middle Park winner Hittite Glory: fairly useful form: impressive winner of maiden at Newbury in May by 1½ lengths from Kawagino: only third to Coconut Penang in minor event at Kempton following month: should stay 7f at least. *R. Hannon*

CAP HORN 3 b.c. Mtoto 134 – Tabyan (USA) 68 (Topsider (USA)) [2002 10m⁵ 10s **65**
Oct 26] sixth foal: brother to smart 1m to 1¼m winner Cap Juluca: dam 6f winner: better effort in maidens when fifth to Lion Hunter at Windsor, racing freely: sold 9,000 gns, sent to Italy. *R. Charlton*

CAPITAL ACCESS 3 b.g. Efisio 120 – Thilda (IRE) (Roi Danzig (USA)) [2002 70: **72 §**
p6g² 6g 5m* 5.7g 5.1d May 31] lengthy, well-made gelding: fair performer: won claimer
at Folkestone in April: barely stays 7f: acts on good to firm going, soft and polytrack:
usually blinkered: sometimes wanders/carries head awkwardly: often races prominently:
unpredictable. *B. J. Meehan*

CAPITANO CORELLI (IRE) 3 b.c. Sadler's Wells (USA) 132 – Ahead 113 **95 p**
(Shirley Heights 130) [2002 10m 10d⁶ 12m* 12s* 12v Nov 9] 52,000Y: big, useful-
looking colt: sixth foal: brother to useful 1½m winner Isadora and half-brother to 3
winners, including smart performer up to 9f in Britain/France Smart Alec (by Diesis):
dam, 1½m winner, half-sister to top-class miler Markofdistinction: useful performer:
made all in maiden at Musselburgh in September and handicap at Doncaster (gamely beat
Sarin by 2½ lengths) in October: well held in November Handicap on latter course final
start: will stay 1¾m: acts on soft and good to firm going: lightly raced, and should yet do
better still. *P. F. I. Cole*

CAPPONICUS (IRE) 2 ch.f. (Feb 15) Woodborough (USA) 112 – Volkova 60 (Green **73**
Desert (USA) 127) [2002 5g p5g* 5.2g³ 5g⁴ 5.1f² 5.2f³ 5g 5m 5m² Jul 29] IR 1,500Y:
lengthy filly: fourth foal: dam, maiden, should have stayed beyond 1m: fair performer:
won claimer at Lingfield in April: likely to prove best at 5f: acts on firm ground and
polytrack: races prominently: tends to hang/carry head awkwardly: none too consistent.
P. S. McEntee

CAPRICCIO (IRE) 5 gr.g. Robellino (USA) 127 – Yamamah 54 (Siberian Express **75**
(USA) 125) [2002 –: 15g 14g⁴ 18m 16.5v Nov 9] fair maiden, lightly raced on Flat nowadays: stays 1¾m: acts on soft ground, probably good to firm: sold 3,500 gns. *C. G. Cox*

CAPRICHO (IRE) 5 gr.g. Lake Coniston (IRE) 131 – Star Spectacle (Spectacular Bid **111**
(USA)) [2002 96: 7d⁵ 7d³ 6m* 7d*ᵈⁱˢ 7d³ 7m* 6g 7f⁴ Oct 10] tall, leggy, useful-looking
gelding: smart handicapper: much improved for new stable in 2002: won at Royal Ascot
(stormed through from well back to beat Border Subject 1¼ lengths in Wokingham) in
June and Goodwood (beat Attache by ¾ length) in August: disqualified after dead-
heating with Mine in Bunbury Cup at Newmarket (rider weighed in 9 lb light) fourth
outing: effective at 6f/7f: acts on firm and good to soft going: has been bandaged hind
joints: has gone freely to post: game and reliable. *J. Akehurst*

*Wokingham Stakes (Handicap), Royal Ascot—Capricho is a comfortable winner from Border Subject,
Chookie Heiton and the unlucky-in-running Crystal Castle (No.7)*

CAPRICIOUS 3 ch.f. Primo Dominie 121 – Megan's Flight 74 (Welsh Pageant 132) **69**
[2002 8.3g 10m⁶ 12.3g⁴ 12m³ 11.7g Oct 16] tall, unfurnished filly: fourth living foal:
half-sister to 6-y-o Magic Flute: dam 1¾m/2m winner, also 2¾m winner over hurdles:
fair maiden: should stay beyond 1½m: raced only on good/good to firm ground. *Lady
Herries*

CAPRICORN RED 2 ch.f. (Jun 10) Rashik 97 – Bella Maggio (Rakaposhi King 119) **–**
[2002 6d 6d Aug 26] small, sturdy filly: second known foal: half-sister to 6-y-o Green
Ginger: dam unraced: last in maiden/seller. *A. Streeter*

CAPRIOLO (IRE) 6 ch.g. Priolo (USA) 127 – Carroll's Canyon (IRE) (Hatim **66 §**
(USA) 121) [2002 80: p13g 12.3f⁵ 12m 16.2m 12d 12g Jul 18] good-topped gelding: fair
handicapper nowadays: effective at 1¼m/1½m: yet to race on heavy going, acts on any
other: visored once, often blinkered: races prominently: carries head high: sometimes
finishes weakly: ungenuine. *J. C. Fox*

CAPTAIN CLIPPER 2 b.c. (May 29) Royal Applause 124 – Collide 102 (High Line **70 p**
125) [2002 6m⁶ Sep 7] 22,000F: rangy colt: has scope: seventh foal: brother to 2001
2-y-o 5f winner Encore Ma Fille and half-brother to fairly useful 1m winner Wolf
Tooth and 4-y-o Collard (both by Wolfhound): dam 1m winner: fair form in maidens at
Thirsk, short of room on second occasion: not sure to stay beyond 1m: type to do better.
R. M. Whitaker

CAPTAIN CLOUDY 2 b.g. (Apr 20) Whittingham (IRE) 104 – Money Supply **70**
(Brigadier Gerard 144) [2002 6m⁵ 6d 6s Oct 25] leggy, good-topped gelding: half-brother
to several winners, including 7f (at 2 yrs) to 1½m winner Credit Squeeze (by Superlative): dam unraced: fair form in maidens: not knocked about at Newbury final start:
should stay at least 7f: acts on soft and good to firm ground. *G. B. Balding*

CAPTAIN CRUSOE 4 b.g. Selkirk (USA) 129 – Desert Girl (Green Desert (USA) **85**
127) [2002 79: 10m p10g² p12g³ Jul 24] strong gelding: fairly useful maiden, lightly
raced: stays 1½m: acts on polytrack and good to firm ground: tongue tied (well held) on
reappearance. *C. A. Horgan*

CAPTAIN DARLING (IRE) 2 b.g. (Apr 17) Pennekamp (USA) 130 – Gale Warning **66 p**
(IRE) (Last Tycoon 131) [2002 p7g Oct 9] sixth living foal: half-brother to useful 1½m/
1¾m winner Takwin (by Alzao) and fairly useful Irish 1995 2-y-o 7f/8.5f winner
Common Spirit (by Common Grounds): dam French 2-y-o 6f winner: 7/1, 7¾ lengths
seventh to Texas Hill in maiden at Lingfield, very slowly away and late headway without
being knocked about: will stay at least 1m: should improve. *R. M. H. Cowell*

CAPTAIN GINGER 2 ch.g. (Feb 17) Muhtarram (USA) 125 – Brand (Shareef **85**
Dancer (USA) 135) [2002 5.7f⁴ 6g* 6m⁵ 7m⁵ 7.1m* 7.9f Oct 10] angular gelding: sixth
foal: half-brother to fairly useful 6f to 1m winner Double Brandy (by Elmaamul): dam
unraced half-sister to useful performer up to 1½m Clever Cliche, from family of
Unfuwain, Nashwan and Nayef: fairly useful performer: won maiden at Brighton in
August and nursery at Warwick in September: should stay 1m: raced only on good ground
or firmer: usually races prominently: gelded after final outing. *I. A. Balding*

CAPTAIN HARDY (IRE) 2 b.g. (Mar 12) Victory Note (USA) 120 – Airey Fairy **73**
(IRE) (Alzao (USA) 117) [2002 6s 5.1d⁶ 7d⁶ 7m⁵ 8g f6g 6d⁴ f6f* p6g³ p7g⁴ p7g Dec 28]
IR 10,000Y: first foal: dam unraced granddaughter of useful sprinter Eloquent Minister:
fair performer: won nursery at Wolverhampton in November: effective at 6f to 1m: acts
on good to soft going, good to firm and all-weather: takes time to warm to task:
sometimes edges left: consistent. *S. Kirk*

CAPTAIN RIO 3 ch.c. Pivotal 124 – Beloved Visitor (USA) 83 (Miswaki (USA) **122**
124) [2002 122: a6f⁴ a6f 8g 6d* 6s² Oct 31]

Asked to compile a list of the top sprinters in training, the average British
racegoer could be forgiven if the name Captain Rio didn't immediately spring to
mind. The horse, who put up the best performance by a British-trained two-year-old
colt in 2001, wasn't seen on a British racecourse in the latest season. Furthermore,
it wasn't until October, almost a year after his crushing win in the Criterium de
Maisons-Laffitte, that Captain Rio fully re-established himself. The race in which
Captain Rio came right back to form was the Bank of Ireland Waterford Testimonial
Stakes at the Curragh. Sent off joint favourite and encountering going softer than
good for the first time since Maisons-Laffitte, Captain Rio thrashed his field, soon
travelling strongly in front and drawing clear on the bridle from over a furlong out
to win from the smart pair One Won One and Kier Park. The eight-length win

*Bank of Ireland Waterford Testimonial Stakes, the Curragh—
Captain Rio bounces back from injury in spectacular fashion*

offically credited to Captain Rio at Maisons Laffitte had seemed over the mark, but there was no call to question the judge's eyesight when the same winning distance was announced at the Curragh.

Captain Rio's first target as a three-year-old had been decided when connections accepted an invitation to compete in the Dubai Golden Shaheen at Nad Al Sheba in March. A below-par fourth in a listed race there earlier that month was followed by an operation to have some teeth removed. Hardly the ideal preparation, and Captain Rio ran poorly in the Golden Shaheen, unable to take up his usual prominent position and never getting into it. Another possible explanation was that he hadn't taken to the dirt surface. Captain Rio was stepped up in trip on his return to Europe, providing his trainer with his first runner in a classic in the Poule d'Essai des Poulains. Captain Rio raced too freely, disputing the lead, and was quickly done with in the straight, the race leaving him with a chipped bone in his knee. Five months on the sidelines meant that Captain Rio missed most of the top sprint races, though he did make the track once more after his win at the Curragh. Returned to Maisons-Laffitte at the end of October for the Group 3 Prix de Seine-et-Oise, Captain Rio failed only by a head, conceding 2 lb to Danehurst, after looking the likely winner most of the way, soon leading from his outside draw and having most of his rivals off the bridle a good way out. Captain Rio was transferred from Richard Whitaker's stable in West Yorkshire to that of David Nicholls in North Yorkshire after the end of the season. Nicholls has a reputation for improving sprinters but Captain Rio already looks good enough to make an impact at the highest level, his best form on a par with that of Nicholls' July Cup winner Continent, whom he looks sure to meet in racecourse competition in 2003.

Captain Rio (ch.c. 1999)			
	Pivotal (ch 1993)	Polar Falcon (b or br 1987)	Nureyev
			Marie d'Argonne
		Fearless Revival (ch 1987)	Cozzene
			Stufida
	Beloved Visitor (USA) (b 1988)	Miswaki (ch 1978)	Mr Prospector
			Hopespringseternal
		Abeesh (b 1982)	Nijinsky
			Lady Bugler

Captain Rio's sire Pivotal was a very smart sprinter and is making a big name for himself as a stallion too. His fee has risen from £10,000 in 2002 to £25,000 in 2003. Kyllachy was among Pivotal's flagbearers in the latest season, when he emulated his sire by winning the Nunthorpe. Other representatives of Pivotal who could cross swords with Captain Rio in 2003 include smart performers Feet So Fast, Needwood Blade, Olivia Grace and Somnus. The strong, good-topped Captain Rio races freely and should prove at least as effective at five furlongs as at six. He showed his form on good to firm going as a two-year-old but clearly revels on going softer than good and, bearing in mind his knee injury, it would come as no surprise to see him doing the majority of his racing under such conditions from now on. Captain Rio will start the new season as arguably the best sprinter in training without a pattern-race penalty and his trainer looks sure to place him to win a good prize before the big Group 1 sprints come along. *R. M. Whitaker*

182

CAPTAIN SAIF   2 b.c. (Mar 8) Compton Place 125 – Bahawir Pour (USA) (Green   **105 p**
Dancer (USA) 132) [2002 7.6m* 7m* 7m* Sep 29] 13,000F, 10,500Y, 35,000 2-y-o: first
foal: dam unraced out of half-sister to US Grade 1 winners De La Rose and Upper Nile:
progressive form: unbeaten in maiden at Lingfield in August and minor events at
Kempton and Ascot in September: beat Weavers Pride by 2 lengths in 4-runner race at
Ascot, not unduly hard ridden to assert final 1f: should stay 1m: smart colt in the making,
and should win more races. *R. Hannon*

CAPTAIN SCOTTLAND   3 b.g. Beveled (USA) – Little Egret 74 (Carwhite 127)   –
[2002 –: p12g 8.5g 7m 7m Sep 17] tall, leggy gelding: no form. *D. J. S. ffrench Davis*

CAPTAIN'S LOG   7 b.g. Slip Anchor 136 – Cradle of Love (USA) 87 (Roberto   **84**
(USA) 131) [2002 92: 10g⁵ 10m⁵ 10s 11.9s* 10m³ 12.6g³ 11.8g* 10s* 10d³ 12m⁴ 10g³
10.1s Oct 22] leggy, rather lightly-made gelding: fairly useful performer: won claimer at
Haydock and claimer/handicap at Leicester in June/July: best at 1¼m/1½m: acts on any
going: has run well when sweating: has started slowly/carried head high/raced freely:
often held up. *M. L. W. Bell*

CAPTAIN VENTI   3 br.g. Ventiquattrofogli (IRE) 118 – Lady Liza 69 (Air Trooper   **95**
115) [2002 86: 7s 7g 8m 6m 6g 6d⁵ 8.1s* 8.1d* 8m* 8.5g³ 8m² 8g⁶ 8s Nov 2] robust
gelding: useful handicapper: won at Haydock, Sandown and Doncaster (dead-heated) in
June: unlucky short-head second to Out For A Stroll at Pontefract in August: well held
final start: stays 8.5f: acts on heavy and good to firm going. *J. J. Quinn*

CAPTIVA   3 b. or br.f. Darshaan 133 – Desert Girl (Green Desert (USA) 127) [2002   –
9.9g 10.2s 11.5m⁵ Jul 2] 34,000Y: smallish filly: fifth foal: half-sister to fairly useful 1997
2-y-o 6f winner Moontabeh (by Mujtahid) and 5-y-o Spanish Star: dam lightly-raced
maiden daughter of St Simon Stakes winner Upend: little form in maidens. *W. Jarvis*

CAPULETTE (IRE)   2 b.f. (Feb 21) Grand Lodge (USA) 125 – Malabarista (FR)   **81**
(Assert 134) [2002 6m⁵ 7.1m 7f* 8m⁴ 7f Oct 21] 26,000Y: good-bodied filly: fourth foal:
half-sister to French 7f winner Epouvantail (by Spectrum) and a 1¼m/11f winner in Italy
by Barathea: dam French 12.5f winner: fairly useful form: won maiden at Yarmouth in
July: well held in nursery at Newmarket final start: bred to stay 1¼m: raced only on going
firmer than good. *W. Jarvis*

CAQUI D'OR (IRE)   4 b.g. Danehill (USA) 126 – Ghaiya (USA) 110 (Alleged   **90**
(USA) 138) [2002 90: 16g⁵ 16.2s 16.4d⁵ 16.2d Aug 10] sturdy, angular gelding: fairly
useful handicapper, lightly raced: creditable efforts in 2002 on reappearance and third
start: stays 2m: acts on soft and good to firm going: usually held up. *J. L. Dunlop*

CARABOSSE   3 b.f. Salse (USA) 128 – Ballet 61 (Sharrood (USA) 124) [2002 51:   **52**
f11g p10g⁴ p10g f8.5g 8.2d Apr 1] leggy, workmanlike filly: modest maiden: stays 1¼m:
acts on polytrack: blinkered last 4 starts. *J. G. Portman*

CARA FANTASY (IRE)   2 b.f. (Feb 14) Sadler's Wells (USA) 132 – Gay Fantasy   **75 p**
(Troy 137) [2002 7f⁴ 8s³ Oct 15] rather leggy, lengthy filly: closely related to fairly useful
1½m/2m winner Fantasy Night (by Night Shift) and useful 1m/1¼m performer Lucky
Guest (by Be My Guest) and half-sister to several winners, including useful 1m to 1½m
winner Son of Sharp Shot (by Sharp Shot): dam unraced sister to dam of Derby winner
Oath: fair form when fourth to Al Jadeed in maiden at Newbury: laboured performance
when favourite for similar event at Ayr (much softer ground) 2 months later: will be suited
by 1¼m+: well worth another chance to confirm debut promise. *J. L. Dunlop*

CARAFE   3 b.f. Selkirk (USA) 129 – Caramba 114 (Belmez (USA) 131) [2002 77p: **85**
8.2d⁶ 8d² 8m 7d* 7.1g Aug 14] rangy, good sort: very good walker: fluent mover: fairly
useful performer: best effort, though found little, second start: made all in 4-runner
maiden at Thirsk in August: below form final outing: stays 1m: acts on good to soft going:
visored third start: not one to trust implicitly. *Sir Michael Stoute*

CARD GAMES   5 b.m. First Trump 118 – Pericardia 60 (Petong 126) [2002 –: 6g⁶ 5d   **64**
5s 5m 7g³ Aug 7] lengthy mare: formerly fairly useful handicapper, modest nowadays:
probably best at 6f/7f: acts on any ground: tried visored earlier in career, usually blinkered
in 2002. *M. W. Easterby*

CARDINAL VENTURE (IRE)   4 b.g. Bishop of Cashel 122 – Phoenix Venture   **86**
(IRE) 69 (Thatching 131) [2002 91: f7g 8s 7f 8f 6g³ 7f 6f⁴ 6m³ 7m⁴ 6g 6g Aug 20] tall,
close-coupled gelding: fairly useful handicapper: effective at 6f to 1m: acts on firm and
good to soft ground: often races prominently. *K. A. Ryan*

CAREL   4 b.c. Polish Precedent (USA) 131 – Castle Peak 90 (Darshaan 133) [2002 78:   **74**
8.2d⁴ 8.3g 8m* 10f 8m* 7m 7.9m 8d 7.6s 6.5d³ Dec 7] fair performer: won minor events

at Musselburgh in May and June: sold from M. Bell 9,000 gns before final start: stays 1¼m: acts on any going: races prominently. *A. Feligioni, Italy*

CARENAGE (IRE)   2 b.f. (Mar 6) Alzao (USA) 117 – Key Change (IRE) 117 (Darshaan 133) [2002 7m 7m⁴ 8.1g⁴ 8s³ Oct 15] smallish, strong filly: has a round action: second foal: half-sister to fairly useful Irish 1¼m winner Calorando (by Green Desert): dam, 1m (at 2 yrs) to 1½m (including Yorkshire Oaks) winner who was second in Irish St Leger, out of half-sister to dam of Kahyasi: fairly useful form: best work finish when third to Craic Sa Ceili in nursery at Ayr: will be well suited by 1¼m+: probably capable of better. *J. L. Dunlop*   **80 p**

CARENS HERO (IRE)   5 ch.g. Petardia 113 – Clear Glade (Vitiges (FR) 132) [2002 73, a61: f9.4g³ f8.5g⁵ f12g 8.1m 8f 8m 7.1g 10.2g f7g f8.5g Dec 20] big, strong gelding: modest performer: on downgrade in 2002: stays 8.5f: acts on firm going, soft and fibresand: tried in blinkers/cheekpieces: bled from nose once at 4 yrs: races freely. *R. Brotherton*   **– a54 d**

CAREQUICK   6 ch.m. Risk Me (FR) 127 – Miss Serlby 65 (Runnett 125) [2002 –: f8.5g f7g Feb 1] leggy mare: maiden: lightly raced and no form since 2000: tried blinkered/tongue tied. *W. M. Brisbourne*   **–**

CAREW   6 b.g. Minster Son 130 – The White Lion 70 (Flying Tyke 90) [2002 12m⁵ 12d⁶ 12.4m 10.1m Aug 16] sixth foal: brother/half-brother to several winning jumpers: dam 1m/9f winner: fair form in maidens/handicap. *C. Grant*   **–**

CARGO   3 b.g. Emarati (USA) 74 – Portvasco 90 (Sharpo 132) [2002 59: p8g f6g² p7g³ p7g⁵ p6g³ 5.1d⁵ 6m² 6.1f 6f⁴ p6g² f6g⁶ 5m* 5d⁶ 5f p7g Nov 19] angular gelding: fair handicapper: won at Sandown in July: effective at 5f to easy 7f: acts on firm ground, good to soft and all-weather: sometimes races freely/finds little. *H. J. Collingridge*   **67**

CARIBBEAN CORAL   3 ch.g. Brief Truce (USA) 126 – Caribbean Star 81 (Soviet Star (USA) 128) [2002 92: 5g² 5g 6d² 5.2g⁴ 6f³ 6f 6f⁶ Oct 12] strong, good sort: useful handicapper: mostly respectable efforts at least in 2002, notably when neck second to Marshman at Haydock third start: effective at 5f/6f: yet to race on soft/heavy going, acts on any other: sometimes wanders, and has refused to run on. *C. F. Wall*   **96**

CARIBBEAN SUN (IRE)   2 b.c. (Apr 10) Grand Lodge (USA) 125 – Carranita (IRE) 111 (Anita's Prince 126) [2002 7d 8.1g Aug 26] first foal: dam 5f/6f winner, including at 2 yrs: well held in maidens. *B. Palling*   **–**

CARIKAR (USA)   3 ch.f. Gulch (USA) – Iviza (IRE) 105§ (Sadler's Wells (USA) 132) [2002 10m⁴ Sep 19] third foal: half-sister to useful but temperamental 1¼m winner Dane (by Doyoun): dam, 2-y-o 7f winner and second in Ribblesdale Stakes, probably ungenuine: 5/1 from 7/2, poor form when fourth of 8 to Light Scent in maiden at Pontefract: visits Mtoto. *M. A. Jarvis*   **49**

CARK   4 b.g. Farfelu 103 – Precious Girl 76 (Precious Metal 106) [2002 73: 5m 5m⁴ 5g³ 6g 5g⁶ 5m⁴ 5m 5m f6s⁶ f5g⁴ f5g⁵ f5f f6g Dec 10] sturdy gelding: fair handicapper: left M. Todhunter after eighth start: raced mainly at 5f: acts on any turf going and fibresand: visored (pulled too hard) seventh start: races prominently: sometimes idles/wanders markedly. *I. Semple*   **66 a61**

CARLTON (IRE)   8 ch.g. Thatching 131 – Hooray Lady 92 (Ahonoora 122) [2002 5m 5f³ 5d 6m 5s³ 5s² 5s* 6s² 6g⁵ 5.9v² 6m 6m f6s² 5g 7d³ 7v Nov 9] sturdy gelding: fairly useful performer: missed 2001 season: won claimer at Sandown in June: effective at 5f (given good test) to easy 1m: acts on fibresand and any turf going: usually blinkered before 2000: consistent. *J. J. Quinn*   **84 a78**

CARLYS QUEST   8 ch.g. Primo Dominie 121 – Tuppy (USA) (Sharpen Up 127) [2002 97: 16.4d Jul 6] leggy gelding: useful performer at best: well held only 8-y-o start: usually visored/blinkered/tongue tied. *J. Neville*   **–**

CARMEN JONES   2 b.f. (Mar 21) Zamindar (USA) 116 – Sipsi Fach 100 (Prince Sabo 123) [2002 7v f7g Nov 26] 5,000Y: angular filly: sixth foal: half-sister to 3 winners, including smart performer up to 1¼m Supply And Demand (by Belmez) and to fairly useful 1m winner Sipsi Fawr (by Selkirk): dam 6f (at 2 yrs) to 1¼m winner: behind in maidens at Doncaster and Southwell. *J. Hetherton*   **–**

CARNAGE (IRE)   5 b.g. Catrail (USA) 123 – Caranina (USA) 85 (Caro 133) [2002 60: f16s² f12g⁵ Dec 27] tall, leggy gelding: modest handicapper: stays 2m: acts on fibresand, soft and good to firm ground. *C. Drew*   **57**

CARNA (IRE)   2 b.f. (May 6) Anita's Prince 126 – Balqis (USA) 93 (Advocator) [2002 5m² 5g² 5m 6.1s 6g Jul 18] IR 11,500Y: leggy filly: half-sister to several winners,   **60**

including useful 1m (at 2 yrs) to 1½m winner who stayed 1¾m Libk (by Kalaglow) and fairly useful 6f (including at 2 yrs) winner Marha (by Shaadi): dam 2-y-o 5f winner: modest maiden: second at Pontefract and Windsor: form only at 5f. *B. Palling*

CARNIVAL DANCER 4 b.c. Sadler's Wells (USA) 132 – Red Carnival (USA) 109 **116**
(Mr Prospector (USA)) [2002 123p: 11.6s⁴ 10m⁵ 10m⁴ 10d Nov 17] strong colt: smart performer, lightly raced: won Scottish Classic at Ayr in 2001: best effort in 2002 when 4¼ lengths fourth to Storming Home in Champion Stakes at Newmarket penultimate start: favourite, well held in Premio Roma final outing: stays 1¼m: acts on good to firm and good to soft going: has had 2 handlers. *Sir Michael Stoute*

CAROLINA SILK (IRE) 3 b.c. Barathea (IRE) 127 – Bold Fashion (FR) (Nashwan **86**
(USA) 135) [2002 95p: 10m² 9.9g 9.9d³ 10m⁵ 10.5d² 10m⁶ 10s Oct 26] big, good sort: fairly useful maiden: will stay 1½m: possibly unsuited by firm going, acts on any other: reportedly finished lame second start: has hung right: tends to carry head high: sold 10,000 gns. *R. Hannon*

CAROLINE'S ROSE 4 bl. or br.f. Fraam 114 – Just Rosie (Sula Bula 109) [2002 **–**
p12g f8g f9.4g Dec 20] second foal: dam winning hurdler: well held in bumper and all-weather maidens. *A. P. Jones*

CAROLLAN (IRE) 3 b.f. Marju (IRE) 127 – Caroline Lady (JPN) (Caro 133) [2002 **68**
7s p8g 10s³ 8.2v⁵ Oct 29] IR 23,000F, IR 30,000Y: sixth foal: half-sister to 3 winners, including 5-y-o Forest Heath: dam French 1½m winner: fair maiden: unlikely to stay beyond 1¼m: raced only on soft/heavy ground on turf. *R. Guest*

CAROLS CHOICE 5 ch.m. Emarati (USA) 74 – Lucky Song 91 (Lucky Wednesday **–**
124) [2002 57, a67: f5s⁵ p5g f5g* 5.7g 5.7d f5g* f6g⁵ f6g f5g³ f5g² f5g³ Dec 13] modest **a63**
performer: won claimer in April and seller in June, both at Wolverhampton: effective at 5f/6f: acts on fibresand, well held (carried head awkwardly) on polytrack: tried blinkered/visored: sometimes swishes tail: usually races prominently. *D. Haydn Jones*

CARONTE (IRE) 2 b.g. (Apr 19) Sesaro (USA) 81 – Go Likecrazy 51 (Dowsing **63**
(USA) 124) [2002 5m 6d⁵ 6m 5g² 5.1d³ f6g 5.1m² 5m² 5m⁵ 5m³ 7.5g⁴ 7m 6d f5g Nov 15] IR 6,400F, IR 8,000Y: sturdy gelding: fourth foal: closely related to 3-y-o Aguila Loco and half-brother to German 9.5f winner Raitera (by Charnwood Forest): dam 2-y-o 5f/6f winner: modest maiden: left B. Meehan after seventh start: seems to stay easy 7.5f: yet to race on extremes of going on turf, some promise on fibresand: effective blinkered or not. *S. R. Bowring*

CAROUBIER (IRE) 2 ch.g. (Mar 1) Woodborough (USA) 112 – Patsy Grimes 95 **60**
(Beveled (USA)) [2002 6.1d 7g⁵ 7.6m 7s Sep 10] 28,000Y: first foal: dam 5f to 7f winner: modest maiden: will need to settle to stay beyond 7.6f. *J. A. Osborne*

CAROUSING 5 b.g. Selkirk (USA) 129 – Moon Carnival 94 (Be My Guest (USA) **–**
126) [2002 88: 16.1m 16m⁶ Sep 29] good-topped gelding: unimpressive mover: fairly useful handicapper in 2001: well held both 5-y-o starts (trained by Mrs D. Thomson on reappearance): tried blinkered. *Mrs J. C. McGregor*

CARPET PRINCESS (IRE) 4 gr. or ro.f. Prince of Birds (USA) 121 – Krayyalei **49**
(IRE) 94 (Krayyan 117) [2002 54: 9m 8m⁶ p10g 11.8g⁴ 15.4m³ 12.1g⁵ Aug 8] smallish, close-coupled filly: poor maiden handicapper: stays 15f: acts on soft and good to firm going: has gone left leaving stall/edged left. *Mrs P. N. Dutfield*

CARRADALE 3 ch.f. Pursuit of Love 124 – Rynavey 67 (Rousillon (USA) 133) **71**
[2002 73: 8.3s⁴ May 10] fair performer, lightly raced: stiff task in handicap only 3-y-o start: should stay 1m: won on firm going on debut, raced on softer than good since: refused to enter stall and withdrawn Jun 16. *Denys Smith*

CARRICK LADY (IRE) 4 ch.f. Fayruz 116 – Mantlepiece (IRE) (Common Grounds **–**
118) [2002 40, a46: 7g May 2] small, compact filly: maiden: well held only 4-y-o outing: blinkered once. *J. Akehurst*

CARRIE POOTER 6 b.m. Tragic Role (USA) – Ginny Binny 113 (Ahonoora 122) **91**
[2002 95: f6g f6g⁴ 6g* 6m 6.1d⁶ 5m 6d 6g 5.9v 5d³ 6s Aug 5] workmanlike mare: fairly useful handicapper: won at Ripon in April: best form around 6f: acts on fibresand and any turf going: usually blinkered: often races prominently: none too consistent. *T. D. Barron*

CARRINGTON DYNASTY 3 b.g. Flockton's Own 98 – Starlite Night (USA) 105 **–**
(Star de Naskra (USA)) [2002 –: p6g p10g Feb 16] no form. *M. Madgwick*

CARROWDORE (IRE) 2 b.c. (May 8) Danehill (USA) 126 – Euromill (Shirley **77**
Heights 130) [2002 6m³ 6d p6g⁶ 7.1m⁴ 8m 8f* p7g Dec 14] small, well-made colt: half-brother to 3 winners, including useful 6f (at 2 yrs) and 1m winner Tadwiga (by Fairy

King): dam, Irish middle-distance stayer, from family of Old Vic: fair performer: won nursery at Goodwood: seems better at 1m than 7f, and should stay further: acts on firm ground and polytrack, well held on good to soft: wore cheekpieces final start. *R. Hannon*

CARROZZINA 3 br.f. Vettori (IRE) 119 – Doliouchka (Saumarez 132) [2002 70: 10.1d 8m⁶ Sep 23] unfurnished filly: fair winner at 2 yrs: well held in face of stiff tasks both 3-y-o starts. *J. G. Given* –

CARSON COUNTRY (USA) 3 b. or br.c. Lord Carson (USA) 121 – New Menu (USA) (Habitony) [2002 a6.5f a5f* a5.5f³ a6f² 5s⁵ 5d 6d a5f Dec 13] second foal: dam unraced: trained by K. McLaughlin on debut: won maiden at Jebel Ali in March: visored, probably flattered when fifth in minor event on soft ground at Sandown on fifth start: stays 6f: tongue tied last 2 appearances: tends to start slowly: looked less than keen penultimate outing. *A. Smith, UAE* **74**

CARTMEL PARK 6 ch.g. Skyliner 117 – Oh My Oh My (Ballacashtal (CAN)) [2002 61§: 5m 5m May 3] tall, lengthy gelding: modest performer at 5 yrs: well held in 2002: effective visored/blinkered or not: temperamental. *M. Todhunter* – §

CARTWHEEL (IRE) 3 b.c. Green Desert (USA) 127 – Carotene (CAN) (Great Nephew 126) [2002 8.1d¹ 9.3s³ 8.5m⁴ f8.5g⁶ 8.3m 8.1m 5.1g Oct 16] rather leggy, lengthy colt: seventh foal: closely related to 1994 2-y-o 6f winner Ginger Tree (by Dayjur) and half-brother to 3 winners, including useful 7f (in UAE)/1m winner Teshami (by Diesis): dam, champion Canadian filly, won up to 1½m: fair maiden: barely stays 9.3f: acts on soft going. *E. J. O'Neill* **71**

CASE HISTORY 2 br.g. (Apr 30) Case Law 113 – Brigadore Gold 51 (Petong 126) [2002 p5g p5g Jun 9] 1,000Y, 600 2-y-o: first foal: dam 7f winner: well held in seller/maiden. *J. J. Bridger* –

CASH 4 b.g. Bishop of Cashel 122 – Ballad Island 83 (Ballad Rock 122) [2002 66: f5s² 5m² f5s³ f6s 5f 5d* f6g³ f6g³ f5g* f5g⁶ f5g* f6g Dec 31] angular gelding: fairly useful on all-weather, fair on turf: won claimer at Catterick and (having left M. Brittain after seventh start) 2 handicaps at Wolverhampton, all in November/December: has won at 6f, best form at 5f: acts on fibresand, good to firm and good to soft ground: races up with pace: genuine and reliable. *Paul Johnson* **68** **a83**

CASHEL DANCER 3 b.f. Bishop of Cashel 122 – Dancing Debut 83 (Polar Falcon (USA) 126) [2002 47: f12g Feb 18] leggy, angular filly: poor maiden. *S. A. Brookshaw* –

CASHEL MEAD 2 b.f. (Apr 13) Bishop of Cashel 122 – Island Mead 86 (Pharly (FR) 130) [2002 5d⁴ 6s* 6d 6g 6.1s* 6g* Oct 28] 2,000Y: leggy filly: half-sister to several winners, including 2-y-o winners Island Prince (6f in 1996, by Prince Sabo) and Jobber's Fiddle (7f in 1994, by Sizzling Melody): dam 2-y-o 7f winner: fairly useful performer: won minor event at Windsor in May and minor event at Nottingham and nursery at Windsor (beat Bond Playboy by neck) in October: will stay 7f: acts on soft going, yet to race on firmer than good. *J. L. Spearing* **89**

CASHMERE 3 ch.f. Barathea (IRE) 127 – Wanton 106 (Kris 135) [2002 69P: 7.5g* 8m⁵ 7g* 7m⁴ 7.6s Sep 10] strong, lengthy filly: fairly useful performer: won maiden at Beverley in June and minor event at Epsom in July: ran respectably last 2 outings: effective at 7f/1m: acted on soft and good to firm going: stud. *J. R. Fanshawe* **86**

CASHNEEM (IRE) 4 b.g. Case Law 113 – Haanem 64 (Mtoto 134) [2002 86: 7m 6d 6f 6m 6m 6m Sep 5] strong gelding: only fair form at best in 2002: stays 7f: acts on good to firm ground, probably on soft: sometimes slowly away: headstrong: sold 4,000 gns. *P. W. Harris* **72**

CASING (IRE) 4 gr.f. Case Law 113 – Singhana (IRE) (Mouktar 129) [2002 41: 6f 6.1v 5.5f 5.1d f5g Jul 11] maiden: no form in 2002. *F. Jordan* –

CASSANDRA 6 b.m. Catrail (USA) 123 – Circo 77 (High Top 131) [2002 53: 9.9m 10m 9.9m 9.9m Sep 24] deep-girthed mare: poor handicapper nowadays: best around 1¼m: acts on soft and good to firm going: quirky. *M. Brittain* **43**

CASSIRER (IRE) 3 ch.c. Zafonic (USA) 130 – Oriane 109 (Nashwan (USA) 135) [2002 89p: 7g 7.9f 10g⁴ 8.5d⁴ 8g Oct 17] strong colt: fairly useful handicapper: best effort when fourth to Rawyaan at Nottingham third start: stays 1¼m: acts on soft going: sold 16,000 gns, sent to France. *Sir Michael Stoute* **90**

CASSIS (USA) 2 b.f. (Feb 6) Red Ransom (USA) – Minstress (USA) (The Minstrel (CAN) 135) [2002 p5g* 6d² 6s⁶ 6m³ 8g Oct 6] $250,000Y: strong, good sort: half-sister to fairly useful 1½m winner Mr Wild (by Wild Again) and several winners abroad: dam minor stakes winner in USA at 8.5f, including at 2 yrs: useful performer: won maiden **103**

at Lingfield in June: best efforts when placed in Cherry Hinton Stakes at Newmarket (short-headed by Spinola) and Mill Reef Stakes at Newbury (1¼ lengths third to Zafeen): reportedly travelled poorly to Ireland third outing: bred to stay beyond 6f (pulled hard when well held at 1m): acts on good to firm going, good to soft and polytrack: bandaged behind last 2 outings. *J. Noseda*

CASTA DIVA (IRE) 3 ch.f. Case Law 113 – Casting Vote (USA) 54 (Monteverdi 129) [2002 74: 7m⁶ 7m⁵ 7s Jun 5] strong filly: fair performer: stayed 7f: acted on good to firm and good to soft going: dead. *C. F. Wall*   **73**

CASTAIGNE (FR) 3 ch.f. Pivotal 124 – Storm Warning 117 (Tumble Wind (USA)) [2002 7g⁶ 7d⁵ 7f⁶ 6m 6m 6g⁴ 8f 7m² 6g 7m⁶ 7f⁵ 7.1f⁶ Sep 27] 280,000 francs Y: lengthy, workmanlike filly: half-sister to 3 winners, including 1999 2-y-o 6f winner Bulletin (by Prince Sabo) and 7f to 8.5f winner Present Situation (by Cadeaux Genereux): dam sprinter: fair maiden: stays 7f: yet to race on soft/heavy going, acts on any other: awkward leaving stall eighth start, very slowly away ninth: has raced freely/found little. *B. W. Duke*   **73**

CASTANET 3 b.f. Pennekamp (USA) 130 – Addaya (IRE) (Persian Bold 123) [2002 78: 8m f8.5s⁶ f12g⁵ f12f f12g⁴ f12g³ Dec 4] rangy, angular filly: modest maiden: stays 1½m: acts on fibresand: visored fourth/fifth starts: sold 5,500 gns. *W. J. Haggas*   **54**

CASTAWAY QUEEN (IRE) 3 ch.f. Selkirk (USA) 129 – Surfing 71 (Grundy 137) [2002 68: 8m⁴ 8g⁵ 10g³ 8.2d² 8g 8.5g² 8.2m⁴ 8m⁶ 8.5m² 8f² 8m⁵ 8f Oct 7] strong, close-coupled filly: fair maiden: stays 8.5f: acts on firm and good to soft going. *W. R. Muir*   **76**

CAST IRON 3 b.g. Efisio 120 – Misellina (FR) 57 (Polish Precedent (USA) 131) [2002 –, a62: p6g f5g p7g⁶ p8g f7g* f8g⁵ f8g⁴ f7g⁴ p7g 7g f8g p7g p7g Dec 18] fair performer on all-weather: left R. Guest after second start: won seller at Southwell in March: left N. Rossiter after ninth outing: effective at 5f, barely at easy 1m: acts on fibresand, well beaten on polytrack/turf: usually blinkered/visored, has worn cheekpieces: sometimes edges left: none too reliable. *J. R. Boyle*   **–** **a65**

CASTLE BELLE 6 ch.m. King's Signet (USA) 110 – Castle Maid 38 (Castle Keep 121) [2002 –: 6.1d 5.7d 5.1g Jul 26] no form. *R. J. Hodges*   **–**

CASTLEBRIDGE 5 b.g. Batshoof 122 – Super Sisters (AUS) (Call Report (USA)) [2002 49§, a–§: 10d 8m 12d 10m³ 10m 10s⁵ 10.2g 10g⁵ Oct 24] neat gelding: poor handicapper: effective at 1m to 10.5f: acts on fibresand, good to firm and heavy going: usually visored/blinkered: unreliable. *M. D. I. Usher*   **49 §** **a– §**

CASTLE GANDOLFO (USA) 3 ch.c. Gone West (USA) – Golden Oriole (USA) (Northern Dancer) [2002 113: p8g* a10f 12m⁶ 8m³ a7f⁵ Dec 26] rather leggy, close-coupled colt: smart performer: landed odds in valuable minor event at Lingfield in April by 2½ lengths from Aramram: always behind in Kentucky Derby at Churchill Downs next time, but ran respectably when never-nearer sixth to Sulamani in Prix du Jockey Club at Chantilly and close third to Umistim in listed race at the Curragh: sold privately from A. O'Brien's stable, below form in Malibu Stakes at Santa Anita final start: stays 1½m: acts on heavy going, good to firm and polytrack: has had 2 handlers: wears crossed noseband. *C. Dollase, USA*   **113**

CASTLE RING 3 b.c. Sri Pekan (USA) 117 – Understudy 60 (In The Wings 128) [2002 61: f8.5g⁵ f9.4g⁴ 10f 12.6m⁶ 10f 16.2d³ 9.9d³ 12m² 8.1m f12g f8g f9.4g Dec 20] strong, useful-looking colt: modest maiden handicapper: effective at 1¼m/1½m: acts on soft ground, firm and fibresand: has worn cheekpieces. *R. Hollinshead*   **53** **a51**

CASTLE RIVER (USA) 3 b.g. Irish River (FR) 131 – Castellina (USA) (Danzig Connection) [2002 77?: 10g 9.9m* 10.4m 9d⁴ 9d³ 8m² 8.5g 8f 8g⁴ p10g p10g Dec 28] close-coupled gelding: fairly useful handicapper: won at Beverley (edged right) in April: left B. Hills 27,000 gns after ninth start: stays 1¼m: acts on good to firm and good to soft going: has found little: tends to race freely: very slowly away final outing. *B. G. Powell*   **84**

CASTLESHANE (IRE) 5 b.g. Kris 135 – Ahbab (IRE) 81 (Ajdal (USA) 130) [2002 83: 11.7f⁴ 12m³ 12.3m* 12g⁶ 10.1m⁴ 10.3f* 9g 11.6m⁶ 10.1d Oct 30] big, strong gelding: fairly useful performer: won handicaps at Chester in August (amateurs) and September and minor event at Windsor (wandered) in October: effective at 9f to 1½m: acts on any going: blinkered (raced freely) first 2 starts at 4 yrs: often forces pace. *S. Gollings*   **90**

CASUAL LOOK (USA) 2 b.f. (May 10) Red Ransom (USA) – Style Setter (USA) (Manila (USA)) [2002 6g³ 7m⁴ 8f* 8g² 7m² Oct 19] big, leggy filly: sixth foal: sister to smart French 1¼m winner Shabby Chic and half-sister to winners in US by Alysheba and Quiet American: dam, US 1m (including at 2 yrs)/8.5f winner out of US Grade 1 2-y-o 1m winner Charleston Rag: useful performer: won maiden at Bath in September: best   **107**

Mr W. S. Farish III's "Casual Look"

efforts when second in Fillies' Mile at Ascot (beaten 1½ lengths by Soviet Song) and Rockfel Stakes at Newmarket (beaten length by Luvah Girl): should stay 1¼m: raced on good going or firmer. *I. A. Balding*

CATCANDO (IRE)   4 ch.g. Catrail (USA) 123 – Tongabezi (IRE) 75 (Shernazar 131)   – [2002 70: 10g 8.2d⁶ 9s 7m 6s p6g 7s Oct 26] strong, quite attractive gelding: fair performer at 3 yrs: lost form in 2002, leaving C. Allen after sixth start: tried tongue tied: sold 5,000 gns. *G. Wragg*

CATCHTHEBATCH   6 b.g. Beveled (USA) – Batchworth Dancer 67 (Ballacashtal (CAN)) [2002 51, a72: f5s* p6g f5g f5g 5.1g 5s f5g 5m 5.3m⁶ 5f 5g⁴ f5g Oct 17] lengthy, sparely-made gelding: fair handicapper on all-weather, modest on turf: won at Southwell in January: effective at 5f/easy 6f: acts on all-weather and good to firm going: tried blinkered: reared as stall opened and unseated sixth start: usually races prominently. *E. A. Wheeler*   **54**   **a76**

CATCH THE CAT (IRE)   3 b.g. Catrail (USA) 123 – Tongabezi (IRE) 75 (Shernazar 131) [2002 70d: 6g 5m 5.9s 6s³ f6g⁵ 5.9d 5g⁴ 5d* 5g 5d⁵ 5m³ 5m 5f Sep 26] well-made gelding: fair handicapper: won at Beverley in July: effective at 5f/6f: acts on soft and good to firm ground: visored/blinkered after fifth start: often races prominently. *J. S. Wainwright*   **65**

CATCH THE FOX   2 b.g. (Apr 2) Fraam 114 – Versaillesprincess (Legend of France (USA) 124) [2002 5m 5d 5s⁴ 5m 6d 6m 8f 8d p7g Nov 19] 8,000Y: leggy, workmanlike gelding: fifth foal: half-brother to 5-y-o Arogant Prince: dam no form: poor maiden on balance: probably stays 6f: difficult ride (withdrawn after bolting eighth intended start). *J. J. Bridger*   **49**

CATEEL BAY   4 ch.f. Most Welcome 131 – Calachuchi 74 (Martinmas 128) [2002 48: f9.4g f8.5g Mar 4] probably of little account nowadays. *Miss J. A. Camacho*   –

CATERHAM COMMON 3 b.g. Common Grounds 118 – Pennine Pink (IRE) 72 **54**
(Pennine Walk 120) [2002 77, a60: f8.5g p7g f9.4g f6g⁶ 7.1f 7.5m⁶ 8m⁵ 7.1m 8m f7g
f8.5g⁵ 10f 8m Jul 26] smallish, sturdy gelding: unimpressive mover: modest performer:
should stay 1¼m: acts on firm going and fibresand, possibly on polytrack: tried blinkered.
D. W. Chapman

CATHY RUAN 2 bl.f. (Apr 24) Robellino (USA) 127 – Q Factor 90 (Tragic Role –
(USA)) [2002 6m 6g Aug 7] second foal: half-sister to 3-y-o Petite Futee: dam 6f (at 2
yrs) to 1m winner: well held in maidens at Windsor (signs of ability) and Leicester.
D. Haydn Jones

CATMINT 2 b.f. (Apr 15) Piccolo 121 – Kitty Kitty Cancan 73 (Warrshan (USA) 117) **84**
[2002 5m³ 5.1f² 5g* 5m* 5g* 6g Oct 18] 800Y, resold 5,000Y: rather leggy filly: second
living foal: dam maiden who stayed 11.6f: fairly useful performer: won maiden at Ripon
in August, minor event at Beverley in September and nursery at Sandown in October: not
disgraced in sales race at Newmarket final outing: will prove best at 5f/6f: raced only on
good ground or firmer: genuine: sold 12,000 gns, and joined J. Unett. *H. Candy*

CAT ONA HIGH (USA) 2 ch.c. (Apr 16) Tabasco Cat (USA) 126 – Uforia (USA) **101 p**
(Zilzal (USA) 137) [2002 6d⁵ 6m² 7g* 8m² 8.1g* Oct 5] $150,000Y: rather lengthy,
good-topped colt: has scope: first foal: dam, ran twice in USA, half-sister to very smart
US performer up to 1m Mr Greeley: useful form: won 13-runner maiden at Leicester (by
short head from Khanjar) in September and 7-runner minor event at Sandown (by head
from Choir Master) in October: good 1½ lengths second of 7 to Saturn in minor event at
Newbury in between: stays 1m: probably capable of better still. *Mrs A. J. Perrett*

CAT'S WHISKERS 3 b.g. Catrail (USA) 123 – Haut Volee (Top Ville 129) [2002 **92**
70: 8.2d⁶ 8m² 8s* 10.4d⁶ 8.5g* 8g* 8g⁵ 10.3s⁵ Oct 25] leggy gelding: fairly useful
handicapper: won at Newcastle, Beverley and Thirsk between June and August: effective
at 1m/1¼m: acts on soft and good to firm going: consistent. *M. W. Easterby*

CATWALK'S FLYER 3 b.f. Mistertopogigo (IRE) 118 – Catwalk Girl 53 (Skyliner **49**
117) [2002 58: 6s⁶ 5m 5f 6m⁵ 5g Jun 27] 800Y: first foal: dam 2-y-o 7f seller winner: poor
maiden: trained by E. Sheehy in Ireland until after reappearance: stays 6f: acts on soft and
good to firm ground: hung left final start. *A. Berry*

CAUGHNAWAGA (FR) 4 b.c. Indian Ridge 123 – Wakria (IRE) (Sadler's Wells **110**
(USA) 132) [2002 104: p10g 7m⁴ a8.5f⁶ May 15] strong, good sort: has plenty of scope:
smart performer: better than ever when 3 lengths fourth to Sea Star in Newmarket
handicap in April: well held in allowance race at Belmont final start: probably best at 7f/
1m: acts on heavy and good to firm going (below form on polytrack on reappearance):
free-going sort who often makes running. *P. Mitchell*

CAUGHT IN THE DARK 2 b.f. (Apr 13) Night Shift (USA) – Captive Heart **85**
(Conquistador Cielo (USA)) [2002 6d⁵ 6m² 5.7m² 6.1m* 6.5g⁶ 6.1s² Oct 23] 5,000Y:
lengthy filly: fifth living foal: half-sister to 15f winner Windfall (by Polish Precedent)
and winners abroad by Pursuit of Love and Serheed: dam, maiden who was best at 7f,
half-sister to Irish Oaks winner Knight's Baroness: fairly useful performer: best effort
when winning maiden at Warwick in September by 6 lengths: travelled well long way in
sales race at Ascot and minor event at Nottingham after: should prove best at 5f/easy 6f:
acts on soft and good to firm ground. *J. L. Dunlop*

CAUGHT OUT 2 b.g. (Feb 21) Ordway (USA) 117 – Catch (USA) (Blushing Groom **63**
(FR) 131) [2002 6m⁶ 6.1f⁵ 6m 7.2g 7.6f⁵ 8m Sep 29] 2,800F, 7,500Y: sparely-made
gelding: fifth foal: half-brother to 3 winners in USA: dam 6.5f winner in USA: modest
maiden: well held in nursery final outing: should stay 1m: unraced on ground firmer than
good. *A. Berry*

CAUSTIC WIT (IRE) 4 b.c. Cadeaux Genereux 131 – Baldemosa (FR) (Lead On **?**
Time (USA) 123) [2002 7.1d 7f 6d 6m Aug 24] leggy, quite good-topped colt: useful
at 2 yrs: reportedly fractured pelvis at 3 yrs: little form in 2002: sold 2,500 gns.
E. A. L. Dunlop

CAUTIOUS 2 gr.g. (Feb 27) Petong 126 – Kind of Shy 61 (Kind of Hush 118) [2002 **59**
5d 5d⁵ 7m 6d Nov 5] 17,000Y: close-coupled, quite good-topped gelding: half-brother to
several winners, including 5-y-o Corunna and 7f winner Kai One (both fairly useful, by
Puissance): dam maiden who stayed 1m: modest maiden: ran poorly last 2 starts, 4
months apart: likely to prove best at 5f/6f. *R. M. Beckett*

CAVERSFIELD 7 ch.h. Tina's Pet 121 – Canoodle 66 (Warpath 113) [2002 –, a59: **55 §**
f8.5g f7g* f8s f6g⁴ f7g f7g f8.5g f7g² f7g f7g 7m³ 8d⁶ f8.5g Dec 26] workmanlike **a59 §**
horse: modest performer: won handicap at Wolverhampton in January: best at 7f/1m:

acts on firm going, soft and fibresand: tried visored, blinkered nowadays: unreliable.
J. M. Bradley

CAYMAN BREEZE 2 b.c. (Jun 2) Danzig (USA) – Lady Thynn (FR) (Crystal Glitters **78**
(USA) 127) [2002 7g⁵ 6g³ 5g² Sep 18] smallish, sturdy colt: sixth foal: half-brother to 3
winners, including 3-y-o Stage By Stage: dam, French 12.5f winner, half-sister to smart
middle-distance performers Lowell and Lady Blessington: fair form in maidens: second
to Bollin Janet at Beverley, tending to carry head awkwardly: probably stays 7f.
E. A. L. Dunlop

CAYMAN EXPRESSO (IRE) 4 b.f. Fayruz 116 – Cappuchino (IRE) 59 (Roi Danzig –
(USA)) [2002 79: 5m 5g 6m Aug 29] leggy, close-coupled filly: has a quick action: fair at
3 yrs: little form in 2002. *R. Hannon*

CAYMAN LODGE (IRE) 3 b.f. Grand Lodge (USA) 125 – Damezao (Alzao (USA) **69 §**
117) [2002 77: 10g 12m 12.3d f12g⁶ 8.3d² 9.1d 11.9d⁴ 11d 13.5m² 11v⁴ 13s⁴ Nov 5] fair
maiden: left M. W. Easterby after seventh start: stays 13.5f: acts on heavy and good to
firm going: hung markedly right sixth outing: free-going sort: usually blinkered of late:
one to treat with caution: sold 1,500 gns. *R. Gibson, France*

CAYMAN SOUND 3 b.f. Turtle Island (IRE) 123 – Kukri (Kris 135) [2002 54p: 8.3m⁶ **72**
8.1m³ p12g⁴ p10g 10d² p12g* 10m⁴ 10.1m Sep 6] good-bodied filly: fair handicapper:
won at Lingfield in July: not sure to stay much beyond 1½m: acts on polytrack, good to
firm and good to soft going: has raced freely: sometimes slowly away (was markedly so
final start). *C. F. Wall*

CAYMAN VENTURE (IRE) 2 b.c. (Mar 24) Entrepreneur 123 – Saninka (IRE) 82 **79**
(Doyoun 124) [2002 6g² 7.1d² p7g² 7d³ 7m³ 7g* 7m⁵ Aug 26] IR 17,000Y: second foal:
dam Irish 12.5f winner: fair performer: placed 5 times prior to winning maiden at
Brighton in August: should stay 1m: acts on polytrack, good to firm and good to soft
going: visored fifth start: sold 15,000 gns. *R. Hannon*

CD EUROPE (IRE) 4 ch.g. Royal Academy (USA) 130 – Woodland Orchid (IRE) **91**
64 (Woodman (USA) 126) [2002 104: f7g³ 7.1g³ 8.3g⁵ 8d 7d 7s³ 7.1d⁴ 7.2v 7d 7g⁴ 8m Jul
30] lengthy gelding: carries little condition: has reportedly had sinus problems: useful at
3 yrs, just fairly useful in 2002: effective at 7f/1m: acts on soft and good to firm going:
sometimes takes good hold (including to post)/looks none too keen: sold 32,000 gns,
joined K. Ryan. *M. R. Channon*

CD FLYER (IRE) 5 ch.g. Grand Lodge (USA) 125 – Pretext (Polish Precedent (USA) **85**
131) [2002 85: p5g⁴ p7g³ 6d 6m* 6d 5.7d² 6s³ 6m 6d⁵ 5.7g⁴ 6m 6g 6m 7m⁴ 6f⁴ 6.1s 7d
Nov 5] lengthy, angular gelding: good walker: fairly useful handicapper: won at Kempton
in June: best at 6f/7f: acts on any turf going and polytrack: didn't handle bend well at
Chester once at 4 yrs: held up. *M. R. Channon*

CEAD MILE FAILTE 7 ch.g. Most Welcome 131 – Avionne 59 (Derrylin 115) [2002 **46**
45: f12g² p13g f12g³ 11.8m f12g 11.8g³ 12.1g⁵ 11.9g⁵ 10m f14.8g Dec 14] poor performer: stays 1½m: acts on fibresand, firm and good to soft ground: has worn cheekpieces:
sometimes carries head awkwardly: usually races prominently. *B. J. Llewellyn*

CEARNACH 4 b.g. Night Shift (USA) – High Matinee (Shirley Heights 130) [2002 **37**
65d: f5g 5m⁴ 5g 5f Sep 25] poor maiden handicapper: effective at 5f to 1m: acts on
fibresand, soft and good to firm ground: tried blinkered/tongue tied: usually races
prominently. *J. M. Bradley*

CEDAR FLAG (IRE) 8 br.g. Jareer (USA) 115 – Sasha Lea (Cawston's Clown 113) –
[2002 –: p10g f16g p12g p12g f12g Mar 14] of little account nowadays. *L. A. Dace*

CEDAR GOLD (IRE) 4 ch.g. Rainbows For Life (CAN) – Miss Roberto (FR) (Don –
Roberto (USA)) [2002 50?: 8.3g Aug 12] seemed to show modest form only 3-y-o start:
well held only run in 2002. *R. J. O'Sullivan*

CEDAR GROVE 5 b.g. Shirley Heights 130 – Trojan Desert 97 (Troy 137) [2002 **54 §**
12s⁶ 12m 14.1d 11.9g 12.4m³ 12g 10d 13.1d⁵ 11.1g 14.1m Jul 27] good-topped gelding:
modest maiden handicapper: stays 1¾m: acts on good to firm going: has flashed tail: tried
tongue tied: unreliable. *John A. Harris*

CEDAR MASTER (IRE) 5 b.g. Soviet Lad (USA) – Samriah (IRE) (Wassl 125) **74**
[2002 78, a?: 9.7m⁴ 10m⁴ 12g⁶ 14m⁵ 16m 16f* p16g⁴ p16g Nov 27] quite attractive
gelding: fair handicapper nowadays: won NH jockeys event at Goodwood in September:
stays 2m: acts on polytrack, firm and good to soft going, probably on soft: sometimes
blinkered/visored: sometimes soon off bridle: tends to hang. *R. J. O'Sullivan*

CEDAR RANGERS (USA)   4 b.g. Anabaa (USA) 130 – Chelsea (USA) (Miswaki   **65 d**
(USA) 124) [2002 55: p8g* 8.2m 8m 8.1m 8.3g 8f p7g f8.5g Dec 20] rather leggy
gelding: fair handicapper at best: won at Lingfield in March: on downgrade after: stays
1m: acts on polytrack and good to firm going. *R. J. O'Sullivan*

CEEPIO (IRE)   4 b.g. Pennekamp (USA) 130 – Boranwood (IRE) (Exhibitioner 111)   **100**
[2002 101d: 6g 7d 6.5g* 6s 6g² Aug 12] lengthy, good-topped gelding: has a quick action:
useful handicapper: won at Ascot in July by 1½ lengths from Royal Millennium:
creditable second to Canterloupe at Windsor final start: races freely, and best efforts
around 6f: acts on soft and good to firm going: races prominently. *T. G. Mills*

CELEBRATION TOWN (IRE)   5 b. or br.g. Case Law 113 – Battle Queen 85   **80 §**
(Kind of Hush 118) [2002 94: 7g 7d 8.1s³ 8.9d 8d 10d⁶ Aug 9] lengthy gelding:
unimpressive mover: fairly useful handicapper: probably best at 7f/1m: acts on good to
firm and heavy going: sometimes on toes: held up: refused to race on reappearance:
untrustworthy: joined N. Richards. *D. Morris*

CELESTIA   2 b.f. (Mar 29) Anabaa (USA) 130 – Divine Quest 81 (Kris 135) [2002   **81**
6g* 5.2f 6.1m³ 7f Oct 2] quite attractive filly: has a round action: third foal: half-sister to
fairly useful 2-y-o 6f winner Ecstatic (by Nashwan) who stayed 9f and a winner in
Holland by Zafonic: dam, 7f winner, sister to smart French sprinter Divine Danse and
half-sister to very smart 6f to 1m performer Pursuit of Love: fairly useful performer: best
effort when winning maiden at Newmarket in June: not discredited in nursery there final
start, disputing lead: races freely, and likely to prove best up to 7f: raced on good going or
firmer. *J. L. Dunlop*

CELTIC BALLET   3 b.f. Celtic Swing 138 – Fairy Feet 78 (Sadler's Wells (USA)   **97**
132) [2002 85p: 8m 9g³ 10g⁶ 10g⁵ 12g⁶ 10m³ 10d⁴ 10.1d* p10g² p10g p10g Nov 23] lengthy,
quite attractive filly: useful performer: won minor event at Yarmouth (idled) in October:
best effort when sixth to Dawn Invasion in Tote Gold Trophy at Goodwood fifth start:
unlucky on penultimate, stiff task final one: stays 1½m: acts on polytrack and soft going,
probably on good to firm: visored (slowly away) sixth outing: has raced freely/found
little: carries head high: quirky. *M. A. Jarvis*

CELTIC CHARMER   3 b.g. Celtic Swing 138 – Hamsah (IRE) 86 (Green Desert   **–**
(USA) 127) [2002 10g p13g⁵ 10m Oct 7] 16,000Y: quite good-topped gelding: fourth
foal: half-brother to fairly useful Irish 1998 2-y-o 5f winner Sparkling Outlook (by
College Chapel): dam, 2-y-o 5f winner, half-sister to Irish 2000 Guineas winner Wassl:
well held in maidens. *M. H. Tompkins*

CELTIC EXIT (FR)   8 b.g. Exit To Nowhere (USA) 122 – Amour Celtique (North-   **–**
fields (USA)) [2002 72d: f8g Jan 24] fair performer at 2 yrs: has deteriorated: blinkered
last 2 starts: sometimes tongue tied. *I. A. Balding*

CELTIC ISLAND   4 b.f. Celtic Swing 138 – Chief Island 62 (Be My Chief (USA)   **92**
122) [2002 92: 10.5m⁶ 12m 10g 11.9d⁶ 10d* 11.9g Aug 20] lengthy, angular filly: fairly
useful performer: won minor event at Ayr in August: stays 1½m: acts on any going:
sometimes slowly away: usually held up. *Mrs M. Reveley*

CELTIC LEGEND   4 b.f. Celtic Swing 138 – No Reprieve (NZ) (Deputy Governor   **–**
(USA) 123) [2002 f12g 16g 8f 5m 6d f8g Dec 4] leggy, plain filly: no form (left
M. Polglase after third start). *Paul Johnson*

CELTIC LEGEND (FR)   3 br.g. Celtic Swing 138 – Another Legend (USA)   **84 ?**
(Lyphard's Wish (FR) 124) [2002 12.5g² 12g⁴ 12d⁶ 11.8g Oct 14] tall gelding: second
foal: brother to French 2000 2-y-o 8.5f winner Boadicea: dam US Grade 2 9f winner:
seemingly fairly useful maiden: second at Fontainebleau in minor event in March then
good fourth of 5 to Meteor Storm in minor event at Saint-Cloud in May: left Mme
C. Head-Maarek and off over 5 months before well held in handicap at Leicester final
start: stays 1½m: raced only on good going or softer: blinkered penultimate outing.
Mrs M. Reveley

CELTIC MAID   3 b.f. Celtic Swing 138 – Native Thatch (IRE) 47 (Thatching 131)   **61**
[2002 76: 6g 10.5m 8m 5m 6s⁶ 6.9s⁴ 8.3g 7.2d Aug 2] leggy filly: modest nowadays:
should stay 1m: probably acts on any going: blinkered (raced freely) final start: sold 1,000
gns. *Mrs M. Reveley*

CELTIC MILL   4 b.g. Celtic Swing 138 – Madam Millie 99 (Milford 119) [2002 78:   **82**
9.3g 8m³ 8g 7.9d 8.1m² 7f* 6.9d⁵ 7g⁴ 7.5m² 7m 7m 7.1m⁴ 7g f7s⁴ f7g* f7s³ f7g* f7g²   **a90**
f7g* Dec 31] tall, leggy gelding: fairly useful performer: won minor events at Catterick
and Wolverhampton and 2 handicaps at Wolverhampton between July and December:

better at 7f than 1m and should prove as effective at 6f: acts on fibresand, firm and good to soft going: has idled markedly: makes running: reliable. *D. W. Barker*

CELTIC PROJECT (IRE)   9 b.g. Project Manager 111 – Diandra (Shardari 134)   **51**
[2002 59d: 13m 13d³ 13s 8m* 11d 8.5g 8.5d 12d⁵ 12g 13f² 10f 10.5f⁶ 11.9m² 12s f12s Nov 30] modest handicapper nowadays: won at Bellewstown in July: well held (all-weather debut) at Wolverhampton final start: effective at 1m, has form at 2m: acts on firm and soft going: tried blinkered/tongue tied. *Edward Sexton, Ireland*

CELTIC ROMANCE   3 b.f. Celtic Swing 138 – Southern Sky 89 (Comedy Star (USA)   –
121) [2002 82: 7s Oct 26] sparely-made filly: fairly useful performer in 2001: well held only 3-y-o start: stays 7f: acts on good to firm and heavy going. *Mrs M. Reveley*

CELTIC ROVER   4 b.g. Celtic Swing 138 – Lady Sabo 69 (Prince Sabo 123) [2002   **39 §**
–§: 8g 5g³ 6m 5g Sep 7] plain gelding: poor maiden: tried blinkered: temperamental. *C. A. Dwyer*

CELTIC SAPPHIRE (FR)   2 b.f. (Apr 29) Celtic Swing 138 – Smart 'n Noble (USA)   **89**
(Smarten (USA)) [2002 6f² 7m³ 7d³ 7.1m⁶ Jul 25] 36,000Y: tall, good-topped filly: has plenty of scope: third foal: sister to smart performer up to 1¼m Celtic Silence, 6f/7f (Chesham Stakes) winner at 2 yrs. dam won 12 races in USA, including Grade 2 7f event: fairly useful maiden: close third to Helm Bank in listed Chesham Stakes at Royal Ascot second start: respectable efforts in similar events after: should stay at least 1¼m: acts on good to firm and good to soft ground. *M. Johnston*

CELTIC SPRITE (IRE)   2 ch.f. (Mar 25) Desse Zenny (USA) – Forest Imp (IRE)   –
(Forest Wind (USA) 111) [2002 7f⁶ 7f f7g Jun 28] small, plain filly: first foal: dam unraced: well held in sellers. *B. S. Rothwell*

CELTIC STYLE   3 b.g. Celtic Swing 138 – Stylish Rose (IRE) 65 (Don't Forget Me   **89**
127) [2002 88p: 12g⁵ Jul 12] tall, leggy gelding: fairly useful form in 4 starts: good fifth of 7 to Reviewer in handicap at Ascot only outing at 3 yrs (subsequently gelded): will stay 1¾m: raced only on good/good to soft going. *M. Johnston*

CELTIC TED   4 b.g. Celtic Swing 138 – Careful Dancer (Gorytus (USA) 132) [2002   –
p10g 11.8g⁶ 10m Jun 4] 1,200Y: angular gelding: fifth foal: half-brother to several winners, including 6f/7f winner Peggy Spencer and 7f winner Victorious (both by Form-idable): dam twice-raced half-sister to smart French performer up to 1½m Darine: well held in seller/maidens. *P. Butler*

CELTIC THATCHER   4 b.g. Celtic Swing 138 – Native Thatch (IRE) 47 (Thatching   **a100 d**
131) [2002 63+, a104: f8.5g³ p6g³ f8.5g² p10g⁶ f8.5g p10g p10g⁶ p8g Dec 21] useful on all-weather: some creditable efforts in 2002, including when placed behind Nose The Trade in minor events at Wolverhampton on first/third outings: well below form last 4 starts: stays 9.4f: better form on fibresand than polytrack: has worn cheekpieces, usually visored. *N. P. Littmoden*

CELTIC VENTURE   7 ch.g. Risk Me (FR) 127 – Celtic River (IRE) (Caerleon (USA)   –
132) [2002 68, a56: 8m 7m 7m f7g 6m Aug 21] good-topped gelding: fair on turf, modest on all-weather: no form in 2002 (trained first 4 starts by R. Wilman). *D. K. Ivory*

CENTURY CITY (IRE)   3 b.c. Danzig (USA) – Alywow (CAN) (Alysheba (USA))   **117**
[2002 96p: 7s² 8m* 7s* 8s² 8g⁵ 8s* 9f³ 9f Dec 1] good-topped, attractive colt: good walker: smart performer: won listed race at Leopardstown (by 2 lengths from Sights On Gold) in April, Mozart EBF Tetrarch Stakes at the Curragh (held Creekview by short head) in May and Goffs International Stakes at the Curragh (beat Common World a neck) in July: good 1½ lengths second to very easy winner Rock of Gibraltar in Irish 2000 Guineas at the Curragh and respectable fifth to No Excuse Needed in Queen Anne Stakes at Royal Ascot (slowly away) in between: sold privately out of A. O'Brien's stable before close third in Grade 3 event at Bay Meadows, then below form in Hollywood Derby final outing: well worth a try at 1¼m: acts on firm and soft going: has worn crossed noseband. *C. B. Greely, USA*

CERALBI (IRE)   4 b.g. Goldmark (USA) 113 – Siwana (IRE) (Dom Racine (FR)   **77**
121) [2002 80: 10g 13.9f⁶ 12g⁵ 9.9m² 12m³ 10s Jul 31] lengthy gelding: fair handicapper: seems best at 1¼m/11f: probably acts on any going: pulled hard penultimate start, found little final one: gelded after. *R. Hollinshead*

CEREUS (USA)   3 ch.g. Gilded Time (USA) – Dayflower (USA) 108 (Majestic Light   –
(USA)) [2002 84+: 9g⁶ 7.5m 8.1d⁶ f8.5g Dec 14] strong, deep-girthed gelding: good mover: fairly useful at 2 yrs, little form in 2002: left B. Hills 6,000 gns and off over 5 months before tailed off on all-weather debut final outing: reportedly broke blood vessel second start. *Ian Williams*

CERTAIN JUSTICE (USA) 4 gr.g. Lit de Justice (USA) 125 – Pure Misk 55 **103**
(Rainbow Quest (USA) 134) [2002 101: 6g⁵ 7.6g⁴ 6f 6s² 6d 6.5g⁶ 7.2d² 7d* 7g⁵ 8s² Nov
2] rather leggy gelding: reportedly suffered hairline fracture of near-fore and underwent
surgery after final 2-y-o start: useful handicapper: won quite valuable race at Newmarket
in August by 1¼ lengths from Barking Mad: good efforts there last 2 starts, particularly
when 2½ lengths second to Pablo on final one (gelded after): stays 1m: acts on soft and
good to firm going: blinkered sixth to eighth starts: has given trouble in preliminaries/
been early to post: seemed ill at ease on track at Epsom fifth outing. *P. F. I. Cole*

CERULEAN 4 ch.g. Polar Falcon (USA) 126 – Billie Blue 63 (Ballad Rock 122) [2002 –
10m 10.1m p13g Oct 4] half-brother to several winners, notably 9-y-o Tumbleweed
Ridge: dam second at 7f on only start: no form. *Dr J. D. Scargill*

CERULEAN ROSE 3 ch.f. Bluegrass Prince (IRE) 110 – Elegant Rose 72 (Noalto –
120) [2002 –: f7g p7g 8m 8.3m 6m 7m 8m 10m Oct 7] workmanlike filly: little form:
tried blinkered/tongue tied. *A. W. Carroll*

CESARE BORGIA (IRE) 2 ch.c. (Feb 24) Dr Devious (IRE) 127 – Prospering 50 **60**
(Prince Sabo 123) [2002 5.1f⁵ 6.1s⁶ 6g 5m⁵ 6g 6m 7.5g⁴ f7g 7g³ 8.2v f8.5g f9.4g Dec 7] **a–**
16,000Y: smallish, strong colt: first foal: dam 7f winner: modest maiden: stays 7.5f: acts
on soft going, probably on firm, well held on fibresand: none too consistent. *A. Berry*

CEZZARO (IRE) 4 ch.g. Ashkalani (IRE) 128 – Sept Roses (USA) (Septieme Ciel **49**
(USA) 123) [2002 65, a?: p10g f12g 11.6d 10d 11.6s⁵ 16.2m⁵ 11.6m* 11.6m 11.9g⁵ 11.8s
11.5s Oct 22] compact gelding: fluent mover: modest nowadays: won seller at Windsor
in July: stays 11.6f: acts on heavy and good to firm going: visored twice: sometimes starts
slowly: sold 1,900 gns. *W. R. Muir*

CHABIBI 3 br.f. Mark of Esteem (IRE) 137 – Nunsharpa 87 (Sharpo 132) [2002 65: **57**
8.1s 7m 10.5d⁴ 9.3d⁶ 7.9m 8.1f⁶ 8f f8.5s Dec 26] leggy, quite good-topped filly: modest
maiden: seems to stay 10.5f: acts on firm and good to soft ground. *T. H. Caldwell*

CHA CHA CHA DANCER 2 ch.g. (May 2) Groom Dancer (USA) 128 – Amber Fizz **53**
(USA) (Effervescing (USA)) [2002 7m⁶ 7g Sep 7] 3,500Y: strong gelding: half-brother
to several winners, notably smart sprinter Cool Jazz (by Lead On Time): dam ran once:
modest form at best in maidens: pulled hard on debut. *G. A. Swinbank*

Kitchwa Stables & Nichols' "Century City"

CHAFFINCH (USA) 2 b.f. (Apr 21) Lear Fan (USA) 130 – Chain Fern (USA) (Blushing Groom (FR) 131) [2002 8m⁴ 7.9f* Oct 12] leggy, quite attractive filly: half-sister to several winners, notably smart 7f to 1¼m (US Grade 1) winner Spanish Fern (by El Gran Senor): dam unraced sister to Irish 1000 Guineas winner Al Bahathri: favourite, confirmed debut promise when winning slowly-run 4-runner maiden at York by short head from Rahaf, very confidently ridden and coming from rear to nose ahead on line under hands and heels: should stay 1¼m: probably a useful performer in the making. *R. Charlton*   **88 p**

CHAIRMAN BOBBY 4 ch.g. Clantime 101 – Formidable Liz 66 (Formidable (USA) 125) [2002 65, a70: 6f 5s³ f6g 5m 5g f6g³ 6f f5g² f5g² f6g³ Nov 26] smallish, sturdy gelding: modest maiden: left J. Quinn after fourth start: effective at 5f/6f: acts on fibresand, soft and good to firm going: has been early to post. *D. W. Barker*   **49 a61**

CHAI WALLA 3 ch.g. In The Wings 128 – Carmita (Caerleon (USA) 132) [2002 9.7m⁴ 10.3m² 10.3s² Oct 25] leggy, lengthy gelding: fifth foal: half-brother to useful 7.5f (in UAE)/1m winner Claranet (by Arazi) and 1m/1½m winner Golden Thunderbolt (by Persian Bold): dam French 1½m listed winner: won maiden at Folkestone (slowly away) in August: much better form (useful) despite lack of experience both runs after, ½-length second to Red Wine in handicap at Doncaster final one: should be suited by 1½m. *H. R. A. Cecil*   **96**

CHAKA ZULU 5 b.g. Muhtarram (USA) 125 – African Dance (USA) (El Gran Senor (USA) 136) [2002 67: 12m⁶ 14.1m³ 14.1m³ f14.8g² 12f⁴ f14.8g² Oct 21] sturdy gelding: modest handicapper: stays 14.8f: acts on firm ground and fibresand: visored twice (also tongue tied second occasion) at 4 yrs: usually held up. *I. Semple*   **60**

CHAKRA 8 gr.g. Mystiko (USA) 124 – Maracuja (USA) (Riverman (USA) 131) [2002 57, a–: 6m 7g 7d 5.7g 5.1f 8.1g 5.7f Sep 16] big gelding: little form in 2002: blinkered final start. *M. S. Saunders*   **–**

CHALCEDONY 6 ch.g. Highest Honor (FR) 124 – Sweet Holland (USA) (Alydar (USA)) [2002 –: p16g⁶ Jan 5] tall, quite good-topped gelding: modest on all-weather: stays 1¾m: tried blinkered: has refused to enter stall: joined R. Rowe, and won over fences. *G. L. Moore*   **53**

CHALCHIHUITLICUE 2 ch.f. (Apr 20) Bijou d'Inde 127 – Miss Chiquita (IRE) 64 (Waajib 121) [2002 5.7g 5g f7g Sep 21] 2,100Y: first foal: dam Irish 1½m winner: well held in maidens/seller. *A. Berry*   **–**

CHALFONT (IRE) 3 b.f. Common Grounds 118 – Pirie (USA) (Green Dancer (USA) 132) [2002 71p: 8.3m³ f8.5s⁶ 8g⁵ 8.3m 8.1d² 8s 10.2g 7g Oct 14] fair maiden handicapper: stays 1m: acts on good to firm and good to soft going: blinkered final start: free-going sort: usually races prominently: none too reliable. *H. Morrison*   **69 §**

CHALLENOR 4 ch.g. Casteddu 111 – Expletive 77 (Shiny Tenth 120) [2002 53: 10.9m⁶ 10m Oct 1] close-coupled gelding: modest performer: stays easy 11f: acts on fibresand and good to firm ground: visored (well held) final 3-y-o start. *Ian Williams*   **52**

CHALOUCHI (USA) 2 ch.f. (Feb 16) Mt Livermore (USA) – Forty Nine Hearts (USA) (Forty Niner (USA)) [2002 6d p6g² a6f⁶ Sep 29] $410,000Y: second foal: dam, 8.5f/9f winner in USA, sister to Belmont Stakes winner Editor's Note and half-sister to 2-y-o Hold That Tiger: best effort in maidens (fair form) when 5 lengths second to Luvah Girl at Lingfield in June, soon off bridle: left J. Gosden after: should stay 1m: visored/blinkered second/third outings. *N. M. O'Callaghan, USA*   **68**

CHAMPAGNE KING 3 b.g. Prince Sabo 123 – Champagne Season (USA) 54 (Vaguely Noble 140) [2002 55: p10g⁵ 11.5f Jun 13] lengthy, well-made gelding: modest maiden: probably stays 1¼m. *P. W. Harris*   **51**

CHAMPAGNE N DREAMS 10 b.m. Rambo Dancer (CAN) 107 – Pink Sensation 69 (Sagaro 133) [2002 10m 7m 7f Jun 1] sturdy mare: fair handicapper in 1999: little form since: blinkered once. *G. A. Harker*   **–**

CHAMPAGNE RIDER 6 b.g. Presidium 124 – Petitesse 55 (Petong 126) [2002 85: f8.5g⁴ f9.4g² 8s² f8.5g⁵ 9.2s⁴ 7d 8v f8.5g f8g f7g⁵ f8.5g Dec 26] leggy, angular gelding: good walker: fairly useful handicapper: on downgrade after first 3 starts in 2002: claimed from K. McAuliffe £8,000 fifth start (off nearly 6 months after): effective at 1m/1¼m: acts on heavy going, good to firm and fibresand: tried blinkered, found little in visor final start: reportedly bled from nose once in 2001: has been early to post/carried head awkwardly. *D. Shaw*   **81 d a90 d**

CHAMPAIN SANDS (IRE) 3 b.g. Green Desert (USA) 127 – Grecian Bride (IRE) (Groom Dancer (USA) 128) [2002 70p: f8g f9.4g² Dec 16] fair form at best in 3 maidens: stays 9.4f: acts on fibresand. *P. W. Harris*   **63 ?**

CHAMPION LION (IRE)   3 b.c. Sadler's Wells (USA) 132 – Honey Bun 51 (Unfu-   **89**
wain (USA) 131) [2002 11g⁵ 12g⁴ 11.8d² 12s² 12d* Jul 3] 150,000Y: strong, close-
coupled colt: second foal: half-brother to very temperamental maiden Carraca (by
Alzao): dam, ran once, half-sister to top-class 1¼m/1½m performer Pilsudski: fairly
useful performer: won maiden at Kempton (beat Passing Interest 7 lengths) in July: will
stay 1¾m+: acts on soft going, yet to race on firmer than good: edged left (reportedly had
breathing problem) second start. *M. R. Channon*

CHAMPION LODGE (IRE)   5 b.g. Sri Pekan (USA) 117 – Legit (IRE) (Runnett   **106 +**
125) [2002 87+: 8g 8d 8.1d² 8.9d* 10d² 10g² 10m⁶ 8g* 9s³ Oct 26] big, rangy gelding:
fluent mover: useful handicapper: better than ever in 2002, winning at York (did well to
overcome wide draw) in June and Newmarket (by ½ length from Tawoos) in October:
good efforts in valuable contests in between and when ½-length third to Dumaran at
Newbury (met bit of trouble) final start: effective at 1m/1¼m: acts on soft and good to
firm going: often visored before fourth outing: sometimes slowly away: game: sold
45,000 gns, sent to USA. *J. A. R. Toller*

CHANCELLOR (IRE)   4 ch.c. Halling (USA) 133 – Isticanna (USA) 96 (Far North   **118**
(CAN) 120) [2002 117: 10d* 10.5s⁴ 10g² 10s* 10.4g⁵ 10m⁵ 10d Nov 17] strong, lengthy
colt: smart performer: won attheraces.co.uk Gordon Richards Stakes at Sandown
(made all to beat Border Arrow 1½ lengths) in April and Royal Whip Stakes at the
Curragh (beat Sights On Gold ¾ length) in August: at least respectable efforts when
fourth to Rebelline in Tattersalls Gold Cup and second to Imperial Dancer (beaten ½
length) in Meld Stakes at the Curragh, fifth to Nayef in International at York and fifth to
Storming Home in Champion Stakes at Newmarket: rare poor effort in Premio Roma
final outing: best around 1¼m: below form on firm going, acts on any other: game and
consistent. *B. W. Hills*

CHANCE REMARK (IRE)   4 ch.f. Goldmark (USA) 113 – Fair Chance (Young   **–**
Emperor 133) [2002 42: 13v 7f 7m Jul 24] no form in 2002. *C. J. Teague*

CHANCIT   3 b.f. Piccolo 121 – Polly Worth 55 (Wolver Hollow 126) [2002 71d: 5.1m   **–**
8g 8.2m f8.5g Jul 12] angular filly: disappointing maiden. *Andrew Reid*

CHANDELIER   2 ch.g. (Feb 27) Sabrehill (USA) 120 – La Noisette (Rock Hopper   **59**
124) [2002 f8.5g 8.3d p8g² f8.5g Dec 2] third foal: half-brother to 3-y-o Stalky: dam
unraced half-sister to 9-y-o Repertory: form only when second in seller at Lingfield:
reportedly lame final start: unlikely to stay beyond 1m: unseated rider start and
withdrawn on intended debut. *M. S. Saunders*

CHANDLER'S SECRET   3 ch.f. So Factual (USA) 120 – Sheila's Secret (IRE) 97   **51**
(Bluebird (USA) 125) [2002 60: p10g f7g² f7g⁵ 6g⁵ f7g⁵ 8.2g 7f 7g 7m Jul 3] modest
performer: best efforts at 7f: acts on fibresand, probably on polytrack: has reared leaving
stall/been slowly away: sold to Spain 1,000 gns and successful over 1m. *C. N. Allen*

CHANDOS PLACE   2 b.c. (Apr 27) Compton Place 125 – Calvanne Miss 48 (Martin-   **84**
mas 128) [2002 6g² 6g* 6.5g⁴ 6s⁶ Oct 25] 9,400Y: fourth foal: half-brother to useful 5f (at
2 yrs) to 7f winner Only For Gold (by Presidium): dam sprinter: fairly useful form: won
maiden at Baden-Baden in September: below-form sixth of 21 in sales race at Doncaster
final start: raced only around 6f. *C. Von Der Recke, Germany*

CHANDRIS   3 b.g. Son Pardo 107 – Dash Cascade (Absalom 128) [2002 60p: 8g³   **64 d**
6.1d 7m 7g Jun 16] plain, quite good-topped gelding: modest maiden at best: stays 1m.
J. A. Glover

---

attheraces.co.uk Gordon Richards Stakes, Sandown—Chancellor finds plenty
under a shrewd front-running ride by Michael Hills; Border Arrow (noseband), Imperial Dancer (rail),
The Whistling Teal (right) and Spanish Don are in vain pursuit

CHANGE OF HEART (IRE) 2 b.f. (Apr 20) Revoque (IRE) 122 – Heart of India **59 ?**
(IRE) (Try My Best (USA) 130) [2002 5m 7.5g 7d³ 7d 7v Nov 9] 10,000Y: unfurnished
filly: fourth foal: half-sister to 2 winners, including useful Irish 6f winner (including at 2
yrs) King of Russia (by Common Grounds): dam unraced half-sister to very smart
sprinter Bolshoi: modest maiden: best effort when never-nearer third in claimer at
Redcar: should stay 1m: sometimes slowly away. *T. D. Easterby*

CHANGE OF IMAGE 4 b.f. Spectrum (IRE) 126 – Reveuse du Soir (Vision (USA)) **56 d**
[2002 65p: 10d 10g³ 9.9g f9.4f f9.7m 13.8g 12s⁶ f11g f16g Dec 17] smallish filly: modest
handicapper, on downgrade: left H. Cecil 11,000 gns after third start in 2002: stays 1¼m:
acts on good to soft going, probably on good to firm: has worn cheekpieces. *J. R. Weymes*

CHANGE PARTNERS (IRE) 2 ch.f. (Feb 25) Hernando (FR) 127 – Favorable **74 p**
Exchange (USA) (Exceller (USA) 129) [2002 8.2m² 8g³ Oct 16] IR 5,500Y: well-made
filly: half-sister to several winners, including useful performer up to 1m Total Love (by
Cadeaux Genereux), 6f winner at 2 yrs, and useful 1½m and 15f winner Shonara's Way
(by Slip Anchor): dam French 1¼m and 1½m winner: fair form in maidens at Nottingham
and Bath (favourite, unsuited by steady pace) in October: will be suited by 1¼m/1½m:
capable of better. *R. Charlton*

CHANGING GUARD (IRE) 3 b.g. Royal Applause 124 – Milne's Way 83 (The **70**
Noble Player (USA) 126) [2002 68: f8s⁵ 10.9g 7f* 8.2d 7.1m 7d⁴ 8d² 8g 6d⁴ Oct 19]
small gelding: fair performer: won maiden at Thirsk in April: left B. Hills 9,500 gns after
seventh start: stays 1m: acts on fibresand, firm and good to soft going. *P. J. Flynn, Ireland*

CHANGING VIEW 2 ch.c. (Apr 21) Lion Cavern (USA) 117 – Change For A Buck **88 p**
(USA) 83 (Time For A Change (USA)) [2002 8.5m* Aug 25] second foal: dam, 1m
winner from 2 starts, daughter of Poule d'Essai des Pouliches winner Pearl Bracelet:
well-backed favourite, won 7-runner maiden at Beverley by length from Lesath, taking
good hold in lead and hanging on turn: will stay at least 1¼m: sold 25,000 gns in October:
should improve. *H. R. A. Cecil*

CHANTESSA SIOUX 4 b.f. Paley Prince (USA) 110 – Legendary Lady (Reprimand **–**
122) [2002 –: p7g 6m 7m Jul 22] no form. *W. G. M. Turner*

CHANTILLY GOLD (USA) 3 ch.f. Mutakddim (USA) 112 – Bouffant (USA) (Aly- **53**
dar (USA)) [2002 66d: f7g⁶ 7f³ 6.1m⁴ 8.2m⁴ 5m 6m 5g⁵ 6.1m⁴ f6g Nov 25] unfurnished
filly: modest maiden handicapper: claimed from J. Given £5,100 fourth start: effective at
5f to 7f: acts on firm going: sometimes slowly away. *J. M. Bradley*

CHANTILLY MYTH 3 b.f. Sri Pekan (USA) 117 – Charolles 82 (Ajdal (USA) 130) **81**
[2002 74: 6d 7f* 7g 7m Jul 27] tall, workmanlike filly: fairly useful performer: won
handicap at Catterick in July: shaped as if something amiss final start: stays 7f: acts on
firm ground. *T. D. Easterby*

CHANTRY FALLS (IRE) 2 br.g. (Jan 18) Mukaddamah (USA) 125 – Woodie **–**
Dancer (USA) (Green Dancer (USA) 132) [2002 6m 8d 7d Nov 5] 7,500Y: tall gelding:
second foal: dam, French maiden, out of smart performer up to 1¼m in Ireland/US Happy
Bride: well held, racing freely, in maidens. *J. R. Weymes*

CHAOS THEORY 7 b.g. Jupiter Island 126 – Indian Orchid (Warpath 113) [2002 **53**
12d⁴ p12g Nov 13] fair handicap hurdler/chaser: better effort in maidens when fourth at
Catterick. *Mrs M. Reveley*

CHAPEL ORCHID 3 b.f. College Chapel 122 – Royal Orchid (IRE) 74 (Shalford **55**
(IRE) 124§) [2002 58p: f6g 6d⁶ f6g 6d 8m 6.9s³ 5.9d⁶ 7.2g⁶ 7m⁵ Jul 27] sturdy filly:
modest maiden: stays 7f: acts on soft and good to firm ground, well beaten both starts on
fibresand: blinkered last 4 starts: sold 800 gns. *T. D. Easterby*

CHAPEL ROYALE (IRE) 5 gr.g. College Chapel 122 – Merci Royale (Fairy King **75**
(USA)) [2002 78: f8s f7s³ f8s² f8s⁴ 7d⁴ 8v⁴ 7m 7g 7.5m³ 8g 9d² 8.5d 7.6g² 7m* 7m² 7m **a66**
8m Sep 29] tall gelding: fair handicapper: ended long losing run at Catterick in August:
effective at 7f to easy 9f: acts on fibresand, soft (probably on heavy) and good to firm
going: tongue tied: comes from off pace. *D. Nicholls*

CHAPTER HOUSE (USA) 3 b.g. Pulpit (USA) 117 – Lilian Bayliss (IRE) 100 **81**
(Sadler's Wells (USA) 132) [2002 8.3m⁴ 7.1g* 7.6m 10.2g 8g⁶ 10s Oct 14] seventh foal:
half-brother to 3 winners, including useful Italian 1998 2-y-o 6f to 1m winner Strike A
Blow (by Red Ransom): dam, 7f (at 2 yrs) and 9f winner, closely related to high-class
French miler Phydilla and half-sister to very smart performer up to 1½m Observation
Post: fairly useful performer: won maiden at Chepstow in August: should stay beyond
1m: raced mainly on good/good to firm going: visored (found little) penultimate start:

has started slowly/hung left: possibly has his share of temperament: sold 57,000 gns, and gelded. *J. H. M. Gosden*

CHARDANE (IRE)   2 b.f. (Feb 14) Danetime (IRE) 121 – Lady Charlotte 75 (Night   **60** Shift (USA)) [2002 5g 5.7f⁴ 5g f5g f6g Nov 22] IR 6,000Y: small, good-bodied filly: first   **a–** foal: dam 2-y-o 5.7f winner: modest maiden: will prove best at bare 5f: acts on firm ground. *Mrs P. N. Dutfield*

CHARENTE (USA)   4 ch.c. Hennessy (USA) 122 – Zalamalec (USA) (Septieme Ciel   **–** (USA) 123) [2002 –, a73d: f9.4g⁶ f12g Feb 2] no form since early-2001: tried visored/ blinkered. *P. G. Murphy*

CHARGE   6 gr.g. Petong 126 – Madam Petoski 61 (Petoski 135) [2002 57, a68: p6g²   **57 §** p7g p6g f6g⁶ 5m⁴ p6g p5g⁶ 5d⁵ 6f⁶ p6g f5s* f6s f6s⁵ f6g Oct 19] fair handicapper on   **a72 §** all-weather, modest on turf: won at Southwell in September: left T. D. Barron 2,300 gns after next start: effective at 5f/6f: acts on soft going, firm and all-weather: blinkered (raced too freely) twice: tongue tied earlier in career: inconsistent. *Mrs L. Stubbs*

CHARGE CARD   4 b.c. Zafonic (USA) 130 – Prophecy (IRE) 109 (Warning 136)   **–** [2002 8.2m 7d Aug 11] 3,500 3-y-o: third foal: brother to useful 6f winner Arabesque and 6-y-o Threat: dam, 2-y-o 5f and (including Cheveley Park) 6f winner who stayed 1m, out of Lancashire Oaks winner Andaleeb: well held in bumper, maiden and seller. *Miss M. E. Rowland*

CHARLATAN (IRE)   4 b.g. Charnwood Forest (IRE) 125 – Taajreh (IRE) 89 (Mtoto   **–** 134) [2002 –: f16g f16.2g 14.1d 15.4m 6d 7m 8m 6d f12f Nov 29] good-topped, workmanlike gelding: little form. *Mrs C. A. Dunnett*

CHARLES SPENCELAYH (IRE)   6 b.g. Tenby 125 – Legit (IRE) (Runnett 125)   **79** [2002 92: f14.8g* 17.2d² 18f f14.8g⁵ 16m⁴ 18m 14.1d Oct 30] trained by P. Cole at 2 yrs: **a66** won Norsk St Leger at Ovrevoll following season (left R. Haugen in Norway after final 5-y-o start): fair form when winning claimer at Wolverhampton in June: stays 17f: acts on fibresand, dirt and soft going. *J. G. M. O'Shea*

CHARLEY BATES (USA)   3 b. or br.g. Benny The Dip (USA) 127 – Vouch (USA)   **114** (Halo (USA)) [2002 86: 10g² 12.3f* 10.5g² 16m³ 13.9m 15g³ 12g Sep 29] big, lengthy,

good-topped gelding: smart performer: won handicap at Chester in May: good efforts in minor event at Haydock (length second of 3 to Legal Approach) and Goodwood Cup (5 lengths third to Jardines Lookout, hung right) in July/August: sweating, below form last 3 starts in Ebor Handicap at York (favourite, headstrong), Prix de Lutece at Longchamp (third of 4 to Savannah Bay) and Tote Exacta Handicap at Ascot (pulled up, reportedly bled from nose): stays 2m: yet to race on soft/heavy going, acts on any other: visored final 2-y-o start: often makes running: quirky: sent to USA. *J. H. M. Gosden*

CHARLEY FARLEY 3 ch.g. Bluegrass Prince (IRE) 110 – Miss Copyforce (Aragon 118) [2002 55: 7g⁴ 6d 6g 7d 6g⁴ 7m 7d 6g² p6g f6g Nov 20] big, lengthy gelding: modest maiden: stays 6f: no form on all-weather: blinkered last 3 starts: inconsistent. *E. A. Wheeler* **55 a–**

CHARLIE GOLF (IRE) 2 b.g. (Mar 23) Cadeaux Genereux 131 – Keepers Dawn (IRE) 103 (Alzao (USA) 117) [2002 p8g p8g Dec 14] second foal: dam, 2-y-o 6f winner, also second in Fred Darling Stakes: only a slight sign of ability in Lingfield maidens. *J. W. Hills* **–**

CHARLIE PARKES 4 ch.g. Pursuit of Love 124 – Lucky Parkes 108 (Full Extent (USA) 113) [2002 98: 5s 5f³ 5.1f 5d 5m⁷ 5m³ 5m 5.1f 5m 5g 5f* Sep 28] strong, lengthy gelding: fairly useful handicapper nowadays: won at Haydock in September: best at 5f: acts on firm going: has had 2 handlers: races prominently: tends to edge left (has seemed not to handle track at Epsom). *E. J. Alston* **92**

CHARLIE SIMMONS (IRE) 4 ch.g. Forest Wind (USA) 111 – Ballinlee (IRE) (Skyliner 117) [2002 68: p10g* 10m 10.5d⁵ Jul 6] big gelding: fair performer: won maiden at Lingfield (edged right) in March: acted on polytrack and good to firm going: refused to enter stall once: dead. *A. P. Jarvis* **78**

CHARLOTTEVALENTINA (IRE) 5 ch.m. Perugino (USA) 84 – The Top Diesis (USA) (Diesis 133) [2002 71d: p5g6 Jan 19] workmanlike mare: one-time fairly useful performer: well held only outing in 2002: visored once. *R. Ingram* **–**

CHARMAWAY 4 b.g. Charmer 123 – Dismiss 95 (Daring March 116) [2002 73: p12g f8.5s Dec 7] tall gelding: seemed to show fair form on debut, well held since. *C. E. Brittain* **–**

CHARMING LOTTE 5 b.m. Nicolotte 118 – Courtisane (Persepolis (FR) 127) [2002 69: 6.1g6 6m⁴ 6m⁴ 6.1d6 5.9d 6m 6m 6g 6s⁴ Aug 30] leggy, angular mare: fair performer: best around 6f: acts on good to firm ground, but all 4 successes on softer than good (acts on heavy): usually visored, blinkered on reappearance: sometimes slowly away: held up. *N. Tinkler* **65**

CHARMING ROSE 3 b. or br.f. Charmer 123 – Punjabi Rose (Nishapour (FR) 125) [2002 8m 8.2m May 10] plain filly: second foal: dam unraced: tailed-off last in newcomers race at Newmarket and maiden at Nottingham, completely failing to handle home turn in latter (bit reportedly slipped through mouth). *P. Howling* **–**

CHARM OFFENSIVE 4 b.f. Zieten (USA) 118 – Shoag (USA) (Affirmed (USA)) [2002 54: f12s² f16s* f16g6 f16g⁵ f16.2g* f14g6 f14.8s 11.8m6 14.1d⁴ 16.2g f16.2g⁵ Jul 12] tall, angular filly: modest handicapper: won at Southwell in January and Wolverhampton in February: stays 2m: acts on good to firm going, good to soft and fibresand: sold 5,200 gns. *S. R. Bowring* **55**

CHARNWOOD STREET (IRE) 3 b.g. Charnwood Forest (IRE) 125 – La Vigie (King of Clubs 124) [2002 64: f8g* p10g f12g⁴ f9.4g⁴ 12d 12m 12.1d6 9d f8s f8.5g6 f12g f9.4s Dec 9] leggy gelding: fair handicapper on all-weather, modest on turf: won at Southwell in February: finds 1m bare minimum nowadays, and stays 1½m: acts on good to soft going and fibresand (below form on polytrack): usually visored. *D. Shaw* **69 d**

CHARTLEYS PRINCESS 4 b.f. Prince Sabo 123 – Ethel Knight (Thatch (USA) 136) [2002 55: p6g p6g f5g f5g6 5m 5g May 20] lengthy filly: modest maiden handicapper at 3 yrs: well held in 2002: sometimes blinkered/visored. *K. R. Burke* **–**

CHASE THE BLUES (IRE) 5 b.g. Blues Traveller (IRE) 119 – Highdrive (Ballymore 123) [2002 –: 8m⁵ 13.8g 12d Nov 5] little form: trained by S. Magnier on reappearance (when blinkered). *R. Wilman* **–**

CHASE THE GOLD 3 ch.c. Greensmith 121 – Rainbow Chaser (IRE) 54 (Rainbow Quest (USA) 134) [2002 46: p10g6 f11g⁵ Feb 21] poor maiden: stays easy 1¼m: acts on all-weather, some promise on turf: bolted to post final start. *J. G. Portman* **48**

CHATEAU BEACH (IRE) 2 b.f. (Feb 4) Danehill (USA) 126 – Heeremandi (IRE) 105 (Royal Academy (USA) 130) [2002 5.7d⁴ 5f* 6m⁴ 5f6 Aug 18] quite attractive filly: **81**

first foal: dam, 2-y-o 6f winner in Ireland, closely related to dam of high-class US filly Flawlessly: fairly useful form: won maiden at Redcar in June: best effort when never-dangerous fourth of 6 to Miss Mirasol in listed event at Newmarket next time: effective at 5f/6f: acts on firm going: sent to USA. *J. H. M. Gosden*

CHATEAU NICOL 3 b.g. Distant Relative 128 – Glensara (Petoski 135) [2002 76: 6f 8g 7f⁵ 8g⁴ 7m Aug 23] fair performer at 2 yrs: mostly below form in 2002: stays 1m: acts on fibresand and good to firm going (yet to race on softer than good). *R. Guest* **?**

CHATER FLAIR 5 b.g. Efisio 120 – Native Flair 87 (Be My Native (USA) 122) [2002 60, a75: f16g f16g f16.2g⁵ Dec 7] rather leggy gelding: fair performer at best: well held both 5-y-o starts: often blinkered/visored. *D. Burchell* **–**

CHECKIT (IRE) 2 br.c. (Mar 18) Mukaddamah (USA) 125 – Collected (IRE) (Taufan (USA) 119) [2002 5m² 6.1d* 6m* 6f³ 7.5d² 6f² 6m² 6d* 7m 7g 8s² Oct 20] IR 5,000Y, resold 24,000Y: well-made colt: has a quick, fluent action: fourth foal: half-brother to 6f (at 2 yrs) and 1¼m winner Witney Royale (by Royal Abjar): dam Irish maiden: useful performer: won maiden at Nottingham and minor event at Pontefract in May and Maurice Lacroix-Trophy at Baden-Baden (short-headed by Easy Way, but awarded race having been bumped) in August: good efforts facing stiff tasks last 3 starts, 3 lengths second to Spartacus in Gran Criterium at Milan final one: should stay 1¼m: acts on firm and soft ground: tough and consistent. *M. R. Channon* **102**

CHEEKY GIRL 2 b.f. (Feb 25) College Chapel 122 – Merry Rous 66 (Rousillon (USA) 133) [2002 5g⁵ 5g 7g 5g 7] 11,000Y: lengthy, good-topped filly: half-sister to several winners, including fairly useful 1994 2-y-o 5f winner Bruton Stream (by Taufan) and 5f (at 2 yrs) and 7.5f winner Clincher Club (by Polish Patriot): dam, 2-y-o 6f winner, half-sister to very smart sprinter Tina's Pet: modest form in maidens: seems to stay 7f. *T. D. Easterby* **62**

CHEEKY LAD 2 b.g. (Apr 8) Bering 136 – Cheeky Charm (USA) 56 (Nureyev (USA) 131) [2002 7m⁵ Jul 12] strong, lengthy gelding: fourth foal: brother to useful French 10.5f winner Calling Card and half-brother to fairly useful 6f (at 2 yrs) to 1m (in Sweden) winner Golden Miracle (by Cadeaux Genereux): dam twice-raced close relative of smart middle-distance colts Mohaajir and Theatrical Charmer out of sister to Dahlia: 7/2 and very green, tailed-off last of 5 in maiden at York, racing freely then eased as though something amiss: subsequently gelded. *B. W. Hills* **–**

CHEENEY BASIN (IRE) 4 ch.g. King's Signet (USA) 110 – Gratclo 65 (Belfort (FR) 89) [2002 79: f6s f7s f6g* f6g² f5g* f6g⁴ f6g* p6g* p6g* 6g 6d⁵ 6m 5g f6g² f6g f6g* f7s² f6g² f5g* Dec 27] leggy gelding: fairly useful on all-weather, fair on turf: won claimer at Southwell, sellers at Wolverhampton (left M. Johnston before)/Southwell, claimer (claimed from J. Akehurst) and handicap at Lingfield, and (having been claimed from N. Littmoden £6,000 after fourteenth start) claimers (claimed at Wolverhampton (left J. Balding £8,000) and Southwell (claimed £13,000) in 2002: effective at 5f to 7f: acts on soft ground and all-weather: has started slowly/wandered/looked less than keen, but seems reformed. *Paul Johnson* **72 + a86**

CHELSEA BLUE (ITY) 4 ch.f. Barathea (IRE) 127 – Indigo Blue (IRE) 56 (Blue-bird (USA) 125) [2002 71: 6g 5g 7f f6s f6g Dec 10] big, strong filly: modest maiden handicapper: stays 6f: raced only on good going or firmer on turf. *J. W. Payne* **59 a–**

CHELSEY MILLER (IRE) 4 ch.f. Up And At 'em 109 – Caradene (IRE) 64 (Ballad Rock 122) [2002 f7s 7d f5g Jun 22] no sign of ability. *Miss S. J. Wilton* **–**

CHEMERAS (IRE) 2 br.g. (Feb 22) Bahhare (USA) 122 – Pink Cashmere (IRE) (Polar Falcon (USA) 126) [2002 6g 7g 7m 6m⁴ 8g⁶ Sep 10] 40,000Y: smallish, quite attractive gelding: third foal: half-brother to useful German 2001 2-y-o 6f winner Medina (by Pennekamp) and 5-y-o Contact: dam unraced half-sister to very smart sprinter Owington: poor maiden: probably stays 1m: sold 2,400 gns, sent to Kuwait. *M. L. W. Bell* **49**

CHENIN NOIR 3 ch.g. Inchinor 119 – Go For Red (IRE) (Thatching 131) [2002 10g p13g Oct 4] strong, lengthy gelding: fourth foal: half-brother to useful 1m (at 2 yrs) to 1½m winner Primary Colours and 4-y-o Pinot Noir (both by Saddlers' Hall): well held in maidens. *W. R. Muir* **–**

CHEQUERHILL (FR) 2 ch.g. (Mar 5) College Chapel 122 – G'Ime A Buzz (Electric 126) [2002 6m Jul 24] 3,000Y: third foal: half-brother to 1999 2-y-o 7f winner Cosmic Buzz (by Cosmonaut): dam bumper/hurdles winner: 14/1 and blinkered, tailed off in maiden at Newcastle. *R. A. Fahey* **–**

CHERCHEUSE (USA) 4 b.f. Seeking The Gold (USA) – Sassy Bird (USA) (Storm **110**
Bird (CAN) 134) [2002 105: 6g⁶ 7d⁴ 6d⁴ 6m 7m Oct 13] $525,000F: second foal: dam,
lightly-raced maiden in US, sister to high-class 7f/1m performer Mukaddamah: smart
performer: won handicap at Fontainebleau, minor events at Toulouse and Cholet and
listed race at Maisons-Laffitte at 3 yrs, and listed race at Le Lion-d'Angers (by ½ length
from By Far) in June: good fourth to Crystal Castle in Prix de Meautry at Deauville in
August: below best last 2 starts in Diadem Stakes at Ascot (got no luck in running at all)
and Prix de la Foret at Longchamp (always behind): effective at 6f/7f: acts on heavy
ground. *H-A. Pantall, France*

CHERISHED NUMBER 3 b.g. King's Signet (USA) 110 – Pretty Average 40 **84**
(Skyliner 117) [2002 66: 7f² 8m⁵ 7m 7m* 8s⁴ 8.3s² 7.2g* 8d* 7.1g⁵ 8.3m⁵ f7s⁴ 7.2g 8s² **a79**
f9.4g f8.5s f8g Dec 17] workmanlike gelding: fairly useful performer: won maiden at
Catterick in May and handicaps at Ayr in July: effective at 7f/1m: acts on any turf going
and fibresand: has worn cheekpieces: sometimes races freely. *I. Semple*

CHEROKEE BAY 2 b.f. (Apr 23) Primo Dominie 121 – Me Cherokee 48 (Persian **83**
Bold 123) [2002 5g* 6.1g 6m³ 6m 6g 8.2s³ Oct 23] 6,200Y: good-topped filly: second
foal: dam, poor maiden who stayed 1½m, half-sister to smart middle-distance stayer
Apache: fairly useful performer: won maiden at Windsor in April: best effort when
staying-on third to Famous Grouse in minor event at Nottingham final start: will probably
stay 1¼m: acts on soft and good to firm ground. *P. W. D'Arcy*

CHERRYCOMBE-ROW 3 gr.f. Classic Cliche (IRE) 128 – Key In The Ring **77**
(Pyjama Hunt 126) [2002 77: 7m 7s³ 8d⁴ 9d² 8.1d³ 9g 8.1m⁵ p10g⁴ p10g² p8g p10g Dec
18] fair handicapper: stays 1¼m: acts on polytrack and heavy going, probably on good to
firm: has worn cheekpieces: sometimes finds little, and temperament under suspicion.
P. R. Hedger

CHESNUT CRACKER 2 ch.f. (Mar 26) Compton Place 125 – Triple Tricks (IRE) **–**
70 (Royal Academy (USA) 130) [2002 f5g Nov 15] 3,000Y: fourth foal: half-sister to
Swedish 6.5f and 1m winner Golden Note (by Efisio): dam, maiden who stayed 1m, out
of sister to smart sprinter Jester: well beaten in maiden at Wolverhampton. *P. C. Haslam*

CHESNUT RIPPLE 3 ch.f. Cosmonaut – Shaft of Sunlight 58 (Sparkler 130) [2002 **64**
66: 10d⁴ 9m⁶ 10g³ 10f 12.3s³ Aug 5] strong filly: modest maiden handicapper: stays
1¼m: acts on soft and good to firm going: has given trouble at stall/taken strong hold/
hung left. *R. M. Whitaker*

CHESTINO 4 ch.c. Bustino 136 – Coir 'a' Ghaill 38 (Jalmood (USA) 126) [2002 –: **71**
10m⁶ 10m 16.4g⁶ 16v Oct 29] workmanlike colt: fair maiden: stays 2m: looked unwilling
final start. *J. G. Portman*

CHETAK (IRE) 2 ch.f. (Mar 24) Halling (USA) 133 – Tithcar 67 (Cadeaux Genereux **77**
131) [2002 7g⁵ 7m³ p7g² p6g³ Nov 19] smallish, rather leggy, plain filly: second foal:
dam effective at 5f to 7f, half-sister to 6-y-o Zindabad: fair maiden: best effort
when head second to Machinist at Lingfield: stays 7f: acts on polytrack and good to firm
ground. *B. W. Hills*

CHEVALIER (IRE) 2 b.c. (Feb 1) Danehill (USA) 126 – Legend Maker (IRE) **115 p**
111 (Sadler's Wells (USA) 132) [2002 8g² 8s* 8v² Nov 2]

It's surely just a matter of time before Aidan O'Brien adds the Criterium
International to his ever-growing list of Group 1 successes. O'Brien has been
responsible for the close second in both runnings of this two-year-old contest at
Saint-Cloud in November, Landseer going down by half a length to Act One in the
first and Chevalier by a neck to Dalakhani in the latest. Whereas Landseer, one
of three O'Brien runners, had a fair amount of big-race experience going into the
Criterium, Chevalier, the trainer's sole representative in 2002, had just a couple of
runs in maidens under his belt. A promising second, coming from behind to split
New South Wales and Napper Tandy, in a decidedly useful race of its type at the
Curragh in October on his debut, Chevalier then forced the pace when landing the
odds by six lengths at Gowran six days later. Forcing tactics were also adopted at
Saint-Cloud, Chevalier holding the advantage until approaching the final furlong,
where favourite Dalakhani took over. To his credit Chevalier stuck to his task really
well, despite always looking likely to come off second best, and pulled five lengths
and more clear of the three other runners, which included Napper Tandy. There is
little doubt that Chevalier will do even better when his stamina is tested more fully

as a three-year-old, and he could make into a high-class performer over a mile and a quarter and more.

Chevalier (IRE) (b.c. Feb 1, 2000)	Danehill (USA) (b 1986)	Danzig (b 1977)	Northern Dancer Pas de Nom
		Razyana (b 1981)	His Majesty Spring Adieu
	Legend Maker (IRE) (b 1994)	Sadler's Wells (b 1981)	Northern Dancer Fairy Bridge
		High Spirited (b 1987)	Shirley Heights Sunbittern

A mile and a half should be well within Chevalier's compass. Although his sire Danehill was a sprinter himself, he is responsible for many who stay much further than he did; and there is plenty of stamina on the dam's side of Chevalier's pedigree. Legend Maker, the dam, showed smart form in France at three gaining the second of her two wins in the mile-and-a-half Prix de Royaumont and going on to finish a good third to Whitewater Affair in the Prix de Pomone, run over an extended thirteen furlongs. Her half-sister Dollar Bird showed useful form at up to a mile and three quarters, and her half-brother Amfortas won the 1996 King Edward VII Stakes. Chevalier's grandam High Spirited, a fairly useful performer who stayed two miles, is a sister to the Ribblesdale Stakes and Park Hill Stakes winner High Hawk, dam of In The Wings, and a half-sister to the dam of Derby winner High-Rise. High Spirited's three-parts sister Infamy won the Sun Chariot Stakes and the Rothmans International. Chevalier's great grandam Sunbittern won her first three races as a two-year-old and was a good fourth in the Cheveley Park, but temperament got the better of her the following year and she refused to race on her last appearance. *A. P. O'Brien, Ireland*

CHEVENING LODGE 4 ch.g. Eagle Eyed (USA) 111 – Meadmore Magic 68 (Mansingh (USA) 120) [2002 55, a68: f7g⁵ f8.5g 7d May 24] strong, close-coupled gelding: fair on all-weather, modest on turf at best: well held in 2002: blinkered/visored. *I. A. Wood* —

CHEVIN 3 ch.f. Danzig Connection (USA) – Starr Danias (USA) (Sensitive Prince (USA)) [2002 7f 7.5g 9d 10g 9.9m⁶ 12m⁶ 16.1m⁶ Oct 2] sparely-made filly: half-sister to 3 winners, including fairly useful 5f (in UAE)/7f winner Yaa Wale (by Persian Bold) and 6f (at 2 yrs) and 1½m winner Potsclose (by Miswaki): dam lightly raced in USA: modest maiden: stays 2m: acts on good to firm going. *R. A. Fahey* — 53

CHEVRONNE 2 b.g. (Apr 3) Compton Place 125 – Maria Isabella (FR) (Young Generation 129) [2002 6s Oct 25] 6,500F, 16,000Y: good-bodied gelding: half-brother to several winners, including 1½m winner Rain In Spain and 7.5f (at 2 yrs) to 10.5f winner in Italy Streisand (both useful, by Unfuwain): dam, French maiden, half-sister to smart French sprinter Titus Livius: 16/1 and backward, well held in maiden at Newbury: gelded after. *L. G. Cottrell* —

CHEYENNE CHIEF 3 b.g. Be My Chief (USA) 122 – Cartuccia (IRE) (Doyoun 124) [2002 –: f5g⁵ f6g 8g 12m⁵ f12g² 14.1f⁵ 12.1g⁶ 13.8f³ 12f⁴ 16.1m 14.1m Oct 5] leggy gelding: modest maiden: stays 1¾m: acts on fibresand and firm going: sometimes blinkered/visored: slowly away/wandered second outing: won over hurdles in November. *G. M. Moore* — 52 a58

CHEYENNE DAWN 2 ch.f. (Mar 29) The West (USA) 107 – Miss Lear (Lear Fan (USA) 130) [2002 5g 5m Apr 24] second foal: dam unraced: well held in maiden/seller. *W. G. M. Turner* —

CHEZ BONITO (IRE) 5 br.m. Persian Bold 123 – Tycoon Aly (IRE) 70 (Last Tycoon 131) [2002 –: 9.7m 10.2f Jul 25] lengthy mare: no form since 2000. *J. M. Bradley* —

CHEZ FORET (IRE) 3 b.c. Charnwood Forest (IRE) 125 – Ezilana (IRE) (Shardari 134) [2002 48: f9.4g f9.4g f11g 12d⁴ 12m⁶ 12m⁶ f12g May 24] quite good-topped colt: poor maiden: seemed to stay 1½m: acted on fibresand and good to firm going: tried visored: dead. *C. N. Kellett* — 38

CHIANTI (IRE) 4 b.c. Danehill (USA) 126 – Sabaah (USA) 65 (Nureyev (USA) 131) [2002 109: 10g² 10m² 10s² 10m 10.1d* 10m² 9.9m⁵ 9.9f⁴ 9m Oct 19] attractive colt: has a quick, fluent action: smart performer: won 4-runner minor event at Epsom in July by 1½ lengths from Nadour Al Bahr: also runner-up 4 times in 2002, including behind Border Arrow in listed race at Kempton on reappearance and Naheef in Winter Hill — 114

Stakes at Windsor on sixth outing: stays 1¼m: acts on firm and soft going: tongue tied: sometimes bandaged in front: early to post/wears crossed noseband: takes good hold/carries head awkwardly: usually races prominently: sent to USA. *J. L. Dunlop*

CHIC 2 ch.f. (Feb 27) Machiavellian (USA) 123 – Exclusive 115 (Polar Falcon (USA) 126) [2002 6m⁴ 7g⁴ Oct 14] lengthy filly: has scope: first foal: dam, 7f (at 2 yrs)/1m (Coronation Stakes) winner, half-sister to 2000 Guineas winner Entrepreneur: favourite, fair form when fourth in maidens at Newmarket (travelled well long way) and Leicester (odds on) 7 weeks apart: not sure to stay much beyond 7f. *Sir Michael Stoute* **75**

CHIC A CHI ACHOO (IRE) 2 ch.f. (Apr 30) Woodborough (USA) 112 – Keen Note 69 (Sharpo 132) [2002 f5s 7f⁵ 6m Jul 2] IR 500Y: ninth foal: half-sister to 3 winners, including 1m seller winner Top Floor (by Waajib): dam, winner in Belgium at 4 yrs, half-sister to useful sprinter Whittingham: well held in claimer/sellers. *P. S. McEntee* **–**

CHICAGO BULLS (IRE) 4 b.g. Darshaan 133 – Celestial Melody (USA) 75 (The Minstrel (CAN) 135) [2002 78: 16g Mar 30] big, strong, good sort: fair maiden: probably stays 2m (stays 21f over hurdles): acts on soft going, yet to race on firmer than good: has carried head awkwardly. *A. King* **75 +**

CHICANERY (IRE) 5 b.g. Irish River (FR) 131 – Deceive 100 (Machiavellian (USA) 123) [2002 50d: f8s⁴ f11s⁶ 7g f8g³ 7g 9g 8.5g* 9m⁶ 10g 8f 8g Oct 5] modest performer: left Mrs L. Stubbs 1,500 gns after fifth start: won handicap at Killarney in July: stays 8.5f: acts on fibresand and good to soft ground: sometimes slowly away. *Mrs Edwina Finn, Ireland* **51**

CHICKASAW TRAIL 4 ch.f. Be My Chief (USA) 122 – Maraschino 53 (Lycius (USA) 124) [2002 52, a46: f12s 7g f8g 10g 8f³ 10m 8.2d 7.9s 10g⁴ 8.1g 8s⁴ 8m² 7f Sep 21] small filly: modest maiden handicapper on turf, poor on all-weather: effective at 1m to 1½m: acts on firm going, soft and fibresand: none too consistent. *R. Hollinshead* **52 a33**

CHICO GUAPO (IRE) 2 b.g. (Feb 9) Sesaro (USA) 81 – Summer Queen 80 (Robellino (USA) 127) [2002 5f 5g⁵ f5s⁵ 5g f5s² f5s Oct 8] IR 24,000F, 22,000Y: good-topped gelding: first foal: dam, 7f winner, half-sister to useful 1m/9f winner Eton Lad: fair maiden: best effort when runner-up in nursery at Southwell: will prove best at bare 5f: acts on fibresand, raced only on good ground or firmer on turf. *J. A. Glover* **65 a75**

CHIEF CASHIER 7 b.g. Persian Bold 123 – Kentfield (Busted 134) [2002 91: p10g⁵ p12g⁶ p10g² p10g 10.1g 10.3f 10s⁴ 10m 10s³ 10.2d³ 10.1d³ 10m⁶ 10g 10d⁶ Oct 14] close-coupled gelding: fairly useful handicapper: best around 1¼m: acts on polytrack, soft and firm going: usually races prominently. *G. B. Balding* **81**

CHIEF MONARCH 8 b.g. Be My Chief (USA) 122 – American Beauty 74 (Mill Reef (USA) 141) [2002 8m⁶ 10f³ 10.4g² 8.9d³ Jun 15] good-topped gelding: fairly useful performer: stayed 1¼m: acted on firm and soft going: dead. *R. A. Fahey* **80**

CHIEF OF JUSTICE 5 b.g. Be My Chief (USA) 122 – Clare Court 89 (Glint of Gold 128) [2002 –: f12g Feb 7] strong, useful-looking gelding: fair handicapper at 3 yrs: well held both starts since. *D. Shaw* **–**

CHIEF WARDANCE 8 ch.g. Profilic 88 – Dolly Wardance (Warpath 113) [2002 65: 12s Mar 21] big gelding: fair handicapper at best, lightly raced: well held only 8-y-o start. *C. N. Kellett* **–**

CHIEF YEOMAN 2 b.g. (Feb 25) Machiavellian (USA) 123 – Step Aloft 87 (Shirley Heights 130) [2002 7m⁴ 8.1m² Sep 18] quite good-topped gelding: second foal: dam, 1¼m winner at 4 yrs, half-sister to smart performers up to 1¼m Starlet and Unknown Quantity: fairly useful form in maidens at Newmarket and Sandown, ½-length second to Orange Touch in latter: gelded after: should stay beyond 1m: probably capable of better. *Sir Michael Stoute* **83 p**

CHIFFON 2 b.f. (Mar 10) Polish Precedent (USA) 131 – Photo Call 73 (Chief Singer 131) [2002 7.1m 8.1f⁴ 8s 8.3d⁶ Oct 28] quite good-topped filly: sixth foal: half-sister to 4-y-o Johannian: dam, 9f (at 2 yrs) and 11f winner, granddaughter of 1000 Guineas second Photo Flash: modest maiden: should stay 1¼m: easily best effort on firm ground. *B. J. Meehan* **64**

CHILI PEPPER 5 b.m. Chilibang 120 – Game Germaine (Mummy's Game 120) [2002 –, a50d: f8g f8g f7g⁵ 7g 10.1m 8d 8s Jul 19] poor nowadays: seems to stay 1m: usually blinkered. *P. R. Wood* **33**

CHILLY COUNTESS 3 b.f. Makbul 104 – Cold Blow 67 (Posse (USA) 130) [2002 8g 8.2g⁶ May 31] 8,000Y: leggy filly: fourth foal: half-sister to 2 winners, notably smart 1m to 1¼m winner Katy Nowaitee (by Komaite): dam, second at 7f at 2 yrs, from family **56**

of Yorkshire Oaks winners Sally Brown and Untold: modest form in maidens at Bath (slowly away) and Nottingham: sold 1,500 gns. *P. W. Harris*

CHIMES AT MIDNIGHT (USA) 5 b.h. Danzig (USA) – Surely Georgies (USA) **106 §** (Alleged (USA) 138) [2002 108§: 10m⁵ 13s² 10s 10.5s 14s⁵ 20m 14g⁶ 12d Aug 2] well-made horse: useful performer: flattered when tenth of 15 in Gold Cup at Royal Ascot sixth start in 2002: finds 10.5f a minimum and stays 14.6f: acts on firm and good to soft going: usually blinkered: inconsistent (often highly tried). *Luke Comer, Ireland*

CHIMICHANGA (IRE) 2 b.g. (Apr 16) Fayruz 116 – Lindas Delight 54 (Batshoof **43** 122) [2002 6d 7v f6g f7s f7g Dec 17] IR 5,000Y: good-topped gelding: brother to 4-y-o Fromsong and 3-y-o Marshallspark, and half-brother to 5-y-o Archon: dam 6f seller winner at 2 yrs (only season to race): poor maiden: should stay 7f: visored final outing. *J. J. Quinn*

CHINA CASTLE 9 b.g. Sayf El Arab (USA) 127 – Honey Plum 57 (Kind of Hush **–** 118) [2002 –, a86: f11s⁴ Jan 15] good-topped gelding: prolific winner on all-weather (has **a73** gained 23 of his 26 victories on fibresand): only fair form from only 4-y-o start: best at 11f to 1¾m: acts on firm going and fibresand: held up. *P. C. Haslam*

CHINA FAIN (IRE) 4 b.f. Emarati (USA) 74 – Oriental Air (IRE) 56 (Taufan (USA) **43** 119) [2002 51: f5g 5m² 5m⁵ p5g 5.5f 5.3d⁵ 5m 5.1m 5g⁴ 5m⁶ Aug 26] sturdy filly: poor maiden: has form at 6f, probably best at sharp 5f: acts on fibresand, good to firm and good to soft ground: visored in 2001: tried tongue tied: often races prominently. *J. M. Bradley*

CHINA RED (USA) 8 br.g. Red Ransom (USA) – Akamare (FR) (Akarad (FR) 130) **–** [2002 74: 10d f8g f8.5g Nov 30] tall gelding: has a fluent, round action: formerly useful handicapper: no form since early in 2001. *J. J. Quinn*

CHIN CHIN 2 b.g. (Feb 21) Inchinor 119 – Twitcher's Delight (Polar Falcon (USA) **85 p** 126) [2002 6s⁴ 6m* 7m 7s* Oct 25] 80,000Y: lengthy, unfurnished gelding: second foal: dam unraced half-sister to useful 1m winner Nuryana, herself dam of very smart miler Rebecca Sharp: fairly useful performer: won maiden at Ripon in June and 20-runner nursery at Newbury (wore cheekpieces on first run for almost 3 months, travelled strongly long way when beating Eastern Magenta a neck) in October: will probably stay 1m: acts on soft and good to firm ground: difficult ride (also gave trouble at stall before poor penultimate effort), but probably capable of better. *M. P. Tregoning*

CHINKARA 2 ch.g. (Mar 11) Desert Prince (IRE) 130 – You Make Me Real (USA) **80** (Give Me Strength (USA)) [2002 7m 8m³ 8m⁶ 8f⁵ 8g⁵ Oct 18] 110,000F, 150,000Y: rangy gelding: has scope: half-brother to several winners, including useful Irish 1998 2-y-o 5f/ 6f winner Camargo (by Brief Truce), later successful in USA, and Irish 9f and 1¾m winner Real Guest (by Be My Guest): dam minor winner in USA: fairly useful maiden: creditable fifth in nursery at Newmarket final start (gelded after): stays 1m: raced on good ground or firmer: sometimes races freely. *B. J. Meehan*

CHIOMARA (IRE) 4 b.f. Namaqualand (USA) – Violet Crown (IRE) 93 (Kefaah **–** (USA) 124) [2002 –: 7f 10m Jun 3] angular filly: no form since 2 yrs. *F. Jordan*

CHISPA 4 b.f. Imperial Frontier (USA) 112 – Digamist Girl (IRE) (Digamist (USA) **87** 110) [2002 94d: f5s f6s f6s⁴ f5s³ f6g f7g f7g⁵ f6g⁶ f5g 6s² 6g³ 5f³ 6g³ 5f 6g* 6s⁴ 7f 6m 5d **a74** 6m 5g 6g 5v Nov 8] lengthy filly: good mover: fairly useful handicapper on turf, fair on all-weather: won at Thirsk in May: left M. Chapman after nineteenth start: best at 5f/6f: acts on soft going, firm and fibresand: tried blinkered: usually races prominently: game. *K. R. Burke*

CHIVALRY 3 b.g. Mark of Esteem (IRE) 137 – Gai Bulga 110 (Kris 135) [2002 61p: **95** 8.3s* 10m* 9.9d* 9.2g* 10m³ 9f 10s⁴ Oct 26] lengthy gelding: has scope: useful performer: won minor events at Hamilton and Windsor, and handicaps at Beverley (apprentices) and Hamilton in June/July: creditable efforts in handicaps last 3 starts, fourth to Demi Beau at Newbury (hampered well inside final 1f) final one: barely stays testing 1¼m: yet to race on heavy going, acts on any other: races freely: has hinted at temperament. *Sir Mark Prescott*

CHIVITE (IRE) 3 b.g. Alhaarth (IRE) 126 – Laura Margaret (Persian Bold 123) **81** [2002 67p: 10.2d³ 12s⁴ 12m⁵ 14g⁵ p13g⁵ Oct 4] well-made gelding: fairly useful maiden: probably stays 1¾m: best efforts on good to soft/soft going: sold 17,000 gns, joined K. Burke and gelded. *Mrs A. J. Perrett*

CHOCOLATE BOY (IRE) 3 b.c. Dolphin Street (FR) 125 – Kawther (Tap On **51** Wood 130) [2002 50: p10g 7g 8g Oct 16] modest maiden: should stay 1m: acts on good to firm going, below form on polytrack. *T. P. McGovern*

Langleys Solicitors Rated Stakes (Handicap), York—
against the backdrop of the shell of the £20m Ebor Stand, due to be opened in 2003,
Chookie Heiton (far side) narrowly beats Trace Clip (centre) and Gateman

CHOIR MASTER (USA) 2 b.g. (Apr 1) Red Ransom (USA) – Performing Arts 104 **97**
(The Minstrel (CAN) 135) [2002 5m⁴ 6d 5.2s⁶ 7m⁵ 8m² 8m³ 8f* 8.1g² 8m³ 7s Oct 25]
smallish gelding: half-brother to several winners, including smart 1995 2-y-o 6f winner
Woodborough (by Woodman) and useful 1997 2-y-o 6f winner Dance Trick (by Diesis):
dam, 2-y-o 5f/6f winner, third in Irish 1000 Guineas: useful performer: gelded after third
start: won nursery at Salisbury in September: best efforts when beaten head by Cat Ona
High in minor event at Sandown and third to Big Bad Bob in listed race at Ascot next 2
starts: will stay 1¼m: acts on firm going, well below form on soft: tried blinkered: sold
70,000 gns, sent to USA. *J. H. M. Gosden*

CHOOKIE HEITON (IRE) 4 br.g. Fumo di Londra (IRE) 108 – Royal Wolff (Prince **113**
Tenderfoot (USA) 126) [2002 103+: 5s 6m² 6f* 6m³ 6m* 7m Jul 27] strong, lengthy
gelding: smart handicapper: won at York (by neck from Trace Clip) in May and Newbury
(by length from Pomfret Lad under confident ride) in July: good third to Capricho in
Wokingham at Royal Ascot in between: rare poor effort in Tote International at Ascot
(reportedly returned home with torn ligaments in off-fore) final start: effective at 5f/6f:
acts on firm and good to soft going: usually ridden prominently before last 3 starts: has
been bandaged in front: game and consistent. *I. Semple*

CHORAL CHIMES (JPN) 2 b.f. (Mar 22) Sunday Silence (USA) – Polent (Polish **82 p**
Precedent (USA) 131) [2002 7m 8m² Sep 3] third foal: half-sister to useful Irish 1¾m
winner Tentpole (by Rainbow Quest): dam, French 13f and 15.5f winner, half-sister to
Oaks winner Snow Bride (dam of Lammtarra) out of Yorkshire Oaks winner and Arc
third Awaasif: still green, better effort in maidens (fairly useful form) when 2 lengths
second of 5 to Flying Wanda at Yarmouth, slowly away and not knocked about once held:
should be suited by 1¼m+: should improve further. *D. R. Loder*

CHORIST 3 ch.f. Pivotal 124 – Choir Mistress (Chief Singer 131) [2002 –: 8.5m* **108**
8.3s² 8s* 8m² 10g* 9.9m⁶ 9.9m 10m² 8f Oct 5] big, angular filly: useful performer:
progressed well in 2002, winning maiden at Beverley, minor event at Newbury, handicap
at Newmarket and listed race at Salisbury (beat Fraulein by 1¾ lengths) between April/
August: mostly good efforts otherwise, notably when ½-length second to Irresistible
Jewel in Blandford Stakes at the Curragh in September: should stay 1½m: acts on soft
and good to firm going (below form on firm final start): unseated to post/cantered loose
on reappearance: has been bandaged near-hind. *W. J. Haggas*

CHORUS 5 b.m. Bandmaster (USA) 97 – Name That Tune 40 (Fayruz 116) [2002 60: **70 §**
f6g⁴ f7g² f7g³ 6m* 5.7g 6.1m f6g⁵ May 20] neat mare: fair handicapper on turf, modest **a54 §**
on all-weather: won apprentice event at Folkestone in April: stays 7f: ran poorly on heavy
going, acts on any other turf and fibresand: sometimes blinkered/visored: reared badly
leaving stall penultimate start: not one to trust. *B. R. Millman*

CHOTO MATE (IRE)   6 ch.g. Brief Truce (USA) 126 – Greatest Pleasure (Be My   **89**
Guest (USA) 126) [2002 87: p10g 8g 7g⁴ 8g 8m⁵ 8f 8d² 8f⁶ 8.3m⁶ 7.1m² 7m⁴ 7.1g⁵ 8g
Oct 24] useful-looking gelding: poor mover (reportedly suffered from knee chips at 3
yrs): fairly useful handicapper: effective at 7f/1m: acts on polytrack (well held twice on
fibresand), firm and good to soft going: has started slowly/carried head high/hung right/
found little. *S. Kirk*

CHRISTALENI   3 ch.f. Zilzal (USA) 137 – El Jazirah (Kris 135) [2002 7d 8.3g⁴ 7f*   **77**
7m Sep 5] 42,000Y: strong, good-bodied filly: second foal: half-sister to useful 1¼m and
13f winner Mount Elbrus (by Barathea): dam unraced sister to Prix de Diane winner
Rafha, herself dam of smart pair Invincible Spirit (sprinter) and Sadian (middle-distance
stayer): fair performer: won maiden at Yarmouth in July by 1¼ lengths from Alqhutub,
soon to fore: well held (reportedly in season) final start: bred to stay further than 1m.
Mrs A. J. Perrett

CHRISTINA SANCHEZ (USA)   2 gr.f. (Apr 20) El Prado (IRE) 119 – Cope's   **– p**
Light (USA) (Copelan (USA)) [2002 6s 7.2s 5g 7v f6g⁶ Nov 18] $140,000Y: lengthy
filly: fifth foal: sister to US winner Miss Jennifer Lynn, third in Grade 1 7f event at 2 yrs,
and half-sister to 2 winners in USA, including 2000 Grade 3 2-y-o 1m winner Zillah The
Hun (by Hawk Attack): dam sprint winner in USA: signs of ability, not knocked about, in
maidens: should be suited by 7f+: remains capable of better. *Sir Mark Prescott*

CHRISTMAS TRUCE (IRE)   3 b.g. Brief Truce (USA) 126 – Superflash (Super-   **84**
lative 118) [2002 74: 12s⁵ 11.6m⁵ 11.9g* 13v* 15g⁶ 16s p12g Nov 23] good-topped
gelding: fairly useful handicapper: won at Carlisle and Hamilton in August: stays 13f:
acts on polytrack, goes well on good going or softer on turf. *M. H. Tompkins*

Cheveley Park Stud's "Chorist"

CHRISTOPHERSSISTER 5 br.m. Timeless Times (USA) 99 – Petite Elite 47 (Anfield 117) [2002 37§, a46§: f7s⁵ f8s f8s f6g⁵ f6g f7g f8g Mar 14] plain mare: poor **– §** performer: effective at 5f to 7f: acts on fibresand, best turf runs on good going or firmer: **a37 §** tried blinkered/tongue tied: often starts slowly: can't be trusted. *N. Bycroft*

CHUNKY O'BRIEN (IRE) 4 b.g. Cois Na Tine (IRE) 101 – Berenice (ITY) **–** (Marouble 116) [2002 –: f8g 12.3g Apr 3] no form: tried blinkered. *K. A. Ryan*

CHURCH FARM FLYER (IRE) 5 b.m. College Chapel 122 – Young Isabel (IRE) **50** (Last Tycoon 131) [2002 –: f8s⁴ f8g² f8g⁶ p8g f8.5g 7d 8d* 10m 10g 8g 8m p10g Jul 10] modest performer: won claimer at Leicester in May: stays 1¼m: acts on good to firm going, good to soft and fibresand. *C. N. Allen*

CHURCH MICE (IRE) 4 br.f. Petardia 113 – Negria (IRE) (Al Hareb (USA) 123) **71** [2002 81: 7d 7f 7m⁵ 8.1s 6m⁵ 7g⁵ 7g 7m⁵ 7m 7.5m⁶ 6d⁵ 7s Oct 26] good-quartered filly: fair performer: effective at 6f/7f: acts on heavy going, good to firm and fibresand: usually visored: none too consistent. *W. H. Tinning*

CHURLISH CHARM 7 b.h. Niniski (USA) 125 – Blushing Storm (USA) 102 (Blushing Groom (FR) 131) [2002 110: 16.2d 14m⁵ 18m Oct 19] good-bodied horse: smart **–** performer at best: well held in 2002: usually visored/blinkered. *J. R. Boyle*

CHYULU HILLS 3 b.f. Dancing High – Explorer (Krisinsky (USA)) [2002 f9.4g **–** f9.4g Feb 4] first foal: dam unraced half-sister to dam of smart 1½m/13f winner Phantom Gold: always behind in maiden/seller at Wolverhampton. *D. J. Wintle*

CIEL 2 b.f. (Mar 24) Rainbow Quest (USA) 134 – River Cara (USA) 86 (Irish River **78 p** (FR) 131) [2002 8m* Sep 19] second foal: half-sister to 3-y-o Araglin: dam, French 2-y-o 1m winner, granddaughter of Musidora winner Fatah Flare: 6/5, won 4-runner maiden at Yarmouth by neck from Golano, hampered early but quickening well to lead 1f out: will be suited by 1¼m+: should improve. *M. L. W. Bell*

CILL DROICHEAD (IRE) 2 b.c. (Apr 13) Entrepreneur 123 – Havinia (Habitat 134) **74** [2002 7.5g p7g³ p8g³ p7g p7g Dec 28] leggy colt: fifth foal: half-brother to 2 winners abroad, notably smart performer up to 1¼m in France/USA Lord Cromby (by Risen Star): dam French 1m winner: fair maiden: best efforts when third at Lingfield: stays 1m: carried head bit high final start. *E. J. O'Neill*

CINEMA PARADISO 8 b.g. Polar Falcon (USA) 126 – Epure (Bellypha 130) [2002 **47** –: f7g f7g f8g f9.4g⁶ f12g 11g* 12.3g p10g 10m⁶ May 1] tall gelding: has a round action: poor handicapper nowadays: won apprentice race at Southwell in April: stays 11f: acts on all-weather, best turf form on good to soft/soft going (has won on firm): below form in blinkers (second run in 24 hrs) seventh start: sometimes races freely. *D. W. Chapman*

CIRCLE OF WOLVES 4 ch.g. Wolfhound (USA) 126 – Misty Halo 93 (High Top **–** 131) [2002 –: 12d 16g Aug 12] rather unfurnished gelding: disappointing maiden. *Bob Jones*

CIRCUIT DANCER (IRE) 2 b.g. (Mar 21) Mujadil (USA) 119 – Trysinger (IRE) **81** (Try My Best (USA) 130) [2002 5g 6g 6m³ 6m⁵ 6f² 5m* Sep 29] IR 46,000F, 16,000Y: tall, leggy gelding: fourth foal: half-brother to 5.7f winner Ulysses Daughter (by College Chapel): dam unraced: fairly useful performer: best effort when winning maiden at Musselburgh by ¾ length from Fanny's Fancy, making all: will prove best at 5f/easy 6f: raced only on good going or firmer: usually races prominently. *A. Berry*

CITA VERDA (FR) 4 b.f. Take Risks (FR) 116 – Mossita (FR) (Tip Moss (FR)) **–** [2002 16s Nov 6] third foal: dam, French maiden, sister/half-sister to smart French middle-distance performers Mansonnien and Tartas: fairly useful performer for A. Hosselet in France at 3 yrs, winning minor event at Saint-Cloud: well held in handicap only British outing: stays 11.5f: acts on heavy ground: fair winning hurdler. *P. Monteith*

CITRINE (IRE) 4 ch.f. Selkirk (USA) 129 – Classic Coral (USA) (Seattle Dancer **81** (USA) 119) [2002 75: 14.4m 14d p16g² 16.4g* 18m 16s Oct 25] tall, leggy filly: fairly useful handicapper: won at Sandown in August: stays 2m: acts on polytrack and probably any turf going: tried visored: races prominently. *C. F. Wall*

CITRONELLA 2 ch.f. (Mar 1) Halling (USA) 133 – Kameez (IRE) 72 (Arazi (USA) **58** 135) [2002 6g 6d⁴ 7m⁶ 7f Sep 17] 40,000Y: first foal: dam, 11f winner, half-sister to smart performers Kalajana (in France at 10.5f) and Kalabo (up to 1½m) from family of Kahyasi: modest maiden: should stay at least 1¼m. *J. W. Hills*

CITRUS MAGIC 5 b.g. Cosmonaut – Up All Night 56 (Green Desert (USA) 127) **54 §** [2002 59: f12s² f16g f12g³ Dec 27] modest maiden handicapper: stays 2m: acts on fibresand, soft and good to firm going: often blinkered: has drifted right/carried head awkwardly: unreliable. *K. Bell*

CITY FAITH 3 b.f. Glory of Dancer 121 – Broughtons Star (Belmez (USA) 131) **73 d**
[2002 83: 7.1m² 8f 10.1s 8.1f⁵ 7m 6m Aug 29] quite plain-topped filly: fair performer at best in 2002: should stay 1m: acts on good to firm and good to soft ground: visored last 2 starts. *G. C. Bravery*

CITY FLITE 2 b.f. (Apr 5) Magic Ring (IRE) 115 – Lady Mabel 34 (Inchinor 119) **43 d**
[2002 5v² 6s⁶ f5g⁴ 6g 5m Aug 22] first foal: dam, maiden, stayed 1m: poor maiden: well held after debut (only start for J. Bethell): visored last 2 starts. *P. D. Evans*

CITY FLYER 5 br.g. Night Shift (USA) – Al Guswa 98 (Shernazar 131) [2002 48, **53**
a57: p8g f9.4g² p10g f8g* f9.4g² f8.5g f8g² 8m² Apr 27] leggy, good-topped gelding: fair **a67**
handicapper on all-weather, modest on turf: won at Southwell in February: stays 1¼m: acts on good to firm going and fibresand: tried visored/tongue tied: sometimes races freely: tends to carry head awkwardly. *Miss J. Feilden*

CITY GENT 8 b.g. Primitive Rising (USA) 113 – Classy Lassy (Class Distinction) **–**
[2002 8g 8m 16m Jul 8] well held in maiden/claimers on Flat. *N. Wilson*

CITY OF LONDON (IRE) 4 ch.g. Grand Lodge (USA) 125 – Penny Fan 58 (Nom- **78 d**
ination 125) [2002 79: f7g 7f⁶ 6m 6d 7m 7m Sep 3] rangy, angular gelding: fair performer at best: on downgrade in 2002: stays 7f: acts on firm going: hung badly left for only win: sent to Sweden. *J. W. Payne*

CITY PLAYER 4 ch.c. Komaite (USA) – Blink Naskra (USA) (Naskra (USA)) [2002 **73**
66: f6g f6g f6g⁶ f7g³ f5g Jun 19] good-topped colt: fair handicapper: stayed 7f: acted on fibresand: sometimes slowly away: dead. *Sir Mark Prescott*

CITY REACH 6 b.g. Petong 126 – Azola (IRE) 63 (Alzao (USA) 117) [2002 50, a71: **57**
f7g⁶ f7g f8.5g p7g p10g⁴ f12g 10g* f8.5g⁴ Nov 18] strong gelding: modest performer: **a63**
won selling handicap at Brighton in October: stays easy 1¼m: acts on any turf going/all-weather: sometimes visored: tongue tied last 4 outings: held up: none too reliable: sold 3,800 gns. *P. J. Makin*

CLANBROAD 4 ch.g. Clantime 101 – Under The Wing 69 (Aragon 118) [2002 74: **–**
6m 6m f6g f6g Nov 26] strong gelding: poor mover: fair handicapper at 3 yrs: well held in 2002: tried visored. *J. J. Matthias*

CLANN A COUGAR 2 ch.g. (Feb 16) Bahamian Bounty 116 – Move Darling (Rock **77**
City 120) [2002 6s² 5m 6d³ 6.1g* 6.1g⁵ 5.7f⁴ 7m⁴ 6m³ p6g 6g Oct 18] leggy, useful-looking gelding: has a quick action: third foal: half-brother to Italian 2000 2-y-o 6f winner Sabrehill Star (by Sabrehill): dam ran twice: fair performer: won maiden at Chepstow in July: in frame in minor event/nurseries after: stays 7f: acts on soft and good to firm going, soundly beaten on polytrack: sold 13,000 gns and gelded. *I. A. Wood*

CLAPTRAP 2 b.c. (Mar 2) Royal Applause 124 – Stardyn (Star Appeal 133) [2002 **–**
p5g p5g f5g Dec 2] 19,000F, 32,000Y: half-brother to several winners, notably very smart 6f (at 2 yrs)/7f winner Young Ern (by Efisio): dam maiden who stayed 1½m: only a little sign of ability in maidens: slowly away first 2 starts. *J. A. Osborne*

CLARETELLE (IRE) 4 ch.f. Ela-Mana-Mou 132 – Kutaisi (IRE) (Soviet Star (USA) **–**
128) [2002 65: 9.9m 8m Sep 5] disappointing maiden: sent to France. *Jane Southcombe*

CLARICE STARLING 4 b.f. Saddlers' Hall (IRE) 126 – Uncharted Waters 68 (Cel- **52**
estial Storm (USA) 132) [2002 72: p12g f12g⁶ f14.8g⁶ p13g Dec 28] strong, good-topped filly: disappointing maiden, modest in 2002: should stay beyond 1½m. *C. A. Cyzer*

CLARINCH CLAYMORE 6 b.g. Sabrehill (USA) 120 – Salu 65 (Ardross 134) **90**
[2002 72: f11s³ f12g f16.2g f16.2g 13s² 13g 12m² 10.5s* 10.9d² 12.1s³ 11.1v³ 12.1g³ 16.2d* 13.1s* 16s² Nov 6] smallish gelding: progressed into a fairly useful handicapper: won at Haydock (amateurs), Beverley and Ayr between June and October: effective at 10.5f (given test) to 2m: acts on heavy going, good to firm and fibresand: held up: reliable. *J. M. Jefferson*

CLARISSE 3 b.f. Salse (USA) 128 – Celia Brady 62 (Last Tycoon 131) [2002 8.3m **76**
8.1m 10s⁶ 10d³ 10m* 11f² 12d Nov 1] angular filly: fourth living foal: half-sister to 1½m winner Stahr (by Liboi): dam effective from 7f to 10.8f: fair handicapper: won at Windsor in June: should stay 1½m: acts on firm and good to soft ground. *H. Candy*

CLASSICAL SONG (IRE) 2 b.f. (Apr 10) Fayruz 116 – Dicci Anno (IRE) 72 **69**
(Classic Music (USA)) [2002 5.7f³ p7g³ p6g⁶ f7s Dec 9] 17,000Y: second foal: half-sister to fairly useful 2001 2-y-o 5f winner Anima Mundi (by Namaqualand): dam, Irish 5f

winner, half-sister to useful 1998 2-y-o 6f/7f winner Smittenby: fair maiden: best effort at Lingfield second start: will probably stay 1m. *P. W. Harris*

CLASSICAL WALTZ (IRE)   4 ch.f. In The Wings 128 – Fascination Waltz 83 (Shy   –
Groom (USA)) [2002 46: 11.6m p12g Aug 9] poor maiden at 3 yrs: well held in 2002.
J. J. Sheehan

CLASSIC CALVADOS (FR)   3 b.g. Thatching 131 – Mountain Stage (IRE) (Pen-   **55**
nine Walk 120) [2002 58p: 7m⁴ 7.9g 6d May 29] big, leggy gelding: modest maiden:
should stay 1m. *Mrs J. R. Ramsden*

CLASSIC CHRON (IRE)   2 b. or br.f. (Mar 29) Danetime (IRE) 121 – Classic   **43**
Goddess (IRE) (Classic Secret (USA) 91) [2002 5d⁴ 5m⁵ 5d 6g Aug 7] IR 14,000Y:
sturdy filly: half-sister to several winners, including fairly useful 2000 2-y-o 6f winner
Blue Goddess (by Blues Traveller): dam unraced from family of Hellenic and Greek
Dance: poor maiden: tends to hang right. *N. Tinkler*

CLASSIC CONKERS (IRE)   8 b.g. Conquering Hero (USA) 116 – Erck (Sun   **56 §**
Prince 128) [2002 58§, a56§: p16g p12g 12.6g 10m 12.3m⁴ 12m 12g 15.8f² p16g Dec 3]
sparely-made gelding: modest handicapper: left Pat Mitchell after second start: effective
at 1½m to 2m: acts on soft going, firm and polytrack: sometimes slowly away/looks far
from keen: untrustworthy. *Miss J. Feilden*

CLASSIC EXAMPLE   3 ch.c. Mark of Esteem (IRE) 137 – Classic Form (IRE) 58   **82**
(Alzao (USA) 117) [2002 p10g⁴ 10g⁵ 10m 12f² 11.6m³ 12d² f12g f9.4g Dec 16] 95,000Y: **a68**
first foal: dam, lightly-raced maiden, sister to Oaks winner Shahtoush and half-sister to
Oaks second Game Plan: fairly useful maiden on turf, fair on all-weather: left E. Dunlop
13,000 gns prior to well held last 3 starts: stays 1½m: acts on firm going, probably on
polytrack: has worn cheekpieces. *Miss S. J. Wilton*

CLASSIC INVESTMENT   2 b.f. (Apr 1) Classic Cliche (IRE) 128 – Tawnais 80   –
(Artaius (USA) 129) [2002 7d 6m p7g Oct 9] 500Y: half-sister to 3 winners, including
4-y-o Talat: dam placed at 7f/1m at 2 yrs: well held in maidens. *Ferdy Murphy*

CLASSIC MILLENNIUM   4 b.f. Midyan (USA) 124 – Classic Colleen (IRE) 79   **58**
(Sadler's Wells (USA) 132) [2002 56: p12g⁵ f12s³ p16g f11g f8g 11.8s* 12f* 11.7g 11.6s⁴
14d* p12g* 13v⁴ 14m⁶ 14m 11.9f Oct 10] lightly-made filly: modest handicapper: left
Pat Mitchell after fourth start: won at Leicester, Pontefract (apprentices), Sandown and
Lingfield between March and July: effective at 1½m/1¾m: acts on soft going, firm and
all-weather: tried blinkered: sometimes slowly away/pulls hard. *W. J. Musson*

CLASSIC ROLE   3 b.c. Tragic Role (USA) – Clare Island 108 (Connaught 130)   **83**
[2002 10g 10s³ 10.1g⁵ 12m 10m⁵ 10s⁴ 12d* p12g² p12g Dec 18] 2,500Y, resold 7,000Y:
half-brother to several winners, including useful 1m (at 2 yrs) and 10.5f winner who
stayed 2m Clare Heights (by Shirley Heights) and fairly useful 1½m winner Island Lake
(by Kalaglow): dam 7f/8.5f winner: fairly useful performer: won maiden at Catterick in
November: stays 1½m: acts on soft going, good to firm and polytrack. *R. Ingram*

CLASSI MAUREEN   2 ch.f. (Mar 10) Among Men (USA) 124 – Hi-Hannah 59 (Red   **48**
Sunset 120) [2002 6.1g f6s 6d Oct 14] 900F: eighth foal: dam, 1m winner, also won over
hurdles: poor maiden. *J. M. Bradley*

CLASSY ACT   4 ch.f. Lycius (USA) 124 – Stripanoora (Ahonoora 122) [2002 74d: –
f7g f8s f8.5g f8.5g⁵ f6g Feb 19] leggy filly: one-time fair performer: little form in 2002:
tried blinkered. *A. Berry*

CLASSY LASSIE (IRE)   2 ch.f. (Mar 20) Goldmark (USA) 113 – Okay Baby (IRE)   **61**
67 (Treasure Kay 114) [2002 5g 5f² 5d² 6d² 5m⁶ Jun 1] IR 2,800Y: first foal: dam 1m
winner: modest maiden: runner-up in claimers/seller: stays 6f: acts on firm and good to
soft ground. *G. A. Swinbank*

CLAUDE (IRE)   4 b.g. Hamas (IRE) 125§ – Tigora (Ahonoora 122) [2002 7.1g Aug   –
8] IR 7,600F, IR 5,300Y: sixth foal: half-brother to 1½m winner Maradi (by Marju): dam
unraced: slowly away and well held in maiden at Chepstow. *Mrs A. J. Bowlby*

CLEAR THOUGHT   3 br.f. Mind Games 121 – Awham (USA) (Lear Fan (USA)   –
130) [2002 –: p8g⁶ p10g 10m 10.9f 10.1m Aug 14] quite good-topped filly: little form:
tried visored. *A. P. Jarvis*

CLEMATIS (USA)   3 b.f. Danzig (USA) – City Dance (USA) (Seattle Slew (USA))   **100 ?**
[2002 7m* 7m³ 7g⁴ 8v Nov 30] $425,000Y: fifth foal: sister to smart Irish 5f and (at 2
yrs) 6f winner Black Rock Desert, closely related to winner in USA by Storm Bird, and
half-sister to winners in Japan (by Deputy Minister) and UAE (by Gone West): dam, 8.5f
minor stakes winner in USA, sister to US Grade 1 9f/1¼m winner Slew City Slew: won

maiden at Salisbury in August: seemingly much the better of last 2 starts in French listed races when 2 lengths fourth to Binya at Maisons-Laffitte, though close up throughout and possibly flattered: stayed 7f: visits King's Best. *J. H. M. Gosden*

CLEVELAND WAY 2 b.g. (Apr 4) Forzando 122 – Fallal (IRE) 47 (Fayruz 116) **59** [2002 f6g⁵ 5g⁴ f6g 6m Aug 16] 12,500Y: third foal: half-brother to 3-y-o Miss C and 4-y-o The Scaffolder: dam maiden who stayed 7f: modest maiden: well held last 2 starts, leaving J. L. Eyre in between: likely to prove best at 5f. *D. Carroll*

CLEVER CLOGS 2 ch.f. (Mar 8) Nashwan (USA) 135 – High Standard 83 (Kris **72 p** 135) [2002 7d p8g² Nov 14] big, lengthy filly: fourth foal: half-sister to fairly useful 7f (at 2 yrs) to 1½m winner Summer Song (by Green Desert): dam, 2-y-o 1m winner who stayed 1½m, out of close relative to Nureyev and half-sister to dam of Sadler's Wells: better effort in maidens when length second to Little Good Bay at Lingfield: will be suited by 1¼m+: should progress further. *E. A. L. Dunlop*

CLEVER CONSUL (IRE) 7 b.g. Acatenango (GER) 127 – Kelvedon (General – Assembly (USA)) [2002 80: 7d 20m Jun 19] fairly useful handicapper at best (lightly raced on Flat): successful at Downpatrick (for second year running) and Leopardstown (by short head from Direct Bearing) in 2001: well held both 7-y-o starts, in Ascot Stakes (Handicap) at Royal Ascot (slowly away) final one: stays 2¼m: acts on good to firm going: tried blinkered. *A. J. Martin, Ireland*

CLIMATE CONTROL (USA) 3 ch.f. Mt Livermore (USA) – Descant (USA) (Nure- **83** yev (USA) 131) [2002 60: 6f² 6.1d 6m* 5.1f² 5m Aug 24] compact filly: fairly useful performer: won maiden at Brighton in May: stays 6f: acts on firm ground: sold 35,000 gns in December. *R. Charlton*

CLIMATE (IRE) 3 ch.g. Catrail (USA) 123 – Burishki 49 (Chilibang 120) [2002 73, **93** a80: p8g²* p7g² 9f³ 8.3m⁴ 9d 8s³ 7.6f* 8m² p7g² Jul 24] strong, compact gelding: fairly useful performer: won maiden at Lingfield in January and minor event at Chester in June: effective at 7f to easy 9f: acts on polytrack, soft and firm going: blinkered last 3 starts: sometimes looks none too keen, but is consistent: gelded after final outing. *R. Hannon*

CLIPPERTON 3 b.g. Mister Baileys 123 – Theresita (GER) (Surumu (GER)) [2002 **87** 67: 8g⁴ 8.1f⁴ 10m 8g* 8f 9d² 9.9m* 10.2d⁵ 10m⁵ 8.1g Oct 5] leggy gelding: has fluent, round action: fairly useful performer: won maiden at Bath in May and minor event at Salisbury in June: stays easy 1¼m: acts on firm and good to soft going: gelded after final start. *I. A. Balding*

CLIQUEY 3 b.g. Muhtarram (USA) 125 – Meet Again (Lomond (USA) 128) [2002 –: **72** 6.1m² 7g⁴ 7g* 8d 8m 8f⁶ 10m 10s Oct 23] fair handicapper: won maiden event at Brighton in June: stays 1m: acts on firm going, well held on fibresand (on debut)/both starts on softer than good: sometimes slowly away. *J. A. Osborne*

CLISDEN (IRE) 4 ch.g. Catrail (USA) 123 – Anita Via (IRE) (Anita's Prince 126) **71** [2002 8.1d⁵ 8.1d⁶ 10m⁴ Jun 17] lengthy gelding: first foal: dam unraced: fair form in maidens: seemed to stay 1¼m: hung left on debut: dead. *B. Palling*

CLOCKING OFF (IRE) 2 b.g. (Feb 14) Night Shift (USA) – Maritana (USA) (Rahy **73** (USA) 115) [2002 5s 5.1d⁵ 5d 6m* 5g² 6g* 6g⁴ 6m* 6g² 6m 7f³ 6f³ 7g Oct 19] 7,500Y: close-coupled gelding: first foal: dam unraced granddaughter of Oaks winner Monade: fair performer: won sellers at Catterick in May and Thirsk in June and nursery at Catterick in August: good efforts in nurseries after when placed: stays 7f: acts on firm going: usually blinkered: has run well when sweating/edgy: sold 9,000 gns, sent to Kuwait. *T. D. Barron*

CLOPTON GREEN 5 b.g. Presidium 124 – Silkstone Lady (Puissance 110) [2002 – § 53: p6g f6s p6g f6g p8g Feb 26] modest handicapper at 4 yrs: no form in 2002: sometimes blinkered: untrustworthy. *J. W. Payne*

CLOTH OF GOLD 5 b.g. Barathea (IRE) 127 – Bustinetta 89 (Bustino 136) [2002 – 64: 14.1d 13.3s May 29] lengthy, quite attractive gelding: lightly-raced maiden on Flat: winning hurdler. *Lady Herries*

CLOUD DANCER 3 b. or br.f. Bishop of Cashel 122 – Summer Pageant 81 (Chief's **86** Crown (USA)) [2002 83p: p7g 7m² 8.2d⁶ 8m* Jun 29] leggy, rather unfurnished filly: fairly useful handicapper: won at Newmarket in June: stays 1m: acts on fibresand and good to firm going, possibly not on good to soft. *D. J. Coakley*

CLOUDY 4 b.f. Ashkalani (IRE) 128 – Shady Leaf (IRE) 56 (Glint of Gold 128) [2002 – 69: f12s Jan 5] lengthy, useful-looking filly: fair maiden at best: well held only run in 2002. *Mrs Lydia Pearce*

CLOWNIN AROUND 3 b.f. Mistertopogigo (IRE) 118 – Pokey's Pet 56 (Uncle – Pokey 116) [2002 –: 7g Jun 5] well held in seller/maidens. *M. Mullineaux*

CLYTHA HILL LASS 3 ch.f. Bluegrass Prince (IRE) 110 – Manhunt 70 (Posse – (USA) 130) [2002 49: 5.1d⁶ 7.1v⁵ 8.2m 8g Jul 24] poor maiden at 2 yrs: little form in 2002. *J. M. Bradley*

COALITION 3 b.g. Polish Precedent (USA) 131 – Selection Board 75 (Welsh Pageant **90** 132) [2002 54p: f12g³ p12g* 12.1d* 12.4m* 14m* 14m⁶ 16m² Oct 1] rather leggy, good-topped gelding: fairly useful performer: won handicaps at Lingfield, Newcastle and Sandown and minor event at Beverley (on third start) in August: will stay further than 2m: acts on all-weather, good to firm and good to soft going: sold 76,000 gns, and gelded. *Sir Mark Prescott*

COASTAL BLUFF 10 gr.g. Standaan (FR) 118 – Combattente (Reform 132) [2002 **84** 94: 5.1f 5d 5f 5s 5m³ 5g³ 5m⁵ 5.2m 5.2m Aug 25] tall, angular gelding: fairly useful handicapper: effective at 5f/6f: acts on soft and firm going: tried blinkered: has had wind operations/worn tongue strap, and is tubed: often races handily: best with strong handling: none too consistent. *N. P. Littmoden*

COAT OF HONOUR (USA) 2 gr.g. (Feb 29) Mark of Esteem (IRE) 137 – Bally- **69** mac Girl 63 (Niniski (USA) 125) [2002 p7g p7g 8g⁵ Oct 24] 40,000Y: third foal: dam, 1½m to 15f winner, closely related to smart stayer Alleluia and half-sister to Last Second and to dam of Alborada, both very smart up to 1¼m: blinkered, best effort in maidens (fair form) when 3 lengths fifth to Redspin at Brighton, racing freely (gelded after): bred to be suited by 1¼m/1½m: very slowly away first 2 starts. *Sir Mark Prescott*

COCCINELLE (IRE) 4 b.f. Great Marquess 115 – Nuit d'Ete (USA) 90 (Super – Concorde (USA) 128) [2002 f12g⁴ f12g⁶ f12g Mar 21] half-sister to 3 winners, including 10-y-o Hugwity and useful Irish 1m/1¼m winner Al Guswa (by Shernazar): dam 2-y-o 5f/6f winner: well held in maidens and a seller. *J. A. Osborne*

COCCOLONA (IRE) 4 b.f. Idris (IRE) 118 – Fair Siobahn (Petingo 135) [2002 59: **46** f12g⁵ f12g⁴ 11.7g May 7] poor performer: stays 1½m: acts on fibresand, soft and good to firm going: tried visored: sometimes slowly away. *D. Haydn Jones*

COCKNEY BOSS (IRE) 3 b.g. General Monash (USA) 107 – Cockney Ground **60 ?** (IRE) (Common Grounds 118) [2002 –: 8.3d 7.1m⁶ 8.1m⁴ 7.1f⁴ 6m Oct 7] tall, angular gelding: poor mover: seemed to show modest form (though may well be flattered) third/ fourth starts: headstrong. *B. R. Millman*

COCKSURE (IRE) 7 b.g. Nomination 125 – Hens Grove (Alias Smith (USA)) [2002 – 11.8g Jul 18] modest handicapper for A. Martin in Ireland at 4 yrs, winning at Down Royal: well held only start since: blinkered at 4 yrs. *B. J. Llewellyn*

COCO LOCO 5 b.m. Bin Ajwaad (IRE) 119 – Mainly Me 76 (Huntingdale 132) **83** [2002 98: 16m 16.2s 16.4d 14v⁶ 18m 16g⁴ Dec 4] tall, workmanlike mare: fairly useful handicapper in 2002: should stay beyond 16.5f: has form on good to firm going, all wins on soft/heavy. *Mrs Lydia Pearce*

COCONUT PENANG (IRE) 2 b.c. (Feb 16) Night Shift (USA) – Play With Fire **98** (FR) (Priolo (USA) 127) [2002 5m² 5g* 6m* 6g⁴ 6m Sep 11] 35,000Y: deep-girthed colt: first foal: dam, French 1½m winner, half-sister to smart performer up to 1½m in France/ US Playact: useful performer: won maiden at Lingfield in May and minor event at Kempton (hung left) in June: respectable fourth in Coventry Stakes at Royal Ascot: off nearly 3 months, raced in unfavoured group when mid-field in sales race at Doncaster final start: stays 6f: raced on good/good to firm going: races up with pace. *B. R. Millman*

COCTAIL LADY (IRE) 2 ch.f. (Feb 5) Piccolo 121 – Last Ambition (IRE) 29 (Cad- **– §** eaux Genereux 131) [2002 6m 6m 5.1d⁶ 5.2f 5.7m 5m f5s³ f6g⁴ f5g⁵ f5g f5g⁵ f5g Dec **a61 §** 10] IR 2,000F, 6,000Y: rather leggy, workmanlike filly: second foal: half-sister to 3-y-o Hawkley: dam, maiden, seemed best at 5f/6f: modest maiden: effective at 5f/6f: acts on fibresand, no form on turf: usually visored: often soon off bridle: not one to trust implicitly. *B. W. Duke*

CODE SIGN (USA) 3 b.g. Gulch (USA) – Karasavina (IRE) (Sadler's Wells (USA) **80** 132) [2002 8f² 8.1s² 10.3m² 9.9m² 9.9f² 9.9f² Oct 5] lengthy gelding: first foal: dam, unraced sister to useful performers Desert Secret (at 2 yrs when 1m winner) and Bincyah (11.5f winner), out of half-sister to Seattle Slew and Lomond: fairly useful maiden: stays 1¼m: acts on firm ground, below best on soft: visored last 2 starts (wandered/found little on penultimate): sold 22,000 gns. *J. H. M. Gosden*

CO DOT UK 4 b.g. Distant Relative 128 – Cubist (IRE) 71 (Tate Gallery (USA) 117) [2002 63: f7s f7g f7g f7g 7.1d 7m Jul 24] seems of little account nowadays. *D. W. Chapman* –

CODROUTZA (FR) 2 ch.f. (Apr 25) Sicyos (USA) 126 – Codreta (FR) (Dark Stone (FR)) [2002 4.5g* 5m 6d⁴ 7.5g³ 8g² 8f² 8d⁶ Nov 4] first known foal: dam, French maiden, third at 9f: trained first/third starts only by B. Moretti, winning newcomers race at La Teste in March: last of 7 in claimer at Leicester on second start (only outing for J. Osborne): placed in minor events at Dax and Toulouse (2) in autumn: stays 1m: acts on firm ground. *H. Carlus, France* ?

CODY 3 ch.c. Zilzal (USA) 137 – Ibtihaj (USA) 97 (Raja Baba (USA)) [2002 –: 10.2d⁶ 11.7d³ 11.7m 16.2g Aug 26] good-topped colt: modest maiden: stays 1½m: acts on good to soft going, pulled up only outing on fibresand. *G. A. Ham* 54

COFFEE TIME (IRE) 3 b.f. Efisio 120 – Petula 103 (Petong 126) [2002 88d: 5d² 5m² 5.1s⁶ 6d⁴ 5.1f³ 5g 5m⁴ 5f 5.1g⁵ 5g⁶ p6g⁴ p7g⁴ p8g⁴ p7g p8g p7g⁴ Dec 28] quite good-topped filly: fairly useful maiden handicapper: effective at 5f to 1m: acts on firm going, good to soft and polytrack: tried blinkered: sometimes slowly away: usually held up: none too genuine. *D. J. S. ffrench Davis* 80 §

COLD CLIMATE 7 b.g. Pursuit of Love 124 – Sharpthorne (USA) 91 (Sharpen Up 127) [2002 80: 6g⁴ 6m 6f 6m 6m⁶ 5.2m 6m 6m³ 6f⁶ 6m⁵ 6f³ 7d⁵ 7s p7g⁴ Nov 14] lengthy gelding: fair handicapper: barely stays 7f: acts on any turf going and polytrack: occasionally visored: usually comes from behind. *Bob Jones* 73

COLD TURKEY 2 b.g. (Apr 27) Polar Falcon (USA) 126 – South Rock 102 (Rock City 120) [2002 6s 7m⁴ 6.1m⁵ 7m⁴ 8s Oct 22] 8,000Y, 10,000 2-y-o: leggy gelding: third foal: dam, 7f/1m winner, out of half-sister to very smart miler Soviet Line: fair maiden: stays 7f: acts on good to firm going, well held on soft: gelded after final start. *W. Jarvis* 67

COLIN COOK 4 b.g. Presidium 124 – Horton Lady 46 (Midyan (USA) 124) [2002 –: f5s f9.4g Feb 11] no form. *D. W. Barker* –

COLISAY 3 b.g. Entrepreneur 123 – La Sorrela (IRE) (Cadeaux Genereux 131) [2002 8m 8f 8m* 8m 8d² 8m* 8.3m² 7m Sep 28] 42,000Y: sturdy gelding: second foal: dam unraced half-sister to smart sprinter Central City: useful performer: won maiden at Kempton in June and handicap at Newmarket (beat Judge Davidson by head) in July, wandering both times (markedly so in latter): at least respectable efforts in similar events last 2 starts, head second to Broadway Score at Windsor on penultimate: stays 1m: acts on good to firm and good to soft going. *A. C. Stewart* 103 +

COLLARD 4 ch.f. Wolfhound (USA) 126 – Collide 102 (High Line 125) [2002 79: p8g f8.5g⁶ 9g³ p10g⁶ f12g* f14.8s⁵ 12g⁶ May 20] workmanlike filly: modest performer: made all in apprentice seller at Wolverhampton (left M. Johnston 7,500 gns) in April: stays 1½m: acts on all-weather and probably any turf going: sold 5,500 gns in July. *J. R. Best* 63

COLLEGE CITY (IRE) 3 b.g. College Chapel 122 – Polish Crack (IRE) (Polish Patriot (USA) 128) [2002 44: f9.4g Jan 7] strong gelding: poor maiden: seems to stay 1m: tried blinkered/visored. *S. J. Magnier* –

COLLEGE DELINQUENT (IRE) 3 br.g. College Chapel 122 – St Cyr Aty (IRE) (Ela-Mana-Mou 132) [2002 73: p6g³ 7m 6f p7g⁵ 6s 6m p7g⁵ p12g p10g Dec 28] quite good-topped gelding: fair maiden handicapper: stays 7f: acts on firm ground, soft and polytrack: blinkered third to seventh outings: left B. Meehan before next start. *K. Bell* 75 ?

COLLEGE HIPPIE 3 b.f. Cosmonaut – Eccentric Dancer 47 (Rambo Dancer (CAN) 107) [2002 65: 5f² 6m³ 5g 5.1m 5g* 5d⁴ 5m f6s⁵ 5m³ 5.1f⁵ 5f Oct 3] plain, angular filly: fair performer: won maiden at Leicester in July: best at 5f: yet to race on soft/heavy going, acts on any other turf: often races prominently. *J. F. Coupland* 67

COLLEGE KING (IRE) 6 b.g. College Chapel 122 – Genetta (Green Desert (USA) 127) [2002 –: 7g May 6] small, sturdy gelding: no form. *M. Brittain* –

COLLEGE MAID (IRE) 5 b.m. College Chapel 122 – Maid of Mourne (Fairy King (USA)) [2002 85: 5s 6f 6g⁶ 6g 6v⁴ 6g 6s 5g⁵ 7.2g⁶ 5d² 6m 6m⁶ 7m⁴ 5.9v 6s* 6s³ 6g⁶ 5m 6d⁴ Oct 15] sturdy mare: fair nowadays: won minor event at Redcar in August: effective at 5f (given test) to 7f: possibly not at best on firm ground, acts on any other: has been mulish in paddock: has edged right: held up: tough: sold 8,200 gns. *J. S. Goldie* 68

COLLEGE QUEEN 4 b.f. Lugana Beach 116 – Eccentric Dancer 47 (Rambo Dancer (CAN) 107) [2002 . 6m* 6d⁴ 6m* 6m⁷ Aug 23] strong filly: fair handicapper: won at Thirsk in July and Folkestone (made all) in August: raced only at 6f: acts on fibresand, good to firm and good to soft going. *S. Gollings* 68

211

COLLEGE ROCK   5 ch.g. Rock Hopper 124 – Sea Aura 89 (Roi Soleil 125) [2002 **79**
79, a47: 7g⁶ 8f⁵ 8.5g⁶ 8m⁴ 8g* 8.1m 8s³ Jun 13] small, sturdy gelding: fair handicapper: **a–**
won at Bath in May: probably best at 1m/9f: acts on fibresand and probably any turf
going: visored: has given trouble in preliminaries/carried head awkwardly. *R. Brotherton*

COLLEGE SONG   2 b.c. (Apr 24) College Chapel 122 – Celt Song (IRE) (Unfuwain **49**
(USA) 131) [2002 6.1m 6m Aug 29] smallish, good-topped colt: fourth foal: half-brother
to smart 1000 Guineas runner-up Princess Ellen (by Tirol), 6f/7f winner at 2 yrs: dam
unraced: poor form in maidens. *W. Jarvis*

COLLEGE STAR   4 b.g. Lugana Beach 116 – Alis Princess (Sayf El Arab (USA) **–**
127) [2002 –: f8s⁴ f8g⁶ f8g f8g⁵ 10.3s⁵ 10m 9.9g 10m f12g f12g⁶ 9.9g 8m Aug 7] tall **a32**
gelding: poor maiden: probably stays 1¼m: acts on soft going, good to firm and fibresand: tried visored: sometimes slowly away. *J. F. Coupland*

COLLIER HILL   4 ch.g. Dr Devious (IRE) 127 – Polar Queen 76 (Polish Precedent **91**
(USA) 131) [2002 8g 10m 11.1s² 13.1g* 12.4s* 11.9g² 12s² 11.9g² 13.1g* 13.1s² 12v
Nov 9] 3,000 3-y-o: strong gelding: poor mover: first living foal: dam, 7f winner, granddaughter of very smart 1m/1¼m performer Roussalka: won bumper on debut: fairly
useful in first season on Flat: won minor events at Ayr and Newcastle, and handicap at
Ayr between May and September: ran as though something amiss final start: stays 13f:
acts on soft going: often held up: reliable. *G. A. Swinbank*

COLNE VALLEY AMY   5 b.m. Mizoram (USA) 105 – Panchellita (USA) 78 (Pancho **60**
Villa (USA)) [2002 56, a49: p10g f9.4g 8g 9.7d⁴ 8.3d² 10g² Aug 13] tall mare: modest **a–**
handicapper: stays 1¼m: acts on firm going, good to soft and all-weather: blinkered
(below form) on reappearance: often makes running. *G. L. Moore*

COLOMBE D'OR   5 gr.g. Petong 126 – Deep Divide 74 (Nashwan (USA) 135) [2002 **–**
42, a60: f11g 9.9g Jul 30] workmanlike gelding: handicapper: well held both 5-y-o starts:
tried blinkered. *M. C. Chapman*

COLONEL COTTON (IRE)   3 b.g. Royal Applause 124 – Cutpurse Moll 76 (Green **95**
Desert (USA) 127) [2002 80: p5g⁵ 6m⁶ 6g² 5g² 6s² 5g² p6g⁴ 5m² 5g² 6g* 6m⁴ 7d⁴ 5g² **a66**
5m* Sep 14] good-topped gelding: useful performer on turf: won maiden at Newmarket
in July and handicap at the Curragh (hung right over 1f out, beat Dancing Mystery short
head) in September: in frame most other starts in 2002: best at 5f/6f: acts on soft and good
to firm going, fair form on polytrack: usually blinkered after seventh start: has looked
none too genuine. *N. A. Callaghan*

COLONEL CUSTER   7 ch.g. Komaite (USA) – Mohican 75 (Great Nephew 126) **54 d**
[2002 –§, a61§: f11s³ f12g³ f11g* f12g f12g 10m f12g f8.5g f12g f11g f12g Dec 26]
tall, angular gelding: modest performer at best: won seller at Southwell in January: on
downgrade after: raced mainly at 11f/1½m: acts on fibresand, lightly raced and little form
on turf: sometimes visored/blinkered/wears cheekpieces: unreliable. *R. Brotherton*

COLONEL KOZANDO   3 b.g. Komaite (USA) – Times Zando 64 (Forzando 122) **57**
[2002 57?: 7m f7g⁴ f7g³ 8.1g f6g² 7.1m⁴ 6d f6g* f7g⁶ f6g p7g f6g* Dec 30] strong,
workmanlike gelding: modest performer: won maiden at Wolverhampton (final start for
Mrs G. Rees) in October: stays 7f: acts on all-weather, and good to firm going: usually
visored/blinkered: has worn cheekpieces: slowly away last 3 outings. *B. G. Powell*

COLONEL KURTZ (USA)   4 b.g. Slip Anchor 136 – Rustaka (USA) 68 (Riverman **43**
(USA) 131) [2002 –: 12f⁵ 12.4g 13.8m² 17.1m 13s 16m Jul 8] big, leggy gelding: poor
maiden handicapper: stays 13.8f: acts on firm going: blinkered last 2 starts (also tongue
tied penultimate). *John Berry*

COLONEL MUSTARD   6 ch.g. Keen 116 – Juliet Bravo 61 (Glow (USA)) [2002 **66**
71: p10g³ f8.5g p8g³ f8.5g 8g 9s p10g⁴ 11.6m³ 11.6m⁶ Jul 29] unfurnished gelding: has a
long stride: fair handicapper: effective at 1m/11.6f: acts on all-weather and firm going:
tried visored: has looked reluctant: sold 5,000 gns. *P. G. Murphy*

COLONEL NORTH (IRE)   6 b.g. Distinctly North (USA) 115 – Tricky 66 (Song **53**
132) [2002 f9.4g 10.9f⁴ Apr 10] modest nowadays: stays 11f: acts on firm ground and **a–**
fibresand: seems effective visored or not: sold 1,500 gns in August. *Andrew Reid*

COLONEL'S DAUGHTER   2 ch.f. (May 18) Colonel Collins (USA) 122 – Clash- **61**
fern (Smackover 107) [2002 5m f5g² f5s³ 5m 5v⁶ 5.9d⁵ 5d³ 5.1m Aug 29] 3,800Y: sturdy
filly: fourth foal: half-sister to fairly useful 2001 2-y-o 5f winner Shuffling Kid (by Rock
City) and 4-y-o Geri Roulette: dam unraced: modest maiden: probably best at 5f: acts on
good to soft ground and fibresand: blinkered last 2 starts, looking difficult ride on first of
them. *E. J. Alston*

COLONEL TELFORD   2 br.c. (Apr 14) Emperor Fountain 112 – Petaz (Petong 126)   **46**
[2002 5g⁶ 5m⁵ 7.5g 6d Aug 26] 2,500Y: quite good-topped colt: second foal: dam well
beaten all 3 starts: poor maiden: should stay at least 6f. *M. E. Sowersby*

COLONIAL SUNRISE (USA)   5 b.g. Pleasant Colony (USA) – Dancing Reef   **52**
(USA) (Danzig (USA)) [2002 8.5m⁴ Apr 25] $87,000F, 25,000Y: good-topped, attractive
gelding: sixth foal: closely related to a minor stakes winner in USA by Pleasant Tap: dam
winning sprinter in USA: fair form in frame in bumpers in 2000/1 (looked difficult ride
final start)/poor maiden hurdler: modest form when fourth to Chorist in Beverley maiden.
T. D. Easterby

COLONNADE   3 b.f. Blushing Flame (USA) 109 – White Palace 80 (Shirley Heights   **–**
130) [2002 51p: 8s 10f Apr 13] lengthy filly: modest form in 3 maidens. *D. Nicholls*

COLORADO FALLS (IRE)   4 b.g. Nashwan (USA) 135 – Ballet Shoes (IRE) 75   **92 d**
(Ela-Mana-Mou 132) [2002 93: 11.9m 13g 15v² 11.9d* 11.9m⁵ 10d³ 14v 14.4g⁶ Aug 26]
useful-looking gelding: fairly useful handicapper at best: won apprentice event at Haydock in July: ran poorly last 2 starts: effective at 1½m, probably at 15f: yet to race on firm
going, acts on any other: has edged left/carried head high. *P. Monteith*

COLOURFUL LADY (USA)   2 b.f. (Apr 5) Quest For Fame 127 – Special Park   **66**
(USA) (Trempolino (USA) 135) [2002 6m⁶ 6g 7.1d* Jul 31] 10,000Y: compact filly: first
foal: dam, French 1m/9f winner, half-sister to US Grade 3 1m winner Wasatch: fair form:
best effort to win maiden at Musselburgh by ½ length from Dark Champion, battling on
well: reportedly suffered from ringworm after: likely to stay at least 1¼m: yet to race on
extremes of going. *P. W. Harris*

COLOURFUL LIFE (IRE)   6 ch.g. Rainbows For Life (CAN) – Rasmara 94§   **–**
(Kalaglow 132) [2002 11.8s Oct 28] big, workmanlike gelding: winning hurdler: behind
in minor event at Leicester on Flat debut. *Mrs M. Reveley*

COLOUR PURPLE   3 b.f. Spectrum (IRE) 126 – Awtaar (USA) 67 (Lyphard (USA)   **–**
132) [2002 47: 10d f12g 12m Apr 22] well-made filly: poor maiden: blinkered (raced too
freely) final start: sent to Barbados. *C. E. Brittain*

COLOUR SERGEANT (USA)   4 ch.g. Candy Stripes (USA) 115 – Princess Afleet   **50**
(USA) (Afleet (CAN)) [2002 55, a60: 8m 8f 8m⁵ 8.5g 7.5m⁶ 7.5d 8g⁵ 8s 8g Aug 27]   **a–**
smallish, lengthy gelding: modest maiden handicapper: stays 8.5f: acts on fibresand, soft
and good to firm going: tried visored. *Don Enrico Incisa*

COLUMBINE (IRE)   4 b.f. Pivotal 124 – Heart of India (IRE) (Try My Best (USA)   **60**
130) [2002 6g 6.1g p7g 6f 6m 6s 6g 7g 5g 5.5s⁴ 5m³ 5s⁴ 5d⁶ 5m 5fg³ 5g 5m³ 5g
5m² 5m⁵ 6g 6m⁶ 6d* f5g f6g Nov 25] lengthy, useful-looking filly: good walker: modest
handicapper nowadays: won at Ayr in October: best at 5f/6f: acts on firm going, soft and
fibresand: tried blinkered: tough. *A. Berry*

COLUMBUS (IRE)   5 b.g. Sadler's Wells (USA) 132 – Northern Script (USA) 95   **–**
(Arts And Letters (USA)) [2002 16.1d Sep 9] fair at 3 yrs in Ireland for A. O'Brien,
winning maiden at Roscommon: tailed off only Flat outing since: stays 2m: blinkered:
has carried head high. *C. Grant*

COLWAY RITZ   8 b.g. Rudimentary (USA) 118 – Million Heiress (Auction Ring   **70**
(USA) 123) [2002 71: 12.3g 9.9m³ 10m³ 12m³ 12.4g⁴ 12g 12f 10g⁶ 12.3m 10.1m⁴ 9d⁴
12.3m² 10.4m* 10.1d⁵ 10m⁵ 10m² 11.9f* 13.8g² 13.8d⁴ Nov 5] big, strong gelding: good
mover: fair performer: won at York (2 apprentice handicaps) and Catterick (minor event)
in September/October: effective at 1¼m to 13.8f: acts on any going except soft/heavy:
tried blinkered: sometimes races freely: usually held up. *W. Storey*

COMANCHE QUEEN   5 ch.m. Totem (USA) 118 – Chess Mistress (USA) 59 (Run   **45**
The Gantlet (USA)) [2002 51: 11.8m⁵ 12d Jul 31] close-coupled mare: poor handicapper:
reportedly lost action final start: effective at 1½m to 2m: acts on firm ground: tried
blinkered. *J. S. Wainwright*

COMBINED VENTURE (IRE)   6 b.h. Dolphin Street (FR) 125 – Centinela 67   **–**
(Caerleon (USA) 132) [2002 –: 10.9m Aug 26] no longer of any account. *G. J. Smith*

COME ON MURGY   5 b.m. Weldnaas (USA) 112 – Forest Song 60 (Forzando 122)   **–**
[2002 37, a55: f9.4g f8.5g f8.5g⁴ f9.4g f8.5g⁵ f8.5g f7g Nov 20] leggy mare: poor nowa-   **a44**
days: stays 8.5f: acts on good to firm going and fibresand: tried blinkered. *A. Bailey*

COMEOUTOFTHEFOG (IRE)   7 b.g. Mujadil (USA) 119 – Local Belle (Bally-   **36**
more 123) [2002 38: f7g³ f7g⁵ 10g f12g Jun 14] small gelding: poor nowadays: effective
at 7f/1m: acts on fibresand, best turf form on good going or firmer: tried blinkered.
Mrs P. Ford

Tote Credit Club Silver Bowl (Handicap), Haydock—
Common World (No.4) eventually finds a way through to overhaul Macaw;
Tahitian Storm (diamonds) and Serieux (rail) are next

COMFORT FACTOR 2 b.g. (Mar 18) Defacto (USA) – Care And Comfort 64 (Most — Welcome 131) [2002 6m 6m Aug 29] 3,000Y: rather angular gelding: second foal: closely related to German 7f winner Gudaut (by Elmaamul): dam 1m winner: behind in maidens. *J. M. P. Eustace*

COMIC TIMES 2 b.f. (Jan 27) Puissance 110 – Glorious Aragon 88 (Aragon 118) — [2002 5m 5m 6f Sep 26] third foal: half-sister to a winner in Spain by Petong: dam 5f winner: little encouragement in maidens. *M. Mullineaux*

COMMANCHE WIND (IRE) 7 b.g. Commanche Run 133 – Delko (Decent Fellow **42** 114) [2002 49: f11g f12g 16g 14m6 17.2d4 Jun 26] poor maiden: stays 17f: acts on firm and good to soft going. *E. W. Tuer*

COMMAND CONTROL 2 ch.g. (Mar 8) Inchinor 119 – Zelda (USA) (Sharpen Up — 127) [2002 6g Sep 9] 13,000F, 25,000Y: half-brother to several winners, including 7-y-o American Cousin and 6f winner (stayed 1¾m) Robzelda (by Robellino): dam once-raced half-sister to Moorestyle: tailed off in maiden: sent to Spain. *J. W. Payne*

COMMANDING 3 ch.g. Pennekamp (USA) 130 – Lady Joyce (FR) (Galetto (FR) **93** 118) [2002 80p: 9f* 8g6 7.1d 8g* 10m3 8m4 10m2 8f* Oct 7] strong gelding: fairly useful performer: won minor event at Kempton and claimers at Ascot and Pontefract between April and October: free-going sort, barely stays 1¼m: possibly best on good going or firmer: tongue tied: gelded after final start. *Mrs A. J. Perrett*

COMMISSAR (IRE) 3 b.g. Common Grounds 118 – Trescalini (IRE) (Sadler's **78** Wells (USA) 132) [2002 10.1g 8m5 10s* Oct 23] IR 220,000Y: fourth foal: half-brother to useful 1¾m/11f winner Fantazia (by Zafonic) and fairly useful Irish 7f/1m winner Machalini (by Machiavellian): dam Irish 2-y-o 1¼m winner: progressive form in maidens, winning at Nottingham by 2 lengths from Frankskips, edging left/carrying head awkwardly: stays 1¼m: reportedly had breathing problem on debut, tongue tied after: sold 22,000 gns. *R. Charlton*

COMMISSION (USA) 2 ch.c. (Apr 27) Gulch (USA) – Accountable Lady (USA) **100 p** (The Minstrel (CAN) 135) [2002 7.1g* 7.1m5 Aug 31] $250,000Y: third foal: closely related to 4-y-o Lots of Love: dam, US 6f to 1m winner and third in Grade 2 7f event, half-sister to dam of high-class French stayer Amilynx: won 4-runner minor event at Sandown in August: still green, useful form when 2 lengths fifth to Foss Way in Solario Stakes on same course, smooth headway to challenge 2f out but no extra and not knocked about (tended to hang): should stay 1m: remains capable of better. *G. A. Butler*

COMMITMENT LECTURE   2 b.f. (Mar 30) Komaite (USA) – Hurtleberry (IRE)   **52**
87 (Tirol 127) [2002 7m 6d Oct 21] 5,800Y: first foal: dam, of (at 2 yrs) to 1m winner:
better effort in maidens (modest form) when seventh to Night Games at Pontefract second
start. *M. Dods*

COMMON CONSENT (IRE)   6 b.m. Common Grounds 118 – Santella Bell (Ballad   **68**
Rock 122) [2002 66: p8g 8d 8.1m⁵ 7g⁶ 8m* Jun 30] smallish mare: fair handicapper: won
at Goodwood in June: has form at 11.5f, best at 1m/9f: acts on firm going and polytrack:
held up: reportedly in foal to Dansili. *S. Woodman*

COMMONDINI (IRE)   3 b.f. Common Grounds 118 – Windini (Windjammer (USA))   **50**
[2002 8.3m 8d 8d⁴ 10f 8d p10g Nov 27] IR 11,000Y: well-made filly: has a quick action:
sister to fairly useful Irish 1m winner Crystal Wind and half-sister to several winners,
including fairly useful Irish 6f winner Faydini (by Fayruz): dam unraced: modest maiden:
seems to stay 1¼m: tried tongue tied. *P. W. Harris*

COMMON THOUGHT (IRE)   3 b.g. Common Grounds 118 – Zuhal 67 (Busted   **81**
134) [2002 69p: 8m* 8m 8d⁴ 8m³ 8m 8m 8f⁵ 10m 8.2s Oct 23] quite attractive gelding:
fairly useful handicapper: won at Ripon in April: stays 1m: best form on going firmer
than good: sold 9,500 gns. *P. W. Harris*

COMMON WORLD (USA)   3 ch.c. Spinning World (USA) 130 – Spenderella (FR)   **112**
(Common Grounds 118) [2002 91p: 8.1d* 8.1d⁶ 10m³ 8s² 10m 9f² 10d⁴ Nov 1] rather
leggy, quite attractive colt: smart performer: won handicaps at Sandown in April and
Haydock (Tote Credit Club Silver Bowl, no run for much of straight, led on line) in May:
best efforts when 1¾ lengths third to Burning Sun in listed race at Royal Ascot and neck
second to Century City in International Stakes at the Curragh third/fourth starts: stays
1¼m: acts on soft and good to firm ground: has hung/carried head awkwardly/found
little: sometimes slowly away. *G. A. Butler*

COMMOYA (IRE)   3 b.c. Great Commotion (USA) 123 – Halvoya 64 (Bay Express   **79**
132) [2002 71: p7g³ 7m 6s* 7s² 7g⁵ Jun 26] fifth reported foal: dam best at 5f: fair
performer: third in maiden at Lingfield in February: won similar event at Cork in May:
stays 7f: acts on soft and good to firm ground, below form on polytrack on reappearance.
Edward Butler, Ireland

COMPANION   4 b.f. Most Welcome 131 – Benazir 91 (High Top 131) [2002 77, a87:   –
p8g f8g p8g 8.3g f8s f8g f7g f9.4s⁵ p10g Dec 21] tall, lengthy, good-topped filly: **a75 d**
fair handicapper: left B. Pearce after fourth start: effective at 1m/easy 1¼m: acts on
all-weather, firm and soft going: sometimes races freely/finds little: on downgrade.
Julian Poulton

COMPLETE CIRCLE   2 ch.f. (Mar 13) Vettori (IRE) 119 – Cockatoo Island 99 (High   **70 p**
Top 131) [2002 6g⁶ Jul 12] half-sister to several winners, including useful performer up
to 1¼m Circle of Light (by Anshan), 7.6f winner at 2 yrs, and useful 1¾m winner Collier
Bay (by Green Desert), latter also Champion Hurdle winner: dam 1½m to 15f winner:
13/2, sixth of 8 to Nasij in maiden at Ascot, slowly away (reportedly found to have been
in season): should do better at 1¼m+. *P. W. D'Arcy*

COMPOS MENTIS   2 b.c. (May 7) Bijou d'Inde 127 – Red Cloud (IRE) 61 (Taufan   **78**
(USA) 119) [2002 7m 7m p7g² Oct 9] 20,000F, 13,000Y: fourth foal: dam, maiden who
stayed 7f and sometimes looked none too keen, half-sister to 5-y-o Cape Town: best effort
in maidens (fair form) when 4 lengths second to Jummana at Lingfield: will stay 1m.
D. Morris

COMPTON ALICE   2 ch.f. (Mar 18) Compton Place 125 – Secret Circle (Magic   **58**
Ring (IRE) 115) [2002 5.7g 5.3m⁴ f6f⁵ 5m Aug 30] 15,000Y: first foal: dam unraced
half-sister to high-class 1m/1¼m performer Bijou d'Inde: modest maiden: should stay at
least 6f. *N. P. Littmoden*

COMPTON AMICA (IRE)   6 gr.m. High Estate 127 – Nephrite 106 (Godswalk   –
(USA) 130) [2002 13.1g May 20] tall, close-coupled mare: fairly useful handicapper for
G. Butler at 3 yrs: well held only Flat start since. *K. Bishop*

COMPTON ARROW (IRE)   6 b.g. Petardia 113 – Impressive Lady 98 (Mr Fluoro-   **71**
carbon 126) [2002 78: 7d 8f 7g⁶ 7g 8g 6m* 7m* 6m⁵ 6g 6s 6f Oct 4] big, rangy gelding:
has a quick action: fair handicapper: won at Pontefract in June and Brighton in July: has
form at 1m, but best at 6f/7f nowadays: acts on soft going, good to firm and fibresand:
tried blinkered: usually tongue tied. *D. Nicholls*

COMPTON AVIATOR   6 ch.g. First Trump 118   Rifada 103 (Fla-Mana-Mou 132)   **75 d**
[2002 76: 7m² 10m 7m 8.9m 10m⁴ 9.9g p8g p7g p10g p10g⁵ Dec 21] lengthy gelding:
fair performer at best: had form at 2m earlier in career, probably best at 7f to 1¼m

nowadays: acts on polytrack, good to firm and good to soft going: blinkered once: tongue tied: held up: on downgrade. *A. W. Carroll*

COMPTON BANKER (IRE)   5 br.g. Distinctly North (USA) 115 – Mary Hinge 100 (Dowsing (USA) 124) [2002 99: 5.2g 5.1f* 5m 5.6m 5m p7g Nov 23] small, strong gelding: useful handicapper: won at Chester (beat James Stark by neck) in May: below form otherwise in 2002: effective at 5f/6f: acts on firm going: tried blinkered: reared as stall opened final start: usually held up. *G. A. Butler*   **98**

COMPTON BAY   2 b.g. (Jan 30) Compton Place 125 – Silver Sun 83 (Green Desert (USA) 127) [2002 5m 6d Aug 26] 500Y: leggy, plain gelding: first foal: dam, 9f winner, half-sister to smart stayer Tioman Island: poor form in maiden/seller. *M. Brittain*   **46**

COMPTON BOLTER (IRE)   5 b.g. Red Sunset 120 – Milk And Honey 102 (So Blessed 130) [2002 117: p10g⁴ p10g Mar 16] smallish gelding: has a quick action: smart performer at best: only useful form at Lingfield both 5-y-o starts, eighth to Adiemus in listed race final one: subsequently off with injured near-fore: stays 1½m: acts on dirt and polytrack, has form on soft going, best turf efforts on good or firmer: blinkered (in USA) once as 3-y-o: has been tongue tied: held up. *G. A. Butler*   **108**

COMPTON CHICK (IRE)   4 b.f. Dolphin Street (FR) 125 – Cecina 100 (Welsh Saint 126) [2002 55: f12g p12g Feb 26] modest maiden handicapper at 3 yrs: well held both 4-y-o starts. *J. W. Mullins*   **–**

COMPTON COMMANDER   4 ch.g. Barathea (IRE) 127 – Triode (USA) 105 (Sharpen Up 127) [2002 99: 10.3f⁵ 12f² 12g 16.1g 10.5d³ p8g* 9.9m⁵ 16.2d 12.3m* 9.2m⁴ 10m⁶ 10s p12g⁵ p10g⁵ Dec 21] smallish-looking gelding: fairly useful performer: won claimers at Lingfield in July and Chester in August: effective at 1m to 1¾m: acts on any turf going and polytrack, effective visored or not: sometimes slowly away: carries head awkwardly: ungenuine and unreliable. *G. A. Butler*   **94 §**

COMPTON DRAGON (USA)   3 ch.c. Woodman (USA) 126 – Vilikaia (USA) 125 (Nureyev (USA) 131) [2002 87P: p8g* 8m⁴ 8m 8m² 7m Jun 19] compact colt: smart performer: won minor event at Lingfield in March impressively: best efforts in 2000 Guineas at Newmarket (seventh to Rock of Gibraltar) and listed race at Kempton (length second to Hero's Journey) third/fourth starts: stays 1m: acts on polytrack and good to firm going: held up. *G. A. Butler*   **109**

COMPTON DRAKE   3 b.g. Mark of Esteem (IRE) 137 – Reprocolor 114 (Jimmy Reppin 131) [2002 f7g⁶ f8.5g f7f Nov 11] 40,000Y: half-brother to several winners, including very smart winner around 1¼m Cezanne (by Ajdal), Irish Oaks winner Colorspin (by High Top, now dam of Opera House and Kayf Tara), and very smart filly up to 1¼m Bella Colora (by Bellypha, now dam of Stagecraft): dam won Lancashire Oaks: always behind in maidens at Wolverhampton: likely to need at least 1¼m: very slowly away on debut: likely to do better. *G. A. Butler*   **– p**

COMPTON DYNAMO   3 b.g. Wolfhound (USA) 126 – Asteroid Field (USA) 123 (Forli (ARG)) [2002 79: p5g² p6g* p5g⁶ p5g* 6m⁴ 6g² 8m 6d⁶ 5.5m² 6m³ 6d 7.1m² 5g 5s Oct 26] rather leggy gelding: useful handicapper: won at Lingfield in February and April: generally respectable efforts at least otherwise, including when runner-up at Salisbury (behind Vanderlin) and Warwick (behind Little Edward) on sixth/ninth outings: claimed from G. Butler £25,000 twelfth start: best at 5f/6f: acts on polytrack, best turf efforts on good/good to firm going: races freely: usually held up. *W. J. Musson*   **101**

COMPTON ECLIPSE   2 ch.c. (Apr 13) Singspiel (IRE) 133 – Fatah Flare (USA) 121 (Alydar (USA)) [2002 7g⁴ p8g Dec 14] 17,500F, 16,000Y: leggy colt: half-brother to several winners, including 6f (at 2 yrs)/7f winner Flavian (by Catrail) and 1¼m winner Refugio (by Reference Point), both fairly useful: dam 6f (at 2 yrs) and 10.5f (Musidora Stakes) winner: well held in Newmarket Challenge Cup and maiden at Lingfield (raced freely). *G. A. Butler*   **–**

COMPTON EMERALD (IRE)   2 ch.f. (Feb 18) Bluebird (USA) 125 – Cheviot Amble (IRE) 105 (Pennine Walk 120) [2002 7m⁶ 7d³ p5g⁴ p8g³ p7g Dec 28] IR 26,000Y: sixth foal: half-sister to smart 1m to 10.4f winner Amalia (by Danehill): dam Irish 6f to 1¼m winner: fair maiden: third at Thirsk and Lingfield (nursery, despite being hampered): will stay beyond 1m: jinked left on bend at Goodwood on debut: soon off bridle final start. *G. A. Butler*   **77**

COMPTON EMPEROR   2 b.c. (Mar 7) Bijou d'Inde 127 – Princess Tara 85 (Prince Sabo 123) [2002 6s² 7.1s* Nov 6] 30,000f, 17,500Y: smallish, useful-looking colt: half-brother to several winners by Risk Me, including useful 1998 2-y-o 5f/6f winner El Tango and fairly useful 5f winner (including at 2 yrs) Bilko: dam, 6f (at 2 yrs) and 1m   **85 p**

winner, half-sister to high-class French sprinter Kind Music: fairly useful form in maidens, winning at Musselburgh by 1¼ lengths from Wozzeck, having travelled very strongly: stays 7f: likely to do better still. *G. A. Butler*

COMPTON PLUME 2 ch.c. (Feb 1) Compton Place 125 – Brockton Flame 72 –
(Emarati (USA) 74) [2002 5g 6m 5g Aug 27] 3,000F, 2,500Y: strong, lengthy colt: third foal: half-brother to 2000 2-y-o 7f and 1¼m winner Trumpington (by First Trump): dam 6f winner (including at 2 yrs): always behind in maidens. *M. W. Easterby*

COMPTON PRINCESS 2 b.f. (Mar 6) Compton Place 125 – Curlew Calling (IRE) **40**
51 (Pennine Walk 120) [2002 5g 6g Sep 9] 4,000Y: fourth foal: dam, ran once, half-sister to smart 1¼m performer Merry Merlin: poor form in maidens 3½ months apart: withdrawn after playing up behind stall in between. *Mrs A. Duffield*

COMPTON STAR 2 ch.c. (May 10) Compton Place 125 – Darakah 78 (Doulab (USA) –
115) [2002 5m 6m Oct 7] 12,000Y: seventh foal: half-brother to 5-y-o Mobo-Baco and 6-y-o Bodfari Signet: dam 5f (at 2 yrs) to 1m winner: slowly away/well held in maidens. *R. J. Hodges*

COMTESSE NOIRE (CAN) 3 b.f. Woodman (USA) 126 – Faux Pas (IRE) 63 **61**
(Sadler's Wells (USA) 132) [2002 67: 7f 8.1m 9.3s³ 10m 10.9g⁴ 10m³ 8g 8m 10.2g⁵ 10m f12g³ Oct 19] angular filly: modest maiden handicapper: stays 11f: acts on soft and good to firm ground, probably on fibresand: has swished tail/carried head high/edged left: free-going sort, and often makes running. *I. A. Balding*

CONCER ETO 3 ch.g. Sabrehill (USA) 120 – Drudwen (Sayf El Arab (USA) 127) **72**
[2002 p8g p6g p5g⁶ 9.2s f8.5g² 8g 10d³ 8.5m⁶ 10m* 7.9s 8.5m* 8f 8.1g* 10m* Oct 3] half-brother to useful 7f/1m winner Concer Un (by Lord Bud): dam won 13f bumper: fair handicapper: won at Brighton (twice, carried head bit high first occasion), Epsom and Chepstow between July and October: effective at 1m/1¼m: acts on fibresand, good to soft and good to firm ground. *S. C. Williams*

CONCHONITA 2 b.f. (Apr 9) Bishop of Cashel 122 – Cactus Road (FR) (Iron Duke –
(FR) 122) [2002 10s Oct 23] half-sister to 6-y-o Danielle's Lad and a winner in Austria by Petardia: dam French 1¼m to 13.5f winner: 33/1, well held in maiden at Nottingham. *B. Palling*

CONCINO (FR) 5 b.g. Zafonic (USA) 130 – Petronella (USA) (Nureyev (USA) 131) –
[2002 ?: 13.8g 16f Jun 11] leggy gelding: little form: tried visored. *Miss A. Stokell*

CONCLUDE (USA) 4 ch.c. Distant View (USA) 126 – Private Line (USA) 105 –
(Private Account (USA)) [2002 107: 10.4g⁶ Jun 14] well-made, quite attractive colt: useful at 3 yrs: ran as though something amiss only 4-y-o start. *J. L. Eyre*

CONCUBINE (IRE) 3 b.f. Danehill (USA) 126 – Bye Bold Aileen (IRE) (Warning **76**
136) [2002 66: p6g 7g 7g* 7g 7d² p7g Oct 31] close-coupled filly: has a quick action: fair **a54**
handicapper: landed gamble at Epsom in July: best effort penultimate start: stays 7f: acts on good to firm and good to soft going: has edged left. *J. R. Boyle*

CONDOLEEZZA (USA) 2 gr.f. (Jan 24) Cozzene (USA) – Rosabella 97 (Niniski **78**
(USA) 125) [2002 7d³ 8.1g² 9f² 8.3d² Oct 28] rather leggy filly: first foal: dam, French 1m (at 2 yrs) to 11.5f (listed race) winner, sister to smart stayer Rubicund: fair form in maidens: placed all starts, short-headed by Desert View at Windsor (dictated pace, hung left) final one: will stay at least 1¼m: acts on firm and good to soft ground. *J. L. Dunlop*

CONFEY CRACKER (IRE) 4 ch.f. Great Commotion (USA) 123 – Our Duchess –
(IRE) 67 (Mansooj 118) [2002 8.5m 10m May 15] sparely-made filly: first foal: dam Irish maiden who stayed 1m: signs of a little ability in maiden/sellers (trained by P. Martin in Ireland only 2-y-o starts): bolted to post and withdrawn once. *E. J. O'Neill*

CONFIDENTIELLE (FR) 3 b.f. Octagonal (NZ) 126 – Dame Modeste (FR) (Iron –
Duke (FR) 122) [2002 10m⁵ f12s⁵ Sep 17] half-sister to several winners in France, notably smart 1¼m/12.5f winner Crnagora (by Esprit du Nord): dam placed at 1¼m in France: well held in 2 maidens. *T. D. Barron*

CONFUZED 2 b.g. (Mar 27) Pivotal 124 – Times of Times (IRE) 78 (Distinctly North –
(USA) 115) [2002 6d Aug 11] 13,500Y: second foal: dam 5f and (including at 2 yrs) 6f winner: 33/1, tailed off in minor event at Windsor (reportedly kicked in stalls). *Andrew Reid*

CONISTON BAY (IRE) 2 b.f. (Apr 28) Lake Coniston (IRE) 131 – Mary Ellen Best **55**
(IRE) 64 (Danehill (USA) 126) [2002 6g⁵ 6g 7m⁶ 6d 6f⁵ 6d Oct 21] IR 1,400Y, 3,500 2-y-o: close-coupled, angular filly: fourth foal: dam, Irish maiden, half-sister to smart Moyglare Stud Stakes winner Gayle Gal: modest maiden: should stay 7f: acts on firm ground. *E. J. Alston*

CONNECT 5 b.g. Petong 126 – Natchez Trace 52 (Commanche Run 133) [2002 88, **92** a75: 5f 5m⁵ 5f 6m 5m 5m 5m⁶ 5.2f 5m³ 5.2m³ 5.1f* 5m² 5.2m³ Sep 17] strong, lengthy **a–** gelding: unimpressive mover: fairly useful handicapper on turf, fair on all-weather at best: won at Chester in August: probably best at 5f: acts on firm going, good to soft and fibresand: sometimes visored/blinkered: sometimes hangs. *M. H. Tompkins*

CONNOR (IRE) 3 ch.g. Alhaarth (IRE) 126 – Ghayah (IRE) (Night Shift (USA)) **85** [2002 87p: 7s⁴ 9d⁵ 8.1m⁶ 8.5f 8.5f⁶ 6.5f Dec 28] strong, rangy gelding: has a quick action: fairly useful performer: left R. Hannon after third outing: should prove best at 7f/1m: acts on soft and good to firm going. *R. B. Hess jnr, USA*

CONQUERING LOVE (IRE) 4 b.g. Pursuit of Love 124 – Susquehanna Days **74** (USA) 68 (Chief's Crown (USA)) [2002 68: 12m 13s⁶ 12g* 12m² 12.1v 11.9g⁴ 12g² 12.1g* 11.9g Aug 20] quite good-topped gelding: not a good walker: fair handicapper: won at Musselburgh in May and Beverley in July: stays 1½m: best form on good/good to firm going: has been mulish to post/raced freely/flashed tail. *B. Ellison*

CONQUESTADORA 4 b.f. Hernando (FR) 127 – Seren Quest 90 (Rainbow Quest **98** (USA) 134) [2002 92p: 14.1m* 14d³ 13.1g 18m 16d Nov 1] workmanlike filly: useful handicapper: won at Salisbury in May: good third to Warrsan at Goodwood next time: off 4 months, below form last 3 starts: should be suited by further than 2m: acts on any ground: held up. *G. A. Butler*

CONSENSUS (IRE) 3 b.f. Common Grounds 118 – Kilbride Lass (IRE) (Lahib (USA) **86** 129) [2002 91: 6m³ 6.1d⁵ 6f 6g Jun 15] leggy filly: unimpressive mover: fairly useful performer: will stay 7f: yet to race on soft/heavy ground, acts on any other: has edged left: seems best held up. *M. Brittain*

CONSIGNIA (IRE) 3 ch.f. Definite Article 121 – Coppelia (IRE) (Mac's Imp (USA) **66** 116) [2002 67: 6m 6s 6.1d 7m⁵ 7m⁵ f7g 6f* f6g² f7g Nov 22] lengthy, rather unfurnished filly: fair performer: left G. Balding after third start and, having won maiden at Catterick in October, J. Hills 8,000 gns after eighth: best around 6f: acts on firm going, good to soft and fibresand: sometimes tongue tied. *D. Haydn Jones*

CONSTANTINE 2 gr.c. (Feb 18) Linamix (FR) 127 – Speremm (IRE) (Sadler's **85 p** Wells (USA) 132) [2002 7.1g 8.2m² 8g* Oct 2] 42,000Y: leggy colt: first foal: dam Italian 11f and 1¾m winner out of half-sister to US Grade 1 1¼m winner Ida Delia: fairly useful form: justified favouritism in maiden at Salisbury by short head from Regal Agenda, leading close home having been under pressure long way: will be suited by 1¼m+: sold 72,000 gns: probably capable of better still. *R. Charlton*

CONSTITUTE (USA) 3 b.f. Gone West (USA) – Appointed One (USA) (Danzig **85** (USA)) [2002 –p: 7m³ 8.1m* 7d 7.1m⁴ 8f Aug 18] rather leggy, useful-looking filly: fairly useful performer: made all in maiden at Warwick in May: respectable efforts in handicaps last 2 starts: stays 1m: acts on good to firm going. *Sir Michael Stoute*

CONSULTANT 6 b.g. Man of May – Avenita Lady 57 (Free State 125) [2002 –: f8s **–** f8.5g² f8.5g⁵ f9.4g f8.5g f8.5g Mar 25] good-bodied gelding: poor performer: stays 1¼m: **a44** acts on fibresand, little form on turf since 2 yrs: often races prominently. *C. N. Kellett*

CONTACT DANCER (IRE) 3 b.g. Sadler's Wells (USA) 132 – Rain Queen **92 p** (Rainbow Quest (USA) 134) [2002 56p: 10d 14.1m* 17.1m³ 14m 18d* 16.5v² Nov 9] well-made gelding: fairly useful handicapper, quite lightly raced: won at Nottingham in May and Pontefract (by 5 lengths from Mandingo Chief) in October: creditable second to enterprisingly-ridden Knavesmire Omen at Doncaster (wandered/well clear of rest) final start (gelded after): stays 2¼m well: acts on heavy and good to firm going: possibly had something amiss fourth outing: type to improve again and win more races at 4 yrs. *J. L. Dunlop*

CONTACT (IRE) 5 br.g. Grand Lodge (USA) 125 – Pink Cashmere (IRE) (Polar **68 d** Falcon (USA) 126) [2002 78: f7s f8g p8g f6g f6g 7g 9.7m³ 10g 7g 6s⁴ 7m³ f6s 6g⁴ 8.5g⁶ 7.5m² 7d f7g⁵ f8.5s⁵ f8.5g² p10g Dec 21] compact gelding: fair handicapper at best: on downgrade and hasn't won since 1999: stays 7f: acts on soft going, good to firm and fibresand: tried blinkered: has worn cheekpieces: sometimes slowly away: often races prominently: untrustworthy. *M. Wigham*

CONTINENT 5 ch.g. Lake Coniston (IRE) 131 – Krisia (Kris 135) [2002 111p: **123** 5s 6g² 6m² 5m 6f 5m 5g² 6m⁵ 6d⁵ 5m⁴ 6m⁶ 5g* 5m Dec 15]

David Nicholls' ability to reap a rich harvest with horses discarded by other stables, shown with Ya Malak in 1997 and Rudi's Pet in 1999 among others, reached new heights when Continent won the July Cup and the Prix de l'Abbaye de

Longchamp, proving himself incontestably one of the best sprinters in training. When Nicholls purchased Continent out of Pascal Bary's stable as a four-year-old for 40,000 guineas at the Newmarket Autumn Sales in 2000, the colt had won one of five starts, a minor event at Chantilly, and had finished last of five, though not disgraced, on his only outing in pattern company, the Prix du Gros-Chene. Gelded soon after joining his new trainer, Continent did not take long revealing that the money had been well spent, including when showing himself capable of winning a good prize when having no luck in running in the Stewards' Cup at Goodwood. Continent duly landed that good prize when running out a neck winner of the Ayr Gold Cup under a confident ride. Seven runs was a fairly light campaign by the standards of a Nicholls' inmate, the majority of which are sprinters—forty-seven of his team's sixty-seven wins during the season came at up to seven furlongs, with only three of his forty individual winners scoring over middle distances. Nicholls follows the dictum that sprinter-milers are able to take more racing than those running over a mile and a quarter or more. Continent, who raced thirteen times between March and December in the latest season, looked a horse to follow as the season got under way. After shaping promisingly off a mark of 100 in a handicap at Doncaster on the opening day of the turf season, he then ran creditably to be runner-up to Reel Buddy at Kempton and Newmarket (Abernant Stakes) and to finish a closing head second to Dominica in the King's Stand Stakes at Royal Ascot, finishing strongly after briefly having to wait for a run, but he had still not got his head in front by the time of the July Cup, and had run below par in the Palace House Stakes, the Duke of York Stakes and the Temple Stakes.

Besides running his horses often, Nicholls is not averse to letting them take each other on. He had at least three runners in a race more than sixty times in the latest season, with the list headed by eight in the handicap contested by Continent at Doncaster in March and seven in similar events at Ripon and Thirsk. For the record, he won six of the ten races in which he had at least five runners, which suggests the practice pays. Nicholls put his feelings and those of Edward St George, owner of Continent and Bahamian Pirate, in perspective after they had contested the Darley July Cup: 'Mr St George doesn't like running two horses in the same race but I don't mind running ten.' Two was quite sufficient at Newmarket, where the Nicholls pair started at 12/1 and 16/1 respectively in a field of fourteen which, incidentally, bore little resemblance to the one shown in an ante-post list published for the race in April, when Johannesburg was 5/1 favourite ahead of Meshaheer and Danehurst, with such as Tendulkar and Western Verse also priced up. Meshaheer and Danehurst were the only ones of the ten quoted in that April list to take part, with Danehurst starting favourite. The original thirteen entries from Aidan O'Brien's stable came down to three, headed by second favourite Landseer, coming back in trip from a mile. Also in the line-up were Malhub and Three Points, first and third in the Golden Jubilee Stakes at Royal Ascot, where Continent, having his second race in five days, had never struck a blow in fifth; Continent's old rival Reel Buddy; and, as mentioned, Bahamian Pirate, winner of the Ayr Gold Cup in 2000 and a consistent performer in pattern races subsequently. The race went pretty much according to plan for Continent, who is not the most straightforward of rides in that he has occasionally been slowly away and needs to be held up and produced late. After travelling well from the start, Continent obtained a dream run against the far

Darley July Cup, Newmarket—a 1,2 for owners Lucayan Stud and trainer David Nicholls as Continent holds Bahamian Pirate; Danehurst and Landseer (No.10) make the frame

Prix de l'Abbaye de Longchamp - Majestic Barriere, Longchamp—
Continent (far side) completes a Group 1 double, putting his nose in front on the line;
Italian-trained Slap Shot (centre) and Zipping (No.8) are close behind

rail with less than a quarter of a mile to go, led just inside the final furlong and always looked like holding his stable companion from there to the line, scoring by half a length with Danehurst a length and a half away third and Landseer fourth. The first two are geldings, and Continent became the first to win the race since Portobello in 1939. The July Cup did not take as much winning as usual—Malhub was below form in seventh—but all credit to Continent and his connections for gaining the day. The closest Nicholls had come to landing the race as a jockey was when second in 1983 on the best horse he rode, Soba. A point of interest before leaving the July Cup. In the run-up to the race hope had been expressed that American-trained pair Morluc, then Caller One might try their luck. In all honesty, hopes of having regular challengers by American horses 'to create real inter-national competition', expressed by clerk of the course Michael Prosser, are not realistic. Prosser seems to think differently: 'We'll still keep trying to entice a top American sprinter. It will happen and, once an American horse does well in this country, others will follow.' Morluc, runner-up in the 2000 and 2001 Hong Kong Sprint but smart at best, is at least a grass specialist, which puts him in a distinct minority among the leading sprinters in the States, where dirt is the predominant surface. There is little incentive to tackle an unfamiliar turf surface at Newmarket, or anywhere else. In June and July in the States and Canada there were eight Grade 2 events, three of them restricted to fillies, at up to seven furlongs. The only one on grass, the Nearctic Handicap at Woodbine, was worth 175,000 dollars to the winner, who happened to be ex-European sprinter Nuclear Debate. The True North Handicap and Triple Bend Handicap on dirt were worth 150,000 dollars and 180,000 dollars to the winner respectively, so crossing the Atlantic for the July Cup worth £145,000 makes little commerical sense, given the other drawbacks, which also include quarantine, acclimatisation and a straight course rather than a turning one.

After a perfect passage in the July Cup, Continent encountered the other extreme in the Nunthorpe Stakes at York on his next start, being forced wide to get a clear run and finishing strongly to be beaten just over a length into fourth behind Kyllachy, running close to his best form. Things did not go Continent's way when he came sixth to Invincible Spirit in the Stanley Leisure Sprint Cup at Haydock either, since he never got in a blow in a race in which the fairly steady early pace militated against those trying to come from behind. Given Continent's require-ments, a field of twenty in the Prix de l'Abbaye de Longchamp-Majestic Barriere meant there could be no guarantee of a trouble-free run. With fifteen of the runners trained outside France, including two each from Sweden and two from Italy, the race had an all-too-familiar look to it, though it lacked two of the best five-furlong specialists Kyllachy and Dominica. The former would surely have had an excellent chance had he been fit enough to take part. Continent started joint favourite with Bahamian Pirate ahead of two-year-olds Mister Links and Wunders Dream, Prix Maurice de Gheest winner May Ball and Zipping, sixth in that race and winner of the Prix de Ris-Orangis. Continent got home by the skin of his teeth in a contest in which only nine lengths or so covered the entire field at the line. Coming through late and fast under strong driving, Continent got up to beat Italian filly Slap Shot by a nose, with Zipping and Bahamian Pirate breathing down their necks in third and fourth. Continent's victory was the first by a gelding in the race since they became eligible to run in 2001. European raiders have made no impact in the Hong Kong Sprint at Sha Tin since its inception in 1999. In the first three years The Trader's fifth in 2001 was the highest placing from twelve runners, who have included Nuclear Debate (twice), Sainte Marine, Bertolini and Nice One Clare. Continent did nothing to improve this miserable record on his only start after the Abbaye, finishing last of fourteen behind All Thrills Too, beaten also by Zipping (fifth), Agnetha (eleventh) and Slap Shot (thirteenth).

Continent (ch.g. 1997)	Lake Coniston (IRE) (b 1991)	Bluebird (b 1984)	Storm Bird
			Ivory Dawn
		Persian Polly (ch 1980)	Persian Bold
			Polyester Girl
	Krisia (ch 1992)	Kris (ch 1976)	Sharpen Up
			Doubly Sure
		Interval (ch 1984)	Habitat
			Intermission

Lucayan Stud's "Continent"

Lake Coniston, the best sprinter of 1995 when he won the July Cup, retired to Coolmore Stud at IR10,000 guineas but is now based in Newmarket where he stands at £2,750, which indicates he has not been a great success. Continent and May Hill Stakes winner Karasta are his only pattern winners in Europe though he has had a Group 1 scorer in Australia. Continent does not take after his dam Krisia in stamina—she won at a mile and a half in France. Continent is her first foal and she has since foaled Risiafon (by Zafonic), successful over five and seven furlongs in France, an unraced three-year-old filly Kalanda (by Desert King), a twice-raced two-year-old Sight Screen (by Eagle Eyed) and a colt by Deploy, a mating programme which suggests she is not that high in the Juddmonte pecking order. Continent's grandam Interval, who was speedy enough to win the Prix Maurice de Gheest and also finished third in the One Thousand Guineas, has produced five other winners, notably Cheyenne Dream, successful in listed company. Continent, an angular gelding, is equally effective at five and six furlongs and acts on firm and soft ground. He has had his tongue tied and has also run well when sweating. Here's hoping he keeps up the good work as a six-year-old, when Nicholls will have a new contender for the top sprints in his yard in the shape of Captain Rio, transferred to him in the winter. *D. Nicholls*

CONTINUOUSLY (USA) 3 b.c. Diesis 133 – Play On And On (USA) (Stop The Music (USA)) [2002 95: 10.3f⁴ 10m Jun 20] quite attractive colt: useful performer: good efforts in listed races at Chester (fourth of 5 to Sohaib) and Royal Ascot (eighth to Burning Sun) in 2002: probably stays 10.3f: raced only on good ground or firmer: sent to USA. *H. R. A. Cecil* **102**

CONTRABAND 4 b.g. Red Ransom (USA) – Shortfall 103 (Last Tycoon 131) [2002 95: 13.9m⁶ 13.9m 12g² 11.9f* Oct 10] good-topped gelding: useful performer, lightly raced: made all in minor event at York in October by 2½ lengths from Team-Mate: had run well in valuable handicaps at York (sixth to Hugs Dancer in Ebor) and Ascot (2½ lengths second to Scott's View in Tote Exacta Stakes) first and third starts: stays 1¾m: yet to race on soft/heavy going, acts on any other: tends to race freely. *W. J. Haggas* **99**

CONTRACT 3 b.g. Entrepreneur 123 – Ispahan 85 (Rusticaro (FR) 124) [2002 8m⁶ 7f³ 7d⁴ 7.1d* 8m 7g Oct 18] 1,500,000 francs Y: leggy, quite attractive gelding: un-impressive mover: closely related to 3 winners by Sadler's Wells, including smart French winner up to 10.5f Cloudings, and half-brother to several winners abroad: dam 6f (at 2 yrs) and 1m (in France) winner: useful performer: won maiden at Thirsk in May and minor event at Sandown (by head from Morpheous, made all) in June: below form last 2 starts: subsequently gelded: will prove best up to 1m: acts on good to soft going. *Sir Michael Stoute* **100**

CONTRACTOR 2 gr.c. (Mar 23) Spectrum (IRE) 126 – Karsiyaka (IRE) (Kahyasi 130) [2002 6g 6m² 7pg³ 7pg* Dec 11] 24,000Y: lengthy colt: first foal: dam unraced half-sister to useful French performer up to 11f Karliyka, herself dam of useful May Hill winner Karasta: fairly useful form: twice shaped well prior to winning maiden at Ling-field by ¾ length from Wages, still seeming bit green: should stay at least 1m: capable of further improvement. *T. G. Mills* **85 p**

CONTRARIAN (IRE) 3 b.f. Mujadil (USA) 119 – Sabaniya (FR) (Lashkari 128) [2002 71: 8.3d⁴ 8d 8.3d³ Jul 19] IR 260,000Y: second foal: sister to fairly useful 2000 2-y-o 5f winner who stayed 1m Chaguaramas: dam, Irish bumper winner, half-sister to grandam of Sinndar: modest maiden: trained at 2 yrs by T. Taaffe in Ireland: stays 1m: raced only on good to soft/soft ground. *L. M. Cumani* **64**

CONTRARY MARY 7 b.m. Mujadil (USA) 119 – Love Street 62 (Mummy's Pet 125) [2002 81: 6m³ 6m* 6d² 7.1d⁶ 7d 7f 6m⁴ 7g 6.1s 7s⁶ 7v⁴ Nov 9] smallish, lightly-made mare: fairly useful performer: won claimer at Doncaster in May: effective at 6f/7f: acts on heavy and good to firm going: has got upset in preliminaries: has wandered: sometimes looks difficult ride (best held up). *J. Akehurst* **84**

CONUNDRUM (IRE) 4 ch.g. Dr Devious (IRE) 127 – Wasabi (IRE) (Polar Falcon (USA) 126) [2002 70: p10g³ 14.4f 12m f9.4s⁴ 10m* 10.1f² 10.1d² 10m³ 12d* 11.9g 12d p12g f9.4s f9.4g f12g Dec 26] fairly useful handicapper on turf, fair on all-weather: won at Leicester in June and Kempton (apprentices) in July: left P. Harris 4,000 gns after twelfth start: stays 1½m: acts on any turf going and all-weather: often tongue tied. *D. W. Chapman* **83 a63**

CONVENT GIRL (IRE) 2 b.f. (Mar 20) Bishop of Cashel 122 – Right To The Top **85**
(Nashwan (USA) 135) [2002 6s⁵ 7d⁴ 7g* 7m² 6.5m 8f⁴ Oct 14] IR 4,500Y, resold IR
8,000Y: big, leggy filly: poor walker: third foal: sister to a winner in Turkey: dam unraced
daughter of smart performer up to around 1m Aim For The Top: fairly useful performer:
won maiden at Leicester in July: best effort when 2 lengths second to Summerland in
minor event at Leicester final start: stays 1¼m: acts on firm going. *Mrs P. N. Dutfield*

CONVEX (USA) 2 b.c. (May 14) Nureyev (USA) 131 – Conical 63 (Zafonic (USA) **81**
130) [2002 5.1d² 6.1m⁴ 6m* 6m⁴ 7.1m Sep 7] neat colt: first foal: dam, maiden in Britain/
USA, half-sister to good middle-distance trio Turners Hill, Wandesta and De Quest: fairly
useful performer: refused to enter stall on intended debut: won maiden at Catterick in
July: creditable efforts in nurseries after: free-going sort, and may prove best up to 7f: yet
to race on extremes of going: visored twice, at least as effective when not: sold 32,000
gns. *Sir Michael Stoute*

CONWY CASTLE 5 b.g. Sri Pekan (USA) 117 – Dumayla 78 (Shernazar 131) [2002 **–**
81: 18s Mar 22] leggy gelding: fairly useful in 2001: tailed off only 5-y-o start: dead.
Mrs S. Lamyman

COODEN BEACH (IRE) 2 b.f. (Mar 26) Peintre Celebre (USA) 137 – Joyful (IRE) **– p**
71 (Green Desert (USA) 127) [2002 7.1m 7g p7g Oct 31] IR 110,000Y: leggy filly: third
foal: dam, Irish 7f winner, half-sister to high-class performer up to 1m Golden Opinion
out of Musidora/Nassau Stakes winner Optimistic Lass: signs of ability, though well held,
in maidens: likely to do better at 1m+. *M. L. W. Bell*

COOKIE CRUMBLE 4 b.f. Never So Bold 135 – Well Tried (IRE) 43 (Thatching **–**
131) [2002 58d: f6g f8.5g f8.5g Feb 25] angular filly: unimpressive mover: modest
performer at 3 yrs: no form in 2002: blinkered final start. *D. McCain*

COOL ALIBI 2 b.f. (Apr 5) Distinctly North (USA) 115 – Alis Princess (Sayf El Arab **–**
(USA) 127) [2002 7d 5g 5g Sep 18] third foal: dam well beaten both starts: well beaten in
maidens. *J. F. Coupland*

COOL BART 2 ch.g. (Mar 5) Cool Jazz 116 – Margaretrose Anna 58 (Handsome **–**
Sailor 125) [2002 6d 6.1m f7g Sep 21] 1,600Y: lengthy, rather unfurnished gelding: first
foal: dam, maiden who stayed 7f, out of half-sister to high-class Irish 1¼m performer
Timarida: tailed off in maidens/seller: tried visored. *B. P. J. Baugh*

COOL BATHWICK (IRE) 3 b.c. Entrepreneur 123 – Tarafa 93 (Akarad (FR) 130) **79**
[2002 79?: 12f³ 12g 10.9g² 14d 16.2m 11.7d² 12m⁵ 11.9g p16g p12g f12g Dec 27] **a67**
useful-looking colt: fair maiden handicapper: stays 1½m: acts on firm and good to soft
going: folded tamely penultimate start. *E. J. O'Neill*

COOLBYTHEPOOL 2 b.c. (May 9) Bijou d'Inde 127 – Alchi (USA) 112 (Alleged **–**
(USA) 138) [2002 7.2g 7.2s 7s f7g Dec 9] workmanlike colt: half-brother to 10-y-o
Pickens and 3 winners in USA: dam French 2-y-o 1m winner and third in Prix Marcel
Boussac: only a little sign of ability. *M. Johnston*

COOL CHRON 3 b.f. Polar Falcon (USA) 126 – Lough Graney (Sallust 134) [2002 **48**
46: 10d 9.9g⁵ 8d⁵ 7.5m 8s* 7.1d⁵ 10m Aug 31] rather leggy, good-topped filly: poor
performer: won claimer at Leicester in July: stays 1m: acts on soft going and fibresand.
N. Tinkler

COOL COUSIN (IRE) 4 b.f. Distant Relative 128 – Nordic Dance (USA) (Graustark) **93**
[2002 74: 6s⁵ 7s³ 7s² 6s 7g⁴ 7s 7g* 6g⁸ 7d 6g 6d² 7d 6s⁴ 7v Nov 10] half-sister to 3
winners, including fairly useful 2-y-o 5f winner Celestial Heights (by Storm Bird): dam
unraced from good family: fairly useful handicapper: much improved when winning at
Tipperary and the Curragh in July: stiff task when well held in Ayr Gold Cup tenth start:
effective at 6f/7f: raced mainly on good going or softer (acts on heavy, ran respectably
once on good to firm): blinkered twice. *M. Halford, Ireland*

COOLERS QUEST 3 b.f. Saddlers' Hall (IRE) 126 – Lucidity 67 (Vision (USA)) **–**
[2002 –: 9m p12g Sep 4] no form. *P. C. Ritchens*

COOLING CASTLE (FR) 6 ch.g. Sanglamore (USA) 126 – Syphaly (USA) (Lyph- **–**
ard (USA) 132) [2002 –: 12g Oct 19] fair 1¼m winner at 3 yrs: lightly raced and no form
since. *Ronald Thompson*

COOLING OFF (IRE) 5 b.m. Brief Truce (USA) 126 – Lovers' Parlour 83 (Beldale **62 §**
Flutter (USA) 130) [2002 77i p12g f16g 12m⁵ 13.1g 11.9g Oct 24] good topped mare:
modest maiden: probably stays 1¾m: acts on heavy and good to firm ground: tried
blinkered/visored: unreliable. *J. R. Jenkins*

COOL QUESTION 2 b.f. (Jan 31) Polar Falcon (USA) 126 – Quiz Time 90 (Efisio **99**
120) [2002 f5g* 5.2f* 6d* 6g⁶ 6m Oct 5] small, close-coupled filly: third foal: half-sister
to a winner up to 9f in Spain by Pursuit of Love: dam, 2-y-o 5f winner, half-sister to useful
1¼m performer Brockette: useful performer: won maiden at Wolverhampton and minor
event at Yarmouth in July and listed race at Ripon (beat Harb by ½ length) in August:
below form in listed race at Ayr (on toes) and Two-Year-Old Trophy at Redcar last 2
starts: effective at 5f/6f: acted on fibresand, firm and good to soft ground: game: stud. *Sir
Mark Prescott*

COOL SINGER 4 b.g. Sea Raven (IRE) 75 – Clean Singer 42 (Chief Singer 131) **53**
[2002 55: 7.5g⁵ 8.1m 7.1d³ 8.3v 9m 7.5m f6g Dec 27] close-coupled, quite good-topped
gelding: modest maiden handicapper: stays 1m: acts on fibresand and good to soft going:
has been early to post. *Jedd O'Keeffe*

COOL SPICE 5 b.m. Karinga Bay 116 – Cool Run 87 (Deep Run 119) [2002 79: **89**
13.8d 11.6g³ 11.7g⁴ 11.7g* 13.1g³ 12.1d* 12g³ 11.8g² 11.8d² 11.9g 13.1g⁴ 11.6m⁶ Oct 7]
good-bodied mare: fairly useful handicapper: won at Bath in May and Chepstow in June:
stays 13f: acts on soft and good to firm going: has raced freely/drifted left: consistent.
B. Pulling

COOL TEMPER 6 b.g. Magic Ring (IRE) 115 – Ovideo 58 (Domynsky 110) [2002 **62**
73, a82: f7g³ f9.4g f8g* 8f 7g 7m 9d 8g³ 9d Aug 23] sturdy gelding: fairly useful handi- **a85**
capper on all-weather, modest on turf: won at Southwell in March: stays easy 1¼m: acts
on fibresand and probably any turf going: has been tongue tied. *J. M. P. Eustace*

COOL TUNE 3 b.g. Piccolo 121 – Agony Aunt 81 (Formidable (USA) 125) [2002 **92**
69p: 5g⁴ 7g f6g* Sep 21] fairly useful form: won handicap at Wolverhampton very
easily in September: may prove best at 5f/6f: acts on fibresand, raced only on good/
good to soft going on turf: sent to Hong Kong, where renamed Epic Enterprise.
J. R. Fanshawe

COOZINHA (IRE) 2 b.f. (Mar 15) Lake Coniston (IRE) 131 – Desert Palace (Green –
Desert (USA) 127) [2002 5.1d 5d⁴ 5m Aug 18] IR 5,500Y: half-sister to 1998 2-y-o 5f
winner Principality and 7f winner Sahara Spirit, both fairly useful and by College Chapel:
dam Irish 5f winner: only a little sign of ability in maidens/minor event. *J. A. Glover*

COPCOURT ROYALE 4 b.f. Rock City 120 – Royal Meeting 44 (Dara Monarch –
128) [2002 –: f9.4g 10g f12g f14.8g Oct 21] modest at 2 yrs: no form since: tried visored.
P. L. Clinton

COPLEY PLACE 2 b.f. (Feb 12) Piccolo 121 – Bangles 83 (Chilibang 120) [2002 5g –
5m Aug 28] good-topped filly: has scope: third foal: dam 5f winner: well beaten in
maidens. *John A. Harris*

COPPERFIELDS LASS 3 b.f. Millkom 124 – Salvezza (IRE) 97 (Superpower 113) **63**
[2002 51p: 8.3m 8.2m⁵ 7d⁵ 8s 7.9m⁴ 8m 8m Sep 19] modest maiden handicapper: should
be suited by 1¼m: acts on good to firm and good to soft ground. *Mrs Lydia Pearce*

COPPERMALT (USA) 4 b.g. Affirmed (USA) – Poppy Carew (IRE) 110 (Danehill **71**
(USA) 126) [2002 73: 10f 10s 10.2v 8.3v Aug 14] fair maiden: barely stays 1¼m: acts on
firm ground, possibly not soft/heavy: has been reluctant at stall: free-going sort: sold
2,500 gns. *P. W. Harris*

COPPINGTON FLYER (IRE) 2 ch.f. (Mar 27) Eagle Eyed (USA) 111 – Miss Flite **73**
(IRE) (Law Society (USA) 130) [2002 5g 5m 6f⁶ 6g⁵ 6s⁴ 7m 6.1m 7g³ 7s 7m 6.1m 6f⁴ 6f² **a57**
f6g⁵ f6f f7g⁵ f7g² f6g p7g⁵ Dec 28] smallish, strong filly: fifth foal: half-sister to 2
winners by Balla Cove, including Irish 1½m winner Dunbrody Cove: dam unraced: fair
maiden: second in nurseries: effective at 6f/7f: acts on firm ground and all-weather.
B. W. Duke

COPPLESTONE (IRE) 6 b.g. Second Set (IRE) 127 – Queen of The Brush (Averof **64 d**
123) [2002 68§, a–§: 12.3g⁵ 13s 12.4m* 13.8m⁶ 13.1g⁴ 12g 16m² 14.1s⁶ 14.4g⁶ 10.1m
16.1d⁶ 16m 14.1m 12g Oct 19] tall gelding: modest handicapper at best in 2002: won
selling event at Newcastle in May: stays 2m: acts on fibresand, firm and good to soft
going: tried visored/tongue tied: not to be trusted. *W. Storey*

COPYBOOK 3 b.c. Danehill (USA) 126 – Easy To Copy (USA) 108 (Affirmed (USA)) **59**
[2002 8f 8f 10d 10.1m⁵ 12m Aug 24] 40,000Y: angular, good-topped colt: closely related
to fairly useful Irish 1996 2 y o 6f winner Desert Ease (by Green Desert) and 4-y-o Lord
Dundee, and half-brother to several winners, notably smart Irish 7f to 1¼m performer
Two-Twenty-Two (by Fairy King): dam, Irish 1m (at 2 yrs) to 1½m winner, sister to Irish

1000 Guineas winner Trusted Partner: modest maiden: stays 1¼m: unseated and ran loose to post before debut: sold 4,500 gns in October. *H. R. A. Cecil*

COPY-CAT 4 b.f. Lion Cavern (USA) 117 – Imperial Jade 105 (Lochnager 132) [2002   **47**
–: 5.3d⁵ 5.3m Jun 25] poor maiden: bred to be best at 5f/6f: sometimes slowly away.
D. R. C. Elsworth

COPYFORCE GIRL 6 b.m. Elmaamul (USA) 125 – Sabaya (USA) 92 (Seattle   **–**
Dancer (USA) 119) [2002 69, a57: f14.8g⁵ Jan 18] angular mare: fair handicapper on turf,
modest on all-weather at 5 yrs: well held only 6-y-o start: tried blinkered: usually tongue
tied. *D. Burchell*

COQUELLES (FR) 6 b.m. In The Wings 128 – La Toja (FR) (Gift Card (FR) 124)   **–**
[2002 10s May 13] ex-French mare: well held in 3 minor events in Britain. *R. M. Stronge*

COQUETRY (USA) 2 b.f. (Jan 27) Distant View (USA) 126 – Souplesse (USA)   **88**
(Majestic Light (USA)) [2002 6d² 6m⁴ 5m* 5m Sep 14] leggy, quite attractive filly: fifth
foal: half-sister to 3-y-o Comfy and a 1m winner in USA by Cox's Ridge: dam, useful
French 1¼m winner, half-sister to smart performer in Britain/USA up to 1½m Eltish from
family of 1000 Guineas winner Wince: fairly useful form: landed odds in maiden at
Haydock in September by 5 lengths: well held in Flying Childers Stakes at Doncaster
next time: effective at 5f/6f: unraced on extremes of going. *Sir Michael Stoute*

CORACLE KING 2 b.g. (Apr 19) Compton Place 125 – Dicentra (Rambo Dancer   **74**
(CAN) 107) [2002 6m² 7g⁵ 7m⁴ 6m⁵ 6g³ 6m⁴ 7g⁵ 6f⁵ f6g⁶ Oct 22] 3,000Y, 17,000 2-y-o:
quite good-topped gelding: second foal: dam lightly-raced half-sister to smart French
middle-distance performer Darine: fair maiden: effective at 6f/easy 7f: raced only on
good going or firmer on turf, below form on fibresand: free-going sort: consistent.
J. J. Quinn

CORANGLAIS 2 ch.g. (Jan 25) Piccolo 121 – Antonia's Folly 64 (Music Boy 124)   **79**
[2002 6f 5d³ 5m³ Jun 14] 23,000Y: compact gelding: good walker: fifth foal: half-brother
to 2-y-o 5f winners Zaragossa (fairly useful in 1998, by Paris House), Antonia's Dilemma
(in 2000, by Primo Dominie) and 3-y-o Bond Domingo: dam 2-y-o 5f winner: fair
maiden: edgy, best effort when ¾-length third to Maugwenna at York final start: subsequently gelded: will prove best at 5f/6f: acts on good to firm and good to soft ground.
T. D. Easterby

CORBEL (USA) 2 b.f. (Jan 29) Diesis 133 – Corsini 88 (Machiavellian (USA) 123)   **77**
[2002 6f² 6d³ Oct 18] angular filly: first foal: dam, 2-y-o 7f winner, out of half-sister to
dam of Eclipse winner Elmaamul (by Diesis): fairly useful form when short-headed by
Rondinay in maiden at Newmarket: evens, only third in similar event at Redcar: should
stay at least 1m. *Sir Michael Stoute*

CORDIAL (IRE) 2 gr.c. (May 10) Charnwood Forest (IRE) 125 – Moon Festival 74   **56 p**
(Be My Guest (USA) 126) [2002 f6g⁶ p7g 7g 7g 7g Oct 24] IR 40,000Y: half-brother to
several winners, including smart Irish 1m/1¼m winner Sita (by Indian Ridge) and
3-y-o Tikkun: dam, maiden who stayed 1¼m, half-sister to high-class middle-distance
performers Sheriff's Star and Moon Madness: mid-field in maidens, not knocked about:
will stay at least 1m: type to do fair bit better in handicaps at 3 yrs. *Sir Mark Prescott*

CORISA (IRE) 2 ch.f. (Apr 6) Be My Guest (USA) 126 – Unalaska (IRE) 65 (High   **–**
Estate 127) [2002 7g Oct 14] IR 4,000Y: smallish filly: unimpressive mover: fourth foal:
half-sister to 3-y-o Only Penang: dam, ran twice in Ireland, half-sister to useful 1989
2-y-o sprinter Makbul: 40/1, soundly beaten in maiden at Leicester. *B. R. Millman*

CORK HARBOUR (FR) 6 ch.g. Grand Lodge (USA) 125 – Irish Sea 66 (Irish River   **81**
(FR) 131) [2002 85: p8g² p8g⁴ p8g 8d 7d 6d 7.6s³ 8g Oct 17] fairly useful handicapper:
best at 7f/1m: acts on polytrack, best on going softer than good on turf: usually blinkered,
visored final start: races prominently: sold 7,500 gns and joined P. Bowen. *Mrs N. Smith*

CORMORANT WHARF (IRE) 2 b.c. (Mar 1) Alzao (USA) 117 – Mercy Bien   **79 p**
(IRE) 63 (Be My Guest (USA) 126) [2002 6m* 6.1s⁶ Oct 23] 13,500F, 10,000Y: fifth
foal, placed at 7f and 1¼m in Ireland, half-sister to smart 7f performer Arjuzah,
herself dam of 4-y-o Malhub: fair form: favourite, overcame greenness to win 16-runner
maiden at Windsor in October by head from Lago d'Orta: sixth to Cashel Mead in minor
event at Nottingham later in month: should stay at least 7f: remains open to improvement.
P. J. Makin

CORNELIAN PRINCE 5 b.g. Sri Pekan (USA) 117 – Silent Girl 75 (Krayyan 117)   **–**
[2002 –: 11.9s Jun 6] tall, lengthy gelding: no form. *A. Senior*

Letherby & Christopher Predominate Stakes, Goodwood—
the ill-fated Coshocton takes advantage of the weight concession from Dubai Destination;
visored Frankies Dream and Highdown make the frame

CORNELIUS 5 b.g. Barathea (IRE) 127 – Rainbow Mountain 71 (Rainbow Quest **115**
(USA) 134) [2002 112: 8s⁴ 8g³ 8m² 8m* 8v³ 8d Nov 17] tall, good-topped gelding: has
an unimpressive, rather round action: smart performer: good 2 lengths second to Keltos
in Prix du Muguet at Saint-Cloud before winning Premio Emilio Turati at Milan in May
by 2½ lengths from Stephant: below best last 2 starts: effective at 1m/1¼m:
acts on good to firm going and heavy ground: has been bandaged behind: usually races
prominently: tends to carry head high. *P. F. I. Cole*

CORRIDOR CREEPER (FR) 5 ch.g. Polish Precedent (USA) 131 – Sonia Rose **91**
(USA) (Superbity (USA)) [2002 92: 5f 5f* 5.1f³ 5f⁶ 6m 5m 5g⁵ 5.2f 5m⁴ 5m 5.2m² 5.1f*
5g 5v Nov 8] useful-looking gelding: fairly useful handicapper: won at Thirsk in May and
Chester in September: effective at 5f/6f: has won on good to soft going, best form on good
or firmer: blinkered once at 3 yrs: tongue tied twice: sometimes finds little. *J. M. Bradley*

CORSICAN SUNSET (USA) 4 b.f. Thunder Gulch (USA) 129 – Miss Evans (USA) **101**
(Nijinsky (CAN) 138) [2002 102: 10d 10.4f³ 12f 10.1g⁶ 10.2g 12d 11.9m⁶ 13.4f⁶ 12d
Nov 2] good-topped filly: useful performer: creditable efforts in 2002 only on second/
third starts, third to Jalousie in listed race at York on former: effective at 1¼m/1½m: yet
to race on heavy going, acts on any other: blinkered fifth outing. *P. F. I. Cole*

CORTON (IRE) 3 b. or gr.g. Definite Article 121 – Limpopo 49 (Green Desert (USA) **–**
127) [2002 88: 8g 12v Nov 9] strong gelding: fairly useful performer at 2 yrs: fell after
clipping another horse on reappearance, never dangerous only start after (nearly 7 months
later): not sure to stay beyond 1m: acts on good to firm going: hung markedly left/carried
head high second start at 2 yrs. *P. F. I. Cole*

CORUNDUM (USA) 3 b. or br.g. Benny The Dip (USA) 127 – Santi Sana 80 (Form- **58**
idable (USA) 125) [2002 76: 10m 6.9g 10m p12g⁴ p16g 11.5m p12g Oct 4] good-bodied
gelding: modest maiden: seems to stay 2m: acts on firm ground and polytrack: tongue
tied last 4 outings. *D. E. Cantillon*

CORUNNA 5 b.g. Puissance 110 – Kind of Shy 61 (Kind of Hush 118) [2002 81: 7f **66 d**
7.6f 6.1f⁴ 7f 7f 6m 7g 6.1m 6d 7m 7m³ 7.1g p8g⁵ p7g⁵ f8.5g Nov 18] tall, rather leggy
gelding: has a quick action: fair performer: on downgrade in 2002: seems to stay 1m: acts
on polytrack, raced mainly on good ground or firmer on turf: tried blinkered: sold 1,800
gns. *A. Berry*

COSHOCTON (USA) 3 b.c. Silver Hawk (USA) 123 – Tribulation (USA) 118 **116**
(Danzig (USA)) [2002 103p: 8m 11g* 12d Jun 8] strong, attractive colt: smart performer:
behind in 2000 Guineas at Newmarket on reappearance, then won listed race at Goodwood in May by 2 lengths from Dubai Destination (who gave 6 lb), making all: well-held
fifth and tiring when falling fatally near finish in Derby at Epsom: stayed 11f: unraced on
extremes of going: free-going sort. *M. A. Jarvis*

COSI FAN TUTTE 4 b.g. Inchinor 119 – Bumpkin 108 (Free State 125) [2002 9.2s² **85**
9.2g³ 8d² 9.9m⁵ 12s² 12.4m² p12g⁵ 8.9m⁴ 10m* 11.9f Oct 10] strong, lengthy gelding:
fairly useful handicapper: won at Nottingham in October: stays 1½m: acts on soft and

good to firm ground: blinkered (claimed from B. Hanbury £15,000) eighth start, visored last 2. *M. C. Pipe*

COSMIC CASE 7 b.m. Casteddu 111 – La Fontainova (IRE) (Lafontaine (USA) 117) **62** [2002 66: 16g 14m² 12m⁴ 13g⁴ 12m³ 16m 12.1v⁶ 12g³ 12m⁵ 14.6m³ 14d⁵ 12g⁵ 14.4g³ 12.1m* 14.1m⁵ 13.8d Nov 5] angular mare: modest handicapper: won at Hamilton in September: has won at 2m, best form at 1½m/1¾m: acts on any going: tried visored earlier in career: usually held up: tough. *J. S. Goldie*

COSMIC MILLENNIUM (IRE) 4 b.g. In The Wings 128 – Windmill Princess 55 **77 §** (Gorytus (USA) 132) [2002 85: 7m 8d⁵ 10m⁴ 7m² 7f 7g* 7m 8g 8g 7m⁶ 7.1m 8.1f³ 7f f8g 7.5s⁶ Dec 30] quite attractive gelding: fair handicapper: won at Yarmouth in July: sold from R. Guest 8,000 gns before final start: probably acts on firm going: visored (started slowly) once, often blinkered nowadays: free-going sort: unreliable. *F. Beluschi, Italy*

COSMIC RANGER 4 b.g. Magic Ring (IRE) 115 – Lismore 61 (Relkino 131) [2002 **–** 44: p12g f12s f14.8g⁵ Feb 2] leggy, useful-looking gelding: maiden: no form in 2002: visored once. *N. P. Littmoden*

COSMIC SONG 5 b.m. Cosmonaut – Hotaria 68 (Sizzling Melody 117) [2002 43: **45** 7m 10m 8g⁴ 10m* 8.5g 10f Sep 26] big mare: poor performer: won seller at Ripon in July: stays 1¼m: acts on good to firm and good to soft going: has given trouble in preliminaries (early to post nowadays): has carried head high: none too consistent. *R. M. Whitaker*

COSMOCRAT 4 b.g. Cosmonaut – Bella Coola 50 (Northern State (USA) 91) [2002 **65 +** 81: 10s 10.2g⁴ Oct 16] fairly useful at 3 yrs: just fair form both 4-y-o outings (slowly away final one): should stay 1¼m: goes well on soft ground. *C. G. Cox*

COSMO (IRE) 2 b.c. (Apr 6) Turtle Island (IRE) 123 – Ewan (IRE) (Indian Ridge **99** 123) [2002 6s² 6m* 6g² Aug 24] IR 16,000Y: close-coupled, good-topped colt: second foal: dam unraced out of half-sister to smart sprinter Ya Malak: useful form: best effort when winning 7-runner event at Salisbury in June by ½ length from Tout Seul (pair clear), quickening well: 1½ lengths second of 25 to same horse in sales race at the Curragh 2 months later: stays 6f: acts on soft and good to firm going. *R. Hannon*

COTEBROOK 3 ch.g. First Trump 118 – Chantelys 52 (Ballacashtal (CAN)) [2002 **65** 64: 9.9m 12.1g⁶ 12.1g⁵ 12f⁵ 14.1s⁴ 12m 16m f8g⁶ f8g Dec 10] angular gelding: fair **a53** maiden handicapper: barely stays 1¾m: acts on soft going and fibresand: sometimes races freely. *J. M. Jefferson*

COTE SOLEIL 5 ch.g. Inchinor 119 – Sunshine Coast 86 (Posse (USA) 130) [2002 **65** 70: 8m 9.3g 9f 9g* 8m² 8.5d* 8g 9.1d⁵ 9m⁵ 9d Oct 18] smallish gelding: fair handicapper: won at Musselburgh in June and Epsom in July: probably best at 1m/9f: acts on any going: tried blinkered/visored: races prominently. *M. L. W. Bell*

COTOPAXI (IRE) 6 b.g. Turtle Island (IRE) 123 – Ullapool (Dominion 123) [2002 **79** 9s² 13.3f⁵ 16.2g² Sep 28] half-brother to several winners, including fairly useful winner up to 1½m Mad Militant (by Vision): dam unraced: fair performer: won 2 claimers at 3 yrs: missed 2001 season: left M. Cunningham (Ireland) after reappearance: stays 2m: acts on any going: sometimes blinkered: tried tongue tied: fairly useful hurdler. *Miss Venetia Williams*

COTTAM GRANGE 2 b.c. (Apr 21) River Falls 113 – Karminski 70 (Pitskelly 122) **60** [2002 6m 7d Oct 18] 5,000Y: unfurnished colt: half-brother to a winner in Norway by Blazing Saddles: dam middle-distance stayer: better effort 4 months apart (modest form) when eighth to Janes Gem in claimer at Redcar second start: likely to be suited by at least 1m: started very slowly on debut. *M. W. Easterby*

COTTAM LILLY 5 b.m. Sabrehill (USA) 120 – Karminski 70 (Pitskelly 122) [2002 **–** 36: 11.9s 11.9s f16m Jun 19] angular mare: maiden: no form in 2002. *J. S. Wainwright*

COTTON HOUSE (IRE) 5 b.m. Mujadil (USA) 119 – Romanovna (Mummy's Pet **101** 125) [2002 107: p6g* a5f a6f 5.5d 6m 6m* 6g 6s 6d Nov 17] lengthy, useful-looking mare: unimpressive mover: useful performer: won minor event at Lingfield in January and listed race at Pontefract (beat Vita Spericolata by neck, overcame slow start and being short of room 2f out) in August: below form last 3 starts: stays 6f: acts on any turf going and polytrack: none too consistent. *M. R. Channon*

COUAL CRYSTAL 3 b.f. Cool Jazz 116 – Indian Crystal 66 (Petong 126) [2002 54: **–** 8.2f May 17] small filly: modest maiden: was usually visored: dead. *J. R. Norton*

COUGHLAN'S GIFT   6 ch.m. Alnasr Alwasheek 117 – Superfrost 49 (Tickled Pink   –
114) [2002 62, a55+: p13g⁵ f11s Jan 22] smallish mare: modest handicapper: probably   **a54**
stays 13f: has form on polytrack and good to firm ground, goes well on soft/heavy:
blinkered (very slowly away) final start: usually claimer ridden: has hung. *J. C. Fox*

COUNSEL'S OPINION (IRE)   5 ch.g. Rudimentary (USA) 118 – Fairy Fortune 78   **101**
(Rainbow Quest (USA) 134) [2002 88: 10m 10g⁵ 10.1d² 12g³ 11.9d⁴ 10m³ 10.3m* 12g
Oct 17] big gelding: useful performer: good efforts in frame in handicaps at Epsom,
Royal Ascot (third to Thundering Surf in Duke of Edinburgh Stakes), Haydock (fourth to
Sun Bird in Old Newton Cup) and Sandown prior to winning minor event at Doncaster
in September by 1½ lengths from Chai Walla, idling: effective at 9f to 1½m: acts on
fibresand, soft and good to firm (well beaten only start on firm) going: sometimes early to
post: tends to race freely: reliable. *C. F. Wall*

COUNT CALYPSO   4 ch.g. King's Signet (USA) 110 – Atlantic Air (Air Trooper   –
115) [2002 65, a82: f6g f7g 6.1m May 10] sturdy, close-coupled gelding: poor walker:
fairly useful handicapper on all-weather, fair on turf at 3 yrs: ran as if something amiss in
2002. *D. J. Coakley*

COUNT COUGAR (USA)   2 b.g. (Jan 8) Sir Cat (USA) 118 – Gold Script (USA)   **73**
(Seeking The Gold (USA)) [2002 5s⁴ 6d⁴ 5g² 5m 7g Sep 7] $10,000Y, resold 3,200Y:
sturdy gelding: poor walker and mover: first foal: dam unraced: fair maiden: best efforts
at 5f: acts on soft ground, probably on good to firm. *T. D. Barron*

COUNT DAVANTI   3 b.c. Puissance 110 – I'm Playing (Primo Dominie 121) [2002   –
5g 7g Oct 14] 1,600Y: sparely-made colt: first foal: dam no worthwhile form: last in
maidens at Leicester (pulled very hard second outing). *M. Mullineaux*

COUNT DE MONEY (IRE)   7 b.g. Last Tycoon 131 – Menominee (Soviet Star   **45**
(USA) 128) [2002 f12g⁵ f16.2g f12g f14.8g May 24] smallish, sturdy gelding: poor form
at 7 yrs: blinkered final start. *Miss S. J. Wilton*

COUNTESS ELTON (IRE)   2 ch.f. (Apr 29) Mukaddamah (USA) 125 – Be Prepared   **57 §**
(IRE) (Be My Guest (USA) 126) [2002 5g 5m 6m 7f f8.5g⁴ 8.2v* f8.5g f7g f7g Dec 17]   **a41 §**
2,800 2-y-o: tall, leggy filly: third live foal: half-sister to 4-y-o Look First: dam unraced:
modest on turf, poor on all-weather: won seller at Nottingham in October: stays 1m: acts
on heavy ground and fibresand: difficult ride: unreliable. *K. A. Ryan*

COUNTESS GUEST (IRE)   2 b.f. (Feb 18) Spectrum (IRE) 126 – Russian Countess   **59**
(USA) 104 (Nureyev (USA) 131) [2002 5.1g⁴ 7m 6m 7g Oct 4] 160,000Y: half-sister to
several winners, including smart 7f (at 2 yrs) and 11.5f winner Crown of Light (by Mtoto)
and useful 7f (at 2 yrs) to 9f winner Alboostan (by Sabrehill): dam French 2-y-o 1m
winner: modest maiden: well held in nursery final start: bred to stay 1m, but races freely.
M. R. Channon

COUNTESS MILETRIAN (IRE)   3 b.f. Barathea (IRE) 127 – Sweet Alma 67   **86**
(Alzao (USA) 117) [2002 10g 11.1s³ 9.9m 8s⁶ 10.1g⁵ 10d³ 10f⁶ 10m* 10g⁵ 10.1m³
10.1m² 8f² 8m² 10f⁵ 10.3s p10g⁴ Nov 13] IR 21,000F, IR 120,000Y: smallish, workmanlike filly: seventh foal: half-sister to fairly useful Irish 1996 2-y-o 6f winner Mubadara
(by Lahib) and a winner (including at 2 yrs) in Turkey by Marju: dam, Irish 1¼m winner,
half-sister to high-class 1m/1¼m performer Montekin: fairly useful performer: won
handicap at Newbury in August: stays 1¼m: unraced on heavy going, acts on any other
turf and polytrack. *M. R. Channon*

COUNT ON US   2 ch.c. (Feb 18) Danehill Dancer (IRE) 117 – Capricious Lady (IRE)   –
(Capricorn Line 111) [2002 7m⁶ 8s p6g Dec 18] fifth foal: half-brother to 1996 2-y-o 7f
winner Buzzby (by Buzzards Bay) and a winner in Italy by Beveled: dam in frame in
bumpers: well held in minor events/maiden. *A. Charlton*

COUNTRY REEL (USA)   2 b.c. (Feb 1) Danzig (USA) – Country Belle (USA)   **109**
108 (Seattle Slew (USA)) [2002 6d* 6g* 6f⁴ Oct 3]
          David Loder took the racing world by surprise in December when announc-
ing that he is to hand in his licence at the end of 2003, partly because he no longer
has 'the same enthusiasm for training as when I started.' Loder's spell in charge of
the Godolphin 'academy', bringing along the pick of the Maktoum family's two-
year-olds, has not been an unqualified success. Two relatively disappointing years
at Evry in France resulted in the stable's relocation to Newmarket for the 2001
season which yielded thirty individual two-year-old winners and a ratio of winners
to runners approaching forty per cent. That wasn't repeated in the latest season
when, of Godolphin Stables' hundred or so blue-blooded juveniles, including

Scottish Equitable Gimcrack Stakes, York—Country Reel makes a quick and successful transition to pattern company, inflicting the first defeat on Mister Links; Membership (rail), Revenue and Fiddlers Reach follow them home

choice lots from the previous year's Keeneland, Saratoga and Newmarket sales, only ten managed to win a race. They recorded a mere fourteen wins between them, all in Britain, Dublin being the stable's only runner abroad, in the National Stakes at the Curragh. The stable made a very slow start and didn't send out its first winner until June 21st—it had no runners at Royal Ascot—and, even more worryingly for 2003, had a disappointing autumn by the standards expected. Champagne Stakes winner Almushahar and Lingfield maiden winner Dubai Lightning were the only successes after August when runners from the stable became few and far between. Around two-thirds of the string never saw a racecourse and, judged by the numbers removed from the Godolphin website in the winter, some of them probably never will.

Loder said in an interview at the start of the season that his 2002 intake was 'the nicest group of horses I have been lucky enough to train in my role with Godolphin. I would like to think that augurs well for the future when they move on to the senior team.' One horse picked out by Loder in that interview was Country Reel who came close to fulfilling Loder's ideal template for a Godolphin juvenile —'three runs, giving the horse a chance to run in a better race, assuming it has won its first two, with plenty left in the tank for a three-year-old career.' Country Reel did win his first two, landing the odds in a maiden at Newmarket in early-August, a highly promising start which led to his being stepped up to pattern company straight away in the Scottish Equitable Gimcrack at York later in the month. It wasn't a vintage renewal but Country Reel justified favouritism, after showing reluctance at the stalls, and his victory from Mister Links, Membership and Revenue, all more experienced, represented useful form. Sprinting looked to be Country Reel's game and he had his third outing in the Middle Park at Newmarket in October. In a strong line-up, Country Reel needed to step up a fair bit on his Gimcrack form and couldn't manage it. Fourth of ten to Oasis Dream, beaten just over five lengths by the winner, represented Country Reel's best effort and he lost no caste in defeat.

The strong, lengthy Country Reel, a fluent mover, was bred by Maktoum Al Maktoum's Gainsborough Farm on similar lines to Anabaa, who developed into a champion sprinter as a four-year-old after being given away by Sheikh Maktoum when written off as a two-year-old with a spinal injury. Like Anabaa, Country Reel is by Danzig, a strong influence for speed (he has sired six July Cup winners); Country Reel is the first foal of Country Belle, a French mile winner (including a listed race and also third in the Group 3 Prix de la Grotte) out of Anabaa's dam, the very smart racemare Balbonella. Balbonella won the Prix Robert Papin and was successful at seven furlongs as a three-year-old before winning another four races in the States as a four-year-old (including the Grade 3 Dahlia Handicap over eight

Maktoum Al Maktoum's "Country Reel"

			Northern Dancer	Nearctic
	Danzig (USA)		(b 1961)	Natalma
	(b 1977)		Pas de Nom	Admiral's Voyage
Country Reel (USA)			(b or br 1968)	Petitioner
(b.c. Feb 1, 2000)			Seattle Slew	Bold Reasoning
	Country Belle (USA)		(b or br 1974)	My Charmer
	(b 1995)		Balbonella	Gay Mecene
			(b or br 1984)	Bamieres

and a half furlongs). Balbonella has bred two other pattern winners, Always Loyal (by Zilzal), successful in Maktoum Al Maktoum's colours in the Poule d'Essai des Pouliches, and the high-class mile-and-a-quarter performer Key of Luck (by a son of Danzig, Chief's Crown). Anabaa won at up to a mile as a three-year-old. That trip may prove within the compass of Country Reel at three, though, like Anabaa, he looks more likely at this stage to make a name for himself at shorter. *D. R. Loder*

COUNTRYWIDE DANCER (IRE) 2 b.f. (Apr 12) Danehill Dancer (IRE) 117 – **61**
Meadow Grass (IRE) (Thatching 131) [2002 5f⁶ 5g⁵ 6.1g 5m 5.1f⁶ 5d* 5d⁵ 6m 6.1m 5m 6f f5g⁴ f6g Oct 19] IR 9,000Y: tall, useful-looking filly: fourth foal: half-sister to Italian 9f/1¼m winner Il Sogno (by Catrail): dam ran 3 times: modest performer: won claimer at Beverley in July, carrying head awkwardly: below form after: should stay 6f: acts on good to soft going, seemingly on firm: tried blinkered: sold 1,500 gns. *A. Berry*

COUNTRYWIDE GIRL (IRE) 3 ch.f. Catrail (USA) 123 – Polish Saga 59 (Polish **–**
Patriot (USA) 128) [2002 67, a–: f6g⁴ 5.1d 6g 6s 6.9s 5.9g 7d Aug 11] leggy, quite good-topped filly: fair at 2 yrs: little form in 2002. *A. Berry*

COUNTRYWIDE PRIDE (IRE) 4 ch.g. Eagle Eyed (USA) 111 – Lady's Dream **–**
85 (Mazilier (USA) 107) [2002 66d: p8g p8g Feb 9] fair maiden at best, possibly temperamental: well held both 4-y-o starts: visored once. *K. R. Burke*

COUNTRYWIDE STAR (IRE) 4 ch.g. Common Grounds 118 – Silver Slipper 67 **54**
(Indian Ridge 123) [2002 70: f7s² f8s f8g⁴ f8g f7g 8.2m Apr 16] sturdy gelding: has a
round action: modest performer: barely stays 1m: acts on all-weather, heavy and good to
firm ground: tried visored. *J. G. Given*

COUNT TALLAHASSEE 5 ch.g. Dervish – Give Me An Answer (True Song 95) –
[2002 10m Apr 27] second foal: dam winning hurdler: well held in bumpers/over jumps/
in seller. *J. Parkes*

COUNT WALEWSKI 2 b.g. (Apr 4) Polish Precedent (USA) 131 – Classic Beauty **74**
(IRE) 65 (Fairy King (USA)) [2002 7f⁶ 7.1m⁵ 7f⁵ 7s⁶ Oct 28] 69,000F, 37,000Y: good-
bodied gelding: third foal: half-brother to 4-y-o King's Crest: dam unreliable 11f winner:
fair maiden: raced freely first 3 starts: should be suited by 1m: gelded after final outing.
J. L. Dunlop

COUNTYKAT (IRE) 2 b.g. (Mar 29) Woodborough (USA) 112 – Kitty Kildare **92**
(USA) 68 (Seattle Dancer (USA) 119) [2002 6g⁴ 6g⁴ f6g* 7m 7.6m⁵ 7.1m* 7.1m⁶ 7m⁵
a8f² a8.5f² Dec 26] 20,000F: lengthy gelding: second foal: brother to 3-y-o Woodboro
Kat: dam, Irish maiden who stayed 7f, out of sister to smart 7f/1m performer Arjuzah
(dam of 4-y-o Malhub): fairly useful performer: won maiden at Southwell in June and
claimer at Haydock (by 4 lengths) in September: at least respectable efforts last 4 starts,
including twice at Nad Al Sheba: stays 8.5f: acts on fibresand/dirt, raced only on good/
good to firm going on turf: visored last 5 appearances: has hung left/carried head awkwardly. *K. R. Burke*

COURAGEOUS DUKE (USA) 3 b.c. Spinning World (USA) 130 – Araadh (USA) **94**
70 (Blushing Groom (FR) 131) [2002 8m 8f 8f⁴ 7.9d³ 8m 8d⁴ 9m² 8g* 8.1m³ 10f* Oct 4]
$150,000F, IR 110,000Y: close-coupled, quite good-topped colt: fifth foal: closely related
to a winner in Japan by Nureyev and half-brother to French 1¼m winner Storm The Altar
(by Storm Bird): dam, maiden, stayed 1¾m: fairly useful performer: won maiden at
Newcastle in August and handicap at Newmarket (beat Macadamia by 1¼ lengths) in
October: stays 1¼m: yet to race on soft/heavy going, acts on any other. *J. Noseda*

COURT ALLIANCE 3 ch.g. Alhijaz 122 – Fairfields Cone (Celtic Cone 116) [2002 –
10g 10s 10m 10.2d⁶ Jul 4] fourth foal: half-brother to 7-y-o Court Shareef and 6-y-o
Kaluana Court: dam lightly raced on Flat and fairly useful over hurdles: little form.
R. J. Price

COURTCARD 3 b.f. Persian Bold 123 – Hafnafah 74 (Shirley Heights 130) [2002 –
8.2m Jun 24] 2,000Y: big, good-bodied filly: sixth foal: half-sister to an Italian 1¼m and
1¾m winner by Taufan: dam 1m winner: well held in maiden at Nottingham: gave good
deal of trouble before start and withdrawn on intended debut and second outing (July 9).
Mrs Lucinda Featherstone

COURT CIRCLE 3 b.g. Lion Cavern (USA) 117 – Chiltern Court (USA) (Topsider **68**
(USA)) [2002 8m⁵ 8d³ 8.3d³ 10m 8.1m⁵ Sep 16] 10,000Y: tall, leggy gelding: second
foal: brother to 1m winner Circlet: dam unraced out of sister to Thatch and Special, latter
dam of Nureyev and grandam of Sadler's Wells and Fairy King: fair maiden: stayed 1m:
acted on good to soft going, probably on good to firm: dead. *J. W. Hills*

COURTELIMORR 2 b.f. (Mar 3) Defacto (USA) – Auntie Fay (IRE) (Fayruz 116) –
[2002 6m 6m 7m Oct 2] 500Y: second foal: half-sister to 4-y-o Gordons Friend: dam of
little account: well held in maidens. *B. S. Rothwell*

COURTESY (USA) 3 b.f. Diesis 133 – Muscadel 103 (Nashwan (USA) 135) [2002 **74**
76p: 10m⁶ p12g⁵ 12.1m Aug 25] fair maiden: stays 1½m: acts on polytrack, showed
promise on good to soft going: sold 7,000 gns in December, sent to France. *Sir Michael
Stoute*

COURT MASTERPIECE 2 b.c. (May 12) Polish Precedent (USA) 131 – Easy **95 p**
Option (IRE) 115 (Prince Sabo 123) [2002 7m⁶ 6g* Aug 21] lengthy, angular colt: has
scope: third foal: half-brother to useful French winner around 5f (including at 2 yrs)
Maybe Forever (by Zafonic) and 6f winner Pride In Me (by Indian Ridge): dam 5f winner,
including at 2 yrs: 5/2, much better effort in maidens (useful form) when winning
6-runner event at York by short head from Arctic Burst, travelling strongly and getting up
near finish: not sure to stay beyond 6f: remains capable of better. *E. A. L. Dunlop*

COURT MATTER (USA) 3 b. or br.g. Red Ransom (USA) – Silent Movie (Shirley –
Heights 130) [2002 8.1s Jun 8] 15,000Y: tall, leggy gelding: half-brother to 3 winners,
notably smart 7f and 1¼m (Sun Chariot Stakes) winner Warning Shadows (by Cadeaux
Genereux): dam, maiden, half sister to very smart 7f to 1¼m performer Noalto: well held
in maiden at Haydock. *M. Johnston*

Queen Alexandra Stakes, Royal Ascot—Cover Up (left) wins at the meeting for the second year in succession, galvanised by Kieren Fallon to overhaul Archduke Ferdinand and Double Honour (right)

COURT MUSIC (IRE) 3 b. or br.f. Revoque (IRE) 122 – Lute And Lyre (IRE) 96 **60** (The Noble Player (USA) 126) [2002 74: 8m 8.2d 7f 7m 5.9s* 6.9g² 7d f8g Nov 25] rather leggy, angular filly: modest performer: won apprentice claimer at Carlisle in July: stays 7f when conditions aren't testing: acts on soft ground: often blinkered/has worn cheekpieces: sometimes slowly away. *T. D. Easterby*

COURT OF APPEAL 5 ch.g. Bering 136 – Hiawatha's Song (USA) (Chief's Crown **84** (USA)) [2002 81: 13.8d³ 10f² 11.9d² 10.1g² 10.3m⁶ 10.4m 12f² 13m⁵ 12s Oct 26] lengthy gelding: fairly useful handicapper: hasn't won since 2000: effective at 1¼m to 1¾m: acts on any turf going: tongue tied: often races prominently: sold 15,000 gns. *B. Ellison*

COURT ONE 4 b.g. Shareef Dancer (USA) 135 – Fairfields Cone (Celtic Cone 116) **39** [2002 –: 12d⁶ 11.6g⁵ 10m 9.9g Oct 2] leggy gelding: shows knee action: poor maiden: stays 11.6f: sometimes slowly away. *R. J. Price*

COURT SHAREEF 7 b.g. Shareef Dancer (USA) 135 – Fairfields Cone (Celtic Cone **101** 116) [2002 92: 14.4f² 16m 16m 18.7f 14d⁶ 14m³ 12g⁵ 11.9g 11.9d³ 13.9m 12m⁶ 14g* 12d⁶ 13.9m 13.4f 12m⁵ Sep 23] small gelding: useful handicapper: won at Sandown in August: career-best effort when 2 lengths seventh to Hugs Dancer in Ebor at York fourteenth start: effective at 1½m to 2m: acts on soft and firm going: carries head high: sometimes slowly away/wanders/finds little: usually held up. *R. J. Price*

COUSTOU (IRE) 2 b.g. (Jan 27) In Command (IRE) 114 – Carranza (IRE) (Lead On **83** Time (USA) 123) [2002 7m⁴ 8.1m³ 6g² 7g* Oct 24] IR 65,000Y: lengthy, good-topped gelding: third foal: half-brother to fairly useful Irish 2000 2-y-o 6f winner Berlin (by Common Grounds): dam French 1m/9.5f winner out of half-sister to Teenoso: fairly useful performer: improved with each outing, making most when winning maiden at Brighton by 2 lengths from Sparky's Mate (gelded after): stays 7f: raced only on good/good to firm going. *M. A. Jarvis*

COVER UP (IRE) 5 b.g. Machiavellian (USA) 123 – Sought Out (IRE) 119 (Rainbow **112** Quest (USA) 134) [2002 109: 18.7f 22.2m* 16m⁶ 15.9g² 18m⁵ 16m⁵ Oct 19] close-coupled, quite good-topped gelding: smart performer: won Queen Alexandra Stakes at Royal Ascot in June by neck from Archduke Ferdinand, despite meeting trouble: best effort when 1¼ lengths second to Boreas in Lonsdale Stakes at York in August: stays 2¾m: acts on firm and good to soft going, probably on heavy: visored once at 3 yrs: sometimes races lazily: usually patiently ridden. *Sir Michael Stoute*

COWBOYS AND ANGELS 5 b.g. Bin Ajwaad (IRE) 119 – Halimah 56 (Be My **63** Guest (USA) 126) [2002 76: f8s⁴ p10g⁶ p7g* f6g² p7g f6g³ f7g⁵ p7g f7g* f8g⁴ f7g³ 7g⁵ **a71** p7g² 7g⁶ 9s 8m⁶ 7d⁴ 7m⁴ p7g* f8.5g* p8g f8.5g Dec 14] fair on all-weather, modest on turf: won claimer at Lingfield in January, minor event at Southwell in March and claimers at Lingfield (claimed from S. C. Williams £7,000) and Wolverhampton in July: effective at 6f to 8.5f: acts on any turf going/all-weather: effective blinkered or not, visored once: sometimes tongue tied: usually races prominently. *Mrs Lydia Pearce*

COZY MARIA (USA) 3 gr. or ro.f. Cozzene (USA) – Mariamme (USA) 66 (Verbatim **105** (USA)) [2002 95: 10m* 9.9d³ 9g⁴ 8m² Jul 26] tall, rather unfurnished filly: useful performer: won maiden at Ripon in April: good efforts last 2 starts, in Prix Chloe at Chantilly (2¼ lengths fourth to Walzerkoenigin) and listed race at Ascot (¾-length second to Fraulein): effective at 1m/1¼m: yet to race on soft/heavy going, acts on any other: races prominently: sent to USA. *J. H. M. Gosden*

CRACOW (IRE) 5 b.g. Polish Precedent (USA) 131 – Height of Secrecy (Shirley **63 §** Heights 130) [2002 99§: 11.6g 14.4d⁵ 11.9g³ 10m 16f Sep 8] rather leggy, useful-looking gelding: useful in 2001: modest form at 5 yrs: rather headstrong, but stays 1½m: yet to race on heavy going, acts on any other: often finds little: not to be trusted. *N. J. Hawke*

CRAFTY CALLING (USA) 2 b.c. (May 2) Crafty Prospector (USA) – Glorious **100 p** Calling (USA) (Nijinsky (CAN) 138) [2002 6m 6d⁴ 6g* Aug 12] tall colt: eighth foal: brother to US Grade 2 11f winner Mr Bluebird and closely related to winners in USA by Jade Hunter and Miswaki: dam, 1m/8.5f winner in USA, out of half-sister to Japan Cup winner Mairzy Doates: useful form: clearly best effort when justifying favouritism in 20-runner maiden at Windsor by 1¼ lengths from Vision of Dreams, quickening on final 1f: has plenty of speed, and not sure to stay 7f: open to further improvement. *P. F. I. Cole*

CRAIC SA CEILI (IRE) 2 b.f. (Mar 28) Danehill Dancer (IRE) 117 – Fay's Song **83** (IRE) 84 (Fayruz 116) [2002 7d 7g 7m⁶ 7.1m² 8m² 8s* 8g⁴ 8s Oct 25] IR 8,000Y: leggy filly: third foal: dam 5f (at 2 yrs) and 6f winner: fairly useful performer: best effort when winning nursery at Ayr in October by 5 lengths from Flake: ran as if something amiss final start: will stay 1¼m: acts on good to firm ground, goes well on soft. *M. R. Channon*

CRAIGMOR 2 br.g. (Mar 24) Polar Falcon (USA) 126 – Western Horizon (USA) 58 **47** (Gone West (USA)) [2002 6m 7d⁶ f6g³ f6g⁶ 7m 6d Aug 26] leggy gelding: third foal: **a57** dam, maiden who stayed 1¾m, out of sister to Ribblesdale winner Nanticious and Stewards' Cup winner Repetitious, latter dam of high-class 7f to 9f winner Indian Lodge: modest maiden on all-weather, poor on turf: stays 7f: acts on fibresand. *B. J. Meehan*

Exors of the late Lord Weinstock's "Cover Up"

CRAIL 2 b.g. (Apr 2) Vettori (IRE) 119 – Tendency 77 (Ballad Rock 122) [2002 7s⁴ **70 p** Oct 25] workmanlike gelding: seventh foal: half-brother to fairly useful 6f to 9f winner Le Sport and 7f winner Dowdency (both by Dowsing): dam 6f winner at 4 yrs: 20/1 and green, 5½ lengths fourth of 12 to Kris Kin in maiden at Doncaster, no extra final 1f: should improve. *C. F. Wall*

CRAIOVA (IRE) 3 b.c. Turtle Island (IRE) 123 – Velvet Appeal (IRE) 101 (Petorius **85** 117) [2002 83p: 7s² 7.1m² 8m² Jul 13] strong, lengthy, attractive colt: has a quick action: fairly useful maiden: will probably stay 1¼m: acts on good to firm going, probably on soft. *B. W. Hills*

CRANMER 3 ch.g. Machiavellian (USA) 123 – True Glory (IRE) 84 (In The Wings **–** 128) [2002 10g Apr 29] first foal: dam, 11f winner, half-sister to 4-y-o Wareed and smart middle-distance performers Jaydoom and Truly A Dream: never on terms nor knocked about in maiden at Windsor. *M. A. Jarvis*

CRANSHAWS (USA) 3 b.c. (Feb 23) Green Dancer (USA) 132 – Highland Ceilidh **90** (IRE) 100 (Scottish Reel 123) [2002 p7g⁶ 7.5g* 7.5g³ 8m* 8m⁵ 9g⁵ 9v Nov 10] well-made colt: seventh living foal: closely related to 1½m winner Nika Nesgoda (by Suave Dancer) and half-brother to 1½m winners Carioca Dream (by Diesis) and Penshiel (by Mtoto), latter fairly useful: dam, 1m (at 2 yrs)/1¼m winner, from family of Halling: fairly useful performer: won maiden at Beverley in July and nursery at Newmarket in August: ran creditably when 5 lengths fifth to Borsieri in Premio Guido Berardelli at Rome penultimate start: will stay 1¼m: acts on good to firm going, ran poorly on heavy: blinkered last 2 starts: sold 65,000 gns. *Sir Mark Prescott*

CRATHORNE (IRE) 2 b.c. (Feb 10) Alzao (USA) 117 – Shirley Blue (IRE) (Shirley **85** Heights 130) [2002 7m⁶ 7d 8g* 8g 8s⁴ Oct 25] 44,000F, 26,000Y: deep-girthed colt: second foal: dam, ran 3 times in France, out of half-sister to smart French performer up to 13.5f Anitra's Dance: fairly useful performer: won maiden at Thirsk in September: good fourth in nursery at Doncaster: will be suited by 1¼m+: acts on soft ground. *J. D. Bethell*

CREATO 2 b.c. (Mar 14) Alzao (USA) 117 – Croalda (IRE) (Darshaan 133) [2002 9v² **63** p10g Dec 3] second foal: dam, Italian maiden, closely related to Italian Oaks third Crodas: modest form in maidens at Milan and Lingfield (14 lengths seventh to Shield): should stay 1½m. *L. M. Cumani*

CREDENZA MOMENT 4 b.c. Pyramus (USA) 78 – Mystoski 35 (Petoski 135) **–** [2002 44: p16g 11.9g⁶ p12g May 28] sparely-made colt: maiden: well held in 2002: tried blinkered/visored. *M. Madgwick*

CREDIBLE (USA) 3 ch.g. Dixieland Band (USA) – Alleged Thoughts (USA) **–** (Alleged (USA) 138) [2002 81: 8d⁶ 12m⁵ 10.9s⁶ Oct 14] small gelding: fairly useful form latter of 2 starts at 2 yrs: well held in 2002: sent to Kuwait. *Mrs L. Stubbs*

CREED (IRE) 2 ch.g. (Mar 29) Entrepreneur 123 – Ardent Range (IRE) (Archway **–** (IRE) 115) [2002 8.1m Sep 6] 29,000F, IR 22,000Y: sturdy gelding: second foal: dam unraced: 50/1 and burly, tailed off in maiden at Haydock. *R. A. Fahey*

CREEKVIEW (USA) 3 b.c. Gone West (USA) – Honfleur (IRE) 100 (Sadler's Wells **108** (USA) 132) [2002 85p: 7s² 9m⁵ 10m Jun 20] $700,000Y: sturdy, angular colt: third foal: closely related to 1m winner Argentan (by Gulch): dam, 1¼m and 13.5f winner, sister to Arc winner Carnegie out of Arc winner Detroit: useful form: won maiden at Gowran only start at 2 yrs: plenty of improvement when short-head second to idling Century City in Tetrarch Stakes at the Curragh (having been off 11 months) and 2½ lengths fifth to Rouvres in Prix Jean Prat at Chantilly: disappointing in listed race at Royal Ascot final start: should be suited by 1¼m+: has worn crossed noseband: sent to Hong Kong, where renamed Successive Gains. *A. P. O'Brien, Ireland*

CREG NY SHEE 3 b.g. Anabaa (USA) 130 – Cos I Do (IRE) (Double Schwartz 128) **–** [2002 7s 10s 10s 8s 7s 10g p10g Dec 21] 2,000Y, re-sold IR 12,500Y: fifth reported foal: dam unraced half-sister to South African Grade 1 11f and 2m winner Devon Air: little form: left P. Mooney in Ireland, gelded and off 6 months, well held in handicap at Lingfield final start. *P. D. Evans*

CREG WILLYS HILL (IRE) 3 b.c. Distinctly North (USA) 115 – Need You Badly **49** 59 (Robellino (USA) 127) [2002 51: f6g f5g⁶ f5g³ f5g³ f5g⁵ Mar 18] poor maiden: should stay 6f: acts on fibresand: blinkered (ran respectably) final start. *R. Ford*

CREME CHARTREUSE (IRE) 3 ch.f. Woodman (USA) 126 – Emerald Dancer **–** (USA) (Green Dancer (USA) 132) [2002 11.8d May 27] leggy, lengthy filly: first foal: dam unraced daughter of smart French filly up to 1½m Stoshka: well beaten in maiden at Leicester, taking strong hold. *R. Charlton*

CRESKELD (IRE) 3 b.g. Sri Pekan (USA) 117 – Pizzazz 47 (Unfuwain (USA) 131) **75** [2002 72: p6g⁵ 7.1m³ 8m 8g⁶ 6d³ 6g⁵ 6m 7m 6m 7.5m 7g 7g³ 7g² f8g* f8g⁵ f8g* Dec 27] **a87** sparely-made gelding: fairly useful handicapper on all-weather, fair on turf: left J. L. Eyre, improved to win at Southwell in November and December: stays 1m: acts on all-weather, soft and good to firm going. *B. Smart*

CRESSEX KATIE 3 b.f. Komaite (USA) – Kakisa 81 (Forlorn River 124) [2002 63: **61** p6g⁵ p6g⁵ f7g⁵ 6s³ 6.1m 6g f6g* f6g³ f5g Dec 13] modest performer: won maiden at Wolverhampton in October: stays 6f: acts on all-weather and soft going: sometimes slowly away. *J. Cullinan*

CRICKETERS CLUB 4 b.g. Dancing Spree (USA) – Alacrity 62 (Alzao (USA) **46** 117) [2002 52: p7g p13g 8.5g⁶ 7m⁴ 10.1m⁴ 7m 10m⁶ 11.6m 11.9g 8.5m Aug 16] strong gelding: has a round action: poor maiden: stays 1¼m: acts on all-weather, good to soft and good to firm going: sometimes visored. *R. Ingram*

CRIMEBUSTERS (IRE) 2 b.f. (Apr 8) Ali-Royal (IRE) 127 – Chardania (IRE) 34 **–** (Rainbows For Life (CAN)) [2002 f5g 5g 5.2f⁵ Jun 24] 2,800Y: sparely-made filly: first foal: dam poor maiden: little form: sent to Holland. *A. Berry*

CRIMSON DANCER 2 b.f. (Mar 18) Groom Dancer (USA) 128 – Crimson Rosella **–** 54 (Polar Falcon (USA) 126) [2002 7.9f 7d Oct 30] tall filly: third foal: half-sister to fairly useful 6f (at 2 yrs)/7f winner Sabo Rose (by Prince Sabo): dam, maiden who probably stayed 1½m, half-sister to high-class sprinter Mr Brooks: well held in maidens. *W. J. Haggas*

CRIMSON SILK 2 ch.g. (Apr 24) Forzando 122 – Sylhall (Sharpo 132) [2002 6g³ **101** 6m* 6m* 6m³ Sep 11] 14,000Y: sturdy gelding: third foal: brother to fairly useful 2001 2-y-o 5f winner Dearest Daisy and half-brother to 4-y-o Galy Bay: dam unraced: useful form: made all in maiden in July and minor event in August, both at Windsor: sweating, excellent narrowly-beaten third of 21 to Somnus in sales race at Doncaster final start: raced only at 6f on good/good to firm ground: races prominently: game. *D. Haydn Jones*

CRIPSEY BROOK 4 ch.g. Lycius (USA) 124 – Duwon (IRE) 55 (Polish Precedent **71** (USA) 131) [2002 72: 10d 8.3g 8d 8g⁴ 8g³ 8m 10f* 10m 10.4f² Oct 10] tall gelding: fair performer: left B. R. Millman after third start: won selling handicap at Redcar in September: races freely, but stays 1¼m: acts on firm and good to soft ground. *N. Tinkler*

CRISTOFORO (IRE) 5 b.g. Perugino (USA) 84 – Red Barons Lady (IRE) (Electric **43 +** 126) [2002 –: 7m 8g 8.5g⁴ 7d² f9.4g* f12g* p13g* Dec 28] big, good-topped gelding: **a71** fair on all-weather, poor form on turf: won maiden at Wolverhampton and handicaps at Southwell and Lingfield (on consecutive days) in December: stays easy 13f: acts on good to soft ground and all-weather: has started slowly: held up. *B. J. Curley*

CRISTOPHE 4 b.g. Kris 135 – Our Shirley 84 (Shirley Heights 130) [2002 53: 16m **–** May 3] quite attractive gelding: maiden: blinkered, well held only 4-y-o start. *A. Crook*

CRITICAL STAGE (IRE) 3 b.g. King's Theatre (IRE) 128 – Zandaka (FR) (Doyoun **62** 124) [2002 –: 8g* 8m⁵ 10s p10g Nov 27] modest performer: clearly best effort when winning apprentice event at Salisbury in June, coming from well off strong pace: will stay 1¼m+. *John Berry*

CROCE DI ORO 6 b.m. Warrshan (USA) 117 – Country Spirit (Sayf El Arab (USA) **–** 127) [2002 10m 9.9g 11.9s May 27] second foal: dam unraced: tailed off in mares bumper in 2000: well held in seller/maiden/claimer. *A. Bailey*

CROESO CROESO 4 b.f. Most Welcome 131 – Croeso-I-Cymru 96 (Welsh Captain **100** 113) [2002 67: 5.7g 5.3d* 5.3m³ 5.3d* 5.7g* 5m⁵ 6g* 5.7f* 5m⁴ 6g Sep 21] sturdy, deep-bodied filly: useful handicapper: better than ever in 2002, winning at Brighton (3 times) and Bath (twice) between June/August: good fourth to The Tatling at Sandown penultimate start: effective at 5f/6f: acts on firm and good to soft going: held up: has started slowly. *J. L. Spearing*

CROP CIRCLE 3 b.g. Magic Ring (IRE) 115 – Surprise Surprise 91 (Robellino (USA) **–** 127) [2002 57: f7g 5.7g 7.1m Sep 21] modest maiden at 2 yrs: well held in 2002. *A. G. Newcombe*

CROSBY DANCER 3 b.g. Glory of Dancer 121 – Mary Macblain 49 (Damister **48** (USA) 123) [2002 48: 12m 10f 7.9g 8.1d 9.9m⁴ 10m 8m 11.5s Oct 22] leggy, angular gelding: poor maiden: stays 1¼m: acts on firm and soft ground: unseated and bolted before start fifth outing. *John A. Harris*

CROSBY DONJOHN 5 ch.g. Magic Ring (IRE) 115 – Ovideo 58 (Domynsky 110) **52 §** [2002 52: 8m⁴ 9.9g 9.2s 8m* 9.2g 9m 10.1d 9m Sep 16] good-bodied gelding: has a round action: modest handicapper: won at Ripon in July: effective at 1m/1¼m: acts on firm going, good to soft and fibresand: usually blinkered: unreliable. *J. R. Weymes*

CROSSED WIRE 4 ch.f. Lycius (USA) 124 – Maze Garden (USA) (Riverman (USA) 131) [2002 10s 11.6g 10m f14.8s* f16.2g² f14.8g⁶ 20m f12g⁴ Oct 5] first foal: dam useful French 1m winner who stayed 1¼m: fair performer: trained at 3 yrs by P. Bary in France, winning minor event at Senonnes-Pouance: won handicap at Wolverhampton in May by 18 lengths: finds 1½m a bare minimum, and stays 2m: acts on fibresand and soft going: effective visored or not. *J. M. P. Eustace* **77**

CROSS PETITION 2 ch.f. (Feb 7) Case Law 113 – Bee Dee Dancer (Ballacashtal (CAN)) [2002 5m 7d 6m⁶ 7g Oct 17] 500Y: heavy-bodied filly: seventh foal: half-sister to 3 winners, including 6f winner Breakin Even (by Chilibang) and 3-y-o Didnt Tell My Wife: dam well beaten only start: well held in maidens/sellers. *T. M. Jones* **–**

CROSSWAYS 4 b.g. Mister Baileys 123 – Miami Dancer (USA) (Seattle Dancer (USA) 119) [2002 74: 9.7m 12m 10g* May 19] fair handicapper: won in Jersey in May: should stay beyond 1½m: acts on firm ground. *P. D. Evans* **68**

CROWN AGENT (IRE) 2 b.g. (Mar 2) Mukaddamah (USA) 125 – Supreme Crown (USA) (Chief's Crown (USA)) [2002 8m⁵ 8g⁶ Oct 16] 15,000Y: half-brother to several winners, including useful performer up to 1¼m in Britain/Scandinavia Tough Guy (by Namaqualand) and fairly useful 2001 2-y-o 1m winner Sir Azzaro (by Charnwood Forest): dam unraced out of US 2-y-o Grade 1 6f winner Share The Fantasy: fair form in maidens: will stay 1¼m. *I. A. Balding* **67**

CROWN CITY (USA) 2 b.f. (Feb 24) Coronado's Quest (USA) 130 – Trisha Brown (USA) (Theatrical 128) [2002 7d Nov 2] $60,000Y: sturdy filly: first foal: dam 8.5f to 1¼m winner in USA, out of half-sister to US Grade 1 9f/1¼m winner Broad Brush: 14/1 and backward, well-held thirteenth of 18 to Aljazeera in maiden at Newmarket, fading: should improve. *M. A. Jarvis* **– p**

CROWN COUNSEL 2 b.c. (Mar 10) Machiavellian (USA) 123 – Confidante (USA) 95 (Dayjur (USA) 137) [2002 7f² 7d³ Oct 15] strong, lengthy colt: has scope: first foal: dam, 7f winner, half-sister to smart 6f/7f performer Wind Cheetah out of close relative to Affirmed: fairly useful form in maidens at Newmarket (promising 5 lengths second of 26 to Desert Star, running on strongly) and Leicester (evens, third to Artistic Lad): should stay 1m: capable of better. *Mrs A. J. Perrett* **85 p**

CROWN FLYER (IRE) 3 ch.g. Barathea (IRE) 127 – Zorette (USA) 66 (Zilzal (USA) 137) [2002 7.5g 12f⁴ 12d 9.9d 12.3s⁶ Aug 5] 15,500F, IR 27,000Y: leggy, close-coupled gelding: fourth foal: half-brother to 3 winners, including 1½m winner Hunters Tweed (by Nashwan): dam twice-raced half-sister to very smart French middle-distance filly Ode: little form. *M. Johnston* **–**

CROW WOOD 3 b.g. Halling (USA) 133 – Play With Me (IRE) 73 (Alzao (USA) 117) [2002 63, a78: 8.2d 7.5m 10.1m² 10d* 10.1s⁵ 10m⁶ 10.3f* 9.2g 10.3d⁵ 9.2v Aug 14] strong, close-coupled gelding: fairly useful handicapper: won at Leicester in May and Chester in July: stays 1¼m: acts on fibresand, soft and firm going: has raced freely: gelded after final outing. *J. G. Given* **80**

CRUAGH EXPRESS (IRE) 6 b.g. Unblest 117 – Cry In The Dark (Godswalk (USA) 130) [2002 60: p10g 9s 8g² 8d p10g⁶ 7g⁴ 8m⁴ 6m² 7m⁶ Sep 3] close-coupled gelding: modest on turf, poor on all-weather: effective at 6f to 1¼m: acts on polytrack, soft and good to firm ground: often blinkered: sometimes tongue tied: takes good hold: has edged left: unreliable: sold 600 gns. *G. L. Moore* **53 §** **a46 §**

CRUISE DIRECTOR 2 b.g. (Jan 30) Zilzal (USA) 137 – Briggsmaid 70 (Elegant Air 119) [2002 p7g 6d f7s⁵ Dec 7] 9,000Y: heavy-topped gelding: fifth foal: closely related to 6-y-o Kez and half-brother to 2 winners, including 5-y-o Reflex Blue: dam 1½m to 2m winner: best effort in maidens when ninth to Machinist at Lingfield on debut, very slowly away: will stay at least 1m: seemed to resent kickback at Wolverhampton final start. *W. J. Musson* **68**

CRUISKEEN LAWN (IRE) 4 b.g. Ashkalani (IRE) 128 – Grand Morning (IRE) 77 (King of Clubs 124) [2002 92: 7s* 8s 7s² 7m 6d⁵ 7d 6s² 7v Nov 10] IR 20,000Y: quite good-topped gelding: half-brother to fairly useful 7f/1m performer Topsy Morning (by Lahib): dam 2-y-o 5f winner: useful performer: won maiden at Gowran at 3 yrs and handicap at Cork in April: best efforts when second in minor event at Naas (behind Mr Houdini) and handicap at the Curragh (behind Senators Alibi): well beaten in quite valuable handicap at Royal Ascot fourth start: best at 6f/7f: acts on soft ground, probably on good to firm: has had tongue tied. *C. Collins, Ireland* **101**

CRUNCHY (IRE) 4 ch.g. Common Grounds 118 – Credit Crunch (IRE) 51 (Caerleon (USA) 132) [2002 60: p10g 11.6g 10g Oct 24] modest handicapper in 2002 (reportedly had breathing problem final start): should stay 1½m: acts on soft and good to firm going: sometimes tongue tied. *J. A. R. Toller* **51**

CRUSOE (IRE) 5 b.g. Turtle Island (IRE) 123 – Self Reliance 72 (Never So Bold 135) [2002 f8s² f8g 8.2v f8.5g f11g f11g³ f12g⁴ f11g Dec 17] small gelding: first foal: dam 7f winner: fair maiden at best: trained by C. Collins in Ireland at 3 yrs: stays 1m: acts on soft ground and fibresand: blinkered once: has worn cheekpieces: on downgrade. *A. Sadik* **73 d**

CRUSTY LILY 6 gr.m. Whittingham (IRE) 104 – Miss Crusty 45 (Belfort (FR) 89) [2002 46, a–: 5d p6g 5.3d 6g 6m 5.1g⁴ 6d 5.1m⁵ 5.3m 6s 6.1m³ Sep 20] smallish, lengthy mare: poor handicapper: left N. Littmoden after sixth start: effective at 5f to 7.5f: acts on firm and good to soft going. *P. D. Evans* **46**

CRUZ SANTA 9 b.m. Lord Bud 121 – Linpac Mapleleaf 69 (Dominion 123) [2002 –: 15d² 16.2g² Aug 15] lengthy mare: poor handicapper, lightly raced on Flat nowadays: stays 2m: acts on fibresand, good to firm and good to soft going: fair hurdler. *Mrs M. Reveley* **47**

CRYFIELD 5 b.g. Efisio 120 – Ciboure 74 (Norwick (USA) 125) [2002 73: 7.1m³ 8.5g 7m³ 7.5g³ f7g⁶ 5.9s³ 7.9d 8.1m 7m⁴ 7g 6.9m⁴ 8.5g* 8.3m* 8.9f 8v Nov 8] good-bodied gelding: fair handicapper: won at Beverley and Hamilton in September: effective at 6f (given good test) to 8.5f: acts on any turf going and fibresand: effective visored or not: free-going sort. *N. Tinkler* **74**

CRYPTOGAM 2 b.f. (Feb 27) Zamindar (USA) 116 – Moss (Alzao (USA) 117) [2002 7m⁵ Sep 23] fourth foal: half-sister to 6-y-o Javelin and useful 1m winner Mossy Moor (by Sanglamore): dam, French 1¼m winner, half-sister to St Leger winner Toulon: 6/1, 4½ lengths fifth of 12 to Spanish Sun in maiden at Kempton, brought wide into straight and not knocked about: will stay 1¼m: sure to do better. *Mrs A. J. Perrett* **73 p**

CRYSTAL BALLET (USA) 2 b.f. (May 9) Royal Academy (USA) 130 – Hot Princess 101 (Hot Spark 126) [2002 6g Jul 12] half-sister to several winners, notably top-class 1m/1¼m winner Rodrigo de Triano (by El Gran Senor), also 6f/7f winner at 2 yrs: dam, Irish 5f to 7f winner, later successful in USA: 9/1, 11 lengths last of 8 to Nasij in maiden at Ascot, slowly away and always behind: sold 60,000 gns in December: probably capable of better. *J. H. M. Gosden* **– p**

CRYSTAL CANYON 5 ch.m. Efisio 120 – Manor Adventure 75 (Smackover 107) [2002 54: f5g p7g f6g 5g³ 5s 5g 5m Jul 16] robust mare: modest maiden handicapper on turf, poor on all-weather: stays 6f: acts on firm going and fibresand: sometimes misses break: none too reliable. *B. Smart* **50 a38**

CRYSTAL CASTLE (USA) 4 b.g. Gilded Time (USA) – Wayage (USA) (Mr Prospector (USA)) [2002 7g³ 8.1m 6m⁴ 7m* 6d* 6m* Sep 28] **120**
Such was Crystal Castle's progress as a four-year-old that, by the season's end, he could rightly be regarded as being among the best six-furlong performers in Europe. Crystal Castle has been quite lightly raced—he had run only five

Tote International Stakes (Handicap), Ascot—an appropriately international flavour as French-trained Crystal Castle gains compensation for an unlucky run in the Wokingham; making the frame behind him are Ghannam, Royal Millennium and Mister Cosmi

Brunswick Diadem Stakes, Ascot—Crystal Castle progresses again to short head Malhub (right), who does particularly well under a penalty; Acclamation (partly hidden by front pair) is third, whilst Polar Way (far left) stays on to grab fourth from Bahamian Pirate (rail)

times before the latest season—and may improve again at five. His trainer John Hammond is best known for his achievements with Arc winners Suave Dancer and Montjeu, but he also did extremely well with another late-developing sprinting gelding, Nuclear Debate, whom he trained to win the King's Stand and Nunthorpe Stakes at five and the Haydock Park Sprint Cup at six. Crystal Castle will reportedly begin his 2003 campaign with a crack at the six-furlong Dubai Golden Shaheen in March, a race that was upgraded to Group 1 status in the most recent season.

Crystal Castle's first two starts in the latest season, third in a seven-furlong minor event at Longchamp in April then well held in a mile rated stakes at Sandown in June (his only outing for Robert Cowell before rejoining Hammond), hardly indicated that significant improvement might be on the cards. However, dropped back to six furlongs in the Wokingham at Royal Ascot—a race he seemed to have been targeted at—Crystal Castle ran really well to finish fourth to Capricho, weaving his way through after a slowish start and then finding his way blocked approaching the final furlong, but for which he would probably have finished upsides the runner-up Border Subject. No such misfortune befell Crystal Castle on his return to Ascot for another big handicap, the seven-furlong Tote International, in July. Looking well treated off the same mark as in the Wokingham, Crystal Castle made the most of racing in the favoured stand-side group to record a half-length success over Ghannam, asserting only near the finish, edging left after being ridden to dispute the lead well over a furlong out. Inaugurated in 1998 with the intention of attracting overseas runners, this was the first time the race had been won by a foreign stable. Handicaps were no longer on the agenda after this and Crystal Castle tackled pattern company on his final two outings, both over six furlongs. He won the Prix de Meautry at Deauville in August, held up but still seeing plenty of daylight in the thirteen-runner field before taking it up well inside the final furlong and beating Swedish Shave by three quarters of a length. Returned to Ascot, Crystal Castle improved again to win the eleven-runner Brunswick Diadem Stakes in September, though he needed all of the 6 lb weight concession to prevail by a short head under a determined Fallon ride from the Golden Jubilee winner and Nunthorpe and Sprint Cup runner-up Malhub.

Crystal Castle (USA) (b.g. 1998)	Gilded Time (USA) (ch 1990)	Timeless Moment (ch 1970)	Damascus
			Hour of Parting
		Gilded Lilly (b 1979)	What A Pleasure
			Luquillo
	Wayage (USA) (b 1984)	Mr Prospector (b 1970)	Raise A Native
			Gold Digger
		Waya (b 1974)	Faraway Son
			War Path

The good-topped Crystal Castle is by the American stallion Gilded Time, winner of the Breeders' Cup Juvenile in 1992 and third in the Breeders' Cup Sprint the following year. Gilded Time has not had many runners in Europe, but he has

Mr J. Raw's "Crystal Castle"

had several winners at graded level in the States, including Mandy's Gold, who won the 2002 Ruffian Handicap. Crystal Castle is the eighth foal out of Wayage, who failed to win from twelve outings in France but is a close relative or half-sister to several winners, including the 1994 American two-year-old Grade 3 winner at five and a half furlongs De Niro. Crystal Castle's grandam is the smart performer Waya, winner of the Prix de l'Opera as a three-year-old before winning Grade 1 events at up to a mile and a half in the States at four and five. Crystal Castle is the best of Wayage's produce, though she is also the dam of the useful performer at up to a mile Secrage (by Secreto), who incidentally also won the Prix de Cabourg—a race won by Crystal Castle—as a juvenile. Secrage is the dam of the smart winner at up to a mile Teapot Row. Crystal Castle's very best form is at six furlongs, but he put up a smart effort when winning the Tote International over seven and will probably prove fully effective back at that trip. Effective on soft and good to firm going, Crystal Castle is usually held up. *J. E. Hammond, France*

CRYSTAL COLLEEN (IRE) 2 gr.f. (Apr 30) Desert King (IRE) 129 – Silver Kristal 81 (Kris 135) [2002 7f f7s f5g⁶ p6g Dec 21] 6,500 2-y-o: small filly: first foal: dam, 7f winner, half-sister to several useful performers, including Irish 1m winner Reina Blanca: modest maiden: seemingly best effort on debut: may prove best around 6f. *R. Guest*   **57**

CRYSTAL CREEK (IRE) 6 b.g. River Falls 113 – Dazzling Maid (IRE) 64 (Tate Gallery (USA) 117) [2002 61: 10.3s 13.8d 12.3g Apr 3] no form in 2002. *D. Nicholls*   **–**

CRYSTAL GIRL 3 b.f. Presidium 124 – Balgownie 43 (Prince Tenderfoot (USA) 126) [2002 –: 9.1g 7m Jul 3] leggy, unfurnished filly: little form. *M. Dods*   **–**

239

CRYSTAL LASS 6 b.m. Ardkinglass 114 – That's Rich (Hot Spark 126) [2002 59, a77: f7s f8s⁵ f7g Mar 18] tall mare: one-time fairly useful performer: no form in 2002: tried blinkered, usually visored nowadays. *R. Brotherton* –

CRYSTAL SOLDIER 4 ch.f. Infantry 122 – Bottle Basher (Le Soleil 96) [2002 –§: p12g f14.8g f9.4g Feb 1] temperamental maiden: has refused to race. *D. Burchell* – §

CRYSTAL STAR 2 ch.f. (Mar 29) Mark of Esteem (IRE) 137 – Crystal Cavern (USA) 89 (Be My Guest (USA) 126) [2002 7.1f* 7s* Oct 26] close-coupled, sparely-made filly: second foal: dam, 2-y-o 7f winner who later won in Canada at 4 yrs, half-sister to Poule d'Essai des Pouliches winner Rose Gypsy: unbeaten in 8-runner maiden at Haydock (by 1½ lengths from Theatre Time, pair clear) in September and 11-runner listed event at Newbury (by head from Garmoucheh, doing well to get up near line having had to be switched) in October: should stay 1m: acts on firm and soft ground: already useful, and open to further progress. *Sir Michael Stoute* — 99 p

CRYSTAL VALKYRIE (IRE) 3 b.f. Danehill (USA) 126 – Crystal Cross (USA) 88 (Roberto (USA) 131) [2002 79: 7.6f 8s⁴ 10.9m⁴ 11m⁴ 10f² 10m³ 10m⁶ 10.2g⁵ 7f 8f p8g⁶ Nov 13] angular filly: fairly useful handicapper: stays 11f: unraced on heavy going, acts on any other turf and fibresand. *B. W. Hills* — 81

CUBAPESKY 2 b.f. (Apr 14) Fleetwood (IRE) 107 – Robert's Daughter (Robellino (USA) 127) [2002 6g 7.6m 6d⁵ p8g f8.5g Dec 20] second foal: dam ran 3 times at 2 yrs: little form. *E. J. O'Neill* —

CUBISM (USA) 6 b.h. Miswaki (USA) 124 – Seattle Kat (USA) (Seattle Song (USA) 130) [2002 101: p6g⁴ p7g 6g⁵ 7g 7d 6g 6g 6m² 6g* 6f⁴ 5.6m Sep 11] smallish, well-made horse: useful handicapper: left J. Osborne before justifying heavy support when beating Forever Times by 2 lengths at York (first success for over 3 years) in August: was effective at 6f/easy 7f: raced mainly on good going or firmer: tried visored: was sometimes tongue tied: was sometimes slowly away/usually held up: dead. *Ian Williams* — 96

CUCHI 2 b.f. (Apr 15) Danzig Connection (USA) – Classic Faster (IRE) (Running Steps (USA) 79) [2002 p5g p5g Nov 23] second foal: dam Italian 7f winner, including at 2 yrs: well held in maidens at Lingfield. *K. O. Cunningham-Brown* —

CUDDLES (FR) 3 b.f. Anabaa (USA) 130 – Palomelle (FR) 112 (Moulin 103) [2002 85: p8g³ 8d 10.1g 8.3m⁶ 10.1m 8g 10g 10s p10g* p8g⁶ p10g Dec 3] leggy filly: fairly useful handicapper on all-weather, fair on turf: won at Lingfield in November: stays 1m: acts on heavy going, good to firm and polytrack: has worn cheekpieces: sometimes looks none too keen. *C. E. Brittain* — 73 a92

CULMINATE 5 ch.g. Afzal 83 – Straw Blade 66 (Final Straw 127) [2002 38?: p10g 11.9g 11.9g 11.9d Jun 13] of little account. *J. E. Long* —

CULTRA (IRE) 3 ch.c. Spectrum (IRE) 126 – Ziggy Belle (USA) (Danzig (USA)) [2002 66p: 6g p7g* 7.1v 6d⁶ 7g 7.1d Aug 8] robust colt: fair performer on all-weather, modest on turf: won minor event at Lingfield in May: below form after, including in visor: will stay 1m: acts on polytrack, raced only on good going or softer on turf: sold 3,000 gns in October. *R. Hannon* — 56 a69

CULZEAN (IRE) 6 b.g. Machiavellian (USA) 123 – Eileen Jenny (IRE) 112 (Kris 135) [2002 96: 8s 8f⁴ 10m 10m 9.9m⁴ 10.2d⁴ Jul 8] leggy gelding: fairly useful handicapper: best around 1¼m nowadays: acts on soft going, good to firm and fibresand: blinkered twice at 4 yrs: tried tongue tied: sometimes fails to go through with effort: usually held up: sold 2,800 gns. *R. Hannon* — 85

CUMBRIAN CARLETON 3 b.g. Polar Falcon (USA) 126 – Fly Dont Run (USA) 59 (Lear Fan (USA) 130) [2002 68: f8.5g 7.9g 8.1s Jun 7] leggy, useful-looking gelding: modest form both starts at 2 yrs: well held in 2002. *T. D. Easterby* —

CUMBRIAN CRYSTAL 3 b.f. Mind Games 121 – Crystal Sand (GER) (Forzando 122) [2002 69p: 6m May 1] unfurnished filly: modest form both 2-y-o starts: well held only run in 2002. *T. D. Easterby* —

CUMBRIAN PRINCESS 5 gr.m. Mtoto 134 – Cumbrian Melody 83 (Petong 126) [2002 60: 12m² f12g f9.4g⁶ 6.1d² f8.5g⁶ 7d 6g 7m f7g⁶ f8.5s⁵ f8.5g Dec 20] leggy, sparely-made mare: modest handicapper: stays 9.4f: acts on fibresand, soft and good to firm going: sometimes wanders/finds little: none too reliable. *M. Blanshard* — 63

CUMBRIAN VENTURE 2 b.c. (Feb 27) Mind Games 121 – Crystal Sand (GER) (Forzando 122) [2002 5s⁵ 5g² 5s³ 6g² 6g* 6g 6m* 5g² 6m⁶ 6f² 6s² Oct 25] 10,000Y, resold 6,400Y: tall, rather leggy colt: second foal: dam unraced: useful performer: won maiden at Newcastle in June and minor event at Ripon in August: mostly good efforts after, — 103 including when ½-length second to Avonbridge in listed event at York penultimate start: clear in unfavoured group when 6 lengths second of 21 to Golden Nun in sales race at Doncaster final one: effective at 5f/6f: acts on firm going, probably on soft: blinkered last 5 starts. *T. D. Easterby*

CUNAS (USA)   3 b.f. Irish River (FR) 131 – Sayyedati 122 (Shadeed (USA) 135)   **86**
[2002 8.3g* 10.1m Sep 17] third foal: half-sister to US 1m winner Djebel Amour (by Mt Livermore) and 2-y-o Almushahar: dam, won 5 Group 1s including Cheveley Park Stakes and 1000 Guineas, half-sister to high-class 1¼m/1½m performer Golden Snake: fairly useful form: won maiden at Windsor (had to be led to start) by ½ length from Miss Brooks, carrying head high: off 10 weeks, failed to make expected progress when last in listed event at Yarmouth (early to post): visits Silver Hawk. *Saeed bin Suroor*

CUPBOARD LOVER   6 ch.g. Risk Me (FR) 127 – Galejade 58 (Sharrood (USA)   **94**
124) [2002 11.6d² 13.3s* 13.3v* 16.4d* 13.9m Aug 21] angular gelding: fairly useful handicapper: better than ever in 2002, winning at Newbury (twice) and Sandown (beat Ranville by length, looked like winning impressively before tiring late on) between May and July: bandaged in front, well held final start: stays 2m: successful on good to firm and fibresand, very best efforts on softer than good: tried blinkered at 2 yrs: has given trouble in preliminaries/sometimes slowly away/pulls hard. *N. J. Henderson*

CURFEW   3 b.f. Marju (IRE) 127 – Twilight Patrol 96 (Robellino (USA) 127) [2002   **101**
77+: 7m 6d³ 6g⁶ 7m² 7m² 7m* 7m* 7m* 7m 7m⁴ Oct 12] useful performer: won handi-caps at Newmarket, Yarmouth and Salisbury (heavily-backed favourite, beat Princess Almora by 2½ lengths) in August/September: bit below form in listed races at Doncaster (first home of those who raced on far side) and Ascot (found little) last 2 starts: stays 7f: yet to race on extremes of going: has had tongue tied: on toes/mulish at start at Doncaster, reportedly due to coming into season: free-going sort: held up. *J. R. Fanshawe*

CURLEW RIVER (IRE)   2 b.g. (Mar 14) Alhaarth (IRE) 126 – Sudden Interest (FR)   **–**
(Highest Honor (FR) 124) [2002 8g Oct 2] IR 38,000Y: fourth foal: half-brother to fairly useful 2000 2-y-o 6f winner There's Two (by Ashkalani) and 1¼m winner After The Blue (by Last Tycoon): dam, French 9f and 10.5f winner, half-sister to very smart 1¼m winner Sudden Love: 20/1, well held in Salisbury maiden. *D. R. C. Elsworth*

CURRENCY   5 b.g. Sri Pekan (USA) 117 – On Tiptoes 107 (Shareef Dancer (USA)   **90**
135) [2002 80: 6d 6m⁵ 6g 6m³ 6d 6m⁶ 6g² 6m* 6m 5.7f² 6m⁴ 6m⁵ 6m³ 6g 7.2g 6g Oct 2] sturdy gelding: fairly useful handicapper: better than ever in 2002, winning at Newcastle in July: raced mainly around 6f: best on good going or firmer: has edged left. *J. M. Bradley*

CUSTOMEYES   3 b.f. Komaite (USA) – Mizog (Selkirk (USA) 129) [2002 –§: 7f Apr   **– §**
11] temperamental maiden: refused to race only 3-y-o outing: withdrawn after unseating to post on intended debut: twice very slowly away. *B. R. Johnson*

CUSTOM MADE   3 ch.g. Zafonic (USA) 130 – Asterita 103 (Rainbow Quest (USA)   **–**
134) [2002: p10g p8g Jan 16] modest maiden at 2 yrs: well held both 3-y-o starts: tried blinkered. *J. R. Best*

CUTBUSH (IRE)   2 b.f. (Apr 28) Mujadil (USA) 119 – Lhotse (IRE) 67 (Shernazar   **56**
131) [2002 5.7f⁶ 5g Oct 4] sixth foal: half-sister to temperamental 6f winner who stayed 1¼m Lobuche (by Petardia) and a winning sprinter in Italy by Danehill Dancer: dam Irish maiden: modest maiden: better effort on debut: dead. *J. S. Moore*

CUTLASS CORAL   3 br.f. Nomination 125 – Cutlass Princess (USA) 41 (Cutlass   **38**
(USA)) [2002 f6g f7g⁴ 6d 8m f6g 7.5m 5g Sep 9] leggy filly: sixth foal: sister to useful sprinter Jimmy Too and half-sister to 5f to 7f winner Princess Efisio (by Efisio): dam poor maiden: poor performer. *R. Hollinshead*

CUT RATE (USA)   4 ch.g. Diesis 133 – Itsamazing (USA) 85 (The Minstrel (CAN)   **80**
135) [2002 71: f8g⁶ p10g³ f12g* 10d⁵ p12g 8d² 10f 10d⁵ 8s 8v f11g⁶ p8g⁴ p10g Dec 11] quite good-topped gelding: fairly useful handicapper: won at Southwell in March: effective at 1m (given test) to 1½m: acts on all-weather and good to soft going, possibly not on firm: tried tongue tied. *K. Bell*

CUT RIDGE (IRE)   3 b.f. Indian Ridge 123 – Cutting Ground (IRE) 85 (Common   **60**
Grounds 118) [2002 6m 5g 6m³ 6s 5.9d⁴ 6g 6m Aug 14] IR 10,000Y: first foal: dam, Irish 9f winner, half-sister to 1m/1¼m winner Stone Ridge (by Indian Ridge): modest maiden: likely to stay 7f: acts on good to firm and good to soft going: hung left final start. *J. J. Quinn*

CYBER BABE (IRE) 5 b.m. Persian Bold 123 – Ervedya (IRE) (Doyoun 124) [2002 –
51d: f12s Jan 2] handicapper: well held only outing in 2002: often visored at 2 yrs.
A. G. Newcombe

CYBER CINDERS 2 ch.f. (Apr 1) Cayman Kai (IRE) 114 – Petticoat Rule (Stanford 52
121§) [2002 5g³ 7.1d 5d⁵ 5d² Jul 31] 2,500Y: fifth foal: dam of little account over hurdles:
modest maiden: beaten head in nursery at Musselburgh final start: will prove best at 5f:
raced only on good/good to soft going: slowly away all starts. *Miss L. A. Perratt*

CYBER SANTA 4 b.g. Celtic Swing 138 – Qualitair Ridge (Indian Ridge 123) [2002 66
59: 12.3g 12f² 12m⁵ 12d 12.4g² 13g 12g² 12g⁶ 9.9g⁴ 12g³ 10m² 12d⁴ 10g³ 14.4g Aug 26] big
gelding: fair handicapper: effective at 1¼m to 13f: acts on firm ground and polytrack:
sometimes slowly away: tends to race freely: consistent. *J. Hetherton*

CYCLONE CONNIE 4 ch.f. Dr Devious (IRE) 127 – Cutpurse Moll 76 (Green 92
Desert (USA) 127) [2002 98: 6f⁴ 6m⁵ 6g² 5.7m² 6m* 5.6m⁴ 5.2f 5m Oct 12] smallish,
sturdy filly: unimpressive mover: fairly useful performer on balance (probably flattered
second start): won maiden at Lingfield in August: close fourth to Halmahera in Portland
Handicap at Doncaster next start: likely to stay 7f: raced only on good going or firmer:
refused to enter stall once at 3 yrs: edged right final start: none too consistent. *C. A. Cyzer*

CYCLONIC STORM 3 b.f. Catrail (USA) 123 – Wheeler's Wonder (IRE) 43 (Sure 76
Blade (USA) 130) [2002 49: 9.2g³ 9.3s² 12.3d 9.3d* 8m* 8d⁵ Aug 3] rather leggy filly:
fair handicapper: won at Carlisle and Salisbury in July: should be suited by 1¼m+: acts
on soft and good to firm going: sometimes slowly away/wanders. *R. A. Fahey*

CYNARA 4 b.f. Imp Society (USA) – Reina 24 (Homeboy 114) [2002 60: 12f⁶ 13g 13v 48
Jun 13] big, good-topped filly: poor performer: probably best at 1m/1¼m: acts on good to
soft and good to firm going, possibly not on soft/heavy: visored/blinkered (below form)
in 2002: has idled. *G. M. Moore*

CYNOSURE 5 b.g. Runnett 125 – Polly Two (Reesh 117) [2002 –: 7f 6f May 13] –
workmanlike gelding: no form. *J. R. Weymes*

CZARINA WALTZ 3 b.f. Emperor Jones (USA) 119 – Ballerina Bay 75 (Myjinski 75
(USA)) [2002 66p: 10m p10g² 10m³ p10g* 10g⁴ p12g³ Oct 9] good-topped filly: fairly **a83**
useful on all-weather, fair on turf: won handicap at Lingfield in July: races freely, but
stays easy 1½m: acts on polytrack, yet to race on extremes of going on turf: has started
slowly: flicked tail under pressure second start. *C. F. Wall*

CZAR WARS 7 b.g. Warrshan (USA) 117 – Dutch Czarina 45 (Prince Sabo 123) 72 d
[2002 72, a89: f6s⁵ f6g⁵ f6g f6g 6m 6m 5d⁵ 6m⁴ 6v 5m f6g 5d f7g³ f6g³ f6g⁴ Dec **a81 d**
20] sturdy gelding: fairly useful on all-weather, fair on turf at best: well below form last 7
starts: effective at 5f to easy 7f: acts on fibresand, firm and soft going: usually blinkered:
tongue tied once: has bled from nose: sometimes drifts left. *J. Balding*

D

DAANA 3 b.f. Green Desert (USA) 127 – Shining Water (USA) (Riverman (USA) 131) 70
[2002 77: 7s² 7m² 8m² May 29] small, strong filly: fair maiden: stays 1m: acts on heavy
and good to firm ground: sold 26,000 gns in December. *J. L. Dunlop*

DABUS 7 b.g. Kris 135 – Licorne 93 (Sadler's Wells (USA) 132) [2002 10m 8.3m 9.9d 45
16.2g⁴ 9.9m Sep 24] small, stocky gelding: useful at 3 yrs, just poor since: stays 2m: acts
on good to firm going. *M. C. Chapman*

D'ACCORD 5 ch.g. Beveled (USA) – National Time (USA) (Lord Avie (USA)) [2002 70
74, a87: 7g 8f 5.3m³ 5.1g 6m² 6d² 5.1g³ 5g² f5g⁴ f6g⁵ p6g⁵ f5g³ f6g³ p5g⁶ Dec 21] tall **a78**
gelding: fair handicapper: best at 5f/6f: acts on fibresand, heavy and good to firm going:
occasionally blinkered/visored: sometimes wanders. *S. Kirk*

DADELAND (IRE) 3 b.f. Desert King (IRE) 129 – Bubbling Heights (FR) (Darshaan 91
133) [2002 85: 7g 7.5m 8.5g⁶ 8g⁶ 11.1d⁴ 10.1m* 10.9d* 10.5d³ 10.6m 10.5g* 10.5v³
Nov 7] leggy, unfurnished filly: fluent mover: fairly useful performer: won handicaps at
Newcastle in July and Ayr in August and (having left M. W. Easterby after eighth start)
minor event at Toulouse in October: well-held third in listed race at Le Croise-Laroche
final outing: will stay 1½m: acts on heavy and good to firm going: blinkered last 6 starts:
sold 42,000 gns in December. *R. Gibson, France*

DADENS ANGEL (IRE) 2 b. or br.f. (Mar 18) Inzar (USA) 112 – Morning Stroll **47**
(Tower Walk 130) [2002 6d 5m⁵ 5.1d 6g Oct 4] 2,500Y: half-sister to 3 winners, including
2-y-o 5f winners Million At Dawn (in 1993, by Fayruz) and Red Ruffian (in 1991, by
Red Sunset), latter useful performer up to 7f in Hong Kong: dam unraced: poor maiden:
probably stays 6f: blinkered last 3 starts. *J. L. Spearing*

DAFA 6 b.g. Deploy 131 – Linpac North Moor 69 (Moorestyle 137) [2002 10m Oct 7] –
stocky gelding: little form. *B. J. Curley*

DAFFODIL GIRL 3 ch.f. Vettori (IRE) 119 – Top Treat (USA) 101 (Topsider (USA)) –
[2002 64: 7.1f 10.2g 7d 6.1d 7f 8g f7g⁵ p10g Dec 30] plain filly: modest maiden at 2 yrs:
little form in 2002: tried in blinkers/cheekpieces. *B. Palling*

DAFNE 3 ch.f. Nashwan (USA) 135 – El Opera (IRE) 100 (Sadler's Wells (USA) 132) **68 §**
[2002 –p: 11.9m* p12g⁶ 11.7m³ 12g⁴ Aug 15] strong filly: fair handicapper: won maiden
event at Brighton in June: stays 1½m: raced only on good/good to firm going on turf:
found little 2 of last 3 starts (blinkered final one): one to treat with caution. *Sir Mark
Prescott*

DAHLIDYA 7 b.m. Midyan (USA) 124 – Dahlawise (IRE) 76 (Caerleon (USA) 132) –
[2002 50, a74: f6s p7g f6s f6s³ f6g f6g f6g⁶ f6g³ f6g⁴ f6g f6g f6g f6g f6g⁶ f6g Dec 10] **a48**
angular mare: poor performer, lightly raced on turf: left P. McEntee after sixth start,
M. Polglase after thirteenth: best at 6f/7f: acts on fibresand, good to firm and good to soft
going: tried blinkered: slowly away, often markedly so, and comes from well behind.
R. Wilman

DAHOAR 3 b.f. Charnwood Forest (IRE) 125 – Glenarff (USA) (Irish River (FR) 131) **66**
[2002 7m 7s² p10g Nov 19] sixth foal: half-sister to several winners, including smart
performer up to 1½m in Britain/Hong Kong Housemaster (by Rudimentary) and smart 6f
(at 2 yrs) and 1m winner Mastermind (by Dolphin Street): dam, French 1m winner, out of
half-sister to very smart French miler Shaanxi: fair form in maidens at Leopardstown and
Tipperary first 2 starts: off 6 months and heavily-backed favourite, well held in similar
event at Lingfield, carrying head awkwardly and finding little: sold 10,000 gns. *J. Oxx,
Ireland*

DAILY TONIC 5 ch.g. Sanglamore (USA) 126 – Woodwardia (USA) 93 (El Gran –
Senor (USA) 136) [2002 53+: f16s Jan 1] close-coupled gelding: modest performer at
best, very lightly raced: well held only 5-y-o start. *N. A. Twiston-Davies*

DAIMAJIN (IRE) 3 b.g. Dr Devious (IRE) 127 – Arrow Field (USA) (Sunshine **83**
Forever (USA)) [2002 74p: 8s³ 8.1f⁵ p8g⁶ 8m² 8s³ 10g³ 10g⁴ 10.2g* 10s p8g p10g Dec **a75 +**
28] unfurnished gelding: fairly useful handicapper: won at Chepstow (final start for
B. Meehan) in September: stays 1¼m: acts on soft and good to firm ground, probably on
polytrack: blinkered fourth to sixth starts: usually races prominently. *B. G. Powell*

DAINTREE AFFAIR (IRE) 2 b.g. (May 16) Charnwood Forest (IRE) 125 – Madam **68**
Loving 99 (Vaigly Great 127) [2002 5.1d 5m 6m⁴ 5d⁶ 5f⁴ 5.1g² 5.1m⁶ Aug 29] IR
12,500Y, 7,500 2-y-o: brother to 2000 2-y-o 6f winner Tuscan and half-brother to several
winners, including 6-y-o Doctor Spin: dam 5f/6f winner, best at 2 yrs: fair maiden: beaten
neck in nursery at Chepstow penultimate start: will prove best at 5f/6f: acts on firm
ground: headstrong: gelded after final start. *M. D. I. Usher*

DAISY BUTTONS (IRE) 3 b.f. Bluebird (USA) 125 – Centella (IRE) (Thatching **57**
131) [2002 57: 12m³ 14.6m⁵ 12.1g³ 12.1g Jun 5] angular filly: modest maiden
handicapper: stays 1½m: acts on good to firm going: sometimes blinkered: looked less
than genuine final start. *T. D. Easterby*

DAISYCUTTER 2 ch.f. (May 7) Zafonic (USA) 130 – Ingozi 91 (Warning 136) **62**
[2002 6.1m⁴ 7g Oct 14] lengthy filly: fifth foal: half-sister to several winners, including
3-y-o Sir George Turner and 6-y-o Tissifer: dam, 7f/1m winner, half-sister to smart 6f/7f
performer Inchinor: modest form when fourth to Bandit Queen in maiden at Nottingham,
not given hard time: flashed tail in paddock and found little in similar event at Leicester.
G. Wragg

DAISY DO (IRE) 2 b.f. (Mar 1) Danehill (USA) 126 – Lothlorien (USA) 80 (Wood- **77**
man (USA) 126) [2002 5m⁶ 5g⁵ 6d 6m⁶ 7m² 8.1g³ 7g² 7m 7f Oct 8] IR 55,000Y: leggy
filly: third foal: half-sister to 4-y-o Miss Devious: dam, 1m winner who stayed 1½m,
sister to smart 1¼m/1½m winner Monsajem out of close relative to Sadler's Wells: fair
maiden: placed 3 times, including in nursery: stays 1m: acts on good to firm ground.
M. R. Channon

DAISY VALENTINE 2 b.f. (Apr 28) My Best Valentine 122 – My Precious Daisy –
(Sharpo 132) [2002 6.1d 5.7g f7g Jul 26] half-sister to 5f winner (including at 2 yrs) Swan

At Whalley (by Statoblest) and 6f seller winner Cairn Dhu (by Presidium): dam Irish 5f/6f winner: no form. *W. G. M. Turner*

DAKHIRA   4 b.f. Emperor Jones (USA) 119 – Fakhira (IRE) 83 (Jareer (USA) 115)   –
[2002 65d: p6g p8g 8.3g 6g 7d 12g 9d Jul 3] disappointing maiden. *D. R. C. Elsworth*

DAKISI ROYALE   5 ch.m. King's Signet (USA) 110 – Marcroft 91 (Crofthall 110)   –
[2002 48: f8s Jan 1] small, sturdy mare: poor maiden at best: well held only 5-y-o start: tried visored/tongue tied. *P. D. Evans*

DAKOTA SIOUX (IRE)   5 ch.m. College Chapel 122 – Batilde (IRE) (Victory Piper   **90**
(USA) 100) [2002 81: 7d 7m 8f 8.3s* 8.3s⁴ 8.1s* 8g* 8m 8.3m³ Sep 2] unfurnished mare: fairly useful handicapper: won at Hamilton, Haydock and Thirsk in May/June: stays 1m: acts on soft and good to firm going: effective blinkered/visored or not: slowly away fifth start. *R. A. Fahey*

DALAKHANI (IRE)   2 gr.c. (Feb 16) Darshaan 133 – Daltawa (IRE) (Miswaki   **116 p**
(USA) 124) [2002 7g* 8d* 8v* Nov 2]
    The second running of the Criterium International was won, like the first, by a French-trained grey colt who ended his first season unbeaten after three appearances. Dalakhani followed Act One, who won the inaugural running of this Group 1 event and went on to show even better form at three in a season cut short by injury, winning the Prix Greffulhe and Prix Lupin and finishing second in the Prix du Jockey Club. There seems no reason why Dalakhani shouldn't go on to at least match Act One's achievements. The form shown by Dalakhani in the Criterium is on a par with that of Act One in the same race, and judged on his pedigree Dalakhani should improve a good deal when given the opportunity to tackle distances of a mile and a quarter and more. A mile and a half should certainly pose no problems for him, and there is every chance that he too will be aimed at the Prix du Jockey Club, a race won by his sire Darshaan, owned like Dalakhani, by the Aga Khan.
    Dalakhani was quickly stepped up in class after making virtually all to win a newcomers race at Deauville in August. Just over three weeks later he started favourite for the Group 3 Prix des Chenes at Longchamp and, ridden with more

Criterium International, Saint-Cloud—Dalakhani and Chevalier pull clear of their rivals

restraint, again won in very good style. Settled in third in a five-runner field, Dalakhani was switched to lead approaching the final furlong and, with his rider looking round several times, drew away to beat Mister Charm by two and a half lengths. It was the best performance by a two-year-old in France up to that stage of the season and Dalakhani was sent off at odds on to take care of his four rivals in the Criterium International run at Saint-Cloud in November. Songlark, also unbeaten in two runs, both of them over a mile at Saint-Cloud and including the Group 3 Prix Thomas Bryon, was the only one of Dalakhani's opponents trained in France. Representing Ireland were Chevalier, the six-length winner of a maiden at Gowran on the second of his two outings, and Napper Tandy, a very close second in the Killavullan Stakes at Leopardstown on his previous start; while the field was completed by the British-trained Governor Brown who had won two of his four starts including the Somerville Tattersall Stakes at Newmarket. On ground much more testing than he had encountered previously, Dalakhani, in contrast to Songlark, settled well as he tracked the leader Chevalier. Dalakhani did take a little time to warm to his task when asked for his effort, as the race began in earnest shortly after the turn into the straight, but came through to take a narrow lead approaching the final furlong, at which point Dalakhani and Chevalier were beginning to pull away from the remainder. Chevalier rallied but Dalakhani's rider always looked to have matters under control and merely pushed out his mount to win by a neck, the pair five lengths clear of third-placed Governor Brown. There was a lot to like about Dalakhani's performance and he was shortened as second favourite, behind Brian Boru, in most ante-post lists for the Derby, though it seems more likely that he will be aimed at Chantilly rather than Epsom. The Prix Greffulhe, won by Act One on his reappearance at three, is the race mentioned as a probable starting point for Dalakhani in his second season.

Dalakhani (IRE) (gr.c. Feb 16, 2000)	Darshaan (br 1981)	Shirley Heights (b 1975)	Mill Reef / Hardiemma
		Delsy (br 1972)	Abdos / Kelty
	Daltawa (IRE) (gr 1989)	Miswaki (ch 1978)	Mr Prospector / Hopespringseternal
		Damana (gr 1981)	Crystal Palace / Denia

Dalakhani won't have the speed to make an impact over a mile at three, as did his illustrious half-brother Daylami (by Doyoun) who won the Poule d'Essai des Poulains. However, Daylami, racing in the colours of Godolphin after his three-year-old days, went on to show much better form at a mile and a quarter to a mile and a half, his victories including the Eclipse, the Man o'War Stakes, the King George VI and Queen Elizabeth Stakes, the Irish Champion and the Breeders' Cup Turf. A sister to Daylami, Daltaiyma, showed useful form at a mile and a quarter in France while a half-brother Daymarti (by Caerleon) showed smart form there, winning a listed race over an extended eleven furlongs in the Provinces, and was later successful in Singapore. Their dam Daltawa, in a short career, won at ten furlongs as a two-year-old and at ten and a half (in a listed race) at three, and she also finished second in the Prix Penelope. The grandam Damana won three races in France at up to a mile and three quarters and is the daughter of a smart half-sister to Raykour, the runner-up in the St James's Palace Stakes and the Hollywood Derby in 1988. Dalakhani looks sure to enhance further the reputation of what is already a highly successful family. *A. de Royer Dupre, France*

DALAL   3 b.f. Cadeaux Genereux 131 – Proudfoot (IRE) (Shareef Dancer (USA) 135)   **54 §**
[2002 63p: 8.2d⁴ 8.3m 10d 8f Jul 17] good-topped filly: modest maiden: should be suited by 1¼m+: blinkered (looked temperamental) final start: sometimes slowly away (appeared reluctant leaving stall second start): untrustworthy. *E. A. L. Dunlop*

DALARAM (IRE)   2 b.c. (Apr 10) Sadler's Wells (USA) 132 – Dalara (IRE) 114   **85** (Doyoun 124) [2002 7f⁴ 7d² 8g³ Sep 7] lengthy, useful-looking colt: very good mover: fifth foal: brother to 6-y-o Daliapour and half-brother to smart but untrustworthy 1½m and 2m winner Dalampour (by Shernazar): dam, won Prix de Royallieu and stayed 15.5f, closely related to Darshaan: fairly useful form in maidens: best effort when length second to Apex Star at Leicester: should be suited by 1¼m+: edgy and noisy in paddock final outing. *Sir Michael Stoute*

DALATI (IRE)   5 b.g. Marju (IRE) 127 – Casbah Girl 79 (Native Bazaar 122) [2002 **45** 8g 5.9d⁵ Jul 19] tall, lengthy, angular gelding: seventh foal: half-brother to 4 winners, including useful sprinter Sabre Rattler (by Beveled) and 5f to 7f winner Mister Bloy (by Dowsing): dam 6f/7f winner: better effort when fifth in seller at Hamilton: will be suited by return to further than 6f. *W. M. Brisbourne*

DALBLAIR (IRE)   3 b.g. Lake Coniston (IRE) 131 – Cartagena Lady (IRE) (Prince **78** Rupert (FR) 121) [2002 62: 10g⁶ 8.2d³ 7.9g⁴ 9.9g⁴ 11f³ 12.1g² 12.3m² 12m* 10g⁵ 11s² 12g² 12.1g² 11.8g Oct 14] rather leggy gelding: fluent mover: fair handicapper: won at Thirsk in July: stays 1½m: acts on firm and soft going: blinkered (raced freely) seventh start: often races prominently. *J. A. Glover*

DALIAPOUR (IRE)   6 b.h. Sadler's Wells (USA) 132 – Dalara (IRE) 114 (Doyoun **114** 124) [2002 119: 13.4f⁴ 16.4m⁵ 14g* 13.3f⁴ 16f Nov 5] small, quite attractive horse: good walker: had a short, fluent action: very smart performer at best: won Coronation Cup at Epsom and Hong Kong Vase at Sha Tin in 2000: best effort at 6 yrs when winning LAWS Curragh Cup in June by 2 lengths from Boreas: respectable fourth to Mubtaker in Geoffrey Freer Stakes at Newbury (reportedly hit head on stalls) next start: below form in Melbourne Cup at Flemington final one: stayed 1¾m: acted on firm and soft going: had worn crossed noseband: usually raced up with pace: to stand at Haras des Chartreux, France, fee €4,800. *Sir Michael Stoute*

DALIYANA (IRE)   3 b.f. Cadeaux Genereux 131 – Dalara (IRE) 114 (Doyoun 124) **80** [2002 10.2d² 11.5g³ 12d² Nov 5] fourth foal: half-sister to 6-y-o Daliapour and smart but headstrong 1½m/2m winner Dalampour (by Shernazar): dam, won Prix de Royallieu and stayed 15.5f, closely related to Darshaan: fairly useful maiden: in frame at Chepstow (minor event), Yarmouth and Catterick: stays 1½m: raced only on good/good to soft ground. *Sir Michael Stoute*

DALRIATH   3 b.f. Fraam 114 – Alsiba 68 (Northfields (USA)) [2002 10g 11.5g⁶ 8m³ **70 d** 9.9m³ 10m 8g 7.9m 8.1g 8g 8m⁶ Oct 3] rangy, angular filly: half-sister to several winners, including useful 9f/1¼m winner Dashiba (by Dashing Blade) and 5-y-o Bond Diamond: dam staying sister to dam of dual Irish St Leger winner Oscar Schindler: fair maiden: well below form last 5 starts: may prove best around 1m: raced only on good/good to firm going: tried visored: sold 1,800 gns. *M. R. Channon*

DAMALIS (IRE)   6 b.m. Mukaddamah (USA) 125 – Art Age (Artaius (USA) 129) **95** [2002 106: 5.5d 5.1g 5.1f 6s 6m² 6d⁶ 5.1f 6.1g³ 7m 6m 5g³ 6f⁵ 6f Oct 12] lengthy, sturdy mare: useful performer: some creditable efforts in 2002 (probably flattered fifth start) including when third to Vita Spericolata in listed race at Chester eighth outing: best at 5f/ 6f: acts on firm and soft going: tried tongue tied: sometimes edgy/on toes/pulls hard/ carries head awkwardly: has run poorly when sweating: none too consistent. *E. J. Alston*

DAMASK DANCER (IRE)   3 b.g. Barathea (IRE) 127 – Polish Rhythm (IRE) 77 **54** (Polish Patriot (USA) 128) [2002 p8g³ f8.5g Nov 16] 68,000Y: first foal: dam, 1m winner at 4 yrs, half-sister to Cheveley Park/Moyglare Stud Stakes winner Capricciosa: much better effort in maidens (modest form) when fifth at Lingfield: ran in snatches next time: will probably stay 1¼m. *Ferdy Murphy*

DAMASK ROSE (IRE)   4 ch.f. Dr Devious (IRE) 127 – Solac (FR) (Gay Lussac **100** (ITY) 116) [2002 100: 12m 16m³ 16.1g 13.9m² 12m 14.6m⁴ Sep 11] sparely-made filly: useful performer: creditable efforts in 2002 when in frame in handicaps at Kempton and York (short-head second to Maycocks Bay in listed rated stakes) and Park Hill Stakes at Doncaster (4¾ lengths fourth to Alexander Three D): probably best at 1¾m/2m: acts on soft and good to firm going: usually held up: sold 42,000 gns in December, sent to USA. *L. M. Cumani*

DAMASQUINER   5 b.m. Casteddu 111 – Hymn Book (IRE) 65 (Darshaan 133) [2002 **–** 50: p6g Jan 9] modest maiden at best: well held only 5-y-o start. *T. E. Powell*

DAME DE NOCHE   2 b.f. (Jan 22) Lion Cavern (USA) 117 – Goodnight Kiss 109 **84** (Night Shift (USA)) [2002 7d 6.1m² 6m Sep 11] 14,000F, 21,000Y: workmanlike filly: third foal: sister to Japanese 7f listed winner Dublin Lion: dam, Irish maiden who was second in Irish 1000 Guineas, temperamentally unsatisfactory: clearly best effort (fairly useful form) when neck second to Striking Ambition in maiden at Nottingham, flashing tail but narrow leader long way: finished lame final start: should stay 7f. *J. G. Given*

DAME MARGARET   2 ch.f. (Feb 15) Elmaamul (USA) 125 – Pomorie (IRE) 67§ **46** (Be My Guest (USA) 126) [2002 7d 8v f8.5f Nov 29] fourth foal: half-sister to German

6.5f and 1¼m winner My Little Princess (by Celtic Swing): dam, 1¼m winner who stayed 2m, became untrustworthy: poor form in maidens. *M. L. W. Bell*

DAME SHARP 3 b.f. Sabrehill (USA) 120 – Dame Helene (USA) (Sir Ivor 135) [2002 **47** 52: f5g f6g⁴ Jan 21] poor maiden: probably best at 6f/7f: acts on fibresand: slowly away last 3 starts (visored first 2). *E. J. Alston*

DANAAN PRINCE (IRE) 2 ch.c. (May 5) Danehill Dancer (IRE) 117 – Classic **74** Queen (IRE) (Classic Secret (USA) 91) [2002 5g p6g p7g⁴ Dec 21] 12,500Y: third foal: half-brother to 5-y-o Blue Hawk: dam well beaten at 2 yrs in Ireland: fair maiden: good fourth to Rifleman in minor event at Lingfield: stays 7f: acts on polytrack. *R. Hannon*

DANAKIL 7 b.g. Warning 136 – Danilova (USA) (Lyphard (USA) 132) [2002 69, a81: **90** p12g² p12g³ p12g 9s 12m⁴ 12d² 12g* 12d⁴ 12m⁵ 12d* 12g* 12v p12g f12s⁵ Dec 9] small gelding: unimpressive mover: fairly useful handicapper: better than ever at 7 yrs, winning at Epsom (twice) and Ascot (amateurs) between July and September: ran poorly last 3 starts: should stay 1¾m: acts on firm going, soft and all-weather: visored once at 5 yrs: usually held up: sometimes hangs, but is genuine and consistent. *S. Dow*

DANAKIM 5 b.g. Emarati (USA) 74 – Kangra Valley 56 (Indian Ridge 123) [2002 **64 d** 65: 5g³ 5m⁵ 6m² 5m 6.1m* 5.1d 5d 5g 6f³ 6f 5m 5g 5m 5m f6g 6g 6f Sep 27] lengthy, good-quartered gelding: modest handicapper: won apprentice event at Nottingham in May: below form last 8 starts: best at 5f/6f: probably acts on any turf going, well beaten on fibresand: tried blinkered: has been early to post/reportedly bled from nose/refused to enter stalls: races prominently. *J. R. Weymes*

DANA POINT (IRE) 10 br.g. Phardante (FR) 123 – Wallpark Princess (Balidar 133) – [2002 13d⁶ Jul 19] probably of little account on Flat nowadays. *L. R. James*

DANASKAYA (IRE) 2 gr.f. (Mar 13) Danehill (USA) 126 – Majinskaya (FR) 110 **106** (Marignan (USA) 117) [2002 6m* 6m² 7g⁴ 6m³ 6f³ Oct 4] small filly: second foal: half-sister to 3-y-o Maskaya: dam, French 1m/1¼m winner, half-sister to dam of very smart French sprinter Kistena: useful performer: won maiden at Naas in July: creditable efforts in frame in Lowther Stakes at York (1¼ lengths second to Russian Rhythm) and

Ballylinch Stud's "Danaskaya"

247

Moyglare Stud Stakes at the Curragh (under a length fourth to Mail The Desert) next 2 starts: blinkered, good 2 lengths third to Airwave in Cheveley Park Stakes at Newmarket final outing: should stay 1m: raced only on good ground or firmer. *J. S. Bolger, Ireland*

DANCE ALL NIGHT 3 b.g. Suave Dancer (USA) 136 – Lyndseylee 96 (Swing Easy — (USA) 126) [2002 54: 6s Aug 24] tall, rather unfurnished gelding: modest maiden: well held only 3-y-o start: may prove best at 5f/6f: ran poorly on fibresand. *A. Bailey*

DANCE CLASS (IRE) 2 b.f. (Mar 13) Desert Prince (IRE) 130 – Dance Ahead 81 **58** (Shareef Dancer (USA) 135) [2002 6d 6m 7g 5g⁵ 6m² Sep 23] IR 40,000Y: strong filly: seventh foal: half-sister to 3 winners, including useful 6f (at 2 yrs) to 9f (in USA) winner Dance Clear (by Marju): dam, 2-y-o 7f winner, out of half-sister to Yorkshire Oaks winners Untold and Sally Brown: modest maiden: good second in nursery at Leicester: best form at 6f: yet to race on extremes of going: carried head awkwardly third start. *Mrs P. N. Dutfield*

DANCE FOR FUN 3 b.f. Anabaa (USA) 130 – Hilaris (Arazi (USA) 135) [2002 **74** p8g* p8g³ Jul 3] first foal: dam unraced out of half-sister to Arc winner Saumarez: fair form: won maiden at Lingfield in May: 1½ lengths third to Start Over in minor event there only subsequent start: likely to stay 1¼m. *P. R. Chamings*

DANCEHALL DARCY 3 ch.f. Bahamian Bounty 116 – Dancing Chimes (London **49** Bells (CAN) 109) [2002 –: 6s 6s⁵ 6.1m 5d 5d⁴ 5s 5.3m 6g Oct 28] poor maiden: effective at 5f/6f: best efforts on good to soft/soft going: has taken good hold. *A. Charlton*

DANCE IN THE DAY (IRE) 4 b.g. Caerleon (USA) 132 – One To One (Shirley **81** Heights 130) [2002 83: 9.9m 12m³ 14d⁶ 14m 11.9g 14m 14v* 12m³ 14.4g² 14m 14f⁶ 13.9f Oct 12] strong gelding: unimpressive mover: fairly useful handicapper: won at Haydock in August: effective at 1½m/1¾m: acts on any going: often held up: looked less than keen tenth outing. *E. J. Alston*

DANCE IN THE SUN 2 b.f. (Apr 29) Halling (USA) 133 – Sunny Davis (USA) 71 **74** (Alydar (USA)) [2002 7g⁵ p8g² Dec 3] lengthy filly: half-sister to several winners, including useful Swedish 1m winner Warming Trends (by Warning), 6f/7f winner in Britain at 2 yrs, and 1½m winner Sunny Chief (by Be My Chief): dam 2-y-o 7f winner: fair form in maidens at Leicester and Lingfield, idling and collared post when short-headed by Treculiar in latter: will probably stay 1¼m. *Mrs A. J. Perrett*

DANCE LESSON 3 b.f. In The Wings 128 – Be Discreet (Junius (USA) 124) [2002 **47** –: 10.2d 12g⁵ 12g 11.9m Aug 28] sturdy filly: half-sister to several winners, including smart 7f/1m performer Gothenberg (by Polish Patriot) and 8-y-o Omaha City: dam won up to 7f in France: poor maiden: seems to stay 1½m. *S. Kirk*

DANCE LIGHT (IRE) 3 b.f. Lycius (USA) 124 – Embracing 91 (Reference Point **73** 139) [2002 p10g⁶ f12g³ 12m⁵ p12g f12g 13.8f* 16g⁸ 16.2g* 15.8f* 17.1f Oct 7] 4,500 2-y-o: angular filly: third foal: half-sister to 5-y-o Hugs Dancer: dam 1½m/1¾m winner: fair performer: won maiden at Catterick and handicaps at Thirsk, Chepstow and Catterick between July and September: reportedly lost a shoe final start: should stay beyond 2m: raced only on good going or firmer on turf: genuine. *T. T. Clement*

DANCE LITTLE LADY (IRE) 5 b.m. Common Grounds 118 – Kentucky Tears — (USA) (Cougar (CHI)) [2002 –: f6s Jan 5] angular mare: modest handicapper in 2000: no form since: tried blinkered. *M. Johnston*

DANCE MASTER (IRE) 4 b.g. Nureyev (USA) 131 – Bay Queen 85 (Damister **68 d** (USA) 123) [2002 72: p10g⁴ p10g⁶ p10g 12s p12g 14.1m 11.6d 11.5m⁶ p10g 11.5m⁵ 16.1d⁶ p16g 14.8m⁵ 14.1m 14.1m f12g⁵ Oct 22] rather leggy, lengthy gelding: unimpressive mover: fair handicapper: on downgrade in 2002: should stay 1¾m: acts on good to firm going and polytrack: tried visored. *J. A. Gilbert*

DANCE OF LIFE 3 b.f. Shareef Dancer (USA) 135 – Regan (USA) 60 (Lear Fan — (USA) 130) [2002 9d 8g 10g⁶ 13.8m 16.2g Aug 26] rather leggy, good-topped filly: second foal: dam, ran twice on Flat, winning hurdler/chaser up to 25f: little form. *S. Gollings*

DANCE ON THE TOP 4 ch.g. Caerleon (USA) 132 – Fern 100 (Shirley Heights 130) **95 d** [2002 93p: 8g⁵ 8m 8.9d p8g⁵ 8f 7.6f 7m Sep 20] close-coupled, good-topped gelding: poor mover: useful handicapper at best: below form after reappearance: finds 1m a bare minimum and stays 1½m: acts on firm going: visored final start: sold 5,500 gns. *E. A. L. Dunlop*

DANCE ROUTINE 3 b.f. Sadler's Wells (USA) 132 – Apogee 113 (Shirley Heights **116** 130) [2002 12g⁶ 10g* 12g* 10.5m² 10g² 12m 12.5g* Oct 5] good-topped, attractive filly:

fourth foal: sister to French 11f winner Light Ballet and half-sister to useful French winner around 1½m who stayed 13.5f Space Quest (by Rainbow Quest): dam, French 1¼m and 1½m (Prix de Royaumont) winner, half-sister to smart French middle-distance performer Daring Miss (by Sadler's Wells): smart performer: won minor event at Longchamp in May, Prix de Royaumont at Chantilly (made all) in June and Prix de Royallieu - Hotel du Golf Barriere at Longchamp (by ¾ length from Trumbaka) in October: also ran well when 2 lengths second to Bright Sky in Prix de Diane at Chantilly and to Pearly Shells in Prix de la Nonette at Deauville in summer: stays 12.5f: raced only on good/good to firm ground: has been bandaged behind: stays in training. *A. Fabre, France*

DANCER POLISH (POL) 4 b.c. Professional (IRE) 73 – Doloreska (POL) (Who **56** Knows 114) [2002 f12g³ f12g⁵ Nov 22] Polish-bred colt: winner of 2 of his 9 starts in native country, including at Warsaw in 2001: modest form both outings on Flat in Britain (won novice hurdle in between): unlikely to stay further than 1½m. *A. Sadik*

DANCES WITH ANGELS (IRE) 2 b.f. (Mar 30) Mukaddamah (USA) 125 – Lady **53** of Leisure (USA) 76 (Diesis 133) [2002 5m 7m⁵ 7m Jul 29] first foal: dam, 1¼m winner, out of sister to Mujadil and half-sister to Fruits of Love: modest form in maidens: should be suited by at least 1m. *Mrs A. L. M. King*

DANCING BAY 5 b.g. Suave Dancer (USA) 136 – Kabayil 75 (Dancing Brave (USA) **96** 140) [2002 93: 13.9g³ 16.1d* Jul 10] useful handicapper: won at Newmarket in July by 3 lengths from Big Moment, despite veering markedly left: stays 2m: best on good ground or softer: has had tongue tied: usually held up (has gone in snatches/hung). *N. J. Henderson*

DANCING BURREN (USA) 2 ch.g. (Apr 15) Irish River (FR) 131 – Pattimech **69** (USA) (Nureyev (USA) 131) [2002 7f 7d⁵ 8.1g⁴ 7.1m Sep 21] IR 35,000Y: smallish gelding: seventh foal: brother to fairly useful 7f/9f winner Riverina and half-brother to 3 winners, including 3-y-o Far Lane: dam, won up to 7f in USA, half-sister to Grand Prix de Paris/Melbourne Cup winner At Talaq: fair maiden: carried head awkwardly third start, well held in nursery final one: free-going sort, likely to prove best up to 7f. *J. L. Dunlop*

DANCING DOLPHIN (IRE) 3 b.f. Dolphin Street (FR) 125 – Dance Model (Unfu- **37** wain (USA) 131) [2002 –: 8.2m p7g 7d 10.1f⁵ 11m 10.1m⁶ 10.1m⁴ 10m⁶ Aug 28] rangy, angular filly: poor maiden: stays 1¼m: form only on ground firmer than good: tried visored. *Julian Poulton*

DANCING FOREST (IRE) 2 br.g. (Jan 28) Charnwood Forest (IRE) 125 – Fauna **72** (IRE) 65 (Taufan (USA) 119) [2002 6s⁴ 7m² 7m⁵ 7m³ 6m³ 7.1m³ 6g 7g Oct 24] 31,000Y: good-topped gelding: second foal: half-brother to 3-y-o Game Leader: dam, maiden who stayed 1m, half-sister to useful 6f to 1m performer Baaderah: fair maiden: below form last 3 starts: effective at 6f/7f: acts on soft and good to firm ground: sold 10,000 gns, and gelded. *R. Hannon*

DANCINGINTHESTREET 2 b.g. (Mar 17) Groom Dancer (USA) 128 – Usk The **79** Way 72 (Caerleon (USA) 132) [2002 5g⁴ 6g⁶ 7.1f* 7d 8g Oct 18] 11,000Y: close-coupled gelding: fifth foal: half-brother to fairly useful Italian 2001 2-y-o 7.5f winner Bod Spectrum (by Spectrum), later successful at 1¼m: dam, 2m winner, sister to Grand Prix de Paris winner Grape Tree Road and closely related to smart stayer Windsor Castle: fair performer: won maiden at Doncaster and minor event at Warwick in June: ran badly last 2 starts (off 2 months in between): should be suited by 1¼m+: acts on firm ground. *M. Johnston*

DANCING KEY 2 ch.f. (Feb 8) Halling (USA) 133 – Fleet Key (Afleet (CAN)) [2002 **74** 7m⁴ 8s Oct 15] first foal: dam, Italian 7f (including at 2 yrs) to 9f winner, out of useful 2-y-o 6f winner/Fillies' Mile fourth Key Tothe Minstrel: fair form when fourth of 5 to Waldmark in minor event at Kempton: well beaten in maiden at Ayr on only subsequent start: should stay at least 1m. *B. W. Hills*

DANCING KING (IRE) 6 b.g. Fairy King (USA) – Zariysha (IRE) (Darshaan 133) **65 ?** [2002 52: 8.2d³ 8d 7f³ Jun 7] lengthy gelding: seemingly fair maiden: stays 1m: acts on firm going and good to soft: often races prominently. *P. W. Hiatt*

DANCING LILY 5 ch.m. Clantime 101 – Sun Follower (Relkino 131) [2002 –, a39: **26** p6g f9 4g⁶ f6g f6g⁶ p7g⁶ p10g p10g 7m 7d 10m 8g 10m 11.6m 11.9g Aug 8] poor maiden: **a37** barely stays easy 1¼m: acts on all-weather, firm and good to soft going: sometimes races freely/hangs. *J. J. Bridger*

DANCING MARY   5 gr.m. Sri Pekan (USA) 117 – Fontenoy (USA) 63 (Lyphard's **47**
Wish (FR) 124) [2002 –, a45: f12s f12g⁵ f16.2g f11g 9.9d⁴ 12.1g⁶ 12.4g 12.1d 9.9m²
8.9m 10m 9.9m Sep 24] leggy, unfurnished mare: poor maiden: stays 1¾m: acts on
fibresand, firm and good to soft going: tried blinkered, often visored. *J. S. Wainwright*

DANCING MYSTERY   8 b.g. Beveled (USA) – Batchworth Dancer 67 (Balla- **102**
cashtal (CAN)) [2002 112: f5s p5g⁴ 5s 5.2g⁴ 5m 5g⁵ 5d 5s 5.7g⁵ 5f 5.2m⁵ 5m⁶ 5m² 5.2f⁶ **a107**
5m⁶ 5m⁶ 5g⁶ 6s Oct 25] close-coupled gelding: useful performer: several respectable
efforts at least in 2002, including when short-head second to Colonel Cotton in handicap
at the Curragh in September: best at 5f: acts on all-weather and any turf ground: occasionally blinkered (not in 2002): has spoilt chance by rearing in stall: takes strong hold and
usually tracks pace. *E. A. Wheeler*

DANCING NELLY   2 b.f. (Mar 17) Shareef Dancer (USA) 135 – Silent Witness **48**
(Inchinor 119) [2002 8g 6s f6f⁶ Nov 11] leggy, unfurnished filly: first foal: dam unraced
half-sister to very smart 1½m to 2¼m performer Busy Flight: poor form in maidens:
should be well suited by 1¼m+: raced freely first 2 starts. *B. W. Hills*

DANCING NUGGET (USA)   2 b.f. (Feb 14) Seeking The Gold (USA) – Shalimar **66 p**
Garden (IRE) 89 (Caerleon (USA) 132) [2002 p7g⁶ Oct 31] first foal: dam, maiden who
stayed 1½m, sister to 5-y-o Bach out of top-class Prix de la Foret/Prix de l'Opera winner
Producer: 14/1, 5 lengths sixth of 11 to Pupillage in maiden at Lingfield, not knocked
about: should improve. *J. W. Hills*

DANCING PEARL   4 ch.f. Dancing Spree (USA) – Elegant Rose 72 (Noalto 120)
[2002 14.1m⁶ Aug 21] 900 3-y-o: fourth foal: half-sister to useful sprinter Bowden Rose
(by Dashing Blade): dam 6f winner: in frame all 3 starts in bumpers: well held in maiden
at Carlisle. *C. J. Price*

DANCING PENNEY (IRE)   4 b.f. General Monash (USA) 107 – Penultimate Cress **36**
(IRE) (My Generation 111) [2002 51d: f8.5g p6g f9.4g 7f 7m 6m 7d 5.7d 5.1f 6.1m Sep
20] angular filly: poor performer: left R. M. Flower after second start: stays 1m: acts on
fibresand and firm going, probably on soft: usually blinkered. *B. Palling*

DANCING PHANTOM   7 b.g. Darshaan 133 – Dancing Prize (IRE) 99 (Sadler's **105**
Wells (USA) 132) [2002 105: 11.9m² 13.1g² 13.1s 16.5v Nov 9] quite attractive gelding:
has a quick action: useful handicapper, lightly raced: creditable efforts in 2002 when
runner-up at York (behind Bourgeois) and Ayr (behind Collier Hill): ran poorly after:
stays 13f: acts on heavy and good to firm going: sometimes edgy/on toes: free-going sort,
and usually races prominently. *M. W. Easterby*

DANCING RIDGE (IRE)   5 b.g. Ridgewood Ben 113 – May We Dance (IRE) 57 **52**
(Dance of Life (USA)) [2002 56: 6d⁵ f5g 5.1d⁵ f7g 5m 6g⁴ 5m³ 5m⁶ Aug 17] good-topped
gelding: modest maiden: effective at 5f/6f: acts on fibresand, firm and good to soft
ground: tried visored: none too consistent. *A. Senior*

DANCING SCHOOL   3 b.g. Danzig Connection (USA) – Drama School 72 (Young **71 d**
Generation 129) [2002 10g⁶ 10g 10.5d 11g f12s Oct 8] good-topped gelding: half-brother
to numerous winners, including 4-y-o Princess Almora and useful 1¼m/1½m winner
Rada's Daughter (by Robellino): dam maiden who stayed 1m: disappointing after
appearing to show fair form in maiden on debut: sold 3,500 gns, sent to Kuwait.
I. A. Balding

DANCING TASSEL   3 b.f. Most Welcome 131 – Delicious 51 (Dominion 123) [2002 **–**
8.1m Sep 16] unfurnished filly: third foal: half-sister to 4-y-o Fantasy Believer: dam
lightly-raced maiden: always behind after slow start in maiden at Warwick. *Lady Herries*

DANCING TILLY   4 b.f. Dancing Spree (USA) – L'Ancressaan 67 (Dalsaan 125) **41**
[2002 –: 9.2s 10g⁵ 8.3v 8f³ 8d⁶ 8f⁵ 10.2f 10.1f 10.5v 8m Oct 5] leggy filly: poor maiden
handicapper: seems to stay 1¼m: acts on firm ground: has looked none too keen.
W. M. Brisbourne

DANCING TSAR   4 b.g. Salse (USA) 128 – Lunda (IRE) 60 (Soviet Star (USA) 128) **–**
[2002 7s: 8.1m 8g 8g p10g 9m 10.9g⁵ Jul 22] small, sparely-made gelding: fair at 3 yrs:
little form in 2002. *J. M. Bradley*

DANCING WATER   3 gr.g. Halling (USA) 133 – Gleaming Water 81 (Kalaglow **76**
132) [2002 86: 8.1f⁴ 8.1d 11m 10m⁵ 10.9m⁶ 10m 9.7m² 12m² 11.9m³ 12.1g⁴ 11f Sep 25]
leggy gelding: has a quick action: fair maiden handicapper: stays 1½m: acts on firm
going: blinkered after third start: often leads nowadays: has looked less than keen: sold
11,000 gns. *R. F. Johnson Houghton*

DANCING WITH HEART   3 ch.f. Dancing Spree (USA) – Heart Broken 78 (Bustino 136) [2002 7.5m 8g Jul 20] fourth foal: dam 6f/7f winner: well held in claimer/seller. *J. R. Norton* —

DAN DARE   3 b.g. Efisio 120 – Daring Ditty (Daring March 116) [2002 6g 8f 6s May 26] half-brother to 3 winners, notably sprinters Bold Edge (very smart) and Brave Edge (useful), both by Beveled: dam twice-raced daughter of useful sprinter Dawn Ditty: well beaten in maidens: dead. *R. Hannon* —

DAN DE LION   3 b.c. Danzig Connection (USA) – Fiorini 54 (Formidable (USA) 125) [2002 –: 10m 7.1m Sep 16] good-bodied colt: no sign of ability. *Jedd O'Keeffe* —

DANDILUM   5 b.g. Dilum (USA) 115 – Renira 60 (Relkino 131) [2002 –: 7f³ 7g 8f 7f⁴ 8g⁴ 8m 10m² 10m Jul 8] leggy, quite good-topped gelding: modest maiden: stays 1¼m: acts on firm and good to soft going: tried blinkered. *J. M. Bradley*   53

DANDOONA   3 b.f. Zafonic (USA) 130 – Speedybird (IRE) 71 (Danehill (USA) 126) [2002 –: 5g 5.3d 6.1m Jun 17] leggy, good-topped filly: no form: looks wayward. *J. D. Czerpak* —

DANDOUN   4 b.c. Halling (USA) 133 – Moneefa 73 (Darshaan 133) [2002 114: 8s* 9m³ 8d Nov 17] useful-looking colt: has a quick, unimpressive action: smart performer: has won 4 of his 8 outings (unraced at 2 yrs), including listed race at Doncaster in March by 3 lengths from Zarin, quickening on under 2f out: good 2 lengths third to Indian Creek in Earl of Sefton Stakes at Newmarket next time: tailed off after 7-month absence in Premio Ribot at Rome final start: stays 9f: acts on soft and good to firm ground: has worn crossed noseband: often tends to be rather edgy in preliminaries: takes strong hold. *J. L. Dunlop*   114

DANDY REGENT   8 b.g. Green Desert (USA) 127 – Tahilla 112 (Moorestyle 137) [2002 52, a–: 7s² 6f⁵ 8d* 8g⁶ 7.9g 7.2d* 8g Aug 26] angular gelding: modest performer: won claimers at Leicester in May and Ayr in August: probably best at 7f/1m: acts on good to firm and heavy going: none too consistent: sold £1,000. *John A. Harris*   64 § a– §

DANEBANK (IRE)   2 b.g. (May 6) Danehill (USA) 126 – Snow Bank (IRE) (Law Society (USA) 130) [2002 7m p7g p7g Oct 16] IR 36,000Y: sixth foal: half-brother to French 10.5f winner Coral Response (by Pursuit of Love): dam, French 1½m/15f winner, half-sister to very smart colts Blue Stag and Oscar, runner-up in Derby and Prix du Jockey Club respectively: modest maiden: should stay 1m: gelded after final start. *J. W. Hills*   64

DANEHILL LAD (IRE)   2 b.g. (Apr 19) Danehill (USA) 126 – River Missy (USA) (Riverman (USA) 131) [2002 p8g Nov 14] 16,000Y: half-brother to numerous winners, including 3-y-o Ticket To Dance and US Grade 2 winner (including at 2 yrs) Miss Golden Circle (by Crafty Prospector): dam, Irish 1¼m winner on only start, half-sister to Fillies' Mile winner Leap Lively, herself dam of Irish 1000 Guineas winner Forest Flower: 20/1 and green, well held in maiden at Lingfield. *S. Dow* —

DANEHILL MISS (IRE)   2 b.f. (May 3) Danehill Dancer (IRE) 117 – Persian Flower (Persian Heights 129) [2002 5m⁴ 5d 7d f6g Nov 18] IR 10,000F, IR 13,000Y: neat, angular filly: fourth foal: half-sister to fairly useful 1999 2-y-o 5f and 7f winner Flowington (by Owington), later successful in USA, and 3-y-o Blooming Lucky: dam lightly raced: well held after showing modest form when favourite for maiden at Beverley on debut. *T. D. Easterby*   50

DANEHILL PRINCE (IRE)   3 ch.c. Danehill Dancer (IRE) 117 – Shragraddy Lass (IRE) 73 (Jareer (USA) 115) [2002 7d³ 7m² 7f⁴ 8m p7g p7g Dec 11] IR 21,000Y: fourth foal: half-brother to a winner up to 7.5f in Italy by Lake Coniston: dam Irish 6f winner: fair maiden at best: well held last 3 starts, including in seller: should stay 1m: acts on good to firm going. *A. P. Jarvis*   70 d

DANEHILL STROLLER (IRE)   2 b.g. (Feb 11) Danetime (IRE) 121 – Tuft Hill 92 (Grundy 137) [2002 p5g* 5d² 5.2f 6d 6m³ Sep 13] 11,500Y: angular gelding: ninth foal: half-brother to 3 winners, including fairly useful 2000 2-y-o 5f winner Da Vinci (by Inzar) and 5f (including at 2 yrs) winner Lady Caroline Lamb (by Contract Law): dam, 2-y-o 6f winner, half-sister to grandam of 3-y-o Bright Sky: fairly useful performer: won maiden at Lingfield in June: unlucky neck second to Sahara Shade in minor event at Beverley: creditable third of 22 to Fleetwood Bay in sales race at Doncaster: effective at 5f/6f: acts on good to firm going, good to soft and polytrack. *R. M. Beckett*   86

DANEHURST   4 b.f. Danehill (USA) 126 – Miswaki Belle (USA) 73 (Miswaki (USA) 124) [2002 117: 6m² 6d³ 5m 5g* 6m 6s* 6d* Nov 17] small, barrel-shaped filly: smart performer: won Big Shuffle Flying Five at the Curragh (from Lady Dominatrix) in September, Prix de Seine-et-Oise at Maisons-Laffitte (from Captain Rio) in October,   118

Big Shuffle Flying Five, the Curragh—
Ireland's most important all-aged sprint sees a 1,2,3 for British-trained fillies Danehurst (right),
Lady Dominatrix (striped sleeves) and Jessica's Dream (second left)

leading close home both times to win by a head, and Premio Umbria at Rome (by 1¼ lengths from Sopran Foldan) in November: ran creditably when placed in Golden Jubilee Stakes at Royal Ascot (second to Malhub) and July Cup at Newmarket (favourite, third to Continent): poor efforts third and fifth starts: effective at 5f/6f: acts on fibresand, soft and good to firm ground: blinkered last 4 starts: stays in training. *Sir Mark Prescott*

DANELOR (IRE) 4 b.c. Danehill (USA) 126 – Formulate 119 (Reform 132) [2002 **90** 94: 8.1d⁴ 7f 8m 10.4m⁶ 10.3d 10d⁴ 10.3m⁶ 8.1f² 7f 8g Oct 24] sturdy, good-bodied colt: fairly useful handicapper: stays 1¼m: yet to race on soft/heavy ground, acts on any other: free-going sort: sold 25,000 gns. *E. A. L. Dunlop*

DANEMERE (IRE) 3 b.f. Danehill (USA) 126 – Kentmere (FR) (Galetto (FR) 118) **90** [2002 79p: 8d³ 8.2f² 8.5s⁵ 8m 7d 6.1m 7.1m Sep 15] good-topped, close-coupled filly: fairly useful performer: best efforts in listed race at Ascot (third to Monturani) and minor event at Nottingham (second to Seihali) in May: stays 1m: acts on any going: free-going sort. *J. W. Hills*

DANESWOOD 3 b.g. Be My Chief (USA) 122 – Floria Tosca § (Petong 126) [2002 **54 §** 60§: 10.2m 8.1d 10m² 11.9m 11.5m⁵ 10.1m* 10m Oct 3] modest performer: left B. R. Millman after second outing: won seller at Yarmouth in September: stays 1¼m: acts on good to firm ground: used to wear blinkers/visor (not since second start): ungenuine. *P. W. D'Arcy*

DANGER BIRD (IRE) 2 ch.f. (Apr 28) Eagle Eyed (USA) 111 – Danger Ahead **51** (Mill Reef (USA) 141) [2002 5.1m 5m⁴ 6m⁵ 6.1m⁴ 6m 6f 7g f6g⁵ Nov 18] IR 6,000F, IR **a54** 3,000Y: leggy filly: sister to a 10.5f winner in Italy, closely related to 1998 2-y-o 5f winner Brockton Saga (by Perugino) and half-sister to 3 winners, including 9-y-o Fairy Prince: dam unraced: modest maiden: races freely and should prove best at 5f/6f: acts on fibresand, raced only on ground firmer than good on turf. *R. Hollinshead*

DANGEROUS DAVE 3 b.g. Superpower 113 – Lovely Lilly (Arrasas (USA) 100) **–** [2002 p6g Nov 14] second foal: dam unraced: 50/1, slowly away and well beaten in maiden at Lingfield. *Jamie Poulton*

DANGEROUS LIAISON 3 b.g. Great Commotion (USA) 123 – Courtisane (Per- **60** sepolis (FR) 127) [2002 75: p5g⁴ p5g⁴ f5g⁶ 5m³ 5.3m 5.1d f5g 5m 7m Jul 3] rather leggy, useful-looking gelding: modest performer: best at 5f: acts on any turf going and polytrack, probably on fibresand: usually blinkered/visored: sometimes hangs right/carries head high: sold 4,500 gns. *C. A. Dwyer*

DANGER OVER 5 b.h. Warning 136 – Danilova (USA) (Lyphard (USA) 132) [2002 **115** 118: 5.5d* 6g⁴ 7m⁴ 6s³ 6d³ 5s⁴ Oct 20] ex-French horse: smart performer: won listed race at Maisons-Laffitte in April by ¾ length from Search For Light: best effort of season when length third to Crystal Castle in Prix de Meautry at Deauville penultimate start: below form (blinkered) in Premio Omenoni at Milan final outing: best at 6f/7f: acts on good to soft going, not discredited on good to firm: sold 85,000 gns, joined J. Osborne. *P. Bary, France*

DANIEL DERONDA 8 b.g. Danehill (USA) 126 – Kilvarnet 78 (Furry Glen 121) – [2002 p13g p10g Apr 10] big, good-topped gelding: fair handicapper at best: lightly raced and no form since 1999: tried blinkered. *Jean-Rene Auvray*

DANIELLE'S LAD 6 b.g. Emarati (USA) 74 – Cactus Road (FR) (Iron Duke (FR) **92** 122) [2002 92, a–: 6d 6v⁴ 6g³ 6f 6g 6.1s* 7v f6g Dec 31] strong gelding: fairly useful **a–** handicapper: won at Nottingham in October by 4 lengths from Taras Emperor: effective at 6f/easy 7f: acts on heavy and good to firm going, well held only all-weather run in 2002: blinkered: tends to get on edge: has run poorly when sweating: often early to post: has wandered/folded tamely: front runner: none too consistent. *B. Palling*

DANI RIDGE (IRE) 4 b.f. Indian Ridge 123 – Daniella Drive (USA) (Shelter Half **92 d** (USA)) [2002 75p: 6d⁵ 7.1d⁶ 7g³ 7m 5.9v⁵ 6m⁶ 6v 6.1f* 7f 7s Oct 26] IR 45,000Y: good-topped filly: has scope: seventh reported foal: sister to useful 7f to 8.5f winner Blomberg and to winner in Japan: dam won 12 races in USA up to 6f: fairly useful performer at best: trained by L. Browne in Ireland only 3-y-o start: won maiden at Catterick in March and minor event at Chester in September: ran poorly last 2 starts: effective at 6f/7f: acts on any going. *E. J. Alston*

DANISH DECORUM (IRE) 3 ch.g. Danehill Dancer (IRE) 117 – Dignified Air **86** (FR) 70 (Wolver Hollow 126) [2002 74: 8.3m² 7.9f 8g⁶ 8f 12f⁴ 13.9f Oct 12] tall gelding: fairly useful performer: best effort on reappearance: seems to stay 1½m: acts on firm going: joined C. Cox. *M. A. Jarvis*

DANISH PAN (IRE) 2 b.f. (Mar 25) Danehill (USA) 126 – Moment of Truth (IRE) **62** (Caerleon (USA) 132) [2002 7m p7g p7g Dec 11] 27,000F, IR 62,000Y, 57,000 2-y-o: first foal: dam unraced half-sister to Pilsudski: modest maiden: best effort on debut: should stay 1m. *J. Noseda*

DANITY FAIR 4 b.f. Cool Jazz 116 – Flute Royale 74 (Horage 124) [2002 33: f7s 6f – 7f Jun 3] of little account. *R. Bastiman*

DANO-MAST 6 b.h. Unfuwain (USA) 131 – Camera Girl (Kalaglow 132) [2002 117: **120** 9g* 13m⁵ 12g² 12g² 9.8g* 10m³ Dec 15] very smart performer: better than ever in 2002, winning listed race at Copenhagen in June, Stockholm Cup International at Taby (by 1½ lengths from Harrier) in September and Prix Dollar Fouquet's Barriere at Longchamp (led 2f out to beat Binary File 2½ lengths) in October: ran well when ½-length third to Precision in steadily-run Hong Kong Cup at Sha Tin final start: effective at 9f to 1½m: acts on soft and good to firm ground: genuine and consistent. *F. Poulsen, Denmark*

DANTON (IRE) 4 ch.g. Cadeaux Genereux 131 – Royal Circle 95 (Sadler's Wells **69** (USA) 132) [2002 74: f9.4g³ 10s⁴ f8g 12.6g⁶ 10m⁵ 10m Aug 16] very tall gelding: fair performer, quite lightly raced: claimed from M. Johnston after reappearance: stays 1¼m: acts on good to firm going, soft and fibresand: carries head awkwardly. *Miss S. J. Wilton*

DANZIG DANCER (IRE) 4 b.g. Barathea (IRE) 127 – Blueberry Walk (Green Desert (USA) 127) [2002 –: f16.2g Jan 19] IR 47,000Y: third foal: half-brother to 1998 2-y-o 7f winner Buona Sera (by Marju) and 9f winner Joondey (by Pursuit of Love), both fairly useful: dam unraced sister to useful stayer Hawait Al Barr: little form (left K. O'Brien, Ireland, after final 3-y-o start). *C. A. Dwyer*

Prix Dollar - Fouquet's Barriere, Longchamp—foreign runners dominate the finish as Dano-Mast, trained in Denmark, beats Binary File from Britain and Eagle Cafe (just off picture) from Japan

DANZIG FLYER (IRE) 7 b.g. Roi Danzig (USA) – Fenland Express (IRE) (Reason- –
able (FR) 119) [2002 –: f9.4g 16f Jun 11] no longer of much account. *M. Mullineaux*

DANZIG STAR 2 b.f. (Mar 23) Danzig Connection (USA) – Julie's Star (IRE) 45
(Thatching 131) [2002 7d 6s 7.6m Aug 21] fifth foal: closely related to 1998 2-y-o 6f
winner Peruvian Star (by Emarati) and half-sister to 9-y-o King of Peru: dam placed twice
at 3 yrs: no promise in maidens. *P. Howling*

DANZIG STYLE (IRE) 3 b.g. Desert Style (IRE) 121 – Aztec Princess (Indian King –
(USA) 128) [2002 7s 7m Apr 12] IR 21,000F: lengthy, good-topped gelding: eighth foal:
half-brother to 3 winners, including 6f to 9.7f winner Montone (by Pennine Walk) and
1¼m winner Pride of May (by Law Society): dam unraced half-sister to Indian Ridge:
claimer ridden, slowly away/tailed off in maidens at Doncaster and Southwell. *B. W. Hills*

DAPHNE ODORA 4 b.f. Elmaamul (USA) 125 – Heavenly Goddess (Soviet Star –
(USA) 128) [2002 41: f8.5g 10.2f[6] Sep 30] probably of little account nowadays.
B. G. Powell

DAPHNE'S DOLL (IRE) 7 b.m. Polish Patriot (USA) 128 – Helietta 78 (Tyrnavos **42**
129) [2002 52, a44: 7g 11.8d 9s 12g 8d 10m 10m 7f Sep 17] big mare: poor handicapper: **a–**
effective at 7f to easy 1¼m: acts on good to firm and heavy going, well held only run on
fibresand. *Dr J. R. J. Naylor*

DARA MAC 3 b.c. Presidium 124 – Nishara (Nishapour (FR) 125) [2002 39: 7m[3] 10f **60**
7m[6] 9d 7.9g 8.5m[2] 8m[4] 9.9m[6] 8m[2] 8.5m[4] Sep 24] modest maiden handicapper: stays 8.5f:
acts on good to firm going: blinkered final start: has started slowly. *N. Bycroft*

DARARA STAR (USA) 3 b.g. Dariyoun (USA) 115 – Tuviah (USA) (Eastern Echo –
(USA)) [2002 65: 10d 14d p12g Jun 29] small, well-made gelding: modest maiden at 2
yrs: well held in 2002. *J. Noseda*

DARASIM (IRE) 4 b.g. Kahyasi 130 – Dararita (IRE) (Halo (USA)) [2002 108: **113**
12.3m* 18.7f 12d[6] 13.9m[5] 14m[2] 12m* 15.9g[3] 18m[3] 12.3g Sep 22] lengthy, quite good-
topped gelding: smart performer: won minor event at Ripon in April and listed rated
stakes at Goodwood (beat The Whistling Teal 1½ lengths) in August: some creditable
efforts otherwise, including third to Boreas in Lonsdale Stakes at York and Doncaster Cup: barely stays 2¼m: probably acts on any going: usually blinkered/visored: best
ridden prominently (can run in snatches): has looked less than keen, and tends to run the
odd poor race. *M. Johnston*

DARCY 8 ch.g. Miswaki (USA) 124 – Princess Accord (USA) 115 (D'Accord (USA)) –
[2002 12m May 16] good-topped gelding: useful for Sir Michael Stoute at 3 yrs: well held
only Flat start since: visored once. *D. C. O'Brien*

DARDANUS 4 ch.g. Komaite (USA) – Dance On A Cloud (USA) 76 (Capote (USA)) **71**
[2002 81: 10m[6] p12g 11.9d[4] Jul 7] good-topped gelding: fairly useful at 3 yrs: just fair
in 2002: should stay beyond 1½m: acts on fibresand, soft and good to firm going:
sometimes visored: has carried head awkwardly: none too consistent: sold 14,000 gns,
joined C. Mann. *R. J. White*

DARE TO RUN 2 b.f. (May 1) Presidium 124 – Kabs Twist (Kabour 80) [2002 f7s –
f7g Dec 17] third foal: sister to 2000 2-y-o winner in Norway: dam unraced: well held in
maiden/seller: slowly away last time. *J. O'Reilly*

DARING CONNECTION 2 b.f. (Feb 21) Danzig Connection (USA) – Daring –
Destiny 113 (Daring March 116) [2002 6v[5] 6m 5f Oct 8] 1,800Y: leggy filly: first foal:
dam winner at 7f but best at 5f/6f: well held in maidens: upset in stall and withdrawn
second intended start. *K. R. Burke*

DARINSKA (IRE) 3 b.f. Zilzal (USA) 137 – Daralbayda (IRE) 102 (Doyoun 124) **105**
[2002 12g* 12g[3] 12m 10d 12.5g[2] 12.5m[4] 10.5v Nov 26] tall, leggy, close-coupled filly:
second foal: dam, French 1½m winner, half-sister to several useful French winners up to
around 1½m out of Prix Minerve winner Daralinsha, herself half-sister to Prix de Diane/
Vermeille winner Daryaba: useful performer: won minor event at Saint-Cloud in April:
creditable efforts afterwards when in frame in Prix de Royaumont at Chantilly (1¼
lengths third to Dance Routine) and listed races at Maisons-Laffitte and Fontainebleau:
travelled well but found little in Ribblesdale Stakes at Royal Ascot third outing: should
stay 1¾m: acts on good to firm going: blinkered except fourth start. *A. de Royer Dupre,
France*

DARJINGLE 3 b.f. Darshaan 133 – Delightful Chime (IRE) 79 (Alzao (USA) 117) **54**
[2002 45: 9.9m 12.1g 16.1m 13.8g[6] 12d Nov 5] leggy filly: modest maiden: barely stays
13.8f: acts on good to firm ground, well held on good to soft: sold 5,500 gns in December.
T. D. Easterby

DARK CHAMPION   2 b.g. (Apr 25) Abou Zouz (USA) 109 – Hazy Kay (IRE) 77   **71**
(Treasure Kay 114) [2002 6g³ 6m⁴ 7.1d² 7m⁵ 7s f8.5f Nov 29] 15,000Y, 48,000 2-y-o:
good-topped gelding: sixth foal: half-brother to 1998 2-y-o 5f winner Clara Blue (by
Alhijaz): dam, disappointing maiden who should have stayed beyond 7f, out of sister to
Middle Park winner Steel Heart: fair maiden: will probably stay 1m: acts on good to firm
ground (probably on soft), well held on fibresand. *P. C. Haslam*

DARK CHARM (FR)   3 b.g. Anabaa (USA) 130 – Wardara 107 (Sharpo 132) [2002   **104**
6g² 6m² 6s* 8m p7g* 7m² 6g² 7f Oct 10] 27,000F: tall, quite good-topped gelding:
first foal: dam, 5f/6f winner, best in France at 5/6 yrs: useful performer: won maiden at
Newbury and handicap at Lingfield in June: off nearly 3 months (reportedly freeze fired)
after latter, then best efforts when second in handicaps at Newbury (beaten ¾ length by
Tudor Wood) and Salisbury (beaten 1½ lengths by Ludynosa): may prove best at 6f/7f:
acts on polytrack, soft and good to firm going. *I. A. Balding*

DARK CUT (IRE)   2 b.g. (Apr 5) Ali-Royal (IRE) 127 – Prima Nox (Sabrehill (USA)   **–**
120) [2002 6f 7.2s f6g Nov 20] IR 2,500F, IR 5,500Y: first foal: dam unraced: well held
in maidens/claimer. *Mrs A. M. Naughton*

DARK DOLORES   4 b.f. Inchinor 119 – Pingin (Corvaro (USA) 124) [2002 43: p7g   **49**
7m⁴ 7d 9.7m⁴ 10.2d³ 10.1g 10m⁵ Jul 22] poor maiden handicapper: stays 1¼m: acts on
good to firm and good to soft ground. *C. Weedon*

DARK FLOWER (IRE)   3 b.f. Sadler's Wells (USA) 132 – Marino Casino (USA)   **78**
(Alleged (USA) 138) [2002 82: 9.9d⁶ 10.2s 12.6m³ p12g² p12g³ p13g⁴ 10.4m⁵ f9.4f⁴ Nov
29] well-made filly: has a quick action: fair maiden: stays 1½m: acts on polytrack, good
to firm and heavy ground: has worn blinkers (raced too freely)/cheekpieces: sold 11,000
gns. *B. W. Hills*

DARK SHADOWS   7 b.g. Machiavellian (USA) 123 – Instant Desire (USA) 86   **–**
(Northern Dancer) [2002 67: 13.8d 12.3g 16.1m 14.1s Jun 16] big, good-topped gelding:
has a high knee action: fair handicapper at best: well held in 2002. *W. Storey*

DARK SHAH (IRE)   2 b.g. (Feb 24) Night Shift (USA) – Shanjah (Darshaan 133)   **74**
[2002 6d⁵ 6m⁴ 5.1g* 5.1g⁴ 7s³ Sep 10] 30,000F: first foal: dam, French 1¼m winner,
sister to 4-y-o And Beyond: fair performer: won maiden at Chepstow in August: good
efforts in nurseries after, though carried head high and found little final start (gelded
after): will prove best up to 7f: acts on soft and good to firm ground: tongue tied second to
fourth starts. *I. A. Balding*

DARK SOCIETY   4 b.g. Imp Society (USA) – No Candles Tonight 74 (Star Appeal   **60**
133) [2002 70: 10d 12f Apr 13] medium-sized, useful-looking gelding: modest maiden
handicapper: stays 1¼m: acts on good to soft going: tried visored: has started slowly/
hung. *A. W. Carroll*

DARK STORM   3 gr.g. Terimon 124 – Norstock 52 (Norwick (USA) 125) [2002 –:   **–**
f7g f9.4g Dec 16] well beaten in maidens. *J. White*

DARK VALONA   3 b.f. Bandmaster (USA) 97 – Valona Valley (IRE) (Reprimand 122)   **–**
[2002 f5g⁶ Mar 18] second foal: dam, ran twice at 2 yrs, out of close relation to smart
Lowther winner Prickle: slowly away and always behind in Wolverhampton seller:
refused to enter stall next intended outing. *R. J. Hodges*

DARK VICTOR (IRE)   6 b.g. Cadeaux Genereux 131 – Dimmer 108 (Kalaglow 132)   **69**
[2002 73, a66: 12s 10d⁴ p10g 9.1s³ 10d f12f f8g f8.5g Nov 30] leggy, workmanlike   **a–**
gelding: fair handicapper: well below form last 6 starts: effective at 1m/1¾m: acts on
fibresand, seems best on going softer than good on turf: sometimes blinkered/visored,
latter for recent wins: usually patiently ridden: quirky. *D. Shaw*

DARLING LOVER (USA)   4 b.f. Dare And Go (USA) 125 – Doris's Secret (USA)   **56**
(Nikoli 125) [2002 6.9d³ 9g⁵ Aug 7] $17,000 2-y-o: half-sister to several winners in
USA, including minor stakes winners by Smile and Known Fact: dam won at 6f/6.5f (at 2
yrs) in USA: trained by C. B. Greely in USA at 3 yrs, best effort when third in maiden at
Hollywood: off a year and tongue tied, better effort in Britain on reappearance
(wandered). *S. J. Magnier*

DARMAGI (IRE)   2 b.f. (Mar 10) Desert King (IRE) 129 – Safe Care (IRE) (Caerleon   **77 p**
(USA) 132) [2002 7g⁵ 8.3d⁵ 7v³ Nov 8] 115,000Y: strong filly: first foal: dam, unraced
half-sister to smart sprinter Lugana Beach, out of half-sister to Mtoto: fair form in
maidens: third to Kingham at Doncaster final start: will be well suited by 1¼m+: likely to
do better. *Mrs A. J. Perrett*

DARWELL'S FOLLY (USA)   7 ch.g. Blushing John (USA) 120 – Hispanolia (FR)   – §
(Kris 135) [2002 –§, a43§: 9g 9.2s May 5] sturdy gelding: temperamental handicapper:
tried blinkered/visored/tongue tied. *P. Monteith*

DARWIN TOWER   4 gr.g. Bin Ajwaad (IRE) 119 – Floria Tosca § (Petong 126)   –
[2002 50: f7s f6g f7g 7g 7f 8m Jul 7] sturdy gelding: little form in 2002: often blinkered/
visored. *B. W. Murray*

DARZAO (IRE)   2 b.f. (Jan 9) Alzao (USA) 117 – Arctic Maid (IRE) 72 (Darshaan   –
133) [2002 7s Sep 10] IR 29,000F: second foal: half-sister to a 1¼m to 11f winner in Italy
by Brief Truce: dam, staying maiden on Flat/winning hurdler: 50/1 and green, tailed off
in maiden at Lingfield. *E. J. O'Neill*

DASAR   2 ch.f. (Feb 18) Catrail (USA) 123 – Rising of The Moon (IRE) 82 (Warning   69
136) [2002 5m* 5m⁴ f7g Nov 15] 8,200Y: close-coupled filly: first foal: fair form: won maiden at Beverley in April: off 6½ months
before well beaten final start: should stay 6f. *M. Brittain*

DASH FOR COVER (IRE)   2 b.g. (Apr 24) Sesaro (USA) 81 – Raindancing (IRE)   81
94 (Tirol 127) [2002 6d² 5.2d³ 6s Jun 12] 9,000Yi third foal. half-brother to fairly useful
2000 2-y-o 5f winner Jack Spratt (by So Factual): dam 2-y-o 6f winner who became
untrustworthy: best effort in maidens (fairly useful form) when third at Newbury: gelded
after disappointing final start: likely to prove best at 5f/6f: raced only on going softer than
good. *R. Hannon*

DASH FOR GLORY   3 ch.g. Bluegrass Prince (IRE) 110 – Rekindled Flame (IRE)   65
(Kings Lake (USA) 133) [2002 59: 9.9m⁴ p10g³ 9.7m 11.9m Sep 6] leggy gelding: fair
maiden: stays 1¼m: acts on good to firm going and polytrack. *M. Blanshard*

DASH FOR GOLD   3 br.f. Highest Honor (FR) 124 – Dashing Water 87 (Dashing   –
Blade 117) [2002 62: 12d⁵ 12m 12m 12.1g 16.2d 10m f12s 13.8f Sep 21] leggy filly:
modest maiden at 2 yrs: little form in 2002: blinkered/visored last 3 starts. *J. Hetherton*

DASHING BEAU (USA)   3 b.g. Beau Genius (CAN) – Full O Cherries (USA) (Full   –
Out (USA)) [2002 –: f8g 8m 12.1g Jul 30] leggy, close-coupled gelding: little form.
T. D. Barron

DASHING GENT   2 ch.c. (May 7) Prince Sabo 123 – Sistabelle (Bellypha 130) [2002   51
5.1d 6.1d p7g 8f f8.5f Nov 29] 3,000Y: half-brother to smart 5f (at 2 yrs) to 1¼m winner
Torch Rouge (by Warning) and to fairly useful 1¼m winner Filmore West (by In The
Wings): dam unraced sister to Bella Colora (dam of Stagecraft) and half-sister to Colorspin (dam of Opera House and Kayf Tara): modest maiden: stays 8.5f: best efforts on
all-weather. *G. L. Moore*

DASHING SPUR (IRE)   2 b.g. (Apr 21) Flying Spur (AUS) – Glamour Stock (USA)   –
(Marfa (USA)) [2002 p7g f8.5s Dec 9] IR 5,000F, IR 9,000Y: second foal: dam, Italian 5f
winner, half-sister to US Grade 2 1m winner Statesmanship: well held in maiden/seller:
gelded after final start. *R. M. Beckett*

DASHING STEVE   3 b.g. Danzig Connection (USA) – Blazing Sunset 55 (Blazing   44
Saddles (AUS)) [2002 f8.5g⁴ 8g 9m 5d 5f⁶ f5g⁵ f6g 5.9g 5m 5s f5g Dec 13] sixth foal:
half-brother to 5f winner Light Evidence (by Factual): dam 5f/6f (at 2 yrs) winner:
poor maiden handicapper: possibly best at 5f/6f: acts on fibresand: tried visored.
M. D. Hammond

DASH OF MAGIC   4 b.f. Magic Ring (IRE) 115 – Praglia (IRE) 64 (Darshaan 133)   57
[2002 53: 10g⁶ 10m⁵ 10m 12g 12.1d 10d⁵ 11.1g⁶ 7.9g⁵ 10.1m 12.1s 9.9m 10f² f12g⁴
f12g³ Dec 27] leggy, quite good-topped filly: modest maiden handicapper: should stay
1½m: acts on firm and good to soft ground, probably on fibresand: tried blinkered/
visored: has looked none too keen. *J. Hetherton*

DAT MY HORSE (IRE)   8 b.g. All Haste (USA) 109 – Toposki (FR) (Top Ville 129)   –
[2002 22.2m Jun 22] fair winning novice hurdler: tailed off when pulled up in Queen
Alexandra Stakes at Royal Ascot on Flat debut. *P. G. Murphy*

DATSME BOY   2 gr.g. (Jan 22) Petong 126 – Telloff (Reprimand 122) [2002 6d⁶ f7g⁶   40
7m Aug 14] 6,500Y: first living foal: dam lightly-raced: half-sister to very smart
performer up to 1½m Highland Chieftain: poor form in claimers/seller: tried blinkered.
B. Palling

DAUNTED (IRE)   6 b.g. Priolo (USA) 127 – Dauntess (Formidable (USA) 125) [2002   a65
46, a61: f12g* f16g³ f14g³ p12g 16g 12.3m f16.2g³ f16.2g³ f14.8g⁴ f14s² f14s* f12s⁵
f12g² f16g⁶ Nov 20] quite good-topped gelding: fair handicapper on all-weather: won at
Southwell in January (amateurs) and September: stays 2m: acts on fibresand: usually

blinkered prior to 2002: sometimes slowly away: usually held up: carries head awkwardly. *R. Wilman*

DAVE BEST (IRE) 2 b.c. (Mar 14) Marju (IRE) 127 – Tajanama (IRE) 52 (Gorytus (USA) 132) [2002 5.1f 5g⁶ 5g 5s 6m³ 7.5g⁴ 7m² 7m⁵ 6g 7m 6m f7g f6g Nov 22] IR 10,000Y: small, sparely-made colt: fourth foal: half-brother to 2 winners in Italy by Mukaddamah: dam Irish 6.5f winner: disappointing maiden, modest at best: barely stays 7f: acts on good to firm going: blinkered (went sharply left leaving stall) third outing: probably none too genuine. *A. Berry* **64 d**

DAVE THE BANK 7 ch.g. Desert Dirham (USA) 108 – L'Ancressaan 67 (Dalsaan 125) [2002 f14.8g Nov 30] of little account. *T. H. Caldwell* **–**

DAVOS 2 gr.g. (Jan 21) Wolfhound (USA) 126 – Misty Goddess (IRE) 63 (Godswalk (USA) 130) [2002 5d 5m 7g⁶ 6.1m 8g f8g² f8.5g³ f7s f7g* Dec 17] 9,000Y: strong, stocky gelding: fifth foal: half-brother to 1m (selling event) and 1¼m winner Imari (by Rock City) and 3-y-o Love In The Mist: dam 7f (at 2 yrs) to 11f winner: modest on all-weather, poor on turf: left Mrs J. Ramsden after second outing: won seller at Southwell in December: will probably stay 1¼m: acts on fibresand and good to firm going: sometimes slowly away (unruly and withdrawn once). *N. P. Littmoden* **38 a61**

DAVY LEESE 2 b.g. (May 8) Overbury (IRE) 116 – Mac's Type (IRE) (Mac's Imp (USA) 116) [2002 6m 6g⁵ 5m Aug 21] 1,800Y: first foal: dam tailed off both starts: poor maiden. *W. Storey* **47**

DAWANA (IRE) 3 ch.f. Halling (USA) 133 – Dawala (IRE) (Lashkari 128) [2002 8g⁴ 10.2d* 10.2g³ 11.9m⁴ 12m⁴ Oct 12] smallish, lengthy filly: fifth foal: half-sister to 1¼m/13f winner Darapour (by Fairy King) and 4-y-o Dawari, both useful: dam, French 1½m winner, closely related to Darshaan and to dam of 6-y-o Daliapour and Dalampour: useful performer: won maiden at Bath in July: best efforts in listed events at Chepstow (third to Albanova) and York (fourth to Alexander Three D) next 2 starts: stays 1½m: yet to race on extremes of going. *Sir Michael Stoute* **98**

DAWARI (IRE) 4 b.g. In The Wings 128 – Dawala (IRE) (Lashkari 128) [2002 99: 13.3m⁵ 12g 12s⁶ a12g a12g³ Dec 15] close-coupled, attractive gelding: useful performer, lightly raced: creditable sixth to Capitano Corelli in November Handicap at Doncaster on third start: sold from Sir Michael Stoute 26,000 gns after next start, third in minor event at Mijas final one: should be suited by further than 1½m: acts on soft going, seemed ill at ease on firm: wore net muzzle on reappearance, visored next 2 starts: has flashed tail/been slowly away/looked none too keen. *P. Haley, Spain* **101**

DAWN ALIBI (IRE) 2 ch.g. (May 12) Ali-Royal (IRE) 127 – Appledorn 99 (Doulab (USA) 115) [2002 5m⁴ 6m² 7f² 7m⁶ 7m 7g⁴ 8g* 8m f7g⁵ f8g⁶ Oct 17] IR 13,000Y: leggy gelding: sixth foal: half-brother to 3 winners, including 4-y-o Lady Pahia and 1m winner Patina (by Rudimentary): dam 6f/7f winner, latter including at 2 yrs: modest performer: claimed from Mrs J. Ramsden £5,200 after third start: won selling nursery at Leicester in September: stays 1m: raced only on good going or firmer on turf (below form on fibresand): blinkered last 5 starts: none too consistent: sold 3,500 gns, sent to Italy. *J. R. Best* **61**

DAWN INVASION (IRE) 3 b.c. Common Grounds 118 – Princess of Zurich (IRE) (Law Society (USA) 130) [2002 88p: 9.9d* 11.6g⁴ 12g* 13.9m⁴ Aug 21] quite good-topped colt: quickly developed into smart performer at 3 yrs, winning minor event at Salisbury in June and Tote Gold Trophy (Handicap) at Goodwood (always well **111**

Tote Gold Trophy (Handicap), Goodwood—Dawn Invasion makes a very lucrative handicap debut, beating Waverley (checked cap), Distinction (second left) and Dune (No.8)

positioned, beat Waverley a neck) in July: good length fourth to Hugs Dancer in Ebor (Handicap) at York final start, run out of second close home: stays 1¾m, at least with emphasis on speed: yet to race on extremes of going: has carried head awkwardly. *Mrs A. J. Perrett*

DAWN ROMANCE (IRE) 4 b. or br.f. Fraam 114 – Whispering Dawn 71 (Then – Again 126) [2002 f9.4g Jan 19] unfurnished filly: modest maiden at 2 yrs: well held only start since. *Mrs H. Dalton*

DAWN'S SHARP SHOT (IRE) 3 b. or br.f. Son of Sharp Shot (IRE) 105 – Dawn **73** Star 94 (High Line 125) [2002 68p: 10m* 10m 10s Oct 23] fair performer, lightly raced: won maiden at Sandown (wandered) in September: took good hold when well held both starts after: will need to learn to settle better to stay 1½m: acts on good to firm going. *J. L. Dunlop*

DA WOLF (IRE) 4 ch.g. Wolfhound (USA) 126 – Lady Joyce (FR) (Galetto (FR) **51** 118) [2002 52: 6f 5m 5s 5.3m⁵ 6f² 5g 7m 5m Sep 2] strong gelding: modest performer: stays 7f: acts on firm going: sometimes blinkered: none too consistent. *D. Nicholls*

DAYGLOW DANCER 4 b.g. Fraam 114 – Fading (Pharly (FR) 130) [2002 95: f8.5g* **95** 8s 8f 7.9f⁶ 8.3s 8.9d 8d² 8f² 8.3m⁴ 7.1m* 7.2g 8m 8g 8.2v 7v Nov 9] rather sparely-made **a103** gelding: useful handicapper: won at Wolverhampton (by head from Diamond Max) in March and Haydock (by 1¼ lengths from Blue Star) in September: well held last 5 starts: effective at 7f to 8.5f: acts on any turf going and fibresand: usually races up with pace. *M. R. Channon*

DAYS OF GRACE 7 gr.m. Wolfhound (USA) 126 – Inshirah (USA) 90 (Caro 133) **65** [2002 72: f6s⁶ f6g 6m 6d p6g³ 6m 5m f6g⁴ f6g² f6g² p7g Dec 30] lengthy mare: fair handicapper: effective at stiff 5f to easy 7f: acts on firm going, soft and all-weather: tried blinkered/visored: usually races prominently. *L. Montague Hall*

DAZZLING BAY 2 b.g. (Mar 1) Mind Games 121 – Adorable Cherub (USA) 58 **73 §** (Halo (USA)) [2002 5s² 5s* 5g⁵ 5v³ 5.9d⁶ 5g⁴ 6m 7f 6m⁵ 6f³ Oct 11] 17,000Y: big, rather leggy gelding: has a round action: sixth living foal: half-brother to Italian 6f to 7.5f winner Marvi Cherub (by Warrshan): dam, maiden bred to stay at least 1m, from family of Singspiel: fair performer: won maiden at Hamilton in May: stays 6f: acts on soft and firm going: tried blinkered: difficult ride: unreliable. *T. D. Easterby*

DAZZLING DAISY 5 b.m. Shareef Dancer (USA) 135 – Mariette 35 (Blushing Scribe – (USA) 107) [2002 –: f11s Jan 10] little form. *N. A. Graham*

DAZZLING QUINTET 6 ch.m. Superlative 118 – Miss Display 47 (Touch Paper **46** 113) [2002 48: 5g² 5g 5s f5g⁶ 5g 5m 5d Aug 23] sturdy mare: poor performer: probably **a30** best at 5f: acts on firm going, good to soft (probably on soft) and fibresand: usually visored prior to 2002: front runner: none too reliable. *C. Smith*

DAZZLING RIO (IRE) 3 b.g. Ashkalani (IRE) 128 – Dazzling Fire (IRE) 78 (Blue- **58** bird (USA) 125) [2002 59: f8s* p10g f9.4g⁶ f11g³ f12g 11.1v⁴ 10.9d⁴ 11s Aug 24] strong, sturdy gelding: modest handicapper: won at Southwell in January: stays 11f: acts on fibresand and soft going. *P. C. Haslam*

D-DAY-SMOKE 8 ch.g. Cigar 68 – Little Pockthorpe (Morston (FR) 125) [2002 8.5d – Aug 14] well beaten in seller/claimer 6 years apart. *A. Streeter*

DEAL IN FACTS 3 ch.f. So Factual (USA) 120 – Timely Raise (USA) (Raise A Man – (USA)) [2002 61d: f6s f8.5g Jan 19] tall, leggy filly: disappointing maiden: blinkered on reappearance. *J. A. Pickering*

DEAR BRIDIE (IRE) 3 ch.f. Entrepreneur 123 – Shebasis (USA) (General Holme **66** (USA) 128) [2002 66p: 8.1m⁴ 8m p10g⁴ 8.1d Jul 5] angular filly: fair maiden: unlikely to stay beyond 1¼m: acts on polytrack and heavy going: blinkered (hampered and unable to recover) second start: sold 5,000 gns, sent to South Korea. *B. W. Hills*

DEBANDY BOY 2 b.g. (Apr 6) Timeless Times (USA) 99 – Judys Girl (IRE) (Simply – Great (FR) 122) [2002 7m 5d 5m 6m 5m 7d Oct 18] sturdy gelding: seventh foal: brother to 1996 2-y-o 7f winner who stayed 1½m Grate Times: dam of little account: little form: tried visored. *J. S. Wainwright*

DEBBIE 3 b.f. Deploy 131 – Elita (Sharpo 132) [2002 10s⁶ f7f⁴ f7g Nov 22] third foal: **61 ?** half-sister to 4-y-o Telori: dam unraced granddaughter of Molecomb and Lowther Stakes winner Flying Legs: clearly best effort in maidens (modest form) when 10 lengths sixth to Behra at Newbury on debut: will probably stay 1½m. *I. A. Wood*

William Hill Great St Wilfrid Stakes (Handicap), Ripon—Deceitful gains reward for a tough campaign; he has a head to spare over Budelli, whilst Artie (No.15) and Gdansk are to the fore in the stand-side group

DEBBIE'S WARNING 6 b.h. Warning 136 – Lomond Blossom 98 (Lomond (USA) 128) [2002 84: p6g 5f 6m 7.1s 7g 6g 10m Jul 29] big, useful-looking horse: poor mover: has reportedly had soft palate operation: one-time smart performer: probably no longer of much account on Flat. *K. C. Bailey* —

DE BLANC (IRE) 2 b.f. (May 4) Revoque (IRE) 122 – Queen's Share (Main Reef 126) [2002 8g* 8s² Oct 13] IR 4,000Y: half-sister to 1994 2-y-o 6f winner Masruf (by Taufan) and 1¼m winner Persian King (by Persian Bold), both fairly useful: dam Irish sprinter: won minor event at Milan in September: useful form when 1¼ lengths second of 13 to Lady Catherine in Premio Dormello there: raced at 1m. *M. G. Quinlan* 98

DECEITFUL 4 ch.g. Most Welcome 131 – Sure Care 62 (Caerleon (USA) 132) [2002 91: p6g⁶ p8g³ p7g³ p7g⁶ 8s⁶ 7.1g⁵ 7f² 7d 5.1f⁶ 6g 7g⁴ 7.1d 7.1m³ 6m 7.6g* 7d 6m* 7m⁵ 6m³ 7m² 6g 8m 7f⁵ 7g Oct 18] leggy, quite good-topped gelding: useful handicapper: won at Chester and Ripon (beat Budelli by head in William Hill Great St Wilfrid) in August: effective at 6f to easy 1m: acts on any all-weather/any turf going: has been early to post/given trouble at stalls: tends to race freely: tough: sent to UAE. *P. D. Evans* 99

DECELERATE 2 ch.c. (Feb 12) Polar Falcon (USA) 126 – Speed To Lead (IRE) 90 (Darshaan 133) [2002 8.3d 8f 6.1g⁵ 8.3m 7s f7g⁴ f8g Dec 27] well-made colt: second foal: half-brother to 3-y-o Elucidate: dam, 2m winner who stayed 2¾m, out of close relative to Poule d'Essai des Poulains winner Fast Topaze: modest maiden: should stay at least 1m: acts on fibresand, well held on soft ground. *I. A. Wood* 58

DECHTIRE (IRE) 3 b.f. Thatching 131 – Derena (FR) (Crystal Palace (FR) 132) [2002 –p: 8.3m² Apr 22] better effort in maidens when 1¾ lengths second to Approaching Storm at Windsor, wandering and still looking green: not certain to stay beyond 1m: sold 7,000 gns. *R. Hannon* 80

DECISIVE 3 b.g. Alhaarth (IRE) 126 – Alys 107 (Blakeney 126) [2002 8f 8.3m 8.1g⁶ 12.4g² 14m⁵ 16.1m³ Oct 2] 78,000Y, 60,000 2-y-o: well-made gelding: closely related to Irish 17f winner Donostia (by Unfuwain) and half-brother to several winners abroad, including useful French stayer Warfield (by Glint of Gold) and German 1000 Guineas winner Princess Nana (by Bellypha): dam French performer up to 1¼m: fair maiden: stays 2m: raced only on good going or firmer. *W. J. Haggas* 72

259

DECO LADY   2 ch.f. (Mar 19) Wolfhound (USA) 126 – Art Deco Lady 51 (Master **65**
Willie 129) [2002 5s⁴ 5.1f⁴ 5m³ p6g f5s 6.5m 6m Sep 30] 2,000F: lengthy filly: has scope:
second foal: dam, maiden, stayed 1¾m: fair maiden: well held in nurseries last 3 starts,
racing freely in visor final one: should stay 6f: acts on firm going, below form on all-
weather. *P. D. Evans*

DECO STAR (IRE)   3 b.g. Dolphin Street (FR) 125 – Ecco Mi (IRE) (Priolo (USA) **57**
127) [2002 p7g⁵ f8.5g⁵ f8.5g⁶ 9.2s⁴ 11.5f² 11.6m 11m² 11.5f 12d⁶ 12g f14g f12g² Dec 27] **a60**
IR 18,000Y: third foal: half-brother to 4-y-o Ecology: dam unraced from very good
family of Sun Princess, Saddlers' Hall and Spectrum: modest maiden handicapper: left
A. Jarvis after tenth start: should stay beyond 11.5f: acts on firm going and fibresand:
visored (ran well) final outing. *I. A. Wood*

DECOY   3 b.f. Double Eclipse (IRE) 122 – Kilcoy (USA) (Secreto (USA) 128) [2002 **84**
–p: 12.1g⁴ 14.1f* 14.1f² 16.2f* 18d² 15g Jul 5] lengthy, unfurnished filly: fairly useful
handicapper: won at Redcar (maiden event) and Warwick in June: reportedly finished
lame (second run in 2 days) final start: stayed 2¼m: acted on firm and good to soft going:
dead. *M. Johnston*

DEDHAM VALE (USA)   2 ch g (Mar 29) Atticus (USA) 121 – Flute of Silver (USA) **69**
(Silver Hawk (USA) 123) [2002 5m⁵ 6d 6m³ 7g⁴ 8m 10m 7g 8g a8g Dec 8] 220,000
francs Y: good-topped gelding: has scope: easy mover: fourth living foal: closely related
to a winner in USA by Alwuhush and half-brother to winner there by Stop The Music:
dam ran 3 times in USA: fair maiden: sold from P. Cole 3,500 gns before final appearance (well beaten): probably stays 1m: yet to race on extremes of going: blinkered (folded
tamely) seventh start. *J. Calderon, Spain*

DEDICATION (FR)   3 gr.f. Highest Honor (FR) 124 – Dissertation (FR) 104 (Sillery **113**
(USA) 122) [2002 6s* 7g² 8g⁶ 7s* 8s² 8g² 7d⁶ 7m* Oct 13] tall filly: first foal: dam,
French 5.5f winner (including at 2 yrs) who stayed 1m, closely related to useful French
stayer Divination and half-sister to smart French/US performer up to 1½m Beau Sultan:
smart performer: won minor events at Maisons-Laffitte at 2 yrs and Fontainebleau in
March, listed race at Deauville (by ½ length from Polygreen) in July and Prix de la Foret
at Longchamp (led inside final 1f to beat Medecis a neck) in October: also ran well when
second to Turtle Bow in Prix d'Astarte (beaten ½ length) and Devious Indian in Prix
Quincey (beaten a nose), both at Deauville in August: effective at 7f/1m: acts on soft and
good to firm going: to join C. Clement in USA. *Mme C. Head-Maarek, France*

DEEKAZZ (IRE)   3 b.f. Definite Article 121 – Lyric Junction (IRE) (Classic Secret **49**
(USA) 91) [2002 54: 9d 7.2g 8m 7.1d 7.9m 7.5m³ 10m² 9m⁴ 10.9s⁵ Oct 14] lengthy,
angular filly: poor maiden: stays 1¼m: best efforts on good going or firmer: usually
blinkered in 2002. *A. Berry*

*Prix de la Foret, Longchamp—Dedication and Medecis (No.7) give trainer Criquette Head-Maarek a 1,2;
Cayoke (No.1) and War Zone (rail) are close behind*

Mme A. Head's "Dedication"

DEEP BLUE 5 b.g. Lake Coniston (IRE) 131 – Billie Blue 63 (Ballad Rock 122) [2002 –
83d: 8d May 1] well-made gelding: fairly useful handicapper at best: well held only 5-y-o
outing: stayed 7f: acted on fibresand, soft and good to firm going: tried visored: dead.
Dr J. D. Scargill

DEEP DALE 6 b.g. Pharly (FR) 130 – L'Oraz (Ile de Bourbon (USA) 133) [2002 –: –
16m 14.1f⁴ 14s 14.6m 16.5g Jul 11] robust gelding: little form. *Mrs S. Lamyman*

DEE PEE TEE CEE (IRE) 8 b.g. Tidaro (USA) – Silver Glimpse 108 (Petingo 135)   **61**
[2002 64: 12.3g 9.9m⁴ 12.4g 12.4s⁵ 11s 9.9m Sep 24] tall gelding: has a round action:
modest handicapper nowadays: stays 1½m: acts on soft and good to firm going.
M. W. Easterby

DEEP END (USA) 2 br.f. (Mar 19) Lord Avie (USA) – Deep Magic (USA) (Gone   **58**
West (USA)) [2002 7.1m 6d 6s f6g² f6g⁶ Nov 30] leggy filly: first foal: dam, ran 3 times,
half-sister to dams of very smart US Grade 1 1¼m winner Skimming and 1000 Guineas
winner Wince: clearly best effort in maidens (fair form) when 6 lengths second to Bond
Royale at Wolverhampton: should stay 7f: acts on fibresand. *R. Charlton*

DEEPER IN DEBT 4 ch.g. Piccolo 121 – Harold's Girl (FR) (Northfields (USA))   **88**
[2002 55, a49: p10g³ p10g⁵ f8.5g* f8.5g* f8.5g f7g³ 8.1m 8m* f9.4f* 8f* 10.4m 8m⁴
8.1m⁴ 8f* 8.2v p8g* Dec 3] fairly useful handicapper: had a good season, winning at
Wolverhampton (3), Yarmouth, Bath, Goodwood (claiming event, left J. Osborne
£12,000) and Lingfield between March and December: effective at 1m/easy 1¼m: acts
on all-weather, firm and soft going: tried blinkered/tongue tied at 3 yrs: often front runner.
J. Akehurst

DEEWAAR (IRE) 2 b.g. (Apr 14) Ashkalani (IRE) 128 – Chandni (IRE) (Ahonoora 122) [2002 6g 6s 7m Aug 26] 2,500Y: sixth foal: half-brother to fairly useful Irish 9f and 1½m winner Chanoud (by Ezzoud) and 3-y-o Arctic Falcon: dam, of no account, sister to smart 1m/1¼m performer Visto Si Stampi: well held in maidens/minor event. *J. S. Moore* —

DEFIANCE 7 b.g. Warning 136 – Princess Athena 119 (Ahonoora 122) [2002 51§: f6g 6m 6.1v⁵ 5.7m 5m³ 5g 6g⁶ Oct 28] tall gelding: poor maiden: best at 5f/6f: acts on good to firm and heavy going: blinkered: unreliable. *A. P. James* **38 §**

DEFINING 3 b.g. Definite Article 121 – Gooseberry Pie 63 (Green Desert (USA) 127) [2002 72p: 7.1g⁶ p10g* 10m* 9.9g p12g* 12m* 12g* 12g* Oct 17] lengthy gelding: has scope: progressive performer: won handicaps at Lingfield (2), minor event at Ripon and handicaps at Newmarket (2) and Thirsk between June and October: useful form to beat Maimana by ¾ length at Newmarket for final success: stays 1½m: acts on polytrack and good to firm going, shaped with promise on fibresand final 2-y-o start: probably capable of further improvement. *J. R. Fanshawe* **101 p**

DEFINITE FLASH (IRE) 4 b.f. Definite Article 121 – Superflash (Superlative 118) [2002 53: p13g f12g⁵ f12g f16,2g Feb 22] maiden: little form in 2002. *G. C. Bravery* —

DEFINITE GUEST (IRE) 4 gr.g. Definite Article 121 – Nicea (IRE) 90 (Dominion 123) [2002 82: 7m 7f⁴ 7m 7m⁴ 7m⁴ 7f 7m 7m⁴ 7m³ 7m⁶ 7g 7d⁴ 8v Nov 8] leggy gelding: fairly useful handicapper: sold from G. Margarson 35,000 gns before final start: should stay 1m: acts on firm and good to soft going: blinkered once: usually held up. *R. A. Fahey* **84**

DEFINITELY SPECIAL (IRE) 4 b.f. Definite Article 121 – Legit (IRE) (Runnett 125) [2002 –: 10m 8.1g 10.2f 10.2g⁴ 10m 8f³ f9.4g Dec 16] modest maiden: barely stays 1m+: raced only on good going or firmer on turf. *J. M. Bradley* **50**

DELACROIX (USA) 2 ch.c. (Apr 26) Gulch (USA) – Line of Thunder (USA) 112 (Storm Bird (CAN) 134) [2002 8s* 10v⁵ Nov 9] brother to high-class US performer Thunder Gulch (won Kentucky Derby and Belmont Stakes) and half-brother to several winners: dam 6f (at 2 yrs) and 7f winner out of high-class 1½m to 14.6f filly Shoot A Line: won maiden at Gowran in October by 1½ lengths from Monsignor Phil: useful form when 5¾ lengths fifth to Alberto Giacometti in Criterium de Saint-Cloud, held up and running on: will stay beyond 1¼m: will improve further. *A. P. O'Brien, Ireland* **102 p**

DELAWARE TRAIL 3 b.g. Catrail (USA) 123 – Dilwara (IRE) (Lashkari 128) [2002 –: 6d Oct 18] big, leggy gelding: well held in 2 maidens. *J. S. Wainwright* —

DELEGATE 9 ch.g. Polish Precedent (USA) 131 – Dangora (USA) 98 (Sovereign Dancer (USA)) [2002 83: 5.3g³ 5.1d⁴ 5s⁶ p5g 5.3d 5d⁴ 5g* 5.1f* 5.2m³ 5m⁶ 5m³ 5g 5g 5v Nov 8] lengthy gelding: poor mover: fairly useful performer: won handicap at Newmarket and claimer at Bath in July: best at 5f nowadays: acts on any turf going: sometimes slowly away/hangs: usually held up. *N. A. Callaghan* **86**

DELGADO 3 b.g. Alhaarth (IRE) 126 – Nur (USA) 74 (Diesis 133) [2002 83: a6g* a8g⁶ a6g⁴ f6s Sep 17] big, strong gelding: fluent mover: fairly useful performer: won minor event at Mijas for J. Brown in Spain in January: well beaten on British return final start: stays 6f: acts on soft going, good to firm and sand: ran poorly in blinkers/tongue strap. *R. Guest* **?**

Buckingham Palace Stakes (Handicap), Royal Ascot—
Demonstrate makes a winning handicap debut; Lunar Leo (behind winner) is second,
in front of Kareeb (right) and Point of Dispute (visor)

DELHAM (IRE)　2 ch.c. (Feb 22) Machiavellian (USA) 123 – Matila (IRE) 98　**67 ?**
(Persian Bold 123) [2002 7f 6.1g⁵ 8m⁵ 7.1m 8m 10f⁵ 10s⁵ Oct 23] IR 8,500Y: tall, leggy,
angular colt: sixth foal: brother to smart 7f (at 2 yrs) to 8.5f winner Easaar and half-
brother to 3 winners, including fairly useful Chafaya (7f, by Mark of Esteem) and 7-y-o
Rayik: dam 6f winner: fair maiden: best effort when fifth at Pontefract sixth start
(possibly flattered): stays 1¼m: acts on firm ground, probably on soft. *J. D. Czerpak*

DELIGHTED (IRE)　3 b.f. Danehill (USA) 126 – Bex (USA) 116 (Explodent (USA))　**74**
[2002 7g⁵ 8.3m⁶ 9d² 8v⁵ 10s Nov 10] rather leggy, quite good-topped filly: half-sister to
several winners (all at least useful), including smart French 1¼m/1½m winners Hijaz (by
Sadler's Wells) and Crimson Quest (by Rainbow Quest), latter also good stayer in Saudi
Arabia: dam 1m to 10.5f winner: fair maiden: 6 lengths second to Sentimental Value at
Ripon third start, final outing for Sir Michael Stoute: stayed 9f: blinkered final outing:
slowly into stride on debut: visits Elusive Quality. *H-A. Pantall, France*

DELLA FRANCESCA (USA)　3 b.c. Danzig (USA) – La Affirmed (USA) (Affirmed　**112**
(USA)) [2002 110p: 8m² 8g 8s³ 10s* 12d⁶ 8d Nov 21] tall, rangy colt: smart performer:
placed in Craven Stakes at Newmarket (2 lengths second to King of Happiness) and Irish
2000 Guineas at the Curragh (4½ lengths third to easy winner Rock of Gibraltar) before
winning Gallinule Stakes at Leopardstown in June by neck from Jammaal, getting on top
close home: always behind in Poule d'Essai des Poulains at Longchamp second start,
never a threat (though not discredited) when 9 lengths sixth to stable-companion High
Chaparral in Irish Derby at the Curragh in June: left A. O'Brien and after nearly 5 months
before well below form final outing (blinkered): stays 1½m: acts on soft and good to firm
going: has worn crossed noseband: races rather lazily. *N. M. O'Callaghan, USA*

DEL MAR SUNSET　3 b.g. Unfuwain (USA) 131 – City of Angels (Woodman　**67**
(USA) 65) [2002 65: f8.5g* 9m 10.3g⁴ 12.3m⁶ 10.9d p8g* f7s³ f9.4g* f8.5f² f8.5s³ p10g　**a93**
Dec 21] fairly useful on all-weather, fair on turf: won maiden at Wolverhampton in April
and handicaps at Lingfield in August and Wolverhampton in October: stays 9.4f: acts on
all-weather: tried blinkered/tongue tied. *W. J. Haggas*

DELPHI　6 ch.g. Grand Lodge (USA) 125 – Euridice (IRE) 66 (Woodman (USA) 126)　**62**
[2002 65: 16s⁶ 14d³ 16d 16d⁶ p13g Dec 28] first foal: dam 9.7f winner who probably
stayed 15f: modest handicapper: left C. Collins, Ireland, €7,000 before final start: stays
2m: acts on firm and soft going. *B. G. Powell*

DEMI BEAU　4 b.g. Dr Devious (IRE) 127 – Charming Life (NZ) (Sir Tristram 115)　**102**
[2002 81: 12m 12m* 12f* 12g 13.9m 10s* Oct 26] tall, close-coupled gelding: useful
performer: much improved in 2002: won handicap at Musselburgh and minor event at
Newmarket in May, and handicap at Newbury (beat Red Carnation gamely by ¾ length
after 3-month break) in October: effective at 1¼m/1½m: yet to race on heavy ground, acts
on any other: reportedly lost action fourth start, folded tamely next time: often makes
running: sold 18,000 gns, joined C. Mann. *W. Jarvis*

DEMOCRACY (IRE)　6 ch.g. Common Grounds 118 – Inonder 31 (Belfort (FR) 89)　**57**
[2002 57: f9.4g³ f9.4g⁴ p12g³ p12g³ 10.9g⁵ 11.9g³ 12d² 12.3m 10d f14.8g 10g p12g
f12g⁵ f12g⁴ Dec 26] modest handicapper: barely stays 1½m: acts on firm going, soft and
all-weather: often visored/blinkered earlier in career: has worn cheekpieces: waited with.
P. G. Murphy

DEMONSTRATE (USA)　4 ch.c. Storm Bird (CAN) 134 – Substance (USA) (Diesis　**112**
133) [2002 –: 6g⁶ 7m* 7m* 7m 7.9m⁵ 7f* 7m⁴ Oct 19] well-made colt: has a quick action:
smart performer: improved substantially in 2002: won maiden at Yarmouth in May and
handicaps at Royal Ascot (Buckingham Palace Stakes by length from Lunar Leo) in
June and Newmarket (impressively by 3 lengths from Barking Mad) in October: good
4¾ lengths fourth to Nayyir in Challenge Stakes at Newmarket final start: better form
at 7f than 1m: raced mainly on going firmer than good: has been led by 2 handlers.
J. H. M. Gosden

DEMOPHILOS　4 b.c. Dr Devious (IRE) 127 – Graecia Magna (USA) 109 (Private　**105**
Account (USA)) [2002 119: 12g Mar 23] good-topped colt: smart performer at 3 yrs,
when second in St Leger at Doncaster: below form in Dubai Sheema Classic at Nad Al
Sheba (reportedly returned home with an injury) only 4-y-o start: races bit freely, but
stays 1¾m: acts on good to firm and good to soft going, ran poorly on firm: has worn
crossed noseband: sometimes slowly away. *Mrs A. J. Perrett*

DENARO (GER)　4 b.c. Dashing Blade 117 – Dapprima (GER) 107 (Shareef Dancer　**107**
(USA) 135) [2002 112: a9.5g² a9.5g⁴ p10g 8g 8s⁶ Jun 29] approx. 22,000Y in
Germany: first foal: dam, German 7f (at 2 yrs) and 1m winner, second in 10.5f Prix de
Flore: smart performer at 3 yrs, winning listed race at Mulheim and Group 2 contest at

Cologne: just useful form in 2002: respectable efforts when ninth to Adiemus in listed race at Lingfield on third start (slowly away) and eighth in Badener Meile at Baden-Baden penultimate one: best around 9f/1¼m: acts on heavy going. *M. Hofer, Germany*

DENISE BEST (IRE) 4 ch.f. Goldmark (USA) 113 – Titchwell Lass 57 (Lead On Time (USA) 123) [2002 –: f8.5s⁴ 11.8d² 10.2v⁴ 12.1d³ 10m Jul 22] poor maiden handicapper: likely to stay beyond 1½m: acts on fibresand, good to firm and heavy going: sometimes slowly away (markedly so final start). *Miss K. M. George* **45**

DENMARK (IRE) 3 b.c. Danehill (USA) 126 – Shamarra (FR) (Zayyani 119) [2002 81p: f8g Dec 17] tall, good sort: has scope: fair form, lightly raced: won maiden at Newcastle on first of 2 starts in 2001: off 13 months, still green and left impression run was needed only outing at 3 yrs: should stay at least 1m. *Sir Mark Prescott* **74**

DENNING (IRE) 3 ch.c. Grand Lodge (USA) 125 – Atyaaf (USA) 48 (Irish River (FR) 131) [2002 8.3g⁴ 10.3m³ 10.5f³ Sep 27] 72,000F, IR 550,000Y: lengthy, unfurnished colt: seventh foal: brother to smart 1998 2-y-o 6f/7f (Solario Stakes) winner Raise A Grand and half-brother to several winners, including 4-y-o Sabana: dam maiden half-sister to smart 6f/7f winner Weldnaas: won maiden at Windsor (slowly away) in August: better form both starts after (ran in snatches/still seemed green penultimate), 5½ lengths third to Akshar in handicap at Haydock (wore crossed noseband) final one, again best work at finish: should stay beyond 10.5f: already useful. *J. Noseda* **96**

DENNIS OUR MENACE 4 b.g. Piccolo 121 – Free On Board 73 (Free State 125) [2002 72: p8g* p8g* p8g² 8d⁵ p8g 8.2d* 8.5s 8m² 8d⁵ 8f⁶ 8d³ 8m p8g 8s p8g* f8g p8g Dec 30] sturdy gelding: fairly useful performer: won maiden/handicap at Lingfield in January/February, minor event at Nottingham in May and handicap at Lingfield in November: best around 1m: acts on soft going and all-weather, probably on firm: held up of late. *S. Dow* **82 a86**

DEN'S-JOY 6 b.m. Archway (IRE) 115 – Bonvin (Taufan (USA) 119) [2002 85: 8s 8.3s 9m 8.3m⁵ 8s 8m 8.3m 8g⁵ 8m 10m⁶ 10m³ 8.9f f9.4s* p10g f9.4g* f9.4g³ f9.4g Dec 14] close-coupled mare: fairly useful handicapper on all-weather, fair on turf: won twice at Wolverhampton in November: reportedly finished lame final outing: best at 1m to 9.4f: acts on firm going, good to soft (probably on soft) and fibresand: visored (below form) once: sometimes slowly away: usually held up. *Miss D. A. McHale* **72 a82**

DEPORTIVO 2 b.c. (Apr 8) Night Shift (USA) – Valencia 79 (Kenmare (FR) 125) [2002 5.1d* 6m* 6f* 5.5g Jul 28] big, well-made colt: has plenty of scope: second foal: half-brother to fairly useful 2001 2-y-o 5f winner Irish Vale (by Wolfhound): dam, second at 1m at 2 yrs only start, half-sister to good middle-distance trio Turners Hill, Wandesta and De Quest: won minor events at Bath and Pontefract and listed race at Newbury, all in June/July: clearly best effort (useful form) when beating Checkit by 1½ lengths in last-named, making all: only eighth of 9 in Prix Robert Papin at Maisons-Laffitte, fly-jumping leaving stall and weakening 2f out: should prove at least as effective at 5f as 6f: acts on firm and good to soft going. *R. Charlton* **107**

DERBY HEIGHTS 9 br.g. Golden Heights 82 – Elvonera (Elvis 96) [2002 10.9m⁵ 10.5m⁶ p13g Aug 9] fourth reported foal: dam unraced: modest form in maidens. *R. J. Smith* **58**

DEREK'S PRIDE (IRE) 4 b.f. General Monash (USA) 107 – Likeness 101 (Young Generation 129) [2002 –: f7s f6g f6g⁵ f7g⁴ 7g 10g³ 7f* 5s* Oct 16] poor handicapper: left J. Parkes after fifth start: won at Down Royal in September and Navan in October: effective at 5f to 7f: acts on firm and soft ground, probably on fibresand: tried blinkered. *P. J. Flynn, Ireland* **46**

DERE LYN 4 b.g. Awesome 73 – Our Resolution (Caerleon (USA) 132) [2002 61?: 13s 18d⁶ Jul 6] leggy, angular gelding: modest maiden on Flat: barely stays 2¼m. *D. Burchell* **50**

DERRYQUIN 7 b.g. Lion Cavern (USA) 117 – Top Berry 87 (High Top 131) [2002 74: 8f 8m Jul 3] good-bodied gelding: fair performer: seems best around 1m: acts on firm and good to soft going: blinkered/visored nowadays: often sweating/edgy: races up with pace. *P. L. Gilligan* **65**

DERWENT (USA) 3 b.c. Distant View (USA) 126 – Nothing Sweeter (USA) (Darby Creek Road (USA)) [2002 90p: 10f³ 10.4m³ 10.1s 10.3m* 11.9m⁴ 10m* 9.9g 10.3m 10f* 10f Oct 4] rangy colt: has a quick action: fairly useful performer: won maiden at Doncaster in June and handicaps at Pontefract in July and September: best form at 1¼m: acts on firm and good to soft ground, possibly not on soft: blinkered after third start: went freely to post/refused to settle final outing. *J. D. Bethell* **94**

264

DES   2 b.g. (Feb 27) Timeless Times (USA) 99 – Song's Best (Never So Bold 135) [2002 **66 d**
5m⁵ 5.1f⁵ 5m 5m Aug 18] 17,000Y: well-made gelding: has a quick action: eighth foal:
half-brother to 3 winners, including useful 1994 2-y-o 5f/6f winner Lennox Lewis (by
Superpower) and 4-y-o Double Fantasy: dam unraced from good sprinting family: fair
maiden: went wrong way after encouraging debut: raced only at 5f on going firmer than
good. *J. J. Quinn*

DESARU (USA)   6 br.g. Chief's Crown (USA) – Team Colors (USA) (Mr Prospector **57 d**
(USA)) [2002 70: 11m 8m⁶ 12.1m⁶ 9.2s 10m 10m 10.9g Sep 19] angular gelding: has a
quick action: modest and on downgrade in 2002: probably stays 1½m: acts on firm going,
probably on soft: visored once: has run in snatches/found little. *D. Nicholls*

DESERT AIR (JPN)   3 ch.c. Desert King (IRE) 129 – Greek Air (IRE) 107 (Ela- **80**
Mana-Mou 132) [2002 71: 8.1d 12.3m³ 11.7d 10m* 9.7m 10m³ 11.9m² 12f³ 10m Sep 23]
close-coupled colt: fairly useful performer: won claimer at Newmarket in July: stays easy
1½m: acts on good to firm going: blinkered (raced freely) penultimate start: joined
M. Pipe. *P. F. I. Cole*

DESERT ALCHEMY (IRE)   3 b.f. Green Desert (USA) 127 – Waffle On 89 (Chief **103**
Singer 131) [2002 80p: 8.3d³ 7d* 8m⁵ 7m* 7f 7m² Oct 12] good-topped filly: useful
performer: won maiden in May and listed race (by 2½ lengths from Roundtree) in July,
both at Goodwood: respectable efforts last 2 starts, second to Secret Garden in listed race
at Ascot final one: better form at 7f than 1m, and should prove effective at 6f: yet to race
on soft/heavy going, acts on any other. *Mrs A. J. Perrett*

DESERT CITY   3 b.g. Darnay 117 – Oasis (Valiyar 129) [2002 73: 10m 10.2g³ 11g **79**
10m³ 11m³ 10m⁶ 9.7m⁵ 11.7g⁶ Oct 16] sturdy gelding: fair maiden handicapper: should
stay 1½m: yet to race on extremes of going: found little last 3 starts: sold 13,500 gns.
R. Hannon

DESERT DANCE (IRE)   2 b.c. (Mar 16) Desert Story (IRE) 115 – Cindy's Star **– p**
(IRE) 68 (Dancing Dissident (USA) 119) [2002 6m Sep 24] IR 30,000F, IR 90,000Y:
leggy, rather unfurnished colt: fifth foal: half-brother to 3 winners, including fairly useful
Irish 2000 2-y-o 7f winner Ducky Divey (by Elbio), later 7f winner in Hong Kong as
Spring Fountain: dam 1m winner: 20/1, never-dangerous thirteenth of 19 to Viera in
maiden at Newmarket: should improve. *G. Wragg*

DESERT DEER   4 ch.c. Cadeaux Genereux 131 – Tuxford Hideaway 102 (Cawston's **118**
Clown 113) [2002 106p: 10m* 10m 8.9m³ 8m² 9f* 8f* Oct 3] big, strong colt: smart
performer: won minor events at Newmarket in May and Newbury (by 4 lengths from
Common World) in September, and listed event at Newmarket (by ½ length from
Masterful, ran on in most tenacious fashion) in October: ran creditably otherwise when
neck second to Duck Row in Park Stakes at Doncaster: effective at 1m/1¼m: raced only
on good going or firmer since debut: shade mulish stall on reappearance: often front
runner: should win a pattern race. *M. Johnston*

Shadwell Stud Joel Stakes, Newmarket—Desert Deer breaks Mister Baileys' course record
and gains his first victory at listed level; Masterful (centre), Sohaib (striped cap), Calcutta (right),
the grey Tikkun and King's Ironbridge follow him home

DESERT DESTINY   2 b.c. (Apr 24) Desert Prince (IRE) 130 – High Savannah 77   **97**
(Rousillon (USA) 133) [2002 7m 7m* 7.1m Aug 31] 170,000Y: leggy, useful-looking
colt: sixth living foal: half-brother to several winners, including smart 1¼m performer
Lady In Waiting (by Kylian), 5f/6f winner at 2 yrs, useful 7f (at 2 yrs)/1m winner Smart
Savannah (by Primo Dominie), and 3-y-o Savannah Bay: dam, maiden who stayed 1½m:
best effort (useful form) when justifying favouritism in maiden at Newmarket in July by
neck from Rainwashed Gold, dictating pace: raced close to strong pace when well beaten
in Solario Stakes at Sandown next time: bred to stay 1m: raced only on good to firm
ground. *D. R. Loder*

DESERT FIGHTER   11 b.g. Green Desert (USA) 127 – Jungle Rose 90 (Shirley   **43**
Heights 130) [2002 48+: 13.8g⁴ᵈ 10f Jun 21] good-topped gelding: poor nowadays: stays
1½m: acts on firm and soft ground: probably best held up. *Mrs M. Reveley*

DESERT FLAME   2 b.c. (May 4) Desert Prince (IRE) 130 – Paradise Soul (USA) 82   **80**
(Dynaformer (USA)) [2002 7.1m⁵ 8f³ 8g⁴ Oct 2] first foal: dam 1¾m/2m winner from
family of Belmez: best effort in maidens (fairly useful form) when third to Island Light at
Kempton, making most: likely to be suited by 1¼m/1½m. *I. A. Balding*

DESERT FORTUNE (IRE)   2 ch.g. (Feb 16) Desert Prince (IRE) 130 – Fairy For-   **67**
tune 78 (Rainbow Quest (USA) 134) [2002 7.2s 7s⁵ 6d Nov 1] IR 100,000F, IR 210,000Y:
heavy-topped gelding: half-brother to several winners, including 5-y-o Counsel's
Opinion and fairly useful 1998 2-y-o 6f winner Halloa (by Wolfhound): dam 7.6f winner:
easily best effort in maidens (fair form) when fifth to Kris Kin at Doncaster, dictating
pace and wandering: gave impression something amiss at Newmarket week later: gelded
after. *M. Johnston*

DESERT FURY   5 b.g. Warning 136 – Number One Spot 71 (Reference Point 139)   **86**
[2002 90: 8d³ p8g 7d 7.1m² 8.5d 10.4f³ 7d 8v f8.5g² f8.5s⁴ Dec 26] small gelding: fairly   **a76**
useful performer: claimed from B. Hanbury £10,000 after sixth start: barely stays 8.5f:
acts on fibresand, soft and good to firm going. *R. Bastiman*

DESERT GIPSY (IRE)   2 b.f. (Feb 24) Desert Story (IRE) 115 – Fureur de Vivre   **38**
(IRE) (Bluebird (USA) 125) [2002 5f 6.1g 7f 6m⁶ Jul 4] IR 3,800Y: leggy filly: first
foal: dam, French maiden, out of sister to 1000 Guineas/Champion Stakes winner Flying
Water: poor maiden: tried blinkered. *T. D. Easterby*

DESERT HEAT   4 b.c. Green Desert (USA) 127 – Lypharitissima (FR) (Lightning   **90**
(FR) 129) [2002 10d⁴ 10.5d² 9.9m² Aug 25] sturdy, good-bodied colt: half-brother to 3
winners, including 7-y-o One Dinar and 9f/1¼m winner Generous Diana, both fairly
useful by Generous: dam unraced sister to Prix de Diane winner Lypharita: fairly useful
form in maidens: best effort when 3 lengths second to Rosa Parks at Haydock second
start, making most: will stay 1½m: yet to race on extremes of going. *H. R. A. Cecil*

DESERTION (IRE)   3 b.f. Danehill (USA) 126 – Sabaah (USA) 65 (Nureyev (USA)   **92**
131) [2002 6g* 8.1m* 8f⁴ 8.1m⁶ 7m⁶ 7m Sep 12] IR 650,000Y: good-topped filly: sixth
foal: sister to 2 winners, notably high-class Irish 2000 Guineas/Irish Derby winner Desert
King, 7f/1m winner at 2 yrs, and half-sister to 3 winners, including 7-y-o Wahj: dam,
lightly-raced maiden, closely related to Queen Elizabeth II Stakes winner Maroof: fairly
useful performer: won maiden at Newcastle in June and minor event at Sandown in July:
seemingly creditable efforts in listed events at Epsom (1½ lengths sixth to Atavus) and
Doncaster (3 lengths seventh to Mamounia) last 2 starts: may prove better at 6f/7f than
1m: raced only on good ground or firmer: raced too freely third/fourth starts: sent to
USA. *Sir Mark Prescott*

DESERT ISLAND DISC   5 b.m. Turtle Island (IRE) 123 – Distant Music (Darshaan   **70**
133) [2002 45: p10g⁴ p12g p10g p10g⁵ 11.6g⁶ 10.2g⁶ 11.9m* 10d⁶ 12.1d⁵ 12g* 12m²
11.8g* 10g³ 12d² 12m⁴ 12m² 10m² 13.3f 12g 9s Oct 25] unfurnished mare: fair handicapper: won at Brighton, Salisbury and Leicester between May and July: effective at
1¼m/1½m: acts on heavy going, good to firm and polytrack: sometimes races freely:
game. *J. J. Bridger*

DESERT LOCH (IRE)   2 b.f. (Mar 31) Desert King (IRE) 129 – Kinlochewe 102   **56**
(Old Vic 136) [2002 6d 7f* 6g² 7.5d⁵ 7g 7m 8m Sep 19] 5,000Y: sturdy, close-coupled
filly: third foal: half-sister to 4-y-o Statue Gallery: dam, 1¼m winner, half-sister to smart
7f/1m performer Ardkinglass: modest performer: won seller at Redcar in June: well held
in nurseries last 3 starts: stays 7.5f: acts on firm and good to soft going: tongue tied.
N. Tinkler

DESERT LORD   2 b.c. (Feb 14) Green Desert (USA) 127 – Red Carnival (USA) 109   **89**
(Mr Prospector (USA)) [2002 6f³ 7d² 7f² 6.1g* 7m Oct 19] lengthy, good-topped colt:

third foal: half-brother to 3-y-o Funfair and 4-y-o Carnival Dancer: dam, 2-y-o 5f/6f (Cherry Hinton) winner who stayed 1m, sister to smart US Grade 1 2-y-o 8.5f winner Golden Attraction and closely related to high-class US Grade 1 9f winner Cape Town: fairly useful form: beaten neck by Stressless in maiden at Chester before landing odds in similar event at Chepstow in September: well beaten in Dewhurst Stakes at Newmarket final start: not sure to stay 1m: acts on firm and good to soft ground. *Sir Michael Stoute*

DESERT OPAL   2 ch.c. (Mar 21) Cadeaux Genereux 131 – Nullarbor (Green Desert – p (USA) 127) [2002 7g⁵ Oct 2] second foal: dam, French 2-y-o 5.5f winner, half-sister to very smart French/US performer up to 1½m Radevore from very good family: 9/1, 7 lengths fifth of 9 to Audience in minor event at Salisbury, never placed to challenge under hands and heels: sure to improve. *J. H. M. Gosden*

DESERT PARTY   3 ch.c. Dancing Spree (USA) – Pharoah's Joy 66 (Robellino (USA) – 127) [2002 7g p10g 7d Jul 11] 6,000Y, 4,200 2-y-o: first foal: dam, 5f and (at 2 yrs) 6f winner, out of half-sister to very smart stayer Band: well held in maidens: blinkered final start. *P. Mitchell*

DESERT QUEST (IRE)   2 b.c. (Apr 11) Rainbow Quest (USA) 134 – Jumilla (USA) 77 P 100 (El Gran Senor (USA) 136) [2002 7s³ Oct 15] third foal: half-brother to French 1¼m winner Jolan's Wish (by Woodman): dam, 2-y-o 6f winner who stayed 1¼m, half-sister to dam of smart pair Hidden Meadow (7f/1m) and Scorned (up to 11f): 9/2 and green, encouraging third of 13, beaten just over a length, ran to stable-companion Mustaneer in maiden at Leicester, patiently ridden and keeping on under considerate handling: should be suited by 1¼m+: likely to do good deal better at 3 yrs. *Sir Michael Stoute*

DESERT QUILL (IRE)   2 ch.f. (Feb 2) In The Wings 128 – Aljood 111 (Kris 135) – [2002 7m Aug 29] 18,000Y: half-sister to several winners, including useful 1998 2-y-o 6f winner Society Snoop (by Warning) and fairly useful 1½m winner Just Grand (by Green Desert): dam, maiden who stayed 1m, fourth in Prix Marcel Boussac: 20/1 and green, outpaced throughout in maiden at Salisbury. *D. R. C. Elsworth*

DESERT ROCK (IRE)   2 b.g. (Mar 22) Desert Style (IRE) 121 – Olympic Rock 62 (IRE) (Ballad Rock 122) [2002 5m 7m⁶ 7d Jul 13] IR 10,000F, 31,000Y: first foal: dam Irish maiden: modest form in maidens at Salisbury, making running: gelded and joined J. Akehurst. *B. R. Millman*

DESERT ROYAL (IRE)   3 ch.g. Ali-Royal (IRE) 127 – Hajat 64 (Mujtahid (USA) 62 d 118) [2002 72: 7.5m⁵ 7.6f 6.1f⁵ 7.2g 7f 7.1d 7m 7g 7d⁵ f7g³ f8.5g f7g f6g Dec 10] leggy, close-coupled, sparely-made gelding: modest performer: on downgrade at 3 yrs: probably best at 7f/1m: acts on any turf going and fibresand: well beaten in blinkers. *A. Bailey*

DESERT ROYALTY (IRE)   2 b.f. (Apr 29) Alhaarth (IRE) 126 – Buraida 64 (Balidar 69 133) [2002 7s³ 7g 8s Oct 25] IR 15,000F, IR 6,000Y, 21,000 2-y-o: close-coupled, good-bodied filly: eighth foal: half-sister to 3 winners, including fairly useful 7f (at 2 yrs) and 9f (in USA) winner Oleana (by Alzao): dam, 6f winner, sister to smart sprinter Carol's Treasure: easily best effort in maidens (fair form) when third to Al Ihtithar at Lingfield: not sure to stay 1m. *E. A. L. Dunlop*

DESERT SPA (USA)   7 b.g. Sheikh Albadou 128 – Healing Waters (USA) (Temper- – ence Hill (USA)) [2002 –, a70: f12g² f11s⁵ f12g³ f12g* f11g⁵ f12g* f12f* f14s⁵ f12g³ a78 f12g⁶ f11g f11g Dec 17] workmanlike gelding: has a round action: fair performer on all-weather: won 3 claimers and seller at Wolverhampton, and amateur handicap and claimer (claimed from P. Makin, fifth start) at Southwell between January and August: found little last 3 starts: best at 1¼m/1½m: acts well on fibresand (all 10 wins on it): blinkered twice at 3 yrs: sometimes looks none too keen. *Andrew Reid*

DESERT SPIRIT (IRE)   2 b.g. (Apr 25) Desert Style (IRE) 121 – Lady Bennington 73 (Hot Grove 128) [2002 5d 5m* 6.1g⁶ 5d 5.1g⁵ 6m³ 6.1m Sep 20] 7,000 2-y-o: quite good-topped gelding: half-brother to several winners, including useful 11f to 1¾m winner Queens Wharf (by Ela-Mana-Mou) and fairly useful Irish 1995 2-y-o 9f winner Sarah's Guest (by Be My Guest): dam, maiden, half-sister to smart performer up to 10.5f Ahohoney: fair performer: won maiden at Sandown (wandered) in July: creditable efforts in nurseries fifth and sixth starts: bred to stay at least 1m, but needs to settle better: withdrawn (gave trouble start) once: none too reliable. *J. R. Best*

DESERT STAR   2 b.c. (Feb 13) Green Desert (USA) 127 – Phantom Gold 119 104 p (Machiavellian (USA) 123) [2002 7m³ 7f* 7m Oct 19] big, deep-girthed colt: has scope: has a fluent, round action: third foal: half-brother to smart 2000 2-y-o 7f winner Flight of Fancy (by Sadler's Wells), later second in Oaks: dam, 1m (at 2 yrs) to 13f winner, from good middle-distance family: useful form: well-backed favourite, won 26-runner maiden

The Queen's "Desert Star"

at Newmarket by 5 lengths from Crown Counsel, leading halfway: only eleventh of 16 to Tout Seul in Dewhurst Stakes at Newmarket later in October, beaten long way out: should stay at least 1m: raced only on ground firmer than good: slowly away on debut: almost certainly remains capable of better. *Sir Michael Stoute*

DESERT TRAPPER (IRE) 2 b.c. (Feb 15) Desert Story (IRE) 115 – Lovely Ali (IRE) 69 (Dunbeath (USA) 127) [2002 5.2s² 6d* 7.1m 6d Oct 14] IR 25,000F, 30,000Y: fourth foal: dam Irish 1m/9f winner at 5 yrs: fair form: won maiden at Ayr in August, leading near finish: well held in nurseries after: should stay at least 7f: acts on soft ground, tended to hang on good to firm: sold 9,000 gns, sent to Kuwait. *B. W. Hills* **74**

DESERT VALENTINE 7 b.g. Midyan (USA) 124 – Mo Ceri 63 (Kampala 120) [2002 61: 12d⁴ 12d 11.6d² p16g Sep 4] tall, lengthy gelding: has high knee action: modest handicapper: probably best at 1¼m/1½m: acts on heavy and good to firm going: has started slowly/found little: tends to race freely. *L. G. Cottrell* **56**

DESERT VIEW 2 b.f. (Mar 22) Sadler's Wells (USA) 132 – Ocean View (USA) 109 (Gone West (USA)) [2002 p7g² 8.3d* Oct 28] second foal: dam, US 5.5f (at 2 yrs) and 6.5f winner, placed in Grade 1 events at 8.5f/9f: fair form in maidens, getting up close home when beating Condoleezza by short head at Windsor: will be suited by 1¼m+: slowly away on debut: carried head high both starts: should do better still. *G. A. Butler* **78 p**

DESERT WOLF 4 b.f. Arrasas (USA) 100 – Rosana Park 83 (Music Boy 124) [2002 10g 7m 7m 12.6m Sep 21] half-sister to 5f (at 2 yrs) to 9.7f winner Saysana (by Sayf El Arab) and 1½m to 17.6f winner Angelica Park (by Simply Great): dam 6f winner: no form (unseated rider and bolted before final start). *J. E. Long* **–**

DESIRE ME 4 b.f. Silca Blanka (IRE) 104 – Dazzle Me (Kalaglow 132) [2002 39: f8g 10g 7f Apr 11] probably of little account nowadays. *A. D. Smith* **–**

268

DESRAYA (IRE) 5 b.g. Desert Style (IRE) 121 – Madaraya (USA) (Shahrastani **76**
(USA) 135) [2002 80d: 6s 6f 6m 7.6f 6m* 6m 5f³ Sep 26] strong, lengthy gelding: fair
handicapper: won at Newmarket in August: best at 5f (given test)/6f: yet to race on heavy
ground, acts on any other: often blinkered/visored: has drifted left. *K. A. Ryan*

DESSERT (USA) 2 br.f. (Feb 27) Storm Cat (USA) – Windsharp (USA) 123 (Lear **69**
Fan (USA) 130) [2002 7m 8m Sep 24] leggy, quite good-topped filly: second foal:
half-sister to smart US Grade 1 9f winner Johar (by Gone West): dam, US Grade 1 winner,
effective at 1¼m to 1¾m: better effort in maidens (fair form) when eighth of 10 to Echoes
In Eternity at Newmarket second start, rearing leaving stall and never a threat: should
stay 1¼m: sent to USA. *E. A. L. Dunlop*

DESTINATION 5 ch.g. Deploy 131 – Veuve (Tirol 127) [2002 –, a66: p13g⁶ p16g **–**
f14g Dec 10] tall, lengthy, angular gelding: modest handicapper: reportedly finished lame **a57**
final outing: best around 1¾m: acts on fibresand: none too reliable. *B. A. Pearce*

DESTRUCTIVE (USA) 4 b. or br.g. Dehere (USA) 121 – Respectability (USA) (His **–**
Majesty (USA)) [2002 61d: 14.1g 16g Aug 12] rangy gelding: disappointing maiden.
J. Mackie

DETENTION 3 b.c. Reprimand 122 – June Fayre (Sagaro 133) [2002 70: 7s 7m 7g **70**
8s² 8.3v⁴ 8m Sep 13] close-coupled, quite attractive colt: fair maiden handicapper: stays
1m: acts on soft going (probably on heavy), below form on good to firm: sold 14,000 gns.
W. J. Musson

DEVANT (NZ) 2 b.f. (Feb 4) Zabeel (NZ) – Frenetic (NZ) (Truly Vain (AUS)) [2002 **79**
8.1g⁵ 8d* Oct 30] third living foal: half-sister to a winner in Australia by Pentire: dam,
Group 2 1m winner in New Zealand, out of half-sister to top-class stayer Buckskin: fair
form: 10/1, won maiden at Yarmouth by ¾ length from Harcourt, gamely regaining lead
close home: will stay at least 1¼m. *M. A. Jarvis*

DEVIL'S TEARDROP 2 ch.c. (Mar 20) Hernando (FR) 127 – River Divine (USA) **67**
59 (Irish River (FR) 131) [2002 p7g 6d⁵ 6m⁴ 7m³ 6.1m³ f6f² f7s⁴ Dec 7] 5,500Y: third **a71**
foal: dam ran once: fair maiden: in frame last 5 starts, finding little on final one: effective at 6f/7f: acts on fibresand and good to firm ground: effective blinkered or not.
D. J. S. Cosgrove

DEVINE LIGHT (IRE) 2 b.f. (Mar 13) Spectrum (IRE) 126 – Siskin (IRE) (Royal **66**
Academy (USA) 130) [2002 p7g⁴ 7.1m 8m⁴ 7.9m Sep 4] 5,000Y: leggy filly: third foal:
half-sister to a 11.5f winner in Germany by Dr Devious: dam unraced close relative to
useful 1m to 1½m performer Lifewatch Vision: fair maiden: well held second/fourth
starts: will stay 1¼m. *A. P. Jarvis*

DEVIOUS BOY 2 br.g. (Feb 5) Dr Devious (IRE) 127 – Oh Hebe (IRE) 74 (Night **99**
Shift (USA)) [2002 6g² 6s* 7g² 5d* 5.9d* 7d² 6m² 6m Sep 30] 9,500Y: small, good-
bodied gelding: first foal: dam, 7f winner, half-sister to smart 1¼m/1½m performer
Poppy Carew: useful performer: won minor events at Hamilton in June and July (2): good
second to Tout Seul and Cumbrian Venture in similar races at Ascot and Ripon: well held
in nursery at Hamilton final start: should stay at least 1m: acts on soft and good to firm
ground: usually races prominently: consistent. *P. C. Haslam*

DEVIOUS LADY (IRE) 3 b.f. Dr Devious (IRE) 127 – Lady Rushmore (IRE) 75 **–**
(Fairy King (USA)) [2002 p10g 8d 12s Nov 1] IR 22,000Y: third foal: half-sister to a
winner in Hong Kong by Marju: dam, Irish maiden, stayed 1½m: well beaten in maidens
(left Mrs A. Perrett 1,800 gns after second start). *G. Keane, Ireland*

DEVISE (IRE) 3 b.g. Hamas (IRE) 125§ – Soreze (IRE) 102 (Gallic League 119) **–**
[2002 80: 5m Aug 31] smallish, close-coupled gelding: fairly useful at 2 yrs: well held
only 3-y-o start: will probably prove best at 5f. *M. S. Saunders*

DEVOLUTION (IRE) 4 b.g. Distinctly North (USA) 115 – Election Special 78 **82**
(Chief Singer 131) [2002 88: 8.1m⁵ 8f 10.9g² p12g⁵ 10.1s* p10g⁴ p10g Dec 21] angular **a88**
gelding: fluent mover: fairly useful handicapper, better on all-weather than turf: won at
Yarmouth (edged left) in October: stays 1¼m: acts on polytrack, soft and good to firm
going: sometimes slowly away: refused to race once as 3-y-o. *J. M. P. Eustace*

DEVON DREAM (IRE) 6 b.g. Paris House 123 – Share The Vision (Vision (USA)) **43**
[2002 48: 7.1m 8f 6m 8.1d² 8g 10g* 12m⁴ 16m Sep 20] leggy gelding: poor handicapper
nowadays: left J. M. Bradley after fifth start: won in Jersey in July: stays 1¼m: acts on
firm and good to soft going: blinkered last 3 starts in Britain. *R. J. Baker*

DEVON FLAME 3 b.g. Whittingham (IRE) 104 – Uae Flame (IRE) (Polish Precedent **–**
(USA) 131) [2002 8.1d 8.3d 7m Aug 15] third foal: brother to 4-y-o Flambe: dam unraced

daughter of smart 1¼m performer On The Staff: well held in seller/maidens (looked wayward last 2 starts). *R. J. Hodges*

DEVONICA 3 br.f. Dr Devious (IRE) 127 – Ann Veronica (IRE) (Sadler's Wells (USA) 132) [2002 7d 9.3s 8m⁶ Jul 8] 16,000Y: third foal: half-sister to 1999 2-y-o 1¼m winner Marjeune (by Marju) and French 13f winner Adina (by Persian Bold): dam unraced from family of Spectrum, Petrushka and Millenary: well held in maidens. *T. D. Barron*   –

DEXTERITY (USA) 4 b.c. Kingmambo (USA) 125 – Diese (USA) 111 (Diesis 133) [2002 7g² 8d² 8.2m* Oct 1] fourth foal: half-brother to 3 winners, notably very smart US performer up to 11f Senure (7f winner in Britain at 2 yrs) and useful winner up to 15f in France Terrazzo (both by Nureyev): dam, French 1¼m/10.5f winner, half-sister to Xaar: fair form in maidens, winning at Nottingham by 5 lengths from True Companion, making most: bred to stay 1¼m: yet to race on extremes of going: raced freely first 2 starts: sold 45,000 gns, sent to France. *R. Charlton*   86

DEXTROUS 5 gr.g. Machiavellian (USA) 123 – Heavenly Cause (USA) (Grey Dawn II 132) [2002 64d: 10.1m 8m⁴ 8g 8.1m 9.9m Aug 24] tall gelding: modest maiden: left J. Mackie after fourth start: stays 1¼m: acts on any going: tongue tied last 4 starts in 2001: sometimes races freely: none too reliable. *N. Tinkler*   61

DHABYAN (USA) 2 b.c. (Mar 1) Silver Hawk (USA) 123 – Fleur de Nuit (USA) (Woodman (USA) 126) [2002 6m² 7d 8f* 7.1m³ 8m³ Sep 20] $150,000F: good-topped colt: second foal: dam, US 6f (at 2 yrs) to 9f (Grade 3 event) winner, out of Poule d'Essai des Pouliches winner Pearl Bracelet: useful performer: won maiden at Kempton in August by 6 lengths: unlucky not to follow up in Solario Stakes at Sandown later in month, meeting plenty of trouble but still beaten less than length by Foss Way: respectable third to Saturn in minor event at Newbury final start, racing freely closer to pace: should stay 1¼m: acts on firm ground. *B. Hanbury*   103 +

DHARKAN (USA) 2 b.c. (Mar 24) King of Kings (IRE) 125 – Meritorious (USA) (St Jovite (USA) 135) [2002 6f 6g* 7m 7g 6.1m⁵ 7g Oct 4] $175,000Y: close-coupled colt: first foal: dam, maiden in USA, out of close relative to dam of 1000 Guineas winner Wince and 7-y-o Ulundi: fair performer: made all in maiden at Southwell in June: ran creditably only once after: stays 6f: raced only on good going or firmer: visored last 3 starts: sold 8,800 gns. *E. A. L. Dunlop*   71

DIAGHILEV (IRE) 3 b.g. Sadler's Wells (USA) 132 – Darara 129 (Top Ville 129) [2002 102: 10m* 10d* 12m 12m⁶ Jun 21] neat, attractive gelding: smart performer: won maiden at Leopardstown in April and Prix La Force at Chantilly (beat Le Fou by short neck) in May: didn't get run of race and not discredited when seventh in Prix du Jockey Club at Chantilly penultimate start: ran poorly after slow start in King Edward VII Stakes at Royal Ascot final one: should prove fully effective at 1½m: acts on soft and good to firm going: wore crossed noseband, had 2 handlers and taken steadily to post (took strong hold/hung off bridle in race) second start at 2 yrs: tends to carry head slightly high: gelded, and sold privately to race in Hong Kong, where renamed River Dancer. *A. P. O'Brien, Ireland*   110

DIAGON ALLEY (IRE) 2 ro.g. (Apr 1) Petong 126 – Mubadara (IRE) 80 (Lahib (USA) 129) [2002 5.9s 6f 8m Oct 2] 7,000Y: 2-y-o: close-coupled gelding: second foal: dam Irish 2-y-o 6f winner out of half-sister to high-class miler Montekin: well held in maidens. *K. W. Hogg, Isle of Man*   –

DIALING TONE (USA) 2 b.f. (Jan 24) Distant View (USA) 126 – Call Account (USA) (Private Account (USA)) [2002 6d⁴ 7m* 7m⁴ Oct 19] leggy, useful-looking filly: first foal: dam, 7f to 8.5f winner in US and third in Grade 2 7f event, half-sister to useful 1m/1¼m performer Keyboogie: won maiden at Redcar in October by 7 lengths: 9/1, useful form when 4 lengths fourth to Luvah Girl in Rockfel Stakes at Newmarket, no extra having travelled well long way: likely to prove best up to 1m: unraced on extremes of going. *Sir Michael Stoute*   100

DIAMOND DAGGER 3 ch.g. Sabrehill (USA) 120 – Diamond Princess 69 (Horage 124) [2002 –: p7g³ p8g² p10g 10.2g 8m 7f 12d p10g⁶ f12g 10d⁵ Oct 28] rangy gelding: poor mover: modest maiden on all-weather, poor on turf: stays 1¼m: acts on polytrack and good to soft going: sold 5,000 gns, sent to Kuwait. *D. W. P. Arbuthnot*   49 / a64

DIAMOND DARREN (IRE) 3 ch.g. Dolphin Street (FR) 125 – Deerussa (IRE) (Jareer (USA) 115) [2002 64: 5.1d 7f 8 1m 9.9g 14.1f⁶ 14d 8d² Jun 21] leggy, close-coupled gelding: poor maiden: stays 1m: acts on firm and good to soft going, some promise on fibresand: usually visored/blinkered at 2 yrs: difficult ride. *John Berry*   48

DIAMOND DECORUM (IRE)   6 ch.g. Fayruz 116 – Astra Adastra (Mount Hagen   **56**
(FR) 127) [2002 67: 7v 7f⁶ 7.1m⁵ 7m 6d 7m⁶ 6g Sep 9] leggy, workmanlike gelding:
fluent mover: modest handicapper: best at 6f/easy 7f: acts on firm and soft going: tried
visored/tongue tied: has been early to post: sometimes races freely/carries head awk-
wardly/hangs right. *J. Hetherton*

DIAMOND GEORGIA (IRE)   5 ch.m. Soviet Lad (USA) – Secret Assignment 71   –
(Vitiges (FR) 132) [2002 f14.8g f16.2g Feb 8] angular mare: disappointing maiden: tried
visored. *P. D. Evans*

DIAMOND GIRL   2 b.f. (Jan 16) Mind Games 121 – Its All Relative 90 (Distant   **60**
Relative 128) [2002 5d³ 5f⁴ 5g⁶ 5m⁵ Jul 13] 24,000Y: first foal: dam, winner at 2 yrs,
raced only around 5f: modest maiden: blinkered, fifth in nursery at York: raced only at 5f:
acts on firm and good to soft ground. *T. D. Easterby*

DIAMOND GREEN (ARG)   4 ch.g. Roy (USA) – Diamond Ring (ARG) (El Basco   **64**
(USA)) [2002 62: f12g³ f9.4g* 10m⁶ 8.2d 8.1d f8g⁴ Dec 27] fair on all-weather, modest   **a72**
on turf: won maiden at Wolverhampton in March: stays 9.4f: acts on fibresand and good
to firm going: visored in 2002: has raced freely: looked none too keen fourth/fifth starts.
B. R. Millman

DIAMOND HALL   9 b.g. Lapierre 119 – Willitwin (Majestic Maharaj 105) [2002   –
f12g⁶ Mar 25] modest winning hurdler/poor chaser: well beaten in Wolverhampton
maiden. *K. R. Burke*

DIAMOND JOBE (IRE)   3 ch.g. College Chapel 122 – Dazzling Maid (IRE) 64   **51**
(Tate Gallery (USA) 117) [2002 59: 5.1d 7f 6g⁵ 7.1d 7d f7g Nov 20] angular gelding:
modest maiden handicapper: probably stays 7f: acts on fibresand, firm and good to soft
going. *J. Hetherton*

DIAMOND JOSHUA (IRE)   4 b.g. Mujadil (USA) 119 – Elminya (IRE) (Sure Blade   –
(USA) 130) [2002 53: f12gᵈ p13g⁶ 10.9d 18d Jul 6] workmanlike gelding: modest maiden
at 3 yrs on Flat: little form in 2002 (reported to have gurgled final start): blinkered once:
winning hurdler. *John Berry*

DIAMOND LOVER (IRE)   3 ch.c. Alhaarth (IRE) 126 – Silent Love (Hansel   **91**
(USA)) [2002 88p: 10m 10.4m⁵ 11.6d⁴ 10d² 8g² 8g p10g⁵ f8g* f8g⁵ Dec 27] big, lengthy
colt: fairly useful handicapper: won at Southwell in December, leading near finish:
effective at 1m/1¼m: acts on all-weather, yet to race on extremes of going on turf:
visored/blinkered last 5 outings: none too reliable. *N. A. Graham*

DIAMOND MAXINE (IRE)   2 b.f. (Apr 29) Turtle Island (IRE) 123 – Kawther   **61 d**
(Tap On Wood 130) [2002 5f 5m³ 5.1d 5m 7s Oct 28] IR 13,000Y: lengthy filly: half-
sister to several winners, including 4-y-o Diamond Max: dam little sign of ability: form
(modest) only when third in maiden at Leicester: refused to race on debut: needs treating
with caution. *P. D. Evans*

DIAMOND MAX (IRE)   4 b.g. Nicolotte 118 – Kawther (Tap On Wood 130) [2002   **107**
109?: f8.5g² 8s⁵ a8.7g 8.3s⁶ 9s 8v Nov 19] angular gelding: smart on all-weather, useful   **a114**
on turf: very good head second to Dayglow Dancer in valuable handicap at Wolverhampton in March: far from discredited when fifth to Dandoun in listed event at
Doncaster next time: below form after: stays 8.5f, probably not testing 9f: acts on
fibresand, best turf efforts on ground softer than good. *P. D. Evans*

DIAMOND MICK   2 ch.c. (May 10) Pivotal 124 – Miss Poll Flinders (Swing Easy   **72**
(USA) 126) [2002 6m 6g 7d Oct 30] big, good-topped colt: half-brother to several
winners, including 3-y-o Distant Diva and 1m (at 2 yrs)/1¼m winner Chilly Lad (by High
Kicker): dam tailed off only start at 2 yrs: green, clearly best effort in maidens (fair form)
when ninth of 18 to Pigeon Point at Newmarket second start: likely to prove best up to
1m. *G. G. Margarson*

DIAMOND ORCHID (IRE)   2 gr.f. (Apr 24) Victory Note (USA) 120 – Olivia's   **75**
Pride (IRE) (Digamist (USA) 110) [2002 6m³ 6s* Jul 2] IR 6,000Y: strong filly: fourth
foal: half-sister to 1998 2-y-o 5f winner Ladycake (by Perugino): dam unraced out of
half-sister to Irish 2000 Guineas winner Northern Treasure: much better effort in maidens
(fair form) when winning at Hamilton by 3 lengths from Aries, racing freely in front and
wandering: stays 6f: acts on soft going: joined D. Carroll. *J. L. Eyre*

DIAMOND RACKET   2 b.g. (Mar 5) Cyrano de Bergerac 120 – Reina 24 (Homeboy   **60**
114) [2002 5m⁵ 6g 5.9d 6d 7g 7d 6m* 6.1m 6g 7d⁴ f5g f6g⁵ f6g⁶ f5g² Dec 27] 8,500Y: **a57**
good-topped gelding: fifth foal: half-brother to 3 winners, including 4-y-o Cynara and
1999 2-y-o 5f winner Richard Ansdell (by Absalom): dam maiden who stayed 7f: modest
performer: won selling nursery at Yarmouth in September: left M. Dods after tenth start:

will prove best at 6f/easy 7f: acts on fibresand, unraced on extremes of going on turf: tried blinkered/visored. *D. W. Chapman*

DIAMOND RIGHT   2 b.f. (Mar 8) Robellino (USA) 127 – Petrikov (IRE) (In The Wings 128) [2002 8m Sep 24] 4,000F, 5,000Y: good-bodied filly: second foal: half-sister to a winner in Holland by Bishop of Cashel: dam unraced daughter of sister to 1000 Guineas/Oaks winner Midway Lady: 66/1 and backward, tailed off in maiden at Newmarket. *M. Wigham*   –

DIAMOND RING   3 b.f. Magic Ring (IRE) 115 – Reticent Bride (IRE) 71 (Shy Groom (USA)) [2002 73: 5g 6d 6d f8g Dec 27] quite good-topped filly: fair performer: creditable effort in 2002 only on second outing: left J. Dunlop only 800 gns before final start: stays 6f: yet to race on extremes of going on turf. *Mrs J. Candlish*   **73**

DIAMOND ROAD (IRE)   5 b.g. Dolphin Street (FR) 125 – Tiffany's Case (IRE) 65 (Thatching 131) [2002 67: p12g⁵ p12g⁴ p13g⁴ p12g 11.6m 10m⁴ 14m 10.9m Sep 16] good-bodied gelding: modest maiden: probably stays easy 13f: acts on polytrack and good to firm going: blinkered third/final starts: free-going sort: has carried head high. *C. A. Horgan*   **62 a52**

DIANA PANAGAEA   3 ch.f. Polar Falcon (USA) 126 – Pandrop (Sharrood (USA) 124) [2002 75: 7m 6g Jul 1] workmanlike filly: fair winner at 2 yrs: well held in handicaps both 3-y-o starts: should stay at least 7f. *A. C. Stewart*   –

DIAPHANOUS   4 b.f. Beveled (USA) – Sharp Venita 84 (Sharp Edge 123) [2002 –: p6g 6.1v² 6m⁶ 6g⁴ f5f f5g² Dec 31] sturdy filly: poor maiden: left N. Berry after reappearance (trained by J. Spearing next start only): will prove best at 5f: acts on fibresand, heavy and good to firm ground: blinkered last 2 starts: withdrawn after breaking out of stall second intended outing: races prominently. *E. A. Wheeler*   **46 +**

DICKIE DEADEYE   5 b.g. Distant Relative 128 – Accuracy 83 (Gunner B 126) [2002 8g 8s Oct 28] fair handicapper: very lightly-raced nowadays: stays 11.6f: goes well on ground softer than good. *G. B. Balding*   **67**

DICK THE TAXI   8 b.g. Karlinsky (USA) – Another Galaxy (IRE) (Anita's Prince 126) [2002 64: f12g* f12g* 16g p12g Oct 31] big, good-topped gelding: won maiden and handicap at Wolverhampton in March: stays 1½m, seemingly not 2m: raced mainly on all-weather (successful over hurdles on heavy ground): sold £16,000 in December. *R. J. Smith*   **74**

DIDDYMU (IRE)   3 b.f. Revoque (IRE) 122 – Family At War (USA) 71 (Explodent (USA)) [2002 66: 10.2g 9.2g 10g p10g⁴ 10g 10.2m* 10.2d³ 9.9d⁴ Jul 5] tall filly: modest handicapper: won at Bath in June: stays 1¼m when emphasis is on speed: acts on good to firm going, good to soft and polytrack: sometimes slowly away: carries head high. *M. R. Channon*   **64**

DIDNT TELL MY WIFE   3 ch.g. Aragon 118 – Bee Dee Dancer (Ballacashtal (CAN)) [2002 73: p7g f7g³ p7g 7.1m p7g⁴ 8.1d⁶ 8m 8g⁵ p7g 7m 7s Oct 25] unfurnished gelding: fair handicapper: left S. Williams after ninth start: stays 1m: acts on all-weather, soft and good to firm going: blinkered (very slowly away) once: sometimes edges left. *C. F. Wall*   **66**

DIDOE   3 br.f. Son Pardo 107 – My Diamond Ring 65 (Sparkling Boy 110) [2002 10m 11.9g 8.2m 8f⁴ 8.3d f8g f6g Dec 10] leggy filly: sixth foal: dam 1m winner: poor maiden: trained first 2 starts by M. Blanshard. *P. W. Hiatt*   **48**

DIFFERENTIAL (USA)   5 b. or br.g. Known Fact (USA) 135 – Talk About Home (USA) (Elocutionist (USA)) [2002 91d: p7g Feb 13] small, sturdy gelding: fairly useful handicapper at best: well held only 5-y-o start: wore net muzzle once at 2 yrs: reportedly bled from nose once at 4 yrs. *B. Smart*   –

DIGDAGA (USA)   3 b. or br.f. Machiavellian (USA) 123 – Baaderah (IRE) 102 (Cadeaux Genereux 131) [2002 p8g p8g² f8.5g³ 12g² 10m² 8m f12g 12.1g⁶ 11.8m 12.1g 8.5m 8.2m 10s 8d 12v f9.4f Nov 29] third foal: half-sister to fairly useful 1m winner Badr Rainbow (by Rainbow Quest): dam 6f (including at 2 yrs) winner who stayed 1m: modest maiden: claimed from M. Channon fifth start: well below form after: stays 1½m: acts on all-weather: tried blinkered/tongue tied (has reportedly had breathing problems). *Mrs S. Lamyman*   **54 d**

DIG EVEN DEEPER   3 ch.g. Jade Hunter (USA) – Alchi (USA) 112 (Alleged (USA) 138) [2002 7.2d 10g Jul 6] closely related to winner in USA by Stuka and half-brother to 3 winners, including 10-y-o Pickens: dam French 2-y-o 1m winner and third in Prix Marcel Boussac: well held in maiden/claimer. *M. Johnston*   –

DIGGER (IRE)   3 ch.g. Danzig Connection (USA) – Baliana 75 (Midyan (USA) 124)   **63**
[2002 71: 6.1f⁶ 6g 6m⁶ 7.1g f8s* f8g 8d Nov 1] big, workmanlike gelding: fair handi-   **a75**
capper: won at Southwell in October: stays 1m: acts on fibresand: tongue tied: carried
head awkwardly penultimate start. *G. B. Balding*

DIGITAL   5 ch.g. Safawan 118 – Heavenly Goddess (Soviet Star (USA) 128) [2002 93:   **97**
8s 8.1d 7m 7d* 8s⁶ 8m³ 7f³ 7.6f 8m³ 9f 7g⁴ 8.2v⁴ 8s⁵ Nov 2] workmanlike gelding: useful
handicapper: won at Newbury in May: ran at least creditably after when in frame,
including third to Zonergem in Mail On Sunday/Tote Mile Final at Ascot ninth start:
effective at 7f/1m (raced too freely at 9f): acts on heavy and good to firm going: has
carried head awkwardly. *M. R. Channon*

DIGNIFIED   2 b.f. (Mar 11) Entrepreneur 123 – Awtaar (USA) 67 (Lyphard (USA)   –
132) [2002 p7g f7g Nov 16] 7,000Y: fifth foal: half-sister to 6f winner Magical River (by
Lahib) and useful 1¼m and 1¾m winner Sharp Stepper (by Selkirk): dam, disappointing
maiden, out of half-sister to Fairy Footsteps and Light Cavalry: well held in maidens.
Mrs C. A. Dunnett

DIHATJUM   5 b.g. Mujtahid (USA) 118 – Rosie Potts 83 (Shareef Dancer (USA) 135)   **51**
[2002 59: 9.7m⁵ p12g 12m 12.6g Jul 5] rather leggy, workmanlike gelding: modest
handicapper: probably stays 1½m: acts on firm and good to soft going: visored/blinkered
nowadays: often slowly away: held up. *R. M. Flower*

DIL   7 b.g. Primo Dominie 121 – Swellegant 84 (Midyan (USA) 124) [2002 –, a73: f7s⁶   –
p7g p6g f6g f6g* f5g⁴ 5g 5.1d f7g f5g³ f6g⁴ f6s f6g⁵ f6s* f5g⁶ f6g f6g f6s³ f6g⁴ f6f² f6g⁶   **a74**
f6g⁴ f6s² Dec 26] lengthy, good-topped gelding: fair performer: left A. Reid to rejoin
former stable after fourth start: won amateur claimer in April and handicap in October,
both at Southwell: effective at 5f/6f: acts on fibresand, lightly raced and little form on turf
since 1999: sometimes visored: tried tongue tied. *Mrs N. Macauley*

DILEER (IRE)   3 b.g. Barathea (IRE) 127 – Stay Sharpe (USA) (Sharpen Up 127)   **86**
[2002 86: 11.1g² 11g⁶ Apr 19] useful-looking gelding: fairly useful form in 3 maidens:
stays 11f: gelded after final start. *M. R. Channon*

DILIGENT LAD   2 b.g. (Apr 12) Secret Appeal – Mohibbah (USA) 86 (Conquistador   –
Cielo (USA)) [2002 6m⁶ 6g 8m Oct 2] 500Y: brother to 5-y-o Secret Conquest: dam 2-y-o
5f winner: well held in maidens: free-going sort. *D. W. Barker*

DILIZA   3 b.f. Dilum (USA) 115 – Little White Lies 78 (Runnett 125) [2002 45: 5.7g   **65**
6m⁶ 8m* 8m⁵ 8.1g Aug 7] fair handicapper: won apprentice event at Salisbury (hung
badly right) in July: much better at 1m than 6f: acts on firm and good to soft going: tends
to be slowly away. *G. B. Balding*

DILLY   4 br.f. Dilum (USA) 115 – Princess Rosananti (IRE) (Shareef Dancer (USA)   –
135) [2002 70, a64: 11.6g 9.7m Apr 23] fair handicapper at 3 yrs: well held both 4-y-o
starts. *P. R. Chamings*

DILSAA   5 ch.g. Night Shift (USA) – Llia 94 (Shirley Heights 130) [2002 56: f16.2g   **45**
14.1d 14.1d 12.3g 11m 12.4m⁴ 11.9s 13.8g³ 14.1f Jun 22] strong, lengthy gelding: poor
performer: stays 1¾m: acts on soft going, firm and fibresand: tried blinkered: sometimes
races freely. *K. A. Ryan*

DILYS   3 b.f. Efisio 120 – Ramajana (USA) (Shadeed (USA) 135) [2002 84: 6g 7.1m⁶   **75 d**
7m f7s p6g 7s Nov 2] smallish, sturdy filly: fair performer at best in 2002: stays easy 7f:
acts on heavy and good to firm going: often races prominently. *W. S. Kittow*

DIMPLE CHAD   3 b.g. Sadler's Wells (USA) 132 – Fern 100 (Shirley Heights 130)   **93**
[2002 67p: 10g³ 10d* 10m 10g Jul 10] rather leggy, quite good-topped gelding: fairly
useful performer: won maiden at Ripon (took good hold) in May: stiffish tasks in listed
race at Royal Ascot (not discredited) and handicap at Newmarket after: reportedly found
to have a minor problem subsequently, and has been gelded: should be suited by at least
1½m: yet to race on extremes of going. *L. M. Cumani*

DIMPLE LIGHTER (IRE)   2 b.c. (Feb 14) General Monash (USA) 107 – Known   **76**
Line 100 (Known Fact (USA) 135) [2002 5d 5d³ 6.1s⁵ 6g 7s Oct 26] 14,000Y: strong colt:
seventh foal: half-brother to 3 winners, including useful 1995 2-y-o 7f winner who stayed
1¾m Story Line (by In The Wings): dam, 1m winner at 2 yrs (better at 1½m), half-sister
to dam of Irish Oaks winner Pure Grain: fair maiden: off over 4 months, creditable eighth
in nursery at Newmarket fourth start: should stay 7f: raced only on good going or softer:
sold 11,000 gns, sent to Kuwait. *B. A. McMahon*

DINOFELIS   4 b.g. Rainbow Quest (USA) 134 – Revonda (IRE) (Sadler's Wells   **52**
(USA) 132) [2002 57: 12m⁵ 10.9m⁶ 10g 10.5d 11.1g 12.1d* 11.1d⁵ 12.1g 12.1s f12s⁵

f14.8g Sep 21] quite attractive gelding: modest handicapper: won at Hamilton in July: should stay 2m: acts on firm and good to soft ground: has pulled hard: sold £500 in December. *W. M. Brisbourne*

DION DEE   6 ch.m. Anshan 119 – Jade Mistress 51 (Damister (USA) 123) [2002 54,   –
a36: 12g 12.6f Jun 26] tall mare: modest handicapper at 5 yrs: well held in 2002.
Dr J. R. J. Naylor

DIONEA (IRE)   3 b.f. Hernando (FR) 127 – Gwydion (USA) 118 (Raise A Cup   53
(USA)) [2002 7.1f⁵ 8s⁴ 8s⁵ Nov 17] smallish, quite attractive filly: half-sister to several
winners, including very smart 7f (including at 2 yrs) winner and 2000 Guineas runner-up
Enrique (by Barathea), and smart French 6f and 1m winner Piperi (by Machiavellian):
dam sprinter: 9 lengths fifth to Jules in maiden at Haydock on debut (only outing for
H. Cecil): better effort after when fourth in minor event at Angers: sold 26,000 gns.
D. Sepulchre, France

DIRECT BEARING (IRE)   5 b.g. Polish Precedent (USA) 131 – Uncertain Affair   100
(IRE) 79 (Darshaan 133) [2002 95: 12d* 16s 14g² 18m² Oct 19] third foal: half-brother
to 2 winners in Ireland, including useful 7f (at 2 yrs) and 9f winner Prize Time (by College
Chapel), 7f winner at 2 yrs: dam, Irish 1¾m winner, out of half-sister to dam of Slip
Anchor: useful performer, lightly raced on Flat: won maiden at Leopardstown and minor
event at Thurles in 2001, and ladies race at the Curragh in July: best effort when
short-head second to Miss Fara in Cesarewitch at Newmarket final start, leading on bridle
4f out and headed only on line: effective at 1½m to 2¼m: acts on good to firm and good
to soft going. *D. K. Weld, Ireland*

DIRECT DESCENDANT (IRE)   3 ch.g. Be My Guest (USA) 126 – Prague Spring   52
66 (Salse (USA) 128) [2002 65?: 8g 9.9g 10f⁶ 11m 11m² 12.4m⁴ 14.1s⁵ f12s Sep 7]
good-topped gelding: good walker: modest maiden handicapper: seems to stay 12.4f: acts
on firm ground: visored (ran poorly) fourth start: won juvenile hurdle in September.
J. J. Quinn

DIRECT REACTION (IRE)   5 b.g. College Chapel 122 – Mary's Way (GR) 78   39
(Night Shift (USA)) [2002 f7g6 f7g f7d⁶ f8.5g⁵ 7d f6s Dec 26] lengthy gelding: modest   a54
handicapper on all-weather, poor on turf: ran in UAE in 2001: stays 1m: acts on firm
going, good to soft and fibresand: usually blinkered/visored: tried tongue tied. *Miss Gay
Kelleway*

DIRTY SANCHEZ   4 b.g. Manhal – Lady Poly (Dunbeath (USA) 127) [2002 11.9g   –
10d p12g Jun 29] second foal: dam, little worthwhile form on Flat, winning selling
hurdler: well beaten in claimer/sellers. *Jamie Poulton*

DISCOED   2 b.f. (Mar 11) Distinctly North (USA) 115 – Lunar Music 67 (Komaite   38
(USA)) [2002 6m⁴ 7f⁵ f7g⁵ 6m f8g f8.5g f7g f5g f7g f5g⁴ Dec 27] 1,400Y: lengthy,
angular filly: first foal: dam 5f winner, including at 2 yrs: poor maiden: left J. Osborne
after sixth start: stays 7f: acts on firm ground, probably on fibresand: sometimes slowly
away. *M. J. Polglase*

DISCO VOLANTE   3 b.f. Sadler's Wells (USA) 132 – Divine Danse (FR) 118 (Kris   105
135) [2002 79p: 8m* 10m² 8g 10g² 10.5v⁶ Oct 25] big, good-topped filly: useful
performer: won maiden at Newbury in April: best efforts when 2 lengths equal-second
to Whim in listed race at Longchamp (after 3-month break) and sixth in Trumbaka in
Prix de Flore at Saint-Cloud last 2 starts: stays 10.5f: yet to race on extremes of going.
J. H. M. Gosden

DISCREET BRIEF (IRE)   2 b.f. (Mar 23) Darshaan 133 – Quiet Counsel (IRE) 81   86 p
(Law Society (USA) 130) [2002 7m³ 8m² 8s² Oct 25] 100,000F: big, good-topped filly:
has plenty of scope: third foal: sister to French 1½m winner Alithini: dam, 1m winner in
Ireland, half-sister to Yorkshire Oaks winner Key Change (by Darshaan): fairly useful
form in maidens: runner-up to Echoes In Eternity at Newmarket and to Richemaur at
Doncaster (gone in coat, beaten 1¾ lengths): should be well suited by 1¼m+: remains
capable of better, and well up to winning races. *J. L. Dunlop*

DISGRACE   2 b.g. (Mar 19) Distinctly North (USA) 115 – Ace Girl 58 (Stanford   –
121§) [2002 5g 6g 6g 7m Jul 7] 500Y: fifth foal: half-brother to 1998 2-y-o 5f winner
Sound's Ace (by Savahra Sound): dam 1m winner: well held in maidens. *A. Berry*

DISPOL CHIEFTAN   4 b.g. Clantime 101 – Ski Baby (Petoski 135) [2002 54: f7g   –
f6s p7g Jan 30] maiden: no form in 2002: tried blinkered/tongue tied. *S. E. Kettlewell*

DISPOL EVITA   3 ch.f. Presidium 124 – She's A Breeze 35 (Crofthall 110) [2002 60:   56 §
p7g* p8g* f7g p7g⁵ 7s 8g 7m p7g⁶ p8g⁴ 10g² 10g 10m³ p10g 11.9m³ 11.9m⁶ 11.5m 10m   a65 §
p10g p10g p10g⁶ p10g⁴ Dec 30] rather leggy, close-coupled filly: fair on all-weather,

modest on turf: won handicap and seller (demoted then reinstated on appeal) at Lingfield in January: stays easy 1½m: acts on all-weather and firm going: often blinkered: often slowly away/looks none too keen (refused to race once at 2 yrs). *Andrew Reid*

DISPOL FOXTROT 4 ch.f. Alhijaz 122 – Foxtrot Pie 77 (Shernazar 131) [2002 53: **74** f11s f9.4g5 f8g3 10g3 9.3g4 11.1g2 10m 9.2v2 9.2s* 9.2s3 8.3g5 9.2d* 9.1d2 7.9g2 9.2v* 10g5 Sep 20] close-coupled filly: bad mover: fair performer: left S. Kettlewell after reappearance: won seller and 2 handicaps between June and August, all at Hamilton: stays 11f: acts on fibresand, best on good ground or softer on turf: has found little/edged right. *T. D. Barron*

DISPOL PETO 2 gr.c. (Mar 12) Petong 126 – Plie 75 (Superlative 118) [2002 5g3 5m **67** 5g* 6s3 6d 6m3 5.9m 6m 6g 6f 7g 6d2 Nov 5] 5,500Y: strong, good-quartered colt: seventh foal: half-brother to 3 winners abroad, including Red Simba (by Absalom), also 7f winner in Britain at 2 yrs: dam, 2-y-o 6f winner, stayed 1m: fair performer: won maiden at Carlisle in May: creditable second in nursery at Catterick: stays 6f: acts on soft and good to firm going: effective blinkered or not: none too genuine. *T. D. Barron*

DISPOL ROCK (IRE) 6 b.g. Ballad Rock 122 – Havana Moon (Ela-Mana-Mou **55 §** 132) [2002 64: f11g5 f12g f12g5 12.3g6 11m 12.4m May 15] tall gelding: modest handicapper: stays 1½m: acts on firm and soft going, probably on fibresand: front runner: temperamental: sold 1,400 gns. *T. D. Barron*

DISPOL VERITY 2 b.f. (Mar 20) Averti (IRE) 117 – Fawley Mist (Suave Dancer **60** (USA) 136) [2002 5g5 f5g4 5f3 5g2 6d3 5.1s4 6v f5g f5g Dec 10] 500Y: small, leggy filly: **a55** first foal: dam unraced half-sister to Park Hill winner Casey: modest maiden: in frame 5 times: left T. D. Barron/off 5 months after fifth start: best form at 5f: acts on fibresand, soft and firm ground: usually races prominently. *W. M. Brisbourne*

DISTANT COUSIN 5 b.g. Distant Relative 128 – Tinaca (USA) (Manila (USA)) **89** [2002 60: 10.9f f14.8s4 12m4 12g* 12g3 14.6m2 14.1m2 12m2 14m4 12s5 14.4g f12g* p12g* 13.8d5 f14g* f14g4 Dec 10] rather leggy gelding: fairly useful handicapper: won at Southwell (3) and Lingfield between June and November: stays 14.6f: acts on soft going, good to firm and all-weather: usually visored. *M. A. Buckley*

DISTANT DIVA 3 b.f. Distant Relative 128 – Miss Poll Flinders (Swing Easy (USA) **63** 126) [2002 86: 6d 5d6 6d 5d 7m 7g p6g Oct 9] good-topped filly: good walker: fairly useful at 2 yrs, just modest in 2002: effective at 5f/6f: acts on soft and good to firm going. *G. G. Margarson*

DISTANT GUEST 5 b.g. Distant Relative 128 – Teacher's Game 64 (Mummy's **–** Game 120) [2002 68: f12s Nov 30] fair handicapper at best: trained by G. Margarson at 3 yrs: won at Laytown in 2001: off 16 months, well beaten at Wolverhampton only start in 2002: should stay beyond 1m: acts on sand and soft going, probably on good to firm: tried blinkered/visored. *John A. Quinn, Ireland*

DISTANT KING 9 b.g. Distant Relative 128 – Lindfield Belle (IRE) 78 (Fairy King **–** (USA)) [2002 7.5m 5f 6m 7d 6f 5m 5m 5g 6d 6s 5m Sep 24] no longer of much account. *G. P. Kelly*

DISTANT LIGHT 2 b.f. (Jan 27) Groom Dancer (USA) 128 – Warning Star 104 **57 p** (Warning 136) [2002 8m6 Oct 2] lengthy, unfurnished filly: third foal: half-sister to winners abroad up to 1m by Zafonic and Lion Cavern: dam 5f (including at 2 yrs)/6f winner: 10/1 and green, 9 lengths sixth to Rocket Force in maiden at Newcastle: sold 8,000 gns: should do better. *M. L. W. Bell*

DISTANT MIST (USA) 3 ch.g. Distant View (USA) 126 – Sage Mist (USA) (Capote **57 d** (USA)) [2002 75: p7g p10g p7g 8g 7m 5.1g 6g Aug 13] just modest at best at 3 yrs: left J. Noseda after second start: best form at 5f: tried visored/tongue tied. *B. G. Powell*

DISTANT PROSPECT (IRE) 5 b.g. Namaqualand (USA) – Ukraine's Affair (USA) **102** (The Minstrel (CAN) 135) [2002 102: 18.7f 16.2s2 20m 16.2m3 18m4 16d4 Nov 1] unfurnished gelding: useful handicapper: as good as ever in 2002, creditable efforts including third to Mana d'Argent at Ascot and fourth to Miss Fara in Cesarewitch at Newmarket (unfortunate, blocked in run 3f out and stayed on strongly in bid to follow up 2001 success) on fourth/fifth outings: effective at 2m to 2½m: acts on any turf going, though all wins on good or softer: has run well when sweating: held up: genuine and consistent. *I. A. Balding*

DISTANT SCENE (USA) 4 b.g. Distant View (USA) 126 – Dangora (USA) 98 **63 d** (Sovereign Dancer (USA)) [2002 65: 6m 5d6 6m6 8m 7g 8m6 7d p6g p7g Dec 30] tall gelding: modest maiden handicapper: stays 7f: yet to race on extremes of going: tried blinkered: has started slowly/raced freely/found little: on downgrade. *T. D. McCarthy*

DISTANT SKY (USA) 5 ch.g. Distant View (USA) 126 – Nijinsky Star (USA) (Nijin- **68** sky (CAN) 138) [2002 75, a59+: p13g³ p16g 16s p13g p16g Dec 3] lengthy, useful-looking gelding: fair maiden handicapper: stays 13f: acts on good to firm going and polytrack: sometimes wears blinkers/cheekpieces. *P. Mitchell*

DISTANT STORM 9 ch.g. Pharly (FR) 130 – Candle In The Wind 90 (Thatching **43 §** 131) [2002 52§: 17.1m 18d 17.2g³ 16f Sep 26] robust gelding: poor handicapper: better at 2m/2¼m than shorter: acts on fibresand, probably on any turf going: blinkered/visored: usually tongue tied: free-going sort: untrustworthy. *B. J. Llewellyn*

DISTILLERY (USA) 4 ch.g. Mister Baileys 123 – Respectable (USA) (Northrop **–** (USA)) [2002 8.1d 10m f8.5g Jul 1] close-coupled gelding: modest form only start at 2 yrs: missed 2001, and well held at 4 yrs. *J. G. M. O'Shea*

DISTINCTION (IRE) 3 b.g. Danehill (USA) 126 – Ivy Leaf (IRE) 76 (Nureyev **108** (USA) 131) [2002 8m⁵ 10d² 10m* 10g⁶ 12g³ 13.9m³ Aug 22] 28,000F, IR 190,000Y: big, strong, good sort: first foal: dam, Irish maiden who stayed 1½m, half-sister to Oaks d'Italia winner Ivyanna: useful performer: won maiden at Newmarket in June: further improvement in handicaps after, third in Tote Gold Trophy at Goodwood (behind Dawn Invasion) and Melrose Stakes at York (beaten 2½ lengths by Total Turtle) last 2 starts: stays 1¾m: unraced on extremes of going. *Sir Michael Stoute*

DISTINCTIVE DANCER (IRE) 4 b. or br.c. Distinctly North (USA) 115 – Resiusa **–** (ITY) (Niniski (USA) 125) [2002 –: p12g Jan 8] well held in maidens. *I. A. Wood*

DISTINCTIVE DREAM (IRE) 8 b.g. Distinctly North (USA) 115 – Green Side **55 §** (USA) 37 (Green Dancer (USA) 132) [2002 68, a61: 5g 7f³ 6m 6s 5.9d⁶ 6d f7g f7g⁴ f6g⁴ **a48 §** p7g Dec 18] strong, lengthy gelding: modest nowadays: effective at 6f to 1m: acts on any turf going and fibresand: often visored/blinkered, effective without: has worn cheek-pieces: sometimes sways away: unreliable. *A. Bailey*

DISTINCTLY ROYAL 4 b.g. Distinctly North (USA) 115 – Hever Golf Queen **–** (Efisio 120) [2002 8g Jun 9] 4,100F, 7,500Y: good-bodied gelding: first foal: dam, 2-y-o 7.5f winner in Sweden, half-sister to smart sprinter Ever Sharp: well held in seller at Ripon. *J. G. FitzGerald*

DISTINCTLYSPLENDID 2 b.g. (Apr 25) Distinctly North (USA) 115 – Shelley **–** Marie 67 (Gunner B 126) [2002 6g⁵ 6m 7d⁶ 8.3d 7g Oct 24] second foal: dam 2-y-o 5f winner: well held, including in seller. *I. A. Wood*

DISTINCTLY WELL (IRE) 5 b.g. Distinctly North (USA) 115 – Brandywell **60** (Skyliner 117) [2002 58: 10m 10f⁴ 11.6s⁵ 10.5s⁶ 10g³ 9.9d 8.3d* 10s* f8s⁶ f12g⁵ 10s Oct 15] angular gelding: modest handicapper: won at Windsor and Ayr in August: effective at 1m to 11.6f: acts on firm going, soft and fibresand: tried visored/blinkered: often on toes/sweating: sometimes races freely: usually races prominently. *B. A. McMahon*

DIVA DANCER 2 ch.f. (May 6) Dr Devious (IRE) 127 – Catina 102 (Nureyev (USA) **42** 131) [2002 5.7g Jul 14] 10,000Y: half-sister to several winners, including 1½m winner Tinashaan (by Darshaan) and 1¼m to 2m winner Life of Riley (by Caerleon), both useful: Irish 2-y-o 6f winner, best at 1m: 11/2 and green, ninth in maiden at Bath. *R. M. Beckett*

DIVA LA VIDA (IRE) 3 ch.f. Perugino (USA) 84 – First Nadia (Auction Ring **37** (USA) 123) [2002 44: 12m 9s 8.5d 10g 13d 8g Aug 27] tall filly: poor maiden: left J. Wainwright after reappearance (reared and got stuck in stall): probably stays 1¼m: tried blinkered. *Patrick Carey, Ireland*

DIVA MARIA 3 b.f. Kris 135 – May Light 62 (Midyan (USA) 124) [2002 8.3g 8.3g⁶ **56** 7s Oct 22] fourth foal: half-sister to fairly useful miler Trio (by Cyrano de Bergerac): dam, maiden who stayed 7f, half-sister to smart middle-distance stayer Torus: modest form in maidens: should stay 1¼m. *B. Smart*

DIVA STAR 2 b.f. (Apr 30) Wizard King 122 – Nightingale (Night Shift (USA)) [2002 **–** 5s 5g Apr 4] IR 3,800Y: quite good-topped filly: first foal: dam little form: well held in minor event/maiden: dead. *P. D. Evans*

DIVINE TASK (USA) 4 ch.c. Irish River (FR) 131 – Set In Motion (USA) (Mr **113** Prospector (USA)) [2002 104: 8g² 8.8g* 8.9g 10m Jun 21] big, lengthy, attractive colt: smart performer: ½-length second to Swiss Law in listed event at Nad Al Sheba prior to winning Keeneland Jebel Hatta there in March by length from Lightning Arrow: well-backed favourite and bandaged in front, only fourteenth in listed rated stakes handicap at Royal Ascot (after 3-month break) final start, though might have made frame but for being badly hampered 1f out: should stay 1¼m: raced only on good/good to firm going. *Saeed bin Suroor*

DIVORCE ACTION (IRE)   6 b.g. Common Grounds 118 – Overdue Reaction (Be   – §
My Guest (USA) 126) [2002 61§: 14.1d Apr 30] sturdy gelding: temperamental handicapper: reluctant to leave stall only 6-y-o start. *R. M. Stronge*

DIVULGE (USA)   5 b.g. Diesis 133 – Avira (Dancing Brave (USA) 140) [2002 p8g   73
p10g⁴ f8.5g 8.3g Apr 29] sturdy gelding: fair performer: probably best around 1m: acts
on polytrack and good to firm going: ran as if something amiss last 2 starts at 3 yrs.
P. J. Hobbs

DIXIE DANCING   3 ch.f. Greensmith 121 – Daylight Dreams 77 (Indian Ridge 123)   75
[2002 –: p6g⁴ 7m f6g⁵ p8g 7g⁴ 8m³ 7.1m³ 7m 7m² p8g² 6m⁶ 7f p6g p7g p8g* Dec 14]
sturdy filly: fair handicapper: won at Lingfield in December: stays easy 1m: acts on good
to firm going and polytrack: free-going sort, usually held up. *C. A. Cyzer*

DIXIE'S DARTS   4 b.g. Mistertopogigo (IRE) 118 – Maestrette 77 (Manado 130)   51
[2002 67: f7g⁴ Jan 21] quite good-topped gelding: maiden: only modest form only 4-y-o
start: best at 6f: acts on polytrack, firm and soft going: sold 1,000 gns. *M. H. Tompkins*

DI YOUNG   2 b.f. (Mar 16) Hernando (FR) 127 – Mo Chos Chle 80 (Indian Ridge 123)   62 p
[2002 p8g Dec 3] IR 16,000Y: second foal: dam, Irish 2-y-o 1m winner from 2 starts,
granddaughter of Oaks runner-up Val's Girl: 50/1, 5 lengths ninth of 12 to Treculiar in
maiden at Lingfield, slowly away and not knocked about: should do better. *J. W. Hills*

DIZZY IN THE HEAD   3 b.g. Mind Games 121 – Giddy 60 (Polar Falcon (USA)   79
126) [2002 79d: 6d* 6f* 6m² 5.1m 6d 6f 5g⁶ 6.1s Oct 29] leggy gelding: fair performer:
won seller at Leicester in May and handicap at Redcar in June: effective at 5f/6f: acts on
any ground: visored: front runner. *J. O'Reilly*

DIZZY KNIGHT   5 b.m. Distant Relative 128 – Top Treat (USA) 101 (Topsider   –
(USA)) [2002 –: 6.1d 5.3d Jun 13] no longer of much account. *B. Palling*

DIZZY TART (IRE)   3 b.f. Definite Article 121 – Tizzy 79 (Formidable (USA) 125)   58
[2002 65: 7.5m 7m 6.1s 8.1m 10m 11.7d 8g Oct 16] rather leggy filly: modest maiden:
seems to stay easy 1¼m: acts on good to firm going: winning hurdler. *Mrs P. N. Dutfield*

DMITRI   2 b.c. (Jan 11) Emperor Jones (USA) 119 – Shining Cloud 73 (Indian Ridge   81
123) [2002 6f⁴ 7m² 7d* 7f² 7m 6m² Aug 24] lengthy colt: first foal: dam 6f winner:
fairly useful performer: won maiden at Folkestone in July: good second in minor event at
Catterick and nursery at Newmarket (beaten ¾ length by Spinsky, edging left) after: may
prove best at 6f/7f: acts on firm and good to soft going: races prominently. *M. L. W. Bell*

DOBERMAN (IRE)   7 br.g. Dilum (USA) 115 – Switch Blade (IRE) 60 (Robellino   48
(USA) 127) [2002 62, a71: f9.4g⁴ f8.5g³ f8.5g f12g⁶ f8.5g² f8.5g⁶ f8.5g⁴ f8.5g⁶   a66
f8.5g 9s 8.1m⁴ f8.5g 8g 9.9g⁶ 8.1g 10m f8g³ f9.4g³ f8.5g 8.5s Dec 26] rangy gelding:
fair handicapper on all-weather, poor on turf: probably best at 1m/easy 1¼m: acts on
fibresand, firm and soft going: often blinkered/visored: tried tongue tied: has been slowly
away: usually amateur ridden/races prominently: sometimes looks none too resolute.
W. M. Brisbourne

DOCDUCKOUT   2 b.g. (Feb 23) Bluegrass Prince (IRE) 110 – Fayre Holly (IRE) 57   59
(Fayruz 116) [2002 6m⁴ p6g p6g Dec 28] 5,200Y resold 14,000Y: third foal: half-brother
to 3-y-o Hollybell and 4-y-o Heaven Forbid: dam, maiden, might have proved best at
5f/6f: modest form in maidens/minor event, all at Lingfield: slowly away on debut.
J. M. P. Eustace

DOCKLANDS DIVA (IRE)   2 b.f. (Apr 30) Desert Prince (IRE) 130 – Mimansa   58
(USA) (El Gran Senor (USA) 136) [2002 5.7m 7m 7s 7g 8s⁴ f8.5g f7g Nov 25] IR
9,500Y: third foal: dam French 13f winner: modest maiden: seems to stay 1m: acts on soft
going, below form on all-weather: sometimes wears cheekpieces. *G. G. Margarson*

DOCKLANDS MAXIMUS (IRE)   2 ch.c. (Apr 20) Danehill Dancer (IRE) 117 –   83
Thats Luck (IRE) (Posen (USA)) [2002 p6g⁵ p7g⁴ 7g³ 6m 6.1m* 7f² p6g³ Oct 9] IR
11,000F, 15,000 2-y-o: workmanlike colt: second foal: dam unraced half-sister to very
smart 1½m performer Quilted: fairly useful performer: won nursery at Warwick in September: good placed efforts in similar events after: effective at 6f/7f: acts on polytrack,
raced only on good going or firmer on turf: edged left third/fourth starts, ran in snatches
penultimate one. *N. P. Littmoden*

DOCKLANDS PRINCESS (IRE)   2 ch.f. (Apr 24) Desert Prince (IRE) 130 –   56
Alamiya (IRE) (Doyoun 124) [2002 6d 5d⁴ 7f Jul 29] IR 15,000Y: sixth foal: half-sister
to fairly useful 9f winner Chrysolite (by Kris) and a 1m/9f winner in Germany by

Fairy King: dam unraced half-sister to high-class French middle-distance performer Altayan: clearly best effort in maidens (modest form) when fourth of 6 to Night Speed at Kempton (subsequently left B. Hills): should stay at least 7f: acts on good to soft ground. *G. G. Margarson*

DOC RYAN'S   8 b.g. Damister (USA) 123 – Jolimo 92 (Fortissimo 111) [2002 16.2g[5] Jul 26] small gelding: well held both runs since 1999: usually blinkered. *B. J. Llewellyn*   –

DOCTOR BRAVIOUS (IRE)   9 b.g. Priolo (USA) 127 – Sharp Slipper (Sharpo 132) [2002 p12g May 28] probably of little account nowadays. *Jamie Poulton*   –

DOCTOR DENNIS (IRE)   5 b.g. Last Tycoon 131 – Noble Lustre (USA) 71 (Lyphard's Wish (FR) 124) [2002 73, a78: p6g[5] f6g[6] f7g[6] f7g 6g[4] 7d[5] p6g[5] 8g 7m Jun 25] good-bodied gelding: fair handicapper: best form at 6f: acts on firm going, soft and all-weather: usually blinkered/visored. *Mrs Lydia Pearce*   **68**

DOCTOR DOVE   8 ch.g. St Enodoc – Saucy Dove (Saucy Kit 76) [2002 f14.8g 12.6m f12g Jun 28] modest form at best in bumpers: failed to complete in points in 2002: well held in claimers/maiden on Flat. *C. J. Price*   –

DOCTOR KOOL   6 ch.g. Local Suitor (USA) 128 – Hasty Sarah 56 (Gone Native) [2002 f9.4g 12.4m 11.8m 14.1m f14.8g Aug 9] fair maiden at best: dead. *K. A. Morgan*   –

DOCTOR SPIN (IRE)   6 b.g. Namaqualand (USA) – Madam Loving 99 (Vaigly Great 127) [2002 108: 5s 6g 5f 5f[5] 6m 6g 6g 6g Sep 20] tall, leggy gelding: usually looks well: fairly useful handicapper nowadays: hasn't won since early in 2000: best at 5f/6f: acts on firm going, below form on soft: blinkered penultimate start: edgy sort, usually sweats: sometimes finds little. *M. W. Easterby*   **94**

DOC WATSON (FR)   2 ch.c. (Feb 23) Dr Devious (IRE) 127 – Blinding (IRE) (High Top 131) [2002 7m[4] 8m[3] 8.1g[3] 8m[2] Sep 23] 70,000F: big, strong colt: sixth foal: half-brother to 3 winners, including 3-y-o Fools Rush In and 1995 2-y-o 5f winner High Priority (by Marju), both fairly useful: dam, ran twice, half-sister to smart 7f/1m performer Hadeer: fairly useful form: fourth in listed race then placed in maidens, edging left when beaten 2 lengths by Albareq at Kempton final start: stays 1m: raced only on good/good to firm ground. *R. Hannon*   **87**

DODGER (IRE)   2 b.g. (Apr 8) Among Men (USA) 124 – Hazy Image (Ahonoora 122) [2002 6m 6g 6m 7g Oct 24] IR 1,000F, IR 2,500Y: small, well-made gelding: half-brother to several winners, including fairly useful Irish 7f (at 2 yrs) to 1¼m winner Irish Empire (by Tirol): dam unraced: well held in maidens: tried blinkered: gelded after final start. *Jamie Poulton*   –

DODONA   4 b.f. Lahib (USA) 129 – Dukrame 76 (Top Ville 129) [2002 64: 9.7m[4] 10d[2] 10d[5] 10m[6] 8g[2] 9.7m[2] 9d[4] 9.9m 9.7g 8.5d[3] p10g[5] Nov 27] modest handicapper: effective at 1m/1¼m: acts on soft and good to firm going: blinkered ninth start: free-going sort: sometimes gives trouble in preliminaries/hangs/carries head awkwardly. *T. D. McCarthy*   **64**

DOL DOL   3 b.f. Danzig Connection (USA) – Namorah (IRE) (River Falls 113) [2002 f7s f6g[5] p5g f7g Feb 21] first foal: dam unraced: well held in sellers/claimer. *K. A. Ryan*   –

DOLFINESSE (IRE)   5 ch.m. Dolphin Street (FR) 125 – Gortadoo (USA) (Sharpen Up 127) [2002 52: 9g[2] f9.4g[4] f9.4g[6] 7g[6] 8g 8m[2] 7.5d 8.5d[5] 8g f8.5g Nov 18] sparely-made mare: poor performer: effective at 7f to 9f: acts on fibresand, heavy and good to firm going: visored: usually races prominently: unreliable. *M. Brittain*   **48 §**

DOLLAR KING (IRE)   4 b.g. Ela-Mana-Mou 132 – Summerhill (Habitat 134) [2002 77+: 7g 8d 8m[6] 8f 7m Aug 14] lengthy, angular gelding: fair handicapper at best at 4 yrs: stays 9f: acts on firm ground: visored final 3-y-o outing and last 3 starts: has worn net muzzle: sold 5,500 gns. *J. Noseda*   **72 ?**

DOLLAR LAW   6 ch.g. Selkirk (USA) 129 – Western Heights (Shirley Heights 130) [2002 66: 8.5g 8.3g* 8g[6] 10s[6] 7d[5] 10g* 10s f9.4g 10s[3] 10d 8s Oct 28] leggy, short-backed gelding: fair handicapper: won at Windsor in April and Southwell in June: effective at 7f to 1¼m: acts on soft ground (well held on fibresand): tongue tied after reappearance: has been taken steadily/alone to post: races freely: has hung left. *R. J. Price*   **72** **a–**

DOLMUR (IRE)   2 b. or br.c. (Mar 9) Charnwood Forest (IRE) 125 – Kawanin 81 (Generous (IRE) 139) [2002 7g 6s 7g* 6g[5] 8g* 7m[4] 8d[4] 7s[4] Oct 25] IR 20,000Y: rather leggy, quite good-topped colt: second foal: dam, lightly-raced maiden, closely related to useful performer up to 1m Intimaa: useful performer: won maiden at Gowran and nursery at Tralee in August: creditable fourth in nursery at Leopardstown and Beresford Stakes at the Curragh next 2 starts: below-form fourth to Makhlab in Horris Hill Stakes at   **103**

Newbury final outing: stays 1m: acts on good to firm and good to soft going. *Anthony Mullins, Ireland*

DOLORES 3 b.f. Danehill (USA) 126 – Agnus (IRE) (In The Wings 128) [2002 87p: **111** 8m⁴ 8d* 8m³ 8g⁴ 8f² 7m⁶ Oct 19] tall, good-topped filly: smart performer: made all in listed race at Goodwood in May: mostly good efforts otherwise, including when length fourth to Kazzia in 1000 Guineas at Newmarket, 2¾ lengths third to Sophisticat in Coronation Stakes at Royal Ascot and ¾-length second to Dress To Thrill in Sun Chariot Stakes at Newmarket: stays 1m: acts on firm and good to soft going, unraced on softer: free-going sort (has worn crossed noseband): consistent. *Mrs A. J. Perrett*

DOLPHINELLE (IRE) 6 b.g. Dolphin Street (FR) 125 – Mamie's Joy (Prince **41 §** Tenderfoot (USA) 126) [2002 54§, a45§: p7g⁴ p10g⁶ p8g* p10g⁵ p10g p10g 10.2g p7g⁴ **a55 §** 8.1m 7d⁶ 8g 8.5d f7g p7g* p7g Dec 18] sturdy gelding: modest on all-weather, poor on turf: won sellers at Lingfield in February and December: effective at 7f/1¼m: below form on heavy going, probably acts on any other turf/all-weather: usually blinkered/visored (wasn't for second success): held up: tends to race lazily: not one to trust. *Jamie Poulton*

DOLZAGO 2 b.g. (Feb 29) Pursuit of Love 124 – Doctor's Glory (USA) 91 (Elmaamul **59 p** (USA) 125) [2002 8d Oct 30] 16,500Y: second living foal: brother to useful 7f (at 2 yrs) to 1¼m winner Courting: dam, 5f (at 2 yrs)/6f winner, half-sister to useful 1½m to 2m winner On Call: 20/1 and very green, 10 lengths tenth to Devant in maiden at Yarmouth, off bridle before halfway (gelded after): will probably stay at least 1¼m: likely to do better. *P. W. Harris*

DOME 4 b.g. Be My Chief (USA) 122 – Round Tower 93 (High Top 131) [2002 60d: **–** 10.2g 11.9g 12m 12d Jul 11] big, good-topped gelding: modest maiden at best: no form at 4 yrs: sometimes visored/tongue tied: has started slowly/looked none too keen. *S. Dow*

Normandie Stud Ltd's "Dolores"

Prix Daniel Wildenstein - Casino Barriere de La Rochelle, Longchamp—
Domedriver (No.5) finishes strongly under a very confident ride from Thierry Thulliez;
the visored Suggestive and Gateman (left) take the minor placings for Britain in a race
previously known as the Prix du Rond-Point

DOMEDRIVER (IRE)   4 b.c. Indian Ridge 123 – Napoli 108 (Baillamont (USA)   **128**
124) [2002 112: 7d⁵ 8m* 8s² 8g² 8g* 8d* Oct 26]
     French-trained Domedriver was the 'champion' who rose without trace,
and, furthermore, had the singular misfortune to earn scant recognition in his
moment of glory. His victory at 26/1 in the NetJets Breeders' Cup Mile at Arlington
was overshadowed by the concentration on the performance of beaten favourite
Rock of Gibraltar. With none of the home-trained runners looking outstanding,
Rock of Gibraltar started odds on and was expected to extend his much-publicised
consecutive winning sequence in Group/Grade 1 events to eight. Six-year-old
Good Journey, winner of three out of three in the current season, and the ex-British
(third in Sinndar's Derby) five-year-old Beat Hollow were the only others in the
fourteen-runner line-up to start at shorter than 14/1. Rock of Gibraltar and Domedriver were joined in the European challenge by Rock of Gibraltar's stable-
companion the Poule d'Essai des Poulains winner Landseer, the French-trained
Poule d'Essai runner-up Medecis and the smart Irish filly Dress To Thrill, unbeaten
in four races in the current season (unusually, there was no British challenge).
     A fatal accident to Landseer entering the straight marred the Breeders' Cup
Mile and the waited-with Rock of Gibraltar lost some momentum when avoiding
his stricken stablemate before finishing very strongly to take second, passing
almost the entire field. Things had gone slightly wrong from the start for Rock of
Gibraltar who was put in an unpromising position after a somewhat sluggish break
and, with a steady pace counting against those held up, was still last but one
entering the short home straight. After such an eye-catching run, he was hailed the
moral victor. Leading American critic Andy Beyer was one who thought Rock of
Gibraltar's performance 'proved his greatness', though he was scathing, as were
the American media in general, of the ride given to the horse. 'Ever since
international racing began we've been seeing your European pinheads lose races
like this. These are not huge European straights where you can make up a ton of
ground . . . any reasonably competent American jockey would have won easily.'

Amid the widespread frustration felt over Rock of Gibraltar's defeat, Domedriver's rider Thierry Thulliez probably appreciated the irony that, only three weeks earlier, his own riding had come in for vitriolic criticism after his mount the Prix du Jockey Club winner Sulamani was set an inordinate amount to do in the home straight in the Prix de l'Arc, a race he probably should have won. Thulliez made no mistake in the Breeders' Cup Mile, riding Domedriver with aplomb, content to keep him tucked in until finding room to make a run on the inside in the home straight. Domedriver showed a fine turn of foot to take advantage of the opening that presented itself and hit the front inside the final furlong. At the line Rock of Gibraltar was three quarters of a length behind him, with Good Journey a nose away third and the previous year's runner-up Forbidden Apple a further length and a quarter away in fourth. Beat Hollow came sixth, with Dress To Thrill and Medecis eighth and ninth.

Interestingly, Domedriver and Medecis were among only four—Islington and Turtle Bow were the others—in the eighteen-strong European challenge for the Breeders' Cup races that ran without the diuretic drug furosemide, traded under the brand name lasix. Pretty well all American horses race on lasix, claimed to be beneficial for those which suffer bleeding in their lungs when racing. None of the European challengers at the latest Breeders' Cup was known to break blood vessels but, as has become the custom, most of their connections (including the major outfits Ballydoyle and Godolphin) unfortunately adopted a 'when in Rome' policy. More can be found on this subject in the essay on Banks Hill in *Racehorses of 2001*, but it is worth reiterating that the use of furosemide is banned for runners in European races and the success of Domedriver—and of the numerous Breeders' Cup challengers from the drug-free Fabre stable over the years—demonstrates that running without standard American medication does no harm to the prospects of European challengers. Europe's strict drugs policy would be more tenable if European-based owners and trainers as a whole took a stand against the use of lasix—and of bute the standard pain-masking drug—by running their horses 'clean' in America.

Domedriver's emergence as a top miler must have come as a surprise to anyone who had followed his career in France, where he had been plying his trade almost exclusively at up to listed and lesser-pattern company. He won a listed event as a two-year-old and another one at three, when third place in a not particularly strong renewal of the Group 3 Prix Quincey at Deauville was his best effort in six

NetJets Breeders' Cup Mile, Arlington—Domedriver shows a good turn of foot as Rock of Gibraltar's record-breaking run comes to a somewhat unlucky end; Good Journey (noseband) is third

outings. Domedriver was a smart performer and a reliable sort, but continued to give the impression in the first half of his four-year-old career that he wasn't up to contesting the most important races for a horse of his type. He beat a useful field to record his first pattern victory in the Group 3 Prix du Chemin du Fer du Nord at Chantilly in June on his second outing, but the runner-up, Italian-trained Altieri, turned the tables next time, when receiving 4 lb, in another Group 3 event, the Prix Messidor at Deauville a month later. When Domedriver was then stepped up to Group 1 company for the first time in the Prix Jacques le Marois at Deauville in August it seemed that the principal reason might be to provide his owners with a runner in an event they sponsored. Only two of the eight starters were sent off at longer odds than Domedriver but he managed to divide the two Group 1 winners in the line-up, Banks Hill and Best of The Bests. Held up as usual, Domedriver couldn't get in a blow at Banks Hill but, in going down by a length and a half, he put up easily the best performance of his career at up to that time. The eleven-runner Group 2 Prix Daniel Wildenstein - Casino Barriere de La Rochelle (formerly the Prix du Rond-Point) at Longchamp on Arc weekend gave Domedriver's rider the opportunity to rehearse his Breeders' Cup tactics. Held up and surprisingly switched inside in the home straight, the very confidently-ridden Domedriver weaved his way through to prevail in a finish of heads with British challengers Suggestive and Gateman, less than a length covering the first five. The bare form was certainly no better than anything Domedriver had recorded before the Prix Jacques le Marois, but the slender winning margin gave a misleading impression. Domedriver had plenty of running left in him and could almost certainly have won by a fair bit further had his jockey started his run earlier.

Niarchos Family's "Domedriver"

		⎧Ahonoora	⎧Lorenzaccio
	⎧Indian Ridge	⎨ (ch 1975)	⎨Helen Nichols
	⎪ (ch 1985)	⎩Hillbrow	⎩Swing Easy
Domedriver (IRE)	⎨	⎧ (ch 1975)	⎧Golden City
(b.c. 1998)	⎪	⎨Baillamont	⎨Blushing Groom
	⎩Napoli	⎩ (b 1982)	⎩Lodeve
	(b 1991)	⎧Bella Senora	⎧Northern Dancer
		⎩ (b 1984)	⎩Sex Appeal

After his triumph in Chicago, Domedriver looked set to put his newly-found status as a top miler on the line in the Hong Kong Mile at Sha Tin in December but he was withdrawn less than a week before the race because of an abscess in his off-hind hoof. It is thought he will stay in training as a five-year-old. His sire, the prolific Indian Ridge, tends to enjoy most success with his three-year-olds and, in particular, with his older horses. Indian Ridge did not stay a mile himself but Domedriver is his second winner of the Breeders' Cup Mile, following the filly Ridgewood Pearl in 1995. Indian Ridge was also represented in the latest season by several other smart or better four-year-olds, including the sprinter Indian Prince, the miler Nayyir, the mile-and-a-quarter performer Indian Creek and the middle-distance stayer High Pitched. Domedriver is the second foal of the French mile- to mile-and-a-quarter winner Napoli, who stayed a mile and a half. Her first foal Forest Rain (by Caerleon) won at up to eleven furlongs in France and her third, the smart three-year-old Tau Ceti (by Hernando), has won at up to a mile and a quarter, over which trip he won the Prix du Prince d'Orange at Longchamp in September. Napoli is a sister to another smart French mile-and-a-quarter performer in D'Arros, winner of La Coupe at Longchamp, while Domedriver's grandam Bella Senora is a sister to the Two Thousand Guineas and Irish Derby winner El Gran Senor and to the top two-year-old of 1977 Try My Best. Domedriver is best at a mile and acts on soft and good to firm going. He is held up to make the best use of his turn of foot.
P. Bary, France

DOMENICO (IRE) 4 b.g. Sadler's Wells (USA) 132 – Russian Ballet (USA) **89**
(Nijinsky (CAN) 138) [2002 83: 14s⁴ 20m 16.4d⁴ 16.2m⁵ 18m Oct 19] strong, close-coupled gelding: seventh foal: half-brother to several winners by Woodman, notably very smart Irish 1¼m to 1¾m winner (also second in Irish Derby) Dr Johnson: dam twice-raced close relative of Try My Best and El Gran Senor: fairly useful performer: won maiden at Thurles in 2001 (left C. O'Brien 78,000 gns after final start): mostly creditable efforts in handicaps in 2002: probably stays 2½m: acts on soft and good to firm ground: blinkered (well beaten) third 3-y-o start: sold 16,000 gns, joined J. Jenkins.
P. R. Webber

DOMINICA 3 ch.f. Alhaarth (IRE) 126 – Dominio (IRE) 99 (Dominion 123) [2002 **115**
105: 5g* 5m⁵ Aug 22] smallish filly: smart performer: 16/1, won King's Stand Stakes at Royal Ascot (beat strong-finishing Continent by head) under well-judged ride, leading under stand rail around halfway and holding on bravely: ran well when under 2 lengths fifth of 17 to Kyllachy in Nunthorpe Stakes at York, only other outing at 3 yrs: best at 5f:

King's Stand Stakes, Royal Ascot—Dominica holds on gamely from Continent, Kyllachy, The Trader (blinkered) and Indian Prince (No.3)

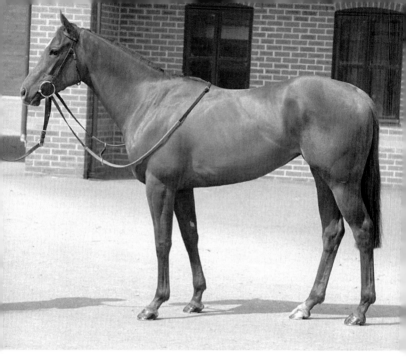

Major & Mrs R. B. Kennard's "Dominica"

yet to race on extremes of going: races prominently: has flashed tail under pressure, but is genuine: stays in training. *M. P. Tregoning*

DOMINION PRINCE   4 b.g. First Trump 118 – Lammastide 93 (Martinmas 128)   –
[2002 –: p16g Jan 23] tall, good-topped gelding: disappointing maiden: said to have had breathing problem only 4-y-o start. *D. Mullarkey*

DOMINION ROSE (USA)   3 b. or br.f. Spinning World (USA) 130 – Louju (USA)   **65 d**
(Silver Hawk (USA) 123) [2002 8.1m² 8.3m 8d³ 7g 10g⁶ p10g 8m 10.2f 12f 12d f8g⁴ f8g⁵ Dec 4] IR 110,000Y: rather leggy, unfurnished filly: has a short, round action: first foal: dam unraced daughter of US winner up to 1m and Grade 1 9f runner-up Secretarial Queen: fair maiden: well below form after fifth outing: probably stays 1¼m: blinkered last 2 starts. *W. R. Muir*

DOMIRATI   2 b.g. (Mar 31) Emarati (USA) 74 – Julia Domna (Dominion 123) [2002   **74 p**
f6g* p6g Dec 18] third foal: half-brother to 5-y-o Vintage Premium: dam, no form, half-sister to very smart 7f/1m performer Norwich: 5/1, won 13-runner maiden at Wolverhampton in November by 1¾ lengths from Tally: favourite, raced much too freely in front in minor event at Lingfield: bred to stay beyond 6f: probably open to improvement. *R. Charlton*

DOMQUISTA D'OR   5 b.g. Superpower 113 – Gild The Lily 83 (Ile de Bourbon   –
(USA) 133) [2002 57d: f9.4g⁶ Jun 22] probably of little account nowadays. *G. A. Ham*

DOM SHADEED   7 b.g. Shadeed (USA) 135 – Fair Dominion 107 (Dominion 123)   **49**
[2002 8.1d 8d 10.2g⁵ 10.9m Sep 21] tall, unfurnished gelding: poor handicapper nowadays: stays 1¼m: acts on fibresand, soft and good to firm going: blinkered (well held) once: has started slowly. *R. J. Baker*

DONA MARIA 2 b.f. (May 4) Titus Livius (FR) 115 – Distant Isle (IRE) (Bluebird **53** (USA) 125) [2002 5m 6m 6.1m 6d Oct 18] fourth living foal: half-sister to 5.7f (at 2 yrs) and 1m winner Entropy (by Brief Truce): dam unraced: modest maiden: best effort final start: stays 6f: sold 500 gns. *A. Berry*

DONATELLO PRIMO (IRE) 3 ch.g. Entrepreneur 123 – Mystical River (USA) **78** (Riverman (USA) 131) [2002 70: f6g* p5g* 5m² 5d 5m p6g⁶ p6g Jul 17] strong gelding: fair performer: won maiden at Southwell in February and handicap at Lingfield in March: effective at 5f/6f: acts on all-weather and good to firm going, probably on heavy: has been early to post/started slowly. *R. Guest*

DONATUS (IRE) 6 b.g. Royal Academy (USA) 130 – La Dame du Lac (USA) **62** (Round Table) [2002 65: p13g⁶ p12g Mar 6] neat gelding: modest maiden handicapper: barely stays easy 13f: acts on firm going, soft and polytrack: visored last 3 starts: none too consistent. *S. Dow*

DON BOLLINGER (IRE) 3 b.c. Petardia 113 – Bollinger Rose (IRE) 60 (Fayruz **–** 116) [2002 7m 6s May 26] 10,000Y: first foal: dam maiden who stayed 6f: tailed off in claimer/maiden. *G. M. McCourt*

DONEGAL DANCER (IRE) 2 ch.g. (Mar 18) Spectrum (IRE) 126 – Unfuwaanah **78** 74 (Unfuwain (USA) 131) [2002 6s⁴ 7d² 7g² 8m 7f³ p7g³ Oct 9] IR 27,000F, 25,000Y: tall gelding: third foal: half-brother to 3-y-o Marjurita and 5-y-o Arizona Lady: dam 7f winner: fair maiden: stays 7f, seemingly not 1m: acts on firm and soft going: usually races prominently: found little final start. *B. W. Hills*

DONEGAL SHORE (IRE) 3 b.c. Mujadil (USA) 119 – Distant Shore (IRE) 71 **90** (Jareer (USA) 115) [2002 98: 6g⁵ 6d⁶ 6m⁶ 7.2g 7f Aug 17] rather leggy colt: fairly useful performer: best efforts at 6f on good ground or softer: tried tongue tied: reportedly had breathing problem final start: sold only 800 gns, joined Mrs J. Candlish. *B. W. Hills*

DON FAYRUZ (IRE) 10 b.g. Fayruz 116 – Gobolino (Don 128) [2002 62: p8g⁴ p8g* **64** p8g² p8g² 10.2g² f8.5g 9s Oct 25] good-topped gelding: modest performer: won seller at Lingfield in February: effective at 1m/1¼m: acts on firm going, soft and polytrack: sometimes finds little. *Mrs A. J. Bowlby*

DON FERNANDO 3 b.c. Zilzal (USA) 137 – Teulada (USA) 61 (Riverman (USA) **93** 131) [2002 93+: 10m⁵ 10.4m² 12m 10g⁵ 10.3m 10f⁶ 8g Oct 17] tall, good-topped colt: fairly useful handicapper: left E. Dunlop after fifth start: effective at 1m/1¼m: acts on firm ground, possibly not on soft: visored once: fairly useful form when successful over hurdles in November/December. *M. C. Pipe*

DON FITZ (ARG) 6 b.g. Fitzcarraldo (ARG) – Luna Donzetta (ARG) (Ahmad **66** (ARG)) [2002 10s⁵ 7m 11.8g 12d 16.4g p16g Sep 4] Argentinian-bred gelding: won 4 races from 7f to 11f out of 14 starts in native country, including Grade 1 event in late-2000: fair form at best in varied company in Britain: blinkered (looked none too keen) final start: dead. *J. A. B. Old*

DONIZETTI (IRE) 2 b.c. (Feb 12) Deputy Minister (CAN) – Festival Song (USA) **91** 87 (Irish River (FR) 131) [2002 6m⁴ 6m* 6g² Oct 16] rather leggy colt: first foal: dam, Irish 5f winner, out of close relative to Preakness winner Summer Squall and half-sister to Belmont/Breeders' Cup Classic winner A P Indy: fairly useful form: landed odds in maiden at Newcastle in October by 5 lengths from Jumhoor, making most: disappointing favourite in minor event at Lingfield final start: should stay 7f. *R. Charlton*

DONNA ANNA 3 b.f. Be My Chief (USA) 122 – Countess Olivia 80 (Prince Tender- **–** foot (USA) 126) [2002 9.9m p12g 10d Aug 5] sister to smart performer up to 1¼m in Britain and in USA Donna Viola and fairly useful Irish 1½m and 1¾m winner Prince Valiant and half-sister to several winners: dam stayed 1¼m: well held in maidens. *C. F. Wall*

DONNA'S DOUBLE 7 ch.g. Weldnaas (USA) 112 – Shadha 57 (Shirley Heights **88** 130) [2002 80, a–: 10d 8v⁵ 8f 10.1m³ 10g⁴ 10.1s* 10.4g* 8g* 7.9m⁴ 10m 10.4m⁶ 8.9m **a–** 9f 10.4f⁵ 12s 8s Nov 6] smallish, workmanlike gelding: fairly useful performer: won 2 handicaps at Newcastle and claimer at York in June: best at 1m/1¼m: acts on firm and soft going, some promise on fibresand: usually held up: has carried head awkwardly. *D. Eddy*

DONNY BOWLING 2 b.f. (Apr 28) Sesaro (USA) 81 – Breakfast Creek 63 **58** (Hallgate 127) [2002 5m* 5m 6g 5g 5f 5m 5f 7f⁶ 7g Oct 19] 1,000Y: leggy, lengthy filly: second foal: dam 2-y-o 5f winner, modest performer: awarded maiden at Beverley in April on technical grounds after finishing second to Razotti: below form in nurseries last 3 starts: best efforts at 5f: raced only on good going or firmer. *M. E. Sowersby*

DON'S LITTLE GEM (IRE) 2 ch.f. (Apr 22) Titus Livius (FR) 115 – Betelgeuse —
86 (Kalaglow 132) [2002 5s f8g f7g Oct 21] 5,500Y: strong filly: half-sister to several
winners, including fairly useful 2000 2-y-o 5f winner Kachina Doll (by Mujadil), later
successful abroad, and 8.5f winner Black Rocket (by Perugino): dam 1¾m winner: well
held in maiden/sellers: sold 3,000 gns. *M. Johnston*

DON'T MATTER 2 b.f. (Mar 25) Petong 126 – Cool Run 87 (Deep Run 119) [2002 **60**
5.7m⁵ 5g⁴ 7.6m 7g Oct 24] sister to useful 6f (at 2 yrs) to 8.5f winner Cool Secret and
half-sister to 5-y-o Cool Spice: dam 1m/1¼m winner: modest maiden: well beaten last 2
starts: should stay at least 6f. *B. Palling*

DON'T SIOUX ME (IRE) 4 b.g. Sadler's Wells (USA) 132 – Commanche Belle 74 **100**
(Shirley Heights 130) [2002 105: 10d 10s Oct 26] deep-girthed gelding: useful performer,
lightly raced: better effort in handicaps in 2002 when seventh to Prize Winner in valuable
race at Sandown (edgy and troublesome beforehand) in July on reappearance: barely
stays 1¾m: acts on firm ground, probably on good to soft: tongue tied final start:
free-going sort: sold only 8,000 gns, joined G. Prodromou. *H. R. A. Cecil*

DON'T TELL ROSEY 2 b.c. (Apr 10) Barathea (IRE) 127 – Patsy Western 81 **71**
(Precocious 126) [2002 6f 6m 6f⁸ 3s² 5f³ 6g 6.1m² Sep 20] 14,000Y: compact colt:
brother to useful 6f (at 2 yrs) to 1m winner in Italy Abe and half-brother to several
winners, notably 8-y-o Granny's Pet and 3-y-o Redback: dam twice-raced 6f winner: fair
maiden: good second in nursery at Nottingham final start, making most: raced only at 5f/
6f: acts on firm and soft going: difficult ride (veered markedly left and ran out second
start). *M. Blanshard*

DONT WORRY BOUT ME (IRE) 5 b.g. Brief Truce (USA) 126 – Coggle 60 **57**
(Kind of Hush 118) [2002 60: 10g⁴ 10.1g Jul 18] modest performer: stays 1½m: acts on
firm ground and fibresand: visored: front runner. *T. G. Mills*

DON'T WORRY MIKE 8 ch.g. Forzando 122 – Hat Hill (Roan Rocket 128) [2002 —
8.1g Jul 5] of little account nowadays. *G. F. Bridgwater*

DORA CORBINO 2 b.f. (Apr 9) Superpower 113 – Smartie Lee 66 (Dominion 123) —
[2002 7.1m Sep 16] quite good-topped filly: sister to 5-y-o Super Dominion and
half-sister to 5f (at 2 yrs) to 8.5f winner Santandre (by Democratic) and 4-y-o Lygeton
Lad: dam, 7f (at 2 yrs) to 1½m winner who stayed 2m, also winning hurdler: 66/1, always
behind in Warwick maiden. *R. Hollinshead*

DORCHESTER 5 b.g. Primo Dominie 121 – Penthouse Lady (Last Tycoon 131) **85**
[2002 85d: 6m 5g⁶ 6m² 6m⁴ 6m³ 6m* 6m² 6m² 6d* 6g 6g 6f 6.1s⁵ Oct 29] good-topped
gelding: fairly useful handicapper: won at Windsor and Newmarket in summer: effective
at 5f/6f: acts on firm going, soft and fibresand: blinkered once at 3 yrs: tends to edge right:
often held up: more consistent nowadays. *W. J. Musson*

DORIS SOUTER (IRE) 2 b. or br.f. (Jan 17) Desert Story (IRE) 115 – Hope And **65 d**
Glory (USA) 87 (Well Decorated (USA)) [2002 5m⁵ 6d 5.3m² 6g 5m 6.5g 7s Oct 25]
10,000F, 12,500Y: well-grown, close-coupled filly: half-sister to several winners,
including 3-y-o Eastern Hope and fairly useful 1¼m winner Saddlers' Hope (by
Saddlers' Hall): dam 2-y-o 6f winner (only season to race): fair maiden: went wrong way
after debut: should stay 6f: acts on good to firm ground. *R. Hannon*

DOROTHY'S FRIEND 2 b.g. (Apr 22) Grand Lodge (USA) 125 – Isle of Flame **64**
(Shirley Heights 130) [2002 7.1g 8g⁶ 7s Oct 15] 210,000Y: useful-looking gelding:
half-brother to several winners, including useful French 9f/1¼m winner Thattinger (by
Salse) and fairly useful 1m winner Burning Impulse (by Cadeaux Genereux): dam
unraced out of close relation to Middle Park winner Balla Cove: modest maiden: should
stay 1¼m: has worn crossed noseband. *R. Charlton*

DOROTHYS SWIFT (IRE) 2 b.f. (Apr 2) Petardia 113 – Verica (USA) (Diesis **62**
133) [2002 5.3f⁵ p6g⁵ 6f⁴ 7m⁴ 6m⁵ f6g⁶ 5.2f⁶ 6f⁴ 7d Aug 9] IR 2,500Y, resold 500Y: leggy
filly: fifth foal: half-sister to a winner abroad by Priolo: dam French 2-y-o 7f winner:
modest maiden: well beaten in sellers last 2 starts: stays 6f: acts on firm ground,
seemingly on polytrack. *Mrs D. Haine*

DOT COM DOT 3 b.f. Monsun (GER) 124 – Number One Spot 71 (Reference Point **61**
139) [2002 8.3g⁵ 8.3d² 8m⁵ 7g⁵ 7.1m² 8g⁵ 8d Nov 1] fourth foal: half-sister to 5-y-o
Desert Fury: dam, 7f winner, closely related to top-class miler Milligram out of 1000
Guineas winner One In A Million: modest maiden: best efforts around 1m: yet to race on
extremes of going. *M. R. Channon*

DOTTIE DIGGER (IRE) 3 b.f. Catrail (USA) 123 – Hint-Of-Romance (IRE) 86 **63**
(Treasure Kay 114) [2002 57: 9m³ 8g 8g 8.3v 9d⁶ 9m² f8.5s 7.1m⁵ 10f⁴ 9.1s f9.4s **a–**

Nov 2] heavy-topped filly: modest maiden: barely stays 1¼m: acts on firm going: tried blinkered/visored: has been restless in stall/wandered. *I. Semple*

DOUBLE ASSEMBLY   2 ch.f. (Apr 8) Presidium 124 – Zamarra 59 (Clantime 101)   **74**
[2002 f5g³ 5.1f* 5g⁶ 6s 5.2d Oct 30] 3,200Y: good-topped filly: poor mover: second foal: dam, lightly-raced maiden at 2 yrs, best at 5f: fair performer: made all in maiden at Chester in May: off 5 months, shaped quite well in sales race at Doncaster penultimate start: disappointing final one: will probably prove best at 5f: acts on firm ground, probably on soft: races prominently. *J. R. Best*

DOUBLE BAILEYS   6 b.g. Robellino (USA) 127 – Thimblerigger 62 (Sharpen Up   –
127) [2002 –: f16s⁶ Jan 4] no longer of much account. *C. P. Morlock*

DOUBLE BLADE   7 b.g. Kris 135 – Sesame 117 (Derrylin 115) [2002 72d: p12g³   **67**
p12g⁵ 12.3g² 12m 11m 16f³ 12.1m⁴ 16m⁴ 12.1m⁵ 14.1m Sep 5] big, angular gelding: fair handicapper: effective at 9f to 2m: acts on firm going, good to soft and polytrack: blinkered (ran poorly) once at 3 yrs: best with waiting tactics: has started slowly/pulled hard/found little: carries head high. *Mrs M. Reveley*

DOUBLE BREW   4 ch.g. Primo Dominie 121 – Boozy 111 (Absalom 128) [2002 80:   **58**
6g 6f* 6f 5.7d⁴ᵈ 5.9d 6m³ 5d 6f⁴ 5.1f² 6g 6g⁶ 6m 6m⁶ 7m 8m 5g p7g f6g⁴ f7g p7g³ p7g   **a64**
f6g² f5g* Dec 31] good-topped gelding: modest performer: won maiden at Thirsk in May and, having been claimed from J. M. Bradley £3,000 ninth start, handicap at Wolverhampton in December: effective at 5f/easy 7f: acts on all-weather, firm and good to soft going: tried blinkered: has won in cheekpieces: carries head high and sometimes finishes weakly. *J. L. Spearing*

DOUBLE CLICK (IRE)   4 ch.g. Ashkalani (IRE) 128 – Santella Bell (Ballad Rock   –
122) [2002 89: f8.5g f7g Nov 20] IR 26,000Y: half-brother to several winners, including useful Irish 1999 2-y-o 7f winner Tender Offer (by Alzao), later 7f/1m winner in USA, and good Hong Kong winner up to 1m Man of Honour (by Marju): dam Irish 1¼m winner: fairly useful winner for D. Hanley in Ireland at 3 yrs: ran badly in 2 sellers in 2002, looking reluctant in blinkers on second start: stays 9f: acts on soft and good to firm ground. *B. J. Curley*

DOUBLE DEMON   2 ch.c. (Apr 10) Double Eclipse (IRE) 122 – Stately Favour 59   –
(Statoblest 120) [2002 7v Nov 8] leggy, workmanlike colt: first foal: dam 5f winner: 33/1, well-beaten eighth of 17 in maiden at Doncaster. *B. R. Millman*

DOUBLE DESTINY   4 b.g. Anshan 119 – Double Gift 68 (Cragador 110) [2002 56:   **58**
8.3g 7m* 7g⁴ 7g 7d² 7g⁴ 8.3m⁵ 7m⁵ 7m 7g 7m Jul 29] modest performer: won maiden at Folkestone in April: stays 1m: acts on good to firm and good to soft ground: tried visored/blinkered: often soon off bridle in rear. *D. K. Ivory*

DOUBLE DIGIT   4 b.f. Timeless Times (USA) 99 – Kagram Queen 64 (Prince   –
Ragusa 96) [2002 –: f5g 6f 5m⁶ f9.4g 15.8m⁶ Aug 6] no form. *I. W. McInnes*

DOUBLE EM   3 b.g. Balnibarbi 95 – Something Speedy (IRE) 53 (Sayf El Arab   –
(USA) 127) [2002 53: 7f 8g 10f⁴ Jun 4] workmanlike gelding: modest maiden at 2 yrs: well held in 2002. *C. W. Fairhurst*

DOUBLE FANTASY   4 b.f. Mind Games 121 – Song's Best (Never So Bold 135)   **74 d**
[2002 71: 6.1d 5.7g² 5.7g 5g 5.7g 6m Oct 7] leggy filly: fair handicapper: below form after second start: effective at 5f/easy 6f: probably acts on any going: tends to start slowly (sometimes markedly so). *B. Smart*

DOUBLE FARE   4 b.f. Mtoto 134 – Double Flutter 92 (Beldale Flutter (USA) 130)   **69**
[2002 69: p8g f9.4g⁴ f12g² p13g* p12g* 12m⁶ 13.1g 12g⁴ f12g⁶ Jun 19] fair on turf,   **a61**
modest on all-weather: won 2 handicaps at Lingfield in March: should stay 1¾m+: acts on all-weather and good to firm going: sold 4,000 gns. *M. R. Channon*

DOUBLE HELIX   3 b.c. Marju (IRE) 127 – Totham 84 (Shernazar 131) [2002 8m 7d²   **72**
7.1s² 10d 8.1d p10g Aug 29] 170,000Y: good-topped colt: sixth foal: half-brother to 3 winners, including useful 1998 2-y-o 6f winner Greensand (by Green Desert) and smart performer in Britain/USA (up to 9.5f) Country Garden (by Selkirk), 7f winner at 2 yrs: dam 11f (in France)/1½m winner: reportedly suffered series of setbacks in 2001: fair maiden: best form at 7f on good to soft/soft going: blinkered last 2 starts: has pulled hard/carried head awkwardly. *B. J. Meehan*

DOUBLE HONOUR (FR)   4 gr.g. Highest Honor (FR) 124 – Silver Cobra (USA)   **116**
(Silver Hawk (USA) 123) [2002 120: 12s* 14.1m³ 16.2d³ 15.5m 22.2m³ 16v* 16m 15g⁶
13.4f⁵ 18m Oct 19] leggy, close-coupled gelding: not a good walker: has round action: smart performer: won minor event at Doncaster (by 4 lengths from Hannibal Lad) in

March and listed race at Hamburg (by 16 lengths from Adlerflieger) in July: ran credit-ably otherwise when third in Sagaro Stakes (behind Give Notice) and Queen Alexandra Stakes (behind Cover Up), both at Ascot on third/fifth outings: stays 2¾m: has form on good to firm going, possibly ideally suited by good or softer: usually races prominently: joined P. Hobbs. *M. Johnston*

DOUBLE M 5 ch.h. First Trump 118 – Girton Degree 41 (Balliol 125) [2002 59: p6g⁵ p6g³ p5g* p5g² p6g* p6g³ p5g 6g 5.7g* p6g⁴ p5g⁵ 5.3m 5.3m 5m 5f p5g Dec 21] modest performer: won handicap/claimer at Lingfield and handicap at Bath in first half of year: best at 5f/easy 6f: acts on good to firm ground and all-weather: usually blinkered/visored. *Mrs L. Richards* **56 a64**

DOUBLE MYSTERY (FR) 2 ch.c. (Mar 18) Starborough 126 – Chene de Coeur (FR) (Comrade In Arms 123) [2002 8d² 10s⁵ Nov 2] smallish, lengthy colt: second foal: half-brother to French 2000 2-y-o 1m winner Coello (by Loup Solitaire): dam, French 5f (at 2 yrs) to 9.5f winner, out of half-sister to very smart middle-distance performer Gunboat Diplomacy: fairly useful form in autumn in maiden at Redcar (1¾ lengths second to Sir Haydn) and listed race at Newmarket (13 lengths fifth to Forest Magic): will be suited by 1½m+: remains capable of better. *M. Johnston* **81 p**

DOUBLE OBSESSION 2 b.c. (Feb 14) Sadler's Wells (USA) 132 – Obsessive (USA) 102 (Seeking The Gold (USA)) [2002 7m³ 7.2g* 7d⁶ Aug 10] 40,000Y: third foal: half-brother to 4-y-o Spy Master and 3-y-o Medallist: dam, 2-y-o 6f winner who stayed 10.4f, out of half-sister to smart performer up to 1½m Beyton: fairly useful form: won maiden in July: only sixth in minor event at Ascot final start: should be suited by 1¼m+: remains capable of better. *M. Johnston* **85 p**

DOUBLE OSCAR (IRE) 9 ch.g. Royal Academy (USA) 130 – Broadway Rosie 101 (Absalom 128) [2002 69, a88: f6s f5g f5g 5g 5g 5d 6g⁵ 6m 5m² 5m 5m Jul 18] good-bodied gelding: modest handicapper nowadays: best at 5f/6f: acts on firm going, soft and fibresand: often blinkered/visored: has had tongue tied: sometimes slowly away: usually held up. *D. Nicholls* **60 a63**

DOUBLE RANSOM 3 b.g. Bahamian Bounty 116 – Secrets of Honour (Belmez (USA) 131) [2002 60: 9.2s⁶ 12.1g 8.3v³ 9.2v* 7.9s* 9s⁵ 8d Nov 1] good-topped gelding: fair performer: won claimer at Hamilton and handicap at Carlisle in July: better than bare result last 2 outings: effective at 1m (given thorough test)/9f: acts on heavy ground, well held on fibresand: blinkered last 5 starts (slowly away final one). *Mrs L. Stubbs* **68**

DOUBLE SPEY 3 b.g. Atraf 116 – Yankee Special 60 (Bold Lad (IRE) 133) [2002 65: f6g⁵ 7s 9.9d 10g 11.9f Oct 10] workmanlike gelding: modest maiden at 2 yrs: little form in 2002: has carried head awkwardly. *P. C. Haslam* **–**

DOUBLE SPLENDOUR (IRE) 12 b.g. Double Schwartz 128 – Princess Pamela 70 (Dragonara Palace (USA) 115) [2002 76: 6m 6.1m⁶ 6m 7m 6m 6m 6m* Aug 23] good-topped gelding: has been hobdayed: fair handicapper: won apprentice race at Newmarket (for second year running) in August: effective at 6f/7f: acts on firm going, soft and fibresand: sometimes slowly away: held up. *P. S. Felgate* **71**

DOUBLEUCEEONE 2 ch.f. (Jan 25) Compton Place 125 – Gunner's Belle 69 (Gunner B 126) [2002 5m⁴ 6m 5d⁶ 7m 8f⁶ Sep 26] 29,000F: half-sister to several winners, including smart 1994 2-y-o sprinter (won Prix Morny) Hoh Magic (by Cadeaux Genereux) and 1m winner Gunner's Daughter (by Pharly): dam 7f to 1¼m winner: modest maiden: disappointing after debut: races freely, and will prove best short of 1m: sold 3,000 gns. *G. C. Bravery* **52 d**

DOVEBRACE 9 b.g. Dowsing (USA) 124 – Naufrage (Main Reef 126) [2002 56: p10g 9g⁴ 7m 8g³ 8d⁴ 8s 9m 10.9g 9.1s⁵ 10g Oct 24] leggy gelding: unimpressive mover: poor handicapper nowadays: effective at 7f to easy 9f: yet to race on heavy going, acts on any other turf: tried blinkered/visored: tends to be slowly away. *A. Bailey* **46**

DOVE TREE (FR) 2 b.f. (Feb 20) Charnwood Forest (IRE) 125 – Quaver (USA) 74 (The Minstrel (CAN) 135) [2002 6m² 7s⁵ Oct 22] sixth foal: half-sister to 3 winners, including fairly useful 2000 2-y-o 1m winner Steel Band (by Kris) and French 8.5f winner Quiver Tree (by Lion Cavern): dam, 7f winner, out of useful performer up to 1m Que Sympatica: 14/1 and green, fairly useful form to win maiden in August, leading over 1f out and holding Eiger by a head: well held on much softer ground next time: bred to stay at least 7f. *H. Candy* **80**

DOWER HOUSE 7 ch.g. Groom Dancer (USA) 128 – Rose Noble (USA) 62 (Vaguely Noble 140) [2002 96: p10g p10g Dec 21] lengthy, rather leggy gelding: one-time useful performer, very lightly raced nowadays. *Andrew Turnell*

DOWHATJEN 3 b.f. Desert Style (IRE) 121 – Cupid Miss (Anita's Prince 126) [2002 **82**
79: 7s 6.1f⁴ 7g* 7m⁶ 6f 7s 6g³ 7g³ 6m 6g⁵ 7m³ 7m⁵ 7d 7.1m* 7f 7s² 7d Nov 5] lengthy
filly: fairly useful performer: won minor event at Brighton in May and claimer at
Warwick in September: best at 7f: yet to race on heavy going, acts on any other: usually
races prominently: tough. *M. R. Channon*

DOWNCLOSE DUCHESS 7 ch.m. King's Signet (USA) 110 – Lucky Love 65
(Mummy's Pet 125) [2002 f12g Mar 25] maiden: well held only run since 1998.
J. W. Unett

DOWNLAND (IRE) 6 b.g. Common Grounds 118 – Boldabsa 96 (Persian Bold 123) **74 §**
[2002 98§: 6s 7d 6d 5.1d 5s 5m 7d³ Oct 30] tall, good sort: useful handicapper in 2001,
just fair in 2002: effective at 6f to 1m: has won on good to firm going, goes very well on
soft/heavy: blinkered last 3 starts at 4 yrs: sometimes early to post/mounted on track:
inconsistent. *R. M. Beckett*

DOWN MEMORY LANE 2 b.c. (Mar 28) Pursuit of Love 124 – Sirene Bleu **84 p**
Marine (USA) (Secreto (USA) 128) [2002 7v² Nov 8] good-bodied colt: has scope:
fifth living foal: half-brother to useful 1¼m to 13.4f winner Flossy (by Efisio) and to 6f
(at 2 yrs) to 1¼m winner Society Girl (by Shavian): dam unraced: 7/1, 5 lengths second
of 17 to Mezuzah in maiden at Doncaster, leading narrowly 2f out: sure to improve.
B. W. Hills

DOWNTHEREFORDANCIN (IRE) 2 b.g. (Apr 11) Groom Dancer (USA) 128 – **58**
Merlin's Fancy 62 (Caerleon (USA) 132) [2002 7.1m 7g 7m⁴ 7g 8.2v³ p8g³ f8g f9.4g³ **a51**
Dec 7] third foal: half-brother to 4-y-o Illusionist: dam, maiden who probably stayed 1m,
half-sister to top-class sprinter Cadeaux Genereux: modest maiden: stays 1m: acts on
fibresand, good to firm and heavy going: blinkered (ran creditably) penultimate outing:
carried head awkwardly third start. *S. Kirk*

DOWNTIME (IRE) 2 ch.g. (May 3) Perugino (USA) 84 – Razana (IRE) 71 (Kahyasi **– p**
130) [2002 6s f6g Nov 18] 28,000Y: third foal: half-brother to 3-y-o Tahitian Storm and
4-y-o Ovambo: dam, winner up to 1½m, including in France, out of half-sister to Irish St
Leger second Rayseka: green, signs of ability in maidens: should stay at least 1m: slowly
away on debut: almost certainly capable of better. *J. R. Fanshawe*

DOWN TO THE WOODS (USA) 4 ch.g. Woodman (USA) 126 – Riviera Wonder **83 §**
(USA) (Batonnier (USA)) [2002 103: f8.5g* a8.7g 8.1d³ 10.4g 10m⁵ 8.1m f8.5g³ 10m
10d f8g Dec 27] tall, angular gelding: good mover: fairly useful nowadays: won
apprentice claimer at Wolverhampton (claimed from M. Johnston £12,000) in March:
stays 1¼m, at least when emphasis is on speed: acts on firm going, soft and fibresand:
blinkered final start at 3 yrs: often tongue tied: takes strong hold: often folds tamely:
unpredictable. *M. J. Polglase*

DO YE KNOW WHA (IRE) 10 b. or br.g. Ajraas (USA) 88 – Norton Princess 76 **–**
(Wolver Hollow 126) [2002 22.2m Jun 22] ex-Irish gelding: winning chaser/fairly useful
handicap hurdler (doesn't always impress with attitude): tailed off in Queen Alexandra
Stakes at Royal Ascot on Flat debut: sold £1,800 in November. *R. Curtis*

DRAGON FLYER (IRE) 3 b.f. Tagula (IRE) 116 – Noble Rocket (Reprimand 122) **103**
[2002 85p: 5m⁴ 5.1f* 5d² 5.2d² 5.1f² 5g 5.1m* Aug 19] small, sturdy filly: useful
performer: won handicap at Chester (bandaged near-fore) in May and minor event at
Nottingham (by ½ length from Funfair Wane) in August: best form when runner-up in
handicap at Windsor (behind Jonny Ebeneezer) and listed race at Chester (behind
Bishops Court) on third/fifth starts, beaten ½ length both times: raced only at 5f: yet to
race on heavy going, acts on any other: often races prominently: game.

DRAGON PRINCE 2 b.g. (Apr 21) Zamindar (USA) 116 – Nawafell 71 (Kris 135) **75 p**
[2002 6g 7d⁶ p6g Nov 19] 40,000F, 22,000Y: smallish, stocky gelding: third foal:
half-brother to 2 winners up to 1½m in Scandinavia by Hernando: dam, 2-y-o 7f winner
(later won in Hungary), half-sister to 4-y-o Storming Home: fair form in maidens, best
effort when sixth of 22 to Blazing Thunder at Newmarket: headstrong, and likely to prove
at least as effective at 5f as 6f/7f: gelded after final start: remains capable of better.
M. A. Jarvis

DRAMA KING 10 b.g. Tragic Role (USA) – Consistent Queen 55 (Queen's Hussar **–**
124) [2002 51: f16.2g Feb 22] sturdy gelding: modest handicapper, lightly raced: well
held only 10-y-o start: often blinkered. *B. J. Llewellyn*

DRAMA OF LIFE (USA) 3 ch.f. Royal Academy (USA) 130 – Hot Princess 101 **61 ?**
(Hot Spark 126) [2002 –p: 7m² Apr 23] seemingly modest form in 2 maidens, soon clear

but tying up markedly final 1f when second at Folkestone in April: sent to Australia. *J. H. M. Gosden*

DRAMA PREMIERE   4 br.f. Emarati (USA) 74 – Dramatic Mood (Jalmood (USA)   –
126) [2002 75: 8.3g p10g May 29] good-topped filly: fair handicapper at 3 yrs: below form both 4-y-o starts: stays 1m: acts on good to soft going: sold 10,000 gns in July. *I. A. Balding*

DRAMATIC MISS   7 b.m. Deploy 131 – Stos (IRE) (Bluebird (USA) 125) [2002   –
9.9m 8.3m f6g f9.4g Jul 20] big, lengthy, deep-girthed mare: second foal: dam unraced: no form. *R. J. Price*

DRAMATIC QUEST   5 b.g. Zafonic (USA) 130 – Ultra Finesse (USA) 107 (Rahy   –
(USA) 115) [2002 108: 11.6m⁴ 13.4f 10.1d 12g 12s p12g Nov 19] rangy gelding: good mover: useful in 2001: well held in 2002: has worn cheekpieces. *Ian Williams*

DRAMRAIRE MIST   3 gr.f. Darshaan 133 – Marie Dora (FR) 86 (Kendor (FR) 122)   **73**
[2002 8.2m⁶ 7m³ 8d⁶ 8.3m 7f⁴ 10.2f³ p12g f9.4g³ Dec 16] 120,000Y: first foal: dam, 1m   **a49**
winner, sister to smart French filly around 1¼m Marie de Ken: fair maiden on turf, modest on all-weather: stays 1¼m: acts on firm ground and fibresand. *B. J. Meehan*

DR COMFORT (USA)   3 ch.g. Spinning World (USA) 130 – Hot Thong (BRZ) (Jar-   **54**
raar (USA) 78) [2002 59: 7m p7g Oct 16] modest form in maidens/claimer. *W. J. Musson*

DR COOL   5 b.g. Ezzoud (IRE) 126 – Vayavaig 78 (Damister (USA) 123) [2002 75:   **82**
11.8s³ 12g² 12m² 12g³ 14m* 14d² 14.4d³ 14g² 16.4g⁴ 16.2g⁵ 13.9f* 14.6s Oct 25] quite good-topped gelding: fairly useful handicapper: better than ever at 5 yrs, winning at Sandown in June and York in October: effective at 1½m to 2m: acts on fibresand and any turf going: tried visored/blinkered early in career: no easy ride (held up and sometimes hangs) but is consistent. *J. Akehurst*

DREAM A DREAM   3 b.f. Emperor Jones (USA) 119 – Thornbury (IRE) (Tender   **52**
King 123) [2002 –: 9d⁶ 9.3s⁵ 11.6m⁶ 8.5d³ 8f⁴ 7g f8.5g 8.1m 10g Oct 14] leggy filly: modest maiden: left Mrs D. Haine before final start: stays 9f: acts on firm and soft ground: visored/blinkered after third outing: races prominently. *G. C. H. Chung*

DREAM FALCON   2 br.g. (Mar 9) Polar Falcon (USA) 126 – Pip's Dream 52 (Glint   –
of Gold 128) [2002 5.7m 7d 6m Aug 14] second foal: half-brother to 4-y-o Dream Magic: dam 1¼m/1½m winner: well held in maidens. *R. J. Hodges*

DREAMIE BATTLE   4 br.f. Makbul 104 – Highland Rossie 67 (Pablond 93) [2002   –
52: f7s f8g⁶ 10m f12f⁵ Nov 29] leggy, quite good-topped filly: maiden: little form in 2002. *R. Hollinshead*

DREAMING DIVA   3 ch.f. Whittingham (IRE) 104 – Any Dream (IRE) 81 (Shernazar   –
131) [2002 71: 7s 8.1f 8.3g 8.1g⁶ Aug 7] strong, lengthy filly: fair winner at 2 yrs: little form in 2002. *J. C. Fox*

DREAM KING (IRE)   2 b.c. (Apr 20) Petardia 113 – Barinia (Corvaro (USA) 124)   –
[2002 7d f8g Nov 26] 8,000 2-y-o: half-brother to several winners, including 7-y-o King Priam and fairly useful Irish 1½m winner Oumaladia (by Waajib): dam French maiden: tailed off in maiden (blinkered)/claimer. *M. J. Polglase*

DREAM MAGIC   4 b.g. Magic Ring (IRE) 115 – Pip's Dream 52 (Glint of Gold 128)   **89**
[2002 80: 8s 10g 8d⁴ 8d² 8.1d³ 8.1s² 8g⁴ 9m⁴ 10d² 10m 10m* 10.3m³ 10.1s² 12v Nov 9] big, good-topped gelding: fairly useful handicapper: won at Sandown in August: stays 1¼m: acts on firm and soft ground: tough and consistent. *M. J. Ryan*

DREAMS FORGOTTEN (IRE)   2 b.f. (Apr 13) Victory Note (USA) 120 – Sevens   **58**
Are Wild 40 (Petorius 117) [2002 5g f5s⁴ 6d 5.3g 7d 7m 8f 8f Sep 26] IR 2,500Y: eighth foal: half-sister to 3 winners, including 8-y-o Falls O'Moness: dam lightly raced and second at 1m: modest maiden: free-going sort, likely to prove best short of 1m: acts on good to firm ground and fibresand. *S. Kirk*

DREAMS OF ZENA   3 b.f. Dreams End 93 – Billan Tara (Nicholas Bill 125) [2002   –
8g 7m 8.1m⁵ 6m 5.3m 10m 7m Sep 23] first foal: dam of little account: no form: tends to hang left. *R. Brotherton*

DRESS TO THRILL (IRE)   3 b.f. Danehill (USA) 126 – Trusted Partner (USA)   **123**
114 (Affirmed (USA)) [2002 104p: 8d* 8g* 8m* 8f* 8d 9f* Dec 1]
Dress To Thrill's success in the Matriarch Stakes at Hollywood Park in December capped a fine year for her, and for her trainer Dermot Weld, whose career and previous foreign victories are detailed extensively in the essay on Melbourne

Cup winner Media Puzzle. A listed winner, and runner-up on her final outing to Quarter Moon in the Moyglare Stud Stakes, from three starts at the Curragh as a two-year-old, Dress To Thrill had already won four of her five races at three before her success in the Matriarch. Talked of as a One Thousand Guineas possible, she was reportedly slow to come to hand and did not reappear until July, when she won a listed race over a mile at Leopardstown. Back over the same course and distance for her next two starts, Dress To Thrill showed improved form in the Desmond Stakes in August, beating Duck Row by a length and a half, and progressed again in the Matron Stakes in September, when she beat Marionnaud convincingly by a length. At Newmarket a month later, she started favourite for the Peugeot Sun Chariot Stakes and never really looked in danger of surrendering her unbeaten record for the year. Travelling strongly up with the steady pace, and the last to come off the bridle, Dress To Thrill knuckled down really well when eventually shaken up to win by three quarters of a length from Dolores. Dress To Thrill met her only defeat later in October when eighth to Domedriver in the Breeders' Cup Mile at Arlington, always around mid-division. Five weeks later, it was back to winning ways stepped up to nine furlongs in the Matriarch, the travelling in the interim clearly having no adverse effect on Dress To Thrill. She put up the best performance on turf all year by a three-year-old filly in North America, responding really well to strong pressure to lead near the finish and beat triple Grade 1-winning filly Golden Apples by a head. The rank outsider Magic Mission was a further length and a half back in third, with ex-French Banks Hill a nose away in fourth. It was reported afterwards that Dress To Thrill is to continue her career in the States with Christophe Clement, and she should continue to do well; she will have more opportunities to add to her Grade 1 success in America than she would have had in Europe.

    An angular filly, Dress To Thrill is from a family her trainer knows well. She is the eighth foal out of the 1988 Irish One Thousand Guineas winner Trusted Partner. Winner of both her two-year-old starts, Trusted Partner ran only three times after her classic success, two of those outings coming at around a mile and a quarter; she gave the impression that she would have stayed a mile and a half given the opportunity. Trusted Partner is a half-sister to the useful performer at up to a mile and a half Easy To Copy, herself the dam of the smart performer at up to a mile and a quarter Two-Twenty-Two. Dress To Thrill's grandam Talking Picture was the leading American juvenile filly in 1973. Trusted Partner produced some useful performers in Ireland before Dress To Thrill, including Blend of Pace, a winner at a mile and a half, and Archive Footage, a winner at that trip and over a mile and three quarters before making into a smart hurdler. Both are by Sadler's Wells and, like all the aforementioned runners—with the exception of Talking Picture—were also trained by Weld. Dress To Thrill's year-younger close-relation the colt Foolish Thought (by Green Desert) showed fairly useful form in four starts for Weld in 2002 without winning, but has since been bought cheaply out of his stable by

Moyglare Stud Farms Ltd's "Dress To Thrill"

		Danzig	Northern Dancer
Dress To Thrill (IRE) (b.f. 1999)	Danehill (USA) (b 1986)	(b 1977)	Pas de Nom
		Razyana	His Majesty
		(b 1981)	Spring Adieu
	Trusted Partner (USA) (ch 1985)	Affirmed	Exclusive Native
		(ch 1975)	Won't Tell You
		Talking Picture	Speak John
		(br 1971)	Poster Girl

Richard Fahey. Trusted Partner foaled a sister and a brother to Dress To Thrill in 2001 and 2002 respectively. Both on her breeding and on the way she finished her race at Hollywood Park, Dress To Thrill should stay further than nine furlongs, though she is not exactly crying out for another step up in trip. The game and genuine Dress To Thrill has won on good to soft going, but her very best form has been shown under firmish conditions. *D. K. Weld, Ireland*

DRINKIN TIME   3 ch.f. Timeless Times (USA) 99 – Mashin Time 73 (Palm Track **63**
122) [2002 68: 6.1d⁶ 6s⁵ 6g⁶ 5.9g³ 5.9g 8m⁶ 6.9g³ 8g⁵ Aug 27] smallish filly:
unimpressive mover: modest maiden: stays 7f: acts on soft and good to firm going:
sometimes looks difficult ride. *T. D. Easterby*

DR JULIAN (IRE)   2 b.g. (Feb 16) Sesaro (USA) 81 – Toda 53 (Absalom 128) [2002 **58**
5.3g f6g² f7g⁶ f7g p8g⁴ f8.5s³ f7g³ Dec 17] IR 5,500Y, 20,000 2-y-o: half-brother to
6-y-o Adelphi Boy: dam, 1¼m seller winner, also won over hurdles: modest maiden:
stays 8.5f: acts on fibresand: blinkered (edged left) last 2 starts, finding little final one.
J. A. Osborne

DR SHARP (IRE)   2 ch.g. (Mar 28) Dr Devious (IRE) 127 – Stoned Imaculate (IRE) **64**
73 (Durgam (USA)) [2002 7g 7.5d² 8.3m⁶ 8s⁵ 8d Oct 21] good-topped gelding: first foal:
dam winning stayer on Flat/over hurdles: modest maiden: creditable fifth in nursery at

Ayr penultimate start: likely to be suited by 1½m+: acts on soft ground: gelded after final outing. *T. P. Tate*

DR STRANGELOVE (IRE)   4 ch.g. Dr Devious (IRE) 127 – Renzola (Dragonara   – Palace (USA) 115) [2002 68§: f12g 7d 12.1m Sep 24] close-coupled, quite attractive gelding: disappointing maiden: left A. Crook before final start: tried visored/blinkered. *M. D. Hammond*

DRURIDGE BAY (IRE)   6 b.g. Turtle Island (IRE) 123 – Lady of Shalott 61 (Kings   – § Lake (USA) 133) [2002 – §: f8.5g Jan 11] useful-looking gelding: temperamental maiden: tried blinkered/visored. *D. G. Bridgwater*

DRURY LANE (IRE)   2 b. or br.c. (Apr 29) Royal Applause 124 – Ghost Tree (IRE)   **84** 88 (Caerleon (USA) 132) [2002 6g 6m³ 6f* Oct 11] IR 62,000Y: rather unfurnished colt: fifth foal: half-brother to 3 winners, including 2000 2-y-o 6f winner Got To Go (by Shareef Dancer) and 1999 2-y-o 7f winner One Step At A Time (by Sabrehill), both useful: dam, 7f winner, sister to very smart Japanese miler Zenno El Cid out of Cheveley Park winner Embla: fairly useful form in maidens, getting on top final 1f when landing odds in 6-runner race at York by 1¾ lengths from Aegean Magic: will probably stay 7f: raced only on good going or firmer. *B. W. Hills*

DRYDEN HOUSE (IRE)   3 b.f. Cadeaux Genereux 131 – For Example (USA) 66   **94** (Northern Baby (CAN) 127) [2002 70p: 8.1d² 8s² 7.1d⁵ 8m* 8.3d* 8m⁴ 7.2g 8v³ Nov 2] lengthy filly: fairly useful performer: won maiden at Pontefract in July and handicap at Windsor (much improved to beat French Mannequin 5 lengths) in August: left M. Jarvis after disappointing seventh start, respectable third to Almond Mousse in listed race at Saint-Cloud final outing: likely to prove best at 7f/1m: has form on good to firm going but may prove best on softer than good: reportedly gurgled third start: sold 72,000 gns. *R. Gibson, France*

DUBAIAN GIFT   3 b.g. Bahamian Bounty 116 – Hot Lavender (CAN) 67 (Shadeed   **86** (USA) 135) [2002 66: p6g f5g* p5g* 5m³ 5d² 5g* 5g⁵ 5m* Sep 7] smallish gelding: fairly useful handicapper: progressed well in 2002, winning at Southwell, Lingfield, Goodwood and Haydock (edged right): seems best at sharp 5f: yet to race on soft/heavy going, acts on any other turf and all-weather: usually races prominently. *I. A. Balding*

DUBAI CREATIVE (IRE)   2 b.g. (Feb 14) Perugino (USA) 84 – Royal Lorna   – (USA) 110 (Val de L'Orne (FR) 133) [2002 6s 8g Oct 2] 26,000F, 60,000Y: half-brother to smart French 1¼m to 13f winner Lycitus (by Lycius) and a winner in New Zealand by Nashwan: dam, 1m/1¼m winner, half-sister to Yorkshire Oaks winner Awaasif from top-class family: well held in maidens at Windsor (for E. Dunlop) and Salisbury nearly 4 months apart. *R. Hannon*

DUBAI DESTINATION (USA)   3 b.c. Kingmambo (USA) 125 – Mysterial (USA)   **119** (Alleged (USA) 138) [2002 119p: 11g² May 21] rangy, quite attractive colt: smart form: won Champagne Stakes impressively by length from Rock of Gibraltar at Doncaster in 2001: reportedly lame behind that autumn and said to have suffered a bruised foot in mid-March: good effort when 2 lengths second to Coshocton (who rec 6 lb) in listed race at Goodwood only 3-y-o start, travelling strongly: may prove best at 1m/1¼m: yet to race on soft/heavy going, seems to act on any other: has worn crossed noseband: reportedly injured near-fore and returned to UAE. *Saeed bin Suroor*

DUBAI DREAMS   2 b.g. (Apr 28) Marju (IRE) 127 – Arndilly 75 (Robellino (USA)   **71 §** 127) [2002 5f⁵ 5.1g 5d² 5.1d⁴ f5g² f5g³ 5g⁴ 7m² 7g⁴ 8m⁶ f8s³ 8m² 10.2f⁴ 8.3d⁵ 7g² f8.5g² p8g* p8g Dec 11] 4,200F, 14,000Y: close-coupled gelding: unimpressive mover: third foal: half-brother to a winner in Japan by Fairy King: dam 6f (including at 2 yrs) to 1m winner: fair performer: runner-up 6 times before winning seller at Lingfield (for B. Meehan) in November: stays easy 1¼m: acts on good to soft going, firm and all-weather: usually blinkered/visored: often forces pace/finishes weakly: not one to trust. *T. J. Etherington*

DUBAI LIGHTNING (USA)   2 br.c. (Feb 13) Seeking The Gold (USA) – Heraklia   **90 p** (USA) (Irish River (FR) 131) [2002 7m² 7p7g* Oct 9] $2,000,000Y: rangy, useful-looking colt: third foal: half-brother to French 1½m winner Cephalonie (by Kris S): dam unraced out of smart French miler Hydro Calido, herself half-sister to Machiavellian and Exit To Nowhere from very good family: still green, confirmed debut promise when landing odds in 16-runner maiden at Lingfield by 1¾ lengths from Zeuss, getting across from widest stall to make running: will stay 1m: useful prospect. *D. R. Loder*

DUBAI NURSE   8 ch.m. Handsome Sailor 125 – Lady Eccentric (IRE) (Magical   – Wonder (USA) 125) [2002 42: 5g 5s⁵ 5s 6m Aug 28] maiden handicapper: no form in 2002: tried blinkered/visored. *A. R. Dicken*

*Champagne Victor Vintage Stakes, Goodwood—a 1,2 for Sheikh Mohammed
as Dublin (trained by David Loder) quickens ahead of Bourbonnais (Mark Johnston);
Sarayat (rail) is third with Norse Dancer fourth*

DUBAI PRINCE (IRE) 3 b.g. Anita's Prince 126 – Balqis (USA) 93 (Advocator) – §
[2002 70: 7s 6f 10f 11m Jul 27] fair maiden at 2 yrs: well both completed outings in
2002: veered left and unseated leaving stall penultimate start, refused to race final one:
one to avoid. *D. Nicholls*

DUBAI SEVEN STARS 4 ch.f. Suave Dancer (USA) 136 – Her Honour 94 (Teenoso 89
(USA) 135) [2002 75: 11.7g 13.1g² 16m⁴ 16.2m 13.1f³ 18m³ Oct 19] leggy, workmanlike
filly: fairly useful maiden handicapper: 7 lb out of handicap and 66/1, best effort when
3½ lengths third to stable-companion Miss Fara in Cesarewitch at Newmarket final start:
stays 2¼m: acts on firm and soft going. *M. C. Pipe*

DUBAI STORM (USA) 2 b. or br.c. (Mar 4) Storm Creek (USA) – Timeless Water –
(USA) (Timeless Moment (USA)) [2002 5m⁶ Jun 3] $100,000Y: half-brother to several
minor winners in USA: dam, US 6f winner, half-sister to US 2-y-o Grade 1 7f winner
Miss Iron Smoke: 11/4, well held in maiden at Leicester. *D. R. Loder*

DUBLIN (IRE) 2 b.c. (May 1) Carson City (USA) – Lustre (USA) 90 (Halo (USA)) 107
[2002 f7g* 7f* 7g* 7m³ 7m Oct 19] quite attractive colt: half-brother to smart 1¼m/1½m
performer Valley of Gold (by Shirley Heights) and fairly useful but ungenuine Irish 1¾m
winner Crystal Hills (by Darshaan): dam, 2-y-o 6f winner who stayed 9f, half-sister to
smart French performer up to 13.5f Whitehaven: useful performer: won maiden at
Wolverhampton, minor event at Newbury (visored, beat Mark of Zorro impressively by
1¼ lengths) and Champagne Victor Vintage Stakes at Goodwood (quickened to lead final
1f, beating Bourbonnais 1¼ lengths), all in July: creditable length third to Refuse To Bend
in National Stakes at the Curragh: ran as though something amiss in Dewhurst Stakes at
Newmarket final start: should stay at least 1m: raced only on good going or firmer on turf:
has worn crossed noseband. *D. R. Loder*

DUBONAI (IRE) 2 ch.c. (May 19) Peintre Celebre (USA) 137 – Web of Intrigue 66 69
(Machiavellian (USA) 123) [2002 7v p10g⁴ p8g Dec 14] unfurnished colt: third foal:
dam, lightly-raced maiden who stayed 7f, half-sister to Yorkshire Oaks winner
Catchascatchcan: best effort in maidens (fair form) when 11 lengths fourth to Shield at
Lingfield: slipped up on debut: should stay 1½m. *Andrew Turnell*

DUBROVSKY 2 ch.c. (Mar 12) Hector Protector (USA) 124 – Reuval 102 (Sharpen 90 p
Up 127) [2002 6m 7.1m* Aug 26] half-brother to several winners, including smart 6f/7f
(latter including at 2 yrs) winner Ardkinglass (by Green Desert) and useful 1¼m winner
Jura (by Rousillon): dam best at 1m: favourite, much better effort in maidens when
winning at Warwick by 2½ lengths from Four Jays, always going well and merely pushed
clear: will stay 1m: useful colt in the making, likely to win more races. *J. R. Fanshawe*

DUCK ROW (USA) 7 ch.g. Diesis 133 – Sunny Moment (USA) (Roberto (USA) 116
131) [2002 114: 9m 7.9f² 8.5d 8d* 8m⁵ 8g² 8m* Sep 12] sturdy, close-coupled gelding:
smart performer: won listed race at the Curragh (by 2½ lengths from Phariseek) in June
and GNER Park Stakes at Doncaster (by neck from Desert Deer) in September: ran
creditably most other starts, including when 1½ lengths second to Dress To Thrill in
Desmond Stakes at Leopardstown (hung left) on penultimate one: effective at 1m/9f: acts
on firm and good to soft going, below form on soft: waited with. *J. A. R. Toller*

DUC'S DREAM 4 b.g. Bay Tern (USA) 86 – Kala's Image 55 (Kala Shikari 125) –
[2002 73: f11g* f12g² f12g f11g* 12.3f 10m 10s 8m 10m f9.4g f11g³ f11g* p10g Dec 14] a73
leggy gelding: fair performer on all-weather, modest on turf: won handicaps at Southwell

294

in February and March and claimer (odds on) there in December: barely stays 1½m: acts on fibresand (below form on polytrack), heavy and good to firm going: blinkered (well held) ninth start. *D. Morris*

DUDLEYS DELIGHT 3 b.f. Makbul 104 – Steadfast Elite (IRE) 58 (Glenstal (USA) 118) [2002 82: a8g⁶ a8g² a6g⁵ 7m³ 6m⁴ f7s 7m* 7m* 7s* p7g Dec 18] leggy, close-coupled filly: fair performer: ran for J. Brown in Spain first 3 starts: won sellers at Yarmouth and Leicester (sold from R. Guest 7,000 gns) in September and claimer at Leicester in October: seems to stay 1m: acts on soft and good to firm ground, no form in Britain on all-weather: bolted to post and withdrawn third intended 2-y-o outing: has been early to post: reportedly broke blood vessel penultimate 2-y-o start. *M. C. Pipe* **65 a?**

DUDS (IRE) 3 ch.g. Definite Article 121 – Domino's Nurse 104 (Dom Racine (FR) 121) [2002 67d: 14g 7.9g 9.3d Jul 19] disappointing maiden: tried blinkered. *F. P. Murtagh* **–**

DUELLING BANJOS 3 ch.g. Most Welcome 131 – Khadino (Relkino 131) [2002 f7s f8g³ f8g³ f12g⁵ 8g 7.9g 8.3v* 8.3s³ f8g 7.9g 8s* Aug 30] 6,800 2-y-o: eighth foal: brother to Norwegian winner up to 1½m Kadimo and half-brother to 3 winners by Komaite, including fairly useful 7.6f to 1¼m winner Mr Teigh: dam no form: fairly useful handicapper on turf, modest form on all-weather: won at Hamilton (maiden event) in June and Ayr in August: should stay 1¼m: acts well on heavy going and fibresand: raced freely/carried head awkwardly third start: sold 25,000 gns. *T. D. Barron* **80 a59**

DUELLO 11 b.g. Sure Blade (USA) 130 – Royal Loft 105 (Homing 130) [2002 76: 10.2g* Apr 30] leggy gelding: has a round action: fair performer in 2001: won seller at Bath only 11-y-o start: effective at 1¼m (given good pace) to 1¾m (when conditions aren't testing): acts on any turf going and fibresand: blinkered once at 3 yrs, visored nowadays: usually held up: has hung/looked less than genuine. *M. C. Pipe* **62 +**

DUE RESPECT (IRE) 2 b.c. (May 11) Danehill (USA) 126 – Stylish (Anshan 119) [2002 7m⁵ 7.1g 7f* Sep 25] IR 125,000F, IR 520,000Y: lengthy, quite attractive colt: has scope: first foal: dam unraced half-sister to very smart sprinter Eveningperformance out of half-sister to Tirol: fairly useful form: early to post, won maiden at Chester by ½ length from Prince Holing, soon allowed to lead and rallying: headstrong (went off too quickly second start), and should prove at least as effective at 6f as 7f: raced only on good ground or firmer. *R. Hannon* **91**

GNER Park Stakes, Doncaster—Duck Row gains his first pattern success at the age of seven; Desert Deer (rail) is worn down in the final fifty yards with the previous year's winner Tough Speed only third this time

DUESCALS (USA) 2 b.f. (Mar 22) Danzig (USA) – Vue (USA) (Mr Prospector – p (USA)) [2002 8.2m Oct 1] big, lengthy filly: sixth foal: half-sister to 3 winners, including smart US 1996 2-y-o Grade 1 7f winner Oath (by Known Fact) and fairly useful Irish 2001 2-y-o 1m winner Venus de Milo (by A P Indy): dam, sprint winner in USA and third in 9f minor stakes, half-sister to Grade 3 9f winner Country Light: 13/8 but very green, slowly away and always behind in maiden at Nottingham: likely to do better. *J. H. M. Gosden*

DUE TO ME 2 gr.f. (Apr 11) Compton Place 125 – Always Lucky 71 (Absalom 128) 58 [2002 6d 6d⁴ 5m⁶ 6.1g 6m Sep 23] 2,800F, 7,000Y: second foal: half-sister to 3-y-o Silver Mascot: dam, 2-y-o 5f/6f winner, out of sister to very smart sprinter Paris House: modest maiden: stays 6f: acts on firm and good to soft going: carried head high penultimate start. *G. B. Balding*

DUFRESNE 2 b.g. (Mar 17) Mind Games 121 – Zihuatanejo (Efisio 120) [2002 7m – 7m 6d Aug 26] second foal: dam unraced out of smart winner up to 1m Rare Roberta: well held in maidens/seller. *A. Dickman*

DUGDALE 2 b.c. (Feb 6) Vettori (IRE) 119 – Coigach 110 (Niniski (USA) 125) [2002 71 f7g⁶ f8.5f⁵ f8.5s⁴ Dec 9] 52,000Y: fourth foal: half-brother to useful 1½m winner Motto (by Mtoto) and to fairly useful 1999 2-y-o 7f winner Aston Mara (by Bering): dam 1m (at 2 yrs) to 14.6f (Park Hill) winner from good staying family: fair form in maidens: will be suited by 1¼m+: raced only on fibresand. *Sir Mark Prescott*

DUKE OF EARL (IRE) 3 ch.c. Ali-Royal (IRE) 127 – Faye 79 (Monsanto (FR) 91 121) [2002 85: 10.3s 8.3m 9m⁴ 11g⁴ 12d⁴ 9.9d² 12m 10g 11.7g³ 12g 10m⁶ 11.9m² 14m³ 14f² 13.9f Oct 12] useful-looking colt: fairly useful handicapper: won at Goodwood in May: probably needs good test at 1¼m, and stays 1¾m: acts on any going: tough: won over hurdles in November. *S. Kirk*

DUKE OF MODENA 5 ch.g. Salse (USA) 128 – Palace Street (USA) 103 (Secreto 103 (USA) 128) [2002 109: 8s 8.3g* 8.1d* 8m 7m 8d 7m 8f⁶ 8g Oct 18] sturdy gelding: useful performer: won minor event at Windsor (beat Thihn by neck) and handicap at Sandown (beat Island Light a head) in April: below form after: effective at 7f/1m: acts on heavy and good to firm going: has been bandaged: usually held up. *G. B. Balding*

DULZIE 5 b.m. Safawan 118 – Dulzura (Daring March 116) [2002 40, a49: f12g³ f11g 34 f12g⁵ f12g Feb 28] small mare: poor performer: stays 1½m: acts on fibresand and firm going. *A. P. Jarvis*

DUMARAN (IRE) 4 b.g. Be My Chief (USA) 122 – Pine Needle 89 (Kris 135) [2002 106 91: 7f³ 7d 7d* 8.5s* 8.1d 8m 8d² 9m 8g 9s* Oct 26] rather leggy gelding: made into useful handicapper in 2002: successful at Goodwood in May, Epsom (beat Thihn by 2 lengths, idled) in June and Newbury (well ridden up with pace, beat Unshakable by short head) in October: effective at 7f to 9f: best efforts on good to soft/soft going: has pulled hard. *I. A. Balding*

DUNASKIN (IRE) 2 b.g. (Mar 21) Bahhare (USA) 122 – Mirwara (IRE) (Darshaan 68 133) [2002 5m⁵ 5s⁶ 5d⁶ 6f 6d² 7m² 8m³ 7.9f⁶ Oct 10] IR 28,000Y: leggy gelding: has traces of stringhalt: second foal: dam unraced half-sister to useful winners around 1¼m Mirjan and Miliana: fair maiden: left K. Ryan after fifth start: good second in nursery at Doncaster next time: stays 1m: acts on good to firm and good to soft ground. *D. Eddy*

DUNCAN DOCK (USA) 3 ch.g. Rakeen (USA) 99 – Smailer (USA) (Smarten 97 p (USA)) [2002 f8g² f8g* Dec 17] $77,000Y: fourth foal: half-brother to 3 winners in USA, including 2-y-o minor stakes winner by Valley Crossing: dam unraced half-sister to smart Greenham Stakes winner Faustus: won maiden (slowly away) in November and minor event in December, both at Southwell: useful form, well ridden in steadily-run race, when beating Hidden Surprise impressively by 3½ lengths in latter: likely to stay 1¼m: should progress further and win more races. *W. J. Haggas*

DUN DISTINCTLY (IRE) 5 b.g. Distinctly North (USA) 115 – Dunbally 57 47 (Dunphy 124) [2002 56: f16s⁴ f12g⁴ f14.8g² f14g f16g Mar 26] poor performer: stays 14.8f: acts on fibresand, well beaten on turf: visored once. *P. C. Haslam*

DUNDONALD 3 ch.g. Magic Ring (IRE) 115 – Cal Norma's Lady (IRE) 87 67 § (Lyphard's Special (USA) 122) [2002 –p: 7.1m³ 7fg⁴ 8.1s 7.2g 6.9g² 8.1d 7m f7f* f7g⁵ a71 § f7g f8.5s⁴ Dec 26] big, leggy gelding: fair performer: first start since leaving K. Ryan, won maiden at Wolverhampton in November: stays 8.5f: acts on good to firm ground and fibresand: tried in visor/cheekpieces: has carried head awkwardly/edged left. *I. Semple*

DUNE 3 b.c. Desert King (IRE) 129 – Flamands (IRE) 92 (Sadler's Wells (USA) 132) 104 [2002 66: 9g² 10g² 12f* 11m³ 12d² 12g⁴ 13.9m⁴ 14m* 12g³ Sep 29] strong, good sort, type to carry condition: useful performer: progressed well at 3 yrs, winning minor event at Thirsk in April and valuable handicap at Haydock (beat Royal Cavalier ½ length) in September: good efforts in handicaps otherwise, third to Scott's View in Tote Exacta Stakes at Ascot final start: stays 1¾m: acts on firm and good to soft going: patiently ridden: tough and consistent: sold 180,000 gns, sent to Saudi Arabia. *R. Charlton*

DUNEDIN RASCAL   5 b.g. Piccolo 121 – Thorner Lane 86 (Tina's Pet 121) [2002 85d: p5g⁵ f5g⁴ p6g² p6g⁴ 5.3f⁵ 6g 5d 5f f6s 6m f5g² f5f p6g² p7g² f7g² Dec 31] smallish gelding: fair handicapper, better on all-weather than turf: stays easy 7f: acts on any turf going/all-weather: blinkered nowadays: held up: none too reliable. *E. A. Wheeler*   **66 a77**

DUNE SAFARI (IRE)   3 br.f. Key of Luck (USA) 126 – Zafaaf 105 (Kris 135) [2002 10.1g³ 10.1m³ May 23] tall filly: fourth foal: half-sister to 5f/6f winner Ashover Amber (by Green Desert) and 5f (at 2 yrs) to 9.4f winner Queens Bench (by Wolfhound), both fairly useful at best: dam 7f/1m winner: modest form in maidens at Newcastle, looking on weak side: sold 800 gns in December. *M. Johnston*   **63 ?**

DUNHILL STAR (IRE)   2 b.c. (May 26) Danehill (USA) 126 – Sueboog (IRE) 109 (Darshaan 133) [2002 p6g* Dec 28] fifth foal: closely related to fairly useful 1¼m winner Sena Desert (by Green Desert) and half-brother to 5-y-o Best of The Bests and to fairly useful 7f winner Baratheastar (by Barathea): dam won Fred Darling Stakes and fourth in Oaks: favourite, won 12-runner maiden at Lingfield by ½ length from Janes Valentine, taking while to warm to task: should stay 1m: open to improvement. *B. W. Hills*   **80 p**

DUNKIRK SPIRIT   4 b.g. Whittingham (IRE) 104 – Ruda (FR) (Free Round (USA)) [2002 –: f9.4g* f12g* f12g* 10g 10.1m 10d f12s Nov 30] big, strong gelding: fair handicapper: won 3 times at Wolverhampton early in year: off 5 months before well beaten last 2 starts: stays 1½m: acts on fibresand, little form on turf. *Mrs Lydia Pearce*   **70**

DUNMIDOE   2 b.f. (Feb 14) Case Law 113 – Rion River (IRE) (Taufan (USA) 119) [2002 p6g 6d 7m⁶ 6.1m 8.2m⁶ Oct 1] leggy filly: half-sister to 3 winners, including 4-y-o Monica Geller and 1999 2-y-o 6f winner Peruvian Jade (by Petong): dam Irish 1¼m winner: modest maiden: seemingly best effort when sixth of 7 at Nottingham final start: appears to stay 1m. *C. Drew*   **62 ?**

DUNN ALMU (IRE)   5 br.g. Hamas (IRE) 125§ – Art Age (Artaius (USA) 129) [2002 56?: p10g⁵ Jan 3] poor maiden nowadays: stays 1¼m: acts on polytrack: sometimes blinkered. *Edward Butler, Ireland*   **42**

DUNN DEAL (IRE)   2 b.c. (Mar 8) Revoque (IRE) 122 – Buddy And Soda (IRE) 75 (Imperial Frontier (USA) 112) [2002 5m 5s³ 5f² 5g* 5d³ 5m 5m 6f⁵ 5s² Nov 6] IR 16,500F: sturdy colt: first foal: dam Irish 7f winner: fair performer: won maiden at Ripon in July: short-headed in seller at Musselburgh final start: best at 5f: acts on firm and soft going: has had tongue tied: tends to hang under pressure. *A. Berry*   **74**

DUPONT   3 b.c. Zafonic (USA) 130 – June Moon (IRE) (Sadler's Wells (USA) 132) [2002 96: p8g³ 8m* 8m* 8g⁴ p10g⁴ 8m Dec 15] useful-looking colt: has a short, round action: smart performer: won Premio Parioli at Rome (by nose from Fisich) and Mehl-Mulhens-Rennen at Cologne (by 2 lengths from Next Desert) in May: creditable efforts after, fourth in St James's Palace Stakes at Royal Ascot (beaten 6 lengths by Rock of Gibraltar) and listed race at Lingfield (5 months later, beaten 1½ lengths by Beauchamp Pilot) and seventh to Olympic Express in Hong Kong Mile at Sha Tin: likely   **115**

Mehl-Mulhens-Rennen, Cologne—Dupont completes a continental Guineas double; Next Desert suffers his only defeat, but does best of the home-trained contingent

Wentworth Racing (Pty) Ltd's "Dupont"

to prove best around 1m: acts on good to firm going and polytrack: sometimes wanders under pressure. *W. J. Haggas*

DURAID (IRE) 10 ch.g. Irish River (FR) 131 – Fateful Princess (USA) 95 (Vaguely **70** Noble 140) [2002 89: 8f 8f 8.5g 8m² 8.9d 7.9d 7.9m⁶ 8m³ 8.5g⁶ Jul 30] workmanlike gelding: has a round action: fair handicapper nowadays: stays 9f: acts on soft and good to firm going (probably on firm), well beaten only start on fibresand: visored once in 1998: tends to carry head high: held up. *Denys Smith*

DURANDANA (FR) 3 b.f. Selkirk (USA) 129 – Damanka (IRE) (Slip Anchor 136) **78** [2002 58: 8.3d 7s* 7g⁴ 7.1d³ 8.5d Sep 11] rather leggy, lengthy filly: fair handicapper: won at Kempton in June: probably best at 7f: acts on soft going: sent to France. *J. R. Fanshawe*

DURKAR STAR (IRE) 4 b.g. Bin Ajwaad (IRE) 119 – Faith Alone 85 (Safawan **–** 118) [2002 –: f6g f5g f5g 6m 6m 5g Jul 3] no form. *M. C. Chapman*

DUSKY BLUE (IRE) 3 b.g. Bluebird (USA) 125 – Massada 106 (Most Welcome **–** 131) [2002 55: 8.2d Apr 1] close-coupled gelding: modest maiden at 2 yrs: well held in handicap only outing in 2002: should stay at least 6f. *Jonjo O'Neill*

DUSKY WARBLER 3 br.g. Ezzoud (IRE) 126 – Bronzewing 103 (Beldale Flutter **106** (USA) 130) [2002 98p: 12m² 16.2m 12.5m⁵ 11.8s* 12v² Nov 9] big, leggy gelding: useful performer: won minor event at Leicester (beat Sundrenched 1½ lengths) in October: creditable 2 lengths second to Red Carnation in listed race at Doncaster final start: should stay beyond 1½m: acts on good to firm going, goes well on soft/heavy. *M. L. W. Bell*

DUST COVER 2 b.c. (Feb 7) Desert Story (IRE) 115 – Convenience (IRE) (Ela- **80 p** Mana-Mou 132) [2002 6g* Sep 2] 36,000F: first foal: dam unraced half-sister to smart sprinter Fire Dome: 12/1, won 13-runner maiden at Folkestone by 1¾ lengths from To The Rescue, travelling comfortably and showing good turn of foot under hands and heels: should stay 1m: probably a useful performer in the making. *P. J. Makin*

DUST FLICKER   3 ch.f. Suave Dancer (USA) 136 – Galaxie Dust (USA) 86 (Blushing Groom (FR) 131) [2002 63p: 10m⁴ 9.9m May 16] strong, close-coupled filly: modest form in maidens: should stay 1½m: slowly away final start: sold 4,500 gns in December. *J. L. Dunlop*   **63**

DUST TO DUST (IRE)   3 ch.g. College Chapel 122 – Poscimur (IRE) (Prince Rupert (FR) 121) [2002 63d: f8.5g* f8g* f9.4g* p10g Jun 9] useful-looking gelding: fair performer: won minor event at Wolverhampton in March and claimers at Southwell/Wolverhampton (claimed from A. Crook £8,000) in May: stayed 9.4f: acted on fibresand and soft going: dead. *J. Balding*   **66**

DUSTY ANSWER   3 b.f. Zafonic (USA) 130 – Dust Dancer 116 (Suave Dancer (USA) 136) [2002 84: 8d² 8d⁵ 7m⁶ Jul 30] smallish, sparely-made filly: has a quick action: useful performer: best efforts in listed races at Ascot (short-head second to Monturani) and Goodwood (fifth to Dolores): off 10 weeks before final start: stays 1m: yet to race on soft/heavy going, acts on any other: seems highly-strung: sold 80,000 gns in December. *J. L. Dunlop*   **97**

DUSTY BANKES   3 ch.f. Greensmith 121 – Heather Honey (Insan (USA) 119) [2002 59d: 8m 8g Jun 17] workmanlike filly: modest at 2 yrs: well held both 3-y-o starts: tried visored. *W. G. M. Turner*   **–**

DUSTY DAZZLER (IRE)   2 ch.f. (Mar 28) Titus Livius (FR) 115 – Satinette 109 (Shirley Heights 130) [2002 p5g* p5g³ 5f* 5m 6m⁴ 5.1f⁵ f5s⁵ p5g³ p5g² p5g* Dec 18] IR 8,500Y: strong, lengthy filly: half-sister to several winners, including 1988 2-y-o 1m winner Code Satin (by Secreto): dam 2-y-o 7f/1m (May Hill Stakes) winner: fairly useful performer: won maiden at Lingfield in March, minor event at Thirsk in April and nursery at Lingfield in December: best at 5f: acts on polytrack (below form on fibresand) and firm ground: often makes running: tends to hang right. *W. G. M. Turner*   **91**

DUSTY DEMOCRAT   4 b.g. Democratic (USA) 101 – Two Shots (Dom Racine (FR) 121) [2002 –: f11s p16g Jan 23] poor maiden: stayed 1m: acted on fibresand: tried visored: had looked none too keen: dead. *W. G. M. Turner*   **–**

DUSTY STAR   3 b.f. Danzig Connection (USA) – Sindos 89 (Busted 134) [2002 –: f8.5g Nov 18] no sign of ability in maiden/sellers. *W. G. M. Turner*   **–**

DUSTY WUGG (IRE)   3 b.f. General Monash (USA) 107 – Welsh Berry (USA) (Sir Ivor 135) [2002 70: f7g 6g 7m 8d f7g³ f8g⁶ Dec 10] leggy filly: has a quick action: fair maiden at best: stays 7f: acts on fibresand, soft and good to firm going: tried blinkered/visored: often slowly away. *A. Dickman*   **64 d**

DUTCH GOLD (USA)   2 ch.c. (Mar 2) Lahib (USA) 129 – Crimson Conquest (USA) 85 (Diesis 133) [2002 6g⁵ 7d⁶ 7.6m² 7m⁵ 8g Sep 28] big, good-topped colt: has plenty of scope: seventh living foal: half-brother to several winners, notably very smart 6f (at 2 yrs) to 1¼m winner Crimplene (by Lion Cavern): dam 2-y-o 6f winner who probably stayed 1¼m: fairly useful maiden: best effort when 1½ lengths second to Big Bad Bob in minor event at Chester: tailed off in Royal Lodge Stakes at Ascot final start: should stay 1m: acts on good to firm going. *C. E. Brittain*   **89**

DUTY PAID (IRE)   2 b.f. (Feb 8) Barathea (IRE) 127 – Local Custom (IRE) (Be My Native (USA) 122) [2002 5m³ 5s* 6m* 7m Oct 19] 15,000F: big, lengthy, rather   **99 +**

Henry Carnarvon Stakes (Albany), Royal Ascot—a competitive field for a new race which acted as a good curtain raiser to Ascot's first 'Royal' Saturday since 1970; there's a close finish between Duty Paid (breastgirth), Luvah Girl (right) and Pearl Dance

unfurnished filly: sister to useful 1m winner Lady Miletrian and half-sister to 3 winners, including 7-y-o Bergen: dam, Irish maiden, half-sister to Middle Park winner Balla Cove: useful form: won maiden at Sandown and listed race at Royal Ascot (19-runner event by head final start: should stay 1m: acts on soft and good to firm ground: bandaged behind all starts. *D. R. C. Elsworth*

DYNAMO MINSK (IRE)   3 b.f. Polish Precedent (USA) 131 – Blazing Glory (IRE)   **62** (Glow (USA)) [2002 8.1m⁴ 9d³ 10.2s f8.5g 8m 8g³ Oct 16] 12,500F, 22,000Y: big, lengthy filly: has plenty of scope: sixth foal: closely related to fairly useful 5f/6f winner La Piazza (by Polish Patriot) and half-sister to several winners: dam Irish 5f winner, including at 2 yrs: modest maiden: stays 1m: acts on good to soft going: tongue tied final start: sold 7,500 gns. *J. W. Hills*

E

EACHY PEACHY (IRE)   3 ch.f. Perugino (USA) 84 – Miss Big John (IRE) (Martin   **54** John) [2002 55: p7g p10g³ 12g³ 10m⁵ 11.6m⁶ 8g p10g p12g 11.5s Oct 22] rather leggy filly: modest maiden: stays easy 1½m: acts on good to firm going, good to soft and all-weather: often slowly away: has carried head high. *J. R. Best*

EAGER ANGEL (IRE)   4 b.f. Up And At 'em 109 – Seanee Squaw (Indian Ridge   **–** 123) [2002 38: f5s f6s f6g f5g³ f5g³ f5g f5g f5g 5m⁵ Jul 29] small, good-quartered filly: **a39** poor maiden: stays 6f: acts on firesand and firm going: tried blinkered. *R. F. Marvin*

EAGLE PARK (IRE)   3 ch.g. Eagle Eyed (USA) 111 – Avidal Park 68 (Horage 124)   **66 d** [2002 66: f8.5g² 10.3s 7f f8.5g³ 7.9g 9.9g 8s 7.1m f8.5g Oct 5] strong gelding: fair maiden at best: on downgrade: should stay at least 1¼m: acts on firm going, soft and fibresand: tried blinkered: sent to Spain. *J. L. Eyre*

EAGLE RISE (IRE)   2 b.c. (Feb 1) Danehill (USA) 126 – Evening Breeze (GER) 99   **108 p** (Surumu (GER)) [2002 8g* 8g* Oct 13] first foal: dam, German 1¼m/1½m performer, closely related to useful German stayer Evening Storm: won maiden at Cologne in September and Ford-Preis des Winterfavoriten (by 2 lengths from Glad Hunter) in October: likely to stay at least 1¼m: should make a smart 3-y-o. *A. Schutz, Germany*

EAGLES HIGH (IRE)   3 ch.g. Eagle Eyed (USA) 111 – Bint Al Balad (IRE) 63   **82** (Ahonoora 122) [2002 71: p8g⁴ p6g³ p8g² p7g* 7s³ 8.5g 7.1s* 8m² 8d* 8.1g* 7.6s 8g Sep 27] sturdy gelding: fairly useful performer: won maiden at Lingfield and handicaps at Chepstow (2) and Brighton between March/August: best at 7f/1m: acts on any turf going and polytrack: tried visored: has been early to post: often races up with pace: consistent: sold 32,000 gns. *R. Hannon*

EAGLES VIEW (IRE)   2 b.f. (Mar 16) Eagle Eyed (USA) 111 – Rock On (IRE)   **59** (Ballad Rock 122) [2002 6s 6g 6d 6f⁶ 7m 6.1m⁶ Sep 20] IR 25,000Y: sturdy, close-coupled filly: third foal: sister to useful 6f (at 2 yrs) to 9f (in Hong Kong) winner Goggles and closely related to 6-y-o Perigeux: dam unraced: modest maiden: likely to prove best at 5f/6f: acts on firm ground. *Mrs P. N. Dutfield*

EAGLET (IRE)   4 b.g. Eagle Eyed (USA) 111 – Justice System (USA) 57 (Criminal   **62 ?** Type (USA)) [2002 –: 8g⁵ 7.1m 7f Apr 20] small, sparely-made gelding: modest maiden at best nowadays: stays 1m: acts on firm ground: tried blinkered. *A. Scott*

EARL OF DUNTON (IRE)   3 b.g. Dr Devious (IRE) 127 – Jade Vine (IRE) (Alzao   **–** (USA) 117) [2002 –: f9.4g Jan 7] no form: tried tongue tied. *S. C. Williams*

EARL SIGURD (IRE)   4 ch.g. High Kicker (USA) – My Kind 59 (Mon Tresor 113)   **–** [2002 64: 10m Apr 22] leggy gelding: modest maiden at 3 yrs: well held only 4-y-o start on Flat: winning hurdler. *L. Lungo*

EARLSTON   2 ch.g. (Mar 14) Fleetwood (IRE) 107 – Mystique Smile 78 (Music Boy   **67** 124) [2002 6g 7.2s⁶ 8g* 8s⁶ Oct 15] 12,000Y: second foal: dam 2-y-o 5f winner who failed to progress: fair performer: best effort when justifying favouritism in seller at Ayr in September by 5 lengths: stays 1m: raced only on good ground or softer: raced freely/hung left second start. *J. S. Goldie*

EARLY MORNING MIST (IRE)   4 b.f. Alzao (USA) 117 – Welsh Mist 102   **86 §** (Damister (USA) 123) [2002 94d: 8.5g³ 8d 10g² 10g⁴ 10f Jun 22] workmanlike filly: fairly useful handicapper: stays 1¼m: acts on soft going, good to firm and polytrack: tried blinkered, visored last 3 outings: irresolute: sold 20,000 gns in July, sent to Saudi Arabia. *M. Johnston*

EASTBOROUGH (IRE)   3 b.g. Woodborough (USA) 112 – Easter Girl (Efisio 120)   **77**
[2002 70, a89: p10g² p8g p8g⁶ 8.3m 9.9g 11g⁶ 9d⁶ 10g⁶ 8.1f⁴ 10.9m* 12f 11.7m⁵ 10d⁴   **a88**
11.7f 10.2g 8g Sep 27] close-coupled, quite good-topped gelding: fairly useful handicapper on all-weather, fair on turf: left A. Jarvis after third outing, J. Portman after ninth:
won at Warwick in July: best form at 1¼m/1½m: acts on all-weather, good to firm and
good to soft going: tried blinkered: held up. *I. A. Wood*

EAST CAPE   5 b.g. Bering 136 – Reine de Danse (USA) 78 (Nureyev (USA) 131)   **64**
[2002 60§: 11m² 10f² 12m* 12f 12f 12g⁶ 12.1d³ 10d³ 12.1g 10.5v² 10.1m* 11s* 10s⁵
9.9m⁵ 12f Oct 7] leggy, useful-looking gelding: modest handicapper: won at Pontefract
in May and Newcastle/Redcar in August: effective at 1¼m/1½m: acts on any going:
visored once in 2001. *Don Enrico Incisa*

EASTERN BLUE (IRE)   3 ch.f. Be My Guest (USA) 126 – Stifen (Burslem 123)   **68**
[2002 68: 6f 6f⁵ 6g⁶ 6g⁵ 7g 7.1m 6.1m Oct 1] sturdy filly: fair performer: left J. Balding
after second outing: stays 6f: acts on firm and good to soft ground. *K. A. Ryan*

EASTERN BREEZE (IRE)   4 b.g. Sri Pekan (USA) 117 – Elegant Bloom (IRE) 84   **100**
(Be My Guest (USA) 126) [2002 86: 10g* 10m⁶ 8g 9s* 10m* 10m³ 9g³ 9m 10m 9f 9s
p10g⁶ p10g* Dec 21] leggy, quite good-topped gelding: useful performer: won maiden
at Leicester and handicaps at Kempton, Newmarket (beat Shafeeq by 2 lengths) and
Lingfield (beat Linning Wine by ¾ length) in 2002: stays 1¼m: acts on soft going, good
to firm and polytrack: edgy sort, has been early to post: has worn crossed noseband.
P. W. D'Arcy

EASTERN DAGGER   2 b.c. (Apr 18) Kris 135 – Shehana (USA) 86 (The Minstrel   **72 p**
(CAN) 135) [2002 6g 7.5d³ 8v⁴ p7g³ Dec 28] leggy colt: half-brother to several winners,
including useful sprinter React (by Reprimand) and 1½m winner Legion of Honour (by
Ahonoora): dam, 2-y-o 9f winner, seemed to stay 1½m: fair form: best effort (went freely
but showed promise previously) when staying-on third in nursery at Lingfield final start:
should stay 1m: acts on polytrack: capable of better. *M. Johnston*

EASTERN GATE   2 b.c. (Apr 13) Elmaamul (USA) 125 – Redgrave Design 77 (Neb-   **–**
biolo 125) [2002 8.3m⁵ 8d f8.5s Dec 9] 5,000Y: half-brother to several winners, notably
useful sprinter Saint Express (by Clantime), also fairly useful 1m winner: dam 2-y-o 5f
winner: behind in maidens/seller. *R. M. Whitaker*

EASTERN HOPE (IRE)   3 b.g. Danehill Dancer (IRE) 117 – Hope And Glory   **84**
(USA) 87 (Well Decorated (USA)) [2002 76: 7f⁵ 7.5g⁴ 7.1m* 8.1d³ 7.1d⁶ 7.5m⁵ 8f Jul 28]
tall, good-topped gelding: fairly useful handicapper: won at Sandown in June: effective at
7f/1m: acts on good to firm and good to soft going: blinkered third to sixth outings:
sometimes races freely/wanders: probably not easiest of rides. *Mrs L. Stubbs*

EASTERN IMAGE (USA)   3 ch.c. Gone West (USA) – My True Lady (USA) (Seattle   **99**
Slew (USA)) [2002 96p: 7m² Apr 16] well-made colt: useful performer: good ½-length
second to Moten Swing in handicap at Newmarket only 3-y-o start: will stay at least 1m:
acts on soft and good to firm going: sent to USA. *J. L. Dunlop*

EASTERNKING   3 ch.f. Sabrehill (USA) 120 – Kshessinskaya 99 (Hadeer 118) [2002   **–**
–: 9m⁶ 16.2d 9.9d 12m 13.8f Sep 21] smallish, sturdy filly: little form. *J. S. Wainwright*

EASTERN MAGENTA (IRE)   2 b.g. (Jan 30) Turtle Island (IRE) 123 – Blue Heights   **86**
(IRE) (Persian Heights 129) [2002 5m⁴ 5s³ 6g* 6s³ 7f 6g⁶ 6g* 6d⁴ 7s² 7v³ Nov 9] IR
8,500F, 10,000Y: well-grown, rather unfurnished gelding: fourth foal: half-brother to
winners abroad by Archway and Fourstars Allstar: dam unraced: fairly useful performer:
won maiden in May and nursery in September, both at Ayr: good efforts in nurseries last
3 starts (gelded after): stays 7f: acts on heavy going: slowly away 3 times: consistent.
Mrs L. Stubbs

EASTERN PROMISE   4 gr.f. Factual (USA) 108 – Indian Crystal 66 (Petong 126)   **49**
[2002 62d: 6f⁵ 5m 6g 5m⁶ 5.9d³ 5g 6f 5g 7m Jul 27] tall, quite good-topped filly:
poor performer: should stay 7f: yet to race on soft/heavy going, acts on any other: tried
visored/blinkered: sometimes wanders: usually races prominently: none too consistent.
T. D. Easterby

EASTERN PROPHETS   9 b.g. Emarati (USA) 74 – Four Love (Pas de Seul 133)   **–**
[2002 45: f8s³ f8g 7d 7m May 2] good-quartered gelding: no form at 9 yrs: often
blinkered/visored before 2002. *Jedd O'Keeffe*

EASTERN ROYAL   3 b.g. Royal Applause 124 – Kentfield (Busted 134) [2002 61:   **52**
7.5g 6s 9m⁶ 8m 7s⁴ f6g Dec 27] leggy gelding: modest performer: should stay 1m: acts
on soft and good to firm going. *Mrs L. Stubbs*

EASTERN SCARLET (IRE)   2 b.g. (Apr 10) Woodborough (USA) 112 – Cuddles   **73**
(IRE) 89 (Taufan (USA) 119) [2002 5d 7g 5m* 6g³ 5m² 5.9m⁵ 6f⁵ p6g Dec 30] IR 7,500F,
20,000Y: good-bodied gelding: third foal: half-brother to a winning sprinter in Italy by
General Monash: dam Irish 5f winner: fair performer: trained by J. Balding on debut: won
maiden at Musselburgh in July: creditable efforts in nurseries next 3 starts: left K. Ryan
before final one: effective at 5f/6f: acts on good to firm going: sometimes carries head
high. *Mrs L. Stubbs*

EASTERN TRUMPETER   6 b.h. First Trump 118 – Oriental Air (IRE) 56 (Taufan   **85**
(USA) 119) [2002 94: f6g f5g p5g⁶ 5f 5d 5g³ 5m⁴ 5g⁵ 5m⁵ 5.1d³ 5m⁶ 5m* 5.2m⁶ 5f 5m
Sep 5] compact horse: fairly useful handicapper: won at Sandown in July: effective at 5f/
6f: acts on fibresand, firm and soft going: held up nowadays. *J. M. Bradley*

EASTERN VENTURE   5 b.g. Last Tycoon 131 – Imperial Jade 105 (Lochnager 132)   **64**
[2002 60: 7.5d³ 8m² 7.1d⁴ Jul 31] smallish gelding: modest maiden handicapper: stays
sharp 1m: acts on good to firm and good to soft going: tried tongue tied: sold 2,200 gns,
sent to Italy. *G. A. Butler*

EASTER OGIL (IRE)   7 ch.g. Pips Pride 117 – Piney Pass (Persian Bold 123) [2002   **66**
69, a59: p8g³ p10g p7g³ p7g p7g² 8.1m² 7.1v⁴ 8m 8.3m 8.1d³ 8g 8.5g 7.1g³ f8.5g⁵ Oct 19]   **a64**
lengthy, good-topped gelding: unimpressive mover: fair handicapper: probably best at 7f/
1m: acts on all-weather and any turf going: usually visored: sometimes soon off bridle/
gets behind: usually apprentice ridden (all wins under strong handling). *I. A. Balding*

EASTER PARADE   2 b.f. (Apr 27) Entrepreneur 123 – Starlet 119 (Teenoso (USA)   **68 p**
135) [2002 7d p8g Nov 27] smallish, leggy filly: closely related to useful 1m (at 2 yrs)
and 13.5f winner Interlude (by Sadler's Wells), and half-sister to several winners,
including useful 1¼m winner Border Comet (by Selkirk): dam, best at 1¼m/1½m at 4
yrs, runner-up in Nassau and Sun Chariot Stakes: fair form when seventh in maidens
at Newmarket and Lingfield: will be suited by 1¼m+: probably capable of better.
R. Charlton

EAST FLARES   2 ch.g. (Feb 26) Environment Friend 128 – Ijada Bianca (Absalom   **–**
128) [2002 7f⁵ f8.5g Sep 21] second foal by thoroughbred sire: dam unraced: well held in
maidens, looking wayward second start. *J. W. Unett*

EAST OF JAVA   4 b.g. Greensmith 121 – Krakatoa (Shirley Heights 130) [2002 71:   **55**
6.1m 5m f5s f6g⁶ 6g Oct 28] workmanlike gelding: modest maiden handicapper: best at
5f/6f: acts on good to firm going, good to soft and fibresand: blinkered twice: has started
slowly: sold 3,500 gns, sent to Kuwait. *P. J. Makin*

EAST RIDING   2 b.f. (Mar 15) Gothenberg (IRE) 117 – Bettynouche 69 (Midyan   **74**
(USA) 124) [2002 6v³ f7g Nov 16] 800Y: tall, leggy filly: first foal: dam 5f (at 2 yrs) and
7f (in France) winner: very green, fair form when third to Harry The Hoover in maiden at
Doncaster: well held in similar event at Wolverhampton week later. *M. Johnston*

EASTWOOD DRIFTER (USA)   5 ch.g. Woodman (USA) 126 – Mandarina (USA)   **–**
105 (El Gran Senor (USA) 136) [2002 11.6d Aug 5] angular, unfurnished gelding: fair
maiden at 3 yrs: well held only run since: blinkered once. *B. G. Powell*

EASY RIDER (IRE)   2 b.c. (Feb 10) Blues Traveller (IRE) 119 – Curie Express (IRE)   **65**
65 (Fayruz 116) [2002 5.1g⁵ 6d² 6s⁶ f6g² 7d⁵ 6m⁵ 8.3m 8d⁵ Nov 1] IR 9,000F, IR
10,000Y: fourth foal: half-brother to 3 winners, including 1998 2-y-o 5f winner Acuria
(by Contract Law) and Italian 5f to 1m winner Dida (by Inzar): dam 2-y-o 5f winner: fair
maiden: best at 5f/6f: acts on fibresand, good to firm and good to soft going. *E. L. James*

EB AAD (USA)   3 b.f. Gone West (USA) – Oumaldaaya (USA) 111 (Nureyev (USA)
131) [2002 7g Apr 19] smallish, quite attractive filly: sixth foal: half-sister to smart 7f (at
2 yrs) to 9f winner Haami and useful 1996 2-y-o 1m winner Asas (both by Nashwan):
dam, 7f (at 2 yrs) and 1¼m (Italian Group 2 event) winner, half-sister to Derby winner
Erhaab: behind in newcomers race at Newbury: sold 12,000 gns in December.
J. L. Dunlop

ECHOES IN ETERNITY (IRE)   2 b.f. (Mar 26) Spinning World (USA) 130 –   **98 P**
Magnificient Style (USA) 107 (Silver Hawk (USA) 123) [2002 8m* Sep 24]
    Godolphin's method for choosing the horses it cherry picks from other
stables hasn't been made public. Nevertheless, if Sheikh Mohammed and his team
had searched through *Timeform* in 2002 for names of two-year-olds from back-end
maidens that should be subject to one of those famous offers that are too good to
refuse, they'd almost certainly have made a note to enquire about Lateen Sails and
Echoes In Eternity. As it happens, it was reported before the end of the season that
both had been purchased to join Godolphin.

Cliff Brants' Champagne Retirement EBF Maiden Fillies' Stakes, Newmarket—Echoes In Eternity makes an impressive winning debut; Discreet Brief is clear of Tease (armlets) and Chaffinch (left)

According to our developing sectional-time analysis, both Lateen Sails and Echoes In Eternity recorded impressive figures in winning Newmarket maidens on their only start. Running in Robert Sangster's colours, Echoes In Eternity seemed very much the stable second string judged by the betting on the Cliff Brants' Champagne Retirement EBF Maiden Fillies' Stakes over a mile in September; she drifted to 10/1 behind Gosden's other runner Felicity, another newcomer who started favourite at 11/4. Echoes In Eternity was in rear to halfway, and had plenty to do when eased out towards the centre of the course to improve, but she proved in a different league once beginning to get the hang of things, scampering clear on meeting the rising ground from the Dip to beat Discreet Brief by three and a half lengths. The race didn't begin in earnest until halfway, which is reflected in a timefigure for the race overall equivalent to a rating of 91. On our interpretation of the sectional times from halfway, however, Echoes In Eternity's performance could be worth a rating of around 106.

		Spinning World (USA) (ch 1993)	Nureyev (b 1977)	Northern Dancer
Echoes In Eternity (IRE) (b.f. Mar 26, 2000)				Special
			Imperfect Circle (b 1988)	Riverman
				Aviance
		Magnificent Style (USA) (b 1993)	Silver Hawk (b 1979)	Roberto
				Gris Vitesse
			Mia Karina (b 1983)	Icecapade
				Basin

There's plenty more to back up the idea that Echoes In Eternity will prove a lot better than the bare form of her Newmarket success. A lengthy filly, she was clearly green at Newmarket, where she pricked her ears and needed to be pushed along firmly to assert her superiority. She is well bred, too. Her dam, Magnificent Style, though difficult to train, made all in the Musidora Stakes at York in 1996, having made her debut only a month earlier. Magnificent Style ran only once in Britain after York, finishing a disappointing sixth in the Ribblesdale Stakes, but she shaped as though she should have been fully effective at a mile and a half. She ran without success in allowance company in the States as a four-year-old when placed at up to ten furlongs. Echoes In Eternity is her second foal after the Storm Cat filly Stylelistick. Echoes In Eternity will stay at least a mile and a quarter. Her sire Spinning World was a top-class miler, winning five Group/Grade 1 events, including at the Breeders' Cup, but he did win a pattern race on soft ground over nine furlongs as a two-year-old on his only start beyond a mile. Spinning World's first crop didn't flourish quite as they once promised in 2002. Tendulkar suffered an injury and another of his best two-year-olds of 2001, Quad's Melody, never ran, but others that had a chance, such as Flat Spin, Common World, King of Happiness and

303

Spinnette, failed to live fully up to expectations. Echoes In Eternity could well put things right in 2003 when she should make the grade in pattern company. *J. H. M. Gosden*

ECOLOGY (IRE) 4 b.c. Sri Pekan (USA) 117 – Ecco Mi (IRE) (Priolo (USA) 127) **112** [2002 9s 8g* 9.8m² 9g³ 8m⁶ 6.8d⁵ 9m 8f Oct 3] useful-looking colt: useful performer for J. Dunlop at 2 yrs: trained by M. Kahn in Sweden in 2001, winning twice, including Norwegian 2000 Guineas at Øvrevoll: best effort (smart form) when winning listed race at same track in May by ½ length from Martellian: just respectable efforts at best afterwards (last in listed race at Newmarket final start): best up to 1m: probably acts on good to firm and good to soft ground. *R. Haugen, Norway*

E C TOO 2 b.f. (Mar 30) Sheikh Albadou 128 – Scarlett Holly 81 (Red Sunset 120) **62** [2002 5m³ May 6] 7,000Y: lengthy filly: half-sister to several winners, including 5-y-o Scarlett Ribbon and 3-y-o Game Guru: dam 6f (at 2 yrs)/7f winner: 25/1, third to Rag Top in maiden at Warwick. *J. L. Spearing*

ECUADOR (IRE) 2 ch.c. (Apr 14) Among Men (USA) 124 – Christle Mill (Pas de – Seul 133) [2002 7.1g 8s Oct 15] 5,200 2-y-o: good-topped colt: half-brother to fairly useful 6f winner Conectis (by River Falls), later 6.5f minor stakes winner in USA, and to a winner in Italy by Mac's Imp: dam ran twice in Ireland at 2 yrs: soundly beaten in maidens: unseated rider and bolted to post second start. *J. G. M. O'Shea*

EDDIES JEWEL 2 b.g. (Mar 22) Presidium 124 – Superstream (Superpower 113) – [2002 6m 7d 6m Sep 8] 500Y: third foal: half-brother to 4-y-o Tommy Smith: dam unraced: well held in maidens. *J. S. Wainwright*

EDDU 4 ch.g. Casteddu 111 – Cabra (Red Sunset 120) [2002 78: p10g² Dec 30] big, **58** lengthy gelding: fair performer at 3 yrs: modest form in seller at Lingfield after 18-month absence in December: stays 1¼m (possibly not 1½m): acts on good to firm ground, probably on polytrack: very edgy/gave trouble stalls final start in 2001. *W. M. Brisbourne*

EDDYS LAD 4 b.g. Lahib (USA) 129 – Glamour Model 78 (Last Tycoon 131) [2002 – 65, a57: f7s³ f7g² f7g⁴ f7g* 8g f8g 8g f7g 7d Oct 15] quite good-topped gelding: modest **a58 d** form when winning maiden handicap at Wolverhampton (final start for J. Balding) in March: on downgrade after: best form at 7f: acts on all-weather, firm and soft going: tried blinkered/visored/tongue tied: has given trouble stall/looked less than keen: sold £1,100. *R. Wilman*

EDE'S 2 ch.g. (Feb 4) Bijou d'Inde 127 – Ballagarrow Girl 66 (North Stoke 130) [2002 **56** 5g⁵ 6g⁶ 8.2v Oct 29] 7,500F, 800Y: lengthy gelding: half-brother to several winners, including 1990 2-y-o 5f winner Northern Nation (by Nomination): dam, maiden, best at 1¼m: modest form when fifth in maiden at Kempton: off over 5 months, well held in seller final start. *W. G. M. Turner*

EDIFICE (JPN) 6 ch.g. Carroll House 132 – Moon Tosho (JPN) (Steel Heart 128) **46** [2002 50: 12m⁵ 9.2s 12.4m⁵ 14.1f⁶ 10f² 10d 12f³ 12m³ 10.1m⁵ 11s⁵ 14.1m⁴ 10.9g Sep 19] smallish, sturdy gelding: poor maiden: stays 1¾m: acts on firm and soft ground: tried blinkered/visored: sometimes slowly away/edges left/looks none too keen. *B. Ellison*

EDITOR IN CHIEF (USA) 3 b.c. Kingmambo (USA) 125 – Cymbala (FR) (Assert **92** 134) [2002 86p: 11.8m* 8f Sep 4] strong, angular colt: fairly useful performer: won handicap at Leicester in April: left J. Dunlop and off over 4 months, well held last of 8 in optional claimer at Del Mar only subsequent outing: almost certainly finds 1m too sharp, and should stay 1¾m: acts on soft and good to firm going: raced up with pace in Britain: carried head awkwardly for only 2-y-o win. *K. Mulhall, USA*

EDMO YEWKAY (IRE) 2 b. or br.c. (Apr 14) Sri Pekan (USA) 117 – Mannequin **80** (IRE) 79 (In The Wings 128) [2002 6f³ 7.2v* 7.5g* 7f 8m 7.9f⁵ Oct 10] IR 14,500Y: rangy colt: has a round action: first foal: dam, maiden who stayed 15.4f, granddaughter of very smart Oaks third The Dancer: fairly useful performer: won maiden at Ayr in June and minor event at Beverley in July: creditable fifth in nursery at York, detached most of way: should stay at least 1¼m: acts on any going. *T. D. Easterby*

EDWARDIAN ERA 3 ch.f. Bering 136 – Charming Life 88 (Habitat 134) [2002 – 9.9m 12s Jun 12] 44,000F: half-sister to several winners, including useful 1¼m and (in France) 11f winner Caerau (by Nashwan) and smart French 5f (at 2 yrs) to 1m winner Run And Gun (by Lomond): dam 7f winner from very good family: well held in maidens: sold 12,000 guineas, sent to Italy. *R. Charlton*

EDWARD'S BROTHER 2 b.c. (Mar 9) Wolfhound (USA) 126 – Dolly Bevan 53 **55** (Another Realm 118) [2002 6d p7g f7s Dec 13] 14,000F, 9,500Y: half-brother to 3 winners, including useful 6f winner Oggi and fairly useful 6f to 1m winner Pengamon (both by Efisio): dam, 2-y-o 6f winner who stayed 1m, half-sister to smart sprinter Pips Pride: modest maiden: will need to settle to stay beyond 7f. *M. Wigham*

EFFECTIVE 2 ch.g. (Apr 17) Bahamian Bounty 116 – Efficacy 62 (Efisio 120) [2002 **68** 5g f5g⁴ 5.3g f6g² Dec 20] 2,200Y: second foal: dam 6f winner at 4 yrs: fair maiden: best effort second in nursery at Wolverhampton after 6 months off: should stay 7f: acts on fibresand. *A. P. Jarvis*

EFFERVESCE (IRE) 4 b.f. Sri Pekan (USA) 117 – Arctic Winter (CAN) (Briartic **80** (CAN)) [2002 77: f6g* f7g³ 6.1d⁵ 5g 5m* 6g² 6g 6m 6d³ 6g 6m³ p7g⁵ p8g* p8g Dec 3] strong filly: fairly useful handicapper: won at Southwell in February, Newcastle in May and Lingfield in November: effective at 5f to easy 1m: acts on all-weather, good to firm and good to soft going: has run well when sweating/edgy: has pulled hard: usually patiently ridden. *M. A. Buckley*

EFFERVESCENT 5 b.m. Efisio 120 – Sharp Chief 71 (Chief Singer 131) [2002 77, **–** a89: f7s² f6g f6g² f7g f8.5g f6g Dec 16] tall mare: fairly useful performer on all-weather, **a89** fair on turf (when last ran in 2001): effective at 6f/7f: acts on fibresand (poorly drawn only run on polytrack): usually waited with. *A. G. Newcombe*

EFFERVESCING 3 ch.g. Efisio 120 – Superspring (Superlative 118) [2002 70, a67: 5m 7g 7f 5.9d⁶ 5s Aug 5] sturdy gelding: fair maiden at 2 yrs: little form in 2002: tried blinkered/visored. *Mrs A. Duffield*

EFFIE GRAY 3 b.f. Sri Pekan (USA) 117 – Rose Bouquet 78 (General Assembly **71 d** (USA)) [2002 69: 8.2d 10f³ 10d 9s 10m 9.7d 9.2m 9.1s 12s³ Nov 6] short-backed, work-manlike filly: fair maiden: well below form after second outing: stays 1½m: acts on firm and soft going: tried visored: very much on edge second/third starts. *P. Monteith*

EFIDIUM 4 b.g. Presidium 124 – Efipetite 54 (Efisio 120) [2002 59: 8m 8f 7f² f7g **55** 5.9d² 7.5d⁵ 6.9d³ 8m⁶ 6s 7m 8g⁵ 8m Sep 19] small gelding: modest performer: probably stays easy 1m: acts on firm going, good to soft and fibresand: usually blinkered nowadays: sometimes slowly away. *N. Bycroft*

EFIMAC 2 b.f. (May 26) Presidium 124 – Efipetite 54 (Efisio 120) [2002 6g 6m 5m⁴ **55** 5g 6.5g f6g* f7g f6s⁴ Dec 26] 1,000Y: small, plain filly: second foal: sister to 4-y-o Efidium: dam 1m winner: modest performer: won claimer at Southwell in November: should stay 7f: acts on fibresand, raced only on good ground or firmer on turf. *N. Bycroft*

EGO 2 b.f. (Jan 9) Green Desert (USA) 127 – Myself 110 (Nashwan (USA) 135) [2002 **107** 6m⁵ 6m* 6m* 6f⁴ Oct 4] tall, lengthy filly: has scope: third foal: half-sister to useful 2000 2-y-o 6f winner Ghayth (by Sadler's Wells): dam, 6f (at 2 yrs) and 7f (Nell Gwyn Stakes)

GNER Conditions Stakes, Doncaster—
Ego shows a good turn of foot to beat Sarayat (left), Avening (right) and Shouting The Odds

winner, half-sister to smart 5f to 7f performer Bluebook out of Queen Mary winner Pushy: useful performer: won maiden at Newmarket in August and minor event at Doncaster (beat Sarayat impressively by 1¾ lengths, idling) in September: creditable 3½ lengths fourth to Airwave in Cheveley Park Stakes at Newmarket, carrying head high: will probably prove best at 5f/6f: raced only on ground firmer than good. *G. Wragg*

EHAB (IRE) 3 b.g. Cadeaux Genereux 131 – Dernier Cri 63 (Slip Anchor 136) [2002 **73** 10m 12d³ 10m⁵ p10g⁶ p10g⁶ f9.4s³ Dec 7] 55,000Y: second foal: dam, French 11f/12.5f winner, half-sister to Mtoto: fair maiden: should be suited by 1½m+: acts on all-weather, yet to race on extremes of going on turf. *P. J. Makin*

EIBH'N ABBIE 3 b.g. Forzando 122 – Brookhead Lady 73 (Petong 126) [2002 69§: **45 §** p6g³ f7g³ f6g² f6g* f5g p7g f7g⁶ p7g f6g⁵ 5d 7m f6g 6d p6g⁴ 7f 7m p7g f7g Oct 5] rather **a61 §** leggy gelding: modest on all-weather, poor on turf: won at Wolverhampton in January: stays easy 7f: acts on all-weather, good to firm and good to soft going: usually visored/blinkered: often soon off bridle: untrustworthy. *P. D. Evans*

EIGER (IRE) 2 b.c. (Apr 6) Indian Ridge 123 – Liffey's Secret (USA) 86 (Riverman **87 p** (USA) 131) [2002 6m² 6f* Sep 21] IR 160,000Y: smallish, useful-looking colt: fifth foal: dam Irish 1¼m winner from family of Shareef Dancer: fairly useful form: confirmed debut promise when landing odds in maiden at Catterick by 4 lengths from Circuit Dancer, taking strong hold and pushed ahead over 1f out: bred to stay at least 7f: capable of better still. *J. J. Quinn*

EIGHT (IRE) 6 ch.g. Thatching 131 – Up To You (Sallust 134) [2002 61, a–: 9d³ 12.1g² **61** 12.1g 12m⁵ 10.2g p13g⁵ Dec 28] workmanlike gelding: modest handicapper on turf, **a46** poor on all-weather: stays 1¾m: acts on polytrack, firm and good to soft going: usually visored/blinkered in 2000. *C. G. Cox*

EIGHT TRUMPS 2 ch.g. (Apr 11) First Trump 118 – Misty Silks 81 (Scottish Reel **–** 123) [2002 5m f6g 8v Nov 8] 5,000F, 500Y: strong gelding: fourth foal: half-brother to 6f winner Misty Boy (by Polar Falcon) and 3-y-o Rodiak: dam, 1m winner, half-sister to useful 1m winner Silk St John: well held in maidens: gelded after final start. *P. R. Wood*

EIRAARDIA (IRE) 3 br.f. Petardia 113 – Eiras Mood 57 (Jalmood (USA) 126) **–** [2002 33: 10g 12m 8g 7d⁴ 8.1d Aug 8] small filly: little form. *P. D. Evans*

EKRAAR (USA) 5 b.h. Red Ransom (USA) – Sacahuista (USA) (Raja Baba (USA)) **121** [2002 125: 12g⁵ 10m² 12s³ 12m⁴ Dec 15] well-made horse: good walker: very smart performer: best efforts in 2002 when 1¼ lengths second to Falbrav in Premio Presidente della Repubblica at Rome in May (off over 5 months after) and 1¾ lengths fourth to Ange Gabriel in Hong Kong Vase at Sha Tin: effective at 1¼m/1½m: acts on firm and soft going, just respectable efforts on dirt: usually blinkered/visored/tongue tied: races prominently: game. *Saeed bin Suroor*

ELA AGORI MOU (IRE) 5 ch.g. Ela-Mana-Mou 132 – La Courant (USA) (Little **69** Current (USA)) [2002 9g² 12m⁴ 12.3g⁵ 14m 13.9f 16s Nov 6] 3,000 3-y-o: strong gelding: half-brother to a winner in USA by Salt Dome: dam US maiden half-sister to National Stakes winner Classic Fame: fair bumper performer: fair maiden on Flat: well held in handicaps last 3 starts: should be suited by 1½m+. *D. Eddy*

ELA ALETHIA 3 b.f. Kris 135 – Artistic Licence (High Top 131) [2002 7g 8m 8.1m **–** f7g Sep 30] 4,800F, 6,500Y: strong, good-topped filly: half-sister to several winners, including 2000 2-y-o 5f winner The Names Bond (by Tragic Role) and 1m winner Around Fore Alliss (by Reprimand): dam, stayed 1¼m, out of half-sister to Oaks winner Circus Plume: little form: wore hood first 2 outings. *T. D. McCarthy*

ELA APHRODITE 4 b.f. Halling (USA) 133 – Darcey Bussell 66 (Green Desert **–** (USA) 127) [2002 8m⁶ Jul 26] 26,000Y: big, good-topped filly: second foal: dam, 7f/1m winner at 4 yrs, half-sister to useful 1½m performer Port Helene: slowly away and always tailed off in listed race at Ascot. *P. W. D'Arcy*

ELA-ARISTOKRATISSA 4 b.f. Danehill (USA) 126 – June Brilly (IRE) (Fayruz **49** 116) [2002 8.1m⁵ 7m May 29] 25,000F: lengthy filly: first foal: dam unraced half-sister to smart Irish winner up to 1½m/high-class hurdler I'm Supposin: better efforts in maidens when fifth at Warwick: reportedly lost action next time. *P. W. D'Arcy*

ELA D'ARGENT (IRE) 3 b.f. Ela-Mana-Mou 132 – Petite-D-Argent 91 (Noalto **66** 120) [2002 74d: 8m p12g 8.3v⁴ 8d* 9.2s² 12m⁴ 11.1g Jul 18] angular, quite good-topped filly: fair performer: won claimer at Ayr (claimed from M. Johnston £6,000) in June: effective at 1m, barely at 1½m: acts on soft and good to firm ground: has been tongue tied: has started slowly: won 2 juvenile hurdles in autumn. *P. Monteith*

ELA FIGURA 2 ch.f. (Apr 10) The West (USA) 107 – Chili Bouchier (USA) (Stop **59** The Music (USA)) [2002 5m 5m 6.1g 5g³ 5.2d f5g6 f5g p5g Dec 18] first foal: dam, no form, out of half-sister to Irish 1000 Guineas winner More So: modest maiden: third in nursery at Sandown: should stay at least 6f. *A. W. Carroll*

ELA JAY 3 b.f. Double Eclipse (IRE) 122 – Papirusa (IRE) (Pennine Walk 120) [2002 **61** –: p8g p12g 16.4g² 16.2g⁴ 16.2m⁵ 15.8f³ 18d⁵ p16g⁵ Dec 3] modest maiden handicapper: left G. Butler after seventh start: stays 2¼m: acts on polytrack, firm and good to soft going: waited with. *H. Morrison*

ELA MARATHONA (IRE) 3 b.c. Doyoun 124 – Peace Melody (IRE) 69 (Classic **67** Music (USA)) [2002 84: f9.4g⁴ p12g⁵ p10g 8m 8g 10f² 9.5m Sep 17] fair maiden: left J. Eustace after third start (trained by P. d'Arcy next outing only): stays 1¼m: unraced on heavy going, acts on any other turf/all-weather. *P. J. Flynn, Ireland*

ELA RE 3 ch.c. Sabrehill (USA) 120 – Lucia Tarditi (FR) (Crystal Glitters (USA) 127) **58** [2002 10s 9d⁵ 11.5g⁴ 10g 10s⁶ 8m 7s⁶ Oct 22] 2,000Y: stout colt: has a round action: fifth foal: half-brother to 2 winners, including useful 7f (at 2 yrs) and 9f (in USA) winner Ettrick (by Selkirk): dam Italian 2-y-o 7f listed winner: modest maiden: barely stays testing 1¼m: acts on soft going. *G. Prodromou*

ELASOUNA (IRE) 2 ch.f. (May 16) Rainbow Quest (USA) 134 – Ebaziya (IRE) 111 **78 P** (Darshaan 133) [2002 7g* Oct 10] sister to smart 1998 2-y-o 7f winner (Moyglare Stud Stakes) who stayed 1½m Edabiya and half-sister to several winners, most notably Irish Oaks and Prix Royal-Oak winner Ebadiyla (by Sadler's Wells) and Gold Cup winner Enzeli (by Kahyasi): dam Irish 7f (at 2 yrs) and 1½m winner: 10/3, won 15-runner maiden at Gowran by short head from Twogoodreasons, green but getting up near post under mainly hands and heels: will be well suited by 1¼m+: sure to improve good deal. *J. Oxx, Ireland*

EL CHAPARRAL (IRE) 2 b.g. (Apr 25) Bigstone (IRE) 126 – Low Line 66 (High **87** Line 125) [2002 7m⁴ 6g 7.1s³ Nov 6] 20,000Y: lengthy gelding: half-brother to several winners, including fairly useful 1995 2-y-o 7f winner Canons Park (by Keen): dam lightly-raced sister to Park Hill winner Quay Line: fairly useful maiden: slowly away when good seventh of 30 to Michelle Ma Belle in sales race at Doncaster second start: pulled hard both other outings: bred to stay 1m: gelded after final start. *M. A. Jarvis*

EL COTO 2 b.c. (Apr 28) Forzando 122 – Thatcherella 80 (Thatching 131) [2002 5s² **85** 5g* 5.1f⁴ 5m³ 6d³ 5m³ 5d* 6m⁴ 6.1s³ Oct 23] 4,000Y: smallish, good-topped colt: fourth foal: half-brother to 7f winner Avery Ring (by Magic Ring): dam, 5f (including at 2 yrs) and 6f winner, half-sister to 6-y-o Pulau Tioman: fairly useful performer: won maiden at Leicester in April and nursery at Haydock in August: effective at 5f (given a test)/6f: acts on soft and good to firm going, possibly on firm: reliable. *B. A. McMahon*

ELDER PRINCESS (IRE) 3 b.f. Houmayoun (FR) 114 – Lanesra (IRE) (Taufan **–** (USA) 119) [2002 –: p10g 14.1m May 10] no form: dead. *T. P. McGovern*

EL DIVINO (GER) 7 b.g. Platini (GER) – Eivissa (GER) (Frontal 122) [2002 **–** 11.9s Jun 6] big, strong gelding: useful performer on Flat in Germany for C. Von Der Recke, successful on 4 occasions: well held only Flat run for current yard: stays 8.5f: acts on heavy and good to firm ground: tried blinkered. *Ian Williams*

ELECTRIQUE (IRE) 2 b.g. (Feb 27) Elmaamul (USA) 125 – Majmu (USA) 105 **65** (Al Nasr (FR) 126) [2002 6.1d 7f f8s⁴ Oct 8] IR 20,000Y: leggy, quite good-topped gelding: has scope: sixth foal: brother to high-class 7f (at 2 yrs) to 1m winner Muhtathir and half-brother to 2 winners, including useful 7f/1m winner Jawla (by Wolfhound): dam won at 1m (May Hill Stakes) at 2 yrs and stayed 1¼m: fair maiden: best effort when fourth to Eva Peron at Southwell: free-going sort, and may prove best up to 1m: acts on fibresand: gelded after final outing. *J. A. Osborne*

ELEGANT SHADOW 2 ch.f. (Mar 16) Grand Lodge (USA) 125 – White Shadow **83 p** (IRE) 87 (Last Tycoon 131) [2002 7g⁶ 7d² Nov 2] good-topped filly: has scope: fourth living foal: half-sister to 3-y-o Shining White: dam, 2-y-o 6f winner, half-sister to smart French middle-distance performer Ordinance: favourite, better effort in maidens (fairly useful when ½-length second of 18 to Aljazeera at Newmarket, travelling strongly and leading penultimate 1f: will probably stay 1m: nervy beforehand on debut: should improve further and win a race. *R. Charlton*

ELEGIA PRIMA 5 ch.m. Mon Tresor 113 – Miss Milton (Young Christopher 119) **–** [2002 11.8d⁵ 14.1d 11.9m⁵ Jul 4] small mare: modest handicapper at best: little form in 2002: blinkered once at 2 yrs. *C. G. Cox*

ELEONOR SYMPSON 3 b.f. Cadeaux Genereux 131 – Anne Bonny 105 (Ajdal **50**
(USA) 130) [2002 p7g⁴ f7g⁵ p8g⁶ 8m f7g⁵ f8g Dec 27] fourth foal: half-sister to 4-y-o
Random Quest and fairly useful 13f winner Who Cares Wins (by Kris): dam 1m/1¼m
winner out of Yorkshire Oaks winner Sally Brown: modest maiden: stays 7f: acts on
fibresand: has worn cheekpieces. *R. M. H. Cowell*

ELFHELM (IRE) 2 b.c. (Feb 19) Perugino (USA) 84 – Symphony (IRE) (Cyrano de **76**
Bergerac 120) [2002 6s 6g f8.5g² Dec 20] 13,000F, IR 15,000Y: second foal: dam
unraced half-sister to useful Irish 5f performer Dairine's Delight: best effort (fair form)
when 4 lengths second of 9 to Greta d'Argent in maiden at Wolverhampton final start,
carrying head high: stays 8.5f. *Edward Butler, Ireland*

EL GIZA (USA) 4 ch.g. Cozzene (USA) – Gazayil (USA) 80 (Irish River (FR) 131) **–**
[2002 –: 14.1m 11.6s May 27] big gelding: little sign of ability. *D. R. C. Elsworth*

EL GRAN LODE (ARG) 7 ch.h. Lode (USA) – La Pastoral (ARG) (Cinco Grande **111**
(USA)) [2002 111: a6g⁶ 6m⁶ 6v* 6.8d⁶ 5.8g⁴ 6m 6s⁴ 6v Nov 10] well-made horse: smart
performer: won Holsten-Trophy at Hamburg in July by 1½ lengths from Monkston Point:
respectable efforts afterwards when fourth to Pistachio in Tahy Open Sprint Championship (won race in 2001) and to Danehurst in Prix de Seine-et-Oise at Maisons-Laffitte:
well beaten in Diadem Stakes at Ascot in between: best at 5f/6f: seems suited by soft/
heavy ground: front runner: none too consistent. *Diego Lowther, Sweden*

ELGRIA (USA) 4 b. or br.g. Distinctly North (USA) 115 – Perfect Swinger (Shernazar **90**
131) [2002 76: 8.5g 10f 10m³ 12m² 12m* 12d² 13.3f* 14m 13.3m² 13.1f* 14m Sep 7]
sturdy gelding: fairly useful handicapper: won at Folkestone, Newbury and Bath (made
all) in summer: should stay 1¾m: acts on polytrack, firm and good to soft going. *S. Kirk*

EL HABEEBA 2 b.f. (Mar 26) Hector Protector (USA) 124 – Habibti 136 (Habitat **49**
134) [2002 6.1d 6g⁶ 7d f6s Dec 13] smallish filly: half-sister to Irish 1994 2-y-o 5f winner
Desert Lily (by Green Desert) and to dam of Derby Italiano winner Morshdi: dam outstanding sprinter: poor form in maidens/nursery. *R. Hannon*

EL HAMRA (IRE) 4 gr.g. Royal Abjar (USA) 121 – Cherlinoa (FR) (Crystal Palace **–**
(FR) 132) [2002 65: f8.5g f9.4g⁵ f8.5g 7g 8.2m f8.5g² 8f 7.5g 7.1v 8.3g 8g f8s f8s Oct 8] **a77 d**
small, strong gelding: fair handicapper on all-weather at best: on downgrade after sixth
start: probably stays 9.4f: acts on fibresand, little form on turf in 2002: tried blinkered/
visored: has given trouble at start/wandered/found little: tends to carry head awkwardly:
sold 7,000 gns. *B. A. McMahon*

ELHEBA (IRE) 3 b. or br.g. Elbio 125 – Fireheba (ITY) (Fire of Life (USA) 113) **–**
[2002 52, a58: p10g⁵ p10g⁶ f8.5g² f9.4g* f8g² f9.4g* f8.5g* f9.4g* f9.4g* 10g 10s **a82**
f9.4g Dec 26] big, leggy gelding: fairly useful on all-weather, modest at best on turf:
won 2 sellers (left J. S. Moore after second one) and 3 handicaps early in year, all at
Wolverhampton: stays 1¼m: acts on soft going and all-weather: blinkered/visored: has
wandered/flicked tail: tough. *R. Wilman*

ELIDORE 2 b.f. (Feb 26) Danetime (IRE) 121 – Beveled Edge 60 (Beveled (USA)) **95**
[2002 5m⁴ 6.1v² 7m* 6f* 6m⁵ 6d⁴ 7s Oct 26] rangy filly: fourth foal: closely related to
3-y-o Bright Edge: dam 6f winner: useful performer: won maiden at Kempton in June
and minor event at Windsor in July: creditable fourth to Cool Question in listed race at
Ripon (made most) penultimate start: well below form final outing: stays easy 7f: acts on
any going: usually races prominently. *B. Palling*

ELIIPOP 4 b.g. First Trump 118 – Hasty Key (USA) (Key To The Mint (USA)) [2002 **–**
68: p8g 9.9m 9d Jul 3] fair maiden at 3 yrs: no form in 2002. *R. J. Price*

ELJOHAR (IRE) 5 ch.h. Nashwan (USA) 135 – Mehthaaf (USA) 121 (Nureyev **89**
(USA) 131) [2002 96: 10.1m* 8m 8f⁵ Oct 4] strong, stocky horse: fairly useful performer:
very lightly raced: won maiden at Yarmouth in August: better at 1¼m than shorter: yet
to race on soft/heavy going, acts on any other: has worn crossed noseband/tongue tie.
J. H. M. Gosden

ELLA CARISA 3 b.f. Elmaamul (USA) 125 – Salty Girl (IRE) 70 (Scenic 128) [2002 **52**
57: 10f 14d 18d 16.2d⁵ 16.2g³ 16.2m 14.1g Oct 2] leggy filly: modest maiden: stays 2m:
raced mainly on good/good to soft going. *A. Charlton*

ELLA FALLS (IRE) 7 ch.m. Dancing Dissident (USA) 119 – Over Swing (FR) (Saint **43**
Cyrien (FR) 128) [2002 55: 21.6m⁵ Apr 22] leggy mare: poor handicapper: stays 2m: acts
on firm going, good to soft and fibresand: tried blinkered. *Mrs H. Dalton*

ELLAMYTE 2 b.f. (Apr 2) Elmaamul (USA) 125 – Deanta In Eirinn (Red Sunset 120) **75**
[2002 5.7d⁶ 6d³ 5m* 5m³ 5g 6.1m⁶ 6g³ 6s Oct 26] 2,000Y: leggy filly: half-sister to

several winners, including 2-y-o winners Welcome Sunset (5f in 1997, by Most Welcome) and Flowing Rio (6f in 2000, by First Trump): dam ran once at 2 yrs: fair performer: won minor event at Windsor in July despite wandering/flashing tail: good efforts after when third in nursery at York and sales race at Newmarket: should stay 7f: acts on good to firm and good to soft going. *H. Morrison*

EL LAYTH (IRE)   2 ch.c. (Feb 12) Hector Protector (USA) 124 – Rose of Shuaib (IRE) 68 (Caerleon (USA) 132) [2002 7m p7g² 7.5d* 7m a8f Nov 28] lengthy colt: first foal: dam, ran 4 times (should have stayed 1¼m), half-sister to useful winner up to 1m in Britain/UAE Man Howa: fair performer: won maiden at Beverley in August: ran poorly in nursery at Chester (left M. Jarvis after) and minor event at Nad Al Sheba last 2 starts: will stay 1¼m: acts on polytrack and good to soft going: hung markedly left on debut. *A. Smith, UAE*   **78**

ELLENDUNE GIRL   4 b.f. Mistertopogigo (IRE) 118 – Perfidy (FR) (Persian Bold 123) [2002 75: 5.1d 6m 5.1g² 5.7g 6m 5.1g Oct 16] quite good-topped filly: fair handicapper: was best at 5f/6f: acted on heavy and good to firm going, probably on fibresand: often slowly away: dead. *D. J. S. ffrench Davis*   **73**

ELLEN MOONEY   3 ch.f. Efisio 120 – Budby 72 (Rock City 120) [2002 78: 8s* 8g 10.5m⁴ 8d 8g⁶ 8.3s⁴ 8d⁴ 8.3g² 10.2g 8.2s 8s 8v Nov 8] workmanlike filly: poor walker: fairly useful performer: won minor event at Doncaster in March: barely stays 10.5f: acts on soft and good to firm going: sometimes slowly away: none too consistent. *B. Smart*   **83**

ELLENS ACADEMY (IRE)   7 b.g. Royal Academy (USA) 130 – Lady Ellen 67 (Horage 124) [2002 111: 5.2g⁵ 6m 6f⁶ 6m Jun 22] big, useful-looking gelding: impresses in appearance: smart at 6 yrs: useful form at best in 2002 (reportedly finished lame final start): best at 5f (given stiff track)/6f: acts on fibresand and firm going, probably on soft: tried blinkered earlier in career: sometimes slowly away/wanders. *E. J. Alston*   **103**

ELLENS LAD (IRE)   8 b.g. Polish Patriot (USA) 128 – Lady Ellen 67 (Horage 124) [2002 114: 5s⁵ 5.2g 6m 5d 6m 5d⁶ 5g² 6g 6g 5.6m Sep 11] sturdy, strong-quartered gelding: smart at 7 yrs: only useful on balance in 2002: best at 5f/easy 6f: probably acts on any going: tried blinkered, including last 3 starts: usually held up. *W. J. Musson*   **98**

ELLE ROYAL (IRE)   3 br.f. Ali-Royal (IRE) 127 – Silvretta (IRE) 73 (Tirol 127) [2002 71: 11.6g 12g 13.1g 10m 11.9d Jun 13] leggy, light-bodied filly: fair maiden at 2 yrs: little form in 2002. *T. P. McGovern*   **–**

ELLOVAMUL   2 b.f. (Apr 9) Elmaamul (USA) 125 – Multi-Sofft 30 (Northern State (USA) 91) [2002 7.1g p7g 7g 7g f8g³ f7s f7g f8g⁴ f8.5g* Dec 31] small, workmanlike filly: fifth foal: half-sister to winner around 1m (including at 2 yrs) Bold State (by Never So Bold) and a winner in Turkey by Magic Ring: dam, maiden who probably stayed 1¾m, out of Cheshire Oaks/Lancashire Oaks winner One Over Parr: modest performer: dead-heated for first in seller at Wolverhampton: should stay 1¼m: acts on fibresand: blinkered fifth to eighth starts. *I. A. Wood*   **54**

ELLPEEDEE   5 b.g. Wolfhound (USA) 126 – Kilvarnet 78 (Furry Glen 121) [2002 a6g a6g* a6g² a6g⁵ 5.1d 7m 5m⁴ 5m³ f6s 6m p7g Oct 16] quite attractive gelding: modest handicapper: won at Mijas in January: left M. Lambert in Spain after fourth start: effective at 5f to 1m: acts on sand and good to firm going, seemingly on soft: sometimes tongue tied in 2001: sold £500 in November. *P. Mitchell*   **50 a?**

ELLWAY HEIGHTS   5 b.g. Shirley Heights 130 – Amina 80 (Brigadier Gerard 144) [2002 61: 14.1d Apr 1] maiden handicapper: well held only 5-y-o start. *W. M. Brisbourne*   **–**

ELLWAY PROSPECT   2 ch.f. (May 25) Pivotal 124 – Littlemisstrouble (USA) (My Gallant (USA)) [2002 5g⁶ 5.7m 5d 8d Oct 21] sparely-made filly: seventh living foal: closely related to 7.5f/9f winner Polar Prospect (by Polar Falcon) and half-sister to 2 winners, including fairly useful 5.7f (at 2 yrs) and 1m winner Ogilia (by Bin Ajwaad): dam minor stakes winner up to 9f in USA: well held after modest form in maiden at Beverley on debut: should stay at least 6f. *G. A. Butler*   **62**

ELMHURST BOY   6 b.h. Merdon Melody 98 – Young Whip (Bold Owl 101) [2002 95: p10g* p10g² p10g⁶ 10g 8.1d 8m 10s⁴ 10d³ 8m Jun 19] good-topped horse: useful on all-weather, fairly useful on turf: won at Lingfield in January: several creditable efforts after, including behind Adiemus in handicap and listed race at same track next 2 starts: effective at 1m/1¼m: acts on polytrack and any turf going: often blinkered/visored earlier in career: carries head high, and sometimes fails to go through with effort. *S. Dow*   **90 a104**

EL MISTI   4 b.f. Elmaamul (USA) 125 – Sherrington 56 (Thatching 131) [2002 49: p7g⁴ p6g f6g p6g³ p5g³ p6g f8g 7m 6d 6m⁵ 8m⁵ 6m 7m⁶ 6.1m f6g Nov 25] quite good-topped filly: poor maiden handicapper: on downgrade: best at 5f to 7f: acts   **47 d**

on heavy going, good to firm and polytrack: sometimes slowly away: difficult ride. *M. D. I. Usher*

ELMUTABAKI 6 b.g. Unfuwain (USA) 131 – Bawaeth (USA) 72 (Blushing Groom (FR) 131) [2002 –: f16s f12s Jan 15] tall, lengthy gelding: unimpressive mover: smart at 3/4 yrs: little form since: tried blinkered/visored. *D. Nicholls* —

ELNAYRAH (USA) 2 b.f. (Feb 3) Danzig (USA) – Ruznama (USA) 105 (Forty Niner (USA)) [2002 6m⁴ Aug 25] third foal: dam, 7f (including at 2 yrs) and 1m winner who stayed 1¼m, out of Musidora winner and Oaks third Last Feather: well-backed favourite, shaped very well when 2½ lengths fourth of 9 to Medeena in maiden at Goodwood, slowly away and not given hard time having moved up going strongly: likely to do significantly better. *B. W. Hills* **75 P**

ELOQUENT SILENCE 2 ch.f. (Feb 22) Nashwan (USA) 135 – Flower Girl 108 (Pharly (FR) 130) [2002 7d p8g* Nov 27] leggy filly: seventh foal: half-sister to 3 winners, including fairly useful 1m winner Roaring Twenties (by Halling) and smart performer up to 14.6f Eco Friendly (by Sabrehill): dam 6f winner, including at 2 yrs: 16/1, much better effort in maidens when beating Toro Bravo by 1¼ lengths at Lingfield in November, dictating slow pace: should stay 1¼m: open to further improvement. *B. W. Hills* **72 p**

EL PEDRO 3 b.g. Piccolo 121 – Standard Rose 52 (Ile de Bourbon (USA) 133) [2002 p8g p8g⁵ f8.5g* p8g 11.6m 8.3s 7m 8m 8m 7d⁴ Oct 15] tall gelding: third living foal: half-brother to a winner in Germany by Interrex: dam 1¼m winner who stayed 2¼m: fair on all-weather, modest on turf: won maiden at Wolverhampton in March: should stay 1¼m: acts on fibresand, best effort on turf on good to soft ground. *M. R. Channon* **51 a65**

EL RAYMONDO 3 b.g. Night Shift (USA) – Alaraby (IRE) 77 (Caerleon (USA) 132) [2002 49: p8g p8g² f7g⁴ p7g⁴ 8.2d p7g³ 6g⁵ 7s p7g p7g 8g 7m p7g⁴ p7g⁶ p6g Dec 30] modest performer: won handicap at Lingfield in February: stays 1m: acts on polytrack: blinkered last 3 starts: usually tongue tied (reportedly had breathing problem fifth start). *M. Blanshard* **58**

ELSAAMRI (USA) 4 b. or br.g. Silver Hawk (USA) 123 – Muhbubh (USA) 108 (Blushing Groom (FR) 131) [2002 103: 12f⁶ Oct 2] quite good-topped gelding: useful performer, lightly raced: reportedly met with minor setback when sent to Dubai after final 3-y-o start: mid-division in handicap at Newmarket only run at 4 years: stays 1½m: acts on firm going, probably on soft: has worn crossed noseband: has edged right/looked bit awkward under pressure. *M. P. Tregoning* **95**

ELSIE B 2 gr.f. (Feb 28) First Trump 118 – Evening Falls 82 (Beveled (USA)) [2002 5m 5g 5d⁶ 5m f5g⁵ 6g f9.4g Dec 7] 4,500Y: small filly: fourth foal: half-sister to 3-y-o Ember Days and 7f (at 2 yrs) to 11f (in France) winner Chimney Dust (by Pelder): dam sprinter: little sign of ability: trained until final start by H. McWilliams. *P. Howling*

EL TALGO (IRE) 3 b.g. Common Grounds 118 – Lovely Me (IRE) 70 (Vision (USA)) [2002 58: f5g 6g 5.9s⁵ 6f 6g 6.1m 5.9g⁵ 5.9g 8.1d Aug 8] leggy gelding: poor maiden: should stay 7f: acts on soft going (no form in 2 outings on fibresand): tongue tied: looked very hard ride final start. *N. Tinkler* **49**

ELUCIDATE 3 ch.f. Elmaamul (USA) 125 – Speed To Lead (IRE) 90 (Darshaan 133) [2002 60: p8g p7g⁴ f7g⁵ f8.5g⁴ f9.4g⁶ 7g 10m 7g² 8g⁶ f8g f7g Nov 22] tall, angular filly: modest performer: left I. Wood after fifth start, C. Dwyer after ninth one: probably stays 8.5f: acts on good to firm going and all-weather. *C. R. Dore* **58**

ELUSIVE CITY (USA) 2 b.c. (Jan 29) Elusive Quality (USA) – Star of Paris (USA) (Dayjur (USA) 137) [2002 p6g*ᵈⁱˢ 6m*ᵈⁱˢ 6g* 6f³ Oct 3] **117**

At one stage, it looked as if Elusive City might be possessed of temperament and merit in equal measure. Winning performances in the Gerrard Investment Management Richmond Stakes at Goodwood in July and the Prix Morny Casinos Barriere at Deauville in August were spoilt by some decidedly recalcitrant behaviour. After making a winning debut in an eleven-runner maiden on the polytrack at Lingfield in July, when he beat Mullion comfortably by three lengths, Elusive City was coltish and had to be led by two handlers in the preliminaries at Goodwood, and then proved most reluctant to enter either the stalls or the winner's enclosure at Deauville. After such behaviour, connections organised a mock 'race day' for Elusive City at Newbury a fortnight before his final outing in the Middle Park Stakes at Newmarket in October. Further familiarisation with the starting stalls procedure and some additional general racecourse experience—he was also sent on a trip to Newmarket—seemed to benefit Elusive City as he gave no trouble when starting a well-supported 6/4 favourite for the Middle Park. He suffered his first defeat when third to Oasis Dream and Tomahawk, beaten a length and a half and a neck. That performance, cruising onto the heels of the leaders around halfway but then unable to quicken, still represents Elusive City's best form. He reportedly returned home with sore shins and a possible challenge for the Breeders' Cup came to nothing. Connections felt that 'the hill caught him out at Newmarket' and Elusive City is set to contest the Poule d'Essai des Poulains, rather than the Two Thousand Guineas.

Elusive City was stripped of both his victories in Britain following the discovery of the prohibited substance omeprazole in post-race samples; he had apparently been treated for stomach ulcers. Elusive City still appeared green in the Richmond Stakes but was soon travelling strongly under restraint after an awkward start and, eased towards the outside, quickened really well to lead just inside the final furlong and record an impressive success; Elusive City had three lengths to spare over Revenue, with Checkit a length further away in third and several other proven useful sorts further back, among them the first and second in the Norfolk Stakes, Baron's Pit and The Bonus King. Elusive City's performance on only his second outing—and first on turf—gave him a good chance in the six-runner Prix Morny. Elusive City's chief rival looked to be the French-trained filly Loving Kindness, favourite following impressive wins on both her starts, including in the Prix de Cabourg on her previous outing. Elusive City started second favourite and put up another convincing performance, albeit without being quite so impressive. The race evolved in similar fashion to Goodwood though, with the waited-with Elusive City enjoying a good run and coming through to lead just over a furlong out. He had to be driven out to beat Zafeen by three quarters of a length, with Loving Kindness two and a half lengths further back in third.

Elusive City's pattern performances came after the death of his owner Prince Ahmed Salman from a heart attack at the age of forty-three five days after Elusive City's debut. Salman was the driving force behind The Thoroughbred Corporation, though he had been involved as an individual owner before that. Hays, owned in partnership with Prince Yazid Saud, was his first pattern winner in the Mill Reef Stakes in 1981, and Lear Fan his first Group 1 winner in the Prix Jacques le Marois in 1984. Salman faded from the racing limelight for a decade before the establishment of The Thoroughbred Corporation in the mid-'nineties. High-profile successes with the likes of Oath in the 1999 Derby and with Royal Anthem, a runaway winner of the Juddmonte International later that season, were among the highlights in Britain. But it was in America that the new organisation made the biggest impact, with numerous Grade 1 winners including the leading three-year-old colts in each of the last two seasons, Point Given's successes in 2001, including the Preakness Stakes and Belmont Stakes, being followed by War Emblem's in the latest season, including the Kentucky Derby and the Preakness Stakes. Also, there

Prix Morny Casinos Barriere, Deauville—
Elusive City overcomes problems at the start to beat Zafeen (rail), Loving Kindness and Zinziberine

was Sharp Cat, successful seven times at the highest level, as well as three owned or part-owned Breeders' Cup winners, Jewel Princess in the 1996 Distaff, Anees in the 1999 Juvenile and Spain in the 2000 Distaff, the last-named retired in 2002 as the all-time leading money-earning female in North America. It was reported shortly after Salman's death that all his racing assets would be sold off, something quickly denied by representatives of The Thoroughbred Corporation, though the breeding side of the operation is to be scaled down as part of a long-term plan already in place. Elusive City and others in the same ownership are set to continue to race in the familiar silks of green and white stripes.

Elusive City (USA) (b.c. Jan 29, 2000)	Elusive Quality (USA) (b 1993)	Gone West (b 1984)	Mr Prospector / Secrettame
		Touch of Greatness (b 1986)	Hero's Honor / Ivory Wand
	Star of Paris (USA) (b 1995)	Dayjur (br 1987)	Danzig / Gold Beauty
		Liturgism (gr 1980)	Native Charger / Cult

Elusive City, who cost 250,000 dollars as a yearling, is from the first crop of Elusive Quality, a sprinter-miler in the States who won two Grade 3 handicaps as a five-year-old, including the Poker Handicap at Belmont, where he broke the world record for a mile on turf. He stood at a fee of only 10,000 dollars in 2002; he'll be standing at three times that fee in 2003. Elusive Quality's only other runner in Britain in 2002 was Nasij, a useful Ascot maiden winner who was third in the Princess Margaret Stakes and in the May Hill Stakes. Elusive Quality is a half-brother to the smart, speedy 1999 two-year-old Rossini (who failed to win at three) and comes from a very good family. Elusive City is the first foal of his unraced dam Star of Paris, a half-sister to the smart performers Young Senor, who won at up to a mile and a quarter in Britain, and Millions, a Grade 3 winner in the States who stayed eight and a half furlongs. Star of Paris is out of a winning half-sister to the triple US Grade 1 winner Coup de Fusil. Elusive City has been raced only on good going or firmer on turf, in addition to his debut on polytrack, the surface incidentally on which his trainer Gerard Butler also introduced Diadem and Challenge Stakes winner Nayyir. Elusive City is a strong, attractive colt—he really took the eye beforehand at Newmarket—and has the physical scope to train on. Provided he remains on his best behaviour, there is every reason to believe he will win more good races. Whether or not that includes the Two Thousand Guineas is a moot point. There are other candidates with stronger claims at present, and Elusive City is not sure to stay a mile anyway. Raced only at six furlongs so far, he has plenty of speed and could easily end up being campaigned back at sprint distances in the second part of his three-year-old career. *G. A. Butler*

ELVINGTON BOY 5 ch.g. Emarati (USA) 74 – Catherines Well 99 (Junius (USA) 124) [2002 84: 5m* 5f² 5f* 5m² 5m 6g 6m 5m² 5m Sep 7] quite good-topped gelding: fairly useful performer: won claimer at Ripon in April and handicap at York in May: barely stays easy 6f: acts on firm going, possibly not on soft: tried visored/tongue tied: has got upset in stall (reared leaving them final start): normally fast starter. *M. W. Easterby* **92**

ELWOOD BLUES (IRE) 3 b.g. Blues Traveller (IRE) 119 – Tolomena 61 (Tolomeo 127) [2002 –: p8g f5g⁶ f12g⁶ 11.9d 17.2d 12d Jul 11] angular gelding: little form: visored last 2 starts (took no interest final one). *S. C. Williams* **–**

EMARATI'S IMAGE 4 b.g. Emarati (USA) 74 – Choir's Image 53 (Lochnager 132) [2002 –: 6m 7.5g 5g 5s* 5m f5s Sep 5] big, good-topped gelding: poor performer, lightly raced: left W. Cunningham before winning handicap at Hamilton in August: best effort at 5f on soft going. *J. O'Reilly* **46**

EMBER DAYS 3 gr.f. Reprimand 122 – Evening Falls 82 (Beveled (USA)) [2002 67: 8.2d 8.3s⁵ 8.3s³ 8g 7.9g* 8.1d* 8d⁶ 9.2s Aug 20] tall, unfurnished filly: fair handicapper: won at Carlisle in June and Chepstow in July: not sure to stay beyond 1m: acts on soft going: wandered/carried head awkwardly penultimate start. *G. C. H. Chung* **76**

EMDAD (USA) 5 b. or br.g. El Gran Senor (USA) 136 – Gumbaru Etsu (USA) (Lear Fan (USA) 130) [2002 p8g Oct 9] $30,000F, IR 140,000Y: second foal: dam unraced: slowly away (carried head awkwardly) in maiden at Lingfield. *D. R. Loder* **–**

EMERALD FIRE   3 b.f. Pivotal 124 – Four-Legged Friend 101 (Aragon 118) [2002   **86**
73: 6d² 6f 6s³ 5g 6.1s⁶ 5v⁴ Nov 8] small, leggy filly: fairly useful handicapper, lightly
raced: effective at 5f (given bit of a test)/6f: seems best on good going or softer (acts on
heavy). *I. A. Balding*

EMERALD GLEN (IRE)   3 b.f. Inzar (USA) 112 – Million At Dawn (IRE) 63   **–**
(Fayruz 116) [2002 f7g 8m 9.2d Jul 25] 3,000Y: neat filly: fifth foal: half-sister to 6f/7f
winner Talaria (by Petardia): dam 2-y-o 5f winner (only season to race): slowly away and
always behind in sellers. *P. C. Haslam*

EMERALD MIST (IRE)   3 b.f. Sacrament 118 – Jade's Gem (Sulaafah (USA) 119)   **–**
[2002 –: 10.9f⁵ 11.7d 12.1d⁵ 12m 16.2g Aug 26] smallish, good-topped filly: little form.
G. B. Balding

EMERGING STAR (IRE)   2 b.g. (Apr 22) Desert Style (IRE) 121 – Feather Star   **74**
(Soviet Star (USA) 128) [2002 6g⁴ 6g 7.5d⁶ 8m⁵ Aug 31] IR 38,000Y: rather leggy gelding: third foal: half-brother to Irish 1999 2-y-o 7f winner Star of Windsor (by Woods of
Windsor) and a winner in Czech Republic by Environment Friend: dam unraced: fair
maiden: not knocked about last 2 starts: should stay 1m: best effort on good to soft
ground. *Mrs J. R. Ramsden*

EMIGRATE   3 b.f. Emarati (USA) 74 – Fly South (Polar Falcon (USA) 126) [2002 64:   **65 d**
6m⁶ p5g⁵ 6.1v f6s f6g⁴ 6g⁵ Oct 28] angular filly: fair maiden: below form after second
start: may prove best around 6f. *P. J. Makin*

EMILY DEE   3 b.f. Classic Cliche (IRE) 128 – Alpi Dora (Valiyar 129) [2002 59: p6g   **–**
5m 6g 7f 6.1v 8.5m 8g⁵ 7g Aug 7] quite good-topped filly: modest maiden at 2 yrs: little
form in 2002: blinkered last 3 starts. *J. M. Bradley*

EMINENT LADY   2 ch.f. (Feb 19) Pennekamp (USA) 130 – Femme Savante 89   **–**
(Glenstal (USA) 118) [2002 5d Aug 14] 26,000Y: third foal: half-sister to 3-y-o Seeking
The Sun and 4-y-o So Sober: dam 2-y-o 6f winner: 14/1, always behind in maiden at
Sandown. *C. F. Wall*

EMINENTLY   3 b.g. Deploy 131 – Lady Clementine 68 (He Loves Me 120) [2002 63:   **63**
11.9d² Jul 19] modest maiden: stayed 1½m: acted on good to soft going, probably on
firm: dead. *R. M. Beckett*

E MINOR (IRE)   3 b.f. Blushing Flame (USA) 109 – Watch The Clock 93 (Mtoto   **78**
134) [2002 54: 11.9d* 11.6m² p12g³ 16.2d² p16g³ p16g* 14f⁶ 12d p13g² p12g Nov 27]   **a86**
rather leggy, lengthy filly: fairly useful handicapper on all-weather, fair on turf: won at
Brighton in June and Lingfield in September: stays 2m: acts on good to firm ground, good
to soft and polytrack: held up: joined T. Wall. *G. A. Butler*

EMLEY   6 b.m. Safawan 118 – Bit of A State 68 (Free State 125) [2002 8f 12m f9.4g   **–**
8m 5m Aug 24] no longer of any account. *N. Wilson*

EMMERVALE   3 b.f. Emarati (USA) 74 – Raintree Venture (Good Times (ITY)) [2002   **62**
63: 6m 7m⁴ 7m² 6.1m Sep 20] angular, unfurnished filly: modest maiden: stays 7f, at least
with emphasis on speed: acts on soft and good to firm going. *J. G. Portman*

EMPEROR OF DREAMS   3 b.c. Emperor Jones (USA) 119 – Girl of My Dreams   **–**
(IRE) 51 (Marju (IRE) 127) [2002 49: f7g p6g 7m Apr 5] rather lengthy, quite attractive
colt: poor maiden at 2 yrs: little form in 2002: blinkered final start: sent to Spain.
R. Hannon

EMPEROR'S CASTLE   3 b.g. Emperor Jones (USA) 119 – Riyoom (USA) 83   **–**
(Vaguely Noble 140) [2002 –: 11.5m Sep 17] no form. *P. C. Haslam*

EMPERORS LOT   2 b.f. (May 6) Emperor Jones (USA) 119 – Westering 54 (Auction   **–**
Ring (USA) 123) [2002 8s Oct 25] 800F: workmanlike filly: third foal: half-sister to
5-y-o Inchinnan: dam maiden: 100/1 and burly, well beaten in maiden at Doncaster.
M. Wellings

EMPEROR STAR   2 b.f. (Feb 26) Emperor Jones (USA) 119 – Blu Tamantara (USA)   **67**
(Miswaki (USA) 124) [2002 p8g⁵ p10g Dec 3] first foal: dam Italian 7f winner: much
better effort in maidens at Lingfield (fair form) when fifth to Face The Storm: should stay
1¼m. *T. G. Mills*

EMPEROR'S WELL   3 ch.g. First Trump 118 – Catherines Well 99 (Junius (USA)   **48**
124) [2002 63: 5.1d 5m⁵ 5s 5m Jul 7] well-made gelding: poor maiden at 3 yrs: raced
only at 5f: acts on good to firm going: visored final start: sometimes slowly away.
M. W. Easterby

EMPIRE PARK   7 b.g. Tragic Role (USA) – Millaine 69 (Formidable (USA) 125)   **60**
[2002 12m 18d Jul 4] leggy, workmanlike gelding: lightly raced on Flat nowadays,
modest form in 2002: probably stays 1¾m: acts on good to firm going, probably on soft:
sometimes blinkered: fair hurdler. *C. R. Egerton*

EMPRESS ALICE   5 b.m. Petoski 135 – Blue Empress (Blue Cashmere 129) [2002   **–**
–: 6g Oct 28] no form. *Dr P. Pritchard*

EMPRESS JOSEPHINE   2 b.f. (Apr 24) Emperor Jones (USA) 119 – Valmaranda   **55**
(USA) (Sir Ivor 135) [2002 p5g p5g⁶ Nov 23] 1,000Y: fifth reported living foal: half-
sister to 3-y-o Kingston Game: dam, Irish 1½m winner at 4 yrs, also successful over
hurdles: better effort in Lingfield maidens (modest form) when sixth to Aventura: may
prove best at 5f. *J. R. Jenkins*

EMPRESS OF AUSTRIA (USA)   4 ch.f. Foxhound (USA) 103 – Falabella (Steel   **–**
Heart 128) [2002 p8g f5g f7g Mar 2] disappointing maiden. *Miss Gay Kelleway*

EMRAN (USA)   2 b.c. (Apr 6) Silver Hawk (USA) 123 – Indihash (USA) 81 (Gulch   **88 p**
(USA)) [2002 7.1m⁶ 7m² 7.2s* Oct 14] rather lengthy, good-topped colt: second foal:
dam, 2-y-o 7f winner, out of smart 6f/7f winner Linda's Magic: fairly useful form in
maidens, winning at Ayr comfortably by 1¼ lengths from Forest Magic: should be suited
by at least 1m: acts on soft and good to firm ground: probably capable of better still.
E. A. L. Dunlop

EMSBOY   3 b.g. Colonel Collins (USA) 122 – Loxley's Girl (IRE) 39 (Lahib (USA)   **–**
129) [2002 f9.4g p7g p12g Nov 13] first foal: dam maiden who stayed 1m: tailed off in
maidens, first 2 for M. Gingell: tried blinkered. *C. Drew*

ENCHANTED   3 b.f. Magic Ring (IRE) 115 – Snugfit Annie 49 (Midyan (USA) 124)   **93**
[2002 84: 7m³ 7m* 7m⁵ 7m⁶ 7m Sep 28] quite good-topped filly: fairly useful performer:
won handicap at Newmarket (edged left) in August: at least respectable efforts after: will
probably stay 1m: raced only on good/good to firm going. *G. G. Margarson*

ENCORE ROYALE   2 b.f. (Apr 1) Royal Applause 124 – Verbena (IRE) (Don't   **56 p**
Forget Me 127) [2002 6g⁶ Aug 7] 18,500Y: second foal: dam French 11f winner: 9/1, 5
lengths sixth of 15 to Fiveoclock Express in maiden at Leicester, no extra final 1f: should
improve. *P. W. Harris*

ENCOUNTER   6 br.g. Primo Dominie 121 – Dancing Spirit (IRE) 72 (Ahonoora 122)   **61**
[2002 68, a–: 7v 8f 8m 7.1m* 7.1m⁴ 7.2g 7.5g⁶ 7g 7m 7g⁴ 7g⁴ 8s 7.5d 7m 8m³ 7.5m 10m   **a–**
10g² Oct 24] lengthy gelding: modest handicapper: won at Musselburgh in May: effective
at 7f to easy 1¼m: probably acts on any turf going, little form on fibresand: sometimes
slowly away: usually held up. *J. Hetherton*

END OF AN ERROR   3 b.f. Charmer 123 – Needwood Poppy 29 (Rolfe (USA) 77)   **–**
[2002 54, a–: f8s⁶ 7g 7d 11.6m⁵ 10g 12m 13.8f 12.1m Sep 24] leggy, close-coupled filly:
modest at 2 yrs: little form in 2002. *M. C. Chapman*

ENDURANCE   3 b.c. Dancing Spree (USA) – Madam Taylor 81 (Free State 125) [2002   **–**
f7g⁵ 7.1g 7.1m f7g 6.1f 6d 8.1s 7m 5.9g f6g⁶ 7.5m Aug 25] 800 2-y-o: workmanlike
colt: sixth living foal: dam 5f (at 2 yrs) to 1½m winner: little form: tried blinkered.
M. Mullineaux

ENDURING FREEDOM   2 b.f. (Feb 25) In The Wings 128 – Feather Bride (IRE)   **74**
(Groom Dancer (USA) 128) [2002 7.5g⁴ 8d³ Sep 29] 21,000Y: fourth foal: half-sister to 3
winners, including 3-y-o Millennium Dragon and fairly useful 1m winner Bless The
Bride (by Darshaan): dam, French 10.5f winner, from family of Breeders' Cup Turf
winner Kotashaan: fair form in frame in newcomers race and minor event at Milan: will
be suited by 1¼m+. *M. L. W. Bell*

EN FIN (FR)   3 b.f. Loup Solitaire (USA) 117 – Isola d'Elba (USA) (Diesis 133) [2002   **59**
8.3m⁵ 8g 8.3d⁵ Oct 14] 140,000 francs Y: second foal: half-sister to French 1m winner
(including at 2 yrs) Loi Martiale (by Homme de Loi): dam, French 9.5f winner (including
at 2 yrs), half-sister to smart French performer up to 9f Signe Divin: modest form in
maidens, off 5 months before final start: will stay at least 1¼m. *J. R. Fanshawe*

ENGULFED (USA)   2 b.f. (Mar 26) Gulch (USA) – Storm Dove (USA) 108 (Storm   **72**
Bird (CAN) 134) [2002 p8g³ f7g⁶ Dec 31] 5,000 2-y-o: fifth foal: closely related to 4-y-o
Good Standing: dam, 6f (at 2 yrs) and 7f winner, out of smart French performer up to
1¼m Daeltown: much better effort in maidens when 2¼ lengths third of 12 to Made In
Japan at Lingfield (slowly away and green): tended to hang and found little at
Wolverhampton later in December. *W. Jarvis*

ENJOY THE BUZZ   3 b.c. Prince of Birds (USA) 121 – Abaklea (IRE) (Doyoun   –
124) [2002 57: 8m f8.5g f7g 8.1m⁶ Jul 20] small, sturdy colt: little form. *J. A. Pickering*

ENSEMBLE   2 b.c. (Feb 19) Polish Precedent (USA) 131 – Full Orchestra 83 (Shirley   –
Heights 130) [2002 5m 6m 7d Aug 23] 13,000Y: strong, useful-looking colt: half-brother
to several winners, including useful 6f (at 2 yrs) and 9f winner Rudimental (by Rudimentary) and fairly useful 1½m winner Anthem (by Saddlers' Hall): dam 1¼m winner:
well held, including in seller. *M. W. Easterby*

ENTRAP (USA)   3 b.f. Phone Trick (USA) – Mystic Lure 70 (Green Desert (USA)   **106**
127) [2002 89: 6m* 6m² 6f* Jun 24] big, rangy filly: useful performer: won minor events
at Kempton (beat Bright Edge by 3 lengths) in May and Yarmouth (beat Simianna by ½
length) in June: good neck second to Purple Haze in similar race at Leicester in between,
bit slowly away: suffered injury to near-hind ankle after Yarmouth: best form at 6f: raced
only on good going or firmer: has idled. *W. J. Haggas*

ENVIOUS   3 ch.g. Hernando (FR) 127 – Prima Verde 81 (Leading Counsel (USA) 122)   **63**
[2002 62: 10.1g⁴ 10g³ May 31] strong, lengthy gelding: modest maiden: stays 1¼m:
visored (raced freely) final start. *R. Allan*

ENVIRO NEWS   4 b.c. Contract Law (USA) 108 – Tina Meena Lisa 38 (Kala Shikari   –
125) [2002 8.5m 8f⁶ 7.5g 8m 7.6f 7.2d 10.1m Aug 16] leggy colt: second reported foal:
dam, maiden, stayed 1½m: showed signs of some ability: dead. *M. Mullineaux*

ENVIRONMENTALIST   3 b.c. Danehill (USA) 126 – Way O'Gold (USA) (Slew   **72**
O' Gold (USA)) [2002 8m⁵ p8g² 10s Oct 26] 220,000Y: quite good-topped colt: has a
quick action: first foal: dam, French maiden, half-sister to 4-y-o Crystal Castle: fair
form in maidens first 2 starts (5½ months apart): should stay 1¼m: edged left on debut.
J. H. M. Gosden

ENVIRONMENT AUDIT   3 ch.g. Kris 135 – Bold And Beautiful 105 (Bold Lad   **84**
(IRE) 133) [2002 78p: 10.3f⁵ 12f² 10d³ 10.2d² 10s* 12g 11.8g Oct 14] rather leggy
gelding: fairly useful performer: left B. Hills 19,000 gns before winning maiden at
Pontefract in July: effective at 1¼m/1½m: yet to race on heavy going, acts on any other:
has started slowly. *J. R. Jenkins*

EOZ (IRE)   2 b.f. (Apr 22) Sadler's Wells (USA) 132 – Greek Moon (IRE) (Shirley   **68 p**
Heights 130) [2002 8g⁵ 7d Nov 2] IR 500,000Y: good-bodied filly: second foal: dam
unraced daughter of smart 1¼m/1½m winner Gay Hellene from family of Pilsudski:
better effort in maidens (fair form) when seventh of 19 to Goodness Gracious at Newmarket on second start: should be suited by 1¼m+. *M. A. Jarvis*

EPHESUS   2 b.c. (Jan 25) Efisio 120 – Composition 82 (Wolfhound (USA) 126) [2002   **75 p**
p7g⁵ Oct 9] 29,000Y: first foal: dam, 2-y-o 6f winner, out of sister to smart sprinter Jester:
12/1 and green, fifth of 15 to Texas Hill in maiden at Lingfield, keeping on after slow
start: should improve. *J. Noseda*

EPICENTRE (USA)   3 b.c. Kris S (USA) – Carya (USA) (Northern Dancer) [2002   **101**
89p: 10.2g* 11m² 9.9m* 12g² 10f³ Jul 28] quite attractive colt: useful performer: won
maiden at Bath (made virtually all, drifting right and giving odd flick of tail) in April and
handicap at Goodwood (beat Harnour by neck) in June: in frame other starts, including
when second in handicap at Newbury (behind Shagraan) and minor event at Ascot
(behind Highest, 3 ran): should prove better at 1½m than shorter: raced only on good
going or firmer: joined R. Frankel in USA. *J. H. M. Gosden*

EPITOME (IRE)   3 b.f. Nashwan (USA) 135 – Proskona (USA) 127 (Mr Prospector   **71**
(USA)) [2002 8f⁵ 8.2x³ p12g² Nov 13] lengthy filly: half-sister to several winners abroad,
including useful French 1m (including at 2 yrs) winner Calista (by Caerleon) and to
grandam of 3-y-o Act One: dam, high-class French 6f/7f performer, half-sister to dam
of Hector Protector and Bosra Sham from family of Lammtarra: fair form in maidens
(reportedly injured on debut): stays 1½m: acts on polytrack and heavy ground.
L. M. Cumani

EQUERRY (USA)   4 b. or br.c. St Jovite (USA) 135 – Colour Chart (USA) 122 (Mr   **120**
Prospector (USA)) [2002 119p: 10d* 10d³ 10s⁴ 10m Oct 19] big, good-topped colt: very
smart performer, lightly raced: made all in La Coupe at Longchamp (beat Sensible by ¾
length) in June: tongue tied, creditable 5 lengths third of 5 to Hawk Wing in Eclipse
Stakes at Sandown next start: well below form last 2, in Grosser Dalmayr-Preis at Munich
and Champion Stakes at Newmarket (blinkered): should stay 1½m: acts on good to firm
and good to soft ground. usually leads. *Saeed bin Suroor*

ERIC LE BEAU (IRE)   3 ch.c. Great Commotion (USA) 123 – Mirmande 66 (Kris   **99**
135) [2002 81p: 8s* 8.1d* 8.1d 8m 10g 9.2s 10d³ 9s⁴ Oct 26] rather leggy, quite good-

topped colt: unimpressive mover: useful performer: won maiden at Leicester in March
and minor event at Sandown in April: some creditable efforts in handicaps after, fourth to
Dumaran at Newbury final start: stays 1¼m: acts on soft going: free-going sort: sold
45,000 gns. *G. C. Bravery*

ERRACHT 4 gr.f. Emarati (USA) 74 – Port Na Blath (On Your Mark 125) [2002 54+: **64**
f6g⁵ p5g f6g f5g⁶ f6g² f6g 5.1d 6g 5.1g² 5g* 5d² 5m⁶ f5s 5.1g 5.1g⁴ f6g f6s Dec 26] **a54**
lengthy filly: modest handicapper: won ladies race at Leicester in August: effective at
5f/6f: acts on all-weather, good to firm and heavy going: has carried head awkwardly.
K. R. Burke

ERRO CODIGO 7 b.g. Formidable (USA) 125 – Home Wrecker (DEN) (Affiliation **57**
Order (USA) 89) [2002 64?: 6f² 6m⁶ 5g 5m 6d Aug 3] strong, good-topped gelding:
modest performer: best at 6f/7f: acts on fibresand and any turf going: visored once at 3
yrs: none too consistent. *F. P. Murtagh*

ERSAAL (USA) 2 ch.c. (Mar 14) Gulch (USA) – Madame Secretary (USA) (Secre- **70**
tariat (USA)) [2002 8m³ 8m⁴ 8g⁶ Oct 24] sturdy colt: closely related to 2 winners, notably
smart 7f/1m (latter Poule d'Essai des Pouliches) winner Ta Rih (by Mr Prospector), and
half-brother to several winners, including useful 6f (including at 2 yrs) and 1m winner
Tabdea (by Topsider): dam, 1m winner in USA, half-sister to useful stayer Zero Watt: fair
form in maidens, in frame at Newcastle and Brighton: raced only at 1m on good/good to
firm ground. *E. A. L. Dunlop*

ERUPT 9 b.g. Beveled (USA) – Sparklingsovereign 53 (Sparkler 130) [2002 52§, a–§: **56 §**
f8g⁶ 8v 8.5m 10m⁴ 10.1s⁵ 10.1m 8g³ 9.9m⁶ 9.1s* Oct 15] plain, leggy gelding: modest **a– §**
performer: won seller at Ayr in October: stays 1¼m: acts on any turf going and fibresand:
sometimes blinkered/visored/tongue tied: sometimes slowly away: moody. *M. Brittain*

ESATTO 3 b.g. Puissance 110 – Stoneydale 83 (Tickled Pink 114) [2002 67, a60: p6g **90**
f5s⁵ f5g⁶ p5g⁵ f5g⁴ f5g 6g 5g³ 6d³ 5s² 5g⁴ 5.3m* 5m* 6d* 5.3m* 5m³ 6g Sep 20] big,
quite good-topped gelding: fairly useful handicapper: left M. Polglase after sixth outing:
much improved in August, winning at Brighton (twice), Carlisle and Ripon, all within 10
days: acts on firm going, soft and all-weather: visored/blinkered first 6 starts:
usually tongue tied: sometimes slowly away: has edged right. *R. Wilman*

ESCALADE 5 b.g. Green Desert (USA) 127 – Sans Escale (USA) (Diesis 133) [2002 **76**
78: f8.5g 8.5g* 10d⁴ 8.9d 9.2g⁴ 8.5g⁵ 8d⁶ 9m 7.9m 8.1f 9g⁵ 10s² 9d² 9s³ f12f⁵ p10g f9.4s² **a63**
f9.4g⁴ p10g² Dec 21] small, compact gelding: fair performer: won minor event at Epsom
in April: effective at 8.5f to 1¼m: acts on any turf going and fibresand: has worn cheekpieces: has found little/wandered, and probably needs exaggerated waiting tactics.
W. M. Brisbourne

ESCAYOLA (IRE) 2 b.g. (Mar 2) Revoque (IRE) 122 – First Fling (IRE) 63 (Last **62**
Tycoon 131) [2002 6s⁶ 6d f6g⁶ Nov 18] 44,000F, IR 40,000Y: good-topped gelding:
half-brother to 2 winners abroad, including Italian 9f/1¼m winner Limoncella (by Most
Welcome): dam, 1½m seller winner, half-sister to smart French middle-distance fillies
Premier Amour and Fleur d'Oranger: modest maiden: best effort on debut: should be
suited by 1m+: gelded after final start. *W. J. Haggas*

ESCENICA (IRE) 3 b.f. Charnwood Forest (IRE) 125 – Scenic Spirit (IRE) (Scenic **?**
128) [2002 76p: 8g³ 10d Oct 21] leggy, quite good-topped filly: showed promise at 2 yrs:
below form both 3-y-o starts: should stay 1¼m: sold 3,500 gns. *C. F. Wall*

ESCORT 6 b.g. Most Welcome 131 – Benazir 91 (High Top 131) [2002 –: 16m⁶ Jun **–**
24] strong, sturdy gelding: fairly useful handicapper at 3 yrs: well held all 3 Flat outings
since. *W. Clay*

ESENIN 3 b.g. Danehill (USA) 126 – Boojum 101 (Mujtahid (USA) 118) [2002 94: **79 §**
7m⁶ 6g 6f 6g 6m 6d 6g³ 7m 5.3m⁵ 6m 5f 6m Oct 7] strong, lengthy gelding: fairly useful
winner at 2 yrs: just fair at best in 2002: should stay 7f: blinkered (slowly away) sixth
outing: tricky ride and can't be trusted: sold 3,000 gns and gelded. *N. A. Callaghan*

ESGRIMA (IRE) 3 b.f. Sadler's Wells (USA) 132 – Lavinia Fontana (IRE) 116 **–**
(Sharpo 132) [2002 7g 9d May 23] second foal: half-sister to useful 2000 2-y-o 6f winner
Oreana (by Anabaa): dam won up to 7f, notably Haydock Park Sprint Cup: never
dangerous in maidens at Kempton and Goodwood. *J. L. Dunlop*

ESHER COMMON (IRE) 4 b.g. Common Grounds 118 – Alsahah (IRE) (Unfuwain **75**
(USA) 131) [2002 92: 7s* 8m² 10m³ 11.6s² 12.1m f12g² Jul 11] tall, good-topped
gelding: fair performer: won seller at Leicester in March: stays 11.6f: acts on heavy and
good to firm going: visored/tongue tied second start: no easy ride (races freely/carries
head high): sold £6,200. *D. E. Cantillon*

ESLIGIER (IRE)   3 ch.f. Sabrehill (USA) 120 – Norbella (Nordico (USA)) [2002   **85**
87+: 5.1f⁵ 6.1d 5.2d⁶ May 29] good-topped filly: fairly useful performer: probably best at
5f: acts on firm and good to soft ground, shaped well on fibresand: races prominently.
B. A. McMahon

ESLOOB (USA)   3 b.f. Diesis 133 – Roseate Tern 123 (Blakeney 126) [2002 104p: **106**
10m* 12s 10.1g* 12g⁶ Jul 20] smallish, sturdy filly: has a fluent, slightly round action:
useful performer: won listed races at Newmarket (by length from Disco Volante) in May
and Newcastle (by ½ length from Lady High Havens, made most in blinkers) in June:
seemed to lose interest when in rear in Oaks at Epsom in between and ran poorly in visor
final start: stayed 1¼m: unraced on heavy going, acted on any other: possibly temperamental: to visit Sadler's Wells. *M. P. Tregoning*

ESPADA (IRE)   6 b.g. Mukaddamah (USA) 125 – Folk Song (CAN) (The Minstrel   **94**
(CAN) 135) [2002 81: 8s 7v 7g² 6m² 8f⁴ 7m* 7g* 7m 7g* 7m 7.6g⁴ 6g Sep 20] strong,
smallish gelding: fairly useful handicapper: won at Catterick (twice) and Chester (beat
Young Rosein 2 lengths) between May and July: effective at 6f (given test) to 1m: acts on
any going: visored once: has raced freely/hung left/found little: sold 17,000 gns, and
joined J. Osborne. *J. A. Glover*

ESPERANCE (IRE)   2 ch.g. (Feb 8) Bluebird (USA) 125 – Dioscorea (IRE) (Pharly   **73**
(FR) 130) [2002 8g 7s³ Oct 25] 48,000F, 50,000Y: good-topped gelding: first foal: dam
unraced half-sister to useful French 1m winner Dirca: better effort in maidens (fair form)
when 10½ lengths third to Barrissimo at Doncaster, taking good hold: gelded after: likely
to prove best up to 1m. *M. H. Tompkins*

ESPRESSO TIME (IRE)   2 b.g. (Apr 30) Danetime (IRE) 121 – Cappuchino (IRE)   **70 d**
59 (Roi Danzig (USA)) [2002 5g³ 5.2s⁴ 5.7m² 6m 6.1g 6f 7g 8g Oct 24] 26,000Y: leggy,
quite good-topped gelding: fifth foal: half-brother to useful 1999 2-y-o 7f winner Blue
Bolivar (by Blues Traveller) and 4-y-o Cayman Expresso: dam 7f winner: fair maiden:
below form after third start: should stay 7f: acts on soft and good to firm going: sold 8,500
gns, and gelded. *R. Hannon*

ESPRIT D'ARTISTE (IRE)   3 ch.g. Selkirk (USA) 129 – Fracci (Raise A Cup   **63**
(USA)) [2002 65p: 10f⁵ 10d⁴ 12.1g Jun 12] big, rangy gelding: modest maiden: stays
1¼m: yet to race on heavy going, acts on any other: blinkered final start: sold 4,500 gns.
C. E. Brittain

ESSAY BABY (FR)   2 b.f. (May 6) Saumarez 132 – Easter Baby (Derrylin 115) [2002   **57**
7.1g⁶ 7g⁷ 8s Oct 26] half-sister to 2m winner Kintbury (by Kylian): dam, winning
hurdler, little form on Flat: modest maiden: should be suited by 1¼m+: slowly away first
2 starts. *P. D. Cundell*

ESSENCE OF DUBAI (USA)   3 br.c. Pulpit (USA) 117 – Epitome (USA) (Summing   **118**
(USA)) [2002 112: a8f* a10f* a10f a12f⁶ a9f³ a9f² a9f* Sep 21] $2,300,000Y: half-
brother to several winners, including minor stakes sprint winner Danjur (by Dayjur) and
smart USA 5f to 1m winner Faltaat (by Mr Prospector): dam won Breeders' Cup Juvenile
Fillies: smart performer: trained by E. Harty in USA at 2 yrs: successful at Nad Al Sheba
in UAE 2000 Guineas (by nose from Firebreak) in February and UAE Derby (by ½ length
from Total Impact, led close home) in March and at Louisiana Downs in Grade 2 Super
Derby (beat Walk In The Snow by 3½ lengths, made all) in September: below form in
Kentucky Derby at Churchill Downs and Belmont Stakes third and fourth starts: stays
1¼m, possibly not 1½m: raced only on dirt: blinkered/visored: has been tongue tied.
Saeed bin Suroor

ESSEQUIBO (IRE)   2 b.g. (Apr 7) Spectrum (IRE) 126 – Far From Home 73 (Habitat   **58**
134) [2002 7d f8.5s⁶ f7g² f8.5g³ Dec 31] IR 30,000Y: tall gelding: has scope: seventh
foal: half-brother to 3 winners, including useful Irish UAE 6f/7.8f winner Poker-B (by
Shalford) and 1999 2-y-o 6f winner Rhode Island (by Doyoun): dam 6f winner: modest
maiden: ran in sellers last 3 starts (blinkered last 2): barely stays 8.5f. *B. J. Meehan*

ESSEX STREET (IRE)   5 b.g. Dolphin Street (FR) 125 – Filet Mignon (USA)   **50**
(Topsider (USA)) [2002 49: 7d 6s 5m³ 6s² 5m 7m 5f⁵ 7g⁵ 5s 5.5s f5g⁴ f6s⁵ Dec 26]
modest maiden: trained by J. Mulhern in Ireland until before last 2 starts: stays 7f: acts on
fibresand, soft and good to firm going: often blinkered/visored. *D. Shaw*

ESSNAAD (USA)   2 b.c. (Mar 25) Swain (IRE) 134 – Shfoug (USA) 106 (Sheikh   **79 p**
Albadou 128) [2002 7m⁶ 8g⁵ Oct 18] first foal: dam 7f (at 2 yrs) to 10.5f winner: fair form
in listed race at Newbury (last of 6) and maiden at Newmarket (settled better, fifth of 16)
2 months apart: will be suited by 1¼m+: probably capable of better. *B. W. Hills*

ESTABELLA (IRE) 5 ch.m. Mujtahid (USA) 118 – Lady In Green (Shareef Dancer —
(USA) 135) [2002 52: 11.8d 14.1d 11.8s Oct 28] fair handicapper at best: well held in
2002. *M. Wellings*

ESTABLISHED 5 gr.g. Not In Doubt (USA) 101 – Copper Trader 53 (Faustus (USA) **49**
118) [2002 51, a–: p16g f16.2g⁵ f14.8g* f12g² f14.8g* f16.2g⁶ f16.2g⁶ f16.2g² f14g
f16g⁴ f14.8g³ 21.6m* 16.2g 11.9g 17.1m 14.1g⁶ 18f 18d 16.4d f14.8s⁶ Dec 13] smallish,
strong gelding: poor performer: won sellers at Wolverhampton in January and February
and handicap at Pontefract in April, stays 21f: acts on firm, good to soft going and all-
weather: tried blinkered: has been reluctant stall/raced lazily. *J. R. Best*

ESTABLISHMENT 5 b.g. Muhtarram (USA) 125 – Uncharted Waters 68 (Celestial **88**
Storm (USA) 132) [2002 85, a76: 18s 12m³ 13.9f 14m⁵ 20m² 16.2m² 16.2m⁴ 16.1d⁵ **a–**
16.2g 18m⁶ 16.5v Nov 9] smallish, workmanlike gelding: fairly useful handicapper on
turf: mostly creditable efforts in 2002, including when second at Ascot twice in summer
(behind Riyadh in Ascot Stakes then Mana d'Argent): effective at 1½m to 2½m: acts on
polytrack, firm and soft going (well beaten on heavy): blinkered (below form) once: has
run well sweating: sometimes races freely (usually held up). *C. A. Cyzer*

ESTEBAN 2 b.g. (Apr 16) Groom Dancer (USA) 128 – Ellie Ardensky 100 (Slip **57 p**
Anchor 136) [2002 8v f7g Nov 26] 26,000Y: tall, unfurnished gelding: third foal: half-
brother to 4-y-o Pole Star : dam, 9f/1¼m winner, closely related to smart performer up to
1½m Lady Shipley out of Lowther Stakes winner Circus Ring: better effort in maidens
(modest form) when seventh to Surdoue at Southwell second start, never dangerous: not
not knocked about: should be suited by 1m+: capable of better still. *J. J. Quinn*

ESTEEMED MASTER (USA) 3 b.c. Mark of Esteem (IRE) 137 – Jasminola (FR) **86**
(Seattle Dancer (USA) 119) [2002 87: 10m⁶ 12.3f⁴ 11m⁶ 12m³ 14m³ Jun 30] sturdy,
close-coupled colt: fairly useful performer: stays 1¾m: yet to race on heavy going, acts
on any other: blinkered/visored 5 of last 7 starts: has hung: lazy but consistent: sold
22,000 gns. *G. A. Butler*

ESTILO 2 b.g. (Mar 15) Deploy 131 – Vilcabamba (USA) (Green Dancer (USA) 132) —
[2002 7m 7d 7.6m Aug 21] second foal: dam won at 9f in French Provinces: well held in
maidens. *R. M. Flower*

ESTIMATE 2 b.f. (Apr 18) Mark of Esteem (IRE) 137 – Mistle Thrush (USA) 90 **82 p**
(Storm Bird (CAN) 134) [2002 7.1m³ Sep 16] tall, unfurnished filly: has scope: fourth
foal: half-sister to smart 1¼m and 14.6f (Park Hill Stakes) winner Mistle Song (by
Nashwan): dam, 1¼m winner, out of half-sister to dam of Kentucky Derby and Belmont
Stakes winner Thunder Gulch: 25/1, 3 lengths third of 14 to Rainbow Queen in maiden at
Warwick, always close up: should stay 1¼m: should improve. *C. E. Brittain*

ESTIMATION 2 b.f. (Mar 11) Mark of Esteem (IRE) 137 – Mohican Girl 112 (Dancing **56**
Brave (USA) 140) [2002 p6g⁶ Jun 1] fourth foal: half-sister to 7.6f to 8.5f winner The
Prince (by Machiavellian) and 4-y-o Fille Genereux: dam, winner up to 11f, half-sister to
Yorkshire Oaks winners Sally Brown and Untold: 16/1, sixth of 10 in Lingfield maiden,
late headway after slow start: should stay at least 1m. *R. M. H. Cowell*

ESTOMAQUE 3 br.g. Mark of Esteem (IRE) 137 – Allespagne (USA) (Trempolino **40**
(USA) 135) [2002 –: p7g 7m 10f 14.1f 12d 12m⁵ 16.2g 10m 11.5m 13.8f⁵ Sep 21]
smallish, close-coupled gelding: poor maiden: seems to stay 2m: blinkered penultimate
start: sold 3,500 gns, sent to Italy. *S. C. Williams*

ESTRELLA LEVANTE 2 ch.c. (Feb 16) Abou Zouz (USA) 109 – Star of Modena **75**
(IRE) (Waajib 121) [2002 7.1m⁴ 8.1g⁶ p5g⁴ Nov 13] 4,000Y, 12,000 2-y-o: second foal:
dam Italian 7f (at 2 yrs) to 1½m winner: fair form in maidens/minor event: will probably
stay 1¼m. *G. L. Moore*

ESTUARY (USA) 7 ch.g. Riverman (USA) 131 – Ocean Ballad 104 (Grundy 137) —
[2002 56, a64: p8g Jan 8] big, workmanlike gelding: modest performer at 6 yrs: well held
only start in 2002: tried tongue tied. *Ms A. E. Embiricos*

ETERNAL BLOOM 4 b.f. Reprimand 122 – Forever Roses 70 (Forzando 122) —
[2002 45: f6s⁶ 6d⁵ f6g Nov 25] maiden: well held in 2002. *M. Brittain*

ETERNAL SPRING (IRE) 5 b.g. Persian Bold 123 – Emerald Waters (Kings Lake **98**
(USA) 133) [2002 107: 11.8s⁵ Oct 28] close-coupled, quite good-topped gelding: useful
performer: fifth of 14 in minor event at Leicester only run in 2002: will stay beyond 1¾m:
acts on heavy going, probably on good to firm: has been taken steadily to post: useful
hurdler. *J. R. Fanshawe*

ETERNELLE 3 b.f. Green Desert (USA) 127 – Eversince (USA) (Foolish Pleasure **90** (USA)) [2002 –p: 9.9m² 10m³ 10m⁵ 10s² f9.4s* p10g Nov 23] lengthy filly: fairly useful performer: won maiden at Wolverhampton (made most) in November: good seventh to Beauchamp Pilot in listed race at Lingfield final start: stays 1¼m: acts on soft and good to firm ground, goes well on all-weather. *Sir Michael Stoute*

ETESAAL (USA) 2 br.c. (Mar 28) Danzig (USA) – Electric Society (IRE) 107 (Law **77** Society (USA) 130) [2002 7d⁵ 7g³ Aug 26] $425,000F, $1,000,000Y: good-bodied colt: third foal: half-brother to a winner in USA by Storm Cat: dam, 1¼m to 12.5f winner in France and later Grade 2 9f/1¼m winner in USA, from family of Salsabil and Marju: fair form in maidens at Newmarket (shaped well when fifth to Quartet) and Newcastle (odds on) in August: will stay at least 1m. *D. R. Loder*

ETHOS 2 b.g. (Apr 18) Emarati (USA) 74 – Leprechaun Lady 57 (Royal Blend 117) **64** [2002 5g⁴ 6.1f³ 7.1f⁴ 6d 7m 7m 7g 6m 8g² 7.5g 10m 8.2v⁴ Oct 29] 15,500Y: rather leggy gelding: half-brother to several winners, including 5-y-o Optimaite: dam winning stayer: modest maiden: best efforts second/third starts: stays 1m: acts on any going. *B. R. Millman*

ETMAL 8 b.g. Unfuwain (USA) 131 – Ekliptik (GER) (Nebos (GER) 129) [2002 10.1m **–** Aug 16] ex-German gelding: won 6 races in Germany for A. Schutz, including handicap at Neuss and minor event at Dortmund at 5 yrs: winning hurdler for C. McCarthy in Ireland in 2000, pulled up only outing there in 2001: tongue tied, well beaten only 8-y-o start: stays 1¼m: acts on sand: has been blinkered. *Mark Campion*

ETOILE DE MOSCOW (IRE) 2 b.c. (Apr 15) Spectrum (IRE) 126 – Moskov- **74** skaya (USA) (Roberto (USA) 131) [2002 8.1g⁶ 6m⁴ 6d³ 7g⁴ Oct 24] 230,000 francs F, 22,000Y: fifth foal: half-brother to a winner in USA by Diesis and to French 9f (at 2 yrs) and 13f winner Empire Celeste (by Barathea): dam French 1m winner (also won in USA), half-sister to Arc winner Trempolino: fair maiden: third at Windsor: should stay 1m: slowly away debut and third start. *B. Hanbury*

ETOILE MONTANTE (USA) 2 ch.f. (Feb 3) Miswaki (USA) 124 – Willstar **115 p** (USA) (Nureyev (USA) 131) [2002 7g* 8m* 8g² Oct 6]
　　　Etoile Montante was unfortunate to come up against the best French two-year-old filly for many years in the Prix Marcel Boussac. Take out Six Perfections, and Etoile Montante would herself have been an impressive and above-average winner of France's top race for two-year-old fillies, pulling as she did five lengths clear of the third horse Luminata. Indeed, in finishing second Etoile Montante ended the year with a higher two-year-old rating than all four of the fillies Criquette Head-Maarek trained to win the Marcel Boussac during the 'nineties: Gold Splash, Macoumba, Loving Claim and Juvenia. Etoile Montante came to the Marcel Boussac as the winner of both her starts, one of only two unbeaten fillies in the ten-runner field. Her two successes had both been gained in ready fashion, the first in a newcomers race over seven furlongs at Deauville in August and the second in a minor event over the Marcel Boussac course and distance on Arc trials day. In neither race did Etoile Montante beat a rival of any real note but she still started second favourite to the odds-on Six Perfections in the Marcel Boussac, and at much shorter odds than her stable-companion Loving Pride, despite that filly having won the Group 3 Prix d'Aumale last time out. The two Head-Maarek fillies led the Marcel Boussac field for most of the way, Etoile Montante proving much the stronger in the straight, staying in front until Six Perfections headed her over a furlong out, Etoile Montante responding by knuckling down well inside the last furlong. In finishing two lengths second to Six Perfections, Etoile Montante had got much closer to the winner than anything else had managed in Six Perfections' two impressive wins at Deauville in the summer.
　　　Etoile Montante fared better than her half-sister Starfan (by Lear Fan), who contested the Marcel Boussac the year before, finishing fourth on what was just her second start. Starfan did not really fulfil that promise in the latest season, gaining her only win in a weak maiden at Yarmouth dropped to six furlongs. Starfan and Etoile Montante were preceded by the twice-raced Distant View filly Prima Centauri who was well beaten on her two starts in France. Their dam Willstar won only in minor company in France over a mile but is well related, being a sister to the French listed winner and Prix de Psyche runner-up Viviana and half-sister to the Kentucky Oaks second Hometown Queen and the American Grade 2 eleven-

furlong winner Revasser. Grandam Nijinsky Star never ran but was a superbly-bred daughter of the champion American three-year-old filly and notable broodmare Chris Evert. Best known of Chris Evert's descendants was grandson Chief's Crown, himself champion at two and then placed in all legs of the American triple crown before a highly successful career as a sire.

		Mr Prospector (b 1970)	Raise A Native
	Miswaki (USA) (ch 1978)		Gold Digger
		Hopespringseternal (ch 1971)	Buckpasser
Etoile Montante (USA) (ch.f. Feb 3, 2000)			Rose Bower
		Nureyev (b 1977)	Northern Dancer
	Willstar (USA) (ch 1993)		Special
		Nijinsky Star (b 1980)	Nijinsky
			Chris Evert

The strong, close-coupled Etoile Montante is likely to prove best at around a mile judged on her breeding and on the fact that she showed a tendency at two to want to get on with things. Etoile Montante made considerable progress in a two-year-old campaign which spanned only little more than a month and looks capable of further improvement at three. If Six Perfections runs in the One Thousand Guineas rather than the French equivalent, and assuming Etoile Montante stays in France (her owner has another potential Guineas filly in Intercontinental), she would hold a leading chance in the Poule d'Essai des Pouliches. *Mme C. Head-Maarek, France*

Mr K. Abdulla's "Etoile Montante"

ETOILE SOLITAIRE (USA)   2 gr.g. (Feb 24) Lit de Justice (USA) 125 – Cydalia   **72**
(USA) 109 (Cresta Rider (USA) 124) [2002 6g 6v Nov 9] $25,000F, 20,000Y: strong,
lengthy gelding: sixth foal: half-brother to a winner in USA by Lear Fan: dam French 7f
winner, including at 2 yrs: better effort in maidens (fair form) when eighth of 18 to Pigeon
Point at Newmarket on debut: refused to enter stalls second intended start: should stay 7f.
M. A. Jarvis

ETON (GER)   6 ch.g. Suave Dancer (USA) 136 – Ermione (Surumu (GER)) [2002   **88**
74d: 12.3m² 10m* 9.9m* 8.3m³ 10f* 10.4f* Oct 11] strong, close-coupled gelding: fairly
useful handicapper: in very good form in September/October, winning at Pontefract
(apprentices), Beverley, Newmarket (apprentices, confidently ridden to beat Graft 2
lengths) and York (briefly carried head awkwardly): probably ideally suited by around
1¼m: acts on firm ground: tried blinkered. *D. Nicholls*

ETTRICK WATER   3 ch.g. Selkirk (USA) 129 – Sadly Sober (IRE) 70 (Roi Danzig   **87**
(USA)) [2002 77: 8m⁴ 8d 8m⁴ 10.1m³ 9.7g³ 8m² 9.2m² Sep 30] strong gelding: fairly
useful maiden: effective at 1m/1¼m: acts on soft and good to firm going: visored last 2
starts: usually patiently ridden: consistent: gelded after final outing. *L. M. Cumani*

EUCALYPTUS (IRE)   5 ch.g. Mujtahid (USA) 118 – Imprecise 64 (Polish Precedent   **59**
(USA) 131) [2002 59: p10g p8g* p8g p7g² p7g³ Dec 18] big, lengthy gelding: poor
mover: modest performer: made all in seller at Lingfield in February: effective at 7f to
easy 1¼m: acts on polytrack, soft and good to firm going: visored last 7 starts: has found
little. *S. Dow*

EURA STAR (IRE)   2 b.f. (Mar 5) Royal Applause 124 – Kentucky Starlet (USA) 69   **76**
(Cox's Ridge (USA)) [2002 7s⁴ 7v f6g² Dec 14] half-sister to several winners, including
useful 5f/6f winner (including at 2 yrs) Pips Magic (by Pips Pride) and 7f winner El
Maximo (by First Trump): dam 7f winner: best effort in maidens (fair form) when 1½
lengths second to Vision of Dreams at Wolverhampton: may prove best up to 7f: acts on
fibresand. *Declan Gillespie, Ireland*

EUROLINK ARTEMIS   5 b.m. Common Grounds 118 – Taiga 69 (Northfields   **68**
(USA)) [2002 75: 10d⁴ 10s⁶ p10g 8.3m 10.1f 10.3d³ 10.1m f8g² f8.5s f8.5g* Dec 13]   **a64**
useful-looking mare: fair performer: wearing cheekpieces, won apprentice minor event at
Wolverhampton in December: stays 1¼m: acts on all-weather, soft and good to firm
going. *Julian Poulton*

EUROLINK ZANTE (IRE)   6 b.g. Turtle Island (IRE) 123 – Lady Eurolink 55 (Kala   **77**
Shikari 125) [2002 77: 8d 7m* 7d 7d 6g⁵ 8m 7.1g 7d p7g Nov 19] fair handicapper: won
at Salisbury in May: stays 1m: acts on soft and good to firm going: none too consistent.
T. D. McCarthy

EURO PREMIUM (IRE)   3 ch.f. Barathea (IRE) 127 – Showing Style (Pas de Seul   **49**
133) [2002 7.1m⁵ 10.3f⁶ 10d⁶ 10m 12f⁶ Oct 8] IR 12,000Y: plain filly: half-sister to
several winners, including Irish 1997 2-y-o 1m winner Kalagold (by Magical Strike) and
8-y-o Style Dancer, both fairly useful: dam unraced: poor maiden: shapes as though will
stay beyond 1½m. *R. A. Fahey*

EURO VENTURE   7 b.g. Prince Sabo 123 – Brave Advance (USA) 98 (Bold Laddie   **56**
(USA)) [2002 76: p6g 6.1f 6m 5.9s 6m f6s Dec 26] sturdy gelding: modest handicapper
in 2002: trained by Mrs H. L. Walton first 5 starts. *R. Wilman*

EVANGELIST (IRE)   2 b.f. (Mar 15) Namaqualand (USA) – Errazuriz (IRE) 94   **68 d**
(Classic Music (USA)) [2002 f5g⁴ 5.1f³ f5g* 6.1g f5g* 6g⁴ 6g² f6g* 6.1g² 6g⁴ 6.1m⁵ f5s⁵
f6s⁵ f6g 6s f6g Nov 20] IR 5,200Y, resold 5,600Y: quite attractive filly: has a quick action:
second foal: half-sister to Italian 7.5f (at 2 yrs) to 1¼m winner Erina (by Mukaddamah):
dam Irish 2-y-o 1m winner: fair performer: won maiden at Wolverhampton in May,
claimer at Southwell in June and nursery at Wolverhampton in July: well below form last
3 starts: stays 6f: acts on good to firm going and fibresand: often races prominently: none
too keen. *A. Berry*

EVA PERON (IRE)   2 b.f. (Feb 16) Alzao (USA) 117 – High Flying Adored (IRE) 85   **79**
(In The Wings 128) [2002 5s⁶ 7.1m³ 7.5g² f8s* Oct 8] 11,000Y: fourth foal: half-sister to
Italian winner around 9f Americaone (by Emperor Jones): dam, 1½m winner, half-sister
to useful French middle-distance performer Mint Crisp: best effort when
justifying favouritism in maiden at Southwell readily by 1¼ lengths from Platinum
Charmer: will stay at least 1¼m: acts on fibresand and good to firm going. *H. Morrison*

EVELYNS LAST   4 b.g. Terimon 124 – Kimbolton Katie 81 (Aragon 118) [2002 10m   **–**
p7g May 28] rather leggy gelding: fourth reported foal: dam 2-y-o 5f winner: well held in
maiden/claimer. *J. W. Payne*

EVENING CHASE (IRE)   4 b.g. Pursuit of Love 124 – Late Evening (USA) (River-   **55**
man (USA) 131) [2002 59, a62: f7g 6.1m² f6g⁶ 6d⁵ 6g f5g⁴ f7g 5m 5s⁵ 6g Aug 23] tall
gelding: modest handicapper: left J. L. Eyre after eighth start: best at 6f/7f: acts on
fibresand, probably on firm and soft going: visored last 4 starts: tongue tied (reportedly
had breathing problem final start at 3 yrs): has edged right/found little. *D. Carroll*

EVENING POST   2 b.g. (Mar 10) Petong 126 – Nevis 61 (Connaught 130) [2002 6d
6g 5m 7s Oct 28] 1,200Y: brother to 6f (at 2 yrs) and 1m winner Naivasha and half-
brother to 3 winners, including 5-y-o Aunt Doris: dam, ran twice, half-sister to very smart
sprinter Paris House: only a little sign of ability in maidens/nursery: gelded after final
outing. *J. R. Boyle*

EVENING PRESS   3 b.f. River Falls 113 – Shiny Kay 65 (Star Appeal 133) [2002 –:   **42**
7g 9m 10.1m⁵ 12.4m⁵ 10m 13.8f 12f Oct 8] good-topped filly: poor maiden handicapper:
should stay 1¼m: raced only on good going or firmer: tried blinkered. *T. J. Etherington*

EVENTUALLY (IRE)   2 ch.c. (Apr 4) Night Shift (USA) – La Menorquina (USA)   **76 d**
65 (Woodman (USA) 126) [2002 6f⁴ 6d⁶ 6m² 6m³ 6m 6m 6m 6s⁵ Oct 22] IR 14,000F,
34,000Y: sturdy, quite attractive colt: first foal: dam, won at 2m and over hurdles, half-
sister to smart Irish 1¼m/1½m performer His Excellence: fair maiden: well below form
after fourth start: bred to stay at least 7f: acts on firm ground: tried tongue tied: sometimes
carries head awkwardly: sold 8,000 gns, sent to Kuwait. *R. Hannon*

EVEREST (IRE)   5 ch.g. Indian Ridge 123 – Reine d'Beaute 97 (Caerleon (USA)   **75**
132) [2002 78: 8.5g 7.1g⁵ 8g² 8v* f8g f9.4g⁴ Dec 14] strong, deep-girthed gelding: fair
handicapper: first start for over 5 months, won 23-runner ladies event at Doncaster in
November: best at 1m/9f: acts on any going, probably on fibresand: has wandered: often
races freely. *B. Ellison*

EVERLAND (IRE)   3 b.g. Namaqualand (USA) – Ukraine's Affair (USA) (The   **62**
Minstrel (CAN) 135) [2002 p12g p10g⁴ Dec 30] IR 6,000F, 10,500Y: seventh foal:
brother to 5-y-o Distant Prospect and half-brother to 3 winners, including 8-y-o Protocol:
dam unraced out of half-sister to Poule d'Essai des Pouliches winner Ukraine Girl: much
better effort in Lingfield maidens (fair form) when under a length fourth to Jade's
Promise, nearest finish: should be suited by 1½m+. *G. C. H. Chung*

EVERMOORE   4 b.f. Thatching 131 – Ganador 67 (Weldnaas (USA) 112) [2002 –:   –
f9.4g Jan 19] little form. *J. S. Moore*

EVERY NOTE COUNTS   2 b.c. (Mar 18) Bluegrass Prince (IRE) 110 – Miss Mirror   **77**
77 (Magic Mirror 105) [2002 6s⁵ 7m³ 6.1m 7g 6s³ p7g f7s* p7g⁴ Dec 28] 6,200Y resold
12,000Y: sixth foal: half-brother to 3 winners, including useful Swedish 1m/1¼m
performer Tragic Love (by Tragic Role): dam 1m winner: fair performer: won maiden at
Wolverhampton in December, dictating pace: should stay 1m: acts on all-weather, soft
and good to firm ground: reportedly had breathing problem third start. *W. Jarvis*

EVERY RIGHT (IRE)   4 b.g. Common Grounds 118 – Incendio (Siberian Express   –
(USA) 125) [2002 –: f5s² f5g⁵ f5g⁶ f6g f7g f7g f5g p6g Mar 16] modest and ungenuine   **a50 d**
maiden: on downgrade: best at bare 5f: acts on fibresand: usually blinkered: tends to pull
hard. *D. W. Chapman*

EVEZIO RUFO   10 b.g. Blakeney 126 – Empress Corina 74 (Free State 125) [2002   – §
–§, a63§: f16s* f14.8g⁴ f16g f16g f16.2g⁵ f16.2g⁶ Mar 4] neat gelding: modest handi-   **a55 §**
capper: won at Southwell in January: effective at 1½m to 2m: acts on firm ground (though
very lightly raced on turf) and fibresand: blinkered/visored: has hung: no easy ride:
unreliable. *N. P. Littmoden*

EVOLUTION BABY (IRE)   2 b.g. (Apr 8) Inzar (USA) 112 – Go Flightline (IRE)   **80**
63 (Common Grounds 118) [2002 7g 6g f6g⁴ f6f* f7f³ Nov 29] 9,200 2-y-o: fourth foal:
half-brother to useful 1999 2-y-o 7f winner On Time (by Blues Traveller): dam 2-y-o 5f
winner: fairly useful performer: banned under non-triers rule on debut: won maiden at
Wolverhampton in November, making most: good third in nursery there final start: stays
7f: acts on fibresand. *John A. Quinn, Ireland*

EWAR VICTORIA (FR)   3 b.f. Valanour (IRE) 125 – Ewar Empress (IRE) 57 (Per-   –
sian Bold 123) [2002 59d: f7g p10g 6g 10g 12m Jul 21] sparely-made filly: modest
maiden at best: well held in 2002: left K. Cunningham-Brown before final start: tried
blinkered. *H. Bidon, France*

EXALTED (IRE)   9 b.g. High Estate 127 – Heavenward (USA) (Conquistador Cielo   **66**
(USA)) [2002 66: 13s⁴ 11.9g 13.1g² 11.9d 14.1s⁴ 13s* 13v⁴ 14.4g 14.1m⁴ Aug 21] good-
topped gelding: has round action: fair performer: won ladies handicap at Hamilton (for

second consecutive year) in June: effective at 1½m/1¾m, possibly not 2m: acts on soft and good to firm ground: 3 of 4 wins at Hamilton. *T. A. K. Cuthbert*

EXCALINOR 2 br.c. (Mar 26) Inchinor 119 – Noble Story 61 (Last Tycoon 131) **61 p** [2002 6v⁵ Nov 9] quite good-topped colt: second foal: dam, ran twice, out of half-sister to dam of Derby winner Shaamit: 6/1, 12½ lengths fifth of 13 to Marinas Charm in maiden at Doncaster: likely to be suited by 1m+: should do better. *P. F. I. Cole*

EXCELLENTO (USA) 2 b.c. (Mar 22) Rahy (USA) 115 – Golden Opinion (USA) **82 p** 127 (Slew O' Gold (USA)) [2002 8f² Sep 26] eighth foal: brother to French 7f winner Dareen and half-brother to 3 winners, including useful 7f winner Meiosis (by Danzig) and fairly useful French 1m winner Goddess of Wisdom (by Sadler's Wells): dam won Coronation Stakes and second in July Cup: weak 9/1-shot, 3 lengths second of 4 to Alasil in maiden at Pontefract, keeping on well: should progress. *D. R. Loder*

EXCELSIUS (IRE) 2 ch.g. (Apr 17) Dr Devious (IRE) 127 – Folgore (USA) 83 **101** (Irish River (FR) 131) [2002 7g* 8s³ Oct 20] second foal: dam, 2-y-o 7f winner, half-sister to smart middle-distance filly Fanjica: won maiden at Milan in September by 7 lengths: plenty of improvement when 3¼ lengths third of 9 finishers to Spartacus in Gran Criterium there, making most and keeping on: gelded after: will be suited by further than 1m. *J. L. Dunlop*

EXCLUSION ZONE 5 ch.g. Exit To Nowhere (USA) 122 – Exclusive Virtue (USA) **88** 94 (Shadeed (USA) 135) [2002 f12g² 11.9s* 10.4g³ f12g² 16.4d³ 11.9g Aug 13] big, good-bodied gelding: fairly useful performer, lightly raced: won claimer at Carlisle (claimed from M. Johnston £10,000) in May: reportedly sustained leg injury when pulled up final start: stays 16.4f: acts on fibresand, raced only on good ground or softer on turf. *A. G. Newcombe*

EXCLUSIVE ACADEMY (IRE) 3 b.f. Royal Academy (USA) 130 – Apprecia- **74 ?** tively (USA) (Affirmed (USA)) [2002 12m 9d 7s 8d 10s⁵ f8.5g³ f8g² f12g³ Dec 7] **a57** 20,000Y: second foal: dam, US maiden, sister to very smart performer up to 1¼m Zoman: seemingly fair maiden on turf, modest on all-weather: left Mrs J. Harrington in Ireland after sixth start: will probably prove best at 1m/1¼m: acts on soft going and fibresand: tried blinkered. *D. J. Wintle*

EXCLUSIVE AIR (USA) 3 ch.g. Affirmed (USA) – Lac Dessert (USA) 91 (Lac **69** Ouimet (USA)) [2002 65p: f8g* f8.5g³ 10.3s⁵ 8s⁵ 9g 9f³ 11m⁶ f8.5s f8g Dec 27] smallish, **a72** good-topped gelding: fair handicapper: won at Southwell in January: should stay 1¼m: acts on fibresand and firm going, probably on soft: gelded after final start. *T. D. Barron*

EXEAT (USA) 6 b. or br.g. Dayjur (USA) 137 – By Your Leave (Private **79 d** Account (USA)) [2002 92d: 7.2g³ 7g 8d* 10.1g⁴ 7.1d 8g³ 7.2d⁵ 10d⁶ 7.2s⁶ 9.1g 9.1s 7s Oct 26] good-topped gelding: unimpressive mover: formerly smart, only fair at best in 2002: won minor event at Ayr in June: stays 9f: acts on soft and good to firm going: blinkered (out of depth) final start, sometimes visored earlier in career: none too genuine: sold 7,000 gns, sent to Spain. *J. S. Goldie*

EXECUTE (FR) 5 ch.h. Suave Dancer (USA) 136 – She's My Lovely (Sharpo 132) **117** [2002 109: 10s* 10d* 10.5g² 9.3m⁴ 8g 9.8g Oct 5] half-brother to several winners, including Tot Ou Tard (up to 1½m, by Robellino) and miler Ing Ing (by Bering), both smart in France: dam unraced half-sister to very smart sprinter/miler Comrade In Arms: smart performer: won all 5 starts at 3 yrs and minor event at Longchamp at 4 yrs: successful in minor event at Compiegne and Prix d'Harcourt at Longchamp (by ¾ length from Sunstrach) in March: best efforts at Longchamp afterwards when ½-length second of 4 to Aquarelliste in Prix Ganay next time and close eighth of 11 under penalty to Dano-Mast in Prix Dollar final start: has won at 1½m but seems best around 1¼m: acts on heavy and good to firm ground. *J. E. Hammond, France*

EXECUTIVE CHOICE (IRE) 8 b.g. Don't Forget Me 127 – Shadia (USA) 53 **46** (Naskra (USA)) [2002 –: 11.9s³ 14.1g² 14.1f 17.2d³ 16d⁵ 16m² 14.1m⁵ 12d f16.2g Nov 18] small gelding: poor performer: stays 17f: acts on soft and good to firm going: has been blinkered: tongue tied: has raced freely. *B. Ellison*

EXECUTIVE NETWORK 4 b.g. Silca Blanka (IRE) 104 – Scene Stealer (Scenic **–** 128) [2002 55?: f16.2f Nov 11] little form: pulled hard only outing in 2002. *A. D. Smith*

EXECUTIVE ORDER 5 b.g. Rainbow Quest (USA) 134 – Exclusive Order (USA) **–** 120 (Exclusive Native (USA)) [2002 8.2d Mar 27] good-topped gelding: fairly useful form in maidens at 3 yrs: well held only start since. *B. Ellison*

EXHIBITION GIRL (IRE) 5 ch.m. Perugino (USA) 84 – Shy Jinks (Shy Groom –
(USA)) [2002 37: f8g 10m Apr 27] angular mare: maiden handicapper: well held both
5-y-o starts. *Andrew Turnell*

EXHIBIT (IRE) 4 b.g. Royal Academy (USA) 130 – Juno Madonna (IRE) (Sadler's **76 d**
Wells (USA) 132) [2002 69: 7m² 8.2m³ 8m 8.1g 7.1g 8.3d Oct 14] good-bodied gelding:
fair maiden at best: on downgrade after second start: stays 1m: raced only on good/good
to firm going prior to final start: has carried head awkwardly: sold 10,000 gns. *R. Hannon*

EXHIBITOR (USA) 3 b.f. Royal Academy (USA) 130 – Akadya (FR) (Akarad (FR) **68**
130) [2002 –p: 8.3m⁵ 8.3d p10g² 10.1f* 10g⁵ Aug 7] lengthy filly: fair handicapper: won
at Yarmouth in July: stayed 1¼m: acted on polytrack and firm going: tended to flash tail:
withdrawn after getting loose at start and taking bad fall fourth intended outing: stud.
J. R. Fanshawe

EXIT TO HEAVEN 2 ch.f. (Apr 24) Exit To Nowhere (USA) 122 – Shona (USA) 60 **63**
(Lyphard (USA) 132) [2002 7m 8m 8g⁵ Oct 16] second foal: dam, lightly-raced maiden,
sister to useful 7f/1m winner Tregaron: modest form in maidens, not knocked about first
2 starts: should stay 1¼m. *J. L. Dunlop*

EXODOUS (ARG) 6 ch.g. Equalize (USA) – Empire Glory (ARG) (Good Manners –
(USA)) [2002 11.6s⁵ 10s⁴ 7m Jun 4] Argentinian-bred gelding: won 3 of 25 starts up to
1½m in native country (third 4 times in Group 1 events in 1999/2000): well beaten in
listed race and minor events for current stable. *J. A. B. Old*

EXOTIC FAN (USA) 4 b. or br.f. Lear Fan (USA) 130 – Green Moon (FR) (Shirley –
Heights 130) [2002 80, a97: p12g p12g³ p12g f12g 11.8g⁵ Jul 6] useful handicapper on **a96**
all-weather: best effort in 2002 when third to Herodotus at Lingfield in February: barely
stays easy 1½m: acts on all-weather: sold 20,000 gns, sent to Saudi Arabia. *R. Guest*

EXOTIC PROFILES 8 ch.m. Minster Son 130 – Ragroyal (Royal Palace 131) [2002 **43**
9.9m f14.8g⁶ Jun 7] winning selling hurdler: blinkered, poor form in maiden and claimer
(missed break): has refused to race over jumps. *Miss K. M. George*

EXPECTED BONUS (USA) 3 b. or br.g. Kris S (USA) – Nidd (USA) 112 (Known **93**
Fact (USA) 135) [2002 96: 12.3f⁵ 10g 9.9m 10m⁶ 12f Oct 2] lengthy gelding: poor
walker: fairly useful performer: generally respectable efforts in 2002: unlikely to stay
beyond 1¼m: held up: tended to wander for pressure as 2-y-o: sold 17,000 gns, joined
S. Williams and gelded. *B. W. Hills*

EXPECTEDTOFLI (IRE) 4 b.f. Mujadil (USA) 119 – Zurarah (Siberian Express –
(USA) 125) [2002 47: p10g p7g 7g⁵ 6d 5s 7m 7f Jul 29] poor maiden. *C. N. Allen*

EXPERTISE 2 ch.f. (Feb 17) Selkirk (USA) 129 – Bacinella (USA) (El Gran Senor **69**
(USA) 136) [2002 8s 7d⁵ 6v⁴ Nov 9] 33,000Y: useful-looking filly: second foal: dam
unraced close relation to 4-y-o Xtra: best effort in maidens (fair form) when fifth of 19 to
Goodness Gracious at Newmarket: should stay 1¼m: raced only on ground softer than
good. *E. A. L. Dunlop*

EXPLODE 5 b.g. Zafonic (USA) 130 – Didicoy (USA) 104 (Danzig (USA)) [2002 –: –
10.3m⁶ 10g⁵ 9s Oct 26] useful winner at 3 yrs: well below form since. *Miss L. C. Siddall*

EXPLORING (IRE) 3 br.g. Charnwood Forest (IRE) 125 – Caribbean Quest 90 **75**
(Rainbow Quest (USA) 134) [2002 69: 7.1m 8.3s 10g 10m⁵ p12g³ 9.9g* 10s Oct 15]
close-coupled, useful-looking gelding: unimpressive mover: fair performer: won
apprentice handicap at Salisbury in October: stays 1¼m: acts on good to firm going, well
below form only start on all-weather: sold 11,000 gns. *R. F. Johnson Houghton*

EXTINGUISHER 3 ch.g. Zamindar (USA) 116 – Xaymara (USA) (Sanglamore **92**
(USA) 126) [2002 100: 6s⁴ 5.5d 6m 6g Sep 21] second foal: dam, French 1m winner,
half-sister to dams of 1000 Guineas winner Wince and very smart US performer up to
1¼m Skimming: useful in France at 2 yrs, winning newcomers race at Saint-Cloud: sold
from Mme C. Head-Maarek 24,000 gns after second start in 2002: shaped as if retaining
ability last 2: stays 7f: raced mainly on good or softer ground. *D. Nicholls*

EXTRA GEAR (USA) 2 ch.c. (May 16) Diesis 133 – Petiteness (USA) (Chief's **80**
Crown (USA)) [2002 8g p8g² p7g³ Dec 21] $170,000Y: third foal: half-brother to 2
winners in USA, including smart performer up to 9f Scorpion (by Seattle Slew): dam,
8.5f/9f winner in USA, half-sister to useful French performer up to 1¼m Mais Oui: fairly
useful form: best effort when length second to Made In Japan in maiden at Lingfield
second start: reared leaving stall next time: should stay 1¼m. *G. A. Butler*

EXTREMIST (USA) 3 b.g. Dynaformer (USA) – Strumming (IRE) 75 (Ballad Rock **86**
122) [2002 70: 10g 11.6m³ 14.1g⁴ 11.9g* 12g* 11.9m 16m Oct 1] tall gelding: fairly

useful performer: won maiden at Brighton and handicap at Epsom in August: stays 1½m: raced only on good going or firmer: usually leads: has hung/found little: sold 18,000 gns. *R. Hannon*

EXUMA 2 ch.f. (Feb 25) Komaite (USA) – Sugar Token 66 (Record Token 128) [2002 **54** 6d 5m⁶ 5m 6m⁵ 7f Oct 8] sister to fairly useful 1995 2-y-o 5f/6f winner Lunar Mist and half-sister to 5f/6f winner Hershebar (by Stanford): dam 6f/7f winner (including at 2 yrs): modest maiden: stays 6f: acts on good to firm going. *G. G. Margarson*

EXZILARATING 2 ch.c. (Feb 26) Zilzal (USA) 137 – Personal Best (IRE) (Kris **77** 135) [2002 7m 6m² 8g² 7s Oct 26] 22,000Y: tall, quite good-topped colt: first foal: dam, French 10.5f winner, granddaughter of Oaks third Last Feather: best efforts (fair form) when runner-up in maidens at Windsor and Salisbury (sweating, raced freely): not sure to stay beyond 1m: acts on good to firm ground, well held on soft. *R. F. Johnson Houghton*

EYAD (IRE) 2 b.c. (Apr 10) Desert Prince (IRE) 130 – Ploy 87 (Posse (USA) 130) **65** [2002 7s p7g⁴ p8g Nov 14] IR 190,000F, IR 300,000Y: good-topped colt: half-brother to several winners, notably Italian miler Poliuto (by Last Tycoon) and 4-y-o Potemkin, both smart: dam, maiden best at 1½m, half-sister to Sun Princess and Saddlers' Hall: best effort in maidens (fair form) when fourth to Twentytwosilver at Lingfield: gave impression something amiss final start: should be suited by 1m+. *E. A. L. Dunlop*

EYECATCHER 5 b.g. Green Desert (USA) 127 – Reuval 102 (Sharpen Up 127) **100** [2002 6g⁴ 7d² 7.1m* 7.1d² 6f² p7g⁴ p7g* p7g³ Dec 28] heavy-topped gelding: useful performer: missed 2001: won minor event at Warwick (idled) in June and handicap at Lingfield (travelled strongly and beat Hand Chime a length) in December: effective at 6f/ 7f: acts on polytrack, firm and good to soft ground: has started slowly, and usually held up: withdrawn after refusing to enter stall fifth intended 5-y-o start (has worn rope halter). *J. R. Fanshawe*

EYES DONT LIE (IRE) 4 b.g. Namaqualand (USA) – Avidal Park 68 (Horage 124) **– §** [2002 51d: 9m 11.1s 11.1g 14g 8.3v 12m⁴ 16s Nov 6] disappointing maiden: tried blinkered/visored/tongue tied. *D. A. Nolan*

EYES OF PARKSTONE 2 ch.c. (Apr 18) The West (USA) 107 – Avinalarf 60 **–** (Fools Holme (USA)) [2002 5m 6m Aug 29] first foal: dam 2-y-o 7f winner: last in minor event at Lingfield: fell fatally on same course next time. *J. J. Bridger*

EYES TO THE RIGHT (IRE) 3 ch.g. Eagle Eyed (USA) 111 – Capable Kate **61** (IRE) (Alzao (USA) 117) [2002 62: p10g³ p8g⁵ p12g 10m 8f 10d p10g p13g f16g Nov 20] sturdy gelding: modest performer: stays 1¼m: acts on good to soft ground, good to firm and all-weather: tried visored/tongue tied: has taken strong hold/started slowly/ wandered. *P. S. McEntee*

EYES WIDE OPEN 4 b.f. Fraam 114 – Dreamtime Quest (Blakeney 126) [2002 –: **44** 10m⁶ p10g 8d⁵ 6m f7g Dec 14] well-made filly: poor maiden, lightly raced: stays 1m: acts on good to firm and good to soft going. *P. F. I. Cole*

EYRE O PLAIN JANE 2 ch.f. (Mar 20) Wolfhound (USA) 126 – Pushkinia (FR) 95 **49** (Pharly (FR) 130) [2002 5f⁶ 5d 7m³ f7g³ f7g⁴ Dec 17] close-coupled filly: half-sister to **a52** several winners, including 8-y-o Lakota Brave and 1m winner who stayed 1½m Shift Again (by Siberian Express): dam French 2-y-o 7f winner: modest maiden: third in sellers at Catterick and Wolverhampton: stays 7f: acts on good to firm going and fibresand. *P. C. Haslam*

EZZ ELKHEIL 3 b.c. Bering 136 – Numidie (FR) (Baillamont (USA) 124) [2002 **85** 85p: 10m⁴ 10.3f⁴ 10d⁵ Aug 11] tall, useful-looking colt: has scope: fairly useful maiden: should stay 1½m: acts on firm going. *J. W. Payne*

F

FABI 7 br.g. Rock City 120 – Shadiyama 58 (Nishapour (FR) 125) [2002 7g f12s Sep **–** 17] lightly raced and seemingly of little account. *F. Watson*

FABRIAN 4 b.g. Danehill (USA) 126 – Dockage (CAN) (Riverman (USA) 131) [2002 **92 ?** 7g⁴ 6d 7s Nov 2] ex-French gelding: half-brother to numerous winners, notably smart 6f (including July Stakes) to 9f winner in Britain/USA Wharf (by Storm Bird): dam, useful French 1m (at 2 yrs) and 9f winner, out close relative to Dahlia: seemingly fairly useful maiden, lightly raced: appeared to put up best effort in minor event at Longchamp on reappearance: sold from A. Fabre 21,000 gns, gelded and off 6 months before British debut final start: best effort at 7f. *D. W. P. Arbuthnot*

FABULOUS JET (FR)   2 ch.g. (Apr 4) Starborough 126 – Jetty (FR) (Fabulous   **82** Dancer (USA) 124) [2002 7d² 8s³ Oct 26] 60,000 francs F, 190,000 francs Y: close-coupled, rather unfurnished gelding: half-brother to 3 winners, including French 1¼m (including at 2 yrs) winner Jet Bond (by Exit To Nowhere): dam, French maiden, out of smart performer up to 1½m Melantha: fairly useful form in maidens at Leicester and Newbury, 3 lengths third of 16 to Zeis in latter (gelded after): will stay 1¼m. *M. R. Channon*

FACE THE JUDGE (USA)   3 b.f. Benny The Dip (USA) 127 – Lyrebird (USA)   **54** (Storm Bird (CAN) 134) [2002 59d: p7g 8m f8.5g³ 10d⁶ 10.1m⁴ 9.9d⁵ 14.1s 15.8f 15.8f   **a49** 12s Nov 6] maiden handicapper, largely disappointing: stays 1¼m (not 2m): acts on firm going, good to soft and fibresand: tongue tied on reappearance: waited with: sold 2,000 gns in December. *A. Berry*

FACE THE LIMELIGHT (IRE)   3 b.g. Quest For Fame 127 – Miss Boniface 112   **76** (Tap On Wood 130) [2002 65: 11.6m³ 10.2g² 12.3f f12g⁴ 10.2g 8.2s Oct 23] leggy, quite good-topped gelding: fair handicapper: below form after third start: acts on fibresand and probably on any turf going, led rideriess to post third start: held up: sometimes flicks tail under pressure: gelded after final outing. *H. Morrison*

FACE THE STORM (IRE)   2 ch.f. (Mar 26) Barathea (IRE) 127 – Atlantic Record   **72** (Slip Anchor 136) [2002 7g p8g³ p8g* p8g Dec 11] IR 120,000Y: fourth foal: half-sister to fairly useful 1¼m winner Santa Isobel (by Nashwan): dam unraced from family of Kayf Tara and Opera House: fair form: best effort when winning maiden at Lingfield in November: well held in nursery there final start: stayed 1m: acted on polytrack: stud. *J. H. M. Gosden*

FACT   2 ch.g. (Mar 5) Factual (USA) 108 – Thalya (Crofthall 110) [2002 p5g p5g⁴ Jun   **59** 9] 2,000Y: fourth foal: half-brother to 4-y-o Fairgame Man: dam unraced: modest form in maidens at Lingfield *J. White*

FACTOR FIFTEEN   3 gr.g. Hector Protector (USA) 124 – Catch The Sun (Kalaglow   **81** 132) [2002 10m 10.5d 10m 12.4g* 13.1s 11.6d⁵ Oct 28] 8,000Y: big, strong gelding: half-brother to several winners, including smart performer up to 2m Tioman Island (by Midyan) and fairly useful 1¼m/1½m winner Remaadi Sun (by Cadeaux Genereux): dam unraced: fairly useful handicapper: won at Newcastle in August: creditable effort at Windsor final start: stays 1½m well: acts on good to soft going: has pulled hard/flashed tail/hinted at temperament. *E. A. L. Dunlop*

FACTORSFORVALUE   2 b.f. (May 7) Entrepreneur 123 – Jeanne Avril 99 (Music   **–** Boy 124) [2002 f5g 6f⁶ 6g 7f⁶ 8.5m⁶ Aug 25] 12,500F, 5,500Y: small, compact filly: half-sister to several winners, including useful 5f/6f winner Mary Hinge (by Dowsing) and fairly useful 6f/7f winner Dark Shot (by Rock City): dam, 6f (including at 2 yrs) winner, sister to Middle Park winner and 2000 Guineas second Mattaboy: well held in maidens/minor event. *Ronald Thompson*

FACT O' THE MATTER   3 b.g. So Factual (USA) 120 – Edgeaway 70 (Ajdal (USA)   **65** 130) [2002 70: 7s 8m 6m 8.3s 7d f9.4g⁴ 11.7m 12m 7g 8.1g 8.3d⁴ 8.2v² f7g* f9.4g⁴ f7g⁵ Dec 31] leggy, close-coupled gelding: fair performer: won maiden at Wolverhampton in November: effective at 7f to 9.4f: acts on heavy going, good to firm and fibresand: tried blinkered: carried head high/hung twelfth start: reportedly had breathing problem eighth outing. *M. Blanshard*

FACTUAL LAD   4 b.g. So Factual (USA) 120 – Surprise Surprise 91 (Robellino   **73** (USA) 127) [2002 88: 6m 7f⁶ 8d⁶ 8f 10.1m 10m³ 9s p8g p10g Dec 21] close-coupled, workmanlike gelding: poor mover: fair performer: probably stays 1¼m: acts on good to firm and good to soft going, possibly not soft: blinkered (hung right) final 3-y-o start: has worn cheekpieces: usually races prominently. *B. R. Millman*

FADDAD (USA)   6 b.g. Irish River (FR) 131 – Miss Mistletoes (IRE) 89 (The Minstrel   **–** (CAN) 135) [2002 –: 14.1d May 18] well-made gelding: one-time fairly useful performer in Ireland: well beaten in 2001/02. *D. C. O'Brien*

FAILED TO HIT   9 b.g. Warrshan (USA) 117 – Missed Again 84 (High Top 131) [2002   **–** –, a69: f12g² f12s² f12g⁵ f12g⁶ f12g² f12g³ p12g p12g f12g⁵ 16g f14.8g f14.8g⁴ f12f*   **a68** f14.8g f14.8g* f12g² Dec 26] lengthy gelding: fair performer: multiple course winner at Wolverhampton, including sellers in November and December: effective at 1½m to 15f: acts on fibresand, lightly raced and little recent form on turf: usually blinkered/visored: sometimes races moodily: needs to dominate. *N. P. Littmoden*

FAILTE (IRE)   4 b.c. Most Welcome 131 – Esh Sham (USA) (Damascus (USA))   –
[2002 –: f8.5g 10d 11.6d 15g Jul 5] IR 4,000Y: lightly-raced ex-Irish colt: half-brother to
3 winners abroad, including Italian 7f/1m winner by Storm Bird: dam ran once: lightly
raced and little form, trained by C. McCarthy in Ireland prior to 2002: visored final start.
L. A. Dace

FAIRFAX FLICKER (IRE)   2 b.f. (May 8) Sri Pekan (USA) 117 – Charwelton 78   –
(Indian Ridge 123) [2002 6f 6m 6d Oct 14] third foal: dam, 2-y-o 6f winner on only start,
sister to useful 6f/7f performer Cheyenne Spirit: never a threat in maidens. *C. R. Egerton*

FAIRGAME MAN   4 ch.g. Clantime 101 – Thalya (Crofthall 110) [2002 91: 5.1f 6g   **79**
5.1f⁵ 5.1d⁵ 5m 6m³ 5m² Sep 18] strong gelding: fair nowadays: placed in claimers at
Yarmouth and Sandown last 2 starts: best at 5f/6f: acts on firm going. *A. Berry*

FAIRLY HIGH (IRE)   2 b.f. (Mar 27) Sri Pekan (USA) 117 – Ecco Mi (IRE) (Priolo   **66**
(USA) 127) [2002 6g 6s² 6s* 7.5d³ f6g⁴ 7d³ 7m f6s Oct 8] 15,500Y: big, strong filly: has
plenty of scope: fourth foal: sister to 4-y-o Ecology: dam unraced from family of Sun
Princess and Saddlers' Hall: fair performer: won maiden at Hamilton in June: claimed
from N. Callaghan sixth start: ran poorly last 2: stays 7.5f: acts on fibresand and soft
ground. *P. G. Murphy*

FAIRMEAD PRINCESS   4 b.f. Rudimentary (USA) 118 – Lessons Lass (IRE) 73   –
(Doyoun 124) [2002 –: f7s May 13] well held, including in seller. *M. J. Gingell*

FAIR MIX (IRE)   4 gr.c. Linamix (FR) 127 – Fairlee Wild (USA) (Wild Again (USA))   **119**
[2002 8s 10g* 10g* 12m 12.5s* 12.5g³ 10g* 12g Oct 6] well-made colt: fourth foal:
brother to useful French performers up to 1m Fairly Grey and Fairlee Mixa: dam 6f (at 2
yrs) to 8.5f winner in USA, including minor stakes: smart performer: won claimer at
Saint-Cloud at 3 yrs (claimed from A. Fabre): much improved in 2002, winning handicaps at Longchamp in April/May, listed race at Deauville in August and La Coupe de
Maisons-Laffitte (by 2 lengths from Jim And Tonic) in September: ran well when eighth
of 16 to Marienbard in Prix de l'Arc de Triomphe at Longchamp final start, though never
a threat: stays 12.5f: acts on heavy and good to firm ground. *M. Rolland, France*

FAIRMORNING (IRE)   3 b.g. Ridgewood Ben 113 – The Bratpack (IRE) (Mister   –
Majestic 122) [2002 10m f12g⁶ f12g Dec 26] smallish, good-topped gelding: second foal:
dam unraced: well beaten in maidens/seller. *J. W. Unett*

FAIR PROMISE   3 b.g. Rudimentary (USA) 118 – Birsay (Bustino 136) [2002 –: p12g   **48**
p13g Aug 9] poor maiden. *D. K. Ivory*

FAIR QUESTION (IRE)   4 b.c. Rainbow Quest (USA) 134 – Fair of The Furze 112   **109**
(Ela-Mana-Mou 132) [2002 113: 12m 16d⁶ May 25] leggy, quite attractive colt: fluent
mover: smart performer at best: won Deutsches St Leger at Dortmund in 2001: best effort
in 2002 when sixth to Adlerflieger in Betty Barclay-Rennen at Baden-Baden final start:
stays 2m: acts on soft and good to firm going: sold 52,000 gns, joined Venetia Williams.
J. L. Dunlop

FAIR SHAKE (IRE)   2 b.g. (Mar 16) Sheikh Albadou 128 – Shamrock Fair (IRE) 77   **60**
(Shavian 125) [2002 6g⁶ 6g 6m Jul 13] 6,200Y, 15,000 2-y-o: close-coupled gelding:
second foal: dam 2-y-o 7f winner: modest maiden: best effort on debut: should stay 7f:
gelded after final start. *D. Eddy*

FAIR STEP   4 ch.f. King's Signet (USA) 110 – Miss Hocroft (Dominion 123) [2002   –
55: 5g 5m Jul 24] unfurnished filly: modest maiden at 3 yrs: well held both starts in 2002,
leaving impression something amiss on final one. *G. A. Swinbank*

FAIRTOTO   6 b.g. Mtoto 134 – Fairy Feet 78 (Sadler's Wells (USA) 132) [2002 60:   –
f16s Jan 14] leggy, plain gelding: modest at 5 yrs: well held only Flat outing in 2002: tried
tongue tied. *D. J. Wintle*

FAIRY LOCH   3 b.f. Sure Blade (USA) 130 – Tremloch (Tremblant 112) [2002 –:   –
8.1m 9.9f Sep 26] unfurnished filly: no sign of ability. *P. C. Ritchens*

FAIRY MONARCH (IRE)   3 b.g. Ali-Royal (IRE) 127 – Cookawara (IRE) (Fairy   **84 d**
King (USA)) [2002 83: 8m⁶ 8d 8m 8f 8f f7g f8g p10g Dec 21] neat gelding: fairly useful
performer at best: well held after reappearance, leaving B. Meehan after second outing
and J. Cullinan after fifth start: stays 1m: yet to race on heavy going, acts on any other:
tried blinkered: difficult ride. *I. W. McInnes*

FAIRY PRINCE (IRE)   9 b.g. Fairy King (USA) – Danger Ahead (Mill Reef (USA)   **67**
141) [2002 68: 7.1m 6d⁶ 6m 6.1m 6m² 6d 6m 5.7f 6m 6.1m Oct 1] lengthy gelding: fair
handicapper: below form last 5 starts: raced mainly at 5f/6f nowadays: acts on firm going

(probably on soft), well beaten only run on fibresand: effective visored/blinkered/hooded or not: sometimes slowly away. *Mrs A. L. M. King*

FAITHFUL WARRIOR (USA)   4 ch.g. Diesis 133 – Dabaweyaa 118 (Shareef   **94**
Dancer (USA) 135) [2002 102p: 8s 8m 8m 8d 8f 8m 7.9m 7.6f³ 8g⁶ Oct 18] good-topped gelding: only fairly useful handicapper in 2002: creditable efforts at Chester and Newmarket (26 ran) last 2 starts (gelded after): free-going sort, but stays 1m: acts on firm and good to soft going: has worn crossed noseband: sometimes on edge: has been early/taken steadily to post: usually waited with. *B. W. Hills*

FAIZA   3 b.f. Efisio 120 – Nanouche (Dayjur (USA) 137) [2002 68: 6f⁶ 6m⁴ 5.7g 5.3m*   **75**
6s Jun 10] smallish, sturdy filly: fair handicapper, lightly raced: won at Brighton in May: stays 6f: acts on good to firm going, possibly not on soft: reportedly hurt back second 2-y-o start: has flicked tail: sold 8,000 gns in December. *R. Hannon*

FALBRAV (IRE)   4 b.c. Fairy King (USA) – Gift of The Night (USA) (Slewpy   **125**
(USA)) [2002 112: 9g* 10m* 12f* 12m³ 12g 11f* Nov 24]

     Frankie Dettori's post-race celebrations have not always been to the taste of his countrymen. For instance, Don Enrico Incisa (who has known him since he was a child) once observed of a Dettori big-race triumph that 'he kissed Hamdan Al Maktoum, Maktoum Al Maktoum and Sheikh Mohammed. The Arabs don't mind because they do kiss each other among the men, but in Italy it is not quite so normal. I think he gets over-excited.' In November 2002, however, came a victory to send all Italians into wild celebration when Falbrav, bred by Azienda Agricola Francesca and owned by Scuderia Rencati, trained by Luciano D'Auria and ridden by Lanfranco Dettori, won the Japan Cup. Super Tassa's 2001 Yorkshire Oaks had been the first Group 1 win by an Italian-trained horse abroad since Tony Bin took the Arc in 1988, but this triumph was of another order altogether. For Falbrav's owner and jockey it was also the second Group 1 success in the space of a week, following Sunstrach's in the Premio Roma. That race was the front-page story on the Italian equestrian newspaper *Lo Sportsman* for two days, followed immediately by another eight days devoted to Falbrav's preparation for the Japan Cup and Falbrav's Japan Cup triumph. There were tears of joy for Dettori and possibly an extra jubilation in the familiar images of him suspended in the air as he performed his flying dismount. The mood was infectious and, with Dettori also having won the 2,000,000-dollar Japan Cup Dirt on Eagle Cafe the day before, that horse's trainer Futoshi Kojima proudly announced that he had recently given the name Frankie to his dog, a Japanese terrier.

     Falbrav was sent off at 195/10 on the Japanese tote in a sixteen-runner field for the Japan Cup that included four other European challengers, all with Group 1 form but relatively unfancied by Japanese backers. They were King George winner Golan (186/10), Champion Stakes winner Storming Home (40/1) and the Prix de l'Opera first and second Bright Sky (169/10) and Irresistible Jewel (63/1). In a

Gran Premio di Milano, Milan—Falbrav draws clear of the tiring Narrative (rail); Hawkeye is third

Japan Cup, Nakayama—a triumph for Italy as Frankie Dettori pounces late on Falbrav; Sarafan (virtually obscured) snatches second from Symboli Kris S (No.7) and Magnaten (rail); Golan (No.3) finishes seventh

steadily-run race, Golan and Irresistible Jewel were disputing third entering the straight but, close up behind them, three others were all going better: a nose and a neck were the final margins (the rider of the runner-up made an unsuccessful objection) as Falbrav got to the front in the last fifty yards and just held off Sir Mark Prescott's former charge Sarafan, now trained in the United States, and local favourite Symboli Kris S, ridden by Olivier Peslier. The second favourite and previous year's winner Jungle Pocket came from much further back to finish fifth, with Golan eventually second of the Europeans to finish, in seventh.

The 4,000,000-dollar Japan Cup took on a somewhat different character in the latest season, run over eleven furlongs instead of a mile and a half, a shorter straight and right-handed instead of left-handed, following a temporary switch to Nakayama from Tokyo, while that course underwent major reconstruction, but one factor remained the same—the going was firm. This was thoroughly in Falbrav's favour judged on the pick of his form on home soil, beginning with his best effort in 2001 when chasing home Morshdi in the Derby Italiano. He failed to progress further as a three-year-old but was unbeaten in Italy on his first three outings in 2002. A minor event at Rome in April got the sequence under way before much improved performances to capture two Group 1 events. On both occasions Falbrav came from behind and had to battle his way up the straight to reel in a Godolphin front-runner inside the final furlong, first Ekraar in course-record time of 1m 57.8 secs (which some consider should be credited as a world record) for the Premio Presidente della Repubblica over a mile and a quarter at Rome in May then Narrative in the mile-and-a-half Gran Premio di Milano in June. In both races, the first two finished clear of the third and the winner's form was high class. In this vein Falbrav would have been a worthwhile candidate for the summer's top middle-distance prizes, but instead he was put away for an autumn campaign, his main target reportedly the Arc. When the Arc came round, Falbrav was indeed in the field but came home a never dangerous though respectable ninth. Perhaps ground conditions weren't ideal for him, but third in the previous month's Prix Foy had been an encouraging return from his summer break and that promise was realised at the second attempt in Japan. Falbrav was ridden by Peslier in the Arc, by Dario Vargiu for most of his Italian starts and in the Foy, and by Dettori for the first time at Nakayama.

The Japan Cup was by a very long way the most important success, but Italian-trained horses made their mark on several other notable occasions in international competition during 2002. Not least of their accomplishments was that of keeping some of their own top prizes at home. Falbrav was in the vanguard, retaining the Gran Premio di Milano for the first time for Italy since 1990. His was only the second Italian Premio Presidente della Repubblica over the same period and, where he had failed in 2001 in keeping the Derby Italiano at home, Rakti succeeded. That was Italy's first victory in the premier domestic classic since 1988. In France, Altieri won the Prix Messidor, Pleasure Place the Prix d'Arenberg and Le Vie dei Colori the Prix La Rochette, the last-named also only just losing out in the Grand Criterium. It wasn't all glory, however. Two examples linger firmly in the memory. In Britain there was the sight of Rakti failing to enter his stall for the Champion Stakes, his jockey giving him a smack around the head and later writing a letter of apology to the *Racing Post*. Earlier in October, amid widespread and prolonged confusion into the result of the Prix de l'Abbaye, the same rider, Mirco Demuro, was led to believe that he had won the race on Italian-trained Slap Shot. With Slap Shot draped in the winner's blanket, Demuro stood on his saddle on entering the winner's enclosure and performed a flying dismount, not quite emulating Dettori, however, as the eventual result of the photo-finish revealed that he had been beaten into second.

Falbrav (IRE) (b.c. 1998)	Fairy King (USA) (b 1982)	Northern Dancer (b 1961)	Nearctic
			Natalma
		Fairy Bridge (b 1975)	Bold Reason
			Special
	Gift of The Night (USA) (b 1990)	Slewpy (b or br 1980)	Seattle Slew
			Rare Bouquet
		Little Nana (ch 1975)	Lithiot
			Nenana Road

Falbrav, who is to be trained by Luca Cumani in 2003, apparently means 'Be Good' in a Milanese dialect and good he certainly was for his Italian connections. Falbrav is a strong, heavy-bodied colt who carries plenty of condition; the weights of all the Japan Cup contestants were published and, at 538 kilograms, he was the heaviest. He is effective at a mile and a quarter to a mile and a half, and has shown useful form on soft and good to soft going, though all of his high-class form was registered on good to firm or firm. There is an obvious inspiration in Falbrav's breeding in the shape of 1996 Arc winner Helissio, who was also by Fairy King out of a mare by Slewpy. Efforts to repeat that particular mating came to nothing, because when confirmation of the whereabouts of Helissio's dam finally came through in 1996 it was to the effect that she had died earlier that year in Saudi Arabia. Bloodstock journalist Tony Morris has reported that there were only two other mares by Slewpy in Ireland, one of which was unable to be covered and the other one Gift of The Night, who produced Falbrav. Fairy King went infertile in 1998 and died the year after that. Falbrav is his dam's fourth foal and fourth Italian winner, following Fanofadiga (by Alzao), Fiur (by Grand Lodge) and Fafinta (by Indian Ridge), and she has since visited Coolmore stallions Night Shift, Alzao, Fasliyev, Montjeu and Galileo, though she didn't get into foal to the first three named. Trained by Pascal Bary, Gift of The Night won her third start as a two-year-old, a minor event over seven and a half furlongs at Deauville, and was second of five in a listed race over a mile. However, she then refused to race in the Prix de Conde, and on her only three-year-old start she was last of seven in the Prix Penelope. Falbrav's grandam Little Nana, contrastingly, won seven of fourteen starts as a two-year-old, five of them claimers, and bounced back from nineteen unsuccessful outings the following season to win three handicaps at around a mile and a quarter from her six starts at four. Third dam Nenana Road was a winner and very well bred, the family luminaries including her half-sister the 1965 Poule d'Essai des Pouliches winner La Sarre. *L. D'Auria, Italy*

FALCON GEORGIE   3 b.f. Sri Pekan (USA) 117 – Georgia Stephens (USA) 64 (The   –
Minstrel (CAN) 135) [2002 43: 7.1g Apr 1] neat filly: poor form on debut at 2 yrs: well below form since. *N. Tinkler*

FALCON GOA (IRE)   4 b.f. Sri Pekan (USA) 117 – Minden (IRE) (Bluebird (USA)   –
125) [2002 69: 5s 6f 6.1d 5g May 10] leggy filly: fair handicapper at 3 yrs: well held in 2002: was effective at 5f/6f: acted on fibresand, good to firm and good to soft going: was usually visored: dead. *N. Tinkler*

FALCON HILL   3 b.g. Polar Falcon (USA) 126 – Branston Jewel (IRE) 95 (Prince   **108 d**
Sabo 123) [2002 102: 6s* 8g 6m 6d 6.5v⁶ 7s⁶ 6v Nov 9] good-topped gelding: useful performer at best: won listed race at Doncaster in March by length from Needwood Blade: ran poorly after, including in blinkers: stays 6f: has form on firm going, very best efforts on soft/heavy: races up with pace: sometimes idles: gelded after final start. *M. Johnston*

FALCON ON THE HILL (USA)   2 b.g. (Feb 25) Southern Halo (USA) – Inca   **75**
Empress (USA) (Sovereign Dancer (USA)) [2002 7g 7.5g³ 7s² Aug 24] second foal: half-

brother to fairly useful 1½m winner Inca Star (by Trempolino): dam, 5f (at 2 yrs) to 8.5f winner in USA, half-sister to very smart German middle-distance horse Germany: fair maiden: 5/1-on, beaten head in minor event at Redcar final start (gelded after): should be suited by 1¼m+. *M. Johnston*

FALLACHAN (USA)   6 ch.g. Diesis 133 – Afaff (USA) (Nijinsky (CAN) 138) [2002   –
78, a84: f8.5g* f8.5g* f8.5g Feb 22] angular, good-topped gelding: fairly useful handi-   **a88**
capper on all-weather: won at Wolverhampton in January/February: stays 8.5f: acts on
fibresand, good to firm and good to soft going (possibly not on soft/heavy): has twice run
poorly when sweating. *M. A. Jarvis*

FALLEN STAR   4 b.f. Brief Truce (USA) 126 – Rise And Fall (Mill Reef (USA) 141)   **112**
[2002 108p: 8m* 9.9m⁴ 8m³ 8f⁴ 8s² Oct 20] rangy filly, good sort: smart performer:
reportedly had joint problem after debut at 3 yrs: won listed contest at Ascot in July by
1¼ lengths from Inglenook: in frame in pattern races after, best efforts when fourth to
Islington in Nassau Stakes at Goodwood next time and when ½-length second to Welsh
Diva in Premio Sergio Cumani at Milan final start: free-going sort, best at 1m: acted on
soft and good to firm going: had proved difficult (swished tail) in preliminaries: carried
head awkwardly. *J. L. Dunlop*

FALLS O'MONESS (IRE)   8 b.m. River Falls 113 – Sevens Are Wild 40 (Petorius   – §
117) [2002 48§, a43§: f7g f8.5g³ f8.5g⁶ Jan 21] sparely-made mare: poor performer: on   **a40** §
long losing run: best at 1m/1¼m: acts on fibresand, firm and soft going: tried blinkered/
visored earlier in career: often slowly away: headstrong and best held up: unreliable.
E. J. Alston

Mr Nicholas Cooper's "Fallen Star"

FAMOUS GROUSE   2 b.c. (Jan 26) Selkirk (USA) 129 – Shoot Clear 111 (Bay   **96 p**
Express 132) [2002 7m² 8.2m* 8.2s* Oct 23] 42,000F, 100,000Y: quite attractive colt:
closely related to a winner in USA by Kris and half-brother to several winners, including
1996 2-y-o sprinter Jhazi (by Arazi) and 1½m winner Shoot Ahead (by Shirley Heights),
both useful: dam, 5f to 7f winner at 2 yrs and fourth in 1000 Guineas, half-sister to
Yorkshire Oaks winners Untold and Sally Brown: useful form: won minor events at
Nottingham in August and October: best effort when beating Lucayan Dancer by 2½
lengths in latter, wandering after leading 3f out: should stay 1¼m: acts on soft and good
to firm ground: probably capable of better still. *R. Charlton*

FANCY LADY   2 ch.f. (Mar 13) Cadeaux Genereux 131 – Ascot Cyclone (USA) 93   **99**
(Rahy (USA) 115) [2002 5s³ 6m² 6s* 6m* 5m⁵ 5m⁴ Oct 12] angular, quite attractive filly:
fluent mover: first foal: dam, 5.7f (at 2 yrs) and 7f winner, half-sister to smart performer
up to 1¼m Magellan and 1000 Guineas runner-up Dabaweyaa: useful performer: won
maiden at Newmarket in July and nursery at Goodwood in August: respectable efforts in
Flying Childers Stakes at Doncaster and Cornwallis Stakes at Ascot last 2 starts: effective
at 5f/6f: acts on soft and good to firm going: usually races prominently. *B. W. Hills*

FANDANGO DREAM (IRE)   6 ch.g. Magical Wonder (USA) 125 – Fandikos   **–**
(IRE) (Taufan (USA) 119) [2002 44: f14.8g 14.1m Aug 21] smallish, angular gelding:
poor handicapper at 5 yrs: well beaten both starts in 2002: tried blinkered/visored.
M. D. I. Usher

FANDANITA (IRE)   3 b.f. Anita's Prince 126 – Fandangerina (USA) (Grey Dawn II   **56**
132) [2002 57: f6s f6g³ f6g³ f6g³ f6g² 5.9s 6g 6.1d Jul 6] modest maiden handicapper:
left N. Littmoden after fifth start: well below form after: should stay 7f: acts on fibresand
and good to firm going (possibly not on soft): has carried head awkwardly: sold 13,000
gns later in July, sent to Australia. *M. L. W. Bell*

FANGIO'S QUEST   3 ch.g. Piccolo 121 – Perioscope (Legend of France (USA) 124)   **64 d**
[2002 76p: 6m 6g 5d⁶ 6d 5v⁵ 5m 6d⁶ 7.9s 6g 5m Sep 2] smallish, strong gelding: modest
performer: gradually lost form after third start, leaving T. Easterby after eighth one: stays
6f: acts on good to soft ground, probably on good to firm: blinkered sixth and seventh
outings: gelded after final one. *J. G. Given*

FANNY BAY (IRE)   3 b.f. Key of Luck (USA) 126 – Disregard That (IRE) (Don't   **–**
Forget Me 127) [2002 76: 7.1m⁵ Apr 13] strong, useful-looking filly: fair maiden at 2 yrs:
off 11 months, well held only outing in 2002. *Mrs P. N. Dutfield*

FANNY'S DREAM (IRE)   2 b.f. (Apr 14) Danetime (IRE) 121 – Roemoor Girl   **–**
(IRE) 59 (Turtle Island (IRE) 123) [2002 f6g f6g Dec 16] IR 5,500Y, 4,800 2-y-o: first
foal: dam, maiden who should have stayed 7f (raced only at 2 yrs), half-sister to smart
Irish sprinter Bradawn Breever: well held in maiden/seller. *S. Kirk*

FANNY'S FANCY   2 b.f. (Mar 23) Groom Dancer (USA) 128 – Fanny's Choice (IRE)   **74 p**
90 (Fairy King (USA)) [2002 5d 5m² Sep 29] 11,000Y: sturdy, good-quartered filly: third
foal: dam, 6f winner, ran only at 2 yrs: favourite, much better effort in maidens 4 months
apart (fair form) when ¾-length second to Circuit Dancer at Musselburgh, no extra late
on: will prove best at 5f/6f: likely to improve further. *C. F. Wall*

FANTASIZE   2 ch.f. (Mar 12) Groom Dancer (USA) 128 – Belle Et Deluree (USA)   **84 p**
(The Minstrel (CAN) 135) [2002 7s⁴ 7g* Oct 14] lengthy, angular filly: half-sister to
several winners, including smart 5f (at 2 yrs) to 7f winner Dazzle (by Gone West) and
useful 1999 2-y-o 7f winner Hypnotize (by Machiavellian): dam French 1m (at 2 yrs) and
1¼m winner: 4/1, fairly useful form when winning 16-runner maiden at Leicester by ½
length from Largo, leading well over 1f out and rallying: will stay 1m: will probably
improve further. *Sir Michael Stoute*

FANTASTIC CHAMPION (IRE)   3 b.g. Entrepreneur 123 – Reine Mathilde (USA)   **97**
123 (Vaguely Noble 140) [2002 –: 10m 8m 11.6m* 11.6s⁶ 16.2m 11.6g³ Jul 8] good-
topped, close-coupled gelding: useful performer: won handicap at Windsor in May: very
good third in minor event at Windsor final start: likely to prove best around 1½m: acts on
soft and good to firm going: sold 37,000 gns, joined Mrs L. Wadham. *P. W. D'Arcy*

FANTASTICO (IRE)   2 b.f. (Apr 5) Bahhare (USA) 122 – Minatina (IRE) 78 (Ela-   **74**
Mana-Mou 132) [2002 7m 8.5d⁴ f8s² 10.2f² 10f³ 10s³ f9.4g⁴ Nov 16] IR 6,000Y:
good-topped filly: fourth foal: half-sister to 5-y-o Yertle: dam, lightly-raced 1¼m winner,
half-sister to 6-y-o Tillerman: fair maiden: in frame all 6 starts after debut: should stay
1½m: acts on fibresand, firm and soft ground. *S. Kirk*

FANTASY ADVENTURER   5 b.g. Magic Ring (IRE) 115 – Delicious 51 (Dominion   **–**
123) [2002 –: f8s Jan 17] tall, leggy gelding: modest maiden at 3 yrs: no form since: tried
blinkered/visored. *J. Cullinan*

FANTASY BELIEVER   4 b.g. Sure Blade (USA) 130 – Delicious 51 (Dominion **99 d**
123) [2002 103: 6g 5.2g 6m⁴ 6m 6m 5m 5f 6m 5m⁶ 5d 5s Oct 26] sturdy gelding: useful
handicapper at best: best effort when fourth at Newmarket third start: creditable efforts in
2002 only on third and sixth starts: effective at 5f/6f: acts on any going: has worn
near-side pricker and hung/carried head awkwardly. *J. J. Quinn*

FANTASY CRUSADER   3 ch.g. Beveled (USA) – Cranfield Charger (Northern   **–**
State (USA) 91) [2002 65d: 9.9g p10g 8.5m 7f 7s Oct 28] fair form when successful at 2
yrs: well held since: tried tongue tied: gelded after final start. *J. Cullinan*

FANTASY HILL (IRE)   6 b.g. Danehill (USA) 126 – Gay Fantasy (Troy 137) [2002   **106**
16m 18.7f* 16.1g 13.9m⁴ 18.7g³ Aug 4] angular gelding: useful handicapper: reportedly
suffered leg injury in September 2000 (has been fired) and missed 2001: better than ever
when winning Tote Chester Cup in May by 2 lengths from Rainbow High: at least
respectable efforts after, including when fourth to Maycocks Bay in listed rated stakes at
York: effective at 1¾m to 2¼m: acts on firm and soft going: usually blinkered: tends to
race freely. *J. L. Dunlop*

FANTASY PARK   5 b.g. Sanglamore (USA) 126 – Fantasy Flyer (USA) (Lear Fan   **51**
(USA) 130) [2002 84?: f16.2g⁶ 17.1m 10.5m³ 15.8f³ f14.8g Sep 30] sturdy gelding:
modest performer nowadays, lightly raced: left G. McCourt after second start: seems to
stay 17f: acts on firm and good to soft going, well held on fibresand: blinkered final
outing: went in snatches (ran well) fourth start. *D. J. Wintle*

FARAUDE   4 b.f. Farfelu 103 – Pennine Star (IRE) 68 (Pennine Walk 120) [2002 55:   **–**
10m 8g 8m 8.1d 10.2f 8m Aug 7] workmanlike filly: modest winner at 3 yrs: no form in
2002. *W. R. Muir*

*Tote Chester Cup (Handicap), Chester—Fantasy Hill wins from the previous year's 1,2
Rainbow High (rail) and High And Mighty (widest) who stays on past Riyadh*

FARAWAY JOHN (IRE) 4 b.g. Farhaan 77 – Indiana Dancer (Hallgate 127) [2002 **48**
59: p12g 11.8s⁶ 12d 12.1g 11.9g Oct 24] poor handicapper nowadays: should stay beyond
1½m: raced only on good going or softer on turf. *G. P. Enright*

FARAWAY LOOK (USA) 5 br.g. Distant View (USA) 126 – Summer Trip (USA) **–**
117 (L'Emigrant (USA) 129) [2002 90: 10s f8.5f f9.4s² f9.4g Dec 26] good-bodied **a76**
gelding: fair handicapper: stays 10.5f: acts on fibresand, best turf effort on good ground:
has carried head high. *J. G. M. O'Shea*

FAR LANE (USA) 3 b.c. Lear Fan (USA) 130 – Pattimech (USA) (Nureyev (USA) **108**
131) [2002 70p: 7s* 8m² 7.9f⁴ 10.1s⁴ 8m² 8m³ 10.3m⁵ 10m² 9f² Oct 5] strong, rangy,
good sort: has a round action: progressed into useful performer: won maiden at Doncaster
in March: very good second in valuable handicaps at Newbury (short headed by
stable-companion Solo Flight in Courage Best Stakes) and Newmarket last 2 starts,
doing even better than result suggests when beaten 1½ lengths by Beauchamp Pilot in
Cambridgeshire in latter, leading unfavoured group throughout and running on really
strongly: stays 1¼m: yet to race on heavy ground, acts on any other: free-going sort (often
wears net muzzle). *B. W. Hills*

FAR NOTE (USA) 4 ch.g. Distant View (USA) 126 – Denoant (USA) (Nureyev (USA) **–**
131) [2002 81: 6m 6f 6m 5d p8g f6s p6g⁵ Nov 14] sturdy, well-made gelding: fairly useful
maiden at 3 yrs: little form in 2002: has worn cheekpieces. *T. J. Etherington*

FAR PAVILIONS 3 b.g. Halling (USA) 133 – Flambera (FR) (Akarad (FR) 130) **94**
[2002 91p: 7m 10.3m 10.5f² Sep 27] good-topped gelding: fairly useful performer, lightly
raced: visored, ran well in handicap at Haydock final start: stays 10.5f: acts on firm going:
ran in snatches/found little final 2-y-o start: sold 14,000 gns, joined G. A. Swinbank and
won both outings over hurdles in December. *Mrs J. R. Ramsden*

FAR REACHING (USA) 3 ch.f. Distant View (USA) 126 – Nimble Feet (USA) 82 **76**
(Danzig (USA)) [2002 8.2g 8m² 8.3g⁴ 7s Sep 10] good-bodied filly: closely related to 3
winners, including useful 1m winners Yamuna (by Forty Niner) and Variety Shop (by Mr
Prospector), and half-sister to several winners, including very smart performer up to 1¼m
Eltish (by Cox's Ridge) and smart sprinter Forest Gazelle (by Green Forest): dam 2-y-o
5f winner: fair maiden: easily best effort on second start: stays 1m: acts on good to firm
going: off bridle some way out last 2 outings: one to treat with caution: sold 70,000 gns in
December. *H. R. A. Cecil*

FAR STORM (USA) 2 ch.c. (Apr 14) Smart Strike (CAN) 121 – Kadeena 76 (Never **61 p**
So Bold 135) [2002 7m 8d Aug 2] $21,000F, 31,000Y: tall, unfurnished colt: second foal:
dam 2-y-o 7f winner out of sister to Derby third Oats: green, modest form in maidens at
Newmarket: has scope to do better at 3 yrs. *I. A. Balding*

FASHIONABLE MAN (USA) 3 ch.c. Unbridled (USA) 128 – Too Chic (USA) **96**
(Blushing Groom (FR) 131) [2002 93p: 12m* 11m 12d⁵ 11.9s² 14.1g² 12m Jun 20] big,
leggy colt: good walker: has a rather splayed action: useful performer: won minor event
at Catterick in April: second in handicaps at Haydock and Salisbury: reportedly lame
final start: stays 1¾m: acts on soft and good to firm going: usually makes running: sold
10,000 gns in November. *M. Johnston*

FASSAN (IRE) 10 br.g. Contract Law (USA) 108 – Persian Susan (USA) (Herbager **–**
136) [2002 f16.2g May 20] fair maiden in Ireland at 3 yrs: poor chaser nowadays:
blinkered only start on Flat in 2002. *A. Crook*

FAST AND FURIOUS (IRE) 5 b.g. Brief Truce (USA) 126 – Zing Ping (IRE) 80 **77**
(Thatching 131) [2002 82: p10g f8.5g 8s⁴ 9g⁵ 7s 8.5d⁶ 9g 9m 9d⁶ Oct 26] fair handicapper: below form on all-weather in Britain first 2 starts: stays 1¼m: acts on fibresand,
heavy and good to firm ground: usually tongue tied. *T. Stack, Ireland*

FAST AND NEAT (IRE) 6 ch.g. Soviet Lad (USA) – Stop The Cavalry (Relko 136) **–**
[2002 8.1g 10m 12d Sep 11] modest handicapper at 3 yrs: well held in 2002. *R. Guest*

FAST CINDY (USA) 3 b.f. Fastness (IRE) 127 – Forever Cindy (ARG) (Forever **73**
Sparkle (USA)) [2002 65: 9.7d 10f 12m⁶ 16.2g⁵ 16m² 16.1m* p16g Oct 16] tall, sparely-
made filly: fair handicapper: won at Newcastle in October: stays 2m: yet to race on soft/
heavy ground, probably acts on any other turf (well held on polytrack debut): sold 11,000
gns. *P. F. I. Cole*

FAST FOIL (IRE) 4 b.f. Lahib (USA) 129 – Fast Chick 93 (Henbit (USA) 130) [2002 **78**
70: p10g³ f8s p8g f7g f9.4g f8.5g⁴ f9.4g 7.1v 8m³ 8.3m* 8.1m⁶ 10g⁴ 8.3m 8m* 8g 10m⁵
9.9m 10m 9m⁶ 10.2g 9.9g² 10d⁴ 12s 10.3v* Nov 8] sparely-made filly: fair performer:
rejoined former trainer (from D. Burchell) after seventh start: won handicaps at Windsor
(2) and Redcar and minor event at Doncaster in second half of 2002: stays 1¼m: acts on

heavy going, good to firm and all-weather: sometimes slowly away: usually dropped out.
M. R. Channon

FAST FORWARD FRED   11 gr.g. Sharrood (USA) 124 – Sun Street 73 (Ile de **52**
Bourbon (USA) 133) [2002 50: p16g⁵ 19.1m⁶ p16g⁵ Jul 17] big, lengthy gelding: shows **a48**
knee action: modest handicapper on turf, poor on all-weather: stays 2¼m: acts on firm
ground and polytrack. *L. Montague Hall*

FAST TRACK (IRE)   5 b.g. Doyoun 124 – Manntika 77 (Kalamoun 129) [2002 70: **84**
p10g f7g f9.4g* f9.4g* f8.5g* f7g Dec 31] lengthy gelding: one-time useful performer:
left G. McCourt, gelded and off 10½ months, best efforts for long time (fairly useful
form) when easily winning 3 handicaps at Wolverhampton in December: effective at 8.5f
to 10.4f: acts on fibresand, firm and good to soft ground. *R. Hannon*

FATEHALKHAIR (IRE)   10 ch.g. Kris 135 – Midway Lady (USA) 126 (Alleged **77**
(USA) 138) [2002 72, a45+: 13.8d* 12m 13.9f³ 16.1m* 16m⁶ 16.1g 16m³ 21g 16d⁴ Aug **a–**
23] leggy, angular gelding: poor mover: fair handicapper: won at Catterick in March and
Newcastle in May: stays 2m: acts on firm going, good to soft and fibresand: visored once
at 4 yrs: all wins on left-handed tracks: held up: tough: fairly useful hurdler/chaser.
B. Ellison

FAT FRANK   2 b.c. (May 7) Alzao (USA) 117 – Bush Rose (Rainbow Quest (USA) **–**
134) [2002 6g 7m Jul 24] quite good-topped colt: third foal: dam unraced half-sister to
smart 1¼m/1½m winner Young Buster: no form in sellers (pulled up and dismounted on
debut). *M. W. Easterby*

FATHER JUNINHO (IRE)   5 b.g. Distinctly North (USA) 115 – Shane's Girl (IRE) **104**
(Marktingo) [2002 100: p12g p12g* Feb 23] strong, close-coupled gelding: has a quick
action: useful handicapper: better than ever when winning at Lingfield in February:
seems best at 1½m: acts on firm and good to soft going (may not take much racing on
former) and polytrack: visored (pulled too hard) once as 3-y-o: has been mulish in
preliminaries: held up, not easiest of rides but has good turn of foot. *A. P. Jarvis*

FATHER SEAMUS   4 b.g. Bin Ajwaad (IRE) 119 – Merry Rous 66 (Rousillon (USA) **–**
133) [2002 43: 11.9g May 2] leggy, workmanlike gelding: maiden: well held only Flat
start in 2002. *P. Butler*

FATHER THAMES   4 b.c. Bishop of Cashel 122 – Mistress Thames 63 (Sharpo 132) **113**
[2002 112: 8.3s* 7.1s⁵ 8m 9m 7s³ Oct 26] strong, lengthy colt: smart performer: won
listed race at Windsor (by 1½ lengths from Bourgainville) in May: just respectable efforts
at best after: effective at 7f/1m: acts on soft and good to firm going: visored final start:
sold 45,000 gns, sent to USA. *J. R. Fanshawe*

FATH (USA)   5 b.h. Danzig (USA) – Desirable 119 (Lord Gayle (USA) 124) [2002 **–**
116: 7.1s⁶ Jun 8] smallish, good-topped horse: wasn't the best of movers: smart performer
at best: won Lennox Stakes at Goodwood in 2001: well held only outing at 5 yrs: was
effective at 5f to 7f, not at 1m: acted on firm and good to soft going: tried tongue tied at 3
yrs: sometimes bandaged/wore crossed noseband/raced freely: game and reliable: to
stand at Rathasker Stud, Co Kildare, Ireland, fee €4,750, Oct 1st. *M. P. Tregoning*

FATIK (USA)   2 br.c. (Apr 16) Gone West (USA) – Muhbubh (USA) 108 (Blushing **94 p**
Groom (FR) 131) [2002 6d³ 6m⁴ Jul 30] neat, attractive colt: closely related to 2 winners
by Mr Prospector, including smart performer up to 7f in UAE/USA Kayrawan (6f winner
in Britain at 2 yrs), and half-brother to 3 winners, including 4-y-o Elsaamri: dam won
Princess Margaret Stakes: shade upset in stall, shaped well on debut: well-backed
favourite, fairly useful form when 6 lengths fifth Elusive City in Richmond Stakes at
Goodwood later in July, recovering from tardy start but fading final 1f: not sure to stay
further than 6f: should improve further and win races if all is well. *M. P. Tregoning*

FATTAAN (IRE)   2 b.c. (Mar 28) Danehill (USA) 126 – Bintalshaati 95 (Kris 135) **–**
[2002 8s Oct 26] sturdy colt: fourth foal: half-brother to 4-y-o Munadil: dam, 1m winner,
out of half-sister to Kentucky Derby winner Winning Colors: 14/1, already well held
when badly hampered over 1f out in maiden at Newbury. *M. P. Tregoning*

FAUTE DE MIEUX   7 ch.g. Beveled (USA) – Supreme Rose 95 (Frimley Park 109) **61**
[2002 74, a63: p7g p6g⁵ f6g p6g³ p6g 6m 6g 7d 6m Jun 3] useful-looking gelding: modest
handicapper: best at 5f/6f: acts on any turf going and polytrack, below form on fibresand:
blinkered twice, including final start: tried tongue tied earlier in career. *S. Kirk*

FAVIA   3 b.f. Mujadil (USA) 119 – Gustavia (IRE) 89 (Red Sunset 120) [2002 6g⁶ 8f **68**
8.3g Aug 12] smallish, good-bodied filly: fourth foal: dam 7f (at 2 yrs)/1m winner:
fair form in maidens at Newmarket and Ascot: unseated leaving stall final outing.
I. A. Balding

FAVOLA 2 b.f. (Feb 28) Royal Applause 124 – Pravolo (Fools Holme (USA)) [2002 **88** 5.7d⁵ 6f² 6.1m* 6g³ 5m* 6.5m 5f Oct 3] 30,000Y: strong, close-coupled filly: half-sister to several winners, including 6-y-o Lionardo: dam, Irish maiden, half-sister to very smart sprinter Sayyaf: fairly useful performer: won maiden at Nottingham in July and nursery at Sandown in August: effective at 5f/6f: acts on good to firm going: races up with pace: sold 28,000 gns, sent to USA. *L. M. Cumani*

FAVORISIO 5 br.g. Efisio 120 – Dixie Favor (USA) 82 (Dixieland Band (USA)) **70 §** [2002 73§: f12s² f14.8g² f12g⁶ f11g f14.8g Dec 16] robust gelding: fair handicapper: stays 14.8f: acts on fibresand and good to firm going: usually visored: has worn cheekpieces: sometimes slowly away: has hung fire/carried head awkwardly: not one to trust. *Miss J. A. Camacho*

FAVOUR 2 b.f. (Apr 8) Gothenberg (IRE) 117 – Prejudice 83 (Young Generation 129) **78 p** [2002 6d* Oct 18] half-sister to several winners by Efisio, including 4-y-o Onlytime Will Tell and fairly useful 7f/1m winner Al Moulouki (later successful up to 1½m in Italy), and to fairly useful 6f to 1m performer Hob Green (by Move Off): dam, maiden miler, half-sister to smart 7f/1m performer Casteddu: 16/1 and green, created good impression when winning 20-runner maiden at Redcar by 3½ lengths from Petite Mac, racing freely then ridden to lead over 1f out: will stay at least 7f: open to fair amount of improvement, and could well prove useful. *Mrs J. R. Ramsden*

FAX TO SOOTY 3 b.g. Factual (USA) 108 – Saltina (Bustino 136) [2002 58: p5g⁶ **55** p6g² p6g* p6g⁴ p8g⁵ p7g 6g p6g 8m p7g 7f Jul 29] lengthy gelding: modest handicapper: won seller at Lingfield in January: below form last 4 starts: probably best up to 7f: acts on good to firm ground, polytrack and probably on fibresand: usually visored/blinkered: sometimes front runner. *J. S. Moore*

FAYMIST (IRE) 3 ch.g. Fayruz 116 – Grave Error (Northern Treat (USA)) [2002 66: **46** f7g 6g³ f6g⁴ 7m 5.9v 5g Sep 7] good-bodied gelding: poor maiden: stays 6f: acts on firm going and fibresand: often blinkered: has been tongue tied: sent to Spain. *J. L. Eyre*

FAYR JAG (IRE) 3 b.g. Fayruz 116 – Lominda (IRE) 80 (Lomond (USA) 128) [2002 **106** 78: 7s 6.1f³ 6m* 6f² 6g⁵ 6m* 6d² 6m Aug 17] close-coupled, quite attractive gelding: useful handicapper: won at Ripon in April and Newmarket in June: very good second to Feet So Fast at Newmarket penultimate start: reared and unseated leaving stall there final outing: seems best at 6f: acts on firm and good to soft going, possibly not on soft. *T. D. Easterby*

FAZZANI (IRE) 4 b.f. Shareef Dancer (USA) 135 – Taj Victory 68 (Final Straw 127) – [2002 –: f8.5g Feb 4] small, useful-looking filly: fairly useful performer at 2 yrs: well held since. *O. Sherwood*

FEABHAS (IRE) 2 b.f. (Apr 12) Spectrum (IRE) 126 – Heike (Glenstal (USA) 118) **100** [2002 5s³ 6s³ 7s³ 7s* 7d* 7g² 8d³ 8d² 8s⁴ Nov 2] half-sister to several winners in Ireland, including 1m winner Father Murphy (by Erins Isle) and fairly useful 5f (at 2 yrs) and 7f winner Fine Project (by Project Manager): dam, useful Irish miler, half-sister to useful Irish 2-y-o performers Cois Na Tine and Eva Luna: useful performer: won maiden in July and nursery in August, both at Galway: placed in C. L. Weld Park Stakes (beaten ½ length by Rag Top) and Beresford Stakes (third to Alamshar and Brian Boru) next 2 starts, both at the Curragh: below form in listed race at Newmarket final outing: stays 1m: raced only on good going or softer. *J. S. Bolger, Ireland*

FEARBY CROSS (IRE) 6 b.g. Unblest 117 – Two Magpies 43 (Doulab (USA) 115) **83** [2002 83: 6g⁴ 6m 6m 6g⁵ 5d 6m³ 6d³ 6m⁶ 6m⁴ 7g 6.1s 7s Nov 2] strong gelding: poor mover: fairly useful handicapper: mostly creditable efforts in 2002: best at 5f (given test)/ 6f: acts on soft and good to firm going: blinkered once at 3 yrs: has swished tail: looked none too keen (hung left) final start: usually held up and suited by strong pace. *W. J. Musson*

FEAST OF ROMANCE 5 b.g. Pursuit of Love 124 – June Fayre (Sagaro 133) [2002 **56 +** –, a79: f6s f6g³ f6g⁶ f6g* p7g³ p6g² f6g² f6g* f6g² 6.1m³ f7s* p6g⁵ f7g⁶ p7g f7g f7g* f6g **a68** f6s Dec 26] sturdy gelding: fair performer: won sellers in February (left N. Littmoden)/ May, claimer in March and (having left J. Osborne after twelfth start) seller in December, all at Wolverhampton: effective at 6f/7f: acts on all-weather and good to firm going: tried blinkered in 2000: tough. *P. Howling*

FEATHER BOA (IRE) 2 b.f. (Apr 10) Sri Pekan (USA) 117 – Dancing Feather 72 **81** (Suave Dancer (USA) 136) [2002 6s⁴ 6d⁶ 6g³ p5g⁵ p6g* 6g* 6g 6f³ 6f⁴ 6g² 6s⁶ Oct 26] leggy, close-coupled filly: second foal: half-sister to 3-y-o Feathers Flying: dam, 1m winner who stayed 1½m, half-sister to 3-y-o Spring Oak: fairly useful performer: won nurseries at Lingfield and Kempton in July: in frame in 3 similar events after: should stay at least 7f: acts on polytrack and firm ground, below form on soft. *M. Blanshard*

FEATHERS FLYING (IRE) 3 b.f. Royal Applause 124 – Dancing Feather 72 (Suave Dancer (USA) 136) [2002 91: 10m 7m³ p10g p10g p8g Dec 21] angular filly: useful performer: at least creditable efforts in 2002 in listed race at Ascot (third to Secret Garden) and handicap at Lingfield on second/third starts: stays easy 1¼m: acts on polytrack, yet to race on extremes of going on turf. *G. A. Butler*   **100**

FEATHERTIME 6 b.m. Puissance 110 – Midnight Owl (FR) (Ardross 134) [2002 58, a–: f11s* Jan 17] leggy, angular mare: modest handicapper: won seller at Southwell in January: stays easy 11f: acts on fibresand, best turf efforts on good to soft/soft going: sold 4,000 gns. *Mrs G. S. Rees*   **63**

FEED THE METER (IRE) 2 b.f. (Apr 9) Desert King (IRE) 129 – Watch The Clock 93 (Mtoto 134) [2002 8s 10s Nov 2] 15,000F, IR 18,000Y, 10,000 2-y-o: big, good-bodied filly: third foal: half-sister to 3-y-o E Minor: dam 2-y-o 6f/7.5f winner who stayed 1¼m: fair form in maiden at Doncaster and listed race at Newmarket (well-held eighth of 10): will be suited by at least 1½m: probably capable of better. *G. C. H. Chung*   **70 p**

FEELING BLUE 3 b.f. Missed Flight 123 – Blues Indigo 103 (Music Boy 124) [2002 6.1m 5.1d⁴ 5m⁵ 5m² 5m³ 5g 5g* 5d 5d² Nov 5] leggy, angular filly: has a splayed action: fifth living foal: half-sister to 3 winners, including 7-y-o Magic Rainbow: dam sprinter: modest performer: won maiden at Newcastle (second run in 3 days) in September: best at 5f: unraced on extremes of going: hung left (possibly amiss) third start: sometimes slowly away: often races prominently. *R. M. Whitaker*   **60 +**

FEET SO FAST 3 ch.g. Pivotal 124 – Splice 114 (Sharpo 132) [2002 89p: 6g² 6g* 6d* 6d* a6g Dec 12]   **119**

There has been no shortage of strange sights at Ascot racecourse—as anyone who has attended the Royal meeting will attest—but that of Australian pop star Natalie Imbruglia performing in front of a crowd of sodden thousands during a torrential downpour on August 10th, 2002, will take some beating. It wasn't quite Woodstock, but those spectators put up easily the gamest display of the day, and one that seemed to confirm that a good percentage of the 23,434 course attendance had turned up principally to admire Ms Imbruglia rather than an event earlier in the day, namely the fourth renewal of the Shergar Cup. And many might say 'who can blame them?' The Shergar Cup, which for the second year was organised as a Great Britain and Ireland versus the Rest of The World jockeys competition, is not something for the racing or betting purists. However, it is a one-off in the racing calendar and any event that is involved in attracting a crowd of 20,000 to a race meeting deserves plenty of praise. Trainers can be relied upon to support almost anything

Tote Exacta Rated Stakes (Handicap), Newmarket—Feet So Fast quickens past Fayr Jag

*Dubai Duty Free Shergar Cup Sprint, Ascot—another impressive performance
as Feet So Fast completes his hat-trick; Ashdown Express and Whitbarrow chase him home*

that leads to increased prize-money, but several who fielded runners at the latest
Shergar Cup ended up being extremely unhappy. After the publicity machine had
been turned full on to gain notoriety for the jockeys' competition and to maintain
interest in it during the afternoon—including the use of It's A Knockout-style
jokers to gain double points—several of the riders entered the spirit of the occasion
so thoroughly that they ended up being accused of employing team tactics rather
than riding each horse on its individual merits. The Rest of The World captain
David Flores, for instance, was criticised for riding one of his mounts directly
opposite to his instructions. The Jockey Club launched an investigation into the
conduct of the meeting, with Malcolm Wallace, their director of regulation, stating
that 'there can be no question of one jockey helping another' and 'there can be no
question of team tactics being allowed to undermine the confidence of the punter.'
For the 2003 Shergar Cup, the jockeys are likely to receive a letter and formal
briefing to remind them of their responsibilities, something which will only serve
to underline the paradox at the heart of the occasion.

The 2002 Blue Square Shergar Cup was won by Great Britain and Ireland,
by 137 points to 110. They held the lead throughout and Richard Hughes rode three
of the six winners. One he missed out on was the horse who put up the best
performance at Ascot that afternoon, Feet So Fast in the Dubai Duty Free Shergar
Cup Sprint. Heightening the day's party atmosphere, favourites won the last two
races on the card, with Feet So Fast particularly well received in the final race, for
which he was sent off at 6/4. Eight of his nine opponents were established as at least
useful performers, but Feet So Fast beat them all in good style, travelling strongly
under Michael Kinane to lead approaching the furlong marker and going on to beat
Ashdown Express by three lengths. Feet So Fast was having only his sixth race and
looked one of the best sprint prospects around. Victory at 66/1 in a Newmarket
maiden the previous November—a rare juvenile winner for trainer Willie Musson
—had suggested that he had a bright future as a three-year-old, which duly materialised with clear-cut successes among his own age group in £29,000 handicaps
at Lingfield in May and Newmarket in July, both times starting favourite. In the
Newmarket race in particular—travelling and quickening impressively—Feet So
Fast left no doubt that he was capable of winning pattern races. He was also well
handicapped for the Stewards' Cup, but insufficient give in the ground meant that
he bypassed that race and was given the opportunity to round off those celebrations
in the Shergar Cup instead.

For those whose interest in British racing that day was not a one-off, the
celebrations over Feet So Fast proved short-lived. The story of a horse that has won
four of his six starts and three out of four in the latest season, all in good style,
should not leave one feeling disappointed, but this one does. His owners will have
turned a tidy profit, but the sport in Britain lost one of its rising stars when Feet
So Fast was sold to Sheikh Rashid bin Mohammed Al Maktoum, son of Sheikh

Mohammed, and was transferred to Dubai in August. The chance to see him in pattern company in 2002 was lost and, having been assiduously steered clear of ground firmer than good by Musson, Feet So Fast did not look the most likely recruit for racing in the Middle East. He began that new phase of his career poorly, wearing a visor in a six-furlong event on dirt at Nad Al Sheba in December, but bounced back with wins in listed races at Abu Dhabi and Nad Al Sheba after the turn of the year, and might still be a major force during the 2003 European turf season.

		Pivotal (ch 1993)	Polar Falcon (b or br 1987)	Nureyev
				Marie d'Argonne
			Fearless Revival (ch 1987)	Cozzene
Feet So Fast (ch.g. 1999)				Stufida
		Splice (ch 1989)	Sharpo (ch 1977)	Sharpen Up
				Moiety Bird
			Soluce (ch 1981)	Junius
				Amatrice

Feet So Fast is a lengthy gelding who has run only at six furlongs, though he should prove effective at five. His three-year-old wins came on good ground, then twice on good to soft. He is by Pivotal, whose reputation went from strength to strength even when deprived of the services of Feet So Fast, notably when Kyllachy landed the Nunthorpe, but also through the likes of Captain Rio, Somnus, US Grade 1 winner Golden Apples and Grade 2 winner Megahertz. In the other half of Feet So Fast's pedigree, third dam Amatrice was an Irish mile-and-a-half winner and a half-sister to Lingfield Oaks Trial winner Gift Wrapped, herself the dam of Royal Lodge winner Reach, and to the grandam of the 2001 Cheveley Park winner Queen's Logic. However, Amatrice's daughter Soluce and granddaughter Splice were progressively speedy sorts, and Feet So Fast might therefore be viewed as sprint-bred pure and simple. Soluce won a Guineas trial in Ireland but flopped in the main event and again on her only two subsequent starts. Splice won the Abernant. Feet So Fast, who is her fourth foal and second winner, following the fairly useful two-year-old five-furlong winner Entwine (by Primo Dominie), made only 8,000 guineas as a yearling. A close relation and contemporary, a filly by Pivotal out of Soluce, made 6,000 at the same stage, while Soluce's 2001 filly by Polar Falcon (Pivotal's sire) fetched the same sum as a foal. *S. Seemar, UAE*

FEIZOR (IRE) 2 ch.f. (Apr 19) Titus Livius (FR) 115 – Blues Queen 85 (Lahib (USA) **53 d** 129) [2002 5g 5m³ 5f³ 5g 5m⁵ 5m f5g Oct 5] IR 8,500Y: second foal: half-sister to 3-y-o Speed Queen: dam, 2-y-o 6f winner, out of half-sister to high-class 1973 2-y-o sprinter The Blues: modest maiden: best efforts when third in seller at Catterick and claimer at Thirsk: will probably prove best at 5f: tried blinkered: looks ungenuine. *R. F. Fisher*

FELICITY (IRE) 2 b.f. (Mar 17) Selkirk (USA) 129 – Las Flores (IRE) 102 (Sadler's **65 p** Wells (USA) 132) [2002 8m Sep 24] big, strong filly: fourth foal: half-sister to 3 winners, including useful 1¼m winner Jaliso (by Machiavellian) and 3-y-o La Paz: dam, 1¼m winner and third in Oaks d'Italia, half-sister to 5-y-o Bach: favourite, raced freely when only ninth of 10 to stable-companion Echoes In Eternity in maiden at Newmarket, fading under considerate handling: has scope, and sure to do better if learning to settle. *J. H. M. Gosden*

FELIX HOLT (IRE) 2 b.g. (Apr 1) Woodborough (USA) 112 – In The Mind (IRE) **–** (Taufan (USA) 119) [2002 5g 5.3g⁵ 8.3d Aug 11] IR 5,200F, 5,000Y: second foal: half-brother to Swedish 1m winner General In Mind (by General Monash): dam unraced: last in maidens. *S. Dow*

FELLOW SHIP 2 b.c. (Feb 14) Elmaamul (USA) 125 – Genoa 96 (Zafonic (USA) **83 §** 130) [2002 5m⁴ 6f 7m 7.1m² p7g³ 7m⁴ 8g³ 8m 10f² 10s Nov 2] close-coupled colt: first foal: dam, possibly temperamental 11.5f winner (in match), granddaughter of Oaks winner Bireme: fairly useful maiden: in frame 6 times: second at Warwick and Pontefract: should stay at least 1½m: acts on firm ground: edgy sort, sometimes pulls hard/finds little: usually held up prior to final start: temperamental. *B. W. Hills*

FENELLA'S LINK 2 gr.f. (Apr 1) Linamix (FR) 127 – Fleet Hill (IRE) 99 (Warrshan **75 p** (USA) 117) [2002 8g² 8d⁴ Oct 30] 90,000F: second foal: half-sister to a winner in USA by Miner's Mark: dam, 2-y-o 6f/7f winner, later stayed 1¼m and successful in USA: in frame in maidens at Dortmund (then left H. Remmert, Germany) and Yarmouth

(1¾ lengths fourth of 13 to Devant): should stay at least 1¼m: should do better. *M. R. Channon*

FEN GYPSY 4 b.g. Nashwan (USA) 135 – Didicoy (USA) 104 (Danzig (USA)) [2002 – 10m⁶ 7s f8g⁶ f12g Dec 2] good-topped ex-French gelding: eighth foal: brother to smart 6f (at 2 yrs) to 8.5f (US Grade 2 event) winner Didina and half-brother to several winners, including smart French winner around 1¼m Espionage (by Zafonic): dam sprinting half-sister to Xaar: fair maiden at 3 yrs for A. Fabre: little form in 2002, including in blinkers/tongue strap: stays 1¼m. *P. D. Evans*

FENWICKS PRIDE (IRE) 4 b.g. Imperial Frontier (USA) 112 – Stunt Girl (IRE) **65** (Thatching 131) [2002 78: f7g f6g 7.2g 7.1s 6m Jun 10] strong, lengthy gelding: fair **a–** handicapper: stays 7f: acts on any turf going, no form on all-weather: visored: has hung. *B. S. Rothwell*

FESTIVE AFFAIR 4 b.g. Mujadil (USA) 119 – Christmas Kiss 82 (Taufan (USA) **57** 119) [2002 65: f6g f6g 5.1d f6g⁶ f6g² f6g Dec 20] modest performer: best at 6f/7f: acts on fibresand and heavy going: tried tongue tied: reportedly bled from nose final start. *B. Smart*

FESTOR 2 ch.c. (Apr 12) Paris House 123 – Miami Dolphin 85 (Derrylin 115) [2002 – 6d Aug 2] half-brother to 7-y-o Happy Days: dam won at 5f/6f as 6-y-o: 25/1, always behind in maiden at Ayr. *A. Berry*

FFYNNON GOLD 5 b.m. Beveled (USA) – Sparklingsovereign 53 (Sparkler 130) **68** [2002 64: 6.1d 6.1m 6.1d* 6g⁴ 6g 6m 6g⁴ 6m 7.1g⁶ p7g Oct 16] fair handicapper: won at Chepstow in June: effective at 6f/7f: acts on fibresand, firm and soft going: sometimes slowly away: has found little: withdrawn after breaking out of stall eighth intended outing. *J. G. Portman*

FIAAFY (USA) 2 b.f. (Feb 18) Gone West (USA) – Yousefia (USA) 84 (Danzig **75 P** (USA)) [2002 5m³ Aug 9] sixth foal: sister to useful 6f (at 2 yrs) and 1m winner Mythical Girl and half-sister to 2 winners, including fairly useful 7f winner Bullsefia (by Holy Bull): dam, 2-y-o 6f winner who stayed 1m (also 5.5f/6.5f winner in US at 4 yrs), sister to Green Desert: 4/1, highly promising 2½ lengths third of 7 to Summer Passion in minor event at Lingfield, running green in rear then finishing best of all: sure to improve considerably, all being well. *D. R. Loder*

FIAMMA ROYALE (IRE) 4 b.f. Fumo di Londra (IRE) 108 – Ariadne 79 (Bustino **63** 136) [2002 68, a52+: p8g⁶ p7g³ f7g* p6g* p6g* f6g³ f7g³ p6g f6g⁴ f5g⁴ 5.3d³ f6g² **a68** f6g³ 5.9s² f5g* 6m⁶ 5f² f6g* f6g⁵ f5g⁴ f5g³ p5g Dec 21] leggy, quite good-topped filly: fair on all-weather, modest on turf: won seller at Wolverhampton, claimer (left Mrs P. N. Dutfield) and apprentice handicap at Lingfield, all in February, and handicaps at Wolverhampton in August/September (claimed from J. Osborne £6,000 after sixteenth start): effective at 5f to easy 7f: acts on any turf going/all-weather: has carried head high/found little: usually races up with pace: tough and consistent. *M. S. Saunders*

FICHE AND CHIPS 3 b.c. Distant Relative 128 – Moorefield Girl (IRE) 57 – (Gorytus (USA) 132) [2002 41: 7.1m f12s⁶ Sep 17] tall colt: poor maiden at 2 yrs: well held in 2002. *A. Dickman*

FIDDLERS CREEK (IRE) 3 b.c. Danehill (USA) 126 – Mythical Creek (USA) **75 p** (Pleasant Tap (USA)) [2002 7.2d⁶ 10.9g* 12.4g⁴ 10m 10.9g⁴ 10.9s⁴ 12s* f12g* f12g* Dec 20] 190,000Y, 3,000 2-y-o: quite good-topped colt: first foal: dam, 1¼m winner in Italy at 2 yrs, out of sister to US Grade 1 winners De La Rose (9f) and Upper Nile (1¼m): fair performer: won seller at Ayr (dead-heated) in July and handicaps at Musselburgh in November and Wolverhampton (2) in December: stays 1½m: acts on fibresand and soft going: probably capable of better still. *R. Allan*

FIDDLERS REACH (CAN) 2 ch.c. (Feb 4) Kingmambo (USA) 125 – Tiny Decision **101** (USA) (Ogygian (USA)) [2002 p6g² 6d² 6g⁵ 6m⁵ 5.7f* 6s* 6v⁴ Nov 13] $75,000F, 500,000 francs Y, resold 75,000Y: lengthy, useful-looking colt: has a quick action: first foal: dam, US 6f (including at 2 yrs) and 1m winner, out of half-sister to very smart 9f/1¼m performer Running Stag: useful performer: fifth in Gimcrack Stakes at York and Mill Reef Stakes at Newbury: landed odds in 4-runner maiden at Bath (by 9 lengths) in September and 5-runner minor event at Yarmouth (best effort, beat Aversham by 5 lengths) in October: respectable fourth to Striking Ambition in listed race at Saint-Cloud: stays 6f: probably acts on any turf going, shaped well on polytrack. *B. J. Meehan*

FIDDLESTICKS 4 b.f. Missed Flight 123 – Fiddling 82 (Music Boy 124) [2002 55: **54** f6g 5m⁴ 6m 5m 6g 7.5m Sep 24] good-topped filly: modest maiden handicapper: below form after second start: should stay 7f: acts on firm and good to soft going. *D. E. Cantillon*

FIDELIS SEMPER (IRE) 2 b.f. (Apr 26) College Chapel 122 – Reflection Time   –
(IRE) (Fayruz 116) [2002 f5g 5m 5g 6d 5.1s Oct 29] IR 3,900Y, 12,000 2-y-o: fifth foal:
half-sister to 7f winner Red Venus (by Perugino) and a 1m winner in Italy by Dolphin
Street: dam unraced: little form. *T. J. Etherington*

FIELD OF VISION (IRE) 12 b.g. Vision (USA) – Bold Meadows 80 (Persian Bold   –
123) [2002 43: 13.8m May 25] of little account nowadays. *Mrs A. Duffield*

FIELD SPARK 2 b.g. (Mar 11) Sillery (USA) 122 – On The Top (High Top 131)   **60**
[2002 7g 7g 7d⁶ 10m Oct 1] IR 10,000Y: good-bodied gelding: sixth foal: half-brother to
3 winners, including 1½m winner Top Rank (by Law Society): dam unraced half-sister to
high-class sprinter Double Schwartz: modest maiden: stays 1¼m. *J. A. Glover*

FIELLA (IRE) 3 b.g. Petorius 117 – Creggan Vale Lass (Simply Great (FR) 122)   **52**
[2002 47: 8.2d⁴ 8.2f⁵ 7.1v 8.2m² 7g Aug 7] smallish gelding: modest maiden: reportedly
finished lame final start: stayed 1m: acted on good to firm and good to soft going: dead.
B. R. Millman

FIENNES (USA) 4 b. or br.g. Dayjur (USA) 137 – Artic Strech (USA) (Arctic Tern   **53**
(USA) 126) [2002 65: f6s⁴ f6s f6g 7g 6g f6g f6g f5g f6g 6.1m⁶ 6m³ f5s 6m f6g² f6g f7g²   **a63**
f7g⁶ f6s Dec 26] small, sparely-made gelding: modest performer: effective at 5f to easy
7f: acts on good to firm going and fibresand: usually visored: tried tongue tied and in
cheekpieces: often claimer ridden. *Mrs N. Macauley*

FIEPES SHUFFLE (GER) 2 b.c. (Feb 28) Big Shuffle (USA) 122 – Fiepe (GER)   **107**
(Zigeunersohn (GER)) [2002 5m* 5v* 5.5g⁶ 6d³ 5m⁶ 6s² Oct 28] approx. 11,200Y in
Germany: workmanlike colt: half-brother to several winners in Germany, including
useful performer (best up to 1m) Fifire (by King of Macedon): dam won in Germany:
useful performer: won maiden at Baden-Baden in May and listed race at Hamburg in
July: sixth in Flying Childers Stakes at Doncaster penultimate start: best effort when
length second of 5 to Zinziberine in Criterium de Maisons-Laffitte, making running: stays
6f: acts on heavy and good to firm ground. *M. Hofer, Germany*

FIERY MINX (IRE) 2 ch.f. (Mar 2) Bahhare (USA) 122 – Gentle Papoose (Com-   –
manche Run 133) [2002 5m p7g⁶ 7g Oct 17] IR 10,000Y: fifth foal: half-sister to 2
winners, including fairly useful 1998 2-y-o 5f/6f winner Cheyenne Gold (by Anita's
Prince), later successful in USA: dam poor Irish maiden: little form: left A. Berry after
debut. *J. R. Best*

FIFE AND DRUM (USA) 5 b. or br.g. Rahy (USA) 115 – Fife (IRE) 95 (Lomond   **72**
(USA) 128) [2002 72: 10f 9.9m 9.9m² 10m³ 10m 10.2g⁶ 10m Oct 1] smallish gelding:
fair handicapper: has won at 1½m, but better at 1¼m: best turf efforts on good going or
firmer (well held on fibresand): tried blinkered: usually races prominently. *J. Akehurst*

FIFTH EDITION 6 b.m. Rock Hopper 124 – Glossary (Reference Point 139) [2002   **62**
40: 11.9g² 12.3m³ 11.9m* 16v⁴ Oct 29] modest handicapper: won amateur maiden event
at Brighton in October: best effort around 1½m: acts on firm and soft going. *R. Guest*

FIGHT THE FEELING 4 ch.g. Beveled (USA) – Alvecote Lady 50 (Touching   **66**
Wood (USA) 127) [2002 10g 10m 8.1d 10g 8m⁶ 10.5g³ 12.3s⁵ 10.5v* 10.2g f12g* f12g³
f12f³ f12g³ f11g⁴ f16.2g³ Dec 7] angular gelding: fourth reported foal: half-brother to a
winner up to 1½m in Italy by Risk Me: dam won 1½m seller: fair handicapper: won at
Haydock in August and Wolverhampton in September: stays 1½m, seemingly not 2m:
acts on heavy going and fibresand. *J. W. Unett*

FIGHT YOUR CORNER 3 b.c. Muhtarram (USA) 125 – Dame Ashfield 90 (Grundy   **111**
137) [2002 114p: 9m 12.3f* 12d⁵ Jun 8] tall, angular, useful-looking colt: smart
performer: won Chester Vase in May going away by 2½ lengths from Sparkling Water:
subsequently changed hands privately and supplemented for Derby, but fractured hind
cannon bone when 20 lengths fifth to High Chaparral at Epsom (swished tail throughout
preliminaries): underwent surgery after and joined Godolphin: will stay 1¾m: acts on
firm and good to soft going: soon off bridle and carried head awkwardly when disappointing in listed race at Newmarket on reappearance. *M. Johnston*

FIG LEAF (FR) 3 b.f. Distant Relative 128 – Shady Leaf (IRE) 56 (Glint of Gold   **75**
128) [2002 81: 9.9g 11.6m 10g⁶ 8.2d 8d³ 6.9m³ 7g⁶ f7g 7s* 7d² 7v⁵ f8.5s⁴ f8g² Dec 27]
tall, useful-looking filly: fair performer: left F. J. Houghton after fifth start and E. O'Neill
after sixth one: won maiden at Yarmouth in October: probably flattered in listed race at
Maisons-Laffitte eleventh outing: best form: at 7f/1m: acts on any turf going and fibresand: often blinkered/visored: often makes running. *P. W. D'Arcy*

FIGLIOLO 2 b.c. (Jan 28) Cadeaux Genereux 131 – Frond 85 (Alzao (USA) 117)   **73**
[2002 6d³ 6m⁴ 6.1m 6m² 7s Oct 25] smallish colt: first foal: dam, 7f winner at 2 yrs (only

season to race), out of useful 1½m winner Fern, herself half-sister to Oaks runner-up Shamshir: fair maiden: should be suited by at least 7f: acts on good to firm and good to soft going, well held in nursery on soft: sold 17,000 gns, sent to Kuwait. *L. M. Cumani*

FIGURA 4 b.f. Rudimentary (USA) 118 – Dream Baby (Master Willie 129) [2002 72: 8.3d 10.2v 9.7m 11.9m⁴ 12g 12f 10s p10g³ Dec 18] big, leggy filly: modest performer nowadays: left C. Cox after third start: may prove best around 1¼m: acts on polytrack and good to firm going, yet to show form on softer than good. *R. Ingram* **64**

FILEUSE 2 b.f. (Apr 6) Primo Dominie 121 – Spinner 59 (Blue Cashmere 129) [2002 f5s p6g f5g Dec 4] sister to 5f (at 2 yrs)/6f winner Seigneurial, later winner in USA, and half-sister to numerous winners, including fairly useful 6f/7f winner Be My Wish (by Be My Chief): dam, sprinter, half-sister to useful 5f performer Clantime: poor form in minor event/sellers. *R. M. Whitaker* **38**

FILIA REGIS (IRE) 2 gr.f. (Mar 19) Presidium 124 – Smooth Princess (IRE) 63 (Roi Danzig (USA)) [2002 5g 5f 7m Aug 16] small filly: first foal: dam 2-y-o 7f seller winner: well beaten in claimer/sellers. *J. G. FitzGerald* **–**

FILLE D'ARGENT (IRE) 3 gr.f. Desert Style (IRE) 121 – Talina (General Assembly (USA)) [2002 62: 8.1m 7m p12g May 29] strong, good sort: modest maiden at 2 yrs: little form in 2002: should stay 1m: acts on firm going: visored 3 starts prior to final one: sold 1,500 gns in October. *Mrs P. N. Dutfield* **–**

FILLE DE BUCHERON (USA) 4 b.f. Woodman (USA) 126 – Special Secreto (USA) (Secreto (USA) 128) [2002 76, a67: f7s⁵ f8s² f8g⁵ Jan 29] strong, angular filly: fair handicapper: stays 1m: acts on fibresand, raced only on going firmer than good on turf: tried visored: carries head high. *S. R. Bowring* **– a70**

FILLE DE FLEURIE 2 ch.f. (Apr 28) Whittingham (IRE) 104 – L'Estable Fleurie (IRE) 76 (Common Grounds 118) [2002 5m 5.7g⁴ 5.1f² 5.1d⁵ Sep 9] 4,000Y: first foal: dam 7f winner: modest maiden: will stay at least 6f. *B. Smart* **63**

FILLE DE JOIE (IRE) 4 b.f. Royal Academy (USA) 130 – Courtesane (USA) (Majestic Light (USA)) [2002 67d: p8g² p7g³ 7m 7g⁶ 7m Aug 26] leggy filly: fair maiden at best: well below form last 3 starts: will probably stay 1¼m: acts on polytrack: tried blinkered: reluctant to go to post and slowly away penultimate start. *R. F. Johnson Houghton* **68 d**

FILLE DE ROI 2 b.f. (May 19) Desert King (IRE) 129 – Western Heights (Shirley Heights 130) [2002 6v p6g Nov 19] half-sister to several winners, including smart 1m/1¼m performer Barathea Guest (by Barathea) and 8-y-o Pinchincha: dam unraced half-sister to useful 1m and 1½m winner Startino: well beaten in maidens. *M. Johnston* **–**

FILLE GENEREUX 4 ch.f. Cadeaux Genereux 131 – Mohican Girl 112 (Dancing Brave (USA) 140) [2002 46: f6s f6g f7g* p7g 6f² 5m² 5.7g* p5g⁶ 5.3d⁴ Jun 13] lengthy filly: modest handicapper: won at Southwell in March and Bath in May: effective at 5f to 8.5f: acts on fibresand, firm and good to soft going: visored (slowly away) on reappearance: tongue tied second start: often races prominently: in foal to Mujtahid. *R. M. H. Cowell* **58**

FINAL DIVIDEND (IRE) 6 b.g. Second Set (IRE) 127 – Prime Interest (IRE) (Kings Lake (USA) 133) [2002 62, a77: p12g³ f12g p12g f12g⁵ 11.9f 12.3g* 12.3m* 11.5m³ 9.9d Jul 12] close-coupled gelding: fair handicapper: won ladies events at Chester and Ripon in June: probably best at 1¼m/1½m: acts on soft and firm going, seems better on polytrack than fibresand: often amateur ridden: none too consistent. *J. M. P. Eustace* **74**

FINAL EXAM (IRE) 5 ch.g. College Chapel 122 – It Takes Two (IRE) (Alzao (USA) 117) [2002 113: 5s 6d³ 6s 7s³ 6.3d 5g² 6s³ Aug 11] robust gelding: smart performer: placed in listed race at Cork, Ballycorus Stakes at Leopardstown, handicap at the Curragh (best effort when 2 lengths second to Serov) and Phoenix Sprint Stakes at the Curragh (½-length third to One Won One): effective at 5f to 7f: acts on soft going (not tried on firmer than good since debut): usually blinkered. *D. K. Weld, Ireland* **113**

FINAL FAZE 3 ch.f. Chaddleworth (IRE) 103 – Fine Fettle (Final Straw 127) [2002 –p: 8f 7d² 8g 8.1g Aug 7] lengthy filly: modest maiden: should stay 1m: tongue tied (below form) last 2 starts. *D. J. Coakley* **59**

FINAL LAP 6 b.g. Batshoof 122 – Lap of Honour 100 (Final Straw 127) [2002 –: f14.8g Sep 21] of little account on Flat nowadays. *S. T. Lewis* **–**

FINANCIAL FUTURE 2 b.c. (Apr 24) Barathea (IRE) 127 – In Perpetuity 90 (Great Nephew 126) [2002 6s³ 6sd³ 8.5d³ 7m³ Sep 24] 36,000Y: brother to 5-y-o Tweed and half-brother to several winners, including winner around 1¼m Baron Ferdinand (by Ferdinand) and 4-y-o Love Everlasting, both smart: dam, 1¼m/11f winner, half-sister to **89**

Shirley Heights: fairly useful maiden: best effort when second past post (placed third after causing interference) at Newmarket final start, beaten 1¼ lengths by Safe From Harm: should be suited by 1¼m+. *M. Johnston*

FINE ARTS 3 b.f. Cadeaux Genereux 131 – Fine Detail (IRE) 93 (Shirley Heights **86** 130) [2002 8.2d 7d² 7d* 8m Jun 22] well-made filly: second foal: dam, 1½m winner on only start, half-sister to French performer up to 12.5f De Quest and US Grade 1 9f/1¼m winner Wandesta, both very smart: fairly useful form: won maiden at Salisbury (raced freely) in June: gave impression something amiss in listed rated stakes at Royal Ascot final outing: should stay 1m: sold 42,000 gns in December. *B. W. Hills*

FINE FRENZY (IRE) 2 b.f. (Apr 18) Great Commotion (USA) 123 – Fine Project **68 d** (IRE) 92 (Project Manager 111) [2002 5g 5m* 5g 6.3g 6.1m 7m⁴ 7g⁵ 8d Nov 1] IR 15,000Y: rather leggy, useful-looking filly: fluent mover: second foal: half-sister to 3-y-o Bezwell's Guest: dam Irish 5f (at 2 yrs) and 7f winner: fair performer: below form after winning maiden at Windsor (hung left) in May: stays 7f: unraced on extremes of going. *J. W. Hills*

FINE LOOKING WOMAN 4 ch.f. Imp Society (USA) – Pity's Pet 62 (Stanford **–** 121§) [2002 –: 6g Oct 28] well beaten in maidens at Southwell and Windsor nearly a year apart. *J. L. Spearing*

FINGER OF FATE 2 br.c. (Feb 7) Machiavellian (USA) 123 – La Nuit Rose (FR) **87** 109 (Rainbow Quest (USA) 134) [2002 6g 7.5g⁵ 7g⁴ f8.5g² 7m* Oct 3] sparely-made colt: first foal: dam, 2-y-o 7f winner, out of Prix de Diane winner Caerlina: fairly useful performer: landed odds in maiden at Brighton by 7 lengths from Java Dawn, dictating pace: free-going sort, likely to prove best at 7f/1m: acts on fibresand, raced only on good/good to firm ground on turf: sold 42,000 gns. *Sir Michael Stoute*

FINISHED ARTICLE (IRE) 5 b.g. Indian Ridge 123 – Summer Fashion 84 (Moore- **100** style 137) [2002 90: 8.1d³ 8g⁴ 8d² 8g* 8m² 8.1d² 8f⁵ 8m 8d⁵ 8f² 9f Oct 5] medium-sized, workmanlike gelding: useful handicapper: won at Goodwood in June: very good second to Heretic in valuable event at Sandown sixth start: pulled too hard in Cambridgeshire at Newmarket final start: acts at 1m/1¼m: acts on firm and good to soft going: often held up: consistent. *D. R. C. Elsworth*

FINMAR 4 b.g. Efisio 120 – Patiala (IRE) (Nashwan (USA) 135) [2002 70§: 9m² 7.1g **64** 10g⁴ 9m³ 7.2d³ 7.9d 9d³ 7.1d² 8.3m³ f7g Nov 15] strong gelding: modest maiden: in frame 7 times in 2002: stays 9f: acts on good to firm and good to soft going, well held on fibresand: sometimes starts slowly. *Miss L. A. Perratt*

FINNFOREST (IRE) 2 ch.g. (Apr 24) Eagle Eyed (USA) 111 – Stockrose (Horage **61** 124) [2002 7.1m 6.1m³ 7.9f⁵ Oct 11] IR 5,000Y, 14,000 2-y-o: well-made gelding: half-brother to several winners abroad, including Italian winner up to 7.5f Pasadilla (by Common Grounds): dam, won 5 times in Germany, half-sister to very smart sprinter Statoblest: modest maiden: stays 1m: raced only on ground firmer than good: raced freely final start (gelded after). *Mrs A. J. Bowlby*

FINNINGLEY CONNOR 2 b.c. (Feb 6) Cosmonaut – Arroganza 62 (Crofthall 110) **68** [2002 5g 5g* 5s⁴ 5d³ 6m⁵ Jul 18] 5,000Y: rather leggy, lengthy colt: seventh foal: half-brother to 3 winners, including 9-y-o Johayro: dam 2-y-o 5f winner: fair performer: won maiden at Musselburgh in May: reportedly lost action final start: should stay 6f: acts on soft ground. *Ronald Thompson*

FIORI 6 b.g. Anshan 119 – Fen Princess (IRE) 72 (Trojan Fen 118) [2002 87: 12s 12m **–** 16.1d Sep 9] close-coupled gelding: has a round action: fairly useful handicapper at 5 yrs: well held on Flat in 2002. *P. C. Haslam*

FIREBREAK 3 b.c. Charnwood Forest (IRE) 125 – Breakaway 98 (Song 132) [2002 **118** 109: a8f² a10f 8g⁶ 8m⁴ 7f* 7m² Oct 19] smallish, leggy, quite attractive colt: smart performer: sold from I. Balding 525,000 gns after final 2-y-o start: beaten nose by Essence of Dubai in UAE 2000 Guineas at Nad Al Sheba in February: in good form on return from 3-month absence after third start, winning Charlton Hunt Supreme Stakes at Goodwood in September by 2½ lengths from Patsy's Double: ran well also when very close fourth to Tillerman in Celebration Mile at Goodwood and 2½ lengths second to Nayyir in Challenge Stakes at Newmarket: stays 1m (never a threat in 1¼m UAE Derby): acts on dirt, firm and soft going. *Saeed bin Suroor*

FIREBURST 3 ch.f. Spectrum (IRE) 126 – Explosiva (USA) 88§ (Explodent (USA)) **–** [2002 f8g p7g Dec 28] half-sister to several winners, including useful 1992 2-y-o 1m winner Brockette (by Bustino) and fairly useful 1994 2-y-o 5f winner Quiz Time (by Efisio): dam 2-y-o 5f winner: well held in maidens. *T. J. Naughton*

FIRE CAT   3 ch.c. Beveled (USA) – Noble Soul 67 (Sayf El Arab (USA) 127) [2002 8g   –
7d Jul 11] fourth living foal: half-brother to winner around 1m Jessinca (by Minshaanshu
Amad): dam lightly-raced 1m winner: well held in maidens at Bath and Folkestone.
A. P. Jones

FIRE DOME (IRE)   10 ch.g. Salt Dome (USA) – Penny Habit (Habitat 134) [2002   **90**
103d, a–: p6g 7g 6m² 6s* 6d³ 6d⁵ 6v 6v Nov 20] rangy gelding: fairly useful nowadays: **a–**
won minor event at Windsor in May: off 5 months, well held in listed races at Doncaster
and Maisons-Laffitte last 2 starts: best form at 6f on good going or softer: tried blinkered/
visored/tongue tied, not recently: usually held up. *Andrew Reid*

FIRE IN ICE   3 b.f. Missed Flight 123 – Boulabas (IRE) 66 (Nashamaa 113) [2002 38:   –
f6s f5g p6g f6g Oct 21] leggy, close-coupled filly: little form at 3 yrs. *B. P. J. Baugh*

FIRE MOON (IRE)   3 b.g. Royal Applause 124 – Welwyn 92 (Welsh Saint 126)   **55**
[2002 60: f9.4g f7g² f8g⁵ f12g f7g 8.2d 9.9m 12m³ 15.8f⁶ 16.1m⁴ 15.8f 12g⁵ f12g f14.8g⁵
f12g Dec 27] smallish, well-made gelding: has a quick action: modest maiden: stays easy
2m: acts on firm ground and fibresand: tried blinkered: has shown reluctance at start:
waited with. *S. R. Bowring*

FIRE NYMPH   2 b.f. (Feb 7) Cois Na Tine (IRE) 101 – Water Pixie (IRE) (Dance of   –
Life (USA)) [2002 f6g⁵ Jun 7] 700Y: fourth foal: half-sister to 1m winner Pix Me Up (by
Up And At 'em): dam unraced: 9/1, well held in seller at Wolverhampton. *K. A. Ryan*

FIRESIDE LEGEND (IRE)   3 b.g. College Chapel 122 – Miss Sandman 86 (Manacle   **55**
123) [2002 56: p10g² f8.5g⁶ f9.4g² p10g f11g Mar 12] modest performer: found little last
2 starts, visored on final one: stays 1¼m: acts on all-weather and soft ground: difficult
ride, and temperament under suspicion. *W. G. M. Turner*

FIRESTONE (GER)   5 b.g. Dictator's Song (USA) – Fatinizza (IRE) (Niniski (USA)   **75**
125) [2002 79?: f6g 9.7m 10m³ 11.6d⁴ 10s 11.7g p7g Oct 31] tall, leggy gelding: fair
handicapper: below form last 3 starts: stays 11.6f: acts on good to firm and good to soft
going: tried blinkered prior to 2001. *A. W. Carroll*

FIRE UP THE BAND   3 b.c. Prince Sabo 123 – Green Supreme (Primo Dominie   **103 p**
121) [2002 p7g* 8s⁵ 6m* 6g⁴ 6f³ 6g³ 5g² Jun 18] 20,000Y: lengthy, good-topped colt:
fourth foal: half-brother to smart sprinter Sampower Star (by Cyrano de Bergerac) and
5-y-o Absent Friends: dam unraced: useful performer: won maiden at Lingfield in February and handicap at Newmarket in April: good efforts in frame in valuable handicaps
all starts after, neck second of 28 to Zargus at Royal Ascot on final one: winner at easy 7f,
probably best at 5f/6f: acts on firm going and polytrack: game: capable of better still.
D. Nicholls

FIREWIRE   4 b.g. Blushing Flame (USA) 109 – Bay Risk (Risk Me (FR) 127) [2002   **72 d**
74: 10m 12m 10m 12s p10g 10g Jul 8] smallish, workmanlike gelding: fair handicapper
at best: stays 1½m: acts on good to firm ground, well beaten on softer than good and on
polytrack: has been slowly away/looked reluctant to race: on downgrade. *N. Hamilton*

FIREWORK   4 b.g. Primo Dominie 121 – Prancing 98 (Prince Sabo 123) [2002 78§:   **71 d**
6f 6m⁵ 6m 6d 7d⁴ p7g Dec 11] quite attractive gelding: good walker: fair maiden: well
below form after second start: left R. Guest after penultimate one: best at 6f/easy 7f: acts
on firm and soft going: usually blinkered/visored: not one to trust implicitly. *J. Akehurst*

FIREY SENORITA (IRE)   5 b.m. Great Commotion (USA) 123 – Spanish Rose   **39**
(Belmez (USA) 131) [2002 –: f14.8s 10d⁶ 11.6s Jun 10] first foal: dam unraced: poor
maiden: trained by F. Flood in Ireland in 2001: stays 1¼m: acts on good to soft going:
blinkered nowadays. *L. A. Dace*

FIROZI   3 b.f. Forzando 122 – Lambast 70 (Relkino 131) [2002 61§: 8g 8m* 6.9g*   **63**
7g⁴ 9m⁴ 7.5m² 8g² 8.5g Sep 18] smallish, workmanlike filly: modest performer: won
selling handicap at Thirsk in July and claimer at Carlisle in August: probably stays 9f:
acts on good to firm going, probably on soft: tried blinkered at 2 yrs: has played up in
preliminaries/wandered under pressure. *R. A. Fahey*

FIRST BALLOT (IRE)   6 b.g. Perugino (USA) 84 – Election Special 78 (Chief Singer   **110**
131) [2002 108: 12m² 13.3m⁴ 22.2m⁵ 16.2m⁶ 14m⁵ 14m⁴ 14.6m⁶ Sep 13] tall, good-
topped gelding: smart handicapper: better than ever when winning at Newmarket in May
by length from Warrsan: respectable efforts at best, including when fourth of 5 to
First Charter in listed race at Goodwood: effective at 1½m to 2½m: acts on firm and
good to soft going: races up with pace (needed early reminders to do so fourth start).
D. R. C. Elsworth

FIRST BASE   3 ch.g. First Trump 118 – Rose Music 86 (Luthier 126) [2002 45: 7m 7f   –
9f⁶ 9m 7m 8g Aug 26] quite good-topped gelding: little form at 3 yrs. *R. E. Barr*

San Miguel March Stakes, Goodwood—
First Charter accounts for Spanish John, Savannah Bay and First Ballot

FIRST CHARTER   3 b.c. Polish Precedent (USA) 131 – By Charter 104 (Shirley   **113**
Heights 130) [2002 94p: 10m* 11.5g⁵ 12m³ 12m² 14m* 14.6m Sep 14] lengthy, quite
attractive colt: smart performer: won maiden at Leicester in April and listed March Stakes
at Goodwood (beat Spanish John by 1½ lengths) in August: also ran well when placed in
King Edward VII Stakes at Royal Ascot (3¾ lengths third to Balakheri) and in Gordon
Stakes at Goodwood (7 lengths second of 4 to Bandari) third/fourth starts: below form in
St Leger at Doncaster (wandered) final outing: stays 1¾m: yet to race on extremes of
going. *Sir Michael Stoute*

FIRST CLASS GIRL   3 b.f. Charmer 123 – Boulevard Girl 80 (Nicholas Bill 125)   **–**
[2002 10.1m May 23] 3,300 2-y-o: tall, quite good-topped filly: half-sister to 4-y-o
Litzinsky and 9-y-o Blenheim Terrace: dam suited by test of stamina: 50/1, well held in
maiden at Newcastle. *C. B. B. Booth*

FIRST EAGLE   3 b.g. Hector Protector (USA) 124 – Merlin's Fancy 62 (Caerleon   **–**
(USA) 132) [2002 –, a55: p8g⁵ p8g³ f7g² f7g² f9.4g³ 8.3g f8g³ f9.4g⁴ f12g⁴ f7g⁴ f7g f7g⁵   **a62**
f8g⁶ f8g⁴ f9.4g Dec 16] rather unfurnished gelding: modest maiden: in frame 9 times in
2002: left S. Kirk after ninth start: stays 1m: acts on all-weather, no form on turf: effective
blinkered or not: has worn cheekpieces. *Mrs N. Macauley*

FIRST FOOTING   2 ch.c. (Feb 26) Inchinor 119 – Laleston 73 (Junius (USA) 124)   **77**
[2002 6g⁵ 7m² 6g* 7v Nov 9] 12,000Y: half-brother to several 5f winners, including 1998
2-y-o winner Ewenny (by Warrshan): dam 5f winner: fair form: best effort in maidens
when winning at Ayr in September by 1¾ lengths from Luke After Me: last in nursery at
Doncaster final start: effective at 6f/7f. *M. L. W. Bell*

FIRST FORTUNE   2 br.g. (Apr 30) Primo Dominie 121 – Jeewan 82 (Touching   **49**
Wood (USA) 127) [2002 7m⁶ 7d Jul 11] 13,000Y: seventh foal: half-brother to 3 winners,
including 3-y-o Woodbury and 7f to 1¼m winner Harry Brown (by Al Hareb): dam 1½m
winner: poor form in maidens at Folkestone: gelded after final start. *P. W. Harris*

FIRST JULIANA   2 b.f. (Apr 16) First Trump 118 – Sweet Wilhelmina 87 (Indian   **– p**
Ridge 123) [2002 6m Aug 29] first foal: dam 7f (at 2 yrs)/1m winner: 10/1, travelled well
until past halfway when last of 13 in maiden at Lingfield: should do better. *D. J. Coakley*

FIRST MAITE   9 b.g. Komaite (USA) – Marina Plata (Julio Mariner 127) [2002 81,   **81**
a88: f8s⁴ f8.5g⁴ f8.5g² f12g f8.5g⁶ f8g⁶ 8s f7g⁴ f7g⁶ 6m f8.5g⁵ 8.2d f6g⁴ 7f⁶ 7.5g⁵ 6v f5g⁴   **a85**
7.5m² 6d 7g⁵ 7.5d² 8.5g f7f* 7.5m⁴ 7m 7g* 7g⁶ 8.2v 8v f8.5s Dec 13] tall, lengthy
gelding: has a round action: fairly useful handicapper: won at Wolverhampton in August
and Leicester (apprentices) in October: acts at 7f to 9f: acts on firesband, good to
firm and soft going (not on heavy): occasionally blinkered/visored: tried tongue tied:
occasionally slowly away/hangs: tough. *S. R. Bowring*

FIRST MOMENT   2 b.f. (Mar 9) First Trump 118 – Watheeqah (USA) 60 (Topsider   **51**
(USA)) [2002 5g 6d 7d Nov 5] 3,200Y: third foal: dam 5f winner: modest maiden: best
effort on debut. *M. Brittain*

FIRST OF MANY   3 b.f. Darshaan 133 – Star Profile (IRE) 100 (Sadler's Wells (USA)   **61**
132) [2002: 8.1m⁴ 9g³ Aug 7] fair form in maiden only outing at 2 yrs: just modest
form in similar events in 2002: should stay 1¼m+. *Sir Michael Stoute*

FIRST ORDAINED (IRE)   3 b.g. Mujadil (USA) 119 – Ordinate (Nashwan (USA)   **63**
135) [2002 76: p7g⁴ p8g⁴ p10g 8.1m 8.3s 8.3s 8.1s⁶ Jun 7] sturdy, lengthy gelding:
unimpressive mover: modest maiden handicapper: left P. Burgoyne before final start:
stays 1m: acts on firm going, soft and all-weather. *D. Nicholls*

345

FIRST OVERTURE   3 b.f. Overbury (IRE) 116 – Ziggy's Viola (IRE) 56 (Roi Danzig   –
(USA)) [2002 8m 8g⁶ 8d Sep 9] first foal: dam, won 1¾m seller, half-sister to smart
performer up to 15f King o' The Mana: no show in maidens. *Mrs A. M. Naughton*

FIRST PRESSURE   2 b.g. (Apr 13) Double Trigger (IRE) 123 – Princesse Lyphard   **71**
36 (Keen 116) [2002 p7g 8s⁵ 7d Nov 2] first foal: dam third at 7f: best effort in maidens
(fair form) when fifth to Midas Way at Newbury: will be well suited by 1¼m+.
J. W. Mullins

FIRST SQUAW   3 b.f. Primo Dominie 121 – Me Cherokee 48 (Persian Bold 123)   –
[2002 11.8d May 27] 3,400F, 7,000Y: heavy-topped filly: first foal: dam, poor maiden
who stayed 1½m, half-sister to smart middle-distance stayer Apache: 200/1 and backward, soon tailed off following very slow start in maiden at Leicester. *Mrs Lucinda
Featherstone*

FIRST TO GO   3 ch.f. First Trump 118 – Port Na Blath (On Your Mark 125) [2002 47:   –
5.9g Jun 27] strong filly: poor maiden: probably stayed 7f: dead. *M. Dods*

FIRST VENTURE   5 b.g. Formidable (USA) 125 – Diamond Wedding (USA) 65   –
(Diamond Shoal 130) [2002 67, a80: p7g p6g f6g p6g⁵ f6g⁵ f3g³ p6g⁰ t6g* f5g³ a8g   **a61**
a6g⁶ a8g a8g a6g² a6g Aug 31] lengthy, useful-looking gelding: modest performer: won
seller at Wolverhampton in March: left C. Allen after next start: best up to 7f: acts on all-
weather/sand, good to firm and good to soft going: often blinkered/visored in Britain.
C. Tinkler, Spain

FIRTH OF LORNE (IRE)   3 b.f. Danehill (USA) 126 – Kerrera 115 (Diesis 133)   **112**
[2002 104p: 8g³ 8g² May 12] sister to French 7.5f winner Talah and half-sister to 3

Sheikh Mohammed's "Firth of Lorne"

winners, including useful 6f performer Shmoose (by Caerleon) and fairly useful 7f winner who stayed 1¼m Kerry Ring (by Sadler's Wells): dam, second in 1000 Guineas and at least as effective at 5f/6f, half-sister to very smart 6f to 1m performer Rock City: smart performer: winner of both starts at Nantes at 2 yrs, namely maiden and listed race: placed in 2002 at Longchamp in Prix de la Grotte (1¼ lengths third to Sophisticat) and Poule d'Essai des Pouliches (stayed on having been slowly away when length second to Zenda): stays 1m. *H-A. Pantall, France*

FISHER ISLAND (IRE) 5 b. or br.m. Sri Pekan (USA) 117 – Liberty Song (IRE) **45 ?**
(Last Tycoon 131) [2002 49: f16.2g f12g³ f12g f12g⁵ Jun 19] tall mare: poor handicapper at best in 2002: reportedly had breathing problem on reappearance and penultimate starts: stays easy 2m: acts on heavy going, good to firm and fibresand: carries head awkwardly. *R. Hollinshead*

FITTLEWORTH (IRE) 2 gr.f. (Apr 21) Bijou d'Inde 127 – Remany 66 (Bellypha **51**
130) [2002 f5g 6.1d⁴ 6.1d f7g² 8g² f8.5g² Oct 19] 1,400Y: sixth foal: half-sister to 1998 2-y-o 6f winner Moon Buzzard (by Polar Falcon): dam, 1¼m and 11.4f winner, half-sister to smart middle-distance stayer Lemhill: modest maiden: runner-up in sellers last 3 starts: stays 8.5f: acts on fibresand, raced only on good/good to soft going on turf: races prominently. *W. G. M. Turner*

FITTONIA (FR) 3 ch.f. Ashkalani (IRE) 128 – Fly For Fame (Shaadi (USA) 126) **66**
[2002 65p: 8m 8.2m⁴ 9.1g⁴ 10d 9.9d⁵ 7.9m⁵ 10m* 10g³ 10m 8.2s Oct 23] lengthy, sparely-made filly: fair handicapper: won at Redcar in September: below form last 2 starts: stays 1¼m: acts on good to firm and good to soft going. *J. D. Bethell*

FIVEOCLOCK EXPRESS (IRE) 2 gr.g. (Mar 11) Woodborough (USA) 112 – **79**
Brooks Masquerade (Absalom 128) [2002 5s⁴ 6g* 6g 6g³ 6d⁶ Nov 1] IR 8,500F, IR 16,000Y: deep-girthed gelding: fourth foal: half-brother to a winner in Greece by Midyan: dam, poor maiden, out of sister to Petong: fair performer: won maiden at Leicester in August: good third in nursery at Windsor penultimate start: should stay 7f: raced only on good going or softer: gelded after final outing. *J. R. Fanshawe*

FIZA (IRE) 3 b.g. Revoque (IRE) 122 – Double Eight (IRE) 77 (Common Grounds **69**
118) [2002 –: 11.6s* 11.6m 12.3d³ f12g 12.3m⁶ 11.9d Aug 8] lightly-made gelding: fair handicapper: won at Windsor in May: below form last 3 starts: will stay at least 1¾m: easily best efforts on going softer than good: won 5,800 gns. *M. L. W. Bell*

FIZZY LIZZY 2 b.f. (Feb 24) Cool Jazz 116 – Formidable Liz 66 (Formidable (USA) **54**
125) [2002 5m⁶ 6m Jul 29] 500Y: second foal: dam 6f winner: modest form when mid-field in maidens, late headway each time: will probably stay 7f. *Jedd O'Keeffe*

FIZZY TREAT 4 b.f. Efisio 120 – Special Guest 67 (Be My Guest (USA) 126) [2002 **59**
63: f7g³ 6.1v f6g* f5g* f6g 6s 5.2f f6s³ 6.1m Sep 20] lengthy filly: fair handicapper on **a79**
all-weather, modest on turf: won at Wolverhampton and Southwell in July: best at 5f/6f: acts on fibresand and heavy ground: sold 27,000 gns in December. *R. Guest*

FLAKE 2 ch.g. (Feb 4) Zilzal (USA) 137 – Impatiente (USA) (Vaguely Noble 140) **72**
[2002 6g f6g⁴ 7d³ 6m⁶ 8d* 8m 8s² 8d⁵ 7v Nov 8] 21,000Y: smallish, close-coupled gelding: closely related to a winner in USA by Theatrical and half-brother to several winners, including useful stayers Eminence Grise and Busy Lizzie (both by Sadler's Wells): dam, French maiden, out of US Grade 1 9f/1¼m winner Sangue: fair performer: won claimer at Newcastle (for W. Haggas) in August: good efforts in nurseries seventh/ eighth starts: will stay at least 1¼m: acts on soft going, possibly not good to firm: usually takes good hold: tends to carry head high. *G. M. Moore*

FLAK JACKET 7 b.g. Magic Ring (IRE) 115 – Vaula 49 (Henbit (USA) 130) [2002 **88**
80: 5.1g 5g 6m³ 5g⁵ 6m* 5g⁴ 6m⁶ 6m⁶ 5m³ 6m⁶ 5.1f 5f 5g⁵ Oct 19] strong gelding: impresses in appearance: fairly useful handicapper: won at York in July and Goodwood (for third year running) in August: not at best last 3 outings: best at 5f/6f: acts on firm and soft going: blinkered once: tongue tied: got very upset in stall final start: sometimes hangs right: often races prominently. *D. Nicholls*

FLAMBE 4 b.g. Whittingham (IRE) 104 – Uae Flame (IRE) (Polish Precedent (USA) **65**
131) [2002 71: f8g⁵ p10g f9.4g² f8.5g³ f8g⁴ 10.3s⁶ f8g* 8m 8f 8d 9f³ 8.1m 8.5g Aug 15] **a72**
good-topped gelding: fair performer: won minor event at Southwell in April: below form last 2 starts: effective at 1m to 9.4f: acts on fibresand and firm going: tongue tied final start: slowly away fifth outing: has been early to post: usually races prominently. *P. C. Haslam*

FLAME DANCER 4 b.c. Dancing Spree (USA) – Madam Taylor 81 (Free State 125) **45 ?**
[2002 f8.5g f12g⁵ f12g f14.8s May 13] fifth living foal: dam 5f (at 2 yrs) to 1½m winner:

347

well held in bumpers in spring: seemingly poor form in seller at Wolverhampton second start on Flat: stays 1½m: raced only on fibresand: blinkered 3 of 4 starts. *M. Mullineaux*

FLAMENCA (USA)   3 b.f. Diesis 133 – Highland Ceilidh (IRE) 100 (Scottish Reel   **49** 123) [2002 –: 11.1s⁶ 13.1d⁴ 12m 8.3d⁶ Jul 19] sturdy filly: poor maiden: probably stays 13f: form only on ground softer than good. *R. Allan*

FLAMENCO BRIDE   2 b.f. (Mar 11) Hernando (FR) 127 – Premier Night 102 (Old   **– p** Vic 136) [2002 7m Sep 5] second foal: half-sister to 3-y-o Sir Brastias: dam, 1½m to 2m winner, half-sister to dam of smart filly up to 1½m Mot Juste: 50/1, always in rear in maiden at Salisbury: should do better at 1¼m+. *D. R. C. Elsworth*

FLAME PRINCESS   2 ch.f. (Apr 27) Bluegrass Prince (IRE) 110 – Rekindled Flame   **41** (IRE) (Kings Lake (USA) 133) [2002 p6g p7g f6g⁴ f6g Dec 16] seventh foal: half-sister to 4-y-o Prince Pyramus, 5-y-o Golden Locket and 6-y-o Goodenough Mover: dam unraced: poor form in maidens/claimer: trained on debut by N. Rossiter: should stay 7f. *J. R. Boyle*

FLAMING SALSA (FR)   3 ch.f. Salse (USA) 128 – Fantastic Flame (IRE) 79   **93** (Generous (IRE) 139) [2002 10g 10.2s² 12.1v* 12 3m³ 13 9m² 12 5v Nov 20] 20,000Y: lengthy filly: first foal: dam, 1¼m winner, sister to smart 1¼m/1½m performer Germano: fairly useful form: won maiden at Chepstow in June: good efforts in handicaps and listed race at Maisons-Laffitte after: stays 1¾m: acts on heavy and good to firm going. *J. H. M. Gosden*

FLAMING SPIRT   3 b.f. Blushing Flame (USA) 109 – Fair Test 95 (Fair Season 120)   **78 §** [2002 74: p8g⁶ f8g⁵ f9.4g³ 9g* 10.9g³ 8.3m 10.2g⁴ 9.9g 9.2g² 10g 9d⁶ 9d 10g 8v p10g Dec 14] lengthy filly: fair handicapper at best: won at Kempton in March: stays 11f: acts on fibresand, best turf efforts on good going: often slowly away: has edged right: sometimes flicks tail under pressure: unreliable. *J. S. Moore*

FLAPDOODLE   4 b.f. Superpower 113 – My Concordia 58 (Belfort (FR) 89) [2002   **60** 55: f5s f5g 5.1g 5d² 5d⁴ 5d 5m* 5.1g³ 5f f5g f5g⁶ f5g Dec 14] modest handicapper: won at   **a51** Folkestone in August: best at 5f: acts on fibresand, firm and good to soft going: effective blinkered or not: has hung: races prominently. *A. W. Carroll*

FLARAN   2 b.c. (May 6) Emarati (USA) 74 – Fragrance (Mtoto 134) [2002 7.1f⁶ 6d 7g   **58** Oct 24] smallish, rather dipped-backed colt: first thoroughbred foal: dam unraced: modest form in maidens: should stay 1m: moved poorly to post on firm ground. *A. C. Stewart*

FLASHFEET   12 b.g. Rousillon (USA) 133 – Miellita 98 (King Emperor (USA))   **–** [2002 –: f8s f8s f8s⁶ f9.4g Feb 11] of little account nowadays. *P. D. Purdy*

FLASH OF GOLD   2 b.f. (Feb 5) Darshaan 133 – Trying For Gold (USA) 103   **73 P** (Northern Baby (CAN) 127) [2002 8g Oct 18] tall, lengthy, unfurnished filly: ninth foal: closely related to useful 1996 2-y-o 1m winner who stayed 1½m Tempting Prospect (by Shirley Heights) and half-sister to smart 1m (at 2 yrs) to 13f winner Phantom Gold (dam of Oaks runner-up Flight of Fancy) and useful 8.5f (US Grade 3 event)/1¼m winner Fictitious (both by Machiavellian): dam, 1½m winner, out of Ribblesdale Stakes winner Expansive: 10/1 and green, shaped very well when 7 lengths seventh of 16 to Calibre in maiden at Newmarket, held up and running on in good style without being knocked about: bred to stay at least 1½m: likely to leave debut form well behind, and should prove useful at least. *Sir Michael Stoute*

FLASH OF MEMORY   5 b.m. Rock Hopper 124 – Mystic Memory 74 (Ela-Mana-   **52** Mou 132) [2002 f12g⁵ f12g⁴ 12f 14g* 18f⁵ 16.2g⁶ 16g 14m 14.1m Sep 5] angular mare: second foal: dam 13.6f to 2m winner, also useful staying hurdler: bumper winner: modest handicapper on Flat: won at Musselburgh in June: left R. Fahey after sixth start: stayed 2¼m: raced only on good going or firmer on turf: dead. *P. D. Niven*

FLAT SPIN   3 b.c. Spinning World (USA) 130 – Trois Graces (USA) (Alysheba   **112** (USA)) [2002 95: 8g* 8m⁵ 8m 8m² 10.3m⁴ 9.9f³ 9m Oct 19] rather leggy, useful-looking colt: easy mover: smart performer: won listed race at Kempton in March by 2½ lengths from Angelus Sunset: best effort after when 2½ lengths second to Where Or When in similar event at Goodwood in August: stays easy 1¼m: raced only on good going or firmer: visored last 4 starts: has been bandaged in front: no easy ride (runs in snatches): sent to USA. *J. L. Dunlop*

FLAT STANLEY   3 b.g. Celtic Swing 138 – Cool Grey 49 (Absalom 128) [2002 –:   **–** 10.1d 14.6v⁵ Nov 8] workmanlike gelding: no form. *R. Bastiman*

FLEDGE   3 b.f. Botanic (USA) – Kitty Kitty Cancan 73 (Warrshan (USA) 117) [2002   **–** 52: 7d⁶ 5.1m 8.1m⁶ 7m Sep 23] useful-looking filly: little form at 3 yrs. *R. M. Beckett*

FLEETWOOD BAY   2 b.c. (Feb 14) Fleetwood (IRE) 107 – Caviar And Candy 47   **85**
(Soviet Star (USA) 128) [2002 5.1g³ 6s² 6d⁵ 7d³ p6g⁴ 6m 7m² 6m* 7s p7g⁴ Nov 13]
3,800F, 11,500Y: smallish, workmanlike colt: has a round action: second foal: dam,
maiden who raced only at 5f/6f at 2 yrs, half-sister to very smart stayer Orchestra Stall:
fairly useful performer: won 22-runner sales race at Doncaster in September by short
head from Queen of Night, making most: creditable fourth in nursery at Lingfield final
start: effective at 6f/7f: acts on polytrack, soft and good to firm going: usually races
prominently. *B. R. Millman*

FLEMMING (USA)   5 ch.g. Green Dancer (USA) 132 – La Groupie (FR) (Groom   **–**
Dancer (USA) 128) [2002 8s 12.1g Aug 8] second foal: brother to French winner around
1¼m Groupinsky: dam French 1m winner: ex-French gelding: maiden: claimed out of
M. Rolland's stable €12,105 after finishing in rear at Saint-Cloud on reappearance: no
encouragement on British debut in handicap only other outing in 2002: stays 1¼m: acts
on soft going. *A. G. Juckes*

FLETCHER   8 b.g. Salse (USA) 128 – Ballet Classique (USA) 84 (Sadler's Wells   **68**
(USA) 132) [2002 74: 12m 14.1m⁴ 12m⁶ 14m 12d 16.5g⁶ 14.1m* 14.1m³ 14.1m⁴ 14.1m   **a–**
p16g 16f 11.8s Oct 15] useful-looking gelding: easy mover: fair handicapper at best: won
at Salisbury (made running) in July: effective at 1½m to 2m: possibly unsuited by heavy
going, acts on any other: visored once: sometimes looks none too keen. *H. Morrison*

FLIGHT OF EAGLES (IRE)   3 gr.g. Paris House 123 – Wisdom To Know (Bay   **–**
Express 132) [2002 74: p5g Apr 10] tall, leggy gelding: fair maiden at 2 yrs: off 9 months
before only start in 2002 (gelded after): tongue tied last 2 starts. *A. Berry*

FLIGHT OF ESTEEM   2 b.c. (Apr 30) Mark of Esteem (IRE) 137 – Miss Up N Go   **79**
(Gorytus (USA) 132) [2002 p8g⁴ p8g⁴ p8g² Dec 14] 16,500F, 35,000Y: half-brother to
several winners, including 4-y-o Trotter's Future and fairly useful 15f winner Mishor
(by Slip Anchor): dam unraced half-sister to dam of Derby winner Oath: fair form in
frame in maidens at Lingfield, short-headed by Nawow final start: will stay at least 1¼m.
P. W. Harris

FLIGHT REFUND   5 ch.g. Missed Flight 123 – Settlement (USA) 75 (Irish River   **33**
(FR) 131) [2002 –: f11s⁵ f12s⁶ f12g f14.8g⁶ Feb 2] angular, workmanlike gelding: poor
maiden: stays 11f. *R. Hollinshead*

FLIGHT SEQUENCE   6 b.m. Polar Falcon (USA) 126 – Doubles 85 (Damister   **88**
(USA) 123) [2002 78: 10m³ 10s* 10f* 10m⁵ Jun 28] good-topped mare: fairly useful
performer, lightly raced: better than ever in 2002, winning minor event at Windsor in May
and Stanley Racing Zetland Gold Cup at Redcar (beat Court of Appeal by head) in June:
barely stays 1½m: acts on firm and soft going: twice visored at 4 yrs: often races
prominently: consistent. *Lady Herries*

FLIGHT TIMES   4 b.g. Timeless Times (USA) 99 – Petite Elite 47 (Anfield 117) [2002   **–**
f7s f7g⁶ 6f 6d f8.5s Dec 26] 1,200F, 2,500Y: seventh foal: brother to 5-y-o Christopherssister and 5f/6f winner E B Pearl, and half-brother to 3 winners: dam maiden who stayed
7f: no form. *N. Bycroft*

FLIGHT TO TUSCANY   4 b.f. Bonny Scot (IRE) 119 – Tuscan Butterfly (Beldale   **32**
Flutter (USA) 130) [2002 38: 10m 8f⁵ 11.9m⁵ 9.7m 11.9g⁶ 10.9m⁶ 10.2g Oct 16] poor
maiden: should stay beyond 1¾m: carries head awkwardly. *J. M. Bradley*

FLIGHTY FELLOW (IRE)   2 ch.g. (May 15) Flying Spur (AUS) – Al Theraab   **82**
(USA) 81 (Roberto (USA) 131) [2002 6g⁵ 6s 6s² 7.2g 5.9s³ 7d* 7m 7g* 7s⁵ Oct 26]
7,000Y: tall, quite good-topped gelding: has scope: eighth foal: closely related to useful
French winners Barsine (6f, including at 2 yrs) and Algallarens (6f/7f), both by Danehill,
and half-brother to 2 winners, including French 1m winner Ebdaa (by Nashwan): dam,
1m winner, best at 1¼m: fairly useful performer: won maiden at Thirsk in August and
nursery at Catterick (hung left) in October: well below best final start: will probably stay
1m: acts on soft ground. *T. D. Easterby*

FLIGHTY MAC   2 g.rf. (Apr 24) Paris House 123 – Stilvella (Camden Town 125)   **41**
[2002 f5s 6d f7g f6s Dec 26] 500Y: seventh foal: half-sister to 1995 2-y-o 5f winner
Pathaze (by Totem) and 3-y-o Tedsdale Mac: dam ran twice: poor maiden. *N. Bycroft*

FLINDERS RANGE (USA)   4 b.g. Pleasant Colony (USA) – Ixtapa (USA) (Chief's   **59**
Crown (USA)) [2002 f12g² 9.7m 10g a12g a12g² a10.5g* a10.5g⁴ a10.5g³ a10.5g a12g⁶
a10.5g* a10.5g⁶ a10.5g* a11g⁵ a10.5g a12g Dec 15] good-topped gelding: sixth foal:
half-brother to 2 winners in France, notably smart French 7.5f (at 2 yrs) and 10.5f winner
Dark Nile (by Riverman): dam, French 1½m winner, half-sister to very smart 1¼m
performer Kefaah: sold from Mme C. Head-Maarek 4,000 gns after only 3-y-o outing:

trained by R. Cowell first 3 starts in 2002 (modest form at best): won minor events at Mijas in July and at Mijas and Dos Hermanas in October: stays 1½m: acts on sand/fibresand, best turf effort on heavy: has had tongue tied. *E. J. Creighton, Spain*

FLINT RIVER   4 b.g. Red Ransom (USA) – She's All Class (USA) (Rahy (USA) 115)   **75** [2002 83: 5g 6m 6f 5m⁵ 5s³ 5m 5g⁶ 5m 7.6g 7m⁴ 6m 8m² 8.1f 6f p10g p10g² Dec 30] close-coupled gelding: fair handicapper: left J. Goldie before penultimate start: effective at stiff 5f to easy 1¼m: acts on firm going, probably on polytrack: tried blinkered: has run well when sweating. *S. Kirk*

FLOORSO'THEFOREST (IRE)   6 ch.g. Forest Wind (USA) 111 – Ravensdale   **–** Rose (IRE) (Henbit (USA) 130) [2002 9g 9.2s⁵ 11.9s 8g 9g 8m Jul 8] angular gelding: little form in 2002. *Miss L. A. Perratt*

FLOPPIE DISK   2 b.f. (Jan 29) Magic Ring (IRE) 115 – Floppie (FR) (Law Society   **82** (USA) 130) [2002 5f³ 5m² 5.1d⁴ 5m² 5m² 5.1d* 5m 5m³ 5m⁵ 5g p5g⁴ p5g Dec 18] 1,600Y: small, strong-quartered filly: half-sister to several winners up to 1m, including 3-y-o Ringmoor Down and Irish 7f winner Still Going On (by Prince Sabo), both fairly useful: dam French 1m winner: fairly useful performer: won maiden at Nottingham in June: mostly creditable efforts after, very stiff tasks on 2 occasions: will prove best at bare 5f: acts on firm and good to soft ground, well held on polytrack: races up with pace. *J. A. Pickering*

FLOREEDA   2 b. or gr.f. (Apr 10) Linamix (FR) 127 – La Sky (IRE) 107 (Law Society   **75 p** (USA) 130) [2002 p7g⁴ 7d³ Nov 2] half-sister to several winners, notably Oaks winner Love Divine (by Diesis), also successful at 1¾m: dam, 1¼m winner (probably stayed 1¾m), closely related to Champion Stakes winner Legal Case: fair form in frame in maidens at Lingfield and Newmarket, third of 19 to Goodness Gracious in latter: will be suited by 1m+: remains capable of better. *H. R. A. Cecil*

FLORENTINE FLUTTER   3 b.c. Machiavellian (USA) 123 – Party Doll 108 (Be   **72** My Guest (USA) 126) [2002 72p: 7.1m* 8s 8d Jun 15] close-coupled, quite attractive colt: fair performer: won maiden at Haydock in April: reportedly lost action when pulled up next time, and ran poorly final start: should stay 1m: acts on good to firm going: has swished tail in preliminaries: sold 7,500 gns. *J. H. M. Gosden*

FLORENZAR (IRE)   4 b.f. Inzar (USA) 112 – Nurse Tyra (USA) (Dr Blum (USA))   **47 +** [2002 –: 10m⁵ 11.9d⁵ May 24] poor maiden. *Miss S. West*

FLORETTE   2 ch.f. (Apr 25) Fleetwood (IRE) 107 – Antum 56 (Hittite Glory 125)   **–** [2002 7g f8s f7g p8g Nov 23] 2,500Y: half-sister to several winners abroad, including French 1½m winner Jarmo (by Jalmood): dam showed ability on debut but didn't progress: well held in maidens/seller. *D. Morris*

FLORIAN   4 b.g. Young Ern 120 – Murmuring 69 (Kind of Hush 118) [2002 56: p8g²   **a63** p7g² p7g³ p8g p7g Mar 27] modest maiden handicapper: stays 1m: form only on   **a63** polytrack: idled second start. *P. Mitchell*

FLORIANA   3 b.f. Selkirk (USA) 129 – Mara River 86 (Efisio 120) [2002 8g⁵ 9.9m⁵   **61 ?** 8.3g 10.3v³ p10g f11g Dec 17] first foal: dam 6f to 1m winner: modest maiden: seemingly best effort on fourth start: appears to stay 1¼m: acts on heavy and good to firm going, well held on all-weather. *I. A. Balding*

FLORIDA (IRE)   4 b.f. Sri Pekan (USA) 117 – Florinda (CAN) (Vice Regent (CAN))   **43** [2002 44: f16s* f16s³ f14.8g² f16g⁵ f16.2g⁵ f14.8g 11.9g 16.2g⁶ 14.1d Oct 30] smallish filly: poor handicapper: won at Southwell in January: stays 2m: acts on fibresand, soft and firm going. *I. A. Wood*

FLOTTA   3 ch.g. Elmaamul (USA) 125 – Heavenly Goddess (Soviet Star (USA) 128)   **78** [2002 8m⁶ 10.4m² 11.7g³ Oct 16] lengthy, plain gelding: third foal: half-brother to 5-y-o Digital: dam unraced: fair form in maidens at Salisbury (started slowly), York and Bath: likely to be better at 1½m than shorter: raced only on good/good to firm going. *M. R. Channon*

FLOW BEAU   5 b.m. Mtoto 134 – Radiance (FR) 115 (Blakeney 126) [2002 33: 10f³   **54** 10m 10.1f* 10.1f 10.1m⁶ 10.9m* 8m 10f Sep 27] modest performer: won sellers at Yarmouth in July and Warwick in August: ran as if something amiss penultimate outing: stays 1¾m: acts on firm and good to soft going: tried blinkered, usually visored: sometimes slowly away (has been markedly so)/races freely/looks less than keen. *J. O'Reilly*

FLOWER BREEZE (USA)   2 ch.f. (Jan 28) Rahy (USA) 115 – Now Showing   **75** (USA) (Golden Act (USA)) [2002 7g 8m³ 8g⁴ 8.3m Oct 7] $47,000F, IR 110,000Y: quite attractive filly: half-sister to several winners in Italy/USA: dam, US 1m/9f winner, including minor stakes: fair maiden: third at Yarmouth: should stay 1¼m: sold 6,500 gns. *M. R. Channon*

FLOWERDRUM (USA) 2 b.f. (May 18) Mister Baileys 123 – Norelands (USA) **64**
(Irish River (FR) 131) [2002 6m f6g³ Oct 22] $13,000Y, resold 12,500Y: third foal: dam
unraced half-sister to 2 minor stakes winners in USA: modest form in maidens at Windsor
and Southwell: will be suited by 7f+. *W. J. Haggas*

FLOWNAWAY 3 b.g. Polar Falcon (USA) 126 – No More Rosies 74 (Warpath 113) **86**
[2002 80: 8g p10g f12g* f14g* Dec 10] strong gelding: has a quick action: fairly useful
handicapper: off 13 months before reappearance: won twice at Southwell in December,
former apprentice event, latter comfortably: stays 1¾m: acts on fibresand, raced only on
good ground or firmer on turf: took strong hold and hung left final 2-y-o start. *W. Jarvis*

FLUENT 3 b.f. Polar Falcon (USA) 126 – Lady Barrister (Law Society (USA) 130) **63**
[2002 64p: f8.5g 7m² 7m⁵ 7f⁶ 6.1m³ 5.9g* 6g Jul 6] lengthy, good-bodied filly: modest
performer: won maiden at Carlisle in June: ran poorly final start: will prove as effective at
7f as 6f: acts on good to firm going, probably on heavy: sold 13,000 gns. *M. L. W. Bell*

FLUR NA H ALBA 3 b.g. Atraf 116 – Tyrian Belle 77 (Enchantment 115) [2002 88: **91 §**
5g³ 6g 7s² 6g 7.2v⁶ 7.1d 5g 7g Aug 15] strong gelding: fairly useful handicapper: placed
at Sandown in April and Epsom in June: well below form last 5 starts: stays 7f: acts on
firm and soft ground: blinkered third to sixth starts: usually races prominently: unreliable:
joined I. Semple. *M. Johnston*

FLY BACK 3 ch.g. Fraam 114 – The Fernhill Flyer (IRE) 71 (Red Sunset 120) [2002 **50**
–: 8m 7m⁴ 10f 8.3v Jun 12] strong gelding: modest maiden: should stay 1m: acts on good
to firm ground. *M. Dods*

FLY BUY DUBAI 3 b.g. Salse (USA) 128 – Her Honour 94 (Teenoso (USA) 135) **–**
[2002 10m 10g p8g 14.1f Jun 13] third foal: half-brother to 1¾m winner Dame Fonteyn
(by Suave Dancer): dam, won all 3 starts at 1¼m/1½m, also a smart but temperamental
staying hurdler: signs of ability in maidens, but well held on handicap debut final start:
bred to be suited by 1½m+: slowly away second outing. *M. L. W. Bell*

FLYING EDGE (IRE) 2 b.g. (Apr 10) Flying Spur (AUS) – Day Is Dawning (IRE) **70 d**
(Green Forest (USA) 134) [2002 6s³ 6g⁶ 6m 7g 7s 7v f8.5g Dec 2] IR 16,500F, 15,000Y:
close-coupled gelding: third foal: brother to fairly useful Irish 7f winner Sa'ed: dam
unraced: fair maiden: best effort on debut: well held in nurseries last 4 starts: likely to
prove best at 5f/6f: acts on soft ground. *J. A. Osborne*

FLYING EXPRESS 2 ch.c. (Mar 21) Air Express (IRE) 125 – Royal Loft 105 (Hom- **94 p**
ing 130) [2002 6m² 6m* 6.1f* Aug 31] 3,500Y: good-topped colt: has scope: closely
related to fairly useful Irish 7f (including at 2 yrs) and 9f winner Sir Slaves (by Salse) and
half-brother to several winners, including 1994 2-y-o 7f winner Wigberto (by Old Vic):
dam 6f/7f winner: progressive form: justified favouritism, making all, in maiden at Ripon
and minor event at Chester in August, latter by 3 lengths from Tug of Love: will probably
stay 7f: raced only on ground firmer than good: should make a useful 3-y-o. *B. W. Hills*

FLYING FAISAL (USA) 4 b.c. Alydeed (CAN) 120 – Peaceful Silence (USA) **59**
(Proper Reality (USA)) [2002 66: f5g⁴ f5g⁵ f5g* f5g⁵ 5.1d⁴ f6g 6f f7g 5m 5g* 5m 5d 5m **a54**
5.7f 6m f5g f6g³ f6s³ Dec 26] sturdy colt: modest performer: won seller at Wolverhampton in February and handicap at Carlisle in July: left B. McMahon 5,000 gns after
twelfth start: effective at 5f to 7f: acts on good to soft going, good to firm and fibresand:
sometimes blinkered/tongue tied before 2002: reportedly bled from nose second start.
J. M. Bradley

FLYING FULMAR 3 ch.f. Bahamian Bounty 116 – West Humble 93 (Pharly (FR) **83**
130) [2002 81: 6g⁴ 7g⁶ 8g⁵ 7g* 7m 7m⁵ Sep 3] leggy, quite good-topped filly: fairly
useful performer: won handicap at Leicester in July: creditable efforts after: stays 7f: acts
on soft and good to firm going. *M. L. W. Bell*

FLYING IN THE DARK (IRE) 3 b.g. Flying Spur (AUS) – Cry In The Dark (Gods- **47**
walk (USA) 130) [2002 p6g f7g f7g⁵ 7m⁴ 10m⁴ 12m 9.9g⁶ 8.2g 8m⁵ 8f 8.2m* 8m 10m
10g Oct 14] IR 6,500Y: quite good-topped gelding: half-brother to fairly useful Irish 6.5f
(at 2 yrs) to 1m winner Classic Express (by Classic Music) and 1m/1¼m winner Cruagh
Express (by Unblest): dam Irish 1m winner: poor performer: won selling handicap at
Nottingham (sold from N. Littmoden 6,500 gns) in June: lost action before falling final
start: stayed 1¼m: acted on good to firm going: blinkered eighth/ninth outings: was
usually tongue tied: dead. *J. Parkes*

FLYING MILLIE (IRE) 4 b.f. Flying Spur (AUS) – Sweet Pleasure 88 (Sweet **95**
Revenge 129) [2002 99: 6d 6m 6m 6d⁵ 6m³ 6g 6f Oct 4] leggy, useful-looking filly: useful
handicapper: creditable ninth in Ayr Gold Cup penultimate start: effective at 5f/6f: acts
on good to firm and good to soft ground: waited with. *R. M. Beckett*

FLYING RIBOT (USA) 2 b.c. (Apr 17) Exclusive Ribot (USA) – Flying Starlet **61**
(USA) (Flying Paster (USA)) [2002 7.1m 6g 6f⁵ 8.2v Oct 29] fifth foal: half-brother to a
winner in USA by Quinton: dam 6f winner in USA: modest maiden: best effort third start:
hampered and unseated rider time before: not sure to stay 1m. *B. W. Hills*

FLYING ROMANCE (IRE) 4 b.f. Flying Spur (AUS) – State Romance 67 (Free **68**
State 125) [2002 56: f12s f12g p12g⁴ f12g* p13g⁵ p12g³ f12g² p13g 11.6g* 10m 11.7g² **a54**
12.3f 13.1g* 13.8m⁵ 12.1d³ 12.1v⁵ 11.9d 11.6m³ p12g² 12.1d* 11.5f p12g 12.1g³ 12m*
12.1m⁴ 12d 12f⁶ 14f f12g 12d* f12g p10g⁴ p13g Dec 28] small, angular filly: fair handicapper on turf, modest on all-weather: won at Wolverhampton, Windsor, Bath, Chepstow,
Salisbury and Newmarket (29 ran) in 2002: effective at 11.6f to 15f: possibly unsuited by
heavy going, acts on any other turf/all-weather: tough. *P. D. Evans*

FLYING SPIRIT (IRE) 3 b.g. Flying Spur (AUS) – All Laughter (Vision (USA)) **78**
[2002 65: 7s⁵ p6g 6f² 7m 9d³ 10.3g² 10d* 10.1m⁴ 10.1m 12f⁵ 10s⁶ Oct 23] quite good-
topped gelding: fair performer: won apprentice minor event at Nottingham in June:
below form last 3 starts (gelded after): stays 1¼m: acts on firm and good to soft going:
tried visored: has raced freely: looks a difficult ride: probably none too trustworthy.
M. H. Tompkins

FLYING TACKLE 4 ch.g. First Trump 118 – Frighten The Life (Kings Lake (USA) **67**
133) [2002 68: 5s 5g⁵ 5.9s 6s⁵ 5m³ 5.9v 5m³ 5m² 5m 5m 5f 5d Nov 5] strong, lengthy
gelding: fair handicapper: below form last 4 starts: best at 5f/6f: acts on good to firm and
heavy going: often visored/blinkered: has wandered. *J. S. Wainwright*

FLYING TRAPEZE (USA) 4 ch.g. Trempolino (USA) 135 – Loen (USA) (Accipiter **55**
(USA)) [2002 73: 8.1d 9.9g 10.2d 10m⁵ 8f Aug 23] strong, quite attractive gelding:
modest form at best in 2002: stays 11f: acts on firm going: tried visored/tongue tied.
B. A. McMahon

FLYING TREATY (USA) 5 br.h. You And I (USA) 118 – Cherie's Hope (USA) **–**
(Flying Paster (USA)) [2002 –, a85: p12g f8g p7g f8.5s* f8.5g² f8.5s* f8g* Dec 27] **a90**
useful-looking horse: has reportedly been hobdayed: fairly useful performer: won
apprentice minor event at Wolverhampton and handicaps at Wolverhampton and Southwell (by 9 lengths) in December: has form up to easy 1½m, probably best around 1m:
better form on fibresand than polytrack, very lightly raced on turf: visored final 4-y-o
outing: usually races prominently. *Miss A. Stokell*

FLYING WANDA 2 b.f. (Apr 13) Alzao (USA) 117 – Royal York 75 (Bustino 136) **87 p**
[2002 7m² 8m* Sep 3] quite good-topped filly: second foal: dam, 1¼m/1½m winner (also
winning hurdler/chaser), out of half-sister to high-class performer up to 1½m Kirtling:
landed odds in 5-runner maiden at Yarmouth by 2 lengths from Choral Chimes, dictating
pace and responding well when challenged: should stay at least 1¼m: should make a
useful 3-y-o. *J. Noseda*

FLY KICKER 5 ch.g. High Kicker (USA) – Double Birthday (Cavo Doro 124) [2002 **–**
38: 12.1g 11.1v 10.1m Aug 16] maiden: well held in 2002. *E. J. Alston*

FLY MORE 5 ch.g. Lycius (USA) 124 – Double River (USA) (Irish River (FR) 131) **76**
[2002 84: 5f 6m⁶ 5f 5g 5d⁵ 6m 6.1m⁶ 5.7g² 5m⁴ 5.1g* 5.7f⁶ 5m 5m 5m Sep 23] very big,
lengthy gelding: fair handicapper: won at Chepstow in July: below form after: probably
better at 5f than 6f: acts on good to firm and good to soft going, not on softer: has folded
tamely. *J. M. Bradley*

FLYOFF (IRE) 5 b.g. Mtoto 134 – Flyleaf (FR) (Persian Bold 123) [2002 f12f f11g **–**
Dec 4] ran twice in France, winning 13.5f 3-y-o event for J-C. Rouget: well held over
hurdles, and in 2 Flat starts in Britain (blinkered). *K. A. Morgan*

FOLEY MILLENNIUM (IRE) 4 ch.c. Tagula (IRE) 116 – Inshirah (USA) 90 (Caro **–**
133) [2002 –: p5g Jun 29] tall, lengthy colt: fairly useful 5f/6f winner at 2 yrs: little form
since: left M. Quinn and off 12 months before only start in 2002. *G. M. McCourt*

FOLIO (IRE) 2 b.g. (Feb 16) Perugino (USA) 84 – Bayleaf 104 (Efisio 120) [2002 **99**
5m² 5s³ 5.1g² 5f* 5.1f* 5g³ 5g⁴ 6f⁴ 6m* 6m⁵ 5m⁵ Oct 12] rather leggy, useful-looking
gelding: first foal: dam 2-y-o 5f winner: useful performer: won maiden at Windsor in July
and minor events at Bath in July and Yarmouth in September: good fifth in Two-Year-Old
Trophy at Redcar and Cornwallis Stakes at Ascot: effective at 5f/6f: acts on firm going,
possibly not on soft: consistent: joined W. Musson. *R. F. Johnson Houghton*

FOLLOW FLANDERS 3 b.f. Pursuit of Love 124 – Pretty Poppy 67 (Song 132) **92**
[2002 74p: 5f* 5m⁵ 5.1m⁴ 6v 6m⁵ 7m 5m⁶ Sep 24] sturdy, angular filly: fairly useful
performer: won minor event at Thirsk in April: best effort when fifth in listed race at

Pontefract in August on fifth outing: effective at 5f/6f: acts on polytrack and firm ground, seemingly not on heavy. *H. Candy*

FOLLOW YOUR STAR 4 ch.g. Pursuit of Love 124 – Possessive Artiste 73 (Shareef **70** Dancer (USA) 135) [2002 70: 10g 12m 11.9d⁴ 12g⁶ 10m 10d 7.5s Dec 30] sturdy gelding: fair maiden handicapper: left P. Hobbs (pulled up on hurdling debut) and returned to former trainer prior to fourth start: sold from P. Harris 3,200 gns after fifth outing: stays 1¼m: best efforts on good/good to firm going: visored (well below form) final 2-y-o start. *F. Beluschi, Italy*

FOODBROKER FOUNDER 2 ch.c. (Feb 5) Groom Dancer (USA) 128 – Nemea **84** (USA) 97 (The Minstrel (CAN) 135) [2002 7.1d⁴ 7d³ 8f² 8g*⁸ 8g Oct 18] 160,000F, 75,000Y: lengthy colt: has scope: third foal: brother to scope 7f/1m winner Lovers Knot: dam 1¼m winner who probably stayed 2m: fairly useful performer: won maiden at Salisbury in October by 3½ lengths from Exzilarating: raced freely when running poorly in nursery at Newmarket final start: should be suited by at least 1¼m: acts on firm and good to soft ground. *D. R. C. Elsworth*

FOOLHARDY 2 ch.f. (Mar 21) Primo Dominie 121 – Rash (Pursuit of Love 124) **72** [2002 6g⁴ 5d* 6g 7m f6g² Oct 21] lengthy filly: has scope: second foal: half-sister to 3-y-o Loveleaves: dam unraced half-sister to useful 2-y-o sprinters Maid For Walking and Maid For The Hills: fair performer: won maiden at Musselburgh in July: creditable second in nursery at Wolverhampton: well held in between: should prove best at 5f/6f: acts on fibresand and good to soft ground: sold 26,000 gns. *W. J. Haggas*

FOOLISH GIFT (FR) 2 b.f. (Apr 1) Barathea (IRE) 127 – Fancy Wrap (Kris 135) **–** [2002 8.3d Oct 28] first foal: dam twice-raced sister to Royal Lodge winner Reach and Oaks d'Italia second Wrapping: 25/1, well held in maiden at Windsor. *W. R. Muir*

FOOLISH WHISPER 3 b.f. Makbul 104 – Whisper Low (IRE) 63 (Shalford (IRE) **46** 124§) [2002 –: 7.5g 8g 5m 7f 6f³ 6d Oct 18] smallish filly: poor maiden: best effort at 6f on firm going. *R. Hollinshead*

FOOL ON THE HILL 5 b.g. Reprimand 122 – Stock Hill Lass 87 (Air Trooper 115) **90** [2002 78: 10f* 10.2v* 10d⁶ 10m⁵ 12m² 12g³ Sep 27] workmanlike gelding: fairly useful handicapper: won at Newbury in May and Chepstow in June: creditable efforts in amateur events at Goodwood and Ascot last 2 starts: stays 1½m: acts on any going: visored last 5 starts in 2001. *L. G. Cottrell*

FOOLS AND HORSES 3 ch.f. Muhtarram (USA) 125 – Lady Phyl 67 (Northiam **–** (USA)) [2002 7d 7.5m 10m Sep 23] second foal: dam 6f winner: well held in seller/ claimers: slowly away on debut: has raced freely: withdrawn after bursting out of stall on intended debut at 2 yrs. *John A. Harris*

FOOLS RUSH IN (IRE) 3 b.g. Entrepreneur 123 – Blinding (IRE) (High Top 131) **94** [2002 87p: f8.5g⁴* p8g⁴ 10m 7g⁵ 8g⁴ 8m Jun 20] tall, good-topped gelding: fairly useful performer: won maiden at Wolverhampton in January: good efforts in handicap at Newmarket and minor event at Thirsk fourth/fifth starts: effective at 7f/1m: acts on fibresand, probably on soft going (best efforts on good): tried tongue tied: sometimes edgy. *T. G. Mills*

FOOTBALL CRAZY (IRE) 3 b.g. Mujadil (USA) 119 – Schonbein (IRE) 60 **101** (Persian Heights 129) [2002 84: 9f 7g 6g⁶ 8m* 9d* 10m* 10d* 10g 10g² 10m⁵ 10g³ Sep 27] lengthy, quite good-topped gelding: useful performer: won claimer at Leicester and handicaps at Sandown (2) and Windsor in June/July: good efforts last 3 starts in handicaps at Newmarket (carried head awkwardly/edged left) and the Curragh and minor event at Ascot (3½ lengths third to Mahroos): stays 1¼m: acts on soft and good to firm going: usually races up with pace. *N. A. Callaghan*

FORBEARING (IRE) 5 b.g. Bering 136 – For Example (USA) 66 (Northern Baby **93** (CAN) 127) [2002 11.9d 12g² 8f 10m⁵ 12g⁵ Sep 29] good-topped gelding: carries plenty of condition: smart in 2000: only fairly useful on belated return: best effort in handicap at Ascot final start: stays 1½m: acts on good to firm going, good to soft and fibresand: has raced freely. *Sir Mark Prescott*

FORCEFUL 2 b.f. (Mar 31) Forzando 122 – Instinction (Never So Bold 135) [2002 **49** 5g 5.1d 6g p5g⁴ f5g³ f5g⁶ f5g Dec 16] 5,200Y: rather leggy filly: fifth foal: half-sister to 5f winner Nickles and a winner in Greece (both by Lugana Beach): dam unraced half-sister to 3-y-o Acclamation: poor maiden: will prove best at 5f/easy 6f: acts on all-weather, raced on good/firmish ground on turf. *J. G. Portman*

FOREIGN ACCENT 3 b.g. Machiavellian (USA) 123 – Rappa Tap Tap (FR) 111 **98** (Tap On Wood 130) [2002 100p: 7m 8s⁴ 10m⁶ Jun 23] tall, good-topped gelding: useful performer: impressive winner of maiden at Doncaster only 2-y-o start: best effort in 2002 when 9½ lengths fourth behind very easy winner Rock of Gibraltar in Irish 2000 Guineas at the Curragh second start, not impressing with attitude under pressure (flashed tail): blinkered, last of 6 in Grand Prix de Paris at Longchamp final outing (gelded after): stays 1m: acts on heavy going: carries head high: joined S. Bray in USA. *J. H. M. Gosden*

FOREIGN AFFAIRS 4 ch.c. Hernando (FR) 127 – Entente Cordiale (USA) (Affirmed (USA)) [2002 117p: 10.3m* 10f² 10s⁶ 12m⁴ 16m⁶ Oct 19] good-topped colt: smart performer: made all in 3-runner minor event at Doncaster in June: best effort after when length fourth to Asian Heights in September Stakes at Kempton penultimate start: has form at 1¾m (failed to stay 2m final start), at least as effective at 1¼m/1½m: acts on good to firm going and fibresand. *Sir Mark Prescott* **114**

FOREIGN EDITOR 6 ch.g. Magic Ring (IRE) 115 – True Precision 84 (Presidium 124) [2002 62, a83: f8s p7g² Jan 8] workmanlike gelding: fair handicapper on all-weather nowadays: stays 1m: acts on fibresand and good to firm going. *J. J. Quinn* **– a75**

FOREST DANCER (IRE) 4 b.g. Charnwood Forest (IRE) 125 – Forest Berries (IRE) (Thatching 131) [2002 88: a8g⁶ a12g a8g² 7.6f 8.1d 8.9d 6.9d 7.6f 8s 7.9m 7g a8g³ a8g* Dec 15] rather leggy gelding: modest form at best in 2002 (trained in Britain fourth to eleventh starts only): won handicap at Mijas in December: stays 1m: acts on firm going, good to soft and sand/fibresand: blinkered (well held) once: sometimes slowly away: has carried head awkwardly. *P. Haley, Spain* **59**

FOREST DREAM 7 b.m. Warrshan (USA) 117 – Sirenivo (USA) 113 (Sir Ivor 135) [2002 ?: f16s⁵ p12g f16g f14g p16g Mar 6] probably of little account nowadays. *L. A. Dace* **–**

FOREST HEATH (IRE) 5 gr.g. Common Grounds 118 – Caroline Lady (JPN) (Caro 133) [2002 88, a79: p10g 10.9g⁶ 10m 10.3m 12f⁵ 14.1m³ 12d 10f 10s Oct 15] quite good-topped gelding: not a good walker: has a short, round action: fair handicapper: on downgrade: effective at 1¼m/easy 1½m: yet to race on heavy going, acts on any other turf and on polytrack: usually blinkered/visored: tried tongue tied: has been bandaged behind: temperamental. *H. J. Collingridge* **75 d**

FOREST LIGHT (IRE) 4 gr.f. Rainbow Quest (USA) 134 – Woodland Garden (Godswalk (USA) 130) [2002 69: f15f 12m⁴ 12m May 16] lengthy, rather leggy filly: fair handicapper: stays 1¾m: acts on firm going: blinkered last 2 starts. *R. F. Johnson Houghton* **66**

FOREST MAGIC (IRE) 2 b.c. (Feb 2) Charnwood Forest (IRE) 125 – Adultress (IRE) (Ela-Mana-Mou 132) [2002 7d⁵ 7.2s² 10s* 10s* Nov 2] 17,500F, 27,000Y: good-topped colt: first foal: dam unraced half-sister to French performer Adaiyka, herself dam of Adilabad (both smart around 1¼m), and to 5-y-o King's Mill: progressive form: won maiden at Nottingham (by 6 lengths) in October and 10-runner listed race at Newmarket (by length from Allergy, pair clear) in November, hanging left in front each time: will stay at least 1½m: raced only on going softer than good: already useful, and open to further improvement. *P. W. D'Arcy* **106 p**

FOREST MOON 4 b.f. Charnwood Forest (IRE) 125 – Moon Watch 64 (Night Shift (USA)) [2002 55: f7g p6g³ p6g p7g f6g f6g⁵ 6m³ 7m 6m Jul 29] smallish, good-bodied filly: modest performer: best at 6f/7f: acts on good to firm ground and all-weather: on downgrade. *Andrew Reid* **52 d**

FOREST PRIZE 3 b.f. Charnwood Forest (IRE) 125 – Midnight's Reward 84 (Night Shift (USA)) [2002 77: 7s⁶ 8m 8s³ 10g⁵ 7.9g² 8.1d⁵ Jul 5] leggy filly: fair performer: effective at 1m/1¼m: acts on soft and good to firm going: unreliable. *T. D. Easterby* **75 §**

FOREST QUEEN 5 b.m. Risk Me (FR) 127 – Grey Cree 64 (Creetown 123) [2002 –: 7.9m Aug 21] no form since 2 yrs: left J. Wainwright and rejoined former trainer prior to only start in 2002. *K. W. Hogg, Isle of Man* **–**

FOREST RAIL (IRE) 2 b.f. (May 14) Catrail (USA) 123 – Forest Heights 81 (Slip Anchor 136) [2002 f5g* f5g* p5g² 5g⁶ Jul 24] third foal: dam, 1½m winner, out of half-sister to Yorkshire Oaks winner Magnificent Star: fair performer: made all in 4-runner seller at Wolverhampton (for D. Morris) in July: good second in nursery at Lingfield: likely to prove best at 5f: acts on all-weather, below form only turf outing: refused to enter stall at Lingfield in December. *R. Wilman* **66**

FOREST RIDGE 3 b. or br.g. Charnwood Forest (IRE) 125 – Away To Me (Exit To Nowhere (USA) 122) [2002 –p: 10.2g 8d⁵ 8g 8m 10g⁵ 12.1g⁴ 11.9m⁴ Oct 3] big, good-topped gelding: fair maiden: probably better at 1¼m than 1½m: yet to race on extremes of going: has pulled hard: sold 13,000 gns. *Mrs A. J. Perrett* **65**

FOREST TUNE (IRE)   4 b.g. Charnwood Forest (IRE) 125 – Swift Chorus (Music **70** Boy 124) [2002 83d: p10g f8.5g* 9.3g 8g f8g* f8g² 10m⁴ 10d Oct 21] well-made, **a83** attractive gelding: fairly useful handicapper on all-weather, fair on turf: won at Wolverhampton in April and Southwell in June: good efforts next 2 starts: effective at 1m/1¼m: acts on soft going, good to firm and fibresand, probably on polytrack: tried blinkered/ tongue tied. *B. Hanbury*

FORETOLD (IRE)   2 b.c. (Feb 22) Darshaan 133 – For Example (USA) 66 (Northern   **– p** Baby (CAN) 127) [2002 7.9f⁴ Oct 12]   IR 170,000Y: fourth foal: half-brother to 5-y-o Forbearing and 3-y-o Dryden House: dam, third at 1¼m in Ireland, closely related to dam of Culture Vulture and half-sister to dams of Zilzal and Polish Precedent: 3/1 and very green, 5¼ lengths last of 4 to Chaffinch in maiden at York, never able to challenge and eased near finish: should do better. *J. Noseda*

FOREVER LOVED   3 ch.f. Deploy 131 – Truly Madly Deeply (Most Welcome 131)   **84** [2002 72: 10g 10m f12g² 11.9d p12g² f12s* f12g⁵ f12s³ f12s* f14.8g* Dec 31] heavy-topped filly: fairly useful performer: won maiden at Southwell in September and 2 handicaps at Wolverhampton in December: stays 15f: acts on all-weather, yet to race on extremes of going on turf. *D. Haydn Jones*

FOREVER MY LORD   4 b.g. Be My Chief (USA) 122 – In Love Again (IRE) 86   **57** (Prince Rupert (FR) 121) [2002 69d: 7m 8.1m 8.5d² 7d 7g³ 7g 10m 9.7g⁶ p10g² 10.9m 10g Oct 24] good-bodied gelding: modest handicapper: left F. J. Houghton after third start: seems to stay easy 1¼m: acts on polytrack, soft and good to firm ground: often blinkered: tried tongue tied: often slowly away, including last 3 starts. *J. R. Best*

FOREVER TIMES   4 b.f. So Factual (USA) 120 – Simply Times (USA) 64 (Dodge   **97** (USA)) [2002 98: 7d 7d 7.6f 6f³ 6f* 6g 6m⁴ 6f² 6m² 6g² 7m⁴ 6m⁴ 6g⁵ 6f⁴ 7f⁶ Oct 10] neat filly: unimpressive mover: useful handicapper: won at Redcar in June: particularly good efforts after when second to Cubism at York tenth start and fifth to Funfair Wane in Ayr Gold Cup: effective at 6f/7f: probably acts on any turf going, well beaten only run on fibresand: tough and consistent. *T. D. Easterby*

FOR EVVA SILCA   3 ch.f. Piccolo 121 – Silca-Cisa 93 (Hallgate 127) [2002 60: p7g   **–** May 28] leggy, quite good-topped filly: modest maiden: off 12 months, well held early start in 2002: may prove best at 5f/6f: best effort on good to firm going: reportedly broke blood vessel final 2-y-o outing: sold 33,000 gns in July. *M. R. Channon*

FOR FREEDOM (IRE)   2 b.f. (Feb 12) King of Kings 125 – Louju (USA)   **78** (Silver Hawk (USA) 123) [2002 6s 7s 7d³ Nov 2]   IR 135,000Y: angular filly: second foal: dam unraced daughter of US Grade 1 9f runner-up Secretarial Queen: 20/1 and sweating, best effort in maidens (fair form) when 2½ lengths third of 18 to Aljazeera at Newmarket: should stay 1m: raced only on ground softer than good. *B. W. Hills*

FORGE VALLEY LADY   3 ch.f. Hamas (IRE) 125§ – Salul (Soviet Star (USA)   **69** 128) [2002 60: f5g 7g* 8f⁵ 7f f8.5g² f8.5g 6.9s* 7m⁴ 7.1d 6m 6.9m 7s f8.5g⁵ f8g p8g f7g⁵ f6g Dec 10] workmanlike filly: fair handicapper: won at Southwell in April and Carlisle (left J. L. Eyre after) in June: effective at 7f to 8.5f: acts on soft and good to firm ground and fibresand: often visored/blinkered: none too consistent. *D. Carroll*

FORMALISE   2 b.g. (Apr 21) Forzando 122 – Esilam 62 (Frimley Park 109) [2002   **85** 6.1g³ 6m* 6d Nov 1] 20,000Y: good-topped gelding: half-brother to several winners, including useful 5f winner (including at 2 yrs) Pure Coincidence and 6-y-o Pure Elegancia (both by Lugana Beach): dam, 2-y-o 5f winner in Britain, won up to 1m in Italy: favourite after promising debut, fairly useful form to win maiden at Windsor in October impressively by 3 lengths from Figliolo: soundly beaten in minor event at Newmarket only subsequent outing (gelded after): raced only at 6f: acts on good to firm ground. *G. B. Balding*

FORMAL PARTY   4 ch.f. Formidable (USA) 125 – Tea Colony (USA) (Pleasant   **–** Colony (USA)) [2002 –: f8g f9.4g Feb 15] maiden: little recent form. *T. D. McCarthy*

FORMERIC   6 ch.g. Formidable (USA) 125 – Irish Limerick 89 (Try My Best (USA)   **62** 130) [2002 –: 7m 8.1d⁶ 8.1m 8d 7.1d⁶ 8.1v⁶ 7g 7m⁵ 6d* Oct 18] big, workmanlike gelding: modest performer: won maiden at Redcar (looked none too keen) in October: possibly best around 6f nowadays: acts on good to firm and good to soft going: visored/ blinkered last 4 starts. *Miss L. C. Siddall*

FORMIDABLE STELLA   6 b.m. Formidable (USA) 125 – Stellajoe 39 (Le Dauphin   **–** 73) [2002 p10g p7g p10g Dec 30] third foal: dam winning selling hurdler: no sign of ability in bumpers: well held in maiden/sellers on Flat. *Miss Z. C. Davison*

FORONLYMO   3 b.g. Forzando 122 – Polish Descent (IRE) (Danehill (USA) 126)   **61**
[2002 70, a82: f6s³ f7s* f6g⁴ f8.5g⁶ f6g³ 7s 7g f6g³ 7m³ f7g³ 8s² 6g p8g⁶ f7s⁴ f6g² f8.5g⁴   **a84 d**
f7g² f8g Nov 25] small gelding: fair handicapper on all-weather, modest on turf: won at
Southwell in January: trained tenth to fourteenth starts only by C. Dore: effective at 6f to
1m: acts on soft going, good to firm and fibresand: effective visored or not: sometimes
wanders under pressure: reportedly returned lame seventh start. *K. R. Burke*

FORT MCHENRY (IRE)   2 b.g. (Feb 29) Danehill Dancer (IRE) 117 – Griqualand   **78**
(Connaught 130) [2002 6m⁴ 7d* 7m³ Jul 26] IR 19,000F, 170,000Y: big, strong, lengthy
gelding: third foal: half-brother to 1994 2-y-o 9.4f winner Shy Paddy (by Shy Groom):
dam ran twice: fair form: green, won maiden at Epsom in July: creditable third in nursery
at Newmarket, pulling hard: edgy, refused to enter stalls next intended outing in August:
subsequently gelded: will need to settle to stay beyond 7f. *N. A. Callaghan*

FORTUNA MEA   2 b.f. (Feb 26) Mon Tresor 113 – Veni Vici (IRE) (Namaqualand   **44**
(USA)) [2002 6d 5.9s⁴ 7.6m⁶ 8g f8.5g* 8.2v Oct 29] angular filly: first foal: dam ran once   **a54**
in Ireland: modest on all-weather, poor on turf: won seller at Wolverhampton in October
despite hanging left: should stay 1¼m: acts on fibresand, well beaten on heavy ground.
W. M. Brisbourne

FORTUNATE DAVE (USA)   3 b.g. Lear Fan (USA) 130 – Lady Ameriflora (USA)   **72**
(Lord Avie (USA)) [2002 p8g f9.4g⁴ p12g³ p10g* 12.6m² 11.6s 11.8m⁴ 12.3d⁶ 12m
14.1d⁵ Oct 18] $4,000Y: leggy, quite good-topped gelding: poor mover: first foal: dam,
US 8.5f winner, half-sister to high-class Japanese performer up to 12.5f Grass Wonder:
fair performer: won seller at Lingfield (left M. Johnston) in March: stays 1¾m: acts on
good to firm going, good to soft and polytrack, probably on fibresand: won over hurdles
in November. *Ian Williams*

FORTUNE BAY   2 b.g. (Mar 8) Forzando 122 – Mazurkanova 63 (Song 132) [2002   **82**
5m² 5.1f* 5.1f³ 5g⁵ 6m 6g Aug 27] 25,000Y: strong gelding: ninth foal: half-brother to
5f/6f winner, including at 2 yrs, Matthew David (by Indian Forest) and 1997 2-y-o 6f
winner Touchanova (by Touch of Grey): dam 2-y-o 6f winner who stayed 7.5f: fairly
useful performer: won maiden at Chester in May: something seemingly amiss final start:
will prove best at 5f: raced only on good going or firmer: sometimes bandaged behind:
sold 12,500 gns in October, sent to Kuwait. *Mrs J. R. Ramsden*

FORTUNE FOUND (IRE)   4 b.f. Fumo di Londra (IRE) 108 – Trillick (IRE) 71   **–**
(Treasure Kay 114) [2002 –: p10g Jan 9] strong filly: no sign of ability in maidens (tongue
tied). *C. G. Cox*

FORTUNE ISLAND (IRE)   3 b.g. Turtle Island (IRE) 123 – Blue Kestrel (IRE) 70   **84**
(Bluebird (USA) 125) [2002 76p: 11.8d 12.3m² p13g* 14.4g³ Aug 26] good-topped
gelding: fairly useful performer: won maiden at Lingfield in August: stays 1¾m: acts on
good to firm going and polytrack, probably on soft: joined M. Pipe. *C. F. Wall*

FORTUNE POINT (IRE)   4 ch.g. Cadeaux Genereux 131 – Mountains of Mist   **80**
(IRE) 80 (Shirley Heights 130) [2002 66: 8g 11.6s p16g 16.2m 8.1d* 10.1g³ 10m² 8d*
8.1g³ 7m² 8.5d 8m⁴ 8s Oct 28] strong, angular gelding: fairly useful handicapper: won at
Chepstow (seller) and Kempton in July: effective at 7f to 1¼m: acts on heavy and good to
firm going: usually visored: tongue tied: wandered (would have won otherwise) seventh
start: temperament under suspicion. *M. C. Pipe*

FORTY FORTE   6 b.g. Pursuit of Love 124 – Cominna (Dominion 123) [2002 78:   **–**
f9.4g f9.4g Oct 5] winning 1m/1¼m handicapper: well beaten both starts in 2002:
free-going front runner. *Miss S. J. Wilton*

FORUM CHRIS (IRE)   5 ch.g. Trempolino (USA) 135 – Memory Green (USA)   **–**
(Green Forest (USA) 134) [2002 14.1d May 18] good-topped gelding: fairly useful
handicapper for M. Johnston at 3 yrs: tailed off only Flat outing since: winning hurdler.
Mrs S. J. Smith

FORUM FINALE (USA)   4 b.f. Silver Hawk (USA) 123 – Silk Masque (USA) 91   **–**
(Woodman (USA) 126) [2002 73: 9m 11.8g f12g⁴ f12f⁵ f16g Nov 20] tall, quite good-
topped filly: fair at 3 yrs for M. Johnston, well held in 2002: left G. McCourt after second
start. *D. J. Wintle*

FORZACURITY   3 ch.g. Forzando 122 – Nice Lady 65 (Connaught 130) [2002 66:   **77 §**
8m 8.2d* 9.2s⁵ 8.3s 7s* 8.1d 8m 7.1m 7s 8.2v⁶ 7v f8.5g Dec 14] strong gelding: fair
handicapper: won at Nottingham in April and Newbury in June: stays 1m: acts on heavy
and good to firm going: visored (ran creditably) final 2-y-o start: has worn cheekpieces:
has looked less than keen: inconsistent. *J. L. Spearing*

FORZA FIGLIO 9 b.g. Warning 136 – Wish You Well 78 (Sadler's Wells (USA) **58**
132) [2002 72: 9s 8m 9d 10g 10m 9.7m 9.9m Aug 14] strong, angular gelding: modest
handicapper at 9 yrs: stays 1½m: acts on soft and good to firm going: tried blinkered/
visored. *R. M. Flower*

FORZA GLORY 3 ch.f. Forzando 122 – Glory Isle 60 (Hittite Glory 125) [2002 57: **54**
p7g 9g 8.2g³ 7m Aug 9] modest maiden: stays 1m: raced mainly on good going or softer
on turf, ran poorly on good to firm final start. *Miss B. Sanders*

FORZANNE WIGMO 2 b.f. (Apr 21) Forzando 122 – Queen of Shannon (IRE) 76 **–**
(Nordico (USA)) [2002 5m⁶ 5.3m Oct 3] second foal: half-sister to 3-y-o Wigmo
Princess: dam 7f/1m winner: well held in maiden/seller: tried tongue tied/blinkered.
A. W. Carroll

FORZNAR RIDGE 2 b.c. (May 30) Forzando 122 – Narbonne 60 (Rousillon (USA) **–**
133) [2002 6s Oct 25] second foal: dam 1m winner: 50/1, well held in maiden at
Newbury. *A. W. Carroll*

FOSS WAY (IRE) 2 ch.c. (Jan 26) Desert Prince (IRE) 130 – Lishaway (FR) (Polish **105**
Precedent (USA) 131) [2002 6d⁴ 6m* 7.1m* 7g⁵ Oct 6] IR 220,000Y: strong, close-
coupled colt: has a quick action: second foal: dam, second at 5.5f in France, closely
related to smart French miler Danzigaway and half-sister to high-class French miler Gold
Away: useful form: won maiden at Goodwood in July and Iveco Daily Solario Stakes at
Sandown (beat Sweet Return by head, staying on strongly from rear to lead final 50 yds)
in August: good 2 lengths fifth to Hold That Tiger in Grand Criterium at Longchamp:
should stay 1m: yet to race on extremes of going: wears crossed noseband: joined
Godolphin. *J. H. M. Gosden*

FOSTON SECOND (IRE) 5 ch.m. Lycius (USA) 124 – Gentle Guest (IRE) (Be My **–**
Guest (USA) 126) [2002 –: f12g 15.4m Apr 23] probably of little account nowadays.
C. Weedon

FOUR EAGLES (USA) 4 b.g. Lear Fan (USA) 130 – Bloomingly (ARG) (Candy **–**
Stripes (USA) 115) [2002 74: 8.3g 8d May 1] close-coupled gelding: good mover: one-
time fair maiden: well held in 2002: tried blinkered. *D. R. C. Elsworth*

FOUR JAYS (IRE) 2 b.g. (Feb 18) Alzao (USA) 117 – Paparazzi (IRE) 68 (Shernazar **82**
131) [2002 6g² 6m² 7.1m² 6m² 6.1m* 7f⁶ f6g³ p7g p6g Nov 27] 2,000F, 11,000Y, 15,000 **a85**
2-y-o: good-bodied gelding: fourth foal: half-brother to a winner in Japan by Seattle
Dancer: dam, Irish maiden who probably stayed 1½m, half-sister to smart French miler
Metal Storm: fairly useful performer: runner-up 4 times prior to winning maiden at
Warwick in September: creditable efforts in nurseries last 3 starts (gelded after): effective
at 6f/7f: acts on all-weather, raced only on good going or firmer on turf. *N. P. Littmoden*

FOUR MEN (IRE) 5 b.g. Nicolotte 118 – Sound Pet (Runnett 125) [2002 –: f8s⁵ Jan **–**
17] tall gelding: poor maiden. *A. Berry*

FOUR OF A KIND 4 b.g. Most Welcome 131 – Pegs 60 (Mandrake Major 122) [2002 **–**
9.2g 11.9s May 27] second foal: dam, third at 1m on 2-y-o debut, well beaten after: no
promise in bumpers, maiden at Hamilton and claimer at Carlisle. *C. W. Thornton*

FOUR RUNS (USA) 3 b.g. Boundary (USA) 117 – Lark Creek (USA) (Meadowlake **–**
(USA)) [2002 6g 6m May 20] 50,000Y: smallish gelding: poor mover: first foal: dam, 6f
(including at 2 yrs) and 7.5f winner in USA, out of half-sister to 1000 Guineas second
Heart of Joy: well held in maiden at Salisbury and claimer at Windsor, slowly away both
times. *R. Charlton*

FOURTH DIMENSION (IRE) 3 b.c. Entrepreneur 123 – Isle of Spice (USA) 74 **88**
(Diesis 133) [2002 59?: 10f 12m² 11.6s 14.1f² 14.1f* 14.1f* 14.1m* 15g⁵ 14m³ 14m²
14f⁵ Oct 5] sturdy colt: fairly useful handicapper: won at Yarmouth in June (twice) and
July: good efforts last 3 starts: will stay 2m: acts on firm going, possibly not on soft.
A. C. Stewart

FOVANT 2 ch.f. (May 13) Night Shift (USA) – Sheppard's Cross 88 (Soviet Star (USA) **78**
128) [2002 5.2d² 5.2s* 5m Jun 19] good-bodied filly: fourth foal: sister to useful 6f (at 2
yrs) to 8.5f winner Sheppard's Watch: dam, 7f winner, out of smart sprinter Cutlers
Corner: fair form: justified favouritism in maiden at Newbury in June by 3 lengths: joint
second favourite, well beaten in Queen Mary Stakes at Royal Ascot: will stay 6f: acts on
soft ground. *M. P. Tregoning*

FOX COTTAGE (IRE) 4 ch.f. So Factual (USA) 120 – Ever So Artful (Never So **36**
Bold 135) [2002 –: p6g⁵ 6f 8f⁴ 8f 7m Jul 4] good-topped filly: poor maiden handicapper:
stays 1m: acts on firm going: usually tongue tied in 2002. *D. W. P. Arbuthnot*

FOXTROTROMEOYANKEE 2 b.g. (Apr 12) Tragic Role (USA) – Hope Chest **56**
70 (Kris 135) [2002 f8.5g 8.2v p8g⁴ Nov 23] 5,000Y: second foal: half-brother to 3-y-o
Liberty Royal: dam, lightly-raced maiden, would have proved best up to 1½m: clearly
best effort (modest form) when never-nearer fourth in seller at Lingfield
(gelded after): should stay 1¼m: acts on polytrack. *M. D. I. Usher*

FOXY ROCKETTE 3 ch.f. Rock City 120 – Absolutley Foxed 45 (Absalom 128) **–**
[2002 –: f8.5g Jan 14] no sign of ability. *C. N. Kellett*

FOYS (FR) 3 b.g. Danehill Dancer (IRE) 117 – Ack's Secret (USA) (Ack Ack (USA)) **73**
[2002 74: 6m² 6f⁴ 6g 7m⁴ a8g⁶ a10.5g³ a10g⁶ a8g⁴ Dec 15] rather sparely-made gelding:
fair maiden: blinkered, creditable fourth in claimer at Salisbury fourth start (final outing
for R. Charlton), keeping on despite giving odd flash of tail: in frame afterwards in minor
event and handicap at Mijas: stays 10.5f: acts on firm ground and sand. *C. Bjorling, Spain*

FRAAMTASTIC 5 b.m. Fraam 114 – Fading (Pharly (FR) 130) [2002 48: f6s* p7g⁴ **43**
p6g⁶ f8g⁶ 6m f7g⁴ 7m⁶ 6m 7d 7m p7g f7g Dec 11] angular mare: poor mover: modest **a52**
performer: won seller at Southwell in January: well held last 6 starts: effective at 6f/7f:
acts on all-weather and good to firm going: usually visored: has worn cheekpieces: on
downgrade. *R. A. Pearce*

FRAGRANT CLOUD 4 b.f. Zilzal (USA) 137 – Stardyn (Star Appeal 133) [2002 –: **37**
8m 8.3d f12f³ Nov 29] poor maiden: stays 1½m: acts on fibresand. *J. R. Best*

FRAGRANT STORM (USA) 3 b.f. Storm Bird (CAN) 134 – Subtle Fragrance **–**
(USA) (Crafty Prospector (USA)) [2002 80: 6s⁴ 6f⁵ 8.3s⁴ 6m Sep 19] smallish, rather
leggy filly: fairly useful at 2 yrs: well held in 2002, leaving M. Johnston after third start.
B. Ellison

FRAGRANT VIEW (USA) 3 ch.f. Distant View (USA) 126 – Musicanti (USA) **99**
(Nijinsky (CAN) 138) [2002 79p: 10g² 10.3f* 10.5m 9.9m⁴ 10g Oct 17] tall, close-
coupled filly: useful performer: won maiden at Chester in May by 3½ lengths from
Highest: creditable efforts when tenth of 15 in Prix de Diane at Chantilly and 4¾ lengths
fourth to Chorist in listed race at Salisbury after: below par in listed race at Newmarket
final start: stayed 1¼m well: acted on firm ground, shaped well on good to soft: stud.
B. W. Hills

FRAMEWORK (USA) 3 b.f. Danehill (USA) 126 – Memories (USA) (Hail The **79**
Pirates (USA) 126) [2002 7g⁴ 8.2d* 10v⁶ 8m⁴ 8.3d Aug 11] big, close-coupled filly: has
plenty of scope: half-sister to several winners, notably high-class 6f/7f performer Russian
Revival (by Nureyev) and smart 1m winner Tobruk (by Red Ransom): dam US Grade 2
2-y-o 9f winner: fair performer: won maiden at Nottingham in April: best effort in
handicaps after when creditable fourth at Newmarket penultimate start: stays 1m, not
testing 1¼m: acts on good to firm and good to soft going: stumbled leaving stall final
outing: races prominently: sold 110,000 gns in December. *J. H. M. Gosden*

FRANCE 2 b.c. (Jan 30) Desert Prince (IRE) 130 – Hyperspectra 91 (Rainbow Quest **101**
(USA) 134) [2002 6m⁵ 7f³ 7g* 7d³ Oct 28] 320,000Y: small, well-made colt: first foal:
dam 1¼m winner out of smart 1m winner Hyabella, herself half-sister to high-class 1¼m
performer Stagecraft: third in maiden at Newmarket before winning similar event at
Limerick in October: blinkered, useful form when narrowly-beaten third to New South
Wales in Killavullan Stakes at Leopardstown: should stay 1m. *A. P. O'Brien, Ireland*

FRANCIS FLUTE 4 b.g. Polar Falcon (USA) 126 – Darshay (FR) 87 (Darshaan 133) **67**
[2002 –: 9m⁵ 8m³ 7.2g 9g⁶ 7.1d⁵ 7.2d⁴ 7.1d 7g* 7m Sep 5] fair performer: won maiden at
Newcastle in August: best at 7f: yet to race on extremes of going on turf (well held only
start on fibresand): rather headstrong. *B. Mactaggart*

FRANCIS OF ASSISI 3 b.g. Sadler's Wells (USA) 132 – Miss Rinjani 83 (Shirley **–**
Heights 130) [2002 10.1m⁵ 12.3g Aug 26] good-topped gelding: fourth foal: brother to
5-y-o St Expedit and half-brother to fairly useful 1998 2-y-o 7f winner Miss Amanpuri
(by Alzao) and 4-y-o Asian Heights: dam 2-y-o 7f winner who stayed 1½m: well held
after slow start in maiden at Yarmouth: pulled up after
cocking jaw on turn in similar event at Ripon later in month: dead. *G. Wragg*

FRANCKEN (ITY) 3 ro.g. Petit Loup (USA) 123 – Filicaia 79 (Sallust 134) [2002 –: **42**
9g³ 9g⁶ 10m Sep 5] poor maiden: probably stays 9f. *Don Enrico Incisa*

FRANCPORT 6 b.g. Efisio 120 – Elkie Brooks 82 (Relkino 131) [2002 80, a67: 5f 6s **71 d**
6f 7f 6d f6s f7g⁵ f7g² f8g Nov 25] big, lengthy gelding: fair handicapper: stays 7f: acts on
all-weather and probably any turf going: tried blinkered, not in 2002: sometimes slowly
away: on downgrade. *K. A. Ryan*

Mr J. J. Devaney's "Frankies Dream"

FRANKIES DREAM (IRE) 3 b.c. Grand Lodge (USA) 125 – Galyph (USA) 72 **115** (Lyphard (USA) 132) [2002 92: p10g² 11.6g 10g* 11g³ 12d 10d* 11.9g⁶ 12m³ 11f² 12g³ Sep 29] sturdy, close-coupled colt: smart performer: won maiden at Lingfield in May and minor event at Newmarket (beat Kayseri 1¾ lengths) in August: good efforts in small fields last 3 starts, neck third to Asian Heights in September Stakes at Kempton, ½-length second to Legal Approach in listed race at Newbury and ¾-length third to Systematic in Cumberland Lodge Stakes at Ascot: stays 1½m: acts on firm and good to soft going: usually visored (not final start): sold 200,000 gns, sent to Saudi Arabia. *T. G. Mills*

FRANKINCENSE (IRE) 6 gr.g. Paris House 123 – Mistral Wood (USA) (Far North **–** (CAN) 120) [2002 f11s 7s 8.5m 8g Sep 7] successful 4 times in Germany for C. Von Der Recke: no form in 2002: sometimes blinkered, including for both wins at 5 yrs. *A. J. Lockwood*

FRANKLIN-D 6 ch.g. Democratic (USA) 101 – English Mint 66 (Jalmood (USA) **–** 126) [2002 35: p10g Jul 20] probably of little account nowadays. *J. R. Jenkins*

FRANKLIN LAKES 7 ch.g. Sanglamore (USA) 126 – Eclipsing (IRE) 93 (Bailla- **–** mont (USA) 124) [2002 –: f8g Feb 21] probably of little account nowadays. *M. R. Bosley*

FRANKLINS GARDENS 2 b.c. (Mar 24) Halling (USA) 133 – Woodbeck 90 (Teri- **84 p** mon 124) [2002 7m² 7.2g* Sep 20] second foal: half-brother to 3-y-o Polar Ben: dam, 7f winner, out of half-sister to Prix de Diane winner Madam Gay: fairly useful form in maidens: 1¼ lengths second to Adekshan at Yarmouth before landing odds at Ayr (still green, idled) later in month by ½ length from Lady Mytton: will stay at least 1m: remains capable of better. *M. H. Tompkins*

FRANK MOR (IRE) 3 ch.g. Common Grounds 118 – Drowsy Maggie (Tumble **73** Wind (USA)) [2002 75: f8.5g² 7s⁴ 7m* 6m 7.9f 7f³ f7g* 7.1d Aug 8] strong gelding: fair performer: won maiden at Southwell in April and handicap at Wolverhampton in June: finished lame final start: best at 7f: acts on fibresand, firm and soft going: often races prominently. *K. A. Ryan*

FRANKSALOT (IRE) 2 ch.g. (Apr 11) Desert Story (IRE) 115 – Rosie's Guest **69** (IRE) (Be My Guest (USA) 126) [2002 5m⁵ 6d³ 6s 6m⁵ 7d² 7m p6g 6g Oct 28] 7,500Y, 15,000 2-y-o: well-grown, close-coupled gelding: third foal: closely related to 3-y-o Northern Desert and half-brother to a winner in Italy by Case Law: dam Irish maiden: fair maiden: second at Folkestone: stays 7f: acts on polytrack, good to firm and good to soft going: gelded after final start. *N. Hamilton*

FRANKSKIPS 3 b.g. Bishop of Cashel 122 – Kevins Lady (Alzao (USA) 117) [2002 **75** 87p] 10g³ 10f⁴ 10m⁴ 10s² f9.4f Nov 29] tall, close-coupled gelding: fair maiden: in frame first 5 starts: left N. Hamilton and tongue tied, reportedly bled from nose on all-weather debut final start: stays 1¼m: acts on firm and soft ground. *Miss B. Sanders*

FRANTIC ANNIE (IRE) 2 b.f. (Mar 18) Among Men (USA) 124 – Queen Sigi (IRE) **63** (Fairy King (USA)) [2002 6f⁵ 7g p7g⁵ Dec 21] IR 8,200F, 15,000Y: rather unfurnished, workmanlike filly: second foal: dam, ran once at 2 yrs, out of half-sister to smart performer up to 2m Harbour Dues: modest form when fifth in maiden at Newmarket (wore net muzzle) and minor event at Lingfield: reportedly lost action in between. *D. W. P. Arbuthnot*

FRASCATI 2 b.f. (Mar 13) Emarati (USA) 74 – Fizzy Fiona (Efisio 120) [2002 f5g⁴ **69** f5g⁴ 5.1m² 5m⁴ 5m² p5g³ 5d² 5.1m⁵ f5s* f5s* 6s Oct 25] 800Y: second foal: dam **a78** unraced: fair performer: won maiden in May, nursery in September and minor event in October, all at Southwell: probably best at 5f: acts on all-weather, good to firm and good to soft going: usually races prominently. *A. Berry*

FRATERNIZE 4 ch.g. Spectrum (IRE) 126 – Proud Titania (IRE) 103 (Fairy King **77** (USA)) [2002 73: p8g³ p10g⁴ p10g 10m 11.7g³ 12m³ 13.3s p12g 11.6d 11.7f* Aug 23] fair performer: won (for first time) weak seller at Bath (bought by M. Pipe 6,600 gns) in August: stays 1½m: acts on firm going, good to soft and polytrack: has raced freely/found little: tends to carry head awkwardly: temperament under suspicion. *S. Dow*

FRAULEIN 3 b.f. Acatenango (GER) 127 – Francfurter 89 (Legend of France (USA) **117** 124) [2002 102p: 10.4m⁴ 10g³ 12m⁴ 10g³ 8m* 9.9m² 10d* Sep 29] big, good-topped filly: smart performer: won listed race at Ascot (beat Cozy Maria ¾ length) in July and E. P. Taylor Stakes at Woodbine in September: best effort when beating Alasha by a length in slowly-run race on latter course: in frame all other starts in 2002: better form at 1m/1¼m than 1½m: unraced on heavy going, acted on any other: was consistent: retired, and reportedly likely to be covered by Kingmambo. *E. A. L. Dunlop*

FRAZZLED 3 b.g. Greensmith 121 – Time For Tea (IRE) 73 (Imperial Frontier (USA) **85** 112) [2002 79: p6g² p6g² p7g* p8g⁶ 6g p8g* p7g p8g³ p7g p8g* p8g⁶ 7d 8f³ 8g p7g f6g **a87** p7g Dec 14] fairly useful performer: won maiden in February, handicap in May and minor event in July, all at Lingfield: better at 7f/1m than shorter: acts on polytrack, soft and firm ground: none too consistent. *C. A. Cyzer*

FREDDIE MERCURY (IRE) 3 ch.g. Eagle Eyed (USA) 111 – So Far Away 48 **– §** (Robellino (USA) 127) [2002 57§, a–§: 5s 6g 5m Aug 22] modest maiden at 2 yrs: well held in blinkers/visor for new trainer in 2002: ungenuine. *D. Shaw*

FREDDY FLINTSTONE 5 b.g. Bigstone (IRE) 126 – Daring Ditty (Daring March **63 d** 116) [2002 76d: p8g⁵ 8m 10m 10.9m Sep 16] close-coupled gelding: good walker: one-time fairly useful maiden: very much on downgrade: left R. Hannon before reappearance: best around 1m: acts on polytrack and firm going (possibly not on softer than good): tried visored. *D. W. P. Arbuthnot*

FREDERICK LUIGI 3 b.g. Bal Harbour 113 – Scented Message (Ivotino (USA)) **–** [2002 82: 12f⁶ 11.6m 12s 14.1f⁴ Jun 24] unfurnished gelding: fairly useful form final 2-y-o start: well held in 2002: visored final outing. *H. Candy*

FRED'S DREAM 3 ch.f. Cadeaux Genereux 131 – Vaguar (USA) (Vaguely Noble **43** 140) [2002 67: 7m 8.2g 7.1v⁴ 8.1d³ f9.4g⁵ 8g Oct 16] poor maiden: effective at 7f/1m: form only on going softer than good. *R. Guest*

FREECOM NET (IRE) 4 b.g. Zieten (USA) 118 – Radiance (IRE) 54 (Thatching **–** 131) [2002 65: p8g8g 7d 7m f8.5g² 10.1f⁶ p10g² f9.4g³ 8.5m f8s p10g* f12g Sep 21] **a65** sturdy gelding: fair performer: won seller at Lingfield (gambled on) in September: stays easy 1¼m: acts on all-weather, mostly well held on turf: none too consistent. *A. P. Jarvis*

Cliveden Stud's "Fraulein"

FREEFOURINTERNET (USA) 4 b.c. Tabasco Cat (USA) 126 – Dixie Chimes **114**
(USA) (Dixieland Band (USA)) [2002 106: 10g⁵ 12m 10.3f* 10m⁵ 10f 8f 8.5d* a8.5f⁶
Dec 8] small, strong, compact colt: good walker: has a quick action: smart performer:
won 4-runner listed race at Chester (by length from Island House) in May: creditable
efforts when fifth to Grandera in Prince of Wales's Stakes at Royal Ascot and eighth to
Beat Hollow in Arlington Million next 2 starts: left B. Meehan after: won optional
claimer at Churchill Downs in November: effective at 8.5f to 1¼m: acts on firm and good
to soft going: blinkered last 7 starts. *C. Simon, USA*

FREEHOLDER 2 ch.f. (Mar 17) Zamindar (USA) 116 – Wild Humour (IRE) 60 **37**
(Fayruz 116) [2002 5m 7m f6s f8.5g⁶ Oct 19] 3,200Y: fourth foal: dam lightly raced at 2
yrs: visored, poor form in claimer/seller last 2 starts: seems to stay 8.5f: acts on fibresand:
sold 600 gns. *W. R. Muir*

FREELOADER (IRE) 2 b.c. (Feb 1) Revoque (IRE) 122 – Indian Sand (Indian King **57**
(USA) 128) [2002 6s 8.1g f7g⁴ Oct 22] 17,000F, 18,000Y: seventh foal: half-brother to
fairly useful Irish 6f (at 2 yrs) and 7f winner Boley Lass and 9-y-o Weetman's Weigh
(both by Archway): dam poor Irish maiden: modest form in maidens: fourth at Southwell:
likely to prove best up to 1m: acts on fibresand. *J. W. Hills*

FREE OPTION (IRE) 7 ch.g. Indian Ridge 123 – Saneena 80 (Kris 135) [2002 –: 7f **92**
7f³ 8g⁵ 8m⁴ 8m³ 8f² 10m⁵ 10.3m 8m 10.1s p8g⁵ Dec 3] strong, lengthy gelding: fairly
useful handicapper: below form last 4 starts: stays 1¼m: acts on firm and good to soft
going (possibly not on soft). *B. Hanbury*

FREE WHEELIN (IRE) 2 b.c. (Feb 9) Polar Falcon (USA) 126 – Farhana 109 **88**
(Fayruz 116) [2002 5d* 5m⁴ 5m Jun 21] 24,000Y: lengthy, useful-looking colt: first foal:
dam 5.5f and (at 2 yrs) 6f winner: fairly useful form: won maiden at Windsor in May:
good fourth to Presto Vento in listed race at Sandown (edgy, early to post): well held in
minor event at Royal Ascot: raced only at 5f. *W. Jarvis*

FREE WILL 5 ch.g. Indian Ridge 123 – Free Guest 125 (Be My Guest (USA) 126) **66**
[2002 79: f12g⁶ 12s 8f⁶ 10m 10.3m 13.8m 8m³ 10m² 7.9d 9d⁴ 9.9d⁶ Jul 22] well-made
gelding: fair performer: stays 1¼m: acts on firm and good to soft ground: none too
consistent. *A. Scott*

FRENCH BRAMBLE (IRE) 4 ch.f. General Monash (USA) 107 – La Mazya (IRE) **45 §**
(Mazaad 106) [2002 51§, a–§: f5s 5m 5g⁶ 6d 5s⁴ 5g 5m 5m⁵ 5m 5d 5m Oct 5] leggy, quite **a– §**
good-topped filly: poor performer: effective at 5f/6f: acts on soft going, good to firm
and fibresand: usually blinkered/visored at 3 yrs: sometimes wanders: untrustworthy.
J. Balding

FRENCH CAT (USA) 4 b. or br.c. Storm Cat (USA) – Shannkara (IRE) (Akarad **–**
(FR) 130) [2002 6m 5g 7.1m 5g 6.1m f5g Oct 17] sturdy, close-coupled colt: third foal:
half-brother to useful 1m winner Swan Knight (by Sadler's Wells) and minor US stakes
winner (second in Grade 2 8.5f event) Tekken (by Nureyev): dam, 1m (at 2 yrs in France)
and 8.5f (Grade 3 event in USA) winner, half-sister to smart/very smart French middle-
distance fillies Sharaniya and Sharaya: little form in USA at 3 yrs (when trained by
H. Tesher) and in Britain in 2002 (left P. Cole after third start): blinkered final start.
I. W. McInnes

Mr Michael Pescod's "Frenchmans Bay"

FRENCH CONNECTION   7 b.g. Tirol 127 – Heaven-Liegh-Grey 90 (Grey Desire   –
115) [2002 –: 10m Apr 16] of little account on Flat nowadays. *B. D. Leavy*

FRENCH GIGOLO   2 ch.c. (Apr 16) Pursuit of Love 124 – French Mist 71 (Mystiko   **77 ?**
(USA) 124) [2002 7.9m 8m³ f8s 8s Oct 22] sturdy colt: second foal: dam, maiden who
stayed 14.6f, half-sister to very smart US performer up to 1¼m Jumron: 66/1, only form
(possibly flattered) when third to St Andrews in steadily-run maiden at Newmarket:
should stay at least 1¼m. *C. N. Allen*

FRENCH GUEST   3 ch.g. Most Welcome 131 – Laleston 73 (Junius (USA) 124) [2002   **49**
–: 8.3g f6g³ Oct 21] smallish, strong, lengthy gelding: modest maiden, lightly raced:
should stay 7f: acts on fibresand. *M. A. Jarvis*

FRENCH HORN   5 b.g. Fraam 114 – Runcina (Runnett 125) [2002 8d⁴ 8d 8d p10g   **82 ?**
Dec 11] workmanlike gelding: winning handicapper: lightly raced nowadays: seemingly
best effort in 2002 on reappearance: should stay 1¼m: best efforts on ground softer than
good. *M. J. Ryan*

FRENCH MANNEQUIN (IRE)   3 gr.f. Key of Luck (USA) 126 – Paris Model   **74**
(IRE) (Thatching 131) [2002 63: 7.1f⁴ 8.2d⁴ 7m⁴ 7g* 7s⁴ 7g 8.2m² f7g⁶ 8.3d² 10m² 8.3m⁴
8.1g Sep 23] sparely-made filly: fair handicapper: won at Newmarket in June: stays
1¼m: seems to act on any turf going: usually visored: races prominently: sold 11,000 gns.
R. M. Beckett

FRENCHMANS BAY (FR)   4 br.c. Polar Falcon (USA) 126 – River Fantasy (USA)   **114**
(Irish River (FR) 131) [2002 118: 7g* 7d* 8g 6.5s 6m 7m³ Oct 19] big, good-topped
colt: smart performer: third to Golan in 2000 Guineas at Newmarket in 2001: found to
have chipped a bone in near-fore knee shortly afterwards and underwent operation: won
maiden at Kempton in April and Prix du Palais-Royal at Longchamp (held rallying
Tempting Fate by short head) in May: best effort after when 4 lengths third to Nayyir in
Challenge Stakes at Newmarket final start, dropped right out and keeping on: will prove
best up to 1m: acts on good to firm and good to soft going: has raced freely. *R. Charlton*

FRENCHMANS LODGE   2 b.c. (Feb 27) Piccolo 121 – St Helena (Monsanto (FR)   **70**
121) [2002 5m 5m⁶ Sep 15] 6,000Y: half-brother to several winners, including 5f
(including at 2 yrs)/6f winner Swino (by Forzando) and 5f (at 2 yrs) to 7f winner Oriel
Girl (by Beveled): dam Italian 5f/6.5f winner: 50/1, much better effort in maidens when
sixth to Peace Offering at Sandown: likely to prove best at 5f/6f. *D. J. S. ffrench Davis*

FRENCH RISK (IRE)   2 b.c. (Mar 16) Entrepreneur 123 – Troyes 81 (Troy 137)   –
[2002 7s Oct 25] 19,000F, IR 20,000Y: strong, lengthy colt: half-brother to several
winners, including fairly useful 9f winner (stayed 1½m) Tromond (by Lomond), now
dam of very smart 1¼m performer Nowhere To Exit, and 3-y-o Jewel of Troyes: dam,
1½m winner, half-sister to Yorkshire Oaks winner Hellenic: 33/1, backward and very
green, tailed off in maiden at Doncaster. *N. A. Graham*

FRENCH TUNE (FR)   4 ch.g. Green Tune (USA) 125 – Guerre de Troie (Risk Me   –
(FR) 127) [2002 10g 14.1s⁶ 10.1g 13v⁶ 10.1d 13.8d Nov 5] strong ex-French gelding:
fairly useful performer at best in France: won maiden at Clairefontaine at 2 yrs: sold from
Mme C. Head-Maarek 150,000 francs after final 3-y-o start: little form in 2002: stays
1¼m: acts on heavy ground: tried blinkered/visored: reportedly had breathing problem
on hurdles debut in August. *Miss S. E. Hall*

FRESH AS A ROSE (USA)   3 ch.f. Rahy (USA) 115 – Kiandra (USA) (Shareef   **90 +**
Dancer (USA) 135) [2002 78p: 8s² 8s² 12v⁴ 10s 9.2m* 10f³ Oct 4] $30,000F, IR 35,000Y:
angular filly: eighth foal: half-sister to several winners in USA, including minor stakes
winner by Bering: dam, ran once in USA, out of half-sister to dam of 2000 Guineas
winner Entrepreneur: fairly useful performer: left T. Stack, won maiden at Hamilton in
September: ran well in handicap at Newmarket final start: effective at 9f to 1½m: acts on
any going: blinkered fourth start. *M. Johnston*

FREYA ALEX   3 b.f. Makbul 104 – Crissem (IRE) 70 (Thatching 131) [2002 58: f7s   **54**
f8.5g³ f7g² f9.4g³ f7g 12m* 9.9g³ 9.3s⁴ 12.1g⁵ 10.9m⁴ f12g⁴ 10g² Oct 14] workmanlike
filly: modest performer: first success in seller at Pontefract in April: stays 1½m: acts on
fibresand and good to firm ground: usually held up/has been slowly away. *R. Hollinshead*

FREYA'S DREAM (IRE)   3 b.f. Danehill Dancer (IRE) 117 – Ruwy 77 (Soviet Star   **90**
(USA) 128) [2002 65: 7m³ 8g* 8g³ 7m* 7.5m* 7.1m* 7m⁵ 7.9m 8g Sep 7] rather leggy,
angular filly: fairly useful handicapper: won at Thirsk in May, Doncaster in June and
Beverley and Sandown (again heavily backed, tended to idle) in July: ran poorly last 2
starts: effective at 7f/1m: acts on good to firm going, below form at 2 yrs on soft: found
less than expected seventh outing. *T. D. Easterby*

FRIAR TUCK   7 ch.g. Inchinor 119 – Jay Gee Ell 78 (Vaigly Great 127) [2002 86: 6f⁶   **80**
6g 6g 6v 6g 5.9v 5g² 5.9d³ 6g⁵ 5m⁵ 5m 5m⁵ 6s² 5.9m³ 5g² 6f* 5m 6f 5v Nov 8] leggy,
lengthy gelding: has reportedly had several wind operations: fairly useful handicapper:
won apprentice event at Redcar in September: best at 5f/6f: acts on any going: none too
consistent. *Miss L. A. Perratt*

FRIDAY'S TAKINGS   3 ch.g. Beveled (USA) – Pretty Pollyanna (General Assembly   **55**
(USA)) [2002 57p: p8g⁵ f8s f9.4g² p10g⁴ f8.5g 10.2g 8d⁴ 7m 8g⁵ 8f⁶ 8.5m 7g 8g f8g*   **a67 +**
f8.5g Dec 20] fair on all-weather, poor on turf: won maiden at Southwell in December by
7 lengths, making most: stays easy 1¼m: acts on all-weather and good to soft ground:
blinkered last 6 starts: usually races up with pace: none too consistent. *B. Smart*

FRIEDA KAHLO (IRE)   2 ch.f. (Apr 3) Indian Ridge 123 – Devil's Bones (USA)   **78**
(Devil's Bag (USA)) [2002 5m 6m² 7f Oct 5] lengthy filly: second foal: dam, French
1¼m/11f winner (later 9f winner in USA), half-sister to 1999 Royal Lodge winner Royal
Kingdom and to dam of high-class Japanese 1m/1¼m performer Agnes Digital: best
effort (fair form) when ¾-length second of 5 to Camlet in maiden at Yarmouth, still
seeming green: looked hard ride when last in listed event at Newmarket final start, free
early on: should stay at least 7f. *G. Wragg*

FRIENDLY ALLIANCE   6 b.g. Shareef Dancer (USA) 135 – Snow Huntress 80   **58**
(Shirley Heights 130) [2002 57: 12d⁵ 14.1m⁴ 18d 15g³ 16.4d³ 14m³ 15.4m² 14.1m⁶ 12g
12m³ Aug 26] tall, workmanlike gelding: modest handicapper: generally creditable
efforts in 2002: effective at 1½m to 2m: acts on good to firm going, good to soft and
polytrack, possibly not fibresand: sometimes hangs left. *R. M. Flower*

FRILLY FRONT   6 ch.m. Aragon 118 – So So 84 (Then Again 126) [2002 –, a74: f5g   **–**
f5g 5g⁵ Mar 28] compact mare: fair performer in 2001: well held in 2002 (off 12 months
before reappearance): blinkered once. *T. D. Barron*

FRIMLEY'S MATTERRY   2 b.c. (Mar 18) Bluegrass Prince (IRE) 110 – Lonely   **68**
Street 93 (Frimley Park 109) [2002 6m 6m⁴ 7m⁴ f7g⁴ f7g⁴ Dec 17] fifth reported foal:
dam 5f/6f winner: fair maiden: probably stays 7f: acts on fibresand, raced only on good to
firm ground on turf: races prominently. *A. P. Jarvis*

FRIXOS (IRE)   2 ch.g. (Apr 6) Barathea (IRE) 127 – Local Lass 106 (Local Suitor   **63**
(USA) 128) [2002 8s 7v⁵ p5g f7s⁵ Dec 9] 15,000Y: big, good-topped gelding: fourth foal:
half-brother to smart 7f to 9f winner Lonesome Dude (by With Approval): dam, 7f winner
and later successful in USA at 5/6 yrs, half-sister to dam of Revoque: modest maiden:
should prove better at 1m+ than shorter: wore cheekpieces final start. *P. F. I. Cole*

FRIZZANTE   3 b.f. Efisio 120 – Juliet Bravo 61 (Glow (USA)) [2002 5g⁵ 5f* 6m Aug   **75 p**
16] fourth foal: closly-related to fairly useful 5f/6f winner Glowing (by Chilibang) and
half-sister to 6-y-o Colonel Mustard: dam 2-y-o 5f winner: fair form: won maiden at
Doncaster in June, plenty to do after halfway but winning shade cleverly in end (reportedly jarred up afterwards): shaped well when mid-division in handicap at Newmarket
final start, soon travelling strongly, then edging left and not given hard time: should stay
6f: slowly away all 3 outings: remains open to improvement. *J. R. Fanshawe*

FRODO   3 b.g. Magic Ring (IRE) 115 – Prompt (Old Vic 136) [2002 77: f6g⁵ p6g 6g³   **73**
6g⁶ a6f a6.5g Nov 21] rather leggy, angular gelding: fair on turf, modest on all-weather: **a55**
left R. White, gelded and off nearly 6 months after fourth outing: should stay 7f: acts on
heavy going and polytrack. *P. L. Rudkin, UAE*

FROGLET   3 b.f. Shaamit (IRE) 127 – Frog 84 (Akarad (FR) 130) [2002 58p: 13.1d²   **83 p**
17.2d* 16.2d⁶ 16.2g* 16f* 14.1m² Aug 7] fairly useful handicapper: generally progressive form in 2002, winning at Carlisle (maiden event), Haydock and Yarmouth in June/
July: ran well when head second to Camzo in ladies race at Yarmouth final start: likely to
prove best at 2m+: acts on firm and good to soft going: found little third outing, flashed
tail fourth start: probably capable of better still. *Sir Mark Prescott*

FROMSONG (IRE)   4 b.c. Fayruz 116 – Lindas Delight 54 (Batshoof 122) [2002   **105**
105: 6g⁶ 5.2g 5g 5d 5m² 5s³ 5d⁵ 5.7g⁴ Jul 14] tall, angular colt: useful performer: best
effort when 1½ lengths second to The Trader in listed race at Kempton in June: below
form last 3 starts: best around 5f: acts on soft and good to firm going: tongue tied (ran
badly) third start. *B. R. Millman*

FRONTIER   5 b.g. Indian Ridge 123 – Adatiya (IRE) (Shardari 134) [2002 8.3s 10.2s   **73**
10f⁴ 8.5d⁶ 8m 10.2g³ 8s⁴ Oct 28] well-made gelding: good walker: useful handicapper at
3 yrs: missed 2001: just fair form in 2002: stays 1¼m: acts on soft and good to firm
ground: tongue tied. *B. J. Llewellyn*

FRONTLINEFINANCIER 2 b.c. (Mar 18) Bluegrass Prince (IRE) 110 – Bunny **47**
Gee (Last Tycoon 131) [2002 5g 7d 7d⁶ Jul 11] fourth foal: half-brother to 1½m seller
winner Bee Gee (by Beveled) and a winner in Sweden by Forzando: dam no form: slowly
away first 2 starts: poor form when sixth in maiden at Folkestone on final one, though
hung badly left. *N. I. M. Rossiter*

FROSTY WELCOME (USA) 3 gr. or ro.f. With Approval (CAN) – Light Ice (USA) **105**
(Arctic Tern (USA) 126) [2002 67p: 7s³ 9d* 10g⁶ 10.1g³ 12g* 12m⁴ 11.9m³ 14.6m 14.6v²
Nov 8] rather leggy, unfurnished filly: quickly improved into a useful performer: won
maiden at Goodwood in May and dead-heated in listed event at Newmarket (joined by
Marani on line) in July: good ½-length second to Pole Star in minor event at Doncaster
final start: stays 14.6f: acts on heavy and good to firm going. *G. Wragg*

FRUIT OF GLORY 3 b.f. Glory of Dancer 121 – Fresh Fruit Daily 92 (Reprimand **84**
122) [2002 91: 8.1d 7m 8f 8.3m* 8.1m³ 9g³ 8.3d³ 7m 7m 8f 6m⁶ 7s p7g³ p7g Dec 11]
sturdy, lengthy filly: fairly useful handicapper: won at Windsor in July: effective at 6f to
easy 9f: acts on polytrack, soft and good to firm going. *M. R. Channon*

FUDGE BROWNIE 6 b.g. Deploy 131 – Carte Blanche 67 (Cadeaux Genereux 131) **47**
[2002 60: 8m⁵ 8g 8.3v⁴ 10.1g⁶ 10.9g Jul 5] workmanlike gelding: poor maiden handicapper nowadays: probably stays 1¼m: yet to race on firm going, probably acts on any
other: none too consistent. *G. A. Swinbank*

FULL EGALITE 6 gr.g. Ezzoud (IRE) 126 – Milva 56 (Jellaby 124) [2002 36, a47: **36**
p16g⁵ f16.2g⁴ f14.8g Apr 8] smallish, sturdy gelding: poor handicapper: stays easy 2m, at
least with emphasis on speed: acts on soft going, good to firm and all-weather: usually
blinkered/visored. *B. R. Johnson*

FULL HOUSE (IRE) 3 br.g. King's Theatre (IRE) 128 – Nirvavita (FR) (Highest **75**
Honor (FR) 124) [2002 84p: 12m 10d⁵ 10.3g³ 12s 10.9m⁵ 10.3f⁴ 12d p10g⁵ 12m² 12.1g⁶
p12g* p10g³ 11.6d Oct 28] useful-looking gelding: fair performer: won amateur minor
event at Lingfield in October: stays 1½m: acts on polytrack and good to firm going,
possibly not on good to soft: tried blinkered: sometimes races too freely: none too
reliable: sold 16,000 gns. *P. F. I. Cole*

FULL KWAI MA (IRE) 2 b.c. (Apr 17) Night Shift (USA) – So Kind 90 (Kind of **62 ?**
Hush 118) [2002 5m 5m⁵ 6f Sep 21] good-bodied colt: has a quick action: seventh foal:
half-brother to useful 1994 2-y-o 5f/6f winner Princely Hush (by Prince Sabo) and 1995
2-y-o 6f winner Sweet Nature (by Classic Secret): dam 6f winner who stayed 7f: modest
form at best in maidens: likely to prove best at 5f/6f. *Miss L. A. Perratt*

FULLOPEP 8 b.g. Dunbeath (USA) 127 – Suggia (Alzao (USA) 117) [2002 68: 16f **–**
16m⁶ Jul 7] useful gelding: lightly raced on Flat nowadays. *Mrs M. Reveley*

FULL SPATE 7 ch.g. Unfuwain (USA) 131 – Double River (USA) (Irish River (FR) **80**
131) [2002 79: 7m⁵ 7f 6m 6m 6d 7.1s 7.1v 6m 6m* 6s* 6m 6g* 6g⁵ 6m⁵ 6f 6m 6m*
6.1s⁴ 5v Nov 8] tall, quite good-topped gelding: fairly useful performer: won handicap at
Doncaster in June, minor event at Hamilton in July and handicaps at Leicester in July
and Newmarket in October: effective at 6f/7f: acts on any going: sometimes slowly away:
usually held up. *J. M. Bradley*

FULROUSCHKA (FR) 4 ch.f. Funambule (USA) 118 – Marouschka (FR) (Mar- **–**
gouillat (FR) 133) [2002 7s 10m 8.3d p10g Nov 27] ex-French filly: seventh foal:
half-sister to 5f (including at 2 yrs) to 1m winner Milzarella (by Mille Balles) and 9f to
13f winner Sharouschka (by Sarhoob), both in France: dam French 1m/9f winner: trained
by R. Crepon at 2 yrs: showed little in maidens/handicap in 2002. *C. A. Horgan*

FULVIO (USA) 2 b.g. (Mar 16) Sword Dance – One Tuff Gal (USA) (Lac Ouimet **64**
(USA)) [2002 7d⁶ 7m⁶ 6m 8.3d 8d 7s f7s² Dec 9] $25,000F: big, strong gelding: first foal:
dam US 6f/7f winner: modest maiden: second in nursery at Wolverhampton: likely to
prove best at 6f/7f: acts on good to firm ground and fibresand: sometimes looks none too
keen. *S. C. Williams*

FUNDAMENTAL 3 ch.g. Rudimentary (USA) 118 – I'll Try 71 (Try My Best (USA) **–**
130) [2002 –: f12g³ f12g Apr 15] strong gelding: modest form: stays 1½m: acts on fibre- **a51**
sand, well beaten on turf: pulled hard on reappearance: stumbled leaving stall final start.
T. P. Tate

FUNFAIR 3 b.c. Singspiel (IRE) 133 – Red Carnival (USA) 109 (Mr Prospector **106**
(USA)) [2002 8.1d³ 10g⁴ 9.3s* 8.1d 7.9m* 9f Oct 5] strong, lengthy colt: second foal:
half-brother to 4-y-o Carnival Dancer (by Sadler's Wells): dam, 2-y-o 5f/6f (Cherry
Hinton) winner who stayed 1m, sister to smart US Grade 1 2-y-o 8.5f winner Golden
Attraction and closely related to high-class US Grade 1 9f winner Cape Town: useful

form: easily landed odds in maiden at Carlisle in June, despite veering markedly left: best effort when winning Bradford & Bingley Rated Stakes (Handicap) at York in August by short head from Muchea: sweating, raced too freely in Tote Cambridgeshire final start: may prove best up to 1m: may prove suited by good ground or firmer: refused to enter stall intended start at 2 yrs. *Sir Michael Stoute*

FUNFAIR WANE 3 b.g. Unfuwain (USA) 131 – Ivory Bride 86 (Domynsky 110) **119**
[2002 101: 7m^4 6d^5 6g 6.1g^6 5.1m^2 7.6m^2 8m^3 6g* Sep 21]

Little has been achieved in the recent history of the most prestigious handicaps to match trainer David Nicholls' hat-trick of Ayr Gold Cups which he completed in 2002. Between 1997 and 2001, Paul Cole won three Lincolns and three Northumberland Plates; Lynda Ramsden won three Chester Cups during the 'nineties; Martin Pipe has won three Ascot Stakes since 1993 and John Gosden four Britannia Handicaps since 1996; Jeremy Glover won four Cambridgeshires between 1987 and 1996. Three successive wins for the same trainer in a race like the Ayr Gold Cup are much rarer. Jack Jarvis was the last before Nicholls to complete the feat at Ayr, winning the 1937 and 1938 runnings and the first after the war in 1946. Jarvis' trio beat forty-eight rivals in all between them. Nicholls' winners had eighty-one rivals, albeit twelve from their own stable (which saddled eight runners in 2000 alone). Funfair Wane started at 16/1 to follow in the footsteps of stable-companions Bahamian Pirate and Continent, like them up against a maximum field in the Tote-sponsored event in late-September. Among Funfair Wane's twenty-seven opponents, Wokingham winner Capricho was backed down to favourite at 15/2. Injaaz was second favourite at 8/1 with Croeso Croeso at 10/1 and Royal Millennium at 11/1. Funfair Wane was given an enterprising ride from trainer's son Adrian, who had also partnered Bahamian Pirate, soon leading the main body of runners towards the stand side, despite a middle draw. Few ever got to him and Funfair Wane held on gamely by a neck from The Tatling, whose trainer Milton Bradley had also had the runner-up in 2001.

Funfair Wane's win in the Ayr Gold Cup was all the more remarkable in that he had joined Nicholls only four starts earlier. He showed useful form for Mick Channon as a two-year-old, winning twice, including in a listed race over seven

*Tote Ayr Gold Cup (Handicap), Ayr—Funfair Wane holds off The Tatling
to give trainer David Nicholls a hat-trick of victories in this highly competitive race;
Abbajabba takes third ahead of Attache (No.6) and Forever Times*

furlongs at Newbury, but it was felt halfway through his three-year-old season that a change of scenery would do him good. 'He's very excitable and I kept him out of the parade ring for as long as I dared, because he was getting geed-up,' said Nicholls after Ayr. Nicholls has made his reputation with sprinters, most of whom have come to him from other yards, and there must be a good chance Funfair Wane will go on to still better things. He put up a smart effort under 9-3 at Ayr, becoming the first to win the race as a three-year-old since 1994, and he won't have to find much improvement to match Bahamian Pirate and Continent by going on to pattern success. He has been placed at up to a mile, but he's clearly best at five and six furlongs. An edgy sort, he has had two handlers and been taken early to post. He has run well when sweating and has yet to race on extremes of ground. *D. Nicholls*

FUNNYGILL BECK (USA) 3 b.f. Exit To Nowhere (USA) 122 – Sandhill (IRE) 96 (Danehill (USA) 126) [2002 f8g 10.2f⁵ 11.7g Oct 16] second foal: dam, 7f winner, half-sister to smart miler Sand Falcon: 50/1, easily best effort in maidens (fair form) when never-nearer fifth at Bath: should stay 1½m: sold 800 gns in December. *G. C. Bravery* **67**

FUNNY GIRL (IRE) 5 b.m. Darshaan 133 – Just For Fun (FR) (Lead On Time (USA) 123) [2002 68: 9d⁵ 7m² 7f Jul 19] compact mare: fair maiden handicapper: effective at 7f, probably 1¼m: acts on firm going: found little final start. *W. R. Muir* **72**

FUNNY VALENTINE (IRE) 4 ch.c. Cadeaux Genereux 131 – Aunt Hester (IRE) 68 (Caerleon (USA) 132) [2002 112: 6m⁶ 5m Oct 12] lengthy, attractive colt: easily best effort (smart form) when third in King's Stand Stakes at Royal Ascot at 3 yrs: off 14 months due to injury, well held both starts in 2002: best form at 5f: acts on any going. *T. G. Mills* **–**

FURNITURE FACTORS (IRE) 2 b.g. (Feb 22) Magic Ring (IRE) 115 – Make Hay (Nomination 125) [2002 5s 5.1d 6m³ 6m 7g³ 7g³ 7m⁴ 7.5g 6m Sep 13] IR 7,000F, 10,000Y: well-made gelding: sixth foal: half-brother to 5f winner Mount Park (by Colonel Collins) and a winner in Japan by Kefaah: dam unraced: fair maiden: well beaten last 2 starts: stays 7f: acts on good to firm going: usually races prominently. *Ronald Thompson* **68**

FURTHER OUTLOOK (USA) 8 gr.g. Zilzal (USA) 137 – Future Bright (USA) (Lyphard's Wish (FR) 124) [2002 110d: 6s 5s⁴ 6g 5m² f5g 6m* 6d³ 6m² 6d² 6s f5g f6f p8g p6g⁵ Dec 30] big, strong gelding: carries condition: useful performer on turf, fair on all-weather: first success since 2000 in claimer at Windsor (claimed from D. Nicholls) in May: good second in handicaps at Kempton and Epsom in June: best at 5f/6f: untried on firm ground of late, acts on any other turf going: has been tongue tied/worn crossed nose-band/bandaged in front: takes strong hold, and usually races up with pace. *Andrew Reid* **100 a77**

FUSILLADE (IRE) 2 ch.g. (Mar 7) Grand Lodge (USA) 125 – Lili Cup (FR) (Fabulous Dancer (USA) 124) [2002 8g Oct 18] IR 100,000Y: sturdy gelding: fifth living foal: half-brother to several winners, including useful Italian sprinter Uruk (by Efisio): dam unraced: 20/1 and burly, last of 16 in Newmarket maiden (gelded after). *M. A. Jarvis* **–**

FUTURE COUP (USA) 6 b.g. Lord At War (ARG) – Holy Moly (USA) (Halo (USA)) [2002 8.5m f9.4g 10f⁶ 12g⁵ 12f* 12m* 10.1d 12f 9.9m 12f⁵ Oct 7] lengthy, quite attractive gelding: modest performer: won claimers at Catterick in July/August: stays 1½m: acts on firm going, good to soft and fibresand: tried blinkered/visored: waited with. *J. R. Norton* **55**

FUTURE FLIGHT 4 b.f. Polar Falcon (USA) 126 – My Branch 111 (Distant Relative 128) [2002 78+: 7m 8m Jul 30] unfurnished filly: poor mover: fair performer at best: well beaten in handicaps in 2002. *B. W. Hills* –

FUTURE KINGS (IRE) 2 b.c. (Apr 19) Desert King (IRE) 129 – Stellar Empress (USA) (Star de Naskra (USA)) [2002 7d p8g Nov 14] IR 200,000Y: sixth foal: half-brother to 3 winners, including useful 1999 2-y-o 6f winner Delphinius (by Dolphin Street) and Irish 7f winner Welsh Queen (by Caerleon): dam Irish 2-y-o 5f/6f winner: well held in maidens. *E. A. L. Dunlop* –

FUTURE PROSPECT (IRE) 8 b.g. Marju (IRE) 127 – Phazania (Tap On Wood 130) [2002 65, a–: 7.5g Jun 12] leggy gelding: has a round action: modest handicapper nowadays: stays 1¼m: acts on firm ground and good to soft: blinkered once: has drifted right/been slowly away. *M. A. Buckley* **57 a–**

FUTURISTIC 2 b.c. (Apr 17) Magic Ring (IRE) 115 – Corn Futures 78 (Nomination 125) [2002 6g 7s 6d Nov 1] quite good-topped colt: brother to useful 1997 2-y-o 6f winner Crazee Mental and half-brother to 3 winners, including 3-y-o Three Days In May and 4-y-o Reap: dam 2-y-o 6f winner: 66/1, easily best effort in maidens (fair form, burly previously) when 10 lengths eighth of 17 to Tante Rose at Newmarket final start, likely to prove best up to 7f: should progress. *J. G. Given* **64 p**

FUTURO VENCEDOR 2 b.g. (Mar 27) Komaite (USA) – Takeall 72 (Another Realm 118) [2002 5m 5m 6m Jul 13] 6,000F, 15,000Y: well-grown, leggy gelding: seventh foal: dam 2-y-o 5f winner: modest maiden: clearly best effort on second start: may prove best at 5f/6f. *M. W. Easterby* **56**

G

GABLESEA 8 b.g. Beveled (USA) – Me Spede (Valiyar 129) [2002 47: 10g 10.3f 12.1s Aug 20] tall gelding: retains little ability: often blinkered/visored. *B. P. J. Baugh* –

GABOR 3 b.g. Danzig Connection (USA) – Kiomi 65 (Niniski (USA) 125) [2002 79: 9f 8.3m 9m 9.1g² 10g* 10.1d⁴ 10.5m⁵ 12m* 12m 10m Aug 30] tall gelding: fairly useful performer: won minor event at Nottingham in June and claimer at Salisbury in July: stays easy 1½m: acts on good to firm and good to soft ground: slowly away final outing: successful over hurdles subsequently. *G. L. Moore* **83**

GAD YAKOUN 9 ch.g. Cadeaux Genereux 131 – Summer Impressions (USA) 70 (Lyphard (USA) 132) [2002 –§: 5g 5d 5g Jul 19] one-time fair 7f winner: has lost his form and become temperamental: tongue tied: visored/blinkered of late. *Mrs G. S. Rees* **– §**

GAELIC PRINCESS 2 b.f. (Feb 11) Cois Na Tine (IRE) 101 – Berenice (ITY) (Maroube 116) [2002 5d⁴ f5s* 5g⁴ 5m 6m³ 5m* 6.5m 5f* 6f Oct 11] 10,000Y: good-bodied filly: fourth foal: half-sister to 6f winner (including at 2 yrs) Berenica (by College Chapel) and 6f (at 2 yrs) and 7f winner The Bomber Liston (by Perugino), both useful in Ireland, latter also winner in Italy: dam unraced: fairly useful performer: won maiden at Wolverhampton (made all) in May and nurseries at Beverley in August and Redcar in September: should stay 6f: acts on fibresand and firm going. *K. A. Ryan* **88**

GAELIC STORM 8 b.g. Shavian 125 – Shannon Princess (Connaught 130) [2002 –: 7m 7v Nov 9] small, sturdy gelding: tubed: smart performer at best, winner of 16 races: lightly raced and no form since 2000. *Ian Emmerson* –

GAELIC SWAN (IRE) 3 b.f. Nashwan (USA) 135 – Scots Lass 79 (Shirley Heights 130) [2002 10d⁴ 12.3g³ f12s² 14.1d Oct 18] rather leggy, lengthy filly: sister to smart 1¼m/1½m winner Mary Stuart and half-sister to several winners, including smart middle-distance stayer Bonny Scot (by Commanche Run) and to dam of Golan: dam 13f winner: promising debut in maiden at Windsor: placed but below that form next 2 starts: ran poorly on handicap debut (reportedly lost a shoe) final start: should be suited by 1¾m+: sold 250,000 gns. *Sir Michael Stoute* **80 ?**

GAGARIN (FR) 2 b.c. (Feb 7) Quest For Fame 127 – Good To Dance (IRE) 115 (Groom Dancer (USA) 128) [2002 7m 8m 10g⁶ Oct 14] 1,000,000 francs Y: quite good-topped colt: sixth foal: half-brother to 3 winners abroad, including useful French 8.5f to 1½m winner Murano (by Royal Academy): dam 2-y-o 1¼m winner in France who stayed 1½m: fair maiden: stiff task, soundly beaten final start: should be suited by 1½m+: sold 4,000 gns. *M. A. Jarvis* **65**

GAINFUL 3 ch.f. Elmaamul (USA) 125 – Regain 86 (Relko 136) [2002 61: 7m 8f 10.2g 12.1g Sep 12] leggy, narrow filly: no form in 2002. *G. F. H. Charles-Jones* –

GALA AFFAIR 3 ch.f. Zilzal (USA) 137 – Sally Slade 80 (Dowsing (USA) 124) [2002 50: 6s 6.1m* 6g p6g 6.1m⁴ Jul 20] modest performer: won handicap at Warwick in June: appeared to run very well final start (edged right): raced only at 5f/6f: best efforts on good to firm ground. *C. A. Cyzer* **55 +**

GALA GOLD 3 b.f. Green Desert (USA) 127 – Melting Gold (USA) 108 (Cadeaux Genereux 131) [2002 65p: 7s 5.1d 9.3s 7f Jun 7] small, plain filly: no form in 2002. *M. Johnston* **–**

GALANDORA 2 b.f. (Mar 22) Bijou d'Inde 127 – Jelabna (Jalmood (USA) 126) [2002 6m 7m 5.7f p7g 7s Oct 28] close-coupled filly: fourth foal: dam, ran once, half-sister to useful 6f to 1m performer Baaderah: modest maiden: soundly beaten in nursery final start: seems to stay 7f: acts on polytrack and firm ground. *Dr J. R. J. Naylor* **54**

GALANT EYE (IRE) 3 ch.g. Eagle Eyed (USA) 111 – Galandria 57 (Sharpo 132) [2002 46: 10d 10f 12.1g⁵ 10.2m 8.5m Jul 16] poor maiden handicapper: stays 1½m: acts on good to firm going: wandered third start. *F. Jordan* **44**

GALANTHUS (USA) 3 ch.f. Rahy (USA) 115 – Tiger Flower 103 (Sadler's Wells (USA) 132) [2002 10g 10m 8.1g 10.1f² 11.7m* 12m³ 12.1g⁵ 14.1m Oct 5] seventh foal: closely related to 1½m winners Zibeth (by Rainbow Quest) and Tiger Lake (by Nashwan), latter fairly useful, and half-sister to 2 winners: dam 1¼m winner who stayed 1½m: modest performer: won handicap at Bath (edged left) in August: stays 1½m: raced only on good going or firmer: blinkered last 2 starts, persistently tried to hang left on final one: waited with. *L. M. Cumani* **59**

GALAPAGOS GIRL (IRE) 4 b.f. Turtle Island (IRE) 123 – Shabby Doll 69 (North-fields (USA)) [2002 80: f7g⁴ f7g⁶ f7g⁶ f8.5g Jul 1] fairly useful for B. Hills at 3 yrs: little form in 2002 (trained by W. Cunningham on reappearance). *J. G. M. O'Shea* **–**

GALAPINO 9 b.g. Charmer 123 – Carousella 62 (Rousillon (USA) 133) [2002 –§: p16g Mar 6] smallish gelding: one-time fairly useful performer, became temperamental: stayed 2½m: acted on any turf going and fibresand: tried visored, was usually blinkered: dead. *Jamie Poulton* **– §**

GALA SUNDAY (USA) 2 b.c. (Apr 3) Lear Fan (USA) 130 – Sunday Bazaar (USA) (Nureyev (USA) 131) [2002 7m² 7m² Sep 7] smallish, well-made colt: half-brother to several winners, notably very smart 1½m winner Perfect Sunday (by Quest For Fame): dam, French 1½m winner, half-sister to US Grade 1 winners Bates Motel (at 1m/1¼m) and Hatim (at 9f): fairly useful form: runner-up in maiden at Goodwood (noisy/green in preliminaries, beaten 1¼ lengths by Wahsheeq) and minor event at Kempton (odds on, beaten neck by Captain Saif): will be suited by 1m+: remains capable of better, and well up to winning a race or 2. *B. W. Hills* **92 p**

GALAXY FACT 2 ch.c. (May 10) Factual (USA) 108 – Miss Petella (Dunphy 124) [2002 5m 5g 5s f5g 5m Aug 18] 1,300Y: workmanlike colt: half-brother to several winners, including fairly useful 7f (at 2 yrs) to 11.4f winner Traceability (by Puissance) and 7f winner Prince Consort (by Clantime): dam of little account: no form: tried blinkered. *A. Berry* **–**

GALAXY FALLON 4 b.f. Dancing Spree (USA) – No Comebacks 70 (Last Tycoon 131) [2002 –: 14g 13.8g May 31] tall, quite good-topped filly: no form. *Mrs A. M. Naughton* **–**

GALAXY FLYER (IRE) 3 ch.g. Flying Spur (AUS) – Classic Delight (USA) 55 (Green Forest (USA) 134) [2002 8m 8m 9.9m Aug 25] 6,000Y: strong gelding: second foal: dam, maiden, stayed 7.5f: well held in 3 maidens. *A. Berry* **–**

GALAXY PASHA (IRE) 3 ch.g. Hector Protector (USA) 124 – Blade of Grass 78 (Kris 135) [2002 –: 10d Aug 5] no encouragement in 2 maidens a year apart. *S. Dow* **–**

GALAXY QUEST (IRE) 2 br.f. (Feb 25) Be My Guest (USA) 126 – Familiar Quest (IRE) 65 (Tirol 127) [2002 5s 5f⁶ 6v³ 7.5m 6d 7d p7g Nov 19] IR 8,000Y: first foal: dam, Irish maiden, stayed 7f: modest maiden: long way below form last 4 starts, twice giving impression something amiss: should stay 7f. *A. Berry* **51 d**

GALAXY SAM (USA) 3 ch.g. Royal Academy (USA) 130 – Istiska (FR) (Irish River (FR) 131) [2002 63: 9m⁵ 11.5f 8s 12m 8m Sep 19] tall, leggy gelding: modest maiden: left A. Berry after reappearance: probably stays 11.5f: acts on firm and good to soft ground. *W. J. Haggas* **63**

GALAXY TEE (IRE) 3 ch.f. Goldmark (USA) 113 – Shepherd's Delight (Prince Sabo 123) [2002 56d: f7s Jan 5] leggy, rather unfurnished filly: modest maiden at best at 2 yrs: well beaten only start in 2002. *A. Berry* **–**

GALAXY THUNDERBIRD 3 ch.g. Bahamian Bounty 116 – Milva 56 (Jellaby **61**
124) [2002 58: 6d 6.1m⁵ 8d 8.5m 7g* 7m f9.4g p7g⁶ Dec 18] strong gelding: modest
performer: left A. Berry after second start: only form in 2002 when fortunate winner of
handicap at Folkestone (runner-up's saddle slipped close home) in September: stays 7f:
acts on soft and good to firm ground: very slowly away final outing. *S. Dow*

GALEY RIVER (USA) 3 ch.c. Irish River (FR) 131 – Carefree Kate (USA) (Lyphard **76**
(USA) 132) [2002 70: 8.1m⁵ 8m⁴ 8m Sep 13] strong, close-coupled colt: fair maiden:
stays 1m: acts on good to firm going, below form only outing on soft. *J. J. Sheehan*

GALFAN 2 ch.g. (Feb 28) Atraf 116 – Clunk Click 72 (Star Appeal 133) [2002 5m **49**
6.1d 6.1g Jul 26] 15,000F, 18,000Y: strong gelding: half-brother to numerous winners,
including French 1990 2-y-o 6f winner Touch And Love (by Green Desert) and 6f (at 2
yrs) and 7f winner Crazy Paving (by Danehill), both useful: dam, maiden, stayed 1½m:
poor form in maidens: stays 6f. *B. Palling*

GALI 6 gr.g. Petong 126 – Wasimah 84 (Caerleon (USA) 132) [2002 40: 7.1g Aug 8] **–**
poor maiden at 5 yrs: well beaten only start (hooded) in 2002: visored once. *C. A. Horgan*

GALLANT BOY (IRE) 3 ch.g. Grand Lodge (USA) 125 – Damerela (IRE) (Alzao **93 +**
(USA) 117) [2002 84p: 8m³ 9g⁶ f7g³ f8.5s* Dec 26] rather leggy, quite good-topped
gelding: easy mover: fairly useful performer: much better than bare result first 2 starts in
2002, heavily-backed favourite in handicap at Goodwood in latter: subsequently sold
from Sir Michael Stoute 12,000 gns and gelded: simple task when winning maiden at
Wolverhampton in December: should stay 1¼m: raced only on fibresand/good going or
firmer: tongue tied last 2 starts. *P. D. Evans*

GALLANT HERO 3 b.c. Rainbow Quest (USA) 134 – Gay Gallanta (USA) 112 **109**
(Woodman (USA) 126) [2002 8m* 10.3f* 10m Jun 20] tall, quite good-topped colt: third
foal: brother to fairly useful 9f winner Gallant: dam, Queen Mary and Cheveley Park
winner who stayed 1m, half-sister to very smart Irish performer up to 1¼m Sportsworld,
from family of A P Indy and Wolfhound: useful performer: won newcomers race at
Newmarket in April and minor event at Doncaster (rallied gamely to beat Wadmaan by
1½ lengths) in June: left firm impression something amiss in listed race at Royal Ascot
final start: likely to prove better at 1½m than 1¼m: raced only on good to firm/firm going.
Sir Michael Stoute

GALLA PLACIDIA (IRE) 4 b.f. Royal Abjar (USA) 121 – Merrie Moment (IRE) **–**
(Taufan (USA) 119) [2002 54: 8g 8d May 27] fair form in maidens at 2 yrs: little form
since. *C. G. Cox*

GALLEON BEACH 5 b.g. Shirley Heights 130 – Music In My Life (IRE) 59 (Law **77**
Society (USA) 130) [2002 92§: p16g 16d 17.1m⁶ 19.1m⁵ 18f³ 18d* 16.2m⁵ 21g⁶ 18.7g⁵
16.1d³ 17.2f* 17.1f* 18d Oct 21] sturdy, deep-girthed gelding: fair handicapper: left
J. Hills after reappearance: won at Chepstow in July, Bath in September and Pontefract in
October: reportedly finished distressed final start: barely stays 21f: acts on firm and soft
going: effective blinkered/visored or not: has been tongue tied: often held up. *A. Streeter*

GALLERY GOD (FR) 6 ch.g. In The Wings 128 – El Fabulous (FR) 111 (Fabulous **109**
Dancer (USA) 124) [2002 113: 12g² 15.5m 12m⁴ 12v³ Nov 4] sturdy gelding: has a quick
action: useful performer: creditable second to Belfortain in listed race at Longchamp on
reappearance: below form in similar events at Newmarket and Nantes last 2 starts, after 4
month-absence in latter: effective at 1½m/1¾m: acts on any going: often sweats/gets on
edge/takes good hold: often leads: joined S. Dow. *G. Wragg*

GALLIVANT 2 b.f. (Mar 26) Danehill (USA) 126 – Gay Gallanta (USA) 112 (Wood- **88**
man (USA) 126) [2002 5m⁴ 6m⁵ 6m² 5g* 6.1m* 6g Sep 21] stocky, good-quartered filly:
has a quick, fluent action: fourth foal: half-sister to 3-y-o Gallant Hero and fairly useful
9f winner Gallant (both by Rainbow Quest): dam, Queen Mary/Cheveley Park winner,
half-sister to very smart Irish performer up to 1¼m Sportsworld from family of A P Indy
and Wolfhound: fairly useful performer: landed odds in maiden at Beverley and minor
event at Chester in August: well held in listed event at Ayr final start: should stay 7f: raced
only on good/good to firm going. *Sir Michael Stoute*

GALORE (IRE) 2 b.f. (Apr 1) Desert Style (IRE) 121 – Rend Rover (FR) (Mon- **48**
seigneur (USA) 127) [2002 6m 5.1f 7g⁵ 7.1m 8.3d Oct 14] IR 4,200Y: lengthy filly:
half-sister to 3 winners, including 6-y-o Rendita: dam Italian 8.5f to 11f winner: poor
maiden: form only on third start. *J. M. Bradley*

GALY BAY 4 b.f. Bin Ajwaad (IRE) 119 – Sylhall (Sharpo 132) [2002 56: f9.4g Jan **–**
25] leggy, unfurnished filly: modest 9f winner at 3 yrs: behind only start in 2002: ran
poorly in blinkers. *A. Bailey*

370

GAME GURU   3 b.g. First Trump 118 – Scarlett Holly 81 (Red Sunset 120) [2002 61,   –
a84: f6s* p7g f6g* 5g 6m⁶ 7m 7g f5g f6g p7g f6g Dec 31] leggy, quite good-topped   **a93**
gelding: fairly useful on all-weather, fair at best on turf: won handicap in January and
minor event in February, both at Southwell: mostly well below form after: has won at 7f,
probably better at 6f: acts on all-weather, yet to race on extremes of going on turf: usually
blinkered. *T. D. Barron*

GAME LEADER (IRE)   3 b.f. Mukaddamah (USA) 125 – Fauna (IRE) 65 (Taufan   –
(USA) 119) [2002 72: 7.1m 7s f6g f6g 6m Aug 21] angular filly: fair performer at 2 yrs:
well below form in 2002 (very edgy on reappearance): stays 6f: acts on firm and good to
soft ground. *D. Haydn Jones*

GAME TIME   3 b.f. Atraf 116 – Real Popcorn (IRE) 52 (Jareer (USA) 115) [2002 64:   **52**
p8g f8.5g⁴ f9.4g² f8g f8g f5g⁵ f5g⁵ f5g f6g f6g Dec 10] unfurnished filly: modest
performer: below form last 4 starts: stays 9.4f: acts on all-weather: sometimes races
freely/carries head high: possibly none too genuine. *R. Brotherton*

GAME TUFTY   6 b.g. Sirgame – Melancolia 77 (Legend of France (USA) 124) [2002   –
45§: f12g Feb 7] workmanlike gelding: pulled up (said to have had breathing problem)
only start in 2002. *P. Howling*

GAMITAS   4 b.f. Dolphin Street (FR) 125 – Driftholme 27 (Safawan 118) [2002 50,   –
a59: f11s f8.5g Jan 21] maiden: no form in 2002. *G. M. McCourt*

GAMRA (IRE)   3 b.f. Green Desert (USA) 127 – Just You Wait (Nonoalco (USA)   **73 p**
131) [2002 8g* 8d Jul 31] sister to smart 6.5f (in USA) to 1m winner Distant Oasis and
7f/1m winner Egypt, closely related to useful 7.5f (at 2 yrs) to 11.5f winner Waiting (by
Polish Precedent) and half-sister to 3 winners, including very smart pair Reprimand
(miler, by Mummy's Pet) and Wiorno (1m to 10.5f winner, by Wassl): dam unraced
daughter of smart 1¼m winner Sleat: fair form: won maiden at Salisbury on debut by ½
length from Sandy City, edging persistently left: similar form when seventh to Selective
in minor event at Kempton following month, weakening having raced freely: sold 35,000
gns in December: should still do better. *J. R. Fanshawe*

GAMUT (IRE)   3 b.c. Spectrum (IRE) 126 – Greektown (Ela-Mana-Mou 132) [2002   **116 p**
83P: 11g* 11.6m² 12m⁴ Sep 13] strong, well-made colt: has quick but unimpressive

Exors of the late Lord Weinstock's "Gamut"

action: smart performer: tongue tied, won maiden at Newbury in April: good efforts when 1¼ lengths second of 4 to Arctic Owl in minor event at Windsor and 3¾ lengths fourth to Systematic in listed race at Doncaster after: should stay beyond 1½m: yet to race on extremes of ground: still lightly raced, and open to further progress. *Sir Michael Stoute*

GANDON 5 ch.g. Hernando (FR) 127 – Severine (USA) 65 (Trempolino (USA) 135) [2002 63: f12g³ f14.8g⁶ 12.1g Jul 26] angular gelding: modest performer: stays 2m: acts on firm ground and fibresand: looked less than keen final start. *P. G. Murphy* **49**

GAP YEAR (USA) 2 b. or br.c. (Apr 6) Majestic Light (USA) – Satan's Satchel (USA) (Devil's Bag (USA)) [2002 7m 7m⁴ 6s f8.5g Dec 2] $60,000F, IR 30,000Y: small colt: sixth foal: half-brother to winners in USA by Dixieland Band and Quiet American, latter minor stakes winner: dam, 6f/7f winner in USA, half-sister to US Grade 2 8.5f winner Sultry Sun, herself dam of US Grade 1 11f/1½m winner Solar Splendor (by Majestic Light): modest maiden: off 4 months, well below form last 2 starts: not sure to stay 1m: acts on good to firm ground: has worn crossed noseband. *J. A. Osborne* **49**

GARDEN SOCIETY (IRE) 5 ch.g. Caerleon (USA) 132 – Eurobid 118 (Ela-Mana-Mou 132) [2002 102: 10.2s 12g 12s⁶ Jul 11] small gelding: useful at best at 4 yrs: well held in 2002: visored penultimate start. *J. A. R. Toller* **–**

GARDOR (FR) 4 b.g. Kendor (FR) 122 – Garboesque (Priolo (USA) 127) [2002 56: f11s² f8s 11g³ 9m May 2] angular gelding: modest maiden handicapper: stays 11f: acts on fibresand, soft and good to firm going. *J. G. FitzGerald* **55**

GARDRUM (IRE) 4 ch.g. Lycius (USA) 124 – Kafayef (USA) 46 (Secreto (USA) 128) [2002 57§: 6v 6.9d 7.1d 8m 7.2d Aug 2] strong gelding: handicapper: refused/virtually refused to race last 2 starts: sometimes blinkered. *Miss L. A. Perratt* **– §**

GARGOYLE GIRL 5 b.m. Be My Chief (USA) 122 – May Hills Legacy (IRE) 68 (Be My Guest (USA) 126) [2002 –: 12.4g 11.1g* 12g 10m 12m³ 10.9d⁶ 12m² 12.1d³ 12d* 13.8m² 10g² 14m* 12.3m 11.9m* 16m⁴ 13.1g³ 16m⁴ 11.9f 13.1s⁶ Oct 15] big, good-topped mare: fair handicapper: improved, and won at Hamilton (seller), Musselburgh (2) and York between May and September: stays 2m: acts on firm and good to soft going: visored second to fifth starts: held up. *J. S. Goldie* **75**

GARMOUCHEH (USA) 2 b. or br.f. (Jan 23) Silver Hawk (USA) 123 – Flowing (USA) 114 (El Gran Senor (USA) 136) [2002 6s 6g² 6m² 8.1g⁴ 7s³ 7f* 7s² Oct 26] 78,000 2-y-o: sturdy filly: sixth foal: half-sister to 3 winners, including useful Irish sprinter Lady Shannon (by Mr Prospector): dam Irish sprinter: useful performer: won nursery at Newmarket in October: best effort when beaten head by Crystal Star in listed event at Newbury final start, staying on well: should stay 1m: acts on firm and soft going. *R. Hannon* **99**

GARROS (USA) 2 b.c. (May 31) Grand Slam (USA) 120 – Affirmatively (USA) (Affirmed (USA)) [2002 5.9d³ 6m³ 7m* 7m Sep 13] $25,000Y: big, lengthy colt: half-brother to several winners abroad, including useful French 1m winner (including at 2 yrs) Mais Oui (by Lyphard): dam, 8.5f/9f winner in USA, daughter of champion US older mare Straight Deal: useful form: best effort when winning maiden at Ascot in July by length from Amandus, well ridden from front: well held in Champagne Stakes at Doncaster final start: should be suited by 1m+: acts on good to firm ground: has scope to make a better 3-y-o. *M. Johnston* **97 p**

GARTER CHAPEL 2 gr.g. (Apr 20) Highest Honor (FR) 124 – Feel Free (IRE) 86 (Generous (IRE) 139) [2002 5.1g May 7] first foal: dam, 9f/1¼m winner, half-sister to smart but untrustworthy performer up to 1¼m Intimate Guest: 8/1, well held in maiden at Bath: sold 8,000 gns in July, resold 1,800 gns in October, sent to Sweden. *R. Hannon* **–**

GARTH POOL (IRE) 5 b.g. Sri Pekan (USA) 117 – Millionetta (IRE) 75 (Danehill (USA) 126) [2002 f6g⁴ f6g² f6g⁵ f6g³ f5g f6g⁶ May 2] good-bodied gelding: useful on all-weather for T. D. Barron in 2000: off over a year, modest form in 2002: was effective at 5f/6f: acted on fibresand, firm and soft going: tried blinkered: often made running: sold £650 in June: dead. *I. A. Wood* **– a64**

GARW VALLEY 3 b.f. Mtoto 134 – Morgannwg (IRE) 86 (Simply Great (FR) 122) [2002 62p: 8m 9.9g⁶ 11.6m⁵ 12m³ 14.1m 12f 11.9g Oct 24] rather leggy filly: fair maiden handicapper: should stay 1¾m: acts on good to firm ground: blinkered final start: sold 3,000 gns. *A. C. Stewart* **73**

GASCON 6 b.g. Beveled (USA) – Lady Roxanne 65 (Cyrano de Bergerac 120) [2002 70, a52+: p6g² p6g p6g⁶ 6m⁵ 5.7g 6g 6m 6m 6.1m Oct 1] modest performer: stays easy 7f: acts on heavy going, good to firm going and polytrack: held up. *D. J. Coakley* **63 a57**

Kennet Valley Thoroughbreds V's "Gateman"

GATEMAN   5 b.g. Owington 123 – Scandalette (Niniski (USA) 125) [2002 6f³ 6g² 7m   **117**
7m* 7d* 8.5s 7f³ 7m² 8g³ 8m Dec 15] big, well-made gelding: progressive for B. Meehan
at 2 yrs: subsequently transferred to USA, winning 2 non-graded races at Keeneland (left
W. E. Walden/gelded after final 4-y-o start): smart form on return to Britain, winning
minor event at Yarmouth and Emirates Airline Minstrel Stakes at the Curragh (by 2½
lengths from One Won One), both in July: ran well when neck second to Meshaheer in
listed race at Newbury and close third to Domedriver in Prix Daniel Wildenstein at
Longchamp (made most) before last in Hong Kong Mile at Sha Tin final start: winner at
9f in USA, probably best at 7f/1m: acts on firm and soft going, well held only outing on
dirt: reportedly finished distressed sixth outing. *M. Johnston*

GAVRILOV (IRE)   3 b.g. Danehill Dancer (IRE) 117 – Elminya (IRE) (Sure Blade   **–**
(USA) 130) [2002 73: 10m May 10] fair maiden at 2 yrs: stayed 7f: acted on firm going and polytrack: dead. *N. A. Callaghan*

GAY BREEZE   9 b.g. Dominion 123 – Judy's Dowry 80 (Dragonara Palace (USA)   **67**
115) [2002 72, a68: f6g f7g f6g p6g² 5.1d⁶ 6m 6g 5m 6g Sep 9] compact gelding: fair   **a49**
handicapper on turf, poor on all-weather: no show last 4 starts: effective at 5f to easy 7f:
acts on any turf going/all-weather. *P. S. Felgate*

GAZEBO   3 ch.f. Cadeaux Genereux 131 – Ferber's Follies (USA) (Saratoga Six   **68**
(USA)) [2002 6f³ 7m⁵ 7s f7g 6d Oct 14] strong filly: fifth living foal: half-sister to useful
6f winner Corndavon and 4-y-o Injaaz (both by Sheikh Albadou), and to multiple winner
in USA by Opening Verse. dam 2-y-o 5.5f winner in USA and third in Grade 2 6f event:
easily best effort (fair form) in Pontefract maiden on debut: left G. Bravery after second
outing: visored final start. *E. A. L. Dunlop*

GAZEILA 3 b.f. Makbul 104 – Liberatrice (FR) (Assert 134) [2002 43: 10g 10d Oct 28] poor maiden at 2 yrs: well held both outings in 2002. *J. J. Bridger* —

GDANSK (IRE) 5 b.g. Pips Pride 117 – Merry Twinkle (Martinmas 128) [2002 86: 5s⁶ 5f 5s⁴ 5.1d² 6s² 5s⁴ 5.9v 5g³ 6g³ 6s² 6m⁴ 6g 6f 5g Oct 17] leggy, lengthy gelding: has a round action: fairly useful handicapper: good fourth to Deceitful in Great St Wilfrid at Ripon eleventh outing: best at 5f/6f: acts on good to firm ground and heavy: sometimes slowly away: has carried head high: seemed reluctant early on penultimate start: none too reliable. *A. Berry* 90

GEE BEE BOY 8 ch.g. Beveled (USA) – Blue And White (Busted 134) [2002 –: 14.1g 11.8s Oct 15] strong gelding: lightly raced and no form since 2000. *G. F. Bridgwater* —

GEESPOT 3 b.f. Pursuit of Love 124 – My Discovery (IRE) (Imperial Frontier (USA) 112) [2002 39: 6g 5.7g³ 6m 6.1v 6d 7m* 7d 7m 7m p7g f6g f8.5g³ p7g* f7g⁵ p7g⁶ Dec 30] small filly: modest performer on all-weather, poor on turf: won sellers at Brighton in July and Lingfield in December: probably stays 8.5f: acts on all-weather, soft and good to firm going: tried visored: none too consistent. *D. J. S. ffrench Davis* 48 a54

GEKKOACCOUNTDOTCOM (IRE) 3 b.g. Grand Lodge (USA) 125 – House Music (IRE) 89 (Thatching 131) [2002 7m 6g 7g⁶ 8.3s p10g 8g⁶ 8m 10d 6m 6m 5.3m Sep 3] 1,600Y: third foal: half-brother to winners abroad by Brief Truce and Lake Coniston: dam, Irish 1½m winner, half-sister to Vintage Crop: modest maiden: stays 1m: acts on good to firm going: blinkered final start. *R. M. Flower* 51 ?

GEM BIEN (USA) 4 b.g. Bien Bien (USA) 125 – Eastern Gem (USA) (Jade Hunter (USA)) [2002 82§: 8f 8.5g* 8d³ 9.1v³ 8.5d* 10.1m³ 8.3m 8m³ 8g Oct 17] rather leggy, quite attractive gelding: fairly useful performer: won handicap in May and minor event in July, both at Beverley: poor efforts last 2 outings: stays 1¼m: acts on soft and good to firm ground: tongue tied once at 3 yrs: difficult ride (carries head awkwardly). *Andrew Turnell* 88

GEMEISTER 2 b.c. (Feb 29) Superlative 118 – Enfant du Paradis (IRE) 52 (Shernazar 131) [2002 7f f6g Oct 5] leggy colt: first reported foal: dam, 1¾m/15f winner, also won over hurdles: tailed off in maidens. *B. P. J. Baugh* —

GEMI BED (FR) 7 b.g. Double Bed (FR) 121 – Gemia (FR) (King of Macedon 126) [2002 p12g p12g p16g³ 12d p16g Jul 17] modest performer: in frame 10 times in France/Belgium at 6 yrs: best effort in Britain in 2002 in apprentice handicap at Lingfield third outing: stays 2m: acts on polytrack: sometimes blinkered. *G. L. Moore* 52

GEMIND 3 b.f. Forzando 122 – Innocent Abroad (DEN) 53 (Viking (USA)) [2002 –: f9.4g⁶ f8.5g p8g f8g Feb 19] of little account. *B. P. J. Baugh* —

GEMINIANI (IRE) 2 b.f. (Feb 8) King of Kings (IRE) 125 – Tadkiyra (IRE) (Darshaan 133) [2002 7m* 7m* Aug 25] IR 60,000Y: angular filly: fourth foal: dam, French 1¼m winner, half-sister to several smart/useful performers, including Princess Royal Stakes winner Tashtiya: useful form: won maiden at Goodwood (by ½ length from Inchberry) and 8-runner Touchdown In Malaysia Prestige Stakes on same course, both in August: beat Mail The Desert by 1¼ lengths in latter, quickening to lead over 1f out: reported in early-September to have been cast in her box: will probably stay 1m: should improve further, all being well. *B. W. Hills* 106 p

GEMINI LADY 2 b.f. (May 1) Emperor Fountain 112 – Raunchy Rita (Brigadier Gerard 144) [2002 f8s 8d⁶ 7d Nov 5] 4,000Y: half-sister to smart 6f/7f winner (latter including at 2 yrs) Daring Destiny (by Daring March): dam ran 3 times: signs of only a little ability in maidens. *Mrs G. S. Rees* —

GEMS BOND 2 b.g. (Feb 27) Magic Ring (IRE) 115 – Jucinda 58 (Midyan (USA) 124) [2002 6f* 5.7f* 6m 6m 8s Oct 25] 19,000Y: leggy, quite good-topped gelding: first foal: dam, 15.4f winner, sister to Goodwood Cup winner Tioman Island: fairly useful performer: won minor events at Newbury in July and Bath (clearly best effort when making all to beat Bond May Day by 3 lengths) in August: well held in sales races/nursery last 3 starts: should stay 7f: acts on firm going. *R. Hannon* 86

GEMTASTIC 4 b.f. Tagula (IRE) 116 – It's So Easy 63 (Shaadi (USA) 126) [2002 62, a57: p6g f6g f5g p6g 6.1g 6f f7g⁶ 8f f5g 5.5f⁵ 5m⁶ 5m⁶ f5s 6.1m f6g⁵ f5g⁴ Dec 27] small, sparely-made filly: poor performer: left P. D. Evans after fourth start: best at 5f/6f: acts on firm going, good to soft and all-weather: reportedly broke blood vessel sixth start. *R. Hollinshead* 43

GENERAL 5 b.g. Cadeaux Genereux 131 – Bareilly (USA) (Lyphard (USA) 132) [2002 69: 11.6d May 25] strong, heavy-bodied gelding: fairly useful hurdler: well held only outing on Flat in 2002. *Mrs N. Smith* —

GENERAL AMNESTY (IRE) 3 b.g. General Monash (USA) 107 – Beautyofthepeace (IRE) (Exactly Sharp (USA) 121) [2002 56: p7g 8.2d 10d⁶ 16.2d* 16g 17.1m⁴ 18d f14.8g Nov 15] leggy, quite good-topped gelding: fair handicapper: left D. Shaw after second outing: won maiden event at Beverley in July by 11 lengths: stayed 17f: acted on good to firm going, good to soft and fibresand: dead. *S. R. Bowring* **65 a–**

GENERAL BATHWICK (IRE) 2 ch.c. (Apr 9) General Monash (USA) 107 – Sweet Finale (Sallust 134) [2002 5.1m 6.1d 6.1s 5.7m⁶ 6.1d 6m 5m⁴ 7m Aug 14] IR 7,000Y: smallish, sturdy colt: seventh foal: dam third at 1m in Ireland: poor maiden: free-going sort, likely to prove best at 5f/6f: acts on good to firm ground: below form only try in blinkers. *B. R. Millman* **44**

GENERAL GORDON 2 ch.c. (Apr 28) Washington State (USA) – Mossalier 57 (Mazilier (USA) 107) [2002 7.1m 7g Oct 24] 800Y: second living foal: dam maiden who stayed 7f: tailed off in maidens. *J. Neville* —

GENERAL HAWK (IRE) 4 b.g. Distinctly North (USA) 115 – Sabev (USA) (Saber Thrust (CAN)) [2002 64: 8f 8f⁴ 7m* 7f 8.1m* 6.9d 8.5g⁴ 7.5m 7.9m* 9m 7.5m* 8m⁵ Oct 5] rather leggy gelding: fair performer: won minor event at Catterick in May then handicaps at Haydock in July and York and Beverley (pulled hard) in September: stays 1m: acts on firm going, probably on fibresand: sometimes slowly away: none too consistent. *R. A. Fahey* **77**

GENERAL JACKSON 5 ch.g. Cadeaux Genereux 131 – Moidart 90 (Electric 126) [2002 63: 14.1m 18s 17.2d⁵ 22.2m 18d 17.2f⁵ Sep 30] big, good-topped gelding: modest maiden at 4 yrs: well held in 2002. *Jane Southcombe* —

GENERAL SMITH 3 b.c. Greensmith 121 – Second Call 67 (Kind of Hush 118) [2002 60: 6g 5.3d³ 6g² 6s⁶ 5.9d⁵ 6.1d³ 5f* 6g⁶ 6m 5m⁴ 6.1m Oct 1] modest handicapper: won at Catterick in July: good fourth at Goodwood penultimate start: effective at 5f/6f: acts on firm going, good to soft and fibresand. *J. M. Bradley* **63**

GENEROUS SHARE 2 ch.f. (Mar 16) Cadeaux Genereux 131 – Marl 94 (Lycius (USA) 124) [2002 6d³ 7m³ 7m⁴ 6g Oct 4] third foal: half-sister to 4-y-o Snow Bunting and 3-y-o Green Line: dam 2-y-o 5f winner but best at 6f: modest form when third in maidens: below best in claimers after: stays 7f: sold 3,000 gns. *R. Hannon* **62**

GENGHIS (IRE) 3 br.g. Persian Bold 123 – Cindy's Baby 36 (Bairn (USA) 126) [2002 12m² 11.7f⁴ Aug 18] IR 16,000F, 35,000Y: rather leggy gelding: fourth foal: brother to 7f (at 2 yrs) and 1¼m winner Karakul and half-brother to winner in Italy by Paris House: dam, maiden, half-sister to smart 6f winner (including at 2 yrs) Two Clubs: better effort in maidens (fairly useful form) when second to Stance at Newbury (slowly away) on debut. *P. R. Webber* **83**

GENIAL GENIE 6 b.g. Sizzling Melody 117 – Needwood Sprite 58 (Joshua 129) [2002 78: f8s⁶ f7g⁶ f7g⁵ 7d³ 7g⁵ 7f 7f 7.6f³ 7g 7f 6.1m⁵ 7.5d 8.2m⁶ 7m 7.1m⁴ 7.1g f8g Nov 26] good-topped gelding: fair handicapper: effective at 7f/1m: acts on fibresand, soft and firm going: tongue tied: sometimes races freely: tends to hang. *R. Hollinshead* **74**

GENTEEL (IRE) 2 b.f. (Apr 18) Titus Livius (FR) 115 – Danseuse Davis (FR) (Glow (USA)) [2002 5s⁴ p5g⁴ 5.1d* p5g⁴ 5f 5.1d 6m⁴ 6m 6f⁶ Jul 29] workmanlike filly: fourth foal: half-sister to fairly useful 5f (at 2 yrs)/6f winner Polly Mills (by Lugana Beach): dam, no form, half-sister to useful stayer Top of The World: modest performer: won seller at Nottingham in April: effective at 5f/6f: acts on good to firm going, good to soft and polytrack: visored (looked none too keen) final outing: none too consistent. *P. D. Evans* **58**

GENTLEMAN VENTURE 6 b.g. Polar Falcon (USA) 126 – Our Shirley 84 (Shirley Heights 130) [2002 97: 10.1g³ 12m 10.1d 12m⁵ 10.1m⁵ 12f 12s Oct 26] tall, quite attractive gelding: useful handicapper: good third at Epsom in April: on downgrade after: effective at 1¼m/1½m: acts on any turf going: usually a free-going sort. *J. Akehurst* **97 d**

GENTLE RESPONSE 2 b.f. (Apr 19) Puissance 110 – Sweet Whisper 63 (Petong 126) [2002 5m² 6g f6s f6g f5g Dec 10] 1,500Y: good-bodied filly: fourth foal: half-sister to 2 winning sprinters, notably 5-y-o Blue Velvet: dam 5f/6f winner at 2 yrs: modest maiden: best effort on debut: likely to prove best at 5f/6f. *B. A. McMahon* **52 d**

GEOFFSTAR   2 b.c. (Apr 4) Groom Dancer (USA) 128 – Skuld (Kris 135) [2002 6m⁶   –
p8g Dec 14] IR 2,000Y, 6,500 2-y-o: fifth living foal: half-brother to fairly useful 1½m
winner Skimra (by Hernando): dam unraced half-sister to Petoski: well held in maidens 4
months apart. *T. G. Mills*

GEOGRAPHY (IRE)   2 ch.g. (Apr 2) Definite Article 121 – Classic Ring (IRE) 50   **62**
(Auction Ring (USA) 123) [2002 7.2s p10g f8.5s⁶ Dec 9] 50,000Y: seventh foal: brother
to German 7f winner Poppaea and half-brother to 3 winners, including 3-y-o Waterside
and 5-y-o Seven No Trumps: dam 2-y-o 7f winner: modest form in maidens: bred to prove
best up to 1m. *P. F. I. Cole*

GEORGE ROMNEY (USA)   3 b.g. Distant View (USA) 126 – Polish Socialite   **70**
(USA) (Polish Navy (USA)) [2002 78: 7g⁵ 8.1d⁴ p8g⁶ 7s 10.9g 7m⁵ 7g 8m p12g⁶ 8d p12g
Nov 19] good-bodied gelding: poor maiden: left P. Cole after fifth start and S. Williams after
fifth start and S. Williams after sixth one: stays 1m: acts on polytrack, soft and good to
firm going: tried in blinkers, tongue strap and cheekpieces. *H. J. Cyzer*

GEORGE STREET (IRE)   4 b.g. Danehill (USA) 126 – Sweet Justice (Law Society   –
(USA) 130) [2002 62: 16.2m 9.9g Oct 2] well-made gelding: modest maiden at 3 yrs:
well held both starts in 2002: often blinkered/visored. *M. C. Pipe*

GEORGE STUBBS (USA)   4 b. or br.g. Affirmed (USA) – Mia Duchessa (USA)   **81**
(Nijinsky (CAN) 138) [2002 82: 8.1d 8.5s⁶ 8.3s² 7.9d 8f 8g* 8.5d 8m² p8g² f8.5g p8g³
p10g Dec 11] leggy, quite good-topped gelding: fairly useful performer: won claimer at
Ripon in August: sold from P. Cole's stable 24,000 gns after ninth start: has won at 1¼m,
raced mainly around 1m in 2002: acts on all-weather, soft and good to firm going (seemed
unsuited by firm going): often makes running. *N. P. Littmoden*

GERI ROULETTE   4 b.f. Perpendicular 119 – Clashfern (Smackover 107) [2002 47:   **60 ?**
f12g⁴ f12s⁴ f12g* f12g 9.9m⁵ 11.7g* 12.4g 10m f12g f12g f14.8s³ f12g⁶ Dec 14] good-   **a52**
topped filly: modest performer: won maiden at Wolverhampton in February and handicap
at Bath in April: no comparable form on turf after: stays 14.8f: acts on fibresand and good
to firm going: often makes running. *E. J. Alston*

GERONIMO   5 b.g. Efisio 120 – Apache Squaw 54 (Be My Guest (USA) 126) [2002   **?**
67: f6s* f7s⁴ f8g⁴ f6g f6g p7g f7g f6g² 6g⁶ p6g f5s⁶ f6g² f6s⁴ f6g² f6s² f6g⁶ f7g⁴   **a71**
Dec 14] sparely-made gelding: fair handicapper on all-weather: won at Southwell (left
M. Wigham) in January: best at 6f/7f: acts on fibresand: tried blinkered: sometimes
slowly away. *Miss Gay Kelleway*

GERT THE FLIRT   4 ch.f. Manhal – Ardross Kala (Ardross 134) [2002 p12g Jun 29]   –
first foal: dam unraced: 33/1, tailed off in Lingfield seller. *G. P. Enright*

GETATEM (IRE)   3 b.g. Up And At 'em 109 – Fiaba 66 (Precocious 126) [2002 66:   **52**
6g 5d 6g 8g 6g 6f⁵ 6f² 5.9g² 5.9g⁵ 5g* Sep 7] small, compact gelding: modest performer:
won maiden handicap at Thirsk in September: effective at 5f/6f: acts on firm ground:
blinkered last 4 starts. *Miss L. A. Perratt*

GET STUCK IN (IRE)   6 b.g. Up And At 'em 109 – Shoka (FR) 86 (Kaldoun (FR)   **85 §**
122) [2002 95: 5s 6m 5f 5m 5.9v 5g* 5m 5m 5m² 5g⁵ 6f Oct 12] leggy, quite attractive
gelding: fairly useful handicapper: won at Ayr (edged right) in July: left impression
something amiss final start: effective at 5f/6f: acts on any going: blinkered once: sometimes reluctant to post/slowly away: best making running: carries head high/finds little:
unreliable. *Miss L. A. Perratt*

GET THE ACCOUNTANT   3 b.f. Vettori (IRE) 119 – Mistitled (USA) 54 (Miswaki   –
(USA) 124) [2002 6m 10m 10m Jul 27] 16,500F, 4,500Y, 15,000 2-y-o: third foal:
half-sister to useful 1999 2-y-o 5f/6f winner Magic of Love and 7f winner Jacobina (both
by Magic Ring): dam 2-y-o 5f winner: well held in 3 maidens. *E. J. O'Neill*

GEZKAT   3 b.f. Petong 126 – Petite Louie 45 (Chilibang 120) [2002 –: p5g 7m 5m 5m²   **42**
Apr 23] close-coupled filly: has a round action: poor maiden: should stay 7f: yet to race
on extremes of going on turf: blinkered second/third starts. *S. C. Williams*

GHANNAM (USA)   3 b.c. Langfuhr (CAN) 124 – Katerina Key (USA) (Key To The   **118**
Mint (USA)) [2002 95: 7f* 7.9f² 8m² 7m² 7f⁴ Aug 17] rather leggy, useful-looking colt:
good walker: smart performer: won maiden at Thirsk in May: good efforts when runner-
up in competitive handicaps at York (beaten length by Macaw), Royal Ascot (beaten neck
by Pentecost in Britannia Stakes) and Ascot (neck second to Crystal Castle in Tote
International) next 3 starts: respectable fourth to Reel Buddy in Hungerford Stakes at
Newbury final outing: likely to prove best at 7f/1m: acts on firm and good to soft going:
sent to USA. *M. P. Tregoning*

GIANFANTI (IRE)   2 b.c. (May 2) Danehill (USA) 126 – That'll Be The Day (IRE)   **98 p**
68 (Thatching 131) [2002 7.5m² 6.3d⁵ 6d* Oct 19] IR 360,000Y: fifth foal: closely related
to Italian winner up to 7.5f That's The Way (by Hamas) and half-brother to 3-y-o
Hiddendale and 6-y-o Majestic Bay: dam, 2-y-o 5f winner, later successful up to 7f in
Italy, half-sister to very smart performer up to 1¼m Candy Glen: useful form: fifth to
Vettriano in valuable minor event at the Curragh: won maiden at Cork by 1½ lengths from
Salt Lake City: should stay at least 7f: capable of better. *A. P. O'Brien, Ireland*

G I BRIDE (IRE)   2 ch.f. (Apr 4) General Monash (USA) 107 – Victim of Love 75   **57**
(Damister (USA) 123) [2002 5g f5s 6m⁵ 5m² 5f³ 5g² 5d³ 5.1m* 5m 5m 5.1g⁴ 5f⁴ 6g⁶ 5g
Oct 19] IR 5,200Y: workmanlike filly: first foal: dam 7f winner, including at 2 yrs:
modest performer: won seller at Bath in August: mostly creditable efforts otherwise,
including in nurseries: likely to prove best at 5f: acts on firm and good to soft going:
consistent: sold 3,600 gns. *A. Berry*

GIFTED FLAME   3 b.g. Revoque (IRE) 122 – Little Lady Leah (USA) (Shareef   **78**
Dancer (USA) 135) [2002 77: 8.1f⁵ 8.2d 7.9f 8m⁶ 10.9g 8g⁴ 8d³ 8.5m* 8f f9.4g 8s Nov 6]
rangy gelding: fair performer: left P. Murphy after fifth start: won handicap at Beverley in
September: effective at 7f/8.5f: acts on firm going, possibly unsuited by softer than good:
visored (well beaten) final start: sometimes races freely. *I. Semple*

GIFT FOUNTAIN   3 b.f. Greensmith 121 – Bright Fountain (IRE) 47 (Cadeaux   **79 d**
Genereux 131) [2002 76p: 9.9m⁴ 10.2s 10g⁴ 8m 10.2f⁵ Sep 16] fair maiden: below form
after reappearance: stays 1¼m: blinkered final start: has carried head high/found little.
H. Candy

GIFT OF GOLD   7 ch.g. Statoblest 120 – Ellebanna 69 (Tina's Pet 121) [2002 83, a–:   **–**
7g 8g⁵ 7.2g f7g Nov 15] good-topped, close-coupled gelding: fairly useful handicapper
in 2001: well held in 2002: tried blinkered. *A. Bailey*

GIGGLE   2 b.f. (Jan 25) Mtoto 134 – Dimple (Fairy King (USA)) [2002 7m³ 8m³ f8s   **67**
7d⁵ f7g* p6g⁶ Oct 9] 6,000Y: smallish, heavy-bodied filly: first foal: dam unraced half-
sister to useful 1½m winner Metronome: fair performer: gamely won seller at Wolverhampton (sold from R. Cowell 9,000 gns) in September: creditable sixth in nursery at
Lingfield: stays 1m: acts on good to firm going and all-weather. *J. M. Plasschaert,
Belgium*

GIG HARBOR   3 b.c. Efisio 120 – Petonica (IRE) 77 (Petoski 135) [2002 7m 8m   **70**
8.1d³ 8.1s⁶ 8.1g³ 8.3g³ 8g² 7s⁶ 7g Oct 14] 30,000F, 72,000Y: good-bodied colt: poor
mover: fifth foal: brother to useful 6f (at 2 yrs) and 7f winner Yorkie George and half-
brother to 4-y-o Bourgainville: dam second at 7f at 2 yrs: fair maiden: below form last 2
starts: stays 1m: acts on good to firm and good to soft going, possibly unsuited by soft:
races prominently: sold 12,000 gns. *B. W. Hills*

GIKO   8 b.g. Arazi (USA) 135 – Gayane 125 (Nureyev (USA) 131) [2002 52: 14.1m   **46**
11.8m 12s 14.1m⁶ 14.4m⁴ 12m 14.1g Oct 2] leggy gelding: has a round action: poor
handicapper nowadays: stays 13f: acts on soft going, good to firm and fibresand: effective
in blinkers, not used since 2000: tried tongue tied. *Jane Southcombe*

GILDED COVE   2 b.c. (Apr 18) Polar Prince (IRE) 117 – Cloudy Reef 57 (Cragador   **68**
110) [2002 f5g² 5m⁵ f6f³ 6g Aug 27] strong colt: fifth foal: half-brother to 3-y-o
Vermilion Creek and a 6f winner by Puissance: dam, maiden, raced only
around 5f: fair form in maidens first 2 starts: off 2 months, below form after: may prove
best at 5f. *R. Hollinshead*

GILDED DANCER   4 b.g. Bishop of Cashel 122 – La Piaf (FR) (Fabulous Dancer   **90**
(USA) 124) [2002 89: f8.5g 8d² 9.2s 8g⁴ 8.2v p10g f8g⁴ Dec 4] small, good-bodied   **a55**
gelding: fairly useful maiden handicapper on turf, modest on all-weather: stays 1m: acts
on good to firm and good to soft ground: none too consistent. *W. R. Muir*

GILDED EDGE   2 ch.f. (Mar 12) Cadeaux Genereux 131 – Palacegate Episode (IRE)   **94 p**
111 (Drumalis 125) [2002 p7g² 6s* Oct 25] lengthy filly: third foal: half-sister to a 6f
winner in Sweden by Danehill: dam 5f winner, including at 2 yrs: favourite and bandaged
hind joints, confirmed debut promise when winning maiden at Newbury in good style by
2 lengths from Lago d'Orta, making most and not having to be put under pressure: may
prove best at 6f/7f: should make useful 3-y-o at least. *J. H. M. Gosden*

GILDEN MAGIC   4 b.g. Magic Ring (IRE) 115 – Have Form (Haveroid 122) [2002   **38**
62d; 8.3g p12g 6g f8g Dec 4] close-coupled gelding: disappointing maiden: left
M. Blanshard after second start. *P. W. Hiatt*

GILLY'S GENERAL (IRE)   2 ch.g. (Feb 28) General Monash (USA) 107 – Good   **72 d**
Aim (IRE) (Priolo (USA) 127) [2002 6g 7.1m⁵ 7m⁶ 6.1m 8.3m 7g Oct 24] IR 9,200F,

6,200Y: sturdy gelding: first foal: dam unraced: disappointing maiden (seemed to show fair form second start): appears to stay 7f: gelded after final outing. *J. W. Unett*

GILT TRIP (IRE) 4 b.g. Goldmark (USA) 113 – Opening Day (Day Is Done 115) – § [2002 –§, a52§: f8.5g f11s f9.4g f7g f11g 11.8s Mar 28] poor performer: stays 11f: acts on fibresand, no form on turf: sometimes blinkered: ungenuine. *M. J. Polglase* — **a43 §**

GIN 2 b.f. (Apr 16) Abou Zouz (USA) 109 – Skedaddle 57 (Formidable (USA) 125) **31** [2002 5s 5.1d⁵ 5f Apr 20] 1,300F, 1,000Y: angular filly: poor mover: third foal: dam, maiden, stayed 1¼m: poor maiden. *M. W. Easterby*

GINGER ICE 2 ch.c. (Apr 19) Bahamian Bounty 116 – Sharp Top 62 (Sharpo 132) **70** [2002 6m 6m⁶ 8g Oct 16] 12,000F: half-brother to several winners, including 3-y-o Aldora and 5-y-o Polar Red: dam 1½m and 2m winner, also won over hurdles: fair form in maidens: raced freely final start, but seems to stay 1m. *G. G. Margarson*

GINGER LADYS SHARP 2 ch.f. (Apr 18) Presidium 124 – Silkstone Lady – (Puissance 110) [2002 6f⁶ 6m⁶ 5m 6.1m 6g Oct 18] 800Y: leggy filly: second foal: sister to 5-y-o Clopton Green: dam unraced: well held in varied company: left J. McConnochie after second start. *D. Morris*

GINGKO 5 b.g. Pursuit of Love 124 – Arboretum (IRE) 83 (Green Desert (USA) 127) **73** [2002 76: 10.3s 10.9g* 10.3m 10s 12m⁵ 10.1d 12d⁵ Jul 13] fair handicapper: won at Warwick in April: stays 1½m: acts on fibresand and good to firm going, seemingly not on softer than good: slowly away fourth start: waited with: none too consistent. *P. R. Webber*

GINNER MORRIS 7 b.g. Emarati (USA) 74 – Just Run (IRE) 45 (Runnett 125) **56 §** [2002 56, a–: f8s 8v 8m² 8.3s 10.9m⁵ 8.1m 9.2g³ 9.1s Oct 15] lengthy gelding: modest **a– §** handicapper: best at 1m/1¼m: acts on heavy ground (probably on good to firm) and fibresand: usually races up with pace: unreliable. *J. Hetherton*

GIOCOSO (USA) 2 b.c. (May 11) Bahri (USA) 125 – Wing My Chimes (USA) (Flying **80 p** Paster (USA)) [2002 8.2v⁴ Oct 29] $9,500Y, 40,000 2-y-o: sixth foal: half-brother to several winners in USA, including 1m/8.5f minor stakes winner Chime After Chime (by Cari Jill Hajji): dam 6f (at 2 yrs) and 1m winner in USA: 16/1, encouraging 4½ lengths fourth of 15 to Bugatti Royale in maiden at Nottingham, finishing well under hands and heels from long way back: should stay at least 1¼m: sure to improve. *B. Palling*

GIRL OF PLEASURE (IRE) 3 b.f. Namaqualand (USA) – Shrewd Girl (USA) 79 **60** (Sagace (FR) 135) [2002 61: 10.2g 11.6s 11.6m⁴ p12g⁵ 16.2d⁴ Jul 12] good-topped filly: modest maiden handicapper: best form around 1½m: acts on good to firm going and polytrack: successful over hurdles later in July. *Mrs P. N. Dutfield*

GIRL'S BEST FRIEND 5 b.m. Nicolotte 118 – Diamond Princess 69 (Horage 124) **66** [2002 77: f8.5g⁴ p10g⁶ p10g Jul 20] tall, lengthy mare: fair handicapper: stays 1¼m: acts on soft going and all-weather: blinkered (very slowly away) final 3-y-o outing: has been tongue tied. *D. W. P. Arbuthnot*

GIULIANI 2 b.c. (Apr 16) Sadler's Wells (USA) 132 – Anka Germania (Malinowski **72 p** (USA) 123) [2002 7d 8.2v⁵ 7v Nov 8] deep-bodied colt: half-brother to very smart US Grade 1 1¼m winner (also second in Breeders' Cup Classic) Deputy Commander (by Deputy Governor) and a winner in Hong Kong by Chief's Crown: dam won 16 races in France/USA, including US Grade 1 1½m winner: clearly best effort in maidens (fair form) when never-nearer fifth to Bugatti Royale at Nottingham: will be suited by 1¼m+: raced only on ground softer than good: looks type to make a better 3-y-o. *L. M. Cumani*

GIUNCHIGLIO 3 ch.g. Millkom 124 – Daffodil Fields (Try My Best (USA) 130) **73** [2002 8m 8m⁶ 8g⁶ 10g² Jun 15] 28,000Y: half-brother to several winners, including 1993 2-y-o 5f/6f winner Petula (by Petong): dam, maiden, stayed 1½m: fair maiden: good second in minor event at Nottingham final start: will stay at least 1½m: raced only on good/good to firm going. *P. J. Makin*

GIUST IN TEMP (IRE) 3 b.c. Polish Precedent (USA) 131 – Blue Stricks (Bluebird **59 ?** (USA) 125) [2002 9s 8m 10m p10g Dec 30] quite attractive colt: fifth foal: half-brother to several winners in Italy, including useful sprinter Della Scala (by Marju): dam, Italian 2-y-o 5f/6f winner, out of half-sister to 2000 Guineas winner Tirol: easily best effort (modest form) on second start: left L. Cumani after next outing. *P. W. Hiatt*

GIVE A LITTLE BACK (IRE) 4 b.g. College Chapel 122 – Daroura (USA) (Forli – (ARG)) [2002 –: p6g f7g 8.2d 6m 10s May 13] big, strong gelding: type to carry condition: no form. *B. J. Curley*

GIVE AN INCH (IRE) 7 b.m. Inchinor 119 – Top Heights (High Top 131) [2002 –: –
16g 13s 16d⁵ 15d 17.5g 18d Oct 21] leggy, sparely-made mare: fair handicapper in 2000:
little form since. *W. Storey*

GIVEAWAY 7 ch.g. Generous (IRE) 139 – Radiant Bride (USA) (Blushing Groom –
(FR) 131) [2002 18s Mar 22] good-topped gelding: lightly raced on Flat: well beaten only
outing in 2002: tried tongue tied. *D. J. Wintle*

GIVE BACK CALAIS (IRE) 4 b.g. Brief Truce (USA) 126 – Nichodoula 65 95
(Doulab (USA) 115) [2002 98: 6m 7m⁶ 7m⁵ 7f⁶ p7g Nov 23] strong, compact gelding:
useful handicapper: good fifth in valuable event at Ascot third start: stays 7f: raced only
on good ground or firmer on turf (lacklustre effort only all-weather outing): blinkered
once at 3 yrs. *P. J. Makin*

GIVE HIM CREDIT (USA) 2 b.c. (Feb 1) Quiet American (USA) – Meniatarra 69
(USA) 68 (Zilzal (USA) 137) [2002 7d 6s⁴ Oct 28] small, sturdy colt: first foal: dam
twice-raced half-sister to Lammtarra out of Oaks winner Snow Bride: better effort in
maidens at Leicester (fair form) when fourth to Soyuz, fading: bred to be suited by 1m+:
sold 13,000 gns. *E. A. L. Dunlop*

GIVEMETHEMOONLIGHT 3 ch.f. Woodborough (USA) 112 – Rockin' Rosie 62
59 (Song 132) [2002 68p: p6g⁴ 6m f6g⁵ f7g³ f8.5s³ Dec 9] sturdy filly: modest maiden:
stays 8.5f: acts on all-weather. *L. G. Cottrell*

GIVE NOTICE 5 b.g. Warning 136 – Princess Genista 108 (Ile de Bourbon (USA) 118
133) [2002 105: 16.2d* 20m⁵ 16m² 15.9g⁵ 20g* Oct 6]
  While a substantial increase in the prize-money on offer for the Prix du
Cadran - Casino Barriere de Cannes Croisette had the desired effect of preventing
yet another single-figure field, it did nothing to raise the quality of the race. The
first of the six Group 1 events on Longchamp's Arc card, the Prix du Cadran lacked
a high-class stayer—the Melbourne Cup seems a more attractive late-season target
for such horses nowadays—and the sixteen that turned up included an assortment
of handicappers and hurdlers who were merely making up the numbers. San
Sebastian, winner of the Cadran in 2000 and placed in the race a further three times

*Prix du Cadran - Casino Barriere de Cannes Croisette, Longchamp—Give Notice has to contend with
  Pushkin's late challenge; Polish Summer (No.1) is disqualified and Cut Quartz is promoted to third*

when trained by John Dunlop, was one of ten home-based runners, while Dunlop himself was responsible for one of the four British challengers, the five-year-old gelding Give Notice.

Had Give Notice lined up for the previous year's Cadran he would himself have been labelled as a handicapper, albeit a useful one, but his progress had continued at such a rate that he was one of the leading contenders for the latest edition, only the Grand Prix de Deauville winner Polish Summer and the nine-year-old Persian Punch starting at shorter odds than Give Notice. Give Notice had shown as early as his first start in the latest season that he had become a force to reckon with in the top staying races, winning the Bovis Homes Sagaro Stakes at Ascot by three and a half lengths from Persian Punch; and he subsequently ran well when four lengths fifth to Royal Rebel in the Gold Cup at Royal Ascot and when a length and a half second to Jardines Lookout in the Goodwood Cup, but had been below par when fifth to Boreas in the Lonsdale Stakes at York. Give Notice didn't need to improve on his best form to win the Cadran. Held up as usual at Longchamp, he stayed on under pressure in the straight to lead halfway through the final furlong and held on by a head from the strong-finishing Pushkin. With little more than four lengths covering the first eleven home, it was hardly surprising that one or two met

Give Notice (b.g. 1997)	Warning (b 1985)	Known Fact (b 1977)	In Reality
			Tamerett
		Slightly Dangerous (b 1979)	Roberto
			Where You Lead
	Princess Genista (b 1985)	Ile de Bourbon (br 1975)	Nijinsky
			Roseliere
		Queen of The Brush (b or br 1977)	Averof
			Little Miss

I. H. Stewart-Brown & M. J. Meacock's "Give Notice"

trouble in running in the closing stages, and both Polish Summer (third) and Persian Punch (fifth) were disqualified for causing interference. The Cadran was Give Notice's last race for the Dunlop stable. In November it was announced that he had been bought to race in Saudi Arabia.

Give Notice, by top miler Warning, has stamina in the bottom half of his pedigree. His dam Princess Genista, a winner at a mile, went on to show useful form over as far as fifteen furlongs, finishing fourth in the Prix Kergorlay; and his grandam Queen of The Brush, a winner at a mile and a half, is a half-sister to the very smart middle-distance stayer Old Country. Princess Genista has also produced a couple of useful performers at up to a mile by Soviet Star, namely Tsarnista and Sovinista, and one by Sure Blade who stays a mile and a half named Tomos. Her three-year-old colt by Elmaamul, Heir To Be, won a two-mile handicap for Dunlop in October. The tall, sparely-made Give Notice, a genuine and consistent sort, stays two and a half miles well and acts on firm and soft going. *J. L. Dunlop*

GIVERAND 3 b.f. Royal Applause 124 – Petersford Girl (IRE) 84 (Taufan (USA) 119) [2002 p6g Dec 18] 10,000F, 1,500Y: third foal: half-sister to 1999 2-y-o 1m winner Storm (by Prince of Birds): dam 6f winner: 33/1, in rear in maiden at Lingfield. *Miss Jacqueline S. Doyle*   –

GIVIMANINCH 2 ch.g. (Mar 1) Inchinor 119 – Tea And Scandals (USA) (Key To The Kingdom (USA)) [2002 6m 6m 6s Oct 25] 16,000Y: half-brother to high-class sprinter Ron's Victory (by General Holme) and French 1m and 9.5f winner The Dude (by Owington): dam French 6f winner: modest form in maidens: raced freely first 2 starts, but should stay 7f: gelded after final start. *D. R. C. Elsworth*   56

GIVRE (IRE) 4 b.g. Houmayoun (FR) 114 – Interj (Salmon Leap (USA) 131) [2002 51: 12.4g⁵ 12m 17.1m Jun 10] strong gelding: modest handicapper: broke down badly at Pontefract in June: stayed 1½m: raced mainly on good going or softer: dead. *R. A. Fahey*   60

GLADSTONE SPIRIT (IRE) 2 b.g. (Apr 16) Woodborough (USA) 112 – Alpencrocus (IRE) (Waajib 121) [2002 5m 7g 6g 5g Jul 6] IR 13,000Y: smallish, strong gelding: fourth foal: half-brother to a winning sprinter in Italy by Forest Wind: dam ran once in Ireland: modest maiden: blinkered, ran poorly in seller final start: free-going sort, likely to prove best at 5f/6f. *J. A. Glover*   53

GLADYS AYLWARD 2 b.f. (Mar 3) Polar Falcon (USA) 126 – Versami (USA) (Riverman (USA) 131) [2002 6g³ 5m³ 7g² 7.9m 6d⁴ 7d* Nov 5] 4,400Y: lengthy, usefullooking filly: second foal: half-sister to 3-y-o Yalla Lara: dam, lightly raced in Italy, sister to useful performers around 1m Underwater and Maze Garden: modest performer: won maiden at Catterick: will stay 1m: yet to race on extremes of going. *T. D. Easterby*   64

GLAMOUR (IRE) 3 b.f. Sadler's Wells (USA) 132 – Golden Reef (USA) (Mr Prospector (USA)) [2002 12.1v⁴ 14.1d⁴ Jul 13] eighth foal: half-sister to fairly useful 1¼m winner Murjana (by Pleasant Colony) and 3 winners in USA: dam, US Grade 2 2-y-o 6f winner, second in Grade 1 2-y-o 7f event: modest form in maidens at Chepstow and Salisbury: raced only on going softer than good. *H. R. A. Cecil*   63

GLAM ROCK 3 ch.f. Nashwan (USA) 135 – Band (USA) (Northern Dancer) [2002 10d* 10g⁴ 12.5g⁵ 12m³ Oct 12] fifth foal: closely related to 2-y-o winners Applaud (5f/6f in 1995, including Cherry Hinton) and Houston Time (7f in 1998), both by Rahy, and 7.5f/1¼m winner Sauterne (by Rainbow Quest), all useful, and half-sister to winner in USA by Seeking The Gold: dam maiden daughter of high-class sprinter Swingtime: useful form: won maiden at Windsor in August: creditable efforts in listed races at Longchamp and Maisons-Laffitte and Princess Royal Stakes at Ascot (3¾ lengths third of 4 to Love Everlasting) after: races freely, and may prove better at 1¼m than 1½m: yet to race on extremes of going: tends to hang right. *J. H. M. Gosden*   102

GLANBEHY (IRE) 2 b.f. (Apr 26) General Monash (USA) 107 – Ron's Secret 92 (Efisio 120) [2002 5g 5g* 5g⁴ 6g 6.1m 7m f6g³ f7g f7g⁴ f7s⁶ f7g⁶ Dec 17] IR 7,000Y: sparely-made filly: third foal: sister to 4-y-o Mon Secret: dam 1m/9f winner: modest performer: won seller at Leicester (for R. Hannon) in July: acts on fibresand: effective blinkered or not: sometimes looks none too keen. *J. A. Glover*   56

GLASS NOTE (IRE) 4 b.f. Spectrum 83 – Alice En Ballade (Tap On Wood 130) [2002 75: p12g 13m⁴ 12g Aug 28] IR 30,000Y: fifth foal: half-sister to French 1½m winner I Am The Chief (by Chief's Crown), later winner in Hong Kong: dam, French 1m winner, half-sister to dam of 1000 Guineas winner Las Meninas: fair performer: stays 13f: 67 acts on good to firm going, well held only outing on polytrack: sold €5,500 in November. *T. Stack, Ireland*

GLENBURN (IRE) 4 br.g. Dr Devious (IRE) 127 – Edwina (IRE) 63 (Caerleon – (USA) 132) [2002 64: 9m 7.1m 8m 7f Jun 3] good-bodied gelding: modest maiden at 3 yrs: well held in 2002: blinkered penultimate start: tongue tied last 3 starts. *I. Semple*

GLENDAMAH (IRE) 5 b.g. Mukaddamah (USA) 125 – Sea Glen (IRE) (Glenstal – (USA) 118) [2002 49: f8s 17.1m Jun 10] probably of little account nowadays. *J. R. Weymes*

GLENHURICH (IRE) 5 b.m. Sri Pekan (USA) 117 – Forli's Treat (USA) (Forli **55** (ARG)) [2002 52: 7v 8f² 9m² 7f² 8g 8f 9.2s³ 8.1m³ 8.8d³ 7.1d 9.1d⁶ 8g⁴ 8s³ 9m 8.3m⁵ Sep 30] lengthy, sparely-made mare: modest maiden handicapper: stays 9f: acts on firm and soft going. *J. S. Goldie*

GLEN PARKER (IRE) 9 ch.g. Bluebird (USA) 125 – Trina's Girl 78 (Nonoalco – (USA) 131) [2002 –: f8s⁶ f11s f11s f8g Jan 24] sturdy, good-bodied gelding: one-time fairly useful performer: no form in 2002: tried visored/blinkered. *R. F. Marvin*

GLENROCK 5 ch.g. Muhtarram (USA) 125 – Elkie Brooks 82 (Relkino 131) [2002 **73 d** 90: f5s f6g 6.1f³ 6f 7v f6g Dec 16] quite good-topped gelding: fairly useful performer at 4 yrs: on downgrade in 2002 (reportedly had chip removed from a hock after second outing): effective at 6f/7f: acts on any turf going and all-weather: has drifted right. *A. Berry*

GLEN VALE WALK (IRE) 5 ch.g. Balla Cove 119 – Winter Harvest (Grundy 137) **57** [2002 57: 10.5s 12g² 12.6m⁵ 12.1g 13.8m⁶ 10.5v 10m⁶ 10.3f⁵ 10m 11.9f² f12g⁴ 12s⁴ Nov 6] leggy gelding: modest handicapper: stays 1½m: acts on firm and soft going, probably on fibresand: tried blinkered: has wandered/found little: tends to race freely: none too consistent. *Mrs G. S. Rees*

GLENVIEWS POLLY (IRE) 2 b.f. (Mar 27) Poliglote 121 – Fun Board (FR) **55** (Saumarez 132) [2002 5g 6f 5g³ f7g* f7g³ f7f⁵ 7m f7g* f6s⁴ f6g² f7g² p7g² f8.5g f7g **a69** f6s² Dec 26] 2,000Y: leggy filly: second foal: dam placed up to 12.5f in France: fair on all-weather, modest on turf: won sellers at Wolverhampton in July (sold from A. Berry 7,750 gns) and September: runner-up in claimers/nursery after: stays 7f: acts on fibresand, best turf effort on good going: tried visored/in cheekpieces. *N. P. Littmoden*

GLENVIEWS PURCHASE (IRE) 2 b.f. (Jan 26) Desert Story (IRE) 115 – White- **74** throat (Artaius (USA) 129) [2002 6s 6m⁵ 5.7g* 6d 7g⁵ Aug 20] IR 37,000F: close-coupled filly: half-sister to 3 winners, including useful 7f (at 2 yrs) to 1¼m winner Resplendent Star (by Northern Baby) and fairly useful 2m winner Woodren (by Woodman): dam lightly-raced half-sister to Assert, Bikala and Eurobird: fair performer: won maiden at Bath in July: 100/1, seemed to run well when fifth of 6 to Bourbonnais in listed race at York final start: should stay at least 1m. *A. Berry*

GLISTENING SILVER 2 b.f. (Jan 22) Puissance 110 – Silver Blessings (Statoblest **49** 120) [2002 5.1d³ 5f⁶ 6.1d* 6m Jun 17] fourth foal: closely related to 3-y-o Secret Spoof: dam unraced half-sister to smart 5f/6f performer Sylvan Barbarosa: poor performer: left A. Berry after winning seller at Chepstow in June: something seemingly amiss only subsequent outing: stays 6f: acts on good to soft ground. *J. Gallagher*

GLITTER AND GLORY 3 b.g. Classic Cliche (IRE) 128 – Veuve (Tirol 127) [2002 **68** –: 10g 12.6m 16.2d f14.8g² f12g² f12f² f12g Dec 2] leggy, close-coupled gelding: has a splayed action: fair maiden: should stay 2m: acts on fibresand: found little final start: refused to enter stall second intended outing in 2002. *C. A. Cyzer*

GLOAMING 4 b.f. Celtic Swing 138 – Kandavu 87 (Safawan 118) [2002 67: p7g 8.5g **74 d** 6.1d* 6d 6f 6g f6g6 5.1g f6s f6g Dec 20] good-topped filly: fair performer at best: won handicap in April and minor event in May, both at Nottingham: on downgrade after: stays 6f: acts on firm going, good to soft and fibresand: blinkered once. *J. Gallagher*

GLOBAL CHALLENGE (IRE) 3 b.g. Sadler's Wells (USA) 132 – Middle Prospect **97** (USA) (Mr Prospector (USA)) [2002 8m 10m* 11.6d² May 25] big, rangy gelding: half-brother to winners in US by El Raggaas and Pleasant Tap: dam unraced: progressive form: won maiden at Pontefract in May: useful effort when second of 5 to In Disguise in minor event at Windsor next time (gelded after): will stay 1½m: yet to race on extremes of going: tends to wander under pressure. *Sir Michael Stoute*

GLOBAL POWER (IRE) 3 ch.c. Spinning World (USA) 130 – Petroleuse 104 – (Habitat 134) [2002 76: 8m Apr 20] angular, useful-looking colt: fair form on debut at 2 yrs: below form both starts after: dead. *W. R. Muir*

GLOBAL PRINCESS (IRE)   3 b.f. Dashing Blade 117 – Brandon Princess (Waajib – 121) [2002 86: 5d 5m 5m Jun 27] rather leggy, quite good-topped filly: fairly useful at 2 yrs: well held in handicaps in 2002: sold 3,000 gns. *I. A. Balding*

GLOBE RUNNER   9 b.g. Adbass (USA) 102 – Scenic Villa (Top Ville 129) [2002 f12g⁶ f16.2g⁶ Feb 22] one-time fair winner up to 1½m: fell fatally over hurdles in April. *Jonjo O'Neill*

GLORIOUS COLOURS   3 ch.f. Spectrum (IRE) 126 – Gaijin 97 (Caerleon (USA) **54** 132) [2002 8g⁶ 7.1m 10g 8.2v³ f8.5g⁵ f9.4f p10g Dec 30] sturdy filly: half-sister to **a46** several winners, notably high-class US 1m/9f performer Hawksley Hill (by Rahy), earlier 7f to 11f winner in Britain: dam, 2-y-o 6f winner, best at 7f: modest maiden: stays 1m: acts on heavy going: raced freely fourth start. *H. Candy*

GLORY AYR   3 b.f. Cool Jazz 116 – Sea-Ayr (IRE) 54 (Magical Wonder (USA) 125) – [2002 f6g Dec 27] first known foal: dam 7.5f/1m winner: slowly away and soon well behind in maiden at Southwell on debut. *B. Ellison*

GLORY DAYS (IRE)   4 ch.c. Lahib (USA) 129 – Gloire (Thatching 131) [2002 76: **66** p7g p6g 6g 6m p7g³ 7d 6m² 7m 6g 6m Aug 21] good-topped colt: fair performer: best at 5f/6f: acts on good to firm going, soft and polytrack: tried blinkered: saddle reportedly slipped penultimate start: sold 1,500 gns, sent to Spain. *R. Hannon*

GLORY QUEST (USA)   5 b.g. Quest For Fame 127 – Sonseri 95 (Prince Tenderfoot **76** (USA) 126) [2002 84: f8s³ f8.5g⁵ f8.5g⁵ f11g⁶ f9.4g p10g f16g 8m⁶ 7g⁴ 8d* 8.1m⁶ 9s⁶ 8m² p8g⁶ f8s³ 8v f8g⁵ f9.4g⁴ f12s³ f14.8g* f14.8g⁵ Dec 31] good-topped gelding: fair handicapper: won at Thirsk in May and Wolverhampton in December: stays 14.8f: acts on firm going, soft and all-weather: has been visored/blinkered: has worn cheekpieces: reliable. *Miss Gay Kelleway*

GLOSSY EYED (IRE)   3 ch.g. Eagle Eyed (USA) 111 – Hi-Gloss (IRE) (Be My Guest – (USA) 126) [2002 –: 8.3v 5.9g Jun 27] no sign of ability: tried blinkered. *C. J. Teague*

GOBLET OF FIRE (USA)   3 b.g. Green Desert (USA) 127 – Laurentine (USA) **105** (Private Account (USA)) [2002 85: 10d* 10.5m³ 12m 10m³ 10g 10g 10.3m² 9.7m* 9m 10.5m⁶ 10.1d³ 10g² 9f³ Oct 5] good-topped gelding: useful performer: won maiden at Nottingham in March and minor event at Folkestone (3 ran) in August: ran well when 1¾ lengths third to Beauchamp Pilot in Tote Cambridgeshire at Newmarket final start, though possibly shade flattered under enterprising ride: gelded after: stays 10.5f: acts on firm and good to soft going: sometimes wears crossed noseband: usually blinkered nowadays. *B. J. Meehan*

GODMERSHAM PARK   10 b.g. Warrshan (USA) 117 – Brown Velvet 68 (Mansingh – (USA) 120) [2002 –, a42: f8s f12g⁴ f16.2g Feb 8] one-time fair performer: well held in 2002: tried blinkered/visored. *P. S. Felgate*

GO FOR SUCCESS (USA)   2 b.g. (Jan 29) Royal Academy (USA) 130 – Barad **70** (Rainbow Quest (USA) 134) [2002 7m 7d Aug 9] unfurnished gelding: second foal: dam unraced close relation to Arazi and Noverre: fair form in mid-division in maidens: should be suited by at least 1m. *E. A. L. Dunlop*

GO GABANA   3 b.g. First Trump 118 – Have Form (Haveroid 122) [2002 64§: f7s² **53 §** p8g⁶ f9.4g³ f8s³ f9.4g⁴ f12g Mar 2] strong gelding: modest maiden: stays 9.4f: acts on fibresand, best turf effort on good going: blinkered/visored nowadays: sometimes slowly away/pulls hard/looks less than keen: unreliable. *N. P. Littmoden*

GO GO GIRL   2 ch.f. (Feb 22) Pivotal 124 – Addicted To Love 73 (Touching Wood **71** (USA) 127) [2002 6m 6m⁵ Sep 13] 15,000Y: third foal: half-sister to 7f/1m winner Unchain My Heart (by Pursuit of Love): dam, 1¼m to 1¾m winner, half-sister to 4-y-o Red Carpet (by Pivotal): better effort in maidens (fair form) when fifth to Tarjman at Goodwood, again forcing pace and no extra final 1f: has plenty of speed, and worth a try at 5f. *L. G. Cottrell*

GOING GLOBAL (IRE)   5 ch.g. Bob Back (USA) 124 – Ukraine Girl 121 (Targo- – wice (USA) 130) [2002 88: 16g 12g Oct 17] smallish, angular gelding: useful winner in 2000: lightly raced on Flat since: tried visored/tongue tied: winning hurdler. *G. L. Moore*

GOLAN (IRE)   4 b.c. Spectrum (IRE) 126 – Highland Gift (IRE) 95 (Generous **129** (IRE) 139) [2002 125: 12m* 10.4g² 12d⁶ 11f Nov 24]

The term 'curate's egg' originated in *Punch* magazine in the 1890s, when a cartoon drawn by George du Maurier featured a timid curate having breakfast in his bishop's home. The bishop's comment 'I'm afraid you've got a bad egg, Mr Jones' received the riposte: 'Oh, no, my Lord, I assure you that parts of it are excellent.' The expression is still in common usage, and Golan's career provided the perfect example. When he was good, as in the Two Thousand Guineas and the King George VI and Queen Elizabeth Diamond Stakes, he was very good indeed. But when he was off key, showing little interest in the Irish Derby and racing moodily in the Breeders' Cup Turf, he was less than satisfactory. Be that as it may, the decision to keep him in training after his classic season proved a wise one in light of his victory at Ascot, which was the best performance of his career.

Golan's connections excepted, nobody had anything to go on in the run-up to the King George as he had not been seen out since finishing sixth in the Japan Cup eight months before. There was no sign of him on the gallops in the spring and in May Sir Michael Stoute announced 'he's being prepared with a back-end campaign in mind and won't run until Ascot.' That he ran at Ascot, only a few days after the death of his owner-breeder Lord Weinstock, was the decision of the Weinstock family. The pick of his form, notably his defeat of Tamburlaine in the Guineas, second to Galileo in the Derby and fourth behind Sakhee in the Prix de l'Arc de Triomphe, put him with a chance in a race universally regarded as the most significant contest in the British calendar most years, but lacking a real top-class performer in the latest running. This is not to imply that the field was weak, since the winners of the Prince of Wales's Stakes (Grandera), Coronation Cup (Boreal), Prix Ganay (Aquarelliste), Dubai Sheema Classic (Nayef) and Hardwicke Stakes (Zindabad) were all running, along with Hardwicke second Storming Home, plus two pacemakers for Grandera. There would have been three more contestants had the ground not been on the firm side, since Sakhee, Millenary and High Pitched were all taken out on the day despite the executive's putting five millimetres of water on overnight. The most significant absentees, though, were the three-year-olds as a whole, making this the first King George since 1969 lacking any of the classic crop. There had been no British-trained three-year-old in the race in 1984 and 2000, and only one from that age group as a whole in 1970 with Nijinsky, 1990 with Belmez and 1997 with Kingfisher Mill. High Chaparral and Sulamani were being 'saved' for the big autumn races while Act One had been retired and Hawk Wing was believed to be heading for York, along with One Thousand Guineas and Oaks winner Kazzia. However, there is no reason to throw hands up in horror and start talking about a decline in the race's relevance. In the 'nineties there were at least three three-year-old challengers most years, including seven Derby winners, and five of the three-year-olds won. Coolmore ran Galileo in 2001, so on the face of it there is no prejudice against the King George in that camp, though they did say one reason for not running High Chaparral was because Galileo had had a hard race at Ascot, which might, in hindsight, have left its mark.

Be that as it may, there are other reasons for Ascot and the racing authorities to keep a close eye on the race's status. Arguably the value of the King George relative to other major prizes at a mile and a half has never been so high as it should be. At one point the situation was deteriorating but that seems to have stopped. In 1982 the King George was worth £126,472 to the winner, the Prix de l'Arc de Triomphe £165,016, the Derby £146,720 and the Irish Derby £104,516. By 1992 these figures had changed to £261,216, £588,929, £355,000 and £328,991. In the

King George VI and Queen Elizabeth Diamond Stakes, Ascot—in a race which attracted no three-year-olds, Golan (left) puts up a career-best effort on his belated return; he wears down Nayef as the pair pull clear, from left to right, Zindabad (third), Aquarelliste (fourth), Storming Home (sixth) and Grandera (fifth)

latest renewals, the values were £435,000, £574,993, £800,400 and £475,068. There is an argument that prize-money is not such a significant issue when a race has enormous prestige, but with the King George some way adrift of the Arc in value, and even further behind the Breeders' Cup Turf, Japan Cup and Hong Kong Vase, there must be some temptation for owners to give the race a miss, even with fully fit horses, and wait for the modern autumn cornucopia. The Grand Prix de Saint-Cloud, run at the end of June, has suffered a decline in competitiveness in recent times, presumably for the same reasons. From 1970 to 1981, thirty-five three-year-olds contested the race, with wins for Gyr, Rheingold, Riverqueen, Shakapour and Akarad and placings for such as Hard To Beat, Ela-Mana-Mou, Policeman and Bikala, all classic colts. From 1990 to 2002, fifteen three-year-olds ran, with only Helissio winning in 1996 and few classic colts taking their chance. The value of the Grand Prix de Saint-Cloud has dropped dramatically in the last decade. Apart from anything else, the allocation of extra funds to age-restricted events such as the Derby and Irish Derby is questionable when, by definition, they are less competitive than those open to all ages. A significant boost in prize-money for the King George, not to mention the Grand Prix de Saint-Cloud, would do no harm at all, and would almost certainly do some good, though the point has not yet been reached where there is a crisis in the offing for the Ascot race.

With any luck, 2003 will see three-year-olds back in the fray in the King George, though their absence from the latest edition did not prevent a marvellous finish. Grandera started 13/8 favourite on the strength of his crushing Royal Ascot victory, ahead of Zindabad and Golan at 11/2. Nayef, fourth in the Prince of Wales's Stakes, was 7/1 and Aquarelliste, below form when third in the Grand Prix de Saint-Cloud last time, 8/1. As a three-year-old Golan had looked as if he was still not fully developed, but he was a revelation at Ascot, really taking the eye (having recovered from a hind-leg infection which had ruled out his possible reappearance in the Eclipse). Golan was also a revelation in the race itself, under a magnificent ride by Kieren Fallon, who had the mount despite having lost it in the Japan Cup. Sir Effendi went straight to the front to do his job as pacemaker for Grandera from Zindabad while Golan, typically, was running a little lazily in last place, further back than intended judged on Stoute's subsequent comments. Zindabad led with five furlongs left, and approaching the home turn Golan was back on the bit and starting to make headway, bumping Grandera as he did so. Nayef looked the most likely winner when he went on with a quarter of a mile to go, with Golan still some way back and looking for a clear passage after being switched to the inside. Over a furlong out, a gap came between the leader and Zindabad and Fallon launched Golan through it like a man possessed. Golan responded splendidly to his rider's firm handling, drawing alongside Nayef a furlong out, heading him with fifty yards left and battling on to beat the equally tenacious runner-up, who drifted right under pressure, by a head. Zindabad was three and a half lengths away third with Aquarelliste, one paced in the closing stages, two lengths back in fourth and Grandera, almost certainly better at a mile and a quarter whatever his connections claimed about the watering having loosened the surface, a never-dangerous fifth. There is no reason to doubt the form—both the first two, proven Group 1 performers, had run the best races of their career, leaving the others behind in what was one of the best big-race finishes of the year. The victory was the highlight of the year for Fallon, whose strength in a finish is second to none. He notched his fifth jockeys' championship with 144 wins, eighteen ahead of Richard Hughes. This was Fallon's lowest winning total—he had scores of 202 in 1997, 204 in 1998, 202 in 1999 and 166 in 2001—and the lowest overall since Steve Cauthen won with 130 in 1984. If Golan showed his jockey to best advantage, he showed his trainer in a fine light too. Getting a horse fit to contest and win a championship event first time out is nothing new—Rock of Gibraltar and Golan himself in the Two Thousand Guineas are two notable recent examples—but no horse had previously won the King George on its seasonal debut. The closest were Lammtarra in 1995 and Swain in 1997, who both won after a single run, while the following year Swain had two runs. The average since the race started in 1951 is between three and four, with Nasram II, Dahlia, Grundy, Pawneese, The Minstrel and King's Theatre ahead of that on five. Golan had had a racecourse work-out at Newmarket a fortnight before Ascot but otherwise all the preparation had been done at home.

Exors of the late Lord Weinstock's "Golan"

Golan and Nayef met again in the Juddmonte International at York in August, with Nayef favourite at 6/4 and Golan at 9/4. A strong gallop, as in the Guineas and the King George, was a help for Golan, enabling him to move through the field and pick off the leaders, but Starbourne, leased as a pacemaker at York, did not do the job efficiently enough. Niggled along turning into the straight, Golan held every chance after looming alongside Nayef, who had gone to the front over two furlongs out, although getting to within a neck of the leader, he was unable to go past and at the finish Nayef was half a length to the good and, if anything, going away. A mile and a quarter almost certainly suits Nayef better than a mile and a half, whereas the reverse applied to Golan, though he lost no caste in defeat, and looked in fine fettle again. Regrettably, that was the last seen of Golan as an effective racehorse. Third favourite for the Prix de l'Arc de Triomphe, he was taken out of the race because his part-owners Coolmore favoured making the Japan Cup his main autumn objective. Golan tackled the Breeders' Cup Turf at Arlington first, starting second favourite to the odds-on High Chaparral. Golan ran a moody race, sluggish from the stalls, racing on and off the bridle and making no impression when switched wide with a lot to do off the home turn. At the line Golan was sixth of eight behind High Chaparral, way below his best, and a similar performance followed in the Japan Cup at Nakayama. The best horse in the race, judged on form in 2002, Golan started sixth favourite at nearly 19/1 in a market in which the local punters paid minimal attention to European form. Rousted along as soon as the stalls opened to hold a prominent position going into the first turn, Golan was unable to quicken after entering the finishing straight in third, eventually dropping back to seventh, under three lengths behind Falbrav. A below-par end to a campaign that had started so well.

			Rainbow Quest	Blushing Groom
	Spectrum (IRE)		(b 1981)	I Will Follow
	(b 1992)		River Dancer	Irish River
Golan (IRE)			(b 1983)	Dancing Shadow
(b.c. 1998)			Generous	Caerleon
	Highland Gift (IRE)		(ch 1988)	Doff The Derby
	(b 1993)		Scots Lass	Shirley Heights
			(b 1982)	Edinburgh

Golan, a rather leggy, close-coupled, attractive colt, who stayed a mile and a half and acted on firm and soft going, has been retired to Coolmore at a fee of €20,000 (around £13,000). That fee is smaller than might be expected for a winner of both the Two Thousand Guineas and the King George; Arc winner Sakhee's fee, for example, is £20,000. The problem with Golan is that his sire Spectrum has not really made the grade despite having had every chance, covering huge books at Coolmore. Spectrum's tally of mares in the last four years has been around six hundred and fifty, yet Golan is his only Group 1 winner in the northern hemisphere. The female side of Golan's pedigree has been covered in previous editions of *Racehorses*. To summarise, Golan's dam ran just three times, winning a mile-and-a-quarter maiden at Newbury. Highland Gift is a half-sister to the Gordon Stakes and Great Voltigeur winner Bonny Scot, also third in the St Leger, and is herself out of a half-sister (who won over thirteen furlongs) to an even stouter stayer Sought Out, winner of the Prix du Cadran. Golan's year-younger half-sister Mount Street (by Pennekamp) won a maiden over a mile and a quarter at Newmarket in June and Highland Gift's two-year-old, Highland Games (by Singspiel), finished tailed off in a similar event on the same course in November. Highland Gift's yearling is a colt by Cadeaux Genereux named Gift Voucher and she produced a filly by Spectrum in April but then was barren to Sadler's Wells. *Sir Michael Stoute*

GOLANO 2 gr.c. (Feb 17) Linamix (FR) 127 – Dimakya (USA) 83 (Dayjur (USA) **85** 137) [2002 8m² 7v² Nov 8] 85,000Y: rather leggy, quite good-topped colt: third foal: half-brother to 1999 2-y-o 6f winner Tereed Elhawa (by Cadeaux Genereux): dam, French 7.5f winner who probably stayed 1¼m, out of smart French/US performer around 1¼m Reloy: fairly useful form when second in maidens at Yarmouth and Doncaster (beaten ¾ length by Kingham in 16-runner race) in the autumn, prominent throughout both times: not sure to stay much beyond 1m. *C. F. Wall*

GOLD BOND (IRE) 3 b.g. Goldmark (USA) 113 – Mujadil Princess (IRE) (Mujadil **63** (USA) 119) [2002 p8g⁶ p8g⁵ p7g⁵ 7s 6d* Jun 14] 8,000Y: second foal: brother to 2000 2-y-o 5f seller winner Sima's Gold: dam unraced: modest performer: 25/1, won handicap at Goodwood (slowly away) in June: probably stays 1m: acts on good to soft going and polytrack. *P. Mitchell*

GOLDEN ARUBA 3 ch.g. Golden Lahab (USA) – Clover Girl (Spin of A Coin 88) **–** [2002 10m⁵ 12d Nov 5] first foal: dam no form: well beaten in maidens. *B. Ellison*

GOLDEN BOUNTY 3 b.c. Bahamian Bounty 116 – Cumbrian Melody 83 (Petong **101** 126) [2002 92: 6m 5g* 6m² 5.2d* 5g 5m 5m Sep 12] good-bodied colt: useful performer: first past post in handicap at Sandown in April and minor event at Newbury (originally demoted after beating Dragon Flyer a head having edged right, but reinstated on appeal) in May: ran poorly final start: barely stays 6f: acts on firm and good to soft going: sometimes swishes tail in paddock. *R. Hannon*

GOLDEN BRIEF (IRE) 4 ch.g. Brief Truce (USA) 126 – Tiffany's Case (IRE) 65 **66** (Thatching 131) [2002 57, a64: p7g⁶ p7g⁶ p7g p7g* f7g 7f* p8g⁵ 7.1g p7g⁶ 7m⁶ 7f 7m **a79** p8g⁴ 7.9m³ 6m 7g⁴ p7g⁵ p7g⁴ p7g* p7g⁶ p7g p7g* Dec 30] strong gelding: fair performer: won minor event at Lingfield in January, handicaps at Lingfield in March, Thirsk in April and Lingfield in November and claimer/handicap at Lingfield in December: best at 7f/easy 1m: acts on firm going and polytrack (little form on fibresand): usually wears blinkers/visor: has been tongue tied: flashes tail: sometimes slowly away. *K. R. Burke*

GOLDEN CHALICE (IRE) 3 ch.g. Selkirk (USA) 129 – Special Oasis (Green **98** Desert (USA) 127) [2002 8.2d² 8m² 8.3d² 8m² 8d* 8m 8d* Jul 13] 110,000Y: rather leggy, close-coupled gelding: first foal: dam unraced half-sister to smart/very smart 1¼m performers One So Wonderful and Alnasr Alwasheek, out of half-sister to Milligram: useful performer: won maiden at Goodwood in June and handicap at Salisbury (beat Ashkelon impressively by 4 lengths) in July: reportedly sustained pelvic injury after, and gelded: should stay 1¼m: yet to race on extremes of going: front runner. *I. A. Balding*

GOLDEN CHANCE (IRE) 5 b.g. Unfuwain (USA) 131 – Golden Digger (USA) 66 – §
(Mr Prospector (USA)) [2002 74§: f11s 10.4m 10g 8.9f f8g⁴ f12g⁶ f11g Dec 17] strong,
sturdy gelding: fair handicapper on his day at 4 yrs: little form in 2002. *M. W. Easterby*

GOLDEN DIXIE (USA) 3 ch.g. Dixieland Band (USA) – Beyrouth (USA) (Alleged **99**
(USA) 138) [2002 6m* 6m* 6m Sep 14] $80,000Y: first foal: dam, useful French 1m
winner and Grade 2 9f winner in USA, half-sister to smart 1¼m performer Flame Valley:
useful performer: reportedly required more than 100 stitches in injury sustained at
home before debut: won maiden at Salisbury (slowly away) in July and minor event at
Newcastle (beat Pic Up Sticks by 1¼ lengths, raced freely early) in August: below form
on handicap debut at Goodwood final start: raced only at 6f on good to firm going.
I. A. Balding

GOLDEN DRAGONFLY (IRE) 4 ch.g. Eagle Eyed (USA) 111 – Shanna (BEL) –
(River Smile (USA)) [2002 49d: f8.5g⁵ f8s⁶ 17.1f Apr 13] probably of little account
nowadays. *P. C. Haslam*

GOLDEN DUAL 2 b.c. (Feb 15) Danehill (USA) 126 – Golden Digger (USA) 66 (Mr **72 p**
Prospector (USA)) [2002 7s⁵ Oct 25] lengthy, good-topped colt: third foal: half-brother
to 3-y-o Naheef and 5-y-o Golden Chance: dam, maiden who failed to progress from only
start at 2 yrs, sister to dam of Irish Oaks/Nassau Stakes winner Lailani and half-sister to
very smart performers Always Fair (at 7f/1m) and Faithful Son (up to 1½m): 4/1, 14
lengths fifth of 12 to Barrissimo in maiden at Doncaster, fading: should do better.
B. W. Hills

GOLDEN FIELDS (IRE) 2 b.f. (Feb 24) Definite Article 121 – Quickstep Queen **50**
(FR) (Pampabird 124) [2002 8d 8g 7.1m Sep 16] lengthy filly: fourth foal: dam unraced:
modest form in maidens: sometimes races freely, but stays 1m. *A. P. Jarvis*

GOLDEN FIGHTER 2 ch.c. (Apr 5) Kendor (FR) 122 – Casting For Gold (IRE) **74 p**
(Hansel (USA)) [2002 7m Aug 23] lengthy, well-made colt: has scope: third foal: half-
brother to useful French 6f (at 2 yrs) and 1m winner Golden Gift (by Cadeaux Genereux):
dam unraced close relative to smart 1990 2-y-o 6f performer Mujtahid and half-sister to
smart middle-distance performers Just Happy and Tanaasa: 33/1, ninth of 16 to Almushahar in maiden at Newmarket, patiently ridden and not given hard time: sure to improve.
E. A. L. Dunlop

GOLDEN FORTUNA 4 b.f. Turtle Island (IRE) 123 – Shady Bank (USA) 62 **63**
(Alleged (USA) 138) [2002 66: f8g p10g³ 11.6d 10g⁴ 11g* Sep 29] fair performer at best:
form in Britain in 2002 only when third in handicap at Lingfield second start (left J. Hills
after next outing): won minor event at Tours in September: stays 11f: acts on good to firm
going and polytrack, probably on fibresand. *J. de Roualle, France*

GOLDEN HEART 2 ch.f. (Feb 5) Salse (USA) 128 – Lonely Heart 101 (Midyan **76**
(USA) 124) [2002 6m⁴ 6m⁶ 7m² 7m⁶ 8g² 8g² 7d⁴ p8g Dec 11] smallish, workmanlike
filly: second foal: half-sister to 3-y-o Ace of Hearts: dam 1¼m winner: fair maiden: in
frame 5 times: stays 1m: yet to race on extremes of going on turf, well held only all-
weather outing. *D. R. C. Elsworth*

GOLDEN HOURS 2 ch.f. (Mar 28) Timeless Times (USA) 99 – Strawberry Pink 87 **53**
(Absalom 128) [2002 5g⁴ 5d 5g 6.1m Sep 20] small, stocky filly: seventh foal: dam, 2-y-o
5f winner, out of very smart sprinter Polly Peachum: modest form in maidens: blinkered,
well held in nursery final start: will prove best at 5f/6f. *T. D. Easterby*

GOLDEN LARIAT (USA) 3 ch.c. Mr Prospector (USA) – Larrocha (IRE) 116 **89**
(Sadler's Wells (USA) 132) [2002 8m² 11.7f* Sep 8] second foal: half-brother to 9f
winner Razkalla (by Caerleon): dam, 1¼m/1½m winner, half-sister to Ardross: fairly
useful form: won maiden at Bath in August: respectable effort in handicap at Kempton
final start: stays 1½m: raced only on ground firmer than good. *Sir Michael Stoute*

GOLDEN LEGEND (IRE) 5 b.g. Last Tycoon 131 – Adjalisa (IRE) 65 (Darshaan –
133) [2002 69, a–: 10s 8g 8.1m 8.1g 8g 10m 10.2f 10.9m 7m Sep 3] useful-looking
gelding: fair handicapper at 4 yrs: little form in 2002: tried tongue tied. *R. J. Price*

GOLDEN LOCKET 5 ch.m. Beveled (USA) – Rekindled Flame (IRE) (Kings Lake **70**
(USA) 133) [2002 73d: f7g f7g* f7g* p7g f6g⁶ f7g 7m⁵ 7f* 7m⁴ f7g Sep 30] tall, **a61**
workmanlike mare: fair on turf, modest on all-weather: won claimer and handicap at
Wolverhampton in March and handicap at Newbury in July: stays 7f: acts on firm going,
good to soft and fibresand: sometimes races freely/carries head awkwardly: usually races
prominently. *A. P. Jarvis*

GOLDEN NUN 2 b.f. (Apr 19) Bishop of Cashel 122 – Amber Mill 96 (Doulab (USA) **98**
115) [2002 5f² 5.1f 6g² 6g⁴ 5g³ 6.1g³ 6m 5.1f* 5.2f 5m² 5.1m 6.5m* 6g⁴ 7f⁴ 6s* 6d² Nov

17] 10,000Y: angular filly: seventh foal: half-sister to 1997 2-y-o 5f winner Salamanca (by Paris House): dam 5f/6f winner, including at 2 yrs: useful performer: won maiden at Chester in July, nursery at Doncaster in September and 21-runner DBS October Yearling Stakes at Doncaster (beat stable-companion Cumbrian Venture by 6 lengths) in October: good length second to Pleasure Place in listed race at Rome final outing: probably best short of 7f: acts on firm and soft ground: swerved markedly left (would probably have won otherwise) sixth start: blinkered thereafter: probably best with exaggerated waiting tactics: somewhat quirky, but also tough and reliable. *T. D. Easterby*

GOLDEN RIDGE   3 ch.f. Salse (USA) 128 – Rubbiyati 56 (Cadeaux Genereux 131)   – [2002 10.2g 8.2m May 10] workmanlike filly: second foal: sister to 4-y-o Alsyati: dam, 8.3f winner at 4 yrs (only season to race), half-sister to high-class miler Air Express (by Salse): well held in maidens at Bath (very slowly away) then Nottingham (blinkered). *B. J. Meehan*

GOLDEN ROD   5 ch.g. Rainbows For Life (CAN) – Noble Form (Double Form 130)   **52 §** [2002 53, a64: f11g p10g² 11.9g f14.8g⁵ 11.8m 12m⁴ 12g f12g Sep 21] close-coupled,   **a64 §** angular gelding: modest handicapper: effective at 1¼m to 1¾m: acts on any turf going/all-weather: has bled from nose: usually races prominently: ungenuine. *P. W. Harris*

GOLDEN SHELL   3 ch.f. Hatim (USA) 121 – Sonnenelle 71 (Sonnen Gold 121)   – [2002 –: 9m 5s 5.9d 9.2v Jul 12] no form: reportedly finished lame on reappearance. *A. C. Whillans*

GOLDEN SILCA   6 ch.m. Inchinor 119 – Silca-Cisa 93 (Hallgate 127) [2002 115:   **115** 8.8g⁵ 8.9g⁴ 8.1d⁴ 9g⁵ 8.5s² 10m⁶ 8g² 9.9m 9.5f⁵ 8m⁵ 10g⁵ 9m* 10g 8d Nov 17] lengthy, sparely-made mare: smart performer: ended long losing sequence in listed event at Newmarket in October, sweeping through to beat Masterful by ½ length: best other efforts in 2002 when fourth to Terre A Terre in Dubai Duty Free at Nad Al Sheba on second outing and 1½ lengths second to Tashawak in Falmouth Stakes at Newmarket on seventh one: best at 1m to 1¼m: acts on firm and soft going: has won when edgy: usually held up: tough. *M. R. Channon*

GOLDEN SKIIS (IRE)   2 ch.f. (Mar 28) Hector Protector (USA) 124 – Ski For Gold   **68 p** 76 (Shirley Heights 130) [2002 7f 8s⁶ Oct 15] third foal: half-sister to 3-y-o Ski For Me: dam, 2-y-o 7f winner who may have proved best around 1¾m, half-sister to US Grade 1 1¼m winner Bequest: fair form, never dangerous, in maidens at Newbury (behind Trade Fair) and Leicester (behind Allergy): will be suited by 1¼m+: should do better. *J. L. Dunlop*

GOLDEN SONATA (USA)   3 b.f. Mr Prospector (USA) – Elissa Beethoven (Royal   **76 +** Academy (USA) 130) [2002 –: 10g 12m² p12g* a8f* Nov 26] tall, leggy filly: fair form: won maiden at Lingfield in September and, having left J. Noseda, allowance race at Churchill Downs in November: effective at 1m to 1½m: acts on polytrack/dirt, raced only on good/good to firm going on turf: hung and looked tricky ride second outing. *W. I. Mott, USA*

GOLDEN SPECTRUM (IRE)   3 ch.c. Spectrum (IRE) 126 – Plessaya (USA)   **86** (Nureyev (USA) 131) [2002 94: 7m² 6g* 7s⁵ 6m 7.1m² 7f 6m 7m 6g⁵ p7g p7g f6g⁴ Dec   **a78** 31] leggy, quite good-topped colt: good mover: fairly useful performer: won maiden at Salisbury in May: good second in handicap at Sandown fifth start: should prove best up to 1m: acts on firm ground and polytrack: tried tongue tied/in cheekpieces: none too consistent. *R. Hannon*

GOLDEN STRANDS   2 ch.f. (Apr 22) Primo Dominie 121 – Rosa Van Fleet (Sallust   – 134) [2002 5m 6g Sep 19] 8,000Y: leggy filly: half-sister to several winners, including useful Irish 9f (at 2 yrs) and 1½m winner Buddy Marvel (by Law Society) and unreliable 1998 2-y-o 6f winner Midnight Orchid (by Petardia): dam, Irish maiden, half-sister to 2000 Guineas winner To-Agori-Mou: well held in maidens: sold 2,200 gns. *A. Berry*

GOLDEVA   3 gr.f. Makbul 104 – Gold Belt (IRE) 61 (Bellypha 130) [2002 85+: 6g²   **102** 8f⁶ 6d* 7m 6m 6v³ Nov 9] leggy filly: has a quick action: useful performer: best effort when winning handicap at Ascot in August: creditable 3¼ lengths third to Tom Tun in listed race at Doncaster final start: best form at 6f: has won on firm going, best efforts on good or softer (acts on heavy). *R. Hollinshead*

GOLD FERVOUR (IRE)   3 b.g. Mon Tresor 113 – Fervent Fan (IRE) 65 (Soviet   – Lad (USA)) [2002 50: 6f 7.2g 7.1d Aug 8] quite good-topped gelding: modest maiden at 2 yrs: well held in 2002: headstrong. *W. M. Brisbourne*

GOLD GUEST   3 ch.c. Vettori (IRE) 119 – Cassilis (IRE) (Persian Bold 123) [2002   **87 +** 91: 6g 7.5m⁵ 7m 8m Jun 20] leggy colt: fairly useful performer: creditable eighth in

Britannia Handicap at Royal Ascot (slowly away) final start: barely stays 1m: acts on soft and good to firm ground: sold 6,000 gns in October. *G. G. Margarson*

GOLD HEART (IRE) 3 b.f. Entrepreneur 123 – Soha (USA) 58 (Dancing Brave (USA) 140) [2002 7g Apr 19] 92,000F, 75,000Y: good-topped filly: poor walker: fifth foal: half-sister to 3 winners, notably smart 1m/9f winner Gold Academy (by Royal Academy): dam, second at 1½m, daughter of Oaks d'Italia winner Paris Royal: 16/1 and unimpressive to post, tailed off in newcomers race at Newbury. *R. Hannon* —

GOLDIE 4 b.f. Celtic Swing 138 – Hotel California (IRE) 58 (Last Tycoon 131) [2002 80: p8g 8.5g⁵ 8m p8g Nov 13] leggy, sparely-made filly: fairly useful at 3 yrs: modest form in 2002: stays easy 8.5f: acts on polytrack, firm and good to soft going: tongue tied (slowly away) on reappearance: sometimes races freely. *D. J. Coakley* **63**

GOLD MEDALLIST 2 ch.c. (Apr 13) Zilzal (USA) 137 – Spot Prize (USA) 108 (Seattle Dancer (USA) 119) [2002 8m⁶ 8g³ 8s Oct 26] tall colt: fourth foal: half-brother to 5-y-o Premier Prize and 4-y-o Prize Dancer: dam, 2-y-o 5f winner, fourth in Oaks: best effort (fairly useful form) when 1¾ lengths third to Constantine in maiden at Salisbury: should be suited by at least 1¼m: acts on good to firm ground, well held on soft. *R. C. Elsworth* **81**

GOLD MILLENIUM (IRE) 8 gr.g. Kenmare (FR) 125 – Gold Necklace 86 (Golden Fleece (USA) 133) [2002 p16g² Nov 27] tall gelding: modest handicapper: short-head second of 14 to High Point at Lingfield, only outing since 2000: stays 16.4f: acts on firm going and polytrack: has idled. *C. A. Horgan* **59**

GOLDON FRIENDSHIP (IRE) 3 b.f. College Chapel 122 – Claire's Thatch (Thatch (USA) 136) [2002 51: 7m 7f f6g Jun 19] angular filly: modest maiden at 2 yrs: no form in 2002 (carried head awkwardly on reappearance). *J. R. Weymes* —

GOLD POINT (IRE) 3 b.g. Goldmark (USA) 113 – Flashing Raven (IRE) (Maelstrom Lake 118) [2002 82: 10g³ p8g 10m² 8.5f⁶ 8.5f² 9f² 8.5f⁴ Sep 11] quite good-topped gelding: fairly useful performer: placed in minor event at Kempton, handicap at Newmarket (left A. Jarvis after) and 2 allowance races at Del Mar: will stay bit beyond 1¼m: acts on firm going. *R. B. Hess jnr, USA* **93**

GOLD RING 2 ch.g. (Feb 8) Groom Dancer (USA) 128 – Indubitable 87 (Sharpo 132) [2002 7d⁶ 8.1g⁵ 8g⁴ 8d³ Nov 1] leggy, workmanlike gelding: half-brother to 1¼m winners Bronzino (by Midyan) and Cugina (by Distant Relative), latter useful: dam 1¼m winner who stayed 1¾m: fairly useful maiden: best effort when fourth to Calibre at Newmarket: well-beaten last of 3 in minor event there final start: will be suited by 1¼m+. *G. B. Balding* **81**

GOLD RIVIERA (USA) 2 ch.c. (May 25) Irish River (FR) 131 – Raj Dancer (USA) (Rahy (USA) 115) [2002 5.7f⁶ 5m² 6.1m 6g Oct 17] $11,000Y, 17,000 2-y-o: good-bodied colt: third foal: half-brother to a winner in USA by Unbridled's Song: dam unraced half-sister to dam of Breeders' Cup Turf winner Kotashaan: clearly best effort (fair form) when 3 lengths second of 4 to Queensway Quay in minor event at Redcar, best work final 1f: last in maiden and nursery after: should stay at least 1m. *M. C. Pipe* **69 ?**

GOLD STANDARD (IRE) 4 ch.g. Goldmark (USA) 113 – Miss Audimar (USA) (Mr Leader (USA)) [2002 86: 14.1m 14.8g 14g⁶ 16f 16m 14.1g⁶ p12g⁴ Oct 4] rather unfurnished gelding: fluent mover: fairly useful handicapper at 3 yrs: on downgrade in 2002: probably best at 1¾m/2m: acts on firm going, probably on polytrack: usually makes running: sold 16,000 gns. *D. R. C. Elsworth* **67 d**

GOLFAGENT 4 b.g. Kris 135 – Alusha 88 (Soviet Star (USA) 128) [2002 8.3s 9.2g 10d 8f f14.8g⁵ f16.2f 14m⁵ 15.8f 17.1f² 18d Oct 21] small gelding: poor maiden handicapper: stays 17f: acts on firm going: usually tongue tied nowadays. *P. D. Evans* **48**

GONDOLIN (IRE) 2 b.g. (Mar 1) Marju (IRE) 127 – Galletina (IRE) 74 (Persian Heights 129) [2002 7f p7g³ Oct 16] workmanlike gelding: first foal: dam, Irish 1¾m/2m winner, also won over hurdles: well-backed favourite, better effort in maidens (fairly useful form) when 3½ lengths third of 16 to Grand Passion at Lingfield, hampered early: gelded after: should be suited by 1¼m+: should progress. *G. A. Butler* **80 p**

GONE'N'DUNNETT (IRE) 3 b.g. Petardia 113 – Skerries Bell 71 (Taufan (USA) 119) [2002 58d: 8.2d 6f⁶ 5.3m⁵ 5f f6g³ 5.3m² 5m³ p5g⁴* 5m 5g 5.3m⁴ 5m⁵ 6m 5f f6g³ f6s⁶ f6g* f5f² f5g⁴ Dec 14] strong gelding: fairly useful on all-weather, modest on turf: won maiden at Lingfield in July and handicap at Southwell in November: best at 5f/6f: best turf efforts on good to firm/firm ground, acts on all-weather: usually blinkered/visored, wore cheekpieces last 3 starts: usually races prominently. *Mrs C. A. Dunnett* **58 a80**

GONE TOO FAR   4 b.g. Reprimand 122 – Blue Nile (IRE) 70 (Bluebird (USA) 125)   **63**
[2002 62: f12s⁵ 14.1d* 14.1d 12m 14d⁴ 16g 17.1m Aug 18] sparely-made gelding:
modest handicapper: made all at Nottingham in April: below form last 2 starts: probably
stays easy 2m: acts on firm and good to soft ground (well held only outing on fibresand):
usually blinkered in 2002: possibly best making running. *M. Dods*

GONFILIA (GER)   2 b.f. Big Shuffle (USA) 122 – Gonfalon (Slip Anchor 136)   **96 p**
[2002 6g* 8s* Nov 3] sister to 3 winners in Germany, notably smart performer up to 9f
Gonlargo (later successful in Hong Kong), and half-sister to 2 winners in Germany,
including useful performer up to 1¼m Gorlor (by Lando): dam unraced sister to useful
stayer Gondolier: 6-length winner of maiden at Dortmund in September and national
listed race at Hanover (in good style, from Bayadere) in November: should stay beyond
1m: joined Godolphin: likely to improve further. *U. Ostmann, Germany*

GOODBYE GOLDSTONE   6 b.g. Mtoto 134 – Shareehan (Dancing Brave (USA)   **67**
140) [2002 –: 9.7m 10m⁴ 11.6s* 11.8m 11.9g Oct 24] sparely-made gelding: fair handicapper, lightly raced: won at Windsor in May: stays 1½m: best on ground softer than good
(acts on heavy). *T. P. McGovern*

GOODBYE MR BOND   2 b.g. (Feb 23) Elmaamul (USA) 125 – Fifth Emerald 54   **–**
(Formidable (USA) 125) [2002 7.1m 7.1m 6g Oct 18] 9,000Y: strong, lengthy gelding:
first foal: dam, 1m winner, out of close relation to smart middle-distance filly Valley of
Gold: no sign of ability. *E. J. Alston*

GOODBYE MRS CHIPS   3 ch.f. Zilzal (USA) 137 – Happydrome (Ahonoora 122)   **55**
[2002 6d² 5s⁶ 7m³ 7m 6g 6g 5.9g 7.5m⁴ 7f³ 7d 8d f8g Nov 26] rather leggy, quite
good-topped filly: fifth foal: sister to 11.5f seller winner Tremor: dam unraced: modest
maiden handicapper: should stay 1m: acts on firm and good to soft ground: tongue tied
last 6 starts. *J. D. Bethell*

GOOD DAY SUNSHINE   2 b.f. (Feb 25) Young Ern 120 – Amathus Glory 76   **30**
(Mummy's Pet 125) [2002 f5g⁴ 5.1d⁶ 5m f5s 6.1d 6d Jun 13] sixth foal: half-sister to 1997
2-y-o 7f seller winner Rock From The Sun (by Rock City) and a winner in Greece by
Rudimentary: dam 2-y-o 5f winner: bad maiden. *W. G. M. Turner*

GOODENOUGH MOVER   6 ch.g. Beveled (USA) – Rekindled Flame (IRE)   **92**
(Kings Lake (USA) 133) [2002 80: 7g² 7.1s 7.1g² 7g* 7m* 7m* 6g⁶ 7f² 8g p7g⁶ p7g²
Nov 27] rangy gelding: fairly useful performer: better than ever in 2002, winning ladies
minor event at Brighton and handicaps at Salisbury (apprentices) and Lingfield in
August/September: has won at 1m, probably best at 6f/7f: acts on polytrack, soft and
good to firm going: front runner. *J. S. King*

GOOD FORM (IRE)   2 b.g. (Apr 26) Danetime (IRE) 121 – Faapette (Runnett 125)   **57**
[2002 6.1s 5m p6g 7.5g³ 8m⁴ 8.3d f8.5s Dec 9] IR 7,000Y: half-brother to several
winners, including Irish 1990 2-y-o 5f winner Bellerofonte (by Tate Gallery) and untrustworthy 11.6f winner Cross Dall (by Blues Traveller): dam Irish 2-y-o 1m winner: modest
maiden: well held in sellers last 2 starts: barely stays 1m: acts on good to firm ground and
polytrack. *R. M. Beckett*

GOOD GIRL (IRE)   3 b.f. College Chapel 122 – Indian Honey (Indian King (USA)   **100**
128) [2002 100: 7m⁶ 6d⁶ 6.1d 5g 5m² 6m⁴ 5f 5g 5.6m 6g 5g⁴ 5s Oct 26] workmanlike
filly: useful performer: mostly creditable efforts in 2002, including when second to Rozel
in handicap at Doncaster in June: best at 5f/6f: acts on good to firm and good to soft
going, ran poorly on soft final start: blinkered nowadays: usually edgy, and sometimes
early to post: usually races up with pace. *T. D. Easterby*

GOOD HEALTH   2 b.f. (Feb 21) Magic Ring (IRE) 115 – Fiddling 82 (Music Boy   **78**
124) [2002 5m⁵ 5s⁵ 5f* 5g⁵ 5m⁵ 5m⁵ 5.1m³ 6.5m Sep 11] 17,000Y: leggy, workmanlike
filly: fifth reported foal: dam, 5f winner, sister to useful sprinter Clantime: fair performer:
won minor event at Redcar in June: good efforts in nurseries sixth/seventh starts:
probably best at 5f: acts on firm and soft ground: often forces pace. *A. Bailey*

GOOD LOSER (IRE)   2 b.g. (Apr 15) Mujadil (USA) 119 – Cockney Star (IRE)   **67**
(Camden Town 125) [2002 6.1g⁶ 7m* 7m 7.1m⁵ Sep 6] IR 8,000Y: third foal: dam
unraced sister to smart Irish mare (best at 1¼m) Cockney Lass: fair form: best effort when
winning claimer at Salisbury (for P. Hobbs) in August: tongue tied, not disgraced final
start: should stay 1m: seemed ill at ease on course at Epsom third outing. *D. Nicholls*

GOODNESS GRACIOUS (IRE)   2 b.f. (Apr 11) Green Desert (USA) 127 – Trois   **89 p**
Graces (USA) (Alysheba (USA)) [2002 7f 7d* Nov 2] leggy filly: third reported foal:
half-sister to 3-y-o Flat Spin: dam, French 1m winner, half-sister to smart French sprinter/
miler Crack Regiment and to Prix de l'Abbaye second La Grande Epoque: 16/1, much

better effort in Newmarket maidens when winning 19-runner race by 2 lengths from Ocean Silk, travelling strongly and running on well having been switched: should stay at least 1m: likely to prove useful at least. *J. L. Dunlop*

GOOD STANDING (USA)   4 b.f. Distant View (USA) 126 – Storm Dove (USA)   **93**
108 (Storm Bird (CAN) 134) [2002 91: f8s² Jan 1] rather leggy filly: fairly useful handicapper: good second at Southwell only start in 2002: may prove best around 1m: acts on fibresand, soft and good to firm going. *B. W. Hills*

GOOD TIMING   4 bl.g. Timeless Times (USA) 99 – Fort Vally 58 (Belfort (FR) 89)   **–**
[2002 61: 7.5d 7m 8g f8g Dec 27] lengthy, sparely-made gelding: maiden handicapper: little form in 2002. *J. J. Quinn*

GOODWOOD HOUSE (IRE)   3 ch.f. Grand Lodge (USA) 125 – Business Centre   **–**
(IRE) 58 (Digamist (USA) 110) [2002 7s⁶ Jun 13] 25,000Y: rather leggy filly: third foal: dam, placed at 6.5f in Ireland, from family of 2000 Guineas winner Doyoun: 20/1, well held in maiden at Newbury: sold 1,500 gns in October, sent to Kuwait. *J. L. Dunlop*

GOODWOOD PRINCE   2 b.g. (Apr 2) Emperor Jones (USA) 119 – Scarlet Lake 60   **84**
(Reprimand 122) [2002 6s³ 6m⁴ 6m² 6m* 6.1s Oct 23] 10,000F, 13,000Y: third foal: half-brother to 4-y-o Polar Kingdom and 3-y-o Maid For Running: dam, lightly-raced half-sister to useful sprinters Maid For The Hills and Maid For Walking: fairly useful form: won maiden at Brighton in August by 3 lengths from Magic Piper: gave impression something amiss final start (gelded after): will stay 7f: acts on soft and good to firm going. *J. L. Dunlop*

GOODWOOD PROMISE   3 b.c. Primo Dominie 121 – Noble Destiny 89 (Dancing   **53**
Brave (USA) 140) [2002 55: 5.7g 6f 6.1m 6.1d 5d⁴ 5f 6g 5d 7g 6g 6m⁶ 6m Sep 4] neat colt: modest maiden: effective at 5f/6f: acts on good to soft ground. *J. M. Bradley*

GOOGOOSH (IRE)   3 b.f. Danehill (USA) 126 – Literary 79 (Woodman (USA) 126)   **–**
[2002 77: 8.3d Aug 11] lengthy filly: fair maiden at 2 yrs: well beaten only start in 2002: has run creditably in blinkers: has raced freely/hung left. *E. A. L. Dunlop*

GOOSE FARM   2 b.f. (Mar 15) Silver Wizard (USA) 117 – Mystical 77 (Mystiko   **–**
(USA) 124) [2002 7m f6s Dec 26] first foal: dam 5f/6f winner: well held in maiden (for G. McCourt) and claimer. *J. W. Unett*

GO POLAR   2 b.f. (May 5) Polar Falcon (USA) 126 – Twilight Patrol 96 (Robellino   **81**
(USA) 127) [2002 6m⁵ 6d³ 6f³ 6f² 5g Oct 5] 11,500F: third foal: half-sister to 3-y-o Curfew: dam 6f (at 2 yrs) to 1m winner: fairly useful maiden: good neck second of 4 to Sharpbill in minor event at Goodwood: last in nursery at Sandown final start: should prove at least as effective at 5f as 6f: acts on firm ground: edged left/flashed tail second outing. *J. Cullinan*

GORDONS FRIEND   4 ch.g. Clantime 101 – Auntie Fay (IRE) (Fayruz 116) [2002   **47**
50: 8m 7g 7f 7.1g⁵ 8m 5.9d 8m* 6.9d 8g Aug 12] smallish gelding: poor performer: won selling handicap at Musselburgh in July: effective at 6f to 1m: acts on good to firm and good to soft going: sometimes visored, including last 4 starts: none too consistent. *B. S. Rothwell*

GORETSKI (IRE)   9 b.g. Polish Patriot (USA) 128 – Celestial Path 101 (Godswalk   **71 d**
(USA) 130) [2002 74: p5g³ f5g³ 5.1d 5s 5m 5m 5g 5.1d 5g² 5s⁶ 5v 5d 5m⁶ 5g 5s³ 5m f5g 5d Nov 5] tall gelding: unimpressive mover: fairly useful handicapper at best, winner of 19 races: only fair at best in 2002: won at 6f, showed best form at 5f: acted on all-weather, best recent turf form on good going or softer: often blinkered earlier in career (well held only try in 2002): sometimes sweated profusely: usually raced prominently: tough. *N. Tinkler*

GORGEOUS GEORGE   3 b.g. Young Ern 120 – Cee Beat § (Bairn (USA) 126) [2002   **–**
8.2v Oct 29] fourth foal: dam temperamental half-sister to useful winner around 7f Sharpalto: 20/1, slowly away and always behind in maiden at Nottingham. *E. A. Wheeler*

GORT NA GCAPPILL   9 b.g. Presidium 124 – Ranipa (Raga Navarro (ITY) 119)   **–**
[2002 f8.5g Jul 26] first foal: dam unraced: tailed off in claimer at Wolverhampton, looking reluctant. *O. O'Neill*

GO SHEEK (IRE)   2 b.f. (Apr 12) Kahyasi 130 – Terrama Sioux (Relkino 131) [2002   **55 p**
6d⁶ 7d Nov 5] IR 9,500Y: half-sister to several winners, including 3-y-o Indian Solitaire and 1½m winner Dakota Brave (by Exactly Sharp): dam unraced: modest form when never-nearer sixth to Night Games in maiden at Pontefract: well held in similar event at Catterick: should do better at 1¼m+. *J. J. Quinn*

GOSHIN'S LAD (USA)   3 b.c. Nicholas (USA) 111 – Maratha (USA) (Devil's Bag   **90**
(USA)) [2002 67p: p8g* p7g⁴ a8.5f⁴ 9f⁵ a7f 8.5f² 11f 8.5g a8f Dec 4] fairly useful

performer: won handicap at Lingfield in January: left G. Butler after next start: creditable efforts in US only when in frame in non-graded event at Aqueduct in February and claimer at Saratoga in August: trained by M. Stidham for fourth outing only, then returned to previous trainer: best efforts at 7f to 8.5f: acts on firm going, polytrack and dirt: tongue tied last 3 outings in Britain. *R. E. Schosberg, USA*

GOSSAMER 3 b.f. Sadler's Wells (USA) 132 – Brocade 121 (Habitat 134) [2002 **118** 114p: 8m 8s* 8m 8g³ 10d⁵ Oct 26]

Gossamer's owner-breeder Gerald Leigh, whose death from cancer was announced in June, entered the racing world relatively late in life after making his fortune as a property developer. Through good judgement and sound business acumen he established himself as one of the most successful thoroughbred breeders in Britain with a smallish broodmare band at Eydon Hall Farm in Northampton-shire, the base for his breeding operation from the early-'eighties after the switch from Cayton Park Stud, purchased by Leigh in 1973. Among the winners bred by Leigh were: Bosra Sham, winner of the Fillies' Mile in 1995 and the One Thousand Guineas and Champion Stakes in 1996; Markofdistinction, successful in the Queen Elizabeth II Stakes in 1990; and Act One, who won the Criterium International in 2001 and the Prix Lupin in the latest season. Leigh also owned Infamy, winner of the Rothman's International in 1988, and Bequest, a Grade 1 winner in the States in 1991. But it was with Gossamer's family that he enjoyed the most success. Canton Silk, one of Leigh's foundation mares at Cayton Park, foaled several winners but the best of her offspring was Gossamer's dam Brocade. Brocade became the first home-bred Group 1 winner for Leigh when winning the Prix de la Foret in 1985, and she went on to become an excellent broodmare. Her most high-profile winner so far is Barathea (erronously reported in Gossamer's essay in *Racehorses of 2001* never to have raced beyond a mile, though he came a non-staying fifth in the Derby). Barathea's successes included the 1993 Irish Two Thousand Guineas and the 1994 Breeders' Cup Mile, the latter win prompting Leigh to reflect: 'It was an overwhelming moment. It drew together all the elements of my involvement in racing and breeding over twenty-five years.'

It seems perhaps fitting, therefore, that Leigh's final winner should be Barathea's sister Gossamer. She ran out a clear-cut winner of the Entenmann's Irish One Thousand Guineas at the Curragh after starting 4/1 favourite in a field of fifteen. Gossamer had flopped when a short-priced favourite to make a winning reappearance in the One Thousand at Newmarket, where she was attempting to retain an unbeaten record after a three-race juvenile campaign culminating in an emphatic victory in the Fillies' Mile at Ascot; the absence of the sidelined Cheveley Park winner Queen's Logic seemed to make Gossamer's task more straightforward, but she managed only a never-dangerous eighth of seventeen to Kazzia at New-market in a muddling race run on good to firm ground. Gossamer more than made amends under much softer conditions at the Curragh, despite failing to impress in

Entenmann's Irish 1000 Guineas, the Curragh—a striking performance from Gossamer; Aidan O'Brien trains five of the next six home, including (from left to right) Quarter Moon, Starbourne and Alstemeria

the paddock beforehand. Travelling strongly under restraint just behind the leaders, Gossamer sprinted clear over a furlong out for a comfortable success by four and a half lengths. Of the next six home, Aidan O'Brien was responsible for five, including Newmarket Guineas fifth Quarter Moon, Starbourne and Alstemeria, who finished second, third and fourth respectively; the Poule d'Essai des Pouliches winner Zenda seemed ill-suited by the ground and finished tailed off. Gossamer's performance suggested she was in for a good season, but she was beaten on her three other outings. Encountering firmish ground again in the Coronation Stakes at Royal Ascot, Gossamer was a very disappointing favourite, trailing in last of eleven behind Sophisticat, after which she was not seen out until early-September. In the Prix du Moulin at Longchamp, taking on colts for the first time, Gossamer finished two lengths third of seven to Rock of Gibraltar, doing all her best work at the finish. Then, on her final outing, tackling a mile and a quarter for the first time in the steadily-run Breeders' Cup Filly And Mare Turf at Arlington in October, Gossamer again ran creditably when two and a half lengths fifth of twelve to Starine, unable to quicken after racing in touch.

		Northern Dancer	Nearctic
Gossamer (b.f. 1999)	Sadler's Wells (USA) (b 1981)	(b 1961)	Natalma
		Fairy Bridge (b 1975)	Bold Reason
			Special
	Brocade (b 1981)	Habitat (b 1966)	Sir Gaylord
			Little Hut
		Canton Silk (gr 1970)	Runnymede
			Clouded Lamp

The Leigh Family - CancerBACUP's "Gossamer"

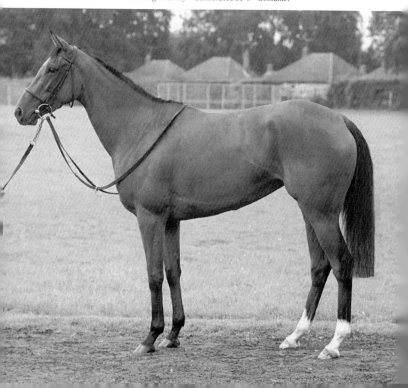

Shortly before his death, Leigh called on thoroughbred breeders to cut the size of stallion books, whose exponential growth, in his opinion, was potentially financially damaging to the bloodstock industry and would also prove detrimental to the future of the thoroughbred itself, as the breed became dominated by too few bloodlines. Leigh suggested that breeders should self-regulate 'by withholding their mares or by insisting that their nomination contracts state the maximum number of mares to be covered.' The economic reality for the majority of breeders is such that Leigh's call seems most unlikely to be heeded, the news late in 2002 that the French racing authorities had rescinded a limit of one hundred and fifty mares for French-based stallions hardly being an encouraging signal. Given Leigh's comments, it is ironic that he sent Brocade back to Sadler's Wells for the mating that produced Gossamer. Sadler's Wells has been one of the most active Flat stallions in Britain and Ireland in recent years. In 2002, for example, he covered one hundred and sixty-four mares. Compare this to 1988, the year Sadler's Wells had his first runners, when the highest number of coverings by a stallion ranked in the top ten by prize-money at the time was Lomond with sixty-eight. Mind you, Sadler's Wells enjoyed the life of Riley in the latest breeding season compared to Turtle Island, who covered an astonishing three hundred and seventy-four predominantly National Hunt mares. The fact that Leigh sent Brocade back to Sadler's Wells is easy to reconcile purely from a breeding point of view. Sadler's Wells has now been the champion sire twelve times and achieved the remarkable feat of siring at least the first three home in three Group 1 races in the latest season. He was responsible for the first three in the Irish One Thousand Guineas, and the first four in the Irish Derby and in the Racing Post Trophy. One more sires' title will put Sadler's Wells level with the legendary eighteenth-century stallion Highflyer, whose total of thirteen titles has not been bettered since. Gossamer's pedigree was detailed extensively in *Racehorses of 2001*, but there are a few other things to add. After a difficult pregnancy in 2001, Brocade has been retired from breeding duties. That final foal, a colt by Nashwan, followed the Green Desert filly Camlet, successful in a maiden at Yarmouth on her racecourse debut in the latest season before coming eighth of eleven, never able to challenge, in the Rockfel Stakes at Newmarket. The small, strong Gossamer will take Brocade's place at stud. Although she made a winning debut on good to firm ground as a two-year-old, subsequent events showed Gossamer to be clearly well suited by good or softer going. She ran well enough on her final outing to suggest she stayed a mile and a quarter. *L. M. Cumani*

GO TECH   2 b.c. (May 20) Gothenberg (IRE) 117 – Bollin Sophie (Efisio 120) [2002 **94** 6m 6m³ 6g* 8g² 8m² 7.2g* 8d⁵ Oct 21] rather leggy, unfurnished colt: shows plenty of knee action: fourth foal: half-brother to 3-y-o Travelling Times and 4-y-o Some Will: dam, little sign of ability, half-sister to smart sprinter Bollin Joanne and 3-y-o Bollin Eric: fairly useful performer: won maiden at Newcastle in August and minor event at Ayr (beat Babodana by short head) in September: pulled hard when well held final start: unlikely to stay beyond 1m: acts on good to firm going. *T. D. Easterby*

GOTHIC BAY   2 b.g. (Mar 28) Gothenberg (IRE) 117 – Greyhill Lady (Grey Desire – 115) [2002 6d 6g 6f Sep 26] fourth foal to thoroughbred sire: dam unraced: well held in maidens. *M. W. Easterby*

GO THUNDER (IRE)   8 b.g. Nordico (USA) – Moving Off (Henbit (USA) 130) – [2002 35: 9.2s 9.2v 10.9g 8.3m 12s Nov 6] no form in 2002: usually tongue tied: tubed. *D. A. Nolan*

GOT TO BE CASH   3 ch.f. Lake Coniston (IRE) 131 – Rasayel (USA) 79§ (Bering **57** 136) [2002 66: 6d 6s 6g 7.6f³ 7.9s³ 8s⁵ 12.3m⁶ 11.9m 12f⁴ Oct 8] strong, lengthy filly: modest maiden handicapper: stays 1½m: acts on firm and soft ground, some promise on fibresand. *W. M. Brisbourne*

GOVERNOR BROWN (USA)   2 ch.c. (Apr 23) Kingmambo (USA) 125 – Miss **104** Mistletoes (IRE) 89 (The Minstrel (CAN) 135) [2002 6g⁴ 7m* 7f* 7m 8v³ Nov 2] $485,000F, $310,000Y: close-coupled, good-topped colt: sixth foal: brother to 1m winner in USA, closely related to smart 7f (at 2 yrs) to 1¼m winner Hattab (by Woodman) and half-brother to fairly useful Irish 1998 2-y-o 1m winner Faddad (by Irish River): dam, Irish 7f and 9f winner, out of half-sister to Le Moss and Levmoss: useful performer: won maiden at York (made all) in September and Somerville Tattersall Stakes at Newmarket (beat Muqbil by ½ length, leading under 2f out and drifting right) in October: ran as

Somerville Tattersall Stakes, Newmarket—Governor Brown upsets the odds laid on Muqbil (striped cap); Hurricane Alan takes third ahead of the grey Marino Marini

though something amiss in Dewhurst Stakes at Newmarket penultimate start: good 5¼ lengths third to Dalakhani in Criterium International at Saint-Cloud: will stay 1¼m: acts on any ground: sent to USA. *P. F. I. Cole*

GRACEFUL EMPEROR 4 b.g. Emperor Jones (USA) 119 – Juvenka (Shirley Heights 130) [2002 –: f16g Feb 14] leggy gelding: little form. *R. M. Stronge* —

GRACIA 3 gr.f. Linamix (FR) 127 – Francia 59 (Legend of France (USA) 124) [2002 –: 8f 10d 8.1d⁴ 9.7d³ 8d 8.3v⁶ 9.9m* 10.1m* 10g p10g Nov 13] lengthy, angular filly: fair handicapper: won at Beverley (apprentice maiden event, carried head awkwardly) in August and Epsom in September: good effort final outing: stays 1¼m: acts on polytrack, good to firm and good to soft going: wandered/flashed tail third start: races prominently. *S. C. Williams* **75 +**

GRACILIS (IRE) 5 b.g. Caerleon (USA) 132 – Grace Note (FR) 99 (Top Ville 129) [2002 93: 16.1m³ 16.2s 20m 16.1g 16.2m Jul 26] heavy-topped gelding: fairly useful handicapper: reportedly lame when tailed off final start: best at 2m+: acts on soft going, good to firm and fibresand: sometimes flashes tail/edges left. *G. A. Swinbank* **90**

GRACIOUS AIR (USA) 4 b.f. Bahri (USA) 125 – Simply Bell (USA) (Simply Majestic (USA)) [2002 49: 9.9m⁴ 9m* 9m 10m⁶ 10.3g² 9.1v⁴ 9.3g² 10.3f 10.1f⁵ 10.3d² 10m⁴ 10g f12g Oct 5] tall, leggy, good-topped filly: modest handicapper: won apprentice maiden event at Redcar in May: ran poorly last 2 starts: stays 1½m: acts on firm and good to soft going. *J. R. Weymes* **64**

GRACIOUS DANCER 2 b.c. (Mar 17) Mark of Esteem (IRE) 137 – Gracious Beauty (USA) 67 (Nijinsky (CAN) 138) [2002 f7s Dec 7] IR 10,000Y: seventh foal: half-brother to useful 1¼m/1½m winner Jazil (by Nashwan) and 11.5f winner who stayed 15f Labeed (by Riverman): dam, maiden who stayed 1¼m, sister to US Grade 1 9f/1¼m winner Maplejinsky and closely related to outstanding sprinter Dayjur: 25/1 and green, eighth to Blue Trojan in Wolverhampton maiden, slowly away and late headway: should improve. *J. A. Osborne* **– p**

GRACIOUS KING 4 ro.c. King's Signet (USA) 110 – Gracious Gretclo 54 (Common Grounds 118) [2002 48: 5.1g 6d May 27] leggy, angular colt: poor maiden at 3 yrs: well beaten in 2002. *R. J. Hodges* —

GRADUATION DAY 2 b.f. (Mar 4) College Chapel 122 – Golden Ciel (USA) (Septieme Ciel (USA) 123) [2002 6.1s² Jun 6] 9,000Y: first foal: dam 2-y-o sprint winner in Italy: 11/2, 3 lengths second to Tout Seul in maiden at Chepstow, keeping on from rear: reportedly suffered from ringworm after: should do better. *P. W. Harris* **69 p**

GRADY 3 ch.c. Bluegrass Prince (IRE) 110 – Lady Sabina 61 (Bairn (USA) 126) [2002 67: p7g p8g⁵ p6g⁵ p6g² 6m p7g p7g⁶ 6m 7.1g Sep 12] modest maiden: probably stays 7f: acts on polytrack: blinkered last 3 appearances. *Miss Jacqueline S. Doyle* **60**

GRAFT 3 b.g. Entrepreneur 123 – Mariakova (USA) 84 (The Minstrel (CAN) 135) **86**
[2002 81p: 10.3s³ 10m 10.2g 10.3f 10f² 10s² Oct 15] quite good-topped gelding: fairly
useful performer: good efforts when runner-up in handicaps at Newmarket and Leicester
last 2 starts: stays 10.3f: acts on firm going, soft and polytrack: ran in snatches/hung left
on reappearance: sold 25,000 gns. *B. W. Hills*

GRAIKOS 2 b.c. (Mar 30) Rainbow Quest (USA) 134 – Grecian Slipper 102 (Sadler's **105 p**
Wells (USA) 132) [2002 8s³ 8g* 8d³ 9d* 10v Nov 9] fifth foal: half-brother to smart
French 9f to 15.5f winner Magna Graecia (by Warning) and Irish 9f winner Fustanella
(by Mtoto): dam, 1m to 11.6f winner, half-sister to Dubai World Cup winner Street Cry
out of Irish Oaks winner Helen Street: won newcomers race at Deauville in August, minor
event at Longchamp in September and Prix de Conde at latter track (beat Silver Gilt and
Garlinote 1½ lengths, just pushed along to improve from last place inside final 1f) in
October: creditable 3¼ lengths third of 5 to Dalakhani in Prix des Chenes at Longchamp
third start: beat only one home in Criterium de Saint-Cloud: should be well suited by
1¼m/1½m: possibly unsuited by heavy going: joined Godolphin: likely to do better as
3-y-o. *A. Fabre, France*

GRAIN OF GOLD 3 b.f. Mr Prospector (USA) – Pure Grain 121 (Polish Precedent **74**
(USA) 131) [2002 57p: 10m² 10g³ 10.2f² Sep 30] leggy, quite attractive filly: fair performer: visored, won maiden at Bath in September: will stay 1½m: raced only on good
ground or firmer. *Sir Michael Stoute*

GRAIN STORM (IRE) 4 b.f. Marju (IRE) 127 – Zuhal 67 (Busted 134) [2002 50: **48**
f8.5g 9f⁴ 8m 9.9d 9.1d Aug 2] lightly-made filly: poor handicapper: stays 9f: best form
on firm going: has been early to post: headstrong. *P. C. Haslam*

GRALMANO (IRE) 7 b.g. Scenic 128 – Llangollen (IRE) 87 (Caerleon (USA) 132) **83**
[2002 89, a96: p10g⁵ p12g⁵ f11g 11.9m* 10f⁴ 11.9d⁴ 10f* 11.9d⁵ Jul 6] strong gelding: **a89**
unimpressive mover: fairly useful handicapper: won at York in May and Redcar in June:
creditable effort at Haydock final start: effective at 1¼m/1½m: acts on all-weather, firm
and good to soft ground: occasionally visored/blinkered earlier in career: edgy sort:
usually races prominently: game: winner over fences November/December. *K. A. Ryan*

GRAMPIAN 3 b.c. Selkirk (USA) 129 – Gryada 93 (Shirley Heights 130) [2002 89: **112**
9g³ 8f³ 10.2g* 12m* 12m⁵ 11.9m² 10d⁵ Nov 1] rather leggy, good-topped colt: smart
performer: in good form in 2002, winning minor events at Bath and Salisbury in May,
beating Mine Host both times: best efforts next 2 starts when fifth to Systematic in King
George V Handicap at Royal Ascot (moved poorly to post) and 2 lengths second of 3 to
Jelani in listed race at Haydock (swished tail under pressure): stays 1½m: raced only on
good going or firmer until final start (below form): has been slowly away: sometimes
races freely/hangs left. *J. G. Given*

GRANADILLA 3 b.f. Zafonic (USA) 130 – Epagris 107 (Zalazl (USA) 120) [2002 **88**
7m⁴ 7s⁴ 7.1m* 8.1m⁵ 8s⁶ Nov 2] quite attractive filly: third foal: half-sister to fairly useful
1¼m winner Krantor (by Arazi): dam 6f (at 2 yrs) and 7f winner who stayed 1m: fairly
useful performer: easily won maiden at Haydock in July: not discredited in listed race at
Sandown next time: may prove better at 6f/7f than 1m: acts on good to firm ground,
disappointing on soft. *H. R. A. Cecil*

GRAN CLICQUOT 7 gr.m. Gran Alba (USA) 107 – Tina's Beauty 41 (Tina's Pet 121) **43**
[2002 52: p7g p10g Dec 30] poor form in cheekpieces both 7-y-o starts. *G. P. Enright*

GRAND AUNT DEE (IRE) 3 b.f. Distant Relative 128 – Willow Dale (IRE) 89 **60**
(Danehill (USA) 126) [2002 64p: 7g⁴ 7m 8.1m 6s 7m⁴ 6m Aug 29] workmanlike filly:
modest maiden: should stay 1m: acts on good to firm ground, well held on soft: sold 2,500
gns, sent to Holland. *D. R. C. Elsworth*

GRAND CRU 11 ch.g. Kabour 80 – Hydrangea 73 (Warpath 113) [2002 –§: f16g Feb **– §**
7] angular gelding: one-time fair performer: no form after 2000: stayed 2m well: acted on
soft going and fibresand: usually visored/blinkered: temperamental: dead. *J. Cullinan*

GRAND DESIRE 3 b.f. Grand Lodge (USA) 125 – Desert Venus 74 (Green Desert **–**
(USA) 127) [2002 12d Jul 9] 1,200F, 9,000Y: third foal: half-sister to useful 5f (at 2 yrs)
and 6f winner Dandy Night (by Lion Cavern): dam, maiden who should have stayed 1m,
out of half-sister to Poule d'Essai des Pouliches winner Dumka (dam of Doyoun): 20/1,
showed nothing after slow start in maiden at Pontefract. *J. Hetherton*

GRANDE DAME (IRE) 3 b.f. Grand Lodge (USA) 125 – Royal Hostess (IRE) (Be **–**
My Guest (USA) 126) [2002 57p: 8.3m 11.6s 10g Jun 17] modest form final start at 2 yrs:
well held in 2002. *I. A. Balding*

GRANDERA (IRE)   4 ch.c. Grand Lodge (USA) 125 – Bordighera (USA) (Aly-   **129**
sheba (USA)) [2002 124: 12g² 10g⁵ 10g* 10m* 12m⁵ 10m* 10.2g³ 10m Dec 15]

'The equine manifestation of the Godolphin ethos'—that, according to his
owners, is Grandera. No previous Godolphin horse has clocked up so many air
miles and Grandera thrived on it, having the World Series title sewn up before the
final event. It was not all plain sailing though, as demonstrated in the Irish Champion Stakes. Talking the hind leg off a donkey probably lies well within Frankie
Dettori's capabilities and, if his post-race remarks are any guide, this race saw him
pull off another formidable act of persuasion. It is a rare thing indeed for a jockey to
pass adverse comment on the willingness of his mount, in public anyway, but there
was no such reticence when Dettori talked about Grandera at Leopardstown. 'He's
a very unusual character,' Dettori summarised. 'He can be such a nightmare, you
don't know what to expect, but at least he goes forward.' That does not always look
to be Grandera's first intention. As a three-year-old, it was possible that a couple of
instances of his wandering under pressure could be put down to discomfort on the
firm ground, but that explanation is not top of the list nowadays. Eye catchingly,
Grandera hung on to the rail when first asked for his effort in the Irish Champion
and, earlier in the latest season, had a good look around him, putting his head firmly
to one side, in the closing stages of the Prince of Wales's Stakes at Royal Ascot. The
most striking aspect of those two races, however, was that he won them. Picking up
three first prizes in all, worth the equivalent of £673,585, £145,000 and £388,734,
Grandera proved a spectacularly successful acquisition.

Grandera's three-year-old campaign, contrastingly, had yielded no major
victories for James Fanshawe, though places in the Prix du Jockey Club, Eclipse
and the Juddmonte International showed that he had the ability. The designated
role for his new owners was that of global adventurer and if Godolphin's sole moti-
vation in their international campaign were financial reward—which it isn't—it
would be easy to see why from a quick look at Grandera's 2002 itinerary: the Prince
of Wales's Stakes offered less than half the money available from all but one of his
seven other assignments. His campaign started off in the Group 3 Dubai City Of
Gold Sponsored By Concord over a mile and a half at Nad Al Sheba in February. In
a seven-runner field, Godolphin and Saeed bin Suroor sent out the first four, but

*Singapore Airlines International Cup, Kranji—Grandera takes this very valuable event,
a new round in the World Series, in good style*

Prince of Wales's Stakes, Royal Ascot—
a fourth win in the race in the last five years for Godolphin and Saeed bin Suroor
as Grandera goes clear of Indian Creek, Banks Hill (rail) and Nayef (hidden by runner-up)

Grandera wasn't the best of them on the day, as he was beaten three and a quarter lengths by Narrative, the winner enjoying the better run through the race. Godolphin's second attempt to get the best out of Grandera ended in failure too, the application of first-time blinkers in the £711,034 Queen Elizabeth II Cup at Sha Tin in April seeing him finish only fifth; starting a short-priced favourite, he raced prominently and failed to settle. But there are plenty of opportunities these days for the high-class horse that is able to keep running and keep travelling, and Grandera's next opportunity resulted in victory in the £673,585 Singapore Airlines International Cup at Kranji. On this occasion, again at a mile and a quarter, he started without the headgear and Dettori rode him with more restraint before leading inside the final furlong for a two-length victory. Placed horses Paolini (from Germany) and Indigenous (from Hong Kong) had smart form aplenty and Grandera was back to his best.

On his return to Europe, Grandera was better than ever. The Prince of Wales's Stakes at Royal Ascot was worth more than £500,000 less than the International Cup, but it was Grandera's best showcase so far. Godolphin had won the first two editions of the race as a Group 1, with Dubai Millennium and Fantastic Light, and Grandera completed the hat-trick in a style that merits comparison. In a representative field of twelve, Grandera started joint-second favourite at 4/1 with Nayef, close behind 7/2-chance Banks Hill. Next in the betting were the improving Mark Johnston-trained Desert Deer, fresh from his nine-length success over some useful rivals in a Newmarket minor event, and Aidan O'Brien's Tattersalls Gold Cup runner-up Bach. Banks Hill, Nayef and Grandera may have been hard to separate in the betting, but they weren't in the race. In a strongly-run race, all the principals had a shot at the lead early in the straight, but only one horse was really attracting the eye and that was Grandera. Coming off the turn close up in seventh, he was on the heels of the leaders two furlongs out and going so strongly that Dettori dropped his hands and took a pull; when pushed along, Grandera surged to a two-length lead at the furlong marker and was five clear (of Indian Creek) at the line, despite carrying his head awkwardly (as our photograph illustrates). Banks Hill and Nayef should have given him a lot more to do, though Grandera was nevertheless a revelation.

'We have found the key to this horse,' reported Dettori, 'He wants fast ground, a strong pace and a mile and a quarter.' And after this performance, who would disagree with him? Possibly his own bosses, because Grandera's next appearance was over a mile and a half in the King George VI and Queen Elizabeth Stakes. While initially a second string to Sakhee, his stablemate's withdrawal when the ground became too firm left the race without a top-notch performer, so Grandera looked worth his chance. He was sent off 13/8 favourite, but managed only fifth of nine. Grandera was edgy in the preliminaries and a bump followed by a couple of stumbles on the home turn seemed to knock the heart out of him because he carried his head high most of the way up the straight, also flashing his tail. He mustered only a token challenge on the outside and then faded right out of contention in the last furlong and a half.

The switch back to a mile and a quarter resulted in two high-class performances to add to those at Kranji and Royal Ascot. At Leopardstown in September for the Ireland The Food Island Irish Champion Stakes, it brought victory, as already mentioned, but that victory was not confirmed until well after the runners had passed the post. Godolphin had a superb record in the race, netting wins in 1998, 1999 and 2001, and the two most recent renewals had been fought out in a pitched battle, virtually head to head, between the two dominant powers, Godolphin and Coolmore. The struggle between the Godolphin older horse and the Coolmore three-year-old took its form in Best of The Bests versus Giant's Causeway in 2000 and Fantastic Light versus Galileo 2001. Two very fine races resulted and another followed in 2002 when Godolphin's Grandera and Best of The Bests were pitched against the Coolmore three-year-old Hawk Wing. Hawk Wing was 11/8-on but, when the start time arrived, there was drama and uncertainty enough over whether he would even run, let alone win. Nearly all the horses at Aidan O'Brien's yard had been coughing in late-summer and most of the runners earlier on the Leopardstown card performed poorly. The misgivings earlier disappointments must have prompted were heightened when, on the way to post, jockey Michael Kinane summoned O'Brien to meet him at the start because he thought Hawk Wing might have spread a plate. The Coolmore team was subject of all the attention in the immediate build-up and it continued in the race as well—right up until the last moment. As in 2000 and 2001, Coolmore fielded a pacemaker, on this occasion Sholokhov who set off at a furious pace, setting up a huge lead: Sholokhov was still ten lengths in front two furlongs out, but Best of The Bests led a furlong out, Hawk Wing led fifty yards out and Grandera was there on the line. Hawk Wing has a tendency to carry his head high and Grandera often puts his in the air but, having looked a very hard ride and destined for third place for most of the straight, the running-on Grandera was finally dragged off the rail and stuck his head down in the final eight or so strides to beat Hawk Wing by the smallest margin.

The Irish Champion was the most dramatic race of the European season. Dettori's reported description was that 'Grandera started to look at the crowd, and then Hawk Wing, and then on the line put his head down and wallop! He's one in a

Ireland The Food Island Champion Stakes, Leopardstown—from left to right, Grandera, Hawk Wing and Best of The Bests provide a thrilling finish

million.' That victory meant that Grandera had captured well over a million (pounds) in win prize-money alone, but he had to settle for place money in the £718,862 Cox Plate at Moonee Valley in Australia in October. With a very short home straight, having to make up his ground on the turn was not ideal for Grandera who was forced to race wide and got into his stride only when it was too late, again carrying his head high as he turned a four-length deficit into one of just over a length to take third place behind Northerly, the top horse in Australasia. Although he had an unassailable lead for the World Series title, Grandera had not finished yet. His bid to justify odds-on favouritism in the £830,618 Hong Kong Cup was ruined by a slow early pace and trouble in running. The travelling was an important factor in the rash of withdrawals and disappointments for British challengers at Hong Kong's international meeting but it is surely safe to assume that that was not the problem for Grandera, who came home seventh, beaten two lengths by the winner Precision. 'The horse needs frequent changes of scenery,' says John Phelan, Grandera's regular work rider. 'Wherever he is, he gets to know the gallops quickly —especially the quickest way home from them. It breaks the routine when he goes somewhere new. Otherwise he might get up to all sorts of tricks.'

Grandera (IRE) (ch.c. 1998)	Grand Lodge (USA) (ch 1991)	Chief's Crown (b 1982)	Danzig
			Six Crowns
		La Papagena (br 1983)	Habitat
			Magic Flute
	Bordighera (USA) (ch 1992)	Alysheba (b 1984)	Alydar
			Bel Sheba
		Blue Tip (b 1982)	Tip Moss
			As Blue

Grandera is a strong, medium-sized, good-topped colt and a fluent mover. Although he ran on well when a close third in the Prix du Jockey Club, he now

Godolphin's "Grandera"

looks best, ridden with waiting tactics, at around a mile and a quarter and is likely to be raced only when the ground is good or firmer. His dam Bordighera and grandam Blue Tip both had their best days over ten and a half furlongs in France, the former when runner-up in a listed race, the latter when winning the Prix Penelope. Blue Tip was easily the most important winner in this family for decades before Grandera came along. Grandera is also easily the best from the third crop of Grand Lodge and his second best offspring overall after the 2000 Derby and Arc winner Sinndar. Grand Lodge's progeny have been a very mixed bag so far, but if he fails to sire another top-notch performer lack of numbers will not be to blame—he has been covering massive books since Sinndar, including a reported one hundred and eighty-three mares in 2002. Grandera remains in training and we would not put it past him to have picked up another top prize even before this book is published. Sometimes edgy in the preliminaries, including on both visits to Ascot in the latest season, he can also take a strong hold to post and a good pace is required in his races to help him settle. The Jamie Spencer-ridden Sydenham did a fine pacemaking job for him in the Prince of Wales's Stakes. Grandera's tendency to carry his head awkwardly was much more marked in 2002 than in 2001 and varied from race to race and during races. Frankie Dettori did a good job in getting the best out of him in 2002, including, as has often been the case abroad, with use of the whip that would be deemed excessive in Britain. Grandera's regular work rider, however, never carries a whip because Grandera will not respond to the use of force on the gallops. 'He's enormously talented but needs everything to go right,' says Dettori. 'We seem to get on quite well.' With Grandera, apparently, that is a rarity. *Saeed bin Suroor*

GRAND FINALE (IRE)   5 b.h. Sadler's Wells (USA) 132 – Final Figure (USA)   –
(Super Concorde (USA) 128) [2002 12v⁵ Nov 5] smart performer at 3 yrs in Ireland, winning minor event at Gowran and 2 listed races at Leopardstown (inflicted only career defeat on Sinndar in first of them): last on both starts in US, in Grade 3 event at Belmont (then left D. Weld) and Grade 2 at Gulfstream (only outing for C. Clement in 2001, reportedly sustained tendon injury afterwards): well held in listed race at Doncaster on British debut, carrying head high: stays 1½m: acts on soft and good to firm going: has been blinkered. *Miss Venetia Williams*

GRAND FOLLY (FR)   2 ch.f. (Mar 9) Grand Lodge (USA) 125 – Folmanie (USA)   **69**
(Blushing John (USA) 120) [2002 6g 7m³ 8g⁶ 8f⁵ 8.3m Oct 7] 110,000 francs Y, 21,000 2-y-o: good-topped filly: second foal: half-sister to French 11f winner Saffirina (by Turtle Island): dam, French 1¼m to 13f winner: fair maiden: should stay 1¼m: acts on firm ground. *J. Cullinan*

GRAND FROMAGE (IRE)   4 ch.g. Grand Lodge (USA) 125 – My First Paige   **83**
(IRE) 53 (Runnett 125) [2002 75: 14.1d⁵ 14.1d³ 16d 12s⁵ 16.2f² 15.9f* 21g Jul 31] quite good-topped gelding: fairly useful handicapper: career-best effort when winning at Chester in July: pulled up reportedly lame final start: better at 1¾m/2m than shorter: acts on firm and good to soft going: visored 3 starts prior to final one. *P. R. Webber*

GRAND GIFT   2 br.f. (Apr 2) Grand Lodge (USA) 125 – Black Velvet Band (Sadler's   **– p**
Wells (USA) 132) [2002 7m Aug 23] $110,000Y: good-topped filly: first foal: dam unraced out of half-sister to smart 1¼m performer Dartrey: 25/1, ninth of 11 to Hold To Ransom in maiden at Newmarket, always towards rear: should improve. *M. A. Jarvis*

GRAND HALO (IRE)   2 b.c. (Feb 4) Grand Lodge (USA) 125 – Band of Angels   **58 p**
(IRE) (Alzao (USA) 117) [2002 6m⁵ 7d⁶ Oct 15] 75,000F, IR 95,000Y: strong, well-made colt: has scope: first foal: dam unraced half-sister to Derby winner Dr Devious: burly, modest form in minor event/maiden, leading 5f in latter: bred to be suited by 1m+: should improve. *B. W. Hills*

GRAND HARBOUR (IRE)   3 b.c. Grand Lodge (USA) 125 – Port Isaac (USA) 64   **72**
(Seattle Song (USA) 130) [2002 71: 10.2g⁵ 8.3s 10g³ 8.3d 9.9m 10m 10.2g Sep 23] fair maiden: below form after third start: should stay beyond 1¼m: acts on ground softer than good: blinkered third/fourth outings: sold 6,000 gns. *R. Hannon*

GRANDHILL (IRE)   2 ch.c. (Apr 19) Grand Lodge (USA) 125 – Just Like Annie   **51**
(IRE) 65 (Mujadil (USA) 119) [2002 6g⁶ f7g⁴ 7g 7m 8g Sep 10] IR 42,000Y: compact   **a60**
colt: second foal: half-brother to 3-y-o Bella Chica: dam, Irish 5f winner, half-sister to smart 6f to 1m performer Pipe Major: modest form in maidens: well held in nurseries last

2 starts: likely to prove best at 6f/7f: best effort on fibresand: sold 3,000 gns, sent to Kuwait. *M. Blanshard*

GRAND IDEAS 3 br.g. Grand Lodge (USA) 125 – Afrafa (IRE) (Lashkari 128) [2002 **74** 10s³ 12d⁵ Nov 5] 26,000 francs Y: second foal: dam, won over hurdles/fences in France, half-sister to useful French performer up to 1½m Afaladja: fair form in maidens at Ayr and Catterick: stays 1½m: raced only on good to soft/soft going. *T. P. Tate*

GRAND ILLUSION (IRE) 3 b.g. Mukaddamah (USA) 125 – Saint Cynthia (Welsh **50** Saint 126) [2002 50: 7m 10m⁵ f12g⁴ 12.6m f12g³ p12g² 14.1f p12g⁵ 11.9m⁴ Jun 25] modest maiden: stays 1½m: acts on polytrack, raced only on good ground or firmer on turf: tried blinkered: sometimes slowly away: edged left final start: has looked none too keen: sold 3,000 gns, sent to Germany. *P. Mitchell*

GRAND (IRE) 2 ch.c. (Mar 2) Grand Lodge (USA) 125 – Easy Pop (IRE) (Shernazar **95** 131) [2002 7d⁶ 7d⁴ 8g* f8.5s* a8.5f³ Oct 6] 20,000Y: good-bodied colt: second foal: half-brother to fairly useful Irish 7f winner All Pop (by Turtle Island): dam unraced half-sister to very smart Irish St Leger third Lord Duke: useful form: won minor events at Newcastle in August and Wolverhampton (simple task, beat Matabele by 23 lengths) in September: changed ownership later in month: creditable 5¾ lengths third to Wando in Grade 2 Grey Breeders' Cup Stakes at Woodbine, then joined W. E. Walden in US: will stay 1¼m: acts on dirt and fibresand, raced only on good/good to soft going on turf. *N. P. Littmoden*

GRAND LASS (IRE) 3 b.f. Grand Lodge (USA) 125 – Siskin (IRE) (Royal Academy **66 ?** (USA) 130) [2002 8.1m 10m 9g Oct 5] 26,000Y: second foal: half-sister to German 11.5f winner Junior Doctor (by Dr Devious): dam unraced close relative of useful 1m to 1½m performer Lifewatch Vision: seemingly fair form in maidens at Sandown: should stay 1½m. *A. C. Stewart*

GRAND MADAM 3 ch.f. Grand Lodge (USA) 125 – Vax Lady 98 (Millfontaine 114) **43** [2002 7.5g⁶ 7.1m⁶ 8.1g 10.2f 10g Aug 7] 35,000Y: sixth foal: half-sister to three 2-y-o winners, including useful 1996 5f winner who became one to treat with caution Vax Star (by Petong) and 1998 6f winner Lord Bergerac (by Cyrano de Bergerac): dam sprinter: poor maiden. *Mrs A. L. M. King*

GRANDMA LILY (IRE) 4 b.f. Bigstone (IRE) 126 – Mrs Fisher (IRE) 94 (Salmon **a71** Leap (USA) 131) [2002 88: f8g 7d f6g f8g f5g⁴ Dec 10] big, lengthy filly: fair handicapper: needs further than 5f, and stays 9.4f: acts on fibresand, well beaten both starts on turf: reportedly bled from nose final start: often races up with pace. *M. C. Chapman*

GRAND PASSION (IRE) 2 b.g. (Mar 10) Grand Lodge (USA) 125 – Lovers' **94** Parlour 83 (Beldale Flutter (USA) 130) [2002 6f³ p7g* p7g² Dec 3] fourth living foal: half-brother to fairly useful 7f (at 2 yrs) to 11f winner Out On A Promise (by Night Shift) and a 7f to 11f winner in Italy by Danehill: dam, lightly-raced maiden, half-sister to high-class 1m/1¼m performer Persian Heights: fairly useful form: won maiden at Lingfield in October by ½ length from Gilded Edge despite racing freely and idling: caught close home when neck second to Splendid Era in minor event there: will probably stay 1m: acts on polytrack, shaped well on good to firm ground. *G. Wragg*

GRAND SLAM (IRE) 7 b.g. Second Set (IRE) 127 – Lady In The Park (IRE) (Last **–** Tycoon 131) [2002 12d 12.1m Sep 2] smallish, useful-looking gelding: well beaten both starts on Flat in 2002, trained by L. Lungo on reappearance: tried blinkered. *A. C. Whillans*

GRAND VIEW 6 ch.g. Grand Lodge (USA) 125 – Hemline 77 (Sharpo 132) [2002 **49** 62, a49: f7g 5m 5m 6f 5g 5m 5g⁶ 6d⁴ 5m 5m⁴ Sep 2] poor performer: trained by **a–** H. McWilliams first 6 starts: best at 5f/6f: acts on all-weather, soft and good to firm going: blinkered first 3 starts in 2001. *T. D. Barron*

GRANGE PRINCE (IRE) 3 b.g. Mujadil (USA) 119 – Cashel Princess (IRE) 91 **50** (Fayruz 116) [2002 60?: 7g 5.3g⁶ 5g⁶ Aug 22] modest maiden: best form at 5f: tried tongue tied. *Mrs L. C. Jewell*

GRANITE CITY 5 ro.g. Clantime 101 – Alhargah (Be My Guest (USA) 126) [2002 **37** 48: 5g 7.1m 5g 7.1g 5s³ 6s 8m 7.2d 6d Aug 3] leggy gelding: poor mover: poor handicapper: barely stays 1¼m: acts on any turf going. *J. S. Goldie*

GRANNY RICH 8 ch.m. Ardross 134 – Weareagrandmother 65 (Prince Tenderfoot **–** (USA) 126) [2002 f14.8s May 13] lightly-raced maiden on Flat: tailed off on return to Flat only start in 2002. *P. M. Rich*

GRA

GRANNY'S PET   8 ch.g. Selkirk (USA) 129 – Patsy Western 81 (Precocious 126)   **106**
[2002 110: 7.1g* 7m³ 7f⁵ 7f⁴ 7m⁴ 7.1g³ 6m³ 7f 7s⁶ Oct 28] angular, close-coupled
gelding: has a quick action: useful performer: won minor event at Warwick in April:
creditable efforts in similar contests/handicap next 6 starts: best at 6f/7f: acts on firm
and soft going: tried blinkered earlier in career: usually held up: has worn cheekpieces.
P. F. I. Cole

GRANUAILE O'MALLEY (IRE)   2 b.f. (Apr 29) Mark of Esteem (IRE) 137 –   **55 p**
Dame Laura (IRE) 100 (Royal Academy (USA) 130) [2002 5m 5.7m⁵ Aug 6] 17,000Y:
second foal: dam, 5f (at 2 yrs)/6f winner, out of smart French 1¼m winner Aunty: modest
form in maidens at Sandown (raced freely) and Bath (fifth to Morning After): should stay
7f: capable of better. *P. W. Harris*

GRASSLANDIK   6 b.g. Ardkinglass 114 – Sophisticated Baby 39 (Bairn (USA) 126)   **60**
[2002 –, a49: f7s f5g³ f5g 5m⁴ 5m* 5g 5g³ f5g 5g⁶ 5g 5m 5m f5s* 5g 5m 6f⁵ f5g⁵ Oct   **a52**
17] lengthy gelding: modest handicapper: won at Musselburgh in May and Southwell in
September: best at 5f/6f: acts on fibresand, good to firm and good to soft going: blinkered
twice at 4 yrs: has found little/carried head awkwardly: sometimes edges left: none too
consistent. *Miss A. Stokell*

GRATE PRIDE   2 b.f. (Feb 14) Charnwood Forest (IRE) 125 – Kanz Pride (USA) 58   **51**
(Lion Cavern (USA) 117) [2002 6m f8s⁴ 8.3m⁶ f8s⁶ f8g⁴ Oct 17] 3,500F, 6,000Y:
smallish, good-bodied filly: has a round action: first foal: dam, ran 3 times, out of smart
winner around 1m (also second in Yorkshire Oaks) Kanz: modest maiden: well below
form in seller final start: stays 1m: acts on fibresand, no form on turf: sold 500 gns.
J. R. Weymes

GRAVIA (IRE)   2 b.f. (Feb 19) Grape Tree Road 122 – Anafi 95 (Slip Anchor 136)   **– p**
[2002 6g Oct 17] rather leggy, quite good-topped filly: half-sister to several winners,
notably useful French performer up to 11.5f Vissinia (by Belmez): dam 1¼m and 1¾m
winner: 20/1, never dangerous in maiden at Newmarket: likely to do better. *G. Wragg*

GREAT AS GOLD (IRE)   3 b.g. Goldmark (USA) 113 – Great Land (USA)   **49**
(Friend's Choice (USA)) [2002 56, a49: f11g⁶ f11g² f12g* 10.3s 12d⁶ 12m f12g 14.6m⁶   **a70**
f12g 16m⁴ f14.8g³ f16g* Dec 17] good-topped gelding: fair on all-weather, poor on turf:
won handicaps at Wolverhampton in March and (having left Miss V. Haigh and off 6
months after tenth start) Southwell in December: stays 2m: acts on good to firm going and
fibresand: effective in blinkers/cheekpieces or not: tried tongue tied: very slowly away on
reappearance/seventh outing: no easy ride. *B. Ellison*

GREATDREAM (IRE)   3 ch.c. Hamas (IRE) 125§ – Simply A Dream (IRE) (Simply   **49**
Great (FR) 122) [2002 64: 7f² 7m 5.9g p12g² 12.1g f12s 11.5s a10g Dec 1] smallish colt: **a61**
modest maiden: sold from E. O'Neill 4,500 gns before final start: seems to stay easy
1½m: acts on all-weather, probably on firm going: blinkered (dropped out tamely on soft
going) final start in Britain. *M. Alvarez, Spain*

GREATER GLORY (IRE)   3 br.c. Mtoto 134 – Folgore (USA) 83 (Irish River (FR)   **64**
131) [2002 70p: 10g⁴ 10.5d 12.3g 12d 11d a7.5g* a10.8g⁶ a9.8g² Dec 26] close-coupled,
good-topped colt: modest performer: failed to confirm promise of only 2-y-o start and left
J. Dunlop after third outing: won minor event at Varese in December: bred to stay 1½m
but clearly effective at 7.5f: acts on sand, best turf effort on soft. *B. Grizzetti, Italy*

GREAT GAME   2 b.c. (Apr 2) Indian Ridge 123 – Russian Grace (IRE) (Soviet Star   **79**
(USA) 128) [2002 6f⁴ 5s² 7m⁵ 6.1g 5g⁶ 23] 57,000Y: useful-looking colt: has scope:
fourth foal: half-brother to useful winner around 1½m Harlequin (by Halling) and Irish
1m/9.5f winner Blue Russian (by Lycius): dam, French 1m winner, half-sister to Poule
d'Essai des Poulains winner No Pass No Sale: fair maiden: off 3 months, well below form
final start: free-going sort, likely to prove best at 5f/6f: acts on firm and soft ground:
found little twice. *R. Hannon*

GREAT NEWS   7 b.g. Elmaamul (USA) 125 – Amina 80 (Brigadier Gerard 144)   **76**
[2002 89, a–: 7g 8.1d 8.5g 8d 9.9g 9.9m³ 10.2d² 8s² 8s Nov 2] tall, angular gelding: fair   **a–**
handicapper nowadays: creditable placed efforts 3 of last 4 starts: stays 1¼m: acts on soft
and good to firm going: races prominently (pulled too hard final start): reportedly bled
from nose sixth start: game. *N. Tinkler*

GREAT ORATION (IRE)   13 b. or br.g. Simply Great (FR) 122 – Spun Gold 106   **–**
(Thatch (USA) 136) [2002 49: 16d 16m⁶ 16g 15.8f Sep 21] angular gelding: has round
action: one-time fair handicapper: no form in 2002: tried visored much earlier in career.
F. Watson

GREAT PYRAMID (IRE) 2 b.c. (Apr 29) Danehill (USA) 126 – Offshore Boom 96 **107** (Be My Guest (USA) 126) [2002 6m² 6g* 7g⁶ 7m 7d Oct 28] IR 550,000Y: small, strong colt: brother to 3-y-o Rock of Gibraltar and half-brother to several winners: dam, Irish 2-y-o 6f winner, out of half-sister to Riverman: useful performer: landed odds in maiden at Cork in August: good 2½ lengths sixth to Hold That Tiger in Grand Criterium at Longchamp: well held in Dewhurst Stakes at Newmarket and Killavullan Stakes at Leopardstown last 2 starts: will stay at least 1m. *A. P. O'Brien, Ireland*

GREAT VIEW (IRE) 3 b.g. Great Commotion (USA) 123 – Tara View (IRE) (Wassl **86 d** 125) [2002 90: 7s 7m 7g⁶ 7d 7s f7g² 8g 8m⁵ f8.5g⁶ 7d* 7m 7m² p7g Dec 18] lengthy gelding: fairly useful performer at best: generally on downgrade in 2002: won seller at Leicester (left B. Meehan after) in August: left Mrs J. Ramsden after penultimate start: barely stays 1m: acts on good to firm going, soft and fibresand: often blinkered/visored: has looked less than keen. *Mrs A. L. M. King*

GREAT WALL 3 b.g. Hector Protector (USA) 124 – Mademoiselle Chloe 106 (Night **52** Shift (USA)) [2002 8s f8.5g³ 9.2s May 5] 800 2-y-o: workmanlike gelding: eighth foal: half-brother to 3 winners, including smart 6f (at 2 yrs) to 1m winner French Fellow (by Suave Dancer), later 1m winner in Hong Kong where renamed Epic Express, and useful 7f/1m performer Black Silk (by Zafonic): dam 2-y-o 5f winner: clearly best effort (modest form) when third in maiden at Wolverhampton. *I. Semple*

GRECIAN GLORY (IRE) 3 ch.f. Zafonic (USA) 130 – Grecian Urn 123 (Ela- **88** Mana-Mou 132) [2002 8.2m* 7d³ 8m⁵ Jun 20] angular, useful-looking filly: half-sister to several winners, including smart 1¼m and 13.3f winner Dark Shell and useful French 1¼m to 12.5f winner Grecian Dart (both by Darshaan): dam French 6.5f (at 2 yrs) to 9f winner: fairly useful form: won maiden at Nottingham in May: good third in minor event at Leicester next time: bit disappointing on handicap debut at Ripon (carried head awkwardly) final start: bred to stay 1¼m: yet to race on extremes of going: sold 37,000 gns in December. *Sir Michael Stoute*

GREEK REVIVAL (IRE) 2 b.c. (Feb 25) Royal Academy (USA) 130 – Las **105** Meninas (IRE) 115 (Glenstal (USA) 118) [2002 5.2s⁵ 5m⁶ 5g* 6d* 6f⁵ 6g p7g* Nov 13] good-topped colt: fourth foal: half-brother to 1¼m winner Swinging Trio (by Woodman): dam won 1000 Guineas: useful performer: won maiden at Warwick (hung right) and minor event at Newmarket in July and nursery at Lingfield (well backed, quickened well to beat Looking Down comfortably by ¾ length) in November: effective at 6f/easy 7f: acts on good to soft going and polytrack. *B. W. Hills*

GREENAWAY BAY (USA) 8 ch.g. Green Dancer (USA) 132 – Raise 'n Dance **71 d** (USA) (Raise A Native) [2002 80, a78: f11s* f11s 8.3s 8.1d 10m 8.1s⁵ 8g f8.5g⁴ Oct 19] quite good-topped gelding: fair performer: won claimer at Southwell (final start for K. Burke) in January: below form after (trained by T. D. Barron next start): stays 11f: acts on fibresand, has form on any turf going, but revels on soft/heavy: usually waited with. *J. J. Quinn*

GREENBOROUGH (IRE) 4 b.g. Dr Devious (IRE) 127 – Port Isaac (USA) 64 **46** (Seattle Song (USA) 130) [2002 –: f9.4g⁵ 11.7g May 7] tall gelding: fair maiden at 2 yrs: poor form since. *Mrs P. Ford*

GREEN CASKET (IRE) 5 b.g. Green Desert (USA) 127 – Grecian Urn 123 (Ela- **76** Mana-Mou 132) [2002 79: 10f 9.9g² Jun 12] fair handicapper: good second at Beverley final start: effective at 1¼m/1½m: acts on soft going, good to firm and fibresand: tried tongue tied: sometimes carries head awkwardly (has reportedly had breathing problems): usually races up with pace. *J. A. Glover*

GREEN CRYSTAL 3 b.f. Green Dancer (USA) 132 – Dunkellin (USA) (Irish River **–** (FR) 131) [2002 57: p10g p7g May 28] close-coupled filly: modest maiden at 2 yrs: should stay at least 1m (badly hampered when tried over 1¼m on reappearance): blinkered (well held) final start: sold 8,000 gns in July. *J. Noseda*

GREEN DOWN 3 ch.f. Greensmith 121 – Marinsky (USA) 63 (Diesis 133) [2002 **–** 8.1g Sep 12] fourth reported foal: dam, ran twice, out of smart French 10.5f winner Indoor: soon tailed off in seller at Chepstow. *W. G. M. Turner*

GREENFIELD (IRE) 4 ch.g. Pleasant Tap (USA) – No Review (USA) (Nodouble **81** (USA)) [2002 f9.4g* p10g⁴ f8.5g 11.5m 10s² 10.2g* 12v¹³ Nov 9] IR 135,000Y: brother to a minor stakes winner in USA: dam US Grade 1 1¼m winner: fairly useful performer: left R. Guest after first start: won maiden at Wolverhampton in January and minor event at Bath in October: good third in November Handicap at Doncaster final start: stays 1½m: acts on all-weather and heavy ground: joined R. T. Phillips. *J. R. Fanshawe*

GREEN GINGER 6 ch.g. Ardkinglass 114 – Bella Maggio (Rakaposhi King 119) **54**
[2002 56: f8g f8.5g² f8.5g f8.5g 8g 10.9m² 10.9m⁵ 10.9m⁵ 11.8s Oct 15] modest
performer: stays easy 11f: acts on good to firm going and fibresand: visored last 4 starts
at 4 yrs: often races up with pace. *A. Streeter*

GREEN GREEN GRASS 4 b.f. Green Desert (USA) 127 – Hulm (IRE) 79 (Mujta- **47**
hid (USA) 118) [2002 –: f5g p6g⁴ f5g² f5g² f5g⁴ f5g Mar 25] smallish, sturdy filly: poor
maiden: best at 5f/6f: acts on all-weather: tried visored: hung left/carried head high third
outing. *N. P. Littmoden*

GREEN HART 3 b.f. Greensmith 121 – Velvet Heart (IRE) 47 (Damister (USA) 123) –
[2002 f9.4g⁶ p10g 12.1d⁴ 11.6s 10m 11.7d 16.2g 11.9g f14.8g Dec 16] second foal: dam,
1¼m seller winner: little form. *A. D. Smith*

GREENHOPE (IRE) 4 b.g. Definite Article 121 – Unbidden Melody (USA) (Chief- **97**
tain II) [2002 85: 16m² 20m 21g² Jul 31] big, useful-looking gelding: useful handicapper:
left J. Osborne and won 3 races over hurdles before returning to Flat better than ever
in 2002: ¾-length second to Hugo Dancer in valuable event at Goodwood final start:
stays 21f: acts on firm going and fibresand: usually races prominently (free-going sort):
consistent. *N. J. Henderson*

GREEN LINE 3 b.g. Green Desert (USA) 127 – Marl 94 (Lycius (USA) 124) [2002 **96**
6m³ 7g² 8f* 8m⁶ 8g⁵ 7m⁴ 6f³ 6g Sep 27] well-made gelding: second foal: half-brother to
4-y-o Snow Bunting: dam, 2-y-o 5f winner, best at 6f: useful performer: won maiden at
Lingfield and handicap at Newmarket in May: mostly good efforts in handicaps after, but
ran poorly final start: effective at 6f to 1m: best efforts on good to firm/firm going: found
little/edged right fifth outing: possibly none too reliable. *Sir Michael Stoute*

GREEN MOOR (IRE) 2 b.g. (Feb 7) Sadler's Wells 121 – Princess Amalie **69 §**
(USA) (Rahy (USA) 115) [2002 7.1v⁴ 8.1g⁵ 8.3m³ 8s Oct 15] IR 75,000Y: close-coupled,
quite good-topped gelding: first foal: dam, lightly raced in USA, half-sister to William
Hill Futurity winner Al Hareb: fair maiden: should stay at least 1¼m: acts on heavy
ground, probably on good to firm: tried visored: ungenuine: sold 8,000 gns, sent to
Kuwait. *M. Johnston*

GREEN 'N' GOLD 2 b.f. (Apr 11) Cloudings (IRE) 112 – Fishki 36 (Niniski (USA) **51**
125) [2002 5f⁶ 7.5g² 7m f7g⁶ 7.5g⁵ 8d³ 7g⁶ f7g Nov 26] angular filly: half-sister to 6f
seller winner Paldost (by Efisio): dam 11.5f to 15f winner, also won over jumps: modest
maiden: trained by A. Crook on debut: stays 1m: acts on fibresand and good to soft going.
M. D. Hammond

GREEN 'PURSUIT 6 b.g. Green Desert (USA) 127 – Vayavaig 78 (Damister (USA) –
123) [2002 57: f6s⁶ 8.5g 8.1d 6d 8.3s Aug 20] of little account nowadays.
W. M. Brisbourne

GREENSLADES 3 ch.c. Perugino (USA) 84 – Woodfield Rose 41 (Scottish Reel 123) **99 p**
[2002 82p: 6m² 6s* 6g* Sep 27] strong, workmanlike colt: useful form:
won maiden at Ayr in August and handicap at Ascot (best effort to beat Magic Glade by
neck) in September: bred to stay 7f, but not short of pace: acts on soft and good to firm
going: capable of better still. *P. J. Makin*

GREENWOOD 4 ch.g. Emarati (USA) 74 – Charnwood Queen 61 (Cadeaux Genereux **92**
131) [2002 93: 6m 5f 6m 5g* 5d³ 5m 5f⁵ 5m⁴ 6f 5s⁵ 5g³ f5g f5g f5g² Dec 17]
strong, lengthy gelding: fairly useful handicapper: won at Salisbury in June: effective at
5f/6f: acts on fibresand, firm and good to soft going: probably best in blinkers: tough.
J. M. P. Eustace

GRETA 3 b. or br.f. Doyoun 124 – Welcome Home 55 (Most Welcome 131) [2002 8f –
10d 7m⁶ 7m 8.1g Sep 23] 14,500Y: first foal: dam 1½m winner: little form. *R. Hannon*

GRETA D'ARGENT (IRE) 2 b.f. (Mar 20) Great Commotion (USA) 123 – Petite- **78**
D-Argent 91 (Noalto 120) [2002 f7g f7s³ f8.5g* Dec 20] IR 15,000Y: third foal: half-
sister to 5-y-o Mana d'Argent and 3-y-o Ela d'Argent: dam 6f (at 2 yrs) and 7f winner:
progressive form in maidens: won at Wolverhampton in December by 4 lengths from
Elfhelm, despite idling in front: should stay at least 1¼m. *M. Johnston*

GREY CLOUDS 2 gr.f. (Mar 5) Cloudings (IRE) 112 – Khalsheva 55 (Shirley Heights **69**
130) [2002 6d² 6g⁴ 7g 8d Oct 21] 21,000 2-y-o: tall, rather leggy, close-coupled filly:
third foal: half-sister to fairly useful Irish 1m winner Moyeala (by Royal Academy) and
3-y-o Red To Violet: dam lightly-raced maiden who should have been suited by test of
stamina: fair form when second in minor event at Haydock: well held after: bred to be
suited by 1¼m+. *A. Berry*

GRO

GREYCOAT 4 ch.g. Lion Cavern (USA) 117 – It's Academic 73 (Royal Academy   –
(USA) 130) [2002 –: p7g 10m Jul 1] little form. *Jean-Rene Auvray*

GREY COSSACK 5 gr.g. Kasakov – Royal Rebeka (Grey Desire 115) [2002 75: 6s⁶   **93**
7v* 6m* 6m 6m⁴ 6m 5.9v 7m² 6v³ 6g⁶ 7.2s³ f8g Dec 27] leggy, workmanlike gelding:
fairly useful performer: better than ever in 2002, winning handicaps at Newcastle and
Pontefract in April: left D. Barker before final start: effective at 6f/7f: acts on heavy and
good to firm going: tried visored early in career: has pulled hard. *I. W. McInnes*

GREY EMINENCE (FR) 5 gr.h. Indian Ridge 123 – Rahaam (USA) 91 (Secreto   **106**
(USA) 128) [2002 98: 6m³ 6f 7.1s 6g² 6m 7d 7f* 6g 7d 7m 7m Aug 30] big, lengthy
horse: useful performer: reportedly split 2 pasterns after final 4-y-o start: won minor
event at Chester in July: best effort when length second to Palace Affair in listed race at
Salisbury previous month: effective at 6f/7f: acts on any turf going: blinkered (edged
right) fifth start: tends to get on edge: sometimes carries head awkwardly: none too
reliable. *R. Hannon*

GREY IMPERIAL (IRE) 4 gr.g. Imperial Frontier (USA) 112 – Petrel 62 (Petong   –
126) [2002 57: p7g 7g Apr 4] modest maiden at best: well held both starts in 2002.
P. W. Harris

GREY MEDALLION 2 gr.g. (Apr 26) Medaaly 114 – Thevetia 65 (Mummy's Pet   **37**
125) [2002 6m 5g 7d f6g Nov 22] 8,800F, 2,000Y: close-coupled gelding: half-brother to
several winners, including 1997 2-y-o 5f winner In Like Flynn (by Magic Ring) and
useful 1993 2-y-o 7f/1m winner In Like Flynn (by Handsome Sailor), later successful
in USA: dam, maiden, should have stayed 7f: poor maiden: should be suited by 7f/1m.
M. Brittain

GREY PEARL 3 gr.f. Ali-Royal (IRE) 127 – River's Rising (FR) 88 (Mendez (FR)   **97**
128) [2002 67: 7f* 10m 8.5s⁶ 8m³ 7m³ 7.6m⁶ Aug 29] sturdy filly: useful performer:
won maiden at Chester in May: best effort when close third to Takes Tutu in handicap at
Goodwood on penultimate start: effective at 7f/1m: acts on firm going, possibly not on
soft: makes running. *Miss Gay Kelleway*

GREY SHOT 10 gr.g. Sharrood (USA) 124 – Optaria 83 (Song 132) [2002 22.2m Jun   –
22] sparely-made gelding: one-time smart stayer: first Flat outing since 1998 when tailed
off in Queen Alexandra Stakes at Royal Ascot. *I. A. Balding*

GRIZEDALE (IRE) 3 ch.g. Lake Coniston (IRE) 131 – Zabeta (Diesis 133) [2002   **100**
89: 7g² 7s⁵ 7m 7d² 8g⁴ 7g³ 7d⁵ 7m 8s³ Oct 14] strong gelding: improved into a useful
performer in 2002: good efforts in frame in handicaps at Newmarket on first, fourth and
fifth starts, head second to Mine in Bunbury Cup on second occasion: barely stays 1m:
acts on heavy and good to firm going: tongue tied: has worn crossed noseband: sold
55,000 gns, joined J. Akehurst. *E. A. L. Dunlop*

GRIZEL 3 b.f. Lion Cavern (USA) 117 – Polska (USA) 103 (Danzig (USA)) [2002 72,
a93: 6s 6d⁶ 5m Jun 28] workmanlike filly: has a quick action: fairly useful on all-weather,
fair on turf over 5f/6f at 2 yrs: well beaten in handicaps in 2002: usually blinkered:
sometimes looks none too keen. *B. J. Meehan*

GROESFAEN LAD 5 b.g. Casteddu 111 – Curious Feeling (Nishapour (FR) 125)   **49**
[2002 63d: f6g 11.1g 10d 8d 8m* 10m⁶ 8g⁴ 7.2d³ 8.1g 8g 7m 8g 8.1g Sep 12]
workmanlike gelding: poor performer: won apprentice handicap at Redcar in July: stays
1¼m: acts on firm going, good to soft and fibresand: tried blinkered/visored, not in 2002.
J. M. Bradley

GROOMS AFFECTION 2 b.c. (May 11) Groom Dancer (USA) 128 – Love And   **60 p**
Affection (USA) (Exclusive Era (USA)) [2002 8s Oct 26] 14,000Y: good-bodied colt:
half-brother to several winners, including 4-y-o Londoner and 3-y-o Always: dam, 5f to
1m winner (second in Grade 1 6f event at 2 yrs), closely related to very smart 1¼m
performer Zoman: 16/1, 3 lengths seventh to Midas Way in maiden at Newbury, never
nearer under considerate handling: should do better. *P. W. Harris*

GROOVEJET 3 b.g. Emperor Jones (USA) 119 – Sir Hollow (USA) (Sir Ivor 135)   **72 d**
[2002 –: f7s³ p8g² p10g³ 7s⁴ p8g⁶ 8.3s p7g 8m 8m f8.5g Oct 5] leggy, quite attractive
gelding: fair maiden: well below form last 5 starts: should stay at least 1¼m: acts on
all-weather and soft going, ran as if amiss on good to firm: visored final start. *J. R. Jenkins*

GROOVY 3 b.f. Shareef Dancer (USA) 135 – Only Yours 113 (Aragon 118) [2002   **87**
7.1d³ 8f³ 8.1g* 10m 8.1g³ 8d⁴ p10g⁵ p8g Nov 23] sturdy filly: third foal: dam 6f (at 2 yrs)
to 1m winner, including Child Stakes and Hungerford Stakes: fairly useful performer:
won maiden at Sandown in August: stays 1¼m: acts on good to soft going and polytrack:
sold 50,000 gns. *J. W. Hills*

407

GROOVY WILLOW (IRE)   3 b.f. Night Shift (USA) – Miss Willow Bend (USA)   **83**
(Willow Hour (USA)) [2002 7s⁵ 7m⁴ 6d² 6m⁵ 5d⁴ 5m⁶ 5.1g* Oct 16] 40,000Y: fifth
foal: half-sister to fairly useful 5f/6f winner (including at 2 yrs) Willow Dale (by Danehill) and 3 winners abroad: dam winning sprinter in USA: fairly useful performer: won
handicap at Bath in October: free-going sort, likely to prove best at 5f/6f: acts on good to
firm and good to soft going: sold 11,000 gns. *D. R. C. Elsworth*

GROUNDSFORDIVORCE (IRE)   4 ch.g. Common Grounds 118 – Nikki's Groom   **–**
(Shy Groom (USA)) [2002 72d: f8s p7g Jan 30] fair maiden at best: blinkered, well
beaten in 2002. *M. Blanshard*

GROUNDSWELL (IRE)   6 b.g. Common Grounds 118 – Fuchsia Belle (Vision   **–**
(USA)) [2002 64: f14.8g 17.1f f14.8g Dec 2] small gelding: modest form at 5 yrs: well
beaten in 2002. *Ferdy Murphy*

GROUND ZERO (IRE)   2 b. or br.g. (Apr 7) Marju (IRE) 127 – Zifta (USA) 82   **79**
(Zilzal (USA) 137) [2002 6m³ 6s³ 6g³ 7.5g⁴ 8m² 7.1m⁴ 8g⁶ 7g³ Oct 19] IR 26,000Y:
quite good-topped gelding: third foal: dam 5f and 7f winner: fair maiden: good efforts in
nurseries fifth/sixth starts (gelded after final one): stays 1m: acts on soft and good to firm
going: consistent. *T. D. Easterby*

GRUB STREET   6 b.h. Barathea (IRE) 127 – Broadmara (IRE) 91 (Thatching 131)   **–**
[2002 40: f12s f12g 9.9m 10m Apr 27] big, lengthy horse: no form in 2002. *M. Brittain*

GRUFF   3 ch.g. Presidium 124 – Kagram Queen 64 (Prince Ragusa 96) [2002 67: f7g   **66**
f6g* f6g f6g 7.5m 6g³ 5g⁴ 6g 6f f6g Jul 20] sturdy gelding: modest handicapper: won at
Southwell in February: stays 6f: acts on firm going, soft and fibresand: races prominently:
none too consistent. *D. W. Barker*

GRUMPYINTMORNING   3 b.g. Magic Ring (IRE) 115 – Grecian Belle 53 (Ilium   **60 p**
121) [2002 6g 7f⁵ 8f³ Oct 7] 1,000F: tall gelding: fourth foal: dam, maiden who stayed
1m: modest form in maidens last 2 starts, third to impressive Zee Zee Top at Pontefract
on final one: stays 1m: raced only on good or firm going: should improve. *A. Dickman*

GUADALUPE (GER)   3 br.f. Monsun (GER) 124 – Guernica (Unfuwain (USA) 131)   **113**
[2002 8s* 11m* 11m³ 11.9m² 12m⁴ 12s² 12m⁶ Dec 15] tall, rather leggy filly: first foal:
dam unraced half-sister to dual Gold Cup winner Royal Rebel: smart performer: won
national listed event at Hoppegarten in April and Oaks d'Italia at Milan (by length from
Bright And Clear) in May: ran well fourth to sixth starts when 5 lengths second to
Islington in Yorkshire Oaks at York, 5 lengths fourth to Pearly Shells in Prix Vermeille at
Longchamp and short-neck second to Black Sam Bellamy in Gran Premio del Jockey
Club at Milan: respectable sixth to Ange Gabriel in Hong Kong Vase at Sha Tin final
outing: stayed 1½m: acted on heavy and good to firm ground: visits Kingmambo.
P. Schiergen, Germany

GUARD   2 b.c. (Apr 5) Night Shift (USA) – Gaijin 97 (Caerleon (USA) 132) [2002 p8g   **–**
Dec 14] half-brother to several winners, notably high-class US 1m/9f performer Hawksley Hill (by Rahy), previously 7f to 11f winner in Britain: dam, 2-y-o 6f winner, best at
7f: 7/1, well held in maiden at Lingfield, weakening after appearing to lose action on final
bend. *N. P. Littmoden*

Oaks d'Italia, Milan—
first and third for Germany as Guadalupe wins from Bright And Clear and Midnight Angel;
Sadowa, in fourth place, does best of the Italian-trained fillies

GUARD DUTY 5 b.g. Deploy 131 – Hymne d'Amour (USA) 58 (Dixieland Band (USA)) [2002 85: 18.7f 20m 18m Oct 19] small gelding: fairly useful handicapper: not discredited in Chester Cup on reappearance: well held after in 2002: stays 2½m: acts on firm and soft going: tried blinkered: tongue tied: has looked none too genuine. *M. C. Pipe* **82**

GUARDED SECRET 5 ch.g. Mystiko (USA) 124 – Fen Dance (IRE) 82 (Trojan Fen 118) [2002 79, a74: p12g* f12g p12g p12g³ p10g³ Aug 29] workmanlike gelding: fair performer: won amateur event at Lingfield (carried head high) in January: stays 1½m: acts on soft going, good to firm, polytrack and probably on fibresand: has pulled hard: sold 10,000 gns, joined J. Mackie. *P. J. Makin* **79**

GUARDIAN SPIRIT 3 b.f. Hector Protector (USA) 124 – Amongst The Stars (USA) 107 (Proctor (USA)) [2002 8m⁶ 8g⁵ 7s p10g Dec 30] 3,500Y: rather leggy filly: sixth foal: half-sister to 3 winners in Germany, including 7.5f to 9f winner Astro Boy (by Surumu): dam, 5f (at 2 yrs) to 11.5f winner, later successful in USA: little form. *H. J. Collingridge* **–**

GUDLAGE (USA) 6 b.g. Gulch (USA) – Triple Kiss 106 (Shareef Dancer (USA) 135) [2002 88§: 8m⁴ 7f⁴ 10.1g⁵ 10g* 8.5g³ 10.5m⁴ Sep 6] strong, lengthy gelding: fair handicapper nowadays: sweating, won amateur event at Pontefract in August: stays 1¼m: acts on good to firm and good to soft going: blinkered (swerved and almost unseated from stall) final 5-y-o outing: tongue tied: has looked none too keen. *M. W. Easterby* **77**

GUERNSEY BOB 4 ch.g. Beveled (USA) – Martian Melody 62 (Enchantment 115) [2002 f7g Dec 2] brother to 5f/6f winner Random and half-brother to 5f/6f winner Mister Raider (by Ballacashtal): dam best at 6f: well held in bumper: last in seller at Wolverhampton. *R. J. Hodges* **–**

GUEST ENVOY (IRE) 7 b.m. Paris House 123 – Peace Mission (Dunbeath (USA) 127) [2002 53, a58: p7g f8g f7g f7g f8.5g⁶ p7g⁶ a10.5g⁵ a8g⁵ a6g* a8g a9g a8g⁵ a8g² a8g⁵ a6g a8g a8g a5.5g a8g Dec 15] sparely-made mare: poor performer nowadays: trained by C. Allen first 6 starts: won amateur race at Mijas in July: left C. Tinkler in Spain after fourteenth outing: stays easy 8.5f: acts on all-weather/sand and any turf going: visored/tongue tied earlier in career: has taken good hold, and usually held up. *J. Bidgood, Spain* **42**

GUEST LINE (FR) 3 ch.g. Ashkalani (IRE) 128 – Double Line (FR) (What A Guest 119) [2002 63: 8m p7g p10g 10g 8g Jul 24] workmanlike gelding: modest maiden: blinkered, soundly beaten in claimer/seller last 2 starts: needs to settle to stay 1m: gave impression ill at ease on firm ground: joined C. Mann, and placed over hurdles in September, then sold 4,000 gns. *B. J. Meehan* **53**

GUILDED FLYER 3 b.g. Emarati (USA) 74 – Mo Ceri 63 (Kampala 120) [2002 43: f8.5g⁶ f9.4g f8.5g⁴ f9.4g* f12g* 12m³ p10g* p10g² p10g³ Dec 3] big, lengthy gelding: fairly useful handicapper on all-weather, fair on turf: vastly improved in second half of 2002, winning at Wolverhampton in June/July and at Lingfield in October: very good placed efforts at Lingfield last 2 starts: stays 1½m: acts on all-weather, yet to race on good or softer going on turf: often makes running. *W. S. Kittow* **69 +
a92**

GUILD'S DELIGHT (IRE) 3 b.g. College Chapel 122 – Tamburello (IRE) (Roi Danzig (USA)) [2002 70: 6g 7g 7s 8m 6.1d 7m⁶ Aug 23] workmanlike gelding: modest maiden: probably stays easy 7f: acts on firm, possibly not on heavy: blinkered (ran creditably) final start: tongue tied fifth outing. *W. S. Kittow* **59**

GUILSBOROUGH 7 br.g. Northern Score (USA) – Super Sisters (AUS) (Call Report (USA)) [2002 76, a95: p10g 8.3g 10m⁴ 8g² 8m⁴ 8.1m Jul 7] close-coupled, workmanlike gelding: fair handicapper: effective at 1m to 1¼m: acts on good to firm going, good to soft and fibresand: visored once as 3-y-o: usually travels strongly: sometimes idles, and best with waiting tactics. *D. Haydn Jones* **78**

GULF (IRE) 3 ch.g. Persian Bold 123 – Broken Romance (IRE) (Ela-Mana-Mou 132) [2002 12g* 13.9m² 16.2m 14.8g⁵ 14.1m⁴ Sep 5] 65,000Y: big, strong gelding: has plenty of scope: fifth foal: brother to smart 7f (at 2 yrs) to 2m winner Romantic Affair and half-brother to 2 winners, including useful 6f to 1½m winner Little Italy (by Common Grounds): dam unraced: useful performer: won maiden at Salisbury in May: creditable efforts after when in frame in minor events at York (2 lengths second of 4 to Mr Dinos) and Salisbury (fourth of 5 to Persian Punch): should stay 2m: raced only on good/good to firm going: raced freely third start. *D. R. C. Elsworth* **101**

GULF SHAADI 10 b.g. Shaadi (USA) 126 – Ela Meem (USA) (Kris 135) [2002 73d: f11g Feb 5] lengthy gelding: has a quick action: poor nowadays: stays easy 1½m: acts on fibresand/any turf going: visored once: tongue tied earlier in career: usually held up (sometimes starts slowly): unreliable. *A. G. Newcombe* **38 §**

GULZAAR 3 b.f. Kris 135 – Kilma (USA) 97 (Silver Hawk (USA) 123) [2002 49: **67** p10g³ 10s⁴ Jul 19] close-coupled filly: fair maiden: best effort when third at Lingfield on reappearance, though flashed tail/carried head high under pressure: stayed 1¼m: acted on polytrack: blinkered both starts in 2002: visits Polish Precedent. *M. P. Tregoning*

GUMLAYLOY 3 ch.g. Indian Ridge 123 – Candide (USA) 74 (Miswaki (USA) 124) **–** [2002 –: 9.1g 7.2g 6m Sep 17] leggy, quite good-topped gelding: no sign of ability: left Miss L. Perratt before final start: raced very freely in blinkers second outing. *J. M. Bradley*

GUMPTION 4 b.g. Muhtarram (USA) 125 – Dancing Spirit (IRE) 72 (Ahonoora 122) **– §** [2002 85: 14d 18s⁶ Jun 6] good-topped gelding: fairly useful maiden handicapper at 3 yrs: well held in 2002: ungenuine: sold 22,000 gns in July, joined K. Bailey. *J. L. Dunlop*

GUNS BLAZING 3 b.g. Puissance 110 – Queen of Aragon 76 (Aragon 118) [2002 **83 d** 81: 5d f6g 5.1s³ 6g 6m 6v 5m 5d 5g 5d⁶ Nov 5] leggy gelding: fairly useful handicapper: below form after third outing, leaving B. McMahon after fourth one: best at 5f: acts on soft and good to firm going: tried blinkered/visored: unreliable: sold 1,300 gns. *D. Shaw*

GURU 4 b.g. Slip Anchor 136 – Ower (IRE) 71 (Lomond (USA) 128) [2002 81?: 14m⁵ **71** p16g Oct 16] unfurnished gelding: fair maiden: stays 1½m: acts on heavy going. *S. Dow* **a–**

GUYS AND DOLLS 3 ch.c. Efisio 120 – Dime Bag 87 (High Line 125) [2002 113: **113** 7m² 8g⁵ 8g* 9g⁵ 10g⁶ Aug 15] leggy, quite good-topped colt: smart performer: creditable efforts when 2½ lengths second to Redback in Greenham Stakes at Newbury and pro- moted fifth to Landseer (beaten 3½ lengths) in Poule d'Essai des Poulains at Longchamp prior to winning listed race at Saint-Cloud in July by head from Green Groom: good 1½ lengths second to Bernebeau in Prix Daphnis at Maisons-Laffitte next time, but demoted to fifth for causing minor interference: reportedly fractured cannon bone when sixth to Highdown in Prix Guillaume d'Ornano at Deauville final start: stayed 1¼m: acted on soft and good to firm going: has wandered: to stand at Haras du Thenney, France, fee €3,500, Oct 1st, live foal. *P. F. I. Cole*

GWENER DDA 4 b.g. Mistertopogigo (IRE) 118 – Good Holidays 60 (Good Times **–** (ITY)) [2002 –: 7.1g 5g Aug 22] third foal: dam maiden who stayed 7f: well held in maidens. *J. M. Bradley*

GYPSY JEWEL 3 b.f. Prince Sabo 123 – Petra's Star 61 (Rock City 120) [2002 f6g⁵ **66** f6g⁴ 6m 7m p6g 6.1v 6d³ f6g³ 5g² f6g² 6s⁴ 6m² 7m f6s 6m 7d f6g² Oct 21] unfurnished **a56** filly: third foal: half-sister to winner in Spain by Aragon: dam ran 3 times: fair maiden on turf, modest on all-weather: should prove best at 5f/6f: acts on soft going, good to firm and fibresand: usually blinkered: sold 7,500 gns, sent to Kuwait. *R. F. Johnson Houghton*

GYPSY MUSIC (IRE) 6 b.m. Treasure Kay 114 – Mighty Special (IRE) (Head For **–** Heights 125) [2002 9.9m 7f 12g f12f Nov 11] lengthy mare: poor maiden at best: well beaten since 2 yrs: tried blinkered/visored: had a foal by Presidium in 2001. *I. W. McInnes*

GYPSY SONG (IRE) 5 b.g. Turtle Island (IRE) 123 – Kate Labelle 58 (Teenoso **–** (USA) 135) [2002 14.1d Apr 1] maiden handicapper: well beaten only Flat outing in 2002. *J. A. Glover*

H

HAAFEL (USA) 5 ch.g. Diesis 133 – Dish Dash 118 (Bustino 136) [2002 64: 11.6d⁶ **68** 12d⁶ 16v p16g* Dec 3] fair performer, lightly raced: well below best in 2002 until winning amateur handicap at Lingfield (blinkered) in December: stays 2m: acts on polytrack, raced on ground softer than good on turf. *G. L. Moore*

HAALIM 4 b. or br.c. Lahib (USA) 129 – Cancan Madame (USA) (Mr Prospector **–** (USA)) [2002 64d: f12s p12g 10g 14.1g Jun 15] no longer of any account. *C. P. Morlock*

HABAYEB (USA) 2 br.c. (Mar 4) Storm Cat (USA) – Gone To Venus (USA) (Gone **80** West (USA)) [2002 7d³ 7.1m Aug 30] $3,300,000Y: rather leggy, quite attractive colt: fourth foal: brother to US Grade 2 8.5f winner Saudi Poetry: dam, 7f winner in USA, half-sister to dam of high-class US 8.5f (including Breeders' Cup Juvenile Fillies) to 1¼m performer Silverbulletday: better effort in maidens (fairly useful form) when third at Doncaster: slowly away and looked difficult ride at Sandown later in August: likely to stay 1m: joined E. Harty in USA. *D. R. Loder*

HADATH (IRE) 5 br.g. Mujtahid (USA) 118 – Al Sylah 118 (Nureyev (USA) 131) **82**
[2002 79: 5s⁵ 6s³ 6s⁴ 7s 7s 7d* 7d* 8d 7d 7m⁶ 8.5d 7d⁶ 7m 7g 7d⁶ 8d 8v Nov 10] lengthy
gelding: has a quick action: fairly useful handicapper: won at Leopardstown and Naas in
June: stiff task and not discredited in Bunbury Cup at Newmarket ninth outing: effective
at 7f/1m: acts on any turf going: tried visored, often blinkered nowadays. *R. J. Osborne,
Ireland*

HADDICE (USA) 3 b.c. Dixieland Band (USA) – Bevel (USA) (Mr Prospector (USA)) **91 d**
[2002 70p: 10.3f³ 10d³ 12.3m 10g⁴ 9.9f⁵ p12g Oct 9] tall, good sort: fairly useful maiden:
below form after second start: not sure to stay much beyond 1¼m: visored final outing:
sold 6,500 gns. *C. E. Brittain*

HADLEIGH (IRE) 6 b.h. Perugino (USA) 84 – Risacca (ITY) (Sir Gaylord) [2002 **58**
66: p10g² p10g⁶ p10g⁵ p8g⁴ p10g 8f⁵ 8m 8.5g⁴ 8.3m 8m Jun 30] leggy horse: modest
performer: won seller at Lingfield in February: effective at 1m/easy 1¼m: acts on soft
going, firm and polytrack: usually visored: sometimes slowly away: usually held up:
sometimes looks none too genuine. *H. J. Collingridge*

HAGLEY PARK 3 b.f. Petong 126 – Gi La High 68 (Rich Charlie (117)) [2002 56, **52**
a62: p5g⁶ p5g³ f5g p6g³ f6g f5g* f5g* 5d⁵ f5g f5f³ f5g f5g³ f5g Dec 27] smallish, **a69**
workmanlike filly: fair performer on all-weather, modest on turf: won 2 sellers at Wolverhampton in March: best at 5f: acts firm and good to soft going (unraced on softer) and
all-weather: often makes running. *J. W. Unett*

HAIKAL 5 b.g. Owington 123 – Magic Milly 60 (Simply Great (FR) 122) [2002 f12s³ **56**
f16g Feb 7] modest maiden handicapper: stays 1½m: acts on fibresand and good to soft
going: blinkered once at 3 yrs: successful over hurdles in April. *E. W. Tuer*

HAILE SELASSIE 2 b.c. (Apr 24) Awesome 73 – Lady of The Realm (Prince Daniel **63**
(USA)) [2002 6g 7f 6g 8d³ Nov 1] well-made colt: third foal: dam ran 3 times: modest
maiden: good third in nursery at Brighton: will probably stay 1¼m: acts on good to soft
going. *B. W. Hills*

HAIL THE KING (USA) 2 gr.c. (Mar 25) Allied Forces (USA) 123 – Hail Kris **60**
(USA) (Kris S (USA)) [2002 p7g Oct 31] $10,000F, 25,000Y: second foal: half-brother
to US 2000 2-y-o Grade 2 6.5f winner Give Praise (by Pioneering): dam 1m winner in
USA: 33/1, 5½ lengths eighth of 12 to Twentytwosilver in maiden at Lingfield.
R. M. Beckett

HAIRY NIGHT (IRE) 3 b.f. Night Shift (USA) – Snowcap (IRE) (Snow Chief **67**
(USA)) [2002 73: 6m 6g 7g⁵ 7g² 7.9s⁶ 6.9g⁴ 8.5m⁵ f8.5s 7d³ Oct 15] small filly: fair
maiden handicapper: stays 7f: acts on soft and good to firm going, possibly not on heavy
(well held only start on all-weather): often races prominently. *M. R. Channon*

HAITHEM (IRE) 5 b.g. Mtoto 134 – Wukk (IRE) (Glow (USA)) [2002 56§: f9.4g **53 §**
f8g f9.4g 8.3d 8.1g f11g f8.5g³ f8.5s Dec 26] close-coupled gelding: modest performer:
re-joined former trainer from R. Wilman after third start: stays 8.5f: acts on good to firm
going and fibresand: blinkered on reappearance: tried tongue tied: sometimes pulls hard/
finds nothing: usually held up: temperamental. *D. Shaw*

HAJEER (IRE) 4 b.g. Darshaan 133 – Simouna (Ela-Mana-Mou 132) [2002 –: p12g³ **53**
f9.4g³ f12g⁴ f12g⁴ f12g f14.8g f14.8s Dec 13] lengthy, angular gelding: modest maiden:
stays 1½m: acts on all-weather: tried blinkered: none too consistent. *P. W. Hiatt*

HAKAM (USA) 3 ch.g. Woodman (USA) 126 – Haniya (IRE) 92 (Caerleon (USA) **70**
132) [2002 p5g 6.1d 8m 8m³ 9m⁶ 12f² 12m⁴ 9.7m³ 12m³ 11.9m³ 11f⁶ 9g⁶ 9d⁴ f9.4s Nov
2] 6,500 2-y-o: small gelding: third foal: brother to fairly useful 1999 2-y-o 7f winner
Atwaar and half-brother to useful 7.6f (at 2 yrs) to 1¼m winner Zulfaa (by Bahri): dam,
1½m winner who stayed 1¾m, half-sister to very smart performer up to 1½m Volochine:
fair maiden handicapper: stays 1½m: acts on firm and good to soft going (well held on
all-weather): improves little: not the easiest of rides, but consistent. *John Berry*

HAKEEM (IRE) 7 ch.g. Kefaah (USA) 124 – Masarrah 91 (Formidable (USA) 125) **51 d**
[2002 61d, a–: 7.5m⁶ 8f 7g³ 8m 8d 8m 8g 8g 7.5m Sep 24] sturdy, lengthy gelding: **a–**
modest performer: probably best at 7f/1m: acts on firm and soft going: sometimes slowly
away: often races prominently: on downgrade. *M. Brittain*

HALAWANDA (IRE) 2 b.f. (Apr 13) Ashkalani (IRE) 128 – Haladiya (IRE) (Dar- **83 p**
shaan 133) [2002 7m² Sep 7] fourth foal: half-sister to useful 9f winner Halawan (by
Muhtarram): dam ran once in France: 16/1, short-head second of 5 to stable-companion
Waldmark in minor event at Kempton, sweeping run from rear to challenge final 1f: will
stay at least 1m: sure to improve and win races. *Sir Michael Stoute*

Tote Trifecta Portland (Handicap), Doncaster—the tough and consistent Halmahera (noseband) gains an overdue big-race success; Injaaz (far side), Kier Park (partly hidden by winner), Cyclone Connie (No.21), Sister In Law (far rail) and Shoeshine Boy (No.17) are all within a length of the winner at the line

HALAWELLFIN HALA   3 ch.c. Kris 135 – Tegwen (USA) 79 (Nijinsky (CAN) **95**
138) [2002 90p: f9.4g* a8f 8g 9.7m² 13.9m Aug 22] tall, rangy colt: useful performer:
landed odds in maiden at Wolverhampton in January: well held at Nad Al Sheba next
time: improved effort after 4-month absence when neck second of 3 to Goblet of Fire in
minor event at Folkestone in August: stiff task when last in handicap at York final start:
should stay at least 1½m: returned to UAE. *C. E. Brittain*

HALCYON MAGIC   4 b.g. Magic Ring (IRE) 115 – Consistent Queen 55 (Queen's **74**
Hussar 124) [2002 67d, a42: p7g p6g 7m 7m⁴ 6g* 6m⁶ 6g 7m* 6m* 6f 6d 7d Oct **a–**
30] sturdy gelding: fair handicapper: left Pat Mitchell after second start, trained by
N. Graham next outing only: won at Ripon in July and on consecutive days at Yarmouth
in September (first an apprentice race): effective at 6f/7f: acts on polytrack, firm and good
to soft going: usually blinkered: tends to hang: seems to go well with forcing tactics.
Miss J. Feilden

HALF GLANCE   3 b.f. Danehill (USA) 126 – Fleeting Glimpse 109 (Rainbow Quest **104**
(USA) 134) [2002 104p: 7m⁵ 10m³ 10.4m⁵ 10.1g⁵ 7f* Jul 17] lengthy filly: easy mover:
useful performer: won May Hill Stakes at Doncaster at 2 yrs: made hard work of landing
odds in minor event over inadequate trip at Yarmouth in July: creditable efforts 3 previous
starts, 1¼ lengths third of 4 to Esloob in listed race at Newmarket, 5¼ lengths last of 5 to
Islington in Musidora Stakes at York and 2½ lengths fifth to Esloob in listed race at
Newcastle: was best at 1¼m on firm going, probably on soft: stud. *H. R. A. Cecil*

HALF HUNTER (USA)   2 ch.g. (Mar 24) Halory Hunter (USA) 126 – Elegant Wish **70**
(USA) (Lyphard's Wish (FR) 124) [2002 f7g⁵ 7d f7g³ f8.5g⁵ Dec 20] $3,500F, $8,000Y,
resold 5,800Y: third foal: half-brother to a winner in US by Ingot's Ruler: dam 6f winner
in US: clearly best effort in maidens (fair form) when 2 lengths third to Web Perceptions
at Southwell: stays 7f: acts on fibresand. *T. D. Barron*

HALF INCH   2 b.f. (Mar 2) Inchinor 119 – Anhaar (Ela-Mana-Mou 132) [2002 5m⁶ **65**
6d⁴ 7g⁴ 7d⁴ 8.3m Oct 7] lengthy filly: half-sister to winning stayers Ellamine (by Warrshan) and Midnight Coup (in Ireland and Jersey, by First Trump): dam bad maiden: fair
maiden: below form last 2 starts, carrying head awkwardly on final one: stays 7f: usually
races prominently. *B. I. Case*

HALLAND PARK LAD (IRE)   3 ch.g. Danehill Dancer (IRE) 117 – Lassalia **64**
(Sallust 134) [2002 77: 8f⁶ 8.3m 9m 10.2g 9d⁵ 8.1s 8g 8f f8.5g 10d* f12g² f12g² Dec 2]
smallish, sturdy gelding: modest handicapper: won seller at Windsor in October: effective
at 1¼m/1½m: acts on fibresand, good to firm and good to soft ground: none too
consistent. *S. Kirk*

HALLAND PARK LASS (IRE)   3 ch.f. Spectrum (IRE) 126 – Palacegate Episode **–**
(IRE) 111 (Drumalis 125) [2002 –: 6m May 20] sparely-made filly: last in 2 maidens/
claimer: has pulled hard/carried head high. *S. Kirk*

HALLINGS OVERTURE (USA)   3 b.g. Halling (USA) 133 – Sonata (Polish Pre- **70 ?**
cedent (USA) 131) [2002 8m 9.9m⁵ 9g p10g Oct 16] $130,000F, 70,000Y: robust gelding:
first foal: dam, unraced, closely related to smart performers up to 7f Russian Bond and

Snaadee: seemingly fair form in maidens/handicap last 2 starts: gelded after: stays 1¼m: acts on polytrack. *C. A. Horgan*

HALLION (IRE) 3 b.c. Halling (USA) 133 – Elisa War (Warning 136) [2002 7m⁴ 8f **89** 8.2g² 7.9d* 10g 7m Aug 1] 27,000F, 65,000Y: sturdy colt: type to carry condition: has a quick action: second foal: dam, French maiden who stayed 1¼m, from family of smart performer up to 1¼m Pollen Count: fairly useful performer: won maiden at York in June: left impression something amiss both runs after: should stay 1¼m: acts on good to soft going. *J. G. Given*

HALMAHERA (IRE) 7 b.g. Petardia 113 – Champagne Girl 67 (Robellino (USA) **102** 127) [2002 96: 5f⁵ 6m 5d⁵ 6m⁶ 5.9v⁴ 6g² 6m 6m³ 5.6m* 6g 5g 6f⁵ Oct 12] rather leggy, good-topped gelding: has a round action: useful handicapper: ended long losing run in Tote Trifecta Portland at Doncaster (finished strongly to beat Injaaz short head) in September: mostly creditable efforts otherwise in 2002, including length second to Bond Boy in Stewards' Cup at Goodwood in August: effective at 5f (given a test)/6f: acts on any going: visored last two 6-y-o starts: sometimes slowly away/carries head awkwardly: held up and best with strong pace: tough and consistent. *K. A. Ryan*

HALO'S RETURN (USA) 3 b.g. Southern Halo (USA) – Una Celebrita (FR) **49** (Dancing Spree (USA)) [2002 5m 5m⁵ 5g 7d Oct 18] $29,000F: rather unfurnished gelding: first foal: dam German 2-y-o 6f winner: never on terms/not knocked about in maidens first 3 starts: well beaten in handicap final outing. *R. A. Fahey*

HAMBLEDEN 5 b.g. Vettori (IRE) 119 – Dalu (IRE) 72 (Dancing Brave (USA) 140) **103** [2002 103: 12m 11.9m⁶ 13.9g² 14m² 13.3f² 14m⁴ 13.9m 13.9m⁴ 13.3f⁴ 16d² Nov 1] tall gelding: useful performer: runner-up in 2002 in handicaps at York and Goodwood, minor event at Newbury and handicap at Newmarket: stays 2m: acts on firm going, soft and fibresand: hung left final 4-y-o outing: takes strong hold: held up: consistent. *M. A. Jarvis*

HAMBLETON JO 2 ch.g. (May 23) Bijou d'Inde 127 – Elegant Rose 72 (Noalto **45** 120) [2002 7g f8.5s⁶ f7g f6g Dec 16] 1,000F: sixth living foal: half-brother to useful sprinter Bowden Rose (by Dashing Blade): dam 6f winner: poor maiden: tried blinkered. *J. R. Weymes*

HAMEEDA 3 b.f. Hector Protector (USA) 124 – Habibti 136 (Habitat 134) [2002 81: **74** 7d⁶ 7g 8.3s⁵ 8m* 7m⁶ Jul 26] strong, sturdy filly: has a quick action: fair performer: won maiden at Brighton in June: stays 1m, at least with emphasis on speed: acts on soft and good to firm going: withdrawn after giving trouble stall on intended reappearance: possibly none too genuine: sent to New Zealand. *R. Hannon*

HAMISH G 5 ch.g. Sure Blade (USA) 130 – Horton Line 89 (High Line 125) [2002 **52** 56: p8g³ p10g⁵ Feb 27] quite good-topped gelding: modest maiden: lightly raced: should stay 1½m: acts on polytrack. *John Berry*

HAMLYN (IRE) 5 gr.g. Lure (USA) 131 – Passamaquoddy (USA) (Drone (USA)) **58** [2002 72d 6.5s 7g⁸ 8.5s 6f⁵ f12f f8.5g⁶ f5g Dec 13] attractive, good-bodied gelding: **a46** modest maiden in 2002 (left D. Pugh after fifth start): ran at Wolverhampton last 3 outings: stays 1m: acts on fibresand, good to firm and good to soft going: tried blinkered/tongue tied: tends to carry head high. *John A. Quinn, Ireland*

HAMMER AND SICKLE (IRE) 5 b.g. Soviet Lad (USA) – Preponderance (IRE) **53** 85 (Cyrano de Bergerac 120) [2002 67: f6g⁵ f5g⁴ f5g p6g 7f² 6f 7m 7g f5g⁴ 5.3m Jun 25] **a48** good-topped gelding: modest performer: effective at 5f to 7f: acts on firm going, soft and fibresand: usually blinkered, visored last 3 starts: tried tongue tied: doesn't find much. *P. S. McEntee*

HAMMER OF THE GODS (IRE) 2 ch.c. (Feb 18) Tagula (IRE) 116 – Bhama **41** (FR) (Habitat 134) [2002 6.1d 6g⁵ 5.1g p7g Jul 20] IR 29,000F: strong colt: has scope: poor mover: half-brother to numerous winners, including very smart 1985 French 2-y-o 7.5f/1m winner Bestebreuje (by Try My Best): dam French 7f to 1¼m winner: poor maiden: has worn tongue strap. *W. G. M. Turner*

HAMMIYA (IRE) 2 b.f. (Jan 27) Darshaan 133 – Albacora (IRE) 98 (Fairy King **64 p** (USA)) [2002 7m Aug 1] unfurnished filly: first foal: dam, French 2-y-o 7.5f winner, closely related to smart French sprinter Pont Aven, herself dam of smart 7f/1m performer Josr Algarhoud (by Darshaan) and smart French sprinter Sainte Marine: 6/1, eighth of 12 to Geminiani in maiden at Goodwood, always mid-field: should do better. *M. P. Tregoning*

HAMPTON LUCY (IRE) 3 b.f. Anabaa (USA) 130 – Riveryev (USA) (Irish River **–** (FR) 131) [2002 –p: 6.1d 5g 8d f6g⁵ p6g f6g* Nov 25] strong, lengthy filly: fair **a65** performer: clearly best effort when winning handicap at Southwell in November, always prominent: will probably stay 7f: acts on fibresand: has swished tail in paddock. *M. A. Buckley*

HAMUNAPTRA 3 ch.g. Alhijaz 122 – Princess Dancer (Alzao (USA) 117) [2002 –: p7g² p7g⁴ 7m² 7g 6g f8s 7m⁴ 8m f7g⁶ Oct 19] stocky gelding: modest maiden: stays 7f: blinkered: sometimes slowly away: none too consistent: sold 1,700 gns. *P. L. Gilligan* — **50**

HANABAD (IRE) 2 b.c. (Mar 15) Cadeaux Genereux 131 – Handaza (IRE) 93 (Be My Guest (USA) 126) [2002 6s² 7g* 7m⁴ 7g⁴ 6.3d Oct 13] lengthy, angular colt: second foal: dam Irish 1m winner: useful performer: landed odds in maiden at Tipperary in August: good keeping-on fourth in National Stakes at the Curragh behind Refuse To Bend and Grand Criterium at Longchamp behind Hold That Tiger, beaten only around a length each time: odds on, well below form in minor event at the Curragh final start: should stay 1m: acts on soft and good to firm ground: tongue tied third and final starts. *J. Oxx, Ireland* — **107**

HANAMI 2 b.f. (Apr 3) Hernando (FR) 127 – Russian Rose (IRE) 82 (Soviet Lad (USA)) [2002 7f 8s* Nov 2] quite attractive filly: first foal: dam 1¼m and 17f winner: 33/1, much better effort in listed races at Newmarket (useful form) when beating Avoidance by 2½ lengths in 7-runner event, leading over 1f out: will stay at least 1¼m: acts on soft going: likely to progress again. *J. A. R. Toller* — **101 p**

HANDA ISLAND (USA) 3 b.g. Pleasant Colony (USA) – Remote (USA) (Seattle Slew (USA)) [2002 85p: 11g³ 12g* 11.9s³ 16.2m⁴ 14.8g⁶ Jul 10] big, strong, close-coupled gelding: has a quick action: useful form: won maiden at Thirsk in May: very good 6½ lengths fourth to Mamool in Queen's Vase at Royal Ascot: ran poorly in listed race at Newmarket final outing: stays 2m: acts on good to firm ground, well held on soft: sold 13,000 gns, joined C. Mann and gelded. *H. R. A. Cecil* — **101**

HAND CHIME 5 ch.g. Clantime 101 – Warning Bell 88 (Bustino 136) [2002 97: 7g² 6s³ 7m 7.1d⁴ 7m⁶ 7m 7.2s³ 7m* 7g p7g⁴ p7g² Dec 14] angular gelding: useful performer: won minor events at Ayr in August and Newcastle (beat Sea Storm a length) in October: good second to Eyecatcher in handicap at Lingfield final start: has won at 1m, but best form at 6f/7f: yet to race on heavy going, acts on any other turf/all-weather: has been bandaged off-hind joint: consistent. *W. J. Haggas* — **97 a102**

HANDFUL (IRE) 3 b.g. Woodborough (USA) 112 – Volkova 60 (Green Desert (USA) 127) [2002 76: f7g* 7.9f 8m⁵ Jun 4] angular gelding: fair form, lightly raced: won maiden at Wolverhampton in April: well below form after: stayed 7f: dead. *W. J. Haggas* — **73**

HANDSHAKE 2 ch.g. (May 27) Most Welcome 131 – Lady Day (FR) (Lightning (FR) 129) [2002 5g 6g⁵ 7.2v² 7.2g⁶ 8g 8g 6m Oct 2] lengthy, good-bodied gelding: half-brother to several winners, including 1995 2-y-o 1m winner Ladykirk (by Selkirk), later stayed 12.4f: dam French 9f to 12.5f winner: modest maiden: well held last 3 starts: should stay at least 1m: acts on heavy going: sold 3,800 gns. *Denys Smith* — **62**

HANDSOME BADSHA (IRE) 4 b.g. Petardia 113 – Cape Shirley (Head For Heights 125) [2002 –: f9.4g⁶ f9.4g p13g Mar 2] maiden handicapper: ran as if possibly amiss final start: often tongue tied. *J. A. Osborne* — **–**

HANNAH PARK (IRE) 6 b.m. Lycius (USA) 124 – Wassl This Then (IRE) 74 (Wassl 125) [2002 58: 16g⁶ Mar 28] workmanlike mare: poor form only run on Flat in 2002: stays 2m: acts on firm and soft going: has been blinkered (including when successful)/visored: has looked none too keen. *P. Monteith* — **42**

HANNAHS FLEET (IRE) 2 ch.f. (Jan 1) Fleetwood (IRE) 107 – Chocolate Souffle (IRE) 68 (Magic Ring (IRE) 115) [2002 7g f7g⁶ 8.2v 7d Nov 5] IR 4,500Y, 4,500 2-y-o: first foal: dam, third at 5.7f at 2 yrs on only start, out of sister to smart sprinter Carol's Treasure: little form, including in seller: trained first 2 starts by J. L. Eyre. *D. Carroll* — **–**

HANNAMIE (IRE) 2 ch.c. (May 2) Alhaarth (IRE) 126 – Bold Timing 73 (Never So Bold 135) [2002 8s⁶ p8g f7g Dec 31] 41,000F, IR 50,000Y: angular colt: fourth foal: dam, 2-y-o 6f winner, became reluctant: best effort in maidens (fair form) when sixth at Newbury: never going well next time. *R. Hannon* — **69**

HANNAVEE 3 br.g. Hamas (IRE) 125§ – Secret Rapture (USA) (Woodman (USA) 126) [2002 –: f9.4g² p12g⁵ 11.6m⁵ 12s⁴ 10f⁴ 8g 9.3d⁴ 8s Jul 31] big, strong gelding: fair maiden handicapper: seems to stay 11.6f: acts on fibresand and firm ground, below form on softer than good: sometimes slowly away/races freely: possibly not straightforward: sold 4,500 gns in October, sent to Kuwait. *S. C. Williams* — **66**

HANNIBAL LAD 6 ch.g. Rock City 120 – Appealing 49 (Star Appeal 133) [2002 100: p10g p12g² f12g⁵ 12s² 14.1m* 13.4f⁵ 13.9f⁶ 12d⁵ 11.9d 12g 12f³ 12s 12f Nov 23] leggy gelding: smart performer: won minor event at Nottingham in April by neck from — **111**

414

Bosham Mill: some stiff tasks after, including when creditable third of 4 to Storming Home in listed race at Newmarket eleventh outing: left W. M. Brisbourne 27,000 gns prior to respectable seventh to Sligo Bay in Hollywood Turf Cup final start: stays 1¾m when conditions aren't testing: acts on any turf going and all-weather: sometimes slowly away: usually held up: tough and game. *D. Vienna, USA*

HANNON (FR) 3 br.c. Exit To Nowhere (USA) 122 – Delphania (FR) (Fabulous **91** Dancer (USA) 124) [2002 61p: 7g⁵ 10g⁴ 10.5d³ 9g 7d⁵ 9g² 7g* 10d² Aug 11] compact colt: fairly useful performer: won maiden at Newmarket in July: stays 1¼m, at least when emphasis is on speed: raced only on good/good to soft going: slowly away on reappearance: has folded tamely. *R. Hannon*

HANS CHRISTIAN (IRE) 2 b.c. (May 10) Danehill (USA) 126 – Mira Adonde **67** (USA) (Sharpen Up 127) [2002 6d⁶ 5m⁶ 5m⁴ f6f Nov 11] IR 36,000Y: angular colt: eighth foal: brother to smart 1996 2-y-o 6f/7f winner Danehill Dancer and useful 6f/7f winner Plaisir d'Amour, and half-brother to 2 winners, including useful Irish 9f/1¼m winner Adonesque (by Sadler's Wells): dam ran once: fair maiden: form only when fourth at Haydock: should stay at least 6f: acts on good to firm ground. *M. Johnston*

HANZANO (IRE) 4 b.c. Alzao (USA) 117 – Movie Legend (USA) (Affirmed (USA)) **103** [2002 a5.5g³ 6d⁴ 6s⁴ 6d 6.8s* 7m 6.8d a8g² a8g² a8g² Oct 31] IR 60,000Y: well-made colt: second foal: half-brother to Irish 5f winner Last Call (by Salse): dam unraced sister to Irish 1000 Guineas winner Trusted Partner: useful performer: won 4 races at 3 yrs and handicap at Ovrevoll in July: tongue tied, mid-division in Tote International Handicap at Ascot sixth outing: second in listed race at Taby (beaten ½ length by Nicki Hill) and handicaps at Jagersro and Ovrevoll last 3 starts: best at 6f to 1m: acts on dirt and soft going. *A. Hyldmo, Norway*

HAPPY CAMPER (IRE) 2 b.g. (Mar 8) Pennekamp (USA) 130 – Happy Dancer **65** (USA) 95 (Seattle Dancer (USA) 119) [2002 5m 5d 5m² 5d* 6.1m* f5s Sep 17] 35,000F, 15,000Y: neat gelding: second foal: dam, 2-y-o 1m winner in France/Italy, out of half-sister to share miler Pater Noster: fair performer: won nurseries at Musselburgh in July and Nottingham in August: effective at 5f/6f: yet to race on extremes of going on turf, well held on fibresand: blinkered last 4 starts. *T. D. Barron*

HAPPY DAYS 7 b.g. Primitive Rising (USA) 113 – Miami Dolphin 85 (Derrylin 115) **–** [2002 –: f16g 13s 16d May 29] probably of no account nowadays. *D. Moffatt*

HAPPY GUEST (IRE) 3 b.g. Be My Guest (USA) 126 – Happy Lucy (IRE) (Alzao **82** (USA) 117) [2002 82: 8.3m p8g³ 8s 8g p10g Jun 29] useful-looking gelding: fairly useful maiden: stayed 1m: acted on polytrack and good to firm going: tongue tied at 2 yrs and on reappearance: tended to be slowly away: sometimes carried head awkwardly: dead. *A. J. Lidderdale*

HAPPY NOTE (IRE) 2 b.g. (Mar 17) Victory Note (USA) 120 – More Mirth (Main **–** Reef 126) [2002 7d 8.3m⁵ f8s 7d f8g Nov 26] 5,000Y: sixth foal: half-brother to a winner in Italy by Danehill Dancer: dam, Irish 1¼m winner, half-sister to useful sprinter Autumn Sunset: signs of just a little ability in maidens/claimers: tried blinkered/tongue tied. *T. P. Tate*

HAPPY UNION 3 b.g. First Trump 118 – Heights of Love 51 (Persian Heights 129) **48** [2002 67: p6g f6g⁶ 5.1d⁶ 6m 5.9g 6g⁶ 7.1d⁵ 6s 10.1m⁶ 8m Sep 19] close-coupled gelding: poor maiden: stays 7f: acts on any turf going: usually visored/blinkered. *K. R. Burke*

HARB (IRE) 2 b.c. (Apr 20) Green Desert (USA) 127 – Ajayib (USA) 84 (Riverman **100** (USA) 131) [2002 5.1g² 6.1m* 6g⁴ 6d² Aug 26] smallish, close-coupled, good-topped colt: second foal: dam, 1m winner, half-sister to high-class US performer up to 1¼m Sky Beauty out of close relative to Dayjur: useful performer: landed odds in maiden at Nottingham in June: best efforts when 2¼ lengths fourth to Mister Links in July Stakes at Newmarket and ½-length second to Cool Question in listed race at Ripon: should stay 7f. *D. R. Loder*

HARBOUR BELL 3 b.g. Bal Harbour 113 – Bellara 65 (Thowra (FR)) [2002 59: **60** 10.2g 7m⁶ 8m⁴ 10.9f* 10d f12g⁵ 11.9m 10.1m⁴ 10g 10d p10g Dec 30] rather sparely-made gelding: modest performer: won seller at Warwick (left B. R. Millman 8,000 gns) in June: stays 11f: acts on firm ground, probably on fibresand: tried blinkered. *J. White*

HARBOUR HOUSE 3 b.g. Distant Relative 128 – Double Flutter 92 (Beldale Flutter **77 d** (USA) 130) [2002 80p: 9g 7.1m 6g² 7f 6d² 5v³ 5.7m 6.1m* 5.9g² 7m 6m 7.6m 5f 7g 6d⁶ f7g p7g p6g Dec 30] leggy gelding: fair handicapper: left M. Channon after ninth start: below form after: best at 6f/7f: acts on heavy and good to firm going, well held on all-weather: blinkered final outing. *J. J. Bridger*

HARCELANTE (FR)   5 b.m. Balleroy (USA) 115 – Hekabe (GER) (Surumu (GER))   –
[2002 –: f8s Jan 1] successful in 3 claimers in France at 3 yrs: no show in Britain: probably stays 10.5f: raced mainly on good going or softer (acts on heavy): tried blinkered.
P. W. Hiatt

HARCOURT (USA)   2 b.c. (Mar 2) Cozzene (USA) – Ballinamallard (USA) 112   **82**
(Tom Rolfe) [2002 8g⁵ 8d² Oct 30] $52,000Y: rangy colt: fourth foal: half-brother to
winners in USA by Pistolet Bleu and Proud Truth: dam French 1m winner: fairly useful
form in maidens: still green (looked likely winner 1f out) when ¾-length second to
Devant at Yarmouth: will probably stay 1¼m. *P. F. I. Cole*

HARD LINES (USA)   6 b.g. Silver Hawk (USA) 123 – Arctic Eclipse (USA) (North-   **39**
ern Dancer) [2002 57: 10.5v⁵ 10.1m³ 10.4m Sep 4] rangy gelding: poor form in 2002:
stays 1¼m well: acts on any turf going: sometimes races freely. *M. D. Hammond*

HARD NOSE (IRE)   2 b.c. (Mar 4) Entrepreneur 123 – Cutlers Corner 111 (Sharpen   **87 p**
Up 127) [2002 7s⁴ 7d* Oct 30] IR 145,000F, IR 185,000Y: well-made colt: closely related
to French 5f winner Natural Beauty (by Scenic), later winner in USA, and half-brother to
3 winners, including useful Irish sprinter Clean Cut (by Formidable) and fairly useful 7f
winner Sheppard's Cross (by Soviet Star): dam 5f winner, including at 2 yrs: favourite,
won maiden at Yarmouth by ½ length from Successor, getting on top well inside final 1f:
will stay 1m: slowly away on debut: useful prospect. *J. H. M. Gosden*

HARDRADA (IRE)   3 b.g. Entrepreneur 123 – Alamiya (IRE) (Doyoun 124) [2002   **88**
8m 8m² 8f⁴ 10m 8.3m² 10.1g² 11.9m⁶ Sep 4] 45,000Y: rangy gelding: fifth foal: half-
brother to fairly useful 9f winner Chrysolite (by Kris) and 1m/9f winner in Germany
by Fairy King: dam unraced half-sister to high-class French middle-distance performer
Altayan: fairly useful maiden handicapper: should stay 1½m: raced only on good going
or firmer: sold 28,000 gns. *R. Charlton*

HARD TO CATCH (IRE)   4 b.g. Namaqualand (USA) – Brook's Dilemma 80   **79**
(Known Fact (USA) 135) [2002 74, a70: p6g² p6g⁶ p7g⁴ p6g⁵ p7g⁶ 6m³ 6f* 6m 5.3d³ 6f   **a76**
6s⁴ 6g³ 5.3g* 5.7f³ 5.3m² 6f 6m Sep 14] close-coupled gelding: fair performer: won
handicap at Yarmouth in June and minor event at Brighton in August: effective at 5f to
7f: acts on all-weather, firm and good to soft going: usually blinkered/visored (effective
without). *D. K. Ivory*

HARD TO KNOW (IRE)   4 b.g. Common Grounds 118 – Lady Fern (Old Vic 136)   –
[2002 –: f12g Jun 28] small, well-made gelding: fair maiden in 2000: well held both Flat
runs since. *P. J. Hobbs*

HAREER   3 b.f. Anabaa (USA) 130 – On The Tide 72 (Slip Anchor 136) [2002 8f* Jun   **81**
24] 42,000F, 240,000Y: third foal: half-sister to useful 1m/1¼m Tier Worker (by Tenby)
who stayed 1½m and fairly useful 1¼m winner Mingling (by Wolfhound): dam, 1m
winner, half-sister to very smart winner up to 1m Rock City: 2/1, won maiden at
Yarmouth by 1¼ lengths from Strathspey, missing break, quickening to lead final 1f and
going away, only outing: visits Zamindar. *J. H. M. Gosden*

HAREWOOD END   4 b.g. Bin Ajwaad (IRE) 119 – Tasseled (USA) (Tate Gallery   –
(USA) 117) [2002 86d: 7d 8m 6d 6f Jun 7] sturdy gelding: fairly useful performer at 3
yrs: has deteriorated considerably: tried blinkered. *A. Crook*

HARIK   8 ch.g. Persian Bold 123 – Yaqut (USA) 77 (Northern Dancer) [2002 53, a85:   –
p12g p16g² f16.2g⁴ Mar 9] rather leggy gelding: fairly useful handicapper on all-weather: **a85**
probably best around 2m: acts on all-weather: visored 3 of last 4 starts: usually tongue
tied. *G. L. Moore*

HARIPUR   3 b.c. Rainbow Quest (USA) 134 – Jamrat Jumairah (IRE) 91 (Polar Falcon   **62**
(USA) 126) [2002 10.4m p13g⁶ p12g⁶ p10g* Dec 30] lengthy, quite good-topped colt:
first foal: dam, 1m winner from 4 starts, half-sister to very smart miler Waajib: modest
form: left A. Stewart after second start (when reportedly had breathing problem): made
all in seller at Lingfield in December: may prove best around 1¼m. *J. Akehurst*

HARLEQUIN DANCER   6 b.g. Distant Relative 128 – Proudfoot (IRE) (Shareef   **59**
Dancer (USA) 135) [2002 54: 6d 8m* 9f 6v⁵ 8m³ 11.1v 8m⁴ 7m⁵ 7.9g 8s⁶ 10.1d Sep 9]
strong, good-topped gelding: modest handicapper: won at Newcastle in May: best around
1m: acts on soft and good to firm going: visored earlier in career: has hung: none too
consistent. *A. C. Whillans*

HARLESTONE BAY   3 b.g. Shaamit (IRE) 127 – Harlestone Lake 78 (Riboboy   **66 p**
(USA) 124) [2002 –: 10g 12g 12d 16m 16m⁵ Oct 1] smallish, sturdy gelding: fair maiden:
best effort in handicap at Nottingham final start: will prove best at 2m+: probably capable
of better still. *J. L. Dunlop*

HARLESTONE GREY 4 gr.g. Shaamit (IRE) 127 – Harlestone Lake 78 (Riboboy **111**
(USA) 124) [2002 101p: 12m 14d² 13.9m 14.1m³ 14.6m³ 14f² Sep 27] tall, lengthy
gelding: smart handicapper: ran particularly well when head second to Warrsan at
Goodwood second start, close third to Persian Punch in minor event at Salisbury and
8-length third to Total Turtle in Mallard Stakes at Doncaster: bred to be well suited by
2m+: acts on firm and good to soft ground. *J. L. Dunlop*

HARLOT 2 b.f. (May 12) Bal Harbour 113 – Queen of The Quorn 53 (Governor **57**
General 116) [2002 p6g p7g Dec 3] 1,000Y: fifth foal: half-sister to 6-y-o Tony Tie and 7f
winner Diamond Olivia (by Beveled): dam 6f/7f winner: modest form in maiden/minor
event at Lingfield. *John Berry*

HARMONIC (USA) 5 b.m. Shadeed (USA) 135 – Running Melody 86 (Rheingold **56**
137) [2002 73: 8f⁶ Jul 17] quite attractive mare: modest form only run on Flat in 2002
(successful over hurdles in August/October): stays 8.5f: acts on soft and good to firm
going: has been sold away/edged right. *G. Prodromou*

HARMONY HALL 8 ch.g. Music Boy 124 – Fleeting Affair 98 (Hotfoot 126) [2002 **62 §**
65: 8m 7.9m⁵ 8m² 8f 8m 8f 8m⁵ 7.1g⁵ 8.1m 7.5m⁴ 8m 8.9f f8g Nov 25] big, lengthy
gelding: modest handicapper: has form at 1½m, races at 7f/1m nowadays: acts on firm
and good to soft going: visored once: sometimes finds little. *J. M. Bradley*

HARNOUR 3 ch.c. Desert King (IRE) 129 – Irish Light (USA) 91 (Irish River (FR) **98**
131) [2002 92: 10g² 10f³ 12.3f 9g 9.9d³ 9.9m² 10g 10g⁶ 10s² 9.7m³ 10.1m² 10.1d⁵ 10.5f⁴
a10f Dec 27] compact colt: useful performer: mostly respectable efforts at least in 2002:
left M. Channon before final start: should stay 1½m: yet to race on heavy going, acts on
any other turf: has run in snatches: carries head awkwardly: often leads. *A. Smith, UAE*

HARRY B 3 b.g. Midyan (USA) 124 – Vilcabamba (USA) (Green Dancer (USA) 132) **52**
[2002 f6g p10g⁶ f12g² 11.6s 10m⁵ 12.1g² 11.9g² 10m⁶ f12g* Sep 30] 4,000Y: first foal: **a59**
dam French 9f winner: modest performer: won claimer at Wolverhampton (claimed
£5,000) in September: will prove best around 1½m: acts on all-weather, best turf efforts
on good going: has edged left. *G. C. Bravery*

HARRY JUNIOR 4 b.g. River Falls 113 – Badger Bay (IRE) 67 (Salt Dome (USA)) **– §**
[2002 –§: 8m Jul 7] temperamental maiden: tried blinkered/visored/tongue tied.
B. W. Murray

HARRY ON THE RUN 2 b.c. (Mar 19) Danzig Connection (USA) – Miss Runaway **67**
73 (Runnett 125) [2002 5m⁵ 5d⁶ p5g⁵ 6d⁴ Jul 11] fifth foal: half-brother to fairly useful
5f/6f winner The Fugative (by Nicholas): dam 6f winner: fair maiden: best effort when
fourth at Epsom: stays 6f: acts on good to soft going and polytrack. *S. Dow*

HARRY THE BEAVER (IRE) 3 b.g. Bigstone (IRE) 126 – Moon River (FR) **70**
(Groom Dancer (USA) 128) [2002 41: 12.1g 10f³ 10f⁵ 10.9g³ f12g⁴ 10m² 9.7m⁶ 10m⁴
Aug 16] fair maiden: effective at 1¼m/1½m: acts on fibresand, raced only on good or
firmer (acts on firm) on turf: consistent: sent to Czech Republic. *M. H. Tompkins*

HARRY THE HOOVER (IRE) 2 b.g. (Mar 29) Fayruz 116 – Mitsubishi Style (Try **88**
My Best (USA) 130) [2002 6g 6v* Nov 9] IR 20,000F, 21,000Y, 5,000 2-y-o: brother to
fairly useful 2001 2-y-o 5f winner Northern Tara and half-brother to 3 winners, including
fairly useful Irish 1992 2-y-o 5f winner Preponderance (by Cyrano de Bergerac): dam
third at 1m in Ireland: 14/1, much better effort in maidens (fairly useful form) when
winning 12-runner race at Doncaster by 4 lengths from Parknasilla, always prominent:
gelded after: not sure to stay much beyond 6f: acts on heavy ground: hung left on debut.
M. D. Hammond

HARVEY LEADER 7 b.g. Prince Sabo 123 – Mrs Leader (USA) (Mr Leader (USA)) **– §**
[2002 –§, a80§: f8g³ f8g 7.9s f8g f8g⁴ f8s f8s⁶ f8s Oct 8] big gelding: fair handicapper: **a66 §**
free-going sort, probably best around 1m: acts on fibresand: has worn crossed noseband:
unreliable. *Miss J. Feilden*

HASANPOUR (IRE) 2 b.c. (Apr 3) Dr Devious (IRE) 127 – Hasainiya (IRE) 109 **88 p**
(Top Ville 129) [2002 7d² Oct 15] tall, useful-looking colt: has scope: fourth foal: half-
brother to 3-y-o Hasik and useful Irish 9f winner Hasikiya (by Green Desert): dam Irish
1¼m winner: 8/1, ½-length second of 5 to Jay Gee's Choice in minor event at Leicester,
staying on under hands and heels: will stay at least 1¼m: sure to progress and win races.
Sir Michael Stoute

HASIK (IRE) 3 b.c. Ashkalani (IRE) 128 – Hasainiya (IRE) 109 (Top Ville 129) **88 p**
[2002 8.1d⁴ 8.3m* 10.3f² Jul 12] third foal: half-brother to useful Irish 9f winner Hasikiya
(by Green Desert): dam Irish 1¼m winner: won maiden at Windsor in June despite
carrying head awkwardly, flashing tail and wandering: plenty of improvement when

short-head second in handicap at Chester final start: should stay beyond 10.3f: already fairly useful, and can probably do better still. *Sir Michael Stoute*

HASINA (IRE)   3 b.f. King's Theatre (IRE) 128 – Smaointeach (IRE) 67 (Green Desert (USA) 127) [2002 77: 8s⁶ 7m⁴ 10v⁶ 7d 8g² 7d⁴ 8.5g² 7d² 8.5d⁵ 7d⁵ 8g 8m 7f 12.5f³ 11g³ 12.5d⁴ 10s² p12g p10g³ Dec 30] fifth foal: half-sister to useful Irish 6f (at 2 yrs) to 8.5f winner Tushna (by Erins Isle): dam, Irish 6f winner, half-sister to useful Irish sprinter Aretha: fairly useful maiden on turf, modest on all-weather: left J. Bolger in Ireland prior to penultimate start: stays 12.5f: acts on firm going, soft and polytrack: blinkered third/fourth starts. *B. W. Duke* **81 a59**

HASTA LA VISTA   12 b.g. Superlative 118 – Falcon Berry (FR) (Bustino 136) [2002 49, a46: 12g 12m 12m⁵ 14g⁴ 14d⁵ 15.8f⁶ Sep 21] compact gelding: has a round action: poor handicapper: effective at 1½m to 2m: acts on any turf going and fibresand: usually blinkered/visored: usually makes running. *M. W. Easterby* **40**

HASTY PRINCE   4 ch.g. Halling (USA) 133 – Sister Sophie (USA) (Effervescing (USA)) [2002 97: 10d 10.5m* 10m⁴ 11m⁵ 10m Sep 21] tall gelding: has a round action: useful handicapper: best effort when winning at Haydock in July by 2½ lengths from Bonaguil: stays 1½m: acts on firm and soft going: sold 18,000 gns, joined Jonjo O'Neill and winner over hurdles. *B. Hanbury* **101**

HATAANA (USA)   3 b.f. Robellino (USA) 127 – Katakana (USA) 106 (Diesis 133) [2002 8.2d 9.9m May 16] good-topped filly: sixth foal: half-sister to a winner in Macau by Arazi: dam 2-y-o 6f winner and third in Coronation Stakes: well held in maidens at Nottingham (upset at start) and Salisbury (refused to settle early): sold 7,500 gns. *M. A. Jarvis* **–**

HATALAN   3 ch.f. Mark of Esteem (IRE) 137 – Elbaaha 97 (Arazi (USA) 135) [2002 74: 7g 10.9g Jul 5] fair maiden at 2 yrs for M. Channon: well beaten in 2002: stays 7f (pulled hard at 10.9f): often finds little and looks wayward. *P. W. D'Arcy* **–**

HATHAAL (IRE)   3 b.c. Alzao (USA) 117 – Ballet Shoes (IRE) 75 (Ela-Mana-Mou 132) [2002 95p: 10d⁴ 10.4d 10.1m* 10.3m⁵ Sep 13] good-topped colt: has a short, un-impressive action: useful performer: won 4-runner minor event at Yarmouth in August by 1¼ lengths from Harnour: on toes/sweating, stiff task when never-dangerous fifth in similar race at Doncaster final start: stays 1¼m: yet to race on extremes of going: visored last 2 outings: sold 40,000 gns, sent to Spain. *Sir Michael Stoute* **100**

HATHA ANNA (IRE)   5 b.h. Sadler's Wells (USA) 132 – Moon Cactus 118 (Kris 135) [2002 115: 20m⁴ 16m⁵ 12m⁵ 16f Nov 5] quite attractive horse: has a round action: smart performer, lightly raced: sweating and edgy, good 3¾ lengths fourth to Royal Rebel in Gold Cup at Royal Ascot on reappearance: found little all starts after, in Goodwood Cup, listed race at Doncaster (respectable fifth to Systematic) and Melbourne Cup (in rear) at Flemington: stays 2½m: acts on firm and good to soft going: visored penultimate 4-y-o start and in 2002: has been bandaged behind: has left Godolphin. *Saeed bin Suroor* **118**

HATTER'S LAD (IRE)   3 b.g. Alzao (USA) 117 – Shamsana (USA) (Nijinsky (CAN) 138) [2002 86p: 12s³ 8m 8d⁶ 7.9s* Jul 31] strong gelding: fairly useful performer: won 4-runner minor event at Carlisle in July: stayed 8.5f: was headstrong and rather wayward: dead. *J. A. Osborne* **84**

HATTINGTON   4 b.g. Polish Precedent (USA) 131 – Ruffle (FR) (High Line 125) [2002 –: 12d* 16m³ 12d³ 12.1g* 13.1f⁴ 12m⁴ 12g² 14.6s⁶ 13.8d² Nov 5] fair handicapper: won amateur events at Salisbury in June and Chepstow in July: left R. Baker after seventh start: effective at 1½m/1¾m: acts on soft and good to firm going: raced freely fifth outing: sometimes looks tricky ride. *M. Todhunter* **70**

HAULAGE MAN   4 ch.g. Komaite (USA) – Texita 65 (Young Generation 129) [2002 63+: 6m 6f* 8m² 6g 7f⁴ 7g⁵ 6d³ 6m² 7g 6m⁴ 7m 8m² Oct 2] tall gelding: fair handicapper: won at Thirsk in May: mainly creditable efforts after: effective at 6f to 1m: acts on firm and good to soft going (yet to race on softer): sometimes slowly away/edges left. *D. Eddy* **79**

HAUNT THE ZOO   7 b.m. Komaite (USA) – Merryhill Maid (IRE) 71 (M Double M (USA)) [2002 –, a66: f8.5s* f8.5g* May 20] tall mare: fairly useful handicapper: won 2 handicaps at Wolverhampton in May: stays 9.4f: acts on fibresand: held up. *John A. Harris* **– a86**

HAVANA (IRE)   6 b.m. Dolphin Street (FR) 125 – Royaltess (Royal And Regal (USA)) [2002 54d: 16g⁶ 16m 16.2g May 11] close-coupled mare: poor maiden handicapper: stays 2m: probably acts on any turf going: tried blinkered: usually tongue tied nowadays: sometimes makes running. *R. Ford* **42**

HAVANTADOUBT (IRE)   2 ch.f. (Mar 13) Desert King (IRE) 129 – Batiba (USA)   **82**
(Time For A Change (USA)) [2002 6d³ 6d² 7.5m* 7g³ 7.1m⁴ 7.5g 10g⁵ 8s⁶ Nov 2] IR
12,500Y, IR 10,500Y: workmanlike filly: second foal: half-sister to Italian 5.5f (including
at 2 yrs) to 7f winner Entrexclusive (by Entrepreneur): dam French 2-y-o 9.5f winner:
fairly useful performer: won maiden at Beverley in June: good efforts in listed races at
Sandown and Baden-Baden (seventh of 8) fifth/sixth starts: likely to prove best at 7f/1m:
acts on good to firm and good to soft ground: often makes running. *J. G. Portman*

HAVOC   3 b.g. Hurricane Sky (AUS) – Padelia (Thatching 131) [2002 80p: 8.2d³ f12s   **68 d**
8v f7g Nov 22] tall, leggy gelding: has a round action: fair maiden: left E. Dunlop 10,000
gns/off 6 months prior to well held last 3 starts: should stay 1¼m: raced only on going
softer than good on turf. *N. Wilson*

HAWAYIL (USA)   3 b.f. Halling (USA) 133 – Avice Caro (USA) 85 (Caro 133) [2002   **59**
61: 10.9g 12.1g⁴ p12g³ 14.1f⁶ 14.1f⁵ p12g 10m⁶ Oct 3] leggy filly: fair maiden handi-   **a65**
capper on all-weather, modest on turf: stays 1½m, not 1¾m: acts on polytrack and firm
ground: sold 3,000 gns. *C. E. Brittain*

HAWK   4 b.g. A P Jet (USA) – Miss Enjoleur (USA) (L'Enjoleur (CAN)) [2002 90§:   **87 §**
p5g 6s 5f 5m⁴ 5g* 5d 5g³ 5m 5m 5m 5m 5g Sep 19] big, good-bodied gelding: fairly
useful handicapper: won at Thirsk in May: below form last 5 starts: best at 5f: acts on firm
going: tongue tied once at 2 yrs: races prominently: unreliable. *D. Nicholls*

HAWKEYE (IRE)   4 b.c. Danehill (USA) 126 – Tea House 107 (Sassafras (FR) 135)   **111**
[2002 122: 10g⁵ 12f³ 10d² 12f 10f⁵ Oct 6] tall, angular, quite good-topped colt: very smart
performer in 2001: just respectable efforts at best at 4 yrs, 1¼ lengths second to Izdiham
in listed event at Sandown and 4½ lengths fifth to The Tin Man in Clement L. Hirsch
Memorial Turf Championship at Santa Anita: best at 1¼m: unraced on heavy going, acts
on any other: blinkered last 3 starts. *M. A. Jarvis*

HAWKLEY   3 ch.g. Arctic Tern (USA) 126 – Last Ambition (IRE) 29 (Cadeaux   **71**
Genereux 131) [2002 54: 10f 8.2m⁵ 8m³ 8.3v* 8m² 10m 9d 8.2s Oct 23] lengthy gelding:
fair performer: won maiden handicap at Hamilton in August: left G. Wragg before below
form last 2 starts (gelded after final one): should stay 1¼m: acts on heavy and good to
firm going. *Miss A. M. Newton-Smith*

HAWKWIND (USA)   3 ro.c. El Prado (IRE) 119 – Pleasantly Quick (USA) (Roanoke   **92**
(USA)) [2002 71: 11s³ 14.1f² 14g² 14.1m* 16m* 16.2g⁶ 18m Oct 19] $160,000Y:
lengthy, rather unfurnished colt: easy mover: first foal: dam, 2-y-o 7f winner in USA,
half-sister to US Grade 3 8.5f winner Forcing Bid, also placed in Grade 1s at 9f/1¼m:
fairly useful performer: won maiden at Carlisle in August and handicap at Goodwood
(carried head high) in September: creditable efforts last 2 starts (visored first occasion):
stays 2¼m: yet to race on heavy going, seems to act on any other: sold 55,000 gns.
J. H. M. Gosden

HAWK WING (USA)   3 b.c. Woodman (USA) 126 – La Lorgnette (CAN) (Val   **127**
de L'Orne (FR) 133) [2002 116p: 8m² 12d² 10d* 10m² 8g² a10f Oct 26]
    When defending himself against the criticism of a wasted career, football
legend George Best has been heard to recall an occasion towards the end of his
playing days when, in a hotel room surrounded by the trappings of his success—
which, as the story goes, included that evening a former Miss World, a plentiful
supply of champagne and several hefty rolls of banknotes—the night porter
bringing him room service looked at him pityingly and said 'Where did it all go
wrong, George?' Public perception can be hard on sporting figures who fail to
deliver all they might have promised, whose achievements in the end don't quite
match their perceived talents. And, those whose reputations soar highest to begin
with can suffer the biggest backlash. Reactions in racing are often no different to
those in other sports and, having caught the public imagination in the spring, and
started clear favourite for the Two Thousand Guineas and the Derby, by season's
end Hawk Wing was in need of rescuing from his detractors. Hawk Wing: an
unlucky second in the Guineas; a fine second in the Derby; winner of the Eclipse; a
short-head second in the Irish Champion Stakes; second in the Queen Elizabeth II
Stakes. Where did it all go wrong?
    If Hawk Wing needed rescuing in the spring, it was from his admirers. As a
two-year-old, when he had won three of his four starts in Ireland, including the
National Stakes at the Curragh, his form had been arguably a little behind that of
Dewhurst winner Rock of Gibraltar (the only horse to have beaten Hawk Wing as a

two-year-old), for example, but Hawk Wing's reputation at Ballydoyle was second to none. At the stable's open day, it wasn't Rock of Gibraltar's or High Chaparral's name—or even that of the top two-year-old of 2001 Johannesburg—that was on trainer Aidan O'Brien's lips. 'It's a dream, but if we have a Triple Crown winner, it's Hawk Wing,' O'Brien was quoted as saying. If the rumour mill was to be believed, O'Brien's remarks stemmed not only from the belief that Hawk Wing was the best horse in his yard, as well as being the best O'Brien had trained, but also from the conviction that he was as good as any trained there in the time of his predecessor at Ballydoyle, Vincent O'Brien, including Nijinsky, the last Triple Crown winner. The public took note! Hawk Wing dominated the ante-post betting on the Guineas without reappearing beforehand, and he started at 6/4 in a field of twenty-two, with Rock of Gibraltar only fourth best at 9/1. 'A new wonder horse?' asked the *Racing Post*'s front page on the morning of the race alongside a picture of Hawk Wing. The media love to label: the annual search for the perfect distillation of the evolution of the racehorse had its first specimen of 2002!

Hawk Wing's spectacular late surge just failed to win him the Guineas, but his reputation blossomed in defeat more than any horse beaten in a classic since Dancing Brave in the Derby in 1986. For most at Newmarket, or among those watching on television either at home or in betting shops, the issue probably wasn't whether or not Hawk Wing should have won the Guineas, but by how far. So, what went wrong? Blanket TV coverage provided by the BBC, Channel 4, who cover the Guineas meeting, and satellite station attheraces, the dedicated Sky racing channel which began broadcasting in May, has brought increased interest in the nuances of the horserace, but, inevitably, different interpretations are still put on events. For some, the explanation for Hawk Wing's defeat at Newmarket lay in the state of the going. The suggestion wasn't that Hawk Wing had failed to cope with the ground, officially good to firm, but that the ground had been firmer on the far side of the course than it had been where Hawk Wing raced in the centre. Newmarket opened a fresh strip of ground on the stand side on Guineas day, but all the riders shunned it in the big race, some doing so in favour of the more 'down-trodden' ground on the far side, where four of the first five raced from the start.

'Ground bias' is a fashionable theory, but, at many meetings throughout a season, trying to establish an advantage for one part of the track over another frequently proves to be like chasing rainbows. The impression that one side of a track is favoured often has another plausible explanation—in the subtle differences to a result that can be accounted for by pace and tactics, the run of the race. Races take different shapes, and the shape of a race early on often gives a strong clue as to how the race might unfold. Racegoers and TV viewers alike have become accustomed to the varieties of fields that head towards them in a race: on straight courses, for example, all the horses cramming to one rail; the field splitting into two groups, one on each rail; or 'rogue' horses racing in isolation from the rest. To give another example: in races in which the field forms an arrowhead up the centre, those on the wings usually prove at a disadvantage. The tip of the arrowhead becomes the 'focal point' of the race, and a disadvantage lies in being the most detached from the focal point once the race begins in earnest, particularly if it is run at something less than a true gallop.

The field soon split into three groups in the Two Thousand Guineas. The early pace wasn't strong, but it was set by Redback in a small, far-side group. Belief in a 'ground bias' can be a powerful incentive for some jockeys to ride more enterprisingly than usual early on so as to secure a position on the part of track considered favoured. This was undoubtedly behind Darryll Holland quickly having Redback across to the far rail from stall sixteen in the Guineas. Other riders were less premeditated, restraining their mounts more than usual early on, while assessing how the race might be shaping up. Such diverse approaches can quickly lead to significant disparities between the pace and momentum of individual groups in the early stages of a race. Not far into the Guineas, it was clear that the largest group up the centre, which included Hawk Wing, was trailing the other two. This spelt danger for the favourite. As the race unfolded, Redback was kicked for home over two furlongs out against the rail, where Rock of Gibraltar, drawn highest in stall twenty-two, began his move in the same group. Soon after, Jamie Spencer, who had dropped Hawk Wing out from stall ten, still seemed under the impression

Sagitta 2000 Guineas Stakes, Newmarket—
a view showing Hawk Wing's domination of the main group (winner off picture, left)

that he had only those in his group to worry about, sitting confidently as Hawk Wing moved easily under him approaching the Dip. Once finally unleashed Hawk Wing responded magnificently, storming clear of his group and producing a turn of foot rarely seen in a classic. The line came too soon. Hawk Wing was still a neck down on his stable-companion Rock of Gibraltar, the two still racing half the width of the track apart. The Guineas field splitting into groups isn't a new phenomenon. Martial and Venture VII raced on opposite rails when divided by a head in the race in 1960. Ground husbandry has also been a topic for discussion in the Guineas before, most recently in the races won by Mark of Esteem and Mister Baileys. Newmarket is reportedly to redouble its efforts to ensure a level playing field in 2003 by trialing more sophisticated equipment designed for testing the racing surface. If the experiment clarifies matters, it will prove worthwhile, though it is more than a strong probability that the run of the race dictated by the tactics of the riders will continue to play a significant part.

Hawk Wing's failure to match Rock of Gibraltar's subsequent success doesn't alter the strong view taken at the time that Hawk Wing was the best horse on the day at Newmarket. In the light of his subsequent record, some tried to play down the impression Hawk Wing had made in the Guineas, making out that the camera angle shown on TV had exaggerated the ground Hawk Wing had made. The sectional times for the race provide independent confirmation, however, of what Hawk Wing achieved at Newmarket and also confirm that the run of the race counted against him compared to Rock of Gibraltar. The sectional times suggest that Naheef was a reluctant leader of Hawk Wing's group, setting a sluggish pace mid-race, and show that Hawk Wing was much the strongest finisher overall, as he came five lengths clear of the remainder of his group, giving the next best of them, the smart Aramram, a 13-lb beating, as we measure it. Hawk Wing made up the equivalent of around 7 lb on Rock of Gibraltar in the final three furlongs, the vast majority of it in the final furlong alone; the lack of pace early on makes that effort look all the more remarkable. What should also be added is that Rock of Gibraltar improved after Newmarket and, though both looked in fine shape on the day, Hawk Wing was perhaps marginally the fitter, having been aimed specifically at the race for longer, Rock of Gibraltar declared a definite runner only a few days beforehand.

Publicly, Aidan O'Brien took defeat for Hawk Wing and the quick end of the 'grand ambition' in his stride. 'Both thought they won so, mentally, the two of them are going to be super after it,' was his immediate response. Privately, the Ballydoyle team as a whole perhaps weren't quite so philosophical. Spencer, who had enjoyed big-race success for Ballydoyle in 2001, and had secured the Hawk Wing ride ahead of Johnny Murtagh, who partnered Rock of Gibraltar, did not figure in the stable's riding arrangements for the Derby or at Royal Ascot, and he wasn't brought fully back into the fold until the autumn. Hawk Wing was the first leg of a disappointing double for twenty-one-year-old Spencer, who was also beaten on the favourite Gossamer in the One Thousand Guineas. He remains a

421

highly promising rider, though, one who'll surely get many more opportunities to show his worth in the classics.

It is a measure of the impression made by Hawk Wing at Newmarket that he was quoted at 3/1-on to beat Rock of Gibraltar in anticipation of a rematch in the Irish Guineas. As things turned out, Rock of Gibraltar wasn't taken on again. For Hawk Wing, debate turned to the Derby—and his prospects of staying a mile and a half. Some doubted that his racing style would allow him to stay at Epsom. 'Hawk Wing: winning the Derby is just out of the question' was the headline over one *Racing Post* article. We had our doubts too, our representative at Newmarket concluding that Hawk Wing had shaped like a horse with more speed than stamina. Differentiating between a horse showing superior speed in relation to the opposition and one showing superior ability isn't easy. For his part, when it came to speculating on stamina Timeform's founder Phil Bull had no time for what he called bluntly 'the idiotic observation that a horse is too fast to stay'. For Bull, performance was simply a measure of ability, and until it was tested in a race stamina was best judged on pedigree. 'If a horse is bred to stay, it usually does; if it isn't, it usually doesn't,' has been the general rule of thumb applied at Timeform. In today's more international pedigrees, stamina is perhaps more difficult to gauge than it once was. That said, on our reading of Hawk Wing's pedigree, there was no cast-iron guarantee that he would stay the Derby trip.

In the circumstances, Hawk Wing's Derby second was all the more praise-worthy because the conditions were the most testing for the race since Teenoso's year in 1983. On firm going, placing the emphasis more on speed, things might have been different, but unexpected and prolonged rain in Derby week forced Michael Kinane—suspended for Newmarket though he had intended to miss the Guineas for the Kentucky Derby anyway—to consider a switch to High Chaparral, and he plumped for Hawk Wing only when asked to commit himself at the two-day declaration stage. Kinane's apparent indecision was reflected in the betting, and Hawk Wing, as short as 11/8 ante-post, lost favouritism for a time on Derby Day, drifting to 3/1 at one point. In the end, the weight of his reputation and the impression he had made at Newmarket helped to force him back to the head of the market and he went off at 9/4, with High Chaparral at 7/2. On firmer going, Hawk Wing would have been a red-hot favourite, and the race he ran in defeat again did as much to enhance his reputation as to detract from it. Put in the stalls last and settled in mid-field, Hawk Wing, towering over his rivals, cruised along without wasting energy pulling for his head. As the field began to become strung out running down towards Tattenham Corner, Hawk Wing was made to bide his time as Murtagh began his move round the outside on High Chaparral. Once in the straight, Hawk Wing continued to move easily, racing in the slipstream of his stable-companion briefly as the pair drew to the fore. Two furlongs out, Kinane began to ask for an effort and soon afterwards Hawk Wing was almost nose to nose with High Chaparral, the pair storming clear. No sooner had he got upsides, however, than Hawk Wing was under pressure and he was quickly beaten off. At the line, eased a touch, Hawk Wing was two lengths down, twelve lengths in front of the remainder.

Hawk Wing's Derby performance was arguably as good as any in defeat in the race in recent memory, but he was essentially outstayed all the same by High Chaparral under the conditions. After some speculation as to his next race, Hawk Wing bypassed a rematch at the Curragh, passing up another chance of classic success in favour of taking on all-aged competition back over shorter distances. Not all those closely involved in the finish of recent Derbys have been able to bounce back quickly from defeat, but Hawk Wing took his race in the conditions at Epsom well enough to tackle the Coral Eurobet Eclipse Stakes at Sandown less than a month later. It is ten years since the Eclipse attracted a field in double figures but the race continues to attract some of the very best around. Without the likes of older horses such as Grandera, Sakhee and Nayef, the Eclipse lacked another horse of Hawk Wing's quality. Hawk Wing became the third three-year-old winner in the last four runnings, following most recently his stable's Giant's Causeway, and he became the first three-year-old to land the odds in the race since Nashwan and Dancing Brave in the 'eighties. Only five runners stood their ground, Noverre and No Excuse Needed the most notable defectors among those from outside the multiple entry from the O'Brien camp. Hawk Wing started at 15/8-on and won

comfortably, cruising up to challenge after his stable-companion the Irish Derby
runner-up Sholokhov had set a slow early pace, and needing only a couple of slaps
to take control under two furlongs out, the field racing up the centre of the track.
Hawk Wing beat Sholokhov by two and a half lengths with Equerry the same
distance away in third, and Imperial Dancer and Indian Creek further behind.

As decisive as it was, Hawk Wing's victory in the Eclipse wasn't the electrifying one which the crowd had come to see. Three starts into his season, as well
as he had done, there was still more of a sense of anticipation than accomplishment
about Hawk Wing. What he had promised in the Guineas wasn't easily forgotten,
and the media and the public expected more. Connections pointed to the going as a
reason for Hawk Wing's failure to draw away in more spectacular style at Sandown.
'He wants it really fast,' said his trainer. Hawk Wing got 'his ground' again in his
next race, the Irish Champion Stakes at Leopardstown on the first Saturday in
September. In the meantime, along with the rest of the Ballydoyle string, Hawk
Wing bypassed the King George, won by the part Coolmore-owned Golan, and he
was also forced to miss the Juddmonte International at York when struck by the
coughing virus which affected many of his stable's horses in late-summer. Hawk
Wing's every move seemed to draw comment for most of the season, and
speculation was rife at Leopardstown as O'Brien saddled his first runners since the
coughing outbreak; the trainer's own physical condition even came in for comment
as his every move was monitored, too. After defeat for his stable's runners earlier
on the card, and with reports of O'Brien looking more gaunt than usual, Hawk
Wing proved easy to back as TV pictures showed his concerned trainer jogging
after him to the start, reportedly having been told that Hawk Wing might have
spread a plate; nerves were clearly frayed. Hawk Wing himself looked in good
shape, though he did froth a little round his mouth in the paddock and got warm
between his legs at the start. After being 2/1-on earlier in the week, Hawk Wing
eased to 11/8-on. He couldn't satisfy the crowd with a victory, but ran a perfectly
creditable race in defeat, waited with in third, as Sholokhov scorched clear, then
taking the measure of Best of The Bests well inside the last furlong, only for
Grandera to get up on his outside in the final stride. Hawk Wing didn't blow
excessively afterwards and Kinane hadn't ridden him with kid gloves, as if he
thought the race might have been needed; almost for the first time in his career
Hawk Wing came under sustained pressure in the closing stages of a race.

Hawk Wing's final chance in Europe to fulfil the expectations of his
supporters came in the Queen Elizabeth II Stakes at Ascot in late-September. In the
absence of Rock of Gibraltar (who travelled to the meeting and would have been a
late substitute had the watered ground turned soft), another stable-companion
Landseer and the likes of Keltos, Gossamer and Noverre, Hawk Wing started odds
on for the third time running, going off at 2/1-on in a field of five. Back at a mile for
the first time since the Guineas, Hawk Wing was again waited with as Sholokhov

set a much steadier pace this time, ignored by the rest. Turning for home Hawk Wing was still moving easily but, as he headed his pacemaker in the straight, he could not match the turn of foot of his fellow three-year-old Where Or When, going down by two lengths, with Tillerman three lengths further back in third.

On the face of it, at the time, Ascot represented Hawk Wing's most humbling reverse and it seemed that perhaps the season he had had, including the virus, had taken a toll. On the other hand, the tactics of the race were puzzling. As with Godolphin, the use of pacemakers has become common practice for the O'Brien stable, yet their deployment doesn't always seem to fit the needs of the horses they are being used to help. In the Guineas, Sholokhov ended up setting the pace for the one group which contained no other O'Brien-trained runner, leaving Hawk Wing stranded in his bunch. At Ascot, Sholokhov dawdled early on and, when he did quicken things up, Hawk Wing wasn't kept in touch with him. If the thinking behind using pacemakers is that a truly-run race suits the best horse, then the pacemaker should set a true gallop, with those meant to benefit from that keeping close enough to be able to take over themselves when it suits. If this doesn't happen, the race still develops into a muddling contest, effectively a sprint. The race that pacemaker Sholokhov and Hawk Wing engineered between them at Ascot wasn't likely to prove of benefit to a horse which had finished second in the Derby.

Hawk Wing had one more race after Ascot, in the Breeders' Cup Classic at Arlington. As had Galileo a year earlier, Hawk Wing was unable to cope with the best home opposition on dirt, slow to break and making a short-lived effort wide before trailing in a well-beaten seventh of twelve behind Volponi. By now, the fanfare which had accompanied Hawk Wing everywhere had died down, and on Breeders' Cup day he was firmly in the shadow of Rock of Gibraltar and High Chaparral. 'There's only one thing worse than being talked about . . .'

Mrs John Magnier's "Hawk Wing"

Hawk Wing had reportedly gone in his coat at Arlington but at least he will have a chance to put the sheen back on his reputation as a four-year-old, as, unusually for a Ballydoyle colt, he stays in training. Which races he might tackle may depend in part on plans for High Chaparral, who also breaks with the Ballydoyle tradition at four. Speed has always been the buzzword with Hawk Wing—he was even talked of as a possible for the July Cup by his trainer—but his effort at Epsom was probably as good as any he has put up, and not many of the races he might tackle at a mile and a half as a four-year-old will test stamina as thoroughly as the Derby did under the prevailing conditions. Hawk Wing will presumably be given another chance at the trip at some stage, though the Tattersalls Gold Cup at the Curragh and the Prince of Wales's Stakes at Royal Ascot, both over a mile and a quarter, might be on the agenda first, as might the Queen Anne Stakes particularly as it is to have Group 1 status for the first time in 2003.

For some, any discussion of Hawk Wing's optimum trip will be over-shadowed by talk of his temperament. The 'Second Coming who keeps coming second' and 'a big girl's blouse' were two of the comments about him which made it into print towards the end of his campaign. Hawk Wing does have a high head carriage but, to our eyes, he has never thrown in the towel at the end of a race and his performance in Ireland ought to have ended any suggestion that the way he carries himself is a sign of faint-heartedness. Hawk Wing's consistency has been hard to fault. He hasn't been out of the first two in his nine races on turf, the last six of which have been Group 1s. Hawk Wing has been asked some big questions, in terms of versatility bigger ones than the likes even of Ballydoyle champions such as Giant's Causeway, Galileo, Rock of Gibraltar and High Chaparral and, if he has come up a little short, it has not been by much.

Hawk Wing (USA) (b.c. 1999)	Woodman (USA) (ch 1983)	Mr Prospector (b 1970)	Raise A Native Gold Digger
		Playmate (ch 1975)	Buckpasser Intriguing
	La Lorgnette (CAN) (b 1982)	Val de L'Orne (b 1972)	Val de Loir Aglae
		The Temptress (b 1973)	Nijinsky La Sevillana

Hawk Wing's rating nudges him ahead of the multiple Group 1 winner Hector Protector as the best son of Woodman to have raced in Europe, though in terms of merit he still rates a bit behind the One Thousand Guineas and Champion Stakes winner Bosra Sham, the best offspring of Woodman. Woodman has been in the upper echelons of those sires capable of producing above-average performers, if not right up among the elite stallions, but he is not everyone's cup of tea as a sire by any means and his reputation for getting some irresolute types was used to knock Hawk Wing as well in some quarters in 2002. Such accusations are easier to make than to justify, though it is true to say that some of Woodman's more high-profile performers, such as Monsajem, Imtiyaz and Sparkling Water, have had their moments. Whatever else, Woodman has been able to get winners over a wide range of distances, though the average winning distance of his progeny in the last three seasons has crept up to nearly ten furlongs, leaving him only just behind the likes of Quest For Fame and Unfuwain, for example, in terms of stamina influence. Hawk Wing's dam La Lorgnette was rated the second best of her sex in her year in the Free Handicap in Canada, where she won the Canadian Oaks and beat the colts in the Queen's Plate over a mile and a quarter. La Lorgnette's best previous representative was the Canadian stakes performer Alexandrina (by Conquistador Cielo), the dam of Thornfield who won the Canadian International as a five-year-old. Physically, Hawk Wing is hard to fault and has the frame to train on as a four-year-old. A big, close-coupled colt, he impresses in appearance and has an equally impressive, flowing action. He wears a crossed noseband and has yet to race on extremes of ground, though there's little to choose between his form on good to firm and good to soft, his Guineas run being on the former. It hardly needs saying that he has yet to live up to the expectations once held of him, but, whatever 2003 holds, he has already shown himself a high-class and versatile racehorse.
A. P. O'Brien, Ireland

HAYDN BOWEN 3 ch.c. Most Welcome 131 – Hi-Li (High Top 131) [2002 –: p13g – 10d Oct 28] no form: tried blinkered. *R. M. Flower*

HAYHAAT (USA) 2 ch.f. (Feb 14) Irish River (FR) 131 – Ball Gown (USA) (Silver **81** Hawk (USA) 123) [2002 7d³ 7m⁵ Aug 29] $220,000F: first foal: dam unraced out of sister to top-class 1982 2-y-o 7f winner Gorytus: green, fairly useful form in minor event at Newmarket (third to Steelaninch, racing freely) and maiden at Salisbury (fifth to Wondrous Story): should stay 1m. *D. R. Loder*

HAZE BABYBEAR 2 b.f. (Jan 29) Mujadil (USA) 119 – River's Rising (FR) 88 **66** (Mendez (FR) 128) [2002 5m 5g⁴ 6m⁶ Sep 8] 10,500Y: half-sister to fairly useful 1996 2-y-o 7f winner Mudflap (by Slip Anchor), 3-y-o Grey Pearl and several winners abroad: dam 1m winner: fair form in maidens: should stay 7f. *R. A. Fahey*

HAZEL'S RIDGE (IRE) 2 ch.f. (Apr 19) Hamas (IRE) 125§ – Claire's Thatch – (Thatch (USA) 136) [2002 5s 6g 7f f6s Dec 26] 1,500Y: smallish filly: half-sister to several winners abroad, including The Imps (by Mac's Imp), 5f seller winner in Britain at 2 yrs, and a winner up to 11f in Italy by Mukaddamah: dam Irish 1½m winner: no form, including in seller. *P. Howling*

HAZIM 3 b.c. Darshaan 133 – Souk (IRE) 98 (Ahonoora 122) [2002 10.5d⁴ 12.6m* **98** 12d⁴ Aug 3] 260,000Y: seventh foal: brother to smart middle-distance stayer Puce, closely related to fairly useful 10.5f winner Shouk (by Shirley Heights) and half-brother to several winners, including useful 1½m winner Seek (by Rainbow Quest): dam 7f winner better at 1m: useful performer: won maiden at Warwick in June by 3 lengths from Stance: not discredited when 2¼ lengths fourth of 5 to Prompt Payment in minor event at Newmarket final start: likely to stay 1¾m. *Sir Michael Stoute*

HAZIMAH (USA) 3 b.f. Gone West (USA) – Elrafa Ah (USA) 105 (Storm Cat (USA)) **67** [2002 74: 8.2m³ 7m³ 7m³ 8.2m⁵ Sep 20] leggy, quite good-topped filly: fair form in maidens: effective at 7f/1m: acted on good to firm going: visits Langfuhr. *M. P. Tregoning*

HAZLEMOORE LANE 3 ch.f. Forzando 122 – Thatcherella 80 (Thatching 131) – [2002 p5g 6m Apr 5] third foal: half-sister to 7f winner Avery Ring (by Magic Ring): dam 5f (including at 2 yrs) and 6f winner: slowly away and always behind in maidens at Lingfield and Folkestone. *E. A. Wheeler*

HAZY MORN 3 gr.f. Cyrano de Bergerac 120 – Hazy Kay (IRE) 77 (Treasure Kay – 114) [2002 51: 5.1d f5g Jun 22] close-coupled filly: poor maiden for N. Hawke at 2 yrs: well held in 2002: tried blinkered. *W. G. M. Turner*

HEADLAND (USA) 4 b. or br.g. Distant View (USA) 126 – Fijar Echo (USA) (In **?** Fijar (USA) 121) [2002 89: f7s f6g² f6g 6m 6.1s f7g p7g p7g Dec 28] well-made gelding: **a95** useful handicapper on all-weather: effective at 6f/7f: ran as if something amiss third/ fourth starts, tongue tied next 2. *J. M. P. Eustace*

HEAD OF COLLEGE (IRE) 2 ch.c. (Feb 8) Ashkalani (IRE) 128 – Ceide Dancer **63** (IRE) 79 (Alzao (USA) 117) [2002 6m 6s 6d³ 7m 7s 7s Oct 28] IR 8,000Y: smallish, sturdy colt: fourth foal: half-brother to 3-y-o Prairie Dunes and a winner in Italy (both by Indian Ridge): dam, 8.5f winner, half-sister to smart winner up to 7f (including Haydock Park Sprint Cup) Lavinia Fontana: modest maiden: stays 7f: best effort on good to soft ground: tried blinkered/tongue tied. *J. L. Dunlop*

HEAD SCRATCHER 4 ch.g. Alhijaz 122 – Sabrata (IRE) (Zino 127) [2002 53: 5.9s – f9.4g Jul 20] probably of little account nowadays. *A. Bailey*

HEAD TO KERRY (IRE) 2 b.g. (Apr 12) Eagle Eyed (USA) 111 – The Poachers – Lady (IRE) (Salmon Leap (USA) 131) [2002 7f p7g p7g 8s Oct 26] 6,500Y: closely related to a 1m winner in Scandinavia by Hamas and half-brother to several winners, including 5-y-o Sir Ninja and fairly useful 1m winner Chalom (by Mujadil): dam, Irish 1¼m/1½m winner, half-sister to very smart 1¼m performer Insatiable: well held in maidens. *D. J. S. ffrench Davis*

HEALEY (IRE) 4 ch.g. Dr Devious (IRE) 127 – Bean Siamsa (Solinus 130) [2002 –: **65 d** 12.4g 10.1m 9f 10g 12m⁴ 12.1s f14s 11.5s f12g⁶ Dec 2] lengthy, quite good-topped gelding: fair performer: left J. Bethell after seventh start: stays 1½m: probably acts on any going: tried blinkered/tongue tied: on downgrade. *C. A. Dwyer*

HEARTBREAKER (IRE) 2 b.g. (Apr 5) In Command (IRE) 114 – No Hard Feelings – (IRE) 86 (Alzao (USA) 117) [2002 5g 7s⁴ Aug 24] 20,000Y: strong gelding: half-brother to several winners, including 1998 2-y-o 5f winner Inca Tern (by Polar Falcon), later 1m winner in USA, and 1½m winner Athletic Sam (by Definite Article), both fairly useful:

dam 5f (at 2 yrs) to 1½m winner: well held in maiden and minor event 4½ months apart. *N. Tinkler*

HEARTHSTEAD PRIDE   3 ch.g. Dr Devious (IRE) 127 – Western Heights (Shirley   **88**
Heights 130) [2002 f8.5g⁴ f9.4g³ f12g² f12g² f12g* 12m² 12m* 14.6m² 14.1m⁵ May 10]
27,000Y: angular gelding: sixth foal: half-brother to several winners, including smart
1m/1¼m performer Barathea Guest (by Barathea) and 6-y-o Dollar Law: dam unraced
half-sister to winner up to 1½m Startino: fairly useful performer: won maiden at Wolverhampton in March and handicap at Pontefract (by 13 lengths) in May: best form at 1½m:
raced only on fibresand/good to firm going: gelded. *M. Johnston*

HEATHER BAY   2 b.f. (Feb 10) Millkom 124 – Jersey Belle 53 (Distant Relative 128)   **–**
[2002 f6g Oct 22] third foal: dam 6f winner: 66/1, tailed off in maiden at Southwell.
J. Balding

HEATHERS GIRL   3 ch.f. Superlative 118 – Kristis Girl 76 (Ballacashtal (CAN))   **–**
[2002 f7g⁶ f8g⁴ f7g f8g f8.5g² f9.4g f8.5g⁵ f8.5g⁵ f9.4g⁶ 7s f8.5g⁴ f8.5g Dec 20] 4,000Y: **a57**
first foal: dam 5f (including at 2 yrs) and 1m winner: modest maiden handicapper: stays
8.5f: acts on fibresand: blinkered (well held) only start on turf. *D. Haydn Jones*

HEATHER VALLEY   6 ch.m. Clantime 101 – Sannavally (Sagaro 133) [2002 –: p6g   **42**
f8s 7g⁶ 7d 6d 6g 6d 6d⁶ Jul 11] poor maiden handicapper: stays 7f: tried visored.
J. Akehurst

HEATHMAN (IRE)   6 b.g. Common Grounds 118 – Dul Dul (USA) (Shadeed (USA)   **–**
135) [2002 –: f8.5g Jan 21] of no account. *R. J. Baker*

HEATHYARDSBLESSING (IRE)   5 b.g. Unblest 117 – Noble Nadia (Thatching   **79 d**
131) [2002 74: 6m 5d 5.1d⁶ 6m 5d 7g Sep 10] quite good-topped gelding: useful winner
at 2 yrs: only fair at best in 2002: stays easy 6f: yet to race on soft/heavy going, probably
acts on any other: has carried head awkwardly. *R. Hollinshead*

HEATHYARDS GUEST (IRE)   4 ch.g. Be My Guest (USA) 126 – Noble Nadia   **–**
(Thatching 131) [2002 60: 8d f12g Dec 2] leggy gelding: one-time modest maiden: well
held in 2002. *Mrs K. Walton*

HEATHYARDS LAD (IRE)   5 b.g. Petardia 113 – Maiden's Dance 65 (Hotfoot   **40**
126) [2002 –: 5.1g 10.2d 12d Jun 11] poor form in 2002. *Dr P. Pritchard*

HEATHYARDS MATE   5 b.g. Timeless Times (USA) 99 – Quenlyn (Welsh Pageant   **45**
132) [2002 –: f8s⁵ f7g⁶ f11s⁵ f8g f7g² f7g f8g 7s Mar 28] sturdy, close-coupled gelding:
poor performer: effective at 7f, probably at 11f: acts on good to firm going and fibresand.
R. Hollinshead

HEATHYARDS SIGNET   4 b.g. King's Signet (USA) 110 – Heathyards Gem 64   **48 §**
(Governor General 116) [2002 61?: f6g⁴ f7g³ f7g² f6g f8.5g f7g f7s 6g 5.9d⁵ 7.6f⁶ 5.1g⁵
6v 5g f6g Nov 15] workmanlike gelding: poor performer: left D. McCain before final
start: barely stays 7f: acts on firm ground, good to soft and fibresand: usually blinkered/
visored: sometimes wears tongue strap: has been slowly away/hung right: inconsistent.
C. L. Popham

HEATHYARDS SWING   4 b.c. Celtic Swing 138 – Butsova 93 (Formidable (USA)   **72**
125) [2002 79: f11s f11s⁵ f11g² f11g* 12s 10g² 10m Jun 4] rather leggy, quite good-
topped colt: fair handicapper: won at Southwell in February: barely stays 11f: acts on
good to firm going, good to soft and fibresand: has flashed tail. *R. Hollinshead*

HEATHYARDS TIPPLE (IRE)   6 b.m. Marju (IRE) 127 – Nikki's Groom (Shy   **–**
Groom (USA)) [2002 f9.4g 9.3g⁵ 12.6g Jul 5] maiden: no form in 2002: tried blinkered.
D. McCain

HEAVEN FORBID   4 b.g. Beveled (USA) – Fayre Holly (IRE) 57 (Fayruz 116) [2002   **56**
54: f5s* f5g f5g Oct 17] modest performer: won claimer at Southwell in January: was
best at 5f: acted on fibresand: dead. *J. G. Portman*

HEAVENLY TIMES   3 ch.f. Timeless Times (USA) 99 – Heavenly Queen (Scottish   **40 +**
Reel 123) [2002 f5g 6g⁴ 7m 5m 7g p6g May 29] 600F: half-sister to several winners,
including 1997 2-y-o 5f winner Heavenly Abstone (by Interrex) and 9f and 1½m winner
Absinther (by Presidium): dam little form: sign of ability in Britain only when fourth of
17 in seller at Leicester second start: tried visored: sent to Holland, and won at 6.5f there
in September. *C. A. Dwyer*

HEAZLE TWIG   2 b.f. (Apr 18) So Factual (USA) 120 – Forest Song 60 (Forzando   **–**
122) [2002 f6g 6d f6g⁴ 7f Jun 22] smallish, workmanlike filly: fifth foal: half-sister to 2

winners, including 5-y-o Come On Murgy: dam, maiden, should have stayed 1m: well held in sellers. *W. G. M. Turner*

HEBENUS 3 b.g. Hamas (IRE) 125§ – Stinging Nettle 90 (Sharpen Up 127) [2002 f7g⁶ f7g 7g⁶ 7f 5.9g* 6m² 7.1d⁶ 6g Sep 9] 12,500Y: lengthy gelding: half-brother to several winners, including useful 2-y-o sprint winners Maid For Walking (in 1994, by Prince Sabo) and Maid For The Hills (in 1995, by Indian Ridge): dam, 2-y-o 6f winner on debut but no form after, half-sister to very smart 7f to 1¼m winner Gairloch: modest handicapper: won at Hamilton in July: best efforts at 6f: acts on good to firm going. *R. A. Fahey* **62**

HECTERINE (IRE) 2 b.f. (Feb 13) Hector Protector (USA) 124 – Half-Hitch (USA) 88 (Diesis 133) [2002 5m a6g⁴ a5.5g* a6g a8g 7g Oct 5] IR 50,000Y: unfurnished filly: has a round action: first foal: dam, 2-y-o 6f winner, daughter of very smart miler Marling: slowly away and soon well outpaced in Queen Mary Stakes at Royal Ascot on debut: best effort when winning maiden at Mijas in July: well held in claimer at Longchamp final start: should stay at least 6f. *E. J. Creighton, Spain* **?**

HECTIC TINA 3 ch.f. Hector Protector (USA) 124 – Tinashaan (IRE) 100 (Darshaan 133) [2002 8.2g⁵ 8g⁷ Jun 16] good-topped filly: second foal: dam, 1½m winner, half-sister to useful stayer Life of Riley: better effort in maidens (fair form) when 5 lengths second to Welsh Diva at Salisbury, again slowly away and staying on: bred to be suited by 1¼m/1½m: has been blanketed for stall entry. *J. R. Fanshawe* **85**

HECTOR'S GIRL 2 ch.f. (Feb 15) Hector Protector (USA) 124 – Present Imperfect 61 (Cadeaux Genereux 131) [2002 6s* 6.5g² Sep 27] 60,000F, 75,000Y: second foal: dam twice-raced half-sister to very smart performer up to 7f College Chapel: won 7f maiden at Lingfield despite meeting interference: plenty of improvement (useful form) when head second of 25 to Sharplaw Venture in sales race at Ascot later in September, drifting left: should be suited by 7f/1m: capable of better still, and should win more races. *Sir Michael Stoute* **95 p**

HECUBA 2 ch.f. (Feb 27) Hector Protector (USA) 124 – Ajuga (USA) 102 (The Minstrel (CAN) 135) [2002 7m 8s⁴ Oct 25] strong, lengthy filly: half-sister to several winners, including smart performers up to 1½m Prolix (by Kris) and Bad Bertrich Again (by Dowsing), and 6-y-o Bangalore: dam, 6f (at 2 yrs) and 7f winner, out of Irish 1000 Guineas and Champion Stakes winner Cairn Rouge: much better effort in maidens (fair form) when fourth of 22 to Richemaur at Doncaster: will be suited by 1¼m+: open to progress. *B. W. Hills* **79 p**

HEFIN 5 ch.g. Red Rainbow 105 – Summer Impressions (USA) 70 (Lyphard (USA) 132) [2002 56: p13g⁶ p12g 13.8d⁴ 14.1d⁴ Apr 30] rather sparely-made gelding: modest handicapper: left S. Williams after second outing: will probably be suited by 2m: acts on good to firm going, good to soft and polytrack. *I. A. Wood* **56**

HEIDELBURG (IRE) 2 b.f. (Apr 28) Night Shift (USA) – Solar Attraction (IRE) 60 (Salt Dome (USA)) [2002 6.1m² 6d³ p7g² f5g* Nov 15] 2,000Y: quite attractive filly: fourth foal: half-sister to 2 winners, including Irish 9f winner Neckar Valley (by Desert King): dam third at 5f in Ireland at 2 yrs: fair form: won maiden at Wolverhampton by 1½ lengths from Percy Douglas: stays 7f: acts on all-weather. *S. Kirk* **76**

HEIR TO BE 3 b.g. Elmaamul (USA) 125 – Princess Genista 108 (Ile de Bourbon (USA) 133) [2002 –p: 10.1m⁴ 14.1m 14.1g³ 16v* 16s³ Nov 6] angular gelding: half-brother to 5-y-o Give Notice: progressive form: won handicap at Nottingham in October: good third in similar event at Musselburgh final start: suited by 2m+: acts on heavy going: useful performer in the making. *J. L. Dunlop* **87 p**

HEKTIKOS 2 ch.c. (Feb 24) Hector Protector (USA) 124 – Green Danube (USA) 92 (Irish River (FR) 131) [2002 7g 7.1f⁴ 8g Oct 16] 40,000F, 48,000Y: sturdy, quite attractive colt: fifth living foal: half-brother to 3 winners abroad, including French 11.4f winner Fabulous Flirt (by Caerleon): dam 7.6f and 1¼m winner: easily best effort in maidens (fair form) when never-dangerous fourth to Crystal Star at Haydock: should be suited by 1m+: sold 7,000 gns. *J. L. Dunlop* **70**

HELDERBERG (USA) 2 b.f. (Feb 8) Diesis 133 – Banissa (USA) (Lear Fan (USA) 130) [2002 7d 8v³ Nov 8] $47,000F, 28,000Y: lengthy, good-topped filly: half-sister to winners in USA by Known Fact and Shananie: dam unraced close relative to St Leger winner Touching Wood: fair form in maiden at Newmarket and minor event at Doncaster, 13 lengths third of 5 to Lady Mytton in latter: should be suited by 1¼m+: has scope to make a better 3-y-o. *C. E. Brittain* **71 p**

HELEN BRADLEY (IRE)   3 ch.f. Indian Ridge 123 – Touraya (Tap On Wood 130)   **81**
[2002 85: 8g 6d 5g p7g⁴ p7g³ 8.3d⁶ 7m p8g⁶ Dec 14] tall, angular filly: fairly useful
performer: stays 1m: acts on polytrack and good to soft going: free-going sort.
N. P. Littmoden

HELICAL GIRL   4 b.f. Presidium 124 – Oubeck 65 (Mummy's Game 120) [2002 40:   **– §**
f7g p7g 7f 10m 8d May 27] temparmental maiden: left R. Cowell after second start:
usually blinkered/visored. *T. T. Clement*

HELLBENT   3 b.g. Selkirk (USA) 129 – Loure (USA) 66 (Lyphard (USA) 132) [2002   **50**
6m⁵ p8g³ 7s Oct 22] 11,000 2-y-o: sixth foal: brother to smart 7f (at 2 yrs) to 1¼m winner
Entice and half-brother to 2 winners abroad, including French winner up to 1½m Culvern
(by Kris): dam, ran 3 times, half-sister to Royal Lodge winner Royal Kingdom and to
dam of high-class Japanese 1m/1¼m performer Agnes Digital: modest form in maidens
first 2 starts: well held final one: slowly away first/third outings, raced freely in between.
J. A. Osborne

HELLOIMUSTBEGOING (USA)   3 b.f. Red Ransom (USA) – Arsaan (USA) 106   **88**
(Nureyev (USA) 131) [2002 76p: 8f* 10m⁵ 9g Jul 31] lengthy, angular filly: fairly useful
form: wearing crossed noseband, won maiden at Newmarket in May by ¾ length from
Code Sign: disappointing after: should stay 1¼m. *E. A. L. Dunlop*

HELLO SWEETY   4 b.f. Shaamit (IRE) 127 – Madam Brady (USA) (Lomond (USA)   **–**
128) [2002 78: 10m 10m 12.1g 10.9m 12d Nov 1] fair performer at 3 yrs: well held in
2002. *G. C. Bravery*

HELLO VEGAS   5 b.g. First Trump 118 – Meet Again (Lomond (USA) 128) [2002 –:   **–**
f16s f14.8g⁴ f14.8g Feb 2] strong, good-topped gelding: no longer of much account. *Mrs
Lydia Pearce*

HELM BANK   2 b.c. (Mar 13) Wild Again (USA) – Imperial Bailiwick (IRE) 104   **97 p**
(Imperial Frontier (USA) 112) [2002 6g* 7m* Jun 19] rather leggy, useful-looking colt:
third foal: half-brother to a winner up to 7.5f in Italy by Efisio: dam 2-y-o 5f (Champion
Flying Childers Stakes) winner): overcame greenness to win minor event at Ayr in
May: 25/1, improved considerably (useful form) to win 12-runner Chesham Stakes at
Royal Ascot by short head from Tomahawk, edging ahead late on: reportedly had minor
problem after: should stay 1m: should improve if all is well. *M. Johnston*

HELMS DEEP   2 b.c. (Feb 16) Royal Applause 124 – Ayunli 81 (Chief Singer 131)   **86**
[2002 6.1m⁵ 6g³ 6m 6.1g² 6g⁶ p7g⁴ Oct 9] 78,000Y: close-coupled colt: third foal:
half-brother to fairly useful 2001 2-y-o 5f winner Ayzal (by Zilzal): dam 8.5f to 15.5f
winner: fairly useful maiden: good sixth of 7 to Zinziberine in Prix Eclipse at Maisons-
Laffitte penultimate start: likely to prove best at 5f/6f: sold 44,000 gns, sent to
USA. *B. J. Meehan*

HELVETIUS   6 b.g. In The Wings 128 – Hejraan (USA) 73 (Alydar (USA)) [2002 70:   **56**
13.3s 17.2d³ Jun 15] tall, leggy gelding: modest handicapper on Flat nowadays: barely
stays 17f: acts on firm and soft going: blinkered once. *P. C. Ritchens*

HENDERSON   3 br.g. Wesaam (USA) 95 – Akatombo (Ilium 121) [2002 7m 6m 6s   **–**
f8g Dec 10] smallish, leggy gelding: has a quick action: first reported foal: dam no form
in 3 starts: well held in maidens: tried blinkered. *D. E. Cantillon*

HENESEYS LEG   2 b.f. (Mar 2) Sure Blade (USA) 130 – Away's Halo (USA)   **–**
(Sunny's Halo (CAN)) [2002 5m 5.7f Jul 25] 2,800Y: closely related to a winning sprinter
in Italy by Kris and half-sister to several minor winners in USA: dam 6f (at 2 yrs)/7f
winner in USA: well beaten in maidens. *C. G. Cox*

HENGROVE   2 b. or br.f. (Mar 9) Fraam 114 – Java Rupiah (IRE) (Hamas (IRE) 125§)   **49**
[2002 5.1g f6f f6g f6g² f6g⁶ Dec 17] first foal: dam ran once: poor maiden: runner-up in
seller at Wolverhampton: should stay 7f: acts on fibresand. *M. S. Saunders*

HENNERWOOD IVY   7 b.m. Tina's Pet 121 – Come On Clover (Oats 126) [2002   **–**
f12s Sep 17] fifth foal: dam of no account: no sign of ability. *R. J. Price*

HENRI MARTIN   2 ch.g. (Apr 5) Inchinor 119 – Bonita 57 (Primo Dominie 121)   **80 §**
[2002 5.2g⁶ 6g² p6g p6g 6s² 7d² 7.9f³ 7g⁴ Oct 19] 44,000Y: workmanlike gelding: fourth foal:
brother to fairly useful 6f winner (including at 2 yrs) Clunie and half-brother to 2 winners,
including 4-y-o Bonito: dam 6f/7f winner: fairly useful maiden: second at Windsor,
Redcar and Epsom: best efforts at 6f/7f: acts on soft going, probably on firm (below form
on polytrack): carries head high: sold 16,000 gns: probably ungenuine. *P. F. I. Cole*

HENRI ROYALE (IRE)   2 gr.c. (Apr 2) Desert King (IRE) 129 – Renzola (Dragonara   **78**
Palace (USA) 115) [2002 7m 7s Oct 25] 65,000F, 100,000 2-y-o: leggy, quite good-

topped colt: half-brother to several winning sprinters, notably smart 1996 2-y-o 5f/6.5f winner Deadly Dudley (by Great Commotion): dam unraced half-sister to dam of very smart French performer up to 1½m Millkom: fair form when seventh to Almushahar in maiden at Newmarket on debut, finishing well: hung left and soon in trouble on much softer ground in similar event at Doncaster 2 months later: will probably stay 1m. *M. L. W. Bell*

HENRY HALL (IRE)   6 b.h. Common Grounds 118 – Sovereign Grace (IRE) 101   **97**
(Standaan (FR) 118) [2002 101: 5.1f 5f⁴ 5d 5m⁶ 5m⁶ 5m⁵ 5.2f⁶ 5m³ 5.2m⁴ 5m² 5m 5s⁶ Oct 26] leggy horse: has a round action: useful handicapper: several creditable efforts in 2002: below best last 4 starts: best at 5f: acts on firm and soft going: visored once: usually waited with. *N. Tinkler*

HENRY ISLAND (IRE)   9 ch.g. Sharp Victor (USA) 114 – Monterana 99 (Sallust   **68 §**
134) [2002 72§, a80§: p16g p12g 11.8s 14.1d 11.6s 14.1d⁶ 14.1g* 16.2m² 14.1m⁶ Jul 13] workmanlike gelding: good mover: fair handicapper: won selling event at Nottingham in June: effective at 1½m, probably at 2¼m: acts on fibresand, soft and good to firm going: tends to sweat: has looked reluctant (particularly over hurdles): reportedly finished lame final start: untrustworthy. *Mrs A. J. Bowlby*

HENRY'S HERO   3 b.g. Pyramus (USA) 78 – Casbatina 71 (Castle Keep 121) [2002   **64**
65: f6s f5s p6g⁶ 5m⁴ 5d 5m 8g 6m² 7g Sep 2] smallish gelding: modest handicapper: was best at 5f/easy 6f: acted on fibresand (probably polytrack), soft and good to firm going: tried visored (hung right): sometimes looked none too keen: was one to treat with some caution: dead. *C. A. Dwyer*

HENRY TUN   4 b.g. Chaddleworth (IRE) 103 – B Grade 59 (Lucky Wednesday 124)   **42 §**
[2002 54, a57: f5s f5g f5g³ f5g* f5g f5g 5d 5m f5g⁴ f5s⁶ f6s 6m f6g f5g* f5g⁶ f5g⁶ f5g⁵   **a60 §**
f5g Dec 31] tall gelding: modest handicapper: left Miss J. Craze after second start: won at Wolverhampton in May and Southwell in October: stays sharp 6f: acts on fibresand and firm going: tried visored/tongue tied (not in 2002): has worn cheekpieces: usually races prominently: sometimes looks reluctant. *J. Balding*

HENRY WINDSOR   2 b.g. (Mar 2) Forzando 122 – Ski Baby (Petoski 135) [2002   **66**
5s⁵ 5g⁵ 5d⁶ 5m² 5g⁶ 5m⁵ 5s 5m⁶ 6d⁴ Oct 21] 8,000Y: strong, close-coupled gelding: fifth foal: half-brother to 5f winner Queens Check (by Komaite): dam unraced half-sister to useful sprinter Deep Finesse and to dam of 7-y-o Halmahera: fair maiden: effective at 5f/6f: acts on good to firm and good to soft going, well held on fibresand. *N. Tinkler*

HERE COMES TOM   4 b.g. Puissance 110 – Young Holly (Risk Me (FR) 127)   **–**
[2002 –: 8.3g p7g⁵ 7d 7d 7m 7f 8.3g Aug 12] of little account. *Jamie Poulton*

HERETIC   4 b.g. Bishop of Cashel 122 – Barford Lady 93 (Stanford 121§) [2002 96:   **114**
8m² 7.1s² 8.1d* 8g⁶ Aug 18] good-bodied gelding: has a short, round action: smart performer, lightly raced: best effort when winning Tote Scoop6 Handicap at Sandown in July by 3 lengths from Finished Article: respectable sixth to Dress To Thrill in Desmond Stakes at Leopardstown final start: likely to prove best up to 1m: acts on soft and good to firm going. *J. R. Fanshawe*

HER EXCELLENCY   3 b.f. Hernando (FR) 127 – Attribute 69 (Warning 136) [2002   **67**
8f⁴ 8.3g Jul 8] second foal: half-sister to 4-y-o Reasoning: dam, maiden daughter of half-sister to Xaar, from family of El Gran Senor: much better effort in maidens (fair form) when fourth to Hareer at Yarmouth on debut: bred to be suited by 1¼m. *G. Wragg*

Tote Scoop6 Handicap, Sandown—Heretic quickens right away to win this £58,000 prize;
Finished Article (rail) and Laggan Minstrel are placed

HERMIT'S HIDEAWAY   5 b.g. Rock City 120 – Adriya 94 (Vayrann 133) [2002 **41**
49: f12s* f12g⁶ 9.9g 10g⁶ 10.9d 8m 8s 8m⁴ Jul 26] useful-looking gelding: modest **a55**
handicapper on all-weather, poor on turf: won apprentice event at Southwell in January:
stayed 1½m: acted on fibresand and probably on any turf going: had sweated/wandered/
found little: was none too consistent: dead. *T. D. Barron*

HERNANDITA   4 b.f. Hernando (FR) 127 – Dara Dee 87 (Dara Monarch 128) [2002   **–**
83: 10d 14d Jun 15] close-coupled filly: fairly useful at 3 yrs for J. Dunlop: well held both
starts in 2002: visored on reappearance. *M. C. Pipe*

HERNE BAY (IRE)   2 b.c. (Mar 27) Hernando (FR) 127 – Charita (IRE) 103 (Lycius   **75**
(USA) 124) [2002 8s f8.5f³ Nov 29] IR 10,000Y: first foal: dam Irish 7f (at 2 yrs)/1m
winner: better effort in maidens (fair form) when never-nearer 3 lengths third to Magenta
Rising at Wolverhampton: should be suited by 1¼m+. *M. Johnston*

HERODOTUS   4 b.g. Zafonic (USA) 130 – Thalestria (FR) 91 (Mill Reef (USA) 141)   **106 §**
[2002 104: p10g p12g* p10g p10g 14.1m⁵ 10.1g 12g 10m 11.9d p10g³ Dec 11] big, good   **a112 §**
sort: smart performer on all-weather, useful on turf: landed gamble in handicap at Lingfield in February by 2 lengths from Hannibal Lad: respectable efforts at best after: seems
to stay easy 1¾m: acts on polytrack, firm and soft going: tried blinkered/tongue tied:
unreliable. *C. E. Brittain*

HERONETTA   3 b.f. Halling (USA) 133 – Trazl (IRE) 88 (Zalazl (USA) 120) [2002   **78**
7g 10.2d³ p12g⁴ 10m³ 11.7g⁴ p12g* Nov 13] 150,000Y: third foal: half-sister to 5-y-o
Three Points: dam, won around 1¾m, from good middle-distance staying family: fair performer: won maiden at Lingfield by 2½ lengths from Epitome despite edging left: should
stay 1¾m: acts on polytrack, unraced on extremes of going on turf. *J. H. M. Gosden*

HERO'S JOURNEY   3 ch.c. Halling (USA) 133 – Zahwa 72 (Cadeaux Genereux   **112**
131) [2002 8m 8m² 8f* 8m* Jun 11] 35,000F, IR 130,000Y: well-made, attractive colt:
second foal: dam, German 7f/1m winner, out of useful Irish 2-y-o sprinter Peace Girl:
smart performer: tongue tied, won maiden at Newbury in May and listed race at Kempton
(beat Compton Dragon by length, despite not travelling with much fluency early on) in
June: raced only on ground firmer than good: looked capable of better,
and was bought by Godolphin in June, but left them in November. *R. Hannon*

HESPERUS (IRE)   3 ch.g. Catrail (USA) 123 – Sweet Pleasure 88 (Sweet Revenge   **–**
129) [2002 –p; 5.7g 5.3m p6g May 29] well-made gelding: little sign of ability: blinkered
in 2002: free-going sort. *R. M. Beckett*

HE'S THE ONE   3 b.g. Salse (USA) 128 – Myth 89 (Troy 137) [2002 10s 10m 10m   **63**
10.9g 14.1g² 14.1m 12.1g 14.1m Oct 5] 37,000Y: angular gelding: half-brother to several
winners, including 4-y-o Vicious Knight and 1m (including at 2 yrs) to 1¾m winner
Midnight Legend (both smart/by Night Shift): dam 1½m to 13.4f winner: modest maiden:
should stay 2m: raced mainly on good/good to firm going: reportedly lame final start.
P. W. Harris

HESTHERELAD (IRE)   3 b.g. Definite Article 121 – Unbidden Melody (USA)   **–**
(Chieftain II) [2002 12m Sep 29] 5,500Y: brother to 4-y-o Greenhope and half-brother to
several winners: dam ran twice in USA: 40/1, soon pulled up (lame) in Musselburgh
maiden. *C. J. Teague*

HETRA HAWK   6 ch.g. Be My Guest (USA) 126 – Silver Ore (FR) 94 (Silver Hawk   **–**
(USA) 123) [2002 –: f12s f12s f12g f8g Feb 21] quite good-topped gelding: unimpressive
mover: no form: blinkered/tongue tied last 2 starts. *W. J. Musson*

HETRA REEF   4 b.g. First Trump 118 – Cuban Reef 54 (Dowsing (USA) 124) [2002   **–**
–: f12s 10.1m Sep 18] smallish, plain gelding: of no account. *W. J. Musson*

HEVER GOLF CHARMER   8 b.g. Precocious 126 – Callas Star (Chief Singer 131)   **–**
[2002 p16g p12g f16.2g Feb 4] sturdy gelding: maiden: well held in 2002: tried blinkered.
N. I. M. Rossiter

HEVER GOLF GLORY   8 b.g. Efisio 120 – Zaius 94 (Artaius (USA) 129) [2002   **– §**
–§, a40§: f9.4g Jan 18] smallish gelding: temperamental handicapper: tried blinkered/
visored. *C. N. Kellett*

HE WHO DARES (IRE)   4 b.g. Distinctly North (USA) 115 – Sea Clover (IRE) 77   **76 d**
(Ela-Mana-Mou 132) [2002 69: 7g² 7d⁶ 8.1d⁶ 8.2m⁵ 8.3d 7d p7g Nov 14] rather leggy,
quite good-topped gelding: fair maiden: below best after second start: probably stays 1m:
acts on heavy going: often tongue tied: sometimes slowly away: pulled hard second start.
A. W. Carroll

HEY PRESTO 2 b.c. (Feb 1) Piccolo 121 – Upping The Tempo (Dunbeath (USA) **74**
127) [2002 5m 5.1f⁴ 5g² 6m 5g⁴ Oct 4] 18,000Y: fourth foal: half-brother to a winner in
Turkey by Forzando: dam unraced half-sister to useful sprinter Up And At 'em: fair
maiden: should stay 6f: raced only on good ground or firmer. *C. G. Cox*

H HARRISON (IRE) 2 b.g. (Apr 13) Eagle Eyed (USA) 111 – Penrose (IRE) 75 **79 §**
(Wolfhound (USA) 126) [2002 5m² 5d³ 5v⁴ 5m 5g³ 5m⁴ 5m⁶ 5f* 5g⁵ p6g⁶ f5g p6g Dec
30] IR 10,500Y: first foal: dam, maiden best at 7f, half-sister to 3-y-o Millstreet: fair
performer: won maiden at Catterick in October: stays easy 6f: acts on firm going, good to
soft and polytrack: irresolute. *R. F. Fisher*

HIBERNATE (IRE) 8 ch.g. Lahib (USA) 129 – Ministra (USA) (Deputy Minister **56 d**
(CAN)) [2002 70, a–: 10m 12.4m 12.3g 11.9d 12f² 12d⁶ 12m⁵ Aug 6] big, angular
gelding: modest handicapper at best in 2002: stays 1½m: acts on firm going, good to soft
and polytrack: occasionally visored: usually front runner: moody. *K. R. Burke*

HIDDEN CAVE 2 b.f. (Apr 27) Bishop of Cashel 122 – Polar Cove (Polar Falcon **–**
(USA) 126) [2002 6d f8.5g Nov 15] fourth foal: dam unraced: well beaten in maiden/
claimer. *K. A. Ryan*

HIDDENDALE (IRE) 3 br.f. Indian Ridge 123 – That'll Be The Day (IRE) 68 **97**
(Thatching 131) [2002 90p: 7m³ 8m 6g⁵ 7m Oct 12] good-bodied filly: useful performer:
good 1¾ lengths third to Misterah in Nell Gwyn Stakes at Newmarket in April: failed to
stay in 1000 Guineas there next time: long way below form in listed races last 2 starts (off
4 months in between): should prove best at 6f/7f: yet to race on extremes of going:
free-going sort, usually wears crossed noseband. *B. J. Meehan*

HIDDEN DRAGON (USA) 3 b.c. Danzig (USA) – Summer Home (USA) (Easy **106**
Goer (USA)) [2002 89p: 7m⁶ 5d Jul 14] $575,000Y: good-topped colt: second foal: dam,
5.5f (at 2 yrs) to 6.5f winner in USA, half-sister to 4-y-o Ice Dancer: useful form: landed
odds in maiden at the Curragh at 2 yrs: very good 4½ lengths sixth to Just James in Jersey
Stakes at Royal Ascot on reappearance: unable to challenge in Rockingham Handicap at
the Curragh only subsequent outing: will stay 1m: sent to Far East. *A. P. O'Brien, Ireland*

HIDDEN FORT 5 ch.g. Mujtahid (USA) 118 – Temple Fortune (USA) 74 (Ziggy's **58 d**
Boy (USA)) [2002 71: f5s³ f6g f6g⁶ f7g f5g³ f5g⁶ p6g f6g⁶ f5g⁶ Apr 20] robust gelding:
modest performer: stays 7f: acts on fibresand, best turf efforts on going firmer than
good: blinkered last 6 starts: tends to race freely: sometimes hangs right: on downgrade.
D. W. Chapman

HIDDEN SMILE (USA) 5 b.m. Twilight Agenda (USA) 126 – Smooth Edge (USA) **–**
(Meadowlake (USA)) [2002 9m 11.6m 10m 12f Oct 7] IR 12,000 3-y-o: lengthy mare:
second foal: dam won around 1m at 2 yrs in USA: fair winner in Ireland for D. Weld at 3
yrs: well held in handicaps in Britain in 2002: stays 7.8f: form only on going firmer than
good: tried blinkered. *F. Jordan*

HIDDEN SURPRISE 3 b.g. Bin Ajwaad (IRE) 119 – Dawawin (USA) 81 (Dixieland **89 p**
Band (USA)) [2002 p8g* f8g² Dec 17] first foal: dam, 8.3f winner from 4 starts, half-
sister to smart German middle-distance performer Saugerties: fairly useful form: won
maiden at Lingfield in October despite very slow start: improved when 3½ lengths second
to Duncan Dock in minor event at Southwell: should stay 1¼m: should continue to
progress. *W. A. O'Gorman*

HIDEAWAY HEROINE (IRE) 3 ch.f. Hernando (FR) 127 – Dulcinea 73 (Selkirk **100**
(USA) 129) [2002 76: 8.2d³ 7m* 8m⁶ 8.1m⁴ 7m² Sep 12] tall, lengthy filly: useful
performer: won 27-runner handicap at Newbury in May by 6 lengths from Cloud Dancer:
ran at least creditably after, including when 7½ lengths sixth to Sophisticat in Coronation
Stakes at Royal Ascot and length second to Mamounia in listed race at Doncaster: stays
1m: much better form on good to firm going than good/good to soft: tongue tied final
2-y-o outing: sent to USA. *J. W. Hills*

HI DUBAI 2 ch.f. (Feb 6) Rahy (USA) 115 – Jood (USA) 87 (Nijinsky (CAN) 138) **88 p**
[2002 7d² Aug 3] sixth foal: sister to top-class 7f (at 2 yrs) to 1½m winner Fantastic
Light, and half-sister to useful 1¼m winner Westbound Road (by Gone West) and UAE
7f winner Madraar (by Mr Prospector): dam, third at 7f (at 2 yrs) and 1¼m, her only
starts, out of Canadian Oaks winner Kamar, herself half-sister to dam of Swain: 5/4 on,
2½ lengths second of 11 to Nayzak in maiden at Newmarket, staying on strongly having
been short of room: should be suited by 1¼m+: sure to improve. *D. R. Loder*

HIGH ACCOLADE 2 b.c. (Apr 22) Mark of Esteem (IRE) 137 – Generous Lady 98 **95**
(Generous (IRE) 139) [2002 7m³ 7f* 7.1m 7m³ Sep 29] 60,000Y: smallish, useful-
looking colt: second foal: half-brother to 3-y-o Summer Wine: dam, Irish 1½m/1¾m

432

winner, half-sister to smart Italian St Leger winner Jape: useful form: won maiden at Newbury in July: good third to To The Rescue in nursery at Ascot final start: will stay at least 1m: raced only on ground firmer than good: carries head high. *R. Hannon*

HIGH ACTION (USA)   2 ch.c. (Jan 27) Theatrical 128 – Secret Imperatrice (USA)   **– p**
(Secretariat (USA)) [2002 7m Aug 23] $150,000Y: strong, close-coupled colt: sixth foal: half-brother to 3 winners, including useful winner around 1½m Octavius Caesar (by Affirmed): dam 6f (at 2 yrs) and 1m (minor stakes) winner: 12/1, well held in maiden at Newmarket: likely to do better. *Sir Michael Stoute*

HIGH AND MIGHTY   7 b.g. Shirley Heights 130 – Air Distingue (USA) 120 (Sir   **96**
Ivor 135) [2002 88: 16g³ 16m⁶ 18.7f³ 20m 16m² 16.2g Sep 28] sturdy, angular gelding: good mover: useful handicapper: best efforts in 2002 when 2 lengths third to Fantasy Hill in Chester Cup on third outing (placed for second year running) and short-headed by Bid For Fame at Newbury: tailed off final outing: stays 2½m: acts on firm and soft going: usually visored. *G. Barnett*

HIGH BEAUTY   5 br.m. High Kicker (USA) – Tendresse (IRE) 60 (Tender King 123)   **–**
[2002 –: f16g 14.1f 11.9s Jun 6] of little account. *S. L. Keightley*

HIGH BOUNCE (USA)   2 ch.g. (Jan 27) Trempolino (USA) 135 – Top Hope 115   **–**
(High Top 131) [2002 f8.5s Nov 2] 14,000Y: half-brother to several winners, including useful 1m winner Free Thinker (by Shadeed) and 2m winner Hetra Heights (by Cox's Ridge): dam, 2-y-o 7f winner, later best at 1½m: 16/1, tailed off in maiden at Wolverhampton (gelded after). *I. A. Balding*

HIGHCAL   5 gr.g. King's Signet (USA) 110 – Guarded Expression 51 (Siberian   **52**
Express (USA) 125) [2002 –: f16g⁵ 16.2g 12g 12m* 14.1f* 12f² 14g⁵ Jun 17] good-bodied gelding: modest handicapper: won at Musselburgh and Redcar within 3 days in June: stays 1¾m: best form on going firmer than good: blinkered final 4-y-o outing. *Ronald Thompson*

HIGH CHAPARRAL (IRE)   3 b.c. Sadler's Wells (USA) 132 – Kasora (IRE)   **130**
(Darshaan 133) [2002 115p: 10m* 10m* 12d* 12d* 12g³ 12d* Oct 26]
    The introduction to *The Bloodstock Breeders' Review* covering 1923 had a somewhat deadpan opening: 'It has been a normal year. Apart from an abortive visit the Derby winner paid to the United States with a view to capturing a prize of £20,000, the regular routine was pursued.' The Derby winner Papyrus (whose owner received £10,825 for his Epsom victory) provided Steve Donoghue, the greatest racing idol of the 'twenties, with his third successive winner of the classic. Donoghue was champion jockey in Britain—sharing the title with the apprentice Charlie Elliott—for the tenth year in a row. Also following 'the regular routine', Alec Taylor was champion trainer for the seventh successive year and Lord Derby was the leading breeder for the fourth time in five years. Even the weather had a familiar ring—'the summer, in the earlier months, was dull, cold and wet . . . there was a deficiency of sunshine for the whole year.' Papyrus's American adventure had to wait to be dealt with in the American section further back in *The Bloodstock Breeders' Review*, the only reference in the main part of the volume being to the contract signed just before the St Leger—in which Papyrus was beaten by the One Thousand Guineas winner Tranquil—to send Papyrus to New York to run a match against the best three-year-old in the States. *The Bloodstock Breeders' Review* explained its 'merely incidental' mention: 'The contract naturally imparted an additional interest to the St Leger.'
    The initiative for the match came from America where it was greeted with much enthusiasm. On the other side of the Atlantic, however, it was said that 'No man of any standing on the English Turf spoke a single word in favour . . . the affair bore too strong a resemblance to a prize fight.' Interest in the match in Britain was at best lukewarm, while there were those who were positively hostile. 'It is sheer prostitution of the Turf,' said one leading trainer. Papyrus met the Kentucky Derby winner Zev, eventually nominated by the New York Jockey Club after plans for a National Trial between him and the Saratoga Cup winner My Own foundered. The Zev-Papyrus match was staged over a mile and a half on dirt at Belmont Park towards the end of the night before turned the track 'ankle deep in sloppy mud' and Zev beat Papyrus by five lengths, Donoghue reporting that Papyrus 'was not the same horse I had ridden in England'. The inquest went on and on, some putting down defeat to the fact that Papyrus's ordinary racing plates—as

*Ballysax Stakes, Leopardstown—High Chaparral gives weight away all round
and spreadeagles his field; stable-companion Twentytwoandchange (dark colours) is next,
followed by Rahn (noseband) and Smuggler's Song*

opposed to Zev's 'clips'—gave him a poor footing under the conditions. Connections themselves attributed the crushing defeat simply to the unfamiliar dirt surface, while there were also the possible effects of travelling to consider. Papyrus was sent to America on the *Aquitania* from Southampton and took seven days by rail, sea and horsebox to reach his destination, going off his feed for the first two or three days on board ship. *The Bloodstock Breeders' Review* summing up of the match is worth recounting: 'That it will live in Turf history is beyond question; that it is the forerunner of other similar enterprises is open to doubt.' Epsom Derby winners, in particular, have been a rare sight on American racecourses since, the two most recent Derby winners Galileo and High Chaparral being only the sixth and seventh respectively to race there since Papyrus.

There was a gap of forty-five years after Papyrus before another Epsom Derby winner crossed the Atlantic for a race, the journey by then taking under eight hours by air. The attraction for the connections of Sir Ivor was the Washington DC International, brainchild of John Schapiro, the president of Laurel racecourse in Maryland. Schapiro, who died in early-2002, did more than anyone to bring about international racing, introducing the event in 1952 and establishing it as the most important American target for European-based horses in the era before the Breeders' Cup. Schapiro went out of his way to attract the Europeans, staging the Washington International on grass over the European classic distance of a mile and a half, and he was rewarded when the Europeans filled first (through British-trained Wilwyn), third and fourth in the inaugural running. There were two Irish Derby winners, Thirteen of Diamonds and Chamier, in the second running and, as the Washington International's prestige grew, Schapiro succeeded for the seventh running in attracting the best horse in Europe, the King George and Prix de l'Arc winner Ballymoss. That horse's defeat didn't seem unduly to deter top-class foreign challengers, but it was another decade before the first Epsom Derby winner was lured. When American-bred Sir Ivor made the journey, it was in the age when the Epsom Derby was still almost universally regarded as the greatest race in the world. The superb Sir Ivor, handy and tractable and possessing a top-class turn of foot, was certainly one of the best horses Europe ever sent for the Washington International and he won easing up, though not before Lester Piggott, riding with supreme confidence, had given Sir Ivor's supporters a few anxious moments when getting boxed in. The Washington International continued to thrive through the 'seventies and early-'eighties, when French challengers in particular did well. But by the time of All Along's victory in 1983, when she won the Prix de l'Arc before completing a hat-trick of big-race wins in North America, the Breeders' Cup was looming. Laurel couldn't compete and the Washington International faded steadily from the spotlight and eventually into oblivion.

Even the Breeders' Cup, instituted in 1984, didn't succeed in attracting an Epsom Derby winner until the 'nineties, by which time the Derby was clinging with increasing desperation to the title of the 'world's premier flat race'. The Derby owed its world-wide status at that time more to tradition than to anything else, its first prize barely getting it into the world's most valuable twenty races in 1990. The Breeders' Cup Classic, the world's richest race, was almost twice as valuable as the Derby. The Derby winner that year, Quest For Fame, was kept in training as a four-year-old, when he finished a good third in the Breeders' Cup Turf (an achievement he repeated as a five-year-old by which time he had been transferred permanently to America). The 1974 Derby winner Snow Knight went on to run three times without success in America as a three-year-old after being transferred to a Canadian trainer that autumn, and he enjoyed a very successful American career as a four-year-old. Two years after Snow Knight, the Derby winner Empery was an intended runner in the Man o'War Stakes but, after losing condition in quarantine, he was forced to miss the race. The 1992 Derby winner Dr Devious, already known to American racegoers as he had contested the Kentucky Derby a month before Epsom, finished fourth, a place behind Quest For Fame, in that year's Breeders' Cup Turf. The 1998 Derby winner High-Rise made one appearance in America, when last of eight in the Manhattan Handicap at Belmont as a five-year-old (he had been nominated as only the third reserve for the Breeders' Cup Turf the year before).

These days it seems there is a prestigious international race somewhere almost every couple of weeks or so, from the start of the racing year to the end. This is the era, not only of Breeders' Cups in America, but of World Cups in Dubai, and richly-endowed Cups in places like Singapore, Japan and Hong Kong. The Epsom Derby, worth £800,400 to the winner in the latest season, remains the most valuable race staged in Europe, but it is no longer the be-all and end-all, as it once was, for a middle-distance three-year-old colt trained in Britain or Ireland. The globalisation of the thoroughbred breeding business has also had an effect on the prestige of the Derby, and on the prestige of its winners, as fashions have moved on from the days when the big middle-distance races were regarded as the prime source of potential stallions. The importance of the American market has been reinforced by the presence of the last two Derby winners at the Breeders' Cup. Both raced for

Derrinstown Stud Derby Trial Stakes, Leopardstown—
High Chaparral continues on the same path as Sinndar and Galileo;
In Time's Eye (left), Ahsanabad (partly hidden by winner) and Nostradamus (rail) make the frame

Ballydoyle, which is controlled by John Magnier, head of the Coolmore breeding empire which has associated studs in America and Australia. Galileo went on to win the Irish Derby and the King George after Epsom, a treble achieved before him only by Nijinsky, Grundy, The Minstrel, Troy, Shergar and Generous. None of the connections of that group felt a need to try to further their horse's reputation by tackling races outside Europe, though, except for Generous, suitable opportunities were much more limited than nowadays. Galileo contested the Breeders' Cup Classic over a mile and a quarter, starting second favourite on his only start on dirt but managing just sixth of thirteen, returning with swollen eyes and sore heels. The outcome with High Chaparral was much happier: under more familiar conditions, he started favourite and won the Breeders' Cup Turf over the Derby trip, becoming only the second Epsom Derby winner—after Sir Ivor—to win as a three-year-old in North America. Coincidentally, the latest One Thousand Guineas and Oaks winner Kazzia also went on to win a Grade 1 event, the Flower Bowl Invitational, in North America.

High Chaparral won the Racing Post Trophy at Doncaster on the last of three outings as a two-year-old and followed the same three-year-old route to Epsom as Galileo and the 2000 Derby winner Sinndar, who was also trained in Ireland. High Chaparral went one better on his reappearance in mid-April than Sinndar, who was beaten under a Group 1 penalty in the listed Ballysax Stakes at Leopardstown. The going was good to firm, in sharp contrast to the heavy ground for the Racing Post Trophy, but odds-on High Chaparral could hardly have been more impressive, giving at least 7 lb and a sound beating to his six rivals, drawing away in the home straight to win by seven lengths from stable-companion Twentytwoandchange. Conditions were similar for the Derrinstown Stud Derby Trial over the same course and distance four weeks later. Conceding weight all round again, High Chaparral landed odds of 5/1-on by a length and a length and a half from two other Epsom Derby entrants, In Time's Eye and Ahsanabad. The style of the victory was not so impressive as in the Ballysax, High Chaparral having to be pushed along to make ground on the home turn after being held up, but he eventually won with something in hand after taking the lead over a furlong out.

High Chaparral was briefly Derby favourite after his Trial win, but neither of his three-year-old performances created anything like the impression made by High Chaparral's stable-companion Hawk Wing when runner-up in the Two Thousand Guineas. Once Hawk Wing was announced a definite Derby runner, he went back to the head of the ante-post betting, with High Chaparral second favourite. With rain lashing Epsom in the days leading up to the race (after the course had begun watering because of fears of firm ground), stable-jockey Michael Kinane must have faced a most difficult choice between the Ballydoyle pair. High Chaparral looked the better bet to get the Derby trip, especially under testing conditions, but Kinane stayed with Hawk Wing, the mount on High Chaparral going to Johnny Murtagh, who had won the Derby on Sinndar. The Derby looked anything but a two-horse race at the time, with the winners of nearly all the principal Derby trials in the line-up of twelve, the same number as in Galileo's Derby and a small field by recent standards (the safety limit is to be reduced from thirty to twenty from 2003). After Hawk Wing at 9/4 and High Chaparral at 7/2, the betting went: 9/2 the runaway Lingfield Trial winner Bandari, 5/1 the principal Godolphin hope Naheef, 8/1 the Chester Vase winner Fight Your Corner and 14/1 bar. Both Bandari and Fight Your Corner had changed hands after winning their trials—joining the Maktoum battalions—and had been supplemented for the Derby at a cost of £90,000 each (details of a heated debate that took place over the Derby entry system can be found in the essay on Bandari). The Godolphin colours were also carried by the Dante winner Moon Ballad, supposedly second best to Naheef at home, and also in the field was Coshocton, conqueror of another one-time Godolphin classic hope Dubai Destination in the listed Predominate Stakes.

After Friday's Oaks had been run on very soft ground—with the first two finishing fourteen lengths clear—conditions dried out somewhat overnight, though the Derby was still run on going softer than good for the first time since Teenoso's year, 1983. The good to soft going, coupled with a very strong pace in the first half mile, had a devastating effect on some of the Derby runners and the finishing distances resembled those at the end of a three-mile steeplechase. The thorough test played into the hands of Murtagh on High Chaparral, who took closer order at the top of the hill after being a little slow to break. Murtagh described afterwards how stamina was always going to be the key to beating Hawk Wing and, rounding Tattenham Corner, he set High Chaparral alight with a couple of cracks of the whip, passing Hawk Wing, whom he had tracked for much of the race, and eventually overtaking the front-running Moon Ballad approaching the two-furlong marker. High Chaparral kept on strongly under pressure in the lead as Hawk Wing briefly drew almost upsides over a furlong out. But, when the crunch came, it was High Chaparral who had the answers. He was well on top at the line, where he had two lengths to spare over Hawk Wing, eased a fraction once clearly held, with twelve lengths back to the very tired Moon Ballad. The 100/1-shot Jelani came fourth, a length behind Moon Ballad, but the finish was marred by the collapse close home, when tiring in fifth, of Coshocton, who was put down. Fight Your Corner, out of contention turning for home and subsequently found to have fractured a hind cannon bone, kept on steadily for fifth, five lengths behind Jelani, and then there was a gap of seventeen lengths to sixth-placed Where Or When, a further two to Naheef, who faded tamely in the straight, and a further twelve to eighth-placed Bandari, who was never travelling. The domination of High Chaparral and Hawk Wing made Aidan O'Brien the first trainer for over half a century—since Dick Carver in 1948 to be precise—to send out the first and second in the Derby at Epsom.

The Derby followed triumphs for Ballydoyle in the season's three major Guineas races for colts in Europe. Rock of Gibraltar and Hawk Wing had come first and second at Newmarket, Landseer had won at Longchamp and Rock of Gibraltar, Century City and Della Francesca had filled first, second and third at the Curragh. Rock of Gibraltar and Landseer were subsequently first and second in the St James's Palace Stakes at Royal Ascot, giving Ballydoyle first and second in all four Group 1 races open to three-year-old colts in Britain and Ireland up to that time. What next? A clean sweep in the Budweiser Irish Derby at the Curragh, though there was no rematch between High Chaparral and Hawk Wing. High Chaparral carries the colours of Michael Tabor, who is not involved in Hawk Wing, and it was always his firm plan that the Derby winner would run at the Curragh. With Hawk Wing waiting for the Eclipse at Sandown the following week, and One Thousand Guineas and Oaks winner Kazzia announced a non-runner, High Chaparral looked likely to face his biggest challenge from France. However, the Prix du Jockey Club winner Sulamani was ruled out some time before the race and the Prix du Jockey Club runner-up Act One, an intended starter, suffered a leg injury that ended his career a week before the Irish Derby. With Act One absent, High Chaparral faced a fairly straightforward task at the Curragh, though the late announcement that the British-trained King Edward VII Stakes winner Balakheri would run added some interest to an event shaping up into a Ballydoyle 'walkover'. In addition to the

Vodafone Derby Stakes, Epsom—the Aidan O'Brien pair, High Chaparral and Hawk Wing, dominate the finish; Moon Ballad is twelve lengths further back in third

3/1-on High Chaparral, Aidan O'Brien saddled the Derby Italiano runner-up Ballingarry, Della Francesca (successful in the Gallinule Stakes since the Irish Guineas) and rank outsider Sholokhov. Balakheri started second favourite at 13/2, then at 15/2 came In Time's Eye, having his first race since the Derrinstown Stud Derby Trial, and 12/1-shot Ballingarry, with the five remaining runners at odds of 20/1, 25/1, 33/1, 40/1 (Della Francesca) and 200/1 (Sholokhov). High Chaparral continued in the footsteps of Sinndar and Galileo by becoming the third successive Derby winner to follow up at the Curragh. Sholokhov soon had the field fairly well strung out, though the gallop appeared no better than fair until past halfway. High Chaparral cruised along in fourth until the home turn and took a little time to warm to his task before quickening to lead a furlong out and drawing away a couple of smacks with the whip inside the final furlong to win by three and a half lengths from Sholokhov. Ballingarry was a further length and a half away third, rallying to touch off British-trained Nysaean, who had looked a big threat approaching the two-furlong marker. The first four were all sons of the record-breaking Sadler's Wells, who has now sired six Irish Derby winners and had the first, second and third in the 1999 edition. Balakheri managed only fifth, possibly feeling the effects of his race at Royal Ascot only nine days previously, with Della Francesca and In Time's Eye coming next. High Chaparral became the fourteenth colt to complete the Derby double at Epsom and the Curragh since 1962, when the Irish version became a race of major international significance when its prize was first boosted by sponsorship. The Irish Derby does not, however, always turn out to be the near-formality that it was for High Chaparral: nine Epsom Derby winners have met with defeat at the Curragh, including Charlottown, Sir Ivor, Empery and Dr Devious, who all started at odds on.

The Irish Derby first three and Hawk Wing all featured in the original multiple entry from Ballydoyle for Britain's most prestigious all-aged middle-distance race, the King George VI and Queen Elizabeth Stakes at Ascot. Some of the post-race comments made by Aidan O'Brien after Galileo's disappointing performance in the Breeders' Cup Classic had hinted that connections might have felt, in hindsight, that a hard race in the King George had prejudiced Galileo's late-season campaign. It was not the greatest surprise, therefore, when an announcement came that High Chaparral would be following a different programme, bypassing the King George to wait for an autumn campaign, as connections of Sinndar had done. What was surprising, however, given the Ballydoyle stranglehold over the colts' classics, was that no challenge at all was forthcoming from the stable for the King George, won in the absence of Ballydoyle's best three-year-olds by British-trained four-year-old Golan, in whom Coolmore had a controlling interest. Another race ruled out of High Chaparral's programme straight after his Derby double was the St Leger, for which he was never even entered. High Chaparral was tailor-made for Doncaster but modern-day commercial considerations make it increasingly unlikely that the Derby winner will be seen in the St Leger. The last time it happened was in 1987 when Reference Point completed the double, but two years later Nashwan's connections spurned the chance of the Triple Crown by bypassing

Budweiser Irish Derby, the Curragh—a relatively straightforward task for High Chaparral;
stable-companions Sholokhov and Ballingarry (rail) come next,
whilst Nysaean completes a 1,2,3,4 for sire Sadler's Wells

John Deere Breeders' Cup Turf, Arlington—the race goes to Europe for the fourth year in succession as High Chaparral becomes the first Epsom Derby winner to take this prize as well; With Anticipation is second, whilst the other horse in the photo is fourth-placed The Tin Man (noseband)

the Leger and little interest has been shown by Derby-winning connections since. High Chaparral's training was interrupted for a time when an outbreak of coughing hit Ballydoyle in early-August. He was reported by his trainer to have become 'very sick', though in the run-up to the Champion Stakes at Leopardstown in early-September he was said to be 'ready if we need him'. In fact, High Chaparral was withdrawn on the day of the race from the Irish Champion—an event for which Hawk Wing was also a declared runner—with his trainer reportedly 'unhappy with the results of the latest blood picture'. The Leopardstown stewards held an inquiry into High Chaparral's withdrawal and requested that O'Brien forward the blood picture to the Keeper of the Match Book. The stewards of the Turf Club later issued a statement confirming that the details had been submitted and were as described by the trainer at the inquiry.

High Chaparral's preparation for the Prix de l'Arc de Triomphe at Long-champ in early-October continued to go anything but smoothly. He missed a planned engagement in the Prix Niel—won by Sinndar on his way to Arc glory—on Longchamp's 'trials day', O'Brien again reporting concerns about the results of blood tests and concluding that High Chaparral 'just isn't quite ready for a race'. Plans for a racecourse gallop also came to nothing, so when High Chaparral lined up as favourite (coupled with pacemaker Black Sam Bellamy) for the Arc he was having his first outing for fourteen weeks. All things considered, he turned in a splendid performance, close up all the way and keeping on with the utmost gameness under the whip, rallying strongly in the closing stages, to go down by three quarters of a length and half a length to Marienbard and Sulamani. Ground conditions were less testing at Longchamp than they had been at Epsom and the Curragh, and the Arc resulted in something of a bunched finish with the first six separated by less than three lengths. As in the Irish Derby, High Chaparral travelled smoothly enough for a long way in the Arc to suggest that he did not necessarily need a very stiff test of stamina to bring out the best in him at a mile and a half, just as well so far as the Breeders' Cup was concerned.

The going on the turf track at Arlington was good to soft, generally thought to be in favour of most of the European challengers, but the tight turns and relatively short straight made the John Deere Breeders' Cup Turf more of a test of speed for High Chaparral than any of the mile and a half races he had encountered in Europe. Interestingly, High Chaparral lost little weight at Longchamp, which indicated to O'Brien that the horse had been fit enough on Arc day, 'although he wasn't sharp enough mentally'. Sir Ivor was second to Vaguely Noble in the Arc before beating America's best turf horses in the Washington International, and High Chaparral earned his place in history—and a prestigious Eclipse award as the best male turf performer—with a high-class effort in the Breeders' Cup Turf. It was said that the American opposition was not up to the usual standard and the other European challenger Golan in the field of eight was expected to prove the biggest danger to odds-on High Chaparral. Golan was off the bridle some way out, however, and the Man o'War Stakes winner With Anticipation and the Canadian International runner-up Falcon Flight gave High Chaparral most to do. Pushed along before the final turn, High Chaparral had to be strongly ridden and quickened well to take the lead inside the final furlong, if anything, in the closing stages with the race won, giving the impression that he was idling. High Chaparral had a length and a quarter and three quarters of a length to spare over With Anticipation and Falcon Flight, with the front-running The Tin Man back in fourth, followed by the Turf Classic winner Denon, Golan and Ballingarry, the last-named sold privately out of O'Brien's stable after winning the Canadian International. High Chaparral's victory was the fourth in a row by a European challenger in the Breeders' Cup Turf, following those of Daylami, Kalanisi and Fantastic Light. Daylami's win was outstanding, but High Chaparral's performance was on a par with those of Kalanisi and Fantastic Light and about average for the race. It was confirmed soon afterwards that both High Chaparral and Hawk Wing—a disappointing seventh in the Breeders' Cup Classic on dirt—would be kept in training as four-year-olds.

In sharp contrast to the notably fluent Galileo, the angular, good-topped High Chaparral is not the best of movers, displaying a moderate, quick action, but those who thought the undulations and gradients of Epsom might find him out in the Derby were well wide of the mark. Some thought they detected a lack of balance about High Chaparral as he rounded the home turn in the Derrinstown Stud Derby Trial, but the run down to and around Tattenham Corner answered any questions about a lack of athleticism, at least on softish going. High Chaparral is something of a rarity for an Epsom Derby winner in that he was purchased at public auction, fetching 270,000 guineas at the Tattersalls Houghton Yearling Sales. In the last quarter of the twentieth century, Grundy, Generous, Dr Devious and Oath were the only Epsom Derby winners to graduate from the yearling sales in Britain and Ireland. Generous went though the sale-ring in Ireland as a foal and a yearling, while Dr Devious, sold at the Newmarket Sales as both a foal and a yearling, was also purchased by Italian interests at the end of his two-year-old career before changing hands for a fourth time before the Derby, bought by Americans whose principal aim had been to win the Kentucky Derby.

High Chaparral is the second Derby winner sired by Sadler's Wells, following Galileo. There is not much to say about Sadler's Wells that hasn't already been said. He was champion sire for the twelfth time—and the eleventh time in succession—and his reign looks set to continue with three of his 2003 classic crop already Group 1 winners and with High Chaparral staying in training. Sadler's Wells also has the advantage of strength of numbers. The produce of his largest book of mares (nearly two hundred covered) will be racing in 2003 as three-year-olds, at which age his offspring usually improve. As well as siring the first four in the Irish Derby in the latest season, Sadler's Wells also had the first four in the Racing Post Trophy and the first three in the Irish One Thousand Guineas. He sired sixteen individual European pattern winners in 2002, which does not include Quarter Moon (a Group 1 winner at two) who was runner-up in three classics. Interestingly, half of Sadler's Wells' pattern winners in 2002, in addition to Quarter Moon, were out of mares by Darshaan, Shirley Heights, Riverman or Doyoun, all descendants of Mill Reef's sire Never Bend. Darshaan, sire of High Chaparral's dam Kasora, topped the list of broodmare sires in 2002, which provided other examples of the results obtained mating Sadler's Wells with daughters of Darshaan, most notably Quarter Moon and the Nassau Stakes and Yorkshire Oaks winner Islington.

High Chaparral is the second offspring out of Kasora, also a 270,000-guinea purchase at Newmarket, where she was purchased from the Aga Khan as an unraced three-year-old at the December Sales. Kasora was the third highest-priced filly at the sale, reflecting her antecedents. High Chaparral's great grandam the Poule d'Essai des Pouliches winner Koblenza was among the mares purchased by the Aga Khan from another leading owner-breeder Mme Francois Dupre in the 'seventies. High Chaparral's grandam Kozana carried the Aga Khan's colours with distinction, winning four races—two of them pattern events—at up to a mile and a quarter and recording high-class placed efforts in top company at a mile (runner-up in the Prix du Moulin) and at a mile and a half (third in the Prix de l'Arc). Kozana, a half-sister to the Prix du Cadran winner Karkour, wasn't so successful for the Aga Khan Studs as she had been on the racecourse, though she did produce seven winners, among them two winners of the One Thousand Guineas Trial at Leopardstown, Kotama and Khanata, and an Italian Two Thousand Guineas runner-up in Khoraz. High Chaparral's dam Kasora is a sister to another of Kozana's winners, the useful mile-and-a-quarter performer Korasoun. Kasora's first foal was by Ridgewood Ben, a smart performer at five furlongs to a mile who owed his opportunity as a stallion partly to the fact that he was a brother to the top filly Ridgewood Pearl. The product was Oriental Ben, a fairly useful handicapper at up to nine furlongs in Ireland.

High Chaparral (IRE) (b.c. 1999)	Sadler's Wells (USA) (b 1981)	Northern Dancer (b 1961)	Nearctic
			Natalma
		Fairy Bridge (b 1975)	Bold Reason
			Special
	Kasora (IRE) (b 1993)	Darshaan (br 1981)	Shirley Heights
			Delsy
		Kozana (br 1982)	Kris
			Koblenza

The decision to keep High Chaparral in training at four may have surprised some, as it is without precedent for a winner of both the Derby and the Irish Derby. However, High Chaparral is not the first dual Derby winner to return as a four-year-old in the Tabor colours, Montjeu having done so with notable success after

Mr M. Tabor & Mrs John Magnier's "High Chaparral"

winning the Prix du Jockey Club and the Irish Derby. Keeping a valuable stallion commodity in training for another year represents a considerable risk, though less so for Coolmore, which already stands Montjeu and Galileo, two other sons of Sadler's Wells cast in the same mould as High Chaparral. Mill Reef, Roberto, Snow Knight (in North America) and Teenoso are the Epsom Derby winners of the last thirty years or so for whom an extra year in training brought the most successes. Henbit, Slip Anchor, Quest For Fame and High-Rise are the only other Derby winners since Mill Reef that have returned as four-year-olds (Quest For Fame and High-Rise also ran at five). The genuine High Chaparral, whose Derby-winning performance has been bettered only by Generous and Galileo in the past fifteen years, stays a mile and a half well. As has been intimated, however, that should not necessarily be taken as a sign that he will prove any less effective brought back to a mile and a quarter. Except in the Derby, he was held up (wears a crossed noseband) and ridden for a turn of foot, usually quickening well after taking a little time to warm to his task. High Chaparral's ability to show his form on going ranging from heavy to good to firm should give his connections a wide choice of options at tour. The King George VI and Queen Elizabeth Stakes, a second crack at the Prix de l'Arc and another trip to the Breeders' Cup look the obvious major targets. *A. P. O'Brien, Ireland*

HIGHCLERE MEMORY (USA)   2 b.f. (Jan 27) Cryptoclearance (USA) – Regal   **62**
State (USA) 122 (Affirmed (USA)) [2002 7g⁶ 7m 7m 7g⁴ Oct 24] tall, leggy filly: eighth foal: half-sister to 3 winners, including useful 1996 2-y-o 6f/6.5f winner Hurricane State (by Miswaki) and 7f/1m winner Eben Naas (by Dayjur): dam, won Prix Morny, half-sister to dam of high-class miler Distant View: modest maiden: blinkered, best effort when fourth in nursery at Brighton, staying on after slow start: will stay at least 1m. *J. L. Dunlop*

HIGH DIVA   3 b.f. Piccolo 121 – Gifted (Shareef Dancer (USA) 135) [2002 65: 10m   **69**
10g p10g² f9.4g⁴ p10g p10g p10g² Dec 30] tall filly: fluent mover: fair maiden handicapper: stays 1¼m: acts on all-weather, raced only on good/good to firm going on turf: tongue tied (ran poorly) once. *J. W. Hills*

HIGH DIVING   2 b.c. (Feb 3) Barathea (IRE) 127 – High And Low 120 (Rainbow   **76 p**
Quest (USA) 134) [2002 7f⁵ 8.3m² Sep 2] sturdy colt: first foal: dam 11.4f winner and second in St Leger: fair form in maidens: eye-catching fifth to Al Jadeed at Newbury: 11/4 on, beaten 10 lengths by Love You Always at Hamilton, still seeming green: likely to be suited by 1¼m+: remains capable of better. *B. W. Hills*

HIGHDOWN (IRE)   3 b.c. Selkirk (USA) 129 – Rispoto 58 (Mtoto 134) [2002 100:   **119**
10g* 11g⁴ 8.5d² 10m⁴ 10f* 10g* Aug 15] leggy, close-coupled colt: smart performer: trained by M. Channon at 2 yrs: won listed events at Newmarket (by short head from Moon Ballad) in May and Newbury (improved form to beat Foreign Affairs 4 lengths) in July then Prix Guillaume d'Ornano at Deauville (beat Shaanmer short head) in August: effective at 1m (given a test) to 1¼m: acts on firm and soft going: wears crossed noseband: edgy type: joined Godolphin. *M. P. Tregoning*

Prix Guillaume d'Ornano, Deauville—Highdown (rail) supplements his two listed-race wins with victory in this Group 2 contest from Shaanmer, suffering his third narrow defeat in a row; Burning Sun (white blaze) runs well under a penalty in third and Without Connexion (right) is fourth

HIGH DRAMA   5 b.g. In The Wings 128 – Maestrale (Top Ville 129) [2002 50: 16g⁵   **44**
14m 15.8f⁶ Oct 8] leggy gelding: poor handicapper: left A. Crook after second start:
seems best at 1¾m/2m: acts on good to firm going: blinkered once: held up. *P. Bowen*

HIGH ESTEEM   6 b.g. Common Grounds 118 – Whittle Woods Girl 80 (Emarati   **71**
(USA) 74) [2002 62: f6s² f6g² f6g² f6g* f5g f6g 5g 5g 5m f6g³ f6g f6g⁵ Dec 10] big
gelding: fair handicapper: won at Southwell in February: best at 6f/7f nowadays: acts on
any turf going and fibresand: has won when sweating: often races prominently: has
looked difficult ride. *M. A. Buckley*

HIGHEST HONOUR (IRE)   2 b.g. (Apr 24) Polish Precedent (USA) 131 – Victoria   **–**
Cross (USA) (Spectacular Bid (USA)) [2002 8g 8s Oct 26] 30,000Y: big, workmanlike
gelding: sixth living foal: closely related to 2 winners, notably top-class sprinter Mozart
(by Danehill), also 7f winner (including at 2 yrs), and half-brother to 2 winners: dam
unraced half-sister to several US graded stakes winners, including Kentucky Derby
winner Sea Hero: well held in maidens: refused to enter stall on intended debut: gelded
after final start. *I. A. Balding*

HIGHEST (IRE)   3 b.c. Selkirk (USA) 129 – Pearl Kite (USA) 106§ (Silver   **123**
Hawk (USA) 123) [2002 98p: 10.3f² 11.8d* 12m² 12g* 11.9g² 14.6m² Sep 14]
        The light blue and dark blue silks of Highclere Thoroughbred Racing
continue to figure prominently at the highest level, and in the latest season the
syndicate came close to gaining a first classic win in Britain when Highest finished
second to Bollin Eric in the St Leger. Very smart though Highest is, he is not the
best horse owned by Highclere. That honour goes to Lake Coniston, a top-class
sprinter who got the syndicate off to a flying start when winning seven races,
including the July Cup, in the mid-'nineties; and not far behind him in terms of
ability comes Petrushka, whose wins in the Irish Oaks, Yorkshire Oaks and Prix de
l'Opera established her as the leading three-year-old filly trained in Britain and
Ireland in 2000. Highest himself has still to win a pattern race—indeed, his only
successes to date have come in a maiden at Leicester and a three-runner minor event
at Ascot—but it is only a matter of time before he does. A big, strong colt with
plenty of scope and only seven runs under his belt, it is not difficult to envisage
Highest making an even better four-year-old, though the colours he carries will
be of a different shade of blue following Highclere's decision to let Highest go to
Godolphin in a private purchase completed in October.
        There is little to be said about the two races Highest won, for both of which
he started at odds on. The second of them, at Ascot, merely confirmed his wellbeing after a fine second to Systematic in the King George V Handicap at the Royal
meeting there. At that stage it seemed as though Highest would be returned to
handicap company, as he looked to be on a handy mark in the Ebor, for which he
was installed favourite following the publication of the weights. However, with
Highest apparently impressing in his work at home, a much bolder policy was
adopted. Highest turned up at York's Ebor fixture for the Great Voltigeur Stakes, in
which he put up a performance that left little room for doubt he'd have won the
Ebor. Not only did Highest turn the tables on Systematic, but he came within a head
of upsetting the odds laid on Bandari, putting in a strong challenge from over three
furlongs out but held towards the finish after probably edging ahead briefly
approaching the final furlong. Highest renewed rivalry with Bandari and close
third Bollin Eric in the St Leger and he showed further improvement, doing easily
the best of the three Sir Michael Stoute-trained runners. Settled in mid-field, he
emerged as the biggest challenger to the winner over a furlong out, and kept on
strongly without ever really looking like pegging back Bollin Eric, who beat him
by a length and a quarter. Highest shaped as though he will stay two miles, which
will give him further options in the next season. However, his new connections will
start by campaigning him over middle distances, with the Dubai Sheema Classic
run over a mile and a half at Nad Al Sheba in March a first target.
        Highest's sire Selkirk was a miler but there is stamina on the dam's side of
Highest's pedigree, his dam Pearl Kite herself being a two-year-old winner over a
mile who was third in the Ribblesdale and showed useful form at up to a mile and
three quarters. Pearl Kite, unlike her son who has proved a genuine and consistent
sort, had her share of temperament, as did her close relation the useful stayer Jaseur.
Highest, a 125,000-guineas yearling, is the fourth foal of Pearl Kite, who is also

Highclere Thoroughbred Racing Ltd's "Highest"

		Sharpen Up	Atan
	Selkirk (USA)	(ch 1969)	Rochetta
	(ch 1988)	Annie Edge	Nebbiolo
Highest (IRE)		(ch 1980)	Friendly Court
(b.c. 1999)		Silver Hawk	Roberto
	Pearl Kite (USA)	(b 1979)	Gris Vitesse
	(b 1991)	Spur Wing	Storm Bird
		(ch 1984)	Equal Change

responsible for a couple of other notable runners in Shamaiel (by Lycius), a smart performer who stayed a mile and three quarters, and Nayyir (by Indian Ridge), a very smart winner at seven furlongs and a mile in the latest season. Highest's gran-dam Spur Wing, a half-sister to the smart Grade 1-placed winner Make Change, won six races in the States including a Grade 3 event over nine furlongs. Highest's great grandam Equal Change, also a winner in the States and second in a Grade 1 event there, is a half-sister to the 1983 Eclipse Stakes winner Solford. Highest has yet to race on soft or heavy going but acts on any other. *Sir Michael Stoute*

HIGHFIELD BOY 3 ch.g. Presidium 124 – Jendor 82 (Condorcet (FR)) [2002 7f 10f⁶ 11.9s May 27] angular gelding: half-brother to 2 winners, including 11f to 17f winner Highfield Fizz (by Efisio): dam 5f (at 2 yrs) and 1m winner who stayed 1½m: well held in maidens/claimer: sold 500 gns in August. *C. W. Fairhurst*

HIGHFIELD JEN 3 ch.f. Presidium 124 – Jendorcet 57 (Grey Ghost 98) [2002 f8.5g Nov 16] first foal: dam, poor maiden, should have stayed 1½m: 33/1, well held in maiden at Wolverhampton. *C. W. Fairhurst*

HIGH FINALE 3 b.f. Sure Blade (USA) 130 – High Velocity 53 (Frimley Park 109) [2002 85: 5d 5d May 25] leggy, workmanlike filly: fairly useful performer at 2 yrs: little form in handicaps in 2002: tried visored. *D. K. Ivory*

444

HIGH FINANCE (IRE) 2 b. or br.f. (May 9) Entrepreneur 123 – Phylella (Persian **68** Bold 123) [2002 p7g⁴ p8g⁴ Dec 14] IR 22,000Y: half-sister to several winners, including useful 6f (at 2 yrs)/7f winner Reunion (by Be My Guest) and fairly useful 1½m winner Speed of Light (by Spectrum): dam won in France (at 1¼m) and USA: fair form in minor event (slowly away) and maiden (beaten 2½ lengths by Nawow) at Lingfield. *J. W. Hills*

HIGHGATE HILL 2 b.g. (Jan 29) Revoque (IRE) 122 – Long View 68 (Persian Bold **– p** 123) [2002 7d Nov 2] big, strong, lengthy gelding: half-brother to several winners, including 1¼m to 2m winner Fearless Wonder (by Formidable) and fairly useful 1997 2-y-o 5f winner Two Williams (by Polar Falcon): dam 9f winner: 50/1, not knocked about when well held in maiden at Newmarket (gelded after): type to do better. *M. H. Tompkins*

HIGHGATES 5 gr.m. Hollington Coral – Connie (Mango Express 106) [2002 f12f **–** p10g Dec 30] first foal: dam unraced: well held in sellers. *Miss E. C. Lavelle*

HIGH HOPE (FR) 4 ch.c. Lomitas 129 – Highness Lady (GER) (Cagliostro (GER)) **91** [2002 105: 12.5m⁵ 12m 14s² 12.5d 10g* 16s p12g* Nov 19] 220,000 francs F, 420,000 francs Y: fourth foal: dam, won Preis der Diana (also successful at 1m at 2 yrs), half-sister to very smart German middle-distance colt Helikon: ex-French performer, useful at best: won minor events at Fontainebleau and Maisons-Laffitte at 3 yrs, and successful in 2002 in similar event at Chateaubriant in July (left R. Gibson after), and amateur handicap at Lingfield (beat High Point a length) in November: stays 15f: acts on polytrack, raced mainly on good going or softer (acts on heavy) on turf: tried blinkered. *G. L. Moore*

HIGH JINKS 7 b.g. High Estate 127 – Waffling 68 (Lomond (USA) 128) [2002 12.3g **48** 16.2g 14d 16g⁴ 16g⁵ f14s⁵ 18d Oct 21] lightly-raced handicapper, just poor nowadays: stays 2m: raced only on good going or softer on turf, and probably acts on fibresand. *R. N. Bevis*

HIGHLAND FLIGHT 4 gr.f. Missed Flight 123 – In The Highlands (Petong 126) **43** [2002 49: p5g f5g⁴ f5g 6f 7g 6f⁵ 6m Jul 3] smallish filly: poor maiden handicapper: seems best at 5f/easy 6f: acts on all-weather and firm going: tried visored/blinkered: none too consistent. *Bob Jones*

HIGHLAND GAIT 3 ch.f. Most Welcome 131 – Miller's Gait 74§ (Mill Reef (USA) **61** 141) [2002 59: 9.9g 10m⁴ 12.3m 14m 9g² 9.9d⁴ 8s 8.3v 8.5m Sep 24] sturdy filly: easy mover: modest maiden: well below form last 3 starts: bred to stay beyond 1¼m: acts on good to firm and good to soft ground, probably not on soft: blinkered final outing: often leads: possibly not straightforward. *T. D. Easterby*

HIGHLAND GAMES (IRE) 2 b.c. (Apr 3) Singspiel (IRE) 133 – Highland Gift **–** (IRE) 95 (Generous (IRE) 139) [2002 7d Nov 2] well-made colt: first foal: half-brother to 3-y-o Mount Street and 4-y-o Golan: dam, 1¼m winner, half-sister to smart middle-distance stayer Bonny Scot and smart 1¼m/1½m winner Mary Stuart: 20/1, tailed off in maiden at Newmarket. *Sir Michael Stoute*

HIGHLAND REEL 5 ch.g. Selkirk (USA) 129 – Taj Victory 68 (Final Straw 127) **92** [2002 106: 8.3g⁴ 8m 8.5s 8g³ 8s Nov 2] leggy gelding: fairly useful performer: ran creditably in 2002 only on reappearance/penultimate start: best around 1m: acts on heavy and good to firm going: races freely: none too reliable. *D. R. C. Elsworth*

HIGHLAND SHOT 4 b.f. Selkirk (USA) 129 – Optaria 83 (Song 132) [2002 57: 6f **74** f8.5g⁶ 8.3d* 8g* 7m⁶ 8.3g⁴ 7m* 8s² 6m⁴ 7m² Sep 5] quite good-topped filly: fair handicapper: won at Windsor in May, Leicester in June and Salisbury in July: effective at 6f to 1m: acts on soft and good to firm going, probably on heavy: sometimes pulls hard: consistent. *I. A. Balding*

HIGHLAND WARRIOR 3 b.c. Makbul 104 – Highland Rowena 59 (Royben 125) **78** [2002 71: 7s 6f⁶ 7m² 8m⁵ 9.1g* 7g⁵ 8s⁵ 7.9m 8m³ 8s⁶ Nov 6] big, leggy colt: fair performer: won maiden at Ayr in May: ran well penultimate outing: effective at 7f to 9f: acts on good to firm and good to soft going: sometimes races freely. *J. S. Goldie*

HIGHLY COMMENDED 2 gr.g. (Mar 21) With Approval (CAN) – High Sevens **–** 90 (Master Willie 129) [2002 7m 8.5d⁵ 10s Oct 23] 11,000F, IR 34,000Y: half-brother to 7f (including at 2 yrs)/1m winner Impulsif (by Diesis): dam, 2-y-o 6f winner, half-sister to smart middle-distance performers Hateel and Munwar: signs of only a little ability in maidens: blinkered debut and final start: gave trouble stalls and looked difficult ride second one: sold 3,700 gns. *M. H. Tompkins*

HIGHLY LIQUID 2 b.f. (Feb 26) Entrepreneur 123 – Premiere Cuvee 109 (Form- **81 p** idable (USA) 125) [2002 6v² Nov 9] 70,000Y: good-topped filly: closely related to useful Italian miler She Bat (by Batshoof) and half-sister to several winners, including useful 7f/ 1m winner Cask (by Be My Chief): dam sprinter: 10/1, backward and green, ¾-length second of 13 to Marinas Charm in maiden at Doncaster, always prominent: sure to do better. *W. Jarvis*

HIGHLY PLEASED (USA) 7 b.g. Hansel (USA) – Bint Alfalla (USA) (Nureyev **45** (USA) 131) [2002 46: p7g f8.5g Sep 21] quite good-topped gelding: poor maiden: left P. Burgoyne before second start: stays 8.5f: acts on firm ground and all-weather: blinkered on reappearance: has reportedly bled from nose. *S. L. Keightley*

HIGHNESS (IRE) 2 ch.f. (Feb 21) Titus Livius (FR) 115 – Highland Crumpet 46 **65** (First Trump 118) [2002 5g⁴ 5.1g² 5f³ 5.1g 5.1d⁵ 5m* 5m* Aug 24] IR 1,200Y: first foal: dam, sprint maiden (ran only at 2 yrs), half-sister to Middle Park winner Stalker: fair performer: won claimer at Folkestone in July and seller at Windsor (made virtually all) in August: likely to prove best at 5f: acts on good to firm going: blinkered (well below form) once: looked none too genuine prior to last 2 starts. *Mrs P. N. Dutfield*

HIGH PADDY 3 b.g. Master Willie 129 – Ivy Edith (Blakeney 126) [2002 –: 10d⁶ **75 ?** p12g 10s⁶ Oct 23] lightly-raced maiden: seemingly easily best effort on reappearance: should stay at least 1½m. *R. Ingram*

HIGH PITCHED 4 ch.c. Indian Ridge 123 – Place de L'Opera 98 (Sadler's Wells **121** (USA) 132) [2002 116p: 12g 13.3m* 12m⁴ 13.3f² Aug 17] good-bodied colt: impresses in appearance: very smart performer: easy winner of listed race at Newbury in May, beating Warrsan by 7 lengths: 1¼ lengths fourth to Zindabad in Hardwicke Stakes at Royal Ascot and 2 lengths second to Mubtaker in Geoffrey Freer Stakes at Newbury (reportedly bled) final start: should stay 1¾m: acts on firm and good to soft going: blinkered (found little) on reappearance: tricky ride (has carried head high/hung left): reluctant to post at Newbury: to continue career in USA. *H. R. A. Cecil*

Mr L. Marinopoulos' "High Pitched"

HIGH POINT (IRE) 4 b.g. Ela-Mana-Mou 132 – Top Lady (IRE) 83 (Shirley Heights 130) [2002 –: p10g p13g* 11.8g⁶ 11.9g p12g⁵ p13g* p12g² p16g* Nov 27] fairly useful performer, lightly raced: won maiden at Lingfield in February, and 2 handicaps there in November (apprentices on first occasion): stays 2m: acts on polytrack: held up: game. *G. P. Enright* **81**

HIGH POLICY (IRE) 6 ch.g. Machiavellian (USA) 123 – Road To The Top 84 (Shirley Heights 130) [2002 61, a84: f16s² f16.2g⁵ f12g⁴ f16g f16.2g² 14.1d⁶ 16g³ 16m² 16m⁵ 14.1d⁶ 14d 14s 14.1m* 16g⁶ 16g³ 16m³ 15.9f⁵ 16v 13.8d³ f14.8g² f14.8g³ f16g⁵ f14g⁶ Dec 10] well-made gelding: fairly useful handicapper on all-weather, modest on turf: won at Nottingham in July: effective at 1¾m to 17f: acts on fibresand, heavy and good to firm going: visored once at 4 yrs, has worn cheekpieces: sometimes slowly away/ flashes tail: held up. *R. Hollinshead* **63 a84**

HIGH POWERED (GER) 3 b.f. So Factual (USA) 120 – High Habit 79 (Slip Anchor 136) [2002 8.2g⁵ 8f⁵ 6d⁶ 10m 8g Aug 13] sixth foal: half-sister to fairly useful 6f winner Alegria (by Night Shift) and winner up to 13f in Scandinavia by Robellino: dam, second at 11.5f, half-sister to smart sprinter Blue Siren: fair maiden: well below form after second outing: left J. Eustace 4,500 gns after third start (blinkered): sold £700 in December. *J. J. Bridger* **67 ?**

HIGH PRAISE (USA) 2 b.f. (Jan 28) Quest For Fame 127 – Stellaria (USA) 98 (Roberto (USA) 131) [2002 7m* 8g³ 8s* Oct 22] half-sister to several winners, notably top-class 6f (at 2 yrs) to 9f winner Observatory (by Distant View): dam 5f (at 2 yrs) to 8.5f (in USA) winner: useful form: won maiden at Salisbury in August and Prix des Reservoirs at Deauville in October, making most and rallying to beat Welcome Millenium a nose in latter: good ½-length third to Loving Pride in Prix d'Aumale at Longchamp in between, headed only well inside final 1f: will be suited by 1¼m+: acts on soft and good to firm ground. *J. H. M. Gosden* **105**

HIGH REACH 2 b.c. (Apr 26) Royal Applause 124 – Lady of Limerick (IRE) (Thatching 131) [2002 6d Oct 14] 13,000F: third foal: half-brother to 2001 2-y-o 5f winner Marechal George (by Deerhound): dam, ran once in USA, out of close relative to smart French 9f performer L'Irresponsable: 12/1 and green, well held in maiden at Windsor, eased once held: should improve. *T. G. Mills* **– p**

HIGH RIDGE 3 ch.c. Indian Ridge 123 – Change For A Buck (USA) 83 (Time For A Change (USA)) [2002 12s 10m Jun 21] first foal: dam, 1m winner from 2 starts, daughter of Poule d'Essai des Pouliches winner Pearl Bracelet: fair form when eighth in maidens at Kempton and Newmarket: sold 2,800 gns in October. *H. R. A. Cecil* **68**

HIGH ROCK HENRY (IRE) 3 ch.g. Pennekamp (USA) 130 – Belsay 68 (Belmez (USA) 131) [2002 65: p10g 10g p10g⁴ 9.7m p8g 10.9m p12g Oct 4] fair maiden handicapper: best effort on reappearance: stays 1¼m: acts on polytrack. *Miss J. Feilden* **71 d**

HIGH SIROCCO 2 ch.g. (Feb 15) First Trump 118 – Amid The Stars 61 (Midyan (USA) 124) [2002 6g 6m 6m⁴ 6m⁶ 7.5g 7m Oct 2] 1,500Y: tall gelding: first foal: dam, maiden, out of half-sister to dam of smart fillies Lemon Souffle (stayed 1m) and Caramba (stayed 1¼m): modest maiden: should stay 7f: raced only on good/good to firm going: none too consistent. *D. W. Barker* **52**

HIGH STRAITS 3 ch.f. Bering 136 – High Summer (USA) 107 (Nureyev (USA) 131) [2002 8m 8.5m⁶ 8.2v¹⁰ 10.3v Nov 8] first foal: dam, 7f winner, sister to dam of Poule d'Essai des Pouliches winner Matiara (by Bering) and half-sister to smart miler Summer View: fair performer: won maiden at Nottingham in October by 7 lengths, drifting left: virtually pulled up final outing: stays 1m: acts on heavy going: very slowly away on debut: sold 62,000 gns. *R. Charlton* **74**

HIGH STREET 2 b.c. (Mar 19) Mark of Esteem (IRE) 137 – Kentmere (FR) (Galetto (FR) 118) [2002 7.1v⁶ 7m⁶ Oct 3] IR 95,000Y: good-topped colt: fourth foal: closely related to 5-y-o Love Bitten and half-brother to 3-y-o Danemere and 4-y-o Love: dam, French 1m (at 2 yrs) and 11f winner, half-sister to Prix de Diane winner Lypharita: only a little sign of ability in maidens. *M. R. Channon* **–**

HIGHSTREET FLIGHT (IRE) 3 br.g. Darnay 117 – La Calera (Corvaro (USA) 124) [2002 –: f8s Jan 10] well held in 3 maidens at Southwell: dead. *J. Nicol* **–**

HIGH SUN 6 b.g. High Estate 127 – Clyde Goddess (IRE) 92 (Scottish Reel 123) [2002 54: 8.3s 8.3g 8g 7.1g³ 7.1d⁶ 8m 7.2d Jul 23] heavy-topped gelding: modest performer: effective at 7f to 1¼m: acts on firm and good to soft going: tried blinkered earlier in career. *P. Monteith* **52**

HIGH TEMPO 4 b.g. Piccolo 121 – Reem Fever (IRE) 79 (Fairy King (USA)) [2002 –
–: f7s Jan 2] of little account. *K. R. Burke*

HILARIOUS (IRE) 2 b.f. (Jan 23) Petorius 117 – Heronwater (IRE) 73 (Ela-Mana- **63**
Mou 132) [2002 5g 5.2f⁵ 6d 8.3m⁵ 8d Oct 21] IR 5,000F, IR 16,000Y: good-topped filly:
first foal: dam, ran twice (better effort at 1½m), half-sister to smart French/US miler Girl
of France out of half-sister to Prix Vermeille winner Walensee: modest maiden: has raced
freely, but will probably stay 1¼m: acts on good to firm and good to soft going.
B. R. Millman

HILBRE ISLAND 2 b.c. (May 3) Halling (USA) 133 – Faribole (IRE) 106 (Esprit du **99**
Nord (USA) 126) [2002 6s² 7m* 7g⁶ 7m⁶ Sep 13] 26,000F, IR 46,000Y: sturdy colt:
half-brother to useful 7f/1m winner Date (by Cadeaux Genereux): dam French 1¼m
winner: useful form: won maiden at Newbury in July, making most: good sixth in Vintage
Stakes at Goodwood (beaten about 3 lengths by Almushahar) and Champagne Stakes at
Doncaster (3¾ lengths behind Dublin) after: free-going sort, but should stay 1m: acts on
good to firm going, showed promise on soft. *B. J. Meehan*

HILL FARM CLASSIC 2 ch.c. (May 20) Meqdaam (USA) – Wing of Freedom –
(Troy 137) [2002 5g 5.1d Apr 30] 500Y: rather leggy colt: sixth foal: half-brother to 1995
2-y-o 5f winner Montrestar (by Mon Tresor) and 6f winner Kustom Kit Kate (by Tragic
Role): dam staying maiden in Ireland: well in rear in maiden/minor event. *P. T. Dalton*

HILL MAGIC 7 br.g. Magic Ring (IRE) 115 – Stock Hill Lass 87 (Air Trooper 115) **73**
[2002 75: 7m 7d 6d⁶ 6m⁵ 7.1g⁴ 6m p8g³ 7.1g 7.1g Sep 23] close-coupled, useful-looking
gelding: fair handicapper: stays easy 1m: acts on firm going, good to soft and polytrack:
visored last 2 outings (hung right first occasion). *L. G. Cottrell*

HILLS OF GOLD 3 b.c. Danehill (USA) 126 – Valley of Gold (FR) 117 (Shirley **98**
Heights 130) [2002 103p: 10.4f 7f⁵ 7d Aug 10] big, lengthy colt: has scope: has a quick,
fluent action: useful form, lightly raced: won minor event at Doncaster at 2 yrs in good
style: form in 2002 only when last of 5 in minor contest at Newbury: should prove better
at 1m/1¼m than shorter: tongue tied final start: sold 8,000 gns. *B. W. Hills*

HILLSWICK 11 ch.g. Norwick (USA) 125 – Quite Lucky 69 (Precipice Wood 123) –
[2002 15.4m 18s 19.1m Jun 22] angular gelding: lightly raced nowadays. *J. S. King*

HILLTIME (IRE) 2 b.g. (Feb 21) Danetime (IRE) 121 – Ceannanas (IRE) 77 (Magical **61**
Wonder (USA) 125) [2002 5g⁴ 5m⁴ 5m⁵ 6m⁵ 5m Jun 1] IR 14,000F: rather unfurnished,
quite attractive gelding: first foal: dam, Irish maiden, stayed 1m: modest maiden: below
form last 2 starts, including in visor: should stay at least 6f. *J. J. Quinn*

HILLTOP WARNING 5 b.g. Reprimand 122 – Just Irene 50 (Sagaro 133) [2002 **92**
101: 7m⁶ 7.9f 7f Jun 1] smallish gelding: useful handicapper at 4 yrs: best effort in 2002
on reappearance: best around 7f: easily best form on good/good to firm ground: blinkered
once at 3 yrs: tends to edge left: has carried head awkwardly: held up. *R. Guest*

HIM OF DISTINCTION 3 br.c. Rainbow Quest (USA) 134 – Air of Distinction **93**
(IRE) 99 (Distinctly North (USA) 115) [2002 93p: 9m 8m⁴ 10d⁵ 12g 12v Nov 9] smallish
colt: fairly useful performer, lightly raced: barely stays 1½m: acts on good to soft going.
J. L. Dunlop

HI NICKY 6 ch.m. High Kicker (USA) – Sharp Top 62 (Sharpo 132) [2002 –: f8s Jan –
1] tall mare: of little account nowadays. *M. J. Polglase*

HIRAETH 4 b.f. Petong 126 – Floppie (FR) (Law Society (USA) 130) [2002 58: f6g –
p7g Feb 13] good-topped filly: one-time fair performer: no form in 2002. *B. Palling*

HIRAPOUR (IRE) 6 b.g. Kahyasi 130 – Himaya (IRE) (Mouktar 129) [2002 107: **100**
12m² 13.3f 18m Oct 19] strong, workmanlike gelding: has a round action: useful
performer: off 10 months, respectable 5 lengths second of 3 to Systematic in 3-runner
minor event at Newbury on belated reappearance: well held in handicaps and Prix du
Cadran at Longchamp after: effective at 1½m to 2¼m: acts on firm and soft going:
blinkered (below form) twice at 4 yrs: effective racing prominently or held up: sold
11,000 gns, and joined I. Williams. *Mrs A. J. Perrett*

HI RED 3 ch.f. Atraf 116 – Red River Rose (IRE) 51 (Red Sunset 120) [2002 75d: **?**
p10g⁶ f8g³ a12g³ 8g³ a8g³ a12g⁶ a12g a12g 11g a12g⁵ a12g⁶ Nov 24] sparely-made filly: fair **a47**
performer at best on turf, poor on all-weather: sold from J. Portman 1,800 gns after
second start: stays 1½m: acts on good to firm going, probably on good to soft and all-
weather/dirt: sometimes blinkered/visored: one to treat with some caution. *H. Crantz,
Sweden*

HIRVINE (FR) 4 ch.g. Snurge 130 – Guadanella (FR) (Guadanini (FR) 125) [2002 –: **69 d**
12f 10d 13s³ 18d 15d Jul 23] big, strong gelding: fair maiden at best: well below form last
2 starts: stays 13f: acts on soft ground. *T. P. Tate*

HISPANIOLA (IRE) 4 ch.f. Barathea (IRE) 127 – Caribbean Quest 90 (Rainbow **–**
Quest (USA) 134) [2002 7f May 4] IR 85,000Y: ex-French filly: first foal: dam, 2-y-o 1m
winner, out of half-sister to smart 1¼m filly Optimistic Lass, herself dam of high-class
sprinter/miler Golden Opinion: placed in maiden, minor event and handicap in French
Provinces at 3 yrs for P. Bary: last in handicap on only outing in 2002: stays 11f: acts on
firm and good to soft ground. *M. W. Easterby*

HISTORIC TREBLE 3 b.c. Lycius (USA) 124 – Alfaaselah (GER) 97 (Dancing **104**
Brave (USA) 140) [2002 81+: 7m⁴ 8.1d 7m p7g* 7m p8g⁴ 6f⁵ 7m² 7m a6f* Dec 27] rather
leggy colt: useful handicapper: won at Lingfield in May and (having left B. Hanbury after
ninth start) Jebel Ali in December: effective at 6f/7f: acts on any turf going and on
polytrack/dirt: blinkered last 3 starts in Britain. *A. Smith, UAE*

HI TECH 3 ch.f. Polar Falcon (USA) 126 – Just Speculation (IRE) 86 (Ahonoora 122) **45**
[2002 7d⁶ 7d⁵ Jul 11] 48,000Y: third foal: half-brother to 4-y-o The Judge and a winner in
Turkey by Sharpo: dam, 2-y-o 6f winner, half-sister to Gold Cup and Irish St Leger
runner-up Tyrone Bridge: poor form in maidens (raced freely): sold 900 gns in August.
M. A. Jarvis

HOBART JUNCTION (IRE) 7 ch.g. Classic Secret (USA) 91 – Art Duo 86 (Artaius **50**
(USA) 129) [2002 p10g⁵ p10g p13g⁶ p12g Mar 6] modest performer, lightly raced on
Flat: probably best around 1¼m: acts on polytrack and firm ground: sometimes blinkered.
J. A. T. de Giles

HO CHOI 3 b.g. Pivotal 124 – Witch of Fife (USA) 91 (Lear Fan (USA) 130) [2002 **102**
102: 8m 7f⁵ 7m⁴ 6d⁴ 7m⁶ 8m⁴ Sep 13] big, good-topped gelding: useful performer:
mostly creditable efforts without making significant impact in pattern/listed races in
2002, including when fourth in Jersey Stakes at Royal Ascot (2¾ lengths behind Just
James) and Shergar Cup Sprint at Ascot (beaten 5¾ lengths by Feet So Fast): below form
in minor event at Doncaster final start (gelded after): needs good test at 6f and stays 1m:
acts on firm and good to soft going: sent to Hong Kong. *Miss L. A. Perratt*

HODAIDA (IRE) 3 b.f. Mtoto 134 – Moonshine Lake 85 (Kris 135) [2002 11s **–**
11.5m⁴ Jul 2] fourth foal: half-sister to 2 winners, including fairly useful winner around
1½m Somayya (by Polar Falcon): dam, 1½m winner who stayed 1¾m, sister to smart
performer up to 10.5f Moon Cactus (dam of Oaks winner Moonshell): well held in
maidens at Goodwood and Yarmouth: visits Kayf Tara. *A. C. Stewart*

HOH BUZZARD (IRE) 2 b.f. (Mar 12) Alhaarth (IRE) 126 – Indian Express 61 **79**
(Indian Ridge 123) [2002 7m 7.6m⁴ 8.2m* Oct 1] IR 27,000F, IR 42,000Y: leggy filly:
fourth foal: half-sister to 2 winners, notably 3-y-o Ashdown Express: dam, 8.5f/1¼m
winner, sister to useful 6f/7f performer Cheyenne Spirit: fair form: won maiden at
Nottingham by ½ length from Change Partners, leading final 50 yds: will stay 1¼m: raced
only on good to firm ground. *M. L. W. Bell*

HOH INVADER (IRE) 10 b.g. Accordion – Newgate Fairy (Flair Path 122) [2002 **58**
78, a–: f16.2g 11.9g⁶ 15.8f⁴ 12m 10.4f Oct 10] tall gelding: fairly useful hurdler/chaser: **a–**
modest maiden on Flat: may prove best at 1¼m/1½m: acts on good to firm going: makes
running. *Mrs A. Duffield*

HOH INVESTOR (IRE) 2 b.g. (Apr 7) Charnwood Forest (IRE) 125 – Uffizi (IRE) **79**
(Royal Academy (USA) 130) [2002 5m⁶ 6s⁵ 6g³ 7d⁵ p6g* p7g³ Dec 14] IR 25,000Y:
close-coupled, quite good-topped gelding: second foal: half-brother to a 1¼m/11f
winner in Italy by Spectrum: dam unraced out of half-sister to Riverman and to grandam
of Rock of Gibraltar: fair performer: off 4 months and gelded, won nursery at Lingfield in
November: stays easy 7f: acts on polytrack, soft and good to firm going: sometimes
slowly away. *I. A. Balding*

HOH'S BACK 3 b.c. Royal Applause 124 – Paris Joelle (IRE) (Fairy King (USA)) **77**
[2002 83: 11.6g f8.5f f9.4g⁵ p8g Dec 14] well-made colt: fair handicapper: stays 9.4f:
acts on all-weather and soft ground. *S. Kirk*

HOH VISS 2 b.c. (Mar 2) Rudimentary (USA) 118 – Now And Forever (IRE) (Kris **55 p**
135) [2002 8s Oct 26] leggy, lengthy colt: second living foal: half-brother to useful 1999
2-y-o 7f winner who stayed 1½m Everlasting Love (by Pursuit of Love): dam unraced
half-sister to smart stayer Witness Box out of close relative to Dahlia: 33/1 and backward,
ninth of 15 to Midas Way in maiden at Newbury, fading: should improve. *S. Kirk*

HOLD ME CLOSE   3 b.f. Most Welcome 131 – With Care 78 (Warning 136) [2002   –
8.1m 10s f12g⁵ May 24] second foal: half-sister to 4-y-o On Guard: dam 7f winner: well
held in maidens/claimer: tongue tied last 2 outings: slowly away on debut. *W. J. Haggas*

HOLD THAT TIGER (USA)   2 b.c. (Feb 25) Storm Cat (USA) – Beware of The   **117 p**
Cat (USA) (Caveat (USA)) [2002 6s* 6d* 6s 7g* a9f³ Oct 26]
    As a million-dollar foal—he cost 1.1 million at the Keeneland November
Sale in 2000—Hold That Tiger had a lot to live up to. With victory in the Grand
Criterium and third place in the Breeders' Cup Juvenile on the credit side there is
no denying he has abundant ability, reflected in his position as one of the market
leaders for the Two Thousand Guineas at the time of writing. He has already
compiled a better record than all but one of the other million-dollar foals sold in
the last six years. King Charlemagne is the only Group 1 scorer in the group of
twelve which also includes another trained by Aidan O'Brien at Ballydoyle, She's
A Beauty, a 1.2 million foal bought at the same sale as Hold That Tiger who
managed only one third place from three starts in her first season. Other colts may
look to have better prospects in the Guineas and the Kentucky Derby, for which
Hold That Tiger is reportedly only a possible contender, but if he progresses the
right way Hold That Tiger should make his presence felt in the best company. One
thing is certain—if he continues with what appears to be his habitual style of
running, no race including him is likely to be dull.
    Hold That Tiger's best performances came on his return from an eight-
week lay-off in the wake of a poor run when short-priced favourite for the Phoenix
Stakes at the Curragh, where he finished last of nine and was found to be suffering
respiratory distress. He faced thirteen rivals in the Grand Criterium - Lucien
Barriere at Longchamp, in what was the biggest field since 1971. Five of them were
pattern winners, namely his stablemate Spartacus, British challengers Checkit and
Foss Way, Italian colt Le Vie dei Colori and the filly Loving Kindness. There were
two others from Ballydoyle, Great Pyramid and Kimberley Mine, continuing
O'Brien's saturation policy, plus the filly Intercontinental, who started favourite;
the Ballydoyle runners were coupled at 7/2. Hold That Tiger briefly ran in snatches
towards the rear and his rider had to bide his time in the straight before switching
the colt wide a furlong and a half out, where he was still last. The runners were well
bunched, but Hold That Tiger still looked to have hardly any chance of playing a
part until he started to make ground hand over fist in astonishing fashion. Sweeping
past his rivals, he caught front-running Le Vie dei Colori in the last thirty yards and

*Grand Criterium - Lucien Barriere, Longchamp—Hold That Tiger (right) displays a remarkable
turn of foot to come from last to first; Italian-trained Le Vie dei Colori (no.12), in second place,
suffers his first defeat as the filly Intercontinental (centre) finishes third*

beat him by half a length going away, with the filly Intercontinental the same distance away third. The twelfth horse was beaten less than five lengths, so there is no reason to think the form is exceptional, but nothing can take away the impression made by Hold That Tiger's acceleration. It was electrifying. The only drawback was the fact that he had had to produce it in the way he did, because this was not the first time Hold That Tiger had dropped himself out. The same had happened when justifying favouritism in a nine-runner maiden at Leopardstown in June on his debut, when he finished very strongly after having only one behind him a furlong out. There were no such problems when he won the Anheuser Busch Railway Stakes at the Curragh—his trainer's fourth consecutive victory in the race—later in the month by a neck from Coventry Stakes runner-up Pakhoes after leading two furlongs out and tending to hang into the runner-up. However, that was not a race from which to draw worthwhile conclusions about racing style because there were only four runners and the pace was muddling, the time 0.6 seconds slower than the next race, which was run over an additional sixty-three yards.

After Longchamp, the possibility still existed that the behaviour of Hold That Tiger was the result of inexperience, but, allowing for the unfamiliar dirt surface and different environment, his run in the Breeders' Cup Juvenile at Arlington did little to allay the suspicion that Hold That Tiger might be a shade quirky. Despite the absence of ante-post favourite Sky Mesa due to injury, the race was as strongly contested as usual. Whywhywhy, favourite on the strength of his success in the Grade 1 Futurity Stakes, headed the home team from Vindication, unbeaten in three starts including a Grade 3 and saddled by leading trainer Bob Baffert, looking for his first win in the event. Toccet, winner of the Grade 1 Champagne Stakes, and the Baffert-trained Kafwain, who had landed the Grade 2 Norfolk Stakes, were also leading contenders. O'Brien ran Tomahawk and Van Nistelrooy as well as Hold That Tiger, who was sent off ahead of the other two in the market as 11/2 third favourite, ridden by Kieren Fallon with Michael Kinane opting for 17/1-shot Tomahawk. Given the habitually ferocious pace in American dirt races, a slow start may not always be the kiss of death over a mile or more, but it is far from helpful and Hold That Tiger did his cause no good by crawling out of the stalls and going to the first turn in last place. He raced wide in the early stages for reasons best known to his rider—perhaps the muddy kickback evident at the meeting, not a pleasant experience for horse or jockey, was a factor—before making progress from halfway. Sixth entering the straight, Hold That Tiger produced a fine run despite being forced to come wide again, finishing five lengths third to clear-cut winner Vindication, who beat Kafwain by two and three quarter lengths after making virtually all.

Immediately after the race O'Brien said: 'We'll definitely look at the Kentucky Derby and maybe we've found the horse for the race.' The so-called 'Run for the Roses' has an astonishing drawing power for the big battalions in Europe, but so far, despite seven attempts since 1999, Godolphin and Ballydoyle representatives have finished no nearer than sixth; O'Brien's pair of Johannesburg and Castle Gandolfo finished eighth and twelfth respectively in the latest running. Even assuming they had the ability and/or stamina, which is debatable, neither of those colts had the battle-hardened experience, gained in the trials on American soil, which seems so necessary for success in the Kentucky Derby, a subject commented on in the essay on Johannesburg in *Racehorses of 2001*. Even if Hold That Tiger were to be sent out to contest a couple of races on dirt in the spring, he would be hard pressed to cope with Vindication at Churchill Downs. At least he should stay the trip, however, despite a remark, presumably tongue-in-cheek, by his part-owner Michael Tabor after the Grand Criterium, when he said: 'The Guineas comes very early on, so we can always drop him in trip after that.' One thing Hold That Tiger will never be, short of a miraculous transformation, is a sprinter.

Hold That Tiger's sire Storm Cat needs no introduction and continued his astonishing career in the latest season with Sophisticat and Van Nistelrooy in Europe, plus top juvenile filly Storm Flag Flying and Grade 1 winner Raging Fever in the States. Storm Cat's yearlings were in massive demand, as usual, with the top lots at Keeneland July and September and at Saratoga all by him. The majority of his runners are not middle-distance performers, but Hold That Tiger comes from a family with reasonable stamina, since his dam Beware of The Cat, a winner of four

Mr M. Tabor & Mrs John Magnier's "Hold That Tiger"

Hold That Tiger (USA) (b.c. Feb 25, 2000)	Storm Cat (USA) (b or br 1983)	Storm Bird (b 1978)	Northern Dancer South Ocean
		Terlingua (ch 1976)	Secretariat Crimson Saint
	Beware of The Cat (USA) (ch 1986)	Caveat (b or br 1980)	Cannonade Cold Hearted
		T. C. Kitten (ch 1969)	Tom Cat Needlebug

races at up to nine furlongs including a minor stakes, is by a Belmont Stakes winner and has already foaled a winner of that race in Editor's Note (by Forty Niner). Another foal, Catfriend (by Capote), picked up listed races over a mile at two and at nine furlongs, while Catnip (by Flying Paster) won a minor stakes and is dam of speedy 1999 juvenile Elaflaak. This is a successful family, one with which Coolmore is well acquainted. Beware of The Cat is a half-sister to Island Kitty, dam of Johannesburg's sire Hennessy (himself by Storm Cat), and to Field Cat, a Grade 1 victor over a mile and a half. Another daughter of T. C. Kitten produced Family Style, champion juvenile filly in the States in 1985. Beware of The Cat's yearling, a filly by Deputy Minister, failed to reach her reserve at the Keeneland July Sale when the bidding stopped at 550,000 dollars. Hold That Tiger, a big, good-topped colt who looks sure to train on, acts on dirt and has raced only on good ground or softer on turf. *A. P. O'Brien, Ireland*

HOLD TO RANSOM (USA) 2 b.f. (Apr 10) Red Ransom (USA) – Wassifa 95 (Sure **91** Blade (USA) 130) [2002 6s³ 6m³ 7m* 8g Sep 28] $95,000Y: strong filly: fluent mover: fourth foal: half-sister to 2 winners in USA by Conte di Savoya: dam, 11f winner in

Britain who later won up to 9f in USA, out of half-sister to Most Welcome: fairly useful form: made all in maiden at Newmarket in August, beating Al Ihtithar by 1¾ lengths: ran poorly in Fillies' Mile at Ascot final start: should stay 1m: acts on soft and good to firm ground. *E. A. L. Dunlop*

HO LENG (IRE) 7 ch.g. Statoblest 120 – Indigo Blue (IRE) 56 (Bluebird (USA) 125) **92 §**
[2002 97§: 6m 6g 7f 7g 7.1d⁵ 7m⁵ 8g* 7.2g 8g² 8.1f⁵ 8m* 7f⁵ 7.9f⁶ 8s Nov 6] leggy, lengthy gelding: fairly useful performer: won 6-runner minor events at Ayr in July and Musselburgh in September: stays 1m: best on good going or firm (acts on firm): often slowly away/rears: has run moodily: unreliable. *Miss L. A. Perratt*

HOLLOW JO 2 b.g. (May 17) Most Welcome 131 – Sir Hollow (USA) (Sir Ivor 135) **–**
[2002 5m 7d 7v Nov 8] strong, lengthy gelding: has scope: seventh living foal: half-brother to 3 winners, including 5-y-o Moon Emperor: dam French 1m winner: well held in minor event/maidens. *J. R. Jenkins*

HOLLYBELL 3 b.f. Beveled (USA) – Fayre Holly (IRE) 57 (Fayruz 116) [2002 68: **87 §**
p5g² p5g* p5g³ p6g⁴ p5g⁵ 6g* 6g³ 6f 5g 6m* 6d 5.7f Aug 18] leggy filly: fairly useful on **a67 §**
turf, fair on all-weather: won seller at Lingfield in February, handicap at Windsor in April and minor event at Kempton in June: effective at 5f/6f: acts on polytrack and good to firm ground (looked ill at ease on firm final start): sometimes slowly away/wanders: unreliable. *J. Gallagher*

HOLLYBUSH (IRE) 3 b.f. Ali-Royal (IRE) 127 – Another Baileys 60 (Deploy 131) **49**
[2002 55: 9.3s 8m 9m 7.2g⁵ 8.1v 7.9m 10s Aug 30] poor maiden at 3 yrs: stays 1m: acts on heavy and good to firm going. *J. S. Goldie*

HOLLY GAMES 3 b.f. Mind Games 121 – Young Holly (Risk Me (FR) 127) [2002 **50**
–: 5.5f 5d³ 5d 5s 6m 6g Oct 28] tall, angular filly: modest maiden: easily best effort at 3 yrs on second outing: races mainly around 5f: acts on good to soft going. *M. R. Bosley*

HOLLY ROSE 3 b.f. Charnwood Forest (IRE) 125 – Divina Luna 96 (Dowsing **60**
(USA) 124) [2002 46: p8g⁵ f8.5g⁶ 7g* 8g 7m 7m Sep 18] modest performer: won apprentice maiden handicap at Brighton in August: stays easy 1m: acts on polytrack, raced only on good/good to firm going on turf: sometimes slowly away: carried head high second start. *D. E. Cantillon*

HOLLYWEST (FR) 2 ch.g. (Mar 25) Sillery (USA) 122 – Hollywood Trick (USA) **–**
(Caro 133) [2002 8.2v p8g Nov 27] sixth foal: closely related to French winner around 1½m Special Effect (by Groom Dancer): dam French 10.5f winner: slowly away and well held in 2 maidens: gelded after. *R. M. Beckett*

HOLLYWOOD HENRY (IRE) 2 b.c. (Feb 26) Bahhare (USA) 122 – Takeshi (IRE) **75**
67 (Cadeaux Genereux 131) [2002 6m 7m² p7g⁵ 8d⁵ 8m 7s³ Oct 26] 40,000F, 32,000Y: well-made colt: fourth foal: dam, maiden who stayed 1m, half-sister to dam of 4-y-o Rebelline: fair maiden: good third in nursery at Doncaster: should stay 1¼m: acts on soft and good to firm going: sold 12,000 gns. *B. W. Hills*

HOLLYWOOD NIGHTS 3 ch.g. Savahra Sound 111 – Sola Mia 78 (Tolomeo 127) **–**
[2002 11m 7.1g Aug 8] brother to 1998 2-y-o 7f seller winner Sounds Solo: dam 2-y-o 6f winner: well held in seller/maiden: slowly away both outings. *B. J. Llewellyn*

HOLME FARM BOY (IRE) 6 b.g. River Falls 113 – Lady Conchita (IRE) (Whist- **–**
ling Deer 117) [2002 10d 12.3m 17.2d Jun 26] modest hurdler: little form on Flat. *G. M. Moore*

HOLY ISLAND 5 b.m. Deploy 131 – Bells 63 (Sadler's Wells (USA) 132) [2002 81: **76**
11.7g³ 10.1s⁶ 12m⁵ 11.9d 11.9m* 10g⁵ 10g⁴ Aug 13] smallish, strong, dipped-backed mare: fair handicapper: won 4-runner event at Brighton in July (pulled hard): stays 11.9f: acts on soft and good to firm going: has shown reluctance at stall/carried head awkwardly: reportedly in foal to Arkadian Hero. *L. M. Cumani*

HOLY ORDERS (IRE) 5 b.g. Unblest 117 – Shadowglow (Shaadi (USA) 126) [2002 **112**
99: 13s* 14s* 14s³ 12g² 10m 16m 16d² 16v Nov 10] smallish straggly gelding: smart performer: won minor events at Navan in April/May: good neck second to Thundering Surf in Duke of Edinburgh Handicap at Royal Ascot and to American Gothic in Irish Cesarewitch (Handicap) at the Curragh: stays 2m: acts on heavy and good to firm going: blinkered in 2002. *W. P. Mullins, Ireland*

HOLYROOD PRINCESS (IRE) 3 b.f. Moshaajir (USA) 77 – Kawarau Queen 67 **–**
(Taufan (USA) 119) [2002 8g 12m Sep 29] strong, workmanlike filly: sixth reported foal: half-sister to a winner in Greece by Distinct Native: dam 1m winner: tailed off in 2 maidens. *A. R. Dicken*

HOME BY SOCKS (IRE)   3 ch.f. Desert King (IRE) 129 – Propitious (IRE) 101   –
(Doyoun 124) [2002 56, a–: f8g Jan 24] leggy, close-coupled filly: modest maiden at 2
yrs: well held only start in 2002. *M. C. Chapman*

HOME COMING   4 br.g. Primo Dominie 121 – Carolside 108 (Music Maestro 119)   –
[2002 –: 6f 8.1g 10m 8m Aug 7] little form. *P. S. Felgate*

HOME FLEET (USA)   2 ch.c. (Apr 10) Gone West (USA) – All At Sea (USA) 124   **71 p**
(Riverman (USA) 131) [2002 p8g⁶ Nov 27] sixth living foal: closely related to useful 1m
winner Insinuate (by Mr Prospector) and half-brother to 3-y-o Stormy Channel and useful
6f/7f winner (both including at 2 yrs) Imroz (by Nureyev): dam won Prix du Moulin
and Musidora Stakes and runner-up in Oaks: 6/1, 2¾ lengths sixth to Face The Storm
in maiden at Lingfield, short of room briefly and not knocked about: should progress.
H. R. A. Cecil

HOMELIFE (IRE)   4 b.g. Persian Bold 123 – Share The Vision (Vision (USA)) [2002   **81**
92: p12g Jan 5] tall, useful-looking gelding: fairly useful handicapper: respectable effort
only run in 2002: will stay beyond 2m: acts on all-weather, best turf form on good going
or softer: has worn net muzzle to post. *P. W. D'Arcy*

HOMESPUN   3 b.f. Reprimand 122 – Home Truth 98 (Known Fact (USA) 135) [2002   **59**
75: 8g 7.9d⁵ 7m⁵ 8.3d Oct 14] leggy filly: just modest maiden in 2002: probably stays 7f:
yet to race on extremes of going: seemed not to handle track at Goodwood once at 2 yrs.
B. W. Hills

HONDURAS   3 b.f. Hernando (FR) 127 – Photo Call 73 (Chief Singer 131) [2002   **71**
7.9d⁴ 10.2d⁴ 12m Jul 25] quite attractive filly: fifth foal: sister to 4-y-o Johannian: dam,
9f (at 2 yrs) and 11f winner, granddaughter of 1000 Guineas second Photo Flash: fair form
when fourth in maidens at York and Chepstow: broke down next time: dead. *M. A. Jarvis*

HONEST OBSESSION (IRE)   4 b.c. Sadler's Wells (USA) 132 – Valley of Gold   **61**
(FR) 117 (Shirley Heights 130) [2002 –: f14g⁴ f16g⁶ 17.1f* 21.6m Apr 22] strong, good-
topped colt: modest handicapper: won at Pontefract in April: pulled up next time: stays
17f: acts on firm ground and fibresand: sometimes carries head awkwardly. *G. C. Bravery*

HONEST WARNING   5 b.g. Mtoto 134 – Peryllys 67 (Warning 136) [2002 76, a65:   –
f8s Jan 5] rather sparely-made gelding: fair handicapper at 4 yrs: last only outing in 2002.
J. R. Best

HONEYMOONER (IRE)   3 ch.f. Pursuit of Love 124 – Bathe In Light (USA) 72   –
(Sunshine Forever (USA)) [2002 47: p10g f11g⁶ Feb 21] poor maiden at 2 yrs: well held
early in 2002. *J. G. Portman*

HONEYPOINT   3 b.f. Robellino (USA) 127 – Short And Sharp 88 (Sharpen Up 127)   –
[2002 53: f7g 10m a9g a10.5g a10.5g a8g Dec 21] dipped-backed filly: won seller on
debut at 2 yrs: well beaten since, leaving D. Morris after second start and C. Tinkler in
Spain after fourth one. *G. Bindella, Spain*

HONEY'S GIFT   3 b.f. Terimon 124 – Honeycroft (Crofter (USA) 124) [2002 56:   **56**
10.9g⁶ 12m⁴ 11.6s⁵ 11.8m Jun 4] rather leggy filly: shows knee action: modest maiden
handicapper: stays 1½m when conditions aren't testing: acts on heavy and good to firm
going. *G. G. Margarson*

HONEYSTREET (IRE)   2 b.f. (Mar 12) Woodborough (USA) 112 – Ring of Kerry   **59**
(IRE) 67 (Kenmare (FR) 125) [2002 5.7m³ 5.1f⁶ 7g 6.1m 6g Oct 17] 3,600Y: sparely-
made filly: first foal: dam Irish maiden who stayed 1¼m, half-sister to useful Irish
performers Northern Pet (stayed 11f) and Propitious (best efforts at 1m): modest maiden:
will stay 7f. *J. S. Moore*

HONEY TRAP (IRE)   2 ch.f. (Feb 12) Dr Devious (IRE) 127 – Goldilocks (IRE)   **50**
(Caerleon (USA) 132) [2002 7m 8g 8.3d Oct 28] first foal: dam, Italian 2-y-o 9f winner,
half-sister to smart 1m winner Dear Daughter: modest form at best in maidens: will stay
at least 1¼m: sold 3,000 gns, sent to Austria. *I. A. Balding*

HONORINE (IRE)   2 b.f. (Mar 14) Mark of Esteem (IRE) 137 – Blue Water (USA)   **66**
104 (Bering 136) [2002 6m³ 6g⁶ 6f³ Sep 27] 47,000Y: leggy filly: second foal: half-sister
to 4-y-o Indian Creek: dam French 1m to 1½m (listed race) winner: fair form in maidens:
third at Thirsk and Redcar: will be suited by at least 1m. *J. W. Payne*

HONOR ROUGE (IRE)   3 ch.f. Highest Honor (FR) 124 – Ayers Rock (IRE) 95 (In   **96**
The Wings 128) [2002 73: 10m* 12m* 11.9m* 12g 12m² 11.9m⁵ 10.3m 12g 10d Oct 14]
good-topped filly: useful handicapper: won at Pontefract, Kempton and Haydock in
June/July: good second at Pontefract first start: below par after: stays 1½m: acts on firm
ground, possibly not on softer than good. *P. W. Harris*

454

HONOR'S LAD 3 ch.g. Sabrehill (USA) 120 – Ackcontent (USA) (Key To Content – (USA)) [2002 –: f6g p5g⁵ f5g 6g 10m 8.2g 7f f8.5g f9.4g⁴ Jul 12] angular gelding: little form: blinkered final start. *C. N. Kellett*

HONOURABLE CHIEF 5 b.g. Be My Chief (USA) 122 – Magic Orb 81 (Primo – Dominie 121) [2002 –: f9.4g⁶ Mar 23] little form on Flat/over hurdles. *G. Prodromou*

HOOPZ 2 gr.f. (Apr 13) Linamix (FR) 127 – Pearl Venture 92 (Salse (USA) 128) [2002 **70 p** 7m Aug 17] 22,000F, 1,100,000 francs Y: third foal: dam 5f (at 2 yrs) to 2m winner: 10/1, 6 lengths fourteenth of 15 in maiden at Newmarket, fading when short of room close home: should improve. *Mrs A. J. Perrett*

HO PANG YAU 4 b. or gr.g. Pivotal 124 – La Cabrilla 89 (Carwhite 127) [2002 63: 5g **56** 7.2g* 7.5g 6.9d 8d⁵ 9m 8.3m 8m Oct 2] close-coupled gelding: modest handicapper: won at Ayr in May: in-and-out form after: seems best at 6f/7f: acts on firm and good to soft going: tried blinkered. *Miss L. A. Perratt*

HORIZON HILL (USA) 2 b.g. (Apr 29) Distant View (USA) 126 – Accadia Rocket **67 p** (USA) (Bold Ruckus (USA)) [2002 5f⁴ 5d³ 6m Jul 13] $55,000Y: rather leggy, lengthy gelding: has scope: fifth foal: half-brother to several winners in North America: dam 4.5f to 1m winner in North America: fair form in maidens: apprentice ridden all 3 starts, travelling strongly before wandering at York on final one: will probably prove best at 5f/ 6f: type to do better, if all is well. *Mrs J. R. Ramsden*

HORMUZ (IRE) 6 b.g. Hamas (IRE) 125§ – Balqis (USA) 93 (Advocator) [2002 67: **87** f8s f7s p7g⁵ f7g⁴ f8g² 8f 8m* 9.2s² 7.6f* 8.5g² 8m p8g³ 10.4g⁴ 10.3f² 8f⁶ 8m 9m **a75** 8.5d⁴ 7.5m* f8s² 7m f8s* 8m³ 7m⁵ f8s⁵ f8g 7g⁴ f8g² 7s⁴ f7s 8s Nov 6] big, heavy-topped gelding: fairly useful performer: won handicaps at Ripon, Chester (by 7 lengths) and, having left D. Nicholls after eighteenth start, Beverley and Southwell between April/ September: best efforts at 7.5f to 9f: acts on all-weather, firm and soft going: usually front runner: tough. *Paul Johnson*

HORSECALLEDCHARLIE 4 ch.g. Charmer 123 – Ordima (Sylvan Express 117) – [2002 –: p13g³ Mar 2] well beaten all starts. *J. Akehurst*

HORTON DANCER 5 b.g. Rambo Dancer (CAN) 107 – Horton Lady 46 (Midyan **47** (USA) 124) [2002 45: f12s⁶ f11s f12g⁵ f16g² 16g² 17.1f⁴ 21.6m³ 16.2g 13.8m³ 14.1f² 18f **a39** 16m f16g f16.2g Dec 7] close-coupled gelding: poor handicapper: left D. Barker after twelfth start: seems to stay 21f: acts on firm going and fibresand: tried visored/tongue tied: often races prominently. *I. W. McInnes*

HOTCALLIE LEGEND 3 b.c. Faustus (USA) 118 – Alice Holt (Free State 125) **75** [2002 57: 9.9s⁵ 11m* 11f Sep 25] fair handicapper: won at Goodwood in June: stays 11f: acts on good to firm ground (shaped well on soft): races prominently. *Mrs A. J. Perrett*

HOTELIERS' DREAM 4 b.f. Reprimand 122 – Pride of Britain (CAN) 67 (Linkage **35** (USA)) [2002 –: 14.1d 11.8d³ 12d Jun 11] poor maiden handicapper: stays 11.8f: acts on good to soft going. *W. S. Kittow*

HOT JAZZ 3 ch.f. Midyan (USA) 124 – Fascinating Rhythm 85 (Slip Anchor 136) **63** [2002 75: 8m⁵ 10m Jul 13] fair maiden at best: probably stayed 1m: dead. *J. R. Fanshawe*

HOT LOVE 3 b.f. Blushing Flame (USA) 109 – Tiama (IRE) 50 (Last Tycoon 131) **59** [2002 a9.5g⁵ 10g 10g⁴ᵈ 8.5d* 9.9m 11.6s f8.5g p12g* 10d 6.9g⁴ 7d² f7g² 8g⁶ 8d f8g f8.5g Dec 20] rather leggy, lengthy filly: second foal: dam, maiden, seemed to stay 9.7f: modest performer: won maiden at Mont-de-Marsan at 2 yrs, claimer at Longchamp (final start for D. Henderson in France) in March and seller at Lingfield (sold from J. Osborne) in June: finds 7f on sharp side, and has won at 1½m: acts on all-weather and good to soft ground: usually blinkered, visored final outing. *Miss Gay Kelleway*

HOT PANTS 4 ch.f. Rudimentary (USA) 118 – True Precision 84 (Presidium 124) – [2002 63: p5g p5g p6g p6g p5g Dec 21] sturdy, close-coupled filly: modest handicapper at 3 yrs: well held in 2002: tried blinkered. *D. K. Ivory*

HOT PRODUXION (USA) 3 ch.g. Tabasco Cat (USA) 126 – Princess Harriet (USA) **72** (Mt Livermore (USA)) [2002 86: 11.9d³ 11.7d³ 16.2m Jul 7] strong, useful-looking gelding: has a quick, fluent action: just fair maiden at 3 yrs (found little first 2 starts): stays 1¼m: blinkered on reappearance: joined J. Mackie. *Mrs A. J. Perrett*

HOT TO TANGO (USA) 3 b.f. Kingmambo (USA) 125 – Polish Treaty (USA) **?** (Danzig (USA)) [2002 8f⁶ a8.5f⁴ a8.5s² 8.5f Dec 27] rangy filly: third foal: dam, won 1m minor stakes in USA, out of half-sister to 1000 Guineas winner Quick As Lightning: modest form when 5¾ lengths sixth to Anoof in maiden at Ascot in July, only outing for

J. Gosden: in frame in similar events after at Keeneland and Churchill Downs (beaten 12 lengths): left J. Hennig before final start: stays 8.5f. *N. J. Howard, USA*

HOUSEPARTY (IRE) 4 b. or br.g. Grand Lodge (USA) 125 – Special Display (Welsh Pageant 132) [2002 93: 9s Oct 26] good-bodied gelding: fairly useful performer at 3 yrs: off over a year before last only run in 2002. *J. A. B. Old* —

HOUSTON PARK (IRE) 3 ch.c. Persian Bold 123 – Harina (Pentotal) [2002 92: 8.3g³ 10.2g* 11g 10m Jun 4] close-coupled colt: fairly useful handicapper: won at Bath in April: stayed 1¼m: acted on soft ground; injured fatally final start. *L. M. Cumani* **84**

HOUT BAY 5 ch.g. Komaite (USA) – Maiden Pool 85 (Sharpen Up 127) [2002 72: p6g* p7g p5g p5g 5.1d 5m 6m 5d² 5m² 5g⁵ 5m² 5m⁵ 5m² 5m⁶ 5f 6f⁵ Oct 12] big, lengthy gelding: fair handicapper: won amateur event at Lingfield in January: left S. Kettlewell after fourth start: best at 5f/easy 6f: acts on firm going, good to soft and all-weather: consistent. *Jedd O'Keeffe* **69**

HOV 2 b.g. (Feb 22) Petong 126 – Harifa (Local Suitor (USA) 128) [2002 6m⁵ Jul 13] 4,600F, 15,000Y: fourth foal: half-brother to 1998 2-y-o 5f winner Landican Lane (by Handsome Sailor) and 11f winner Lindisfarne Lady (by Jupiter Island), both selling winners: dam unraced: 25/1, 3 lengths fifth of 19 to Somnus in maiden at York, keeping on from rear: should improve if all is well. *J. J. Quinn* **69 p**

HOWARDS HEROINE (IRE) 3 ch.f. Danehill Dancer (IRE) 117 – Romangoddess (IRE) (Rhoman Rule (USA)) [2002 61§, a52§: f8.5g* f9.4g* f8.5g² f9.4g 8.3s⁶ f8.5g 7f* 8d⁴ 7.9g 12f 9m 7f f7s 12s Nov 6] good-topped filly: fair on all-weather, modest on turf: won seller and handicap at Wolverhampton in January/February and seller at Redcar in June: below form after, leaving I. Semple following twelfth start: stays 9.4f: acts on fibresand, firm and good to soft going: visored (below form) once at 2 yrs: sometimes early to post/slowly away: usually forces pace: one to treat with caution. *Paul Johnson* **55 §** **a70 §**

HOWARDS HERO (IRE) 3 gr.g. Paris House 123 – Gold Braisim (IRE) 77 (Jareer (USA) 115) [2002 59: 8g 5d 6g 5g⁴ 5m² 5d 5m⁵ 6s 5g³ 7f 7f⁵ 6f⁶ f5g³ 6d⁴ f5f⁵ f5g* f5g* Dec 31] tall gelding: modest performer: left I. Semple after eleventh start: won 2 handicaps at Wolverhampton in December: best at 5f: acts on good to firm going, good to soft and fibresand: blinkered/visored third to eighth outings. *Paul Johnson* **61**

HOWARD'S LAD (IRE) 5 b.g. Reprimand 122 – Port Isaac (USA) 64 (Seattle Song (USA) 130) [2002 52§, a45§: 7g 6d May 10] rangy gelding: temperamental handicapper: usually blinkered/visored. *I. Semple* **– §**

HOW DO I KNOW 4 gr.f. Petong 126 – Glenfield Portion 86 (Mummy's Pet 125) [2002 91: p5g Feb 9] leggy filly: fairly useful handicapper at 3 yrs: well held on all-weather debut only run at 4 yrs: stays 6f: yet to race on extremes of going on turf. *G. A. Butler* **–**

HOWE TIMELY 5 b.g. Timeless Times (USA) 99 – Adder Howe (Amboise 113) [2002 –: 8.5m 14.1f⁶ May 17] seems of little account. *N. Bycroft* **–**

HOWLE HILL (IRE) 2 b.c. (Apr 1) Ali-Royal (IRE) 127 – Grandeur And Grace (USA) 75 (Septieme Ciel (USA) 123) [2002 6m³ p7g² 7m* 7.1m³ 8g* 8d² Nov 1] 3,200F, IR 6,700Y, 15,000 2-y-o: leggy colt: third foal: dam second at 1m in Ireland: useful performer: won maiden at Salisbury in August and nursery at Newmarket (overcame poor run to beat Impersonator by neck) in October: odds on, 5 lengths second of 3 to Blaise Castle in minor event at Newmarket (sweating) final start: stays 1m: acts on polytrack, unraced on extremes of going on turf: free-going sort. *A. King* **98**

HOW'S THINGS 2 b.g. (Mar 24) Danzig Connection (USA) – Dim Ots 92 (Alhijaz 122) [2002 7d 7g f6s⁵ f7f⁴ Nov 29] good-topped gelding: first foal: dam 5f (at 2 yrs) and 6f winner: modest maiden: fourth in nursery at Wolverhampton: likely to stay 1m. *D. Haydn Jones* **62**

HUB HUB 4 b.c. Polish Precedent (USA) 131 – Ghassanah 73 (Pas de Seul 133) [2002 69d: 11.6d 8d 7d f7g² f8.5g⁶ f7g⁶ f8.5g⁴ 8.5d f8.5g Dec 20] modest maiden nowadays: effective at 7f/1m: acts on good to firm going, good to soft and fibresand: sometimes visored/blinkered: none too reliable. *W. R. Muir* **53**

HUFFLEPUFF (IRE) 3 b.f. Desert King (IRE) 129 – Circle of Chalk (FR) 74 (Kris 135) [2002 81: 6g 6f⁶ 5g 5.1f* 5g 5.2m 5f* 6g⁶ Oct 18] neat filly: useful performer: won handicap at Bath in July and Newmarket (beat Madame Maxine by 1½ lengths) in October: good 3 lengths sixth to Needwood Blade in listed event at Newmarket final start: free-going sort and should be at least as good back at 5f as 6f: yet to race on soft/ **102 +**

heavy going, acts on any other: weakened as if amiss sixth start: usually forces pace. *J. L. Dunlop*

HUGH THE MAN (IRE) 3 b.g. Hamas (IRE) 125§ – Run To Jenny 105 (Runnett 125) [2002 64?: p8g² f8g f8.5g f9.4g Oct 21] close-coupled, good-topped gelding: modest maiden: not sure to stay beyond 1m: acts on polytrack (well held in 4 starts on fibresand): visored (looked reluctant) second outing. *N. P. Littmoden* **56**

HUGS DANCER (FR) 5 b.g. Cadeaux Genereux 131 – Embracing 91 (Reference Point 139) [2002 83: 13.9f² 20m 11.9g* 16.1g⁴ 16.2m⁴ 21g* 13.9m* 18m⁵ Oct 19] work-manlike handicapper: better than ever in 2002, winning quite valuable events at Carlisle in June, Goodwood (Marriott Hotels Goodwood Stakes for second year running) in July, and Tote Ebor at York (beat Pole Star ¾ length) in August: good fifth to Miss Fara in Cesarewitch at Newmarket final outing: effective at 1½m to 21f: best form on good going or firmer: blinkered/visored only once in 2002: waited with: has raced lazily/idled in front: tough and consistent. *J. G. Given* **101**

HUGWITY 10 ch.g. Cadeaux Genereux 131 – Nuit d'Ete (USA) 90 (Super Concorde (USA) 128) [2002 69, a79: 8g⁶ 10m² 10d f12g³ p12g² p10g² 10.1f³ 11.6m 10.1m² 10m³ p12g² 9.7g p10g 16m f12s Oct 8] big, good-topped gelding: modest performer nowadays: effective at 1m to easy 1½m: acts on firm going, good to soft and all-weather. *G. C. Bravery* **61**

HUJA (IRE) 2 b.f. (Feb 21) Alzao (USA) 117 – Nasanice (IRE) 97 (Nashwan (USA) 135) [2002 7d* 7m³ 8g⁴ Sep 28] close-coupled filly: has a quick action: first foal: dam Irish 9f winner: useful form: won maiden at Kempton in July: better efforts after when just over a length third to Gemíniani at Goodwood and 3¾ lengths fourth to Soviet Song in Fillies' Mile at Ascot: not sure to stay much beyond 1m. *Sir Michael Stoute* **102**

HULA BALLEW 2 ch.f. (Mar 4) Weldnaas (USA) 112 – Ballon 63 (Persian Bold 123) [2002 7.5m 7g 8d⁵ 8m³ 8s Oct 15] 4,000Y: smallish filly: first foal: dam, maiden who stayed 1m (winning hurdler), out of half-sister to smart performer up to 1¼m Bengal Fire and to Grade 1 1½m winner in USA Kings Island: modest maiden: clearly best effort when third at Musselburgh: should stay 1¼m: acts on good to firm ground. *M. Dods* **60**

HUMDINGER (IRE) 2 b.f. (Mar 18) Charnwood Forest (IRE) 125 – High Finish 58 (High Line 125) [2002 p7g⁶ Dec 21] 3,000Y: third foal: half-sister to 3-y-o Rainbow End and 1999 2-y-o 6f winner Conclusion (by Prince Sabo), later winner at 1m/1¼m in Sweden: dam, lightly-raced maiden, half-sister to smart performers Munwar (up to 1½m) and Hateel (up to 1¾m): 50/1, staying-on 5 lengths sixth to Rifleman in minor event at Lingfield: will stay at least 1m: open to progress. *D. J. Coakley* **60 p**

Tote Ebor (Handicap), York—the versatile Hugs Dancer copes well with the step back in trip and just holds off Pole Star (third left) and Barathea Blazer (partly hidden by winner); Dawn Invasion (rail) is fourth

HUME'S LAW 4 b.c. Puissance 110 – Will Be Bold 79 (Bold Lad (IRE) 133) [2002 –: –
7.1g 7.1m 5f 6f 6d 7.1m 5g 7m 7.1s⁶ 8.2d⁴ 7.1m⁶ 8d⁵ 6d 6.1d 5.7g⁶ Jul 14] probably of
little account nowadays. *A. Berry*

HUMID CLIMATE 2 ch.c. (Apr 12) Desert King (IRE) 129 – Pontoon 89 (Zafonic **63 p**
(USA) 130) [2002 8g Oct 2] first foal: dam, 2-y-o 7f winner on only outing, half-sister to
smart performer up to 9f in Britain/USA Wharf: 20/1 and green, never-dangerous seventh
to Foodbroker Founder in maiden at Newbury: likely to do better. *Mrs A. J. Perrett*

HUMOURESQUE 2 b.f. (Apr 2) Pivotal 124 – Miswaki Belle (USA) 73 (Miswaki **76 p**
(USA) 124) [2002 6s⁴ f6g³ f7s² f7g² Dec 31] fourth foal: half-sister to 4-y-o Danehurst:
dam, second at 7f at 3 yrs on only start, closely related to smart performer up to 1m
Dazzle: best efforts in maidens when runner-up at Wolverhampton, beaten 3 lengths by
Just A Glimmer final start: will be suited by 1m: should progress. *Sir Mark Prescott*

HUNGRY HORACE 5 b.h. Reprimand 122 – Lucky Mill 50 (Midyan (USA) 124) –
[2002 6m 6f⁵ 8.1d 6m 6d 6g 6m Sep 19] sparely-made horse: third foal: brother to 6-y-o
Oh No Not Him: dam sprint maiden: little form: blinkered penultimate start, seemingly
amiss in visor final start. *M. Mullineaux*

HUNTER'S MARK (USA) 2 b.f. (Mar 18) Titus Livius (FR) 115 – Manfath (IRE) – p
65 (Last Tycoon 131) [2002 7g Aug 22] third foal: half-sister to very smart US 1m/9f
winner The Deputy (by Petardia), also 7f winner in Britain at 2 yrs: dam staying maiden:
20/1, last of 12 in maiden at Folkestone, racing freely and eased when weakening: should
do better. *J. W. Hills*

HUNT IN PAIRS 3 b.g. Pursuit of Love 124 – Emily-Mou (IRE) 80 (Cadeaux **53**
Genereux 131) [2002 7s 7m⁵ 7f 10f 7f Jun 3] 11,500F, 27,000Y: tall, lengthy, useful-
looking gelding: second foal: half-brother to 1¾m seller winner Dangerous Deploy (by
Deploy): dam, 1¼m winner, from family of Time Charter and Nicholas Bill: form
(modest) only in maiden at Catterick second start: bred to be suited by 1m+: has taken
strong hold/found little: refused to enter stall on intended debut, and withdrawn after
causing trouble in stall once. *Mrs J. R. Ramsden*

HURRICANE ALAN (IRE) 2 b. or br.c. (Mar 12) Mukaddamah (USA) 125 – Bint **102**
Al Balad (IRE) 63 (Ahonoora 122) [2002 5.1d³ 5.3g* 5.1g* 6.3g* 5.2f⁶ 6m³ 6f² 6m* 7f³
Oct 2] IR 13,000Y: neat colt: fourth foal: half-brother to 3-y-o Eagles High: dam twice-
raced sister to Nell Gwyn winner A-To-Z: useful performer: won maiden at Brighton and
minor event at Bath in May, sales race at the Curragh in June and listed race at the Curragh
(beat Mombassa by 1½ lengths) in September: creditable ¾-length third to Governor
Brown in Somerville Tattersall Stakes at Newmarket final start: stays 7f: acts on firm
going: tough and consistent. *R. Hannon*

HURRICANE COAST 3 b.g. Hurricane Sky (AUS) – Tread Carefully 51 (Sharpo **77**
132) [2002 70: 8.2d 10g 7m*ᵈⁱˢ 7.1d⁴ 7f² 7f* 7d⁴ Oct 18] tall gelding: fair performer:
first past post in handicap at Newcastle (subsequently disqualified) in July and maiden at
Redcar in September: stays 7f: acts on firm and good to soft going: edgy sort: has carried
head awkwardly: tends to edge left. *T. D. Easterby*

HURRICANE FLOYD (IRE) 4 ch.g. Pennekamp (USA) 130 – Mood Swings **104**
(IRE) 77 (Shirley Heights 130) [2002 110: 6s 6g 7m 6m 6s⁶ 6m 6g 7m² 7m 6g⁴ 8d 6g 7f
Oct 3] smallish, sturdy gelding: has a quick action: useful handicapper: best effort in 2002
when second to Albashoosh at York in July: favourite, respectable fourth to Bond Boy in
Stewards' Cup at Goodwood following month: raced mainly at 6f/7f: acts on good to firm
ground, probably not on softer than good: visored (missed break) once: usually tongue
tied. *D. Nicholls*

HURRICANE LOVE (USA) 2 b.f. (Feb 19) Quiet American (USA) – Outlasting – p
(USA) (Seattle Slew (USA)) [2002 6f Sep 8] $575,000Y: fifth foal: half-sister to 2
winners, including US Grade 3 9f winner Fortitude (by Cure The Blues): dam, 1¼m/1½m
winner in USA, out of Breeders' Cup Juvenile Fillies winner Outstandingly: 14/1, slowly
away and green, mid-field in 21-runner maiden at Kempton: sure to improve. *B. W. Hills*

HUSKY (POL) 4 b.g. Special Power – Hallo Bambina (POL) (Neman (POL)) [2002 **54**
9g² 7m⁴ f6g⁵ f6g f7g Dec 17] Polish-bred gelding: winner of 3 of 15 starts in native
country, runner-up in 9f event at Warsaw in May: modest form first 2 starts in Britain,
leaving J. Osborne after first of them: well held after. *R. M. H. Cowell*

HUWAIDAH 2 b.f. (Mar 14) Shareef Dancer (USA) 135 – Romoosh 69 (Formidable **65 p**
(USA) 125) [2002 7g 6d⁶ f6f⁶ Nov 11] smallish filly: third foal: half-sister to 1½m winner
Ramzain (by Alzao): dam, 1¼m winner, half-sister to smart 6f/7f performer Unblest: fair

form without being knocked about in maidens: will be well suited by 1m+: remains capable of better. *G. A. Butler*

HYDE PARK (IRE)   8 b.g. Alzao (USA) 117 – Park Elect (Ahonoora 122) [2002 60: 7d 7f 7g 7.1g⁶ 7f 6d 8m⁵ 7m Jul 24] robust gelding: handicapper: little form in 2002: blinkered once. *D. Nicholls*   –

HYPERACTIVE (IRE)   6 b.g. Perugino (USA) 84 – Hyannis (FR) (Esprit du Nord (USA) 126) [2002 52: 7g² 8m 6g⁶ 6v f7g⁶ 7m⁶ Jul 27] rather dipped-backed gelding: poor performer nowadays: stays easy 1m: acts on firm and good to soft going: tried blinkered. *B. Ellison*   49

HYPERSONIC   5 b.g. Marju (IRE) 127 – Hi-Li (High Top 131) [2002 –: p10g 7d⁶ 7d⁵ 7m 8d⁴ 10m Aug 28] poor maiden: left C. Popham after reappearance (blinkered): stays 1m: acts on heavy going. *B. R. Millman*   49

HYPOTHESIS (IRE)   5 b.g. Sadler's Wells (USA) 132 – Surmise (USA) 75 (Alleged (USA) 138) [2002 –: f12g 12.6g 16.4d 13.8m 16.2m Aug 26] close-coupled gelding: of little account. *Ian Williams*   –

I

IAMBACK   2 b.f. (Apr 9) Perugino (USA) 84 – Smouldering (IRE) (Caerleon (USA) 132) [2002 7f⁶ 7d 6m³ 6m⁶ 8g³ 8m³ 8.3d Oct 14] leggy filly: half-sister to several winners, including 1999 2-y-o 6f winner Camp Fire (by Lahib) and 2001 2-y-o 1m winner Almost Famous (by Grand Lodge), both fairly useful in Ireland: dam once-raced half-sister to Irish 2000 Guineas winner Flash of Steel: modest maiden: stays 1m: acts on good to firm and good to soft ground: blinkered (pulled hard) fourth start: ungenuine. *R. Guest*   51 §

I AM TROUBLE (IRE)   2 b.f. (Jan 29) Darnay 117 – Secret Combe (IRE) 81 (Mujadil (USA) 119) [2002 f5g⁵ f5g⁵ 5.1d⁴ f5s⁵ 5v⁶ 6m⁶ 6m 6g Aug 7] compact filly: has a round action: first foal: dam, 2-y-o 6f winner, stayed 7f: poor maiden: stays 6f: acts on good to firm and good to soft going. *J. S. Moore*   36

IBTECAR (USA)   2 b.c. (Mar 25) Seeking The Gold (USA) – Balanchine (USA) 131 (Storm Bird (CAN) 134) [2002 7d Aug 9] small colt: fourth foal: closely related to smart French 1¼m/10.5f winner Gulf News (by Woodman): dam, Oaks and Irish Derby winner, also 7f winner at 2 yrs: 12/1, pulled hard when well held in maiden at Newmarket: wore crossed noseband. *D. R. Loder*   –

ICANNSHIFT (IRE)   2 b.c. (Feb 29) Night Shift (USA) – Cannikin (IRE) 82 (Lahib (USA) 129) [2002 6g* 7m* 7d³ 7s Oct 25] IR 40,000F, 21,000Y: small, good-bodied colt: first living foal: dam, Irish 2-y-o 6f winner, half-sister to useful Irish performer up to 1½m Tout A Coup: useful performer: won maiden at Pontefract in July and minor event at Yarmouth in August: best effort when close third to Jay Gee's Choice in minor event at Leicester: faded when seventh in Horris Hill Stakes at Newbury final start: likely to prove best at 6f/7f: acts on soft and good to firm ground. *P. W. Harris*   96

I CAN'T REMEMBER   8 br. or gr.g. Petong 126 – Glenfield Portion 86 (Mummy's Pet 125) [2002 48: 9.2d 12d⁴ 12.1s Aug 20] small, compact gelding: poor performer: stays 1¾m: acts on firm going, soft and fibresand: tried visored/blinkered/tongue tied. *Miss Lucinda V. Russell*   34

ICARESSA   4 b.f. Anabaa (USA) 130 – Dance Quest (FR) 117 (Green Dancer (USA) 132) [2002 –: p8g³ 7m 7m Aug 14] angular filly: modest maiden: stays 1m: form only on polytrack. *W. Jarvis*   56

ICEALION   4 b.g. Lion Cavern (USA) 117 – Icecapped 91 (Caerleon (USA) 132) [2002 –: f6s f9.4g Jan 25] angular, workmanlike gelding: no form. *M. W. Easterby*   –

ICECAP   2 b.f. (May 16) Polar Falcon (USA) 126 – Warning Light (High Top 131) [2002 7m⁶ Sep 23] sister to fairly useful 1m winner Polar Challenge and half-sister to 3 winners, including 6f (at 2 yrs) to 1m winner Twilight Patrol (by Robellino) and 1¼m winner Illumination (by Saddlers' Hall), both useful: dam unraced from family of Nash-wan and Unfuwain: 20/1, 4½ lengths sixth of 12 to Spanish Sun in maiden at Kempton, going on well after being short of room and switched: sure to do better. *M. L. W. Bell*   72 p

ICE CRACKER   3 b.f. Polar Falcon (USA) 126 – Blessed Honour 77 (Ahonoora 122) [2002 8.3m 8.3m² 9m p8g 8m* 8g Oct 14] 13,500 2-y-o: lengthy filly: third foal: sister to useful 1999 2-y-o 6f/7f winner Icicle (stays 8.5f) and half-sister to 11f winner Invincible   65

(by Slip Anchor): dam, 2-y-o 7f winner on only start, half-sister to smart middle-distance stayer Sacrament: fair performer: won minor event at Brighton in October: stays 1m: raced only on good/good to firm going on turf, below form on polytrack: carries head awkwardly: possibly has her share of temperament. *Mrs A. J. Bowlby*

ICE DANCER (IRE)   4 b.g. Sadler's Wells (USA) 132 – Tappiano (USA) (Fappiano (USA)) [2002 112: 20g 10d* Oct 28] good-topped gelding: smart performer: won listed race at Leopardstown (for second year running) in October by 2 lengths from In Time's Eye, making all: stays 1½m (below form over 2½m in Prix du Cadran on belated reappearance): acts on heavy and good to firm going: front runner (often pacemaker at 3 yrs). *A. P. O'Brien, Ireland*   **115**

ICED DIAMOND (IRE)   3 b.c. Petardia 113 – Prime Site (IRE) (Burslem 123) [2002 10g 10g 8f p8g² p7g³ 7m* 7m 8m 7m 7f⁶ 7g 8.2s Oct 23] IR 4,100F, IR 4,000Y, 9,500 2-y-o: good-topped colt: fourth foal: brother to 1998 2-y-o 5f winner Sammal and Italian 7f (including at 2 yrs)/1m winner Artaserse: dam, Irish maiden, best at 1m: fair performer: won maiden at Folkestone in June: stays 1m: acts on firm going and polytrack: visored/blinkered once each: wandered for lady rider: sold 17,000 gns. *Mrs A. J. Perrett*   **71**

ICE PALACE   2 ch.f. (Apr 11) Polar Falcon (USA) 126 – White Palace 80 (Shirley Heights 130) [2002 6m² Aug 29] fourth foal: half-sister to useful 7f (including at 2 yrs) winner Palatial (by Green Desert): dam 1m winner: 7/2, shaped very well when 1½ lengths second of 15 to Avonbridge in maiden at Lingfield (winner, third and fourth all successful next time), slowly away and running on well without being knocked about: useful performer in the making, sure to win races. *J. R. Fanshawe*   **83 P**

ICONIUM (IRE)   3 b.c. Be My Guest (USA) 126 – Monoglow (Kalaglow 132) [2002 9d 8m⁵ 10m 12.1g 10.3g⁶ 14.1m 11m⁵ Jul 27] 12,000Y: quite attractive colt: unimpressive mover: sixth living foal: closely related to German 1m winner May I Say (by Night Shift) and half-brother to 2 winners, including fairly useful Irish 1m/1¼m winner Monongahela (by Caerleon): dam third at 1½m in Ireland: fair maiden: should prove better at 1¼m+ than shorter: visored fifth outing: found little last 2 starts: possibly none too genuine. *E. J. O'Neill*   **69**

I CRIED FOR YOU (IRE)   7 b.g. Statoblest 120 – Fall of The Hammer (IRE) (Auction Ring (USA) 123) [2002 104, a–: p10g³ p10g² 8s³ 10m⁵ 10.4m 9f 9s⁵ 12v Nov 9] strong, angular gelding: useful handicapper: mostly creditable efforts in 2002, including very close third (promoted to second) to Adiemus in listed Winter Derby at Lingfield and third to Zucchero in Lincoln at Doncaster (off 3 months after): effective at 7f (given test) to 1¼m: acts on polytrack (well beaten both starts on fibresand) and probably any turf going: tried visored/blinkered earlier in career: usually tracks pace: game. *J. G. Given*   **106**

IDLE CHATTER   2 b.f. (Feb 5) Spectrum (IRE) 126 – Elfin Laughter 76 (Alzao (USA) 117) [2002 7d 7g 6g Sep 2] fourth foal: half-sister to UAE 6f winner Joyous Gift (by Cadeaux Genereux) and 4-y-o Smirk: dam 2-y-o 7.5f/1m winner: well held in maidens. *M. L. W. Bell*   **–**

IDLE POWER (IRE)   4 b. or br.g. Common Grounds 118 – Idle Fancy 79 (Mujtahid (USA) 118) [2002 95+: 7f⁵ 7m⁵ 7d 7g² 7m 7m 6g 7m³ 7m⁵ 7f* Oct 5] rather leggy, close-coupled gelding: fairly useful handicapper: won at Newmarket in October: stays 7f when conditions aren't testing: acts on firm and good to soft going: has worn cheekpieces: sold 35,000 gns. *P. W. Harris*   **94**

IF   3 b.f. Emperor Jones (USA) 119 – Mighty Flash 81 (Rolfe (USA) 77) [2002 7.1g³ 8m 10.2f Sep 30] ninth foal: half-sister to 1993 2-y-o 7f winner Mighty Forum (by Presidium), later smart up to 8.5f in USA: dam staying sister to Derby third Mighty Flutter: form (modest) only in maiden at Chepstow on debut: should stay 1m. *B. R. Millman*   **58**

IF BY CHANCE   4 ch.g. Risk Me (FR) 127 – Out of Harmony 79 (Song 132) [2002 63, a68: f6s² p5g f6g f6g⁴ f6g⁵ 5.1d f5g f6g⁴ 6m⁵ 7f 6.1m* p6g p6g 6d 6m f6s f6g⁵ f6s Dec 26] strong, close-coupled gelding: poor mover: fair on all-weather, modest on turf: made all to win seller at Nottingham in July: left M. Buckley £800 before penultimate outing: best at 5f/easy 6f: acts on heavy going, good to firm and fibresand: often visored/blinkered: unreliable. *I. W. McInnes*   **59 §**   **a67 §**

IF I CAN DREAM (IRE)   2 ch.f. (Feb 8) Brief Truce (USA) 126 – Only In Dreams 78 (Polar Falcon (USA) 126) [2002 6g f5g⁵ 5m 5.1g⁵ 5.1f⁴ f5s f5g Nov 22] first foal: dam, 2-y-o 7f winner, stayed 1m: modest maiden: may prove best at 5f: acts on fibresand and firm ground: tried blinkered: tends to hang. *B. J. Meehan*   **60**

I GOT RHYTHM   4 gr.f. Lycius (USA) 124 – Eurythmic 58 (Pharly (FR) 130) [2002 50+: 16g* 12.4g⁶ May 6] leggy filly: has a round action: modest performer: won handicap   **51**

at Musselburgh in March: stays 2m: acts on soft going, good to firm and fibresand. *Mrs M. Reveley*

IJTIHAD 2 b. or br.c. (Jan 31) Darshaan 133 – Asfurah (USA) 108 (Dayjur (USA) 137) [2002 6d Nov 1] smallish, quite good-topped colt: first foal: dam, 2-y-o 5f/6f (Cherry Hinton) winner, half-sister to smart US 6f/7f performer Istintaj: 7/1, well held in maiden at Newmarket. *M. P. Tregoning* –

IKAN (IRE) 2 br.f. (Feb 20) Sri Pekan (USA) 117 – Iktidar 80 (Green Desert (USA) 127) [2002 5m 5d⁴ 6m⁶ 6m⁵ 5.1f² 6m* 7f 6.3d³ 6s² 6v Nov 13] workmanlike filly: unimpressive mover: second foal: half-sister to 3-y-o To The Woods: dam, Irish maiden who stayed 1m, out of half-sister to Sheikh Albadou: fairly useful performer: won nursery at Newmarket in September: best efforts when third in valuable minor event at the Curragh and second (to Miguel Cervantes) in listed race at Doncaster eighth/ninth starts: last in listed race at Saint-Cloud final start: will stay 7f: acts on firm ground and soft. *N. P. Littmoden* 91

IKBAL 4 ch.c. Indian Ridge 123 – Amaniy (USA) 96 (Dayjur (USA) 137) [2002 64: f6g² f5g⁶ f6g* Feb 4] lengthy colt: modest performer: won maiden at Wolverhampton in February (clear when broke down ½f out): stayed 8.5f: acted on fibresand, good to firm and good to soft going: dead. *E. J. Alston* 64

IKENGA (IRE) 3 ch.f. Spectrum (IRE) 126 – Thistle Hill (IRE) 58 (Danehill (USA) 126) [2002 88: 7.5m² 8.2f⁵ 7.1m⁶ 7.1d⁵ Jun 14] small, good-bodied filly: poor mover: fairly useful performer: below form after reappearance: stays 7.5f: acts on good to firm and good to soft going, possibly not on firm: usually races up with pace: sometimes flashes tail. *M. L. W. Bell* 87

IKTINAS 3 b.c. Unfuwain (USA) 131 – Midway Lady (USA) 126 (Alleged (USA) 138) [2002 82: 10.3f⁵ 8f³ May 25] good-topped colt: fairly useful maiden: stayed 1m: acted on firm going: tongue tied at 3 yrs: dead. *B. Hanbury* 82

IL CAVALIERE 7 b.g. Mtoto 134 – Kalmia (Miller's Mate 116) [2002 81: 16m 14.4g 17.5g 16s Nov 6] good-topped gelding: fair handicapper in 2002: stays 2m: acts on firm going, probably on good to soft. *Mrs M. Reveley* 70

IL DESTINO 7 b.g. Casteddu 111 – At First Sight (He Loves Me 120) [2002 52: 9.2s f8.5g May 24] lengthy gelding: fair performer at best: well held in 2002: probably best around 1¼m: acts on good to firm and good to soft going: blinkered/visored once each: broke blood vessel once. *J. G. M. O'Shea* –

ILE MICHEL 5 b.g. Machiavellian (USA) 123 – Circe's Isle (Be My Guest (USA) 126) [2002 87: 8.3g 8d 7m³ 8g⁶ 8m 7.1g Oct 5] good-topped gelding: fairly useful handicapper: effective at 7f/1m: raced mainly on good going or firmer: has hung left/carried head high. *Lady Herries* 80

ILLEGAL IMMIGRANT (CZE) 3 br.g. Thatching 131 – Silindhra (GER) (Windwurf (GER)) [2002 –: 11m 10.1m Aug 7] no form: tried visored. *Julian Poulton* –

ILLEGAL (IRE) 3 b.g. Eagle Eyed (USA) 111 – Lady Bodmin (IRE) (Law Society (USA) 130) [2002 66: 8.2d⁵ 10f f9.4g p10g f12g 8.1m⁶ 8.1m⁵ 7g⁴ 7.1m⁶ 8s⁵ 8g 7m f8g Oct 22] leggy gelding: fair handicapper: left N. Littmoden after fourth start: stays 1m: acts on soft and good to firm going, well held on all-weather: often visored in 2002, blinkered penultimate start: carried head awkwardly/edged right for only success. *M. J. Polglase* 68 a–

ILLUSIONIST 4 b.g. Mujtahid (USA) 118 – Merlin's Fancy 62 (Caerleon (USA) 132) [2002 63, a70: f8g⁶ 10s f8g f8g f8g Nov 25] quite attractive gelding: modest performer: well below form after reappearance: probably best around 7f: acts on good to firm and good to soft going: usually visored nowadays: has looked hard ride/less than keen. *Mrs N. Macauley* – a54

ILLUSIVE (IRE) 5 b.g. Night Shift (USA) – Mirage 60 (Red Sunset 120) [2002 68, a93: f6g p7g p5g⁶ f6g⁵ p5g² f5g⁴ f6g³ p6g⁴ p5g⁴ p6g⁵ f6g² 5.1d³ f6g³ 5f⁴ p6g² 5g 5m p7g f6g f6f f6g p5g³ Dec 21] fair performer: best at 5f/6f: acts on firm going, good to soft and all-weather: usually blinkered: on a lengthy losing sequence, and sometimes looks none too keen. *M. Wigham* 70 a79

ILLUSTRATOR 2 b.c. (Mar 20) Sadler's Wells (USA) 132 – Illusory 81 (Kings Lake (USA) 133) [2002 7.1m³ 8s² 8s³ Oct 26] smallish, quite good-topped colt: half-brother to several winners, including smart 1m/9f winner Phantom Quest (by Rainbow Quest), useful 7f (including at 2 yrs) winner Sensory (by Selkirk) and 4-y-o Trace Clip: dam, 6f winner, sister to Lowther winner Kingscote: placed in maidens at Haydock and Leicester 111 (short-headed by Allergy pair long way clear) on first 2 starts: smart form when 3 lengths third to Brian Boru in Racing Post Trophy at Doncaster, having been short of room: should stay 1¼m: acts on soft ground, shaped well on good to firm: fitted with blanket for stall entry: sure to win races. *Sir Michael Stoute*

ILLUSTRIA 2 b.f. (Apr 15) Seeking The Gold (USA) – Noble Rose (IRE) 113 **92** (Caerleon (USA) 132) [2002 6s⁴ 6m² 6m* 7m⁵ Aug 25] leggy filly: third living foal: dam, 7f (at 2 yrs) to 14.6f (Park Hill Stakes) winner, half-sister to 3-y-o Simeon out of half-sister to US Grade 1 9f winner Talinum: fairly useful form: justified favouritism in maiden at Newbury in August: good 4 lengths fifth to Geminiani in Prestige Stakes at Goodwood, though never dangerous: should stay 1¼m: acts on good to firm ground, shaped well on soft. *M. R. Channon*

ILLUSTRIOUS DUKE 4 b.g. Dancing Spree (USA) – Killick 69 (Slip Anchor 136) **–** [2002 –, a76: f8s⁴ f8s f8.5g³ f7g² f7g* f7g f8.5g* f8.5g⁶ f8g³ 8.3g f6g 7g f7g Dec 31] **a81** workmanlike gelding: fairly useful on all-weather: made all to win minor event and handicap at Wolverhampton in February: effective at 7f to 8.5f: acts on fibresand, little form on turf: played up in stall/ran moody race sixth outing: usually races prominently. *M. Mullineaux*

ILOVETURTLE (IRE) 2 b.g. (May 12) Turtle Island (IRE) 123 – Gan Ainm (IRE) **72 d** 92 (Mujadil (USA) 119) [2002 5d 6g⁵ 6g³ f7g³ 7.5d* 7.2g⁴ 7m 7.5g 8s 7v⁶ Nov 9] IR 10,000Y: tall gelding: second foal: dam, Irish 2-y-o 7f/1m winner, half-sister to useful Irish performer up to 1¾m Bamford Castle: fair performer: won maiden at Beverley in July: well below form in nurseries last 4 starts (gelded after final one): should stay at least 1m: acts on good to soft going, probably on fibresand. *M. Johnston*

ILTON 3 ch.g. Dr Devious (IRE) 127 – Madame Crecy (USA) (Al Nasr (FR) 126) **53** [2002 52: 12f⁵ f12g 12.1g 9f⁴ 9.9g 7.5m⁴ 7.9s 8.1d⁶ 8g Aug 26] strong gelding: modest maiden: seems to stay 1½m: acts on firm going: tried tongue tied: has carried head awkwardly: sold 3,000 gns. *J. D. Bethell*

I'M ALL HEART 4 b.f. Minshaanshu Amad (USA) 91§ – Fizzy Fiona (Efisio 120) **–** [2002 f8.5g 8.1d Jun 3] 1,500Y: first foal: dam unraced: no show in maidens at Wolverhampton and Chepstow, pulled up in latter. *J. W. Unett*

IMAN ANGEL 3 b.f. Fayruz 116 – Biba (IRE) (Superlative 118) [2002 7s f7g f8g Nov **–** 26] 2,000Y: second foal: dam maiden half-sister to useful sprinter Farhana (by Fayruz): well beaten in maidens/seller. *C. N. Allen*

Sodexho Prestige Scottish Classic, Ayr—
Imperial Dancer beats Sohaib (right) and the visored Border Arrow in this four-runner contest

IMBIBING (IRE)   3 ch.c. Halling (USA) 133 – Polar Fizz (Polar Falcon (USA) 126)   **101**
[2002 83p: 10m⁶ 9m² 9g² 10.4d⁴ 8m 8.1m* 9.9m³ 10f* 10.4m² Aug 21] leggy, useful-
looking colt: useful performer: won maiden at Sandown in July and handicap at Newbury
(by 1¼ lengths from Waverley) in August: good second to Leadership in handicap at York
final start: stays 10.4f: acts on firm and good to soft going: tends to wander. *R. F. Johnson
Houghton*

I'M MAGIC   2 ch.f. (Mar 1) First Trump 118 – Crystal Magic 92 (Mazilier (USA) 107)   **69**
[2002 5m² 5.1d² 6g⁴ 7m⁴ 7m² 6g 8d⁶ Nov 1] rather leggy filly: third foal: half-sister to 6f
winner O B Comfort (by College Chapel): dam, 2-y-o 5f winner, out of sister to high-class
sprinter Petong: fair maiden: stays 7f: unraced on extremes of going. *R. Hannon*

IMOYA (IRE)   3 b.f. Desert King (IRE) 129 – Urgent Liaison (IRE) (High Estate 127)   **94**
[2002 84: 8g⁴ 10g* Apr 15] fairly useful performer: good fourth to Kootenay in listed
event at Kempton on reappearance, then won Windsor maiden following month comfortably, making most: not seen out again: should stay beyond 1¼m: acts on heavy and good
to firm going. *B. J. Meehan*

IMPASTO (FR)   2 ch.c. (Mar 2) Grand Lodge (USA) 125 – Marie Loup (FR) 92 (Wolf-   **–**
hound (USA) 126) [2002 8s Oct 15] 40,000Y, 70,000 2-y-o: smallish, strong colt: first
foal: dam, half-sister to dam of 5-y-o Marienbard: 33/1, soundly beaten
in maiden at Leicester: sold 3,500 gns. *P. F. I. Cole*

IMPELLER (IRE)   3 ch.g. Polish Precedent (USA) 131 – Almaaseh (IRE) 63   **93**
(Dancing Brave (USA) 140) [2002 86: 8g² 8.1d 8f 8g³ 8m³ 7f 7m² 8.1m 8f⁴ 7m 8g² Oct
24] tall gelding: fairly useful performer: stays 1m: acts on good to firm going: blinkered
penultimate start (well below form): tends to race freely: none too consistent. *W. R. Muir*

IMPERIAL DANCER   4 b.c. Primo Dominie 121 – Gorgeous Dancer (IRE) (Nordico   **119**
(USA)) [2002 105: 8s 10g* 10d³ 9.9d* 10m³ 11.8g⁵ 10d⁴ 10g* 10g* 10s³ 10m⁴ 9.8g 10m
10d⁴ Nov 17] smallish, angular colt: smart performer: won Coral Eurobet Rosebery
Stakes (Handicap) at Kempton in April, listed race at Goodwood (by head from Island
House) in May and Sodexho Prestige Scottish Classic at Ayr (by length from Sohaib) and
Meld Stakes at the Curragh (beat Chancellor by ½ length) in July: respectable fourth of 5

Imperial Racing's "Imperial Dancer"

to Hawk Wing in Eclipse Stakes at Sandown seventh outing: seems best around 1¼m: acts on heavy and good to firm going: sometimes carries head awkwardly: usually held up: tough. *M. R. Channon*

IMPERIAL EYE (IRE) 4 b.f. Eagle Eyed (USA) 111 – Capellino (IRE) 76 (Imperial – Frontier (USA) 112) [2002 73: 10m p7g f6g Dec 10] ex-Irish filly: second foal: dam, Irish 5f winner (ran only at 2 yrs), out of useful Queen Alexandra Stakes winner Easy To Please: fair maiden handicapper for J. Bolger in Ireland: well held in 2002: stays 1m: acts on any going: sometimes tongue tied. *John R. Upson*

IMPERIAL ROCKET (USA) 5 b. or br.g. Northern Flagship (USA) 96 – Starsa- **76 d** whirl (USA) (Star de Naskra (USA)) [2002 10s 12g 10g⁵ 10d⁶ 12.1m 10.4m 10m Sep 20] good-topped gelding: fairly useful for R. Hannon in 2000: on downgrade in 2002: should stay 1½m: acts on firm and soft going, raced freely on heavy: blinkered final start. *Mrs A. L. M. King*

IMPERSONATOR 2 b.g. (Jan 27) Zafonic (USA) 130 – Conspiracy 98 (Rudi- **94 p** mentary (USA) 118) [2002 6s³ 7f 8m⁴ 8g² 7v* Nov 9] good-bodied gelding: has a long, round stride: second foal: half-brother to 3-y-o In Disguise: dam, 2-y-o 5f winner, closely related to high-class sprinter Gayane out of very smart filly up to 1¼m Roussalka, herself half-sister to Oh So Sharp: fairly useful form: beaten neck in nursery at Newmarket before winning similar event at Doncaster by 4 lengths from Sewmore Character: will probably stay 1¼m: acts on heavy going, possibly not firmer than good: upset in stall second start: has scope to do better still as 3-y-o. *J. L. Dunlop*

IMPISH JUDE 4 b.f. Imp Society (USA) – Miss Nanna 56§ (Vayrann 133) [2002 59: **55** 8m f8.5s 10g 11.8g³ 13v³ Aug 14] leggy filly: modest maiden: stays 13f: probably acts on any turf going. *J. Mackie*

IMPORTANT BOY (ARG) 5 ch.g. Equalize (USA) – Important Girl (ARG) (Candy **61** Stripes (USA) 115) [2002 10m 10.2g⁵ 11.9g² 16.2m⁵ p12g Oct 4] Argentinian-bred gelding: won 3 times on dirt in native country from 1m to 10.5f early in 2001: modest form on Flat in Britain: blinkered on reappearance: wandered third start. *J. A. B. Old*

Godolphin's "Imtiyaz"

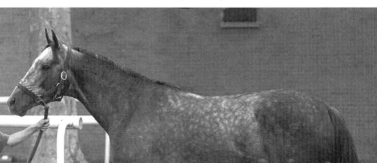

IMPRESSIVE FLIGHT (IRE) 3 b.f. Flying Spur (AUS) – Certain Impression **105 p**
(USA) (Forli (ARG)) [2002 6f* 6.1d³ 5f 6g² 6d³ 6m* 6g Sep 21] IR 2,200Y: lengthy filly:
fifth foal: half-sister to 1m winner in Italy by Petardia: dam unraced: quickly developed
into useful performer, winning maiden at Thirsk in April and handicap at Newmarket
(beat Pic Up Sticks by neck, stall having opened fractionally earlier than others) in
August: raced in disadvantaged group when well held in Ayr Gold Cup final start: will
prove best at 5f/6f: acts on firm and good to soft going: type to win a good handicap.
T. D. Barron

IMPREVUE (IRE) 8 ch.m. Priolo (USA) 127 – Las Bela 75 (Welsh Pageant 132) **55 d**
[2002 58, a68: p13g p12g p13g 12m⁴ 9.7m 11.9g 11.9m⁵ 11.6s 12.6f⁶ Jun 26] lengthy **a68 d**
mare: fair on all-weather, modest on turf: on downgrade in 2002 (won over hurdles in
July): has form at 2m, possibly best at 1¼m/1½m: acts on polytrack, firm and soft ground:
blinkered: sometimes slowly away/wanders: held up. *R. J. O'Sullivan*

IMPULSIVE AIR (IRE) 10 b.g. Try My Best (USA) 130 – Tracy's Sundown (Red **44 §**
Sunset 120) [2002 54§: 8m 9.9g 10.1g 10m 9.2g 10m 10.1m 9m Sep 16] strong gelding:
unimpressive mover: poor performer nowadays: effective at 1m to 11f: acts on firm going, good to soft and fibresand: tried visored early in career: untrustworthy. *J. R. Weymes*

IMPULSIVO 2 ch.g. (Feb 27) Millkom 124 – Joytime (John de Coombe 122) [2002 **59 p**
7.1g⁵ Sep 23] 2,000Y: half-brother to 3 winners, including 3-y-o Major Laugh and 1½m/
1¾m winner All The Joys (by Adbass): dam ran once: 66/1 and green, 2½ lengths fifth to
Aegean Line in maiden at Chepstow: will be suited by 1m+: should do better. *Simon
Earle*

IMTIHAN (IRE) 3 ch.c. Unfuwain (USA) 131 – Azyaa 101 (Kris 135) [2002 –p: 8s **83**
9.9g* 10m 12s³ 12m² 12.3m* 12g 12.3m⁵ Aug 17] good-topped colt: good mover: fairly
useful handicapper: won at Beverley in May and Ripon in July: will probably stay 1¾m:
acts on soft and firm going: ran in snatches final start. *B. W. Hills*

IMTIYAZ (USA) 3 ro.c. Woodman (USA) 126 – Shadayid (USA) 122 (Shadeed **116**
(USA) 135) [2002 96: 10.4f* 9m² 8.9m⁴ 9.9f² Sep 25] leggy colt: smart performer: won
3-runner listed race at York (by 6 lengths from L'Oiseau d'Argent) in May: good short-
neck second to Rouvres in Prix Jean Prat at Chantilly next time: creditable efforts last 2
starts in listed events at York (fourth to Binary File) and Goodwood (more patiently
ridden when head second of 4 to Rawyaan): stays 10.4f: acts on firm and soft going:
effective visored or not: tongue tied last 2 starts: often makes running. *Saeed bin Suroor*

INABA 3 b.g. Forzando 122 – White Hare 56 (Indian Ridge 123) [2002 5m 7.5g 7m 6s **–**
5.9g 5m 8m Jul 26] tall gelding: second foal: dam third at 1m: well held all starts: tried
blinkered: probably wayward. *Mrs M. Reveley*

IN A SILENT WAY (IRE) 2 b.f. (Jan 23) Desert Prince (IRE) 130 – Pray (IRE) **77**
(Priolo (USA) 127) [2002 6m² 6m* 6m⁵ 6.5m 5f⁴ Oct 3] IR 130,000Y: lengthy, useful-
looking filly: second foal: dam unraced half-sister to smart performer up to 9f in Britain/
USA Anshan: fair performer: landed odds in maiden at Goodwood in June: respectable
efforts in nurseries last 2 starts: races freely, and may prove best at 5f/6f: raced only on
ground firmer than good: sometimes early to post. *M. A. Jarvis*

INCA MOON 2 b.f. (Mar 4) Sheikh Albadou 128 – Incatinka 63 (Inca Chief (USA)) **58**
[2002 5.1d⁴ 5.7f⁵ f6g⁵ 8.3d³ f8.5g Oct 19] 7,500Y: second foal: dam, maiden, should have
stayed 7f: modest maiden: third in seller at Windsor: stays 1m: acts on firm and good to
soft going, below form on fibresand. *I. A. Balding*

INCH AGAIN 2 ch.c. (Apr 27) Inchinor 119 – Spoilt Again 91 (Mummy's Pet 125) **92**
[2002 7.1m⁴ 7.5d⁴ 8m* 8g* 8s Oct 26] 8,200F, IR 26,000Y: tall, good-topped colt: has
scope: half-brother to several winners, including useful 7f to 9f winner High Spirits (by
Great Commotion) and 1¼m and 1¾m winner Teen Jay (by Teenoso): dam, 9f/1¼m
winner, out of Park Hill winner Reload: fairly useful performer: won maiden at Yarmouth
in August and minor event at Ayr (dictated pace, beat King's Protector by 2 lengths) in
September: tailed off in Racing Post Trophy at Doncaster final start: should be suited by
at least 1¼m: acts on good to firm ground. *M. H. Tompkins*

INCHALONG 7 b.m. Inchinor 119 – Reshift 94 (Night Shift (USA)) [2002 –: 8m 7g **–**
May 6] small mare: unimpressive mover: fair handicapper in 1999: has shown little since:
visored. *M. Brittain*

INCHBERRY 2 b.f. (May 6) Barathea (IRE) 127 – Inchyre 102 (Shirley Heights 130) **90**
[2002 5.1d⁴ 7m² 8.3s*ᵈⁱˢ 8d² Oct 21] good-topped filly: second living foal: closely related
to useful 1¼m/1½m winner Inchiri (by Sadler's Wells): dam, 1m winner who stayed
1½m, half-sister to smart performer up to 1m Inchinor: fairly useful form: easily won

maiden at Hamilton in August (disqualified after failing dope test): creditable 6 lengths second of 5 to Battle Chant in listed race at Pontefract next time: will be suited by 1¼m/ 1½m: acts on soft and good to firm going. *G. A. Butler*

INCH BY INCH   3 b.f. Inchinor 119 – Maid Welcome 81 (Mummy's Pet 125) [2002   **58** 52: 7.1f f9.4g⁴ 8.2f 7g p6g² Jul 17] smallish filly: modest maiden handicapper: effective at 6f, barely stays 9.4f: acts on all-weather: blinkered last 3 starts: sometimes looks none too keen. *P. J. Makin*

INCHCOONAN   4 b.f. Emperor Jones (USA) 119 – Miss Ivory Coast (USA) (Sir Ivor   **67** 135) [2002 64: p8g* f7g* f7g* f7g* f7g³ 7.6f² f8.5g² 6.9s 7m⁴ 6s⁶ 6m 7.1m Sep 29]   **a81** strong filly: fairly useful handicapper on all-weather, fair on turf: completed 4-timer early in year at Lingfield (apprentices), Wolverhampton (2) and Southwell: best form at 7f/ 1m: acts on all-weather and firm going, probably not on soft: sometimes idles in front. *K. R. Burke*

INCHDURA   4 ch.g. Inchinor 119 – Sunshine Coast 86 (Posse (USA) 130) [2002 92:   **105** 8g 8m³ 8m 8f³ 7f* 7m³ 7m² 7m* 7m 7f 7f² Oct 10] quite attractive gelding: useful handi-capper: improved in 2002, and won at Newbury in August and Goodwood (neck from Vanderlin) in September: good second to Surprise Encounter at York final outing: better form at 1m than 7f: best on going firmer than good: sometimes tongue tied earlier in career: sometimes edgy: tough and reliable: sold 56,000 gns. *R. Charlton*

INCH HIGH   4 ch.g. Inchinor 119 – Harrken Heights (IRE) (Belmez (USA) 131)   **–** [2002 –: 8.3d 13v⁶ 7.1m Sep 16] no form. *J. S. Goldie*

INCHING   2 b.f. (Apr 12) Inchinor 119 – Tshusick 81 (Dancing Brave (USA) 140)   **65** [2002 p6g f6g³ p6g³ Dec 28] fourth foal: half-sister to 3 winners, including 4-y-o Liberty Bound and 5-y-o Tribal Prince: dam, 7f winner, out of useful sprinter Infanta Real: fair maiden: may prove best at 5f/6f. *R. M. H. Cowell*

INCHINNAN   5 b.m. Inchinor 119 – Westering 54 (Auction Ring (USA) 123) [2002   **?** 78: 8.5g⁴ Apr 24] small mare: fair handicapper at 4 yrs: stays 10.5f: has form on firm going, seems at very best on soft/heavy. *C. Weedon*

INCH ISLAND (IRE)   2 b.g. (Apr 21) Turtle Island (IRE) 123 – Persian Light (IRE)   **66** 52 (Persian Heights 129) [2002 5s³ 5m³ 5g 5m 6d³ 7s⁶ Oct 26] IR 14,500F, IR 6,500Y: useful-looking gelding: sixth foal: half-brother to 2 winners, including Irish 7f and 8.5f winner Peru Girl (by Petardia): dam, Irish maiden, best at 6f to 1m: fair maiden: effective at 5f/6f: acts on good and good to firm ground: continually flicked tail in parade second outing: free-going sort. *J. J. Quinn*

INCHNADAMPH   2 b.g. (Apr 25) Inchinor 119 – Pelf (USA) 79 (Al Nasr (FR) 126)   **64** [2002 7.5g⁵ 7m 8v Nov 8] 8,000Y: half-brother to several winners, including useful Irish 6f and (at 2 yrs) 7f winner Pelmeny (by Machiavellian) and fairly useful but ungenuine middle-distance performer House of Riches (by Shirley Heights): dam Italian 7f winner: modest maiden: clearly best effort on debut: should stay at least 1m. *J. G. FitzGerald*

INCH PERFECT   7 b.g. Inchinor 119 – Scarlet Veil 75 (Tyrnavos 129) [2002 95:   **80** 13.8d⁵ 11.9m 12m⁶ 11.9m 12.1v* 11.9g⁶ 14.8g⁶ Jul 20] tall, good-topped gelding: fairly useful handicapper nowadays: won at Hamilton in June: stays 1¾m: acts on any turf going and fibresand: tongue tied once: has idled, and usually held up: tough. *R. A. Fahey*

INCLINE (IRE)   3 b.g. Danehill (USA) 126 – Shalwar Kameez (IRE) (Sadler's Wells   **89** (USA) 132) [2002 –: f8.5g⁶ 8.3m⁴ 8m 7.1g³ 7m 7s* 8d* 7v³ Nov 9] fairly useful per-former: won maiden at Yarmouth in October and apprentice handicap at Newmarket in November: stays 1m: acts on heavy and good to firm going. *T. G. Mills*

INCORPORATION   3 b.g. In The Wings 128 – Danishkada 119 (Thatch (USA) 136)   **–** [2002 10.5d 10f 12s 14.1f⁶ 13.8m Aug 6] 150,000Y: good-topped gelding: half-brother to smart French performer up to 6.5f Danakal (by Diesis) and 1m/9f winner in USA by Lyphard: dam won Grand Criterium but failed to train on: well held in maidens/ handicaps: blinkered (raced freely final start): sold 2,400 gns. *R. Charlton*

INDEFINITE STAY   4 b.g. Beveled – Wassl's Sister (Troy 137) [2002 –:   **–** 10.2d 11.8g Jul 18] tall gelding: modest maiden at 2 yrs: no form since. *W. R. Muir*

INDELIBLE   3 br.f. Polar Falcon (USA) 126 – Ink Pot (USA) 73 (Green Dancer   **58** (USA) 132) [2002 63. f8g f7g³ f6g 8.2d² 10m⁶ 7.5m⁵ 9m 7f 8g⁵ 8.3v⁵ 8f 7f⁵ 8m 7f⁴ 8.5m   **a49** 7d³ 7s f8.5s f6g Dec 10] small filly: has a round action: modest maiden handicapper: stays 1m: acts on firm ground, good to soft and fibresand. *J. Hetherton*

INDEPENDENCE HALL (IRE) 5 b.g. Sadler's Wells (USA) 132 – Fruition 89   –
(Rheingold 137) [2002 –: p16g 16f Sep 26] fairly useful 1½m winner at 3 yrs: little form
since. *J. E. Long*

IN DEPTH (USA) 4 b.f. Defensive Play (USA) 118 – Popularity (USA) 58 (Blushing   –
Groom (FR) 131) [2002 58: f12g Feb 11] modest form in maiden at Wolverhampton on
debut: well held both runs since: blinkered on reappearance. *Mrs H. Dalton*

INDIAN BAZAAR (IRE) 6 ch.g. Indian Ridge 123 – Bazaar Promise 58 (Native   **59**
Bazaar 122) [2002 67: 5.1g 5m 5.1d 5.1d⁶ 5g 5m 5m 5.7g⁵ 5m 5.1g 5g 5m 5.3m 5m⁵ 5m⁴
5f Sep 25] big, good-topped gelding: modest handicapper: best at 5f: acts on soft and
good to firm going: blinkered (not discredited) final start. *J. M. Bradley*

INDIAN BEAT 5 ch.g. Indian Ridge 123 – Rappa Tap Tap (FR) 111 (Tap On Wood   **52**
130) [2002 68: p10g p10g 10.2g⁵ 12m 10.2d 18d³ 16.2g² 18.7g⁶ 14.1m 16f Sep 26] leggy,
useful-looking gelding: modest maiden handicapper: barely stays 2¼m: acts on good to
firm and good to soft going: well held when visored/blinkered: looked sure to win before
idling markedly seventh outing. *C. L. Popham*

INDIAN BLAZE 8 ch.g. Indian Ridge 123 – Odile (Green Dancer (USA) 132) [2002   **70 §**
76: p7g⁵ p8g 8.5g 8.1m 8m⁵ p8g⁴ 8s⁶ 8.3m⁴ 8.3m⁵ 7m⁵ 8d⁴ 7m 8m p7g p10g⁴ Dec 30]
workmanlike gelding: fair handicapper: effective at 7f/1m: acts on any turf going/all-
weather: tried blinkered: takes good hold: often hangs right: untrustworthy.
D. R. C. Elsworth

INDIAN COUNTRY 3 ch.c. Indian Ridge 123 – Arethusa 101 (Primo Dominie 121)   **107**
[2002 5s² 6m* 6d 7f² 6m⁴ 6f⁵ Jul 20] 88,000Y: strong, lengthy, good sort: first foal: dam
2-y-o 5f/6f winner: useful performer: won maiden at Newmarket in April: best effort
when 3¾ lengths fourth to Malhub in Golden Jubilee Stakes at Royal Ascot: hung left
when only fair fifth in listed event at Newbury final start: best form at 6f on going firmer
than good. *J. Noseda*

INDIAN CREEK 4 br.c. Indian Ridge 123 – Blue Water (USA) 104 (Bering 136)   **119**
[2002 117: 9m* 10.5s⁶ 10m² 10d⁵ 10.4g⁴ 10m⁶ 10m Dec 15] tall, useful-looking colt:

Mr Seymour Cohn's "Indian Creek"

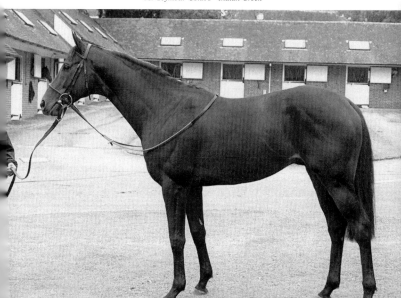

smart performer: won Weatherbys Earl of Sefton Stakes at Newmarket in April by head from Island House: good efforts after only when in frame in Prince of Wales's Stakes at Royal Ascot (5 lengths second to Grandera) and Juddmonte International Stakes at York (3½ lengths fourth to Nayef): stays 1¼m: acts on good to firm and good to soft going: reportedly pulled a muscle second start: sometimes slowly away/tends to be soon off bridle in rear, and may not have ideal attitude. *D. R. C. Elsworth*

INDIAN DRIVE (IRE)   5 b.g. Indian Ridge 123 – Daniella Drive (USA) (Shelter   – Half (USA)) [2002 –: f7g f7g Mar 2] disappointing maiden: tried blinkered and tongue tied. *E. J. Alston*

INDIAN GIFT   3 ch.f. Cadeaux Genereux 131 – Vanishing Trick (USA) 80 (Gone   **64** West (USA)) [2002 58: 7f 8.5g⁵ 8m⁴ 6.9g 8d f12g Dec 4] strong filly: modest maiden: left E. Dunlop after fourth start: should stay 1¼m: tried blinkered. *W. J. Musson*

INDIAN HAVEN   2 ch.c. (Feb 21) Indian Ridge 123 – Madame Dubois 121 (Legend   **99** of France (USA) 124) [2002 6m* 6g⁶ 7m⁵ 7m Oct 19] 62,000Y: tall, good-bodied colt: has plenty of scope: half-brother to several winners, including useful 2000 2-y-o 6f and 1m (Gran Criterium) winner Count Dubois (by Zafonic) and useful 1¼m winner Place de L'Opera (by Sadler's Wells), herself dam of 4-y-o High Pitched: dam won Park Hill Stakes: useful form: won maiden at Yarmouth in July: good efforts when 4½ lengths sixth to Country Reel in Gimcrack Stakes at York (hampered halfway) and 3 lengths fifth to Almushahar in Champagne Stakes at Doncaster: well held in Dewhurst Stakes at Newmarket: should stay 1m: raced on good/good to firm going: sold 95,000 gns. *P. W. D'Arcy*

INDIAN MAIDEN (IRE)   2 br.f. (Apr 21) Indian Ridge 123 – Jinsiyah (USA) 98   **68** (Housebuster (USA)) [2002 6m 6g³ 6g f6g² Nov 30] IR 22,000Y: first foal: dam, 7f winner who stayed 8.5f, out of half-sister to Kentucky Derby winner Winning Colors: fair maiden: good second at Wolverhampton final start: should prove as effective at 5f as 6f: acts on fibresand. *M. S. Saunders*

INDIAN MUSIC   5 b.g. Indian Ridge 123 – Dagny Juel (USA) 75 (Danzig (USA))   **69 d** [2002 77: f6s4 f6s⁶ f5g² f6g² f5g⁶ f6g f5g 5g⁴ 6m f5g 7.2g 8g f6g² f6g⁵ f6g³ f6g³ 5.9s⁶ f6g* 5s⁴ 5m³ 6s f6s f6g f5g f6g⁶ f5g f7g⁴ Dec 17] strong, stocky gelding: fair performer: on downgrade in 2002, though won seller at Wolverhampton in August: below form after: effective at 5f/6f: acts on fibresand, probably any turf going: sometimes blinkered/wears cheekpieces/slowly away: wayward. *A. Berry*

INDIAN PLUME   6 b.g. Efisio 120 – Boo Hoo 68 (Mummy's Pet 125) [2002 96:   **94** f8.5g⁵ f7g⁶ 8f* 8m⁵ 8m⁶ 8g³ 7m 8g Oct 18] smallish, sturdy gelding: fairly useful handicapper: won at Brighton in April: effective at 7f to 8.5f: acts on any going: front runner: game: sold 15,000 gns, sent to USA. *T. G. Mills*

INDIAN PRINCE (IRE)   4 ch.g. Indian Ridge 123 – Lingering Melody (IRE) 59   **121** (Nordico (USA)) [2002 112: 5m 5g⁵ 5d³ 5g 5m³ Aug 22] sturdy gelding: very smart performer: good efforts in 2002 when 1¼ lengths fifth of 15 to Dominica in King's Stand Stakes at Royal Ascot (not clear run) and length third of 17 to Kyllachy in Nunthorpe Stakes (improved form) at York: was best at 5f on good or firmer going: sometimes started slowly (reared at stall opened when last in King George Stakes at Goodwood fourth outing): was headstrong: was none too reliable: dead. *B. J. Meehan*

INDIAN SHORES   3 b.f. Forzando 122 – Cottonwood 80 (Teenoso (USA) 135) [2002   **57** 66: 5m⁴ 5f 5m³ 5d³ 6g⁴d 5g 5d Oct 14] neat filly: modest maiden: best at 5f/6f: acts on firm and good to soft going, ran poorly on fibresand: has been awkward at stall (unseated leaving stall on second outing)/slowly away: usually races prominently: found little third start. *E. J. Alston*

INDIAN SILK (IRE)   4 b.f. Dolphin Street (FR) 125 – Scammony (IRE) (Persian   **53** Bold 123) [2002 74: f8s 10d f8.5g⁶ p10g Nov 27] modest form in handicaps in 2002 (left M. Polglase after second start and returned to former trainer): stays 1m: acts on heavy going, good to firm and fibresand: blinkered final run: sometimes tongue tied. *J. A. Osborne*

INDIAN SOLITAIRE (IRE)   3 b.g. Bigstone (IRE) 126 – Terrama Sioux (Relkino   **91** 131) [2002 91p: p10g 1ig⁴ 12d³ 14s⁵ 14m⁴ 11.9g 11.8g² 12s⁵ 12v Nov 9] good-bodied gelding: fairly useful handicapper: mostly creditable efforts in 2002: left Mrs A. Perrett 32,000 gns after fifth start: stays 1¾m: acts on firm and soft ground: wandered fourth outing: held up: gelded after final appearance. *R. A. Fahey*

INDIAN SPARK   8 ch.g. Indian Ridge 123 – Annes Gift (Ballymoss 136) [2002 112:   **112** 5s⁴ 6f* 5m⁴ 6f 5m³ 5g 6g 6m⁴ 5.6m 5m⁵ 6s Oct 25] close-coupled gelding: poor mover (reportedly fractured off-fore joint earlier in career): smart performer: won minor event at Thirsk in April: good efforts when fourth to Kyllachy in Palace House Stakes at Newmarket next time and to Needwood Blade in handicap at York in September: best at 5f/6f: acts on any going: waited with. *J. S. Goldie*

INDIAN STEPPES (FR) 3 b.f. Indian Ridge 123 – Ukraine Venture 96 (Slip Anchor 72 136) [2002 8.2d 8.3m⁵ 8.3g⁶ 8.2m⁴ 10m⁵ 9.7g⁵ p8g⁶ 7s² p7g² f7f² f6g² f7g² f6g* Dec 27] 11,000Y: angular filly: first foal: dam, 1¼m winner, should have proved as effective over further: fair performer: won maiden at Southwell in December: effective at 6f to 1¼m: acts on soft going, good to firm and all-weather: has worn cheekpieces. *Julian Poulton*

INDIAN SUN 5 ch.g. Indian Ridge 123 – Star Tulip 99 (Night Shift (USA)) [2002 67d: – f12s² f11s⁶ f11g³ f12g⁴ f12g⁵ f12g³ 12s 11g Apr 2] angular gelding: modest performer: **a51** effective at 11f, probably at 2m: acts on fibresand and any turf going: tried blinkered/ visored earlier in career: tongue tied: often held up. *P. D. Evans*

INDIAN TRAIL 2 ch.c. (Apr 10) Indian Ridge 123 – Take Heart 84 (Electric 126) 80 [2002 6g⁶ 6s³ 7d Nov 2] 38,000Y: strong, useful-looking colt: sixth foal: half-brother to 3 winners, including useful 1¼m winner Lonely Heart (by Midyan) and 5-y-o Mac Be Lucky: dam 7f to 1¼m winner: fairly useful maiden: third to Zabaglione at Newbury: well below form at final start: should stay 7f. *D. R. C. Elsworth*

INDIAN WARRIOR 6 b.g. Be My Chief (USA) 122 – Wanton 106 (Kris 135) [2002 54 56: f6s³ p6g p7g⁵ p6g p6g³ p6g 6m 6f 7m 7f³ 5.9v³ 6m⁶ p7g Oct 16] small gelding: modest performer: probably best at 6f/7f: acts on any turf going and all-weather: tried visored, usually blinkered: often starts slowly: held up. *W. J. Musson*

INDIAN WELCOME 3 ch.g. Most Welcome 131 – Qualitair Ridge (Indian Ridge 73 123) [2002 10s 8.1d³ 10m² 10s p12g Nov 13] 10,000Y: big gelding: second foal: half-brother to 4-y-o Cyber Santa: dam little worthwhile form: fair maiden: stays 1¼m (raced freely at 1½m): acts on good to firm and good to soft going, probably on polytrack: slowly away second outing. *H. Morrison*

INDIGO BEACH (IRE) 6 b.g. Rainbows For Life (CAN) – Sandy Maid (Sandy 50 ? Creek 123) [2002 p12g f12g³ Mar 25] sturdy gelding: modest at best and untrustworthy on Flat and over hurdles: tried tongue tied/blinkered. *P. S. McEntee*

IN DISGUISE 3 ch.g. Nashwan (USA) 135 – Conspiracy 98 (Rudimentary (USA) 103 118) [2002 78: 10.3s² 10f* 12m² 11.6d* 10.4d 11.6g* 12m³ 12f 13.1s Oct 15] lengthy gelding: had a fluent, round action: useful performer: won maiden at Pontefract in April and minor events at Windsor in May (carried head awkwardly) and July (beat Maimana by a head): stayed 1½m: acted on firm and soft going: tended to hang: sometimes swished tail, but was game enough in a finish: often made running: dead. *J. L. Dunlop*

INDIUM 8 b.g. Groom Dancer (USA) 128 – Gold Bracelet § (Golden Fleece (USA) – 133) [2002 74: p16g f11s⁴ Jan 17] tall, leggy gelding: fair performer at 7 yrs: well held on Flat in 2002. *D. E. Cantillon*

INDRAPURA STAR (USA) 2 b.g. (May 7) Foxhound (USA) 103 – Royal Recall – (USA) (Native Royalty (USA)) [2002 7d Aug 11] $10,000F, 24,000Y: half-brother to numerous winners in USA, including If Memory Serves (by Youth), also useful 7f to 1¼m winner in Britain: dam 6f winner in USA: 25/1, well held in maiden at Leicester: sold 4,000 gns. *E. A. L. Dunlop*

INDUCEMENT 6 ch.g. Sabrehill (USA) 120 – Verchinina 99 (Star Appeal 133) 84 [2002 86: 11.6s* 12g 16.4d 11.8d⁶ Aug 11] tall, good-topped gelding: has a fluent, round action: fairly useful performer: won claimer at Windsor (left Mrs A. Perrett) in June: will probably prove best at 1¼m/1½m: acts on soft and good to firm going. *R. M. Stronge*

INDULENE (IRE) 2 b.c. (Apr 23) Alhaarth (IRE) 126 – Don't Care (IRE) 93 (Nordico 62 (USA)) [2002 p6g Dec 28] IR 20,000F, IR 21,000Y, 24,000 2-y-o: second foal: dam 5f/6f winner in Ireland: 14/1 and tongue tied, 6 lengths eighth of 11 to Wages in Lingfield maiden, fading having been briefly short of room. *D. Carroll*

INEXPENSIVE 6 b.m. Puissance 110 – Sojourn 87 (Be My Guest (USA) 126) [2002 39 –: p8g 7f f9.4g f9.4g 7d p7g May 28] poor performer: stays 8.5f: acts on fibresand, firm and good to soft going: tried blinkered/tongue tied. *I. A. Wood*

INFINITE RISK 3 gr.g. Vettori (IRE) 119 – Dolly Bevan 53 (Another Realm 118) 59 [2002 61?: p8g⁴ p7g 10f Apr 11] modest maiden: well held after reappearance: seems to stay 1m: acts on polytrack, raced only on good to firm/firm going on turf: gelded. *R. Hannon*

IN FOR THE CRAIC (IRE)   3 b.g. Our Emblem (USA) 114 – Lucky State (USA)   **64**
(State Dinner (USA)) [2002 –: p10g* 10f⁵ 11.6m⁴ p10g⁵ f9.4g 10d⁴ 12g f12g p10g Dec
30] modest performer: won maiden at Lingfield in March: stays 11.6f: acts on polytrack
(below form on fibresand) and good to firm going, probably on good to soft: tends to
wander. *S. Kirk*

INFRA RED   3 ch.c. Most Welcome 131 – Flying Wind 51 (Forzando 122) [2002 –:   **–**
8.5m⁵ 8m Jul 8] good-bodied colt: tailed off in maidens. *C. Grant*

INGLENOOK (IRE)   5 b.h. Cadeaux Genereux 131 – Spring 112 (Sadler's Wells   **113**
(USA) 132) [2002 112: 8d³ 8g² 9g⁵ 8m² 9m Oct 19] lengthy horse: reportedly suffers
from knee problems: smart performer: creditable efforts in 2002 only when second in
Badener Meile at Baden-Baden (to Touch Down) in May and listed event at Ascot (beaten
1¼ lengths by Fallen Star) in July: effective at 1m to 10.5f: acts on heavy and good to
firm going: sometimes bandaged in front: often races prominently: sold only 10,000 gns.
J. L. Dunlop

INGLEWOOD   2 ch.c. (Mar 7) Fleetwood (IRE) 107 – Preening 62 (Persian Bold   **–**
123) [2002 7.1s Nov 6] half-brother to 3-y-o White Cliffs (by Cloudings) and 2-y-o 5f
Alpha (by Primo Dominie): dam, 1½m winner, half-sister to smart 7f/1m winner Hadeer:
50/1, soon outpaced in Musselburgh maiden. *C. W. Thornton*

INGLIS DREVER   3 b.g. In The Wings 128 – Cormorant Creek 73 (Gorytus (USA)   **87**
132) [2002 65p: 9.9d² 10m* 9d² 10.3m³ Aug 30] good-bodied gelding: fairly useful
handicapper: won apprentice event at Nottingham in August by 5 lengths despite wandering markedly: tends to race freely, but should stay 1½m: acts on good to firm and good to
soft going, possibly not on heavy. *Sir Mark Prescott*

IN GOOD TIME   3 b.g. Classic Cliche (IRE) 128 – Primum Tempus 49 (Primo Domi-   **–**
nie 121) [2002 –: 10.5d 7f Jun 11] workmanlike gelding: well held in 3 maidens/
handicap: sold 2,800 gns. *E. J. Alston*

INISHOWEN (IRE)   3 b.g. Alhaarth (IRE) 126 – Naaman (IRE) 61 (Marju (IRE)   **82 d**
127) [2002 89p: 8g 8.1d 6.1d 7d 8f 7f p7g Oct 16] compact gelding: has a quick action:
fairly useful performer: well below form after reappearance, leaving B. Hills following
fourth outing: probably stays 1m: tried visored (raced freely)/tongue tied: appeared not to
be at ease on soft going (though ran well) final 2-y-o start: sold 1,700 gns, sent to Kuwait.
R. M. Beckett

INITIATIVE   6 ch.g. Arazi (USA) 135 – Dance Quest (FR) 117 (Green Dancer (USA)   **37**
132) [2002 –: f7s f11s⁵ 10m 11.9s⁶ 10f⁴ 10m 15.8f Oct 8] smallish, leggy gelding: poor
performer: stays 11f, seemingly not 2m: acts on firm going: tried blinkered. *J. Hetherton*

INJAAZ   4 ch.f. Sheikh Albadou 128 – Ferber's Follies (USA) (Saratoga Six (USA))   **99**
[2002 99: 7m 7g 8d⁴ 7d 6m⁴ 6v 6m* 5.6m² 6g 5g Oct 17] rangy, unfurnished filly: has a
fluent, round action: useful handicapper: won at Goodwood in August by 1¾ lengths
from Alpen Wolf: good short-head second to Halmahera in Portland at Doncaster next
time: effective at 6f to 1m: acts on firm and good to soft going, possibly not on heavy:
carries head awkwardly: none too consistent. *J. L. Dunlop*

INJUN   3 ch.g. Efisio 120 – Lassoo 87 (Caerleon (USA) 132) [2002 –: f7g f8g⁶ f8g⁶ 10g   **–**
7.9g p12g Sep 4] little form: left C. Thornton after fifth start. *Miss A. M. Newton-Smith*

IN LOVE   2 b.f. (May 10) Unfuwain (USA) 131 – Nemesia 111 (Mill Reef (USA) 141)   **82 p**
[2002 8m 8s* Oct 15] 45,000Y: half-sister to several winners, including fairly useful
1½m winner Rafiya (by Halling): dam, 1¼m and 13.5f winner, closely related to smart
1¼m performer Elegant Air: better effort in maidens (fairly useful form) when winning
at Ayr by head from Karathaena, patiently ridden and staying on well to lead near finish:
will be well suited by 1¼m+: acts on soft going: sure to improve further. *E. A. L. Dunlop*

IN LUCK   4 b.f. In The Wings 128 – Lucca (Sure Blade (USA) 130) [2002 72: p10g⁵   **72**
11.6g 11.5m⁵ 11.9m 11.5m² 10.5f³ 10s 12d² Nov 1] lengthy filly: unimpressive mover:
fair maiden handicapper: stays 1½m: acts on good to firm and good to soft going: sometimes pulls hard. *C. E. Brittain*

INNOCENT (IRE)   4 b.g. Lure (USA) 131 – Miss Declared (USA) (Alleged (USA)   **–**
138) [2002 41: p7g 8d May 27] tall, good-topped gelding: maiden: well held in 2002.
J. A. Osborne

INNOVATION   2 b.f. (Apr 6) Salse (USA) 128 – I Will Lead (USA) (Seattle Slew   **68 p**
(USA)) [2002 7d⁶ Nov 2] tall filly: has scope: third foal: half-sister to useful 1¼m winner
Stay Behind (by Elmaamul): dam unraced half-sister to Rainbow Quest: 8/1, 8½ lengths

sixth of 19 to Goodness Gracious in maiden at Newmarket, travelling strongly long way and not knocked out: sure to improve. *R. Charlton*

INSIGNIFICANCE   2 b.c. (Mar 30) Bishop of Cashel 122 – Summer Pageant 81   –
(Chief's Crown (USA)) [2002 7d 7g 6g f7g Oct 22] IR 5,500Y: brother to 3-y-o Cloud Dancer and 4-y-o Rock Concert and half-brother to 2 winners, including 1¼m winner Join The Parade (by Elmaamul): dam 1½m winner out of half-sister to Sun Princess and Saddlers' Hall: well beaten in minor event/maidens: tongue tied at Southwell final start. *John A. Quinn, Ireland*

IN SPACE (USA)   3 ch.g. Sky Classic (CAN) – Thrilling Day 112 (Groom Dancer   –
(USA) 128) [2002 97: 7m 7m 6g Sep 21] strong, close-coupled gelding: fluent mover: useful at 2 yrs for S. Woods: well held in minor event/handicaps in 2002. *D. Nicholls*

INSPECTOR BLUE   4 ch.g. Royal Academy (USA) 130 – Blue Siren 113 (Bluebird   –
(USA) 125) [2002 63?: 7m 10s 8.1m f8.5g 10m 9.7m 14.1m Aug 21] leggy, quite good-topped gelding: modest maiden at 3 yrs: well held in 2002, leaving C. Dwyer after reappearance. *N. P. Littmoden*

INSPECTOR GENERAL (IRE)   4 b.g. Dilum (USA) 115 – New Generation 91   **85 d**
(Young Generation 129) [2002 96: 8s 8s⁴ 7.1d⁵ 7.2v 7g⁶ p8g 8.5g⁴ 12g⁴ 8m 10.4f⁴ 9s f8g²
f8.5g³ f8.5g² Dec 26] good-topped gelding: unimpressive mover: fairly useful performer: on downgrade after third start, leaving P. Cole after eleventh: probably stays 1¼m: acts on firesand, firm and soft ground: tried blinkered. *T. D. Barron*

INSPECTOR HECTOR (IRE)   2 b.g. (Apr 21) Hector Protector (USA) 124 –   **64**
Sombre Lady (Sharpen Up 127) [2002 p8g f7g⁴ Nov 26] 8,500Y: half-brother to several winners abroad, including useful Italian performer up to 11f Mon Alexandrino (by Ezzoud) and US 1m winner Final Tango (by Danehill), 7f winner in Britain at 2 yrs: dam French winner around 9f: better effort in maidens (modest form) when fourth to Surdoue at Southwell: should stay 1m. *M. Blanshard*

IN SPIRIT (IRE)   4 b.g. Distinctly North (USA) 115 – June Goddess (Junius (USA)   **70 ?**
124) [2002 74: p7g Dec 30] fair performer at 3 yrs: down field only run in 2002: stays 1¼m: acts on firm going and fibresand: sometimes blinkered. *D. J. S. Cosgrove*

INSTANT HIT   3 b.c. Indian Ridge 123 – Pick of The Pops 109 (High Top 131) [2002   **64**
8m 9.2g 10s 8.3s⁴ 8m⁵ 7g Oct 4] 100,000Y: eighth foal: half-brother to 3 winners, including 1996 2-y-o 8.3f winner Fascinating Rhythm (by Slip Anchor) and 9-y-o Migwar (by Danehill): dam, 2-y-o 7f winner and second in Fillies' Mile, from excellent family: modest maiden: stays 1m: acts on good to firm going: tongue tied: races prominently: dropped away tamely fourth start: sold 3,500 gns. *M. L. W. Bell*

INSTANT THOUGHT (USA)   2 ch.f. (Mar 13) Kris S (USA) – Nimble Mind   **69 p**
(USA) 103 (Lyphard (USA) 132) [2002 8s Oct 25] useful-looking filly: third foal: dam, 2-y-o 1m winner in France and later second in US Grade 3 events up to 11f, sister to smart performer up to 10.4f Skimble, herself dam of very smart US 1¼m performer Skimming: 16/1 and backward, 10 lengths ninth of 22 to Richemaur in maiden at Doncaster, never a threat: should do better. *H. R. A. Cecil*

INTANGIBLE (USA)   3 ch.f. Diesis 133 – Flamboyance (USA) 94 (Zilzal (USA)   **86**
137) [2002 72p: 8.3m³ 9.9g 10g 12d Nov 1] fairly useful performer, lightly raced: stays 1¼m, probably not 1½m: acts on soft and good to firm going. *H. R. A. Cecil*

INTEGRATION   2 b.c. (May 10) Piccolo 121 – Discrimination 72 (Efisio 120) [2002   **57**
7.1m 7d p7g Oct 31] 11,000Y: smallish, quite attractive colt: first foal: dam, 7f winner, sister to useful 6f/7f performer Onlytime Will Tell: modest form in maidens: bred to prove best up to 7f. *P. W. Harris*

INTELLIBET ONE   2 b.f. (Apr 29) Compton Place 125 – Safe House 81§ (Lyphard   **74**
(USA) 132) [2002 5s* p5g² 5m³ 5.1f⁶ 5.2f 5.2f⁵ 5m³ 5.9m² 5m 6m Sep 30] leggy filly: half-sister to several winners, including fairly useful 1988 2-y-o 1m winner Ivory Tower (by Shirley Heights), later successful in USA, and 9f seller winner Northern Rainbow (by Rainbow Quest): dam temperamental 11f winner: fair performer: won maiden at Doncaster in March: good efforts when placed in nurseries at Musselburgh (final start for P. D. Evans) and Hamilton seventh/eighth starts: stays 6f: acts on good to firm going, soft and polytrack. *P. Monteith*

INTELLIBET TWO   2 b.g. (Apr 30) Tina's Pet 121 – Pondicherry (USA) 64 (Sir   **49**
Wimborne (USA) 118) [2002 5m 5.1f p5g⁶ 6m 5.2f Jun 24] 650Y: angular gelding: fifth living foal: half-brother to 3 winners, including 5f and (at 2 yrs) 6f winner Kirsch (by Wolfhound) and 1m (at 2 yrs) and 1¼m (in France) winner Teresa Balbi (by Master Willie): dam 7f winner: poor maiden: tried blinkered. *P. D. Evans*

INTERCEPTOR 2 ch.c. (May 11) Hector Protector (USA) 124 – Moorish Idol 90 **82 p**
(Aragon 118) [2002 8m⁵ 8g* Oct 16] 14,000Y: brother to a winner in Norway and
half-brother to several winners, including useful Scandinavian performer up to 1½m
Duty Time (by Night Shift), 7f/1m winner in Britain at 2 yrs: dam 2-y-o 6f winner who
probably stayed 1m: fairly useful form: justified favouritism in maiden at Bath by ½
length from Golden Heart (pair clear), leading 1f out: will probably stay 1¼m: capable of
better still. *J. W. Hills*

INTERCESSION 2 ch.f. (Mar 6) Bluebird (USA) 125 – Intercede (Pursuit of Love **90 p**
124) [2002 7m 8.3d 7m* Aug 26] 11,500Y, resold IR 16,000Y: good-bodied filly: first
foal: dam unraced half-sister to Interval (very smart at 6f to 1m) and Interim (smart up to
1½m) out of smart 1m/9f winner Intermission: progressive form in maidens: clearly best
effort when winning at Folkestone by 11 lengths from First Footing, quickening clear
over 1f out: reportedly suffered from ringworm after: should stay 1m: carried head high
second start: useful performer in the making. *P. W. Harris*

INTERCONTINENTAL 2 b.f. (Mar 19) Danehill (USA) 126 – Hasili (IRE) **105 p**
(Kahyasi 130) [2002 6.5g* 7g* 7g³ Oct 6]
  Owing to significantly fewer opportunities, and perhaps also a bolder
approach by owners and trainers, the temptation to run fillies in the top open events
for two-year-olds in France is greater than in Britain and has regularly been yielded
to. There is only one race above Group 3 level restricted to fillies in France—the
Group 1 Prix Marcel Boussac—whereas in Britain there are five such races,
including two Group 1s, the Cheveley Park Stakes and Fillies' Mile. In the last fifty
years fillies have won one running of the Dewhurst Stakes, with the French-trained
Torbella III in 1957 and, since it was initiated in 1961, one running of the Racing
Post Trophy, with Noblesse when it was run as the Timeform Gold Cup in 1962;
Fillies' Mile winners Ivanka and Fairy Heights both finished second in the Racing
Post Trophy in the early-'nineties. In contrast, fillies have made hay against the
colts in France, highlighted by fifteen victories in the Prix Morny, eleven in the Prix
de la Salamandre and eight in what has usually been the toughest of them all, the
Grand Criterium—Apollonia in 1955, Bella Paola in 1957, Hula Dancer in 1962,
Silver Cloud in 1966, Treizieme in 1983, Alydar's Best in 1984, Femme Elite in
1985 and Danishkada in 1986. Perhaps the practice is in decline, because Intercontinental was the first filly to contest the Grand Criterium since 1989, though
fillies won six other pattern events against colts during the year through Ela Merici
(Prix du Bois), Loving Kindness (Prix de Cabourg) and Zinziberine (Prix Eclipse
and Criterium de Maisons-Laffitte); Italian-trained Pleasure Place took the Prix
d'Arenberg and British-trained Never A Doubt the Prix Robert Papin.
  Intercontinental ran a smashing race to come third to Hold That Tiger in the
Grand Criterium, one which suggests she should add further to her family's kudos
as a three-year-old. The reduction in distance of the event in 2001 made it more
appealing for the right type of filly—the Prix Marcel Boussac is over a mile. With
Khalid Abdulla represented by the equally promising Etoile Montante in the longer

*Prix de la Potiniere, Deauville—Intercontinental makes a promising debut
an hour and a half before her sister Banks Hill wins the Jacques le Marois*

race, the Grand Criterium seemed the sensible option for Intercontinental, since seven furlongs was likely to suit her better than a mile as a juvenile. She arrived at Longchamp in October with a big reputation as the winner of both her starts in good style, a newcomers race over six furlongs at Deauville in August and a minor event over the course and distance of the Grand Criterium in September, when she scarcely came off the bridle in defeating Matakana by two lengths. The level of public confidence in Intercontinental was such that she started 17/10 favourite to beat thirteen rivals, most of whom had better form and were more battle hardened. Inexperience may have contributed to her undoing. After travelling strongly behind Le Vie dei Colori, and looking full of running when produced to challenge a furlong out, Intercontinental made no further progress once let down, finishing half a length and the same behind Hold That Tiger and Le Vie dei Colori. The experience should have done her a lot of good, though, and Intercontinental looks just the type to train on.

Intercontinental (b.f. Mar 19, 2000)	Danehill (USA) (b 1986)	Danzig (b 1977)	Northern Dancer
			Pas de Nom
		Razyana (b 1981)	His Majesty
			Spring Adieu
	Hasili (IRE) (b 1991)	Kahyasi (b 1985)	Ile de Bourbon
			Kadissya
		Kerali (ch 1984)	High Line
			Sookera

    Intercontinental's breeding provided reason for optimism even before she raced. She is a sister to two high-class performers in Banks Hill and Dansili, whose pedigrees have been dealt with in detail in recent editions of *Racehorses*. Hasili certainly throws impressive-looking stock—Dansili was described as strong, good-topped, Banks Hill is strong, lengthy and carries plenty of condition and Intercontinental is strong and good-bodied, also the type to carry plenty of condition. She should make into a fine-looking three-year-old. The mare's three-year-old, Heat Haze (by another son of Danzig, Green Desert) won the listed Prix Coronation over a mile at Maisons-Laffitte in September. Hasili's 2001 foal, another colt by Danehill, will be watched with interest; she was barren to the same sire in 2002 and returned to him. Banks Hill stays a mile and a quarter and Dansili was best at a mile, over which trip he would have won the Breeders' Cup Mile with better luck in running. There is no guarantee that Intercontinental will be fully effective at a mile, but, with time, she could well be so. It will come as no surprise to see her line up for the One Thousand Guineas, especially if the ground is on the firm side, placing the emphasis on speed. Dansili and Banks Hill seemed suited by such conditions, and Intercontinental's connections are of the opinion that she will follow suit—so far she has raced only on good going. While she has quite a bit to find on form, the same applies to most of the other hopefuls other than Six Perfections, and it would be dangerous to underestimate her. *A. Fabre, France*

INTERNATIONALGUEST (IRE) 3 b.c. Petardia 113 – Banco Solo (Distant Relative 128) [2002 73: 7.1g 8.3s* 8m³ 8g³ 8g 10s* 8.2v* Oct 29] tall, close-coupled colt: useful handicapper: won at Windsor in May and Nottingham (2) in October: all out to beat Oakley Rambo by neck on final occasion: stays 1¼m: acts on good to firm going, goes particularly well on soft/heavy: blinkered/visored. *G. G. Margarson*   **100**

INTERSTICE 5 b.h. Never So Bold 135 – Mainmast 63 (Bustino 136) [2002 p7g p7g f7g⁵ 8.1m 9s p10g⁶ 12g 12.1s⁴ 10.9g³ 12s² f12g³ f12g* Dec 27] 5,000Y: half-brother to several winners, including fairly useful 1½m winner Progression (by Reprimand) and 7f (at 2 yrs) to 1½m winner Instantaneous (by Rock City): dam ran twice: winner twice in Czech Republic: modest handicapper in Britain: won at Southwell in December: stays easy 1½m: acts on soft ground and all-weather: takes strong hold. *A. G. Newcombe*   **50 a61**

INTER VISION (USA) 2 b.c. (May 12) Cryptoclearance (USA) – Fateful (USA) 90 (Topsider (USA)) [2002 5f² 5s² 5.1m* 5m* 5.1f* 5g 5g Aug 21] $20,000Y: tall colt: sixth foal: half-brother to 3 winners, including smart 7f/1m winner Fatefully (by Private Account) and fairly useful 6f/7f performer Dark Mile (by Woodman): dam, 6f (at 2 yrs) and 7f winner, out of half-sister to US Grade 1 7f winner Devil's Orchid: useful performer: won maiden at Chester and minor event at Ripon in June and minor event at Chester in July: stiff tasks, well held in Molecomb Stakes at Goodwood and listed race at   **96**

York last 2 starts: may prove best at 5f: yet to race on heavy ground, seems to act on any other. *A. Dickman*

INTHAAR 5 b.g. Nashwan (USA) 135 – Twafeaj (USA) 110 (Topsider (USA)) [2002 –, a58: f12s³ f12s⁵ f11g f12g⁵ f12g 7s f9.4g⁶ 8.3g 8g f12g⁶ f12g⁵ Jul 11] poor performer: **a45** stays 1½m: acts on fibresand, lightly raced and well beaten on polytrack/turf: blinkered/visored. *R. Brotherton*

IN THE ARENA (USA) 5 ch.g. Cadeaux Genereux 131 – Tajfah (USA) (Shadeed – (USA) 135) [2002 –: f8s Jan 1] big, strong gelding: fair 7f winner in 2000: has shown nothing since. *D. Shaw*

IN THE CLOUDS 2 b.g. (May 28) Cloudings (IRE) 112 – Tread Carefully 51 (Sharpo – 132) [2002 7.1v 8.5m 8.1m Sep 6] leggy gelding: fifth foal: half-brother to 3-y-o Hurricane Coast: dam, maiden who stayed 1m, half-sister to high-class stayer and Champion Hurdle winner Royal Gait: no encouragement in maidens. *T. D. Easterby*

IN THE FRAME (IRE) 3 b.g. Definite Article 121 – Victorian Flower (Tate Gallery **82** (USA) 117) [2002 69: 10m 10m 10g⁵ 8m* 8d⁵ 7g 7.6m² 7g 8.1g⁶ 9g² Oct 5] quite good-topped gelding: fairly useful handicapper: won at Salisbury in June: ran well final start, best at 1m/9f: acts on firm and good to soft going: sometimes carried head awkwardly at 2 yrs: sold 21,000 gns. *R. Hannon*

IN THE GLOAMING (IRE) 2 b.f. (Apr 26) Avarice – Katherine Kath (Merdon **40** Melody 98) [2002 6v³ 6g⁵ 5g⁵ 6d 5s Nov 6] first foal: dam showed little in Irish bumpers: poor maiden. *D. Moffatt*

IN THE GREEN 3 b.g. Greensmith 121 – Carn Maire 83 (Northern Prospect (USA)) – [2002 72: 6g 6f 6d 6g 5m 5f 5d 5g 5m Aug 28] good-topped gelding: has a short action: fair performer for R. Fahey at 2 yrs: little form in 2002: visored final start. *J. J. Quinn*

IN THE STARS (IRE) 4 ch.g. Definite Article 121 – Astronomer Lady (IRE) **68** (Montekin 125) [2002 60: p12g p13g⁴ Dec 28] fair maiden: gelded and off 14 months before creditable efforts both starts in 2002: stays 13f: acts on polytrack. *P. R. Webber*

IN TIME'S EYE 3 b.c. Singspiel (IRE) 133 – Irish Edition 83 (Alleged (USA) 138) **112** [2002 92p: 10m² 12d 9g* 10d² Oct 28] tall colt: has scope: half-brother to several winners, notably Belmont Stakes winner Go And Go and smart Irish 1¼m winner Off'n'Away (both by Be My Guest): dam, Irish 9.5f winner, half-sister to Breeders' Cup Classic second Twilight Agenda and to dam of Media Puzzle: smart performer, lightly raced: straightforward task when landing odds in maiden at Fairyhouse in October: much better form behind High Chaparral first 2 starts when length second in Derrinstown Stud Derby Trial at Leopardstown and 9½ lengths seventh in Irish Derby at the Curragh, and when 2 lengths second to Ice Dancer in listed race at Leopardstown final outing: at least as effective at 1½m as 1¼m: acts on good to firm and good to soft going (promising effort on soft on debut). *D. K. Weld, Ireland*

INTO THE BLUE (IRE) 3 b.g. Blues Traveller (IRE) 119 – Lux Aeterna (Sandhurst – Prince 128) [2002 p8g⁶ p10g 10g 7g 8m Aug 29] 8,000F: IR 3,500Y: tall gelding: half-brother to 3 winners, including 1m winner Rhapsody In White (by Contract Law): dam ran twice in Ireland: little sign of ability in maidens. *T. M. Jones*

INTO THE BREEZE (IRE) 2 b.c. (May 7) Alzao (USA) 117 – Catalane (USA) **93** (Septieme Ciel (USA) 123) [2002 6f 6.1s³ p6g* Jul 10] 14,000Y: good-bodied colt: third foal: half-brother to French 2000 2-y-o 1m winner La Fontainiere (by Kaldoun): dam, French 5f (at 2 yrs) to 7f winner, out of sister to smart sprinter King's Signet: fairly useful form: clearly best effort when winning maiden at Lingfield by 1¼ lengths from Wathiq, quickening well final 1f: suffered minor injury after: should prove best up to 1m. *J. W. Hills*

INTRICAT 2 ch.c. (Mar 10) Bluegrass Prince (IRE) 110 – Noble Soul 67 (Sayf El – Arab (USA) 127) [2002 7d 7g Jul 18] fifth living foal: half-brother to 6-y-o Jessinca: dam lightly-raced 1m winner: no show in maidens. *A. P. Jones*

INTRICATE WEB (IRE) 6 b.g. Warning 136 – In Anticipation (IRE) 93 (Sadler's **87** Wells (USA) 132) [2002 91, a99: f7s f7g⁴ f7g⁶ 6s 7f 8f 7f 7.9s² 7.9d⁶ 10g* 10m* 12s f8g⁴ **a93** p10g Dec 21] sturdy, angular gelding: fairly useful handicapper: won at Ripon (dead-heated) in July and Redcar in October: effective at 7f to easy 1¼m: well beaten on heavy going, acts on any other on turf and on fibresand: tried blinkered/visored, not since 2000: sometimes slowly away. *E. J. Alston*

INTRODUCING (USA) 2 b.f. (Mar 31) Deputy Minister (CAN) – Interim 117 **81 p** (Sadler's Wells (USA) 132) [2002 7g² Oct 14] smallish filly: shows knee action: third foal: half-sister to useful 1¼m/1½m winner Staging Post (by Pleasant Colony), later smart up to 1¾m in USA: dam, 1m to 1½m (US Grade 2) winner, half-sister to very smart 6f to 1m performer Interval: 20/1, 1½ lengths second of 17 to Star Sensation in maiden at Leicester, staying on strongly under hands and heels: should be suited by 1¼m/1½m: sure to improve. *B. W. Hills*

IN TUNE 2 b.g. (Apr 26) Distinctly North (USA) 115 – Lingering 96 (Kind of Hush **61** 118) [2002 6d p7g p6g p8g p7g Dec 28] half-brother to 5f (at 2 yrs)/6f winner Jobie (by Precocious): dam 2-y-o 5f winner: modest maiden: stays 7f: acts on polytrack: sometimes slowly away. *P. Mitchell*

INVADER 6 b.h. Danehill (USA) 126 – Donya 74 (Mill Reef (USA) 141) [2002 87§, **95 §** a96§: f8.5g* f8.5g 8d 8d* 7g⁶ 8.9d⁶ 8m² 7m 8f 7.6f 8m Sep 14] big, strong horse: carries **a97 §** condition: useful handicapper: won at Wolverhampton in February and Ripon in May: good ½-length second to Norton in Royal Hunt Cup at Royal Ascot, never headed on far side: lacklustre efforts after: best at 1m/easy 1¼m: acts on firm going, good to soft and all-weather: effective blinkered/visored or not: has worn crossed noseband: sometimes finds little: often soon off bridle: untrustworthy. *C. E. Brittain*

INVENTING PARADISE (USA) 4 ch.f. Mr Prospector (USA) – Miesque (USA) **96** 133 (Nureyev (USA) 131) [2002 105: 8d 6s 6m Aug 18] rather leggy filly: sister to high-class miler Kingmambo and smart 6f/7f performer Miesque's Son, closely related to useful 1m winner Moon Is Up (by Woodman) and half-sister to very smart 1m and 10.5f winner East of The Moon (by Private Account): dam top-class miler: useful performer, lightly raced: won minor event at Maisons-Laffitte at 2 yrs: good efforts in frame there in Prix de Seine-et-Oise and listed race last 2 starts in 2001: respectable efforts at best at 4 yrs, getting bit worked up in paddock when down field in listed race at Pontefract final outing: effective at 6f/7f: raced mainly on good going or softer: sent to USA. *J. E. Hammond, France*

Moyglare Stud Farm's "In Time's Eye"

INVER GOLD 5 ch.h. Arazi (USA) 135 – Mary Martin (Be My Guest (USA) 126) **69**
[2002 74: f9.4g* p12g f9.4g⁶ f9.4g⁶ f9.4g⁶ f11g⁴ f12g² f12g² 12d⁴ f12g* 11.9d⁵ 12d **a82**
11.8g⁴ 12d³ 12m⁵ 9s f11g⁵ Nov 26] lengthy horse: poor mover: fairly useful handicapper
on all-weather, fair on turf: won at Wolverhampton in January, March and June: stays
1½m: acts on all-weather, good to firm and good to soft going: often takes while to warm
to task. *A. G. Newcombe*

INVERMARK 8 b.g. Machiavellian (USA) 123 – Applecross 117 (Glint of Gold 128) **117**
[2002 114: 20m 16.4m² 20m Jun 20] tall, workmanlike gelding: very smart performer
at best: won Prix du Cadran at Longchamp in 1998, and second in Gold Cup at Royal
Ascot in 1999: missed 2000 (reportedly due to suspensory trouble): back to near best last
2 starts in 2002, ½-length second to Akbar in Henry II Stakes at Sandown and 5 lengths
seventh to Royal Rebel in steadily-run Gold Cup at Royal Ascot (unable to be covered up
and took strong hold): stayed 2½m: acted on heavy and good to firm going: sweating and
edgy on reappearance: seemed best held up: difficult ride (flashed tail under pressure):
retired. *J. R. Fanshawe*

INVERNESS 2 ch.g. (Feb 13) Inchinor 119 – Inimitable 66 (Polish Precedent (USA) **62 p**
131) [2002 f8d⁵ f2d⁶ Oct 24] 10,000Y: second foal: half-brother to 3 y o Royal Approval:
dam, 1¼m winner, out of half-sister to Melbourne Cup winner Jeune: modest form in
maidens: not knocked about when sixth to Coustou at Brighton (gelded after): should stay
at least 1¼m: remains capable of better. *J. R. Fanshawe*

INVESTMENT AFFAIR (IRE) 2 b.c. (Apr 25) Sesaro (USA) 81 – Superb In- **– p**
vestment (IRE) (Hatim (USA) 121) [2002 6g⁶ Aug 7] IR 7,000Y: fourth living foal:
half-brother to useful 1m (at 2 yrs) to 15f winner Cool Investment (by Prince of Birds)
and 1998 2-y-o 7f seller winner Investment Hero (by Imperial Frontier): dam champion
2-y-o filly in Czechoslovakia: 7/1, disputed lead until 2f out when well held in maiden at
Newcastle: should do better. *M. Johnston*

INVICTA 3 b.f. Distant Relative 128 – Blue Zulu (IRE) 94 (Don't Forget Me 127) **78**
[2002 10s 10s⁴ 10m* 10.5m³ 12d 9.9m³ 8g³ 10s p10g⁴ Dec 11] second foal: dam, 1m
winner (stayed 1¼m), half-sister to smart pair Showbrook (sprinter) and Smarginato
(at 1m/1¼m): fair performer: won maiden at Ripon in June: unlikely to stay beyond
10.5f: acts on polytrack, best turf efforts on good going or firmer: tried tongue tied.
J. R. Fanshawe

INVINCIBLE SPIRIT (IRE) 5 b.h. Green Desert (USA) 127 – Rafha 123 (Kris **121**
135) [2002 115: 6m⁴ 6f* 5m⁵ 6m⁶ 6m* Sep 7]

Trainer John Dunlop needed invincible spirit in more ways than one in
2002. In February, he was rushed to hospital from his yard in Arundel with a ruptured aorta, reportedly within minutes of death, and in recuperation he was afflicted by
a 'superbug' followed by dangerously low haemoglobin levels. Happily, Dunlop's
recovery allowed him to pass a career milestone of three thousand winners worldwide when Rahwaan won at Chepstow in June and, though the stable's three-yearolds in general were a low-key bunch in 2002, Invincible Spirit and the other older
horses compensated with some notable highlights. The five-year-olds Millenary
and Give Notice won major prizes, while Invincible Spirit, a former invalid himself
before a successful comeback in 2001, completed his own recuperation with two
pattern-race victories at the same age.

Invincible Spirit capped his career with victory in the Group 1 Stanley
Leisure Sprint Cup at Haydock in September. Looking in outstanding shape, he
nonetheless started at 25/1 in a field of fourteen, which included the July Cup
winner Continent and the Prix Maurice de Gheest winner May Ball plus favourite
Nayyir and St James's Palace Stakes runner-up Landseer. In the event, none of
those rivals ran to form on the day and it was the Golden Jubilee winner Malhub
that came closest to preventing Invincible Spirit pulling off a surprise. In a muddling contest, which saw many in the field pulling for their heads as the Japanese
challenger Air Thule set a steady pace up the centre of the course, Invincible Spirit
was soon moving typically well just off the pace. Malhub looked to have beaten
him to the punch when seemingly in control at the head of affairs approaching the
final furlong, but Invincible Spirit responded gamely to jockey John Carroll's
driving to come out the better by a short head with Three Points two lengths back in
third. On the day, Invincible Spirit, who gave his rider a first Group 1 winner, beat
Malhub fairly and squarely, but, very smart though it is, the form doesn't measure

up to Malhub's subsequent effort in finishing second in the Diadem Stakes at Ascot, conceding weight all round.

It may be easy to say now, but Invincible Spirit should never have started at 25/1 at Haydock. Presumably, he hadn't been himself when only sixth in the Golden Jubilee Stakes at Royal Ascot on his previous start, and he had shown himself better than ever in the spring. As a result of a penalty for his Group 3 success in the Boland Stakes at the Curragh on his final start as a four-year-old, he was up against it at the weights in minor pattern company at the start of the year. He conceded weight all round when two lengths fourth to Reel Buddy in the Abernant Stakes at Newmarket on his reappearance in April and followed that effort with a win in the Group 3 Duke of York Stakes (to be Group 2 in 2003) in May. Invincible Spirit had to concede 5 lb to most of his eleven rivals at York, but he showed a good turn of foot to get the better of Mugharreb by a neck under Michael Kinane. He didn't get the best of runs when only fifth of eleven behind four-length winner Kyllachy in the Temple Stakes over five furlongs at Sandown on his next start.

Invincible Spirit is the third son of Green Desert to have emulated his sire in winning the Haydock Sprint Cup. Of the first two, Sheikh Albadou died in 1999 and Tamarisk proved a flop at stud before returning to the track, so there's room for a sprint stallion by Green Desert, who received another timely boost in 2002 when Oasis Dream won the Middle Park Stakes. Invincible Spirit, who will be at the Irish National Stud in 2003 at a fee of €10,000, Oct 1st terms, is certainly bred well enough to make a successful sire. His dam Rafha won the Prix de Diane for Henry Cecil and has proved a notable success at stud. Her first six foals to race have all been useful or better. Her third, Sadian (by Shirley Heights), was the best of them prior to Invincible Spirit and won the John Porter Stakes and the Ormonde Stakes, while Fnan (by Generous) and Aquarius (by Royal Academy) were useful over a distance of ground, as was Al Widyan (by Slip Anchor) at around a mile and a half. Three-year-old Massarra (by Danehill), the only filly out of Rafha to have raced, was useful at six/seven furlongs in the latest season, when two-year-old Voyager (by Green Desert), Rafha's seventh foal to race, also showed some promise. Invincible Spirit's grandam Eljazzi has also produced the smart middle-distance stayer Chiang Mai. Invincible Spirit never raced much beyond seven furlongs and

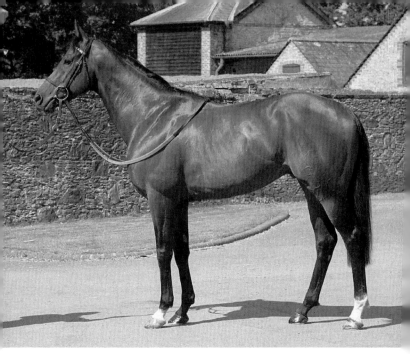

Invincible Spirit (IRE) (b.h. 1997)	Green Desert (USA) (b 1983)	Danzig (b 1977)	Northern Dancer
			Pas de Nom
		Foreign Courier (b 1979)	Sir Ivor
			Courtly Dee
	Rafha (b 1987)	Kris (ch 1976)	Sharpen Up
			Doubly Sure
		Eljazzi (b 1981)	Atraius
			Border Bounty

showed his best form at six. He won seven of his seventeen races, the first two as a juvenile, when he also started favourite for the Middle Park. Despite suffering a broken pelvis in the spring as a three-year-old, he was only once raced on ground other than good or firmer afterwards. A strong, well-made sort, a typical sprinter in appearance, Invincible Spirit had a powerful, round action. Usually equipped with a crossed noseband, he was waited with in his races. *J. L. Dunlop*

INVITADO (IRE) 3 ch.g. Be My Guest (USA) 126 – Lady Dulcinea (ARG) (General (FR)) [2002 –: 12.1g 9.9g 12f Jul 17] leggy gelding: little form: tried blinkered. *J. G. FitzGerald* —   **–**

INVITATION 4 b.g. Bin Ajwaad (IRE) 119 – On Request (IRE) 53 (Be My Guest (USA) 126) [2002 84: 10f 10m 10s 10.2v² 10.1d⁶ 10d* 9.2s³ 10s* 10s 10d Nov 1] angular gelding: fairly useful handicapper: won at Newmarket in August and Leicester in October: likely to prove best short of 1½m: raced mainly on good going or softer (acts on heavy): sometimes races freely/carries head high: none too consistent. *A. Charlton*   **85**

IN XANADU (IRE) 3 b.g. Persian Bold 123 – Dromoland (Cadeaux Genereux 131) [2002 72p: 8.2d² 8m 8d⁵ 7d⁴ 7.6m 10.2g² 10s Oct 23] small gelding: fair maiden handi-   **75**

capper: effective at 1m/1¼m: acts on good to soft going, below form on good to firm: visored/blinkered last 2 starts: gelded after final start. *J. L. Dunlop*

INZACURE (IRE)   4 b.g. Inzar (USA) 112 – Whittingham Girl 58 (Primo Dominie   **59** 121) [2002 –: 6m⁴ 5.1d 6g 6m Jun 29] small gelding: modest handicapper: stays 6f: acts on soft ground and fibresand: broke blood vessel reappearance/final start. *R. M. Beckett*

INZARMOOD (IRE)   4 b.f. Inzar (USA) 112 – Pepilin (Coquelin (USA) 121) [2002   **46 §** –, a42: f8s³ f8.5g f8s f9.4g⁴ f11g² p12g Mar 25] neat filly: poor maiden: stays 11f: acts on fibresand: visored/blinkered: sometimes flashes tail: inconsistent. *K. R. Burke*

IONA   3 b.f. Celtic Swing 138 – Circe 73 (Main Reef 126) [2002 8.3m 8.1m 10g⁵ 12f 12.1g Jul 30] rather leggy filly: seventh foal: half-sister to 3 winners, including fairly useful 9f to 1½m winner My Learned Friend (by Broken Hearted): dam 1m winner who stayed 1¼m: little sign of ability: visored final start. *R. M. Beckett*

IONIAN SPRING (IRE)   7 b.g. Ela-Mana-Mou 132 – Well Head (IRE) (Sadler's   **89** Wells (USA) 132) [2002 89: 10d* 10.1g⁵ 10.4f³ 10m 10s⁶ 12v Nov 9] sturdy gelding: fairly useful handicapper: won at Nottingham in March: stays easy 1½m: acts on firm going, good to soft and fibresand: tends to edge left: waited with. *C. G. Cox*

IPANEMA BEACH   5 ch.m. Lion Cavern (USA) 117 – Girl From Ipanema 106   **62** (Salse (USA) 128) [2002 65: f8g f6g² Feb 2] lengthy, angular mare: modest performer: effective at 6f to 8.5f: acts on fibresand, best turf run on good going: visored (ran creditably) final start. *Andrew Reid*

I PROMISE YOU   5 b.g. Shareef Dancer (USA) 135 – Abuzz 101 (Absalom 128)   **–** [2002 64, a61: p8g⁴ p10g² p10g f8g p7g p7g⁵ 8m p10g⁶ 7m⁶ 8d Dec 3] small, sturdy   **a57** gelding: modest performer: sold from C. Brittain 1,200 gns before final start: effective at 7f to easy 1¼m: acts on firm going and all-weather: blinkered in Britain. *M. Mureddu, Italy*

IPSA LOQUITUR   2 b.f. (Feb 4) Unfuwain (USA) 131 – Plaything 69 (High Top   **69 p** 131) [2002 p8g⁴ Dec 14] sister to 1½m and 2m winner Little Acorn, and half-sister to 2 winners, including 1¾m selling winner Slip of The Tongue (by Slip Anchor): dam lightly-raced 1m winner: 33/1, shaped well when fourth of 12 to Made In Japan in maiden at Lingfield, held up travelling well before staying on strongly under hands and heels (reportedly found to be lame): should be suited by 1½m+: should improve. *S. C. Williams*

IRIE RASTA (IRE)   3 ch.g. Desert King (IRE) 129 – Seeds of Doubt (IRE) (Night   **81** Shift (USA)) [2002 62: 10g 11.6m 11.6s⁴ 11.8m⁵ 14d* 14m* 16.2d³ 14g⁵ 11.7f 12m⁶ 14.4m² 14m 14.1g Oct 2] big, strong gelding: fairly useful handicapper: won at Goodwood (maiden event) in June and Haydock in July: likely to stay 2m: acts on good to firm and good to soft going: on toes/keen in preliminaries for latter win: found little last 2 starts: gelded after final outing. *S. Kirk*

IRISH BLESSING (USA)   5 b.g. Ghazi (USA) – Win For Leah (USA) (His Majesty   **–** (USA)) [2002 –: 14.1d 14.1d f16.2g 16.2m Jun 17] sturdy, angular gelding: fair performer at best: no form since 3 yrs (had breathing problem penultimate start): usually blinkered. *F. Jordan*

IRISH CREAM (IRE)   6 b.m. Petong 126 – Another Baileys 60 (Deploy 131) [2002   **–** –, a50: f12g³ f12g* f12g⁶ f12g⁴ f14.8g f14.8g f12g⁶ f12g* f14.8g Jul 1] small, work-   **a50** manlike mare: modest performer: won amateur handicap at Wolverhampton in February and claimer there in June: best at 1½m: acts on fibresand and heavy going: visored/blinkered: tried tongue tied: reportedly had breathing problem fifth start. *J. L. Spearing*

IRISH DISTINCTION (IRE)   4 b.g. Distinctly North (USA) 115 – Shane's Girl   **65** (IRE) (Marktino) [2002 73d: 10m p12g* 12d 10.9m² f14.8g⁵ f10.4g⁶ 10.4f* Oct 10] good-bodied gelding: fair performer: rejoined former trainer from S. Earle after reappearance: won seller at Lingfield in August and claimer at York (subsequently joined M. Pipe £10,000) in October: stays 1½m: acts on firm going and polytrack, probably on fibresand: sometimes races freely/flashes tail. *A. P. Jarvis*

IRISH FLOWER (IRE)   5 b.m. Zieten (USA) 118 – Sally St Clair (Sallust 134) [2002   **99** 7g² 6d⁶ 7d³ 7m 8g 6g Sep 11] raw-boned, useful-looking mare: half-sister to numerous winners, notably smart winner up to 11f in Ireland/UAE Doreg (by Fools Holme): dam, winner in Canada, half-sister to smart sprinter Superlative: useful performer: won apprentice race at Clairefontaine and handicap at Longchamp at 4 yrs: ran well first 3 starts in 2002, including when placed in minor event at Longchamp and listed race (½-length third to Chercheuse) at Le Lion d'Angers: well beaten in handicaps last 3 starts, first of them Tote International at Ascot: effective at 6f to 1m: acts on good to firm and good to soft ground: has had tongue tied: blinkered final start. *R. Gibson, France*

IRMA LA DOUCE (IRE) 3 b. or br.f. Elbio 125 – Eves Temptation (IRE) (Glenstal **62** (USA) 118) [2002 7s 6m² 5m³ 5g⁵ 6m⁶ 6.9m Aug 21] neat filly: fourth foal: sister to 5-y-o Budelli: dam unraced: modest maiden: stays 6f: acts on good to firm going. *M. R. Channon*

IRON DRAGON (IRE) 4 b.g. Royal Academy (USA) 130 – Kerry Project (IRE) 79 **48** (Project Manager 111) [2002 –: 10m 10.1m 10m 9.2g⁵ 15.8m⁵ Aug 6] quite attractive gelding: poor nowadays: probably stays 1¼m, not 2m: tongue tied prior to 2002. *Mrs M. Reveley*

IRON LAD (IRE) 2 b.c. (Apr 15) Mukaddamah (USA) 125 – Truffle Pig (Formidable **96** (USA) 125) [2002 5g⁵ 5m⁴ 6m² 6.1s* 6d⁵ 7d³ 6g⁴ 7.2g³ 7f⁵ 7s⁶ Oct 25] IR 13,000F, IR 24,000Y: leggy colt: second foal: dam, German 7.5f winner, sister to useful 2-y-o in Britain/performer up to 9f in USA Take A Left: useful performer: won maiden at Chepstow in June: best efforts when close third to Go Tech in minor event at Ayr and 7 lengths sixth to Makhlab in Horris Hill Stakes at Newbury eighth/final starts: effective at 6f/7f: acts on soft and good to firm going: sold 62,000 gns, sent to USA. *M. G. Quinlan*

IRON MOUNTAIN (IRE) 7 b.g. Scenic 128 – Merlannah (IRE) (Shy Groom (USA)) **73** [2002 86. p12g p12g 10f Oct 2] good-topped gelding: handicapper: fair form at 7 yrs only on reappearance: off 8½ months before final start: stays 11.5f: acts on polytrack, firm and soft going: blinkered once at 2 yrs: has wandered: usually held up. *Mrs L. C. Jewell*

IRON WARRIOR (IRE) 2 b.c. (May 7) Lear Fan (USA) 130 – Robalana (USA) **58** (Wild Again (USA)) [2002 5m 7v f8g⁴ᵈ Nov 25] IR 24,000F, IR 24,000Y: workmanlike colt: has scope: fourth foal: half-brother to a winner in US by Bahri: dam, 8.5f winner in US, out of half-sister to Dowsing and US Grade 1 9.5f winner Fire The Groom, latter dam of Stravinsky: best effort (modest form) when well-held fourth in minor event at Southwell (disqualified after rider failed to weigh in): should stay beyond 1m. *G. M. Moore*

Moyglare Stud Farms Ltd's "Irresistible Jewel"

Ribblesdale Stakes, Royal Ascot—Irresistible Jewel finishes to some tune after being switched to the outside and overhauls Shadow Dancing (centre), Red Rioja (left), Fraulein (spots) and Alexander Three D (noseband)

IRONY (IRE) 3 gr.g. Mujadil (USA) 119 – Cidaris (IRE) (Persian Bold 123) [2002 102: 6d⁴ 7f³ 8m³ 7m 7m 6m Sep 4] good-topped gelding: useful performer: creditable third in listed events at Newmarket and Kempton (beaten 2½ lengths by Hero's Journey) second/third starts: well below form after, including in Jersey Stakes at Royal Ascot next time (subsequently left J. Osborne): seems to stay easy 1m: acts on firm and good to soft going: tongue tied last 2 outings: has worn crossed noseband: often early to post: usually races up with pace. *I. A. Balding* **105**

IROQUOIS CHIEF (USA) 3 b.c. Known Fact (USA) 135 – Celtic Shade (Lomond (USA) 128) [2002 66p: f7g² 6.1f³ 7m⁴ 6f² f6g* f7g⁵ 6f⁶ f6g 6s 7m 7m⁵ 6g 7m 7m⁶ f6g p8g² 8g f8.5g p7g f6g Dec 20] good-topped colt: fair performer: won claimer at Wolverhampton (claimed from M. Bell) in June: stays easy 1m: acts on firm going and all-weather: visored final outing: tried tongue tied: on downgrade. *C. N. Kellett* **69 d**

IRRAWADDY (USA) 2 g.r.c. (May 4) Nureyev (USA) 131 – Jewel of The Mile (USA) (Spectacular Bid (USA)) [2002 5s* 5m 6f⁶ Oct 3] $650,000Y: quite good-topped colt: closely related to a winner in USA by Dixieland Band and half-brother to several winners abroad: dam unraced half-sister to dam of very smart French performer up to 11f Welkin: useful form: won 3-runner maiden at Tipperary in May: 33/1, clearly best effort when 6¾ lengths sixth to Oasis Dream in Middle Park Stakes at Newmarket, leading for nearly 4f: bred to stay at least 7f: acts on firm ground, successful on soft: hung when well held in Norfolk Stakes at Royal Ascot second start. *A. P. O'Brien, Ireland* **105**

IRRESISTIBLE 2 b.f. (Mar 12) Cadeaux Genereux 131 – Polish Romance (USA) 83 (Danzig (USA)) [2002 5g² 5g* 6m* 6g² 7m⁶ Oct 19] sturdy, lengthy filly: second foal: dam 7f winner out of US Grade 1 2-y-o 7f/1m winner Some Romance: useful performer: won minor event at Newcastle in August and nursery at York (idled) in September: best efforts when 1½ lengths second to Airwave in listed event at Ayr and 5¼ lengths sixth to Luvah Girl in Rockfel Stakes at Newmarket (faded): barely stays 7f: raced only on good/ good to firm ground: sometimes bandaged hind joints. *M. L. W. Bell* **96**

IRRESISTIBLE JEWEL (IRE) 3 b.f. Danehill (USA) 126 – In Anticipation (IRE) 93 (Sadler's Wells (USA) 132) [2002 78p: 8s³ 10s* 12m* 12d 11.9m⁵ 10m* 10g² 11f Nov 24] tall, lengthy, angular filly: has scope: fourth foal: half-sister to 3 useful winners in Ireland, including 1m winner Legal Jousting (by Indian Ridge) and 1m to 1½m winner Diamond Trim (by Highest Honor): dam Irish 1½m/1¾m winner: smart performer: won maiden at Naas and Ribblesdale Stakes at Royal Ascot (by ¾ length from Shadow Dancing) in June and Aga Khan Studs Blandford Stakes at the Curragh (beat Chorist ½ length) in September: ran well when 4 lengths second to Bright Sky in Prix de l'Opera at Longchamp penultimate start, well held in Japan Cup at Nakayama final outing: should be as effective at 1½m as 1¼m: successful on soft ground, very best efforts on good/good to firm. *D. K. Weld, Ireland* **115**

IRVINGTON (IRE) 4 br.c. Lahib (USA) 129 – Snoozy Time 65 (Cavo Doro 124) [2002 81: p10g 10g 10f 10.2d 10s² 10m² 10g⁵ 10m* 10g Aug 8] rangy colt: fairly useful handicapper: won at Windsor in July: stays easy 1¼m: acts on polytrack, soft and good to firm ground: blinkered last 4 starts: sold 15,000 gns, sent to USA. *R. Hannon* **82**

481

Mollers Racing's "Island House"

ISA'AF (IRE) 3 b.c. Darshaan 133 – Shauna's Honey (IRE) 88 (Danehill (USA) 126) **61**
[2002 8m 8.3d May 7] 85,000F, 200,000Y: neat colt: first foal: dam, Irish 7f winner who
stayed 1m, half-sister to smart performer up to 1½m Ahohoney: better effort in maidens
when ninth at Newbury (wore crossed noseband) on debut: slowly away next time: sold
2,000 gns in September. *A. C. Stewart*

ISAZ 2 b.c. (Mar 29) Elmaamul (USA) 125 – Pretty Poppy 67 (Song 132) [2002 5m **86**
6m² 6d⁵ Oct 14] 18,000Y: good sort: half-brother to several sprint winners, including
3-y-o Follow Flanders and 4-y-o Kyllachy: dam 2-y-o 5f winner who stayed 7.6f: fairly
useful form in maidens: best effort when 2 lengths second to Marching Band at Newbury,
staying on: favourite, only fifth at Windsor: will probably stay 7f. *H. Candy*

ISCHIA 3 ch.f. Lion Cavern (USA) 117 – Royal Passion 78 (Ahonoora 122) [2002 64: **–**
7.5m 9.9m 7f May 11] unfurnished filly: modest maiden at 2 yrs: disappointing for new
trainer in 2002. *Mrs J. R. Ramsden*

ISENGARD (USA) 2 b. or br.f. (Feb 13) Cobra King (USA) 122 – January Moon **75 p**
(USA) (Apalachee (USA) 137) [2002 6m p5g* Nov 13] IR 95,000Y: third foal: sister to
fairly useful 7f (at 2 yrs) and 8.5f (in USA) winner Lunar Sovereign: dam, winning
sprinter in USA, half-sister to useful Irish sprinter Flawless Image: much better effort in
maidens (fair form) when winning at Lingfield by 3½ lengths from Redwood Star: should
stay at least 6f: should improve further. *B. J. Meehan*

ISHELA (IRE) 3 gr.f. Barathea (IRE) 127 – Lalandria (FR) (Highest Honor (FR) 124) **51**
[2002 10m³ 10m Oct 7] IR 25,000Y: sturdy filly: second foal: dam French 11f to 13.5f
winner: modest form in maiden at Pontefract on debut: well held in similar event
following month. *H. R. A. Cecil*

482

ISHTAK   3 ch.f. Nashwan (USA) 135 – Colorsnap (Shirley Heights 130) [2002 9.9m⁴ **90**
10g³ 12m* 14.6m⁵ 12g Sep 27] 500,000Y: tall, lengthy filly: half-sister to several
winners, including useful performer up to 1½m Croeso Cariad (by Most Welcome) and
fairly useful Irish 1997 2-y-o 6f/7f winner Photogenic (by Midyan): dam unraced half-
sister to Irish Oaks winner Colorspin, herself dam of Opera House and Kayf Tara: fairly
useful performer: won maiden at Kempton in July: good fifth in Park Hill Stakes at
Doncaster next time, though folded tamely: tailed off in listed event at Ascot final
start: barely stayed 14.6f: raced only on good/good to firm going: visits Kingmambo.
J. H. M. Gosden

ISLA AZUL (IRE)   2 ch.f. (Feb 16) Machiavellian (USA) 123 – Nuryana 107 (Nureyev **74 p**
(USA) 131) [2002 6f 7m 7g⁶ Oct 14] compact filly: sister to very smart 7f/1m winner
Rebecca Sharp and half-sister to several winners, including smart 1m and 11.5f winner
Mystic Knight (by Caerleon): dam 1m winner out of half-sister to 1000 Guineas winner
On The House: progressive form in maidens: never-nearer sixth to Star Sensation at
Leicester, not at all knocked about: raced freely second start, but bred to stay 1m: almost
certain to do better still. *G. Wragg*

ISLAND DESTINY   3 ch.f. Kris 135 – Balnaha 67 (Lomond (USA) 128) [2002 79: **60 d**
7m 8.3d 8m 7g 6f 6.9g Aug 5] quite attractive filly: has a round action: disappointing
maiden in 2003, finding little last 4 starts: tried blinkered: needs treating with caution.
G. Wragg

ISLAND FLIGHT   3 b.f. Missed Flight 123 – Island Mead 86 (Pharly (FR) 130) [2002 **–**
57?: 12d³ 12m 9.9m f12g 12m 8.5m 10f Sep 27] smallish, unfurnished filly: little form:
ran as though something amiss fifth start: tried blinkered. *C. W. Thornton*

ISLAND HOUSE (IRE)   6 ch.h. Grand Lodge (USA) 125 – Fortitude (IRE) (Last **118**
Tycoon 131) [2002 118: 9m² 10.3f² 9.9d² 11.8g* 12d⁴ 12g³ 10.9g* 10d* 10d Nov 17] tall,
quite good-topped horse: smart performer: won listed events at Leicester in June, Ayr in
September (beat Vintage Premium by short head) and Newmarket (beat Parasol by 5
lengths) in November: creditable efforts otherwise in 2002 when head-second in Earl of
Sefton Stakes at Newmarket (to Indian Creek) and listed race at Goodwood (to Imperial
Dancer) and when 1¼ lengths third of 4 to Warrsan in minor event at Newmarket in July:
finds 9f a bare minimum and stays 1½m: acts on any going: has idled/edged left: carried
head awkwardly last 2 starts: reliable. *G. Wragg*

ISLAND LADY (IRE)   2 b.f. (Apr 16) Hernando (FR) 127 – Prosperous Lady (Prince **–**
Tenderfoot (USA) 126) [2002 8s Oct 26] IR 30,000F, IR 18,000Y: sturdy filly: ninth
foal: half-sister to 3 winners, notably smart 7f (including at 2 yrs)/1m winner Eurolink
Thunder (by Fairy King): dam unraced: 25/1 and backward, well held in maiden at Newbury. *J. W. Hills*

ISLAND LIGHT   4 b.g. Inchinor 119 – Miss Prism 60 (Niniski (USA) 125) [2002 **96**
85p: 8f* 8.1d² 8m 8.1d 8m⁵ 9.2s 8g* Oct 17] well-made gelding: useful handicapper:
won at Pontefract (well-backed favourite) in April and Newmarket (beat Quantum Leap
by length in 30-runner event) in October: should stay 1¼m: acts on firm and soft going.
A. C. Stewart

ISLAND LIGHT (USA)   2 ch.c. (Apr 20) Woodman (USA) 126 – Isla Del Rey (USA) **94 p**
103 (Nureyev (USA) 131) [2002 7.5d⁵ 8f* 8m⁶ Sep 20] leggy colt: third foal: half-brother
to 3-y-o L'Oiseau d'Argent: dam, 6f (in UAE)/7f (including at 2 yrs in Ireland) winner:
overcame greenness to win maiden at Kempton in September, quickening well to lead
final 1f: improved when sixth of 7 to Saturn in minor event at Newbury: stays 1m: should
make a useful 3-y-o. *E. A. L. Dunlop*

ISLAND MINT (USA)   3 b.f. Hennessy (USA) 122 – Mintecy (USA) (Key To The **69 §**
Mint (USA)) [2002 80?: f8g p10g 7g 7g 8f 10f⁵ 7g⁶ 10s Nov 1] useful-looking filly: fair
maiden: left B. Meehan after second start: stays 1¼m: acts on firm ground, well beaten
both starts on all-weather: refused to race fifth outing. *G. M. O'Neill, Ireland*

ISLAND OF PARADISE   3 b.f. Turtle Island (IRE) 123 – Mighty Squaw 58 (Indian **61**
Ridge 123) [2002 61: f7g 7m 8g² 8m⁴ 8.1d⁶ 10f⁴ 10g 14.1m⁶ 12m 10.2g Sep 23] angular
filly: modest maiden handicapper: stays 1¼m: acts on firm and good to soft going, ran
poorly on fibresand. *B. R. Millman*

ISLAND RAPTURE   2 b.f. (Apr 23) Royal Applause 124 – Gersey (Generous (IRE) **79**
139) [2002 7m⁵ 7m² 7s² 6.5g Sep 27] 25,000Y: second foal: dam once-raced half-sister to
smart performer up to 1¾m Jahafil: fair maiden: runner-up at Salisbury (beaten neck by
Wondrous Story, tending to wander) and Lingfield (made most, beaten ¾ length by Lucky
Date): will probably stay 1m: acts on soft and good to firm ground. *Mrs A. J. Perrett*

ISLAND SAINT 2 b.c. (Feb 1) Efisio 120 – Kembla 59 (Known Fact (USA) 135) **77**
[2002 6m⁵ 6.1s⁶ Jun 6] 20,000Y: neat colt: fourth foal: half-brother to 3 winners abroad,
including useful French performer up to 1¼m Quit Rent (by Fairy King): dam, 2-y-o 5.7f
winner who later won in Italy, half-sister to Urgent Request (very smart performer up to
1½m in Britain/USA) and Sanmartino (smart, stayed 2m): fair form when never-nearer
fifth of 18 to Cap Ferrat in maiden at Newbury: favourite, well held in similar event at
Chepstow. *J. L. Dunlop*

ISLAND SOUND 5 b.g. Turtle Island (IRE) 123 – Ballet 61 (Sharrood (USA) 124) **–**
[2002 109: 10m⁵ 9f⁵ 10s Oct 26] lengthy, angular gelding: has round action: useful
performer at 4 yrs: well held in 2002: visored once. *D. R. C. Elsworth*

ISLAND STAR (IRE) 2 b.g. (Apr 8) Turtle Island (IRE) 123 – Orthorising (Aragon **71**
118) [2002 f7g p7g p8g⁶ Dec 3] IR 2,000F, 12,000Y: fifth foal: half-brother to 3 winners,
including fairly useful Italian 2001 2-y-o 6f winner Magnitudo (by Sri Pekan) and 1999
2-y-o 5f winner Shalarise (by Shalford): dam unraced: fair form in maidens: best effort
when sixth to Treculiar at Lingfield: will need to settle to stay beyond 1m: gelded after
final start. *P. W. Harris*

ISLE OF MULL 3 gr.f. Elmaamul (USA) 125 – Sinking Sun 72§ (Danehill (USA)
126) [2002 8.2v⁶ f8.5g f8g Nov 26] second foal: half-sister to 2000 2-y-o 7f winner
Caspian (by Spectrum): dam, untrustworthy maiden who stayed 1¼m, half-sister to very
smart performer up to 1½m Urgent Request: well held in maidens. *Miss Gay Kelleway*

ISLINGTON (IRE) 3 b.f. Sadler's Wells (USA) 132 – Hellenic 125 (Darshaan **123**
133) [2002 100p: 10g* 10.4m* 12s 9.9m* 11.9m* 12g⁵ 10d³ Oct 26]
Lord Weinstock's business judgement as head of GEC was legendary, and
anyone seeking confirmation that his assessment of thoroughbreds was of similar
standing need look no further than his success as a breeder and his opinion of
Islington. Soon after seeing her for the first time on a racecourse at Newbury in
April, he wryly said: 'I wouldn't hesitate in putting Islington forward as the nearest
I've seen to perfection in a filly. Indeed, she's so perfect that, rather than race her, I
should have her home as a pet.' Racing should be delighted that Lord Weinstock
raced Islington, since she developed into the best of her sex in Britain, putting
together a run of cracking performances to win the Vodafone Nassau Stakes at
Goodwood and the Aston Upthorpe Yorkshire Oaks at York, and to finish fifth in
the Prix de l'Arc de Triomphe at Longchamp. Moreover, together with Golan, she
provided a handsome epitaph to their owner-breeder, who died aged seventy-seven
a few days before the King George VI and Queen Elizabeth Stakes. Together with
his father-in-law Sir Michael Sobell, then his son Simon who died in 1996, Lord
Weinstock bred twenty-three Group 1 winners at the Ballymacoll Stud in Ireland,
purchased in the early-'sixties, including outstanding performers in Troy (rated
137), Pilsudski (134), Sallust (134), Admetus (133), Homeric (133), Reform (132)
and Sun Princess (130); Simon Weinstock owned, though did not breed, another
top performer in Ela-Mana-Mou (132). Owner-breeders of this type, including also
the late Lord Howard de Walden, are a disappearing species, since they made few
concessions to the fashionable modern trend towards speed and breeding horses
likely to be suited by a mile to a mile and a quarter. Nor did their operations suffer
from over-stocking, unlike those of the Maktoums, Lord Weinstock, for example,
tending to have fewer than forty mares and a similar number of horses in training
at any one time. The majority of his stud's horses have always been far from
precocious, suited by middle distances, tough, and well-built if occasionally on
the plain side, with anything puny being a rarity. Islington is an exemplar of the
Weinstock methods. She is not perfection in looks, for all that Lord Weinstock
said—close-coupled, quite attractive is our description. She was lightly raced as a
two-year-old, showing great promise when a close third to Protectress in a listed
race at Newmarket in October on the second of her two starts. And she is well suited
by a mile and quarter to a mile and a half.
Although entered in the One Thousand Guineas, Islington was never
seriously considered for that event and started her campaign in a sixteen-runner
maiden race at Newbury, going off at odds on and confirming her promise by
beating Fragrant View a length and a half after a muddling pace. With no reference
to the value of the form, she was immediately made 8/1 favourite with the major
firms for the Oaks and was soon down to 5/1, and then as short as 5/2 after the

Tattersalls Musidora Stakes at York the following month. Odds on again, she put in only a workmanlike display at York, showing what was to become a persistent characteristic in racing freely behind the leaders before going on three furlongs out and having to be given reminders to keep her up to her work because of a tendency to idle in front. At the line Islington had a length in hand over Spinnette with Alexander Three D third. Islington did not start favourite at Epsom, being replaced by Kazzia, and as far as she was concerned the race is best forgotten. Involved in some scrimmaging before halfway, she travelled better than any bar Kazzia, tried to go with that filly from the turn but soon dropped away, finishing over eighteen lengths back in eighth. The very soft going, rather than any lack of stamina, looked the most likely cause of this substandard display, but it later transpired that Islington had come back very sore, needing several weeks to recover. Her race-course rehabilitation began in the Nassau at Goodwood at the start of August, just a few days after she had been found to have a minor infection in a foot. Second favourite in a field of ten behind Oaks and Irish Oaks runner-up Quarter Moon, with Ascot listed winner Fallen Star and Tarfshi, successful in the Pretty Polly Stakes at the Curragh, close behind her in the betting, Islington outclassed her rivals. Always travelling strongly, she was shaken up to go ahead over two furlongs out, accelerated clear in eye-catching style and was fully seven lengths ahead before being eased to win by four from 33/1-shot Sulk, with the favourite, not showing her best form, half a length further back.

Islington had two things to prove in her next race later in the month, the Yorkshire Oaks—whether she stayed a mile and a half, and whether she was good enough to beat Kazzia. The outcome was conclusive on both counts. The ground at Goodwood—and for the Musidora, for that matter—had been good to firm and conditions were exactly the same at York. The market suggested it was a two-horse race, with Kazzia 7/4 and Islington 2/1, followed by Quarter Moon at 8/1, Ribblesdale Stakes winner Irresistible Jewel, below her best in the Irish Oaks, 9/1 and Sulk 16/1. The others, including the last two Oaks d'Italia winners, Guadalupe and Zanzibar, were 20/1 and upwards. Starbourne, who had not gone fast enough when making the running for Golan the day before, did the reverse this time on behalf of Quarter Moon, going off like a scalded cat and being virtually ignored by the other jockeys. Islington was always travelling supremely well behind second-placed Kazzia, was sent on over two furlongs out and quickened clear, staying on strongly to beat Guadalupe by five lengths with Sulk a head away third and the tiring Kazzia fourth. Kazzia was not in the form she had shown at Epsom but even that form wasn't so good as Islington's in the Yorkshire Oaks. Her scintillating display provided Sir Michael Stoute with his seventh success in the race and encouraged thoughts that Islington might give the Weinstock colours another prominent showing in the Prix de l'Arc de Triomphe—their horses had finished second or third six times, through Homeric in 1972, Troy in 1979, Ela-Mana-Mou in 1980, Sun Princess in 1983 and Pilsudski in 1996 and 1997. Initially there was a possibility that Islington would take on her own sex in the shorter Prix de l'Opera but she duly went for the Arc and ran creditably without making the frame. After racing more freely than ideal in second place, she led with a couple of furlongs to go but was soon struggling and could keep on only at one pace under strong pressure to finish fifth, around two lengths behind Marienbard. Despite her hard race, and the fact that she had been on the go since April, Islington was sent to Arlington for the Breeders' Cup Filly & Mare Turf at the end of the month, when she was the only Breeders' Cup runner from Britain or Ireland racing

Vodafone Nassau Stakes, Goodwood—Islington makes up for a disappointing run in the Oaks and has plenty to spare over Sulk (right), Quarter Moon (dark colours, white sleeves) and Fallen Star (spots)

Aston Upthorpe Yorkshire Oaks, York—another scintillating display as Islington wins by five lengths from Guadalupe (fourth left), Sulk (second right) and Kazzia (partly hidden by winner), who loses her unbeaten record

without lasix. Her stablemate Golan, along with Aidan O'Brien's seven runners plus Zenda and Kazzia, were all administered the anti-bleeding drug, though the French challengers, including Domedriver, were not. Using lasix and any other medication may be more of a double-edged sword than some people imagine, since the smart German horse Caitano was refused a licence to stand at stud in Germany because he had raced on lasix, and has been sent instead to Russia. Racing on softish ground for the first time since the Oaks, Islington did not reproduce her best form at Arlington but wasn't discredited, ridden with more restraint than usual after breaking a bit slowly and staying on in the straight to be third without posing a threat to the length-and-half winner Starine.

Islington (IRE) (b.f. 1999)	Sadler's Wells (USA) (b 1981)	Northern Dancer (b 1961)	Nearctic
			Natalma
		Fairy Bridge (b 1975)	Bold Reason
			Special
	Hellenic (b 1987)	Darshaan (br 1981)	Shirley Heights
			Delsy
		Grecian Sea (ch 1978)	Homeric
			Sea Venture

Islington is to stay in training. Although very smart, she is not one of the top ten horses to have raced for the Sobell-Weinstock team over the years—she is slightly below her dam Hellenic in ability for one—and her prospects of beating the top colts are not exceptional. Equally, her trainer is a past master at finding the right opportunities for his horses and it is to be hoped Islington rewards her connections' boldness. Her female family is even better than Golan's and, as a daughter of Sadler's Wells, her prospects as a broodmare when the time comes for her to be retired are excellent. Hellenic was a high-class filly, successful in the Ribblesdale

Stakes and Yorkshire Oaks and runner-up to Snurge in the St Leger. In contrast to Islington, who wasn't able to show anything like her best form on soft going at Epsom, Hellenic did not have a good action and needed give in the ground; she was withdrawn from the Irish Oaks on the day of the race because of the firmish conditions, even though she was ante-post favourite. Predictably for one with her racing record, Hellenic has been given every opportunity at stud, visiting Sadler's Wells seven times and Caerleon, Danehill, Green Desert and Royal Academy once each. The results have been impressive, as she has produced three other winners, notably smart stayer Election Day, third in the 1997 Gold Cup, and very smart mile-and-a-quarter performer Greek Dance, winner of the Group 1 Grosser Dallmayr-Preis (Bayerisches Zuchtrennen) in Germany and runner-up in similar events in Britain, France, Ireland and Hong Kong. Election Day is at stud in Colombia and Greek Dance proved infertile when retired to stand in Germany. Both are by Sadler's Wells, as are Hellenic's next two foals after Islington, the fillies Olympienne and Greek Flame. She foaled a colt by Danehill named Grecian Mount in 2002 and was tested in foal to Sadler's Wells again. There are plenty of other stakes performers in the pedigree but nothing exceptional. The grandam Grecian Sea and great grandam Sea Venture were both in the frame in Group 3 races and, maintaining the Ballymacoll continuity, fourth dam Knighton House was a sister to Reform, while fifth dam Country House is also fifth dam of Golan. *Sir Michael Stoute*

ISOBEL SCARLETT 3 b.f. Emperor Jones (USA) 119 – Key West (FR) (Highest Honor (FR) 124) [2002 p6g 8.3m⁵ 8f p12g p10g p10g p7g Dec 28] third foal: half-sister to 4-y-o Among Women: dam unraced: modest maiden: has worn cheekpieces: edged right second start. *T. D. McCarthy* **55**

ISOLDE'S IDOL 2 ch.f. (Feb 14) Night Shift (USA) – Atmospheric Blues (IRE) 91 (Double Schwartz 128) [2002 p5g 6m 6d* Aug 8] 14,000Y: smallish, strong filly: fourth foal: dam, 2-y-o 5f winner, later 1m winner in Italy: 25/1, clearly best effort in maidens (fair form) when winning at Haydock by ½ length from Monte Mayor Lad, under pressure by halfway but edging ahead final 75 yds: should stay 7f: acts on good to soft ground. *C. F. Wall* **72**

IS SHE EC (IRE) 2 ch.f. (Feb 19) Flying Spur (AUS) – La Duse 66 (Junius (USA) 124) [2002 f6g 6.1g 6m Jul 2] IR 5,500F, 7,000Y: half-sister to 3 winners, including 10-y-o Blushing Grenadier and 1m winner Cindy's Star (by Dancing Dissident): dam third at 1½m: well held in sellers/maiden. *J. L. Spearing* **–**

ISTANBUL (IRE) 3 b.g. Revoque (IRE) 122 – Song of The Glens (Horage 124) [2002 7s 8.2m⁶ 8.1m 10.2g 16.2g Aug 26] 75,000Y: half-brother to several winners, including 2000 Prix Morny winner Bad As I Wanna Be and 5-y-o Musical Heath (both by Common Grounds): dam, maiden, out of half-sister to 2000 Guineas winner Right Tack: poor maiden: tried blinkered. *B. J. Meehan* **44**

I SWEAR 3 b.c. Barathea (IRE) 127 – Karlafsha (Top Ville 129) [2002 83p: 10d³ 10d³ May 29] leggy, quite attractive colt: has scope: good walker: fairly useful maiden, lightly raced: yet to race on extremes of going: hung markedly left on reappearance: sent to USA. *J. L. Dunlop* **81**

ITALIAN AFFAIR 4 ch.f. Fumo di Londra (IRE) 108 – Sergentti (IRE) 76 (Common Grounds 118) [2002 50: f5s f6s⁶ f6g f5g 5.3f⁶ 5m 5g 7f 5.7d² 5m² 5d² 5m 5.1f 6d* 6m⁴ 7f³ 6d² p7g Dec 18] leggy filly: modest performer on turf, poor on all-weather: won ladies selling handicap at Thirsk in August: best at 5f/6f: acts on firm going, good to soft and fibresand. *A. Bailey* **62**
a36

ITALIAN COUNSEL (IRE) 5 b.g. Leading Counsel (USA) 122 – Mullaghroe (Tarboosh (USA)) [2002 –: 11.9m Oct 3] of no account on Flat. *B. J. Llewellyn* **–**

ITALIAN MIST (FR) 3 b.g. Forzando 122 – Digamist Girl (IRE) (Digamist (USA) 110) [2002 73: p5g⁶ 7g 6m p7g p7g 5d 7d Oct 15] fair maiden at 2 yrs: on downgrade in 2002, leaving B. Meehan after third start: should stay 6f: acts on good to firm going and polytrack: blinkered first 3 starts in 2002: sometimes carries head awkwardly: untrustworthy. *Mrs A. J. Bowlby* **58 d**

ITCANBEDONE AGAIN (IRE) 3 b.c. Sri Pekan (USA) 117 – Maradata (IRE) 68 (Shardari 134) [2002 68: 10.3s 8f 8.1s³ 7g⁶ 9f* 10s⁴ 11.9m⁵ 10.3f Sep 25] tall, good-topped colt: unimpressive mover: fair handicapper: won at Redcar in June: barely stays 1½m: acts on any going: consistent. *R. Hollinshead* **71**

ITCH 7 b.g. Puissance 110 – Panienka (POL) 70 (Dom Racine (FR) 121) [2002 8v⁶ f6g **41**
7m 5.9d 9.2d⁶ 7.9g 5.9v 8.3s⁵ Aug 20] good-bodied gelding: poor performer nowadays:
probably stays 9f: acts on fibresand and heavy going: tried visored. *R. Bastiman*

I T CONSULTANT 4 b.g. Rock City 120 – Game Germaine (Mummy's Game 120) **60**
[2002 68, a64: p6g f6g⁶ f6g 6m 6m 5.1g⁶ f6g⁵ Nov 15] modest handicapper: best at **a53**
5f/6f: acts on fibresand, yet to race on extremes of ground on turf: blinkered last 2 starts
(seemed none too keen final one): tongue tied third outing: sometimes slowly away.
A. G. Newcombe

ITEMISE (USA) 2 ch.f. (Feb 14) Kris S (USA) – Company Binness (USA) (Seattle **87**
Dancer (USA) 119) [2002 6m⁴ 7s⁵ 8m* 7m Sep 29] $75,000Y: quite good-topped filly:
third foal: dam unraced daughter of US Grade 3 8.5f winner Summer Secretary: fairly
useful form: won maiden at Goodwood in September despite wandering under pressure:
far from disgraced in nursery at Ascot final start: should stay at least 1¼m: acts on soft
and good to firm ground. *M. Johnston*

I TINA 6 b.m. Lycius (USA) 124 – Tintomara (IRE) (Niniski (USA) 125) [2002 62: **57 §**
p12g p10g³ p13g⁶ p12g⁵ 9.9m 10d 10m⁴ 10m 10.2f 10.2g 10.9m 10.9m Sep 16] modest **a53 §**
performer: well below form last 3 starts: best around 1¼m: acts on polytrack, soft and
firm going: tried visored, blinkered in 2002: has pulled hard/carried head high, and seems
best held up: unreliable. *J. G. Portman*

ITNAB 2 b.f. (Mar 12) Green Desert (USA) 127 – Midway Lady (USA) 126 (Alleged **76 p**
(USA) 138) [2002 7d⁶ Aug 3] ninth foal: sister to smart 6f (including at 2 yrs) winner
Haafiz and useful 7f/1m winner Umniyatee, and half-sister to 3 winners: dam won 1000
Guineas and Oaks: 7/1, 7 lengths sixth to Nayzak in maiden at Newmarket, slowly away
then staying on when hampered final 1f: should improve. *B. Hanbury*

ITSABOY 2 b.c. (Apr 20) Wizard King 122 – French Project (IRE) 84 (Project **58**
Manager 111) [2002 6g⁵ 6d p6g f7g Dec 17] 900F: second foal: dam, maiden who stayed
1½m, winning hurdler: modest maiden: well beaten in nursery final start: should stay at
least 1m. *J. R. Boyle*

ITS ALL EURS (IRE) 2 b.f. (Apr 10) BaratheA (IRE) 127 – Brief Sentiment (IRE) **67**
96 (Brief Truce (USA) 126) [2002 7d f7s⁴ p6g Dec 28] good-topped filly: first foal: dam
Irish 2-y-o 7f winner who stayed 1¼m: easily best effort in maidens (fair form) when
fourth of 12 to Every Note Counts at Wolverhampton: found little final outing: should
stay 1m. *R. Hannon*

ITS ALL PINK (IRE) 2 gr.f. (Apr 10) Victory Note (USA) 120 – Chickamauga **49**
(USA) (Wild Again (USA)) [2002 5s² f5g³ p5g⁶ Apr 10] small filly: second foal: dam ran
once: poor maiden: placed in sellers: raced only at 5f. *J. S. Moore*

ITSANOTHERGIRL 6 b.m. Reprimand 122 – Tasmim 63 (Be My Guest (USA) **67**
126) [2002 69, a–: f11g p12g⁶ 10s³ 11g Apr 2] leggy mare: fair handicapper: best at 1m **a–**
(given test) to 1¼m: has form on good to firm going, goes very well on soft/heavy, well
below form on fibresand/polytrack: blinkered nowadays: has hung left. *M. W. Easterby*

IT'S A WIZARD 2 b.g. (Apr 1) Wizard King 122 – Axed Again (Then Again 126) **57 §**
[2002 5s 5m 5f 7f⁴ 7d⁴ 7d² 8.3s⁴ 7m 8g Sep 10] 4,000Y: well grown, leggy gelding: good
mover: third living foal: half-brother to 2001 2-y-o 5f/6f winner It'safact (by So Factual)
and a winner abroad by Timeless Times: dam, no sign of ability, sister to Stewards' Cup
winner For The Present: modest maiden: in frame 4 times, including in sellers/nursery:
stays 7f: acts on good to soft ground: tried blinkered: wayward and temperamental:
gelded after final start. *P. D. Evans*

IT'S DEFINITE (IRE) 3 b.g. Definite Article 121 – Taoveret (IRE) (Flash of Steel **81**
120) [2002 11g 11.1s⁵ p10g* 12m 10.9m⁴ 12d² 10.1g³ 11.9g 12f p10g Dec 14] 16,000Y:
big, lengthy gelding: second foal: brother to 7f to 9f winner in Italy: dam, won 15 times in
Italy up to 1¼m, out of half-sister to smart Greenham Stakes winner Faustus: fairly useful
performer: won maiden at Lingfield in June, making all: stays 1½m: acts on good to firm
going, good to soft and polytrack: visored (ran poorly) last 2 starts. *A. P. Jarvis*

ITS ECCO BOY 4 ch.g. Clantime 101 – Laena 72 (Roman Warrior 132) [2002 78: **71**
6m² 7f 6.1f⁵ 6.9d³ 7g 6g⁶ 7m³ f7f 6m² 6m⁵ 7m⁴ Sep 18] tall, useful-looking gelding:
fair maiden: best at 6f/7f: acts on firm and good to soft going (below form only start on
all-weather): visored second/third starts. *K. R. Burke*

ITSONLYAGAME 2 b.c. (May 23) Ali-Royal (IRE) 127 – Mena 58 (Blakeney 126) **62 ?**
[2002 7m 8f³ 8g Oct 18] fourth foal: half-brother to 3-y-o My Maite and 4-y-o Komena:
dam maiden who probably stayed 11.5f: seemingly modest form in maidens: third of 4 at
Goodwood: will probably stay 1¼m. *R. Ingram*

IT'S OUR SECRET (IRE)   6 ch.g. Be My Guest (USA) 126 – Lady Dulcinea   **79**
(ARG) (General (FR)) [2002 76: 8.2m⁵ 8.3g³ 7f² 8m p8g⁴ 7m³ 8g² 9m* 8m⁶ Sep 18]   **a70**
sturdy, lengthy gelding: fair handicapper: won at Ripon in August: effective at 7f to easy
1¼m: acts on fibresand, soft and firm going: tried visored, not since 1999: consistent.
M. H. Tompkins

IT'S SMEE AGAIN   4 ch.f. Mizoram (USA) 105 – Mountain Dew (Pharly (FR) 130)   **38**
[2002 –: 7d 7f 7f 7m⁶ 10m⁵ 12f⁶ Jul 17] tall filly: poor performer: stayed 1¼m: acted on
good to firm going: dead. *Ronald Thompson*

IT'S THE LIMIT (USA)   3 b.c. Boundary (USA) 117 – Beside (USA) (Sportin' Life   **100**
(USA)) [2002 –p: 12m* 13.3m³ 12m* Sep 23] tall, rather leggy colt: useful performer,
lightly raced: won maiden at Newmarket (4 ran, made all) in July and minor event at
Kempton (beat Zaajel short head) in September: good third to Windermere in handicap at
Newbury in between: will stay 1¾m: raced only on good to firm ground after debut.
Mrs A. J. Perrett

ITS WALLACE JNR   3 b.g. Bedford (USA) 109 – Built In Heaven (Sunley Builds   **53 ?**
102) [2002 10s 10d 11.9g⁵ 16.2g 16.2m⁴ 11.9m Oct 3] first foal: dam ran in bumper/2
hurdles: modest maiden: seems to stay 2m: won over hurdles in December. *Miss S. West*

ITS YOUR BID   4 b.f. Dilum (USA) 115 – By Arrangement (IRE) 60 (Bold Arrange-   **53**
ment 127) [2002 58: 13.1g⁵ 14d⁴ 12d⁴ 14m 14.1m 11.9m p16g² 16f² p16g² Dec 3] modest
handicapper: stays 2m: acts on polytrack, firm and good to soft going, well beaten on soft/
heavy: tried visored. *S. Woodman*

IT WAS MEANT TO BE   3 b.f. Distant Relative 128 – Belle Vue 78 (Petong 126)   **–**
[2002 62, a69: f7s³ f6g* Jan 25] rather dipped-backed filly: fair performer: won claimer   **a74**
at Wolverhampton in January: effective at 6f, barely at 1m: acts on good to firm going,
good to soft and all-weather: tends to wander/carry head awkwardly, but is consistent:
sent to USA. *P. C. Haslam*

IVANIA   2 ch.f. (Jan 24) First Trump 118 – Antonia's Choice 73 (Music Boy 124) [2002   **81**
5g 5.1g² 5.1f* 5g² 5m 5.1f⁴ 5.2f 5g² Aug 1] 15,500Y: good-topped filly: has a quick
action: first foal: dam 2-y-o 5f winner out of half-sister to very smart sprinter Bolshoi:
fairly useful performer: won maiden at Chester in May: clearly best efforts when
runner-up in listed race at Beverley (beaten ¾ length by On The Brink) and nursery at
Goodwood: likely to prove best at 5f: raced only on good ground or firmer: inconsistent.
A. Berry

IVAN'S BABY (IRE)   3 b. or br.f. Distinctly North (USA) 115 – Alexander Goddess   **– §**
(IRE) (Alzao (USA) 117) [2002 61d: p6g p6g p5g f6s p6g⁶ Jan 30] temperamental maiden:
best at 5f/6f: acts on firm going and polytrack, below form both starts on fibresand:
effective blinkered/visored or not. *B. A. Pearce*

IVORSAGOODUN   3 b.f. Piccolo 121 – Malibasta 83 (Auction Ring (USA) 123)   **61**
[2002 61: 8.1m 10f 10g 9.7g⁶ 12m⁴ 16.2m 9.9g⁶ 11.8s³ 14.1d³ f16.2g Nov 18] smallish,
sturdy filly: modest maiden: should stay easy 2m: acts on firm and soft going, unraced on
heavy: blinkered (edgy, ran creditably) final 2-y-o start: consistent. *Mrs P. N. Dutfield*

IVORY BAY   3 b.g. Piccolo 121 – Fantasy Racing (IRE) 86 (Tirol 127) [2002 78d: f8g⁶   **55**
f7g f6g² 8g* 7g 9.9m³ 9.2s⁶ 7m 6v 6g 8g 6f⁵ 8.5m 7m 8m³ 7.1m³ 7.5m* 6g 7m 7d Oct
18] rather leggy gelding: has a quick action: modest performer: won maiden handicap at
Musselburgh in March and claimer at Beverley in August: effective at 7.5f, probably at
1¼m: acts on fibresand and firm going, possibly not on soft: blinkered (found nothing)
once at 2 yrs: none too reliable. *J. Hetherton*

IVORY DAWN   8 b.m. Batshoof 122 – Cradle of Love (USA) 87 (Roberto (USA) 131)   **65**
[2002 70: p5g⁶ 6m 6g p6g⁶ 7m 8m p10g 6m⁵ 7m 6m 6.1m Oct 1] leggy, workmanlike
mare: fair handicapper: on a lengthy losing run: probably best at 6f: possibly unsuited by
heavy going, acts on any other on turf and on polytrack: has run creditably when visored:
usually held up. *D. K. Ivory*

IVORY'S JOY   7 b.m. Tina's Pet 121 – Jacqui Joy 63 (Music Boy 124) [2002 107d: 5d   **99**
5m⁴ 5.1d* 5.1f⁶ 5g 5m³ Jul 26] leggy mare: useful performer: won handicap at Chepstow
in July by short head from Welsh Emperor: not discredited after: stays easy 6f: acts on
fibresand, firm and good to soft ground: has won in blinkers, tried only once since 2 yrs:
usually bandaged: usually waited with. *D. K. Ivory*

IVORY VENTURE   2 b.f. (Feb 8) Reprimand 122 – Julietta Mia (USA) 72 (Wood-   **54**
man (USA) 126) [2002 7f³ 5g² 5.7f⁶ 6d 5m⁶ 5m⁴ 5.1d⁶ Sep 9] 3,000Y: first foal: dam,
2-y-o 7f winner, granddaughter of champion US sprinter My Juliet: modest maiden:
should stay at least 6f: acts on firm and good to soft ground. *D. K. Ivory*

I WANT YOU NOW (IRE) 4 ch.f. Nicolotte 118 – Christle Mill (Pas de Seul 133) –
[2002 –: f12g⁵ Mar 25] IR 8,000Y: seventh foal: half-sister to fairly useful 1997 2-y-o
6f winner Conectis (by River Falls), later minor 6.5f stakes winner in USA, and winner
in Italy by Mac's Imp: dam ran twice in Ireland at 2 yrs: well held in 3 maidens.
D. J. S. Cosgrove

I WISH 4 ch.f. Beveled (USA) – Ballystate 71 (Ballacashtal (CAN)) [2002 58?: p8g² **72**
p7g⁵ p8g p7g³ p7g* 8.3d³ 8d 5.3d⁶ 7g⁴ 6m⁵ 8.3m⁵ 7m³ 7m⁵ 6m 5.1g* 6m 6d⁴ Oct 14]
tall, leggy filly: fair handicapper: won at Lingfield (edged left) in April and Chepstow in
September: effective at 5f to 1m: acts on good to firm going, good to soft and polytrack:
headstrong. *M. Madgwick*

IWO JIMA (IRE) 2 b.c. (May 3) Desert King (IRE) 129 – Allegheny River (USA) **61**
(Lear Fan (USA) 130) [2002 7.1m Sep 7] 22,000Y: closely related to very smart 6f winner
(including at 2 yrs) Danetime and useful Irish performer up to 7f Dane River (both by
Danehill) and half-brother to 3 winners: dam Irish 7f winner: 33/1, ninth of 16 to Jay
Gee's Choice in maiden at Haydock, never better than mid-field. *N. P. Littmoden*

IZDIHAM (IRE) 3 ch.c. Nashwan (USA) 135 – Harayir (USA) 119 (Gulch (USA)) **112**
[2002 8m³ 10f* 10m² 10d* 12m³ Jul 30] good-bodied colt: third foal: brother to 1½m
winner Moonjaz: dam, 6f (Lowther Stakes at 2 yrs) to 1m (1000 Guineas) winner, granddaughter of Irish Oaks winner Give Thanks: smart performer: won maiden at Newbury in
May and listed race at Sandown (shade comfortably by 1¼ lengths from Hawkeye,
having wandered when first in front) in July: good 1½ lengths second to Burning Sun in
listed race at Royal Ascot in between, just respectable fair third of 4 to Bandari in Gordon
Stakes at Goodwood final outing, finding little: best form at 1¼m: acts on firm and good
to soft going. *M. P. Tregoning*

IZMAIL (IRE) 3 b.g. Bluebird (USA) 125 – My-Lorraine (IRE) 77 (Mac's Imp **84 §**
(USA) 116) [2002 94: 6g 5g 5.1f* 5g 7.1m 7g Aug 15] useful-looking gelding: fairly
useful performer: creditable effort in 2002 only when fourth in handicap at Chester: will
prove best at 5f/easy 6f: acts on firm and good to soft going: visored (fourth/fifth starts):
sometimes slowly away/races freely: not to be trusted: sold 15,000 gns. *E. A. L. Dunlop*

IZZET MUZZY (FR) 4 ch.g. Piccolo 121 – Texanne (BEL) 66§ (Efisio 120) [2002 –
68, a92: f7g 5.1d 5g 5.1d⁶ 7f f7g f5g f7s Nov 30] good-bodied gelding: unimpressive
mover: fairly useful handicapper at best on all-weather, modest on turf: little form in
2002, leaving R. Wilman after second start: stays easy 7f: acts on any turf going and
fibresand: has been visored. *D. Shaw*

J

JABAAR (USA) 4 gr.g. Silver Hawk (USA) 123 – Sierra Madre (FR) 119 (Baillamont **106**
(USA) 124) [2002 85p: 10m⁴ 10g* 12g 10m⁴ Sep 21] strong, lengthy gelding: useful
form, very lightly raced: reportedly suffered stress fracture of pelvis at 3 yrs: won handicap at Newmarket (28 ran, beat Pretrail impressively by 3 lengths) in May: creditable
efforts after in Duke of Edinburgh Handicap at Royal Ascot (favourite) and Courage Best
Handicap at Newbury (fourth to Solo Flight) in September: effective at 1¼m/1½m: won
maiden on good to soft going, but raced on good or firmer otherwise: has worn crossed
noseband: sold 35,000 gns, joined D. Nicholls and gelded. *E. A. L. Dunlop*

JABULANI (IRE) 3 b.g. Marju (IRE) 127 – Houwara (IRE) (Darshaan 133) [2002 **77 d**
79p: f9.4g* p8g 10g⁵ 9d 8m 10.5d⁶ 9m 10.5f⁶ 8m Oct 5] tall gelding: fair performer at
best: won maiden at Wolverhampton in February: below form last 4 starts (claimed from
W. Jarvis after first occasion): stays 9.4f: acts on fibresand and good to soft going:
sometimes wears crossed noseband: edgy sort, sometimes too headstrong. *G. M. Moore*

JACARANDA (IRE) 2 ch.g. (Jan 22) Bahhare (USA) 122 – Near Miracle (Be My **80**
Guest (USA) 126) [2002 6f 6m³ 7.2m* 8m 7f⁶ 8.3d p7g Nov 13] 10,000F, 29,000Y:
unfurnished gelding: half-brother to ungenuine 5f (at 2 yrs) to 7f winner Footprints
(by College Chapel) and several winners abroad: dam Irish 7f winner: fairly useful
performer: won maiden at Epsom in August: well beaten in nurseries last 2 starts: stays
7f: acts on firm going: usually races prominently. *B. J. Meehan*

JACINTO 2 b.g. (Feb 3) Komaite (USA) – Times Zando 64 (Forzando 122) [2002 6m **56**
6d⁵ 5m⁴ 5m 7d 6.1s f8g⁵ Nov 26] 12,500 2-y-o: small gelding: fourth foal: brother to
3-y-o Colonel Kozando and 6f (including at 2 yrs) winner Captain Kozando: dam 2-y-o
7f/1m winner: modest maiden: stays 1m: acts on fibresand. *T. H. Caldwell*

JACKAMVIC 3 ch.f. Dancing Spree (USA) – Pinup 44 (Risk Me (FR) 127) [2002 – p10g p10g p10g f12g p12g⁵ Jun 1] first foal: dam 6f winner: well held, including in seller. *B. G. Powell*

JACK DAWSON (IRE) 5 b.g. Persian Bold 123 – Dream of Jenny 73 (Caerleon **86** (USA) 132) [2002 80: 12m⁴ 16f² 13g* 16m* 11.9d 14.6m⁵ 16.2m⁵ 16.2d⁴ 13.3m⁶ 16.2m² 14m 16m² Sep 29] neat gelding: fairly useful handicapper: won at Hamilton in May and Musselburgh in June: effective at 13f to 2m: acts on good to soft going, though seems ideally suited by good or firmer: often held up: tough and consistent. *John Berry*

JACK DURRANCE (IRE) 2 b.c. (Apr 3) Polish Precedent (USA) 131 – Atlantic **– p** Desire (IRE) 100 (Ela-Mana-Mou 132) [2002 p7g Dec 21] first foal: dam 1m/1¼m winner: signs of ability in minor event at Lingfield, prominent until outpaced 2f out: likely to improve. *M. Johnston*

JACKIE'S BABY 6 b.g. Then Again 126 – Guarded Expression 51 (Siberian Express **–** (USA) 125) [2002 –: f5f⁶ f5g f5g f5g⁶ Dec 31] big, good-topped gelding: only fair **a64** handicapper in 2002: best at 5f: best efforts on fibresand/good going or firmer: sometimes wanders. *J. M. Bradley*

JACK OF TRUMPS (IRE) 2 b.c. (Mar 24) King's Theatre (IRE) 128 – Queen **60** Caroline (USA) 67 (Chief's Crown (USA)) [2002 6m 7d 7d⁶ Oct 30] 45,000F, 160,000Y: strong colt: sixth foal: half-brother to 3 winners, including 6-y-o Blackheath and 1¼m winner Regal Reprimand (by Reprimand): dam maiden who stayed 10.5f: green, modest form in maidens: best effort when sixth at Yarmouth: should stay at least 1m. *G. Wragg*

JACKSMILES 3 b.g. Puissance 110 – Cassiar 84 (Connaught 130) [2002 –: 8m 6g 8d **–** Jul 7] no sign of ability: tried blinkered. *J. J. Bridger*

JACK THE TRACK (IRE) 3 b.g. Barathea (IRE) 127 – Babushka (IRE) (Dance of **78** Life (USA)) [2002 88: 10m 7.9m 8m p8g⁶ Oct 16] good-topped gelding: fair performer: will stay 1¼m: acts on polytrack and good to firm going, well held on soft: blinkered (found little) penultimate start/carried head high final one: sold 5,000 gns, sent to Kuwait. *J. Noseda*

JADARAH (USA) 2 b.f. (Mar 31) Red Ransom (USA) – Crafty Example (USA) **62** (Crafty Prospector (USA)) [2002 5m⁶ Jun 3] strong, well-made filly: sixth foal: sister to top-class miler Intikhab and half-sister to a winner in US by Bates Motel: dam, ran once, out of sister to top-class miler Polish Precedent from very good family: 3/1, burly and wearing crossed noseband, sixth of 7 in maiden at Sandown, not knocked about when losing action momentarily: looked capable of better. *D. R. Loder*

JADEERON 3 b.g. Green Desert (USA) 127 – Rain And Shine (FR) 78 (Rainbow **64** Quest (USA) 134) [2002 59: 7m⁵ 6d 7g⁵ p6g⁵ 8.5g⁶ 8m³ 8g³ 10m⁵ f8.5s 7m Sep 17] useful-looking gelding: modest maiden handicapper: stays 8.5f: acts on good to firm going and polytrack: tried blinkered/tongue tied: sold 8,000 gns. *B. Hanbury*

JADE FOREST (IRE) 2 gr.f. (Mar 24) Charnwood Forest (IRE) 125 – Jade Vine **–** (IRE) (Alzao (USA) 117) [2002 7g⁶ Jun 18] 3,500Y: second foal: dam, ran once at 2 yrs in Ireland, out of useful Irish 2-y-o 5f/6f winner Grey Dream: 25/1, well held in maiden at Thirsk. *J. L. Eyre*

JADE'S PROMISE 3 b.g. Definite Article 121 – Zacinta (USA) (Hawkster (USA)) **71** [2002 60: p8g⁴ p10g p13g⁴ f12g p12g² p10g⁴ p10g* Dec 30] fair performer: won maiden at Lingfield in December: stays 13f: acts on polytrack. *J. R. Best*

JADE STAR (USA) 2 b.f. (Feb 27) Jade Hunter (USA) – Danzig's Girl (USA) **61** (Danzig (USA)) [2002 p6g 6.1m p6g Dec 21] 7,000 2-y-o: third foal: dam, 7f winner at 2 yrs in USA, daughter of US Grade 3 winner up to 9f Squan Song: modest maiden: best effort on debut: left J. Poulton after next outing. *Miss Gay Kelleway*

JADE WARRIOR 3 b.g. Sabrehill (USA) 120 – Jade Pet 90 (Petong 126) [2002 70: **50 ?** p8g f9.4g f7g 10m 11.8d 7.1s 7m 8s 9.9d⁶ 11.8s 10g Oct 24] big, lengthy gelding: fair form in maidens at 2 yrs: disappointing in 2002: not sure to stay much beyond 7f: tried blinkered. *P. Howling*

JAGGER 2 gr.c. (Feb 25) Linamix (FR) 127 – Sweetness Herself 106 (Unfuwain **67 p** (USA) 131) [2002 6g Oct 17] 45,000Y: quite attractive colt: first foal: dam 1½m to 16.5f winner: 16/1 and green, 7 lengths thirteenth of 18 to Pigeon Point in maiden at Newmarket, not dangerous and tending to hang: likely to be suited by 1¼m+: should do better. *G. A. Butler*

JAGUAR 6 b.g. Barathea (IRE) 127 – Oasis (Valiyar 129) [2002 f11g⁶ f14.8g 11.6m –
9.7m Jul 29] strong, deep-girthed gelding: fair maiden at 3 yrs: well held on Flat in 2002.
J. R. Best

JAHANGIR 3 b.g. Zamindar (USA) 116 – Imperial Jade 105 (Lochnager 132) [2002 **68**
73: p6g² 6m 6g⁵ p6g 7m 6g 7d 5m p6g p6g Dec 30] close-coupled, useful-looking
gelding: fair maiden: probably stays easy 7f: acts on polytrack, raced mainly on good/
good to firm going on turf: sometimes early to post/gives problems at stall: blinkered (ran
poorly) once: usually held up. *W. R. Muir*

JAHASH 4 ch.g. Hernando (FR) 127 – Jalsun (Jalmood (USA) 126) [2002 55: 14.1f **58**
18d 15.4m⁴ 16g⁵ 17.1m 14.1m* 16.1d 16m 14.1d Oct 18] leggy, quite good-topped
gelding: modest handicapper: won at Yarmouth in August: stays 17f: acts on good to firm
and good to soft going: effective with or without blinkers: very slowly away fourth start:
sometimes runs in snatches/looks reluctant: sold 15,000 gns. *Sir Mark Prescott*

JAILHOUSE ROCKET 5 gr.g. Petong 126 – Selvi (Mummy's Pet 125) [2002 47: **48**
p13g f7g⁴ 10g⁴ 8.3s⁶ 7d 8m⁶ 6.1m Jul 13] poor performer nowadays: left Miss B. Sanders
after fifth start: seems to stay easy 1¼m: acts on soft and good to firm going: blinkered
last 6 outings. *C. R. Dore*

JAIR OHMSFORD (IRE) 3 b.g. Hamas (IRE) 125§ – Harry's Irish Rose (USA) **68 p**
(Sir Harry Lewis (USA) 127) [2002 8s f8.5g⁴ 8.3d 8.3s⁴ 8.1d Jun 14] IR 13,500F,
11,000Y: second foal: dam unraced half-sister to high-class miler Recitation: fair form:
caught the eye last 2 outings, in handicap at Sandown final one, behind for much of way,
late headway not knocked about: may prove best up to 1m: raced only on good to soft/soft
going on turf: almost certainly capable of better, assuming all is well. *W. J. Musson*

JAKARTA (IRE) 3 b.f. Machiavellian (USA) 123 – Lunda (IRE) 60 (Soviet Star **79**
(USA) 128) [2002 7g 8d 11.5g 7m* 7.6m⁵ 7d⁵ 8f⁴ 7d Nov 5] 135,000Y: smallish, sturdy
filly: has a quick action: second foal: half-sister to 4-y-o Dancing Tsar: dam, maiden,
half-sister to performers up to 1½m Luso (very smart) and Needle Gun/Cloud Castle
(both smart): fair performer: won maiden at Brighton in August: found 7f a minimum,
and stayed 1m: acted on firm and good to soft going: reportedly made a noise second
start, tongue tied next time: visits Mark of Esteem. *C. E. Brittain*

JAKEAL (IRE) 3 b.g. Eagle Eyed (USA) 111 – Karoi (IRE) (Kafu 120) [2002 90: 7m **77**
8m 7.9f 6f⁴ 6m⁴ 6m⁶ 7g 7.5m⁶ 6m 7.1d* 8.1m⁵ 7g³ 7d 7s Oct 25] IR 4,500F, IR 7,500Y:
strong gelding: half-brother to 1996 2-y-o 5f winner Rusty (by Shalford) and Irish 6.5f
winner Lions Den (by Desert Style): dam Irish 9f and 9.5f winner: fairly useful for
E. Lynam in Ireland at 2 yrs: fair handicapper in 2002, winning at Beverley in August:
probably best around 7f: acts on firm and good to soft ground: has been awkward leaving
stall: has worn severe bridle. *N. Tinkler*

JAKE BLACK (IRE) 2 b.g. (Apr 25) Definite Article 121 – Tirhala (IRE) (Chief **72**
Singer 131) [2002 8d⁵ 8v⁶ Nov 8] IR 30,000Y: third living foal: dam, Irish 2-y-o 6f
winner, half-sister to high-class 1¼m performer Timarida: fair form in maidens at Redcar
and Doncaster: should stay 1¼m. *J. J. Quinn*

JALB (IRE) 8 b.g. Robellino (USA) 127 – Adjacent (IRE) 82 (Doulab (USA) 115) **66**
[2002 f16.2g⁵ f16.2g² f16.2g* 14.1d* f14.8g⁵ f16.2f Aug 16] strong, well-made gelding:
fair handicapper: won at Wolverhampton in March and Nottingham in April: broke down
final start: stayed easy 2m: acted on soft going, good to firm and fibresand: blinkered last
5 starts: tongue tied in 2002: carried head awkwardly: dead. *P. G. Murphy*

JALOUHAR 2 b.g. (Feb 3) Victory Note (USA) 120 – Orient Way (IRE) 61 (Danehill **67**
(USA) 126) [2002 6g⁶ 7.2g⁵ 7g³ 7m⁶ 7m 6f⁶ Sep 27] 26,000F, 16,000 2-y-o: smallish,
rather leggy gelding: first foal: dam, Irish maiden, best at 7f: fair maiden: below form
in nurseries last 2 starts: stays 7f: raced on good going or firmer: races prominently.
K. R. Burke

JALOUSIE (IRE) 4 b.f. Barathea (IRE) 127 – Duende 75 (High Top 131) [2002 105: **108**
10.4f* 11.9d⁴ 12g 10m² 12g⁵ 10.3v⁵ Nov 8] well-made filly: useful performer: won listed
race at York in May by head from Salim Toto: respectable efforts after only when fourth
to Mellow Park in Lancashire Oaks at Haydock and second to Maid of Dawkins in
valuable listed race at Longchamp (worn down close home): effective at 1¼m to 1¾m:
acts on soft going, good to firm and fibresand: races prominently. *C. F. Wall*

JAMAICAN FLIGHT (USA) 9 b.h. Sunshine Forever (USA) – Kalamona (USA) **59 d**
(Hawaii) [2002 60d: f16s⁵ f16.2g* f16.2g² f16g² f16.2g² f16g² f16g⁶ f16g f16g³ 17.1f⁵
21.6m² 16.2g⁵ 16d³ 17.1m⁴ 18f⁴ 16.2g 12m⁵ 16f² 16.1d⁶ 16d⁵ 18m⁵ Sep 19] leggy horse:
modest handicapper nowadays: won at Wolverhampton in January: finds 1½m bare

minimum and stays 21f: acts on any turf going/fibresand: tried in visor, better without: has been too free to post/given trouble start: usually front runner: on downgrade. *Mrs S. Lamyman*

JAMES DEE (IRE) 6 b.g. Shalford (IRE) 124§ – Glendale Joy (IRE) (Glenstal (USA) 118) [2002 65: f7s f6g 8.1m f7g 10g Jul 8] one-time fairly useful 7f winner: no form in 2002: sometimes looks wayward. *Mrs P. Ford* –

JAMES DRUMMOND 3 b.g. Shaddad (USA) 75 – Miss Drummond 59 (The Brianstan 128) [2002 9.3s Jun 16] half-brother to 1996 2-y-o 5f winner Molly Drummond (by Sizzling Melody), later winner in Denmark: dam, 2-y-o 5f/6f winner, out of sister to high-class sprinter Petong: 66/1, always tailed off after very slow start in maiden at Carlisle. *B. Mactaggart* –

JAMES STARK (IRE) 5 b.g. Up And At 'em 109 – June Maid 56 (Junius (USA) 124) [2002 92: f5s f6g* p6g f6g f6g⁶ p5g f6g p5g f6g 5s² 6g 6m 5.1f² 5f 6m 5.1f 6d⁵ 5d 5.5m⁴ 6m 6g f5g* f6g f5g⁵ f6g⁶ Dec 31] leggy gelding: has a quick, fluent action: useful handicapper on all-weather, fairly useful on turf: won at Wolverhampton in January and Southwell in November: has form at 7.5f, probably best at 5f/6f: acts on any turf going/ all-weather: effective blinkered/visored or not: usually races prominently: tends to wander: unpredictable. *N. P. Littmoden* 89 § a97 §

JAMESTOWN 5 b.g. Merdon Melody 98 – Thabeh 57 (Shareef Dancer (USA) 135) [2002 74, a76: f8.5g* p10g 7.1m⁴ 7.1g 7.5g 7.9g 9.9d 7.5d⁵ 8.5g p7g f8.5g Dec 26] workmanlike, close-coupled gelding: fair performer at best: won amateur handicap at Wolverhampton (drifted right) in January: best at 7f to 8.5f: acts on all-weather, firm and soft going: on downgrade. *C. Smith* 75 d

JAMIERA (IRE) 2 b.f. (Apr 10) Compton Place 125 – Cafe Solo 51 (Nomination 125) [2002 6g 5m 6.1d⁵ p6g 5m 5.1m³ 5v⁴ 5m⁶ 6g f5g f7g⁵ 8.2v Oct 29] IR 5,000Y: third foal: dam 6f/7f winner: modest maiden: best effort on third start: probably stays 7f: acts on heavy going and all-weather: tried tongue tied/visored: sometimes finds little. *P. D. Evans* 62 d

JAMMAAL 5 b.h. Robellino (USA) 127 – Navajo Love Song (IRE) 43 (Dancing Brave (USA) 140) [2002 115: 10v⁶ 10s² 10g⁶ 10s³ 11s Oct 20] strong, close-coupled horse: carries condition: smart performer: best effort in 2002 when neck second of 5 to Della Francesca in Gallinule Stakes at Leopardstown in June: respectable efforts last 2 starts in Royal Whip Stakes at the Curragh and handicap at Naas: effective at 1¼m to 1½m: seems suited by good ground or softer (acts on heavy): blinkered. *D. K. Weld, Ireland* 113

JAM TODAY 2 b.f. (Apr 9) Elmaamul (USA) 125 – Sonic Sapphire 67 (Royal Academy (USA) 130) [2002 5m 6d 5g Jul 30] 1,500F, 4,200 2-y-o: angular, rather unfurnished filly: first foal: dam, looked less than keen only start (fourth at 1m at 2 yrs), out of sister to Middle Park winner/2000 Guineas runner-up Lycius: modest form in maidens: best effort on second start: will stay 7f. *M. C. Chapman* 58

JAN BRUEGHEL (USA) 3 ch.g. Phone Trick (USA) – Sunk 94 (Polish Navy (USA)) [2002 82p: 6m⁶ 5m⁵ 8m 6.5v⁵ 9m⁶ 8g⁶ 7.5s 8g Oct 31] big, strong gelding: fair maiden: left P. Cole after third outing: below form after next start: stays 6.5f: acts on heavy and good to firm going. *W. P. Browne, Ireland* 70 d

JANES GEM (IRE) 2 b.f. (Feb 12) Among Men (USA) 124 – Kingdom Queen (IRE) 65 (Night Shift (USA)) [2002 6s⁶ 6m⁵ f8s⁵ 7d* f7g³ 7v f8.5g f8.5s⁴ f8.5g⁴ Dec 31] lengthy filly: first foal: dam 1¼m winner who stayed 15f: modest performer: won claimer at Redcar in October: left C. Thornton after next start: stays 8.5f: acts on soft going, good to firm and fibresand. *A. Bailey* 54

JANES VALENTINE 2 b.f. (Mar 29) My Best Valentine 122 – Jane Herring (Nishapour (FR) 125) [2002 p6g² Dec 28] fifth foal: dam lightly-raced half-sister to useful but temperamental 5f/6f performer Sylvan Breeze: 50/1, ½-length second to Dunhill Star in Lingfield maiden, slowly away and headway from rear to challenge final 1f: should improve. *J. R. Boyle* 74 p

JANNADAV (IRE) 2 b.f. (Apr 17) Barathea (IRE) 127 – Sweet Alma 67 (Alzao (USA) 117) [2002 6m³ p7g⁴ f7g* Nov 16] IR 25,000Y: eighth foal: sister to 3-y-o Countess Miletrian and half-sister to fairly useful Irish 1996 2-y-o 6f winner Mubadara (by Lahib) and a winner in Turkey by Marju: dam, Irish 1¼m winner, half-sister to high-class 1m/ 1¼m performer Montekin: fair form: best effort when winning maiden at Wolverhampton by neck from Shadowfax, getting up near finish: will be suited by at least 1m: should progress. *J. A. Osborne* 72 p

JANOUEIX (IRE)   3 b.g. Desert King (IRE) 129 – Miniver (IRE) (Mujtahid (USA)   **70**
118) [2002 59p: p10g² f9.4s p12g p7g Dec 28] fair maiden: stays 1¼m, possibly not
1½m: form only on polytrack: visored final start. *G. A. Butler*

JARALA   3 b.f. Mtoto 134 – Al Raja 79 (Kings Lake (USA) 133) [2002 9d 12.1d⁶   **64**
12.4m⁴ 12m Aug 24] 600F, 2,500Y: leggy, workmanlike filly: eighth foal: dam 1½m
winner: modest maiden: should stay 1¾m: raced too freely final start. *Mrs L. Stubbs*

JARDINES LOOKOUT (IRE)   5 b.g. Fourstars Allstar (USA) 122 – Foolish   **119**
Flight (IRE) 57 (Fools Holme (USA)) [2002 119: 13.9f³ 20m 16m* 15.9g⁶ 18m⁴
16f Nov 5]

So attached is the stayer Jardines Lookout to his companion Henry the
Shetland pony that Flemington racecourse agreed the pair could enter the winner's
circle together if 30/1-shot Jardines Lookout won the Melbourne Cup. With
Jardines Lookout held up and staying on late for seventh to Media Puzzle, Henry
never looked like enjoying his 'fifteen minutes of fame'. Connections were critical
of Australian jockey Patrick Payne for setting Jardines Lookout too much to do,
though the jockey's version of events was that his mount couldn't go the early pace.
The Melbourne Cup, contested on very firm going, was the second-fastest ever run
and the strong pace should have been ideal for out-and-out stayer Jardines Lookout.
A repeat of his best form—as represented by victory under similar conditions over
the same trip in the Goodwood Cup—would have seen Jardines Lookout in the
frame at Flemington and he is well worth another tilt at the race. The JPMorgan
Private Bank Goodwood Cup is the only race Jardines Lookout has won since his
three-year-old days and it was run at an end-to-end gallop. With Persian Punch
stretching the field from the start, Jardines Lookout had his bottomless stamina
brought fully into play and, driven ahead over three furlongs out, he won by a
length and a half from Give Notice, with the only three-year-old in the line-up
Charley Bates a further three and a half lengths away third. The course record was
lowered by almost two seconds. Ground conditions had been similar for the Gold
Cup at Royal Ascot but Jardines Lookout, starting third favourite, never looked like
repeating his good third of the previous year, finishing only ninth. The explanation
offered afterwards by his trainer was that the gelding had been girthed too tightly at
the start, returning badly chafed. Jardines Lookout also finished in the frame in the
latest season in the Yorkshire Cup, not at all discredited when third to Zindabad
over a trip short of his best, and in the Doncaster Cup, in which he ran a little in
snatches when fourth to Boreas. The Lonsdale Stakes at York, a race in which
Jardines Lookout was just touched off by Persian Punch in 2001, provided him with
an opportunity to follow up his Goodwood Cup win—he started favourite—but his
pacemaker didn't set a strong enough gallop and the race began in earnest all too
late, Jardines Lookout managing only sixth.

The leggy, sparely-made Jardines Lookout, named after a suburb of Hong
Kong, is by Fourstars Allstar, who pulled off a successful American challenge for

*JPMorgan Private Bank Goodwood Cup—Jardines Lookout gains a deserved pattern-race victory,
beating Give Notice and Charley Bates*

			Compliance		Northern Dancer
	Fourstars Allstar (USA)		(b 1978)		Sex Appeal
	(b 1988)		Broadway Joan		Bold Arian
Jardines Lookout (IRE)			(ch 1979)		Courtneys Doll
(b.g. 1997)			Fools Holme		Noholme II
	Foolish Flight (IRE)		(b 1982)		Fancifool
	(ch 1991)		Black Crow		Sea Hawk II
			(b 1974)		Cafe Au Lait

the Irish Two Thousand Guineas in 1991. The dam of Jardines Lookout, Foolish Flight, was lightly raced in Ireland and is a daughter of the stoutly-bred, modest winning handicapper Black Crow, who stayed a mile and three quarters. Black Crow's best offspring was Dark Raven, the top juvenile hurdler of 1985/6. Jardines Lookout, who sometimes hangs under pressure, shows knee action and has won on soft going, but nearly all his best performances have come on good going or firmer. He is best at two miles plus and needs a strong gallop. *A. P. Jarvis*

JARJOOR 2 b.c. (Feb 28) Alhaarth (IRE) 126 – Neptunalia 70 (Slip Anchor 136) **71** [2002 7s 8g⁴ 8s Nov 6] 31,000F, 115,000Y: has a quick action: fourth foal: half-brother to 4-y-o Beechy Bank and 7f winner Jabuka (by Shareef Dancer): dam, 1½m winner, half-sister to very smart performer up to 1½m Glory of Dancer: best effort in maidens (fair form) when fourth to Redspin at Brighton, racing freely: stays 1m: raced only on good going or softer: carried head awkwardly final outing. *M. A. Jarvis*

JARRAAF 2 ch.c. (Feb 1) Desert Story (IRE) 115 – Bee Off (IRE) 59 (Wolfhound **60** (USA) 126) [2002 6m Jul 29] IR 46,000F, 37,000Y: first foal: dam, Irish maiden who stayed 7f, half-sister to Nell Gwyn winner Thrilling Day: 8/1, seventh of 15 to Crimson Silk in maiden at Windsor: sold 6,000 gns. *M. P. Tregoning*

JARV (IRE) 4 b.f. Inzar (USA) 112 – Conditional Sale (IRE) (Petorius 117) [2002 60: **53 §** 7g 7m 7d⁴ 8.1g 7m Jul 22] modest handicapper: was best around 1m: acted on soft and good to firm going: usually blinkered: unreliable: dead. *J. Akehurst*

JASMICK (IRE) 4 ch.f. Definite Article 121 – Glass Minnow (IRE) 59 (Alzao (USA) **96** 117) [2002 88: 12m⁶ 12g⁶ 12g⁴ 14.4d* 14m 16.2d⁵ 13.9m Aug 21] smallish filly: useful handicapper: won at Kempton in July by head from Scott's View (pair clear): below form after: best at 1½m/1¾m: acts on firm and good to soft going. *H. Morrison*

JASMINE BREEZE 3 b.f. Saddlers' Hall (IRE) 126 – Regal Peace 94 (Known Fact **–** (USA) 135) [2002 61p: 9.9m May 16] lengthy, rather unfurnished filly: modest form in maiden at Newmarket only 2-y-o start: only tenth (raced freely) in similar event only outing in 2002. *W. Jarvis*

JAVA 3 b.f. Rainbow Quest (USA) 134 – Island Jamboree (USA) (Explodent (USA)) **82 p** [2002 8.2m² 11s⁵ 8.5f* Dec 8] big, good-bodied, imposing filly: sixth foal: sister to high-class winner up to 1¼m in Britain and USA Fiji and half-sister to smart 1½m winner Capri (by Generous): dam, won 10 times in USA from 6f to 8.5f, also second in Grade 1 9f event at 5 yrs: burly, better effort in maidens in Britain (fairly useful form) when 1½ lengths second to Kirov at Nottingham on debut in May: tongue tied, found little at 11f on soft ground at Goodwood following month: left H. Cecil and off 6 months, won maiden at Hollywood in December: bred to stay 1¼m+, but may prove best around 1m: acts on firm going: likely to do better still. *N. D. Drysdale, USA*

JAVA DAWN (IRE) 2 b.f. (Feb 26) Fleetwood (IRE) 107 – Krakatoa (Shirley Heights **60** 130) [2002 7d⁴ 6m 6s⁶ 7g⁵ 7m⁵ 7m⁵ 8m 7m² 7g Oct 24] fourth foal: half-sister to a winner in Greece by King's Signet: dam temperamental and of little account over hurdles: modest maiden: stays 7f: acts on good to firm going: slowly away final start: none too genuine. *Miss D. A. McHale*

JAVELIN 6 ch.g. Generous (IRE) 139 – Moss (Alzao (USA) 117) [2002 –: 10f* 10m⁴ **70** 12.6f* 12.6g² 12m Aug 25] strong gelding: fair handicapper: won at Nottingham in May and Warwick in June: stays 12.6f: acts on firm and good to soft going (some promise on fibresand). *Ian Williams*

JAWHARI 8 b.g. Lahib (USA) 129 – Lady of The Land 75 (Wollow 132) [2002 70: **88** f5g* f6g⁵ 5.3f³ 5d* 5.3g² 6g* 6m* 6d⁴ 6g² 5.3m³ Aug 19] small, sturdy gelding: has a **a80** quick action: fairly useful handicapper: won at Wolverhampton in February and 3 apprentice races at Goodwood in May/June: has form at 7.6f, probably ideally suited by 5f/6f: acts on all-weather, soft and good to firm ground: blinkered (raced freely) once. *T. G. Mills*

JAWLEYFORD COURT 3 b.f. Moshaajir (USA) 77 – Mrs Jawleyford (USA) 58 – (Dixieland Band (USA)) [2002 7d 9d 12m 16.2d Jul 22] lengthy, good-topped filly: second foal: dam, 2m winner, also won over hurdles: no form. *C. Smith*

JAWWALA (USA) 3 b.f. Green Dancer (USA) 132 – Fetch N Carry (USA) (Alleged (USA) 138) [2002 84p: 7.1m⁵ 10d 10f 12d⁴ 14.1s² 16m⁵ f12s Oct 8] leggy, close-coupled, sparely-made filly: fair handicapper: stays 1¾m (raced freely at 2m): acts on soft going: sometimes takes good hold: sold 15,000 gns. *J. W. Payne* 75

JAYANJAY 3 b.g. Piccolo 121 – Morica 88 (Moorestyle 137) [2002 78: 6m 5d⁴ 6f 5s³ 6d² 6d⁴ 5m³ 6m⁵ 6m⁵ 5m 6f⁵ 5m⁶ p6g⁴ Oct 8] close-coupled gelding: fairly useful handicapper: best at 5f/6f: acts on polytrack, firm and soft going: sometimes slowly away. *N. Hamilton* 83

JAYCAT (IRE) 4 ch.f. Catrail (USA) 123 – Improviste (CAN) (The Minstrel (CAN) 135) [2002 56: 8.3g 11.8d 9.2g 7.9g Aug 5] unfurnished filly: modest maiden at best: no form since fourth 3-y-o start: blinkered once at 3 yrs. *W. M. Brisbourne* –

JAYED (IRE) 4 b. or br.g. Marju (IRE) 127 – Taqreem (IRE) 73 (Nashwan (USA) 135) [2002 f8.5g 6g 10m May 15] 3,200 3-y-o: third foal: half-brother to useful 7f winner who stayed 1¼m Ma-Ariif (by Alzao): dam, middle-distance maiden, half-sister to Ibn Bey and Roseate Tern: well held in maidens/seller (pulled hard). *M. Bradstock* –

JAY GEE'S CHOICE 2 b.c. (Mar 20) Barathea (IRE) 127 – Llia 94 (Shirley Heights 130) [2002 6m² 7d³ 7f³ 7.1m* 7d* 7s Oct 25] sturdy, well-made colt: sort to carry condition: has a quick action: fourth foal: half-brother to 3-y-o Kootenay and 5-y-o Dilsaa: dam, 2-y-o 7f winner who stayed 1½m, out of smart performer up to 9f Llyn Gwynant: fairly useful performer: won maiden at Haydock in September and minor event at Leicester (by ½ length from Hasanpour) in October: should stay 1m: acts on firm and good to soft ground, folded tamely on soft: usually races prominently. *M. R. Channon* 94

JAY JAY LASS 2 b.f. (Feb 7) Bold Fort 100 – Suelizelle 54 (Carnival Dancer 117) [2002 f6g May 24] first known foal: dam, maiden who ran only at 2 yrs, probably stayed 6f: 33/1, always behind in maiden at Wolverhampton. *D. Burchell* –

JAZAN (IRE) 3 b.f. Danehill (USA) 126 – Babita 107 (Habitat 134) [2002 94?: 7f³ 8.5m² 8.1m⁵ 8s³ 9.9m 8.3d⁴ p8g f8g³ p10g Dec 18] good-bodied filly: fair maiden on turf, modest on all-weather: stayed 8.5f: acted on fibresand, firm and soft ground: blinkered (faded over 1¼m) final outing: visits Best of The Bests. *C. E. Brittain* 74 a57

JAZMEER 3 ch.f. Sabrehill (USA) 120 – Saabga (USA) 83 (Woodman (USA) 126) [2002 83: 9m 7m 8m³ 8.3m² 8.5m* Aug 24] lengthy filly: fairly useful performer: found to have fractured a pastern and had 2 screws inserted after winning on second of 2 outings at 2 yrs: good placed efforts in handicaps before winning minor event at Beverley in August: stayed 8.5f: raced only on good to firm going: raced too freely on reappearance: wore crossed noseband final start: visits In The Wings. *M. P. Tregoning* 88

*Manchester Evening News July Trophy Stakes, Haydock—only three runners,
but a good-quality field as Derby fourth Jelani beats Grampian (left) and Bollin Eric*

JAZZAAM   3 ch.f. Fraam 114 – Aldwick Colonnade 62 (Kind of Hush 118) [2002 –:   **63 ?**
8.3m 6s 10m f8.5g 10.1g 10d⁴ Aug 11] leggy filly: well beaten until seemed to show
modest form in maiden at Windsor final start: seems to stay 1¼m. *M. D. I. Usher*

JAZZ BEAT (IRE)   3 b.c. Darshaan 133 – Hint of Humour (USA) 93 (Woodman   **113**
(USA) 126) [2002 80p: 10s* 10m⁵ 12d 9.5f² 10f² 9f Sep 22] tall, useful-looking colt:
second foal: half-brother to Irish 8.5f winner National Honour (by Nashwan): dam, Irish
7f winner, out of Italian Group 3 1¼m winner High Competence: won minor event at
Cork in June: good efforts after when 3¾ lengths fifth to Burning Sun in listed race
at Royal Ascot, ¾-length second to Mananan McLir in Grade 2 American Derby at
Arlington and nose second to Chiselling in Secretariat Stakes at Arlington, caught near
line on last 2 occasions: below form in Grade 2 Jamaica Handicap at Belmont final start:
seems best around 1¼m (well held in Irish Derby over 1½m): acts on firm and soft going:
sent to Hong Kong. *D. K. Weld, Ireland*

JAZZ MESSENGER (FR)   2 bl.g. (Feb 27) Acatenango (GER) 127 – In The   **67 p**
Saltmine (FR) (Damister (USA) 123) [2002 p7g⁶ Oct 16] third known foal: half-brother
to a 1m winner in Germany by Damister: dam German 7f/1m winner: 33/1, 8 lengths
sixth to Grand Passion in maiden at Lingfield, carrying head awkwardly but keeping on
from rear: should improve. *G. A. Butler*

JAZZY MILLENNIUM   5 ch.g. Lion Cavern (USA) 117 – Woodcrest 82 (Niniski   **60**
(USA) 125) [2002 65: 6m⁴ 6g 7m 7m 7m 6g 6g* 6m⁵ 5m Aug 26] quite attractive gelding:
modest performer: won selling handicap at Brighton in August: better at 6f than 7f, and
should be effective at 5f: acts on firm and soft going: blinkered nowadays: races up with
pace. *B. R. Millman*

JEANNIE WIZ   2 b.f. (Apr 21) Wizard King 122 – One For Jeannie 68 (Clantime 101)   **54**
[2002 6d⁶ 7.2g 7f⁶ Sep 25] strong, lengthy filly: third foal: half-sister to fairly useful 2001
German 2-y-o 5f winner One For Us (by Superlative): dam 5f/6f winner: modest form in
minor event at Haydock and maiden at Ayr first 2 starts: will probably stay 1m. *A. Bailey*

JEDEYDD   5 b.g. Shareef Dancer (USA) 135 – Bilad (USA) (Riverman (USA) 131)   **90**
[2002 95: 7f 8d 7m⁵ 7m 7g* 7m⁶ 8.3m³ 7m 8g⁶ Oct 24] lengthy gelding: fairly useful
handicapper: won at Leicester in July: effective at 7f/1m: acts on firm ground, probably
not on softer than good: sold 13,000 gns, and joined M. Dods. *B. Hanbury*

JEEPSTAR   2 b.g. (Mar 6) Muhtarram (USA) 125 – Jungle Rose 90 (Shirley Heights   **66 p**
130) [2002 5m⁶ 5d⁴ 5m 7m⁴ Sep 5] 22,000Y: unfurnished gelding: half-brother to several
winners, including 4-y-o Patsy's Double: dam lightly-raced 1¼m winner: half maiden:
best effort when fourth in nursery at Redcar final start, good late headway: will be suited
by 1m+: has given trouble in preliminaries: open to further improvement. *T. D. Easterby*

JEFFREY ANOTHERRED   8 b.g. Emarati (USA) 74 – First Pleasure 73 (Dominion   **57**
123) [2002 72, a–: 7v 6s⁵ 7.1g 7.2g⁴ 7.5g 5.9s 7.2v³ 6.9d 7.2d⁵ Jul 23] small gelding: **a–**
modest handicapper nowadays: on a lengthy losing run: stays 7.6f: acts on heavy going,
probably good to firm: sometimes blinkered/visored: usually held up: none too
reliable. *M. Dods*

JELANI (IRE)   3 b.c. Darshaan 133 – No Rehearsal (FR) (Baillamont (USA) 124)   **115**
[2002 98p: 10.4f⁵ 12d⁴ 11.9m* Jul 14] big, good-topped colt: smart performer, lightly
raced: best effort when winning 3-runner listed event at Haydock in July by 2 lengths
from Grampian: found to have suffered tendon injury: 15 lengths fourth to High Chaparral in Derby at Epsom previous outing: stays 1½m: yet to race on heavy going, acts on
any other: stays in training, but not expected to return before autumn. *Andrew Turnell*

JELBA   4 b.f. Pursuit of Love 124 – Gold Bracelet § (Golden Fleece (USA) 133) [2002   **79**
87: p7g p8g⁶ p7g* p7g² p10g 6m⁴ 7g⁵ 6d⁴ 7d⁶ 7g 6.9d 7m 7m⁶ 8.1m p8g* p7g⁵ p8g²   **a95**
Dec 21] tall, quite good-topped filly: useful handicapper on all-weather, fair on turf: won
at Lingfield in February and November, better than ever when beating Marnie 2 lengths
in latter: effective at 6f to 1m: acts on firm ground, good to soft and all-weather (best
form on polytrack): blinkered twice, visored nowadays: often slowly away: held up, and
sometimes finds little. *N. P. Littmoden*

JELLYHEAD   2 b.c. (Feb 3) Distinctly North (USA) 115 – Homebeforemidnight (Fools   **–**
Holme (USA)) [2002 p5g Nov 23] 2,800Y, resold 3,600Y: third foal: dam lightly-raced
half-sister to smart sprinter Roman Prose: 100/1, well beaten in maiden at Lingfield.
Mrs S. A. Liddiard

JEPAJE   5 b.g. Rambo Dancer (CAN) 107 – Hi-Hunsley 82 (Swing Easy (USA) 126)   **44**
[2002 52d: f7g p7g f7g³ f7g f6g Feb 8] poor nowadays: stays 7f: acts on fibresand (function
on polytrack), heavy and good to firm going: tried blinkered: sometimes awkward
leaving stall/twice unseated after finishing line: none too consistent. *A. Bailey*

JERPAHNI   3 b.f. Distant Relative 128 – Oublier L'Ennui (FR) 79 (Bellman (FR) 123)   **49** §
[2002 58§: 6m f8.5s 9.3s 8.2g² 10d f12g 10m 8g Oct 16] tall, leggy filly: poor maiden:
left T. Wall after sixth start: stays 1m: tried blinkered/visored: has given plenty of trouble
in preliminaries: not an easy ride: one to treat with caution. *P. D. Evans*

JERVAULX FLICKA   3 b.f. Magic Ring (IRE) 115 – Tirolina (IRE) (Thatching 131)   **41**
[2002 –: 8g 7m 6m 6f³ Jun 3] lengthy filly: second foal: dam, unraced half-sister to useful
Irish sprinter Sharp Point, out of half-sister to 2000 Guineas winner Tirol: poor maiden:
blinkered last 2 starts. *C. W. Fairhurst*

JESSICA'S DREAM (IRE)   4 b.f. Desert Style (IRE) 121 – Ziffany 68 (Taufan   **112**
(USA) 119) [2002 114: 5m⁵ 5s* 5g 5.1f³ 5g³ 5m 5g³ 5g Oct 6] smallish, workmanlike
filly: smart performer: won Kerry Group Ballyogan Stakes at Cork in June by ½ length
from Miss Beabea: good close third to Agnetha in King George Stakes at Goodwood on
fifth start, despite meeting trouble: has won at 6f, but best at 5f: winner on firm ground,
very best efforts on good ground or softer: tough and genuine: sold 115,000 gns in
December. *J. G. Given*

JESSIE   3 ch.f. Pivotal 124 – Bold Gem 68 (Never So Bold 135) [2002 77: 7.6f 7m 8m   **57**
8d 8s⁴ 7d Oct 18] lengthy filly: fair performer at 2 yrs, modest in 2002: seems best around
1m: acts on soft going, probably on firm. *Don Enrico Incisa*

JESSIE MACDOUGALL   2 br.f. (Apr 29) Overbury (IRE) 116 – Miss Crusty 45   **53**
(Belfort (FR) 89) [2002 5d* 6f⁴ 7d⁶ f7f f7g⁴ Sep 21] leggy filly: fourth foal: half-sister to
6-y-o Crusty Lily: dam 1m winner: modest performer: won claimer at Haydock in May:
well below form last 3 starts (visored last 2): likely to prove best at 5f/6f: acts on firm and
good to soft ground: possibly ungenuine. *P. D. Evans*

Peter Onslow and Derek Hilton's "Jessica's Dream"

JESSINCA   6 b.m. Minshaanshu Amad (USA) 91§ – Noble Soul 67 (Sayf El Arab   –
(USA) 127) [2002 42, a59: 6.1m Sep 20] smallish, sturdy mare: modest handicapper on
all-weather, poor on turf in 2001: well held only start at 6 yrs: tried visored. *A. P. Jones*

JEVINGTON GREY   3 gr.g. Bal Harbour 113 – Bercheba (Bellypha 130) [2002 –:   –
12g 10g 14.1m p13g 12m 16.4g⁶ Aug 22] well held in maidens/handicaps. *R. M. Flower*

JEWEL OF INDIA   3 ch.c. Bijou d'Inde 127 – Low Hill (Rousillon (USA) 133) [2002   **93**
73: f7g⁵ 6f⁴ 8.3s* 7g* f8g* 8m⁵ 8m f8.5g³ 9.2m⁵ 8s* p8g* Dec 30] leggy, sparely-made
colt: fairly useful performer: won minor events at Hamilton/Leicester and handicap at
Southwell within 10 days in July, handicap at Leicester in October and (having left Sir
Mark Prescott) minor event at Lingfield in December: stays 1m (raced too freely at 9f):
acts on all-weather and soft going, probably on good to firm: effective blinkered or not:
sometimes slowly away. *P. J. Hobbs*

JEWEL OF TROYES (IRE)   3 ch.f. Bijou d'Inde 127 – Troyes 81 (Troy 137) [2002   **75 §**
10.5d 10s⁴ 10g* 11.7d⁴ 10.1d 10d³ 11.5m² f9.4g f16.2g Nov 18] IR 42,000Y: half-sister   **a– §**
to fairly useful 9f winner (stayed 1½m) Tromond (by Lomond), now dam of very smart
1½m performer Nowhere To Exit, and to several winners by Risk Me, including 9f/1¼m
winner Trojan Risk: dam, 1½m winner, half-sister to Yorkshire Oaks winner Hellenic:
fair performer: won maiden at Ayr in May by 11 lengths: left M. Bell after seventh outing:
stayed 1¼m: unraced on extremes of going on turf, ran as if amiss both starts on
fibresand: often found little: needed treating with caution: dead. *R. Brotherton*

JEZADIL (IRE)   4 b.f. Mujadil (USA) 119 – Tender Time (Tender King 123) [2002   **49**
52, a63: p16g 12.4g² f12s 12.1m³ 12g⁴ Oct 19] sparely-made filly: poor performer: stays
1½m, not 2m: acts on firm going, soft and fibresand: blinkered (well below form) once:
folded tamely final start: none too consistent. *Mrs L. Stubbs*

JIMJONPADDAL (IRE)   3 b.g. Key of Luck (USA) 126 – Rich Heiress (IRE) 49   **76**
(Last Tycoon 131) [2002 76, a62: 7s 8f 6g 5s⁴ 6s³ 7g 6.2d 6.5s Aug 21] fair maiden on
turf, modest on all-weather: left J. M. Bradley after third start: effective at 5f, stays 1m:
acts on soft going, good to firm and polytrack: sometimes blinkered. *M. V. Manning,
Ireland*

JIM LAD   2 b.g. (Mar 23) Young Ern 120 – Anne's Bank (IRE) 77 (Burslem 123) [2002   –
6s p7g 7d 6m 5.7f 8f⁵ 8f 6g Oct 18] 1,100Y: sixth foal: dam Irish 7f (at 2 yrs)/1m winner
who should have stayed 1½m: signs of only a little ability: tried blinkered/visored.
Dr J. R. J. Naylor

JIMMY MORSE   4 b.g. Chaddleworth (IRE) 103 – Sea Crossing (FR) 50 (Kala Shikari   **44**
125) [2002 10m 7m⁶ p5g 6m 7d Aug 11] third known foal: dam 1m seller winner: poor
maiden: dead. *J. White*

JINGLING GEORGIE   3 b.f. Ali-Royal (IRE) 127 – Golden Daring (IRE) (Night   –
Shift (USA)) [2002 51: 10m 8.1d 11.6m Jul 15] modest at best at 2 yrs: no form in 2002.
B. Palling

J M W TURNER   3 b.c. Forzando 122 – Noor El Houdah (IRE) 61 (Fayruz 116) [2002   **73**
80, a95: 6g 6g 6g 5g 5d 6m 5m 5.9m² f7s² 5m⁵ 6m⁵ 6f p7g² f6g* p7g⁴ p7g f6g* Dec 31]   **a105**
sturdy colt: useful handicapper on all-weather, fair on turf: better than ever in 2002,
winning twice at Wolverhampton in December (beat Massey by 3½ lengths on second
occasion): best form at 6f/7f: acts on all-weather and firm going: usually blinkered/
visored: races freely, and best held up. *N. P. Littmoden*

JOB RAGE (IRE)   8 b. or br.g. Yashgan 126 – Snatchingly (Thatch (USA) 136) [2002   **39**
f16g⁴ 17.2d² 11.1g⁵ 12.1d 16d⁴ 16g Aug 12] tall gelding: poor maiden handicapper: stays
17f: acts on soft going. *A. Bailey*

JOCKO GLASSES   5 ch.g. Inchinor 119 – Corinthia (USA) (Empery (USA) 128)   –
[2002 –: 12g⁶ Jul 11] lengthy gelding: fairly useful winner at 3 yrs: well held both Flat
runs since. *Mrs M. Reveley*

JODEEKA   5 ch.m. Fraam 114 – Gold And Blue (IRE) (Bluebird (USA) 125) [2002   **84 §**
97: 6d⁴ 5f 5.1d 5.1m³ 5g 5d 5m 5g 5m f6s f5g* f6g⁴ p6g f5g f5g Dec 17] strong, close-
coupled mare: only fairly useful handicapper in 2002, though won at Wolverhampton in
November: best form around 5f: acts on fibresand, good to firm and good to soft going:
tried visored: unreliable. *J. A. Glover*

JODONSTAY   2 b.f. (May 5) Komaite (USA) – Cliburnel News (IRE) 76 (Horage   –
124) [2002 5.1s f6f Nov 11] first foal: dam 6f (at 2 yrs) to 2m winner: last in maidens.
D. Shaw

JOE BEAR (IRE) 2 ch.c. (Apr 28) Peintre Celebre (USA) 137 – Maharani (USA) **79 p**
(Red Ransom (USA)) [2002 6d p8g* Nov 14] 11,000 2-y-o: quite attractive colt: third
foal: half-brother to 4-y-o Lucefer: dam, second at 8.5f in Germany, sister to smart 1994
2-y-o Sri Pekan: better effort in maidens (fair form) when winning at Lingfield by head
from Tropical Coral: backward/slowly away on debut: will stay at least 1¼m: should
improve. *P. Mitchell*

JOELY GREEN 5 b.g. Binary Star (USA) – Comedy Lady 46 (Comedy Star (USA) **68**
121) [2002 62, a59: p10g⁴ p10g* p10g² f12g⁵ p10g⁶ 10.9f 10m⁴ 11.9g* 11.9g 16.5g⁵ **a79**
12.1g 11.9g⁴ p12g² 11.9g³ p12g⁶ f14.8g* f12g² p13g² Dec 28] tall, workmanlike gelding:
fair performer: won handicap at Lingfield in January, claimer at Brighton (ladies) in
May, and minor event at Wolverhampton (amateurs) in December: stays 15f: acts on all-
weather, raced only on good ground or firmer on turf: usually blinkered/visored:
sometimes slowly away/races freely/looks less than easy ride. *N. P. Littmoden*

JOE TAYLOR (CAN) 4 b.g. Known Fact (USA) 135 – Shore Mist (USA) (Coastal **–**
(USA)) [2002 53d: f11s Jan 17] smallish gelding: maiden: tongue tied (pulled up) only
run in 2002. *C. N. Kellett*

JOHANNESBURG (USA) 3 b.c. Hennessy (USA) 122 – Myth (USA) (Ogygian **116**
(USA)) [2002 127: 7s² a10f 6m Jun 22]
    The wheels might have come off after the Kentucky Derby plan backfired,
but there is no danger of Johannesburg's ending up on the scrapheap. Although
his reputation has been severely dented, Johannesburg's exploits at two were still
relatively fresh in the mind and will ensure that he is well supported when returned
to the States for a third time to take up stallion duties at Coolmore's Ashford Stud,
his fee set at 30,000 dollars. The top two-year-old in Europe after gaining six
straight wins, including those in the Phoenix Stakes, Prix Morny and the Middle
Park, Johannesburg maintained his unbeaten record and also established himself
as the best two-year-old to race in America in 2001 with a smooth success in the
Breeders' Cup Juvenile. He was only the second European-trained two-year-old,
after Arazi, to receive an Eclipse award. Who would have thought that Johannesburg's seventh win would be his last? Things might have been different if a more
conventional approach to Johannesburg's three-year-old career had been adopted.
His trainer Aidan O'Brien certainly held the view that the tilt at the Kentucky
Derby was a mistake. Johannesburg, ridden by Gary Stevens as Michael Kinane
was suspended, was a never dangerous eighth of eighteen behind War Emblem.
'The combination of training him on bad ground in our wet spring and trying to
stretch his stamina too far just bottomed him out.' Johannesburg looked a shadow
of the colt who carried all before him at two when trying to restore his reputation in
the Golden Jubilee Stakes at Royal Ascot. Although he couldn't have looked in
better shape, Johannesburg drifted alarmingly in the betting, though still going off
favourite, and was in trouble passing halfway, eventually beating only three of his
eleven rivals. Johannesburg's reappearance effort, when a short-head second to the
very smart four-year-old filly Rebelline in the Gladness Stakes at the Curragh,
turned out to be his best as a three-year-old. On the soft ground that day, Johannesburg tired after looking to be full of running two furlongs out and was caught in
the last stride. It was a disappointing performance, but not one which gave any
indication at the time that Johannesburg, who blew excessively in the unsaddling
enclosure, might have failed to train on.

				Storm Bird
	Hennessy (USA)	Storm Cat		Terlingua
	(ch 1993)	(b or br 1983)	Island Kitty	Hawaii
Johannesburg (USA)			(ch 1976)	T C Kitten
(b.c. 1999)		Ogygian		Damascus
	Myth (USA)	(b 1983)		Gonfalon
	(b 1993)	Yarn		Mr Prospector
		(b or br 1987)		Narrate

    Johannesburg's pedigree, fully documented in an expansive essay in
Racehorses of 2001, is one which will make plenty of appeal to breeders in the
States. His sire Hennessy, who also stands at Ashford, raced only at two, winning
four times and also finishing a close second in the Breeders' Cup Juvenile; Johan-
nesburg's dam Myth, a sprint winner, is a half-sister to another Ashford stallion
Tale of The Cat (by Hennessy's sire Storm Cat), who was smart at up to nine

furlongs but best at seven, and to the Phoenix Stakes and Middle Park Stakes winner Minardi. This is a pedigree very much tailored for speed, of which Johannesburg had plenty, and although he won the Breeders' Cup Juvenile over an extended mile it was optimistic to think that he would prove as effective over a mile and a quarter in the Kentucky Derby. A well-made colt and a good walker, Johannesburg, who wore a crossed noseband, acted on dirt, good to firm and good to soft going. *A. P. O'Brien, Ireland*

JOHANNIAN 4 b.c. Hernando (FR) 127 – Photo Call 73 (Chief Singer 131) [2002 **110** 108: 10m³ 10.4f* 10.3g² 10m 10.3m² 10.4m 10.4m⁵ 10.9g⁴ Sep 21] quite good-topped colt: unimpressive mover: smart performer: won handicap at York in May by ½ length from Pasithea: good second of 3 to Foreign Affairs in minor event at Doncaster in June: well below form last 2 starts: effective at 1¼m/1½m: acts on firm and soft going: sometimes bandaged off-hind: sold 80,000 gns. *M. A. Jarvis*

JOHAYRO 9 ch.g. Clantime 101 – Arroganza 62 (Crofthall 110) [2002 60: 5g 7.1m⁶ **44 §** 6d⁵ 7.1g 7f 6m⁶ 5m 6m 5m Aug 22] close-coupled gelding: has a quick action: poor handicapper: effective at 5f to sharp 7f: possibly unsuited by soft/heavy going, acts on any other: occasionally blinkered/visored: usually races up with pace: unreliable. *J. S. Goldie*

JOHN FOLEY (IRE) 4 b.g. Petardia 113 – Fast Bay (Bay Express 132) [2002 49§: **– §** f9.4g 16.2m⁶ Jul 7] big gelding: temperamental maiden: tried blinkered/visored. *P. S. Felgate*

JOHNNY OSCAR 5 b.g. Belmez (USA) 131 – Short Rations (Lorenzaccio 130) [2002 **91** 91p: 16.2s⁴ 13.9g⁵ 16.1d⁵ Jul 10] tall, leggy gelding: fairly useful handicapper: good efforts first 2 outings in 2002: likely to prove best at 2m+: acts on firm and soft going: sold 12,000 gns. *J. R. Fanshawe*

JOHNNY REB 4 b.g. Danehill (USA) 126 – Dixie Eyes Blazing (USA) 56 (Gone **–** West (USA)) [2002 69d: 8m 7m 9.9g 6.1m Jul 13] strong gelding: fair handicapper in 2001: well held in 2002, running as though something amiss on occasions: tried tongue tied earlier in career. *J. G. Given*

JOHNNY STACCATO 8 b.g. Statoblest 120 – Frasquita (Song 132) [2002 53§, a–§: **– §** p10g f16g 10.9g Apr 1] leggy gelding: modest handicapper on his day at 7 yrs: well held in 2002: tried visored earlier in career. *C. Drew*

JOHN O'GROATS (IRE) 4 b.g. Distinctly North (USA) 115 – Bannons Dream (IRE) **101 p** (Thatching 131) [2002 81: 5f⁶ 5f⁴ 6g⁵ 5s 5.1f 5m⁶ 5g 6m⁴ 5g* 5d² 5m⁴ 5.1f³ 5m⁴ 5m* 6g* 6f Oct 12] tall, close-coupled, good-topped gelding: useful performer, much improved in 2002: won handicap at Pontefract in August and minor event at Sandown and 27-runner Tote (Ayr) Silver Cup in September, last-named by length from Blue Velvet: effective at 5f/6f: acts on firm and soft going: has worn crossed noseband: has been early to post: held up: type to improve further. *M. Dods*

JOHN'S CHAMP (IRE) 2 b.g. (Apr 23) Mujadil (USA) 119 – Big Buyer (USA) 67 **57** (Quest For Fame 127) [2002 6s 6m p7g 8m⁵ f8.5s f7g⁵ Dec 17] 17,000F, 15,000Y: first foal: dam, ran 3 times (should have stayed beyond 1¼m), granddaughter of Irish Oaks winner Regal Exception: modest maiden: best effort at 1m on good to firm going: visored final start. *A. P. Jarvis*

Tote (Ayr) Silver Cup (Handicap)—the much improved John O'Groats comes with a strong run to beat Blue Velvet, Adweb (No.22) and Tayif (far side)

JOHNSON'S POINT   4 ch.f. Sabrehill (USA) 120 – Watership (USA) (Foolish   **73**
Pleasure (USA)) [2002 65: 9.9m⁶ 9.9g³ 11.9d 12m² 12.1d⁴ 12m* 12.1g⁴ 12.1d² 14m²
11.9m⁶ 13.9f² Oct 12] sturdy filly: fair handicapper: won at Doncaster in July: at least
creditable efforts after: stays 1¾m: acts on firm and good to soft going: usually blinkered:
held up: reliable: successful over hurdles in October. *M. W. Easterby*

JOHNSON'S DIAMOND (IRE)   4 b.g. Tagula (IRE) 116 – Toshair Flyer 88   **62**
(Ballad Rock 122) [2002 63: 8m 5d 6m² 6g² 5m⁵ 6m 6d³ f7g⁴ Dec 14] sparely-made
gelding: modest maiden: seems best at 5f/6f: acts on firm ground, good to soft and fibresand. *E. J. Alston*

JOHN'S TREASURE (IRE)   2 b.g. (Feb 7) Entrepreneur 123 – Misallah (IRE)   **–**
(Shirley Heights 130) [2002 7.2g Sep 20] 3,000Y: fourth living foal: dam, in frame up to
12.5f in France, closely related to dam of very smart miler Almushtarak: 66/1, tailed off
in maiden at Ayr. *P. C. Haslam*

JOINT INSTRUCTION (IRE)   4 b.g. Forzando 122 – Edge of Darkness 62 (Vaigly   **56 +**
Great 127) [2002 70d: f7s⁶ p6g⁴ p5g³ a6g a6.8g⁵ 5.8m² a6g 5.8g⁶ a6.8g⁵ a6g⁴ a6.8g²
a6s* a6s⁴ Nov 30] smallish, sturdy gelding: modest performer at best nowadays: left
D. Nicholls after third start: won handicap at Taby in November: probably best around 6f:
acts on any turf going and dirt/all-weather: tried visored: has found little/flashed tail.
Y. Brandt, Sweden

JOINT STATEMENT   3 b.g. Barathea (IRE) 127 – Gena Ivor (USA) (Sir Ivor 135)   **91**
[2002 6g 10g 8f 9.1g⁶ 7s 7g 8m³ 8g² 7.2g³ 8m⁶ 8m⁵ 8m⁶ 8.1m* 8m* 8f* 8m* 8g³ 8.1g⁴
8g* Oct 24] 15,000F, 21,000Y: strong, lengthy gelding: sixth foal: half-brother to fairly
useful 1997 2-y-o 5f winner Call To Order (by Reprimand), later successful in USA, and
unreliable 7f winner Ivor's Deed (by Shadeed): dam 6f to 8.5f winner in USA: progressed
into a fairly useful performer in second half of year, winning handicaps at Haydock,
Goodwood and Bath and minor events at Leicester and Brighton in September/October:
stays 1m: acts on firm going. *M. R. Channon*

JOKESMITH (IRE)   4 b.g. Mujadil (USA) 119 – Grinning (IRE) (Bellypha 130)   **95**
[2002 102: 12g 10d 10.4m 9s Oct 26] leggy, lengthy gelding: useful performer:
respectable efforts at Royal Ascot and Sandown first 2 starts: stays 1¼m: acts on soft
and good to firm ground: has worn crossed noseband: reportedly had breathing problem
penultimate 3-y-o start: sold 15,000 gns, joined K. Ryan. *B. J. Meehan*

JOLLANDS   4 b.g. Ezzoud (IRE) 126 – Rainbow Fleet 66 (Nomination 125) [2002   **–**
74d: 10s f14.8g 11.6g 10m Jul 16] quite good-topped gelding: fair performer at best: no
form in 2002: tried visored. *R. Curtis*

JONALTON (IRE)   3 b.g. Perugino (USA) 84 – Vago Pequeno (IRE) (Posen (USA))   **47**
[2002 44: f12g 14.1m⁶ 12.3m⁶ Jun 19] poor maiden: stays 1¾m: acts on good to firm
going, probably on fibresand. *Mrs P. Sly*

JONES'FOLLY (IRE)   3 b.g. Anita's Prince 126 – Dame's Folly (IRE) (Kings Lake   **51**
(USA) 133) [2002 49: 8.2g⁵ 8g 8.1d* 8s 8.1g Sep 12] modest performer: won seller at
Chepstow in July: stays 1m: yet to race on ground firmer than good: looked tempera-
mental for win and on final start: joined S. Treacy in Ireland. *B. Palling*

JONESY   4 b.g. Emperor Jones (USA) 119 – Don't Jump (IRE) 71 (Entitled 126) [2002   **–**
–: f7s Jan 2] last in maidens/seller. *J. Gallagher*

JONI WIKABE (IRE)   3 b.g. Nicolotte 118 – Shoot To Kill 64 (Posse (USA) 130)   **–**
[2002 –: f7g⁶ 5.7g p7g 7f 8m 10d Oct 28] probably of little account. *R. M. H. Cowell*

JONLOZ   5 ch.g. Presidium 124 – Stratford Lady 48 (Touching Wood (USA) 127)   **–**
[2002 44: 16.2g 11.9s⁶ 13.8g 14.1f 16.2g Aug 15] sparely-made gelding: of little account
nowadays. *J. R. Norton*

JONNY EBENEEZER   3 b.g. Hurricane Sky (AUS) – Leap of Faith (IRE) 65   **97**
(Northiam (USA)) [2002 84: 7s⁵ 6m 6g⁵ 5d* 7s* 6g 6d 8g² 7m 6m* 6g Sep 27] tall
gelding: useful handicapper: won at Windsor in May, Epsom in June and Goodwood (beat
Roses of Spring by ¾ length) in September: effective at 5f to 1m: acts on soft and good to
firm going: sometimes awkward leaving stall/wanders: races up with pace. *I. A. Wood*

JOOLS   4 b.g. Cadeaux Genereux 131 – Madame Crecy (USA) (Al Nasr (FR) 126) [2002   **95 ?**
72: 7f 8.3g⁶ 9f 6m² 7m 6m⁴ 6m 10m⁶ 6d⁴ 6m 8.3s⁵ 8m² 8v Nov 19] rather leggy gelding:
seemingly useful performer: left Mrs N. Macauley after third start: won handicaps at
Windsor in June and Newmarket in August: contested French listed races last 3 starts,
appearing to run very well when fifth at Craon and short-neck second at Longchamp:

effective at 6f to 8.3f: acts on soft going, good to firm and fibresand: visored (not discredited) final 3-y-o outing. *P. D. Evans*

JORDANS ELECT 2 ch.g. (May 22) Fleetwood (IRE) 107 – Cal Norma's Lady (IRE) 87 (Lyphard's Special (USA) 122) [2002 7.2s⁶ 8s Nov 6] fifth foal: half-brother to several winners, including 1997 2-y-o 6f winner Magical (by Magic Ring), later Grade 3 1m winner in USA, and 1999 2-y-o 5f winner Sabre Lady (by Sabrehill), both fairly useful: dam 2-y-o 6f/7f winner who stayed 1¼m: green, well held in maidens. *I. Semple*

JOROBADEN (FR) 2 gr.c. (Mar 10) Poliglote 121 – Mercalle (FR) 108 (Kaldoun (FR) 122) [2002 7s⁴ Oct 25] 700,000 francs Y: close-coupled, quite good-topped colt: seventh foal: half-brother to 2 winners, including Japanese Group 1 1¼m winner Fabulous La Fouine (by Fabulous Dancer), also second in Japan Cup: dam French 1m to 2½m (Prix du Cadran) winner: 16/1, green and burly, 10½ lengths fourth of 12 to Barrissimo in maiden at Doncaster, staying on without being knocked about: will be suited by 1¼m+: sure to do better. *C. F. Wall* **75 p**

JORVICK 2 br.g. (Feb 14) Deploy 131 – Petra's Star 61 (Rock City) 120) [2002 8m f8.5g⁶ 7g Oct 17] 7,800Y, 12,000 2-y-o: fourth foal: half-brother to a winner in Spain by Aragon: dam ran 3 times: no sign of ability: tried visored. *C. A. Dwyer* **–**

JOSEPH WILLIAM (IRE) 3 b.g. College Chapel 122 – Murroe Star (Glenstal (USA) 118) [2002 –: 10m Aug 31] lengthy gelding: little sign of ability. *C. N. Kellett* **–**

JOSHUAS BOY (IRE) 2 ch.c. (Apr 27) Bahhare (USA) 122 – Broadway Rosie 101 (Absalom 128) [2002 6d⁶ 7.1m 5g Oct 19] IR 21,000F, 40,000Y: big, strong colt: has plenty of scope: half-brother to several winners, notably smart 6f winner Eastern Purple (by Petorius): dam Irish 5f to 7f winner: seemingly modest form in maiden at Haydock on debut: well beaten after: kicked in paddock before second start. *K. A. Ryan* **59 ?**

JOUVERT 2 ch.c. (Jan 11) Grand Lodge (USA) 125 – Polygueza (FR) 78 (Be My Guest (USA) 126) [2002 6m 6m 6d 6g Oct 28] 38,000Y: well-made colt: third foal: half-brother to an Italian winner around 7f (including at 2 yrs) by Barathea: dam, Irish 7f winner, half-sister to useful Irish miler Lepoushka: fair maiden: best effort when seventh at Windsor second start: last in nursery final one: should stay at least 7f. *R. Hannon* **68**

JOVIAL LAD (IRE) 6 b.g. Soviet Lad (USA) – Vital Spirit 65 (Tachypous 128) [2002 –: f7g f7g Feb 1] no form after 1999: tried blinkered: dead. *W. Jenks* **–**

JOYCE'S CHOICE 3 b.g. Mind Games 121 – Madrina 70 (Waajib 121) [2002 72: 5v 5d 5d⁴ f5g Dec 17] leggy, unfurnished gelding: fair performer at 2 yrs: below best in 2002: best form at 5f: acts on firm and soft going. *A. Berry* **60**

JOYFUL ILLUSION 3 br. or b.f. Robellino (USA) 127 – Sharp Falcon (IRE) 76 (Shaadi (USA) 126) [2002 –: 10m 12g 10.2f Sep 16] small, good-topped filly: has a markedly round action: no form. *M. D. I. Usher* **–**

JOYFULL DREAM (FR) 4 ch.f. Midyan (USA) 124 – Villa Maria Pia (FR) (Alwasmi (USA) 115) [2002 43d: f8g f7g⁶ 14f Oct 3] of little account nowadays. *Miss G. Lee, Ireland* **–**

J R STEVENSON (USA) 6 ch.g. Lyphard (USA) 132 – While It Lasts (USA) 78 (Foolish Pleasure (USA)) [2002 99: 8g 10.3f 8g 8.5s⁴ 8m 8d* 7m 8g 8g⁶ 8.2v 8s f8.5g⁵ Nov 18] strong, close-coupled gelding: has a quick action: fairly useful handicapper: won at Newmarket in July: effective at 1m/1¼m: acts on soft and good to firm going: tried visored: held up/often finds trouble. *M. Wigham* **92**

JUAN CARLOS (IRE) 3 ch.g. Ashkalani (IRE) 128 – Mimansa (USA) (El Gran Senor (USA) 136) [2002 9g 12d 10m 8.5m Aug 16] IR 12,000Y: second foal: dam French 13f winner: well held in maidens/claimer: tried visored. *B. Gubby* **–**

JUBILEE 2 ch.f. (Mar 6) Selkirk (USA) 129 – Royal Passion 78 (Ahonoora 122) [2002 7d Nov 2] leggy, angular filly: sixth foal: half-sister to 9-y-o Tadeo and 4-y-o Attache: dam 1¼m winner: 20/1, 8 lengths eighth of 18 to Aljazeera in maiden at Newmarket, off bridle by halfway: should do better. *B. J. Meehan* **65 p**

JUBILEE GIRL (IRE) 2 b.f. (Mar 26) Desert Prince (IRE) 130 – Hopping Higgins (IRE) 103 (Brief Truce (USA) 126) [2002 5d⁵ 5.2f⁵ 6d⁶ 7v Nov 9] first foal: dam best at 2 yrs when Irish 5f winner: modest maiden: soundly beaten in nursery final start: not sure to stay 7f: acts on firm and good to soft ground. *M. A. Jarvis* **56**

JUBILEE PRINCE 2 b.g. (Mar 13) Petong 126 – Efficacious (IRE) 49 (Efisio 120) [2002 6m Jun 30] 3,000Y: second foal: dam maiden who stayed 1½m: 25/1, tailed off in maiden at Goodwood. *A. E. Jones* **–**

JUBILEE STREET (IRE) 3 b.g. Dr Devious (IRE) 127 – My Firebird (Rudimentary (USA) 118) [2002 p8g 7g³ 7.5g⁵ 7g 7d 9g⁵ Oct 5] 38,000F, IR 74,000Y: big gelding: has scope: first foal: dam twice-raced half-sister to useful sprinters Rosselli and Dancing Music: fair maiden: barely stays 9f: raced freely third outing: sold 7,500 gns. *I. A. Balding* **75**

J'UBIO 3 b.f. Bijou d'Inde 127 – Eternal Triangle (Barachois (CAN)) [2002 43: p7g⁶ p8g⁴ f7g⁴ f8g³ f8g⁵ p7g 11.7d Sep 9] poor maiden: stays 1m: acts on all-weather: sometimes looks none too keen. *B. A. Pearce* **35**

JUDGE DAVIDSON 3 b.c. Royal Applause 124 – Without Warning (IRE) (Warning 136) [2002 90p: 8m 7m² 7.1d⁵ 8m² 8f* 8.1m² 8f* Sep 26] good-bodied colt: useful performer: won handicap at Kempton in August by 2½ lengths from Free Option, and minor event at Goodwood in September (cosily by ½ length from Summer View): stays 1m: acts on firm and good to soft going: hung right for 2-y-o win: sent to Hong Kong, where renamed Shanghai King. *J. R. Fanshawe* **108**

JUDGEMENT (IRE) 3 gr.c. Kendor (FR) 122 – Fleur d'Oranger 110 (Northfields (USA)) [2002 8m* 10g³ 10.3f⁵ Jun 1] IR 130,000Y: close-coupled colt: good mover: half-brother to several winners, including useful French/US performer up to 1¼m Wedding Ring (by Never So Bold) and fairly useful 7m winner Orangerie (by Darshaan): dam French 6f (at 2 yrs) and 1¼m winner who stayed 1½m: fairly useful form: won maiden at Newbury in April by 1½ lengths from Pagan Dance: didn't improve as much as expected when 8 lengths third to Highdown in listed event at Newmarket following month: ran poorly (reportedly had breathing problem) final start: bred to be suited by 1¼m+: bandaged behind/blanketed for stall entry all 3 starts. *J. H. M. Gosden* **93**

JUDHOOR 2 b.f. (Jan 14) Alhaarth (IRE) 126 – Almurooj 54 (Zafonic (USA) 130) [2002 6s² 6g* 7s⁴ 6.5m 6f³ Oct 12] leggy, close-coupled filly: first foal: dam, ran 4 times (best effort at 6f), half-sister to smart 7f performer Munir out of Lowther Stakes/Irish 1000 Guineas winner Al Bahathri: fairly useful performer: won maiden at Goodwood in July: best effort when 3 lengths third to Avonbridge in listed event at York: should stay 1m: acts on firm and soft going. *B. W. Hills* **93**

JUDIAM 5 b.m. Primo Dominie 121 – Hoist (IRE) 75 (Bluebird (USA) 125) [2002 59: p5g Mar 27] tall, leggy mare: modest handicapper: best at 5f: acts on heavy ground and all-weather. *C. A. Dwyer* **52 +**

JUDICIOUS (IRE) 5 b.g. Fairy King (USA) – Kama Tashoof 72 (Mtoto 134) [2002 92: 7.2g* 8m 7.9m⁴ 6m Sep 7] big, good-topped gelding: useful handicapper: won at Ayr in July by length from Up Tempo: suffered leg injury at Haydock final start: effective at 7f/1m: acted on any ground: probably best with exaggerated waiting tactics: dead. *I. Semple* **97**

JUFISCEA 3 b.g. Efisio 120 – Jucea 77 (Bluebird (USA) 125) [2002 59: 6g 8.2g 6.1d Jul 6] modest maiden for M. Channon at 2 yrs: well held in 2002: will probably stay 7f. *J. L. Spearing* **–**

JULES (IRE) 3 b.f. Danehill (USA) 126 – Before Dawn (USA) (Raise A Cup (USA)) [2002 8d 8m⁵ 8.5m 7.1f* 8v Nov 2] smallish filly: half-sister to numerous winners, including 1½m winners Pompeii (fairly useful, by Salse) and Blue Saddle (useful in France, by Sadler's Wells): dam, champion US 2-y-o filly in 1981, Grade 1 winner at 6f/7f: fair form: won maiden at Haydock in September by 6 lengths from King David: very stiff task, behind in listed race at Saint-Cloud final start: may prove best at 6f/7f: acts on firm ground: raced freely third outing. *J. H. M. Gosden* **76**

JUMBO'S FLYER 5 ch.g. Jumbo Hirt (USA) 90§ – Fragrant Princess (Germont) [2002 –: 8m 7.9g 8.3g Jul 18] close-coupled, sturdy gelding: fair handicapper at 3 yrs: lightly raced and well held on Flat since: visored final start. *F. P. Murtagh* **–**

JUMEIRAH DREAM (USA) 3 ch.c. Diesis 133 – Golden Vale (USA) (Slew O' Gold (USA)) [2002 76: 8.1f² 8.5g² a8f⁶ Oct 31] close-coupled colt: fairly useful maiden: left E. Dunlop and off 6 months after second outing: likely to stay beyond 8.5f: acts on firm going: pulled too hard final 2-y-o start. *M. Al Kurdi, UAE* **82**

JUMHOOR (IRE) 2 b.c. (Mar 25) Bahhare (USA) 122 – West of Eden (Crofter (USA) 124) [2002 6g 6m² 7g³ Oct 24] IR 115,000F, IR 175,000Y: sturdy, attractive colt: has scope: half-brother to 3 winners, including 4-y-o Tempting Fate and useful 1m (at 2 yrs)/1¼m winner Clapham Common (by Common Grounds): dam unraced: fair form in maidens: placed at Newcastle and Brighton, racing freely and wandering in latter: should stay 1m. *E. A. L. Dunlop* **77**

JUMMANA (FR) 2 ch.f. (Apr 27) Cadeaux Genereux 131 – Forty Belles (USA) (Forty Niner (USA)) [2002 p7g* 7s⁴ Oct 26] 350,000 francs Y: tall, angular filly: third **96 p**

foal: dam French maiden half-sister to smart French performer up to 1½m Bayourida: useful form: raced freely when winning maiden at Lingfield in October easily by 4 lengths from Compos Mentis: favourite, close fourth to Crystal Star in listed event at Newbury, running green and tiring having quickened to lead over 1f out: likely to prove best up to 7f: remains a good prospect, sure to win more races. *G. A. Butler*

JUNGLE LION 4 ch.g. Lion Cavern (USA) 117 – Star Ridge (USA) (Storm Bird **72** (CAN) 134) [2002 83: 8f f7s⁵ f8.5g³ 7f f9.4g² 7d f8s³ f8s Oct 8] lengthy, quite good-topped gelding: fair form in 2002: unlikely to stay further than 9.4f: acts on soft going and fibresand: visored last 6 starts: tongue tied: has worn near-side pricker: raced freely/hung left penultimate start: none too consistent. *J. O'Reilly*

JUNIKAY (IRE) 8 b.g. Treasure Kay 114 – Junijo (Junius (USA) 124) [2002 83: 10g **71** 10d⁴ 12g 9.9m⁶ 12.6g⁴ 10.1d⁴ 9m 9.9m⁶ 12m⁴ 10m 8f p10g² p10g Dec 21] workmanlike gelding: fair handicapper: barely stays 1½m: acts on polytrack, soft and good to firm going: tried blinkered early in career: usually held up. *R. Ingram*

JUNIPER (USA) 4 b.c. Danzig (USA) – Montage (USA) (Alydar (USA)) [2002 105: **?** 6d Jul 11] well-made, good sort: useful performer at best, lightly raced: stiff task and well-held last of 14 in July Cup at Newmarket on only outing in 2002: will stay beyond 6f: unraced on extremes of going: slowly away final 3-y-o start. *A. P. O'Brien, Ireland*

JUNKANOO 6 ch.g. Generous (IRE) 139 – Lupescu 102 (Dixieland Band (USA)) **66** [2002 66p: 14.1d* Mar 27] strong, good-topped gelding: useful bumper winner/fairly useful hurdler: fair handicapper on Flat, lightly raced: won at Nottingham on only Flat run of 2002: should stay beyond 2m: acts on soft ground: usually slowly away in 2001: twice reportedly distressed over hurdles, though won easily in November. *Mrs M. Reveley*

JUST A GIGOLO 2 b.g. (Apr 29) Inchinor 119 – Courtisane (Persepolis (FR) 127) **50** [2002 6m 7.9m 8g⁵ 7d Oct 18] 12,500Y, 4,500 2-y-o: neat gelding: half-brother to several winners, including 3-y-o Dangerous Liaison and 5-y-o Charming Lotte: dam French 2-y-o 7f winner: modest maiden: likely to prove best short of 1m: tongue tied after debut. *N. Tinkler*

JUST A GLIMMER 2 b.f. (Apr 16) Bishop of Cashel 122 – Rockin' Rosie 59 (Song **68** 132) [2002 6m p7g⁵ 6s⁶ f6f³ f7g³ f7g* Dec 31] 3,000Y: lengthy filly: eighth foal: **a87** half-sister to 4-y-o Another Diamond and fairly useful 1999 2-y-o 6f winner Rule of Thumb (by Inchinor): dam 5f winner: fairly useful on all-weather, fair on turf: won maiden at Wolverhampton in December by 3 lengths from Humouresque, making all: stays 7f: acts on fibresand and soft ground: sometimes slowly away. *L. G. Cottrell*

JUSTALORD 4 b.g. King's Signet (USA) 110 – Just Lady 72 (Emarati (USA) 74) **?** [2002 72d: f5g f5g f5g⁵ f5g⁴ f5g² f5g² 5m f5g³ p5g⁵ 5m f5g² f5s³ f6g f5g⁴ f5g f5f* f5g² **a85** p5g* Dec 21] lengthy gelding: fairly useful on all-weather: won handicaps at Wolverhampton (made all) in November and Lingfield (carried head awkwardly throughout) in December: races mainly at 5f: acts on firm ground, soft and all-weather: has worn cheekpieces. *J. Balding*

JUST A MARTIAN (FR) 2 b.c. (Apr 23) Marju (IRE) 127 – Stamatina (Warning **80** 136) [2002 7.1m 7f⁴ 8s p7g³ p8g³ Nov 19] 14,000Y: first foal: dam Italian 7f to 9f winner: fairly useful maiden: third in nurseries at Lingfield: stays 1m: acts on polytrack and firm ground. *W. R. Muir*

JUST ARTHUR 4 b.g. Aragon 118 – Spark Out (Sparkler 130) [2002 –: 8.1d Jun 3] **–** leggy gelding: probably of little account. *P. D. Evans*

JUSTBETWEENFRIENDS (USA) 3 ch.f. Diesis 133 – Just Cause (Law Society **85 d** (USA) 130) [2002 12g³ 12m² 12d⁵ f12g Nov 25] leggy, useful-looking filly: eighth foal: closely related to useful 1994 2-y-o 7f/1m winner (later stayed 11f) Jural (by Kris) and half-sister to 3 winners, including useful 1995 2-y-o 1m winner Committal (by Lycius), later 6f to 1½m winner in France/USA: dam unraced: promising debut (fairly useful form) when third in maiden at Thirsk in May: regressed: sold 4,500 gns. *M. Johnston*

JUST EMERALD 3 ch.f. Emarati (USA) 74 – Bichette 66 (Lidhame 109) [2002 65: **51** p7g p10g p8g³ p10g 8.3s p7g 7g 8d⁵ 8.5g 10m 8m Sep 3] good-topped filly: modest **a55** maiden: ran poorly last 3 starts: stays easy 1m, seemingly not 1¼m: acts on polytrack and soft ground: tried blinkered: sometimes races freely: inconsistent. *G. L. Moore*

JUSTE POUR L'AMOUR 2 ch.g. (Feb 12) Pharly (FR) 130 – Fontaine Lady 41 **84** (Millfontaine 114) [2002 7d 7m⁵ 7d⁶ 7m* 7m⁴ Sep 29] sturdy, workmanlike gelding: third foal: dam 5f/6f winner: fairly useful performer: won nursery at Doncaster in

505

September, making all despite flashing tail: creditable fourth in similar event at Ascot: will be suited by at least 1m: acts on good to firm going. *M. J. Ryan*

JUST ERN 3 ch.g. Young Ern 120 – Just Run (IRE) 45 (Runnett 125) [2002 61: f8.5g **54** 8g 5.9s⁶ 5.9g⁶ 5g⁴ 6g⁵ f6g Dec 10] compact gelding: modest maiden handicapper: **a–** effective at 5f, probably at 1m: raced mainly on going firmer than good on turf, below form both runs on fibresand: sometimes hangs left. *P. C. Haslam*

JUST FLY 2 b.g. (Feb 5) Efisio 120 – Chrysalis 66 (Soviet Star (USA) 128) [2002 p7g⁵ **81** f6f⁵ f7g² f8.5s⁵ p7g² p6g* Dec 30] 12,000Y: first foal: dam, maiden who stayed 1m, out of half-sister to Arc winner Saumarez: fairly useful performer: won nursery at Lingfield by head from Whippasnapper: stays 7f: acts on all-weather. *S. Kirk*

JUST JAMES 3 b.g. Spectrum (IRE) 126 – Fairy Flight (IRE) 86 (Fairy King (USA)) **110** [2002 84p: 6g 6f* 6g⁴ 7m* 7m 7m Jul 27] strong, compact gelding: not the best of walkers: smart performer: something seemingly amiss on reappearance: won handicap at Newmarket (came with remarkable run) in May and Jersey Stakes at Royal Ascot (beat Steenberg by neck, again finishing strongly) in June: respectable efforts after in Chipchase Stakes at Newcastle (sixth to Tedburrow) and Tote International Stakes (Handicap) at Ascot (slowly away and eased when unable to get on terms): better at 7f than 6f: acts on firm and soft going: held up: has shown signs of temperament, and gelded after final outing. *J. Noseda*

JUST JENNIFER 2 b.f. (Feb 1) Emperor Jones (USA) 119 – Highest Bid (FR) **68** (Highest Honor (FR) 124) [2002 6m 6f 6g 7s Oct 28] leggy, quite good-topped filly: third foal: dam, French 7.5f (at 2 yrs) to 1¼m winner, half-sister to US Grade 1 winner at 9f/ 1¼m Janet (by Emperor Jones): fair maiden: best effort when eleventh of 30 in sales race at Newmarket third start: should stay 7f: well held on soft ground: visored last 2 outings. *P. W. D'Arcy*

JUST MAGICAL 5 b.m. Emperor Jones (USA) 119 – Magnetic Point (USA) 60 **63 d** (Bering 136) [2002 63p: p6g p7g f8.5g 10m 7d 6v⁴ 8.1m f6g⁴ 7m 6d⁶ 6m⁴ f6g f6g f8.5g⁶ Dec 13] big, lengthy mare: modest performer at best: effective at 6f to 1m: acts on heavy going, good to firm and all-weather: sometimes blinkered: on downgrade. *A. B. Coogan*

JUST MICHAEL 3 b.c. Bluegrass Prince (IRE) 110 – Plucky Pet 50 (Petong 126) **88** [2002 61: f5g a6g² 5.8d⁵ a6g* a6g² a6g*] Sep 19] small, well-made colt: good walker: modest performer in Britain (sold from A. Berry after reappearance): fairly useful form in Sweden, winning maiden at Taby in August and handicap at Jagersro in September: probably best around 6f: acts on heavy going, good to firm and dirt: some promise on fibresand: has been blinkered. *T. Persson, Sweden*

Jersey Stakes, Royal Ascot—Just James makes a successful transition from handicap company, finishing strongly to beat Steenberg (far side) and Meshaheer

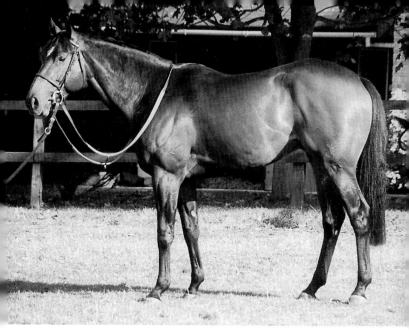

Lucayan Stud's "Just James"

JUST MY HOBBY   3 b.f. Kris 135 – Noble Peregrine (Lomond (USA) 128) [2002 —
10.2g 9.9m 11.8d 8.2g 10m f12g f12f⁶ Nov 11] angular, quite attractive filly: has a round
action: fifth foal: half-sister to 3 winners, including useful winner up to 11.5f Nobelist
(by Bering) and 4-y-o Wannabe Around: dam, Italian 1¼m winner, half-sister to smart
performer up to 1¼m Amrak Ajeeb: well held all starts. *M. Blanshard*

JUST NICK   8 b.g. Nicholas (USA) 111 – Just Never Know (USA) (Riverman (USA)   **83**
131) [2002 92+: 8m 8g 7d 8d⁵ 8d 8f 8d³ 8.3m 7.6s p8g Oct 9] smallish, good-topped
gelding: fairly useful handicapper at best: effective at 1m/9f: acted on heavy and good to
firm going: often slowly away: usually held up: dead. *W. R. Muir*

JUST ONE SMILE (IRE)   2 b.f. (Jan 28) Desert Prince (IRE) 130 – Smile Awhile   **68**
(USA) (Woodman (USA) 126) [2002 6g³ 7.5m³ 6m⁶ Aug 17] IR 18,000Y: lengthy,
useful-looking filly: has scope: second foal: half-sister to a winner in Japan by Lure: dam
once-raced sister to useful performer up to 1½m Gypsy Passion: fair form in maidens:
third at Doncaster and Beverley: likely to be suited by 1¼m/1½m. *T. D. Easterby*

JUST PERRY (IRE)   3 b.g. Perugino (USA) 84 – Bella More (IRE) (Law Society   **67**
(USA) 130) [2002 10f* 8m 12.3m⁵ Jun 20] 4,000Y: good-topped gelding: second foal:
dam, 2-y-o 9f winner in Italy, half-sister to very smart middle-distance performer
Infantry: won maiden at Redcar in May: slowly away and still looked green when below
that form in minor event/handicap after. *G. A. Swinbank*

JUST SAPPHIRE (IRE)   3 b.f. Entrepreneur 123 – Enthrone (USA) (Diesis 133)   —
[2002 p6g p8g⁶ f7g 8m 10d 7m Jul 3] 8,000Y: first foal: dam ran twice: no form: tried
visored. *D. K. Ivory*

JUST SAY YES (IRE)   2 b.f. (Apr 19) Bahhare (USA) 122 – Lyphards Goddess   **73**
(IRE) (Lyphard's Special (USA) 122) [2002 6d 7g² 7m⁴ 7g* 7m⁴ 7m² 10m⁶ Oct 1] IR
24,000Y: leggy filly: seventh foal: half-sister to 3 winners, including 6-y-o Route Sixty
Six: dam, lightly-raced Irish maiden, half-sister to useful 1988 2-y-o 5f winner Petrilla:

fair performer: won maiden at Catterick in July: creditable efforts in nurseries last 3 starts: stays 1¼m: yet to race on extremes of going: consistent. *M. R. Channon*

JUST SERENADE 3 ch.f. Factual (USA) 108 – Thimbalina 63 (Salmon Leap (USA) **66 d** 131) [2002 66: 8.2d⁴ 10g 8.1m⁶ 7m³ 7m 7.1m 7s² 8.1d 7d 7g 7m 10m 8m 8m Sep 19] workmanlike filly: fair maiden handicapper: below form after seventh start: stays 7f: acts on soft and good to firm ground: tried blinkered/visored. *M. J. Ryan*

JUST SUPERB 3 ch.g. Superlative 118 – Just Greenwich 65 (Chilibang 120) [2002 **–** 8m 8.1g 10s f9.4g Dec 16] fourth foal: dam 6f/7f winner at 2 yrs: well beaten in 4 maidens. *P. A. Pritchard*

JUST THE JOB TOO (IRE) 5 b. or br.g. Prince of Birds (USA) 121 – Bold **–** Encounter (IRE) 69 (Persian Bold 123) [2002 –, a59: f12s* f12g³ f11g⁵ f16.2g* f16g* **a60** f16.2g³ p16g⁵ f16g f16.2g May 20] good-topped gelding: modest performer: won seller at Southwell in January and handicaps at Wolverhampton/Southwell in February: stays 2m: acts on all-weather, poor form on turf: tongue tied penultimate start: sometimes idles in front: drifted right fourth outing. *P. C. Haslam*

JUST THE TRICK (USA) 3 b. or br.f. Phone Trick (USA) – Tammi's Pal (USA) **–** (Lear Fan (USA) 130) [2002 40: p5g f5g³ p5g f5g⁴ f5g⁶ f3g 3.1d 3.1f 3s f6g Aug 9] **a48** workmanlike filly: modest performer: won seller at Wolverhampton in February: best at 5f: acts on fibresand, best turf effort on good to firm going: usually blinkered, tried visored: sold 1,000 gns in November. *W. R. Muir*

JUST WIZ 6 b.g. Efisio 120 – Jade Pet 90 (Petong 126) [2002 45, a84: f9.4g² f9.4g³ **46** f8.5g⁴ 10.9m 10m 8g⁶ 9.7m⁶ f12g⁶ f8.5f⁵ f9.4g² f9.4g³ f9.4g² Dec 26] small gelding: **a85** fairly useful handicapper on all-weather, poor on turf: best at 8.5f to 9.4f: acts on fibresand, best turf form on good going or firmer: blinkered/visored earlier in career: usually held up. *N. P. Littmoden*

JUST WOODY (IRE) 4 br.g. Charnwood Forest (IRE) 125 – Zalamera 45 (Rambo **41 §** Dancer (CAN) 107) [2002 63§: 9g 9.2s⁵ 11.1g 7.9s⁵ May 27] poor performer: likely to prove best around 1m: acts on soft and good to firm going: inconsistent. *P. Monteith*

JUTHJOOR (IRE) 4 b.g. Marju (IRE) 127 – Deyaajeer (USA) 64 (Dayjur (USA) **–** 137) [2002 –: f12s f11g Mar 12] well held in claimer/sellers: tried blinkered. *J. O'Reilly*

JUWWI 8 ch.g. Mujtahid (USA) 118 – Nouvelle Star (AUS) (Luskin Star (AUS)) [2002 **89** 97, a101: f5s² f6g f6g f6g⁶ 5s⁶ 6s⁴ 6m 5g May 10] robust gelding: useful handicapper on **a102** all-weather, fairly useful on turf: ran well on reappearance: generally at least respectable efforts after: best at 5f/6f: acts on fibresand and any turf going: has reportedly bled: usually claimer ridden: usually slowly away and gets behind. *J. M. Bradley*

K

KAFIL (USA) 8 b. or br.g. Housebuster (USA) – Alchaasibiyeh (USA) 85 (Seattle **–** Slew (USA)) [2002 –: p7g f6g⁵ p6g p7g p6g 7f 5d p6g⁶ 9m 10m Jul 22] leggy gelding: of little account nowadays. *J. J. Bridger*

KAGOSHIMA (IRE) 7 b.g. Shirley Heights 130 – Kashteh (IRE) 79 (Green Desert **–** (USA) 127) [2002 73: 16.1m 16d⁶ 16.2s Jun 6] deep-bodied gelding: fair handicapper at best: well held in 2002: visored nowadays. *J. R. Norton*

KAHALAH (IRE) 3 b.f. Darshaan 133 – Alyakkh (IRE) 78 (Sadler's Wells (USA) **77** 132) [2002 10g 10g⁵ 12d* 14.4g⁴ Aug 26] leggy filly: half-sister to several winners, including 5-y-o Mutakarrim and useful 7f (at 2 yrs) to 1¼m winner Nafisah (by Lahib): dam, 1m winner who stayed 1¼m, out of Irish 1000 Guineas winner Al Bahathri: fair performer: fortunate to win maiden at Pontefract in July from prematurely-eased True Courage: good fourth in handicap at Newcastle (raced freely) final start: seemed to stay 1¾m: slowly away second outing: visits Alhaarth. *J. L. Dunlop*

KAIETEUR (USA) 3 b.c. Marlin (USA) 124 – Strong Embrace (USA) (Regal **117** Embrace (CAN)) [2002 93p: 10g* 10d² 12m⁴ 10d² 10s* 10m Oct 19] big, strong, well-made colt: has scope: smart performer: won minor event at Kempton in March and Grosser Dallmayr-Preis at Munich (by 2 lengths from Noroit) in August: also creditable ¾-length second to Burning Sun in Prix Eugene Adam at Maisons-Laffitte on fourth outing: increasingly on edge in preliminaries before below form in Champion Stakes at Newmarket final start: probably best around 1¼m (took strong hold in King Edward VII Stakes at Royal Ascot over 1½m): acts on soft and good to firm ground, probably on firm: usually races prominently. *B. J. Meehan*

KAISER (IRE) 2 b.g. (Mar 28) Barathea (IRE) 127 – Emerald Waters (Kings Lake **59 p**
(USA) 133) [2002 8d Oct 30] sixth foal: half-brother to fairly useful 1m (at 2 yrs) and 2m
winner Persian Waters and 5-y-o Eternal Spring (both by Persian Bold): dam Irish 11f
winner: 12/1 and green, 10 lengths eleventh of 13 to Devant in maiden at Yarmouth
(gelded after): should improve. *J. R. Fanshawe*

KALAMAN (IRE) 2 b.c. (May 22) Desert Prince (IRE) 130 – Kalamba (IRE) (Green **78 P**
Dancer (USA) 132) [2002 7d⁴ Oct 15] useful-looking colt: fifth foal: half-brother to 3
winners, notably top-class winner up to 1½m Kalanisi (by Doyoun): dam third at 9f (at 2
yrs) and 1¼m in France: 5/1, lethargic and green, promising 4 lengths fourth of 13 to
stable-companion Artistic Lad in maiden at Leicester, travelling comfortably in mid-field
after slow start and keeping on without being given hard time: should stay at least 1m:
type to improve considerably. *Sir Michael Stoute*

KALAMBARI (IRE) 3 b.g. Kahyasi 130 – Kalamba (IRE) (Green Dancer (USA) **93**
132) [2002 10m⁵ 10.1g² 12g* 12m⁶ 15g³ 13.1s⁵ Oct 15] leggy, useful-looking gelding:
fourth foal: half-brother to 2 winners, notably top-class winner up to 1½m Kalanisi (by
Doyoun): dam third at 9f (at 2 yrs) and 1¼m in France: fairly useful form: won maiden at
Catterick in May: creditable efforts in handicaps last 3 starts: unlikely to stay beyond 15f:
acts on soft and good to firm ground: blinkered last 4 outings: held up: sold 20,000 gns.
Sir Michael Stoute

KALOU (GER) 4 b.c. Law Society (USA) 130 – Kompetenz (IRE) (Be My Guest **87 ?**
(USA) 126) [2002 10d² 11v⁶ 10m³ 11s⁶ 11m⁴ 10d 11g² 10d⁵ 10.1s Oct 22] ex-German
colt: half-brother to winners in Germany by Platini and Komtur: dam ran twice in
Germany: useful performer at best: won maiden at Cologne at 3 yrs and ran well when
third in national listed race at Baden-Baden next start: in frame in handicaps and minor
event in 2002 prior to leaving A. Trybuhl after eighth outing: always behind in handicap
at Yarmouth on British debut: stays 11f: acts on heavy and good to firm going: tried
blinkered. *B. J. Curley*

KALUANA COURT 6 b.m. Batshoof 122 – Fairfields Cone (Celtic Cone 116) [2002 **61**
63: 15f⁶ 14.1d 18d⁵ 17.2g⁴ 14m* 21g 17.1m 16.2m⁴ 16m Sep 20] strong, good-topped
mare: modest handicapper: won at Sandown in July: should stay beyond 17f: acts on good
to firm going, probably not on softer than good: usually held up. *R. J. Price*

KAMAKAZI KNIGHT (IRE) 3 b.g. Night Shift (USA) – Kaskazi (Dancing Brave **–**
(USA) 140) [2002 –: 12g May 5] no sign of ability. *R. M. Flower*

KAMALA 3 b.f. Priolo (USA) 127 – Fleeting Vision (IRE) 79 (Vision (USA)) [2002 **68**
11.7m³ 12.1d⁴ 12m⁶ 12.4m⁵ 11.7f² 12.1g f14.8g³ Sep 21] first foal: dam, Irish 1½m to
2¼m winner, out of half-sister to St Leger winner Snurge: fair maiden: claimed from
M. Johnston £6,000 after fifth start: will stay beyond 14.8f: acts on firm going, good to
soft and fibresand: looks difficult ride: possibly has suspect attitude. *R. Brotherton*

KAMA'S WHEEL 3 ch.f. Magic Ring (IRE) 115 – Tea And Scandals (USA) (Key **43**
To The Kingdom (USA)) [2002 51: f8g f6g⁶ f7g 10m 7f 7m 8m² 8.3s 8m 8d Nov 1]
workmanlike filly: poor maiden: stays 1m: acts on good to firm ground (unproven on
softer than good) and fibresand: edgy sort: often slowly away. *John A. Harris*

KANDYMAL (IRE) 4 ch.f. Prince of Birds (USA) 121 – Gentle Papoose (Comman- **–**
che Run 133) [2002 49: 10.9m 7.5d Jul 5] angular, sparely-made filly: maiden: well held
in 2002: visored once at 3 yrs. *J. A. Glover*

KANGA 3 b.f. Primo Dominie 121 – Princess Zara (Reprimand 122) [2002 7.1f 6d² 6g⁴ **59**
f7g² f7g⁶ Dec 14] sparely-made filly: first foal: dam unraced: modest maiden: stays 7f:
acts on fibresand and good to soft going. *N. P. Littmoden*

---

*Grosser Dallmayr-Preis, Munich—a Group 1 success for the Brian Meehan-trained Kaieteur over Noroit,
Imperial Dancer (dark colours) and Equerry (rail), as Ifag Mannheim suffers an accident*

KANGARILLA ROAD 3 b.g. Magic Ring (IRE) 115 – Kangra Valley 56 (Indian **88 p**
Ridge 123) [2002 56: 5.1d² 5m* 5m³ 5g* 5f 5m 5g³ 5g* 5m⁶ 5f⁵ 5f⁶ Oct 11] leggy, good-
topped gelding: fairly useful handicapper: progressed well in 2002, winning at Catterick
in April, Thirsk in May and York in August: good efforts last 2 starts: will prove best at
5f: acts on firm ground: waited with nowadays: sometimes races freely: type to improve
further at 4 yrs. *Mrs J. R. Ramsden*

KANZINA 3 b.f. Machiavellian (USA) 123 – Kanz (USA) 115 (The Minstrel (CAN) **?**
135) [2002 72: p5g⁵ p7g 7.1f 7d 6g³ 8d Nov 1] smallish filly: unimpressive mover:
disappointing maiden: bred to stay at least 1m: blinkered (very slowly away) final start.
R. Hannon

KANZ WOOD (USA) 6 ch.g. Woodman (USA) 126 – Kanz (USA) 115 (The **61**
Minstrel (CAN) 135) [2002 69, a76: f8s² f7s* f7s⁶ f7g⁴ f7g⁴ f7g⁶ f7g² 8.3g 7m² 7d 7g⁶ **a71**
8.3s f8s 8f Sep 25] strong gelding: has reportedly had wind operation: fair performer on
all-weather, modest on turf: won seller at Southwell in January: effective at 7f/1m: acts
on good to firm going, good to soft and fibresand: tongue tied (ran as if amiss) penultimate start: often slowly away: has carried head high: none too reliable. *A. W. Carroll*

KAPALUA (USA) 2 b.f. (May 8) King of Kings (IRE) 123 – Numero Privee (USA) **–**
(Private Account (USA)) [2002 7m 7d Nov 2] 80,000Y: sixth foal: half-sister to 2
winners, including French 11f winner Private Party (by Fabulous Dancer): dam, placed
at 3 yrs in France, out of US Grade 2 9f winner Quixotic Lady: well held in maidens.
B. W. Hills

KAPAROLO (USA) 3 ch.g. El Prado (IRE) 119 – Parliament House (USA) (General **89**
Assembly (USA)) [2002 73p: 10g² 12.1m² 11.6m⁶ 12s² 14.1d* 14g 16m⁵ 14.6s² Oct 25]
strong gelding: fairly useful performer: won 4-runner maiden at Salisbury in July: good
second in handicap at Doncaster final start (gelded after): stays 14.6f: acts on soft and
good to firm going: has worn crossed noseband. *Mrs A. J. Perrett*

KARAKAL (GER) 6 bl.h. Dashing Blade 117 – Kardia (Mister Rock's (GER)) [2002 **106**
108: 10s⁴ 10g* 9.9d⁵ May 23] half-brother to smart German 1m to 1¼m performer
Kalatos (by Big Shuffle): dam German 7f (at 2 yrs) to 11f winner, half-sister to German
Group 1 1½m winner Kamiros: useful performer: lightly raced nowdays but won listed
race at Munich in May by 2 lengths from Adare Manor: creditable 9 lengths fifth to
Imperial Dancer in similar event at Goodwood later in month: stays 11f: raced mainly on
good going or softer. *Dr Andreas Bolte, Germany*

KARAKUM 3 b.g. Mtoto 134 – Magongo 103 (Be My Chief (USA) 122) [2002 75: **–**
p10g 10.2g 10.2g f12g Sep 30] close-coupled gelding: fair form in 2 maidens at 2 yrs:
well held in 2002, leaving M. Jarvis after reappearance: should stay at least 1¼m:
blinkered penultimate start. *A. J. Chamberlain*

KARAMAH 3 b.f. Unfuwain (USA) 131 – Azdihaar (USA) 81 (Mr Prospector (USA)) **74**
[2002 78p: 7g⁶ 6d⁵ Nov 1] well-made filly: promising second in maiden at Newmarket
on sole 2-y-o start (off 15 months after): much better effort in 2002 when fifth to
Zabaglione in minor event at Newmarket: visits Sakhee. *J. L. Dunlop*

KARAOKE (IRE) 2 b.c. (Mar 23) Mujadil (USA) 119 – Kayoko (IRE) 74 (Shalford **70**
(IRE) 124§) [2002 7.1g 6d 8g f7g³ f7f Nov 29] 21,000Y: first foal: dam, 6f winner,
half-sister to 8-y-o Proud Native: fair maiden: third in nursery at Wolverhampton: barely
stays 1m: acts on fibresand. *S. Kirk*

KARAOKE KING 4 ch.c. King's Signet (USA) 110 – Brampton Grace 80 (Tachy- **61**
pous 128) [2002 6g⁵ 6g⁴ 6g⁶ 5m 5f p12g p6g p8g p7g⁴ᵈ Dec 30] half-brother to German
7f winner Private Imp (by Risk Me): dam 5f (at 2 yrs) and 6f winner: modest maiden:
stays 7f: acts on polytrack: sometimes makes running. *J. E. Long*

KARATHAENA (IRE) 2 b.f. (May 1) Barathea (IRE) 127 – Dabtara (IRE) 88 (Kah- **82**
yasi 130) [2002 7m 8s² Oct 15] 42,000F, IR 25,000Y: good-bodied filly: second foal: dam
Irish 9f winner out of useful Irish performer up to 1¾m Dabtiya: much better effort in
maidens (fairly useful form) when beaten head by In Love at Ayr, leading 2f out, hanging
left and worn down close home: should stay 1¼m. *J. W. Hills*

KAREEB (FR) 5 b.g. Green Desert (USA) 127 – Braari (USA) 97 (Gulch (USA)) **94**
[2002 87: 7g 8g² 7d 7d⁶ 8s⁵ 7m³ 8g⁵ 7d⁵ 8m⁶ 7d 7m⁵ 7.1m 8m 7f⁶ 7s Nov 2] smallish,
robust gelding: fairly useful handicapper: probably better at 7f than 1m: acts on firm and
soft going: tried blinkered at 3 yrs: held up, and best in strongly-run race: hard to win
with. *W. J. Musson*

KARITSA 4 b.f. Rudimentary (USA) 118 – Desert Ditty 67 (Green Desert (USA) 127) **–**
[2002 56: f6s f6g p6g Feb 6] lengthy filly: fair winner at 2 yrs: no form in 2002.
G. L. Moore

KARLI 2 b.f. (Apr 13) Superpower 113 – Saraswati 55 (Mansingh (USA) 120) [2002 **49** 6s 6m[5] Oct 2] 1,200Y: good-topped filly: sixth foal: half-sister to 3 winners, including fairly useful 1997 2-y-o 5f winner Alfiglia (by Alhijaz), later 6f winner in Sweden: dam, disappointing maiden, closely related to Norfolk Stakes winner Petillante: poor form in maidens. *D. W. Barker*

KARLINIGHT (IRE) 2 b.f. (Feb 18) Night Shift (USA) – Karlinaxa (Linamix (FR) **–** 127) [2002 5f Apr 10] 350,000 francs Y: good-bodied filly: second foal: dam, French maiden who stayed 1¼m, half-sister to smart French performers Karmifira (up to 9f) and Karmousil (stayer): 33/1 and burly, well held in maiden at Warwick. *R. J. White*

KARMINSKEY PARK 3 b.f. Sabrehill (USA) 120 – Housefull 81 (Habitat 134) **71 §** [2002 64: f5g 6d 5g[2] 5m[3] 5g 5g[3] 5.1f 6s[4] 6s[2] 7d 7s p6g[3] Nov 14] heavy-bodied filly: fair maiden: seems to stay 6f: acts on polytrack, firm and soft going: sometimes flashes tail under pressure, and probably ungenuine. *T. J. Etherington*

KARTUZY (JPN) 2 b.f. (Apr 27) Polish Precedent (USA) 131 – Marienbad (FR) **– p** (Darshaan 133) [2002 7.1v[5] 8s Oct 25] big, strong, good sort: fourth foal: brother to 2 winners, notably 5-y-o Marienbard: dam, French 1m winner (including at 2 yrs), out of half-sister to very smart winner up to 1m Sakura Reiko: signs of ability in maidens: looks type to do better. *M. A. Jarvis*

KARYON (IRE) 2 b.f. (Feb 22) Presidium 124 – Stealthy 73 (Kind of Hush 118) **46** [2002 6s f8g[5] Nov 25] 2,100Y: good-topped filly: seventh foal: sister to a 5f (at 2 yrs) to 7.5f winner in Italy and half-sister to 1999 2-y-o 6f winner Stealthy Times (by Timeless Times): dam 1m winner: poor form in maiden at Leicester and minor event at Southwell. *P. C. Haslam*

KASAMBA 3 b.f. Salse (USA) 128 – Kabayil 75 (Dancing Brave (USA) 140) [2002 **80** 78: 9f 8.1d[3] 7.9f 8.1d[4] 8d[2] 8s[5] 10.2g 10s Oct 23] quite good-topped filly: has a quick action: fairly useful performer: stays 1¼m: best form on good going or softer (acts on soft): sometimes carries head awkwardly under pressure: not easy to predict. *C. G. Cox*

KASS ALHAWA 9 b.g. Shirley Heights 130 – Silver Braid (USA) 101 (Miswaki **–** (USA) 124) [2002 56, a50: p10g f9.4g f8g 9m Sep 16] good-topped gelding: modest handicapper at 8 yrs: no form in 2002: sometimes blinkered. *D. W. Chapman*

KASTHARI (IRE) 3 gr.g. Vettori (IRE) 119 – Karliyka (Last Tycoon 131) **113** [2002 10g[4] 10s* 10.2s[3] 13.9m[2] 14.6m[2] 12s Oct 26] tall, rather unfurnished gelding: third foal: half-brother to useful 2000 2-y-o 7f/1m winner Karasta (by Lake Coniston) and fairly useful 9f winner Karaliyfa (by Kahyasi): dam won at 8.5f to 11f in France: smart performer: won maiden at Windsor in May: best efforts when runner-up to Total Turtle in Melrose Handicap at York (hung left under strong pressure when beaten short head) and Mallard Handicap at Doncaster (beaten 3 lengths): well held in St Simon Stakes at Newbury final outing (on toes): gelded after: will stay 2m: acts on soft ground, very best efforts on good to firm. *Sir Michael Stoute*

KASTINA 3 b.f. Lancastrian 126 – Kit 34 (Green Ruby (USA) 104) [2002 –: f9.4g p7g **–** Feb 20] no sign of ability in 3 maidens. *M. J. Gingell*

KATAHOLIC 3 b.c. Bluegrass Prince (IRE) 110 – Langton Herring (Nearly A Hand **–** 115) [2002 10g 10m 10g[5] 6d 7m 8m Jun 27] half-brother to several winners, including useful but untrustworthy sprinter Sylvan Breeze (by Sulaafah) and fairly useful 2000 2-y-o 7f/8.5f winner Pathan (by Pyramus): dam unraced: no form: left I. Wood after third start: blinkered (very stiff task) fourth/fifth outings. *G. A. Ham*

KATANDI 3 b.f. In The Wings 128 – Maid of Kashmir (IRE) 94 (Dancing Brave **83** (USA) 140) [2002 9.9g 12f[2] 12m[2] 12d p12g[3] Nov 13] small, strong filly: third foal: sister **a71** to UAE 1m to 2m winner Shaalayn and half-sister to useful 1¼m winner Bezzaaf (by Machiavellian): dam Irish 1¼m winner who stayed 1½m: fairly useful form on turf, fair on all-weather: runner-up in maidens at Pontefract and Kempton: stayed 1½m: acted on firm going, probably on polytrack: blinkered/visored last 4 starts: visits Mtoto. *M. P. Tregoning*

KATCH ME KATIE 3 br.f. Danehill (USA) 126 – Miss Toot 72 (Ardross 134) [2002 **77** 7g[3] 8.3m[2] 9m* 8m Jun 22] leggy, useful-looking filly: seventh living foal: half-sister to very smart 7f/1¼m winner Kool Kat Katie and smart 8.3f (at 2 yrs) and 1¼m winner who stayed 1½m Kalypso Katie (both by Fairy King): dam 1¼m/15f winner on only starts: fair form in maidens, making hard work of landing odds at Musselburgh in June, drifting left: stiff task, running creditably when badly hampered in listed rated stakes at Royal Ascot final start: should be suited by 1¼m+: sent to France. *J. Noseda*

KATDOGAWN   2 b.f. (Feb 19) Bahhare (USA) 122 – Trempkate (USA) (Trempolino **90**
(USA) 135) [2002 5.7d* 5m 6m³ 6m⁶ Sep 5] smallish, lengthy filly: good mover:
first foal: dam, French 2-y-o 9f winner, out of smart performer up to 7f Glen Kate: fairly
useful performer: won maiden at Bath in May: creditable eighth in Queen Mary Stakes at
Royal Ascot next time: below best after (slowly away final outing): should stay at least
7f: sold 10,000 gns, sent to USA. *R. Hannon*

KATES SON (IRE)   5 ch.g. Fayruz 116 – Kates Choice (IRE) 86 (Taufan (USA) 119) **55**
[2002 61, a55: p10g f11g p8g² p10g² 9.7m p10g⁵ f8.5g p10g³ Jul 3] strong, lengthy
gelding: modest maiden handicapper: effective at 7f to 1¼m: acts on firm ground and
polytrack, seemingly not fibresand: visored third to seventh starts. *Noel T. Chance*

KATHAKALI (IRE)   5 b.g. Dancing Dissident (USA) 119 – Shes A Dancer (IRE) **49**
(Alzao (USA) 117) [2002 63, a76: p8g p10g p8g⁵ p10g⁶ p10g* 9.7m 10m f8.5g⁴ 10g⁵ **a69**
May 31] angular gelding: fair on all-weather, poor on turf: won seller at Lingfield in
April: effective at 1m/easy 1¼m: acts on all-weather, soft and good to firm going: tried
visored: none too consistent: sold £5,500 and gelded. *S. Dow*

KATHIES PET   7 b.m. Tina's Pet 121 – Unveiled 76 (Sayf El Arab (USA) 127) [2002 **61**
34. 10.2g 8d³ 7d⁴ 7.1v² 8g* 6m⁶ 7m³ 7.1g³ 8.3d⁰ Aug 5] rather leggy mare: modest
performer: won claimer at Salisbury and handicap at Brighton in June: effective at 7f/1m:
acts on fibresand, good to firm and heavy ground. *R. J. Hodges*

KATHINKA   3 b.f. Bin Ajwaad (IRE) 119 – Promissory (Caerleon (USA) 132) [2002 **82**
69?: 8.2d* 7d⁵ 9g⁶ 10.1m³ 10d Oct 14] leggy, quite good-topped filly: fairly useful
performer: won handicap at Nottingham in June, despite wandering: stays 1¼m: acts on
good to firm and good to soft going: reportedly had breathing problem third start.
C. E. Brittain

KATHOLOGY (IRE)   5 b.g. College Chapel 122 – Wicken Wonder (IRE) 71 (Distant **93**
Relative 128) [2002 96d: 6d⁴ 5.3g* 5d 6d* 6m 5m 6g 5.2f³ 5m² 5.6m 6g 5s Oct 26]
smallish, sturdy gelding: fairly useful handicapper: won at Brighton in May and Salisbury
in June: good placed efforts eighth/ninth starts: effective at 5f/6f: acts on soft and good to
firm going: usually races prominently. *D. R. C. Elsworth*

KATIES CHIMES (IRE)   5 b.m. African Chimes 100 – The Monks Sister (IRE)   **–**
(Tony Nobles (USA)) [2002 –: p13g Jan 9] little sign of ability. *R. Ingram*

KATIES DOLPHIN (IRE)   4 ch.f. Dolphin Street (FR) 125 – Kuwah (IRE) 77 (Be   **–**
My Guest (USA) 126) [2002 49: 7.1m⁶ 7f 6f 7f 7m 8m 8d 8m Jul 27] leggy, close-coupled
filly: maiden handicapper: little form in 2002: sometimes blinkered/visored: sold 1,500
gns. *A. Berry*

KATIES TIGHT JEANS   8 b.m. Green Adventure (USA) 119 – Haraka Sasa (Town   **–**
And Country 124) [2002 –: 7.1g⁴ 7.1g Sep 23] little form. *R. E. Peacock*

KATINA (USA)   3 b.f. Danzig (USA) – Alisidora (IRE) 105 (Nashwan (USA) 135) **68** +
[2002 6f⁶ 6s 7m p7g Nov 19] IR 290,000Y: quite good-topped filly: first foal: dam, Irish
1½m winner, out of half-sister to dams of Warning, Commander In Chief and Rainbow
Quest: won maiden at Redcar in June: ran well in handicap at Lingfield final outing: will
stay 1m: soon off bridle penultimate start. *M. Johnston*

KATIYPOUR (IRE)   5 ch.g. Be My Guest (USA) 126 – Katiyfa (Auction Ring **79**
(USA) 123) [2002 73: p10g³ 8.3g² 8m* 7d 8d³ 8g⁵ 8f³ 8.1m⁶ f8s⁴ f8g² 8s f9.4g* p8g³ f8g²
Dec 27] quite attractive gelding: fair performer: won claiming handicap at Bath in
June, and (having left P. Webber following eighth start) handicap at Wolverhampton in
November: stays 1¼m: acts on all-weather, best turf efforts on good ground or firmer:
effective visored or not: has looked ill at ease at Epsom: carries head high. *T. D. Barron*

KATMANDU   3 b.g. Sadler's Wells (USA) 132 – Kithanga (IRE) 117 (Darshaan 133) **73**
[2002 10s⁴ 12d⁶ p12g⁶ p12g³ Dec 14] third foal: brother to 4-y-o Milan: dam, won St
Simon Stakes and third in Irish St Leger, out of half-sister to dam of Kahyasi: fair form in
maidens: should stay 1¾m: acts on soft going and polytrack. *L. M. Cumani*

KAT SLATER (IRE)   3 b.f. Eagle Eyed (USA) 111 – Janiokey (Grundy 137) [2002   **–**
–: 11.1v Jun 12] no form in claimers/maidens: tried blinkered: refused to enter stall
intended debut. *G. A. Swinbank*

KATY O'HARA   3 b.f. Komaite (USA) – Amy Leigh (IRE) 78 (Imperial Frontier   **–**
(USA) 112) [2002 66: f6s² f6s² p6g³ f6g² Mar 14] good-bodied filly: fair performer: **a76**
creditable efforts in handicaps in 2002: will prove best at 5f/6f: acts on all-weather: has
idled in front. *Miss S. E. Hall*

KAVI (IRE) 2 ch.g. (Apr 13) Perugino (USA) 84 – Premier Leap (IRE) 56 (Salmon **64** Leap (USA) 131) [2002 5m 5s 6g³ 7.5d² 7m⁵ 7.5g* 10m f8.5g⁴ f8g* f9.4g² Dec 7] **a70** 3,500Y: small, strong, close-coupled gelding: fourth foal: half-brother to a winner up to 11f in Italy by Sri Pekan: dam Irish 11f and hurdles winner: fair on all-weather, modest on turf: won selling nursery at Beverley in September and claimer at Southwell in November: should stay at least 1¼m: acts on fibresand, good to firm and good to soft going. *P. C. Haslam*

KAWAGINO (IRE) 2 b.g. (Mar 9) Perugino (USA) 84 – Sharakawa (IRE) (Darshaan **99** 133) [2002 6m² 6g³ 7d⁵ 7d⁵ 6m Sep 20] IR 9,500Y: angular, deep-bodied gelding: fourth reported foal: half-brother to smart 7f (at 2 yrs) and 1m (in UAE) winner Rabi (by Alzao) and fairly useful 1998 2-y-o 1m winner Ebinzayd (by Tenby): dam unraced out of Prix Vermeille winner Sharaya: useful maiden: best effort when 3¾ lengths third to Statue of Liberty in Coventry Stakes at Royal Ascot: not disgraced when seventh in Mill Reef Stakes at Newbury: should stay 7f: acts on good to firm ground. *Mrs P. N. Dutfield*

KAWANBAIK 3 ch.f. Inchinor 119 – Sky Music 85 (Absalom 128) [2002 49: 8.2d **–** 8.2m 7.1m 10m Oct 3] angular filly: poor maiden: left K. McAuliffe after second start: tried blinkered. *J. S. Moore*

KAY KAY GIRL 2 b.f. (Mar 18) Piccolo 121 – Poly Blue (IRE) 82 (Thatching 131) **–** [2002 6m 6m Aug 25] lengthy filly: first foal: dam, 2-y-o 6f winner, out of half-sister to dual Gold Cup winner Sadeem: in rear in maidens: dead. *M. R. Channon*

KAYO NOBILE (USA) 2 b. or br.g. (May 17) Torrential (USA) 117 – Nobile Decre- **–** tum (USA) (Noble Decree (USA) 127) [2002 7m 7m 6m Sep 4] $1,200F, $15,000Y, 8,000 2-y-o: half-brother to several winners, notably smart 9f to 1½m performer Triarius (by Trempolino): dam maiden in USA: last in maiden/sellers. *T. Keddy*

KAYSERI (IRE) 3 b.c. Alzao (USA) 117 – Ms Calera (USA) (Diesis 133) [2002 90p: **107** 10f* 12.3f³ 12m 10m 10d² 12m³ 12m⁶ Sep 13] stocky colt: useful performer: won minor event at Pontefract in April: good efforts when placed after in Chester Vase (3½ lengths third to Fight Your Corner) and minor events at Newmarket (1¾ lengths second to Frankies Dream on first occasion, 7 lengths third to The Whistling Teal on second one): stays 1½m: acts on firm and good to soft going: has been bandaged off-hind: sent to UAE. *M. A. Jarvis*

KAYTASH 3 b.f. Silverdale Knight 65 – Lady Swift (Jalmood (USA) 126) [2002 8m **–** 10.5m 12f Jul 17] first foal: dam of little account: tailed off in maidens/claimer. *K. W. Hogg, Isle of Man*

KAZZIA (GER) 3 b.f. Zinaad 114 – Khoruna (GER) (Lagunas) [2002 105p: 8m* **121** 12s* 11.9m⁴ 10s* 10d⁶ Oct 26]

Godolphin's practised policy of purchasing promising two-year-olds with a view to the classics has had its share of disappointments, including recently Bad As I Wanna Be, Henri Lebasque, Inchlonaig, Rumpold, West Order and, in the States, Worldly Manner and Comeonmom, none of whom so much as placed in a stakes race at three. But there have been some even more notable success stories, namely Balanchine, successful in the One Thousand Guineas and Irish Derby, another Guineas winner in Cape Verdi, and Island Sands, who landed the Two Thousand Guineas. Now another can be added to the list—Kazzia. Bought out of Andreas Wohler's stable on Sheikh Mohammed's judgement after winning the Group 3 Premio Dormello in Milan decisively from Kootenay on the second of her two starts as a juvenile, she developed into one of the best of her sex, showing tenacity and versatility to win the One Thousand Guineas at a mile, the Oaks at a mile and a half and the Flower Bowl Invitational at a mile and a quarter.

Kazzia, who had won a maiden race at Hoppegarten before winning at Milan, started her classic campaign in one of the Dubai 'trials', finishing a head second to the Cherry Hinton winner Silent Honor, who failed to run in Europe during the year, reportedly due to a breathing problem, and was retired in September. Even after that effort the runner-up's connections—Sheikh Mohammed possibly excepted—apparently had no great hopes of her for the Sagitta One Thousand Guineas. At the time, Godolphin's general manager Simon Crisford said 'she will want one and a quarter miles plus on soft ground', and after the Guineas he revealed: 'When Kazzia shipped in I told the boss she could win the Italian Oaks, finish second in the French Guineas or fourth here, and told him those were the choices!' The decision to run Kazzia at Newmarket was Sheikh Mohammed's though, at 14/1, she was only joint-sixth favourite in a field of seventeen. In the absence of Queen's Logic, ruled out on the day by lameness found earlier in the week, the 11/8 market leader was Fillies' Mile winner Gossamer, making her reappearance along with six others, including Quarter Moon, winner of the Moyglare Stud Stakes and part of a four-horse contingent trained by Aidan O'Brien, and Sulk, successful in the Prix Marcel Boussac. There were six runners from the Nell Gwyn Stakes, including the winner Misterah at 7/1 and fourth-placed Alasha at 6/1. Soon travelling well disputing the lead with Lahinch at only a steady gallop to halfway, Kazzia took a definite advantage entering the final furlong and kept on strongly while some of her opponents encountered a bit of trouble getting through as the field bunched. At the line Kazzia had a neck to spare over the Nell Gwyn seventh Snowfire with Alasha the same distance away third and 66/1-shot Dolores fourth. The Guineas was a poor renewal but given her breeding, backed up by the opinion of her connections, Kazzia was clearly going to have a big say in the Vodafone Oaks.

The going at Newmarket was good to firm and Kazzia had no problems with it, but conditions at Epsom on Oaks day, after heavy rain over the two preceding days following watering earlier in the week, were very different. The soft going placed a premium on stamina and undoubtedly disadvantaged some among the fourteen runners, but Kazzia coped splendidly with everything. The field included just about all the best fillies with pretensions to staying the trip in Britain and Ireland at the time—Margarula was still an unknown quantity—though there were no French contenders. Quarter Moon, fifth at Newmarket before finishing second to Gossamer in the Irish One Thousand Guineas, tried her luck again, as did Snowfire, and new rivals for the favourite included the first three from the Musidora Stakes—well-bred winner Islington, Spinnette and Alexander Three D —along with Cheshire Oaks winner Shadow Dancing, Mellow Park, who had won the Lupe Stakes impressively, and Newmarket's Pretty Polly Stakes winner Esloob. Islington and Mellow Park started joint-second favourites but neither played a part in the finish as Kazzia, ridden for stamina, was immediately sent on from Irish Guineas third Starbourne. Kazzia had all her rivals off the bit when forging clear, brought to the stand side early in the straight, and she kept on resolutely when Quarter Moon came from some way back to challenge in the final furlong, winning all out by half a length. The rest, headed by Shadow Dancing, were fourteen lengths and more away. Frankie Dettori once again showed superb judgement and initiative in the saddle. Kazzia was the first to win the One Thousand Guineas and Oaks since Salsabil in 1990, and before long her connections expressed the intention of trying to make her the first to win the so-called fillies' triple crown since Oh So Sharp in 1985. When the entries for the St Leger were published in July, Kazzia was installed 3/1 favourite. By that time she had bypassed the Irish Oaks, in which Quarter Moon was second to Margarula, and had her sights set on the Yorkshire Oaks. The betting

Sagitta 1000 Guineas Stakes, Newmarket—the ex-German Kazzia holds off Snowfire, Alasha and Dolores

Vodafone Oaks, Epsom—Kazzia (left) completes a classic double last achieved by Salsabil in 1990; Quarter Moon is well clear of the others, who are led home by Shadow Dancing (right) and Starbourne (centre) as Islington (rail) weakens into eighth

suggested the race was a virtual match between Kazzia and Islington, who had bounced back with a facile victory in the Nassau Stakes. Kazzia was favourite at 7/4 with Islington at 2/1, but it was the latter who triumphed, taking over from her rival over two furlongs out and drawing clear as Kazzia struggled, losing her action and finishing over five lengths fourth after Guadalupe and Sulk passed her close home. Kazzia returned stiff, though some of the other explanations for her performance were intriguing to say the least. Dettori claimed the ground was too firm, though she had won under similar conditions at Newmarket. Crisford said she was not race-fit after her eleven-week break, though she looked straight enough beforehand. More significant, perhaps, was the news that Kazzia had a quarter-crack before York, which might well have had some effect. In any event, on the balance of form, she would have found Islington difficult to cope with even if fully fit. Unfortunately, Kazzia suffered further foot trouble early in September with an abscess and, despite the best attempts, she could not be made ready for the St Leger or the Prix Vermeille, which was mentioned as a possible alternative target.

Kazzia's next appearance was on the other side of the Atlantic. American turf races for fillies are well endowed, but not that competitive on the whole, relying heavily on European and ex-European runners to make them worthy of their status. In the latest season, Kazzia, Dress To Thrill and ex-Europeans Dublino, Golden Apples and Starine all notched a Grade 1 event, two in the case of Golden Apples. The Flower Bowl Invitational Stakes at Belmont Park in October offered an extreme instance, since all seven runners had connections with Europe. Kazzia started second favourite behind ex-French England's Legend, second to Lailani in the race the year before, with another ex-French mare Starine, who had not run for four months, next in the betting. Tarfshi was a second British challenger while French-trained Turtle Bow and the ex-British pair Mot Juste (second in the Irish Oaks and Prix de l'Opera in 2001) and Sunstone completed the field. Ridden this time by Jorge Chavez, Kazzia raced in her usual style, setting off in front and defying the others to catch her. They weren't up to the job—she was a length and a half ahead early in the straight and kept on gamely to hold off Turtle Bow by a neck. Kazzia had a realistic chance on this form in the Breeders' Cup Filly & Mare Turf, though she had to be supplemented for the race at a cost of 90,000 dollars. Having suffered a second quarter-crack in the run-up to the Flower Bowl, she sustained another abscess on a foot and missed a couple of days' work in the week before the Breeders' Cup. In the event she did not do herself justice at Arlington, showing some reluctance to enter the stalls and dropping away once headed a furlong out to finish sixth to Starine, who had finished fourth in the Flower Bowl when probably needing the run. A month afterwards Kazzia's retirement was announced.

Kazzia is the first German-bred to win a British classic or indeed a British Group 1 of any description. There was little in her pedigree to suggest she would prove up to such a standard, and nothing to suggest she would be able to win a top-grade race at a mile. Her sire Zinaad is well bred, by one classic winner in Shirley Heights out of another in Time Charter, and, despite being hard to train,

Kazzia (GER)
(b.f. 1999)

		Shirley Heights (b 1975)	Mill Reef
	Zinaad (b 1989)		Hardiemma
		Time Charter (b 1979)	Saritamer
			Centrocon
	Khoruna (GER) (b 1991)	Lagunas (b 1981)	Ile de Bourbon
			Liranga
		Khora (b 1984)	Corvaro
			Kandia

showed smart form at up to two miles, putting up his most noteworthy performance when landing the Jockey Club Stakes. He has not been popular at stud, covering only thirty-six mares in his best season, in 1997, and single-figure books on average in more recent years. Kazzia, an angular filly, is his solitary black-type winner from over sixty runners, and his fee in the latest season was €4,000. Khoruna, the dam, was an ordinary performer who won small races over seven furlongs at two and over eleven furlongs as a four-year-old but she is doing a lot better as a broodmare. Both her previous foals are winners, including the year-older filly Kimbajar (by Royal Abjar), successful in listed races over a mile at three and over seven furlongs and a mile in the latest season. The next dam, Khora, did not race but is a half-sister to Kamiros, winner of the Europa Preis and Deutsches St Leger, out of a good filly in Kandia, whose tally included the 1976 Aral-Pokal over a mile and a half. Another of Khora's half-sisters produced Kazoo, winner of the German One Thousand Guineas for Sheikh Mohammed in 1991. There is little doubt that the St Leger trip would have been within Kazzia's compass, but even at her best she would have found Bollin Eric a tough opponent to beat. Kazzia is not one of the best of the eleven fillies who have notched the two classics restricted to their sex in Britain in the last fifty years. On the contrary, she is the lowest rated of the group comprising Petite Etoile (134 in 1959), Bella Paola (131 in 1958), Oh So Sharp (131 in 1985), Salsabil (130 in 1990), Meld (128 in 1955), Never Too Late II (128 in 1960), Sweet Solera (127 in 1961), Mysterious (127 in 1973), Altesse Royale (126 in 1971) and Midway Lady (126 in 1986). However, Kazzia did become the first One Thousand Guineas winner in the last six years to win again after Newmarket. Fillies with her qualities are hard to find and she deserves the utmost praise. Her career at stud begins with a visit to Singspiel. *Saeed bin Suroor*

KEBREYA (USA) 3 ch.g. Affirmed (USA) – Minifah (USA) 69 (Nureyev (USA) 131) [2002 66: 12m⁶ 12m⁶ 12.4g 12.6m⁴ Sep 21] well-made gelding: fair maiden: best effort on reappearance: stays 1½m: acts on good to firm going: refused to settle second start, ran as if something amiss next time: sold 10,500 gns, gelded and joined M. Dods. *J. L. Dunlop* **72**

KEEN HANDS 6 ch.g. Keen 116 – Broken Vow (IRE) (Local Suitor (USA) 128) – [2002 10g 6g f7s² f7g⁴ f7g² f6g f6g f7g³ f7g f7g f7g f6g f7g f8g⁴ f8.5g⁶ f8g f8.5g* f9.4f f8s f6g⁵ f6s² f8.5g Oct 19] compact gelding: fair handicapper: in-and-out form in 2002, winning at Wolverhampton in July: effective at 6f to easy 1m: acts on fibresand, no recent form on turf: used to wear visor (equipped only once in 2002): tends to drift left: held up. *Mrs N. Macauley* **a74**

KEEPER 3 ch.c. Hector Protector (USA) 124 – Mary Martin (Be My Guest (USA) – 126) [2002 10g Jul 6] 1,600Y: half-brother to several winners, including smart performer up to 7f Marina Park (by Local Suitor), later successful in USA, and 5-y-o Inver Gold: dam unraced: 40/1 and tongue tied, tailed off in claimer at Leicester. *Mrs P. Sly*

KEEPERS HILL (IRE) 3 b.f. Danehill (USA) 126 – Asnieres (USA) (Spend A 99 Buck (USA)) [2002 95: 6d⁵ 5m* 5g 5g⁵ 5.5f* Dec 4] unfurnished filly: useful performer: won maiden at Naas in July: stiff tasks and creditable efforts next 2 starts in King George Stakes at Goodwood (ninth to Agnetha) and Flying Five at the Curragh (3¾ lengths fifth to Danehurst): left M. Halford, Ireland prior to winning allowance race at Hollywood in December: should stay 6f: acts on firm going. *R. J. Frankel, USA*

KEEP IKIS 8 ch.m. Anshan 119 – Santee Sioux (Dancing Brave (USA) 140) [2002 65 66: 17.1m 16m⁵ 15.8f² 18d Oct 21] leggy, short-backed mare: fair handicapper: needs at least 2m: acts on firm and good to soft going: patiently ridden. *Mrs M. Reveley*

KEETCHY (IRE) 3 b.g. Darshaan 133 – Ezana (Ela-Mana-Mou 132) [2002 76p: 86 10.5m 11g⁵ 14s² 14.1d² 14m⁵ 14.6s Oct 25] rather leggy, unfurnished gelding: fairly useful maiden handicapper: should be suited by further than 1¾m: acts on soft going, probably on good to firm: visored (ran creditably, though looked difficult ride) penultimate start. *J. L. Dunlop*

KELBIO (IRE)   2 br.f. (Feb 10) Elbio 125 – Blackdabronze (IRE) 47 (Damister (USA)   **58**
123) [2002 6s 6d⁶ 6g 6d 7g 7s f6g Oct 22] first living foal: dam, ran twice in Ireland, out
of half-sister to Derby third Rankin: modest maiden: blinkered, well held at Southwell
final start: best efforts at 6f on good to soft going. *John A. Quinn, Ireland*

KELBURNE (USA)   5 b.g. Red Ransom (USA) – Golden Klair 115 (Damister (USA)   **109**
123) [2002 90: 8f⁴ 10m* 10.4f⁴ 8.1m* 8m⁶ 10.4m 8m⁴ Aug 15] big, strong, lengthy
gelding: has a quick action: smart performer: better than ever in 2002, winning handicaps
at Newmarket (edged left) in May and Sandown (beat Broadway Score a head) in June:
also ran well when sixth in Royal Hunt Cup at Royal Ascot and when close fourth to
Priors Lodge in listed event at Salisbury final outing: effective at 1m/1¼m: acts on firm
ground, not discredited on good to soft: sometimes flashes tail: has run well when
sweating: usually waited with. *I. Semple*

KELLS (IRE)   4 b.g. Dilum (USA) 115 – Elizabethan Air 55 (Elegant Air 119) [2002   **82**
9s* f9.4s³ f11g f9.4s Dec 7] fairly useful handicapper on turf, fair on all-weather: won   **a68**
apprentice race at Newbury in October: well below that form after: should stay 1¼m: acts
on soft going, probably on fibresand: reportedly had breathing problem penultimate start.
P. W. D'Arcy

KELLY'S TUNE   3 b.f. Alhaarth (IRE) 126 – Roxy Music (IRE) 63 (Song 132) [2002   **63 d**
7g 7g⁴ 6m³ 7d 7.1m p7g Dec 11] 9,500F, 22,000Y: smallish, sturdy filly: sixth foal:
half-sister to fairly useful 5f (at 2 yrs) to 8.5f winner Foot Battalion (by Batshoof) and a
winner in Greece by Lahib: dam 2-y-o 7f winner: modest maiden at best: ran poorly last 3
starts: stays 7f: has worn cheekpieces. *A. P. Jarvis*

KELPIE (IRE)   3 b.f. Kahyasi 130 – Darrouzett 98 (Darshaan 133) [2002 10.5g⁵   **80**
12.5s⁵ 12.5d³ 10.2g⁶ 11.6d p10g⁵ p12g p12g⁴ p10g* Dec 18] first foal: dam, Irish 9f/
1¼m winner, out of half-sister to top-class American middle-distance performer Creme
Fraiche: fairly useful form: left H-A. Pantall in France after third start: won handicap at
Lingfield in December readily by 4 lengths: probably better at 1¼m than 1½m: stays easy
1½m: acts on polytrack and good to soft going. *I. A. Balding*

KELSEAS KOLBY (IRE)   2 b.g. Perugino (USA) 84 – Notre Dame (IRE)   **64**
(Classic Music (USA)) [2002 6s³ 5m 5m Sep 24] IR 5,400Y: leggy gelding: second foal:
dam unraced half-sister to useful Irish performers Mysterious Ways (stayed 7f) and
Crown Regent (stayed 1m): modest maiden: best effort when third at Redcar: should stay
7f. *J. A. Glover*

KELSEY ROSE   3 b.f. Most Welcome 131 – Duxyana (IRE) (Cyrano de Bergerac   **97**
120) [2002 93: f7g⁴ 6g⁶ 5m⁶ 6d³ a6g 6d² 7s⁴ 6g 6f⁴ 6m 7f² 7m 6d 7m Sep 18] leggy
filly: useful performer: probably best effort when length third to Lady Dominatrix in
listed race at Ascot in May: below form after eighth outing: tried visored: best at 5f/6f:
acts on fibresand, firm and soft going: sometimes edgy: tends to hang right. *P. D. Evans*

KELTECH GOLD (IRE)   5 b.g. Petorius 117 – Creggan Vale Lass (Simply Great   **–**
(FR) 122) [2002 67, a–: 8.3m 7m 7.1g Jul 26] heavy-topped gelding: fair handicapper at
best: well held in 2002: tried blinkered: tongue tied: joined S. Treacy in Ireland.
B. Palling

KELTIC FLUTE   3 b.g. Piccolo 121 – Nanny Doon (Dominion 123) [2002 53: 7m⁶ 7f   **49**
8.2m 7m² 10m 8m 8.1m Sep 16] poor maiden: left D. Morris after sixth start: likely to
prove best up to 1m: acts on good to firm going, probably on fibresand: sometimes
blinkered. *Mrs Lucinda Featherstone*

KELTIC FLYER (IRE)   3 b.g. Farhaan 77 – Indiana Dancer (Hallgate 127) [2002   **–**
8m 8m 10d Aug 5] IR 3,000Y: quite good-topped gelding: fourth reported thoroughbred
foal: brother to 4-y-o winner Faraway John: dam unraced: no sign of ability in maidens.
G. P. Enright

KELTOS (FR)   4 gr.c. Kendor (FR) 122 – Loxandra 76 (Last Tycoon 131) [2002   **132**
116: a10f 8m* 8m* May 18]

For a measure of the considerable improvement Keltos showed from three
to four, compare the two appearances he made in Britain. The first of those was as a
three-year-old in the St James's Palace Stakes, in which he started at 33/1 and
finished sixth behind Black Minnaloushe. Eleven months later, Keltos was back for
the Juddmonte Lockinge Stakes, in which he put up one of the performances of the
season, indeed the best by an older horse in Europe all year by our reckoning. The
three who completed the frame behind him at Newbury—Noverre, Olden Times
and No Excuse Needed—had all finished in front of him at Royal Ascot in the St

Juddmonte Lockinge Stakes, Newbury—Keltos puts up the best performance by an older horse all year in Europe, showing a really good turn of foot to go clear of Noverre, Olden Times and No Excuse Needed (far side)

James's Palace. The field for the Lockinge was probably as competitive as any edition since the race was awarded Group 1 status in 1995, though that was not really reflected in a one-sided market which had Noverre as the odds-on favourite ahead of Olden Times at 8/1 and Keltos on 9/1 along with No Excuse Needed and Swallow Flight.

Keltos was held up at Newbury, a change of tactics from his three-year-old days when he tended to be ridden more prominently. With the field still well grouped three furlongs out and collectively starting to drift towards the stand rail, finding a way through never looked like being easy, particularly with Olden Times' rider seeming intent on keeping Keltos boxed in. But when a gap finally appeared approaching the final furlong, Keltos showed a really good turn of foot to put distance between himself and his rivals, passing the post three and a half lengths clear of Noverre, who appeared to attempt to bite the winner as he went by. Keltos put up a top-class effort, comfortably the best seen in the race recently, and one which promised to make him very hard to beat in the top mile contests during the remainder of the year. As it turned out, he never raced again. He missed the Prix Jacques le Marois with a virus and his retirement was announced in early-September after he had suffered a fetlock problem. His curtailed campaign prevented a clash with Rock of Gibraltar and a potential resolution of the question as to which was the better horse; for all his string of Group 1 wins, Rock of Gibraltar never came up against a rival so good as Keltos, and it is possible to argue that the *bare* form of Rock of Gibraltar's easy successes never quite matched up to the form shown by Keltos at Newbury.

The improvement Keltos showed in the Lockinge did not come entirely out of the blue. He was supplemented for the race at a cost of £12,000 after stepping up on his three-year-old form to win the Prix du Muguet at Saint-Cloud early in May. Patiently ridden, he came from well back early in the straight to win going away by two lengths from British-trained Cornelius. There had been just a short head between them when they had also finished first and second in the Prix Perth over the same course and distance the previous November.

Keltos is much the best offspring of his sire Kendor, who won the Grand Criterium and the Poule d'Essai des Poulains. Kendor has been a regular among the top dozen sires in France, but his only Group 1 winner prior to Keltos was the 1997

Prix Morny winner Charge d'Affaires. Keltos is not the first good miler to emerge from the dam's side of his pedigree. His grandam Northshiel is a half-sister to Waajib who, like Keltos, improved considerably from three to four; as a four-year-old Waajib won the Prix du Rond-Point and the following season added both the Diomed Stakes and Queen Anne Stakes. Northshiel herself won only a seven-furlong maiden at Chepstow as a two-year-old but she bred a handful of useful performers: Boloardo, third in the Gordon Richards Stakes, the Lingfield Oaks Trial winner Asterita, the Italian Group 2 winner Special Nash, the Cambridgeshire runner-up Halland, and Rasm who was third in a handicap at Royal Ascot in the latest season. Loxandra, the dam of Keltos, was no better than fair, winning a mile maiden at Newcastle for Henry Cecil. She too, however, is compiling a good record as a broodmare. Her first foal Iridanos (by Sabrehill) was a useful miler in France, where he made the frame in several pattern races. Next came Kresna (by Distant Relative), a winner in Greece, and Keltos is followed by the three-year-old Loxias (by Saumarez), who won a couple of listed events in the French Provinces at around a mile and a half in the latest season. Loxandra's two-year-old Krataios, a full brother to Iridanos, finished second in a newcomers race at Deauville in the autumn on his only start.

			Kenmare	Kalamoun
		Kendor (FR)	(gr 1975)	Belle of Ireland
		(gr 1986)	Belle Mecene	Gay Mecene
Keltos (FR)			(b 1982)	Djaka Belle
(gr.c. 1998)			Last Tycoon	Try My Best
		Loxandra	(b 1983)	Mill Princess
		(b 1991)	Northshiel	Northfields
			(ch 1984)	Coryana

Mr Gary A. Tanaka's "Keltos"

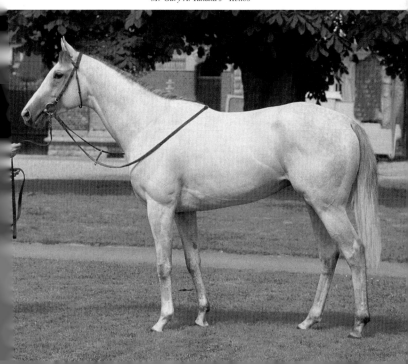

While some greys do eventually turn almost white in their later years, the close-coupled, useful-looking Keltos did so unusually early. He won six of his ten starts, on ground ranging from heavy to good to firm, and all his wins came at a mile. His only defeats at that trip were when promoted to fifth on Noverre's disqualification in the Poule d'Essai des Poulains (Keltos started favourite for that race on his pattern-race debut) and in the St James's Palace. Keltos made his reappearance in the latest season in the Dubai World Cup in which he finished a never dangerous and well-held eighth; he can easily be forgiven that since he faced a stiff task on the form he had shown up until then, and it was also his first and only attempt both on dirt and at a mile and a quarter. Keltos is to stand at Airlie Stud in Ireland at a fee of €10,000, Oct 1st. *C. Laffon-Parias, France*

KENLEY LASS (IRE) 2 b.f. (Mar 20) Danetime (IRE) 121 – Big Fandango (Bigstone (IRE) 126) [2002 5m² 5m² p5g⁶ 6.1s 5.1d⁵ 5g⁵ 5.7m⁴ 6.1m⁴ 6g 6m* 7d p6g f6g⁵ Nov 22] IR 4,000Y: quite attractive filly: first foal: dam unraced half-sister to useful performer up to 1m Elegant Warning: modest performer: won seller at Lingfield in September: stays 6f: acts on all-weather and good to firm going, well held on softer than good: sometimes slowly away/looks none too keen: has run creditably when sweating. *Mrs P. N. Dutfield* **63 a52**

KENNET 7 b.g. Kylian (USA) – Marwell Mitzi 50 (Interrex (CAN)) [2002 73, a59: p13g* p12g Mar 25] leggy, plain gelding: modest handicapper: won at Lingfield in March: probably best at 1½m/1¾m: acts on soft going, good to firm and all-weather: tried blinkered/visored earlier in career. *P. D. Cundell* **61**

KENNINGTON 2 ch.c. (Mar 12) Compton Place 125 – Mim 39 (Midyan (USA) 124) [2002 p8g Nov 27] 42,000F, 130,000Y: second foal: dam, little sign of ability, half-sister to smart performers Norton Challenger (from 6f to 1m) and Young Hal (at 5f/6f): weak 10/1-shot, better than bare result in maiden at Lingfield (seventh to Face The Storm), travelling well and short of room twice in straight: sure to improve. *J. H. M. Gosden* **68 p**

KENNY THE TRUTH (IRE) 3 b.g. Robellino (USA) 127 – Just Blink (IRE) (Fairy King (USA)) [2002 7.1m 8g 8g 10g 6d f8g f8.5g Dec 13] IR 10,000F, 10,000Y: smallish, robust gelding: first foal: dam ran twice at 4 yrs: little form. *A. Dickman* **–**

KENNYTHORPE BOPPY (IRE) 4 ch.g. Aragon 118 – Spark (IRE) 79 (Flash of Steel 120) [2002 54: 12.4m 11.9s³ 17.2d 16g 9.9m Aug 25] tall, leggy gelding: poor maiden nowadays: stays 1½m: acts on soft and good to firm going: visored/blinkered last 6 starts. *J. S. Wainwright* **44**

KEN'S DREAM 3 b.c. Bin Ajwaad (IRE) 119 – Shoag (USA) (Affirmed (USA)) [2002 69: f7g⁴ 7m⁵ 10g* 10m* 10m 10.9m* 14f⁵ Oct 2] workmanlike colt: fairly useful handicapper: won at Nottingham in June/July and at Warwick in September: well held in listed race at Newmarket final start: stays easy 11f: acts on soft and good to firm ground: tends to race freely (has worn crossed noseband). *Ms A. E. Embiricos* **89**

KENT 7 b.g. Kylian (USA) – Precious Caroline (IRE) 60 (The Noble Player (USA) 126) [2002 50, a72: f16.2g⁴ f16g² f12g* f14g⁶ 14.1d⁴ 16d* 15g* 16.5g⁴ 17.1m 12m p16g 13.8g² 16v³ Oct 29] very big gelding: fair performer: has gained 7 wins at Southwell, including minor event in February: also won handicaps at Ripon in May and Warwick in July: effective at 1½m to 2m: acts on fibresand, firm and good to soft going: usually blinkered/visored: sometimes runs in snatches/hangs/finds little. *P. D. Cundell* **69 a78**

KENTISH ROCK 7 b.g. Rock Hopper 124 – Capel Lass (The Brianstan 128) [2002 p10g Jan 23] probably of little account. *Mrs L. C. Jewell* **–**

KENTUCKY BLUE (IRE) 2 b.c. (Feb 17) Revoque (IRE) 122 – Delta Town (USA) (Sanglamore (USA) 126) [2002 6s² 7g* 7.5d* 7m² Jul 26] IR 12,000Y: lengthy, good-topped colt: has scope: third foal: dam French maiden daughter of smart French performer up to 1¼m Daeltown: fairly useful performer: won maiden at Thirsk in June and nursery at Beverley in July: creditable head second in minor event at Thirsk final start: will stay at least 1m: acts on soft and good to firm going. *T. D. Easterby* **90**

KENTUCKY BOUND (IRE) 4 b.g. Charnwood Forest (IRE) 125 – Blown-Over 41 (Ron's Victory (USA) 129) [2002 –: f6g f8g Mar 14] rather leggy gelding: of little account nowadays. *J. O'Reilly* **–**

KENTUCKY BULLET (USA) 6 b.g. Housebuster (USA) – Exactly So (Caro 133) [2002 46§, a64§: f12g* p12g f12g² 11.9f f14.8s² 11.8m f12g f12g Nov 22] leggy, angular gelding: modest handicapper on all-weather: won amateur race at Wolverhampton in February: stays 14.8f: acts on fibresand, no form on turf in 2002: rarely blinkered/tongue tied nowadays: sometimes hangs/flashes tail: ungenuine. *A. G. Newcombe* **– § a51 §**

KENTUCKY KING (USA) 2 b.c. (Mar 13) Tale of The Cat (USA) 113 – Anna's **91 p**
Honor (USA) (Alleged (USA) 138) [2002 7d* Aug 3] $75,000F, $32,000Y: strong,
lengthy colt: fifth foal: half-brother to a winner in USA by Phone Trick: dam, French
7f (at 2 yrs) to 1½m (listed race) winner, half-sister to useful French 6.5f/7f winner
Savannah's Honor: 11/1, backward and green, won 11-runner maiden at Doncaster by
length from Desert Lord, showing willing attitude to get up near finish: had minor
problem after: will be suited by 1m+: useful prospect at least, sure to win more races.
M. Johnston

KEPLER (USA) 3 ch.c. Spinning World (USA) 130 – Perfect Arc (USA) 120 (Brown **97**
Arc (USA)) [2002 94P: p8g⁵ 7m⁶ 9g 10s³ 10m⁶ 11.8g 10.1d f8.5f* f8.5g* f8.5s⁵ p10g²
Dec 3] strong colt: has quick, fluent action: useful performer: won 2 handicaps at
Wolverhampton in November: stays 1¼m: acts on all-weather and heavy going, probably
on good to firm: blinkered (folded very tamely) seventh start. *P. F. I. Cole*

KERALA (IRE) 3 b.f. Mujadil (USA) 119 – Kalisz (IRE) (Polish Precedent (USA) **–**
131) [2002 –: 6.1d 6m May 24] small filly: well held in 3 maidens. *Don Enrico Incisa*

KERENSAS PRINCE 3 b.g. Rislan (USA) 57 – Skippy (Emarati (USA) 74) [2002 **–**
10g Oct 14] second known foal: dam unraced: 66/1, last in seller at Leicester. *A. D. Smith*

KERNEL DOWERY (IRE) 2 b.g. (Apr 8) Sri Pekan (USA) 117 – Lady Dowery **74**
(USA) (Manila (USA)) [2002 p8g⁵ p8g² p8g Dec 3] 5,500Y: half-brother to several
winners, including 4-y-o Pivotable: dam French 11f winner: fair form in maidens at
Lingfield: best effort when staying-on second to Face The Storm: raced at 1m on
polytrack: held up: gelded after final start. *P. W. Harris*

KESTLE IMP (IRE) 4 b.f. Imp Society (USA) – Dark Truffle 69 (Deploy 131) [2002 **–**
–: 11.8s Mar 28] little form after debut: tried visored. *M. R. Ewer-Hoad*

KESTRAL 6 ch.g. Ardkinglass 114 – Shiny Kay 65 (Star Appeal 133) [2002 72+, a52: **–**
8m 8s 10m 9m 9m Sep 16] leggy, angular gelding: fair handicapper in 2001: no form in
2002, pulled up (reportedly lame) final outing: tried tongue tied at 4 yrs. *T. J. Etherington*

KETAN 2 ch.g. (Mar 17) Zilzal (USA) 137 – Vivid Imagination (USA) (Raise A Man **93**
(USA)) [2002 5f* 5f* 6m³ Aug 17] rangy gelding: has scope: fluent mover: seventh foal:
half-brother to 4-y-o Stormy Voyage and a winner in USA by Rahy: dam, US 2-y-o 5f to
1m (Grade 3 event) winner (also winner over 6f at 3 yrs), half-sister to high-class multiple
Grade 1-winning filly up to 9f Serena's Song, dam of 3-y-o Sophisticat: fairly useful form
in minor events: landed odds at Thirsk and Redcar in May, hanging left both times: off 3
months, good 1½ lengths third to Cumbrian Venture at Ripon: will stay at least 7f: played
up at start for both wins and withdrawn once having given trouble. *M. Johnston*

KEW 3 b.g. Royal Applause 124 – Cutleaf 81 (Kris 135) [2002 50: f9.4g⁵ p10g p10g **46**
10f 12g p12g³ 11.9d 11.6m 11.6m² 12m⁴ 12g⁶ 11.9m Oct 3] poor maiden: probably
stays 1½m: acts on good to firm going and polytrack: sometimes visored/blinkered.
J. J. Bridger

KEW GREEN (USA) 4 b. or br.g. Brocco (USA) 124 – Jump With Joy (USA) **90**
(Linkage (USA)) [2002 78p: 8d 10f² 10.5s* 12d 12s⁴ 10m² 10.1s Oct 22] rangy gelding:
has scope: fairly useful handicapper: won at Haydock in June: stays 10.5f, probably not
1½m: acts on firm and soft ground: tongue tied second start: wandered penultimate
outing: sometimes races bit freely. *W. J. Haggas*

KEY ONEOTHREE (USA) 2 b.f. (Feb 19) Entrepreneur 123 – Wallflower (Polar **59**
Falcon (USA) 126) [2002 f5s⁵ p5g³ f5g⁴ 7.1d³ 7.2g 5.9d³ 7g⁴ f7f 7d² 7m⁴ 7g⁴ 8m⁶ 7d Oct
18] 700F: lengthy, angular filly: second foal: half-sister to 3-y-o The Leather Wedge:
dam, ran once, half-sister to dam of very smart sprinter Pivotal: modest maiden: in frame
8 times, including nurseries and seller: stays 7f: acts on all-weather, yet to race on
extremes of going on turf: sold 1,500 gns. *A. Berry*

KEY TO THE CITY (IRE) 8 b.g. Shalford (IRE) 124§ – Green Wings (General **–**
Assembly (USA)) [2002 –: f9.4g Feb 18] fair performer in 1999: well held 3 starts since:
sometimes blinkered/finds little. *C. P. Morlock*

KEY VIRTUE (USA) 3 ch.f. Atticus (USA) 121 – Questionablevirtue (USA) (Key **78**
To The Mint (USA)) [2002 72: 8g² 8s³ 9.9m² 10.2d⁵ 8m³ 8.1m 6m 7g Oct 14] leggy filly:
good mover: fair maiden: well below form last 3 starts: likely to prove best up to 1m: acts
on soft and good to firm ground: tends to race freely/carry head high: sold 20,000 gns.
Mrs A. J. Perrett

KEZ 6 b.g. Polar Falcon (USA) 126 – Briggsmaid 70 (Elegant Air 119) [2002 77: 11.7g² **84**
11.5m* 10g³ 10.1f* 11.5m⁴ 10g 11.7f 10.1m Sep 18] lengthy gelding: has a quick action:

fairly useful handicapper: won at Yarmouth in May (idled) and June: effective at 1¼m/ 1½m: acts on firm going, probably on good to soft: visored once: usually held up. *P. R. Webber*

KHABIR (USA)   2 br.c. (Feb 10) Gulch (USA) – Jafn 104 (Sharpo 132) [2002 7m⁵ 6g⁴ 7d² 8g⁴ 7g² Oct 2] good-bodied colt: second foal: half-brother to 3-y-o Waraqa: dam 7f/ 1m winner: fairly useful maiden: travelled strongly long way when fourth to Mysterinch in nursery at Newcastle fourth start: likely to prove best up to 1m: unraced on extremes of going. *B. Hanbury*   **86**

KHAIZARANA   2 b.f. (Apr 26) Alhaarth (IRE) 126 – Ta Rib (USA) 116 (Mr Prospector (USA)) [2002 7m Aug 23] angular filly: third foal: half-sister to 3-y-o Mawaheb: dam 7f and 1m (Poule d'Essai des Pouliches) winner: 20/1 and green, 5½ lengths seventh of 11 to Hold To Ransom in maiden at Newmarket: joined E. Dunlop: open to improvement. *D. R. Loder*   **72 p**

KHALED (IRE)   7 b.g. Petorius 117 – Felin Special (Lyphard's Special (USA) 122) [2002 44: 10.1m⁶ 10g³ 10m 10.1f 12.6m 10m Jul 22] tall gelding: poor performer nowadays: seems to stay 2m: acts on good to firm going and fibresand: blinkered (well held) final start: tried tongue tied earlier in career: has hung right. *Mrs D. Haine*   **43**

KHALKEVI (IRE)   3 b.c. Kahyasi 130 – Khalisa (IRE) 113 (Persian Bold 123) [2002 10.5g* 12g* 12m 10m* Jun 23] second foal: dam, won Prix Cleopatre and Prix Chloe, should have stayed beyond 10.5f: smart performer: won newcomers race at Fontaine-bleau at 2 yrs, minor event at Maisons-Laffitte in April, Prix Hocquart at Longchamp (beat demoted Louveteau ¾ length) in May and Juddmonte Grand Prix de Paris at Longchamp in June: did really well to beat Shaanmer a head in last-named race, having to come from last after stumbling badly over 4f out: only defeat when ninth of 15 to Sulamani in Prix du Jockey Club at Chantilly: stayed 1½m: acted on good to firm going, successful on soft: retired after fracturing off-hind pastern in racecourse workout in late-July. *A. de Royer Dupre, France*   **117**

KHALKISSA (USA)   2 b.f. (Jan 20) Diesis 133 – Khamsin (USA) (Mr Prospector (USA)) [2002 6m Aug 4] fourth foal: half-sister to useful 1998 2-y-o 6f winner Subeen (by Caerleon) and fairly useful French 1999 2-y-o 9f winner Different View (by Arazi): dam, second at 11f in France, half-sister to US Grade 1 1¼m winner Storm Trooper and May Hill/Musidora winner Marillette: 6/1, 9 lengths seventh to Illustria in maiden at Newbury: should stay at least 1m: should improve. *D. R. Loder*   **63 p**

KHAMS-ALHAWAS (IRE)   3 gr.f. Marju (IRE) 127 – Bint Shadayid (USA) 109 (Nashwan (USA) 135) [2002 10g³ 10d* 12f² 11.9d³ 10g Aug 27] angular, unfurnished filly: first foal: dam, 2-y-o 6f/7f winner and third in 1000 Guineas (stayed 1¼m), daughter of 1000 Guineas winner Shadayid: fairly useful performer: won maiden at Pontefract in July: good efforts in handicaps next 2 starts: stayed 1½m: acted on firm and good to soft going: visits Machiavellian. *J. L. Dunlop*   **93**

Juddmonte Grand Prix de Paris, Longchamp—Khalkevi takes his record to four wins from five career starts with a narrow success over Shaanmer; Without Connexion is third

KHAMSUN 2 b.f. (Apr 22) Shaamit (IRE) 127 – Marie d'Island (FR) (Turtle Island – (IRE) 123) [2002 7m 7g Oct 14] small filly: first foal: dam unraced: well held in maidens. *B. A. McMahon*

KHANJAR (USA) 2 ch.c. (Feb 16) Kris S (USA) – Alyssum (USA) (Storm Cat **96 +** (USA)) [2002 7g² 8f⁴ Oct 2] $1,200,000Y: sturdy, attractive colt: first foal: dam, US 6f/7f (minor stakes) winner, out of champion 2-y-o US filly who later won Grade 1s at 8.5f/9f Althea, a very good family: useful form: short-headed by Cat Ona High in maiden at Leicester (had 2 handlers and were crossed noseband): hung right when fourth of 6 to Lateen Sails in similar event at Newmarket: should stay beyond 1m: well up to winning races. *D. R. Loder*

KHAYSAR (IRE) 4 b.g. Pennekamp (USA) 130 – Khaytada (IRE) 111 (Doyoun 124) **–** [2002 –: 12d f14s 12f Oct 3] small gelding: maiden on Flat: little form in 2002. *D. Morris*

KHAYYAM (USA) 4 b.g. Affirmed (USA) – True Celebrity (USA) (Lyphard (USA) **71 d** 132) [2002 82: 8.1d⁵ 8s⁵ 8m⁶ 8.5d 12g³ 10.1m² 12g 10.2g 9s Oct 25] well-made gelding: only fair at best in 2002: left P. Cole after sixth start: probably stays 1½m: acts on good to firm going, some promise only outing on fibresand: tongue tied second outing: usually races prominently: not one to trust implicitly. *S. Gollings*

KHUCHN (IRE) 6 b.h. Unfuwain (USA) 131 – Stay Sharpe (USA) (Sharpen Up 127) **42** [2002 –: 11g⁴ 10m⁶ 10m⁵ 9.9d 12.3s⁴ 10.1m Aug 16] strong, good-topped horse: poor performer: probably stays 11f: acts on fibresand, heavy and good to firm going: tried tongue tied (reportedly had breathing problem final start). *M. Brittain*

KHULOOD (USA) 2 ch.f. (May 19) Storm Cat (USA) – Elle Seule (USA) 122 (Exclu- **102 p** sive Native (USA)) [2002 6m* 6m⁵ 7f* Oct 5] tall, leggy filly: fluent mover, with a light action: half-sister to several winners, including high-class 6f (July Cup) winner Elnadim (by Danzig), very smart 6f (at 2 yrs) to 1m (Irish 1000 Guineas) winner Mehthaaf (by

Mr Hamdan Al Maktoum's "Khulood"

Nureyev) and French 1990 2-y-o 7.5f winner Only Seule (by Lyphard), herself dam of very smart Prix de la Foret winner Occupandiste: dam, French 1m (Prix d'Astarte) to 10.5f winner, half-sister to dam of Dubai Millennium out of outstanding broodmare Fall Aspen: useful form: impressive winner of maiden at Ascot in July and listed event at Newmarket (warm and carrying little condition) in October, making all to beat Soldera by 4 lengths in latter: carried head awkwardly when disappointing in minor event at Salisbury in between: will stay 1m: smart filly in the making. *J. L. Dunlop*

KHUZDAR (IRE) 3 ch.c. Definite Article 121 – Mariyda (IRE) (Vayrann 133) [2002 **83** 10g* 11.8d Aug 11] 8,000F, 35,000Y: second living foal: half-brother to 1998 2-y-o 7f winner Spontaneity (by Shalford): dam, Irish 1½m/1¾m winner, half-sister to dam of very smart 1¼m performer Manndar: fair form when winning maiden at Southwell in April by 1½ lengths from No Question: off over 4 months, pulled too hard in minor event next time: sold 2,500 gns in November. *M. R. Channon*

KICKBACK 2 b.c. (Mar 22) High Kicker (USA) – Moniques Venture (Midyan (USA) **–** 124) [2002 6m 7m 6m p8g Nov 23] second foal: dam no form: no sign of ability, including in sellers. *B. A. Pearce*

KID'Z'PLAY (IRE) 6 b.g. Rudimentary (USA) 118 – Saka Saka (Camden Town **72** 125) [2002 81: 8v 8.3s 10g 10.9g* 10s 12s Nov 6] fair handicapper: won amateur event at Ayr (sixth win in Scotland) in September under good ride from Mrs C. Williams: best at 9f (given test) to 1½m: acts on any going: has been early to post: looked most temperamental once as 4-y-o: often leads. *J. S. Goldie*

KIER PARK (IRE) 5 b.h. Foxhound (USA) 103 – Merlannah (IRE) (Shy Groom **112** (USA)) [2002 114: 6g³ 6d² 5g* 5m 5s⁶ 5d⁴ 5.6m³ 6d³ 6s⁶ 6v Nov 20] tall, quite good-topped horse: smart performer: reportedly split pastern after only 3-y-o outing: won minor event at Beverley in May by 3 lengths from Borders: best effort at 5 yrs when close third to Halmahera in Portland Handicap at Doncaster on seventh start: effective at 5f to 6.5f: acts on soft and good to firm going: wore cheekpieces last 2 outings: none too consistent. *M. A. Jarvis*

KIKOI (IRE) 2 b.f. (Mar 24) Alzao (USA) 117 – Kimono (IRE) (Machiavellian (USA) **–** 123) [2002 p6g Jun 1] first foal: dam twice-raced daughter of smart 1½m winner Kiliniski: 25/1, slowly away and always behind in maiden at Lingfield. *M. Blanshard*

KILCULLEN LAD (IRE) 8 b.g. Fayruz 116 – Royal Home 69 (Royal Palace 131) **61** [2002 73d: 5s⁴ 5g 5m³ 6g p6g⁵ 5m⁵ 5f⁴ 6f Sep 28] smallish, workmanlike gelding: modest handicapper: best at 5f/6f: unraced on heavy going, acts on any other turf and polytrack: usually blinkered/visored. *P. Mooney, Ireland*

KILKENNY CASTLE (IRE) 6 b.g. Grand Lodge (USA) 125 – Shahaamh (IRE) 85 **91** (Reference Point 139) [2002 88: p8g⁴ p10g² p10g² p10g* 10m* 10m 10m⁴ 8m 10.4m 8f 10m³ 10m 8g Oct 18] big gelding: fairly useful performer: won minor event at Lingfield in March and handicap at Newbury in April: stays 1¼m: acts on good to firm going and polytrack: slowly away and raced too freely penultimate start: held up. *S. Dow*

KILLALA (IRE) 2 b.g. (Mar 25) Among Men (USA) 124 – Hat And Gloves (Wolver **66** Hollow 126) [2002 6s 5.9d² Jun 26] IR 8,000F, IR 15,000Y: fifth foal: half-brother to 3 winners, including fairly useful 1995 Irish 2-y-o 6.5f winner Daddy's Hat (by Dancing Dissident): dam Irish maiden: better effort in maidens (fair form) when ¾-length second of 11 to Logsdail at Carlisle: gelded after: should stay 7f. *M. H. Tompkins*

KILLARNEY 4 gr.f. Pursuit of Love 124 – Laune (AUS) 68 (Kenmare (FR) 125) [2002 **42** 65: 10m³ 12.1m Sep 24] lengthy, deep-girthed filly: fair maiden at 3 yrs: only poor form in sellers in 2002: stays 1¼m: acts on good to firm ground: blinkered (raced freely and ran poorly) final 3-y-o outing: has hung left. *Miss Kate Milligan*

KILLERBY KATE (IRE) 2 b.f. (Apr 14) Desert Story (IRE) 115 – Reet Petite **–** (Thatching 131) [2002 6f 7.5m 7m 6d Aug 26] IR 13,500Y, 12,000Y: good-topped filly: half-sister to several winners, including 6f to 7f winner Al Reet (by Alzao) and Irish 5f and 7f winner Fleet Petite (by Posen), both fairly useful: dam Irish 1m winner: little form: blinkered in sellers last 2 starts. *T. D. Easterby*

KILLING JOKE 2 b.c. (Feb 9) Double Trigger (IRE) 123 – Fleeting Vision (IRE) 79 **73 ?** (Vision (USA)) [2002 9f³ 10f Oct 7] 24,000Y: lengthy colt: second foal: dam, Irish 1½m to 2¼m winner, out of half-sister to St Leger winner Snurge: seemingly fair form when 5½ lengths last of 3 to Amundsen in maiden at Redcar, running wide on bend: well held in similar event at Pontefract: will be suited by 1½m+. *J. G. Given*

KILMEENA LAD 6 b.g. Minshaanshu Amad (USA) 91§ – Kilmeena Glen (Beveled **64** (USA)) [2002 73+: 6m 6d Jun 11] good-quartered gelding: modest handicapper: lightly raced in 2002: effective at 6f to easy 1m: acts on any turf going: tried blinkered: tends to edge left: has run well sweating: has reared leaving stall. *J. C. Fox*

KILMEENA STAR 4 b.c. So Factual (USA) 120 – Kilmeena Glen (Beveled (USA)) **–** [2002 51, a–: 6g p7g 7d 5.3m 6d⁵ 7f 5.3m 10m 8.2m Oct 1] maiden: little form in 2002. *J. C. Fox*

KILMENY (IRE) 4 b.f. Royal Abjar (USA) 121 – Mouchez Le Nez (IRE) 41 (Cyrano **61** de Bergerac 120) [2002 74, a87: 8.1m 8g 10v 8m⁵ 8g 8.1v 10.9m* f9.4g Nov 16] robust **a64** filly: modest performer: won claiming handicap at Warwick (claimed from H. Morrison £8,000) in September: stays 11f: acts on good to firm going and fibresand. *M. C. Pipe*

KINABALU (IRE) 2 b.g. (Apr 2) Danetime (IRE) 121 – Highly Fashionable (IRE) **63** 68 (Polish Precedent (USA) 131) [2002 6d 7m f7s f8.5g⁵ Dec 20] IR 14,000Y, 7,500 2-y-o: fourth foal: half-brother to 2 winners, including Irish 8.5f winner Langkawi Bay (by Blues Traveller): dam 2-y-o 7f winner: modest maiden: best effort final start: stays 8.5f. *J. S. Moore*

KINAN (USA) 6 b.g. Dixieland Band (USA) – Alsharta (USA) (Mr Prospector (USA)) **68** [2002 70: f8.5g f7g³ Feb 8] quite attractive gelding: fair handicapper: was probably best around 6f/7f: acted on all-weather, best on good going or softer on turf: sometimes started slowly: was possibly no easy ride: dead. *T. D. Barron*

KINCOB (USA) 2 b.f. (Mar 19) Kingmambo (USA) 125 – Gossamer (USA) (Seattle **63** Slew (USA)) [2002 7m⁴ 7.1m p7g Oct 9] leggy, unfurnished filly: fourth live foal: closely related to 4-y-o Translucid: dam, won up to 9f in USA, from excellent family: modest maiden: fourth at Salisbury: possibly amiss final start: should stay 1¼m. *J. L. Dunlop*

KIND EMPEROR 5 br.g. Emperor Jones (USA) 119 – Kind Lady 56 (Kind of Hush **59 §** 118) [2002 60§: 7m⁵ 10.1m³ 8m 8m 6m 8.9f f8g Nov 20] leggy, sparely-made gelding: modest handicapper: seems to stay easy 1¼m: acts on firm and soft going (well held on all-weather): visored twice, refusing to race first occasion: hung markedly right once at 4 yrs: often races freely: unreliable. *P. L. Gilligan*

KINDLELIGHT DEBUT 2 b.f. (Apr 21) Groom Dancer (USA) 128 – Dancing **71** Debut 83 (Polar Falcon (USA) 126) [2002 p7g⁶ p7g⁴ p8g⁶ Nov 14] third foal: dam, maiden who stayed 1¼m well, out of half-sister to 2000 Guineas winner Entrepreneur: fair form in maidens at Lingfield: will probably stay 1¼m: edged left on debut: found little final run. *D. K. Ivory*

KINDNESS 2 ch.f. (Mar 27) Indian Ridge 123 – Kissing Gate (USA) 62 (Easy Goer **64** (USA)) [2002 6d 5s⁴ 7.1m 7m⁵ 7m 8f³ 8.3m Oct 7] second foal: half-sister to 1m to 1½m winner in Sweden by Green Desert: dam, 2-y-o 8.5f winner, half-sister to very smart 5f/ 6f performer Keen Hunter and smart performers up to 1¼m Altibr and Marnor: modest maiden: likely to prove best up to 1m: acts on firm and soft going: sold 6,000 gns. *R. Hannon*

KIND OF LOVING 3 ch.f. Diesis 133 – Gentilesse 81 (Generous (IRE) 139) [2002 **64** 63p: p10g⁵ 8s⁴ 10m 8.5s⁶ 8f⁴ 10s⁴ 8g⁶ 8d² Nov 7] smallish filly: modest maiden: left J. Dunlop after third start: effective at 1m/1¼m: acts on polytrack, firm and soft ground. *V. Kennedy, Ireland*

KING AT LAST 3 b.g. Zamindar (USA) 116 – Louis' Queen (IRE) 102 (Tragic Role **–** (USA)) [2002 8m Aug 24] 10,000Y: good-topped gelding: third foal: half-brother to 1999 2-y-o 6f winner Princess Louise (by Efisio) and winner in Hong Kong at 1m by Lycius: dam 5f (at 2 yrs) to 1m winner: 14/1, showed little in maiden at Newmarket. *Mrs A. J. Perrett*

KING COM 3 ch.g. King's Signet (USA) 110 – Comhail (USA) (Nodouble (USA)) **–** [2002 p10g f8.5g 6.1d 6s May 26] 1,000F, 2,200Y: rangy, angular gelding: sixth foal: closely related to 2 winners, including 1m winner Polarize (by Polar Falcon) and half-brother to a winner in Germany by Unfuwain: dam ran twice: only a little sign of ability in maidens. *T. T. Clement*

KING CREOLE 3 b.c. Slip Anchor 136 – Myrrh (Salse (USA) 128) [2002 70p: 8f **72** 12g³ 14.1s⁴ 11.9m⁵ p12g⁴ 10s Oct 23] strong, well-made colt: has a quick action: fair maiden handicapper: stays 1¾m: acts on soft going: sold 11,000 gns. *J. Noseda*

KING DARSHAAN 2 b.c. (Apr 12) Darshaan 133 – Urchin (IRE) (Fairy King **74** (USA)) [2002 10s p8g⁴ p8g³ Nov 27] second foal: dam unraced half-sister to smart sprinter Lugana Beach out of half-sister to Mtoto: fair form in maidens: third at Lingfield: should be suited by 1¼m/1½m: tends to be slowly away. *P. R. Hedger*

KING DAVID   3 b.g. Distant Relative 128 – Fleur Rouge 71 (Pharly (FR) 130) [2002   **76** 58p: 7s⁴ 7.1f² f7g⁵ f8.5g* Nov 16] well-made gelding: fair performer: reportedly found to have split a pastern after only 2-y-o start: won maiden at Wolverhampton in November: stays 8.5f: bit slowly away/hung left on reappearance: raced freely then reportedly lost action penultimate start. *J. A. Osborne*

KING EIDER   3 b. or br.g. Mtoto 134 – Hen Harrier 94 (Polar Falcon (USA) 126)   **96** [2002 68p: 10f² 12.6m* 12d² 12d³ 11.9g* 13.1f⁶ 14m* 14.1f² 16s² Oct 25] smallish, good-topped gelding: useful handicapper: won at Warwick in May, Brighton in August and Sandown in September: good efforts at Redcar and Newbury last 2 starts: stays 2m: unraced on heavy going, acts on any other turf. *J. L. Dunlop*

KINGFISHERS BONNET   6 b.m. Hamas (IRE) 125§ – Mainmast 63 (Bustino 136)   **–** [2002 40: 8.3v⁶ 10f 10m 10m Jul 8] of little account nowadays. *J. M. Bradley*

KING FLYER (IRE)   6 b.g. Ezzoud (IRE) 126 – Al Guswa 98 (Shernazar 131) [2002   **83** 90, a–: 12m 16m 14.1d² 14m⁴ p16g³ 14.8g⁵ 14 8m³ 14 8m⁴ 14m 16m⁴ 14.1f* 13.9f¹ Oct   **a72** 12] leggy, workmanlike gelding: fairly useful handicapper on turf, fair on all-weather: won at Redcar in September: finds 1¾m a minimum nowadays and stays 2¼m: acts on firm and good to soft going: blinkered once: tongue tied: held up: consistent. *Miss J. Feilden*

KING HALLING   3 b.c. Halling (USA) 133 – Flower Fairy (FR) (Fairy King (USA))   **76** [2002 10d⁵ p10g* 10.1m⁶ 10f⁴ p12g 10s Oct 23] big, good-bodied colt: first live foal: dam unraced half-sister to smart French/US performer up to 10.5f Golden Arches: fair performer: won maiden at Lingfield in July: stays 1¼m: acts on polytrack, firm and good to soft going: reportedly finished distressed fourth start, well held after: sold 17,000 gns. *B. Hanbury*

KINGHAM   2 ch.g. (Apr 17) Desert Prince (IRE) 130 – Marie de Flandre (FR) 109   **86 p** (Crystal Palace (FR) 132) [2002 7v* Nov 8] rather sparely-made gelding: closely related to fairly useful 1¼m winner Count of Flanders (by Green Desert) and half-brother to several winners, notably 8-y-o Solo Mio: dam, French 1¼m winner, half-sister to Prix Morny winner Sakura Reiko: 9/2, green and nervy, won 16-runner maiden at Doncaster by ¾ length from Golano, gradually recovering from slow start to lead final 1f under mostly firm hands and heels: likely to stay at least 1½m: joined Mrs Mary Hambro: should do better. *J. H. M. Gosden*

KING HARSON   3 b.g. Greensmith 121 – Safari Park 43 (Absalom 128) [2002 80+:   **88** 7m 6g 5g 7.5m² 6m² 7.1g⁴ 7m 7.2g⁵ 7.1f² 6f 7s Oct 25] close-coupled, good-bodied gelding: fairly useful handicapper: effective at 6f to 7.5f: acts on any turf ground: sometimes visored/blinkered (not last 8 starts): usually races prominently: has looked none too keen. *J. D. Bethell*

KING NICHOLAS (USA)   3 b.g. Nicholas (USA) 111 – Lifetime Honour (USA)   **68** (Kingmambo (USA) 125) [2002 –p: 6m 7.9g³ f7g² 8.1s² Jun 7] good-topped gelding: modest maiden handicapper: stays 1m: acts on soft going and fibresand: flashed tail penultimate start. *M. A. Jarvis*

KING OF ADOC   3 ch.c. Dr Devious (IRE) 127 – Urchin (IRE) (Fairy King (USA))   **–** [2002 49: f8s⁶ Jan 5] poor maiden: stays 7f: blinkered last 3 starts. *S. Kirk*

KING OF HAPPINESS (USA)   3 ch.c. Spinning World (USA) 130 – Mystery Rays   **114** (USA) 122 (Nijinsky (CAN) 138) [2002 105p: 8m* 8m 8g 7m² Jun 29] rather leggy, good-topped colt: smart performer, lightly raced: favourite: won Macau Jockey Club Craven Stakes at Newmarket in April comfortably by 2 lengths from Della Francesca: best subsequent effort when short-head second of 6 to Atavus in steadily-run Criterion Stakes at Newmarket final outing: got worked up in preliminaries when below par behind Rock of Gibraltar in 2000 Guineas at Newmarket (11/2, only ninth) and St James's Palace Stakes at Royal Ascot (eighth of 9) in between: will prove best up to 1m: raced only on good/good to firm going. *Sir Michael Stoute*

KING OF PERU   9 br.g. Inca Chief (USA) – Julie's Star (IRE) 45 (Thatching 131)   **59** [2002 68, a77: f5s f6s f5g f5g 5g⁵ p6g⁴ 5s 5m² 5.9d 5d³ 5m⁴ 6f* 5m* 5m Aug 28] tall, leggy gelding: has a quick action: modest performer: won seller at Catterick in July and apprentice handicap at Musselburgh in August: effective at 5f to 7f: acts on all-weather, soft and hard going: effective blinkered/visored or not: often a weak finisher. *D. Nicholls*

KING OF TARA (IRE)   4 b.c. Fairy King (USA) – La Bella Fontana (Lafontaine   **115** (USA) 117) [2002 116: 10d 10d⁶ 10d² 10s⁶ 10g⁵ Sep 3] good-topped colt: smart performer: ran well when short-neck second to Cheshire in Grand Prix de Vichy third start: below form otherwise in 2002, including in Gordon Richards Stakes at Sandown on reappearance: stays 1¼m: yet to race on firm ground, probably acts on any other turf: blinkered last 3 starts and once at 3 yrs: has carried head high: possibly not one to trust implicitly. *F. Doumen, France*

KING PRIAM (IRE)　　7 b.g. Priolo (USA) 127 – Barinia (Corvaro (USA) 124) [2002 **86 d** 95d: f8s² p12g⁶ f9.4g³ f11s* f8.5g³ p12g f11g³ f12g³ f11g³ f12g 8s³ 10d 8d 10.3f 8m 12f⁶ 12g³ 12g f11g² 11.9g 13d⁵ f9.4g f12g f9.4s⁶ f11g f12g⁵ f12g Dec 27] sturdy gelding: poor mover: fairly useful handicapper: won at Southwell in January: on downgrade after eleventh outing: effective at 1m (given test) to 1½m: probably acts on any turf going/ all-weather: usually blinkered: tried tongue tied: tends to get behind: has bled from nose: unreliable. *M. J. Polglase*

KING REVO (IRE)　　2 b.g. (Feb 18) Revoque (IRE) 122 – Tycoon Aly (IRE) 70 (Last **78** Tycoon 131) [2002 6g 7g 7s* 7m⁵ p8g⁵ f7f⁵ Nov 29] IR 13,500F, 6,500Y: tall, useful-looking gelding: has scope: third foal: half-brother to 5-y-o Chez Bonito: dam third at 1m in Ireland only start: fair performer: won minor event at Redcar in August: creditable efforts in nurseries after: stays 1m: acts on soft ground, good to firm and polytrack: tends to race freely. *P. C. Haslam*

KING'S BALLET (USA)　　4 b.c. Imperial Ballet (IRE) 110 – Multimara (USA) **–** (Arctic Tern (USA) 126) [2002 94: 6g 5f 5d 5g 7d Nov 5] strong, lengthy colt: fairly useful handicapper at 3 yrs: well held in 2002. *J. S. Goldie*

KING'S CHAMBERS　　6 ch.g. Sabrehill (USA) 120 – Flower Girl 108 (Pharly (FR) **–** 130) [2002 37: f16s⁵ f12s Jan 15] maiden: well held in 2002: used to wear blinkers. *J. Parkes*

KINGS COLLEGE BOY　　2 b.g. (Mar 26) College Chapel 122 – The Kings Daughter **62** 79 (Indian King (USA) 128) [2002 6m 6m 6s 6d⁶ Oct 14] 18,500Y: well-made gelding: half-brother to several winners, including fairly useful 5f/6f winner The Kings Ransom (by Cadeaux Genereux) and 3-y-o Wicked Uncle: dam 5f/6f winner: modest maiden: likely to prove best at 5f/6f: acts on soft and good to firm ground: blinkered (ran well) final start. *R. A. Fahey*

KING'S CONSUL (USA)　　3 b.c. Kingmambo (USA) 125 – Battle Creek Girl (USA) **–** (His Majesty (USA)) [2002 11.8s Oct 28] $5,300,000Y: tall, good-topped colt: brother to 2 winners in USA, notably very smart Grade 2 9f winner Parade Ground, closely related to winner in USA by Forty Niner and half-brother to numerous winners, notably US Grade 2 8.5f (at 2 yrs)/9f winner Tricky Creek (by Clever Trick): dam 6f (at 2 yrs) and 8.5f winner in USA: evens favourite, successful debut in maiden at Belmont only 2-y-o start (for E. Harty): weak 12/1-shot, tailed off on British debut in minor event at Leicester: blinkered/visored both outings: joined D. Loder. *Saeed bin Suroor*

KING'S CREST　　4 b.g. Deploy 131 – Classic Beauty (IRE) 65 (Fairy King (USA)) **78** [2002 83: 12s 11g 10m 8.5g 12g⁶ 10d* 9.9d* 11.1g² 13d³ 10.3d⁶ 12.3g⁵ 10g* 13.9f f9.4s **a–** Dec 7] medium-sized gelding: fair handicapper: won at Pontefract, Beverley (both ladies races), Hamilton and Ripon in summer: probably best up to 13f: acts on firm and good to soft going, below form in 3 starts on fibresand: reared stall fourth outing: usually held up: game. *R. A. Fahey*

Macau Jockey Club Craven Stakes, Newmarket—King of Happiness shortens in the 2000 Guineas betting after a striking display against Della Francesca, Sweet Band, Compton Dragon and Flat Spin (rail)

KINGSCROSS   4 ch.g. King's Signet (USA) 110 – Calamanco 71 (Clantime 101)   **89**
[2002 76p: 6.1g² 6m 6d* 6m 6d* 6.5g³ 6d² 6g 6g 7g 5s⁴ Oct 26] strong, good-bodied
gelding: fairly useful handicapper: improved at 4 yrs, and won at Goodwood in May and
Epsom in July: effective at 5f to 6.5f: acts on good to soft going, probably on soft: refused
to enter stall once in 2002: usually held up. *M. Blanshard*

KINGSDON (IRE)   5 b.g. Brief Truce (USA) 126 – Richly Deserved (IRE) (Kings   **64**
Lake (USA) 133) [2002 74: 8.5m 10m* 10m 7.9s 9.9g⁵ f11g⁵ 10m² 9.2g* 9.2d 9.9g²
9.2v* 10.1m* 9d⁶ 10.9m 9d Oct 18] sturdy, useful-looking gelding: modest performer:
won seller at Ripon, claimers at Hamilton (2) and seller at Newcastle between April/
August: probably best at 1m to 10.5f: seems to act on any turf going: visored/blinkered:
tongue tied: sometimes finds little. *J. G. FitzGerald*

KING'S ENVOY (USA)   3 b.g. Royal Academy (USA) 130 – Island of Silver (USA)   **–**
107 (Forty Niner (USA)) [2002 73p: 10.9g 11.6m 11.9g May 10] tall gelding: fair form in
maidens at 2 yrs: well held in 2002: visored final start. *E. A. L. Dunlop*

KING SILA (IRE)   3 b.c. Desert King (IRE) 129 – Sil Sila (IRE) 116 (Marju (IRE)   **–**
127) [2002 10.2d 12.1g Sep 12] second foal: dam 7f (at 2 yrs) and 10.5f (Prix de Diane)
winner: well held in maidens at Bath (slowly away) and Chepstow: tongue tied: sent to
Spain. *B. Smart*

KING SILCA   5 b.g. Emarati (USA) 74 – Silca-Cisa 93 (Hallgate 127) [2002 7m p8g   **61**
8.1m 8.3m 7d 7m⁴ Jul 22] lengthy gelding: modest handicapper: stays 7f, worth a try back
at 6f: yet to race on firm going, seems to act on any other: blinkered (raced freely/carried
head awkwardly) last 3 starts: virtually bolted to post once: sold £1,200 in August.
G. L. Moore

KING'S IRONBRIDGE (IRE)   4 b.c. King's Theatre (IRE) 128 – Dream Chaser   **106**
92 (Record Token 128) [2002 114: 8s³ 7.1g* 7m 8f⁶ Oct 26] tall, good sort: easy
mover: won Craven Stakes at Newmarket in 2001: only useful since, winning minor
event at Chepstow in August by 2½ lengths from Late Night Out: below even that form
last 3 starts, running badly final outing: unlikely to stay beyond 1m: acts on soft and good
to firm ground (unraced on heavy): has raced freely/found little. *B. J. Meehan*

KING'S MILL (IRE)   5 b.g. Doyoun 124 – Adarika (Kings Lake (USA) 133) [2002   **105**
96: 12f⁴ 10d* 10d⁴ 12g 9s⁶ Oct 26] rangy gelding: poor walker, but good mover: useful
handicapper: won at Sandown in June by 2½ lengths from Linning Wine: good fourth to
Prize Winner in valuable event there next time: best form at 1¼m: acts on firm and soft
going: usually held up. *N. A. Graham*

KING'S MOUNTAIN (USA)   2 b.g. (May 2) King of Kings (IRE) 125 – Statistic   **83**
(USA) (Mr Prospector (USA)) [2002 8.5d* 7d 7g p7g Dec 3] fifth foal: half-brother to
winner in USA by Housebuster: dam, 7f winner in USA, out of close relative to Nureyev
and half-sister to dam of Sadler's Wells: fairly useful form when winning maiden at
Killarney in July: below that level after, leaving D. Wachman and gelded before final
appearance: should stay at least 1¼m. *Mrs A. L. M. King*

KINGS OF ALBION (USA)   2 b.c. (Mar 11) King of Kings (IRE) 125 – Akadya   **– p**
(FR) (Akarad (FR) 130) [2002 8m 7f Oct 3] $260,000F, 550,000Y: quite attractive colt:
seventh foal: half-brother to 3 winners, including useful French 1¼m/1½m winner Aka
Lady (by Sanglamore): dam French 1¼m (at 2 yrs) and 12.5f (listed race) winner: signs
of a little ability in maidens: likely to do better at 1¼m/1½m. *R. Hannon*

KING SOLAR (USA)   2 b.c. (Jun 10) King of Kings (IRE) 125 – Solar (CAN) 109   **72**
(Halo (USA)) [2002 6g³ 7d 7m⁴ 6.1m⁵ 7s p6g Nov 19] $25,000Y: 43,000 2-y-o:
close-coupled, unfurnished colt: half-brother to several winners, including 1993 2-y-o 7f
winner Fayrooz (by Gulch): dam, half-sister to El Gran Senor and Try My Best, unbeaten
in 3 starts up to 7f at 2 yrs in Ireland: fair maiden: will probably stay 1m: unraced on
extremes of going on turf, probably acts on polytrack. *R. Hannon*

KING SOLOMON (FR)   3 gr.c. Simon du Desert (FR) 116 – All Square (FR) (Holst   **109 ?**
(USA) 119) [2002 99: 12m⁵ 11f⁵ 12g⁴ 11.8s⁴ Oct 28] good-topped colt: useful performer:
seemingly better than ever when 4 lengths fifth of 6 to Asian Heights in September Stakes
at Kempton on reappearance, but didn't repeat the form after in listed race at Newbury,
Cumberland Lodge Stakes at Ascot and minor event at Leicester: stays 1½m: acts on soft
and good to firm going: races prominently: sold 88,000 gns, and joined Venetia Williams.
P. F. I. Cole

KING'S PROTECTOR   2 b.c. (Feb 22) Hector Protector (USA) 124 – Doliouchka   **88 p**
(Saumarez 132) [2002 7.9m* 8g² Sep 21] 8,000Y, 18,000 2-y-o: rather leggy, lengthy
colt: second foal: half-brother to 3-y-o Carrozzina: dam 9f winner in France: overcame

greenness to win maiden at York in September: better effort (fairly useful form) when 2 lengths second of 4 to Inch Again in minor event at Ayr: will stay at least 1¼m: should do better still. *T. D. Easterby*

KINGS SIGNAL (USA)   4 b.c. Red Ransom (USA) – Star of Albion 61 (Ajdal   **74** (USA) 130) [2002 76: 8d May 22] good-topped colt: fair performer: stays 1m: acts on firm and good to soft going: usually held up. *J. J. Sheehan*

KING'S THOUGHT   3 b.c. King's Theatre (IRE) 128 – Lora's Guest 99 (Be My   **81** Guest (USA) 126) [2002 76P: 8f³ 8m* 10.3m 8g p10g⁶ Nov 14] angular, good-topped colt: has scope: fairly useful performer: won maiden at Leicester in June: has form at 1¼m, but free-going sort and may prove best up to 1m: acts on firm going, probably on soft and polytrack: wears crossed noseband: sold 22,000 gns. *E. A. L. Dunlop*

KINGSTON BLUE   3 b.g. Bluegrass Prince (IRE) 110 – Miss Pokey (Uncle Pokey   **–** 116) [2002 45: 12m Apr 22] long-backed gelding: poor form at 2 yrs: well held in seller only outing in 2002. *W. G. M. Turner*

KINGSTON GAME   3 b.c. Mind Games 121 – Valmaranda (USA) (Sir Ivor 135)   **– §** [2002 55: f7g 8.5g f8.5g⁵ f8.5g 10.2g f9.4s* f8.5g f12g f9.4s f8.5g Dec 20] workmanlike   **a55 §** colt: modest performer: left A. Berry after second start: won apprentice handicap at Wolverhampton in May: poor efforts after: stays 9.4f: acts on fibresand: often blinkered/visored: sometimes mulish/slowly away: inconsistent. *Miss K. M. George*

KINGSTON WISH (IRE)   3 b.g. Mujadil (USA) 119 – Well Wisher (USA) (Sangla-   **–** more (USA) 126) [2002 69: f6g f8g Dec 4] leggy gelding: fair maiden for A. Berry at 2 yrs: well held in 2002. *Ian Emmerson*

KINGS TO OPEN   5 b.g. First Trump 118 – Shadiyama 58 (Nishapour (FR) 125)   **–** [2002 53: f8.5g⁴ f12g⁶ f9.4g Feb 8] angular, workmanlike gelding: maiden: well held in 2002: tried blinkered: usually tongue tied. *P. W. Hiatt*

KINGS TOPIC (USA)   2 ch.c. (Mar 26) Kingmambo (USA) 125 – Topicount (USA)   **–** (Private Account (USA)) [2002 7f 7s 8d Oct 30] $85,000Y: deep-bodied colt: seventh foal: closely related to a winner in USA by Forty Niner and half-brother to US minor 6f stakes winner Laguna Seca (by Seattle Slew): dam US Grade 2 1m winner: well beaten in maidens. *G. Wragg*

KING'S WELCOME   4 b.g. Most Welcome 131 – Reine de Thebes (FR) 67 (Dar-   **102** shaan 133) [2002 97: 11.9m⁴ 11.8g² 12d* 13.9m Aug 21] rather leggy, quite good-topped gelding: useful handicapper, lightly raced: won at Ascot in August by ¾ length from Miss Fara, taking a while to settle: ran poorly in Ebor at York final start: should stay 1¾m: acts on heavy and good to firm going: genuine. *C. W. Fairhurst*

KINKY BOOTS   2 b.f. (Mar 12) The West (USA) 107 – Kinkajoo 53 (Precocious 126)   **43** [2002 p5g³ f5g 5m f6g Nov 20] half-sister to 6-y-o Sharoura and 9f winner Eyelets Echo (both by Inchinor): dam lightly raced: poor form when third in claimer at Lingfield: well held after, off 7 months before final start. *J. S. Moore*

KINNESCASH (IRE)   9 ch.g. Persian Heights 129 – Gayla Orchestra (Lord Gayle   **–** (USA) 124) [2002 12s⁵ Mar 23] small gelding: fairly useful performer at best: missed 2001: well held in minor event at Doncaster only outing in 2002. *P. Bowen*

KINNINO   8 b.g. Polish Precedent (USA) 131 – On Tiptoes 107 (Shareef Dancer   **–** (USA) 135) [2002 53: 12d⁶ 10.2f⁵ Jul 25] sturdy gelding: modest at best: well held in 2002: often blinkered. *G. L. Moore*

KINSMAN (IRE)   5 b.g. Distant Relative 128 – Besito 79 (Wassl 125) [2002 79, a92:   **71** 8.2m 7m⁴ 7m 8f⁴ p8g³ p8g p8g⁶ p8g p8g p10g Dec 28] leggy, useful-looking gelding: fair   **a79** performer: effective at 7f to easy 1¼m: acts on firm going, soft and all-weather: tried in blinkers/visor/cheekpieces/tongue tie: has broken blood vessel, reportedly had breathing problem: has started slowly/carried head high/hung badly right: held up. *T. D. McCarthy*

KIPPAX BLUES (IRE)   4 b.c. Grand Lodge (USA) 125 – Bird In Blue (IRE) 57   **–** (Bluebird (USA) 125) [2002 –: f7s Jan 5] leggy colt: well beaten in 4 maidens: tongue tied. *J. L. Eyre*

KIRISNIPPA   7 b.g. Beveled (USA) – Kiri Te (Liboi (USA) 76) [2002 –, a69: f16s⁴   **–** f16.2g⁶ f14g⁴ p16g 10f 14.1d May 18] tall gelding: modest handicapper: stays easy 2m: **a58** acts on fibresand, no recent form on turf: tried blinkered/visored: sometimes slowly away. *A. P. Jones*

KIRKBY'S TREASURE   4 br.g. Mind Games 121 – Gem of Gold 52 (Jellaby 124)   **79** [2002 75: 7d* 7.1m⁴ 6m 7f³ 8.3g 7g 7.9s* 7.2v 6.9d 7m 6m 7g 7m f7g⁴ 7g Oct 19] tall, leggy gelding: has a round action: fair performer: won handicap at Catterick in March and minor event at Carlisle in June: below form after: stays 1m: well held on heavy going, acts on any other turf and fibresand: often hangs left. *A. Berry*

KIRKHAM ABBEY 2 b.g. (Mar 15) Selkirk (USA) 129 – Totham 84 (Shernazar 131) [2002 8g 8.2v f7g⁶ Nov 16] 82,000Y: brother to smart performer in Britain and USA up to 9.5f Country Garden, 7f winner at 2 yrs, and half-brother to 2 winners, including useful 1998 2-y-o 6f winner Greensand (by Green Desert): dam 11f (in France)/1½m winner: well held in maidens: gelded after final start. *M. A. Jarvis* —

KIRK WYND 2 b.f. (Mar 22) Selkirk (USA) 129 – Abbey Strand (USA) 78 (Shadeed (USA) 135) [2002 7s⁶ 8.1f² Sep 28] unfurnished, quite attractive filly: sister to 7f winner Celtic Cross and half-sister to several winners, including 3-y-o Right Approach and useful 9f/1¼m winner New Assembly (by Machiavellian): dam, 1m winner, half-sister to winner up to 10.5f Church Parade and middle-distance stayer Castle Rising, both smart: favourite, better effort in maidens (early form) when beaten 1½ lengths by Blackwater Angel at Haydock, collared final 1f after dictating pace: will probably stay 1¼m. *Sir Michael Stoute* 76

KIROV 3 b.f. Darshaan 133 – Dance To The Top 107 (Sadler's Wells (USA) 132) [2002 72p: 8.2m* 8g⁵ 10m⁴ 10.5m⁶ Jul 14] leggy filly: fairly useful performer, lightly raced: won maiden at Nottingham in May: stays 1¼m: raced only on good/good to firm going: slowly away (well held) final start. *Sir Michael Stoute* 87

KIROVSKI (IRE) 5 b.g. Common Grounds 118 – Nordic Doll (IRE) 71 (Royal Academy (USA) 130) [2002 91: 10.1g* 10.4m² 9.9m³ 10.4m⁴ 10m³ 9f⁵ p10g² Nov 23] tall, quite attractive gelding: smart handicapper, better than ever in 2002, winning at Epsom in April by 3 lengths from Nadour Al Bahr: good efforts all starts after, including fifth to Beauchamp Pilot in Cambridgeshire at Newmarket and short-head second to same horse in listed event at Lingfield last 2: effective at 1m/1¼m: acts on polytrack, firm and soft going: usually held up nowadays: consistent. *P. W. Harris* 111

KIR ROYALE (IRE) 2 b.f. (Apr 17) Desert King (IRE) 129 – Mountain Hop (IRE) (Tirol 127) [2002 6g⁶ 6.1m 7.5m Aug 24] IR 5,000Y: close-coupled filly: fourth living foal: sister to German 7.5f (at 2 yrs) and 1¼m winner Poccino: dam lightly-raced half-sister to 3-y-o Mr Dinos: form in maidens only when sixth at Doncaster: tongue tied and reportedly hung left final appearance. *J. A. Glover* 66

KIRTLE 3 b.f. Hector Protector (USA) 124 – Kyle Rhea 104 (In The Wings 128) [2002 81p: 8.2d* 10d² 8f³ 8.5f* 9d⁴ 8f⁴ Oct 3] smallish filly: useful performer: won maiden at Nottingham in April: good second in handicap at Windsor next time, then left J. Fanshawe: won allowance race at Del Mar in July: good fourth to Wonder Again in Grade 2 at Saratoga next time: stays 1¼m: acts on firm and good to soft going. *R. B. Hess jnr, USA* 101

KISHARI (FR) 3 ch.f. Kris 135 – Reema (Nashwan (USA) 135) [2002 10m³ 9.9m 10m⁴ Jun 26] unraced granddaughter of top-class sprinter Habibti: fair form in maidens: raced only at 1¼m on good to firm ground: visits Agnes World. *M. A. Jarvis* 76

KISMET 4 b.f. Tirol 127 – Belamcanda (Belmez (USA) 131) [2002 –: 8v⁵ 10.1g⁵ 10m May 24] little form. *Don Enrico Incisa* —

KISMET QUEEN (IRE) 2 b.f. (May 13) Desert King (IRE) 129 – Kiya (USA) 85 (Dominion 123) [2002 5.9s⁶ 7g⁴ 7.1m⁶ 8f⁴ f8g³ Nov 26] 8,000Y: leggy, angular filly: seventh foal: half-sister to a 1m winner in USA by Night Shift and a winner in Sweden by Sharrood: dam, best at 1m, half-sister to smart 1993 2-y-o Lemon Souffle: fair maiden: stays 1m: acts on firm ground and fibresand. *C. W. Thornton* 66

KISS CURL 4 ch.f. Beveled (USA) – Laquette (Bairn (USA) 126) [2002 –: p7g 10d Jun 13] of little account. *M. Madgwick* —

KISSING TIME 5 b.m. Lugana Beach 116 – Princess Athena 119 (Ahonoora 122) [2002 67d: p5g⁴ 5.7g² 5.3g 5g* 5m* 5.3d 5m⁵ p5g* 5.2m 5.1m³ 6m³ 5m 5m⁴ 5.1g Sep 12] tall mare: fair handicapper: won at Beverley and Musselburgh in June, Lingfield in July and Pontefract in August: stays easy 6f: acts on all-weather, good to firm and good to soft going: often blinkered/visored early in career: consistent. *M. R. Channon* 74

KISS THE RAIN 2 b.f. (Feb 11) Forzando 122 – Devils Dirge 68 (Song 132) [2002 5g 6s⁵ f6f⁴ Nov 11] 10,000Y: small filly: sixth foal: sister to very smart 5f (including at 2 yrs)/6f winner Superior Premium and half-sister to 2 winning sprinters by Phountzi: dam maiden who probably stayed 7f: modest form in maidens: not sure to stay much beyond 6f. *W. S. Kittow* 63

KISTLER (USA) 3 b. or br.f. Honor Grades (USA) – Time For A Buck (USA) (Dam- **68** ascus (USA)) [2002 7.1g⁵ 6m² 7s 7f p7g Nov 14] $92,000Y: fifth foal: closely related to a winner in USA by Pine Bluff and half-sister to French 1m winner Miss Chantilly (by Fabulous Dancer): dam unraced daughter of high-class sprinter Swingtime: fair maiden: second at Yarmouth: well held after: very slowly away on debut. *B. J. Meehan*

KITALI (IRE) 2 b.f. (Jan 22) Atraf 116 – Mari-Ela (IRE) 60 (River Falls 113) [2002 – § 5m⁶ 5m 5m p5g 7.1m 6.1m Aug 19] 5,000Y: good-topped filly: first foal: dam, 2-y-o 7f seller winner, half-sister to useful performer up to 1m Scarteen Fox: temperamental maiden: tried visored: often slowly away: one to avoid. *Mrs P. N. Dutfield*

KITTYLEE 3 b.f. Bal Harbour 113 – Courtesy Call (Northfields (USA)) [2002 –: f8g – 14.1m 9.3s f12g Jul 11] probably of little account. *R. M. Whitaker*

KLANCYLADY 4 ch.f. Clantime 101 – Mrs Skinner 53 (Electric 126) [2002 5g 6d – 12d Nov 5] third reported foal: dam, maiden, stayed 1m: well beaten in maidens. *C. W. Thornton*

KNAVESMIRE OMEN 3 b.g. Robellino (USA) 127 – Signs 91 (Risk Me (FR) 127) **100** [2002 73: f8s⁴ p8g⁵ f8.5g 9.1g 8g³ 10g 12m* 12.3m⁴ 12.6m* 12d* 12s* 12.3m² 11.9g 12.3m⁶ 14m 16m* 16.2g 12f* 13.9f 14.6s* 16.5v* Nov 9] sturdy gelding: poor mover: useful performer: much improved, and had a fine year, winning handicaps at Musselburgh, Warwick (apprentices), Newmarket, Pontefract, Yarmouth and Doncaster (2, beat Contact Dancer by 6 lengths on second occasion): also won claimer at Newmarket eighteenth start: stays 2m: acts on any going: blinkered once at 2 yrs: usually races prominently: looked reluctant in past, but very game nowadays. *M. Johnston*

KNIGHT CROSSING (IRE) 4 b.g. Doyoun 124 – Princess Sarara (USA) (Trem- **56** polino (USA) 135) [2002 57: 9.3g 6.9d⁵ 6m⁵ 6m 6g 6f Oct 11] close-coupled gelding: modest maiden: seems effective from 6f to 1¼m: acts on soft and good to firm going. *Mrs A. Duffield*

KNIGHTED 6 b.g. Bigstone (IRE) 126 – Missed Again 84 (High Top 131) [2002 77: – 16.2g May 11] leggy gelding: has a markedly round action: fair handicapper at best, lightly raced: tailed off only run in 2002. *T. D. Easterby*

KNIGHT GENERAL MAC 3 b.g. Presidium 124 – Agnes Jane (Sweet Monday – 122) [2002 8m 9.9m Aug 25] 3,200Y: sixth foal: dam unraced: well beaten in maidens. *N. Bycroft*

KNIGHT'S EMPEROR (IRE) 5 b.g. Grand Lodge (USA) 125 – So Kind 90 (Kind – of Hush 118) [2002 65: 8.1m Jul 7] rangy, good sort: maiden handicapper on Flat: blinkered once: winning hurdler/chaser. *J. L. Spearing*

KNOCKAINEY FARMER (IRE) 3 b.g. Balla Cove 119 – High State 72 (Free – State 125) [2002 f5g f6g f7g Feb 8] IR 600Y, 7,500 2-y-o: half-brother to 3 winners, including useful performer up to 1m Highborn (by Double Schwartz) and fairly useful 6f performer Macs Maharanee (by Indian King): dam 9f seller winner: well held in maidens at Wolverhampton: dead. *P. S. Felgate*

KNOCKDOO (IRE) 9 ch.g. Be My Native (USA) 122 – Ashken (Artaius (USA) – 129) [2002 55: 14.1d⁵ 16f 13s⁵ Jun 19] modest handicapper in 2001: well held in 2002, leaving J. J. O'Neill after second start: tried visored. *J. S. Goldie*

KNOCKEMBACK NELLIE 6 b.m. Forzando 122 – Sea Clover (IRE) 77 (Ela- **51 d** Mana-Mou 132) [2002 65: 5.7g 5.1d 5g 5.5f³ 5.1d⁶ 5m 5.1f⁶ 5.1m 5m 5.3m 5f f6g Dec 10] smallish mare: handicapper, on the downgrade: stays 6f: acts on firm and soft going: usually blinkered: has had tongue tied: often reluctant: one to avoid. *J. M. Bradley*

KNOCKTOPHER ABBEY 5 ch.g. Pursuit of Love 124 – Kukri (Kris 135) [2002 **75** 82: p10g 8.1g³ 10m⁴ 10m 10m⁵ 11.7g Oct 16] angular, plain gelding: fair handicapper: stays 1¼m: seems unsuited by soft/heavy going, acts on any other turf and polytrack: blinkered last 3 starts. *B. R. Millman*

KNOTTY ASH GIRL (IRE) 3 ch.f. Ashkalani (IRE) 128 – Camisha (IRE) 82 **65 ?** (Shernazar 131) [2002 76: 6.9d 8m⁴ f9.4g² 10m 12.3m³ 10s 8g⁴ f9.4g Nov 16] smallish, close-coupled filly: seemingly fair maiden: probably stays easy 1½m: acts on heavy going, good to firm and fibresand. *B. A. McMahon*

KNOTTY HILL 10 b.g. Green Ruby (USA) 104 – Esilam 62 (Frimley Park 109) – [2002 –: f8g f6g⁵ 7g 7f⁵ 8.3v 7.6f 6f 7m 8m⁵ Jul 26] of little account. *R. Craggs*

KNOWLE PARK (IRE) 3 br.f. Woodborough (USA) 112 – Nagida 94 (Skyliner – 117) [2002 6m f7g Nov 22] 4,500Y: fifth foal: half-sister to 5-y-o Love You Too and 1997

2-y-o 7f winner Chief Blade (both by Be My Chief): dam won Wokingham: well held in maidens at Lingfield (slowly away) and Wolverhampton. *M. S. Saunders*

KNOWN MANEUVER (USA) 4 b.g. Known Fact (USA) 135 – Northern Maneuver **79 d** (USA) (Al Nasr (FR) 126) [2002 73: 10m* 12m 10d 11.9g 10.4m 12f Sep 21] smallish gelding: fair performer: won minor event at Nottingham in April: no form after, leaving P. Cole after next start (gave impression something amiss): stays 1½m: acts on fibresand and good to firm going. *M. C. Chapman*

KOHIMA (IRE) 2 ch.f. (Mar 14) Baratrea (IRE) 127 – Albenita (IRE) (Alzao (USA) **63** 117) [2002 7d Aug 3] IR 30,000F, 21,000Y: half-sister to several winners, including fairly useful Irish 7f winner Girl In Pearls (by Soviet Lad): dam Irish 2-y-o 5f winner: 66/1 and tongue tied, eighth to Nayzak in maiden at Newmarket, short-lived effort. *G. C. Bravery*

KOKOPELLI STAR 3 b.f. Hernando (FR) 127 – Celebrity 101 (Troy 137) [2002 –: **–** 8.2m 10s 10m 9.9d Jul 12] little form: bred to be suited by 1¼m+. *B. Smart*

KOMALUNA 4 ch.g. Komaite (USA) – Sugar Token 66 (Record Token 128) [2002 **–** 41: f6s Jan 2] lengthy gelding: maiden: well beaten only outing in 2002. *D. Shaw*

KOMASEPH 10 b.g. Komaite (USA) – Starkist 81 (So Blessed 130) [2002 –§, a35§: **– §** f6s Jan 22] workmanlike gelding: temperamental nowadays: tried blinkered/visored: sometimes tongue tied. *R. F. Marvin*

KOMATI RIVER 3 b.g. Wesaam (USA) 95 – Christening (IRE) (Lahib (USA) 129) **58** [2002 8.2v p12g Dec 14] second foal: dam unraced out of half-sister to smart middle-distance stayers Bright Finish and Shining Finish: modest form in maidens at Nottingham and Lingfield. *J. Akehurst*

KOMEDERA 3 b.g. Danzig Connection (USA) – Musica 82 (Primo Dominie 121) **–** [2002 56: 6d 6f Apr 13] good-bodied gelding: modest maiden at 2 yrs: well held in 2002. *D. Nicholls*

KOMENA 4 b.f. Komaite (USA) – Mena 58 (Blakeney 126) [2002 –: 8.3g⁵ 8m 8f p10g **60 §** 8m³ 7m 8.3m 7m 6m Sep 19] tall, lengthy filly: modest performer nowadays: stays 1m: form only on good ground or firmer: has been edgy/reluctant stall/raced too freely: one to treat with caution. *J. W. Payne*

KONICA 3 b.f. Desert King (IRE) 129 – Haboobti (Habitat 134) [2002 57: 5.1d f7g⁶ **55** f8.5s² 10g f8.5g f6g f9.4f 6.1m Sep 20] good-bodied filly: modest maiden handicapper: should stay 1¼m: acts on fibresand, best turf form on going softer than good. *P. S. Felgate*

KONKER 7 ch.g. Selkirk (USA) 129 – Helens Dreamgirl 95 (Caerleon (USA) 132) **–** [2002 76: p10g 10d Oct 21] unfurnished gelding: fair handicapper on Flat at best, lightly raced. *Mrs M. Reveley*

KOOL (IRE) 3 b.g. Danehill Dancer (IRE) 117 – New Rochelle (IRE) 65 (Lafontaine **104** (USA) 117) [2002 87: 6m 7m⁵ 7d⁵ 6s⁴ 6d 6.1m⁹ 7d* 7d* 8f² 7m Sep 28] well-made gelding: useful performer: won claimer at Warwick in July and handicaps at Kempton and Leicester in July/August, final one by 2 lengths from Royal Quarters: ran respectably in Tote Trifecta Handicap at Ascot final outing (gelded after): effective at 6f/7f, very enterprisingly ridden when tried at 1m, but stays trip when emphasis is on speed: acts on firm and good to soft going: has worn crossed noseband. *P. F. I. Cole*

KOOTENAY (IRE) 3 ch.f. Selkirk (USA) 129 – Llia 94 (Shirley Heights 130) [2002 **109** 100: 8g* 8m 9.9d² 8.5s* 8g³ 8s³ 8s Nov 2] rather unfurnished filly: useful performer: won listed races at Kempton (by 1¼ lengths from Red Liason) in March and Epsom (beat Golden Silca by 4 lengths) in June: creditable third after in Falmouth Stakes at Newmarket (3 lengths behind Tashawak) and Premio Sergio Cumani at Milan (beaten 3½ lengths by Welsh Diva): was probably best around 1m: acted on soft going, below form on good to firm: often front runner: genuine: stud. *J. L. Dunlop*

KOSMIC LADY 5 b.m. Cosmonaut – Ktolo 80 (Tolomeo 127) [2002 55, a–: p10g **56** p8g⁴ p10g f8.5g 8.3g⁴ 10.2g 8.1m 8d⁴ 8.1s 8g* 8.1g 8m² 8.3m 8.3d 8m⁴ 8.3m 8.1g Sep **a43** 12] strong, lengthy mare: modest on turf, poor on all-weather: won seller at Brighton in June: barely stays 1¼m: acts on soft going, good to firm and all-weather: tried blinkered earlier in career: usually tongue tied: occasionally carries head high. *P. W. Hiatt*

KOTORI (IRE) 3 gr.g. Charnwood Forest (IRE) 125 – La Kermesse (USA) 58 (Storm **–** Bird (CAN) 134) [2002 –: 6d 6s 5.7g 5f Sep 25] no form. *M. S. Saunders*

KOURNAKOVA (IRE) 3 b.f. Sadler's Wells (USA) 132 – Bermuda Classic 98 **106** (Double Form 130) [2002 102p: 7s² 8s⁶ 12s 10g⁵ 12d 10m⁶ 9.5d* Oct 12] strong, good-topped filly: type to carry condition: useful performer: won listed race at Gowran in

October by 1½ lengths from Desert Trail: creditable efforts earlier at the Curragh in listed race (2 lengths second to Rum Charger), Irish 1000 Guineas (6¾ lengths sixth to Gossamer) and Pretty Polly Stakes (4½ lengths fifth behind Tarfshi): probably stayed 1¼m (well held in Oaks and Irish Oaks both attempts at 1½m): acted on soft going: blinkered fourth start: had worn crossed noseband: visits Danehill. *A. P. O'Brien, Ireland*

KRIS KIN (USA) 2 ch.c. (Mar 5) Kris S (USA) – Angel In My Heart (FR) 119 (Rainbow Quest (USA) 134) [2002 7f 7s* Oct 25] $275,000Y: angular, useful-looking colt: on weak side at 2 yrs: half-brother to useful 7f/1m winner Venturer (by Gone West): dam, French 1m/1¼m (Prix de Psyche) winner, half-sister to Prix de la Salamandre winner Common Grounds: burly and green on debut: 5/1, plenty of improvement (fairly useful form) when winning maiden at Doncaster by 2½ lengths from Presenter, leading over 1f out: likely to stay 1¼m: slowly away both starts: should continue to progress. *Sir Michael Stoute* **81 p**

KRISTAL DANCER (IRE) 2 b.f. (Apr 11) Charnwood Forest (IRE) 125 – Kristal's Paradise (IRE) 100 (Bluebird (USA) 125) [2002 7d 7m Sep 5] third foal: dam 1¾m/2m winner: signs of ability in maidens at Kempton and Salisbury: capable of better at 1¼m+. *J. L. Dunlop* **– p**

KRISTAL FOREST (IRE) 3 b.g. Charnwood Forest (IRE) 125 – Kristal's Paradise (IRE) 100 (Bluebird (USA) 125) [2002 8m 8f 10f³ 12d 12.4m² 16g Aug 27] big, rangy, unfurnished gelding: second foal: dam 1¾m/2m winner: fair maiden: stays 12.4f: acts on firm going: sold 12,000 gns, and joined Mrs S. Lamyman. *J. L. Dunlop* **77**

KRISTENSEN 3 ch.g. Kris S (USA) – Papaha (FR) 103 (Green Desert (USA) 127) [2002 71: 8.2d² 12.3m* 12.3f⁵ 10m⁵ 11.9d 9.9g⁶ 10.3f³ 12.3g⁶ 9m 10.1d² 10m⁴ 11.9f³ 10d² 10.3s⁴ f12s* f12s² Dec 7] smallish, sturdy gelding: fairly useful handicapper: won at Ripon in April, and (having been claimed from Mrs J. Ramsden ninth start) Wolverhampton in November: stays 1½m: yet to race on heavy going, acts on any other turf/fibresand: has worn cheekpieces: occasionally edgy: slowly away seventh outing, raced freely eighth: usually patiently ridden: consistent. *D. Eddy* **85**

KRISTOFFERSEN 2 ch.c. (Feb 24) Kris 135 – Towaahi (IRE) (Caerleon (USA) 132) [2002 p8g⁵ Dec 14] first foal: dam unraced out of Fillies' Mile and Yorkshire Oaks winner Untold: 25/1, fair form when fifth of 12 to Nawow in maiden at Lingfield, slowly away and staying on: should improve. *W. Jarvis* **72 p**

KRUGERRAND (USA) 3 ch.g. Gulch (USA) – Nasers Pride (USA) (Al Nasr (FR) 126) [2002 94: 7.6f 7d 8m² 7.1m* 6m⁶ 7.1f⁴ 8f⁴ 7v Nov 9] big, lengthy, attractive gelding: fairly useful performer: won minor event at Warwick in July: left M. Bell 32,000 gns before well held final run (gelded after): stays 1m: acts on firm and good to soft going: tongue tied final start at 2 yrs: headstrong, and has worn crossed noseband: has wandered/carried head high. *W. J. Musson* **92**

KRYPTON 2 b.g. (Apr 12) Kylian (USA) – Tiama (IRE) 50 (Last Tycoon 131) [2002 5.1g f5g⁶ p7g Jun 22] 4,800Y: third foal: half-brother to 3-y-o Hot Love: dam maiden who seemed to stay 9.7f: well held in maidens: slowly away first 2 starts. *P. D. Cundell* **–**

KRYSTAL MAX (IRE) 9 b.g. Classic Music (USA) – Lake Isle (IRE) (Caerleon (USA) 132) [2002 72, a79: p5g p7g Feb 9] smallish, good-topped gelding: one-time fairly useful performer: gained all but one of his 17 successes on all-weather: said to have bled from nose final start: was effective at 5f to easy 7f: acted on all-weather, firm and good to soft going: blinkered once at 2 yrs: reportedly retired. *P. S. McEntee* **–**

KULACHI (IRE) 3 b.c. Royal Applause 124 – Silly View (IRE) 75 (Scenic 128) [2002 96: 7m 7m³ 7d 8m 6d 7.1m² 7m 6f² 6.1m⁴ 6m⁵ 6g 6g Sep 27] tall, rather leggy colt: has a fluent, round action: fairly useful performer: effective at 6f/7f: acts on firm going: effective visored or not: sent to UAE. *M. R. Channon* **92**

KUMAKAWA 4 ch.g. Dancing Spree (USA) – Maria Cappuccini 70 (Siberian Express (USA) 125) [2002 –§, a86d: f8s⁵ f8s⁵ f11s⁵ f8g³ f6g f7g³ f6g f7g f7g⁵ f8g* f8g³ p8g f8g f9.4s 10.1m f8g f8.5g Dec 13] tall gelding: modest performer: won claimer at Southwell (final start for M. Polglase) in March: stays 9.4f: acts on soft going, good to firm and fibresand: well held run on polytrack: tried visored/blinkered: has been edgy/reluctant stall/looked difficult ride: unreliable. *D. K. Ivory* **– § a60 §**

KUNDALILA 4 b.f. River Falls 113 – Kalou 71 (K-Battery 108) [2002 –: 11.1s 8.3s 11.1g 13g May 18] maiden, no longer of any account. *D. A. Nolan* **–**

KUNDOOZ 3 b.g. Sabrehill (USA) 120 – Reem Albaraari 81 (Sadler's Wells (USA) 132) [2002 97: 10g 12m 12m⁴ 10m Sep 21] sturdy, well-made gelding: useful performer, lightly raced: best effort when 1½ lengths fourth to Royal Cavalier in handicap at **105**

Doncaster on third start: well held in King George V Handicap at Royal Ascot and Courage Best Handicap at Newbury on second and final appearances: stays 1½m: yet to race on extremes of going: has been bandaged: sweating/edgy first 2 outings (reared leaving stall/raced freely on reappearance): sent to UAE. *M. A. Jarvis*

KUPKAKEKATIE 3 b.f. Saddlers' Hall (IRE) 126 – Miss Laetitia (IRE) (Entitled 126) [2002 10m 10.2d 10g 14.1d Oct 30] strong, lengthy filly: fourth living foal: half-sister to 1¼m seller winner Diletia (by Dilum): dam of little account: no form. *N. A. Graham* — **–**

KUSTER 6 b.g. Indian Ridge 123 – Ustka 60 (Lomond (USA) 128) [2002 95: 10g⁴ 10m May 4] good-bodied gelding: unimpressive mover: fairly useful handicapper: reportedly sustained small injury in June: best at 1¼m/1½m: acts on firm and soft going: blinkered last 3 starts at 5 yrs and final one in 2002. *L. M. Cumani* — **89**

KUSTOM KIT FOR HER 2 b.f. (Feb 27) Overbury (IRE) 116 – Antonias Melody 86 (Rambo Dancer (CAN) 107) [2002 10s f6g Nov 20] first foal: dam 6f (including at 2 yrs)/7f winner: poor form in maiden at Nottingham and claimer at Southwell. *S. R. Bowring* — **37**

KUT O ISLAND (USA) 4 br.g. Woodman (USA) 126 – Cherry Jubilee (USA) (Coastal (USA)) [2002 59: p10g 8d 10s⁶ 10g 10g⁵ 9s⁴ 9v⁴ 12s 10s 7g* 8s² 8s* 8s* 7v* 7.5s⁶ Nov 20] lightly raced in Britain (modest form at best), leaving D. Arbuthnot (only start for that stable) after reappearance: won 4 handicaps at Munich in autumn, first 2 amateur events: best at 7f/1m: acts on heavy ground: tried blinkered/tongue tied. *W. Figge, Germany* — **?**

KUTUB (IRE) 5 b.h. In The Wings 128 – Minnie Habit (Habitat 134) [2002 123: 12g⁵ 12s⁶ 12d Jul 9] compact, attractive horse: very smart performer: improved in second half of 2001, winning Grosser Dallmayr-Preis at Munich, Preis von Europa at Cologne, Gran Premio del Jockey Club at Milan, all Group 1s, and Singapore Gold Cup (Handicap) at Kranji: conceding weight all round, creditable 2½ lengths fifth to Marienbard in Jockey Club Stakes at Newmarket in May, switched then hampered final 1f: ran poorly after in Coronation Cup at Epsom (hung left, said by rider to have lost action) and Princess of Wales's Stakes at Newmarket (looked none too keen): stayed 1½m: acted on good to firm going but went well on good or softer: tried blinkered, visored last 9 starts: tongue tied final outing: to stand at Haras du Thenney, France, fee €4,000, special live foal. *Saeed bin Suroor* — **122**

KUWAIT BIRD 6 b.g. Cosmonaut – Loadplan Lass 63 (Nicholas Bill 125) [2002 16g Aug 12] tall, leggy, shallow-girthed gelding: little form. *Mrs A. M. Naughton* — **–**

KUWAIT DAWN (IRE) 6 b.m. Pips Pride 117 – Red Note (Rusticaro (FR) 124) [2002 71d: f6s Jan 4] big, lengthy mare: poor mover: fair performer at best: on downgrade: tried visored. *D. Nicholls* — **–**

KUWAIT FLAVOUR (IRE) 6 b.g. Bluebird (USA) 125 – Plume Magique (Kenmare (FR) 125) [2002 –: f9.4g f12g f12g 7f Apr 11] small, stocky gelding: maiden, no longer of any account. *Mrs D. Haine* — **–**

KUWAIT SAND 6 b.g. Lugana Beach 116 – Soon To Be 84 (Hot Spark 126) [2002 –: f5g Feb 15] maiden, no longer of any account. *G. A. Ham* — **–**

KUWAIT THUNDER (IRE) 6 ch.g. Mac's Imp (USA) 116 – Romangoddess (IRE) (Rhoman Rule (USA)) [2002 49§: 8g⁵ f8.5g² 8m³ 8g 8.5d f12f f7g f11g⁵ Dec 4] rather leggy, quite good-topped gelding: poor mover: poor performer: effective at 7f to easy 1½m: acts on firm going, good to soft and fibresand: sometimes visored: tried tongue tied: usually a weak finisher, and can't be trusted. *D. Carroll* — **47 § a43 §**

KUZI 3 br.f. Bin Ajwaad (IRE) 119 – Petonellajill 73 (Petong 126) [2002 –: f8.5g f7g Mar 15] leggy, unfurnished filly: no form: tried visored. *M. Mullineaux* — **–**

KYDA (USA) 4 b.f. Gulch (USA) – Trampoli (USA) 115 (Trempolino (USA) 135) [2002 75: 9.2g⁶ 9.2v⁶ 11.9g 11.9m⁶ 9.9d 11.1d* 12.1g⁵ 12s³ 13v² 14.8m f12s 13.1s 14.6s³ 16.5v⁶ Nov 9] quite good-topped filly: fair handicapper: won at Hamilton in July: stays 14.6f: yet to race on firm going, acts on any other turf: tried visored. *M. Moore* — **78**

KYLE OF LOCHALSH 2 gr.c. (May 20) Vettori (IRE) 119 – Shaieef (IRE) 66 (Shareef Dancer (USA) 135) [2002 6m 6m⁶ 6g Oct 18] leggy colt: half-brother to 1995 2-y-o 5f winner Capture The Moment (by Keen) and several winners abroad: dam 1m winner out of half-sister to Shergar: modest maiden: reportedly lame when last in sales race at Newmarket final start. *G. G. Margarson* — **57**

KYLKENNY   7 b.g. Kylian (USA) – Fashion Flow (Balidar 133) [2002 66: f12g* **84**
f12g* f11g² f12g* f12g² 12s 10m² 10m 10m 11.7f² 12.3m⁵ 10f² 10f 10d* 12v⁴ f12s⁴
Dec 7] angular, workmanlike gelding: fairly useful handicapper: better than ever at 7 yrs,
winning at Southwell (3 times, first one for amateurs) in January/February and Pontefract
in October: ran as if amiss final outing: effective at 1¼m/easy 1½m: acts on fibresand,
firm and good to soft going. *H. Morrison*

KYLLACHY   4 b.c. Pivotal 124 – Pretty Poppy 67 (Song 132) [2002 111: 5.2g* **129**
5m* 5m* 5g³ 5m* Aug 22]
        There was nothing in Kyllachy's three-year-old career to suggest he would
develop into a sprint champion but his form in defeating Malhub in the Victor
Chandler Nunthorpe Stakes was clearly the best of the season over sprint distances
and well up to standard for a champion in the last decade. Unfortunately, having
revealed the extent of his ability, Kyllachy did not race again due to injury—the
Prix de l'Abbaye would have been at his mercy on his Nunthorpe form. Kyllachy
started the season as a smart performer with a record of two wins from seven starts.
Successful in a maiden at Chepstow at two and a handicap at Sandown off a mark
of 90 on his reappearance at three, he had run well to be second in a listed race at
Deauville and fourth in a well-contested minor event at Nottingham, though his
final run when fourth in a handicap at Ascot suggested his improvement had
probably run its course. Kyllachy reappeared in a competitive showcase handicap
at Newbury in April, not in a conditions event, but the style of his victory made it
apparent that better races were there for the taking. Carrying 9-3, he made smooth
progress to lead a furlong out and left the others for dead, beating Trace Clip by a
length and three quarters and recording a timefigure equivalent to a rating of 120,
which wasn't surpassed among the season's sprinters until Malhub recorded 122
in the Diadem at the end of September. Kyllachy's principal weapon, shown to

Victor Chandler Palace House Stakes, Newmarket—Kyllachy (far side) justifies strong support
but snatches the spoils only by a short head from Smokin Beau (noseband),
with Bahamian Pirate the same margin away in third

Victor Chandler Nunthorpe Stakes, York—Kyllachy secures the title of champion sprinter after being switched from a high draw to come up near the rail; Malhub (striped cap) is second, in front of Indian Prince (spots on sleeves), Continent (left), Dominica (behind winner) and Lady Dominatrix (star on cap)

particularly good effect at Newbury, was a fine turn of foot, and unlike one of his principal rivals for the sprinting title Continent he did not need to be held up for most of the race before producing his hallmark acceleration. Horses who are waited with are more likely to encounter trouble than those like Malhub who bowl along in front, Kyllachy proving the point when stepped up in grade in the Victor Chandler Palace House Stakes at Newmarket. Starting favourite at 2/1 in a field of twelve, he had to be switched to obtain a run entering the final furlong and burst through on the stand rail to touch off front-running Smokin Beau by a short head with Bahamian Pirate close up third. If that victory was earned by the skin of his teeth, Kyllachy's success in the Group 2 Tripleprint Temple Stakes at Sandown early in June definitely was not—he put up an electrifying display in a race as strongly contested as one or two Group 1 sprints during the year. Soon travelling strongly on the bridle off the pace, Kyllachy sprinted past the leaders to beat the penalised Vision of Night by four lengths, with Invincible Spirit, Continent and Bahamian Pirate among those further back, albeit none of them at their best on the day. His rider Jamie Spencer later recounted that Kyllachy 'felt like a Porsche against a fleet of Minis', a view with which it was easy to concur.

Royal Ascot follows soon after the Temple, and a week before Kyllachy's next target, the King's Stand Stakes, Cheveley Park Stud bought a half share for a reported £500,000, with the proviso of an additional payment of £500,000 if Kyllachy should be placed in a Group 1, plus another £200,000 for each Group 1 he won. Judged on his Sandown performance, Kyllachy looked close to unbeatable at Ascot and started favourite at 11/10. For some reason, however, he ran below form and failed to enjoy the best of runs in finishing a head and half a length behind Dominica and Continent, only just ahead of The Trader, Indian Prince and Olivia Grace. With the July Cup ruled out because of its six-furlong trip, the first possibility of Cheveley Park's having to make an extra payment arrived with the Nunthorpe at York. Even though reopposed by Dominica, Kyllachy started

536

favourite to beat sixteen opponents, also including Danehurst, Malhub, Continent and Bahamian Pirate. The decision by clerk of the course John Smith to place the stalls against the far rail rather than in the centre did not please Spencer, Kyllachy's regular rider in the latest season, or Richard Hills, rider of Malhub. However, it would have made little material difference wherever the stalls had been placed due to the size of the field. Spencer decided to go for what he presumed to be firmer ground on the farthest rail from the stands, dropping out Kyllachy, drawn fifteen, and tacking across virtually the whole width of the course. Last after a furlong, Kyllachy was asked to improve at halfway and produced his characteristic acceleration under fairly hard driving—Spencer received a one-day ban for using his whip from above the shoulder, as he had at Royal Ascot—to get up and beat Malhub (drawn sixteen) by half a length. Indian Prince at 33/1 was the same distance away third, followed by Continent and Dominica. Given the way the race was run, Kyllachy's performance, and Malhub's for that matter, was first rate but Kyllachy came out of the race jarred up with bruising behind his off-fore knee, a problem which had reportedly affected him after his reappearance as a three-year-old. He could not be got ready in time for the Abbaye and was retired to Cheveley Park, where breeders were reported to be keen to book his services at £7,500.

Kyllachy (b.c. 1998)	Pivotal (ch 1993)	Polar Falcon (b or br 1987)	Nureyev	
			Marie d'Argonne	
		Fearless Revival (ch 1987)	Cozzene	
			Stufida	
	Pretty Poppy (b 1988)	Song (b 1966)	Sing Sing	
			Intent	
		Moonlight Serenade (br 1987)	Crooner	
			March Moonlight	

Thurloe Thoroughbreds V & Cheveley Park Stud's "Kyllachy"

Kyllachy is the first champion sprinter not to be tried over further than the minimum trip at any stage in his career since Sandford Lad in 1973, though Flirting Around raced only over five in his championship season, 1975, and Lochsong was undoubtedly best at five when she notched her titles in 1993 and 1994. Kyllachy is by a specialist sprinter in Pivotal, also at Cheveley Park Stud and standing at £25,000 in 2003, over four times his fee on retirement from racing. Successful in the King's Stand Stakes and Nunthorpe Stakes as a three-year-old, Pivotal was bred to get at least a mile and sires some horses effective at up to a mile and a quarter, including the very smart ex-Irish filly Golden Apples, winner of the Beverly D Stakes and Yellow Ribbon Stakes in the latest season. Like his son, Pivotal did not race again after York. Kyllachy, a strong, well-made individual purchased for 36,000 guineas at Doncaster as a yearling, is likely to be a much more straight-forward proposition as a sire. His dam Pretty Poppy stayed seven furlongs but gained her only success over five as a two-year-old and has produced five other winners with Henry Candy, all at five furlongs, headed by Borders (by the miler Selkirk), placed in listed events at Dortmund and Kempton. It will be interesting to see if Pretty Poppy's two-year-old Isaz turns out to be purely and simply a five-furlong performer as well; he's by Elmaamul, who is more of a stamina influence than Pretty Poppy's earlier mates. Kyllachy's grandam Moonlight Serenade was a sister to smart sprinter Blackbird. A reliable sort who did not race on firm going but seemed to act on any other, Kyllachy had been tried in a crossed noseband. *H. Candy*

KYLMAX   3 b.g. Classic Cliche (IRE) 128 – Dame Lorraine 56 (Damister (USA) 123)   –
[2002 –: 10.1m⁶ 10f 16d 13.8f⁶ 15.8f Sep 21] very tall, lengthy gelding: third living foal: dam maiden who stayed 1m: little form: tried blinkered: dead. *H. A. McWilliams*

L

LA BAYADERE   2 b.f. (Apr 18) Sadler's Wells (USA) 132 – Oriental Mystique 97   –
(Kris 135) [2002 7d Aug 3] 375,000Y: sixth foal: sister to 4-y-o Xtra, closely related to useful 7f (including at 2 yrs) winner Mandarina (by El Gran Senor), and half-sister to useful 1997 2-y-o 6f winner who later won in Australia Sky Rocket (by Storm Cat): dam, 7f/1m winner, half-sister to dam of Derby runner-up City Honours: 25/1 and very green, well held in maiden at Newmarket. *D. R. Loder*

LA BELLE CLARE (IRE)   4 ch.f. Paris House 123 – Sarah-Clare 67 (Reach 122)   **61**
[2002 5g* 5.3m Sep 3] third living foal: half-sister to smart 6f/7f performer Nice One Clare (by Mukaddamah): dam 1m/1¼m winner: won maiden at Folkestone (edged right) in August: well below that form in minor event at Brighton following month, carrying head awkwardly: will stay 6f: sold 5,000 gns. *J. W. Payne*

LABRETT   5 b.g. Tragic Role (USA) – Play The Game 70 (Mummy's Game 120)   **84**
[2002 93: 6s 6m 7g 6d⁶ 7g* 7m² 7m 7.9m² 7.1m³ 8m⁵ 7f⁴ 8g 8v 8f8g⁵ f8.5s³ Dec 13]   **a82**
good-topped gelding: fairly useful performer: won minor event at Wolverhampton in July: probably best at 7f/easy 1m nowadays: acts on fibresand, firm and soft going: usually blinkered earlier in career (only once since 2000): has worn cheekpieces: tongue tied after fourth start: has swished tail/had 2 handlers in preliminaries: sometimes slowly away: usually set plenty to do. *Miss Gay Kelleway*

LABRUSCA   3 b.f. Grand Lodge (USA) 125 – Catawba 98 (Mill Reef (USA) 141)   **58 p**
[2002 9.9m³ Sep 13] sister to fairly useful 9.4f winner Tyler's Toast and 1½m winner Fraternity and half-sister to several winners, notably very smart Yorkshire Oaks winner Catchascatchcan (by Pursuit of Love): dam, 1¼m winner, out of Ribblesdale winner Catalpa: 10½ lengths third to Blue Leader in maiden at Goodwood, travelling smoothly but unable to quicken: should progress. *H. R. A. Cecil*

LA CAMPANELLA (IRE)   2 b.f. (Apr 22) Tagula (IRE) 116 – Dawn Chorus (IRE)   **83**
(Mukaddamah (USA) 125) [2002 5g⁴ 5m³ 6d* 6d⁴ 6m 6.3g 6g 6g⁵ 6.5m⁴ 6.1m⁴ 6m* 6f 7f p6g⁵ 6g⁶ 6.1s⁵ Oct 23] IR 12,000Y: rather leggy, workmanlike filly: second foal: half-sister to useful Irish 7f (at 2 yrs) to 1¼m winner Solid Approach (by Definite Article): dam unraced half-sister to smart performer in Scandinavia up to 1½m Barrier

Reef: fairly useful performer: won minor event at Brighton in May and nursery at Leicester in September: good efforts in nurseries/minor event last 3 starts: best form at 6f: acts on good to firm going, soft and polytrack: edgy sort: often races up with pace: tough and consistent: sold 11,000 gns, sent to USA. *M. R. Channon*

LA CORUJERA   2 b.f. (Feb 5) Case Law 113 – Aybeegirl 66 (Mazilier (USA) 107)   **68**
[2002 f5g⁶ 5m² 5.2f 5m⁴ f5s⁴ᵈ 7f² 6d² Oct 21] 3,200Y: workmanlike filly: first foal: dam 2-y-o 5f winner: fair maiden: in frame in nurseries fourth to sixth starts: effective at 5f to 7f: acts on fibresand, firm and good to soft going: edgy sort, sometimes early to post. *T. D. Barron*

LADIES KNIGHT   2 b.g. (Apr 23) Among Men (USA) 124 – Lady Silk 67 (Prince   **48**
Sabo 123) [2002 f8.5g⁵ f8s 6g 5.2d f6g f5g f5g f5g³ Dec 27] 11,500F, 8,000Y: leggy, angular gelding: second foal: dam 6f winner: poor maiden: best efforts at 5f/6f: acts on fibresand. *D. Shaw*

LA DOLFINA   2 b.f. (May 2) Pennekamp (USA) 130 – Icecapped 91 (Caerleon (USA)   **67**
132) [2002 7m 8m 8.1m⁵ 6.5g Sep 27] 16,000Y: rather leggy, angular filly: half-sister to several winners, including useful 1999 2-y-o 6f/7f winner Goodwood Blizzard (by Inchinor) and fairly useful Irish 1997 2-y-o 7f winner Have Merci (by High Estate): dam 1½m and 2m winner: fair maiden: seems to stay 1m: raced freely second start. *J. G. Portman*

LADY ALRUNA (IRE)   3 ch.f. Alhaarth (IRE) 126 – In Tranquility (IRE) (Shalford   **68**
(IRE) 124§) [2002 76p: 7m 6.1g² 6m⁴ 6m p6g⁵ Dec 18] fair maiden: should stay 7f: raced only on good/good to firm going: hung right penultimate start. *P. J. Makin*

LADY ANSELL   3 b.f. Puissance 110 – Rare Indigo 80 (Timeless Times (USA) 99)   **–**
[2002 73: p5g 5m Apr 24] tall, unfurnished filly: fair at 2 yrs: well held both outings in 2002: sold €1,500 in November. *A. Berry*

LADY ARNICA   3 b.f. Ezzoud (IRE) 126 – Brand (Shareef Dancer (USA) 135) [2002   **–**
–: 10s Oct 23] lengthy, angular filly: well held in 2 maidens. *A. W. Carroll*

LADY AT LEISURE (IRE)   2 ch.f. (Apr 13) Dolphin Street (FR) 125 – In A Hurry   **55**
(FR) (In Fijar (USA) 121) [2002 5g⁶ 5m³ f5g f8.5g Dec 31] 2,000Y: leggy, quite   **a–**
good-topped filly: half-sister to 3 winners abroad: dam third at 6f in Sweden: modest maiden: should stay 6f: well held on fibresand. *W. G. M. Turner*

LADY BASE   4 b.f. Blushing Flame (USA) 109 – Lady Marguerrite (Blakeney 126)   **–**
[2002 –: f12g⁶ f12g Mar 4] lengthy, angular filly: little form in 3 maidens: visored both 4-y-o starts. *W. S. Kittow*

LADY BEAR (IRE)   4 b.f. Grand Lodge (USA) 125 – Boristova (IRE) 79 (Royal   **103**
Academy (USA) 130) [2002 87§: f7g f8.5g² 8s* 10g 8g 7.6g⁶ 8g* 8g* 8m³ 9f 8s⁵ Oct 20] useful-looking filly: useful performer: won handicaps at Doncaster (randombet.com Spring Mile) in March, Ripon in August and Ayr (beat Ho Leng by 1½ lengths in Tote Ayrshire Handicap) in September: creditable third to Welsh Diva in listed rated stakes at Ascot ninth start: best at 1m/1¼m: acts on good to firm going, heavy and fibresand: sometimes visored, usually blinkered in 2002: saddle slipped fourth/fifth starts: often slowly away/gets behind: quirky. *R. A. Fahey*

LADY BETAMBEAU (IRE)   2 b.f. (May 6) Grand Lodge (USA) 125 – Boristova   **63 p**
(IRE) 79 (Royal Academy (USA) 130) [2002 6f⁶ Oct 5] IR 8,500Y, 45,000 2-y-o: neat filly: fourth foal: sister to 4-y-o Lady Bear: dam, Irish 2-y-o 9f winner, half-sister to useful Irish middle-distance stayer Judicial Field: 7/1, never dangerous sixth of 8 to Rondinay in maiden at Newmarket: will be suited by 1m+: sure to improve. *L. M. Cumani*

LADYBIRD LOVER   6 ch.m. Clantime 101 – Miss Brightside 41 (Crofthall 110)   **–**
[2002 f5g f6g 8g Apr 3] second foal: dam, maiden, effective from 5f to 7f: well held in maidens (reportedly bled from nose final start). *P. R. Wood*

LADY BIRGITTA   4 b.f. Emperor Jones (USA) 119 – Badiane (USA) (Green Forest   **79 d**
(USA) 134) [2002 91: p10g f8.5g² f8.5g³ 7.1m⁴ 8.5g 9d⁴ f8.5g⁶ 7m 8s p7g⁴ 8s f9.4g f9.4g   **a92 d**
f7g Dec 31] angular filly: fairly useful handicapper on all-weather, fair on turf at best: left R. Guest after sixth start, M. Usher before penultimate one: probably best around 1m/9f: acts on all-weather, good to firm and good to soft ground: on downgrade. *K. R. Burke*

LADY BLANCHE   5 b.m. Pyramus (USA) 78 – Lady Antoinette (Pharly (FR) 130)   **42**
[2002 7s f9.4g 8m 10m 8.2m⁴ f8g Dec 4] 1,000Y: fifth reported foal: dam unraced: poor maiden. *D. Morris*

LADY BOXER   6 b.m. Komaite (USA) – Lady Broker 54 (Petorius 117) [2002 88+:   **82 ?**
6s[6] 7.1g[6] 8.1d[5] 7g 7.1s[4] 6m[6] 5.9v 7.2d[6] Jul 23] close-coupled mare: seemingly still fairly
useful performer in 2002, though generally well held: finished lame final start: effective
at 6f to 7.6f: goes well on soft/heavy ground: has been early to post: sometimes slowly
away: usually comes from off pace. *M. Mullineaux*

LADY CATHERINE   2 ch.f. (Feb 18) Bering 136 – Queen Catherine (Machiavellian   **101 p**
(USA) 123) [2002 5.5d[4] 7d[4] 8g* 8.3g* 8s* Oct 13] first foal: dam useful French 1m
winner, including at 2 yrs: useful form: completed hat-trick in minor event at Clairefontaine in August, listed race at Craon (by short neck from Shedabad) in September and
Premio Dormello at Milan (came from rear, led final 1f to beat De Blanc 1¼ lengths)
in October: stays 1m: acts on soft going: joined Godolphin: should do better still.
H.-A. Pantall, France

LADY DE BATHE   3 b.f. Robellino (USA) 127 – Langtry Lady 91 (Pas de Seul 133)   **51**
[2002 70: p7g p7g[6] p10g[5] f12g[5] Mar 2] sparely-made filly: modest maiden handicapper:
left I. Balding after second outing: stayed 1¼m: acted on polytrack and soft going: dead.
J. R. Best

LADY DEVIKA   3 b.f. Sri Pekan (USA) 117 – The Frog Lady (IRE) 52 (Al Hareb   **73 d**
(USA) 123) [2002 54p: 7m[4] 8.2d[4] 7m 7.5g[4] 7.1v[3] p8g 8s[6] 6m Aug 21] strong filly: fair
form on reappearance, but disappointing after: stays 1m: visored (tailed off) final start.
R. Hannon

LADY DOMINATRIX (IRE)   3 b.f. Danehill Dancer (IRE) 117 – Spout House   **112**
(IRE) 55 (Flash of Steel 120) [2002 89: 8s[6] 6g* 7m[4] 6d* 6f[3] 6s[6] 6m[3] 6d 5m[6] 5g[2] 5.2f*
Sep 21] tall, leggy filly: smart performer: won minor event at Leicester in April, listed
race at Ascot (beat Approval by short head) in May and Dubai International Airport
World Trophy at Newbury (beat Smokin Beau by short head despite carrying head shade
awkwardly) in September: at least creditable efforts otherwise in Duke of York Stakes at
York (¾-length third to Invincible Spirit) fifth start, Nunthorpe Stakes at York (sixth to
Kyllachy) on ninth and Flying Five at the Curragh (head second to Danehurst) on tenth:
effective at 5f/6f: yet to race on heavy going, acts on any other: often makes running.
Mrs P. N. Dutfield

LADY DOUBLE U   2 b.f. (Mar 22) Sheikh Albadou 128 – Bollin Victoria 51 (Jalmood   **–**
(USA) 126) [2002 5m May 6] sturdy filly: half-sister to several winning sprinters,
including fairly useful 1999 2-y-o 5f winner First Blood (by Rambo Dancer) and 6f
winner Lady Rock (by Mistertopogigo): dam, ran only at 2 yrs, third at 7f: 16/1,
never-dangerous eighth in maiden at Warwick: moved poorly to post. *B. R. Millman*

LADY DRUE (IRE)   3 b.f. Darnay 117 – Sharkiyah (IRE) 75 (Polish Precedent   **–**
(USA) 131) [2002 10g 10s p12g Jun 9] 1,000Y: first foal: dam, maiden (best efforts at 7f),
out of a useful Irish sprinter: well held in maidens. *A. P. Jarvis*

LADY DULCET   2 b.f. (Apr 23) Thowra (FR) – Freedom Weekend (USA) (Shah-   **–**
rastani (USA) 135) [2002 6s Oct 25] second living foal: dam, behind in maidens, out
of half-sister to champion 1980 US 2-y-o Heavenly Cause: 100/1, last in maiden at
Newbury. *D. Burchell*

LADY EL EE   3 b.f. Komaite (USA) – Mountain Harvest (FR) 64§ (Shirley Heights   **37**
130) [2002 51: 8g 5m 6d 6f[4] 8d[5] 9.2v[5] 7.2g 9m Aug 22] strong filly: poor maiden: should
stay 7f: blinkered final start. *Miss L. A. Perratt*

LADY FRANPALM (IRE)   2 b.f. (Mar 16) Danehill Dancer (IRE) 117 – Be Nimble   **50**
(Wattlefield 117) [2002 5g[3] 6m p5g p6g Dec 18] IR 2,000Y: leggy filly: eighth foal:
half-sister to 3 winners, including 5f (including at 2 yrs) and 6f winner Trentesimo (by
Imperial Frontier): dam, Irish 7f winner, half-sister to smart sprinter Carol's Treasure:
modest maiden: should stay 6f. *M. J. Haynes*

LADY GLYDE   2 b.f. (Jan 28) Inchinor 119 – Happy And Blessed (IRE) (Prince Sabo   **45**
123) [2002 5s[3] 5g[5] 6d[5] 7f[4] Jun 13] angular filly: second foal: dam unraced daughter of
useful 2-y-o sprinter Bless The Match: poor form in sellers. *W. G. M. Turner*

LADY HIGH HAVENS (IRE)   3 b.f. Bluebird (USA) 125 – Blanche Dubois   **101**
(Nashwan (USA) 135) [2002 102: 8m 10.1g[2] 12g 10d[4] 10g 8m Sep 28] close-coupled,
workmanlike filly: useful performer: creditable effort in 2002 only when ½-length
second to Esloob in listed event at Newcastle: left P. d'Arcy after fifth start: stays 1¼m:
yet to race on soft/heavy going, acts on any other: has worn crossed noseband: races
prominently: sold 230,000 gns in December, reportedly for stud. *J. Noseda*

Dubai International Airport World Trophy, Newbury—previously run as a listed race, this Group 3 contest goes to Lady Dominatrix, who holds off Smokin Beau (right)

LADY HURRICANE 2 b.f. (Feb 15) Deploy 131 – Tatouma (USA) 79 (The Minstrel (CAN) 135) [2002 5g 6d³ f6g³ 7.5g 6m⁵ f7g⁴ 7g f8s Sep 17] small, quite good-topped filly: half-sister to fairly useful 1994 2-y-o 7f winner Trimming (by Thatching) and a winner up to 1m in Germany by Dowsing: dam 2-y-o 5f/6f winner: poor maiden: probably stays 7f: acts on fibresand, unraced on extremes of going on turf: tried visored. *W. G. M. Turner* **39**

LADY INCH 4 b.f. Inchinor 119 – Head Turner 61 (My Dad Tom (USA) 109) [2002 –: f12g 14.1d f11g Dec 4] little form: tried visored/tongue tied. *S. L. Keightley* **–**

LADY JEANNIE 5 b.m. Emarati (USA) 74 – Cottonwood 80 (Teenoso (USA) 135) [2002 64, a54: p8g 9.7m⁶ 7g 8.3m 10g⁴ 8.3d 11.6g Aug 12] sturdy mare: modest handicapper: stays 1¼m: acts on polytrack and good to firm ground: often forces pace. *M. J. Haynes* **60 a–**

LADY JONES 5 b.m. Emperor Jones (USA) 119 – So Beguiling (USA) 49 (Woodman (USA) 126) [2002 65: p13g Jan 9] fair handicapper at 4 yrs: blinkered, pulled up (said to have knocked herself leaving stall) only 5-y-o start. *P. L. Gilligan* **–**

LADY JUSTICE 2 b.f. (May 24) Compton Place 125 – Zinzi (Song 132) [2002 6f 6d⁶ Nov 1] rather lengthy filly: half-sister to several winners, including smart 5f/6f (latter including at 2 yrs) winner Sarcita (by Primo Dominie) and useful 1999 2-y-o 5f winner Mrs P (by First Trump): dam Irish 5f winner: bandaged behind, fair form in maidens at Newmarket, sixth to Tante Rose on second occasion: not sure to stay beyond 6f. *W. Jarvis* **67**

LADY KINVARRAH (IRE) 4 b.f. Brief Truce (USA) 126 – Al Corniche (IRE) 62 (Bluebird (USA) 125) [2002 79: 10f⁶ 10d³ 10.1f⁵ 10.2d⁴ p10g Aug 9] fair performer: stays 1¼m: acts on firm and good to soft going: blinkered final start: sometimes slowly away/races freely: sold 4,200 gns. *P. J. Makin* **73**

LADY LAKSHMI 2 ch.f. (Mar 2) Bahhare (USA) 122 – Polish Honour (USA) 61 –
(Danzig Connection (USA)) [2002 6d Nov 1] 14,000Y: sturdy filly: sixth living foal:
half-sister to 2 winners abroad, including 8.5f to 11.5f winner in France and Ireland
Salsicaia (by Pursuit of Love): dam ran once: 50/1 and very green, always behind in
maiden at Newmarket. *R. Guest*

LADY LAP DANCER 4 b.f. Shareef Dancer (USA) 135 – Jelabna (Jalmood (USA) 41
126) [2002 42+: 10.1s 14g 15.8m⁴ 16g Aug 12] small filly: poor maiden: stays 2m: acts
on good to firm going. *Mrs M. Reveley*

LADY LAUREATE 4 b.f. Sir Harry Lewis (USA) 127 – Cyrillic 88 (Rock City 120) 79
[2002 79: 16m² 16.2g² 11.6m⁵ 18m Oct 19] small, sparely-made filly: fair handicapper:
possibly needs further than 1½m nowadays, and stays 17f: acts on firm and soft going:
usually held up. *G. C. Bravery*

LADY LE MANS 2 br.f. (Apr 25) Fraam 114 – Scenic Air (Hadeer 118) [2002 5s 5g 51
f5g³ f5s⁶ 6d⁶ 6g⁴ 6m* 7g⁴ 7m 7d 7m 7g⁶ Aug 22] IR 2,200Y: leggy, plain filly: third foal:
dam ran twice: modest performer: left M. Polglase after second appearance: won seller at
Yarmouth (for R. Wilman) in July: trained next start only by D. Morris: best effort final
outing: stays 7f: acts on good to firm going and fibresand: tried blinkered/visored: sold
1,200 gns in October, and rejoined R. Wilman. *P. S. McEntee*

LADY LENOR 4 b.f. Presidium 124 – Sparkling Roberta 55 (Kind of Hush 118) 57
[2002 58: f5g 5m⁶ 5s 6s⁵ 6g² 6m 6d Oct 15] tall filly: modest maiden handicapper: raced
only at 5f/6f: acts on soft going (probably on heavy), good to firm and fibresand: has
started slowly/drifted left/carried head awkwardly. *Mrs G. S. Rees*

LADY LIESEL 2 b.f. (Feb 3) Bin Ajwaad (IRE) 119 – Griddle Cake (IRE) 62 (Be My 63
Guest (USA) 126) [2002 6s 6d 5.7g³ 6m⁶ 6g⁶ 7m 5.1d 7f p6g⁶ p7g p8g p6g p5g p6g a60
Dec 30] 700Y, 2,600 2-y-o: fifth foal: dam, maiden who stayed 1½m, half-sister to smart
middle-distance performers Bonny Scot and Mary Stuart, and to dam of Golan: modest
maiden: stays easy 7f: acts on good to firm going and polytrack. *J. J. Bridger*

LADY LINDSAY (IRE) 3 ch.f. Danehill Dancer (IRE) 117 – Jungle Jezebel 107 105
(Thatching 131) [2002 82p: 7g³ 8d² 7m³ 8m⁴ Jul 26] rather leggy, lengthy filly: useful
performer, lightly raced: at least creditable efforts (despite not having run of race) all
starts in 2002, including in listed events at Goodwood (1¼ lengths second to Dolores) and
Ascot (1¼ lengths fourth to Fraulein) and Criterion Stakes at Newmarket (½-length
third to Atavus on third outing): effective at 7f/1m: yet to race on extremes of going: held
up. *R. Guest*

LADY LINKS 3 b.f. Bahamian Bounty 116 – Sparky's Song 63 (Electric 126) [2002 100
95: 7m⁵ 7m⁵ 6m* 6d⁵ 6g 7s⁵ 6d Aug 10] strong, angular filly: useful performer: won
listed race at Newbury in May by ¾ length from Golden Bounty: seemed to run well
when 2¾ lengths fourth to Dedication in similar event at Deauville, easily best other
effort: barely stays 7f: yet to race on firm ground, acts on any other: has been bandaged
in front: usually races prominently: none too reliable: sold 105,000 gns in December.
R. Hannon

LADY LLANOVER 2 ch.f. (Feb 24) Halling (USA) 133 – Francia 59 (Legend of 60
France (USA) 124) [2002 7m Aug 12] fourth foal: half-sister to 3-y-o Gracia and 5-y-o
Suave Performer: dam 7f (at 2 yrs) and 1¼m winner: 20/1, never-dangerous seventh to
Bush Cat in maiden at Folkestone: should be suited by 1¼m+. *S. C. Williams*

LADY MCNAIR 2 b.f. (Mar 21) Sheikh Albadou 128 – Bonita Bee 50 (King of Spain 89
121) [2002 p7g³ 7d* 7m* 7m* 8.1m* 7f³ 8d⁴ Oct 21] workmanlike filly: fourth foal:
half-sister to a 7f/8.5f winner in Italy by Petong: dam, maiden, best effort at 6f: fairly
useful performer: won maiden at Brighton, nurseries on same course and Newbury and
minor event at Sandown (beat Rainwashed Gold ½ length) in July/August: below form
last 2 starts: stays 1m, at least with emphasis on speed: acts on good to firm and good to
soft ground. *P. D. Cundell*

LADY MYTTON 2 ch.f. (Mar 2) Lake Coniston (IRE) 131 – The In-Laws (IRE) 90 84 +
(Be My Guest (USA) 126) [2002 6d 7m 7.2g² 7f³ 8s⁵ 8v* Nov 8] 15,000Y: big, lengthy
filly: has scope: first foal: dam, 2-y-o 7f winner, stayed 1¼m: fairly useful performer:
raced alone when winning 5-runner minor event at Doncaster in November by 9 lengths
from Albanov: stays 1m: acts on any going. *A. Bailey*

LADY NATILDA 2 ch.f. (Apr 3) First Trump 118 – Ramajana (USA) (Shadeed 64
(USA) 135) [2002 7.1m 5.7f³ f6g* f6g Dec 20] 4,500F, 10,000Y: third foal: half-sister

to 3-y-o Dilys and German 7f winner Ramondia (by Monsun): dam 6f (at 2 yrs) and 1m winner in Germany: modest performer: made all in maiden at Wolverhampton in October: well beaten in nursery there final outing: likely to prove best at 6f/7f: acts on fibresand and firm ground. *D. Haydn Jones*

LADY NETBETSPORTS (IRE)   3 b.f. In The Wings 128 – Auntie Maureen (IRE)   **74**
73 (Roi Danzig (USA)) [2002 76: 10m⁴ 10.5d⁶ f12s 8.2s 12d⁶ f9.4f Nov 29] leggy filly: **a–**
fair maiden: stays 1½m: acts on any turf ground, below form both starts on fibresand. *B. S. Rothwell*

LADY OF GDANSK (IRE)   3 ch.f. Danehill Dancer (IRE) 117 – Rebecca's Girl   **68**
(IRE) (Nashamaa 113) [2002 –: p8g³ p7g⁴ 6s* 6m 6g 7s p7g p5g⁵ Dec 21] big, lengthy   **a58**
filly: fair performer on turf, modest on all-weather: won maiden at Doncaster in March: below form after: may prove best up to 7f: acts on soft going and on polytrack. *H. J. Collingridge*

LADY OF TA'PINU   3 ch.f. Greensmith 121 – Pitcairn Princess (Capricorn Line 111)   **– §**
[2002 –§: 8m Jun 4] no sign of ability: has looked reluctant/refused to enter stall: one to avoid. *C. N. Kellett*

LADY OF THE BRAES   3 b.f. Mind Games 121 – Mary From Dunlow 49 (Nicholas   **–**
Bill 125) [2002 –: 5g 9.1g 8d Sep 9] no sign of ability. *Miss L. A. Perratt*

LADY OF THE INN (IRE)   3 ch.f. Hamas (IRE) 125§ – Faakirah (Dragonara Palace   **67**
(USA) 115) [2002 55: p8g p8g⁴ 10.9g 8.2f* 8m* 9.3g 8d 8g Aug 7] fair handicapper: won at Nottingham (selling event, sold from B. Meehan 10,500 gns) and Newcastle in May: best form around 1m: acts on firm going, some promise on polytrack: usually front runner: joined M. Pipe, successful over hurdles in October. *D. Nicholls*

LADY OF WINDSOR (IRE)   5 ch.m. Woods of Windsor (USA) – North Lady   **47 §**
(Northfields (USA)) [2002 –§: f8.5g² f8.5g f8g f7g³ 7.1d³ Jul 1] sturdy, lengthy mare: poor performer: stays 8.5f: acts on firm going, soft and fibresand: sometimes visored/ blinkered: sometimes slowly away: ungenuine: reportedly in foal to Lake Coniston. *I. Semple*

LADY PAHIA (IRE)   4 ch.f. Pivotal 124 – Appledorn 99 (Doulab (USA) 115) [2002   **79**
81: 7f⁶ 8g⁶ 8.3s³ 7g* 8m 7f 7m 8g 7m 7f p7g p8g² Dec 14] tall, leggy filly: fair handicapper: won (for second successive year) at Goodwood in June: effective at 7f/1m: acts on polytrack, firm and good to soft going (probably on soft): sometimes hangs left: best held up. *A. P. Jarvis*

LADY PAN JAMMER (IRE)   2 b.f. (Feb 13) Marju (IRE) 127 – Crystal City (Kris   **61**
135) [2002 6m⁴ 7.2v⁵ 6m 7m⁶ 8f 8f² 7.9f⁴ 8s Oct 25] IR 36,000F, IR 42,000Y: leggy, close-coupled filly: fifth foal: half-sister to 3 winners, including useful 1998 2-y-o 5f/6f winner Acicula (by Night Shift) and 4-y-o Stoli: dam, French 5f/7f winner, out of Yorkshire Oaks winner Untold: modest maiden: good efforts in nurseries sixth/seventh starts: should stay 1¼m: acts on firm going, well held on soft/heavy: visored last 3 starts: sometimes carries head awkwardly: sold 10,500 gns, sent to USA. *M. R. Channon*

LADY PAST TIMES   2 b.f. (Feb 5) Tragic Role (USA) – Just A Gem (Superlative   **–**
118) [2002 5.1f 5d 5m Sep 6] 5,500Y: quite good-topped filly: second foal: dam unraced sister to Oaks third Pearl Angel: well held in maidens. *E. J. Alston*

LADY PEKAN   3 b.f. Sri Pekan (USA) 117 – Cloudberry 88 (Night Shift (USA))   **–**
[2002 87: 5g 5f 6m⁶ 5f Sep 28] smallish, strong filly: fairly useful at 2 yrs: well below form in 2002. *J. Balding*

LADY PERCY   2 ch.f. (May 2) Double Trigger (IRE) 123 – Dundeelin 46 (Dunbeath   **–**
(USA) 114) [2002 7g 6s f7g Nov 26] small filly: first foal: dam 2-y-o 5f seller winner: well held in maidens. *B. R. Millman*

LADY PROTECTOR   3 b.f. Sri Pekan (USA) 117 – Scared (Royal Academy (USA)   **42**
130) [2002 5f 5.1d 6m 7g 8d f6g⁵ f6g⁶ Dec 27] 8,000Y: second foal: half-sister to 4-y-o Lord Protector: dam unraced: poor maiden: stays 6f. *D. W. P. Arbuthnot*

LADY SHOPPER   2 b.f. (Apr 6) Merdon Melody 98 – Young Whip (Bold Owl 101)   **–**
[2002 7m Aug 1] sturdy, workmanlike filly: sister to 3 winners, notably 6-y-o Elmhurst Boy: dam unraced: 50/1 and burly, always behind in maiden at Goodwood. *S. Dow*

LADY'S SECRET (IRE)   3 b.f. Alzao (USA) 117 – Kaaba (Darshaan 133) [2002   **111**
88p: 11.5g⁴ 11.9d* 10s² 11.9d² 12d³ 11.9m 14f³ 12s Oct 26] useful-looking filly: smart performer: won maiden at Brighton in May: best efforts when 1½ lengths second to Mellow Park in Lancashire Oaks at Haydock (edged left) and 7 lengths third to Margarula

Mrs E. Roberts & Nick Roberts' "Lady's Secret"

in Irish Oaks at the Curragh fourth/fifth starts: should stay 1¾m: acts on soft ground, possibly not ideally suited by firmer than good: carried head awkwardly penultimate outing. *B. W. Hills*

LADYSTGEORGE   3 b.f. Mind Games 121 – Indiahra 76 (Indian Ridge 123) [2002   –
f6g⁶ f6g Nov 20] second foal: dam 5f (at 2 yrs) and 1m winner: well held in maidens on fibresand, slowly away both times. *M. Mullineaux*

LADY STRATAGEM   3 gr.f. Mark of Esteem (IRE) 137 – Grey Angel (Kenmare   –
(FR) 125) [2002 61: 8.3d⁶ 8.3s 6m 9d 9.9m Sep 24] sturdy filly: has a round action: modest maiden at 2 yrs: little form in handicaps in 2002, leaving R. Hannon after third start: successful over hurdles in October. *E. W. Tuer*

LADY SUNRIZE   3 ch.f. Whittingham (IRE) 104 – Scenic Air (Hadeer 118) [2002   **41**
8.3g 7s 6m f6g⁴ f6g Nov 20] 520 2-y-o: second foal: dam ran twice: poor maiden: slowly away first 2 outings. *Mrs A. L. M. King*

LADY TILLY   5 b.m. Puissance 110 – Lady of Itatiba (BEL) (King of Macedon 126)   –
[2002 –: 10.9g⁶ 6m⁵ Sep 30] workmanlike mare: maiden, no longer of much account. *B. Mactaggart*

LADY TWO K (IRE)   5 b.m. Grand Lodge (USA) 125 – Princess Pavlova (IRE)   **96**
(Sadler's Wells (USA) 132) [2002 85: 14d* 13.3v² 13.9g* 15v* 13.9m³ 13.9m Aug 21] sturdy, lengthy mare: useful handicapper: won at Haydock, York and Ayr (3 ran, by 11 lengths from Colorado Falls) in May/June: creditable third to Maycocks Bay in listed rated stakes at York penultimate start: stays 15f: yet to race on firm going, acts on any other: often held up: reportedly in foal to Bertolini. *J. Mackie*

LADY VALENTE (USA)   2 b.f. (Jan 13) Labeeb 124 – Homeward Angel (USA)   –
(Lyphard (USA) 132) [2002 5m Jul 1] sixth foal: closely related to a minor stakes winner

544

in USA by Lear Fan and half-sister to winners in USA by Affirmed and River Special: dam 8.5f winner in USA: 12/1, tailed off in minor event at Windsor. *R. Hannon*

LADY WARD (IRE)   4 b.f. Mujadil (USA) 119 – Sans Ceriph (IRE) 75 (Thatching   –
131) [2002 64, a–: p8g Jan 9] leggy filly: modest performer at 3 yrs: well held only run on Flat in 2002: tried blinkered: successful over hurdles in April. *M. H. Tompkins*

LADYWELL BLAISE (IRE)   5 b.m. Turtle Island (IRE) 123 – Duly Elected (Persian   57 §
Bold 123) [2002 52§: p7g p7g p6g⁶ p6g* p6g⁵ 6g p7g⁵ 6m 6m 7d 6.1d 10d⁴ 8g 7m* 8.3m 7f⁴ 8d 7m p10g⁴ 9.7g 8m 10g Oct 24] sturdy mare: modest performer: won seller at Lingfield in March and apprentice handicap at Newbury in July: effective at 6f to easy 1¼m: acts on all-weather, firm and good to soft going: blinkered once: often slowly away: sometimes races freely: unreliable. *J. J. Bridger*

LADY WEST   2 b.f. (Apr 2) The West (USA) 107 – Just Run (IRE) 45 (Runnett 125)   55
[2002 f5g² 5m f5s May 13] lengthy filly: sixth foal: half-sister to 3 winners by Emarati, including 1995 2-y-o 5f winner Just Lady: dam ran twice: modest form when second to Willhewiz in maiden at Southwell: well held after. *W. G. M. Turner*

LADY ZONDA   3 b.f. Lion Cavern (USA) 117 – Zonda 100 (Fabulous Dancer (USA)   95
124) [2002 7.1g⁴ 10f⁴ 8d⁴ 8g⁶ 8.1d 8m* 9m 8.1m⁴ 8f³ 7.1f* 7m⁶ 8d⁵ Oct 15] tall, lengthy, rather sparely-made filly: sixth foal: half-sister to 3 winners, including smart 6f (at 2 yrs) to 1m (in UAE) winner Zoning (by Warning): dam, 5f to (in USA) 8.5f winner, out of half-sister to Oh So Sharp: useful performer: won handicaps at Salisbury in August and Haydock (best effort, beat King Harson by 1¾ lengths) in September: effective at 7f/1m: unraced on soft/heavy going, acted on any other: headstrong: had edged right/found little: visits Mark of Esteem. *M. R. Channon*

L'AFFAIRE MONIQUE   3 b.f. Machiavellian (USA) 123 – Much Too Risky 87   101
(Bustino 136) [2002 73p: 10.2s* 12d⁶ 11.9m Aug 22] angular, unfurnished filly: useful performer, lightly raced: won maiden at Chepstow (beat Flaming Salsa 6 lengths) in June: far from discredited when sixth to Margarula in Irish Oaks at the Curragh next time: stays 1½m: acts on soft ground, well held only start on firmer than good (listed race at York). *Sir Michael Stoute*

LAFI (IRE)   3 ch.c. Indian Ridge 123 – Petal Girl 96 (Caerleon (USA) 132) [2002 7d⁴   80 p
8g* Aug 7] 180,000Y: good-topped colt: fourth foal: half-brother to very smart 1½m performer Mutamam (by Darshaan) and useful Scandinavian filly up to 9f Pretty Girl (by Polish Precedent): dam, 1m winner, half-sister to Mtoto: confirmed debut promise when winning maiden at Pontefract by ½ length from Strathspey, going freely and leading inside final 1f: not sure to stay much beyond 1m: type to progress again. *A. C. Stewart*

LAGGAN BAY (IRE)   2 b.c. (May 15) Alzao (USA) 117 – Green Lucia 116 (Green   78
Dancer (USA) 132) [2002 5s⁶ 7m³ 7.1d² 7m⁵ 8m⁵ 8f² 10f⁴ 8.3d⁵ 8g Oct 18] small colt: fluent mover: half-brother to numerous winners, including smart 1½m performer Luchiroverte (by Slip Anchor) and useful performer up to 2m Ravensmoth (by Warning), 7f winner at 2 yrs: dam, placed in Irish and Yorkshire Oaks, half-sister to Old Vic: fair maiden: should be suited by 1¼m+: acts on firm and good to soft ground: raced freely only try in blinkers. *R. Hannon*

LAGGAN MINSTREL (IRE)   4 b.g. Mark of Esteem (IRE) 137 – Next Episode   92
(USA) (Nijinsky (CAN) 138) [2002 84: 7f⁴ 8.3g² 8.1d⁶ p8g 8g² 7d³ 8s³ 8m 8.1d³ 8f 8m 8.3m 8f⁶ 8g⁵ 7d Nov 5] tall, close-coupled gelding: fairly useful handicapper: mostly creditable efforts at least in 2002, leaving R. Hannon 12,000 gns before final start (trainer fined, rider suspended and horse banned 40 days under 'non-triers' rule, trainer's and horse's penalties later quashed): stays 1m: acts on fibresand, firm and good to soft ground: carries head high: usually held up: gelded after final start. *N. P. Littmoden*

LAGO   4 b.g. Maelstrom Lake 118 – Jugendliebe (IRE) (Persian Bold 123) [2002 52:   59
10m 13v² 13s⁶ 16.2g* 16.2m⁴ Jul 16] robust gelding: modest handicapper: won at Beverley in July: stays 2m: acts on good to firm and heavy ground. *M. W. Easterby*

LAGO DI VARANO   10 b.g. Clantime 101 – On The Record 72 (Record Token 128)   80
[2002 88: 6g 5d⁴ 5.1d 6g 7m 6s⁶ Aug 5] strong gelding: fairly useful performer: showed form only once in 2002: best at 5f/6f: acts on any going: visored/blinkered: normally races up with pace. *R. M. Whitaker*

LAGO D'ORTA (IRE)   2 ch.c. (Mar 4) Bahhare (USA) 122 – Maelalong (IRE) 77   86
(Maelstrom Lake 118) [2002 6s³ 6m² 6s² Oct 25] approx. 10,300Y in Italy: good-topped colt: third foal: half-brother to a 1m to 11f winner in Italy by Brief Truce: dam Irish 2-y-o 5f winner: fairly useful maiden: placed at Lingfield, Windsor and Newbury, best effort when beaten 2 lengths by Gilded Edge on last-named course: should stay at least 7f: acts on soft and good to firm ground. *C. G. Cox*

LAGUDIN (IRE) 4 b.g. Eagle Eyed (USA) 111 – Liaison (USA) (Blushing Groom   **109 §**
(FR) 131) [2002 112: 10g⁴ 9m 10d³ p10g³ p10g⁴ Dec 11] good-topped, quite attractive
gelding: useful performer: respectable efforts in 2002 when in frame in listed races at
Kempton (fourth to Border Arrow, reportedly sustained minor injury and off over 6
months after), Newmarket (third to Island House) and Lingfield (third to Beauchamp
Pilot): edged left and found little when running poorly final outing (gelded after): best
around 1¼m: acts on soft going and polytrack: has worn crossed noseband: tends to flash
tail: has gone freely, and probably best waited with: not to be trusted. *L. M. Cumani*

LAHAAY 5 ch.g. Lahib (USA) 129 – Jasarah (IRE) 70 (Green Desert (USA) 127) [2002   **–**
74, a66: p8g Jan 8] quite good-topped gelding: fair handicapper at best: well held only
start in 2002. *J. Akehurst*

LAHBERHORN (USA) 3 ch.c. Affirmed (USA) – Skiable (IRE) (Niniski (USA)   **75**
125) [2002 71p: 9d 8m* 8m 10.5v f7g Oct 5] strong colt: fair performer: made all in
maiden at Ripon in July: left B. Hills 6,500 gns before final start: stayed 1m: acted on
firm going: dead. *A. G. Newcombe*

LAHINCH (IRE) 3 b.f. Danehill Dancer (IRE) 117 – Dublah (USA) (Private Account   **104**
(USA)) [2002 104: 7m* 8m 6s⁵ 6m⁶ 5g Oct 6] strong, deep-girthed filly: useful performer: won listed race at Leopardstown in April by ¾ length from Marionnaud: creditable 3¼
lengths seventh to Kazzia in 1000 Guineas at Newmarket (headed 1f out) next time but
below form after: stays 1m: acts on soft and good to firm going: often wears crossed
noseband. *A. P. O'Brien, Ireland*

LAHOOQ 3 b.c. Indian Ridge 123 – Woodsia 97 (Woodman (USA) 126) [2002 96p: **?**
8m Aug 15] well-made, attractive colt: has a fluent, slightly round action: useful form:
tongue tied, pulled too hard but far from discredited (appeared to run to 98) when 5
lengths last of 9 behind Priors Lodge in listed event at Salisbury only 3-y-o start: all 3
outings at 1m, should prove as effective at 7f: joined K. McLaughlin in UAE. *Saeed bin
Suroor*

LAIS 2 ch.f. (Apr 7) Inchinor 119 – Night Transaction 59 (Tina's Pet 121) [2002 f6g p7g   **–**
p8g Nov 23] sixth live foal: half-sister to 5-y-o Prime Recreation and 6f winner
(including at 2 yrs) Silca Key Silca (by Polar Falcon), both fairly useful: dam 1m winner:
only a little sign of ability in maidens/seller. *G. C. H. Chung*

LAISSEZALLER (USA) 3 gr. or ro.c. End Sweep (USA) – Laissez Faire (USA)   **102**
(Talinum (USA)) [2002 95: p10g² p10g³ a9f Apr 13] close-coupled, useful-looking colt:
useful performer: good efforts when placed behind Adiemus in minor event and listed
race (wandered and beaten short head, demoted to third) at Lingfield early in year: put
down after fracturing off-hind leg in Wood Memorial Stakes at Aqueduct: stayed 1¼m:
acted on firm going, good to soft and polytrack: unseated and got loose before second
outing at 2 yrs, upset in stall and withdrawn next intended one. *Mrs A. J. Perrett*

LAKATOI 3 b.f. Saddlers' Hall (IRE) 126 – Bireme 127 (Grundy 137) [2002 –p: 12m²   **82 d**
11.4f⁵ 11.9d³ 14s⁴ 12.1d² 13.8m² 12d³ 12m⁵ Sep 23] good-bodied filly: fairly useful
maiden: below form after second outing: stays 13.8f: acts on firm and good to soft going:
races prominently. *B. W. Hills*

LAKE EYRE (IRE) 3 b.f. Bluebird (USA) 125 – Pooh Wee 71 (Music Boy 124)   **48**
[2002 57: f6g f8g⁴ 5d⁴ 5.1m⁵ 5d 6d⁴ 5f f5g Dec 13] poor maiden handicapper: effective at   **a43**
5f to 7f: acts on good to firm going, good to soft and fibresand: visored on reappearance:
gave trouble start fifth outing. *D. Shaw*

LAKELAND PADDY (IRE) 5 b.g. Lake Coniston (IRE) 131 – Inshad 81 (Indian   **56**
King (USA) 128) [2002 –: 7g 7.1s 6m 7m Jul 4] rather unfurnished gelding: modest
handicapper nowadays: probably stays 7.6f: acts on heavy and good to firm going.
M. Blanshard

LAKELANDS LADY (IRE) 2 ch.f. (Apr 21) Woodborough (USA) 112 – Beautyof-   **67**
thepeace (IRE) (Exactly Sharp (USA) 121) [2002 6.1g* 6s⁴ 6.1m⁶ 7g⁶ 8d f7g* f7g* f8g*   **a85**
Dec 27] IR 3,000F, 2,000 2-y-o: close-coupled, unfurnished filly: fifth foal: half-sister to
3-y-o General Amnesty and 6-y-o Windshift: dam unraced: fairly useful on all-weather,
fair on turf: won maiden at Nottingham in June and nurseries at Wolverhampton in
November and Southwell (2) in December: not extended to beat Magenta Rising by 3
lengths at last-named track final outing: effective at 7f/1m: acts on fibresand, soft and
good to firm ground: usually races up with pace. *S. R. Bowring*

LAKE OF DREAMS 3 b.g. Polish Precedent (USA) 131 – Rainbow Lake 113   **–**
(Rainbow Quest (USA) 134) [2002 10s p12g Nov 13] 5,500 3-y-o: fifth foal: brother
to smart 13f/1¾m winner Brimming (by Generous) and fairly useful 1999 2-y-o 1m
winner who stayed 1½m Unaware (by Unfuwain), latter subsequently successful in

Switzerland: dam 1¼m and 1½m (Lancashire Oaks) winner: well beaten in maidens at Newbury (slowly away) and Lingfield. *Dr J. R. J. Naylor*

LAKE 'O' GOLD   3 ch.f. Karinga Bay 116 – Ginka 57 (Petoski 135) [2002 12f⁴ p12g **69** p13g³ Oct 4] third foal: dam, maiden, out-and-out stayer: best effort in maidens when third at Lingfield, racing freely: stays 13f. *J. W. Mullins*

LAKE VERDI (IRE)   3 ch.c. Lake Coniston (IRE) 131 – Shore Lark (USA) (Storm **81** Bird (CAN) 134) [2002 88: 6g 5d 5f 7s Nov 2] quite good-topped colt: fairly useful at 2 yrs: ran respectably at best in 2002: stays 7f: acts on firm and good to soft going: sometimes tongue tied. *B. Hanbury*

LA KOCA (FR)   4 b.f. Thatching 131 – Green Maid (USA) (Green Dancer (USA) **47** 132) [2002 44: p7g⁴ p8g⁵ p7g f8.5s 10g 7g Jul 11] poor maiden handicapper: probably best around 7f: acts on polytrack: visored last 2 starts. *H. J. Collingridge*

LAKOTA BRAVE   8 ch.g. Anshan 119 – Pushkinia (FR) 95 (Pharly (FR) 130) [2002 **69** –, a87: f9.4g p7g* p7g² p7g² p7g⁵ p7g* f7g* 7m* 8.1m⁶ p7g³ 7g p7g* f7g* p7g³ f8.5s⁴ **a97** p7g³ p8g* p8g⁴ Dec 30] useful performer on all-weather, fair on turf: won claimers at Lingfield in January and February (2, left C. Allen after second one) and Wolverhampton in March, handicap at Southwell in April, claimer at Lingfield (first run after leaving J. Osborne) in October, handicap at Wolverhampton in November and minor event at Lingfield in December: best at 7f/easy 1m: acts on all-weather, raced only on good going or firmer on turf: tried tongue tied: tends to race freely, and is held up: tough and consistent. *N. P. Littmoden*

LALAPAANZI (IRE)   2 b.f. (Mar 28) Night Shift (USA) – Sharp Deposit (Sharpo **57** 132) [2002 6m⁴ 6g⁵ 6.1m⁶ Aug 19] 19,000F, 17,000Y: smallish, quite good-topped filly: fifth living foal: half-sister to 3 winners, including useful 1998 2-y-o 6f winner Rose of Mooncoin (by Brief Truce) and a winner up to 1m in Italy by Tenby: dam unraced: modest maiden: raced only at 6f on good/good to firm ground. *R. M. Beckett*

LAMBADORA   4 ch.f. Suave Dancer (USA) 136 – Lust (Pursuit of Love 124) [2002 **–** 55: f12s⁶ f14.8g Apr 8] tall, good-topped filly: modest maiden handicapper at 3 yrs: well held on Flat in 2002, leaving Miss J. Camacho after reappearance: should stay beyond 2m: acts on good to firm going and fibresand: won over hurdles in April/May (then joined Miss K. Marks). *J. G. M. O'Shea*

LAMBROOK   3 b.g. Emarati (USA) 74 – Shalverton (IRE) (Shalford (IRE) 124§) **–** [2002 54, a45: p8g⁵ f8g Jan 29] modest maiden at 2 yrs: little form in 2002 (reportedly had breathing problem final start). *W. R. Muir*

LA MONDOTTE (IRE)   4 b.f. Alzao (USA) 117 – Saucy Maid (IRE) 69 (Sure Blade **61** (USA) 130) [2002 60§, a66§: p12g 10.9f* 11.9g⁵ May 2] modest handicapper: won at Warwick (first run after leaving J. Osborne) in April: should stay 1¾m: acts on fibresand and firm going, probably on soft: blinkered on reappearance: tongue tied last 2 outings: has looked a difficult ride. *A. M. Hales*

LA MOULINE (IRE)   2 ch.f. (Feb 8) Nashwan (USA) 135 – Lamarque (IRE) (Nure- **86 p** yev (USA) 131) [2002 7m³ 10.2f* Sep 30] tall filly: has scope: first foal: dam unraced close relative to Arc winner Carnegie out of Arc winner Detroit: fairly useful form in listed race at Newbury (third to Muqbil) and maiden at Bath, still green when landing odds by 6 lengths from Fantastico in latter: will be suited by 1½m+: had 2 handlers in preliminaries at Newbury: almost certainly capable of better. *G. A. Butler*

LAMPOS (USA)   2 b. or br.c. (Mar 15) Southern Halo (USA) – Gone Private (USA) **67** (Private Account (USA)) [2002 6d 6m 7.1m 7.1m³ 8g 8d² p8g Nov 19] $50,000F, 50,000 2-y-o: good-topped colt: fourth foal: half-brother to winners by Conquistador Cielo and Phone Trick, both in USA: dam, 8.5f winner in USA, half-sister to US Grade 1 1m (including at 2 yrs)/8.5f winner Ogygian: fair maiden: good second in nursery at Brighton: stays 1m: yet to race on extremes of going on turf, well held on polytrack: visored last 2 starts. *N. A. Graham*

LA MUETTE (IRE)   2 b.f. (Feb 19) Charnwood Forest (IRE) 125 – Elton Grove **83** (IRE) (Astronef 116) [2002 7f⁶ 8.3d* Oct 28] 25,000Y: second foal: dam, French 9f and 10.5f winner, half-sister to smart French middle-distance performers Fleur d'Oranger and Premier Amour: better effort in maidens (fairly useful form) when winning at Windsor by short head from Largo, always prominent and running on gamely: will stay 1¼m. *Mrs A. J. Perrett*

LA MYSTIQUE   3 b.f. Most Welcome 131 – Dismiss 95 (Daring March 116) [2002 **–** 7g 8.2v f8.5g Nov 16] 3,000F: sixth foal: sister to fairly useful 6f winner La Modiste and half-sister to 7f winner Mystery (by Mystiko): dam 1m/1¼m winner: well held in maidens: has worn cheekpieces. *Miss Gay Kelleway*

LAMZIG 3 b.g. Danzig Connection (USA) – Lamsonetti 68 (Never So Bold 135) [2002 –: 7f 6m 6s 6.9d 10.9d⁶ 9m 7f Sep 21] workmanlike gelding: little form: tried visored. *M. Todhunter*

LANA 2 gr.f. (Feb 29) Linamix (FR) 127 – Beaming 93 (Mtoto 134) [2002 6m⁵ 5.7d³ 7m Jul 13] 21,000F: lengthy filly: fifth foal: half-sister to French 10.5f/1½m winner Tunnel Topics (by Sri Pekan): dam, 6f (at 2 yrs) and 1m winner, out of smart 2-y-o sprinter Glancing: fair form in minor event at York and maiden at Bath first 2 starts: reportedly lost action final outing: should stay at least 1m. *J. G. Given* **72**

LANARK BELLE 2 b.f. (May 6) Selkirk (USA) 129 – Anodyne 100 (Dominion 123) [2002 6d 7m 6g Sep 9] closely related to fairly useful 1993 2-y-o 5f winner Stimulant (by Sharpo) and half-sister to several winners, including 4-y-o Adiemus: dam 6f winner, including at 2 yrs: clear signs of ability in maidens at Thirsk, Salisbury and Newcastle, not at all knocked about final start: should stay 1m: will do better. *Sir Mark Prescott* **– p**

LANCER (USA) 10 ch.g. Diesis 133 – Last Bird (USA) (Sea Bird II 145) [2002 61§, a–§: 11.8s 12.3g³ 12.4m 11.8m² 14.1g⁴ 10.9m 12.1s* 11.6m 12.4g⁵ 16.2g f14s 12.1m Sep 24] workmanlike gelding: modest handicapper: won apprentice race at Hamilton in July: effective at 1½m to 15f: acts on any turf going and fibresand: blinkered twice, usually visored: tends to start slowly/look none too keen: held up: not one to trust. *Mrs Lydia Pearce* **58 §** **a– §**

L'ANCRESSE (IRE) 2 b.f. (Jan 13) Darshaan 133 – Solo de Lune (IRE) (Law Society (USA) 130) [2002 7m* 7m⁵ Oct 19] leggy, good-topped filly: sixth foal: sister to 1¼m winner (stayed 2m) Qaatef and French 1m (including at 2 yrs) and 1¼m (Prix Saint-Alary) winner Cerulean Sky, both smart, and half-sister to 2 winners in France: dam, French 11f winner, half-sister to E P Taylor Stakes winner Truly A Dream (by Darshaan) and very smart stayer Wareed: impressive winning debut in minor event at Newbury in September by 2½ lengths from Rainbow City: some improvement (useful form) when 4¾ lengths fifth to Luvah Girl in Rockfel Stakes at Newmarket, off bridle by halfway: will be suited by 1¼m+: remains capable of better. *R. Charlton* **98 p**

L'ANCRESS PRINCESS 5 b.m. Rock City 120 – Premier Princess 45 (Hard Fought 125) [2002 –: f14.8g Dec 31] smallish mare: of no account. *G. A. Ham* **–**

LANDESCENT (IRE) 2 b.g. (Feb 13) Grand Lodge (USA) 125 – Traumerei (GER) 70 (Surumu (GER)) [2002 5s³ 6d⁶ 6g p7g 8m 7m 7f 7g* f7g⁴ Nov 15] 160,000Y: smallish, sturdy gelding: half-brother to several winners, including 1¼m/1½m winner Backcloth (by Scenic) and Irish 1¼m/11f winner Tertia (by Polish Patriot), both useful: dam Irish stayer: fair performer: won nursery at Brighton in October, leading last stride: should stay 1m: acts on soft ground and fibresand: tried blinkered: difficult ride: none too consistent: sold 11,500 gns. *B. J. Meehan* **74**

LAND GIRL 4 b.f. General Monash (USA) 107 – Charming Madam (General Holme (USA) 128) [2002 –: 8.3g 11.1s 11.7d⁶ 12.6m Sep 21] no form. *J. G. M. O'Shea* **–**

LANDING STRIP (IRE) 2 b.g. (Mar 28) Dolphin Street (FR) 125 – Funny Cut 70 (IRE) (Sure Blade (USA) 130) [2002 f5g² 6s May 26] IR 7,500Y: second foal: half-brother to a winner in Sweden by Malvernico: dam Swedish 1m/1¼m winner: fair form when second in maiden at Southwell: well beaten in minor event at Windsor later in month: subsequently gelded. *J. M. P. Eustace* **70**

LAND 'N STARS 2 b.g. (Feb 25) Mtoto 134 – Uncharted Waters 68 (Celestial Storm (USA) 132) [2002 6g Oct 4] fourth foal: half-brother to 5-y-o Establishment: dam 1¼m/1½m winner: 66/1 and green, last in maiden at Lingfield. *C. A. Cyzer* **–**

LAND OF FANTASY 3 ch.g. Hernando (FR) 127 – Height of Folly 81 (Shirley 75 Heights 130) [2002 74: p8g³ p12g³ p10g* p10g⁵ 10g⁴ 8.1d 10.3m 10.9m⁶ p8g Dec 30] close-coupled, quite good-topped gelding: fair performer: won maiden at Lingfield in February: should stay 1½m: acts on polytrack. *D. K. Ivory* **75**

LANDOFHEARTSDESIRE (IRE) 3 b.f. Up And At 'em 109 – Ahonita 90 (Aho- 60 noora 122) [2002 75: 7s 7v 6g 9m 9.3d 10m 8s 8.3d 7.5m 6g* 7f² 8f f6g 7s f8g⁵ f8.5s f6g⁶ **a50** f7g Dec 17] smallish, good-topped filly: half-sister to several winners, including 5-y-o Vita Spericolata and 1½m/1¾m winner Special Risk (by Simply Great): dam 2-y-o 5f winner: fair at 2 yrs in Ireland for D. Gillespie, first past post in claimers at Sligo and Down Royal (blinkered, demoted a place): only modest nowadays: won handicap at Newcastle in September: effective at 6f, barely at 1m: acts on fibresand, firm and soft going: tried blinkered, visored after sixth start. *J. S. Wainwright*

LANDRFUN 7 b.g. Lugana Beach 116 – Basic Fun (Teenoso (USA) 135) [2002 10d⁶ – p10g 12g 16.2m Sep 16] small gelding: one-time modest handicapper: stayed 1½m: acted on firm going and all-weather: was effective visored or not: dead. *H. J. Collingridge*

LANDSEER   3 b.c. Danehill (USA) 126 – Sabria (USA) (Miswaki (USA) 124)   **125**
[2002 115: 8g³ 8g* 8g² 6d⁴ 6m 8f* 8d Oct 26]

'Is there a better hand?' was the rhetorical question asked by a Coolmore advertisement on October 23rd, the question written above an illustration of the ace of spades, ace of hearts and ace of clubs. The cards each carried the name of a horse—'All are Two Thousand Guineas winners. All retire to Coolmore for 2003.' —and the horses were Golan, Rock of Gibraltar and Landseer. Three days later, sadly, the hand was reduced to a pair. About to enter the straight in the Breeders' Cup Mile, poised to challenge and perhaps to put up the performance of his career, Landseer staggered to a sickening standstill on three legs; he had broken his off-fore and had to be put down.

It is unfair, but there is a good chance that this race and the part he played in the far less serious downfall of Rock of Gibraltar—who had to avoid his stricken stablemate—are what Landseer will be remembered for most. A classic winner he was, but not quite in the same class as Golan or Rock of Gibraltar, more a king of clubs than the ace. Landseer's 'Guineas' was the Gainsborough Poule d'Essai des Poulains. The thirteen-runner field at Longchamp in May was a representative one, including seven pattern winners, but apparently without star potential except that of favourite Shaanmer, impressive in an unbeaten two-year-old campaign. Another Fabre-trained colt Bowman had won the Prix de Fontainebleau over the same course and distance four weeks earlier in a very tight finish from Medecis and Landseer. As well as Landseer, Aidan O'Brien fielded a second string for the Poulains in Della Francesca and a pacemaker in Sahara Desert, while Godolphin was double-handed with Firebreak and Waldenburg. Michael Kinane rode a fine race on Landseer, grabbing a position on the rail before producing Landseer halfway up the straight; Kinane's performance looked all the better when viewed next to that of Yutaka Take on Bowman, who finished best of all, coming from last to be beaten into third place, a length and three quarters behind the winner. Splitting the pair was Medecis, whom Landseer held off by a length.

When Landseer and Bowman met again in the St James's Palace Stakes at Royal Ascot, Landseer was sent off at 13/2 and Bowman at 4/1, with neither reckoned to be in the same class as 5/4-on shot Rock of Gibraltar. That particular assessment proved thoroughly justified. Landseer got first run on Rock of Gibraltar but found that it made no difference, going down by a length and three quarters, though, in the process, beating Bowman and his six other rivals by four lengths and more. At this stage of the season, it has become a familiar routine for it to be said of one or more of Ballydoyle's miling or middle-distance stars that he or she also possesses all the speed necessary for the July Cup. For most, however, that assertion goes untested. Speedy horses such as Stravinsky and Mozart have taken their place in the line-up, but, apart from them, the July Cup has been left to the Ballydoyle second and third division. In the latest season, Landseer lined up for the July Cup seemingly more because he was available for a substandard renewal and had very little to lose, than because he looked an especially likely candidate for sprinting. He managed fourth, beaten little over two lengths, but ran well below his

Gainsborough Poule d'Essai des Poulains, Longchamp—
Landseer is given an excellent ride by Michael Kinane as they beat Medecis,
the strong-finishing Bowman (right), Firebreak (rail) and Shaanmer

Mr M. Tabor & Mrs John Magnier's "Landseer"

form at a mile and shaped as if the trip was too short. On firmer ground in the Haydock Park Sprint, he fared a good deal worse, though his stable's runners were under something of a cloud at around that time; Landseer had been forced to miss the Jacques le Marois in the meantime reportedly because of coughing and had also suffered a kidney infection. Over a mile, however, Landseer was undoubtedly a very smart performer and a highly successful one too, and, in addition to the Poulains, he brought home a £240,000 first prize from the Grade 1 Shadwell Keeneland Turf Mile in October. Starting second favourite, the Edgar Prado-ridden Landseer quickened past favourite Beat Hollow inside the final furlong and then held off the strong-finishing Touch of The Blues by a neck. On form, a bit more would have been needed for Landseer to have reached a place in the Breeders' Cup Mile.

			Danzig (b 1977)	Northern Dancer
		Danehill (USA) (b 1986)		Pas de Nom
			Razyana (b 1981)	His Majesty
Landseer (b.c. 1999)				Spring Adieu
			Miswaki (ch 1978)	Mr Prospector
		Sabria (USA) (b 1991)		Hopespringseternal
			Flood (b or br 1983)	Riverman
				Hail Maggie

Better over a mile than shorter and untried over further, Landseer acted on firm going and on soft. He sometimes flashed his tail under pressure. He was by

Danehill, sire also of Rock of Gibraltar and second only to Sadler's Wells in so many of the 2002 sire lists. Landseer came from a famous family on the dam's side, that of Generous and Triptych who are both descended from his fourth dam Margarethen. Landseer's dam Sabria had a 2002 two-year-old called Ikhtyar (by Unfuwain) in training with John Gosden, but he did not see the racecourse. Sabria's next progeny is a 2001 colt by Entrepreneur reportedly called Truman and she was covered by Danehill's son Dansili in 2001. Landseer was a well-made, attractive colt and a powerful galloper. He was named after the nineteenth century artist Sir Edwin Landseer and, bearing in mind the fate of Landseer the racehorse, it is hard not to be struck by a sad irony when remembering the artist's most famous painting, the magnificent, indomitable Monarch Of The Glen. *A. P. O'Brien, Ireland*

LANE COVE (IRE) 3 b.f. Turtle Island (IRE) 123 – Shining Creek (CAN) (Bering 136) [2002 54: 5.1m Aug 6] modest maiden at 2 yrs: well held only start in 2002. *P. J. Makin* —

LANGFORD 2 ch.g. (Mar 25) Compton Place 125 – Sharpening 72 (Sharpo 132) [2002 6s 6m 6m⁶ 7g⁵ 8m² 8.3m² Oct 7] 24,000F, 18,000Y: well-made gelding: fifth foal: half-brother to 1m (at 2 yrs) to 11.5f winner Sharp Riposte (by Robellino) and 1¼m/11f winner Strange Pursuit (by Pursuit of Love), both in France: dam 6f (at 2 yrs)/7f winner: fair maiden: runner-up in nurseries at Yarmouth and Windsor: not sure to stay much beyond 1m: acts on good to firm going: gelded after final start. *M. H. Tompkins* **72**

LANOS (POL) 4 ch.g. Special Power – Lubeka (POL) (Milione (FR) 62) [2002 f12g⁶ 10f 7f⁵ 8.3m f14.8g⁵ f11g⁶ f12g² Dec 26] angular, unfurnished ex-Polish gelding: winner of 5 races in native country, 3 of them (listed events) at 3 yrs: fair form in Britain in 2002 (left J. Osborne after fourth outing), winning seller at Wolverhampton in December: stays 1½m: acts on firm going and fibresand: tried blinkered/tongue tied. *R. Ford* **70**

LANZADOR (ARG) 4 b.c. Rudy's Fantasy (USA) 93 – La Senal (ARG) (Cambremont 121) [2002 a8.5f⁵ a7.5f² a8.5f⁶ a9f² 10m³ p10g 8.9g⁵ 8g⁵ Dec 15] neat ex-Argentinian colt: half-brother to winner in Argentina by Long Johns: dam unraced: fairly useful maiden: second 5 times from 6 starts in native country at 2/3 yrs: trained by Paul Smith, Belgium first 6 outings in 2002: third at Sandown in June: stays 1¼m: acts on dirt and good to firm going: often tongue tied. *D. J. Selvaratnam, UAE* **82**

LANZLO (FR) 5 b. or br.g. Le Balafre (FR) 116 – L'Eternite (FR) (Cariellor (FR) 125) [2002 –: 14.1m Aug 15] lightly-raced maiden on Flat: fair hurdler. *P. J. Hobbs* —

LAPADAR (IRE) 3 b. or br.f. Woodborough (USA) 112 – Indescent Blue 63 (Bluebird (USA) 125) [2002 52, a80: f7g 12d 12.3m⁴ 12f⁵ 12m⁵ 11.9g 14g⁴* 12.4s 14g⁶ f12g² 13s⁶ 12m* 16.2g 14m Aug 22] rather leggy filly: fairly useful on all-weather, modest on turf: won minor event in May and handicap in July, both at Musselburgh: stays 1¾m: acts on fibresand, good to firm and good to soft going: tried visored/tongue tied: tried to run out fourth outing. *J. R. Weymes* **60 a82**

LA PAZ 3 b.f. Nashwan (USA) 135 – Las Flores (IRE) 102 (Sadler's Wells (USA) 132) [2002 70p: 10g 12f* 12f 12.5v² Nov 20] strong, lengthy filly: useful performer, lightly raced: won maiden at Kempton in August: best effort when 2 lengths second to Moon Search in listed race at Maisons-Laffitte final start: stays 12.5f: acts on any going. *J. H. M. Gosden* **102**

LA PERLA 3 gr.f. Royal Applause 124 – Lammastide 93 (Martinmas 128) [2002 69§: f6s⁴ f6s⁵ f7g f7g f6g⁴ Feb 12] leggy filly: modest performer: effective at 6f, barely at 1m: acts on firm ground, good to soft and fibresand: often blinkered: tends to hang/finish weakly: ungenuine. *M. J. Polglase* **55 §**

LARA BAY 2 b.f. (Mar 3) Polish Precedent (USA) 131 – Way O'Gold (USA) (Slew O' Gold (USA)) [2002 8.1g⁵ 8m Sep 11] 75,000Y: close-coupled, quite attractive filly: dam, French maiden, half-sister to 4-y-o Crystal Castle: green, fair form when last of 5 in maiden at Chepstow: well beaten in similar event at Doncaster 2 weeks later: should stay 1¼m. *I. A. Balding* **66**

LARA FALANA 4 b.f. Tagula (IRE) 116 – Victoria Mill 59 (Free State 125) [2002 60: p8g⁶ 9.9m⁶ 8g⁴ 8g⁵ 7g 10.2f⁶ 9.9m* 10.2g⁴* 9.7g⁴ 10m* 10m⁵ p12g⁵ p10g⁶ Nov 27] smallish, good-topped filly: fair performer: won handicaps at Salisbury and Chepstow in August and minor event at Nottingham in September: left J. Osborne after next start: stays 1¼m: acts on firm going, good to soft and polytrack: blinkered (folded tamely) fifth start: has worn tongue tie. *Miss B. Sanders* **71 a65**

LA REINE ROXANNE 3 b.f. Cyrano de Bergerac 120 – Sylvandra 81 (Mazilier (USA) 107) [2002 40: f6g f6g Apr 15] small, strong filly: poor maiden: blinkered final start. *L. R. James* –

LARGO (IRE) 2 ch.f. (Apr 14) Selkirk (USA) 129 – Lady of The Lake 104 (Caerleon (USA) 132) [2002 7m 7m⁴ 7g² 8.3d² Oct 28] close-coupled, quite attractive filly: has a short action: second foal: dam, winner at 2m/17f, out of smart performer up to 9f Llyn Gwynant: fairly useful maiden: made most when short-headed by La Muette at Windsor final start: will stay at least 1¼m: reared leaving stall/veered right under pressure penultimate start. *J. L. Dunlop* **83**

LARGS 2 ch.f. (Feb 9) Sheikh Albadou 128 – Madam Zando 51 (Forzando 122) [2002 5m Jul 16] 1,600Y: second foal: dam maiden who stayed 7f: 50/1, always behind in maiden at Beverley. *J. Balding* –

LARK IN THE PARK (IRE) 2 ch.f. (Feb 24) Grand Lodge (USA) 125 – Jarrayan 64 (Machiavellian (USA) 123) [2002 7f⁵ 8.3d 6.1m Sep 16] IR 15,000Y: lengthy filly: first foal: dam, maiden best at 6f at 2 yrs, half-sister to useful UAE sprinter Moonis out of half-sister to smart 1¼m performer Husyan: backward in maidens, best effort (modest form) when never-dangerous ninth at Warwick final start: sold 7,500 gns. *M. L. W. Bell* **50**

LARKY'S LOB 3 b.g. Lugana Beach 116 – Eucharis 41 (Tickled Pink 114) [2002 f7g* f7g* f6g⁶ 7s 7m 8m f8g f7g⁶ f6g f6g f6s⁶ Dec 26] 3,200Y, 3,200 2-y-o: leggy, plain gelding: half-brother to 3 winners, including 5f winners Chalice (by Governor General) and Barbara's Cutie (by Tina's Pet): dam maiden who stayed 1m: fair performer: won sellers at Southwell (made all) in January and February: left J. Given after seventh start: likely to prove best at 6f/7f: acts on fibresand, no form on turf: tried in visor/cheekpieces. *R. Wilman* **a64**

LA ROSE 2 b.f. (Feb 23) Among Men (USA) 124 – Marie La Rose (FR) (Night Shift (USA)) [2002 6m p6g Jul 17] 40,000F: fourth foal: half-sister to French 1m (at 2 yrs) and 1¼m winner Contemporary Art (by Blushing Flame) and French winner up to 1½m Danni La Rose (by Lycius): dam French 1¼m winner out of half-sister to French Group 1 winners Le Nain Jaune, Indian Rose and Vert Amande: slowly away and well held in maidens: visored second start: joined J. Unett. *M. P. Tregoning* –

LAROUSSE 4 ch.f. Unfuwain (USA) 131 – Allespagne (USA) (Trempolino (USA) 135) [2002 70: 11.7g 14.1d⁶ 14.6m⁴ 14.1m 12g² 16.2m 10s 16g⁴ 14.1m 11.5m 17.2f⁴ 15.8f Oct 8] big, lengthy filly: modest handicapper: generally below form after fifth start: stays 1¾m: probably acts on any going: tends to race freely. *S. C. Williams* **61 d**

LASANGA 3 ch.g. Zamindar (USA) 116 – Shall We Run 59 (Hotfoot 126) [2002 p10g⁴ Nov 19] 55,000Y: 18,000 2-y-o: sixth foal: half-brother to 3 winners, including 4-y-o Bannister and 1999 2-y-o 5f/6f winner Roo (by Rudimentary), both useful: dam, lightly-raced maiden, half-sister to very smart but temperamental sprinter Dead Certain: 50/1, 4 lengths fourth of 14 to Scent of Victory in maiden at Lingfield, racing freely in rear, headway widest of all and not unduly punished when no further impression: sure to progress. *Lady Herries* **60 p**

LASCOMBES 3 b.g. Bluebird (USA) 125 – Arinaga (Warning 136) [2002 96: 8g⁶ 7.5m⁴ 8g³ May 30] close-coupled, quite attractive gelding: fairly useful performer: never a threat in 2002, though won disappointing when sixth to Flat Spin in listed race on reappearance: may prove best around 7f: acts on soft and good to firm going: visored (ran poorly) final 2-y-o start: has been slowly away/run in snatches: one to treat with caution: sold 6,200 gns. *J. Noseda* **90 §**

LASER CRYSTAL (IRE) 3 b.f. King's Theatre (IRE) 128 – Solar Crystal (IRE) 110 (Alzao (USA) 117) [2002 f6p: 8.3d⁶ 10.2d 10d³ 10m⁴ 11.7g p8g Nov 23] fair maiden: should stay 1½m: yet to race on extremes of going: looked unwilling (saddled reportedly slipped) second start. *D. R. C. Elsworth* **67**

LAS RAMBLAS (IRE) 5 b.g. Thatching 131 – Raise A Warning 57 (Warning 136) [2002 74: 6s 6g 6g 6v 5.9s⁵ 5m⁵ 5.9v⁶ 5g 7.2d 6s 5.9m⁵ 5g 7.1m 6m³ 6d Oct 15] compact gelding: poor mover: modest performer nowadays: best around 6f: acts on fibresand and any turf going: blinkered once, effective visored or not: usually tongue tied: none too consistent. *D. A. Nolan* **59**

LASSITUDE 2 ch.f. (Feb 14) Efisio 120 – Lassoo 87 (Caerleon (USA) 132) [2002 6f⁵ Sep 26] half-sister to temperamental 7f/1m winner Mustang (by Thatching) and to 1½m winner Sioux (by Kris): dam, placed up to 11f, half-sister to very smart middle-distance colt Apache: 25/1, 7 lengths fifth to Yafoul in maiden at Pontefract: likely to stay at least 1m: should improve. *B. W. Hills* **58 p**

LAST CHANCE SALOON   3 b.g. Reprimand 122 – Bala Monaafis (IRE) (In The   –
Wings 128) [2002 f6g f7g f7g f12g 10f May 13] 1,500F: good-topped gelding: second
foal: half-brother to 1m (at 2 yrs) to 11f winner Academic Record (by Royal Academy):
dam, twice-raced maiden, out of sister to dam of Salsabil and Marju: little form.
M. W. Easterby

LA STELLINA (IRE)   4 b.f. Marju (IRE) 127 – Supportive (IRE) (Nashamaa 113)   **85**
[2002 100: 5d 6g 5g 5g* 5m 6f* f6f p7g³ p7g Dec 28] IR 50,000Y: fourth foal: closely
related to German 6f/7f winner Porcellina (by Last Tycoon) and half-sister to 5f (at 2 yrs)
and 6f winner Grand Lad and Irish 5f winner Galloway Boy (both useful and by
Mujtahid): dam fairly useful Irish 5f performer: fairly useful handicapper: won at Tralee
in August and Listowel in September, then left D. Weld 16,000 gns: best effort in Britain
when third at Lingfield: stays 7f: acts on polytrack, raced mainly on good going or firmer:
usually blinkered, has worn cheekpieces. *C. A. Dwyer*

LAST EXHIBIT   4 b.f. Royal Academy (USA) 130 – Noirmant (Dominion 123) [2002   **72**
67: p6g³ Jan 16] fair performer, lightly raced: will stay 7f: acts on polytrack, once raced
on turf: starts slowly. *R. Guest*

LAST GESTURE   3 b.g. Jester 119 – Suile Mor 65 (Satin Wood 117) [2002 56: p8g   **48**
f6s f7g⁴ 8.2m 8d Jul 7] poor performer: stayed 1m: acted on good to firm going and   **a36**
fibresand: blinkered after reappearance: dead. *Jean-Rene Auvray*

LAST IMPRESSION   4 b.f. Imp Society (USA) – Figment 75 (Posse (USA) 130)   –
[2002 –: 5m 6f 5m 5s 5.9d Jul 19] no longer of any account. *J. S. Goldie*

LAST MASTER   3 b.c. Master Willie 129 – Oatfield 69 (Great Nephew 126) [2002   **85**
–p: 10m* 12d⁶ 11.7d² 10.1d³ Jul 4] fairly useful performer, lightly raced: won maiden at
Leicester in April: at least respectable efforts last 2 starts: should stay 1¾m: yet to race on
extremes of going. *H. Candy*

LASTOFTHECASH   6 b.g. Ballacashtal (CAN) – Blue Empress (Blue Cashmere   –
129) [2002 –: p16g Jan 5] no form. *Dr P. Pritchard*

LASTOFTHEWHALLEYS   4 b.f. Noble Patriarch 115 – Pride of Whalley (IRE)   –
61 (Fayruz 116) [2002 6f 9.2s⁶ 5d Jul 1] strong filly: poor winner at 2 yrs: no form in
2002. *K. W. Hogg, Isle of Man*

LAST SYMPHONY   5 b.g. Last Tycoon 131 – Dancing Heights (IRE) 80 (High   –
Estate 127) [2002 71d: 9g Mar 28] leggy gelding: fair performer: well held only 5-y-o
start: tried visored. *Denys Smith*

LA SYLPHIDE   5 ch.m. Rudimentary (USA) 118 – Primitive Gift 38 (Primitive   –
Rising (USA) 113) [2002 ?, a71: 6s May 5] workmanlike mare: shows knee action: fair
performer at 4 yrs, lightly raced: well held only 5-y-o start. *Mrs A. Duffield*

LA TANIA   3 b.f. Polish Precedent (USA) 131 – Highsplasher (USA) (Bucksplasher   –
(USA)) [2002 56: 8.3m 10g p12g Oct 4] modest maiden: should stay 1¼m: sent to Saudi
Arabia. *C. F. Wall*

LATE ARRIVAL   5 b.g. Emperor Jones (USA) 119 – Try Vickers (USA) 72 (Fuzz-   **66**
buster (USA)) [2002 52: f7g³ f11g⁵ f8.5g f9.4s 8m 7.5d* 6.9d² 7.5d⁴ 8.5g 8.5d⁴ 7m⁶   **a52**
7.5m* 8.3m⁶ f8g f8.5g⁶ Dec 20] tall gelding: fair handicapper on turf, modest on
all-weather: trained by A. Crook first 4 starts: won at Beverley in July (selling event) and
September: effective at 7.5f to 1¼m: acts on firm going, good to soft and fibresand:
visored once, usually blinkered. *M. D. Hammond*

LATE CLAIM (USA)   2 ch.g. (Jan 29) King of Kings (IRE) 125 – Irish Flare (USA)   **83**
(Irish River (FR) 131) [2002 7m⁵ 7.2g² 7g* 7.1m 7s⁶ Oct 25] $210,000F: good-topped
gelding: first foal: dam, lightly-raced French maiden, out of half-sister to very smart
performers Hatoof (at 1m to 1½m) and Irish Prize (in USA up to 9f): fairly useful
performer: won maiden at Chester in August: creditable sixth of 20 in nursery at Newbury
(gelded after): will be well suited by at least 1m: acts on soft and good to firm going:
looks type to train on. *B. W. Hills*

LATE DECISION (USA)   2 ch.c. (Mar 30) Gone West (USA) – Larrocha (IRE) 116   **81 p**
(Sadler's Wells (USA) 132) [2002 8m⁴ Sep 11] leggy, quite attractive colt: third foal:
closely related to 3-y-o Golden Lariat and half-brother to 9f winner Razkalla (by
Caerleon): dam, 1¼m and 1½m (Galtres Stakes) winner and third in Prix Vermeille,
half-sister to Ardross: 8/1 and green, 7 lengths fourth of 13 to Silver Gilt in maiden at
Doncaster, keeping on from rear without being knocked about: wore crossed noseband:
will probably stay 1¼m: sure to improve. *D. R. Loder*

LATEEN SAILS 2 ch.c. (Mar 2) Elmaamul (USA) 125 – Felucca 94 (Green Desert **106 P** (USA) 127) [2002 8f* Oct 2]

'Dante's time performances establish him as a brilliant two-year-old. My racefigure records cover only a few years, but I am convinced he is the fastest two-year-old that has been seen for a very long time.'

Time marches on, but the appreciation of what time study can reveal about racehorses and horseraces lags behind. More than half a century on from Phil Bull's words on Dante written in *Best Horses of 1944* about the following year's Derby winner, time is still perceived as the poor relation of form, despite the proof of its value. Reporting of course records, and remarking about the times of two maiden races over the same distances on a card, are about as far as a lot of media coverage goes on the topic. In such a climate, it was perhaps inevitable that the relative clamour which greeted the prospect of a new dimension to time study—sectional timing—would fade from its first introduction at Newmarket in 1998. The difficulties involved in interpreting the times inevitably meant that early attempts at analysis would be superficial, a point discussed in the essay on Tamarisk in *Racehorses of 1997*.

As with race times, comparing one sectional time with another, like for like, is at best of limited use. To reach meaningful conclusions, the data needs to be processed and adjustments made. And, if the resulting figures are to be of practical use to the racing public, they need to be presented, not in the shape of advanced maths, but as ratings on the same scale as a set of timefigures for the races as a whole and a set of form ratings for the runners involved.

Newmarket's enterprise in introducing official sectional timing on the Rowley Mile course and putting the recording of such times on a more professional footing has finally afforded the opportunity for the beginnings of worthwhile study. During the rebuilding of the new grandstand, the course was also excavated and cables put down, with the result that, since the course's re-opening in April 2000, all horses running on the Rowley Mile have been fitted with transponders in the saddle cloths which provide electronically the time it takes each horse to cover a certain part of each race. The number of races run in this period isn't extensive, especially when account is taken of the number of different distances involved, but it has provided enough information for some reasonably confident conclusions to be drawn. The two-year-old Lateen Sails is one horse to come out well from our initial findings. Lateen Sails recorded an overall timefigure equivalent to a rating of 106 in making a winning debut in the JRA London Office's 10th Anniversary Maiden over a mile at Newmarket in October, when he beat Powerscourt by a length and a quarter in a field of six. Such a timefigure in a maiden race is eye-catching in itself, particularly for a debutante, but, by our calculations, on sectional times he looks significantly better still, his figures for the second half of the race equating to an average timefigure worth a rating of around 116, which immediately puts him in the pattern-race bracket. Whether or not Lateen Sails eventually matches up, the example demonstrates the advantage sectional times can have over race-performance times. A race-performance time is dictated to some degree by the pace of a race, and may well—and often does—underplay a horse's true ability, particularly if the horse isn't asked to assert until late on. Sectional

JRA London Office's 10th Anniversary Maiden, Newmarket—
Lateen Sails creates a very good impression on his only outing for Henry Cecil;
Powerscourt, Musanid (striped cap) and Khanjar are well clear of the two other runners

timing isn't always so limiting. Potentially, it is the icing on the cake of time study, and it is to be hoped other courses follow Newmarket's example in providing an accurate bank of data. The announcement that all courses will return electronic overall times for races for the first time in 2003 is a welcome one, as is the additional option of sectional times. The more courses for which sectional timing is also available, the more sectional times can be used in evaluating the horse population.

Lateen Sails is entitled to be considered an unusually promising horse, even leaving aside the findings from his sectional times. He was given a large P after Newmarket anyway on the grounds of the style of his victory and his physical scope. A strong, lengthy colt, he started at 5/1 and overcame fairly obvious signs of his inexperience to win most decisively, short of room as his rider kept him in behind for a little longer two furlongs out before switching him to the right. Lateen Sails knuckled down in willing style, despite edging left once in front. In the end, he was much too good for the more experienced Powerscourt, who paid a compliment to the form subsequently.

Lateen Sails (ch.c. Mar 2, 2000)	Elmaamul (USA) (ch 1987)	Diesis (ch 1980)	Sharpen Up / Doubly Sure
		Modena (b 1983)	Roberto / Mofida
	Felucca (ch 1990)	Green Desert (b 1983)	Danzig / Foreign Courier
		Bloudan (ch 1985)	Damascus / Chain Store

Lateen Sails is the fourth foal of Felucca, who raced only five times for Henry Cecil, winning a maiden at Newmarket over six furlongs at two and being placed over seven furlongs at three, showing quite useful form. Some members of the immediate family have seemed quite fragile. Of Felucca's first three foals, all by Zafonic, the only one to reach the racecourse, Luconic, was a winning sprinter in Scandinavia after two runs in Britain. Among the unraced pair, the three-year-old Night Sky did seem highly regarded in the spring before being reported as dead in August. Lateen Sails's second dam, the unraced Bloudan, is a half-sister to Al Bahathri and produced Radevore, a very smart performer at up to a mile and a half in France and the States.

Lateen Sails was bought from Khalid Abdulla by Godolphin after Newmarket and will winter in Dubai. On pedigree, he is far from sure to stay a mile and a half but, if he remains sound, he could well prove a live candidate for the Two Thousand Guineas (33/1 with the Tote at the time of writing), and other good races at up to a mile and a quarter later on. He showed a markedly round action to post at Newmarket, and fairly remarkable finishing speed in the race! *H. R. A. Cecil*

LATE NIGHT OUT 7 b.g. Lahib (USA) 129 – Chain Dance 88 (Shareef Dancer (USA) 135) [2002 116: 7.1d³ 8.5d⁵ 8m⁶ 7m 7.1g² 7m Sep 6] compact gelding: has had knee problems: smart performer at best: creditable third to Reel Buddy in listed race at Haydock in May: on downgrade after: barely stays 8.5f when conditions are testing: acts on soft and good to firm going: fifth (poor form) on hurdling debut in October: subsequently sold 24,000 gns, and sent to USA. *W. Jarvis* **113 d**

LATENSAANI 4 b.g. Shaamit (IRE) 127 – Intoxication 73 (Great Nephew 126) [2002 49: 11.9f* 11.9g² 14.1f³ 12.3m p16g⁶ 15.4m⁵ 16.2g Aug 15] neat gelding: modest handicapper: won ladies race at Brighton in April: stays 2m: acts on firm ground, probably on polytrack: blinkered (went freely) final start: joined G. M. Moore, won 3 times over hurdles in autumn. *W. J. Haggas* **56**

LATEST EDITION 2 b.f. (Mar 17) Charnwood Forest (IRE) 125 – Star of The Future (USA) 100 (El Gran Senor (USA) 136) [2002 6m⁵ 6f* Oct 5] good-topped filly: has scope: eighth foal: closely related to fairly useful 7f winner Starry Eyed (by Warning) and half-sister to useful 7f winner Big Future (by Bigstone): dam, 7f (at 2 yrs)/1m winner, half-sister to US Grade 2 9f winner Man From Eldorado: fairly useful form: won 21-runner maiden at Kempton in September by 1¾ lengths from Yafoul: never travelling fluently when favourite for nursery at Newmarket final start: should stay 1m: probably remains capable of better. *Mrs A. J. Perrett* **81 p**

LATEST MOMENT (USA) 3 br.g. Quest For Fame 127 – Estala (Be My Guest (USA) 126) [2002 10m* Jun 4] tall, good-topped gelding: fourth foal: half-brother to **94 p**

useful 7f/1m winner Entail (by Riverman): dam, useful French 2-y-o 9f winner who stayed 10.5f, half-sister to French performers Erudite (smart up to 2m) and Danefair (useful up to 1½m): wearing crossed noseband, won maiden at Sandown by 5 lengths from Sunday's Well, forging clear from over 1f out: should stay at least 1½m: coltish in paddock/at start, and was subsequently gelded: looks a useful prospect at least if all is well. *Mrs A. J. Perrett*

LAUD KARELIA   3 b.c. Royal Applause 124 – Finlandaise (FR) (Arctic Tern (USA) 126) [2002 10f 10d 10.3m⁵ 10m 11.6g Aug 12] 40,000Y: smallish, sturdy colt: half-brother to several winners, including smart German performer up to 2m Flying Dream (by Most Welcome) and useful 1½m winner Dream of Nurmi (by Pursuit of Love): dam French 1m/9f winner: signs of just a little ability. *A. C. Stewart*   –

LAUREL DAWN   4 gr.g. Paris House 123 – Madrina 70 (Waajib 121) [2002 84d, a90: p5g⁵ 5m⁴ 5m* 5g* 5g⁶ 5g⁶ 6g 5.7m³ 5m⁵ 5g⁴ 5g⁵ 5m³ 5m 5g 5f² 5m⁶ 5m f5g f5g Dec 17] leggy, plain gelding: fairly useful performer: won handicaps at Musselburgh and Beverley in May: best at 5f: acts on firm going and all-weather: usually races prominently: none too consistent. *A. Berry*   **81 a85**

LAURO   2 b.f. (Mar 12) Mukaddamah (USA) 125 – Lapu-Lapu 62 (Prince Sabo 123) [2002 6m* 7m³ 7.5g⁴ 7g 6d Nov 5] 1,100Y: strong filly: first foal: dam, 1m/1¼m winner, became one to avoid: fair performer: won maiden claimer at Haydock in July: in frame in minor events: off 2 months, well below form last 2 starts: will stay 1m: yet to race on extremes of going: often slowly away. *Miss J. A. Camacho*   **71**

LAUTREC (SWI)   2 ch.c. (Mar 30) Peintre Celebre (USA) 137 – La Venta (USA) (Drone (USA)) [2002 7m 8m 8g Oct 18] good-topped colt: good walker: sixth foal: half-brother to fairly useful 1m winner Oberon's Mistral (by Fairy King) and French 1998 2-y-o 1m/9f winner La Pascua (by Caerleon), later successful in USA: dam, 6.5f winner in France, sister to dam of Dancing Brave: twelfth in maidens, best effort (fair form) at Newmarket on final start: likely to be suited by 1¼m+. *J. L. Dunlop*   **65**

LAVINIA'S GRACE (USA)   2 b.f. (Feb 23) Green Desert (USA) 127 – Lesgor (USA) 106 (Irish River (FR) 131) [2002 5d² 5v³ 5g³ 7s* 6.5s 6s⁵ Nov 18] 95,000Y: small, leggy filly: first foal: dam, French 1¼m winner, out of New Zealand Oaks winner Let's Sgor: placed in maidens for M. Channon before 3 starts: won 4-runner minor event at Le Lion d'Angers in August: stays 7f: raced only on good ground or softer. *H-A. Pantall, France*   **66**

LAVYS DREAM   3 b.f. Lugana Beach 116 – Gaelic Air 65 (Ballad Rock 122) [2002 52d: f6g 5s f6g f6g f5g Jul 11] poor maiden: well held in 2002: hung markedly left leaving stall final 2-y-o outing. *M. J. Polglase*   –

LAW BREAKER (IRE)   4 ch.g. Case Law 113 – Revelette (Runnett 125) [2002 72, a78: p8g⁶ p7g f7g* p8g p6g⁴ f7g² f6g* f6g⁶ f7g f6g* 7m⁴ 5.1m⁴ 6m* 6m 6f f6g* 5d p6g 5g² f5g² 6m 5m 5d 5m 6d⁵ 5d 5m³ 5m 5g 5d⁵ 5g⁴ 7v f6g f5g* f6g* Dec 16] useful on all-weather, fairly useful on turf: improved and had a good year: won seller at Wolverhampton (left J. Cullinan after next start), handicap/minor event at Southwell and handicaps at Windsor (apprentices) and Wolverhampton (3, beat Sir Desmond impressively on final occasion): effective at 5f to easy 7f: acts on soft going, good to firm and all-weather: effective visored or not: usually races up with pace: sometimes hangs/finds little: usually ridden by apprentice B. Reilly: very tough. *J. A. Gilbert*   **89 a96**

LAW COMMISSION   12 ch.g. Ela-Mana-Mou 132 – Adjala 89 (Northfields (USA)) [2002 69, a62: 6g 7m 8d 7m⁶ 8m² 7m 8.1m⁶ 7g Oct 14] small, sturdy gelding: modest handicapper nowadays: effective at 6f to easy 1m: acts on all-weather, best recent form on good going or firmer: sometimes starts slowly/hangs: held up. *S. Kirk*   **60**

LAWLESS   2 ch.g. (Mar 19) Case Law 113 – Oh My Oh My (Ballacashtal (CAN)) [2002 5g⁶ 5d 5g Aug 12] workmanlike gelding: half-brother to 3 winning sprinters, including 6-y-o Cartmel Park: dam sprint maiden: modest form in maidens: likely to prove best at 5f/6f. *M. Todhunter*   **53**

LAW MAKER   2 b.g. (Apr 8) Case Law 113 – Bo' Babbity 75 (Strong Gale 116) [2002 5f⁶ Jun 21] 40,000Y: half-brother to several winners, including 6-y-o Abbajabba and useful sprinter Blue Iris (by Petong): dam, 2-y-o 5f winner, half-sister to high-class sprinter Anita's Prince: 5/1, well held in maiden at Redcar: subsequently gelded. *C. W. Fairhurst*   –

LAWOOD (IRE)   2 gr.c. (May 8) Charnwood Forest (IRE) 125 – La Susiane (Persepolis (FR) 127) [2002 6m² 6s² 6d² 6s Aug 11] good-topped colt: has a quick action: fifth foal: half-brother to 3-y-o Mahsusie: dam, won 1½m bumper, half-sister to useful 1¼m winner Gisarne: fairly useful form when runner-up in maidens at Leopardstown and the   **89**

Curragh (beaten 1½ lengths by Pakhoes) first 2 starts: below that in similar events at Haydock and the Curragh: should stay 7f: acts on soft and good to firm ground. *Francis Ennis, Ireland*

LAWRENCE OF ARABIA (IRE) 2 b.g. (May 21) Desert King (IRE) 129 – Cumbres (FR) (Kahyasi 130) [2002 7d 6d f8.5s⁴ Nov 2] IR 9,000Y: tall, close-coupled gelding: has scope: shows knee action: fourth foal: half-brother to French 10.5f winner Ouroumtsi (by Sin Kiang): dam unraced half-sister to Montjeu: never going pace after slow start in maidens: likely to do better at 1¼m/1½m. *Sir Mark Prescott* **57 p**

LAYAN 5 b.m. Puissance 110 – Most Uppitty 69 (Absalom 128) [2002 55, a44: f6s f5s⁵ f6s 5m³ 5m⁶ 6f² 6d 6f³ 5m 6m 6v 5m⁴ 5g 6.1m 6f 6d⁶ Oct 18] smallish, workmanlike mare: modest maiden: raced only at 5f/6f: well held on heavy going, acts on any other turf and fibresand: has found little: unreliable. *Miss L. C. Siddall* **53 §** **a34 §**

LAY DOWN SALLY (IRE) 4 ch.f. General Monash (USA) 107 – Sally Fay (IRE) 66 (Fayruz 116) [2002 54: p6g³ f5g p7g p5g f5g⁴ 6m p7g* 5.3d² 5.3m* 7m⁵ p5g⁴ 6g⁴ 6m 5.3m⁴ f7g p7g Dec 11] sturdy filly: modest performer: won claimer at Lingfield in May and handicap at Brighton in June: effective at 5f to 7f: acts on all-weather, soft and good to firm going: effective blinkered or not: has worn cheekpieces: usually slowly away: has looked less than keen. *J. White* **62**

LAZZAZ 4 b.g. Muhtarram (USA) 125 – Astern (USA) 67 (Polish Navy (USA)) [2002 55: p8g⁴ p8g⁵ f12s f9.4g³ f12g³ f12g² 10m 10.9m f9.4s f12f³ f9.4g* p10g⁶ Dec 30] modest performer on all-weather: won maiden at Wolverhampton in December: effective at 9.4f, barely stays 1½m: acts on all-weather, no turf form in 2002: tried blinkered. *P. W. Hiatt* **–** **a55**

LEADERSHIP 3 b.c. Selkirk (USA) 129 – Louella (USA) (El Gran Senor (USA) 136) [2002 84p: 9m⁵ 10.5d* 12m³ 10.4m³ 10.4m* 12m² Sep 7] well-made, attractive colt: smart performer: won handicaps at Haydock (by 5 lengths from Salute) in May and York (beat Imbibing ½ length in quite valuable event, made all) in August: ran well all other starts, including when close third in King George V Handicap at Royal Ascot (to Systematic) and John Smith's Cup at York (to Vintage Premium when favourite) and when neck second to Asian Heights in September Stakes at Kempton: stays 1½m: acts on good to firm and good to soft going: sold privately, and joined Godolphin. *Sir Michael Stoute* **115**

LEAHSTAR 3 ch.f. In The Wings 128 – Moondance (Siberian Express (USA) 125) [2002 9.2m⁶ 10s Oct 23] first foal: dam unraced half-sister to top-class French performer up to 1½m Freedom Cry: tailed off in maidens. *Miss L. C. Siddall* **–**

LEAPING CHARLIE 6 b.g. Puissance 110 – Impala Lass 81 (Kampala 120) [2002 66: 5m 5g 5m 5m 5m Aug 16] leggy, angular gelding: fair handicapper at 5 yrs: poor form in 2002: effective at 5f/6f: acts on fibresand and any turf going: blinkered once. *Mrs A. Duffield* **45**

LEARNED LAD (FR) 4 ch.g. Royal Academy (USA) 130 – Blushing Storm (USA) 102 (Blushing Groom (FR) 131) [2002 74: p12g p12g 12g 8.1m 8g² 8.3m³ 9m³ 8f⁵ 9m 8m 8m 8m p10g* p10g* p10g³ Dec 28] big gelding: fair handicapper: won at Lingfield in November and December: effective at 1m, barely at 1½m: acts on polytrack, firm and good to soft going. *Jamie Poulton* **68** **a71**

LEATHERBACK (IRE) 4 b.g. Turtle Island (IRE) 123 – Phyllode (Pharly (FR) 130) [2002 85: 10s⁴ 10g May 3] strong, useful-looking gelding: fairly useful handicapper: best form at 1¼m: goes well on soft/heavy going: visored when refusing to enter stall on intended debut: wandered on reappearance. *N. A. Callaghan* **82**

LEDGENDRY LINE 9 b.g. Mtoto 134 – Eider 80 (Niniski (USA) 125) [2002 –: 17.1f² 16.1m⁵ 18f Jun 24] good-topped gelding: modest handicapper: stays 17f: acts on any going: usually held up, and has found little. *Mrs M. Reveley* **60**

LEEN 5 b.m. Distant Relative 128 – St James's Antigua (IRE) 79 (Law Society (USA) 130) [2002 49: 7f 8m 16.2m 12.1m Jun 25] of little account nowadays. *M. J. Polglase* **–**

LE FANTASME 4 b.g. Fairy King (USA) – La Splendide (FR) (Slip Anchor 136) [2002 72: p7g 8d p8g² 8.5g³ 8g⁴ p8g⁶ 8.5d p7g⁵ f8.5s Dec 7] strong gelding: fair handicapper: stays 8.5f: acts on soft going (yet to race on firmer than good) and polytrack: sometimes races freely. *S. Dow* **69** **a72**

LEGAL APPROACH 3 b.c. Zafonic (USA) 130 – Legaya 94 (Shirley Heights 130) [2002 100p: 10.5g* 11.6m³ 11f* Sep 21] lengthy colt: smart performer, lightly raced: won minor event at Haydock (by length from Charley Bates, 3 ran) in July and listed race at Newbury (dictated, then responded really well to beat Frankies Dream ½ length) in September: odds on, creditable 3¼ lengths third of 4 to Arctic Owl in minor event at **116**

Windsor in between: probably stays 11.6f: yet to race on heavy going, acts on any other. *M. Johnston*

LEGAL COUP   4 gr.f. Contract Law (USA) 108 – What A Coup (Malicious) [2002 –: –
f12g Feb 19] no form. *B. A. Pearce*

LEGALIS (USA)   4 ch.g. Gone West (USA) – Loyalize (USA) 105 (Nureyev (USA)   83
131) [2002 7.5g a6.5f⁶ a6f* a5.5f⁶ f8g f6g* Dec 14] first live foal: dam, 2-y-o 5f/6f
winner, out of smart French/US performer around 1¼m Reloy: fair form in France at 2
yrs for D. Loder: won maiden at Nad Al Sheba at 3 yrs, and handicap there in March:
left J. Sadler 15,000 gns and gelded, better effort in Britain when winning handicap at
Wolverhampton in December: stays 6f: acts on good to soft ground, dirt and fibresand.
K. A. Ryan

LEGALITY   2 b.f. (Apr 27) Polar Falcon (USA) 126 – Lady Barrister (Law Society   77
(USA) 130) [2002 7d⁶ 8d² f8s* 7f Oct 2] lengthy filly: sister to 6f winners Eloquent (at 2
yrs in 1997) and 3-y-o Fluent and half-sister to several winners, including fairly useful
1m winner (in Italy) who stayed 1¾m Edipo Re (by Slip Anchor): dam unraced: fair
performer: clearly best effort when winning maiden at Southwell in September: mid-
field in nursery at Newmarket final start: stays 1m: acts on fibresand: sold 10,500 gns.
M. L. W. Bell

LEGAL SET (IRE)   6 gr.g. Second Set (IRE) 127 – Tiffany's Case (IRE) 65 (Thatch-   84
ing 131) [2002 80: p6g* p6g⁵ p5g* p5g 5s⁵ p6g 6m* 6g 6g 6m⁴ 6m 5m 6f f5g p6g³
Dec 30] rather leggy, close-coupled gelding: fairly useful performer: won minor event/
handicap at Lingfield and handicap at Doncaster in first half of year: has form at 1m, best
at 5f/6f: acts on heavy going, good to firm and polytrack: tried visored/tongue tied:
usually makes running: reportedly had breathing problem once at 5 yrs: sometimes looks
none too keen. *K. R. Burke*

LEGAL VENTURE (IRE)   6 ch.g. Case Law 113 – We Two (Glenstal (USA) 118)   –
[2002 –: 5d 5m 5m Sep 18] small, sturdy gelding: modest at 4 yrs: lightly raced and little
form since: usually blinkered/visored previously. *Julian Poulton*

LEGENDAIRE (USA)   5 gr.g. Fly Till Dawn (USA) – Iolani 59 (Alzao (USA) 117)   56
[2002 –: p7g p6g³ p7g p6g p6g 7f Apr 11] modest maiden: stays 1m: acts on good to
firm going and polytrack: tried blinkered: usually races prominently (free-going sort).
D. K. Ivory

LEGENDARY LOVER (IRE)   8 b.g. Fairy King (USA) – Broken Romance (IRE)   55
(Ela-Mana-Mou 132) [2002 69, a–: 11.6s 11.6s⁴ 10g Jul 8] strong, rangy gelding: poor
mover: modest performer, lightly raced: best at 1¼m/1½m: acts on soft and good to firm
going: tried visored: not one to trust implicitly. *J. R. Jenkins*

LEGGIT (IRE)   4 b.f. Night Shift (USA) – Scales of Justice 85 (Final Straw 127)   47 §
[2002 60§: p8g f9.4g 9.9m 10f 9s 10g 8m⁵ 7m Jul 22] unreliable maiden: stays 1¼m: acts
on firm ground and fibresand: visored once, blinkered last 2 starts: tried tongue tied: tends
to hang. *Andrew Reid*

LEGION OF HONOUR (IRE)   3 b.c. Danehill (USA) 126 – Total Chic (USA) (Far   84
North (CAN) 120) [2002 9f⁵ 10f⁴ 10g² 10d⁶ f8.5f Nov 11] 80,000Y, 200,000Y: ex-
Irish colt: half-brother to 2 winners abroad, including Italian 9f (at 2 yrs) to 11f winner by
Nashwan: dam, winning sprinter in USA, half-sister to US Grade 3 8.5f winner Smart
Style: fairly useful maiden: best effort when fourth at Listowel in October: left
A. O'Brien, tailed-off last on British/handicap debut at Wolverhampton final outing:
stays 1¼m. *Miss S. J. Wilton*

LE GRAND VIZIER   3 br.g. Doyoun 124 – Just Visiting 85 (Superlative 118) [2002   –
10m 10s⁶ Oct 23] first foal: dam 2-y-o 5f/6f winner: well held in 2 maidens. *J. R. Jenkins*

LEIGHTON (IRE)   2 b.g. (Feb 10) Desert Story (IRE) 115 – Lady Fern (Old Vic 136)   89
[2002 6m 6m² 7.5g* 7f⁴ Oct 10] 20,000Y: second foal: dam
unraced out of US 2-y-o Grade 1 6f/7f winner Mrs Warren: fairly useful form: won
maiden at Beverley in September despite idling and hanging left: carried head awkwardly
when creditable fourth of 5 to Prince Tum Tum in minor event at York: stays 7.5f: raced
only on good ground or firmer. *J. D. Bethell*

LEISURELY WAY   3 b.f. Kris 135 – Arietta's Way (IRE) 71 (Darshaan 133) [2002   71 p
8.2v² Oct 29] first foal: dam, ran 4 times, sister to useful performer up to 1½m Rubhahunish and half-sister to smart performers Court of Honour (up to 2m) and Single Empire
(by Kris, up to 1¾m): fair form when neck second to Princess Miletrian in maiden at
Nottingham, keeping on well from off pace: will stay beyond 1m: should improve.
P. R. Chamings

LEITRIM LAKES (IRE) 2 b.g. (Apr 18) Mujadil (USA) 119 – Mystical Jumbo 94
(Mystiko (USA) 124) [2002 6s p5g³ f6g⁴ p7g* Dec 14] IR 16,500F, 47,000Y: first foal:
dam unraced half-sister to useful German performer up to 9.5f Siberian Grey: fairly
useful performer: won maiden in November and nursery (beat Agilis by head) in
December, both at Lingfield: stays easy 7f: acts on polytrack: game. *B. J. Meehan*

LEITRIM ROCK (IRE) 2 b.g. (Feb 19) Barathea (IRE) 127 – Kilshanny 70 (Groom 83 d
Dancer (USA) 128) [2002 5g⁵ 5s* 5m⁵ 6g 7.1m 6m f7g³ 6g f6f⁶ Nov 11] 33,000Y: quite
good-topped gelding: second foal: brother to Italian 2001 2-y-o 7f winner Golden Gables:
dam, 1½m winner, out of smart 1½m performer Kiliniski: fairly useful at best: won minor
event at Windsor in May: creditable fifth to Presto Vento in listed race at Sandown next
time: very disappointing after, leaving B. Meehan before eighth start: should stay at least
7f: acts on soft and good to firm ground: tried blinkered: unreliable. *D. W. P. Arbuthnot*

LEMAGURUT 2 b.f. (May 23) Mukaddamah (USA) 125 – Fervent Fan (IRE) 65 61
(Soviet Lad (USA)) [2002 6.1m 6f³ 6d Oct 18] leggy filly: second foal: dam 2-y-o 6f
winner: modest form: third in maiden at Catterick: bred to stay 1m. *W. M. Brisbourne*

LEMARATE (USA) 5 b.g. Gulch (USA) – Sayyedati 122 (Shadeed (USA) 135) –
[2002 63: f6s f7g² f8s² f8g f7g⁴ f8.5g⁴ f7g f7g³ 9m 8f 8.3v f8.5g f7g Dec 31] quite a51
attractive gelding: modest maiden handicapper: effective at 7f to 8.5f: acts on fibresand,
no turf form in 2002: sometimes blinkered. *D. W. Chapman*

LE MERIDIEN (IRE) 4 ch.f. Magical Wonder (USA) 125 – Dutch Queen (Ahonoora 67
122) [2002 61: 5m 7f 5g⁴ 6g⁵ 5m* 5s² 5.1d⁵ 6d 5m 6s 7m² 6g³ Sep 9] robust filly: fair
performer: won apprentice handicap at Beverley in June: effective at 5f to 7f: acts on firm
and soft going: often visored/tongue tied. *J. S. Wainwright*

LEMON BRIDGE (IRE) 7 b.g. Shalford (IRE) 124§ – Sharply (Sharpman) [2002 – §
77: 12m 12m 11.9d 14.1m 16m Sep 14] formerly fairly useful winner up to 1¾m: well
held in 2002 (finished lame final start): blinkered third (refused to race)/fourth starts. *Ian
Williams*

LENGAI (USA) 3 br.g. Dixieland Band (USA) – La Pepite (USA) (Mr Prospector –
(USA)) [2002 85: 10m 10m 10m 9.1g Sep 20] close-coupled, quite good-topped gelding:
unimpressive mover: fairly useful maiden at 2 yrs: well held in 2002, leaving E. Dunlop
9,000 gns after third outing: resold 5,500 gns after final start, sent to Kuwait. *J. G. Given*

LENNEL 4 b.g. Presidium 124 – Ladykirk 78 (Slip Anchor 136) [2002 75: 8f 8.3g 8.1d 68
10g 10.3g³ 9.1d⁴ Aug 2] leggy, close-coupled gelding: fair performer: effective at 1m/
1¼m: seems to act on any going: blinkered last 2 starts. *A. Bailey*

LEO BOY (USA) 2 b.c. (Jan 27) Danehill (USA) 126 – Leo Girl (USA) 100 (Seattle 79
Slew (USA)) [2002 6f 8f⁶ 8g⁴ Oct 2] rather leggy, lengthy colt: first foal: dam, French
1¼m and (listed race) 10.7f winner, out of smart French miler Navratilovna: fair form in
maidens: best effort when sixth at Kempton: raced freely when fourth at Salisbury: not
sure to stay much beyond 1m. *J. L. Dunlop*

LEOMINDA 3 b.f. Lion Cavern (USA) 117 – Arminda (Blakeney 126) [2002 6.1d⁴ 67 +
7.5g⁶ 5f³ 6g² 6g Jul 20] tall, quite good-topped filly: has scope: half-sister to several
winners, including fairly useful 7f (at 2 yrs) to 1½m winner Carburton (by Rock City) and
4-y-o Marshal Bond: dam unraced half-sister to high-class 1¼m/1½m performer Madam
Gay: fair maiden: should stay at least 7f: yet to race on soft/heavy going, probably acts on
any other. *J. A. Glover*

LEONARDO DE VINCI (IRE) 2 b.c. (Apr 19) Sadler's Wells (USA) 132 – Andro- 70
maque (USA) 111 (Woodman (USA) 126) [2002 7.1v³ 7d⁴ 8g⁶ Sep 7] IR 28,000Y: strong,
close-coupled colt: fifth foal: half-brother to a 9f winner in Hong Kong by Danehill: dam
1m winner and awarded 9f Prix de l'Opera: fair form in maidens: best effort on debut:
should be suited by 1m+. *K. A. Ryan*

LEONICA 3 b.f. Lion Cavern (USA) 117 – South Shore 102 (Caerleon (USA) 132) 75 +
[2002 92: 8.1m* May 6] quite attractive filly: fairly useful performer in 2001: didn't have
to be at best to win maiden at Warwick (wore crossed noseband) only 3-y-o start, edging
right: unlikely to stay beyond 1m: raced only on good/good to firm going: refused to enter
stall intended debut. *M. L. W. Bell*

LEONIE SAMUAL 7 b.m. Safawan 118 – Hy Wilma 52 (Jalmood (USA) 126) [2002 45
10.2g 8d⁴ 7d³ 10m⁶ Jun 25] angular mare: reportedly has no tongue: poor performer:
stays 1m: acts on soft going: sometimes slowly away. *R. J. Hodges*

LEONORA TRUCE (IRE) 3 b.f. Brief Truce (USA) 126 – Eleonora d'Arborea 78 –
(Prince Sabo 123) [2002 53: f7s³ f7s⁶ p6g² p5g* f5g⁴ p6g 5m 5s 7m f8s p10g f9.4g⁵ a60

f8.5g* f8g f8.5g² f9.4g⁵ f8.5g Dec 20] rather leggy filly: modest performer: won handicap at Lingfield in February, and (having left K. McAuliffe after sixth start) seller at Wolverhampton in November: winner at 5f, best at 8.5f to easy 1¼m: acts on all-weather and good to firm ground: usually visored/blinkered before seventh outing. *N. P. Littmoden*

LEONOR DE SOTO 2 b.f. (Apr 26) Fraam 114 – Wings Awarded 67 (Shareef Dancer (USA) 135) [2002 6.1d⁴ 6.1g³ 6m 7s 7.1m⁵ 6m³ 6g⁴ f6g³ f8.5s² f8.5g* Dec 31] 6,500Y: sparely-made filly: first foal: dam 1m and 1½m winner: modest maiden: dead-heated for first in seller at Wolverhampton: will stay 1¼m: acts on soft going, good to firm and fibresand. *M. R. Channon* — **54**

LEOPARD SPOT (IRE) 4 b.g. Sadler's Wells (USA) 132 – Savoureuse Lady 111 (Caerleon (USA) 132) [2002 86: 11.9s⁴ 18d Jul 6] close-coupled, attractive gelding: useful maiden at best for A. O'Brien in Ireland at 2/3 yrs: has deteriorated: blinkered once. *Jonjo O'Neill* — **–**

LEOPHIN DANCER (USA) 4 b.g. Green Dancer (USA) 132 – Happy Gal (FR) (Habitat 134) [2002 70: p12g f12s p12g p13g f9.4g 10g⁶ 9m⁴ 10m 10m⁵ 10g 10.9g 9.2d⁴ 15.8m³ 11.9g³ 12m³ 16.2m 12.1m 11.9m⁵ 11.9g⁵ Oct 24] tall, leggy gelding: modest maiden: seems to stay 2m: acts on firm and good to soft going: usually tongue tied: free-going sort: has looked no easy ride. *P. W. Hiatt* — **55 a–**

LEO'S LUCKYMAN (USA) 3 b. or br.c. Woodman (USA) 126 – Leo's Lucky Lady (USA) (Seattle Slew (USA)) [2002 103p: a10f 7m⁵ 9g 10.3f³ 10.3g* Jun 8] big, strong, attractive colt: has scope: useful performer: won 3-runner minor event at Doncaster in June by 1¼ lengths from Johannian, rallying well: creditable efforts previous 2 starts, 1¾ lengths third to Gallant Hero in similar race at Doncaster: stays 1¼m: acts on firm and good to soft going: blinkered first 2 outings: tried tongue tied: often makes running: sent to UAE. *M. Johnston* — **105**

LEOZIAN 4 b.g. Lion Cavern (USA) 117 – Alzianah 102 (Alzao (USA) 117) [2002 89: 5g 5.2m a6f³ a5f Dec 13] strong, stocky gelding: only fair form at 4 yrs, leaving R. White after second outing: best at 5f: acts on firm and soft going, and on dirt: edgy sort. *P. L. Rudkin, UAE* — **77**

LERMONTOV (USA) 5 b. or br.g. Alleged (USA) 138 – Prospect Dalia (USA) (Mr Prospector (USA)) [2002 93: 10m⁵ 12m 10f⁶ 10g⁵ 10.3m⁴ 12g⁵ 10.4m 9.9g* 10m⁵ 10.3m 10m 8s⁶ Oct 28] lengthy, sparely-made gelding: fairly useful handicapper: left W. Muir before gaining first win since 2 yrs at Beverley in August: effective at 1¼m/1½m: acts on firm and soft going: blinkered final start: sometimes takes strong hold (has worn crossed/dropped noseband): usually held up: consistent: sent to USA. *R. A. Fahey* — **87**

LE RUBAN BLEU (IRE) 3 ch.g. Bluebird (USA) 125 – Minervitta (Warrshan (USA) 117) [2002 –: f8s 8s 7s Oct 22] smallish gelding: no form. *H. J. Collingridge* — **–**

LESATH (USA) 2 b.g. (Apr 16) Mister Baileys 123 – Green Moon (FR) (Shirley Heights 130) [2002 8.5m² 8.1g² 8d³ Oct 18] $26,000F, 30,000 2-y-o: half-brother to several winners, including useful French winner up to 10.5f Golfe Juan (by Lyphard) and 4-y-o Exotic Fan: dam, French 11f winner, half-sister to smart French 1¼m winner Glity: fairly useful maiden: best effort when beaten head by Atahuelpa at Chepstow on second start: odds on, only third to Sir Haydn at Redcar (gelded after): will stay 1¼m. *J. R. Fanshawe* — **89**

LESLEY (IRE) 2 b.f. (May 7) Sesaro (USA) 81 – Haysel (IRE) (Petorius 117) [2002 7m 7.5g Sep 18] IR 500Y: first foal: dam unraced: well beaten in claimer/maiden. *Mrs P. N. Dutfield* — **–**

LET ME TRY AGAIN (IRE) 2 b.c. (Apr 13) Sadler's Wells (USA) 132 – Dathiyna (IRE) (Kris 135) [2002 7.1m 7g⁵ 8s Oct 26] IR 90,000Y: good-bodied colt: second foal: brother to 3-y-o Sadlers Law: dam, unraced, out of very smart 6f/7f winner Dafayna, herself half-sister to 2000 Guineas winner Doyoun: best effort in maidens (fairly useful form) when fifth to Cat Ona High at Leicester: should stay 1¼m. *T. G. Mills* — **81**

LET'S CELEBRATE 2 b.g. (Mar 26) Groom Dancer (USA) 128 – Shimmer 55 (Bustino 136) [2002 6d 6f⁵ p7g 7.1m 8m f6g f5g Dec 4] rather unfurnished gelding: fifth living foal: half-brother to 3-y-o Young Lion: dam, maiden, bred to stay 1½m, from family of Nashwan, Nayef and Unfuwain: poor maiden: best efforts at 6f: acts on fibresand and firm ground. *C. E. Brittain* — **45**

LET'S PARTY (IRE) 2 b.f. (Apr 22) Victory Note (USA) 120 – Mashoura (Shareef Dancer (USA) 135) [2002 6d² 6g 6d⁴ p7g Oct 31] IR 26,000Y: second living foal: dam French 1m winner out of useful sprinter Massorah: fair maiden: stays 6f, possibly not 7f: best efforts on good to soft ground. *R. Hannon* — **69**

Premio Primi Passi, Milan—Europe's first pattern race of the year for two-year-olds falls to Le Vie dei Colori (left), who gains the fourth of his six wins; he accounts for Golden Jade, the British-trained Checkit and Golden Devious

L'EVANGILE   4 b.f. Danehill (USA) 126 – Dubai Lady 78 (Kris 135) [2002 105: **98** 11.8g² 16.2d⁶ 14.1f* 15.5d⁵ 14g 13.9m 12f 18m 17v Nov 3] workmanlike filly: has a powerful, round action: useful performer: made all in maiden at Nottingham in May: quite highly tried on several occasions otherwise (probably flattered second start): should stay beyond 2m: acts on good to soft going, and may not take repeated racing on firmer than good: none too consistent. *J. W. Hills*

LEVANTINE (IRE)   5 b.g. Sadler's Wells (USA) 132 – Spain Lane (USA) 115 (Seek- **77** ing The Gold (USA)) [2002 a8f 8g 8m⁴ 7.1g p8g p7g p8g f9.4s Dec 7] first foal: dam, **a–** French sprinter, closely related to US Grade 1 9f/1¼m winner Marquetry: fair performer at best: trained at 2 yrs by D. Loder, making all in minor event at Saint-Cloud: trained for 3-y-o reappearance only by Saeed bin Suroor: won handicap at Abu Dhabi in 2001: left K. McLaughlin, UAE, 18,000 gns after second start in 2002: below form last 5 outings: stays 8.5f: acts on soft going, good to firm and dirt: has been visored, including when successful. *S. Dow*

LE VIE DEI COLORI   2 b.c. (Feb 25) Efisio 120 – Mystic Tempo (USA) 76 (El **110** Gran Senor (USA) 136) [2002 5g* 6m* 5.5m* 6f* 6m* 7m* 7g² Oct 6] workmanlike colt: third foal: half-brother to a winner in Italy by Alhijaz: dam, 6f winner (including at 2 yrs), half-sister to dam of Queen Mary winner Shining Hour: smart performer: won newcomers race, minor event and listed race (all at Rome), Premio Primi Passi (by ½ length from Golden Jade) and minor event, both at Milan, and Prix La Rochette Royal Thalasso Barriere (beat Il Barone by neck) at Longchamp between April and September: best effort when ½-length second of 14 to Hold That Tiger in Grand Criterium at Longchamp, making most and keeping on gamely: stays 7f: raced only on good ground or firmer: mulish at stalls last 2 starts: tough. *R. Brogi, Italy*

LEWIS ISLAND (IRE)   3 b.c. Turtle Island (IRE) 123 – Phyllode (Pharly (FR) 130) **94** [2002 85: 8.3m⁵ 9m³ 11g² 12s* 12m⁶ 12g⁶ 12m³ 11.8g Oct 14] angular, lengthy colt: fairly useful handicapper: won at Kempton in June: mostly creditable efforts otherwise, including when sixth to Systematic in King George V Stakes at Royal Ascot next start: will stay beyond 1½m: acts on soft and good to firm going: has worn crossed noseband: usually races prominently: sold 86,000 gns, joined N. Twiston-Davies and fairly useful form over hurdles, successful in December. *T. G. Mills*

LEXI'S HOSS (USA) 2 b. or br.f. (Apr 19) Siphon (BRZ) 130 – Da River Hoss **72**
(USA) (River Special (USA)) [2002 p6g³ 7g⁴ 8.3m² 7.1m⁵ Oct 19] $70,000Y: second foal:
dam unraced half-sister to dual Breeders' Cup Mile winner Da Hoss: fair maiden: good
fifth in nursery at Catterick: stays 1m: acts on polytrack, raced only on good/good to firm
ground on turf. *J. Nicol*

LEYAALY 3 ch.f. Night Shift (USA) – Lower The Tone (IRE) 74 (Phone Trick (USA)) **–**
[2002 10g p8g May 29] 18,000Y, 2,800 2-y-o: second foal: sister 4-y-o More Sirens:
dam, Irish 1m winner, half-sister to useful 1m/1¼m performer Pantar: tailed-off last in
maidens. *B. A. Pearce*

LIAM'S STORY (IRE) 2 gr.c. (Mar 28) Desert Story (IRE) 115 – Sweet Class **74**
(Rusticaro (FR) 124) [2002 8.3d 8g 7.1m⁵ Sep 7] IR 26,000F, IR 20,000Y: eighth foal:
half-brother to winners abroad by Cyrano de Bergerac and Don't Forget Me: dam
unraced: easily best effort (fair form) when fifth to Jay Gee's Choice in maiden at
Haydock: should stay at least 1m. *J. G. Given*

LIBERTY BOUND 4 b.f. Primo Dominie 121 – Tshusick 81 (Dancing Brave (USA) **61**
140) [2002 62, a69: f5g* f5g* f5g³ 5m⁶ May 23] workmanlike filly: fairly useful **a85**
handicapper on all-weather, only modest on turf: won at Wolverhampton in February and
March: raced only at 5f/6f: acts on fibresand, good to firm and heavy going: visored once:
sold 6,000 gns in November. *D. Shaw*

LIBERTY ROYAL 3 b.c. Ali-Royal (IRE) 127 – Hope Chest 70 (Kris 135) [2002 **91 +**
83p: p8g² 10m f8.5g⁶ p10g Dec 21] fairly useful form, lightly raced: off 7 months, raced
freely and shaped as if retaining all his ability last 2 starts: ran creditably over 1¼m, but
may well prove best around 1m: raced only on all-weather/good to firm going. *P. J. Makin*

LIBERTY SEEKER (FR) 3 ch.g. Machiavellian (USA) 123 – Samara (IRE) 108 **77**
(Polish Patriot (USA) 128) [2002 8m 10s³ f12g³ Nov 25] 120,000Y: angular gelding: first
foal: dam, miler, half-sister to smart middle-distance stayer Lille Hammer: much better
effort in maidens at Newbury (6 months after debut) when third to Behra: disappointing
at Southwell final run: should stay 1½m. *M. R. Channon*

LIBRE 2 b.g. (Feb 17) Bahamian Bounty 116 – Premier Blues (FR) 35 (Law Society **75**
(USA) 130) [2002 5g⁶ 5m 7.1m⁵ 7g 8.3d² 8s² 8d Nov 1] 9,500F, 13,500Y, 19,000
2-y-o: second foal: dam, maiden, stayed 1¾m: fair maiden: good second in nurseries at
Pontefract and Doncaster sixth/seventh starts: stays 1m: has form on good to firm ground,
very best efforts on softer than good: blinkered (ran poorly) final start: usually wears
tongue strap: often slowly away: sometimes looks none too keen. *F. Jordan*

LIEUDAY 3 b.g. Atraf 116 – Figment 75 (Posse (USA) 130) [2002 68: 7m³ 6.9d 7.2g **61**
7g⁶ 6s⁵ 8.1m 6g f6g Sep 30] rather leggy gelding: modest maiden: effective at 6f/7f: acts
on soft and good to firm ground: visored last 2 starts. *J. L. Eyre*

LIEUTENANT DUNBAR 2 ch.g. (Feb 14) Wolfhound (USA) 126 – Hickleton **61**
Lady (IRE) 64 (Kala Shikari 125) [2002 5m p7g⁴ 8d f7f⁶ 7s⁴ 8m⁵ 6g 7g⁵ a7g² Dec 8]
14,000Y: smallish, strong gelding: third foal: half-brother to 1m winner Pleasure Dome
(by Most Welcome) and 6f (at 2 yrs) and 1¼m winner En Grisaille (by Mystiko): dam 7f/
1m winner: modest maiden: sold from J. Eustace 6,700 gns before second in minor event
at Dos Hermanas: stays 1m: acts on polytrack/sand and soft going, probably on good to
firm: visored last 2 starts in Britain. *M. Alvarez, Spain*

LIFE ESTATES 2 b.c. (Apr 9) Mark of Esteem (IRE) 137 – Chepstow Vale (USA) 97 **–**
(Key To The Mint (USA)) [2002 f5s 6s 6s Nov 9] close-coupled colt: half-brother to
several winners, including useful French performer up to 10.5f Amiarma (by Unfuwain),
7.5f winner at 2 yrs: dam 7f 2-y-o 5f/6f winner who stayed 1m: no form: sweating and on
edge last 2 starts. *J. G. FitzGerald*

LIFE IS BEAUTIFUL (IRE) 3 b.f. Septieme Ciel (USA) 123 – Palombella (FR) **65**
(Groom Dancer (USA) 128) [2002 65: 7m⁵ 7m 8.2f 9.3s* 10m 9.3g 10g⁴ 12.1g* 12.1d³
12.4g⁶ 12.1g 12.1m* 13.8g⁴ Oct 19] smallish, sturdy filly: fair performer: won handicaps
at Carlisle in May and Beverley (seller) in July, and seller at Beverley in September:
stays 1½m: acts on soft and good to firm ground: sometimes early to post: usually leads.
W. H. Tinning

LIFFEY (IRE) 2 br.c. (Apr 5) Desert Prince (IRE) 130 – Toujours Irish (USA) (Irish **83 p**
River (FR) 131) [2002 7m⁶ Aug 2] IR 65,000Y: sturdy colt: second foal: dam unraced
half-sister to smart French 9f to 1½m winner Athyka, herself dam of US Grade 1 9f
winner Atticus: 6/1 and very green, 5 lengths sixth of 10 to Wahsheeq in maiden at
Goodwood, weakening final 1f: should do better. *P. F. I. Cole*

LIFTED WAY 3 b.c. In The Wings 128 – Stack Rock 111 (Ballad Rock 122) [2002 **80** 8.3m 8m 10m² 9.9f⁶ 9g² Oct 5] fourth foal: half-brother to 6f winner Exorcet (by Selkirk): dam, best at 5f/6f, also won at 1m: fairly useful maiden: reportedly rapped a joint penultimate start: will probably stay 1½m. *P. R. Chamings*

LI GALLI (USA) 2 b. or br.f. (Mar 10) Nureyev (USA) 131 – Redwood Falls (IRE) **57** 107 (Dancing Brave (USA) 140) [2002 5d May 25] $400,000Y: smallish filly: third foal: half-sister to 1¼m to 1½m winner Karpasiana (by Woodman): dam, French 1¼m winner, out of smart French middle-distance stayer Robertet: weak 11/2-shot, 6 lengths eighth of 11 to Silca Boo in maiden at Haydock: wore crossed noseband. *G. A. Butler*

LIGHT BRIGADE 3 b.g. Kris 135 – Mafatin (IRE) 74 (Sadler's Wells (USA) 132) **–** [2002 59: f6g 8.3s 11.5f⁵ 14.1f f12g⁶ Nov 22] modest maiden at 2 yrs: little form in 2002: tried visored. *J. M. P. Eustace*

LIGHT OF ARAGON 4 b.f. Aragon 118 – Light The Way 72 (Nicholas Bill 125) **41** [2002 f8g f7g p8g 7m⁶ 8.1m 7d⁵ 7f Jun 7] small filly: poor maiden: stays 7f. *I. A. Wood*

LIGHT ON THE WAVES 6 b.m. Greensmith 121 – Roof Dancer (Martinmas 128) **51** [2002 f16.2g f12g² p12g Mar 6] modest peformer, lightly raced (missed 2000/2001 seasons): won seller at Wolverhampton in February: reportedly bled from nose final start: stays 17f: acts on fibresand: has carried head awkwardly/flashed tail. *M. C. Pipe*

LIGHT PROGRAMME 8 b.g. El Gran Senor (USA) 136 – Nashmeel (USA) 121 **–** (Blushing Groom (FR) 131) [2002 56: f14.8s 10.5s 14.1g Jun 15] sturdy gelding: modest at 7 yrs: well held in 2002. *A. L. Forbes*

LIGHTSABRE 2 ch.f. (Apr 28) Polar Falcon (USA) 126 – Heavenly Ray (USA) 97 **55** (Rahy (USA) 115) [2002 p8g p7g f8.5g Dec 20] second foal: closely related to smart 1m (at 2 yrs in France) and 1¼m winner (in USA) Megahertz (by Pivotal): dam 7f/1m winner: modest form in Lingfield maidens first 2 starts: made much of running when well held final outing: will need to settle much better to stay beyond 1m. *Sir Mark Prescott*

LIGHT SCENT (USA) 3 ch.g. Silver Hawk (USA) 123 – Music Lane (USA) (Mis- **93** waki (USA) 124) [2002 93p: 10m 10.4m 11.9d 10m* 10d Oct 14] strong, close-coupled gelding: fairly useful performer: won maiden at Pontefract in September: stays 1¼m: acts on soft and good to firm going: visored last 2 outings (raced freely/folded tamely final one): went in snatches second start: sold 38,000 gns, joined J. Akehurst, and gelded. *Sir Michael Stoute*

LIKELY LADY (IRE) 3 b.f. Revoque (IRE) 122 – Harmer (IRE) 72 (Alzao (USA) **52** 117) [2002 51: p7g⁵ p6g p6g p8g⁴ 8.2d 7.9g 8m* 8.1d 8d² 8m⁴ 8m 8.5m f8.5g⁵ f8.5g Nov **a44** 30] quite attractive filly: modest performer: won seller at Pontefract (carried head high) in June: left N. Littmoden after twelfth start: stays 1m: acts on good to firm going, good to soft and all-weather: races freely. *D. Burchell*

LILAC 3 ch.f. Alhijaz 122 – Fairfield's Breeze (Buckskin (FR) 133) [2002 8.3m 10s **–** 10m p12g Jul 3] smallish, plain filly: third foal: dam winning pointer/hunter chaser: no form. *R. J. Price*

LILARDO 5 b. or br.m. Son Pardo 107 – Jimlil 99 (Nicholas Bill 125) [2002 f16g* **58** 16m f12g⁴ f12s* f12g⁶ Oct 19] modest performer, lightly raced (missed 2000/2001 seasons): won sellers at Southwell in June and Wolverhampton (handicap) in September: stays 2m: acts on fibresand: tongue tied: races prominently. *B. Palling*

LILIAN 2 b.f. (Mar 31) First Trump 118 – Lillibella 64 (Reprimand 122) [2002 p6g **60 p** Nov 19] second foal: dam 5f/6f winner: 33/1, 6 lengths tenth of 12 to Leitrim Lakes in maiden at Lingfield, soon pushed along: will probably improve. *I. A. Balding*

LILLAN 5 b.m. Hernando (FR) 127 – Lillemor (Connaught 130) [2002 12d f12g Dec **–** 7] fair maiden at 3 yrs for G. Butler: well beaten both starts in 2002 (first one for M. Manning in Ireland): visored final outing. *D. Carroll*

LILLIAN VIOLET 3 b.f. Beveled (USA) – Grey Twig 68 (Godswalk (USA) 130) **–** [2002 –: 7d 10.1m 11.5s Oct 22] little form. *M. J. Ryan*

LILLIES BORDELLO (IRE) 3 b.f. Danehill Dancer (IRE) 117 – Lunulae (Tumble **–** Wind (USA)) [2002 81: 7g 6d 6g f5g Nov 20] lengthy, quite good-topped filly: fairly useful performer at 2 yrs: no form in 2002, leaving E. Lynam in Ireland after third start: effective at 5f/6f. *K. A. Ryan*

LILL'S STAR LAD 4 ch.g. Kasakov – Lady Khadija (Nicholas Bill 125) [2002 8g **–** 8m 10.3m Jun 29] first foal: dam of no account: no sign of ability. *Mrs S. Lamyman*

LILY OF THE GUILD (IRE)   3 ch.f. Lycius (USA) 124 – Secreto Bold (Never So   **65**
Bold 135) [2002 53§: 5.7g p6g² 7g 6m* 6m⁶ 6.1m⁵ 7g Oct 14] close-coupled filly: fair
handicapper: won at Salisbury in August: stays 6f: acts on good to firm going and
polytrack: has swished tail/hung markedly/pulled hard: none too consistent. *W. S. Kittow*

LIMBO LAD   3 b.g. Millkom 124 – Bumble Boogie (IRE) (Bluebird (USA) 125) [2002   **56**
58: f8s² f9.4g³ f7g⁶ f7g⁵ 9.9m⁵ 12.1g⁶ 12.1s⁴ 10m* 10f Sep 27] modest handicapper: won   **a54**
apprentice selling race at Ripon (edged right) in August: stays 1¼m: acts on fibresand
and good to firm going. *P. C. Haslam*

LINBY LAD (IRE)   2 ch.g. (Apr 1) Dolphin Street (FR) 125 – Classic Look (IRE) 58   **75**
(Classic Music (USA)) [2002 6g² 7m³ 8m* 7.9f² Oct 10] IR 5,500F, IR 5,000Y: useful-
looking gelding: third foal: half-brother to useful Italian performer up to 1¼m Bishi Bashi
(by Topanoora): dam, maiden who should have stayed 1m, half-sister to useful performer
up to 1m Brief Glimpse: fair performer: won maiden at Musselburgh in September,
dictating pace and rallying: good second in nursery at York final start: will probably stay
1¼m: raced only on ground firmer than good. *J. J. Quinn*

LINCOLN DANCER (IRE)   5 b.g. Turtle Island (IRE) 123 – Double Grange (IRE)   **108**
(Double Schwartz 128) [2002 107: 7d² 7.1s³ 7d 7d Aug 10] compact, sturdy, attractive
gelding: poor mover: has reportedly had chipped fetlock: useful form first 2 starts in
2002: 3 lengths second to Scotty's Future in Victoria Cup at Ascot on first occasion:
probably best at 6f/7f: goes well on ground softer than good: has worn stick-on shoes:
sold 11,500 gns, joined D. Nicholls and gelded. *M. A. Jarvis*

LINCOLN DEAN   6 b.g. Mtoto 134 – Play With Me (IRE) 73 (Alzao (USA) 117) [2002   **– §**
52§, a–§: 7.9g 11.1v⁵ 9.2g 7.9g Aug 5] small, sturdy gelding: temperamental performer:
tried visored: tongue tied. *F. P. Murtagh*

LINCOLN IMP   3 b.g. Lion Cavern (USA) 117 – Chain Dance 88 (Shareef Dancer   **56**
(USA) 135) [2002 8m 7m³ May 2] strong, quite attractive gelding: fourth foal: half-
brother to 7-y-o Late Night Out: dam, 2-y-o 6f winner who stayed 1¼m, refused to race
last 2 starts: modest form in newcomers race at Newmarket and maiden at Redcar: dead.
W. Jarvis

LINDEN'S LADY   2 b.f. (Mar 25) Compton Place 125 – Jubilee Place (IRE) 76   **79**
(Prince Sabo 123) [2002 f5g 5f³ 5m⁶ 5g⁵ 6f² 6g* f7f 6g³ 6f* 6s Oct 25] 4,800Y, resold   **a–**
4,000Y: third foal: half-sister to a 5f and 7.5f winner in Italy by So Factual: dam 2-y-o 6f
winner: fair performer: won maiden at Newcastle in August and nursery at Pontefract in
October: stays 6f: acts on firm ground, well beaten on soft/fibresand. *J. R. Weymes*

LINDINIS (USA)   4 b.c. Distant View (USA) 126 – Annual Dance (USA) (Nostalgia   **57**
(USA)) [2002 53: f12g² Feb 18] modest maiden: stayed 1½m: dead. *S. Kirk*

LINE IN THE SAND   3 b.g. (Feb 24) Royal Applause 124 – Second Secret (Second   **–**
Set (IRE) 127) [2002 p8g Dec 14] IR 15,000F, IR 16,000Y, 5,000 2-y-o: first foal: dam
tailed off in 2 sellers: 50/1, last of 12 in maiden at Lingfield. *Miss B. Sanders*

LINENS FLAME   3 ch.g. Blushing Flame (USA) 109 – Atlantic Air (Air Trooper   **61**
115) [2002 9.9m 9.9f 10m⁶ Oct 7] half-brother to several winners, including 6f winner
Count Calypso (by King's Signet) and 7f (including at 2 yrs)/1m winner Mullitover (by
Interrex), both fairly useful: dam Italian 1¼m winner: best effort in maidens when sixth
at Windsor (raced freely). *B. G. Powell*

LINGO (IRE)   3 b.g. Poliglote 121 – Sea Ring (FR) (Bering 136) [2002 53p: 7s* 10m   **101**
10m* 12.3f² 10.1s* 9.9m⁴ 12g⁵ 12s Oct 26] strong gelding: useful handicapper: won at
Doncaster in March, Pontefract in May and Epsom (beat Systematic by 2½ lengths) in
June: creditable efforts at Goodwood (length fourth to Macaw) and Newmarket (got very
poor run when fifth behind Defining) next 2 starts: probably better at 1¼m than 1½m, at
least when conditions are testing: has form on firm going, but leaves impression may
prove ideally suited by good or softer: held up. *Mrs J. R. Ramsden*

LINNING WINE (IRE)   6 b.g. Scenic 128 – Zallaka (IRE) (Shardari 134) [2002   **85**
p12g² p10g* 10m² 10d² 10m 11.6m 10.1d⁴ 8v³ p10g² p10g² p12g* p10g² Dec 21] lengthy   **a104**
gelding: second foal: half-brother to useful 1¼m/1½m winner Zalal (by Darshaan): dam,
French 11f winner, granddaughter of Petite Etoile: fairly useful bumper winner: useful
performer on all-weather on Flat, fairly useful form on turf: won maiden at Lingfield in
February, and handicap there (by 1¾ lengths from Alessandro Severo) in December: very
good second to Eastern Breeze at same track final outing: will prove best at 1¼m/1½m:
acts on polytrack, good to firm and good to soft going: found little fourth to sixth starts:
held up. *B. G. Powell*

LINUS 4 b.g. Bin Ajwaad (IRE) 119 – Land Line (High Line 125) [2002 65: 14.1d **58 §**
13.3s 12d 16.4d⁴ 11.8g² 16.2m 12.1m⁵ f12g 14.1d⁴ f14.8g⁶ Nov 30] quite attractive
gelding: unimpressive mover: modest maiden: claimed from S. Kirk £6,000 fifth start:
stays 1¾m: acts on soft and good to firm going: blinkered (looked none too keen) final
outing: sometimes slowly away/wanders. *G. A. Ham*

LIONARDO 6 b.h. Lion Cavern (USA) 117 – Pravolo (Fools Holme (USA)) [2002 **86**
78: a8f⁴ a9f* 10g a9f* a9f a9f⁶ 8d* 8.1m 8.3s⁴ 9m³ 12d a10g a10f Dec 27] sturdy horse:
fairly useful handicapper: won at Jebel Ali in January/February and Goodwood in May:
effective at 1m (given test) to 1¼m: acts on dirt and any turf going. *A. Smith, UAE*

LIONEL ANDROS 4 b.g. Lion Cavern (USA) 117 – Guyum (Rousillon (USA) 133) **50**
[2002 50: 5m³ 6m 5.1g 6d⁶ f5g⁵ 5.7d³ 5.3m 5.1d⁴ 6m² 5.1g³ 5.7m³ 5s 5g Sep 7] tall, leggy
gelding: modest maiden: claimed from R. Hodges £10,000 eleventh start: stays 5.7f: acts
on fibresand, goes well on going firmer than good on turf: blinkered once: sometimes
slowly away. *K. A. Ryan*

LION HUNTER (USA) 3 b.c. Quest For Fame 127 – Prodigious (FR) (Pharly (FR) **90**
130) [2002 8s³ 10f² 10.1m² 12.3m⁵ 10m* Oct 7] tall, rather leggy colt: half-brother to
several winners abroad, including very smart French 1¼m/1½m winner Public Purse (by
Private Account) and US Grade 1 1¼m winner Super Staff (by Secretariat): dam French
1m/1¼m winner: fairly useful performer: off 3½ months, made all in maiden at Windsor
in October by 6 lengths from Rajasthan: should stay 1½m: yet to race on heavy ground,
acts on any other: has found little: sold 32,000 gns. *B. W. Hills*

LION'S DOMANE 5 b.g. Lion Cavern (USA) 117 – Vilany 87 (Never So Bold 135) **74 §**
[2002 67, a54: f7g⁵ 7.1m³ 7.1g* 7.5g 7.1g 7g⁶ 7m⁴ 7m f7s 7.1m⁵ p7g Dec 11] strong, **a– §**
workmanlike gelding: fair handicapper on turf: won at Musselburgh in May: best around
7f: acts on firm going and fibresand: visored once at 4 yrs: has been equipped with net
muzzle: usually leads: unreliable *I. Semple*

LIPSTICK 3 b.f. Zamindar (USA) 116 – Final Shot 91 (Dalsaan 125) [2002 99p: 8g **103**
6m² 7m⁴ 7m⁴ Aug 22] rather angular filly: useful performer: reportedly suffered an
overreach in April: well held in Poule d'Essai des Pouliches at Longchamp following
month: at least creditable efforts in listed races at York on second and fourth starts, neck
second to Palace Affair on former occasion, 5½ lengths fourth to Suggestive on latter:
barely stays 7f: raced only on good/good to firm going: usually held up. *M. R. Channon*

LIQUIDAMBAR 3 ch.f. Atraf 116 – Precious Ballerina 66 (Ballacashtal (CAN)) **–**
[2002 49: 10f 6m 7f 10g Oct 14] leggy, close-coupled filly: poor maiden: well held at 3
yrs. *J. R. Norton*

LIQUID FORM (IRE) 2 b.g. (Feb 14) Bahhare (USA) 122 – Brogan's Well (IRE) **80**
(Caerleon (USA) 132) [2002 f7g⁵ 7d³ 8d 8m* 7.1m 8m Sep 12] 14,500Y: first foal: dam
unraced half-sister to 2 useful performers: fairly useful performer: best effort when
winning maiden at Goodwood in August: well held in nurseries last 2 starts (sweating on
final one): stays 1m: acts on good to firm ground. *B. Hanbury*

LISA'S LOONEY 3 b.f. Bahamian Bounty 116 – Starfida (Soviet Star (USA) 128) **42**
[2002 44§: p6g 5m 5.3m 5.1d⁴ 6s⁴ 6f 6g 6m 6g Oct 28] strong, close-coupled filly: poor
maiden: stays 6f: acts on soft and good to firm ground: tried visored: sometimes slowly
away (has gone right leaving stall). *Mrs C. A. Dunnett*

LISHTAR (IRE) 3 b.g. Mtoto 134 – Lilissa (IRE) (Doyoun 124) [2002 79p: 10f* May **95**
17] quite attractive gelding: confirmed promise of only 2-y-o start when winning maiden
at Newbury in May by 5 lengths from Scent of Victory: stayed 1¼m: acted on firm going:
dead. *Sir Michael Stoute*

LISIANSKI (IRE) 4 b.g. Fairy King (USA) – Tough Lady 91 (Bay Express 132) **95**
[2002 82: 5f³ 6m⁴ 5m⁵ 5m 5g* 5g Oct 28] quite good-topped gelding: useful handicapper:
better than ever in 2002, winning at Catterick in October by 5 lengths from Texas Gold:
probably best at 5f/6f on good going or firmer: usually visored: hung (possibly something
amiss) fourth start: occasionally slowly away: joined M. Magnusson. *D. W. P. Arbuthnot*

LISSAHANELODGE 3 br.g. Grand Lodge 125 – Lissahane Lass (Daring **–**
March 116) [2002 10s 10m 8d⁶ 9.9m Sep 13] third foal: dam, maiden on Flat, won at 2m
over hurdles: well held in maidens. *P. R. Hedger*

LISSOME (USA) 3 b.f. Lear Fan (USA) 130 – Miss Otis (USA) (One For All (USA)) **–**
[2002 –: 8.3m 9.9m 10.2f Jul 25] little form. *I. A. Balding*

LISTEN KID (USA) 3 b.g. Royal Academy (USA) 130 – Prosper (USA) (Affirmed **–**
(USA)) [2002 8.2m 8.3d Oct 14] big, good-topped gelding: second foal: dam, winner in

USA, half-sister to US Grade 1 1¼m runner-up Dearly Loved: little sign of ability in maidens. *Mrs A. J. Bowlby*

LISZT (USA) 5 ch.h. Woodman (USA) 126 – Pushkina (USA) (Nureyev (USA) 131) **74**
[2002 p10g⁶ 6f⁵ p5g 10s p12g⁶ May 28] $300,000Y: first foal: dam unraced close relative to useful Irish 1m winner Chanzi out of sister to US Grade 1 9f/1¼m winner Fiesta Gal: fair maiden: barely stays 1½m: acts on firm going and polytrack: slowly away third/fourth outings. *G. L. Moore*

LITANY 3 b.f. Colonel Collins (USA) 122 – Hymn Book (IRE) 65 (Darshaan 133) **73**
[2002 –§: 10d* 12m⁵ 14.6m* 11.8d* 11.8m* 11.8g⁴ Jul 6] leggy filly: unimpressive mover: fair handicapper: won at Nottingham, Doncaster and Leicester (twice) between April and June: stays 14.6f: yet to race on extremes of going: tried visored: often makes running. *John A. Harris*

LITERACY (USA) 2 b.f. (Apr 5) Diesis 133 – Tuviah (USA) (Eastern Echo (USA)) **68**
[2002 7m² 7g 7m⁵ 6m⁶ Aug 28] $80,000F, $105,000Y: close-coupled filly: second foal: dam, placed several times in USA, half-sister to 7-y-o Duck Row: fair maiden: second at Yarmouth: should stay at least 1m: raced only on good/good to firm going. *C. E. Brittain*

LITERAL TRUTH 2 ch.g. (Feb 13) So Factual (USA) 120 – High Cut 84 (Dashing **45**
Blade 117) [2002 6g f8g Oct 17] second foal: dam, lightly-raced maiden who should have stayed beyond 7f, out of half-sister to smart sprinter Blue Siren: well held in claimer/seller: sold 3,500 gns, sent to Spain. *J. M. P. Eustace*

LITEWSKA (IRE) 2 b.f. (Feb 23) Mujadil (USA) 119 – Old Tradition (IRE) 76 **86**
(Royal Academy (USA) 130) [2002 5g 5m* 6g² 6m⁶ 6g⁶ 6s p6g³ Dec 30] IR 40,000Y: rather leggy, unfurnished filly: first foal: dam, ran twice, out of sister to Cheveley Park/1000 Guineas winner Ma Biche: fairly useful performer: won maiden at Salisbury in June: good second in nursery at Leicester next time: should stay 7f: acts on good to firm going and polytrack. *R. Hannon*

LITHUANIAN (AUS) 4 br.c. Nureyev (USA) 131 – Doe (USA) (Hansel (USA)) **78 p**
[2002 p6g² Dec 18] second foal: dam unraced sister to high-class 1½m performer Fruits of Love and half-sister to Mujadil: 11/4 favourite, short-head second of 14 to Manicani in maiden at Lingfield, travelling strongly but looking green in front under pressure: should stay 7f, but doesn't look short of speed: sure to improve and win a race. *W. J. Haggas*

LITIGIOUS 5 b.m. Mtoto 134 – Kiomi 65 (Niniski (USA) 125) [2002 f12g f12g⁵ 10d **–**
Apr 30] poor maiden in 2000: no form in 2002: tried visored. *A. Senior*

LITTLE AMIN 6 b.g. Unfuwain (USA) 131 – Ghassanah 73 (Pas de Seul 133) [2002 **85 §**
92: 8m 8m 8m 8.3g* 10.1m 8.9m 8m² f12g 8g f8.5f⁴ f9.4g Nov 30] smallish, well-made **a75 §**
gelding: has marked knee action: fairly useful performer on turf, fair on all-weather: claimed from T. D. Barron £8,000 on reappearance: won minor event at Windsor in August: has won at 1½m, probably best at 1m/1¼m: acts on fibresand, good to firm and good to soft going: collided with rail early/reportedly lost action fifth start: unreliable. *P. W. Hiatt*

LITTLE BITTYDANCER (IRE) 6 ch.m. Pips Pride 117 – Glowing Touch (IRE) **–**
(Glow (USA)) [2002 –: 6g 7d 7m 6.1m 6m 5.9m⁶ Sep 2] IR 400Y: third reported foal: dam poor Irish maiden: little form (trained by L. Woods in Ireland prior to 2002): tried blinkered. *P. W. Hiatt*

LITTLE BRAVE 7 b.g. Kahyasi 130 – Littlemisstrouble (USA) (My Gallant (USA)) **69 §**
[2002 –, a78: p16g³ p16g f16g³ f16.2g⁵ 16g⁴ 14.4m⁴ 16f* 16m 17.2d p12g p16g⁵ f16.2f⁵
p16g⁵ Nov 27] lengthy gelding: fair handicapper: won at Thirsk (looked reluctant early but made most) in May: stays 2¼m: acts on all-weather, firm and soft going: effective visored or not: temperamental. *J. M. P. Eustace*

LITTLE CALLIAN 4 ch.f. Charmer 123 – Eucharis 41 (Tickled Pink 114) [2002 **?**
61d: p6g 5.1d 5m⁶ 5g 5d 5.1d³ 5s⁶ 5.3m 5m⁵ 8.3m Jul 22] disappointing maiden: tried visored/tongue tied. *T. M. Jones*

LITTLE DAISY 4 ch.f. Factual (USA) 108 – Twice In Bundoran (IRE) 70 (Bold **–**
Arrangement 127) [2002 –: 6m 6d Oct 18] strong filly: no form (left J. Balding after reappearance). *K. A. Ryan*

LITTLE DOUBT (USA) 2 b.g. (Mar 12) Affirmed (USA) – Little Fuzzy (USA) (Turn **–**
And Count (USA)) [2002 7m 10.2f⁵ 10f Oct 7] lengthy gelding: half-brother to numerous winners in USA, including Breeders' Cup Juvenile second It'sali'Iknownfact (by Known Fact): dam minor stakes winner in USA: well held in maidens: sold 2,800 gns, sent to Kuwait. *Sir Mark Prescott*

LITTLE EDWARD 4 gr.g. King's Signet (USA) 110 – Cedar Lady (Telsmoss 91) **101**
[2002 76: 5.7d 5m* 5.5m* 6g 5.2f² 5m 5.6m 5m Sep 29] angular gelding: useful handicapper: won twice at Warwick (impressively by 3 lengths from Compton Dynamo on
second occasion) in July: best effort when length second to Talbot Avenue at Newbury in
August: raced only at 5f/6f: acts on firm going: reportedly went lame fourth start: refused
to enter stall once. *B. G. Powell*

LITTLE FEAT 7 b.m. Terimon 124 – Run On Stirling (Celtic Cone 116) [2002 12.6m³ –
Jun 17] second foal: dam poor maiden hurdler: fairly useful bumper winner: remote third
in maiden at Warwick, slowly away. *Ian Williams*

LITTLE FOX (IRE) 7 br.m. Persian Bold 123 – Dance Land (IRE) (Nordance **55**
(USA)) [2002 55, a62: p10g⁶ p12g* p12g p12g⁵ p8g p10g⁴ 11.7g⁵ p10g p10g Aug 29] **a65**
fair handicapper on all-weather, modest on turf: won at Lingfield in February: stays 13f:
acts on polytrack and firm going. *J. J. Bridger*

LITTLE GOOD BAY 2 b.c. (Apr 13) Danehill (USA) 126 – Brave Kris (IRE) 104 **79 p**
(Kris (USA) [2002 p7g² p8g* Nov 14] first foal: dam, 1m winner, out of half-sister to
Lowther Stakes winner Kingscote: fair form in maidens at Lingfield: second to Splendid
Era before beating Clever Clogs by length, quickening out of trouble then edging left:
stays 1m: should improve. *J. H. M. Gosden*

LITTLE IN WELSH 2 b.f. (Apr 3) Distinctly North (USA) 115 – Time Clash 67 –
(Timeless Times (USA) 99) [2002 p6g f6g f7g Dec 17] third foal: dam 2-y-o 6f winner:
little form in sellers. *B. Palling*

LITTLE JOHN 6 b.g. Warrshan (USA) 117 – Silver Venture (USA) (Silver Hawk **57 §**
(USA) 123) [2002 63§: 12m 12g³ 12m⁶ 14.1f 12g 13.1d³ 12m³ 14d² 15.8f⁵ 13d³ 15d⁴
12m 14.1m 16m⁶ 12f⁵ 12s⁵ Nov 6] big, lengthy gelding: modest maiden handicapper:
in frame numerous times: effective at 1½m to easy 2m: acts on any going: occasionally
blinkered/visored: has run creditably when sweating profusely: held up: shirker.
Miss L. A. Perratt

LITTLE LOUIS 2 b.g. (Mar 28) Defacto (USA) – Naufrage (Main Reef 126) [2002 **53**
5.1d f5g f5g⁴ 5.1f f6g² 5d⁵ f7g² f6g⁴ f6g³ 6.1g⁴ 6.1m f7g⁴ f6s f6g⁵ f6g⁴ f5g⁵ f6s⁵ Dec **a60**
26] 1,750Y: smallish, workmanlike gelding: half-brother to 9-y-o Dovebrace and 1¼m/
1½m winner Kismetim (both by Dowsing): dam unraced: modest performer: in frame 8
times prior to winning seller at Wolverhampton in December: stays 7f: acts on fibresand,
best turf effort on good going: blinkered after second outing: tough. *P. D. Evans*

LITTLE MALVERN 2 b.f. (Mar 6) Piccolo 121 – Little Emmeline 52 (Emarati **88**
(USA) 74) [2002 5m² 5g⁴ 5.1f³ 5m* 6m⁴ 6.1m* 5.1g⁶ 6f² Oct 5] 16,000Y: close-coupled
filly: has a quick action: fourth foal: half-sister to 4-y-o Spice Island, 2001 2-y-o 6f
winner Splendid Rose (by Prince Sabo) and 11f winner Preposition (by Then Again):
dam 2-y-o 5f winner: fairly useful performer: won maiden at Catterick in August and
nursery at Nottingham in September: excellent second in nursery at Newmarket final
start: will prove best at 5f/6f: raced only on good going or firmer: sometimes troublesome
in preliminaries: sold 45,000 gns, sent to USA. *R. M. Beckett*

LITTLEMISSATTITUDE 3 ch.f. Common Grounds 118 – Last Look (Rainbow **75**
Quest (USA) 134) [2002 9d² p10g² 10.9m³ 10m 11.5m* 10m² 12f 10.9s² p10g p8g p10g
Dec 14] leggy, sparely-made filly: first foal: dam unraced out of half-sister to very smart
sprinter/miler Pursuit of Love: fair performer: won claimer at Yarmouth (final start for
Mrs A. Perrett) in September: stays 11.5f: acts on polytrack, soft and good to firm going:
has worn cheekpieces. *K. R. Burke*

LITTLE MISS TRICKY 3 br.f. Magic Ring (IRE) 115 – Mistook (USA) (Phone –
Trick (USA)) [2002 7g 6s 8m 8.3d 7m Sep 23] 7,000Y: second foal: dam unraced: little
sign of ability. *P. Mitchell*

LITTLE NOBBY 3 b.g. Makbul 104 – Simply Style (Bairn (USA) 126) [2002 55: **49**
f7g⁵ 8.1f 8.2g 7m⁵ 8m Oct 2] angular, close-coupled gelding: poor maiden: stays 7f: acts
on soft going, good to firm and fibresand. *R. Hollinshead*

LITTLE OAK (IRE) 4 b.f. Tagula (IRE) 116 – Blue Goose (Belmez (USA) 131) –
[2002 –: 7.1m 6v Jun 12] little form. *G. A. Swinbank*

LITTLE RICHARD (IRE) 3 b.g. Alhaarth (IRE) 126 – Intricacy 65 (Formidable **59**
(USA) 125) [2002 f8g p10g³ p10g f12g³ 10.9g 12m² f12g³ f12g* 16m² 14.1f 16.2g⁶ f14g
Nov 25] 12,000Y: small, workmanlike gelding: fifth foal: half-brother to 2m winner Faith
Again (by Namaqualand) and winner in Italy by Taufan: dam 1½m/1¾m winner: modest
performer: won claimer at Wolverhampton (sold from A. Jarvis £6,000) in May: stays
2m: acts on fibresand and good to firm going: visored after fifth start. *J. C. Tuck*

LITTLE ROBS' GIRL   3 ch.f. Cosmonaut – David James' Girl 65 (Faustus (USA)   –
118) [2002 54: 6f f7g 8m⁶ 6g 7.6f 8g 8.1d 10g f12g 11.5s⁵ Oct 22] sparely-made filly: no
form: left R. Hollinshead after seventh outing. *M. Mullineaux*

LITTLE SNIP   5 ch.m. Farmer Jock 72 – Shemust (Deadly Nightshade 107) [2002   –
f12f⁵ Aug 16] fifth reported foal: dam unraced: reluctant stalls, tailed off in seller at
Wolverhampton. *John Allen*

LITTLE TASK   4 b.g. Environment Friend 128 – Lucky Thing (Green Desert (USA)   –
127) [2002 –: 10.9d Jun 21] smallish, close-coupled gelding: fair winner at 2 yrs: little
form since: tried blinkered. *J. S. Wainwright*

LITTLE TOBIAS (IRE)   3 ch.g. Millkom 124 – Barbara Frietchie (IRE) (Try My   **54 d**
Best (USA) 130) [2002 68: 7.5m 7m⁶ 7f 7.9g 8g³ 7.9s 7m Sep 23] smallish, good-topped
gelding: modest maiden at best in 2002: probably stays 1m: acts on good to firm going:
successful over hurdles in October. *Andrew Turnell*

LITTLETON AMETHYST (IRE)   3 ch.f. Revoque (IRE) 122 – Sept Roses (USA)   **43**
(Septieme Ciel (USA) 123) [2002 p6g 8.3m 8.1m⁶ f7g 8g 6m f11g³ Dec 4] IR 17,000F,
14,000Y, 15,000 2-y-o: close-coupled, angular filly: second foal: half-sister to 4-y-o
Cezzaro: dam, French maiden, half-sister to high-class Prix de Diane winner Harbour:
poor maiden: left R. White after sixth start: may prove best short of 11f: acts on fibresand
and good to firm ground. *T. J. Naughton*

LITTLETON ARWEN (USA)   2 b.f. (Jan 30) Bahri (USA) 125 – Jathibiyah (USA)   **94 p**
89 (Nureyev (USA) 131) [2002 7g³ p7g* Oct 31] 250,000 francs Y: rangy, attractive filly:
has scope: ninth foal: half-sister to 3 winners, including fairly useful 7f (including at 2
yrs) winner Ashjar (by Kris): dam, 2-y-o 7f winner who stayed 1¼m, closely related to
Irish 1000 Guineas winner Ensconse: odds on, confirmed promise when winning 13-
runner maiden at Lingfield by 3½ lengths from Heidelburg, taking good hold and merely
shaken up to quicken clear: should stay 1m: drifted right/flashed tail on debut: useful
performer in the making. *T. G. Mills*

LITTLETON BOREAS (USA)   3 b. or br.c. Foxhound (USA) 103 – Susita Song   –
(USA) (Seattle Song (USA) 130) [2002 52: p8g 8.2f 7g Aug 7] leggy colt: modest maiden
at 2 yrs: dead. *R. J. White*

LITTLETON BOUNTY (IRE)   3 b.g. Bahamian Bounty 116 – Take Heart 84   **74**
(Electric 126) [2002 8.1f² 8.1d⁴ 9.2g a10f Dec 27] 8,500Y, 22,000 2-y-o: well-made,
quite attractive gelding: fifth living foal: half-brother to 3 winners, including useful 1¼m
winner Lonely Heart (by Midyan): dam 7f and 1¼m winner: fair form when in frame in
maiden at Warwick and minor event at Sandown: left R. White and off 7 months before
final start. *P. L. Rudkin, UAE*

LITTLETON GILDOR   2 b.g. (Mar 12) Mind Games 121 – Millie's Lady (IRE)   **55**
(Common Grounds 118) [2002 5g 6g 5m Aug 21] 8,500Y: fifth living foal: brother to
4-y-o Milly's Lass: dam unraced: modest form at best in maidens: likely to prove best at
5f/6f: sent to UAE. *R. J. White*

LITTLETON TZAR (IRE)   3 b.g. Inzar (USA) 112 – Solo Symphony (IRE) 67   **74**
(Fayruz 116) [2002 74: 6.1m 6g⁵ a6f³ a8f Dec 27] small gelding: fair maiden: left
R. White after second outing: should stay 7f: acts on fibresand/dirt, firm and soft going.
P. L. Rudkin, UAE

LITTLETON ZEPHIR (USA)   3 b.f. Sandpit (BRZ) 129 – Miss Gorgeous (IRE) 76   **59**
(Damister (USA) 123) [2002 10.3s⁴ 8.1f 8.3m 10g* 10m f12g f8.5g² f8.5g⁶ Dec 20]
$4,500Y: sturdy filly: fourth foal: dam 6f (at 2 yrs)/7f winner: modest handicapper: won
at Brighton in August: left R. White after fifth start: stays 1¼m: acts on fibresand.
T. J. Naughton

LITTLETON ZEUS (IRE)   3 ch.g. Woodborough (USA) 112 – La Fandango (IRE)   **45**
51 (Taufan (USA) 119) [2002 45: f8.5g⁴ 7m 8.3g⁶ 11.9g May 2] poor maiden: probably
stays 9.4f: acts on fibresand, soft and good to firm going: visored final 2-y-o start: has
looked headstrong. *R. J. White*

LITTLE TUMBLER (IRE)   7 b.m. Cyrano de Bergerac 120 – Glass Minnow (IRE)   **53**
59 (Alzao (USA) 117) [2002 62: 10g 9m 9d⁶ 9m p10g⁵ 10m⁶ 10m 8f 9g p10g Dec 18]
neat mare: modest handicapper: probably best at 9f/1¼m: has form on good to soft
ground, but goes well (all 3 wins) on going firmer than good and acts on polytrack:
sometimes slowly away. *S. Woodman*

LITTLE VENICE (IRE)   2 b.f. (Mar 6) Fumo di Londra (IRE) 108 – Petrine (IRE)   **71**
(Petorius 117) [2002 6m 6g³ 6g 7g³ 6d³ 7d³ Nov 5] IR 6,500Y: half-sister to fairly useful

1999 2-y-o 5f winner Imperialist (by Imperial Falcon) and winners abroad by Simply Great and Kefaah: dam ran 4 times in Ireland: fair maiden: best efforts at Pontefract and Catterick last 2 starts: effective at 6f/7f: yet to race on extremes of going. *C. F. Wall*

LITZINSKY 4 b.g. Muhtarram (USA) 125 – Boulevard Girl 80 (Nicholas Bill 125) **76** [2002 81: 18s⁴ 16.1m⁴ 16.2s Jun 6] rather leggy, lengthy gelding: fair handicapper: stays 2¼m well: has form on good to firm going, very best efforts on soft. *C. B. B. Booth*

LIVELY FELIX 5 b.g. Presidium 124 – Full of Life 85 (Wolverlife 115) [2002 –: **–** 10.3g f5g 8.2m 6.1g⁵ Jul 5] maiden, no longer of much account. *W. Clay*

LIVELY LADY 6 b.m. Beveled (USA) – In The Papers 87 (Aragon 118) [2002 84, **67 §** a–: 5s⁴ 6g 5d 5d 5g Oct 28] sturdy mare: poor mover: fair nowadays: effective at 5f/6f: **a– §** acts on good to firm and heavy going, probably on fibresand: usually visored/blinkered: sometimes slowly away: usually held up: tends to wander: unreliable. *J. R. Jenkins*

LIVE THE DREAM 4 b.f. Exit To Nowhere (USA) 122 – Inveraven 53 (Alias Smith **47 +** (USA)) [2002 57: 16f⁴ Sep 26] angular filly: poor form only outing on Flat in 2002: better at 1¾m/2m than shorter: acts on firm going: fairly useful hurdler. *M. C. Pipe*

LIVING DAYLIGHTS (IRE) 3 b.f. Night Shift (USA) – Shesadelight 67 (Shirley **56** Heights 130) [2002 8m 9.9m⁴ 10m 12d Nov 1] 45,000Y: fifth foal: half-sister to several winners, including 11.7f winner Tikopia (by Saddlers' Hall) and untrustworthy 1¼m/ 1¾m winner Total Delight (by Mtoto), both fairly useful: dam, maiden who stayed 2m, sister to very smart middle-distance performer Infamy from family of In The Wings and High-Rise: modest maiden: should be suited by 1½m+. *J. L. Dunlop*

LIVIUS (IRE) 8 b.g. Alzao (USA) 117 – Marie de Beaujeu (FR) 108 (Kenmare (FR) **78 d** 125) [2002 89: p12g p12g p12g² 12m 12.3f 12m 11.5m 12s 12m 11.9d⁵ 11.5f⁶ 14.8m⁴ p12g 10.9m f12g³ f8.5g³ f9.4s⁶ p10g Dec 30] big gelding: one-time fairly useful per- former, on downgrade in 2002: stays 1½m: acts on all-weather, firm and soft ground: tried blinkered/visored/tongue tied: often sweats: usually held up: often finds little: not one to trust. *C. A. Dwyer*

LIVY (IRE) 2 ch.g. (Apr 19) Titus Livius (FR) 115 – Shalerina (USA) (Shalford (IRE) **51** 124§) [2002 6d 7g 5g 6d⁶ f5g* f6g* f6f⁵ f5g* p5g⁴ Dec 18] IR 23,000Y: useful-looking **a77** gelding: third foal: half-brother to fairly useful Irish 2000 2-y-o 7f winner Calumet Spice (by Mujadil): dam, well beaten only 2 starts (at 2 yrs), granddaughter of US Grade 1 9f winner Sugar And Spice: fair on all-weather, modest on turf: won seller and claimer (for J. Glover) at Wolverhampton in October and nursery (by 7 lengths from Tirailleur) in November: left P. D. Evans before final outing: best at 5f: acts on all-weather, raced only on good/good to soft going on turf: tried blinkered/tongue tied: races prominently. *M. Salaman*

LIZZIE DRIPIN 2 b.f. (Apr 26) Overbury (IRE) 116 – Edithmead (IRE) 73 (Shardari **–** 134) [2002 10g 8s Oct 25] leggy filly: third living foal: dam, lightly-raced maiden, should have been suited by 1¾m+ (also maiden over hurdles): no sign of ability. *C. Smith*

LLOYD 3 b.g. Glory of Dancer 121 – Broughtons Bird (Exhibitioner 111) [2002 **57 §** 77§: 5m⁶ f6g⁴ f5g⁵ f6g⁵ f6g Sep 30] strong gelding: modest maiden: stays 6f: acts on fibresand: visored third start: usually tongue tied (not final outing): has carried head high, and difficult ride: not to be trusted: joined J. Plasschaert in Belgium. *J. O'Reilly*

LOBATICA (GER) 3 ch.f. Acatenango (GER) 127 – Lebrija (GER) (Windwurf **102** (GER)) [2002 10m* 10g* 12f⁴ 11g³ 11m² 14.6m⁶ 10g Oct 27] smallish filly: first foal: dam unraced: useful performer: won maiden and minor event at Milan in May: credit- able efforts when 1¼ lengths fourth to Kardthea in Premio Mario Incisa there next time and neck second to Luttje Lage in listed race at Merano fifth start: stays 1½m (well below form in Park Hill Stakes at Doncaster penultimate outing): acts on firm going. *Frau M. Rotering, Germany*

LOBLITE LEADER (IRE) 5 b.g. Tirol 127 – Cyrano Beauty (IRE) (Cyrano de **–** Bergerac 120) [2002 54: 13s 14.1d 12s f16g Nov 20] good-topped gelding: handicapper: well held in 2002. *G. A. Swinbank*

LOBOS (SWI) 3 ch.g. Rainbow Quest (USA) 134 – Lady of Silver (IRE) (Caerleon **74** (USA) 132) [2002 8m⁴ 10m 8m³ 8.5m³ 8.2m p10g p8g p7g² Dec 28] 100,000Y: sparely-made gelding: second foal: half-brother to French 1m (including at 2 yrs) and 10.5f winner Lady Dadar (by Dadarissime): dam, French 2-y-o 7f winner, half-sister to smart French 1984 staying 2-y-o Hello Bill: fair maiden: left E. Dunlop 10,000 gns after sixth start: effective at 7f and should stay 1¼m+: acts on polytrack, raced only on good to firm going on turf: reportedly lame second outing. *S. Dow*

LOCHARIA 3 b.f. Wolfhound (USA) 126 – Lochbelle 70 (Robellino (USA) 127) **86**
[2002 91: 5m 5.2d⁴ 5g 6m⁵ 6f⁶ Aug 18] sturdy filly: fairly useful performer: seemingly
best effort in 2002 when fifth to Palace Affair in listed race at York penultimate start:
stays 6f: acts on good to firm and good to soft going: sold 15,000 gns in December.
Mrs L. Stubbs

LOCH INCH 5 ch.g. Inchinor 119 – Carrie Kool 69 (Prince Sabo 123) [2002 63: 5f f5f **–**
Nov 29] smallish gelding: handicapper: well held both runs in 2002: visored once, often
blinkered. *J. M. Bradley*

LOCH LAIRD 7 b.g. Beveled (USA) – Daisy Loch (Lochnager 132) [2002 69: p6g **62**
7g³ 7d* 6d⁵ 7.1s² 6g² 7m 6m 7m 7.1g Sep 12] lengthy gelding: modest handicapper: won
at Brighton in May: best at 6f/7f: acts on firm and soft ground, probably on polytrack:
tried visored/blinkered (not in 2002): has carried head awkwardly. *M. Madgwick*

LOCH MAREE 3 b.f. Primo Dominie 121 – Aurora Bay (IRE) (Night Shift (USA)) **53**
[2002 65d: f7g 7.1m 6g 5g³ 6d 5s 5v f6g Dec 27] angular, quite good-topped filly: modest
maiden: well held last 4 starts: barely stays 6f: best efforts on good ground: usually
blinkered in 2002. *M. W. Easterby*

LOCHRIDGE 3 ch.f. Indian Ridge 123 – Lochsong 129 (Song 132) [2002 87p: 8d⁶ **96 p**
7m* 6d 7m 6g³ 6f⁶ Oct 1] workmanlike, rather unfurnished filly: useful performer: won
maiden at Salisbury (edged left) in June and handicap at Newmarket (beat Birjand by ½
length) in October: best form at 6f: acts on firm going: should progress further, and type
to win a good handicap. *I. A. Balding*

LOCK INN 3 b.g. Dolphin Street (FR) 125 – Highest Bid (FR) (Highest Honor (FR) **56**
124) [2002 –: p12g⁴ f11g² f12g⁶ f12g 11.6m p13g p12g f16g⁶ Dec 17] modest maiden:
below form after second start, leaving Miss D. McHale after fifth one: barely stays easy
1½m: acts on all-weather: tried blinkered. *Miss Z. C. Davison*

LOCKSTOCK (IRE) 4 b.g. Inchinor 119 – Risalah (Marju (IRE) 127) [2002 67: 8g³ **81**
8g³ 8.1m² 7.1v* 8.1m³ 7g² 7.1g* f7f³ 7.1m 8m Sep 29] quite good-topped gelding: **a72**
fairly useful handicapper on turf, fair on all-weather: won at Chepstow in June and July:
effective at 7f to 9.4f: acts on heavy ground, good to firm and fibresand: blinkered after
second start: has been slowly away. *M. S. Saunders*

LOCOMBE HILL (IRE) 6 b.g. Barathea (IRE) 127 – Roberts Pride 62 (Roberto **83**
(USA) 131) [2002 64: 7v² 8.3s³ 7g* 9.9m 8.5d 7g* 8m⁵ 8d* 8s* 7.6f 7.9m 9.1g⁶ 8.9f 7v
Nov 9] very big, rather dipped-backed gelding: fairly useful handicapper: won at Thirsk
(2), Doncaster and Redcar between June/August: best at 7f/1m: acts on good to firm and
heavy going: takes good hold: tended to race up with pace second half of year. *D. Nicholls*

LOCOMOTIVE 3 b.g. Bin Ajwaad (IRE) 119 – Saluti Tutti 77 (Trojan Fen 118) **68**
[2002 65p: 10g 9.2g 11.8m 8.1d² f8s Sep 17] quite good-topped gelding: poor mover: fair
maiden: stays 1m: acts on good to soft going: sent to Saudi Arabia. *C. F. Wall*

LODESTONE (IRE) 4 b.g. Distant Relative 128 – Magnetic Point (USA) 60 (Bering **–**
136) [2002 –: f5g⁴ Apr 26] little form. *J. M. Bradley*

LODGE KEEPER 2 ch.c. (Feb 7) Grand Lodge (USA) 125 – Aunt Tate (Tate Gallery **92**
(USA) 117) [2002 6g⁵ 7g³ 7m* 8m³ 8m⁴ 8f² Sep 17] 26,000Y: well-made colt: fourth
foal: half-brother to 3-y-o Border Artist and French 12.5f winner Devious Aunty (by Dr
Devious): dam twice-raced daughter of smart French 1¼m winner Aunty: fairly useful
performer: won maiden at Catterick in August: good second to Choir Master in nursery at
Salisbury: will probably stay 1¼m: raced only on good going or firmer: consistent: sold
96,000 gns, sent to Bahrain. *E. A. L. Dunlop*

LODGER (FR) 2 ch.c. (Mar 18) Grand Lodge (USA) 125 – Light River (USA) (Irish **68 p**
River (FR) 131) [2002 8g Oct 18] 210,000Y: first foal: dam unraced granddaughter of
Prix Fille de l'Air winner Liastra: 20/1, never-dangerous tenth of 16 to Persian Majesty in
maiden at Newmarket: should do better. *J. Noseda*

LOGIQUE (IRE) 3 b.c. Revoque (IRE) 122 – Logstown (IRE) 98 (Keen 116) [2002 **61**
10g 10.5d 12s 14.1m⁴ 14.1g³ 14.1m⁶ 12.6m⁵ 11.9m³ Oct 3] 15,000Y: tall colt: second
foal: dam, Irish 9f/11f winner, also successful over hurdles: modest maiden handicapper:
stays 1½m: acts on good to firm going: wandered/carried head awkwardly final start.
C. F. Wall

LOGISTICAL 2 b.c. (Mar 17) Grand Lodge (USA) 125 – Magic Milly 60 (Simply **73**
Great (FR) 122) [2002 5s⁴ 5m² 5.1g* 6m⁶ 6g 7d⁶ 7g⁶ 8f⁶ 7g³ Oct 24] 22,000Y: close-
coupled colt: half-brother to several winners, including 9-y-o Westcourt Magic and fairly
useful 5f (at 2 yrs) to 1½m winner Batswing (by Batshoof): dam 2-y-o 1m winner: fair

performer: won maiden at Bath in May: good third in nursery at Brighton: stays 7f: acts on good to firm ground, probably on soft: sold 27,000 gns. *W. R. Muir*

LOGO'S DREAM 3 b.g. Mind Games 121 – Yukosan 69 (Absalom 128) [2002 53: – 5.1d f8.5s 7d Oct 15] close-coupled gelding: modest maiden: left B. McMahon after reappearance: best form at 5f. *J. White*

LOGSDAIL 2 b.g. (May 2) Polish Precedent (USA) 131 – Logic 94 (Slip Anchor 136) **88** [2002 5m⁵ 5.9d* 6m⁶ 7m* 8m Sep 12] big, good-topped gelding: has plenty of scope: second foal: dam, maiden ran only at 2 yrs (bred to stay at least 1¼m), half-sister to useful 1½m winner Port Helene, herself dam of smart French middle-distance stayer Helen of Spain: fairly useful performer: won maiden at Carlisle in June and nursery at York (best effort, beat New Wish a length) in August: should stay at least 1m: acts on good to firm and good to soft going: held up. *Mrs J. R. Ramsden*

L'OISEAU D'ARGENT (USA) 3 ch.g. Silver Hawk (USA) 123 – Isla Del Rey **107** (USA) 103 (Nureyev (USA) 131) [2002 8m* 10.4f² 8m* 8m³ 7m³ Aug 22] big, strong, lengthy gelding: second foal: dam, 6f (in UAE)/7f (including in Ireland at 2 yrs) winner: useful form: won maiden at Kempton in May and minor event at Doncaster (rallied to beat Love Regardless by head) in July: creditable efforts in listed events other starts, 5 lengths third to Suggestive at York final one (gelded after): free-going sort, will prove best up to 1m: raced only on good to firm/firm going. *Sir Michael Stoute*

LOLANITA 4 b.f. Anita's Prince 126 – Jimlil 99 (Nicholas Bill 125) [2002 f12g f8.5g³ **42** f7g Dec 2] third foal: sister to 1m seller winner Lilanita and half-sister to 5-y-o Lilardo: dam 6f (at 2 yrs) and 1m winner: poor form in claimer (carried head high)/sellers at Wolverhampton. *B. Palling*

LONDOLOZI LAD (IRE) 3 b.g. Ali-Royal (IRE) 127 – Ashdown (Pharly (FR) **40** 130) [2002 38: p8g* f8.5g* f8g f12g 9.2g⁶ 8.5m 8m 10m f16g Dec 17] small gelding: **a49** poor handicapper: won at Lingfield and Wolverhampton in January: below form after: not sure to stay beyond 8.5f: acts on all-weather. *P. C. Haslam*

LONDON BY NIGHT (USA) 2 br.g. (Apr 13) Mt Livermore (USA) – Sheena's Gold – (USA) (Fast Gold (USA)) [2002 7f 8f⁴ 8s Oct 15] IR 55,000Y: good-topped gelding: sixth foal: closely related to smart 1998 US Grade 1 2-y-o 8.5f winner The Groom Is Red (by Runaway Groom) and half-brother to a winner there by Known Fact: dam, 8.5f winner in USA, from family of Blushing Groom: well held in maidens: gelded subsequently. *T. G. Mills*

LONDONER (USA) 4 ch.g. Sky Classic (CAN) – Love And Affection (USA) **101** (Exclusive Era (USA)) [2002 104: 9.9m 11m⁶ 7m 7m⁴ 7.9f* p10g p7g Dec 28] tall, rather unfurnished gelding: useful handicapper: won at York in October by head from Nashaab: effective at 7f, barely at 1½m: yet to race on soft/heavy going, acts on any other turf (well held on polytrack last 2 outings). *S. Dow*

LONDON MIXTURE 2 b.g. (Apr 29) Mind Games 121 – Surrealist (ITY) (Night – Shift (USA)) [2002 6d Oct 21] 10,000Y: close-coupled gelding: third foal: closely related to 3-y-o Mitsuki: dam unraced half-sister to smart Italian 5f to 1m winner Arranvanna: 25/1 and backward, tailed off in maiden at Pontefract. *J. D. Bethell*

LONDONNETDOTCOM (IRE) 2 ch.f. (Apr 24) Night Shift (USA) – Hopeful Sign **101** (Warning 136) [2002 7d* 7g² 8m⁶ Sep 12] 42,000F, 190,000Y: good-topped filly: has scope: second foal: dam, ran once, closely related to smart 7f/1m winner Greensmith and half-sister to Queen's Vase winner Infrasonic and to dam of St Leger winner Toulon: useful form: won maiden at Kempton in July: best effort when 4 lengths second to Six Perfections in Prix du Calvados at Deauville: found little when only sixth in May Hill Stakes at Doncaster: should stay 1m. *M. R. Channon*

LONE CHIEF (USA) 3 b.g. Cozzene (USA) – Alcando 113 (Alzao (USA) 117) [2002 – 89: 7.5m Jul 16] neat gelding: fairly useful at 2 yrs: well held in claimer only outing in 2002: stayed 7f: raced only on going firmer than good: had run well when sweating/edgy: dead. *T. D. Barron*

LONE PIPER 7 b.g. Warning 136 – Shamisen 86 (Diesis 133) [2002 71: f6g f5g⁶ 5m **60** 5m 6f⁵ 5g 5m³ 5m 5m 5m⁶ 5g 5m 5m f5g⁵ Oct 17] small, close-coupled gelding: poor mover: modest handicapper: successful at 7f, raced mainly at 5f/6f nowadays: acts on fibresand, firm and soft going: tried visored/tongue tied: has found little: held up: sold 2,100 gns. *Jedd O'Keeffe*

LONER 4 b.g. Magic Ring (IRE) 115 – Jolis Absent 57 (Primo Dominie 121) [2002 –: **58** p7g p7g⁶ 7.5m² f7g f8.5s⁴ p7g Dec 30] strong gelding: modest handicapper, lightly raced **a50**

nowadays: stays 7.5f: acts on soft and good to firm going, probably on all-weather: blinkered (found little) second start. *M. Wigham*

LONG GOODBYE (IRE)   3 ch.c. Dr Devious (IRE) 127 – Lady Nessa (USA) (Al   **102** Nasr (FR) 126) [2002 99p: 12m 11.5g² 12m 10d³ 10d 10d* Dec 1] quite good-topped colt: useful performer: placed in Derby Trial at Lingfield (13 lengths second to Bandari, finished strongly under hands and heels) in May and minor event at Rome (first start since leaving P. Cole) in September: won minor event at Naples in December: saddle slipped (had jinked left leaving stall) on reappearance, and stiff tasks in Derby Italiano and Premio Roma (both at Rome) other 2 outings: should be suited by 1½m: acts on good to soft going. *L. Camici, Italy*

LONGING LOOK   2 b.f. (Mar 12) Whittingham (IRE) 104 – Admire 77 (Last Tycoon   **42** 131) [2002 f8s f7g f7g⁶ Nov 25] 7,500Y: first foal: dam, 2-y-o 1m winner, became temperamental: poor maiden: sixth in seller at Southwell: should stay 1m. *J. G. Portman*

LONGMEADOWS BOY (IRE)   2 b.g. (Apr 29) Victory Note (USA) 120 – Karoi   **58** (IRE) (Kafu 120) [2002 5.9d⁶ 6m 7g 7m 7g⁵ f8.5g⁶ f8.5f Nov 29] IR 17,000F, IR 7,000Y, 10,000 2-y-o: half-brother to 3 winners, including 3-y-o Jakeal: dam Irish 9f/9.5f winner: modest maiden: stays 7f: unraced on extremes of going, some promise on fibresand. *A. Berry*

LONG TALL SALLY (IRE)   3 b.f. Danehill Dancer (IRE) 117 – Miss Galwegian   **71** (Sandford Lad 133) [2002 69: p6g p6g 5.1m⁴ 6m⁴ 6m* 6g⁴ 7f p6g⁴ 6d² 6m⁵ 6g⁵ 6m³ p5g² Dec 21] lengthy, unfurnished filly: fair performer: won maiden at Catterick in May: effective at 5f, barely stays 7f: acts on polytrack, firm and good to soft ground: consistent. *D. W. P. Arbuthnot*

LONG WEEKEND (IRE)   4 b.c. Flying Spur (AUS) – Friday Night (USA) (Trem-   **52** polino (USA) 135) [2002 45: f6s⁵ f7s⁵ f6g⁶ f6g² f7g⁴ f7g⁶ f6g³ f6g⁵ p6g⁶ 5s⁴ 6s⁶ 6m⁴ 6d   **a56** 6g f6g f6g p6g Dec 30] sturdy, angular colt: modest maiden: best form at 6f: acts on good to firm ground and fibresand: usually blinkered/visored. *D. Shaw*

LONGWOOD SUNSHINE   3 b.g. Komaite (USA) – Brown Velvet 68 (Mansingh   **–** (USA) 120) [2002 f8.5g Jun 14] brother to 6-y-o Sunley Sense, closely related to 4-y-o Sunley Scent, and half-brother to several winners up to 1m: dam (possibly short runner) half-sister to Sonic Lady: well held in maiden at Wolverhampton. *S. Kirk*

LOOKALIKE   3 b.f. Rainbow Quest (USA) 134 – Balalaika 108 (Sadler's Wells (USA)   **96** 132) [2002 9.9m² 10.2s³ 10m* 10.2g 8d* 8s Nov 2] quite good-topped filly: first foal: dam, 9f winner who stayed 1½m, sister to high-class 1¼m performer Stagecraft from family of Opera House and Kayf Tara: useful performer: won maiden at Kempton in June and minor event at Leicester (beat Mahsusie by ½ length) in October: well-held last in listed races fourth and final starts: effective at testing 1m, will stay 1½m: acts on soft and good to firm going. *L. M. Cumani*

LOOK AND LEARN (FR)   7 ch.g. Rock Hopper 124 – Lailati (USA) 66 (Mr Pros-   **–** pector (USA)) [2002 –: f14s Sep 5] fairly useful winner in France in 1998: no show 3 starts since. *A. G. Newcombe*

LOOK AWAY NOW   3 ch.g. Timeless Times (USA) 99 – Petite Elite 47 (Anfield   **62** 117) [2002 66+: 6m 6g 6.1f⁶ p7g 7g 7m 7m⁶ 8m Sep 19] strong gelding: modest maiden: stays 7f: raced only on good going or firmer on turf, showed promise on fibresand: tried blinkered/tongue tied: none too consistent. *W. A. O'Gorman*

LOOK EAST   3 b.g. Ezzoud (IRE) 126 – College Night (IRE) 54 (Night Shift (USA))   **–** [2002 8m 10g 8m f12g 7m 11.5m f12g 11.5s Oct 22] lengthy gelding: first foal: dam, 6f winner, half-sister to dam of Prix Vermeille winner and Arc runner-up Leggera: little form: tried visored. *Mrs C. A. Dunnett*

LOOK FIRST (IRE)   4 b.g. Namaqualand (USA) – Be Prepared (IRE) (Be My Guest   **89** (USA) 126) [2002 71: p12g² f11g p12g f12g p10g f12g² 11.6d³ 11.1g⁵ f12g 10g 16m²   16.4d* 16f⁴ 15.4m* 16.2m³ 16f* 16m⁵ 17.2f² p16g³ Oct 16] leggy gelding: fairly useful handicapper: left A. Jarvis after fifth start: won at Folkestone (2) in July and Kempton in September: stays 17f: acts on all-weather, firm and soft going: tried visored: held up: used to look none too keen. *I. A. Wood*

LOOK HERE NOW   5 gr.g. Ardkinglass 114 – Where's Carol 67 (Anfield 117) [2002   **79** 71: f6g 7m 6m f6g* f6g 7g⁶ 6s* f6s* 7g² f6g 7v Nov 9] workmanlike gelding: fair performer: won minor events at Southwell (2) and handicap at Ayr between June and September: stays 7f: acts on fibresand, has form on good to firm ground, but goes well on softer than good: has looked none too keen in past. *B. A. McMahon*

LOOK HERE'S CAROL (IRE)   2 ch.f. (Mar 14) Safawan 118 – Where's Carol 67   **71** (Anfield 117) [2002 5.1f 6f² 7m² Oct 5] leggy filly: third living foal: half-sister to 5-y-o Look Here Now and 6-y-o Now Look Here: dam 2-y-o 6f winner: fair form when runner-up in maidens at Pontefract and Redcar: stays 7f: raced only on ground firmer than good. *B. A. McMahon*

LOOKING DEADLY   8 b.m. Neltino 97 – Princess Constanza (Relkino 131) [2002   **–** 10.9g Jul 22] poor hurdler: well held in seller at Ayr. *F. P. Murtagh*

LOOKING DOWN   2 ch.f. (Feb 26) Compton Place 125 – High Stepping (IRE)   **85** (Taufan (USA) 119) [2002 6.1g⁵ 6d⁴ 7.1f² 6m² 7m* 7m 6.5g 6s⁴ p7g² p8g² Nov 19] 3,500Y: lengthy filly: fourth foal: half-sister to 5-y-o Bint Habibi: dam unraced: fairly useful performer: won nursery at Goodwood in August: good second in nurseries at Lingfield last 2 starts: stays easy 1m: acts on polytrack and firm going, probably on soft. *R. Hannon*

LOOKING FOR LOVE (IRE)   4 b.f. Tagula (IRE) 116 – Mousseux (IRE) (Jareer   **78** (USA) 115) [2002 81: 8s 7m f7g⁵ 8d 8.3d⁵ 7d² 7.1m³ 7.1v³ 7m³ 7f² 7m³ 7m² 7s Nov 2] leggy filly: fair handicapper: has form at 1¼m, but races mainly around 7f: acts on any turf going: often races prominently: reliable. *J. G. Portman*

LOOP THE LOUP   6 b.g. Petit Loup (USA) 123 – Mithi Al Gamar (USA) 68 (Blush-   **87** ing Groom (FR) 131) [2002 91: 14.4f 16m 13.9f 20m 14.6m* 14.1f³ 13.9f 14.6s Oct 25] smallish, workmanlike gelding: fairly useful handicapper: won at Doncaster in June: should stay at least 2m: acts on firm and soft going: effective blinkered or not: ran in snatches penultimate start: usually held up. *Mrs M. Reveley*

LOOSE CHIPPINS (IRE)   4 b.f. Bigstone (IRE) 126 – Fortune Teller (Troy 137)   **53** [2002 –: 10s⁶ p12g 12m⁵ 11.9m Oct 3] tall, rangy filly: modest maiden handicapper: barely stays 1½m: has started slowly. *G. L. Moore*

LORD ADVOCATE   14 br.g. Law Society (USA) 130 – Kereolle (Riverman (USA)   **–** 131) [2002 –: 13s 13s 10.9g⁵ 13m⁶ Sep 30] of no account nowadays. *D. A. Nolan*

LORD ASHMORE   3 ch. or gr.g. Greensmith 121 – Flair Lady 55 (Chilibang 120)   **–** [2002 58: 5.1d 6m 8.1d 5.1f Jul 25] modest maiden: no form in 2002: tried visored. *W. G. M. Turner*

LORD CHAMBERLAIN   9 b.g. Be My Chief (USA) 122 – Metaphysique (FR) (Law   **51** Society (USA) 130) [2002 –: 10.3s 8v 11.9f 10m 11.9g 10d⁵ 9s⁴ 8.3v² 8f⁸ 9.2s⁵ 10m 9.7m 8.1g 10m Aug 28] big gelding: modest handicapper: won amateur maiden event at Redcar in June: best form at 1m/1¼m: acts on any going: usually blinkered: very slowly away fifth start: none too consistent. *J. M. Bradley*

LORD CONYERS (IRE)   3 b.f. Inzar (USA) 112 – Primelta 55 (Primo Dominie   **46** 121) [2002 51: f7s⁶ p6g f6g 5.9d 7f⁴ 7.2d² 7d⁵ 9m 10m⁴ Aug 31] leggy filly: poor maiden: left Miss V. Haigh after third start: stays 1¼m: acts on good to firm going, good to soft and fibresand: tried visored/blinkered. *B. Ellison*

LORD DUNDEE (IRE)   4 ch.c. Polish Precedent (USA) 131 – Easy To Copy (USA)   **93** 108 (Affirmed (USA)) [2002 87: 14s* Jun 7] tall, well-made colt: fairly useful form in 2 maidens, winning at Haydock (visored/shade coltish in paddock) in June by 2 lengths from Keetchy: subsequently underwent minor surgery on knee: had looked a useful prospect. *H. R. A. Cecil*

LORD EUROLINK (IRE)   8 b.g. Danehill (USA) 126 – Lady Eurolink 55 (Kala   **91** Shikari 125) [2002 87: 10m 10g⁶ 12d³ 10g² 11.5m² 11.9m³ 10m⁵ 12.3m 10.1m 12g 10.1s⁵ Oct 22] strong, lengthy gelding: fairly useful handicapper: effective at 1¼m/easy 1½m: acts on fibresand, firm and soft going: usually visored in 2000: tried tongue tied: often held up. *M. H. Tompkins*

LORD FERNANDO   3 ch.g. Forzando 122 – Lady Lacey 66 (Kampala 120) [2002   **60** 65: 8.2d 7m 8.3s² 7.1m⁵ 8g⁴ 8.3g 8.3d 8g Sep 27] smallish, sturdy gelding: modest maiden handicapper: stays 1m: acts on soft and good to firm going: handled bend none too comfortably at Sandown fourth outing: none too consistent. *G. B. Balding*

LORD INVINCIBLE   4 b.g. Dancing Spree (USA) – Lady Broker 54 (Petorius 117)   **–** [2002 45: f6g f9.4g 6m 6d May 10] workmanlike gelding: no longer of any account. *M. Mullineaux*

LORD JIM (IRE)   10 b.g. Kahyasi 130 – Sarah Georgina 79 (Persian Bold 123) [2002   **85** 96+: 8.1m 12d⁴ 20m 16.1g 16.4d⁶ 21g Jul 31] good-bodied gelding: fairly useful handi-capper: effective at 1½m, probably at 2¾m: acts on firm and soft going, probably on fibresand: sometimes blinkered/visored. *G. A. Butler*

LORD KINTYRE 7 b.g. Makbul 104 – Highland Rowena 59 (Royben 125) [2002 **95**
113: 5.2g 5.1f⁴ 5d⁴ 5m 5f 5.2f 5m⁶ 5m Oct 12] good-topped gelding: useful handicapper
nowadays: raced only at 5f/6f: acts on any going: has started slowly/been awkward stall.
B. R. Millman

LORD LAHAR 3 b.g. Fraam 114 – Brigadiers Bird (IRE) (Mujadil (USA) 119) [2002 **–**
7d Jun 11] second foal: brother to useful 6f (at 2 yrs) to 1m winner Lady Lahar: dam
unraced: seventh in maiden at Salisbury, outpaced from halfway. *M. R. Channon*

LORD LIAM (USA) 4 b.g. Foxhound (USA) 103 – Crackling Sike 77 (Salse (USA) **–**
128) [2002 58d, a–: p13g f8.5g Mar 15] maiden: well held in 2002. *T. Keddy*

LORD MELBOURNE (IRE) 3 b.g. Lycius (USA) 124 – Adana (IRE) (Classic **73**
Music (USA)) [2002 52: f7g f7g* p7g* f8.5g⁶ 7m* 7.6f⁵ 7.1m f7g⁵ 7f f7f⁵ 7m 7d Sep
11] sturdy gelding: fair handicapper: won at Wolverhampton, Lingfield and Catterick
between February/April: stays 7.6f: acts on firm ground and all-weather: blinkered penultimate start: sometimes takes good hold: tends to carry head high: has flicked tail under
pressure: sold 8,200 gns. *J. A. Osborne*

LORD MERLIN (IRE) 3 b.g. Turtle Island (IRE) 123 – My-O-My (IRE) 105 (Waajib **–**
121) [2002 96: 7m 6g 6v⁶ 7s Nov 2] strong gelding: useful at 2 yrs: below form in 2002,
leaving W. Musson after second start. *J. G. Given*

LORD MISTRAL 3 b.g. Makbul 104 – South Wind 62 (Tina's Pet 121) [2002 f8.5g **–**
Apr 29] 3,200Y, 7,000 2-y-o: first foal: dam, maiden who stayed 1½m, out of half-sister
to Yorkshire Oaks winners Sally Brown and Untold: slowly away and never dangerous in
maiden at Wolverhampton. *B. R. Millman*

LORDOFENCHANTMENT (IRE) 5 ch.g. Soviet Lad (USA) – Sauvignon (IRE) **61 §**
63 (Alzao (USA) 117) [2002 63: 7f 6f 7.5g 7.5g² 7g 7g 7g² 7.5d 7m⁶ 7.5m 7.5m 8m 7s
Oct 26] strong gelding: modest handicapper: stays 7.5f: acts on heavy and good to firm
going: sometimes visored earlier in career: tried tongue tied: untrustworthy. *Don Enrico
Incisa*

LORD OF LOVE 7 b.g. Noble Patriarch 115 – Gymcrak Lovebird 84 (Taufan (USA) **–**
119) [2002 –: 12.1g Aug 8] of little account nowadays. *D. Burchell*

LORD OF METHLEY 3 gr.g. Zilzal (USA) 137 – Paradise Waters 73 (Celestial **66**
Storm (USA) 132) [2002 70: 10d 10.3g⁵ 7.9g 10g⁴ a8f Dec 27] leggy, good-topped
gelding: fair maiden handicapper: stays 1¼m: acts on soft ground. *R. M. Whitaker*

LORD OF THE EAST 3 b.g. Emarati (USA) 74 – Fairy Free (Rousillon (USA) 133) **78**
[2002 67: 5.1d⁴ 5d 6d⁶ 6d 6g 6g² 6m* 6m* 6.1m⁶ 7d 6m p6g f6g p7g Dec 30] lengthy,
rather unfurnished gelding: fair performer: won handicap and claimer at Epsom in
August: left B. R. Millman, below form on all-weather last 3 starts (reportedly had
breathing problem on first occasion): effective at 5f/6f: acts on firm and soft ground:
blinkered (raced too freely) once: usually tongue tied: has looked wayward. *P. Howling*

LORD OF THE INN 2 b.g. (Feb 12) Efisio 120 – Tarneem (USA) 87 (Zilzal (USA) **88**
137) [2002 5s 5m 5m 5.1f³ p5g* 5g³ 5d* 5g⁶ 5m⁵ 5m 5f Oct 3] 38,000F, 15,000Y:
lengthy, good-quartered gelding: second foal: half-brother to Italian winner up to 13.5f
Kris's Bank (by Inchinor): dam 1m winner: fairly useful performer: won nurseries at
Lingfield in July and Sandown in August: should stay 6f: acts on polytrack and good to
soft going, probably on firm: sold 20,000 gns, sent to Kuwait. *B. J. Meehan*

LORD PIERCE 4 b.g. Tragic Role (USA) – Mirkan Honey 83 (Ballymore 123) [2002 **–**
94: p12g Jan 5] good-bodied gelding: fairly useful at 3 yrs: well held only start in 2002.
M. Johnston

LORD PROTECTOR (IRE) 4 b.g. Nicolotte 118 – Scared (Royal Academy (USA) **103**
130) [2002 95: f8.5g⁴ 8s 7d 7d² 7s² 7m 7d³ 7.2g⁵ 7d 6g 7g* a6g³ a8g² Dec 15] lengthy **a93**
gelding: useful handicapper: won 30-runner event at Newmarket in October by ½ length
from Millennium Force: several creditable efforts earlier in year (unlucky fourth start),
including third to Mine in Bunbury Cup at Newmarket: sold from D. Arbuthnot 43,000
gns before placed in minor events at Mijas and Dos Hermanas last 2 starts: effective at 7f/
1m, probably at 6f: acts on fibresand/sand, soft and good to firm ground: held up: often
bandaged: sometimes carries head awkwardly. *E. J. Creighton, Spain*

LORD STRADBROKE (USA) 3 b.g. Lear Fan (USA) 130 – Encorenous (USA) **?**
(Diesis 133) [2002 72p: 10m 7.9g⁶ p10g 7d a12g² a10s* a12s² Dec 22] strong, lengthy
gelding: modest performer at best: disappointing for M. Jarvis and sold 3,500 gns after
fourth start: won maiden at Taby in December: stays 1½m: acts on dirt, best turf effort on
soft ground. *M. Kahn, Sweden*

LORETO ROSE 3 b.f. Lahib (USA) 129 – Pinkie Rose (FR) (Kenmare (FR) 125) **71**
[2002 p5g p7g³ p6g⁵ 5g p10g⁵ Jun 9] 18,000Y: sixth foal: half-sister to 1999 2-y-o 6.8f
winner Love Letters (by Pursuit of Love): dam French 1½m winner from very good
French family: fair form: banned for 40 days under non-triers rule second start: gambled
on, best effort when close fifth on handicap debut at Lingfield final outing, dropped right
out and looking to have plenty of running left in her when short of room close home: stays
1¼m: acts on polytrack (inadequate trip only run on turf). *G. A. Butler*

LOST AT SEA (IRE) 4 b.g. Exit To Nowhere (USA) 122 – Night At Sea 107 (Night **59**
Shift (USA)) [2002 77: 8v 10m 7.1m 7g 7m⁶ f7g⁵ 7.9g Jun 27] strong, good-bodied
gelding: modest nowadays: stays 7f: acts on fibresand and firm going, possibly not on
heavy: has been tongue tied: headstrong. *K. R. Burke*

LOST SPIRIT 6 b.g. Strolling Along (USA) – Shoag (USA) (Affirmed (USA)) [2002 **62**
63, a71: p13g⁵ p12g⁵ p12g p12g³ p12g p12g⁵ p13g f12g 12.3g² 11.9g 11.8m 12f* 12g² **a49**
12.6f 11.1g* 11.1d² 12.3g⁴ 11.6g³ 12.1m⁶ 12.1m⁵ Sep 2] strong gelding: modest handicapper: won at Catterick in June and Hamilton (apprentices) in July: stays 13f: acts on
soft going, good to firm and all-weather: blinkered twice at 2 yrs: free-going front runner:
sometimes drops out tamely: claimer ridden. *P. W. Hiatt*

LOTS OF LOVE (USA) 4 b.g. Woodman (USA) 126 – Accountable Lady (USA) **93**
(The Minstrel (CAN) 135) [2002 102: p10g 8f⁶ 8g 7s³ 8s 7v* a7f a10f Dec 27] lengthy **a89**
gelding: unimpressive mover: fairly useful handicapper: well held on dirt at Jebel Ali last 2 starts: effective at 7f/
1m: goes well on soft/heavy going and acts on polytrack: blinkered last 3 outings: has
been slowly away/edged left: tends to carry head awkwardly: usually takes a while to
warm to task. *M. Johnston*

LOTS OF MAGIC 6 b.g. Magic Ring (IRE) 115 – Pounelta 91 (Tachypous 128) **67**
[2002 95: 7g 6d 7m⁶ 8m 7g Oct 14] tall, quite good-topped gelding: fluent mover: has had
wind operation: very smart 3-y-o, just fair nowadays: seems to stay easy 1m: acts on firm
going, probably not on softer than good: tried tongue tied: has been early to post: has
found little. *S. Kirk*

LOTUS EATER 3 gr.f. Linamix (FR) 127 – La Adrada (Arazi (USA) 135) [2002 –: **–**
p7g 8g Jun 16] leggy, quite good-topped filly: well beaten in maidens (looked none too
keen final start). *S. C. Williams*

LOUD AND PROUD 3 b.g. Polish Precedent (USA) 131 – Echo Cove (Slip Anchor **–**
136) [2002 42: 14.1m 10.9g⁵ 9f⁵ 12m Jul 1] sparely-made gelding: poor maiden: tried
blinkered/tongue tied. *R. A. Fahey*

LOUGH BOW (IRE) 4 b.g. Nicolotte 118 – Gale Force Seven (Strong Gale 116) **58**
[2002 –: 10.5s 8f 9.9g* 10.5g⁴ 12.3s² 12m² 12.3m 12s* Nov 6] quite good-topped
gelding: modest handicapper: won at Beverley in July and Musselburgh in November:
stays 1½m: acts on soft and good to firm going: visored/blinkered after second start.
M. W. Easterby

LOUGHLORIEN (IRE) 3 b.g. Lake Coniston (IRE) 131 – Fey Lady (IRE) (Fairy **70**
King (USA)) [2002 69§: 5d* 5m⁴ 6g⁶ 5s³ 6g* 5g² 5g² 5m 5f⁵ 5g 6d 5d Oct 14] close-
coupled, good-topped gelding: fair performer: won minor event in March and handicap
in May, both at Catterick: effective at 5f/6f: acts on any going: often blinkered/visored at
2 yrs: sometimes slowly away/hangs. *K. A. Ryan*

LOUIS GEORGIO 3 b.c. Royal Applause 124 – Swellegant 84 (Midyan (USA) 124) **71**
[2002 61: p5g* p6g 5.3d 5.3m² 5.3m³ 6m 6f a6g Dec 1] smallish, quite attractive colt: fair
performer: won maiden at Lingfield in January: sold from J. Noseda 8,500 gns before
final start: should stay 6f: acts on polytrack and good to firm ground: got very worked up
in stall final 2-y-o start. *J. H. Brown, Spain*

LOUIS NAPOLEON 2 b.c. (Feb 20) Indian Ridge 123 – Napoleon's Sister (IRE) **84 p**
101 (Alzao (USA) 117) [2002 p7g 8s* Nov 6] first foal: dam, 1¼m winner, half-sister to
Derby winner Oath and high-class performer up to 10.5f Pelder: better effort in maidens
(fairly useful form) when winning at Musselburgh by 1¼ lengths from Beau Artiste:
likely to stay at least 1¼m: should continue to improve. *G. A. Butler*

LOUISVILLE (IRE) 3 b.c. Grand Lodge (USA) 125 – Megastart (USA) (Private **97**
Account (USA)) [2002 8s* 12d Jun 8] close-coupled, good-topped colt: sixth foal: half-
brother to 1m/9f winner Megascene (by Scenic) and 9.5f/1¼m winner Abikan (by Erins
Isle), both useful in Ireland: dam Irish maiden from family of Secretariat: won maiden at
the Curragh in May by 3½ lengths from Samer: wearing crossed noseband, well-beaten

ninth of 12 in Derby at Epsom only start after: should stay at least 1¼m: joined N. Meade, Ireland. *A. P. O'Brien, Ireland*

LOUP CERVIER (IRE) 5 b.g. Wolfhound (USA) 126 – Luth d'Or (FR) (Noir Et Or 125) [2002 –: 12.1g 11.6d Aug 5] quite good-topped gelding: maiden, no longer of much account. *S. Dow* —

LOU'S WISH 5 b.g. Thatching 131 – Shamaka 53 (Kris 135) [2002 41, a49: f12s f9.4g⁶ f14.8g Sep 21] of little account nowadays. *M. J. Polglase*

LOUVOLITE (IRE) 3 b.f. Fayruz 116 – Non Dimenticar Me (IRE) 63 (Don't Forget Me 127) [2002 81: 5g Jun 9] strong, well-made filly: fairly useful performer, lightly raced: well held only 3-y-o start: raced only at 5f on good/good to firm ground: hung left second 2-y-o outing. *J. A. Glover* —

LOVE APPEAL (IRE) 3 ch.f. Singspiel (IRE) 133 – Royale (IRE) 102 (Royal Academy (USA) 130) [2002 9.9m⁵ 10.2s⁴ 10.2d* Jul 4] 45,000Y: first foal: dam, Irish 7f/1m winner, out of unraced half-sister to top-class sprinter Double Form: fairly useful form in maidens, winning at Chepstow by 1¼ lengths from Daliyana: stays 1¼m: sent to race in USA: looks capable of better still. *J. L. Dunlop* — **82 p**

LOVE BITTEN (IRE) 5 b.g. Darshaan 133 – Kentmere (FR) (Galetto (FR) 118) [2002 p12g 11.6d¹ 13.3s 12m* 12d Jul 4] smallish, leggy gelding: modest handicapper: won at Newmarket in June: stays 1¾m: best on good ground or firmer: tends to wander. *J. Akehurst* — **62**

LOVE EVERLASTING 4 b.f. Pursuit of Love 124 – In Perpetuity 90 (Great Nephew 126) [2002 112: 13.3m⁶ 12d⁵ 12m* 11.9m 14.6m 12g* 12m* Oct 12] tall, lengthy filly: smart performer: won listed races at Newbury (for second successive year, by length from Salim Toto) in August and Ascot (beat Treble Heights by ¾ length) in September and Princess Royal Willmott Dixon Stakes at Ascot (4 ran, beat Bright And Clear by 1¼ lengths) in October: below form in Yorkshire Oaks at York and Park Hill Stakes at Doncaster in between: better around 1½m than shorter, and should stay at least 1¾m: yet to race on heavy going, acts on any other: tends to race lazily. *M. Johnston* — **110**

LOVE IN THE MIST 3 gr.f. Pursuit of Love 124 – Misty Goddess (IRE) 63 (Godswalk (USA) 130) [2002 67: p10g⁴ f8.5g⁴ f9.4g⁴ f9.4g⁵ Feb 25] modest performer: stays 1¼m: acts on good to soft going and all-weather: looked less than keen final start. *N. P. Littmoden* — **57**

LOVE (IRE) 4 b.g. Royal Academy (USA) 130 – Kentmere (FR) (Galetto (FR) 118) [2002 66d: 5m 6d 7f* 5s f8.5g Dec 20] rather leggy, lengthy gelding: modest handicapper: form in 2002 only when winning at Listowel in September: reportedly had breathing problem at Wolverhampton final start: stays 9f: best efforts on good going or firmer: often blinkered as 3-y-o: sometimes tongue tied. *Edward Butler, Ireland* — **58 a?**

LOVE IS BLIND (IRE) 2 b.c. (Apr 3) Ali-Royal (IRE) 127 – Dawn's Folly (IRE) 47 (Bluebird (USA) 125) [2002 6m 6.1d⁴ 6.1g² f6f* 7m* 7.1m² 7.1m⁴ 6g² 6f⁵ Oct 12] 25,000 2-y-o: smallish, leggy colt: second foal: half-brother to 3-y-o Red Eagle: dam, Irish maiden (probably stayed 7f), out of half-sister to high-class miler Be My Guest: fairly useful performer: won maiden at Wolverhampton (hung right) and nursery at Lingfield in August: good efforts in nursery/minor events next 3 starts: effective at 6f/7f: acts on fibresand and good to firm going: often makes running: sold 67,000 gns, sent to USA. *Miss E. C. Lavelle* — **94**

LOVE KISS (IRE) 7 b.g. Brief Truce (USA) 126 – Pendulina 102 (Prince Tenderfoot (USA) 126) [2002 –: 12.4g May 6] tall gelding: no longer of much account. *W. Storey* —

Princess Royal Willmott Dixon Stakes, Ascot—Love Everlasting knuckles down well to beat Bright And Clear (rail) and Glam Rock; Dawana is last of the four runners

LOVELEAVES 3 b.f. Polar Falcon (USA) 126 – Rash (Pursuit of Love 124) [2002 **93**
84p: 8.3m* 8.5s⁴ 7s³ Oct 28] strong, rangy filly: has scope: fairly useful performer: made
all in maiden at Windsor in May: best effort when fourth to Kootenay in listed race at
Epsom following month: unlikely to stay beyond 8.5f: yet to race on firm ground,
probably acts on any other. *M. A. Jarvis*

LOVELY SPARK (BEL) 5 gr.m. Abbey's Grey – Spark Haven (Hot Spark 126) **49**
[2002 ?: p5g⁶ p6g 5g² 5.5g 5.5f⁴ 5.5m Sep 30] Belgian-bred mare: ran in Britain first 2
outings in 2002: best at 5f/6f: acts on any turf going, dirt and polytrack. *Andre Hermans,
Belgium*

LOVELY YOU (IRE) 2 b.c. (May 2) Fayruz 116 – Lovely Me (IRE) 70 (Vision **63**
(USA)) [2002 6s 6.1g 6g⁴ Oct 4] IR 18,500F, IR 27,000Y, 27,000 2-y-o: fourth foal:
half-brother to 4-y-o Red Millennium: dam maiden who stayed 7f: modest maiden: best
effort when fourth to Stormont at Lingfield: stays 6f: sold 6,200 gns. *Miss E. C. Lavelle*

LOVE ON REQUEST 2 b.f. (Feb 20) Revoque (IRE) 122 – Search For Love (FR) **– p**
(Groom Dancer (USA) 128) [2002 6s⁶ Oct 28] 7,500Y: leggy filly: first foal: dam unraced
out of sister to Prix de la Salamandre winner Noblequest and half-sister to dam of Pursuit
of Love: 16/1, never-dangerous sixth of 16 to Zietory in maiden at Leicester: should do
better. *J. G. Given*

LOVE REGARDLESS (USA) 3 b. or br.c. Storm Bird (CAN) 134 – Circus Toons **112**
(USA) (Wild Again (USA)) [2002 98P: 8m 8m² 8g* 10f⁵ 8s⁴ 8.5s* 7m Oct 19] leggy colt:
smart performer: well held in 2000 Guineas at Newmarket on reappearance: made all in
Jaguar-Meile at Cologne (beat Touch Down by 2 lengths) in August and Grosser Preis der
Landeshauptstadt Dusseldorf at Dusseldorf (by 4 lengths from Lips Lion) in October:
creditable ½-length fourth to Royal Dragon in Oppenheim-Meile at Cologne in between,
but below form when seventh to Nayyir in Challenge Stakes at Newmarket final outing:
best around 1m (well below form in Secretariat Stakes at Arlington over 1¼m): acts on
firm and soft ground. *M. Johnston*

LOVE'S DESIGN (IRE) 5 b. or br.g. Pursuit of Love 124 – Cephista 61 (Shirley **75**
Heights 130) [2002 83, a91: p8g p8g⁵ f8.5g³ f7g⁴ 8f 8d p8g⁵ p8g³ 8g⁶ 7m² 7.6s 8m⁵ 8m⁴ **a90 d**
p7g p7g p8g Dec 3] fairly useful at best on all-weather, fair on turf: well below par last 5
starts on all-weather: best at 7f to 8.5f: acts on firm going, good to soft and all-weather:
visored: free-going type, usually waited with: has shown signs of temperament. *Miss
J. Feilden*

LOVES TRAVELLING (IRE) 2 b.g. (Mar 6) Blues Traveller (IRE) 119 – Fast **63**
Love (IRE) (Second Set (IRE) 127) [2002 6s 6m 5.3m³ 7g⁵ p8g Nov 19] IR 7,500Y: first
foal: dam unraced: best effort when fifth at Brighton: seems better at 7f than shorter.
J. W. Hills

LOVE THEE FOREVER 3 ch.f. Millkom 124 – Exceptional Beauty 94 (Sallust **–**
134) [2002 –: 7m 7g f6g⁵ Jul 26] plain, leggy filly: well held in maidens. *N. P. Littmoden*

LOVE THING 4 b.f. Phountzi (USA) 104 – Devils Dirge 68 (Song 132) [2002 68: 6f **68**
6d⁶ 6g* 6m 6g 7m 6m³ 6g³ 6m⁵ 6f 6m Oct 7] lengthy, rather unfurnished filly: unimpressive mover: fair handicapper: won at Doncaster in June: best at 6f: acts on firm and good
to soft going: tried blinkered, usually visored: edgy sort: has stamina. *R. A. Fahey*

LOVE TUNE 4 b.f. Alhijaz 122 – Heights of Love 51 (Persian Heights 129) [2002 **52 d**
61d: f5g 5s³ 5m 5m 5g May 30] small filly: modest maiden: form in 2002 only on second
start: effective at 5f/6f: acts on fibresand, soft and good to firm going: tried visored.
K. R. Burke

LOVE YOU ALWAYS (USA) 2 ch.c. (Feb 14) Woodman (USA) 126 – Encorenous **98 p**
(USA) (Diesis 133) [2002 8.3m* 7m³ Sep 29] $52,000Y: third foal: half-brother to 3-y-o
Lord Stradbroke: dam unraced half-sister to very smart German 7f/1m performer Royal
Abjar: useful form: won maiden at Hamilton in September by 10 lengths from High
Diving, overcoming greenness to storm clear final 2f: evens, 3 lengths third of 4 to
Captain Saif in minor event at Ascot, more patiently ridden and unable to quicken: should
stay at least 1¼m: joined Godolphin: remains capable of better. *M. Johnston*

LOVE YOU TOO 5 ch.m. Be My Chief (USA) 122 – Nagida 94 (Skyliner 117) [2002 **88 §**
82: 6m 6m 6g 6m² 6d 6m* 7f⁴ 6m 7m 7m Sep 12] big, close-coupled mare: fairly useful
handicapper: won at Windsor in July: temperamental displays last 3 starts, refusing to
race first occasion and virtually doing same next 2: effective at 6f/7f: acts on firm
going: usually visored/blinkered: been early to post: has started slowly/looked lazy: one
to avoid. *D. K. Ivory*

Niarchos Family's "Loving Kindness"

LOVING KINDNESS (USA) 2 b.f. (Mar 7) Seattle Slew (USA) – Coup de Genie **111**
(USA) 114 (Mr Prospector (USA)) [2002 6g* 6d* 6g³ 7g Oct 6] rangy filly: fourth foal:
closely related to useful 7f (in France) to 9f (US Grade 3 event) winner Glia and US
Grade 3 9f/9.5f winner Snake Mountain (both by A P Indy): dam, French 6f/7f winner
(including Prix Morny and Prix de la Salamandre) and third in 1000 Guineas, sister to
Machiavellian from top-class family: smart performer: won newcomers race at Maisons-
Laffitte in July and Prix de Cabourg at Deauville (impressively by 4 lengths from
Together, drawing clear under minimal pressure) in August: disappointing favourite in
Prix Morny at Deauville (3¼ lengths third to Elusive City): found little when tenth of 14
in Grand Criterium at Longchamp: should stay 7f: joined Godolphin. *P. Bary, France*

LOWE GO 2 b.g. (Feb 7) First Trump 118 – Hotel California (IRE) 58 (Last Tycoon **72**
131) [2002 6.1s⁴ 6m 7d² 8.3d⁴ 8g Oct 18] 10,000F, 23,000Y: sixth foal: brother to
Italian winner up to 11.5f Populous and half-brother to 4-y-o Goldie: dam 2-y-o 7.5f
winner: fair maiden: second at Folkestone: stays 1m: best efforts on going softer than
good. *J. G. Portman*

LOWESWATER (USA) 3 b.c. Nureyev (USA) 131 – River Empress (USA) (River- **–**
man (USA) 131) [2002 102: 7m 7f May 25] strong, close-coupled colt: useful at 2 yrs:
ran badly at Newmarket in European Free Handicap (favourite, raced freely, reportedly
lost action) and listed race in 2002: should stay 1m: raced only on going firmer than good:
has had 2 handlers/been on toes. *J. H. M. Gosden*

LOWRY (USA) 4 b. or br.g. Gulch (USA) – Aviara (USA) (Cox's Ridge (USA)) **–**
[2002 –: f12g Oct 22] no form. *J. S. King*

LOYAL (GER) 2 b.g. (Apr 19) Bluebird (USA) 125 – La Luganese (Surumu (GER)) **65**
[2002 p7g 7s Oct 25] IR 95,000Y: big, good-topped gelding: eighth foal: brother to smart

German performer up to 1¼m La Blue and half-brother to 3 German winners, including smart 1¼m/1½m performer Lomita (by Niniski): dam, ran twice, from family of high-class German 1½m performers Lomitas and Lavirco: eighth in maidens, better effort (fair form) at Lingfield on debut: swished tail beforehand when well beaten at Doncaster: gelded after. *Sir Michael Stoute*

LOYAL TYCOON (IRE)   4 br.g. Royal Abjar (USA) 121 – Rosy Lydgate 53 (Last Tycoon 131) [2002 85: 6s 6g 6m⁴ 6m 6d 6m 6m⁵ 6m* 5.9m* 7m² 6m 6f⁶ Oct 8] robust, close-coupled gelding: fairly useful performer: won minor events at Catterick and Hamilton (edged right) in August/September: effective at 6f/7f: acts on soft and good to firm going: visored last 5 starts: sometimes starts slowly/finds little. *D. Nicholls*   **87**

LUCAYAN DANCER   2 b.c. (Mar 27) Zieten (USA) 118 – Tittle Tattle (IRE) 80 (Soviet Lad (USA)) [2002 6.1d² 6g* 7m² 8g⁶ 8m 7.6f² 7f³ 8.2s² Oct 23] 23,000F, 58,000Y: leggy colt: has a markedly round action: first foal: dam, Irish 1½m winner, one to treat with caution: fairly useful performer: won maiden at Brighton in May: creditable efforts in minor events last 3 starts: stays 1m: acts on firm and soft ground. *E. A. L. Dunlop*   **88**

LUCAYAN LEGACY (IRE)   3 b.g. Persian Bold 123 – Catherinofaragon (USA) (Chief's Crown (USA)) [2002 81: 10m 10d⁶ 10m 9.9d Jul 12] useful-looking gelding: fairly useful at 2 yrs: well beaten in 2002. *D. Nicholls*   **–**

LUCAYAN MONARCH   4 ch.g. Cadeaux Genereux 131 – Flight Soundly (IRE) 78 (Caerleon (USA) 132) [2002 71: f8s* f8s⁶ f8s 7g³ 8m⁵ 7.1m² 6f 6g⁵ 6d² 6m⁶ 6d⁴ 7g f5g⁵ 7m³ 7m 7.1g⁴ 5m³ 7g 7s⁴ 8v⁶ 6v Nov 9] lengthy gelding: fair performer: won seller at Southwell in January: successful at 9.4f, best form at 6f: acts on fibresand, firm and soft going: sometimes starts slowly away. *R. Wilman*   **76**

LUCEBALL (IRE)   2 b.f. (Apr 29) Bluebird (USA) 125 – Mysterious Plans (IRE) (Last Tycoon 131) [2002 5.1g⁵ 5d 5m⁶ 5g f5s 6m⁵ 6g⁵ Oct 28] 13,000Y, 23,000 2-y-o: fifth foal: half-sister to 2 winners abroad, including French 1m/1¼m winner Ti For Too (by Exit To Nowhere): dam, French 10.5f winner, sister to smart French sprinter Monde Bleu and half-sister to high-class sprinter Sayf El Arab: modest maiden: will stay 7f: acts on good to firm ground, well beaten (in blinkers) on fibresand. *E. L. James*   **56**

LUCEFER (IRE)   4 b.g. Lycius (USA) 124 – Maharani (USA) (Red Ransom (USA)) [2002 75?: 9.2s 7f 7.2d 6m* p7g² p7g Dec 18] leggy, close-coupled gelding: modest nowadays: won handicap at Yarmouth in September: effective at 6f/7f: acts on polytrack, firm and soft ground: tried blinkered/tongue tied: has carried head high. *G. C. H. Chung*   **55**

LUCID DREAMS (IRE)   3 b.g. Sri Pekan (USA) 117 – Scenaria (IRE) (Scenic 128) [2002 –: 7.9g⁵ 8g⁴ 7f⁴ 7.9g⁵ 7m⁶ 7g² 6m 7g⁴ Sep 2] rather leggy, good-topped gelding: modest maiden handicapper: left Mrs K. Walton after fourth start: probably best at 7f/1m: acts on firm going: has edged left. *M. Wigham*   **51**

LUCINDI   2 b.f. (Mar 11) Tamure (IRE) 125 – Miss Petronella (Petoski 135) [2002 6g 8s⁴ 8s⁶ Nov 6] 600F: fourth foal: dam unraced: easily best effort in maidens when 6 lengths fourth to In Love at Ayr: not knocked about final outing: will be suited by 1¼m+. *C. W. Thornton*   **70**

LUCINI (IRE)   3 ch.f. Selkirk (USA) 129 – Aunt Hester (IRE) 68 (Caerleon (USA) 132) [2002 6s 8g Jun 16] 11,000Y: seventh foal: half-sister to several winners, notably smart 5f/6f winner Funny Valentine (by Cadeaux Genereux): dam 2-y-o 5f winner: well held in maidens at Newbury (slowly away) and Salisbury. *D. R. C. Elsworth*   **–**

LUCKY ARCHER   9 b.g. North Briton 67 – Preobrajenska 93 (Double Form 130) [2002 67: 8g² 8g⁵ 8m² 9m⁴ 8m 8.5m⁵ Aug 16] smallish, well-made gelding: fair performer: best around 1m: acts on firm and good to soft going: blinkered once at 3 yrs: often races up with pace. *Ian Williams*   **74**

LUCKY BREAK (IRE)   4 ch.g. Brief Truce (USA) 126 – Paradise Forum 78 (Prince Sabo 123) [2002 69: p8g⁴ p10g⁴ p10g⁵ p8g⁶ 9.7m 10d 9.9m 8m Sep 5] small gelding: fair maiden handicapper: stays easy 1¼m: acts on firm going and polytrack. *C. A. Horgan*   **–** **a65**

LUCKY COVE   6 gr.g. Lugana Beach 116 – Port Na Blath (On Your Mark 125) [2002 45?: f6s f6s f6g Jan 29] of little account. *N. Tinkler*   **–**

LUCKY DATE (IRE)   2 ch.f. (Apr 4) Halling (USA) 133 – Hesperia (Slip Anchor 136) [2002 7s* 6.5g Sep 27] 70,000Y: third foal: dam, useful 11f/1½m winner in France/Italy, from very good family of champion US filly Go For Wand: fairly useful form when winning 14-runner maiden at Lingfield in September by ¾ length from Island Rapture, leading near finish despite wandering/swishing tail: well held in sales race at Ascot later   **81 p**

in month (joined M. Magnusson after): will be well suited by 1m+: should still do better. *D. W. P. Arbuthnot*

LUCKY FOR GEORGE   4 b.c. Theatrical Charmer 114 – Jeedamaya 57 (Taufan   –
(USA) 119) [2002 –: 10g f16.2g Jul 26] sparely-made colt: of no account. *T. T. Clement*

LUCKY HEATHER (IRE)   5 b.m. Soviet Lad (USA) – Idrak 68 (Young Generation   –
129) [2002 47: p12g 11.6m Jul 22] probably of little account nowadays. *R. J. Baker*

LUCKY JACASA   3 b.f. Whittingham (IRE) 104 – Lucky Dip 68 (Tirol 127) [2002   57
62: 5.1d³ 6g 5.1s⁵ 6.1v 5.5f 6.1d 5g 5d 5g⁵ 5g 6d Oct 18] modest maiden: best form at 5f:
acts on soft ground: tried blinkered. *Mrs P. N. Dutfield*

LUCKY JUDGE   5 b.g. Saddlers' Hall (IRE) 126 – Lady Lydia 66 (Ela-Mana-Mou   68
132) [2002 78: 16g⁴ Mar 28] close-coupled gelding: fair handicapper: stays 2m: acts on
any going: visored once: has carried head high. *G. A. Swinbank*

LUCKY LEO   2 b.g. (Apr 5) Muhtarram (USA) 125 – Wrong Bride (Reprimand 122)   70
[2002 7s⁴ 8.2v⁶ 7.1s⁴ f6g p8g Dec 11] third foal: dam once-raced half-sister to smart   a–
sprinter Funfair Wane: fair maiden: reportedly finished lame final start: should stay 1m:
raced only on soft/heavy ground on turf, well held on all-weather. *M. R. Channon*

LUCKY LUCKY BOB (USA)   5 b.g. Alleged (USA) 138 – Alloy (FR) 98 (Pharly
(FR) 130) [2002 p10g p10g f7g p8g p10g⁵ 14.1d Mar 27] $110,000Y, 3,000 4-y-o:
half-brother to 2 winners abroad by Cure The Blues, including smart French winner
around 1¼m Fast Cure, later Grade 1 placed in USA: dam, French 1m winner, half-sister
to high-class miler Noalcoholic: little sign of ability (reportedly lost action second start/
bled from nose next one/left N. Berry after fifth). *E. A. Wheeler*

LUCKY MAN   3 b.c. Robellino (USA) 127 – Vannozza 58 (Kris 135) [2002 74: f7s⁶   72
f9.4g³ p12g² 12.3m⁶ p12g⁵ 12d⁶ 10m Aug 16] leggy, plain colt: fair maiden: stays easy
1½m: acts on good to firm going, good to soft and all-weather: sold 5,500 gns, sent to
Kuwait. *G. C. Bravery*

LUCKY RING   2 b.g. (Apr 5) Magic Ring (IRE) 115 – Name That Tune 40 (Fayruz   –
116) [2002 5.1m Aug 6] 500Y: third foal: half-brother to 5-y-o Chorus: dam sprint
maiden: 20/1, well beaten in seller at Bath. *R. J. Hodges*

LUCKY ROMANCE   3 b.f. Key of Luck (USA) 126 – In Love Again (IRE) 86 (Prince   61
Rupert (FR) 121) [2002 68p: p7g² p7g⁶ 6.1m f6s Oct 8] tall filly: modest maiden: barely
stays easy 7f: acts on all-weather: has looked none too keen: headstrong and a tricky ride.
R. F. Johnson Houghton

LUCKY'S SON (IRE)   5 gr.g. Lucky Guest 109 – April Wind 91 (Windjammer   –
(USA)) [2002 50, a–: 5g Oct 5] good-topped gelding: modest performer at 4 yrs: well
held only 5-y-o start. *Julian Poulton*

LUCKY STAR   5 b.m. Emarati (USA) 74 – Child Star (FR) 58 (Bellypha 130) [2002   52
46, a?: f8.5g⁵ f8.5g f6g p7g⁶ 5g 8m 5.9d² 5.9v 5m* 5d 5m 6m 5d⁵ f6g⁶ f6g⁴ Dec 10] leggy   a38
mare: modest performer: trained by J. Unett first 3 starts: won claimer at Catterick in
August: effective at 5f to 8.5f: acts on fibresand, firm and good to soft going: visored once
at 5 yrs: often races prominently. *J. Balding*

LUCKY UNO   6 b.g. Rock City 120 – Free Skip 68 (Free State 125) [2002 f8g Mar 21]   – §
big gelding: temperamental maiden: blinkered once. *R. Wilman*

LUCKY VALENTINE   2 b.f. (Apr 14) My Best Valentine 122 – Vera's First (IRE) 69   55 p
(Exodal (USA)) [2002 6f⁶ Sep 17] third foal: dam 2-y-o 7f seller winner: 20/1 and green,
6 lengths sixth to To The Rescue in maiden at Salisbury: should improve. *G. L. Moore*

LUDYNOSA (USA)   3 b.f. Cadeaux Genereux 131 – Boubskaia (Niniski (USA) 125)   98
[2002 74p: 7g* 8.2f³ 8.1d 7m 6m³ 6g* 6g 7v Nov 15] strong, well-made filly: has a quick
action: useful performer: won maiden at Newmarket in May and handicap at Salisbury
(beat Dark Charm by 1½ lengths) in October: not discredited in listed race at Newmarket
penultimate outing: effective at 6f to 1m: acts on firm going: found little fifth start: tail
swisher. *L. M. Cumani*

LUKE AFTER ME (IRE)   2 b.g. (Mar 2) Victory Note (USA) 120 – Summit Talk   70 d
(Head For Heights 125) [2002 6g² 6d f8.5f f7g Dec 17] IR 22,000F, 8,500Y: angular,
good-topped gelding: seventh foal: half-brother to 3 winners, including 1m/1¼m winner
Talk Back (by Bob Back): dam Irish 7.5f winner: fair form when second in maiden at Ayr:
showed little in similar events/nursery after. *P. C. Haslam*

LULUWA (IRE)   3 b. or br.f. Zafonic (USA) 130 – Affection Affirmed (USA)   72
(Affirmed (USA)) [2002 83p: 8.3m² 9m⁵ 8m⁴ Aug 29] strong, lengthy filly: fair maiden:

free-going sort, should prove at least as effective at 7f as 1m: yet to race on extremes of going: sold 105,000 gns in December, sent to USA. *H. R. A. Cecil*

LUMBER JILL (USA) 4 b. or br.f. Woodman (USA) 126 – Bineyah (IRE) 109 **75** (Sadler's Wells (USA) 132) [2002 11.6g 13.1g[6] 11g[6] 14d[6] 16s Jul 29] fifth foal: closely related to UAE 1¼m winner Mowjood (by Mr Prospector): dam 11.5f winner and second in Yorkshire Oaks, out of half-sister to Seattle Slew and Lomond: fair performer: successful in minor event at Lyon Parilly and handicap at Craon in 2001 for C. Laffon-Parias in France: trained by P. Webber first 2 starts in 2002: probably flattered in listed race at Leopardstown penultimate start: stays 13f: acts on soft going: blinkered final outing. *Andrew Slattery, Ireland*

LUMIERE DU SOLEIL 4 b.f. Tragic Role (USA) – Pounelta 91 (Tachypous 128) **59** [2002 55: f6s f7s* f8s[4] f8g f8g* f8.5g Mar 4] tall filly: modest performer: won maiden and handicap at Southwell in January/February: effective at 7f/1m: acts on good to firm going, good to soft and fibresand: usually blinkered/visored: tried tongue tied: usually races prominently. *K. A. Ryan*

LUMINATA (IRE) 2 ch.f. (Apr 25) Indian Ridge 123 – Smaoineamh (Tap On Wood **103** 130) [2002 5s[2] 6s[2] 6d[3] 6s* 6g* 6s 7g[2] 8g[3] Oct 6] rather leggy, useful-looking filly: good walker: sister to useful Irish 1999 2-y-o 6f winner Aretha and half-sister to 3 winners in Ireland, including useful 1m winner Dathuil (by Royal Academy): dam, Irish 6f (at 2 yrs) to 1¾m winner, half-sister to top-class sprinter Double Form: useful performer: won maiden at the Curragh and listed race at Leopardstown (by neck from Daganya) in July: good placed efforts in Moyglare Stud Stakes at the Curragh (beaten head by Mail The Desert) and Prix Marcel Boussac at Longchamp (7 lengths third to Six Perfections) last 2 starts: stays 1m: raced only on good going or softer. *J. S. Bolger, Ireland*

LUNA MOTH (USA) 3 b.f. Silver Hawk (USA) 123 – Night And Dreams (USA) **65** (Fappiano (USA)) [2002 78p: 10d[5] Jul 9] strong, well-made filly: fair maiden: found little when disappointing only 3-y-o start: sent to Australia. *E. A. L. Dunlop*

Mr D. H. W. Dobson's "Luminata"

LUNA NOVA 4 b.g. Aragon 118 – Lucidity 67 (Vision (USA)) [2002 –: 9.2s 10f 16m Jul 8] little form: tried blinkered. *D. Moffatt* —

LUNAR LEO 4 b.g. Muhtarram (USA) 125 – Moon Mistress 82 (Storm Cat (USA)) [2002 98: 6m 7m² 7m 8m 7m* 7m⁴ 8f Oct 5] sturdy gelding: useful handicapper: won at Chester (by length from Inchdura) in August: ran well otherwise when second to Demonstrate in Buckingham Palace Stakes at Royal Ascot: stiff task/never threatened in Grade 2 Kelso Breeders' Cup Handicap at Belmont final start: best at 6f/7f: acts on good to firm going and polytrack: usually tongue tied: often early to post. *S. C. Williams* **103**

LUNAR LORD 6 b.g. Elmaamul (USA) 125 – Cache (Bustino 136) [2002 64: f16.2g³ f12g⁵ f16.2g 11.9g 10.2d* 12.3g³ 12d* f12g p13g Dec 28] close-coupled gelding: modest handicapper on turf, poor on all-weather: won at Bath (amateurs) in May and Epsom in July: barely stays 2m: acts on heavy going and fibresand, probably on good to firm. *D. Burchell* **64 a47**

LUNAR LUSTRE (IRE) 2 ch.f. (Apr 6) Desert Prince (IRE) 130 – Green Rosy (USA) (Green Dancer (USA)) 132) [2002 6m 7s Sep 10] 230,000F: half-sister to several winners, notably French/US 7f (at 2 yrs) to 1½m winner Majorien (by Machiavellian) and French 9f (at 2 yrs) to 1½m winner America (by Arazi), both smart: dam French 1½m winner: well held in maidens. *J. Noseda* —

LUNCH PARTY 10 b.g. Beveled (USA) – Crystal Sprite 74 (Crystal Glitters (USA) 127) [2002 56: 7g 7f⁴ 7m 7g Jun 5] good-bodied gelding: modest performer: stays 1m: acts on firm and soft going, probably on fibresand: tried tongue tied: has been early to post/slowly away: usually races prominently. *R. A. Fahey* **52**

LUNDY'S LANE (IRE) 2 b.c. (Feb 28) Darshaan 133 – Lunda (IRE) 60 (Soviet Star (USA) 128) [2002 8m³ 8g² Oct 18] lengthy, good-topped colt: third foal: half-brother to 4-y-o Dancing Tsar and 3-y-o Jakarta: dam, maiden, half-sister to good performers up to 1½m Luso, Needle Gun and Cloud Castle: fairly useful form in minor event at Salisbury and maiden at Newmarket, 1½ lengths second of 16 to Calibre in latter: should do better as 3-y-o at 1¼m+. *C. E. Brittain* **92 p**

LUPINE (IRE) 3 b. or br.f. Lake Coniston (IRE) 131 – Prosaic Star (IRE) 81 (Common Grounds 118) [2002 82: 6m⁴ 6.1d 6m³ 7d⁶ 7d³ 7m 6m Sep 19] lengthy, unfurnished filly: fairly useful performer: stays 7f: yet to race on extremes of going. *M. R. Channon* **84**

LURRAMIO 2 b.g. (Apr 17) Key of Luck (USA) 126 – Carreamia 62 (Weldnaas (USA) 112) [2002 f5g⁵ 5m² f6g⁴ 5m 6d³ 6.1m 7g⁵ 8.2v² Oct 29] 1,500Y: close-coupled, workmanlike gelding: first foal: dam, maiden, should have stayed 1m: modest maiden: in frame in 4 sellers: should stay 1¼m: acts on fibresand, good to firm and heavy ground: blinkered (played up in stall, ran poorly) fourth outing: folded tamely sixth: temperamental: sold 6,000 gns, sent to Kuwait. *J. G. Given* **58 §**

LUVAH GIRL 2 b.f. (Feb 28) Alzao (USA) 117 – Girl of My Dreams (IRE) 51 (Marju (IRE) 127) [2002 6m⁴ p6g* 6m² 6m² 7m* Oct 19] good-bodied filly: has a quick action: second foal: dam 7f winner: smart performer: won maiden at Lingfield in June: changed ownership by 1¼ lengths second of 6 to Russian Rhythm in Princess Margaret Stakes at Ascot (tended to edge left but battled on well) fourth start: off nearly 3 months before winning 11-runner Owen Brown Rockfel Stakes at Newmarket by length from Casual Look: should stay 1m: acts on polytrack, raced only on good to firm going on turf: races prominently (made all for both wins): to join Jenine Sahadi in USA. *R. Charlton* **110**

Owen Brown Rockfel Stakes, Newmarket—Luvah Girl makes all and is too strong for Casual Look; Yesterday (white blaze) is third with Dialing Tone fourth

LUXI RIVER (USA) 2 b.c. (Apr 16) Diesis 133 – Mariella (USA) 106 (Roberto **69** (USA) 131) [2002 7.5g⁴ 8m⁵ f8.5s² Nov 2] 6,000Y: big, close-coupled colt: half-brother to several winners, including fairly useful 1½m winner Duke of Warsaw (by Danzig): dam 1½m/1¾m winner out of Oaks winner Monade: fair form in maidens: 2 lengths second to Platinum Charmer at Wolverhampton: should be well suited by 1¼m+. *N. A. Graham*

LUXOR 5 ch.g. Grand Lodge (USA) 125 – Escrime (USA) 92 (Sharpen Up 127) [2002 **60** 58: 12.3g 10f 9.2v 10.3f* 10.5g⁵ 10m² 10m⁵ 10m³ 9d 10.4m 10.3f 10m* Oct 1] rangy gelding: fluent mover: modest handicapper: won at Chester in July and Nottingham in October: stays 1½m: acts on firm going, probably not on soft/heavy: tried visored/tongue tied: headstrong front runner: sometimes flashes tail/finds little. *W. M. Brisbourne*

LYCHEEL 4 ch.g. Lycius (USA) 124 – Talon d'Aiguille (USA) (Big Spruce (USA)) – [2002 52, a59: p10g³ p10g f11s³ f11g f8g* f8.5g⁵ f8.5g Mar 15] modest handicapper: **a56** won apprentices maiden event at Southwell in February: stays 1¼m: acts on all-weather and good to firm going: tried blinkered: sometimes slowly away. *W. R. Muir*

LYCIAN (IRE) 7 b.g. Lycius (USA) 124 – Perfect Time (IRE) (Dance of Life (USA)) **69** [2002 63, a71: 10g 10m² 10m³ 10.2d⁶ 10m² 10m 10.1m² 10m f8g p10g⁶ p10g⁵ Dec 30] **a58** tall, angular gelding: fair handicapper: left J. Toller 5,000 gns after eighth start: effective at 1m/1¼m: acts on all-weather, best on good going or firmer on turf. *Mrs L. Stubbs*

LYCIAT SPARKLE (IRE) 4 b.g. Lycius (USA) 124 – Benguiat (FR) (Exceller **36** (USA) 129) [2002 36: 12m f12g 8f 10g³ 10.5g 10m 9.9g³ 10.1m 10.9m⁵ 9m Sep 16] angular, close-coupled gelding: poor maiden handicapper: stays 1¾m: acts on good to firm going: has been awkward leaving stall: headstrong. *Mrs G. S. Rees*

LYDIA'S LOOK (IRE) 5 b.m. Distant View (USA) 126 – Mrs Croesus (USA) (Key **61** To The Mint (USA)) [2002 65, a53: 6g 5s³ 6g 5.1m⁵ 5d⁴ 5d⁴ 5m* 6m 6.1m Oct 1] **a–** close-coupled mare: modest handicapper: won at Hamilton in August: effective at 5f/ 6f: acts on fibresand, firm and soft going: none too reliable. *T. J. Etherington*

LYGETON LAD 4 b.g. Shaamit (IRE) 127 – Smartie Lee 66 (Dominion 123) [2002 **75 +** 56: f9.4g 10.9f³ 10d 10.9m* 8m* 10.1f³ p10g² 10.3f⁴ 8g* 7m 8.1g 10m p7g³ p8g* p7g* **a89** p8g² p7g² p8g³ p8g² Dec 30] fairly useful handicapper on all-weather, fair on turf: won apprentice races at Warwick and Newmarket in June, ladies race at Newmarket in July and twice at Lingfield in November: winner at 11f, probably best at 7f/1m: goes well on all-weather, raced mainly on good going or firmer on turf: usually tongue tied: has been early to post/given trouble at start. *Miss Gay Kelleway*

LYNBURG 5 b.g. Bonnova's Lad – The Cross (Sallust 134) [2002 p12g 10m p12g – p16g p13g Oct 4] smallish, angular gelding: third reported foal: dam of little account: little form, leaving J. Long after third start. *J. R. Boyle*

LYNCHPIN (USA) 3 b.g. Royal Academy (USA) 130 – Shenandoah Snow (CAN) – (Secretariat (USA)) [2002 6m 7g 12f⁶ 11.5f⁶ 12m 10.1m Aug 14] $87,000F: useful-looking gelding: sixth foal: half-brother to 3 winners in USA: dam ran once: little form: tried blinkered/tongue tied: twice had breathing problem: dead. *W. J. Haggas*

LYNX 2 gr.f. (Jan 31) Linamix (FR) 127 – Gharība 112 (Final Straw 127) [2002 7d p7g⁵ **67** Dec 3] leggy filly: half-sister to several winners, including useful Italian sprinter Reinaldo (by Green Desert) and fairly useful 6f to (in USA) 1m winner Promptly (by Lead On Time): dam, won Nell Gwyn Stakes, half-sister to smart performers Braashee (up to 2m) and Adam Smith (up to 1¼m): better effort (fair form) when 6 lengths fifth of 10 to Splendid Era in minor event at Lingfield: slowly away on debut: will probably stay 1m. *Sir Michael Stoute*

LYRICAL LAD 3 b.g. Primo Dominie 121 – Lyrical Bid (USA) 77 (Lyphard (USA) **62** 132) [2002 64?: 8.2d 10f⁶ 10f⁴ p12g 10f⁴ p12g 10.9m³ 10m² 9.7m 10.9m 10m Oct 1] smallish gelding: modest maiden handicapper: stays 11f: acts on firm going and polytrack: sometimes slowly away: possibly has his share of temperament: sold 3,500 gns, sent to Spain. *P. W. Harris*

LYRICAL WAY 3 b.g. Vettori (IRE) 119 – Fortunate (Reference Point 139) [2002 59: **62** 8.1m p10g³ 10g² 10d⁵ 10m² 9.9m 9.7g 10m⁵ 12d 10m² Oct 3] leggy gelding: modest maiden handicapper: stays 1¼m: acts on good to soft ground, good to firm and polytrack: blinkered (raced freely/found little) final start. *P. R. Chamings*

LYRIC MAESTRO 3 b.g. Merdon Melody 98 – Dubitable 59 (Formidable (USA) **62** 125) [2002 77: 10d 9m 12m 12d 10.1m⁵ Sep 18] good-bodied gelding: modest maiden: reportedly suffered knee injury after final 2-y-o start: stays 1½m: visored last 3 starts. *S. Dow*

LYSANDER'S QUEST (IRE) 4 br.g. King's Theatre (IRE) 128 – Haramayda (FR) **60** (Doyoun 124) [2002 –: 11.6m 9.9m 12m⁵ 12d² 14m² 11.9f f12g p12g p16g Nov 27] tall gelding: modest maiden handicapper: stays 1¾m: acts on good to firm and good to soft going, probably on polytrack: has been slowly away. *L. Montague Hall*

LY'S WEST 2 ch.g. (Apr 17) The West (USA) 107 – Lysithea 63 (Imperial Fling (USA) – 116) [2002 6.1d p5g May 28] lengthy gelding: seventh foal: half-brother to 5f (at 2 yrs) and 12.5f winner Lying Eyes (by Interrex): dam 6f seller winner: well held in maidens. *W. G. M. Turner*

M

MA BELLE BLEUE 3 b.f. Bluegrass Prince (IRE) 110 – My Bonus 79 (Cyrano de – Bergerac 120) [2002 66d: f6s f7g Feb 14] small filly: disappointing maiden: tried blinkered/visored. *Miss A. Stokell*

MABEL RILEY (IRE) 2 b.f. (Apr 4) Revoque (IRE) 122 – Mystic Dispute (IRE) **66** (Magical Strike (USA) 114) [2002 5.7d 6s p5g⁶ 6m⁵ 7d⁶ 7s 7g³ 6f f6g 6d f6g⁴ Dec 13] 13,000Y: third foal: half-sister to fairly useful 2000 2-y-o 7f/1m winner Specific Sorcerer (by Definite Article), later successful up to 1¼m in Hong Kong: dam unraced half-sister to smart middle-distance performer Trakady: fair maiden: best effort when third in nursery at Lingfield: barely stays 7f: acts on good to soft ground, probably on all-weather: tried blinkered: none too reliable. *B. J. Meehan*

MABROOKA (USA) 3 b. or br.f. Bahri (USA) 125 – Barakat 93 (Bustino 136) [2002 **81** 10m⁵ 10m⁴ 10g⁴ 11.7f³ 11.7d* Sep 9] leggy, useful-looking filly: half-sister to several winners, including useful 1¼m performer Ta Awun (by Housebuster) and fairly useful 1½m winner Mumaris (by Capote): dam, winner around 1¾m, half-sister to Ibn Bey and Roseate Tern from family of Teleprompter: fairly useful performer: won maiden at Bath in September: stays 1½m: raced freely third start, found little fourth: sold 7,000 gns in December. *A. C. Stewart*

MABRUM (IRE) 3 b.c. Alhaarth (IRE) 126 – Absaar (USA) 76 (Alleged (USA) 138) **57** [2002 –p: 8.2d 10g 10m Jun 4] lengthy, rather lightly-made colt: unimpressive mover: modest maiden: probably stays 1¼m: yet to race on extremes of going. *J. L. Dunlop*

MAC 2 ch.g. (Mar 14) Fleetwood (IRE) 107 – Midnight Break 78 (Night Shift (USA)) **71** [2002 7m 7m⁴ p8g⁵ Nov 14] 18,500Y: good-bodied gelding: third foal: half-brother to 3-y-o Bobby Kennard: dam 5f/6f winner: fair form in maidens: off 3½ months before final start (gelded after): stays 1m. *M. P. Tregoning*

MACADAMIA (IRE) 3 b.f. Classic Cliche (IRE) 128 – Cashew 80 (Sharrood (USA) **91** 124) [2002 82p: 8m⁶ 9.9d⁶ 10m 10m* 10m⁴ 10f² Oct 4] lengthy filly: fairly useful performer: won minor event at Newmarket in August: creditable efforts in handicaps last 2 starts, second to Courageous Duke at same track final one: stays 1¼m: raced mainly on good ground or firmer: changed legs several times penultimate outing. *J. R. Fanshawe*

MACAW (IRE) 3 b.c. Bluebird (USA) 125 – No Quest (IRE) – Rainbow Quest (USA) **106** 134) [2002 88: 8g 7m 6m 7.9f* 8.1d² 7.9d 10g³ 8g* 9.9m* 9f⁴ 9f³ 12f Dec 28] smallish, good-topped colt: useful performer: generally progressive form in 2002, winning handicaps at York in May, Newmarket in July and Goodwood (by ¾ length from Tertullian in quite valuable event) in August: left J. Goldie: ran well when 3½ lengths fourth to Finality in Grade 2 Jamaica Handicap at Belmont, best effort in US last 3 starts: effective at 1m/1¼m: acts on any going: likeable sort. *B. Tagg, USA*

MAC BE LUCKY 5 b.g. Magic Ring (IRE) 115 – Take Heart 84 (Electric 126) [2002 **63** 67: f8.5g² f7s⁴ f8.5g² f9.4g f8g⁵ 12.5g³ 9g* 11d 7v⁵ 6v a9g⁴ Dec 22] strong, lengthy gelding: modest performer: sold from I. Semple 2,100 gns at fifth start: won maiden at Herxheim in April, then left C. Von Der Recke after next outing: stays 9f: acts on fibresand, very best turf form on ground softer than good. *Mme S. Braem, Belgium*

MACDUNE (FR) 4 b.g. Machiavellian (USA) 123 – Sandhill (IRE) 96 (Danehill – (USA) 126) [2002 67: f6g p8g 7.9g 6.1m Jul 13] small, lightly-made gelding: fair maiden at 3 yrs: well held in 2002. *G. C. Bravery*

MACEO (GER) 8 ch.g. Acatenango (GER) 127 – Metropolitan Star (USA) 84 – (Lyphard (USA) 132) [2002 79: 13.1s Oct 15] good-topped gelding: smart performer at best when raced in Germany: lightly raced on Flat nowadays: successful over hurdles in November. *Mrs M. Reveley*

MACHINIST (IRE)   2 br.c. (Apr 21) Machiavellian (USA) 123 – Athene (IRE) 83   **82 p**
(Rousillon (USA) 133) [2002 6g³ p7g* Oct 16] fifth foal: half-brother to useful French 9f
(at 2 yrs) and 1½m (Prix de Royaumont) winner Side Saddle (by Saddlers' Hall) and
French 11f to 15.5f winner Last Roman (by Salse): dam, 1¼m winner, half-sister to
high-class hurdler Landing Light out of smart 1¼m/1½m winner Gay Hellene: better
effort in Lingfield maidens (fairly useful form) when winning 15-runner event by head
from Chetak, getting up near finish: will stay at least 1¼m: should continue to progress.
Sir Michael Stoute

MACHRIHANISH   2 b.c. (Mar 24) Groom Dancer (USA) 128 – Goodwood Lass   **56 ?**
(IRE) 71 (Alzao (USA) 117) [2002 7.1m 8m 6g 7.1s⁶ Nov 6] 5,000Y, 12,500 2-y-o: quite
good-topped colt: second foal: half-brother to 2001 2-y-o 7.5f winner Silent Gift (by
Brief Truce): dam 7f (at 2 yrs) and 1½m winner: seemingly modest form in maiden at Ayr
on third start: should stay at least 1m: twice slowly away. *Miss L. A. Perratt*

MACHYNLETH   2 b.c. (Apr 11) Machiavellian (USA) 123 – Tanami 111 (Green   **74**
Desert (USA) 127) [2002 5g* 6m⁵ 7m Sep 14] compact colt: third living foal:
half-brother to UAE 6f winner Tangram (by Indian Ridge): dam, 2-y-o 5f/6f winner,
second in Cheveley Park Stakes: fair form: won maiden at Ripon in April: off over 4
months having reportedly thrown a splint, well held in minor event there (had breathing
problem) and nursery at Doncaster after: sent to UAE. *M. R. Channon*

MAC MELODY (IRE)   2 b.f. (Mar 15) Entrepreneur 123 – Milly of The Vally 93   **91**
(Caerleon (USA) 132) [2002 5s* 6m² 7.5d* a7f 8f⁴ 8f Nov 29] 4,200Y: second foal:
half-sister to 3-y-o Scott's View: dam, 1½m winner, half-sister to 4-y-o Bosham Mill out
of smart 1½m performer Mill On The Floss: fairly useful performer: won at Milan in
maiden in May and (having finished second to Coconut Penang in minor event at
Kempton) listed race in July: left M. Quinlan: fourth in restricted event at Santa Anita,
probably best effort in US after: stays 1m: acts on firm and soft going. *R. B. Hess jnr, USA*

MAC NIGHT (IRE)   2 b.c. (Apr 28) Night Shift (USA) – Rosy Lydgate 53 (Last   **79**
Tycoon 131) [2002 5s* 5m³ 6m⁴ 5m* 6g⁶ 5m* 6m Nov 9] IR 31,000F, 16,000Y: leggy
colt: third foal: half-brother to 4-y-o Loyal Tycoon: dam maiden half-sister to smart
performer up to 11f Supreme Sound and useful stayer Top Cees: fair performer: won
maiden at Milan in May and (having left M. Quinlan after third start) minor events at
Leghorn in July and November: third in minor event at Windsor, only outing in Britain:
seems best at 5f: acts on soft and good to firm ground. *A. Macchi, Italy*

MACONACHIE   3 b.g. Bahamian Bounty 116 – Madurai 71 (Chilibang 120) [2002   **62**
69: 6m 6g 6g 6d 6g³ Oct 28] useful-looking gelding: modest maiden: effective at 5f/6f:
acts on heavy ground: sold 5,000 gns, sent to Kuwait. *J. L. Dunlop*

MAC'S JEWEL   3 ch.c. Bijou d'Inde 127 – Elabellou (IRE) 41 (Ela-Mana-Mou 132)   **61 d**
[2002 67: 8.2d⁵ 10d⁵ 10g 7m 10m⁵ p10g 12.1g 8.1d 9.9m f12g Sep 30] sturdy, close-
coupled colt: bad mover: modest maiden at best at 3 yrs: left W. O'Gorman after sixth
start: stays 1¼m: acts on all-weather, good to firm and good to soft going. *T. H. Caldwell*

MAC'S TALISMAN (IRE)   2 ch.c. (Mar 12) Hector Protector (USA) 124 – Inherent   **69 p**
Magic (IRE) 95 (Magical Wonder (USA) 125) [2002 p7g⁵ p7g⁵ Dec 11] 4,000Y: fourth
foal: dam 5f winner, including at 2 yrs: encouraging fifth in claimer (slowly away) and
maiden at Lingfield, not knocked about when beaten 4¼ lengths by Contractor in latter:
will stay 1m: remains open to improvement. *W. A. O'Gorman*

MADAAR (USA)   3 b.c. Spinning World (USA) 130 – Mur Taasha (USA) 108 (River-   **66**
man (USA) 131) [2002 8f 9g⁵ f9.4g Dec 16] fourth foal: half-brother to smart performer
up to 1m Iftitah (by Gone West), 7f winner at 2 yrs, and 4-y-o Mahroos: dam, 7f/1m
winner, out of Criterion Stakes winner Linda's Magic: better effort in maidens for Sir
Michael Stoute when eighth to Helloimustbegoing at Newmarket on debut: sold 2,000
gns, slowly away and looked less than keen (first race for 6 months) final outing: tended
to run in snatches second start. *P. D. Evans*

MADAME BOULANGERE   3 b.f. Royal Applause 124 – Jazz 76 (Sharrood (USA)   **100**
124) [2002 91: 8.1d 6m³ 7d 6m* 6m⁵ 7m⁶ 6m³ 6g 6g Oct 18] leggy, useful-looking
filly: useful performer: won minor event at Windsor in July by length from Simianna:
creditable efforts next 3 starts, slowly away when 4 lengths third to Smokin Beau in listed
race at Goodwood: effective at 6f/7f: unraced on extremes of going: usually races
prominently: sold 50,000 gns, sent to USA. *R. Hannon*

MADAME EZZIE   3 b.f. Ezzoud (IRE) 126 – Daanat Nawal (Machiavellian (USA)   **45**
123) [2002 10g 10d f9.4g⁵ f9.4f⁴ 8m f9.4g f12f Nov 11] 3,800Y: second foal: half-sister
to winner in Spain by Petong: dam unraced out of half-sister to Breeders' Cup Sprint winner Smile: poor maiden: left P. Gilligan after fifth start: seems to stay 9.4f. *J. D. Czerpak*

MADAME JONES (IRE) 7 ch.m. Lycius (USA) 124 – Gold Braisim (IRE) 77 **75**
(Jareer (USA) 115) [2002 72, a79: f7g 8f 6.9d⁶ 7m 8m³ 8d³ f8g⁵ 8m Jul 16] tall mare: fair
handicapper: failed to add to 12 wins of 2001: probably best at 7f to 8.5f: acts on
all-weather and probably any turf going: wears visor (tried blinkered): often takes good
hold. *P. D. Evans*

MADAME MARIE (IRE) 2 b.f. (Feb 8) Desert King (IRE) 129 – Les Trois Lamas **63**
(IRE) (Machiavellian (USA) 123) [2002 7d 6g 7s⁵ Sep 10] 280,000 francs Y: third foal:
dam, French 1½m winner, half-sister to smart French winner up to 10.5f Cloudings:
modest maiden: will stay at least 1¼m. *S. Dow*

MADAME MAXI 8 ch.m. Ron's Victory (USA) 129 – New Pastures (Formidable **77**
(USA) 125) [2002 61, a–: 8.3d² 8.3s² 10m⁶ 8m 8.1g* 8.3m³ 7.1m⁵ 8m f8.5g Oct 19] **a–**
angular mare: shows knee action: fair handicapper: won apprentice event at Sandown in
August: effective at 7f/1m: acts on firm and soft going (no form on fibresand): tried
blinkered in 1999: often races up with pace. *H. S. Howe*

MADAME MAXINE (USA) 3 b. or br.f. Dayjur (USA) 137 – Political Parody **89**
(USA) (Doonesbury (USA)) [2002 69: f6g⁴ p6g* p6g⁴ 6g⁶ p5g² 5.1m² 5g 5g 5m* 5m 5s
5f² f5g³ Nov 20] smallish filly: fairly useful handicapper: won at Lingfield in January and
Goodwood in August: effective at 5f/6f: acts on all-weather and firm going: blinkered
(ran well) last 2 starts. *B. J. Meehan*

MADAME ROUX 4 b.f. Rudimentary (USA) 118 – Foreign Mistress (Darshaan 133) **58 d**
[2002 65: 6.1d⁴ 6f f7g 6.1m 5.7m⁶ 6g 6.1m Sep 20] angular filly: modest maiden: on
downgrade at 4 yrs, leaving G. Wragg after fifth start: stays 7f: acts on good to soft going:
has wandered. *Miss J. A. Camacho*

MADAMOISELLE JONES 2 b.f. (Feb 24) Emperor Jones (USA) 119 – Tiriana **52**
(Common Grounds 118) [2002 p5g³ p5g⁵ 5.1g 6s⁵ 6g⁶ 6.1g Aug 8] 2,500Y: first foal:
dam, French maiden, half-sister to useful 1996 2-y.-o 5f winner Head Over Heels: modest
maiden: should stay 7f: acts on soft ground and polytrack. *H. S. Howe*

MAD CAREW (USA) 3 ch.g. Rahy (USA) 115 – Poppy Carew (IRE) 110 (Danehill **–**
(USA) 126) [2002 70: 10m Jun 17] sturdy gelding: fair maiden at 2 yrs: well held only
outing in 2002: sold 6,000 gns in November. *P. W. Harris*

MADDIE'S A JEM 2 b.f. (Mar 10) Emperor Jones (USA) 119 – Royal Orchid (IRE) **68 p**
74 (Shalford (IRE) 124§) [2002 6.1s⁴ Oct 23] 3,000Y: second foal: dam, maiden who
stayed 7f, out of half-sister to smart sprinter Mistertopogigo: 66/1, 4¼ lengths fourth of
16 to Cashel Mead in minor event at Nottingham, staying on after slow start: will stay 7f:
should improve. *J. R. Jenkins*

MADDORA (IRE) 3 b.f. Mark of Esteem (IRE) 137 – Almuhtarama (IRE) 84 (Rain- **–**
bow Quest (USA) 134) [2002 63: p10g 12g Jul 19] modest maiden at 2 yrs: well held in
2002: blinkered (raced freely) final start: visits Lujain. *M. P. Tregoning*

MADE IN JAPAN (JPN) 2 b.g. (Apr 16) Barathea (IRE) 127 – Darrery 98 (Darshaan **82 p**
133) [2002 p8g* Dec 14] 55,000Y: fourth foal: half-brother to useful 1998 2-y-o 7f
winner Al Waffi (by Fairy King) and to 7f winner in Greece by Green Desert: dam, 1¼m/
1½m winner, out of smart performer up to 1m Flamenco: 3/1 from 5/1, fairly useful form
when winning 12-runner maiden at Lingfield by length from Extra Gear, staying on really
well to lead close home (first winner with first runner for trainer): should stay 1¼m: sure
to improve. *M. A. Magnusson*

MADELINE BASSETT (IRE) 4 b.f. Kahyasi 130 – Impressive Lady 98 (Mr Fluoro- **87**
carbon 126) [2002 85+, a95: 9g 10g³ 9.5m 10m⁶ 11.5m⁴ 10.3f⁴ 8.9f p10g* p10g⁵ p10g³ **a93**
Dec 14] smallish filly: fluent mover: fairly useful handicapper: won apprentice race at
Lingfield in November: effective at 1¼m/1½m: acts on soft going, good to firm and
polytrack: tried visored: waited with: sometimes finds little. *G. A. Butler*

MADERNO (USA) 3 ch.g. Nureyev (USA) 131 – Mr P'S Princess (USA) (Mr Pros- **109**
pector (USA)) [2002 6s* 7m³ 6d⁴ 6s⁴ 6d⁵ 7m Dec 15] sturdy, good-topped gelding: third
foal: brother to very smart 1999 2-y.-o 5f/6f winner (including Phoenix Stakes/Prix
Morny) Fasliyev and half-brother to winner at 1¼m and 2m in USA/UAE Dubai To
Dubai (by Kris S): dam unraced half-sister to very smart US Grade 1 9f winner Menifee,
also runner-up in Kentucky Derby/Preakness Stakes: useful performer: won maiden at
the Curragh in March: best effort when 2¾ lengths third to Redback in Greenham Stakes
at Newbury next time: left A. O'Brien, Ireland and renamed Chinook before final outing:
stays 7f: acts on good to firm going, possibly on soft. *P. C. Kan, Hong Kong*

MAD GENIUS 3 b.g. Makbul 104 – Rinca (Unfuwain (USA) 131) [2002 –: f8.5g Mar **–**
9] tailed-off last in maidens/claimer. *T. H. Caldwell*

MADIBA   3 b.g. Emperor Jones (USA) 119 – Priluki 65 (Lycius (USA) 124) [2002 69p: **81**
7m f8.5g³ 8.2d² 9.9s² 12g³ 12f⁴ p12g² p12g³ 14m⁴ p12g⁴ Oct 9] leggy, useful-looking
gelding: fairly useful maiden: stays 1¾m: acts on soft going, good to firm (probably on
firm) and all-weather: gelded after final start: consistent. *S. Dow*

MADIES PRIDE (IRE)   4 b.f. Fayruz 116 – June Lady (Junius (USA) 124) [2002 52:   **58**
5m⁵ 5m² 5.1g f5g Oct 17] angular filly: modest handicapper: probably best at 5f: acts on
good to firm going: has looked wayward. *J. J. Quinn*

MADRASEE   4 b.f. Beveled (USA) – Pendona 72 (Blue Cashmere 129) [2002 70: p5g   **79**
p6g⁴ p6g* p5g 5.3f* 5m³ 5.3g⁵ p6g³ 6m 6d² p6g⁴ 5.3g² 5m³ 5f* 5g p7g p5g³ Dec 21] fair
handicapper: won at Lingfield (apprentices) in February, Brighton in April and Goodwood in September: effective at 5f/6f: acts on firm going, soft and polytrack: usually
races prominently: consistent. *L. Montague Hall*

MAEDANCE   2 br.f. (Jan 16) Groom Dancer (USA) 128 – Maestrale (Top Ville 129)   **73**
[2002 6m⁵ 6m⁵ 7m⁶ 8m 8f⁴ Sep 26] good-topped filly: fifth foal: half-sister to 3 winners,
including useful 1m winner Ebony Heights (by Polar Falcon) and 7f to 1¼m winner
Birthday Venture (by Soviet Star): dam unraced half-sister to high-class middle-distance
performer Head For Heights: fair maiden: will stay at least 1¼m: raced only on ground
firmer than good. *G. B. Balding*

MAFRUZ   3 ch.c. Hamas (IRE) 125§ – Braari (USA) 97 (Gulch (USA)) [2002 6s² 6m³   **75**
7g⁴ 7g* 8s Nov 2] fourth foal: closely related to useful 2000 2-y-o 5.7f/6f winner Shaard
(by Anabaa) and 5-y-o Kareeb: dam 2-y-o 6f winner: fair performer: left B. Hills 10,000
gns before winning maiden at Leicester in October: should stay 1m: acts on soft and good
to firm going. *R. A. Fahey*

MAGDALEON   4 b.f. Lion Cavern (USA) 117 – Magdala (IRE) (Sadler's Wells (USA)   **–**
132) [2002 51: f12s⁶ Jan 5] leggy, lengthy filly: modest maiden at 3 yrs: well held only
4-y-o start: sold €5,000 in November. *R. Ford*

MAGELTA   5 b.g. Magic Ring (IRE) 115 – Pounelta 91 (Tachypous 128) [2002 73: f7s   **61**
p8g* p10g p8g³ p8g⁶ Feb 26] big, useful-looking gelding: modest performer: won seller
at Lingfield in January: stays 1m: acts on good to firm going, good to soft and all-weather:
visored final start: often tongue tied. *R. M. H. Cowell*

MAGENTA RISING (IRE)   2 ch.f. (Apr 4) College Chapel 122 – Fashion Queen   **79**
(Chilibang 120) [2002 6d f8.5s³ f8.5g*ᵈⁱˢ f8.5f* f8.5g⁵ f8g² Dec 27] IR 500Y: fourth
foal: dam ran twice: fair performer: first past post in maiden at Wolverhampton (beat Mr
Mischief by short head, disqualified due to jockey deliberately impeding that horse) in
November: won similar event there later in month by 2 lengths from Princess Shoka:
stays 8.5f: acts on fibresand: tongue tied on debut. *P. W. D'Arcy*

MAGGIE'S PET   5 b.m. Minshaanshu Amad (USA) 91§ – Run Fast For Gold (Deep   **57**
Run 119) [2002 10.2f f8.5g² f8g⁵ Dec 4] second foal: dam poor winning hurdler: left
G. McCourt after debut: slowly away when second in maiden at Wolverhampton, best
effort: should stay at least 1¼m. *K. Bell*

MAGHANIM   2 b.c. (Mar 10) Nashwan (USA) 135 – Azdihaar (USA) 81 (Mr Pros-   **107**
pector (USA)) [2002 7m² 7m* 7g Oct 6] lengthy, quite attractive colt: has scope: fourth
foal: brother to German 7f winner Mosaahim and half-brother to useful French 1999
2-y-o 6.5f winner Sand Pigeon (by Lammtarra): dam, 7f winner, half-sister to 1000
Guineas winner Shadayid and smart performer up to 7f Fath: useful form: shaped well
when second to Almushahar in maiden at Newmarket: landed odds in minor event at
Doncaster in September by 2½ lengths from Magistretti, racing freely early and quickening clear: something probably amiss when well beaten in Grand Criterium at Longchamp:
should stay 1m. *J. L. Dunlop*

MAGHAS (IRE)   8 ch.g. Lahib (USA) 129 – Rawaabe (USA) 87 (Nureyev (USA)   **48**
131) [2002 47: f5s f5s f5g³ f6g f5g f5g f5g³ f5g⁴ Dec 31] poor performer: left G. Stack,
Ireland, after second start, R. Marvin (and off 8 months) after fifth one: best at 5f: acts on
heavy ground and fibresand: usually blinkered prior to last 6 starts: none too consistent.
J. M. Bradley

MAGICAL BAILIWICK (IRE)   6 ch.g. Magical Wonder (USA) 125 – Alpine   **59**
Dance (USA) 62§ (Apalachee (USA) 137) [2002 –: 12.1g⁶ Aug 8] modest handicapper:
stays 1½m: acts on heavy and good to firm ground: often blinkered. *R. J. Baker*

MAGICAL DAY   3 ch.f. Halling (USA) 133 – Ahla 90 (Unfuwain (USA) 131) [2002   **54** §
52: 10m 8m³ 11.1v³ 10.3f³ 10m 10.9m Sep 16] rather leggy filly: modest maiden: should
stay 1½m: acts on any going: flashed tail and looked unwilling third start: untrustworthy.
W. G. M. Turner

MAGICAL FIELD 4 ch.f. Deploy 131 – Ash Glade (Nashwan (USA) 135) [2002 **59** p13g² p8g⁶ p10g³ 10g 10s 12d Nov 1] first foal: dam unraced close relative to 7-y-o Ulundi and half-sister to 1000 Guineas winner Wince: modest maiden: ran once for M. Zilber in France at 3 yrs: should be suited by 1½m+: acts on polytrack. *Mrs M. Reveley*

MAGICAL MYTH 3 b.f. Robellino (USA) 127 – Sinking (Midyan (USA) 124) [2002 **–** 50p: 8d 12d Nov 5] sturdy, good-quartered filly: has scope: signs of ability only on sole 2-y-o outing when trained by D. Nicholls. *J. G. Given*

MAGIC AMOUR 4 ch.g. Sanglamore (USA) 126 – Rakli 84 (Warning 136) [2002 7g **57** 10m 7m 7f 10s 10.9g 6m³ 6f 6d Oct 18] strong, lengthy gelding: third foal: half-brother to 7f (at 2 yrs) to 9f winner Agiotage and French/US 1m/9f winner Flinch (both by Zafonic): dam, ran once, out of useful half-sister to Xaar: modest maiden: stays easy 6f: acts on firm going. *Ian Williams*

MAGIC ARROW (USA) 6 b.g. Defensive Play (USA) 118 – Magic Blue (USA) **–** (Cure The Blues (USA)) [2002 –: f16g Dec 4] seems of little account nowadays. *Ian Emmerson*

MAGIC BENGIE 3 b.g. Magic Ring (IRE) 115 – Zinzi (Song 132) [2002 56: 7m Apr **–** 5] good-topped gelding: has scope: modest maiden at best. *Mrs L. Stubbs*

MAGIC CHARM 4 b.f. Magic Ring (IRE) 115 – Loch Clair (IRE) 53 (Lomond (USA) **–** 128) [2002 44: f12s⁵ p12g f9.4g* f12g⁶ f9.4g f8g⁵ 11g 10m Sep 19] angular filly: poor **a44** handicapper: won at Wolverhampton in January: left N. Littmoden after sixth start: probably best around 9f/1¼m: acts on firm going and all-weather: usually visored/ blinkered in 2002: sometimes looks away. *A. G. Newcombe*

MAGIC COMBINATION (IRE) 9 b.g. Scenic 128 – Etage (Ile de Bourbon (USA) **79** 133) [2002 11.9g 14d* 16.1d* 17.5g Sep 20] leggy gelding: one-time useful handicapper, fair nowadays: missed 2001 season: won at Haydock (flashed tail/carried head high) in July and Newcastle (idled) in September: stays 2m: acts on heavy and good to firm going: blinkered once at 4 yrs. *L. Lungo*

MAGIC EAGLE 5 b.g. Magic Ring (IRE) 115 – Shadow Bird 70 (Martinmas 128) **–** [2002 56, a76: p5g f6g² p6g⁵ f6g f6g f6g⁵ f6s f8s f6s f6g Dec 10] quite good-topped **a68 d** gelding: fair performer on all-weather: left G. L. Moore after fifth start: best form at 6f: acts on soft going, good to firm and all-weather: usually races prominently: on downgrade. *R. Wilman*

MAGIC FEATHERS 4 b.g. Anabaa (USA) 130 – Plume Magique (Kenmare (FR) **–** 125) [2002 50: 12.4m 13.8m May 25] modest maiden at 3 yrs: well held both starts in 2002: tried blinkered. *M. E. Sowersby*

MAGIC FLUTE 6 ch.m. Magic Ring (IRE) 115 – Megan's Flight 74 (Welsh Pageant **78** 132) [2002 71: 8g 8g* 8.3m⁶ 8g 8f 8m 7.1g Sep 23] good-bodied mare: fair handicapper: won at Bath (for second successive year) in July: best around 1m: acts on good to firm and good to soft going: has been tongue tied: bled from nose final 5-y-o start: tends to race freely. *R. J. Baker*

MAGIC GLADE 3 b.g. Magic Ring (IRE) 115 – Ash Glade (Nashwan (USA) 135) **98 p** [2002 7g³ f6g* 6m³ 6g² 6f³ Oct 12] second foal: dam unraced close relative to 7-y-o Ulundi and half-sister to 1000 Guineas winner Wince: useful and progressive form: made all in maiden at Wolverhampton in July: placed in competitive handicaps at Ascot (second to Greenslades) and York (third to The Tatling, travelled strongly long way, again carried head high/wandered) last 2 starts: likely to prove best at 5f/6f: acts on fibresand, raced only on good going or firmer on turf: probably capable of better still. *R. Charlton*

MAGIC HANNE 3 ch.f. Magic Ring (IRE) 115 – Sunfleet 59 (Red Sunset 120) [2002 **55** –: 8s f7g³ 5.9s³ 7f 6.9s 5.9g 5.9g f6g Dec 27] rather leggy filly: modest maiden: should stay 1m: acts on soft going and fibresand. *G. C. H. Chung*

MAGIC LODGE 3 b.g. Grand Lodge (USA) 125 – Samsung Spirit 79 (Statoblest **–** 120) [2002 67: 8g 8g 9.9g 7m 14.1f 7.2d⁵ Jun 21] sturdy gelding: fair maiden at 2 yrs: no form in 2002: tried blinkered. *J. R. Weymes*

MAGIC MAID 3 b.f. Presidium 124 – Mrs Magic (Magic Mirror 105) [2002 –: 6m **–** Jul 26] no form. *H. S. Howe*

MAGIC MAMMA'S TOO 2 b.g. (Apr 5) Magic Ring (IRE) 115 – Valona Valley **58** (IRE) (Reprimand 122) [2002 7g⁵ 7.1d⁶ f6g⁶ Oct 17] 2,200Y: rather leggy gelding: third foal: dam ran twice at 2 yrs: modest form in maidens: trained first 2 starts by H. McWilliams: likely to prove best up to 1m. *T. D. Barron*

MAGIC MISTRESS 3 b.f. Magic Ring (IRE) 115 – Sight'n Sound 63 (Chief Singer **79**
131) [2002 8f 7f⁵ 7.1d* 8.2s⁵ 7s⁵ 8v⁴ Nov 8] tall filly: second foal: dam, 13f winner, half-
sister to smart performers Grey Shot (stayer) and Night Shot (sprinter): fair performer:
won maiden at Chepstow in July: best efforts around 7f: acts on soft going. *S. C. Williams*

MAGIC MOON 3 gr.g. So Factual (USA) 120 – Moon Magic 62 (Polish Precedent **78**
(USA) 131) [2002 10m³ 10f⁵ 10.2d⁵ May 31] strong gelding: fourth foal: half-brother to
a winner abroad by Be My Chief: dam once-raced half-sister to Moon Madness and
Sheriff's Star: fair form in maidens: raced freely last 2 starts, carrying head high final one:
dead. *Lady Herries*

MAGIC MUSIC (IRE) 3 b.f. Magic Ring (IRE) 115 – Chiming Melody 71 (Cure **77**
The Blues (USA)) [2002 67: 8.2m 6s 6g 7m 7f⁴ 6.9g 7m² 6.1m* 6d³ Oct 14] tall, plain
filly: fair handicapper: won at Nottingham in September: effective at 6f/7f: probably acts
on any going. *Mrs H. Dalton*

MAGIC MYTH (IRE) 2 b.f. (Apr 21) Revoque (IRE) 122 – Family At War (USA) **81**
71 (Explodent (USA)) [2002 5d⁶ 6f⁵ 6d⁵ 5v* 6d* 6g⁴ 6g⁵ Sep 19] IR 30,000Y: quite
good-topped filly: has scope: seventh foal: sister to 3-y-o Diddymu and half-sister to 3
winners by Common Grounds, notably smart 5f winner (including at 2 yrs) Flanders: dam
2-y-o 5f winner: fairly useful performer: won maiden at Hamilton in July and nursery at
Newmarket in August: good efforts in nurseries at York and Ayr last 2 starts: will stay 7f:
acts on heavy going: blinkered third start. *T. D. Easterby*

MAGIC PIPER 2 ch.g. (Feb 9) Piccolo 121 – Magical Dancer (IRE) 53 (Magical **81**
Wonder (USA) 125) [2002 5m³ 5m 5g⁴ 6m⁴ 6g³ 6m² 5m 5.1f⁶ Sep 16] 25,000F, 32,000Y:
close-coupled gelding: first foal: dam, 1m winner, half-sister to smart sprinter Don't
Worry Me: fairly useful maiden: below form 3 of last 4 starts: effective at 5f/6f: raced
only on good going or firmer. *R. Hannon*

MAGIC RAINBOW 7 b.g. Magic Ring (IRE) 115 – Blues Indigo 103 (Music Boy **73**
124) [2002 85: p6g p5g⁴ f6g² 5f⁴ 5.1g 6m 6f 5g⁵ Jul 30] leggy gelding: poor mover: fairly **a89**
useful on all-weather, fair on turf: effective at 5f to easy 7f: seems unsuited by soft/heavy
going, acts on any other turf/all-weather: sometimes starts slowly. *M. L. W. Bell*

MAGIC RED 2 ch.c. (Mar 17) Magic Ring (IRE) 115 – Jacquelina (USA) 66 (Private **71 d**
Account (USA)) [2002 6d 5.1g 6m² 7d 6m 8g 8s Oct 22] 5,500F, 7,000Y: big, rather leggy
colt: has a round action: half-brother to fairly useful 1¼m winner Eyeballs Out
(by Polar Falcon): dam, ran 3 times (should have stayed 1¼m), half-sister to smart
sprinter Zarani Sidi Anna: fair maiden: soundly beaten after second to Indian Haven at
Yarmouth in July: should stay at least 7f: acts on good to firm ground: tried visored.
M. J. Ryan

MAGIC SONGBIRD 3 b.f. Magic Ring (IRE) 115 – Winsong Melody (Music **–**
Maestro 119) [2002 50: f5g f6g Jan 25] modest maiden at 2 yrs: no form in 2002.
C. A. Dwyer

MAGIC SOUND 4 ch.g. Savahra Sound 111 – Ace Girl 58 (Stanford 121§) [2002 52: **–**
8.5m6 10m 6.1g Jul 5] lengthy gelding: modest maiden at 3 yrs: no form in 2002: visored
once. *M. J. Polglase*

MAGIC STONE 2 br.g. (Feb 24) Magic Ring (IRE) 115 – Ridgewood Ruby (IRE) 77 **–**
(Indian Ridge 123) [2002 5.7m 6.1d 5.7f Jul 25] first foal: dam, maiden who stayed 7f,
out of half-sister to dam of Ridgewood Pearl: well held in maidens. *A. Charlton*

MAGIC TRICK 3 b.c. Magic Ring (IRE) 115 – Les Amis 70 (Alzao (USA) 117) [2002 **76**
91: 8g 7.6f 8f 7d⁵ 8m⁵ 7f³ 7m⁵ 7m 7d p7g Nov 14] big, well-made colt: fair performer:
probably stays 1m: acts on firm going, good to soft and polytrack: has worn cheekpieces:
sometimes sweating/on toes: has hung left. *B. W. Hills*

MAGIC WARRIOR 2 b.c. (Apr 11) Magic Ring (IRE) 115 – Clarista (USA) 67 (Riva **67**
Ridge (USA)) [2002 5.2g⁶ 6d p7g⁶ p7g p6g* p7g³ f6g⁶ Dec 20] 1,500Y: half-brother to
several winners, including useful 7f winner (including at 2 yrs) Indhar and fairly useful 5f
(at 2 yrs) and 7f winner Huntswood, later successful at 7.5f to 10.5f in Italy (both by
Warning): dam, maiden who stayed 1¼m, half-sister to Derby winner Teenoso: fair
performer: won seller at Lingfield in November: effective at 6f/7f: acts on polytrack, well
beaten on turf. *S. L. Keightley*

MAGIQUE ETOILE (IRE) 6 b.m. Magical Wonder (USA) 125 – Shes A Dancer **–**
(IRE) (Alzao (USA) 117) [2002 –: 7d Jun 11] good-bodied mare: modest maiden
handicapper at 4 yrs: no form since: tried blinkered/visored. *Dr J. R. J. Naylor*

MAGISTRETTI (USA) 2 b.c. (Mar 5) Diesis 133 – Ms Strike Zone (USA) (Deputy **96**
Minister (CAN)) [2002 7.1d* 7d² 7m² 8g⁵ Sep 28] $150,000F, IR 170,000Y: big, strong

colt: has scope: first foal: dam, 8.5f winner in USA, out of sister to Damister: useful performer: won maiden at Sandown in June: runner-up in listed race at Newmarket (beaten 5 lengths by Surbiton) and minor event at Doncaster (beaten 2½ lengths by Maghanim): sweating, edgy and free to post, creditable effort when just under 6 lengths fifth to Al Jadeed in Royal Lodge Stakes at Ascot, racing freely in front: bred to stay further than 1m: yet to race on extremes of going. *N. A. Callaghan*

MAGNIFICO 3 b.c. Mark of Esteem (IRE) 137 – Blush Rambler (IRE) (Blushing **103**
Groom (FR) 131) [2002 8m 8.2g* 8m* Jun 21] strong, quite attractive colt: half-brother to several winners, including smart 1m (at 2 yrs) and 1½m winner Rambling Rose (by Cadeaux Genereux) and useful 1¼m winner Kiftsgate (by Kris): dam Irish 1½m winner: progressive form: played up in stall/tailed off on debut, then won maiden at Nottingham in May and minor event at Newmarket (useful form to beat Krugerrand ¾ length, led well inside final 1f) in June: will be suited by 1¼m: looked open to further improvement. *Sir Michael Stoute*

MAGNUSSON 4 b.g. Primo Dominie 121 – Nunsharpa 87 (Sharpo 132) [2002 79+: **–**
7m 6g 6g 6m 6g 6d f8s Sep 5] tall gelding: fair at 3 yrs: no form in 2002. *M. Wigham*

MAHLSTICK (IRE) 4 b.g. Tagula (IRE) 116 – Guv's Joy (IRE) 72 (Thatching 131) **52 +**
[2002 43: p6g⁵ f8g p7g⁶ p6g 6g⁴ 7m 8m 7m⁴ 8f 6g⁶ Oct 28] good topped gelding: modest maiden: best at 6f/7f: acts on polytrack, best turf efforts on good going or firmer: tried visored. *D. W. P. Arbuthnot*

MAHROOS (USA) 4 ch.g. Kingmambo (USA) 125 – Mur Taasha (USA) 108 (River- **107**
man (USA) 131) [2002 8m* 10.1d* 10g* 10m³ a8.5f² Dec 26] quite attractive gelding: third foal: closely related to smart performer up to 1m Iftitah (by Gone West), 7f winner at 2 yrs: dam, 7f/1m winner, out of smart 7f winner Linda's Magic: useful performer: runner-up in newcomers race at Chantilly at 2 yrs for D. Loder: unraced at 3 yrs (refused to enter stall intended reappearance): won maiden at Newmarket in August and minor events at Epsom (beat Persian King by 1¼ lengths) and Ascot (beat Goblet of Fire by length despite flashing tail) in September: left J. Gosden prior to good short-head second to Northern Rock in minor event at Nad Al Sheba final start: effective at 8.5f/1¼m: acts on dirt, good to firm and good to soft going: takes strong hold. *K. P. McLaughlin, UAE*

MAHSUSIE (IRE) 3 gr.f. Mukaddamah (USA) 125 – La Susiane (Persepolis (FR) **103**
127) [2002 97: 5s² 7m³ 6s 6s 6g 8g 8d² 7s⁴ Oct 26] big, good-topped filly: useful performer: won maiden at Leopardstown and listed race at the Curragh in May 2001: best efforts when short- kept second to Serov in handicap at the Curragh and ¾-length third to Lahinch in listed event at Leopardstown first 2 starts in 2002: left F. Ennis, Ireland, after sixth one: seems to stay 1m: acts on soft and good to firm going: blinkered fourth outing: sold 60,000 gns: sent to USA. *K. Bell*

Moyglare Stud Stakes, the Curragh—Mail The Desert (No.6) makes virtually all and just holds on from Luminata (far side) and Pearl Dance; Danaskaya (left) is fourth

MAIDEN VOYAGE 4 b.f. Slip Anchor 136 – Elaine Tully (IRE) 80 (Persian Bold **54** 123) [2002 47: 14.1d 14.1d³ 16.2g³ 12m⁶ 12.3g² 9.2s⁵ Jun 19] lengthy, good-bodied filly: modest maiden handicapper: stays 2m: acts on good to firm and good to soft ground. *Mrs J. R. Ramsden*

MAID FOR A MONARCH 2 b.f. (Apr 16) King's Signet (USA) 110 – Regan (USA) **–** 60 (Lear Fan (USA) 130) [2002 7s 7.2g p7g Oct 9] third foal: dam, ran twice on Flat, winning hurdler/chaser up to 25f: well held in maidens. *J. G. Given*

MAID FOR FREEDOM (USA) 4 gr.f. Trempolino (USA) 135 – Spectacular Native **72** (USA) (Spectacular Bid (USA)) [2002 64: p8g* Feb 27] leggy, unfurnished filly: fair performer, lightly raced: won maiden at Lingfield only 4-y-o start: stays 1m: acts on polytrack: sent to USA. *G. A. Butler*

MAID FOR RUNNING 3 b.f. Namaqualand (USA) – Scarlet Lake 60 (Reprimand **74** 122) [2002 80: 9f 9m May 6] close-coupled filly: fairly useful 5f winner at 2 yrs: fair form in 2002 only on reappearance: probably stays 9f: acts on good to firm going, probably on firm (though carried head high on it): sold 11,500 gns in December. *G. A. Butler*

MAID FOR THE AISLE 2 ch.f. (Mar 29) College Chapel 122 – Debutante Days 83 **–** (Dominion 123) [2002 7g Jul 24] 13,000Y: first foal: dam, 1¼m to 12.4f winner, also useful hurdler: 20/1, well beaten in maiden at Leicester. *J. G. Given*

MAID TO PERFECTION 3 b.f. Sadler's Wells (USA) 132 – Maid For The Hills **102** 101 (Indian Ridge 123) [2002 84p: 10f⁶ 7.1d⁴ 10d* 10g⁶ 12d³ 12.5v Nov 20] leggy, finely-made filly: useful performer: won handicap at Leicester in August by short head from Able Baker Charlie: best effort when 1¼ lengths third to Kiltubber in listed race at Milan penultimate start: stayed 1½m: acted on good to soft going: stud. *J. L. Dunlop*

MAIL THE DESERT (IRE) 2 b.f. (Jan 23) Desert Prince (IRE) 130 – Mail Boat **103** (Formidable (USA) 125) [2002 6d* 6m⁴ 7s⁴ 7.1m³ 7s 7m² 7g* Sep 1] IR 54,000Y:

Mr John Livock's "Mail The Desert"

good-topped filly: third foal: dam unraced half-sister to smart 1¼m/1½m performer Dry Dock: useful performer: won minor event at Windsor in May and Moyglare Stud Stakes at the Curragh (gamely made most, by head from Luminata) in September: in frame in 3 listed races and Prestige Stakes at Goodwood (1¼ lengths second to Geminiani) in between: will stay 1m: acts on good to firm ground, possibly not on soft: goes well with forcing tactics. *M. R. Channon*

MAIMANA (IRE) 3 b. or br.f. Desert King (IRE) 129 – Staff Approved 94 (Teenoso (USA) 135) [2002 79: 9.9g³ 12s* 12.6m* 11.6g² 13.5s⁶ 12g² 12v⁵ Nov 9] good-topped filly: useful performer: won maiden at Kempton and minor event at Warwick in June: good efforts when 7½ lengths sixth to Bernimixa in Prix de Pomone at Deauville and ¾-length second to Defining in handicap at Newmarket fifth/sixth starts: barely stayed 13.5f: acted on heavy and good to firm going: visits Indian Ridge. *M. A. Jarvis* **105**

MAINPOWER (IRE) 2 b.c. (Apr 18) Lake Coniston (IRE) 131 – Chipewyas (FR) (Bering 136) [2002 6d Oct 14] 2,000Y, resold 2,600Y: first foal: dam unraced: 66/1, always behind in maiden at Windsor. *R. M. Flower* **–**

MAIRI'S WEDDING 3 b.f. Atraf 116 – Crofters Ceilidh 101 (Scottish Reel 123) [2002 59: 5.1m f5g⁶ 5s 5g f5g⁶ 6.1m² 6.1m⁶ 6.1m f6g f7g Oct 19] small filly: modest maiden: left B. McMahon 2,000 gns after seventh start: should stay 7f: acts on firm and good to soft ground (little form on fibresand). *J. L. Spearing* **51 a–**

MAI SCENE 2 ch.f. (May 5) Among Men (USA) 124 – Scenicris (IRE) 73 (Scenic 128) [2002 6m f8.5f Nov 29] 2,500Y: unfurnished filly: first foal: dam, 1m winner, out of sister to 2000 Guineas winner Bolkonski: tailed off in maidens at Thirsk and Wolverhampton. *R. Hollinshead* **–**

MAI TAI (IRE) 7 b.m. Scenic 128 – Oystons Propweekly 74 (Swing Easy (USA) 126) [2002 46, a64: f7g f7g f8g⁶ f8g 8.5m 7g² f8.5g 8g² 8f⁶ 10m 8g 7.9g⁴ 8.5g* f8g f11g² Dec 4] good-bodied mare: modest performer: won amateur handicap at Beverley in August: effective at 7f, probably at 11f: acts on soft going, good to firm and fibresand: sometimes visored/blinkered: none too consistent. *G. M. Moore* **53**

MAJBORAH (IRE) 3 b.f. Entrepreneur 123 – Safka (USA) 104 (Irish River (FR) 131) [2002 p10g 6m p12g Sep 4] 20,000Y: closely related to smart 6f (at 2 yrs) and 1m winner Speedfit Too (by Scenic) and half-sister to several winners, including useful Irish 1994 2-y-o 7f winner Sannkaya (by Soviet Star): dam, 2-y-o 5f winner, half-sister to smart performer up to 1m Safawan: well held in Lingfield maidens: sold 3,000 gns in December. *C. E. Brittain* **–**

MAJESTIC BAY (IRE) 6 b.g. Unfuwain (USA) 131 – That'll Be The Day (IRE) 68 (Thatching 131) [2002 93: 11.8s Oct 28] sturdy gelding: fairly useful handicapper at best: well held only start in 2002: blinkered once as 4-y-o. *J. A. B. Old* **–**

MAJESTIC HORIZON 2 b.c. (Apr 4) Marju (IRE) 127 – Jumairah Sunset 67 (Be My Guest (USA) 126) [2002 7d² Jul 9] 160,000Y: well-made colt: has a quick action: third foal: dam, 7f winner, closely related to smart 1m/9f performer Fanaar: 11/2 and backward, promising ½-length second of 12 to Tycoon Hall in maiden at Newmarket, seeming sure to win when leading under 2f out but running green and caught on line: wore crossed noseband: should do better and win races if all is well. *D. R. Loder* **96 p**

MAJESTIC QUEST (IRE) 4 b.g. Piccolo 121 – Teanarco (IRE) 94 (Kafu 120) [2002 55, a–: f6g⁴ p6g⁶ p10g f7g³ f7g p7g p6g f7⁵ 8.3s 6d 7d Jun 11] close-coupled gelding: modest performer: left P. D. Evans after seventh start: stays easy 7f: acts on all-weather and firm going: has been early to post: on downgrade. *D. Burchell* **50 d**

MAJESTIC TIMES (IRE) 2 b.c. (Apr 5) Bluebird (USA) 125 – Simply Times (USA) 64 (Dodge (USA)) [2002 7.2s² 6m Sep 13] 24,000Y: well-made colt: third foal: half-brother to 3-y-o Welsh Emperor and 4-y-o Forever Times: dam ran twice at 2 yrs: fair form when second to Pure Speculation in maiden at Ayr and eleventh to Fleetwood Bay in sales race at Doncaster (short of room), slowly away each time: will probably stay 1m: capable of better. *T. D. Easterby* **79 p**

MAJHOOL 3 b.g. Mark of Esteem (IRE) 137 – Be Peace (USA) (Septieme Ciel (USA) 123) [2002 71d: 6m³ p6g* 6d⁵ 5m p6g* 5.1f⁴ 7.6m⁵ Aug 21] tall gelding: fair handicapper: won at Lingfield in May and July: best at 5f/6f: acts on firm ground and polytrack: has been early to post. *G. L. Moore* **74**

MAJHUD (IRE) 2 b.f. (Jan 25) Machiavellian (USA) 123 – Winsa (USA) 80 (Riverman (USA) 131) [2002 7m⁵ 7m³ 7d⁴ Nov 2] leggy, useful-looking filly: first foal: dam, 1½m winner, sister to high-class miler Bahri and half-sister to very smart 1996 2-y-o 7f winner Bahhare: fairly useful form in maidens: in frame at Kempton and Newmarket: should be suited by 1m+. *J. L. Dunlop* **80**

MAJIK 3 ch.g. Pivotal 124 – Revoke (USA) 70 (Riverman (USA) 131) [2002 p7g 8s **70** 8.1f 6s* 6g* 7g 6.1m⁴ 6m⁴ f6g* p7g⁶ Nov 14] close-coupled gelding: seventh foal: half-brother to fairly useful winner up to 7f (including in UAE) First Principle (by Rudimentary): dam maiden half-sister to very smart French/US 1½m performer Contested Bid: fair handicapper: won at Haydock/Brighton in June and Southwell in October: should stay 7f: acts on soft going, good to firm and fibresand: reportedly had breathing problem third start. *D. J. S. ffrench Davis*

MAJOR ATTRACTION 7 gr.g. Major Jacko 78 – My Friend Melody (Sizzling **59** Melody 117) [2002 64: 11m* 12g 10.9d 11.5f² 12.3m³ 10.5m² 12m 12f* 14.1m Oct 5] sturdy gelding: modest handicapper: won at Redcar in May and Catterick in September: probably stays 13f: acts on fibresand and firm going, not on softer than good: tried blinkered/visored: sometimes slowly away: held up. *W. M. Brisbourne*

MAJOR CAVELLI (IRE) 2 b.c. (Apr 29) Entrepreneur 123 – Eljazzi 92 (Artaius **75 §** (USA) 129) [2002 5.3f² 5m* 6m⁵ 6m 7g 6g⁶ Oct 28] 40,000F, IR 90,000Y: strong, well-made colt: closely related to useful Irish 1½m winner Chamela Bay and smart performer up to 2m Chiang Mai (both by Sadler's Wells) and half-brother to several winners, notably Prix de Diane winner/good broodmare Rafha (by Kris): dam 2-y-o 7f winner who stayed 1¼m: fair performer: won maiden at Newmarket in April: off 4 months after third start: below form on return, reportedly finishing lame when favourite for seller fifth outing: should stay at least 7f: raced on good ground or firmer: very slowly away fourth start: probably ungenuine: sold 6,500 gns, sent to Holland. *N. A. Callaghan*

MAJORITY RULE (IRE) 3 b.g. Sadler's Wells 132 – Lady Liberty (NZ) **90** (Noble Bijou (USA)) [2002 12f* 10.2s⁶ 16.2m 11.7g⁵ Jul 14] good-topped gelding: half-brother to smart 1996 2-y-o 7f/1m winner Equal Rights (by Royal Academy) and to winners in Australia by Bluebird and Sir Tristram: dam Australian Group 1 1½m winner: fairly useful performer: won maiden at Newmarket in May: stiff tasks after, including when eighth in Queen's Vase at Royal Ascot third outing: probably stays 2m: acts on firm ground, well beaten on soft: ran in snatches in visor/blinkers last 2 starts: sold 13,000 gns. *J. H. M. Gosden*

MAJOR LAUGH 3 ch.c. Colonel Collins (USA) 122 – Joytime (John de Coombe **77** 122) [2002 92: f6s⁵ 6g 6.1d May 18] big, strong colt: fairly useful at 2 yrs: fair form first 2 outings in 2002, then left B. Hills: may prove better at 7f than 6f: acts on firm going, good to soft and all-weather: sold 6,800 gns in July. *W. Jarvis*

MAJOR SPECULATION (IRE) 2 b.c. (Apr 5) Spectrum (IRE) 126 – Pacific **85** Grove 89 (Persian Bold 123) [2002 7m p7g* 5m⁴ 6m³ 7.1m⁵ Sep 7] 65,000F, 70,000Y: smallish, sturdy colt: third foal: half-brother to Irish 6f winner John Dorans Melody (by Bluebird) and 2001 2-y-o 6f winner Caroline Island (by Catrail), both fairly useful: dam, 2-y-o 7f/1m winner, half-sister to useful French performer around 1¼m All Glory: fairly useful performer: idled when winning maiden at Lingfield in July: creditable efforts in minor event/nurseries after: stays 7f: acts on polytrack, raced only on good to firm going on turf. *G. A. Butler*

MAKAM (IRE) 2 b.f. (Apr 28) Green Desert (USA) 127 – Simaat (USA) 72 (Mr **68** Prospector (USA)) [2002 8.1f³ 7g Oct 14] angular filly: sixth foal: closely related to useful 7f winner Al Ihsas and fairly useful 1998 2-y-o 7.5f winner Samut (both by Danehill) and half-sister to a winner in Spain by Last Tycoon: dam 1m winner: much better effort in maidens (fair form) when third to Blackwater Angel at Haydock: sold 21,000 gns, sent to USA. *J. H. M. Gosden*

MAKARIM (IRE) 6 ch.g. Generous (IRE) 139 – Emmaline (USA) (Affirmed (USA)) **80 d** [2002 89§, a92§: 14.4m⁵ 14.1d 14m 12m 13.3f 15.4m⁶ Jul 29] tall gelding: fairly useful handicapper at best: creditable effort in 2002 only on reappearance: stays 2m: acts on fibresand and firm ground: blinkered once: usually held up: has hung badly right: no battler. *M. R. Bosley*

MAKE MY HAY 3 b.g. Bluegrass Prince (IRE) 110 – Shashi (IRE) 79 (Shaadi (USA) **51** 126) [2002 –: p10g 8.1f 8.2f 11.6m 12d⁴ 8.3d 11.8s f12g f11g⁶ Dec 4] leggy, sparely- **a–** made gelding: modest maiden: ran poorly last 4 starts, running none too keen final one: better at 1½m than shorter: acts on good to firm and good to soft going, no form on all-weather. *J. Cullinan*

MAKHLAB (USA) 2 b.c. (Feb 8) Dixieland Band (USA) – Avasand (USA) **112 p** (Avatar (USA)) [2002 7d 6d* 7m* 8m³ 7s* Oct 25]
Recent winners of the Vodafone Horris Hill Stakes have hardly gone on to set the world alight, but the latest winner Makhlab looks to have a better chance than most of making further progress. He won at Newbury in quite good style and

has the physical scope to train on. Tirol was the last Horris Hill winner to achieve classic success, when winning the Two Thousand Guineas in 1990, and Makhlab is also due to take the classic trail, though the Irish Guineas is reportedly more likely to be his principal target.

Down the field in a well-contested maiden at Newmarket in July on his debut, Makhlab got off the mark in a similar event at Pontefract in August, keeping on gamely to beat Fiddlers Reach by a short head, the pair finishing well clear of the rest. This useful effort made Makhlab look very well treated on his next outing in a seven-runner nursery at Chester later that month. He ran away with the race, not needing to repeat his Pontefract form to win easily by five lengths from Bond May Day. Makhlab was clearly capable of holding his own in better company, but he did not make the transition straight away. Tried at a mile for the first time, he finished only third of five to Rimrod in a listed event at Goodwood in September before confirming earlier impressions in the ten-runner Horris Hill. Dropped back to seven furlongs, and racing on the softest ground he had encountered, Makhlab showed at Newbury that he was still on the upgrade, producing a smart performance to beat Zaide by two and a half lengths. Held up, Makhlab travelled strongly before quickening in good style after being switched to obtain a run up the rail approaching the two-furlong pole; he led entering the final furlong and was soon in control. The form of the Horris Hill was confirmed by time analysis, Makhlab achieving a timefigure equivalent to a rating of 115, a time performance bettered or equalled in the two-year-old division only by Oasis Dream, Tout Seul, Tomahawk and Elusive City.

			Neartic
	Dixieland Band (USA)	Northern Dancer (b 1961)	Natalma
	(b 1980)	Mississippi Mud (b 1973)	Delta Judge
Makhlab (USA)			Sand Buggy
(b.c. Feb 8, 2000)		Avatar (ch 1972)	Graustark
	Avasand (USA)		Brown Berry
	(b 1985)	Sandy Blue (ch 1970)	Windy Sands
			Blue Nola

Makhlab, a rangy, good sort who went through the ring as a yearling for 700,000 dollars, is by the American sire Dixieland Band whose best runners in Europe have been the Prix de Diane winner and Arc runner-up Egyptband and the dual Gold Cup winner Drum Taps. Makhlab's dam Avasand, successful at six and nine furlongs in minor company as a three-year-old in the States, is out of the Grade 2 Hollywood Oaks winner Sandy Blue, as well as being a half-sister to the American Grade 3 winner Window Seat and to the dam of the Criterium de Saint-Cloud winner Miserden. Makhlab is Avasand's sixth foal. Four of her previous foals have won, and three of those are closely related to Makhlab, notably the champion turf mare Possibly Perfect (by Northern Baby), whose Grade 1 wins included the Beverly D Stakes at nine furlongs and the Yellow Ribbon Stakes at a mile and a quarter. Makhlab is not short of speed, but he should stay a mile on pedigree. The going could prove more of a hindrance to Makhlab's progress as a three-year-old; though he won on good to firm going at Chester, Makhlab's best effort by far was on soft in the Horris Hill. *B. W. Hills*

MAKINDI 2 br.f. (May 11) Makbul 104 – Indian Flower 87 (Mansingh (USA) 120) **63** [2002 5g⁶ 6.1m² f6g Nov 20] eleventh known foal: dam, 5f winner, also successful in USA: best effort (modest form) when 6 lengths second to Favola in maiden at Nottingham: will stay 7f: signs of temperament in preliminaries (withdrawn once). *J. A. Pickering*

MAKING WAVES (IRE) 3 b.f. Danehill (USA) 126 – Wavey 93 (Kris 135) [2002 **70** –p: 7g May 3] leggy, useful-looking filly: twice raced maiden: much better effort when seventh at Newmarket on only 3-y-o outing, again taking strong hold: sold 22,000 gns in December. *J. H. M. Gosden*

MAKTAVISH 3 b.g. Makbul 104 – La Belle Vie 73 (Indian King (USA) 128) [2002 **89** 97: 6s 5g⁶ 5.1f 5.2d⁵ 6m³ 6m 5.1f 5.1f⁵ 5m 5m⁵ 7f 5g* 5d³ 5v⁵ f5g⁶ f6f³ f5g⁴ f5g Dec 17] close-coupled gelding: useful at 2 yrs, just fairly useful in 2002: won claimer at Sandown (left B. R. Millman £10,000) in October: best at 5f: acts on fibresand, firm and soft going: has worn cheekpieces: usually races prominently. *I. Semple*

MAKULU (IRE) 2 b.c. (Apr 3) Alzao (USA) 117 – Karinski (USA) (Palace Music **69**
(USA) 129) [2002 6d 6s⁵ 6m 8.3m 8.3d⁶ p8g⁶ Dec 11] 30,000Y: rather leggy, useful-
looking colt: fourth foal: half-brother to 2000 2-y-o 1m winner Branicki (by Spectrum)
and 1999 2-y-o 6f winner Pekanski (by Sri Pekan), both fairly useful: dam unraced: fair
maiden: stays 1m: acts on soft going, probably on good to firm/polytrack: blinkered
(shaped well) final outing. *B. J. Meehan*

MALAAH (IRE) 6 gr.g. Pips Pride 117 – Lingdale Lass 60 (Petong 126) [2002 54, **48**
a72: p8g p6g* p7g³ p6g 5.1g p6g 7f⁵ 6g f5g f6g Dec 10] good-topped gelding: modest on **a61**
all-weather, poor on turf: won at Lingfield in March: stays 1m: acts on firm going and
polytrack: blinkered/visored. *Julian Poulton*

MALADERIE (IRE) 8 b.g. Thatching 131 – Native Melody (Tudor Music 131) **43**
[2002 50, a42: p7g f7g⁵ 9g⁶ 12.3g 10m 7g⁴ 9.9g 5d Jul 1] close-coupled gelding: poor
performer: stays 7f: acts on firm and soft going: usually blinkered/visored: has had
tongue tied. *M. Dods*

MALAHIDE EXPRESS (IRE) 2 gr.g. (Apr 19) Compton Place 125 – Gracious **76**
Gretclo 54 (Common Grounds 118) [2002 f6g² 5.1d⁵ f5g⁴ f5s f8.5g⁶ f6g* p5g f5g⁴ f6s⁵
p5g Dec 18] 10,500Y, 38,000 2-y-o: angular gelding: second living foal: dam, maiden
who stayed 6f, sister to useful 6f/7f performer Rich Ground: fair performer: won maiden
at Southwell in October: will prove best at 5f/6f: acts on all-weather (some promise
only run on turf): sometimes pulls hard/hangs: has run well in blinkers/cheekpieces.
N. P. Littmoden

MALAKAL (IRE) 6 b.g. Shernazar 131 – Malmada (USA) (Fappiano (USA)) [2002 **55**
–: 8.5d* Jul 31] fair maiden for J. Oxx in Ireland in 1999: first form for current yard when
winning handicap at Galway in July: stays 1¼m: successful over hurdles in September.
B. J. Curley

MALAPROPISM 2 ch.g. (Feb 16) Compton Place 125 – Mrs Malaprop 83 (Night **83**
Shift (USA)) [2002 6m 5s² 5m³ 5.1m³ 6m³ 5.2g² 5m* 5d² 5m 5m⁵ 5g² 5.2d³ Oct 30]
well-made gelding: first foal: dam, 5f (at 2 yrs)/6f winner, half-sister to useful performer
up to 1½m Black Monday: fairly useful performer: won maiden at Redcar in July: placed
in 3 nurseries: best form at 5f: acts on soft and good to firm going: tends to hang/
carry head awkwardly: consistent. *M. R. Channon*

MALARKEY 5 b.g. Mukaddamah (USA) 125 – Malwiya (USA) (Shahrastani (USA) **77**
135) [2002 78: 14.1m* 14m 14m* 16m³ 13.9f p16g⁶ Nov 27] tall, rather angular gelding:
has a high knee action: fair handicapper: won at Salisbury in August and Sandown in
September: stays 17f: acts on soft going, good to firm and all-weather: blinkered once at
4 yrs, has worn cheekpieces: has found little. *P. R. Hedger*

MALCHIK 6 ch.g. Absalom 128 – Very Good (Noalto 120) [2002 –, a61: f8.5g* **–**
f9.4g* f9.4g⁴ f9.4g³ f12g⁶ f8.5g f8.5g Mar 15] leggy gelding: modest on all-weather: won **a56**
seller and claimer at Wolverhampton in January: was effective at 8.5f to easy 1½m: acted
on good to firm going, good to soft and fibresand: blinkered once: sometimes wandered:
was none too consistent: dead. *P. Howling*

MALEYNA 2 ch.f. (Feb 4) Elmaamul (USA) 125 – Tereyna 58 (Terimon 124) [2002 **61**
6g 7.6m⁴ Aug 21] first foal: dam, maiden who stayed 5f, half-sister to smart performer
up to 1½m Jack Jennings: better effort in maidens (modest form) when fourth to Captain
Saif at Lingfield: will be suited by 1¼m+. *R. F. Johnson Houghton*

MALHUB (USA) 4 b. or br.c. Kingmambo (USA) 125 – Arjuzah (IRE) 110 **126**
(Ahonoora 122) [2002 115: 6f* 6m* 6d 5m² 6m² 6m² Sep 28]
In mid-June, celebrations of the Queen's Golden Jubilee were in full swing
and as part of those celebrations Royal Ascot was extended to five days. Of all the
changes in the course of fifty years, Royal Ascot must have been among the things
that changed least—horses and hats, carriages and curtsies, some aspects have not
changed at all. Back in 1952 though, the Gold Cup was the most valuable event of
the week, worth £10,822 as against today's £127,600; with inflation, that £10,822
would have been £188,844 fifty years later and in prize money terms the race has
now been overtaken by the meeting's other Group 1 events. The 1952 Gold Cup
winner, Aquino II, who took 'a devil of a lot of driving', does not however sound
too dissimilar to his 2002 counterpart. In the saddle on Aquino was Gordon
Richards, on his way to a double century for the season for the last time, but none of
that year's top trainers had more than sixty-three wins. Most pertinently perhaps for
the Queen are the owners' tables. Although the monarch had a modest season in
1952, she had a genuine classic candidate in Aureole who went on to be second in

Golden Jubilee Stakes, Royal Ascot—in a race previously run as the Cork And Orrery Stakes and upgraded to Group 1, Malhub shows improved form in beating Danehurst, Three Points (No.10) and Indian Country

the 1953 Derby; the year after that, when Aureole won the King George VI and Queen Elizabeth Stakes, the Queen was the season's leading owner. In 2002, she was thought to have a classic horse in Right Approach, but he flopped in his trials in the spring and was not seen again. The 1952 owners' table was dominated by owner-breeders and, illustrating how success in bloodstock is founded on the work of generations, as well as fabulous wealth, it was headed by the Aga Khan, the present Aga Khan's grandfather. Third in the list was Aquino II's owner, the Maharanee of Baroda from India.

For Royal Ascot 2002, the Cork And Orrery Stakes was upgraded, renamed and moved to the Saturday in order to provide a Group 1 event on every day of the meeting. The Golden Jubilee Stakes, as it was now known, was the second-most valuable contest of the week (behind the St James's Palace). The Queen could not muster a runner, though she did have two at the meeting in Green Line, who started a heavily-backed favourite when sixth in the Britannia Handicap, and Approval who was ninth in the Jersey. Fittingly perhaps, or inevitably, the Golden Jubilee was won instead by a horse representing the sport's dominant power of recent years, the Maktoum family. Malhub was one of three in the field owned by Sheikh Hamdan, the others being Mugharreb and Misraah; the family's Godolphin operation had Three Points and the Maktoums' Coolmore rivals sent over the previous year's top juvenile Johannesburg, bidding to get his career back on track after defeat in the Kentucky Derby. Johannesburg was generally priced at 6/4 in the morning but, while he still went off favourite, he was weak in the market and did so at 3/1, and that despite four non-runners, including the American challenger Caller One, dual winner of the Dubai Golden Shaheen. With the signs ominous for Johannesburg, it brought most of the remaining eleven runners into the equation. Malhub, a very promising sort twelve months earlier but now with plenty to prove following two wind operations, was a 16/1 chance and sported Sheikh Hamdan's third colours; both of the owner's retained jockeys rejected him and the mount went to Kevin Darley. Setting a new track record nine days earlier when 11/10-on in a Yarmouth minor event provided some encouragement for Malhub's prospects and he was always in the front rank in the Golden Jubilee Stakes. Three Points was there as well, with Danehurst and outsider Indian Country throwing down challenges, but Malhub was a length up at the furlong marker and had extended his advantage by another half length at the line.

All in all, the field for the Golden Jubilee, arguably like that for the Jubilee pop concert at Buckingham Palace, did not look as inspiring as it might have. The winner's form was no more than average by normal Group 1 sprinting standards, but he did improve on it afterwards and, as it turned out, the winners of the July Cup, Haydock Sprint Cup and the Abbaye were among his Royal Ascot victims. Malhub also ran in the first two of those races. The July Cup was a wash-out, with good to soft ground against him, his trainer John Gosden justifiably voicing exasperation that the supplementary entry stage had been six days before the race, at a time when the going was open to major change. Malhub got his favoured ground in three starts afterwards though, and ran well to finish runner-up in all three. He was cut down late on by Kyllachy in the Nunthorpe at York (over five furlongs), and very late on by both Invincible Spirit in the Haydock Park Sprint Cup and Crystal Castle in the Diadem at Ascot. Carrying a 6-lb penalty and finishing two and a half lengths clear of the third horse, Malhub's performance in the Diadem was a career best, and he also recorded the fastest timefigure by a sprinter—equivalent to a rating of 122—all season. He was due to appear again in the Hong Kong Sprint at Sha Tin in December, but, like several others from Europe, was withdrawn due to sickness after travelling there.

Malhub (USA) (b. or br.c. 1998)	Kingmambo (USA) (b 1990)	Mr Prospector (b 1970)	Raise A Native / Gold Digger
		Miesque (b 1984)	Nureyev / Pasadoble
	Arjuzah (IRE) (b 1990)	Ahonoora (ch 1975)	Lorenzaccio / Helen Nichols
		Saving Mercy (b 1980)	Lord Gayle / Fair Darling

Malhub, bred by Sheikh Hamdan, is by the 1993 St James's Palace winner Kingmambo, the son of Mr Prospector and Miesque who is warranting plenty of attention in his own right as a stallion. Malhub and Russian Rhythm helped make up for the virtual non-appearance of what had promised to be his best performer in 2002, Dubai Destination. Kingmambo stood at a fee of 200,000 dollars in the latest season. Malhub's dam is the smart seven-furlong winner Arjuzah and his grandam is the Rockfel Stakes and Lincoln Handicap winner Saving Mercy. Paradise Bird and Affaire d'Amour, two half-sisters to Saving Mercy, merit a mention, the former as grandam of Molecomb Stakes winner Lady Alexander and the latter as dam of US Grade 1 winners Mourjane and Anka Germania, herself the dam of dual Grade 1 winner Deputy Commander. Malhub is Arjuzah's third foal, following two Dayjur colts, the useful sprinter Mutaakkid and Italian winner Ajyaal. The three-year-old Shatarah (by Gulch) ended 2002 a fair maiden, while Arjuzah's 2000 and 2002 offspring are a filly (called Nebraas) and colt by Green Desert. Malhub is a quite attractive colt and a fluent mover who acts on firm going. He had two wind operations, as already mentioned, and has had his tongue tied throughout the last two seasons. He remains in training and it seems that, after an announcement in October that the fifth day at Royal Ascot is not after all going to be a one-off, the Golden Jubilee Stakes will be back as well, the title presumably considered no more anachronistic than many other aspects of the Royal meeting. *J. H. M. Gosden*

MALLARD (IRE) 4 b.g. Tagula (IRE) 116 – Frill (Henbit (USA) 130) [2002 49: f8.5g* 11.6d f8.5g p10g³ Dec 21] workmanlike gelding: fair performer, lightly raced: won amateur handicap at Wolverhampton in April: left D. Cantillon and off 7 months after next outing: may prove best up to 1¼m: acts on all-weather, raced only on good to soft going on turf: sometimes makes running. *J. G. Given* **67**

MALLIA 9 b.g. Statoblest 120 – Pronetta (USA) (Mr Prospector (USA)) [2002 54§, a65§: f6s* f6s⁵ f6s⁵ f6g f6g* f6g² f6g f6g² f6g² f6g 6m f6g f7g 6s f6s Sep 17] lengthy, dipped-backed gelding: modest performer: won claimers at Southwell in January and February: best at 6f: acts on any turf going/fibresand: blinkered/visored: has started slowly/edged right: held up: sometimes finds little: unreliable. *T. D. Barron* **– §** **a60 §**

MALMAND (USA) 3 ch.g. Distant View (USA) 126 – Bidski (USA) (Explosive Bid (USA)) [2002 60p: 8.5g⁵ 8.3s 7.1m⁶ 7.9g 8g f7g f9.4f f8.5s⁵ Dec 26] compact, quite attractive gelding: modest maiden: left M. Jarvis after fourth start: stays 8.5f: acts on fibresand, soft and good to firm going: has worn cheekpieces/visor. *R. Brotherton* **57**

MALTESE FALCON 2 b.c. (May 3) Mark of Esteem (IRE) 137 – Crime Ofthecentury 80 (Pharly (FR) 130) [2002 6d* Oct 14] fifth foal: half-brother to 7-y-o Tussle and 4-y-o Senior Minister: dam, 5f winner, out of Cherry Hinton winner Crime of Passion: 12/1, made good impression when winning 21-runner maiden at Windsor by ½ length from Soyuz, travelling strongly, leading 2½f out and keeping on well despite running green/edging left: will improve. *P. F. I. Cole* **82 p**

MAMA JAFFA (IRE) 2 ch.f. (Apr 14) In The Wings 128 – Harir (Kris 135) [2002 7.2g⁶ 7f 8.3d Oct 28] 15,000Y: tall, useful-looking filly: fourth foal: half-sister to a winner in Greece by Polar Falcon: dam unraced half-sister to smart stayer Shaya: easily best effort in maidens (modest form) when sixth at Ayr: should stay at least 1½m. *K. R. Burke* **58**

MAMBEE (IRE) 2 b.f. (Apr 17) Sesaro (USA) 81 – Besito 79 (Wassl 125) [2002 5.1d **45 §** 5m 6m 6d 5f Jul 10] IR 6,000Y: strong, close-coupled filly: half-sister to several winners, including 5-y-o Kinsman: dam 2m winner: poor maiden: tried visored: probably temperamental. *J. A. Glover*

MAMCAZMA 4 gr.g. Terimon 124 – Merryhill Maid (IRE) 71 (M Double M (USA)) **94** [2002 74: 10s 14.4f³ 14.1d² 12g⁴ 12s 14.8g* 14.8m* 16.1d² 14.8m* 13.9m* Sep 8] strong, lengthy gelding: fairly useful handicapper: better than ever at 4 yrs, winning at Newmarket (3 times) and York (beat Flaming Salsa a neck) between July/September: best form at 1¾m/2m: acts on fibresand, soft and firm going: waited with: sometimes carries head awkwardly, but game. *D. Morris*

MAMEYUKI 3 ch.f. Zafonic (USA) 130 – Musetta (IRE) 107 (Cadeaux Genereux **80 ?** 131) [2002 81: 7m 8s⁵ Nov 2] leggy filly: fairly useful performer at best, lightly raced: stiff tasks in Nell Gwyn Stakes and listed race (pulled hard) at Newmarket over 6 months apart in 2002: should stay at least 1m: acts on good to firm going. *C. E. Brittain*

MAMMA'S BOY 7 b.g. Rock City 120 – Henpot (IRE) 68 (Alzao (USA) 117) [2002 **40** 60: 7.1m 7f 7.1g 7.1d 8m⁴ 9m Sep 16] sturdy gelding: poor performer nowadays: winner 6 times at Musselburgh in prime: probably stays 9f: acts on any turf going: blinkered once at 4 yrs: usually held up. *A. Berry*

MAMMAS F-C (IRE) 6 ch.m. Case Law 113 – Wasaif (IRE) 79 (Lomond (USA) **64 §** 128) [2002 71, a–: f5g 5m 6f 5m 5.7g p5g³ 5g⁶ 6g 5.5f² 6g 5.1m 5f 6m² 6m³ 5.1m 6m 6m **a46 §** 5.1g⁴ 6m 6.1m⁴ Sep 20] strong, good-bodied mare: modest handicapper on turf, poor on all-weather: effective at 5f to easy 7f: acts on firm going, soft and all-weather: usually held up: unreliable: sold £6,800. *J. M. Bradley*

MAMMEE BAY 3 b.c. Distant Relative 128 – Cormorant Bay 55 (Don't Forget Me **78** 127) [2002 10g⁵ 10d⁵ f9.4f* f12g Oct 17] 13,000F, 30,000Y: well-made colt: half-brother to 1m winner Glen Ogil (by Thatching) and German winner up to 1¼m Dance Again (by Shareef Dancer): dam, maiden who stayed 1¼m, half-sister to top-class 1¼m filly Cormorant Wood: fair performer: won maiden at Wolverhampton in August: stayed 1¼m: acted on fibresand: dead. *W. J. Haggas*

MAMOOL (IRE) 3 b.c. In The Wings 128 – Genovefa (USA) 107 (Woodman (USA) **118** 126) [2002 101: 11.5g⁴ 16.2m² 12v⁵ 14.6m⁴ Sep 14] good-topped colt: smart performer: won Queen's Vase at Royal Ascot in June by ½ length from Mr Dinos, kicking clear early

Queen's Vase, Royal Ascot—Mamool (rail) holds on admirably from Mr Dinos and Ancestor (right)

in straight and holding on bravely: ran well when 4¾ lengths fourth to Bollin Eric in St Leger at Doncaster final start: stays 2m: acts on soft and good to firm ground, below par (in German Derby) on heavy: has worn crossed noseband. *Saeed bin Suroor*

MAMORE GAP (IRE)   4 b.c. General Monash (USA) 107 – Ravensdale Rose (IRE)   **80** (Henbit (USA) 130) [2002 89: 7f 10.1g 8.5d³ 10m⁴ 10m² 9m⁶ 8g Aug 27] smallish, useful-looking colt: fairly useful performer: reportedly finished lame final start: barely stays 1¼m: acts on firm and good to soft ground. *R. Hannon*

MAMOUNIA (IRE)   3 b.f. Green Desert (USA) 127 – Maroussie (FR) 115 (Saumarez   **101** 132) [2002 81: 7m* 8m 7.1m² 8m² 8d* 9g* 8f² 8.1m³ 7m* 8f⁶ 7m Oct 19] rather leggy, quite good-topped filly: useful performer: improved, and had a good season, winning maiden at Doncaster in May, handicaps at Newmarket/Goodwood in July and listed race at Doncaster (by a length from Hideaway Heroine) in September: creditable sixth behind Dress To Thrill in Sun Chariot Stakes at Newmarket penultimate start: effective at 7f to 9f: acts on firm and good to soft going: effective held up or making running: reliable. *B. W. Hills*

MANAAR (IRE)   2 b.c. (Apr 11) Titus Livius (FR) 115 – Zurarah (Siberian Express   **81** (USA) 125) [2002 6g² 6g² Aug 7] good-quartered colt: half-brother to several winners, including fairly useful Irish 1995 2-y-o 6f winner Magarah (by Magical Strike) and 1999 2-y-o 5f winner Porcini (by Alzao): dam unraced half-sister to very smart 7f/1m performer Gabr: fairly useful form when second in maidens at Newmarket and Newcastle, beaten 1¾ lengths by Go Tech in latter: not sure to stay much beyond 6f. *J. Noseda*

MANA D'ARGENT (IRE)   5 b.g. Ela-Mana-Mou 132 – Petite-D-Argent 91 (Noalto   **101** 120) [2002 96: 11.9m 12m⁶ 12m⁴ 11.9m² 12g 20m³ 11.9d 16.2m* 21g³ 18.7g⁴ 16.2d* 13.9m 13.9m 14.6m 16.2g* 18m 16s⁴ 16.5v⁵ Nov 9] small gelding: good walker: unimpressive mover: useful handicapper: all 4 successes at Ascot, including in July, August (beat Moon Emperor 15 lengths) and September (beat Cotopaxi ½ length): seems suited by 2m+ nowadays (stays 21f): acts on any turf going and fibresand: sometimes blinkered/visored: held up nowadays: sometimes wanders: runs the odd below-par race: tough. *M. Johnston*

MANA-MOU BAY (IRE)   5 b.g. Ela-Mana-Mou 132 – Summerhill (Habitat 134)   **84** [2002 99: 8s 8.3g⁶ 8f 8m* 8m 8.5d* 12g⁴ 8m 12s Oct 26] good-topped gelding: fairly useful nowadays: won claimers at Pontefract in May and Epsom in July: left D. Nicholls before final start: stays easy 1½m: acts on good to firm and good to soft going: effective visored or not: held up nowadays. *B. Ellison*

MANANIYYA (IRE)   2 ch.f. (Apr 9) Ashkalani (IRE) 128 – Madiriya 119 (Diesis   **83 p** 133) [2002 7m² Sep 23] seventh foal: half-sister to 3 winners, including very smart British/US 9f/1¼m winner Manndar (by Doyoun): dam 1m (at 2 yrs) to 1½m winner: 13/2 and green, ½-length second of 12 to Spanish Sun in maiden at Kempton, keeping on well: should prove suited by 1¼m/1½m: likely to make a useful 3-y-o. *Sir Michael Stoute*

MANA POOLS (IRE)   3 b.f. Brief Truce (USA) 126 – Pipers Pool (IRE) 94 (Mtoto   **72** 134) [2002 53: 8m 8m² 8.2g* 8g* 10m³ 8m 8.5g 8m 9d⁶ 10g² p10g³ p10g² Dec 21] good-topped filly: fair handicapper: won at Nottingham in June and Leicester in July: stays 1¼m: yet to race on heavy going, acts on any other turf and all-weather: blinkered/visored: usually held up. *J. A. Glover*

MANDARIN SPIRIT (IRE)   2 b.c. (Feb 26) Primo Dominie 121 – Lithe Spirit   **55 p** (IRE) 74 (Dancing Dissident (USA) 119) [2002 f7s⁶ f5g Dec 16] 14,000Y, 36,000 2-y-o: half-brother to 3-y-o Blythe Spirit and 2000 2-y-o 6f winner Berezina (by Brief Truce): dam, maiden who stayed 1m, out of half-sister to smart 7f/1m performers Bog Trotter and Poteen: slowly away but some promise in 2 maidens at Wolverhampton: should stay 1m: sure to do better. *Sir Mark Prescott*

MANDELSON (USA)   3 ch.g. Spinning World (USA) 130 – Draconienne (USA)   **–** (Trempolino (USA) 135) [2002 52: 8.2d f12g 14.1m 10d 11.6m 12d Sep 2] modest maiden at 2 yrs: little form in 2002 (left J. Cullinan after fifth outing): tried blinkered. *J. G. Coogan, Ireland*

MANDINGO CHIEF (IRE)   3 b.c. Flying Spur (AUS) – Elizabethan Air 55 (Elegant   **79** Air 119) [2002 11.1s³ 12.3m⁴ 12d⁵ 14m⁴ 14m 18d² Oct 21] second foal: half-brother to 4-y-o Kells: dam 1m winner: fair maiden: left E. O'Neill after fourth start: stays 2¼m: acts on soft and good to firm going: has wandered: sold 28,000 gns. *P. W. D'Arcy*

MANDOLIN (IRE)   3 b.f. Sabrehill (USA) 120 – Russian Countess (USA) 104   **69** (Nureyev (USA) 131) [2002 7g May 3] 130,000Y: sturdy, lengthy filly: sister to useful performer up to 1¼m Alboostan, 7.5f/1m winner at 2 yrs, and half-sister to several winners, including smart 1½m performer Crown of Light (by Mtoto), 7f winner at 2 yrs: dam French 2-y-o 1m winner: green/very short to post, 7 lengths ninth to Ludynosa in maiden at Newmarket, taking strong hold up with leaders: looked likely to do better. *H. R. A. Cecil*

MANDOOB 5 b.g. Zafonic (USA) 130 – Thaidah (CAN) 105 (Vice Regent (CAN)) **71** [2002 71: f12g⁴ f9.4s f9.4g⁴ 10m⁴ 9s 12m⁵ 11.9d² 11.8s² f12f* f12g* f14.8s² Dec 13] big, **a74** close-coupled gelding: fair performer: won minor event and handicap at Wolverhampton in November: barely stays 14.8f: acts on fibresand/any turf ground: tongue tied in 2002 (also blinkered first 2 starts): has given trouble at stall/been slowly away/hung under pressure. *B. R. Johnson*

MANDOWN 3 b.g. Danehill Dancer (IRE) 117 – Golden Decoy 73 (Decoy Boy 129) **48** [2002 58: p8g f8g⁵ f9.4g Dec 20] poor maiden, lightly raced: probably stays 1m. *J. S. Moore*

MANDY'S COLLECTION 3 ch.f. Forzando 122 – Instinction (Never So Bold **–** 135) [2002 52: f5g² p5g 5m f5g⁵ 6.1d f6g⁴ 5g f5g f5g⁴ f5g³ Dec 31] modest maiden **a58** handicapper: should be suited by 6f: acts on fibresand, little form on turf in 2002. *A. G. Newcombe*

MAN EATER 2 gr.f. (Feb 3) Mark of Esteem (IRE) 137 – Desert Delight (IRE) (Green **74** Desert (USA) 127) [2002 5m⁴ 6d 5m² 5d³ 5.1f² 5.2f 5m⁶ 5.1g³ 5.1d² 5f⁵ Oct 3] 32,000Y: rather leggy filly: fourth foal: half-sister to 3 winners, including fairly useful 1999 2-y-o 6f winner Alphilda (by Ezzoud): dam unraced half-sister to May Hill winner Intimate Guest: fair maiden: in frame 6 times, including in nursery: form only at 5f: acts on firm and good to soft going: usually races prominently. *R. Hannon*

MANE FRAME 7 b.g. Unfuwain (USA) 131 – Moviegoer 104 (Pharly (FR) 130) **–** [2002 f16g Feb 7] rangy gelding: one-time fairly useful handicapper: always behind on only Flat outing since 2000: successful over hurdles in March. *H. Morrison*

MAN FROM HAVANA (USA) 3 b.g. Green Dancer (USA) 132 – Charmie Carmie **79** (USA) (Lyphard (USA) 132) [2002 75: 10m 10g⁴ 11.6m³ 10m³ 11.9g⁴ p12g⁵ p10g⁵ Oct **a73** 16] tall gelding: fair maiden: left P. Cole after third start: stays 11.6f: acts on firm and soft going: shied at whip on debut: has hung badly left/raced freely. *S. Dow*

MANGUS (IRE) 8 b.g. Mac's Imp (USA) 116 – Holly Bird (Runnett 125) [2002 49§, **– §** a66§: p5g⁶ f5g f5g f5g² f5g⁵ 5s f5g 5m f5g f5g Dec 13] workmanlike gelding: modest **a55 §** handicapper on all-weather: raced mainly at 5f: acts on fibresand: tried tongue tied: sometimes starts slowly: not an easy ride, and not one to trust. *K. O. Cunningham-Brown*

MANIATIS 5 b.h. Slip Anchor 136 – Tamassos 67 (Dance In Time (CAN)) [2002 103: **108** 12g⁶ 12d* 12g⁴ 13.3f⁶ 12s⁵ Oct 26] tall, good sort: usually looks well: useful performer: won minor event at Goodwood in May by 2½ lengths from Xtra: creditable fourth in listed race at Lyon Parilly next time: below form at Newbury in Geoffrey Freer Stakes and St Simon Stakes last 2 starts: effective at 1½m/1¾m: acts on soft and good to firm going: has been taken steadily to post/blanketed for stall entry: tends to race freely up with pace: sold 16,000 gns, joined M. Hammond. *Mrs A. J. Perrett*

MANICANI (IRE) 4 ch.g. Tagula (IRE) 116 – Pluvia (USA) (Raise A Native) [2002 **82** 74+: 8.1d 8m 8g 6g³ 6d 7m⁶ 8.1d² p5g³ 7g³ 8m 8f 7s³ 7f⁶ 7.1g p7g p6g* Dec 18] tall, useful-looking gelding: fairly useful performer: won maiden at Lingfield in December: effective at 6f/1m: acts on polytrack, firm and good to soft going: tried tongue tied: usually held up: sometimes finds little. *I. A. Balding*

MANIKATO (USA) 8 b.g. Clever Trick (USA) – Pasampsi (USA) (Crow (FR) 134) **49** [2002 40: p12g⁶ p10g p13g⁴ 11.9f² 11.9g 9d⁴ 10.1g 8.1g 10m 9.9g 10g Oct 24] close- **a43** coupled gelding: poor handicapper: stays 1½m: acts on firm going, good to soft and all-weather: sometimes visored earlier in career. *R. Curtis*

MANNORA 2 b.f. (Jan 28) Prince Sabo 123 – Miss Bussell 65 (Sabrehill (USA) 120) **49** [2002 5.1g 5.1d 6g Oct 18] 13,500Y: workmanlike filly: first foal: dam, 1m winner, granddaughter of high-class sprinter Abergwaun: poor maiden: free-going sort, and likely to prove best at 5f/6f. *P. Howling*

MANNY 2 b.g. (Feb 3) Emarati (USA) 74 – Needwood Nymph 45 (Bold Owl 101) **43** [2002 6m 6m f5g⁵ Oct 5] 2,900Y, resold 1,000Y: leggy gelding: ninth foal: half-brother to 3 winners, including 1¾m and 15.4f winner Needwood Spirit (by Rolfe): dam 1½m winner: poor maiden: refused to enter stall intended debut: may prove best at 5f: acts on fibresand. *A. Berry*

MAN OF DISTINCTION   4 b.g. Spectrum (IRE) 126 – Air of Distinction (IRE) ?
99 (Distinctly North (USA) 115) [2002 72: p8g* 8.1d p8g² 8d⁴ Aug 23] rather leggy, **a99**
useful-looking gelding: useful on all-weather: best effort when winning handicap at
Lingfield in June by 2½ lengths from Port Moresby: stays 1m: acts on polytrack, firm and
good to soft going: has been slowly away. *G. A. Butler*

MAN OF KENT   2 b.c. (May 7) Paris House 123 – Club Elite 57 (Salse (USA) 128)   37
[2002 f5g 5f 5f 6m⁶ 7f⁵ 7f f5g³ 6g Aug 7] 500Y: close-coupled colt: second foal: dam
staying maiden: free-going sort, and barely stays 7f: acts on fibresand,
raced on good going or firmer on turf. *Ronald Thompson*

MAN OF THE NIGHT   6 b.g. Clantime 101 – Forbidden Monkey 47 (Gabitat 119)   67
[2002 8.1d 10.9m⁴ 10m² 12.1g* 12d⁵ 10.2g Sep 23] fair handicapper, lightly raced:
missed 2000/2001 seasons: won at Chepstow in August: best efforts at 1½m: acts on firm
and soft going: tried blinkered/tongue tied. *Jonjo O'Neill*

MAN O'MYSTERY (USA)   5 b.g. Diesis 133 – Eurostorm (USA) 104 (Storm Bird   113
(CAN) 134) [2002 115: 10g 8m 10s* 10.4m 9m⁴ p10g⁵ Nov 23] sturdy, lengthy gelding:
unimpressive mover: smart performer: won minor event at Newbury in May by head
from Chianti: ran creditably otherwise only when fourth to Golden Silca in listed event at
Newmarket, though finding little: stays 10.4f: acts on good to firm going, probably on
soft/polytrack: held up. *J. Noseda*

MANORBIER   6 ch.g. Shalford (IRE) 124§ – La Pirouette (USA) 73 (Kennedy Road   92
(CAN)) [2002 95+: f6g 5s 6g 5f 6m⁴ 6g² 6m⁴ 6d² 6g 6.1d⁵ 6g 6m Aug 17] strong, close-
coupled gelding: poor mover: fairly useful handicapper: probably best at 6f: acts on firm
going, soft and fibresand: held up. *K. A. Ryan*

MANOR FROM HEAVEN   4 ch.f. Most Welcome 131 – Manor Adventure 75   –
(Smackover 107) [2002 –: 6.1v 10m 8g Aug 7] leggy filly: little form. *P. T. Dalton*

MANORSON (IRE)   3 ch.c. Desert King (IRE) 129 – Familiar (USA) 96 (Diesis 133)   101
[2002 83p: p10g* 10.3s* 12d⁵ May 15] sturdy colt: useful performer: won maiden at
Lingfield and handicap at Doncaster (by 3 lengths from In Disguise, pair well clear) in
March: creditable 5 lengths fifth to Sulamani in listed race at Chantilly final start, making
much of running: stays 1½m: acts on soft ground and polytrack: joined M. Magnusson.
D. W. P. Arbuthnot

MANOUBI   3 b.g. Doyoun 124 – Manuetti (IRE) 86 (Sadler's Wells (USA) 132) [2002   88
10m 10m* 11.9d² 11.6m² Oct 7] good-topped gelding: first foal: dam, maiden who would
have been suited by 1½m, daughter of Prix Saint-Alary winner Rosefinch, herself out of
Oh So Sharp: fairly useful form: won maiden at Windsor in July: at least creditable efforts
after, off 2 months before 5 lengths second to Castleshane in minor event there final start,
pulling hard: will stay at least 1¾m: yet to race on extremes of going: gelded after final
outing. *Sir Michael Stoute*

MANQUE NEUF   3 b.g. Cadeaux Genereux 131 – Flying Squaw 102 (Be My Chief   68
(USA) 122) [2002 12f⁵ 10.5d³ 12d³ 10g Aug 7] 67,000Y: third foal: half-brother to 8.5f
winner Flying Carpet (by Barathea): dam 2-y-o 5f/6f winner: fair maiden: stays 1½m:
sold 16,000 gns. *J. D. Bethell*

MAN THE GATE   3 b.g. Elmaamul (USA) 125 – Girl At The Gate 53 (Formidable   75
(USA) 125) [2002 61: 8g⁴ 8.5g³ 8s* 8d 10.2g³ 10m³ p10g⁴ Oct 31] fair handicapper: won
at Leicester in July: stays 1¼m: acts on soft going, good to firm and polytrack (some
promise on fibresand). *P. D. Cundell*

MANTLES PRIDE   7 b.g. Petong 126 – State Romance 67 (Free State 125) [2002 78:   73
8v² 7f 8m⁶ 8.3g³ 8d 7g Jun 8] useful-looking gelding: fluent mover: fair handicapper:
best around 7f/1m: acts on any turf going: usually visored/blinkered: sometimes slowly
away, very much so third start: reportedly broke blood vessel once as 6-y-o: tends to carry
head awkwardly: probably best with strong handling: none too consistent. *M. Dods*

MANX FIZZ   2 b.f. (Jan 23) Efisio 120 – Stica (IRE) (In The Wings 128) [2002 5s 6v⁴   55
5v⁵ 5.9g⁴ 5.9s 7m⁴ 7.5m⁶ 7.5g² 8m⁵ 8.3m⁴ Sep 30] 1,900Y, 6000 2-y-o: smallish, strong
filly: first foal: dam unraced half-sister to useful Irish winner up to 11f Lacinia: modest
maiden: stays 1m: acts on heavy and good to firm going: often forces pace. *J. Hetherton*

MANX GYPSY   4 b.f. Puissance 110 – Najariya (Northfields (USA)) [2002 6f 9.2s 5d   –
Jul 1] workmanlike filly: little form. *K. W. Hogg, Isle of Man*

MANX MINI   2 b.f. (May 14) Distinctly North (USA) 115 – Octavia (Sallust 134)   –
[2002 5s 5.1d Apr 1] half-sister to numerous winners, including fairly useful 6f to 1m

winner Ryefield (by Petong) and 1¼m to 2m winner Kinoko (by Bairn): dam maiden: well beaten in sellers. *K. W. Hogg, Isle of Man*

MANZONI   6 b.g. Warrshan (USA) 117 – Arc Empress Jane (IRE) (Rainbow Quest   –
(USA) 134) [2002 68: 16.1m 12f⁶ 12.1m³ Jun 25] small gelding: fair handicapper at 5 yrs: little form in 2002: tried blinkered, visored once. *M. W. Easterby*

MAPLE HOUSE   3 ch.f. Emperor Fountain 112 – Strathrusdale (Blazing Saddles   –
(AUS)) [2002 54: 6s 6g Jun 18] smallish, sparely-made filly: modest maiden at 2 yrs: well held in 2002. *M. W. Easterby*

MARABAR   4 b.f. Sri Pekan (USA) 117 – Erbaya (IRE) (El Gran Senor (USA) 136)   **83**
[2002 81: 6m⁵ 7m⁶ 6d² 5.5m 6m 6f 7v Nov 9] big, close-coupled filly: fairly useful handicapper, lightly raced: effective at 6f/7f: acts on good to firm and good to soft going. *P. J. Makin*

MARABELLO   2 b.g. (Feb 22) Robellino (USA) 127 – Mara River 86 (Efisio 120)   **78 d**
[2002 5d³ 5m 6s 7m Aug 4] 10,500Y: leggy, close-coupled gelding: second foal: dam 6f to 1m winner: fair form when third to Rockets 'N Rollers in minor event at Ascot: disappointing after: should stay 7f. *I. A. Balding*

MARAKABEI   4 ch.f. Hernando (FR) 127 – Kirsten 77 (Kris 135) [2002 –: 11 7g⁶   **72**
11.9m³ 12.3s* 12.1s* 12.1m 16s²ᵈ Oct 25] smallish filly: fair handicapper: won at Ripon and Hamilton (apprentices) in August: stays 2m: best efforts on soft going. *R. Guest*

MARAKASH (IRE)   3 b.g. Ashkalani (IRE) 128 – Marilaya (IRE) 96 (Shernazar   **73**
131) [2002 77p: f8.5g² 7.5g² f9.4g³ f8.5g Nov 16] first foal: dam, 9f and 10.5f winner, out of half-sister to smart French middle-distance performers Madaiyn and Malakim: fair maiden: left Sir Michael Stoute 16,000 gns and gelded, weakened alarmingly from halfway final start: should stay 1¼m: acts on fibresand and soft going. *M. R. Bosley*

MARANI   4 ch.f. Ashkalani (IRE) 128 – Aquamarine 89 (Shardari 134) [2002 106:   **105**
12g* 11.9m Aug 22] tall, leggy filly: useful performer, lightly raced: dead-heated in listed race at Newmarket (joined Frosty Welcome on line) in July: reportedly struck into when last in similar event at York: stayed 1½m: acted on firm going: stud. *J. H. M. Gosden*

MARANILLA (IRE)   3 b.c. Desert King (IRE) 129 – Queen Moranbon (USA) 65   **109**
(Bering 136) [2002 94: 10g* 12m 10.5g* 10m⁶ 10g 10.8s p10g⁶ Nov 23] leggy, workmanlike colt: useful performer: won Group 3 events at Frankfurt (by 1½ lengths from Whispered Secret) in April and Bremen (Walther J Jacobs-Rennen) (by 1¼ lengths from Ammonias) in June: just respectable efforts at best after, leaving E. O'Neill after fifth outing: should stay 1½m (below form in Derby Italiano when tried): probably acts on polytrack, best turf efforts on good or softer going. *P. W. D'Arcy*

MARBLE LODGE (IRE)   2 ch.f. (Feb 23) Grand Lodge (USA) 125 – Marble Halls   –
(IRE) (Ballad Rock 122) [2002 7s 7g Oct 14] second foal: half-sister to 3-y-o Waverley: dam twice-raced half-sister to high-class sprinter Hallgate and to dam of smart sprinter Mistertopogigo: well held in maidens. *H. Morrison*

MARCH ALONE   3 b.f. Alzao (USA) 117 – I Will Lead (USA) (Seattle Slew (USA))   **58 p**
[2002 p12g⁶ Dec 14] 7,000 3-y-o: second foal: half-sister to useful 1¼m winner Stay Behind (by Elmaamul): dam unraced half-sister to Rainbow Quest: 16/1, 6 lengths sixth of 16 to Theatre in maiden at Lingfield, not given hard time after slow start: will probably improve. *Mrs A. J. Perrett*

MARCHING BAND (USA)   2 b.c. (Jan 26) Dixieland Band (USA) – More Silver   **101**
(USA) 90 (Silver Hawk (USA) 123) [2002 7d⁶ 6m* 6g* 7m Oct 19] smallish, well-made colt: first foal: dam 5f (at 2 yrs) and 8.5f (in USA) winner: useful form: won maiden at Newbury (by 2 lengths from Isaz) in September and minor event at Salisbury (beat Love Is Blind by neck) in October: good ninth of 16, beaten over 7 lengths by Tout Seul, in Dewhurst Stakes at Newmarket: will probably prove best at 6f/7f: yet to race on extremes of going. *J. H. M. Gosden*

MARCUS AURELIUS (IRE)   3 b.g. Alzao (USA) 117 – Kaguyahime (Distant   –
Relative 128) [2002 85p: 6s 6g 5v 5g Oct 19] strong gelding: has a quick action: fairly useful at 2 yrs: little form in 2002: tried blinkered/tongue tied. *T. D. Barron*

MARDOOF   2 gr.c. (Apr 15) Piccolo 121 – Cumbrian Melody 83 (Petong 126) [2002   **79**
5f² 5m³ p5g³ 5g² 5m* 5g⁴ 5m⁴ 5f⁵ Sep 27] 47,000F, 76,000Y: useful-looking colt: halfbrother to several winners, including 3-y-o Golden Bounty and 7f winner Titanium Honda (by Doulab): dam 2-y-o 5f/6f winner: fair performer: made all in maiden at Carlisle in August: raced only at 5f: acts on firm going and polytrack: probably best ridden up with pace: consistent. *M. R. Channon*

MARENGO 8 b.g. Never So Bold 135 – Born To Dance 76 (Dancing Brave (USA) **60** 140) [2002 57, a61: f7s⁶ f6g f6g⁴ f6s* f6g⁵ f6g⁵ f6g³ f7g* f7g f7g² 6.1g⁴ 7m f7g **a78** f5g 6m 6.1m 6m 7g 7g⁴ 7g 7g 6m 7m⁵ 6m f8s* 7.1g f8s² 8.9f⁶ f8.5f⁶ f8g³ f8g² f8g f8g⁵ Dec 27] small gelding: fairly useful on all-weather, modest on turf: successful in 2 sellers and 2 handicaps at Southwell in 2002: effective at 6f to 9f: acts on fibresand, firm and soft going: tried visored: has seemed reluctant: often held up: carries head high: very tough. *M. J. Polglase*

MARE OF WETWANG 4 ch.f. River Falls 113 – Kudos Blue (Elmaamul (USA) **46** 125) [2002 42: 12.3g⁴ 12f 11.1g⁵ 16d 13v⁴ 11.6m 12g 12d f14s Sep 5] sparely-made filly: **a–** poor performer: probably stays 1¾m: acts on fibresand, heavy and good to firm ground: has started slowly. *J. D. Bethell*

MARFOOQ (USA) 2 ch.c. (Apr 3) Diesis 133 – Fabulous Fairy (USA) 75 (Alydar **78** (USA)) [2002 6m⁶ 7f⁵ Oct 3] $120,000F, 320,000Y: useful-looking colt: fourth living foal: half-brother to fairly useful 1998 2-y-o 6f winner Truly Bewitched (by Affirmed): dam, 1¼m winner, out of 1000 Guineas winner Fairy Footsteps: fair form in maidens at Newbury and Newmarket (unimpressive to post, fifth of 26 to Desert Star) 4½ months apart: should stay 1m. *E. A. L. Dunlop*

MARGARET'S FANCY (IRE) 2 ch.f. (Feb 19) Ali-Royal (IRE) 127 – Danalia **73** (IRE) 78 (Danehill (USA) 126) [2002 5m⁶ 5f* 6m* a6.5f³ 8f⁶ Oct 25] 4,000F: second foal: half-sister to temperamental 1¼m winner Mujalia (by Mujtahid): dam, Irish 2-y-o 5f winner, half-sister to smart middle-distance performer Trakady: fair perfrmer: won seller at Catterick and nursery at Redcar in July, latter by ½ length from Miss Ceylon: left P. Haslam: ½-length third in non-graded stakes at Fairplex in September, better effort in US: best up to 6.5f: acts on firm going and on dirt. *P. G. Aguirre, USA*

MARGARITA TIME (IRE) 2 ch.f. (Mar 30) Grand Lodge (USA) 125 – Brillantina **–** (FR) (Crystal Glitters (USA) 127) [2002 6d 7s⁶ p7g Oct 31] IR 30,000F: fifth foal: sister to 3-y-o Orinocovsky and half-sister to 3 winners abroad: dam German 7.7f winner: only a little sign of ability in maidens/minor event. *B. J. Meehan*

MARGARULA (IRE) 3 b.f. Doyoun 124 – Mild Intrigue (USA) 91 (Sir Ivor 135) **120** [2002 81: 10s* 10s² 12m* 10s 9.5s⁵ 10g⁴ 12d* 10m⁶ 14m⁶ Sep 14]

In upsetting the odds laid on Quarter Moon in the Darley Irish Oaks at the Curragh in July, 33/1-shot Margarula became the longest-priced winner ever of the race, while also providing her jockey Kevin Manning with his first victory in a classic. Margarula's odds seemed an accurate reflection of her chance beforehand, as she looked exposed as no more than useful after eleven appearances. All three of

Darley Irish Oaks, the Curragh—
33/1-shot Margarula becomes the longest-priced winner in the history of the race;
Quarter Moon (rail) has to settle for second in another classic, whilst Lady's Secret takes third

Ecurie Wildenstein's "Margarula"

her wins in that period had come in handicap company, the last of them quite a hard-fought one off a mark of 87 over the Oaks distance at Leopardstown in May.

Margarula, also successful in a nursery at Thurles on the last of her five starts at two and at Cork in March on her reappearance at three, was below form in a handicap and a listed event on her two starts after Leopardstown; but then she acquitted herself well tried in pattern-race company for the first time, finishing fourth to Tarfshi in the Pretty Polly Stakes over a mile and a quarter at the Curragh. It was an improved performance from Margarula, but not one which suggested a fortnight later that she was likely to trouble such as Quarter Moon, who had finished second in both the Irish One Thousand Guineas and the Oaks at Epsom, and the Ribblesdale winner Irresistible Jewel. However, the step back up to a mile and a half, combined with conditions which placed much more emphasis on stamina than on her previous attempt at a mile and a half, brought out the best in Margarula. In a race run at a strong pace, set by Quarter Moon's stable-companions Kournakova and Starbourne, Margarula was dropped out last and didn't begin to make any significant progress until approaching the straight. The decision by Manning to stick to the rail paid off handsomely, with Margarula travelling well, on the heels of the leaders over two furlongs out, as Quarter Moon quickened ahead. Margarula had to wait for a clear run briefly, and when sent in pursuit she found plenty to peg back the favourite just inside the final furlong, going on to win by a length as the pair pulled six lengths clear of the remainder. Margarula's performance stood head and shoulders above anything she had achieved previously, and, as it turned out, her form never reached such heady heights subsequently, though she reportedly suffered from the cough before her next appearance. The return to a mile and a quarter to take on Grandera, Hawk Wing and company in the Champion

Stakes at Leopardstown looked far from ideal for Margarula, and not surprisingly she trailed home sixth of seven. The mile and three quarters of the Irish St Leger at the Curragh a week later should have suited her though, and it was disappointing that she should again finish a well-held sixth. In those last two races Margarula carried the Wildenstein colours after they purchased a half share in her following the Irish Oaks.

		Mill Reef	Never Bend
	Doyoun	(b 1968)	Milan Mill
	(b 1985)	Dumka	Kashmir II
Margarula (IRE)		(br 1971)	Faizebad
(b.f. 1999)		Sir Ivor	Sir Gaylord
	Mild Intrigue (USA)	(b 1965)	Attica
	(b 1985)	Mild Deception	Buckpasser
		(b 1970)	Natashka

Margarula, bought as a yearling for IR 33,000 guineas, is the eighth foal of Mild Intrigue and her fifth winner, the useful Irish 1998 two-year-old Wild Heaven (by Darshaan) and the fairly useful stayer High Intrigue the pick of her previous foals. Mild Intrigue raced for John Dunlop's stable and won a mile-and-a-quarter maiden at Sandown at three on her debut. She faced a stiffish task and was beaten a fair way in five subsequent starts, but did enough to say that she probably stayed a mile and a half. A half-sister to the useful Grimesgill and the stakes winner Determined Bidder, Mild Intrigue is from an outstanding family. Her dam Mild Deception, a winner at up to a mile in the States, is a daughter of the top-class Natashka who has also produced the high-class animals Arkadina (herself runner-up in the Irish Oaks), Blood Royal, Gregorian and Truly Bound, as well as the smart Ivory Wand, herself the dam of the very smart performer around a mile and a half Gold And Ivory. Margarula, a small, workmanlike filly, acts on soft and good to firm ground. *J. S. Bolger, Ireland*

MARGERY DAW (IRE)   2 b.f. (May 9) Sri Pekan (USA) 117 – Suyayeb (USA)   **70 p**
(The Minstrel (CAN) 135) [2002 p8g³ Dec 14] IR 5,400F, 1,200Y: fifth foal: sister to a winner up to 11f in Italy and half-sister to 3 winners, including fairly useful 1m winner Dr Martens (by Mtoto): dam unraced half-sister to US Grade 1 9f/1¼m winner Cutlass Reality: 20/1, fair form when 1½ lengths third of 12 to Nawow in maiden at Lingfield: should improve. *M. P. Tregoning*

MARGOLD (IRE)   2 ch.f. (Feb 23) Goldmark (USA) 113 – Arcevia (IRE) 85   **67**
(Archway (IRE) 115) [2002 8.2m⁴ 7d⁵ Nov 5] 3,200Y: first foal: dam 11f winner: better effort in maidens when 3½ lengths fourth of 7 to Hoh Buzzard at Nottingham. *R. Hollinshead*

MARIENBARD (IRE)   5 b.h. Caerleon (USA) 132 – Marienbad (FR) (Darshaan   **129**
133) [2002 119: 12g⁴ 12g* 12s⁴ 12m* 12g* 12g* Oct 6]
Covered up and gradually edging closer to get his head in front well inside the final furlong—Marienbard's run in the latest Prix de l'Arc de Triomphe mirrored the longer-term progress he showed to emerge from the second division of Godolphin's middle-distance horses. In fact, when the season opened he was almost unconsidered as a candidate for top honours. When it was over, he had won the most important race in Europe. Godolphin needed a horse in Europe to emerge from the shadow of 2001 Arc winner Sakhee, and Marienbard was the one who stepped forward.

Among all of Godolphin's middle-distance performers at the end of 2001, Marienbard ranked only joint-fifteenth on Timeform ratings, behind Sakhee, Fantastic Light, Ekraar, Tobougg, Grandera, Kutub, Best of The Bests, E Dubai, Express Tour, Give The Slip, State Shinto, Street Cry, Alexius and Mutafaweq. Among their 2002 team, only dirt performer Street Cry, the Dubai World Cup winner, ended up with a higher Timeform rating. Also highly relevant during 2001 was the question of whether Marienbard was a middle-distance performer at all because the shortest trip he encountered as a four-year-old was twelve and a half furlongs (once) and he also appeared in the Melbourne Cup over two miles and the Gold Cup over two and a half. As a five-year-old, though, he was campaigned exclusively at a mile and a half. Saeed bin Suroor also reported that 'Marienbard is a different horse this year, more mature and mentally relaxed.' Marienbard's un-

Sagitta Jockey Club Stakes, Newmarket—Marienbard (right) shows a fine turn of foot to sweep past virtually the entire field; the previous year's winner Millenary is second, ahead of Storming Home (noseband), Zindabad (rail) and Kutub (hidden by winner)

expected development as a five-year-old provided another spectacular vindication of the Maktoum family's policy of keeping horses in training, not just a vindication of that policy but reason to celebrate it. 'Monochrome monotonie', however, was how one French newspaper saw it after the Arc, likening Marienbard variously to a Kleenex, a disposable razor and another rabbit produced from Saeed bin Suroor's hat. Some wounded French pride might have been understandable—it is now three years in a row that they have failed to keep their greatest prize at home, and that is unprecedented.

An additional cause for pique, of course, among the home contingent at Longchamp was the narrow defeat of their champion Sulamani. Some whistling was heard afterwards; something stronger might have been in the air eight days after that when it was announced that Sulamani had himself been bought by Godolphin. Carrying the famous Niarchos colours, Sulamani had been beaten on his debut but won all four starts since, including the Prix du Jockey Club and the Prix Niel. In a sixteen-runner Arc field, however, he was shaded for favouritism by the Derby and Irish Derby winner High Chaparral, who had been coughing in late-summer and then missed the Prix Niel because of an unsatisfactory blood count. The Nassau Stakes and Yorkshire Oaks winner Islington headed the classic fillies, and all three of these three-year-olds had a major say after the Ballydoyle pacemaker Black Sam Bellamy led the field rounding the home turn. Islington and High Chaparral were poised to strike first, followed by Califet, who was travelling astoundingly well for a 131/1-shot, the previous year's runner-up Aquarelliste, Marienbard and Manhattan Cafe. Sulamani, whose own pacemaker was unable to get anywhere near the front, was travelling strongly too, but five lengths or so further back with only three horses behind him. It was Islington who struck for home and led for most of the straight, but High Chaparral and Califet were reeling her in by fractions, Marienbard was challenging on their outside, closely attended by Aquarelliste, and Sulamani was coming widest and apparently fastest of all. There was little to choose between the six of them a furlong and a half out, but Marienbard and Sulamani emerged in front, the younger horse having hung persistently early in the straight and then edged to his right in the closing stages, battle-hardened Marienbard proving the stronger in the final hundred yards. The margin between them was three quarters of a length, with half a length and the same back to High Chaparral and Califet. Incidentally, adding to an atmosphere of exasperation and disappointment for some French television viewers was an

606

experiment in broadcasting the sounds picked up by a microphone attached to one of the jockeys. Dominic Boeuf was the jockey in question on board Aquarelliste and, as described afterwards in *Paris-Turf*, things began well when he had 'words of tenderness and immense affection' for his mount in the preliminaries, though when the race was in progress the experiment proved more controversial with 'his words concerning the Japanese jockey' [on Manhattan Cafe].

The 2002 Arc was indeed a race of high emotions, one to set the pulse racing, but it was below the normal standard in terms of form, despite the also-rans including 2001 Prix du Jockey Club winner Anabaa Blue and dual Italian Group 1 and subsequent Japan Cup winner Falbrav, the pair having finished second and third respectively to Aquarelliste in the Prix Foy; September Stakes winner Asian Heights; Japanese Group 1 winner Manhattan Cafe; and German challenger Boreal who four months earlier had won the Coronation Cup. Marienbard was sent off at 158/10 on the pari-mutuel and Boreal at 105/1, despite Boreal having finished in front of Marienbard twice in three meetings in 2002. On Marienbard's reappearance in the Sheema Classic at Nad Al Sheba in March the margin between them was a head, Marienbard short of room and coming off just the worse in a tight battle for the places, though neither had a chance against the smooth winner Nayef. At Epsom in June for the Coronation Cup, Marienbard finished twelve lengths behind Boreal, the track and the soft ground possible explanations for a poor display. That, however, was the nadir of Marienbard's season and the zenith for Boreal, and when they met for a third time, at Baden-Baden five weeks before the Arc, the tables were turned decisively as Marienbard registered his third success of the campaign and his second German Group 1 in a row. The German double had been initiated in the WGZ Bank-Deutschlandpreis at Dusseldorf in July, run at a sound pace, in which Marienbard came from last of six to justify favouritism by a length and a half from veteran Yavana's Pace. The Grosser Preis von Baden in September should have been a good deal more demanding, but wasn't. A tighter finish might also have been anticipated after a pedestrian early pace that saw the eight-runner field enter the home straight closely bunched. Marienbard showed easily the best turn of foot to surge clear and win eased by two and a half lengths from Salve Regina, the German Oaks winner and German Derby runner-up; favourite Boreal was only sixth.

Those achievements on foreign soil might have escaped the attention of British onlookers but domestic racegoers had been warned because that turn of foot and the prospect of a transformed Marienbard had both been on display at

Grosser Preis von Baden, Baden-Baden—Marienbard gains a comfortable victory over German Oaks winner Salve Regina (striped cap), Noroit, Califet (checks), Samum (left) and Boreal (right)

Prix de l'Arc de Triomphe - Lucien Barriere, Longchamp—Marienbard accounts for Derby winners Sulamani (far side) and High Chaparral (striped cap), with Califet (checks) in fourth

Newmarket in May when he won the Sagitta Jockey Club Stakes. The early pace was not strong but Marienbard came with a striking run from the back of the field under Jamie Spencer to lead in the shadow of the post. The next four in this nine-runner field were Millenary, Storming Home, Zindabad and Kutub—no mean collection. Marienbard had been sent off a 9/1 chance, carrying Godolphin's second colours, and afterwards Sheikh Mohammed remarked: 'We will take it step by step, but his best trip is a mile and a half. He was working well in Dubai, and Kutub was short of a race, so we thought Marienbard would run well, though we didn't expect that.' It was not the last time that Sheikh Mohammed had to revise his expectations for Marienbard.

Godolphin's policy of keeping horses in training did not extend to Marienbard after the Arc, as he was retired shortly afterwards to take up stallion duties at East Stud in Japan, still under the Darley Stud banner. He was bred by Mr Saif Ali and raced for him as a three-year-old, trained by Michael Jarvis. His dam Marienbad carried Sheikh Mohammed's colours though and was trained by Andre Fabre. She ran only five times, winning minor events over a mile at Evry on her debut at two and at Clairefontaine at three. To state that she made the frame in a listed race flatters her rather, because she was last of four on that occasion as a juvenile and also brought up the rear in an eight-runner listed race to end her career at three. Marienbad had been bought for 2,100,000 francs as a yearling, her attractiveness boosted by the records of two half-sisters to her dam Marie de Fontenoy, one the Prix Morny winner and Poule d'Essai des Pouliches runner-up Sakura Reiko and the other the dam of Prix Royal-Oak winner Top Sunrise; another half-sister is the dam of very smart 2001 stayer Solo Mio. Marie de Fontenoy herself did not achieve much as a racehorse, quickly despatched to the Provinces where she won a maiden over a mile and a quarter. Marienbard's great grandam Primula won three times over a mile. Marienbard is Marienbad's second foal, following the modest winner Genscher (by Cadeaux Genereux) and preceding two fillies by Polish Precedent, the unraced Zacheta and the 2002 two-year-old Kartuzy, who showed a little promise in two starts for Marienbard's original trainer. Her yearling filly is by Carnegie, another Sheikh Mohammed-owned Arc winner now in Japan.

A big, good-topped horse, Marienbard was too backward and green to run at all as a two-year-old. His development at five has provided a very late triumph for his sire Caerleon, who died in 1998. Caerleon's progeny have been popular in Japan, with their effectiveness on a firm surface having something to do with it, and

Godolphin's "Marienbard"

	Caerleon (USA) (b 1980)	Nijinsky (b 1967)	Northern Dancer / Flaming Page
Marienbard (IRE) (b.h. 1997)		Foreseer (b or br 1969)	Round Table / Regal Gleam
	Marienbad (FR) (b 1991)	Darshaan (br 1981)	Shirley Heights / Delsy
		Marie de Fontenoy (ch 1983)	Lightning / Primula

Marienbard probably fits the mould, his high-class efforts in the latest season all coming on good ground or firmer, although he showed smart form to be runner-up in the St Simon Stakes on heavy ground as a three-year-old. Marienbard clearly didn't stay two and a half miles in the 2001 Gold Cup and his form when winning that season's Yorkshire Cup over a mile and three quarters was nothing like so good as that shown in 2002 over a mile and a half. He wore a visor or blinkers throughout his last two campaigns. *Saeed bin Suroor*

MARIINSKY 3 gr.g. Royal Applause 124 – Mainly Dry (The Brianstan 128) [2002 **106** 100p: 5m* 5m⁶ 5m⁶ 5g 6g 5m³ 6g Dec 7] rangy gelding: useful performer: won listed event at Haydock in April by length from Online Investor, making most: creditable sixth in Palace House Stakes at Newmarket (behind Kyllachy) and listed race at Kempton next 2 starts: left B. Meehan after fourth outing (slowly into stride): sent to Hong Kong and renamed Speed Lord: third in handicap at Happy Valley in November: best at 5f: acts on good to firm going: *I. W. Allan, Hong Kong*

Mrs J. S. Bolger's "Marionnaud"

MARIKA   4 b.f. Marju (IRE) 127 – Nordica 99 (Northfields (USA)) [2002 102: 7g² 6s*   **103**
6g⁵ 6m³ Aug 18] tall, strong filly: has marked knee action: useful performer, lightly
raced: won listed race at Haydock (beat Palace Affair by short head) in June: creditable
efforts in Chipchase Stakes at Newcastle (fifth to Tedburrow) and listed race at Pontefract
(third to Cotton House) after: effective at 6f to 1m: acts on soft and good to firm going
(probably on firm): has sweated/been on toes/had 2 handlers in paddock: early (and free)
to post final start. *G. Wragg*

MARINAS CHARM   2 b.f. (Mar 5) Zafonic (USA) 130 – Marina Park 112 (Local   **83 p**
Suitor (USA) 128) [2002 5d² 5g³ 6v* Nov 9] small filly: third foal: half-sister to 3-y-o
Rheinpark and 4-y-o Super Canyon: dam 5f to 7f performer: fairly useful form: off 5
months after debut: best effort when winning maiden at Doncaster by ¾ length from
Highly Liquid, gamely regaining lead near finish: will stay 7f: raced only on good ground
or softer: should improve further. *M. Johnston*

MARINKA   4 b.f. Pivotal 124 – Roxy Hart (High Top 131) [2002 –: p8g f12f Nov 29]   **–**
no form. *D. Haydn Jones*

MARINO MARINI (USA)   2 gr.c. (Apr 2) Storm Cat (USA) – Halo America (USA)   **106**
123 (Waquoit (USA)) [2002 6s* 5s* 5m³ 6s² 7f⁴ 7m Oct 19] $1,800,000Y: tall, quite
good-topped colt: has plenty of scope: first foal: dam won 15 times in USA, including
Grade 1 8.5f event: useful performer: won maiden at Cork in April and 4-runner listed
race at the Curragh (by 2½ lengths from Luminata) in May: best efforts when ½-length
second to Spartacus in Phoenix Stakes at the Curragh and under 6 lengths seventh to
Tout Seul in Dewhurst Stakes at Newmarket: reportedly lame and missed engagement at
Arlington later in October: stays 7f: acts on soft and good to firm going: has had 2
handlers in preliminaries. *A. P. O'Brien, Ireland*

MARINO TINO (IRE) 3 ch.f. Fayruz 116 – Zestino (Shack (USA) 118) [2002 –: f8g **43** f8g² f8g⁴ f8.5g⁶ f9.4g⁵ f7g⁴ f7g f8g⁴ 8m 7f⁶ 8m Jul 27] poor maiden: left Miss V. Haigh after eighth start: stays 9.4f: acts on fibresand and firm going: tried blinkered. *B. Ellison*

MARINO WOOD (IRE) 3 ch.f. Woodpas (USA) 85 – Forgren (IRE) (Thatching **36** 131) [2002 47: f5g f6g 6g 5m f6g² 6g f6g 5s⁵ 5g 10m f6g Nov 25] lengthy filly: poor **a40** maiden: claimed from R. Wilman £3,000 fifth start: effective at 5f/6f: acts on firm going and fibresand: tried blinkered: sometimes slowly away. *C. N. Kellett*

MARIONNAUD (IRE) 3 b.f. Spectrum 83 – Raghida (IRE) 102 (Nordico (USA)) **111** [2002 99: 7m² 7s³ 8m* 8s 6.3d* 8g⁶ 6s⁵ 8g⁴ 8m² 7.5m* 8s³ 10d³ Oct 28] small filly: good walker: third foal: dam, Irish 2-y-o 5f winner, half-sister to 3-y-o Sholokhov: smart performer: won last 4 starts at 2 yrs, notably listed race at Leopardstown: won Derrinstown Stud 1000 Guineas Trial at Leopardstown (by head from Aqualina) in May, valuable handicap at the Curragh in June and Coolmore Stud Home of Champions Concorde Stakes at Tipperary (by head from Patsy's Double) in October: some creditable efforts otherwise, including won sixth to Tashawak in Falmouth Stakes at Newmarket and length second behind Dress To Thrill in Matron Stakes at Leopardstown sixth/ninth starts: effective at 6f to 1m: acts on soft and good to firm going: carries head high: tough. *J. S. Bolger, Ireland*

MARISKA 3 b.f. Magic Ring (IRE) 115 – Prima Silk 82 (Primo Dominie 121) [2002 **–** 65: 8.3s May 27] useful-looking filly: fair maiden in 2001: tailed off only 3-y-o start. *G. G. Margarson*

MARITIME BLUES 2 b.c. (Mar 13) Fleetwood (IRE) 107 – Dixie d'Oats 66 (Alhijaz **47** 122) [2002 7d 6g 6m Oct 7] small colt: first foal: dam, maiden, stayed 1¼m: poor form in maidens. *G. C. Bravery*

MARITUN LAD 5 b.g. Presidium 124 – Girl Next Door 58 (Local Suitor (USA) 128) **54 §** [2002 –: f5s p5g³ f5g f5g f5g⁶ p6g 5s² 5s⁶ 5m 5.1d 5f Jul 15] good-topped gelding: modest handicapper: effective at 5f/6f: acts on all-weather and soft going: often blinkered/visored: sometimes slowly away: unreliable. *D. Shaw*

MARJURITA (IRE) 3 b.f. Marju (IRE) 127 – Unfuwaanah 74 (Unfuwain (USA) **77** 131) [2002 81: p5g 7m 6m 6f p7g⁴ 7f⁶ p7g* 7m⁶ 6.9m* p8g³ p8g* 8f³ 8.1g⁵ 7d* 7s⁶ p7g p8g³ p10g⁵ Dec 14] leggy, lengthy filly: fair performer: won handicaps at Lingfield and Redcar, and minor events at Carlisle and Lingfield between July and October: stays 1m: acts on firm ground, soft and polytrack: well below form when sweating. *N. P. Littmoden*

MARKER 2 ch.g. (Apr 12) Pivotal 124 – Palace Street (USA) 103 (Secreto (USA) **99** 128) [2002 6g* 6d⁵ 6g² Sep 19] half-brother to several winners, including 4-y-o Palace Affair and 5-y-o Duke of Modena: dam 6f/7f winner: useful performer: won maiden at Windsor in July: best effort when ½-length second to Eastern Magenta in nursery at Ayr, leading briefly final 1f: raced only at 6f. *G. B. Balding*

MARKET AVENUE 3 b.f. Factual (USA) 108 – The Lady Vanishes (Robin Des Pins **68** (USA) 119) [2002 62: 7m 6g 8m⁴ 10f* 10m³ 9.3g⁴ 11m² 10m⁵ 10.1m Aug 16] lengthy, angular filly: has a quick action: fair handicapper: won at Redcar in June: barely stays 11f: acts on firm and good to soft going: has pulled hard/hung left. *R. A. Fahey*

MARKING TIME (IRE) 4 b.g. Goldmark (USA) 113 – Tamarsiya (USA) (Shah- **–** rastani (USA) 135) [2002 57: f12f⁴ f11g f14.8g⁴ Dec 14] smallish gelding: only poor **a40** form on belated return in 2002: should stay 2m: acts on good to firm going. *K. R. Burke*

MARK IT 3 b.g. Botanic (USA) – Everdene (Bustino 136) [2002 –p: p8g 10m 8g 8.3s⁵ **61** 8m⁴ 10.2m 10g⁶ Jul 6] modest maiden: should stay 1¼m: acts on soft going, probably on good to firm: has started slowly: sold 7,000 gns later in July, joined D. Cantillon, and successful twice over hurdles in November. *Mrs A. J. Perrett*

MARK OF ZORRO (IRE) 2 b.g. (Feb 12) Mark of Esteem (IRE) 137 – Sifaara **93** (IRE) (Caerleon (USA) 132) [2002 6d* 7f² 7.1g² 8m⁵ 8.2s⁴ Oct 23] 31,000F, 75,000Y: well-made gelding: third foal: dam, ran twice in France at 3 yrs, out of very smart 7f to 9f (US Grade 2 event) winner Royal Touch: fairly useful performer: won minor event at Kempton in July: best effort when beaten ½ length by Commission in similar race at Sandown third start: should stay 1m: acts on firm and good to soft ground: blinkered (hampered, ran respectably) final start: gelded after. *R. Hannon*

MARLO 3 b.c. Hector Protector (USA) 124 – Tender Moment (IRE) 78 (Caerleon **86** (USA) 132) [2002 95: 7s 6f 8d 7g 7d* 7d⁶ f7g⁴ Nov 15] good-topped colt: fairly useful handicapper: won at Yarmouth in October: should stay 1m: acts on fibresand, best turf form on ground softer than good. *B. W. Hills*

MARMADUKE (IRE)   6 ch.g. Perugino (USA) 84 – Sympathy 77 (Precocious 126)   **70**
[2002 63, a57: p10g f8g⁴ f16g* f16g⁴ 18s³ 12g⁵ f14.8g* 16m⁶ 16.2m³ p16g* Jul 17] tall
gelding: fair handicapper: won at Southwell in February, Wolverhampton in May and
Lingfield in July: effective at 1½m, seemingly at 2¼m: acts on all-weather and probably
any turf going: tried visored: tends to race freely. *M. Pitman*

MARNIE   5 ch.m. First Trump 118 – Miss Aboyne 64 (Lochnager 132) [2002 68, a75:   **63**
p7g 8g 8g³ 8m* 8.5d⁶ 7m⁴ 8f 8f³ p7g² p8g² p7g Dec 30] sturdy, lengthy mare: fair handi-   **a66**
capper: won at Bath in June: stays 1m: acts on firm going, good to soft and polytrack.
J. Akehurst

MAROMA   4 b.f. First Trump 118 – Madurai 71 (Chilibang 120) [2002 12m 10.1d 10g   **–**
Sep 20] fair maiden at 2 yrs for J. Dunlop: trained in Czech Republic at 3 yrs, winning 3
times at Velka Chuchle in first half of year: well beaten in 2002 (trained by A. Newcombe
on reappearance): seems to stay 1¾m. *I. Semple*

MAROMITO (IRE)   5 b.g. Up And At 'em 109 – Amtico (Bairn (USA) 126) [2002   **84**
79, a66+: 5d 5m* 5m 5g 5.2f 5.3m⁵ Aug 19] well-made gelding: fairly useful handicapper   **a–**
on turf: won at York in June: left R. Bastiman after next start: not knocked about last 2
outings: best at bare 5f: acts on firm going, good to soft and fibresand: sometimes sweats/
on edge/early to post: has hung left: usually a front runner: joined C. Dore. *G. A. Butler*

MARON   5 b.g. Puissance 110 – Will Be Bold 79 (Bold Lad (IRE) 133) [2002 –, a67d: **–**
p6g p6g⁶ p6g f6g f6g f6g 6d 10.5s 6v 6v 5s⁴ 7m Jul 27] rather leggy gelding: modest   **a56 d**
performer: on downgrade: stays easy 6f: acts on all-weather and any turf going: tried
blinkered/tongue tied: often slowly away. *A. Berry*

MAROONED (IRE)   2 ch.f. (Apr 10) Definite Article 121 – No Islands (Lomond   **50**
(USA) 128) [2002 5m 6f⁵ 7d 7m 6m 6m Sep 23] workmanlike filly: seventh foal: half-
sister to 3 winners, including 6-y-o Medelai: dam ran once: modest maiden: free-going
sort, not sure to stay 1m. *M. Blanshard*

MAROTTA (FR)   3 gr.f. Highest Honor (FR) 124 – Mistra (IRE) 104 (Rainbow Quest   **115**
(USA) 134) [2002 10m 10d* 10m* 10.5m⁵ 10g³ 10g³ 10g* Oct 27] 450,000 francs Y,
600,000 francs 2-y-o: second foal: dam, French 10.8f winner, half-sister to useful miler
Pescara: smart performer: unraced at 2 yrs: won minor event at Chantilly in April, Prix
Saint-Alary at Longchamp (by neck from Bright Sky) in May and Premio Lydia Tesio at
Rome (by 3½ lengths from Choc Ice) in October: also ran creditably when never-nearer
fifth to Bright Sky in Prix de Diane at Chantilly, 2½ lengths third to Pearly Shells in
Prix de la Nonette at Deauville and 4¾ lengths third to Bright Sky in Prix de l'Opera at
Longchamp: raced only around 1¼m: unraced on extremes of ground: held up. *R. Gibson,
France*

MARRAKECH (IRE)   5 ch.m. Barathea (IRE) 127 – Nashkara (Shirley Heights 130)   **100**
[2002 103: p10g 11.9m⁴ 12m 12f⁴ 12g Oct 17] tall mare: useful handicapper: creditable
efforts in 2002 when fourth at Haydock and Newmarket (behind Blagovest): should
stay beyond 1½m: acts on firm and good to soft going: refused to settle final outing.
P. W. Harris

MARREL   4 b.g. Shareef Dancer (USA) 135 – Upper Caen (High Top 131) [2002 60:   **50**
f16.2g⁶ f12g³ 15g 16.4d⁵ 16f⁵ 12m⁶ p12g f14.8g³ Dec 14] strong, workmanlike gelding: **a55**
modest performer: left B. Hanbury after sixth start: stays 2m: acts on fibresand, best turf
efforts on ground firmer than good: tried visored, usually blinkered: none too consistent.
S. L. Keightley

*Prix Saint-Alary, Longchamp—Marotta has enough in hand to hold off the strong-finishing Bright Sky;
Summertime Legacy is third*

Mrs A. E. Oppenheimer's "Marotta"

MARSAD (IRE) 8 ch.g. Fayruz 116 – Broad Haven (IRE) (Be My Guest (USA) 126) **102** [2002 99: 7f 6m* 6d³ 6m 6m 6g 6f 6s Oct 25] lengthy, good-topped gelding: useful handicapper: well backed when winning 30-runner event at Newmarket (for second year running, beat Peruvian Chief by short head) in May: ran creditably next and sixth starts: effective at 6f/easy 7f: acts on any going: has run creditably when sweating. *J. Akehurst*

MARSHAL BOND 4 b.g. Celtic Swing 138 – Arminda (Blakeney 126) [2002 75, **70** a62: 9.9g⁵ 9.9d Jul 12] workmanlike gelding: fluent mover: fair handicapper: stays 1¼m: **a–** seems to act on any turf going (below best on fibresand): blinkered final 3-y-o start: usually races prominently. *B. Smart*

MARSHALL (FR) 2 b.c. (Apr 26) Anabaa (USA) 130 – Monitrice (FR) (Groom **107** Dancer (USA) 128) [2002 8g⁴ 7.5s* 10v³ Nov 9] fifth foal: closely related to French 1½m winner Mysterieux (by Petit Loup) and half-brother to French 12.5f winner Monitoring (by Linamix): dam lightly-raced half-sister to smart French 7f/1m performer Malaspina: won minor event at Deauville in October: improved again when just over 2 lengths third to Alberto Giacometti in Criterium de Saint-Cloud final start: should stay 1½m: raced only on good going or softer. *C. Laffon-Parias, France*

MARSHALLSPARK (IRE) 3 b.g. Fayruz 116 – Lindas Delight 54 (Batshoof 122) **78** [2002 75: 5s⁵ 5m 6.1f* 6f⁶ 6m³ 7f² 5.1f⁵ 6m³ Aug 9] sturdy, lengthy gelding: fair handicapper: won at Chester in May: effective at 6f/easy 7f: acts on firm ground, good to soft and fibresand: blinkered (inadequate trip) seventh start. *R. A. Fahey*

MARSHALL WARNING 2 b.g. (Apr 19) Averti (IRE) 117 – Spring Sunrise 59 **53** (Robellino (USA) 127) [2002 6s 7.1g 5.7f³ Sep 30] first winner: best effort in maidens (modest form) when third of 4 at Bath: will probably stay 7f: reluctant stall/soon under pressure debut. *C. G. Cox*

MARSHMAN (IRE) 3 ch.g. College Chapel 122 – Gold Fly (IRE) (Be My Guest **90** (USA) 126) [2002 81: 7d³ 7g³ 6d* 6m⁴ 6.1m⁵ 6g 7v p7g* p7g⁶ p7g⁴ Dec 28] good-topped **a100** gelding: useful handicapper on all-weather, fairly useful on turf: won at Haydock in July and Lingfield (all-weather debut, beat J M W Turner by ¾ length) in November: effective at 6f/7f: yet to race on heavy going, seems to act on any other turf/polytrack: reliable. *M. H. Tompkins*

MARTHA'S ROSE 2 b.f. (May 10) Forzando 122 – Marjorie Rose (IRE) 67 (Magical **39** Strike (USA) 114) [2002 5g 6d 7f Jun 11] 700Y: first foal: dam 5f/6f winner: poor form in sellers. *B. S. Rothwell*

MARTIN HOUSE (IRE) 3 b.g. Mujadil (USA) 119 – Dolcezza (FR) (Lichine (USA) **97** 117) [2002 89: 10g⁵ 8.1d 8m 10g 10.5d² Aug 8] tall, leggy gelding: useful handicapper: best efforts at Haydock when eighth to Common World in quite valuable event second start and second of 4 to Muwassi final one: stays 1¼m: acts on good to firm and good to soft going, probably on soft: visored (pulled hard) penultimate start: has run respectably when sweating: sold 25,000 gns and gelded. *J. D. Bethell*

MARTIN'S PEARL (IRE) 5 gr.g. Petong 126 – Mainly Dry (The Brianstan 128) **51** [2002 56: f11s p10g⁴ p10g f8g² f8g³ f8.5g f11g f8.5g Mar 15] lengthy gelding: modest maiden: effective at 1m/1¼m: acts on all-weather and good to firm ground: tried blinkered: has started slowly (unseated as stall opened on reappearance): none too trustworthy: sold 2,400 gns, sent to Holland. *W. R. Muir*

MARTIN'S SUNSET 4 ch.g. Royal Academy (USA) 130 – Mainly Sunset (Red **62 §** Sunset 120) [2002 80§: 8d 10s 10g p10g* 9.7m 12m³ 14m 12d⁶ 17.2f³ f14.8g f12f Nov 11] sparely-made gelding: fairly useful at 3 yrs, just modest in 2002: won seller at Lingfield in July: stays easy 1½m: acts on firm ground, soft and polytrack: sometimes blinkered/visored: usually soon off bridle: has found little: unreliable. *W. R. Muir*

MARTON MERE 6 ch.g. Cadeaux Genereux 131 – Hyatti 74 (Habitat 134) [2002 **47** 54: 8m 12.1m 7.5d⁴ 9.9d 7m⁶ 6d Aug 3] angular gelding: poor performer: reportedly bled from nose final start: stays 1¼m: acts on firm and good to soft going. *A. J. Lockwood*

MARWELL'S KRIS (IRE) 6 b.g. Kris 135 – Marwell 133 (Habitat 134) [2002 **62** p6g* p6g³ 5g 5g³ 6f⁵ 7f p7g Dec 11] IR 40,000Y: half-brother to several winners, notably very smart miler Marling (by Lomond) and very smart sprinter/miler Caerwent (by Caerleon): dam champion sprinter and fourth in 1000 Guineas: modest performer: won claimer at Lingfield in January: well held in seller there final start (gelded after): stays 6f: acts on firm going and polytrack. *Andre Hermans, Belgium*

MARY BOONE 3 b.f. Dr Devious (IRE) 127 – Tolmi 122 (Great Nephew 126) [2002 **65** 8f⁶ 8.1m Sep 16] smallish, good-bodied filly: half-sister to several winners, including useful performers Double Dagger (up to 1¾m, by Reference Point) and Unreal City (up to 1¼m, by Rock City): dam second in 1000 Guineas: better effort in maidens 4 months apart when 5 lengths sixth to Helloimustbegoing at Newmarket. *H. R. A. Cecil*

MARY DOLL (IRE) 3 b.f. Distinctly North (USA) 115 – Robin Red Breast 74 (Red **43 §** Alert 127) [2002 54d: f5g f6g f6g 5m⁴ f5g 5d 5m 6d 6d 5g 5g³ 5m Jul 7] angular filly: poor maiden handicapper: form only at 5f: acts on good to firm ground: tried blinkered: sometimes slowly away: unreliable. *D. W. Chapman*

MARYINSKY (IRE) 3 b.f. Sadler's Wells (USA) 132 – Blush With Pride (USA) **100** (Blushing Groom (FR) 131) [2002 107p: 8m 8s 12s 8m 8m⁴ 10m Sep 15] close-coupled, good-topped filly: has a quick, unimpressive action: useful performer: failed to make expected progress from 2 to 3 yrs (highly tried first 4 starts, including in 1000 Guineas at Newmarket and Oaks at Epsom), though not discredited when 4½ lengths fourth to Dress To Thrill in Matron Stakes at Leopardstown penultimate start, making most: bred to be suited by 1¼m+: acts on soft and good to firm going: sometimes slowly away. *A. P. O'Brien, Ireland*

MARY JANE 7 b.m. Tina's Pet 121 – Fair Attempt (IRE) (Try My Best (USA) 130) **75** [2002 67, a60: 5.1d 5m 5m* 5g 5m² 5f 5g 5m 5m⁴ 5g⁵ 5.1m² 5g 5d⁴ 5d* 5m⁴ 5m 5m⁶ 5f⁵ **a–** f5g Nov 16] smallish, sturdy mare: fair handicapper: won at Redcar in May and Thirsk (apprentices) in August: has won at 6f, best at 5f: acts on any turf going and fibresand: blinkered once at 3 yrs: has edged left: often front runner: tough. *N. Tinkler*

MARY'S BABY 2 b.f. (Mar 8) Magic Ring (IRE) 115 – Everdene (Bustino 136) [2002 **72** 6m⁴ 6m⁵ 6s⁶ Sep 10] sixth foal: half-sister to 5f (at 2 yrs) to 7.5f winner Hever Golf Express (by Primo Dominie): dam, French 1¼m winner, half-sister to useful sprinter Great Deeds: fair form in maidens: not sure to stay 7f: acts on soft and good to firm ground. *Mrs A. J. Perrett*

MARZELLE (FR) 4 b.f. Sillery (USA) 122 – Marzipan (IRE) 74 (Green Desert **68 d** (USA) 127) [2002 76: p8g⁶ a10g⁵ 10.5s⁴ p10g p12g 11.6g 11.7g 11.7g⁴ 13.1g 12g p13g⁵ f12f5 Dec 7] tall, workmanlike filly: fair maiden handicapper: stays 11.7f: acts on soft and good to firm going: often slowly away: tends to wander: on downgrade. *S. Dow*

MASAADER (USA) 2 gr.f. (Mar 30) Wild Again (USA) – Futuh (USA) 95 (Diesis **88** 133) [2002 6m⁴ 6g² 6d* Nov 1] compact filly: half-sister to several at least useful winners, including smart 6f (at 2 yrs) and 1¼m (in UAE) winner Tamhid (by Gulch) and 1997 2-y-o 6f (Middle Park Stakes) winner Hayil (by Dayjur): dam 2-y-o 6f winner: fairly useful form in maidens: second at Newmarket and won (readily, by 1½ lengths from Regent's Secret) at Brighton: will probably prove best at 6f/7f. *E. A. L. Dunlop*

MASANI (IRE) 3 b.c. Indian Ridge 123 – Masawa (IRE) 86 (Alzao (USA) 117) [2002 **116** 83: 8m³ 7s³ 9.5g* 10s⁴ 9d² 8.5s⁴ 8g* Sep 1] fourth foal: half-brother to fairly useful Irish 7f winner Masakala (by Cadeaux Genereux): dam Irish 1m winner out of Poule d'Essai des Pouliches winner Masarika: smart performer: won maiden at Gowran in May and ladbrokes.com EBF Irish Cambridgeshire (Handicap) at the Curragh (by head from Moratorium) in September: may prove best around 1m: acts on soft ground: blinkered (best efforts) last 3 starts: sold 250,000 gns in October, sent to Hong Kong, where renamed Beverly Green. *J. Oxx, Ireland*

MASHHOOR (USA) 4 b.g. Thunder Gulch (USA) 129 – Memorive (USA) 81 (River- **–** man (USA) 131) [2002 52: f14.8s 16f Sep 8] modest maiden at best: left B. Llewellyn after reappearance: tried blinkered. *Mrs Barbara Waring*

MASIDEHA (IRE) 3 b.f. Selkirk (USA) 129 – Masafiya (IRE) 80 (Shernazar 131) **97** [2002 10g 12m⁴ 12d² 12m* 13m³ Sep 30] tall, lengthy filly: has a round action: second foal: dam, Irish maiden who raced only around 1¼m, half-sister to smart performer up to 1½m Massyar out of Poule d'Essai des Pouliches winner Masarika: useful form: made all in maiden at Catterick in August: best effort when 1¾ lengths third to Robandela in handicap at Hamilton final start: stays 13f: yet to race on extremes of going: sold €20,000. *Sir Michael Stoute*

MASKAYA (IRE) 3 b.f. Machiavellian (USA) 123 – Majinskaya (FR) 110 (Marignan **92** (USA) 117) [2002 91: 7s 5g⁶ 5d 6m a6s² a6f 5.5f Dec 22] smallish filly: first foal: dam, French 1m/1¼m winner, half-sister to dam of very smart French sprinter Kistena: fairly useful performer: won minor event at Navan at 2 yrs: best efforts when sixth to Zargus in Balmoral Handicap at Royal Ascot and (having left J. Burns after fourth outing) when second in allowance race at Churchill Downs in October: effective at 5f (given test), probably at 7f: acts on good going, good to firm and sloppy dirt: blinkered (ran poorly) final 2-y-o start. *A. M. Stall jnr, USA*

MASONIC DREAM (IRE) 2 ch.f. (Feb 15) Grand Lodge (USA) 125 – Licentious **–** 45 (Reprimand 122) [2002 7m⁴ 7d 7.1m Sep 16] IR 18,500Y: third foal: half-sister to 4-y-o Perestroika: dam twice-raced half-sister to Prix Morny winner Hoh Magic: well held in maidens. *E. A. L. Dunlop*

MASONRY (IRE) 2 b.c. (Feb 24) Grand Lodge (USA) 125 – Tumble (Mtoto 134) **73** [2002 p8g⁴ p10g³ f8.5g⁶ Dec 14] IR 54,000Y, resold IR 120,000Y: third foal: half-brother to 2000 2-y-o 7f winner Night Fall (by Night Shift): dam, prolific winner around 1m/ 1¼m in French Provinces, half-sister to smart middle-distance performer Angel Falls: well backed, fair form when in frame in maidens at Lingfield won by Face The Storm and by Shield: ran as if something amiss final outing: stays 1¼m. *P. F. I. Cole*

MASSALANI (IRE) 3 b.c. Ashkalani (IRE) 128 – Massatixa (FR) (Linamix (FR) 127) **116** [2002 7g⁴ 8m May 4] well-made colt: first foal: dam, placed at 7.5f/1m at 2 yrs in France (her only starts), sister to Prix Jacques le Marois winner Miss Satamixa: smart performer: won maiden at Clairefontaine and minor event at Chantilly at 2 yrs, and listed event at Maisons-Laffitte (comfortably held off Zipping by ½ length) in April: raced in disadvantaged group when respectable eighth, beaten 6 lengths by Rock of Gibraltar, in 2000 Guineas at Newmarket: not seen out again: stays 1m: yet to race on extremes of going. *A. Fabre, France*

MASSARRA 3 b.f. Danehill (USA) 126 – Rafha 123 (Kris 135) [2002 99: 7m² 8g 6f³ **99** 6d* 6m 6m⁶ 5f⁵ Oct 4] small, lengthy filly: useful performer: won minor event at Newmarket (beat Affaire Royale by length) in August: creditable efforts otherwise only when length second to Misterah in Nell Gwyn Stakes at Newmarket and third to Ashdown Express in listed event at Newbury: headstrong, and was probably best at 6f/7f: acted on firm and good to soft going: blinkered (soon struggling) final start: often edgy: wore crossed noseband with pace: stud. *J. L. Dunlop*

MASSEY 6 br.g. Machiavellian (USA) 123 – Massarand (USA) (Nureyev (USA) 131) **60** [2002 –, a78: f8s³ f8s⁴ f7s* f7g* f7g f7g² f7g³ 7.1m* 7m 6m² 7g 7g³ 7.5d 7m f6g² p7g **a95** f6g² Dec 31] useful handicapper on all-weather, modest on turf: better than ever in 2002, winning at Southwell (twice) and Musselburgh in first half of year: successful at 1½m, but almost certainly best at 6f/7f: acts on fibresand and good to firm going: often visored in 2000: front runner. *T. D. Barron*

MASSIGANN (IRE) 3 ch.c. Selkirk (USA) 129 – Masslama (FR) 114 (No Pass No **117 p**
Sale 120) [2002 8d² 8d* 8g* 8.3s* 8g⁴ Oct 5] fifth foal: half-brother to French 1995
2-y-o 1m winner Massoura (by Shernazar) and French 1½m winner Marsakara (by Turtle
Island): dam won Prix des Reservoirs and Prix Vanteaux and stayed 10.5f well: smart
performer: won minor events at Vichy in July and Deauville in August then listed race at
Craon (by length from Dionello) in September: ran well when ¾-length fourth to
Domedriver in Prix Daniel Wildenstein at Longchamp final start, running on strongly to
be nearest at finish: should stay 1¼m: blinkered all starts: should improve further, and
capable of winning a pattern race. *A. de Royer Dupre, France*

MASTER COOPER (IRE) 8 b.g. Kahyasi 130 – Arabian Princess (Taufan (USA) **82 d**
119) [2002 82: p12g⁴ p12g⁶ 10g 13d³ 14g 10g 12g 10g Oct 31] leggy gelding: fairly
useful handicapper at best: left D. Elsworth after second start: well below form last 4
outings: stays 13f: acts on good to firm going, good to soft and polytrack: often blinkered
earlier in career. *E. Tyrrell, Ireland*

MASTER CORBIN 3 b.g. Mind Games 121 – Cafe Solo 51 (Nomination 125) [2002 **–**
8m 6s⁵ 7g f6s Oct 8] 24,000Y, 16,000 2-y-o: sturdy gelding: second foal: dam 6f/7f
winner: little form. *P. T. Dalton*

MASTER ELLIS (IRE) 3 b.g. Turtle Island (IRE) 123 – Take No Chances (IRE) 94 **–**
(Thatching 131) [2002 – . 10.3s 8.2d Apr 1] tall gelding: little form. *P. D. Evans*

MASTER FELLOW 4 ch.g. First Trump 118 – Take Charge (Last Tycoon 131) **–**
[2002 47: f11s Jan 17] sparely-made gelding: modest maiden at best: well held only
outing in 2002: blinkered last 3 starts. *J. G. Given*

MASTERFUL (USA) 4 b.c. Danzig (USA) – Moonlight Serenade (FR) (Dictus (FR) **114**
126) [2002 119: 9g² 8f² 9m² Oct 19] good-bodied colt: smart performer: respectable
runner-up all 3 starts in 2002, behind Desert Deer then Golden Silca in listed events at
Newmarket last 2, beaten ½ length each time: stays 1¼m: yet to race on soft/heavy going,
acts on any other: tended to hang third start at 3 yrs. *Saeed bin Suroor*

MASTER IN LAW (IRE) 3 ch.c. Polish Precedent (USA) 131 – Clara Bow (USA) **93**
(Coastal (USA)) [2002 85: 9m⁴ 10.2g³ 12m 9f 10s Oct 26] leggy colt: fairly useful
performer: best efforts in listed race at Newmarket (fourth to Playapart) in April and
minor event at Bath (third to Grampian, tended to wander) in May: should stay beyond
1¼m: acts on soft and good to firm going (tailed off on heavy): tongue tied: sold 800 gns,
sent to Italy. *G. C. Bravery*

MASTER JONES 5 b.g. Emperor Jones (USA) 119 – Tight Spin (High Top 131) **– §**
[2002 f14.8s 12m 17.1m Jun 10] lengthy, angular gelding: temperamental maiden: tried
blinkered. *Mrs H. L. Walton*

MASTER MCGHEE 3 ch.g. Beveled (USA) – Sandra Dee (IRE) 60 (Be My Guest **–**
(USA) 126) [2002 f6g 5d Aug 7] first foal: dam maiden who stayed 7f: tailed off in
maidens at Wolverhampton and (seemingly something amiss) Sandown. *E. A. Wheeler*

MASTER MCGRATH (IRE) 4 b.g. Common Grounds 118 – Darabaka (IRE) **79**
(Doyoun 124) [2002 75p: 17.5g² Sep 20] lengthy, workmanlike gelding: fair performer,
lightly raced: ran well only 4-y-o start (edged left): will stay further than 17.5f: acts on
soft going: visored last 2 starts: has swished tail: withdrawn after getting trapped beneath
stall Oct 25. *M. C. Pipe*

MASTER NIMBUS 2 b.g. (Apr 19) Cloudings (IRE) 112 – Miss Charlie 59 (Pharly **67**
(FR) 130) [2002 6m 5g⁴ 6s Oct 25] 1,500F, 4,600Y: strong, angular gelding: second foal:
half-brother to a 6f winner in Sweden by Tragic Role: dam 7f winner: better effort in
maidens (fair form) when fourth of 17 to Bollin Janet at Beverley: well beaten in sales
race at Doncaster final start: should stay at least 6f. *J. J. Quinn*

MASTERPOINT 2 ch.g. (Mar 12) Mark of Esteem (IRE) 137 – Baize 95 (Efisio 120) **91**
[2002 5g³ 6f* 6g 6m⁴ 7.2g⁶ 8g Oct 18] strong gelding: second foal: dam, 2-y-o 5f winner
(later 5f/6f winner in USA), sister to useful sprinter Bayleaf: fairly useful performer: won
maiden at Newmarket in May: best effort after when fourth in nursery at York: likely to
prove best at 5f/6f: raced only on good going or firmer. *M. Johnston*

MASTER RATTLE 3 b.g. Sabrehill (USA) 120 – Miss Primula 81 (Dominion 123) **58**
[2002 7.1g 6g⁶ 6s⁶ 6s 5.3m p6g Dec 18] 32,000Y, 3,500 2-y-o: half-brother to several
winners, including useful Irish 5f/6f winner Tinker Amelia (by Damister) and fairly
useful German winner up to 7.5f Magic Grey (by Petong): dam 5f/6f winner: modest
maiden: well held last 3 starts: likely to prove best at 5f/6f. *Jane Southcombe*

MASTER ROBBIE 3 b.g. Piccolo 121 – Victoria's Secret (IRE) 70 (Law Society **91 d**
(USA) 130) [2002 95: 5m 5g⁴ 6g 5g⁴ 5g 5m 6m 5s 5v Nov 8] tall, close-coupled gelding:

fairly useful handicapper: generally on downgrade: effective at 5f/6f: acts on good to firm going. *M. R. Channon*

MASTER T (USA)   3 b.g. Trempolino (USA) 135 – Our Little C (USA) (Marquetry (USA) 121) [2002 67: p8g⁴ f9.4g⁵ p10g* p8g* 10f⁴ 10.2g⁶ 11.9d⁵ 10m⁴ p10g² p10g⁴ Dec 21] sparely-made gelding: fair performer: won 2 claimers at Lingfield in February: stays 1¼m: acts on firm going and polytrack: tongue tied third to eighth starts. *G. L. Moore*   **66 a73**

MASTER TYSON (IRE)   2 b.g. (May 9) College Chapel 122 – Molvina (ITY) (Final Straw 127) [2002 5.1g⁴ 5.1g 6m f6g f5g Dec 27] IR 4,000Y, 4,500 2-y-o: good-bodied gelding: fourth foal: dam, ran once in Italy at 2 yrs, half-sister to useful Irish 1997 2-y-o 5f winner Danyross (later winner in USA): well held in maidens/nursery/seller: tried visored. *Mrs N. Macauley*   **–**

MATABELE   2 ch.g. (Mar 1) Muhtarram (USA) 125 – Newala 61 (Royal Academy (USA) 130) [2002 7m 8m 8.5s² Sep 7] 21,000Y: rather unfurnished gelding: first foal: dam, second at 7f/1m, out of close relative to smart Irish/US performer up to 1¼m Casey Tibbs: signs of ability in maidens and minor event (23 lengths second of 4 to Grand at Wolverhampton): gelded after final start: difficult to assess. *W. J. Haggas*   **?**

MATCHSTICKS   2 b.c. (Feb 4) Case Law 113 – Up All Night 56 (Green Desert (USA) 127) [2002 7m 7.2s 8.3m⁴ 8g⁶ Sep 19] 4,400F, 9,000Y: third foal: dam maiden daughter of Oaks runner-up Vielle: modest maiden: fourth at Hamilton: well held in seller final start: stays 1m: acts on soft and good to firm ground: sold 1,000 gns. *Miss L. A. Perratt*   **60**

MATERIAL WITNESS (IRE)   5 b.g. Barathea (IRE) 127 – Dial Dream (Gay Mecene (USA) 128) [2002 86§, a74§: p8g² p8g p8g⁴ p10g f8g³ 8d⁶ 7g⁵ 7d⁴ 7s* 7d² 8g⁶ 7g² 7d⁶ 7g⁵ 7.1m* 7g 7s³ p7g* p7g⁵ p7g Dec 14] angular gelding: fairly useful handicapper: showed more resolution than in past, and won at Goodwood in June, Sandown in September and Lingfield in November: best at 7f/1m: acts on soft going, good to firm and polytrack, probably on fibresand: sometimes blinkered/visored (not after second start in 2002): carries head high: usually front runner: consistent. *W. R. Muir*   **91**

MATHMAGICIAN   3 ch.g. Hector Protector (USA) 124 – Inherent Magic (IRE) 95 (Magical Wonder (USA) 125) [2002 43: f7g f6g f8g⁵ f11g 7.5m 8m⁶ 9.9g Jul 30] strong gelding: little form at 3 yrs: tried blinkered. *R. F. Marvin*   **–**

MATINEE LOVER   2 b.f. (May 15) Theatrical Charmer 114 – Classic Artiste (USA) 56 (Arctic Tern (USA) 126) [2002 5.1d p5g⁵ 6m⁶ f7g 6s Oct 31] first foal: dam ran 4 times at 2 yrs: little form: left Miss J. Feilden after fourth start. *Seamus Fahey, Ireland*   **–**

MATRIARCHAL   2 ch.f. (Mar 29) Presidium 124 – Mayor 86 (Laxton 105) [2002 6m⁵ 6d 6s 6.1m Sep 20] 1,000Y: neat filly: sixth foal: sister to a winner in Singapore and half-sister to 11-y-o Nineacres: dam best at 6f: modest maiden: well held in nursery final start: raced only at 6f. *N. Tinkler*   **51**

MATSIENG   3 b.f. Woodborough (USA) 112 – Ty High (IRE) (High Line 125) [2002 7g⁴ 7m 8g 7f 7.1m⁶ 10m Oct 3] 1,000Y: fifth foal: dam, ran 3 times, bred to stay at least 1¼m: poor maiden: should stay at least 1m. *R. Guest*   **35**

MATTY TUN   3 b.g. Lugana Beach 116 – B Grade 59 (Lucky Wednesday 124) [2002 63: f5s⁶ f5g 5d⁵ 5m* 5s² 5v 5d* 5g 5m⁵ 5f⁴ 5v³ f5g* Dec 17] strong gelding: fairly useful performer: left Miss J. Craze after second start: won maiden at Newcastle in May and handicaps at Sandown in August and Southwell (carried head high, hung markedly right) in December: raced mainly at 5f: acts on any turf going and fibresand: tried tongue tied: sometimes slowly away/races freely. *J. Balding*   **84**

MAUGWENNA   2 b.f. (Mar 14) Danehill (USA) 126 – River Abouali (Bluebird (USA) 125) [2002 6g³ 5m* 5.1f⁵ Jun 29] 50,000F, 60,000Y: quite attractive filly: fluent mover: first foal: dam unraced out of sister to dam of Saffron Walden, Dolphin Street and Insight, and to dam of Sequoyah, all Group/Grade 1 winners: fair form: justified favouritism in maiden at York in June by ½ length from Night Speed: hampered and lost action final start: should stay at least 6f: sometimes early to post. *J. Noseda*   **79**

M'AULD SEGOISHA (IRE)   4 gr.f. Dolphin Street (FR) 125 – September Tide (IRE) 58 (Thatching 131) [2002 70: 7m 6s² 6g 6.9s⁴ 6.9g³ 5.9v 6m f6s⁶ Oct 8] strong filly: modest maiden: effective at 6f (given good test) to 7.5f: acts on soft and good to firm going, probably on fibresand: visored fifth to seventh starts: tongue tied: has carried head awkwardly: none too reliable. *J. G. FitzGerald*   **61**

MAUMEE (IRE)   4 b.c. Indian Ridge 123 – Moy Water (IRE) 87 (Tirol 127) [2002 108: 7s 7m 9d³ 8.5s 10g⁵ 8g² 8m 10.5f² Sep 21] IR 68,000Y: good-topped colt: second   **108**

foal: half-brother to useful 1999 German 2-y-o sprinter Mona Em (by Catrail): dam Irish 1m (at 2 yrs) and 9f winner out of half-sister to smart sprinter Governor General: useful performer: creditable efforts in 2002 when third to Masnada and fifth to Mkuzi, both in handicaps at Leopardstown, and second to Blatant in listed race at Tralee on third/fifth/ sixth starts: well held in handicap at Royal Ascot second outing: stays 1¼m: acts on soft and good to firm going: usually blinkered: sent to USA. *D. K. Weld, Ireland*

MAUNBY ROCKER   2 ch.g. (Jan 31) Sheikh Albadou 128 – Bullion 85 (Sabrehill   **73**
(USA) 120) [2002 6g 6m 5.9s* 5.9s³ 7.1m f6s⁶ f7g f8g⁴ Nov 26] 15,000Y: small gelding: **a64**
first foal: dam 2-y-o 1m winner: fair on turf, modest on all-weather: 50/1-winner of
maiden at Carlisle in July: some creditable efforts after: stays 1m: acts on soft going and
fibresand: sometimes carries head awkwardly. *P. C. Haslam*

MAUNBY ROLLER (IRE)   3 b.g. Flying Spur (AUS) – Brown Foam (Horage 124)   **62**
[2002 p8g² f8.5g⁴ f8g² 8m 8.3m Sep 30] strong gelding: modest maiden handicapper:
stays 1m: acts on all-weather: has carried head awkwardly/run in snatches/found little.
P. C. Haslam

MAUNSELL'S ROAD (IRE)   3 b.g. Desert Style (IRE) 121 – Zara's Birthday (IRE)   **78**
71 (Waajib 121) [2002 74: 8.1f³ 10g² 10.9m p10g⁴ 8.1m⁴ 9.7m³ 8f⁵ 12f* 12f³ 10.4f⁵ Oct
10] strong, close-coupled gelding: fair performer: won claimer at Salisbury in September:
stays 1½m: acts on firm going, probably on polytrack: blinkered (raced freely) fourth
start: has edged left: joined L. Lungo. *S. Kirk*

MAUREEN ANN   2 b.f. (Jan 28) Elmaamul (USA) 125 – Running Glimpse (IRE) 84   **60 ?**
(Runnett 125) [2002 7m 8.3d⁴ p8g Nov 14] fourth foal: half-sister to 4-y-o Another
Glimpse: dam, 5f (at 2 yrs)/6f winner, half-sister to smart 1¼m/1½m performer Captain
Horatius: modest maiden: form only when fourth to La Muette at Windsor, nearest finish:
free-going sort, but should stay 1¼m: wore hood all starts: veered right leaving stall on
debut. *Miss B. Sanders*

MAURI MOON   4 b.f. Green Desert (USA) 127 – Dazzling Heights 99 (Shirley   **102**
Heights 130) [2002 104: 8.2d* 7m³ 7f⁶ 7m³ 7m 7s Oct 26] angular, quite attractive filly:
useful performer: won 4-runner minor event at Nottingham in June: at least respectable
efforts next 3 starts, third to Desert Alchemy in listed race at Goodwood on last of them:
best efforts at 7f/1m: yet to race on heavy going, acts on any other: has worn rope halter/
given trouble in preliminaries (has had 2 handlers in paddock and been accompanied by
expert in stall entry): sometimes finds little. *G. Wragg*

MAWAHEB (IRE)   3 ch.f. Nashwan (USA) 135 – Ta Rib (USA) 116 (Mr Prospector   **89**
(USA)) [2002 11.1g* 9.9d⁵ 12.6m² 12d² 10.5m⁵ Sep 7] rangy, good-topped filly: second
foal: dam 7f/1m (Poule d'Essai des Pouliches) winner: fairly useful performer: won
maiden at Kempton in April: creditable efforts last 3 starts: stayed 12.6f: acted on good to
firm and good to soft going: carried head high third outing: visits Green Desert.
E. A. L. Dunlop

MAWHOOB (USA)   4 gr.g. Dayjur (USA) 137 – Asl (USA) 114 (Caro 133) [2002 79:   **–**
f12g 10m 8f 8.2d 7.1m 7m 9.7g f8s f8g f9.4s⁶ Nov 2] good-bodied gelding: has a round
action: maiden handicapper: little form in 2002: tried visored. *Mrs N. Macauley*

MAXILLA (IRE)   2 b. or br.f. (Apr 29) Lahib (USA) 129 – Lacinia 107 (Groom   **68**
Dancer (USA) 128) [2002 6s 6v p6g⁴ Nov 19] IR 30,000Y: rangy filly: third foal: dam
Irish 6f (at 2 yrs) and 11f winner: easily best effort in maidens (fair form) when 3¼
lengths fourth to Leitrim Lakes at Lingfield: should stay at least 7f. *L. M. Cumani*

MAXIMINUS   2 b.c. (Apr 20) The West (USA) 107 – Candarela 41 (Damister (USA)   **–**
123) [2002 7f Sep 17] fourth foal: dam, maiden, half-sister to useful 1¼m performer
Game Ploy: 50/1, always behind in maiden at Salisbury. *M. Madgwick*

MAXIM (IRE)   3 b.c. Zamindar (USA) 116 – Lavanda 60 (Soviet Star (USA) 128)   **49**
[2002 p8g 7s⁵ Oct 22] 4,000F, 12,000Y: second foal: half-brother to 1m winner in Spain
by Bin Ajwaad: dam once-raced daughter of half-sister to Miesque: poor form in maidens
(raced freely final start). *W. A. O'Gorman*

MAX'S MICRO (IRE)   3 b.g. Inzar (USA) 112 – Guess Who 76 (Be My Guest (USA)   **–**
126) [2002 50: f9.4g⁵ f9.4g⁶ f9.4g Jan 21] maiden: little form in 2002: tried visored.
P. D. Evans

MAYAN PRINCESS (IRE)   2 b.f. (Mar 3) Perugino (USA) 84 – Tendermark (Prince   **–**
Tenderfoot (USA) 126) [2002 8g 7d f6g Nov 18] 2,000Y: big, leggy filly: closely related
to UAE 7f winner Mystery Hill (by Danehill) and 7f and 1¼m winner Monica's Choice
(by Shaadi) and half-sister to 2 winners: dam Irish 7f and (at 2 yrs) 1m winner: last in
maidens. *N. P. Littmoden*

618

Prix Maurice de Gheest, Deauville—a career-best effort from May Ball (No.5),
who takes over from the Japanese raider Air Thule; Nayyir (rail) does well to finish so close in third

MAY BALL 5 b.m. Cadeaux Genereux 131 – Minute Waltz (Sadler's Wells (USA) 132) **115**
[2002 104: 7.1d 7.1s⁴ 6s² 6.5s* 6m⁵ 5g 7m Oct 13] big, strong mare: smart performer:
better than ever at 5 yrs, winning Prix Maurice de Gheest at Deauville (beat Air Thule ¾
length) in August: creditable fifth to Invincible Spirit in Sprint Cup at Haydock (took
good hold ridden patiently) next start: below form at Longchamp after in Prix de
l'Abbaye and Prix de la Foret: effective at 6f to 1m: acts on soft and good to firm going,
probably on heavy: often races prominently: none too consistent. *J. H. M. Gosden*

MAYBE BABY (IRE) 3 b.g. Lake Coniston (IRE) 131 – Nadedge (IRE) 78 (Petorius **43**
117) [2002 53: f5g 8.2g f6g⁶ 6g 6d 5s⁴ 5m Aug 22] leggy, sparely-made gelding: poor
maiden: stays 6f: acts on fibresand and soft going: tried visored. *J. L. Eyre*

MAYCOCKS BAY 4 b.f. Muhtarram (USA) 125 – Beacon (High Top 131) [2002 81: **100**
10d* 10.3m⁶ 10s² 10g⁵ 12g² 13.9m* Jul 13] strong, compact filly: useful handicapper:
won at Nottingham in April and York (listed rated stakes from 13 lb out of weights, beat
Damask Rose by short head) in July: stays 1¾m: acts on soft and good to firm going,
below form only outing on fibresand: has worn crossed noseband: wandered third start:
usually takes good hold: often held up: consistent: reportedly in foal. *M. L. W. Bell*

MAYFAIR MAUNDY 2 ch.f. (Apr 20) The West (USA) 107 – Mayfair Ballerina 53 **43**
(King's Signet (USA) 110) [2002 f6g p7g 6m⁵ 6m 6g Oct 4] first foal: dam, maiden who
ran only at 2 yrs, best at 5f: poor maiden. *W. G. M. Turner*

MAY I SAY (IRE) 6 b.m. Night Shift (USA) – Monoglow (Kalaglow 132) [2002 –: **–**
11.8d 11.8m 10g 10m Jun 25] close-coupled mare: winner in Germany in 2000: no form
since: tried blinkered/visored. *R. Brotherton*

MAY PRINCESS 4 ch.f. Prince Sabo 123 – Mim 39 (Midyan (USA) 124) [2002 61d: **–**
8m 7m 7f Jul 29] quite good-topped filly: disappointing maiden: tried blinkered.
D. Morris

MAY QUEEN MEGAN 9 gr.m. Petorius 117 – Siva (FR) (Bellypha 130) [2002 50, **43**
a43: f9.4g 8g 10f 9.7m⁶ 9d Jul 3] leggy mare: poor handicapper: reportedly lame final **a–**
start: effective at 1m/1¼m: acts on fibresand, firm and soft going: blinkered once at 3 yrs:
held up. *Mrs A. L. M. King*

MAYREAU LEGEND (IRE) 3 b.g. Distinctly North (USA) 115 – Crystal River **55**
(Jester 119) [2002 62: 7s 8.3s 8.3v⁶ 5.9d* f7g⁵ p7g 6.9g⁵ 7m 7s Oct 26] sturdy gelding: **a61**
modest performer: won seller at Carlisle in June: stays 7f: acts on fibresand and good to
soft going, possibly on soft (soon detached only start on polytrack): tried visored/
blinkered: sold 2,200 gns, sent to Kuwait. *M. H. Tompkins*

MAYS MIRACLE 3 ch.f. Inchinor 119 – Merryhill Maid (IRE) 71 (M Double M **–**
(USA)) [2002 f7g 7m 10g 10.9f Jun 26] compact filly: fifth foal: half-sister to 3 winners,
including 4-y-o Mamcazma and 7-y-o Haunt The Zoo: dam winning sprinter: last in
maidens/seller. *P. Howling*

MAYVILLE'S MAGIC (USA) 3 b.f. Gone West (USA) – Gallanta (FR) (Nureyev **80**
(USA) 131) [2002 p6g* 8d 6m⁴ 5.2g³ 5d p8g p6g⁶ Oct 9] $725,000Y: close-coupled,

good-topped filly: closely related to several winners, including smart 1994 Queen Mary/Cheveley Park winner Gay Gallanta (by Woodman), and half-sister to 3 winners, including very smart Irish performer up to 1¼m Sportsworld (by Alleged): dam, French 5.5f to 1m winner, from very good family: fairly useful performer: won maiden at Lingfield in April: likely to prove best at 6f/7f: acts on polytrack and good to firm going: visored fourth start: has had 2 handlers/raced freely: sent to USA. *G. A. Butler*

MAYZIN (IRE)   2 b.g. (May 11) Fayruz 116 – Peep of Day (USA) (Lypheor 118)   **66**
[2002 6m 6m 6s⁵ Oct 28] IR 5,200F, IR 8,000Y: fourth foal: closely-related to 1992 2-y-o 5f winner Aberlady (by Sizzling Melody): dam French 9f winner: fair maiden: raced only at 6f. *B. Palling*

MAZEED (IRE)   9 ch.g. Lycius (USA) 124 – Maraatib (IRE) 93 (Green Desert (USA)   **–**
127) [2002 p10g f16.2g⁶ f12g Feb 22] no longer of much account. *Miss K. M. George*

MAZEPA (IRE)   2 b.c. (May 17) Indian Ridge 123 – Please Believe Me 93 (Try My   **98**
Best (USA) 130) [2002 5.1d* 5m* 5d² 5m⁴ 6g⁶ p7g⁵ Dec 14] rangy, good-topped colt: has a quick action: sixth foal: brother to 4-y-o Autumnal and useful 5f (at 2 yrs) to 7f winner Lord Pacal, and half-brother to 8-y-o Storyteller: dam 2-y-o 5f winner: useful performer: won maiden at Nottingham and minor event at Newmarket in April: creditable efforts in Norfolk Stakes at Royal Ascot (fourth to Baron's Pit), July Stakes at Newmarket (sixth to Mister Links) and (after 5-month break) nursery at Lingfield last 3 starts: barely stays 7f: acts on polytrack, yet to race on extremes of going on turf. *N. A. Callaghan*

MAZURY (USA)   3 b.g. Langfuhr (CAN) 124 – Assurgent (USA) (Damascus (USA))   **65 d**
[2002 68p: f6s³ f8.5g² f8g* 7.5m 6m⁶ 8m 7m 7g f6s f8s Sep 17] unfurnished gelding: fair performer at best: won maiden at Southwell in January: left M. Johnston 7,000 gns after fifth outing: should stay 1¼m: acts on fibresand and good to soft going: on downgrade. *M. C. Chapman*

MCBAIN (USA)   3 br.c. Lear Fan (USA) 130 – River City Moon (USA) (Riverman   **91**
(USA) 131) [2002 80: 9g 10g 12.6m³ 10d* 10.1s³ 9.9d⁴ 10.4m 10.3m⁶ 10d 12s⁴ p12g* p12g⁴ p10g⁴ Dec 21] leggy colt: fairly useful performer: won handicap at Windsor in May and minor event at Lingfield in November: effective at 1¼m/1½m: yet to race on firm going, acts on any other turf and polytrack. *R. F. Johnson Houghton*

MCCRACKEN (IRE)   6 b.g. Scenic 128 – Sakanda (IRE) (Vayrann 133) [2002 –:   **–**
f12g⁶ f16g Feb 5] fairly useful at best: left N. Meade in Ireland 12,000 gns after only 5-y-o start: well held in 2002: tried blinkered. *Mrs A. L. M. King*

MCGILLYCUDDY REEKS (IRE)   11 b.m. Kefaah (USA) 124 – Kilvarnet 78   **77 d**
(Furry Glen 121) [2002 79: 11.9m 10d⁵ 11.9m⁴ 12d 10f 9.9m 11.9m⁴ 10.3d 9.9g³ 11.9m 10.3m 10m 10.4f 10.3v⁶ Nov 8] small mare: fair handicapper: best at 1¼m/1½m: acts on fibresand and any turf going: has worn tongue strap: takes good hold: held up: on downgrade. *Don Enrico Incisa*

MCLAREN   3 ch.g. Lion Cavern (USA) 117 – Calendula 75 (Be My Guest (USA) 126)   **–**
[2002 10s 10.2d p10g p12g Aug 29] 14,000Y: first foal: dam, 1¼m and 1½m winner, daughter of smart middle-distance stayer Sesame, herself half-sister to Gold Cup winner Celeric: no form. *Lady Herries*

MCQUEEN (IRE)   2 ch.c. (Mar 14) Barathea (IRE) 127 – Bibliotheque (USA) 79   **– p**
(Woodman (USA) 126) [2002 p7g Dec 11] second reported foal: dam, 1m winner, out of half-sister to very smart 6f to 1m performer Lycius: 16/1, slowly away and not knocked about once held in maiden at Lingfield: open to improvement. *Sir Michael Stoute*

MCQUILLAN   5 b.g. Maledetto (IRE) 103 – Macs Maharanee 85 (Indian King (USA)   **–**
128) [2002 43: 6g f8g Dec 4] maiden: well beaten in 2002 (reportedly had breathing problem last start). *P. S. Felgate*

MEASURE UP   3 ch.g. Inchinor 119 – Victoria Blue (Old Vic 136) [2002 74: 7.1g³ 7m   **84**
p7g⁴ 7d⁶ 8d² f9.4f² 8.2s³ Oct 23] strong, lengthy gelding: fairly useful maiden on turf, fair   **a71**
on all-weather: races freely, but seems to stay 9.4f: acts on all-weather, soft and good to firm going: sometimes carries head awkwardly: gelded after final start. *M. L. W. Bell*

MEDALLIST   3 b.c. Danehill (USA) 126 – Obsessive (USA) 102 (Seeking The Gold   **93**
(USA)) [2002 10m⁴ 8.1d* 9d⁴ 10m⁶ 10d³ 8g Oct 18] lengthy colt: second foal: closely related to fairly useful 2000 2-y-o 6f winner Spy Master (by Green Desert): dam, 2-y-o 6f winner who stayed 10.4f, out of half-sister to smart performer up to 1½m Beyton: fairly useful performer: won maiden at Haydock in May: best effort when third to Port Moresby in handicap at Newmarket (edged left): unlikely to stay beyond 1¼m: yet to race on extremes of going: sold 15,000 gns, and joined B. Ellison. *Sir Michael Stoute*

MEDECIS   3 ch.c. Machiavellian (USA) 123 – Renashaan (FR) (Darshaan 133) [2002   **119**
104p: 8s* 8g² 8g² 8g* 8g⁵ 7m² 8d 8f Dec 26] fifth foal: half-brother to 3 winners in
France, including useful performer up to 1½m Renaleon (by Generous): dam, French 1m
and (at 2 yrs) 9f winner, out of half-sister to dam of dual Gold Cup winner Royal Rebel:
smart performer: won listed race at Saint-Cloud in March and Prix de la Jonchere at
Chantilly (comfortably by 1½ lengths from Jubilation) in June: good second at Longchamp in between in Prix de Fontainebleau (beaten neck by Bowman) and Poule d'Essai
des Poulains (beaten length by Landseer) and also ran creditably when 4¾ lengths fifth
to Banks Hill in Prix Jacques le Marois at Deauville and neck second to Dedication in
Prix de la Foret at Longchamp fifth/sixth outings: respectable ninth to Domedriver in
Breeders' Cup Mile at Arlington penultimate start, then left Mme C. Head-Maarek: will
stay 1¼m: acts on soft going: held up: consistent. *R. E. Mandella, USA*

MEDEENA (IRE)   2 b.f. (Feb 12) Green Desert (USA) 127 – Tanouma (USA) 114   **82**
(Miswaki (USA) 124) [2002 6m³ 6m* 6g Sep 21] leggy, angular filly: sister to useful
1995 2-y-o 6f/7f winner Tamnia and half-sister to several winners, including 1m (at 2 yrs)
to 13f winner Azzilfi (by Ardross) and 1¼m to 15f winner Khamaseen (by Slip Anchor),
both smart: dam 6f (at 2 yrs)/7f winner: fairly useful form: won maiden at Goodwood in
August readily by 1½ lengths from So Dear: 9/2, possibly amiss when last in listed event
at Ayr: free-going sort, not sure to stay much beyond 6f. *J. L. Dunlop*

MEDELAI   6 b.m. Marju (IRE) 127 – No Islands (Lomond (USA) 128) [2002 –:   **–**
f14.8g³ f12g Feb 22] close-coupled mare: poor performer: seems to stay 21f: acts on   **a31**
fibresand: blinkered final start. *A. G. Juckes*

MEDIA BUYER (USA)   4 b. or br.g. Green Dancer (USA) 132 – California Rush   **–**
(USA) (Forty Niner (USA)) [2002 61: f7g f9.4g 8.1d 11.6m 8m Aug 7] small, sturdy
gelding: modest maiden at 3 yrs: no form in 2002: tried blinkered. *R. J. Price*

MEDIA PUZZLE (USA)   5 ch.g. Theatrical 128 – Market Slide (USA) 94 (Gulch   **117**
(USA)) [2002 116: 13s 14s³ 10s⁴ 12g 12s 12d 16m³ 12g* 16f* Nov 5]
      When Captain Scott finally reached the South Pole in January 1912, he
found that Amundsen had already beaten him to be the first man to reach it. Without
wishing to disparage Scott's achievement in any way, various European trainers are
going to know how Scott felt, if, on winning one of the top prizes halfway round the
world, they find the inscription 'trained by D. K. Weld, Ireland' already on the
trophy. For Dermot Weld, Antarctica is the only continent out of bounds for his
racehorses; he harbours an ambition to train a winner in Africa one day, having
already been successful in Europe, America, Asia and Australasia. In 1990, Weld
became the first and (despite Godolphin's and Coolmore's attempts to win a Kentucky Derby) so far only European-based trainer to win an American triple crown
race when Go And Go won the Belmont Stakes. A year later 33/1-shot Additional
Risk paved the way for European challenges at Hong Kong's International meeting
when winning the Hong Kong Invitation Bowl. But it was Vintage Crop's win in
the Melbourne Cup in 1993, the first in Australia's most valuable race by a horse
trained outside Australasia, which must rank as probably Weld's greatest international success.
      There have been annual attempts by European-based stables to emulate
Vintage Crop but none succeeded—until the latest season when Weld was back
again, this time with Media Puzzle. What made his second success all the more
praiseworthy was that Weld has made only selective challenges for the Melbourne
Cup. Vintage Crop returned to Flemington twice after his win, finishing seventh
(accompanied by stable-companion Cliveden Gail who was well beaten) and then
third, but, until Media Puzzle and Vinnie Roe contested the latest Melbourne Cup,
the stable had not had a runner in the race since 1995. 'Pick and choose your races.
Like the Indians, you have to go in, attack, and get out. I do that pretty well, learning
when to attack and when not to. I don't fight every battle; I choose my battle-
grounds.' That was how Weld summed up his philosphy of raiding international
prizes, one which contrasts with Godolphin's approach, for example, which has
seen them send eight horses for the Melbourne Cup in the last five runnings.
      If Dermot Weld's stable housed a potential Melbourne Cup winner, then for
much of the year it seemed to be Vinnie Roe who looked the yard's obvious
candidate. A narrow defeat in the Gold Cup was his only setback in his last eight
races before being sent to Melbourne, and a second Irish St Leger win before he left

*Tooheys New Melbourne Cup (Handicap), Flemington—
an emotional victory for jockey Damien Oliver on board Media Puzzle,
who provides Dermot Weld with his second win in 'the race that stops a nation'*

justified his position, both as top weight at Flemington on 9-4 and as ante-post favourite. Meanwhile, Media Puzzle had finished third in a handicap at the Curragh the day before the Irish St Leger, but the fact that he too was heading 'down under' was given just a passing mention in reports on his stable-companion. Media Puzzle had had a much lower profile all season; in his two previous starts he had finished last in handicaps at the Curragh and Galway, and had shown his best form when finishing eighth under 10-0 in the Duke of Edinburgh Stakes at Royal Ascot. He was well down the Melbourne Cup weights as a result, so much so that he was flown out to Australia with no guarantee of making the cut for the final field.

Whilst Vinnie Roe gave his stable cause for concern by initially failing to regain weight lost during his journey to Australia, Media Puzzle was clearly thriving. He was given a preparatory race in the listed Geelong Cup a couple of weeks before the big race and won it in course-record time, thereby earning a penalty which would be enough to secure him a place in the Melbourne Cup field. The Weld pair were two of a record eight 'internationals' in the Cup. Godolphin's trio comprised Irish St Leger runner-up Pugin (purchased after his run at the Curragh, and much better off at the weights with Vinnie Roe), Beekeeper, a creditable sixth in the Caulfield Cup in his preparatory race, and the Gold Cup fourth Hatha Anna, a Group 2 winner at Flemington in 2001. They were joined from Britain by the Sir Michael Stoute-trained Curragh Cup winner Daliapour, and the Alan Jarvis-trained Goodwood Cup winner Jardines Lookout, both near the top of the weights. The eighth runner trained outside Australasia was Helene Vitality, representing Hong Kong. The Weld stable companions headed the betting, Vinnie Roe at 9/2 and Media Puzzle (his odds tumbling after Geelong) at 11/2, ahead of the New Zealand gelding Distinctly Secret, Pugin and Beekeeper, the only others at shorter than 12/1.

Media Puzzle and Vinnie Roe were ideally placed turning for home, Vinnie Roe yielding up the lead two furlongs out as Media Puzzle took a decisive three-length advantage. The 40/1-shot Mr Prudent cut Media Puzzle's winning margin to two lengths at the line, and was just ahead of Beekeeper and the keeping-on Vinnie Roe. Jardines Lookout fared best of the other Europeans in a never-dangerous seventh. There have been harsh words in the Australian media for the European contenders for the Melbourne Cup in the past, either for their jockeyship or simply because their presence denied the chance of Australian horses running. In contrast, there seemed to be universal acclaim for Dermot Weld's training prowess on this occasion. Weld had spent some time as a vet in Australia earlier in his career as well as being assistant to trainer Tommy Smith. The fact that Media Puzzle was partnered by an Australian jockey, Damien Oliver, must have helped too, though that was only part of the story. Oliver's brother Jason had been killed in a race-course fall just a week earlier and, by way of a tribute, Damien, wearing his brother's breeches in the race, raised his whip to the sky as he passed the post.

Media Puzzle (USA) (ch.g. 1997)	Theatrical (b 1982)	Nureyev (b 1977)	Northern Dancer
			Special
		Tree of Knowledge (b 1977)	Sassafras
			Sensibility
	Market Slide (USA) (ch 1991)	Gulch (b 1984)	Mr Prospector
			Jameela
		Grenzen (ch 1975)	Grenfall
			My Poly

Details of Media Puzzle's pedigree can be found in the essay on his two-year-old half-brother Refuse To Bend (by Sadler's Wells) though, as a point of interest, Media Puzzle's dam is a half-sister to the dam of another of Dermot Weld's landmark foreign winners Go And Go. The Melbourne Cup had apparently been the long-term plan for Media Puzzle ever since he finished fourth in the St Leger. However, a fractured pelvis afterwards necessitated over four months box rest and he ran only twice as a four-year-old, winning a minor event at the Curragh and finishing second in the listed Saval Beg Stakes at Leopardstown. The big, strong, lengthy Media Puzzle is a fluent mover who has never raced on heavy going but acts on any other, though he evidently goes particularly well on firm ground. The

Mr Michael W. J. Smurfit's "Media Puzzle"

MED

Melbourne Cup was only the second time he had tackled two miles and he doesn't need such a searching test of stamina. Media Puzzle's best efforts in the latest season came when blinkered; the headgear was left off on those two occasions when he finished last, and on his first three outings which, for the record, came in a couple of minor events at Navan and a handicap at Cork.

Dermot Weld's international approach was partly born of necessity: 'In Ireland I was finding it very hard to beat Vincent O'Brien in the major races, so I decided to look around the world.' The Melbourne Cup was not the only big foreign prize won by the stable in 2002. Dress To Thrill beat some of America's best turf fillies to win the Matriarch Stakes at Hollywood in December, while earlier in the year Jazz Beat lost out by just a nose in another Grade 1 event, the Secretariat Stakes at Arlington. All this was a far cry from Dermot Weld's first venture into top-flight international competition; in his very first season as a trainer in 1972 he sent Boreen to the States for the Washington DC International, only for the horse to slip up shortly before halfway. Racing history would have been very different if Weld had decided to stick to Galway and Tralee from then on. *D. K. Weld, Ireland*

MEDKHAN (IRE) 5 ch.g. Lahib (USA) 129 – Safayn (USA) 82 (Lyphard (USA) – 132) [2002 –: f12g f16.2g Feb 4] disappointing maiden: tried blinkered. *F. Jordan*

MEDOOZA 5 b.m. Night Shift (USA) – Seastream (USA) (Alleged (USA) 138) [2002 **49** f12g3 f11g Mar 12] good-bodied mare: poor maiden, lightly raced: stays 1½m: acts on fibresand. *G. C. Bravery*

MEDUSA 2 b.f. (Feb 16) Emperor Jones (USA) 119 – Diebiedale 58 (Dominion 123) – [2002 7d Nov 2] third foal: dam, maiden who stayed 1m, half-sister to useful 5f/6f performer Welsh Mist: 33/1, well held in maiden at Newmarket. *D. Morris*

MEELUP (IRE) 2 ch.g. (Mar 5) Night Shift (USA) – Centella (IRE) (Thatching 131) **74** [2002 5m5 5.1g3 6m3 7m5 7m5 7s5 7s2 7g2 p7g3 Oct 31] 30,000Y: sturdy, deep-girthed gelding: unimpressive mover: fifth foal: half-brother to 5f seller winner Cameo (by Statoblest) and 5-y-o Serpico: dam placed at 6f at 2 yrs in Ireland: fair maiden: placed 5 times, including in nursery: stays 7f: acts on polytrack, soft and good to firm going: races prominently: gelded after final start. *R. Hannon*

MEGAROLE 3 b.g. Tragic Role (USA) – Our Megan (Puissance 110) [2002 8.1d – 7.5m 8.1m Sep 16] unfurnished gelding: first foal: dam unraced: soundly beaten in claimers/maiden. *B. P. J. Baugh*

MEHMAAS 6 b.g. Distant Relative 128 – Guest List 85 (Be My Guest (USA) 126) **72** [2002 72: 8f2 7.1g 7f5 7.5g3 7.5m5 8.5d2 9m5 8.5d2 7.5d* 8.5g 7m2 7.5m 7m 7.9m4 7.5m **a66** 8m5 8m3 7g 8v2 f8g6 f8g4 Nov 26] smallish, sturdy gelding: fair handicapper: won at Beverley in July: effective at 7f/1m: acts on any turf going and fibresand: usually visored, has been blinkered: often front runner: tough. *R. E. Barr*

MEILLAND (USA) 2 b.c. (Apr 5) Carson City (USA) – Cherokee Rose (IRE) 122 **76** (Dancing Brave (USA) 140) [2002 6d2 6.1m3 Sep 20] rather unfurnished colt: fourth foal: half-brother to 3-y-o Bowman and French 9f winner Moyesii (by Diesis): dam 6f (Haydock Park Sprint Cup) to 7f winner: fair form in maidens at Thirsk and Nottingham (6½ lengths third to Oasis Dream), missing break both times: should stay 7f. *D. R. Loder*

MEILLEURE LOI (FR) 5 b.m. Homme de Loi (IRE) 120 – Ti Bout de Zan (FR) (Ti – King (FR) 121) [2002 10m 12.1d 10g 10g Jul 8] third foal: half-sister to 2 winners in France, including 5f (at 2 yrs) to 11f winner Ballezan (by Balleroy): dam French 7f (at 2 yrs) and 11.5f winner: won minor event at Saint-Cloud at 3 yrs: fairly useful form in listed races next 3 starts: left J-C. Rouget (France) before no form in 2002: stayed 1½m: acted on heavy going: slowly away final start: dead. *K. C. Bailey*

MEIYING 4 br.f. Cyrano de Bergerac 120 – Hong Kong Girl 94 (Petong 126) [2002 – § –§: f6g Apr 15] no form: reluctant to race first 2 outings at 3 yrs. *A. G. Newcombe*

MELLINO 2 b.f. (Jan 31) Robellino (USA) 127 – Krista 73 (Kris 135) [2002 5m4 6m **62** 6m4 7.5g6 6g Aug 27] strong, quite attractive filly: first foal: dam, 1m winner, half-sister to useful German performer up to 1m Tristano: modest maiden: should stay 1m: raced only on good/good to firm going. *T. D. Easterby*

MELLOW PARK (IRE) 3 b.f. In The Wings 128 – Park Special (Relkino 131) [2002 **114** 7p: 9.9d* 12s6 11.9d* 12d 11.9m Aug 21] robust, attractive filly: usually takes the eye: smart performer: won listed event at Goodwood (by 11 lengths from Kootenay) in May and Lancashire Oaks at Haydock (by 1½ lengths from Lady's Secret, ran in snatches) in

Lancashire Oaks, Haydock—Mellow Park (right) gains a pattern win; Lady's Secret is second

July: well held otherwise in Oaks at Epsom (joint-second favourite, seemed not to cope with track when sixth to Kazzia), Irish Oaks at the Curragh and Yorkshire Oaks (visored) at York: will stay 1¾m: best efforts on good to soft going. *J. Noseda*

MELMOTT 2 ch.g. (Jan 18) Piccolo 121 – Time For Tea (IRE) 73 (Imperial Frontier –
(USA) 112) [2002 p7g p8g Dec 14] second foal: half-brother to 3-y-o Frazzled: dam, maiden who stayed 1¼m, out of useful half-sister to Kalaglow: well held in minor event and maiden at Lingfield. *C. A. Cyzer*

MELODIAN 7 b.h. Grey Desire 115 – Mere Melody 88 (Dunphy 124) [2002 9ld: f8g **71 d**
7v⁵ 8.1d 8d 10.1s⁴ 10g 8.9f Oct 12] leggy horse: fair handicapper: on downgrade: stays 1m: has won on firm ground, best efforts on softer than good: usually blinkered, visored once: often races up with pace. *M. Brittain*

MELODY MASTER (IRE) 2 b.c. (May 2) Woodborough (USA) 112 – Tabasco **62**
Jazz 65 (Salse (USA) 128) [2002 5.1g⁵ 5f³ 6g 7.1m⁵ 6.1m 7g p7g⁶ Nov 19] IR 3,000Y: useful-looking colt: second foal: dam, maiden best at 7f/1m, out of useful sprinter Melody Park: modest maiden: stays 7f: acts on polytrack, raced only on good ground or firmer on turf. *M. J. Ryan*

MELOGRANO (IRE) 2 ch.g. (Mar 30) Hector Protector (USA) 124 – Just A Treat **80**
(IRE) 47 (Glenstal (USA) 118) [2002 p7g p7g 8.2v² 8v Nov 8] 14,500Y: sixth foal: half-brother to 3 winners, including 1997 2-y-o 6f winner Special Treat (by Wolfhound) and 7f winner Goes A Treat (by Common Grounds), both fairly useful: dam 2-y-o 5f winner: 50/1, easily best effort in maidens (fairly useful form) when 3½ lengths second to Bugatti Royale at Nottingham, never nearer: something seemingly amiss final start: should stay 1¼m: acts on heavy ground. *R. M. Beckett*

MELROSE PLACE (IRE) 2 b.f. (Apr 14) Danetime (IRE) 121 – Negria (IRE) (Al **84**
Hareb (USA) 123) [2002 5s⁵ p5g³ 5.1m⁴ 5.2f³ 6m⁵ 5g* 5.1f* 6m⁴ 5f³ 5m Oct 12] 18,000 2-y-o: good-quartered filly: third foal: half-sister to 4-y-o Church Mice: dam, German 2-y-o 6f winner, half-sister to useful 1996 2-y-o sprinter Miss Stamper: fairly useful performer: won maiden at Folkestone and nursery at Bath in September: good efforts in nurseries at Newmarket next 2 starts: will prove best at 5f/easy 6f: acts on firm going: sometimes flashes tail: has been heavily bandaged hind joints: sold 5,000 gns, sent to Kuwait. *N. A. Callaghan*

MELS BABY (IRE) 9 br.g. Contract Law (USA) 108 – Launch The Raft (Home –
Guard (USA) 129) [2002 38: 9g Mar 28] of little account nowadays. *J. L. Eyre*

MELSTAIR   7 b.g. Terimon 124 – Kevins Lady (Alzao (USA) 117) [2002 –: 8m 12m   –
Sep 29] sturdy gelding: no sign of ability. *A. R. Dicken*

MELUSINA (IRE)   2 b.f. (Apr 7) Barathea (IRE) 127 – Moon Masquerade (IRE) 69   **56**
(Darshaan 133) [2002 8g p7g 8.3d Oct 28] 11,000Y: first foal: dam, maiden who stayed
1¾m, sister to useful middle-distance stayer Shaandar from family of Sheriff's Star and
Moon Madness: modest form at best in maidens: should be suited by 1¼m+. *Mrs
A. J. Perrett*

MEMAMEDA   6 b.m. Cigar 68 – Mamzooj (IRE) (Shareef Dancer (USA) 135) [2002   –
31: f8s Jan 17] of little account nowadays. *K. A. Ryan*

MEMBERSHIP (USA)   2 ch.c. (Mar 11) Belong To Me (USA) – Shamisen 86 (Diesis   **103**
133) [2002 5.1f³ 6m* 6g⁶ 6g 5.2f² 6g³ 6f³ 5g² 6f Oct 3] $35,000Y: big, strong, lengthy
colt: has plenty of scope: has a quick action: fifth foal: half-brother to 7-y-o Lone Piper
and 5-y-o Wind Chime: dam, 2-y-o 7f winner, half-sister to smart miler Enharmonic:
useful performer: won minor event at Yarmouth in May: third to Country Reel in
Gimcrack Stakes at York (beaten 1½ lengths) and to Sir Edwin Landseer in listed event at
Kempton (beaten ½ length): blinkered, creditable eighth of 10 to Oasis Dream in Middle
Park Stakes at Newmarket (edged right) final start: races freely, and will prove best at 5f/
6f: raced on good going or firmer. *C. E. Brittain*

MENTAL PRESSURE   9 ch.g. Polar Falcon (USA) 126 – Hysterical 68 (High Top   –
131) [2002 74: 13.9f May 15] rangy gelding: fair handicapper: broke leg at York in May:
stayed 2m: didn't race on soft/heavy going, acted on any other: usually held up: was most
consistent: dead. *Mrs M. Reveley*

MENTRO (IRE)   3 b.f. Entrepreneur 123 – Sudden Interest (FR) (Highest Honor (FR)   **65**
124) [2002 10.2f⁴ 10s³ p12g Nov 13] IR 80,000Y: third foal: half-sister to fairly useful
2000 2-y-o 6f winner There's Two (by Ashkalani) and 1¼m and 1½m winner After The
Blue (by Last Tycoon): dam, French 9f and 10.5f winner, half-sister to very smart 1¼m/
1½m winner Sudden Love: fourth to Mexican Hawk in maiden at Bath on debut: below
that form both starts after. *H. R. A. Cecil*

MENUHIN   2 b.c. (Feb 14) Royal Academy (USA) 130 – Child Prodigy (IRE) 87   **87**
(Ballad Rock 122) [2002 6d⁶ 6m³ 6m³ 8.1g² f8.5g* 8s Oct 15] 65,000Y: first foal: dam,
6f (at 2 yrs) and 1m (in USA) winner, half-sister to 5-y-o Kutub: fairly useful performer:
won maiden at Wolverhampton in September, battling on well to get on top near finish:
should stay 1¼m: acts on fibresand and good to firm going, well held on softer than good:
sold 75,000 gns, sent to USA. *Sir Mark Prescott*

MERCURIOUS (IRE)   2 ch.f. (Apr 5) Grand Lodge (USA) 125 – Rousinette (Rou-   **48**
sillon (USA) 133) [2002 6g 6d 6.1s Oct 23] IR 9,000Y, 10,500 2-y-o: sister to 3-y-o
Treetops Hotel and half-sister to 3 winners, including fairly useful Irish performer up to
1½m Renvyle Rose (by Rainbows For Life): dam twice-raced half-sister to useful
performer up to 1½m Rosananti: poor maiden: should stay at least 1m. *J. Mackie*

MERDIFF   3 b.c. Machiavellian (USA) 123 – Balwa (USA) 101 (Danzig (USA)) [2002   **68**
–: 11s⁶ p10g Jul 3] fair maiden: unlikely to stay beyond 1¼m: sold 3,000 gns. *M. A. Jarvis*

MERELY A MONARCH   3 b.g. Reprimand 122 – Ruby Princess (IRE) 70 (Mac's   **60**
Imp (USA) 116) [2002 69: 7s⁶ f7g 6g 8m f6s f8g f7g* f7g³ f7g Dec 17] sparely-made
gelding: modest performer: won seller at Southwell in November: should stay 1m: acts
on fibresand, probably on soft going. *I. A. Wood*

MERENGUE   2 b.f. (Mar 11) Salse (USA) 128 – Swing And Brave (IRE) 70 (Arctic   –
Tern (USA) 126) [2002 5d 5g 7.1f f6g 7.1s Nov 6] smallish, leggy filly: first foal: dam,
1¼m winner in Italy, half-sister to Gimcrack winner Chilly Billy: well held in maidens/
nursery. *T. J. Etherington*

MEREWOOD (USA)   3 ch.f. Woodman (USA) 126 – Imperial Bailiwick (IRE) 104   **74**
(Imperial Frontier (USA) 112) [2002 7d 9.3s² 10.3m³ 10g 10d Jul 23] sturdy, angular
filly: second foal: half-sister to a winner up to 7.5f in Italy by Efisio: dam 2-y-o 5f
(including Flying Childers Stakes) winner: fair maiden: should stay 1½m: slowly away
first 2 outings (markedly so on debut): pulled hard last 2 (also carried head high final
one). *M. Johnston*

MERLIN'S DANCER   2 b.c. (Feb 13) Magic Ring (IRE) 115 – La Piaf (FR) (Fabulous   **78**
Dancer (USA) 124) [2002 6g 6.1d³ 5f² 6m³ Aug 2] 22,000F, 30,000Y: good-bodied colt:
unimpressive mover: fifth foal: half-brother to a winner in Turkey by Primo Dominie:
dam, French 2-y-o 7.5f winner, later won up to 1¼m in US and second in Grade 3 event:
fair maiden: good third in nursery at Goodwood final start, hanging right: effective at 5f/
6f: acts on firm and good to soft going. *W. R. Muir*

MERLIN'S GIFT 2 b.g. (May 20) Wizard King 122 – Formosanta (USA) (Believe It – (USA)) [2002 5s 5g Jul 5] 3,200Y: half-brother to several winners, including 1996 2-y-o 8.5f winner Premier and 7f to 8.5f winner Farnham (both by Rainbow Quest): dam, maiden in USA, half-sister to Cherry Hinton winner Turkish Treasure: headstrong and well held in maidens (gelded after latter one). *Bob Jones*

MERLINS MALLARD 2 b.f. (Mar 14) Silver Wizard (USA) 117 – Defy Me 75 – (Bustino 136) [2002 7g 8.1g Sep 12] eighth foal: dam 2-y-o 5f winner: well held in maidens. *A. D. Smith*

MERLINS PROFIT 2 b.g. (Mar 30) Wizard King 122 – Quick Profit 78 (Formidable **60** (USA) 125) [2002 5g 6g⁵ 6g 8g⁴ 8m Oct 2] 13,000Y: rather unfurnished gelding: half-brother to several winners, including fairly useful 1996 2-y-o 5f winner Smokey Pete and 6-y-o Rogue Spirit: dam 7f winner: modest maiden: barely stays 1m. *M. Todhunter*

MERRYVALE MAN 5 b.g. Rudimentary (USA) 118 – Salu 65 (Ardross 134) [2002 – 70, a–: f11s⁵ 10.5s Jun 7] leggy gelding: modest handicapper: left J. M. Jefferson after **a52** reappearance: stays 1¾m: acts on fibresand, heavy and good to firm going: blinkered once in 2001: has found little. *R. Bastiman*

MERSEY MIRAGE 5 b.g. King's Signet (USA) 110 – Kirriemuir 51 (Lochnager **68 §** 132) [2002 f6g p6g f7g⁵ 6m³ 6m 6m 6g Jul 18] neat gelding: fair handicapper: effective at 6f/7f: acts on firm, good to soft going and fibresand: tried visored/blinkered: usually races prominently: unreliable. *T. D. Barron*

MERSEY SOUND (IRE) 4 b.g. Ela-Mana-Mou 132 – Coral Sound (IRE) 67 (Glow **77** (USA)) [2002 96: p12g* p12g 10m 10d 16.4d 12f 10.2g⁵ p12g³ Oct 31] rather leggy, quite attractive gelding: reportedly suffered hairline fracture of fetlock at 3 yrs: only fair form in 2002: won maiden at Lingfield (looked none too keen) in January: stays 1½m well: acts on firm ground and polytrack: tried visored. *D. R. C. Elsworth*

MESHAHEER (USA) 3 b.c. Nureyev (USA) 131 – Race The Wild Wind (USA) 121 **115** (Sunny's Halo (CAN)) [2002 113: 8m 7m³ 6d 7m³ 7m* 7m⁶ Oct 13] rather unfurnished colt: has a round action: smart performer: won listed race at Newbury in September by

Godolphin's "Meshaheer"

neck from Gateman: ran well otherwise in 2002 when close third to Just James in Jersey Stakes at Royal Ascot second start: stays 7f: raced mainly on good/good to firm going: tongue tied second to fifth starts: has worn crossed noseband: has raced freely. *Saeed bin Suroor*

MESMERIC (IRE)   4 b.c. Sadler's Wells (USA) 132 – Mesmerize (Mill Reef (USA) 141) [2002 111: 13.4f² 14.6m⁵ 12g 11.8s³ Oct 28] good-topped colt: smart performer: creditable effort in 2002 only when second to Supremacy in listed rated stakes at Chester in August: should stay 1¾m: yet to race on heavy going, acts on any other: visored fifth to ninth 3-y-o starts: sometimes carries head awkwardly: unseated on way to post once as 3-y-o: often held up. *E. A. L. Dunlop*   **111**

MESMERISED   2 b.f. (Apr 9) Merdon Melody 98 – Gracious Imp (USA) (Imp Society (USA)) [2002 5m 5f* 5m⁶ 5m² 6m* 6m 6d⁴ 6g 6d⁶ 6g⁶ 5.9m 7f 6s Oct 25] 4,800Y: leggy, workmanlike filly: second foal: sister to 3-y-o Sophies Symphony: dam no form: fair performer: won claimer at Thirsk in May and seller at York in June: below form last 4 starts: should stay 7f: acts on firm and good to soft ground: edgy type. *A. Berry*   **73 d**

MESMERIST (USA)   2 b.f. (Apr 23) Green Desert (USA) 127 – Mesmerize (Mill Reef (USA) 141) [2002 5f⁵ 6g⁴ 6m² 8d Oct 21] angular filly: half-sister to several winners, 4 of them smart, including 1990 2-y-o 6f winner Mujtahid (by Woodman) and 4-y-o Mesmeric: dam unraced: fair maiden: off 3 months, ran poorly in nursery at Pontefract final start: should stay 1m: acts on good to firm ground: sold 47,000 gns. *M. Johnston*   **65**

MESMERIZING (IRE)   2 b.g. Dr Devious (IRE) 127 – Mesenzana (IRE) (Mac's Imp (USA) 116) [2002 8v Nov 21] second foal: dam Italian 2-y-o 6f winner: well-held ninth of 10 in maiden at Milan (gelded after). *L. M. Cumani*   **–**

METALICO   3 b.f. Piccolo 121 – Pewter Lass 56 (Dowsing (USA) 124) [2002 59: 7.1f Apr 10] leggy, close-coupled filly: modest maiden: acted on fibresand: dead. *I. A. Wood*   **–**

METEOR STRIKE (USA)   8 ch.g. Lomond (USA) 128 – Meteoric 102 (High Line 125) [2002 –§: f11s Jan 17] big, lengthy gelding: temperamental performer: tried blinkered. *P. D. Evans*   **– §**

METICULOUS   4 gr.g. Eagle Eyed (USA) 111 – Careful (IRE) 59 (Distinctly North (USA) 115) [2002 –: f12g 8g 8.5m 6m⁶ 6m 6g 6g 5m 5g 5g Sep 18] leggy, quite good-topped gelding: little form. *M. C. Chapman*   **–**

MEXICAN HAWK (USA)   3 b. or br.f. Silver Hawk (USA) 123 – Viva Zapata (USA) 116 (Affirmed (USA)) [2002 10g³ 10.2f* 8f 10g Oct 17] $390,000Y: leggy, quite good-topped filly: half-sister to several winners abroad, including useful French/UAE performer up to 1m Viva Nureyev (by Nureyev): dam French sprinter: shaped very well on debut, then won maiden at Bath (5 months later) in September: useful form when seventh behind Dress To Thrill in Sun Chariot Stakes at Newmarket next time: gave impression something amiss in listed race there final start: at least as effective around 1m as 1¼m. *G. A. Butler*   **98**

MEXICAN PETE   2 b.g. (Apr 15) Atraf 116 – Eskimo Nel (IRE) 75 (Shy Groom (USA)) [2002 5f 6m 7m⁶ 8.3m p8g⁶ Nov 23] second living foal: dam, 1¼m/1½m winner, also useful hurdler: modest maiden: should stay 1¼m. *R. M. Beckett*   **59**

MEXICAN ROCK   6 b.g. Rock City 120 – Pink Mex (Tickled Pink 114) [2002 7d f6g p8g Dec 21] well-made gelding: fairly useful in 1999: well beaten since (missed 2001 season): blinkered last 2 starts: tried tongue tied. *R. Guest*   **–**

MEXICAN (USA)   3 b.c. Pine Bluff (USA) – Cuando Quiere (USA) (Affirmed (USA)) [2002 78: 12f² 11.5g⁶ 10d 11.7f² 10.3m⁵ 13.9m 10m⁶ 7f³ 7g³ 7s³ Oct 22] quite attractive colt: fairly useful maiden: barely stays easy 1½m: acts on firm going, probably on good to soft: blinkered/visored last 4 starts: tongue tied next time: has wandered markedly/found little: not one to trust implicitly: sold 13,000 gns, and joined M. Hammond. *C. E. Brittain*   **83**

MEZEREON   2 b.f. (Mar 24) Alzao (USA) 117 – Blown-Over 41 (Ron's Victory (USA) 129) [2002 6g Oct 17] quite good-topped filly: third foal: dam, lightly-raced maiden, half-sister to very smart sprinter Piccolo and smart miler Tahilla: 25/1, 7 lengths twelfth of 18 to Pigeon Point in maiden at Newmarket, never on terms. *W. J. Haggas*   **63**

MEZUZAH   2 b.c. (Mar 17) Barathea (IRE) 127 – Mezzogiorno 108 (Unfuwain (USA) 131) [2002 7m⁷ 7v* Nov 8] lengthy colt: half-brother to half-brother to 3-y-o Monturani and useful 6f/7f winner Monnavanna (by Machiavellian): dam, 7f (at 2 yrs) and 1¼m winner, third in Oaks: favourite, confirmed promise when beating Down Memory Lane by 5   **94 p**

lengths in maiden at Doncaster (carried head bit awkwardly and possibly still needed experience): will stay at least 1m: potentially at least useful. *G. Wragg*

MEZYA (USA) 3 b.f. Gulch (USA) – Aljawza (USA) 86 (Riverman (USA) 131) [2002 82 7g⁵ 8.2m³ 8d³ 7f⁴ 10f³ 10m* Aug 17] rather leggy, attractive filly: fourth foal: closely related to fairly useful 6f (at 2 yrs) to (in France/UAE) 1m winner Ishtihar (by Woodman) and 1m winner Elsundus (by Gone West): dam, Irish 2-y-o 6f winner, half-sister to smart Queen Mary/Cheveley Park winner Gay Gallanta and very smart Irish 1¼m performer Sportsworld: won handicap at Ripon in August: stayed 1¼m: acted on firm and good to soft going: visits Intikhab. *J. H. M. Gosden*

M FOR MAGIC 3 ch.g. First Trump 118 – Celestine 62 (Skyliner 117) [2002 72: – 6.1f 6g 8.3s 5.7d Jun 15] useful-looking gelding: fair maiden at 2 yrs: no form in 2002: sometimes blinkered. *J. L. Spearing*

MIA FOOL 3 ch.f. Cosmonaut – Young Annabel (USA) 71 (Cahill Road (USA)) [2002 – f8g f8g Dec 10] 700Y: first foal: dam 7f winner: well beaten in 2 maidens at Southwell. *G. G. Margarson*

MIAMI EXPLORER 2 b.f. (Mar 1) Pennekamp (USA) 130 – Elaine Tully (IRE) 80 – (Persian Bold 123) [2002 6m 7d 7.6m Aug 29] fourth foal: dam, 1m to 1¾m winner, also fairly useful staying hurdler: well held in maidens/minor event: looks wayward. *H. Morrison*

MIA'S REFORM 3 b.g. Lugana Beach 116 – Lady Caroline Lamb (IRE) 68 (Contract 51 Law (USA) 108) [2002 53: 5d 5m 5m⁵ 5f⁴ 5m⁴ 5d⁶ 5m 6f 5f 5m³ 5s f5g² Dec 27] smallish gelding: modest maiden: left H. McWilliams before final start: best at 5f: acts on fibresand, firm and good to soft ground: blinkered once at 2 yrs. *S. R. Bowring*

MI CASTANO (IRE) 3 ch.g. Fayruz 116 – Tadasna (IRE) (Thatching 131) [2002 57: 53 8.2d⁵ f7g⁶ Apr 26] useful-looking gelding: modest maiden: reportedly finished lame final start: stays 7f: acts on fibresand and good to soft going. *N. P. Littmoden*

MICE IDEAS (IRE) 6 ch.g. Fayruz 116 – Tender Encounter (Prince Tenderfoot 42 (USA) 126) [2002 38, a60d: f12s 12.1g 8.1g 10.9m 11.8s Oct 15] tall, angular gelding: poor performer: left O. O'Neill after second start, B. Doran after fourth: seems best at 1¼m/1½m: acts on good to firm going, soft and fibresand: has taken fierce hold: sometimes looks none too keen: usually held up. *Mrs A. J. Bowlby*

MICHAEL MAHER 3 b.c. Indian Ridge 123 – Well Proud (IRE) (Sadler's Wells 84 (USA) 132) [2002 –p: 8.1d² 10f³ 8.2g² 8m³ 7s* 7g Oct 18] tall, quite good-topped colt: fairly useful performer: won maiden at Lingfield in September: barely stays 1¼m: acts on firm and soft going: headstrong: sold 40,000 gns. *M. A. Jarvis*

MICHAELS DREAM (IRE) 3 b.g. Spectrum (IRE) 126 – Stormswept (USA) 74 72 (Storm Bird (CAN) 134) [2002 68d: 8.2d 9.9m 10f 12g 14.1f⁴ 12.1g⁴ 10f² 9.9d⁵ 12f³ 11.1d³ 10.9d 14.1s³ 10m³ 12.1g* 9.9m³ 14.1m² 12f* 11.9f⁴ 12s² Nov 6] smallish gelding: fair handicapper: won at Beverley in September and Catterick in October: finds 1¼m a minimum, and stays 1¾m: acts on firm going, good to soft and fibresand: usually visored/ blinkered (effective without): often races freely: tough and consistent. *J. Hetherton*

MICHAELS GIRL 3 ch.f. Bluebird (USA) 125 – Bonnie Lassie 74 (Efisio 120) ? [2002 66d: f6s f7g f6g 5d 5.1m f8g 8m 10m Jun 24] smallish, strong filly: fair at 2 yrs: no form in Britain in 2002, though later won over 1¼m in Spain. *M. C. Chapman*

MICHELLE MA BELLE (IRE) 2 b.f. (Mar 21) Shareef Dancer (USA) 135 – April 90 Magic (Magic Ring (IRE) 115) [2002 5.7m 5m³ 5.1f* 6m² 6.5m⁵ 6m⁴ 6g* 6s³ Oct 26]

£100000 Tattersalls Autumn Auction Stakes, Newmarket—Michelle Ma Belle provides trainer Sylvester Kirk with his biggest winner; Morning After (spots on sleeves), Ellamyte (hooped cap) and Swift Alchemist (hooped sleeves) are next home

10,000 2-y-o: smallish filly: first foal: dam unraced: fairly useful performer: won maiden at Bath in August and valuable sales race at Newmarket (beat Morning After by length in 30-runner event) in October: good third to Miguel Cervantes in listed race at Doncaster final start: stays 6f: acts on firm and soft ground: usually waited with. *S. Kirk*

MICKLEY (IRE) 5 b.g. Ezzoud (IRE) 126 – Dawsha (IRE) 75 (Slip Anchor 136) **83 d** [2002 80d: p13g² f14.8g* f12g* f12g⁵ f12g* f14g* f12g⁴ f16.2g p12g⁵ 15f² 12g 14.4m 11.9m 15.4m Jul 29] tall, short-backed gelding: fairly useful handicapper: won at Wolverhampton (3, including apprentices) and Southwell in January/February: below form last 5 starts: barely stays 2m: acts on firm going, good to soft and all-weather: occasionally visored/blinkered: carries head awkwardly/sometimes idles: often races prominently. *P. R. Hedger*

MICKLOW MAGIC 4 b.f. Farfelu 103 – Scotto's Regret (Celtic Cone 116) [2002 **71** 75: 8f² 8g 8m⁵ 6.9m 10.4m Sep 4] strong, workmanlike filly: fair handicapper: stays 1m: acts on firm going, well held on heavy. *C. Grant*

MIDAS WAY 2 ch.c. (Apr 4) Halling (USA) 133 – Arietta's Way (IRE) 71 (Darshaan **92 p** 133) [2002 8m 8s* Oct 26] rather leggy colt: second foal: dam, ran 4 times, sister to useful performer up to 1½m Rubhahunish and half-sister to smart performers Court of Honour (up to 2m) and Single Empire (up to 1¾m): considerably handled on debut: 10/1, plenty of improvement (fairly useful form) when winning maiden at Newbury by 1¾ lengths from Titurel, leading final 1f: will be suited by 1¼m+: acts on soft ground: should continue to progress. *R. Charlton*

MIDDLEHAM PEACOCK (IRE) 2 b.g. (Feb 12) Revoque (IRE) 122 – Alexanders **97** Way (FR) 83 (Persian Heights 129) [2002 f5s 7.1d* 7.2g* 6g* Jul 22] 3,000Y: third foal: half-brother to an Italian 1¼m winner by Definite Article: dam, Irish 9f maiden, half-sister to 3-y-o Millstreet: useful form: won maiden at Musselburgh and nurseries at Ayr (2) in July: odds on, beat Evangelist by 1¼ lengths final start despite hanging right: effective at 6f/7f: yet to race on ground firmer than good: sold to race in Hong Kong, where renamed Delightful Win. *P. C. Haslam*

MIDDLEMISS (IRE) 2 b.f. (Mar 17) Midhish 109 – Teresa Deevey 50 (Runnett – 125) [2002 6g 8.3d f8.5g Oct 19] half-sister to 1994 2-y-o 6f winner Euro Rebel (by Roi Danzig) and 1992 2-y-o 7f winner Yeveed (by Wassl): dam twice-raced 6f winner: well held in claimer/sellers. *J. W. Mullins*

MIDDLETHORPE 5 b.g. Noble Patriarch 115 – Prime Property (IRE) 60 (Tirol 127) **77** [2002 71: 12s* 13.8d² 12.3g 12d⁵ 12.1v³ 10d 12s Nov 6] rather sparely-made gelding: poor mover: fair handicapper: made all in apprentice race at Doncaster in March: stays 13.8f: acts on heavy going, well beaten on firmer than good/fibresand: blinkered: unseated exiting paddock on 4-y-o reappearance: tends to wander. *M. W. Easterby*

MIDDLETON GREY 4 gr.g. Ashkalani (IRE) 128 – Petula 103 (Petong 126) [2002 – 70, a91: f8.5g³ f7g² f8.5g³ p10g f7g 8g 8d 7d 6d f6g f8.5s² f8g³ Dec 27] leggy gelding: **a91** fairly useful on all-weather: probably best at 7f to 8.5f: acts on all-weather, little turf form in 2002: tried blinkered/visored: has run well in cheekpieces. *D. W. P. Arbuthnot*

MIDGES PRIDE 2 b.c. (Mar 11) Puissance 110 – It's All Academic (IRE) 91 (Mazaad **58** 106) [2002 f6g f7g Dec 31] 8,500Y: third living foal: half-brother to 7f winner Warrior King (by Fairy King): dam 2-y-o 5f winner: modest form in maidens at Wolverhampton, seeming green. *Mrs A. Duffield*

MIDHISH TWO (IRE) 6 b.g. Midhish 109 – Tudor Loom (Sallust 134) [2002 –: – § p6g p6g 6d 6f Jun 13] leggy gelding: has a quick action: temperamental nowadays: tried blinkered/visored. *P. Mitchell*

MIDNIGHT CHIEF 2 b.g. (May 9) Bluegrass Prince (IRE) 110 – Midnight Romance **53** (Inca Chief (USA)) [2002 f8.5s Dec 9] first foal: dam, lightly-raced maiden, half-sister to smart 1½m to 2¼m performer Quick Ransom: 33/1, 15¾ lengths eighth of 12 to Rifleman in maiden at Wolverhampton, slowly away. *A. P. Jarvis*

MIDNIGHT COUP 6 br.g. First Trump 118 – Anhaar (Ela-Mana-Mou 132) [2002 –: **47** 21.6m 16.2m⁴ 16.2f⁴ 16.2m⁴ 15g* 16.2g³ 17.1m⁵ 14m* 16.2m⁶ 16m 16f Sep 26] good-topped gelding: poor nowadays: won in Jersey in July and August: stays 17f: acts on firm and good to soft going: races prominently. *B. G. Powell*

MIDNIGHT CREEK 4 b.g. Tragic Role (USA) – Greek Night Out (IRE) 54 (Ela- **73** Mana-Mou 132) [2002 76: 14.1d 11.9g⁴ p16g* 18d⁶ p16g⁴ 16.4g³ 14m 16m⁶ 16f p12g **a79** p16g Oct 16] leggy gelding: fair handicapper: won at Lingfield in June: barely stays

2¼m: acts on polytrack, soft and good to firm going: tried tongue tied: carries head awkwardly: probably not one to trust implicitly: sold 8,500 gns, joined G. A. Swinbank. *Mrs A. J. Perrett*

MIDNIGHT FIZZ 2 gr.f. (Feb 5) Forzando 122 – Mrs Dawson 52 (Sharrood (USA) –
124) [2002 6g f7g Jun 28] fifth foal: dam 1m winner: last in maiden/seller. *D. Shaw*

MIDNIGHT PARKES 3 b. or br.g. Polar Falcon (USA) 126 – Summerhill Spruce 70 **87**
(Windjammer (USA)) [2002 63p: 6m³ 6f³ 6m* 6m* 6m⁵ 6.1s 5v Nov 8] strong, lengthy
gelding: type to carry condition: fairly useful performer: won maiden at Pontefract in
May and handicap at Ripon in June: raced mainly at 6f: easily best form on going firmer
than good: races prominently. *M. A. Jarvis*

MIDNIGHT PEBBLES 3 ch.f. Pebble Powder – Midnight Mischief (Bairn (USA) –
126) [2002 6m p8g 7s Oct 26] second reported foal: dam well beaten both starts: well
held in maidens/claimer. *Mrs C. A. Dunnett*

MIDNIGHT SONG (USA) 2 ch.g. (Mar 2) Hennessy (USA) 122 – Gratify (USA) **66**
(Miswaki (USA) 124) [2002 6f⁵ 6f⁵ Jun 1] $150,000Y: strong, sturdy gelding: first foal:
dam 2-y-o 5f winner in USA from 2 starts: fair form in maidens: should stay 7f.
E. A. L. Dunlop

MIDNIGHT SPECIAL (IRE) 2 b.f. (Feb 19) Danetime (IRE) 121 – Daffodil Dale **75**
(IRE) 78 (Cyrano de Bergerac 120) [2002 5g 5m² p5g² 5g⁵ 5.1m 5m* 5f² 5g p5g⁴ Oct 31]
6,500Y: useful-looking filly: second foal: half-sister to 3-y-o Bacchanalia: dam Irish
2-y-o 5f winner who stayed 1m: fair performer: left J. L. Eyre after third start: won
maiden at Musselburgh in September: best at bare 5f: acts on polytrack, raced only on
good going or firmer on turf: has been bandaged on hind joints: front runner. *D. Carroll*

MIDNIGHT WATCH (USA) 8 b.g. Capote (USA) – Midnight Air (USA) 111 (Green –
Dancer (USA) 132) [2002 –: p10g f11s 15.4m Apr 23] leggy gelding: no longer of much
account. *M. A. Allen*

MIDSHIPMAN 4 b.c. Executive Man 119 – Midler (Comedy Star (USA) 121) [2002 –
80, a109: f8.5g² p10g Feb 23] good-topped colt: useful on all-weather: easily better effort **a104**
in 2002 when creditable 1½ lengths second to Nose The Trade in minor event at Wolverhampton: effective at 1m to 1½m: acts on fibresand (ran poorly on polytrack): races
prominently: joined H. Cyzer. *P. W. D'Arcy*

MI FAVORITA 4 b.f. Piccolo 121 – Mistook (USA) (Phone Trick (USA)) [2002 39, **44**
a44: 6f 6f⁴ 7f 5.9g 6g 6v 7g⁶ 7f⁴ Sep 27] small filly: poor maiden: stays 1m: acts on firm
going, good to soft and good to firm: tried blinkered/visored. *Don Enrico Incisa*

MIGHTY ATEM (IRE) 2 ch.g. (Mar 17) Up And At 'em 109 – Perfectly Entitled **60**
(IRE) (Entitled 126) [2002 5g⁵ 5d⁴ 5.3g 5m 5d⁵ 5d⁴ 5g³ 6m 5.1s 5s Nov 6] IR 6,000F, IR
7,000Y, resold 5,800Y: strong, close-coupled gelding: fifth foal: brother to 1999 2-y-o 5f
winner Slick Willie: dam soundly beaten both starts: modest maiden: probably best at 5f:
acts on good to firm and good to soft ground: upset preliminaries only try in visor: sold
4,000 gns, sent to Spain. *N. Tinkler*

MIGHTY MAX 4 b.g. Well Beloved 86 – Jokers High (USA) (Vaguely Noble 140) **47**
[2002 –: f9.4g f9.4g 12.6m 11.6m 10.2g⁶ f12f⁴ Aug 16] poor maiden: stays 1¼m.
G. A. Ham

MIGHTY PIP (IRE) 6 b.g. Pips Pride 117 – Hard To Stop 77 (Hard Fought 125) [2002 **49**
68d: p8g² p8g⁴ p10g 8g⁵ 9s⁵ 8.1g⁴ 8.1d⁶ 10m 10m² 10m⁴ 10f⁶ 12f⁶ Oct 7] poor nowadays:
stays 1¼m: acts on heavy going, good to firm and polytrack: tried blinkered/tongue tied.
M. R. Bosley

MIGLDI MAGLDI 3 b.f. Halling (USA) 133 – Lloc 79 (Absalom 128) [2002 10g³ **?**
8.2m⁴ p8g Oct 9] 14,000Y: quite good-topped filly: second foal: dam, 5f winner (including at 2 yrs), half-sister to July Cup winner Compton Place: best effort in maidens when
third at Windsor in April. *I. A. Balding*

MIGUEL CERVANTES (USA) 2 b.c. (Feb 3) Danzig (USA) – Warm Mood (USA) **102**
(Alydar (USA)) [2002 5g* 6m⁴ 6f 5m² 6s* Oct 26] close-coupled colt: fourth foal:
half-brother to useful 1999 2-y-o 5f (Norfolk Stakes) winner Warm Heart (by Diesis):
dam, unbeaten in 4 starts from 6f to 1m in USA, daughter of champion Canadian sprinter
Summer Mood: useful performer: won maiden at the Curragh in July and listed race at
Doncaster (beat Ikan by 2½ lengths) in October: creditable efforts in between in Mill Reef

Stakes at Newbury, Middle Park Stakes at Newmarket (hinted at temperament beforehand) and listed race at Tipperary (neck second to Shizao): should stay 7f: acts on firm and soft ground. *A. P. O'Brien, Ireland*

MIGWAR 9 b.g. Unfuwain (USA) 131 – Pick of The Pops 109 (High Top 131) [2002 –§: f12g Mar 21] deep-girthed gelding: temperamental nowadays: sometimes blinkered/visored. *R. Craggs*

MIKE SIMMONS 6 b.g. Ballacashtal (CAN) – Lady Crusty (Golden Dipper 119) [2002 f16g Mar 26] maiden handicapper: well held only start on Flat since 2000: winning hurdler. *L. P. Grassick*

MILAN 4 b.c. Sadler's Wells (USA) 132 – Kithanga (IRE) 117 (Darshaan 133) [2002 129: 10s May 6] rather leggy, useful-looking colt: high-class performer at 3 yrs, winning Great Voltigeur Stakes at York and Rothmans Royals St Leger at Doncaster: pulled up in listed race at the Curragh only 4-y-o outing, having fractured off-fore cannon bone: effective at 1½m, should stay 2m: wears crossed noseband: held up: genuine: stays in training. *A. P. O'Brien, Ireland*

MILK AND SULTANA 2 b.f. (Apr 8) Millkom 124 – Premier Princess 45 (Hard Fought 125) [2002 f7g f7g⁵ Dec 31] fifth foal: half-sister to 9.4f winner Rosie Jaques (by Doyoun): dam winning stayer on Flat/over hurdles: better effort in maidens at Wolverhampton (fair form) when 7½ lengths fifth of 12 to Just A Glimmer: bred to stay at least 1¼m: troublesome in stall on debut. *W. M. Brisbourne*

MILL DOT KOM 3 ch.g. Millkom 124 – Bear To Dance 46 (Rambo Dancer (CAN) 107) [2002 46§, a51§: p8g Jan 8] modest maiden: stays 7f: acts on fibresand and good to firm going: visored once: has wandered under pressure: one to have reservations about. *W. G. M. Turner*

MILL EMERALD 5 b.m. Old Vic 136 – Milinetta (Milford 119) [2002 12.4m May 15] unfurnished mare: maiden: well held only Flat run since 2000: tried visored: won over hurdles in May/June. *Mrs M. Reveley*

MILLENARY 5 b.h. Rainbow Quest (USA) 134 – Ballerina (IRE) 88 (Dancing Brave (USA) 140) [2002 124: 12g² 12m³ 12d* 12d³ 14m⁵ 12s⁵ Oct 20] leggy, attractive horse:

Princess of Wales's UAE Equestrian And Racing Federation Stakes, Newmarket—
Millenary responds in typically game fashion to overcome Mubtaker (left); Yavana's Pace is third

Mr L. Neil Jones's "Millenary"

good walker: fluent mover: very smart performer: creditable placed efforts in Jockey Club Stakes at Newmarket (neck second to Marienbard) and Hardwicke Stakes at Royal Ascot (length third to Zindabad) prior to winning Princess of Wales's Stakes at Newmarket in July, beating Mubtaker a neck, reeling in runner-up close home: rare lacklustre efforts in Pokal at Cologne, Irish St Leger at the Curragh and Gran Premio del Jockey Club at Milan last 3 starts: effective at 1½m (given a truly-run race) and likely to stay 2m: acts on firm going, has won on soft: seemed unsuited by course at Epsom second start at 4 yrs: game: stays in training. *J. L. Dunlop*

MILLENIUM MOONBEAM (USA) 5 b.c.g. Phone Trick (USA) – Shywing (USA) 70 (Wing Out (USA)) [2002 85: 7d 7.1d 7m 8.3g 7m 7g 8.1g Aug 7] rangy gelding: one-time useful performer, just fair nowadays: stays 1m: acts on good to firm and good to soft ground: tried blinkered/tongue tied: often starts slowly: one to treat with some caution. *G. G. Margarson*

MILLENNIUM BUG 6 b.m. Rock Hopper 124 – So Precise (FR) (Balidar 133) [2002 – 47: p12g Feb 2] probably no longer of any account. *M. Madgwick*

MILLENNIUM DRAGON 3 b.c. Mark of Esteem (IRE) 137 – Feather Bride (IRE) 112 (Groom Dancer (USA) 128) [2002 97p: 8g⁴ 7m* 7f* 7m⁵ 6d⁵ 7m⁴ 7m² 7m Oct 19] tall, quite attractive colt: usually impresses in appearance: smart performer: won minor event and listed race (beat Indian Country by 3 lengths) at Newmarket in May: creditable efforts after when 2¾ lengths fifth to Continent in July Cup at Newmarket and 5 lengths second to Suggestive in listed race at York on fifth/seventh starts: probably better at 6f/7f than

Sheikh Hamdan bin Mohammed Al Maktoum's "Millennium Dragon'

1m: acts on firm and good to soft ground, seemingly not on heavy: sometimes has rope halter/blanket for stall entry: usually races handily: joined Godolphin. *M. A. Jarvis*

MILLENNIUM FORCE 4 b.g. Bin Ajwaad (IRE) 119 – Jumairah Sun (IRE) 98   **113** (Scenic 128) [2002 90: 8s⁴ 7d⁶ 7g* 8m 7d 7m* 8m 7m³ 7m³ 7m* 7g² 7s* 6v⁶ Nov 9] tall, lengthy gelding: smart performer: improved, and won handicaps at Lingfield in May, Newcastle in July and Ascot (Tote Trifecta Stakes, beat Mr Mahoose gamely by ½ length) in September, and minor event at Doncaster (beat Resplendent Cee 8 lengths) in October: best at 7f/1m: yet to race on firm going, acts on any other: visored (ran well) once at 3 yrs: held up: occasionally edges left: reliable. *M. R. Channon*

MILLENNIUM HALL 3 b.g. Saddlers' Hall (IRE) 126 – Millazure (USA) 71 (Day-   **75** jur (USA) 137) [2002 75: 9g 11.6g⁵ 11.6m² 11.9m⁶ 10s⁴ 8.2v⁴ Oct 29] leggy gelding: has a quick action: fair maiden: left L. Cumani after third start: stays 11.6f: yet to race on firm ground, acts on any other: gelded after final outing. *I. Semple*

MILLENNIUM KING 3 b.g. Piccolo 121 – Zabelina (USA) 57 (Diesis 133) [2002   **74 d** 85: 6s 6m 6.1m³ 6g 5m 5m 7g Oct 4] smallish gelding: fairly useful winner on debut: generally disappointing since (left W. Jarvis after fifth start): stays 6f: lost all chance by rearing as stall opened final 2-y-o outing. *J. M. Bradley*

MILLERS WEIR (IRE) 3 ch.g. Lake Coniston (IRE) 131 – Isca 66 (Caerleon (USA)   **62 d** 132) [2002 62: 7d 8m 6g 7.5s 7d 6s f5g Nov 30] 21,000F, 2,900 3-y-o: fourth foal: half-brother to 3 winners, including useful Italian 6f (at 2 yrs) and 1m winner Sonda (by Dolphin Street) and 4-y-o Type One: dam, maiden, should have been suited by further than 1m: modest maiden at 2 yrs: well below form after reappearance, including on all-weather/British debut at Wolverhampton final outing: stays 6f: acts on firm and good to soft going: tried blinkered. *Edward Sexton, Ireland*

MILLIONFORMERTHYR   6 b.m. Mon Tresor 113 – Regal Salute 68 (Dara Mon-   –
arch 128) [2002 p16g Jan 5] no longer of any account. *Mrs L. C. Jewell*

MILLION PERCENT   3 b.c. Ashkalani (IRE) 128 – Royal Jade 82 (Last Tycoon   89
131) [2002 96: p7g⁶ p5g f7g 5s 6g 5f 6d⁶ 6f 6f 6m² 5.7f⁴ 6g 5s Oct 26] small, strong colt:
fairly useful performer: best around 6f: acts on firm ground, good to soft and polytrack:
sometimes slowly away. *K. R. Burke*

MILLKOM ELEGANCE   3 b.f. Millkom 124 – Premier Princess 45 (Hard Fought   49
125) [2002 52: 10d⁵ 10d² 10m⁴ f12g 9.3s 12.1g 10g⁵ Aug 26] small, quite good-topped
filly: poor maiden handicapper: stays 1¼m: acts on good to soft and good to firm going.
K. A. Ryan

MILL REGENT   2 ch.g. (Feb 23) Prince Sabo 123 – Milinetta (Milford 119) [2002   53
5m⁵ 5m 7.5g⁵ 7g² 8g⁵ 7.5g⁵ Sep 18] rather leggy gelding: half-brother to 1993 2-y-o 1m
winner Mill Force (by Forzando): dam winning hurdler: modest maiden: best efforts in
selling nurseries last 2 starts: barely stays 1m: raced only on good/good to firm ground:
sold 6,000 gns, sent to Kuwait. *J. G. Given*

MILLSTREET   3 ch.g. Polish Precedent (USA) 131 – Mill Path (Mill Reef (USA)   112
141) [2002 86: 12d² 10g* 10g² 12d³ 12g² 10m² 12f² 12d* Oct 13] leggy gelding: closely
related to useful 1m winner Desert Track (by Green Desert) and half-brother to 2 winners,
including useful 6f (at 2 yrs)/7f winner Queen's View (by Lomond): dam, ran once, from
family of Teenoso: smart performer: won maiden at the Curragh in June and listed race
there (by 2 lengths from Starbourne) in October: creditable placed efforts in between,
including second in listed races at Leopardstown (beaten ½ length by Vinnie Roe on fifth
start and 1½ lengths by Sights On Gold on sixth one): stays 1½m: acts on firm and good
to soft going: reliable: joined Godolphin. *J. Oxx, Ireland*

MILLYBAA (USA)   2 b.f. (Mar 22) Anabaa (USA) 130 – Millyant 114 (Primo   66 p
Dominie 121) [2002 6d⁶ Oct 14] third foal: dam, 5f performer, half-sister to very smart
sprinter Prince Sabo: 8/1, 4 lengths sixth of 21 to Maltese Falcon in maiden at Windsor,
travelling well in rear and keeping on under hands and heels: sure to improve. *R. Guest*

MILLY FLEUR   2 ch.f. (Feb 5) Primo Dominie 121 – My Cadeaux 93 (Cadeaux   60 p
Genereux 131) [2002 6m⁵ Sep 24] first foal: dam, 6f winner, closely related to very
smart sprinter Prince Sabo and half-sister to smart sprinter Millyant (by Primo Dominie): joint
favourite, 3 lengths fifth of 19 to Viera in maiden at Newmarket: likely to do better.
R. Guest

MILLY LAHIB (IRE)   2 b.f. (Feb 29) Lahib (USA) 129 – Treadmill (IRE) 51 (High   64
Estate 127) [2002 5.7f² 6g 5.7f f7g⁶ Nov 26] IR 4,000Y: second foal: half-sister to a 2-y-o
winner in Italy by Mujtahid: dam ran 3 times at 2 yrs in Ireland: modest maiden: best
effort when staying-on second at Bath: should stay 7f. *D. J. Coakley*

MILLY'S LASS   4 b.f. Mind Games 121 – Millie's Lady (IRE) (Common Grounds   67 d
118) [2002 –: 6.1d 5.7g⁴ 5.7g 5g 5g 5.5f 5d p5g⁶ f5g 5.1g f5g Dec 13] sparely-made
filly: fair handicapper: effective at 5f/6f: acts on any turf going and polytrack: has worn
cheekpieces: sometimes starts slowly: on downgrade. *J. M. Bradley*

MIMAS GIRL   3 b.f. Samim (USA) 84 – Cocked Hat Girl 47 (Ballacashtal (CAN))   43
[2002 7m⁶ f7g⁴ 6.1m⁴ f8.5g 5.9s 6.1m Jun 17] fourth foal: half-sister to 6f and (at 2 yrs)
7f winner Rex Is Okay (by Mazilier): dam placed up to 12.5f: poor maiden: should stay
7f: blinkered (slowly away) final start. *S. R. Bowring*

Tote Trifecta Stakes (Handicap), Ascot—the consistent Millennium Force holds off the unlucky
Mr Mahoose, with Royal Millennium (No.5), Mister Cosmi (rail) and Give Back Calais clear of the others

Ladbrokes Bunbury Cup, Newmarket—a controversial contest as Mine is awarded the race outright after dead-heating with Capricho (left), the latter being disqualified for running without his weight cloth; Grizedale (white blaze) is next

MIMIC 2 b.f. (Apr 17) Royal Applause 124 – Stripanoora (Ahonoora 122) [2002 6g **63** p5g³ Nov 13] 42,000Y: angular filly: half-sister to several winners, including smart 1m (at 2 yrs) to 1½m winner Naked Welcome (by Most Welcome) and fairly useful 1996 2-y-o 5f/6f winner Olympic Spirit (by Puissance), later winner in US including at 1m: dam maiden who stayed 1m: modest form in maidens at Newmarket and Lingfield, third to Isengard in latter: will probably stay 7f. *R. Guest*

MINASHKI (IRE) 3 b.c. Ashkalani (IRE) 128 – Blushing Minstrel (IRE) 85 (Nicholas **106** (USA) 111) [2002 95: 7s⁴ 6d* 6s 5d⁵ 5.1f 5g Oct 6] well-made colt: useful performer: best effort when winning listed race at Cork in May by 2½ lengths from Mr Houdini: well held in similar event at Chester (poorly drawn, final start for H. Rogers) fifth outing: effective at 5f/6f: acts on soft and good to firm going. *K. Prendergast, Ireland*

MINDAHRA 4 b.f. Mind Games 121 – Indiahra 76 (Indian Ridge 123) [2002 –: f5g **–** Mar 12] no form: tried visored. *M. Mullineaux*

MINDANAO 6 b.m. Most Welcome 131 – Salala 83 (Connaught 130) [2002 79: 10.9g **76** 10s³ 10d⁶ 16s f14g Dec 10] leggy mare: fair performer: below form after second start, leaving F. Murtagh before final outing: effective at 1¼m (given a test) to 1¾m: acts on any going: held up. *I. Semple*

MIND BOBBY 2 b.c. (Feb 7) Mind Games 121 – Young Holly (Risk Me (FR) 127) [2002 f6g p6g Dec 28] third foal: dam unraced: well beaten in maidens at Wolverhampton and Lingfield. *J. M. Bradley*

MIND CONTROL 3 gr.f. Mind Games 121 – Islandreagh (IRE) (Knesset (USA) **–** 105) [2002 f5g f6g f5g⁶ 5m f5g 5f 8s 5m Aug 17] big, lengthy filly: second foal: dam no worthwhile form over jumps: no form. *M. J. Polglase*

MINDEROO 4 b.g. Efisio 120 – Mindomica 63 (Dominion 123) [2002 61: f8.5g 10d **58** 7d f6g⁶ 6g* 7.2d⁶ 6d 5g f5g⁶ f6s⁴ Dec 26] quite good-topped gelding: modest performer: won maiden at Catterick in July: left B. Hills 5,800 gns after sixth start: probably best at 6f: acts on fibresand and good to soft ground: blinkered third to sixth outings (tongue tied last 2 occasions): has worn cheekpieces: sometimes flashes tail, and temperament under suspicion. *J. M. Bradley*

MIND THE SILVER 5 gr.g. Petong 126 – Marjorie's Memory (IRE) 76 (Fairy King **– §** (USA)) [2002 –§: 8.2d May 18] temperamental handicapper: fatally injured only 5-y-o start: tried visored/blinkered. *R. Lee*

MINE FOREVER 3 br.g. Royal Academy (USA) 130 – Overseas Romance (USA) **–** (Assert 134) [2002 49: 8m Sep 19] tall, sparely-made gelding: poor maiden at 2 yrs: well held only outing in 2002 (blinkered): has looked wayward. *D. McCain*

636

MINE HOST 3 b.c. Elmaamul (USA) 125 – Divina Mia 66 (Dowsing (USA) 124) **96** [2002 92: 8s³ 10.1g² 10.2g² 12m² 12m 10g Jul 10] good-topped colt: has scope: useful performer: runner-up in minor events at Epsom (behind Swing Wing), Bath and Salisbury (behind Grampian both times): best form at 1¼m: acts on good to firm going: sometimes goes freely: sent to Hong Kong. *M. L. W. Bell*

MINE (IRE) 4 b.c. Primo Dominie 121 – Ellebanna 69 (Tina's Pet 121) [2002 82: 8v **99** 7f⁵ 7d² 7.1d* 7g³ 7d* 7m 6g 6g 7m Sep 28] tall, useful-looking colt: useful handicapper: improved, and won at Sandown (by 2 lengths from Bouncing Bowdler) in June and Ladbrokes Bunbury Cup at Newmarket (dead-heated with disqualified Capricho) in July: best around 7f: acts on firm and good to soft going, well below form on heavy: visored last 5 starts. *J. D. Bethell*

MINELLY 2 b.f. (Mar 2) Defacto (USA) – Lady Liza 69 (Air Trooper 115) [2002 6g **42 §** 7.5g³ 7.5g f8s Sep 5] 1,000Y: small filly: has a markedly round action: half-sister to 3-y-o Captain Venti: dam 1m winner: poor maiden: third in seller: should stay 1m: probably temperamental. *M. E. Sowersby*

MINESHAFT (USA) 3 b. or br.c. A P Indy (USA) 131 – Prospectors Delite (USA) **109** (Mr Prospector (USA)) [2002 8m⁴ 8m* 10g⁴ 8m 9g³ 8m⁶ 8m² a8f* a8.2f* Dec 20] tall, good-topped colt: fifth foal: brother to smart US Grade 1 8.5f/1¼m winner Tomisue's Delight and half-brother to 2 winners, including smart Irish 6f (at 2 yrs) and 7f winner Monashee Mountain (by Danzig): dam, US Grade 1 winner around 1m, from very good US family: useful performer: won maiden at Newmarket in May: mostly creditable efforts after, including when fourth (promoted a place) to Bernebeau in Prix Daphnis at Maisons-Laffitte and 2 lengths second to Tikkun in minor event at Doncaster on fifth/ seventh starts: left J. Gosden, won allowance race at Churchill Downs in November and optional claimer at Fair Grounds in December: likely to prove best at 1m/1¼m: acts on dirt, showed little to suggest he acts on good/good to firm going on turf. *N. J. Howard, USA*

MINGORA (USA) 3 b.f. Mtoto 134 – Silk Braid (USA) 105 (Danzig (USA)) [2002 **83** 89p: 11.5g⁵ May 11] good-bodied filly: fairly useful form when second in maiden at Newmarket (trained by D. Loder) at 2 yrs and 9¼ lengths fifth to Birdie in listed race at Lingfield (visored, carried head awkwardly early on), only outing in 2002: visits Halling. *Saeed bin Suroor*

MING THE MERCILESS 2 b.c. (Apr 1) Hector Protector (USA) 124 – Sundae **74** Girl (USA) 75 (Green Dancer (USA) 132) [2002 6g 6d³ 6g Sep 19] 29,000Y: big, strong colt: has plenty of scope: first foal: dam, 2-y-o 6f winner, half-sister to South American Grade 1 winner Faaz from excellent North American family: best effort in maidens (fair form) when 11 lengths third to Makhlab at Pontefract: gave impression something amiss at Ayr final start: should stay at least 7f. *J. G. Given*

MINGUN (USA) 2 b. or br.c. (Apr 29) A P Indy (USA) 131 – Miesque (USA) 133 **97 P** (Nureyev (USA) 131) [2002 7g² Oct 31] half-brother to several at least useful winners, notably high-class miler Kingmambo (by Mr Prospector) and very smart Poule d'Essai des Pouliches/Prix de Diane winner East of The Moon (by Private Account): dam top-class miler: 10/1, promising neck second of 24 to stable-companion Alberto Giacometti in newcomers race at the Curragh (pair 3 lengths clear), leading over 1f out until well inside last: open to good deal of improvement, and sure to win races at 3 yrs. *A. P. O'Brien, Ireland*

MINIHAHA 4 ch.f. First Trump 118 – Indian Lament 52§ (Indian Ridge 123) [2002 **72** 71: p10g 9s² 10s 9d² 8d 8g 10g 9g Oct 5] workmanlike filly: fair performer: barely stays 1¼m: yet to race on heavy going, acts on any other: races prominently: none too consistent: sold 5,000 gns, sent to Kuwait. *Mrs A. J. Perrett*

MINI LODGE (IRE) 6 ch.g. Grand Lodge (USA) 125 – Mirea (USA) 104 (The **–** Minstrel (CAN) 135) [2002 –: f11s⁵ f11g Feb 5] tall, close-coupled gelding: one-time fairly useful handicapper: stayed 1½m: acted on any turf going: tried visored: was usually held up: dead. *J. G. FitzGerald*

MINIRINA 2 b.f. (Jan 27) Mistertopogigo (IRE) 118 – Fabulous Rina (FR) (Fabulous **65** Dancer (USA) 124) [2002 5f⁵ 5d⁵ 5m⁴ 5m⁵ f5g³ 5d⁵ 5m² Aug 28] leggy, rather un-furnished filly: half-sister to several winners, including useful 1m winner Tom Dougal (by Ron's Victory) and 7f/1m winner Dispol Diamond (by Sharpo): dam French 1¼m winner: fair maiden: will probably stay 6f: acts on good to firm going and fibresand. *C. Smith*

MINNE'S LAST 3 b.f. So Factual (USA) 120 – Minne Love 67 (Homeric 133) [2002 **–** 7m 7.1v Jun 14] half-sister to several winners, including sprinter Micro Love (by Vaigly

Great) and 7f winner Sumthinelse (by Magic Ring), both fairly useful: dam 6f (at 2 yrs) and 1m winner: well held in claimers. *L. G. Cottrell*

MINNIE BLOO MIN (IRE)   3 b.f. Blues Traveller (IRE) 119 – White Jasmin 53   **42** (Jalmood (USA) 126) [2002 49: p6g⁶ p8g f8g 5m 7f May 11] good-bodied filly: poor performer: left Miss V. Haigh after second start: stays 6f: acts on all-weather, probably on good to firm going. *G. Prodromou*

MINSTREL HALL   3 b.f. Saddlers' Hall (IRE) 126 – Mindomica 63 (Dominion 123)   **57** [2002 8g⁴ 10m⁶ 9.9g 12.1g³ 11.1v* 12.1m Sep 2] tall, unfurnished filly: fourth living foal: half-sister to 4-y-o Minderoo: dam, 7f winner (including at 2 yrs), half-sister to Fred Darling winner/Oaks fourth Sueboog, herself dam of very smart 1m/1¼m performer Best of The Bests: modest performer: won claimer at Hamilton (final start for C. Thornton) in June: stays 1½m: acts on heavy and good to firm going. *P. Monteith*

MINT APPROVAL (USA)   3 gr. or ro.g. With Approval (CAN) – Mint Bell (USA)   **–** (Key To The Mint (USA)) [2002 –: 7m Apr 5] no form: tried blinkered. *B. J. Meehan*

MINUSCOLO   4 b.f. Piccolo 121 – Wrangbrook (Shirley Heights 130) [2002 –: f8.5g⁵   **–** Jan 11] fair maiden at 2 yrs: little form since: blinkered (very slowly away) only 4-y-o start. *J. A. Osborne*

MI ODDS   6 b.g. Sure Blade (USA) 130 – Vado Via 56 (Ardross 134) [2002 62, a87:   **a94** 11.6d 10m f12g* p12g⁶ p10g Dec 3] fairly useful handicapper on all-weather: trained by I. Williams first 2 starts: career-best effort when winning at Wolverhampton (made most) in October: effective at 9.4f to 1½m: acts on fibresand and good to firm going. *Mrs N. Macauley*

MIRACLE ISLAND   7 b.g. Jupiter Island 126 – Running Game 81 (Run The Gantlet   **63** (USA)) [2002 63, a72: f8g⁵ p10g⁶ p13g⁵ f14g³ 18s* 16g 16m⁴ 16f⁶ f16g² 16.4d p13g f14.8g² f14.8g² Dec 14] tall gelding: modest performer: won handicap at Doncaster in March: effective at 1¼m to 2¼m: acts on all-weather, soft and firm going: visored once early in career: sometimes tongue tied: not one to trust implicitly. *K. R. Burke*

MIRAFIORI (IRE)   3 br.f. Inzar (USA) 112 – Monaco Lady 83 (Manado 130) [2002   **–** 47: f9.4g Jan 19] sparely-made filly: poor performer: should stay beyond 1m: races only on good going or firmer on turf, below form on fibresand. *G. C. H. Chung*

MIRANT   3 b.c. Danzig Connection (USA) – Ingerence (FR) (Akarad (FR) 130) [2002   **81** 10m⁶ 10.2g³ p12g⁴ 14m⁴ Jul 4] 7,500F, 41,000Y: tall, useful-looking colt: third foal: half-brother to smart performer up to 7f Pan Jammer (by Piccolo), 5f/6.3f winner at 2 yrs, and 1¼m winner Kiss Me Kate (by Aragon): dam, French maiden, half-sister to smart French middle-distance filly La Monalisa: fairly useful maiden: stays 1¾m: acts on good to firm going: hung badly left final start: joined M. Pipe. *E. A. L. Dunlop*

MIRELA (IRE)   3 b.f. Charnwood Forest (IRE) 125 – Topseys Tipple (IRE) 76 (Hatim   **81** (USA) 121) [2002 72: 8m 10s 8.5d 10g 9.5g* 8d³ 9d² p10g Nov 13] IR 19,000Y: fourth foal: half-sister to 3 winners, including fairly useful Irish 1997 2-y-o 6f/7f winner Maduka (by Paris House) and 1¼m winner Miss Moselle (by Zieten): dam Irish 9f winner: fairly useful handicapper: won at Gowran in October: bit below form on all-weather/British debut at Lingfield final outing: stays 9.5f: raced mainly on good going or softer on turf (acts on soft). *J. S. Bolger, Ireland*

MISAAYEF (USA)   2 b. or br.f. (Feb 2) Swain (IRE) 134 – Zakiyya (USA) (Dayjur   **78 p** (USA) 137) [2002 7m⁶ Sep 20] rather lengthy, useful-looking filly: fourth foal: half-sister to a winner in USA by A P Indy: dam 8.5f winner in USA: 6/1 and backward, 5 lengths sixth of 7 to L'Ancresse in minor event at Newbury: bandaged off-hind joint: will be suited by 1m+: should improve. *Sir Michael Stoute*

MISBEHAVIOUR   3 b.g. Tragic Role (USA) – Exotic Forest 66 (Dominion 123)   **56** [2002 70: p6g 7.1f 8m 6m 7s⁴ 7d 7m 6.1d 7m Aug 23] leggy, unfurnished gelding: modest maiden: stays 7f: acts on soft ground: visored sixth start. *J. G. Portman*

MISCHIEF   6 ch.g. Generous (IRE) 139 – Knight's Baroness 116 (Rainbow Quest   **46 §** (USA) 134) [2002 45§: 11.9d³ 12.1g 14.1m² Aug 21] compact gelding: poor performer: effective at 1½m to easy 2m: acts on fibresand and any turf going: sometimes blinkered/visored: has looked reluctant to race: unreliable. *K. Bell*

MISCK (IRE)   3 ch.f. Desert King (IRE) 129 – Sedra 116 (Nebbiolo 125) [2002 –p: **79** 10d² 10m 12.1g* Sep 12] smallish, sturdy filly: fair performer: won maiden at Chepstow in September: stayed 1½m: acted on good to soft going: dead. *J. L. Dunlop*

MISHEAD   4 ch.g. Unfuwain (USA) 131 – Green Jannat (USA) (Alydar (USA)) [2002   –
–: f16s Jan 4] little form. *M. C. Chapman*

MISHKA   4 b.g. Mistertopogigo (IRE) 118 – Walsham Witch 61 (Music Maestro 119)   **71**
[2002 81§, a71§: p7g⁴ p6g* p6g² p6g* f5g⁶ 5g 6.1m p6g² 6d⁶ p7g⁶ f6f p5g⁴ Dec 21]   **a79**
strong, close-coupled gelding: fair performer: won maiden and handicap at Lingfield
early in year: best recent form around 6f: acts on heavy going, good to firm and all-
weather: blinkered/visored: carries head awkwardly: often races prominently: formerly
unreliable. *Julian Poulton*

MI SOMBRERO   3 ch.f. Factual (USA) 108 – Rose Elegance 83 (Bairn (USA) 126)   –
[2002 8m 7s 7m 8.3d 10d f8.5s Dec 13] third foal: sister to 2000 2-y-o 6f winner Myhat:
dam 1m/1¼m winner: no form: slowly away first 2 outings. *D. K. Ivory*

MISRAAH (IRE)   5 ch.g. Lure (USA) 131 – Dwell (USA) 96 (Habitat 134) [2002   **114**
120+: 6f⁵ 5m⁴ 6m 6g⁴ 6d Jul 11] close-coupled, useful-looking gelding: smart performer:
respectable efforts at best in 2002, including in Duke of York Stakes (fifth to Invincible
Spirit), Temple Stakes at Sandown (fourth to Kyllachy) and Chipchase Stakes at
Newcastle (fourth to Tedburrow, not clear run): effective at 5f to 7f: acts on firm and good
to soft going: blinkered final start: has worn crossed noseband: often mulish in
preliminaries (sometimes mounted on track/in saddling box): sometimes races freely:
usually waited with: joined J. Sadler in UAE. *Sir Michael Stoute*

MISS AMAZER   3 b.f. Shaamit (IRE) 127 – Kiss On Time (Lead On Time (USA)   **47**
123) [2002 63d: 5.1m 8.2m 6s 10g⁶ 10m 8m³ 8f⁵ f8g f12g f9.4g Dec 16] poor maiden   **a38**
handicapper: left J. M. Bradley after third start: stays 1m, not 1½m: acts on firm going,
probably on fibresand: has looked less than keen. *C. G. Cox*

MISS ANABAA   3 b.f. Anabaa (USA) 130 – Midnight Shift (IRE) 73 (Night Shift   **85 +**
(USA)) [2002 6s³ 6d* 6v 6v Nov 20] first foal: dam, 6f winner, half-sister to very smart
sprinter Owington: confirmed debut promise when winning maiden at Salisbury in July
by 3 lengths from Groovy Willow, very free early and quickening well: off 4 months, stiff
tasks in listed races at Cologne and Maisons-Laffitte, appearing to run well when ninth to
Welsh Emperor on latter course: raced only at 6f on ground softer than good. *R. Guest*

MISS ASSERTIVE   2 b.f. (Mar 10) Zafonic (USA) 130 – Self Assured (IRE) 97 (Aho-   **88**
noora 122) [2002 6m p7g³ 7s³ 8m⁵ 6.5m³ 7f³ 6d* 7s⁵ Oct 26] 7,500Y: leggy, workmanlike
filly: fourth foal: dam 7f winner and second in May Hill Stakes, out of half-sister to very
smart sprinter Sayyaf: fairly useful performer: justified favouritism in maiden at
Pontefract in October: good third in listed races at Newmarket third and sixth starts: ran
creditably final one: stays 7f: acts on firm and soft ground. *N. P. Littmoden*

MISS BEABEA (IRE)   3 ch.f. Catrail (USA) 123 – Lady Ellen 67 (Horage 124)   **105**
[2002 102: 6d⁵ 8s 5s² 6m 5d⁴ 6d² 6s⁴ 6g⁵ 5g⁶ 5g⁶ 6d⁴ Oct 13] IR 15,000Y: lengthy, angular
filly: sixth foal: half-sister to 3 winners, notably 8-y-o Ellens Lad and 7-y-o Ellens
Academy: dam, placed over 5f at 2 yrs, half-sister to Indian Ridge: useful performer: won
minor event at Leopardstown and listed race at the Curragh in 2001: several creditable
efforts in 2002, including in Ballyogan Stakes at Cork (½-length second to Jessica's
Dream), minor event at Leopardstown (neck second to D'Anjou) and Phoenix Sprint
Stakes at the Curragh (length fourth to One Won One) on third/sixth/seventh starts:
slowly away, well held in Golden Jubilee Stakes at Royal Ascot fourth outing: effective
at 5f (given test) to 7f: acts on soft and good to firm ground. *K. Prendergast, Ireland*

MISS BEETEE (IRE)   4 b.f. Brief Truce (USA) 126 – Majestic Amber (USA)   –
(Majestic Light (USA)) [2002 –: f8.5g⁶ f7s Jan 17] probably of little account nowadays.
S. C. Williams

MISS BROOKS   3 b.f. Bishop of Cashel 122 – Crimson Rosella 54 (Polar Falcon   **81**
(USA) 126) [2002 8.3g² 8.2m⁶ f7g* p7g f8g Dec 4] 15,500Y, 20,000Y: second foal:
half-sister to fairly useful 6f (at 2 yrs)/7f winner Sabo Rose (by Primo Dominie): dam,
maiden who probably stayed 1½m, half-sister to high-class sprinter Mr Brooks and to
dam of Middle Park winner First Trump: fairly useful performer, lightly raced: won
maiden at Wolverhampton in October: races freely, and may prove best at 6f/7f: acts on
all-weather: hung second start. *W. J. Haggas*

MISS C   3 b.f. Tachyon Park 87 – Fallal (IRE) 47 (Fayruz 116) [2002 69, a62: f5g f5g   –
f5g 5m 5m 5g 5d 5f f6g f5s Sep 5] unfurnished filly: fair performer at 2 yrs: little form in
2002. *R. Hollinshead*

MISS CASH   5 b.m. Rock Hopper 124 – Miss Cashtal (IRE) (Ballacashtal (CAN))   **39**
[2002 35: 16.2g 13.8m 14.1f 16f⁴ 14.1f⁶ 16m Jul 7] workmanlike mare: poor maiden:
stayed 2m: acted on firm going: dead. *M. E. Sowersby*

Tote Cesarewitch (Handicap), Newmarket—Miss Fara (far side) gives Martin Pipe his second win in the race in three years as she and apprentice Ryan Moore catch the Irish challenger Direct Bearing close home; one of Pipe's four other runners, Dubai Seven Stars, comes third in the largest field for the race since 1952

MISS CEYLON 2 b.f. (Jan 19) Brief Truce (USA) 126 – Five Islands 62 (Bairn (USA) 126) [2002 f5g⁵ 5g⁶ 5.9d⁴ 5m³ 5g³ 6m² 5g* 5d² 6m⁵ 5m 6s Oct 25] 500Y: angular, close-coupled filly: fourth foal: half-sister to winners abroad by Clantime and Danehill Dancer: dam 2-y-o 5f winner: fair performer: won maiden at Beverley in July: good second in nursery at Haydock next time: left G. M. Moore after penultimate start: effective at 5f/6f: acts on good to firm and good to soft ground. *Miss A. Stokell* **75**

MISS CHAMPERS (IRE) 2 b. or br.f. (Jan 2) Grand Lodge (USA) 125 – Katherine Gorge (USA) (Hansel (USA)) [2002 f6d 6.5g 6s f6s* f7s* f7g² f6g⁴ Dec 20] 25,000Y: leggy filly: second foal: half-sister to a winner in Spain by Petardia: dam unraced daughter of useful sprinter Katies First: fairly useful on all-weather, fair on turf: won nurseries at Wolverhampton in November and December: should stay 1m: acts on fibresand, raced on good ground or softer on turf. *R. Hannon* **66 a83**

MISS COLDUNELL 3 b.f. Zilzal (USA) 137 – Beau's Delight (USA) (Lypheor 118) [2002 8.2m 10m Oct 7] small, close-coupled filly: eighth foal: half-sister to several winners, including useful 1¾m winner Zaforum and 1½m/13f winner Lady Coldunell (both by Deploy): dam maiden who should have stayed at least 1m: never dangerous in maidens at Nottingham (gave trouble in preliminaries) and Windsor. *N. A. Callaghan* **–**

MISS CORNICHE 3 b.f. Hernando (FR) 127 – Miss Beaulieu 106 (Northfields (USA)) [2002 81p: 10g² 10.1m* 10.5v Oct 25] useful performer: won listed event at Yarmouth by ½ length from Persian Lass: respectable seventh to Trumbaka in Prix de Flore at Saint-Cloud final start: barely stays 10.5f: yet to race on firm going, acts on any other: has been bandaged on near-hind: has raced freely. *G. Wragg* **104**

MISS CROISETTE 3 ch.f. Hernando (FR) 127 – Miss Riviera 103 (Kris 135) [2002 60p: 10m p12g⁵ Nov 13] strong filly: fair form: off 11 months before reappearance: best effort in maiden at Lingfield only other 3-y-o start: stays 1½m: sold 6,000 gns. *G. Wragg* **69**

MISS DAMASK (IRE) 4 b.f. Barathea (IRE) 127 – Startino 111 (Bustino 136) [2002 70+: f8s* f8s* f8g f8g² 8.2d² 8m 8.3m⁵ 8m* 8g⁵ Oct 14] big, rangy filly: fairly useful on all-weather, fair on turf: won minor event/handicap at Southwell in January and handicap at Salisbury in September: barely stays 9.4f: acts on good to soft going, good to firm and fibresand: often races freely: sold 17,000 gns, sent to Saudi Arabia. *J. A. Osborne* **70 a80**

MISS DEVIOUS (IRE) 4 ch.f. Dr Devious (IRE) 127 – Lothlorien (USA) 80 (Woodman (USA) 126) [2002 50, a47: f16s 16g 11.9f 11.9m 11.8d 14m⁴ 14f* 10s³ Nov 1] good-topped filly: poor handicapper: left Miss J. Feilden 2,200 gns after fifth start: won apprentice race at Thurles in October: races freely, but stays 2m: acts on fibresand, soft and firm going: has been blinkered/hooded. *Francis Ennis, Ireland* **46**

MISSED A NOTE 2 br.g. (Apr 21) Missed Flight 123 – Out of Harmony 79 (Song 132) [2002 6d⁴ 6d⁴ 7f Jun 13] 1,000Y: half-brother to several winners, including fairly **47**

useful 5f/6f winner Mijas (by Risk Me): dam 2-y-o 5f winner: poor maiden: lost action final start. *W. G. M. Turner*

MISS FARA (FR) 7 ch.m. Galetto (FR) 118 – Faracha (FR) (Kenmare (FR) 125) **100**
[2002 90: 14m⁶ 11.9d 11.8g³ 12d² 11.7f³ 16.2g³ 18m* Oct 19] leggy, angular mare: useful handicapper: 12/1, better than ever when winning 36-runner Tote Cesarewitch at Newmarket in October by short head from Direct Bearing, staying on strongly from mid-field to lead on line: stays 2¼m: acts on firm and good to soft going: reliable. *M. C. Pipe*

MISS FAYE 2 b. or br.f. (May 5) Puissance 110 – Bingo Bongo 60 (Petong 126) [2002 **–**
6.1g 6d Oct 14] second reported foal: half-sister to 6f winner Grace (by Buzzards Bay): dam ungenuine maiden: slowly away and well beaten in maidens. *J. M. Bradley*

MISS FLEURIE 2 b.f. (Feb 7) Alzao (USA) 117 – Miss Sancerre 95 (Last Tycoon **–**
131) [2002 6g⁴ Jul 31] good-topped filly: second foal: dam, 2-y-o 7f winner, out of sister to very smart sprinter Cyrano de Bergerac: 9/2, backward and very green, 13 lengths last of 4 to Judhoor in maiden at Goodwood: sold 1,800 gns. *G. Wragg*

MISS FLIRTATIOUS 5 b.m. Piccolo 121 – By Candlelight (IRE) 84 (Roi Danzig **51**
(USA)) [2002 75: f6s p6g f5g f6g f5g 6m Jun 24] tall, useful-looking mare: modest handicapper nowadays: effective at 5f/6f: acts on firm going, good to soft and fibresand: often blinkered/visored: has missed break, did so badly final start: races prominently. *D. Haydn Jones*

MISS GEORGE 4 b.f. Pivotal 124 – Brightside (IRE) 99 (Last Tycoon 131) [2002 84: **81**
5m f5g f6f⁴ f5g p7g Dec 28] big, workmanlike filly: fairly useful performer: effective at 5f/6f: acts on firm going and fibresand: tried in cheekpieces: has hung left. *D. K. Ivory*

MISS GIGI 3 br.f. Deploy 131 – Sunley Sinner 93 (Try My Best (USA) 130) [2002 78: **78**
10.3s⁶ 10g³ 10m 9g* 10m⁴ 10m⁴ 9.7m⁴ 9.7g⁴ 12m⁴ 10.2g⁶ 12.6m² 10.5f² 14f⁴ 11.8g⁴ f12g⁶ 11.6d Oct 28] quite attractive filly: fair performer: won maiden at Ripon in July: mostly creditable efforts in handicaps after: barely stays 1¾m: acts on firm and soft ground (below form on fibresand): usually patiently ridden. *M. R. Channon*

MISS GLORY BE 4 b.f. Glory of Dancer 121 – Miss Blondie (USA) (Stop The Music **64**
(USA)) [2002 42, a56: p10g³ f9.4g* f8g⁴ f11g³ f9.4g⁴ f9.4g 10g 9.9m² p10g* 10f* p10g³ 10s 10.1f⁶ f9.4s f9.4g⁶ f9.4g² f8.5g* f8.5g Dec 26] modest handicapper: won at Wolverhampton, Lingfield and Nottingham in first half of year, and at Wolverhampton (idled markedly in front) in December: effective at 8.5f, barely stays 11f: acts on all-weather and firm going: sometimes carries head awkwardly. *Miss Gay Kelleway*

MISS GRACE 2 ch.f. (Apr 8) Atticus (USA) 121 – Jetbeeah (IRE) 95 (Lomond (USA) **68 p**
128) [2002 6d⁵ Nov 1] leggy filly: sixth foal: closely related to useful 7f/1m performer Dazilyn Lady (by Zilzal), 6f winner at 2 yrs, and half-sister to winner in USA by Quiet American: dam 1m winner: 33/1 and green, 7 lengths fifth of 17 to Tante Rose in maiden at Newmarket, finishing well: sure to improve. *B. W. Hills*

MISS GRIMM (USA) 3 ch.f. Irish River (FR) 131 – Gretel 100 (Hansel (USA)) **–**
[2002 69: 9f 8f⁶ 9g f6g p10g Dec 30] first foal: dam 2-y-o 7f winner who stayed 1m: modest maiden: off course 12 months before reappearance: sold from J. Oxx, Ireland 13,000 gns after third start: blinkered, well held on all-weather in Britain last 2 outings: tongue tied second/third starts. *R. Guest*

MISS HOLLY 3 b.f. Makbul 104 – Seraphim (FR) 48 (Lashkari 128) [2002 8v³ 10m² **73**
12m⁴ 13.8f² 10.9d² 11.8g⁴ 12m* Aug 28] third living foal: dam 1¾m winner who stayed 17.5f: fair performer: won handicap at Catterick in August: will stay 1¾m: acts on good to firm and good to soft going. *M. Johnston*

MISSIE 2 ch.f. (Apr 30) Compton Place 125 – About Face (Midyan (USA) 124) [2002 **–**
5g 6d Oct 18] 2,600Y: good-topped filly: fourth foal: half-sister to fairly useful 7f winner Indian Giver (by Cadeaux Genereux): dam unraced half-sister to high-class 1m/1¼m performer Bijou d'Inde: well held in maidens: unruly at start and withdrawn in between. *G. A. Swinbank*

MISSILE TOE (IRE) 9 b.g. Exactly Sharp (USA) 121 – Debach Dust 64 (Indian **66**
King (USA) 128) [2002 63, a–: 9.7m 10d³ᵈ 10s³ 10s⁴ 10m* 10g 9m⁶ 10s⁴ 10s⁴ 8.5d² Sep **a–**
11] good-topped gelding: poor walker: fair handicapper: won at Nottingham in June: stays 1¼m: acts on firm and soft going: tried blinkered/visored (not since 1996): pulls hard. *D. Morris*

MISS INFORM 4 b.f. So Factual (USA) 120 – As Sharp As 64 (Handsome Sailor **44**
125) [2002 51, a56: 5d 5.7d 5.1f 5.1m 5g⁵ Aug 22] poor maiden: raced only at 5f/6f: acts on fibresand and any turf going. *A. Charlton*

MISSING   3 b.f. Singspiel (IRE) 133 – Misbelief 107 (Shirley Heights 130) [2002 55p: **57**
7.1m^4 8g 10m 9.9d^3 12f 16g 11.9f Oct 10] workmanlike filly: modest maiden: should be
suited by 1½m+: acts on good to firm going: blinkered final start. *T. D. Easterby*

MISSION TO MARS   3 b.g. Muhtarram (USA) 125 – Ideal Candidate 80 (Celestial   **69 §**
Storm (USA) 132) [2002 –: p10g^3 12m^4 11.6g 10.2g^5 14.1f^3 11.7d 13.8m^5 16.4g 16.2g
12f^4 Sep 17] quite good-topped gelding: fair maiden: stays 1¾m: acts on firm going:
sometimes looks none too keen: one to treat with caution. *C. A. Cyzer*

MISS ISSY (IRE)   2 b.f. (Apr 8) Victory Note (USA) 120 – Shane's Girl (IRE) (Mark-   **64**
tingo) [2002 6f 7m f8.5g^3 Dec 20] third foal: half-sister to 5-y-o Father Juninho and 4-y-o
Irish Distinction: dam unraced: modest form in maidens: third at Wolverhampton: stays
8.5f: acts on fibresand: tends to pull hard. *A. P. Jarvis*

MISS JAISY (IRE)   2 b.f. (Apr 28) Revoque (IRE) 122 – Million At Dawn (IRE) 63   –
(Fayruz 116) [2002 5.7g 6m 5.1m 7g Oct 17] 6,500 2-y-o: sixth foal: half-sister to
6-y-o Talaria: dam 2-y-o 5f winner (only season to race): well held in maidens/sellers.
J. S. Moore

MISS JINGLES   3 b.f. Muhtarram (USA) 125 – Flamingo Times 60 (Good Times   **60**
(ITY)) [2002 57: 8.2d 11.6m 8m 6f f6g* p7g^5 6.1m^3 7m 6.1g 6m^5 f6g^2 f7g^4 f6g^5 p7g p6g   **a73**
f8.5s^0 p8g Dec 21] leggy filly: fair handicapper on all-weather, modest on turf: won at
Southwell in June: effective at 6f to 8.5f: acts on good to firm ground and all-weather:
tends to get behind. *J. A. Gilbert*

MISS JOJO (IRE)   2 b. or br.f. (Apr 12) Darnay 117 – Rose Tint (IRE) (Salse (USA)   –
128) [2002 6.1g^6 6m 7.5d 6d f8.5s Dec 9] IR 1,400F, IR 3,500Y: small, close-coupled
filly: third foal: half-sister to 4-y-o Amelia: dam poor maiden: little form, including in
sellers: tried visored and in cheekpieces. *B. S. Rothwell*

MISS KRISS KROSS (IRE)   2 ch.f. (Mar 17) Kris 135 – Miss Salsa Dancer 64   **55**
(Salse (USA) 128) [2002 5s^6 6.1g^5 6g 7m 8f^5 6d Oct 14] IR 62,000F: leggy, lengthy filly:
first foal: dam, 1m winner, out of close relative to Norfolk Stakes winner Magic Mirror:
modest maiden: will need to settle to stay beyond 1m: sold 3,800
gns, sent to Sweden. *Mrs J. R. Ramsden*

MISS MANETTE   5 br.m. Dilum (USA) 115 – Lucy Manette 53 (Final Straw 127)   –
[2002 –: 8m Jul 8] little form. *P. Monteith*

MISS MIRASOL   2 b.f. (Mar 20) Sheikh Albadou 128 – Play The Game 70 (Mummy's   **92**
Game 120) [2002 5d^5 6f* 6m* 5.2f 7s 6m 6g^5 Sep 21] 18,000Y: well-grown, unfurnished
filly: half-sister to several winners, including fairly useful 1997 2-y-o 5f winner Lets Be
Fair (by Efisio) and 5-y-o Labrett: dam 2-y-o 5f winner: fairly useful performer: won
maiden at Redcar and listed event at Newmarket (by 1¾ lengths from Bishop's Lake) in
June: creditable fifth to Airwave in listed event at Ayr final start: likely to prove best at 5f/
6f: acts on firm ground: edgy sort. *K. A. Ryan*

MISS MOUGINS   4 b. or br.f. Polar Falcon (USA) 126 – Miss Bergerac (Bold Lad   –
(IRE) 133) [2002 61: 8g Apr 3] rangy, rather unfurnished filly: disappointing both starts
since eye-catching debut (ran as if something amiss only 4-y-o start). *G. Wragg*

MISS NOTERIETY   2 b.f. (Apr 28) Victory Note (USA) 120 – Mystic Maid (IRE)   –
62 (Mujtahid (USA) 118) [2002 8m 6f 5s Nov 6] 800Y: unfurnished filly: second foal:
dam, third once at 5f, out of half-sister to high-class French 1¼m performer Creator: well
beaten in maidens/seller. *C. J. Teague*

MISS OCEAN MONARCH   2 ch.f. (Apr 28) Blue Ocean (USA) 87 – Faraway Grey   **53 d**
99 (Absalom 128) [2002 7m^6 7.5g* f7g 7.5g f7g f7g Sep 30] 3,800Y: angular filly: half-
sister to 3 winners, including fairly useful 5f/6f winner Royal Dream (by Ardkinglass):
dam 2-y-o 5f winner who stayed 1m: modest performer: won seller at Beverley (for
M. Channon) in July: well held after: should stay 1m. *D. W. Chapman*

MISS OPULENCE (IRE)   3 b.f. Kylian (USA) – Oriental Splendour 85 (Runnett   **86**
125) [2002 74: 8s^2 8g 9f 8g 8g^4 7m 8.9d^4 10f 9.2s* 9.2s* 9.9d 9g^5 10g^6 Sep 20] good-
topped filly: fairly useful handicapper: left Miss V. Haigh after fifth start: won twice at
Hamilton within 7 days in June/July: stays 9.2f: acts on soft going, possibly not on firmer
than good: sometimes slowly away. *B. Ellison*

MISSOURI   4 b.f. Charnwood Forest (IRE) 125 – Medway (IRE) 60 (Shernazar 131)   **86**
[2002 84: 16m^5 16f^6 13.9g 13.3m^5 14.8m^2 14.6m 17.5g Sep 20] big, rather unfurnished
filly: fairly useful handicapper: raced only on good going or firmer: stays 2m: sometimes
races freely. *M. H. Tompkins*

MISS PEACHES 4 b.f. Emperor Jones (USA) 119 – Dear Person (Rainbow Quest –
(USA) 134) [2002 54: 8.3d May 7] quite good-topped filly: modest maiden at 3 yrs: well
held only 4-y-o start. *G. G. Margarson*

MISS PHANTINE (IRE) 4 ch.f. Be My Guest (USA) 126 – Rosananti 107 (Blush- –
ing Groom (FR) 131) [2002 –: f12s Jan 2] no form. *A. G. Newcombe*

MISS PINKERTON 3 b.f. Danehill (USA) 126 – Rebecca Sharp 122 (Machiavellian **104**
(USA) 123) [2002 81p: 8g³ 8m 7d² 7d⁴ 8d² 8.1m* 8f Oct 5] rather angular, unfurnished
filly: useful performer: won listed race at Sandown in August by ½ length from Mythic:
good second to Kithira in similar event at Deauville previous outing: stiff task and below
form in Sun Chariot Stakes at Newmarket final start: stays 1m: acts on good to firm and
good to soft ground: races prominently. *G. Wragg*

MISS PITZ 4 b.f. Cadeaux Genereux 131 – Catch The Sun (Kalaglow 132) [2002 75: **86**
10d² 10.3f³ 10.4f p10g² 12.1d 9d³ p10g⁵ p8g 10g* 10g* 12.6m³ 10d 12d⁴ Nov 1] leggy **a84**
filly: fairly useful handicapper: won at Leicester (apprentices, first run after leaving
E. Dunlop) and Ayr in September: barely stays 1½m: acts on soft going, firm and polytrack: sometimes races freely: sold 20,000 gns. *M. C. Pipe*

MISS REBECCA 4 b.f. Prince Sabo 123 – Bint Baddi (FR) (Shareef Dancer (USA) –
135) [2002 8.2m 8g 7g⁵ 6s⁶ Aug 30] smallish filly: maiden: little form: sent to Spain.
N. Tinkler

MISS SAMANTHA 4 b.f. Emarati (USA) 74 – Puella Bona 60 (Handsome Sailor **47**
125) [2002 –: f9.4g² f8g f7g f6g 9.7d 8m p6g² Dec 30] poor maiden: left M. Usher before
final start (blinkered): best effort at 6f: acts on polytrack. *K. R. Burke*

MISS SOOTY 2 b.f. (Apr 26) Sooty Tern 79 – Dawn Bell 55 (Belfort (FR) 89) [2002 –
p5g 6d f6g Dec 16] smallish filly: fifth reported foal: dam 6f winner: well held in maiden/
sellers. *J. M. Bradley*

MISS SUTTON 4 b.f. Formidable (USA) 125 – Saysana 63 (Sayf El Arab (USA) 127) –
[2002 –, a50: 11.6g 11.7g f7g 5.1d p7g p10g⁵ 7.1g⁵ 8.1g p10g Dec 30] lengthy filly: no
longer of much account. *G. F. H. Charles-Jones*

MISS T 3 b.f. Sabrehill (USA) 120 – Pourville (USA) (Manila (USA)) [2002 –p: 9.9m –
Apr 25] big, useful-looking filly: well held in maiden/claimer: dead. *J. R. Fanshawe*

MISS TAKEORTWO (IRE) 2 b.f. (Mar 25) Danehill Dancer (IRE) 117 – Princess **95**
Leona (IRE) (Naiyli (IRE)) [2002 5m⁴ 5.1f⁵ 5g⁴ 5m* 6g* 6.1g* 6g 5m 6g³ 7f Oct 5]
IR 8,000Y: unfurnished filly: first foal: dam unraced: useful performer: won maiden at
Pontefract and nursery at Leicester in July and nursery at Chester (beat Evangelist by 4
lengths) in August: good third to Airwave in listed event at Ayr penultimate start: stays
6f, possibly not 7f: raced only on good ground or firmer: sometimes slowly away/flashes
tail: sold 16,000 gns, sent to USA. *K. A. Ryan*

MISS TRIGGER 2 ch.f. (Mar 8) Double Trigger (IRE) 123 – Saint Navarro 77 (Raga –
Navarro (ITY) 119) [2002 8.3d Oct 28] 2,600Y: sixth foal: dam best at 5f: 25/1, always
behind in maiden at Windsor. *W. R. Muir*

MISS TRINITY 2 b.f. (Mar 24) Catrail (USA) 123 – Rosy Sunset (IRE) (Red Sunset **60**
120) [2002 5m⁴ f5g² 6.1m³ 6s⁵ 5.1s Oct 29] 15,000Y: sixth foal: half-sister to several **a69**
winners, including 3-y-o Pagan Sky and useful 6f (including at 2 yrs) winner Evening
Promise (by Aragon), later Grade 3 winner in US: dam, lightly-raced maiden, half-sister
to 3-y-o Bandari: fair maiden: second at Southwell: left B. McMahon and off 3 months
before below form (blinkered) final start: effective at 5f/6f: acts on fibresand and good to
firm going, possibly not on soft. *S. L. Keightley*

MISS TWTI 2 b.f. (Feb 23) Ali-Royal (IRE) 127 – Gargren (IRE) (Mujtahid (USA) **82 ?**
118) [2002 5g³ 5f 5m* 5.1d* 5.1f⁵ f5s 6.1s Oct 23] 6,000Y: angular filly: second foal:
dam unraced: fairly useful performer: made all in claimer at Leicester in June and minor
event at Chepstow (clearly best effort, beat The Kiddykid by length) in July: something
possibly amiss last 3 starts: will prove best at 5f: acts on good to firm and good to soft
going: usually races prominently. *B. Palling*

MISS ULUWATU (IRE) 3 b.f. Night Shift (USA) – Miss Kinabalu 50 (Shirley **72**
Heights 130) [2002 64: 12m² 12.6m 12.1d² 11.5f p12g 9.9d* 10m p10g Aug 21] close-
coupled filly: has a quick action: fair performer: minor event at Beverley in July: effective
at 1¼m/1½m: acts on good to firm and good to soft going. *E. J. O'Neill*

MISS VALENTINE 3 b.f. Cosmonaut – Miss Mariner (Rock Hopper 124) [2002 –: –
8m f6g 7.5m Jul 16] no form. *J. F. Coupland*

MISS WHITT (IRE) 2 b.f. (Mar 4) Whittingham (IRE) 104 – Cupid Miss (Anita's — Prince 126) [2002 6s Jul 31] closely related to 2 winning sprinters by Fayruz, including Diamond Promise (also successful at 2 yrs), and half-sister to several winners, including 3-y-o Dowhatjen: dam Irish 6f (at 2 yrs) and 1m winner: 20/1, well held in maiden at Leicester: dead. *B. Palling*

MISS WIZZ 2 b.f. (Apr 27) Wizard King 122 – Fyas 52 (Sayf El Arab (USA) 127) **55** [2002 6g 5m³ 6g 5f 5s Nov 6] lengthy filly: fifth foal: dam 2-y-o maiden who stayed 7f: modest maiden: third in seller: should stay at least 6f. *W. Storey*

MISS WOODY 3 b.f. Bin Ajwaad (IRE) 119 – Miss Doody 63 (Gorytus (USA) 132) — [2002 6s 8g⁶ 7m⁶ 10g 11.6m Jul 15] 2,400Y: fifth foal: half-sister to 1999 2-y-o 6f/7.5f seller winner Dispol Magic (by Magic Ring) and winner up to 10.5f in Italy by Mukaddamah: dam 6f (at 2 yrs) and 1¼m winner: little form. *P. Butler*

MISS YOU 2 ch.f. (Mar 11) Grand Lodge (USA) 125 – Miss Queen (USA) (Miswaki **73** (USA) 124) [2002 6f⁴ p7g 8g Oct 24] IR 40,000F, IR 300,000Y: rather unfurnished filly: first foal: dam, US 6f winner, half-sister to useful 6f/7f winner Tajannub out of half-sister to Derby third Star of Gdansk: fair form when fourth to Rondinay in maiden at Newmarket: well held in similar events after, raced freely final start; should stay 7f. *N. A. Callaghan*

MISS ZALLY 2 b.f. (May 9) Timeless Times (USA) 99 – Ohnonotagain 45 (Kind of **48** Hush 118) [2002 f5g 5g 5m 5m 5d³ 7.5g 7d⁴ 6d⁵ f8s 7.5g Sep 18] 3,000Y: small filly: has a markedly round action: second foal: dam sprint maiden: poor maiden: seems to stay 7.5f: acts on good to firm and good to soft going: hung left first 2 starts: unseated rider in paddock/got loose beforehand sixth outing: sold 800 gns. *M. E. Sowersby*

MISTERAH 3 b.f. Alhaarth (IRE) 126 – Jasarah (IRE) 70 (Green Desert (USA) 127) **105** [2002 103: 7m* 8m⁶ 8m⁴ 8g⁵ Jul 10] sturdy filly: useful performer: won Shadwell Stud Nell Gwyn Stakes at Newmarket (beat Massarra by a length) in April: creditable efforts after in 1000 Guineas at Newmarket (3 lengths sixth to Kazzia), Coronation Stakes at Royal Ascot (3½ lengths fourth to Sophisticat) and Falmouth Stakes also at Newmarket (4¾ lengths fifth to Tashawak): stayed 1m: acted on good to firm and good to soft going: raced freely: visits Kingmambo. *M. P. Tregoning*

MISTER ARJAY (USA) 2 b.c. (Mar 20) Mister Baileys 123 – Crystal Stepper (USA) **76 p** (Fred Astaire (USA)) [2002 p6g* Dec 18] $9,000F, 36,000Y: half-brother to several winners in USA, including minor stakes winner up to 1m Dash For Daylight (by Cherokee Run): dam, 8.5f/9f winner in USA, half-sister to US Grade 3 7f winner Carborundum: 7/1 and green, won 10-runner minor event at Lingfield by ½ length from Aegean Magic, slowly away but leading final 1f: should stay at least 7f: sure to improve. *G. A. Butler*

MISTER BENJI 3 b.g. Catrail (USA) 123 – Katy-Q (IRE) 58 (Taufan (USA) 119) **73** [2002 88: 7s 7.6f 7d 6s 6m⁴ 6g 5g 5m Aug 21] quite good-topped gelding: fairly useful at 2 yrs: just fair form at best in 2002: stays 6f: acts on good to firm and good to soft going: blinkered last 2 starts. *J. G. Given*

TNT July Stakes, Newmarket—Mister Links wins his third race in a row; Tacitus (No.9) and The Bonus King (rail) follow him home

MISTER CHISUM   6 b.g. Sabrehill (USA) 120 – Anchor Inn 48 (Be My Guest   –
(USA) 126) [2002 8.3d 9.2d Jul 25] well beaten on Flat in maiden and seller (slowly
away) at Hamilton. *R. Bastiman*

MISTER CLINTON (IRE)   5 ch.g. Lion Cavern (USA) 117 – Thewaari (USA) 68   **67**
(Eskimo (USA)) [2002 74: p8g⁶ p7g p7g⁵ p8g⁶ p6g p7g⁵ 7d⁵ 7d³ 7m 7m 7f⁴ 7f⁶ 8g⁴ 10m⁶
8f² 7m 9.7g 7g⁵ 8m 6.1m Oct 1] tall, lengthy gelding: fair handicapper: effective at 6f
to 1m: acts on firm going, good to soft and polytrack: tried blinkered/visored: held up.
D. K. Ivory

MISTER COSMI   3 b.c. Royal Applause 124 – Degree 81 (Warning 136) [2002 107:   **114**
7m⁶ 7m⁵ 8.1d 7m⁴ 6d 8g* 7m⁴ 8s⁵ 7d⁵ 6d Nov 17] leggy colt: fluent mover: smart
performer: won listed race at Baden-Baden (beat Alinorus 2½ lengths) in August: ran
well otherwise when fourth in Tote International Handicap (behind Crystal Castle) and
Tote Trifecta Handicap (behind Millennium Force), both at Ascot: below form in pattern
races in Italy last 3 outings: best at 7f/1m: acts on firm and soft going: blinkered after
second start: sometimes slowly away: possibly needs things his own way nowadays, and
seems best racing prominently. *M. Johnston*

MISTER DOC   4 ch.g. Most Welcome 131 – Red Poppy (IRE) 58 (Coquelin (USA)   –
121) [2002 61?: 16g 12.3g Apr 3] little form: tried blinkered. *D. W. Barker*

MISTER EMCEE   2 b.c. (Apr 29) Whittingham (IRE) 104 – Oh Whataknight 85   –
(Primo Dominie 121) [2002 5d 5m 5f f6g f5g Dec 27] 3,600Y: second foal: dam, 2-y-o 5f
winner, didn't train on: well held in maidens/sellers. *H. A. McWilliams*

MISTER H   5 b.g. Thowra (FR) – Sicilian Vespers 44 (Mummy's Game 120) [2002   –
f12g Feb 18] brother to 1¾m winner Bellara: dam, 7f seller winner, also won over
hurdles: slowly away and well held in maiden at Wolverhampton. *J. Cullinan*

MISTER LINKS (IRE)   2 b.c. (Mar 30) Flying Spur (AUS) – Lady Anna Livia   **109**
(Ahonoora 122) [2002 5s⁵ 6s* 6g* 6g² 6m² 5g Oct 6] IR 14,000F, 27,000Y: tall, good
sort: half-brother to several winners, including fairly useful 1990 2-y-o 7f winner Plan of

Coriolan Links Partnership III's "Mister Links"

Action (by Krayyan), later successful in Italy, and Irish 9f winner Karoi (by Kafu): dam won in Holland: useful performer: won maiden at Kempton and minor event at Newbury in June and TNT July Stakes at Newmarket (beat Tacitus ½ length) in July: good ½-length second in Gimcrack Stakes at York (to Country Reel) and sales race at Doncaster (behind Somnus, conceding weight all round) next 2 starts: not discredited when tenth of 20 in Prix de l'Abbaye de Longchamp: stays 6f: acts on soft and good to firm ground: genuine. *R. Hannon*

MISTER MAL (IRE) 6 b.g. Scenic 128 – Fashion Parade (Mount Hagen (FR) 127) **86** [2002 92, a–: 6s 6g 6m⁶ 6g 6f 6g 6m 6m⁴ 7m 5v 6f⁶ f7g⁴ f6g³ Dec 14] big, strong, lengthy **a74** gelding: fairly useful handicapper on turf, fair on all-weather: left D. Nicholls after seventh start: best at 6f/7f: acts on firm ground, soft and fibresand: has worn cheekpieces: often unruly at stall, and has been withdrawn after giving trouble to post: sometimes slowly away: free-going sort, usually races prominently. *R. A. Fahey*

MISTER MIND 4 b.c. Mind Games 121 – Madam Bold (Never So Bold 135) [2002 – 6f 7d 5s Jun 5] leggy colt: little form: tried blinkered. *M. Brittain*

MISTER MOUSSAC 3 b.g. Kasakov – Salu 65 (Ardross 134) [2002 –: 9g⁶ 8.3v⁵ 8m **46** 12f⁵ 12s Nov 6] tall, unfurnished gelding: poor maiden: barely stays 1½m: acts on firm ground, free-going sort. *R. Bastiman*

MISTER RAMBO 7 b.g. Rambo Dancer (CAN) 107 – Ozra 63 (Red Alert 127) **79** [2002 77d: 7v⁶ 8m⁴ 8f² 7.6f² 8.3g⁶ 8.3s⁵ 7d² 8m⁵ 6.9d⁴ 7m⁶ 7m⁴ 7.2g⁴ 8m Sep 29] strong, lengthy gelding: fair handicapper: won at Musselburgh in April and York in September: effective at 7f/1m: probably acts on any turf going: tried blinkered: usually races up with pace: sometimes carries head awkwardly/finds little. *D. Nicholls*

MISTER RUSHBY 2 b.g. (Mar 28) Hamas (IRE) 125§ – Final Rush 66 (Final Straw **55 §** 127) [2002 f5g f5g 6g 5s 5f 7f⁵ 7m* 7g 7m* 7m 7f 7d f7g f8g Dec 27] 5,500F, 7,000Y: **a– §** close-coupled gelding: half-brother to several winners abroad, including useful French miler Chrysalu (by Distant Relative): dam lightly raced: modest performer: trained first, second and twelfth starts by Miss V. Haigh, third to eleventh by B. Ellison: won sellers at Catterick in July and August: should stay 1m: acts on soft and good to firm ground, no form on all-weather: unreliable. *D. W. Chapman*

MISTER SANDERS 4 ch.g. Cosmonaut – Arroganza 62 (Crofthall 110) [2002 48: 7f – 6m 7g 12.4m 8.3v Jun 12] leggy gelding: maiden: well held in 2002: tried visored/blinkered: probably none too genuine. *R. M. Whitaker*

MISTER SWEETS 3 ch.g. Nashwan (USA) 135 – Keyboogie (USA) 97 (Lyphard **64** (USA) 132) [2002 12d f6g⁵ f8g² f8g² f6g³ Dec 27] 3,000 3-y-o: first foal: dam, 1¼m winner, daughter of US Grade 2 9.5f winner Key Dancer: modest maiden: should stay at least 1¼m: acts on fibresand. *M. C. Chapman*

MISTER WATERLINE (IRE) 3 b.g. Mujadil (USA) 119 – Cree's Figurine 63 **68 d** (Creetown 123) [2002 65, a74: p6g p5g⁴ p6g⁶ 6g⁵ 6f⁵ 7m⁵ 6m 6d 6v⁶ 5.7d⁵ 6g 6.1d **a72 d** 5g⁶ f6g⁴ f6s f6g f8g Nov 20] leggy, angular gelding: fair maiden: below form after fourth outing, leaving P. D. Evans after fourteenth one: effective at 5f/easy 6f: acts on firm ground and all-weather: tried blinkered/visored/tongue tied: has been early to post. *K. A. Ryan*

MIST 'N RAIN 3 b.f. Ezzoud (IRE) 126 – Uncharted Waters 68 (Celestial Storm – (USA) 132) [2002 66p: p10g 9.9m 10d p12g 11.6m 12m Aug 6] tall, lengthy filly: fair form only outing at 2 yrs: well held in 2002: headstrong. *C. A. Cyzer*

MIST OF TIME (IRE) 3 b.f. Danehill (USA) 126 – Lothlorien (USA) 80 (Woodman **57** (USA) 126) [2002 72p: 10s⁵ 8.1g Aug 14] angular filly: fair form only 2-y-o start: disappointing in 2002: sold 10,000 gns in December. *J. H. M. Gosden*

MISTRAL SKY 3 b.c. Hurricane Sky (AUS) – Dusk In Daytona 64 (Beveled (USA)) **54** [2002 –: 7d³ 10g Aug 7] modest maiden: stays 7f. *P. Mitchell*

MISTRESS ELLIE 3 b.f. Royal Applause 124 – Ellie Ardensky 100 (Slip Anchor **63** 136) [2002 7g 8m 8.1g 8.3m p10g³ Dec 21] 16,000Y: useful-looking filly: second foal: half-sister to 4-y-o Pole Star: dam, 9f/1¼m winner who stayed 1½m, closely related to smart performer up to 1½m Lady Shipley: modest maiden: left G. Butler 8,000 gns after second start: stays 1¼m: acts on polytrack. *J. Nicol*

MISTRESS MOUSE 3 br.f. Mistertopogigo (IRE) 118 – Perfidy (FR) (Persian Bold – 123) [2002 –: p6g Feb 13] little form. *T. M. Jones*

MISTRESS PAGE   4 b.f. Beveled (USA) – Pallomere 85 (Blue Cashmere 129) [2002   –
7s p8g 6g Oct 28] sister to 1m winner Inclination and half-sister to 3 winners abroad: dam
1m winner: no show in maidens. *E. A. Wheeler*

MISTY DANCER   3 gr.g. Vettori (IRE) 119 – Light Fantastic 66 (Deploy 131) [2002   73
75: 10g³ 8g³ 10m 7.1d Jul 5] good-topped gelding: fair maiden: barely stays 1¼m: acts
on good to firm going: races freely. *G. L. Moore*

MISTY EYED (IRE)   4 gr.f. Paris House 123 – Bold As Love (Lomond (USA) 128)   103
[2002 112: a6f 6f 5m 5g 6d 5g⁵ 5m 5m Sep 12] smallish, strong, useful-looking
filly: smart at 3 yrs, just useful form at best in 2002, mainly in pattern company: best
effort when fifth to Agnetha in King George Stakes at Goodwood: effective at 5f/6f: yet
to race on soft/heavy going, acts on any other turf, ran poorly on dirt on reappearance.
Mrs P. N. Dutfield

MISTY MAGIC   5 b.m. Distinctly North (USA) 115 – Meadmore Magic 68 (Man-   –
singh (USA) 120) [2002 –: p6g f6g p6g f6g p6g Mar 16] neat mare: no longer of much
account. *D. K. Ivory*

MISTY MAN (USA)   4 ch.g. El Gran Senor (USA) 136 – Miasma (USA) 92 (Lear   –
Fan (USA) 130) [2002 56+: 10g 10g 11.6s 8g f9.4f 8.3d Oct 14] lengthy, angular gelding:
disappointing maiden: tried visored. *Miss J. Feilden*

MITAWA (IRE)   3 b.f. Alhaarth (IRE) 126 – Susquehanna Days (USA) 68 (Chief's   –
Crown (USA)) [2002 73+: 12.3f 8d 8m f8s Sep 17] strong filly: fair at 2 yrs: well held in
2002: sold 27,000 gns in December. *B. W. Hills*

MITCHAM (IRE)   6 br.g. Hamas (IRE) 125§ – Arab Scimetar (IRE) (Sure Blade   107
(USA) 130) [2002 99: 6g⁸ 5.1m³ 5m 6m⁴ 5m Sep 29] strong gelding: usually impresses
in appearance: useful handicapper: won at Kempton in April by 2½ lengths from Sussex
Lad: subsequently below form, off 4 months through injury after next start: best at 5f/6f:
acts on good to firm going, probably on soft: blinkered final 4-y-o outing: has found little:
none too consistent. *T. G. Mills*

MITCHELLA (IRE)   3 ch.f. Persian Bold 123 – Maysoura (Nishapour (FR) 125)   75
[2002 8.3m⁴ 8.2g³ 8g³ 9d Jul 3] unfurnished filly: sixth foal: dam ran twice in France: fair
maiden: should be suited by 1¼m: has found little: sold €7,500. *L. M. Cumani*

MITREBEENJANE   3 b.f. Beveled (USA) – Jane Herring (Nishapour (FR) 125)   –
[2002 –: 8d 7m 6d 6m Aug 26] no form. *D. J. S. ffrench Davis*

MITSUKI   3 b.f. Puissance 110 – Surrealist (ITY) (Night Shift (USA)) [2002 86: 5m⁵   91 §
5.1g⁶ 6d⁴ 5g 5m 5f⁴ 6g 5g⁴ 6.1m 5.2m⁵ 6f 6f Oct 12] big filly: fairly useful handicapper:
effective at 5f/6f: acts on firm going, possibly not on good to soft: unreliable. *J. D. Bethell*

MIXED MARRIAGE (IRE)   4 ch.g. Indian Ridge 123 – Marie de Flandre (FR) 109   57
(Crystal Palace (FR) 132) [2002 65: p10g p12g p13g⁴ Dec 28] quite attractive gelding:
modest maiden handicapper: probably stays 13f: acts on polytrack (unraced on fibresand), best turf efforts on good going. *G. L. Moore*

MIZHAR (USA)   6 b. or br.g. Dayjur (USA) 137 – Futuh (USA) 95 (Diesis 133) [2002   84 d
88: p5g² p7g p5g⁶ p5g⁵ 6f* 7m² 6m² 5d f5g f7s⁵ Nov 30] sturdy gelding: fairly useful at
best in 2002: won seller at Pontefract in April: below par after fourth start, leaving
D. Nicholls after seventh: best at 5f/6f: acts on all-weather, firm and good to soft going:
usually blinkered/visored. *J. J. Quinn*

MIZILLABLACK (IRE)   3 b.f. Eagle Eyed (USA) 111 – Sketch Pad 78 (Warning   95
136) [2002 93: 5m³ 5.1g² 6m⁶ 5d 5m⁶ 5g⁵ 6g 6g Oct 2] strong filly: useful performer:
good third in listed events at Haydock (2 lengths behind Mariinsky) and Bath (beaten 1¾
lengths by Swiss Lake) in April: well below form after next start: effective at 5f/6f: acts
on firm going: blinkered (bolted to post) fifth outing: sold €40,000. *Mrs P. N. Dutfield*

MIZINKY   2 b.f. (May 11) El Conquistador 109 – Miss Pimpernel 62 (Blakeney 126)   –
[2002 p5g Apr 10] first foal: dam, 3m hurdle winner, maiden on Flat: 25/1, last in claimer
at Lingfield. *W. G. M. Turner*

MJOLNIR   5 gr.g. Casteddu 111 – Myjinka 56 (Myjinski (USA)) [2002 p8g⁶ f6g Dec   –
10] maiden: tried tongue tied. *N. A. Graham*

MOARBAN (IRE)   2 b.c. (Apr 28) Bahhare (USA) 122 – Suave Star 48 (Suave   87
Dancer (USA) 136) [2002 7f² 7g⁴ Oct 2] 75,000F, 150,000Y: leggy, useful-looking colt:
third foal: dam, maiden (ran only at 2 yrs), out of half-sister to Oaks winner Fair Salinia:
fairly useful form when 6 lengths second to Trade Fair in maiden at Newbury: favourite,
only fourth in minor event at Salisbury: will stay 1m. *M. R. Channon*

MOAT STAR (IRE)   2 b.g. (Jan 27) Whittingham (IRE) 104 – Miss Divot (IRE) 67   –
(Petardia 113) [2002 5s f5g 5f May 11] IR 5,400F, IR 6,000Y: first foal: dam only form
from 4 starts at 7f when third on debut: well held in maidens/claimer: tried blinkered.
K. A. Ryan

MOAYED   3 b.g. Selkirk (USA) 129 – Song of Years (IRE) 89 (Shareef Dancer (USA)   **91**
135) [2002 91: 9d⁵ 10.1m² 8f 8.1g p10g f9.4g Dec 26] 120,000Y: third foal: half-brother
to a winner in Hong Kong by Pursuit of Love: dam, maiden, stayed 1½m: fairly useful
performer: won maiden at Tipperary in 2001: left D. Weld, Ireland 5,500 gns after
reappearance: stays 9f: acts on heavy and good to firm going: blinkered last 2 starts at 2
yrs: tried tongue tied: sometimes slowly away. *B. R. Johnson*

MOBIL-ONE DOT COM   4 b.g. Magic Ring (IRE) 115 – Not So Generous (IRE)   **45**
68 (Fayruz 116) [2002 49: 5v³ 5m 5.9d 5s Aug 20] tall gelding: poor maiden: likely to
prove best at 5f (given test)/6f: acts on heavy and good to firm going. *J. S. Goldie*

MOBO-BACO   5 ch.g. Bandmaster (USA) 97 – Darakah 78 (Doulab (USA) 115   **62**
[2002 55: 7s³ 10.9f² 9.7m* 10d 10.9m 8m 8.1g² Jul 5] good-bodied gelding: modest
handicapper: won at Folkestone in April: best at 1m/1¼m: acts on fibresand and probably
any turf going: has wandered: often races prominently. *R. J. Hodges*

M'OUCHTY CRUA   2 b.c. (Feb 13) Octagonal (NZ) 126 – Pedestal (High Line 125)   **79**
[2002 6d⁴ 7m³ Jul 12] 27,000Y: small, well-made colt: eighth foal: half-brother to 3
winners, including useful 7f to 8.5f winner Lionize (by Storm Cat): dam once-raced
half-sister to Precocious and Jupiter Island: fair form in maidens at Haydock and York:
should stay at least 1¼m. *M. H. Tompkins*

MODEM (IRE)   5 b.g. Midhish 109 – Holy Water (Monseigneur (USA) 127) [2002   **45**
53, a41: f7s f7g f8g⁴ f7g⁵ p7g³ p8g f6g⁵ 7s⁶ 6m 7m 7f⁵ 8g Jun 9] sturdy gelding: poor   **a49**
performer: probably best at 7f/1m: acts on soft going, firm and all-weather: tried
blinkered, visored nowadays. *D. Shaw*

MOJALID   3 b. or br.g. Zafonic (USA) 130 – Affair of State (IRE) 99 (Tate Gallery   **105**
(USA) 117) [2002 8f³ 9.9m* 11.8g* 11m² a12f⁴ a10f⁶ Dec 27] 150,000Y: quite good-
topped gelding: sixth foal: half-brother to several winners, including fairly useful 6f
winner who stayed 1m Diplomat (by Deploy): dam 2-y-o 5f/6f winner: useful performer:
won maiden at Salisbury in June and handicap at Leicester (by 1½ lengths from King's
Welcome) in July: good short-head second to Optimaite in handicap at Newbury next
time (final outing for M. Tregoning): better effort for new stable when creditable fourth
in similar event at Nad Al Sheba: stays 1½m: acts on dirt, raced only on good going or
firmer on turf: has worn crossed noseband: has wandered/reared leaving stall: tends to
carry head awkwardly. *K. P. McLaughlin, UAE*

MOJO   6 gr.g. Mtoto 134 – Pepper Star (IRE) (Salt Dome (USA)) [2002 –: f8.5g 16m   –
7d 13.8g May 31] angular gelding: no form: left G. M. Moore after reappearance.
Miss A. Stokell

MOJO MAN   3 b.g. Millkom 124 – Prima Sinfonia 64 (Fairy King (USA)) [2002 70:   **67 +**
7.9f May 16] sturdy gelding: fair maiden: shaped well only 3-y-o start (gelded after): will
be suited by 1¼m+: acts on firm and soft ground. *R. Hannon*

MOLAAF   3 b.f. Shareef Dancer (USA) 135 – Amber Fizz (USA) (Effervescing   **59**
(USA)) [2002 75: 7m⁵ 6m⁴ 6m 7m 7.1m 6m⁵ f6s Sep 5] lengthy, sparely-made filly:
modest maiden: stayed 7f: raced only on good/good to firm going on turf: usually
blinkered in 2002: had run well when sweating: pulled hard/found nothing fifth outing:
stud. *C. E. Brittain*

MOLLY   3 b.f. Efisio 120 – Mohican 75 (Great Nephew 126) [2002 f8g f8g⁶ 8g Apr   –
3] half-sister to 7-y-o Colonel Custer: dam 1½m winner at 5 yrs: well held in maidens.
C. W. Thornton

MOLLY BE   2 ch.f. (Jan 31) First Trump 118 – Broughton Singer (IRE) 61 (Common   –
Grounds 118) [2002 p7g f7s Dec 7] third foal: half-sister to fairly useful 8.5f (at 2 yrs)
and 9.7f winner Keltic Bard (by Emperor Jones): dam 9f winner: well held in claimer/
maiden. *W. J. Musson*

MOLLY ELLEN (IRE)   3 b.f. Fayruz 116 – Magic Melody 62 (Petong 126) [2002   **66**
73: 7m p7g 6g* 6s 7m Jun 25] IR 43,000Y: first foal: dam, maiden best at 6f at 2 yrs,
half-sister to useful sprinters Rosselli, Heather Bank and Dancing Music: fair performer:
trained at 2 yrs by D. Weld in Ireland: won minor event at Brighton in May: effective at
6f/7f: acts on good to firm ground, well held on softer than good: has been blinkered

(including for win), visored final start: tongue tied last 3: sold 8,000 gns, sent to South Korea. *D. E. Cantillon*

MOLLY MALONE 5 gr.m. Formidable (USA) 125 – Pharland (FR) (Bellypha 130) **43**
[2002 60: 5.1g 5.7g p7g 6f 7m Jul 4] leggy, workmanlike mare: poor maiden handicapper: stays 1m: acts on good to firm going, possibly not on softer than good: tried blinkered/visored: has started slowly/drifted right. *J. C. Tuck*

MOLLY MONASH (IRE) 2 b.f. (Feb 21) General Monash (USA) 107 – Moody **40**
Lover (Jalmood (USA) 126) [2002 6.1d⁶ 7f⁶ 7m 7f 7g f6g⁶ f7g f9.4g⁶ Dec 7] IR 1,000F, IR 3,200Y: sixth living foal: half-sister to a winner abroad by Pennine Walk: dam unraced: poor maiden: stays 7f: acts on firm going and fibresand. *J. S. Moore*

MOLLYOBRIEN (IRE) 2 b.f. (Apr 5) Bluebird (USA) 125 – Madaraka (USA) 84 **65**
(Arctic Tern (USA) 126) [2002 5s 6s 7s 6d 6g 5.5s f5g Dec 16] IR 8,500F, IR 7,500Y: third foal: dam Irish 1¼m winner: fair maiden: well held at Wolverhampton final start: stays 6f: raced only on good going or softer on turf. *P. Henley, Ireland*

MOLLY'S SECRET 4 b.f. Minshaanshu Amad (USA) 91§ – Secret Miss 55 **51**
(Beveled (USA)) [2002 61: p12g p10g⁶ 10f 11.5m 9m³ 9m⁵ 10.2f³ p10g* 8.5d 10.2g **a59**
f9.4g² p10g Dec 18] modest handicapper: won at Lingfield in August: best form around 9f/1¼m: acts on all-weather and firm ground: has taken good hold/carried head awkwardly: difficult ride. *C. G. Cox*

MOLOKO (USA) 3 b. or br.f. Boundary (USA) 117 – Future Starlet (USA) (Theat- **64**
rical 128) [2002 54: f8.5g* f9.4g⁵ p8g 8.5m⁵ 10m⁵ Oct 3] modest handicapper: won at Wolverhampton in June: stays 1¼m: acts on fibresand and good to firm going: tried tongue tied. *J. W. Hills*

MOLOTOV 2 b.g. (May 17) Efisio 120 – Mindomica 63 (Dominion 123) [2002 6g **68**
f6f³ f7g⁵ f6s* Dec 26] fifth living foal: brother to 4-y-o Minderoo and half-brother to 3-y-o Minstrel Hall: dam, 7f winner, half-sister to Fred Darling winner/Oaks fourth Sueboog, herself dam of 5-y-o Best of The Bests: fair maiden: won claimer at Wolverhampton by 2 lengths from Glenview Polly: should stay 7f: acts on fibresand, some promise only run on turf. *C. W. Thornton*

MOMENT 3 ch.f. Nashwan (USA) 135 – Well Away (IRE) (Sadler's Wells (USA) **79**
132) [2002 59p: 7g² May 3] smallish, sturdy filly: better effort in maidens when 1½ lengths second to Ludynosa at Newmarket, only 3-y-o start, rallying: stud. *J. H. M. Gosden*

MOMENTOUS JONES 5 b.g. Emperor Jones (USA) 119 – Ivory Moment (USA) **52**
(Sir Ivor 135) [2002 50: 15.4m³ 11.9g May 2] leggy gelding: modest maiden handicapper: stays 2m: acts on heavy and good to firm going: has started slowly. *M. Madgwick*

MONACLE 8 b.g. Saddlers' Hall (IRE) 126 – Endless Joy 90 (Law Society (USA) **40**
130) [2002 36: f12s³ f16g⁴ f16g³ f16g² Feb 14] big gelding: blind on his off-side: poor handicapper: stays 2m: acts on fibresand and firm ground: tried blinkered: has been slowly away/looked ungenuine. *John Berry*

MONASH LADY (IRE) 4 ch.f. General Monash (USA) 107 – Don't Be That Way **74 d**
(IRE) (Dance of Life (USA)) [2002 65, a76: p12g p12g⁵ p10g³ p12g p12g 10d* 9.9g*
10f² p10g⁴ 12.3g 12d 10m p10g p10g Dec 21] workmanlike filly: fair handicapper: won at Windsor and Beverley (ladies) in May: well below par last 5 starts: effective at 1¼m/1½m: acts on firm going, good to soft and polytrack: sometimes slowly away. *J. S. Moore*

MONCHIQUE 2 br.f. (Apr 30) Makbul 104 – Steadfast Elite (IRE) 58 (Glenstal **55**
(USA) 118) [2002 5m 5.1f 5.2f 5v³ 6.1m Aug 26] 10,000Y: tall, leggy filly: third foal: sister to 2000 2-y-o 6f winner Ebullience and 3-y-o Dudleys Delight: dam, 5f (at 2 yrs) to 11f winner, also successful over hurdles: modest maiden: trained by A. Berry first 2 starts: should stay 6f: acts on any turf going: reared leaving stall final start: sold 1,000 gns. *J. G. Given*

MONDURU 5 b.g. Lion Cavern (USA) 117 – Bint Albadou (IRE) 91 (Green Desert **53**
(USA) 127) [2002 53: f9.4g⁴ f8.5g⁴ 7f³ 10.9m 8f 9g Oct 5] good-topped gelding: modest maiden: stays easy 1¼m: acts on fibresand and any turf going: tried blinkered: sometimes carries head high. *Miss G. Browne*

MONEYBAGS (IRE) 2 b.c. (May 14) Petorius 117 – Creggan Vale Lass (Simply **–**
Great (FR) 122) [2002 7g Oct 24] IR 7,500F: sixth living foal: brother to 5-y-o Keltech Gold and half-brother to a winner in Turkey by Ile de Chypre: dam poor Irish maiden: 25/1, well held in maiden at Brighton. *B. Palling*

MONICA GELLER 4 b.f. Komaite (USA) – Rion River (IRE) (Taufan (USA) 119) **60**
[2002 86, a59+: p8g p10g p12g 8m 8g 12d 10.3v Nov 8] leggy filly: modest handicapper: **a52**
left C. Allen after third start: stays 9f: acts on all-weather, soft and good to firm going:
tried visored: sometimes slowly away. *J. W. Payne*

MONKSFORD 3 b.g. Minster Son 130 – Mortify (Prince Sabo 123) [2002 73: 7.1m⁵ **70**
8m³ 9.2g² 10g² 9.3s⁴ 9m⁵ 8.3d* 8g 9.1g 8.3m Sep 30] leggy gelding: fair performer: won
maiden at Hamilton in July: stays easy 9f: acts on firm and good to soft going: has
wandered: races prominently: sold 8,000 gns. *Denys Smith*

MONKSTON POINT (IRE) 6 b.g. Fayruz 116 – Doon Belle (Ardoon 124) [2002 **111**
114: 6d* 5m³ 5g 6.3d 6v² 6.1g⁴ 6d⁶ 6g 6v Nov 9] sturdy, good sort: smart performer: won
listed race at Windsor (beat Patsy's Double by 2 lengths) in May: creditable efforts after
in Temple Stakes at Sandown (third to Kyllachy), Holsten-Trophy at Hamburg (second to
El Gran Lode) and Prix de Meautry at Deauville (sixth to Crystal Castle): effective at 5f/
6f: has form on good to firm ground, goes very well on softer than good: wears visor: has
been bandaged: has been early to post. *D. W. P. Arbuthnot*

MON PERFORMER 8 ch.g. Mon Tresor 113 – Hot Performer (Hotfoot 126) [2002 **–**
f14s 12.1m Sep 24] leggy, good-topped gelding: has been freeze fired on shins: very
lightly raced, and no form. *D. W. Barker*

MON PETIT DIAMANT 2 b.f. (Mar 14) Hector Protector (USA) 124 – Desert Girl **54**
(Green Desert (USA) 127) [2002 7.1g 6.1m 6g 7d f6s Nov 2] smallish filly: sixth foal:
half-sister to fairly useful 1997 2-y-o 6f winner Moontabeh (by Mujtahid) and 5-y-o
Spanish Star: dam, lightly-raced maiden, out of St Simon Stakes winner Upend: modest
maiden: clearly best effort second start: should stay at least 7f. *M. Wigham*

MON PETITE (IRE) 3 ch.f. General Monash (USA) 107 – Wide Outside (IRE) 50 **53**
(Don't Forget Me 127) [2002 57: 7m⁶ 5d 6d⁶ 6g² 7f 7.9g 8m² 7.9s⁵ 8m 7.9m 8m 7f 7s f6g
Nov 15] small filly: modest handicapper: stays 1m: acts on good to firm and good to soft
going: often visored/blinkered: none too consistent. *J. A. Glover*

MONSAL DALE (IRE) 3 ch.g. Desert King (IRE) 129 – Zanella (IRE) 87 (Nordico **59**
(USA)) [2002 65: 8d⁵ 8g⁴ 8m f12g Dec 14] strong gelding: modest maiden: left J. Toller/
off 3 months after third start: stays 1m: yet to race on extremes of going on turf: has
started slowly/raced freely. *B. J. Llewellyn*

MON SECRET (IRE) 4 b.g. General Monash (USA) 107 – Ron's Secret 92 (Efisio **54**
120) [2002 65: p7g* f8.5g⁵ p7g 7.1m² 8d 7.5g 6.9d⁶ 7m 7m 8s 7.5m 8m⁶ Oct 2] sparely-
made gelding: modest handicapper: won apprentice event at Lingfield in February: stays
1m: acts on polytrack, good to soft and good to firm ground. *J. L. Eyre*

MONSIEUR BOND (IRE) 2 ch.c. (Mar 6) Danehill Dancer (IRE) 117 – Musical **109**
Essence 65 (Song 132) [2002 6m² 6m* 6d* 6m⁵ 6m² 6m³ Oct 5] 10,000F, 36,000Y:
close-coupled, useful-looking colt: closely related to 4-y-o Up Tempo and half-brother
to 3 winners: useful performer: won maiden at Pontefract in July and
minor event at Windsor in August: good placed efforts in Mill Reef Stakes at Newbury
(¾-length second to Zafeen) and Two-Year-Old Trophy at Redcar (third to Somnus) last
2 starts: will probably stay 7f: yet to race on extremes of going. *B. Smart*

MONSIEUR BOULANGER 2 ch.c. (Apr 3) Compton Place 125 – Songsheet 74 **91**
(Dominion 123) [2002 5g⁶ 5f* 5m⁴ 6d² 6m* 5.2f 6.1f⁴ 6m Sep 11] 12,500F, 26,000Y:
rather leggy, good-topped colt: second foal: dam best at 5f: fairly useful performer: won
maiden at Kempton in April and minor event at Goodwood in June: best effort when
runner-up in listed race at Epsom: likely to prove best at 5f/6f: acts on firm and good to
soft ground: sold 25,000 gns: sent to USA. *R. Hannon*

MONTANA 2 b.c. (Mar 9) Puissance 110 – Mistral's Dancer (Shareef Dancer (USA) **85 ?**
135) [2002 6m³ 5g⁶ Aug 27] 11,000Y: tall colt: half-brother to several winners, including
3-y-o Brocketeer and fairly useful 5f (at 2 yrs) to 11.6f winner Queen's Pageant (by Risk
Me): dam, maiden, best at 7f: 2/1-on, seemed to show fairly useful form when 3¼ lengths
last of 3 to Salcombe in newcomers event at Ascot in July, fading: again favourite, only
sixth of 8 to Tilak in minor event at Ripon following month: took strong hold both starts,
and will need to learn to settle. *R. Hannon*

MONTANA BLUE 5 b.m. Batshoof 122 – Mountain Bluebird (USA) 79 (Clever **?**
Trick (USA)) [2002 14d 13.5g* 12g⁵ 11.6s Jun 10] 8,000Y: half-sister to several winners,
including useful stayer Anchor Clever (by Slip Anchor): dam 1m winner: won handicaps

at Sterrebeek (2) and Ostend in 2001 and another handicap at Ostend in May: well held in claimer at Windsor final start: seems to stay 2½m: acts on firm ground and dirt: often visored/blinkered. *Paul Smith, Belgium*

MONTANA MOON (IRE)   3 b.g. Ajraas (USA) 88 – Batilde (IRE) (Victory Piper – (USA) 100) [2002 64, a57: 5f 7m 7m 8.1m Sep 6] small gelding: modest maiden at 2 yrs: well held in 2002: tried visored. *R. A. Fahey*

MONTE CARLO (IRE)   5 b.g. Rainbows For Life (CAN) – Roberts Pride 62   **84** (Roberto (USA) 131) [2002 –: f12g8 16g4 14.4m 14d May 23] big, close-coupled gelding: had a quick action: useful at 2/3 yrs: just fairly useful in 2002: won minor event at Wolverhampton in March: stayed 2m: winner on fibresand/good to firm going, best form on softer than good: dead. *L. Montague Hall*

MONTECASSINO ABBEY (IRE)   3 b.g. Danehill (USA) 126 – Battle Mountain   **84** (IRE) (Dancing Brave (USA) 140) [2002 77: 7g5 7m 7.1m4 p7g3 8g3 8d* 8m 7g 8m4 8m5   **a93** 7.1m5 8f3 p7g8 Dec 11] sturdy gelding: fairly useful performer: won maiden at Brighton in July and handicap at Lingfield (wore cheekpieces) in December: effective at 7f/1m: acts on polytrack, good to soft and good to firm going: effective visored or not: often races freely: has found little. *P. W. Harris*

MONTECRISTO   9 br.g. Warning 136 – Sutosky 78 (Great Nephew 126) [2002 95:   **84** 13s 14s 11.9d 11.9g 12d* 11.9d* 13.1g* a16g4 12g4 18m 16s6 f16g6 Dec 4] leggy, sparely-made gelding: fairly useful performer: won apprentice handicap at Epsom and small-field minor events at Carlisle and Ayr in July: effective at 1½m to 2m: acts on good to firm going, heavy and fibresand/dirt: held up: has won twice for lady rider. *R. Guest*

MONTE MAYOR LAD (IRE)   2 b.c. (Feb 26) Sesaro (USA) 81 – Alcalali (USA)   **76** 96 (Septieme Ciel (USA) 123) [2002 7g4 6d2 6m Sep 13] 14,000Y: good-bodied colt: first foal: dam, maiden on Flat who was fourth in Ribblesdale Stakes, winning hurdler: fair maiden: second to Isolde's Idol at Haydock: should stay 7f. *D. Haydn Jones*

MONTESSORI MIO (FR)   3 b.g. Robellino (USA) 127 – Child's Play (USA)   **61** (Sharpen Up 127) [2002 63: 12.3m3 12.1g May 21] good-topped gelding: modest maiden handicapper: barely stays 1½m: acts on fibresand and good to firm going: joined Mrs M. Reveley. *M. Johnston*

MONTE VERDE (IRE)   2 b.f. (Mar 10) Whittingham (IRE) 104 – Anita's Love   **60** (IRE) 53 (Anita's Prince 126) [2002 5g4 5.1g3 6.1d6 5.1m f5s p6g3 Dec 21] IR 4,400Y: smallish filly: fifth foal: closely related to 1998 2-y-o 5f winner Thornaby Girl (by Fayruz): dam sprint maiden: modest maiden: stays easy 6f: acts on polytrack, best turf efforts on good going. *B. Palling*

MONTEZ (USA)   3 ch.c. Royal Academy (USA) 130 – Omara (USA) 87 (Storm Cat   **64** (USA)) [2002 7m4 6g 7s6 Oct 22] 180,000Y: rangy, angular colt: first foal: dam, won around 1¼m, half-sister to smart performer up to 1½m Etizaaz, out of half-sister to Swain: best effort in maidens when fourth to Clematis at Salisbury on debut: tongue tied (stumbled and all but fell) second start: sold 4,000 gns. *J. Noseda*

MONTMARTRE (IRE)   2 b.f. (May 3) Grand Lodge (USA) 125 – French Quarter   **74** (Ile de Bourbon (USA) 133) [2002 6m4 7m* Jul 2] IR 10,000Y: tall, unfurnished filly: seventh foal: half-sister to 3 winners, including 7f/1m winner Broughton's Pride (by Superpower): dam, French 1¼m to 11.5f winner, half-sister to high-class performer up to 1¼m Executive Pride: fair form: justified favouritism in 4-runner maiden at Yarmouth by length from Literacy: looked open to improvement. *N. A. Callaghan*

MONTOSARI   3 ch.g. Persian Bold 123 – Sartigila 67 (Efisio 120) [2002 p10g 8.1m   **51** 7m 8m5 8d f12g4 Dec 2] third foal: half-brother to 4-y-o Alfano: dam 6f and 1m winner: modest maiden handicapper: barely stays 1½m: acts on all-weather and good to firm ground. *P. Mitchell*

MONTOYA (IRE)   3 b.g. Kylian (USA) – Saborinie 56 (Prince Sabo 123) [2002 74?:   **71** p8g p8g 10.3s4 10g3 11.6g2 11.6s3 11g 11.9d3 f12g 8.3d4 10g2 9s Oct 25] close-coupled   **a–** gelding: fair maiden handicapper: stays 1½m: acts on firm and soft ground: often races prominently. *P. D. Cundell*

MONTURANI (IRE)   3 b.f. Indian Ridge 123 – Mezzogiorno 108 (Unfuwain (USA)   **112** 131) [2002 77P: 7m2 8d* 10f* 10f* 10.5m Jun 9] big, good-topped filly: has scope: smart performer: won listed races at Ascot (by short head from Dusty Answer) and Newbury (by 1¼ lengths from Protectress, quickened clear over 2f out and seemed to idle) in May:

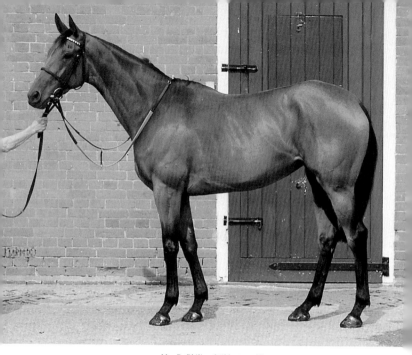

Mrs R. Philipps' "Monturani"

only ninth in Prix de Diane at Chantilly final start: suffered stress fracture of off-hind after: stays 1¼m: yet to race on soft/heavy going, acts on any other: stays in training. *G. Wragg*

MOONA'S MAGIC (IRE) 3 b.f. Inzar (USA) 112 – Moona (USA) 73 (Lear Fan (USA) 130) [2002 58: 8.1m 10g May 31] leggy filly: modest maiden: well held both 3-y-o starts. *J. M. Bradley*   –

MOON AT MIDNIGHT 2 b.c. (Apr 17) Night Shift (USA) – Mashmoon (USA) 80 (Habitat 134) [2002 5s⁴ 5s⁴ 5m* 5f⁴ 6g² 6d⁶ 5.1d² 5v* 6m⁵ 9v Nov 10] 17,000F, 21,000Y: strong, useful-looking colt: half-brother to several winners, including fairly useful winner around 1m Talathath (by Soviet Star): dam, 6f (at 2 yrs) and 1m winner, half-sister to very smart French middle-distance filly Galla Placidia: fairly useful performer: won maiden at Folkestone in April and minor event at Ayr in June: good second in minor events at Ayr (short-headed by Helm Bank) and Bath: left M. Channon and off 4½ months before soundly beaten in listed race at Leopardstown (tongue tied) final start: stays 6f: acts on good to firm and heavy going. *R. J. Osborne, Ireland*   **86**

MOON AT NIGHT 7 gr.g. Pursuit of Love 124 – La Nureyeva (USA) 83 (Nureyev (USA) 131) [2002 60: 8.1m* 10m 7.1g 8f 8m Sep 5] leggy gelding: modest handicapper: won amateur event at Warwick in June: stays 1m: acts on firm and good to soft going: visored once at 6 yrs: front runner: none too consistent. *W. S. Kittow*   **54**

MOON BALLAD (IRE) 3 ch.c. Singspiel (IRE) 133 – Velvet Moon (IRE) 108 (Shaadi (USA) 126) [2002 98p: a9f* a10f⁴ 10g² 10.4f* 12d³ 9.9m* 10m² Oct 19] The team of horses which made the annual transfer from the David Loder 'nursery' to the Godolphin set-up after the 2001 turf season looked as formidable as usual. In the event, however, only Moon Ballad, a once-raced maiden at the end   **124**

of 2001, made a significant impact in the latest season. Dubai Destination, Silent Honor and Kriskova, all among those from the Loder stable in the 'top hundred' two-year-olds in *Racehorses of 2001*, managed just a single outing between them for Godolphin in 2002, while Moon Ballad developed into a very smart performer in a seven-race campaign.

Moon Ballad passed the post first in a maiden at Newmarket in September on his only start at two but carried his nearest challenger across the track, resulting in the placings being reversed. He soon made up for that demotion in his second season, winning a minor event at Nad Al Sheba on his return by a wide margin and finishing a creditable fourth to stable-companion Essence of Dubai in the UAE Derby before being sent to Britain. Moon Ballad lined up as a 13/2 chance for the Convergent Dante Stakes at York in May twelve days after finishing a short-head second to Highdown (purchased by Godolphin later in the season) in a listed race at Newmarket. Jamie Spencer, who was on board for all Moon Ballad's races in Britain in the latest season, dictated the pace and they were always in control after quickening clear around three furlongs out. Runner-up Bollin Eric stayed on really well to be beaten a length and a quarter, with Balakheri a further three quarters of a length back in third and Where Or When fourth. The Dante hadn't looked a particularly strong renewal beforehand and, unusually, the result made little impact on the ante-post market for the Derby, Moon Ballad being available at as long as 33/1, around double the odds of his stable-companion Naheef. The bookies were unimpressed with Moon Ballad's performance and connections seemed in agreement, Godolphin's Simon Crisford saying 'If he'd been ready, Naheef would have been our Dante runner and he remains number one in the pecking order.' The Godolphin camp clearly expected Naheef to show himself a different horse in the Derby from the one who flopped in the Two Thousand Guineas and Frankie Dettori's decision to partner him, rather than Moon Ballad, helped to make Naheef 5/1 fourth favourite, Moon Ballad sent off at 20/1 on the day. The ride on Moon Ballad was Jamie Spencer's first in the Derby and coincided with his twenty-second birthday. Interestingly, Spencer has yet to ride a winner at Epsom, from admittedly limited opportunities, but he and Moon Ballad led home the British-based challenge in the Derby, Moon Ballad finishing fourteen lengths third to High Chaparral, twelve lengths behind runner-up Hawk Wing. Increasingly on edge during the preliminaries and setting a breakneck pace up the hill, Moon Ballad was sent on again rounding the home turn but had no answer when the two Ballydoyle contenders appeared alongside. As in the Guineas, Naheef faded tamely once push came to shove and finished seventh.

Off the course for over three months following his very hard race at Epsom, Moon Ballad was returned to ten furlongs in the Select Stakes at Goodwood in September. Starting at odds on, he justified punters' faith in him with an impressive performance, running on well under just hands and heels after being allowed to dictate the pace and, despite being eased near the line, still having two and a half lengths to spare over runner-up Sir George Turner, breaking the course record in the process. Moon Ballad was aimed at the Champion Stakes at Newmarket the following month, his final race of the season, and Dettori again passed him over, this time favouring Noverre. In fairness, the pair looked fairly evenly matched on form beforehand, but it was Moon Ballad who again came out best of the

Convergent Dante Stakes, York—Moon Ballad is comfortably holding Bollin Eric (white star on face), Balakheri, Where Or When (left) and Jelani (rail)

Godolphin runners. Starting favourite at 5/2, with Noverre at 9/2, Moon Ballad put up a career-best performance in finishing half a length second to Storming Home. Tracking the third Godolphin runner Equerry, Moon Ballad took over approaching the final two furlongs and kept on really well after the winner edged ahead of him just under a furlong later. Noverre finished three quarters of a length back in third, with Equerry fading to finish ninth.

Moon Ballad (IRE) (ch.c. 1999)	Singspiel (IRE) (b 1992)	In The Wings (b 1986)	Sadler's Wells
			High Hawk
		Glorious Song (b 1976)	Halo
			Ballade
	Velvet Moon (IRE) (b 1991)	Shaadi (b 1986)	Danzig
			Unfurled
		Park Special (b 1984)	Relkino
			Balilla

The strong, lengthy Moon Ballad impresses in appearance. A 350,000-guinea yearling, he is from the first crop of Singspiel, who improved with every season that he raced and gained five Group 1 victories in his last seven outings, including the Japan Cup and Dubai World Cup. Moon Ballad's dam Velvet Moon, a somewhat quirky individual, won three times over six furlongs as a two-year-old (including the Lowther Stakes) and also won a listed event at a mile and a quarter as a three-year-old. Moon Ballad is Velvet Moon's third living foal, the only other one to make the track being the first of those, the useful Velvet Lady (by Nashwan), who raced only as a three-year-old, winning a mile maiden after finishing sixth in the One Thousand Guineas on her second start. Velvet Moon, who was sold for 875,000 guineas in foal to Daylami in December as part of the dispersal of the late

Godolphin's "Moon Ballad"

MOO

Fahd Salman's Newgate Stud, is a half-sister to the In The Wings pair Central Park and Mellow Park. The former was very smart, numbering the Vintage Stakes at Goodwood and the Derby Italiano at Rome among his wins. He ended his career with a second in the Melbourne Cup. The smart Mellow Park was campaigned in pattern company over middle distances in the latest season and won the Lancashire Oaks. Moon Ballad's grandam Park Special was lightly raced and gained her only victory in a maiden over a mile and a quarter in Ireland.

Moon Ballad may have inherited some of his dam's temperament. He did, as already stated, become increasingly on edge before the Derby and carried his head a bit high in the UAE Derby. He has also edged left under pressure on occasions, though, encouragingly, seemed to become more straightforward as the year went on. Usually a front runner, Moon Ballad has so far shown his very best form at around a mile and a quarter, though he may yet prove capable of showing comparable form at a mile and a half given the opportunity under less testing conditions than at Epsom. He has yet to race on soft or heavy ground but acts on any other turf going and on dirt. He was tongue tied on his last six appearances and visored on the first four of those. The Dubai World Cup will reportedly be the starting point for Moon Ballad's four-year-old campaign. He will probably need to progress further to win but, however he fares at Nad Al Sheba, appeals as the type his stable should do well with in 2003. *Saeed bin Suroor*

MOON COLONY   9 b.g. Top Ville 129 – Honeymooning (USA) (Blushing Groom (FR) 131) [2002 55: f14.8s 14.1d 14.1g Jun 15] quite attractive gelding: one-time fairly useful handicapper: no form in 2002: tried blinkered. *A. L. Forbes*   –

MOON EDGE   3 gr.f. Beveled (USA) – Zamoon (Zambrano) [2002 f9.4g⁴ Dec 16] fourth reported foal: half-sister to 6f winner Moon Fairy (by Interrex): dam unraced: 6/1, 7¾ lengths fourth of 13 to Red Storm in maiden at Wolverhampton. *M. P. Tregoning*   43

MOON EMPEROR   5 b.g. Emperor Jones (USA) 119 – Sir Hollow (USA) (Sir Ivor 135) [2002 108: 12s³ 16.2d 14d⁵ 20m 16.1d³ 14m³ 16.2d² 13.9m 16.2g⁴ 16d⁶ Nov 1] tall, close-coupled gelding: useful performer: mostly creditable efforts in 2002 (though flattered in Gold Cup at Royal Ascot fourth start), including in handicaps at Goodwood (third to Scott's View in Prestige Stakes) and Ascot (15 lengths second to Mana D'Argent) on sixth/seventh outings: stays 2m: acts on soft and good to firm going: held up: very free to post sixth start. *J. R. Jenkins*   105

MOON JAGUAR (IRE)   2 b.c. (Mar 3) Bahhare (USA) 122 – Top of The Form (IRE) 79 (Masterclass (USA) 116) [2002 p7g 7d f7g f8.5g⁶ Dec 20] 25,000F, 21,000Y, 40,000 2-y-o: first foal: dam, 5f (including at 2 yrs)/6f winner, half-sister to useful 5f performers Double Quick and Speedy James: modest form in maidens: stays 8.5f. *J. G. Given*   52

MOONLIGHT DANCER   4 b.g. Polar Falcon (USA) 126 – Guanhumara (Caerleon (USA) 132) [2002 73, a61+: 8m 8g Jun 9] lengthy, quite attractive gelding: fair form at 3 yrs: well held in 2002. *K. R. Burke*   –

MOONLIGHTING   5 b.m. Lugana Beach 116 – White Flash 39 (Sure Blade (USA) 130) [2002 –: p12g p10g⁵ p10g p10g 11.9m May 15] form (modest) only on second outing: blinkered/visored last 4 starts. *B. R. Johnson*   a51

MOONLIGHT SONG (IRE)   5 b.m. Mujadil (USA) 119 – Model Show (IRE) 82 (Dominion 123) [2002 57, a71d: f7g⁴ f6g⁵ f7g⁴ f7g f7g⁶ 6g 7.2v* 8m⁶ 7m 8.3g³ 6.9s³ 7m 7.1m 7g f7g⁶ f7g 6v f6g Nov 25] modest handicapper: won at Ayr in June: effective at 7f/easy 1m: acts on fibresand, heavy and good to firm going: usually races prominently: none too consistent. *John A. Harris*   63 a53

MOON MAN   2 b.g. (Mar 3) Cosmonaut – Little Unknown (Known Fact (USA) 135) [2002 f6g f7g Nov 25] 500Y: fifth living foal: dam unraced: slowly away and always behind in claimer/seller at Southwell. *P. D. Evans*   –

MOON MASTER   4 b.c. Primo Dominie 121 – Sickle Moon (Shirley Heights 130) [2002 43: f8g Feb 7] poor maiden: probably stayed 1¼m: tried blinkered: dead. *J. A. Osborne*   –

MOONRAKING   9 gr.g. Rusticaro (FR) 124 – Lunaire (Try My Best (USA) 130) [2002 –§, a39§: f12g f16g f16.2g Feb 8] close-coupled gelding: moody performer: usually blinkered/visored. *W. Clay*   – §

MOON ROCKET (IRE)   2 b.c. (Apr 27) Alzao (USA) 117 – Osmunda (Mill Reef (USA) 141) [2002 6m 8.1g 7.1m⁴ f7f Nov 29] IR 26,000Y: good-bodied colt: half-brother   63 to several winners, including useful 1½m to 2m winner Rum Pointer (by Turtle Island) and fairly useful stayer Icecapped (by Caerleon): dam Irish 1¼m winner: best effort (still burly, modest form) when fourth in maiden at Warwick: never going well in nursery final start: should be suited by 1¼m+. *R. Hannon*

MOON ROYALE   4 ch.f. Royal Abjar (USA) 121 – Ragged Moon 72 (Raga Navarro (ITY) 119) [2002 53: 8m 7g 8g 8m⁵ 8m 12d 8g⁵ 10f 9.1s Oct 15] close-coupled filly: poor handicapper: should stay 1¼m: acts on good to firm going: none too consistent. *Denys Smith*   **45**

MOONSHINE BEACH   4 b.g. Lugana Beach 116 – Monongelia 98 (Welsh Pageant 132) [2002 9.9m³ 10g⁶ p13g² 14.6s Oct 25] leggy gelding: half-brother to 3 winners, including 13f/2m winner Hattaafeh (by Mtoto): dam 1m to 1¼m winner: fair maiden: stays 13f: acts on good to firm ground and polytrack: looked none too keen third start. *P. W. Hiatt*   **73**

MOONSPRITE   2 b.f. (Apr 7) Seeking The Gold (USA) – Moonshell (IRE) 117 (Sadler's Wells (USA) 132) [2002 7g³ 8s³ Oct 26] lengthy filly: third foal: half-sister to 4-y-o Alunissage: dam, 1m (at 2 yrs) and 1½m (Oaks) winner, sister to 5-y-o Hatha Anna and half-sister to smart performer up to 15f Ocean of Storms: third in minor event at Newmarket and maiden at Newbury, staying on having been short of room when beaten 2 lengths by Midas Way in latter: should be suited by 1¼m+: potentially useful, and sure to win races. *E. A. L. Dunlop*   **82 p**

MOORTOP LADY   3 b.f. Mtoto 134 – Octavia Girl 104 (Octavo (USA) 115) [2002 44: p8g⁶ f9.4g⁵ Feb 4] poor maiden in 2001: well held both 3-y-o starts. *J. L. Eyre*   **–**

MOOT (FR)   3 b.f. Mtoto 134 – Arusha (IRE) 84 (Dance of Life (USA)) [2002 p10g⁵ f9.4g p10g 10g 16.2g Aug 26] fifth foal: dam, 2-y-o 1m winner, half-sister to 2000 Guineas winner Don't Forget Me: poor maiden: stays 1¼m. *J. A. Osborne*   **48**

MOPPY MAY (IRE)   3 b.f. Alhaarth (IRE) 126 – Lacinia 107 (Groom Dancer (USA) 128) [2002 –: f8g⁵ f8g 7m May 16] poor maiden: should stay 1¼m: visored final start. *T. G. Mills*   **45**

MOQUI MARBLE (GER)   6 b.g. Petit Loup (USA) 123 – Margo's New Hope (USA) (Cannonade (USA)) [2002 –: 7.1m p7g p10g³ f9.4g Dec 9] won 3 of his 4 starts in Germany at 3 yrs and handicap at Dusseldorf in 2000 for P. Rau: left John Berry after second start in 2002: modest form on all-weather last 2 starts: stays 1¼m: acts on heavy ground and polytrack: tried visored/tongue tied. *D. E. Cantillon*   **59**

MORAHIB   4 ch.c. Nashwan (USA) 135 – Irish Valley (USA) (Irish River (FR) 131) [2002 –: 10d⁵ 7.5g* 8g⁴ Aug 26] strong, well-made colt: quite useful form: won maiden at Beverley in June, making all: good fourth to Lady Bear in handicap at Ripon final start: seems better around 1m than further: raced only on good or softer ground. *M. P. Tregoning*   **90**

MOREOVER (IRE)   4 b.f. Caerleon (USA) 132 – Overcall (Bustino 136) [2002 69: 14.1d Mar 27] strong, good-bodied filly: fair maiden at 3 yrs: well held only 4-y-o start: blinkered (pulled hard) once. *M. W. Easterby*   **–**

MORE SIRENS (IRE)   4 ch.f. Night Shift (USA) – Lower The Tone (IRE) 74 (Phone Trick (USA)) [2002 78: p10g 8f* 8f³ 7.1m⁵ 8g² a8g a7.5g⁵ Dec 12] tall, good-topped filly: fairly useful handicapper on turf, fair on all-weather/dirt: won at Thirsk in April: left P. Webber 38,000 gns after fifth outing: stays 1m: acts on firm and soft going, ran respectably on dirt: usually races prominently. *M. Hussain, UAE*   **91 a73**

MORGAN LE FAY   7 b.m. Magic Ring (IRE) 115 – Melody Park 104 (Music Boy 124) [2002 –, a60: f7s³ f6s³ f8s⁶ f6g³ f7g² f7g³ 6f 7f Jun 1] leggy mare: poor performer: left Don Enrico Incisa after sixth start: effective at 6f/7f: acts on fibresand, firm and good to soft ground: usually visored nowadays: sometimes slowly away. *N. Tinkler*   **– a49**

MORGAN THE RED   2 ch.g. (May 31) Presidium 124 – Warning Bell 88 (Bustino 136) [2002 8.1m 7.9f⁶ 8d⁴ Oct 18] good-topped gelding: half-brother to several winners, including 5-y-o Hand Chime and fairly useful 1m/1¼m winner Virtual Reality (by Diamond Shoal): dam 1¼m winner: best effort in maidens (fair form) when fourth to Sir Haydn at Redcar: should stay at least 1¼m. *T. D. Easterby*   **73**

MORIBURNS (IRE)   2 b.c. (Apr 26) Goldmark (USA) 113 – Coffee Bean (Doulab (USA) 115) [2002 8.3m 7.1m 8g Sep 19] 6,500Y: good-bodied colt: brother to 3-y-o Tioga Gold and half-brother to several winners, including 1m/1¼m winner Java Red (by Red Sunset): dam poor Irish maiden: well held, including in seller. *Miss L. A. Perratt*   **–**

MORITAT (IRE) 2 b.c. (Apr 18) Night Shift (USA) – Aunty Eileen (Ahonoora 122) – [2002 6g[6] Aug 21] IR 25,000Y: good-topped colt: closely related to 2 winners, including 5f winner Moving Image (by Nordico), and half-brother to several winners, including 5-y-o The Tatling: dam unraced half-sister to smart sprinter Lugana Beach: 16/1, well held in maiden at York. *P. S. McEntee*

MORNING AFTER 2 b.f. (Feb 18) Emperor Jones (USA) 119 – Oneforthedicth 84 (USA) 79 (With Approval (CAN)) [2002 p6g[3] 5.7m* 7m[2] 6g[2] Oct 18] 1,500Y: first foal: dam 1m/1¼m winner: fairly useful form: won maiden at Bath in August: runner-up to Zingari in nursery at Yarmouth and Michelle Ma Belle in 30-runner sales race at Newmarket: stays 7f: raced only on good ground or firmer on turf, shaped well on polytrack. *J. R. Fanshawe*

MORNING LIGHT 2 b.g. (Feb 3) Danehill Dancer (IRE) 117 – Edge of Darkness – 62 (Vaigly Great 127) [2002 6g 5g Sep 18] 13,500Y: workmanlike gelding: fifth foal: half-brother to 4-y-o Joint Instruction and fairly useful 1½m/1¾m winner Salford Flyer (by Pharly): dam 1¼m to 2m winner: tailed off in maidens. *B. S. Rothwell*

MORNING SKY (IRE) 3 b.f. Machiavellian (USA) 123 – Dizzy Heights (USA) – (Danzig (USA)) [2002 79p: 8.3d 7m May 18] leggy, quite good-topped filly: fair at 2 yrs: slowly away and soundly beaten in handicaps in 2002: sold 9,000 gns in December. *E. A. L. Dunlop*

MORNINGTON FLYER 2 b.g. (Apr 15) Abou Zouz (USA) 109 – Cartuccia (IRE) ? (Doyoun 124) [2002 7m f8s 10f Oct 7] 8,000F, 4,800Y: leggy, angular gelding: unimpressive mover: second foal: dam unraced half-sister to Derby/Irish Derby second City Honours: well held in maidens: sent to Holland, and won at 6.5f there. *S. L. Keightley*

MORNIN RESERVES 3 b.g. Atraf 116 – Pusey Street Girl 87 (Gildoran 123) [2002 86 55: 9m 5d* 6g[3] 5s[5] 5v* 5g* 5.1f* 5g 5g Sep 19] tall, angular gelding: improved into a fairly useful handicapper: won at Hamilton, Ayr, Carlisle and Chester between May/July: easily best form at 5f: acts on any ground: usually leads. *D. A. Nolan*

MORPHEOUS 3 b.c. Halling (USA) 133 – Vilany 87 (Never So Bold 135) [2002 8m[5] 100 7.5g* 7.1d[2] 6d 7.9m Aug 22] 52,000Y: big, good-topped colt: fifth foal: half-brother to several winners, including 5-y-o Lion's Domane: dam 7f winner: useful performer: won maiden at Beverley in May: best effort when head second to Contract in minor event at Sandown next time: stays 1m: acts on good to soft going: sent to Hong Kong. *J. J. Quinn*

MORRIS DANCING (USA) 3 b.g. Rahy (USA) 115 – Summer Dance 86 (Sadler's 57 d Wells (USA) 132) [2002 75: f9.4g[3] f9.4g 8.2d 12.3m f8s f12f f12g Nov 22] fair maiden at 2 yrs: on downgrade in 2002. *B. P. J. Baugh*

MORRO CASTLE (USA) 4 b. or br.c. Kris S (USA) – Fuerza (USA) (Distinctive 94 Pro (USA)) [2002 83: 10m 10g[3] 8.5g[2] 10m[2] 8m[4] 8.1d 10.4m 8d[6] 9m 8.1f* 9f 8g Oct 18] big, good-topped colt: fairly useful handicapper: won at Haydock in September: creditable efforts otherwise when in frame, including fourth to Norton in Hunt Cup at Royal Ascot, drifting right: effective at 1m/1¼m: acts on firm going: blinkered fifth to eighth outings: races prominently: broke through stall and withdrawn once at 4 yrs: none too consistent: sold 18,000 gns, sent to Saudi Arabia. *C. E. Brittain*

MORSON BOY (USA) 2 b.c. (Feb 24) Lear Fan (USA) 130 – Esprit d'Escalier 79 p (USA) (Diesis 133) [2002 8m[4] 8m[5] 8v[4] Nov 8] 62,000Y: tall, leggy colt: has a powerful, round action: fifth foal: closely related to 3-y-o Spanish John and 2 winners in USA by Sunshine Forever, notably Grade 3 8.5f winner Gastronomical: dam maiden in USA: fair form in maidens: first home on stand side at Doncaster final start: will be suited by 1½m+: capable of better, and should win races. *M. Johnston*

MORVERN (IRE) 2 ch.g. (Apr 5) Titus Livius (FR) 115 – Scotia Rose (Tap On Wood 64 ? 130) [2002 6s 7m[2] 6g Oct 17] IR 20,000F, 21,000Y: strong gelding: half-brother to several winners, including fairly useful 1997 2-y-o 1m winner Herminius (by Ballad Rock) and 14.6f to 2¼m winner Amiarge (by Reference Point): dam Irish 1½m winner: modest maiden: runner-up in slowly-run match for minor event at Leicester: not sure to stay 1m. *J. G. Given*

MOSCOW (IRE) 3 ch.g. Cadeaux Genereux 131 – Madame Nureyev (USA) (Nureyev – p (USA) 131) [2002 8.2v[4] Oct 29] IR 290,000Y: half-brother to several winners, including US Grade 3 11f winner Miss Universal (by Lycius), earlier useful 1m/1¼m performer in Britain: dam French 2-y-o 6f winner: shaped as though in need of outing/experience when remote fourth to High Straits in maiden at Nottingham, soon recovering from slow start and not knocked about once tiring (gelded after): should improve. *J. H. M. Gosden*

MOSSY MAZE   3 b.f. Zamindar (USA) 116 – Moss (Alzao (USA) 117) [2002 7m – Aug 15] third foal: half-sister to 6-y-o Javelin and useful 1m winner Mossy Moor (by Sanglamore): dam, French 1¼m winner, half-sister to St Leger winner Toulon: considerately handled in maiden at Salisbury: sold 3,000 gns in December. *Mrs A. J. Perrett*

MOSTARSIL (USA)   4 ch.g. Kingmambo (USA) 125 – Naazeq 80 (Nashwan (USA)   58 § 135) [2002 89: f9.4g p10g 10m 10s 14.1m 10.2f* 10.2f² 11.7f³ 10.9m³ 8.1g⁵ 10.2g 10f³ 11.8s f12g Nov 22] useful-looking gelding: fairly useful at 3 yrs, modest in 2002: trained by J. O'Keefe first 2 starts: won seller at Bath in July: effective at 1m to 1½m: acts on firm going: blinkered/visored/wore cheekpieces last 3 starts: has hung/found little: sold £4,000. *J. G. M. O'Shea*

MOST DEFINITELY (IRE)   2 b.g. (Apr 18) Definite Article 121 – Unbidden   58 Melody (USA) (Chieftain II) [2002 6g⁵ 7m⁵ 7g 7m Oct 2] 6,500Y: leggy gelding: brother to 4-y-o Greenhope and half-brother to numerous winners, including 7f/1m winner Great Melody (by Pips Pride): dam ran twice in USA: modest maiden: should stay 1m: raced only on good/good to firm going. *T. D. Easterby*

MOST-SAUCY   6 br.m. Most Welcome 131 – So Saucy 59 (Teenoso (USA) 135)   66 [2002 66, a86: p10g³ f7s³ p8g² p7g⁴ p8g² p7g² p8g* 8f⁴ p8g 7.9s p8g² 8.3g⁶ 8.3m* 8.3m⁴   a78 p8g p8g⁵ f8.5s³ Dec 26] lengthy mare: fair performer: won minor event at Lingfield in April and handicap at Windsor in July: best at 7f/1m: acts on firm going, soft and all-weather: usually held up: tough and consistent. *I. A. Wood*

MOTEN SWING   3 b.g. Kris 135 – Lady Bankes (IRE) 69 (Alzao (USA) 117) [2002   85 75: 6g³ 7m* 7.9f 8m 7.1d 6g² 7d⁶ 7m 7f 7s Nov 2] sturdy, good-bodied gelding: fairly useful performer: won handicap at Newmarket in April: effective at 6f/7f: acts on good to firm going, probably on soft: blinkered seventh (found little)/eighth starts: gelded after final one. *R. Hannon*

MOTHER CORRIGAN (IRE)   6 gr.m. Paris House 123 – Missed Opportunity (IRE) – (Exhibitioner 111) [2002 –: f6g Nov 25] leggy, angular mare: modest handicapper at 4 yrs: little form since: visored/blinkered. *M. Brittain*

MOTH HIL (USA)   3 b.c. Danzig (USA) – Siyadah (USA) 106 (Mr Prospector (USA)) – [2002 –: 11.8g⁵ 11g Apr 19] strong colt: well held in maidens. *J. L. Dunlop*

MOUJOUDH (IRE)   2 b.c. (Apr 8) Mujadil (USA) 119 – Modelliste (Machiavellian   77 (USA) 123) [2002 5m³ 5d² 6f* 6m³ 7g³ 5.9s² 7.1m 6g⁵ Oct 2] angular colt: third foal: half-brother to fairly useful 2000 2-y-o 1m winner Samara Middle East (by Marju): dam, 1m winner in UAE, closely related to smart 7f winner Beraysim out of half-sister to Belmont/Preakness winner Risen Star: fair performer: won maiden at Redcar in June: creditable efforts in minor events/nurseries after bar penultimate start: stays 7f: acts on firm and soft ground: withdrawn after getting very upset/trapped in stall intended second start: difficult ride: sold 18,000 gns, sent to USA. *M. R. Channon*

MOUNT ABU (IRE)   5 b.h. Foxhound (USA) 103 – Twany Angel (Double Form   108 130) [2002 123: 6m 7m 7d⁴ Nov 2] rather leggy, quite attractive horse: usually takes the eye: very smart at 4 yrs: won Prix de la Foret at Longchamp at 4 yrs: not seen until September in 2002, and only useful form at best: well below par when favourite in Premio Chiusura at Milan final start: best at 6f (given trip of a test)/7f: has form on good to firm ground, but all wins on good to soft/soft: waited with. *J. H. M. Gosden*

MOUNT BENGER   2 ch.c. (May 7) Selkirk (USA) 129 – Vice Vixen (CAN) (Vice   73 Regent (CAN)) [2002 p7g⁶ f7s³ Dec 13] 32,000Y: half-brother to several winners, including smart 1¼m/1½m winner Cunning (by Bustino) and useful 6f (at 2 yrs) and 1m winner Mushraaf (by Zafonic): dam unraced out of half-sister to smart French 9f to 11f winner Lichine: better effort in maidens (fair form) when third to Every Note Counts at Wolverhampton: should be suited by 1m+. *R. M. Beckett*

MOUNT HESSE (FR)   3 ch.c. Midyan (USA) 124 – Minaudeuse (USA) (The Minstrel   87 p (CAN) 135) [2002 p7g⁴ 8s⁴ 8.3d⁵ 8m⁴ 8m* 8f* 8s² Nov 6] 520,000 francs Y: rather leggy colt: fourth foal: brother to French 1m winner Hequus and half-brother to French winner up to 1¼m Hazida (by Exit To Nowhere): dam won over 1¼m in France: progressive form: won handicap at Doncaster in July and minor event at Salisbury in September: creditable 6 lengths second to Parting Shot in handicap at Musselburgh final outing: will stay 1¼m: acts on firm and soft going, some promise on polytrack: should make a useful 4-y-o. *G. Wragg*

MOUNT HILLABY (IRE)   2 b.f. (Apr 25) Mujadil (USA) 119 – Tetradonna (IRE)   79 102 (Teenoso (USA) 135) [2002 5m⁵ 5g 7g⁷ Oct 19] IR 25,000Y: good-topped filly:

fourth living foal: half-sister to 7-y-o Alberich and fairly useful 10.5f winner Broadway Legend (by Caerleon): dam, second in Nell Gwyn Stakes but disappointing after, stayed 1½m: fair form: off nearly 6 months before winning maiden at Catterick in October readily by 1½ lengths from Cabeza de Vaca: should be suited by at least 1m. *B. W. Hills*

MOUNT JOY 3 br.c. Mtoto 134 – Nightitude 93 (Night Shift (USA)) [2002 102p: 7m² **61** 7d³ 7d³ a7f a10f⁶ Dec 13] sturdy, lengthy colt: maiden: useful form both 2-y-o starts: beaten at odds on first 2 outings in 2002, finding little/carrying head high (left Saeed bin Suroor after): free-going sort, will need to settle to stay beyond 1m: has been tongue tied. *P. L. Rudkin, UAE*

MOUNT OLYMPUS 3 b.f. Primo Dominie 121 – Penthouse Lady (Last Tycoon 131) **–** [2002 7d 6f 7g 7.2d Jul 23] third foal: sister to 5-y-o Dorchester: dam unraced half-sister to very smart French/US middle-distance performer Louis Cyphre and smart French performer up to 1m Psychobabble: no form in sellers/claimers. *W. Storey*

MOUNT PEKAN (IRE) 2 b.c. (May 5) Sri Pekan (USA) 117 – The Highlands (FR) **68** (High Line 125) [2002 7.2s 7.1m 7.2g⁴ 7.2s Oct 14] IR 10,000F, 15,500Y: leggy colt: half-brother to several winners abroad, including French 9.5f/10.5f winner Gandals (by Bigstone): dam French 2-y-o 9f winner: best effort in maidens (fair form) when fourth to Franklins Gardens at Ayr, dictating pace: bred to stay at least 1m. *J. S. Goldie*

MOUNTRATH ROCK 5 b.m. Rock Hopper 124 – Point of Law (Law Society (USA) **38 §** 130) [2002 45§: p16g⁴ p13g f16.2g p16g⁴ 12d Sep 11] small mare: poor handicapper: stays easy 2m: acts on firm going, good to soft and polytrack: usually visored/blinkered/tongue tied: sometimes slowly away: has been reluctant to race: not one to trust. *Miss B. Sanders*

MOUNT ROYALE (IRE) 4 ch.g. Wolfhound (USA) 126 – Mahabba (USA) 74 **52** (Elocutionist (USA)) [2002 60: 8m 7.1m 7f⁶ 7f 7.1g f7g⁵ 8g 9.1s 7s f7g³ f7g⁶ Dec 2] close-coupled gelding: has knee action: modest performer: stays 7f: acts on fibresand, soft and good to firm going: sometimes blinkered/visored: tongue tied. *N. Tinkler*

MOUNTSORREL (IRE) 3 b.g. Charnwood Forest (IRE) 125 – Play The Queen **50** (IRE) (King of Clubs 124) [2002 7g f8.5g f8.5g⁶ 10.9f² 12m² 16.4g⁵ f12s⁴ f12f⁶ Nov 29] 6,000F, 32,000Y: angular gelding: sixth foal: half-brother to several winners, including 8-y-o Salty Jack and 1998 2-y-o 5f winner Franco Mina (by Lahib), both fairly useful: dam, Irish 7f winner, out of Coronation Stakes winner Orchestration: modest maiden: claimed from W. Muir £6,000 fifth start and same amount from J. Best before final one: stays 1½m: acts on firm going and fibresand: has worn cheekpieces. *T. Wall*

MOUNT STREET (IRE) 3 b.f. Pennekamp (USA) 130 – Highland Gift (IRE) 95 **87 ?** (Generous (IRE) 139) [2002 82P: 12g 10g* 9.9m 10.3m Sep 11] leggy filly: fairly useful performer: won maiden at Newmarket in June by 2½ lengths from Trekking: last in handicap and minor event after: should stay 1½m. *Sir Michael Stoute*

MOUNT SUPERIOR (USA) 6 b.g. Conquistador Cielo (USA) – Zum Solitair **–** (USA) (Vice Regent (CAN)) [2002 f7g⁵ f8g 7g Jul 23] $125,000Y: fourth foal: closely related to winner in USA by Miswaki: dam winning sprinter in USA at 2 yrs: formerly trained by D. Oughton in Hong Kong where known as Partiking: only win at Sha Tin in 2000: little form there in 2001 or in Britain in 2002: stays 7f: raced mainly on good/good to firm going on turf, well beaten only start on dirt: tried blinkered. *P. W. D'Arcy*

MOUSEHOLE 10 b.g. Statoblest 120 – Alo Ez 100 (Alzao (USA) 117) [2002 79: 5f **74 d** 5.1g 5g² 5.1d² 5d 5f 5m 5f 5m 5f 6m 5f Sep 26] strong gelding: fair handicapper: races mainly at 5f nowadays: acts on firm and good to soft going: successful in blinkers, not tried since 1996: often soon off bridle: on downgrade. *R. Guest*

MOVE IT 2 ch.c. (Feb 28) Cadeaux Genereux 131 – Midnight Shift (IRE) 73 (Night **77** Shift (USA)) [2002 6s⁵ 6d 6v⁵ Nov 9] IR 230,000Y: sturdy colt: second foal: dam, 6f winner, half-sister to very smart sprinter Owington: fair form when fifth to Zabaglione in maiden at Newbury: well held in similar events after, though not at all knocked about at Doncaster final start: will probably stay 7f: raced only on ground softer than good. *R. Charlton*

MOVIE KING (IRE) 3 ch.g. Catrail (USA) 123 – Marilyn (IRE) 72 (Kings Lake **88** (USA) 133) [2002 67: p7g⁵ f8g p10g* p10g* 9g³ 8.3m* 7.9f³ 8m 10m⁶ 8m 15.9g Aug 20] workmanlike gelding: fairly useful performer: won maiden/handicap at Lingfield and handicap at Windsor between February/April: has won at 1¼m, best form at 1m: acts on polytrack and firm going, probably on fibresand: races prominently. *A. P. Jarvis*

MOVING EXPERIENCE (IRE)   5 b.m. Nicolotte 118 – Sound Performance (IRE) **82**
63 (Ahonoora 122) [2002 72: 8m 8g⁴ 9m⁵ 8m³ 9m* 8g³ 10.1m* 10m⁵ 10.3m Sep 14]
fairly useful handicapper: better than ever in 2002, winning at Goodwood and Epsom
in August: stays 1¼m: acts on soft going, good to firm and probably on polytrack: sold
22,000 gns, sent to USA. *D. W. P. Arbuthnot*

MOWGLI BRADDAN   2 b.f. (Jan 5) El Dimagio – Yuppy Girl (IRE) 61 (Salt Dome
(USA)) [2002 f6f f6g Nov 30] first foal: dam, maiden who stayed 1¼m, not one to trust:
well held in maidens at Wolverhampton. *Mrs G. S. Rees*

MOYANNA (IRE)   2 b.f. (Apr 24) Sri Pekan (USA) 117 – Certain Impression (USA) **69**
(Forli (ARG)) [2002 6m² 6d⁴ Aug 23] smallish filly: sixth foal: half-sister to 3-y-o
Impressive Flight and a 1m winner in Italy by Petardia: dam unraced: fair form in
maidens at Thirsk: will stay at least 7f. *T. D. Barron*

MOYNE PLEASURE (IRE)   4 b.c. Exit To Nowhere (USA) 122 – Ilanga (IRE) 92 **79**
(Common Grounds 118) [2002 69, a87: f8.5g* f8g* f7g³ f8.5g* f8.5g⁴ f8.5g⁴ 10m³
f9.4g⁶ 9s 8m⁵ p7g 8g* 8g⁴ 10.1d* 9m f8s⁵ 10m³ 10f 7m⁶ f12s³ 11.9f f8g⁶ 12g*
f8g⁶ 16s⁵ 12v f14.8g f12g f9.4g⁶ Dec 14] small, sparely-made colt: fair performer: won
claimers at Wolverhampton and Southwell (for J. Osborne) in January, Wolverhampton
(for K. Burke) in February (trained by J. Unett fifth start only) and Newcastle (for
N. Littmoden) in August, handicap at Newcastle in September and claimer at Catterick
in October: well held last 4 starts: effective at 1m, probably at 2m: well beaten on heavy
going, acts on any other turf and on fibresand: usually claimer ridden: tough. *Paul
Johnson*

MOZZARELLA   2 ch.f. (May 4) King's Signet (USA) 110 – Martine 68 (Clantime   –
101) [2002 6d Oct 18] 800Y twice: first foal: dam maiden who stayed 7f: 100/1, well held
in maiden at Redcar. *Don Enrico Incisa*

MR BLUE SKY (IRE)   3 b.c. Blues Traveller (IRE) 119 – Faypool (IRE) (Fayruz **58**
116) [2002 72, a82: p7g f7g f9.4g³ f9.4g⁵ Jul 20] useful-looking colt: fairly useful at best
at 2 yrs, just modest in 2002: stays 1m: acts on heavy ground and all-weather: tongue tied
last 2 starts: sold 2,200 gns. *G. C. H. Chung*

MR BOUNTIFUL (IRE)   4 b.g. Mukaddamah (USA) 125 – Nawadder 73 (Kris 135) **64 +**
[2002 58: p7g p7g² p6g p6g 7.1m⁵ 6m 6.1m⁴ 6m 5m² 7m* 7m 6g⁶ 6m² 6.1m Oct 1]
angular gelding: has a fluent, rather exaggerated action: modest handicapper: won at
Catterick in August: effective at 5f to 7f: acts on polytrack, soft and good to firm going:
sometimes slowly away. *M. Dods*

MR CHESTNUT TREE   3 b.g. Forzando 122 – Sure Flyer (IRE) (Sure Blade (USA)   –
130) [2002 56: f8g 8g 9.9m 7.9g 10f 10m Jun 20] good-topped gelding: modest maiden
at 2 yrs: well held in 2002: tried visored. *Mrs A. M. Naughton*

MR COMBUSTIBLE (IRE)   4 b.c. Hernando (FR) 127 – Warg (Dancing Brave **121**
(USA) 140) [2002 121: 12m⁵ Apr 20] big, strong, rangy colt: very smart performer: won
Chester Vase and Geoffrey Freer Stakes at Newbury at 3 yrs, when also creditable fourth
to Galileo in Derby at Epsom and respectable third to Milan in St Leger at Doncaster:
creditable 2¾ lengths fifth to Zindabad in John Porter Stakes at Newbury (reportedly
sustained joint injury) only 4-y-o outing: stayed 14.6f: acted on firm going, probably on
heavy: tended to hang left final 3-y-o start: to stand at Beechbrook Stud, Co Wicklow,
Ireland. *B. W. Hills*

MR COSPECTOR   5 b.g. Cosmonaut – L'Ancressaan 67 (Dalsaan 125) [2002 69:   –
p16g Dec 3] tall gelding: formerly fair 7f winner: well beaten only Flat run in 2002: won
over fences later in December. *D. L. Williams*

MR DINOS (IRE)   3 b.c. Desert King (IRE) 129 – Spear Dance (Gay Fandango **117**
(USA) 132) [2002 89p: 11.1g³ 12m* 13.9m* 16.2m² 16.1g² 15g* 14.6m⁵ 15.5v*
Oct 27]
    For the first time since 1985 the first three to pass the post in the Prix
Royal-Oak were all three-year-olds, and leading them home in this Group 1 contest
was a colt who had made remarkable progress since finishing third in a maiden on
his seasonal reappearance. The game front-runner Mr Dinos, the colt in question,
may be open to still further improvement, especially given the opportunity to tackle
distances in excess of two miles, and he should continue to make a significant
impact in the top staying races in 2003, including the Gold Cup.

Prix Royal-Oak, Longchamp—three-year-olds fill the first three places for the first time since 1985 as Mr Dinos makes all to win from Sulk and Morozov, though the last-named is demoted; Clety (rail) is fourth

After easily justifying favouritism at Newmarket in April on his third start in maidens, Mr Dinos followed up in a minor event at York and then went on to finish second in both the Queen's Vase at Royal Ascot and the Northumberland Plate at Newcastle, beaten half a length by Mamool in the former and a head by Bangalore in the latter. Mr Dinos showed smart form at Newcastle, on his only start in handicap company, and he didn't need to improve on it to gain his first pattern-race success, trouncing four rivals by ten lengths and more in the Group 3 Prix Berteux-Etalon Marchand de Sable at Vichy. More was required from Mr Dinos in the Royal-Oak, however, even though it was a rather substandard renewal. His six rivals at Longchamp included one other British challenger, the Yorkshire Oaks third Sulk, while the home-trained runners included three who had run well over the course earlier in October, Morozov winning the Prix Hubert de Chaudenay, and Cut Quartz and Clety fourth and sixth past the post respectively in the Prix du Cadran. Mr Dinos, probably having to do a bit too much up front when fifth, beaten nearly ten lengths behind Bollin Eric, in the St Leger on his previous start, was able to dictate matters more easily in the Royal-Oak, gradually stepping up the pace from the approach to the straight. Sulk proved the only serious threat from thereon, almost getting upsides after two furlongs out to mount a serious challenge, but Mr Dinos kept on too strongly for her, forging clear to win by two and a half lengths. There was a further four lengths back to third-placed Morozov, who was demoted to sixth for causing interference close home.

Mr Dinos (IRE) (b.c. 1999)	Desert King (IRE) (b 1994)	Danehill (b 1986)	Danzig Razyana
		Sabaah (ch 1988)	Nureyev Dish Dash
	Spear Dance (b 1982)	Gay Fandango (ch 1972)	Forli Gay Violin
		Lancette (b 1971)	Double Jump Persian Union

Mr Dinos is closely related to Risk Material (by Danehill), a smart winner at up to a mile and a quarter (including the Derrinstown Stud Derby Trial) who stayed a mile and three quarters, and a half-brother to several winners, including Bahi (by Tate Gallery), a useful performer both in Ireland and Australia. Bought for 42,000 guineas as a two-year-old, having fetched IR 40,000 guineas the previous year, Mr Dinos is the tenth foal of Spear Dance, a mare who won over seven furlongs and a mile in Ireland at three. Spear Dance, out of a maiden half-sister to the Gimcrack winner Golden Horus, is a sister to the 1981 Jersey Stakes winner Rasa Penang. The good-topped Mr Dinos, who acts on heavy and good to firm ground, is a thoroughly likeable individual, not only very game but also most reliable. The St Leger is the only race in which he has failed to reach a place in nine outings. *P. F. I. Cole*

MR ED (IRE) 4 ch.g. In The Wings 128 – Center Moriches (IRE) 74 (Magical Wonder **80** (USA) 125) [2002 69: 13.3s³ 14.1m² 14d³ 16.2m² 16.4g 12m* 13.3f 11.9f Oct 10] angular gelding: fairly useful handicapper: won at Goodwood in August: finished last final outing: effective at 1½m to 2m: acts on soft and good to firm going: sometimes slowly away: has wandered. *P. Bowen*

MR FITZER   3 b.g. Robellino (USA) 127 – Tiszta Sharok 81 (Song 132) [2002 –: f8g   –
p12g f11g Feb 14] big gelding: no form. *M. C. Chapman*

MR FLEMING   3 b. or br.g. Bin Ajwaad (IRE) 119 – Fabulous Night (FR) (Fabulous   56
Dancer (USA) 124) [2002 p8g⁴ p10g f8g Dec 10] first foal: dam, third at 12.5f in France,
out of half-sister to Prix Jacques le Marois winner Miss Satamixa: modest form in
maidens at Lingfield first 2 starts: beaten long way out final outing. *Dr J. D. Scargill*

MR FORTYWINKS (IRE)   8 ch.g. Fools Holme (USA) – Dream On 54 (Absalom   70
128) [2002 73: 16m 16.1m 13s⁵ 16.5g* 15d* 16d² 16g 17.5g 14.6s⁴ 16.5v⁴ Nov 9]
sparely-made gelding: fair handicapper: won at Doncaster (amateurs) and Ayr in July:
probably better at 1¾m/2m than shorter nowadays: has form on firm going, probably best
on good or softer, and acts on fibresand: tried tongue tied: tends to sweat: usually races up
with pace: sometimes runs in snatches. *B. Ellison*

MR GEORGE SMITH   5 b.g. Prince Sabo 123 – Nellie's Gamble 66 (Mummy's   –
Game 120) [2002 –: f6s Jan 22] no longer of much account. *R. Wilman*

MR GISBY (USA)   4 b. or br.g. Chief's Crown (USA) – Double Lock 104 (Home   64
Guard (USA) 129) [2002 63: p10g⁶ f8.5g f12g³ f16.2g² f16g³ Dec 17] lengthy gelding:
modest maiden: left D. Elsworth after reappearance: effective at 1½m to 2m: acts on
fibresand, raced only on good/good to firm going on turf. *S. C. Williams*

MR HAWKEYE (USA)   3 ch.g. Royal Academy (USA) 130 – Port Plaisance (USA)   69 ?
(Woodman (USA) 126) [2002 7g 11.9g³ 10m 11.5m Sep 17] tall, rather raw-boned
gelding: first foal: dam, won at 1½m in France, later successful in USA: easily best effort
second start (raced freely/hung left): edgy/sweating third outing, visored final one: sold
2,500 gns. *W. J. Haggas*

MR LEAR (USA)   3 b.g. Lear Fan (USA) 130 – Majestic Mae (USA) (Crow (FR)   65
134) [2002 49: f8g* p8g³ 8g⁴ 8g⁶ 8.2g p7g Jun 29] sturdy gelding: fair handicapper: won   a72
at Southwell (by 16 lengths, only outing there) in February: should stay 1¼m: acts on
fibresand: raced freely/looked less than keen second outing. *T. D. Barron*

MR MAHOOSE (USA)   4 b.g. Rakeen (USA) 99 – Golden Hen (USA) (Native   106
Prospector (USA) 90) [2002 105p: 7d 8.5g 7f* 6m⁵ 7m³ 7m² 7f Oct 3] tall, quite good-
topped gelding: useful handicapper: won at Yarmouth in July: best effort and unlucky
when ½-length second to Millennium Force in Tote Trifecta Stakes at Ascot (tended to
edge right): again didn't have race run to suit when creditable seventh to Demonstrate at
Newmarket final start: best at 6f/7f: acts on firm and good to soft ground: has been edgy/
sweating/led by 2 handlers in preliminaries (mulish on fourth start): ridden patiently, and
ideally suited by truly-run race: sent to UAE. *W. J. Haggas*

MR MALARKEY (IRE)   2 b.g. (Apr 22) Pivotal 124 – Girl Next Door 58 (Local   –
Suitor (USA) 128) [2002 f6f p7g Oct 9] fourth foal: half-brother to 5-y-o Maritun Lad:
dam 6f winner, including at 2 yrs: well held in maidens. *Mrs C. A. Dunnett*

MR MIDAZ   3 ch.g. Danzig Connection (USA) – Marmy 43 (Midyan (USA) 124)   63
[2002 67: 8m 7g⁵ 8.2g 7.1d⁴ 6.9d 7m f6s Oct 8] good-bodied gelding: modest maiden
handicapper: should stay 1m: acts on firm and good to soft ground: tried blinkered:
usually races prominently: sold 2,800 gns. *Jedd O'Keeffe*

MR MISCHIEF   2 b.g. (Apr 21) Millkom 124 – Snow Huntress 80 (Shirley Heights   82
130) [2002 6d f8.5g* f8.5g* Dec 2] 3,000F, 4,000Y: half-brother to 3 winners, including
6f winner Friendly Alliance and 8-y-o Zorro: dam 1¼m/1½m winner: fairly useful form:
won maiden (awarded race) and nursery (beat Bishops Finger by 4 lengths) at
Wolverhampton in November/December: will be suited by 1¼m/1½m. *P. C. Haslam*

MR MONROE   3 b.c. Mistertopogigo (IRE) 118 – Highland Heights (IRE) (Lomond   –
(USA) 128) [2002 43: f8g Feb 7] smallish, quite good-topped colt: poor maiden. *C. Smith*

MR MONTAGUE (IRE)   10 b.g. Pennine Walk 120 – Ballyewry (Prince Tenderfoot   –
(USA) 126) [2002 f14.8g⁶ Jan 18] lengthy gelding: winning hurdler: maiden on Flat,
lightly raced: stayed 1¾m: acted on good to firm going: tried blinkered: dead.
C. N. Kellett

MR OBOE   4 b.g. Charnwood Forest (IRE) 125 – Miss Clarinet (Pharly (FR) 130)   59
[2002 –: 10.9f 10m³ May 1] lengthy gelding: modest maiden, lightly raced: stays 1¼m:
acts on good to firm going. *Andrew Turnell*

MR PERTEMPS 4 b.g. Primo Dominie 121 – Amber Mill 96 (Doulab (USA) 115) **64**
[2002 58: 8.2d⁵ 6.1v f5g 6s 6d 6g 6m⁶ Jul 22] tall, lengthy gelding: modest maiden: stays
7f: raced mainly on good going or softer on turf: tried tongue tied: has carried head high:
joined R. Fahey. *S. C. Williams*

MR PIANO MAN (IRE) 4 gr.g. Paris House 123 – Winter March (Ballad Rock 122) **–**
[2002 –: p6g Jan 23] leggy, close-coupled gelding: modest maiden at 2 yrs: no form since.
J. L. Eyre

MR PICCLES 2 b.g. (Apr 12) Piccolo 121 – Brigadiers Bird (IRE) (Mujadil (USA) **48**
119) [2002 7m 7d 5g⁶ 5.1m⁴ 7m⁵ 6d 5.1g Sep 23] close-coupled gelding: third foal:
half-brother to useful 6f (at 2 yrs) to 1m winner Lady Lahar (by Fraam): dam unraced:
poor maiden: well below form last 2 starts: probably stays 7f: yet to race on extremes of
going: visored 3 of last 4 outings. *M. R. Channon*

MR POP IDOL 2 b.c. (Mar 30) Mistertopogigo (IRE) 118 – Diamond Time (Clantime **77**
101) [2002 5s⁶ 5g² 5.2f Jul 20] 1,600Y, resold 4,200Y: strong colt: second foal: dam
lightly raced in bumpers/over hurdles: fair maiden: second at Kempton in March: good
tenth in sales race at Newbury: likely to prove best at 5f: sent to UAE. *B. A. McMahon*

MR RICCIOLO (IRE) 3 b.g. Highest Honor (FR) 124 – Just Rainbow (FR) (Rainbow **–**
Quest (USA) 134) [2002 –: 10g 10m 10g May 31] leggy, workmanlike gelding: well held
in maidens: has looked wayward. *B. J. Curley*

MR SANDANCER 3 b.g. Zafonic (USA) 130 – Um Lardaff (Mill Reef (USA) 141) **96**
[2002 102: 9m⁵ 10.4m⁴ 11.6m³ 10.3m³ 10s p8g Dec 21] strong, attractive gelding: good
walker: useful performer: respectable efforts at best in 2002: well below form last 4 starts,
leaving J. Given before final one: stays 1¼m: acts on good to firm going, possibly not
softer than good: slowly away fourth/fifth starts, visored on first occasion. *P. Mitchell*

MRS CUBE 3 ch.f. Missed Flight 123 – Norska 67 (Northfields (USA)) [2002 41: **42**
5.1m 6f 6.1v 8m 7g 7m⁵ 7m⁴ 8f f6g Nov 25] well-grown filly: poor maiden handicapper:
stays 7f: acts on good to firm going. *J. M. Bradley*

MRS KANNING 3 ch.f. Distant View (USA) 126 – Red Hot Dancer (USA) (Seattle **–**
Dancer (USA) 119) [2002 61: 11.6m Apr 22] small, good-bodied filly: modest maiden at
2 yrs: well held only outing in 2002. *M. H. Tompkins*

MR SMITHERS JONES 2 br.g. (Mar 4) Emperor Jones (USA) 119 – Phylian 77 **–**
(Glint of Gold 128) [2002 6s p6g Nov 19] close-coupled, quite good-topped gelding:
third living foal: half-brother to 1999 2-y-o 7f seller winner Summertime Joy (by Muhtarram), later winner abroad: dam 1¼m/11f winner: well held in maidens. *S. C. Williams*

MRS PICKLES 7 gr.m. Northern Park (USA) 107 – Able Mabel 77 (Absalom 128) **–**
[2002 –: f16.2g Jan 11] handicapper: well held both starts on Flat since 1999: tried
blinkered: successful over hurdles in February. *M. D. I. Usher*

MR SPLIFFY (IRE) 3 b.g. Fayruz 116 – Johns Conquerer (IRE) 74 (Conquering **74**
Hero (USA) 116) [2002 65: f5s³ f5g p6g f5g f5g³ 5f 6g⁶ 5d 5m 5f⁴ 5f* 5m³ 6d⁴ 5d⁴ 5f 5m⁵
5g² 5m⁵ 5f³ Oct 3] close-coupled gelding: unimpressive mover: fair handicapper: won at
Catterick in June: left M. Chapman after sixteenth start: barely stays 6f: acts on fibresand,
firm and good to soft ground: visored final outing: has bolted/been early to post: usually
races prominently: no easy ride. *K. R. Burke*

MRS PLUM 3 b.f. Emarati (USA) 74 – Aubade (Henbit (USA) 130) [2002 72: p6g **–**
8.2f f7g f8.5g Dec 13] disappointing maiden: left D. Morris after third start. *I. A. Wood*

MRS POOTERS (IRE) 3 b.f. Petardia 113 – Mrs Hooters (Glint of Gold 128) [2002 **61**
66: 7m 8.3d 8.3d⁵ 10.2g 11.6d Oct 28] modest maiden: stays 8.3f: acts on heavy going:
has carried head awkwardly/edged left. *D. W. P. Arbuthnot*

MRS TIGGYWINKLE 4 b.f. Magic Ring (IRE) 115 – Upper Sister (Upper Case **– §**
(USA)) [2002 47§: 6d 5g 6g May 31] sparely-made filly: ungenuine maiden: sometimes
blinkered at 2 yrs. *Miss L. A. Perratt*

MR STYLISH 6 b.g. Mazilier (USA) 107 – Moore Stylish 65 (Moorestyle 137) [2002 **68 §**
83: 5g 6m⁵ 6m 6g 6m⁵ p6g⁴ 6m 6v 5.7m⁴ 6g 5.7g³ 5.1g⁶ 5.7m⁴ 6m f6g⁵ f6s⁴ 6d f7g*
f7g p7g⁶ Dec 11] lengthy gelding: fair performer: won seller at Southwell in November:
effective at 6f/7f: acts on fibresand and any turf going: tried blinkered (reportedly bled
from nose), visored/tongue tied nowadays: hung markedly right sixth outing: carries head
awkwardly: unreliable. *J. S. Moore*

MR TOAD (IRE)   3 b.g. Marju (IRE) 127 – Zany (Junius (USA) 124) [2002 99: 6.1d² **98**
6g 6f⁴ 6.1m 6m* 6g⁵ 6f⁶ Oct 12] good-topped gelding: good mover: useful performer:
won claimer at Yarmouth in September by length from Sir Northerndancer: creditable
fifth to Greenslades in handicap at Ascot next time: best at 5f/6f: acts on soft and good to
firm going: usually tongue tied at 2 yrs: has worn crossed noseband: carries head
awkwardly: headstrong, and suited by waiting tactics: has found little: sold 44,000 gns,
sent to USA. *J. A. Osborne*

MR TOP FLIGHT (IRE)   3 b.g. Night Shift (USA) – Native Rhythm (IRE) 71   **66**
(Lycius (USA) 124) [2002 55: 8.1s 7.9g 7.9s⁴ 10g f8s 8m⁶ 8.5m³ f8.5g³ f9.4g² Oct 21]
workmanlike gelding: fair maiden handicapper: stays 9.4f: acts on fibresand, soft and
good to firm going: has gone freely, including in blinkers fifth start: has flashed tail/
wandered: sold 7,800 gns. *Mrs G. S. Rees*

MR UPPITY   3 b.g. Shareef Dancer (USA) 135 – Queenfisher 101 (Scottish Reel 123)   –
[2002 8m p8g 7g 8.3d 10.1m⁵ 8f Sep 30] 2,500Y: second foal: dam 5f (at 2 yrs) and 7f
winner: little form. *Julian Poulton*

MR WENSLEYDALE   3 b.g. Alzao (USA) 117 – Third Watch 114 (Slip Anchor   **77 +**
136) [2002 61: f9.4g² 8g³ 7.1f* 7m² 7.1m* 8g² 7s 8f 8f* 8.5f⁵ 8.5f⁶ 9f³ 9f Nov 3] close-
coupled, good-topped gelding: fair performer: won handicaps at Warwick in April and
May: left R. Cowell after seventh outing: won claimer at Del Mar in August: not
discredited in Grade 3 event at Bay Meadows final start: effective at 7f/1m: acts on firm
going, probably on soft and fibresand: visored (ran respectably) seventh outing: has
carried head awkwardly. *M. Chew, USA*

MR WHIZZ   5 ch.g. Manhal – Panienka (POL) 70 (Dom Racine (FR) 121) [2002 69:   **54**
6.1g 6m 6s 7.1s 6g 6d 8d 10m⁴ 10.2g Aug 26] lengthy gelding: modest performer: seems
to stay 1¼m: tried visored: sometimes slowly away. *M. R. Bosley*

MUBAAH   3 ch.c. Cadeaux Genereux 131 – Numuthej (USA) 50 (Nureyev (USA)   **95**
131) [2002 64p: 6f⁶ 6m² 6f² 5g 6d⁵ 7m 7f a6f* a7f⁴ Dec 19] sparely-made colt: useful
performer: won maiden at Kempton in April and (having left A. Stewart after seventh
outing) handicap at Nad Al Sheba in December: best form at 6f/7f: acts on firm going,
good to soft and dirt. *P. L. Rudkin, UAE*

MUBADALAH (USA)   2 gr.f. (Mar 14) Dumaani (USA) 115 – Dish Dash 118   **78**
(Bustino 136) [2002 7g⁴ 7.6m⁵ 7m⁵ Oct 5] close-coupled, workmanlike filly: closely
related to high-class miler Maroof (by Danzig) and half-sister to several winners,
including useful 1995 2-y-o 7f winner Mawwal (by Elmaamul) and to dam of Irish 2000
Guineas/Irish Derby winner Desert King: dam won Ribblesdale Stakes: easily best effort
in maidens (fair form) when fourth to Summitville at Newmarket: should stay at least 1m:
sold 46,000 gns in December. *N. A. Graham*

MUBAHATH (IRE)   3 b.c. Sadler's Wells (USA) 132 – Greek Moon (IRE) (Shirley   **68**
Heights 130) [2002 10m 10s⁶ 10s⁵ Oct 26] 400,000Y: first foal: dam unraced half-sister
to very smart hurdler Landing Light out of smart winner up to 1½m Gay Hellene:
blinkered, best effort in maidens when fifth to Behra at Newbury, hanging left again and
looking less than keen under pressure: stays 1¼m: temperament under suspicion: sold
10,000 gns. *J. H. M. Gosden*

MUBEEN (IRE)   2 ch.c. (Jan 25) Barathea (IRE) 127 – Fernanda 95 (Be My Chief   **94**
(USA) 122) [2002 6d⁴ 6g* 7d⁶ 8m* 8m⁴ Sep 13] 50,000Y: smallish, sturdy colt: second
foal: dam, 6f (at 2 yrs) and 1m (in France) winner, half-sister to smart performer up to 1m
Chipaya: fairly useful performer: won maiden at Ripon in June and minor event at
Salisbury (beat St Pancras a neck) in August: respectable fourth of 5 to Rimrod in listed
race at Goodwood final start: stays 1m: yet to race on extremes of going. *E. A. L. Dunlop*

MUBKERA (IRE)   3 ch.f. Nashwan (USA) 135 – Na-Ayim (IRE) 68 (Shirley Heights   **100**
130) [2002 86p: 11.5g³ 12m 12g⁵ 10m² 10.1m Sep 17] quite good-topped filly: useful
performer: best effort when 2 lengths second to Averted View in listed rated stakes at
Brighton in August: effective at 1¼m/1½m: raced only on good/good to firm going: visits
Almutawakel. *E. A. L. Dunlop*

MUBTAKER (USA)   5 ch.h. Silver Hawk (USA) 123 – Gazayil (USA) 80 (Irish   **123**
River (FR) 131) [2002 123: 12d² 13.3f* Aug 17]
　　　　Mubtaker had appeared to be over his problems when completing a full
season in 2001, after being restricted to just three starts in the previous two, but
difficulties resurfaced in 2002 and he managed only two appearances. At least
Mubtaker was in good form for both those runs, not only maintaining his record of

Stan James Geoffrey Freer Stakes, Newbury—
very smart performances from Mubtaker (right) and High Pitched

never having finished out of the first three, but also gaining his first pattern-race victory. Mubtaker developed into a very smart performer and won three listed races as a four-year-old but he began the latest season in Dubai acting as lead horse for Nayef, who won the Sheema Classic there in March. Mubtaker himself didn't appear on a racecourse until July, in the Princess of Wales's Stakes at Newmarket. It was a race he looked all set to win when taking over approaching the final furlong, before his lack of a recent race began to tell and Millenary collared him close home. Mubtaker was sent off a short-priced favourite to go one better in the Stan James Geoffrey Freer Stakes at Newbury the following month, the second favourite being High Pitched, who had won a listed event over the course and distance in May. The race went as the betting suggested. Mubtaker was still on the bridle as he improved to lead over two furlongs out and was always doing enough to hold High Pitched's challenge, winning by two lengths, the rider on the runner-up accepting things close home. Some ambitious plans were made for Mubtaker subsequently but they didn't come to fruition. He missed the Canadian International reportedly because his blood wasn't quite right and the Breeders' Cup Turf because of coughing; and after failing to impress in his work he was also taken out of the Hong Kong Vase. It is to be hoped that Mubtaker is able to complete a full programme in 2003, for there are more good races to be won with this thoroughly reliable individual.

Mubtaker is a half-brother to three winners in Australia, and to Crystal Downs (by Alleged), who showed useful form over seven furlongs and a mile for Aidan O'Brien, including when second in the Prix Marcel Boussac and fourth in the 1999 Irish One Thousand Guineas. Their dam Gazayil, a seven-furlong maiden race winner at two and later successful in Australia, is a half-sister to the smart mile-and-a-quarter winner Husyan. The grandam Close Comfort is an unraced half-sister to Ancient Regime, the leading French two-year-old filly of 1980, while the great grandam Caterina, a half-sister to the high-class middle-

Mr Hamdan Al Maktoum's "Mubtaker"

Mubtaker (USA) (ch.h. 1997)	Silver Hawk (USA) (b 1979)	Roberto (b 1969)	Hail To Reason Bramalea
		Gris Vitesse (gr 1966)	Amerigo Matchiche II
	Gazayil (USA) (ch 1985)	Irish River (ch 1976)	Riverman Irish Star
		Close Comfort (b 1979)	Far North Caterina

distance colt Scottish Rifle, won the Nunthorpe Stakes. Mubtaker, a lengthy individual, is an unimpressive mover but he does act well on firm going. He is also effective on ground softer than good and gained his first win, in a maiden at Newbury at three years, on heavy. The extended thirteen furlongs of the Geoffrey Freer is the longest trip Mubtaker has tackled so far, and while he will probably stay a bit further the likelihood is that he will continue to be campaigned at around a mile and a half. *M. P. Tregoning*

MUCHEA   8 ch.h. Shalford (IRE) 124§ – Bargouzine 67 (Hotfoot 126) [2002 105:   **105**
7.5g³ 7f 8g 7d 7.6g² 8g 8.1d² 8.1m³ 8m 8m⁵ 8.1d 7.9m² 8f³ 8m 7.9m² 8d* 8m* 8g 8f³ 9f
Oct 5] good-topped horse: useful performer: won minor event at Thirsk in August and
handicap at Doncaster (beat Calcutta by ¾ length) in September: several respectable
efforts at least otherwise, including when short-head second to Funfair in Bradford &
Bingley Rated Stakes at York fifteenth start: stays 1m: acts on any going: sometimes
visored at 6 yrs: sometimes sweats: has been bandaged: usually held up: tough.
M. R. Channon

MUCKY BUSINESS 2 b.c. (Apr 20) Lahib (USA) 129 – Berliese (IRE) (High Estate **68** 127) [2002 7f 8g 8g Oct 18] 15,000Y: tall colt: first living foal: dam once-raced sister to Chester Vase winner High Baroque: best effort in maidens (fair form) when eleventh of 16 to Calibre at Newmarket final start, fading: not sure to stay further than 1m. *T. G. Mills*

MUDDY WATER 6 b.m. Salse (USA) 128 – Rainbow Fleet 66 (Nomination 125) **–** [2002 51, a63: f9.4g⁶ f8g⁴ p7g p8g f8.5g 7m 8m⁵ 8g Jun 9] smallish, sturdy mare: modest performer at 5 yrs: little form in 2002: tried blinkered. *R. Wilman*

MUFFIT (IRE) 3 b.f. Alhaarth (IRE) 126 – Calash (Indian King (USA) 128) [2002 **47** 63, a56: p7g³ p6g 8.2f 7g 7g 5g 6g 7g f11g Dec 4] smallish, sturdy filly: poor performer: claimed from P. Howling £5,100 third outing, left M. Polglase after eighth: stays 8.5f: acts on heavy going, good to firm and all-weather: has carried head awkwardly/found little. *Paul Johnson*

MUFREH (USA) 4 b.c. Dayjur (USA) 137 – Mathkurh (USA) 97 (Riverman (USA) **67** 131) [2002 65+: f8.5g 7s f6g* f7g³ Dec 17] fair performer, lightly raced: won handicap at Southwell in December: probably best at 6f: acts on fibresand: sometimes slowly away. *A. G. Newcombe*

MUGHARREB (USA) 4 b.c. Gone West (USA) – Marling (IRE) 124 (Lomond **115** (USA) 128) [2002 117: 6f² 6m 6f² 6m* 6m² 7m⁵ 7m Sep 20] strong colt: impresses in appearance: very good mover: smart performer: won 4-runner minor event at Yarmouth in August: ran creditably otherwise when runner-up in Duke of York Stakes (beaten neck by Invincible Spirit) and listed race at Newbury (beaten neck by Ashdown Express) on first/third starts: best form at 6f: acts on firm going: joined J. Sadler in UAE. *B. Hanbury*

MUHAREB (USA) 3 ch.c. Thunder Gulch (USA) 129 – Queen of Spirit (USA) **99** (Deputy Minister (CAN)) [2002 76: f8s² f9.4g* p10g³ 9g⁶ 12.3f³ 12d* 16.2m 10g 14m³ 12.3m* 11.9m* 12g⁶ Sep 29] rather leggy, lengthy colt: useful handicapper: won at Wolverhampton in January, Goodwood in May, Ripon (beat Knavesmire Omen by ¾ length) in August and York (dead-heated with Scott's View, who met trouble) in September: probably best at 1½m/1¾m: acts on firm ground, good to soft and all-weather: has run well sweating: races prominently. *C. E. Brittain*

MUJADILLY 4 b.f. Mujadil (USA) 119 – Casbah Girl 79 (Native Bazaar 122) [2002 **43** –: f7g⁵ p7g f8g⁴ f8g f7g⁴ Mar 26] workmanlike filly: poor maiden handicapper: best form at 7f: acts on fibresand, probably on polytrack. *W. M. Brisbourne*

MUJA FAREWELL 4 ch.f. Mujtahid (USA) 118 – Highland Rhapsody (IRE) 78 **93** (Kris 135) [2002 94: 5f 5m 5g⁴ 5.1f 5m⁶ 6g Aug 3] strong, lengthy filly: fairly useful handicapper: best at 5f: acts on firm and good to soft going: sometimes on toes/early to post: reportedly bled from nose on reappearance. *T. D. Barron*

MUJAGAIN 3 b.g. Mujadil (USA) 119 – Spoilt Again 91 (Mummy's Pet 125) [2002 **56** 5.7g* 6m⁴ May 20] 10,000F, 10,000Y: eighth foal: half-brother to several winners, including useful 7f to 9f winner High Spirits (by Great Commotion): dam 9f/1¼m winner: 50/1-winner of claimer at Bath: still seemed green/unable to get a run in similar event at Windsor (claimed to join J. M. Bradley £9,000) later in May: will stay 6f. *B. Gubby*

MUJARAD (USA) 2 b.c. (Mar 28) King of Kings (IRE) 125 – Happy Result (USA) **81 p** (Diesis 133) [2002 7d⁵ 7d⁴ Nov 2] $130,000F, IR 150,000Y: well-made colt: has a quick action: half-brother to several winners, notably useful 1996 2-y-o 1m winner in France and Italy Happy Dancer (by Seattle Dancer): dam, lightly-raced maiden, half-sister to smart miler Pater Noster: better effort in maidens (fairly useful form) when fourth of 22 to Blazing Thunder at Newmarket, travelling well long way: should stay 1m: open to improvement. *J. H. M. Gosden*

MUJASINA (IRE) 3 b.c. Mujadil (USA) 119 – Camassina (IRE) 62 (Taufan (USA) **–** 119) [2002 70: p8g Jan 23] rather leggy, workmanlike colt: fair at 2 yrs: well held only start in 2002. *J. L. Eyre*

MUJFOUR (IRE) 3 b.g. Mujadil (USA) 119 – Symbolise (IRE) (Nashwan (USA) **–** 135) [2002 8.5m 8.1g 7m Sep 17] IR 7,000Y: first foal: dam unraced out of sister to smart French/US 7.5f to 9f winner Sha Tha: well held in maiden/sellers. *M. R. Channon*

MUJKARI (IRE) 6 ch.g. Mujtahid (USA) 118 – Hot Curry (USA) (Sharpen Up 127) **54 §** [2002 54d: 10m⁶ 12m 10m 9.9g p7g* f7g f9.4g p7g⁴ p7g⁴ Dec 18] lengthy gelding: modest performer: won claimer at Lingfield in October: effective at 7f to easy 13f: acts on firm going, good to soft and all-weather: visored/blinkered: got loose and withdrawn on intended reappearance: sometimes looks none too keen: untrustworthy. *J. M. Bradley*

MUKLAH (IRE) 3 b.f. Singspiel (IRE) 133 – Maraatib (IRE) 93 (Green Desert (USA) 127) [2002 101: 8m Sep 13] small, strong, lengthy filly: useful in 2001: well held in minor event at Doncaster only 3-y-o start: stayed 7f: raced only on good going or firmer: visits Silver Hawk. *B. W. Hills* –

MULABEE (USA) 3 br.g. Gulch (USA) – Shir Dar (FR) (Lead On Time (USA) 123) [2002 84p: 9m 8.1g f7g Dec 31] useful-looking gelding: fairly useful at 2 yrs: well held in handicaps in 2002: off 5 months after reappearance, left E. Dunlop 5,000 gns before final outing. *R. Brotherton* –

MULAN PRINCESS (IRE) 2 b.f. (Jan 19) Mukaddamah (USA) 125 – Notley Park 71 (Wolfhound (USA) 126) [2002 5m³ 5g⁶ 6m 6.1s⁴ 6.1g² 7d 6g³ 7m⁶ 7m³ 6.1m³ 6g⁴ f7g⁵ f8.5g⁴ Dec 20] 9,000Y: leggy filly: first foal: dam, maiden who stayed 7.5f, half-sister to smart sprinter Notley: fair maiden: second at Nottingham: left Mrs P. N. Dutfield after eleventh start: effective at 6f to 8.5f: acts on soft going, good to firm and fibresand: consistent. *T. J. Naughton* **66**

MULDOON (IRE) 3 b.c. Fumo di Londra (IRE) 108 – Caroline's Mark (On Your Mark 125) [2002 53: f6s⁶ f7g² f7g f7g p6g⁵ f6g f7g 6g* 5.7g² 6d 5.7d 5.1f f5g f6g Nov 15] small colt: poor mover: modest on turf, poor on all-weather: won seller at Leicester in April: stays 7f: acts on soft going and all-weather: blinkered after sixth start: none too consistent. *B. Palling* **53 a48**

MULLER (IRE) 2 gr.g. (Jan 22) Bigstone (IRE) 126 – Missie Madam (IRE) (Kenmare (FR) 125) [2002 7s 6g 8g Sep 19] IR 7,000Y: first foal: dam, ran twice in Ireland, half-sister to smart Irish sprinter Antinnaz: no sign of ability: trained in Ireland by T. Stack first 2 starts. *J. S. Haldane* –

MULLION 2 b.g. (Apr 3) Reprimand 122 – Royal Jade 82 (Last Tycoon 131) [2002 6d 5.2d⁶ 5.7m³ p6g* 6m² 8m Sep 20] leggy, rather unfurnished gelding: good mover: third foal: half-brother to 3-y-o Million Percent and 4-y-o Xaloc Bay: dam, 7f winner, half-sister to smart sprinter Averti: fairly useful performer: awarded maiden at Lingfield in July on disqualification of Elusive City: best effort when short-headed by Fancy Lady in nursery at Goodwood: stays 6f, probably not quite 1m: acts on polytrack and good to firm going. *B. W. Hills* **89**

MULRAJ 3 b.g. Sayaarr (USA) – Elizabeth Ann (Octogenarian 69) [2002 p8g Feb 23] first reported foal: dam unraced: missed break and always detached in maiden at Lingfield. *M. D. I. Usher* –

MULSANNE 4 b.g. Clantime 101 – Prim Lass 65 (Reprimand 122) [2002 –: 10g 7.1m 6.1g Jul 5] no form. *P. A. Pritchard* –

MULTAKA (USA) 2 b.f. (May 2) Gone West (USA) – Wasnah (USA) 96 (Nijinsky (CAN) 138) [2002 7m 7f 7d Nov 2] tall, rather leggy filly: has scope: closely related to very smart 1996 2-y-o 7f winner who stayed 1¼m Bahhare (by Woodman) and half-sister to 2 winners by Riverman, notably high-class 6f (at 2 yrs) and 1m winner who stayed 10.4f Bahri: dam, maiden who should have stayed 1½m, half-sister to dam of Breeders' Cup Distaff winner Ajina: fair form in maidens: not knocked about last 2 starts: type to do better. *J. L. Dunlop* **66 p**

MULTICOLOUR 2 ch.f. (May 15) Rainbow Quest (USA) 134 – Raymouna (IRE) (High Top 131) [2002 8s p7g⁵ Oct 31] 26,000Y, 7,000 2-y-o: angular filly: half-sister to 3 winners, including smart Irish performers Rayouni (by Zayyani) and Raiyoun (by Doyoun), both 1m winners including at 2 yrs: dam, Irish 1m winner, half-sister to smart performer up to 1¾m Rayseka: better effort in maidens (modest form) when fifth to Littleton Arwen at Lingfield, slowly away: should stay at least 1¼m. *R. Hannon* **64**

MULTIPLOY 3 b.f. Deploy 131 – Multi-Sofft 30 (Northern State (USA) 91) [2002 56: 10d⁴ f12g 11.8m 11.9d 12m⁵ 13.8f² 11.9g 14.1d f16.2g³ Nov 18] close-coupled filly: modest maiden: stays 2m: acts on firm going, good to soft and fibresand: visored fourth start: edgy type: sold 4,700 gns. *I. A. Wood* **52**

MUMBLING (IRE) 4 ch.g. Dr Devious (IRE) 127 – Valley Lights (IRE) (Dance of Life (USA)) [2002 89: 10g 12m 10g 12.1v 12m⁴ 10.5d* 12g* 12m² 12m* 12.3m² 13.1g 12f⁵ Oct 3] strong, lengthy gelding: fairly useful performer: won claimers at Haydock and Doncaster and handicap at Pontefract in summer: effective at 10.5f to 1¾m: acts on soft and good to firm going: blinkered once. *M. H. Tompkins* **89**

MUNADIL   4 ch.c. Nashwan (USA) 135 – Bintalshaati 95 (Kris 135) [2002 86: 10.3f   –
8d 8.1m 10.3f Sep 25] angular, good-topped colt: fluent mover: fairly useful performer at
3 yrs: well held in 2002. *P. R. Webber*

MUNDO RARO   7 b.g. Zafonic (USA) 130 – Star Spectacle (Spectacular Bid (USA))   **45**
[2002 54: f8g 8.5m⁵ 7m 7g May 6] robust gelding: poor nowadays: stays 8.5f: acts on
fibresand, good to firm and good to soft going: blinkered last 2 starts: tongue tied in 2002.
J. G. FitzGerald

MUNGO PARK   8 b.g. Selkirk (USA) 129 – River Dove (USA) 86 (Riverman (USA)   **73 §**
131) [2002 85§: 5s 5f 5g⁴ 5d 5g⁴ 5m² 5g 5g³ 5m³ 5m⁶ 5m³ 5m 5m 5f Sep 26] big
gelding: impressed in appearance: had a round action: one-time fairly useful performer:
placed several times in 2002: was effective at 5f/6f: acted on any going: was occasionally
visored/blinkered: was sometimes unruly stall: was best held up as long as possible:
irresolute: dead. *M. Dods*

MUNQITH (USA)   3 b.c. Bahri (USA) 125 – Indihash (USA) 81 (Gulch (USA))   **82**
[2002 82p: 7m³ 8m⁵ 8f⁵ Oct 7] good-topped colt: has a quick action: fairly useful maiden:
better form at 7f than 1m: found nothing final start: sold 2,500 gns, sent to Holland.
E. A. L. Dunlop

MUQBIL (USA)   2 ch.c. (Feb 26) Swain (IRE) 134 – Istiqlal (USA) (Diesis 133)   **106 P**
[2002 7m* 7f² Oct 2]
          It's about time John Dunlop's yard had another three-year-old to crow
about. Since Millenary's win in the St Leger in 2000, Castle Stables has gone two
seasons without a runner in the Two Thousand Guineas, the Derby or the St Leger.
Colts of classic potential in the yard don't always tend to be highly tried as
two-year-olds and are often given plenty of time to mature. Millenary ran twice
without winning in his first season, while the stable's last Derby winner Erhaab and
Epsom seconds Silver Patriarch and Sakhee all did their winning outside pattern
company as juveniles. It says much for the promising Muqbil that he was asked to
make his debut in a listed event, the Scottish & Newcastle Pub Enterprises Stakes
at Newbury in August. The race is currently restricted to horses sired by winners at
a mile and a half plus, and it had a fairly illustrious history in its days as the
Washington Singer Stakes, when it was won by Rodrigo de Triano and Lammtarra
amongst others. Muqbil launched its new manifestation in fine style. Starting at 4/1,
he brushed aside his five rivals in a matter of strides once asked to improve from
last and stormed away in the final furlong to beat Pinkerton by five lengths,
recording useful form—confirmed by time analysis—for a debutant, particularly
given the lack of early pace.
          On the strength of his debut, Muqbil started at 5/4-on in a field of five for the
Somerville Tattersall Stakes at Newmarket when next seen out in October. Again
patiently ridden, Muqbil was unsuited by a race which turned into even more of a
sprint. This time, however, he was up against more speedily-bred rivals, and, in the
circumstances, did equally well in defeat, crossed by Governor Brown as he was
tapped for speed in the Dip then rallying strongly without being knocked about,
beaten only half a length conceding the winner 3 lb.

*Scottish & Newcastle Pub Enterprises Stakes (Washington Singer), Newbury—
Muqbil quickens impressively; left in his wake are Pinkerton (left), La Mouline (second right),
Doc Watson and Theatre Time (right)*

		Nashwan	Blushing Groom
	Swain (IRE)	(ch 1986)	Height of Fashion
Muqbil (USA)	(b 1992)	Love Smitten	Key To The Mint
(ch.c. Feb 26, 2000)		(b 1981)	Square Angel
		Diesis	Sharpen Up
	Istiqlal (USA)	(ch 1980)	Doubly Sure
	(b 1993)	Wasnah	Nijinsky
		(b 1987)	Highest Trump

On balance, Muqbil should stay a mile and a half as a three-year-old. Muqbil's dam the unraced Istiqlal is a half-sister to Bahri, who was second to Halling in the Juddmonte International over ten furlongs but put up his most memorable effort when winning the Queen Elizabeth II Stakes over a mile. Her other half-brother of note was Bahhare, the joint-top two-year-old of 1996 who showed he stayed a mile and a quarter when third to Pilsudski in the Champion Stakes. Istiqlal's dam Wasnah was second in the Pretty Polly Stakes at Newmarket over a mile and a quarter and should have stayed a mile and a half. The only previous foal out of Istiqlal was the fairly useful Hureya (by Woodman), a winner over a mile and untried over further. Muqbil's sire Swain should, however, prove a fairly strong influence for stamina. He started his career by winning three times over a mile and three quarters and one of his two King George successes was achieved in gruelling conditions. Swain's sire Nashwan, who died in 2002, has proved quite a strong influence for stamina himself. Swain was unraced at two and got better and better with age, so it is most encouraging that three of his twelve runners on turf in Britain from his first crop were winners as two-year-olds, with Muqbil the first of them. Muqbil takes more after Nashwan in colour and markings and he moves with similar ease too. A good walker, he showed a flowing action to post at Newbury. He did tend to hang right in the Dip at Newmarket, probably due to inexperience, and will almost certainly benefit from another run beforehand if he is to tackle the Guineas. He is quoted at around 25/1 for Newmarket and at an attractive-looking 33/1 for the Derby at the time of writing. A lengthy, attractive colt, Muqbil remains a fine prospect, and should make his mark in good company. *J. L. Dunlop*

MUQTADI (IRE) 4 b.g. Marju (IRE) 127 – Kadwah (USA) 80 (Mr Prospector (USA)) [2002 p8g 8g 7m 6.1m f6s 7d f5g p7g5 Dec 30] quite attractive gelding: fairly useful winner at 2 yrs: little form in 2002 (trained by K. Morgan on reappearance): blinkered last 6 starts. *C. R. Dore* —

MURDINGA 3 br.g. Emperor Jones (USA) 119 – Tintinara (Selkirk (USA) 129) [2002 65: p10g 10m3 Oct 7] tall, rather unfurnished gelding: fair maiden: stays 1¼m: acts on good to firm going: has raced freely. *Lady Herries* — 73

MUREEFA (USA) 3 b.f. Bahri (USA) 125 – Mata Cara 98 (Storm Bird (CAN) 134) [2002 9m 10m2 Aug 31] fourth living foal: half-sister to 2 winners, including fairly useful 1½m winner Liefling (by Alleged): dam, 7f winner, out of Musidora winner Fatah Flare: better effort in maidens when 1½ lengths second to Tanaji at Ripon, racing freely: slowly away on debut: visits In The Wings. *J. H. M. Gosden* — 73

MURGHEM (IRE) 7 b.h. Common Grounds 118 – Fabulous Pet (Something-fabulous (USA)) [2002 108: 16.4m 11.8g2 14g4 12m3 13.3f 14f* 14.5g2 11.8s6 17v5 p12g Nov 14] rangy horse: smart performer: beat sole rival Harlestone Grey by 1¼ lengths in minor event at Haydock in September: some creditable efforts otherwise, including when 1½ lengths second to Island House in listed race at Leicester on second start, fourth in Curragh Cup (2½ lengths behind Daliapour) on third and second in listed race at Cologne (short-head behind Tempelwachter) on seventh: stays 14.5f: acts on any ground: blinkered twice: usually races up with pace. *M. Johnston* — 112

MURGHOB 3 b.c. Lycius (USA) 124 – Jamrat Samya (IRE) 79 (Sadler's Wells (USA) 132) [2002 8m 10s 8.2g 10f3 9.9d5 11.7m4 11s 10.9m2 10m Oct 1] first foal: dam, ran once, out of sister to Flame of Tara, herself dam of Salsabil and Marju: fair maiden handicapper: stays 11.7f: acts on firm ground: sold 22,000 gns, and joined P. Hughes, Ireland. *A. C. Stewart* — 74

MURRAY 3 b.g. Darshaan 133 – Melisendra (FR) (Highest Honor (FR) 124) [2002 10.3s* 12m4 15g4 Sep 19] leggy, quite attractive gelding: first foal: dam, useful French 5.5f (at 2 yrs) to 1m winner, out of smart French middle-distance performer Noble Tiara: — 96 useful form when winning maiden at Doncaster in March by 6 lengths from Shanook: below that level both starts after, off 4½ months after second outing: should stay at least 1½m: joined S. Seemar in UAE. *M. R. Channon*

MURRENDI (IRE) 4 b.g. Ashkalani (IRE) 128 – Formaestre (IRE) 56 (Formidable **64** (USA) 125) [2002 68: p10g p10g5 10.1d6 11.6m5 Jul 29] workmanlike gelding: modest handicapper: stays easy 1¼m: acts on good to firm going, good to soft and polytrack: tends to race freely. *R. J. O'Sullivan*

MURTAKEZ 2 b.g. (Mar 29) Alhaarth (IRE) 126 – Raaqiyya (USA) (Blushing Groom **58** (FR) 131) [2002 6g5 6m Aug 14] good-topped gelding: fifth foal: half-brother to Irish 6f winner Samawi (by Pennekamp): dam unraced half-sister to French fillies up to 1m Maximova, Vilikaia and Navratilovna, all at least smart: modest form in maidens, racing freely second start (subsequently gelded). *M. P. Tregoning*

MURZIM 3 b.g. Salse (USA) 128 – Guilty Secret (IRE) 109 (Kris 135) [2002 59?: **83** 12g* 10.9g2 12.3m5 14.1m2 p16g2 11.9g 16.2g3 14m* 11.7m2 10.1g4 10.9s* 11.8s6 11.6d Oct 28] angular, quite attractive gelding: fairly useful performer: won minor event at Musselburgh in March, handicap at Sandown in July and claimer at Ayr in October: claimed from G. Butler £12,000 penultimate start: effective at 11f to 2m: acts on polytrack, soft and good to firm going: effective blinkered/visored or not: has raced very freely/carried head awkwardly. *J. Gallagher*

MUSALLY 5 ch.g. Muhtarram (USA) 125 – Flourishing (IRE) 85 (Trojan Fen 118) **68** [2002 f9.4g f14.8g6 f16.2f Nov 11] fairly useful at 3 yrs: fair form at best on return in 2002: stays 1¼m. *W. Jenks*

MUSANID (USA) 2 ch.c. (Feb 8) Swain (IRE) 134 – Siyadah (USA) 106 (Mr **100** Prospector (USA)) [2002 7g3 8f3 Oct 2] good-bodied colt: has a fluent, round action: second foal: dam, 1¼m winner, out of Yorkshire Oaks winner Roseate Tern (also third in Oaks and St Leger), herself half-sister to high-class middle-distance performer Ibn Bey: third in maidens at Leicester and Newmarket, beaten 2½ lengths by Lateen Sails on latter course (useful form), taking strong hold to post and once racing and no extra final 1f: bred to be suited by 1¼m+: well up to winning races. *Sir Michael Stoute*

MUSAWAH (USA) 2 b.f. (Apr 28) Gulch (USA) – Haniya (USA) 92 (Caerleon (USA) **63 p** 132) [2002 6m Aug 4] fourth foal: closely related to fairly useful 1999 2-y-o 7f winner Atwaar (by Woodman) and half-sister to useful 7.6f (at 2 yrs) to 1¼m winner Zulfaa (by Bahri): dam, 1½m winner, half-sister to very smart performer up to 1½m Volochine: 16/1, 9 lengths eighth of 16 to Illustria in maiden at Newbury, not knocked about when fading: should improve. *J. L. Dunlop*

MUSH (IRE) 5 b.g. Thatching 131 – Petite Jameel (IRE) (Ahonoora 122) [2002 75, **80** a–: 8g 7.9d5 8.1m2 8m6 8d* 8d 8.3m* 7.9m 8m 8s p7g2 Dec 30] quite good-topped geld- **a66** ing: fairly useful handicapper on turf, fair on all-weather: won at Newmarket in August and Hamilton in September: effective at 7f/1m: acts on polytrack, firm and good to soft going: has been slowly away: carries head awkwardly: free-going sort. *N. P. Littmoden*

MUSICAL DANNY 5 b.g. Rambo Dancer (CAN) 107 – Musical Princess 66 (Cavo **–** Doro 124) [2002 12g3 14.1f4 12d5 13.8m 12m 10s Oct 15] brother to 1¼m/1½m winner Sing And Dance and half-brother to 2 winners, including fairly useful 9f to 10.5f winner Drummer Hicks (by Seymour Hicks): dam 1½m to 2m winner at 5 yrs: well held in maidens/handicaps. *J. R. Weymes*

MUSICAL FAIR 2 b.f. (Mar 8) Piccolo 121 – Guarded Expression 51 (Siberian **–** Express (USA) 125) [2002 5g 6m 6d Oct 18] 9,000Y: fourth foal: half-sister to 6-y-o Jackies Baby and 5-y-o Highcal: dam ran 4 times at 5f/6f at 2 yrs: no form in maidens. *J. A. Glover*

MUSICAL FLUTE 3 b.f. Piccolo 121 – Stride Home 78 (Absalom 128) [2002 68d: **–** p7g p7g p10g 10.2g Apr 30] disappointing maiden. *M. Madgwick*

MUSICAL HEATH (IRE) 5 b.g. Common Grounds 118 – Song of The Glens **87 d** (Horage 124) [2002 87: 8.3g* 8g p8g 8.3m5 9m 10m 8f4 8m6 8g Oct 17] lengthy, angular gelding: fairly useful handicapper at best: won at Windsor in April: below par last 5 starts: stays 8.5f: acts on good to firm going: tried tongue tied: usually races prominently: sold 2,000 gns. *P. W. Harris*

MUSICAL KEY 2 b.f. (Apr 20) Key of Luck (USA) 126 – Musianica 92 (Music Boy **71** 124) [2002 5m4 5m 5p4 5m6 Aug 28] close-coupled filly: half-sister to several winners, including 7f (at 2 yrs) to 1¼m winner Mensa (by Rudimentary) and 6f winner (including at 2 yrs) Volata (by Flying Spur), both smart and later successful in Hong Kong as

Industrialist and Firebolt respectively: dam 2-y-o 6f winner: fair maiden: should stay at least 6f. *M. H. Tompkins*

MUSICAL MAYHEM (IRE) 9 b.g. Shernazar 131 – Minstrels Folly (USA) (The **73 d** Minstrel (CAN) 135) [2002 –: 14.1d⁴ 13.3s 18s 16.2m Jun 17] lightly-raced peformer: fair at best on Flat in 2002, form only on reappearance: stays 2m: acts on heavy going: tried blinkered: won over hurdles in July. *D. J. Wintle*

MUSICAL SLEUTH 3 ch.g. Piccolo 121 – My Dear Watson (Chilibang 120) [2002 **66** 7.1g⁵ 7m³ f6g⁴ 6s³ 6m⁵ 5g² 5f Oct 3] 14,500Y, resold 20,000Y: second foal: dam twice-raced half-sister to smart sprinter Sizzling Melody: fair maiden: stays 7f: races freely. *G. C. Bravery*

MUSIC BOOK 2 b.f. (Feb 19) Piccolo 121 – Big Story 50 (Cadeaux Genereux 131) **–** [2002 7.1g Sep 12] fourth foal: half-sister to 1998 2-y-o 6f winner who probably stayed 1¾m Scoop (by Scenic): dam ran twice: 66/1, last in maiden at Chepstow. *Jane Southcombe*

MUSIC CLUB (USA) 3 b.f. Dixieland Band (USA) – Long View (USA) (Damascus **107** (USA)) [2002 93p: 10d* 10.5m Jun 9] big, useful-looking filly: has a fluent, round action: useful form in 3 outings: won listed race at Longchamp (made all to beat Marche de Paix 3 lengths) in May: 11/2, respectable 7½ lengths eighth to Bright Sky in Prix de Diane at Chantilly, only subsequent outing: will probably stay 1½m: yet to encounter extremes of going: sent to USA. *J. H. M. Gosden*

MUSIC MAID (USA) 4 b.f. Inzar (USA) 112 – Richardstown Lass (IRE) (Muscatite **58** 122) [2002 69: 8.3g 8.5g⁵ 8.3d 7m 7m⁵ 7g 8f Aug 23] angular filly: modest handicapper: stays 8.5f: acts on firm going, probably on soft: has swished tail/wandered. *H. S. Howe*

MUSTANEER (USA) 2 b.c. (Feb 18) Gone West (USA) – Market Booster (USA) **80 p** 117 (Green Dancer (USA) 132) [2002 7s* Oct 15] $700,000Y, resold IR 150,000Y: lengthy colt: third foal: dam 1¼m/1½m performer in Ireland/US: weak 11/2-shot, won 13-runner maiden at Leicester by ½ length from Meelup, getting up well inside final 1f: will stay at least 1m: sure to progress. *Sir Michael Stoute*

MUSTAWA (USA) 3 b.g. Wild Again (USA) – Tatwij (USA) 94 (Topsider (USA)) **–** [2002 8m Apr 18] sturdy, useful-looking gelding: eighth foal: half-brother to fairly useful 6f winner Masafah (by Cadeaux Genereux) and 1¼m winner Azihaam (by Cozzene): dam 2-y-o 5f winner who probably stayed 1m: short to post, well held in maiden at Ripon. *E. A. L. Dunlop*

MUST BE LOVE (IRE) 2 b.f. (Apr 15) Turtle Island (IRE) 123 – Shalstayholy **57** (IRE) 84 (Shalford (IRE) 124§) [2002 5s 6g⁵ 6.1d⁴ 8.3d⁵ 7g f6s³ f7g 7s Oct 28] 5,000Y: small filly: first foal: dam 5f to 7f winner: modest maiden: in frame in claimers: may prove best at 7f/1m: acts on fibresand, raced only on good going or softer on turf: sold 1,400 gns. *J. G. Portman*

MUST BE MAGIC 5 b.g. Magic Ring (IRE) 115 – Sequin Lady (Star Appeal 133) **64** [2002 66: p10g⁶ p10g² p10g³ p10g 10.3s 9.7m⁶ 8.5g 10m⁶ 9s⁴ p10g 9m 8d² 8d⁴ 9m⁴ 8m⁵ 8m* 8.9f Oct 12] smallish, good-topped gelding: modest handicapper: won at Kempton in September: best at 1m/1¼m: acts on soft going, good to firm and polytrack: effective visored or not. *H. J. Collingridge*

MUTABARI (USA) 8 ch.g. Seeking The Gold (USA) – Cagey Exuberance (USA) **55** (Exuberant (USA)) [2002 –, a51: f8.5g f9.4g⁶ f9.4s⁵ f9.4g³ 8d⁵ 7d* 7.1g* 7m 7m f7g² 6.9d f7s f8s f8g⁵ Oct 22] rangy gelding: fluent mover: modest performer: won claimers at Salisbury and Musselburgh in June: effective at 7f, barely at 1¼m: acts on fibresand and any turf: effective visored or not: sometimes slowly away. *J. L. Spearing*

MUTABASSIR (IRE) 8 ch.g. Soviet Star (USA) 128 – Anghaam (USA) 80 (Diesis **63** 133) [2002 70: p8g⁴ f8.5g⁶ p8g² p7g p8g⁵ 8f 8f p7g p7g* p7g⁴ Dec 30] modest performer: claimed from G. L. Moore third start: won claimer at Lingfield in December: stays easy 1m: acts on all-weather, very best efforts on turf on good going or firmer: has started slowly. *Andrew Reid*

MUTADARRA (IRE) 9 ch.g. Mujtahid (USA) 118 – Silver Echo (Caerleon (USA) **45 §** 132) [2002 52§: p12g⁶ f12g f12g Feb 8] tall, angular gelding: poor handicapper: stays 1½m: yet to race on heavy going, acts on any turf and polytrack: tried blinkered early in career: held up and tends to hang: unreliable: won twice over hurdles in October. *J. W. Mullins*

MUTAJJEB (IRE) 2 b.c. (Feb 29) Darshaan 133 – Nightlark (IRE) 85 (Night Shift **67 ?** (USA)) [2002 8.1m⁶ 10s⁶ Oct 23] IR 26,000Y: second foal: half-brother to 3-y-o

Nightwatchman: dam, 1½m winner, half-sister to smart 9f to 11f performer Overbury from family of Vintage Crop: seemingly fair form when last of 6 to Orange Touch in maiden at Sandown: well held on much softer ground next time: should stay at least 1¼m. *E. A. L. Dunlop*

MUTAKARRIM   5 ch.g. Mujtahid (USA) 118 – Alyakkh (IRE) 78 (Sadler's Wells (USA) 132) [2002 112: 10m 12s⁴ 14g⁴ 12s² 12f² 11s⁴ Oct 20] good-topped gelding: smart performer: ran at least respectably all starts in 2002, including when 6 lengths second of 4 to Storming Home in listed race at Newmarket on penultimate one: stays 1½m, possibly not 1¾m: acts on any going: usually blinkered: fairly useful hurdler. *D. K. Weld, Ireland*   **112**

MUTARAFAA (USA)   3 b.g. Red Ransom (USA) – Mashaarif (USA) (Mr Prospector (USA)) [2002 76: f8g* 7s 9g f8.5g⁴ f7s Sep 7] strong gelding: fair performer: won maiden at Southwell in February: off 4½ months before final outing: stays 8.5f: acts on fibresand and good to firm going. *D. Shaw*   **74**

MUTARASED (USA)   4 b. or br.g. Storm Cat (USA) – Sajjaya (USA) 97 (Blushing Groom (FR) 131) [2002 88: 8d Jul 31] small, stocky gelding: fairly useful handicapper at 3 yrs: always behind only 4-y-o start: sent to UAE. *R. J. White*   **–**

MUTARED (IRE)   4 b.g. Marju (USA) – Shahaada (USA) 57 (Private Account (USA)) [2002 78+: 10.3s f8.5g* 8m 7g³ 7m⁴ 10.2d² 11.9d 9d 7m 8.1g 8.5g f8.5g⁴ f7s p8g f6s* Dec 26] lengthy gelding: fairly useful handicapper: won amateur events at Wolverhampton in April and December: left Gay Kelleway after eleventh start: effective at 6f to 1¼m: acts on good to firm going, soft and all-weather: tried blinkered/visored: has left stall awkwardly: often amateur ridden. *N. P. Littmoden*   **80**
a84

MUTASAWWAR   8 ch.g. Clantime 101 – Keen Melody (USA) 60 (Sharpen Up 127) [2002 65: p6g p5g f5g³ f5g f5g³ f5g 5.1d* 5.3f f5g* f5g 5g 5d⁶ 5s 5.3g⁴ 5m f5g³ 5.3m 5.1g 5f f6s Oct 8] lengthy gelding: modest handicapper: won at Nottingham and Southwell in spring: effective at 5f/easy 6f: acts on any turf going/all-weather: has won in blinkers: has been awkward leaving stall: often races prominently: none too consistent. *J. M. Bradley*   **64**

MUTAWAQED (IRE)   4 ch.g. Zafonic (USA) 130 – Waqood (USA) 75 (Riverman (USA) 131) [2002 82p: p7g* p7g³ 7.6s 7m 8g⁴ 8s p7g² Dec 28] strong, heavy-bodied gelding: fairly useful handicapper: won at Lingfield in January: left D. Arbuthnot before running well there final outing: effective at 6f to 1m: acts on all-weather, best effort on turf on good going: tried visored, usually blinkered/tongue tied: sometimes slowly away: tends to idle/carry head awkwardly: suited by waiting tactics. *M. A. Magnusson*   **86**
a90

MUTAYAM   2 b.c. (Mar 16) Compton Place 125 – Final Shot 91 (Dalsaan 125) [2002 5.7f 6g 5m Aug 28] 40,000F, 120,000Y: half-brother to several winners, including 5f (at 2 yrs)/6f winner Double Action (by Reprimand) and 6f (including at 2 yrs) winner Sir Nicholas (by Cadeaux Genereux), both smart: dam won Ayr Gold Cup: well held in maidens: sold 1,500 gns. *M. R. Channon*   **–**

MUTINY   4 ch.g. Selkirk (USA) 129 – Indian Love Song 68 (Be My Guest (USA) 126) [2002 –: 10.3s 14.1d f9.4g 16f f12g Nov 25] little form: left B. Meehan after third outing: tried blinkered. *B. W. Duke*   **–**

MUWAJAHA   2 b.f. (Apr 17) Night Shift (USA) – Maraatib (IRE) 93 (Green Desert (USA) 127) [2002 6g³ Oct 17] IR 31,000Y: small, close-coupled filly: half-sister to several winners, including useful 5f/6f winner (including at 2 yrs) Khasayl (by Lycius) and 3-y-o Muklah: dam 5f (including at 2 yrs)/6f winner: 7/2, close third of 18 to Pigeon Point in maiden at Newmarket, staying on well once switched: will probably stay 7f: sure to improve and win a race or 2. *B. W. Hills*   **87 p**

MUWASSI   3 b.c. Grand Lodge (USA) 125 – Sardonic 105 (Kris 135) [2002 10m² 8.5m* 8m⁴ 10.5d* 9.9g⁵ a8f a9f Dec 19] 260,000Y: quite good-topped, angular colt: second foal: half-brother to 4-y-o Satyr: dam, 1¼m winner, daughter of smart performer up to 13f Sardegna from very good family of Slip Anchor: useful performer: won maiden at Beverley (slowly away) in June and 4-runner handicap at Haydock (beat Martin House by 3½ lengths) in August: left Sir Michael Stoute after next start: well held in handicaps on dirt at Nad Al Sheba after: will probably stay 1½m: yet to race on extremes of going on turf: often raced freely in Britain. *E. Charpy, UAE*   **99**

MUYASSIR (IRE)   7 b.g. Brief Truce (USA) 126 – Twine (Thatching 131) [2002 88, a74: p8g⁵ p8g⁵ p7g p8g⁵ 8m 8g 8m⁴ 8g² 8m⁴ 9m⁴ 8.5g 10m p10g Dec 28] compact, deep-bodied gelding: fairly useful handicapper on turf, fair on all-weather: effective at 1m/1¼m: acts on firm going and polytrack: tried blinkered/tongue tied: often races handily. *Miss B. Sanders*   **84**
a73

MYAHS MIRACLE   4 b.f. Never So Bold 135 – My Ducats (IRE) (Red Sunset 120)   –
[2002 6g f8.5g Nov 18] second reported foal: dam no worthwhile form: tailed off in
maiden/seller. *D. J. Wintle*

MY AMERICAN BEAUTY   4 ch.f. Wolfhound (USA) 126 – Hooray Lady 92   **92**
(Ahonoora 122) [2002 87+: 5f 5f 5d 5g⁴ 5m³ 5g² Jul 19] big, lengthy filly: fairly useful
handicapper: good efforts at Ascot (close third to Brave Burt) and Pontefract (¾-length
second to Budelli) last 2 starts: should stay 6f: acts on firm going, possibly not soft: edgy
sort. *T. D. Easterby*

MY BAYARD   3 ch.g. Efisio 120 – Bay Bay 101 (Bay Express 132) [2002 –: f7g f7g   **61**
f11g² Dec 17] modest maiden: stays 11f: acts on fibresand: tried tongue tied. *J. O'Reilly*

MY BEST SIDE   4 b.g. Mistertopogigo (IRE) 118 – So Precise (FR) (Balidar 133)   –
[2002 f16g Jun 19] half-brother to 11f winner Crystal Park (by Head For Heights)
and winner in Sweden by Elegant Air: dam ran once: well beaten in Southwell seller.
Mrs C. A. Dunnett

MY BOLD BOYO   7 b.g. Never So Bold 135 – My Rosie (Forzando 122) [2002 37:   **38**
10.5g⁶ 10m Sep 3] sturdy, close-coupled gelding: poor handicapper: barely stays 1½m:
acts on firm going, probably on soft. sometimes blinkered earlier in career: won twice
over hurdles in October. *K. Bishop*

MY BROTHER   8 b.g. Lugana Beach 116 – Lucky Love 65 (Mummy's Pet 125)   **61 §**
[2002 54: 6d² 5.7d 6m 6g 5d⁶ 5f 7f Sep 17] modest handicapper: best at 5f/6f: best
form on good/good to soft ground: visored once as 5-y-o: sometimes starts slowly.
Dr J. R. J. Naylor

MY DAISYCHAIN   2 ch.f. (Mar 12) Hector Protector (USA) 124 – Dayville (USA)   **73 ?**
86 (Dayjur (USA) 137) [2002 6f⁴ 7m² 7s 7.1s⁵ Nov 6] lengthy filly: second foal: half-
sister to Irish 5f winner Alexander Ballet (by Mind Games): dam, 6f winner (including at
2 yrs), half-sister to smart filly up to 1¼m in Britain/USA Spanish Fern out of sister to
Irish 1000 Guineas winner Al Bahathri: fair maiden: seemingly best effort when 7 lengths
second of 3 to Puma in minor event at Ascot: well held in listed event at Newbury next
time: will stay at least 1m. *M. Johnston*

MY DANCER (IRE)   3 b.f. Alhaarth (IRE) 126 – Dance Land (IRE) (Nordance
(USA)) [2002 79: 6g p5g 6.1f 7s Jun 5] strong, lengthy filly: fair performer at 2 yrs: well
held in 2002. *R. Hannon*

MY FAS (USA)   2 b. or br.c. (Feb 24) King of Kings (IRE) 125 – Granny Kelly (USA)   **79**
60 (Irish River (FR) 131) [2002 7m² 7m⁶ 7.1f⁵ Sep 28] $70,000F, 150,000Y: rather leggy,
useful-looking colt: has a quick, fluent action: second foal: half-brother to fairly useful
2001 2-y-o 6f and 7.5f winner Six Hitter (by Boundary): dam, third at 7f at 2 yrs in
Ireland, from family of Northern Dancer: fair maiden: second at York: disappointing
favourite at Haydock final start: likely to prove best up to 1m. *M. A. Jarvis*

MY GIDDY AUNT (IRE)   2 b.f. (Jan 15) Danehill (USA) 126 – Regal Portrait (IRE)   **57**
57 (Royal Academy (USA) 130) [2002 p7g 7d Nov 2] unfurnished filly: fourth foal:
half-sister to useful Italian sprinter King's Ivory (by Lake Coniston) and 3-y-o Atarama:
dam, lightly-raced maiden, half-sister to high-class pair High Estate and King's Theatre:
modest form when tenth of 15 in maiden at Lingfield: edgy and attended by 2 handlers,
well beaten in similar event at Newmarket 2 weeks later. *J. H. M. Gosden*

MY GIRL PEARL (IRE)   2 b.f. (Feb 10) Sri Pekan (USA) 117 – Desert Bloom (FR)   **65**
(Last Tycoon 131) [2002 f5g⁶ 5f⁴ 6.1s 5.3g³ 7.5m⁵ 6m⁶ 5.7f⁵ 7m³ 6g 6.1m 7m Sep 17]
4,000Y: angular, unfurnished filly: first foal: dam, second at 7.5f in France, daughter of
useful 5f performer Desert Dawn: fair maiden: third at Brighton and Newbury (nursery):
stays 7f: acts on firm going, probably on fibresand: none too consistent. *J. M. Bradley*

MY GODSON   12 br.g. Valiyar 129 – Blessit 79 (So Blessed 130) [2002 7g May 6]   –
sturdy gelding: no longer of any account. *F. Watson*

MY JODIE   2 b.f. (Apr 28) Bluegrass Prince (IRE) 110 – Sally Green (IRE) 79   **57**
(Common Grounds 118) [2002 6.1m⁵ 6g p6g Nov 19] 1,000Y: lengthy filly: first foal:
dam, 5f/6f (latter at 2 yrs) winner, half-sister to smart miler Soviet Bureau: modest
maiden: should stay at least 7f. *M. G. Quinlan*

MY LAST BEAN (IRE)   5 gr.g. Soviet Lad (USA) – Meanz Beanz (High Top 131)   **76**
[2002 73: f12s⁴ f12g² p13g f12g* f12g* 12s⁵ 13g⁶ 13.3s 11.9d² 13s f14s f12g² Dec 27]
fair performer: won maiden in February and apprentice handicap at Wolverhampton and
Southwell in March: stays 13f: acts on fibresand and soft going: usually blinkered
nowadays: races prominently. *B. Smart*

MY LINE   5 b.g. Perpendicular 119 – My Desire 88 (Grey Desire 115) [2002 58p: **72**
12.4g* 13g 16d⁴ 14.1s* 14d⁴ 14.1s* 14.4g⁴ 14.4g⁵ 14.6s Oct 25] lengthy gelding: fair
handicapper: won at Newcastle and Carlisle (twice, edged markedly left first occasion)
between May and July: will stay beyond 2m: acts on soft going: has a low head carriage.
Mrs M. Reveley

MY LOVELY   4 b.f. Dolphin Street (FR) 125 – My Bonus 79 (Cyrano de Bergerac   **–**
120) [2002 5s⁵ p6g Dec 30] won both starts at 2 yrs: little form in 2 runs 6 months apart in
2002. *D. J. S. Cosgrove*

MY LUCY LOCKET (IRE)   4 b.f. Mujadil (USA) 119 – First Nadia (Auction Ring   **96 §**
(USA) 123) [2002 88: 7m 8d 8.3s* 8.1m⁶ 7.1d 8d 8.3m² 8m 8g p10g p10g p8g⁵ p8g⁵ Dec   **a89 §**
30] rather leggy, angular filly: unimpressive mover: useful handicapper on turf, fairly
useful on all-weather: won at Windsor in May: good head second to Shaiyzima at same
course in August: best form at 1m: probably acts on any turf going/polytrack: sometimes
hangs (markedly so on occasions): inconsistent. *R. Hannon*

MY MAITE (IRE)   3 b.g. Komaite (USA) – Mena 58 (Blakeney 126) [2002 6m⁴ 7g⁵   **70**
8m⁶ 6m⁶ 7m 8.5m⁵ 8m⁶ 10m p10g* p10g⁵ Dec 28] third foal: brother to 4-y-o Komena: **a73**
dam maiden who probably stayed 11.5f: fair performer: won handicap at Lingfield in
October: stays 1¼m: acts on good to firm going and polytrack: tongue tied fourth to ninth
starts/visored last 2. *R. Ingram*

MY MAN FRIDAY   6 b.g. Lugana Beach 116 – My Ruby Ring 72 (Blushing Scribe   **54**
(USA) 107) [2002 45: 7f⁶ 7m* 7m 7m⁶ 7.1g 6g⁴ 6g⁴ 7m 5.9m⁴ p7g Oct 16] modest
handicapper: won at Brighton in June: effective at 6f/7f: acts on polytrack and probably
any turf going: has edged right/found little/carried head high/flashed tail. *P. W. Hiatt*

MY MATE WHITEY (IRE)   3 ch.g. Millkom 124 – Imagery (Vision (USA)) [2002   **–**
p8g f9.4g 10d⁶ 12s Jun 12] 9,000Y: workmanlike gelding: closely related to winner
up to 9f in Italy by Cyrano de Bergerac: dam no form: little form. *K. Bell*

MY MELLORS (USA)   2 b.c. (Feb 16) Woodman (USA) 126 – Breath Taking (FR)   **66 p**
119 (Nureyev (USA) 131) [2002 7f Oct 3] 3,500,000 francs Y: smallish, attractive colt:
closely related to French 1993 2-y-o 6.5f winner Arabian Sky (by Fappiano) and half-
brother to 3 winners, including smart French/US performer up to 8.5f Borodislew (by
Seattle Slew): dam French 5f to 6.5f winner, including at 2 yrs: 12/1, 12 lengths tenth of
26 to Desert Star in maiden at Newmarket, fading: should improve. *H. R. A. Cecil*

MYND   2 b.g. (Mar 24) Atraf 116 – Prim Lass 65 (Reprimand 122) [2002 6m 5.1s³   **65**
p5g⁵ Nov 13] 12,000Y: workmanlike gelding: third foal: brother to 3-y-o Primarosa: dam,
maiden, might have proved best at 5f/6f and hinted at temperament: fair form in maidens:
third at Nottingham: should stay 6f. *R. M. Whitaker*

MY ONLY SUNSHINE   3 b.g. First Trump 118 – Fiveofive (IRE) 61 (Fairy King   **93**
(USA)) [2002 76: 6m² 6g 6m² 6d⁴ Jul 9] dipped-backed gelding: fairly useful handicapper: good efforts in 2002 when in frame at Newmarket, including fourth to Feet So
Fast: effective at 6f/7f: yet to race on extremes of going: sometimes carries head high/
wanders. *G. G. Margarson*

MY PETAL   6 gr.m. Petong 126 – Najariya (Northfields (USA)) [2002 –: 6f 5.7g   **–**
May 7] tall mare: fairly useful winner at 2 yrs: lightly raced since: tried blinkered.
J. M. Bradley

MY PLEDGE (IRE)   7 b.g. Waajib 121 – Pollys Glow (IRE) 91 (Glow (USA)) [2002   **62**
64: p12g² 12g 11.6m 12g* 12m⁴ p12g Oct 31] modest handicapper: made all at
Folkestone in August: should stay 1¾m: acts on polytrack, good to firm and good to soft
going: has worn tongue strap: often slowly away: sometimes races freely. *C. A. Horgan*

MY RAGGEDY MAN   3 b.g. Forzando 122 – Ragged Moon 72 (Raga Navarro   **102**
(ITY) 119) [2002 81: p8g² p7g 9g⁵ 9f⁶ p8g 7g* 7d* 7m² 9m⁶ 8m⁵ 7f 8.1g² Oct 5] smallish,
sturdy gelding: useful handicapper: won at Brighton in May and Epsom in July: best
effort when 2 lengths second to Perfect Storm at Sandown final start: effective at 7f to 9f:
acts on polytrack, soft and firm going: blinkered once, effective visored or not: tried
tongue tied: sometimes races lazily: sent to UAE. *R. Hannon*

MY RETREAT (USA)   5 b.g. Hermitage (USA) – My Jessica Ann (USA) (Native   **76 d**
Rythm) [2002 88: f7s* f7s f8.5g 7.1m f8.5g 9.3g⁵ 8.3g 8.1d f8.5g f8.5g Dec 14] sturdy
gelding: fair performer: won minor event at Southwell in January: effective at 7f to easy
9.4f: acts on heavy going and fibresand: blinkered (below form) once: usually waited
with: on downgrade. *I. Semple*

MYRTLE MEG   4 b.f. Chocolat de Meguro (USA) 98 – Barefoot Landing (USA)   –
(Cozzene (USA)) [2002 12m Aug 16] first foal: dam, poor novice hurdler, out of half-
sister to smart performer up to 1½m Triarius: well held in maiden at Catterick: sold 800
gns, sent to Kuwait. *M. Johnston*

MYRTUS   3 ch.g. Double Eclipse (IRE) 122 – My Desire 88 (Grey Desire 115) [2002   –
10f May 13] lengthy gelding: third foal: half-brother to 5-y-o My Line: dam, suited by
thorough test of stamina, also winning stayer over hurdles: always behind in Redcar
maiden. *Mrs M. Reveley*

MY SHARP GREY   3 gr.f. Tragic Role (USA) – Sharp Anne 74§ (Belfort (FR) 89)   **64**
[2002 54: 7s 8m² 8.5g 8m⁴ 8g² p10g³ 8g⁴ p7g Oct 31] modest maiden: best at 1m/1¼m:
acts on good to firm going and polytrack. *A. Charlton*

MYSTERI DANCER   4 b.g. Rudimentary (USA) 118 – Mystery Ship 105 (Decoy   **79**
Boy 129) [2002 83: p10g p10g² p10g⁶ p10g p8g³ 10g² 10m 9m 11.6m⁴ p8g p10g Dec 11]
fair performer: stays easy 1½m: acts on all-weather, firm and soft going: tried in visor/
cheekpieces: has started slowly: often takes good hold. *R. J. O'Sullivan*

MYSTERINCH   2 b.c. (Apr 29) Inchinor 119 – Hakone (IRE) 78 (Alzao (USA) 117)   **98**
[2002 6f 7.1m⁴ 7m⁴ 8d² 8g* 8m* Sep 12] 7,000Y: good-topped colt: fourth foal: half-
brother to 2 winners, including Irish 1¼m winner Casa Que Canta (by Robellino): dam,
Irish maiden (stayed 1m), sister to smart 9f to 1½m performer Cicerao: useful performer:
won nurseries at Newcastle in August and Doncaster (beat only other horse to race far
side Go Tech by 1¼ lengths) in September: will stay 1¼m: acts on good to firm and good
to soft ground. *N. P. Littmoden*

MYSTERIOUS FORCE   3 b.f. Forzando 122 – Mystique (Mystiko (USA) 124)   –
[2002 60: f7s f7g 9d Aug 23] modest performer at 2 yrs: well held in 2002 (left D. Barker
after second start). *G. M. Moore*

MYSTERIUM   8 gr.g. Mystiko (USA) 124 – Way To Go 69 (Troy 137) [2002 62:   **57**
p13g⁴ f12g³ f12g⁴ p13g² p12g 11.9f³ 11.9g³ 9.9g 12g 16.2m* 14.1f⁴ 16.2f³ 16.2m³
17.2g* 14.8g 17.1m⁶ 14.1m 16.2m² 15.9f² 17.1f³ p16g Oct 16] tall, leggy gelding:
modest handicapper: won at Warwick and Bath in summer: stays 17f: acts on firm going
and all-weather: usually visored: sometimes slowly away: held up: has hung left/looked
none too keen. *N. P. Littmoden*

MYSTERY PIPS   2 b.f. (Feb 18) Bin Ajwaad (IRE) 119 – Le Shuttle 49 (Presidium   –
124) [2002 f6g f6g Oct 19] second foal: dam, sprint maiden, out of sister to very smart 5f
performer Paris House: tailed off in maiden/claimer. *J. D. Czerpak*

MYSTICAL CHARM (IRE)   3 ch.f. Indian Ridge 123 – Manazil (IRE) 98 (Generous   –
(IRE) 139) [2002 6g 7f 7f f6g Nov 25] IR 17,000Y: lengthy filly: first foal: dam, 1m/1¼m
winner, half-sister to 5-y-o Takamaka Bay: little form. *J. G. Given*

MYSTIC FOREST   3 b.g. Charnwood Forest (IRE) 125 – Mystic Beauty (IRE) (Alzao   **81**
(USA) 117) [2002 75: 9g 10m 9m p12g* p12g² 11.9d⁵ p12g² 11.7g⁴ 16s³ p12g p12g Nov   **a84**
23] leggy gelding: fairly useful handicapper: won at Lingfield in June: stays 2m: acts on
polytrack and soft ground: blinkered final start: sometimes soon off bridle. *B. J. Meehan*

MYSTIC MAN (FR)   4 b.g. Cadeaux Genereux 131 – Shawanni 105 (Shareef Dancer   **84**
(USA) 135) [2002 74: 8v 8.3s 9.3g 7.5g² 6.9d* 8.3d* 7.6g³ 8g² Aug 26] strong, angular
gelding: fairly useful performer: left W. Storey after third start: won handicap at Carlisle
and minor event at Hamilton in July: stays 8.3f: acts on soft and good to firm going:
sometimes tongue tied: tends to race freely. *K. A. Ryan*

MYSTIC MILE (IRE)   3 gr.f. Sadler's Wells (USA) 132 – Delage (Bellypha 130)   **94**
[2002 10d* 10g 11.6d* 12.5v⁵ Nov 20] IR 300,000Y: big, lengthy filly: third living foal:
closely related to German 1m winner Doctor Biba (by Classic Music): dam unraced
half-sister to very smart performer up to 7f College Chapel: fairly useful form: won
maiden in August and handicap in October, both at Windsor, latter by 1½ lengths from
Sergeant Cecil: creditable promoted fifth to Moon Search in listed race at Saint-Cloud
final start: stays 12.5f: raced only on good or softer going. *M. A. Jarvis*

MYSTIC STAR   2 b.f. (May 16) Young Ern 120 – Tocco Jewel 44 (Reesh 117) [2002   –
6m f7g 5.3m Oct 3] second foal: dam 1m winner: soundly beaten in sellers. *J. S. Moore*

MYSTIC VENTURE (IRE)   3 b.g. Woodborough (USA) 112 – Paganina (FR)   **48**
(Galetto (FR) 118) [2002 62: f7s⁴ f7g² f6g⁴ f7g² f7g* 7g 7m 7f f7s 7d f6g³ f7g² 6d f7g⁵   **a62**
f8g Nov 25] smallish, quite good-topped gelding: modest performer: won seller at

676

Southwell in March: stays 7f: acts on fibresand, firm and soft going: tried visored: has been slowly away: often makes running. *K. A. Ryan*

MYSTIC WITCH 3 b.f. Mistertopogigo (IRE) 118 – Walsham Witch 61 (Music **57** Maestro 119) [2002 49: 5d 5.9s 7f 8m 5m⁴ 5f² 5m² 5g 5m 5g 5g⁶ 5f Sep 26] smallish filly: modest maiden handicapper: stays 6f: acts on firm ground: blinkered after third start. *E. J. Alston*

MYSTIFY (FR) 2 ch.f. (Mar 20) Selkirk (USA) 129 – Mytilene (IRE) 103 (Soviet **–** Star (USA) 128) [2002 7m Jul 7] 10,000Y: second foal: half-sister to 1¼m winner Coruscating (by Highest Honor): dam, 2-y-o 7f winner, out of smart performer up to 1½m Dancing Meg: 33/1 and very green, soundly beaten in maiden at Redcar. *M. W. Easterby*

MY SWEETHEART (IRE) 2 b.f. (Feb 26) Up And At 'em 109 – Selkirk Flyer **–** (Selkirk (USA) 129) [2002 5.3g 5.1f 6m f6f 6m 5.3m f8.5g 6.1s Oct 23] IR 1,000F, IR 2,200Y: first foal: dam unraced: no sign of ability: visored (swerved badly left leaving stall) third start: sent to Kuwait. *J. D. Czerpak*

MY TESS 6 br.m. Lugana Beach 116 – Barachois Princess (USA) 62 (Barachois **–** (CAN)) [2002 72, a90: f7s³ f6g f7g² f7g Mar 14] big, strong, lengthy mare: fairly useful **a89** performer: was best at 7f to easy 8.5f: acted on fibresand, soft and good to firm going: usually raced up with pace: sometimes wandered: dead. *B. A. McMahon*

MYTHIC 3 ch.f. Zafonic (USA) 130 – Fetlar (Pharly (FR) 130) [2002 70p: 8.2m* 8m⁵ **103** 8f 8.1m² 8f⁵ 10g³ 10d Nov 1] big, lengthy filly: useful performer: won maiden at Nottingham in June: mostly creditable efforts after, including in listed race at Sandown (½-length second to Miss Pinkerton) then Sun Chariot Stakes (3½ lengths fifth behind Dress To Thrill) and listed race (2½ lengths third to Salim Toto), last 2 at Newmarket: stays 1¼m: acts on firm ground (well below best on good to soft): has been equipped with rope halter and given trouble in stall (refused to enter on intended reappearance): unseated leaving stall third outing (led to post). *J. R. Fanshawe*

MYTHICAL CHARM 3 b.f. Charnwood Forest (IRE) 125 – Triple Tricks (IRE) 70 **63** (Royal Academy (USA) 130) [2002 8.2g⁶ 8g⁵ 8.1m⁶ f12g² Dec 7] good-topped filly: has scope: third foal: half-sister to Swedish winner up to 1m Golden Note (by Efisio): dam, maiden who stayed 1m, out of sister to smart sprinter Jester: modest maiden: left J. Gosden 2,200 gns after third outing: stays 1½m: acts on fibresand and good to firm going: tongue tied (awkward leaving stall) third start. *B. R. Johnson*

MYTHICAL KING (IRE) 5 b.g. Fairy King (USA) – Whatcombe (USA) 88 **67** (Alleged (USA) 138) [2002 88: 10.9g 10m 10f 10.2v⁵ 10g 12.1g 10m 10.2g³ 10m⁶ 10.2g⁴ 10.3f 11.9g⁶ Oct 24] deep-girthed gelding: fair handicapper nowadays: best at 1¼m/1½m: acts on firm and good to soft going: possibly needs to dominate. *B. Palling*

MYTTON'S AGAIN 5 b.g. Rambo Dancer (CAN) 107 – Sigh 75 (Highland Melody **61** 112) [2002 76: f8s⁶ f8s² p8g* f8.5g f8.5g⁶ Feb 11] sparely-made gelding: fair handi- **a71** capper on all-weather, modest on turf: won at Lingfield in January: effective at 6f (given test) to 8.5f: acts on firm going, soft and all-weather: effective blinkered or not: usually held up: none too consistent: sold 1,600 gns. *A. Bailey*

MYTTON'S MAGIC (IRE) 2 br.g. (Apr 21) Danetime (IRE) 121 – Maldinion 88 **–** (Dominion 123) [2002 5.9d Jun 26] IR 4,000F, IR 2,400Y, 10,500 2-y-o: second foal: dam, lightly raced in Ireland (best effort at 7f), out of half-sister to Mummy's Pet: 25/1, well held in maiden at Carlisle. *A. Bailey*

MYTTONS MISTAKE 9 b.g. Rambo Dancer (CAN) 107 – Hi-Hunsley 82 (Swing **55** Easy (USA) 126) [2002 62, a44: p7g p8g 8f⁶ 9.7g Sep 2] leggy, workmanlike gelding: **a41** modest handicapper on turf, poor on all-weather: effective at 7f/1m: acts on firm going, good to soft, and all-weather: tried blinkered. *R. J. Baker*

MYTTON'S QUEST (IRE) 2 ch.g. (May 20) Grand Lodge (USA) 125 – Fleeting **62** Quest (Rainbow Quest (USA) 134) [2002 6d 8g⁴ 8.3m³ 10f⁶ 7g f8.5g f7g f6g Dec 16] IR **a48** 15,500F, 10,000 2-y-o: good-bodied gelding: third foal: half-brother to 2 winners, including Irish 7f winner Marko Jadeo (by Eagle Eyed): dam unraced half-sister to Oaks second Bourbon Girl: modest maiden on turf, poor on all-weather: should stay at least 1¼m: acts on good to firm ground and fibresand: blinkered (not disgraced) final outing: gave impression something amiss sixth/seventh starts. *A. Bailey*

MY VALENTINE 3 gr.g. Samim (USA) 84 – Sea Farer Lake 74 (Gairloch 122) [2002 **67** 8g p8g⁶ f8 5g⁴ 8 5g f9 4s⁴ f8g² f9.4s³ f9.4g² Dec 20] half-brother to 3 winners, including 7-y-o Smooth Sailing: dam 1m (at 2 yrs) and 1¼m winner: fair maiden: should stay 1½m: acts on fibresand. *P. R. Chamings*

MY YORKSHIRE ROSE 2 b.f. (Mar 24) Bishop of Cashel 122 – Gloriana 78 (Form- –
idable (USA) 125) [2002 8s Oct 25] 1,700Y: third foal: half-sister to 3-y-o Thunderclap:
dam, 1m/9f winner who stayed 1½m, also winning hurdler: 100/1 and backward, well
beaten in maiden at Doncaster. *T. J. Etherington*

N

NAAHY 2 ch.c. (Mar 7) Bahamian Bounty 116 – Daffodil Fields (Try My Best (USA) **91**
130) [2002 5m² 5m³ 7g* 7d² 7.2g² 7m 7m* 7.1m* 8m⁵ 7f² Sep 25] 36,000Y: quite attractive colt: half-brother to several winners, including 1999 2-y-o 6f winner Petary and 1993
2-y-o 5f/6f winner Petula (both useful/by Petong): dam Irish maiden: fairly useful
performer: won maiden at Thirsk in June and nurseries at Goodwood and Sandown in
August: creditable efforts in listed race and minor event (7 lengths second to Binanti) at
Goodwood last 2 starts: barely stays 1m: acts on firm and good to soft ground: front
runner: didn't handle sharp left-hand turn at Catterick sixth outing: genuine and reliable.
M. R. Channon

NABOKOV 3 ch.g. Nashwan (USA) 135 – Ninotchka (USA) 110 (Nijinsky (CAN) –
138) [2002 f8s f12g f12g Mar 25] second foal: dam 1½m winner: well beaten in maidens.
Sir Mark Prescott

NADESZHDA 2 ch.f. (Feb 24) Nashwan (USA) 135 – Ninotchka (USA) 110 (Nijinsky –
(CAN) 138) [2002 p7g p7g 8.3d Oct 28] third foal: dam 1½m winner: well held in
maidens, tending to start slowly and pull hard. *Sir Mark Prescott*

NADOUR AL BAHR (IRE) 7 b.g. Be My Guest (USA) 126 – Nona (GER) (Cortez **111**
(GER)) [2002 102: 10.1g² 10.1g² 10.1d² 10m² 10m³ 10m 9f 10m² Oct 12] tall, close-
coupled gelding: unimpressive mover: smart performer: ran at least respectably most
7-y-o starts, including in handicaps at Kempton (1¼ lengths second to Imperial Dancer in
Rosebery Stakes) on reappearance and Ascot (neck second to Prize Winner) on fourth
start, and when third to Naheef in Winter Hill Stakes at Windsor: better form at 1¼m than
1½m: acts on any going: tailed off in blinkers final 5-y-o start: sometimes slowly away/
races freely/wanders, and is held up: none too genuine. *T. G. Mills*

NAFSIKA (USA) 2 b.f. (Apr 2) Sky Classic (CAN) – Exotic Beauty (USA) (Java **54**
Gold (USA)) [2002 6.1m 7d 6.1m⁴ 6f Oct 7] 20,000Y: lengthy, sturdy filly: fourth foal:
half-sister to a winner in USA by Uncounted For: dam 1m winner in USA: modest
maiden: should stay 1m. *B. A. McMahon*

NAHEEF (IRE) 3 b.c. Marju (IRE) 127 – Golden Digger (USA) 66 (Mr Prospector **117**
(USA)) [2002 109: 8m 12d 10m* 12m⁶ Sep 7] unfurnished, quite attractive colt: smart
performer: won private trial at Nad Al Sheba in April by 6 lengths before well held in
2000 Guineas at Newmarket (appeared to try to bite a rival) and Derby at Epsom (5/1
fourth favourite): best effort when winning Winter Hill Stakes at Windsor in August by
1½ lengths from Chianti, asserting final 1f despite briefly hanging left: stays 1¼m (beaten
before stamina became issue both starts at 1½m, in September Stakes at Kempton on
second occasion): yet to race on extremes of going. *Saeed bin Suroor*

NAJAABA (USA) 2 b.f. (Jan 28) Bahhare (USA) 122 – Ashbilya (USA) (Nureyev **57**
(USA) 131) [2002 6.1g⁶ 6.1m⁶ 7g Oct 14] smallish, sturdy filly: first foal: dam, unraced
sister to useful Dewhurst Stakes third Zentsov Street, out of half-sister to dam of
Bakharoff and Emperor Jones: best effort in maidens (modest form) when sixth to Bandit
Queen at Nottingham second outing: should stay 7f. *M. R. Channon*

NAJDA (IRE) 4 b.f. Halling (USA) 133 – Danishkada 119 (Thatch (USA) 136) [2002 –
–: 12s 10v 7s 10d 10g 8m 5d 7g 7f Sep 21] maiden: little form in 2002: trained by K. Ryan
fifth to seventh starts: visored/blinkered last 3. *Andrew Lee, Ireland*

NAJ-DE 4 ch.g. Zafonic (USA) 130 – River Jig (USA) 98 (Irish River (FR) 131) [2002 **59 d**
68: p10g p12g p10g⁴ 10.9f 8.5g p12g 9d 8.1d⁴ 8d 8m 7m⁵ 8m⁴ p10g Dec 30] close-
coupled gelding: modest maiden: stays 1¼m: acts on good to firm going, good to soft and
polytrack: blinkered (ran respectably) once at 3 yrs: on downgrade. *S. Dow*

NAJEEBON (FR) 3 ch.c. Cadeaux Genereux 131 – Jumairah Sun (IRE) 98 (Scenic **81**
128) [2002 8d⁴ 8m 6m* 6f⁴ Oct 11] lengthy, well-made colt: third foal: half-brother to
1999 2-y-o 6f winner Joonayh (by Warning) and 4-y-o Millennium Force: dam 1¼m
winner who stayed 1½m: fairly useful performer: won maiden at Yarmouth in September:
easily best effort final outing: may prove best at 6f/7f: acts on firm going. *M. R. Channon*

TFMCyntergy Ltd Winter Hill Stakes, Windsor—
Naheef returns to form after flopping in two classics; Chianti follows him home

NAJWA LIBNAAN (KSA) 2 b.f. (Feb 17) Tasso (USA) – Cloette 69 (Damister – (USA) 123) [2002 5.7m Jun 26] first known foal: dam, 7f winner, half-sister to smart performer up to 1½m French Fellow: 20/1, always outpaced in maiden at Bath: sent to Saudi Arabia. *C. F. Wall*

NAKED OAT 7 b.g. Imp Society (USA) – Bajina (Dancing Brave (USA) 140) [2002 – § 53§, a81§: f12g f11g Feb 28] smallish, strong gelding: fairly useful performer at best: well held both 7-y-o starts: tried blinkered: unreliable. *B. Smart*

NAKOTA 2 ch.f. (Apr 12) Emarati (USA) 74 – Naulakha (Bustino 136) [2002 7.5g 6d – Oct 14] 2,200Y: fifth foal: half-sister to 2000 2-y-o 6f winner Galaxy Returns (by Alhijaz): dam lightly-raced sister to smart winner up to 11.5f N C Owen: well held in maidens. *B. Smart*

NAKWA (IRE) 4 b.g. Namaqualand (USA) – Cajo (IRE) (Tirol 127) [2002 70: 8m **56** 8.1v 8s 8m f12g³ Dec 14] tall gelding: modest handicapper in 2002: stays 1½m: acts on fibresand, good to firm and good to soft ground: often makes running: has reportedly broken blood vessels. *E. J. Alston*

NANDOO 3 b.f. Forzando 122 – Ascend (IRE) (Glint of Gold 128) [2002 60: 10m⁵ 10d **60 d** 10m 12m 14.1m⁵ 16.2m 14.1g⁴ Oct 2] modest maiden handicapper: on downgrade: stays 1¾m: acts on good to firm ground: sold 5,000 gns. *P. W. Harris*

NANETTE 4 b.f. Hernando (FR) 127 – No Restraint 84 (Habitat 134) [2002 60: 10d³ **71 d** 10m p12g⁴ 10g p12g Oct 9] fair maiden, lightly raced: below form after reappearance: best effort at 1¼m: acts on good to soft going. *I. A. Wood*

NARBAYDA (IRE) 3 b.f. Kahyasi 130 – Noufiyla 68 (Top Ville 129) [2002 10m⁴ p10g **68** Jun 29] sister to fairly useful 2m winner Noufari and half-sister to 3 winners, notably very smart 1¼m/1½m (Princess Royal Stakes) winner Narwala (by Darshaan): dam placed at 1½m: much better effort in maidens when never-dangerous fourth at Ripon: looked ill at ease on track at Lingfield later in month: will stay 1½m: sold €20,000 in November. *Sir Michael Stoute*

NARRATIVE (IRE) 4 b.c. Sadler's Wells (USA) 132 – Barger (USA) (Riverman **117** (USA) 131) [2002 a10f* 12g* 12g 14m* 12f² 12m 12s⁵ Sep 22] strong, lengthy, good-bodied colt: smart performer: ran twice at 2 yrs for J. Oxx in Ireland, winning maiden at Gowran: missed 2001: much improved in 2002, winning handicap and Concord Dubai

679

Godolphin's "Narrative"

City of Gold (by 3¼ lengths from Grandera), both at Nad Al Sheba, in January/February, and Premio Carlo d'Alessio at Rome (eased to beat Kanaris 8 lengths) in May: best effort when 3 lengths second to Falbrav in Gran Premio di Milano fifth start: below form in King George VI and Queen Elizabeth Stakes at Ascot (sweating profusely, acted as pacemaker) and Preis von Europa at Cologne last 2: effective at 1½m/1¾m: yet to race on heavy going, acts on any other turf/dirt: has been tongue tied: usually front runner. *Saeed bin Suroor*

NASHAAB (USA) 5 b.g. Zafonic (USA) 130 – Tajannub (USA) 104 (Dixieland Band (USA)) [2002 94: a7f³ a8.5f³ a8f⁵ a8f⁴ a8f⁶ 8s² 8m 8.1d⁶ 8f 8m⁴ 8f⁴ 7.9m³ 8m 9f⁶ 7.9f² 8g⁴ 8s Nov 2] small, quite attractive gelding: useful handicapper on turf, fairly useful on all-weather: below best for P. Rudkin at Nad Al Sheba first 5 starts: good efforts after when in frame, including fourth to Smirk at Goodwood (William Hill Mile on tenth start), third to Funfair (Bradford & Bingley Stakes) and second to Londoner at York, and unlucky close fourth of 26 to Champion Lodge at Newmarket (weaved through to be first home of those drawn low): best form at 1m/9f: acts on fibresand, firm and soft going: visored final 4-y-o start: has been bandaged in front: often slowly away: held up: tough. *R. M. Beckett* **103 a82**

NASHIRA 4 ch.f. Prince Sabo 123 – Aldevonie 75 (Green Desert (USA) 127) [2002 –: 10f 8m Jun 3] fair 5f winner at 2 yrs: lightly raced and modest form at best since. *M. Blanshard* **57**

NASIJ (USA) 2 ch.f. (Apr 18) Elusive Quality (USA) – Hachiyah (IRE) 91 (Generous (IRE) 139) [2002 7m² 6g* 6m³ 8m³ 7m Oct 19] rather leggy, quite attractive filly: second foal: dam, 1¼m winner, closely related to useful performer up to 1½m Mutawwaj and **101**

680

Mr Hamdan Al Maktoum's "Nasij"

half-sister to useful performer up to 1m Hiwaya: useful performer: won maiden at Ascot in July: good third in Princess Margaret Stakes at Ascot (6¼ lengths behind Russian Rhythm) and May Hill Stakes at Doncaster (beaten 2¾ lengths by Summitville, despite trouble in running): ran poorly in Rockfel Stakes at Newmarket final outing: should stay 1¼m: raced only on good/good to firm ground. *E. A. L. Dunlop*

NASIYKA (FR) 3 b.f. Doyoun 124 – Nasaraya (FR) (Dancing Brave (USA) 140) – [2002 6g f9.4s Nov 2] €9,000 3-y-o: third foal: dam, French 1¼m winner, half-sister to Prix du Jockey Club winner Natrown: well held in maidens within 6 days. *P. D. Evans*

NASSARO (IRE) 2 gr.c. (Mar 4) Linamix (FR) 127 – Dawnsio (IRE) 102 (Tate **75** Gallery (USA) 117) [2002 p7g³ p7g 7v Nov 8] half-brother to several winners, 3 at least useful, notably high-class 5f/6f (latter including at 2 yrs) winner Namid (by Indian Ridge): dam Irish sprinter: best effort in maidens (fair form) when third to Dubai Lightning at Lingfield, slowly away: should stay 1m. *Sir Michael Stoute*

NASSAU NIGHT 3 b.g. Bahamian Bounty 116 – Leave At Dawn (Slip Anchor 136) **45** [2002 –p: p8g⁵ p8g f8.5g² f9.4g³ f8g* 7g f7g f7g 8m 8g 10.1m³ Aug 14] modest **a63** performer: won minor event at Southwell in March: probably stays 1¼m: acts on all-weather and good to firm going: sold 4,000 gns, sent to Denmark. *R. M. H. Cowell*

NASTY NICK 3 gr.g. Petong 126 – Silver Spell 54 (Aragon 118) [2002 –: 7d 5d 5m – ' 6m 8.2v Oct 29] no form: tried blinkered/visored. *Julian Poulton*

NATHAN BRITTLES (USA) 2 ch.g. (May 4) Cat's Career (USA) – Doc's Answer **54** (USA) (Dr Schwartzman (USA)) [2002 5v⁶ 5m⁵ Aug 28] $3,000Y: fifth foal: half-brother to 3 winners abroad, 2 in USA: dam U3 maiden, out of half sister to dam of Nuclear Debate: modest form in maidens: slowly away second start. *T. D. Barron*

681

NATIAIN 3 ch.g. Danzig Connection (USA) – Fen Princess (IRE) 72 (Trojan Fen 118) – [2002 –: 8g 12.3m Jun 20] big, strong gelding: well held in maidens/handicap: sold 2,000 gns in November. *P. C. Haslam*

NATIVE TITLE 4 b.g. Pivotal 124 – Bermuda Lily 78 (Dunbeath (USA) 127) [2002 **89** 87: 7g⁴ 8.3g 7m⁵ 6m* 6g 6m⁶ 6m⁵ 6m 5.7f² 5f⁶ Sep 28] big, close-coupled gelding: has reportedly had wind operation: fairly useful handicapper: won at Leicester in June: reportedly lame final start: has form at 1m, likely to prove best at 5f/6f: acts on firm and soft going: blinkered eighth start. *M. Blanshard*

NATMSKY (IRE) 3 b.g. Shadeed (USA) 135 – Cockney Lass 117 (Camden Town – 125) [2002 48, a71: f6g⁶ f8g³ f6g 7.5m f6g f8g Dec 10] quite good-topped gelding: **a63** modest maiden on all-weather: barely stays 1m: acts on fibresand and good to firm going: blinkered/visored most starts in 2002: has been slowly away: usually races up with pace. *K. A. Ryan*

NATSMAGIRL (IRE) 5 b.m. Blues Traveller (IRE) 119 – Top The Rest (Top Ville – § 129) [2002 45§: f7g f8g f8g f8g 9.9m 10m May 1] small, sparely-made mare: temperamental performer: tried visored. *R. E. Barr*

NATSTELLE (IRE) 2 b.g. (Apr 11) Sesaro (USA) 81 – Baliana 75 (Midyan (USA) **68** 124) [2002 5d⁴ 5v² 6g³ 6f Oct 7] 8,000F, 4,000Y: fifth foal: closely related to 3-y-o Digger and half-brother to 7f (at 2 yrs)/1m winner Bali Dance (by Rambo Dancer): dam unreliable sprinter: fair maiden: gave impression something amiss final start: stays 6f: acts on heavy ground: sent to Spain. *J. L. Eyre*

NATURAL DANCER 3 b.f. Shareef Dancer (USA) 135 – Naturally Fresh 91 (Thatching 131) [2002 –: 9d 10d 9.9d⁶ 8.5g p10g Dec 18] workmanlike filly: poor mover: little form. *C. N. Allen*

NATURE (IRE) 3 b.f. Bluebird (USA) 125 – Nawaji (USA) 45 (Trempolino (USA) – 135) [2002 49: f8g 6g 10g 10g 8m Sep 19] maiden: well held in 2002. *B. A. Pearce*

NAUGHTY GIRL (IRE) 2 b.f. (Feb 6) Dr Devious (IRE) 127 – Mary Magdalene 78 **79** (Night Shift (USA)) [2002 5g³ 5m² 5.1d² 5.1f⁶ May 9] IR 32,000Y: smallish, sturdy filly: first foal: dam, 5f winner, half-sister to useful sprinter Roger The Butler: fair maiden: short-headed by Arran Pilot in minor event at Nottingham third start: something possibly amiss at Chester final one: should stay 6f: acts on good to firm and good to soft ground. *M. L. W. Bell*

NAUGHTY NELL 3 b.f. Danehill Dancer (IRE) 117 – Hana Marie 101§ (Formidable **76 +** (USA) 125) [2002 69p: p6g* p6g* 6.5g 6m Aug 16] fairly useful form on all-weather, fair **a89** on turf: won maiden and handicap at Lingfield in June/July: should prove as effective at 5f as 6f: acts on polytrack, seemingly on good to firm going. *J. Noseda*

NAUTICAL STAR 7 b.g. Slip Anchor 136 – Comic Talent 105 (Pharly (FR) 130) **51** [2002 51: 12.3g* 12.4g 11.9s⁴ 13v³ 13s² 16d 13v⁵ 15d Jul 23] good-topped gelding: formerly useful, modest nowadays: won selling handicap at Ripon in April: stays 2m: acts on firm and soft going: tried visored: usually leads. *A. C. Whillans*

NAUTICAL WARNING 7 b.g. Warning 136 – Night At Sea 107 (Night Shift – (USA)) [2002 –, a81: p8g p8g Feb 2] sturdy gelding: fairly useful handicapper on all-weather in 2001: well held both 7-y-o starts (said to have finished lame final one): tried visored, blinkered nowadays. *Jamie Poulton*

NAVADO (USA) 3 b.c. Rainbow Quest (USA) 134 – Miznah (IRE) 102 (Sadler's **97** Wells (USA) 132) [2002 10g⁶ 10.5d² 10d² 11.6m* 11.9m³ Sep 4] tall, good-bodied colt: sixth foal: closely related to 2 winners by Nashwan, including useful Irish performer up to 1¾m Geisha Girl, 7f winner at 2 yrs, and half-brother to 6-y-o Zindabad: dam, 7f/1m 2-y-o 6f winner, closely related to dam of US champion turf mare Flawlessly: useful performer: won handicap at Windsor in July by ¾ length from Playback: creditable third to dead-heaters Scott's View and Muhareb in similar event at York final start, again dictating (raced freely early): unlikely to stay further than 1½m: yet to race on extremes of going. *Sir Michael Stoute*

NAVALE (FR) 3 gr.f. Baryshnikov (AUS) – Nabita (FR) (Akarad (FR) 130) [2002 10g **74** 12g⁴ 12f³ p12g Sep 10] 380,000 francs Y: half-sister to several winners, including fairly useful French 10.5f winner Neiges Eternelles (by Exit To Nowhere): dam 13f winner in France: fair maiden: stays 1½m: joined A. King. *J. H. M. Gosden*

NAVARRE SAMSON (FR) 7 b. or br.g. Ganges (USA) 119 – L'Eternite (FR) – (Cariellor (FR) 125) [2002 52+: 16.2g⁴ Jul 26] leggy, close-coupled gelding: modest performer: dead. *P. J. Hobbs*

NAVIASKY (IRE) 7 b. or br.g. Scenic 128 – Black Molly (IRE) (High Top 131) [2002 **93 §** 80: 8.3g 7m* 6f* 7d 7d 6f² 7m* 8m² 8m 7m 8m 7g⁴ 8f⁵ 7.9m 7.1m p7g p7g Nov 27] big, strong gelding: fairly useful performer: won seller and claimer (claimed from D. Nicholls £6,000, trained by R. Spicer next start only) at Redcar in May and handicap at Kempton in June: refused to race last 4 outings (often reluctant to post/slowly away), leaving C. Dore before penultimate one: effective at 6f to 1m: acts on firm and good to soft going: best held up: has been banned from racing. *I. A. Wood*

NAWADER (USA)   6 b. or br.h. Silver Hawk (USA) 123 – Music Lane (USA) (Miswaki (USA) 124) [2002 46: f8s Jan 1] strong, good-topped horse: maiden handicapper. *M. C. Chapman*   –

NAWOW   2 b.g. (Mar 26) Blushing Flame (USA) 109 – Fair Test 95 (Fair Season 120) [2002 p8g⁵ p8g* Dec 14] 4,200Y: brother to 3-y-o Flaming Spirt and half-brother to 3 winners, including Irish 7f winner Bestbeteastwood (by Chief Singer): dam 5f winner, including at 2 yrs: better effort in maidens at Lingfield (fair form) when beating Flight of Esteem by short head in 12-runner race, leading near finish: will stay 1¼m. *P. D. Cundell*   **79**

NAYEF (USA)   4 b.c. Gulch (USA) – Height of Fashion (FR) 124 (Bustino 136) [2002 129: 12g* 10.5s³ 10m⁴ 12m² 10.4g* Aug 20]   **129**

Acts to follow do not get much harder than those that preceded Marcus Tregoning and Nayef. For Tregoning, the daunting task has been to take over at Kingwood House Stables from Major Dick Hern, his employer, mentor and friend, and a training legend. Nayef will not have felt any weight of history or burden of expectation on his shoulders, but a great deal has been expected of him nonetheless since the day he was foaled, a half-brother to Nashwan and Unfuwain and the final foal of the outstanding broodmare Height of Fashion. Both horse and trainer have done fine jobs of following in those famous footsteps, achievements that were particularly poignant and fitting in 2002, a year that saw the deaths of Dick Hern in May, at the age of eighty-one, and of Unfuwain in January and Nashwan in July.

Dick Hern was one of the outstanding British Flat trainers of his generation and sent out the winners of sixteen British classics, winning each of those races at least twice. The Tregoning-trained Shadow Dancing, incidentally, bred by Hern and his long-time stable-jockey Willie Carson, was third in the 2002 Oaks. Among Hern's classic winners were three in the Derby, the last of them Nashwan. Tregoning has yet to win a classic of any sort, so there is some irony in his strongly influencing the decision to pass up a shot at the 2001 Derby with Nayef, a course of action that seems to have contributed to his reputation as a trainer. That and the horse's triumphant return in the second half of that season when winning four pattern races on the trot, finishing off with a Champion Stakes victory that established him once again among the top handful of his generation. Nayef, a failure in the Two Thousand Guineas, ended the season rated higher than Golan, the Guineas winner.

Which was the better horse, Nayef or Golan, became an ongoing issue in 2002, but not before Nayef had already justified the decision to keep him in training by winning at Nad Al Sheba in March with the British turf season only a few days

Juddmonte International Stakes, York—Nayef (right) gains revenge over his King George conqueror Golan; Noverre and Indian Creek complete the frame

old. Generally speaking, 'racehorses to race' seems to be the motto of the Maktoum operation these days, and more specifically for their star performers it is one of 'racehorses to race in the Dubai World Cup'. As one of the very best, Nayef was trained for the World Cup in 2002, arriving the previous November and reportedly doing all of his work thereafter on the Nad Al Sheba dirt track. Until, that is, three days before the World Cup when he was rerouted to the Dubai Sheema Classic over a mile and a half on turf. With Sheikh Hamdan's best horse Sakhee there to do battle in the World Cup—and 5/2-on to win it with the British bookmakers—this decision was understandable, but Sheikh Hamdan might well have regretted the switch when Sakhee was beaten into third behind Street Cry. The signs did not look good for Nayef either when he severely disappointed his trainer on the first of three late pieces of exercise on the turf track. The race itself, however, offered no cause for concern as Nayef led on the bridle two furlongs out and went on to beat Hong Kong's 50/1-shot Helene Vitality by two lengths, with Boreal and Marienbard close up in third and fourth. Nayef may get his chance in the main event in 2003.

Preparing Nayef for his latest turf campaign in Europe, Tregoning faced a task that would have been more familiar to his mentor. None of the top middle-distance prizes was out of bounds for Nayef, who always looked the type to make good physical progress from three to four. Speaking before the Sheema Classic, Tregoning reported that 'Nayef has given me a fantastic feel all winter and he's a totally different horse from last year. He's fifteen kilos heavier and has filled his frame on his neck and across his quarters.' However, Nayef's European campaign began with below-par efforts in both the Tattersalls Gold Cup at the Curragh (at 11/8-on) and the Prince of Wales's Stakes at Royal Ascot. Soft ground was given as an explanation for the Irish effort, although he had already won twice on soft or heavy. But the ground at Royal Ascot was good to firm and Nayef performed even

Mr Hamdan Al Maktoum's "Nayef"

further below his best, leaving some pundits to speculate on his next start that the ground might be too firm!

If Tregoning needed any inspiration to bring Nayef back to his peak for that next assignment, the King George VI and Queen Elizabeth Stakes, he might have found it in Dick Hern's five victories in the race, with the three-year-olds Troy, Petoski and Nashwan and the four-year-olds Brigadier Gerard and Ela-Mana-Mou. Nayef failed to add his name to the illustrious list of King George winners, but he could not have come much closer. Sent off 7/1 fourth favourite in a field of nine, which included a stable companion as pacemaker, he looked the winner when moving up smoothly to lead two furlongs out but succumbed by a head as Golan kept up a sustained challenge on his inside in the closing stages. Nayef had now lost their two meetings—he had finished some six lengths behind in the Guineas—but if further confirmation were needed after the King George that there was next to nothing between them, it came when the pair met again in the Juddmonte International Stakes at York in August. With the style of their performances in the King George suggesting that Nayef would be the better suited by the step back in trip, he was sent off 6/4 favourite with Golan the 9/4 second favourite, but the matter was not nearly so clear cut in running. In a seven-runner field that, like the King George, lacked any significant challenge from the three-year-olds, Nayef as usual travelled strongly and took over the running with two furlongs remaining. Golan once again laid down the strongest challenge, earlier though than in the King George. The pair of them fought it out over the final furlong before Nayef emerged victorious by half a length. Those behind the first two—Noverre, Indian Creek, Chancellor, Golan's pacemaker Starbourne and No Excuse Needed—did not on the day represent much of a threat and the winner's form was nowhere near that achieved by wide-margin winners Sakhee and Royal Anthem in two of the previous three runnings. The sight of two high-class performers reproducing their best form almost to the pound, as they once again went head to head, was in its own way just as satisfying.

To be at or near the top of the tree at two, three and four years is extremely rare, as indicated by the fact that Nayef is the first Timeform champion two-year-old to go on to win a Group 1 contest as a four-year-old. Triptych was the top two-year-old filly in 1984 and went on the win the Champion Stakes at four, five Group 1s at five and the Coronation Cup at six. With nearly three months remaining of the British turf season, Nayef should have had an opportunity to add to his record after the International, but he did not get it. He was withdrawn from the Arc in the week of the race, connections preferring an attempt to emulate Brigadier Gerard by achieving consecutive victories in the Champion Stakes. Nayef would have been a short-priced favourite at Newmarket but, unfortunately, a coughing virus was in circulation at Tregoning's stable for over a month and Nayef finally succumbed to it four days before the Champion. Following the deaths of his half-brothers (Unfuwain due to a neurological condition; Nashwan due to complications after a leg operation), there is no doubt that there is a career for Nayef as a stallion, probably a highly popular one, at Sheikh Hamdan's Nunnery Stud at Newmarket, where both Unfuwain and Nashwan stood. However, Nayef races on, a decision to celebrate. Nashwan's racing career came to a close in, for many, highly unsatisfactory circumstances, but ducking the challenge and premature retirement are charges you don't find levelled often at the Maktoums nowadays and they will not be levelled at Sheikh Hamdan over Nayef.

			Mr Prospector (b 1970)	Raise A Native
	Gulch (USA) (b 1984)			Gold Digger
			Jameela (b or br 1976)	Rambunctious
Nayef (USA) (b.c. 1998)				Asbury Mary
			Bustino (b 1971)	Busted
	Height of Fashion (FR) (b 1979)			Ship Yard
			Highclere (b 1971)	Queen's Hussar
				Highlight

When he does take his place at stud, Nayef will again have plenty to live up to. Nashwan (by Blushing Groom) sired a dual King George winner in Swain and, although lacking a star performer in recent years, he still figures highly when his progeny are assessed by median rating. Unfuwain (by Northern Dancer) did well with less obvious opportunities and had a fine year in 2000 with classic-winning fillies Petrushka and Lahan, which earned him better mares for what turned out to be his final covering season. Nayef's dam Height of Fashion died in 2000. She had five daughters, and easily the most important prize to have come from their offspring is the 1999 Premio Ribot, won by Oriental Fashion, a daughter of the useful mile- and mile-and-a-quarter winner Wijdan (by Mr Prospector). A once-raced daughter of Height of Fashion, Deyaajeer (by Dayjur), had a useful representative during the latest season in Al Mohallab.

Nayef is a rangy, imposing colt who impresses in appearance and is a good mover with a long stride. He is effective at a mile and a quarter and at a mile and a half. Unraced on firm going, he acts on good to firm and heavy. Comparisons may be odious, but they have always been obvious in Nayef's case. In terms of their highest ratings, Nayef falls short of both Nashwan and Unfuwain, by 6 lb and 2 lb respectively, but Unfuwain never won a Group 1 race and Nayef is now only one short of Nashwan's four successes at that level, admittedly with many more opportunities. A more pressing issue during the latest season was the comparison between Nayef and Golan, and this Annual rates both the same, almost equal horses at a mile and a half but with Nayef holding a slight edge over the extended mile and a quarter of the International. Nayef's two-year-old season was arguably something of a false dawn, but only so far as the classics were concerned. Since the middle of his three-year-old season, he has more than made good any shortfall and his brightest hour may still lie ahead of him. *M. P. Tregoning*

NAYYEL   3 b.c. Zafonic (USA) 130 – The Perfect Life (IRE) 106 (Try My Best (USA)   **–**
130) [2002 94p: 8.1d⁵ 8f Oct 4] smallish, strong, angular colt: fairly useful winner at 2 yrs: disappointing both 3-y-o outings: should stay 1m: sold 5,500 gns. *J. L. Dunlop*

NAYYIR   4 ch.g. Indian Ridge 123 – Pearl Kite (USA) 106§ (Silver Hawk (USA)   **125**
123) [2002 p7g* p10g⁶ 8.1d⁴ 8.5g* 8.5d* 8g⁴ 7m* 6.5s³ 6m 7m* Oct 19]
Few horses came from nowhere and went somewhere faster in 2002 than the four-year-old Nayyir. After a belated debut success in an all-weather maiden at Lingfield in March, he progressed to win a Group 3 race by June, and continued his improvement from there, winning two more pattern races, including the Group 2 Victor Chandler Challenge Stakes at Newmarket on his final start.

Nayyir barely broke sweat when 100/30-on at Lingfield on polytrack and he won with great authority in much better company in the Challenge Stakes too. In a field of sixteen, he started co-second favourite at 7/1, alongside Demonstrate and Reel Buddy in the betting behind the three-year-old Firebreak, a 4/1-shot. Nayyir's odds had drifted from 5/1, possibly because of rumours that he had worked poorly in his final gallop, but it wasn't long before he dispelled any doubts in the race as to his well-being, travelling smoothly from the start and producing his customary turn

Vodafone Diomed Stakes, Epsom—
Nayyir announces his arrival in pattern company by trouncing his field;
Highdown (No.9) stays on past Wannabe Around, whilst Cape Town and Late Night Out (rail) come next

*Victor Chandler Challenge Stakes, Newmarket—Nayyir shows an impressive turn of foot;
Firebreak and Frenchmans Bay follow him home*

of foot as the field opened up in front of him over a furlong out. His rider Eddie
Ahern didn't need to use his whip as Nayyir strode clear to beat the favourite by
two and a half lengths with Frenchmans Bay in third. Nayyir's performance showed
him to be better than ever and he would have been one of the favourites for his final
intended run of the season, the Hong Kong Mile in December, from which he was
withdrawn a few days beforehand because of a severe attack of diarrhoea.

      Nayyir's turn of foot stood him in good stead throughout his first season. He
used it to effect in winning under a remarkably confident ride in a handicap at
Beverley in May, cruising past almost the entire field in a matter of strides before
his jockey Shane Kelly took a pull inside the last, then nudged Nayyir to lead near
the post. On the strength of his Beverley success (gained off a BHB mark of just
83), Nayyir started 5/1 joint favourite when stepped up to pattern company for the
first time in the Vodafone Diomed Stakes at Epsom on Derby Day. An open-looking
race turned into exactly the opposite as Nayyir trounced his eight opponents, held
up again as usual and quickening away after two furlongs out to beat the three-year-
old Highdown by three lengths. Judged on his Epsom form, Nayyir would have had
an outstanding chance under a penalty in the Royal Hunt Cup later in the month, but
he tackled the Queen Anne Stakes at Royal Ascot instead. He ran only respectably

Mr Abdulla Al Khalifa's "Nayyir"

to finish fourth to No Excuse Needed and was dropped back to seven furlongs for his next outing, the Theo Fennel Lennox Stakes at Goodwood in August. He faced no easy task under a Group 3 penalty for Epsom, but won in customary style, quickening through on the rail to beat the three-year-old Redback by half a length.

Nayyir's pedigree has taken on a healthy shine since he was sold for 15,000 guineas as a yearling and resold for 57,000 guineas as a two-year-old, with his year-younger half-brother Highest (by Selkirk) also giving the dam a considerable boost in 2002. Further details of their dam's family can be found in Highest's essay. Nayyir's sire Indian Ridge had a resurgence in 2002 with Breeders' Cup Mile winner Domedriver also among his representatives. Indian Ridge has also been responsible for sprinters such as Cassandra Go and Namid, and it wouldn't be a surprise to see Nayyir mix sprinting with miling again in 2003. He ran creditably when a close third to May Ball in the Prix Maurice de Gheest over six and a half furlongs at Deauville in August, held up in a race in which it paid to race handily and staying on strongly after being short of room at one point; and he started favourite when down the field in a muddling renewal of the Sprint Cup at Haydock in September

Nayyir (ch.g. 1998)	Indian Ridge (ch 1985)	Ahonoora (ch 1975)	Lorenzaccio
			Helen Nichols
		Hillbrow (ch 1975)	Swing Easy
			Golden City
	Pearl Kite (USA) (b 1991)	Silver Hawk (b 1979)	Roberto
			Gris Vitesse
		Spur Wing (ch 1984)	Storm Bird
			Equal Wing

A lengthy, angular gelding, Nayyir, who isn't the best of movers in his slower paces and shows a round action once racing, acts on soft and good to firm going, as well as polytrack. His debut was reportedly delayed due to a series of niggling problems, including a foot abscess, but he stood up admirably to a ten-race, first campaign. Apparently, his health caused great concern in Hong Kong, but connections are aiming him at a trial in Dubai in March before he tackles a race at the World Cup meeting. Hopefully, he'll be a regular in good races for some time to come. *G. A. Butler*

NAYZAK (USA)   2 b.f. (Feb 13) Silver Hawk (USA) 123 – Mamlakah (IRE) 104   **91 p**
(Unfuwain (USA) 131) [2002 7d* Aug 3] third foal: half-sister to fairly useful Irish 7f/ 1m winner Al Mamaaliq (by Gulch): dam 2-y-o 7f/1m (May Hill Stakes) winner: 13/2, won 11-runner maiden at Newmarket by 2½ lengths from Hi Dubai, switched over 2f out and quickening in good style: will stay at least 1m: useful performer in the making, assuming all is well. *Sir Michael Stoute*

NDOLA   3 b.g. Emperor Jones (USA) 119 – Lykoa (Shirley Heights 130) [2002 –: 5m 8.2v Oct 29] rather leggy, quite good-topped gelding: well beaten in maidens. *B. J. Curley*

NEAR DUNLEER (IRE)   7 b.m. Soviet Lad (USA) – Clipper Queen 66 (Balidar   **59 §**
133) [2002 65§: 13d 12s⁴ 11g² 12d³ 12g⁴ f12f² Nov 29] fourth foal: half-sister to fairly useful Irish 6f to 9f winner Short Shift (by Mac's Imp): dam 6f winner: modest performer: won handicaps at Galway (only 4-y-o start) and Wexford (twice, at 5/6 yrs): well backed, below form when second in seller at Wolverhampton on British debut: stays 13f: acts on heavy and good to firm going: inconsistent. *M. Hourigan, Ireland*

NEARLY A FOOL   4 b.g. Komaite (USA) – Greenway Lady (Prince Daniel (USA))   **74**
[2002 94: 6m 7.6f 7d 7.6g 7.1g³ p8g f7g Dec 7] close-coupled gelding: fairly useful at 3 yrs: just fair in 2002: stays 7f: acts on any ground: has been edgy. *A. Bailey*

NEARLY A SMURF   2 ch.f. (May 24) Emarati (USA) 74 – Lime Brook 56 (Rapid   **–**
River 127) [2002 5g Jul 6] sixth foal: half-sister to 1½m winner Needwood Spitfire (by Rolfe): dam winning sprinter: 66/1, well held in seller at Leicester. *J. A. Pickering*

NEBULAE (IRE)   4 b.f. Unfuwain (USA) 131 – Three Stars 93 (Star Appeal 133)   **–**
[2002 82: 7.1m 8.3s Jun 10] 105,000Y: sister to Irish Oaks winner Bolas and 1½m winner who stayed 2m One For Baileys, and half-sister to several winners: dam 1½m winner from staying family: fairly useful form at 3 yrs for J. Oxx in Ireland, winning maiden at Roscommon: sold 33,000 gns then well held both starts in 2002: will stay beyond 1½m: acts on soft and good to firm going: usually tongue tied. *G. A. Butler*

Bentinck Stakes, Newmarket—Needwood Blade takes this well-contested listed race from Orientor (middle of picture, spots on body and cap), Acclamation (noseband), Resplendent Cee (dark sleeves, light stars) and Bahamian Pirate (black colours)

NEEDWOOD BLADE 4 ch.c. Pivotal 124 – Finlaggan 83 (Be My Chief (USA) 122) **117** [2002 111: 6s² 6m³ 6d³ 6d* 7m 6m* 5m⁴ 5.2f⁴ 6g* Oct 18] strong, compact colt: usually takes the eye: smart performer: won minor event at Doncaster in August, handicap at York (by neck from Royal Millennium) in September and listed event at Newmarket (beat Orientor by length) in October: ran at least respectably most other starts, including over inadequate trip seventh/eighth, fourth to Lady Dominatrix in Group 3 at Newbury second occasion: best at 6f/7f: acts on any turf going: tough and genuine. *B. A. McMahon*

NEEDWOOD MERLIN 6 b.g. Sizzling Melody 117 – Enchanting Kate (Enchant- **–** ment 115) [2002 10m 12f Jul 17] close-coupled gelding: modest maiden handicapper in 1999: tailed off both runs since. *K. W. Hogg, Isle of Man*

NEEDWOOD MISSILE 6 b.g. Sizzling Melody 117 – Sea Dart 55 (Air Trooper **–** 115) [2002 –: 10.2g Aug 8] well beaten in maiden/seller. *J. L. Spearing*

NEEDWOOD MYSTIC 7 b.m. Rolfe (USA) 77 – Enchanting Kate (Enchantment **64** 115) [2002 70: p12g⁴ p12g⁴ 11.9f 11.9m⁴ 11.8m 12d³ 11.9d* 12d 12.1g 14.1m⁴ 14.1m* **a53** 16.2m f14.8g⁵ Sep 30] smallish, workmanlike mare: modest performer: won ladies minor event at Brighton in June and amateur handicap at Carlisle in August: effective at 1½m/ 1¾m: acts on firm going, soft and polytrack: tried tongue tied: used to make running, but often slowly away nowadays. *Mrs A. J. Perrett*

NEEDWOOD TRICKSTER (IRE) 5 gr.g. Fayruz 116 – Istaraka (IRE) (Darshaan **–** 133) [2002 –, a56: f6s⁵ f6g f6g 7f 10m⁵ 8.1g 8.1d Jul 12] close-coupled gelding: poor **a42** nowadays: barely stays 7f: acts on fibresand and probably any turf going: tried blinkered/ tongue tied. *R. Brotherton*

NEEDWOOD TROOPER 5 br.g. Puissance 110 – Blueit (FR) 101 (Bold Lad (IRE) **58** 133) [2002 –: 6m 6m⁵ 5d⁵ 6f Jun 4] modest maiden: effective at 5f/6f: acts on good to firm and good to soft ground: tried blinkered. *S. J. Magnier*

NEGLIGEE 3 gr.f. Night Shift (USA) – Vax Star 96 (Petong 126) [2002 94: 6g 6d Jul **87 +** 9] small, sturdy filly: fairly useful performer: raced only at 6f, should prove as effective at 5f: yet to race on extremes of going: has hung badly left: usually makes running: sold 22,000 gns. *B. W. Hills*

NELLIE MAY (IRE) 3 b.f. Kylian (USA) – Oriental Air (IRE) 56 (Taufan (USA) **–** 119) [2002 8.2d 5.7g 6m 6.1v 7m 5g 7m 6.1m Sep 20] quite good-topped filly: fourth foal: half-sister to 6-y-o Eastern Trumpeter: dam, 5f winner, half-sister to useful sprinter Sunset Reigns: little form. *J. M. Bradley*

NELLIE MELBA 3 b.f. Hurricane Sky (AUS) – Persuasion 79 (Batshoof 122) [2002 **70** 68: f8g* 9m 8m³ May 29] leggy filly: fair performer: won maiden at Southwell in January: will be suited by 1¼m: acts on good to firm going, good to soft and all-weather: carries head high. *D. J. Coakley*

NELSONS FLAGSHIP 4 b.g. Petong 126 – Marie's Crusader (IRE) (Last Tycoon **–** 131) [2002 –: p13g Feb 6] small, strong gelding: bad maiden. *Miss E. C. Lavelle*

NEMINOS (IRE) 3 b.c. Lake Coniston (IRE) 131 – Bandit Girl 70 (Robellino (USA) **–** 127) [2002 67: 5s 7s 10s 6d⁶ Oct 18] 7,000Y: second foal: dam, 7f/1m winner, half-sister to smart 5f to 7f performer Blue Siren: fair maiden at 2 yrs: little form in 2002, including at Redcar final start: best effort at 8.5f on soft ground: tongue tied last 2 starts. *Ms J. Morgan, Ireland*

Mr D. M. James's "Never A Doubt"

NEMO FUGAT (IRE) 3 b.g. Danehill Dancer (IRE) 117 – Do The Right Thing 71 **93** (Busted 134) [2002 91: 7m* 7m 6f 6f* 6f 7m 6m 6g 7g Oct 18] strong, lengthy gelding: fairly useful performer: won minor event at Newmarket (awarded race) in April and handicap at Newbury (beat Forever Times ½ length) in July: effective at 6f/7f: yet to race on soft/heavy going, acts on any other: tried blinkered: has edged right: joined D. Nicholls and gelded. *R. Hannon*

NEOCLASSIC 2 b.c. (Jan 25) Peintre Celebre (USA) 137 – Pure Grain 121 (Polish **– p** Precedent (USA) 131) [2002 7d Nov 2] 300,000Y: lengthy, useful-looking colt: third foal: half-brother to smart 7f (at 2 yrs) and 10.5f winner Goncharova (by Gone West) and 3-y-o Grain of Gold: dam 7f (Prestige Stakes at 2 yrs) to 1½m (Irish/Yorkshire Oaks) winner: 20/1 and bandaged behind, not given hard time when tenth of 22 to Blazing Thunder in maiden at Newmarket: should prove suited by 1¼m+: almost certain to improve. *J. H. M. Gosden*

NEPTUNE 6 b.g. Dolphin Street (FR) 125 – Seal Indigo (IRE) 93 (Glenstal (USA) **37** 118) [2002 32: f12s³ p12g* f16g p16g³ f16g 10.2d 12d 12d⁶ 11.6g⁴ p12g f12g⁵ f14.8g **a49** f16g Nov 20] leggy gelding: poor performer: won amateur handicap at Lingfield in January: stays 2m: acts on all-weather, firm and good to soft going: has given trouble at stall/looked difficult ride. *J. C. Fox*

NEPTUNE'S GIFT 3 b.f. Lugana Beach 116 – Not So Generous (IRE) 68 (Fayruz **–** 116) [2002 60: p5g⁶ f5g² f5g³ f16g² p5g f5g⁴ f6g f5g⁴ f6g f5g f5s f6g f5g Nov 22] modest **a60 d** handicapper: well beaten last 5 starts, leaving A. Reid before penultimate one: effective at 5f/easy 6f: acts on good to firm ground and fibresand: usually visored: has worn cheekpieces: usually races up with pace: sometimes wanders. *I. W. McInnes*

690

NERINA PRINCESS (IRE) 3 b.f. Key of Luck (USA) 126 – Finessing (Indian King **40**
(USA) 128) [2002 8.3g 11.6m⁴ 11m 16.2g 10d Oct 28] half-sister to several winners,
including 11f winner Sir Edward Henry (by Taufan) and 1½m winner Soviet King (by
Soviet Lad): dam Irish maiden: poor maiden: stays 11.6f. *J. S. Moore*

NETTLETON KNIGHT 4 b.g. Beveled (USA) – Mybella Ann (Anfield 117) [2002 **–**
–: f8g 7f 7f 8.1g Aug 8] lengthy, workmanlike gelding: little form. *J. M. Bradley*

NEUTRAL NIGHT (IRE) 2 b.f. (Apr 9) Night Shift (USA) – Neutrality (IRE) **58**
(Common Grounds 118) [2002 5m 5.3m f5g f6g⁶ f6s Dec 26] first foal: dam unraced:
modest maiden: best effort when sixth at Wolverhampton: should stay 1m: acts on fibresand. *R. Brotherton*

NEVADA DESERT (IRE) 2 b.g. (Mar 31) Desert King (IRE) 129 – Kayanga (Green **75**
Desert (USA) 127) [2002 6f⁶ 7.1m⁵ 7.5d⁵ 7g³ 8g 7g Sep 7] useful-looking gelding:
second foal: dam, placed at 3 yrs in Italy, out of half-sister to Prix du Jockey Club
winner Natroun: fair maiden: clearly best effort when third at Chester: should stay 1m.
R. M. Whitaker

NEVEN 3 b.g. Casteddu 111 – Rose Burton 42 (Lucky Wednesday 124) [2002 6m⁴ **73**
7.2d² 6g⁴ 8.3v 8.1m 7d f7g* Dec 17] 1,100Y: lengthy gelding: first foal: dam 1m seller
winner: fair performer: won handicap at Southwell (all-weather debut) in December:
should stay 1m: acts on fibresand and good to soft ground: hung left/found little third
outing. *T. D. Barron*

NEVER A DOUBT 2 b.f. (Mar 28) Night Shift (USA) – Waypoint 95 (Cadeaux Gener- **107**
eux 131) [2002 5g² 5.1g² 5m* 5m² 6d⁴ 5.5g* Jul 28] 42,000Y: lengthy, useful-looking
filly: second foal: dam, 6f/7f winner, out of smart 5f performer Princess Athena: useful
performer: won maiden at Sandown in June and Prix Robert Papin at Maisons-Laffitte
(beat Zinziberine by head, racing freely and quickening to lead 1f out) in July: in frame in
between in Queen Mary Stakes at Royal Ascot (3½ lengths second to Romantic Liason)
and Cherry Hinton Stakes at Newmarket (fourth to Spinola): effective at 5f/6f: yet to race
on extremes of going. *B. W. Hills*

NEVER FORGET BOWIE 6 b.g. Superpower 113 – Heldigvis 63 (Hot Grove 128) **50**
[2002 5d 5.9d⁴ 9.2d³ 8.3v³ 5s 9m⁴ 8.3m 9.1s⁴ Oct 15] little form over hurdles: modest
maiden handicapper on Flat: stays 9f: acts on heavy and good to firm going. *R. Allan*

NEVER PROMISE (FR) 4 b.f. Cadeaux Genereux 131 – Yazeanhaa (USA) 68 **66 d**
(Zilzal (USA) 137) [2002 66: 10g² 9.9m 10m 10.2v 7m 8.3g* 7d 8.5d 8m f8s 7f 10g 7s
Oct 28] smallish filly: fair handicapper: made all at Windsor in July: ran poorly after:
stays 1¼m: acts on good to firm ground: visored/blinkered: has raced freely/found little.
J. Neville

NEVINSTOWN (IRE) 2 b.c. (Mar 14) Lahib (USA) 129 – Moon Tango (IRE) 81 **–**
(Last Tycoon 131) [2002 7g 8d 8d f6g p7g Dec 21] IR 12,500F, IR 28,000Y, 37,000 2-y-o:
first foal: dam, 6f winner, half-sister to useful 1996 2-y-o 6f winner Elegant Warning:
signs of just a little ability in maidens/minor event, including at Wolverhampton and
Lingfield. *Niall Moran, Ireland*

NEW CALADONIA (USA) 3 ch.g. Trempolino (USA) 135 – Tea Cozzy (USA) **–**
(Irish River (FR) 131) [2002 63: 8s 8g 14.1m 8.1m f6g Oct 17] rather sparely-made
gelding: modest maiden at 2 yrs: no form in 2002. *D. Shaw*

NEWCORP LAD 2 b.c. (Mar 30) Komaite (USA) – Gleam of Gold (Crested Lark 78) **72**
[2002 6m 7.1v² 7.9f⁴ 8s 7v Nov 9] second reported foal: brother to 1998 2-y-o 5f seller
winner Ok Maite, later 6f winner in Sweden: dam no form: fair maiden: well beaten in
nurseries last 2 starts: stays 1m: acts on any ground. *Mrs G. S. Rees*

NEW CURRENCY (USA) 2 b.c. (Feb 3) Touch Gold (USA) 127 – Ceirseach (IRE) **83**
100 (Don't Forget Me 127) [2002 6s⁶ 7s* 10s⁴ Nov 2] useful-looking colt: second foal:
half-brother to fairly useful Irish 7.5f (at 2 yrs) and 9f winner Laoch Na Mara (by Sea
Hero): dam, Irish 7f (at 2 yrs) and 9.6f winner, half-sister to smart Irish performer up to
1½m Project Manager: fairly useful form: won maiden at Gowran in June: creditable 12
lengths fourth to Forest Magic in listed race at Newmarket: stays 1¼m: raced only on soft
ground. *J. S. Bolger, Ireland*

NEW DESIGN (IRE) 2 ch.f. (Feb 14) Bluebird (USA) 125 – Ashirah (USA) (House- **93**
buster (USA)) [2002 5s⁵ 6s⁴ 6s⁴ 6s⁶ 5g⁸ 5s² 6g³ 5.2f 5m² 5m⁵ Oct 6] 28,000F, 26,000Y:
well-made filly: first foal: dam unraced out of close relation to Unfuwain and half-sister
to Nachwan and Nayef: fairly useful performer: won maiden at Bellewstown in July:
good efforts after when placed: ran in listed race at Newbury eighth start: effective at 5f/
6f: acts on soft and good to firm ground. *D. Wachman, Ireland*

Sheikh Mohammed's "New South Wales"

NEW DIAMOND 3 ch.g. Bijou d'Inde 127 – Nannie Annie 60 (Persian Bold 123) **75 p**
[2002 6m p8g* Oct 9] 16,000F: half-brother to 2 winners abroad by Risk Me, including
Swedish winner up to 1½m Brandon Express: dam ran 3 times at 2 yrs: better effort in
maidens when winning at Lingfield by 9 lengths from Rare Quality: likely to improve
further. *J. M. P. Eustace*

NEW FOUNDATION (IRE) 2 b.f. (Mar 21) College Chapel 122 – Island Desert **89**
(IRE) 55 (Green Desert (USA) 127) [2002 5f* 5.2g⁴ 6d² 5g 5.1f⁴ 5.2f⁴ 5.2f⁶ 5g⁶ 5m 6g
Sep 21] IR 30,000Y: leggy filly: good mover: fifth foal: half-sister to 3-y-o Roundtree
and 1997 2-y-o 5.7f winner Brandon Frank (by Beveled), later winner abroad: dam
maiden who stayed 1½m: fairly useful performer: won maiden at Warwick in April: best
efforts when fourth of 24 to Presto Vento in sales race at Newbury sixth start and eighth
of 14 to Wunders Dream in Flying Childers Stakes at Doncaster ninth one: effective at 5f/
6f: acts on firm and good to soft going, unraced on softer: sometimes hangs. *R. Hannon*

NEWFOUNDLAND (USA) 2 ch.c. (Feb 24) Storm Cat (USA) – Clear Mandate **100**
(USA) 117 (Deputy Minister (CAN)) [2002 6s* 6d⁴ 7g⁵ 8g Sep 28] $3,300,000Y: close-
coupled, quite good-topped colt: second foal: dam US Grade 1 1m/1¼m winner: useful
performer: landed odds in maiden at Fairyhouse in May: best efforts when last of 4 to
stable-companion Hold That Tiger in Railway Stakes at the Curragh and fifth to Dublin
in Vintage Stakes at Goodwood: well held in Royal Lodge Stakes at Ascot: should stay
1m: raced only on good going or softer: has worn crossed noseband/had 2 handlers: sent
to USA. *A. P. O'Brien, Ireland*

NEW OPTIONS 5 b.g. Formidable (USA) 125 – No Comebacks 70 (Last Tycoon **75**
131) [2002 99, a104: a5g* a5.8d⁶ a6g⁴ a6g a5.5g⁵ 7s 7s p7g p7g p7g Dec 28] useful in
2001: only fair in 2002, winning minor event at Jagersro in May: left R. Haugen in
Norway after fifth start: stays easy 7f: acts on good to firm ground, polytrack and dirt:
usually blinkered in Scandinavia. *W. J. Musson*

NEWRYMAN   7 ch.g. Statoblest 120 – With Love (Be My Guest (USA) 126) [2002 –:   –
12.4g Aug 7] of little account. *G. P. Kelly*

NEW SEEKER   2 b.c. (Mar 1) Green Desert (USA) 127 – Ahbab (IRE) 81 (Ajdal   **76 p**
(USA) 130) [2002 7f⁵ Sep 21] IR 30,000Y: half-brother to several winners, including
5-y-o Castleshane and useful 1m (in UAE) to 1¼m winner Labeq (by Lycius): dam, 7f
winner, out of half-sister to Fairy Footsteps and Light Cavalry: 16/1, 10 lengths fifth of 12
to Trade Fair in maiden at Newbury: wore crossed noseband: should improve. *C. G. Cox*

NEW SOUTH WALES   2 b.c. (Mar 4) In The Wings 128 – Temora (IRE) 90 (Ela-   **104 p**
Mana-Mou 132) [2002 8g* 7d* Oct 28] third foal: brother to fairly useful Irish 1½m
winner Tempter: dam, 9f (in USA)/1¼m winner, sister to very smart 1m/1¼m performer
Ela Romara: won maiden at the Curragh (by ¾ length from Chevalier) and Killavullan
Stakes at Leopardstown (by head from Napper Tandy, edging left after quickening to lead
over 1f out), both in October: will stay at least 1¼m: joined Godolphin: should make a
smart 3-y-o. *J. Oxx, Ireland*

NEWTONIAN (USA)   3 ch.c. Distant View (USA) 126 – Polly Adler (USA) (House-   –
buster (USA)) [2002 10.4m⁶ Sep 8] $160,000Y: well-made colt: second foal: half-brother
to a winner in USA by Holy Bull: dam unraced half-sister to Breeders' Cup Juvenile
Fillies winner Epitome: always behind in maiden at York. *J. H. M. Gosden*

NEW WISH (IRE)   2 b.g. (Feb 11) Ali-Royal (IRE) 127 – False Spring (IRE) (Petorius   **90**
117) [2002 6f² 6g 7g* 7g 7m² 7.2g⁴ Sep 20] IR 10,000F, IR 45,000Y: rather leggy, good-
topped gelding: fourth foal: half-brother to fairly useful 7f (at 2 yrs) to 11f (in Italy)
winner Henry Joy (by Scenic) and 4-y-o Rumore Castagna: dam unraced: fairly useful
performer: won maiden at Epsom in July: creditable efforts after, particularly when
second in nursery at York: should stay 1m: raced only on good ground or firmer.
M. R. Channon

NEXT DESERT (IRE)   3 b.c. Desert Style (IRE) 121 – Night Petticoat (GER)   **122**
116 (Petoski 135) [2002 107p: 8.5s* 8m² 11d* 12v* Jul 7]
    The latest crop of German three-year-olds, particularly the colts, were a
substandard lot on the whole, but Next Desert stood out as much the best of them.
Not only is he unbeaten against fellow German rivals, but none of his compatriots
has managed to finish closer than three lengths to Next Desert in any of his five
wins. The only blot on Next Desert's record came in the Mehl-Mulhens-Rennen, the
German Two Thousand Guineas in May, when he was beaten two lengths into
second place by the smart British-trained colt Dupont, though there was no real
disgrace in that. For one thing, a mile was right up Dupont's street as he had already
won the Italian Guineas and was to go on to finish fourth to Rock of Gibraltar in
the St James's Palace Stakes. Subsequent events also showed Next Desert to be a
much better horse over longer distances, and there is a chance that the good to firm
ground (he has raced mainly under much softer conditions otherwise) was not ideal
for him.
    Next Desert had already shown plenty of ability at two, winning a maiden at
Cologne by four lengths and a national listed race at Dortmund by seven on his only
two outings. That form put him just behind Timeform's top German two-year-old
of 2001 Flying Dash, and ahead of the best two-year-old filly Kazzia. Next Desert
made his reappearance at Krefeld, in the Dr Busch Memorial, a Group 3 over an
extended mile. He landed the odds by four lengths from Orfisio, third top in the
German rankings the previous season. Following defeat in the German Guineas, the
Derby was the obvious target for Next Desert, though there were stamina doubts to
be allayed first. Looking at the dam's side of his pedigree, there should have been
little doubt about Next Desert's staying middle distances. A daughter of Petoski,
Night Petticoat won the Preis der Diana, the eleven-furlong German Oaks, and
finished second in the German St Leger. The doubts stemmed from Next
Desert's sire the six- and seven-furlong performer Desert Style, whose most notable
offspring have been best at up to a mile, including the French/Irish Two Thousand
Guineas winner Bachir, the Free Handicap winner Cape Town and the speedy filly
Jessica's Dream.
    Any stamina doubts were dispelled in no uncertain terms when Next Desert
won one of the main trials for the Derby, the Oppenheim-Union-Rennen at Cologne
in June over eleven furlongs. Next Desert drew readily clear inside the final furlong
for another four-length win, this time over Levirat, his performance suggesting the

BMW Deutsches Derby, Hamburg—Next Desert continues his domination of the German classic crop, defeating the fillies Salve Regina and Tomori to provide trainer Andreas Schutz with a clean sweep

extra furlong at Hamburg would cause him no problem. None of the other trials revealed any German colts to rival Next Desert's Derby claims and he was sent off the 26/10 favourite in a field of seventeen. His nearest rivals in the betting were the only runner trained outside Germany—the Queen's Vase winner Mamool representing Godolphin—and one of the two fillies in the line-up, Salve Regina. Also trained by Andreas Schutz, Salve Regina was a sister to the 2000 Deutsches Derby winner Samum and was still unbeaten after winning the Preis der Diana. Despite its date in early-July, the heavy ground that prevailed for the Deutsches Derby was not untypical of recent runnings; five of the last seven renewals have been run on either soft or heavy going. Next Desert made light of the conditions, though, with a most authoritative win, having the race sewn up when sent into the lead from just off the pace on the home turn and keeping on resolutely in the straight. Andreas Schutz took a leaf out of Aidan O'Brien's book by saddling the first three home, a remarkable feat by any standards but one Schutz had already accomplished in the race two years earlier. Salve Regina ran on for second, three lengths behind the winner, with another four back to Tomori, the other filly in the race. The remainder were routed, with a further eight lengths to the fourth horse, just ahead of Mamool in fifth, while the last passed the post more than sixty lengths adrift of Next Desert. If the race was a triumph for Next Desert's trainer, it had no little significance for his rider, Andrasch Starke, either. Just days earlier he had returned from a six-and-a-half-month worldwide ban imposed by the Hong Kong Jockey Club after testing positive for cocaine at the International meeting at Sha Tin the previous December.

Next Desert had proved conclusively that he was the best three-year-old in Germany, and the best colt there by some way. Apart perhaps from the Coronation Cup winner Boreal, he seemed to have little to fear from the older horses in Germany as well, but he never got the chance to prove himself against his elders. He missed the Grosser Preis von Baden (in which Salve Regina finished second to Marienbard) but was reported to be still on course for a crack at the Prix de l'Arc de Triomphe. However, in September came news that Next Desert had been retired for the season in order to give him time to recover from a fetlock problem.

Next Desert (IRE) (b.c. 1999)	Desert Style (IRE) (b 1992)	Green Desert (b 1983)	Danzig
			Foreign Courier
		Organza (b 1985)	High Top
			Canton Silk
	Night Petticoat (GER) (b 1993)	Petoski (b 1982)	Niniski
			Sushila
		Nightrockette (b 1983)	Rocket
			Nightlife

Next Desert's sire and dam have already been discussed. Next Desert is the first foal of Night Petticoat, the pick of seven winners out of Nightrockette, a winner over seven furlongs and a mile in ordinary company in Germany. Nightrockette had already been represented by one of her descendants in the Deutsches Derby before the latest season, as she was the grandam of third-placed Near Honor in 2001. Great grandam Nightlife also won in Germany, but her dam was a filly named Nigeria, who was a six-furlong winner at Pontefract as a two-year-old for Charlie Elsey. Nightlife's half-sisters included the 1983 Preis der Diana winner Novelle. Next Desert went through the ring at Baden-Baden as a yearling but was bought back for 160,000 marks.

There was a time when German champions were content to remain just that, but nowadays they are campaigned more frequently on the international stage. Hopefully, Next Desert will get the opportunity to prove himself outside the relatively small pond he has dominated so far. Reportedly fully recovered from his setback by the end of the year, he has the makings of a high-class four-year-old. *A. Schutz, Germany*

NEXT FLIGHT (IRE) 3 b.g. Woodborough (USA) 112 – Sans Ceriph (IRE) 75 (Thatching 131) [2002 76: 9g 11m 10m p10g f11g p12g Dec 14] good-bodied gelding: fair maiden: mostly well held in 2002: stays 1¼m: acts on polytrack. *A. P. Jarvis* **64**

NIAGARA (IRE) 5 b.g. Rainbows For Life (CAN) – Highbrook (USA) 88 (Alphabatim (USA) 126) [2002 79: p10g p10g⁵ 9.2v⁵ 9m³ 9.2v² 12.3m 12g* p12g Oct 9] stocky gelding: fair on turf, modest on all-weather: won 4-runner minor event at Folkestone in September: stays easy 1½m: acts on any turf going and polytrack: usually races prominently. *M. H. Tompkins* **78** **a63**

NICE BALANCE (USA) 7 b.g. Shadeed (USA) 135 – Fellwaati (USA) (Alydar (USA)) [2002 –, a39+: f8s² f7s³ f8s² f8g f8g f7g f12g 12f Jul 17] big gelding: seemingly modest form first 2 starts only in 2002: acts on fibresand: best recent efforts in blinkers, also tried visored/tongue tied: sometimes rears start, often slowly away: tends to hang right: untrustworthy. *M. C. Chapman* **– §** **a51 ?**

NICHOL FIFTY 8 b.g. Old Vic 136 – Jawaher (IRE) 60 (Dancing Brave (USA) 140) [2002 60: f16s³ f12s f16s 12.3g 12f 16m⁵ 16.2g 12.1m* 10d 12f⁴ 15d³ 12m 12m⁴ 14.1m⁵ Aug 21] workmanlike gelding: modest performer: left D. Nicholls before winning claimer at Beverley in June: effective at 1½m to 17f: acts on fibresand, soft and firm going: tried blinkered/visored: has edged right: sometimes slowly away. *N. Wilson* **46** **a52**

NICIARA (IRE) 5 b.g. Soviet Lad (USA) – Verusa (IRE) (Petorius 117) [2002 –: f11g f16g f16g Mar 26] lengthy gelding: no longer of much account. *M. C. Chapman* **–**

NICKEL SUNGIRL (IRE) 2 b.f. (May 9) Petorius 117 – Sharp Hint 60 (Sharpo 132) [2002 5g 5f⁶ 6d f5g f5g³ Dec 16] IR 2,000Y: leggy filly: first foal: dam, maiden, best at 5f: poor maiden: made running when third at Wolverhampton (reportedly finished distressed): will prove best at 5f/6f: acts on fibresand and firm ground. *R. Hollinshead* **49**

NICKLETTE 3 b.f. Nicolotte 118 – Cayla (Tumble Wind (USA)) [2002 67: p8g² p7g³ p8g* 10.3s p8g 8.1m 7.1m p7g 7g f8.5g p7g p7g p6g Dec 30] tall, workmanlike filly: fair performer: won maiden at Lingfield in February: stays 1m: acts on polytrack: has worn cheekpieces: on downgrade. *C. N. Allen* **66 d**

NICO 2 ch.c. (Mar 20) Komaite (USA) – Mamoda (Good Times (ITY)) [2002 5m 6m 7m 7d⁵ Aug 23] 3,500F, 2,000Y: third foal: half-brother to a 9f winner in Denmark by Noble Patriarch: dam unraced out of half-sister to Champion Stakes winner Swiss Maid: modest maiden: best effort when fifth in seller at Thirsk: will probably stay 1m: acts on good to soft going: sent to Holland. *M. W. Easterby* **53**

NICOLETA POWER (IRE) 2 b.f. (May 14) Grand Lodge (USA) 125 – Oiche Mhaith 74 (Night Shift (USA)) [2002 6d 6g 6d 8g 5m⁴ Sep 5] 10,000Y: quite good-topped filly: fifth foal: half-sister to winners in Italy up to 7.5f by Catrail and Thatching: dam Irish 6f winner: little form: tried blinkered: sent to Cyprus. *T. D. Easterby* **–**

NIEMBRO 2 b.g. (Apr 3) Victory Note (USA) 120 – Diabaig 76 (Precocious 126) [2002 7m Jul 28] fifth foal: half-brother to 4-y-o Ailincala: dam 1m winner: 66/1, always behind in maiden at Newmarket. *Mrs Lydia Pearce* **–**

NIEVE LADY 3 b.f. Komaite (USA) – Nikoola Eve 69 (Roscoe Blake 120) [2002 71: p5g⁴ p5g² f5g* p5g⁴ 6m f6g⁴ 5s 6s* p7g⁶ 6g f6g 7s p7g⁶ f7g f5g p7g⁴ Dec 30] leggy filly: fair performer: won maiden at Southwell in March and handicap at Windsor in June: stays easy 7f: acts on all-weather and soft ground: has been mounted on track. *D. Shaw* **67**

NIFTY ALICE 4 ch.f. First Trump 118 – Nifty Fifty (IRE) 97 (Runnett 125) [2002 69d: 5m⁴ 5m 5g 5v 5m 5d 5m Aug 6] leggy, lengthy filly: modest handicapper: best at 5f: acts on firm and good to soft going: usually races up with pace: tends to wander: none too consistent. *E. J. Alston* **53**

NIFTY DAN 3 b.g. Suave Dancer (USA) 136 – Nifty Fifty (IRE) 97 (Runnett 125) [2002 45: 8g 9.2s* 9.2g 10.9g⁶ 10s Oct 14] good-bodied gelding: modest handicapper: won handicap at Hamilton in May: should stay at least 1¼m: acts on soft going: sold 1,000 gns. *E. J. Alston* **52**

NIFTY MAJOR 5 b.g. Be My Chief (USA) 122 – Nifty Fifty (IRE) 97 (Runnett 125) **65 d**
[2002 74d: p5g⁴ p5g³ p5g* p5g⁶ p6g 5g⁶ 5m 6s 5g⁴ 6g 6f 5.9s 5m 5m⁵ 5g 5s 5m 5g f5g
f5g⁶ Dec 27] tall, workmanlike gelding: fair performer: won claimer at Lingfield in
January: on downgrade after, leaving A. Berry and off 3 months after eighteenth start:
best at 5f: acts on polytrack, soft and firm going: usually blinkered/visored: sometimes
slowly away: tends to hang right/carry head high: has twice refused to race: untrustworthy. *S. R. Bowring*

NIFTY NORMAN 8 b.g. Rock City 120 – Nifty Fifty (IRE) 97 (Runnett 125) [2002 **46**
–: f7s f6g f6g** 6d 6v 5m f6g 6d 5m Aug 16] leggy, angular gelding: modest performer: **a54**
won amateur claimer at Southwell in April: effective at 5f/6f: acts on fibresand/sand,
best turf form on good or softer (acts on heavy): tried visored/tongue tied, often blinkered
earlier in career: has been early to post/reared stall. *N. Wilson*

NIFTY ROY 2 b.g. (Apr 29) Royal Applause 124 – Nifty Fifty (IRE) 97 (Runnett 125) **50**
[2002 6v² 6d⁶ 6g⁵ 6g⁶ 7.2s Oct 14] 26,000Y: sixth foal: half-brother to 3 winners,
including 5-y-o Nifty Major and 8-y-o Nifty Norman: dam 2-y-o 5f winner: modest
maiden: bred to prove best at 5f/6f: raced only on good ground or softer. *A. Berry*

NIGELS DREAM (IRE) 3 b. or br.g. Turtle Island (IRE) 123 – Black Orchid (IRE) –
(Persian Bold 123) [2002 p13g⁶ p12g Sep 4] second foal: dam unraced out of half-sister
to very smart sprinter Indian Ridge: little form in Lingfield maidens. *M. D. I. Usher*

NIGEL'S LAD (IRE) 10 b.g. Dominion Royale 112 – Back To Earth (FR) (Vayrann –
133) [2002 75: 18s 17.1f Apr 13] sturdy gelding: fair handicapper in 2001: well held both
starts in 2002 (though won over hurdles in between): visored once. *P. C. Haslam*

NIGHT ARRANGEMENT 2 ch.f. (Apr 2) Night Shift (USA) – By Arrangement –
(IRE) 60 (Bold Arrangement 127) [2002 6m 7m Aug 12] third foal: half-sister to 3-y-o
Turbo and 4-y-o Its Your Bid: dam 1m to 2m winner: always behind in maidens: tongue
tied debut, reportedly had breathing problem second start. *J. L. Dunlop*

NIGHT BEAUTY 2 b.f. (May 15) King of Kings (IRE) 125 – Kymin (IRE) 78 **80**
(Kahyasi 130) [2002 8g 8s³ Oct 25] 100,000Y: big, good-topped filly: has scope: first
foal: dam, disappointing staying maiden on Flat (winning hurdler), half-sister to smart
middle-distance stayer Book At Bedtime from good family: better effort in maidens
(fairly useful form) when third of 22 to Richemaur at Doncaster, leading 3f out until over
1f out: should stay at least 1¼m. *E. A. L. Dunlop*

NIGHT CAP (IRE) 3 ch.g. Night Shift (USA) – Classic Design (Busted 134) [2002 **68**
55: p5g³ f6g* p6g* f7g 7f² 8g 6g³ 7g 6m⁵ 6.1m p7g⁴ p7g p6g Dec 3] fair performer: won
handicaps at Southwell and Lingfield in March: left Sir Mark Prescott after fifth start:
best at 6f/7f: acts on all-weather and firm going: sometimes slowly away: none too
consistent. *T. D. McCarthy*

NIGHT CITY 11 b.g. Kris 135 – Night Secret 86 (Nijinsky (CAN) 138) [2002 –§, **– §**
a45§: f12g Jan 25] sturdy gelding: well held only 11-y-o start: tried blinkered/visored.
A. G. Juckes

NIGHT DIAMOND 5 b.g. Night Shift (USA) – Dashing Water 87 (Dashing Blade **69**
117) [2002 10s² 8.3m 12d* 12.6m² 12.1g⁶ 11.6d⁴ 11.8s p13g Nov 13] good-topped
gelding: fair handicapper: won amateur event at Salisbury in July: stays 1½m: acts on soft
and good to firm going: effective visored or not: usually tongue tied: sold only 500 gns.
M. C. Pipe

NIGHT DRIVER (IRE) 3 b.g. Night Shift (USA) – Highshaan (Pistolet Bleu (IRE) **76**
133) [2002 76: 10g⁵ 10d p10g* 10.3f⁶ 10.3d 10.9m 10f* 10.2g 10d⁵ Oct 21] big, strong **a82**
gelding: fairly useful on all-weather, fair on turf: won maiden at Lingfield in July and
minor event at Pontefract in September: stays 1¼m: acts on polytrack and firm going: has
taken good hold: inconsistent: sold 20,000 gns. *B. W. Hills*

NIGHT FLIGHT 8 gr.g. Night Shift (USA) – Ancestry (Persepolis (FR) 127) [2002 **88 d**
92: f6g⁵ 5s 6g⁵ 5f 5f 5g 6g 6g 6d⁶ 6m 6m³ 5g 5m² 6f⁶ 5m 5v f5f⁴ Nov 29] good-bodied
gelding: fairly useful handicapper in first half of 2002: best at 5f/easy 6f: acts on soft
going, firm and fibresand: tried in blinkers and cheekpieces. *R. A. Fahey*

NIGHT FLYER 7 b.g. Midyan (USA) 124 – Scandalette (Niniski (USA) 125) [2002 –
f9.4g 10.9m Sep 21] angular, good-quartered gelding: fairly useful handicapper in 1999:
well beaten both starts since. *J. W. Unett*

NIGHT GAMES 2 b.f. (Feb 1) Mind Games 121 – Miss Beverley (Beveled (USA)) **78**
[2002 5m 6.1m³ 6m 7m² 6d* Oct 21] 10,000Y: angular filly: first foal: dam unraced out

of half-sister to very smart Lockinge Stakes winner Motavato: fair performer: justified favouritism in maiden at Pontefract by 2 lengths from La Corujera: effective at 6f/7f: yet to race on extremes of going: sold 26,000 gns, sent to USA. *A. C. Stewart*

NIGHTGLADE (IRE)   6 b.g. Night Shift (USA) – Woodland Garden (Godswalk (USA) 130) [2002 14.1f 12.1m Jun 25] small, sturdy gelding: maiden handicapper: well beaten both starts since 2000. *B. W. Murray* –

NIGHT KISS (FR)   2 ch.f. (Jan 12) Night Shift (USA) – Roxy (Rock City 120) [2002 5.7d 6.1d⁵ 6m 6m 5m 6m² 5.1g⁵ 7g* 8s p6g³ p7g⁴ p8g³ Nov 23] first reported foal: dam unraced half-sister to Irish 1000 Guineas second Goodnight Kiss (by Night Shift): modest performer: won 26-runner seller at Newmarket in October: stays 7f, seemingly not 1m: acts on polytrack, and good to firm and good to soft going: consistent. *R. Hannon* **61**

NIGHT MAIL   2 b.c. (Apr 11) Shaamit (IRE) 127 – Penlanfeigan (Abutammam 85) [2002 7v Nov 8] leggy colt: second foal: dam unraced: 100/1 and backward, well beaten in maiden at Doncaster. *M. W. Easterby* –

NIGHT MARKET   4 ch.g. Inchinor 119 – Night Transaction 59 (Tina's Pet 121) [2002 64: p8g 7m⁵ 7f³ 7g⁵ 8.2d 8.3m² 8.3g⁵ 8f 8f⁵ f8.5s⁵ 8.5g 8m⁵ f8g⁴ f8g³ Nov 20] strong gelding: fair maiden handicapper: stays 9f: acts on fibresand and firm going: has raced freely. *B. Smart* **66**

NIGHT MIST (IRE)   2 b.f. (Jan 19) Alzao (USA) 117 – Night Mirage (USA) 80 (Silver Hawk (USA) 123) [2002 7.5g² 8.3m* Sep 30] workmanlike filly: first foal: dam 9f winner: fairly useful form: landed odds in maiden at Hamilton by 4 lengths from Lexi's Hoss: should be suited by 1¼m/1½m: remains open to improvement. *M. Johnston* **80 p**

NIGHT OMEN (IRE)   5 ch.g. Night Shift (USA) – Propitious (IRE) 101 (Doyoun 124) [2002 46: f5g p7g Jan 23] heavy-topped gelding: maiden: well held both 5-y-o outings. *S. C. Williams* –

NIGHT PROSPECTOR   2 b.c. (Jan 25) Night Shift (USA) – Pride of My Heart 74 (Lion Cavern (USA) 117) [2002 5g² 5.2f² Jul 17] 32,000F, 54,000Y: first foal: dam, 7f winner, half-sister to smart sprinter Northern Goddess (by Night Shift): odds on, better effort in maidens 2 months apart when ½-length second to Riva Royale at Yarmouth on second outing, leading until inside final 1f: should stay 7f. *J. W. Payne* **86**

NIGHT RUNNER   3 b.c. Polar Falcon (USA) 126 – Christmas Kiss 82 (Taufan (USA) 119) [2002 65: 7f⁵ 6g² 7m 5g* 6m* 5d³ 6.1m² 6g⁶ 6g 6f Oct 12] leggy, unfurnished colt: fairly useful performer: won maiden at Beverley and handicap at Newcastle in July: stays 7f: acts on good to firm going, probably on soft: usually blinkered: type to do well again at 4 yrs. *T. D. Easterby* **88 p**

NIGHT SHIFT BLUE'S (IRE)   3 b.g. Night Shift (USA) – Tommelise (USA) (Dayjur (USA) 137) [2002 75: f6g⁴ 6g² 6g 8m 5.9v 6m³ 6f f6g² f7g* f6s⁵ f7g f6g* f5g Dec 10] smallish, close-coupled gelding: fair performer: won seller at Southwell (sold from M. Johnston 7,000 gns) in October and handicap there in November: effective at 6f/7f: acts on good to firm going, heavy and fibresand: blinkered/visored after fourth outing. *M. J. Polglase* **64 a71**

NIGHT SIGHT (USA)   5 b.g. Eagle Eyed (USA) 111 – El Hamo (USA) (Search For Gold (USA)) [2002 64§, a94§: f11s³ f12g² p10g f11g⁵ f11g* f12g⁴ 11g² 12m* 10.3m* 11.9m³ 12f* 12g* 12g⁵ 11.9d 10d⁶ 10d⁵ 13.9m 11.9m 12m 12f⁴ 10f³ Oct 2] smallish, stocky gelding: fluent mover: fairly useful handicapper: won at Southwell, Catterick and Doncaster (3) in first half of year: best at 1¼m/1½m: acts on fibresand, probably on any turf going: blinkered once: sometimes slowly away/races freely: often held up: tough. *M. C. Chapman* **91**

NIGHT SPEED (IRE)   2 ch.c. (Mar 5) Night Shift (USA) – Dead Certain 123§ (Absalom 128) [2002 5m⁵ 5m² 5m 5d* 5g 5d 6m⁵ 5m³ p6g Oct 16] 37,000Y: strong colt: brother to useful 1998 2-y-o 5f/6f winner Deadly Nightshade and 5-y-o True Night, closely related to 2 winners by Sadler's Wells, including useful Irish 7f/1¼m winner Hamad, later successful up to 11f in Hong Kong, and half-brother to a winner by Alzao: dam, won Cheveley Park Stakes, became temperamental: fairly useful performer: made all in maiden at Kempton in July: best effort after when close third to Arzoo in nursery at Musselburgh: likely to prove best at 5f: acts on good to firm and good to soft going, well held on polytrack: effective blinkered or not: front runner: sold 25,000 gns, sent to USA. *B. J. Meehan* **81**

NIGHT WARRIOR (IRE)   2 b.g. (May 11) Alhaarth (IRE) 126 – Miniver (IRE) 71 (Mujtahid (USA) 118) [2002 p8g³ p8g Dec 3] IR 14,000Y: second foal: dam, ran once in **71**

Ireland at 2 yrs, half-sister to high-class performer up to 1½m Legal Case and useful performer up to 1¾m La Sky (dam of Oaks winner Love Divine): fair form in maidens: will be suited by 1¼m+. *M. P. Tregoning*

NIGHTWATCHMAN (IRE)   3 b.g. Hector Protector (USA) 124 – Nightlark (IRE)   **62** 85 (Night Shift (USA)) [2002 53: f12g² 11.6m p12g⁵ f12g* 14m⁵ 12d³ 12.1d⁴ Aug 14]   **a67** smallish, strong gelding: fair on all-weather, modest on turf: won handicap at Southwell in June: stays 1¾m: acts on all-weather, good to firm and good to soft going: gelded after final start. *W. R. Muir*

NIGHT WOLF (IRE)   2 gr.g. (Apr 16) Indian Ridge 123 – Nicer (IRE) 113 (Pennine   **– p** Walk 120) [2002 8m⁴ 8f⁴ Sep 16] 140,000Y: fourth living foal: dam 6f (at 2 yrs) and Irish 1000 Guineas winner: green, signs of ability in minor event at Salisbury and maiden at Bath, losing lead when running wide on bend in latter (gelded after): should do better. *M. R. Channon*

NIGRASINE   8 b.h. Mon Tresor 113 – Early Gales (Precocious 126) [2002 88: p8g⁵   **86** p10g 8s 6g⁶ 6m 6f³ 8.3g* 8m 7.9d 7m Aug 7] close-coupled horse: fluent mover: fairly useful nowadays: won handicap at Hamilton in May: left J. L. Eyre before final start: best at stiff 6f to 1m: acts on any turf going, probably on polytrack: visored/blinkered: sometimes wanders. *D. Carroll*

NIJMAH   2 ch.f. (Feb 8) Halling (USA) 133 – Star Ridge (USA) (Storm Bird (CAN)   **71** 134) [2002 6m⁵ 7m⁴ 8m⁴ 7.1m⁶ Sep 21] half-sister to several winners, including smart 7f/ 1m winner On The Ridge (by Risk Me) and fairly useful 2001 2-y-o 1m winner Five Stars (by Bahamian Bounty): dam ran twice in France: fair maiden: should stay 1¼m: sold 5,500 gns. *H. R. A. Cecil*

NIKITIN   3 b.g. Emarati (USA) 74 – Choral Sundown 81 (Night Shift (USA)) [2002   **52 d** 72, a55: p8g⁴ f7g³ f8g 9.9g 8d 7g f8.5g Jun 14] rather sparely-made gelding: modest maiden at best in 2002: left R. Beckett after second outing: usually visored/blinkered. *G. J. Smith*

NIMBLE TRAVELLER (IRE)   3 b.f. Blues Traveller (IRE) 119 – Be Nimble   **–** (Wattlefield 117) [2002 –: 5g 8d 7g Jun 7] unfurnished filly: little form. *K. R. Burke*

NIMBUS TWOTHOUSAND   2 b.f. (Apr 17) Cloudings (IRE) 112 – Blueberry   **– §** Parkes 71 (Pursuit of Love 124) [2002 6m 7.5g Sep 18] 500Y: first foal: dam, second at 6f from 3 starts, half-sister to useful sprinters Lucky Parkes, My Melody Parkes and Summerhill Parkes: no form: wayward. *P. R. Wood*

NIMELLO (USA)   6 b.g. Kingmambo (USA) 125 – Zakota (IRE) (Polish Precedent   **91 §** (USA) 131) [2002 111: 8s 10g 8m 7.9f 8d³ 10.2s⁵ 8s⁴ 7.9m⁵ 8d³ 8d* 9.2s 7.2s 8g Oct 18] smallish, well-made gelding: formerly smart handicapper, just fairly useful nowadays: won at Leicester in August: best around 1m: has won on firm going, goes particularly well on softer than good and fibresand: tried blinkered: tends to carry head high/wander: unreliable: sold 7,000 gns, joined K. Ryan. *P. F. I. Cole*

NINEACRES   11 b.g. Sayf El Arab (USA) 127 – Mayor 86 (Laxton 105) [2002 88:   **73 §** f5s⁵ p5g⁴ f6g p6g⁵ f5s p5g 6m 5m 5m⁵ 5g 5g⁶ 5f 5m 5.1g f6g 5f³ 6.1m f6g f5g f5g⁵   **a85 §** f6g² f5g⁵ f6g⁴ f6s Dec 26] angular, workmanlike gelding: fairly useful handicapper on all-weather, fair on turf: gradually deteriorated after winning at Lingfield in January: best at 5f/6f: unraced on heavy, acts on any other turf going and all-weather: tried visored, blinkered nowadays: has given trouble at stall: untrustworthy. *J. M. Bradley*

NIRVANA   3 b.f. Marju (IRE) 127 – Charming Life (NZ) (Sir Tristram 115) [2002 78p: **82** 10.1g² 10m³ 12m² 11.7g* Oct 19] unfurnished filly: fairly useful performer: won maiden at Bath in October: stayed 1½m: raced only on good or firmer going: stud. *J. L. Dunlop*

NISR   5 b.g. Grand Lodge (USA) 125 – Tharwa (IRE) 63 (Last Tycoon 131) [2002 87:   **85** f7s⁶ p7g⁵ p7g³ f7g Mar 14] lengthy gelding: fairly useful performer, lightly raced: reportedly had shoulder problem final start: should stay 1m: acts on firm, good to soft going and polytrack. *J. W. Payne*

NITEOWL DREAM   2 ch.f. (Feb 9) Colonel Collins (USA) 122 – Nite-Owl Dancer   **59** 75 (Robellino (USA) 127) [2002 5s³ 5m³ 6m f6g² 7d 7s⁵ Aug 24] tall, leggy filly: third foal: half-sister to 5-y-o Nite-Owl Mate and 4-y-o Nite-Owl Fizz: dam 5f winner: modest maiden: below form after second at Wolverhampton: stays 6f: acts on fibresand, good to firm and soft ground: blinkered (very slowly away) final start. *J. O'Reilly*

NITE-OWL FIZZ   4 b.g. Efisio 120 – Nite-Owl Dancer 75 (Robellino (USA) 127)   **74** [2002 67: f8s f8g² f8.5g* f8g f8s⁴ Sep 17] fair handicapper on all-weather: won at

Wolverhampton in July: unlikely to stay beyond 8.5f: acts on fibresand, lightly-raced on turf: usually races prominently. *J. O'Reilly*

NITE-OWL MATE   5 b.g. Komaite (USA) – Nite-Owl Dancer 75 (Robellino (USA) 127) [2002 –: f7g f5s² f6g Sep 30] smallish, angular gelding: modest performer: best at 5f/6f: tried blinkered: often tongue tied. *J. O'Reilly*   – **a62**

NIVERNAIS   3 b.g. Forzando 122 – Funny Wave 65 (Lugana Beach 116) [2002 76p: 5d³ 6f 7f³ 5d 6.1s Oct 29] fairly useful handicapper: stays 7f: acts on firm and good to soft going: visored (below form) penultimate outing. *H. Candy*   **83**

NO ARGUMENT   3 b.g. Young Ern 120 – As Sharp As 64 (Handsome Sailor 125) [2002 58: f8.5g 7m 7.1m 8f May 13] maiden: well held in 2002. *D. W. Chapman*   –

NOBILISSIME   3 b.f. Halling (USA) 133 – Keswa 94 (Kings Lake (USA) 133) [2002 73p: 8m* 8m⁶ 8f³ 8f⁴ 8f 6.5f Dec 27] fairly useful performer: won handicap at Yarmouth in May: got too worked up (sweating, edgy and took strong hold) next time, then left W. Jarvis: creditable efforts when in frame in non-graded events at Del Mar and Santa Anita after: bred to be suited by 1¼m/1½m: raced only on good or firmer going. *Kathy Walsh, USA*   **82**

NOBLE ACADEMY (USA)   3 ch. or ro.g. Royal Academy (USA) 130 – Aristo-cratique 71 (Cadeaux Genereux 131) [2002 79: p6g⁴ 6g 6d³ 5m³ 6f 5.1s 5m p6g³ p6g 8m 6g Aug 7] lengthy gelding: poor mover: fair handicapper: stays 6f: acts on firm ground, good to soft and polytrack: visored seventh start: has drifted left. *R. Hannon*   **75 a77**

NOBLE CALLING (FR)   5 b.h. Caller I D (USA) – Specificity (USA) 103 (Alleged (USA) 138) [2002 65, a–: 10.2g³ 11.6d 10.2d⁴ 17.2d 9m² 8.1m 10m 10.2f² 8.1g² 10m⁵ 8f Sep 25] angular horse: modest performer: effective at 1m to easy 1½m: acts on firm and good to soft ground: sometimes blinkered/visored: often slowly away: no easy ride. *R. J. Hodges*   **59**

NOBLE CHALLENGE   6 ch.g. Formidable (USA) 125 – What A Challenge 70 (Sallust 134) [2002 10.2g Apr 30] tailed off (finished lame) in Bath seller. *C. J. Drewe*   –

NOBLE CYRANO   7 ch.g. Generous (IRE) 139 – Miss Bergerac (Bold Lad (IRE) 133) [2002 53§: 12.4g 11.1g³ 11.9s 14.1g 10g* 10.5g² 10.1m⁶ 12.1m⁶ 10m² 12f² 11.9f Oct 10] tall, angular gelding: modest handicapper: won apprentice race at Pontefract in July: finds 1¼m bare minimum and stays 1¾m: acts on any turf going and fibresand: sometimes takes long time to warm up/finds little: unreliable. *Jedd O'Keeffe*   **55 §**

NOBLE LADY   2 ch.f. (Mar 24) Primo Dominie 121 – Noble Destiny 89 (Dancing Brave (USA) 140) [2002 f5g⁴ Dec 2] sister to useful 5f winner (including at 2 yrs) Noble One and half-sister to several winners, including fairly useful 1¼m winner Maiden Castle (by Darshaan): dam, 2-y-o 7f winner, disappointing at 3 yrs: 9/1, green and ridden by 7-lb claimer, 9 lengths fourth of 13 to Beauvrai in maiden at Wolverhampton, keeping on from rear: sure to improve. *Sir Mark Prescott*   **65 p**

NOBLE LOCKS (IRE)   4 ch.g. Night Shift (USA) – Imperial Graf (USA) (Blushing John (USA) 120) [2002 65: f8s* f8g³ p7g f8.5g⁴ f7g* f8.5g² f8.5g⁵ f7g³ f7g* f6g* f7g* f6g⁴ f8.5g³ f6s⁶ f6s f8s f8.5g³ f8.5s³ f7g⁵ f8.5g⁴ Dec 26] smallish gelding: fair handicapper: won at Southwell (4 times) and Wolverhampton between January and July: left K. Ryan after seventeenth start: probably best at 6f/7f: acts on fibresand and heavy ground: tried tongue tied/blinkered (not in 2002): front runner. *J. W. Unett*   – **a69**

NOBLE NICK   3 b. or br.g. Primo Dominie 121 – Pericardia 60 (Petong 126) [2002 78§: 7m* 6m⁶ 5g² 5d³ 5g⁵ 6d 5g⁴ 5g 5f Oct 3] useful-looking gelding: fairly useful performer: made all in maiden at Catterick in April: effective at 5f to easy 7f: acts on firm going, good to soft and fibresand: races freely: often looked none too keen at 2 yrs. *D. Nicholls*   **89**

NOBLE PASAO (IRE)   5 b.g. Alzao (USA) 117 – Belle Passe (Be My Guest (USA) 126) [2002 78: f8.5g 10m 8d⁶ 9.9g* 9.9m 9.9d³ 11.8d⁵ 12.1m² 12f³ p12g² 14.6s⁵ Oct 25] close-coupled gelding: has a round action: fairly useful handicapper: better than ever in 2002, winning at Beverley in June and Lingfield in October: effective at 1¼m to 14.6f: acts on firm going, soft and all-weather: blinkered once: has raced freely: usually held up. *Andrew Turnell*   **87 a82**

NOBLE PENNY   3 b.f. Pennekamp (USA) 130 – Noble Form (Double Form 130) [2002 7g 8f 8g⁴ p10g p12g⁶ 10m 8f Sep 30] 32,000Y: well-made filly: half-sister to 3   **59**

winners, including 5f/6f winner Noble Patriot (by Polish Patriot) and 5-y-o Golden Rod:
dam French 1m and 10.5f winner: modest maiden: seems to stay 1¼m: sold 800 gns.
J. W. Hills

NOBLE PURSUIT   5 b.g. Pursuit of Love 124 – Noble Peregrine (Lomond (USA)   **83**
128) [2002 89: 7d 8.3s* 8g 8m⁶ 8.5d 8d⁶ 8.3g⁴ 7.6s⁴ 8m⁵ 8s f7s⁴ p7g Dec 28] workmanlike gelding: fairly useful performer: won minor event at Windsor in June: left
T. Mills 21,000 gns after ninth start: effective at 7f/1m: acts on fibresand, soft and good to
firm ground: sometimes slowly away/races freely: consistent. *N. P. Littmoden*

NOBLE VIEW (USA)   3 ch.f. Distant View (USA) 126 – Proud Lou (USA) (Proud   **–**
Clarion) [2002 68: 7.1g 9.9g 10.2f⁶ Sep 16] leggy filly: fair maiden at 2 yrs: little form in
2002: sold 21,000 gns in December. *B. W. Hills*

NO BORROWING (IRE)   2 b.f. (Feb 22) Tagula (IRE) 116 – Tisima (FR) 61 (Selkirk   **–**
(USA) 129) [2002 6d Aug 5] IR 3,800Y: second foal: sister to 3-y-o Queen Charlotte:
dam, lightly-raced maiden, likely to have proved best up to 1m: 20/1, tailed off in maiden
at Windsor. *Mrs P. N. Dutfield*

NO DISRUPTION (IRE)   2 b.g. (Apr 26) Lahib (USA) 129 – Angela's Venture (GER)   **47**
(Simply Great (FR) 122) [2002 5d 5m 5m Jul 29] 10,000Y, 15,000 2-y-o: well-made
gelding: fourth foal: half-brother to 2 winners abroad by Waajib: dam 7f winner in
Germany: poor form in maidens: probably needs further than 5f. *T. D. Barron*

NOD'S NEPHEW   5 b.g. Efisio 120 – Nordan Raider 81 (Domynsky 110) [2002 64:   **75**
f8s* p8g* f8s* f8g⁵ f7g⁴ f9.4g* 10.9g f9.4g² 7.9g 8.1v⁴ 8.5g⁶ p10g f8g Oct 17] lengthy   **a83**
gelding: fairly useful performer on all-weather, fair on turf: won seller at Southwell and
handicaps at Lingfield (apprentices), Southwell and Wolverhampton early in year: stays
9.4f: acts on heavy going, good to firm and all-weather: tongue tied in 2002: usually
tracks pace. *D. E. Cantillon*

NO EXCUSE NEEDED   4 ch.c. Machiavellian (USA) 123 – Nawaiet (USA)   **123**
(Zilzal (USA) 137) [2002 121: 8.9g 8m⁴ 8g* 8g⁴ 10.4g 10m⁵ Sep 7]
Stable-companions No Excuse Needed and Tough Speed, first and third
respectively in the Queen Anne Stakes at Royal Ascot in June, are to continue their
racing careers in the States following a season which ended on a low for the former
and saw the latter without a win. No Excuse Needed did at least give his stable a
third successive Queen Anne victory, following those of Kalanisi and Medicean,
giving the best performance of his career in the process.

Like Medicean, No Excuse Needed had won the Celebration Mile at Goodwood in his three-year-old season, but he began his four-year-old campaign in
Dubai where he finished tailed off in the Dubai Duty Free, reportedly having lost a
hind shoe. The experience did him no lasting harm and he quickly showed himself
none the worse on his return to Britain, coming an encouraging fourth to Keltos in
the Lockinge Stakes at Newbury despite meeting trouble in running. It was then on
to Royal Ascot for a competitive, though substandard, renewal of the Queen Anne,
on which the betting was very open. Nayyir and Frenchmans Bay, winners on their
previous starts of the Diomed Stakes and Prix du Palais-Royal respectively, were
bracketed at the head of the market at 5/1 with Best of The Bests, successful in the

*Queen Anne Stakes, Royal Ascot—a hat-trick of wins in the race for Sir Michael Stoute
as No Excuse Needed (rail) holds Tillerman by a short head; Stoute's other runner Tough Speed is third,
with Nayyir (left) fourth*

Prix d'Ispahan on his previous start and the only Group 1 winner in the line-up, at 11/2 and No Excuse Needed next in the betting at 13/2. No Excuse Needed, waited with as usual, had everything go right for him. The strong pace took its toll on the pacesetters, and those who were patiently ridden came to the fore in the closing stages. Enjoying a clear passage this time, No Excuse Needed hung left onto the stand rail under pressure after improving rapidly to lead over a furlong out before keeping on gamely as the unlucky-in-running Tillerman finished very strongly, the pair pulling three lengths clear of Tough Speed. The jubilant reaction by Tillerman's rider on passing the post turned out to be wishful thinking, the photograph showing that No Excuse Needed had held on by a short head. The Queen Anne, a race being raised to Group 1 status in 2003, when it will no longer be the curtain-raiser to the Royal meeting or open to three-year-olds, proved to be the highpoint of No Excuse Needed's season. He managed only fourth, almost six lengths behind Rock of Gibraltar, in the Sussex Stakes at Goodwood on his next outing, and was even further below form on his last two starts, both over a mile and a quarter. Probably unsuited by the good to soft going when well held in the 2001 Champion Stakes on his first run at the trip, No Excuse Needed had the ground in his favour on

		Mr Prospector	Raise A Native
	Machiavellian (USA)	(b 1970)	Gold Digger
	(b or br 1987)	Coup de Folie	Halo
No Excuse Needed		(b 1982)	Raise The Standard
(ch.c. 1998)		Zilzal	Nureyev
	Nawaiet (USA)	(ch 1986)	French Charmer
	(ch 1991)	Greenland Park	Red God
		(ch 1976)	Centre Piece

Maktoum Al Maktoum's "No Excuse Needed"

both his outings over the distance in 2002, but was again disappointing. Reportedly struck into when trailing home last of seven in the International at York, No Excuse Needed was then a never dangerous fifth of seven in the Champion Stakes at Leopardstown.

No Excuse Needed is the third foal of Nawaiet, and so far the only one to have raced. A winner over six furlongs in France, Nawaiet is a daughter of the very smart sprinter Greenland Park, who also produced a filly every bit as good as herself in Fitnah, winner of the Prix Saint-Alary and Prix de la Nonette and second in the Prix de Diane and Prix Vermeille. No Excuse Needed, who has a quick action, is an imposing-looking individual, rangy and quite attractive. Usually waited with, he acts on good to firm ground. *Sir Michael Stoute*

NOFAN (IRE) 2 b.c. (May 2) Marju (IRE) 127 – Auntie Maureen (IRE) 73 (Roi Danzig (USA)) [2002 7f 8.2s⁶ Oct 23] fourth foal: half-brother to 6f (in Ireland at 2 yrs) and 8.5f (in USA) winner Coney Kitty (by Lycius) and 2m winner Intrum Morshaan (by Darshaan), both useful: dam Irish 9f/1¼m winner from family of Halling: no sign of ability. *J. D. Czerpak* —

NO GROUSE 2 b.g. (Apr 6) Pursuit of Love 124 – Lady Joyce (FR) (Galetto (FR) 118) [2002 p7g p8g f8.5g² Dec 20] 15,000F, 20,000Y: fourth foal: half-brother to 3-y-o Commanding and 4-y-o Da Wolf: dam unraced half-sister to smart French/US middle-distance performers Lady Blessington and Lowell: easily best effort (fair form) when ½-length second to Toro Bravo in maiden at Wolverhampton: gelded after: will probably stay 1¼m. *J. W. Hills* 73

NO ILLUSIONS 3 b.g. Bluegrass Prince (IRE) 110 – Dancing Years (USA) 56 (Fred Astaire (USA)) [2002 53: p10g p12g p10g⁵ f12g 14.1m 16m⁶ p12g p13g⁶ Dec 28] sparely-made gelding: modest maiden: seems to stay 2m: acts on polytrack, firm and soft going: often visored. *R. Ingram* 53

NO LANGUAGE PLEASE (IRE) 8 ch.g. Arapahos (FR) 117 – Strong Language 58 (Formidable (USA) 125) [2002 46: f16g f16g⁴ p16g 15.4m⁶ Apr 23] strong, lengthy gelding: poor handicapper: stayed 2m: acted on firm going and fibresand: sometimes started slowly: dead. *R. Curtis* 39

NO LOOKING BACK (IRE) 2 b.g. (Apr 18) Revoque (IRE) 122 – Chloe (IRE) 79 (Green Desert (USA) 127) [2002 5m 7.5g⁶ 6g⁴ Aug 7] small, angular gelding: second foal: dam, lightly-raced Irish maiden (best effort at 8.5f), out of smart Irish 1½m performer Eileen Jenny: modest maiden: will probably stay 1m. *T. D. Easterby* 55

NO MERCY 6 ch.g. Faustus (USA) 118 – Nashville Blues (IRE) 94 (Try My Best (USA) 130) [2002 54, a74: p7g p7g p7g f6g⁴ f7g³ f8g 6m f7g² 7m 7d f7g f6g f7g p7g f8g f6g Nov 26] big, lengthy gelding: fair performer: has won at 1¼m, best at 7f/1m: acts on fibresand and any turf going: usually blinkered/visored: tried tongue tied: usually races prominently: unreliable. *B. A. Pearce* – § a65 §

NON ULTRA (USA) 2 ch.f. (Mar 14) Peintre Celebre (USA) 137 – Susun Kelapa (USA) 94 (St Jovite (USA) 135) [2002 6g⁶ 5g³ 5m 7m⁶ 6m Sep 23] IR 52,000Y: leggy filly: first foal: dam, Irish 1m (at 2 yrs) and 9f winner, out of half-sister to dam of Green Tune and Pas de Reponse: modest maiden: below form in nurseries last 2 starts, blinkered on final one: bred to stay at least 1¼m: raced only on good/good to firm ground. *B. J. Meehan* 63

NOOSA COURT (USA) 3 b.f. Hansel (USA) – Mahmoud Dancer (USA) (Moment of Hope (USA)) [2002 9.2g 6.9d⁴ f9.4g³ f8g Dec 10] third foal: half-sister to a winner in USA by Entropy: dam placed in USA: modest maiden: off 4 months before well beaten final start: stays 9.4f: acts on fibresand and good to soft ground. *G. A. Swinbank* 55

NO QUESTION 3 b.f. Salse (USA) 128 – Opalette 75 (Sharrood (USA) 124) [2002 77: 10g² 12.1m³ 14.1f³ May 17] smallish filly: fair maiden: seems barely to stay 1¾m: acts on fibresand and firm going: sold 10,000 gns. *B. W. Hills* 75

NORCROFT LADY 4 b.f. Mujtahid (USA) 118 – Polytess (IRE) (Polish Patriot (USA) 128) [2002 –: 7m Jul 2] big, useful-looking filly: fairly useful winner at 2 yrs: little form since. *G. G. Margarson* –

NO REFUGE (IRE) 2 ch.c. (Apr 20) Hernando (FR) 127 – Shamarra (FR) (Zayyani 119) [2002 f6g 6d p7g Oct 31] 11,000Y: rather leggy colt: third foal: half-brother to 2001 2-y-o 6f winner Denmark (by Danehill): dam unraced half-sister to small performer up to 1½m Shantaroun: modest form in maidens, not knocked about final start: will be suited by 1¼m+: type to do fair bit better in handicaps. *Sir Mark Prescott* 59 p

NORMA SPEAKMAN (IRE) 2 ch.f. (Apr 14) Among Men (USA) 124 – Bride Bank **46**
(IRE) (Statoblest 120) [2002 6g 6g² 7f² 7d Oct 18] IR 1,000F, 2,800Y: workmanlike filly:
first foal: dam unraced: poor maiden: runner-up in sellers: left A. Berry and off 4 months
before final start: will probably stay 1m: acts on firm ground. *E. W. Tuer*

NORSE DANCER (IRE) 2 b.c. (Apr 3) Halling (USA) 133 – River Patrol 96 (Rousil- **101 p**
lon (USA) 133) [2002 7m* 7m* 7g⁴ 8g⁴ 8s Oct 26] 26,000F: big, rangy, good sort: has a
quick action: fifth foal: half-brother to 3 winners, including fairly useful 1¼m winner
Regal Patrol (by Red Ransom): dam, 1¼m winner, half-sister to smart middle-distance
stayer Dry Dock from family of Bireme and Buoy: useful performer: won maiden at
Salisbury in June and minor event at Ascot (beat Pinkerton by 2 lengths) in July: good
fourth in Vintage Stakes at Goodwood (2¼ lengths behind Dublin) and Royal Lodge
Stakes at Ascot (beaten around 4 lengths by Al Jadeed): below-form seventh in Racing
Post Trophy at Doncaster: should be suited by 1¼m/1½m: acts on good to firm going,
possibly not soft: has scope to make a better 3-y-o. *D. R. C. Elsworth*

NORTH BY NORTHEAST (IRE) 4 ch.g. Polish Precedent (USA) 131 – Catalonda **73**
(African Sky 124) [2002 6f 7m⁵ 8.1d³ 6f³ 7m³ 8.3m 7g⁵ 7m 7g³ 8m Sep 23] 92,000Y: tall,
rather leggy gelding: half-brother to several winners, including smart winner around 1m
Fanaar (by Unfuwain) and useful French performer up to 1¼m Alamtara (by Cadeaux
Genereux): dam Irish 2-y-o 5f winner: fair maiden handicapper: stays 7f: acts on firm
going: sometimes slowly away: races freely. *J. W. Payne*

NORTHERLY (AUS) 6 b.g. Serheed 92 – North Bell (AUS) (Bellwater (FR) 117) **129**
[2002 128: 7d² 9g* 10g² 6.5f⁵ 7.1g⁴ 8g* 9d* 10d* 12g* 10.2g* Oct 26] high-class
gelding: confirmed himself the top performer in Australia in 2002, winning 6 races,

Carlton Draught Caulfield Cup (Handicap), Caulfield—
Northerly confirms his status as Australia's top performer

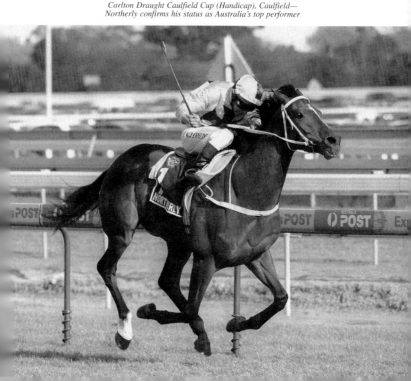

namely Group 2s at Caulfield in March and Flemington in September, Emirates Racing Association Underwood Stakes at Caulfield later in September, then Group 2 at Flemington, Carlton Draught Caulfield Cup at Caulfield (beat Fields of Omagh a short neck) and Carlton Draught Cox Plate at Moonee Valley, all in October: gaining second consecutive win in race when beating Defier and Grandera by a length and a neck for last success, leading inside final 1f: stays 1½m: acts on firm and good to soft going: has worn blinkers. *F. Kersley, Australia*

NORTHERN CASTLE (IRE) 4 b.g. Distinctly North (USA) 115 – Dunbally 57 (Dunphy 124) [2002 f12g Jan 24] no sign of ability. *P. C. Haslam*   **–**

NORTHERN DESERT (IRE) 3 b.c. Desert Style (IRE) 121 – Rosie's Guest (IRE) (Be My Guest (USA) 126) [2002 76p: 8.2d* 7m² 7.6f² 8m 7g⁵ᵈ 7m⁵ 6m⁴ Sep 18] lengthy, quite good-topped colt: useful performer: won maiden at Nottingham in March: mostly creditable efforts after, including when 6 lengths fifth to Suggestive in listed race at York and 3 lengths fourth to Welcome Friend in minor event at Yarmouth last 2 starts: effective at 6f to 1m: acts on firm and good to soft going, probably on soft: tends to swish tail in preliminaries: has edged left: sold 15,000 gns in November. *G. Wragg*   **103**

NORTHERN EXPOSURE 3 ch.f. Polar Falcon (USA) 126 – Lucky Round 82 (Auction Ring (USA) 123) [2002 –: 8.1g⁶ 10m⁶ Aug 31] strong filly: seemingly best effort in maidens when sixth at Sandown on reappearance. *John Berry*   **58 ?**

NORTHERN FLEET 9 b.g. Slip Anchor 136 – Kamkova (USA) 62 (Northern Dancer) [2002 62: 16.4d 14.1m Aug 15] quite good-topped gelding: modest handicapper in 2001: no form in 2002: tried blinkered. *P. R. Hedger*   **–**

NORTHERN FRIEND 2 b.g. (Apr 4) Distinctly North (USA) 115 – Pharaoh's Joy 66 (Robellino (USA) 127) [2002 6g 7.5g⁴ 6g 6.1m 6m² 7f⁴ 6f Oct 7] 10,000Y: small gelding: second foal: dam, 5f/6f winner (latter at 2 yrs), out of half-sister to very smart stayer Band: modest maiden: in frame in nurseries fifth (visored)/sixth starts: stays 7f: raced only on good ground or firmer. *J. A. Glover*   **54**

NORTHERN GAMES 3 b.g. Mind Games 121 – Northern Sal 59 (Aragon 118) [2002 67: 7m⁴ 6f 6f³ f6g² 6.1g* 6m⁴ 6.1m p6g f6g³ f6g f6f f6g Dec 16] leggy, useful-looking gelding: fairly useful performer: won maiden at Warwick in July: effective at 6f/7f: acts on firm going, good to soft and all-weather: often races prominently: slowly away last 2 starts: inconsistent. *A. Berry*   **83**

NORTHERN GOLD 4 b.g. Goldmark (USA) 113 – Scottish Royal (IRE) (Night Shift (USA)) [2002 59: f7g² f9.4g f9.4g* f8.5g² f12g² Jun 14] modest performer: won seller at Wolverhampton in April: barely stayed 1½m: raced only on fibresand: dead. *J. G. Given*   **62**

NORTHERN MOTTO 9 b.g. Mtoto 134 – Soulful (FR) (Zino 127) [2002 –: 16g 14m Apr 11] leggy gelding: modest handicapper in 2000: lightly raced and little form on Flat since: sometimes visored/blinkered. *J. S. Goldie*   **–**

NORTHERN NYMPH 3 b.g. Makbul 104 – Needwood Sprite 58 (Joshua 129) [2002 80: 7s² 10.5m⁶ 10m³ 12.3f 10.5d⁴ 8s 14m⁶ 16.2g² 11.8d³ 14.1m⁵ Aug 19] good-topped gelding: fairly useful performer: stays 2m: acts on fibresand, soft and good to firm going. *R. Hollinshead*   **87**

NORTHERN RULER 2 gr.g. (Apr 11) Lugana Beach 116 – Aimee Jane (USA) 76 (Our Native (USA)) [2002 7m f8s f5g⁶ Dec 27] 900Y: eighth living foal: half-brother to 1998 2-y-o 6f winner Dispol Safa (by Safawan) and a winner up to 15f in Germany by Niniski: dam ungenuine 1½m winner, also successful over hurdles: showed little in maidens (for A. Crook) and seller. *A. Dickman*   **–**

NORTHERN SVENGALI (IRE) 6 b.g. Distinctly North (USA) 115 – Trilby's Dream (IRE) (Mansooj 118) [2002 68§, a62§: f5s³ p6g² f6s⁴ p6g 6g 5.9s 9s 5d 5s⁶ 5m 5m⁴ 5m 5g Sep 19] small, sturdy gelding: modest handicapper at best in 2002: left T. D. Barron after fifth start: effective at 5f to easy 7f: acts on any turf going/all-weather: sometimes blinkered (not in 2002): tongue tied last 5 starts: has been slowly away: on downgrade. *D. A. Nolan*   **57 d**

NORTHERN TIMES (USA) 5 ch.g. Cahill Road (USA) – Northern Nation (USA) (Northrop (USA)) [2002 49: f12s f8.5g⁴ f8.5g f8g 7s Mar 28] compact gelding: poor performer: stays easy 15f: acts on fibresand and good to soft going: usually blinkered/visored: sometimes slowly away. *R. Brotherton*   **46**

Royal Hunt Cup (Handicap), Royal Ascot—Norton gains easily his biggest success;
Invader (far side), Beauchamp Pilot (No.15), Morro Castle, Sea Star (No.6),
Kelburne (No.8) and One More Round come next

NORTHERN TRIO (FR) 5 b.g. Aragon 118 – Northern Notion (USA) (Northern –
Baby (CAN) 127) [2002 f11g⁶ f7g Feb 12] workmanlike gelding: poor maiden: stayed
11f: acted on fibresand: dead. *Mrs Barbara Waring*

NORTH (IRE) 4 br.g. Mukaddamah (USA) 125 – Flamenco (USA) 116 (Dance Spell –
(USA)) [2002 60: 8.5d f12s 10f Sep 27] little form. *D. W. Chapman*

NORTH LANDING (IRE) 2 b.g. (Apr 11) Storm Bird (CAN) 134 – Tirol Hope **69**
(IRE) 100 (Tirol 127) [2002 6m⁵ 7d² 8g 8g Sep 20] 23,000Y: leggy, quite good-topped
gelding: easily best effort (fair form) when neck second
to Flighty Fellow in maiden at Thirsk, making most: should stay 1m: gelded after final
start. *M. Johnston*

NORTH POINT (IRE) 4 b.g. Definite Article 121 – Friendly Song 48 (Song 132) **73**
[2002 79: p10g f9.4g 14.4f 10s 11.5m 10m 10m³ 9d* 10d⁴ 10.1g* 10m³ 12m Sep 13]
smallish, useful-looking gelding: fair handicapper: won at Kempton (amateurs) and
Epsom (apprentices) in July: left A. Jarvis 14,500 gns before final start: stays 1¼m: acts
on good to firm and good to soft going: visored fourth start. *R. Curtis*

NORTHSIDE LODGE (IRE) 4 b.g. Grand Lodge (USA) 125 – Alongside 58 (Slip **89**
Anchor 136) [2002 71: p10g² 10m* 10f⁵ p10g* 9.9g² 10.1g⁴ 10m* 10d p10g* 10.1m*
10.4f² Oct 11] good-topped gelding: fairly useful handicapper: won at Pontefract,
Lingfield (twice, awarded race on first occasion), Nottingham and Yarmouth between
April and September: would have won with clear run at York final start: best around
1¼m: acts on polytrack, raced mainly on good going or firmer on turf: has worn blinkers
(including when successful): often held up: tough and consistent. *P. W. Harris*

NORTON (IRE) 5 ch.g. Barathea (IRE) 127 – Primrose Valley 99 (Mill Reef (USA) **109**
141) [2002 98: 8s⁶ 8g³ 7.6g* 8m* 7m 8d³ 10.4m³ 9m Sep 13] strong, useful-looking
gelding: useful performer: better than ever in 2002, winning minor event at Lingfield in
May and Royal Hunt Cup (Handicap) at Royal Ascot, drifting right when beating Invader
by ½ length in latter: at least respectable efforts in handicaps otherwise, including when
third at Ascot (behind Bouncing Bowdler) and York (behind Leadership) in August:
refused to enter stalls in Cambridgeshire: effective at 7f to 10.4f: yet to race on heavy
going, acts on any other: game and consistent. *T. G. Mills*

NORWOOD ORIGO 3 ch.g. Elmaamul (USA) 125 – Miller's Creek (USA) 62 (Star **75 d**
de Naskra (USA)) [2002 68: 11.8g⁴ 11.8m³ 11.1s⁴ 11.5f⁴ 11.9m³ 11.7d 14.1g⁵ 10.1m⁴

12m 10.9m Sep 16] smallish gelding: fair maiden: below form last 5 starts: stays 1½m: acts on good to firm ground: sold 2,800 gns, sent to Kuwait. *M. L. W. Bell*

NOSE THE TRADE 4 b.g. Cyrano de Bergerac 120 – Iolite 85 (Forzando 122) [2002 **103** 107: f8.5g* f8.5g* f8.5g⁶ 7m³ 7d³ 8m⁶ 7m 7.1d³ 7.1m⁴ 7m 9f 7g a9f³ Dec 14] strong, sturdy gelding: useful performer: easy winner of minor events at Wolverhampton in January (by 1½ lengths from Midshipman) and February: ran at least respectably most starts after, including when third in handicaps at Newmarket (behind Sea Star) and Ascot (behind Scotty's Future in Victoria Cup): left J. Osborne 36,000 gns before third in Grade 3 handicap at Hollywood final start: probably best at 7f to 9f: acts on good to firm going, good to soft (probably on soft) and fibresand/dirt: blinkered once: sometimes slowly away: usually held up. *M. Puhich, USA*

NOSEY NATIVE 9 b.g. Cyrano de Bergerac 120 – Native Flair 87 (Be My Native – (USA) 122) [2002 44+, a–: 14.1m 14.1d⁵ Oct 30] leggy gelding: little form in 2002: tried visored. *Mrs Lydia Pearce*

NOSY BE 4 b.g. Cyrano de Bergerac 120 – Blossomville (Petong 126) [2002 67d: p7g⁴ **58** f7g³ p5g⁶ 6g 6m Aug 21] modest maiden: effective at 5f to easy 7f: acts on firm ground and all-weather: tried visored: has been slowly away/hung: sold £800. *P. J. Makin*

NOT AMUSED (UAE) 2 ch.c. (Mar 18) Indian Ridge 123 – Amusing Time (IRE) **75 p** 104 (Sadler's Wells (USA) 132) [2002 7s⁵ Oct 15] big, lengthy colt: has plenty of scope: first foal: dam, French 1¼m winner who stayed 12.5f, sister to smart performer up to 1¼m Musalsal, out of Prix Robert Papin winner Ozone Friendly: 9/1 and backward, 2½ lengths fifth of 13 to Mustaneer in maiden at Leicester, slowly away but every chance over 1f out: sure to improve. *B. W. Hills*

NOTANOTHER 2 b.f. (Feb 14) Inchinor 119 – Select Sale (Auction Ring (USA) 123) **68** [2002 6.1m² Jul 27] 24,000Y: half-sister to several winners, notably smart 1½m performer Private Tender (by Shirley Heights): dam unraced half-sister to Ribblesdale Stakes winner Queen Midas: 20/1, neck second of 9 to Takes Two To Tango in maiden at Nottingham, green after slow start but keeping on well: will be suited by 7f+. *J. A. Osborne*

NOTATION (IRE) 8 b.g. Arazi (USA) 135 – Grace Note (FR) 99 (Top Ville 129) **– §** [2002 35§: 12d Jul 31] quite good-topped gelding: temperamental performer: usually blinkered. *D. W. Chapman*

NOTHING DAUNTED 5 ch.g. Selkirk (USA) 129 – Khubza 86 (Green Desert **87** (USA) 127) [2002 103: 8s 7m 7d 6g 7g² 7g 8m 6d 7.2s² 6g 7s Oct 26] quite attractive gelding: fluent mover: only fairly useful nowadays: left D. Nicholls after eighth start: best around 7f: acts on soft and good to firm going: visored once: none too consistent: joined P. Monteith in December. *I. Semple*

NO TIME (IRE) 2 b.c. (Mar 31) Danetime (IRE) 121 – Muckross Park 41 (Nomina- **102** tion 125) [2002 6g⁴ 6g⁴ 5m⁵ 5.1f² 5d² 5g 6d⁵ 5m⁴ 6g* 6.1f⁶ 5m 6m² 6f⁶ 6s⁴ 6v Nov 13] 5,800Y, 10,000 2-y-o: close-coupled, good-topped colt: fourth foal: half-brother to winners abroad by Petardia and Mac's Imp: dam, sprint maiden, sister to useful performer up to 1m Nominator: useful performer: won maiden at Warwick in June and nursery at York in August: best effort when ½-length second to B A Highflyer under 9-10 in nursery at Hamilton twelfth start: effective at 5f/6f: acts on firm and good to soft ground: wanders under pressure: none too consistent. *M. J. Polglase*

NOTIONAL (IRE) 6 b.m. Lucky Guest 109 – Sportin' Notion (USA) (Sportin' Life **–** (USA)) [2002 –: f12g Jun 22] disappointing maiden handicapper: tried blinkered. *A. Sadik*

NOT PROVEN 3 br.g. Mark of Esteem (IRE) 137 – Free City (USA) (Danzig (USA)) **–** [2002 70: 10.1s Jun 5] useful-looking gelding: modest maiden at 2 yrs: well held only outing in 2002. *J. G. FitzGerald*

NOT SO DUSTY 2 b.c. (Apr 30) Primo Dominie 121 – Ann's Pearl (IRE) 81 (Cyrano **67 p** de Bergerac 120) [2002 f5g³ Dec 2] third foal: brother to 3-y-o Sadie Sadie and half-brother to 4-y-o Sal's Gal: dam 5f winner (including at 2 yrs): 5/1, 8 lengths third to Beauvrai in maiden at Wolverhampton, good early speed: should improve. *P. J. Makin*

NOTTY BITZ (IRE) 2 b. or br.g. (Mar 23) Darnay 117 – Riskie Things 62 (Risk Me **81** (FR) 127) [2002 5s⁵ 5g* 5s² 5m⁴ 6.1v⁴ 6d* 6m⁴ 6s Oct 25] 500Y: lengthy gelding: first foal: dam 5f/6f winner, including at 2 yrs: fairly useful performer: won maiden at Musselburgh in March and nursery at Pontefract in July: off 3½ months, well held in sales race at Doncaster final start: should stay 7f: acts on heavy and good to firm going: flashes tail under pressure. *J. S. Moore*

NOUL (USA) 3 ch.c. Miswaki (USA) 124 – Water Course (USA) (Irish River (FR) **74** 131) [2002 6s³ 8s⁴ 9d 8g⁵ 7s 7d f7g* Dec 14] \$55,000F, IR 110,000Y: ex-Irish colt: closely related to a winner in USA by Woodman and half-brother to 3 winners, including 5-y-o Paradise Garden and useful 1½m winner Star of The Course (by Theatrical): dam unraced: fair performer: left K. Prendergast 10,000 gns after fourth start: won maiden at Wolverhampton in December: stays 1m: acts on fibresand, raced only on good going or softer on turf: has started slowly. *K. A. Ryan*

NOUVEAU CHEVAL 7 b.m. Picea 99 – Freeracer (Free State 125) [2002 16m – 11.9d⁵ 12g Jun 16] leggy mare: fair performer in 1999: below form all 3 runs since. *S. Woodman*

NOVATINO 4 b.g. Bustino 136 – Alghabrah 70 (Lomond (USA) 128) [2002 p12g 12s – p12g 10m 11.9m Oct 3] big, workmanlike gelding: seventh foal: half-brother to winner in Italy by Dominion: dam maiden who stayed 1m: little form. *D. R. C. Elsworth*

NOVERRE (USA) 4 b.c. Rahy (USA) 115 – Danseur Fabuleux (USA) 106 **123** (Northern Dancer) [2002 125: 8.9g² 8m² 8g² 10.4g³ 8f⁶ 10m³ 8m Dec 15]

A healthy appetite for racing is an admirable quality in a racehorse, but in the Lockinge Stakes at Newbury in May it looked for one moment as though Noverre had more of an appetite for the hindquarters of the passing Keltos! Sent off at odds on, Noverre ran a thoroughly satisfactory race in every other respect in the Lockinge, taking over from his pacemaker Summoner over two furlongs out and, despite having no chance with Keltos inside the final furlong, beating the remainder comfortably enough. The ease with which he was brushed aside probably startled Noverre as much as it did the betting public and it was possibly that which caused him to think about savaging the winner. Noverre's errant behaviour wasn't apparent on his six other starts in the latest season and, though he failed to add another victory to his record, he showed himself almost as good as ever.

Successful four times as a two-year-old, including in the July Stakes and the Champagne Stakes, Noverre developed into a high-class three-year-old but ended that season with only a single win to his name, a notable one admittedly in the Sussex Stakes at Goodwood. He also passed the post first in the Poule d'Essai des Poulains at Longchamp but was disqualified after testing positive for a banned substance which had been administered to treat the arthritic problems to which he is reportedly prone. Noverre also finished a creditable second in races at the highest level either side of the Lockinge. On the first occasion, he did his best work in the final furlong when beaten three quarters of a length by Terre A Terre in the Dubai Duty Free over almost nine furlongs at Nad Al Sheba in March. That effort marked Noverre out as a likely type for good races at a mile and a quarter but, before taking that route, he attempted a repeat in the Sussex Stakes at Goodwood in July, leading briefly inside the final furlong before Rock of Gibraltar sauntered past to record his sixth successive Group 1 win. Noverre was stepped up in trip at York in the International Stakes, in which a reproduction of his season's best form was good enough to secure third place, two lengths behind the winner Nayef, Noverre travelling well under restraint but able only to keep on when let down. Unfortunately, Noverre's easiest assignment of the campaign coincided with his first below-par effort when only sixth to Good Journey in the Atto Mile on firm ground at Woodbine in September, though the run of the race did count against the waiting tactics employed on him. Noverre's retirement plans had already been announced before his final two outings, which resulted in a creditable one and a quarter lengths third to Storming Home in the Champion Stakes at Newmarket in October and a below-form eighth in the Hong Kong Mile at Sha Tin in December. Noverre will be at the Kildangan Stud in Ireland in 2003, standing at a fee of €15,000 on a special live foal basis.

The pedigree of Noverre has been covered in depth in previous editions of *Racehorses*. There is nothing to add, though it is worth restating that he is closely related to the outstanding 1991 two-year-old Arazi (by Rahy's sire Blushing Groom). It is to be hoped that Arazi's failure to make more of an impact at stud will not have an adverse effect on the support Noverre receives as a stallion. A rather

Godolphin's "Noverre"

Noverre (USA) (b.c. 1998)	Rahy (USA) (ch 1985)	Blushing Groom (ch 1974)	Red God / Runaway Bride
		Glorious Song (b 1976)	Halo / Ballade
	Danseur Fabuleux (USA) (b 1982)	Northern Dancer (b 1961)	Nearctic / Natalma
		Fabuleux Jane (ch 1974)	Le Fabuleux / Native Partner

angular, good-quartered colt with a fluent, quick action, Noverre was mostly consistent in a twenty-one race career, in which he passed the post out of the first three on only four occasions. Tough and game, he was a smart two-year-old and trained on to prove himself effective at a mile to a mile and a quarter. He acted on dirt, good to firm going and probably on soft. He wore a crossed noseband and was tongue tied when putting up his very best efforts. *Saeed bin Suroor*

NOWELL HOUSE 6 ch.g. Polar Falcon (USA) 126 – Langtry Lady 91 (Pas de Seul 133) [2002 95: 10d 11.9m 13s 12d 13.1s³ 12s³ Oct 26] smallish, lengthy gelding: fairly useful handicapper nowadays: stays 13f: seems best on good ground or softer: visored (well below form) final 5-y-o outing: has pulled hard/carried head awkwardly/wandered. *M. W. Easterby* **82**

NOW LOOK HERE 6 b.g. Reprimand 122 – Where's Carol 67 (Anfield 117) [2002 111: 6g 7s 6v Nov 9] tall, leggy gelding: unimpressive mover: smart performer at 5 yrs: well held in 2002: blinkered once. *B. A. McMahon* **–**

NOW THEN SOPHIE 2 ch.f. (Feb 21) Keen 116 – Rachels Eden (Ring Bidder 88) **49**
[2002 5f⁵ 5v⁴ 5.6m⁴ 5g⁶ Jul 6] 1,200Y: sixth foal: half-sister to 4-y-o Billie H and a
winner in Germany by Risk Me: dam ran once: poor maiden: should stay 1m: acts on firm
ground: carries head awkwardly: difficult ride. *A. Berry*

NUGGET (IRE) 4 b.g. Goldmark (USA) 113 – Folly Vision (IRE) 58 (Vision (USA)) **–**
[2002 46: p12g p13g f16.2g Feb 4] strong, sturdy gelding: maiden: little form in 2002:
blinkered final start. *P. Mitchell*

NUIT SOMBRE (IRE) 2 b.g. (May 4) Night Shift (USA) – Belair Princess (USA) **84**
(Mr Prospector (USA)) [2002 5v⁴ 6d* 7g* 6g⁵ 8m 6m⁵ 8s⁶ Oct 25] 20,000F, 7,200Y,
44,000 2-y-o: good-topped gelding: half-brother to several winners, including French
10.5f and 1½m winner Bel Amix (by Linamix): dam, 6f winner in USA, out of multiple
US Grade 1 winner Bold'n Determined: fairly useful performer: won maiden at Ayr
in July and nursery at Newcastle (very easily) in August: lacklustre effort in nursery
at Doncaster final outing: stays 7f: acts on good to firm and good to soft ground.
M. Johnston

NULL AND VOID 3 b.g. Zamindar (USA) 116 – Nullarbor (Green Desert (USA) **75**
127) [2002 6s³ 6f 6g³ 7g³ 8.2m⁶ f7g Dec 14] first foal: dam, French 2-y-o 5.5f winner,
sister to dam of 2-y-o Lateen Sails and half-sister to very smart French/US performer up
to 1½m Radevore: fair maiden: off 5 months and left R. Charlton 8,500 gns before
running poorly final start (gelded after): stays 7f: best effort on good ground: possibly
temperamental. *D. W. Chapman*

NUMBER TEN 3 ch.f. Polish Precedent (USA) 131 – Flower Girl 108 (Pharly (FR) **69**
130) [2002 10d⁵ 8.1g³ 8.1m⁵ 8.3d Oct 14] lengthy filly: sixth foal: half-sister to 3
winners, including fairly useful 1m winner Roaring Twenties (by Halling) and smart
performer up to 14.6f Eco Friendly (by Sabrehill): dam 6f winner, including at 2 yrs: fair
maiden: may prove better at 1m than 1¼m: yet to race on extremes of going: sold 10,000
gns. *M. A. Jarvis*

NUMITAS (GER) 2 b.c. (Feb 6) Lomitas 129 – Narola (GER) (Nebos (GER) 129) **88**
[2002 7.2g⁴ 7m* 7m² 8.2m³ Aug 19] approx. 62,000Y in Germany: leggy, workmanlike
colt: half-brother to several winners, including useful German winner up to 11f National
Academy (by Royal Academy): dam German 11f winner: fairly useful performer: won
maiden at Folkestone (beat Big Bad Bob ¾ length) in July: creditable efforts in minor
events at Yarmouth and Nottingham after: will be suited by 1¼m/1½m: raced only on
good/good to firm going. *Sir Mark Prescott*

NURSLING (IRE) 3 b.f. Kahyasi 130 – Medicosma (USA) 80 (The Minstrel (CAN) **57**
135) [2002 10s 12f⁴ 10m Oct 7] 9,000Y: seventh foal: sister to 1m (at 2 yrs) and 1½m
performer Macca Luna, and half-sister to 3 winners, including Irish 2m/2¼m winner
Luna Fleur (by Shardari): dam, 1½m/2m winner, half-sister to Park Hill winner Eva
Luna, herself dam of 2-y-o Brian Boru: signs of ability in maidens (not at all knocked
about final start): bred to be suited by 1½m+: sold 2,200 gns in December. *A. C. Stewart*

NUTMEG (IRE) 5 ch.m. Lake Coniston (IRE) 131 – Overdue Reaction (Be My **–**
Guest (USA) 126) [2002 49, a–: f7g³ f7g* f7g f7g⁴ f7g f7g² f7g² f6g⁴ f7g Jul 11] modest **a62**
performer: won maiden at Southwell in January: best at 7f: acts on fibresand, firm and
good to soft going: tried blinkered. *M. H. Tompkins*

NUTTY (IRE) 2 b.f. (Mar 12) Sri Pekan (USA) 117 – Mitra (IRE) 98 (Archway (IRE) **–**
115) [2002 7.1m Jul 20] IR 5,000Y: first foal: dam, Irish 2-y-o 1m winner, half-sister
to useful Irish 7f winner Mr Houdini: 33/1, soundly beaten in maiden at Warwick.
Mrs P. N. Dutfield

NUZZLE 2 b.f. (Apr 2) Salse (USA) 128 – Lena (USA) (Woodman (USA) 126) [2002 **71**
7.1g² Sep 23] first foal: dam unraced: weak 7/1-shot, ½-length second of 15 to Aegean
Line in maiden at Chepstow, finishing well from rear: will stay at least 1m: sold 18,000
gns in October. *Sir Michael Stoute*

NYSAEAN (IRE) 3 b.c. Sadler's Wells (USA) 132 – Irish Arms (FR) (Irish River **119**
(FR) 131) [2002 83p: 10g* 10.4f³ 10.2s* 12d⁴ 10s* 12s³ Oct 26] good-topped colt: smart
performer: won maiden at Windsor (by a neck from Burning Sun) in April, minor event at
Chepstow (made all to beat Suleiman by neck) in June and listed race at Deauville (beat
Tripat impressively by 5 lengths) in August: also ran creditably when 5 lengths fourth to
High Chaparral in Irish Derby at the Curragh and length third to The Whistling Teal in St
Simon Stakes at Newbury, both times seeming to find stamina stretched having looked

Jeffen Racing's "Nysaean"

big threat: may prove best at 1¼m: best form on soft/good to soft ground (seemed unsuited by firm second start). *R. Hannon*

NZAME (IRE)   4 b.g. Darshaan 133 – Dawnsio (IRE) 102 (Tate Gallery (USA) 117)   – [2002 82: 12s Jun 12] close-coupled gelding: fairly useful handicapper at 3 yrs: well held only 4-y-o start: sometimes visored. *Miss S. J. Wilton*

O

OAKLEY RAMBO   3 br.c. Muhtarram (USA) 125 – Westminster Waltz (Dance In   **96** Time (CAN)) [2002 81: 8m⁶ 8f⁴ 7d² 7.1g⁶ 7m⁶ 8f² 8.1m 8f* 8g 8.2v² p7g p10g p7g Dec   **a87** 14] leggy colt: useful handicapper on turf, fairly useful on all-weather: won at Newbury in September: stays 1m: acts on polytrack and any turf ground. *R. Hannon*

OAKSY   2 b. or br.g. (Apr 27) Turtle Island (IRE) 123 – Safe Secret 50 (Seclude (USA))   – [2002 f6g 6g⁶ 5.9s⁶ 8m 8.3d Oct 14] 4,500Y: third foal: half-brother to 3-y-o The Mog and a 5f/6f winner (including at 2 yrs) in Italy by General Monash: dam, maiden on Flat who seemed to stay 1½m, winning hurdler: well held, including in seller: tried blinkered: sold 500 gns. *G. C. Bravery*

OAKWELL ACE   6 b.m. Clantime 101 – Fardella (ITY) (Molvedo 137) [2002 57:   **50** 6m 6g 6g⁶ 6g 6m⁵ Jul 25] modest performer: races mainly at 6f nowadays: acts on soft and firm going, below form on fibresand: tried visored: has been slowly away/carried head awkwardly. *J. Balding*

OARE KITE 7 b.m. Batshoof 122 – Portvasco 90 (Sharpo 132) [2002 57, a46: f6s f6g^4 f6g^3 Feb 2] close-coupled mare: modest handicapper: was effective at 5f to 1m: acted on firm going, soft and fibresand: usually wore visor/blinkers: sometimes carried head awkwardly/wandered/found little: dead. *P. S. Felgate*   – **a46**

OARE PINTAIL 5 b.m. Distant Relative 128 – Oare Sparrow 75 (Night Shift (USA)) [2002 –: p6g Jan 3] smallish, sturdy mare: one-time modest maiden. *R. M. Beckett*

OASES 3 ch.g. Zilzal (USA) 137 – Markievicz (IRE) 73 (Doyoun 124) [2002 92p: 6m^4 7s^3 8m 8d 8g^6 p8g 7g^6 7d 7.1m^4 7m f6g p7g^2 Dec 30] rather leggy, quite good-topped gelding: useful form in listed races first two 3-y-o starts: disappointing after, leaving B. Meehan after tenth start: effective at 6f/7f: acts on heavy and good to firm ground: tried blinkered/visored: often races freely. *D. Shaw*   **95 d**

OASIS DREAM 2 b.c. (Mar 30) Green Desert (USA) 127 – Hope (IRE) (Dancing Brave (USA) 140) [2002 6m^5 7.1m^2 6.1m* 6f* Oct 3]   **122**
Oasis Dream kept his light hidden under a bushel for most of the year, contesting maiden races at Salisbury and Sandown before winning one at Nottingham, and seemingly deceiving his trainer for a time into thinking seven furlongs might suit him better than six. The victory of Oasis Dream in the Shadwell Stud Middle Park Stakes at Newmarket in October, though, revealed him with crystal clarity as a very smart colt, the best of his age in Europe, and one who should take high rank at three. John Gosden rarely entertains angels unawares, and considering the level of Oasis Dream's bare form was at least 20 lb behind that of the other leading contenders in the ten-runner Middle Park it was significant that, with his stable in top form, there was strong market support for Oasis Dream. He started co-third favourite behind Prix Morny winner Elusive City and Aidan O'Brien's main hope Tomahawk, alongside Country Reel and Zafeen, successful respectively in the Gimcrack and the Mill Reef. Oasis Dream's maiden race performances had consisted of two promising displays in defeat as favourite, including when racing freely and losing out by three and a half lengths to Rimrod over seven furlongs at Sandown, and an easy odds-on victory at Nottingham, where he made all against four rivals. Oasis Dream looked a horse with speed in excess of stamina and he had no trouble lying close up at Newmarket, racing strongly behind the O'Brien pacemaker Irrawaddy before leading over two furlongs out and running on with great relish to see off Tomahawk by a length and a half, with Elusive City a neck away third, followed at a respectful distance by Country Reel and Zafeen. Tomahawk went on to finish a length and a quarter second to Tout Seul in the Dewhurst Stakes, and our interpretation of the form of the Middle Park and the Dewhurst puts Oasis Dream narrowly at the top of the tree. The Middle Park time clipped half a second off the track record for six furlongs set by Lycius in the same race in 1990, and records were also set over a mile by Desert Deer and over five furlongs for two-year-olds by Valiant Romeo. With the ground firmer than the official good to firm, and some assistance from the wind (though not so much as in 1990), conditions were favourable for fast times but Oasis Dream's time was also significant in terms of its time value, his timefigure equivalent to a

Shadwell Stud Middle Park Stakes, Newmarket—Oasis Dream shows much improved form in a strong renewal; Tomahawk and Elusive City (partially obscured by winner) are his closest pursuers

rating of 121, the best recorded by a two-year-old all season. Having the form of the Middle Park confirmed by the time analysis boosts confidence in Oasis Dream's prospects, but at what distance will he prove effective? He races freely, like a sprinter, and is able to quicken, yet immediately after the Middle Park Gosden said: 'He's the fastest two-year-old at Manton and probably the fastest two-year-old in Europe over six furlongs. Next season it's more likely he'll be a French Guineas horse—it's an easier mile at Longchamp.' Jimmy Fortune, who rode Oasis Dream, remarked that 'I think seven furlongs may not be beyond him, but a mile might stretch him.' With opportunities for top sprinters, particularly three-year-olds, so thin on the ground early in the season it may well be worth aiming Oasis Dream at the Poule d'Essai des Poulains, even though that race's standing is some way below that of the Two Thousand Guineas. However, it's the prospect of seeing Oasis Dream in some of the top sprints, the Golden Jubilee Stakes at Royal Ascot and the July Cup for starters, that looks the most mouthwatering for 2003.

Oasis Dream (b.c. Mar 30, 2000)	Green Desert (USA) (b 1983)	Danzig (b 1977)	Northern Dancer Pas de Nom
		Foreign Courier (b 1979)	Sir Ivor Courtly Dee
	Hope (IRE) (b 1991)	Dancing Brave (b 1983)	Lyphard Navajo Princess
		Bahamian (ch 1985)	Mill Reef Sorbus

In the wake of the decline in trade at the select yearling sales in the States, many stallion fees there have been cut for 2003 or at least remained static—Point

Mr K. Abdulla's "Oasis Dream"

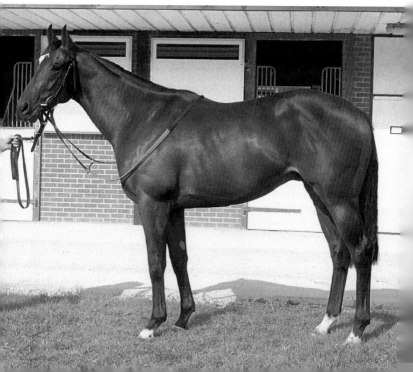

Given is down from 125,000 dollars to 75,000 dollars, Deputy Minister from 150,000 to 100,000, Rahy from 100,000 to 80,000 and Dixieland Band from 75,000 to 60,000. The situation is different in Europe, where the bloodstock market seemingly remains buoyant and fees for sires such as Pivotal (£10,000 up to £25,000), Indian Ridge (€60,000 up to €75,000) and the sire of Oasis Dream, Green Desert (£40,000 up to £60,000), are all on the rise. If breeders are aiming for runners with prospects of being fully effective at a mile to a mile and a quarter, where most of the prize money is to be found for three-year-olds and upwards, it is odd that Green Desert's fee should be soaring by fifty per cent. Although he had form at a mile himself he was undoubtedly best at sprint distances and the average distance of races won by his progeny aged three and up is just under a mile. Only one of his twelve leading winners in terms of race grading, White Heart in the States, has won over further than a mile at the top level and most, including Owington, Sheikh Albadou, Tamarisk and Invincible Spirit, have been at their best over five or six furlongs. Oasis Dream seems to take after his sire, though there is stamina on the distaff side of his pedigree. His once-raced dam Hope is a sister to Irish Oaks winner Wemyss Bight, dam of Arlington Million winner Beat Hollow, and the grandam Bahamian won the Lingfield Oaks Trial. Hope has produced two other winners, both smart—Zenda (by Zamindar), successful in the Poule d'Essai des Pouliches and runner-up in the Coronation Stakes and Queen Elizabeth II Challenge Cup, the latter over nine furlongs, and listed winner Hopeful Light (by Warning), who was best at up to a mile. Oasis Dream, a strong, good-bodied, attractive colt, looks the part and very much took the eye before the Middle Park. He has raced only on ground firmer than good, and was twice blanketed for stall entry. *J. H. M. Gosden*

OBEE GOOD 4 b.g. Zambrano – Tout de Val 41 (Tout Ensemble) [2002 –: 9.9g 11.9g 12d 7g Aug 8] of no account. *W. G. M. Turner* –

OBE ONE 2 b.g. (Apr 14) Puissance 110 – Plum Bold 83 (Be My Guest (USA) 126) [2002 5s⁵ 5m³ 5m* 5f³ 5f² 5m⁶ 5.1f³ 5g² 6m 5m⁴ 5g⁴ Oct 19] 10,000Y: leggy gelding: brother to fairly useful 1m winner Pomona (later smart up to 1¼m in USA) and half-brother to several winners, including useful Italian sprinter Plumbird (by Statoblest): dam 6f winner: fair performer: won maiden at Musselburgh in May: mostly creditable efforts in minor events/nursery after: raced mainly at 5f on going firmer than good. *A. Berry* **79**

OBLIGE 2 b.f. (Jan 24) Robellino (USA) 127 – Acquiesce (Generous (IRE) 139) [2002 6g³ 7m⁵ 7g* 7.1m⁵ 8g⁵ Sep 28] strong filly: has a round action: second foal: half-sister to fairly useful 2001 2-y-o 7f winner I Do (by Selkirk): dam unraced half-sister to smart 2000 2-y-o 6f winner Endless Summer out of sister to Dewhurst dead-heater Scenic: useful performer: won maiden at Brighton in August and nursery at Haydock (made all) in September: best effort when 4 lengths fifth to Soviet Song in Fillies' Mile at Ascot final start, detached on home turn but staying on strongly despite hanging markedly right: should stay 1¼m: raced only on good/good to firm going. *I. A. Balding* **101**

OCARINA 2 ch.g. (May 27) Piccolo 121 – Nanny Doon (Dominion 123) [2002 5f 7g Jul 24] 10,500 2-y-o: fifth foal: half-brother to winner around 9f Lord Harley (by Formidable) and a winner abroad by Alflora: dam well beaten both starts: last in maidens. *P. G. Murphy* –

OCCAM (IRE) 8 ch.g. Sharp Victor (USA) 114 – Monterana 99 (Sallust 134) [2002 48, a41: f12g⁴ f12g² f12g⁴ p16g 12s 12.3g 11.9f⁵ 14.1g³ 15d⁵ 10.2f³ 12d⁵ Jul 31] leggy gelding: poor performer: probably stays 15f: acts on soft going, good to firm and fibresand: tried visored: sometimes starts slowly/races freely/looks none too keen. *A. Bailey* **48 a45**

OCEAN AVENUE (IRE) 3 b.g. Dolphin Street (FR) 125 – Trinity Hall 67 (Hallgate 127) [2002 –: p10g⁵ 11m⁴ 12m* 12m* 11f Sep 25] fair handicapper: made all at Folkestone and Salisbury in August: stays 1½m: acts on good to firm going: has raced freely: gelded after final outing. *C. A. Horgan* **76**

OCEAN LOVE (IRE) 4 b.f. Dolphin Street (FR) 125 – Scuba Diver (Kings Lake (USA) 133) [2002 45: p10g 7d 10d Jun 13] workmanlike filly: poor maiden at 3 yrs: little form in 2002: tried blinkered. *C. Weedon* –

OCEAN SILK (USA) 2 b. or br.f. (Mar 5) Dynaformer (USA) – Mambo Jambo (USA) (Kingmambo (USA) 125) [2002 7d² Nov 2] $190,000Y: quite good-topped filly: first foal: dam, French 1½m winner from 2 starts, sister to useful French performer around 1¼m Indigo Myth: 10/1, shaped well when 2 lengths second of 19 to Goodness Gracious **83 p**

in maiden at Newmarket, keeping on after very slow start: should be suited by 1¼m/1½m: sure to improve and win races. *J. H. M. Gosden*

OCEAN SONG   5 b.m. Savahra Sound 111 – Marina Plata (Julio Mariner 127) [2002   **36**
53d: f16s⁶ f16.2g f9.4g* f12g⁴ f8g f9.4g* f9.4g⁵ f9.4g⁶ f8g 10m 9.9m 8f 8f 9.9g 9.9g⁴   **a56**
10m Aug 19] rangy mare: modest on all-weather, poor on turf: won maiden and handicap
at Wolverhampton early in year: has form at 1¾m, but best recent efforts around 9f/1¼m:
acts on good to soft going and fibresand: usually blinkered. *S. R. Bowring*

OCEAN SONG (USA)   2 ch.c. (Feb 8) Woodman (USA) 126 – Ocean Ridge (USA)   **78**
115 (Storm Bird (CAN) 134) [2002 6m⁵ Jul 30] smallish, strong colt: first foal: dam, 5.5f
(Prix Robert Papin)/6f winner at 2 yrs who later stayed 1m, out of smart 6f performer
Polar Bird: 3½ lengths fifth of 9 to Foss Way in maiden at Goodwood, unable to quicken. *D. R. Loder*

OCEAN SPIRIT (USA)   3 b.g. Rahy (USA) 115 – Clear Attraction (USA) (Lear Fan   **75**
(USA) 130) [2002 8m⁶ 9m 10.1m p12g 12m⁴ 11.7g Oct 16] very big, lengthy gelding:
second foal: brother to fairly useful 1¼m winner Purple Heather: dam once-raced half-
sister to excellent broodmare Height of Fashion out of 1000 Guineas/Prix de Diane
winner Highclere: fair maiden: stays 1½m: acts on good to firm going: visored last 3
starts: has worn crossed noseband/been coltish/swished tail: jinked right and unseated
entering straight at Yarmouth third outing: didn't impress with finishing effort last 2: sold
16,000 gns, sent to UAE. *Sir Michael Stoute*

OCEAN STAR   3 ch.c. Lycius (USA) 124 – Limerick Belle (IRE) 98 (Roi Danzig   **72**
(USA)) [2002 10g³ 10g 10m⁵ 12.3f a8f a7f⁵ 8.9g a10f* a8f⁶ Dec 27] well-made colt:
second foal: dam, fairly useful 5f/6f winner, later 5f winner in UAE: fair performer: left
M. Channon after fourth start and off nearly 6 months: won maiden at Jebel Ali in
December: stays 1¼m: acts on dirt: tried blinkered, wore cheekpieces for win. *M. Al
Kurdi, UAE*

OCEAN TIDE   5 b.g. Deploy 131 – Dancing Tide (Pharly (FR) 130) [2002 82: 14d⁴   **87**
16m² 16.2s* 14.4s³ 15.9f⁶ 16m⁴ 16s 16.5v Nov 9] angular gelding: fairly useful handicapper: better than ever in 2002, winning at Haydock in June and Musselburgh (after
2½-month absence) in September: stays 2m: acts on any going: visored: usually races
prominently. *R. Ford*

OCKER (IRE)   8 br.g. Astronef 116 – Violet Somers (Will Somers 114§) [2002 f6g   **–**
Apr 15] leggy gelding: fairly useful at 6 yrs: behind only start since: tried blinkered/
visored. *Mrs N. Macauley*

OCTANE (USA)   6 b.g. Cryptoclearance (USA) – Something True (USA) 119 (Sir   **87**
Ivor 135) [2002 71: p12g* p10g⁴ f12g⁵ 16g 11.9m⁶ 13g³ 10.5s² 12g³ 12g 11.9g 12.3g²
14v⁴ 13.3m 14m³ 15.9f* 13.1s 16s⁵ p12g⁵ Nov 14] good-bodied gelding: fluent mover:
fairly useful handicapper: won at Lingfield in February and Chester in September: stays
2m: acts on all-weather and firm going, seemingly on soft: tried blinkered/tongue tied:
has refused to enter stall/twice failed stall tests: usually held up. *W. M. Brisbourne*

OCTENNIAL   3 gr.c. Octagonal (NZ) 126 – Laune (AUS) 68 (Kenmare (FR) 125)   **68**
[2002 76: 6g⁶ 6m⁵ 7s 6d⁴ 7g Jul 18] leggy, unfurnished colt: fair handicapper: not sure to
stay beyond 6f: acts on fibresand and good to firm going: visored (reportedly lost action)
final start: tends to carry head high, and possibly none too genuine: sold 3,500 gns in
August. *R. Hannon*

OCTOBER MIST (IRE)   8 gr.g. Roselier (FR) – Bonny Joe (Derring Rose 97) [2002   **76**
12d³ Nov 5] useful hurdler, winning chaser: fair form when third in maiden at Catterick:
should stay 1¾m. *Mrs M. Reveley*

OCTOBER MOON   2 b.f. (Mar 7) Octagonal (NZ) 126 – Moon Carnival 94 (Be My   **– p**
Guest (USA) 126) [2002 6s Oct 28] 33,000Y: good-bodied filly: half-sister to 5-y-o
Carousing and fairly useful 1998 2-y-o 7f winner Distant Moon (by Distant Relative):
dam, won around 1½m, half-sister to Sheriff's Star and Moon Madness: 14/1, 10 lengths
seventh of 16 to Zietory in maiden at Leicester, left behind final 2f: likely to stay at least
1m: should improve. *W. Jarvis*

OEUF A LA NEIGE   2 b.c. (Mar 17) Danehill (USA) 126 – Reine de Neige 96 (Kris   **71**
135) [2002 7m 6m³ p7g Oct 16] fourth foal: half-brother to 1999 2-y-o 5f winner Stylish
Beauty (by Night Shift): dam, 1m winner, half-sister to dam of Fantastic Light: fair form
in maidens: third at Windsor: will probably stay 1m. *E. A. L. Dunlop*

OFF HIRE   6 b.g. Clantime 101 – Lady Pennington 51 (Blue Cashmere 129) [2002 65,   **69**
a69: f5g² f5g f5g f5g 5m* 5m⁴ 5g 5m f5g³ f5g² Dec 13] leggy, angular gelding: fair handi-

capper: won at Beverley in July: probably best at 5f: acts on any turf going/fibresand: visored: races prominently. *C. Smith*

OFFICER'S PINK 2 ch.f. (Mar 17) Grand Lodge (USA) 125 – Arethusa 101 (Primo Dominie 121) [2002 7m 5g² 5g Sep 2] 54,000Y: lengthy filly: second foal: half-sister to 3-y-o Indian Country: dam 2-y-o 5f/6f winner: easily best effort in maidens (fair form) when second to Gallivant at Beverley: saddle slipped final start: will be suited by 6f+. *P. F. I. Cole* **72**

OFFTOWORKWEGO 2 b.g. (Apr 18) Fraam 114 – Hi Hoh (IRE) (Fayruz 116) [2002 6g 5m⁶ 5d⁵ 5m* Aug 22] 23,000Y: sturdy gelding: second foal: brother to 3-y-o Zinging: dam of little account: fair performer: won seller at Musselburgh (claimed to join P. Monteith) by 1¼ lengths from Blue Jannessa, leading 2f out: will prove best at 5f/6f: unraced on extremes of going. *Mrs J. R. Ramsden* **65**

OFFWITHTHEFAIRIES 2 b.f. (Apr 16) Farfelu 103 – My Ruby Ring 72 (Blushing Scribe (USA) 107) [2002 5.3g 5.1m⁵ 6m Sep 4] 2,200Y: half-sister to 2 winners, including 6-y-o My Man Friday: dam 6f winner: poor form in maiden/sellers: may prove best around 5f: very slowly away first 2 starts. *W. R. Muir* **46**

OH BOY (IRE) 2 b.c. (Mar 27) Tagula (IRE) 116 – Pretty Sally (IRE) 51 (Polish Patriot (USA) 128) [2002 6m Sep 20] IR 19,000F, 24,000Y: good-topped colt: third foal: half-brother to Italian 5f/6f winner, including at 2 yrs, Pretty Gio (by Ali-Royal): dam, placed in 6f sellers, half-sister to smart performer in Britain/US up to 9.5f Unanimous Vote: 33/1, in rear in maiden at Newbury: has scope to do better. *R. Hannon* **– p**

OH NO NOT HIM 6 b.g. Reprimand 122 – Lucky Mill 50 (Midyan (USA) 124) [2002 50§: 8f 8m³ 7.9g⁶ 8.5m 8.3s⁶ 9d Aug 23] poor performer: stays 8.5f: acts on soft and good to firm going: tried blinkered: often slowly away: has refused to race/looked reluctant: unreliable. *W. M. Brisbourne* **44 §**

OH SO DUSTY 4 b.f. Piccolo 121 – Dark Eyed Lady (IRE) 82 (Exhibitioner 111) [2002 71: 6.1d 7m p7g⁵ 8g 8f³ 8f⁴ 9.7m f9.4s p10g² Dec 18] smallish, sturdy filly: modest nowadays: stays 1¼m: acts on polytrack and firm ground: blinkered twice at 2 yrs. *N. P. Littmoden* **57**

OH SO ROSIE (IRE) 2 b.f. (Apr 4) Danehill Dancer (IRE) 117 – Shinkoh Rose (FR) 67 (Warning 136) [2002 5s p5g⁵ 5g 5m⁵ f5s 5d 6m² 5.2f⁴ 6.1d³ 7m⁵ 6g* 6g* 7m⁵ 7f* 7m Sep 29] IR 4,600F, IR 650Y: small, angular filly: third foal: dam third at 9f in Ireland: fairly useful performer: hung left when winning nurseries at Leicester (seller) and Windsor in August: clearly best effort when winning sales race at Fairyhouse (came from rear to beat Jemmy John 1½ lengths) in September: effective at 6f/7f: acts on soft and firm going: tried visored: has twice spoilt chance with slow start: tough. *J. S. Moore* **81**

OILEANACH (IRE) 5 ch.m. Erins Isle 121 – Noorajo (IRE) (Ahonoora 122) [2002 –: 11.9g May 2] third foal: sister to Irish 1½m to 2m winner Traditional: dam placed at 1m in Ireland: little form (left J. Bolger in Ireland after final 4-y-o start): blinkered once. *T. P. McGovern* **–**

OK PAL 2 b.c. (Apr 4) Primo Dominie 121 – Sheila's Secret (IRE) 97 (Bluebird (USA) 125) [2002 5m⁶ 5d* 6f Sep 8] fourth foal: half-brother to 3 winners, including 4-y-o Olivia Grace and 5-y-o Our Fred: dam 5f winner (including at 2 yrs) who stayed 6f: fairly useful form when winning maiden at Sandown in August by 3 lengths from Queen's Victory, making most: virtually pulled up in listed event at Kempton only subsequent outing (found to have suffered muscle strain behind): will prove best at 5f/6f: remains open to improvement. *T. G. Mills* **94 p**

OKTAN (IRE) 10 b.h. Dance of Life (USA) – Sharp Dresser (USA) (Sharpen Up 127) [2002 6.8s³ 6.8d³ 5.8m² 5.8g³ 7f Sep 26] smart performer, has won 10 races: returned from stud duties and at least as good as ever over shorter trips in 2002: placed in Scandinavia first 4 starts, including very good length third to Pistachio in Taby Open Sprint Championship penultimate outing: well below form in Supreme Stakes at Goodwood final start: raced mainly at 1m/1¼m but evidently at least as effective at around 6f: acts on soft and good to firm ground. *Ms C. Erichsen, Norway* **111**

OLD BAILEY (USA) 2 gr.c. (Mar 18) Lit de Justice (USA) 125 – Olden Lek (USA) (Cozzene (USA)) [2002 5g* 5f 5m 5d⁵ 7m 6f f6s⁵ f7g* f7g³ Dec 17] $8,000Y, resold 3,200Y: good-topped colt: third foal: half-brother to a winner in USA by Wild Again: dam, French 1¼m winner, later won in USA: modest performer: won maiden at New-castle in May and nursery at Wolverhampton in December: stays 7f: acts on fibresand, firm and good to soft ground. *T. D. Barron* **63**

OLD CALIFORNIA (IRE) 3 b.c. Sadler's Wells (USA) 132 – Turban 80 (Glint of **102**
Gold 128) [2002 89p: 11.8g* 11.9s* 16.2m 14.8g⁴ 15g² Sep 19] tall, quite good-topped,
attractive colt: easy mover: useful performer: won maiden at Leicester in April and
handicap at Haydock (beat Fashionable Man by 5 lengths) in June: off 2 months, ran well
when length second to Allinjim in handicap at Ayr final start, though wandered/carried
head awkwardly: should stay at least 2m: acts on soft going: sold 85,000 gns, joined
M. Pipe and won over hurdles in December. *J. L. Dunlop*

OLDEN TIMES 4 b.c. Darshaan 133 – Garah 107 (Ajdal (USA) 130) [2002 121: 8m³ **120**
May 18] big, good-topped colt: takes eye in appearance: good walker: very smart
performer: won Prix Jean Prat at Chantilly in 2001: creditable 5 lengths third to Keltos in
Lockinge Stakes at Newbury only 4-y-o start: reportedly suffered hairline fracture of
pelvis while being prepared for Sussex Stakes: best around 1m/9f: yet to race on extremes
of going: tended to hang left second start at 3 yrs: stays in training. *J. L. Dunlop*

OLDENWAY 3 b.g. Most Welcome 131 – Sickle Moon (Shirley Heights 130) [2002 **80**
62: 8m² 8g² 10f² 10m³ 12.3f* 9d* 12.3g⁴ 12g Jul 31] lengthy gelding: fairly useful
performer: won handicap at Chester and minor event at Musselburgh (made all) within 3
days in June/July: effective at 9f to 1½m: acts on firm and good to soft going (well held
only start on heavy): tends to race freely: consistent. *R. A. Fahey*

OLD HARRY 2 b.g. (Mar 22) Case Law 113 – Supreme Thought 68 (Emarati (USA) **67 ?**
74) [2002 6m⁴ 6s Oct 25] 1,700F, 2,500Y: first foal: dam 6f winner: seemingly fair form
in maidens over 2 months apart: bred to prove best up to 1m. *L. G. Cottrell*

OLD LATIN 2 b.c. (Jan 14) Zafonic (USA) 130 – Classic Form (IRE) 58 (Alzao **101 p**
(USA) 117) [2002 7g* 8m² Oct 13] 220,000F: second foal: dam, lightly-raced maiden,
sister to Oaks winner Shahtoush and half-sister to Oaks second Game Plan: useful form:
very easy winner of newcomers race at Maisons-Laffitte in September: good ½-length
second of 5 to Campsie Fells in minor event at Longchamp following month: will stay at
least 1¼m: joined Godolphin: likely to improve further. *A. Fabre, France*

OLD TOM (IRE) 2 ch.g. (Apr 30) Bering 136 – Lovely Lyca 76 (Night Shift (USA)) **56 §**
[2002 6.1s 7g⁵ 7g⁶ 7m f8s f7g² f8.5s⁵ f8.5g Nov 18] 5,000Y, 22,000 2-y-o: third foal:
half-brother to 4-y-o Polish Off: dam, 1m and 1½m winner, out of half-sister to Old Vic:
modest maiden: runner-up in seller at Wolverhampton: should stay 1m: acts on fibresand:
visored last 3 starts: sometimes edges left. *R. M. H. Cowell*

OLIMOLIMOO (IRE) 3 gr.g. Ali-Royal (IRE) 127 – Classy 59 (Kalaglow 132) **85**
[2002 81: 10s⁶ 10d³ 10g⁴ 11.6d³ p12g Dec 14] good-topped gelding: fairly useful maiden:
stays 11.6f: acts on good to soft going. *M. J. Haynes*

OLIRANAR 6 gr.g. Gran Alba (USA) 107 – April Rain (Lepanto (GER)) [2002 –: **–**
f12g f12g⁶ Feb 15] no form. *J. R. Best*

OLIVIA GRACE 4 ch.f. Pivotal 124 – Sheila's Secret (IRE) 97 (Bluebird (USA) **117**
125) [2002 103p: f6g⁵ p5g² 6.1d⁵ 5g⁶ 5g 5m² 5m* Oct 12] sturdy, good-quartered filly:
smart performer: best effort when winning handicap at Ascot in October under big weight
by 2 lengths from Trace Clip: ran at least respectably most other starts, second to Bishops
Court in listed race at Doncaster on penultimate: has won at 6f, best form at 5f: acts on
good to soft going, good to firm and all-weather: usually races prominently. *T. G. Mills*

*ladbrokes.com Handicap, Ascot—Olivia Grace puts up a smart performance under top weight;
Trace Clip, the grey Pic Up Sticks and Peruvian Chief (visor) are the next three home*

OLIVIA ROSE (IRE) 3 b.f. Mujadil (USA) 119 – Santana Lady (IRE) 72 (Blakeney **71**
126) [2002 74: f6s p7g f8.5g³ f6g 7s⁶ 7.5m² 7m 9.2g 8d³ 8m* 7f³ 8.3s³ 9m⁴ 8d 8.5d Aug
14] lengthy filly: fair performer: won claimer at Leicester (subsequently left M. Johnston)
in June: probably best around 1m: acts on fibresand and any turf going. *Mrs Lydia Pearce*

OLNEY LAD 3 b.g. Democratic (USA) 101 – Alipampa (IRE) (Glenstal (USA) 118) **71**
[2002 8.3d⁴ 9.9m⁴ 10g 10m Oct 1] angular gelding: sixth foal: brother to a winner in
Greece and half-brother to 1m to 10.5f winner Petuntse (by Phountzi): dam unraced: fair
maiden: will stay 1½m. *R. Guest*

OLYMPIC PRIDE (IRE) 4 b.f. Up And At 'em 109 – So Far Away 48 (Robellino **–**
(USA) 127) [2002 –: p12g f8g f8g 7g 8d May 27] no form. *C. N. Allen*

OMAHA CITY (IRE) 8 b.g. Night Shift (USA) – Be Discreet (Junius (USA) 124) **105**
[2002 8g* 7m⁵ 7.1d 8m 7d 8m⁶ 7.9m⁶ 7.6f⁶ 8.9m⁵ 8f⁴ 8g Oct 18] strong gelding: useful
handicapper: missed 2001 season: at least as good as ever at 8 yrs, winning at Goodwood
(50/1, beat Laggan Minstrel by head) in May: trained sixth to tenth starts by D. Nicholls,
creditable sixth in William Hill Mile at Goodwood (behind Smirk) and Bradford &
Bingley Stakes at York (behind Funfair) first 2 occasions: returned to former trainer:
effective at 7f/1m: has won on good to soft ground, best form on good or firmer: sometimes edgy/on toes: usually handy/on toes. *B. Gubby*

OMAIMAH 3 b.f. Mark of Esteem (IRE) 137 – Gracious Beauty (USA) 67 (Nijinsky **68**
(CAN) 138) [2002 8.3m³ 8m⁴ 8.1g p7g³ Dec 28] sixth foal: half-sister to useful 1¼m/
1½m winner Jazil (by Nashwan) and 11.5f winner who stayed 15f Labeed (by Riverman):
dam, maiden who stayed 1¼m, sister to Grade 1 1¼m winner Maplejinsky (dam of
champion US older mare Sky Beauty) and closely related to outstanding sprinter Dayjur:
fair maiden: third at Windsor and, having left E. Dunlop, Lingfield: should stay beyond
1m: acts on polytrack and good to firm going. *M. R. Channon*

OMBUDSMAN 2 b.g. (Mar 7) Eagle Eyed (USA) 111 – Council Rock 74 (General **66**
Assembly (USA)) [2002 5.7f³ 5m³ 6m² 5m³ 7g⁶ Oct 4] leggy gelding: brother to fairly
useful 2001 2-y-o 5f winner Horoscope and half-brother to several winners, notably
smart 2000 2-y-o 5f winner Superstar Leo (by College Chapel): dam, maiden best at
1¼m, out of Nassau Stakes winner Dancing Rocks: fair maiden: second at Lingfield:
stays 7f: raced only on good going or firmer: visored third/fourth starts: sold 9,000 gns.
W. J. Haggas

OMEY STRAND (IRE) 3 b.g. Desert Style (IRE) 121 – Ex-Imager (Exhibitioner **54**
111) [2002 71, a56: f8g⁶ 7.1m f7g 6d³ 7f⁵ 7.1v⁶ 6m 8.1d² 8.1d 8g² 8m 7g 7d Aug 11]
strong gelding: modest maiden: stays 1m: acts on fibresand, good to firm and good to
soft going: usually blinkered/tongue tied: has run in snatches: reportedly had breathing
problem third start. *J. M. Bradley*

OMNISCIENT (IRE) 3 br.f. Distinctly North (USA) 115 – Mystic Shadow (IRE) 80 **57**
(Mtoto 134) [2002 77: 7s 11.6m 8.1m 7m³ 7m 8.2m 8m 10g Oct 14] quite good-topped
filly: modest performer: probably stays 1m: acts on good to firm going: blinkered sixth
start: best form racing up with pace: sometimes puts head in air/wanders: sold 900 gns.
Mrs P. N. Dutfield

ONCE (FR) 2 gr.c. (Mar 8) Hector Protector (USA) 124 – Moon Magic 62 (Polish **78**
Precedent (USA) 131) [2002 7m⁶ 7.1m² f8.5g³ Sep 30] 30,000Y: leggy, quite good-
topped colt: fifth foal: half-brother to a winner abroad by Be My Chief: dam once-raced
half-sister to Moon Madness and Sheriff's Star: best effort (fair form) when 2½ lengths
second to Sri Diamond in maiden at Warwick: should be suited by 1¼m/1½m.
M. L. W. Bell

ONCE SEEN 2 b.g. (Jan 15) Celtic Swing 138 – Brief Glimpse (IRE) 108 (Taufan **73**
(USA) 119) [2002 6m 7.1g⁵ 8g Oct 18] 11,000Y: close-coupled gelding: first foal: dam 5f
(at 2 yrs) to 7f winner: fair maiden: probably stays 1m. *R. M. Beckett*

ON EDGE 3 b.c. Zafonic (USA) 130 – Gull Nook 120 (Mill Reef (USA) 141) [2002 **93 +**
8m⁶ 10.5m* Jul 14] 220,000Y: tall, rather leggy colt: half-brother to several winners,
notably top-class 1¼m/1½m winner Pentire (by Be My Guest) and smart performer up to
1¾m Spring (by Sadler's Wells): dam, 10.5f/1½m (Ribblesdale) winner, from family of
Shirley Heights: made promising debut, then useful form when winning maiden at
Haydock (over 2 months later) by 8 lengths from Shaiyzima, dictating pace: will stay
1½m: joined P. Brette in UAE. *Saeed bin Suroor*

ONE DINAR (FR) 7 b.g. Generous (IRE) 139 – Lypharitissima (FR) (Lightning (FR) **46**
129) [2002 70, a74: f9.4g⁶ p8g 7d 7v 8.5m 10m⁵ 8m p10g f12g⁴ f8.5g* Nov 18] big **a56**
gelding: has a markedly round action: modest nowadays: left D. Nicholls after seventh

start (trained by Mrs D. Haine next outing only): won seller at Wolverhampton in November: best at 1m/9f: acts on any turf going and fibresand: visored (too free) once in 1999: has won when sweating: sold 5,700 gns. *G. C. H. Chung*

ONE DOMINO 5 ch.g. Efisio 120 – Dom One 92 (Dominion 123) [2002 16g 14m* 16.2g 14g³ 14.1f Jun 3] quite good-topped gelding: modest handicapper, lightly raced: missed 2001 season: won at Musselburgh in April: stays 1¾m: acts on firm and soft going: visored/blinkered nowadays. *M. Dods* **60**

ONE FOR ME 4 br.f. Tragic Role (USA) – Chantallee's Pride (Mansooj 118) [2002 62: p8g 8.5g 9.9m 8.1m 10s f8.5g* p13g Dec 28] modest handicapper: won maiden event at Wolverhampton in July: should stay 1¼m: acts on fibresand and good to firm going: tongue tied final start: sometimes slowly away. *Jean-Rene Auvray* **48 a57**

ONEFORTHEBOYS (IRE) 3 b.g. Distinctly North (USA) 115 – Joyful Prospect (Hello Gorgeous (USA) 128) [2002 –: 7s 6.2d f12g Dec 14] ex-Irish gelding: fourth foal: half-brother to Irish 9f winner Joyful Music (by Accordion): dam maiden: little form: left T. Stack and off over 4 months before final start: tried tongue tied: gelded after final outing. *R. Ford* **–**

ONEFOURSEVEN 9 b.g. Jumbo Hirt (USA) 90§ – Dominance (Dominion 123) [2002 14.1s³ 16.2g 14.1s² 17.1m f14s 18d⁶ Oct 21] angular gelding: shows knee action: modest handicapper: stays 2¼m: acts on soft going, good to firm and fibresand: tried blinkered. *P. C. Haslam* **54 a–**

ONE LAST DANCE 2 b.g. (Feb 27) Groom Dancer (USA) 128 – Sparkling (Kris 135) [2002 7g 7m 7d⁴ 7g Oct 17] 35,000F: lengthy, useful-looking gelding: first foal: dam unraced close relative to smart performer up to 1¼m Port Lucaya out of half-sister to Oaks winner Diminuendo: poor maiden: should stay 1m: sold 6,500 gns, sent to Spain. *W. R. Muir* **44**

ONE LAST TIME 2 b.g. (Apr 29) Primo Dominie 121 – Leap of Faith (IRE) 65 (Northiam (USA)) [2002 5m⁵ 6d³ 5m² 6m⁴ 6g⁴ 6g⁵ 6d Nov 1] 8,000F, 20,000Y: good-topped gelding: has scope: has a quick action: good walker: fifth foal: half-brother to 3-y-o Jonny Ebeneezer: dam 2-y-o 5f/6f winner who stayed 1¼m: fairly useful performer: won maiden at Salisbury in May: best efforts when 1½ lengths second to Revenue in minor event at Royal Ascot and fifth of 30 to Michelle Ma Belle in sales race at Newmarket: stays 6f: yet to race on extremes of going: slowly away first 2 starts (seemed ill at ease on course when third at Epsom): gelded after final outing. *R. Hannon* **93**

ONE MIND 4 b.c. Mind Games 121 – Cafe Solo 51 (Nomination 125) [2002 49: 6d May 27] good-topped colt: poor maiden: tongue tied, reportedly had breathing problem only 4-y-o start: better form at 6f than 7f. *R. Hannon* **49**

ONE MORE HYMN (IRE) 2 b.g. (Mar 23) General Monash (USA) 107 – Maz (IRE) 48 (Cyrano de Bergerac 120) [2002 5m³ 5.3f⁴ 6g⁶ 7m p6g⁴ Dec 21] IR 15,000F, IR 14,000Y: third foal: dam 7f winner: modest maiden: left R. Hannon before good fourth in seller at Lingfield final outing: should stay 7f: acts on firm going and polytrack: sometimes races freely/finds little. *S. L. Keightley* **59**

ONE MORE ROUND (USA) 4 b.c. Ghazi (USA) – Life of The Party (USA) (Pleasant Colony (USA)) [2002 110: 8m 8.5s 7m* 7m 8.5d² Oct 26] first foal: dam US maiden daughter of Fred Darling winner Top Socialite: smart performer: unraced at 2 yrs: won maiden at Galway and handicap at the Curragh in 2001, and valuable handicap at Leopardstown (by 2 lengths from Triple Gold) in September: ran creditably otherwise at 4 yrs when seventh to Norton in Royal Hunt Cup (Handicap) at Royal Ascot on reappearance and ½-length second to Capsized in non-graded handicap at Arlington in October: found little/wandered (something possibly amiss) in Tote Trifecta Stakes (Handicap) at Ascot penultimate start: stays 8.5f: acts on good to firm and good to soft going: blinkered last 3 starts. *D. K. Weld, Ireland* **112**

ONE OFF 2 b.g. (Apr 17) Barathea (IRE) 127 – On Call 103 (Alleged (USA) 138) [2002 7.1m 7.1f 6g 7v f9.4g⁵ Nov 16] well-made gelding: first foal: dam 1½m to 2m winner: modest form at best in maidens: should be suited by 1¼m+: gelded after final start. *Sir Mark Prescott* **58**

ONE WAY TICKET 2 ch.c. (Mar 7) Pursuit of Love 124 – Prima Cominna 86 (Unfuwain (USA) 131) [2002 6m⁵ 6s³ 7v Nov 8] lengthy, workmanlike colt: third foal: dam, 2-y-o 6f winner, out of sister to very smart sprinter Primo Dominie: best effort in maidens (fair form) when 7 lengths third to Gilded Edge at Newbury: not knocked about final start: should stay at least 7f: has scope to do better as 3-y-o. *R. Charlton* **74 p**

ONE WON ONE (USA) 8 b.g. Naevus (USA) – Havards Bay (Halpern Bay (USA)) **111**
[2002 113: a8f 7s⁶ 8m⁴ 6s³ 5s 8d* 7s² 8d 7d² 7d 8g² 6s* 8g⁵ 6g² 6m² 8m 7.5m 6d²
7m 7v⁶ Nov 10] good-topped, attractive gelding: smart performer: won listed race at
Leopardstown (for second year running, beat Mr Houdini by ½ length) in June and
Phoenix Sprint Stakes at the Curragh (got up on post to short-head Bahamian Pirate) in
August: some good efforts otherwise, including in Ballycorus Stakes at Leopardstown
(second to Rum Charger on seventh start), Minstrel Stakes (second to Gateman on ninth),
listed race (second to Osterhase on fourteenth) and Boland Stakes (second to Polar Way
on fifteenth), all at the Curragh: well beaten in Challenge Stakes at Newmarket on
penultimate outing: effective at 6f to 1m: acts on any turf going, well beaten both starts
on dirt: blinkered twice: held up: genuine and very tough. *Ms J. Morgan, Ireland*

ON GUARD 4 b.g. Sabrehill (USA) 120 – With Care 78 (Warning 136) [2002 75: f8s³ **67**
f9.4g⁵ f11s f9.4g f11g⁴ f11g⁴ 8.5g f9.4g⁶ 10m⁶ 10m³ 10g⁶ 10.9m² 10g⁶ 11.9m⁶ p10g **a73**
f9.4g⁵ f8.5g² f9.4s² f8.5g³ f9.4g⁶ f9.4g Dec 16] neat gelding: fair handicapper: left Mrs
N. Macauley after eighth start: best at 1m to 11f: acts on good to firm going, good to soft
and fibresand: usually visored for previous stable: tends to hang/carry head awkwardly:
held up: not one to trust implicitly. *P. G. Murphy*

ONLINE INVESTOR 3 b.c. Puissance 110 – Anytime Baby 56 (Bairn (USA) 126) **101 d**
[2002 95: 5m² 6g⁶ 6m⁵ 7m 6d⁴ 6m⁵ 5g 5.6m 5f⁴ 5m Oct 12] leggy, quite good-topped
colt: useful performer: good length second to Mariinsky in listed event at Haydock in
April: ran respectably at best after: probably stays 6f: acts on firm going, probably good
to soft: blinkered (pulled too hard) sixth outing: bolted before start once as 2-y-o: often
slowly away. *C. G. Cox*

ONLY FOR GOLD 7 b.g. Presidium 124 – Calvanne Miss 48 (Martinmas 128) [2002 **66**
89, a57: f7g f7g 7.6f 7g 8.1s 7.6f 6v² 6.9m 7m 8.1f f8.5g⁴ Dec 20] rangy gelding: fair on **a55**
turf, modest on all-weather: effective at 6f, barely at 1m: acts on heavy going, good to
firm and fibresand: visored once at 4 yrs: usually races handily. *A. Berry*

ONLY FOR SUE 3 ch.g. Pivotal 124 – Barbary Court (Grundy 137) [2002 62p: 8m **50**
f7g⁴ f7f⁵ Nov 11] rather leggy, angular gelding: modest maiden: should stay 1m: acts on
fibresand. *W. S. Kittow*

ONLY JUST IN TIME 2 ch.f. (Jan 1) Bahamian Bounty 116 – Badger Bay (IRE) 67 **–**
(Salt Dome (USA)) [2002 p6g Dec 21] 4,000Y: third foal: dam unreliable maiden who
stayed 1m: 25/1, well beaten in seller at Lingfield. *D. K. Ivory*

ONLY ONE LEGEND (IRE) 4 b.g. Eagle Eyed (USA) 111 – Afifah 66 (Nashwan **68 §**
(USA) 135) [2002 81: 5m 6f 7m 6f* 6m 6m⁶ 5m⁴ 5g 5m 5m 6m³ 6f⁴ 6.1m² f6g⁶ f6g² f6g² **a76 §**
Dec 14] lengthy gelding: fair handicapper: won at Catterick in June: best at 5f/6f: acts on
fibresand, firm and good to soft ground: usually blinkered, and has worn cheekpieces: has
found little: inconsistent. *T. D. Easterby*

ONLY PEARL 3 ch.f. Presidium 124 – Samana Cay 52 (Pharly (FR) 130) [2002 8g **–**
10f 12.4g Aug 7] small filly: second foal: dam 2-y-o 7f seller winner: well held in sellers/
claimer. *J. R. Norton*

ONLY PENANG (IRE) 3 b.f. Perugino (USA) 84 – Unalaska (IRE) 65 (High Estate **87**
127) [2002 77: 9f 9.9g 10g 8.1d⁵ 8.3m³ 8m³ 8.2s* p8g Nov 23] leggy filly: fairly useful
handicapper: won at Nottingham (first start for 2½ months) in October: stays 1m: acts on
firm and soft ground, probably on polytrack: blinkered (raced freely) third start.
B. R. Millman

ONLYTIME WILL TELL 4 ch.g. Efisio 120 – Prejudice 83 (Young Generation **105**
129) [2002 86, a73: 6g² 7d 6m 8d 6f² 6d* 6m 6g² Jun 29] lengthy, useful-looking gelding: **a–**
useful handicapper: better than ever in 2002, winning at Epsom in June by 1¾ lengths
from Further Outlook: fared clearly best of those who raced on far side when tenth in
Wokingham at Royal Ascot next start, then very good short-head second to Ragamuffin
at Newcastle final one: best at 6f/7f: acts on fibresand and any turf going: sometimes
slowly away/wanders. *D. Nicholls*

ONLY WORDS (USA) 5 ch.g. Shuailaan (USA) 122 – Conversation Piece (USA) **40**
(Seeking The Gold (USA)) [2002 41: 13.8m 12m 9.9m 9.9m Aug 25] sturdy gelding:
poor maiden handicapper: stays 1¼m: acts on good to firm going: tried tongue tied: won
over hurdles in October. *A. J. Lockwood*

ON MY HONOUR 4 b.f. Pyramus (USA) 78 – Princess Matilda 110 (Habitat 134) **–**
[2002 –: p7g 9g⁶ p8g 7f 11.7f 10m Sep 3] little form: tried blinkered. *J. C. Fox*

ON POINT 2 b.f. (Jan 29) Kris 135 – Odette 72 (Pursuit of Love 124) [2002 f5g f6g⁵ **60 p**
p6g⁶ Dec 28] first foal: dam, 5f/5.7f winner, half-sister to useful 6f/7f performer Cabal-

lero out of Queen Mary Stakes winner On Tiptoes: modest form in maidens, shaping as though in need of race first 2 starts: races freely, and may prove best at 5f/6f: capable of better. *Sir Mark Prescott*

ON PORPOISE 6 b.g. Dolphin Street (FR) 125 – Floppie (FR) (Law Society (USA) 130) [2002 –: f8.5g Dec 13] lengthy gelding: modest performer at 4 yrs: lightly raced since, and well held only 6-y-o start. *P. W. D'Arcy* —

ONTARIO (USA) 2 ch.c. (Feb 4) Storm Cat (USA) – Flying Fairy 79 (Bustino 136) [2002 5s³ 5s* 5m⁴ 6.3s* 6s⁵ 6f 7m⁶ Oct 19] strong, close-coupled colt: eighth foal: closely related to useful 1999 Irish 2-y-o 6f winner Admiral's Cup (by Bluebird) and half-brother to 2 winners, notably top-class miler Desert Prince (by Green Desert): dam, maiden who stayed 1½m, out of 1000 Guineas winner Fairy Footsteps: useful performer: won maiden at the Curragh (by head from Pakhoes) in May and 4-runner Anglesey Stakes there (by 1½ lengths from Spartacus) in July: reportedly found to be coughing after next start: creditable efforts when 7 lengths seventh to Oasis Dream in Middle Park Stakes and 5¼ lengths sixth to Tout Seul in Dewhurst Stakes at Newmarket: will stay 1m: acts on soft and firm ground: wears crossed noseband. *A. P. O'Brien, Ireland* — 107

ON THE BRINK 2 b.f. (Jan 22) Mind Games 121 – Ocean Grove (IRE) 84 (Fairy King (USA)) [2002 5m² 5g* 5g* 5m Jun 19] 10,000Y: well-grown, useful-looking filly: good mover: second foal: sister to 2000 2-y-o 5f winner Night Gypsy: dam 2-y-o 6f winner who stayed 1m: fairly useful performer: won minor event at Thirsk in May and listed contest at Beverley (led close home, beat Ivania by ¾ length) in June: creditable twelfth of 19 in Queen Mary Stakes at Royal Ascot: should stay 6f: raced on good/good to firm going: wears crossed noseband. *T. D. Easterby* — 83

ON THE FAIRWAY (IRE) 3 b.f. Danehill Dancer (IRE) 117 – Asta Madera (IRE) 67 (Toca Madera 111) [2002 54p: 5.1d* 5.1m 6d 6g⁴ 5d 6g⁴ 5.6s⁴ 6.9s⁵ 6g p7g⁶ f6g 6m Oct 7] tall filly: modest handicapper: won at Nottingham in April: left T. Easterby 2,500 gns after eighth start: best at 5f/6f: acts on soft going: none too consistent. *J. J. Bridger* — 62 d

ON THE LEVEL 3 ch.f. Beveled (USA) – Join The Clan 95 (Clantime 101) [2002 6m⁵ 5g 6f 6d Oct 18] third foal: dam 5f/6f winner: little form in maidens. *Mrs N. Macauley* —

ON THE LINE 4 ch.f. Alhijaz 122 – Join The Clan 95 (Clantime 101) [2002 –: 5.1d f6g Jun 28] poor maiden: tried visored. *Mrs N. Macauley* — 34

ON THE TRAIL 5 ch.g. Catrail (USA) 123 – From The Rooftops (IRE) (Thatching 131) [2002 58, a65: f7s⁴ f7g² f6g* p6g* f6g* f6g p6g f6g f6g f6g f7g f6g⁵ f6s⁶ f6s³ f6g f5g⁶ f7g⁴ f6g* f7g² f6g* Dec 20] strong gelding: fair performer: won handicaps at Wolverhampton (twice) and Lingfield in January and sellers at Southwell and Wolverhampton in December: has won at 7f, best at 6f: acts on good to soft ground, good to firm and all-weather: sometimes tongue tied: often takes strong hold/makes running. *D. W. Chapman* — a68

ON TOPHEEMEE 2 b.f. (Apr 16) Mistertopogigo (IRE) 118 – Heemee 81 (On Your Mark 125) [2002 5m 5m 6f Sep 21] 500Y: half-sister to 1995 2-y-o 5f winner Dancing Rainbow (by Rambo Dancer) and 4-y-o Picture Mee: dam 2-y-o 5f winner: showed little in maidens: pulled up on debut: tried blinkered. *C. J. Teague* —

ON YOUR MARKS (IRE) 5 ch.g. Forest Wind (USA) 111 – Felicitas (Mr Fluorocarbon 126) [2002 68: p10g⁶ p13g Mar 2] half-brother to several winners, including 7f to 9f winner Markskeepingfaith and 1¼m winner Keeping The Faith (both by Ajraas), both fairly useful in Ireland: dam, third at 13f and 2m on Flat, winning hurdler in Ireland: fair handicapper at 4 yrs: only modest form at Lingfield in 2002: stays 1¼m: acts on good to firm ground: tried blinkered/tongue tied. *T. Carmody, Ireland* — 57

ONYX KNIGHT 3 b.g. Awesome 73 – Lady of The Realm (Prince Daniel (USA)) [2002 –: p8g f8.5g f8g 9.9m Apr 25] little form. *J. Neville* —

OOPSIE DAISY 3 b.f. Singspiel (IRE) 133 – Oops Pettie 93 (Machiavellian (USA) 123) [2002 8m⁴ 8f⁴ 8m³ p8g⁵ Nov 13] 47,000Y: angular filly: first foal: dam, 1¼m winner who stayed 1½m, half-sister to useful 1m/1¼m filly Moselle: fairly useful maiden: will be suited by 1¼m+: acts on good to firm going and polytrack: could well make a useful handicapper at 4yrs. *J. R. Fanshawe* — 81 p

OOPS (IRE) 3 b.g. In The Wings 128 – Atsuko (IRE) (Mtoto 134) [2002 10m 10f 12s⁵ 12.3m³ 16.2g⁵ 11.9g⁶ Aug 5] IR 190,000Y: fourth foal: half-brother to 3 winners, including 11f and 1½m winner Triphenia (by Ashkalani): dam, second at 1m at 2 yrs in Ireland, closely related to very smart French middle-distance performer Muroto: fair maiden: should stay 1¾m. *J. G. Given* — 79

OPAL'S HELMSMAN (USA)   3 b.g. Helmsman (USA) 121 – Opal's Notebook **43**
(USA) (Notebook (USA)) [2002 –: 8.5m 13.8f 10f 8f Oct 7] poor maiden: tried visored.
A. Dickman

OPEN ARMS   6 ch.g. Most Welcome 131 – Amber Fizz (USA) (Effervescing (USA)) **73**
[2002 62: p10g² p12g* p10g* p16g² 12g⁴ 11.5m⁶ 11.8g p16g⁴ p12g³ p12g² p12g³ p16g⁴
p12g⁴ Dec 18] strong gelding: fair handicapper: won twice at Lingfield in February:
effective at 1¼m to easy 2m: acts on polytrack, good to firm and good to soft going:
blinkered (well held) once: consistent. *Mrs A. L. M. King*

OPEN GROUND (IRE)   5 ch.g. Common Grounds 118 – Poplina (USA) (Roberto **59**
(USA) 131) [2002 58: 11.8m 16.2m 19.1m⁴ 16.2m* 13.8d Nov 5] lengthy gelding:
modest handicapper: won at Warwick in July: stays 19f: acts on heavy and good to firm
going. *Ian Williams*

OPENING CEREMONY (USA)   3 br.f. Quest For Fame 127 – Gleam of Light (IRE) **87**
81 (Danehill (USA) 126) [2002 87p: 8d⁴ 7.1m⁵ 10m Aug 17] fairly useful performer:
disappointing in 2002 (pulled too hard all starts): should stay 1¼m: sold 11,000 gns in
October. *Mrs A. J. Perrett*

OPEN OUTCRY   3 ch.g. Bluegrass Prince (IRE) 110 – Bowden Rose 100 (Dashing **47**
Blade 117) [2002 10g 10f 10s 11.6m f12g Jul 20] 21,000Y: well-made gelding: first foal:
dam 5f and (including at 2 yrs) 6f winner: poor maiden. *M. Blanshard*

OPEN WARFARE (IRE)   4 b. or br.f. General Monash (USA) 107 – Pipe Opener 58 **45 §**
(Prince Sabo 123) [2002 60§, a–§: 5m 5g 5g³ 5v⁵ 5m² 8m⁴ 5.9s⁵ Jul 31] small, strong filly: **a– §**
has a round action: poor performer: stays 6f: acts on heavy and good to firm going: has
been early to post: refused to race on 3-y-o reappearance: untrustworthy. *G. A. Swinbank*

OPERA GLASS   2 b.f. (Apr 25) Barathea (IRE) 127 – Optaria 83 (Song 132) [2002 6m³ **84**
7m² 7m³ Sep 20] tall, lengthy filly: has scope: half-sister to several winners, including
10-y-o Grey Shot and smart sprinter Night Shot (by Night Shift): dam 2-y-o 5f winner:
fairly useful maiden: best effort when third to L'Ancresse in minor event at Newbury
(blinkered in paddock before being mounted, but not in race) final start: should stay 1m:
edged left last 2 starts. *I. A. Balding*

OPERA KNIGHT   2 ch.c. (Mar 12) In The Wings 128 – Sans Escale (USA) (Diesis **74**
133) [2002 7m⁶ 8.3s⁶ 8m⁶ Sep 24] 45,000Y: good-bodied colt: sixth foal: half-brother to
3 winners, including useful 1m winner West Escape (by Gone West) and fairly useful
2001 2-y-o 7f winner Sequin (by Green Desert): dam, French 11f winner, out of Prix de
Diane winner Escaline: fair maiden: bred to be suited by 1¼m+: pulled hard/looked none
too keen second start. *M. L. W. Bell*

OPERASHAAN (IRE)   2 b.c. (Feb 19) Darshaan 133 – Comic Opera (IRE) (Royal **–**
Academy (USA) 130) [2002 8m Sep 23] 32,000F, 26,000Y: second foal: dam, ran once at
2 yrs, half-sister to dam of Derby second City Honours: 25/1, always behind in maiden at
Kempton. *T. T. Clement*

OPTIMAITE   5 b.g. Komaite (USA) – Leprechaun Lady 57 (Royal Blend 117) [2002 **97 §**
98§: 14.1m³ 14d 10.1d³ 10.3m* 10m⁴ 12d 11m* 10.1d⁶ 12m⁶ 11.9f⁴ Oct 10] tall, workmanlike gelding: easy mover: useful handicapper: won at Doncaster (beat Takamaka Bay
by head) in June and Newbury (beat Mojalid by short head) in August: effective at 1¼m,
barely at 1¾m: acts on firm and good to soft going: visored (reluctant to race) once:
tongue tied: often bloody away: has hung right/found little: ungenuine. *B. R. Millman*

ORAKE PRINCE   3 b.g. Bluegrass Prince (IRE) 110 – Kiri Te (Liboi (USA) 76) [2002 **59**
51: 10m p12g f8.5g 8.1d⁵ 8g 8g² f7g 10d⁶ Oct 28] modest maiden: should stay 1¼m: **a–**
blinkered after second start. *J. G. Portman*

ORANGE TOUCH (GER)   2 b.c. (Feb 3) Lando (GER) 128 – Orange Bowl (General **84 p**
Assembly (USA)) [2002 7m⁵ 8.1m* Sep 18] approx. 40,000Y in Germany: well-made
colt: closely related to 2 winners in Germany by Acatenango, including 1½m winner
Oriental Night, and half-brother to several winners, including 1½m winner Eurotwist (by
Viking): dam unraced half-sister to smart French 1¼m performer Nero Zilzal: better
effort in maidens (fairly useful form) when winning at Sandown by ½ length from Chief
Yeoman, making all: will stay at least 1¼m: raced freely on debut: should continue to
progress. *Mrs A. J. Perrett*

ORANGETREE COUNTY (IRE)   4 b.f. Dolphin Street (FR) 125 – Empress Kim **37**
(Formidable (USA) 125) [2002 39: f5g 7g May 6] poor maiden. *C. A. Dwyer*

ORANGE TREE LAD   4 b.g. Tragic Role (USA) – Adorable Cherub (USA) 58 **58**
(Halo (USA)) [2002 64: f6s⁶ p7g³ f8g p7g f9.4g⁶ f8.5g⁶ Mar 15] close-coupled gelding:

modest maiden: left A. Crook after fifth start: stays 9.4f: acts on all-weather, soft and good to firm ground: sold 3,500 gns in March. *P. R. Hedger*

ORANGINO   4 b.g. Primo Dominie 121 – Sweet Jaffa 73§ (Never So Bold 135) [2002   **51** 46+: 6d 6f³ 8f 6s⁶ 5.9d⁵ 7m² Jul 27] unfurnished gelding: unimpressive mover: modest maiden: stays 7f: acts on soft and good to firm going: blinkered last 3 starts in 2001. *J. S. Haldane*

ORAPA   3 b.c. Spectrum (IRE) 126 – African Dance (USA) (El Gran Senor (USA) 136)   **–** [2002 8m 10s May 27] big, long-backed colt: closely related to fairly useful 1¼m winner Congo Man (by Rainbow Quest) and half-brother to fairly useful 1996 2-y-o 6f winner Telemania (by Mujtahid) and 5-y-o Chaka Zulu: dam, Irish maiden, daughter of Irish Oaks runner-up Fleur Royale: tailed-off last (something presumably amiss) in maidens at Newmarket and Windsor (tongue tied). *Sir Michael Stoute*

ORDINARY HERO (IRE)   2 b.c. (Apr 12) Anabaa (USA) 130 – Mare Aux Fees   **68** (Kenmare (FR) 125) [2002 6d 6d 6g⁵ Aug 12] 32,000Y: rather leggy, quite attractive colt: brother to French 1m winner Albula and half-brother to 3 winners abroad, notably 6-y-o The Mask: dam French 10.5f winner: fair maiden: free-going sort, and not sure to stay 7f: sold 11,000 gns, sent to Norway. *D. W. Hills*

ORIENTAL EMPRESS   3 b.f. Emperor Fountain 112 – Beijing (USA) 89 (Northjet   **83** 136) [2002 –: 10f⁶ 14.1f³ 14g² 13.1d* 16d* 16.2d* f16.2g⁴ 14.1s* 16g* 17.5g³ 14.1d 16s⁶ Oct 25] small, angular filly: fairly useful handicapper: won at Ayr (maiden event), Musselburgh, Chepstow, Redcar and Ripon in summer, first 2-named handicaps races: stays 17.5f: acts on soft ground (some promise on firm): has found little. *C. W. Thornton*

ORIENTAL MIST (IRE)   4 gr.g. Balla Cove 119 – Donna Katrina (Kings Lake   **54** (USA) 133) [2002 73d: 10.3s 14m 9.2s³ 11.1g⁴ 8g 13v 13s⁴ 9.2s 12.1d 10.9g⁴ Jul 22] leggy gelding: modest performer: seems barely to stay easy 15f: acts on heavy and good to firm going: visored final start. *Miss L. A. Perratt*

ORIENTAL MOON (IRE)   3 ch.f. Spectrum (IRE) 126 – La Grande Cascade (USA)   **62 §** (Beaudelaire (USA) 125) [2002 70: 6.1d 8.3s 8m⁶ 8.2d 8m⁵ 10.1m² 10g⁴ 9.7m⁵ 11.9m   **a59 §** f12s p10g Dec 18] leggy filly: modest maiden handicapper: stays 1¼m: acts on good to firm going, seemingly on polytrack: unreliable. *G. C. H. Chung*

ORIENTOR   4 b.c. Inchinor 119 – Orient 106 (Bay Express 132) [2002 118: 6s³ 6m⁶   **116** 6f⁴ 5m 6m⁴ 5g⁶ 6g² Oct 18] close-coupled colt: smart performer: creditable efforts in 2002 when fourth to Invincible Spirit in both Duke of York Stakes (beaten a length) in May and Sprint Cup at Haydock (beaten 2¼ lengths) in September, sixth to Continent in Prix de l'Abbaye at Longchamp and length second to Needwood Blade in listed event at Newmarket: best form at 6f: acts on any going: held up: tough and reliable. *J. S. Goldie*

ORINOCOVSKY (IRE)   3 ch.c. Grand Lodge (USA) 125 – Brillantina (FR) (Crystal   **77** Glitters (USA) 127) [2002 78p: 10g 8.5g p10g 8.1f* 10.2d² 10m 8.2m⁵ Jul 27] fair handicapper: won at Warwick in June: stays 1¼m: acts on firm and good to soft going: blinkered (ran respectably) third start: free-going sort: sold 25,000 gns in October. *P. F. I. Cole*

ORIOLE   9 b.g. Mazilier (USA) 107 – Odilese 82 (Mummy's Pet 125) [2002 49: 8.5m   **38** 7f 8m 8d⁶ 7m 10.1m⁴ 7m 10m Sep 19] leggy gelding: poor performer: stays 1¼m: acts on any turf going and fibresand: tried blinkered/visored. *Don Enrico Incisa*

ORION'S BELT   2 ch.g. (Apr 21) Compton Place 125 – Follow The Stars 86 (Sparkler   **65** 130) [2002 6m⁶ 5m 6g 5g⁵ 6g 6g Oct 28] 20,000Y, 15,000Y: half-brother to numerous winners, including useful 5f (at 2 yrs) to 1¼m winner Brigante di Cielo (by Robellino) and fairly useful 5f (at 2 yrs)/6f winner Montserrat (by Aragon): dam 8.5f and 1¼m winner: fair maiden: below form in nurseries last 2 starts (gelded after): effective at 5f/6f: raced only on good/good to firm going. *G. B. Balding*

ORLANDO SUNRISE (IRE)   5 ch.m. Dolphin Street (FR) 125 – Miss Belgravia   **–** (USA) (Smarten (USA)) [2002 58: 12.6m Jul 20] workmanlike mare: modest maiden handicapper at 4 yrs: well held only 5-y-o start: tried blinkered. *Ian Williams*

ORMELIE (IRE)   7 gr.g. Jade Hunter (USA) – Trolley Song (USA) (Caro 133) [2002   **–** –: 10.1m⁵ 12m⁵ Aug 16] leggy, lightly-made gelding: unimpressive mover: useful handicapper at 5 yrs: very lightly raced and well held since (lame final start): blinkered once. *C. A. Dwyer*

ORNELLAIA (IRE)   2 b.f. (Apr 27) Mujadil (USA) 119 – Almost A Lady (IRE) 70   **56** (Entitled 126) [2002 6s f6g f6f⁴ Nov 11] 26,000Y: fifth foal: half-sister to useful 2001 2-y-o 6f and 1m winner Henri Lebasque (by Sri Pekan) and 4-y-o Thanks Max: dam, second at 1m at 2 yrs in Ireland, half-sister to very smart 1¼m performer Insatiable: modest maiden: fourth at Wolverhampton: should stay 7f. *J. A. Osborne*

OR ROYAL (FR) 11 ro.g. Kendor (FR) 122 – Pomme Royale (FR) (Shergar 140) [2002 73, a67: f16.2g* f16.2g⁴ f16g² f16.2g* f16.2g⁵ 16.2m f16.2g² f16.2f⁴ f14.8g f16.2f Nov 11] workmanlike gelding: fair handicapper on all-weather: won at Wolverhampton in February and April: stays 2m: acts on fibresand: blinkered/visored early in 2001: has carried head awkwardly: refused to race final start: one to treat with caution. *R. Lee* — § a70 §

ORRY (USA) 3 b.f. Marlin (USA) 124 – Popi Vlahos (USA) (Exactly Sharp (USA) 121) [2002 7m³ 8.3g 9g⁴ 5.9g 8g 7m Aug 28] $45,000Y: good-bodied filly: second foal: half-sister to a winner in USA by Devil His Due: dam 8.5f winner in USA: disappointing maiden: should stay at least 1m: sent to Italy. *M. R. Channon* 58 d

ORTHODOX 3 gr.c. Baryshnikov (AUS) – Sancta 106 (So Blessed 130) [2002 73: 10m 11m⁴ May 18] tall, rather leggy colt: fairly useful maiden: will stay 1½m: raced only on good/good to firm going. *G. L. Moore* 81

OSCAR PEPPER (USA) 5 b.g. Brunswick (USA) 119 – Princess Baja (USA) (Conquistador Cielo (USA)) [2002 73, a103: f6g f7s⁵ p8g f7g⁶ 8m³ 8f³ 8f* 8d⁵ 9f* 10f⁵ 8.5d² 9.9d 8s 9m 10.1d⁴ 8m⁵ 8m⁴ 10d⁴ f8.5g² f8g⁶ Dec 4] close-coupled, useful-looking gelding: useful handicapper on all-weather, fair on turf: won at Redcar in May and June: good second at Wolverhampton penultimate start: stays 1¼m: acts on fibresand, firm and good to soft ground: tried blinkered/visored: has been slowly away: usually held up. *T. D. Barron* 78 a96

OSCIETRA 6 b.m. Robellino (USA) 127 – Top Treat (USA) 101 (Topsider (USA)) [2002 37: 12m 9.2s 11.9s⁵ 11.9s⁶ 9.2s⁴ 12.1d² 11.1g⁴ 12.1d⁵ 11.1d 12.1s 12.1m Sep 2] good-topped mare: poor handicapper: stays 1½m: probably best on good going or softer: tried visored/blinkered: none too reliable. *W. M. Brisbourne* 37

O'SO NEET 4 b.g. Teenoso (USA) 135 – Unveiled 76 (Sayf El Arab (USA) 127) [2002 p10g 14.1m 10m 7d Jun 11] neat gelding: disappointing maiden: tried blinkered. *J. C. Fox* —

OSTARA (IRE) 5 b.g. Petorius 117 – Onde de Choc (USA) (L'Enjoleur (CAN)) [2002 61d: f7g p6g f7g* f7g⁵ f8.5g f6g 7g⁴ 8f 7m* 7d* p7g² 7.5g⁴ 7m⁴ 8m 7d* 7m 7f f7f 7m Sep 6] tall gelding: fair handicapper: won at Wolverhampton, Brighton (twice), then left R. Spicer), Beverley, Doncaster and Kempton between February and July: was effective at 7f/1m: acted on soft going, good to firm and all-weather: blinkered once as 2-y-o: was ridden by claimer Claire Stretton for last 5 successes: dead. *C. R. Dore* 72

OSTERHASE (IRE) 3 b.g. Flying Spur 72 – Ostrusa (AUT) (Rustan (HUN)) [2002 92: 7m⁶ 5s 6g² 5d² 6g* 7m⁶ 5g* 6d Oct 13] third foal: half-brother to fairly useful Irish 6f winner Ostarrichi (by Approach The Bench): dam won in Austria: smart performer: improved in 2002, winning listed race in August (by ½ length from One Won One) and handicap (by short head from Reilly Mac) in September, both at the Curragh: well below form in listed race there final start: best at 5f/6f: acts on good to firm and good to soft ground: races prominently: blinkered last 6 starts. *J. E. Mulhern, Ireland* 111

OTHER ROUTES 3 ch.g. Efisio 120 – Rainbow Fleet 66 (Nomination 125) [2002 47: 7m³ 7g 7s 7g⁶ 6.1d p7g² 7g 7g³ 8m² 8f* 8g* 8d³ Nov 1] fair handicapper: won twice at Bath in autumn, apprentice maiden event first occasion: stays 1m: acts on firm going, good to soft and polytrack: sometimes blinkered: has wandered. *G. L. Moore* 66

OTOTOTM 2 b.c. (Apr 21) Mtoto 134 – Najmat Alshemaal (IRE) 98 (Dancing Brave (USA) 140) [2002 7.1g 8g 8v Nov 8] fourth foal: half-brother to 1¼m/1½m winner Emteyaz (by Mark of Esteem): dam 1¼m winner who stayed 14.6f: only a little sign of ability in maidens: likely to do better at 1¼m+. *A. C. Stewart* — p

OTYLIA 2 ch.f. (May 10) Wolfhound (USA) 126 – Soba 127 (Most Secret 119) [2002 6d 6f⁶ Sep 26] 25,000Y: smallish, strong, lengthy filly: closely related to fairly useful 1998 2-y-o 7f/1m winner Spitzbergen (by Polar Falcon), later successful at 6f to 10.5f in Spain, and half-sister to several winners, including 1993 2-y-o 6f winner French Gift (by Cadeaux Genereux) and 7.6f winner Water Well (by Sadler's Wells), both useful, and to dam of very smart performer up to 1¼m Dark Moondancer: dam sprinter: poor form in maidens. *A. Berry* 49

OULTON BROAD 6 b.g. Midyan (USA) 124 – Lady Quachita (USA) (Sovereign Dancer (USA)) [2002 –: p12g⁴ f16g p13g 11.1v* 11.1d⁶ Jul 25] poor handicapper: won amateur race at Hamilton (first run since leaving M. Ewer-Hoad) in July: stays 1½m: acts on heavy going and all-weather: visored once at 3 yrs: fair hurdler, successful in October. *R. Ford* 48

OUNDLE SCOUNDREL (FR)   3 b.g. Spinning World (USA) 130 – Tidal Treasure   **80 d**
(USA) (Crafty Prospector (USA)) [2002 66?: 8f* 8.1d 8s 7.6f⁴ 8g p7g Dec 30] quite
good-topped gelding: fairly useful form when making all in maiden at Thirsk in May:
disappointing after, leaving M. Johnson before final start: stays 1m: acts on firm going:
blinkered fourth start: races freely. *P. W. Hiatt*

OUR CHELSEA BLUE (USA)   4 ch.f. Distant View (USA) 126 – Eastern Connec-   **73**
tion (USA) (Danzig Connection (USA)) [2002 79: f5g² 5m² 5.3d⁶ 5g⁵ 5.1m⁶ f5g f5f   **a59**
p7g² p7g Dec 30] fair maiden on turf, modest on all-weather: left T. Mills 7,000 gns after
fifth start: stays easy 7f: acts on good to firm going and all-weather: tried tongue tied:
sometimes pulls hard. *C. A. Dwyer*

OUR DESTINY   4 b.g. Mujadil (USA) 119 – Superspring (Superlative 118) [2002 65:   **47**
f12s f11g⁴ f12g 10f 8g 10m p12g f14.8g⁵ f12g Dec 26] big, strong, lengthy gelding: poor
nowadays: left M. Buckley 1,400 gns after fifth start: stays 11f: acts on firm going, soft
and fibresand: often visored: has raced freely. *D. Burchell*

OUR FRED   5 ch.g. Prince Sabo 123 – Sheila's Secret (IRE) 97 (Bluebird (USA) 125)   **71 §**
[2002 85, a89: p5g p5g² f5g² f6g³ p5g³ 5m² 6g 5g 5s 5m⁴ 5.1d 5m² 5f⁵ Aug 18] lengthy   **a83 §**
gelding: fairly useful handicapper on all weather, fair on turf: barely stays easy 6f: acts
on soft going, good to firm and all-weather: often blinkered/visored: usually races up
with pace: unreliable. *T. G. Mills*

OUR GLENARD   3 b.c. Royal Applause 124 – Loucoum (FR) 93 (Iron Duke (FR)   **63 ?**
122) [2002 72: 7s 7g⁶ f9.4g 10d 10.9g p10g 8f f8g⁶ Nov 26] smallish, sturdy colt: modest
maiden handicapper: reportedly had breathing problem third/fourth outings, unseated
and bolted to post when pulled up fifth one: left B. Hills 3,000 gns after seventh: seems to
stay easy 1¼m: acts on good to firm going, probably on polytrack: sometimes slowly
away. *S. L. Keightley*

OUR IMPERIAL BAY (USA)   3 b.g. Smart Strike (CAN) 121 – Heat Lightning   **85**
(USA) (Summer Squall (USA)) [2002 p10g² f12g* 12m⁴ 11m⁵ 14m 14.1g⁴ 14m 16m
11.8s* 11.6d⁴ Oct 28] $50,000Y: tall gelding: second foal: closely related to winner in
USA by Miswaki: dam, placed in USA, half-sister to very smart Irish performer up to
1¼m Fair Judgment and smart stayer Orpheus: fairly useful performer: won maiden at
Southwell in March and claimer at Leicester in October: best form around 1½m: acts on
fibresand, soft and good to firm ground: sometimes blinkered: has raced lazily/hung left.
Mrs A. J. Perrett

OUR KRISSIE   4 b.f. Kris 135 – Shehana (USA) 86 (The Minstrel (CAN) 135) [2002   **56**
65: 12.4s⁶ 14.1f 16m⁵ 14.1s³ 17.1m Aug 18] workmanlike filly: modest maiden handicapper: probably stays 2m: acts on soft and good to firm going: tried blinkered. *C. Grant*

OUR LADY   2 b.f. (Mar 6) Primo Dominie 121 – Polytess (IRE) (Polish Patriot (USA)   **62**
128) [2002 6m⁵ 6m⁶ 6m⁵ Sep 18] second foal: half-sister to 4-y-o Norcroft Lady: dam,
second at 1¼m in France, out of close relative to smart French 9f to 11f winner Lichine:
modest form in maidens: should stay 7f: slowly away first 2 starts, unseated rider and
bolted before final one. *G. G. Margarson*

OUR LITTLE ANGEL   2 b.f. (Apr 30) Makbul 104 – Crown Angel (USA) 51 (The   **44**
Minstrel (CAN) 135) [2002 5g⁶ p5g⁴ f5g 5m 5.3m f5g Dec 4] 500Y: sixth foal: half-sister
to a winner abroad by Terimon: dam maiden who stayed 1m: poor maiden: raced only at
5f: very slowly away fifth start. *W. G. M. Turner*

OUR MONOGRAM   6 b.g. Deploy 131 – Darling Splodge (Elegant Air 119) [2002   **61**
57: 16.2g 16m 17.1m² 19.1m² Jun 22] big gelding: modest handicapper: effective at 2m
to 19f: acts on firm and good to soft going: has weakened. *R. M. Beckett*

OUR OLD BOY (IRE)   2 br.c. (May 11) Petorius 117 – Minzal Legend (IRE) 84
(Primo Dominie 121) [2002 5d f6f 5m⁶ Sep 19] IR 1,200F, IR 1,600Y, 6,500 2-y-o: small
colt: third foal: dam Irish 2-y-o 5f winner: well held in maidens. *J. G. Given*

OUR PLACE (IRE)   3 b.g. Distinctly North (USA) 115 – Simplyhectic (IRE) (Simply
Great (FR) 122) [2002 12m 12d⁴ p12g Jul 20] IR 4,000F: lengthy, good-topped gelding:
third foal: dam unraced half-sister to useful French middle-distance performer Flanaghan
Cocktail: well beaten in maidens: missed break badly on debut. *A. P. Jarvis*

OUR ROSY   4 ch.f. First Trump 118 – Cadeau Elegant 64 (Cadeaux Genereux 131)   –
[2002 –: f7s p7g Jan 30] little form. *G. G. Margarson*

OUR SION   2 b.g. (Mar 28) Dreams End 93 – Millfields Lady 75 (Sayf El Arab (USA)   –
127) [2002 5.1g f6f Aug 16] 500Y: second foal: dam 6f (at 2 yrs, seller) and 1m winner:
last in maidens. *R. Brotherton*

OUR TEDDY (IRE) 2 ch.c. (Mar 14) Grand Lodge (USA) 125 – Lady Windley (Bail- **101**
lamont (USA) 124) [2002 6s⁶ 7m* 7d⁴ 8g² 6m 7g 10v Nov 9] 55,000F, 84,000Y:
unfurnished colt: fifth foal: half-brother to 5-y-o Waseyla and a winner up to 11f in Italy
by Dr Devious: dam, French 11f winner, out of top-class French middle-distance
performer Northern Trick: useful performer: won maiden at Newmarket in June: best
efforts when second in listed race at Deauville (beaten 2 lengths by Snipewalk) and eighth
(on penultimate start) in Grand Criterium at Longchamp: stays 1m: best form on good
ground. *G. G. Margarson*

OUR WEDDINGPRESENT (USA) 3 ch.g. Known Fact (USA) 135 – All A Lark **–**
(General Assembly (USA)) [2002 49: f9.4g⁵ 11.9g f12g May 24] leggy, workmanlike
gelding: maiden: well held in 2002: visored (pulled hard) final start. *M. C. Pipe*

OUR WOL 3 b.g. Distant Relative 128 – Lady Highfield 62 (High Kicker (USA)) **51**
[2002 6m p8g⁵ f7g³ f7f f7g Dec 17] second foal: dam temperamental 1¼m winner:
modest maiden: will probably prove best at 7f/1m: acts on all-weather: has worn cheekpieces. *G. G. Margarson*

OUTEAST (IRE) 2 b.f. (Apr 24) Mujadil (USA) 119 – Stifen (Burslem 123) [2002 **70**
5m² 5m* 5g Jun 5] 16,000Y: angular filly: half-sister to numerous winners, including 5f
(at 2 yrs) and 6f winner Ruzen (by Fayruz) and 2000 2-y-o 6f winner Where's Jasper
(by Common Grounds), both fairly useful: dam unraced: fair form: reportedly suffered
overreach when winning maiden at Redcar in May: free to post when last of 11 in
listed race at Beverley: raced only at 5f on good/good to firm ground: sold 4,500 gns.
M. Johnston

OUT FOR A STROLL 3 b.g. Zamindar (USA) 116 – The Jotter 99 (Night Shift **83**
(USA)) [2002 67: 5f 7m⁵ 8m² 8m* 8.1m² 8m³ 8g 8.2v Oct 29] sturdy, deep-girthed
gelding: fairly useful handicapper: off nearly 4 months after reappearance: won at Newcastle (awarded race) in July and Pontefract in August: best at 7f/1m: acts on good to firm
going. *S. C. Williams*

OUT OF SEASON (IRE) 3 ch.f. Brief Truce (USA) 126 – Red Partridge (Solinus **40**
130) [2002 58: f7g 5.3d 6m 5.1f 5g Oct 5] poor maiden: will probably stay 1m: tried
visored/tongue tied. *W. G. M. Turner*

OUT OF THIS WORLD 3 ch.f. Beveled (USA) – Martian Melody 62 (Enchant- **65**
ment 115) [2002 59p: p7g⁵ 6.1m 7m 6m* 7m 6.1m Oct 1] fair performer: won selling
handicap at Lingfield in August: stays 7f: acts on all-weather and good to firm going: has
been awkward leaving stall: reportedly bled from nose twice in 2002. *S. Kirk*

OUT OF TUNE 2 ch.g. (Apr 10) Elmaamul (USA) 125 – Strawberry Song 87 (Final **–**
Straw 127) [2002 p8g p8g Dec 14] 12,000Y, 12,000 2-y-o: brother to fairly useful 1999
2-y-o 5f/6f winner Ebba and 5f winner (including at 2 yrs) Sans Rivale and half-brother
to 3-y-o Strawberry Sands: dam 1¼m winner: signs of just a little ability in maidens at
Lingfield: gelded after final outing. *C. Weedon*

OVAL OFFICE 3 ch.f. Pursuit of Love 124 – Pushy 112 (Sharpen Up 127) [2002 8s* **99**
8.1d* Jul 5] lengthy, useful-looking filly: half-sister to numerous winners, including
smart performer up to 7f Bluebook (by Secretariat), and useful 7f performer Myself and
fairly useful 1¼m winner Nanda (both by Nashwan): dam, 2-y-o 5f (Queen Mary)
winner, half-sister to Jupiter Island and Precocious: justified favouritism in 5-runner
maiden at Goodwood in June and 4-runner minor event at Sandown in July, latter by neck
from Trojan Princess: raced only around 1m: stud. *H. R. A. Cecil*

OVAMBO (IRE) 4 b.g. Namaqualand (USA) – Razana (IRE) 71 (Kahyasi 130) [2002 **114**
108: 13.4f³ 16.4m⁶ 12m² 12m⁴ 12v³ Nov 9] sturdy gelding: smart performer: at least
creditable efforts in 2002 when third to St Expedit in Ormonde Stakes at Chester, neck
second to Xtra in listed event at Newmarket and fourth to Darasim in listed rated stakes at
Goodwood: effective at 1½m/1¾m: acts on firm going, well below form on heavy:
usually held up: reliable. *P. J. Makin*

OVERBOARD (IRE) 3 b.f. Rainbow Quest (USA) 134 – Up Anchor (IRE) 114 (Slip **73**
Anchor 136) [2002 10g 12m² 10.2s⁶ 12.1v³ Jun 14] leggy filly: fifth foal: closely related
to 1997 2-y-o 7f winner Fleetwood (by Groom Dancer) and 7f (at 2 yrs) to 1½m winner
Sailing (by Arazi), both useful, and half-sister to smart performer up to 1½m Red Sea (by
Barathea), 6f (Coventry Stakes) winner at 2 yrs: dam 1m (at 2 yrs) to 12.5f (St Simon
Stakes) winner: fair maiden: stays 1½m: acts on good to firm going, probably on heavy:
looked difficult ride second start. *P. F. I. Cole*

OVERLOAD (USA) 3 b.f. Forest Wildcat (USA) 120 – Magical Avie (USA) (Lord **–**
Avie (USA)) [2002 85: p7g 8.3g⁵ 7m Sep 12] good-topped filly: fairly useful performer
at 2 yrs: little form in 2002: sent to USA. *C. R. Egerton*

OVERRIDE (IRE) 2 b.c. (Apr 27) Peintre Celebre (USA) 137 – Catalonda (African **75**
Sky 124) [2002 7f⁶ 5m* 5g 6m⁶ 7g* p7g⁶ Nov 13] 30,000Y: rather leggy, quite attractive
colt: closely related to useful 1m winner Wealthy Star (by Soviet Star) and half-brother to
several winners, including smart 1m winner Fanaar (by Unfuwain): dam Irish 2-y-o 5f
winner: fair performer: won maiden at Pontefract (idled) in August and nursery at
Lingfield in October: stays 7f: raced only on good going or firmer on turf, probably acts
on polytrack. *J. M. P. Eustace*

OVERSTRAND (IRE) 3 b.c. In The Wings 128 – Vaison La Romaine 100 (Arctic **86**
Tern (USA) 126) [2002 10.2g 10f³ 10.2d² p12g² 11.7m* 14g⁶ 12m³ 12.1m³ 11.8g Oct 14]
35,000Y: lengthy colt: half-brother to numerous winners, including smart German/New
Zealand middle-distance performer Vialli (by Niniski) and fairly useful 9.4f to 2m winner
Roman Hideaway (by Hernando): dam 7.5f winner in France: fairly useful performer:
won maiden at Bath (edged left/idled) in June: should stay 1¾m: acts on firm going, good
to soft and polytrack: consistent: sold 24,000 gns. *Mrs A. J. Perrett*

OVER THE TWEED 5 b.m. Presidium 124 – Nicolini 56 (Nicholas Bill 125) [2002 **–**
11.9s May 27] 3,200Y: sixth known foal: dam 10.4f to 1½m winner: well beaten in
claimer at Carlisle. *J. S. Haldane*

OWN LINE 3 b.g. Classic Cliche (IRE) 128 – Cold Line 74 (Exdirectory 129) [2002 **58**
9g⁵ 10s³ 12m 15.8f⁵ 17.1f⁴ 18d f12g⁵ Dec 2] good-topped gelding: half-brother to
bumpers/hurdles winner Give Best (by Dunbeath): dam, 1½m winner, half-sister to high-
class 2m hurdler Past Glories: modest maiden handicapper: will prove best at 2m+: acts
on firm going and fibresand: should win races, given good test of stamina. *J. Hetherton*

OYSTER ISLAND (IRE) 2 b.c. (Feb 9) Mind Games 121 – Food of Love 109 (Music **–**
Boy 124) [2002 6m Oct 7] 36,000Y: fifth living foal: half-brother to 3 fairly useful
winners, including 3-y-o Tough Love: dam 5f (including at 2 yrs) winner: 10/1 and
visored, slowly away when well beaten in maiden at Windsor: sold 3,500 gns, sent to
Kuwait. *I. A. Balding*

OZ 3 ch.g. Kris 135 – Arletty 63 (Rainbow Quest (USA) 134) [2002 10g 10s May 27] **–**
22,000Y: first foal: dam, maiden who stayed 1½m, half-sister to high-class miler Shavian
(by Kris) and Gold Cup winner Paean: never dangerous in maidens at Windsor. *W. Jarvis*

P

PABLO 3 b.c. Efisio 120 – Winnebago 63 (Kris 135) [2002 7.1g² 7.5g³ 7d* 7.1d* 7m **112 p**
7g³ 8s* Nov 2] good-bodied colt: first foal: dam, 13f winner, half-sister to very smart
middle-distance colt Apache: smart performer: progressed really well in first season,
winning maiden at Goodwood in May and handicaps at Sandown in July and Newmarket
in November: best effort when beating Certain Justice by 2½ lengths on last-named,
always going well and soon on top once asked from Dip: stays 1m: acts well on soft going
(ran poorly on good to firm): genuine: capable of better still, and should win a good prize
or 2 at 4 yrs. *B. W. Hills*

PACHARA 3 b.g. Mind Games 121 – Miss Mercy (IRE) 62 (Law Society (USA) 130) **102**
[2002 98: 6g² 7m a5.5s⁴ 5.5f² Dec 7] well-made gelding: useful performer: runner-up at
3 yrs in minor event at Leicester (beaten ½ length by Lady Dominatrix) in April and
(having been sold from M. Bell 20,000 gns after second outing, then gelded) allowance
race at Hollywood in December: stays 6f (raced freely when well held at 7f): acts on firm
and good to soft going, well below form on heavy. *S. Shulman, USA*

PACIANO (IRE) 2 b.g. (Apr 23) Perugino (USA) 84 – Saucy Maid (IRE) 69 (Sure **81**
Blade (USA) 130) [2002 6m⁴ 6d 6d³ Nov 1] IR 10,000Y, 16,000 2-y-o: fourth foal:
closely related to fairly useful 2001 2-y-o 6f winner Sophorific (by Danehill) and half-
brother to 2 winners, including 4-y-o La Mondotte: dam, maiden who stayed 1¼m,
half-sister to dam of Pilsudski: best effort in maidens (fairly useful form) when third to
Masaader at Brighton, edging right: should be suited by 7f/1m. *C. G. Cox*

PACIFIC ALLIANCE (IRE) 6 b.g. Fayruz 116 – La Gravotte (FR) (Habitat 134) **38**
[2002 66d: 8g 8.1g 10.2f⁴ 8g Aug 12] fairly useful handicapper at 4 yrs: poor on Flat in
2002: seems best around 1m: acts on good to firm and good to soft going: blinkered: often
races prominently: successful over hurdles in October. *M. Wigham*

PACIFIC OCEAN (ARG) 3 b.c. Fitzcarraldo (ARG) – Play Hard (ARG) (General
(FR)) [2002 7g Oct 14] half-brother to 3 winners in Argentina, including Group 2

12.5f winner Omar's Play (by Ahmad): dam unraced: well held in maiden at Leicester.
B. R. Millman

PACIFIC PADDY (IRE) 2 ch.c. (Feb 21) Tagula (IRE) 116 – Lady From Limerick **90**
(IRE) 61 (Rainbows For Life (CAN)) [2002 6m 7d p7g* 7d 7.5g* 7m⁴ 8g* Sep 20]
5,500Y: good-topped colt: first foal: dam, sprint maiden, from family of Oaks winner
Ramruma: fairly useful performer: won maiden at Lingfield in July, minor event at
Beverley (pulled hard/drifted right) in August and nursery at Ayr (beat Rutters Renegade
1½ lengths) in September: stays 1m: yet to race on extremes of going on turf, acts on
polytrack: sometimes bandaged in front. *I. A. Balding*

PACKIN EM IN 4 b.c. Young Ern 120 – Wendy's Way 53 (Merdon Melody 98) [2002 **–**
7m 7d Jul 10] modest maiden at 2 yrs: unraced in 2001: no form at 4 yrs. *J. R. Boyle*

PADDY MUL 5 ch.h. Democratic (USA) 101 – My Pretty Niece (Great Nephew 126) **52**
[2002 38: f12g² f16g 12.3g 16m* 14g⁵ 16f 14g³ 14.1f³ 16d⁴ 16m 15d 12.4g⁶ 16.1d² 16m⁵
15.8f 15.8f⁵ Oct 8] sparely-made horse: modest performer: won amateur claimer at
Musselburgh in May: stays 2m: acts on firm going, soft and fibresand: tried visored:
tongue tied: reportedly had breathing problem second start. *W. Storey*

PADDYWACK (IRE) 5 b.g. Bigstone (IRE) 126 – Millie's Return (IRE) 71 (Ballad **94**
Rock 122) [2002 –, a71d: f5s p6g⁵ p5g* f5g³ f6g⁵ f5g* p5g* 5.3f² 5m 5g³ 5g **a88**
5.1f* 5g² 6g f5g 5.1f⁶ 5m² 5f 6g 5m 5.1f 5m 5.1f 5m² 5f* 5g³ 5d* f5g⁵ f5g² f5g Dec
10] small gelding: fairly useful handicapper: had a fine year, winning at Lingfield (2),
Wolverhampton (2), Chester, York and Pontefract: career-best effort to beat Time N Time
Again by 2½ lengths on last-named track in October: best at 5f: acts on firm going, good
to soft and all-weather: blinkered: has edged left: tough. *D. W. Chapman*

PADDY WINALOT (IRE) 2 ch.g. (Apr 12) College Chapel 122 – Six Penny Express **56 ?**
(Bay Express 132) [2002 6s⁴ 5m 7g Aug 12] IR 18,000Y: good-topped gelding:
half-brother to several winners, including useful 5f (at 2 yrs in Ireland) and 6.5f (in
Germany) winner Nashcash (by Nashamaa) and 1997 2-y-o 6f winner Madame Claude
(by Paris House): dam Irish maiden: seemingly best effort in maidens (modest form)
when fourth of 5 at Hamilton: likely to prove best at 5f/6f: very slowly away second start.
D. Nicholls

PAGAN DANCE (IRE) 3 b.g. Revoque (IRE) 122 – Ballade d'Ainhoa (FR) (Al Nasr **93**
(FR) 126) [2002 8m² 8.1m² 9m* 10m 10.3s³ Oct 25] 9,000F, 32,000Y: strong, quite
attractive gelding: first foal: dam, French 10.5f and 1½m winner, half-sister to smart
French winner up to 13f Oa Baldixe: fairly useful form: won maiden at Newbury in
August, wandering and colliding with rail final 1f: good 2½ lengths third to Red Wine in
handicap at Doncaster (squeezed out late on) final start (gelded after): stays 1¼m: acts on
soft and good to firm ground: has looked far from easy ride (carries head awkwardly).
Mrs A. J. Perrett

PAGAN PRINCE 5 br.g. Primo Dominie 121 – Mory Kante (USA) (Icecapade (USA)) **81**
[2002 69: 7g 8m³ 8d 8g² 7.9d² 8.5d* 9m 8g f8g* f8.5f Nov 11] leggy gelding: fairly
useful handicapper: won at Beverley in July and Southwell (apprentices, drifted left) in
October: races at 1m/9f: acts on soft going, good to firm and fibresand: consistent.
J. A. R. Toller

PAGAN SKY (IRE) 3 ch.g. Inchinor 119 – Rosy Sunset (IRE) (Red Sunset 120) **87**
[2002 8d² 7m* 8.1m² 8d⁶ 8.1m⁵ 10.3m 10.4f Oct 11] 33,000F, IR 65,000Y: fifth foal:
half-brother to 3 winners, including useful 6f (including at 2 yrs) winner Evening Promise
(by Aragon), later Grade 3 winner in USA: dam, lightly-raced maiden, half-sister to 3-y-o
Bandari: fairly useful performer: won maiden at Goodwood in June: should stay 1¼m
(beaten before trip became issue last 2 starts): acts on good to firm going: has started
slowly: gelded after final start. *J. A. R. Toller*

PAGAN STORM (USA) 2 ch.g. (Jan 23) Tabasco Cat (USA) 126 – Melodeon (USA) **80**
(Alydar (USA)) [2002 6m⁶ 7.1m⁵ 7f⁴ 8g³ Oct 24] $70,000F: lengthy, sparely-made
gelding: fluent mover: half-brother to several winners abroad, including useful Seeing
(by Secreto), third in Premio Regina Elena: dam unraced: fairly useful maiden: close third
to Redspin at Brighton (gelded after): stays 1m: raced only on good ground or firmer.
Mrs A. J. Perrett

PAGAN WOLF 2 b.g. (May 19) Wolfhound (USA) 126 – Sharp Girl (FR) 114 **–**
(Sharpman) [2002 7d 6v Nov 9] 6,400F: half-brother to several winners, including fairly
useful 7f and 1¼m winner Robsart (by Robellino) and to 9f winner Newscaster (by
Bluebird): dam French 1¼m winner: well held in maidens at Newmarket (slowly away)
and Doncaster. *W. Jarvis*

PAGEANT   5 br.m. Inchinor 119 – Positive Attitude 82 (Red Sunset 120) [2002 52, a60d: f7g f7g⁵ f7g³ f7g 8m* 7m 8.1g 8g* 8g 7m⁵ 8g 8.1g* 8m 9g f8.5g f7g⁵ p7g Dec 18] rather leggy, useful-looking mare: modest on turf, poor on all-weather: won sellers at Ripon (2, first apprentice handicap) and Chepstow (edged left) between June and September: effective at 7f/1m: acts on fibresand and probably any turf going: often front runner: has looked none too keen: unreliable. *J. M. Bradley*   **54 §**
a39 §

PAGE NOUVELLE (FR)   4 b.f. Spectrum (IRE) 126 – Page Bleue (Sadler's Wells (USA) 132) [2002 –: 8.3s⁵ 7d 9.1v² 9m 8.5g⁴ 12.3m³ 10g 10.5f 10.2g Oct 16] strong, lengthy filly: has round action: fair performer: finds 1m a minimum, barely stays 1½m: probably best on good ground or softer. *W. M. Brisbourne*   **79**

PAID UP   4 b.g. Mind Games 121 – Indian Summer 78 (Young Generation 129) [2002 53: f6s⁵ f5g⁴ 5m⁶ 5m² 5g⁴ 6f 5m 5m a6g a6g a9g³ Nov 17] small, sparely-made gelding: modest maiden on turf, poor on all-weather: left M. W. Easterby after eighth start: seems to stay 9f: probably acts on any turf going and sand/fibresand: blinkered all 3 starts in Britain in 2003: none too consistent. *C. Tinkler, Spain*   **51**
a39

PAILITAS (GER)   5 b.g. Lomitas 129 – Pradera (GER) (Abary (GER) 119) [2002 8.5g Sep 18] ex-German gelding: won maiden at Baden-Baden and handicap at Gelsenkirchen in 2001: well held only Flat run in 2002: stays 1m: has reportedly had breathing problems. *Ian Williams*   **–**

PAINTBRUSH (IRE)   2 b.f. (Jan 27) Groom Dancer (USA) 128 – Bristle 96 (Thatch (USA) 136) [2002 5d 6f Jun 11] 8,000Y: good-bodied filly: half-sister to several winners, 3 of them useful, including 1¼m winner Premier Generation (by Cadeaux Genereux) and 7f winner (including at 2 yrs) Rakis (by Alzao): dam Irish 2-y-o 8.5f winner: poor form in maidens. *Mrs L. Stubbs*   **48**

PAIRING (IRE)   4 ch.g. Rudimentary (USA) 118 – Splicing 82 (Sharpo 132) [2002 80: f8s* f8s* p10g 8d 10f 10m² 10s 11.9d 8d 10.1g 9m 10s⁵ 10.1s a12g Dec 15] smallish, lengthy gelding: useful handicapper on all-weather, fairly useful on turf: won twice at Southwell in January: sold from H. Morrison 16,000 gns before final start: effective at 1m/1¼m: acts on fibresand and good to firm going: blinkered (raced too freely) seventh start: on edge/took strong hold to post ninth outing: often races up with pace: none too consistent. *J. H. Brown, Spain*   **82**
a96

PAKHOES (IRE)   2 b.c. (Apr 27) College Chapel 122 – Park Charger 105 (Tirol 127) [2002 6s² 5s² 6s* 6g² 6d² Jun 30] 130,000Y: strong, close-coupled colt: fourth foal: half-brother to 3 winners, including 7f/1m winner Stage Presence (by Selkirk) and 3-y-o Rum Charger: dam Irish 1m/1¼m winner: useful performer: won maiden at the Curragh in May: best efforts when beaten neck by Statue of Liberty in Coventry Stakes at Royal Ascot and Hold That Tiger in Railway Stakes at the Curragh last 2 starts: should stay 7f: raced on good going or softer. *D. K. Weld, Ireland*   **108**

PALACE AFFAIR   4 ch.f. Pursuit of Love 124 – Palace Street (USA) 103 (Secreto (USA) 128) [2002 112: 6s 5.1g² 7g⁴ 6s² 6g* 5d* 6m* 6m 6g Oct 18] quite good-topped filly: smart performer: at least as good as ever in 2002, winning listed races at Salisbury (by length from Grey Eminence), Sandown (by 2½ lengths from Boleyn Castle) and York (for second successive year, by neck from Lipstick) in June/July: below form last 2 starts (shaped as though something amiss penultimate): effective at 5f to 7f: acts on good to firm and good to soft going, probably on soft: blinkered at 2 yrs: tends to carry head awkwardly. *G. B. Balding*   **113**

PALACEGATE TOUCH   12 gr.g. Petong 126 – Dancing Chimes (London Bells (CAN) 109) [2002 59, a68: f7s f7g⁶ f6g⁶ f7g f6g 6f³ f6g⁵ 7g f7s 7f² 7g⁴ 7g⁴ 5.9d⁶ f7g³ 5.9d 7m² 6d² 6s⁶ f7g f6g Dec 10] tall, good-topped gelding: modest performer: successful 33 times in career: best at: 6f/7f: acts on firm going, soft and fibresand (probably on polytrack): formerly blinkered/visored (tried only once since 2000): tends to hang left/race with head high: often claimer ridden: tough. *A. Berry*   **62**
a56

PALAIS (IRE)   7 b.g. Darshaan 133 – Dance Festival 101 (Nureyev (USA) 131) [2002 –: 10g⁶ 14.1m Jul 13] of little account on Flat. *John A. Harris*   **–**

PALAMEDES   3 b.g. Sadler's Wells (USA) 132 – Kristal Bridge 75 (Kris 135) [2002 78p: 9.9f³ 11.7g⁵ Oct 16] fair maiden: should be suited by 1½m+. *P. W. Harris*   **75**

PALANZO (IRE)   4 b.g. Green Desert (USA) 127 – Karpacka (IRE) 99 (Rousillon (USA) 133) [2002 108: 6g⁴ 6f² 7g⁶ 6g 7m 7m³ 7.9f⁴ Oct 11] lengthy gelding: useful performer: creditable fourth to Reel Buddy in minor event at Kempton on reappearance: ran respectably at best after: effective at 6f/7f: probably acts on any going: blinkered (ran   **106 §**

poorly) penultimate 3-y-o start: sometimes slowly away, very much so fourth outing: ungenuine: sold 36,000 gns. *P. W. Harris*

PALATIAL POISE   4 b.f. Rock Hopper 124 – Kamaress 85 (Kampala 120) [2002 –: 14.1s⁵ 16.2g Aug 15] angular filly: little form. *N. Bycroft*   –

PALAWAN   6 br.g. Polar Falcon (USA) 126 – Krameria 72 (Kris 135) [2002 77: p5g²   **85**
p6g* p5g* p5g³ f5g² p5g⁵ p5g⁴ p6g 5m* 5.1g³ 5.1g⁶ 5s Jun 10] lengthy gelding: fairly useful performer: won 2 handicaps at Lingfield in January and minor event at Folkestone in April: has won at 7f, races at 5f/6f nowadays: acts on all-weather, raced mainly on good or firmer ground on turf: visored once in 2001. *I. A. Balding*

PALLIUM (IRE)   14 b.g. Try My Best (USA) 130 – Jungle Gardenia (Nonoalco (USA)   –
131) [2002 –: 5g May 30] no longer of any account. *D. A. Nolan*

PALM BEACH (IRE)   3 ch.c. Pennekamp (USA) 130 – Crystal Bright 75 (Bold Lad   –
(IRE) 133) [2002 7m 7d 10m Jun 17] closely related to useful 1m/1¼m winner Wainwright (by Bering) and half-brother to 3 winners, notably smart performer up to 1m Crystal Gazing (by El Gran Senor): dam, placed at 5f at 2 yrs in Britain, later won up to 9f in USA: well held in maidens (reportedly wrong behind final start). *D. J. S. Cosgrove*

PALOMO (IRE)   3 b. or br.g. Petardia 113 – Miss Barcelona (IRE) 53 (Mac's Imp   –
(USA) 116) [2002 –: f9.4g f9.4g Jan 21] well held in minor event/maidens (visored/tongue tied final start). *R. M. Beckett*

PALUA   5 b.g. Sri Pekan (USA) 117 – Reticent Bride (IRE) 71 (Shy Groom (USA))   **91 §**
[2002 91§: p12g* 18s 16m⁴ 18.7f 20m 16m² 18m Oct 19] tall, useful-looking gelding: fairly useful handicapper: won maiden at Lingfield in February: creditable effort after only when second to Hawkwind at Goodwood after 3-month break. stays 2¼m: unraced on heavy, acts on any other turf going and polytrack: tried blinkered: has worn crossed noseband: tends to wander/carry head high: ungenuine: sold 11,000 gns, joined E. Lavelle. *I. A. Balding*

PANCAKEHILL   3 ch.f. Sabrehill (USA) 120 – Sawlah (Known Fact (USA) 135)   **70**
[2002 63: 10m* 8m⁶ 10g 10m 9.3g p8g² 8.5g p8g* p10g p10g³ p8g f8g p12g p10g Dec   **a72**
14] quite good-topped filly: fair performer: won handicap at Southwell in April and seller at Lingfield (sold from G. Butler 7,000 gns) in October: stays 1¼m: acts on good to firm going and polytrack: tried blinkered: reared twice leaving stall third start: sometimes wanders/finds little: tail swisher. *D. K. Ivory*

PANCAKE ROLE   2 b.g. (Mar 7) Tragic Role (USA) – My Foxy Lady 37 (Jalmood   –
(USA) 126) [2002 7g f8.5g⁴ 8.2s Oct 23] tall gelding: third foal: dam sprint maiden: signs of just a little ability in maiden/minor events. *D. Haydn Jones*

Stanley Racing Summer Stakes, York—third listed-race win in a row for Palace Affair (left), who holds on from Lipstick; Lady Dominatrix is third

PANGLOSSIAN (IRE) 2 b.f. (Feb 8) Barathea (IRE) 127 – Overcall (Bustino 136) **65**
[2002 8s⁵ 7d⁵ Nov 5] IR 16,000Y: sister to useful French 11.5f winner Cruzeiro (later
winner in Hong Kong) and half-sister to several winners, including smart 7f (at 2 yrs) to
11f winner Overbury (by Caerleon): dam, Irish 1½m winner, sister to dam of high-class
stayer Vintage Crop: fifth in maidens, better effort behind In Love at Ayr on debut, racing
freely: should be suited by 1¼m+. *M. Johnston*

PANGO 3 ch.g. Bluegrass Prince (IRE) 110 – Riverine (Risk Me (FR) 127) [2002 77: **79**
8m² 8.1d* 8d⁵ 10m⁶ 8.5d 9g p10g² f11g² Nov 26] rather unfurnished gelding: fluent
mover: fair performer: won minor event at Chepstow in June: stays 11f: acts on firm
going, good to soft (hung right on soft final 2-y-o start) and all-weather. *H. Morrison*

PANJANDRUM 4 b.g. Polar Falcon (USA) 126 – Rengaine (FR) (Music Boy 124) **–**
[2002 54+, a69: p5g p5g³ Jan 30] lengthy, sparely-made gelding: fair performer on all- **a70**
weather: effective at 5f/easy 6f: acts on all-weather: visored 4 of last 5 starts: sold 900
gns. *Andrew Reid*

PANPIPES (USA) 2 ch.f. (May 10) Woodman (USA) 126 – Forest Treasure (IRE) 94 **69**
(Brief Truce (USA) 126) [2002 5d³ a6.5f Dec 19] $40,000Y: first foal: dam 5f winner at 2
yrs and third in Cherry Hinton: 1¾ lengths third of 8 to Bollin Jeannie in maiden at
Thirsk: left M. Johnston: well held in similar event at Nad Al Sheba 3½ months later.
K. P. McLaughlin, UAE

PANTONE 2 b.f. (May 4) Spectrum (IRE) 126 – Tinashaan (IRE) 100 (Darshaan 133) **71**
[2002 5m³ 7m² 7.5d³ 7.1m 7v p8g⁴ Nov 19] quite good-topped filly: third foal: dam, 1½m
winner, half-sister to useful stayer Life of Riley: fair maiden: will probably stay 1¼m:
acts on polytrack, good to firm and good to soft ground: looked less than keen fourth start:
lazy sort. *M. Johnston*

PANTS 3 b.f. Pivotal 124 – Queenbird 90 (Warning 136) [2002 78d: 6m⁶ p7g⁵ 6s⁵ 7g **68**
7m 7m⁵ p7g³ 7f⁵ 7m 6m² 7.6m⁶ 7m³ 8m⁵ 8m 7g² f6g² f7g p7g Dec 28] sparely-made filly:
fair maiden handicapper: best at 6f/7f: acts on good to soft ground, good to firm and
all-weather: visored (below form) once: often slowly away: has reared leaving stall/hung.
Andrew Reid

PAOLINI (GER) 5 ch.h. Lando (GER) 128 – Prairie Darling (Stanford 121§) [2002 **121**
121: 10g² 10m 10f⁶ 12d⁶ 10m² Dec 15] strong, good-bodied horse: carries plenty of
condition: very smart performer: ran well in 2002 when 2 lengths second to Grandera in
Singapore Airlines International Cup at Kranji on reappearance, close sixth to Beat
Hollow in Arlington Million (not clearest of runs) third start and short-head second to
Precision in Hong Kong Cup at Sha Tin (led over 1f out): still going well when badly
hampered on home turn in Prince of Wales's Stakes at Royal Ascot second start: effective
at 1¼m/1½m: acts on firm going, not at best on soft: blinkered in 2002: attempted to bite
rival once at 4 yrs: stays in training. *A. Wohler, Germany*

PAPERWEIGHT 6 b.m. In The Wings 128 – Crystal Reay 59 (Sovereign Dancer **–**
(USA) [2002 –, a70: 11.7g f14.8s 13.1g 11.8d⁶ 12.1d⁶ f14.8g p10g⁵ Jul 3] modest **a63**
handicapper: stays 1½m: acts on any turf/all-weather: tried blinkered/visored/tongue
tied: sometimes runs lazily. *Miss K. M. George*

PAPINGO 4 b.f. Charnwood Forest (IRE) 125 – Maracuja (USA) (Riverman (USA) **–**
131) [2002 –: f9.4s 12d f14.8s Dec 13] tall filly: no form. *K. R. Burke*

PAPUA 8 ch.g. Green Dancer (USA) 132 – Fairy Tern 109 (Mill Reef (USA) 141) **–**
[2002 p12g Jan 5] tall gelding: one-time useful handicapper: well held only run since
1999: tried visored/blinkered. *J. White*

PARACHUTE 3 ch.g. Hector Protector (USA) 124 – Shortfall 103 (Last Tycoon 131) **58**
[2002 62p: f9.4g⁶ Jun 22] big, strong, lengthy gelding: has scope: modest maiden: should
be suited by 1¼m/1½m: acts on soft going and fibresand: has started slowly. *Sir Mark
Prescott*

PARADISE EVE 2 b.f. (Apr 20) Bahamian Bounty 116 – Twilight Time (Aragon **46**
118) [2002 5g⁶ May 31] 2,200Y: fourth foal: half-sister to winning sprinters abroad by
Forzando and Pivotal: dam unraced: 13/2, hung right throughout when sixth in maiden at
Catterick. *T. D. Barron*

PARADISE GARDEN (USA) 5 b.g. Septieme Ciel (USA) 123 – Water Course **52**
(USA) (Irish River (FR) 131) [2002 44+: 12g⁶ 10.5s 12.3m 10.1g² 12.6g⁵ 10g Aug 7] tall
gelding: fluent mover: modest handicapper: barely stays 1½m: acts on good to firm and
good to soft going: blinkered final start. *P. L. Clinton*

PARADISE VALLEY   2 b.c. (Mar 15) Groom Dancer (USA) 128 – Rose de Reve   **72**
(IRE) (Persian Heights 129) [2002 7d⁴ 7.5d⁴ 7.1m³ 7m⁵ f7g⁵ 7m⁶ 7.1m² 7g f7g Dec 9]   **a64**
3,000Y: good-bodied colt: third foal: dam, won around 1m in France (including at 2 yrs)/
USA, half-sister to Irish 1000 Guineas/Irish Oaks runner-up Kitza and smart 1985 2-y-o
5f performer Marouble: fair maiden on turf, modest on all-weather: runner-up in nursery
at Warwick: should stay 1m: acts on fibresand, yet to race on extremes of going on turf.
A. P. Jarvis

PARADISO PARADIS (IRE)   4 b.f. Tagula (IRE) 116 – Shanamara (IRE) 77 (Sher-   **–**
nazar 131) [2002 –: 6f 9m 12g⁵ 10g 6m f12s² f12g Sep 30] angular filly: little form:
tongue tied after third start. *Miss A. Stokell*

PARAGON OF VIRTUE   5 ch.g. Cadeaux Genereux 131 – Madame Dubois 121   **88**
(Legend of France (USA) 124) [2002 84: p10g* p10g² p10g⁶ 10g 12f p12g p10g p12g*
Nov 27] lengthy gelding: fairly useful performer: won maiden in January and claimer in
November, both at Lingfield: stays 1½m: acts on soft going, good to firm and polytrack.
P. Mitchell

PARALLEL UNIVERSE   3 b.f. Hector Protector (USA) 124 – Fextal (USA) (Alleged   **59**
(USA) 138) [2002 12f³ May 25] rather lengthy filly: sixth foal: half-sister to 3 useful
performers, including French/US miler Eubee (by Common Grounds) and 2000 2-y-o 1m
winner Autumn Rhythm (by Hernando): dam, unraced, out of Canadian Oaks winner
Northernette, herself sister to Storm Bird: 12 lengths third to Majority Rule in maiden at
Newmarket, under pressure long way out, only outing. *H. R. A. Cecil*

PARASOL (IRE)   3 br.c. Halling (USA) 133 – Bunting 102 (Shaadi (USA) 126) [2002   **105**
107: 8m 10.1m* 10d² Nov 1] big, rangy colt: usually takes the eye: easy mover: useful
performer: behind in 2000 Guineas at Newmarket on reappearance: simple task in
2-runner minor event at Epsom (made all, tended to carry head high) in August: creditable
5 lengths second to Island House in listed event at Newmarket final start: stays 1¼m: acts
on soft and good to firm going: visored in 2002: tends to hang: joined D. Loder. *Saeed bin
Suroor*

PARDISHAR (IRE)   4 b.g. Kahyasi 130 – Parapa (IRE) (Akarad (FR) 130) [2002   **–**
105: 10.1g 10m May 4] useful at 3 yrs: soundly beaten both 4-y-o starts. *G. L. Moore*

PARISIAN ABBY   2 b.f. (Feb 26) Paris House 123 – Plentitude (FR) (Ela-Mana-Mou   **–**
132) [2002 5m 5f 5m Aug 21] 800Y, resold 500Y: first foal: dam unraced: well held in
maidens/seller. *H. A. McWilliams*

PARISIAN EIRE (IRE)   3 gr.g. Paris House 123 – La Fille de Feu (Never So Bold   **–**
135) [2002 –: 6.1d 8.2f 10.9f Jun 26] no form. *N. A. Smith*

PARISIAN ELEGANCE   3 b.f. Zilzal (USA) 137 – Tshusick 81 (Dancing Brave   **–**
(USA) 140) [2002 90: 5.1m 6g 6d³ 5g 5.1f 6m f6g Oct 17] sturdy, good-quartered filly:
fairly useful performer at 2 yrs: little solid form in 2002: effective at 5f/6f: acts on soft
going, good to firm and fibresand: tried tongue tied: sold 52,000 gns in December.
R. M. H. Cowell

PARISIEN STAR (IRE)   6 ch.g. Paris House 123 – Auction Maid (IRE) (Auction   **91**
Ring (USA) 123) [2002 94: 8g⁶ 10.1d 10m² 9m* 10m² 10m³ 10.1m 9f 10.4f 10.1d⁶
Oct 30] leggy gelding: poor mover: fairly useful handicapper: won at Goodwood in June:
effective at 1m/1¼m: possibly unsuited by heavy going, acts on any other turf: very
slowly away eighth start: held up. *J. R. Boyle*

PARIS KNIGHT (IRE)   4 b.g. Paris House 123 – Bykova (Petoski 135) [2002 –:   **–**
f9.4s 11.6m Jul 15] little form. *B. J. Llewellyn*

PARIS MUSIC   2 b.g. (Apr 14) Paris House 123 – Sky Music 85 (Absalom 128) [2002   **–**
6d 7d f6g Nov 20] 1,000Y: poor walker: fourth foal: half-brother to 5-y-o Polar Haze:
dam 6f/7f winner: well held in maidens/claimer. *R. Bastiman*

PARIS PIPER (IRE)   3 gr.g. Paris House 123 – Winter March (Ballad Rock 122)   **54**
[2002 5g⁴ 6f 6d⁵ f7g Dec 17] IR 15,000Y: workmanlike gelding: third foal: dam Irish
2-y-o 6f winner: modest maiden: left Mrs A. Naughton after third start: likely to prove
best at 5f/6f: well held on fibresand. *D. Carroll*

PARK CITY   3 b.c. Slip Anchor 136 – Cryptal (Persian Bold 123) [2002 –: p8g³ p8g⁵   **63**
f8g⁵ f8.5g 8.1d 8.3m⁵ 8g⁶ Jul 6] poor mover: modest maiden: will stay 1¼m+: acts on
polytrack, good to firm and good to soft going: sold 10,000 gns, joined P. Hobbs and won
over hurdles in December. *P. Howling*

PARKER   5 b.g. Magic Ring (IRE) 115 – Miss Loving 89 (Northfields (USA)) [2002 **82 d**
86, a81: p8g³ f7g² 7d⁵ 7.1m* 7.6f p7g 7m 7g 7.6g 7m 7.1g Sep 23] neat gelding: fluent
mover: fairly useful performer: won minor event at Musselburgh in April: below form
last 5 starts: effective at 7f/easy 1m: acts on all-weather, best turf form on good ground or
firmer: often blinkered nowadays: usually races prominently. *B. Palling*

PARKLAND (USA)   2 ch.c. (Apr 28) Distant View (USA) 126 – Victorian Style 88 **96**
(Nashwan (USA) 135) [2002 6m³ 6g* 6m³ 7f² Oct 10] second foal: closely related to
French 1½m winner Dickensian (by Miswaki): dam, 1m winner in Britain/USA, out of
half-sister to top-class 1997 2-y-o Xaar: useful form: won maiden at Newcastle in
September, making most: best effort when neck second of 5 to Prince Tum Tum in minor
event at York: should stay 1m: raced only on good ground or firmer. *R. Charlton*

PARKNASILLA   2 b.g. (Jan 25) Marju (IRE) 127 – Top Berry 87 (High Top 131) **79**
[2002 5g 7g 6v² Nov 9] close-coupled gelding: ninth foal: half-brother to 3 winners,
including 7-y-o Derryquin: dam 1m winner: easily best effort in maidens when 4 lengths
second to Harry The Hoover at Doncaster (edgy): should stay at least 1m. *M. W. Easterby*

PARKSIDE (IRE)   6 b.g. Common Grounds 118 – Warg (Dancing Brave (USA) 140) **–**
[2002 –: 10s⁶ Oct 15] one-time fairly useful performer: lightly raced nowadays.
W. R. Muir

PARKSIDE PURSUIT   4 b.g. Pursuit of Love 124 – Ivory Bride 86 (Domynsky 110) **86**
[2002 75, a–: 5m 5.1g 5m⁵ 5.7g⁶ 6g 6.1m* 6d* 6g* 6m⁵ 6d² 6m 6g 6m 6f 7.2g 6g Oct 2] **a–**
lengthy, dipped-backed gelding: fairly useful handicapper: better than ever in 2002,
winning at Nottingham, Salisbury and Ayr in summer: best at 5f/6f: acts on firm and good
to soft going (below form on soft/fibresand): often held up. *J. M. Bradley*

PARK STAR   2 b.f. (Apr 18) Gothenberg (IRE) 117 – Miriam 59 (Forzando 122) [2002 **–**
f5g³ f5g* 6.1g p5g⁵ 5d⁶ f5s f5s 7f f6s Oct 8] 33,000Y: leggy, good-topped filly: fourth foal: **a61**
half-sister to 3 winning sprinters, including 4-y-o Viewforth and 5-y-o United Passion:
dam 5f winner, including at 2 yrs: modest performer: won maiden at Southwell in May:
well held last 5 starts: best at 5f: acts on all-weather, little form on turf: tried visored.
D. Shaw

PARK STREET (USA)   2 b.c. (Jan 28) Mr Prospector (USA) – Sunlit Silence (USA) **81 p**
(Trempolino (USA) 135) [2002 p6g³ Dec 28] $475,000Y: second foal: dam, 6f to 8.5f
winner in USA, half-sister to US Grade 3 6.5f winner Madame Pandit: evens, promising
2-length third of 11 to Wages in maiden at Lingfield, bumped start and taking while to
settle before running on well: sure to improve and should win similar event. *G. A. Butler*

PARLIGHT   3 b.f. Woodborough (USA) 112 – Skedaddle 57 (Formidable (USA) 125) **40**
[2002 f8g³ f7g f7g 9.9g 8m 10d Oct 28] 2,000F, 800Y: workmanlike filly: second foal:
dam, maiden, stayed 1¼m: poor maiden: visored/blinkered last 3 starts (found little final
one). *K. R. Burke*

PARNASSIAN   2 ch.g. (Mar 16) Sabrehill (USA) 120 – Delphic Way 63 (Warning 136) **65**
[2002 5.1d⁴ 5.1g⁶ 6m 7m 7s³ 7v Nov 9] angular gelding: first foal: dam, disappointing
maiden, half-sister to 4-y-o Palace Affair: fair maiden: best effort when staying-on third
to Chin Chin in nursery at Newbury: will be well suited by at least 1m: acts on soft
ground. *G. B. Balding*

PARSIFAL   3 b.c. Sadler's Wells (USA) 132 – Moss (USA) (Woodman (USA) 126) **67**
[2002 85: 10.5d⁴ 10m 14.1m⁴ 14.1m f12g Oct 21] rangy colt: has a quick action: fair
maiden: left L. Cumani after second start: stays 10.5f: acts on good to soft going: sold
7,500 gns. *J. G. Given*

PARTING SHOT   4 b.g. Young Ern 120 – Tribal Lady 80 (Absalom 128) [2002 71: **83**
7m 7.5g 7g⁶ 7g² 7.5m* 7f⁵ 7m 7.5d 7g 7.5m 7m⁶ 8.5g² 7.5m⁴ 9d* 8s* 8v⁵ Nov 8] quite
good-topped gelding: fairly useful handicapper: won at Beverley, Redcar and Musselburgh in 2002, improved effort on last-named course: stays 9f: acts on any going: usually
races prominently. *T. D. Easterby*

PARTY PLOY   4 b.g. Deploy 131 – Party Treat (IRE) 69 (Millfontaine 114) [2002 74: **65**
12m 13.1g³ 12.4s³ 11.9d³ 13s² 12.1d² 13.1g² p12g⁶ 10.9g⁵ Sep 19] small gelding: poor
mover: fair handicapper: barely stays testing 1¾m: acts on soft going, good to firm and
all-weather: visored last 4 starts (found little first 3 occasions). *K. R. Burke*

PASADA LLAMADA   3 b.g. College Chapel 122 – First Play 59 (Primo Dominie **–**
121) [2002 –: f7g 10.9d Aug 2] workmanlike gelding: no form. *J. R. Weymes*

PAS DE PROBLEME (IRE) 6 ch.g. Ela-Mana-Mou 132 – Torriglia (USA) (Nijinsky – (CAN) 138) [2002 61: 12.3g⁶ 12.3m 16.5g Jul 11] sparely-made gelding: modest handicapper at 5 yrs: well held in 2002. *A. L. Forbes*

PAS DE SURPRISE 4 b.g. Dancing Spree (USA) – Supreme Rose 95 (Frimley Park **63** 109) [2002 68: 7g² 8g³ 8.3m⁶ 7m 7m 7.1g p7g Dec 28] modest maiden handicapper: effective at 7f/1m: acts on polytrack, good to firm and good to soft going: blinkered once at 3 yrs. *J. G. Portman*

PASITHEA (IRE) 4 b.f. Celtic Swing 138 – Midnight's Reward 84 (Night Shift **101** (USA)) [2002 90: 10.5m³ 10.4f² 10g* 10.1d 10.3m³ 10.4m 12g³ Jul 20] leggy, useful-looking filly: has a quick action: useful performer: won handicap at Ayr in May by 2 lengths from Altay: best effort when fourth (promoted) to dead-heaters Marani and Frosty Welcome in listed event at Newmarket final start, making running: effective at 1¼m/ 1½m: acts on any going: usually held up. *T. D. Easterby*

PASO DOBLE 4 b.g. Dancing Spree (USA) – Delta Tempo (IRE) (Bluebird (USA) **67** 125) [2002 77: 8g 6d f9.4g⁵ p7g⁶ Dec 28] fair maiden handicapper: stays 1m: acts on firm going and polytrack: usually races prominently. *B. R. Millman*

PASSANDO 2 b.f. (Feb 10) Kris 135 – Iota 83 (Niniski (USA) 125) [2002 7g Oct 2] **– p** 7,500Y: third foal: dam 14.6f to 2m winner: 33/1 and green, well-held eighth of 9 in minor event at Salisbury: should do better at 1¼m+. *I. A. Balding*

PASSA NOVA (IRE) 2 b.g. (Apr 7) Mujadil (USA) 119 – Passing Beauty 83 (Green **64** Desert (USA) 127) [2002 5m⁶ 6m 6m³ 7.5g Aug 15] IR 26,000F, 16,500Y: strong, lengthy gelding: has scope: has a quick action: first foal: dam 1m winner in France: modest maiden: visored, third at Newcastle, best effort: should stay 7f: sold 3,200 gns, sent to Kuwait. *Mrs J. R. Ramsden*

PASSE PIED 2 gr.g. (Apr 19) Linamix (FR) 127 – La Fazenda (Warning 136) [2002 – 8m⁶ 7g 7g Sep 10] workmanlike gelding: first foal: dam unraced half-sister to 2 useful performers up to 1¾m in France out of smart Spanish filly Teresa (winner of Spanish 1000 Guineas and Oaks): well held in maidens/seller. *S. C. Williams*

PASSERINE 4 b.f. Distant Relative 128 – Oare Sparrow 75 (Night Shift (USA)) [2002 – 57d: 6d 5m 10m Apr 27] smallish, good-topped filly: modest maiden at best: no form in 2002: tried blinkered. *J. R. Weymes*

PASSING GLANCE 3 b.c. Polar Falcon (USA) 126 – Spurned (USA) 91 (Robellino **101** (USA) 127) [2002 94p: p8g 9g⁴ 8.3g³ 9.9g⁵ 9g* 8m 9.9m 9m³ 8m² 8m⁴ 7.1f³ 8f* 7.9f³ 8s⁴ Nov 2] tall, rather leggy colt: useful performer: won handicap at Goodwood (beat Imbibing by ¾ length) in May and minor event at Newmarket (beat Finished Article by 2 lengths) in October: ran at least respectably most other starts: effective at 7f, barely at 1¼m: acts on firm and soft going, well held only start on polytrack: front runner: has worn crossed noseband/carried head awkwardly: consistent. *I. A. Balding*

PASSING INTEREST (USA) 3 b.c. Defensive Play (USA) 118 – Intimate (USA) **76** (Topsider (USA)) [2002 p10g 12d² 12s⁶ 12s Nov 1] close-coupled colt: easy mover: third foal: dam, 6f/6.5f winner in USA at 4 yrs, half-sister to dam of smart 1998 2-y-o 7f winner Auction House: best effort in maidens when second at Kempton: left Mrs A. Perrett 42,000 gns after and trained next start only by R. Hannon: stays 1½m. *D. T. Hughes, Ireland*

PASSIONATE 2 b.f. (Feb 6) Woodborough (USA) 112 – Runs In The Family 69 **56** (Distant Relative 128) [2002 5m 5g 6m⁴ 6m² 5g⁵ 6g⁴ 7g 6d 8g 7d⁵ p8g Nov 23] 2,400Y: smallish, sturdy filly: first foal: dam 5f and (at 2 yrs) 6f winner: modest maiden: best form at 5f/6f: unraced on extremes of going on turf: sometimes slowly away/hangs: none too consistent. *Mrs P. N. Dutfield*

PASSION FOR LIFE 9 br.g. Charmer 123 – Party Game 70 (Red Alert 127) [2002 **– §** 86§: 6g 6m 7m 6m 6d 6m 6d Oct 14] good-topped gelding: unimpressive mover: fairly useful handicapper in 2001: little form in 2002: tried blinkered earlier in career: temperamental. *J. Akehurst*

PASTEL 3 ch.f. Lion Cavern (USA) 117 – Dancing Spirit (IRE) 72 (Ahonoora 122) **82** [2002 95: 7m⁶ 6d 6m⁵ May 6] smallish, close-coupled filly: has a quick action: useful at 2 yrs: just fairly useful in 2002: effective at 5f/6f: yet to race on extremes of going: seems effective blinkered or not: races prominently. *B. J. Meehan*

PASTICHE 8 b.m. Kylian (USA) – Titian Beauty (Auction Ring (USA) 123) [2002 –: – f8g f9.4s May 13] modest winner in 1997: produced a foal in 1999: no form since: tried visored. *Mrs L. C. Jewell*

PATAVELLIAN (IRE)   4 b.g. Machiavellian (USA) 123 – Alessia 91 (Caerleon   **91**
(USA) 132) [2002 71: 7m³ 8.1m³ 9s 10.2d p10g 7.1g* 7.1g* 6f* Oct 4] tall, sparely-made
gelding: fairly useful performer: blinkered when winning handicap and minor event at
Chepstow and handicap at Newmarket (beat Eyecatcher by 2½ lengths) in autumn:
effective at 6f/7f: acts on firm going: sweating/edgy/leery at Newmarket: tends to race
freely: much improved. *R. Charlton*

PATAVIUM PRINCESS (IRE)   2 ch.f. (Apr 2) Titus Livius (FR) 115 – Goodnight   **80**
Girl (IRE) (Alzao (USA) 117) [2002 f5g* 5m² 5m³ 5m* Jul 13] 6,200Y: rather leggy,
useful-looking filly: fifth foal: half-sister to winners in Italy by Imp Society (5f to 7f) and
Namaqualand (1m/9f): dam unraced: fairly useful form: won maiden at Southwell in
April and nursery at York in July: off 2 months (reportedly had sore shins), beat Frascati
by ½ length in latter, drifting left: will stay 6f: acts on fibresand, raced only on good to
firm going on turf. *T. D. Easterby*

PATH OF HONOUR (IRE)   3 b.f. Marju (IRE) 127 – Zorilla (Belmez (USA) 131)   **35**
[2002 –: 11.1g 8.2g⁶ 12.1g 8.3v 12m Jul 1] poor maiden. *M. Johnston*

PATIENTES VIRTIS   3 ch.f. Lion Cavern (USA) 117 – Alzianah 102 (Alzao (USA)   **–**
117) [2002 –: f6g² p7g⁶ 5d 6g p6g f6g² f6g³ f6g* 5.9g f6g f6g f8.5s⁶ Dec 13] angular   **a67**
filly: fair handicapper: won at Wolverhampton (flashed tail) in July: well below form
after: best efforts at 6f: acts on all-weather, no form on turf. *Miss Gay Kelleway*

PATRICIAN FOX (IRE)   4 b.f. Nicolotte 118 – Peace Mission (Dunbeath (USA)   **59 §**
127) [2002 67§, a–§: 5m 5g 5m³ 5g 5s⁵ Jun 26] rather unfurnished filly: unimpressive
mover: modest handicapper: stays 6f: acts on any turf going, probably on fibresand: tried
visored/tongue tied: unreliable. *J. J. Quinn*

PATRICIA PHILOMENA (IRE)   4 br.f. Prince of Birds (USA) 121 – Jeewan 82   **58**
(Touching Wood (USA) 127) [2002 59: f8s f9.4g 7d⁵ 8f 7f⁶ 8f 8f 12m⁶ 10.9g* 12d² 12m²   **a–**
11s⁴ 12.1m³ 14.1m² 16m* 15.8f⁴ 17.1f⁶ 16v⁶ p13g Nov 13] leggy, close-coupled filly:
modest performer: won seller at Ayr (dead-heated) in July and handicap at Musselburgh
in September: stays 17f: acts on firm and soft going. *T. D. Barron*

PATRICKS DAY   2 b.c. (Mar 4) Wizard King 122 – Honour And Glory 46 (Hotfoot   **–**
126) [2002 6f 7d f8.5g Nov 15] workmanlike colt: sixth foal: half-brother to unreliable 6f
selling winner Unfortunate (by Komaite): dam, poor maiden, half-sister to smart sprinter
Singing Steven: well held in maidens/claimer: looked headstrong second start, tongue
tied third one. *J. Balding*

PATRIVALOR (USA)   4 b.g. Diesis 133 – False Image (USA) 79 (Danzig (USA))   **55 §**
[2002 57: p8g⁵ p7g⁶ 8f⁴ 7.1m⁴ 7f 7.1d 8g³ 7m 8m Sep 19] strong, sturdy gelding: modest
maiden: stays 1m: acts on polytrack and firm going: blinkered/tongue tied: finds little:
can't be trusted: sold 800 gns. *M. Dods*

PATSEA   3 b.f. Puissance 110 – Alana's Ballad (IRE) (Be My Native (USA) 122) [2002   **–**
f6g f5g 6.1m Jul 13] 850Y: first foal: dam of little account: no form in sellers/claimer.
B. P. J. Baugh

PAT'S MIRACLE (IRE)   2 ch.f. (Feb 12) College Chapel 122 – Exemplaire (FR)   **43**
(Polish Precedent (USA) 131) [2002 6m 7g 6m⁴ Aug 9] second foal: dam placed up to 11f
in France: form in sellers only when 9 lengths fourth to Queens Jubilee at Lingfield:
should stay 7f. *John Berry*

PATSY CULSYTH   7 b.m. Tragic Role (USA) – Regal Salute 68 (Dara Monarch 128)   **54**
[2002 52, a–: 5m 7m 7f 5.9d 6.1m 7.2d⁴ 6.9s⁵ 8.5d² Aug 14] useful-looking mare: modest   **a–**
performer: effective at 5f (given test) to 8.5f: acts on any turf going, well held on
fibresand: usually visored prior to last 4 starts. *Don Enrico Incisa*

PATSY'S DOUBLE   4 b.g. Emarati (USA) 74 – Jungle Rose 90 (Shirley Heights 130)   **107**
[2002 112: 7m⁴ 7.1d² 6d² 7.1s² 6m 7f² 7f³ 7m 7m⁵ 7f² 7.5m² 7s⁵ Oct 28] tall, useful-
looking gelding: unimpressive mover: useful performer: runner-up 6 times in 2002,
including in listed races at Haydock (beaten 1½ lengths by Reel Buddy and ½ length by
Warningford on second/fourth starts), Supreme Stakes at Goodwood (beaten 2½ lengths
by Firebreak on tenth) and Concorde Stakes at Tipperary (beaten head by Marionnaud on
eleventh): effective at 6f to 7.5f: acts on firm and soft going: tends to sweat: races
prominently: consistent. *M. Blanshard*

PAULA LANE   2 b.f. (Mar 10) Factual (USA) 108 – Colfax Classic 48 (Jareer (USA)   **54**
115) [2002 5.1m⁶ 6d 6s 7d p8g² f8.5g³ Dec 2] second reported foal: dam 7f winner:

modest maiden: placed in seller/nursery: should stay 1¼m: best efforts on all-weather. *R. Curtis*

PAULA'S PRIDE   4 ch.f. Pivotal 124 – Sharp Top 62 (Sharpo 132) [2002 74d: 9.7d*   **69** 12d p10g6 Dec 18] strong filly: fair handicapper: won at Folkestone in July: stays 1¼m: **a76** acts on polytrack, firm and soft going: blinkered (ran poorly) once at 3 yrs: sometimes finds little: none too consistent. *J. R. Best*

PAULUKE   3 b.f. Bishop of Cashel 122 – Beacon Blaze 85 (Rudimentary (USA) 118) –   **–** [2002 12g 11.9d 10.2s5 14.1g 11.7g Oct 16] 600F, 3,000 2-y-o: good-topped filly: first foal: dam, 1m winner, half-sister to useful performer up to 1½m Clever Cliche: little form: tried blinkered: has refused to enter stall. *N. J. Hawke*

PAVEMENT GATES   2 b.f. (Mar 13) Bishop of Cashel 122 – Very Bold 57 (Never   **71** So Bold 135) [2002 5d6 6f3 6v* 5.9m 6m4 7f 8s Oct 15] leggy filly: fifth foal: half-sister to Italian winner up to 11f Rainbow King (by Puissance): dam 5f winner: fair performer: won maiden at Hamilton in June: should stay beyond 6f: acts on any turf ground. *W. M. Brisbourne*

PAVLA (USA)   5 ch.m. St Jovite (USA) 135 – Big E Dream (USA) (Persian Bold 123)   **58** [2002 62: 8s 12d 13s4 14d 13m4 16d 12d 14v5 16d 16d 11.9f6 12d 12f4 13.5f* 14g 13m 12g f14.8g Nov 30] modest handicapper: won at Fairyhouse in September: well held at Wolverhampton final start: stays 13.5f: acts on firm and soft going: has run well blinkered (not tried for long time). *Edward Sexton, Ireland*

PAWAN (IRE)   2 ch.c. (May 6) Cadeaux Genereux 131 – Born To Glamour (Ajdal   **80** (USA) 130) [2002 7m4 Jul 4] half-brother to several winners, including 6-y-o Sailing Shoes and fairly useful Irish 2001 2-y-o 7.5f winner Hot Trotter (by Halling): dam Irish 2-y-o 6f winner: 33/1 and green, 2 lengths fourth of 13 to Hilbre Island in maiden at Newbury, staying on from rear. *E. A. L. Dunlop*

PAWN BROKER   5 ch.g. Selkirk (USA) 129 – Dime Bag 87 (High Line 125) [2002   **– §** 116§: 10d6 12s5 Jun 7] tall, leggy, angular gelding: smart performer at best: well held in Gordon Richards Stakes at Sandown and Coronation Cup at Epsom in 2002: stays 1½m: acts on any going: tends to find little: blinkered last 2 starts in 2001: one to leave alone nowadays. *D. R. C. Elsworth*

PAWN IN LIFE (IRE)   4 b.g. Midhish 109 – Lady-Mumtaz (Martin John) [2002 67+:   **–** p6g f6g 6s f6g 6g 6s f6s f6s* f6g f6g5 f7g3 Dec 17] lengthy gelding: modest handicapper: **a62 +** won at Southwell in October: stays 7f: acts on all-weather, no form on turf: reared violently just before stall opened on reappearance, slowly away next time. *T. D. Barron*

PAX   5 ch.g. Brief Truce (USA) 126 – Child's Play (USA) (Sharpen Up 127) [2002 –: 5s   **83** 6m* 7f2 6m* 6f 5f3 6f2 6g 6m5 6d* 6m 5m 6g5 6f Oct 4] tall gelding: fairly useful handicapper: won at Southwell and Leicester in April and Pontefract in July: probably best at 6f/easy 7f: acts on firm and good to soft going: often blinkered in 2001. *D. Nicholls*

PAYS D'AMOUR (IRE)   5 b.h. Pursuit of Love 124 – Lady of The Land 75 (Wollow   **84 d** 132) [2002 94: 6g5 6m 6m 6d4 6g6 7m 7m 7m 5g 6d p7g6 Oct 16] strong horse: unimpressive mover: fairly useful handicapper at best: on the downgrade in 2002: best at 6f/7f: acts on firm and soft going: usually races prominently: sold 8,500 gns. *R. Hannon*

PAY THE SILVER   4 gr.g. Petong 126 – Marjorie's Memory (IRE) 76 (Fairy King   **81** (USA) 80, a75: p10g6 p12g f12g5 f9.4g 10g 10d 10m 9m* 10.1d5 10.1g2 9m3   **a64** 9.9g 10.1m4 8.5d* 10f 9g4 10d Oct 14] close-coupled, good-bodied gelding: fairly useful handicapper on turf, modest on all-weather: left A. Jarvis after fourth start: won at Goodwood in June (amateurs, edged left) and Epsom in September: best at 9f/1¼m: acts on good to firm going, soft and polytrack (probably on fibresand): tried visored: often races freely (usually held up). *I. A. Wood*

PAY TIME   3 ch.f. Timeless Times (USA) 99 – Payvashooz 78 (Ballacashtal (CAN))   **–** [2002 58: f5g6 5d 5d6 6g f6g Nov 20] modest maiden at 2 yrs: little form in 2002: tried tongue tied: reared as stall opened second outing. *M. Brittain*

PEACE   2 b.f. (Feb 5) Sadler's Wells (USA) 132 – Virtuous 92 (Exit To Nowhere   **78 P** (USA) 122) [2002 8.3d3 Oct 28] first foal: dam, 2-y-o 1m winner who stayed 11.5f, out of half-sister to 2000 Guineas winner Entrepreneur (by Sadler's Wells): 5/1, shaped most promisingly when narrowly-beaten third of 12 to Desert View in maiden at Windsor, travelling well and staying on under hands and heels having been hampered and carried left: will stay at least 1¼m: sure to improve considerably and win races. *J. R. Fanshawe*

Willmott Dixon Cornwallis Stakes, Ascot—Peace Offering (left), the least exposed member of the field, beats Speed Cop (noseband), Revenue (armlets), Fancy Lady (right) and Folio (breastgirth)

PEACE FLAG (USA)   2 ch.f. (Feb 28) Gold Fever (USA) 119 – Fold The Flag (USA)   **82 p**
(Raja Baba (USA)) [2002 6m³ 7g* Oct 18] $50,000F: quite-good topped filly: half-sister to several winners in USA: dam, 6f (including at 2 yrs) to 7f (minor stakes) winner in USA, half-sister to smart filly up to 1¼m Flagbird and US Grade 1 winners Prospectors Delite and Runup The Colors: shaped well when third to Illustria in maiden at Newbury: landed odds in slowly-run 4-runner Newmarket Challenge Cup 2½ months later by neck from Thingmebob, dictating pace but still looking green and all out having edged right: withdrawn after refusing to enter stall in between: will probably stay 1m: remains capable of better. *J. H. M. Gosden*

PEACE IN THE VALLEY   2 ch.f. (Feb 2) Timeless Times (USA) 99 – Fort Vally 58   **48**
(Belfort (FR) 89) [2002 6m 5m 6d 6f⁵ Sep 21] lengthy, plain filly: fourth foal: sister to 7f winner Time Vally: dam 1m/9f winner: poor maiden: should stay 7f: acts on firm ground: sold 1,200 gns, sent to Israel. *A. Berry*

PEACE KEEPER (IRE)   2 b.g. (Mar 6) Bahhare (USA) 122 – Break For Peace   **73**
(IRE) 65 (Brief Truce (USA) 126) [2002 5m⁵ 5.2f⁴ 5m³ 7g 6g⁴ Oct 21] IR 31,000Y, 18,000 2-y-o: quite attractive gelding: first foal: dam, sprint maiden, half-sister to useful Irish 5f performer Soreze: fair maiden: stays 6f: acts on fibresand, raced only on good going or firmer on turf: worked up in preliminaries (threw rider leaving paddock) on debut, led most of way to start next time: slowly away last 2 outings: sold 10,000 gns. *W. Jarvis*

PEACE OFFERING (IRE)   2 b.c. (Apr 28) Victory Note (USA) 120 – Amnesty   **105 p**
Bay 63 (Thatching 131) [2002 6g 5m* 5m* Oct 12] IR 8,000Y: 20,000 2-y-o: second foal: dam won 1m seller: progressive type: won maiden at Sandown in September and 11-runner Willmott Dixon Cornwallis Stakes at Ascot in October: 8/1 and still green, beat Speed Cop by ½ length in latter, travelling well just off pace and getting on top final 1f despite hanging markedly right: will prove best at 5f/6f: hung left on debut: should make a smart 3-y-o and win more races. *T. G. Mills*

PEAK PARK (USA)   2 b. or br.c. (Feb 23) Dynaformer (USA) – Play Po (USA) (Play   **–**
On (USA)) [2002 7f Sep 21] $35,000Y: third foal: half-brother to a winner in US by Brocco: dam, 8.5f/9f winner in US, half-sister to US Grade 2 6f winner (also second in 7f Grade 1 event) Penny's Reshoot: 33/1, always rear in maiden at Newbury. *J. A. R. Toller*

PEAK PRACTICE   4 b.f. Saddlers' Hall (IRE) 126 – High Habit 79 (Slip Anchor   **–**
136) [2002 –: 11.8g Apr 4] well held in maidens: headstrong. *J. J. Bridger*

PEARL DANCE (USA)   2 b.f. (May 21) Nureyev (USA) 131 – Ocean Jewel (USA)   **102**
(Alleged (USA) 138) [2002 6d* 6m³ 6d³ 7g³ 8g⁴ Oct 6] $290,000Y: sturdy filly: has a quick action: half-sister to several winners, including useful German performer up to 2m Ocean Sea (by Bering) and fairly useful 1½m winner Tjinouska (by Cozzene): dam unraced: useful performer: won maiden at Goodwood in May: close third in Cherry Hinton Stakes at Newmarket (to Spinola) and Moyglare Stud Stakes at the Curragh (to Mail The Desert) and about 7 lengths fourth in Prix Marcel Boussac at Longchamp (behind Six Perfections) last 3 starts: will probably stay 1¼m: yet to race on extremes of going. *J. H. M. Gosden*

PEARLY BROOKS   4 b.f. Efisio 120 – Elkie Brooks 82 (Relkino 131) [2002 77:   **68**
6.1m² 7f 6m f6s f6g³ Dec 10] sturdy filly: fair performer, lightly raced: left R. White after fourth outing: should stay 7f: acts on good to firm going, probably on soft and fibresand. *T. J. Naughton*

736

Mr George Strawbridge's "Pearl Dance"

PEARLY GATES (IRE) 4 b.f. Night Shift (USA) – Pearl Shell (USA) (Bering 136) **95** [2002 104: 6m Apr 16] neat filly: useful performer: eighth of 9 in listed contest at Newmarket only 4-y-o start: stays 7f: acts on good to firm and good to soft going (ran poorly on soft). *G. A. Butler*

PEARLY SHELLS 3 b.f. Efisio 120 – Piffle 87 (Shirley Heights 130) [2002 8g² **121** 10.5g* 10g* 12m* 10g* 12m* Sep 15]

Pau-based trainer Francois Rohaut enjoyed a memorable season thanks mainly to the exploits of a couple of three-year-old fillies whose careers had begun with a defeat in the French Provinces early on in the year. By summer's end Pearly Shells and Turtle Bow were performing successfully on a far bigger stage and had conquered Deauville, Longchamp and Saint-Cloud, a far cry from La Teste de Buch and Mont-de-Marsan where they had made their respective debuts. Turtle Bow developed into a smart filly and won five races, including the Prix Cleopatre and Prix d'Astarte, but Pearly Shells, who also won five times, turned out even better.

Pearly Shells, a late developer according to her trainer, never stopped improving and was unbeaten after her first outing. Staying in the Provinces to win a maiden at Dax and a listed event at Marseille Borely, both in May, Pearly Shells made her first appearance on the Parisian circuit the following month, in the Group 2 Prix de Malleret at Saint-Cloud. Tackling a mile and a half for the first time, Pearly Shells edged ahead a furlong and a half from home and kept on gamely to hold on by a short neck from Ana Marie. On her previous start Ana Marie had finished fourth, half a length and one place behind Turtle Bow, in the Prix de Diane,

737

Prix de la Nonette Royal Barriere, Deauville—the progressive Pearly Shells has two lengths to spare over the Prix de Diane runner-up Dance Routine, with the grey Marotta third

although the placings were reversed following the latter's demotion. Pearly Shells faced at least as stiff a task on her next outing, in the Prix de la Nonette Royal Barriere at Deauville in August, even though the race was a Group 3 event. With pattern-race winners escaping penalties it also attracted the Prix de Royaumont winner Dance Routine and the Prix Saint-Alary winner Marotta, who had also finished second and fifth respectively in the Prix de Diane. Pearly Shells was not at all inconvenienced by the step back to a mile and a quarter and put that pair firmly in their place, taking up the running over a furlong out and running on strongly to win by two lengths from Dance Routine, with Marotta half a length back in third. Having already taken care of the second, third, fourth and fifth from the Prix de Diane, Pearly Shells was sent off favourite to overcome its winner, Bright Sky, and nine others, including Ana Marie, in the Prix Vermeille - Hermitage Barriere de la Baule at Longchamp in September. She did so in decisive fashion, and in a time which was a record for the race. While Bright Sky was tackling a distance as far as a mile and a half for the first time and couldn't sustain her effort in the straight, Pearly Shells ran on strongly in pursuit of Ana Marie, who had taken it up around two furlongs out. Collaring the leader well inside the final furlong, Pearly Shells had put a length and a half between them on reaching the line, where she was three and a half lengths clear of third-placed Bright Sky. Pearly Shells, still very much on the upgrade, wasn't entered for the Prix de l'Arc de Triomphe, but she now looked well worth her place in the field and initially connections favoured supplementing her for the race. However, they eventually decided against it and Pearly Shells was retired for the season. She is to stay in training, though, and reportedly the Arc will be her main target in 2003.

Pearly Shells (b.f. 1999)	Efisio (b 1982)	Formidable (b 1975)	Forli
			Native Partner
		Eldoret (b 1976)	High Top
			Bamburi
	Piffle (b 1984)	Shirley Heights (b 1975)	Mill Reef
			Hardiemma
		Fiddle-Faddle (b 1976)	Silly Season
			Fiddlededee

Pearly Shells' story can hardly be described as a rags to riches one given that it had taken a bid of IR 265,000 guineas to secure her at the Goffs Orby Sale in 2000, a figure which far exceeded anything that had been paid previously for a yearling by Efisio. Efisio, though hardly fashionable, has done quite well at stud given the opportunities he's had. He stayed a mile but his only Group 1 winners prior to Pearly Shells, namely Hever Golf Rose, Pips Pride and Tomba, were better at shorter. Pearly Shells has made up into a lengthy, good-topped individual and she must have taken the eye in the sale-ring; her pedigree on the dam's side, where there is stamina, would also have made plenty of appeal to prospective purchasers. The dam Piffle had already been responsible for three winners from five previous foals including Frenchpark (by Fools Holme), a smart performer at up to a mile and a half in both Europe and the USA who gained his most notable victory in the 1994 Hollywood Turf Cup. Piffle herself raced five times in Britain for John Dunlop, winning a mile-and-a-half minor event at Salisbury and also showing fairly useful form at two miles before being sold for 31,000 guineas at the 1987 December Sales. Piffle's full brother El Conquistador was a thorough stayer, and a useful one at that, probably best known for having unseated his rider when bumped two furlongs out

738

Prix Vermeille - Hermitage Barriere de la Baule, Longchamp—
Pearly Shells gains her fifth successive victory, drawing away from Ana Marie (rail), Bright Sky (noseband),
Guadalupe (third left) and Albanova (right)

by Royal Gait in the 1988 Gold Cup, leading to Royal Gait's controversial disqualification. Their dam Fiddle-Faddle, a fairly useful winner at up to two miles, is a daughter of the Park Hill Stakes third Fiddlededee and a half-sister to the Cesarewitch and Irish St Leger winner Mountain Lodge, the last named the dam of the 2000 Gold Cup third Compton Ace. Pearly Shells, raced only on good and good to firm ground, still has some improvement to find if she is to fare anything like so well in 2003, when she will also have to compete with the colts. *F. Rohaut, France*

PEARSON GLEN (IRE) 3 ch.g. Dolphin Street (FR) 125 – Glendora (Glenstal (USA) 118) [2002 8g⁶ 9m* 7.9g 10f 7.9g 11m⁵ 9d⁵ 10m² Sep 5] IR 3,000F, IR 4,500Y (twice), 15,000 2-y-o, resold 2,500 2-y-o: good-topped gelding: half-brother to Irish 7f winner Caduga (by Dancing Dissident) and 3 winners abroad: dam ran 3 times in Ireland: fair performer: won maiden at Musselburgh (drifted left) in April: effective at 9f to 11f: acts on good to firm and good to soft going. *G. A. Swinbank* **65**

PEARTREE HOUSE (IRE) 8 b.g. Simply Majestic (USA) – Fashion Front (Habitat 134) [2002 94: 10.4f 8.5d f8.5g Jul 26] rangy gelding: fairly useful handicapper in 2001: well held on Flat in 2002: tried visored: successful over hurdles in August. *Mrs M. Reveley* **–**

PEASE BLOSSOM (IRE) 3 b.f. Revoque (IRE) 122 – Saneena 80 (Kris 135) [2002 63: 8.2d⁵ 9.2g⁵ p12g⁶ 11.8g⁵ 12.1d⁵ 10.9g 11.5s² Oct 22] tall, useful-looking filly: modest maiden: should stay 1½m: acts on soft going, probably on polytrack: sold 6,000 gns, joined T. McCourt in Ireland. *M. H. Tompkins* **63**

PEDLER'S PROFILES 2 br.g. (May 5) Topanoora 118 – La Vie En Primrose 104 (Henbit (USA) 130) [2002 7.1g 6s Oct 25] 6,500 2-y-o: rather dipped-backed gelding: half-brother to winning stayer Influence Pedler (by Keen): dam 1¼m winner: well held in maidens. *Miss K. M. George* **104**

PEDRO JACK (IRE) 5 b.g. Mujadil (USA) 119 – Festival of Light (High Top 131) [2002 76, a85: f6g⁶ f6g⁶ f6g* f6g 6f⁴ 6m 6m³ 6m² 6f 6m 6g⁴ 6f³ 6f² f6g⁴ f6g⁴ p7g Dec 14] tall gelding: fairly useful handicapper: won at Wolverhampton in February: best around 6f: acts on all-weather, best on good ground or firmer on turf: tried blinkered/visored/tongue tied: sometimes slowly away (very reluctant to race when tailed off final start): temperament under suspicion. *B. J. Meehan* **86**
a89

PEGGY LOU 2 b.f. (Mar 17) Washington State (USA) – Rosemary Nalden (Great Commotion (USA) 123) [2002 5.7g 8.1g f8s 8d Nov 1] first foal: dam unraced: little promise in maidens/nursery. *J. Neville* **–**

PELLI 4 b.f. Saddlers' Hall (IRE) 126 – Pellinora (USA) (King Pellinore (USA) 127) [2002 37: f7g f8g f11g Mar 12] workmanlike filly: has a round action: maiden: no form in 2002. *P. Howling* **–**

PENELEWEY 2 b.f. (Mar 25) Groom Dancer (USA) 128 – Peryllys 67 (Warning 136) [2002 6m⁶ 7m³ Aug 29] fourth foal: half-sister to 5-y-o Honest Warning and a winner in Belgium by Primo Dominie: dam, maiden who stayed 1m, half-sister to smart sprinter Cragside: fair form in maidens, third to High Praise at Salisbury: will need to settle better to stay 1m. *H. Candy* **67**

PENERAK 2 b.c. (Feb 26) Primo Dominie 121 – Ansellady 67 (Absalom 128) [2002 –
5.1m 7.1g f5g Dec 4] 800F, 3,000 2-y-o: fourth foal: half-brother to 2000 2-y-o 5f winner
Miss Verity (by Factual): dam 6f winner: well held in sellers/maiden. *A. G. Juckes*

PENGUIN BAY 6 b.g. Rock Hopper 124 – Corn Lily 78 (Aragon 118) [2002 73d: **53**
11m⁴ 12m 16m 10g f14s Sep 17] modest maiden: left Mrs M. Reveley after third start:
should stay 2m: acts on firm going: tried tongue tied. *N. Wilson*

PENNEECK 2 ch.c. (May 22) Pennekamp (USA) 130 – Orange Hill 75 (High Top –
131) [2002 7s 8v Nov 8] 14,000Y: sturdy colt: half-brother to 3 winners, including 7f (at
2 yrs) and 1¼m winner Jackson Hill (by Priolo) and 1½m and 15f winner Old Provence
(by Rainbow Quest): dam won Cesarewitch: well beaten in maidens. *N. A. Graham*

PENNELESS DANCER 3 b.g. Pennekamp (USA) 130 – Villella (Sadler's Wells **59**
(USA) 132) [2002 69: f9.4g⁴ f7g 7f 8s⁵ 7d³ 7m Aug 23] modest maiden: stays 7f: acts
on fibresand, good to firm and good to soft going: tends to edge left: sold £4,500.
M. Blanshard

PEN NOTE 2 b.g. (Apr 10) Victory Note (USA) 120 – Penny Hasset 73 (Lochnager –
132) [2002 5f May 11] 3,500Y: sixth foal: half-brother to fairly useful 1999 2-y-o 5f/6f
winner Happy Times (by Timeless Times): dam 5f/6f winner: 25/1, well beaten in claimer
at Thirsk. *M. W. Easterby*

PENNY CROSS 2 b.f. (Mar 18) Efisio 120 – Addaya (IRE) (Persian Bold 123) [2002 **69 p**
6d⁴ Nov 1] good-topped filly: has scope: fourth foal: half-sister to 4-y-o Priors Lodge:
dam once-raced daughter of half-sister to smart 7f/1m performer Hadeer: 25/1, 6½
lengths fourth of 17 to Tante Rose in maiden at Newmarket, keeping on without being
knocked about: should do better. *M. Johnston*

PENNY HA'PENNY 3 b.f. Bishop of Cashel 122 – Madam Millie 99 (Milford 119) **80**
[2002 51: 6m⁵ 6s² 5v⁴ 5d⁵ 5m² 6s 5g* 5m* 5f 5d* Oct 14] tall, lengthy filly: fairly useful
performer: won maiden at Beverley (made all) and handicaps at Newcastle (raced alone)
and Ayr in autumn: effective at 5f/6f: acts on soft and good to firm ground: has hung left.
D. W. Barker

PENNY PASS (IRE) 3 b.g. Pennekamp (USA) 130 – Belle Etoile (FR) (Lead On Time –
(USA) 123) [2002 7.1m 7dᵈ 6.9dᵈ 10m Sep 5] 85,000Y: big, rather unfurnished gelding:
second foal: half-brother to useful Irish 1¼m winner Starlight Venture (by Hernando):
dam, French 7.5f winner, half-sister to useful French performer at 6f to 1m Matin de
Printemps: signs of a little ability in maidens first 3 starts: should be suited by 1m+:
joined M. Pipe. *Sir Mark Prescott*

PENNY PICTURES (IRE) 3 b.c. Theatrical 128 – Copper Creek 78 (Habitat 134) **96**
[2002 83: 10.5d 10g⁵ 12.3m* 12.3f² 11.7g² 11.8g³ 9.9g⁴ Aug 15] close-coupled, quite
good-topped colt: useful performer: won handicap at Ripon in June by 5 lengths from
Dalblair: creditable efforts after: stays 1½m: acts on firm going, yet to race on soft/heavy:
free-going front runner: sold 50,000 gns in October. *J. G. Given*

PENNY VALENTINE 2 ch.f. (Feb 28) My Best Valentine 122 – Precision Finish 63 **52**
(Safawan 118) [2002 5m⁶ 5d⁶ 6m f6g⁵ f6g p6g⁶ Dec 30] first foal: dam, maiden, likely to
have proved best at 1m: modest maiden: stays 6f: acts on all-weather: slowly away first 3
starts. *J. Cullinan*

PENRIC 2 b.g. (Mar 2) Marju (IRE) 127 – Nafhaat (USA) 91 (Roberto (USA) 131) **57 ?**
[2002 7m 7d 7.1m Sep 16] IR 30,000Y: neat gelding: brother to useful 7f winner
Qhazeenah and half-brother to several winners, including smart 1¼m to 14.6f (Park Hill)
winner Ranin (by Unfuwain) and useful 7f/1m winner Ghalib (by Soviet Star): dam, 1½m
winner, out of sister to US Grade 1 1¼m winner Sisterhood: modest form at best in
maidens: gave trouble at stall on debut. *C. G. Cox*

PENSACOLA (IRE) 3 b.f. Pennekamp (USA) 130 – Silly Imp (IRE) 90 (Imperial **83**
Frontier (USA) 112) [2002 8g² 12m Jun 29] 26,000F, 700,000 francs Y: rather leggy, lengthy
filly: first foal: dam, Irish 5f/7f winner who stayed 1m, half-sister to dam of Racing
Post Trophy winner Seattle Rhyme: ½-length second to Ashgar Sayyad in maiden at
Newcastle: looked likely to improve. *M. P. Tregoning*

PENSION FUND 8 b.g. Emperor Fountain 112 – Navarino Bay 102 (Averof 123) **79**
[2002 85, a77: 10f 10.5s⁴ 8.9d 9.9d 10.5v⁴ 10.1m⁵ 10.4m Sep 4] tall gelding: fair
handicapper: effective at 7f to 1¼m: unproven on heavy going, acts on any other turf and
fibresand: blinkered twice (including when racing freely/finding little penultimate start):
has been slowly away: not an easy ride. *M. W. Easterby*

*Britannia Stakes (Handicap), Royal Ascot—Pentecost puts up a useful performance
to beat Ghannam (striped cap), Shot To Fame (left) and Wing Commander (No.15)*

PENTECOST   3 ch.g. Tagula (IRE) 116 – Boughtbyphone 62 (Warning 136) [2002   **104**
90: 7m 8.1d² 8g² 8m* 8.1d⁵ 7m 8m 7.9m 8.1m Sep 15] sturdy, close-coupled gelding:
useful handicapper: 25/1, best effort when winning Britannia Stakes at Royal Ascot in
June by neck from Ghannam: probably best at 1m: yet to race on soft/heavy going, acts
on any other: visored (well held) final 2-y-o start: has been bandaged/worn dropped
noseband: sometimes slowly away: raced freely/found little final start: none too consistent. *I. A. Balding*

PENTLAND (JPN)   4 br.g. Pentire 132 – Lay Claim (USA) (Mr Prospector (USA))   **–**
[2002 84: p12g p10g f11g 8f 10.1m Aug 16] smallish, good-bodied gelding: fairly useful
performer at best: well held in 2002, leaving J. L. Eyre before final start (visored).
D. Carroll

PENWELL HILL (USA)   3 b.g. Distant View (USA) 126 – Avie's Jill (USA) (Lord   **–**
Avie (USA)) [2002 58?: 8.2d 6g 8m 10f 12f 10.9d Aug 2] quite good-topped gelding:
little form. *T. D. Barron*

PEPPERCORN (GER)   5 b.g. Big Shuffle (USA) 122 – Pasca (GER) (Lagunas)   **110**
[2002 115: 8.1d⁶ 8m 8s 8g 8s⁵ 8.5s⁴ 8d* 7d Nov 2] smallish, leggy, close-coupled
gelding: smart performer: not quite force of old for new stable in 2002 (including an
attaces Mile at Sandown on reappearance), best effort when around 1¼ lengths fifth
to Royal Dragon in Oppenheim-Meile at Cologne fifth start then won amateur event at
Fontainebleau in October: raced mainly at around 1m: acts on good to firm and heavy
ground: blinkered once at 3 yrs and final outing: third on hurdling debut in November.
F. Doumen, France

PEPPERONI (IRE)   3 b.g. Nicolotte 118 – Enchantica 67 (Timeless Times (USA)   **105**
99) [2002 96: 6f⁵ 5.1f² 6m² 5.1m⁶ Aug 19] strong, lengthy gelding: useful performer:
creditable efforts in 2002 when runner-up in handicap at Chester (beaten ½ length by
Dragon Flyer, left T. Easterby and off 3 months after) and minor event at Yarmouth
(beaten head by Mugharreb): effective at 5f/6f: raced only on good going or firmer on
turf, showed signs of promise on fibresand: races prominently: carried head awkwardly
final start: sent to Hong Kong. *J. Noseda*

PEPPER ROAD   3 ch.g. Elmaamul (USA) 125 – Floral Spark 69 (Forzando 122)   **58**
[2002 58: 5.9s 7f 8m* 8s 7.1m⁶ 8.1m 7.5m 7d Oct 18] modest handicapper: won at
Musselburgh in June: stays easy 1m: acts on firm and good to soft going: sometimes
slowly away/races freely/wanders: probably best held up. *R. Bastiman*

PEPPIATT   8 ch.g. Efisio 120 – Fleur du Val (Valiyar 129) [2002 59: f8g 7.9s 6g² 5.9s   **63**
8m⁵ 6.9g Aug 5] robust gelding: modest handicapper: effective at 6f to 7.5f: acts on any
turf going, well beaten on fibresand: tried blinkered: sometimes slowly away: none too
consistent. *N. Bycroft*

PEQUENITA   2 b.f. (Feb 14) Rudimentary (USA) 118 – Sierra Madrona (USA) (Wood-   **– p**
man (USA) 126) [2002 7m⁵ Sep 18] third foal: dam, ungenuine 3m hurdle winner,
half-sister to Oaks third Poquito Queen: weak 8/1-shot, 7¼ lengths fifth of 7 to Shuhood
in maiden at Yarmouth, not knocked about once fading: should do better. *J. G. Given*

PER AMORE (IRE)   4 ch.g. General Monash (USA) 107 – Danny's Miracle (Super-   **84**
lative 118) [2002 96: 12m⁵ Jun 26] IR 14,000Y: half-brother to several winners, including
Lordan Velvet (by Lord Americo), successful up to 11.5f in Germany/Norway: dam
unraced: fairly useful performer at 3 yrs, winning maiden at Cork and apprentice
handicap at Tipperary for K. Prendergast in Ireland: blinkered (has won over hurdles in
them), fifth in handicap at Kempton only Flat start in 2002: probably stays 1½m: acts
on soft and good to firm ground. *P. J. Hobbs*

741

PERCHANCER (IRE) 6 ch.g. Perugino (USA) 84 – Irish Hope (Nishapour (FR) 125) [2002 72§, a67§: p10g f11s f9.4g⁵ f12g f16.2g 10m* 9.9g 10m 10g⁶ 12m 10.4m 10.9g Sep 19] strong gelding: fair handicapper on turf, modest on all-weather: won at Pontefract (apprentices) in May: stays easy 11f: acts on fibresand, firm and soft ground: tried visored/blinkered: often slowly away (sometimes markedly so) held up/finds little: has hung: one to be wary of. *P. C. Haslam* **72 §** **a56 §**

PERCHANCE TO WIN 5 b.m. Pelder (IRE) 125 – French Plait (Thatching 131) [2002 67: 6.9g⁵ 8f³ 7m 7f⁶ Sep 21] modest maiden: stays 1m: acts on soft and firm going. *R. Guest* **62**

PERCY DOUGLAS 2 b.c. (Apr 14) Elmaamul (USA) 125 – Qualitair Dream 80 (Dreams To Reality (USA) 113) [2002 5d⁶ 5g⁴ 6m 5g 5m 5g 5f⁵ 5m f5g² f5g² f5g* p6g Dec 30] 2,000Y, 500 2-y-o: good-topped colt: half-brother to 6-y-o Swynford Welcome and 9-y-o Swynford Dream: dam 2-y-o 6f winner who stayed 1m: fair on balance: seemed to run very well in face of stiff tasks fourth to sixth starts: landed odds in maiden at Wolverhampton in December: will prove best at 5f/easy 6f: acts on good to firm ground and fibresand: wears cheekpieces: tends to wander. *Miss A. Stokell* **76**

PEREGIAN (IRE) 4 b.g. Eagle Eyed (USA) 111 – Mo Pheata (Petorius 117) [2002 ?: p8g³ p8g f8.5g 7m⁴ p7g Dec 30] stocky gelding: type to carry condition: fairly useful at 2 yrs, modest nowadays: stays 1m: acts on firm going, good to soft and polytrack: tried blinkered: usually races prominently: has hung. *J. Akehurst* **56**

PERESTROIKA (IRE) 4 ch.g. Ashkalani (IRE) 128 – Licentious 45 (Reprimand 122) [2002 81: 14.4m² 13.9f 16.2m 16.2d⁵ 14m f12s⁵ f14g Dec 10] leggy gelding: fairly useful handicapper at best: ran creditably on reappearance: left E. Dunlop 8,500 gns after fifth start, and ran poorly last 2: better at 1¾m than shorter, and should stay 2m: acts on firm going. *B. Ellison* **88 d**

PERFECT ECHO 3 ch.f. Lycius (USA) 124 – Perfect Timing 107 (Comedy Star (USA) 121) [2002 f7f³ f9.4g⁶ Dec 16] sister to useful 5f (at 2 yrs)/7f winner Perfect Peach, and half-sister to 6f winner Perfect Brave (by Indian Ridge) and a winner abroad by Belfort: dam sprinter: green, better effort in maidens at Wolverhampton (modest form) when third to Dundonald, slowly away: should stay 1m. *M. P. Tregoning* **53**

PERFECT EVENING (IRE) 2 b.f. (Apr 14) Sadler's Wells (USA) 132 – Ivy (USA) (Sir Ivor 135) [2002 8s Oct 26] sister to 2-y-o 7f winners Ivrea (in 1989) and Iviza (in 1992), both later useful at 1¼m/1½m, and half-sister to 3 winners, notably smart Oaks d'Italia winner Ivyanna (by Reference Point): dam placed twice at 2 yrs in USA: 25/1, last in maiden at Newbury. *J. W. Hills* –

PERFECT LOVER (IRE) 4 ch.g. Pursuit of Love 124 – Elabella (Ela-Mana-Mou 132) [2002 –: p7g p6g 7d 5s Jun 14] heavy-topped gelding: no form. *D. J. S. ffrench Davis* –

PERFECTLY HONEST 4 b.f. Charnwood Forest (IRE) 125 – Carina Clare (Slip Anchor 136) [2002 51: f12s² f12g 11.8s Mar 28] good-topped filly: modest maiden: should stay 1¾m: acts on fibresand and good to firm going: blinkered in 2002: sold 3,800 gns. *B. Smart* **56**

PERFECT NIGHT 2 b.f. (Mar 21) Danzig Connection (USA) – Blissful Night (Cadeaux Genereux 131) [2002 7v³ p8g Nov 27] rather leggy filly: first foal: dam unraced half-sister to smart French middle-distance stayer North Col: better effort in maidens (shaped well, fair form) when third to Mezuzah at Doncaster: should stay at least 1m. *R. Charlton* **74**

PERFECT PICTURE 3 b.g. Octagonal (NZ) 126 – Greenvera (USA) (Riverman (USA) 131) [2002 7.1s⁶ 9.3s 9m² 16m⁶ f12f f16.2g Dec 7] 45,000Y: leggy, lengthy gelding: sixth foal: half-brother to 6-y-o Royal Rebel: dam, maiden in France, half-sister to useful French performer up to 7f Way West: fair maiden: tailed off after third start: should be suited by 1½m+: tongue tied last 2 outings. *M. Johnston* **67** **a–**

PERFECT PUNCH 3 b.g. Reprimand 122 – Aliuska (IRE) 70 (Fijar Tango (FR) 127) [2002 p7g p7g⁵ p10g⁶ Mar 27] 20,000Y: third foal: half-brother to fairly useful 2000 2-y-o 6f winner Goodie Twosues (by Fraam) and 5-y-o Altay: dam, Irish 5f winner, ran only at 2 yrs: modest form in maidens: stays 1¼m: raced only on polytrack. *C. F. Wall* **62**

PERFECT SETTING 2 b.g. (Feb 7) Polish Precedent (USA) 131 – Diamond Park (IRE) 91 (Alzao (USA) 117) [2002 5m² Sep 15] 12,000Y: fifth foal: half-brother to 1998 2-y-o 5f winner Key (by Midyan) and 1999 2-y-o 5f winner Pop Shop (by Owington): dam, disappointing maiden, stayed 1¼m: favourite but green, promising ½-length second **85 p**

PER

of 14 to Peace Offering in maiden at Sandown, travelling comfortably in front after slowish start, then wandering under pressure: sure to improve and win a race. *P. J. Makin*

PERFECT STORM 3 b.c. Vettori (IRE) 119 – Gorgeous Dancer (IRE) (Nordico (USA)) [2002 85: 8g³ 8m⁶ 8.1m 8f² 8.1g* 9s Oct 26] lengthy colt: useful handicapper: best effort when winning at Sandown in October by 2 lengths from My Raggedy Man: stays 1m: raced only on good ground or firmer prior to final start. *M. Blanshard* **102**

PERFIDIOUS (USA) 4 b.g. Lear Fan (USA) 130 – Perfolia (USA) 104 (Nodouble (USA)) [2002 70, a79: f11g² f12g⁴ 11.8s 12g 11.6d 12g p10g*dis 10.3f⁶ 10.1g⁶ 9.7m² 10g³ 10m⁵ p10g² f9.4g² Dec 14] sturdy gelding: fair handicapper on all-weather, modest on turf: failed dope test and disqualified after being first past post at Lingfield in June: barely stays 1½m: acts on all-weather and good to firm going: often makes running/wanders. *J. R. Boyle* **64 a77**

PERIGEO (IRE) 3 b.c. Sadler's Wells (USA) 132 – Lacandona (USA) 71 (Septieme Ciel (USA) 123) [2002 11g⁴ 10.5d³ 12.3g* 13.1g 11.8g Oct 14] robust colt: second foal: half-brother to 2000 2-y-o 1m winner Baranova (by Caerleon): dam, lightly-raced maiden who stayed 1¼m, granddaughter of Canadian Horse of the Year Fanfreluche: fairly useful performer: won maiden at Ripon in August: good seventh to Collier Hill in handicap at Ayr next time: likely to prove best at 1¼m/1½m: raced only on good/good to soft going: sold 35,000 gns. *J. H. M. Gosden* **91**

PERIGEUX (IRE) 6 b.g. Perugino (USA) 84 – Rock On (IRE) (Ballad Rock 122) [2002 58, a78: p5g⁶ p6g f5g² p5g f5g f5g f5g⁵ 5.3f⁴ 5.1g 5m 6f 5g⁴ 5d 5m 5.1f f6g 5m 5m 10.4f Oct 10] small, good-bodied gelding: modest on all-weather, poor on turf: left J. M. Bradley before penultimate start: best at 5f/6f: acts on all-weather, good to firm and good to soft going (probably on soft): tried visored, usually blinkered: tongue tied last 2 starts: sometimes slowly away: often races prominently: none too reliable. *C. N. Kellett* **47 a52**

PERIPHERAL (USA) 2 b. or br.f. (Mar 12) Boundary (USA) 117 – Stand From Under (USA) (First Albert (USA)) [2002 6m* 7d⁴ 6.1m³ 7f* 7f Oct 2] $62,000F, $160,000Y: leggy filly: sister to a winner in USA and half-sister to several winners there: dam unraced half-sister to dam of 4-y-o Fair Mix: fairly useful performer: won maiden at Doncaster (tended to carry head high) in June and nursery at Chester (made most) in September: stays 7f: acts on firm and good to soft going: joined J. Sadler in UAE. *M. R. Channon* **81**

PERLE D'AZUR 3 b.f. Mind Games 121 – Pearls (Mon Tresor 113) [2002 91: 6.1d 7s 7f Jul 13] leggy filly: fairly useful at 2 yrs: well held in 2002 (pulled up penultimate start). *A. Berry* **–**

PERLE DE SAGESSE 5 b.m. Namaqualand (USA) – Pearl of Dubai (USA) (Red Ransom (USA)) [2002 –, a47: p16g f8g Feb 12] of little account nowadays. *Julian Poulton* **–**

PERPETUITY 4 ch.g. Timeless Times (USA) 99 – Boadicea's Chariot (Commanche Run 133) [2002 65: f9.4g Mar 25] lengthy, quite good-topped gelding: fair maiden at 3 yrs: well held only 4-y-o outing: blinkered (looked unwilling) once. *Mrs H. Dalton* **–**

PERPETUO 5 b.m. Mtoto 134 – Persian Fountain (IRE) 67 (Persian Heights 129) [2002 81: 12.3g f12f³ 12g 11.9g² 12g Jul 19] sparely-made mare: poor mover: fair handicapper: reportedly had back trouble in between last 2 starts (said to have finished lame final one): stays 1¾m: acts on soft and firm going: has wandered: usually comes from off pace. *R. A. Fahey* **68**

PERSARIO 3 b.f. Bishop of Cashel 122 – Barford Lady 93 (Stanford 121§) [2002 6s⁵ 7g* Jun 5] fifth foal: sister to 4-y-o Heretic and closely related to 8-y-o Warningfront, both smart: dam 7f/1m winner: confirmed debut promise when winning maiden at Southwell by short head from Bubble Up, travelling comfortably, switched 2f out, then quickening under pressure, despite running green (carried head high): will stay 1m: looked likely to improve further. *J. R. Fanshawe* **82**

PERSEPHONE HEIGHTS 2 br.f. (Mar 22) Golden Heights 82 – Jalland (Jalmood (USA) 126) [2002 7.1m⁶ 7g⁶ f8g⁶ Nov 25] second foal by thoroughbred sire: dam unraced: best effort (modest form) in maiden at Warwick on debut, very slowly away: should stay at least 1m. *D. J. Coakley* **62**

PERSHAAN (IRE) 2 br.f. (Feb 12) Darshaan 133 – Persian Fantasy 94 (Persian Bold 123) [2002 7f 8s⁶ Oct 25] unfurnished filly: fifth foal: closely related to useful 1¾m/2m winner Height of Fantasy (by Shirley Heights) and half-sister to 3-y-o Persian Lightning and to dam of 2-y-o Big Bad Bob: dam 1½m winner who stayed 2m: better effort in **74 p**

743

maidens (fair form) when sixth of 22 to Richemaur at Doncaster: will be well suited by 1¼m+: almost certainly capable of further improvement. *J. L. Dunlop*

PERSIAN BANDIT (IRE)   4 b.g. Idris (IRE) 118 – Ce Soir (Northern Baby (CAN)   **46**
127) [2002 ?: a6g 7f⁴ 8.1g³ p7g Dec 11] poor nowadays: won 2 handicaps at Mijas in 2001: left E. Creighton, Spain, after reappearance: stays 1m: acts on sand, firm and soft going: tried blinkered/visored: carries head high: has looked none too cooperative. *J. R. Jenkins*

PERSIAN EMBERS   3 gr.f. Blushing Flame (USA) 109 – Podrida 48 (Persepolis   **74**
(FR) 127) [2002 12.1v² 12d⁴ 12d⁵ Aug 3] fourth living foal: dam, thorough stayer on Flat, also winning hurdler: clearly best effort in maidens when second at Chepstow: mulish to post final start: will stay at least 1¾m. *I. A. Wood*

PERSIAN FACT   3 b.g. Greensmith 121 – Forest Song 60 (Forzando 122) [2002 61:   **–**
8g 7m f7g f6g Nov 20] good-topped gelding: modest maiden at 2 yrs: well held in 2002: tried visored. *K. R. Burke*

PERSIAN FAYRE   10 b.g. Persian Heights 129 – Dominion Fayre 49 (Dominion   **–**
123) [2002 68, a–: 7f 8g 7.1g 7.2d⁶ 8g Sep 7] sturdy gelding: fair performer in 2001: little form in 2002. *A. Berry*

PERSIAN JASMINE   2 b.f. (May 8) Dynaformer (USA) – Rumpimpumpy 80 (Shirley   **79 p**
Heights 130) [2002 7m* Aug 12] first foal: dam, maiden at 2 yrs in Britain but later Grade 2 9f winner in USA, half-sister to Irish 1000 Guineas winner Classic Park: favourite, won 10-runner maiden at Folkestone by ½ length from Daisy Do, switched right then running on under pressure to lead final 1f: will stay at least 1m: sure to improve. *P. W. Harris*

PERSIAN KING (IRE)   5 ch.g. Persian Bold 123 – Queen's Share (Main Reef 126)   **98**
[2002 –: 10g⁴ 10m 10.1m* 10.1m 10.1d² Sep 11] useful performer: won minor event at Epsom in August: good 1¼ lengths second to Mahroos in similar race there final start: probably stays 1¾m: acts on good to firm and good to soft ground: tried tongue tied (has reportedly had a wind operation): fair hurdler, successful twice in autumn. *J. A. B. Old*

PERSIAN LASS (IRE)   3 ch.f. Grand Lodge (USA) 125 – Noble Tiara (USA) 110   **103**
(Vaguely Noble 140) [2002 8m⁶ 9.9m* 12s 12m⁵ 11.7g⁴ 10g* 10m⁴ 10.5m² 10.1m² 10m⁵ 9f 10g⁴ Oct 17] 19,000F, 100,000Y: leggy filly: half-sister to several winners in France, including 7f (at 2 yrs) to 10.5f winner On Credit (by No Pass No Sale), herself dam of very smart stayer Stowaway: dam French 10.5f and 12.5f winner: useful performer: won maiden at Salisbury in May and handicap at Sandown in August: creditable efforts after, including in listed races at Yarmouth (unlucky ½-length second to Miss Corniche) and Newmarket (fourth to Salim Toto, had plenty to do) on ninth/final starts: best form around 1¼m: acts on soft and good to firm ground, probably on firm: awkwardly leaving stalls penultimate start: takes good hold, and is patiently ridden: consistent. *P. W. Harris*

PERSIAN LIGHTNING (IRE)   3 b.g. Sri Pekan (USA) 117 – Persian Fantasy 94   **97**
(Persian Bold 123) [2002 73p: 8m* 10m² 10.1g* 12.3g³ 10m³ 11.9m² 13.1g⁶ 11.8g³ Oct 14] strong, angular gelding: useful performer: progressed steadily in 2002, winning handicap at Leicester in April, minor event at Newcastle in June and handicap at Haydock (by 1½ lengths from Duke of Earl) in September: creditable third to Sharpcut in handicap at Leicester final start: barely stays 13f: raced mainly on good/good to firm ground: free-going sort: consistent. *J. L. Dunlop*

PERSIAN MAJESTY (IRE)   2 b.c. (Feb 12) Grand Lodge (USA) 125 – Spa   **94 P**
(Sadler's Wells (USA) 132) [2002 8g* Oct 18] 36,000Y: rangy, attractive colt: first foal: dam unraced half-sister to very smart 1½m performer Sandmason (by Grand Lodge) out of smart close relation to Slip Anchor: well-backed 8/1-shot, though backward and green (shade upset in stall), won 16-runner maiden at Newmarket by ½ length from Regal Agenda, staying on well to lead final 1f: will be suited by 1¼m+: useful prospect at least, sure to go on to better things. *P. W. Harris*

PERSIANO   7 ch.g. Efisio 120 – Persiandale (Persian Bold 123) [2002 107: 7m 8g⁵   **101**
8.2d³ Jun 10] big, lengthy gelding: unimpressive mover: useful performer: creditable effort in 2002 only when fifth to Omaha City in handicap at Goodwood in May: reportedly broke down badly final start: best at 7f/1m: probably unsuited by soft/heavy going, acted on any other: visored once as 4-y-o: retired. *J. R. Fanshawe*

PERSIAN PEARL   3 b.f. Hurricane Sky (AUS) – Persian Fountain (IRE) 67 (Persian   **–**
Heights 129) [2002 73: 8.1f⁶ 6d 5d 5m f5s 5m Sep 23] sturdy filly: fair at 2 yrs: well held in 2002. *B. A. McMahon*

PERSIAN PRIDE (IRE)   4 ch.g. Barathea (IRE) 127 – Glenarff (USA) (Irish River **84**
(FR) 131) [2002 96d: 10m p12g Jul 24] strong, compact gelding: fairly useful nowadays:
stays 1½m: acts on good to firm and good to soft going. *P. W. Harris*

PERSIAN PUNCH (IRE)   9 ch.g. Persian Heights 129 – Rum Cay (USA) 75 **117**
(Our Native (USA)) [2002 124: 16.2d² 13.9f⁴ 16.4m³ 20m⁶ 16m 13.3f³ 14.1m*
18m² 20g⁵ᵈ 16m* Oct 19]

'Reports of my death are greatly exaggerated.' The words of the famous
cable to Associated Press from Samuel Langhorne Clemens (Mark Twain) have
been applied to comebacks of many kinds down the years. The front-running,
staying veteran Persian Punch performed his own notable comeback in the latest
season after connections reportedly considered retiring him when he finished last
of nine in the Goodwood Cup in the summer. 'If he turns in the same sort of run as
he did at Goodwood, then that will probably be it,' said trainer David Elsworth
before Persian Punch lined up for the Geoffrey Freer Stakes at Newbury in
mid-August (an engagement chosen in preference to the Prix Kergorlay and the
Lonsdale Stakes). Racing over a barely adequate trip and with a new jockey in
Martin Dwyer, Persian Punch staved off retirement with a creditable third to
Mubtaker, typically making it a good test and battling on well.

*Catisfield Hinton And Stud
Conditions Stakes, Salisbury—short heads
separate Persian Punch, Warrsan (right)
and Harlestone Grey (left)*

The following month Persian
Punch won his first race of the season, a
minor event at Salisbury, where he came
again under Dwyer to beat Warrsan and
Harlestone Grey in a finish of short
heads. The Doncaster Cup came next and
Persian Punch ran a cracker to finish
runner-up to Boreas, beaten a length and
a quarter and recording as good an effort
as he had put up since winning the
Goodwood Cup and the Lonsdale Stakes
and finishing third in the Melbourne Cup
the previous season. Persian Punch had
given the impression he was probably as
good as ever when in the frame in the
Sagaro Stakes, the Yorkshire Cup and the
Henry II Stakes (a race he has won three
times) on his first three outings but, in the
end, he had taken much longer than usual
to find his very best form. Another hiccup
in the Prix du Cadran at Longchamp in
October, when disqualified from fifth for causing interference, was followed by an
extremely popular victory in the Jockey Club Cup at Newmarket in October.
Persian Punch got the better of another splendid tussle with Boreas, cutting out the
donkey work and then answering Dwyer's every call to hold on by three quarters of
a length for his second win in the race and the tenth pattern-race success of his long
and honourable career. That record, however, does not include a Group 1 victory
and Persian Punch was only sixth in the latest Gold Cup (his sixth appearance in the
event), though the race was nothing like so strongly run as the year before, when he
was just touched off by Royal Rebel.

*Jockey Club Cup, Newmarket—Persian Punch (left) gains his tenth pattern-race success,
reversing Doncaster Cup placings with Boreas; Spanish John (striped cap) and Pole Star (right) are next*

Mr J. C. Smith's "Persian Punch"

		Persian Bold	Bold Lad
	Persian Heights	(br 1975)	Relkarunner
	(ch 1985)	Ready And Willing	Reliance II
Persian Punch (IRE)		(b 1971)	No Saint
(ch.g. 1993)		Our Native	Exclusive Native
	Rum Cay (USA)	(b 1970)	Our Jackie
	(ch 1985)	Oraston	Morston
		(ch 1978)	Orange Cap

    The big, strong Persian Punch is a grand stamp of animal who impresses in appearance and has a powerful, round action. As we have said before, many a jumps trainer must have cast an envious eye over him. His own trainer has had several notably game and durable jumpers through his yard in his time, most famously Desert Orchid, but he must have had well-nigh as much satisfaction from training the admirably tough Persian Punch. 'If he was a jumper you would say that he is just about coming to his best,' Elsworth said of the nine-year-old in the latest season, a clear indication that Persian Punch will be around for at least another season, and probably longer, provided he keeps his form. There is little to add to the details of his pedigree that have appeared in earlier editions of *Racehorses*, except to record that Rum Cay's eighth foal, the three-year-old Wadmaan (by Singspiel), reached the racecourse in the latest season, finishing runner-up in a minor event over an extended mile and a quarter at Doncaster in June, making the running and battling on gamely. As his record suggests, Persian Punch stays very well and his very best efforts in the latest season came at two miles plus; the Cup races bring his renowned battling qualities fully into play and represent his best chance of adding further pattern-race successes. He acts on any going. *D. R. C. Elsworth*

PERSUADE 4 ch.g. Lure (USA) 131 – Shapely (USA) 81 (Alleged (USA) 138) [2002 **71 §**
83§: p8g p10g f7g 8s 8.3g 7g 7m 8.5d f7f 8g* 9.1g⁴ a7f⁵ a8g⁴ a7.5g Dec 12]
leggy gelding: fair nowadays: left R. White after eighth start: won seller at Thirsk in
September: effective at 6f to 9f: acts on all-weather/any turf going: visored (slowly away)
sixth outing: sometimes tongue tied: has raced freely/hung left: sometimes finds little:
unreliable. *K. R. Burke*

PERTEMPS BIANCA 2 b.f. (Feb 11) Dancing Spree (USA) – Bay Bianca (IRE) **73 d**
(Law Society (USA) 130) [2002 5s* 5s* 5f 7f f6g f7g f7g⁵ f8.5s⁵ f8.5g Dec 31] leggy
filly: fourth foal: half-sister to a winner in Greece by Lead On Time: dam German 6f
winner: fair performer: won maiden seller at Doncaster (for A. D. Smith) in March and
minor event at Newcastle in April: well below form after: should stay 1m: acts on soft
ground: tried visored. *K. R. Burke*

PERTEMPS GILL 4 b.f. Silca Blanka (IRE) 104 – Royal Celerity (USA) (Riverman **–**
(USA) 131) [2002 39: 7d 10g f8.5s Dec 13] close-coupled, sparely-made filly: maiden:
well held in 2002, including in blinkers. *A. D. Smith*

PERTEMPS MAGUS 2 b.f. (Mar 22) Silver Wizard (USA) 117 – Brilliant Future 58 **70**
(Welsh Saint 126) [2002 5s² 5g* Apr 1] sparely-made filly: fifth living foal: dam 1½m/
hurdles winner: fair form: won maiden at Warwick by head from Rowan Express, leading
halfway: will stay at least 6f. *A. D. Smith*

PERTEMPS SIA 2 b.c. (Apr 24) Distinctly North (USA) 115 – Shamrock Dancer **41**
(IRE) 36 (Dance of Life (USA)) [2002 7m 5.7f 7d⁵ 8g 8.1g Sep 12] sparely-made colt:
third foal: dam third at 8.5f: poor maiden: fifth in seller at Newmarket: tongue tied after:
looked hard ride final start. *A. D. Smith*

PERTEMPS WIZARD 2 br.c. (Feb 6) Silver Wizard (USA) 117 – Peristyle 59 (Tolo- **55**
meo 127) [2002 f6g⁶ f6g⁴ 5.7m 10m Oct 1] lengthy colt: sixth reported foal: dam, maiden
who stayed 1½m, winning hurdler: modest maiden: left J. Osborne after third outing:
should stay at least 7f: acts on fibresand, well held on turf. *F. Jordan*

PERTINACIOUS 2 gr.f. (May 17) Petong 126 – Petit Peu (IRE) (Kings Lake (USA) **44**
133) [2002 5m 6m 7f⁴ 7.5g 7m Jul 24] 6,800Y: leggy, unfurnished filly: sixth foal: sister
to 1¼m winner Silvery and half-sister to 2 winners abroad: dam, ran once over hurdles in
Ireland, half-sister to smart performer up to 1m Petardia (by Petong): poor maiden: stays
7f: raced only on good ground or firmer: tried blinkered. *T. D. Easterby*

PERU GENIE (IRE) 5 b.g. Perugino (USA) 84 – High Concept (IRE) (Thatching **66**
131) [2002 71: 6m 6s 5m 5d 6.2d 5g² 6g 5g⁴ 5m³ 6f³ 6f* f6g f6g Dec 16] good-topped
gelding: fair handicapper: won at Fairyhouse in September: well held at Wolverhampton
last 2 starts: stays 6f: acts on firm and good to soft ground: usually blinkered: has worn
tongue strap. *Michael McElhone, Ireland*

PERUVIA (IRE) 2 b.f. (Feb 29) Perugino (USA) 84 – Dane's Lane (IRE) (Danehill **80**
(USA) 126) [2002 7g³ 7m⁵ 7m³ 7f Oct 2] IR 30,000F, 20,000Y: strong, close-coupled
filly: fifth foal: sister to fairly useful 7f/1m winner (including at 2 yrs) Hoh Steamer, later
successful in USA, and half-sister to 2000 2-y-o 5f winner Distinctly Chic (by Distinctly
North): dam unraced: fairly useful maiden: third to Saturn at Newmarket third start: well
below form in nursery there final one: should stay 1m. *R. Hannon*

PERUVIAN CHIEF (IRE) 5 b.g. Foxhound (USA) 103 – John's Ballad (IRE) **99**
(Ballad Rock 122) [2002 94: f5s* f6g⁶ p5g⁵ f6g* p5g* f6g 5s 6g 6m² 5g⁵ 6d⁵ 5m 6f³ 6m⁵ **a104**
6m⁶ 6m³ 5m² 5f⁶ 6g⁵ 6m 7.6f² 6m³ f6g 5m* 5m⁴ Oct 12] good-topped gelding: useful
handicapper: won at Southwell in January, Wolverhampton/Lingfield in February and
Ascot (beat Budelli by 1¼ lengths for first success on turf) in September: ran creditably
most other starts, including at Ascot (second to Brave Burt), Goodwood (best of those
on stand side when fifth to Bond Boy in Stewards' Cup) and York (third to Needwood
Blade) on seventeenth/nineteenth/twenty second: effective at 5f to sharp 7.6f: acts on all-
weather, firm and soft going: sometimes blinkered, visored all wins in 2002: has hung:
tough and consistent. *N. P. Littmoden*

PERUVIAN WAVE (USA) 4 b. or br.g. Alydeed (CAN) 120 – Polish Devil (USA) **49**
(Devil's Bag (USA)) [2002 58: f5s⁶ f6g f6g f5g⁴ Feb 1] strong gelding: poor maiden
handicapper: effective at 5f/6f: acts on fibresand, easily best turf run on good going: tried
blinkered: carries head high: has started slowly/hung left/folded tamely. *P. D. Evans*

PETALITE 4 gr.f. Petong 126 – Veuve Hoornaert (IRE) 88 (Standaan (FR) 118) [2002 **–**
53, a63: f7s³ p7g² f6g p7g f6g Feb 20] modest maiden: stays easy 7f: acts on all-weather and **a58**
good to firm going: very unruly at flip start and refused to race final outing. *M. A. Jarvis*

PETANA 2 br.f. (Mar 23) Petong 126 – Duxyana (IRE) (Cyrano de Bergerac 120) – [2002 f5g 5g May 10] 3,000Y, resold 6,500Y: sixth foal: sister to fairly useful 6f winner Vista Alegre and half-sister to 3-y-o Kelsey Rose: dam unraced: last in maidens: hung badly right throughout on second start. *Mrs G. S. Rees*

PETER'S IMP (IRE) 7 b.g. Imp Society (USA) – Catherine Clare 58 (Sallust 134) **51** [2002 65d, a–: 8.5m⁴ 10m² 9.9g² 12g² 12f 12.3m⁵ 10.3f⁶ 11.1d Jul 25] good-bodied gelding: modest handicapper: stays 1½m: acts on firm and soft going: sometimes blinkered/visored. *A. Berry*

PETER THE GREAT (IRE) 3 b.g. Hector Protector (USA) 124 – Perfect Alibi – (Law Society (USA) 130) [2002 78: 11.7g 10s Oct 26] fair maiden at 2 yrs: well held in 2002: should stay at least 1¼m: gelded after final start. *R. M. Beckett*

PETITE BLEU 2 b.f. (Mar 31) Vettori (IRE) 119 – Blue Lamp (USA) 68 (Shadeed **49** (USA) 135) [2002 6m 7.5m⁶ 6d 6d 6m⁵ Sep 3] 4,500Y: smallish, good-topped filly: second foal: half-sister to fairly useful 2001 2-y-o 1m winner More Specific (by Definite Article): dam maiden who stayed 1¼m: poor maiden: probably stays 7.5f. *J. G. Given*

PETITE FUTEE 3 b.f. Eflsto 120 – Q Factor 90 (Tragic Role (USA)) [2002 60: 8.1m⁵ **67** 8.3s³ 10m⁴ 11.6m 10.9g⁵ 10g* 10m* 10.2g⁴ 10g 10m⁴ 10m⁶ Oct 7] small, stocky filly: fair performer: won handicap at Leicester and claimer at Newmarket, both in August: stays 11f: acts on soft and good to firm going: played up in stall and left it riderless fourth outing: often soon off bridle/flashes tail. *D. Haydn Jones*

PETITE MAC 2 b.f. (Apr 24) Timeless Times (USA) 99 – Petite Elite 47 (Anfield **68** 117) [2002 6m 6g⁶ 5m⁶ f5g³ 6m 5m⁵ 5g² f5s⁶ 6d² f5g⁵ Dec 10] 1,500Y: small filly: ninth **a59** foal: sister to 2 winning sprinters, including 5-y-o Christopherssister, and half-sister to 3 winners, including fairly useful 7f winner (including at 2 yrs) who stayed 8.5f Effervescence (by Efisio): dam maiden who stayed 7f: fair maiden on turf, modest on all-weather: effective at 5f/6f: acts on fibresand, good to soft and good to firm going: usually races prominently. *N. Bycroft*

PETONGSKI 4 b.g. Petong 126 – Madam Petoski 61 (Petoski 135) [2002 79: 7f 6f **75 §** 7.2g 6m 5.9s² 6s 6s 7.5m f6s 6d³ f6g f6s f6g Nov 15] good-bodied gelding: fair handi- **a– §** capper: best recent efforts at 6f on ground softer than good: tried visored/blinkered: reportedly had breathing problem tenth start: sometimes hangs right/flashes tail: unreliable. *D. W. Barker*

PETRIE 5 ch.g. Fraam 114 – Canadian Capers 70 (Ballacashtal (CAN)) [2002 –: f6g – Mar 23] of little account nowadays. *B. G. Powell*

PETROLERO (ARG) 3 gr.c. Perfect Parade (USA) – Louise (ARG) (Farnesio – (ARG)) [2002 8.1m⁶ 8.2m 7g Oct 14] tall colt: third foal: dam unraced: little form in maidens. *B. R. Millman*

PETRULA 3 ch.g. Tagula (IRE) 116 – Bouffant (High Top 131) [2002 79: 7g 7.6f⁴ 7m⁴ **85** 7g² 7.6f³ 6g² 7.5m³ 7.9s² 7.6g 8.1m² 7.1f 8s⁴ 8.2v Oct 29] good-bodied gelding: fairly useful performer: stays 1m: acts on firm and soft going: veered right leaving stall/edged left for only success: sometimes finishes weakly: joined K. Ryan. *A. Berry*

PETRUS (IRE) 6 b.g. Perugino (USA) 84 – Love With Honey (USA) (Full Pocket **93 d** (USA)) [2002 82: p8g* p8g³ p8g* f8.5g f7g² 7g p8g 7.6s 7m 7g f8.5g p7g³ Dec 18] smallish, compact gelding: fairly useful handicapper: won at Lingfield in January/February: well below form last 7 starts: best at 7f/1m: acts on all-weather, probably best on good going or firmer on turf: tried blinkered/tongue tied: has worn net muzzle to post/been taken down early. *C. E. Brittain*

PETUNTSE 8 b.g. Phountzi (USA) 104 – Alipampa (IRE) (Glenstal (USA) 118) – [2002 59: 11m May 2] tall gelding: modest handicapper at 7 yrs: well held only outing on Flat in 2002: retired. *Mrs M. Reveley*

PEYTO PRINCESS 4 b. or br.f. Bold Arrangement 127 – Bo' Babbity 75 (Strong **85** Gale 116) [2002 79: 6f⁴ 6m⁵ 6.1d² 7m 6g 6m⁵ 6s⁴ 7m 6m 6g 6.1s Oct 29] strong, lengthy filly: fairly useful performer: flattered when second to Bright Edge in listed race at Nottingham in May: effective at 5f/6f: yet to race on heavy going, acts on any other turf: sometimes wanders: none too consistent: joined M. Buckley. *C. W. Fairhurst*

PHAEDRA (IRE) 2 b.f. (Feb 12) Marju (IRE) 127 – Sopran Marida (IRE) (Darshaan **86** 133) [2002 6f⁵ 6.1m 6.5g 8g³ 8d⁴ Nov 1] 22,000Y: leggy, lengthy filly: unimpressive mover: third foal: half-sister to fairly useful 2000 2-y-o 6f winner Millenium Princess (by Eagle Eyed): dam, Italian 7f and 9f winner, half-sister to useful Italian performer up to 1½m/US Grade 2 9f winner Sopran Mariduff: fairly useful maiden: best effort when third to Howle Hill in nursery at Newmarket: will stay 1¼m: acts on good to soft going: sent to USA. *G. C. Bravery*

PHAMEDIC (IRE) 2 b.f. (Apr 14) Imperial Ballet (IRE) 110 – Beeper The Great 62 (USA) (Whadjathink (USA)) [2002 6g 7g⁴ 7.5d³ 7m⁴ 7g² 8g 8m⁵ 7f⁵ Oct 8] IR 21,000F, IR 18,000Y: tall, leggy filly: second foal: half-sister to Italian 2001 2-y-o 1m winner Paula Smith (by Red Ransom): dam unraced half-sister to Prix Marcel Boussac winner Tropicaro: modest maiden: second in nursery at Newcastle: should stay 1¼m: acts on good to soft ground, probably on firm: blinkered (found little) sixth start: has hung/ carried head awkwardly. *T. D. Easterby*

PHANTOM STOCK 2 b.g. (Mar 30) Alzao (USA) 117 – Strike Alight (USA) (Gulch – (USA)) [2002 7m 6m 6m Sep 24] 24,000Y: good-bodied gelding: fifth foal: half-brother to useful 1m winner Cyber World (by Robin des Pins): dam, 1m winner in USA, sister to smart 1¼m winner Flame Valley out of sister to Prix de la Salamandre winner Common Grounds: well held in maidens. *W. Jarvis*

PHARAOH HATSHEPSUT (IRE) 4 b.f. Definite Article 121 – Maid of Mourne 47 (Fairy King (USA)) [2002 64d: 7v 6f 8.3s 7.2g 8.3m⁴ 10s 7s Oct 26] good-topped filly: poor performer: effective at 6f to easy 1m: acts on heavy and good to firm going: none too consistent. *R. A. Fahey*

PHARAOH'S HOUSE (IRE) 5 b.g. Desert Style (IRE) 121 – Cellatica (USA) 67 – (Sir Ivor 135) [2002 16m Jul 8] strong, lengthy gelding: has a round action: maiden: well held only 5-y-o outing: tried blinkered. *R. Allan*

PHARLY'S GOLD 2 ch.f. (Mar 20) Pharly (FR) 130 – Hoop La (Final Straw 127) 51 [2002 8.3d⁶ 7m f8s Oct 8] 3,200F, 3,000Y: fourth foal: half-sister to a winner in Turkey by Charmer: dam, lightly-raced maiden, half-sister to smart performer up to 1¼m Desert Shot: easily best effort in maidens (modest form) when sixth at Windsor: should stay at least 1¼m. *M. G. Quinlan*

PHAROAH'S GOLD (IRE) 4 b.g. Namaqualand (USA) – Queen Nefertiti (IRE) 69 61 (Fairy King (USA)) [2002 88d: f7s² f6g* p7g⁶ p7g f6g⁴ p6g f7g⁶ 6s 6v⁴ 7m⁶ f6s 7.1g 7s⁴ 7d f7g³ p7g⁵ f7g² Dec 17] smallish, strong gelding: fair performer: won minor event at Southwell in January: raced mainly at 6f/7f: acts on soft going, good to firm and all-weather: usually visored: often slowly away: none too consistent. *D. Shaw*

PHASE EIGHT GIRL 6 b.m. Warrshan (USA) 117 – Bugsy's Sister (Aragon 118) 26 [2002 14.1f 16d³ 15d Jul 23] small mare: bad performer, lightly raced (missed 2001 season): won over hurdles in August. *J. Hetherton*

PHECKLESS 3 ch.g. Be My Guest (USA) 126 – Phlirty (Pharly (FR) 130) [2002 43: 69 p8g³ p7g² 8.2d p7g² 7g* 6g 8m p6g 7m³ 7g 6d p7g² f8g f6g Dec 16] fair performer: a75 won claimer at Southwell in June: stays 7f: acts on polytrack and good to firm going: sometimes slowly away: none too consistent. *R. F. Johnson Houghton*

PHILATELIC LADY (IRE) 6 ch.m. Pips Pride 117 – Gold Stamp (Golden Act – (USA)) [2002 –: 10g Apr 29] fairly useful handicapper at best: well held both outings since 2000: withdrawn after refusing to enter stalls Jun 3. *M. J. Haynes*

PHILBOY 3 b.g. Young Ern 120 – Just Lady 72 (Emarati (USA) 74) [2002 62: f5g 5d⁶ 54 5m 7m⁵ 6g 6d² 6g⁴ 6v³ 6f⁶ 5.9d 5.9g 5.9s 5m 5m⁶ 5g Sep 7] angular gelding: modest maiden: effective at 5f/6f: acts on soft and good to firm ground, well held both starts on fibresand (blinkered first occasion): often visored: has had tongue tied. *C. W. Fairhurst*

PHILGIRL 3 ch.f. Bijou d'Inde 127 – Ballagarrow Girl 66 (North Stoke 130) [2002 60: f6g f6g 8m 9.2s 8.2f⁶ 5.9s 7f⁶ 6.9s⁶ 7f 7.2d⁵ 6.9g 6s⁴ 7.1m Sep 16] leggy filly: little form in 2002: probably stays 1m: acts on any going. *C. W. Fairhurst*

PHILO (IRE) 2 b.g. (Mar 10) Desert Prince (IRE) 130 – Silly Imp (IRE) 90 (Imperial 58 ? Frontier (USA) 112) [2002 7m p7g f7s p6g Dec 28] 21,000Y: second foal: dam, Irish 5f and 7f winner, half-sister to dam of Racing Post Trophy winner Seattle Rhyme: form in maidens (modest) only when ninth at Lingfield final start, having been reluctant to go to post: swerved badly right start on debut, pulled hard second outing. *M. Blanshard*

PHILOSOPHIC 8 b.g. Be My Chief (USA) 122 – Metaphysique (FR) (Law Society – (USA) 130) [2002 f16.2g f14.8s p16g Jul 17] fair staying handicapper in 1999 (reportedly bled from nose final start): well beaten in 3 starts since (visored final one). *Mrs L. C. Jewell*

PHINDA FOREST (IRE) 3 br.f. Charnwood Forest (IRE) 125 – Shatalia (USA) 63 (Shahrastani (USA) 135) [2002 8d⁶ 10m 10.5d p10g p10g 8.1g Sep 12] tall, close-coupled filly: has a round action: half-sister to French 1m/1¼m winner Miss Adelaide (by Exit To Nowhere): dam French 1¼m/11f winner: modest maiden: needs further than 1m, and should be suited by 1½m+. *I. A. Balding*

PHNOM PENH (IRE)   3 b.g. Alhaarth (IRE) 126 – Crystal City (Kris 135) [2002 —
p6g 8m 10s 10m 8d Nov 1] IR 44,000F, 92,000Y: fifth foal: half-brother to useful 1998 2-y-o 5f/6f winner who stayed 7f Acicula (by Night Shift), 4-y-o Stoli and 1½m winner Crystal Flite (by Darshaan): dam, French 10.5f winner, out of Yorkshire Oaks winner Untold: no form (trained by J. Noseda on debut). *Miss J. Feilden*

PHOEBE BUFFAY (IRE)   5 b.m. Petardia 113 – Art Duo 86 (Artaius (USA) 129)   **70 d**
[2002 74: p8g⁵ f8g p10g f8g³ p10g f8.5g p8g p10g⁴ 8.2m 8.1m f8.5g⁵ p10g 8f⁵ 8m 9.7m³ Jun 28] close-coupled mare: fair handicapper: best form at 7f/1m: acts on good to firm going and all-weather: blinkered (well held) once: sometimes slowly away/carries head awkwardly: on downgrade: sold 4,000 gns. *C. N. Allen*

PHOENIX NIGHTS (IRE)   2 b.c. (May 4) General Monash (USA) 107 – Beauty —
Appeal (USA) (Shadeed (USA) 135) [2002 f6g 7d Nov 5] 15,000Y: smallish, workman-like colt: fourth foal: half-brother to 1999 2-y-o 5f winner Agua Caballo (by Petorius) and 3 y o Beauteous: dam unraced: well held in maidens. *A. Berry*

PHOENIX REACH (IRE)   2 b.c. (Mar 5) Alhaarth (IRE) 126 – Carroll's Canyon   **83 +**
(IRE) (Hatim (USA) 121) [2002 7m² Jun 27] IR 16,000F, 36,000Y: seventh foal: half-brother to 6-y-o Capriolo, Irish 1½m winner The Director (by Prince Rupert) and a winner in Greece by Revoque: dam unraced half-sister to Arc winner Carroll House: 10/1, head second of 9 to Norse Dancer in maiden at Salisbury leading from 2f out until near finish (edged right): suffered split pastern and not seen again: will stay 1m. *I. A. Balding*

PHOTO FLASH (IRE)   3 ch.f. Bahamian Bounty 116 – Zoom Lens (IRE) 65 (Caer-   **76**
leon (USA) 132) [2002 69: 8f⁴ 10.2g f8.5g 8g* 10.1m 8m² 8g Oct 14] leggy, unfurnished filly: fair performer: won handicap at Brighton in August: stays 1m: acts on firm ground: blinkered last 4 starts. *J. L. Dunlop*

PHOTOGRAPHER (USA)   4 b. or br.g. Mountain Cat (USA) – Clickety Click (USA)   —
(Sovereign Dancer (USA)) [2002 90?: 10g 12g Apr 24] close-coupled gelding: fairly useful performer at best: well held both 4-y-o starts. *Mrs N. Smith*

PHRED   2 ch.g. (May 3) Safawan 118 – Phlirty (Pharly (FR) 130) [2002 f6f 6m 8.3d⁴   **62**
7s⁵ 7v⁵ Nov 9] tall gelding: fourth foal: half-brother to 3-y-o Pheckless and 5f (at 2 yrs) to 1½m winner Pheisty (by Faustus): dam tailed off both starts: modest maiden: stays 1m: acts on heavy going. *R. F. Johnson Houghton*

PHYLOZZO   6 ch.m. Michelozzo (USA) 127 – Phyllida Fox (Healaugh Fox) [2002   —
7.6f Jul 12] sparely-made mare: poor maiden at 3 yrs: tailed off only run since. *C. J. Price*

PHYSICAL FORCE   4 b.g. Casteddu 111 – Kaiserlinde (GER) (Frontal 122) [2002   —
63: p16g* p12g⁴ f16.2g³ p16g⁴ p16g⁶ 12g 14.1g f11g f12g f14.8g³ Dec 31] leggy gelding: **a68**
fair handicapper: won amateur event at Lingfield in January: well below form last 5 starts, sold out of J. Best's stable 1,000 gns after second of them: effective at 1½m to 2m: acts on all-weather: blinkered once at 3 yrs: has started slowly/carried head awkwardly/flashed tail. *D. W. Chapman*

PICATRIP   2 b.f. (Feb 27) Piccolo 121 – Transylvania 85 (Wolfhound (USA) 126)   —
[2002 6s 6d 6m 6.1s f6g Nov 22] 1,000Y: first foal: dam 7f/1m winner: little form, including in seller. *P. R. Hedger*

PICCATUNE   2 b.f. (May 10) Piccolo 121 – Musica 82 (Primo Dominie 121) [2002   **73**
5m 5g⁶ f5s* 5m³ 5f* 5m⁵ 5m 5.2f 6g⁵ 5f 5.1g* 5g⁵ f5s² 5m f6s 6g Oct 18] 6,000Y: good-   **a81**
topped filly: unimpressive mover: third foal: half-sister to fairly useful 1999 2-y-o 5f winner Coco de Mer (by Prince Sabo): dam 5f winner, including at 2 yrs: fairly useful on all-weather, fair on turf: won claimer at Wolverhampton in May, minor event at Catterick in June and nursery at Chepstow in August: best at 5f: acts on fibresand and firm ground (unraced on softer than good): visored 5 of last 6 starts: usually races up with pace: joined M. Johnston. *C. A. Dwyer*

PICCLED   4 b.g. Piccolo 121 – Creme de Menthe (IRE) (Green Desert (USA) 127)   **80 +**
[2002 67: f6g f5s² f5g* 5g² 5f f5g* 5f 5g 5m 5m 5g 5f² f5g* Dec 10] good-topped   **a97**
gelding: useful handicapper on all-weather, fairly useful on turf: won at Southwell in February, May and December (beat Sundried Tomato by 1½ lengths after 10-week break): best at 5f: acts on fibresand, firm and good to soft going: sometimes slowly away. *E. J. Alston*

PICCOLEZZA 3 b.f. Piccolo 121 – Sound Check 62 (Formidable (USA) 125) [2002 –
75p: 6g 5m p6g Oct 9] rather leggy filly: fair winner at 2 yrs: well held in 2002.
D. E. Cantillon

PICCOLITIA 4 ch.f. Piccolo 121 – Miss Laetitia (IRE) (Entitled 126) [2002 51: 9m –
7m 6m 8.1g 8.1d 8.5m⁶ 8g 10m Sep 19] lengthy, workmanlike filly: modest maiden
at 3 yrs: little form in 2002 (trained first 5 starts by J. M. Bradley): tried blinkered.
N. A. Graham

PICCOLO CATIVO 7 b.m. Komaite (USA) – Malcesine (IRE) 46 (Auction Ring **52**
(USA) 123) [2002 61, a–: 6g 6.9s 5.9v 7f 6d Oct 15] smallish mare: modest handicapper: **a–**
barely stays 1m: acts on good to firm going, heavy and fibresand: has flashed tail/drifted
left: has gone well fresh. *Mrs G. S. Rees*

PICCOLO LADY 3 b.f. Piccolo 121 – Tonic Chord 49 (La Grange Music 111) [2002 –
63: 7g 8.5m f6g Oct 17] workmanlike filly: modest maiden at 2 yrs: well held in 2002.
M. Wigham

PICKENS (USA) 10 b.g. Theatrical 128 – Alchi (USA) 112 (Alleged (USA) 138) –
[2002 –, a62: f12s f16s f11s⁴ f16g f12g⁴ f16g f14g⁵ f12g⁶ f14g² f12g⁴ Mar 21] stocky **a49**
gelding: poor performer: effective at 11f to 2m: raced only on fibresand at Southwell
since 1997: tried blinkered/tongue tied earlier in career: sometimes slowly away/races
freely. *Don Enrico Incisa*

PICKETT POINT 4 b.g. Magic Ring (IRE) 115 – Bay Runner (Bay Express 132) –
[2002 –: p12g p12g Jan 12] no form: tried blinkered. *J. J. Bridger*

PICKPOCKET 2 ch.c. (May 19) Paris House 123 – Sabo Song 67 (Prince Sabo 123) **48**
[2002 5g 5f 5s 5m³ 6m 5m 5m 5s Nov 6] 1,400Y: third living foal: dam 2-y-o 5f winner:
poor maiden: probably stays 6f: acts on soft and good to firm ground: tongue tied after
debut. *H. A. McWilliams*

PICKWICK AYR 3 b.g. Bijou d'Inde 127 – Ayr Classic (Local Suitor (USA) 128) **43**
[2002 58: 7f 8m 7.1m 8s 8g f9.4s f12g f9.4g⁵ Dec 16] angular gelding: poor maiden: left
J. Goldie after fourth start: stays 7f: acts on good to firm ground, probably on fibresand.
I. A. Wood

PIC N MIX (IRE) 2 b.f. (Mar 16) Piccolo 121 – Kingdom Princess 69 (Forzando 122) **54**
[2002 5d 6.1g⁶ 7.5m⁴ 8s Oct 15] 7,500Y: leggy filly: third foal: sister to a 1m/9f winner in
Denmark and half-sister to 3-y-o Short Respite: dam 7f/1m winner: modest maiden: off
nearly 4 months before well held in nursery final start: should stay 1m: acts on good to
firm ground. *C. W. Thornton*

PICOBELLA (IRE) 4 b.f. Piccolo 121 – Chelsea Classic (IRE) 53 (Classic Music –
(USA)) [2002 –: f8.5g⁶ Mar 25] sturdy filly: well beaten in maidens/claimer. *R. J. White*

PICPOUL (BEL) 3 b.c. Fabulous White (FR) – A Nous Cinq (FR) (Ataxerxes (GER)) **?**
[2002 8f* 10d* 11g⁵ 8.5d⁶ Jul 4] Belgian-bred colt: won maiden at Ostend at 2 yrs and
minor events at Groenendaal in April/May: well held in claimer at Epsom in July: stays
1¼m. *Paul Smith, Belgium*

PICTURE MEE 4 b.f. Aragon 118 – Heemee 81 (On Your Mark 125) [2002 55d: –
f8s Jan 1] quite attractive filly: modest performer at 3 yrs: well held only 4-y-o start.
B. S. Rothwell

PIC UP STICKS 3 gr.c. Piccolo 121 – Between The Sticks 83 (Pharly (FR) 130) **101**
[2002 89: 7m³ 7g⁴ 6g³ 6g⁵ 7s 6m³ 6m² 7m 6m² 6m² 6f² 6g 6g⁴ 5m³ Oct 12] tall colt: has a
quick, fluent action: useful handicapper: in frame 10 times in 2002, including when
runner-up at Newmarket (behind Impressive Flight) and Kempton (behind Toldya) on
tenth/eleventh starts and fourth at Ascot (behind Greenslades) on penultimate: best form
around 6f: acts on firm and good to soft ground: reliable. *M. R. Channon*

PIE HIGH 3 ch.f. Salse (USA) 128 – Humble Pie 92 (Known Fact (USA) 135) [2002 **96**
74: f7s² p7g⁵ f7g* f8.5g⁴ 8m⁶ 7.1m² 8.2d⁴ p7g 7f² 7.2d* 7m² 7d* 7d³ 7.9m 10m⁵ 8s 7f⁴
7g Oct 18] small, sturdy filly: useful performer: won handicap at Southwell in January
(left N. Littmoden after next start), minor event at Ayr in July and handicap at Newmarket
in August: good fourth to Demonstrate in handicap at Newmarket penultimate start:
effective at 7f to 8.5f: acts on firm ground, good to soft and all-weather: often races
prominently: genuine and reliable. *M. Johnston*

PIERPOINT (IRE) 7 ch.g. Archway (IRE) 115 – Lavinia (Habitat 134) [2002 66: f6s **54 §**
p5g f6g f5g p6g 6.1g⁵ 6m 6m 5d⁴ 5.3d² 5d⁴ 5.1g 5m⁵ 5m⁶ 5g⁴ 5.3m⁶ 6g 6m 7.5m⁵ 8m Oct **a41 §**
2] smallish gelding: poor mover: modest handicapper on turf, poor on all-weather: best at

5f/6f: acts on firm going, good to soft and fibresand: normally visored/blinkered: has been slowly away: usually races prominently: unreliable. *J. M. Bradley*

PIETER BRUEGHEL (USA)   3 b.g. Citidancer (USA) – Smart Tally (USA) (Smarten (USA)) [2002 101: 6f⁴ 7f* 7.6m³ 6m 8f⁵ 7m³ Oct 5] neat gelding: useful performer: won handicap at Chester (beat Marshallspark by 2½ lengths) in June: stays easy 7f: acts on firm and good to soft ground (well held on heavy): possibly needs to dominate: sold 38,000 gns, joined D. Nicholls. *P. F. I. Cole*   **100**

PIETRA DURA   3 b.f. Cadeaux Genereux 131 – Bianca Nera 107 (Salse (USA) 128) [2002 84p: 7m⁵ 8m 8g 9.5s² 10g Jun 29] 600,000Y: smallish filly: first foal: dam, 2-y-o 5f to 7f (including Lowther and Moyglare Stud Stakes) winner, didn't train on: useful performer: won maiden at Leopardstown at 2 yrs: ran at least creditably in 2002 in listed races at Leopardstown (close fifth to Lahinch) and Gowran (second to Fionns Folly): stiff tasks otherwise, including in 1000 Guineas at Newmarket and Poule d'Essai des Pouliches (missed break) at Longchamp: stays 9.5f: acts on soft and good to firm ground: blinkered final outing: has worn crossed noseband. *A. P. O'Brien, Ireland*   **96**

PIETRO SIENA (USA)   4 b. or br.c. Gone West (USA) – Via Borghese (USA) 116 (Seattle Dancer (USA) 119) [2002 82p: 7m 8.5g 7.1g⁴ p8g⁵ Oct 16] useful-looking colt: fairly useful handicapper, lightly raced: stays 1m: acts on heavy going and polytrack, probably on good to firm: sold 12,500 gns. *E. A. L. Dunlop*   **83**

PIGEON POINT (IRE)   2 b.f. (Apr 6) Victory Note (USA) 120 – Mevlana (IRE) (Red Sunset 120) [2002 5d³ 7d² 7d⁶ 6g² 6m³ 6.5m 6g* Oct 17] IR 22,000Y: leggy filly: half-sister to several winners, including fairly useful Irish 2000 2-y-o 6f winner Ladylishandra (by Mujadil) and French winner up to 11f Abu'l Fazl (by Legend of France): dam, French 11f/1½m winner, sister to smart Irish 1¼m/1½m performer Dancing Sunset: fairly useful performer: won 18-runner maiden at Newmarket by neck from Masaader, leading over 1f out: unlucky second in nursery at Windsor fourth start: should stay 7f: unraced on extremes of going. *R. Hannon*   **89**

PIGGY BANK   6 b.m. Emarati (USA) 74 – Granny's Bank 88 (Music Boy 124) [2002 5g Mar 28] tall, lengthy mare: one-time fair handicapper. *M. W. Easterby*   **–**

PIHELPLINE   2 ch.c. (Apr 4) Paris House 123 – What Happened Was 82 (Deploy 131) [2002 5.6m⁵ 6m 5m 6v Nov 9] first foal: dam 2-y-o 5f and 7f winner: no form in maidens. *A. Berry*   **–**

PIKESTAFF (USA)   4 ch.g. Diesis 133 – Navarene (USA) (Known Fact (USA) 135) [2002 63: f7s⁶ f12s³ f11g⁵ f8g⁵ f11g* f11g⁴ 11g⁶ 10m May 1] sturdy gelding: modest performer: won seller at Southwell in March: stays 1½m: acts on fibresand: none too consistent: sold 3,000 gns in August. *T. D. Barron*   **52**

PILGRIM GOOSE (IRE)   4 ch.g. Rainbows For Life (CAN) – Across The Ring (IRE) (Auction House (USA) 123) [2002 48§, a45§: f11s 11.9m² 12g Oct 19] poor maiden: left M. Tompkins after reappearance: stays 1½m: acts on fibresand, raced mainly on good going or firmer on turf: effective blinkered or not: carries head awkwardly: has found little: ungenuine. *J. R. Best*   **41 §**

PILGRIM PRINCESS (IRE)   4 b.f. Flying Spur (AUS) – Hasaid Lady (IRE) 69 (Shaadi (USA) 126) [2002 49, a52: f7g⁶ f5g⁵ f6g³ 6f* 6s² 6f² 6g⁴ 6d⁵ 6s 6m⁴ 5s 6g 6d f5g⁵ Dec 13] rather angular, good-quartered filly: fair handicapper: won at Thirsk in April: effective at 6f/7f: acts on fibresand, firm and soft going: tried blinkered: races prominently: has found little: has been early to post: none too consistent. *E. J. Alston*   **67**

PILGRIM SPIRIT (USA)   2 b. or br.f. (Apr 1) Saint Ballado (CAN) – Oshima (USA) (Mr Prospector (USA)) [2002 p7g⁵ Oct 31] 380,000Y: fourth foal: dam, 1m/9f winner in USA, sister to smart French/US performer up to 9f Sha Tha, herself dam of very smart 1¼m performer State Shinto: 4/1 and green, 5 lengths fifth of 11 to Pupillage in maiden at Lingfield, late headway without being knocked about: sure to improve. *J. H. M. Gosden*   **64 p**

PILIBERTO   2 br.g. (Apr 11) Man of May – Briska (IRE) 69 (River Falls 113) [2002 f6g f7g f7g f5g Dec 4] 600 2-y-o: first foal: dam 2-y-o 7f winner: well held in maidens/ sellers. *C. N. Kellett*   **–**

PILLAGER   5 b.g. Reprimand 122 – Emerald Ring 74 (Auction Ring (USA) 123) [2002 –: p12g 10m Apr 27] big, good-topped gelding: no longer of much account. *Mrs A. J. Bowlby*   **–**

PINCHANINCH   5 ch.g. Inchinor 119 – Wollow Maid 73 (Wollow 132) [2002 72, a–: 14.1d 11.6d 11.6s 11.6s⁸ 14.1g⁵ 12.6f 11.6m⁵ 12.1g² 16.2g 12m⁶ Sep 13] small, lengthy   **52**

gelding: modest handicapper nowadays: stays 1½m: acts on any turf going: blinkered twice in 2000: ran thoroughly moody race final 4-y-o start. *J. G. Portman*

PINCHBECK 3 b.g. Petong 126 – Veuve Hoornaert (IRE) 88 (Standaan (FR) 118) **83** [2002 61p: 6f 5m 5g* 6d* 6d* 6m⁶ 6m* 6m 6m 5g 5v Nov 8] strong, good sort: fairly useful handicapper: won at Carlisle, Haydock (apprentices) and Ripon in May and Doncaster in July: should stay 7f: acts on good to soft and good to firm ground: gelded after final outing. *M. A. Jarvis*

PINCHINCHA (FR) 8 b.g. Priolo (USA) 127 – Western Heights (Shirley Heights **89** 130) [2002 95: 8g 10m⁵ 10.3f 10f 10f⁶ 10m⁴ 10.4m 10m² 10d² 10m 10.3m⁴ 10.1m³ 8.9f³ 10.1s³ 10.1d³ Oct 30] workmanlike gelding: fairly useful handicapper: stays 1¼m: acts on fibresand and any turf going: tried visored earlier in career: usually held up: tough and consistent. *D. Morris*

PINES OF ROME 2 b.c. (Jan 28) Charnwood Forest (IRE) 125 – Ninfa di Cisterna **44** (Polish Patriot (USA) 128) [2002 6d 6.1s p8g Nov 23] 5,700F, 10,000Y: first foal: dam, Italian 5f/6f winner (including at 2 yrs), out of half-sister to Poule d'Essai des Poulains winner Victory Note: poor form, including in seller. *G. G. Margarson*

PINHEIROS STAR 4 b.g. Mtoto 134 – Octavia Girl 104 (Octavo (USA) 115) [2002 **–** p10g p12g p13g f12g Mar 25] 8,000 2-y-o: brother to useful winner around 1½m Toto Caelo, and half-brother to several winners, including 7f/1m winner Festival Mood (by Jalmood) and 1m (at 2 yrs) and 15f winner Lofty Lady (by Head For Heights), both fairly useful: dam 2-y-o 6f winner who later stayed 1m: no form in maidens/claimer. *G. C. H. Chung*

PININI 3 b.f. Pivotal 124 – Forget Me (IRE) (Don't Forget Me 127) [2002 8m 7f 8f⁶ 6g **63 d** 7g 7m p10g⁶ 11.9m 8m⁶ f8.5g f12g⁶ Oct 21] 6,000F, 5,800Y: fifth foal: half-sister to winner in Italy by Lear Fan: dam French/Italian 5f (at 2 yrs) to 1m winner: modest maiden handicapper: barely stays 1¼m: acts on polytrack, raced only on good going or firmer on turf: tried visored. *Mrs C. A. Dunnett*

PINJARRA 3 b.f. Petong 126 – Hoh Dancer 66 (Indian Ridge 123) [2002 –p: 8f **–** 10.1m⁶ 8m Sep 19] lengthy filly: well held in maidens/handicap: sold 800 gns, sent to Kuwait. *J. A. R. Toller*

PINJARRA PARK 3 gr.g. Petong 126 – Hattaafeh (IRE) 79 (Mtoto 134) [2002 p12g **–** Sep 4] first foal: dam 13f and 2m winner: started very slowly when tailed off in maiden at Lingfield. *N. P. Littmoden*

PINKERTON 2 b.c. (Jan 30) Alzao (USA) 117 – Dina Line (USA) 60 (Diesis 133) **96** [2002 6f⁵ 6s* 7m⁶ 7m² 7m² 7m³ 7s³ Oct 22] 32,000Y: close-coupled, quite attractive colt: first foal: dam, 1m winner, half-sister to smart US 6f/7f performer Gold Land out of half-sister to very smart miler Soviet Line: useful performer: won 18-runner maiden at Windsor in June by 10 lengths from Fairly High, soon leading: failed to repeat that form fully, and ran poorly (found little) final start: may prove best at 6f/7f: acts on good to firm going, best effort on soft. *R. Hannon*

PINK FIZZ 2 b.f. (Jan 26) Efisio 120 – Pennine Pink (IRE) 72 (Pennine Walk 120) **–** [2002 f8g Nov 26] 15,000F, 350 2-y-o: fourth foal: half-sister to fairly useful 5f (at 2 yrs) and 1¼m winner Never Diss Miss (by Owington) and 3-y-o Caterham Common: dam 1m/1¼m winner: slowly away and well held in claimer at Southwell. *J. G. Portman*

PINK TRIANGLE (IRE) 2 b.f. (Feb 21) Sesaro (USA) 81 – Sperrin Mist 83 (Camden **38** Town 125) [2002 5m 5m Apr 24] IR 3,800F, IR 4,000Y: workmanlike filly: half-sister to several winners, including 5f (at 2 yrs) to 1¼m winner L'Uomo Classics (by Indian King): dam 2-y-o 5f winner: poor form in maiden/seller. *J. J. Quinn*

PINOT NOIR 4 b.g. Saddlers' Hall (IRE) 126 – Go For Red (IRE) (Thatching 131) **80 d** [2002 80: 12m² 12m 13.3v⁵ 10m* 11.9d³ 10g 10.9m 10m 13.8d Nov 5] rather leggy, useful-looking gelding: fairly useful performer: on downgrade after reappearance, though won claimer at Brighton in June: left H. Morrison after fifth start: fell when seeming to jump path early on penultimate one: stays 1½m: acts on firm going: blinkered (downed tools) once: possibly temperamental. *G. J. Smith*

PIOUS 3 b.f. Bishop of Cashel 122 – La Cabrilla 89 (Carwhite 127) [2002 74p: f6g³ 6d **74** 6s⁶ 6g* 7d Aug 3] compact filly: fair handicapper: won at Leicester in July: best form at 6f: acted on fibresand: stud. *J. R. Fanshawe*

PIPE DREAM 6 b.g. King's Signet (USA) 110 – Rather Warm 103 (Tribal Chief 125) **44** [2002 –: p7g f6g p6g⁴ 7g May 10] poor maiden: stayed 1m: acted on good to firm going and polytrack: blinkered last 2 outings: dead. *Jean-Rene Auvray*

PIPE MUSIC (IRE) 7 b.g. Mujadil (USA) 119 – Sunset Cafe (IRE) 68 (Red Sunset **48** 120) [2002 48: f16s² f16.2g f16.2g² f16g f16.2g⁵ Mar 4] compact gelding: poor performer: stays 2m: acts on good to firm ground, good to soft and fibresand: often blinkered/visored: tried tongue tied. *P. C. Haslam*

PIPER 2 ch.g. (Mar 19) Atraf 116 – Lady-H (Never So Bold 135) [2002 5g 5m 5m 6m – Oct 2] 6,000Y: first foal: dam, ran once in bumper, half-sister to dam of smart sprinter Tadeo: well held in maidens. *D. W. Barker*

PIPER DREAM 4 b.g. Contract Law (USA) 108 – Good Fetch 66 (Siberian Express – (USA) 125) [2002 39: f11s Jan 5] leggy gelding: maiden: tailed off only 4-y-o start: blinkered. *J. Balding*

PIP'S BRAVE 6 b.g. Be My Chief (USA) 122 – Pipistrelle 62 (Shareef Dancer (USA) – § 135) [2002 p12g f14.8g 11.9d p16g Jul 17] tall, lengthy gelding: unimpressive mover: modest on his day at 4 yrs: well beaten in 2002 (reportedly had breathing problem final start): sometimes blinkered. *L. A. Dace*

PIPS MAGIC (IRE) 6 b.g. Pips Pride 117 – Kentucky Starlet (USA) 69 (Cox's Ridge – (USA)) [2002 86: 5m 6g 6g 6m 6g 6m 7m Sep 8] good-bodied gelding: fairly useful at 5 yrs: little form in 2002. *J. S. Goldie*

PIPS SONG (IRE) 7 ch.g. Pips Pride 117 – Friendly Song 48 (Song 132) [2002 80: **78** f6s p6g⁴ p6g p6g f6g f6g* 6.1g f7g* f6g f6g² 6g* 6m 5g³ 6g f6s⁴ f6g f7g 5g⁵ f6s⁴ Nov 2] **a74** lengthy gelding: poor mover: fair handicapper: left Dr J. Scargill after third start: won at Wolverhampton in March/April and Windsor in July: effective at stiff 5f to 7f: acts on all-weather, all turf wins on good ground or softer: tried blinkered/visored: has been awkward leaving stall. *P. W. Hiatt*

PIQUET 4 br.f. Mind Games 121 – Petonellajill 73 (Petong 126) [2002 75, a54: p8g **a52 ?** 5.3d 6m 5d 6g 6m f7g 5g p7g p7g p10g³ Dec 30] unfurnished filly: modest at best in 2002, leaving R. Hannon after reappearance: stays easy 1¼m: acts on any turf going and polytrack (below form on fibresand): has started slowly/edged left. *J. J. Bridger*

PIRANDELLO (IRE) 4 ch.g. Shalford (IRE) 124§ – Scenic Villa (Top Ville 129) **72** [2002 73: 10m 10f⁴ 12g 12g 10g 14m⁶ 14.1d p12g f16.2g p10g⁶ p10g Dec 21] fair maiden **a59** handicapper on turf, modest on all-weather: seems to stay easy 1½m: acts on any turf going, probably on polytrack. *Miss K. B. Boutflower*

PIRI PIRI (IRE) 2 b. or br.f. (Apr 6) Priolo (USA) 127 – Hot Curry (USA) (Sharpen **71** Up 127) [2002 6s⁶ 7f³ 6g⁶ Oct 18] 1,500F: rather leggy, workmanlike filly: half-sister to several winners, including 5-y-o Bold Ewar and 6-y-o Mujkari: dam 1m winner in USA: fair form: best effort when sixth of 30 to Michelle Ma Belle in sales race at Newmarket final start: should stay 1m. *M. G. Quinlan*

PIRLIE HILL 2 b.f. (Jun 8) Sea Raven (IRE) 75 – Panayr (Faraway Times (USA) – 123) [2002 f5g Nov 15] 1,800Y: sister to 6-y-o Ptarmigan Ridge and half-sister to 7f winner Miss Pigalle (by Good Times): dam unraced: last in maiden at Wolverhampton, very slowly away. *Miss L. A. Perratt*

PIROUETTES (IRE) 2 b.f. (Feb 21) Royal Applause 124 – Dance Serenade (IRE) **73** 54 (Marju (IRE) 127) [2002 7f 7g⁴ 6d Nov 1] IR 28,000Y: big, lengthy filly: has scope: first foal: dam lightly-raced half-sister to smart Irish performer up to 1¼m Pre-Eminent: best effort in maidens (fair form) when fourth to Fantasize at Leicester: not sure to stay 1m. *J. H. M. Gosden*

PISTE BLEU (FR) 2 b.f. (Feb 24) Pistolet Bleu (IRE) 133 – Thamissia (FR) (River- **65** man (USA) 131) [2002 6m 6f 6.1m Oct 1] third reported foal: dam unraced half-sister to smart French 7.5f (at 2 yrs) to 1¼m winner Varxi: fair form at best in maidens, fading each time: bred to be suited by 1m+. *R. M. Beckett*

PIVOTABLE 4 ch.f. Pivotal 124 – Lady Dowery (USA) (Manila (USA)) [2002 57+, **57** a75: f6s⁵ f7g⁵ f6g* f6g f6g⁶ f6g⁴ 6f⁵ 6m³ 6d 6g 6d Jul 3] big, lengthy filly: modest **a68** performer: won claimer at Southwell in January: stays easy 7f: acts on soft ground (probably on firm) and fibresand: tried visored: has raced freely: joined R. Fahey 6,000 gns in July, re-sold €11,000 in November. *K. R. Burke*

PIVOT D'AMOUR 3 ch.f. Pivotal 124 – Miss Loving 89 (Northfields (USA)) [2002 – 56: 5d 6g 6.9s f6g⁶ Jun 22] leggy, plain filly: little form at 3 yrs. *J. J. Quinn*

PLACATE 4 b.f. Rainbow Quest (USA) 134 – Princess Borghese (USA) 82 (Nijinsky – (CAN) 138) [2002 75: p8g⁵ p12g f7g Feb 15] close-coupled, quite good-topped filly: **a47** disappointing maiden: should prove better at 1½m than shorter. *G. G. Margarson*

PLATEAU 3 b.g. Zamindar (USA) 116 – Painted Desert 89 (Green Desert (USA) 127) **98**
[2002 94: 6d⁵ 5.2g* 5g Aug 21] good-bodied gelding: useful performer, lightly raced:
won 4-runner handicap at Yarmouth in July by short head from Baralinka: well held only
start after: effective at 5f/6f: yet to race on extremes of going: has worn crossed noseband:
sold 38,000 gns in October, and gelded. *B. W. Hills*

PLATINUM BOY (IRE) 2 b.c. (Apr 28) Goldmark (USA) 113 – Brown Foam **49**
(Horage 124) [2002 f5g⁶ 5f 6m⁶ f7g³ 7m⁴ 8d⁶ 7.5g f8g p8g⁵ f9.4g* Dec 7] IR 2,200Y: **a65**
compact colt: seventh foal: half-brother to 6f/7f winner Diamond Rachael and fairly
useful 1m/8.5f winner Pass The Rest (both by Shalford): dam ran twice: fair on all-
weather, poor on turf: won seller at Wolverhampton: stays 9.4f: acts on all-weather and
good to firm going: blinkered (below form) once: sometimes edges left. *K. A. Ryan*

PLATINUM CHARMER (IRE) 2 b.g. (Feb 4) Kahyasi 130 – Mystic Charm **76**
(Nashwan (USA) 135) [2002 5m⁵ 8g² 8m f8s² 8s³ f8.5s* f8g⁴ Nov 25] IR 17,000Y: **a79**
compact gelding: second foal: half-brother to a winner up to 10.5f in Italy by Elmaamul:
dam unraced: fair performer: won maiden at Wolverhampton in November: will be suited
by 1¼m+: acts on fibresand and soft going. *K. A. Ryan*

PLATINUM DUKE 3 br.g. Reprimand 122 – Princess Alaska (Northern State (USA) **92**
91) [2002 81: f7g³ f7g* p8g⁵ 10.3s 8m f8g² 7m* 8d* 7f* 7f* f7g* 7f⁴ 7.5m* 7m* 8m⁵
7m* 7m 7.1m³ Sep 21] tall, close-coupled gelding: fairly useful performer: had an
excellent year, winning seller at Southwell, claimers at Salisbury, Ripon, Catterick and
Beverley, minor event at Redcar and handicaps at Wolverhampton, Redcar and Catterick
between February and August: effective at 7f/1m: acts on fibresand, firm and good to soft
going: has been bandaged: tough and consistent: sold 25,000 gns, sent to USA. *K. A. Ryan*

PLATONIC 3 b.f. Zafonic (USA) 130 – Puce 112 (Darshaan 133) [2002 79: 7.1g 7m **77**
8m³ 9.9m⁵ 10m⁶ 11.9d⁶ 10.2g Oct 16] leggy, light-bodied filly: fair maiden handicapper:
probably stays 1¼m: acts on good to firm ground: sent to France. *L. M. Cumani*

PLAYAPART (USA) 3 b.c. Theatrical 128 – Spotlight Dance (USA) (Miswaki (USA) **110**
124) [2002 107p: 9m* 10.3f³ 11g⁶ May 21] rather leggy, quite attractive colt: has a long,
round action: smart performer: won listed race at Newmarket in April by ¾ length from
Wahchi: creditable 1¼ lengths third to Sohaib in similar event at Chester next time:
reportedly thought to have swallowed tongue when last in another listed race at Goodwood final outing: will probably stay 1½m: acts on firm going, good to soft and
polytrack: held up: sent to USA. *G. A. Butler*

PLAYBACK (IRE) 3 b.c. Revoque (IRE) 122 – Sound Tap (IRE) (Warning 136) **90**
[2002 81: 10g⁴ 10g 9.9s⁴ 12m³ 12d* 11.6m² 12f⁵ 12m³ 14m⁴ 10g⁶ 15m² Sep 29] leggy, good-
topped colt: fairly useful performer: won handicap at Salisbury in July: left R. Hannon
before final start: stays 15f: acts on firm and soft ground: blinkered after second outing:
has started slowly/hung: reliable. *P. Favero, Italy*

PLAYFUL DANE (IRE) 5 b.g. Dolphin Street (FR) 125 – Omicida (IRE) (Danehill **44**
(USA) 126) [2002 5m⁶ 5m 5m 5g⁵ Sep 9] 10,500Y: good-topped gelding: second foal:
half-brother to winner in Germany by Platini: dam unraced: poor form in maidens: raced
only at 5f. *W. S. Cunningham*

PLAYFUL SPIRIT 3 b.f. Mind Games 121 – Kalimat 74 (Be My Guest (USA) 126) **76 d**
[2002 88: 6m 7g 8m⁶ 7g⁵ 7m 8.1m 8m 7.6m 8.1m 7f⁵ 7g 7g Dec 17] leggy filly: fairly
useful at 2 yrs: fair form at best in 2002: below par last 6 starts, leaving P. Harris 3,000
gns before final one: stays 7f: acts on good/good to firm going: tried visored: races freely:
tricky ride. *S. R. Bowring*

PLAYING CARD 2 ch.c. (Mar 31) First Trump 118 – Poleaxe (Selkirk (USA) 129) **61**
[2002 5d⁵ 5.1f 5m f5g 7g Oct 17] 2,200Y: second foal: dam, ran twice, out of unraced
half-sister to Kris and Diesis: modest maiden: well beaten in sellers last 2 starts: raced
mainly at 5f: acts on firm and good to soft ground: sold 2,000 gns, sent to Spain.
I. A. Balding

PLAY MISTY (IRE) 3 b.f. Dr Devious (IRE) 127 – Mystic Step (IRE) 90 (Fairy **51**
King (USA)) [2002 56: p7g² p8g f6g p10g² f12g f8g p10g Dec 30] modest maiden: left
John Berry after fifth outing: seems to stay easy 1¼m: acts on all-weather, soft and good
to firm going: sometimes blinkered. *B. R. Johnson*

PLAY THAT TUNE 2 ch.f. (Jan 26) Zilzal (USA) 137 – Military Tune (IRE) (Nash- **80 +**
wan (USA) 135) [2002 7d² 7m⁴ Aug 1] 14,000Y: strong filly: fourth foal: half-sister to
fairly useful French 11f winner Filly Bergere (by Sadler's Wells): dam unraced half-sister
to Prix Saint-Alary winner Muncie and Prix Royal-Oak winner Mersey: favourite,
fairly useful form in maidens at Kempton (2 lengths second to Londonnetdotcom) and

Goodwood (fourth to Geminiani), racing freely both times: will need to settle to stay 1m. *H. R. A. Cecil*

PLAY THE FLUTE 2 ch.f. (Apr 21) Piccolo 121 – Son Et Lumiere (Rainbow Quest **47** (USA) 134) [2002 6m 7m 8.1g Sep 12] 11,000Y: half-sister to several winners, including useful miler Sonatina (by Distant Relative), 6f winner at 2 yrs: dam, maiden, out of smart miler Soprano: poor form in maidens. *M. Blanshard*

PLAYTIME BLUE 2 b.g. (Mar 26) Komaite (USA) – Miss Calculate 67 (Mummy's **67** Game 120) [2002 6d 7g⁶ f6f² f5s³ p6g f6g Oct 21] 8,000 2-y-o: lengthy, good-quartered gelding: has scope: fourth foal: brother to 4-y-o Sandles: dam 4-y/7f winner: fair maiden: second at Wolverhampton: effective at 5f/6f: acts on fibresand: edged left second/third starts. *M. D. I. Usher*

PLAZZOTTA (IRE) 5 b.g. Sri Pekan (USA) 117 – Porte Des Iles (IRE) 76 (Kris 135) **–** [2002 –: f5s⁶ f6s f6g f6g f7g⁶ Feb 12] good-topped gelding: no form. *M. C. Chapman*

PLEADING 9 b.g. Never So Bold 135 – Ask Mama 83 (Mummy's Pet 125) [2002 61: **–** 6f⁶ p7g 8g Jul 19] smallish, good-topped gelding: modest performer in 2001: little form in 2002: usually blinkered/visored. *M. A. Buckley*

PLEASE THE PRINCE (IRE) 2 b.c. (Mar 9) Desert Prince (IRE) 130 – Inner Door **–** (IRE) (King of Clubs 124) [2002 7s⁶ Oct 16] approx. 29,000Y in Italy: second foal: dam won up to 1½m in Italy: well held in minor event at Milan. *C. F. Wall*

PLEASURE 7 ch.m. Most Welcome 131 – Peak Squaw (USA) 75 (Icecapade (USA)) **–** [2002 56§: 5.9d f5s Sep 5] unfurnished mare: modest handicapper in 2001: well held both 7-y-o starts: sometimes blinkered. *P. R. Wood*

PLEASURE TIME 9 ch.g. Clantime 101 – First Experience 58 (Le Johnstan 123) **63** [2002 66: 5m² 5.1d 6.1m 5m 5m f5s Sep 5] leggy, good-topped gelding: modest handicapper: best at 5f: acts on fibresand, best turf form on good going or firmer: effective blinkered, visored nowadays: front runner. *C. Smith*

PLEINMONT POINT (IRE) 4 b.g. Tagula (IRE) 116 – Cree's Figurine 63 (Cree- **62** town 123) [2002 67: 7f⁵ 6.1m⁴ 7s 6.1v 7.1g 6g⁵ p6g² p6g⁴ p7g Dec 28] big, workmanlike gelding: modest maiden handicapper: stays 7f: acts on heavy going, good to firm and polytrack: blinkered last 4 starts: tried tongue tied. *P. D. Evans*

PLUMBAGO (IRE) 2 b.f. (Feb 8) Mujadil (USA) 119 – Bint Alhabib (Nashwan **58 d** (USA) 135) [2002 6.1d³ 7f² 7f⁶ f7g³ 8d 8.3d f8g Oct 17] tall, unfurnished filly: fourth foal: dam, last on only start, half-sister to 6-y-o Gallery God: modest maiden: placed in sellers: well below form last 3 starts: stays 7f: best effort on firm going: blinkered/tongue tied penultimate outing. *P. D. Evans*

PLUM BEAUTIFUL 4 b.f. Wolfhound (USA) 126 – Miss Haversham 81 (Salse **54** (USA) 128) [2002 56: p7g² 7s f8.5s Dec 9] modest maiden: left C. Cyzer £1,000 after reappearance: probably stays 9.4f: acts on all-weather, best turf efforts on good to firm going. *D. Burchell*

PLUTOCRAT (USA) 5 ch.g. Silver Hawk (USA) 123 – Satin Velvet (USA) 103 (El **74** Gran Senor (USA) 136) [2002 8g* 7.5g a8f⁶ 8g p7g p7g f7g* f7g p7g Dec 30] first foal: dam, 7f winner, half-sister to smart performer up to 9f Satin Flower, herself dam of Middle Park winner Lujain: fair handicapper: won at Abu Dhabi in January and (having left S. Seemar, UAE, 6,000 gns after third start) Wolverhampton in November: stays 9f: acts on dirt/fibresand, raced only good ground or firmer on turf: has won in cheekpieces: has been slowly away. *Mrs L. Stubbs*

PLYMSOLE (USA) 3 ch.f. Diesis 133 – Pump (USA) (Forli (ARG)) [2002 79p: 8m **84** 8f⁵ 8m² 9.9m⁵ 8g Sep 27] rather leggy filly: fairly useful handicapper, lightly raced: stays 1¼m: raced only on good going or firmer. *J. L. Dunlop*

POCKET STYLE (IRE) 3 b.f. Desert Style (IRE) 121 – Practical 95 (Ballymore **55** 123) [2002 64: 7.9g⁴ 9.3s 8m³ 8m 10g⁶ f8g Nov 26] small, workmanlike filly: modest maiden: stays 1m: acts on good to firm going: has started slowly/hung under pressure. *C. Grant*

POINT OF DISPUTE 7 b.g. Cyrano de Bergerac 120 – Opuntia (Rousillon (USA) **101** 133) [2002 101: 7m⁴ p8g 7m 7f⁵ Aug 17] tall gelding: useful handicapper: creditable efforts in 2002 only on first and final starts, fourth to Demonstrate in Buckingham Palace Stakes at Royal Ascot on former occasion: best at 6f/7f: acts on all-weather, firm and good to soft going: visored: has tended to sweat/get on edge: has been early to post: often held up: tends to carry head awkwardly/wander/find little: less than trustworthy nowadays. *P. J. Makin*

POKER SCHOOL (IRE)   8 b.g. Night Shift (USA) – Mosaique Bleue (Shirley   **–**
Heights 130) [2002 –, a58: f12s⁶ f12s⁶ f12g⁶ f12g⁴ Jan 24] smallish, sturdy gelding: poor   **a45**
performer: effective at 1½m to 2m: acts on fibresand, little form on turf since 1997: tried
blinkered/visored/tongue tied. *M. R. Bosley*

POLANSKI MILL   3 b.g. Polish Precedent (USA) 131 – Mill On The Floss 117 (Mill   **–**
Reef (USA) 141) [2002 9g 10s Oct 26] 65,000Y: brother to winner in Spain, closely
related to useful performer around 1¼m Hatta's Mill (by Green Desert) and half-brother
to several winners, including 4-y-o Bosham Mill and to dam of 3-y-o Scott's View: dam
7f (at 2 yrs) and 1½m winner: slowly away and well held in maidens: gelded after final
start. *C. A. Horgan*

POLAR BEAR   2 ch.c. (May 4) Polar Falcon (USA) 126 – Aim For The Top (USA)   **73 p**
111 (Irish River (FR) 131) [2002 5g 5.1s⁵ f6g³ Nov 30] 21,000Y: half-brother to several
winners, including 1993 2-y-o 7f winner/Fillies' Mile second Dance To The Top and
fairly useful 1¼m winner Aim High (both by Sadler's Wells): dam 6f (at 2 yrs) to 8.5f
winner: slowly away and better than result in maidens: nearest at finish under considerate
handling (edged left) when third to Ronnie From Donny at Wolverhampton: should stay
1m: reportedly had breathing problem on debut: capable of better, and should win a race
or 2. *W. J. Haggas*

POLAR BEAUTY (IRE)   5 b.m. Distinctly North (USA) 115 – How Gorgeous   **–**
(Frimley Park 109) [2002 56: 8.1m 5.5f Jun 26] lengthy mare: modest maiden at 4 yrs:
gave impression something amiss both 5-y-o starts. *M. F. Harris*

POLAR BEN   3 b.g. Polar Falcon (USA) 126 – Woodbeck 90 (Terimon 124) [2002   **106 +**
86p: 6g⁴ 7.1s* 7d⁵ 7m* Sep 24] rather leggy, useful-looking gelding: useful performer:
successful in minor events at Haydock (beat Heretic ¾ length) in June and Newmarket
(showed decent turn of foot in 4-runner affair, beat Tumbleweed Ridge by length) in September: unlikely to stay beyond 7f: acts on soft and good to firm going. *J. R. Fanshawe*

POLAR DANCE (USA)   4 gr. or ro.g. Nureyev (USA) 131 – Arctic Swing (USA)   **–**
(Swing Till Dawn (USA)) [2002 –: f7g² p7g f9.4g³ f7g⁵ f9.4f f9.4g⁴ f8.5s Dec 26] modest   **a54 §**
maiden: stays 9.4f: acts on fibresand: has hung markedly left. *J. W. Unett*

POLAR FORCE   2 ch.c. (Feb 17) Polar Falcon (USA) 126 – Irish Light (USA) 91   **105**
(Irish River (FR) 131) [2002 5.2g* 5.1f⁵ 5m³ 5m 5m² 5.2f⁵ 5g⁵ 6s³ 6d³ 6m 6s Oct 26]
31,000Y: neat colt: second foal: half-brother to 3-y-o Harnour: dam, 1m winner, out of
half-sister to smart US 6f/7f performer Gold Land: useful performer: won minor event at
Newbury in April: placed 4 times after, running particularly well in Phoenix Stakes at the
Curragh (beaten ½ length by Spartacus) and listed event at Ripon eighth/ninth starts:
should stay 7f: has form on firm ground, goes well on softer than good: sometimes finds
little. *M. R. Channon*

POLAR HAZE   5 ch.g. Polar Falcon (USA) 126 – Sky Music 85 (Absalom 128) [2002   **55**
52, a60: f6g³ f6g⁵ f6g 5.9s⁶ 6.1m 5m 6s f5s⁵ f6s* f6g f5g³ f6g Dec 10] lengthy, good-   **a60**
quartered gelding: modest performer: won seller at Southwell in September: best at 5f/6f:
acts on firm ground, soft and fibresand: usually visored: has hung left. *Miss S. E. Hall*

POLAR IMPACT   3 br.c. Polar Falcon (USA) 126 – Boozy 111 (Absalom 128) [2002   **80**
76+: 5s* 6m⁴ 6d³ 6s⁵ 6m³ 6m⁶ 5d⁴ 5v Nov 8] strong, short-backed colt: fairly useful
performer: won maiden at Newcastle in April: raced only at 5f/6f: acts on soft and good
to firm going, ran as if something amiss on firm: has been early to post. *A. Berry*

POLAR KINGDOM   4 b.g. Pivotal 124 – Scarlet Lake 60 (Reprimand 122) [2002   **83**
101: 6m⁵ 6.3d 7.2g 7g 8g 7.6s² 8g 8s Oct 28] rangy gelding: usually leads well: fairly
useful handicapper nowadays: effective at 6f (given bit of a test) to 7.6f: acts on soft
going: tried visored/blinkered/tongue tied. *W. J. Haggas*

POLAR RED   5 ch.g. Polar Falcon (USA) 126 – Sharp Top 62 (Sharpo 132) [2002   **–**
106: 12v Nov 9] good-topped gelding: has a round action: smart performer at best:
visored, well held only 5-y-o outing on Flat: blinkered first 3 starts at 2 yrs: smart hurdler.
M. C. Pipe

POLAR ROCK   4 ch.f. Polar Falcon (USA) 126 – South Rock 102 (Rock City 120)   **–**
[2002 66: p7g 7.1m 6d 9d Jul 3] lengthy, rather unfurnished filly: fair maiden at 3 yrs:
well held in 2002. *M. Salaman*

POLAR TRYST   3 ch.f. Polar Falcon (USA) 126 – Lovers Tryst 91 (Castle Keep 121)   **68**
[2002 65: 10d⁶ 10.1f⁴ 12m⁵ 11f⁴ Sep 25] leggy, lengthy, unfurnished filly: fair maiden:
stays 1½m: acts on firm and good to soft ground. *Lady Herries*

Aon MacDonagh Boland Stakes, the Curragh—the Amanda Perrett-trained Polar Way extends his unbeaten record to four with a length-and-a-half success over One Won One; Tender Cove is third

POLAR WAY 3 ch.g. Polar Falcon (USA) 126 – Fetish 85 (Dancing Brave (USA) **112 p** 140) [2002 7s* 6m* 6f* 6m* 6m⁴ Sep 28] medium-sized, angular, workmanlike gelding: fourth living foal: half-brother to useful French 1m winner Front Bench (by Arazi): dam, 1m winner who stayed 10.5f, out of Irish 1000 Guineas second Bold Fantasy: smart form: won first 4 starts, namely maiden at Newbury in June, minor events at Kempton in July/ August and Aon MacDonagh Boland Stakes at the Curragh (beat One Won One by 1½ lengths) in September: creditable 3¾ lengths fourth to Crystal Castle in Diadem Stakes at Ascot, short of room after 2f out: raced only at 6f/7f: slowly away second outing: likely to do better still. *Mrs A. J. Perrett*

POLDEN CHIEF 2 br.g. (May 3) Atraf 116 – Maid of Mischief (Be My Chief (USA) **54** 122) [2002 6m⁶ 6m 7.1g Sep 12] second foal: half-brother to 5f (at 2 yrs) and 7f winner Naughty Knight (by King's Signet): dam unraced: modest form in maidens: will probably stay 1m: swished tail/edged left on debut. *G. B. Balding*

POLE STAR 4 b. or br.g. Polar Falcon (USA) 126 – Ellie Ardensky 100 (Slip Anchor **111** 136) [2002 103: 10f² 10m² 10m⁴ 13.9m² 16m⁴ 14.6v* Nov 8] tall, angular gelding: smart performer: won minor event at Doncaster in November by ½ length from Frosty Welcome: good efforts otherwise in 2002, particularly when ¾-length second to Hugs Dancer in Ebor (Handicap) at York and 4 lengths fourth to Persian Punch in Jockey Club Cup at Newmarket previous 2 starts: effective at 1¼m and stays 2m: acts on any going: usually held up: reliable. *J. R. Fanshawe*

POLGAMES (IRE) 2 b.f. (Jan 29) Mind Games 121 – Polgwynne 48 (Forzando 122) **–** [2002 6m 6d Oct 21] second foal: dam 7f winner: well held in maidens. *B. R. Millman*

POLICASTRO 4 b.g. Anabaa (USA) 130 – Belle Arrivee 87 (Bustino 136) [2002 66: **64** p12g⁵ p10g Dec 21] modest maiden: should stay 1¾m: acts on all-weather and heavy ground: tried tongue tied. *P. Mitchell*

POLISH BARON (IRE) 5 b.g. Barathea (IRE) 127 – Polish Mission (Polish Pre- **79** cedent (USA) 131) [2002 73: 11.6s³ f14.8g* 16.4d² f14s* f14.8g* 14.1d Oct 30] useful-looking gelding: fair performer: unbeaten in 3 starts on fibresand, namely claimers at Wolverhampton/Southwell and handicap at Wolverhampton between July/September: barely stays 2m: acts on soft going, good to firm and fibresand: reliable. *J. White*

POLISH CORRIDOR 3 b.g. Danzig Connection (USA) – Possibility 59 (Robellino **77** (USA) 127) [2002 63: 10g² 9.9m⁴ 12.1g³ 11f⁴ 10f* 11m³ 12m⁴ Jul 18] tall gelding: has scope: fair handicapper: won at Pontefract in June: probably best at 1¼m/11f: raced only on good going or firmer: has run in snatches. *M. Dods*

POLISHED 3 ch.g. Danzig Connection (USA) – Glitter (FR) 70 (Reliance II 137) **–** [2002 9.9m Sep 13] half-brother to several winners, notably top-class French 1½m

758

performer Village Star (by Moulin) and smart French 1¼m/1½m performer For Valour (by Trempolino): dam 1¼m winner: reluctant at start and very slowly away when last in maiden at Goodwood. *K. O. Cunningham-Brown*

POLISH EMPEROR (USA)   2 ch.c. (Feb 2) Polish Precedent (USA) 131 – Empress   **82 p** Jackie (USA) (Mount Hagen (FR) 127) [2002 6s* Jun 12] IR 34,000Y: closely related to 1995 2-y-o 7f winner Jezyah (by Chief's Crown) and half-brother to several winners, including useful 6f (including at 2 yrs)/7f winner Tajannub (by Dixieland Band): dam, 5f to 8.5f winner in USA, half-sister to Derby third Star of Gdansk: 7/2, won 20-runner maiden at Kempton by neck from Clann A Cougar, getting on top final 1f: reportedly suffered muscle injury after: should improve. *P. W. Harris*

POLISH FLAME   4 b.g. Blushing Flame (USA) 109 – Lady Emm (Emarati (USA)   **71 p** 74) [2002 71: 13s* 16.2g* 17.5g⁴ Sep 20] lightly-raced handicapper, fair form: won at Hamilton and Beverley in May: shaped well at Ayr when next seen out: will stay beyond 17f: acts on heavy going: probably capable of better still. *Mrs M. Reveley*

POLISH LEGEND   3 b.g. Polish Precedent (USA) 131 – Chita Rivera 61 (Chief   **56** Singer 131) [2002 11.7f 8m Aug 29] 10,000Y: third foal: half-brother to useful but untrustworthy performer up to 1½m Sunstone (by Caerleon): dam, staying maiden, half-sister to Oaks winner Lady Carla: better effort in maidens when eighth of 18 at Salisbury second start: should be suited by further than 1m: slowly away on debut. *R. J. Baker*

POLISH LEGION   9 b.g. Polish Precedent (USA) 131 – Crystal Bright 75 (Bold Lad   **71** (IRE) 133) [2002 68: 6m 6g 7m 5g 5g* 6g 5g² 5m 6f* 7f⁵ 6d 6d Oct 19] big gelding: fair handicapper: trained in 2001 by Miss A. McMahon in Ireland: left S. Keightley after third 9-y-o outing: won at Cork in August and Listowel in September: best at 5f/6f: acts on any going: has looked hard ride. *Hugh O'Driscoll, Ireland*

Mr D. I. Russell's "Pole Star"

POLISH OFF 4 b.g. Polish Precedent (USA) 131 – Lovely Lyca 76 (Night Shift (USA)) **67**
[2002 87: 8d 8.3s 7g 8g 9.9g 8m³ 7.9m⁵ 8m 8.1m 7.1m⁶ 7d Oct 15] strong gelding: fairly
useful winner at 3 yrs: only fair in 2002: effective at 1m to 10.4f: acts on firm and good to
soft going: tried tongue tied: has started slowly: sold 2,500 gns. *R. M. Beckett*

POLISH SUMMER 5 b.h. Polish Precedent (USA) 131 – Hunt The Sun (Rainbow **120**
Quest (USA) 134) [2002 114: 10g* 12m² 14g² 12.5g* 12m⁴ 20g³ᵈ 12m⁵ Dec 15] strong,
good sort: first foal: dam, placed at 1¼m in France, sister to very smart middle-distance
stayers Sunshack and Raintrap: very smart performer, lightly raced prior to 2002: won
minor event at Chantilly in June and Grand Prix de Deauville (beat Califet a neck) in
August: ran well when 2 lengths second to Ange Gabriel in Grand Prix de Saint-Cloud
second start and when 1¾ lengths fourth of 5 to Aquarelliste in Prix Foy at Longchamp
fifth outing: visored, creditable 4¼ lengths fifth to Ange Gabriel in Hong Kong Vase
at Sha Tin final start: may prove best at 1½m to around 2m (faded, hung right and
disqualified over 2½m after third past post, beaten under length, in Prix du Cadran at
Longchamp penultimate start): has form on soft ground, best efforts on good/good to
firm: reliable: stays in training. *A. Fabre, France*

POLKA PRINCESS 2 b.f. (Feb 13) Makbul 104 – Liberatrice (FR) (Assert 134) **72**
[2002 5g f5g f6g³ f6g* f7g* f7g* f7f³ 7f* 7f⁴ f6f Nov 11] small, angular filly: third foal:
dam maiden half-sister to smart French 1989 2-y-o 5.5f winner Zinarelle: fair performer:
won 2 sellers at Wolverhampton in June and nurseries on same course (first run after
leaving D. Coakley) in August and Catterick in September: stays 7f: acts on fibresand,
raced only on good going or firmer on turf: seemed to run moodily final start. *I. A. Wood*

POLLY FLINDERS 4 b.f. Polar Falcon (USA) 126 – So True 116 (So Blessed 130) **–**
[2002 65: 10.9g 8g p10g Dec 18] rangy filly: fair maiden at 3 yrs: well held in 2002:
reportedly broke blood vessel final start. *G. B. Balding*

POLLY PLUNKETT 2 b.f. (Mar 6) Puissance 110 – Expectation (IRE) 59 (Night **68**
Shift (USA)) [2002 6m 6f³ 6g⁴ 6m 6.1m⁴ 6f² 6f 6d⁶ Oct 21] 7,000Y, resold 2,000Y:
strong, angular filly: second foal: dam, sprint maiden, granddaughter of Irish 1000
Guineas winner Front Row: fair maiden: best effort when second in nursery at Haydock:
raced only at 6f: acts on firm and good to soft ground: sold only 1,000 gns. *A. Berry*

POLLYS ANGEL 3 b.f. Makbul 104 – Wayzgoose (USA) 76 (Diesis 133) [2002 8.1s **–**
Jun 8] lengthy filly: fifth foal: dam once-raced daughter of smart French 10.5f winner
Indoor: tailed off in maiden at Haydock. *W. Clay*

POLONAISE 4 b.f. Pivotal 124 – Vallauris 94 (Faustus (USA) 118) [2002 p8g f9.4g **–**
p12g 8.5d⁶ 8.5d 9m Aug 16] fair maiden at 2 yrs: no form in 2002, leaving I. Balding
1,000 gns after third start: tried blinkered. *Daniel O'Connell, Ireland*

POLYPHONY (USA) 8 b.g. Cox's Ridge (USA) – Populi (USA) (Star Envoy (USA)) **–**
[2002 18s Jun 6] tall gelding: fair winner at 3 yrs: lightly raced and well held on Flat since
(poor maiden hurdler/chaser). *D. C. O'Brien*

POLYSONIC 2 b.f. (Mar 25) Zafonic (USA) 130 – El Opera (IRE) 100 (Sadler's Wells **53**
(USA) 132) [2002 6m⁶ 6m⁶ Aug 14] 28,000Y: good-bodied filly: third foal: half-sister to
3-y-o Dafne and fairly useful 1¼m winner Rainshine (by Rainbow Quest): dam, 7f
winner who stayed 1¼m well, closely related to smart sprinter Pharaoh's Delight: modest
form in maidens: dead. *R. M. H. Cowell*

POMFRET LAD 4 b.g. Charge de Bergerac 120 – Lucky Flinders 77 (Free State 125) **111**
[2002 107: 5m 5g 6m² Jul 4] tall, good-topped gelding: smart performer, lightly raced:
best effort when length second to Chookie Heiton in handicap at Newbury in July: not
disgraced in Palace House Stakes at Newmarket on reappearance: behind in King's Stand
Stakes at Royal Ascot next time: races freely, and should prove as effective at 5f as 6f: yet
to race on extremes of ground. *P. J. Makin*

POMME D'OR 4 b.f. Celtic Swing 138 – Glitter (FR) 70 (Reliance II 137) [2002 –: **–**
p12g 14.1f⁵ f14.8g Jun 7] angular filly: of no account: sent to France. *K. O. Cunningham-*
Brown

POMME SWINGER (FR) 4 b.f. Celtic Swing 138 – Tarte Aux Pommes (USA) **45**
(Local Talent (USA) 122) [2002 –: 8.1m 8g 6m Jun 26] leggy, sparely-made filly: poor
maiden: sent to France. *K. O. Cunningham-Brown*

PONDERON 2 ch.c. (Mar 11) Hector Protector (USA) 124 – Blush Rambler (IRE) **– p**
(Blushing Groom (FR) 131) [2002 8g Oct 18] half-brother to several winners, including
smart 1m (at 2 yrs) to 1½m winner Rambling Rose (by Cadeaux Genereux) and useful
1¼m winner Kiftsgate (by Kris): dam Irish 1½m winner: 25/1, burly and green, never-

dangerous thirteenth of 16 in maiden at Newmarket: will probably do better. *R. F. Johnson Houghton*

PONGEE 2 b.f. (Mar 22) Barathea (IRE) 127 – Puce 112 (Darshaan 133) [2002 6m 6g **72 p** 6f 8d⁴ Oct 21] quite attractive filly: second foal: dam 1¼m/1½m winner who stayed 14.6f: fair maiden: clearly best effort when close fourth of 20 to Arcalis in nursery at Pontefract, still green and checked when weaving through: will be well suited by 1¼m+: slowly away 3 times: capable of better still. *L. M. Cumani*

PONT NEUF (IRE) 2 b.f. (Mar 16) Revoque (IRE) 122 – Petite Maxine 70 (Sharpo **67** 132) [2002 p7g 8.3d² f8s² 7f Oct 2] 13,000Y: tall, angular filly: fourth foal: half-sister to fairly useful 5f (including at 2 yrs)/6f performer Pipadash and a 6.5f and 1m winner in Sweden (both by Pips Pride): dam, maiden who stayed 7f, out of smart 2-y-o 5f winner Penny Blessing: fair maiden: runner-up at Windsor and Southwell: should stay 1¼m: acts on fibresand, firm and good to soft ground. *J. W. Hills*

POOKA'S DAUGHTER (IRE) 2 b.f. (Jan 31) Eagle Eyed (USA) 111 – Gaelic's **59** Fantasy (IRE) (Statoblest 120) [2002 5.7d 6m 5m 7m 6m 8.3d* 8d f7g f8g⁶ f6g⁴ Dec 16] IR 5,200Y: first foal: dam, Italian 1m winner, half-sister to smart performers Bachir (at 1m) and Albuhera (at 1m/1¼m): modest performer: won seller at Windsor in October on final outing for Mrs P. N. Dutfield: respectable fourth in seller at Wolverhampton: stays 1m: acts on fibresand and good to soft going, probably on good to firm: none too consistent. *J. M. Bradley*

POP GUN 3 ch.g. Pharly (FR) 130 – Angel Fire (Nashwan (USA) 135) [2002 7s⁶ 7.1g **56** f8.5g 8.5g 9.1d 12m f14s⁴ 10m³ Oct 3] fourth foal: half-brother to fairly useful 1m winner Shall We Dance (by Rambo Dancer): dam unraced granddaughter of Arc winner All Along: modest maiden handicapper: should prove best at 1¼m/1½m: acts on fibresand and good to firm ground. *B. W. Hills*

POPOCATEPETL (FR) 3 br.f. Nashwan (USA) 135 – Dimakya (USA) 83 (Dayjur **66** (USA) 137) [2002 66p: 11.1g⁵ 10f⁶ 14.1f³ 12.4m³ 12m f12s⁴ p13g⁴ Oct 4] leggy, quite **a–** good-topped filly: fair maiden on turf: probably stays 1¾m: acts on firm and good to soft going, well held on all-weather. *B. W. Hills*

POPPYLINE 2 b.f. (May 17) Averti (IRE) 117 – Shalverton (IRE) (Shalford (IRE) **65** 124§) [2002 5m 5.7f² 6m 6f 7g⁴ Oct 19] close-coupled filly: second foal: dam, ran 3 times, half-sister to smart 1995 2-y-o sprinter Kahir Almaydan: fair maiden: in frame at Bath and Catterick (nursery): stays 7f: raced only on good going or firmer. *W. R. Muir*

POP THE AUCTIONEER (IRE) 2 b.g. (Mar 6) Sesaro (USA) 81 – Cora-B (IRE) **53** 58 (Digamist (USA) 110) [2002 5.1g 5.1f 5m⁴ 7m 6.1m⁶ 6g f6s f8.5s Dec 9] IR 4,500F, **a–** 1,600Y: sturdy, close-coupled gelding: third foal: dam showed a little ability in Ireland: modest maiden: effective at 5f/6f: acts on good to firm going, well beaten on fibresand. *E. J. Alston*

POP THE CORK 5 ch.g. Clantime 101 – Hyde Princess 75 (Touch Paper 113) [2002 **70 d** 75, a–: 5m⁶ 5m⁵ 5m 5g 5m 5m 5m⁵ 5m 5m Aug 28] strong-quartered gelding: fair **a–** handicapper: on the downgrade in 2002: raced mainly at 5f: acts on firm and good to soft going: visored final start: reportedly broke blood vessel final 3-y-o outing: races prominently: has carried head high. *R. M. Whitaker*

POP UP AGAIN 2 ch.f. (Mar 5) Bahamian Bounty 116 – Bellair (Beveled (USA)) **71** [2002 5m 6m² 6s⁵ Oct 25] 2,600F, 1,800Y: unfurnished filly: first foal: dam unraced daughter of Free Handicap winner Lyric Dance: fair form: ½-length second to Riska King (pair clear) in maiden at York: raced on unfavoured far side when fifth of 21 to Golden Nun in sales race at Doncaster: should stay 7f: acts on soft and good to firm ground. *J. D. Bethell*

PORAK (IRE) 5 ch.g. Perugino (USA) 84 – Gayla Orchestra (Lord Gayle (USA) 124) **84** [2002 78, a69: 10s⁵ 10g 12m 12m* 12g p12g Nov 23] big gelding: fairly useful **a66** handicapper on turf, fair form on all-weather: off 4 months, career-best effort when winning amateur event at Goodwood in September: acts at 1¼m/1½m: acts on heavy and good to firm going, lightly raced on all-weather. *G. L. Moore*

PORLEZZA (FR) 3 ch.f. Sicyos (USA) 126 – Pupsi (FR) (Matahawk 127) [2002 97: **110** 5.5g 5g² 5m* 5g⁴ 5m 5g³ 5g Oct 6] strong filly: fourth foal: half-sister to useful French 10.5f and 1½m winner Ponte Brolla (by Highest Honor): dam won around 1¼m in France: smart performer: successful in newcomers race at Chantilly and listed event at Deauville at 2 yrs: won Prix du Gros-Chene at Chantilly in June by neck from Maybe Forever: creditable efforts afterwards when 2 lengths fourth to Agnetha in King George Stakes at Goodwood and when 1¾ lengths third to Ziria in Prix du Petit Couvert and 2½ lengths seventh to Continent in Prix de l'Abbaye, both at Longchamp: effective at 5f/6f: acts on soft and good to firm going. *Y. de Nicolay, France*

PORTACASA 3 b.f. Robellino (USA) 127 – Autumn Affair 100 (Lugana Beach 116) **72**
[2002 49: 6m 8.1s 10f 9.9d* 9.9d² 8.5m⁴ 10.5g* 9.9d* 10g² 10.5d⁴ 10.4m 10g Sep 20]
leggy filly: fair handicapper: won at Beverley (twice, idled second occasion) and
Haydock (in between) in July: stays 10.5f: acts on good to firm and good to soft going:
usually blinkered/visored (has won without). *R. A. Fahey*

PORT ALGARVE (SAF) 2 b.f. (Mar 25) Desert King (IRE) 129 – Raahat Algharb –
(USA) (Gone West (USA)) [2002 6d 6d Nov 1] first foal: dam, well beaten at 2 yrs both
starts, out of half-sister to 4-y-o Street Cry: well beaten in maidens (reportedly fractured
left cannon bone in latter). *W. J. Haggas*

PORTICHOL PRINCESS 2 b.f. (Apr 24) Bluegrass Prince (IRE) 110 – Barbrallen –
38 (Rambo Dancer (CAN) 107) [2002 f8.5s Dec 9] first foal: dam of little account: behind
in maiden at Wolverhampton. *Mrs L. C. Jewell*

PORT MORENO (IRE) 2 b.c. (Apr 7) Turtle Island (IRE) 123 – Infra Blue (IRE) **54**
(Bluebird (USA) 125) [2002 5.1g 6.1m 5.7f⁵ 7.1g⁶ 8m 7s f7g Dec 9] IR 4,000Y, 7,200
2-y-o: rather sparely-made colt: fourth foal: half-brother to 9f winner Claim Gebal Claim
(by Ardkinglass): dam little form: modest maiden: seems to stay 7f: acts on firm ground.
J. G. M. O'Shea

PORT MORESBY (IRE) 4 b.g. Tagula (IRE) 116 – Santana Lady (IRE) 72 (Blake- **98**
ney 126) [2002 96, a86: p12g 10.5s³ p8g² 10m⁶ 8.1d p12g⁴ 10m* 10d* 10d⁵ 9f 9s 8s⁶ **a86**
p10g³ p12g Nov 19] compact, good-bodied gelding: useful handicapper on turf, fairly
useful on all-weather: won twice at Newmarket within 6 days in July/August, beating
Pinchincha both times, by neck on latter occasion: effective at 1¼m/easy 1½m: acts on
firm going, soft and all-weather: tried blinkered/tongue tied: usually held up.
N. A. Callaghan

PORTO ELOUNDA (IRE) 2 b.f. (Mar 31) Desert King (IRE) 129 – Stay Sharpe – §
(USA) (Sharpen Up 127) [2002 5.7d 6.1g f5g 8m Sep 17] leggy, unfurnished filly:
half-sister to several winners, including useful 1m/1¼m winner Manazil (by Generous)
and 5-y-o Takamaka Bay: dam unraced half-sister to dam of Indian Skimmer: no form:
left C. Egerton after third start (blinkered): temperamental. *R. J. Osborne, Ireland*

PORT ST CHARLES (IRE) 5 b. or br.g. Night Shift (USA) – Safe Haven (Blakeney **79**
126) [2002 74: 6.1g* 6m 7m 6d⁴ 6d⁴ 6m 6m² 6d⁶ 6.5g⁵ 5g p6g p8g p7g² Dec 30] tall
gelding: fair handicapper: won at Warwick in April: stays 7f: acts on polytrack, heavy
and good to firm going: free-going sort: sometimes finds little/wanders. *P. R. Chamings*

POSITIVE IMAGE 3 b.f. Positive Statement (USA) – Wensley Rose 53 (Aragon –
118) [2002 6g Oct 28] sixth reported foal: dam, sprint maiden, ran only at 2 yrs: behind
when losing action and pulled up in maiden at Windsor: dead. *Miss Z. C. Davison*

POSITIVE PROFILE (IRE) 4 b.g. Definite Article 121 – Leyete Gulf (IRE) (Slip **87**
Anchor 136) [2002 68, a80: p16g* f16.2g³ f16g* 18s² 16g 15f³ 16m⁶ 13.9f 14m 17.5g⁵ **a92**
18m f16g³ Dec 4] angular gelding: fairly useful handicapper: won at Lingfield and
Southwell early in year: 9 lb out of weights, seemed to run well when eighth to Miss Fara
in Cesarewitch at Newmarket penultimate start: stays 2¼m: acts on soft ground, firm and
all-weather: sometimes slowly away/carries head high/flicks tail: waited with: placed
over hurdles. *P. C. Haslam*

POTEMKIN (IRE) 4 ch.c. Ashkalani (IRE) 128 – Ploy 87 (Posse (USA) 130) [2002 **114**
112: 12m⁶ 12g 11.6s² 10m* 12m⁵ 10f⁵ 10m³ Aug 23] big, strong, good sort: smart
performer: won 4-runner Brigadier Gerard Stakes at Sandown in June by length from The
Mask, ducking right in front then idling: creditable efforts when ¾-length second to Asian
Heights in listed race at Windsor previous start and 6¼ lengths fifth to Zindabad in
Hardwicke Stakes at Royal Ascot on fifth outing: below form last 2: effective at 1¼m/
1½m: acts on soft and good to firm ground: often wears crossed noseband: has got worked
up in preliminaries: often races up with pace: tends to hang. *R. Hannon*

POT LUCK 5 b.g. Be My Guest (USA) 126 – Cremets 94 (Mummy's Pet 125) [2002 –
p16g Oct 16] rangy, quite attractive gelding: modest maiden at best: well held only start
since 3 yrs. *Mrs P. Sly*

POT OF GOLD (FR) 4 gr.g. Kendor (FR) 122 – Golden Rainbow (FR) (Rainbow –
Quest (USA) 134) [2002 61: f11s⁶ 10.1s 7.9g Aug 5] modest maiden at 3 yrs: well held in
2002: tried blinkered. *J. G. FitzGerald*

POTSDAM 4 ch.g. Rainbow Quest (USA) 134 – Danilova (USA) (Lyphard (USA) **56**
132) [2002 63: f12g 8.5s 7m 7d f12g Dec 14] modest maiden: trained by John Berry on
reappearance only: stays 9f: has been tongue tied: free-going sort. *Niall Moran, Ireland*

Brigadier Gerard Stakes, Sandown—Potemkin is allowed to keep the race after a lengthy inquiry; The Mask (right) avoids the trouble in which Imperial Dancer and Tarfshi (left) suffer interference

POTTED SHRIMP (USA) 3 ch.c. Prized (USA) – Mint Callee (USA) (Key To The Mint (USA)) [2002 48: f9.4g f8.5g 12m⁶ 9.2s 9.9g 8m 8d⁶ 8.1d Aug 8] small colt: little form at 3 yrs. *A. Berry* **–**

POTWASH 2 b.f. (Apr 26) Piccolo 121 – Silankka 70 (Slip Anchor 136) [2002 5m⁶ 5g³ 7m² 7g² 6g⁶ 7d⁵ 7s⁴ 6.5v⁵ Nov 13] 1,200F, 2,600Y: second foal: sister to 2001 2-y-o 5.7f winner Piccolo Party, later successful up to 1¾m abroad: dam, 1½m/13f winner, out of half-sister to Ibn Bey and Roseate Tern: fair maiden: claimed from M. Channon after second in seller at Folkestone fourth start: mostly creditable efforts in French claimers after: stays 7f: acts on soft and good to firm ground. *Andre Hermans, Belgium* **70**

POUSSIN (IRE) 4 b.c. Alzao (USA) 117 – Paix Blanche (FR) (Fabulous Dancer (USA) 124) [2002 115: 10d³ 9.3m² 10m 10s⁵ 10g⁶ Sep 17] tall, rather leggy, quite good-topped colt: smart performer: ran well at Longchamp first 2 starts, just under length third to Execute in Prix d'Harcourt and ½-length second of 4 to Best of The Bests in Prix d'Ispahan: disappointing afterwards, including in Prince of Wales's Stakes at Royal Ascot third outing: best around 1¼m: acts on heavy and good to firm ground. *E. Lellouche, France* **117**

POWDER RIVER 8 b.g. Alzao (USA) 117 – Nest 65 (Sharpo 132) [2002 –: p13g³ p13g f12g⁵ Mar 15] modest performer, lightly raced nowadays: stays 13f: acts on poly-track, soft and good to firm going. *A. G. Newcombe* **54**

POWERSCOURT 2 b.c. (Apr 1) Sadler's Wells (USA) 132 – Rainbow Lake 113 (Rainbow Quest (USA) 134) [2002 7d² 8f² 7.5s* 8s² Oct 26] **112 p**

Powerscourt won't have to produce much out of the ordinary in his second season to better the subsequent achievements of Lermontov and Castle Gandolfo, the two previous Aidan O'Brien-trained colts to finish second to stable-companions in Doncaster's Racing Post Trophy. Lermontov, beaten by Aristotle in the 1999 edition, has won only one race since, a handicap at Beverley off a BHB mark of 76 in the latest season; while Castle Gandolfo, caught near the finish by High Chaparral in 2001, landed the odds in a valuable minor event on the polytrack at

Lingfield on his three-year-old reappearance but failed to progress and was sold to race in the States. There's no reason why Powerscourt himself shouldn't do well at three. A good-topped colt, he has the scope to improve on his already smart form, particularly when given the opportunity to tackle much longer distances. Powerscourt had three runs under his belt, all in maidens, when he turned up at Doncaster in October. A short-head second to stable-companion Macedonian King when favourite at Naas on his debut, Powerscourt then showed useful form in finishing a length-and-a-quarter second to the highly promising Lateen Sails at Newmarket before unimpressively landing the odds at Punchestown, where he veered left under pressure after hitting the front well inside the final furlong. Powerscourt showed no wayward tendencies in the Racing Post Trophy and led from over two furlongs out until collared by Brian Boru, who had met trouble in running, inside the final furlong, going down by a length and a quarter.

Powerscourt (b.c. Apr 1, 2000)	Sadler's Wells (USA) (b 1981)	Northern Dancer (b 1961)	Nearctic / Natalma
		Fairy Bridge (b 1975)	Bold Reason / Special
	Rainbow Lake (b 1990)	Rainbow Quest (b 1981)	Blushing Groom / I Will Follow
		Rockfest (ch 1979)	Stage Door Johnny / Rock Garden

Rainbow Lake, the dam of Powerscourt, ran six times as a three-year-old for Henry Cecil and completed a hat-trick of wins with an impressive performance in the Lancashire Oaks. She started favourite for both the Yorkshire Oaks and Park Hill Stakes subsequently, but proved most disappointing in both. Rainbow Lake, who should have stayed beyond a mile and a half, produced five foals prior to Powerscourt, two of them winners. The first of them was Brimming (by Generous), who showed smart form around a mile and three quarters for Cecil as a three-year-old; while the second was a close relative of Powerscourt, Unaware (by the Northern Dancer stallion Unfuwain), who was a fairly useful winner over a mile at two, and subsequently won at up to a mile and a half in Switzerland. Rainbow Lake, a half-sister to several winners including useful performers Best Rock, the nine-year-old Rock Falcon (who has now become a thorough rogue) and Vertex, is a daughter of Rockfest, who won at seven furlongs and a mile as a two-year-old. Rockfest ran in three middle-distance pattern races, her best placing coming when second in the Lingfield Oaks Trial. Powerscourt's great grandam Rock Garden showed fairly useful form up to a mile, gaining her sole success at that distance. Powerscourt, a good-topped colt who has worn a crossed noseband, will stay at least a mile and a half. On the limited evidence available, it would appear that he acts on firm ground as well as on soft. *A. P. O'Brien, Ireland*

POYLE HEATHER 2 b.f. (Apr 6) Air Express (IRE) 125 – Hithermoor Lass 75 (Red Alert 127) [2002 7g⁶ p7g Oct 16] half-sister to numerous winners, including sprinter Poyle George (by Sharpo) and 6f/7f performer State of Caution (by Reprimand), both smart: dam maiden who stayed 7f: well held in minor event/maiden: raced freely both starts. *J. G. Portman* —

POYLE JENNY 3 b.f. Piccolo 121 – Poyle Amber 55 (Sharrood (USA) 124) [2002 –: 10g 10s Oct 23] no sign of ability. *G. Barnett* —

POYLE JOSH 2 b.g. (May 9) Danzig Connection (USA) – Poyle Jezebelle 58 (Sharpo 132) [2002 86: 5f 5m 6f⁵ 6.1m Aug 6] 2,600Y: third foal: dam, 6f winner, sister to smart sprinter Poyle George: modest maiden: best effort when third in seller: raced only at 5f: blinkered final start: ungenuine: sold 500 gns. *W. G. M. Turner* 50 §

POYLE MAGIC 3 b.g. Magic Ring (IRE) 115 – Poyle Fizz (Damister (USA) 123) [2002 86: 6f 5m 6f⁵ 6.1m Jul 20] leggy gelding: fairly useful performer: seems to stay easy 6f: acts on firm going: sold 900 gns. *W. G. M. Turner* 82 ?

POYLE PICKLE 4 b.f. Piccolo 121 – Hithermoor Lass 75 (Red Alert 127) [2002 –: 7g 6.1d Jun 3] little sign of ability. *M. S. Saunders* —

PRADO 3 b.g. Hernando (FR) 127 – Harefoot 92 (Rainbow Quest (USA) 134) [2002 8m⁴ Apr 17] quite attractive gelding: has a round action: fourth foal: half-brother to smart 1m/1½m winner Zarfoot (by Zafonic) and winner in Japan by Last Tycoon: dam 11.5f 83

winner out of Irish Oaks and Park Hill winner Swiftfoot: 2 lengths fourth to Gallant Hero
in newcomers race at Newmarket, not knocked about once clearly held: looked sure to
progress, particularly at 1¼m+, but reportedly injured afterwards: subsequently gelded.
L. M. Cumani

PRAETORIAN FORCE   3 b.g. Atraf 116 – Zaima (IRE) 92 (Green Desert (USA)   **56 ?**
127) [2002 –: p7g 7m⁶ 6m 5g Sep 7] little form (left K. McAuliffe after second start):
tried visored/blinkered. *J. M. Bradley*

PRAGUE   4 b.g. Cyrano de Bergerac 120 – Basenite (Mansingh (USA) 120) [2002 –:   **68**
p10g⁴ Jul 3] best effort in maidens when fourth at Lingfield only 4-y-o start: stays 1¼m:
acts on polytrack. *J. R. Boyle*

PRAGUE EXPRESS   3 ch.g. Shaddad (USA) 75 – Express Girl 75 (Sylvan Express   **–**
117) [2002 42: 9.1d Aug 2] strong gelding: poor form on debut: well held since.
M. Todhunter

PRAIRIE DUNES (IRE)   3 br.g. Indian Ridge 123 – Ceide Dancer (IRE) 79 (Alzao   **80**
(USA) 117) [2002 6s⁶ 7d⁴ 6s³ 7.2d* 7.1d 7g² 7.1g 7m⁵ 8s³ Aug 30] IR 80,000Y: sturdy,
useful-looking gelding: third foal: brother to Italian winner up to 7.5f Indiana Max: dam,
8.5f winner, half-sister to smart winner up to 7f (including Haydock Park Sprint Cup)
Lavinia Fontana: fairly useful performer: won maiden at Ayr in June: smoothish at 1m:
acts on soft and good to firm going: visored/blinkered last 4 starts: often slowly away: has
wandered: sold 18,000 gns. *J. Noseda*

PRAIRIE FALCON (IRE)   8 b.g. Alzao (USA) 117 – Sea Harrier (Grundy 137)   **90**
[2002 90: 16g 16m² 16m³ 18.7f 13.9g⁶ 16.4d 15.9f 14.8g³ 15.9f* 14.6m 14f⁵ Sep 28]
attractive gelding: good mover: fairly useful handicapper: won at Chester in August:
effective at 13f to 2¼m: acts on firm and soft going: often races prominently. *B. W. Hills*

PRAIRIE WOLF   6 ch.g. Wolfhound (USA) 126 – Bay Queen 85 (Damister (USA)   **99**
123) [2002 100: 10.1g 8.5g⁴ 8.9d 9m⁵ 9.9m* 11m³ 10.1d 10m⁴ Oct 12] big, strong
gelding: useful handicapper: won quite valuable contest at Goodwood in July by neck
from Robandela: below form last 2 starts: stays 1¼m: acts on firm going, good to soft and
fibresand: often sweating/on edge. *M. L. W. Bell*

PRAYERFUL   3 b.f. Syrtos 106 – Pure Formality 84 (Forzando 122) [2002 10g 10d⁴   **47**
f12g Nov 25] workmanlike filly: fifth foal: half-sister to 3 winners, including 1m winner
Ritual (by Selkirk): dam 2-y-o 6f winner: best effort when fourth in seller at Windsor,
slowly away. *B. N. Doran*

PRAYERS FOR RAIN (IRE)   3 b.f. Darshaan 133 – Whispered Melody 68 (Primo   **91**
Dominie 121) [2002 85: 10.4m 10v⁵ 9d⁶ 10.1m* 8.5m³ 10.3m 10.5f* Sep 28] angular
filly: unimpressive mover: fairly useful performer: won minor event at Newcastle in July
and handicap at Haydock (beat Miss Gigi by ½ length) in September: stays easy 1¼m:
acts on any going: has raced freely. *M. A. Jarvis*

PRAY SILENCE   2 ch f (Feb 25) In Command (IRE) 114 – Loose Talk 68 (Thatching   **56**
131) [2002 p5g⁵ f5g Dec 2] third foal: half-sister to a winner in Greece by Common
Grounds: dam, sprint maiden, closely related to dam of Irish 1000 Guineas winner
Classic Park and half-sister to smart 5f performer Easy Option: better effort in maidens
(modest form) when 6 lengths fifth to Aventura at Lingfield, slowly away: still looked
green next time. *W. Jarvis*

PRECASTER   3 ch.g. Factual (USA) 108 – Caspian Morn 63 (Lugana Beach 116)   **63**
[2002 10m 11m⁴ 12.3g⁶ 13.8f³ f12f⁴ f12f* f11g* Dec 17] 5,400Y: smallish, sturdy
gelding: first foal: dam 6f winner: modest performer: won seller at Wolverhampton and
claimer at Southwell in November/December: should stay 2m: acts on fibresand, raced
only on good ground or firmer on turf. *P. C. Haslam*

PRECIOUS BANE (IRE)   4 b.g. Bigstone (IRE) 126 – Heavenward (USA) (Con-   **62**
quistador Cielo (USA)) [2002 16f 14d 14.1m⁵ Aug 21] IR 12,000Y, 20,000 2-y-o, 10,000
3-y-o: half-brother to several winners, including 1m/9f winner Girlie Set (by Second Set)
and 9-y-o Exalted: dam ran once in USA: well held in claimer/minor event/maiden.
B. P. J. Baugh

PRECIOUS FREEDOM   2 b.c. (Mar 11) Ashkalani (IRE) 128 – Prayers'n Promises   **68**
(USA) (Foolish Pleasure (USA)) [2002 5m⁶ 7g⁴ 6s³ f6g 6g³ 7s⁶ 6d Oct 14] sturdy colt:
half-brother to several winners, including very smart sprinter Nabeel Dancer (by Northern Dancer) and useful 1990 2-y-o 6f winner Anjiz (by Nureyev), latter later successful in
US: dam US Grade 1 winner at 6f/7f at 2 yrs: fair maiden: will probably stay 1m: acts on
soft ground, well below form on fibresand: sold 11,000 gns. *E. A. L. Dunlop*

PRECIOUS JOOLS   2 ch.f. (Apr 17) Bijou d'Inde 127 – Balinsky (IRE) 55 (Skyliner   –
117) [2002 7d⁶ Nov 5] 3,200Y: second foal: dam, maiden who stayed 7f, sister to smart
sprinter Blyton Lad: sixth in maiden at Catterick: dead. *B. Smart*

PRECIOUS MYSTERY (IRE)   2 ch.f. (Mar 25) Titus Livius (FR) 115 – Ascoli   –
(Skyliner 117) [2002 6m 8d 8v Nov 8] 8,000F, 5,200Y: fifth foal: half-sister to 2 winners,
including 5-y-o Spencer's Wood: dam Irish winner up to 1¼m and over hurdles: signs of
just a little ability in maidens. *J. Nicol*

PRECISELY (IRE)   7 b.g. Petorius 117 – Indigent (IRE) 54 (Superlative 118) [2002   –
f6g f8g Mar 14] modest at 3 yrs: well held both starts since: often blinkered.
N. I. M. Rossiter

PREEN   3 b.f. Lion Cavern (USA) 117 – Made of Pearl (USA) 107 (Nureyev (USA)   79
131) [2002 72p: 8.2d² 9d* 10g⁵ Aug 7] leggy filly: fair performer: won handicap at
Kempton in July: effective at 1m/9f: acted on good to soft going: stud. *J. R. Fanshawe*

PREFERRED (IRE)   4 b.g. Distant Relative 128 – Fruhlingserwachen (USA) (Irish   78
River (FR) 131) [2002 78: 10m 11.7g 10f May 17] sturdy gelding: fair handicapper: stays
1¼m: acts on firm going. visored (ran creditably but found little) final 3-y-o start: joined
O. Sherwood. *R. Hannon*

PREMIER ACCOUNT   4 b.g. Mark of Esteem (IRE) 137 – Gemaasheh (Habitat   48
134) [2002 61: 8v f7g 7.9s⁶ May 27] useful-looking gelding: poor mover: modest maiden
handicapper: stays 9.4f: acts on heavy going and fibresand. *R. A. Fahey*

PREMIER AMBITIONS   4 b.g. Bin Ajwaad (IRE) 119 – Good Thinking (USA)   47
(Raja Baba (USA)) [2002 60: f8g⁶ f8.5g f8.5g 8m⁶ 7.5g 7g Jun 8] modest handicapper on   a64
all-weather, poor on turf: won at Southwell in January: best effort at 1m: acts on soft
going, good to firm and fibresand: blinkered (half-reared leaving stalls) final start: sold
4,700 gns. *W. J. Haggas*

PREMIER BARON   7 b.g. Primo Dominie 121 – Anna Karietta 82 (Precocious 126)   94
[2002 91, a–: 7f* 6m 7g 7d⁴ 8f 7d Aug 10] smallish gelding: fairly useful handicapper: a–
won at Doncaster in June: was probably best at 6f/7f: acted on fibresand, firm and soft
going: tried blinkered in 2000: dead. *P. S. McEntee*

PREMIER PRIZE   5 ch.m. Selkirk (USA) 129 – Spot Prize (USA) 108 (Seattle   106
Dancer (USA) 119) [2002 105: 8.1d³ 9g³ 10.4f⁶ 8m³ 9.9m 9.9m Aug 14] big, strong,
lengthy mare: useful performer: reportedly had bone chips removed from hind legs early
in 2001: best efforts in 2002 when third in attheraces Mile at Sandown (2 lengths behind
Swallow Flight) and listed race at Goodwood (beaten length by Fraulein) on first/fourth
starts: ran poorly last 2 outings: effective at 1m/1¼m: acts on good to firm and good to
soft going: edgy sort: sometimes hangs/finds little: races freely, and usually waited with.
D. R. C. Elsworth

PREPARE FOR WAR (IRE)   3 b.f. Marju (IRE) 127 – Fadaki Hawaki (USA) 60   –
(Vice Regent (CAN)) [2002 10m Jun 21] 52,000F: fourth foal: half-sister to 5-y-o Sutton
Common and French 1¼m winner Premiership (by Zinaad): dam, maiden who stayed
1m, closely related to smart 1990 2-y-o sprinter Mujadil and half-sister to high-class 1½m
performer Fruits of Love: well held in maiden at Newmarket, only outing. *L. M. Cumani*

PRESENTER (IRE)   2 ch.c. (Mar 13) Cadeaux Genereux 131 – Moviegoer 104   76 P
(Pharly (FR) 130) [2002 7s² Oct 25] IR 160,000Y: big, unfurnished, rather raw-boned
colt: has plenty of scope: half-brother to several winners, including 7-y-o Mane Frame
and 5-y-o Salim: dam, 7f winner, half-sister to dam of Oaks winner Lady Carla: 5/1 and
green, 2½ lengths second of 12 to Kris Kin in maiden at Doncaster, staying on well having
been held up and short of room: will stay at least 1m: type to make a much better 3-y-o.
J. H. M. Gosden

PRESENT 'N CORRECT   9 ch.g. Cadeaux Genereux 131 – Emerald Eagle 78   47
(Sandy Creek 123) [2002 48: f5g p6g 5m³ 7m³ 5g 5m⁶ 6g 5.1d³ f6g Aug 9] workmanlike   a38
gelding: poor performer: effective at 5f to 7f: acts on any turf going/fibresand: has started
slowly. *J. M. Bradley*

PRESSIONAGE   3 b.f. Puissance 110 – My Girl 39 (Mon Tresor 113) [2002 47: 8.3m   –
Jul 29] poor maiden: missed break and well beaten only 3-y-o start. *H. S. Howe*

PRESTO VENTO   2 b.f. (Mar 23) Air Express (IRE) 125 – Placement (Kris 135)   103
[2002 5.1g* 5g* 5m* 5m⁶ 6d 5.2f* 5g⁶ 6m 6.5g³ 6m Oct 5] 18,500Y: close-coupled filly:
fluent mover: third foal: dam unraced close relative to smart French sprinter Pole
Position: useful performer: won maiden at Bath in April, minor event at Salisbury in May,
listed contest at Sandown (by length from Arran Pilot, drifting left) in June and 24-runner

Weatherbys Super Sprint, Newbury—Presto Vento, one of only three to race towards the stand rail, wins going away and gives trainer Richard Hannon his fourth success in the race; Wunders Dream and Sir Edwin Landseer (spots on cap) fight it out for the minor honours

Weatherby's Super Sprint at Newbury (easily best effort, raced virtually alone, beat Wunders Dream 2½ lengths) in July: not discredited in sales races at Ascot and Redcar (seventh to Somnus) last 2 starts: best at 5f/6f: acts on firm and good to soft going. *R. Hannon*

PRESUMPTIVE (IRE) 2 b.c. (Mar 4) Danehill (USA) 126 – Demure (Machiavellian (USA) 123) [2002 6m Sep 20] leggy, useful-looking colt: first foal: dam unraced half-sister to very smart 6f/7f performer Diffident out of smart French 6f to 7f winner Shy Princess: 15/2 and very green, 5½ lengths ninth of 12 to Marching Band in maiden at Newbury, late headway under considerate handling: will improve. *J. Noseda* **75 p**

PRESUMPTUOUS 2 ch.g. (Mar 8) Double Trigger (IRE) 123 – T O O Mamma's (IRE) 50 (Classic Secret (USA) 91) [2002 7m 7.1d 7m Aug 6] 500Y: third foal: dam, 9.4f and 11f winner (also successful over hurdles), half-sister to useful sprinter Whittingham: behind in maidens. *A. Berry* **–**

PRETENCE (IRE) 2 b.c. (Apr 15) Danehill (USA) 126 – Narva (Nashwan (USA) 135) [2002 p7g⁴ Oct 16] second foal: dam unraced half-sister to high-class performer up to 1½m Predappio: 14/1 and visored, 7 lengths fourth of 16 to Grand Passion in maiden at Lingfield: will stay 1m: should improve. *J. Noseda* **71 p**

PRETRAIL (IRE) 5 b.g. Catrail (USA) 123 – Pretty Lady 98 (High Top 131) [2002 95: p10g⁴ p10g³ f12g⁶ 10g² 11.9m⁵ 10s a10.5g a10.5g* a10.5g⁵ a12g² Dec 15] strong, deep-bodied gelding: has a round action: fairly useful performer: generally creditable efforts in 2002: sold from P. D'Arcy 4,200 gns after sixth start: won minor event at Mijas in November: stays 1½m: acts on good to firm going, good to soft and all-weather/sand: visored fourth/sixth starts: sometimes slowly away. *M. Lambert, Spain* **90**

PRETTY CLEAR (USA) 3 b.f. Mr Prospector (USA) – Seven Springs (USA) 114 (Irish River (FR) 131) [2002 89: 7.1g² 7m² 6g* Sep 7] small, leggy filly: sister to high-class miler Distant View: fairly useful form at 2 yrs: just fair in 2002, winning maiden at Thirsk in September: effective at 6f/7f: raced only on good/good to firm going: free-going sort: stud. *H. R. A. Cecil* **71**

PRETTY FLY GUY (IRE) 6 ch.g. Forest Wind (USA) 111 – Achtung Lady (IRE) 53 (Warning 136) [2002 13.8g f11g Jun 20] little form: has virtually refused to race. *J. Parkes* **–**

PRETTY KOOL 2 b.f. (Mar 11) Inchinor 119 – Carrie Kool 69 (Prince Sabo 123) [2002 7d Nov 2] 16,000Y: good-topped filly: fourth foal: sister to 5-y-o Loch Inch and half-sister to 2000 2-y-o 5f winner Screamin' Georgina (by Muhtarram): dam 2-y-o 5f winner who stayed 7f: 50/1, backward and bandaged in front, well held in maiden at Newmarket. *S. C. Williams* **–**

PRETTY PEKAN (IRE) 2 b.f. (Apr 26) Sri Pekan (USA) 117 – Pretty Precedent (Polish Precedent (USA) 131) [2002 5d 7.1m 7s 6.5g 8s Oct 22] 10,000Y: second foal: half-sister to 2000 2-y-o 1m winner Gilda (by Goldmark): dam unraced out of useful 1m/1¼m winner Pretty Pol: signs of only a little ability in varied company. *G. G. Margarson* **–**

PRETTY PROSPECT (IRE) 2 b.f. (Mar 29) Titus Livius (FR) 115 – Force Divine (FR) (L'Emigrant (USA) 129) [2002 6.1d 5m⁶ 6g⁶ Jun 18] 2,000F, IR 2,500Y: small **–**

filly: first foal: dam French 6f (at 2 yrs) to 1¼m winner: well held, including in seller. *J. A. Glover*

PRICKLY POPPY   4 b.f. Lear Fan (USA) 130 – Prickwillow (USA) 75 (Nureyev (USA) 131) [2002 72: p8g f7g f8.5g p12g 10.9m Sep 21] fair maiden at 3 yrs: well held in 2002. *A. G. Newcombe*

PRIDE OF BRIXTON   9 b.g. Dominion 123 – Caviar Blini 80 (What A Guest 119) [2002 –, a76: f5g⁶ Jan 19] lengthy gelding: fair performer in 2001: below form only 9-y-o start: visored once. *Andrew Reid*

PRIDE OF KINLOCH   2 ch.f. (Mar 2) Dr Devious (IRE) 127 – Stormswept (USA)   **69** 74 (Storm Bird (CAN) 134) [2002 6m⁶ 5.9d² Jul 25] sixth foal: half-sister to 1m winners Amico (by Efisio) and Stormswell (by Persian Bold): dam, 2-y-o 5f winner, closely related to Colonel Collins, Lit de Justice and Commander Collins: better effort (fair form) when 1¼ lengths second to Devious Boy in minor event at Hamilton, making most: will stay 7f. *J. Hetherton*

PRIDE OF PERU (IRE)   5 b.m. Perugino (USA) 84 – Nation's Game 51 (Mummy's Game 120) [2002 42, a52: f6g 6f 6f 5s Jun 3] tall mare: poor maiden: well held in 2002: tried blinkered. *M. Brittain*

PRIDE OF THE PARK (FR)   3 b.g. Marju (IRE) 127 – Taj Victory 68 (Final Straw   **53 d** 127) [2002 –: f9.4g⁴ f11g* f11g* f12g⁶ f9.4g 10g f12g 10g f12g f9.4g 10g f12g Jul 20] angular gelding: modest performer: won handicap and claimer (final start for P. Haslam) at Southwell in February: below form after: stays 11f: acts on fibresand: tried visored/blinkered: sometimes races freely. *Mrs N. Macauley*

PRIDEWAY (IRE)   6 b.m. Pips Pride 117 – Up The Gates (Captain James 123) [2002   **64 §** 57d: f7g f8.5g f7g⁶ f7g⁶ f9.4g* f9.4g² f9.4g⁵ f8g* p8g⁵ f8.5g 8g* f7g 8.3v² 8g 9m⁶ 7.6f³   **a54 §** 8.3g² 8.3d³ 7.9g 8.1v⁵ f8s f8.5s f8.5g⁵ Dec 26] leggy, sparely-made mare: modest handicapper: won at Wolverhampton, Southwell (apprentices) and Ayr in first half of year: effective at 7f to 9.4f: acts on any turf going and fibresand, probably on polytrack: usually blinkered nowadays: tried tongue tied: sometimes starts slowly/hangs/looks less than keen: unreliable. *W. M. Brisbourne*

PRIMA FALCON   3 b.c. (Apr 30) Polar Falcon (USA) 126 – Prima Silk 82 (Primo   **–** Dominie 121) [2002 7d Oct 30] third foal: dam 5f to 7f winner: 25/1 and very green, well held in maiden at Yarmouth. *G. G. Margarson*

PRIMA PATRONA   2 b.f. (Feb 21) Hector Protector (USA) 124 – Ballet Rambert 69   **59** (Rambo Dancer (CAN) 107) [2002 7m⁵ 7.5g³ 7m³ 8g⁶ 7s Oct 28] small filly: first foal: dam, 2-y-o 5f winner, didn't train on: modest form in maidens: soundly beaten in nursery final start: stays 7.5f. *Mrs A. J. Perrett*

PRIMAROSA   3 ch.f. Atraf 116 – Prim Lass 65 (Reprimand 122) [2002 52: f12g 8.2g   **47** 10g 12m⁵ 16m Sep 20] leggy filly: poor performer: stays 1½m: acts on heavy going, good to firm and fibresand. *John A. Harris*

PRIMA STELLA   3 br. or gr.f. Primo Dominie 121 – Raffelina (USA) (Carson City   **77** (USA)) [2002 67: f6g* 6.1f⁴ f6g 6s² 7.1d 6.1m² 6m 6m⁶ 7m f6g³ 6m 6d f5g Dec 27] leggy filly: fair handicapper: won at Wolverhampton in April: left B. R. Millman 12,000 gns before final start: free-going sort, best at 5f/6f: acts on firm going, soft and fibresand. *J. Balding*

PRIME ATTRACTION   5 gr.m. Primitive Rising (USA) 113 – My Friend Melody   **63** (Sizzling Melody 117) [2002 10.3m⁴ 10.5m⁴ 8.3d⁵ 11.8g 10.9m 10.5f⁵ Sep 28] lengthy mare: second foal: half-sister to 7-y-o Major Attraction: dam unraced: fair bumper winner: modest maiden on Flat: should prove suited by 1½m+: slowly away first 2 outings. *W. M. Brisbourne*

PRIME CUT   3 ch.c. Hector Protector (USA) 124 – Filly Mignonne (IRE) (Nashwan   **73 ?** (USA) 135) [2002 7.1s 10m 7f³ Jul 17] strong, good-topped colt: second foal: half-brother to fairly useful 7f (including at 2 yrs) winner Sauce Tartar (by Salse): dam, lightly-raced maiden, from family of Warning and Rainbow Quest: seemingly best effort in maidens when third at Yarmouth: sold 2,500 gns in October. *N. A. Callaghan*

PRIME OFFER   6 b.g. Primo Dominie 121 – Single Bid 68 (Auction Ring (USA)   **70** 123)) [2002 71: p7g f7g² p8g* p7g p7g⁴ 7m⁴ f8.5g p8g p7g³ a6g a12g⁴ a8g a6g⁵ a8g⁴ᵈ a8g³ Dec 15] useful-looking gelding: fair handicapper: won at Lingfield in February: left D. Morris after ninth outing, C. Tinkler in Spain after thirteenth: stays easy 1m: acts on all-weather and firm going: blinkered eighth start: usually races prominently. *J. Bidgood, Spain*

PRIME RECREATION   5 b.g. Primo Dominie 121 – Night Transaction 59 (Tina's   **89 d**
Pet 121) [2002 84: f5s* f5s f5g 5d 5s* 5.1f 5m 5g 5g f5g f5g Dec 10] strong, rangy
gelding: fairly useful performer: won handicap at Southwell in January and minor event
at Windsor in June: well below form last 6 starts: best at 5f: acts on fibresand and heavy
going: has been slowly away/found little/edged left: usually travels strongly. *P. S. Felgate*

PRIME TRUMP   4 b.g. First Trump 118 – Maristax 74 (Reprimand 122) [2002 78:   **68 §**
11.7g 10g⁴ 10m 12g⁶ 12m² 10d Oct 21] angular gelding: fair maiden handicapper: stays
1½m: acts on good to firm going: visored (folded tamely) third start: often races
prominently: tricky ride: untrustworthy: sold 7,000 gns. *P. W. Harris*

PRIMO DANCER   3 b.g. Primo Dominie 121 – Whittle Woods Girl 80 (Emarati   **–**
(USA) 74) [2002 –: f12g Mar 21] lengthy gelding: no form: tried blinkered. *R. Wilman*

PRIMO DAWN   3 b.g. Primo Dominie 121 – Sara Sprint (Formidable (USA) 125)   **70**
[2002 69: p8g⁴ p7g f7g* Jul 11] big, lengthy gelding: fair performer: won claimer at
Southwell in July: stays 1m: acts on all-weather. *N. P. Littmoden*

PRIMO ROSE   2 b.f. (Mar 11) Primo Dominie 121 – My Dear Watson (Chilibang   **–**
120) [2002 6d p5g Nov 13] 10,500Y: third foal: dam, ran twice, half-sister to smart
sprinter Sizzling Melody: well beaten in maidens. *R. Guest*

PRIMROSE ALLEY (IRE)   2 ch.f. (Apr 26) Flying Spur (AUS) – Sliding (Formid-   **55**
able (USA) 125) [2002 5m 6m p8g Nov 23] IR 4,000Y: close-coupled filly: second foal:
half-sister to a 1m winner in Denmark by Sri Pekan: dam unraced half-sister to 4-y-o
Suggestive: modest form in maidens: may prove best up to 7f. *J. G. Portman*

PRIMROSE AND ROSE   3 b.f. Primo Dominie 121 – Cointosser (IRE) 66 (Nordico   **60 d**
(USA)) [2002 72, a59: p6g f5g³ f6g* f6g f5g² p6g f6g 5.3m⁴ 5.3d p6g 6g 5m 5d⁵ 5m 6m
5m f5g f6g p7g Dec 11] plain, sparely-made filly: modest handicapper: won at Wolverhampton in January: well held most starts after: best at 5f/easy 6f: acts on all-weather,
soft and good to firm ground: usually races prominently. *J. J. Bridger*

PRINCE ADJAL (IRE)   2 b.c. (Mar 10) Desert Prince (IRE) 130 – Adjalisa (IRE) 65   **–**
(Darshaan 133) [2002 6g p6g 8.3m Sep 2] fifth foal: half-brother to 3 winners, including
smart Irish performer up to 9f Access All Areas (by Approach The Bench), 5f/6f winner
at 2 yrs: dam, Irish maiden who stayed 1m, half-sister to Irish 2000 Guineas second
Adjareli: tailed off in maidens: tried blinkered. *B. W. Hills*

PRINCE ALBERT   4 ch.g. Rock City 120 – Russell Creek 80 (Sandy Creek 123) [2002   **54**
51: p8g 8.3g 10m³ 8.3d⁵ Aug 5] leggy, lengthy gelding: modest maiden handicapper:
stays 1¼m: acts on soft and good to firm ground. *J. R. Jenkins*

PRINCE ATRAF   3 b.g. Atraf 116 – Forest Fantasy 61 (Rambo Dancer (CAN) 107)   **86 d**
[2002 88: 7s³ 8g 10m 12s⁶ 10d 8g 10.2g f12g⁴ Dec 20] useful-looking gelding: fairly
useful performer: below form after reappearance: should stay 1m: acts on any going: tried
blinkered/in cheekpieces: has carried head high: not one to trust implicitly. *B. R. Millman*

PRINCE CYRANO   3 b.g. Cyrano de Bergerac 120 – Odilese 82 (Mummy's Pet 125)   **109**
[2002 100: 5m 6g⁶ 6m 5d⁶ 5m⁴ Jul 26] quite good-topped gelding: useful handicapper:
clearly best efforts at 3 yrs at York (sixth to Artie in William Hill Trophy) and Royal
Ascot (seventh to Capricho in Wokingham) second/third starts: effective at 5f/6f: acts on
firm and good to soft going: blinkered (very slowly away/looked wayward) on debut:
sometimes bandaged behind: takes strong hold (often wears severe noseband/early to
post): carried head awkwardly final start: none too reliable. *W. J. Musson*

PRINCE DAYJUR (USA)   3 b. or br.g. Dayjur (USA) 137 – Distinct Beauty (USA)   **–**
(Phone Trick (USA)) [2002 104: 6m⁴ 6m Sep 18] close-coupled, quite attractive gelding:
useful at 2 yrs: well held both 3-y-o starts (gelded after): should stay 7f: raced on good/
good to firm going. *J. Noseda*

PRINCE DIMITRI   3 ch.g. Desert King (IRE) 129 – Pinta (IRE) (Ahonoora 122)   **60**
[2002 64: 7f 7f³ 8f 9m² 8.5m* 9.3d³ 8g⁵ Aug 12] close-coupled gelding: modest handicapper: won apprentice race at Beverley in July: barely stays easy 9f: acts on good to firm
going: takes good hold/races prominently: has hung left: joined M. Pipe, won over
hurdles in December. *D. Nicholls*

PRINCE DOMINO   3 b.c. Primo Dominie 121 – Danzig Harbour (USA) (Private   **78 ?**
Account (USA)) [2002 86: 7m 8f 7.1m 7f⁴ f8g 7s p7g Nov 14] leggy, useful-looking colt:
fairly useful at 2 yrs: just fair at best in 2002: stays 7f: acts on firm and soft going: tried
tongue tied: usually races prominently. *G. L. Moore*

PRINCE DU SOLEIL (FR)   6 b.g. Cardoun (FR) 122 – Revelry (FR) (Blakeney   **58 §**
126) [2002 69: f8s 8g 10s 8.3m³ 8.3m 8s⁶ 8m³ Sep 5] quite attractive gelding: modest

handicapper: probably best around 1m: acts on heavy and good to firm going: visored once in 2001: often tongue tied: ungenuine. *J. R. Jenkins*

PRINCE HECTOR 3 ch.g. Hector Protector (USA) 124 – Ceanothus (IRE) 61 **90** (Bluebird (USA) 125) [2002 86p: 7m 9g 8d* Jun 15] strong, close-coupled gelding: fairly useful performer: won handicap at Bath in June by length from Thesaurus: said to have been injured after: may prove best around 1m: sold 13,000 gns to soft going: sold 13,000 gns in October, joined W. Haggas and gelded. *Mrs A. J. Perrett*

PRINCE HOLING 2 ch.g. (Mar 31) Halling (USA) 133 – Ella Mon Amour 65 (Ela- **90** Mana-Mou 132) [2002 7m⁴ 8m² 7.1g³ 7f² Sep 25] 32,000Y: rangy gelding: half-brother to several winners, including 6-y-o Pulau Tioman and 1½m winner Myosotis (by Don't Forget Me): dam, maiden who stayed 9f, out of half-sister to very smart sprinter Sayyaf: fairly useful maiden: best effort when ½-length second to Due Respect at Chester final start: stays 1m: acts on firm ground, unraced on softer than good: slowly away on debut/ third outing: tongue tied last 3 starts. *B. Hanbury*

PRINCE IVOR 2 b.c. (Mar 2) Polar Falcon (USA) 126 – Mistook (USA) (Phone **66** Trick (USA)) [2002 6g 7.1m⁶ 8f 8g¹ 8s⁶ p8g Dec 11] 19,000Y: third foal: dam unraced: fair maiden: fourth at Bath: stays 1m: acts on good to firm going, well held on soft. *R. Hannon*

PRINCELY VENTURE (IRE) 3 ch.c. Entrepreneur 123 – Sun Princess 130 (Eng- **98 p** lish Prince 129) [2002 82P: 10.5d* 12d Jun 30] strong, lengthy colt: has scope: confirmed promise of only 2-y-o start when beating Navado by 3½ lengths in maiden at Haydock in May (showed useful form): didn't take eye beforehand and disappointing when last in Irish Derby at the Curragh following month: should prove suited by 1½m+: raced only on good to soft going: stays in training, and should still be capable of better. *Sir Michael Stoute*

PRINCE MILLENNIUM 4 b.g. First Trump 118 – Petit Point (IRE) 78 (Petorius **54** 117) [2002 52: 8.1m 7m⁴ 8.3v² 8s⁴ f8s 8.1m 7.5m 8.3m⁶ Sep 30] neat gelding: modest maiden handicapper: probably stays 1¼m: acts on heavy and good to firm ground: usually blinkered/visored in 2001: has carried head high. *W. M. Brisbourne*

PRINCE MINATA (IRE) 7 b.g. Machiavellian 123 – Aminata 98 (Glenstal **54** (USA) 118) [2002 67, a75: f8s f9.4g f9.4g f9.4g f8.5g f8.5g f8.5g f8.5g⁶ f8.5g 8.3g⁵ 8f **a58** f9.4g⁵ 8m 8g 8m f8.5g* 9m 10m f9.4g 10m f8.5g f8g⁶ Dec 27] sturdy gelding: modest handicapper: won amateur event at Wolverhampton in June, making most: stays 8.5f: acts on fibresand, firm and soft going: tried tongue tied: has reportedly broken blood vessels: none too consistent. *P. W. Hiatt*

PRINCE NICHOLAS 7 ch.g. Midyan (USA) 124 – Its My Turn 80 (Palm Track **46** 122) [2002 –: 12s 12.4m 13.8m 14.1m Aug 21] sparely-made gelding: poor handicapper: stays 1½m: acts on heavy going. *K. W. Hogg, Isle of Man*

PRINCE NUREYEV (IRE) 2 b.c. (Mar 7) Desert King (IRE) 129 – Annaletta 89 **94** (Belmez (USA) 131) [2002 7m⁴ 7.1d* 7f³ 7d Aug 10] IR 50,000Y: quite good-topped colt: first foal: dam French 1½m winner from family of very smart performer up to 1½m Annus Mirabilis: landed odds in 4-runner maiden at Sandown in July: better efforts (fairly useful form) on starts either side, in listed race at Royal Ascot and minor event at Ascot: should be suited by 1¼m/1½m: acts on firm and good to soft ground: reportedly off colour final start. *B. R. Millman*

PRINCE OF BLUES (IRE) 4 b.g. Prince of Birds (USA) 121 – Reshift 94 (Night **96** Shift (USA)) [2002 88§, a79§: f5s⁴ p6g⁵ f5s⁴ f6g* f5g* p5g f6g⁴ f6g² f6g* f5g² 5s³ 5.2g⁶ **a100** 5m 5.1f 5f² Jun 4] good-topped, useful-looking gelding: poor mover: useful handicapper: better than ever in 2002, winning 3 times at Wolverhampton early in year: good head second to Salviati at Redcar final start: effective at 5f/6f: acts on firm going, soft and all-weather: often blinkered/visored in 2001: sometimes slowly away: usually races prominently: more resolute at 4 yrs. *N. P. Littmoden*

PRINCE OF GOLD 2 b.c. (May 30) Polar Prince (IRE) 117 – Gold Belt (IRE) 61 **77** (Bellypha 130) [2002 6g⁴ 7.5g³ 7m³ 7.9f² 8v f9.4g⁶ Nov 16] 15,000Y: good-topped colt: half-brother to several winners, including 3-y-o Goldeva and 5-y-o Royal Cavalier: dam 1m winner: fair maiden: second at York: stays 1m: acts on firm going, probably on heavy and fibresand. *R. Hollinshead*

PRINCE OF MY HEART 9 ch.h. Prince Daniel (USA) – Blue Room 70 (Gorytus **58** (USA) 132) [2002 81d: p10g⁵ p8g p10g 10m 8.3g May 17] tall horse: only modest handicapper nowadays: stays 1½m: acts on polytrack: visored once at 5 yrs. *J. Neville*

PRINCE OF PERSIA   2 b.g. (Apr 19) Turtle Island (IRE) 123 – Sianiski (Niniski   **56**
(USA) 125) [2002 7.2g 7g 7v Nov 8] 6,500Y: sixth foal: half-brother to 1998 2-y-o 7f
winner Sweet Compliance (by Safawan) and useful 7f (at 2 yrs) to 11f winner Sick As A
Parrot (by Casteddu): dam lightly raced: modest maiden: best effort on debut: slowly
away first 2 starts. *D. Nicholls*

PRINCE OMID (USA)   5 b.g. Shuailaan (USA) 122 – Matilda The Hun (USA)   **–**
(Young Bob (USA)) [2002 –: f9.4g 10.9g 10m Jul 16] no longer of much account. *Mrs
Merrita Jones*

PRINCE PROSPECT   6 b.g. Lycius (USA) 124 – Princess Dechtra (IRE) 65 (Belly-   **59 §**
pha 130) [2002 61, a72: f8s³ f8s³ f8s² f8.5g⁶ f8.5g f8.5g f8.5g³ f8g² f9.4s⁴ 7.9s⁴ f8g 7.9g   **a71 §**
10d 10.5v⁶ f8g f9.4s⁵ f12f³ f12g² f12g⁴ f12g f12g⁵ f12g³ Dec 26] sturdy gelding:
unimpressive mover: fair on all-weather, modest on turf: stays easy 1½m: acts on firm
going, good to soft and fibresand: visored once at 2 yrs: often soon off bridle: tends to
edge left: has flicked tail: untrustworthy. *Mrs L. Stubbs*

PRINCE PYRAMUS   4 b.g. Pyramus (USA) 78 – Rekindled Flame (IRE) (Kings   **65**
Lake (USA) 133) [2002 83d: 5v⁶ 5.9s 6m³ 6m 6g 6m⁶ 6f 6f 7s² Oct 28] well-made
gelding: usually takes the eye: fair nowadays: stays 7f: acts on any going: has worn
blinkers, including last 4 starts: has started slowly. *E. J. Alston*

PRINCE'S PASSION   3 b.f. Brief Truce (USA) 126 – Green Bonnet (IRE) (Green   **80**
Desert (USA) 127) [2002 80: 7g² p7g⁶ 7g² 8g⁶ 8f p8g⁵ p8g⁴ Dec 14] small, good-
bodied filly: fairly useful performer: stays easy 1m: acts on firm going and polytrack.
D. J. Coakley

PRINCESS ALMORA   4 b.f. Pivotal 124 – Drama School 72 (Young Generation   **87**
129) [2002 88: 7.6f 6m 7.1d³ 7.1m⁴ 7g 7m³ 8d⁵ 7m⁶ 7m² 7.1m 11f⁴ 8m⁶ 6f⁶ 6f Oct 12]
rather unfurnished filly: fairly useful handicapper: trained on reappearance by P. Harris:
several creditable efforts after: probably best at 6f/7f (flattered in 11f listed event at
Newbury eleventh start): yet to race on soft/heavy going, acts on any other: usually held
up. *D. K. Ivory*

PRINCESS ANOUSHKA   4 b.f. Prince Sabo 123 – Malwiya (USA) (Shahrastani   **–**
(USA) 135) [2002 p10g p10g 8.3g 6m Aug 26] 11,000Y: fourth foal: half-sister to 5-y-o
Malarkey and winners abroad by Polish Patriot and Be My Chief: dam unraced daughter
of very smart French filly up to 10.5f Masmouda: no form. *J. R. Boyle*

PRINCESS BLUEGRASS   2 ch.f. (Feb 8) Bluegrass Prince (IRE) 110 – Lavender   **–**
Della (IRE) 66 (Shernazar 131) [2002 7.1m Sep 16] workmanlike filly: second foal: dam,
maiden who stayed 1½m, out of half-sister to very smart French middle-distance stayer
Hard To Sing: 40/1, always behind in maiden at Warwick. *J. A. R. Toller*

PRINCESS CYRANO   3 b.f. Cyrano de Bergerac 120 – Odile (Green Dancer (USA)   **–**
132) [2002 8.3m 6s 10m 9.7d 7g 7m 11.5m Sep 17] sister to 5f (at 2 yrs) and 7f winner
Cyro and half-sister to several winners, including 1m winner Odilex (by Mummy's Pet):
dam ran once: no form: visored twice (unseated first occasion on fifth outing).
Miss D. A. McHale

PRINCESS ELECTRA (IRE)   3 b.f. Lake Coniston (IRE) 131 – Elect (USA) 113   **69**
(Vaguely Noble 140) [2002 66: f7g f8g⁴ f8.5g² 7s⁵ 7.1f³ 7m⁴ f7g⁴ 6g³ 6s 6g 8m² 7f² 8m   **a62**
8.5m 7g Oct 19] tall, angular filly: fair handicapper on turf, modest on all-weather:
effective at 6f to easy 8.5f: acts on fibresand and any turf going: usually blinkered/
visored: slowly away and went right leaving stall penultimate outing. *K. A. Ryan*

PRINCESS ERICA   2 b.f. (Apr 23) Perpendicular 119 – Birichino (Dilum (USA)   **62**
115) [2002 6s⁴ 7.5g⁶ f5s² 6v⁴ Nov 9] big, good-topped filly: first foal: dam unraced:
modest maiden: second at Southwell: may prove best up to 7f: acts on fibresand, raced on
good going or softer on turf. *T. D. Easterby*

PRINCESS ESME (IRE)   3 b.f. Ela-Mana-Mou 132 – Tijuana Tango (CAN) 53   **–**
(Tejano (USA)) [2002 10.2s 12.3g f12s Sep 17] IR 15,500Y: second foal: half-sister to 5f
to 7.5f winner in Italy by Distant Relative: dam Irish maiden: well beaten in maidens.
B. S. Rothwell

PRINCESS FAITH   2 b.f. (Jan 20) Polar Prince (IRE) 117 – Crissem (IRE) 70 (Thatch-   **–**
ing 131) [2002 8s f6g Nov 18] lengthy, good-topped filly: second foal: half-sister to 3-y-o
Freya Alex: dam 2-y-o 5f winner who stayed 7f: well held in maidens. *R. Hollinshead*

PRINCESS GRACE   3 b.f. Inchinor 119 – Hardiprincess (Keen 116) [2002 –: 9.3s⁶   **45**
10m 12f⁶ 16.4g³ 14.1m Sep 3] leggy, angular filly: poor maiden handicapper: barely stays
2m. *M. L. W. Bell*

PRINCESS LILLI 3 b.f. Vettori (IRE) 119 – Move Darling (Rock City 120) [2002 –: **47**
10g 9.3s[6] 11.6m[4] 11.6m[6] 10.2f 10.1f Jul 29] leggy, unfurnished filly: poor maiden: seems
to stay 11.6f: visored (raced too freely) penultimate start. *Mrs D. Haine*

PRINCESS MAGDALENA 2 ch.f. (Feb 27) Pennekamp (USA) 130 – Reason To **76**
Dance 96 (Damister (USA) 123) [2002 6m 7.1g[2] 6.5g Sep 27] 20,000Y: third foal:
half-sister to fairly useful 9f winner Stands To Reason (by Hernando) and untrustworthy
1¼m selling winner Twist (by Suave Dancer): dam 5f (at 2 yrs) and 6.5f (in USA) winner
who stayed 1¼m: easily best effort (fair form) when 2½ lengths second to Assraar in
maiden at Chepstow, prominent throughout: gave impression something amiss in sales
race at Ascot final start: should stay 1m: hung left on debut. *L. G. Cottrell*

PRINCESS MARIANNE 2 b.f. (Feb 2) Shareef Dancer (USA) 135 – Adeptation **–**
(USA) (Exceller (USA) 129) [2002 7.1s f7g f7g Nov 26] 12,000F: third foal: half-sister
to 3-y-o Retirement: dam, French 1¼m/1½m winner, out of US Grade 1 9f winner Adept:
well held in maidens. *K. A. Ryan*

PRINCESS MILETRIAN (IRE) 3 b.f. Danehill (USA) 126 – Place of Honour (Be **73**
My Guest (USA) 126) [2002 80: 8.1g[2] 10m 8.1m 8.3d[3] 8.2v* p8g Nov 13] useful-looking
filly: fair performer: won maiden in October: stays 1m: acts on heavy and
good to firm going: has raced freely. *G. L. Moore*

PRINCESS MONIQUE 3 b.f. Muhtarram (USA) 125 – Royal Recreation (USA) **–**
(His Majesty (USA)) [2002 p8g p10g Mar 25] 800Y: seventh foal: half-sister to fairly
useful 1½m winner Royal Diversion (by Marju) and winner in USA by Lycius: dam Irish
maiden who stayed 2m: behind in maidens at Lingfield. *Jamie Poulton*

PRINCESS PETARDIA (IRE) 3 b. or br.f. Petardia 113 – Coolrain Lady (IRE) 74 **–**
(Common Grounds 118) [2002 76: p7g 8.3d 7m 7s 7m 7m Jul 16] leggy filly: has a quick,
fluent action: fair performer at 2 yrs: little form in 2002: tried blinkered. *R. Hannon*

PRINCESS PUD (IRE) 4 b.f. Topanoora 118 – Blue Kestrel (IRE) 70 (Bluebird **–**
(USA) 125) [2002 –: 7g 10f 11.8d 6.1g 16.2g 11.9g[6] Aug 13] IR 9,000Y: second foal:
dam Irish 7f to 9f winner: no form: trained by M. Halford in Ireland before 2002: tried
blinkered. *B. N. Doran*

PRINCESS SABAAH (IRE) 2 br.f. (Mar 6) Desert King (IRE) 129 – Sound Tap **90**
(IRE) (Warning 136) [2002 6g[2] 6d* 6f[2] 7.1m Jul 25] IR 31,000F, IR 30,000Y: second
foal: half-sister to 3-y-o Playback: dam French 6f to 1m winner: fairly useful form: won
maiden at Goodwood in June: best effort when second of 4 to Elidore in minor event at
Windsor next time: should stay 1m: acts on firm and good to soft ground: sold 17,000 gns
in December. *R. Hannon*

PRINCESS SERENA (USA) 3 gr.f. Unbridled's Song (USA) 125 – Serena's Sister **48**
(USA) (Rahy (USA) 115) [2002 7g 6s[6] 7m[6] p7g 8m a8f[4] a8.5s Dec 20] useful-looking
filly: fluent mover: second foal: dam twice-raced sister to champion US filly Serena's
Song, herself dam of 3-y-o Sophisticat: poor maiden: left B. Meehan after fifth outing:
races freely. *A. McKeever, USA*

PRINCESS SHOKA (IRE) 2 b.f. (Feb 15) Definite Article 121 – Shoka (FR) 86 **72**
(Kaldoun (FR) 122) [2002 6g 7g[3] 8.3d[4] 7.6m[2] 7.1m 8.3m[4] f8.5f[2] f7g[6] Dec 9] IR 21,000Y:
leggy filly: seventh foal: half-sister to 3 winners, including 6-y-o Get Stuck In: dam 10.6f
winner: fair maiden: second at Lingfield and Wolverhampton: barely stays 8.5f: acts on
fibresand, yet to race on extremes of going on turf. *R. Hannon*

PRINCESS SOFIE 3 b.f. Efisio 120 – Dust 61 (Green Desert (USA) 127) [2002 84: **–**
5m 5d 5g 5.1f Aug 31] small, well-made filly: fairly useful performer at 2 yrs: little form
in 2002: sold 4,000 gns in December. *T. D. Easterby*

PRINCESS SOPHIE 4 b.f. Tragic Role (USA) – Octavia (Sallust 134) [2002 12.1g **–**
11.9s 12m 14d Jul 1] little sign of ability. *K. W. Hogg, Isle of Man*

PRINCESS SPEEDFIT (FR) 2 b.f. (Feb 2) Desert Prince (IRE) 130 – Perfect Sister **72**
(USA) (Perrault 130) [2002 6m 6g[5] 7s[5] 7f Oct 2] 28,000F, 72,000Y: quite attractive filly:
has a round action: eighth foal: half-sister to 3 winners, including smart French/UAE
1¼m to 1½m winner Sibling Rival (by Quest For Fame): dam, French 11f winner, sister
to very smart French/US middle-distance performer Frankly Perfect: fair maiden: should
be suited by at last 1m: acts on soft ground: slowly away first 2 starts. *G. G. Margarson*

PRINCESS TAVERY 2 b.f. (Feb 12) Emperor Jones (USA) 119 – Thanks And Praises **47**
(USA) (Diesis 133) [2002 5g 5g 5.2f[6] 5m f7g[4] f8.5g[3] f9.4g Nov 16] 2,200Y: close-
coupled, good-topped filly: first foal: dam unraced: poor maiden: broke leg final start and
will reportedly not race again: stayed 8.5f: acted on fibresand. *H. S. Howe*

PRINCES STREET   4 b.g. Sri Pekan (USA) 117 – Abbey Strand (USA) 78 (Shadeed   **74**
(USA) 135) [2002 66: 5f⁶ 6f⁴ 5s⁵ 6m⁴ 6f² 6m⁴ 6m* 6m³ 6d³ 5m 6s² 6d⁵ 6m 6m 6m⁴ 7m
Sep 6] smallish gelding: fair performer: won handicap at Windsor in June: best at 5f/6f:
acts on any going: usually tongue tied: sometimes reluctant at start/slowly away: free-
going sort: has found little/carried head high, but is consistent: sold 10,000 gns.
G. G. Margarson

PRINCESS VALENTINA   2 b.f. (Apr 9) My Best Valentine 122 – Sandkatoon (IRE)   **–**
(Archway (IRE) 115) [2002 5m 6s p5g 5.1d 6m Aug 9] neat filly: second reported foal:
half-sister to a winner in Italy by Beveled: dam ran 3 times: little sign of ability. *J. White*

PRINCES THEATRE   4 b.g. Prince Sabo 123 – Frisson (Slip Anchor 136) [2002   **64**
74: p8g 7.5g 10f 8m⁴ 7m² 8s 9m 8.5g 8m Oct 2] good-topped gelding: modest maiden
handicapper: best at 7f/1m: acts on good to firm going: tried tongue tied: reportedly bled
from nose on reappearance. *G. P. Kelly*

PRINCE TULUM (USA)   3 ch.g. Bien Bien (USA) 125 – Eastsider (USA) (Diesis   **–**
133) [2002 74: p7g² f8.5g* p8g 10.1g⁴ 10.4d 7g f9.4g p8g⁶ f7g³ f8.5s* f9.4g⁵ Dec 26]   **a91**
fairly useful performer on all-weather in 2002: won maiden in March and handicap in
December, both at Wolverhampton: stays 8.5f (flattered over 1¼m fourth start): yet to
race on extremes of going on turf, acts on all-weather: has been awkward leaving stalls.
N. P. Littmoden

PRINCE TUM TUM (USA)   2 b.c. (Mar 26) Capote (USA) – La Grande Epoque   **97 p**
(USA) 120 (Lyphard (USA) 132) [2002 6m³ 7m³ 7.1m* 7f* Oct 10] lengthy, quite
attractive colt: sixth living foal: half-brother to 3 winners, including smart French/UAE
6f/7f performer Matelot (by Riverman) and useful 1m winner Grand Maitre (by Gone
West): dam French sprinter: useful form: twice withdrawn (unseated rider to dust on
second occasion) prior to debut, when ridden by lad in paddock: won maiden at Warwick
in September and minor event at York (by neck from Parkland, leading over 2f out and
keeping on gamely) in October: should stay at least 1m: raced only on ground firmer than
good: capable of better still. *J. L. Dunlop*

PRINCE ZAR (IRE)   2 b.g. (Apr 10) Inzar (USA) 112 – Salonniere (FR) 88 (Bikala   **–**
134) [2002 6m Aug 29] IR 8,500Y: sixth foal: half-brother to 3 winners, including fairly
useful 1¼m winner Kissair (by Most Welcome), also winner of Triumph Hurdle: 25/1
and green, well held in maiden at Lingfield. *C. G. Cox*

PRINGIPESSA'S WAY   4 b.f. Machiavellian (USA) 123 – Miss Fancy That (USA)   **69**
99 (The Minstrel (CAN) 135) [2002 72: 9.9m 8.1m 9d 8m⁵ 8.3m 8m⁵ 8m 8g⁶ Oct 14]
close-coupled filly: fair maiden handicapper: probably stays 1¼m: acts on good to firm
going: blinkered third start: sometimes finds little: swishes tail. *P. R. Chamings*

PRINS WILLEM (IRE)   3 b.g. Alzao (USA) 117 – American Garden (USA)   **84**
(Alleged (USA) 138) [2002 69p: 7m 11.6m* 11.6g⁴ 10d³ 12.1g* 12m³ 12g Jul 12] sturdy
gelding: progressed into a fairly useful handicapper: won at Windsor in April and
Beverley in June: reportedly struck into final outing: will stay at least 1¾m: acts on good
to firm and good to soft going: sometimes tongue tied. *J. R. Fanshawe*

PRINTSMITH (IRE)   5 br.m. Petardia 113 – Black And Blaze (Taufan (USA) 119   **53**
[2002 56: 8m 7.9s³ 8.5g 8f Jun 24] leggy, unfurnished mare: modest handicapper: stays
1m: has form on good to firm ground, but best efforts (and all wins) on good or softer:
none too consistent. *J. R. Norton*

PRIORS DALE   2 b.c. (Feb 27) Lahib (USA) 129 – Mathaayl (USA) 79 (Shadeed   **77 p**
(USA) 135) [2002 8s⁵ Oct 26] IR 38,000Y: third living foal: brother to 1m winner
Alikhlas and half-brother to useful Irish 9f winner Nasanice (by Nashwan): dam 6f and
1¼m winner: 33/1, 5 lengths fifth of 16 to Zeis in maiden at Newbury, keeping on without
being knocked about: should improve. *K. Bell*

PRIORS LODGE (IRE)   4 br.c. Grand Lodge (USA) 125 – Addaya (IRE) (Persian   **113**
Bold 123) [2002 115: 9m⁴ 8.1d⁵ 8g 8m² 7f* 7m³ 8m* 8m 9.9m⁴ Sep 14] close-coupled,
quite attractive colt: usually impresses in appearance: smart performer: won minor event
at Newbury (by neck from Umistim) in July and listed race at Salisbury (by ¾ length from
Bourgainville) in August: ran at least respectably most other starts, including in Lennox
Stakes (third to Nayyir) and Celebration Mile (not beaten far when last of 7 behind
Tillerman) at Goodwood on sixth/eighth: effective at 7f, barely at 9f: acts on good to firm
going, probably on soft: game and consistent. *R. Hannon*

PRISSY (IRE)   2 b.f. (May 3) Desert Story (IRE) 115 – Practical 95 (Ballymore 123)   **–**
[2002 6f 7.5g Jul 6] 600Y: half-sister to several winners, including fairly useful 6f winner

Be Practical (by Tragic Role): dam Irish 9f/1¼m winner: well held in maiden/seller. *C. J. Teague*

PRIVATE BENJAMIN 2 b. or gr.g. (Mar 5) Ridgewood Ben 113 – Jilly Woo 60 **75** (Environment Friend 128) [2002 5.2d 6s⁶ 6m² 6m 6m⁴ 6m 6m⁶ 6f² 6m⁶ 6f Oct 5] angular gelding: has a round action: first foal: dam maiden who stayed 1¼m: fair maiden: second at Goodwood and Salisbury: will probably stay 7f: acts on firm going: sometimes looks difficult ride. *D. R. C. Elsworth*

PRIVATE CHARTER 2 b.c. (Apr 12) Singspiel (IRE) 133 – By Charter 104 (Shirley **90 p** Heights 130) [2002 7d² Nov 2] lengthy colt: half-brother to several winners, including 1½m winner Careful Timing (by Caerleon) and 2000 2-y-o 6f winner Ridge Runner (by Indian Ridge), both fairly useful: dam, 2-y-o 7f winner who seemed to stay 1½m, out of Time Charter: 20/1, shaped well when 1¼ lengths second of 22 to Blazing Thunder in maiden at Newmarket, travelling smoothly and leading from 2f out until inside final 1f: likely to be suited by 1¼m/1½m: useful prospect, should win races. *B. W. Hills*

PRIVATE POSSESSION (USA) 2 b.c. (Feb 13) Belong To Me (USA) – Salon Prive **78** (USA) (Private Account (USA)) [2002 p7g² Jul 20] 90,000Y: fourth foal: half-brother to a 1m winner in Hong Kong by Sheikh Albadou and French 1½m winner Tustarta (by Trempolino): dam, French maiden, half-sister to Prix Morny winners Regal State and Seven Springs, latter also dam of high-class miler Distant View: 4/1, considerate introduction when ¾-length second of 13 to Armada Grove in maiden at Lingfield, always well there: joined R. Rudkin in UAE. *D. R. Loder*

PRIVATE SEAL 7 b.g. King's Signet (USA) 110 – Slender 79 (Aragon 118) [2002 **– §** 49§, a54§: p8g p10g⁵ p10g⁶ 10.1m p12g p10g⁶ Dec 30] workmanlike gelding: poor **a49 §** performer: stays 11.5f: acts on firm going and polytrack: tried blinkered: usually tongue tied: has carried head awkwardly/flashed tail: can't be trusted. *Julian Poulton*

PRIVATE TREATY 4 b.f. Contract Law (USA) 108 – Inbisat 68 (Beldale Flutter **–** (USA) 130) [2002 f8.5s Dec 26] dam disqualified 1¾m winner: fifth foal: dam promise in bumpers/over hurdles, and tailed off on Flat debut (tongue tied). *S. A. Brookshaw*

PRIX STAR 7 ch.g. Superpower 113 – Celestine 62 (Skyliner 117) [2002 78, a–: 5m³ **80** 6m² 6s⁴ 6f⁶ 6m 6m 6m f6s 6.1s 7d⁵ Nov 5] angular gelding: fairly useful handicapper: **a–** won at Hamilton in May: has form at 7f, best at 5f/6f: acts on fibresand and any turf going: often visored (though effective without). *C. W. Fairhurst*

PRIZE DANCER (FR) 4 ch.g. Suave Dancer (USA) 136 – Spot Prize (USA) 108 **78** (Seattle Dancer (USA) 119) [2002 81: 14m 14.1m⁵ p16g 16f³ 14.1m 14.1m 18m⁴ Sep 19] useful-looking gelding: fair handicapper: left D. Elsworth after fifth start: stays 17f: acts on firm going: free-going sort: sold 2,500 gns, sent to Spain. *M. E. Sowersby*

PRIZE RING 3 ch.g. Bering 136 – Spot Prize (USA) 108 (Seattle Dancer (USA) 119) **79** [2002 8m⁴ 10.1g³ 10m⁵ 12f² 12f⁴ 10s 8v Nov 8] tall, quite attractive gelding: third foal: half-brother to 5-y-o Premier Prize and 4-y-o Prize Dancer: dam, 2-y-o 5f winner, fourth in Oaks: fair maiden: left D. Elsworth 18,000 gns before final start: races freely, but stays 1½m: acts on firm ground. *Mrs J. R. Ramsden*

PRIZE WINNER 4 b.c. Mtoto 134 – Rose Show (Belmez (USA) 131) [2002 108: **113** 10g⁵ 10m³ 12d³ 10.1d⁵ 10m 10d* 10m* 8d 9m Dec 15] small colt: smart handicapper: neck winner at Sandown (beat Champion Lodge in Pentax 'Digital Binocular' Stakes) and Ascot (beat Nadour Al Bahr, gamely made all) in July: left J. Noseda before penultimate outing: effective at 1¼m/1½m: yet to race on firm going, acts on any other: genuine and consistent. *S. Woods, Hong Kong*

PROCESSION 3 b.f. Zafonic (USA) 130 – Applaud (USA) 105 (Rahy (USA) 115) **72** [2002 71: 8.3m³ 7.1m 8.5g³ p10g³ 9.3g Jun 27] fair maiden: stays easy 1¼m: acts on all-weather, raced only on good going or firmer on turf: visored last 2 starts (edged left on penultimate, found little final one): has been edgy. *Sir Michael Stoute*

PROFLUENT (USA) 11 ch.g. Sunshine Forever (USA) – Proflare (USA) 101 (Mr **–** Prospector (USA)) [2002 13.8g 16f Jun 11] winner in France at 5 yrs: well held both Flat starts since: useful hurdler/chaser at best, only fair nowadays. *Mrs M. Reveley*

PROJECT RED (IRE) 2 b.c. (Mar 15) Danehill Dancer (IRE) 117 – Mini Project **59** (IRE) 94 (Project Manager 111) [2002 6g 6m 7f 7g f8s⁴ 8.3d Oct 14] IR 13,000F, 13,000Y: fourth foal: dam lightly-raced 2-y-o 6f winner who stayed 11f: modest maiden: finished lame final start: stays 1m: acts on fibresand and firm ground: shows signs of waywardness. *S. Kirk*

PROMISED (IRE) 4 b.f. Petardia 113 – Where's The Money 87 (Lochnager 132) – [2002 89: 5m 7m 5v p7g f6s p7g Dec 30] short-backed, leggy filly: fairly useful handicapper at best: well held in 2002: visored once. *N. P. Littmoden*

PROMISING (FR) 4 ch.f. Ashkalani (IRE) 128 – Sea Thunder 83 (Salse (USA) 128) **56** [2002 –: 8g⁶ 6m 6m³ 7m³ 7m⁴ 7f 7f² 6g 7.5m 7m³ 7m 7d 10m Aug 19] strong, lengthy filly: modest maiden handicapper: stays 7f: acts on firm going: often races prominently: none too consistent. *M. C. Chapman*

PROMISING KING (IRE) 2 ch.c. (Feb 26) Desert King (IRE) 129 – Bazaar Promise – 58 (Native Bazaar 122) [2002 5.1g 5g 6m Oct 7] 32,000F, IR 70,000Y: half-brother to several winners by Indian Ridge, including useful sprinter Cheyenne Spirit and 8.5f/1¼m winner Indian Express: dam temperamental sister to smart sprinter Crofthall: well held in maidens: twice slowly away. *G. A. Butler*

PROMOTE 6 gr.g. Linamix (FR) 127 – Rive (USA) (Riverman (USA) 131) [2002 –: – f8.5g⁶ f8.5g⁶ f7g 8m 7m 9.7g Sep 2] one-time fairly useful 1m winner: little form in 2002, often finding little: tongue tied. *Ms A. E. Embiricos*

PROMPT PAYMENT (IRE) 4 b. or br.f. In The Wings 128 – Lady Lucre (IRE) 73 **99** (Last Tycoon 131) [2002 87: 12m 10v² 10g* 12s* 12d* 12g⁶ Sep 27] tall filly: useful performer: won minor event at Leicester and handicap (beat Cosi Fan Tutte by 3 lengths) and minor event (beat Mawaheb by 1¼ lengths) at Newmarket in summer: making headway in listed event at Ascot final start when losing footing/nearly falling approaching home turn: effective at 1¼m/1½m: acts on heavy going: has been blanketed for stall entry: flashes tail: has taken strong hold/appeared to hang fire. *J. R. Fanshawe*

PROPERTY ZONE 4 b.g. Cool Jazz 116 – Prime Property (IRE) 60 (Tirol 127) **46** [2002 43: f11s⁴ f12s* f11s 9.9g⁴ 10f⁶ 13.8m f11g⁵ Dec 4] smallish, workmanlike gelding: **a51** modest handicapper: won at Southwell (edged right/idled) in January: left M. Easterby after sixth start: effective at 1¼m/1½m: acts on firm ground and fibresand: usually races prominently. *C. Grant*

PROPRIUS 2 b.g. (Mar 14) Perpendicular 119 – Pretty Pollyanna (General Assembly **47** (USA)) [2002 8g 7d f7g Nov 26] 13,000Y: sixth foal: brother to useful 1m (including at 2 yrs) winner Peculiarity, and half-brother to 3 winners, including 3-y-o Friday's Takings: dam unraced: poor form in maidens: gelded after final start. *B. Smart*

PROSERPINE 3 b.f. Robellino (USA) 127 – Hymne d'Amour (USA) 58 (Dixieland **92** Band (USA)) [2002 95p: 9.9m⁵ 11.7g⁶ 12s Oct 26] fairly useful performer: disappointing after shaping well on reappearance: should stay at least 1½m: yet to race on firm going, seems to act on any other. *M. P. Tregoning*

PROSPECTOR JOHN (USA) 6 b.h. Unbridled (USA) 128 – Ataentsic (USA) **62** (Hold Your Peace (USA)) [2002 12d 14m 10g 9.9m 12.3m Aug 30] $270,000Y: fifth foal: half-brother to winner in USA by Manila: dam 6f to 8.5f winner in USA (including at 2 yrs), half-sister to Nell Gwyn Stakes winner and 1000 Guineas runner-up Heart of Joy: modest handicapper: trained by D. Weld in Ireland in 1999: unplaced twice in USA later at 3 yrs and again in 2000 (missed 2001): stays 1½m: acts on good to firm going: blinkered: tried tongue tied. *G. L. Moore*

PROSPECTOR'S COVE 9 b.g. Dowsing (USA) 124 – Pearl Cove 63 (Town And **46** Country 124) [2002 64d, a52d: 10f⁵ 10m⁴ 8m 10m 10.1f 10.9g³ 10.2g 8m⁵ Aug 19] workmanlike gelding: poor performer: stays 11f: acts on fibresand and any turf going: has run poorly when visored: often slowly away: tends to wander: usually held up. *J. M. Bradley*

PROSPECTS OF GLORY (USA) 6 b.h. Mr Prospector (USA) – Hatoof (USA) **89** 124 (Irish River (FR) 131) [2002 a7f⁵ 10g⁶ 14.1m³ p12g*¹ 12m 16m³ 13.1s Oct 15] rather sparely-made horse: first foal: dam 1m to 1¼m winner (including 1000 Guineas and Champion Stakes) and second in Breeders' Cup Turf: fairly useful performer: unraced prior to 2002: left P. Brette, UAE, 17,000 gns after second start: won maiden at Lingfield in August: flattered in listed race next time: should stay 1¾m: acts on good to firm ground and polytrack. *E. J. O'Neill*

PROTAGONIST 4 b. or br.g. In The Wings 128 – Fatah Flare (USA) 121 (Alydar **71** (USA)) [2002 71: 14.4f⁵ 14.4m May 6] leggy gelding: fair maiden, lightly raced: probably stays 1¾m. *P. R. Webber*

PROTECTION MONEY 2 ch.g. (Apr 26) Hector Protector (USA) 124 – Three **66** Piece (Jaazeiro (USA) 127) [2002 8m 8g 7g Oct 24] half-brother to several winners, notably Poule d'Essai des Poulains winner Victory Note (by Fairy King), 6f winner at 2 yrs, and useful 1½m performer Dance So Suite (by Shareef Dancer): dam Irish maiden:

clearly best effort in maidens (fair form) when eighth of 13 at Bath second start: will probably stay 1¼m. *J. A. Osborne*

PROTECTOR 5 b.g. Be My Chief (USA) 122 – Clicquot 101 (Bold Lad (IRE) 133) – [2002 18s 15f Apr 10] strong, well-made gelding: fair at 3 yrs: well beaten both Flat starts since (blinkered final one). *C. J. Price*

PROTECTORATE 3 ch.f. Hector Protector (USA) 124 – Possessive Lady 62 (Dara 88 Monarch 128) [2002 91: 8g 6g 6.1d* 8.1d 8.5s 10.4d 6g 8s p8g p7g p7g⁵ p8g Dec 14] tall, angular filly: fairly useful performer: won minor event at Nottingham in May: needs test at 6f, and stays 1m: acts on polytrack, raced only on good ground or softer on turf: blinkered/visored 4 of last 6 outings. *I. A. Wood*

PROTECTRESS 3 ch.f. Hector Protector (USA) 124 – Quota 102 (Rainbow Quest 110 (USA) 134) [2002 103p: 10f² May 17] medium-sized, quite good-topped filly: won listed race at Newmarket only 2-y-o start: reportedly had minor setback (an infection) in spring: smart form when 1¼ lengths second to Monturani in similar event at Newbury, sole outing at 3 yrs: stayed 1¼m: wore boots on front legs at Newbury: stud. *H. R. A. Cecil*

PROTOCOL (IRE) 8 b.g. Taufan (USA) 119 – Ukraine's Affair (USA) (The Minstrel 45 (CAN) 135) [2002 50, a32: f12g f16g 11.8s 10f⁵ 10m⁴ 9.9g⁶ 10.5s³ 12.3m 13s⁴ 9.9g a– 14.1m 10g 14.1m 10m Sep 19] rather leggy gelding: poor handicapper: effective at stiff 1¼m to 17f: acts on heavy going, good to firm and fibresand: visored once in 1999: usually tongue tied: not one to trust implicitly. *Mrs S. Lamyman*

PROUD BEAUTY (IRE) 2 b.f. (Apr 9) Danehill (USA) 126 – Honey Bun 51 (Unfu- 84 wain (USA) 131) [2002 6s² 5m 8f⁴ Sep 20] 50,000Y: leggy, quite attractive filly: third foal: half-sister to 3-y-o Champion Lion: dam once-raced half-sister to top-class 1¼m/ 1½m performer Pilsudski: fairly useful form: in frame in maidens at Leopardstown and Belmont: mid-field in Queen Mary Stakes at Royal Ascot (then left A. O'Brien in Ireland) in between: should stay beyond 1m. *T. A. Pletcher, USA*

PROUD BOAST 4 b.f. Komaite (USA) – Red Rosein 97 (Red Sunset 120) [2002 93: 104 6g 5m 5.1f 5d² 5m 6m* 5m* 6m⁴ 5f³ 6d 5m 5m 5f* Oct 4] rather leggy, angular filly: useful performer: better than ever at 4 yrs, winning handicaps at York and Newcastle (Northern Rock Gosforth Park Cup, beat Salviati by ½ length) in June and listed race at Newmarket (beat Smokin Beau by head) in October: only a few creditable efforts other-wise, including when third to Boleyn Castle in Hong Kong Jockey Club Sprint at Ascot: effective at 5f/6f: has form on good to soft ground, but best efforts on good to firm/firm: usually held up. *Mrs G. S. Rees*

PROUD CAVALIER 6 b.g. Pharly (FR) 130 – Midnight Flit 89 (Bold Lad (IRE) 133) – [2002 –: 10m p10g Jul 10] no longer of much account. *Jean-Rene Auvray*

PROUD CHIEF 5 ch.g. Be My Chief (USA) 122 – Fleur de Foret (USA) 61§ (Green – Forest (USA) 134) [2002 66§: 6g 7.5g 5m 7m 6m f5g 7s f8.5g Nov 18] small, strong gelding: fair handicapper on his day at 4 yrs: well held in 2002: tried blinkered/visored. *J. Parkes*

PROUDEST MONKEY (IRE) 3 b.c. Darnay 117 – Champagne Truffle (IRE) 45 (Priolo (USA) 127) [2002 –: f6g⁴ f9.4g Apr 8] IR 3,000F, IR 7,500Y: first foal: dam unraced out of useful Irish middle-distance performer Hazy Bird: poor maiden: better effort in sellers at Wolverhampton in 2002 on reappearance: tried blinkered. *John A. Quinn, Ireland*

PROUD NATIVE (IRE) 8 b.g. Imp Society (USA) – Karamana (Habitat 134) [2002 102 108: 6f⁵ 6f 6m⁴ 5d 5.7m⁵ 5m⁵ 5m 5m* 5g² Oct 5] sturdy gelding: poor walker/mover: useful performer: simple tasks when winning claimers at Bath in August and Sandown in September: only a couple of creditable efforts otherwise, fourth to Proud Boast in Gosforth Park Cup (Handicap) at Newcastle: barely stays 6f: possibly not at best on heavy going, acts on any other: blinkered (well held) once: edgy sort: usually early to post: sometimes bandaged in front: usually waited with. *D. Nicholls*

PROUD PROTECTOR (IRE) 3 ch.g. Hector Protector (USA) 124 – Hooray Lady – 92 (Ahonoora 122) [2002 62: 7f f12g May 2] plain, angular gelding: disappointing maiden. *T. D. Easterby*

PROUD RULER (IRE) 2 b.c. (Mar 1) Spectrum (IRE) 126 – La Pellegrina (IRE) 73 – (Be My Guest (USA) 126) [2002 6s Jun 7] third foal: half-brother to 1m winner Native Force (by Indian Ridge): dam, disappointing maiden who stayed 1¼m, closely related to 1000 Guineas winner Las Meninas: 7/1 and green, last of 8 in maiden at Goodwood: sold 7,000 gns. *J. H. M. Gosden*

UAE Equestrian And Racing Federation Rous Stakes, Newmarket—
Proud Boast (far side) notches her most important success, beating Smokin Beau by a head;
Autumnal is third in an unusually small field for the race

PROUD VICTOR (IRE)   2 b.g. (Apr 14) Victory Note (USA) 120 – Alberjas (IRE)   **64**
(Sure Blade (USA) 130) [2002 f5g* p6g⁴ Dec 18] 7,000 2-y-o: fifth foal: half-brother to
2 winners by Shalford, including 5-y-o Shalbeblue: dam once-raced daughter of very
smart sprinter Street Light: modest form: overcame slow start to win seller at Southwell
in December: fourth in minor event at Lingfield: should stay 7f. *D. Shaw*

PROUD WESTERN (USA)   4 b.g. Gone West (USA) – Proud Lou (USA) (Proud   **55**
Clarion) [2002 73: p8g⁵ 7d 8s 6m 8.5g 7f⁶ f8g f8g⁶ Nov 25] fair maiden at 3 yrs: modest
form in 2002: stays 1m: acts on fibresand and soft going: blinkered once. *B. Ellison*

PROVENDER (IRE)   3 b.g. Ashkalani (IRE) 128 – Quiche 83 (Formidable (USA)   **70**
125) [2002 75: p7g 6g³ f7g² 8.2m 8g⁴ p8g f6s³ f6g⁶ Oct 17] good-topped gelding: fair   **a73**
maiden: unlikely to stay beyond 1m: acts on good to firm going and all-weather:
blinkered final start (gelded after): free-going sort. *Sir Mark Prescott*

PROVEN (USA)   3 br.c. Benny The Dip (USA) 127 – Night Fax (USA) (Known Fact   **107**
(USA) 135) [2002 96p: 10g* 12m 9.8m³ 12s Oct 26] strong, angular colt: useful
performer: won minor event at Newbury in April by length from Miss Corniche, despite
idling: respectable effort after only when 3 lengths third to Without Connexion in listed
race at Longchamp (after 4½-month break), making most: should be suited by 1½m+
(well held in St Simon Stakes at Newbury on second occasion): acts on heavy going,
probably on good to firm: visored (reportedly broke blood vessel in Derby Italiano
at Rome) second outing: wears crossed noseband: joined P. Rudkin in UAE.
J. H. M. Gosden

PSYCHIC (IRE)   3 b.f. Alhaarth (IRE) 126 – Mood Swings (IRE) 77 (Shirley Heights   **72**
130) [2002 60P: 6.1d⁵ 5g* 6f p7g² 7g³ 7m³ 7m Sep 5] sturdy, lengthy filly: fair performer:
won maiden at Beverley in May: stays 7f: acts on firm going and polytrack. *M. L. W. Bell*

PTAH (IRE)   5 b.g. Petardia 113 – Davenport Goddess (IRE) (Classic Secret (USA)   **–**
91) [2002 50: p16g f16.2g Feb 4] small gelding: no form in 2002: tried blinkered.
J. L. Eyre

PTARMIGAN RIDGE   6 b.h. Sea Raven (IRE) 75 – Panayr (Faraway Times (USA)   **93 §**
123) [2002 94§: 5d 5m³ 5g⁶ 5m³ 5m³ 5f 6m 5m⁴ 5m⁵ 5g 5v² Nov 8] quite good-topped
horse: fairly useful handicapper: best at 5f: acts on heavy and good to firm going: not one
to trust implicitly. *Miss L. A. Perratt*

PUGIN (IRE)   4 b.c. Darshaan 133 – Gothic Dream (IRE) 113 (Nashwan (USA)   **121**
135) [2002 115: 13s 14g* 14m² 16f Nov 5]
     A late addition to the Godolphin team in its latest bid to win the Melbourne
Cup, Pugin reportedly suffered a slight setback in his preparation, kicking a panel
in his box and twisting a plate, and failed by a long way to do himself justice at
Flemington. According to his rider, Pugin also returned jarred on his first outing on
firm ground. Pugin had shown very smart form for John Oxx in Ireland previously,
and judged on his performance on his final start there, when second in the Irish St
Leger at the Curragh, looked well treated in the Melbourne Cup, in which he
received 12 lb from Vinnie Roe. At level weights in the Irish St Leger, the front-
running Pugin had stuck on gamely after being headed by Vinnie Roe around a

furlong out and the latter was all out to beat him a length and a half. Pugin finished a long way behind fourth-placed Vinnie Roe in the Melbourne Cup but will be one to reckon with in good races over a mile and three quarters and more if he returns to his Irish St Leger form in 2003. There's no reason why he shouldn't. Unraced at two and with only ten appearances all told under his belt, Pugin looked a colt still on the upgrade at the Curragh.

Both of Pugin's wins in his first season, in a maiden at Navan and a listed race at the Curragh, were over a mile and a quarter, but he showed better form over further subsequently. On his next two starts, both at the Curragh, Pugin finished fourth behind four-length winner Galileo in the Irish Derby and a head second to Vinnie Roe in another listed event. He was then fifth in the St Leger at Doncaster. Pugin had just two outings in the latest season prior to the Irish St Leger. He was off for four months after pulling a muscle in his back when well held on his reappearance and returned to justify favouritism in the six-runner listed Ballycullen Stakes at Fairyhouse in August without needing to run up to his best. Allowed to dictate in a steadily-run race at Fairyhouse, Pugin kept on gamely to hold off stable-companion Dibiya by a neck.

		Shirley Heights (b 1975)	Mill Reef
	Darshaan (br 1981)		Hardiemma
		Delsy (br 1972)	Abdos
Pugin (IRE) (b.c. 1998)			Kelty
		Nashwan (ch 1986)	Blushing Groom
	Gothic Dream (IRE) (b 1991)		Height of Fashion
		Dark Lomond (b 1985)	Lomond
			Arkadina

Pugin is by the Prix du Jockey Club winner Darshaan and from a very good family. There is plenty of stamina in his pedigree and he should prove fully effective at two miles and more. His dam Gothic Dream showed smart form over a mile and a half for Oxx, including when placed in the Ribblesdale Stakes and Irish Oaks. She reportedly finished lame on her only outing over further, when last of eight in the Irish St Leger. Pugin's grandam Dark Lomond succeeded where both he and Gothic Dream had failed, winning the Irish St Leger in 1988. The next dam Arkadina, placed in the Irish One Thousand Guineas, the Oaks and the Irish Oaks, is a sister to the Queen's Vase and Jockey Club Cup winner Blood Royal. Pugin is Gothic Dream's third foal and her second winner, her first foal Gothic Theme (by Zafonic) having won a two-mile maiden at Clonmel in 1999. Pugin's year-younger half-sister Chartres (by Danehill) showed useful form over a mile and a quarter in Ireland in the latest season after making a winning debut over seven furlongs. Pugin, a strong colt easily picked out in the preliminaries because of his stringhalt (a condition causing an exaggerated bending of the hind leg), raced only on good going and softer prior to the Irish St Leger, winning on soft on his debut. He has been blanketed for stalls entry. *Saeed bin Suroor*

PULAU PINANG (IRE) 6 ch.m. Dolphin Street (FR) 125 – Inner Pearl (Gulf Pearl 117) [2002 97: p10g² p10g³ p10g³ p10g 10.4f⁵ 12g 10.2g⁴ 9.9m Aug 14] leggy mare: useful performer: best efforts in 2002 in handicaps at Lingfield first 3 starts: creditable efforts in listed races at York (fifth to Jalousie) and Chepstow (fourth to Albanova) after: best at 1¼m/1½m: acts on polytrack (some promise on fibresand), firm and good to soft going: usually tongue tied: free-going sort: held up: suffered from fibrillating heart fifth start at 5 yrs. *G. A. Butler*   **98 a101**

PULAU TIOMAN 6 b.h. Robellino (USA) 127 – Ella Mon Amour 65 (Ela-Mana-Mou 132) [2002 112: 8.5d 8m 8m 8m⁴ 8m⁶ Sep 12] compact horse: smart in 2001: useful at best in 2002, seemingly creditable effort when fourth to Summer View in handicap at Pontefract: very best form at 7f/8.5f: acts on any going: held up: reportedly suffered breathing problem third start. *M. A. Jarvis*   **103 ?**

PULSAAR 3 br.g. Hamas (IRE) 125§ – Sure Victory (IRE) 75 (Stalker 121) [2002 62§: p5g⁴ 5.1d² 5f⁵ 5.3m 5m⁴ Jun 28] modest maiden: effective at 5f/easy 6f: acts on polytrack, good to firm and good to soft going, probably on firm: tried blinkered (too free)/visored: has wandered: usually races up with pace: not to be trusted. *R. M. Beckett*   **62 §**

PUMA (IRE) 2 b.c. (Apr 3) Catrail (USA) 123 – Rahwah 73 (Northern Baby (CAN) 127) [2002 6m* 7.1d* 7f* 7m 8g 7m* 7s Oct 25] IR 23,000Y, 37,000 2-y-o: strong, good sort: half-brother to several winners, including useful 6f and (at 2 yrs) 7f winner Pepperdine (by Indian Ridge): dam 1½m winner: useful performer: won maiden at Windsor in June, minor events at Sandown and Ascot in July and another minor event at Ascot (3-runner race, beat My Daisychain by 7 lengths) in October: probably stays 1m: acts on firm and good to soft ground, well held on soft: sometimes sweats/swishes tail in paddock: sold 160,000 gns, sent to USA. *R. Hannon*

PUNISHMENT   11 b.h. Midyan (USA) 124 – In The Shade 89 (Bustino 136) [2002 **74 §** 76§: p10g 11.6d³ f12g⁶ f14.8g Jul 1] workmanlike horse: smart performer at best: just fair form in latter years: was effective at 1m to easy 13f: acted on any turf going and fibresand: visored final start in 1999: was tongue tied: dead. *K. O. Cunningham-Brown*

PUPILLAGE (USA)   2 ch.f. (Mar 17) Spinning World (USA) 130 – Shadowlawn **83** (Glint of Gold 128) [2002 5m⁴ f6g⁴ p7g* p7g Nov 13] $15,000Y: rather leggy filly: half-sister to French 10.5f winner Soleil Levant (by Blushing John): dam unraced close relative to Dante winner Simply Great and Prix Royal-Oak winner Star Lift and half-sister to Arc winner Sagace: fairly useful performer: off 5 months, won maiden at Lingfield in October readily by 2½ lengths from Alexander Ridge: slowly away/badly hampered final outing: will stay 1m: acts on polytrack. *M. A. Jarvis*

PUPPET PLAY (IRE)   7 ch.m. Broken Hearted 124 – Fantoccini (Taufan (USA) **74** 119) [2002 72, a82: f6g f7g⁴ f6g 7m 6g⁴ 7m 7m 8g² 8.1m* 8m f7s Nov 2] workmanlike mare: fair handicapper: made all at Warwick in September: effective at 6f to 1m: acts on firm going and fibresand: tried blinkered: races prominently: has idled/found little: difficult to predict. *E. J. Alston*

PUP'S PRIDE   5 b.g. Efisio 120 – Moogie 103 (Young Generation 129) [2002 46, a64: **–** f8s* f9.4g⁴ f8g² f7g* p7g⁵ f8.5g² f7g⁴ f8.5g⁵ f8.5g² f8.5g² f8g⁴ f7g* f8.5g³ f6g 7m f7g⁴ **a70** f7g⁵ f6s f8g⁴ f8g Oct 22] good-topped gelding: fair performer on all-weather: won handicap and claimer at Southwell (left R. Fahey after ninth start) and minor event at Wolverhampton early in year: probably needs further than 6f nowadays, and stays 9.4f: acts on fibresand (bit of promise on polytrack) and good to firm going: often visored/blinkered: sometimes slowly away/gets behind: has found little/wandered/carried head high: consistent. *Mrs N. Macauley*

PURE BRIEF (IRE)   5 b.g. Brief Truce (USA) 126 – Epure (Bellypha 130) [2002 **–** –: 15g] Jul 5] poor maiden at 3 yrs: well held both Flat outings since: winning hurdler. *A. Streeter*

PURE ELEGANCIA   6 b.m. Lugana Beach 116 – Esilam 62 (Frimley Park 109) [2002 **65** 72: 5.7g p5g* p5g⁴ 5g p5g⁴ 5g Dec 21] rather leggy, workmanlike mare: fair handicapper: **a70** won at Lingfield in June: barely stays sharp 6f: acts on firm going and all-weather: tried visored/blinkered: very slowly away fourth outing at 5 yrs: none too consistent. *G. A. Butler*

PURE MIRACLE   3 b.f. Royal Applause 124 – Deerlet 64 (Darshaan 133) [2002 –: **–** 8m⁴ 10m 15.8f Oct 8] sparely-made filly: no form. *R. A. Fahey*

PURE MISCHIEF (IRE)   3 b.g. Alhaarth (IRE) 126 – Bellissi (IRE) 77 (Bluebird **61** (USA) 125) [2002 92: p10g³ f9.4g² f8g 8.3d f7g 10d³ p12g Nov 19] fairly useful maiden at 2 yrs, only modest in 2002 (left E. Dunlop 3,000 gns after third start): stays 1¼m: acts on all-weather and heavy going. *Miss J. Feilden*

PUREPLEASURESEEKER (IRE)   3 ch.f. Grand Lodge (USA) 125 – Bianca **–** Cappello (IRE) (Glenstal (USA) 118) [2002 –: 10.2g Apr 30] only a little sign of ability. *P. F. I. Cole*

PURE SPECULATION   2 b.f. (May 17) Salse (USA) 128 – Just Speculation (IRE) **80** 86 (Ahonoora 122) [2002 7d⁵ 6m 7g² 7.2s* 8m⁴ Sep 12] fourth foal: half-sister to 4-y-o The Judge and a 1m/9f winner in Turkey by Sharpo: dam, 2-y-o 6f winner, half-sister to Gold Cup and Irish St Leger runner-up Tyrone Bridge: fairly useful performer: won maiden at Ayr in August: raced freely when good fourth of 18 in nursery at Doncaster: stays 1m: acts on soft and good to firm going. *M. L. W. Bell*

PURPLE HAZE (IRE)   3 b.f. Spectrum (IRE) 126 – Isticanna (USA) 96 (Far North **103** (CAN) 120) [2002 92p: 7m 7d⁵ 6m* 8m⁶ 7m⁵ Jul 30] leggy, attractive filly: useful performer: won minor events at Leicester in May (beat Miss Pinkerton by 1¼ lengths) and June (beat Entrap by neck): below form final start: best at 6f/7f: yet to race on extremes of going: often edgy in preliminaries (has had 2 handlers): has been very early to post: free-going sort, usually races prominently. *G. A. Butler*

PURRING (USA)   3 ch.f. Mountain Cat (USA) – Memory's Gold (USA) 68 (Java **79** Gold (USA)) [2002 7d³ 7g* 8g Sep 7] good-topped filly: third foal: half-sister to smart

French 5.5f (at 2 yrs) and 1m winner Ronda (by Bluebird): dam, 7.6f winner, out of sister to Mill Reef: fair performer: won maiden at Thirsk in June: well-held last in listed race at Hamburg and handicap at Thirsk subsequently. *M. Johnston*

PUSHKIN (IRE) 4 b.c. Caerleon (USA) 132 – Palmeraie (USA) (Lear Fan (USA)   **116**
130) [2002 111: 12d³ 12g⁴ 15d² 15.5d* 14g* 15g⁴ 15.5g 20g² Oct 6] leggy colt: first foal: dam once-raced half-sister to dam of Peintre Celebre: smart performer: won listed race at Longchamp (by short neck from Miraculous) in June and Prix Maurice de Nieuil at Maisons-Laffitte (by 1½ lengths from Polish Summer) in July: ran well when head second to Give Notice in Prix du Cadran at Longchamp final start, staying on strongly from rear: effective at 1½m to 2½m: raced mainly on good/good to soft ground: held up: consistent. *E. Lellouche, France*

PUTRA KU (IRE) 2 b.c. (Apr 30) Sri Pekan (USA) 117 – London Pride (USA) 106   –
(Lear Fan (USA) 130) [2002 f6g p7g Dec 21] sixth foal: brother to 2000 2-y-o 7f winner Pekan's Pride and half-brother to German 1m winner Bremen Rose (by Shadeed): dam 1m winner and third in Fred Darling Stakes only outings in Britain (also ran 3 times in USA): well beaten in maiden/minor event. *P, F, I, Cole*

PUTRA PEKAN 4 b.c. Grand Lodge (USA) 125 – Mazarine Blue 65 (Bellypha 130)   **112**
[2002 105: 8m³ 8.1d* 8.1m⁴ 8m 9f³ 9f 9s 8s Nov 2] good-topped colt: good walker: smart performer: better than ever in first half of 2002, winning Jubilee Stakes (Handicap) at Kempton (by 1¼ lengths from Heretic) and minor event at Haydock (by 2 lengths from Muchea) in May: good fourth to Kelburne in handicap at Sandown next time: below par after: best form around 1m, though worth another try at 7f: acts on good to firm and good to soft going: often blinkered: free-going sort. *M. A. Jarvis*

PYRAM BAY 4 b.f. Pyramus (USA) 78 – Navarino Bay 102 (Averof 123) [2002 –:   –
p8g p6g Jan 16] well beaten in maiden/claimer. *C. A. Dwyer*

PYRRHIC 3 b.g. Salse (USA) 128 – Bint Lariaaf (USA) (Diesis 133) [2002 61p: 10m⁵   **83 d**
10m⁶ 10.5d 9m² 8d² 8.3d p8g p10g p8g p6g p5g Dec 21] smallish gelding: disappointing maiden: left M. Johnston 12,500 gns after fifth start: should stay 1½m: acts on good to firm and good to soft going: blinkered last 3 starts: ungenuine. *R. M. Flower*

Q

QABAS (USA) 2 b.c. (May 26) Swain (IRE) 134 – Classical Dance (CAN) (Regal   **75 p**
Classic (CAN)) [2002 7v⁴ Nov 8] $130,000F: good-topped colt: third foal: half-brother to fairly useful 1999 2-y-o 6f winner With Iris (by Schossberg): dam unraced half-sister to top 1982 2-y-o Danzatore: 9½ lengths fourth to Mezuzah in maiden at Doncaster, slowly away and keeping on without being knocked about: should do better. *A. C. Stewart*

QAZWEEN 3 b.c. Primo Dominie 121 – Be My Lass (IRE) (Be My Guest (USA) 126)   **96**
[2002 7m² 8m 6m⁵ 6m² 7d⁶ p7g* p6g 7.1g² 7.6m⁴ 7d* 7f² a6.5f⁶ a7f Dec 13] 29,000F, 72,000Y: leggy colt: has a quick action: half-brother to 1997 2-y-o 6f winner who became temperamental Behold (by Prince Sabo), 1½m winner My Lass (by Elmaamul), both fairly useful, and a winner in Greece by Polar Falcon: dam, French 11f winner at 4 yrs, half-sister to smart middle-distance performers Bonne Ile and Ile de Nisky: useful performer: won minor event at Lingfield in June and handicap at Epsom in September: left M. Channon after good effort next time: effective at 6f/7f: acts on polytrack, firm and good to soft going: sometimes races freely. *A. Smith, UAE*

QOBTAAN (USA) 3 b.g. Capote (USA) – Queen's Gallery (USA) 98 (Forty Niner   **46**
(USA)) [2002 8m p8g f9.4s f8.5s⁴ Dec 26] big, strong gelding: second foal: dam, French 2-y-o 6.5f winner (second in 7f Prix du Calvados), closely related to US Grade 1 9f/1¼m winner Marquetry and smart French sprinter Spain Lane: left M. Jarvis after debut, A. Chamberlain before final start: blinkered, form only when fourth in maiden at Wolverhampton: should stay 1¼m: slowly away on debut. *M. R. Bosley*

QUAKERESS (IRE) 7 b.m. Brief Truce (USA) 126 – Deer Emily (Alzao (USA)   –
117) [2002 f12g f12g f16g Mar 26] lightly-raced performer nowadays: well held in 2002: tried blinkered. *R. Brotherton*

QUALITAIR WINGS 3 b.g. Colonel Collins (USA) 122 – Semperflorens (Don 128)   **78**
[2002 67: 8m 7m⁴ 8f⁶ 7g 8.5g⁵ 8s⁶ 8g⁶ 9d 8.1m³ 8m* 8.5m² 8f⁵ 7g* 8d⁴ 8s⁴ p7g p8g⁴   **a73**
Dec 3] lengthy, quite good-topped gelding: fair handicapper: won at Yarmouth (maiden event) in September and Catterick in October: stays 8.5f, at least when conditions aren't

testing: yet to race on heavy going, acts on any other turf and polytrack: tends to wander. *J. Hetherton*

QUALITY SLEEP (IRE) 3 b.f. Mukaddamah (USA) 125 – Blue Bell Lady 75 **– §** (Dunphy 124) [2002 43§: 8.1d 6s 8.1d 5.1f Jul 25] poor maiden at 2 yrs: no form in 2002: blinkered final start: ungenuine. *R. J. Price*

QUANTICA (IRE) 3 b.g. Sri Pekan (USA) 117 – Touche-A-Tout (IRE) (Royal **85** Academy (USA) 130) [2002 77: 5s 5.1s⁴ 6s⁶ 5v² 6m 5d² 5d* 5g 5g 6f 6.1s³ Oct 29] very tall, workmanlike gelding: fairly useful handicapper: found guilty under non-triers rule on reappearance: won at Windsor in August: effective at 5f/6f: acts on heavy ground: usually tongue tied: hung markedly third start. *N. Tinkler*

QUANTUM LADY 4 b.f. Mujadil (USA) 119 – Folly Finnesse 80 (Joligeneration **–** 111) [2002 76, a57: p6g⁶ p7g 5.1d Mar 27] sparely-made, angular filly: fair on turf, modest on all-weather at 3 yrs: little form in 2002. *I. A. Wood*

QUANTUM LEAP 5 b.g. Efisio 120 – Prejudice 83 (Young Generation 129) [2002 **81** 80: 6g 8d 8d⁴ 8.1m* 7.9d⁴ 7.9m* 9m⁵ 7.1g 8g² 8s Oct 28] quite good-topped gelding: fairly useful handicapper: won at Sandown in June and York (despite not taking turn well) in July: seems best at 1m/9f: acts on good to firm and good to soft going, possibly not soft. *S. Dow*

QUARTER MASTERS (IRE) 3 b.g. Mujadil (USA) 119 – Kentucky Wildcat 64 **45** (Be My Guest (USA) 126) [2002 –: 10.5d 11.1g³ Jul 18] workmanlike gelding: form (poor) only when third in apprentice handicap at Hamilton final start: tried tongue tied: gelded. *G. M. Moore*

QUARTER MOON (IRE) 3 b.f. Sadler's Wells (USA) 132 – Jude 53 (Darshaan **120** 133) [2002 106p: 8m⁵ 8s² 12s² 12d² 9.9m³ 11.9m⁶ 10g Oct 6]

Often a bridesmaid but never a bride. As a three-year-old anyway. Quarter Moon gained a Group 1 success as a juvenile in the Moyglare Stud Stakes but she couldn't get her head in front in the latest season, during which she finished runner-up in three classics before a series of hard races took their toll on her form in the second part of the season. Quarter Moon proved anything but straightforward to train or to ride, her trainer announcing before her reappearance in the One Thousand Guineas that she had had 'a few little setbacks and, as a result, is a bit fresh'. Quarter Moon took some holding early on at Newmarket and was left with plenty of ground to make up after her rider finally got her settled. She stayed on for fifth to Kazzia, doing best of her stable's four runners and being beaten only about a length and a half. Quarter Moon also came out best of her stable's five runners (who filled five of the first seven places) in the Irish One Thousand Guineas but, increasingly on edge beforehand, again took a while to settle before eventually staying on to finish second to British-trained Gossamer, beaten four and a half lengths.

Quarter Moon's performance at the Curragh confirmed the impression that, so far as her distance requirements were concerned, she was probably more of an Oaks filly, though her intractability was something of a worry, and there were questions about how she might cope with the undulations and gradients at Epsom. The gangling Quarter Moon, again on edge and taking a good hold on the way to post, did not handle the descent to Tattenham Corner very well but was full of running once in line for home and made up a lot of ground to challenge before going down by half a length to Kazzia, with the third Shadow Dancing fourteen lengths back. This was a tremendous performance by Quarter Moon who, in the absence of Kazzia, deservedly started at odds on next time for the Irish Oaks, a race her trainer has yet to win. O'Brien had run four at Epsom and two more of those, fourth-placed Starbourne and eleventh-placed Kournakova, also accompanied Quarter Moon to post at the Curragh. They ensured that the Irish Oaks was run at a good pace—most of the runners were off the bridle before the home turn—and Quarter Moon took over from them and struck for home early in the straight. She forged a couple of lengths clear only to be collared inside the final furlong by 33/1-shot Margarula. Quarter Moon went down by a length but, with six lengths less to third-placed Lady's Secret, she ran almost up to the form she showed at Epsom. The rest of Quarter Moon's campaign was an anti-climax. She was not affected by the coughing which hit Ballydoyle in the summer and, despite being in season, finished third

Mrs Richard Henry & Mrs John Magnier's "Quarter Moon"

to Islington when a late replacement for stablemate Sophisticat in the Nassau Stakes at Goodwood, where she was unwilling to go to post and had to be led part of the way by her trainer. Quarter Moon was retired after finishing unplaced in the Yorkshire Oaks and the Prix de l'Opera and begins her career as a broodmare with a visit to Danehill.

Quarter Moon (IRE) (b.f. 1999)	Sadler's Wells (USA) (b 1981)	Northern Dancer (b 1961)	Nearctic
			Natalma
		Fairy Bridge (b 1975)	Bold Reason
			Special
	Jude (b 1994)	Darshaan (br 1981)	Shirley Heights
			Delsy
		Alruccaba (gr 1983)	Crystal Palace
			Allara

The tall, leggy, sparely-made Quarter Moon carried very little condition when in training (her portrait was taken at Coolmore very late in the year when she had gone in her coat). She is the first foal of the modest maiden Jude, also represented on the racecourse in the latest season by Quarter Moon's sister the useful Yesterday, who looks the type to do better still at three. Jude might not have been any great shakes on the racecourse—she was unplaced on all four of her starts—but she is well connected, being a sister to the unlucky Irish Oaks third Arrikala and to the useful Irish mile-and-a-half winner Alouette, who is the dam of dual Champion Stakes winner Alborada. Jude is also a half-sister to several winners, notably the Nassau and Sun Chariot winner Last Second and the Don-caster Cup winner Alleluia. The racing record of Quarter Moon's grandam, the ex-Aga Khan filly Alruccaba, is of little or no consequence compared to her achievements at stud, but, for the record, she ran as a two-year-old, gaining her only win in a six-furlong maiden at Brighton. Quarter Moon's great grandam Allara, another who was only lightly raced, won at seven furlongs in the French Provinces and is a half-sister to the dams of Aliysa and Nishapour. Quarter Moon showed her best form at a mile and a half and acted on soft and good to firm going. Given her manifest flightiness, her classic performances reflect great credit on those who were most closely involved with her at Ballydoyle. *A. P. O'Brien, Ireland*

QUARTER TO 3 gr.f. Chocolat de Meguro (USA) 98 – Miss Lakeland (Pongee 106) – [2002 7g p12g 7m Aug 15] fourth reported foal: dam of little account over jumps: well held, including in seller. *W. de Best-Turner*

QUARTET (USA) 2 b.c. (Mar 8) Quest For Fame 127 – Ninette (USA) 101 (Alleged **94 p** (USA) 138) [2002 7d* 8m⁵ Sep 20] good-bodied colt: third foal: half-brother to French 1m winner Summer Shrill (by Summer Squall): dam, 9f (in USA)/1¼m winner, half-sister to top-class miler Observatory: won maiden at Newmarket in August by head from Tresillian, leading final 1f: improved when 4½ lengths fifth to Saturn in minor event at Newbury: will be suited by 1¼m/1½m: useful performer in the making. *R. Charlton*

QUATREDIL (IRE) 4 b.f. Mujadil (USA) 119 – Quatre Femme 76 (Petorius 117) – [2002 67d: p8g Jan 9] leggy filly: one-time fair handicapper. *J. S. Moore*

QUEBECK 4 b.g. Rainbow Quest (USA) 134 – Purbeck (IRE) (Polish Precedent – (USA) 131) [2002 78: p12g⁶ 10d 12m Apr 17] rather leggy gelding: fair maiden at 3 yrs: well held in 2002: stayed 1½m: acted on firm going, below form on soft: dead. *W. J. Musson*

QUEDEX 6 b.g. Deploy 131 – Alwal (Pharly (FR) 130) [2002 83, a–: 10s 14s⁶ 14d⁵ Jul **82** 5] neat gelding: has a round action: fairly useful handicapper: lightly-raced nowadays: **a–** probably stays 2¼m: acts on soft and good to firm going: sold £1,700, joined R. J. Price and gelded. *E. L. James*

QUEENBORO CASTLE (FR) 3 b.f. Night Shift (USA) – Magic Motion (USA) – (Green Dancer (USA) 132) [2002 –: 8m⁵ 6.9d 8m 5m Aug 17] sturdy filly: well held in maidens: dead. *M. A. Barnes*

QUEEN CHARLOTTE (IRE) 3 ch.f. Tagula (IRE) 116 – Tisima (FR) 61 (Selkirk **66** (USA) 129) [2002 8.2m 9.3s 7f² 6.9m 6m* 7d f8g⁶ Nov 20] 4,500 2-y-o: strong filly: first foal: dam, lightly-raced maiden, likely to have proved best up to 1m: fair performer: won maiden at Catterick in August: stays 1m: acts on fibresand, raced mainly on good to firm/firm going on turf: sometimes races freely. *A. Crook*

QUEEN EXCALIBUR 3 ch.f. Sabrehill (USA) 120 – Blue Room 70 (Gorytus **66** (USA) 132) [2002 12g⁶ 12d⁴ 10g³ p10g 10s Oct 23] rather leggy filly: half-sister to 9-y-o Prince of My Heart: dam 7f winner who stayed 1m: fair maiden: ran poorly in handicaps last 2 starts: stays 1½m: raced only on good going or softer on turf. *H. R. A. Cecil*

QUEEN G (USA) 3 b. or br.f. Matty G (USA) 119 – Neieb (USA) 64 (Alleged (USA) – 138) [2002 f8g⁴ 10g 8.2m f12g f11g⁴ f16g Dec 17] $7,500Y, 27,000 2-y-o: second foal: **a55** dam, 1¾m winner, half-sister to dam of top-class miler Observatory: modest maiden: stays 11f: acts on fibresand. *K. R. Burke*

QUEEN OF NIGHT 2 b.f. (Mar 12) Piccolo 121 – Cardinal Press (Sharrood (USA) **83** 124) [2002 6m⁵ 6m 6s* 6m² Sep 13] 9,500Y: tall filly: third living foal: half-sister to 6-y-o Supreme Salutation: dam maiden half-sister to smart sprinter Coquito's Friend: fairly useful performer: won maiden at Redcar (drifted right) in August by 1¼ lengths from Henri Martin: good short-head second of 22 to Fleetwood Bay in sales race at Doncaster, having been hampered at start: will probably stay 7f: looked hard ride second start. *T. D. Barron*

QUEENS BENCH (IRE) 5 ch.m. Wolfhound (USA) 126 – Zafaaf 105 (Kris 135) – [2002 63: 10d Jul 9] lengthy mare: modest performer at 4 yrs: well beaten only run in 2002. *P. C. Haslam*

QUEENSBERRY 3 b.g. Up And At 'em 109 – Princess Poquito (Hard Fought 125) **66** [2002 –: f7g³ p7g f8.5g⁵ 8f f8.5g⁵ Dec 20] heavy-topped gelding: fair maiden: stays 8.5f: acts on fibresand, no form on turf. *A. P. Jarvis*

QUEEN'S COLLEGE (IRE) 4 b.f. College Chapel 122 – Fairy Lore (IRE) 89 – (Fairy King (USA)) [2002 46: p7g⁶ Jan 23] sparely-made filly: maiden handicapper: well held only run in 2002. *M. L. W. Bell*

QUEEN'S GIFT (IRE) 2 b.f. (Jan 30) Alzao (USA) 117 – Monarchy (IRE) (Common **55** Grounds 118) [2002 5g⁴ 5g³ 5.1f⁵ 6g⁴ 6d² 5f 5m⁶ 6m³ 7.5g⁶ f8g* f8.5g⁵ Oct 19] 12,000Y: angular filly: first foal: dam, ran twice, out of half-sister to high-class miler Second Set (by Alzao): modest performer: won seller at Southwell in October: should stay 1¼m: acts on fibresand and firm ground: sometimes hangs: sold 3,000 gns. *M. R. Channon*

QUEENS JUBILEE 2 ch.f. (Mar 19) Cayman Kai (IRE) 114 – Miss Mercy (IRE) 62 **71** (Law Society (USA) 130) [2002 5m³ 5g⁵ 6.1g⁴ 5.3m³ 6m* 6g² 6.5m 6s p7g Dec 14] 4,000Y: lengthy filly: fourth foal: half-sister to 3-y-o Pachara and 6f winner That's Jazz (by Cool Jazz): dam, 2-y-o 6f winner, out of sister to smart dam of 4-y-o Malhub: fair performer: won seller at Lingfield in August: well held last 3 starts, leaving M. Bell before final one: will prove best at 5f/6f: acts on good to firm going: visored for win and next 3 appearances. *J. M. P. Eustace*

QUEENSLAND (IRE) 4 ch.f. Dr Devious (IRE) 127 – Fairy Fortune 78 (Rainbow — Quest (USA) 134) [2002 8.3d p10g p12g Dec 14] half-sister to several winners, including 5-y-o Counsel's Opinion and fairly useful 1998 2-y-o 6f winner Halloa (by Wolfhound): dam 7.6f winner: well held in maidens/minor event. *J. R. Jenkins*

QUEEN'S LODGE (IRE) 2 ch.f. (Feb 13) Grand Lodge (USA) 125 – Manilia (FR) **88 p** (Kris 135) [2002 6m* 7m Aug 25] third foal: half-sister to a 2-y-o winner in Italy by Salse: dam French 10.7f winner: fairly useful form: won maiden at Newmarket in July by short head from Stormont: reportedly pulled muscles when last of 8 in Prestige Stakes at Goodwood: will probably stay 1m: remains capable of better. *L. M. Cumani*

QUEEN'S LOGIC (IRE) 3 ch.f. Grand Lodge (USA) 125 – Lagrion (USA) 68 **103 +** (Diesis 133) [2002 125: 7m* Apr 20]

　　And it had all been going so well. Promoted to the head of the ante-post market for the One Thousand Guineas following a scintillating victory in the Cheveley Park Stakes, Queen's Logic maintained that position through seven trouble-free months only to miss the race after she was found to be lame on her near-fore the day before it was due to take place. Queen's Logic was sound again shortly after but, unfortunately, her troubles were far from over. Coughing put paid to plans to run her in the Irish equivalent; and when a lot of mucus was discovered to be in Queen's Logic's lungs after she had coughed, following a routine canter in July, it was decided to retire her. So, Queen's Logic goes to stud the unbeaten winner of five races, the last of which came in the Dubai Duty Free Stakes (Fred Darling) at Newbury in April. Queen's Logic looked head and shoulders above the seven who opposed her at Newbury and didn't need to run anywhere near her best to land the odds in what essentially was a warm-up for the Guineas. Fit enough though not right in her coat, Queen's Logic, waited as usual, won less impressively than had seemed likely when she eased to the front over a furlong out, Roundtree finishing with a rattle to get to within a couple of lengths of her. It was a satisfactory enough reappearance, though not one to set the pulse racing in the way her performance in the Cheveley Park most definitely had. Sophisticat, runner-up to Queen's Logic in both the Queen Mary and the Lowther, had to settle for second place yet again in the Cheveley Park, beaten seven lengths. With Sophisticat going on to win the Coronation Stakes after finishing third in the Poule d'Essai des Pouliches, Queen's Logic's connections were left to reflect on what might have been had Queen's Logic enjoyed a trouble-free three-year-old campaign. It must have been particularly galling for her trainer Mick Channon, who three years earlier

Dubai Duty Free Stakes (Fred Darling), Newbury—the previous year's top two-year-old filly Queen's Logic doesn't have to be hard ridden to maintain her unbeaten record; Roundtree (stripes) and Shiny are placed

had the misfortune to lose another leading One Thousand Guineas contender Bint Allayl when that filly broke a shoulder on the gallops.

Queen's Logic (IRE) (ch.f. 1999)	Grand Lodge (USA) (ch 1991)	Chief's Crown (b 1982)	Danzig
			Six Crowns
		La Papagena (br 1983)	Habitat
			Magic Flute
	Lagrion (USA) (ch 1989)	Diesis (ch 1980)	Sharpen Up
			Doubly Sure
		Wrap It Up (ch 1979)	Mount Hagen
			Doc Nan

Queen's Logic, whose pedigree was detailed fully in *Racehorses of 2001*, is the fifth foal of Lagrion, a sister to the Middle Park runner-up Pure Genius. A maiden who stayed a mile and a half, Lagrion produced two minor winners before Queen's Logic, the mile-and-a-quarter winner Tulsa (by Priolo) and the nine-furlong to mile-and-a-half winner in Italy, Carlo Bank (by Lahib). Queen's Logic's year younger half-sister Chatifa (by Titus Livius), an IR 380,000-guinea yearling, was in training with Marcus Tregoning but did not race. On pedigree, Queen's Logic should have stayed a mile, and possibly even further. She acted on soft and good to firm going. *M. R. Channon*

QUEENS MUSICIAN 4 b.g. Piccolo 121 – Queens Welcome 60 (Northfields (USA)) **65** [2002 52: 8m 8f² 8.1m 8d² 7m³ 8s⁵ 10s 9m² 9.9m⁴ 8m⁴ 9d Oct 18] short-backed gelding: fair maiden handicapper: probably stays 1¼m: acts on firm and soft going: blinkered once at 3 yrs: has found little: sold 12,000 gns. *G. A. Swinbank*

QUEENS RHAPSODY 2 b. or br.c. (Mar 26) Baryshnikov (AUS) – Digamist Girl **69** (IRE) (Digamist (USA) 110) [2002 6s⁵ 6g⁴ 7d⁴ Nov 5] 16,000Y: third foal: half-brother to 4-y-o Chispa: dam, winning sprinter in Belgium, half-sister to dam of 4-y-o Ange Gabriel: best effort in maidens (fair form) when fourth to First Footing at Ayr second start: should stay 7f. *A. Bailey*

QUEEN'S VICTORY 2 b.f. (Mar 25) Mujadil (USA) 119 – Gibaltarik (IRE) 68 **93** (Jareer (USA) 115) [2002 5.2f² 5m⁵ 5d² 5.2f 5d² 5.1f* 6f⁵ Sep 8] 35,000Y: lengthy filly: unimpressive mover: fourth foal: half-sister to useful 1998 2-y-o 5f winner Patriot (by Whittingham) and 3-y-o Vintage Style: dam, twice-raced 2-y-o 5f winner, half-sister to Mill Reef Stakes winner Kahir Almaydan: fairly useful performer: best efforts when fifth to Romantic Liason in Queen Mary Stakes at Royal Ascot and 1¾ lengths second to Bella Tusa in listed event at Sandown second/third starts: landed odds in maiden at Bath in August: respectable effort final appearance: likely to prove best at 5f: acts on firm and good to soft going: found little/ducked violently left fifth start. *M. R. Channon*

QUEENSWAY QUAY 2 b.c. (Apr 14) Royal Applause 124 – Ballad Island 83 (Ballad **91 p** Rock 122) [2002 6m* 5m* Sep 5] 11,500F, 14,000Y: lengthy, unfurnished colt: half-brother to several winners, including 5f (at 2 yrs)/6f winner Warning Time (by Warning), later successful in USA, and 7f winner Savoyard (by Sayf El Arab), both useful: dam 7f/1m (including at 2 yrs) winner: fairly useful form, making nearly all, when winning maiden at Lingfield (by 7 lengths from Ombudsman) in August and minor event at Redcar (by 3 lengths from Gold Riviera, hanging right) in September: likely to prove best at 5f/6f: sold 50,000 gns, sent to USA: remains open to improvement. *P. J. Makin*

QUE GUAPO 3 b.c. Hector Protector (USA) 124 – Queen Linear (USA) (Polish Navy **?** (USA)) [2002 8.2g 7.9d 7f⁵ Jul 17] 20,000Y: big, good-bodied colt: fourth foal: half-brother to 1m winner Ellway Queen (by Bahri) and winner in USA by Miner's Mark: dam, 5f winner in USA, half-sister to very smart winner up to 1¼m Hardgreen: signs of some ability in maidens at Nottingham, York (still not fully wound up) and Yarmouth (tongue tied, always last of 5). *H. Akbary*

QUERIDA ROSE (IRE) 2 b.f. (May 12) Desert Story (IRE) 115 – Sanctuary Cove **63 d** (Habitat 134) [2002 5.1f 5d⁶ 5m 5.1f² 5.1f⁶ 6g 5d⁵ 5.1m f5s 5m f5g f5g Dec 16] IR 8,000Y: small, sparely-made filly: half-sister to 3 winners, including 6-y-o Bundy and 1¼m seller winner Hiding Place (by Saddlers' Hall): dam Irish maiden: modest maiden: below form after fifth start: free-going sort, and will prove best at 5f/6f: acts on firm and good to soft going: tried visored. *B. S. Rothwell*

QUEST FOR GLORY (IRE) 3 b.c. Fayruz 116 – Moyhora (IRE) (Nashamaa 113) **74 §** [2002 87: f7g p6g p6g p5g f6g³ p5g 6.1f² 7.5m⁶ 7g⁵ 6m p6g³ 6m⁴ 5g 5g 7m 6m f6s² 6.1m* f6s f6g f6g Nov 26] close-coupled colt: fair performer: won minor event at Nottingham in October: stays easy 7f: acts on firm ground and all-weather: usually visored/blinkered after tenth start: tried tongue tied: often races prominently. *G. C. Bravery*

QUEST ON AIR   3 b.g. Star Quest 79 – Stormy Heights 62 (Golden Heights 82) [2002 –: 8.3d 10s 8.2g6 10d 8f Sep 8] little form. *J. R. Jenkins*   **–**

QUIBBLE   5 ch.g. Lammtarra (USA) 134 – Bloudan (USA) (Damascus (USA)) [2002 55: f14.8g Dec 2] fairly useful maiden at 3 yrs for A. Fabre in France: modest form at best in Britain since: tried blinkered. *A. Bailey*   **–**

QUICK   2 b.c. (Mar 15) Kahyasi 130 – Prompt (Old Vic 136) [2002 p10g6 p8g Dec 14] 9,000Y: third foal: half-brother to 3-y-o Frodo and a winner in Greece by Efisio: dam, ran once, half-sister to smart 1¼m winner Baron Ferdinand out of half-sister to Shirley Heights: better effort in maidens at Lingfield (fair form) when sixth to Shield, slowly away and wandering: went left leaving stall next time: should stay at least 1½m. *R. M. H. Cowell*   **66**

QUICK FLIGHT   2 ch.f. (Apr 14) Polar Falcon (USA) 126 – Constant Delight 80 (Never So Bold 135) [2002 5g3 5g* 5f3 7.1m* 6d 6m4 Aug 16] 2,000F, 7,000Y: fifth foal: half-sister to 1994 2-y-o 6f winner Corio (by Sharpo) and 7f (at 2 yrs)/1m seller winner Princess of Hearts (by Prince Sabo): dam 9f winner: fair performer: won maiden at Catterick in May and minor event at Musselburgh in June: stays 7f: acts on firm and good to soft ground. *J. R. Weymes*   **72**

QUICKS THE WORD   2 b.g. (Mar 9) Sri Pekan (USA) 117 – Fast Tempo (IRE) 74 (Statoblest 120) [2002 5m 5g 5g5 5s3 6d 5g2 5m3 5m6 5m6 6d2 Oct 14] 11,000F, 12,000Y: rather leggy gelding: first foal: dam, 2-y-o 5f winner, half-sister to useful performer up to 1½m Maralinga: fair maiden: good placed efforts in minor event/nurseries: effective at 5f/6f: acts on soft and good to firm going: consistent. *C. W. Thornton*   **70**

QUIET READING (USA)   5 b.g. Northern Flagship (USA) 96 – Forlis Key (USA) (Forli (ARG)) [2002 –, a63: f11g* f12g5 f12g2 p12g 10f 10g2 f11g4 9d 10d f9.4f2 f8s5 f8g* f9.4s* f8.5g2 f8.5s2 Dec 26] big, lengthy gelding: fair on all-weather, poor on turf: won seller at Southwell in January and handicaps at Southwell (amateurs)/Wolverhampton in November/December: best form around 1m/9f: acts on fibresand and any turf going: occasionally blinkered, usually visored. *M. R. Bosley*   **44 a74**

QUIET STORM (IRE)   2 b.f. (Mar 10) Desert Prince (IRE) 130 – Hertford Castle (Reference Point 139) [2002 6f6 p6g2 p7g3 Dec 11] 100,000F: fourth foal: half-sister to 3 winners, including useful 7f (including at 2 yrs)/1m winner Safarando (by Turtle Island) and Italian 1¼m winner Alher (by Alzao): dam thrice-raced daughter of Irish 1000 Guineas winner Forest Flower: fair form in maidens: placed twice at Lingfield, unlucky on first occasion: will stay 1m. *G. Wragg*   **77**

QUIET TIMES (IRE)   3 ch.g. Dolphin Street (FR) 125 – Super Times (Sayf El Arab (USA) 127) [2002 f5g* f7g 5d f5g 7f f6g 5m3 5m 5d 5s* 6s f5s2 5f 5d2 f5g f6g f6g* Dec 10] strong gelding: first foal: dam well beaten in 3 starts: fair performer: won maiden at Southwell and handicaps at Ripon (selling event) and (having left T. Easterby after fourteenth start) Southwell in 2002: best at 5f/6f: acts on fibresand, soft and good to firm going: usually blinkered/visored after fifth start: none too reliable. *K. A. Ryan*   **67**

QUIET TRAVELLER (IRE)   4 b.g. Blues Traveller (IRE) 119 – Quietly Impressive (IRE) 66 (Taufan (USA) 119) [2002 76: 8m6 10m6 8m2 8.3g 8m 9f2 9g4 10f3 8g3 9m2 10g 8.3m4 7.9m 10.3m 10m 8.9f f8.5g Nov 16] tall, quite good-topped gelding: fair handicapper: left Miss L. Perratt before final start (reportedly finished lame): effective at 1m to easy 1¼m: acts on firm and good to soft going: blinkered once: sometimes slowly away (seemed reluctant thirteenth start): usually held up. *I. Semple*   **77**

QUINN   2 ch.c. (Feb 3) First Trump 118 – Celestine 62 (Skyliner 117) [2002 5d 6m6 5g Aug 5] 5,200Y: lengthy colt: fourth living foal: half-brother to 7-y-o Prix Star and 6-y-o Ringside Jack: dam 5f (at 2 yrs) to 7f winner: well held in maidens. *C. W. Fairhurst*   **–**

QUINTA LAD   4 b.g. Alhijaz 122 – Jersey Belle 53 (Distant Relative 128) [2002 58, a–: f7g 6f 7m 6d4 7m 6f 7.5d 9.2v 12g Oct 19] quite good-topped gelding: poor maiden: left I. Balding after eighth start: stays 7f: acts on soft going, firm and fibresand: tried tongue tied. *J. R. Norton*   **42 a–**

QUINTA SPECIAL (IRE)   3 b.f. Spectrum (IRE) 126 – Al Galop (USA) (Affirmed (USA)) [2002 10g 10m 8.3m 8s2 8.3v 7g f8.5g 8g2 f9.4s2 f12f4 f9.4f* f9.4s4 f9.4g6 Dec 26] 320,000 francs Y: unfurnished filly: first foal: dam, French 11f winner, half-sister to US Grade 1 1½m winner Both Ends Burning: fair on all-weather, modest on turf: won maiden at Wolverhampton in November: probably best at 1m/1¼m: acts on soft going and fibresand. *G. G. Margarson*   **63 a67**

QUINTOTO   2 b.g. (Mar 3) Mtoto 134 – Ballet 61 (Sharrood (USA) 124) [2002 7m⁵ 8s   **70**
f9.4g Nov 16] 55,000Y: smallish, stocky gelding: half-brother to several winners, notably
5-y-o Island Sound and useful 1¼m and 11.6f winner Serge Lifar (by Shirley Heights):
dam, maiden, half-sister to May Hill winner Satinette: best effort in maidens when fifth
to Garros at Ascot (wore crossed noseband): off 3 months after: bred to be suited by
1¼m+, but tends to race freely: gelded after final start. *T. G. Mills*

QUITE A CASE   2 b.f. (Feb 14) Case Law 113 – Munequita (Marching On 101) [2002   **–**
f6g f8.5g Nov 15] 500Y: eighth living foal: half-sister to 3 winners, including 1994 2-y-o
5f winner Monkey Adel and 1993 2-y-o 5f/6f winner Monkey's Wedding (both by
Skyliner and fairly useful): dam ran once at 2 yrs: well held in maiden/claimer. *B. Palling*

QUITE A NIGHT   3 b.c. Night Shift (USA) – Ellebanna 69 (Tina's Pet 121) [2002 75:   **78 d**
p7g² p7g⁵ 7d⁶ 8m⁵ 7m 8m 8f p7g p10g Oct 31] fair maiden: below form after reappearance: likely to prove best at 7f/1m: acts on polytrack: sometimes tongue tied: has hinted
at temperament: sold 11,000 gns. *J. W. Hills*

QUITE FRANKLY   4 b.g. Environment Friend 128 – Four-Legged Friend 101   **–**
(Aragon 118) [2002 –: f9.4s 11.8m p12g Jun 22] leggy, close-coupled gelding: no form:
tried blinkered. *Dr J. D. Scargill*

QUITE HAPPY (IRE)   7 b.m. Statoblest 120 – Four-Legged Friend 101 (Aragon   **50**
118) [2002 –: 5g 5m 5d 5f⁴ 5m Jul 24] sturdy mare: modest handicapper: best form at 5f
on good going or firmer: tried visored/blinkered earlier in career. *W. J. Musson*

QUITE REMARKABLE   3 b.g. Danzig Connection (USA) – Kathy Fair (IRE) 46   **71 §**
(Nicholas Bill 125) [2002 73§: p7g p6g 7s* 8f⁶ Apr 11] workmanlike gelding: fair on   **a58 §**
turf, modest on all-weather: won handicap at Leicester in March: stays 7f: acts on soft
and good to firm ground: sometimes carries head high/folds tamely: played up and
withdrawn final intended outing: unreliable. *A. D. Smith*

QUITO (IRE)   5 b.r. Machiavellian (USA) 123 – Qirmazi (USA) 113 (Riverman   **78**
(USA) 131) [2002 6g⁵ a6f 5g³ 5g 8.5g⁴ 5m f8s⁴ 7m⁶ f8s⁴ 7.5m f6s⁵ f6g* f6g* f6s* 7d² 7v   **a91**
p7g f6g f6g Dec 16] tall, angular rig: fairly useful handicapper on all-weather, fair on turf:
left J. Sadler in UAE 3,500 gns after second start: won at Wolverhampton (twice) and
Southwell in the autumn: has form at 8.5f, but probably best around 6f: acts on good to
soft ground, good to firm and dirt/fibresand: usually blinkered: tried tongue tied: has been
sweating/edgy: races prominently. *D. W. Chapman*

QUITTE LA FRANCE   4 b.f. Saddlers' Hall (IRE) 126 – Tafila 101 (Adonijah 126)   **84**
[2002 80: 10d² 11.9m³ 13s⁵ 12m⁴ 16.2s³ 20m 11.9m² 11.8d⁴ 10g⁶ 14m Sep 7] strong filly:
poor mover: fairly useful handicapper: stays 2m: acts on soft and good to firm going:
blinkered (unseated after 2f) once at 3 yrs: sometimes flashes tail/finds little: sold 3,000
gns, sent to Spain. *J. G. Given*

QUIT THE PACK (IRE)   4 b. or br.g. Grand Lodge (USA) 125 – Treasure (IRE) 72   **–**
(Treasure Kay 114) [2002 67: 12.3g f14s f14.8g Sep 21] ex-Irish gelding: second foal:
dam third at 1¼m in Ireland: fair maiden at best: no form in 2002: tried blinkered/visored.
R. N. Bevis

R

RAASED   10 b.g. Unfuwain (USA) 131 – Sajjaya (USA) 97 (Blushing Groom (FR)
131) [2002 8g May 31] tall gelding: probably of little account nowadays. *F. Watson*

RACHEL   2 ch.f. (Feb 24) Spectrum (IRE) 126 – Agnus (IRE) (In The Wings 128)   **– p**
[2002 8s Oct 15] strong, close-coupled filly: has scope: third foal: half-sister to 3-y-o
Dolores: dam, Belgian 7f (at 2 yrs) and 9f winner, half-sister to smart performer up to 1m
Wavy Run: 14/1 and backward, missed break completely and always well in rear in
maiden at Leicester: type to do better. *Mrs A. J. Perrett*

RACINGFORMCLUB BOY   3 ch.g. Blushing Flame (USA) 109 – Sonoco 61 (Song   **42**
132) [2002 53: p10g p8g⁵ f9.4g⁵ p7g p10g 8.2d 10m 8f 16m 8m⁴ 11.9d 10.9f⁴ 11.6m
10m 10.1m⁶ 10d Oct 28] angular gelding: bad mover: poor maiden: stays 11.6f: acts on
all-weather, firm and good to soft ground: tried visored/blinkered: very slowly away final
outing. *P. S. McEntee*

RADDIT (IRE)   3 b.g. Thatching 131 – Smart Display (Elegant Air 119) [2002 p10g   **–**
13.8f⁴ 13.8m⁴ Jul 24] IR 15,000Y: third living foal: half-brother to French 1¼m winner
Pedraza (by Glauco): dam unraced: well beaten in maidens. *J. W. Unett*

RADIANT BRIDE   2 ch.f. (Jan 26) Groom Dancer (USA) 128 – Radiancy (IRE) 77   **61**
(Mujtahid (USA) 118) [2002 p8g⁵ Dec 14] second foal: half-sister to a winner in Italy by
Emperor Jones: dam, ran twice (second at 7f), half-sister to useful stayer Upper Strata,
herself dam of smart performer up to 12.5f Lord of Men (by Groom Dancer): 14/1, 6¾
lengths fifth of 12 to Made In Japan in maiden at Lingfield, flashing tail and no extra.
D. W. P. Arbuthnot

RADIANT SKY (IRE)   4 ch.f. Spectrum (IRE) 126 – Shakey (IRE) (Caerleon (USA)   **–**
132) [2002 62: p12g Jan 8] modest maiden at 3 yrs: tried blinkered. *L. G. Cottrell*

RADLEY PARK (IRE)   3 b.g. Vettori (IRE) 119 – Livry (USA) (Lyphard (USA) 132)   **79 ?**
[2002 10m⁴ 10m p12g⁵ Sep 10] 36,000F, 30,000Y: half-brother to several winners,
including 8-y-o Sophomore: dam, French 11f winner, half-sister to very smart middle-
distance performer Defensive Play: easily best effort (fair form) when 1¼ lengths fourth
to Manoubi in maiden at Windsor on debut: should stay 1½m: sold 7,500 gns, joined
E. Tuer. *P. J. Makin*

RAED   9 b.g. Nashwan (USA) 135 – Awayed (USA) 108 (Sir Ivor 135) [2002 43§: f11s   **– §**
Jan 17] sturdy gelding: well beaten only start in 2002. *Mrs A. M. Naughton*

RAFFERTY (IRE)   3 ch.c. Lion Cavern (USA) 117 – Badawi (USA) 103 (Diesis 133)   **93**
[2002 80: 7.1g* 8g 7.6f* 7d³ 8m 8d⁵ 9.9m 7f 7g Oct 18] angular colt: fairly useful
performer: won maiden at Warwick in April and handicap at Chester in May: probably
stays 1m: yet to race on soft/heavy going, acts on any other. *C. E. Brittain*

RAFFLESTONE   3 b.g. Atraf 116 – Annie Hall (Saddlers' Hall (IRE) 126) [2002 p8g   **–**
p10g Feb 13] first foal: dam behind on only start: slowly away and well held in maidens
at Lingfield. *L. Montague Hall*

RAFTERS MUSIC (IRE)   7 b.g. Thatching 131 – Princess Dixieland (USA) (Dixie-   **83**
land Band (USA)) [2002 85: f5s³ f6g² f6g⁴ p7g⁵ f6g³ f6g³ 6g 6m³ 6d 7f 6d 6m³ 6.5g 6.1s
f6g f7s⁶ f5g⁴ f6s⁴ Dec 26] good-bodied gelding: fairly useful handicapper: effective at 5f
to 7f: acts on all-weather and any turf going: tried blinkered/tongue tied earlier in career:
tends to hang: often claimer ridden: usually held up. *B. W. Hills*

RAGAMUFFIN   4 ch.g. Prince Sabo 123 – Valldemosa 81 (Music Boy 124) [2002 90:   **89**
6s 5s 6g² 6g 6g 6s⁵ 6g* 6d² 6m 6m⁶ 6s³ 6m 7.2s 7m 6g Sep 20] sturdy gelding: fairly
useful handicapper: won at Newcastle in June: well held last 4 starts: effective at 5f/6f:
acts on soft and good to firm ground: usually blinkered nowadays: held up. *T. D. Easterby*

RAGASAH   4 b.f. Glory of Dancer 121 – Slight Risk 72 (Risk Me (FR) 127) [2002 55:   **54 d**
p10g⁴ f11s p12g 11.9m 10s 12.1d p16g 10m⁶ 12.3m Aug 30] sparely-made filly: modest
performer at best: generally on downgrade in 2002: probably stays easy 1½m: acts on
all-weather, good to firm and good to soft going: reportedly lost action once as 3-y-o and
second outing 2002: sometimes looks difficult ride. *Miss Gay Kelleway*

RAGHBA (USA)   3 b.f. Gulch (USA) – Manwah (USA) 72 (Lyphard (USA) 132)   **71**
[2002 12m² 12s⁴ 12.3g² Aug 26] lengthy, unfurnished filly: has knee action: fifth foal:
dam, middle-distance maiden, closely related to Unfuwain and half-sister to Nayef (by
Gulch) and Nashwan: fair form in frame in maidens at Doncaster, Newmarket and Ripon:
raced only at 1½m: wore crossed noseband: visits Marju. *M. P. Tregoning*

RAG TOP (IRE)   2 ch.f. (Feb 3) Barathea (IRE) 127 – Petite Epaulette 80 (Night Shift   **101**
(USA)) [2002 5m* 5.2f* 6s* 5m³ 7g5 7g* Oct 5] 28,000F, 60,000Y: strong, useful-
looking filly: has scope: poor mover: fifth foal: sister to 2-y-o winners Dress Code (5f in
2000) and Seamstress (7f in 2001) and half-sister to 2-y-o 5f winners Shalford's Honour
(in 1997, by Shalford) and Lady Sarka (in 1999, by Lake Coniston): dam, 5f winner, ran
only at 2 yrs: useful performer: won maiden at Warwick and minor event at Newbury in
May, listed race at Naas in June and C. L. Weld Park Stakes at the Curragh (comfortably
by ½ length from Feabhas, leading over 1f out) in October: creditable efforts when third
to Romantic Liason in Queen Mary Stakes at Royal Ascot and fifth to Six Perfections in
Prix du Calvados at Deauville: stays 7f: acts on firm and soft ground: races prominently.
R. Hannon

RAHAF (USA)   2 b.c. (Apr 5) Theatrical 128 – Gozo Baba (USA) (Raja Baba (USA))   **94**
[2002 5m² 6f² 6d² 5.9d² 7.9f² Oct 12] $90,000Y: leggy, rather unfurnished colt: eighth
foal: brother to a winner in USA and half-brother to 3 winners there: dam maiden
half-sister to US Grade 1 9f winner Tango Dancer: fairly useful maiden: runner-up all
starts: seemed not to go through with effort in nursery on fourth one: short-head second
of 4 to Chaffinch at York final one, dictating slow pace: should stay
1¼m: acts on firm and good to soft ground. *M. Johnston*

RAHEEL (IRE)   2 ch.c. (Jan 22) Barathea (IRE) 127 – Tajawuz 82 (Kris 135) [2002   –
7.1m Aug 30] first foal: dam 1¼m winner from family of Rainbow Quest: 16/1 and very
green, well held in Sandown maiden, tending to carry head high: sold 8,000 gns.
E. A. L. Dunlop

RAHJEL SULTAN   4 b.g. Puissance 110 – Dalby Dancer 71 (Bustiki) [2002 57: 6m   –
6m 5m 6s⁵ f9.4s⁵ Nov 2] big, heavy-topped gelding: modest maiden at best: little form in
2002. *B. A. McMahon*

RAHLEX (IRE)   4 ch.g. Rahy (USA) 115 – Lady Express (IRE) (Soviet Star (USA)   **51**
128) [2002 55: f6s* f6g⁶ f6g⁶ f8g⁵ 7g2 8m p6g* 6f⁶ Jun 7] lengthy, sparely-made   **a60**
gelding: modest performer: won maiden at Southwell in January and claimer at Lingfield
in May: best around 6f: acts on all-weather and firm going: tongue tied in 2002. *Ronald
Thompson*

RAHWAAN (IRE)   3 b.c. Darshaan 133 – Fawaakeh (USA) 84 (Lyphard (USA) 132)   **100**
[2002 78p: 10.2g2 12g2 12.1d* 13.3f⁴ 16.1d* 14m 16s Oct 25] medium-sized, lengthy
colt: useful performer: won maiden at Chepstow in June and handicap at Newmarket
(beat Mamcazma short head) in August, on both occasions dictating pace: stays 2m: acts
on firm and good to soft going, possibly not on soft: ran as if amiss penultimate start,
seemed to try to bite a rival and again well held final outing: sold 33,000 gns. *J. L. Dunlop*

RAHY'S SON (USA)   3 ch.g. Rahy (USA) 115 – Rose Crescent (USA) (Nijinsky   –
(CAN) 138) [2002 10.1f 13.8m⁵ 11.7f 10m 10d Oct 28] $175,000Y, 800 3-y-o: half-
brother to numerous minor winners abroad: dam, US Grade 3 11f winner, sister to Ile de
Bourbon and half-sister to Rose Bowl, both top class: well held, including in sellers: tried
blinkered/tongue tied. *P. S. McEntee*

RAINBOW CHASE (IRE)   4 b.g. Rainbow Quest (USA) 134 – Fayrooz (USA) 74   –
(Gulch (USA)) [2002 82d: f14s Sep 17] tall, leggy, light-bodied gelding: lightly-raced
and disappointing maiden: stays 11f: tried blinkered. *S. J. Magnier*

RAINBOW CITY (IRE)   2 b.f. (Mar 25) Rainbow Quest (USA) 134 – Greektown   **85 p**
(Ela-Mana-Mou 132) [2002 7m² Sep 20] quite good-topped filly: sister to smart 1¼m and
13f winner Multicoloured and closely related to useful 7f (at 2 yrs) and 1¼m winner
Athens Belle (by Groom Dancer): dam, French 1¼m/1½m winner, half-sister to Prix du
Cadran winner Sought Out (by Rainbow Quest) and to grandam of Golan: 7/1 and
bandaged off-hind joint, 2½ lengths second of 7 to L'Ancresse in maiden at Newbury,
staying on well under considerate handling: will be well suited by 1¼m+: sure to improve
and win races. *Sir Michael Stoute*

RAINBOW DASH (IRE)   3 b.c. Rainbow Quest (USA) 134 – High Spirited 80   **81**
(Shirley Heights 130) [2002 10g⁵ 10d 10.5d⁵ Aug 8] 210,000Y: angular colt: half-brother
to several winners, including French 10.5f and 1½m winner Legend Maker (by Sadler's
Wells) and 1½m winner Amfortas (by Caerleon), both smart, and useful performer up to
1¾m Dollar Bird (by Kris): dam, 1¾m and 2m winner, sister to dam of In The Wings and
half-sister to dam of High-Rise: best effort in maidens (fairly useful form) when 7¾
lengths fifth to Rosa Parks at Haydock (edgy) final start: will be suited by 1½m+: sold
7,000 gns. *Sir Michael Stoute*

RAINBOW D'BEAUTE   3 ch.f. Rainbow Quest (USA) 134 – Reine d'Beaute 97   –
(Caerleon (USA) 132) [2002 –p: p13g* 10g p12g2 p12g Nov 23] close-coupled filly: **a88**
fairly useful performer, lightly raced: won maiden at Lingfield in October: ran well
penultimate start and better than bare result final one: stays 13f: acts on polytrack: sold
36,000 gns. *M. A. Jarvis*

RAINBOW END   3 ch.f. Botanic (USA) – High Finish 58 (High Line 125) [2002   **101**
10m* 16.2m 12g⁴ 10g 10d Nov 1] 9,000F, 15,000Y: sturdy, useful-looking filly: second
foal: half-sister to 6f (at 2 yrs) and 1¼m (in Sweden) winner Conclusion (by Prince Sabo):
dam, lightly-raced maiden, half-sister to smart performers Munwar (up to 1½m) and
Hateel (up to 1¾m): useful form: won maiden at Sandown (gave trouble stall) in June:
easily best effort when third past post behind Marani in listed race at Newmarket (edged
right, demoted to fourth): may prove ideally suited by around 1¼m: raced only on good/
good to firm going. *D. R. C. Elsworth*

RAINBOW HIGH   7 b.h. Rainbow Quest (USA) 134 – Imaginary (IRE) 94   **121**
(Dancing Brave (USA) 140) [2002 117: 12s⁴ 12m 18.7f² 20m Jun 20]
Excess devalues: just ask university entrance boards trying to differentiate
between the various annual levels of A-level passes. Their problem has a parallel in
racing, too. More and more horses each season seem to be putting up what would

traditionally have been considered exceptional weight-carrying efforts in handicaps. By all accounts, to solve their problem universities are thinking of looking elsewhere for indicators as to how well students might cope with higher education, or at least looking more closely at the different backgrounds against which A-level passes are achieved. Some of today's better weight-carrying efforts in handicaps need putting in a wider context too. Those that should carry most kudos are those achieved in handicaps with the widest weight range and in the most truly-run races. Rated stakes, with their limited weight range, and those open handicaps in which the featherweights have been balloted out, do not provide so tough a test for the top weights. And, when the authorities decided to raise the minimum riding weight from 7-7 to 7-10, it perhaps should have compensated by raising the top weights allowed accordingly. The question of the pace of races is out of their hands, of course, but the strength of the gallop inevitably has an affect on the reliability of the form. Weight-carrying performances in which the form is backed up by an equivalent timefigure, suggesting a well-run race, are generally more valid than those that aren't.

The now-retired Rainbow High twice put up apparently exceptional weight-carrying efforts in the Tote Chester Cup, firstly when winning the race for the second time in three years in 2001 and again when runner-up in the latest season. The Chester Cup is an open handicap and Rainbow High carried 9-13 to victory as a six-year-old when the weight range went down to 7-10. He carried the same weight and again faced some opponents carrying a featherweight when beaten two lengths by Fantasy Hill in attempting a third victory in four runnings in May. Despite good-sized fields, however, on neither occasion did he have to cope with a fierce, end-to-end gallop, as borne out by the modest timefigures. Very smart though the form looked, Rainbow High found it hard going in better company, lack of success in his case, however, possibly explained more by his own quirkiness as by the idea that Chester form flattered him greatly. Rainbow High's only pattern success came in the Jockey Club Cup at Newmarket in 1999, when the race cut up to three runners. His other credits include seconds in the Doncaster Cup in 1999 and 2001 and a third in the Goodwood Cup, also in 2001. Rainbow High managed no better than seventh in three attempts in the Gold Cup, and he had his final outing in the 2002 renewal of that event, finishing second last, presumably not himself.

Rainbow High (b.h. 1995)	Rainbow Quest (USA) (b 1981)	Blushing Groom (ch 1974)	Red God
			Runaway Bride
		I Will Follow (b 1975)	Herbager
			Where You Lead
	Imaginary (IRE) (b 1990)	Dancing Brave (b 1983)	Lyphard
			Navajo Princess
		Bold Fantasy (b 1974)	Bold Lad
			Ribot's Fantasy

Rainbow High has been retired to the Louella Stud, Leicestershire, at a fee of £1,250, October 1st. He is the first foal of the mile-and-a-quarter winner Imaginary, a half-sister to the Lowther Stakes winner Kingscote, dam of the smart pair Rainbow Corner (second in the Poule d'Essai des Poulains) and the five-year-old Welcome Friend. Just one of Imaginary's subsequent foals has made it to the racecourse so far, Imaginative (by Last Tycoon) winning at up to eleven furlongs in France and over hurdles in Britain. Grandam Bold Fantasy was second in the Irish One Thousand Guineas and was out of a sister to Ragusa, the outstanding Irish Derby, King George, St Leger and Eclipse winner. A compact, quite attractive horse, who tended to carry plenty of condition, Rainbow High won five of his thirty-three races. Unraced on heavy going, he acted on any other and stayed two and a quarter miles. He wasn't the easiest of rides, usually racing freely and sometimes finding little. Though none too reliable in his final two seasons, he was, overall, an asset to racing, playing a colourful part in the long-distance scene.
B. W. Hills

RAINBOW QUEEN   2 b.f. (Feb 1) Rainbow Quest (USA) 134 – Dazzle 116 (Gone West (USA)) [2002 7.1m* 8g Sep 28] good-topped filly: has scope: has a round action: second foal: half-sister to 2001 2-y-o 6f winner Wish (by Danehill): dam, best at 2 yrs when 5f/6f winner (later 7f winner and third in 1000 Guineas), half-sister to dam of 4-y-o   **92 p**

Danehurst: well-backed favourite, fairly useful form when winning 14-runner maiden at Warwick in September by 3 lengths from Ayun, drawing clear final 1f: 6/1, well held in Fillies' Mile at Ascot later in month: should stay at least 1m: almost certainly remains capable of better. *Sir Michael Stoute*

RAINBOW RIVER (IRE)   4 ch.g. Rainbows For Life (CAN) – Shrewd Girl (USA)   **64** 79 (Sagace (FR) 135) [2002 72, a75: f11g f7g⁴ f12g f11g 12.3g⁴ 8f 10g 11.6d 10.1m 12g   **a59** 10g 9.9d 8.5d 8g² f8s 8.5g⁵ 9.9m f8g f8g² f11g* f12g⁶ f14g⁵ f11g f12g Dec 27] close-coupled gelding: shows plenty of knee action: modest handicapper: won at Southwell in November: stays 1½m: acts on fibresand, firm and soft going: sometimes visored/blinkered at 3 yrs: sometimes races freely/hangs right: none too consistent. *M. C. Chapman*

RAINBOW STAR (FR)   8 b. or br.g. Saumarez 132 – In The Star (FR) (In Fijar   **–** (USA) 121) [2002 f14.8g Sep 30] of little account on Flat nowadays. *Mrs P. Ford*

RAINSTORM   7 b.g. Rainbow Quest (USA) 134 – Katsina (USA) 98 (Cox's Ridge   **51** (USA)) [2002 56: f8.5g 9.9g 10.2d 12.3g 12.3m 10d³ 8g⁴ 9.9g 8.1g* 10m³ 10.5m 10.9g Sep 19] stocky gelding: modest handicapper: won ladies race at Chepstow in August: stays easy 11f: acts on fibresand and firm going, probably on soft: tried visored: sometimes forces pace: none too consistent. *W. M. Brisbourne*

RAINWASHED GOLD   2 b.c. (Jan 22) Rainbow Quest (USA) 134 – Welsh Autumn   **108** 107 (Tenby 125) [2002 7m² 8m* 8.1m² 8m² 8m² Oct 12] smallish, sturdy colt: first foal: dam French 1m winner, including at 2 yrs, half-sister to 6-y-o Tillerman: useful performer: landed odds in maiden at Newmarket in August: runner-up all other starts, in listed races at Goodwood (beaten 1¼ lengths by Rimrod, carrying head awkwardly) and Ascot (below best when beaten 3½ lengths by Big Bad Bob) last 2 outings: will stay at least 1¼m: raced only on good to firm going: wore blanket for stall entry at Ascot. *Mrs A. J. Perrett*

RAISE A MELODY (IRE)   3 ch.f. Hector Protector (USA) 124 – Dumayla 78   **70** (Shernazar 131) [2002 –: f8.5g⁴ 7.1g 8.3m⁶ 11.6s f12g² f16.2f* f14.8g³ f14.8g⁶ Dec 31] fair handicapper: won at Wolverhampton in November: stays 2m: acts on fibresand. *A. J. Lidderdale*

RAISED THE BAR (USA)   3 ch.f. Royal Academy (USA) 130 – Barari (USA)   **85** (Blushing Groom (FR) 131) [2002 71: 9.2s² 9d 10.9m* 11.9m Jul 4] leggy, angular filly: fairly useful performer: won handicap at Warwick in June: tailed off final outing: not sure to stay beyond 11f: acts on soft and good to firm going: sent to Australia. *M. Johnston*

RAISON GARDE (IRE)   3 b.f. Ashkalani (IRE) 128 – Didjala (USA) (Irish River   **96** (FR) 131) [2002 86: 8m* 10.4d 10f⁶ 10g³ 12.3m⁴ 10.5m⁴ 12g⁴ Oct 17] big, strong, lengthy filly: useful handicapper: won at Pontefract in May by neck from Golden Chalice: at least respectable efforts in frame last 4 starts: effective at 1m to 1½m: acts on soft and good to firm ground: has been heavily bandaged in front: reportedly lost action third start: off bridle some way out penultimate outing. *J. G. FitzGerald*

RAJAB   3 br.c. Selkirk (USA) 129 – Putout 69 (Dowsing (USA) 124) [2002 94p: 6m³   **102** 7m⁴ 6f 6m⁴ 5.1d⁶ Jul 4] tall, quite good-topped colt: has scope: useful performer: good 1½ lengths third to Fire Up The Band in handicap at Newmarket in April (made most): lost action under pressure and below form after: will prove best at 5f/6f: acts on good to firm going, possibly not on heavy: joined E. Charpy in UAE. *M. Johnston*

RAJAH EMAN (IRE)   4 b.g. Sri Pekan (USA) 117 – Jungle Book (IRE) (Ballad   **–** Rock 122) [2002 82: 10.9g 10g f9.4g 8m Jun 21] lengthy, rather sparely-made gelding: unimpressive mover: fairly useful at 3 yrs: no form too 2002: visored last 2 starts. *C. A. Dwyer*

RAJAM   4 b.g. Sadler's Wells (USA) 132 – Rafif (USA) 68 (Riverman (USA) 131)   **–** [2002 102: 12d 11.9m⁶ 12.3g Aug 4] useful performer at best: reportedly suffered from breathing problem at 3 yrs: well held in 2002: tried blinkered. *A. C. Stewart*

RAJASTHAN (IRE)   3 b.g. Spectrum (IRE) 126 – Sherkova (USA) (State Dinner   **80** (USA)) [2002 8f 10m³ p10g² 10m² 10.1s Oct 22] quite good-topped gelding: sixth foal: half-brother to 3 winners, including 1m winner Russian Party (by Lycius) and 2m winner Norma's Lady (by Unfuwain): dam unraced half-sister to Prix de Diane winner Lady In Silver: fairly useful form when placed in maidens: stiff task and well held in handicap final start: stays 1¼m: acts on polytrack and good to firm going: found little third outing: sold 13,000 gns, sent to Kuwait. *J. R. Fanshawe*

RAKAYEB (USA)   3 ch.f. Gone West (USA) – Matiya (IRE) 116 (Alzao (USA) 117)   **–** [2002 10d Jul 10] second foal: dam, 7f (at 2 yrs) and 1m (Irish 1000 Guineas) winner, probably stayed 10.5f: 10/1 and tongue tied, pulled too hard when last in maiden at Kempton: sold 18,000 gns in December. *B. Hanbury*

RAKTI 3 b.c. Polish Precedent (USA) 131 – Ragera (IRE) (Rainbow Quest (USA) 134) **118**
[2002 11d* 10.5m* 12m* 10g* 11s⁶ 10s³ 10d Nov 17] tall, good-topped colt: third foal: half-brother to Italian winner up to 10.5f Riksha (by Zilzal): dam lightly-raced daughter of Italian 1000 Guineas/Oaks third Smageta: smart performer: won first 4 starts at Rome in 2002, namely minor event (by 8 lengths) in March, listed race (by 7 lengths) in May and 16-runner Derby Italiano in May and another listed event in September: best effort when beating Ballingarry by 1½ lengths in Derby Italiano, leading virtually on bridle over 3f out before being ridden out: below form last 3 starts, reportedly suffering from temperature on first occasion: should prove at least as effective at 1¼m as 1½m: acts on good to firm and good to soft going: refused to enter stall for Champion Stakes at Newmarket sixth intended outing: joined M. Jarvis. *B. Grizzetti, Italy*

RAMBLER 2 b.f. (May 16) Selkirk (USA) 129 – Rahaam (USA) 91 (Secreto (USA) **70**
128) [2002 7d p8g p8g⁵ Dec 3] tall, quite good-topped filly: half-sister to several at least useful winners, including Cassandra Go (won at 7f but best at 5f, by Indian Ridge) and 1996 2-y-o 6f winner (later successful in USA) Verglas (by Highest Honor), both smart: dam 7f winner who stayed 1¼m: blinkered, best effort in maidens (fair form) when fifth to Treculiar at Lingfield, edging left: not sure to stay beyond 1m: twice slowly away. *J. H. M. Gosden*

RAMBLIN' MAN (IRE) 4 b.g. Blues Traveller (IRE) 119 – Saborinie 56 (Prince –
Sabo 123) [2002 54: f12s Jan 17] neat gelding: modest maiden at best. *P. D. Evans*

RAMBO NINE 5 b.g. Rambo Dancer (CAN) 107 – Asmarina 50 (Ascendant 96) –
[2002 –: f7g⁴ f12g Feb 19] of little account. *S. R. Bowring*

RAMBO WALTZER 10 b.g. Rambo Dancer (CAN) 107 – Vindictive Lady (USA) –
(Foolish Pleasure (USA)) [2002 71d: f12g f11g⁶ f8.5g⁵ f8.5g f9.4g³ f9.4g Apr 20] **a55**
smallish, sturdy gelding: prone to lameness: fair performer: well below form since first half of 2001: stays 1½m: acts on heavy going, good to firm and fibresand: visored once: tongue tied last 4 starts. *Miss S. J. Wilton*

RAMPANT (IRE) 4 b.g. Pursuit of Love 124 – Flourishing (IRE) 85 (Trojan Fen 118) –
[2002 89: 11.6d May 25] tall, useful-looking gelding: fairly useful performer at 3 yrs: shaped as if something amiss only run in 2002. *R. M. Beckett*

RAMPART 5 b.g. Kris 135 – Balliasta (USA) (Lyphard (USA) 132) [2002 50: f6g f6s² **57 §**
f6g f7g f6g 7v f6g³ f6g f6d* 5g 7m 6v⁶ 6s 5.9d Jun 26] strong, workmanlike gelding: **a50 §**
modest performer: won amateur minor event at Hamilton in May: probably best at 6f: acts on fibresand and good to soft going: tried blinkered, usually visored: sometimes slowly away/races freely: unreliable: sold 1,900 gns. *D. Shaw*

RANDOM QUEST 4 b.g. Rainbow Quest (USA) 134 – Anne Bonny 105 (Ajdal **103**
(USA) 130) [2002 94: 11.9m 20m⁴ 18.7g* 16.2d 18m 16d 14.6v³ Nov 8] leggy, useful-looking gelding: useful handicapper, lightly raced: won at Chester in August by 2 lengths from Ranville: ran creditably otherwise in 2002 only when fourth to Riyadh in Ascot Stakes and ninth behind Miss Fara in Cesarewitch (fifth outing) at Newmarket: stays 2½m: winner on soft ground, best form on good/good to firm: often races prominently: none too consistent. *P. F. I. Cole*

RANDOM TASK (IRE) 5 b.h. Tirol 127 – Minami (IRE) (Caerleon (USA) 132) **78 d**
[2002 –: f6g* f6g* f7g³ f6g² f6g⁵ f6g* f6g³ f6g f7g⁵ 6d f6g⁶ Oct 19] good-topped horse: fair performer at best: won seller at Wolverhampton and claimers at Southwell and Wolverhampton in first half of season: off 4½ months after seventh start (reportedly fractured bone in foreleg): effective at 6f/7f: acts on soft ground and fibresand: tried blinkered, visored nowadays: on downgrade. *D. Shaw*

RANEEN NASHWAN 6 b.g. Nashwan (USA) 135 – Raneen Alwatar 80 (Sadler's **81**
Wells (USA) 132) [2002 –: p12g² p12g Feb 9] lengthy, angular gelding: fairly useful handicapper: lightly raced: stays 1½m: acts on soft, good to firm ground and polytrack. *R. J. Baker*

RANI TWO 3 b.f. Wolfhound (USA) 126 – Donya 74 (Mill Reef (USA) 141) [2002 **63**
7m⁵ 7.6f* 10.1m³ 8d³ 7.6m⁴ 8.1m⁶ 8g Oct 19] 2,000 2-y-o: sister to winner in Greece, closely related to useful 1995 2-y-o 6f winner Jedaal (by Soviet Star) and half-sister to several winners, including 10.5f/1½m winner Altaweelah (by Fairy King) and 6-y-o Invader, both useful: dam twice-raced half-sister to Rothmans International winner French Glory out of Prix de Diane winner Dunette: modest performer: won maiden at Chester in July: should stay 1¼m. *W. M. Brisbourne*

Derby Italiano, Rome—Rakti becomes the first since Tisserand in 1988 to keep the prize at home; Ballingarry and Fisich are second and third

RANSOM O'WAR (USA) 2 b.c. (Mar 22) Red Ransom (USA) – Sombreffe 71 **86** (Polish Precedent (USA) 131) [2002 7.1m² 7.1m³ 7s² f8g* p7g Dec 3] $160,000F, 60,000Y: close-coupled, good-topped colt: fourth foal: half-brother to 3 winners, including useful Irish 1m winner Madame Cerito (by Diesis) and fairly useful Irish 1¼m winner Uliana (by Darshaan): dam, 7f winner, closely related to smart performers up to 7f Russian Bond and Snaadee: fairly useful performer: won minor event at Southwell in November by 5 lengths from Town Called Malice: stays 1m: acts on fibresand (some promise on polytrack), soft and good to firm going. *M. Johnston*

RANVILLE 4 ch.g. Deploy 131 – Kibitka (FR) (Baby Turk 120) [2002 102p: 20m **105** 16.4d² 16.2m 18.7g² 14.6m⁴ Sep 13] heavy-bodied gelding: poor mover: useful handicapper: lightly raced in 2002: good efforts when second at Sandown (beaten length by Cupboard Lover) and Chester (beaten 2 lengths by Random Quest): stays 2¼m: acts on heavy going and good to firm: races prominently: genuine. *M. A. Jarvis*

RANWAY (IRE) 2 ch.g. (Mar 21) Piccolo 121 – Disallowed (IRE) 76 (Distinctly **39** North (USA) 115) [2002 6.1d 6m⁴ 7d 6m Sep 3] IR 12,500F, IR 11,000Y: leggy, close-coupled gelding: poor mover: second foal: dam, 9f winner who was also successful over hurdles, half-sister to useful winner up to 1¾m Ferny Hill: poor maiden: form only when fourth in seller at Brighton: should stay 7f. *M. R. Channon*

RAPHAEL (IRE) 3 b.f. Perugino (USA) 84 – Danny's Miracle (Superlative 118) **80** [2002 75: 7.5m³ 7.6f 8m⁴ 7f³ 7.5m 7m⁶ 8g 7m³ 7m 7.5m⁵ 7g³ 7s* 7v⁶ Nov 9] leggy, quite good-topped filly: fairly useful handicapper: won apprentice race at Doncaster in October: effective at 7f/1m: acts on firm and soft ground: blinkered (below form) ninth start. *T. D. Easterby*

RAPID DEPLOYMENT 5 b.g. Deploy 131 – City Times (IRE) 65 (Last Tycoon **88** 131) [2002 95: 16d 18m 16v Nov 10] rangy gelding: has scope: fairly useful handicapper: won Irish Cesarewitch at the Curragh at 4 yrs: best effort in 2002 when respectable tenth in Cesarewitch at Newmarket second start: probably stays 2¼m: acts on soft and good to firm going: went in snatches/found little once at 3 yrs. *P. Hughes, Ireland*

RAPID LINER 9 b.g. Skyliner 117 – Stellaris (Star Appeal 133) [2002 –: f16s 5.7m⁶ **–** 6.1m 7m 6g Aug 13] maiden: tried visored/blinkered. *J. Gallagher*

RAPPAREE (USA) 4 b.f. Red Ransom (USA) – Pixie Erin 110 (Golden Fleece **–** (USA) 133) [2002 78: 10d 10s May 13] sturdy filly: fair performer at 3 yrs: well beaten in 2002, in blinkers final start. *J. W. Hills*

RAPSCALLION (GER) 3 b.g. Robellino (USA) 127 – Rosy Outlook (USA) 79 **100** (Trempolino (USA) 135) [2002 107: 8m 11f⁶ 8s⁴ Nov 2] leggy, unfurnished gelding: useful performer: won Horris Hill Stakes at Newbury at 2 yrs: lightly raced in 2002 (off 4 months after 2000 Guineas on reappearance), best effort when 8 lengths fourth to Smirk in listed race at Newmarket final outing (gelded after): should be fully effective at 1m (well held at 11f): goes well on ground softer than good: sometimes sweating: tends to edge left, but is game. *J. M. P. Eustace*

RAPT (IRE) 4 b.g. Septieme Ciel (USA) 123 – Dream Play (USA) (Blushing Groom   –
(FR) 131) [2002 70, a78: f8s p7g⁶ p6g⁴ f6g⁶ 8.3g f7s³ 7m May 15] leggy, useful-   **a72**
looking gelding: fair handicapper: effective at 6f/7f: acts on all-weather and good to firm
going: visored (ran creditably) second start: sold £3,600. *P. W. D'Arcy*

RAPTOR (IRE) 4 ch.g. Eagle Eyed (USA) 111 – Ahakista (IRE) (Persian Bold 123)   –
[2002 43?: 16m May 3] strong, lengthy gelding: poor maiden at best: tried visored.
J. R. Weymes

RARE DESTINY (IRE) 2 b.g. (Mar 19) Mujadil (USA) 119 – Jamaican Law (IRE)   –
(Case Law 113) [2002 5d 6m 6g Sep 19] 29,000Y: close-coupled gelding: first foal: dam,
ran 4 times at 2 yrs, half-sister to useful 1997 2-y-o sprinter Bay Prince (by Mujadil): only
a little sign of ability in maidens. *A. Berry*

RARE QUALITY 4 b.f. Chaddleworth (IRE) 103 – Pink Mex (Tickled Pink 114)   **45**
[2002 –p: p8g² 12d⁶ p12g Dec 18] poor maiden: stays 1m: acts on polytrack. *R. Guest*

RASHIK 8 ch.h. Cadeaux Genereux 131 – Ghzaalh (USA) 87 (Northern Dancer) [2002   **58**
59: f11g³ f12g² Feb 7] useful-looking horse; has been to stud: modest performer
nowadays: stays 1½m: acts on fibresand. *A. Streeter*

RASHIQA (USA) 3 b.f. Diesis 133 – Umniyatee 104 (Green Desert (USA) 127)   **80**
[2002 8m² 7.9d² 7.6f⁴ 8s⁶ 7.1m 6d Nov 1] sturdy, lengthy filly: half-sister to 3 winners,
including useful 7f winner (including at 2 yrs) Meshhed (by Gulch) and useful 7f (at
2 yrs) and 1m winner Jarah (by Forty Niner): dam, 7f/1m winner, daughter of 1000
Guineas/Oaks winner Midway Lady: fairly useful maiden: effective at 7f/1m: acts on soft
and good to firm going: has found little: sold 35,000 gns. *B. Hanbury*

RASID (USA) 4 b.g. Bahri (USA) 125 – Makadir (USA) (Woodman (USA) 126)   **95**
[2002 88p: 10m² 10g² 10s* 10d⁶ Nov 1] rangy gelding: useful performer, very lightly
raced: landed odds in maiden at Ayr in October after 5-month break: well beaten in listed
event at Newmarket final outing: not sure to stay beyond 1¼m: acts on soft and good to
firm ground. *E. A. L. Dunlop*

RASM 5 b.g. Darshaan 133 – Northshiel 85 (Northfields (USA)) [2002 10s³ 10m³   **106**
10.4m Jul 13] tall, leggy gelding: good walker: fluent mover: useful performer, lightly
raced (reportedly injured tendon final 3-y-o outing): good 2 lengths third to Ulundi in
listed rated stakes at Ascot on second start: poor effort in John Smith's Cup (Handicap) at
York next time (reportedly unsettled by parade): subsequently sold privately: stays 1¼m,
possibly not 1½m: acts on good to firm going, some promise on soft. *A. C. Stewart*

RATBARRY (IRE) 3 ch.g. Woodborough (USA) 112 – Ever So 78 (Mummy's Pet   –
125) [2002 f6g f5g 7m⁶ Jul 26] IR 1,700Y, resold IR 2,500Y, 5,500 2-y-o: unfurnished
gelding: half-brother to 3 winners, including sprinter Ever So Artistic (by Claude Monet):
dam 2-y-o 6f winner: well beaten in maidens/seller: left R. Fahey after second start.
D. Nicholls

RATHMULLAN 3 ch.g. Bluegrass Prince (IRE) 110 – National Time (USA) (Lord   **46**
Avie (USA)) [2002 8m 6g 7g p6g 7d 6m⁶ 7g⁵ Aug 7] workmanlike gelding: half-brother
to several winners, including 5-y-o D'Accord, Kildee Lad (by Presidium) and Malibu
Man (by Ballacashtal), all fairly useful sprinters: dam ran twice at 2 yrs: poor maiden:
stays 7f: tried blinkered: slowly away third outing: looked hard ride in apprentice event
final start. *E. A. Wheeler*

RATIFIED 5 b.g. Not In Doubt (USA) 101 – Festival of Magic (USA) 73 (Clever   –
Trick (USA)) [2002 44: 16.2g Aug 15] good-bodied gelding: probably of little account
nowadays. *M. C. Chapman*

RATIO 4 ch.c. Pivotal 124 – Owdbetts (IRE) 69 (High Estate 127) [2002 106: 7.1g⁴ 8g   **93**
8s* 6v⁶ Nov 20] angular, quite good-topped colt: useful performer at 3 yrs: only fairly
useful form in 2002, leaving I. Balding after second start: won minor event at Angers in
October: not discredited in listed race at Maisons-Laffitte following month: stays 1m:
acts on soft and good to firm going: troublesome in stall and withdrawn on intended
reappearance. *J. E. Hammond, France*

RAVENGLASS (USA) 3 b.c. Miswaki (USA) 124 – Urus (USA) (Kris S (USA))   **73**
[2002 72: 8.3d⁶ 10s² Oct 23] fair form in 3 maidens: stays 1¼m: raced only on good to
soft/soft going: sold 38,000 gns. *J. H. M. Gosden*

RAVE ON (ITY) 3 b.f. Barathea (IRE) 127 – Kalliopina (FR) (Arctic Tern (USA)   **73**
126) [2002 73: 8.3m 7m 8.3m 8m 10.1m Sep 6] rather leggy filly: fair maiden at 2 yrs:
well held in 2002: bred to stay at least 1m: raced only on good to firm going. *R. Hannon*

RAWWAAH (IRE)   2 ch.c. (Mar 7) Nashwan (USA) 135 – Muhaba (USA) 96 (Mr   **– p** Prospector (USA)) [2002 8m Sep 5] first foal: dam, 2-y-o 1m winner, sister to US Grade 2 9f winner Sahm out of 1000 Guineas, Oaks and Irish Derby winner Salsabil: weak 20/1-shot, always in rear in minor event at Salisbury: should improve. *J. L. Dunlop*

RAWYAAN   3 b.c. Machiavellian (USA) 123 – Raheefa (USA) 75 (Riverman (USA)   **117** 131) [2002 94p: 10g* 10g⁴ 9.9m⁵ 9m* 9.9f* Sep 25] close-coupled, quite attractive colt: has a round action: smart performer: progressed well in 2002, winning handicaps at Nottingham and Goodwood, and listed event (beat Imtiyaz by head in 4-runner race) at Goodwood: good efforts in handicaps both other starts: likely to stay 1½m: yet to race on soft/heavy ground, acts on any other: visored last 3 outings: has worn crossed noseband. *J. H. M. Gosden*

RAYANA (FR)   4 b.f. Midyan (USA) 124 – High Kash (FR) (Highest Honor (FR) 124)   **52** [2002 39: p8g 10g 10.9m 8d* 8f* Jul 17] lengthy, plain filly: modest handicapper: won at Pontefract and Yarmouth in July: stays 1m: acts on firm and good to soft going. *T. T. Clement*

RAYBAAN (IRE)   3 b.g. Flying Spur (AUS) – Genetta (Green Desert (USA) 127)   **81** [2002 79: 7m 10m 10.2g² 10m 10.9m² p12g² 11m* 10m⁶ 12m⁶ 10m⁴ 11.5m Sep 17] strong gelding: fairly useful handicapper: won at Redcar in July: stays easy 1½m: acts on soft going, good to firm and polytrack: visored (ran poorly) final start. *M. H. Tompkins*

RAYIK   7 br.g. Marju (IRE) 127 – Matila (IRE) 98 (Persian Bold 123) [2002 54§, a66§:   **52** p13g p13g p12g⁶ p13g² p12g² 11.9f 11.9g 11.9d⁶ p12g² p12g⁶ 11.6m⁴ 11.9g* p12g p16g   **a58** p12g³ p12g⁵ p13g⁶ Dec 28] sparely-made gelding: modest performer: won selling handicap at Brighton in August: stays 13f: acts on all-weather and good to firm going: tried visored/tongue tied earlier in career: sometimes pulls hard: none too reliable. *G. L. Moore*

RAYMOND'S PRIDE   2 b.g. (Feb 26) Mind Games 121 – Northern Sal 59 (Aragon   **78** 118) [2002 6g 5g² f5g² 5d² 5g 5f² f6s⁴ Nov 2] second foal: brother to 3-y-o Northern   **a71** Games: dam 2-y-o 5f winner: fair maiden: runner-up 4 times, hanging right when short-headed at Catterick penultimate start: likely to prove best at 5f: acts on firm going, good to soft and fibresand: usually races prominently. *A. Berry*

RAYWARE BOY (IRE)   6 b.g. Scenic 128 – Amata (USA) (Nodouble (USA)) [2002   **– §** 49§: 13v 12.1d Jul 5] leggy, short-backed gelding: temperamental handicapper: visored/blinkered. *D. Shaw*

RAZOTTI (IRE)   2 b.f. (Mar 30) Raphane (USA) 102 – Zalotti (IRE) 84 (Polish   **62** Patriot (USA) 128) [2002 5m*ᵈⁱˢ 5g 6g⁶ Sep 19] IR 6,000F, 5,000Y: sturdy filly: third foal: half-sister to 2000 2-y-o 5f winner Celotti (by Celtic Swing): dam 5f winner, including at 2 yrs: modest form: best effort when winning maiden at Beverley in April (disqualified for failing dope test): should stay 6f. *N. Tinkler*

RAZZLE (IRE)   3 b.f. Green Desert (USA) 127 – Organza 105 (High Top 131) [2002   **68** –p: 8v⁶ 7f⁶ 8d⁵ 7m⁶ 10g² 10m⁶ Sep 20] lengthy filly: fair maiden: stays 1¼m: best efforts on good/good to soft going: blinkered last 3 starts (wandered final one). *J. L. Dunlop*

REACH FOR THE MOON (USA)   2 b. or br.f. (Jan 22) Pulpit (USA) 117 –   **103 p** Chancey Squaw (USA) (Chief's Crown (USA)) [2002 6g* 8g³ Sep 28] $1,650,000Y: quite attractive filly: third foal: half-sister to high-class Japanese 1m/1¼m performer Agnes Digital (by Crafty Prospector): dam, US 1m winner, half-sister to Royal Lodge winner Royal Kingdom out of half-sister to Blushing Groom: won maiden at Cork in August by 4 lengths from Spring Clean: missed Moyglare Stud Stakes at the Curragh next intended outing due to coughing: 2 handlers in preliminaries and taken steadily to post, 3 lengths third to Soviet Song in Fillies' Mile at Ascot, bumped by winner 2f out then staying on well: not sure to stay much beyond 1m: capable of better still. *A. P. O'Brien, Ireland*

REACHFORYOURPOCKET (IRE)   7 b.g. Royal Academy (USA) 130 – Gema-   **48** asheh (Habitat 134) [2002 52d, a68d: p10g² p7g* f9.4s³ 10f 7d⁴ p7g* 9s 6g³ 7m² 6m⁶   **a61** p6g⁶ 10m⁴ p10g Aug 29] modest handicapper on all-weather, poor on turf: won at Lingfield (apprentices) in February and June: effective at 6f to 1¼m: acts on firm going, good to soft and all-weather: tried blinkered/visored/tongue tied earlier in career: sold 4,000 gns, sent to Kuwait. *M. D. I. Usher*

READY TO ROCK (IRE)   6 b.g. Up And At 'em 109 – Rocklands Rosie (Muscatite   **–** 122) [2002 61, a67: f5g p6g Mar 6] fair handicapper at 5 yrs: well held in 2002: usually blinkered. *J. S. Moore*

REAL AMBITION (IRE)   3 b.g. Fayruz 116 – Mauradell (IRE) (Mujadil (USA)   **66**
119) [2002 77: f6s⁶ p6g f6g³ p5g³ Feb 9] sturdy gelding: fair maiden at 2 yrs: bit below
best in 2002: was effective at 5f/6f: acted on good to firm going and all-weather: usually
blinkered: sometimes wandered: dead. *R. Wilman*

REAL ESTATE   8 b.g. High Estate 127 – Haitienne (FR) (Green Dancer (USA) 132)   **–**
[2002 9.9g 11.7g Oct 16] of little account on Flat nowadays. *J. S. King*

REAP   4 b.g. Emperor Jones (USA) 119 – Corn Futures 78 (Nomination 125) [2002 54:   **–**
p10g⁶ p10g³ f9.4g* p10g⁴ f8.5g* f8.5g* f8.5g³ p8g³ f9.4g f8.5s⁵ Dec 13] rather leggy,   **a75**
good-topped gelding: fair handicapper on all-weather: won at Wolverhampton in
February, March and April: stays 1¼m: acts on all-weather: tried visored at 2 yrs:
sometimes slowly away/wanders. *Mrs Lydia Pearce*

REAR WINDOW   8 b.g. Night Shift (USA) – Last Clear Chance (USA) (Alleged   **47**
(USA) 138) [2002 50: 16.4d 14.1m³ 14.1m³ 12.1g⁴ 14.1m Aug 25] compact gelding: poor
handicapper: was effective at 1½m to easy 2m: acted on good to firm going, heavy and
fibresand: tried visored/blinkered/tongue tied earlier in career: dead. *M. J. Ryan*

REASONING   4 ch.f. Selkirk (USA) 129 – Attribute 69 (Warning 136) [2002 65:   **50 d**
f8.5g* f8s f8g 7.5g 8f 7g Jul 11] sparely-made filly: modest performer: won maiden at
Wolverhampton in January: well held in handicaps after (reportedly bled from nose final
start): effective at 1m/1¼m: acts on good to firm, good to soft ground and fibresand:
visored second start. *B. S. Rothwell*

REBANNA   2 ch.f. (Apr 29) Rock City 120 – Fuwala (Unfuwain (USA) 131) [2002 7g   **–**
Oct 14] plain, lengthy filly: has a round action: first foal: dam no form: 100/1, well beaten
in maiden at Leicester. *J. Balding*

REBATE   2 b.c. (Apr 4) Pursuit of Love 124 – Aigua Blava (USA) (Solford (USA) 127)   **77**
[2002 6s 7m⁶ 7d² 7d⁴ 7m³ 8.3d Oct 14] lengthy colt: fifth foal: half-brother to fairly useful
7f (at 2 yrs) and 1¼m winner Bettron (by Alnasr Alwasheek) and 2m winner Aquavita
(by Kalaglow): dam, tailed off only start, half-sister to Cesarewitch winner Captain's
Guest: fair maiden: creditable efforts in nurseries fourth/fifth starts: should stay at least
1m: acts on good to firm and good to soft going. *R. Hannon*

REBEL CLOWN   4 gr.g. King's Signet (USA) 110 – Castle Cary 69 (Castle Keep   **–**
121) [2002 7.1g f12s Sep 17] third foal: half-brother to 1996 2-y-o 5f winner Blazing
Castle (by Vague Shot): dam 6f winner: well beaten in 2 maidens. *N. J. Hawke*

REBELLE   3 b. or br.g. Reprimand 122 – Blushing Belle 74 (Local Suitor (USA) 128)   **71**
[2002 –: f8.5g⁵ 10m⁶ f12g⁴ f12g* p12g² 11.8m³ f12g⁵ p12g⁴ 14.1m³ 12m³ 16.2g² 16.2m³
15.8f² 15.8f⁵ f16g* p16g³ f16g² Dec 17] tall, close-coupled gelding: fair handicapper:
improved during 2002, and won at Southwell in May and November (wandered): stays
2m: acts on firm going and all-weather: reliable. *I. A. Wood*

REBELLINE (IRE)   4 b.f. Robellino (USA) 127 – Fleeting Rainbow 65   **122**
(Rainbow Quest (USA) 134) [2002 112: 7s* 10s* 10.5s* May 26]

Not only did Rebelline win all three of her starts in what turned out to be her
final season, but she took three notable scalps in the process. Johannesburg, Milan
and Nayef were the beaten favourites in those races, and their failures tended to
overshadow the performances of this grand filly, who was not far below the leading
members of her sex in Europe. It's just a pity that Rebelline's season was cut short.
She was still improving at the time of her last race, in May, and could well have
gone on to show even better form but for the recurrence of an old muscle injury in
her hip which eventually forced her retirement in October. Rebelline reportedly
suffers from arthritis and must have been far from easy to train, her achievements in
a restricted career reflecting great credit on her trainer Kevin Prendergast.

Rebelline was never risked on ground firmer than good and showed that she
was very much at home in the mud when winning a maiden on heavy going on the
first of her two starts at two; all five of her subsequent successes came on either
good to soft or soft. At three, Rebelline won a listed event at Leopardstown and the
Pretty Polly Stakes at the Curragh; and she was better still at four when each of the
races she contested took place at the Curragh. Dropped back to seven furlongs
for her reappearance, in the Castlemartin/La Louviere Studs Gladness Stakes,
Rebelline upset the odds laid on Johannesburg despite not getting the best of runs,

*Tattersalls Gold Cup, the Curragh—Rebelline (No.9) and Declan McDonogh
are fortunate to obtain a gap; they overhaul Bach, with Nayef third*

quickening smartly once finding room to collar the favourite in the last stride.
Johannesburg's stable-companion Milan looked the one Rebelline had to beat when
she was returned to a mile and a quarter in the Peintre Celebre EBF Mooresbridge
Stakes, but sadly he suffered a fractured cannon bone before the home turn and it
was his pacemaker Shoal Creek who gave Rebelline most to do. Rebelline moved
into second early in the straight and took over a furlong out, but she had to work
hard to maintain her advantage, having three quarters of a length to spare at the line.
The Tattersalls Gold Cup, Ireland's first Group 1 event of the season for horses
above the age of three, was next on the agenda for Rebelline, and it provided her
with her stiffest test since the Champion Stakes at Newmarket on her final start as a
three-year-old. Rebelline, who had failed to do herself justice then, renewed rivalry
with Nayef, Tobougg and Indian Creek, the first three home in the Champion; and
the four others in the line-up at the Curragh included Bach and Chancellor, that pair
successful in a listed race and a Group 3 contest respectively on their previous
starts. Nayef started at odds on, having his first race since winning the Dubai
Sheema Classic two months earlier. Next in the betting were Tobougg at 4/1 and
Rebelline and Bach, both at 7/1. Rebelline was given a daring waiting ride by
Declan McDonogh, who partnered the filly in all of her races. Fortunately for
McDonogh, a gap appeared which enabled him to switch his mount off the rail
inside the last furlong, and Rebelline responded really well to catch the front-
running Bach and win going away by two lengths, with Nayef only third. It was a
fitting swansong for a very smart filly, one who possessed a good turn of foot and
was thoroughly genuine.

		Roberto	Hail To Reason
	Robellino (USA)	(b 1969)	Bramalea
	(b 1978)	Isobelline	Pronto
Rebelline (IRE)		(b 1971)	Isobella
(b.f. 1998)		Rainbow Quest	Blushing Groom
	Fleeting Rainbow	(b 1981)	I Will Follow
	(b 1989)	Taplow	Tap On Wood
		(b 1984)	Fighting

Rebelline appeared not to stay on her only attempt at a mile and a half, in
the Irish Oaks, but her performance over an extended mile and a quarter in testing
conditions in the Tattersalls Gold Cup suggested she would have been worth
another try at the trip. Her dam Fleeting Rainbow should have stayed a mile and a
half but she, too, had only one attempt at the trip. Fleeting Rainbow was a strong-
finishing third in a mile-and-a-quarter maiden on good to soft ground on her second

Lady O'Reilly's "Rebelline"

start, before disappointing over a mile and a half on good to firm next time and not being seen out again. Rebelline, a 28,000-guinea foal who fetched IR 68,000 guineas as a yearling, is the fifth offspring of Fleeting Rainbow and is her second winner. Fleeting Rainbow's first foal Quws, a full brother to Rebelline and also trained by Prendergast, was a smart and consistent performer who stayed eleven furlongs. He, too, gained his most important wins at the Curragh, in the Blandford Stakes and Gallinule Stakes. The next dam Taplow is an unraced daughter of the useful miler Fighting. The family is a good one, and there seems no reason why Rebelline should not make another significant contribution to its success as a broodmare. *K. Prendergast, Ireland*

REBORN (IRE)   4 b.f. Idris (IRE) 118 – Tantum Ergo 106 (Tanfirion 110) [2002 48: –
10.1m May 29] leggy filly: poor maiden at 3 yrs. *N. P. Littmoden*

RECEIVED WISDOM (USA)   4 b.c. Gone West (USA) – Sleep Easy (USA) 116   **60**
(Seattle Slew (USA)) [2002 54+: p8g² p10g Feb 26] modest form from 4 starts: stayed
1m: acted on all-weather: dead. *Edward Butler, Ireland*

RECEIVEDWITHTHANX (IRE)   3 b.c. Celtic Swing 138 – Sabrata (IRE) (Zino   **?**
127) [2002 86: f6g f9.4g⁶ 7s a10.5g⁶ a8g² a8g* a8g* 8s⁵ a10.5g² a8g* a8g³ a10g* a8g³
Dec 15] fairly useful performer at 2 yrs: left A. Dickman after third start: in good form
afterwards, winning minor events at Mijas in July (2) and September and Dos Hermanas
in December: stays 1¼m: acts on firm going and sand: found little last 2 starts in Britain.
C. Tinkler, Spain

798

RECIPROCAL (IRE)　　4 gr.f. Night Shift (USA) – African Light 65§ (Kalaglow 132)　　–
[2002 88: 8.3d 7d 8m Aug 15] tall filly: fairly useful handicapper at 3 yrs: has reportedly
had breathing problems: tried visored/tongue tied. *D. R. C. Elsworth*

RECOUNT (FR)　　2 b.g. (Mar 28) Sillery (USA) 122 – Dear Countess (FR) (Fabulous　　**61 p**
Dancer (USA) 124) [2002 7f 7.6m⁶ 6m Aug 29] 250,000 francs Y: good-topped gelding:
third foal: half-brother to a winner in Spain by Kaldoun: dam placed around 1½m in
France: left Mrs J. Ramsden after debut: better effort in maidens after (modest form)
when sixth to Captain Saif at Lingfield: said to have been found lame behind after final
start (connections originally found guilty under non-triers' rule, but horse's ban and
trainer's fine quashed on appeal, rider's suspension reduced from 10 to 7 days): should
stay at least 1m: almost certainly capable of better. *J. R. Best*

RECTANGLE (IRE)　2 ch.g. (Apr 11) Fayruz 116 – Moona (USA) 73 (Lear Fan　　**81 p**
(USA) 130) [2002 5.6m² 5m⁴ 5g* Aug 12] 7,500Y: close-coupled gelding: half-brother
to several winners, including 2000 2-y-o 5f winner Rare Old Times (by Inzar): dam 7f
winner: fairly useful form: best effort when winning maiden at Thirsk by ¾ length from
Mardoof, making all: likely to prove best at 5f/6f: capable of better still. *D. Nicholls*

RED ADDICK (IRE)　　3 gr.g. Grand Lodge (USA) 125 – Glad's Night (IRE) 54　　–
(Sexton Blake 126) [2002 p8g 8s 10m p12g⁶ 8.1d Jul 4] 4,500Y: third foal: half-brother
to winner in Italy by Welsh Term: dam, staying maiden on Flat, won Irish bumper: well
held in maidens/sellers: sometimes slowly away: visored last 2 starts. *M. R. Ewer-Hoad*

REDBACK　　3 ch.c. Mark of Esteem (IRE) 137 – Patsy Western 81 (Precocious　　**116**
126) [2002 107+: 8g³ 7m* 8m³ 8g 7m 7m² 8m² 7m Oct 19]
　　Redback wasn't the proverbial 'horse in a million' like Rock of Gibraltar,
but on a more modest scale his was a remarkable career too, it representing even
more of a departure from convention than Rock of Gibraltar's. Unusually for a
classic horse, Redback had ten races as a two-year-old, making his debut in April
and racing regularly until late-October. Although his classic campaign was slightly
less hectic, it started in March and again ended in October, by its end bringing
Redback's career to eighteen races. Redback's outing in the Two Thousand Guineas
was his thirteenth and came almost a year to the day after he had been beaten in a
maiden on the course. Despite four wins in the interim, including on his latest run
in the Lane's End Greenham Stakes, a recognised Guineas trial, Redback went off
at 25/1 at Newmarket. Under an enterprising ride from Darryll Holland, he belied
his odds, soon in front overall on the far rail and not dropping away once Rock of
Gibraltar came by. Redback held on for a clear-cut third, a neck and a length and a
quarter behind the winner and Hawk Wing. In doing so, Redback became the most
often-raced horse to reach the first three in the Guineas since Tap On Wood won it
in 1979 on his sixteenth start.
　　As a two-year-old, Redback met with two defeats over five furlongs before
winning a minor event over the trip at Windsor. He finished fourth over six furlongs
in the Coventry Stakes at Royal Ascot and in the Railway Stakes at the Curragh
before stepping up to seven furlongs to win a listed event at Newmarket and the
Solario Stakes at Sandown. His sole success as a three-year-old, in the Greenham at
Newbury, came on his second start of the season. At 5/1 in a field of ten, Redback
led three furlongs out and ran on with plenty of enthusiasm to beat Guys And Dolls
by two and a half lengths. After Newmarket, a fourth race in six weeks seemed to
take its toll on Redback, who managed only ninth in the Poule d'Essai des Poulains
at Longchamp. He was again below par when second favourite for the Jersey Stakes
at Royal Ascot, but bounced back with two efforts at Goodwood in August, both on
a par with any he put up in his career. Redback went down by half a length to Nayyir
in the Lennox Stakes over seven furlongs on the first occasion and was then beaten
even more narrowly in a blanket finish to the Celebration Mile later in the month,
trying to make all but failing by a neck to hold Tillerman's late burst. Redback's
next outing, down the field in the Challenge Stakes at Newmarket, turned out to be
his last. He was sold and retired to stand at the Tally-Ho Stud, Co Westmeath,
Ireland for €6,500, October 1st terms.
　　Redback is the best colt from the first two crops of the exceptional miler
Mark of Esteem, and he is of similar merit to his sire's best filly to date, the One
Thousand Guineas winner Ameerat. Redback and the listed winner Millennium
Dragon kept Mark of Esteem's reputation ticking over in 2002, and the likes of the

		Darshaan	Shirley Heights
Redback (ch.c. 1999)	Mark of Esteem (IRE) (b 1993)	(br 1981)	Delsy
		Homage	Ajdal
		(b 1989)	Home Love
	Patsy Western (ch 1986)	Precocious (b 1981)	Mummy's Pet
			Mrs Moss
		Western Air (ch 1967)	Sound Track
			Peggy West

unbeaten filly Crystal Star will be trying to do the same in 2003. Redback's dam, Patsy Western, a twice-raced six-furlong winner, has a useful record at stud. Her best produce apart from Redback is the smart eight-year-old Granny's Pet (by Selkirk), and she has also produced the above-average trio Western General (by Cadeaux Genereux), Abe (by Barathea) and Way Out Yonder (by Shirley Heights). Western General won at a mile, Abe was successful up to a mile in Italy and Way Out Yonder scored at a mile and three quarters. Patsy Western is a half-sister to the Queen Anne Stakes winner Mr Fluorocarbon and to the grandam of Barathea Guest, who, like Redback, was successful in the Greenham before taking third in the Guineas. The strong, close-coupled Redback, who cost 40,000 guineas as a yearling, was effective at seven furlongs and a mile. He never encountered firm ground but acted on any other, though his effort on heavy when third in the Racing Post Trophy as a two-year-old—his only outing on ground softer than good—wasn't up with his best. A tough sort, if not altogether consistent, Redback will do racing another service if he goes on to produce a few like himself. *R. Hannon*

RED BEAUFIGHTER 2 b.g. (Mar 12) Sheikh Albadou 128 – Tart And A Half 83 **65** (Distant Relative 128) [2002 p8g⁶ Dec 14] 2,800F: second foal: dam 2-y-o 5f winner who stayed 7f: 12/1, 7¼ lengths sixth of 12 to Made In Japan in maiden at Lingfield, soon niggled along. *N. P. Littmoden*

RED BLOODED (IRE) 5 b.g. River Falls 113 – Volkova 60 (Green Desert (USA) –
127) [2002 p8g p10g f16.2g Apr 20] IR 12,000Y: second foal: dam, maiden, should have
stayed beyond 1m: modest maiden: trained in Ireland at 3 yrs: off 18 months, well held in
3 starts on all-weather in Britain. *Mrs L. C. Jewell*

RED BULL (IRE) 3 ch.g. Woodborough (USA) 112 – Maz (IRE) 48 (Cyrano de Ber- **63 d**
gerac 120) [2002 72: f7g² f8.5g 6.5v 7s 8s 7g 5d Jul 10] IR 9,000F, IR 10,000Y: first
living foal: dam 7f winner: modest handicapper: well held after reappearance at Wolverhampton: not bred to stay beyond 7f: possibly temperamental. *John A. Quinn, Ireland*

RED CAFE (IRE) 6 ch.m. Perugino (USA) 84 – Test Case 90 (Busted 134) [2002 61: **38**
f12g f12g⁶ f12g⁴ f11g⁶ f16g Mar 26] leggy mare: poor nowadays: stays 1½m (raced too
freely at 2m): acts on heavy going, good to firm and fibresand: tried blinkered/visored:
sometimes slowly away/looks none too keen/hangs left: usually held up. *P. Howling*

RED CARNATION (IRE) 4 b.f. Polar Falcon (USA) 126 – Red Bouquet (Refer- **103**
ence Point 139) [2002 103: 10.4f⁴ 11.6s³ 12g⁴ 11.9d 10g⁵ 12g 10s² 12v* Nov 9] lengthy,
sparely-made filly: useful performer: mostly creditable efforts in 2002, winning listed
race at Doncaster in November by 2 lengths from Dusky Warbler: in frame in handicaps
at Royal Ascot (fourth behind Thundering Surf in Duke of Edinburgh Stakes) and
Newbury (¾-length second to Demi Beau) third and seventh starts: stays 1½m: acts on
any going: often slowly away/carries head awkwardly/wanders, but is consistent.
M. A. Jarvis

RED CARPET 4 ch.c. Pivotal 124 – Fleur Rouge 71 (Pharly (FR) 130) [2002 113: **109**
7m² 6m 7f 7m⁵ Oct 19] tall, close-coupled colt: good mover: useful performer, lightly
raced: reportedly suffered lameness after finishing fifth in 2000 Guineas at Newmarket
on final start at 3 yrs: ½-length second of 5 to Warningford in Leicestershire Stakes at
Leicester in April: off further 5 months, only creditable effort on return when fifth to
Nayyir in Challenge Stakes at Newmarket final outing: stays 1m: acts on firm and good
to soft ground: carried head awkwardly second start: often makes running. *M. L. W. Bell*

RED CHARGER (IRE) 6 ch.g. Up And At 'em 109 – Smashing Pet (Mummy's Pet –
125) [2002 56+: f5s 5.1g 5m 5s May 26] tall gelding: handicapper: little form in 2002:
tried blinkered/visored. *D. Nicholls*

RED CHIEF (IRE) 2 b.g. (Apr 23) Lahib (USA) 129 – Karayb (IRE) 93 (Last Tycoon **78**
131) [2002 7m⁵ 7m³ 8.1m* 8.3d Oct 14] IR 22,000F, IR 75,000Y: angular gelding: third
foal: half-brother to useful French 1¼m winner Ghyraan (by Cadeaux Genereux): dam 6f
(at 2 yrs)/7f winner: fair performer: won maiden at Haydock in September: well held in
nursery final start: will probably stay 1¼m: acts on good to firm ground. *M. L. W. Bell*

RED CHINA 3 ch.g. Inchinor 119 – Little Tramp (Trempolino (USA) 135) [2002 69: **68 d**
p6g p5g³ p5g* 5d 5.3m p5g p6g 5d 5f 5.1g f7g⁶ f5g f5g Dec 13] fair performer: won
maiden at Lingfield in April despite flicking tail under pressure: well held in handicaps
after: best at 5f/6f: acts on polytrack, soft and good to firm ground, below form on
fibresand: sometimes slowly away (reared and unseated leaving stall final 2-y-o start).
M. Blanshard

RED DELIRIUM 6 b.g. Robellino (USA) 127 – Made of Pearl (USA) 107 (Nureyev –
(USA) 131) [2002 –, a71: f8s⁴ f7g* f7g* f7g⁴ f7g* f8.5g² f8g⁵ f8.5g⁴ f7g⁵ f9.4s⁶ 8d f7g⁵ **a66 §**
f7g f8s f8g f7g² f8.5g f7g* f8.5g³ Dec 14] small, sturdy, close-coupled gelding: fair
performer on all-weather: won sellers at Wolverhampton (3) and Southwell in 2002:
effective at 7f to 8.5f: acts on fibresand, lightly raced on turf nowadays: tried visored,
usually blinkered nowadays: tried tongue tied earlier in career: bled from nose once at 5
yrs: inconsistent. *R. Brotherton*

RED DIAMOND 3 b.g. Mind Games 121 – Sandicroft Jewel (Grey Desire 115) [2002 –
61: f7g 6.1f 8m 8.1g f8g Dec 4] leggy, close-coupled gelding: modest maiden at 2 yrs:
well held in 2002 (left A. Berry after second start): tried blinkered. *Miss K. M. George*

REDDING 2 b.c. (Feb 9) Puissance 110 – My Girl 39 (Mon Tresor 113) [2002 5s 5g² **91**
5m* 5m* 5m⁴ 5g⁵ 5g² 5m 5m² 5m Oct 12] 1,700Y, resold 6,000Y: leggy, close-coupled
colt: second foal: dam sprint maiden: fairly useful performer: won maiden at Haydock in
April and minor event at Doncaster in May: best efforts in minor event at Ripon and
Flying Childers Stakes at Doncaster (tenth of 14) seventh/eighth starts: likely to prove
best at 5f: acts on good to firm going: sold 13,000 gns, sent to USA. *B. A. McMahon*

RED EAGLE (IRE) 3 b.f. Eagle Eyed (USA) 111 – Dawn's Folly (IRE) 47 (Bluebird **62**
(USA) 125) [2002 61: p5g⁵ p5g f5g⁵ f5g Jan 29] modest performer: won handicap at
Wolverhampton in January: will prove best at 5f: acts on good to soft ground and all-
weather. *A. Berry*

RED FLYER (IRE)   3 br.g. Catrail (USA) 123 – Marostica (ITY) (Stone 124) [2002   **55**
67: p8g³ f8g³ p7g 6f 6f 9.2v³ 7.9s f12g Nov 22] close-coupled gelding: modest maiden:
stays 9f: acts on all-weather and any turf going: often slowly away: sometimes carries
head high: won over hurdles in November. *P. C. Haslam*

RED FOREST (IRE)   3 b.c. Charnwood Forest (IRE) 125 – High Atlas 65 (Shirley   **63**
Heights 130) [2002 80: p10g⁵ 9g 8.5d 8g* 7g f6g Sep 21] medium-sized colt: fair   **a76**
performer on all-weather, modest on turf: won seller at Leicester (left B. Hills 8,500 gns)
in July: well below form after: stays easy 1¼m: acts on soft ground and all-weather:
tongue tied (ran poorly) second/third starts. *W. Clay*

RED FRED   2 ch.g. (May 3) Case Law 113 – Mississipi Maid 47 (All Systems Go 119)   **51**
[2002 5s⁵ f5g⁴ f5g² p5g² 5f⁵ 5m⁶ f5s⁶ f7g 5.1g⁶ 6m Sep 4] well-grown gelding: third foal: **a54**
half-brother to a winner up to 7.5f in Italy by Interrex: dam third at 6f at 2 yrs: modest
performer: won seller at Wolverhampton in March: probably stays 6f: acts on all-weather
and firm going: visored 5 of last 7 starts. *P. D. Evans*

RED FURY (USA)   5 ch.g. Rahy (USA) 115 – Hatoof (USA) 124 (Irish River (FR)   **–**
131) [2002 f12s Jan 22] 3,000 3-y-o: second foal: half-brother to 6-y-o Prospects of
Glory: dam, French 1m (won 1000 Guineas) to 1½m (second in Breeders' Cup Turf)
performer: well beaten in maiden at Southwell: dead. *Ian Williams*

RED GALAXY (IRE)   2 b.f. (Mar 14) Tagula (IRE) 116 – Dancing Season (Warrshan   **91**
(USA) 117) [2002 5m* 5m* 5m Jun 19] IR 5,500Y: lengthy, well-made filly: third foal:
dam unraced half-sister to smart but temperamental 1½m winner Out of Shot: won
maiden at Musselburgh (hung right much of way) and minor event at Ripon, both in
April: fairly useful form when seventh of 19 to Romantic Liason in Queen Mary Stakes
at Royal Ascot: will stay 6f: joined D. Arbuthnot. *A. Berry*

RED HALO   3 b.c. Be My Guest (USA) 126 – Pray (IRE) (Priolo (USA) 127) [2002   **71**
75p: 8.5g⁴ 12g⁵ 11.9d⁴ 13.3s⁶ 14d 14.1d³ p16g⁵ Sep 4] fair maiden: probably stays easy
2m: acts on soft ground, good to firm and polytrack: tends to race freely: has found little:
won 3 juvenile hurdles in August. *M. C. Pipe*

RED HOT POLKA (IRE)   2 b.c. (Mar 25) Marju (IRE) 127 – Mochara (Last Fan-   **68**
dango 125) [2002 8.3d 6m⁶ 6f⁴ 8.3m p8g Nov 19] 18,000 2-y-o: half-brother to 3 winners,
notably smart 5f to 1m winner Cool Edge (by Nashamaa): dam second at 5f at 2 yrs in
Ireland: fair maiden: barely stays 1m: acts on polytrack, firm and good to soft ground.
P. Mitchell

REDISCOVERY   3 b.g. Octagonal (NZ) 126 – Life Watch (USA) (Highland Park   **–**
(USA)) [2002 11.7f⁶ Aug 18] 620,000 francs Y: fourth foal: half-brother to fairly useful
Irish 13f winner Life Match (by Polish Precedent): dam twice-raced sister to Poule
d'Essai des Pouliches second Duckling Park: 7/1, sixth of 8 in maiden at Bath: sold
22,000 gns. *J. H. M. Gosden*

RED LIASON (IRE)   3 ch.f. Selkirk (USA) 129 – Red Affair (IRE) 95 (Generous   **103**
(IRE) 139) [2002 95p: 8g² 8s³ 7s* 8m 6.5g² 6d² 6g Oct 18] big filly: useful performer:
won 5-runner listed event at Epsom in June by 2½ lengths from Terfel: also ran well when
3¾ lengths third to Portella in Henkel-Rennen at Dusseldorf (had stamina stretched) in
May and second in Grosser Preis von Berlin at Hoppegarten (beaten short head by
Toylsome) in July: likely to prove best at 6f/7f: acts on soft and good to firm going:
free-going type, and seems suited by forcing tactics. *J. L. Dunlop*

RED LIGHT LADY   3 br.f. Timeless Times (USA) 99 – Sparkling Roberta 55 (Kind   **–**
of Hush 118) [2002 6m⁶ 6g⁴ 8.1d 10g Aug 26] sparely-made filly: third foal: dam 1m
winner who stayed 1¾m: well held all starts. *G. A. Harker*

RED LION   6 ch.g. Lion Cavern (USA) 117 – Fleur Rouge 71 (Pharly (FR) 130) [2002   **72 d**
69: 5s 6m² 6m 6f 7m⁶ 7f³ 7g 7.5g 7f 6d⁴ 7f⁴ 7m 6m 7.5m 9m 8.9m Sep 13] useful-looking
gelding: fair performer: below form last 5 starts, reportedly broke blood vessel final one:
stays 7f: probably acts on any going: tried blinkered: usually held up. *S. Gollings*

RED LION (FR)   5 ch.g. Lion Cavern (USA) 117 – Mahogany River (Irish River (FR)   **74**
131) [2002 73: f16.2g 12d³ 12d² 11.8g² 12m* 12.3m⁶ 12m 12g Sep 27] big, rather angular
gelding: fair handicapper: won amateur event at Epsom in August: below form after:
effective at 1½m to 2m: acts on good to firm and good to soft going: sometimes slowly
away. *B. J. Meehan*

RED MAGIC (FR)   4 b. or br.c. Grand Lodge (USA) 125 – Ma Priere (FR) (Highest   **–**
Honor (FR) 124) [2002 ?: 8m 10.1m⁶ Aug 16] big, strong, close-coupled colt: useful form

at 2 yrs: third in claimer at Aqueduct for C. Clement in 2001: well held in Britain both starts in 2002, in visor final outing: probably stays 8.5f. *M. C. Pipe*

RED MILLENNIUM (IRE)   4 b.f. Tagula (IRE) 116 – Lovely Me (IRE) 70 (Vision   **101** (USA)) [2002 102: 5.2g³ 5.1g⁵ 5g 5m⁴ 5d 5.5m⁵ 5g 5g Sep 10] quite attractive, good-quartered filly: good third in handicap at Newbury on reappearance: below best after, leaving A. Berry after fifth start: raced only around 5f: acts on firm and soft going: races prominently. *D. W. P. Arbuthnot*

RED MITTENS   5 ch.m. Wolfhound (USA) 126 – Red Gloves 83 (Red God 128§)   **32** [2002 –: f7g³ f12g f18g⁵ 7f 8m 8m Jul 26] small, sparely-made mare: poor maiden. *R. E. Barr*

RED MOOR (IRE)   2 gr.g. (Apr 25) Eagle Eyed (USA) 111 – Faakirah (Dragonara   **–** Palace (USA) 115) [2002 5.1m 6m Aug 17] IR 6,000F, IR 6,000Y: leggy gelding: closely related to fairly useful Irish 1996 2-y-o 5f winner Klinsman (by Danehill), later successful in USA, and half-brother to several winners, including 11.5f winner Henrietta Holmes (by Persian Bold): dam ran twice: burly and green, well held in maidens: gelded after final start. *R. Hollinshead*

RED OPAL (IRE)   3 b.f. Flying Spur (AUS) – Tamaya (IRE) (Darshaan 133) [2002   **83** 81: 6m* 6m³ 7d² 5d⁵ 7m 6m⁴ 6g⁶ 5f 6f* 6.1s p7g Nov 14] rather leggy, good-topped filly: fairly useful performer: won maiden at Folkestone in April and minor event at York in October: stays 7f: acts on firm and good to soft going: often races prominently: sold 11,000 gns. *R. Hannon*

REDOUBLE   6 b.g. First Trump 118 – Sunflower Seed 70 (Mummy's Pet 125) [2002   **49 +** 65, a–: 10m 10m Aug 28] good-topped gelding: fair handicapper at 5 yrs: only poor form in 2002: stays 1¾m: yet to race on heavy going, acts on any other turf. *E. L. James*

REDOUBTABLE (USA)   11 b.h. Grey Dawn II 132 – Seattle Rockette (USA) (Seattle   **66 §** Slew (USA)) [2002 66§, a78§: f6s f8.5g f7g f6g 6m 7g f7g 6.1m³ 7.1d* 7.5d 6m² 6g⁵ 6g   **a– §** f6g Sep 30] small, sturdy horse: fair handicapper: won at Musselburgh in July: effective at 6f/easy 1m: acts on any turf going/all-weather: occasionally blinkered: sometimes slowly away: unreliable. *D. W. Chapman*

RED PASSION (USA)   2 b.f. (Apr 27) Seeking The Gold (USA) – Lovers Knot 117   **– p** (Groom Dancer (USA) 128) [2002 7s Oct 22] first foal: dam 7f/1m (including Falmouth Stakes) winner: weak 8/1-shot and very green, tailed off in minor event at Yarmouth: should do better. *Sir Michael Stoute*

RED RACKHAM (IRE)   2 b.c. (Feb 8) Groom Dancer (USA) 128 – Manarah 76   **62 p** (Marju (IRE) 127) [2002 p10g Dec 3] IR 45,000Y: second foal: dam, Irish 1½m winner, half-sister to smart Irish 1¼m winner Muakaad: 14½ lengths eighth to Shield in maiden at Lingfield, very slowly away and green: will stay at least 1½m: should do better. *J. Nicol*

RED RAMONA   7 b.g. Rudimentary (USA) 118 – Apply 87 (Kings Lake (USA) 133)   **– §** [2002 86§: p12g Jan 30] lengthy gelding: formerly useful handicapper: has become most ungenuine (refused to race only outing in 2002): tried blinkered. *J. Akehurst*

RED RIOJA (IRE)   3 b.f. King's Theatre (IRE) 128 – Foreign Relation (IRE) 57   **107** (Distant Relative 128) [2002 98: 8s 12s⁵ 12m³ 12d⁵ 9.9m 10g⁵ 10.1m⁵ Sep 17] smallish, quite attractive filly: useful performer: fifth to Kazzia in Oaks at Epsom prior to best effort when 1¼ lengths third to Irresistible Jewel in Ribblesdale Stakes at Royal Ascot: left E. O'Neill prior to running respectably in Prix de la Nonette at Deauville and listed event at Yarmouth (behind Miss Corniche) last 2 starts: stays 1½m: acts on soft and good to firm going. *P. W. D'Arcy*

RED RIVER REBEL   4 b.g. Inchinor 119 – Bidweaya (USA) 45 (Lear Fan (USA)   **80** 130) [2002 74: 11.9g 12f⁴ 14.1d 12m³ 12.3g² 12.1g² 12.1m* 12.3m³ 14.1f⁴ 13.9f⁶ Oct 12] tall, leggy gelding: fairly useful handicapper: won at Beverley in August: barely stays 1¾m: acts on good to firm and good to soft going (no show only start on fibresand). *J. R. Norton*

RED ROONEY   3 b.g. Astronef 116 – Mica Male (ITY) (Law Society (USA) 130)   **–** [2002 55d: 7.1v 10m Jun 25] strong gelding: no form since 2-y-o debut: tongue tied on reappearance. *P. Butler*

RED ROSIE (USA)   4 b.f. Red Ransom (USA) – Do's Gent (CAN) (Vice Regent   **83** (CAN)) [2002 81: 10g 10m p10g⁶ 9m Jun 26] workmanlike filly: fairly useful performer: stays 1¼m: acts on good to firm ground and polytrack: sometimes makes running: sold 5,500 gns in December. *Mrs A. J. Perrett*

Tote Scoop6 November Stakes (Handicap), Doncaster—the last big race of the turf season and Red Wine (nearside) and Bollin Nellie fight out a rousing finish in the heavy ground.

RED SATIN (IRE)   3 b.c. Mujadil (USA) 119 – Satinette 109 (Shirley Heights 130)   **48**
[2002 –: 11.8m² 11.9d⁴ 12d 14.1s 12m Aug 28] strong, lengthy colt: poor maiden handicapper: stays 1½m: acts on good to firm going: reportedly had breathing problem third
start, tongue tied after. *J. A. Glover*

RED SCORPION (USA)   3 ch.g. Nureyev (USA) 131 – Pricket (USA) 111 (Diesis   **63**
133) [2002 60: f7.9d 8g⁵ Jul 11] 4,500 2-y-o: stocky gelding: first foal: dam, 1m (at 2 yrs)/
1¼m winner and second in Oaks, sister to Diminuendo: modest form in maidens at York
and Doncaster (still green). *W. M. Brisbourne*

REDSPIN (IRE)   2 ch.c. (Feb 19) Spectrum (IRE) 126 – Trendy Indian (IRE) 71   **82**
(Indian Ridge 123) [2002 7f p7g³ 8g* 10s Nov 2] IR 44,000F, 37,000Y: leggy colt: first
foal: dam ran once: fairly useful form: won maiden at Brighton in October by ½ length
from Golden Heart: stays 1m: acts on polytrack, soundly beaten (in listed race) on soft.
J. W. Hills

RED STORM   3 ch.f. Dancing Spree (USA) – Dam Certain (IRE) 61 (Damister (USA)   **57**
123) [2002 60: 7s 8g 10g 12s f9.4f⁶ f9.4g* p10g Dec 18] modest performer: left
M. Brassil, Ireland, after fourth start: best effort at 3 yrs when winning maiden at
Wolverhampton in December: stays 1¼m: acts on fibresand and probably any turf
going: blinkered (well held) once. *J. R. Boyle*

RED SUN   5 b.g. Foxhound (USA) 103 – Superetta 65 (Superlative 118) [2002 –, a60:   **–**
f14s³ Sep 17] modest handicapper: should stay 2m: acts on fibresand. *A. Streeter*   **a53**

REDSWAN   7 ch.g. Risk Me (FR) 127 – Bocas Rose 106 (Jalmood (USA) 126) [2002   **70 §**
72§: 8.3s³ p7g³ f7g p7g Dec 18] big, workmanlike gelding: fair performer: best at 7f/1m:
acts on firm going, soft and all-weather: sometimes blinkered/tongue tied (not since
2000): held up: often races freely/finds little: bled from nose several occasions in 2001:
unreliable. *A. W. Carroll*

RED TO VIOLET   3 b.f. Spectrum (IRE) 126 – Khalsheva 55 (Shirley Heights 130)   **85**
[2002 77p: 10d 8m 8.2d³ 7g 8.3s² 8m⁶ 8g 8g Sep 7] fairly useful performer: won minor
event at Nottingham in July and handicap at Doncaster in August: should prove as effective at 7f as 1m: acts on soft and good to firm going: pulled
too hard in blinkers second outing, visored sixth to ninth starts. *J. A. Glover*

RED VELVET   4 ch.f. So Factual (USA) 120 – Amber Fizz (USA) (Effervescing   **–**
(USA)) [2002 –: 6m May 6] strong filly: well held in maiden at Newbury and claimer at
Doncaster over a year apart. *D. K. Ivory*

RED VINTAGE 3 ch.c. Most Welcome 131 – Ninety-Five 70 (Superpower 113) **?**
[2002 p8g p8g³ 8f⁵ 8f⁵ a6.5f* 8.5f⁶ a6f* a6f* a7f² a6.5f* Dec 29] 7,000Y: second foal:
dam 5f winner: left W. O'Gorman after second outing: won maiden at Hollywood
in July and (after being claimed out of Kathy Walsh's stable $62,500 after sixth start)
claimers at Del Mar in August and Santa Anita in October/December: claimed again for
$62,500 after final success: best at 6f/7f: acts on dirt: blinkered last 7 outings.
M. Machowsky, USA

RED WINE 3 b.g. Hamas (IRE) 125§ – Red Bouquet (Reference Point 139) [2002 **101**
7p5f: f8s* p10g⁴ 8.1d 8.1f² 8g 7d f8.5g* 10m 10.2g⁴ 11f³ f12g² 11.7g* 10.3s* 12v* Nov
9] workmanlike gelding: useful performer: improved during 2002, winning maiden at
Southwell and handicaps at Wolverhampton, Bath and Doncaster (twice, beat Bollin
Nellie by head in Tote Scoop6 November Stakes second occasion, pair 9 lengths clear):
effective at 1¼m/1½m: acts on any turf going/all-weather: blinkered (well beaten) sixth
start: tough and reliable. *J. A. Osborne*

RED WIZARD 2 b.g. (Apr 25) Wizard King 122 – Drudwen (Sayf El Arab (USA) **81**
127) [2002 6m⁴ 6f* 7.1f⁵ 7.5g³ 6m² p6g 6g Oct 18] 4,000Y, 18,000 2-y-o: quite good-
topped gelding: eighth foal: half-brother to 3-y-o Concer Eto and useful 7f/1m winner
Concer Un (by Lord Bud): dam won 13f bumper: fairly useful performer: won minor
event at Yarmouth in June: best effort after when second in nursery at Newmarket: likely
to prove best at 6f/7f: acts on firm going: usually races prominently. *W. A. O'Gorman*

RED WOOD 4 b.g. Kris 135 – Pearl Venture 92 (Salse (USA) 128) [2002 –: f9.4g May **–**
20] well held in maidens/seller/claimer: dead. *A. W. Carroll*

REDWOOD STAR 2 b.f. (Apr 14) Piccolo 121 – Thewaari (USA) 68 (Eskimo **64**
(USA)) [2002 p5g² p6g Dec 28] 2,000F, 6,800Y: sixth living foal: half-sister to 5-y-o
Mister Clinton and 1¼m winner Moonshift (by Cadeaux Genereux): dam 7f winner:
modest form in maidens at Lingfield: beaten 3½ lengths by Isengard on debut: will
probably stay 7f. *P. L. Gilligan*

REEDS RAINS 4 b.f. Mind Games 121 – Me Spede (Valiyar 129) [2002 –: 5g 5m 5s **–**
Jun 26] lightly-made filly: fair 5f winner at 2 yrs: little form since: tried blinkered/
visored. *D. A. Nolan*

REEFS SIS 3 ch.f. Muhtarram (USA) 125 – Horseshoe Reef 88 (Mill Reef (USA) **103**
141) [2002 91: 8f⁵ 6.1f 7m 8.1d⁶ 8m³ 7d* 8.5f⁶ Sep 14] small, sparely-made filly: useful
handicapper: sweating and unimpressive in appearance, won at Newmarket in July by
neck from Aldora, having had to wait for gap: also creditable third to Tashawak in listed
rated stakes at Royal Ascot previous start: left E. Alston before final outing (below form):
effective at 6f to 1m: acts on good to firm and good to soft going: usually held up.
Kathy Walsh, USA

REEL BUDDY (USA) 4 ch.c. Mr Greeley (USA) 122 – Rosebud 80 (Indian Ridge **116**
123) [2002 113: 6g* 6m* 7.1d* 6f⁶ 6d 8g³ 7f* 8m³ 7m Oct 19] big, strong, close-coupled
colt: smart performer: better than ever in 2002, winning minor event at Kempton and
listed race at Newmarket (both narrowly from Continent) in April, listed race at Haydock
in May and Stan James Hungerford Stakes at Newbury (beat Umistim by short head) in
August: also good third in Sussex Stakes (beaten 4 legths by Rock of Gibraltar, pulling

*Stan James Hungerford Stakes, Newbury—fourth success of the season for Reel Buddy,
who just holds the renewed challenge of stable-companion Umistim (rail);
Gateman (left) takes third ahead of Ghannam (striped cap)*

Speedlith Group's "Reel Buddy"

hard) and Celebration Mile (beaten narrowly behind Tillerman) at Goodwood: effective at 6f to easy 1m: acts on good to firm and good to soft ground: usually held up for turn of foot (rather headstrong): genuine. *R. Hannon*

REFA'AH (IRE) 3 b.f. Lahib (USA) 129 – Shurooq (USA) 94 (Affirmed (USA)) — [2002 79: 7f⁵ Jul 17] rather unfurnished filly: fair form on second of 2 runs in maidens at 2 yrs: disappointing in weak event at Catterick on firm going only run in 2002, carrying head awkwardly (reportedly lost a shoe): should stay 1m. *E. A. L. Dunlop*

REFERENDUM (IRE) 8 b.g. Common Grounds 118 – Final Decision (Tap On   **60 d** Wood 130) [2002 74d: f6s⁶ f5s⁴ f7s f6s⁴ f6g² p6g 7d 6f 5m⁴ 5m Aug 16] good-topped gelding: has a fluent, round action: modest form at best in 2002: generally on downgrade: best at 5f/6f: acts on firm going, good to soft and fibresand: tried blinkered/visored: sometimes on toes/slowly away: has won for amateur. *D. Nicholls*

REFLEX BLUE 5 b.g. Ezzoud (IRE) 126 – Briggsmaid 70 (Elegant Air 119) [2002   **48** 76: p12g 14.1d 16m 14.1m 14m 16f⁵ Sep 8] lengthy, angular gelding: fair handicapper at 4 yrs: poor in 2002: probably stays 2m: acts on firm and good to soft going, well held twice on polytrack: sometimes blinkered/visored: none too reliable. *R. J. Price*

REFRACT 4 b.g. Spectrum (IRE) 126 – Sofala 103 (Home Guard (USA) 129) [2002   — –: f8s⁶ f7g Feb 12] angular gelding: fair form only run in 2002: well held in 2002. *D. E. Cantillon*

REFUSE TO BEND (IRE)   2 b.c. (Mar 17) Sadler's Wells (USA) 132 – Market **110 p**
Slide (USA) 94 (Gulch (USA)) [2002 7g* 7m* Sep 15]

The form of Ireland's most valuable two-year-old race, the Aga Khan Studs National Stakes, tends to vary from year to year. The latest winner Refuse To Bend, who lived up to his name when holding off Van Nistelrooy and Dublin, put up a performance that was just a little better than average for recent renewals. More significantly, however, Refuse To Bend looks very much the type to improve again at three and it would come as no surprise to see him follow in the footsteps of three of the last six National Stakes winners—Desert King, King of Kings and Sinndar—by adding a classic victory to his record.

Recently deposed ante-post Two Thousand Guineas favourite Van Nistelrooy, the world's most expensive yearling sold at auction in 2001, started a short-priced favourite at the Curragh in September for 'Team Ballydoyle', with Dublin, from the Godolphin 'nursery' of David Loder, second favourite. Van Nistelrooy and Dublin, both unbeaten in their first three starts, were already pattern winners, while 7/1-shot Refuse To Bend had won a Gowran maiden in good style on his only start, in mid-August. The early pace in the National Stakes, which was run on good to firm going, wasn't strong and connections of both Van Nistelrooy and Dublin felt afterwards that their colts had been disadvantaged by the way the race was run. But Refuse To Bend, who went a bit freely early on and gradually took closer order to lead over a furlong out, deserved plenty of credit for his own display, keeping on well under pressure as the second and third stayed on strongly, challenging on either flank. At the line, Refuse To Bend had three quarters of a length to spare over Van Nistelrooy with Dublin a neck away third and Hanabad a short head away fourth, a position he also filled on his next start, in the Grand Criterium at Longchamp. Van Nistelrooy suffered two further defeats before the end of the season, when third in the Royal Lodge and fifth in the Breeders' Cup Juvenile, while Dublin ran as if something amiss when last in the Dewhurst on his only subsequent outing. Refuse To Bend was put away straight after the National Stakes.

Aga Khan Studs National Stakes, the Curragh—Refuse To Bend ends Ballydoyle's sequence of wins in the race as he runs on gamely to get the better of Van Nistelrooy (No.10); Dublin (far side) and Hanabad finish third and fourth

Refuse To Bend (IRE) (b.c. Mar 17, 2000)	Sadler's Wells (USA) (b 1981)	Northern Dancer (b 1961)	Nearctic
			Natalma
		Fairy Bridge (b 1975)	Bold Reason
			Special
	Market Slide (USA) (ch 1991)	Gulch (b 1984)	Mr Prospector
			Jameela
		Grenzen (ch 1975)	Grenfall
			My Poly

Refuse To Bend was one of three two-year-old Group 1 winners for his sire Sadler's Wells in the latest season; the two others Brian Boru (Racing Post Trophy) and Alberto Giacometti (Criterium de Saint-Cloud) were both sent out by Bally-doyle. The offspring of Sadler's Wells usually improve from two to three, while Refuse To Bend's dam Market Slide and his grandam Grenzen both trained on well. Market Slide won a maiden from four starts in Ireland as a two-year-old and developed into a fairly useful sprinter there as a three-year-old (winning the valuable Scurry Handicap over six and a half furlongs); she was then returned to North America where she continued to do well over sprint distances, finishing third in the Grade 3 First Lady Handicap over six furlongs at Gulfstream Park as a five-year-old. Refuse To Bend's modestly-bred grandam Grenzen was ranked among the best of her sex at up to nine furlongs as a three- and four-year-old in North America, training on well after being placed in graded company at two. Grenzen won three times at Grade 2 level, in the Santa Maria Handicap, the Santa Monica Handicap and the Santa Susana Stakes, and was also runner-up in the Grade 1

Kentucky Oaks. Grenzen was acquired for the Moyglare Stud after her racing career and has done extremely well, the pick of her nine winners being Twilight Agenda, a useful winner in Ireland as a three-year-old who improved out of all recognition on dirt in North America, winning numerous graded races at up to a mile and a quarter, including the Grade 1 Meadowlands Cup Handicap, and finishing runner-up in both the Santa Anita Handicap and the Breeders' Cup Classic. Grenzen's winners also included the Alleged filly Irish Edition, who went on to become the dam of Belmont Stakes winner Go And Go and was represented in the latest season by the Derrinstown Stud Derby Trial runner-up In Time's Eye. The dam of Refuse To Bend, Market Slide, is by Nayef's sire Gulch, who has been represented by a number of winners who have stayed further than might have been expected, given that he won the Breeders' Cup Sprint. Market Slide began her career as a broodmare with a visit to Theatrical, producing a stayer in Media Puzzle, who finished fourth in the St Leger and won the two-mile Melbourne Cup for Refuse To Bend's stable in the latest season as a five-year-old. Market Slide's second foal Ripple of Pride, a year-older sister to Refuse To Bend, won a maiden at Limerick over a mile and a half in the latest season, also for Weld. Refuse To Bend will probably stay a mile and a half as a three-year-old, though, judged on his National Stakes victory under conditions which placed the emphasis on speed, he is not likely to be crying out for middle distances, at least in the first part of the next season. He is generally quoted at odds of 12/1 for the Two Thousand Guineas and 25/1 for the Derby at the time of writing. *D. K. Weld, Ireland*

REGAL AGENDA (IRE) 2 b.c. (Feb 24) Ali-Royal (IRE) 127 – Hidden Agenda (FR) 55 (Machiavellian (USA) 123) [2002 8g² 8g² Oct 18] quite good-topped colt: second foal: dam, maiden who stayed 11f, out of smart 7f/1m winner Ever Genial: fairly useful form when runner-up in maidens at Salisbury (short-headed) and Newmarket (beaten ½ length by Persian Majesty): will probably stay 1¼m: mulish at stall at Newmarket. *H. R. A. Cecil*   **93**

REGAL AIR (IRE) 4 b.f. Distinctly North (USA) 115 – Dignified Air (FR) 70 (Wolver Hollow 126) [2002 60§, a–§: 5m 6g 8f 5s Oct 16] neat filly: poor maiden: left L. James after third start: best at 5f/6f: acts on soft going, good to firm and fibresand: sometimes blinkered/visored/tongue tied: unreliable. *Francis Ennis, Ireland*   **45 §** **a– §**

REGAL ALI (IRE) 3 ch.g. Ali-Royal (IRE) 127 – Depeche (FR) (Kings Lake (USA) 133) [2002 –: 8m³ 10m⁶ 12m⁵ 14.1m 13.8f⁴ 12f f14.8g Dec 14] smallish, close-coupled gelding: poor maiden handicapper: barely stays 1¾m: acts on firm going, well beaten (raced freely) only all-weather outing: tried blinkered at 2 yrs. *John Berry*   **46**

REGAL APPLAUSE 3 b.f. Royal Applause 124 – Panchellita (USA) 78 (Pancho Villa (USA)) [2002 –: 10m Jul 22] leggy, rather unfurnished filly: well held in maidens/handicap. *G. L. Moore*   **–**

REGAL GALLERY (IRE) 4 b.f. Royal Academy (USA) 130 – Polistatic 53 (Free State 125) [2002 –: p10g⁴ p10g* p10g p10g⁵ 12g 9m p10g⁴ p10g Aug 21] lengthy filly: modest performer: won maiden at Lingfield in February: should stay 1½m: acts on polytrack, raced only on good/good to firm going on turf: tongue tied penultimate start: ran as though something amiss third outing. *C. A. Horgan*   **55** **a63**

REGAL MELODY 4 b.f. Mistertopogigo (IRE) 118 – Edensong (Lochnager 132) [2002 6m 6f 6g⁶ 7f 5m Oct 2] good-topped filly: second foal: dam unraced: no form in maidens/handicaps. *M. Todhunter*   **–**

REGAL SONG (IRE) 6 b.g. Anita's Prince 126 – Song Beam 84 (Song 132) [2002 93§, a–§: f5g 5s 5g 6g 5s* 5.9v 6s 6v⁵ 5d 5g 5v Nov 8] useful-looking gelding: fairly useful handicapper: won at Hamilton in July (raced alone on far rail much of way): little form otherwise in 2002: best at 5f/6f: acts on fibresand, probably on good to firm going but revels on soft/heavy: usually blinkered: often races prominently: hung right sixth start: weak finisher: inconsistent. *T. J. Etherington*   **89 §** **a– §**

REGAL VINTAGE (USA) 2 ch.c. (Feb 7) Kingmambo (USA) 125 – Grapevine (IRE) 88 (Sadler's Wells (USA) 132) [2002 7d Nov 2] $700,000Y, resold IR 420,000Y: strong colt: first foal: dam, 9.5f and 11f winner in USA, half-sister to smart performer up to 1½m Theatre Script out of half-sister to high-class sprinter Committed: 20/1, well beaten in maiden at Newmarket: type to do better. *B. J. Meehan*   **– p**

REGENCY RED (IRE) 4 ch.g. Dolphin Street (FR) 125 – Future Romance (Distant **55** Relative 128) [2002 37: f8g 11.9f⁴ 11.9g⁴ 10f⁶ 14.1g 11.9m² 12.6m³ 14.1m² 15.8m* 15.8f **a–** 18d Oct 21] modest performer: left M. Usher prior to winning seller at Catterick in August: seems suited by 2m: acts on firm going: sometimes carries head awkwardly/finds little (seemed to throw away winning chance eighth outing). *R. Ford*

REGENT'S SECRET (USA) 2 br.c. (Mar 16) Cryptoclearance (USA) – Misty **84** Regent (CAN) (Vice Regent (CAN)) [2002 5s² p5g² 6d⁶ 6d³ 7g² 7m² 6d² Nov 1] $27,000F, 35,000Y: leggy, useful-looking colt: first foal: dam, winning sprinter in USA, second in minor stakes: fairly useful maiden: runner-up 5 times: effective at 6f/7f: acts on polytrack, good to firm and soft going. *R. Hannon*

REGIMENTAL DANCE 2 b.f. (Mar 14) Groom Dancer (USA) 128 – Enlisted (IRE) **63** 83 (Sadler's Wells (USA) 132) [2002 7g 7d* 7f² 7f Oct 8] second foal: dam 1¼m winner: modest performer: won seller at Thirsk (sold from Sir Mark Prescott 6,500 gns) in August: good second in nursery at Catterick: should be suited by 1¼m/1½m: acts on firm and good to soft ground. *D. Nicholls*

REINE CLEOPATRE (IRE) 2 b.f. (Feb 27) Danehill (USA) 126 – Nomothetis (IRE) **–** (Law Society (USA) 130) [2002 7.5v Nov 21] approx. 78,000Y in Italy: first foal: dam once-raced half-sister to very smart 1½m performer Posidonas: ninth of 10 in maiden at Milan. *L. M. Cumani*

REINE INDIENNE (IRE) 3 b.f. College Chapel 122 – Mystic Maid (IRE) 62 (Muj- **49** tahid (USA) 118) [2002 60: f5g p7g f7g⁵ f7g⁴ f6g⁴ 7m f6g May 2] small filly: poor maiden: stays 7f: acts on fibresand: visored last 5 starts: sometimes slowly away/races very freely: looked none too keen third outing. *M. J. Gingell*

REJUVENATE (IRE) 2 ch.c. (Jan 26) Grand Lodge (USA) 125 – Nawara 75 (Welsh **74 p** Pageant 132) [2002 p8g⁴ Nov 14] IR 50,000Y: half-brother to several winners, including very smart 6f (at 2 yrs) to 1m winner Alhijaz (by Midyan) and useful 7f (at 2 yrs) and 9f winner Wijara (by Waajib): dam 1¼m winner: 2 lengths fourth to Joe Bear in maiden at Lingfield, slowly away and running on: will improve. *Mrs A. J. Perrett*

RELATIVE DELIGHT 4 b.f. Distant Relative 128 – Pasja (IRE) (Posen (USA)) **–** [2002 –: 11g 14.1d 13.8g⁵ 16f Jun 11] angular filly: modest maiden at 2 yrs: little form since. *John A. Harris*

RELATIVE HERO (IRE) 2 ch.g. (Mar 27) Entrepreneur 123 – Aunty (FR) 114 **–** (Riverman (USA) 131) [2002 6m May 18] 10,000Y: smallish gelding: closely related to 2 winners by Sadler's Wells, including useful Irish 1988 2-y-o 5f/6f winner Kyra, and half-brother to 3 winners, including useful 5f (at 2 yrs) and 6f winner Dame Laura (by Royal Academy): dam, French 1¼m winner, half-sister to Ebor winner Crazy: 20/1, well held in maiden at Newbury. *H. Morrison*

RELLIM 3 b.f. Rudimentary (USA) 118 – Tycoon Girl (IRE) 74 (Last Tycoon 131) **–** [2002 70: p5g³ f5s² f5g⁴ f6g⁴ f5g* f5g⁴ f5g² 6m⁵ 5.1m 5m 5d f5g⁶ f5f⁵ f5g⁵ f5g p5g **a74** Dec 21] tall, angular filly: fair performer: left B. Meehan after third start: won maiden at Southwell in February: headstrong, and best at 5f: acts on all-weather, little form on turf in 2002: effective blinkered or not: reportedly bled from nose final start: usually makes running. *R. Wilman*

REMAINS OF THE DAY 3 ch.g. Prince Sabo 123 – Pussy Foot 83 (Red Sunset **55** 120) [2002 51: 5g³ 5v 5.9g³ 5.9v 6m⁴ f5s⁵ 5g 5g² 6f⁴ 7d f7g⁵ Oct 22] strong gelding: modest maiden: effective at 5f/6f: acts on fibresand, best turf form on good ground: effective blinkered or not, visored (below form) final start: sometimes looks none too keen: sold 6,800 gns, sent to Kuwait. *T. D. Barron*

REMEDY 3 gr.f. Pivotal 124 – Doctor Bid (USA) (Spectacular Bid (USA)) [2002 68: **72** f12g f8g⁶ f8.5s⁵ f8.5g* Dec 26] tall, rather unfurnished filly: fair performer: won handi-cap at Wolverhampton in December: should stay beyond 8.5f: acts on soft ground and fibresand: effective blinkered or not: has been slowly away: difficult ride, and possibly none too genuine. *Sir Mark Prescott*

REMEMBER STAR 9 ch.m. Don't Forget Me 127 – Star Girl Gay (Lord Gayle **–** (USA) 124) [2002 36: 12d Jun 11] of little account nowadays. *A. D. Smith*

REMEMBRANCE 2 b.c. (Feb 29) Sabrehill (USA) 120 – Perfect Poppy 73 (Shareef **70** Dancer (USA) 135) [2002 7g 7m⁴ 7.9m⁶ Sep 4] good-topped colt: first foal: dam 1½m winner: fair form in maidens: fourth at Salisbury: should stay 1¼m. *J. M. P. Eustace*

REMINISCENT (IRE) 3 b.g. Kahyasi 130 – Eliza Orzeszkowa (IRE) 69 (Polish **75** Patriot (USA) 128) [2002 72: 10m⁵ 12m 8.5g p10g⁶ 10.2g f14s³ f14s² 11.9m⁶ f12g² f12f² f16g² p16g³ f14.8s* f14.8g⁴ Dec 16] rather leggy gelding: fair handicapper: won at Wolverhampton in December: stays 2m: acts on all-weather, raced only on good going or firmer on turf: blinkered/visored after fourth start: consistent. *R. F. Johnson Houghton*

RENAISSANCE LADY (IRE)   6 ch.m. Imp Society (USA) – Easter Morning (FR)   **53**
(Nice Havrais (USA) 124) [2002 65: 14.1m⁶ 14.1d⁵ May 18] small, sparely-made mare: modest handicapper: probably in need of both runs in 2002: effective at 1¾m to 21f: best on good ground or firmer: has been early to post/fitted with net muzzle: best form forcing pace: has won 4 times at Warwick. *D. W. P. Arbuthnot*

RENATA'S PRINCE (IRE)   9 b.g. Prince Rupert (FR) 121 – Maria Renata (Jaazeiro   –
(USA) 127) [2002 45, a39: f11s Jan 10] probably of little account nowadays. *M. D. I. Usher*

RENDITA (IRE)   6 b.m. Waajib 121 – Rend Rover (FR) (Monseigneur (USA) 127)   **38**
[2002 42, a63d: p10g f8g³ f9.4g² f7g⁶ f8.5g² f9.4g³ f8.5s³ 8d 8.1g⁴ Aug 8] poor   **a48**
handicapper: left D. Haydn Jones after eighth start: stays 9.4f: acts on fibresand, good to firm ground and probably on polytrack: usually blinkered/visored: sometimes slowly away. *J. M. Bradley*

RENEE   4 b.f. Wolfhound (USA) 126 – Montserrat 81 (Aragon 118) [2002 –: p7g f8g²   **45**
f7g 9m 10.1m f8.5g² f8s Sep 17] modest maiden handicapper on all-weather, poor on   **a54**
turf: probably stays 1¼m: acts on good to firm ground and fibresand, probably polytrack. *M. L. W. Bell*

REN'S MAGIC   4 gr.g. Petong 126 – Bath 76 (Runnett 125) [2002 –: p10g p8g p10g⁵   **55**
p10g 11.9f⁶ 11.9g 10.1m² 10.9g⁶ 11.5f³ 11.6g² 10m 9.9g⁵ p13g³ Dec 28] modest maiden handicapper: stays 13f: acts on firm going and polytrack: tried visored/tongue tied: tends to hang left. *J. R. Jenkins*

RENZO (IRE)   9 b.g. Alzao (USA) 117 – Watership (USA) (Foolish Pleasure (USA))   **81 §**
[2002 78§: 18s⁵ 16g 14d 20m Jun 19] strong gelding: has been hobdayed: fairly useful handicapper, lightly raced on Flat nowadays: below form after reappearance: stays 2¼m: acts on any going: tried blinkered earlier in career: usually carries head high: held up: unreliable and ungenuine. *John A. Harris*

REPEAT (IRE)   2 ch.g. (Feb 14) Night Shift (USA) – Identical (IRE) (Machiavellian   **74**
(USA) 123) [2002 5m³ 6g⁴ 5.3g⁵ p5g⁶ f7f 7m² 7m³ 6m 7g 8.3d f7g⁶ f6s Dec 13] IR   **a64**
10,000Y: tall, close-coupled gelding: first foal: dam unraced half-sister to smart 7f/1m performer Darnay: fair maiden on turf, modest on all-weather: placed in nurseries sixth and seventh (drifted left) starts: left F. J. Houghton after tenth: best form at 7f: acts on good to firm going and all-weather: tongue tied final outing. *K. A. Ryan*

REPENT AT LEISURE   2 b.g. (Apr 11) Bishop of Cashel 122 – Sutosky 78 (Great   –
Nephew 126) [2002 5.3g⁴ 7d Jul 11] 4,000F: sixth living foal: closely related to 9-y-o Montecristo and half-brother to 3 winners, including fairly useful 7f winner Dancing Sioux (by Nabeel Dancer): dam best at 1m/1¼m: well held in maidens. *W. G. M. Turner*

REPERTORY   9 b.g. Anshan 119 – Susie's Baby (Balidar 133) [2002 117: 5g⁵ 5g 5d³   **112**
6g⁴ 5d 5m* 5g 5.1m² 5g* 5.2f 5m 5g* 6v⁴ Nov 9] tall, angular gelding: smart performer: won minor events at Newmarket in July and Leicester in September, and handicap at Newmarket (beat Artie by 1¾ lengths under top weight, edging left) in October: trail-blazing front runner, best at 5f: acts on any going: game. *M. S. Saunders*

REPLACEMENT PET (IRE)   5 b.m. Petardia 113 – Richardstown Lass (IRE)   **53**
(Muscatite 122) [2002 51: 14.1d 10m⁵ f8.5g 9.7d 10.2f 10m³ 10.2g* 10.2g⁶ 10.4m⁶ 10.9m 10g Oct 24] modest performer: won seller at Chepstow in August: stays 1¼m: acts on all-weather and probably any turf going: blinkered/visored: has worn tongue strap: none too consistent. *H. S. Howe*

REPUBLICAN LADY   10 b.m. Battle Hymn 103 – Sweet Helen (No Mercy 126)   –
[2002 f12g 14.1m Aug 7] plain mare: lightly raced and little form. *C. Drew*

REPULSE BAY (IRE)   4 b.g. Barathea (IRE) 127 – Bourbon Topsy 108 (Ile de   – §
Bourbon (USA) 133) [2002 84d: 16m 10s⁵ Oct 15] big, good-topped gelding: has a fluent, rather round action: fairly useful maiden at 2/3 yrs: has become temperamental: tried visored. *J. S. Goldie*

REQUESTOR   7 br.g. Distinctly North (USA) 115 – Bebe Altesse (GER) (Alpenkonig   –
(GER)) [2002 8s f11g Nov 26] smallish, good-bodied gelding: fair performer in 2000: well held both starts since: tried blinkered. *J. G. FitzGerald*

RESCIND (IRE)   2 b.f. (Apr 22) Revoque (IRE) 122 – Sunlit Ride (Ahonoora 122)   **52**
[2002 5g 6.1g 5.9g² 7g⁶ 6.1m⁵ 7f⁶ Sep 21] 5,000F, 8,000 2-y-o: leggy filly: half-sister to

3 winners in Italy, including winner up to 9f Tenby Ride (by Tenby): dam, second at 1¼m in Ireland, out of sister to 2000 Guineas winner Bolkonski: modest maiden: runner-up at Hamilton: should stay 7f: raced on good ground or firmer. *Jedd O'Keeffe*

RESEARCHED (IRE)   3 b.g. Danehill (USA) 126 – Sought Out (IRE) 119 (Rainbow **106** Quest (USA) 134) [2002 –p: 10g* 12.3f6 11.9g3 10m Sep 21] sturdy, good sort: useful performer, lightly raced: landed odds in maiden at Windsor in April (edged right, reportedly finished lame): very good ½-length third to Spectrometer in Knavesmire Handicap at York in August: seemed unsuited by step back in trip next time (gelded after): stays 1½m: best effort on good ground: went in snatches when well held in Chester Vase second start. *Sir Michael Stoute*

RESEARCHER   3 ch.f. Cosmonaut – Rest 70 (Dance In Time (CAN)) [2002 61: **68** 12m* 14.1m 11.8d May 27] lengthy, angular filly: has scope: fair performer: won handicap at Beverley in April: stays 1½m (raced freely at 1¾m): acts on good to firm going: sold 11,500 gns, and joined Venetia Williams. *R. M. Beckett*

RESILIENCE   2 b.f. (Mar 8) Most Welcome 131 – Ahstone Queen 66 (Presidium 124) **51** [2002 5s 5m 5f5g5 f6g 6d3 6m3 6m2 5.3m5 6.1g f5g 7d Oct 18] 3,200Y: angular filly: second foal: dam 6f (including at 2 yrs)/7f winner: modest maiden: below form last 4 starts, leaving P. D. Evans after second of them: stays 6f: acts on fibresand and good to firm going: visored after second outing: sometimes carries head awkwardly. *J. Balding*

RESILIENT   5 b.g. Last Tycoon 131 – Alilisa (USA) (Alydar (USA)) [2002 f6g f7g **– §** Mar 21] small, sturdy gelding: modest maiden in 2000 for W. Haggas: should have stayed 1¼m: acted on fibresand: looked unrideable on reappearance: dead. *T. D. Barron*

RESONATE (IRE)   4 b.c. Erins Isle 121 – Petronelli (USA) (Sir Ivor 135) [2002 7g4 **85** 6g 6m5 7m3 7g 7s* Oct 26] useful-looking colt: fifth foal: half-brother to Irish 9f winner Benelli (by Grand Lodge): dam useful Irish 2-y-o 6f/1m winner: fairly useful performer: trained in Ireland first 5 starts at 2 yrs, then by R. Feligioni in Italy until after second outing in 2002: simple task in claimer at Doncaster final outing: effective at 6f, probably at 1¼m: acts on soft and good to firm going: joined A. Newcombe. *M. A. Jarvis*

RESPLENDENT CEE (IRE)   3 ch.c. Polar Falcon (USA) 126 – Western Friend **112** (USA) (Gone West (USA)) [2002 104: 6d2 6d5 7m5 7m4 6m2 7m* 6g4 7s2 Oct 26] rangy, quite attractive colt: fluent mover: smart performer: won minor event at Redcar in October by 8 lengths from Amaranth: particularly good efforts when in frame both starts after, 1¾ lengths fourth to Needwood Blade in listed event at Newmarket and second to easy winner Millennium Force in minor event at Doncaster: barely stays testing 7f: acts on firm and soft going: edged right second outing. *P. W. Harris*

RESPLENDENT FLYER (FR)   4 b.g. Danehill (USA) 126 – Zehoor Alsafa (USA) **–** (Wild Again (USA)) [2002 8g p10g Jul 3] lightly-raced maiden. *P. W. Harris*

RESPLENDENTLY   2 b.c. (Mar 5) Piccolo 121 – Llyn Gwynant 115 (Persian Bold **73** 123) [2002 6d3 p6g6 f6g Nov 30] 13,000Y: half-brother to several winners, including useful 2m/17f winner Lady of The Lake (by Caerleon) and fairly useful 1994 2-y-o 7f winner Llia (by Shirley Heights): dam best at 1m/9f: fair form in maidens first 2 starts (reportedly jarred up and suffered from ringworm after third at Epsom): should stay 7f. *P. W. Harris*

RESSOURCE (FR)   3 b.c. Broadway Flyer (USA) 121 – Rayonne (Sadler's Wells **–** (USA) 132) [2002 12d 9g p13g Aug 9] 145,000 francs Y: fifth foal: half-brother to French 1m winner Cloth of Gold (by Kendor): dam winner in France around 11f: well held in France for A. Spanu, and in maiden at Lingfield on British debut. *G. L. Moore*

RETAIL THERAPY (IRE)   2 b.f. (Mar 20) Bahhare (USA) 122 – Elect (USA) 113 **–** (Vaguely Noble 140) [2002 6m p7g f7g Nov 26] IR 42,000F, IR 77,000Y: half-sister to several winners, including US Grade 3 8.5f winner Aquaba (by Damascus) and fairly useful 7f/1m winner (latter including at 2 yrs) in Britain/UAE Select Few (by Alzao): dam 1¼m/1½m winner: behind in maidens. *M. A. Buckley*

RETIREMENT   3 b.g. Zilzal (USA) 137 – Adeptation (USA) (Exceller (USA) 129) **79** [2002 71: 8m5 8.3s2 7s3 8m f8.5g2 p10g4 9.1g2 8s Nov 2] leggy, quite attractive gelding: unimpressive mover: fair handicapper: stays 1¼m: acts on all-weather, soft and good to firm going: has edged left. *M. H. Tompkins*

RETURN OF AMIN   8 ch.g. Salse (USA) 128 – Ghassanah 73 (Pas de Seul 133) [2002 **–** –: f7g Jun 20] one-time useful 6f/7f performer: little form since 2000: usually blinkered nowadays, has been visored. *D. W. Chapman*

REVAMP (IRE) 5 b.g. Shalford (IRE) 124§ – Golden Weaver (Reference Point 139) – [2002 f9.4g Apr 20] first foal: dam unraced: well held in seller at Wolverhampton. *D. McCain*

REVEILLEZ 3 gr.g. First Trump 118 – Amalancher (USA) 85 (Alleged (USA) 138) **89** [2002 63p: 6m 8.3d 11.5m² 11.5f* 12f* 11.9m⁴ 12f Oct 2] tall, angular gelding: fairly useful handicapper: won at Yarmouth in June and Ascot (beat Tasneef by neck, edging right) in July: disappointing final start: stays 1½m: acts on firm going. *J. R. Fanshawe*

REVELINO (IRE) 3 b.g. Revoque (IRE) 122 – Forelino (USA) 62§ (Trempolino **90** (USA) 135) [2002 82: 10g⁴ 8.3m 10.2g² 10m* 10d Oct 14] useful-looking gelding: fairly useful performer: won handicap at Windsor in October, hanging violently right when hitting front: not sure to stay beyond 1¼m: acts on soft and good to firm going: sold 26,000 gns, and joined Miss S. Wilton. *E. A. L. Dunlop*

REVENANTE (USA) 3 b.f. Known Fact (USA) 135 – Avira (Dancing Brave (USA) **?** 140) [2002 8.1m* 9f* Dec 26] leggy filly: third foal: half-sister to 5-y-o Divulge: dam twice-raced half-sister to useful performer up to 1m Tatsfield: successful in maiden at Warwick (by short head from Can't Buy Me Love, overcoming inexperience) in September and, having been sold from Mrs A. Perrett 12,000 gns, allowance race at Santa Anita (by a head, leading in straight) in December: will stay 1¼m: should improve again. *D. Vienna, USA*

REVENGE 6 b.g. Saddlers' Hall (IRE) 126 – Classic Heights (Shirley Heights 130) – [2002 –: 16v Oct 29] lengthy, quite good-topped gelding: poor mover: fair maiden at 4 yrs: well beaten both Flat runs since: blinkered last 5 starts. *C. G. Cox*

REVENUE (IRE) 2 ch.c. (Feb 27) Cadeaux Genereux 131 – Bareilly (USA) (Lyphard **103** (USA) 132) [2002 5.1m² 5m² 6.1f² 5m* 6m* 6g⁴ 5m² 5m³ Oct 12] 33,000Y: smallish,

The Royal Ascot Racing Club's "Revenue"

sturdy, lengthy colt: fourth foal: dam, unraced close relative to Prix de Diane second Baya, out of sister to Triptych: useful performer: won Windsor Castle Stakes at Royal Ascot (by 1½ lengths from One More Time) in June and Gerrard Investment Management Richmond Stakes at Goodwood (awarded race after finishing 3 lengths second to Elusive City) in July: good efforts in frame after in Gimcrack Stakes at York, Flying Childers Stakes at Doncaster (length second to Wunders Dream) and Cornwallis Stakes at Ascot (third to Peace Offering): effective at 5f/6f: raced only on good going or firmer: genuine and reliable. *M. L. W. Bell*

REVIEWER (IRE)　4 b.g. Sadler's Wells (USA) 132 – Clandestina (USA) 98 **82** (Secretariat (USA)) [2002 80: 12.6g* 12g* 14m⁶ Jul 30] rangy gelding: fairly useful handicapper: won at Warwick (amateurs) and Ascot (tended to idle), both in July: should stay 1¾m: acts on good and good to firm going: tried blinkered in 2000: held up: carries head awkwardly. *H. Morrison*

REVOLVING (USA)　2 b. or br.f. (Apr 5) Devil's Bag (USA) – Mims Return (USA) **79** (Woodman (USA) 126) [2002 5m 5g* 5m⁶ Jun 4] $50,000Y: rather leggy, close-coupled filly: fourth foal: half-sister to a winner in Japan by Dehere: dam unraced half-sister to dam of Breeders' Cup Sprint winner Elmhurst from family of Alydar: best effort (fair form) when winning 5-runner maiden at Goodwood in May by 3½ lengths from Sir Edwin Landseer, making all: heavily bandaged behind, last of 6 in listed event at Sandown: should stay 6f: joined K. McLaughlin in UAE. *M. Johnston*

REX IS OKAY　6 ch.g. Mazilier (USA) 107 – Cocked Hat Girl 47 (Ballacashtal **–** (CAN)) [2002 77, a61: f8g⁴ f8g⁵ f7g⁶ Feb 7] quite good-topped gelding: modest form on **a56** all-weather in 2002: probably best at 6f/7f: acts on fibresand: often blinkered: usually forces pace: ran moody race final start: refused to enter stall in April and was banned from racing from stalls until October. *S. R. Bowring*

REZZAGO (USA)　2 b.c. (Apr 4) Night Shift (USA) – Western Friend (USA) (Gone **63 p** West (USA)) [2002 6d⁵ Oct 14] 65,000Y: fifth foal: half-brother to 3 winners, notably 3-y-o Resplendent Cee: dam once-raced sister to smart performer up to 1m in Britain and USA Gold Land: 6/1, 8½ lengths fifth of 21 to Turn Around in maiden at Windsor, good late work after slow start: will stay at least 7f: sure to do better. *P. W. Harris*

RHEINPARK　3 ch.g. Cadeaux Genereux 131 – Marina Park 112 (Local Suitor (USA) **68** 128) [2002 75: 6d³ 6f 7m* f7s 7m f5g Dec 27] smallish gelding: fair performer: made all in claimer at Newmarket (left M. Johnston £6,000) in August: stays 7f (with emphasis on speed): acts on soft and good to firm ground, well held on fibresand: front runner. *J. R. Best*

RHEINPFALZ　3 b.f. Slip Anchor 136 – Pfalz 101 (Pharly (FR) 130) [2002 f9.4g Dec **–** 20] fifth foal: half-sister to 10.8f winner Come Together (by Mtoto): dam 1m winner who seemed to stay 1¼m: 13/2, tailed off in maiden at Wolverhampton. *J. R. Fanshawe*

RHETORIC (IRE)　3 b.g. Desert King (IRE) 129 – Squaw Talk (USA) (Gulch (USA)) **–** [2002 –p: 7.1m 10.2g 14.1m May 10] quite attractive gelding: little form: blinkered (soon clear, folded tamely) final start: sold 7,500 gns. *J. H. M. Gosden*

RHICONICH (IRE)　3 gr.g. Ashkalani (IRE) 128 – Snowing 88 (Tate Gallery (USA) **–** 117) [2002 6s p6g f6g² 5d 5d f8.5s f7g 7s Oct 28] third foal: half-brother to 4-y-o The **a62** Trader: dam Irish 5f winner: modest maiden: well held last 5 starts: bred to prove best at 5f/6f: form only on all-weather. *M. Blanshard*

RHINEFIELD LASS　2 ch.f. (Apr 28) Bijou d'Inde 127 – Rhinefield Beauty (IRE) **–** 52 (Shalford (IRE) 124§) [2002 5m 8s 5s Nov 6] first foal: dam sprint maiden: well held in maidens/seller. *J. S. Goldie*

RHODAMINE (IRE)　5 b.g. Mukaddamah (USA) 125 – Persian Empress (IRE) 51 **–** (Persian Bold 123) [2002 64: 10.1s 10.9m Jun 17] smallish, leggy gelding: has a quick, fluent action: modest handicapper at 4 yrs: off 11 months, well held in 2002. *J. L. Eyre*

RHOSSILI (IRE)　2 b.g. (Mar 15) Perugino (USA) 84 – Velinowski (Malinowski **58** (USA) 123) [2002 7g 6m⁶ 8d Aug 2] 5,000Y: strong gelding: half-brother to several winners, including fairly useful Irish 1¼m winner Masters of War (by Sri Pekan) and 1992 2-y-o 5f/6f winner Nicki-J (by Jareer): dam unraced: form in maidens (modest) only when seventh at Thirsk on debut: gelded after final start. *Bob Jones*

RHUM RUNNER　2 b.c. (May 2) Petong 126 – Crosby Sue (Hotfoot 126) [2002 6f 6g **49** 7g⁴ f7g² 7.5d⁶ p7g f7g 7g Oct 17] 2,500Y: leggy, quite good-topped colt: third foal: dam **a66** unraced: fair maiden on all-weather, poor on turf: second at Wolverhampton: left Mrs D. Haine before final start: stays 7f: acts on all-weather, best turf effort on good going: sold 7,500 gns. *G. C. H. Chung*

RHYME 3 b.g. Magic Ring (IRE) 115 – Pretty Thing 83 (Star Appeal 133) [2002 11.6m – Jul 15] 5,000F: 12,000Y, 11,000 2-y-o: half-brother to several winners, including 6-y-o Bergamo: dam best at 1½m: always behind in seller at Windsor. *J. A. Osborne*

RHYTHM 2 ch.c. (Mar 28) Fleetwood (IRE) 107 – Emaline (FR) 105 (Empery (USA) – 128) [2002 6.1m p7g Oct 9] 15,000Y, 16,000 2-y-o: good-bodied colt: half-brother to several winners, including smart 1991 2-y-o 5f winner Magic Ring (by Green Desert) and 11.5f to 2m winner Monarda (by Pharly): dam French 2-y-o 7f winner: well held in maidens: sold 500 gns. *Miss E. C. Lavelle*

RHYTHMICAL ROAD (USA) 2 b.c. (Mar 8) Dance Brightly (CAN) – Senita Lane 62 (CAN) (Ascot Knight (CAN) 130) [2002 6m⁴ Jul 3] $50,000F, $320,000Y: second foal: half-brother to useful 2001 2-y-o 5f winner Latin Lynx (by Forest Wildcat): dam US 2-y-o winner around 6f, including minor stakes: 13/8 on, persistently tried to hang right when 5 lengths fourth of 6 to Indian Haven in maiden at Yarmouth. *D. R. Loder*

RHYTHM OF LIFE 3 ch.f. Dr Devious (IRE) 127 – Nashville Blues (IRE) 94 (Try 78 My Best (USA) 130) [2002 55: 7.1g 6f³ 7m* 7m³ 8.1m* 8g⁵ 8f⁶ Oct 7] lengthy, angular filly: fair performer: won maiden at Redcar in May and handicap at Sandown in September: bred to stay 1¼m: raced only on good going or firmer: withdrawn after refusing to enter stall intended fourth outing: sent to USA. *J. W. Hills*

RIANATTA (IRE) 3 b.f. Nicolotte 118 – Asturiana (Julio Mariner 127) [2002 p8g 53 p6g 8.3m 6m 8.3s 7m 7d 6.1m⁵ 6g 7m 8f Sep 8] 2,800Y: half-sister to several winners, including 5f winner (including at 2 yrs) Twice In Bundoran (by Bold Arrangement) and 1½m winner Spirit of Tenby (by Tenby): dam lightly-raced: modest maiden: well held last 3 outings (reportedly had breathing problem on second occasion): barely stays 1m: has edged right. *P. Butler*

RIBBON OF LIGHT 4 b.g. Spectrum (IRE) 126 – Brush Away (Ahonoora 122) – [2002 47: 10.9m 10.9g Jul 5] angular, attractive gelding: maiden handicapper. *Ian Williams*

RIBBONS AND BOWS (IRE) 2 gr.f. (Feb 13) Dr Devious (IRE) 127 – Nichodoula 91 65 (Doulab (USA) 115) [2002 6g 6d* 7d 7.1m² 8m⁶ 6m³ 8m Sep 12] 14,000Y: leggy, angular filly: fourth foal: half-sister to 3 winners, including 4-y-o Give Back Calais: dam, 7f/1m winner, half-sister to very smart 9f to 1½m performer Terimon: fairly useful performer: won maiden at Salisbury in June: unlucky short-head second to Sister Bluebird in listed event at Sandown following month: should stay 1¼m: yet to race on extremes of going. *C. A. Cyzer*

RICH AFFAIR 2 br.f. (Apr 11) Machiavellian (USA) 123 – Much Too Risky 87 77 p (Bustino 136) [2002 7m Aug 17] sister to 3-y-o L'Affaire Monique and smart 1m to 13.5f winner Whitewater Affair and half-sister to several winners, including very smart 7f (at 2 yrs) to 1½m winner Little Rock (by Warning): dam 2-y-o 7f/1m winner: 25/1, 4 lengths seventh of 15 to Almaviva in maiden at Newmarket: should do better. *Sir Michael Stoute*

RICHARD 2 b.c. (Mar 18) Distinctly North (USA) 115 – Murmuring 69 (Kind of Hush 67 118) [2002 5g⁵ 5g⁴ May 21] neat colt: fourth reported foal: dam 6f winner: fair form in maidens: likely to prove best at 5f: slowly away both starts. *S. Dow*

RICH DANCER 2 b.f. (Apr 3) Halling (USA) 133 – Fairy Flight (IRE) 86 (Fairy 70 p King (USA)) [2002 7d⁶ Nov 2] 27,000Y: leggy filly: second foal: half-sister to 3-y-o Just James: dam, Irish 2-y-o 6f winner, sister to useful sprinter King of The East: 33/1 and green, 6 lengths sixth of 18 to Aljazeera in maiden at Newmarket, keeping on from rear: will improve. *J. D. Bethell*

RICHEMAUR (IRE) 2 b.f. (Feb 2) Alhaarth (IRE) 126 – Lady President (IRE) 72 89 p (Dominion 123) [2002 7.5g⁴ 8s* Oct 25] 50,000Y: leggy, workmanlike filly: fifth foal: half-sister to fairly useful Irish 1997 2-y-o 5f winner Dress Design (by Brief Truce) and a winner in Japan by Keen: dam Irish sprinting half-sister to smart 1m/1¼m performer Citidancer: much better effort in maidens (fairly useful form) when winning 22-runner event at Doncaster by 1¾ lengths from Discreet Brief, quickening on over 1f out: not sure to stay much beyond 1m: should improve further. *M. H. Tompkins*

RICHENDA 4 b.f. Mister Baileys 123 – Forget Me (IRE) (Don't Forget Me 127) – [2002 8f 8.2d p7g 8d 10m 8m Aug 7] small, close-coupled filly: fair maiden at 2 yrs: well held in 2002: visored final start. *Mrs Lucinda Featherstone*

RICH PICKINS (USA) 3 b.c. Smart Strike (CAN) 121 – Palace Weekend (USA) 70 (Seattle Dancer (USA) 119) [2002 p8g³ f9.4g² 8.1m⁴ p7g p10g⁴ p10g* Dec 21] first foal: dam unraced half-sister to Kentucky Derby runner-up Tejano Run and smart US Grade 2

8.5f winner More Royal: fair performer: won handicap at Lingfield in December: stays 1¼m: acts on polytrack: tried visored: wore cheekpieces last 2 starts. *N. A. Graham*

RIDE THE TIGER (IRE)   5 ch.g. Imp Society (USA) – Krisdaline (USA) 98 (Kris S (USA)) [2002 52: p10g f12g* f12g⁵ f12g f11g³ f12g³ 12.3g 10m³ f12f⁶ f14.8g⁵ f12f²   **54** Nov 29] modest handicapper: won seller at Wolverhampton (left M. Usher 3,600 gns) in January: stays 1½m: acts on firm going and all-weather: reportedly finished lame fourth/fifth starts: difficult ride (sometimes hangs markedly left and runs in snatches). *R. Wilman*

RIDGEBACK   2 ch.c. (Feb 25) Indian Ridge 123 – Valbra (Dancing Brave (USA)   **– p** 140) [2002 6d Oct 14] sixth foal: half-brother to 9.7f winner Valfonic (by Zafonic) and French 6f winner Valiantly (by Anabaa): dam twice-raced half-sister to dam of 5-y-o Continent: 8/1, mid-field in maiden at Windsor, not given hard time when fading: should improve. *B. W. Hills*

RIDGE MANOR (IRE)   3 b.c. Charnwood Forest (IRE) 125 – Tony's Ridge (Indian   **–** Ridge 123) [2002 –p: p10g p12g Nov 27] useful-looking colt: well held in maidens/claimer. *B. G. Powell*

RIDGEWAY (IRE)   7 b.g. Indian Ridge 123 – Regal Promise (Pitskelly 122) [2002   **81** 81+: 8m 8.5g⁶ 8.9d 8.5d³ 8m* 8m² 8g⁶ 7.9m Sep 8] tall gelding: fairly useful handicapper, lightly raced: first win for over 4 years at Doncaster in July: effective from 1m to 1½m: acts on heavy and good to firm going: blinkered fourth/last 3 starts: none too consistent. *M. W. Easterby*

RIDGEWAY LAD   4 ch.g. Primo Dominie 121 – Phyliel (USA) 82 (Lyphard (USA)   **69** 132) [2002 78: 6d⁴ 7m 7f 6f⁴ May 13] good-bodied gelding: fair maiden: stays 7.5f: acts on firm and good to soft going: blinkered last 2 starts: slowly away last 3 outings: sold 2,800 gns. *T. D. Easterby*

RIDICULE   3 b.g. Piccolo 121 – Mockingbird 64 (Sharpo 132) [2002 60: 6g 5.9s 6f*   **82** 5g* 6f² 5m 5m⁵ 6s* 5g 6d⁶ 5f⁶ Oct 3] tall, lengthy, useful-looking gelding: has scope: fairly useful performer: won handicaps at Redcar (amateur maiden event) and Mussel-burgh in June and minor event at Pontefract in August: effective at 5f/6f: acts on firm and soft going: visored last 4 starts: slowly away (lost all chance) sixth outing: sold 14,000 gns. *T. D. Easterby*

RIESLING   4 b.f. Slip Anchor 136 – Our Aisling 82 (Blakeney 126) [2002 8f⁵ 10d 7.5g   **–** 12.1d 9.2g Jul 18] lengthy filly: fourth foal: half-sister to 9.4f winner Madam Lucy (by Efisio): dam won up to 2m: no form. *J. A. Glover*

RIFIFI   9 ch.g. Aragon 118 – Bundled Up (USA) (Sharpen Up 127) [2002 –, a70: f5g⁴   **– §** f5g² f6g³ f5g f6g f6g f6g f6s Sep 17] small, sturdy gelding: poor mover: fair per-   **a70 d** former: stays 7f: acts on fibresand: temperamental nowadays (refused to race penultimate start): one to leave alone. *R. Wilman*

RIFLEMAN (IRE)   2 ch.c. (Apr 28) Starborough 126 – En Garde (USA) 82 (Irish   **86 p** River (FR) 131) [2002 f7g³ f8.5s* p7g⁸ Dec 21] 450,000 francs Y, 20,000 2-y-o: first foal: dam, 2-y-o 5.7f winner who stayed 1¼m, half-sister to top-class miler Observatory: fairly useful form when winning 12-runner maiden at Wolverhampton and 10-runner minor event at Lingfield (by 1¼ lengths from Just Fly) in December: stays 8.5f: acts on all-weather: should continue to progress. *Mrs A. Duffield*

RIGADOON (IRE)   6 b.g. Be My Chief (USA) 122 – Loucoum (FR) 93 (Iron Duke   **49** (FR) 122) [2002 55: 17.1f³ Apr 13] tall gelding: poor handicapper: best at 2m+: acts on firm ground, possibly not softer than good: blinkered. *M. W. Easterby*

RIGHT APPROACH   3 b.c. Machiavellian (USA) 123 – Abbey Strand (USA) 78   **104** (Shadeed (USA) 135) [2002 103P: 10d³ 10.4f May 15] leggy, useful-looking colt: fluent mover: useful performer: won minor event at Newmarket, first of 2 starts at 2 yrs: 11/8 favourite (having been heavily backed for Derby), beaten 6½ lengths when only third of 4 behind Simeon in Classic Trial at Sandown in April, taking fierce hold under restraint and not knocked about after tending to edge left: tongue tied, presumably amiss when remote eighth of 9 in Dante Stakes at York following month: not sure to stay beyond 1¼m: acts on good to soft going: slowly away both outings at 2 yrs: stays in training. *Sir Michael Stoute*

RIGHTY HO   8 b.g. Reprimand 122 – Challanging 95 (Mill Reef (USA) 141) [2002   **52** 49: 12.3g 9.9g³ 10.1g 9.9d⁶ 12d³ 12.1m³ 12.1m⁶ 14.1m Oct 5] tall, leggy gelding: modest performer: effective at 1¼m to 2m: acts on any going: often visored earlier in career: usually races prominently. *W. H. Tinning*

RILEYS DREAM   3 b.f. Rudimentary (USA) 118 – Dorazine 77 (Kalaglow 132)   **75** [2002 5.1d* 6d* 6s⁴ Aug 7] unfurnished filly: fifth foal: dam, 7f to 10.5f winner, out of half-sister to St Leger winner Bruni: fair form: won maiden at Nottingham in June (slowly away/hung markedly left) and minor event at Pontefract in July: disappointing (found little) final start (disqualified after finishing eighth of 10): will stay 7f. *M. R. Channon*

RILEYS ROCKET   3 b.f. Makbul 104 – Star of Flanders (Puissance 110) [2002 –:   **55** 6.1d 8.2g⁴ 7.1m⁴ 7f³ 10g 8g f6g² f7f f7g⁶ f8g Dec 10] leggy, angular filly: modest maiden: **a50** stays 1m (raced freely at 1¼m): acts on good to firm going and fibresand: sometimes slowly away. *R. Hollinshead*

RIMATARA   6 ch.g. Selkirk (USA) 129 – Humble Pie 92 (Known Fact (USA) 135)   **40 §** [2002 58d: f8g f7g³ f7g³ 7d 6m 7f a6g a10.5g a8g a8g⁵ a7g² a8g⁵ a8g² Dec 1] good-   **a45 §** topped gelding: poor performer: left M. W. Easterby after sixth start: probably best at 7f/ 1m: acts on sand/fibresand: usually blinkered/visored in Britain: races prominently/ carries head awkwardly: not to be trusted. *C. Tinkler, Spain*

RIMROD (USA)   2 b.c. (Apr 21) Danzig (USA) – Annie Edge 118 (Nebbiolo 125)   **111** [2002 5m 6d⁴ 7.1m* 8m* 7m Oct 19] quite attractive colt: unfurnished at 2 yrs: brother to 3 winners, including smart 1996 2-y-o 5f/6f winner (later second in Poule d'Essai des Pouliches) Seebe and fairly useful 1¼m winner Skillington, and half-brother to several winners, notably high-class 7f/1m (latter including at 2 yrs) winner Selkirk (by Sharpen Up): dam, 5f and 7f winner in Britain, later won up to 11f in USA: smart performer: won maiden at Sandown (by 3½ lengths from Oasis Dream) in August and listed race at Goodwood (beat Rainwashed Gold by 1¼ lengths, pair 6 lengths clear of Makhlab) in September: only eighth to Tout Seul in Dewhurst Stakes at Newmarket (supplemented) final start: stays 1m: acts on good to firm going: reportedly struck into on debut. *I. A. Balding*

Mr George Strawbridge's "Rimrod"

RING DANCER   7 b.g. Polar Falcon (USA) 126 – Ring Cycle 64 (Auction Ring   **62 §**
(USA) 123) [2002 80§: 5m³ 6m⁴ 6.1f 5m⁵ 6m⁶ Jun 28] useful-looking gelding: modest
nowadays: effective at 5f to easy 7f: acts on firm going, good to soft and fibresand: often
slowly away: refused to race once as 6-y-o: tends to carry head high: not to be trusted
implicitly. *Mrs L. Stubbs*

RINGING HILL   3 b.f. Charnwood Forest (IRE) 125 – Not Before Time (IRE) (Polish   **88 p**
Precedent (USA) 131) [2002 8m² 10m² 10g* Sep 10] 55,000Y: lengthy filly: fifth foal:
half-sister to 3 winners, including smart 1m (at 2 yrs) and Musidora winner Time Away
(by Darshaan) and fairly useful 1¼m and 12.5f winner Original Spin (by Machiavellian):
dam unraced daughter of top-class 1¼m/1½m performer Time Charter: fairly useful
form: second in maidens at Kempton prior to winning similar event at Leicester in
September by 3½ lengths from Razzle: will be suited by 1½m+: remains open to
improvement. *H. Candy*

RINGMOOR DOWN   3 b.f. Pivotal 124 – Floppie (FR) (Law Society (USA) 130)   **74**
[2002 81: 7m Aug 24] smallish, strong, angular filly: won maiden at Kempton on first of
2 starts at 2 yrs: off 11 months before eleventh in handicap at Newmarket on only run of
2002. will probably stay 1m. *P. J. Makin*

RING OF DESTINY   3 b.c. Magic Ring (IRE) 115 – Canna (Caerleon (USA) 132)   **98**
[2002 71: 7m² 8.3m⁶ 8.1d⁵ 9.9m* 10d⁵ 10g* 10d⁴ 12m³ 12.3m* 10.3m 10f² Sep 26] quite
attractive colt: won maiden at Salisbury in June and Ripon in July and August
(beat Colway Ritz by 1½ lengths): probably best at 1½m: acts on firm and good to soft
going. *P. W. Harris*

RINGSIDE JACK   6 b.g. Batshoof 122 – Celestine 62 (Skyliner 117) [2002 73:   **70**
12.3g³ 9.9m² 10g 10.3f 10.1m⁴ 10s⁵ 12.4s² 13s* 11.9g 12.1s⁵ f12s 14.6s Oct 25] quite
good-topped gelding: fair handicapper: won apprentice event at Hamilton in June: well
below form after: should stay 1¾m: acts on any going, though all 4 wins on softer than
good: effective visored or not. *C. W. Fairhurst*

RINGWOOD (USA)   4 b.g. Foxhound (USA) 103 – Tewksbury Garden (USA) (Wolf   **60**
Power (SAF)) [2002 72d: f6g f7g* f8.5g⁶ f7g⁵ f7g f8.5g f7g⁶ 8.2m⁶ Apr 16] smallish,
useful-looking gelding: modest performer: won maiden at Wolverhampton in January:
left J. Unett after sixth start: stays 1m: acts on fibresand, firm and good to soft going: tried
in visor/net muzzle earlier in career. *P. S. Felgate*

RIOJA   7 ch.g. Anshan 119 – Executive Flare (Executive Man 119) [2002 57: p8g p6g⁶   **52**
p7g⁶ p8g⁵ p8g⁴ p6g⁵ 6g 5.7d⁶ f8.5g Jun 28] all, useful-looking gelding: modest performer: mostly below form in 2002, leaving M. Wigham after sixth start: best at 6f/7f:
acts on all-weather, soft and good to firm going: blinkered sixth start. *D. Burchell*

RIO'S DIAMOND   5 b.m. Formidable (USA) 125 – Rio Piedras 86 (Kala Shikari   **59**
125) [2002 56: f8g* f8g² f9.4g⁶ f8.5g⁶ f7g⁵ f7g p7g p10g 8m⁶ 10.1m f8s p7g Dec 11]
small mare: modest handicapper: won at Southwell in January: below form after fifth
start: effective at 7f/1m: acts on all-weather and any turf going except soft/heavy: visored
twice: has idled/hung left. *M. J. Ryan*

RIPCORD (IRE)   4 b.g. Diesis 133 – Native Twine 114 (Be My Native (USA) 122)   **– §**
[2002 66§: 8m 7d 8m p10g 12.1g Jul 26] big, lengthy, good-topped gelding: temperamental maiden handicapper nowadays. *Lady Herries*

RIPPLE EFFECT   2 ch.f. (Apr 15) Elmaamul (USA) 125 – Sharp Chief 71 (Chief   **88**
Singer 131) [2002 6m² p6g⁴ 7s Oct 26] leggy filly: seventh foal: half-sister to 2 winners,
including 5-y-o Effervescent: dam, 6f winner, half-sister to smart performer up to 1½m
Dashing Blade: shaped well and showed fairly useful form when 2½ lengths second to
Wimple in minor event at Salisbury: well below that level in similar event at Lingfield
(hampered) and listed race at Newbury (something possibly amiss) after: should stay at
least 7f: acts on good to firm ground. *I. A. Balding*

RISKA KING   2 b.c. (Feb 21) Forzando 122 – Artistic Licence (High Top 131) [2002   **80**
f5g³ 5g⁴ 6m* 7m 6s 6d³ 7v⁴ p6g⁵ p7g Dec 14] 11,000F, 6,800Y: smallish, good-bodied
colt: half-brother to 3 winners, including 2000 2-y-o 5f winner The Names Bond (by
Tragic Role) and 1m winner Around Fore Alliss (by Reprimand): dam maiden who
stayed 1¼m: fairly useful performer: won maiden at York in September: mostly creditable efforts in sales race/nurseries after: barely stays 7f: acts on polytrack, good to firm
ground and heavy: blinkered/visored last 4 starts (swerved left leaving stall final one).
R. A. Fahey

RISKER (USA)   3 b.g. Gone West (USA) – Trampoli (USA) 115 (Trempolino (USA)   **78**
135) [2002 78: 10.3s 9.9m 12.3f f12g³ Jul 1] small, quite attractive gelding: good mover:

fair performer: stays 1½m: acts on good to firm going and fibresand: sold 10,000 gns, and joined P. Hobbs. *M. Johnston*

RISK TAKER   2 ch.c. (Jan 17) Rainbow Quest (USA) 134 – Post Modern (USA) **91 p** (Nureyev (USA) 131) [2002 7f⁶ 8m³ Sep 11] close-coupled colt: first foal: dam unraced sister to Oaks winner Reams of Verse and half-sister to Eclipse winner Elmaamul: better effort in maidens (fairly useful form) when 3 lengths third to Silver Gilt at Doncaster: should be suited by 1¼m+: useful prospect, should win races. *B. W. Hills*

RISKY REWARD   3 b.f. First Trump 118 – Baroness Gymcrak 62§ (Pharly (FR) 130) **43** [2002 55: 8.2d 7m 7f⁴ 10f 8m⁶ 7g 8g 11m³ 12.1g⁴ 9.2v 10m³ Aug 31] strong filly: poor maiden: stays 1½m: acts on heavy and good to firm going: usually blinkered. *T. D. Easterby*

RISQUE SERMON   4 b.g. Risk Me (FR) 127 – Sunday Sport Star 96 (Star Appeal **68 d** 133) [2002 68: p6g³ p6g⁴ p7g 6d p6g 6d Jul 4] quite good-topped gelding: fair handicapper: well held after second start: best at 5f/6f: acts on polytrack and firm going, well held on softer than good: tongue tied. *Miss B. Sanders*

RISUCCHIO   3 ch.g. Thatching 131 – Skip To Somerfield 79 (Shavian 125) [2002 69: **59** f6g² f7g f6g f6g Oct 21] close-coupled, unfurnished gelding: modest maiden handicapper: visored (well held after lay-off) final start: stays 6f: acts on fibresand, best turf effort on good going: sold 500 gns. *B. S. Rothwell*

RITA'S ROCK APE   7 b.m. Mon Tresor 113 – Failand 36 (Kala Shikari 125) [2002 **82** 87, a69: 5g 5.1g 5g 5m* 5m 5m 5g 5.3m⁴ 5m⁵ 5.1f⁴ 5f f5g f5g² Dec 31] workmanlike **a71** mare: fairly useful handicapper on turf, fair on all-weather: won at Salisbury in June: best at 5f: acts on firm going, good to soft and fibresand: usually makes running: has reportedly bled from nose: tough. *R. Brotherton*

RIVAL (IRE)   3 b.g. Desert Style (IRE) 121 – Arab Scimetar (IRE) (Sure Blade (USA) **64 §** 130) [2002 79: 6s 6f 8g 6.1v 5.7m⁵ 7m Jul 3] rather leggy, quite good-topped gelding: fair maiden at 2 yrs: just modest in 2002: may prove best at 6f/7f: best effort on good to firm going: blinkered last 3 starts: not one to place much faith in: sold 3,000 gns. *P. F. I. Cole*

RIVA ROYALE   2 b.f. (Feb 5) Royal Applause 124 – Regatta (Mtoto 134) [2002 5s² **88** 6m 5.2f* 5g 5.2f⁵ Aug 17] close-coupled, useful-looking filly: third foal: half-sister to a winner in Turkey by Muhtarram: dam unraced half-sister to smart sprinter Notley: fairly useful performer: won maiden at Yarmouth in July: best effort when fifth to Speed Cop in listed event at Newbury: likely to prove best at 5f/6f: acts on firm and soft going. *I. A. Wood*

RIVELLI (IRE)   3 b.f. Lure (USA) 131 – Kama Tashoof 72 (Mtoto 134) [2002 66: **70** 8.2d⁵ 8.2d⁴ 8.2d 7g 7m Aug 19] strong filly: fair maiden: well below form after second start: not sure to stay beyond 1m: acts on good to soft going, showed promise on good to firm on debut: blinkered (looked none too keen) final start: sold 2,000 gns in December. *P. F. I. Cole*

RIVER ANGEL   2 b.f. (Mar 16) River Falls 113 – Latin Beat (Puissance 110) [2002 **–** 6f 7m⁶ 7m 8d f8.5g f8g Nov 26] first foal: dam unraced: poor maiden. *G. M. Moore*

RIVER BLEST (IRE)   6 b.g. Unblest 117 – Vaal Salmon (IRE) (Salmon Leap (USA) **–** 131) [2002 –: f7g⁵ f6g Feb 14] tall, angular gelding: probably of little account nowadays. *Mrs A. Duffield*

RIVERBLUE (IRE)   6 b.g. Bluebird (USA) 125 – La Riveraine (USA) 90 (Riverman **66** (USA) 131) [2002 77, a62: 10d f8.5g 11.7g May 7] rather leggy gelding: fair handi- **a–** capper: stays 1½m: acts on heavy going, good to firm and fibresand: tried visored at 3 yrs: tongue tied on reappearance: sometimes gets behind. *D. J. Wintle*

RIVERBOAT DANCER   2 b.f. (Apr 13) Muhtarram (USA) 125 – South Wind 62 **72** (Tina's Pet 121) [2002 6m⁵ 6d* Jul 11] second foal: dam, maiden who stayed 1½m, out of half-sister to Yorkshire Oaks winners Sally Brown and Untold: better effort in maidens (fair form) when winning 7-runner event at Epsom by 1¼ lengths from Atheer, dictating pace: should stay at least 1m: slowly away on debut. *S. Dow*

RIVER CAPTAIN (USA)   9 ch.g. Riverman (USA) 131 – Katsura (USA) (Northern **48 ?** Dancer) [2002 14.4g⁵ 16.1d Sep 9] close-coupled gelding: poor form at best in 2002: stayed 1½m: acted on fibresand: sometimes wore tongue strap/blinkers: dead. *A. Scott*

RIVER CELEBRE (IRE)   2 ch.c. (Apr 4) Peintre Celebre (USA) 137 – Diavolina **94** (USA) (Lear Fan (USA) 130) [2002 6g² 7m 7m² 7f² a5f⁵ a7.5f* a8f³ Nov 28] 40,000Y: good-topped colt: half-brother to several winners, including 6f (at 2 yrs) to 1m (in USA) winner Polish Spring (by Polish Precedent) and French 1¼m/1½m winner Go Boldly (by

Sadler's Wells), both useful: dam French 1¼m winner: fairly useful performer: runner-up in maidens/minor event in Britain, leaving B. Hills after fourth start: won 4-runner minor event at Nad Al Sheba in November: stays 7.5f: acts on dirt, raced only on good ground or firmer on turf: blinkered fifth start. *S. Seemar, UAE*

RIVER DAYS (IRE)   4 b.f. Tagula (IRE) 116 – Straw Boater 89 (Thatch (USA) 136)   **64**
[2002 72: 6f 5m 5m⁴ 5g f5g f6s* f6g³ 5f f6g f6g⁵ Dec 7] eighth foal: half-sister to 3 winners, including useful 1997 2-y-o 1m winner Taverner Society (by Imp Society): dam 9.4f winner: modest handicapper: trained by J. Hayden in Ireland in 2001: won at Wolverhampton in September: best at 5f/6f: acts on firm going (below form on softer than good) and fibresand: blinkered final start: tongue tied earlier in career. *I. Semple*

RIVER ENSIGN   9 br.m. River God (USA) 121 – Ensigns Kit (Saucy Kit 76) [2002   **48**
63d: f9.4g³ f9.4g⁶ f8.5g² f9.4g² f8.5g³ f9.4g² 10g⁴ f9.4s f8.5g 9.1s Oct 15] small mare: has stringhalt: poor handicapper: effective at 8.5f to bare 1½m: acts on fibresand and heavy going: possibly needs to dominate. *W. M. Brisbourne*

RIVER FALCON   2 b.c. (Feb 29) Pivotal 124 – Pearly River 72 (Elegant Air 119)   **73**
[2002 6d 6d³ 6g 6d 6s Oct 26] 18,000Y: fourth foal: half-brother to 1999 2-y-o 7f winner Another Pearl (by Ezzoud) and 3-y-o Rumbunctious: dam, 7f (at 2 yrs) and 1½m winner, out of half-sister to Roseate Tern and Ibn Bey: fair maiden: third at Ayr: should stay at least 7f. *J. S. Goldie*

RIVER LARK (USA)   3 b.f. Miswaki (USA) 124 – Gold Blossom (USA) (Blushing   **–**
John (USA) 120) [2002 7m 7f 7m⁴ p5g 7d 6m Aug 14] $10,000Y, resold $20,000Y, 38,000 2-y-o: second foal: dam, 8.5f/9f winner in US, half-sister to smart 5f performer Welsh Note: well held in maidens/minor event/handicaps. *C. A. Dwyer*

RIVER NYMPH   4 ch.f. Cadeaux Genereux 131 – La Riveraine (USA) 90 (Riverman   **–**
(USA) 131) [2002 71: p7g p7g 8.2m 8m May 1] leggy, angular filly: fair maiden at 3 yrs: little form in 2002. *P. Howling*

RIVER OF FIRE   4 ch.g. Dilum (USA) 115 – Bracey Brook (Gay Fandango (USA)   **58**
132) [2002 58: 10d⁵ 11.5m 10.9d⁴ 12.1s² 10g 11.5s⁴ 14.1d² f16.2g⁴ f14g³ f14g² f14.8g² f14.8g Dec 31] modest handicapper: stays 14.8f: acts on soft going, good to firm and fibresand: usually visored nowadays: reportedly lost action second outing. *J. M. P. Eustace*

RIVER REINE (IRE)   3 br.f. Lahib (USA) 129 – Talahari (IRE) (Roi Danzig (USA))   **80**
[2002 80: 10m⁴ 11m 11.9m³ 10d 10g f12g 14.6s Oct 25] big, good-bodied filly: fairly useful handicapper: well held after fourth start: stays 1½m: acts on good to firm and heavy going: sold 8,000 gns, joined E. Tuer. *B. W. Hills*

RIVER TERN   9 b.g. Puissance 110 – Millaine 69 (Formidable (USA) 125) [2002   **51 §**
61d: 5m⁶ 5.7g 5m 5g⁴ 5f 5m 5.1f 5m⁵ 5m⁴ 5m 5f Sep 25] tall gelding: has a high knee action: modest nowadays: best at 5f/easy 6f: acts on firm and good to soft going: usually visored/blinkered at 3 yrs: often starts slowly: held up: unreliable. *J. M. Bradley*

RIYADH   4 ch.g. Caerleon (USA) 132 – Ausherra (USA) 106 (Diesis 133) [2002 95:   **103**
18.7f⁴ 20m* 16.1g 16.2d⁶ 13.9m 18m Oct 19] lengthy, angular gelding: poor mover: useful handicapper: favourite, won Ascot Stakes at Royal Ascot by head from Establishment: well held last 3 starts, tailed off in Cesarewitch at Newmarket final one: stays 2½m: has form on good to soft going, but best efforts on good or firmer: usually blinkered/visored: tends to hang. *M. C. Pipe*

Ascot Stakes (Handicap), Royal Ascot—the visored Riyadh keeps up trainer Martin Pipe's good record in the race, holding off the strong-finishing Establishment, with Mana d'Argent (right) in third

ROAN RAIDER (USA) 2 gr. or ro.c. (Mar 1) El Prado (IRE) 119 – Flirtacious –
Wonder (USA) (Wolf Power (SAF)) [2002 8.2v f8.5g Nov 15] $70,000Y: first foal: dam
minor sprint stakes winner in USA: well held in maiden and (visored) claimer: sold 800
gns. *J. M. P. Eustace*

ROASSI (IRE) 3 ch.f. Pennekamp (USA) 130 – Virelai 72 (Kris 135) [2002 53: p10g –
Jun 1] useful-looking filly: modest maiden at best, lightly raced: will need to settle to stay
1m: slowly away (well held) only run in 2002: sold 1,000 gns, sent to Spain. *C. E. Brittain*

ROBANDELA (USA) 5 b.g. Kingmambo (USA) 125 – Yemanja (USA) (Alleged **102**
(USA) 138) [2002 91: 10g 12g² 12m² 10d 9.9m² 12d⁵ 11.9g⁶ 14m 10.3m 13m* 12f²
10m* 12g Oct 17] big, good-topped gelding: useful handicapper: won at Hamilton in
September and Ascot (career-best effort when beating Nadour Al Bahr by 6 lengths) in
October: was effective at 1¼m to 13f: acted on any turf going and fibresand: blinkered/
visored: dead. *M. Johnston*

ROBBED (IRE) 3 b.c. Inzar (USA) 112 – Evocative (IRE) (Double Schwartz 128) –
[2002 8s 8.1g Sep 12] IR 12,000Y: third foal: dam placed up to 7f in Ireland: well held in
claimer/seller. *J. A. Osborne*

ROBBIE CAN CAN 3 b.g. Robellino (USA) 127 – Can Can Lady 82 (Anshan 119) **71**
[2002 66p: 7.1m² 7m 9.9g⁶ 9.1g³ 10g 12.3m 10m² 10g³ 11.5m³ p16g⁶ 14.1d³ Oct 30]
leggy, useful-looking gelding: fair maiden: stays easy 2m: acts on polytrack and good to
firm going. *J. G. Given*

ROBBIES DREAM (IRE) 6 ch.g. Balla Cove 119 – Royal Golden (IRE) (Digamist –
(USA) 110) [2002 –, a64: f8s f9.4g f9.4g f8g⁵ f7g⁴ f8g³ f8.5g⁵ f9.4f⁴ f8s* f8s² Sep 17] **a63**
small, sparely-made gelding: poor mover: modest handicapper on all-weather: won at
Southwell in September: stays 8.5f: acts on turf, lightly raced on turf: tried visored:
tongue tied: sometimes looks none too keen. *R. M. H. Cowell*

ROBBO 8 b.g. Robellino (USA) 127 – Basha (USA) (Chief's Crown (USA)) [2002 67: **60 +**
18d⁴ Oct 21] small gelding: useful chaser: modest form only run on Flat in 2002: best at
15f+: acts on fibresand and heavy ground: usually blinkered before 2001. *Mrs M. Reveley*

ROBBO'S ROCKET (IRE) 2 b.f. (Mar 17) Perugino (USA) 84 – Jus'chillin' (IRE) **69 d**
60 (Elbio 125) [2002 5.1m⁴ 5g* p5g⁴ 5m³ 5g⁵ 5.2f⁵ f5g⁵ 6m² 6d⁵ 6m³ 7m⁴ 6f³ 6g³ 7m² 6g
6m 6f p8g Nov 23] IR 4,500Y: close-coupled filly: first foal: dam, maiden who stayed
6f, half-sister to useful Irish 1m and 1½m winner Bay Empress: fair on turf, modest on
all-weather: won seller at Beverley in May: ran poorly last 4 starts (trained by R. Wilman
second and third of them, then returned to former trainer): stays 7f: acts on firm and good
to soft ground: sometimes blinkered/visored: sent to Spain. *P. S. McEntee*

ROBE CHINOISE 3 b.f. Robellino (USA) 127 – Kiliniski 119 (Niniski (USA) 125) **103**
[2002 77: 9.9m² 9.9g* 12.3d² 11.7g* 14g³ 11.9m⁵ 13.4f⁴ 14f⁴ Oct 2] rather leggy,
useful-looking filly: useful performer: won maiden at Beverley in May and minor event at
Bath in July: good efforts when after third in handicap at Goodwood (4¼ lengths
behind Scott's View) and Chester (1¼ lengths fourth to Supremacy in listed rated stakes
on penultimate start, taking while to settle): forced pace when below form in listed race at
Newmarket final outing: stays 1¾m: yet to race on soft/heavy going, acts on any other.
J. L. Dunlop

ROBESPIERRE 2 b.c. (Apr 12) Polar Falcon (USA) 126 – Go For Red (IRE) –
(Thatching 131) [2002 5g Oct 4] fifth foal: half-brother to useful 1m (at 2 yrs) to 1½m
winner Primary Colours (by Saddlers' Hall) and 4-y-o Pinot Noir: dam unraced: 50/1 and
tongue tied, well held in maiden at Lingfield. *H. Morrison*

ROBINIA PARKES 2 b.f. (Apr 14) Robellino (USA) 127 – Lucky Parkes 108 (Full **85**
Extent (USA) 113) [2002 5d* 6d³ 6d⁴ 6d⁴ 7.1m³ 7f Oct 2] neat filly: easy mover: third
foal: half-sister to 4-y-o Charlie Parkes: dam prolific 5f winner: fairly useful performer:
won maiden in May and minor event in July, both at Haydock: good efforts in frame in
nurseries after: will prove best at 6f/7f: acts on good to soft and good to firm going: sent
to Bahrain. *M. A. Jarvis*

ROBIN SHARP 4 ch.c. First Trump 118 – Mo Stopher 47 (Sharpo 132) [2002 –, a73: –
f8s 7g f6g 7d f8g f6g⁴ Dec 10] strong colt: modest handicapper: best at 6f/7f: acts on **a59**
fibresand, little form on turf. *W. Jarvis*

ROBOASTAR (USA) 5 b. or br.g. Green Dancer (USA) 132 – Sweet Alabastar **46**
(USA) (Gulch (USA)) [2002 –: f12g⁴ 14.1g Jun 15] useful-looking gelding: poor at best
nowadays: stays 1½m: acts on soft going and fibresand: has refused to race over hurdles.
P. G. Murphy

ROBWILLCALL   2 b.f. (Jan 20) Timeless Times (USA) 99 – Lavernock Lady (Don't   **75**
Forget Me 127) [2002 5g⁴ 5d* 5g³ 5s* 6s⁴ 5g 5.9m³ 5m⁵ 6m 6s Oct 25] 1,600Y: first foal:
dam no form: fair performer: won maiden at Hamilton in May and minor event at Carlisle
in June: barely stays 6f: acts on soft and good to firm ground: usually races prominently.
A. Berry

ROCCIOSO   5 br.g. Pelder (IRE) 125 – Priory Bay 54 (Petong 126) [2002 –: p12g Feb   **–**
2] leggy gelding: no form. *J. C. Fox*

ROCHES FLEURIES (IRE)   2 b.f. (Apr 30) Barathea (IRE) 127 – Princess Cara-   **–**
boo (IRE) (Alzao (USA) 117) [2002 6m⁶ 6d 6d Oct 18] close-coupled filly: first foal: dam
unraced half-sister to Fillies' Mile winner Fairy Heights and smart 1½m performer
Persian Brave: little sign of ability in maidens. *Andrew Turnell*

ROCINANTE (IRE)   2 b.g. (Mar 1) Desert Story (IRE) 115 – Antapoura (IRE) 82   **73 d**
(Bustino 136) [2002 5.1m* 5m⁴ 6s 6s⁵ 5g 7m Aug 4] 17,000Y: sturdy gelding: good
walker: second foal: half-brother to fairly useful 2001 2-y-o 6f/7f winner Richest Vein
(by Ali-Royal): dam, Irish 1¾m/2m winner and useful staying hurdler, half-sister to
useful French performer up to 9f Ancysar: fair performer: raced alone when winning
maiden at Nottingham in April: deteriorated after: should stay at least 6f: acts on good to
firm ground: blinkered last 2 starts: one to treat with caution. *R. M. Beckett*

ROCK CONCERT   4 b.f. Bishop of Cashel 122 – Summer Pageant 81 (Chief's Crown   **62**
(USA) [2002 59: 8f 10m⁶ 11.6s 10m⁴ 8.1m³ 8.3m 7m 9.9m² 10m 11.9f f8g* f8.5s² f8.5s²   **a65**
Dec 13] deep-girthed filly: fair performer: left H. Candy 7,800 gns after sixth start: won
maiden at Southwell in December: effective at 1m/1¼m: acts on firm going, good to soft
and fibresand: visored fourth to seventh starts (wandered/found little but ran creditably
on 2 occasions). *I. W. McInnes*

ROCKERFELLA LAD (IRE)   2 b.c. (May 14) Danetime (IRE) 121 – Soucaro   **–**
(Rusticaro (FR) 124) [2002 5.9s 7g 6d⁶ Aug 23] IR 4,500Y: good-topped colt:
half-brother to several winners, including fairly useful 5f/6f (including at 2 yrs) winner
Miss Fit (by Hamas): dam, ran 4 times in Ireland, out of half-sister to high-class sprinter
Abergwaun: best effort in maidens (modest form) when sixth to Sheriff Shift at Thirsk:
may prove best at 5f/6f. *K. A. Ryan*

ROCKET FORCE (USA)   2 ch.c. (May 27) Spinning World (USA) 130 – Pat Us   **87 p**
(USA) (Caucasus (USA) 127) [2002 7m⁴ 8m* Oct 2] $50,000F, $220,000Y: well-made
colt: half-brother to several winners abroad, including US Grade 3 9f winner Silver Fox
(by Pleasant Colony): dam, US maiden, half-sister to dam of US Grade 1 winners A
Phenomenon (at 7f) and Roanoke (at 9f): landed odds in maiden at Newcastle by 6
lengths from Blackwater Fever, travelling strongly and quickening clear over 1f out: not
sure to stay much beyond 1m: useful prospect, should win more races. *E. A. L. Dunlop*

ROCKET RIDGE   2 b.c. (Mar 27) Brief Truce (USA) 126 – Lunar Ridge (Indian   **–**
Ridge 123) [2002 5d 7f 6g 8d f8g Oct 17] smallish, strong colt: second foal: dam unraced
half-sister to US Grade 3 6.5f winner Wrekin Pilot: little sign of ability: tried visored:
swerved and unseated rider second start. *C. W. Fairhurst*

ROCKET SHIP (IRE)   2 b.c. (Mar 1) Pennekamp (USA) 130 – Rock The Boat 52   **85 p**
(Slip Anchor 136) [2002 7.9f* Oct 11] 50,000Y: good-topped colt: fifth foal: half-brother
to 3 winners, including useful 1m (including at 2 yrs) winner Heavenly Whisper (by
Halling) and 5f (including at 2 yrs) winner Gipsy Moth (by Efisio): dam, maiden half-
sister to Kerrera and Rock City, out of Musidora Stakes winner Rimosa's Pet: landed odds
in 7-runner maiden at York by 2½ lengths from Prince of Gold, asserting final 1f having
been pushed along soon after halfway: will be well suited by 1¼m/1½m: useful prospect,
likely to win more races. *R. Charlton*

ROCKETS 'N ROLLERS (IRE)   2 b.c. (Mar 24) Victory Note (USA) 120 – Holly   **99**
Bird (Runnett 125) [2002 5m* 5d* May 1] IR 16,500Y: good-topped colt: half-brother to
several winners, including 5f (including at 2 yrs)/6f winner Blue Holly and Irish 2000
2-y-o 1m winner Wayfarer (both by Blues Traveller), both fairly useful: dam Irish 7f and
1½m winner: useful form: won maiden at Windsor (slowly away) in April and minor
event at Ascot in May, beating Mazepa by 2½ lengths in latter: likely to stay 6f: wandered
both starts. *R. Hannon*

ROCK FALCON (IRE)   9 ch.g. Polar Falcon (USA) 126 – Rockfest (USA) 104   **§§**
(Stage Door Johnny) [2002 f7s May 13] useful handicapper in 1999: has refused to race
last 5 outings on Flat/over jumps: a thorough rogue who should be avoided. *R. J. Hodges*

ROCKING RINGO   3 b.g. Mazaad 106 – Dalgorian (IRE) (Lancastrian 126) [2002   **–**
–: f8.5g Jan 14] well beaten in sellers/maiden. *C. N. Kellett*

ROCK OF GIBRALTAR (IRE)   3 b.c. Danehill (USA) 126 – Offshore Boom **133**
96 (Be My Guest (USA) 126) [2002 118: 8m* 8s* 8g* 8g* 8g* 8d² Oct 26]

Some are born great, some achieve greatness and some have greatness thrust upon 'em. And then there are those for whom, in an age of instant celebrity, 'greatness' often seems more a function of mass media coverage. 'Great' is a word that was traditionally used sparingly. Only one British monarch has always been accorded the accolade and, in recording the deeds of Britain's racehorses in these pages, the adjective *great* has always been used with precision: only a dozen or so horses have merited the description in over half a century. In some other spheres, however, historical perspective counts for little, especially when television and tabloid newspapers set the agenda, its broadcasters and writers bombarding the nation with superlatives: 'Great shot!' 'Great goal!' 'Great performance!' Alfred the Great did appear in fourteenth place in a BBC opinion poll conducted in late-2001 to find the 'Greatest Briton'—a title eventually awarded, after a series of part-history, part-talent-show TV programmes in 2002, to Sir Winston Churchill. The top hundred included Britons from a period reaching back two thousand years, but it had a disproportionate number of meretricious 'celebrities' from the world of show business, most of whom will do well to make the list if the exercise is repeated in ten or twenty years time. If nothing else, the list illustrated a genuine confusion in the public mind about what constitutes 'greatness'. Many voters seemed to regard 'famous' as synonymous with 'great'; the 'latest' was also the 'greatest'.

G. K. Chesterton described history as 'a hill or high point of vantage, from which alone men see . . . the age in which they are living.' The disadvantage of not knowing the past was that they did not know the present. The same criticism might be levelled at some modern commentators on horseracing to whom events from more than a decade ago seem lost in a no-man's-land of ignorance. Eyebrows should have been raised at the constant comparisons in the latest season between Horse of the Year Rock of Gibraltar and that paragon Mill Reef. Mill Reef was one of the greats, his Timeform rating of 141 bettered only by half a dozen others among the hundreds of thousands of horses dealt with in *Racehorses* down the years. He fulfilled the definition of greatness consistently used in these pages, being 'a horse of such superlative merit as to make him, or her, far superior to the general run of classic winners.' Mill Reef's fourteen-race career was ended by a training injury as a four-year-old, but it included some stunning performances, among them winning the King George by six lengths (from Ortis who had won the Hardwicke at the

Sagitta 2000 Guineas Stakes, Newmarket—
stable-companions Rock of Gibraltar (nearest camera) and Hawk Wing
race in different groups; there's just a neck between them at the finish

Royal meeting by eight), the Arc by three, the Prix Ganay by ten, the Eclipse by four (from Caro, rated 133), the Coventry Stakes by eight and the Gimcrack by ten. Mill Reef was beaten only twice, once as a two-year-old and by Brigadier Gerard, another of the greats, in the Two Thousand Guineas, after which he recorded six consecutive Group 1 victories (Derby, Eclipse, King George, Arc, Ganay and Coronation Cup), the only horse to do so since the official pattern system was introduced in 1971.

Until the latest season, that is, when the remarkable Rock of Gibraltar, winner of the Grand Criterium and the Dewhurst at the end of a fairly busy two-year-old campaign, extended his winning sequence in Group 1s to seven with successive victories in the Two Thousand Guineas, the Irish Two Thousand Guineas, the St James's Palace Stakes, the Sussex Stakes and the Prix du Moulin, all over a mile. Another Ballydoyle colt Giant's Causeway achieved five straight Group 1 victories, including the St James's Palace and the Sussex, in 2000 when he also proved himself at around a mile and a quarter, including the Eclipse, the International at York and the Irish Champion in his five-timer. Giant's Causeway's achievements helped to make the summer of 2000 unforgettable, but he wasn't the best horse in training, or even the best three-year-old of his year, those titles belonging to Dubai Millennium and Sinndar respectively. Most appreciations in the media of horses like Giant's Causeway ('The Iron Horse') and Rock of Gibraltar ('The Rock') rely almost entirely on subjective judgement, rather than on an objective assessment of the form-book. Such horses tend to be judged largely on the prestige of the races they win, or how they stir the emotions, rather than on the actual quality of their performances. Unlike Giant's Causeway, Rock of Gibraltar, who won nearly all his races with something in hand, was almost certainly the best horse of his year in Europe, but on any rational reading of the form-book he was not an outstanding champion in historical terms, despite his run of consecutive Group 1 victories. As for those comparisons with Mill Reef, Rock of Gibraltar took nothing away from Mill Reef except a record. What made Mill Reef a great horse in our book was not winning six Group 1 races in a row, but his performances in those races.

Despite landing two of the most prestigious events in the juvenile calendar, Rock of Gibraltar was rated 9 lb below the top two-year-old of 2001, his stablemate Johannesburg, while another stablemate Hawk Wing was ante-post favourite for the Sagitta Two Thousand Guineas over the winter. A mile looked likely to prove within Rock of Gibraltar's compass as a three-year-old—though on pedigree he couldn't be guaranteed to stay much further—and he was reported at the beginning of April to be a possible for the Poule d'Essai des Poulains at Longchamp. Johannesburg was bound for the Kentucky Derby and Hawk Wing, the subject of glowing reports from Ballydoyle, was to spearhead an intended three- or four-horse challenge by the stable for the Two Thousand Guineas. Rock of Gibraltar was the subject of a late switch to Newmarket after reportedly working impressively at Ballydoyle in the week leading up to the race. With stable-jockey Michael Kinane suspended, Jamie Spencer was on 6/4 favourite Hawk Wing, with Johnny Murtagh (originally booked for Tendulkar) taking the mount on Rock of Gibraltar, who started fourth favourite at 9/1, behind also the Craven Stakes winner King of

Entenmann's Irish 2000 Guineas, the Curragh—much more clear-cut this time for Rock of Gibraltar; Century City (right) and Della Francesca (left) help make it a 1,2,3 for Aidan O'Brien, with Foreign Accent (spots on cap) in fourth

Happiness (11/2) and French-trained Massalani (7/1), who had beaten the previous season's top-rated French juvenile Zipping in the Prix Djebel. There were twenty-two runners in all—though half of them started at 50/1 or longer—and none looked in better shape beforehand than the quartet from Ballydoyle, which also included the close Dewhurst third Tendulkar, a 16/1-shot, and Gran Criterium winner Sholokhov, the last-named said to be acting largely as a pacemaker. Massalani was among the others to take the eye, while 50/1-shot Aramram, winner of the Thirsk Classic Trial, stood out on looks even in such a field. The race before the Guineas, a thirty-runner sprint handicap, was dominated by those who raced on the far side and, when the Guineas field broke from the stalls, the runners split into three groups to begin with, some of those in the centre eventually joining five who had gone straight to the far rail. Those five included the eventual first, third, fourth and fifth, Rock of Gibraltar (drawn highest of all), the Greenham winner Redback, Zipping and European Free Handicap winner Twilight Blues. Rock of Gibraltar, who'd been held up, headed the front-running Redback entering the final furlong, and just held a striking late surge by Hawk Wing, the pair separated by half the width of the track. The margin was a neck, with Redback a length and a quarter away in third, Zipping a further two and a half lengths back in fourth and Twilight Blues a neck further behind in fifth, a length ahead of Aramram, who was second home in the main group. The way the race developed made the latest Guineas a somewhat unsatisfactory renewal, with Hawk Wing looking most unlucky, having a huge amount to do two furlongs out but bursting clear of the main group inside the final furlong and only just failing to get up. The running of the Two Thousand Guineas is discussed in greater detail in the essay on Hawk Wing, suffice to record here that, notwithstanding the merit of the first two home, it was no more than an average renewal in terms of form.

With the prize-money, if not all the kudos, from the Two Thousand Guineas safely in the bag, Rock of Gibraltar was aimed at a Guineas double in the Entenmann's Irish Two Thousand Guineas three weeks later. Hawk Wing was by now earmarked for Epsom but 'Team Ballydoyle' still supplied eight of the eleven five-day declarations at the Curragh. Four of the eight eventually lined up, 7/4-on shot Rock of Gibraltar joined by Century City (6/1 second favourite), Della Francesca and Nostradamus, and opposed by Sights On Gold, runner-up to Century City in the Leopardstown Guineas Trial, Ahsanabad, third to High Chaparral in the Derrinstown Stud Derby Trial, and the only British challenger Foreign Accent, who had finished down the field in the Greenham. Rock of Gibraltar toyed with his rivals, scarcely knowing he had had a race in victory. Always moving easily, he cruised through from the back of the field to win as Kinane pleased, by a length and a half and three lengths from Century City and Della Francesca. For trainer Aidan O'Brien it was his fourth Irish Two Thousand Guineas winner in six years and the second year running that he had saddled the first three in the race. Having also won the Poule d'Essai des Poulains with Landseer, O'Brien also became the first trainer to complete the English, French and Irish Two Thousand Guineas treble in the same season.

Rock of Gibraltar became only the fifth horse to complete the Anglo-Irish Two Thousand Guineas double, following Right Tack in 1969, Don't Forget Me in 1987, Tirol in 1990 and Rodrigo de Triano in 1992. Although the Irish Two Thousand Guineas used to be a relatively parochial affair—Right Tack earned three times as much at Newmarket as he did at the Curragh—its elevation to a race of international significance has not led to the Guineas double being tackled so often as you might think. Only five other Two Thousand Guineas winners have gone on to attempt it, High Top, Nebbiolo, To-Agori-Mou, Lomond and Island Sands. Three of them were beaten at odds on, illustrating that victory is anything but a formality for an English Guineas winner. In fact, the subsequent careers of English Guineas winners in general in their classic season have tended to be anti-climactic in recent times, for various reasons. The Anglo-Irish Guineas double was just the start for Rock of Gibraltar, though. Following in the footsteps of Right Tack, Don't Forget Me and Rodrigo de Triano, the last-named also having taken in the Derby, Rock of Gibraltar appeared next at Royal Ascot in the St James's Palace Stakes. Only Right Tack had achieved the treble, Don't Forget Me and Rodrigo de Triano both finishing fourth. Rock of Gibraltar faced anything but a straightforward task on form, though he started at 5/4-on. He was up against his very smart stablemate Landseer and the Fabre-trained Bowman, a fast finishing third to Landseer in the Poule d'Essai des Poulains. Bowman was sent off second favourite at 4/1 in a field of nine for the St James's Palace which also included Dupont, who had landed the Guineas double in Italy and Germany, and three who had finished behind Rock of Gibraltar at Newmarket, Aramram, ninth-placed King of Happiness and eleventh-placed Where Or When. Rock of Gibraltar and Landseer provided another first and second in a Group 1 for Ballydoyle, whose classic colts were carrying all before them (High Chaparral and Hawk Wing had filled the first two places in the Derby). The patiently-ridden Rock of Gibraltar gave arguably his best performance, producing an excellent turn of foot to sweep aside Landseer entering the final furlong, winning largely under hands and heels by a length and three quarters, the first two pulling clear. Aramram came third, four lengths behind Landseer, with Dupont a neck away fourth, just ahead of Where Or When and Bowman. The early stages of the St James's Palace were not run at a breakneck gallop by any means, making Rock of Gibraltar's effort in cutting down the leaders in such striking style even more praiseworthy. Handicappers who rigidly adhere to the result, accepting the relationship between the horses as they cross the line in a race, are victims of self-imposed limitations. To say Rock of Gibraltar was 'probably better than anyone was able to rate him', as more than one leading handicapper did, is an abdication of responsibility. Rock of Gibraltar was a better horse than was simply reflected by the results of most of his races. Using time analysis to support observation and traditional handicapping methods, it is possible to quantify with a fair degree of accuracy how much better a horse like Rock of Gibraltar is than the bare result. We have rated Rock of Gibraltar as a four-length winner of the St James's Palace.

Rock of Gibraltar was relaxed in the preliminaries at Royal Ascot and settled very well in the race, showing not the slightest sign that the racing programme set for him might be starting to take its toll. The St James's Palace was the tenth race of Rock of Gibraltar's career which had begun with success in a maiden at the Curragh in the April of his two-year-old days. Landseer had made his debut even earlier, beaten at odds on in a blanket finish at Leopardstown before getting off the mark in May at Gowran. Both represented their stable in the Coventry Stakes at Royal Ascot, where Landseer won at 20/1 with 10/1-shot Rock of Gibraltar, repeatedly denied a run and one of the worst sufferers in an unsatisfactory race, back in sixth. Landseer's six races as a two-year-old included two good efforts in Group 1 company, including almost beating Rock of Gibraltar in the Dewhurst. The careers of both Rock of Gibraltar and Landseer, who landed a second big win as a three-year-old in the Turf Mile at Keeneland in October, were a credit to their trainer, who firmly believes in running the pick of his horses in the races designed to test the best two-year-olds, a policy that some think can damage a horse's classic potential. Thanks largely to Aidan O'Brien and Ballydoyle, the leading two-year-old that trains on to win a classic is no longer an endangered species.

Having showered the stock superlatives on Rock of Gibraltar at Royal Ascot, the reviewers might well have had to reach for a thesaurus after his next race, but for the fact that Michael Kinane virtually did their job for them. Rock of Gibraltar continued his triumphal progress with another splendid performance in

St James's Palace Stakes, Royal Ascot—Rock of Gibraltar produces an excellent turn of speed to account for yet another stable-companion, Landseer

Sussex Stakes, Goodwood—Rock of Gibraltar is much too good for the previous year's winner Noverre;
Reel Buddy takes third ahead of No Excuse Needed and the pacemaker Sahara Desert

the Sussex Stakes at Goodwood, his first encounter with some of the leading older milers, headed by Noverre and No Excuse Needed who had filled the first two places in the race as three-year-olds the previous year. The field of five included a pacemaker for odds-on Rock of Gibraltar, who would have faced a sterner test had the French-trained four-year-old Keltos, impressive conqueror of Noverre in the Lockinge, taken up his Sussex entry. Rock of Gibraltar could, however, do no more than win with ease against the best of those that took him on—and win with ease he did, closing effortlessly on the bridle after being waited with and cruising past Noverre inside the final furlong. Rock of Gibraltar treated the opposition like handicappers, winning without turning a hair by two lengths from Noverre, though the fact that the subsequent Hungerford winner Reel Buddy was only another two lengths behind in third limited the view that could be taken of the bare form. Kinane's post-race comment that Rock of Gibraltar had put up a 'great performance' and proved himself 'the ultimate racehorse' was widely reported, as was the trainer's announcement that either the Nunthorpe or the International at York was next on Rock of Gibraltar's agenda. The International trip looked likely to stretch Rock of Gibraltar's stamina to its limit, while the Nunthorpe offered the prospect of his tackling just about the sharpest test of the remaining top sprints. Either race would have given an opportunity to discover something new about Rock of Gibraltar, and an impressive victory might have added a little credence to the 'ultimate racehorse' tag.

In the end, Rock of Gibraltar missed York altogether in favour of a short rest, amid concerns over an outbreak of coughing in his stable. Rock of Gibraltar never caught the infection but there was nonetheless concern when he reappeared on the second Sunday in September in the NetJets Prix du Moulin de Longchamp. The stable's runners were still under a cloud after a number of reverses at Leopardstown the previous day, when the Coronation Stakes winner Sophistical had finished distressed and Hawk Wing had been beaten when an uneasy favourite for the Irish Champion; Landseer had beaten only one home in the Sprint Cup at Haydock. Bowman and the Irish One Thousand Guineas winner Gossamer were the other three-year-olds in the Moulin line-up (excepting Sahara Desert, acting for a third successive race as Rock of Gibraltar's pacemaker). With Keltos sidelined by illness and injury in August, which was to lead to premature retirement, the representatives of the classic generation faced their biggest challenge in the Moulin from the Prix Jacques le Marois winner Banks Hill. But neither she nor any of the others could prevent Rock of Gibraltar from extending his sequence of successive Group 1 victories to seven. He pounced in typical style, after looking to have plenty to do early in the straight, to win readily by half a length from Banks Hill, whose rider inadvertently struck Rock of Gibraltar over the head with his whip in the closing stages. Gossamer came a further length and a half behind in third, a neck ahead of Proudwings. One footnote to the Moulin was that armchair viewers in Britain did not have the chance to see Rock of Gibraltar's historic victory live because the BBC, which holds the rights to French racing, was committed to showing World Superbikes from Holland. The crowd at Longchamp also looked pitifully small.

The curtain effectively came down on Rock of Gibraltar's European racing career with the Prix du Moulin. He was declared for the Queen Elizabeth II Stakes at Ascot later in September, but only with the intention of replacing Hawk Wing if the going turned soft. Rock of Gibraltar accompanied Hawk Wing to Ascot and was galloped after racing as part of his preparation for the Breeders' Cup. The build-up to Arlington included speculation about whether Rock of Gibraltar would run in the Mile (on turf) or in the Classic (a mile and a quarter on dirt). Giant's Causeway had been touched off in the Classic in 2000 and Galileo had represented Ballydoyle in the race in 2001 (Hawk Wing was the stable's runner in 2002), but it always looked a fairly safe bet that Rock of Gibraltar would be kept to a mile. Arlington's sharp turf course is only a mile round with a run-in of just over a furlong and a half, but there seemed no reason to think that it would inconvenience Rock of Gibraltar, a straightforward, tractable racehorse with plenty of speed who could be put anywhere in a race. His reputation for invincibility preceded him to America, the record-breaking Breeders' Cup trainer D. Wayne Lukas, for example, saying that he was glad he didn't have a runner in the Mile because Rock of Gibraltar was 'a monster'. With only a short run of a hundred and twenty-five yards to the first turn, an inside draw was considered essential by the Americans and there was some concern when Rock of Gibraltar was drawn ten, towards the outside, in the field of fourteen, though he fared better than stablemate Landseer who was allotted stall thirteen. Sent off at odds on for the fifth race in a row, Rock of Gibraltar fractionally missed the break after becoming a little restless in the stalls and was at the back of the field going into the first turn. The runners usually go faster in the first half of the Mile than they did in the latest renewal and it was a little surprising that Kinane, riding a little over confidently, was content to remain on the rail at the rear of the field for most of the back straight. As the race began in earnest approaching the home turn Rock of Gibraltar was still last but one and, to compound matters, he had to dodge the stricken Landseer who suffered a fatal injury entering the straight. Once in the clear and fully opened out, Rock of Gibraltar unleashed a tremendous run down the outside, sprinting past rival after rival, and making up five or six lengths on the leader, Good Journey. He was making no further ground on the winner as the post was reached, however, and finished three quarters of a length adrift of the more handily ridden Domedriver.

Inevitably, the critics rounded on Kinane at Arlington, particularly the American experts who were vitriolic (the view of one of them is reproduced in the essay on Domedriver). Another way of looking at Kinane's handling of his mount,

NetJets Prix du Moulin de Longchamp, Longchamp—
Rock of Gibraltar becomes the first horse to win seven Group 1 races in succession since the European pattern was introduced in 1971; Banks Hill is second and Gossamer (right) snatches third from Proudwings

however, is that he employed more or less the same tactics that had proved successful in most of Rock of Gibraltar's earlier races and was simply unlucky the way the race went. Even after the steadier than usual early pace, Rock of Gibraltar might still have won—though only narrowly—had the momentum of his finishing run not been affected by the sudden manoeuvre to avoid Landseer. Punters were left to lick their wounds but Rock of Gibraltar's failure to extend his run of consecutive Group 1s scarcely harmed his reputation or his stud value. Rock of Gibraltar was widely hailed as the moral victor of the Breeders' Cup Mile, though it seemed incongruous that defeat in a race he was expected to win should be hailed in some quarters as his finest moment, one newspaper going so far as to ask whether any race had ever witnessed such equine heroics! His inclusion as one of the four nominees in the Eclipse awards for Horse of the Year in the US was greeted with derision by leading trainer Bob Baffert. Unlike his stable-companion Hawk Wing, probably still best remembered at the end of the season for his unfortunate Guineas defeat, Rock of Gibraltar needed no prop to support his reputation. Hawk Wing might have been regarded by many close to Ballydoyle as the better horse for much of the season, but the durable and reliable Rock of Gibraltar kept on delivering the goods, thriving on his work and looking more impressive with almost every race. In a splendid campaign, he trained on into a top-class performer, one of the best milers of the last fifteen years or so. He was held up to make fullest use of an excellent turn of foot which became one of the hallmarks of his three-year-old career. He wasn't beholden to the state of the going, showing form on ground ranging from soft to good to firm. It goes almost without saying that the hardy *Timeform* epithet 'tough, genuine and consistent' fits Rock of Gibraltar to a T. He won ten of his thirteen races, his only other defeat, apart from those in the Coventry and Breeders' Cup Mile, coming when Dubai Destination beat him comfortably by a length in receipt of 4 lb in the Champagne Stakes at Doncaster. Few at that time, outside his connections, could possibly have envisaged Rock of Gibraltar's scaling the heights he subsequently reached.

The close-coupled, medium-sized Rock of Gibraltar is by no means an imposing individual and he appeared not to grow much between two and three. Both he and the ill-fated Landseer were sired by the prolific Danzig stallion Danehill, a high-class sprinter who also finished third in the Two Thousand Guineas. By coincidence, Landseer's Poule d'Essai des Poulains win came on the day that another top horse by Danehill, the leading sprinter of 2001 Mozart, died at Coolmore. Rock of Gibraltar will replace him there in the next season, standing alongside Danehill, who was runner-up to Sadler's Wells in most of the sires' tables for 2002. There is no disgrace in having to play second fiddle to Sadler's Wells, though Danehill did have the distinction of outscoring his illustrious fellow Coolmore stallion by twenty-four victories to twenty-two—only one other stallion recorded double figures—in European pattern races in the latest season. Aquarelliste, Banks Hill, Danehurst, Dress To Thrill, Irresistible Jewel and Spartacus were also among Danehill's thirteen individual European pattern scorers in 2002.

Rock of Gibraltar is out of Offshore Boom and is aptly-named, the British colony earning notoriety as a 'tax free' betting haven when Victor Chandler set up there in 1999. Offshore Boom, who has the same grandsire—Northern Dancer—as Danehill, was weeded out of the Moyglare Stud as a twelve-year-old in 1997 when Rock of Gibraltar's trainer, together with his wife and father-in-law, picked her up for only IR 11,000 guineas, carrying her sixth foal. That offspring, a filly by Definite Article subsequently named D'Articleshore, passed through the sale-ring as a foal for only 3,500 guineas before enjoying plenty of success in Turkey and becoming Offshore Boom's fifth winner. Offshore Boom, a useful two-year-old herself when successful over six furlongs in Ireland, visited six different stallions in her time at Moyglare Stud and the best of the rest of a motley collection of winners before Rock of Gibraltar was probably the modest Irish mile- to mile-and-a-quarter winner Eloquent Way, a daughter of the sprinter Dowsing. Offshore Boom was represented in the latest season by a two-year-old full brother to Rock of Gibraltar, the useful Great Pyramid (also in training with O'Brien), and there is also a yearling colt by Danehill. Their grandam Push A Button won a minor race over six furlongs as a two-year-old and bred five winners in all, including the one-time useful sprinter-miler Winning Venture and the Irish mile-and-a-quarter winner Outside

Sir Alex Ferguson & Mrs John Magnier's "Rock of Gibraltar"

Pressure, who was successful in listed company. Of more significance, however, is that Push A Button was a half-sister to the top-class racehorse and sire Riverman.

Rock of Gibraltar (IRE) (b.c. 1999)	Danehill (USA) (b 1986)	Danzig (b 1977)	Northern Dancer Pas de Nom
		Razyana (b 1981)	His Majesty Spring Adieu
	Offshore Boom (ch 1985)	Be My Guest (ch 1974)	Northern Dancer What A Treat
		Push A Button (b 1980)	Bold Lad River Lady

The Coolmore stallions, whom Rock of Gibraltar joins in 2003, work hard for a living and Rock of Gibraltar's sound constitution looks sure to be tested. Galileo covered one hundred and fifty-seven mares in his first season at Coolmore in 2002 and was also 'shuttled' to cover in the southern hemisphere. Given Danehill's standing in Australasia, where he made his name as a top sire—he has been champion five times—long before he became established as such in Europe, it seems likely that dual-hemisphere covering seasons will be on the agenda for Rock of Gibraltar. His part-owner Sir Alex Ferguson, who bought a share in the horse for an undisclosed sum after the Coventry Stakes, is no stranger to sporting success, but he will surely never make a more lucrative signing than the one that resulted in Rock of Gibraltar carrying his racing colours. *A. P. O'Brien, Ireland*

ROCKON ARRY 3 b.g. Aragon 118 – Rockstine (IRE) 61 (Ballad Rock 122) [2002 50: f6s⁴ 6d 7.1v Jun 14] strong, workmanlike gelding: modest maiden at 2 yrs: well held, including in seller, in 2002: reportedly had breathing problem second 2-y-o start. *K. Bell* –

ROCKSPUR (IRE) 2 b.f. (Feb 1) Flying Spur (AUS) – Over The Rocks (Salmon Leap (USA) 131) [2002 5.1d⁵ 6m 5.7g⁵ 6g 7.5g 6g³ f6g⁵ p8g Nov 23] IR 1,000F, IR 59 §

830

4,200Y: seventh foal: half-sister to winners in Italy and Hong Kong, both at 1m by Case Law: dam, ran once, half-sister to Derby third Rankin: modest maiden: stays 6f: yet to race on extremes of going on turf, below form on all-weather: visored last 3 starts: usually starts slowly. *Mrs P. N. Dutfield*

ROCK THE NATION   3 b.f. Makbul 104 – Miss Sarajane 74 (Skyliner 117) [2002   **55 ?** 6f⁶ f7g 8.2m⁶ 10m 8m Sep 19] 650F: lengthy, sparely-made filly: third foal: dam effective at 1m to 1¼m: modest maiden: left D. Shaw and off 4 months after third start: stays 1m: slowly away first 2 outings. *J. G. Given*

RODEO DRIVE (IRE)   2 b.f. (Feb 26) Spectrum (IRE) 126 – Royalsadler's (IRE)   **68 d** (Sadler's Wells (USA) 132) [2002 5g f6g³ 6g* 6d 6g 7d* 7m 7.1m³ 8m⁶ 7f 7g p8g Nov 19] 11,500F, 27,000Y: rather leggy, close-coupled filly: second foal: dam unraced: fair performer: won maiden at Leicester in June and nursery at Newmarket in August: ran badly last 3 starts: probably stays 1m: acts on good to soft and good to firm going: sold 6,000 gns. *N. A. Callaghan*

RODIAK   3 b.g. Distant Relative 128 – Misty Silks 81 (Scottish Reel 123) [2002 59:   **52** 8.2d 7f⁶ 8.1s 6.1v⁶ 7m⁴ 7m 11.5s* Oct 22] good-topped gelding: poor mover: modest performer: upped in trip, won selling handicap at Yarmouth in October: stays 11.5f: acts on heavy going, probably on good to firm: tried visored/blinkered (not at Yarmouth): tended to hang fourth outing/carried head high next time. *Bob Jones*

RO ERIDANI   2 b.f. (Mar 5) Binary Star (USA) – Hat Hill (Roan Rocket 128) [2002   **–** 7m Oct 5] well-made filly: half-sister to several winners, including 7f winner City Rocket (by King of Spain) and 1998 2-y-o 6f winner Missing Ted (by Formidable): dam ran 4 times: 50/1, well held in maiden at Redcar. *T. J. Etherington*

ROGER ROSS   7 b.g. Touch of Grey 90 – Foggy Dew 45 (Smoggy 115) [2002 –§,   **– §** a44§: 8d 9s 7d 8g Jun 17] small, good-bodied gelding: temperamental handicapper: often blinkered. *R. M. Flower*

ROGUE SPIRIT   6 b.g. Petong 126 – Quick Profit 78 (Formidable (USA) 125) [2002   **58 §** –§: p13g p16g* p12g p12g⁴ f16.2g Jul 12] modest performer: won seller at Lingfield in January: left R. Strange after next start: stays easy 2m: acts on good to firm going, good to soft and polytrack: tried blinkered (including at Lingfield): sometimes rears badly stall, including when unseating third outing: unreliable. *S. L. Keightley*

ROI DE DANSE   7 ch.g. Komaite (USA) – Princess Lucy 42 (Local Suitor (USA) 128)   **–** [2002 –, a56: 8.3g Apr 15] lengthy, workmanlike gelding: modest performer at 6 yrs: well held only outing in 2002: tried visored earlier in career. *Miss Z. C. Davison*

ROISTERER   6 ch.g. Rudimentary (USA) 118 – Raffle 82 (Balidar 133) [2002 26,   **–** a35: f5s³ f6g Feb 5] poor maiden handicapper: best at 5f/6f: acts on soft going, good to   **a35** firm and fibresand: often blinkered: has started slowly/raced freely. *D. W. Chapman*

ROJABAA   3 b.g. Anabaa (USA) 130 – Slava (USA) (Diesis 133) [2002 47: 10m f8.5g   **45** p10g 11.7f⁵ 8f 10g 10d Oct 28] lengthy gelding: poor maiden: appears to stay 1¼m. *W. G. M. Turner*

ROLEX FREE (ARG)   4 ch.g. Friul (ARG) – Karolera (ARG) (Kaljerry (ARG))   **?** [2002 a9f² a12.5f a10f* 12f a12.5f p10g⁶ Dec 11] fifth known foal: half-brother to winners in Argentina by Ski Champ and Il Corsano: dam unraced: winner of maiden and minor event from 11 outings in Argentina (unraced at 2 yrs): well held in minor event at Lingfield on British debut final outing: won at 1m and 1¼m: acts on dirt and firm ground. *Mrs L. C. Taylor*

ROLLER   6 b.g. Bluebird (USA) 125 – Tight Spin (High Top 131) [2002 58, a55: f8.5g   **49 §** f8s³ f8.5g⁵ f8g f8.5g⁵ 7v⁴ 7m⁵ 8.3s⁶ 8d f8.5s Dec 26] useful-looking gelding: poor mover: poor performer: effective at 7f to easy 1¼m: has form on firm going/fibresand, but goes well on softer than good (acts on heavy): usually blinkered: sometimes pulls hard/starts slowly/runs in snatches: irresolute. *J. M. Bradley*

ROMAN BOY (ARG)   3 ch.c. Roy (USA) – Roman Red (USA) (Blushing Groom   **72** (FR) 131) [2002 6.1d 7g² 8.1d² 7m² 8.1m* 8.1g⁴ 8f Sep 17] half-brother to several winners in Argentina/USA: dam unraced daughter of Argentinian 1000 Guineas winner Manzanera: fair performer: won maiden at Warwick (despite drifting right) in July: stays 1m: acts on good to firm and good to soft ground: races freely. *B. R. Millman*

ROMAN CHIEF   3 b.c. Forzando 122 – Red Cloud (IRE) 61 (Taufan (USA) 119)   **– §** [2002 47§: f9.4g Jun 22] poor maiden at 2 yrs: well held only outing in 2002: virtually refused to race in blinkers second 2-y-o start. *D. Haydn Jones*

ROMANCING   3 b.f. Dr Devious (IRE) 127 – Polish Romance (USA) 83 (Danzig   **79** (USA)) [2002 f9.4g⁴ p10g⁶ 10d² 8.3d⁴ Jul 19] first foal: dam, 7f winner, not one to trust implicitly: fair form in maidens: best effort when second at Pontefract: stays 1¼m: sometimes flashes tail: temperament under suspicion. *Sir Mark Prescott*

ROMAN EMPIRE 2 b.g. (Apr 1) Efisio 120 – Gena Ivor (USA) (Sir Ivor 135) [2002 6m 6d 7d Nov 5] 6,200 2-y-o: lengthy, good-bodied gelding: seventh foal: half-brother to fairly useful 1997 2-y-o 5f winner Call To Order (by Reprimand) and unreliable 7f winner Ivor's Deed (by Shadeed): dam won up to 9f in USA: signs of a little ability in maidens, starting slowly each time. *T. J. Etherington* —

ROMAN KING (IRE) 7 b.g. Sadler's Wells (USA) 132 – Romantic Feeling 88 (Shirley Heights 130) [2002 92: 12m 12m 10g 10.5s⁵ 10.1d⁵ Jul 4] sturdy gelding: fairly useful handicapper at best: well held in 2002. *Mrs M. Reveley* —

ROMAN MISTRESS (IRE) 2 ch.f. (Apr 7) Titus Livius (FR) 115 – Repique (USA) 88 (Sharpen Up 127) [2002 5d⁴ 5s* 5m² 5.2f 6m 6m² 7m³ 6m⁵ 5m³ 7f 6g Oct 17] 17,000Y: smallish, angular filly: seventh foal: half-sister to useful Irish 5f winner Give A Whistle (by Mujadil): dam, 6f/7f winner, half-sister to high-class 7f to 9f performer Indian Lodge: fair performer: won maiden at Newcastle in June: mostly creditable efforts after: barely stays 7f: acts on soft and good to firm going: blinkered last 6 starts: weak finisher. *T. D. Easterby* 77

ROMANNIE (BEL) 3 b.f. Piccolo 121 – Green Land (BEL) 72 (Hero's Honor (USA)) [2002 –: 7m 10g 11.8m⁶ 11.6m 12m⁶ 10g³ f9.4g² 11m 8m⁶ 9m f11g Dec 17] poor maiden: stays 1½m: acts on good to firm going and fibresand: reportedly found to have sore shins on reappearance. *G. M. Moore* 46

ROMAN QUINTET (IRE) 2 ch.c. (Apr 9) Titus Livius (FR) 115 – Quintellina 83 (Robellino (USA) 127) [2002 7m³ 7.1g p6g⁴ Dec 28] 15,000F, 9,200Y: second foal: half-brother to fairly useful Irish 2001 2-y-o 7f winner Nutley King (by Night Shift): dam 2-y-o 7f winner: best effort in maidens (fair form) when fourth at Lingfield: likely to prove best at 5f/6f. *D. W. P. Arbuthnot* 73

ROMANTIC LIASON 2 b.f. (Jan 12) Primo Dominie 121 – My First Romance 61 (Danehill (USA) 126) [2002 p5g* 5m* 6m³ Aug 22] 108 p
    The latest season saw Pat Eddery pass Lester Piggott to go into second place behind Sir Gordon Richards on the all-time jockeys' list in Britain. Eleven-times champion Eddery equalled Piggott's total of 4,493 domestic winners on Romantic Liason in the Queen Mary Stakes at Royal Ascot, leaving him with 377 to go to reach Richards' total. Eddery is still going strongly at fifty and showed his appetite for winners by continuing to ride after the end of the turf season in an attempt—he failed by one—to reach a hundred winners in a season for the twenty-ninth time (Piggott previously held the record for most centuries with twenty-five). Eddery enjoyed something of an armchair ride on Romantic Liason at Royal Ascot, where the pair turned what had looked a wide-open renewal into a one-horse race. It was a typical Queen Mary field with the vast majority of the nineteen runners looking open to improvement, including Romantic Liason, who had made a winning debut in a maiden on the polytrack at Lingfield at the end of May. It would have been unthinkable a few years ago that a two-year-old pattern winner would start out on the all-weather—Dublin and Elusive City were others who began their careers in similar fashion in the latest season. Romantic Liason dominated her rivals at Royal Ascot as clearly as she did in the paddock, putting up one of the best performances

Queen Mary Stakes, Royal Ascot—Romantic Liason enables Pat Eddery to equal Lester Piggott's career total of winners; Never A Doubt hangs on for second in front of Rag Top (rail) and Speed Cop

in the Queen Mary in recent times, quickening most impressively and winning by three and a half lengths and a neck from Never A Doubt and the favourite Rag Top. The well-made Romantic Liason had lots of physical scope and she changed hands after Royal Ascot, bought by Sheikh Mohammed in a private deal which guaranteed she would stay with her present trainer until the end of her two-year-old days. Romantic Liason looked purely and simply a two-year-old five-furlong filly on her Queen Mary performance and she did not quite see out the sixth furlong when third in the Lowther Stakes at York on her only subsequent start. Travelling strongly under restraint (ridden by Dettori) she looked sure to capitalise when the odds-on Russian Rhythm met trouble in running in the last two furlongs. But Romantic Liason couldn't hold off the extricated Russian Rhythm after leading inside the final furlong, and was run out of second close home by Danaskaya. Romantic Liason looked in excellent shape at York and it was surprising to see her put by for the season. She will be back under the Godolphin banner as a three-year-old when she should be a force to be reckoned with in sprint pattern races.

Romantic Liason (b.f. Jan 12, 2000)	Primo Dominie (b 1982)	Dominion (b 1972)	Derring-Do
			Picture Palace
		Swan Ann (ch 1971)	My Swanee
			Anna Barry
	My First Romance (b 1992)	Danehill (b 1986)	Danzig
			Razyana
		Front Line Romance (ch 1987)	Caerleon
			Bottom Line

Sheikh Mohammed's "Romantic Liason"

Romantic Liason, a 70,000-guinea yearling, is bred for speed, by the very smart sprinter Primo Dominie out of the twice-raced Danehill mare My First Romance who is the dam of another Queen Mary winner in Romantic Myth (by Mind Games). Romantic Liason is the fourth foal out of My First Romance. All four have won, and Romantic Liason became the dam's third Royal Ascot winner, following the success on the opening day of the latest Royal meeting of the fairly useful Zargus (by Zamindar) in the five-furlong Balmoral Handicap. My First Romance's first foal Power Packed (by Mind Games' sire Puissance) won over five furlongs as a juvenile and was successful at six as a four-year-old in Sweden. *B. J. Meehan*

ROMANY FAIR (IRE) 3 b.g. Blues Traveller (IRE) 119 – Fantasticus (IRE) 78 – (Lycius (USA) 124) [2002 –: f9.4g f8g⁵ 12g⁶ May 18] little form. *W. S. Cunningham*

ROMANY NIGHTS (IRE) 2 b.g. (Feb 23) Night Shift (USA) – Gipsy Moth 99 **80** (Efisio 120) [2002 5.6m* 5.2f⁴ 5f³ 5m⁴ 6m Sep 13] 8,000 2-y-o: first foal: dam, 5f performer, half-sister to useful 1m winner Heavenly Whisper from family of Kerrera and Rock City: tardy useful performer: won maiden at Doncaster in June: good efforts in nurseries at Kempton and Sandown third and fourth outings: should stay at least 6f: raced only on ground firmer than good: sold 7,500 gns. *R. M. Beckett*

ROMANY PRINCE 3 b.g. Robellino (USA) 127 – Vicki Romara 83 (Old Vic 136) **101** [2002 10s⁵ 12s* 12f² 14f³ 16s Oct 25] 42,000F: rangy gelding: has scope: first foal: dam, 2m winner, half-sister to very smart Lowther/Nassau Stakes winner Ela Romara: useful performer: won maiden at Newmarket in August: very good head second to Starzaan in handicap at Kempton following month: well held final outing: should stay 2m: won on soft going, best runs on firm. *D. R. C. Elsworth*

ROMIL STAR (GER) 5 b.g. Chief's Crown (USA) – Romelia (USA) (Woodman **71** (USA) 126) [2002 f12g² 12g² f12s⁴ f12s² Dec 9] first foal: dam placed in Germany around 1m/9f: won maiden at Dortmund at 3 yrs and handicap at Hanover at 4 yrs when trained by P. Rau in Germany: fair form in 2002: stays 1½m: acts on heavy going and fibresand. *R. D. Wylie*

RONDINAY (FR) 2 ch.f. (Mar 17) Cadeaux Genereux 131 – Topline (GER) (Acate- **77** nango (GER) 127) [2002 6s⁵ 6m⁵ 6d 6f* 7s Oct 26] 1,000,000 francs Y: strong, close-coupled filly: fifth foal: half-sister to German 1m winner Tabita (by Alzao) and 1¼m/11.5f winner in Germany/France Titus Manius (by Be My Guest): dam, German 1¼m/1½m winner, half-sister to German performers Turfkonig (very smart up to 1½m) and Tryphosa (smart at 1m/1¼m): fair performer: dictated pace when winning maiden at Newmarket in October: well held in listed event at Newbury final start: should stay at least 7f: acts on firm ground: found little third outing. *R. Hannon*

RONNIE FROM DONNY (IRE) 2 b.c. (Feb 28) Eagle Eyed (USA) 111 – New **76** Rochelle (IRE) 65 (Lafontaine (USA) 117) [2002 5s³ 5s⁶ f5g² 5m 5.1f⁴ 6g 7m f6s f6g* **a81** f6s² Dec 13] 9,500Y: sturdy, useful-looking colt: fourth foal: closely related to 1999 2-y-o 1m seller winner Tower of Song (by Perugino) and half-brother to 3-y-o Kool: dam, Irish 1¾m winner at 5 yrs, sister to smart 1½m to 2m performer Shambo: fairly useful on all-weather, fair on turf: left J. Given before winning maiden at Wolverhampton in November: ran well final start: best at 5f/6f: acts on firm ground, soft and fibresand: often races up with pace: sometimes wanders. *B. Ellison*

RON'S PET 7 ch.g. Ron's Victory (USA) 129 – Penny Mint 79 (Mummy's Game 120) – [2002 6s, a70: f7s p8g² f8.5g f7g⁵ f7g⁵ p8g f7g⁴ f7g⁶ 8m Apr 27] tall gelding: modest **a62 d** performer: below form after second start: effective at 7f/1m: acts on all-weather: blink-ered: usually tongue tied: tends to carry head high: usually races prominently. *P. D. Evans*

ROOFER (IRE) 4 b.f. Barathea (IRE) 127 – Castlerahan (IRE) (Thatching 131) **70 d** [2002 78: 8s 10.9g⁴ 11.6g 11.7g 10m 10.2d 9m 8m 9g Oct 5] tall, rather angular filly: fair maiden handicapper: generally on downgrade in 2002, leaving B. R. Millman after sixth outing: stays 9f: acts on soft and good to firm going: tongue tied second to sixth starts (breathing problem on reappearance): tends to start slowly/carry head awkwardly. *Miss K. M. George*

ROOFTOP 6 b.g. Thatching 131 – Top Berry 87 (High Top 131) [2002 –: 8f 12f 12m – 12.4g Aug 7] one-time fair maiden: no form since 2000: often visored/blinkered prior to 2002. *W. Storey*

ROOFTOP ROMANCE 3 ch.f. Pursuit of Love 124 – Singer On The Roof 62 **37** (Chief Singer 131) [2002 –: f7s p6g⁶ f6g p5g⁵ p5g 5d 5.3m 7f 5.9d 6g Jul 6] angular filly: poor maiden: bred to stay 1m: visored. *D. Shaw*

ROOKWITH (IRE)   2 b.c. (Mar 7) Revoque (IRE) 122 – Resume (IRE) 69 (Lahib **60** (USA) 129) [2002 6g 7g[6] 7.5d[6] 7.1d[5] 7m[6] 8m 6f[6] f7g[2] p7g p7g Dec 14) 16,000Y: tall colt: **a72** first foal: dam, Irish 1½m and 2m winner, half-sister to useful 6f to 1m performer Baaderah: fair maiden on all-weather, modest on turf: second at Southwell: should stay at least 1m: acts on firm going, good to soft and all-weather: blinkered last 5 starts. *J. D. Bethell*

ROOM ENOUGH   2 b.g. (Apr 1) Muhtarram (USA) 125 – Salsita (Salse (USA) 128) **–** [2002 7d f7g Nov 16] 8,000F, 6,000Y: close-coupled gelding: fourth foal: half-brother to 2000 2-y-o 7f winner Nun Left (by Bishop of Cashel): dam won 3 times (including at 2 yrs) in Spain: well held in maidens. *R. M. Beckett*

ROPES OF TIME (IRE)   3 b.f. Sadler's Wells (USA) 132 – Twine (Thatching 131) **–** [2002 77: 12m[4] 11.9d[6] 14d 12.6m[4] Jun 22] sister to Irish 1¾m winner Martial Eagle, and half-sister to several winners, including very smart winner around 1¼m Alderbrook (by Ardross, also won Champion Hurdle) and smart 7f to 9f winner Restructure (by Dane-hill): dam unraced: fair maiden at 2 yrs for A. O'Brien in Ireland: well held in 2002: blinkered final start. *J. W. Hills*

ROPPONGI DANCER   3 b.f. Mtoto 134 – Ice Chocolate (USA) 77 (Icecapade **44** (USA)) [2002 –: 12d 12m[3] 14.1f 12m Jul 1] small, quite good-topped filly: poor maiden: stays 1½m. *Mrs M. Reveley*

ROSA PARKS   3 b.f. Sadler's Wells (USA) 132 – Free At Last 115 (Shirley Heights **103** 130) [2002 12m[2] 10.5d* 11.9m[2] 10.1m[3] 10g 12d[2] 10d[6] Nov 17] good-topped, attractive filly: fifth foal: sister to fairly useful 1¼m winner Freedom Now and half-sister to 1¼m

The Leigh Family's "Rosa Parks"

winner Coretta (by Caerleon), later smart winner up to 1½m in USA, and useful 1¼m winner Trumpet Sound (by Theatrical): dam, 2-y-o 7f winner and fourth in 1000 Guineas (later stakes winner up to 1½m in USA), half-sister to Barathea and Gossamer (both by Sadler's Wells): useful performer: won maiden at Haydock in August: best efforts after when placed in listed races at York (2½ lengths second to Alexander Three D), Yarmouth (¾-length third to Miss Corniche) and Milan (length second behind Kiltubber): stays 1½m: yet to race on extremes of going: sent to USA. *L. M. Cumani*

ROSE D'OR (IRE) 3 b.f. Polish Precedent (USA) 131 – Gold Rose (FR) (Noblequest (FR) 124) [2002 65p: 10g 10g 8.2m⁴ 8.2m³ 8m⁵ 8.2v⁵ p10g Nov 27] tall, leggy filly: fair maiden: stays 1¼m: acts on good to firm ground, found little on heavy: blinkered final outing. *J. L. Dunlop* — 69

ROSE HEDGE (GER) 2 gr.f. (Apr 7) Highest Honor (FR) 124 – Roseate Wood (FR) 110 (Kaldoun (FR) 122) [2002 6f Sep 8] approx. 62,000Y in Germany: second foal: dam German 5f/6f winner who stayed 1m: 7/1, made running when well held in maiden at Kempton: likely to do better. *M. R. Channon* — – p

ROSEMEAD MARY 3 b.f. Keen 116 – Arasong 76 (Aragon 118) [2002 43: 7f 9.3s May 27] poor maiden at 2 yrs: last on both outings in 2002: tried blinkered. *M. Dods* — –

ROSE OF AMERICA 4 ch.f. Brief Truce (USA) 126 – Kilcoy (USA) (Secreto (USA) 128) [2002 81: 8g 7g 7m 8d 7m 8g 8m² 7.1m* 8m² 8.9f 8s⁵ Nov 6] big, strong filly: fairly useful handicapper: won at Musselburgh in September: best at 7f/1m: acts on firm going: free-going sort: has edged right/carried head awkwardly: held up. *Miss L. A. Perratt* — 81

ROSES FLUTTER 3 b.f. Son Pardo 107 – Silent Scream (IRE) (Lahib (USA) 129) [2002 –: 7f 5m Jul 18] well held in maidens/handicap: tried tongue tied: wayward and probably ungenuine. *P. R. Wood* — – §

ROSES OF SPRING 4 gr.f. Shareef Dancer (USA) 135 – Couleur de Rose (Kalaglow 132) [2002 82: f6g f5g p6g 6g 6g 6g 7m 5m² 6m 6f 6m² 5m* 5f 5m⁴ 5.1g f6g p6g³ f5g p5g* Dec 21] lengthy filly: fairly useful handicapper: won at Leicester in September, and dead-heated at Lingfield in December: best at 5f/easy 6f: acts on firm ground and all-weather: visored once: has won in cheekpieces: tongue tied after sixth start: sometimes slowly away/carries head high: usually races prominently. *R. M. H. Cowell* — 80

ROSE TEA (IRE) 3 ro.f. Alhaarth (IRE) 126 – Shakamiyn (Nishapour (FR) 125) [2002 10f⁶ 10m⁵ p10g 10m 11.8s Oct 15] 41,000Y: leggy, plain filly: fifth foal: half-sister to 11f to 2m winner Shakiyr (by Lashkari) and winner in Turkey by Marju: dam unraced half-sister to high-class French middle-distance performer Shakapour and to dam of Derby winner Shahrastani: edgy, easily best effort (fair form) when fifth in maiden at Sandown second start: ran as though something amiss penultimate outing: should stay at least 1½m. *N. A. Graham* — 69 ?

ROSETTA 5 b.m. Fraam 114 – Starawak 68 (Star Appeal 133) [2002 43+: f7g⁴ f8.5g⁶ p7g p6g Feb 6] leggy, sparely-made mare: bad maiden: effective at 6f to 1m: acts on good to firm ground, well held on softer than good: sometimes gets behind. *R. J. Hodges* — 29

ROSETTA ROEBUCK 2 b.f. (Apr 24) Fleetwood (IRE) 107 – Alwal (Pharly (FR) 130) [2002 7m⁵ 8s Oct 25] big, workmanlike filly: fourth foal: half-sister to 6-y-o Quedex: dam won 4 races in Holland, including Dutch Oaks: green, modest form when fifth in maiden at Folkestone: off 4 months, soundly beaten in similar event at Doncaster. *A. P. Jarvis* — 57

ROSEWINGS 2 b.f. (Mar 6) In The Wings 128 – Calvia Rose (Sharpo 132) [2002 8g 8g 7d⁶ Nov 5] IR 12,000Y: third foal: dam, unraced, closely related to 8.5f to 1¼m winner Dusty Dollar and half-sister to 1m to 11f winner Kind of Hush, both smart: modest form at best in maidens: should be suited by 1¼m+. *M. H. Tompkins* — 59

ROSEWOOD BELLE (USA) 4 ch.f. Woodman (USA) 126 – Supreme Excellence (USA) (Providential 118) [2002 70: 11.6d 13.1g 16m Jun 24] workmanlike filly: fair maiden at 3 yrs: well held in 2002: visored final start. *W. R. Muir* — –

ROSEY GLOW 2 b.f. (Feb 28) Elmaamul (USA) 125 – Red Rosein 97 (Red Sunset 120) [2002 5m⁵ 5m³ 5s 5g⁶ 7g Oct 19] 32,000 2-y-o: quite good-topped filly: fifth foal: half-sister to 3 winners, including 4-y-o Proud Boast and 6-y-o Young Rosein: dam, tough sprinter, won Wokingham: modest maiden: likely to prove best at 5f/6f: sometimes gives trouble in preliminaries (withdrawn as a result once): wore hood final start: needs treating with caution. *Mrs G. S. Rees* — 58

ROSIE'S POSY (IRE)   3 b.f. Suave Dancer (USA) 136 – My Branch 111 (Distant **84** Relative 128) [2002 86p: 8g⁶ 7g 7.1d⁶ 7d Jul 9] rather leggy, close-coupled filly: fairly useful form: easily best effort in 2002 when sixth in listed event at Kempton on reappearance: should stay 1¼m: sold 2,200 gns. *B. W. Hills*

ROSIE'S RESULT   2 ch.g. (Apr 10) Case Law 113 – Precious Girl 76 (Precious **73 d** Metal 106) [2002 5g 5m* 5f² 5m⁵ 5.1f 5g⁶ 5m Sep 16] sparely-made gelding: third foal: half-brother to 4-y-o Cark: dam 5f/6f winner, including at 2 yrs: fair performer: won maiden at Ripon in April: well below form last 3 starts (visored final one): raced only at 5f on good going or firmer. *M. Todhunter*

ROSIE STARLIGHT (IRE)   4 b.f. Tagula (IRE) 116 – Idrak 68 (Young Generation **58** 129) [2002 58: 5m⁴ 5.1d² 5m Jun 24] small filly: modest maiden: effective at 5f/6f: acts on firm and good to soft ground. *D. Nicholls*

ROSI'S BOY   4 b.g. Caerleon (USA) 132 – Come On Rosi 77 (Valiyar 129) [2002 109: **106 §** 9m 10.3f⁴ 9.9d⁶ 10s Nov 5] smallish, well-made gelding: useful performer: not entirely discredited in listed races at Chester and Goodwood second and third starts: left J. Dunlop before final outing: effective at 1m/1¼m: acts on firm and good to soft going: tried visored/blinkered: held up: has been reluctant to go to post/behind stalls: temperamental. *J-P. Delaporte, France*

ROSKILDE (IRE)   2 br.c. (Mar 13) Danehill (USA) 126 – Melisendra (FR) (Highest **98** Honor (FR) 124) [2002 6d⁵ 6s² 6d³ 7m* 7f³ 8g⁴ 8m* 7m⁶ Sep 15] rather angular colt: second foal: half-brother to 3-y-o Murray: dam, useful French 5.5f (at 2 yrs) to 1m winner, out of smart French middle-distance performer Noble Tiara: useful performer: won maiden at Redcar in July and minor event at Salisbury (by 1¼ lengths from Alasil, dictating pace) in September: creditable sixth of 7 to Refuse To Bend in National Stakes at the Curragh: stays 1m: acts on firm going, probably on soft. *M. R. Channon*

ROSSELLINI (USA)   2 b.f. (Feb 5) Spinning World (USA) 130 – Camilla B (USA) **78 p** (Chief's Crown (USA)) [2002 7f Oct 3] $250,000: quite good-topped filly: second foal: dam unraced half-sister to very smart miler Among Men: 14/1 and burly, not given hard time after chasing leaders when ninth of 26 to Desert Star in maiden at Newmarket: sure to do better. *Sir Michael Stoute*

ROSSELLI (USA)   6 b.g. Puissance 110 – Miss Rossi (Artaius (USA) 129) [2002 **66 §** 103d: 6f³ 6d⁶ 5g⁶ 6f 7.1s⁵ 6m 7g 7.1d 5.7g² 6g⁵ 6.1g 6v 5.7f 7.2s⁵ 6m 7m 5.1f 6m² 7m⁴ 6f³ f6g Nov 26] tall, good-topped gelding: one-time useful miler: suffered suspensory and sesamoid injuries in 1999: fair on balance nowadays: stays 7f: acts on any ground: usually races prominently: sometimes blinkered/visored (not in 2002): has had tongue tied: sometimes early to post: unreliable. *A. Berry*

ROSS GELLER   2 ch.g. (Apr 4) Case Law 113 – Enchanting Eve 67 (Risk Me (FR) **–** 127) [2002 6d 7g Oct 17] 800F: angular gelding: first foal: dam 5f (at 2 yrs) to 1m winner who stayed 1¼m: well held in sellers. *C. N. Allen*

ROS THE BOSS (IRE)   3 b.f. Danehill (USA) 126 – Bella Vitessa (IRE) (Thatching **80** 131) [2002 –: 5g 7m² 8m* 8.1m³ 7d p7g* p7g³ Nov 14] fairly useful performer: won handicap at Brighton in September and minor event at Lingfield in October: effective at 7f/1m: acts on good to firm going and polytrack: sold 50,000 gns. *G. A. Butler*

ROTARY   2 b.c. (Feb 18) Robellino (USA) 127 – Tarry 65 (Salse (USA) 128) [2002 **59** f5g⁵ 6g f8s⁵ 10s Oct 23] 5,000Y: second foal: dam, 7f (at 2 yrs) and 1¾m winner, also won over hurdles: modest maiden: should stay at least 1¼m: acts on fibresand: sold 8,000 gns, sent to Kuwait. *I. A. Balding*

ROTHERAM (USA)   2 b.g. (Feb 22) Dynaformer (USA) – Out of Taxes (USA) (Out **69** of Place (USA)) [2002 7.1d³ 7m⁴ 8m 8g Oct 18] $35,000F, $100,000Y: tall, useful-looking gelding: first foal: dam, 1m/8.5f winner in US, out of half-sister to dam of US Grade 1 9f/1¼m winner Astra: fair maiden: well beaten in nursery final start: will be suited by 1¼m/1½m: gelded after final outing. *P. F. I. Cole*

ROTUMA (IRE)   3 b.g. Tagula (IRE) 116 – Cross Question (USA) 84 (Alleged (USA) **58** 138) [2002 69: f8g p7g 9m 9.9m* 14.1m 11.1v² Jun 12] smallish, useful-looking gelding: modest performer: won claimer at Beverley in April: stays 1¼m, probably not testing 11f: acts on any going: blinkered last 3 starts. *M. Dods*

ROUBERIA (IRE)   3 ch.f. Alhaarth (IRE) 126 – Robinia (USA) 90 (Roberto (USA) **54 +** 131) [2002 64p: p7g Nov 19] rather leggy filly: fair form in maidens at 2 yrs: signs of retaining that ability only 3-y-o start: should be suited by 1m+: possibly capable of better. *G. A. Butler*

ROUGH SEAS (IRE)   3 b.g. Royal Applause 124 – Hebrides (Gone West (USA))   –
[2002 51: f5s f6g Jan 21] compact gelding: modest form in maidens at 2 yrs for B. Hills:
soundly beaten in handicaps in 2002. *J. O'Reilly*

ROUNDTREE (IRE)   3 b.f. Night Shift (USA) – Island Desert (IRE) 55 (Green   **98 §**
Desert (USA) 127) [2002 98: 7m² 8m 7g³ 7d⁴ 6m* 5.1f 7m² 6m 7m 6v Nov 9] small,
strong filly: useful performer: made hard work of landing odds in minor event at
Newmarket in June: ran well when second in Fred Darling Stakes at Newbury (finished
strongly when beaten 1¾ lengths by Queen's Logic) and listed race at Goodwood (didn't
find much when beaten 2½ lengths by Desert Alchemy: stays 7f: acts on good to firm and
good to soft going: sometimes edgy/swishes tail: ungenuine: sent to USA. *R. Hannon*

ROUSING THUNDER   5 b.g. Theatrical 128 – Moss (USA) (Woodman (USA) 126)   **52**
[2002 66: 10d 11.5m 12.6f 11.5f⁴ 11.6m³ 12g⁵ 14.1m³ 12m 14.1m⁴ 15.8f⁴ 14.1d Oct 18]
leggy gelding: modest handicapper: left W. Musson after eighth start: will prove best
short of 2m: acts on firm going: tried visored/blinkered: reportedly had breathing problem
final start: often races freely. *W. Storey*

ROUTE BARREE (FR)   4 ch.g. Exit To Nowhere (USA) 122 – Star Des Evees (FR)   **78 d**
(Moulin 103) [2002 83: p10g⁶ p12g⁶ 14.4f⁴ 14.4m 14d 12s 12d 11.9m* 14.1m⁵ p16g³
14.1g⁵ Oct 2] quite attractive gelding: fair performer: on downgrade in 2002, though won
minor event at Brighton in July: stays 2m: acts on polytrack, best efforts on good going or
firmer: tried visored at 3 yrs: carries head awkwardly/sometimes wanders: sold 10,500
gns. *S. Dow*

ROUTE SIXTY SIX (IRE)   6 b.m. Brief Truce (USA) 126 – Lyphards Goddess (IRE)   **63**
(Lyphard's Special (USA) 122) [2002 65: 6.9s* 8.1v³ 7.9m 9m⁵ 7.9m Sep 8] close-
coupled mare: modest handicapper: won at Carlisle in July: stays 9f: acts on any going:
blinkered once: waited with. *Jedd O'Keeffe*

ROUVRES (FR)   3 b.c. Anabaa (USA) 130 – Riziere (FR) (Groom Dancer (USA)   **117**
128) [2002 106: 8g* 9.3g* 9m* Jun 2] third foal: half-brother to useful performer up to

Mr A. Head's "Rouvres"

1¼m Rizerie (by Highest Honor), 7f winner at 2 yrs: dam, French 1m winner, half-sister to useful French miler Comillas: smart performer: won minor event at Longchamp at 2 yrs when also 3 lengths second to Act One in Prix Thomas Bryon at Saint-Cloud: unbeaten in 2002 in minor event at Longchamp in April, Prix de Guiche (by short neck from Rashbag) there in May and Prix Jean Prat at Chantilly (battled on to lead well inside final 1f, beat dead-heaters Imtiyaz and Shaanmer short neck) in June: stays 9.3f: acts on soft and good to firm going: sent to USA. *Mme C. Head-Maarek, France*

ROVERETTO 7 b.g. Robellino (USA) 127 – Spring Flyer (IRE) 66 (Waajib 121) [2002 **64** p16g p12g 16.1m⁶ 16v Oct 29] fair maiden handicapper: will stay beyond 2m: acts on soft and good to firm going: fairly useful hurdler. *Mrs M. Reveley*

ROWAN EXPRESS 2 b.f. (Mar 9) Air Express (IRE) 125 – Nordico Princess 71 **72 §** (Nordico (USA)) [2002 5g² 5f⁵ 5g³ 5d 5.3g⁶ f5g* 5m 5m³ 5.1m⁴ f5s* f5s p6g* 6s⁴ 6d⁶ **a78 §** Nov 5] 4,200Y: close-coupled filly: third foal: half-sister to 2000 2-y-o 5f winner Nordic Sabre (by Sabrehill) and to temperamental 1999 2-y-o 5f/6f winner City Princess (by Rock City): dam, 5f/6f winner, out of close relative to Dewhurst winner/2000 Guineas runner-up Wind And Wuthering: fair performer: won seller at Wolverhampton in July and nurseries at Southwell in September and Lingfield in October: effective at 5f/6f: acts on all-weather, soft and good to firm ground: blinkered/visored after second start: ungenuine. *M. H. Tompkins*

ROWAN LAKE (IRE) 2 b.f. (May 11) Lake Coniston (IRE) 131 – Kind of Cute 52 **56** (Prince Sabo 123) [2002 5g 6m f7g⁶ 6g² 6d p6g⁶ Dec 21] 3,000Y: smallish filly: fifth foal: closely related to useful French 1¼m to 11f winner Abou Safian (by Bluebird) and 4-y-o Travelling Band: dam, third at 6f at 2 yrs (only season to race), sister to Mill Reef Stakes winner Princely Hush: modest maiden: second in claimer at Lingfield: stays 6f: acts on polytrack, best turf effort on good going. *Andrew Reid*

ROXANNE MILL 4 b.f. Cyrano de Bergerac 120 – It Must Be Millie 66 (Reprimand **93** 122) [2002 71, a61: 5.1g⁶ 5.1d* 5s 5m⁴ 5.1m* 5d* 5.2m 5f⁶ 5.2m* 5m⁵ 5m 5.2m 5m 5d **a–** Oct 21] sturdy filly: fairly useful handicapper: improved, and won at Nottingham (2, edged left on both occasions), Hamilton and Yarmouth between May and August: best at 5f: acts on fibresand, soft and good to firm going: sometimes slowly away: often claimer ridden: races prominently/travels strongly. *M. D. I. Usher*

ROYAL APPROVAL 3 b.c. Royal Applause 124 – Inimitable 66 (Polish Precedent **78** (USA) 131) [2002 70: 10m 10d 9.9m⁵ 10m* 11f Sep 25] rather leggy, quite attractive colt: fair handicapper: won at Brighton in September: stays 1¼m: acts on good to firm going, yet to race on soft/heavy. *J. L. Dunlop*

ROYAL ARTIST 6 b.g. Royal Academy (USA) 130 – Council Rock 74 (General **64** Assembly (USA)) [2002 95d: f8s f7s f7g f7g* f7g⁴ f7g f7g 7.1m 6m 7g 6m Aug 16] workmanlike gelding: modest handicapper nowadays: left Miss J. Craze after third outing: won at Wolverhampton in February: stays easy 8.5f: acts on fibresand and firm going, probably on good to soft: sometimes blinkered: sometimes very mulish at start/slowly away: none too reliable: banned from Flat races started from stalls until March 2003. *M. Brittain*

ROYAL AURA (USA) 2 ch.f. (May 5) Royal Academy (USA) 130 – Barari (USA) **83** (Blushing Groom (FR) 131) [2002 7.5m² 7f⁶ Aug 31] tall, quite good-topped filly: has scope: half-sister to several winners, including 6f to 1¼m (US Grade 1 event) winner White Heart (by Green Desert) and 7.5f (at 2 yrs) to 1½m winner Kind Regards (by Unfuwain), both smart: dam unraced half-sister to very smart French/US performer up to 10.5f Colour Chart, herself dam of Breeders' Cup Juvenile Fillies winner Tempera and 4-y-o Equerry: fairly useful form when 1¾ lengths second to Approach in maiden at Beverley, dictating pace: gave impression something amiss later in month. *M. Johnston*

ROYAL AXMINSTER 7 b.g. Alzao (USA) 117 – Number One Spot 71 (Reference **45** Point 139) [2002 48: f12g³ 11m³ p12g⁴ 12m³ 10m⁴ 12m Sep 13] useful-looking gelding: **a48** poor maiden handicapper: should stay beyond 1½m: acts on all-weather and firm going: tried blinkered. *Mrs P. N. Dutfield*

ROYAL BEACON 2 b.c. (Jan 31) Royal Applause 124 – Tenderetta (Tender King **97** 123) [2002 5s² 6f* 6g⁵ 5d⁵ 5g 6g 6m² 5m Sep 19] 22,000F, 46,000Y: tall, strong colt: sixth foal: half-brother to 3 winners, including 5-y-o Al Ghabra: dam Irish 2-y-o 6f and 1m winner: useful performer: won maiden at York in May: quite highly tried after, running well when fifth in Coventry Stakes at Royal Ascot (next start) and second in minor event at Yarmouth: stays 6f: acts on firm going: usually races up with pace. *M. Johnston*

ROYAL BEAU (IRE)   3 b.f. Fayruz 116 – Castlelue (IRE) (Tremblant 112) [2002 46: **46**
f7s p6g⁴ f7g Jan 14] rather leggy, close-coupled filly: poor maiden: stays 7f: acts on good
to firm going and polytrack (well held in 3 starts on fibresand). *D. Nicholls*

ROYAL CASCADE (IRE)   8 b.g. River Falls 113 – Relative Stranger (Cragador **58**
110) [2002 –, a64: f9.4g² f8.5g³ f8.5g* f8.5g³ 7s f7g f9.4g⁵ 7.9s* f7g f8.5g f9.4g⁴ 8g⁶ f7s **a63**
8m⁵ f8.5g² f8.5g⁶ f8.5g⁴ Dec 14] lengthy gelding: moderate performer: won minor event at
Wolverhampton in February and apprentice handicap at Carlisle in May: effective at 7f to
9.4f: raced mainly on fibresand, also acts on soft and good to firm going: sometimes
blinkered: often gets behind early on. *B. A. McMahon*

ROYAL CASTLE (IRE)   8 b.g. Caerleon (USA) 132 – Sun Princess 130 (English **62**
Prince 129) [2002 –: 16f* 18f 16m* 16d³ f16.2f² 16d⁶ 16m⁵ f16.2f³ Nov 11] sturdy, **a66**
lengthy gelding: good mover: fair performer: won claimers at Redcar in June and Musselburgh in July: left M. Tompkins after latter win: stays 18.7f: acts on firm ground and
fibresand, below form on softer than good: visored once: none too reliable. *Mrs K. Walton*

ROYAL CAVALIER   5 b.g. Prince of Birds (USA) 121 – Gold Belt (IRE) 61 (Belly- **97**
pha 130) [2002 86, a–: 11.9m* 10.3f² 11.9m 10f 13.9g 12m⁵ 14m² 12m* 12f³ 12s 12v **a–**
Nov 9] sturdy gelding: useful handicapper: better than ever in 2002, winning at Haydock
in April and Doncaster (beat Solo Flight by neck) in September: well held last 2 starts:
stays 1¾m: acts on fibresand and any turf going: usually waited with. *R. Hollinshead*

ROYAL DANDY   2 ch.f. (Apr 8) Dolphin Street (FR) 125 – Supergreen (Superlative **–**
118) [2002 5s 5m Apr 22] 500Y: big, leggy filly: eighth reported foal: dam unraced: well
held in maidens: sent to Holland. *M. W. Easterby*

ROYAL DIGNITARY (USA)   2 b. or br.c. (Feb 9) Saint Ballado (CAN) – Star **89**
Actress (USA) (Star de Naskra (USA)) [2002 7.1m* 8.1m⁴ Aug 30] $425,000Y: fourth
foal: half-brother to winners in USA by Phone Trick and You And I: dam, ran twice in
USA, half-sister to US Grade 1 9f winner Dreamy Mimi: fairly useful form: favourite,
won maiden at Sandown in July by neck from Bint Alhaarth, dictating pace: visored, only
a little improvement when last of 4 to Lady McNair in minor event on same course:
should stay beyond 1m. *D. R. Loder*

ROYAL ENCLOSURE (IRE)   4 b.g. Royal Academy (USA) 130 – Hi Bettina 96 **50 §**
(Henbit (USA) 130) [2002 54, a59: f11s f9.4g⁴ f9.4g⁴ f9.4g f9.4g f8.5g 9g⁵ Mar 28]
close-coupled gelding: modest handicapper: effective at 1m/1¼m: acts on fibresand, firm
and good to soft going: blinkered/visored: tongue tied nowadays: often goes in snatches,
and looks a difficult ride. *P. D. Evans*

ROYAL EXPRESSION   10 b.g. Sylvan Express 117 – Edwins' Princess 75 (Owen **54 §**
Dudley 121) [2002 55: f16s⁵ f16s⁴ f16s f16.2g Feb 8] tall gelding: modest handicapper:
stays 2¼m: acts on firm ground, soft and fibresand: tried blinkered/visored: very slowly
away penultimate start/looked reluctant final one: untrustworthy. *G. M. Moore*

ROYAL FASHION (IRE)   2 b.f. (Jan 19) Ali-Royal (IRE) 127 – Fun Fashion (IRE) **62**
64 (Polish Patriot (USA) 128) [2002 p5g² f6g³ f5g⁵ f5g² f5g² 5.3m* 5.2f³ 5.2f 5m³ 6m⁶
f6f Nov 11] IR 2,000Y: neat filly: first foal: dam Irish maiden who stayed 1m: modest
performer: trained by B. R. Millman on debut, by A. Reid next 8 starts: won maiden at
Brighton in July: best form at 5f: acts on firm going and all-weather: sometimes led to
post. *Miss S. West*

ROYAL GLEN (IRE)   4 b.f. Royal Abjar (USA) 121 – Sea Glen (IRE) (Glenstal **–**
(USA) 118) [2002 –: 8g 7f Sep 27] rather leggy filly: modest at 2 yrs: little form since.
I. Semple

ROYAL GRAND   2 ch.c. (Mar 24) Prince Sabo 123 – Hemline 77 (Sharpo 132) [2002 **71**
5m⁵ 5m⁴ 5m f6g* Dec 20] 10,000Y: small, leggy colt: half-brother to several winners,
including 6-y-o Grand View and fairly useful 11.6f winner Heart of Armor (by Tirol):
dam 7f winner: fair performer: trained first 2 starts by H. McWilliams: best effort when
winning nursery at Wolverhampton: should stay 7f. *T. D. Barron*

ROYAL HEIGHTS   2 b. or br.f. (Feb 3) Bin Ajwaad (IRE) 119 – Lunchtime (USA) **63**
(Known Fact (USA) 135) [2002 6g² 6m Oct 5] 4,000Y: first foal: dam, ran twice in
France, half-sister to dam of very smart 1½m/1¾m performer Mons out of US Grade 1
2-y-o 8.5f winner Arewehavingfunyet: ¾-length second to Bella Tusa in maiden at
Goodwood, flashing tail: tailed off in sales race at Redcar over 3 months later (reportedly
had nasal discharge). *A. P. Jarvis*

ROYAL INDULGENCE   2 b.g. (Mar 30) Royal Applause 124 – Silent Indulgence   **75**
(USA) (Woodman (USA) 126) [2002 8f³ 7m⁴ 8m⁶ 6g 6d Oct 14] 62,000Y: third foal:
brother to 3-y-o Tudor Wood and half-brother to 2000 2-y-o 6f winner In The Woods (by
You And I), later useful in Scandinavia: dam placed in USA: fair maiden on balance:
trained first 4 outings by M. Channon: likely to prove best at 6f/7f: acts on firm ground:
gelded after final start. *M. Dods*

ROYAL INSULT   5 ch.g. Lion Cavern (USA) 117 – Home Truth 98 (Known Fact   **–**
(USA) 135) [2002 80: f7s⁵ p10g Dec 30] close-coupled gelding: fairly useful performer
at best: stayed 1m: acted on good to firm going: tried visored: dead. *K. R. Burke*

ROYAL IVY   5 ch.m. Mujtahid (USA) 118 – Royal Climber (Kings Lake (USA) 133)   **60**
[2002 64, a–: f6g⁶ 6m 7g⁵ 7d³ 8.1m 7d⁵ 6g³ 6m 7m⁴ 8f Sep 25] small mare: has a quick   **a–**
action: modest handicapper on turf: effective at 6f to 1m: acts on polytrack, firm and good
to soft going: tried blinkered. *J. Akehurst*

ROYAL LADY (IRE)   3 b.f. Royal Academy (USA) 130 – Shahoune (USA) (Blushing   **59**
Groom (FR) 131) [2002 65: 6m⁵ 8m Jun 24] close-coupled, good-topped filly: lightly-
raced maiden: fair form at 2 yrs: below that level in tongue tie in 2002: stays 7f: sent to
France. *R. Guest*

ROYAL MILLENNIUM (IRE)   4 b.c. Royal Academy (USA) 130 – Galatrix 72   **111**
(Be My Guest (USA) 126) [2002 102: 8g³ 9m 7.9f⁵ 8.5s 7m 7g 6.5g² 7m³ 7g* 7d 7f⁵ 6m²
6m² 6g⁶ 7f³ 7m³ 7m Oct 19] lengthy, angular colt: unimpressive mover: smart performer:
won minor event at Goodwood in August by 1¾ lengths from Vanderlin: mostly good
efforts after, including second to Smokin Beau in listed event at Goodwood on thirteenth
start and third to Millennium Force in Tote Trifecta Stakes (Handicap) at Ascot on
penultimate one: effective at 6f to 1m: acts on firm going, probably on soft: has run well
when sweating: held up: tough. *M. R. Channon*

ROYAL MINSTREL (IRE)   5 ch.g. Be My Guest (USA) 126 – Shanntabariya (IRE)   **90**
(Shernazar 131) [2002 90: 12m² 12.1m² Aug 24] strong, lengthy gelding: fairly useful
performer: ran creditably in handicap at Newmarket and minor event at Goodwood in 2002,
though hung and looked none too hearty in latter: probably best at 1¼m/1½m: acts on
firm and soft going: blinkered once in 2000: tends to carry head high. *M. H. Tompkins*

ROYAL MIRAGE (IRE)   3 ch.f. Lycius (USA) 124 – Cariellor's Miss (FR) (Cariellor   **66 d**
(FR) 125) [2002 60: 10m* 10m f7g 11.6d* 11.6s 10d⁵ 10m 11.6m 10.1f 6g 10.1m 10m³
8m Sep 3] tall, rather leggy filly: fair performer at best: won seller at Southwell (left
M. Bell 10,000 gns) in April and minor event at Windsor in May: below form after: stays
11.6f: acts on good to firm going, good to soft and fibresand: blinkered/visored tenth/
eleventh outings: sometimes hangs left/carries head awkwardly: sold 1,900 gns, joined
M. Hourigan in Ireland. *Andrew Reid*

ROYAL MYSTERY   3 ch.f. King's Signet (USA) 110 – Miss Caradon (IRE) (Prince   **44**
Rupert (FR) 121) [2002 f8.5g 10g 10.2g⁴ Apr 30] third foal: dam no sign of ability: poor
maiden: not sure to stay further than 10.2f. *H. S. Howe*

ROYAL PARTNERSHIP (IRE)   6 b.g. Royal Academy (USA) 130 – Go Honey   **–**
Go (General Assembly (USA)) [2002 53: 12.1g 11.6d f14.8g⁶ f14.8g* f16.2g f8g³ f14.8g   **a53**
p12g Dec 18] tall, angular gelding: modest handicapper on all-weather: won amateur
race at Wolverhampton in November: stays 15f: acts on fibresand, soft and good to firm
ground: often visored. *D. L. Williams*

ROYAL POPPY   4 b.f. Mind Games 121 – Never So True 52 (Never So Bold 135)   **–**
[2002 –: 10g 9.2g 12.4g 10.1m 7.1m Sep 16] lengthy, rather unfurnished filly: probably
of little account. *H. A. McWilliams*

ROYAL PORTRAIT   2 b.f. (May 2) Perugino (USA) 84 – Kaguyahime (Distant   **– p**
Relative 128) [2002 6m 6s 7v Nov 8] sturdy filly: fourth foal: half-sister to 3-y-o Marcus
Aurelius: dam, French 9f winner, half-sister to high-class 1m/1¼m performer Bijou
d'Inde: signs of a little ability in maidens at Newbury, Leicester and Doncaster: capable
of better. *J. L. Dunlop*

ROYAL PRODIGY (USA)   3 ch.g. Royal Academy (USA) 130 – Prospector's Queen   **77**
(USA) (Mr Prospector (USA)) [2002 77: p8g* 8.1d 10g p12g 10.1m Aug 16] rather
leggy, close-coupled gelding: fair performer: landed odds in maiden at Lingfield in
February: well beaten after: stays 1m: acts on polytrack and good to soft going:
sometimes wears crossed noseband: visored final start: got stirred up beforehand and ran
as if something amiss second start: joined M. Pipe. *J. Noseda*

ROYAL QUARTERS (IRE)   3 ch.c. Common Grounds 118 – Queen Canute (IRE)   **109**
(Ahonoora 122) [2002 93p: 7m⁴ 7m 6d 7d² 7m⁶ 7.6m* 7m² 8.5d⁴ Oct 26] unfurnished,
quite attractive colt: useful performer: won minor event at Chester in August by ¾ length
from Funfair Wane: also ran well when in frame in Greenham Stakes at Newbury (fourth
to Redback), handicap at Leicester (second to Kool), listed race at Epsom (beaten head by
Atavus) and non-graded handicap at Arlington (fourth to Capsized): stays 8.5f: acts on
good to firm and good to soft going, yet to race on soft/heavy: blinkered (below form
third) outing. *B. J. Meehan*

ROYAL RACER (FR)   4 b.g. Danehill (USA) 126 – Green Rosy (USA) (Green   **78 d**
Dancer (USA) 132) [2002 78: p12g⁵ p12g f14g 12g 12.3f 9s⁶ 8.3m 8d⁶ 8g p10g³ p10g⁵
9d Oct 18] rangy gelding: fair handicapper at best: on downgrade after reappearance in
2002: stays 1½m: acts on good to soft ground and polytrack: has worn crossed noseband:
reportedly lost action second start. *J. R. Best*

ROYAL REBEL   6 b.g. Robellino (USA) 127 – Greenvera (USA) (Riverman   **124 §**
(USA) 131) [2002 123§: 18.7f 16.4m 20m* Jun 20]
        News that Royal Rebel is to miss the 2003 season with a leg injury may turn
out to be a mixed blessing for punters—and for jockey Johnny Murtagh. For the
second year running, the moody and unreliable Royal Rebel consented to put his
best foot forward in the Gold Cup at Royal Ascot and confounded the 2002
form-book by pulling off another narrow victory under another outstanding ride
from Murtagh. Murtagh's 'reward' for his latest performance in galvanising Royal
Rebel, and playing his part in a magnificent horserace that provided a thrilling
spectacle, was a four-day suspension for using his whip with 'excessive force and
frequency'. Murtagh was said to have struck Royal Rebel fourteen times from two
furlongs out and, after also being suspended for excessive use of the whip on Royal
Rebel twelve months earlier, described himself as 'very disillusioned, I've won the
Gold Cup and it's a total anti-climax . . . I've done my best for the owner and
trainer. Who am I riding for—the people sitting at home?' Royal Rebel's owner,
BHB chairman Peter Savill, was surprisingly called before the stewards, in the light
of Murtagh's evidence, to recount the instructions he had given to the jockey before
the latest Gold Cup. Savill was found to be 'not in breach of Jockey Club instruction
H9 with regard to his responsibilities as an owner' but Murtagh might have felt that
the owner had not backed him strongly enough and reportedly told trainer Mark
Johnston in the heat of the moment: 'Don't ring me next year for Royal Rebel'.
        Johnston also found himself before the Royal Ascot stewards, asked to
explain Royal Rebel's improvement in form compared with his latest run behind
stablemate Akbar (a last-minute withdrawal from the Gold Cup through lameness)
in the Henry II Stakes at Sandown where he had finished eighth, beaten twenty-two
lengths. After also hearing evidence from the BHB handicapper, the stewards noted
that Royal Rebel was better suited by the extra distance and that his 'known form'
was over two and a half miles at Ascot. The trainer was candid with the assembled
media: 'It's all in the mind with this one and when he's in the right mood he's a very
good horse . . . he clearly loves coming here.' On Murtagh's suspension, Royal
Rebel's owner later hit the nail on the head: 'There wasn't a person at Ascot who
didn't think it was a brilliant ride and the BBC didn't receive a single complaint.
There needs to be more flexibility in the whip rules.' The current whip rules—
among the tightest in the world—may be well-intentioned but they continue to do
more harm than good for racing's image. Bans on top jockeys in big races guarantee
headlines which portray racing as a cruel sport. In the vast majority of such cases
nowadays, however, it is arguably the rules themselves—not the jockeys—which
bring racing into disrepute. If the Royal Ascot stewards had not been compelled by
Jockey Club guidelines to hold an inquiry, the subsequent furore over Murtagh's
riding of Royal Rebel—who won only because his jockey kept riding hard—would
have been avoided. Frankie Dettori was also suspended for four days for his use of
the whip on close third Wareed, but the finish of the latest Gold Cup was patently
not one which made the viewing public wince. Nor did it raise any animal welfare
issues, since neither Royal Rebel nor Wareed showed signs of distress or was found
to be badly marked afterwards.
        Royal Rebel arrived at Royal Ascot without a victory in seven outings since
his Gold Cup success the previous year when, in common with runner-up Persian

Gold Cup, Royal Ascot—Royal Rebel returns to form with a vengeance to win the race for a second time, rallying splendidly under an outstanding ride from Johnny Murtagh to beat Vinnie Roe and Wareed

Punch, he had shown tremendous battling qualities to scramble home by a head, the first two clear. Royal Rebel's latest campaign began in the Chester Cup, connections suggesting that the tight track might 'give him something to think about'. Under top weight of 10-1, and starting at 20/1, Royal Rebel beat only three home in an eighteen-runner field. He was refitted with a visor in the Henry II Stakes, for which he was also a 20/1-shot, but he took little interest, skulking in the rear for much of the way before belatedly passing three beaten rivals. The visor was discarded again in the Gold Cup, as it had been the previous year, but, even with Murtagh taking over from Darryll Holland and Eddie Ahern (who had ridden him in his first two races), Royal Rebel was still sent off at 16/1, twice the odds he had been twelve months earlier. The 5/2 favourite was the Irish-trained four-year-old Vinnie Roe, successful in the Irish St Leger and the Prix Royal-Oak at three and unbeaten in his last five races. Then, in a field of fifteen, came the principal Godolphin representative Wareed at 13/2, the previous year's third Jardines Lookout at 7/1 and the Henry II Stakes runner-up Invermark at 8/1, followed by 10/1 chances Persian Punch and Sagaro Stakes winner Give Notice. Roused from the stalls and given a couple of backhanders early on, Royal Rebel wasn't given the chance to dawdle at the back and he held a prominent position all the way. Niggled along when Persian Punch's rider stepped up the gallop from around three quarters of a mile out, Royal Rebel was in the firing line all the way up the home straight. The waited-with Vinnie Roe challenged strongly from over a furlong out, with hard-ridden Wareed making his run between the first two inside the final furlong. Royal Rebel answered his rider's urgings splendidly to edge ahead close home, cocking his ears as Murtagh put his whip down in the shadow of the winning post. The margin over Vinnie Roe was a neck, with Wareed a further length away in third, followed by the second Godolphin runner Hatha Anna, Give Notice and Persian Punch. Approximately nine lengths covered the first twelve home in a Gold Cup that wasn't anything like so strongly run as the previous year's edition which had provided a searching test of stamina. The first to win successive Gold Cups since Drum Taps in 1992 and 1993, Royal Rebel met with a training setback whilst being prepared for the Goodwood Cup and wasn't seen out again. He is due to miss the whole of the forthcoming season due to a leg problem, but connections are reportedly still hopeful he could resume racing in 2004.

The pedigree of the good-topped Royal Rebel is of largely academic interest and was detailed in *Racehorses of 2001*. His dam, the French maiden Greenvera, had two other runners in 2002, the four-year-old Greenfire (by Ashkalani), who showed nothing in bumpers, and the three-year-old Perfect Picture (by Octagonal),

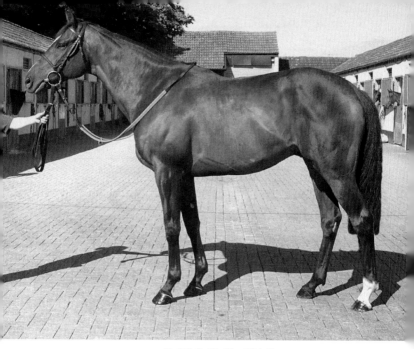

Mr P. D. Savill's "Royal Rebel"

		Roberto	Hail To Reason
	Robellino (USA)	(b 1969)	Bramalea
	(b 1978)	Isobelline	Pronto
Royal Rebel		(b 1971)	Isobella
(b.g. 1996)		Riverman	Never Bend
	Greenvera (USA)	(b 1969)	River Lady
	(ch 1989)	Greenway	Targowice
		(br 1978)	Gracious

who ran several times for Johnston's stable, showing fair form when second in a nine-furlong maiden at Redcar in September but then finishing tailed off in three outings over longer distances, two of them over two miles. Greenway's two-year-old Yoshka (by Grand Lodge) was also in training at Kingsley House but wasn't seen out. Royal Rebel, who is a good-topped gelding, acts on firm and good to soft going, but the biggest consideration with him is not the state of the going, nor is it the application or otherwise of different types of headgear (he has worn blinkers and a visor, and, of course, didn't wear either in his Gold Cups). Royal Rebel's ratio of good efforts to distinctly ordinary ones makes him—plainly and simply—not one to trust. *M. Johnston*

ROYAL REPRIMAND (IRE)   7 b.g. Reprimand 122 – Lake Ormond (Kings Lake   **45 §**
(USA) 133) [2002 59§: 7d 6f 8m 7f 8g 7m⁴ 6s 8d⁵ Sep 9] close-coupled, good-topped gelding: poor maiden: effective at 7f to 1¼m: acts on firm and soft going: tried visored: unreliable. *R. E. Barr*

ROYAL ROBBIE   4 b.g. Robellino (USA) 127 – Moogie 103 (Young Generation   –
129) [2002 –: p10g f14g p12g p12g Jun 29] probably of little account. *P. Butler*

ROYAL ROBE (IRE) 2 gr.g. (Mar 9) King of Kings (IRE) 125 – Sallanches (USA) **80**
(Gone West (USA)) [2002 6d 6m² 7.1m 6.1m Sep 16] IR 155,000F, IR 180,000Y:
close-coupled gelding: fluent mover: second foal: dam, French 9.5f winner, half-sister to
Arlington Million winner Mill Native: fairly useful maiden: second in minor event at
Newmarket: well held in Solario Stakes at Sandown and nursery at Warwick after: races
freely, but should stay 7f. *B. J. Meehan*

ROYAL ROMEO 5 ch.g. Timeless Times (USA) 99 – Farinara (Dragonara Palace –
(USA) 115) [2002 74: 7g 6g 6d 5.7d 5d 5m Aug 30] good-bodied gelding: unimpressive
mover: fair 5f/6f winner at best: well held in 2002: sometimes blinkered. *J. M. Bradley*

ROYAL SPIN 3 b.g. Prince Sabo 123 – Cabaret Artiste (Shareef Dancer (USA) 135) **68 ?**
[2002 8m May 6] 18,000Y: fourth foal: half-brother to 1997 2-y-o 7f winner Misalliance
(by Elmaamul) and 6-y-o Cabaret Quest: dam unraced: 10/1, shaped better than result
suggests when ninth of 14 to L'Oiseau d'Argent in maiden at Kempton, in group of 5
clear when clipping heels and nearly falling 1½f out, eased (reportedly finished lame):
sold 3,000 gns in October, joined J. Osborne. *A. C. Stewart*

ROYAL STAMP (USA) 3 br.c. With Approval (CAN) – Louis d'Or (USA) (Mr **105**
Prospector (USA)) [2002 10m* 10.3g³ Jun 8] leggy, quite attractive colt: second foal:
dam unraced half-sister to US Grade 1 1¼m/Grade 2 1½m winner Louis Le Grand: useful
form: won maiden at Newmarket in April comfortably by 2 lengths from Zaajel: far from
discredited when 1¼ lengths last of 3 to Leo's Luckyman in minor event at Doncaster
next time (possibly still bit green): should stay 1½m: looked a smart prospect.
J. H. M. Gosden

ROYAL STORM (IRE) 3 b.c. Royal Applause 124 – Wakayi 87 (Persian Bold 123) **92**
[2002 72: 7d⁴ 7d⁴ 7.1m* 7.5m⁴ 7m 6m⁶ 8.5g² 8f⁴ 8f⁵ 7f* 7.1g* 7g Oct 18] tall, lengthy
colt: fairly useful performer: won maiden at Warwick in June and handicaps at Goodwood in September and Sandown in October: best around 7f on good going or firmer.
Mrs A. J. Perrett

ROYAL TARRAGON 6 b.m. Aragon 118 – Lady Philippa (IRE) 77 (Taufan (USA) –
119) [2002 37: p7g 6f 7.1m 7g 7.2d 7g 7m Sep 4] quite good-topped mare: bad maiden:
tried blinkered/visored. *W. de Best-Turner*

ROYAL TASK 2 b. or br.f. (Mar 29) Tragic Role (USA) – Formidable Task 61 **45**
(Formidable (USA) 125) [2002 6f 5g 5f 7.5g Sep 18] eighth living foal: dam, should have
stayed further than 6f, out of sister to Highclere: poor maiden. *Miss S. E. Hall*

ROYAL TIME 2 b.f. (Apr 5) Emperor Jones (USA) 119 – Anytime Baby 56 (Bairn – p
(USA) 126) [2002 6m 7g 6m Aug 31] 1,000Y: good-topped filly: third foal: closely
related to 2000 2-y-o 5f winner Acorn Catcher (by Emarati) and half-sister to 3-y-o
Online Investor: dam 5f winner: signs of ability in maidens, showing early speed each
time: probably capable of better. *T. D. Barron*

ROYAL TRIGGER 2 b.c. (Mar 14) Double Trigger (IRE) 123 – Jeronime (USA) **67**
81 (Sauce Boat (USA)) [2002 7s⁶ 7d Nov 2] leggy, lightly-made colt: second known
thoroughbred foal: dam 2-y-o 5f winner: fair form, not knocked about, in maidens at
Doncaster and Newmarket: likely to be suited by 1¼m+. *B. W. Hills*

ROYAL TWIST (USA) 2 ch.g. (Jan 8) Royal Academy (USA) 130 – Musical Twist **63**
(USA) 97 (Woodman (USA) 126) [2002 6g 6g³ Jul 20] 21,000Y: big, strong gelding: first
foal: dam, maiden (stayed 1m), out of Cherry Hinton/Fred Darling winner Musicale:
much better effort in maidens (modest form) when 8 lengths third to Wizard of Noz at
Haydock: will stay 1m. *T. P. Tate*

ROYAL WINDMILL (IRE) 3 b.g. Ali-Royal (IRE) 127 – Salarya (FR) (Darshaan **51**
133) [2002 74: 5m 10.5s 7f 6f f6g⁴ 8g⁵ 7.1m 7m³ 7m 6f Oct 8] leggy gelding: just modest
form in 2002, leaving F. P. Murtagh after second start: should stay at least 1m: acts on
firm going, probably on fibresand. *M. D. Hammond*

ROY MCAVOY (IRE) 4 b.g. Danehill (USA) 126 – Decadence (Vaigly Great 127) **68**
[2002 –: p7g² p7g p7g³ f8.5s² p6g³ p7g⁵ Dec 28] fair maiden: trained by J. Best second
start only: effective at 6f to 8.5f: acts on all-weather: consistent. *C. A. Cyzer*

ROZEL (IRE) 5 ch.m. Wolfhound (USA) 126 – Noirmart (Dominion 123) [2002 104: **104**
5.1g 5m 5m* 5.1f 5g 5.6m Sep 11] lengthy mare: useful performer: won handicap at
Doncaster in June by 1½ lengths from Good Girl: behind otherwise: raced only at 5f: has
form on soft ground, best efforts on firmer than good: visored final outing, blinkered
previous 4: sent to USA. *R. Guest*

RUBY GOLIGHTLY (IRE)   3 b.f. Alhaarth (IRE) 126 – Rhoman Ruby (IRE)   –
(Rhoman Rule (USA)) [2002 10m⁶ p12g Sep 4] fourth foal: half-sister to fairly useful
1¼m winner Rhythmicall (by In The Wings) who stayed 1¾m, and winner in Spain by
Brief Truce: dam Irish 7f to 8.5f winner: sixth in maiden at Windsor on debut: broke down
at Lingfield next time: dead. *Mrs L. Richards*

RUBY LEGEND   4 b.g. Perpendicular 119 – Singing High 87 (Julio Mariner 127)   62
[2002 52: 11m 8f 14.1f 11.8g⁶ 9d³ 10.4m² 8m* 8.9f Oct 12] leggy gelding: modest
handicapper: won at Newcastle in October: stays 1¼m: acts on good to firm and good to
soft going: blinkered last 4 starts. *Mrs M. Reveley*

RUBY WEDDING   4 b.f. Blushing Flame (USA) 109 – First Sapphire (Simply Great   78
(FR) 122) [2002 60p: p12g² p13g³ 14.1m² 16f² 16m² 18d 16.5v Nov 9] fair maiden: stays
2m (raced freely at 2¼m): acts on firm ground and polytrack. *Mrs A. J. Perrett*

RUDDINGTON GRANGE   2 gr.f. (Mar 13) Bahamian Bounty 116 – Rain Splash   45
74 (Petong 126) [2002 5m 6.1g 5m 6.1m Sep 20] 20,000Y: leggy filly: fifth foal: sister
to a 1m winner in Hong Kong: dam, 5f (at 2 yrs) and 6f winner, half-sister to smart
performer up to 1m Muchea: poor maiden: tried blinkered. *J. Balding*

RUDE AWAKENING   8 b.g. Rudimentary (USA) 118 – Final Call 79 (Town Crier   –
119) [2002 47, a63: 5.9d 7m Jul 27] sturdy gelding: fair performer at best: was best at 5f/
6f: acted on fibresand, firm and soft going: occasionally blinkered/visored: carried head
high: usually raced prominently: dead. *T. A. K. Cuthbert*

RUDETSKI   5 b.g. Rudimentary (USA) 118 – Butosky 71 (Busted 134) [2002 60: 8s⁵   48
9.1d 8.1v 10.1m 9d Aug 23] big, lengthy gelding: poor handicapper: probably stays 11f:
acts on any going: has been early to post/worn crossed noseband/taken fierce hold.
M. Dods

RUDIK (USA)   5 b. or br.g. Nureyev (USA) 131 – Nervous Baba (USA) (Raja Baba   92 d
(USA)) [2002 93: 6s³ 6g 7d 6m 6g⁶ 6g⁴ 6d 7m⁵ 7g 5.9v³ 6g⁶ 7.2d³ 7m 7m 7.2g⁶ Sep 21]
compact gelding: fairly useful handicapper: last won in 1999: generally on downgrade
after reappearance in 2002, though fifth in Tote International at Ascot on eighth start:
stays 7f: acts on heavy and good to firm going: visored tenth/eleventh starts: tongued tied:
sold 5,800 gns. *D. Nicholls*

RUDI'S PET (IRE)   8 ch.g. Don't Forget Me 127 – Pink Fondant (Northfields (USA))   113
[2002 105: 5s 5.1m² 5m⁶ 5.1f 5g⁴ 5d³ 5m 5d* 5m³ 5m 5g² 5m Aug 22] strong gelding:
smart performer: almost back to very best in 2002, and won listed Vodafone 'Dash' Rated
Stakes (Handicap) at Epsom in June by 1½ lengths from Watching: good efforts last 2
starts, short-headed by Agnetha in King George Stakes at Goodwood and ninth to
Kyllachy in Nunthorpe Stakes at York: best at 5f: acts on firm and good to soft going:
usually blinkered/visored, but effective when not: has been early to post/bandaged in
front: sometimes slowly away (has been markedly so)/hangs left: usually races
prominently. *D. Nicholls*

RUDOOD (USA)   2 b.c. (Jan 20) Theatrical 128 – Kardashina (FR) (Darshaan 133)   86 p
[2002 7.5d⁴ 7.1m² Sep 21] 220,000Y: rather leggy colt: first foal: dam, 11f to 12.5f
winner in France, half-sister to smart French pair Karmifira (at 1m/9f) and Karmousil (up
to 15f): odds on, something seemingly amiss on debut: fairly useful form when head
second to Prince Tum Tum in maiden at Warwick, again racing freely and just caught
having led 1f out: should stay at least 1¼m: likely to do better still. *A. C. Stewart*

*Vodafone 'Dash' Rated Stakes (Handicap) Epsom—Rudi's Pet is on his own down the centre
as Watching (rail), Repertory (spots on cap), Lord Kintyre (No.6) and Bishops Court (noseband)
battle it out for the minor placings*

RUE DE PARIS 2 br.g. (Apr 29) Paris House 123 – Innocent Abroad (DEN) 53 **57** (Viking (USA)) [2002 5f 5s⁵ 5.6m³ 5m 5m 5g 5m 5f⁴ 5s Nov 6] 1,300F, 1,600Y: leggy, good-topped gelding: fourth foal: dam maiden who stayed 1m: modest maiden: likely to prove best at 5f/6f: acts on firm and soft going: sometimes gives trouble in preliminaries (withdrawn as a result once). *N. Bycroft*

RUFIJI RIVER 3 b.g. Hernando (FR) 127 – Jadirah (USA) 68 (Deputy Minister **54** (CAN)) [2002 61: 14.1m⁴ 14.1f Jun 4] lengthy gelding: modest maiden: probably stayed 1¾m: dead. *J. L. Dunlop*

RUISSEC (USA) 3 b. or br.f. Woodman (USA) 126 – Jadana (Pharly (FR) 130) [2002 – –: 6.1d 8.2d p12g 10.2m 8.1m 10m Sep 15] close-coupled filly: good mover: little form: tried blinkered/visored. *J. W. Hills*

RULE BRITANNIA 3 b.f. Night Shift (USA) – Broken Wave 103 (Bustino 136) [2002 **79 p** 10m⁶ 10d³ 9.9m* Aug 25] quite good-topped filly: closely related to French 1¼m winner Bressay (by Nureyev), later successful in USA, and half-sister to 9f winner Stormy Crest (by Catrail) and French 1¼m and 15f winner Levallois (by Trempolino): dam, won up to 15f in Britain/France, out of Oaks third Britannia's Rule: progressive form: won maiden at Beverley in August by 4 lengths from Desert Heat: should stay 1½m: raced quite freely in steadily-run race second outing: should be capable of better still. *J. R. Fanshawe*

RUMBUNCTIOUS 3 b. or br.f. Charnwood Forest (IRE) 125 – Pearly River 72 **78** (Elegant Air 119) [2002 8.3m 8.1m 8.3m⁶ 8g² f8.5s² f7g* Sep 30] 10,000Y: third foal: half-sister to 1999 2-y-o 7f winner Another Pearl (by Ezzoud): dam, 7f (at 2 yrs) and 1½m winner, out of half-sister to Roseate Tern and Ibn Bey: fair performer: won handicap at Wolverhampton (idled in front) in September: not sure to stay further than 8.5f: acts on fibresand, raced only on good/good to firm going on turf. *P. J. Makin*

RUM CHARGER (IRE) 3 b.f. Spectrum (IRE) 126 – Park Charger 105 (Tirol 127) **106** [2002 103: 7s* 8g 8s 7s* 7.5m 7m 7v Nov 10] smallish, lengthy filly: useful performer: won listed race at the Curragh (by 2 lengths from Kournakova) in May and Ballycorus Stakes at Leopardstown (by ¾ length from One Won One) in June: below best otherwise in 2002, including in Challenge Stakes at Newmarket penultimate outing: should stay 1m: goes well on soft ground: blinkered final start: sent to USA. *D. K. Weld, Ireland*

RUM DESTINY (IRE) 3 b.g. Mujadil (USA) 119 – Ruby River (Red God 128§) – [2002 93: 5g 5.1f 5.1s 5g 5m 5g 5.1f⁵ 5d⁶ 5m 6m Sep 3] small gelding: unimpressive mover: fairly useful at 2 yrs, generally well held in 2002: best at 5f: acts on firm and good to soft going: blinkered seventh start: sold 3,000 gns. *A. Berry*

RUMORE CASTAGNA (IRE) 4 ch.g. Great Commotion (USA) 123 – False Spring – (IRE) (Petorius 117) [2002 –: f7s 7.1m 6m 8m Jul 8] fairly useful at 2 yrs: little form since, leaving S. Kettlewell after reappearance: sent to Kuwait. *R. Wilman*

RUNAWAY STAR 5 ch.m. Superlative 118 – My Greatest Star 93 (Great Nephew **55** 126) [2002 45: f12g p13g⁵ p16g² 14.1d² p10g⁴ 12g 14.1d* 12m⁶ 11.6m² 12.1d⁴ 12g* 14.4g Aug 26] workmanlike mare: modest handicapper: won at Nottingham in June and Pontefract in July: effective at 1¼m to 2m: acts on good to firm going, good to soft and polytrack. *W. J. Musson*

RUNNING FOR ME (IRE) 4 ch.f. Eagle Eyed (USA) 111 – Running For You (FR) **?** (Pampabird 124) [2002 –, a60d: f6s f6s a6g* a6g* 5.8s a6g 7m² a6g² a6g³ a6g⁵ a6s a6s Nov 30] leggy, unfurnished filly: modest performer at best in Britain: won handicaps at Taby in May/June: stays 6f: acts on dirt/fibresand and good to firm ground. *T. Persson, Sweden*

RUN ON 4 b.c. Runnett 125 – Polar Storm (IRE) 76 (Law Society (USA) 130) [2002 **53** 56: 5g f6g 5.7d⁶ 7.1v 6m* 6g⁵ 5m 5.1g⁶ 6m Sep 19] robust colt: modest handicapper: won at Yarmouth in July: stays 6f: acts on fibresand, good to firm and good to soft going: sometimes tongue tied/slowly away. *D. G. Bridgwater*

RUPESH (IRE) 2 ch.f. (May 4) Fayruz 116 – Maricica (Ahonoora 122) [2002 5m 6g **57** 5.1f 6m 7.5g Sep 18] IR 8,500Y, resold 13,000Y: half-sister to useful 5f winner (including at 2 yrs) Cortachy Castle (by Pips Pride): dam Irish 1m winner: modest maiden: well held in nurseries last 2 starts: best efforts at 5f: raced only on good going or firmer. *D. W. P. Arbuthnot*

RUSH ABOUT (IRE) 3 ch.c. Kris 135 – Rachrush (IRE) (Sadler's Wells (USA) 132) **79** [2002 77p: 10g⁶ p12g³ f12s⁴ 10m² 10s Oct 26] good-bodied colt: fair maiden, lightly raced: stays 1½m: acts on polytrack, good to firm and good to soft ground: found little final start: sold 14,000 gns, joined Miss K. Marks. *H. R. A. Cecil*

RUSHCUTTER BAY 9 br.g. Mon Tresor 113 – Llwy Bren (Lidhame 109) [2002 **101 §** 117d: 5m 6g³ 5m 5s⁴ Jun 15] close-coupled gelding: impresses in appearance: smart performer at best, just useful nowadays: effective at 5f/6f: acts on firm and soft going: effective visored or not: has twice reportedly bled from nose, including once as 8-y-o: tends to wander/look none too keen: unreliable. *P. L. Gilligan*

RUSHMORE (USA) 5 b.g. Mt Livermore (USA) – Crafty Nan (USA) (Crafty **–** Prospector (USA)) [2002 7s Oct 26] strong, workmanlike gelding: fairly useful performer in 2000, winning 4 times: well held in claimer only run since. *P. F. I. Cole*

RUSKIN BAY 3 b.g. Muhtarram (USA) 125 – Mossy Rose 78 (King of Spain 121) **–** [2002 9g Oct 5] half-brother to 7-y-o Browning (by Warrshan): dam 6f/1m winner: slowly away and broke down on debut: dead. *M. P. Tregoning*

RUSSIAN DUNE (IRE) 3 b.g. Danehill (USA) 126 – Russian Ribbon (USA) 86 **76** (Nijinsky (CAN) 138) [2002 7p: 8.1d⁶ 7g³ 10d³ 11.9g⁴ p12g Oct 9] quite attractive gelding: fair maiden: seems to stay 1½m, should be at least as effective at shorter: raced only on good going or softer on turf: has worn crossed noseband: sold 10,000 gns, sent to Kuwait. *E. A. L. Dunlop*

RUSSIAN FOX (IRE) 5 ch.g. Foxhound (USA) 103 – La Petruschka (Ballad Rock **46 §** 122) [2002 66d: f6s f5s f6g 6f⁴ 5.1g 5s 5.3m⁴ 5d 6f⁵ 5m Sep 2] close-coupled gelding: poor performer: best at 5f/6f: acts on firm and good to soft going: often blinkered/visored nowadays: tends to race prominently: wayward and untrustworthy. *D. Nicholls*

RUSSIAN PRINCESS (IRE) 2 b.f. (Apr 20) Mujadil (USA) 119 – Romanovna **74** (Mummy's Pet 125) [2002 6s⁴ 6m³ Aug 17] IR 23,000Y: small filly: fourth foal: sister to 2 winners, notably 5-y-o Cotton House: dam maiden out of half-sister to Eclipse winner Connaught: better effort in maidens (fair form) when third of 20 to Flying Express at Ripon: may well prove best short of 1m. *P. W. Harris*

RUSSIAN RELATION (USA) 2 b.c. (Mar 24) Kris S (USA) – Tereshkova (USA) **78 p** 113 (Mr Prospector (USA)) [2002 7.5g² Jul 30] third foal: brother to 2001 2-y-o 7f winner Kriskova and half-brother to French 1½m winner Russian Range (by St Jovite): dam, 6f (at 2 yrs in France) to 1m (in UAE) winner, sister to Middle Park winner and 2000 Guineas runner-up Lycius: 11/8 on but green, ¾-length second of 7 to Cranshaws in maiden at Beverley, leading briefly final 1f: should stay at least 1m. *D. R. Loder*

RUSSIAN RHAPSODY 5 b.m. Cosmonaut – Hannah's Music 85 (Music Boy 124) **96** [2002 100: 8d⁵ 7g⁶ 8d⁶ 7f⁴ 7g⁴ 8g p7g Nov 23] good-topped mare: useful performer: some respectable efforts in 2002: well held in handicaps last 2 starts: best at 7f/1m: acts on any turf ground. *M. A. Jarvis*

RUSSIAN RHYTHM (USA) 2 ch.f. (Feb 12) Kingmambo (USA) 125 – Balis- **113 p** troika (USA) (Nijinsky (CAN) 138) [2002 6m* 6m* 6m* 6f² Oct 4]
    In the heyday of children's adventure comics suspense was created— stimulating the next week's sales—by leaving the heroes and heroines precariously placed at the end of each episode of the main strip cartoons. No matter how improbable a predicament—cornered by man-eating tigers, clinging one-handed over a precipice—the hero or heroine was, of course, guaranteed to emerge unscathed. But fathoming the means of escape or rescue could cause some head-scratching among readers, and sometimes among the writers themselves. The story goes that one writer left his hero in such an impossible position that he couldn't think of a plausible way of extricating him. In desperation, he started the following week's episode with the words 'In a bound, Jack was free!' Even trainer Sir Michael Stoute, who must have thought he had seen it all in a long racing career, was left scratching his head after a Houdini-like performance by Russian Rhythm in the Peugeot Lowther Stakes at York in August. In Stoute's words, Russian Rhythm 'overcame the impossible', pocketed against the far rail a furlong out before being extricated and responding magnificently to win going away from Irish-trained Danaskaya and the Queen Mary winner Romantic Liason. Any victory, let alone such a clear-cut one, looked improbable when front-running Wunders Dream, winner of the Molecomb at Goodwood, suddenly veered off a true line at the two-furlong marker, hanging left and causing Russian Rhythm's rider Kieren Fallon to snatch up to avoid a collision, just as he was beginning a run against the far rail. Forced to drop back and losing valuable momentum, Russian Rhythm was then kept hemmed against the rail behind Wunders Dream by her main rival Romantic Liason whom Frankie Dettori quickly moved up on the outside of

*Peugeot Lowther Stakes, York—Russian Rhythm shortens as favourite for the 2003 Guineas
after overcoming trouble in running to burst through between the grey Danaskaya and Romantic Liason;
Wimple (No.5) and Wunders Dream are the only other runners*

the leader approaching the final furlong. A little wider, 50/1-shot Wimple with
Danaskaya on her right, widest of all, were also throwing down a challenge, the
pair also beginning to drift across towards Romantic Liason. Entering the final
furlong, Russian Rhythm was last of the five runners with seemingly nowhere to
go. Switched three wide as Wunders Dream weakened, Russian Rhythm effected a
most unlikely escape by quickening in amazing style through the narrowing gap
between Wimple and Romantic Liason. Russian Rhythm got through in the nick of
time, hitting the front about fifty yards out and being well on top at the line, a length
and a quarter and a neck ahead of Danaskaya and Romantic Liason, the latter not
quite seeing out the six furlongs, with Wimple fourth and non-staying Wunders
Dream last. Had she not been hampered two furlongs out, Russian Rhythm would
certainly have won by a fair bit further. For a five-runner race, the Lowther produced plenty of drama and the stewards had quite a bit to ponder. Though deciding
to leave the placings unaltered, the riders of Wunders Dream (Michael Fenton) and
Danaskaya (Kevin Manning), who was found to have interfered with Wimple,
picked up suspensions of four days and two days respectively for careless riding.

Russian Rhythm's victory in the Lowther extended her unbeaten run to
three, following victories in a maiden at Newmarket in June (over the more
experienced Fancy Lady, who won next time at the July meeting) and in the
Princess Margaret Stakes at Ascot at the end of July. An imposing individual with
the scope to progress, the waited-with Russian Rhythm looked of tremendous
potential when winning the Princess Margaret in good style by a length and a
quarter from Luvah Girl, the pair clear. As low as 10/1 straight afterwards in ante-
post betting on the One Thousand Guineas, Russian Rhythm was down to 5/2 in
places after the Lowther as her reputation soared to new heights. She looked certain
to take plenty of beating in any of the remaining top domestic two-year-old races
chosen for her, and looked a most exciting classic prospect, having the looks and
pedigree of a filly with the potential to be even better at three. Russian Rhythm was
eased to 5/1 after a surprising defeat on her final start in the Cheveley Park Stakes
at the hands of Airwave. There were only six runners, including Danaskaya and
Wimple, and the early pace was muddling. Odds-on Russian Rhythm went down
by a length and a half, seemingly beaten fairly and squarely on the day after edging
ahead two furlongs out before being beaten for speed by Airwave. Russian Rhythm,
afterwards found to have come into season at Newmarket, was so impressive at
Ascot and York that it would be wrong to dismiss her classic chances

849

because of her defeat in circumstances that played to the winner's strengths. Russian Rhythm has so much to recommend her and, all things being equal, is sure to be there or thereabouts back at Newmarket on May 4th.

		Mr Prospector (b 1970)	Raise A Native / Gold Digger
	Kingmambo (USA) (b 1990)	Miesque (b 1984)	Nureyev / Pasadoble
Russian Rhythm (USA) (ch.f. Feb 12, 2000)		Nijinsky (b 1967)	Northern Dancer / Flaming Page
	Balistroika (USA) (ch 1988)	Balidaress (gr 1973)	Balidar / Innocence

Russian Rhythm is a big, good-topped filly with plenty of scope and she is from an excellent family. By the miler Kingmambo, one of America's most fashionable sires, Russian Rhythm fetched 370,000 dollars as a foal and 440,000 guineas when resold as a yearling. Her dam, the unraced Balistroika, is superbly bred, being a half-sister to the Cheveley Park winners Desirable (the dam of One Thousand Guineas winner Shadayid) and Park Appeal (the dam of Lockinge winner Cape Cross and grandam of Diktat) and the Irish Oaks winner Alydaress, among others. Russian Rhythm's Princess Margaret and Lowther victories made Balistroika the fifth daughter of the remarkable Balidaress to be represented by a pattern winner, Alydaress and minor winner Salidar being the dams of Group 3 winners Allurement and Bin Ajwaad respectively. On pedigree, Russian Rhythm looks most likely to be a miler—her dam is similarly bred to Shadayid who was by

Cheveley Park Stud's "Russian Rhythm"

Nijinsky's son Shadeed—but her year-older close relation the useful French filly Balade Russe (by another son of Mr Prospector, Gone West) won at nine furlongs as a two-year-old and was campaigned at middle distances in the latest season, seeming to run well in the face of a very stiff task when eleventh in the Prix de Diane. Balistroika has also had two winners in America, Alawal (by another son of Mr Prospector, Miswaki) and Ive Gota Bad Liver (by Mt Livermore), the former successful at up to nine furlongs and the latter at up to seven, as well as a winner in Japan, the sprinter Zenno Keima (by Gone West). Russian Rhythm has raced so far only on going firmer than good. *Sir Michael Stoute*

RUSSIAN SOCIETY   2 b.f. (Feb 11) Darshaan 133 – Russian Snows (IRE) 113   **82 p**
(Sadler's Wells (USA) 132) [2002 7m³ 8g² Sep 10] leggy, good-topped filly: second foal: dam, 1¼m to 12.5f (Prix de Royallieu) winner who was second in Irish Oaks, out of Irish 1000 Guineas winner Arctique Royale from good family: fairly useful form in maidens at Newmarket and Leicester, caught close home and clear of rest when ½-length second to Time Honoured in latter: should stay at least 1¼m: capable of better. *D. R. Loder*

RUST EN VREDE   3 b.g. Royal Applause 124 – Souveniers (Relko 136) [2002 72:   **57**
6m 8.2g 7.9d 10m² 12f p10g Dec 21] tall gelding: fair maiden at 2 yrs: modest in 2002, leaving J. L. Eyre after third start: should stay beyond 7f. *D. Carroll*

RUSTLE IN THE WIND   2 b.f. (Jan 25) Barathea (IRE) 127 – Night Owl 73 (Night   **70 p**
Shift (USA)) [2002 6m³ Oct 2] 40,000Y: rather leggy filly: first foal: dam, headstrong maiden who stayed 6f, half-sister to 10-y-o Lord Jim and smart French performer up to 10.5f Audacieuse: 7/1, 5¾ lengths third of 11 to Donizetti in maiden at Newcastle, keeping on after racing freely: should do better. *M. R. Channon*

RUTLAND CHANTRY (USA)   8 b.g. Dixieland Band (USA) – Christchurch (FR)   **74**
88 (So Blessed 130) [2002 79: 10m⁶ 10d.6 11.6d⁵ 12.3g⁵ 9.9g⁴ 12.1d⁵ 9.9d⁴ 9.9g*
11.6d 11.8g* 12m⁶ 10g⁵ 12g⁶ 10s 10d Oct 21] robust gelding: fair performer: won ladies handicap at Beverley in July and minor event at Leicester in August: effective at 1¼m/ 1½m: acts on fibresand, best recent turf form on good going or softer (acts on heavy): tried blinkered earlier in career: usually races prominently: tough. *S. Gollings*

RUTTERS RENEGADE (IRE)   2 b.f. (Apr 2) General Monash (USA) 107 – Penul-   **82**
timate Cress (IRE) (My Generation 111) [2002 6m⁴ 5g² 6s² 6g* 7m² 7m* 8g² 8m* Sep
29] IR 3,500Y: leggy, quite good-topped filly: fourth foal: sister to 4-y-o Dancing Penney: dam unraced: fairly useful performer: improved steadily, winning seller at Newcastle in June and nurseries at Redcar and Musselburgh in September: stays 1m: acts on soft and good to firm ground: consistent. *G. A. Swinbank*

RUWAYA (USA)   3 b. or br.f. Red Ransom (USA) – Upper Class Lady (USA) (Upper   **80**
Nile (USA)) [2002 –: 11.5m² 10.9m² p13g² 14.1m² 12.3m⁴ 14f 12d⁴ f16g Dec 4] small-
ish, angular filly: fairly useful maiden: stayed 1¾m: acted on good to firm going and polytrack: tried visored/in cheekpieces: sometimes ran in snatches: visits Lujain. *C. E. Brittain*

RYAN'S BLISS (IRE)   2 b.f. (Apr 18) Danetime (IRE) 121 – Raja Moulana 75 (Raja   **69**
Baba (USA)) [2002 7.6m 7m 7.1m⁴ p6g p7g Dec 14] 4,500Y: ninth foal: half-sister to useful Italian performer up to 1¼m Futurballa (by Taufan), also 6f to 8.5f winner in Britain at 2 yrs, and 2000 2-y-o 5f winner Sing A Song (by Blues Traveller): dam 7f winner: fair maiden: stays 7f. *T. D. McCarthy*

RYAN'S GOLD (IRE)   4 b.g. Distant View (USA) 126 – Kathleen's Dream (USA)   **–**
(Last Tycoon 131) [2002 71: 9.3g 10.1d 9m 12m⁶ Sep 29] close-coupled gelding: fair maiden at best: little form at 4 yrs: tried blinkered. *B. Mactaggart*

RYAN'S QUEST (IRE)   3 b.f. Mukaddamah (USA) 125 – Preponderance (IRE) 85   **58**
(Cyrano de Bergerac 120) [2002 67: 5m 5.1m 5m p5g⁴ 5.3d p5g⁴ p5g⁵ f5g p5g Dec 21]
neat filly: modest maiden: raced only at 5f: acts on firm ground and polytrack: looked none too keen once at 2 yrs. *K. R. Burke*

RYDERS STORM (USA)   3 b. or br.g. Dynaformer (USA) – Justicara 113 (Rusti-   **–**
caro (FR) 124) [2002 94: 10.2g⁵ 9g 11.9s⁴ Jun 8] strong, angular gelding: fairly useful performer at 2 yrs for M. Johnston: well held on Flat in 2002: blinkered final start: joined M. Pipe, won 3 times over hurdles in autumn, but ran poorly next outing. *P. F. I. Cole*

RYE N DRY (IRE)   2 ch.f. (May 23) Timeless Times (USA) 99 – Inonder 31 (Belfort   **–**
(FR) 89) [2002 5g 7f 7m Oct 5] workmanlike filly: sixth foal: half-sister to 3 winners by Common Grounds, including 1997 2-y-o 5f to 7.5f winner Chips and 6f (at 2 yrs)/7f winner Aretino, both fairly useful: dam poor maiden: well held in maidens. *A. Berry*

RYME INTRINSECA   3 ch.f. Hector Protector (USA) 124 – Star And Garter 75   **88**
(Soviet Star (USA) 128) [2002 7g 7d 8d* 8f³ 10m Aug 28] workmanlike filly: second
foal: dam, maiden who stayed 7f at 2 yrs (didn't train on), half-sister to smart miler
Inchmurrin (dam of Inchinor) and to dam of smart miler Balisada: fairly useful
performer: won maiden at Bath in May: good third in listed event at Bath penultimate
start: free-going sort, not sure to stay beyond 1m: acts on firm and good to soft going.
M. R. Channon

RYMER'S RASCAL   10 b.g. Rymer 121 – City Sound 63 (On Your Mark 125) [2002   **66 §**
77, a–: 7d⁶ 8.5m⁶ 8.3g⁵ 8m 8d 8.1m 6.9g 8g* 8.3s* 8g² 8g Sep 7] sturdy gelding: fair   **a– §**
performer: won selling handicaps at Thirsk and Hamilton in August: best at 7f/easy 1m:
acts on any going: takes good hold and usually waited with: sometimes finds little/looks
less than keen: unreliable nowadays. *E. J. Alston*

S

SAAFEND ROCKET (IRE)   4 b.g. Distinctly North (USA) 115 – Simple Annie   **53**
(Simply Great (FR) 122) [2002 68, a77: f8.5g⁶ p8g 8m 8.3g p7g⁵ p8g 8.3d f8.5g Oct 19]   **a67**
fair performer on all-weather, modest on turf in 2002: left Andrew Reid following
seventh start: stays 8.5f: acts on fibresand, raced mainly on good or firmer ground on turf:
visored/blinkered once each at 3 yrs: sometimes carries head high. *R. Lee*

SABADILLA (USA)   8 b.g. Sadler's Wells (USA) 132 – Jasmina (USA) (Forli   **92 ?**
(ARG)) [2002 11.6g⁶ 12d³ 12g Oct 17] strong, lengthy gelding: has a short, round action:
smart performer at best, lightly raced in recent years: seemingly fairly useful form first 2
starts in 2002: stays 1½m: acts on firm and soft going, below best only outing on dirt
(blinkered, for E. Charpy in UAE at 7 yrs): reportedly bled from nose final outing.
M. R. Bosley

SABANA (IRE)   4 b.g. Sri Pekan (USA) 117 – Atyaaf (USA) 48 (Irish River (FR) 131)   **69**
[2002 74: 7f 7f⁶ 7g 7.5g 6m 7.1d 7.2g 7.1g 6m 6g² 6g⁴ 6m⁴ f6g⁴ 6m³ f6s² f6g⁴ f6g⁵ f6g   **a60**
f6f Nov 29] quite attractive gelding: fair handicapper on turf, modest on all-weather:
effective at 6f to 1m: acts on firm going, good to soft and fibresand: blinkered twice:
sometimes wanders: consistent. *J. M. Bradley*

SABO PET   2 b.c. (Feb 21) Prince Sabo 123 – Jade Pet 90 (Petong 126) [2002 5d² May   **72**
30] 20,000Y: fourth foal: half-brother to smart 7f to 9.4f winner Hail The Chief (by Be
My Chief), later Grade 2 1¼m winner in USA, and 6-y-o Just Wiz: dam, 5f winner,
half-sister to dam of smart sprinter Sampower Star: 3/1, ¾-length second of 13 to Streaky
in maiden at Goodwood, keeping on well under hands and heels: reportedly split a cannon
bone after. *P. W. Harris*

SABRE DANCE   3 ch.g. Sabrehill (USA) 120 – Anna Karietta 82 (Precocious 126)   **60**
[2002 62p: 8g⁶ 9.7m⁶ 12.1g⁶ Sep 12] leggy, unfurnished gelding: modest form in 4
maidens: sold 3,000 gns, sent to Kuwait. *H. Candy*

SABREEZE   4 ch.g. Sabrehill (USA) 120 – Zipperti Do 70 (Precocious 126) [2002   **–**
72: 8.2m 7f 8g Aug 27] quite good-topped gelding: fair maiden at 3 yrs: well held in
2002: shaped as though something amiss penultimate start, leaving P. Harris afterwards.
M. Blanshard

SABRELINE   3 ch.f. Sabrehill (USA) 120 – Story Line 98 (In The Wings 128) [2002   **64**
58: 7m² f7g 10m 11.6d⁶ 12d p12g f12g² f12g Dec 4] modest maiden: stays 1½m: acts on   **a57**
fibresand, yet to race on extremes of going on turf. *D. W. P. Arbuthnot*

SACHIKO   4 b.f. Celtic Swing 138 – Leap of Faith (IRE) 65 (Northiam (USA))   **–**
[2002 54: 10g 8.3d⁵ 8d⁴ 9d 7m⁶ Oct 5] modest maiden at 3 yrs: well held in 2002.
W. de Best-Turner

SACHO (IRE)   9 b.g. Sadler's Wells (USA) 132 – Oh So Sharp 131 (Kris 135) [2002   **–**
–: 11.9m May 14] smart performer at best: very lightly raced through injuries, and tailed
off only run in 2002. *John A. Harris*

SACRED LOVE (IRE)   2 ch.f. (Mar 29) Barathea (IRE) 127 – Abstraction (Rainbow   **69 p**
Quest (USA) 134) [2002 8g 8d⁵ Oct 30] IR 150,000Y: close-coupled, angular filly:
half-sister to several winners, including useful 6f (at 2 yrs) to 9f (in Germany) winner
Blueberry Forest (by Charnwood Forest): dam unraced sister to very smart French
performer up to 12.5f De Quest and half-sister to US Grade 1 9f/1¼m winner Wandesta:

fair form in maidens: not knocked about when fifth to Devant at Yarmouth: should do better at 1¼m/1½m. *E. A. L. Dunlop*

SACREMENTUM (IRE) 7 b.g. Night Shift (USA) – Tantum Ergo 106 (Tanfirion 110) [2002 –, a38: f14.8g f12g Jun 22] good-bodied gelding: probably of little account nowadays. *R. J. Smith* —

SACSAYHUAMAN 3 b.f. Halling (USA) 133 – La Dolce Vita 76 (Mazilier (USA) 107) [2002 8.3m³ 8g³ 7.1m³ 8.5m 8g⁴ Oct 14] lengthy filly: first foal: dam 5f (at 2 yrs) and 7f winner: fair maiden: stays 1m: raced only on good/good to firm going: edged left on debut: flicked tail in paddock/mounted on track second start. *R. M. Beckett* **69**

SADDAD (USA) 3 ch.c. Gone West (USA) – Lite Light (USA) (Majestic Light (USA)) [2002 112p: 5m³ Sep 12] strong, lengthy, attractive colt: smart form: won Flying Childers Stakes at Doncaster on last of 3 starts at 2 yrs: off 12 months (reported in spring to have suffered a setback), 1½ lengths third to Bishops Court in listed race at Doncaster on return: speedy, and likely to prove best at 5f: wore crossed noseband/started bit slowly last 2 outings at 2 yrs. *Sir Michael Stoute* **112**

SADHAKA 3 b.f. Slip Anchor 136 – Secretilla (USA) 61 (Secreto (USA) 128) [2002 63p: 10.2d⁴ 9.5d 10m 9m 7d Nov 12] fair form when sixth in maiden at Milan only start at 2 yrs and fourth to Windermere in similar event at Bath: left L. Cumani, well beaten for new stable. *L. Riccardi, Italy* **72**

SADIE SADIE 3 b.f. Primo Dominie 121 – Ann's Pearl (IRE) 81 (Cyrano de Bergerac 120) [2002 46: 5d* 5m f6g 5v Nov 8] fair performer, lightly raced: won maiden at Sandown in August, despite idling: well held in handicaps after: likely to prove best at 5f/6f. *P. J. Makin* **74**

SADIKA (IRE) 2 b.f. (Mar 23) Bahhare (USA) 122 – Nordica 99 (Northfields (USA)) [2002 p8g Nov 27] half-sister to several winners, including useful 7f winner (including at 2 yrs) who stayed 1½m (fourth in Oaks) Sueboog (by Darshaan), now dam of 5-y-o Best of The Bests, and useful 6f and 1m winner Marika (by Marju): dam 6f and 1m winner: green, eighth to Face The Storm in Lingfield maiden, carrying head bit high. *I. A. Balding* **55**

SADLERS LAW (IRE) 3 b.c. Sadler's Wells (USA) 132 – Dathiyna (IRE) (Kris 135) [2002 –p: 8.1f⁶ 8m 10.2g* 10d⁵ Jun 10] fair performer: won minor event at Bath in May: should prove at least as effective at 1m as 1¼m: free-going sort (pulled hard/found little final start): has hung: sold 14,000 gns. *J. W. Hills* **76**

SAD MAD BAD (USA) 8 b.g. Sunny's Halo (CAN) – Quite Attractive (USA) (Well Decorated (USA)) [2002 –: 16v² Oct 29] workmanlike gelding: modest handicapper in 1999: well held since: tried blinkered: fairly useful chaser. *Mrs M. Reveley* —

SAFE FROM HARM (USA) 2 ch.c. (Mar 1) Mt Livermore (USA) – Not So Careless (USA) (Desert Wine (USA)) [2002 7m* Sep 24] $375,000Y: big, strong colt: has plenty of scope: seventh foal: brother to very smart US Grade 1 9f winner Subordination and half-brother to winners in USA by French Deputy and Prized: dam, 6.5f winner in US, half-sister to top-class 1½m performer in Britain/US Cacoethes: 2/1 favourite, made all in 9-runner maiden at Newmarket, beating Financial Future by 1¼ lengths: useful prospect, sure to win more races. *Sir Michael Stoute* **92 p**

SAFE SHOT 3 b.g. Salse (USA) 128 – Optaria 83 (Song 132) [2002 52: 9m 12m Sep 29] modest form on second 2-y-o start, little show since, leaving Mrs D. Thomson after reappearance. *Mrs J. C. McGregor* —

SAFFRON HEIGHTS 4 b.f. Shirley Heights 130 – Persia (IRE) (Persian Bold 123) [2002 –: p12g p12g 10d⁶ Aug 11] lightly-raced maiden: seemingly modest form final start: tongue tied (slowly away) on debut. *C. A. Horgan* **59 ?**

SAFINAZ 4 gr.f. Environment Friend 128 – Safidar 83 (Roan Rocket 128) [2002 41: f9.4g² f9.4g² f9.4g³ f8g⁴ f9.4g f8.5g f9.4g³ 7.5g⁵ 9.9g 12g Jun 18] modest maiden: stays 1¼m: acts on fibresand. *Mrs N. Macauley* **50**

SAFRANINE (IRE) 5 b.m. Dolphin Street (FR) 125 – Webbiana (African Sky 124) [2002 55d: f6g f5g* f5g³ f5g 5m³ 5d³ 6g 5s* 5g 5d⁵ 5g⁴ 5m 5m⁵ Sep 23] rather leggy mare: modest handicapper: made all at Southwell in March and Hamilton in June: has won at 6f, possibly best at 5f: yet to race on heavy ground, acts on any other turf and fibresand: tried blinkered/visored. *Miss A. Stokell* **61**

SAGA BOY (IRE) 2 b.g. (Feb 11) Efisio 120 – Caribbean Dancer 71 (Shareef Dancer (USA) 135) [2002 7d⁶ Oct 18] 17,000Y: first foal: dam lightly-raced 1m winner: 16/1, 2 lengths sixth of 16 to Janes Gem in claimer at Redcar, plugging on from rear: should stay 1m: sold 7,000 gns. *C. F. Wall* **57**

SAGES END (IRE) 2 b.c. (Mar 15) College Chapel 122 – Celtic Guest (IRE) (Be My **56**
Guest (USA) 126) [2002 5.1d⁴ 6g³ Aug 7] second foal: dam unraced: modest form in
maidens at Nottingham and Newcastle 4 months apart. *T. D. Easterby*

SAGITTARIUS 6 b.h. Sadler's Wells (USA) 132 – Ste Nitouche (FR) (Riverman **112**
(USA) 131) [2002 117: 12g 13.4f² May 9] big, leggy horse: has a quick action: smart performer, lightly raced: much the better effort in pattern races in 2002 when length second
to St Expedit in Ormonde Stakes at Chester: stays 13f: acts on any ground. *R. Haugen,
Norway*

SAGUARO 8 b.g. Green Desert (USA) 127 – Badawi (USA) 103 (Diesis 133) [2002 **47**
–, a52: f8.5g* f9.4g f9.4g² f9.4g⁶ 10.9m³ f8.5g⁴ 11.8g⁵ f9.4f Aug 16] modest on all- **a58**
weather, poor on turf: won seller at Wolverhampton in March: stayed 9.4f: acted on fibresand and firm going: tried visored: dead. *R. Lee*

SAHARA DESERT 3 b.c. Green Desert (USA) 127 – Apache Star 96 (Arazi (USA) **109**
135) [2002 94p: 7m⁵ 8g 8g 6d 8g⁵ 8g⁵ 7.5m⁶ Oct 6] 140,000Y: well-made colt: good
mover: first foal: dam 7f (at 2 yrs) to 9f winner from family of very smart miler Rebecca
Sharp: useful performer: first past post in minor event at Newmarket (beat Nemo Fugat
by neck, demoted to fifth for causing interference) in April: creditable eighth to Continent
in July Cup at Newmarket fourth start: acted as pacemaker in Group 1 events most other
starts in 2002: creditable efforts when seventh in St James's Palace Stakes at Royal Ascot
and fifth, beaten 3 lengths by Rock of Gibraltar, in Prix du Moulin de Longchamp on
third/sixth outings: below form final appearance: stays 1m: acts on soft and good to firm
going: often wears crossed noseband. *A. P. O'Brien, Ireland*

SAHARA SHADE (USA) 2 ch.f. (Mar 27) Shadeed (USA) 135 – Tadwin 109 (Never **79**
So Bold 135) [2002 6m* 6m 5d* 5m Jul 13] $20,000Y: good-topped filly: sister to useful
1997 2-y-o 5f (Queen Mary) winner Nadwah and half-sister to several winners, including
fairly useful 5f and (including at 2 yrs) 6f winner Iltimas (by Dayjur): dam, 5f (at 2 yrs)
and 6f winner, half-sister to smart sprinter Reesh: fair form: won maiden at Newcastle in
May and minor event at Beverley (by neck from Danehill Stroller) in July: below form in
nursery final start: will probably prove best at 5f/6f: joined S. Keightley. *T. D. Barron*

SAIF MAJROUR 6 b.g. Darshaan 133 – Garconniere (Gay Mecene (USA) 128) [2002 **–**
f12g⁵ Mar 25] fairly useful bumper winner for P. Webber at 4 yrs: well held in maiden at
Wolverhampton. *M. J. Gingell*

SAIF SAREEA 2 b.c. (Mar 18) Atraf 116 – Slipperose 72 (Persepolis (FR) 127) [2002 **54**
5f⁶ 6.1d⁵ 5.1d⁶ 5v² 6s⁵ 6g⁶ 5g f5g f6s Oct 8] 17,000Y: leggy colt: eighth foal: closely **a–**
related to 7-y-o Yorkies Boy: dam 11.5f winner: modest maiden: effective at 5f/6f: acts
on heavy going, below form on fibresand: blinkered final start. *A. Berry*

SAIHOOK 3 ch.c. Halling (USA) 133 – Agama (USA) 44 (Nureyev (USA) 131) [2002 **74**
8g³ 9.9d⁴ 8.5m 9.9f⁴ 8g³ Dec 15] angular colt: third foal: half-brother to 6f (at 2 yrs) to
9f winner Can Can Lady (by Anshan) and useful 1997 2-y-o 7f/1m winner Setteen (by
Robellino): dam poor form in 2 starts in Britain at 2 yrs, then won over 13.5f in France as
3-y-o: fair form in maidens: left M. Jarvis before final outing: stays 1¼m: acts on firm
going: has worn crossed noseband. *A. Smith, UAE*

SAILING SHOES (IRE) 6 b.g. Lahib (USA) 129 – Born To Glamour (Ajdal (USA) **73 §**
130) [2002 67§: f6s f6g 5d* 5f 5m³ 5s 5g 5m 6f Sep 7] smallish gelding: fair handicapper: **a– §**
won at Thirsk in May: effective at 5f/6f: acts on any turf going, except possibly heavy:
tried blinkered/visored/tongue tied: seems to need to dominate, and can't be trusted.
D. Nicholls

SAILING THROUGH 2 b.c. (Apr 3) Bahhare (USA) 122 – Hopesay 84 (Warning **65 p**
136) [2002 6d⁶ 7.1m⁶ 8g⁶ Oct 2] 23,000F, 47,000Y: rangy colt: second foal: half-brother
to fairly useful 2001 2-y-o 6f winner Road To Justice (by Danehill Dancer): dam maiden
who stayed 6f: fair form in maidens: free-going sort, likely to prove best short of 1m: has
scope to do better as 3-y-o. *T. G. Mills*

SAILOR'S VALENTINE (USA) 3 b.f. Irish River (FR) 131 – Vashon (USA) **69**
(Seattle Dancer (USA) 119) [2002 9d⁵ p12g⁶ 12f⁶ Sep 23] first foal: dam, 8.5f winner in
USA (including minor stakes) out of half-sister to Arlington Million/Japan Cup winner
Golden Pheasant: best effort in maidens (fair form) when sixth at Lingfield on second
outing (left J. Gosden after): should stay 1¾m. *J. K. Hennig, USA*

SAIL WITH THE TIDE (IRE) 2 b.f. (Feb 23) Charnwood Forest (IRE) 125 – Good **89**
Relations (Be My Guest (USA) 126) [2002 7.9m⁵ f8s³ 8v² 8v⁵ Nov 22] 2,000Y: smallish
filly: half-sister to several winners, including 1990 2-y-o 7f winner Affair of Honour (by
Ahonoora) and fairly useful 1m winner Tacoma Heights (by Taufan): dam, Irish 7f and

1½m winner, half-sister to high-class performer up to 1½m Montekin: fairly useful maiden: 1½ lengths second to Shelini at Doncaster: creditable fifth to Vallee Enchantee in listed race at Saint-Cloud later in November: should stay 1¼m: acts on heavy ground. *M. G. Quinlan*

SAINT ALEBE   3 b.g. Bishop of Cashel 122 – Soba Up 74 (Persian Heights 129)   **79**
[2002 10d⁴ 10d⁴ 9g⁴ 10s² Oct 26] 8,000Y: tall, good-topped gelding: poor mover: second foal: dam, 1¼m/1½m winner, half-sister to dam of very smart 1¼m/1½m performer Dark Moondancer out of high-class sprinter Soba: fair maiden: good second at Newbury final start: will be well suited by 1½m+. *D. R. C. Elsworth*

SAKAMOTO   4 b.g. Celtic Swing 138 – Possessive Lady 62 (Dara Monarch 128)   **–**
[2002 –: 6f May 13] tall, good-topped gelding: no longer of much account. *R. C. Spicer*

SAKHEE (USA)   5 b.h. Bahri (USA) 125 – Thawakib (IRE) 108 (Sadler's Wells   **128**
(USA) 132) [2002 136: a10f* a10f³ 10s² Aug 10]
  An austere-sounding critic of yesteryear once observed that 'the human knee is a joint and not an entertainment'. Sadly, in 2002, it turned out to be a very similar story with the equine knee belonging to Sakhee. His was a damaged joint and the best horse in training from 2001 was undermined. He might have been described as an also ran in the latest season, except that he was far more notable by his absence. Sakhee did win his warm-up contest for the Dubai World Cup but, after a sorry display in the main event itself, the remainder of his career was comprised of just one more race. He cast a long shadow over the latest European middle-distance events, as no horse proved capable of the form he had shown in breathtaking victories in the Juddmonte International and the Arc. In the end, alas, that included Sakhee himself. There were several false dawns, when he was apparently waiting in the wings, but in the wings he stayed. For European racegoers in 2002, the entertainment provided by Sakhee was largely confined to reading about his next big-race target and then in reading why he failed to turn up.
  The decision to keep Sakhee in training gained nothing like the reward it deserved. Connections were not left entirely out of pocket, however. The Concord Conditions Stakes at Nad Al Sheba in February was a suitable warm-up race for the Dubai World Cup four weeks later when Sakhee faced only four rivals and two of them were his pacemakers! Amid high excitement, he won. Actually, it was an impressive enough performance as Sakhee beat the smart Atlantis Prince (one of the pacemakers) by nine lengths, and he was sent off at 5/2-on with British bookmakers in the Dubai World Cup over the same course and distance. Disappointingly and surprisingly, this time he lost by nearly nine lengths. Third place and £419,580 at prevailing exchange rates might suggest that Sakhee had not run too badly, but the rating for that run was easily his worst since his two-year-old days and some 25 lb below his best. On the form he showed on his debut on dirt (which was a bit below his turf form), when touched off by Tiznow in the previous October's Breeders' Cup Classic, Sakhee should have won the latest Dubai World Cup. After moving up to challenge entering the straight, however, he was immediately eclipsed by stablemate Street Cry and overrun by 66/1-shot Sei Mi as well as in the final furlong. Though he would not have been the first to sustain an injury running in Dubai, Sakhee was reportedly 'fine' immediately after this defeat. The top European middle-distance events were on his agenda, but he did not appear in any of them. After pleasing in a racecourse gallop at Sandown in July, he was ante-post favourite for the King George and did make it to the final declaration stage but was withdrawn on the day when the going was considered too firm. When he did appear, it was in the Prix Gontaut-Biron at Deauville in August and, at pari-mutuel odds of 5/1-on, Sakhee was beaten a length by Wellbeing, unable to quicken after travelling just as well as the winner on the home turn. Frankie Dettori missed the ride because of chicken pox, which was not so bad in hindsight because this was a poor way to remember the champion racehorse of 2001.
  It was clear at an early stage that Godolphin were having plenty of problems in getting Sakhee ready for those European races. Apparently it was the knee injury sustained in the 2000 Derby that caught up with him. 'His knee problem meant we couldn't risk him on the firm ground that has prevailed for so long,' said Godolphin racing manager Simon Crisford. 'Since the Breeders' Cup he has not been the Sakhee that we know,' said Dettori. Now retired to stand at Nunnery Stud

Godolphin's "Sakhee"

Sakhee (USA) (b.h. 1997)	Bahri (USA) (b 1992)	Riverman (b 1969)	Never Bend
			River Lady
		Wasnah (b 1987)	Nijinsky
			Highest Trump
	Thawakib (IRE) (b 1990)	Sadler's Wells (b 1981)	Northern Dancer
			Fairy Bridge
		Tobira Celeste (b 1971)	Ribot
			Heavenly Body

in Norfolk at a fee of £20,000, Sakhee is a strong, good-topped horse who carried condition and had a round action. He was effective at a mile and a quarter and at a mile and a half. Although the ground was clearly vitally important to him after his injury, he had earlier won the Dante Stakes on firm. His Arc win came on soft, the Juddmonte International on good and he also showed top-class form, though short of his best, on dirt in the Breeders' Cup. Sakhee's American-based sire Bahri continues to have a very limited number of racecourse representatives, thirteen (and four winners) during the latest British turf season. Sakhee is far and away his best offspring. On the other side of the pedigree, dam Thawakib is a half-sister to King George, St Leger and Champion Stakes runner-up Celestial Storm and to the dam of the very smart middle-distance filly River Memories. Sakhee is Thawakib's third foal and third winner, the year-older Nasheed (by Riverman) having been a smart winner over seven furlongs (as a two-year-old) and a mile and a quarter. Thawakib's 2002 two-year-old Weqaar (a filly by Red Ransom) made the frame in three maiden races. *Saeed bin Suroor*

856

SALADIM (IRE)   3 b.c. Lahib (USA) 129 – Wathbat Mtoto 88 (Mtoto 134) [2002   **84**
8m⁴ 9.3s³ 8.1g* 10.3m⁵ 11.9d Aug 8] useful-looking colt: third foal: half-brother to UAE
6f winner Wathbat Mujtahid (by Mujtahid): dam, 1¼m winner who stayed 1½m, from
family of Stravinsky: fairly useful performer: won maiden at Warwick in July: good fifth
in handicap at Doncaster penultimate start: should stay 1½m: acts on good to firm going,
disappointing on softer than good: started slowly on debut: joined A. Smith in UAE.
M. A. Jarvis

SALAMAN (FR)   10 b.g. Saumarez 132 – Merry Sharp (Sharpen Up 127) [2002 18s⁵   **–**
19.1m Jun 22] lengthy gelding: lightly-raced handicapper nowadays: tried blinkered/
visored/tongue tied. *D. C. O'Brien*

SALCOMBE   2 ch.c. (Jan 9) Elmaamul (USA) 125 – West Devon (USA) (Gone West   **100**
(USA)) [2002 6m* 7g² 7m⁴ Sep 13] well-made colt: first living foal: dam unraced sister
to smart 5f performer Western Approach and half-sister to very smart performer up to
1¼m Tinners Way: won 3-runner newcomers event at Ascot in July despite wandering:
useful form when ¾-length second to Bourbonnais in listed race at York and 2¾ lengths
fourth to Almushahar in Champagne Stakes at Doncaster: will probably stay 1m.
B. W. Hills

SALERNO   3 ch.g. Mark of Esteem (IRE) 137 – Shamwari (USA) 63 (Shahrastani   **47 +**
(USA) 135) [2002 71: 6g 8m f6g f6g⁶ Nov 20] rather unfurnished gelding: fair form in
maidens at 2 yrs (reportedly underwent wind operation after final start): just poor form
in 2002, leaving M. Tregoning after reappearance: should stay 1m: has had tongue tied.
Miss Gay Kelleway

SALFORD EXPRESS (IRE)   6 ch.h. Be My Guest (USA) 126 – Summer Fashion   **49**
84 (Moorestyle 137) [2002 110: f12g f9.4g 8g f11g 8m f8g 7m Aug 6] leggy horse:
one-time smart performer: sometimes blinkered. *D. W. Chapman*

SALFORD LIGHTNING   4 b.g. Most Welcome 131 – Heresheis 69 (Free State   **–**
125) [2002 f12s p12g p13g Feb 6] 2,000 3-y-o: sixth foal: half-brother to several winning
stayers, including useful Athenry (by Siberian Express): dam 1½m to 2m winner: well
held in 3 maidens (slowly away on debut). *J. Cullinan*

SALIERI   2 b.f. (Mar 21) Silver Wizard (USA) 117 – Queen of Tides (IRE) 62 (Soviet   **51**
Star (USA) 128) [2002 p7g⁵ Jul 24] first foal: dam, maiden, best effort on debut at 2 yrs at
7f: 25/1, 10 lengths fifth of 10 to Pacific Paddy in maiden at Lingfield, slowly away and
never dangerous. *S. Dow*

SALIM   5 b.g. Salse (USA) 128 – Moviegoer 104 (Pharly (FR) 130) [2002 58§, a68§:   **– §**
f8.5g p8g⁶ p8g p8g p12g 9s 10s Jun 13] useful-looking gelding: irresolute performer:
tried blinkered/visored. *J. E. Long*

SALIM TOTO   4 b.f. Mtoto 134 – Villasanta (Corvaro (USA) 124) [2002 80: 11.6g²   **107**
12g* 10.4f² 10.5s⁵ 12d* 10.2g² 12m² 11.9m 10g* 12s Oct 26] quite good-topped filly:
useful performer: much improved in 2002, winning handicaps at Epsom in April (by
8 lengths from Dr Cool) and June (Vodafone Rated Stakes by 5 lengths from Solo
Flight) and listed race at Newmarket (beat Zee Zee Top by 2 lengths) in October: effective
at 1¼m/1½m: unraced on heavy going, acts on any other turf: front runner: genuine: visits
Singspiel. *H. Morrison*

*Lanwades Stud Severals Stakes, Newmarket—a third win of the season for the much improved front-running
Salim Toto, who beats Zee Zee Top (spots) and Mythic (partially obscured by second)*

SALINOR 2 ch.c. (Feb 1) Inchinor 119 – Salanka (IRE) 68 (Persian Heights 129) **61**
[2002 7s 7g Oct 24] 70,000F, 70,000Y: sturdy colt: fifth foal: brother to useful 1998
2-y-o 7f winner Penmayne and half-brother to fairly useful 7f (at 2 yrs) to 1½m winner
Kaiapoi (by Elmaamul): dam 1¼m winner: modest form, never dangerous, in maidens at
Leicester and Brighton: will stay at least 1m. *A. C. Stewart*

SALIX DANCER 5 b.g. Shareef Dancer (USA) 135 – Willowbank 66 (Gay Fandango **50**
(USA) 132) [2002 61d: p12g² p13g³ p13g⁴ p16g 16.2g⁵ 14.1m⁴ 14.1g 16g³ 18d³ Oct 21]
tall, angular gelding: had stringhalt: modest maiden handicapper: left Pat Mitchell
after third start: stayed 2¼m: acted on heavy going, good to firm and polytrack: dead.
H. J. Collingridge

SALKA'S RING 2 b.f. (Apr 28) Magic Ring (IRE) 115 – Nikki Noo Noo 58 (Preco- **–**
cious 126) [2002 5.1m Aug 6] fifth foal: dam 5f (at 2 yrs) to 1m winner: 12/1 and reluctant
to post, tailed off in seller at Bath. *R. J. Hodges*

SALLY TRAFFIC 3 b.f. River Falls 113 – Yankeedoodledancer (Mashhor Dancer **57**
(USA)) [2002 43: 6g 5m* 5d³ 6d³ 5f³ 5m 6f 5d² 5g⁶ 5d³ 6f⁵ f6g Oct 17] small, sturdy
filly: modest handicapper: won at Musselburgh (maiden event) in April: barely stays 6f:
acts on firm and good to soft ground. *R. M. Whitaker*

SALOME'S ATTACK 2 b. or br.f. (Mar 5) Anabaa (USA) 130 – Silver Cobra (USA) **90**
(Silver Hawk (USA) 123) [2002 5m³ 5g³ 6d² 6d² 7m⁴ 7.8g* 8g² 8d* Nov 4] 650,000
francs F: rather leggy filly: half-sister to several winners, including 4-y-o Double Honour
and useful 1½m winner Silversword (both by Highest Honor): dam, French 11f and 1½m
winner, sister to US Grade 1 9f winner Silver Ending: fairly useful performer: in frame in
maidens/minor event for M. Channon first 5 starts: won minor events at Tours in
September and Toulouse in November: stays 1m: yet to race on extremes of ground:
sometimes wanders. *H-A. Pantall, France*

SALSA 4 b.g. Salse (USA) 128 – Lana Turrel (USA) (Trempolino (USA) 135) [2002 **–**
63: 8f 8g May 31] leggy gelding: modest handicapper at 3 yrs: well held in 2002. *M. Dods*

SALSALINO 2 ch.c. (Apr 17) Salse (USA) 128 – Alicedale (USA) (Trempolino (USA) **95**
135) [2002 6m³ 6m* 7.1m⁶ Aug 31] 10,000Y, 25,000 2-y-o: fourth foal: half-brother to
1999 2-y-o 6f winner Ocean Rain (by Lake Coniston): dam placed at 1m/9f in France:
won maiden at Salisbury in August: improved (useful form) when about 4 lengths sixth
to Foss Way in Solario Stakes at Sandown: will stay at least 1m: raced only on good to
firm ground. *A. King*

SAL'S GAL 4 b.f. Efisio 120 – Ann's Pearl (IRE) 81 (Cyrano de Bergerac 120) [2002 **67**
73: 5d 6s f6g f5g* f7g⁴ f6g* f6g⁵ f6g⁶ Dec 20] smallish, workmanlike filly: fair performer: won handicap at Southwell in October and claimer at Wolverhampton (claimed from
P. Makin £6,000) in December: effective at 5f to 7f: acts on fibresand, good to firm and
good to soft going. *N. P. Littmoden*

SALTRIO 4 b.c. Slip Anchor 136 – Hills' Presidium (Presidium 124) [2002 101p: **109**
10.3m 12g 15.5s² 15.5v Nov 22] tall, angular, attractive colt: useful performer: off nearly
12 months before reappearance: easily best effort when short-neck second to Roman
Saddle in listed race at Maisons-Laffitte penultimate start, making most: stays 15.5f: acts
on soft and good to firm ground: pulled hard second start: joined J. Pease, France.
J. H. M. Gosden

SALTY JACK (IRE) 8 b.h. Salt Dome (USA) – Play The Queen (IRE) (King of **88**
Clubs 124) [2002 92: p8g⁴ p7g p8g 8g 7d 8.3s 8.1d⁵ 8f² 8f Aug 18] small horse: has a
round action: fairly useful handicapper: best at 7f/1m: acts on any turf going and all-
weather: best patiently ridden. *D. R. C. Elsworth*

SALUEM 5 b.m. Salse (USA) 128 – Pat Or Else 72 (Alzao (USA) 117) [2002 82: 12m³ **79**
12m 11.6d 12g² 20m 12.1d 13d² 11.9g f9.4g f11g Nov 26] small, workmanlike mare: fair **a–**
handicapper on turf: stays 14.5f: acts on soft and good to firm going, well held on
fibresand: blinkered (ran well) seventh start: none too consistent. *R. Guest*

SALUTE (IRE) 3 b.g. Muhtarram (USA) 125 – Alasib 93 (Siberian Express (USA) **99**
125) [2002 91: 10m 10.5d² 12m 10g² 9f 10s⁵ Oct 26] lengthy, quite attractive gelding:
useful handicapper: mostly creditable efforts in 2002, runner-up at Haydock and Newmarket (to Bonecrusher) and eighth in Cambridgeshire at Newmarket penultimate start:
best form at 9f/1¼m: acts on firm and soft going: edgy type (got particularly worked up
third outing). *J. M. P. Eustace*

SALVE REGINA (GER) 3 ch.f. Monsun (GER) 124 – Sacarina (Old Vic 136) [2002 **115**
8.5v* 11g* 11m* 12v² 12d² 12g² 12s² Sep 22] approx. 86,000Y in Germany: third foal:
sister to high-class German middle-distance performer Samum and half-sister to German

7f (at 2 yrs) and 11.5f winner Sandino (by Platini): dam unraced: smart performer: won maiden at Dusseldorf in March, listed race at Mulheim in May and Ostermann Preis der Diana at latter track (by 2½ lengths from Midnight Angel) in June: runner-up afterwards in Deutsches Derby at Hamburg (beaten 3 lengths by Next Desert but clear of remainder), Credit Suisse Private Banking Pokal at Cologne (beaten ½ length by Yavana's Pace), Grosser Preis von Baden (beaten 2½ lengths by Marienbard) and Preis von Europa at Cologne (beaten ¾ length by Well Made): stays 1½m: acts on heavy and good to firm ground: consistent: stays in training. *A. Schutz, Germany*

SALVIATI (USA) 5 b.g. Lahib (USA) 129 – Mother Courage 67 (Busted 134) [2002 **100** 95: 5d 5m⁴ 5f* 5m² 5m 5m 5f 6g 5.2f 5m 5m 5.2m⁶ Sep 17] sturdy gelding: useful handicapper: won at Redcar in June: fine second in Gosforth Park Cup at Newcastle later in month: below form last 4 starts: barely stays 6f: acts on firm and good to soft ground: sometimes slowly away: reportedly had breathing problem ninth start: travels strongly, and usually held up. *J. M. Bradley*

SALVINO (USA) 3 b.c. Lear Fan (USA) 130 – Fairy Fable (IRE) 95 (Fairy King **92** (USA)) [2002 7m⁴ 8.1s* Jun 8] $120,000Y: strong, well-made, attractive colt: sixth foal: half-brother to 3 winners abroad, including Fabricate (by Crafty Prospector), also 9.6f winner in Ireland: dam Irish 2-y-o 7f winner: won maiden at Haydock in June by 11 lengths from Code Sign: bandaged near-hind joint on debut: sent to USA: looked a useful performer in the making. *W. J. Haggas*

SAMAN 3 ch.c. Samim (USA) 84 – Redspet (Tina's Pet 121) [2002 54: 5.9s 8.2g 7f – f7g Jul 11] smallish colt: modest maiden at 2 yrs: no form in 2002: usually blinkered. *S. R. Bowring*

SAMARARDO 5 b.g. Son Pardo 107 – Kinlet Vision (IRE) 56 (Vision (USA)) [2002 – 50: f12s Jan 5] leggy gelding: modest performer at 4 yrs: stayed 2m: acted on soft going, good to firm and fibresand: tried visored, blinkered (well held) only outing on Flat in 2002: usually raced prominently: dead. *N. P. Littmoden*

SAMARA SONG 9 ch.g. Savahra Sound 111 – Hosting (Thatching 131) [2002 54, a–: **46** 7.5m 8m 7.5d⁶ 8.1g⁵ 7f Sep 17] lengthy gelding: poor handicapper nowadays: best at 7f/ **a–** 1m: acts on firm going, good to soft and fibresand: tried blinkered/visored early in career: occasionally slowly away/looks none too keen: best held up. *Ian Williams*

SAMAR QAND 3 b.f. Selkirk (USA) 129 – Sit Alkul (USA) 73 (Mr Prospector **56** (USA)) [2002 8.2m 10d 12f⁵ Aug 18] leggy, quite good-topped filly: fifth foal: half-sister to fairly useful 7f winner Fine Melody (by Green Desert): dam once-raced sister to Middle Park winner and 2000 Guineas runner-up Lycius: modest form in maidens at Nottingham (missed break), Windsor and Kempton (not given unduly hard time): not bred to need further than 1¼m: sold 3,000 gns in December. *E. A. L. Dunlop*

SAMBA BEAT 3 ch.f. Efisio 120 – Special Beat 65 (Bustino 136) [2002 56: f9.4g² f9.4g³ f9.4g² f8g* f8.5g³ f9.4g f8g f6g f9.4s f7g Dec 17] fair handicapper: won maiden **a66 d** event at Southwell in February: left J. Hills 4,000 gns after seventh outing: well held after, including in blinkers: will stay at least 1¼m: acts on fibresand, well beaten on turf. *R. F. Marvin*

SAMBAMAN 2 b.g. (Feb 13) Groom Dancer (USA) 128 – Guest of Anchor (Slip **66** Anchor 136) [2002 6s 7d 7d⁴ 7m 8.3m Oct 7] 20,000Y: first foal: dam, French 11.5f to 1¾m winner, out of smart performer up to 1¼m Intimate Guest: fair maiden: well held in nurseries last 2 starts: should be well suited by 1m+: acts on good to soft ground. *W. R. Muir*

SAMBUCAN DAZE (IRE) 2 b.c. (Apr 7) Mujadil (USA) 119 – Non Dimenticar Me **– p** (IRE) 63 (Don't Forget Me 127) [2002 6d Nov 1] 46,000Y: tall, rather leggy colt: fourth foal: half-sister to useful 1999 2-y-o 5f/6f winner Master Fay (later 7f winner in Hong Kong, by Fayruz), 3-y-o Louvolite and 4-y-o Zarin: dam 5f winner who stayed 7f: 20/1 and green, late headway when tenth of 17 to Tante Rose in maiden at Newmarket: should do better. *J. D. Bethell*

SAMEEAH (IRE) 6 br.m. Perugino (USA) 84 – Kayrava (Irish River (FR) 131) – [2002 f12s Jan 2] lightly raced and no sign of ability. *Miss J. Feilden*

SAMHARI (USA) 3 ch.c. Indian Ridge 123 – Cambara 97 (Dancing Brave (USA) **107** 140) [2002 106: 8s* 8s² Nov 2] strong, close-coupled colt: useful performer, lightly raced: trained at 2 yrs by D. Loder: 6 lengths second in private trial at Nad Al Sheba in April: landed odds in minor event at Ayr by 4 lengths, tending to wander and idle in front: creditable 5 lengths second to Smirk in listed race at Newmarket following month: likely to prove best at 7f/1m: acts on heavy going: tongue tied last 2 starts: sometimes bit slowly away: hung right penultimate outing. *Saeed bin Suroor*

SAMMAX (IRE) 3 b. or br.g. Mujadil (USA) 119 – Run Bonnie (Runnett 125) [2002 **57** 59: 5d² 5.1d³ f5g² 5g 5.1d³ 5f f5g 5g 5m a8g³ a6g* a5.5g⁴ Dec 8] neat gelding: modest performer: left N. Tinkler after ninth start: won minor event at Dos Hermanas in November: stays 6f: acts on good to firm and good to soft ground, and on sand: tried visored: usually tongue tied. *C. Tinkler, Spain*

SAMMY'S SHUFFLE 7 b.g. Touch of Grey 90 – Cabinet Shuffle (Thatching 131) **68** [2002 52, a64: p10g² p10g* p10g⁵ p10g⁵ p10g⁴ 10m 10.1g 10m* 10m² p10g² Aug 29] fair handicapper: won at Lingfield in January and Newmarket (amateurs) in July: effective at 1¼m/easy 1½m: acts on firm going, soft and polytrack: blinkered: held up. *Jamie Poulton*

SAMMY'S SISTER 3 gr.f. Touch of Grey 90 – Northwold Star (USA) 71 (Monte- **–** verdi 129) [2002 p7g Dec 28] fifth foal: dam thorough stayer: 25/1, slowly away and always behind in maiden at Lingfield. *Jamie Poulton*

SAMSARA 4 ch.g. Pivotal 124 – Fire Lily (Unfuwain (USA) 131) [2002 60, a48. f7g **53** 7g⁵ 8m 5g³ 6m Sep 19] modest maiden handicapper: stays 7f: acts on good to firm going: **a–** tried blinkered: sold 3,500 gns. *P. F. I. Cole*

SANBENITO (IRE) 2 b.g. (Mar 12) Elbio 125 – Inter Madera (IRE) (Toca Madera **90** 111) [2002 5m* 6m² 5g² 6d 6s* 6m Sep 11] 10,000Y: big, strong gelding: has plenty of scope: third foal: brother to Irish 7f winner Faithfulbond: dam unraced half-sister to smart Irish 1m/9f performer Scottish Memories: fairly useful performer: won maiden at Pontefract in May and minor event at Ripon (idled) in August: best effort when 2½ lengths second to Willhewiz in minor event at Beverley third start: will prove best at 5f/6f: acts on soft and good to firm ground: sold 38,000 gns. *Mrs J. R. Ramsden*

SANDERSTEAD 3 b.g. So Factual (USA) 120 – Charnwood Queen 61 (Cadeaux **44** Genereux 131) [2002 60: 8m 10f 7f⁵ 6f⁴ f7g 7.5m⁵ 10.1m² 9.9m Aug 24] close-coupled gelding: has a short, round action: poor maiden: left T. Easterby after sixth start: stays 1¼m: acts on firm and good to soft going: usually blinkered. *K. A. Morgan*

SANDGATE CYGNET 2 ch.f. (Apr 29) Fleetwood (IRE) 107 – Dance of The Swans **66** (IRE) 69 (Try My Best (USA) 130) [2002 6d⁴ 5v* 5.9m⁶ Sep 2] 1,000Y: second foal: dam 2-y-o 5f winner who later stayed 7f: fair form: won maiden at Hamilton in August despite racing freely, hanging and idling: again looked tricky ride when sixth in nursery there next time: likely to prove best at 5f/6f: acts on good to firm and heavy ground. *I. Semple*

SAND HAWK 7 ch.g. Polar Falcon (USA) 126 – Ghassanah 73 (Pas de Seul 133) **53** [2002 –, a71: 7d³ f7g⁵ Apr 8] workmanlike gelding: modest performer: probably best **a64** around 7f: acts on fibresand, heavy and good to firm going: blinkered/visored: has been slowly away: usually patiently ridden: has found little: has bled from nose. *D. Shaw*

SAN DIMAS (USA) 5 gr.g. Distant View (USA) 126 – Chrystophard (USA) (Lypheor **–** 118) [2002 44: 12.1d Jul 19] strong gelding: maiden handicapper on Flat: tried blinkered/ visored: won over hurdles in October. *R. Allan*

SANDLES 4 b.g. Komaite (USA) – Miss Calculate 67 (Mummy's Game 120) [2002 **66** 67: p12g 10.9f Apr 10] tall, useful-looking gelding: fair performer: stays easy 1½m: acts on firm going, soft and all-weather: has worn crossed noseband/tongue strap. *Miss K. M. George*

SANDORRA 4 b.f. Emperor Jones (USA) 119 – Oribi 59 (Top Ville 129) [2002 44: 9d **–** 8.9m 7.5m Sep 24] big, leggy filly: modest maiden at best: no form in 2002. *M. Brittain*

SANDPOINT 6 b.m. Lugana Beach 116 – Instinction (Never So Bold 135) [2002 52, **–** a39: f6s Jan 2] modest maiden at 5 yrs: well held only 6-y-o start: visored once. *J. G. Given*

SANDRONE (IRE) 2 b.f. (Mar 6) In Command (IRE) 114 – Florinda (CAN) (Vice **64** Regent (CAN)) [2002 5m 6d 6.1m⁴ 6.1g⁶ f7f² 7m 8v f8.5g³ Nov 15] 18,000F, IR **a73** 20,000Y: good-topped filly: has scope: half-sister to several winners, including useful 1997 2-y-o 5f winner Diligence (by Dilum) and 1m/9f winner Canadian Fantasy (by Lear Fan): dam unraced half-sister to smart performer up to 1½m Insan: fair maiden on all-weather, modest on turf: best effort when second to Bakewell Tart in nursery at Wolverhampton: should prove best at 7f/1m: acts on fibresand and good to firm ground. *B. J. Meehan*

SANDY BAY (IRE) 3 b.g. Spectrum (IRE) 126 – Karinski (USA) (Palace Music **69** (USA) 129) [2002 8.1d⁶ 8m⁴ 10.2d⁴ 10g⁶ 11.8s Oct 15] IR 40,000Y: rather leggy, useful-looking gelding: third foal: brother to 2000 2-y-o 1m winner Branicki and half-brother to 1999 2-y-o 6f winner Pekanski (by Sri Pekan), both fairly useful: dam unraced half-sister to Italian Group 3 1¼m winner Riverullah: fair maiden: stays 1¼m: sold 8,500 gns. *R. F. Johnson Houghton*

SANDY CITY (IRE)   3 gr.f. Green Desert (USA) 127 – City Fortress (Troy 137) **72**
[2002 8.3m 8g² 8g⁵ 8.3g⁵ 9.9m⁴ 8g 8d Oct 19] leggy, unfurnished filly: sister to smart performer up to 1½m Desert Boy, later Hong Kong Horse of the Year as Oriental Express, and half-sister to 3 winners, including high-class US 1m/9f performer Fastness (by Rousillon): dam French 1¼m and 12.5f winner: fair maiden: left Sir Michael Stoute after fifth start, and well beaten subsequently: shapes as if will stay 1½m: blinkered final outing: dropped away tamely third outing: sold 130,000 gns. *J. Oxx, Ireland*

SANDY GROUND (FR)   7 b.m. Cricket Ball (USA) 124 – Song of Tonga (FR) **43**
(Dancer's Image (USA)) [2002 42: p10g f9.4g⁵ p7g 9.7m p10g⁵ 10.1g p10g⁶ p12g Aug 29] poor performer: stays 1¼m: acts on all-weather, good to soft and good to firm going: tried blinkered. *J. E. Long*

SANDY LADY (IRE)   3 b.f. Desert King (IRE) 129 – Mamma's Too 104 (Skyliner **91**
117) [2002 86: 8g⁵ 7g 7d⁴ 8d* 8m 7d 8s 8f* 8m p10g³ p8g³ p8g Dec 30] leggy, close-coupled filly: fairly useful performer: won minor event at Goodwood in May and handicap at Kempton in September: probably best at 1m: acts on soft going, firm and polytrack: took too strong a hold to post sixth start. *R. Hannon*

SANGIOVESE   3 b.g. Piccolo 121 – Kaprisky (IRE) (Red Sunset 120) [2002 61: 8m **69**
p10g⁶ 10.2g² 10.2m² Jun 26] fair maiden handicapper: barely stays 1¼m, and should be as effective at 1m: below form on polytrack, raced only on good/good to firm going on turf: tends to race freely. *B. R. Millman*

SANGITA   4 ch.f. Royal Academy (USA) 130 – Saquiace (USA) (Sagace (FR) 135) **47**
[2002 f11s f16g 8f 10.1f 14.1m 14m³ 11.9m 16.2m* 15.8f 15.8f p12g Nov 27] angular filly: fourth foal: half-sister to 3 winners, including useful German performer up to 1½m Sky Dancing (by Exit To Nowhere): dam French 10.5f to 15f winner: modest for A. Wohler in Germany at 3 yrs: poor handicapper: won apprentice event at Warwick in September: stays 2m: acts on firm and good to soft going. *John Berry*

SAN HERNANDO   2 b.g. (Feb 11) Hernando (FR) 127 – Sandrella (IRE) (Darshaan **69 p**
133) [2002 8s 8d Oct 30] leggy, quite attractive gelding: shows knee action: first foal: dam unraced half-sister to 4-y-o Storming Home: fair form in maidens at Leicester and Yarmouth: gelded after: should do better at 1¼m+. *E. A. L. Dunlop*

SAN JUAN MATIA   2 br.f. (Apr 13) Makbul 104 – The Lady Vanishes (Robin Des **65 ?**
Pins (USA) 119) [2002 6m 6m⁵ Oct 7] 1,000Y: second foal: half-sister to 3-y-o Market Avenue: dam unraced: very slowly away on debut: 66/1, fair form when fifth of 16 to Formalise in maiden at Windsor nearly 3 months later: should stay at least 7f: withdrawn at start in October. *Dr J. R. J. Naylor*

SAN LUIS REY   2 b.f. (Apr 13) Zieten (USA) 118 – Shavya (Shavian 125) [2002 5.1f² **75**
5m* 5m 5.1f⁴ 5d⁴ Aug 3] 370,000 francs Y: lengthy, good-topped filly: has scope: fourth foal: half-sister to 2 winners in France by Midyan, including smart performer up to 7f Swedish Shave: dam unraced: fair performer: won maiden at Leicester in June: well beaten in Queen Mary Stakes at Royal Ascot (edgy, hung right) next time: failed to last home after making running in nurseries last 2 starts: will prove best at 5f: acts on firm ground, probably on good to soft: sold 20,000 gns. *Mrs J. R. Ramsden*

SAN MARCO (IRE)   4 b.g. Brief Truce (USA) 126 – Nuit Des Temps (Sadler's Wells **80**
(USA) 132) [2002 81: 8d 8g 8g³ 7s 8d² p10g p12g p10g Dec 28] IR 7,000Y: third foal: **a74**
half-brother to useful Irish winner around 7f (including at 2 yrs) Mrs Evans (by College Chapel): dam, ran once in Ireland, half-sister to useful French performer up to 1¼m Night Watch: fairly useful maiden handicapper: left C. Collins, Ireland, after fifth start: likely to prove best short of 1½m: acts on firm and good to soft going, probably on polytrack: usually blinkered: has worn cheekpieces. *Mrs P. Sly*

SAN SEBASTIAN   8 ch.g. Niniski (USA) 125 – Top of The League 85 (High Top **101**
131) [2002 120: 15d⁴ 15.5d⁶ 22.2m⁴ 20g Oct 6] sturdy gelding: very smart performer at best: just useful form for new stable in 2002, fourth in Queen Alexandra Stakes at Royal Ascot third start and probably flattered when mid-division in Prix du Cadran at Longchamp final one (made winning debut over hurdles in between): best at 2m+: acts on any going: usually blinkered/visored: tends to wander. *M. Rolland, France*

SANTA AMARO (IRE)   2 ch.c. (Apr 3) College Chapel 122 – Forest of Arden (Tap **–**
On Wood 130) [2002 f6g⁶ 6.1d Jun 3] 3,000Y: half-brother to several winners, including

useful 6f (at 2 yrs)/7f winner Forest Cat (by Petorius): dam Irish 7f winner: well held in maiden/seller. *D. Haydn Jones*

SANTA CATALINA (IRE)   3 br.f. Tagula (IRE) 116 – Bui-Doi (IRE) 58 (Dance of   **55**
Life (USA)) [2002 60: 7s 8m p6g⁴ f7g² 8d f8g³ f8.5s Dec 13] modest maiden: barely stays
1m: acts on all-weather: tried tongue tied and in cheekpieces. *J. J. Matthias*

SANTA SOPHIA (IRE)   2 gr.f. (Feb 4) Linamix (FR) 127 – Samara (IRE) 108 (Polish   **79**
Patriot (USA) 128) [2002 7m³ 7m Aug 29] small filly: second foal: dam, miler, half-sister
to smart middle-distance stayer Lille Hammer: much better effort in maidens (fair form)
when third to Geminiani at Goodwood: should stay at least 1m. *J. L. Dunlop*

SANTA VIDA (USA)   4 b.f. St Jovite (USA) 135 – Castellina (USA) (Danzig Con-   **–**
nection (USA)) [2002 64: 10m Jun 4] modest maiden handicapper at 3 yrs: well held only
run in 2002. *Jonjo O'Neill*

SANTIBURI LAD (IRE)   5 b.g. Namaqualand (USA) – Suggia (Alzao (USA) 117)   **66**
[2002 76: 8v 7f 8m 9.3g 9f 8.3v⁵ 7.9g² 8m⁴ 8m⁴ 8.3g⁶ Jul 18] leggy gelding: fair
performer: effective at 7f to 9f: acts on fibresand and any turf going. *N. Tinkler*

SANTISIMA TRINIDAD (IRE)   4 b.f. Definite Article 121 – Brazilia 63 (For-   **92**
zando 122) [2002 77: 8f 7f⁴ 8m⁶ 7.5g* 7.2v² 7g 7m 7.6f⁴ 7m 7.2g* 7g⁶ 7d* p7g Nov
23] lengthy, useful-looking filly: fairly useful handicapper: much improved, and won at
Beverley in June, Ayr in September and Catterick in November: effective at 7f/1m:
probably acts on any turf going: game. *T. D. Easterby*

SANTUZZA'S BEAUTY (GER)   2 b.f. (Feb 23) Bluebird (USA) 125 – Salviostra   **–**
(GER) (Cagliostro (GER)) [2002 8.3d p10g Dec 3] approx. 40,300Y in Germany: sixth
known foal: half-sister to 3 winners, including German performer up to 11f Sachsenking
(by High Estate) and Italian 1m/9f (including at 2 yrs) winner Strawberry Fields (by
Tenby), both useful: dam German 1¼m/11f winner: only a little sign of ability in maidens
(wandered on debut). *M. R. Channon*

SAORSIE   4 b.g. Emperor Jones (USA) 119 – Exclusive Lottery (Presidium 124) [2002   **53 §**
64§: p10g f8.5g 8.1d 7d⁴ p8g 14.1m² 14.1m Aug 15] tall, close-coupled gelding: modest
handicapper: stays easy 1¾m: acts on soft and good to firm going: tried blinkered: has
been mounted on track/early to post: has pulled hard/looked difficult ride: not one to trust
(banned from Flat racing from stalls until 2003). *J. C. Fox*

SAPHILA (IRE)   2 b.f. (Mar 31) Sadler's Wells (USA) 132 – Fanny Cerrito (Gulch   **– p**
(USA)) [2002 8.5s⁶ Oct 27] 1,600,000 francs Y: first foal: dam unraced daughter of US
Grade 1 9f/1¼m winner Sabin: favourite, well-held sixth of 13 in newcomers race at
Milan: will probably do better. *L. M. Cumani*

SAPIENTI (GER)   6 b.h. Konigsstuhl (GER) – Sapientissima (Try My Best (USA)   **99**
130) [2002 a9.5g² p10g 8g⁴ 8s³ 8g 9g 8v² 8v⁵ a9.5g³ a9.5g* Dec 21] fifth foal: brother to
1994 German 2-y-o 6.5f winner Septuagesima and half-brother to a winner in Germany
by Windwurf: dam unraced: useful performer: successful in minor events at Mulheim and
Neuss and handicap at Gelsenkirchen in 2001: creditable efforts in 2002 when in frame in
listed races at Neuss and Cologne first/third starts: below form in similar event at
Lingfield in between: won minor event at Neuss in December: best up to 11f: acts on dirt,
raced mainly on good going or softer on turf. *H. Steinmetz, Germany*

SAPONI (IRE)   4 b.g. Indian Ridge 123 – Taking Liberties (IRE) 57 (Royal Academy   **58 p**
(USA) 130) [2002 f8g³ Dec 4] 8,000 3-y-o: first foal: dam once-raced sister to smart 1996
2-y-o 7f/1m winner Equal Rights out of Australian Group 1 1½m winner Lady Liberty:
11/4, 2 lengths third to Rock Concert in maiden at Southwell, not knocked about after
leading briefly 2f out: should do better. *W. J. Haggas*

SAPPERDOT   5 b.g. St Ninian 104 – Beau Gem (Kalaglow 132) [2002 14.1m Aug 21]   **–**
first foal: dam winning pointer: 66/1, well held in maiden at Carlisle. *F. Watson*

SAPPHIRE ALLISE   2 b.f. (Feb 5) Royal Applause 124 – Paradise News 51 (Sure   **55**
Blade (USA) 130) [2002 5m⁵ 6.1g p5g 5g⁵ 5.2f p6g Dec 21] 2,800Y: third foal: half-sister
to 5f winners abroad by Ezzoud (at 2 yrs) and Pivotal: dam, 5f winner at 2 yrs, half-sister
to useful performer up to 1½m Musetta: modest maiden: will prove best at 5f/6f: best
efforts on good going/polytrack. *D. K. Ivory*

SARABANDE   3 ch.f. Nashwan (USA) 135 – Western Reel (USA) 95 (Gone West   **73**
(USA)) [2002 –p: 8m 8.3g f8.5s⁴ f8.5g f8.5g² p10g Oct 31] leggy filly: fair maiden
handicapper: should stay 1¼m: acts on fibresand: slowly away fourth start. *B. W. Hills*

SARANGANI   6 b.g. Polish Precedent (USA) 131 – Height of Folly 81 (Shirley Heights   **112**
130) [2002 97: 11.9m 16m* 13.9f* 13.9m Aug 21] big, good-topped gelding: smart

handicapper: trained by I. Balding in 2001: better than ever when winning at Ripon (raced freely) in April and York (by 2 lengths from Hugs Dancer, barely came off bridle) in May: broke down fatally in Ebor at York: was effective at 1¼m to 2m: acted on any going: tongue tied last 7 starts at 5 yrs: had worn crossed noseband: was genuine. *M. W. Easterby*

SARATOV 4 b.g. Rudimentary (USA) 118 – Sarabah (IRE) 83 (Ela-Mana-Mou 132) **93**
[2002 102: 10.4f 12d⁶ May 27] big, lengthy, good-topped gelding: has a round action: useful handicapper at best: only fairly useful form at best in 2002: probably stays 1½m: acts on firm ground, probably on good to soft: blinkered final 3-y-o outing: looks none too keen nowadays: sold 28,000 gns. *G. A. Swinbank*

SARAYAT 2 br.c. (Feb 22) Polar Falcon (USA) 126 – Montserrat 81 (Aragon 118) **103**
[2002 6d³ 6d² 7g³ 6m⁴ Oct 5] 62,000Y: useful-looking colt: has a fluent, round action: third foal: half-brother to 3-y-o Terfel: dam 5f (at 2 yrs) and 6f winner: useful performer: won maiden at Leicester in May: in frame all starts after, including when 1¾ lengths third to Dublin in Vintage Stakes at Goodwood (rider dropped whip when still battling for second) and just over 2 lengths fourth to Somnus in Two-Year-Old Trophy at Redcar: will prove best at 6f/7f: unraced on extremes of going: races prominently. *M. A. Jarvis*

SARDIS (IRE) 3 b.c. Priolo (USA) 127 – Punta Gorda (IRE) (Roi Danzig (USA)) **55**
[2002 67p: p10g⁶ 10d⁵ 11.6m 9d 8g Jun 16] good-topped colt: modest maiden handicapper: well held last 3 outings: probably stays 1¼m: acts on good to soft going: visored second to fourth starts: sold 800 gns. *Mrs A. J. Perrett*

SARENA PRIDE (IRE) 5 b.m. Persian Bold 123 – Avidal Park 68 (Horage 124) **68**
[2002 74: p12g³ p12g 10m⁴ p12g³ 10m 10.9m p12g⁶ Oct 9] fair handicapper: **a73**
stays easy 1½m: acts on firm going, soft and polytrack: usually blinkered: tends to be slowly away/race freely. *R. J. O'Sullivan*

SARENA SPECIAL 5 b.g. Lucky Guest 109 – Lariston Gale 81 (Pas de Seul 133) **54**
[2002 –: 6.1v* Jun 14] angular gelding: modest performer: won maiden handicap at Chepstow in June: stays 7f: acts on heavy and good to firm ground: usually blinkered (not at Chepstow). *J. D. Frost*

SARIBA 3 b.f. Persian Bold 123 – En Vacances (IRE) 90 (Old Vic 136) [2002 9d **–**
12.6m 11.9g⁶ 11.9m 11.7d⁵ Sep 9] first living foal: dam, 2m winner, half-sister to smart performer up to 1¼m Invited Guest: well held in maidens/handicap. *A. Charlton*

SARIN 4 b.g. Deploy 131 – Secretilla (USA) 61 (Secreto (USA) 128) [2002 67: 11.9d⁴ **88**
12d⁴ 12.1g⁴ 14.1m⁶ 11.5m* 12s² Oct 26] fairly useful handicapper: won at Yarmouth in September: stays 1½m: acts on soft and good to firm ground. *L. M. Cumani*

SARI (USA) 3 gr.f. Cozzene (USA) – Yamuna (USA) 103 (Forty Niner (USA)) [2002 **63**
–p: 6m³ 7.1m Aug 26] close-coupled filly: fluent mover: has run only 3 times: off 10½ months, modest form when 5 lengths third to Golden Dixie in maiden at Salisbury on reappearance, tending to edge left: well held (soon pushed along) in similar event final run: sold 18,000 gns in December. *Mrs A. J. Perrett*

SARN 3 b.g. Atraf 116 – Covent Garden Girl 67 (Sizzling Melody 117) [2002 70, a–: 8f **59**
7m 7.6f 8.1s⁵ 8m 7.9g³ 10.3f 8g 8.1v 8g 10.2g 8d² Nov 1] smallish gelding: modest **a–**
nowadays: stays 1m: acts on any turf going, well beaten on fibresand: none too consistent. *A. Bailey*

SARRAAF (IRE) 6 ch.g. Perugino (USA) 84 – Blue Vista (IRE) (Pennine Walk 120) **89 §**
[2002 90: 8f² 8g³ 7d⁵ 7g 8.9d 8d⁴ 8g² 8.1d 7m³ 7m 7g 8.5m* 8d³ 8m⁴ 8g 7.1m 6f* 7f **a78 §**
6f⁵ 5d⁶ 7s* f7g f9.4g f8g f5g f7g⁴ Dec 31] 64,000Y: strong, lengthy gelding: third foal: half-brother to 1996 2-y-o 7f winner Smugurs (by Masterclass): dam unraced half-sister to smart sprinter Polykratis: fairly useful performer on turf, fair on all-weather: trained by K. Prendergast in Ireland at 5 yrs: won claimer at Epsom in August and minor events at Catterick (apprentices, first start after leaving I. Semple) and Leicester in October: effective at 6f to 9f: acts on any going: usually held up: blinkered (raced freely) fifteenth start: often held up/finds little: untrustworthy. *Paul Johnson*

SARREGO 3 b.g. Makbul 104 – Simmie's Special 75 (Precocious 126) [2002 85: 6.1d **78**
6m⁵ 5m⁴ 5f f7g Dec 7] close-coupled gelding: fair performer, lightly raced: best at 5f: acts on good to firm going: decidedly edgy penultimate start. *R. Hollinshead*

SARSON 6 b.g. Efisio 120 – Sarcita 111 (Primo Dominie 121) [2002 5.1g⁵ 6.1m⁵ 5.1d⁴ **71**
5g² 5s 6g Jun 21] neat gelding: has a quick action: fair handicapper: ran poorly penultimate start, pulled up final one: effective at 5f to 7f: acts on heavy going, good to firm and fibresand. *J. M. Bradley*

SARTORIAL (IRE) 6 b.g. Elbio 125 – Madam Slaney 92 (Prince Tenderfoot (USA) **114** 126) [2002 115: 6f⁶ 5.2f⁵ 6m Sep 28] big, strong gelding: smart performer, lightly raced (has been difficult to train): best effort at 6 yrs when strong-finishing 1½ lengths fifth to Lady Dominatrix in Dubai International Airport World Trophy at Newbury in September: never better than mid-division in Diadem Stakes at Ascot final outing: stays 6f: acts on fibresand, firm and good to soft going: has been bandaged in front: visored final 4-y-o start: free-going sort. *P. J. Makin*

SASARAM (IRE) 3 ch.g. Indian Ridge 123 – Flaming June (USA) 69 (Storm Bird **–** (CAN) 134) [2002 73: 10f 10d Jun 15] fair form only outing at 2 yrs: reportedly suffered from colic after, and also displaced his colon: well held in 2002 (tongue tied second start): sold 4,200 gns in October, sent to Kuwait. *M. P. Tregoning*

SASHA 5 ch.g. Factual (USA) 108 – Twice In Bundoran (IRE) 70 (Bold Arrangement **39** 127) [2002 46: 7f 6f 5.9d 7m 6d⁶ Aug 3] sparely-made gelding: poor maiden: stays 7.5f: acts on soft going, good to firm and fibresand: tried blinkered. *R. E. Barr*

SASHAY 4 b.f. Bishop of Cashel 122 – St James's Antigua (IRE) 79 (Law Society **62** (USA) 130) [2002 50, a56: p12g³ f12g² f16 2g* f16.2g* 14.4f 16m¹ᵖ 16f⁴ 16m⁵ 17.2d **a67** f16.2g⁶ f14.8g³ f14.8g² Dec 31] close-coupled filly: fair handicapper: won at Wolverhampton (twice) and Nottingham early in year: effective at 1½m to 2m: acts on all-weather and good to firm ground: reliable. *C. G. Cox*

SASPYS LAD 5 b.g. Faustus (USA) 118 – Legendary Lady (Reprimand 122) [2002 **76** 12.1g⁵ 9.2g⁵ 10d⁵ 11.9d 10.1g⁶ Jun 28] 700Y, resold 500Y: good-bodied gelding: second foal: dam little form: fair maiden: should stay 1½m: raced on good/good to soft going: fair hurdler, won in August/September. *W. M. Brisbourne*

SATELCOM (USA) 2 b.c. (Apr 20) Alhaarth (IRE) 126 – Tommelise (USA) (Dayjur **75 p** (USA) 137) [2002 6m 5m⁴ 5g p6g p7g* Dec 28] $3,000F, 48,000 2-y-o: rather leggy, unfurnished colt: second foal: half-brother to 3-y-o Night Shift Blue's: dam, French 6f winner, closely related to US Grade 2 1½m winner Ampulla: confirmed promise and showed fair form when winning 15-runner nursery at Lingfield by nose from Agilis: will stay 1m: acts on polytrack: probably capable of better yet. *Noel T. Chance*

SATTAM 3 b.c. Danehill (USA) 126 – Mayaasa (USA) 70 (Lyphard (USA) 132) [2002 **–** 75p: 7s Oct 22] smallish, stocky colt: burly and green, seventh in maiden at Doncaster at 2 yrs, only outing for D. Loder (wore crossed noseband): fourth to Naheef in private trial at Nad Al Sheba in April: easy-to-back favourite, well held in maiden at Yarmouth 6 months later: left Godolphin shortly after. *Saeed bin Suroor*

SATU NUSA 3 b.c. So Factual (USA) 120 – Tarry 65 (Salse (USA) 128) [2002 78: 8g **65** 10m⁵ 10m p10g⁶ 10m 8.3g² 8m f8s 8.2s Oct 23] neat colt: fair maiden: well below form last 3 outings: barely stays 1¼m: acts on good to firm and good to soft going, some promise on polytrack: tongue tied fourth start, visored last 4: seems a difficult ride: sold 5,000 gns. *G. C. Bravery*

SATURN (IRE) 2 b.c. (Feb 16) Marju (IRE) 127 – Delphinus (Soviet Star (USA) **111 p** 128) [2002 8d⁶ 7m* 8m* 7m⁵ Oct 19]
        In the night sky, Saturn is the furthest planet from Earth visible to the naked eye, though it can be discerned from the stars around it only because it is dimmer. When brought into sharper focus, it's a more impressive sight, offering the most spectacular ring system in the solar system, made up of ice particles from broken satellites. There's probably more than meets the eye to Saturn, the racehorse, too. He didn't shine so brightly as some in the Dewhurst Stakes at Newmarket in October, but in finishing fifth of sixteen behind Tout Seul ran a fine race all the same for an inexperienced horse stepping back in trip and facing much his stiffest task. He was tapped for speed when the leaders quickened then stayed on strongly late on, beaten under four lengths. Saturn was supplemented for the Dewhurst having won his two previous starts. After showing only fair ability when sixth in a maiden at Newmarket on the July course in August on his debut, he improved considerably to win a similar event over seven furlongs there later in the month, quickening well to beat Flying Wanda by just over a length after meeting some trouble. Saturn improved again when returned to a mile the following month for the Haynes, Hanson and Clark Stakes, a well-established conditions event at Newbury, where he again quickened best to beat Cat Ona High by a length and a half, despite

still seeming green in front. The Racing Post Trophy was reported to be his end-of-season target at the time, but connections clearly had a change of heart.

Saturn (IRE) (b.c. Feb 16, 2000)	Marju (IRE) (br 1988)	Last Tycoon (b 1983)	Try My Best Mill Princess
		Flame of Tara (b 1980)	Artaius Welsh Flame
	Delphinus (b 1991)	Soviet Star (b 1984)	Nureyev Veruschka
		Scimitarra (ch 1984)	Kris Fanghorn

Saturn was one of the more expensive of Marju's yearlings sold in 2001, purchased for IR 100,000 guineas on behalf of Highclere Thoroughbreds. The sum probably owed more to Saturn's looks than his pedigree, though he is not badly bred by any means. His dam Delphinus, who won a handicap over a mile and a quarter on soft ground for Andre Fabre in France, is a daughter of Scimitarra. Scimitarra won the Lupe Stakes for Henry Cecil, but is probably best remembered for her run in the Oaks, when she started favourite and led two furlongs out only to break down, eventually pulled up behind the winner Unite. Scimitarra had been bought at the end of her two-year-old season by Sheikh Mohammed for 620,000 guineas from Baroness Thyssen, who also owned Scimitarra's half-brother the top-class sprinter Double Form. Saturn's great grandam Fanghorn was third in the Poule d'Essai des Pouliches. Whether or not Saturn will turn out to be good enough,

Highclere Thoroughbred Racing V's "Saturn"

or to stay well enough, to line up at Epsom remains to be seen. Marju came second to Generous in the Derby before reverting to a mile to win the St James's Palace Stakes and he has not proved a notable influence for stamina at stud, the average distance of races won by his progeny being between eight and nine furlongs. It is interesting that his dam's only other foal to race, the Irish-trained Glocca Morra (by Catrail) began the year in a bumper and staying maidens on the Flat but didn't win until dropped to seven furlongs, at which trip he won twice at the Curragh in the autumn. Saturn did take quite a strong hold through the early stages of the Dewhurst and connections may be tempted to let him have a crack at the Guineas, though a race like the Dee Stakes at Chester could be an ideal early-season target. Saturn should stay at least a mile and a quarter. A good-topped colt, with plenty of scope, though an early foal, Saturn gave the impression at two that he was green and immature, and the best of him is almost certainly still to come. He made his debut on good to soft ground and raced only on good to firm afterwards. *M. L. W. Bell*

SATYR 4 b.g. Pursuit of Love 124 – Sardonic 105 (Kris 135) [2002 79: f9.4g⁵ p10g² **73** 10d 10m 11.6d 9s 9m² 8d⁴ 10 4m⁵ 10.9m 10m³ 8.9f² 9s Oct 25] quite good-topped gelding: fair handicapper: stays easy 11f: acts on polytrack and firm going, probably on good to soft: has awkward head carriage: often held up. *W. J. Musson*

SAVANNAH BAY 3 ch.c. In The Wings 128 – High Savannah 77 (Rousillon (USA) **109** 133) [2002 105p: 9m 10.1g³ 16.2m⁶ 14.8g² 14m³ 15g* 15g⁵ Oct 5] good-topped colt: useful performer: won 4-runner Prix de Lutece at Longchamp in September by ½ length from Swing Wing, having been last and off bridle early in straight: good efforts otherwise when placed in listed races at Newmarket (1¼ lengths second to Spanish John) and Goodwood (third behind First Charter) and when 2 lengths fifth of 6 to Morozov in Prix Hubert de Chaudenay at Longchamp: should stay 2m: raced only on good going or firmer: blinkered second start, tongue tied next 3: has worn crossed noseband. *B. J. Meehan*

SAVE THE PLANET 5 b.m. Environment Friend 128 – Geoffreys Bird (Master Willie **34** 129) [2002 39: 14m⁵ 16m May 3] big, strong, lengthy mare: poor maiden: stays 2m: acts on firm ground: tried blinkered/visored. *P. Monteith*

SAWWAAH (IRE) 5 ch.g. Marju (IRE) 127 – Just A Mirage 76 (Green Desert (USA) **91** 127) [2002 10.3m⁴ 8.9m 9.1g* Sep 20] big, useful-looking gelding: fairly useful per- former, lightly raced: left E. Dunlop 6,500 gns after reappearance: won claimer at Ayr in September: stays 1¼m: acts on soft and good to firm ground. *D. Nicholls*

SAXE-COBURG (IRE) 5 b.g. Warning 136 – Saxon Maid 108 (Sadler's Wells (USA) **74 d** 132) [2002 a8f² a6f⁴ a8f⁵ a8f 7m p10g³ f9.4s p10g Dec 21] first foal: dam, 1½m/1¾m winner, out of Oaks third Britannia's Rule: fair performer: won maiden at Jebel Ali at 4 yrs: generally on downgrade in 2002: sold 6,000 gns from J. Sadler in UAE after fourth start: stays easy 1¼m: acts on dirt and polytrack: tried blinkered. *Mrs L. Stubbs*

SAYIT 3 b.g. Sayaarr (USA) – Wigit (Safawan 118) [2002 50: p10g p8g³ p8g⁵ f9.4g⁵ **58** p8g² 8g 10.2m⁶ 8.1d 8.5m 10m* 11.9m Sep 3] modest on turf, poor on all-weather: won **a48** handicap at Brighton in August, wandering and carrying head high: likely to prove best at 1m/9f: acts on polytrack and good to firm going. *M. D. I. Usher*

SAY WHAT YOU SEE (IRE) 2 b.c. (Apr 25) Charnwood Forest (IRE) 125 – Aster **58** Aweke (IRE) 87 (Alzao (USA) 117) [2002 6m 7m⁵ 7.1g Sep 23] IR 22,000Y: fourth foal: dam, Irish 9f winner, half-sister to smart performer up to 1½m in Ireland/USA Baba Karam: best effort in maidens (modest form) on debut: should stay 1m. *J. W. Hills*

SCALADO (USA) 3 ch.c. Mister Baileys 123 – Lady di Pomadora (USA) (Danzig **81** Connection (USA)) [2002 73: p8g* 7s² 8m³ p7g 8f Sep 27] smallish, strong colt: fairly useful performer: won maiden at Lingfield in January: good efforts in handicaps next 2 starts: left R. Charlton 28,000 gns after fourth outing: will stay 1¼m: acts on good to firm going, good to soft and polytrack: carried head awkwardly third start. *R. J. Osborne, Ireland*

SCALLOWAY (IRE) 2 b.g. (Apr 7) Marju (IRE) 127 – Zany (Junius (USA) 124) **68** [2002 6d 6g² 6g⁶ 7.1m⁵ 7m 6.1m⁵ 7m 7.1m 7.1m⁴ Sep 21] IR 19,000F, 24,000Y: strong, compact gelding: has scope: brother to 3-y-o Mr Toad and half-brother to several winners, including useful Irish 1997 2-y-o 7f/8.5f winner Magical Minty (by Magical Wonder), later 9f winner in Hong Kong: dam Irish 9.5f/1¼m winner: fair maiden: bit below form last 3 starts: should stay 1m: acts on good to firm ground: effective blinkered or not. *J. A. Osborne*

SCARLET FANTASY 2 b.c. (May 8) Rudimentary (USA) 118 – Katie Scarlett 70 –
(Lochnager 132) [2002 6d 8s Oct 26] 2,000Y: sixth foal: half-brother to 3 winners,
including fairly useful 1998 2-y-o 6f winner Scarlett's Boy and 7f/1m winner Antarctic
Storm (both by Emarati): dam, 1¼m winner, also successful over hurdles: well held in
maidens at Windsor (started very slowly) and Newbury (wandered markedly having
made early running). *E. A. Wheeler*

SCARLET RIBBONS 3 b.f. Anabaa (USA) 130 – Scarlet Plume 103 (Warning 136) **80**
[2002 95: 7m 8.2f⁴ 6m⁵ Jun 4] workmanlike filly: fairly useful performer: bred to stay
1m: acts on firm going: very worked up in stall final outing: sold 25,000 gns in December.
J. L. Dunlop

SCARLET SECRET 2 ch.f. (Apr 20) Piccolo 121 – Rise 'n Shine 67 (Night Shift **53**
(USA)) [2002 5m⁵ 6m² 6m p6g Dec 28] first foal: dam, 5f winner, half-sister to useful
French sprinter Touch And Love: modest maiden: second at Brighton: likely to prove best
at 5f/6f. *C. A. Cyzer*

SCARLETTI (GER) 5 ch.g. Master Willie 129 – Solidago (USA) (Decies 129) [2002 –
8g Sep 21] brother to German 9f winner Sam Lowry and half-brother to 3 winners in
Germany: dam, lightly raced in USA, half-sister to Grand Prix de Paris winner Swink:
winner of 3 races in Germany for B. Hellier, including handicap at Mulheim in 2001:
tongue tied, well held in handicap at Ayr on British Flat debut: stays 9f: acts on soft
ground: fair form over hurdles. *Jonjo O'Neill*

SCARLETT RIBBON 5 b.m. Most Welcome 131 – Scarlett Holly 81 (Red Sunset **95**
120) [2002 95, a104: 7.1s³ 7.1d 6v Aug 9] quite good-topped mare: useful performer:
form in 2002 only on reappearance (edged left): stays 7f: goes well on fibresand, best turf
efforts on soft/good to soft going: free-going sort. *P. J. Makin*

SCARPIA 2 ch.g. (Apr 14) Rudimentary (USA) 118 – Floria Tosca § (Petong 126) **55**
[2002 6m⁵ 6.1m⁵ 6m Oct 7] 4,400F, IR 10,000Y: fifth foal: brother to Swedish sprint
winner Tremendous Girl and half-brother to 3-y-o Daneswood: dam, ran 3 times, one to
avoid: modest form at best in maidens: will probably stay 7f. *E. L. James*

SCARROTTOO 4 ch.g. Zilzal (USA) 137 – Bold And Beautiful 105 (Bold Lad (IRE) **81**
133) [2002 70: 7.1g³ 7g 7m⁴ 7f⁶ 7m 7m* 7m³ 7m⁵ 7g⁶ 7m 7m² 7.1g⁵ 7g⁵ 8s Oct 28]
strong gelding: fairly useful handicapper: won at Folkestone in July: stays 7f: acts on firm
ground and fibresand: has worn tongue strap (not in 2002). *S. C. Williams*

SCARTEEN SISTER (IRE) 4 ch.f. Eagle Eyed (USA) 111 – Best Swinger (IRE) **37 ?**
(Ela-Mana-Mou 132) [2002 54: f9.4g³ 7m 8.3d 8m 9m⁵ f9.4s⁴ f8g f9.4g Dec 16] poor **a48**
maiden: left R. Beckett after reappearance: stays 9.4f: acts on firm ground and fibresand:
effective blinkered/visored or not: tends to wander. *I. A. Wood*

SCARY NIGHT (IRE) 2 b.g. (Mar 11) Night Shift (USA) – Private Bucks (USA) **67**
(Spend A Buck (USA)) [2002 5.1g³ 5g⁶ f6g* 5d⁶ f7f⁴ f6s² f6g f6s³ Dec 26] IR 6,000Y:
tall, good-topped gelding: fifth foal: half-brother to winners in USA (by Naevus) and
Japan (by Common Grounds): dam, won in USA, half-sister to smart performers Irish
Shoal (sprinter) and Hibernian Gold (at 1¼m): fair performer: won seller at Wolverhampton (then left M. Channon) in May: creditable efforts when in frame in nursery/
claimers after: effective at 6f/7f: acts on fibresand: usually races prominently. *J. Balding*

SCENIC LADY (IRE) 6 b.m. Scenic 128 – Tu Tu Maori (IRE) (Kings Lake (USA) **63**
133) [2002 61: 11.9g p10g 10d² 9s² 12s³ 10g 12d⁵ 10m 11.9m² 9m² 11.9g³ 10m⁶ 10.3m
Sep 14] smallish mare: modest handicapper: effective at 9f (given test) to 1¾m: acts on
firm and soft going: blinkered twice as 4-y-o: reluctant to post ninth start: sometimes
slowly away. *L. A. Dace*

SCENT AHEAD (USA) 3 b.g. Foxhound (USA) 103 – Sonseri 95 (Prince Tender- –
foot (USA) 126) [2002 60: 5g 5m 5m 5g 5d f6g⁵ Oct 21] modest maiden at 2 yrs: little
form in 2002: tried blinkered. *Mrs G. S. Rees*

SCENTED AIR 5 b.m. Lion Cavern (USA) 117 – Jungle Rose 90 (Shirley Heights **58**
130) [2002 52: f9.4g² f8.5g* f8.5g² f7g⁴ f7g f8.5g f8.5g 8f 8.1d* 9.2g⁶ 8.5d 8f 8m⁶ 8m
f7g Sep 30] leggy, plain mare: modest handicapper: won at Wolverhampton (amateurs)
in January and Chepstow in July: best at 1m/easy 1¼m: acts on fibresand, firm and soft
going: visored once: sometimes slowly away: often looks difficult ride: not one to trust
implicitly: successful over hurdles in October. *P. W. Hiatt*

SCENT OF VICTORY (IRE) 3 b. or br.g. Polish Precedent (USA) 131 – Dayanata **94**
(Shirley Heights 130) [2002 8m² 8m³ 10f² 12d 10s p10g* f12s³ f12g³ Dec 20] 85,000Y:
big, lengthy gelding: half-brother to several winners, including very smart 1m (at 2 yrs)
to 12.5f winner Courteous (by Generous): dam unraced sister to Prix du Jockey Club

winner Darshaan: fairly useful performer: off 5 months and gelded after fourth start: won maiden at Lingfield (wandered) and minor event at Wolverhampton late in year: will stay 1¾m: acts on firm going, good to soft and all-weather. *P. F. I. Cole*

SCHEDULE B   4 ch.g. Dancing Spree (USA) – Jolizal 52 (Good Times (ITY)) [2002 52d: f11s f8s f12s⁵ f12g 10m 11.9s f12g³ f12g³ 11.8g f14.8g⁶ f12g⁶ f14.8g Oct 21] close-coupled gelding: poor maiden: seems to stay 1½m: acts on fibresand: none too consistent. *R. Hollinshead*   **a49**

SCHEMATIC   2 ch.g. (Jan 26) Brief Truce (USA) 126 – Swissmatic 54 (Petong 126) [2002 5m⁴ 5v³ 5m* 6g⁶ f5s f6g f5g Dec 4] unfurnished gelding: first foal: dam, ran 4 times and best effort at 6f, half-sister to useful sprinter in Britain/Scandinavia Prime Match: easily best effort (fair form) when winning seller at Musselburgh in June: left W. M. Brisbourne after fifth start: should stay 6f: has given plenty of trouble in preliminaries and twice been withdrawn at start: temperamental. *Mrs L. Williamson*   **65 §**

SCHOLAR   2 ch.c. (Feb 11) Primo Dominie 121 – Hardiprincess (Keen 116) [2002 7f 7m 8m⁶ f8s Sep 5] 5,000Y: tall, rather unfurnished colt: third foal: closely related to 1¼m winner Anne-Sophie (by First Trump): dam well beaten both starts: poor maiden: visored final start: sold 2,000 gns, sent to Kuwait. *J M P Eustace*   **46**

SCHOOL DAYS   3 b.f. Slip Anchor 136 – Cradle of Love (USA) 87 (Roberto (USA) 131) [2002 77: p10g⁴ 9m f8.5g 8m³ 7.9g* 7.9m* Aug 21] angular filly: fair handicapper: left M. Bell prior to winning twice at Carlisle in August: best around 1m: acts on polytrack, yet to race on extremes of going on turf: visored third start (stirrup leather broke): has carried head awkwardly. *R. Wilman*   **76**

SCHUSCHEMIGA   3 ch.f. Rock City 120 – Bahrain Queen (IRE) (Caerleon (USA) 132) [2002 44: f8g Feb 12] sparely-made, rather leggy filly: poor maiden. *J. Balding*   **–**

SCIPPIT   3 ch.g. Unfuwain (USA) 131 – Scierpan (USA) 86 (Sharpen Up 127) [2002 63?: 9m 8m 7.1m 8.9m 7f Sep 21] close-coupled gelding: modest maiden at 2 yrs: little form in 2002: should stay 1m: visored penultimate start. *F. Watson*   **–**

SCISSOR RIDGE   10 ch.g. Indian Ridge 123 – Golden Scissors 76 (Kalaglow 132) [2002 44, a62: p8g p8g f9.4g⁵ f8.5g⁴ p10g f8.5g³ f8.5g f7g 10.2g 7d Jun 11] sparely-made gelding: modest performer: stays 8.5f: acts on all-weather: tried blinkered earlier in career: sometimes soon off bridle. *J. J. Bridger*   **–**
a51

SCONCED (USA)   7 ch.g. Affirmed (USA) – Quaff (USA) 115 (Raise A Cup (USA)) [2002 57§: f16s* f16.2g² f14.8g⁶ f16g⁴ f16g⁵ 14.1d 12.3g 14m 11.9s May 27] leggy gelding: modest handicapper: won at Southwell in January: stays 2m: acts on fibresand: visored/blinkered: tends to run in snatches. *M. J. Polglase*   **–**
a52

SCOOBY WHO (IRE)   2 b.g. (Apr 30) Brief Truce (USA) 126 – Miss Butterfield (Cure The Blues (USA)) [2002 6m⁵ 5.2g³ 7m⁴ Aug 7] IR 10,000Y: half-brother to several winners, including 4-y-o Zozarharry: dam poor maiden: best effort (fair form) when third to Blazonry in maiden at Yarmouth: not sure to stay 7f: troublesome in paddock/at start when well backed for seller on debut: sold 1,200 gns. *D. Morris*   **70**

SCOTISH LAW (IRE)   4 ch.g. Case Law 113 – Scotia Rose (Tap On Wood 130) [2002 70: 10m p8g 8.1m Jun 22] close-coupled gelding: fair handicapper: stays 1¼m: acts on good to firm going, possibly not on soft: has drifted right. *P. R. Chamings*   **65**

SCOTMAIL PARK   3 b.g. Presidium 124 – Miss Tri Colour 37 (Shavian 125) [2002 54: 8m 7.9g 10s² Aug 5] close-coupled gelding: poor maiden: seems to stay 1¼m: acts on soft ground: often slowly away. *G. M. Moore*   **46**

SCOTTIE YORK   6 b.g. Noble Patriarch 115 – Devon Dancer 73 (Shareef Dancer (USA) 135) [2002 16m² 11.9s⁵ 16f 14g Jun 17] leggy, workmanlike gelding: modest maiden: stays 2m: acts on soft and good to firm going: visored final start. *P. Monteith*   **51**

SCOTTISH KNIGHT   4 b.g. Marju (IRE) 127 – Scottish Eyes (USA) (Green Dancer (USA) 132) [2002 61: p10g f9.4g⁴ f12g f9.4g p8g 8.2d 9s 8f Jun 21] modest maiden at best: on downgrade: unlikely to stay beyond 1¼m: acts on good to soft going and fibresand: sometimes races freely. *M. R. Bosley*   **58 d**

SCOTTISH RIVER (USA)   3 b.g. Thunder Gulch (USA) 129 – Overbrook 95 (Storm Cat (USA)) [2002 107: a10f 8m³ 8.3s⁵ 7d May 22] strong gelding: useful performer: gelded and reportedly had soft palate operation before reappearance: creditable efforts in 2002 only on second/third starts, fifth to Father Thames in listed race at Windsor in latter: probably stays 1m: acts on soft and good to firm going: often races up with pace: joined K. McLaughlin in UAE. *M. Johnston*   **99**

SCOTT'S VIEW   3 b.g. Selkirk (USA) 129 – Milly of The Vally 93 (Caerleon   **121**
(USA) 132) [2002 71: p10g³ 11.6m* 12g* 12.1d* 14.4d² 12.3f* 14m* 14g* 14g³
13.4f³ 11.9m* 12g* 12s⁴ Oct 26]

'Johnston in tough and progressive horse shocker'—what's new or surprising about the story of Scott's View? Middleham trainer Mark Johnston has
turned out so many horses in similar mould that the success of Scott's View could
hardly take anyone unawares. Those that preceded him by making striking progress
through the handicap ranks for Kingsley House stables really are too numerous to
mention but they include stalwarts Branston Abby, Quick Ransom, Star Rage and
Yavana's Pace and, in recent years alone, multiple winners of pattern or listed class
such as Gaelic Storm, Kind Regards, Murghem, Riberac and Systematic. In 1994,
Star Rage won nine handicaps to equal the then twentieth-century record for handicap wins in a season, improving from a Timeform rating of 41 to one of 81, and in
1998 Spirit of Love won five times while taking his rating from —p to 121. So
Scott's View falls short by some Johnston standards in winning eight races (seven
of them handicaps) in 2002 and in improving his rating from 71 to 121. However,
his eighth success was very nearly the year's best performance in a British handicap
and the fact that Scott's View broke no new ground for Kingsley House does not
prevent his being exceptional by the standards of virtually every other stable.

Scott's View ran thirteen times in the latest season—after four starts at
two—and at eleven different courses, winning at seven of them. He won around
pronounced left turns and right turns, on sharp tracks and galloping tracks; he won
when making the running and when held up late. Off the course from January until
late-June, his first six wins came in quick succession. The first three were in
handicaps over a mile and a half at Windsor, Catterick and Beverley and—after a
hiccup at Kempton—they were followed by a minor event over that trip at Chester
and two more handicaps, a £29,000 event and a rated stakes, over a mile and three
quarters at Goodwood. The first three wins came within twelve days; those at
Goodwood over five days at the Glorious meeting. It was breathless stuff and sent
Scott's View shooting up the ante-post lists for the Ebor, for which after Goodwood
he was as short as 9/2 favourite.

It was somewhat ironic therefore that, in a campaign of such achievement,
most of the words written about Scott's View concerned a race he never ran in:
there was a maximum field of twenty-two in the Ebor and Scott's View, at number
twenty-three, just missed a place. Twelve horses that did get a run had lower BHB
handicap marks than the ante-post favourite but eleven of the twelve were set to
carry more weight than Scott's View by virtue of being older horses conceding him
weight for age. A widespread debate ensued in the letters pages between those who
defended or damned the Ebor entry system, until Johnston himself effectively
called 'this correspondence is closed' when finally persuaded that the current
method is arguably the correct one. At York, incidentally, the three-year-olds also
have the Melrose Rated Stakes as an alternative over the Ebor trip the following
day. Scott's View's missing the Ebor was, said Johnston, 'a particularly bitter pill to
swallow'. His absence might have seemed less significant when Scott's View was
beaten twice that month, once before the Ebor and once after it, but he was ridden
rather too forcefully (four days after Goodwood) on the first occasion and still ran a
fine race off his revised mark on the second, when third to Supremacy in a rated
stakes at Chester. Even that effort, however, would be surpassed by the end of the
season.

*ladbrokes.com Prestige Stakes (Handicap), Goodwood—the ultra progressive Scott's View
wins the first of two handicaps at the Glorious Goodwood meeting, beating stable-companion Darasim,
Moon Emperor (rail), Hambleden and First Ballot*

Tote Exacta Stakes (Handicap), Ascot—Scott's View puts up one of the best handicap performances of the year to win his eighth race, readily going clear of Contraband (right) and Dune (black sleeves)

Back at York, over a mile and a half in a rated stakes in early-September, Scott's View dead-heated for first with Muhareb and was most unlucky not to win outright, hemmed in through the penultimate furlong. He had been due to run off a mark 5 lb lower in the Ebor. At the end of September, though, came the crowning glory of Scott's View's season when he took the £40,600 Tote Exacta Stakes (Handicap) at Ascot. His first success of the season was off a BHB mark of 70; this was off 105. It was a good renewal of the Tote Exacta, known as the Krug Trophy when Quick Ransom was successful in 1992 and the Coral Eurobet Stakes when Kind Regards won it in 2000, both for Johnston. Amazingly, for a horse registering his eighth victory of the season, Scott's View won it easily. He set the pace for his second success at Goodwood but, and this is where he differs from many of his stable companions, he is usually ridden with more restraint. At Ascot, he was held up in mid-division and cruising on the heels of the leaders a furlong out, before being pushed along to win by two and a half lengths from Contraband. The form demanded that he be given his chance in a listed or pattern race. Opportunities at Newmarket the following week were passed up, Johnston explaining that 'I didn't want to push the boat out too often or too soon.' When Scott's View was seen again it was for the final time in 2002. He produced his only significant disappointment when, starting 7/2 second favourite, he was beaten eleven lengths into fourth behind The Whistling Teal in the St Simon Stakes at Newbury. It remains possible that a busy season had finally caught up with him, but it is also worth bearing in mind that he was not proven on the soft ground. He was below form on heavy going on his final outing as a two-year-old, but he acts on firm and good to soft ground and his third place on polytrack in January looked a creditable effort at the time. Although Scott's View showed smart form to win twice over a mile and three quarters at Goodwood, he put up clearly his best effort over a mile and a half and connections showed no interest in running him in the Cesarewitch. Scott's View sometimes wanders and idled in front at Beverley and for his first win at Goodwood. A small, rather leggy gelding, he is a lot better than he looks, and remarkably tough—a great credit to his stable.

		Selkirk (USA) (ch 1988)	Sharpen Up (ch 1969)	Atan
				Rocchetta
Scott's View (b.g. 1999)			Annie Edge (ch 1980)	Nebbiolo
				Friendly Court
		Milly of The Vally (b 1994)	Caerleon (b 1980)	Nijinsky
				Foreseer
			Mill On The Floss (ch 1983)	Mill Reef
				Milly Moss

Selkirk, the sire of Scott's View, has sired smart performers across a wide variety of distances, in the latest season ranging from five-furlong performer The Trader to Scott's View and St Leger runner-up Highest. Scott's View's dam, grandam and great grandam all won at around a mile and a half with, respectively,

Milly of The Vally taking a maiden at Thirsk, Mill On The Floss the Lingfield Oaks Trial and Milly Moss the Cheshire Oaks. Scott's View is Milly of The Vally's first foal and the next, Mac Melody (by Entrepreneur), showed fairly useful form in 2002, winning a listed race at Milan, before being transferred to the United States. Mac Melody made only 4,200 guineas as a yearling—Scott's View made 21,000 —but this family is packed with good winners as Milly Moss also figures in the pedigrees of pattern winners Madame Dubois, Count Dubois, High Pitched, Lady High Havens, Daggers Drawn, Endorsement, Samsaam and Steward. Mill On The Floss, who refused to enter the stalls for the Oaks but was runner-up in the Ribblesdale, has produced a couple of useful middle-distance performers but is also responsible for Bosham Mill, who is smart at his best but was also notably less willing to put his best foot forward in the latest season than was Scott's View. *M. Johnston*

SCOTTY'S FUTURE (IRE)   4 b.g. Namaqualand (USA) – Persian Empress (IRE)   **105**
51 (Persian Bold 123) [2002 94p: 8s⁵ 10g 7d* 8m 7m⁶ 7d 7m 8m 8d 8g 7m Sep 28] close-coupled, quite good-topped gelding: useful handicapper: won Sony Victoria Cup at Ascot in May by 3 lengths from Lincoln Dancer, still last under 3f out and producing fine turn of speed: eye-catching effort/no luck in running when eighth in Bunbury Cup at Newmarket sixth start: well held after: probably best at 7f (given a test)/1m: acts on firm and soft ground: has been bandaged in front: edgy/taken steadily to post eighth outing, very much on toes penultimate start: slowly away/looked reluctant final outing: held up: temperament under suspicion. *D. Nicholls*

SCRAMBLE (USA)   4 ch.g. Gulch (USA) – Syzygy (ARG) (Big Play (USA)) [2002   **56**
66, a56: p12g f8s 8.2d 8f 8.3s 8f⁶ 8m 9f 8f² 10.1g* 10d 10.1g 8.5g² 8.5g² f8s³ 8m f8g*   **a61**
f8.5s f7g⁴ Dec 17] long-backed gelding: modest handicapper: won amateur events at Newcastle in June and Southwell (made all) in November: stays 1¼m: acts on any going/ fibresand: tried blinkered: often tongue tied: has worn cheekpieces. *B. Ellison*

SCRAPPY DOO   2 b.g. (Apr 26) Petong 126 – Maziere 45 (Mazilier (USA) 107)   **45 §**
[2002 5g 5g⁶ 7f³ 7.5g⁶ 7m⁵ 7g p8g f8g Nov 26] 5,800Y: good-topped gelding: fourth foal: half-brother to 1999 2-y-o 5f winner More Magic (by Cyrano de Bergerac): dam, poor maiden, half-sister to very smart performer up to 1½m in France/USA Millkom: poor maiden: trained by B. Ellison second to sixth outings, then returned to former trainer: stays 7f: acts on firm ground: blinkered/visored last 4 starts: tail flasher: ungenuine. *Miss V. Haigh*

SCRAPS   2 b.g. (Apr 11) Wolfhound (USA) 126 – Jamarj 113 (Tyrnavos 129) [2002 f5g   **62**
5f⁴ 5m⁶ 6m³ May 23] 6,000Y, resold 12,000Y: quite good-topped gelding: poor mover: ninth living foal: half-brother to a winner in Turkey by Pursuit of Love: dam best at 1m/ 9f: modest maiden: should stay 7f: raced only on going firmer than good on turf, well held on fibresand. *T. D. Easterby*

SCRAVELS   3 ch.g. Elmaamul (USA) 125 – Defined Feature (IRE) 91 (Nabeel Dancer   **46**
(USA) 120) [2002 63d: 9.9g³ 12.1g 10m 8.2m 12m 10g Aug 7] small, workmanlike gelding: modest maiden: well held after reappearance: stays 1¼m: best efforts on good/ good to firm going: blinkered (ran poorly) once. *Dr J. D. Scargill*

SCREAMING EAGLE (IRE)   3 b.f. Sadler's Wells (USA) 132 – Ducking 71 (Rep-   **79 +**
rimand 122) [2002 65p: 10.9g* 12m⁴ 14m 12d 15.5v Nov 22] fair handicapper: won at Warwick in April: flattered in face of stiff task in listed race at Saint-Cloud final start: stays 1½m: acts on good to firm going: blinkered in 2002: free-going sort. *J. L. Dunlop*

SCULPTOR   3 b.g. Salse (USA) 128 – Classic Colleen (IRE) 79 (Sadler's Wells (USA)   **70 §**
132) [2002 p8g⁵ p8g² p10g³ 11.8m⁶ 14.6m⁴ 12.1g p10g³ p8g⁵ p10g* 9.9d³ 10m³ 8m⁶ Aug   **a78 §**
16] 35,000F, 34,000Y: big, lengthy gelding: type to carry condition: has plenty of scope: second foal: half-brother to 4-y-o Classic Millennium: dam, maiden who stayed 1¾m, half-sister to very smart miler Alhijaz: fair performer: won minor event at Lingfield in July: should stay 1½m: acts on polytrack, raced mainly on good going or firmer on turf: effective blinkered/visored or not: has run in snatches/found little/edged left: one to treat with caution: sold 15,000 gns, joined C. Mann. *G. A. Butler*

SCURRA   3 b.g. Spectrum (IRE) 126 – Tamnia 106 (Green Desert (USA) 127) [2002   **72 d**
77: 8s 12m⁵ 7g⁴ f7g⁶ 8.5g⁴ 8g³ 6.9g⁶ 9m f8.5g f7g⁶ 10d Oct 28] leggy gelding: fair maiden: left R. Hollinshead after second start: well below best after fifth one: should stay 1¼m: acts on heavy ground: sometimes slowly away: ran well but failed to handle bend at Epsom fifth outing: sold 1,200 gns. *R. Wilman*

SCYTHIAN 2 b.c. (Apr 15) Selkirk (USA) 129 – Sarmatia (USA) (Danzig (USA)) **81**
[2002 5g 6.1s p5g⁶ 6d³ 5m* 5m² 5g Oct 5] 12,000Y: fifth foal: brother to useful 7f winner
(including at 2 yrs) Cybinka and half-brother to 1½m winner Seeker (by Rainbow Quest):
dam unraced half-sister to Kris and Diesis: fairly useful performer: won maiden at
Windsor in July: good neck second in nursery at Sandown: will prove best at 5f/6f: acts
on good to firm ground. *R. Hannon*

SEABORNE 3 b.f. Slip Anchor 136 – Jezebel Monroe (USA) 98 (Lyphard (USA) 132) **87**
[2002 62p: 12m* 12.6m⁶ 14.1g* 14g⁴ 14.1m⁴ Aug 19] leggy, lengthy filly: fairly useful
performer: won 4-runner events at Folkestone (maiden) in April and Salisbury (handicap,
despite edging right/flicking tail) in June: stays 1¾m: yet to race on extremes of going:
pulled hard/carried head high second start (wore crossed noseband). *R. Charlton*

SEA DANZIG 9 ch.g. Roi Danzig (USA) – Tosara 84 (Main Reef 126) [2002 49§, **51 §**
a62§: 9s 12d 9m 11.6d* 11.7f 16f⁶ 12m f14.8g p12g p12g p16g Dec 3] big, plain gelding:
modest handicapper: won amateur event at Windsor in August: stays 1¾m: possibly
unsuited by heavy going, acts on any other turf and fibresand: often blinkered/visored:
unreliable. *J. J. Bridger*

SEAFIELD TOWERS 2 ch.c. (Mar 12) Compton Place 125 – Midnight Spell 79 **72**
(Night Shift (USA)) [2002 6v³ 6d⁵ 5m² 5.9m⁴ 6m 6g 5m⁴ 6m³ Sep 30] 9,000F, 11,000Y:
third foal: half-brother to a winner in Sweden by Piccolo: dam 5f winner: fair maiden:
placed at Carlisle and Hamilton (nursery): will stay 7f: acts on good to firm and good to
soft ground. *Miss L. A. Perratt*

SEA HAZE 5 ch.g. Emarati (USA) 74 – Unveiled 76 (Sayf El Arab (USA) 127) [2002 **–**
–: p7g Jan 12] modest handicapper in 2000: lightly raced and no form since: blinkered
once. *R. J. Baker*

SEA HOLLY (IRE) 2 b.g. (Mar 23) Barathea (IRE) 127 – Mountain Holly 69 (Shirley **– p**
Heights 130) [2002 7m f8s⁵ Sep 5] 3,400F: tall gelding: has a round action: second foal:
dam lightly-raced half-sister to smart performers up to 1½m Earlene and Foyer: clear
signs of ability in maidens at Salisbury and Southwell (edgy): should do better at 1¼m/
1½m. *G. G. Margarson*

SEAHORSE BOY (IRE) 5 b.g. Petardia 113 – Million At Dawn (IRE) 63 (Fayruz **–**
116) [2002 f12g f5g Dec 31] angular, quite good-topped gelding: modest maiden at 3 yrs:
well held both runs in 2002: tried visored/blinkered. *Mrs A. C. Tate*

SEA JADE (IRE) 3 b.f. Mujadil (USA) 119 – Mirabiliary (USA) 74 (Crow (FR) 134) **56**
[2002 –: 6g 6.1m⁶ 6g⁶ 7.9s² 7g³ 8.5m² 8m Sep 3] workmanlike filly: modest maiden
handicapper: stays 8.5f: acts on soft and good to firm going: sometimes flashes tail.
J. W. Payne

SEALED BY FATE (IRE) 7 b.g. Mac's Imp (USA) 116 – Fairy Don (Don 128) **–**
[2002 48+, a–: 5f 5g 6f 5.9s 6m⁵ Aug 25] big, workmanlike gelding: modest performer at
6 yrs: little form in 2002: usually visored/blinkered earlier in career. *J. S. Wainwright*

SEAL OF OFFICE 3 ch.c. Mark of Esteem (IRE) 137 – Minskip (USA) 64 (The **94 ?**
Minstrel (CAN) 135) [2002 9d* 8g 8d p8g⁶ Dec 21] seventh foal: half-brother to 3
winners, including useful French 10.5f winner Minority (by Generous) and smart French/
US performer up to 11f Skipping (by Rainbow Quest): dam, 2-y-o 5f winner, half-sister
to very smart middle-distance performer St Hilarion: fairly useful form: won newcomers
race at Compiegne in June: left P. Bary in France 18,000 gns and off 5 months, never
dangerous in minor event at Lingfield: stays 9f. *J. Cullinan*

SEA MARK 6 gr.g. Warning 136 – Mettlesome (Lomond (USA) 128) [2002 91: 8f **–**
10.3m 8.5m 8.5d Jul 5] big, rangy gelding: has a round action: carries condition: fairly
useful handicapper at best: well held in 2002: blinkered final start. *C. Grant*

SEAN'S HONOR (IRE) 4 b.f. Mukaddamah (USA) 125 – Great Land (USA) **– §**
(Friend's Choice (USA)) [2002 59§, a53§: f5s⁴ Jan 4] good-quartered filly: modest
performer on her day at 3 yrs: usually visored: ungenuine. *Miss J. F. Craze*

SEA PLUME 3 b.f. Slip Anchor 136 – Fine Quill (Unfuwain (USA) 131) [2002 –: **70**
10d⁵ 10m³ 11.7f⁵ Aug 18] fair maiden: third at Nottingham (shaped well): will be well
suited by 1¾m+: sometimes edgy/flashes tail. *Lady Herries*

SEA PRINCE 3 ch.g. Bering 136 – Gersey (Generous (IRE) 139) [2002 –: 10g f12g **–**
11.9m⁶ Jun 25] big, leggy gelding: little form in 5 runs: tried visored/blinkered.
I. A. Balding

SEARCH PARTY (FR) 3 b.g. Efisio 120 – Hunt The Thimble (FR) (Relkino 131) **–**
[2002 53: 14.1f f12g Jun 20] rather leggy gelding: modest maiden at 2 yrs: no form in
2002. *T. D. Easterby*

SEASHORE 2 b.f. (Mar 2) Prince Sabo 123 – Florentynna Bay 61 (Aragon 118) [2002 **81 §**
5s⁶ 6s* 6m 5g* 6d 6m 5g 6s Oct 25] 500Y: leggy filly: closely related to 6f winner
Charnwood Queen (by Cadeaux Genereux) and half-sister to several winners, including
smart 7f/1m performer Sunstreak (by Primo Dominie): dam, 2-y-o 5f winner, half-sister
to smart sprinter Superpower: fairly useful performer: won maiden in June and nursery in
July, both at Haydock: ran as though something amiss 2 of last 3 starts: will prove best at
5f/6f: acts on soft ground: has worn blinkers and cheekpieces: unreliable. *K. A. Ryan*

SEA SQUALL 2 b.f. (Apr 22) Piccolo 121 – City Times (IRE) 65 (Last Tycoon 131) **60 d**
[2002 6m⁵ 7g 6.1m f6g f6g⁴ f7g f7g f6s⁶ Dec 26] 500Y: fifth foal: half-sister to 5-y-o
Rapid Deployment and a winner in Turkey by Bin Ajwaad: dam, maiden best up to
7.6f, half-sister to smart middle-distance performer Water Boatman: modest maiden: ran
poorly last 3 starts: should stay 7f: acts on fibresand and good to firm ground: often
visored/wears cheekpieces: inconsistent. *J. L. Spearing*

SEA STAR 4 b.c. Distant Relative 128 – Storm Card (Zalazl (USA) 120) [2002 91: **111**
7m* 7d⁴ 7.9f* 8m⁵ 8m⁶ 8v Nov 2] good-bodied colt: smart performer: much improved,
and won handicap at Newmarket in April and listed rated stakes at York (by 1½ lengths
from Duck Row, dictated pace) in May: creditable efforts at Ascot in Royal Hunt Cup
and listed event (sixth to Fallen Star) next 2 starts: left H. Cecil, well beaten in Prix
Perth at Saint-Cloud final outing: stays 1m: acts on firm and good to soft going: has been
bandaged fore joints: sometimes on toes/takes strong hold to post. *C. Laffon-Parias,
France*

SEA STORM (IRE) 4 b.g. Dolphin Street (FR) 125 – Prime Interest (IRE) (Kings **94**
Lake (USA) 133) [2002 92: 7f 8.5g 8d⁶ 7g⁵ 8m 7g⁶ 7g⁵ 7.1m³ 7m³ 7.2g² 7.1m³ 7m² p7g* **a102**
p7g⁵ p7g* Dec 28] big, strong gelding: useful on all-weather, fairly useful on turf:
won minor event at Lingfield in November and handicap on same course (career-best
effort, beat Mutawaqed by 1½ lengths) in December: better form at 7f than 1m, and
should prove effective at 6f: acts on polytrack and firm ground, probably on soft: often
wanders: consistent. *R. F. Fisher*

SEA TERN 2 b.f. (Mar 7) Emarati (USA) 74 – Great Tern 59 (Simply Great (FR) 122) **–**
[2002 6f 8g Oct 16] first foal: dam winner around 1¾m: always behind in maidens.
N. M. Babbage

SEA THE WORLD (IRE) 2 b.g. (May 5) Inzar (USA) 112 – Annie's Travels (IRE) **71**
(Mac's Imp (USA) 116) [2002 f5s f6g f5g³ f5g² p5g⁵ Dec 18] 8,000 2-y-o: second living
foal: half-brother to 4-y-o Travel Tardia: dam unraced: fair maiden: second in nursery at
Southwell: should stay 6f: acts on fibresand: hung last 2 starts. *D. Shaw*

SEA TOP 3 gr.g. Highest Honor (FR) 124 – Anotheranniversary 95 (Emarati (USA) **50 d**
74) [2002 50: p5g⁴ f5g⁵ p6g² p7g p5g⁵ f6g 6g 5m⁵ 5.1d 7s 7g 6m Aug 26] modest maiden:
stays 6f: acts on all-weather and good to firm going, below form on softer than good: on
downgrade. *B. G. Powell*

SEATTLE PRINCE (USA) 4 gr.c. Cozzene (USA) – Chicken Slew (USA) (Seattle **63**
Slew (USA)) [2002 86: 10g 12d 12d⁶ 13.3m 12m 14m 16f⁴ 16f³ 11.9g* Oct 24] strong,
quite attractive colt: fairly useful handicapper at best: modest in 2002, winning apprentice
event at Brighton in October: stays 2m: acts on firm and soft going: tried visored/
blinkered at 3 yrs: has carried head awkwardly/drifted left: sold 13,000 gns. *R. Hannon*

SEA WORLD (IRE) 2 b.g. (Mar 25) Dolphin Street (FR) 125 – Shuckran Habibi **–**
(Thatching 131) [2002 d6⁶ 6m Jun 17] IR 700Y: half-brother to several winners,
including 5f (at 2 yrs) and 8.5f winner My Tyson (by Don't Forget Me): dam ran once:
well held in sellers. *M. J. Haynes*

SEA YA MAITE 8 b.g. Komaite (USA) – Marina Plata (Julio Mariner 127) [2002 44, **–**
a77: f8s⁶ f8s⁶ f8g f8.5g f8g³ f8g f8.5g f9.4s² f9.4g² f8g Jun 20] tall, rangy gelding: poor **a58 §**
mover: modest on all-weather: stays 9.4f: acts on fibresand: tried blinkered/tongue tied:
sometimes slowly away/runs lazily: inconsistent. *S. R. Bowring*

SEBRING 3 ch.g. Hurricane Sky (AUS) – Carmenoura (IRE) (Carmelite House (USA) **68**
118) [2002 73: p10g⁴ 11.6g 8f 10s 10.1f⁴ 8d 8g 10.1m* 10.1m⁶ 10f³ Sep 26] close-
coupled gelding: fair performer: won claimer at Yarmouth in August: stays 1¼m: acts on
polytrack and firm going: blinkered (below best) fourth to sixth starts. *N. A. Callaghan*

SEBULBA (IRE) 4 b. or br.g. Dolphin Street (FR) 125 – Twilight Calm (IRE) (Hatim **–**
(USA) 121) [2002 61d: f8s Jan 1] fair performer at 2 yrs: well beaten only outing in 2002:
blinkered/visored last 4 starts: sent to Macau. *J. G. Given*

SECOND MINISTER 3 ch.g. Lion Cavern (USA) 117 – Crime of Passion 115 **66 d**
(Dragonara Palace (USA) 115) [2002 79: 6s 8d⁶ 8.1f f8g f6g⁴ Dec 27] big, leggy gelding:

fair maiden: left J. Eustace 7,000 gns after third outing: likely to prove best at 5f/6f: acts on good to firm ground: on downgrade. *T. D. Barron*

SECOND PAIGE (IRE)   5 b.g. Nicolotte 118 – My First Paige (IRE) 53 (Runnett 125) [2002 76, a–: 10m 11.6d⁵ 11.5m⁴ 12m 12g 11.5m⁶ 12f Oct 7] tall gelding: fair handicapper at best: on downgrade in 2002 (reportedly had breathing problem final start): stays 1¾m: acts on good to firm and soft going: usually blinkered nowadays: has found little. *N. A. Graham*   **66 d**

SECOND TO GO (USA)   2 b. or br.f. (Apr 22) El Prado (IRE) 119 – Sharp Tradition (USA) 65 (Sharpen Up 127) [2002 7m 7m³ 8.1f⁵ Sep 28] $50,000Y: smallish, useful-looking filly: half-sister to several winners in USA: dam ran once at 2 yrs in Britain and later 8.5f winner in USA: fair form in maidens: best effort on debut: fly-jumped and stumbled leaving stall final start: should stay 1¼m. *E. A. L. Dunlop*   **75**

SECOND VENTURE (IRE)   4 b.g. Petardia 113 – Hilton Gateway (Hello Gorgeous (USA) 128) [2002 73: 7v 6m⁶ 7d 6g 6m f6g 5.9g² 5g⁶ 6g³ 6m 6s³ 7.1m³ f8s⁶ 6d* f7g f6g f7g Dec 17] good-topped gelding: fair performer on turf, modest on all-weather: won maiden at Redcar in October: stays 7f: acts on soft and good to firm going, modest form on fibresand: effective visored or not: difficult ride. *J. R. Weymes*   **66 a52**

SECOND WIND   7 ch.g. Kris 135 – Rimosa's Pet 109 (Petingo 135) [2002 67: 7m 7g⁶ 7g p8g⁶ 7.5g⁴ 7m⁶ 8m² p7g⁴ 8d 7m⁶ 8.5m f8s⁴ f8s Oct 8] lengthy, workmanlike gelding: unimpressive mover: fair on turf, modest on all-weather: effective at 7f, barely at 1¼m: acts on all-weather and on any turf going: usually tongue tied: sometimes sweating: reportedly bled from nose third outing: looked most reluctant leaving stall eleventh start: sometimes hangs right/finds little: one to treat with caution: sold 1,000 gns. *C. A. Dwyer*   **67 § a60 §**

SECRET CONQUEST   5 b.m. Secret Appeal – Mohibbah (USA) 86 (Conquistador Cielo (USA)) [2002 62: 7.1m 7g 7m³ 8m² f7g Nov 20] strong mare: modest handicapper: barely stays 1m: has won on good to soft going, best efforts on good or firmer: often blinkered. *G. M. Moore*   **56**

SECRET EXPLORER (IRE)   3 br.g. Blues Traveller (IRE) 119 – Mystery Bid (Auction Ring (USA) 123) [2002 11g 10.2g 10s³ Nov 1] 42,000Y, 10,000 2-y-o: half-brother to several winners, including 1998 2-y-o 7f winner Spy (by Mac's Imp) and 1½m winner Secret Service (by Classic Secret) who stayed 2m: dam, Irish maiden, stayed 1½m: left G. McCourt after second start: off 6 months, first form (fair) in maidens when third at Clonmel final start. *L. P. Greene, Ireland*   **79**

SECRET FLUTTER (IRE)   3 b.f. Entrepreneur 123 – Spend A Rubble (USA) – (Spend A Buck (USA)) [2002 73: 12g 11.8d f14s 11.6d Oct 28] well-made filly: fair form on debut: well held since. *J. G. Portman*   **–**

SECRET FORMULA   2 b.f. (Apr 8) So Factual (USA) 120 – Ancient Secret (Warrshan (USA) 117) [2002 7d⁵ 7g³ 7m⁵ 7.1m⁴ 7m² 6f* Oct 11] tall, leggy filly: fourth foal: sister to 4-y-o Artifact and half-sister to 1999 2-y-o 6f (including in USA) winner Secret Spice and 2001 2-y-o 8.5f winner Old Opium (both by Dilum): dam unraced half-sister to smart stayer Primitive Rising: fairly useful performer: best efforts in nurseries last 2 starts, winning at York by short head from B A Highflyer: effective at 6f/7f: acts on firm going. *S. Kirk*   **85**

SECRET GARDEN (IRE)   3 b.f. Danehill (USA) 126 – Chalamont (IRE) 88 (Kris 135) [2002 8.2m² 9d⁴ 8.2m* 8.1g⁵ 7m* a9f² 8.5f* Dec 13] good-bodied filly: second foal: dam, 2-y-o 6f winner, half-sister to Gold Cup winner Gildoran out of Cheveley Park winner Durtal, herself half-sister to Arc winner Detroit: won maiden at Nottingham in September and listed race at Ascot (useful form when beating Desert Alchemy by 5 lengths) in October: respectable 4 lengths second to Sentimental Value in non-graded stakes at Hollywood following month: left J. Gosden, won optional claimer on same course in December: barely stays 9f: acts on firm going: flashed tail fourth outing. *S. Bray, USA*   **106**

SECRET JEWEL (FR)   2 b.f. (Mar 24) Hernando (FR) 127 – Opalette 75 (Sharrood (USA) 124) [2002 8g Oct 16] second foal: dam 1¼m winner: 11/1, 11 lengths seventh of 16 to Interceptor in maiden at Bath, late headway after very slow start: will be well suited by 1¼m+: almost certain to do better. *Lady Herries*   **51 p**

SECRETO DREAMS (IRE)   3 b.g. Distinctly North (USA) 115 – Whittingham Girl 58 (Primo Dominie 121) [2002 69: f6g⁵ 6g⁵ 6m² May 16] tall, leggy gelding: fair maiden: stayed 6f: acted on soft going and fibresand: was sometimes slowly away: dead. *M. Wigham*   **71**

SECRET PRIDE   2 b.f. (Mar 19) Green Desert (USA) 127 – Talented 112 (Bustino   **89**
136) [2002 6m² 5m* 6m⁴ Sep 5] fifth foal: half-sister to fairly useful 2001 2-y-o 7f winner
Zaeema (by Zafonic): dam, 1¼m (including Sun Chariot Stakes) winner who stayed
1½m, half-sister to dam of 5-y-o Three Points out of half-sister to very smart
middle-distance performer Richard of York: fairly useful form: won maiden at Lingfield
in August by 1¼ lengths from Stormont, pair clear: raced freely when fourth of 6 to
Wimple in minor event at Salisbury next time: likely to prove best at 5f/6f. *B. W. Hills*

SECRET SENTIMENT   4 b.f. Mark of Esteem (IRE) 137 – Sahara Baladee (USA)   **43**
79 (Shadeed (USA) 135) [2002 56: p6g p12g f12s 10m 8.1m 9m 10m 6d 8m 8.5g
f8.5s Dec 13] tall, useful-looking filly: poor maiden handicapper: should stay 1¼m.
A. B. Coogan

SECRET SPOOF   3 b.g. Mind Games 121 – Silver Blessings (Statoblest 120) [2002   **83**
76: 6s² 6m² 5g⁵ Jun 27] sturdy gelding: fairly useful handicapper: will prove best at 5f/6f:
acts on soft and good to firm going. *T. D. Easterby*

SECRET SPRING (FR)   10 b.g. Dowsing (USA) 124 – Nordica 99 (Northfields   **?**
(USA)) [2002 9s 9m⁶ 9.9m 10m Aug 28] leggy gelding: useful handicapper in 2000: little
form in 2002. *Mrs L. Richards*

SECRET STYLE   7 b.g. Shirley Heights 130 – Rosie Potts 83 (Shareef Dancer (USA)   **–**
135) [2002 –: f14.8g f16g f16.2g Feb 22] lightly raced and no form on Flat since 2000:
has won in blinkers. *R. Hollinshead*

SECURON DANCER   4 b.f. Emperor Jones (USA) 119 – Gena Ivor (USA) (Sir Ivor   **–**
135) [2002 49: 12m 16.4d Jul 11] tall, workmanlike filly: unimpressive mover: poor
maiden handicapper at 3 yrs: well held in 2002 (reported to have moved badly throughout
when pulled up final start). *R. Rowe*

SEDUCTIVE DANCE   2 b.f. (Mar 25) Groom Dancer (USA) 128 – Sedova (USA)   **–**
(Nijinsky (CAN) 138) [2002 7s Sep 10] 16,000F, 25,000Y: ninth foal: sister to useful
1¼m winner Segovia and half-sister to 2 winners, including useful 1¼m winner Dovaly
(by Lycius): dam French 1½m winner: 50/1, last in maiden at Lingfield. *R. M. Beckett*

SEEKING THE SUN (IRE)   3 b. or br.g. Petardia 113 – Femme Savante 89 (Glen-   **77**
stal (USA) 118) [2002 90: 7g 6d 7.1f 7s⁵ Oct 25] useful-looking gelding: fairly useful
performer at 2 yrs: only fair form in handicaps in 2002: probably stays 7f: very best
efforts on good to soft going: failed to handle bend at Warwick once at 2 yrs: sold 7,000
gns. *C. F. Wall*

SEEL OF APPROVAL   3 br.g. Polar Falcon (USA) 126 – Petit Point (IRE) 78 (Petor-   **85**
ius 117) [2002 68: 5d 6m* 6m* 6g³ Oct 2] fairly useful performer: won handicaps at
Lingfield and Kempton (tended to idle) in September: stays 6f: acts on good to firm
going. *R. Charlton*

SEEMS SO EASY (USA)   3 b.f. Palmister (USA) – I'm An Issue (USA) (Cox's   **51 ?**
Ridge (USA)) [2002 –: 6f 6m⁴ 5g Jul 6] smallish, strong filly: seemingly best effort in
maidens (modest form) when fourth at Ripon (played up behind stall and unseated
beforehand): stays 6f: blinkered/tongue tied last 2 starts. *S. J. Magnier*

SEFTON LODGE   3 b.g. Barathea (IRE) 127 – Pine Needle 89 (Kris 135) [2002 –p: **45**
7s 7.1m 7s⁵ Oct 22] sturdy, quite attractive gelding: poor maiden: left J. Noseda 3,000
gns and off 6 months after second start: slowly away on debut: tried tongue tied.
S. L. Keightley

SEGSBURY BELLE   7 b.m. Petoski 135 – Rolling Dice (Balinger 116) [2002 f12s   **–**
Jan 22] 3,000 4-y-o: fourth foal: half-sister to a winning chaser: dam winning chaser:
slowly away in maiden at Southwell. *Miss G. Browne*

SEIGNOSSE (IRE)   4 b.g. College Chapel 122 – How Ya Been (IRE) (Last Tycoon   **88**
131) [2002 75: 5f⁴ 5m* 5m* 5g² 6d 5m Jun 1] strong, workmanlike gelding: fairly useful
handicapper: won at Ripon (apprentices) and Epsom in April: pulled up (seemingly
lame) final start: speedy, and was almost certainly best at 5f: acted on firm going: dead.
I. A. Balding

SEIHALI (IRE)   3 b.c. Alzao (USA) 117 – Edwina (IRE) 63 (Caerleon (USA) 132)   **111**
[2002 87p: 8.2f* 7m 8d* Jul 5] tall, quite attractive colt: smart performer: lightly raced:
won minor event at Nottingham in May and steadily-run 4-runner minor event at
Salisbury (by 3 lengths from Bestam, gave odd flick of tail) in July: will prove best up to
1m: acts on firm and good to soft going: most coltish before second start (travelled strongly long
way when seventh in Jersey Stakes at Royal Ascot): has worn crossed noseband/had 2
handlers: joined A. Smith in UAE. *A. C. Stewart*

SELECTIVE   3 b.c. Selkirk (USA) 129 – Portelet 91 (Night Shift (USA)) [2002 86p: **101**
7m* 7.6f⁶ 7d² 6g 7.1d 8d* 8g⁵ 8.1m* Sep 15] good-bodied colt: useful performer: won
maiden at Southwell in April, minor event at Kempton in July and handicap at Sandown
(showed good turn of foot to beat Petrula by ½ length with bit to spare) in September:
stays 1m when emphasis is on speed: yet to race on soft/heavy going, probably acts on
any other turf: tends to carry head awkwardly. *A. C. Stewart*

SELF EVIDENT (USA)   2 b. or br.c. (Mar 18) Known Fact (USA) 135 – Palisade   **87 p**
(USA) 87 (Gone West (USA)) [2002 6g 7f⁴ 8g* Oct 16] first foal: dam 7f (at 2 yrs) and
1m (in USA) winner, half-sister to smart performer up to 1¼m Boatman: progressive
form in maidens: won at Bath by 3½ lengths from Wozzeck despite edging right:
free-going sort, unlikely to stay much beyond 1m: useful prospect. *Mrs A. J. Perrett*

SELKIRK GRACE   2 b.c. (Apr 26) Selkirk (USA) 129 – Polina 69 (Polish Precedent   **92 p**
(USA) 131) [2002 8g³ Oct 18] 33,000Y: tall, angular colt: has scope: fourth foal: half-
brother to 1999 2-y-o 7f winner Sally Gardens (by Alzao) and a winner in Japan by
Spectrum: dam, second at 1m, out of Yorkshire Oaks winner Sally Brown: 20/1, promising length third of 16 to Persian Majesty in maiden at Newmarket (got upset in stall),
battling on well: will probably stay 1¼m: sure to improve and win a race. *E. A. L. Dunlop*

SELTON HILL (IRE)   5 b.g. Bin Ajwaad (IRE) 119 – Ivory Gull (USA) 80 (Storm   **47**
Bird (CAN) 134) [2002 p10g p13g 12.3g 10m May 10] one-time fair maiden handicapper: dead. *N. A. Callaghan*

SEMAH'S PARC   4 b.g. Pure Melody (USA) 77 – Semah's Dream 39 (Gunner B 126)   **–**
[2002 12m 10s 12d Nov 5] second foal: dam maiden who probably stayed 7f: well held in
maidens. *Mrs A. M. Naughton*

SEMENOVSKII   2 b.g. (Apr 8) Fraam 114 – Country Spirit (Sayf El Arab (USA) 127)   **82**
[2002 5s 5m⁶ 5s⁴ 5g² 6d* 6m² 6m 6m 6g Sep 19] 12,500F, 16,000Y: strong gelding: fifth
foal: half-brother to 5f (at 2 yrs) and 1m winner Millennium Magic (by Magic Ring): dam
unraced: fairly useful performer: made all in maiden at Haydock in July: below form last
3 starts: stays 6f: acts on good to firm and good to soft going: moved poorly to post/
reportedly finished lame second start: sold 12,500 gns. *A. Berry*

SEMIGOLD (USA)   2 b.c. (Feb 26) Seeking The Gold (USA) – Shmoose (IRE) 106   **72**
(Caerleon (USA) 132) [2002 5.7m* 6m 5.1g Aug 26] smallish, lengthy colt: first foal:
dam, 2-y-o 6f winner, half-sister to 3-y-o Firth of Lorne out of smart sprinter/1000
Guineas second Kerrera: fair form when winning maiden at Bath in June: failed to repeat
it in Richmond Stakes at Goodwood and nursery at Chepstow (reared start): should stay
at least 6f: joined J. Sadler in UAE. *M. R. Channon*

SEMPERGREEN   2 ch.f. (Feb 1) Hector Protector (USA) 124 – Star Tulip 99 (Night   **65 p**
Shift (USA)) [2002 6d⁶ May 23] third foal: half-sister to 5-y-o Indian Sun and 4-y-o
Texas Gold: dam 6f winner, including at 2 yrs: 7/1 and green, 3 lengths sixth of 13 to
Pearl Dance in maiden at Goodwood, handling downhill gradients none too well and not
knocked about: reportedly suffered minor injury after: should do better if all is well.
J. L. Dunlop

SEMPER PARATUS (USA)   3 b.c. Foxhound (USA) 103 – Bletcha Lass (AUS)   **80**
(Bletchingly (AUS)) [2002 66: 7m 5.3m² 5.3d* 6s* 5m p6g 6f³ 7m⁶ 7.1g 7m 6g Sep 27]
close-coupled colt: unimpressive mover: fairly useful handicapper: won at Brighton in
May and Kempton in June: stays 7f: yet to race on heavy ground, acts on any other turf:
blinkered after reappearance. *G. C. Bravery*

SEMPRE SORRISO   2 b.f. (Feb 7) Fleetwood (IRE) 107 – Ever Genial 117 (Brig-   **–**
adier Gerard 144) [2002 6d 5.7m Aug 6] 10,000Y: closely related to a winner abroad
by Groom Dancer and half-sister to several winners, including fairly useful 5f and 7f
winner Present Laughter (by Cadeaux Genereux): dam 7f/1m winner, including May Hill
and Hungerford Stakes: behind in minor event/maiden: finished lame second start.
A. Charlton

SENDINTANK   2 ch.g. (Mar 20) Halling (USA) 133 – Colleville 97 (Pharly (FR) 130)   **55**
[2002 5.1d p5g 5m 5.9m Sep 2] first foal: dam 7f (at 2 yrs) to 1½m winner: modest
maiden: best effort second start: should be well suited by 1m+. *S. C. Williams*

SENIOR MINISTER   4 b.g. Lion Cavern (USA) 117 – Crime Ofthecentury 80   **–**
(Pharly (FR) 130) [2002 102: 6m 6d⁶ 5m 7.1d 5m 6.1f⁴ 5g⁵ 5g Oct 19] good-topped
gelding: useful performer at best, lightly raced: reportedly fractured pelvis after final
2-y-o start, and ran only once in 2001: little form in 2002, leaving J. Eustace 6,000 gns
after fourth start: blinkered third outing: had something go amiss first and fourth outings.
P. W. Hiatt

SENNEN COVE   3 ch.g. Bering 136 – Dame Laura (IRE) 100 (Royal Academy   **67**
(USA) 130) [2002 78: 7g 7m 8m⁵ 8.2d⁵ p6g⁶ Dec 18] close-coupled gelding: fair maiden:
off 7 months before final start: free-going sort, probably better at 6f/7f than 1m: acts on
good to firm and good to soft going. *H. Morrison*

SENOBAR   4 b.f. Mtoto 134 – Elegantissima 57 (Polish Precedent (USA) 131) [2002   **–**
f7g 6g 7.1m Aug 26] first foal: dam, maiden who stayed 1m, out of close relation of
Pebbles: soundly beaten in maidens: very slowly away on debut. *Mrs N. Macauley*

SENOR BENNY (USA)   3 br.c. Benny The Dip (USA) 127 – Senora Tippy (USA)   **78**
(El Gran Senor (USA) 136) [2002 7g³ Jul 20] fifth foal: half-brother to 3 winners in USA,
including Grade 3 8.5f winner Tippity Witch (by Affirmed): dam, French 9f listed winner,
later won in USA: 7/4 favourite and better for race, 3¼ lengths third to Hannon in maiden
at Newmarket, caught flat-footed when pace increased and drifting right before finishing
strongly: bred to stay 1m+: seemed sure to do better. *J. H. M. Gosden*

SENORITA (IRE)   2 b.f. (Mar 20) Spectrum (IRE) 126 – Princess Natalie 78 (Rudi-   **–**
mentary (USA) 118) [2002 5m May 6] 28,000Y: lengthy, useful-looking filly: first foal:
dam 5f winner (including at 2 yrs): 6/1, green and backward, last of 7 in minor event at
Doncaster. *T. D. Easterby*

SENOR MIRO   4 b.g. Be My Guest (USA) 126 – Classic Moonlight (IRE) (Machia-   **60**
vellian (USA) 123) [2002 76: 7m p7g³ Jul 17] leggy, useful-looking gelding: modest
maiden, lightly raced: claimed £3,000 and joined J. Akehurst after final start: stays 7f: yet
to race on extremes of going: sometimes races freely: tongue tied/flashed tail final 3-y-o
outing. *R. F. Johnson Houghton*

SENOR PEDRO   2 b.c. (Mar 29) Piccolo 121 – Stride Home 78 (Absalom 128) [2002   **60**
7.1g 7f 8.3d p7g f7g² f8.5s* Dec 18] sixth foal: brother to 2000 2-y-o 5.7f winner Magical
Flute and half-brother to fairly useful 1¼m to 11.6f winner Pedro Pete (by Fraam): dam
5f (at 2 yrs) to 1¼m winner: modest performer: won seller at Wolverhampton: should stay
1¼m: acts on fibresand and firm ground. *M. R. Channon*

SENOR SOL (USA)   2 b.c. (Apr 1) El Prado (IRE) 119 – One Moment In Time (USA)   **89**
(Magesterial (USA) 116) [2002 6s 7m⁴ 7f² 8d* Aug 2] $155,000Y: big, good-bodied colt:
fifth foal: half-brother to winners in USA by Numerous and Slew City Slew: dam 6f to
1m winner in USA: fairly useful performer: won maiden at Newmarket by head from
Mysterinch: will be suited by 1¼m/1½m: acts on firm and good to soft ground, probably
on soft. *P. F. I. Cole*

SENOR TORAN (USA)   2 b.g. (Mar 30) Barathea (IRE) 127 – Applaud (USA) 105   **75 p**
(Rahy (USA) 115) [2002 8s⁴ 8s Oct 26] big, strong gelding: third foal: dam 2-y-o 5f/6f
(Cherry Hinton) winner: better effort in maidens (fair form) when fourth to Allergy at
Leicester: not sure to stay further than 1m: gelded after final start: has scope to make a
better 3-y-o. *P. F. I. Cole*

SENTIMENTAL VALUE (USA)   3 ch.f. Diesis 133 – Stately Star (USA) (Deputy   **107**
Minister (CAN)) [2002 75p: 10g⁵ 10g⁵ 8g³ 9d* 8m* 8m² 8f² 8.5f³ 8f* a9f* a8.5f³ Dec
18] rather leggy, quite attractive filly: useful performer: won maiden and handicap at
Ripon in June: left H. Cecil after next start: successful in non-graded events at Santa
Anita and Hollywood (by 4 lengths from Secret Garden) in October/November: will
prove best at 1m/1¼m: acts on dirt, firm and good to soft going, shaped well on soft on
debut: blinkered last 8 starts: races prominently. *K. Mulhall, USA*

SENTINEL   3 ch.c. Hector Protector (USA) 124 – Soolaimon (IRE) 71 (Shareef Dancer   **100**
(USA) 135) [2002 p7g f7g* f8.5g⁵ p12g* p10g* 12s* 12m* 12g⁵ Jul 31] well-made colt:
third reported foal: half-brother to useful 1m (at 2 yrs) and 1¼m (in USA) winner Reduit
(by Lion Cavern): dam, maiden who should have stayed 1½m, half-sister to smart French
performer up to 10.5f Audacieuse and useful stayer Lord Jim: progressive handicapper:
won at Lingfield (2), Newbury and Salisbury in May/June: beat Imtihan in good style by
1¼ lengths at Salisbury, despite hanging right: good fifth to Dawn Invasion in Tote Gold
Trophy at Goodwood final start: subsequently found to have had minor problem with
off-fore fetlock: will stay 1¾m: acts on soft going, good to firm and all-weather: has
carried head awkwardly and races lazily. *G. A. Butler*

SENTRY (IRE)   2 b.c. (Mar 10) In Command (IRE) 114 – Keep Bobbin Up (IRE) 76   **79 p**
(Bob Back (USA) 124) [2002 7f 8s⁴ Oct 26] IR 33,000F, 50,000Y: strong, lengthy colt:
has scope: has a quick action: third foal: half-brother to Irish 6f (at 2 yrs) to 1m winner
Flying Boat (by Desert Style): dam Irish 2-y-o 7f winner: much better effort in maidens
(fair form) when fourth of 16 to Zeis at Newbury, staying on without being knocked
about: should stay 1¼m: capable of better. *J. H. M. Gosden*

SENZA SCRUPOLI 2 ch.g. (Apr 8) Inchinor 119 – Gravette 79 (Kris 135) [2002 — p
7.5s Nov 13] approx. 22,000Y in Italy: seventh foal: half-brother to 3 winners abroad,
including Italian winner up to 1½m Oro Nero (by Alzao): dam, 1m winner, half-sister to
very smart performer up to 1¾m Welsh Guide: well-held ninth of 10 in minor event at
Milan (gelded after): likely to do better. *L. M. Cumani*

SEPTEMBER HARVEST (USA) 6 ch.g. Mujtahid (USA) 118 – Shawgatny (USA) 38 §
83 (Danzig Connection (USA)) [2002 –, a44: f8g f8g⁶ f11g² 8d⁵ 18m⁶ 12.1m Sep 24] tall,
angular gelding: poor handicapper: effective at 1m (given a test) to 1½m: acts on firm
going, soft and fibresand: tried blinkered/visored: tends to get behind. *Mrs S. Lamyman*

SEQUENTIAL 3 b.c. Rainbow Quest (USA) 134 – Dance Sequence (USA) 105 (Mr 98
Prospector (USA)) [2002 10m³ 12g⁵ 10f* 12.3g* 10.3m Aug 30] tall, quite attractive
colt: second foal: half-brother to fairly useful stayed 2000 2-y-o 5f winner Dance On (by Caerleon): dam, 2-y-o 6f (Lowther Stakes) winner who stayed 1m, sister to smart US juveniles
Souvenir Copy and Gold Tribute: useful performer: won maiden at Redcar in June and
handicap at Chester (by ¾ length from Octane, despite starting slowly and looking hard
ride) in August: tailed-off last final start: stays 1½m: raced on good going or firmer. *Sir
Michael Stoute*

SEQUIN SLIPPERS (IRE) 2 b.f. (Feb 26) Revoque (IRE) 122 – Strutting (IRE) 95 74 d
(Ela-Mana-Mou 132) [2002 7g 7g³ 7d⁶ 7s⁶ 6f 7.5s⁵ f7g Nov 26] IR 35,000Y: fourth foal:
half-sister to smart Irish 7f/1¼m winner Chiming (by Danehill): dam 7f (at 2 yrs) and
1¼m winner: fair maiden: below form after third at Tipperary: left K. Prendergast,
Ireland, 1,000 gns after sixth outing: should stay 1m. *K. A. Ryan*

SERAPH 2 ch.g. (Apr 7) Vettori (IRE) 119 – Dahlawise (IRE) 76 (Caerleon (USA) —
132) [2002 f6g f6g 6g 7m f8s Sep 5] 2,500F, IR 5,000Y: workmanlike gelding: half-
brother to several winners, including 6f winner Denton Lad (by Prince Sabo) and 1995
2-y-o 7f winner Alfayza (by Danehill): dam 2-y-o 6f winner: little form: left P. McEntee
before final start: tried blinkered. *R. Wilman*

SERBELLONI 2 b.c. (Mar 29) Spectrum (IRE) 126 – Rose Vibert (Caerleon (USA) 73 p
132) [2002 8d⁶ Oct 30] third foal: brother to 4-y-o Sky Quest: dam unraced out of smart
7f performer Premier Rose: weak 20/1-shot and green, 5 lengths sixth of 13 to Devant in
maiden at Yarmouth, best work late on: should do better. *P. W. Harris*

SERGEANT CECIL 3 ch.g. King's Signet (USA) 110 – Jadidh 64 (Touching Wood 82
(USA) 127) [2002 69: p10g 12g 12m 14d⁶ 10.2g² 12.1g³ 14.1g² 11.7g² 11.6d² Oct 28]
fairly useful maiden handicapper: left J. W. Mullins after fourth start, good placed efforts
subsequently: at least as effective at 1½m as 1¾m: yet to race on extremes of going on
turf: waited with: wandered penultimate start. *B. R. Millman*

SERGEANT SLIPPER 5 ch.g. Never So Bold 135 – Pretty Scarce (Handsome 53 §
Sailor 125) [2002 62, a56: f5g f5g f5g 5g f5g² f5g² 5v f5g² 6.1m⁴ 5m⁴ 5m f5g 5s⁶ f5s
f6g⁶ f5g Dec 13] workmanlike gelding: modest handicapper: raced only at 5f/6f: acts on
fibresand, good to firm and heavy going: tried blinkered, usually visored: often slowly
away: untrustworthy. *C. Smith*

SERIEUX 3 b.c. Cadeaux Genereux 131 – Seranda (IRE) (Petoski 135) [2002 100: 7m 109
7m* 8.1d⁴ 7m 7m Sep 28] strong, lengthy, useful-looking colt: useful handicapper: won
at York in May by 1¼ lengths from White Rabbit: creditable fourth to Common World at
Haydock next start: well held after 4-month break last 2 outings: unlikely to stay beyond
1m: yet to race on extremes of going: free-going sort, possibly best making running: sold
46,000 gns. *B. W. Hills*

SERIOUS TRUST 9 b.g. Alzao (USA) 117 – Mill Line 71 (Mill Reef (USA) 141) —
[2002 21: 11.9m Jul 16] of little account nowadays. *Mrs L. C. Jewell*

SEROTONIN 3 b.c. Baratheas (IRE) 127 – Serotina (IRE) 73 (Mtoto 134) [2002 64p: 97
11g² 12g² 10s* 10m* 11.8g⁵ 10.1m⁴ Aug 25] big, angular colt: useful performer: won
maiden at Windsor in May and 5-runner minor event at Newbury (by short head from
Shahzan House) in July: ran as though something amiss final start: may prove best around
1¼m: acts on soft and good to firm going: sold 68,000 gns, joined J. O'Neill. *R. Charlton*

SEROV (IRE) 4 ch.g. Mujtahid (USA) 118 – Title Roll (IRE) 107 (Tate Gallery 99
(USA) 117) [2002 87: 5s* 5s 6s⁶ 5g³ 5d 5g* 6m 6g Sep 1] fourth foal: half-brother to
fairly useful 6f winner (including at 2 yrs) Young Josh (by Warning): dam effective at 5f
to 7f: useful handicapper: won at the Curragh in March and July: well held at Ripon and
the Curragh last 2 starts: best at 5f/6f: acts on soft and good to firm ground: sometimes
blinkered, including for second win. *T. Stack, Ireland*

SERPICO (IRE)   5 ch.h. Bluebird (USA) 125 – Centella (IRE) (Thatching 131) [2002   **?**
a12g a8g² a12g³ a9g* a10.5g* a12g³ a8g* a12g³ p8g a12g a10.5g² a12g a8g³ a11g⁵
a10.5g Nov 17] third foal: half-brother to 5f seller winner Cameo (by Statoblest): dam
placed at 6f at 2 yrs in Ireland: fair maiden in Ireland for C. O'Brien at 3 yrs: raced mainly
at Mijas for current stable, winning 2 minor events and handicap between March and
June: mid-division in handicap at Lingfield ninth start: effective at 1m, stays 1½m: had
form on good to firm and good to soft ground in Ireland, raced mainly on sand since: has
been blinkered/visored/tongue tied. *E. J. Creighton, Spain*

SERRAFINA   2 ch.f. (Mar 18) Bluegrass Prince (IRE) 110 – Josifina (Master Willie   **–**
129) [2002 6m Jul 17] first living foal: dam refused to enter stall only intended Flat
outing, later winner over hurdles: 33/1, ninth of 15 in maiden at Kempton. *B. De Haan*

SERRAVAL (FR)   4 ch.f. Sanglamore (USA) 126 – Saone (USA) (Bering 136) [2002   **78 d**
f11g 10m³ 9.9m* 10.3m 10s 9f 12g 11.9g 10.3f Jul 13] ex-French filly: fourth foal:
half-sister to 3 winners in France, including 1m winner State (by Petit Loup) and 9.5f
winner Salers (by Lead On Time): dam once-raced half-sister to smart French/US
middle-distance stayer Special Price out of half-sister to Allez France: fair handicapper:
trained by H. Van de Poele in 2001: won at Beverley in April: generally on downgrade
after: should stay 1½m: acts on soft and good to firm ground: reportedly lost action fourth
start: visored 2 of last 3 starts. *B. S. Rothwell*

SERVICE   2 ch.f. (Feb 8) College Chapel 122 – Centre Court 74 (Second Set (IRE)   **65 §**
127) [2002 5.2f* 5d⁶ 6g⁵ 5g³ 5m² 6m⁴ 6m 7g 7v p6g⁵ Dec 21] 6,000F: sparely-made filly:
first foal: dam, 2-y-o 5f winner, from family of very smart sprinter College Chapel: fair
performer: won seller at Yarmouth in June: left W. Haggas after sixth start, and showed
little subsequently: effective at 5f/6f: acts on firm ground: wore cheekpieces final start:
tail flasher: unreliable. *J. Akehurst*

SESARY (IRE)   2 b.f. (Mar 29) Sesaro (USA) 81 – Dunfern (Wolver Hollow 126) [2002   **72 ?**
6f⁴ 6d⁶ 6m² 6g 7s 6m Sep 23] IR 5,500Y: close-coupled filly: fifth foal: half-sister to
fairly useful Irish 7f winner (including at 2 yrs) Canaima (by Rainbows For Life): dam,
7f winner in Ireland, half-sister to useful performer up to 1m Pilot Jet: seemingly showed
fair form when 3½ lengths second to Zafeen in maiden at Salisbury: modest at best
otherwise: bred to stay 7f, but races freely: sold 500 gns. *Mrs P. N. Dutfield*

SEVEN MOONS (JPN)   2 br.f. (Feb 22) Sunday Silence (USA) – Moon Is Up (USA)   **– p**
104 (Woodman (USA) 126) [2002 7g Oct 14] good-bodied filly: second foal: dam,
French 1m winner, closely related to Kingmambo and half-sister to East of The Moon,
out of Miesque: 9/2, well held after chasing leaders over 4f in maiden at Leicester: sent to
USA: should do better. *H. R. A. Cecil*

SEVEN NO TRUMPS   5 ch.g. Pips Pride 117 – Classic Ring (IRE) 50 (Auction Ring   **108 d**
(USA) 123) [2002 101: 5s* 5m 6s 6g 5.6m 5g 6s Oct 25] rangy, good-topped gelding:
useful handicapper: won at Doncaster in March by a length from James Stark: generally
on downgrade after: at least as effective at 5f as 6f: acts on any going: blinkered once at 3
yrs: edgy sort: tends to carry head high. *B. W. Hills*

SEVEN SPRINGS (IRE)   6 b.g. Unblest 117 – Zaydeen (Sassafras (FR) 135) [2002   **–**
–, a59: f5s f6g³ f5g f6g⁶ f6g 6m 5.1d² 7.1m⁶ 5g f5f Nov 29] tall, workmanlike gelding: **a49**
poor performer: stays 6f: acts on fibresand and any turf going: tried visored: sometimes
early to post/slowly away. *R. Hollinshead*

SEWMORE CHARACTER   2 b.c. (Feb 16) Hector Protector (USA) 124 – Kyle   **83**
Rhea 104 (In The Wings 128) [2002 6g 6d 7g³ 7s 7v² Nov 9] 21,000Y: angular colt:
second foal: brother to 3-y-o Kirtle: dam, 1¼m/11.4f winner, half-sister to smart
performer up to 1¾m Applecross, herself dam of Invermark and very smart winner up to
1¾m Craigsteel: fairly useful maiden: good second to Impersonator in nursery at
Doncaster: should be suited by 1¼m/1½m: acts on heavy ground, unraced on firmer than
good. *M. Blanshard*

SEWMUCH CHARACTER   3 b.g. Magic Ring (IRE) 115 – Diplomatist 69 (Domin-   **76**
ion 123) [2002 75§: 7s 7.1m³ 7.6f 6s² 6s 7d* 7g⁴ 7.1g 8s 8f Oct 7] big, good-topped
gelding: fair performer: won maiden at Folkestone in July: best at 6f/7f: acts on soft and
good to firm going: usually races prominently: looked none too keen final start: none too
reliable. *M. Blanshard*

SEYED (IRE)   2 b.c. (Feb 2) Desert Prince (IRE) 130 – Royal Bounty (IRE) 80 (Gener-   **– p**
ous (IRE) 139) [2002 6m⁵ Jun 1] 180,000Y: leggy, useful-looking colt: first foal: dam,
2-y-o 7.5f winner, daughter of smart half-sister to Prix du Cadran winner Sought Out: 6/1
and green, fifth of 6 in minor event at Kempton, hanging right and fading. *D. R. Loder*

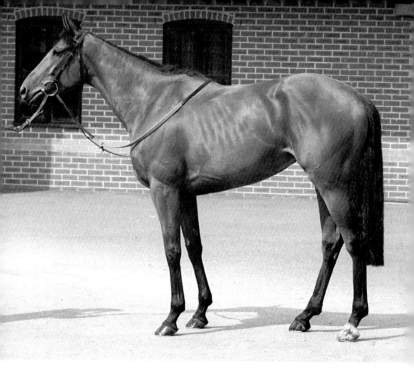

Mrs Hugh Dalgety & Partners' "Shadow Dancing"

SEYMOUR (IRE)   3 ch.f. Eagle Eyed (USA) 111 – Twany Angel (Double Form 130)   –
[2002 78: 6s 5.1d⁵ Apr 1] 10,000Y: ex-Irish filly: closely related to 5-y-o Mount Abu and
fairly useful 5f (in Ireland at 2 yrs) to 1m (in USA) winner Melleray and half-sister to 3
winners: dam French maiden: well held in 2002: raced only at 5f/6f: best efforts on soft/heavy going. *B. A. McMahon*

SHAAMEL (USA)   3 ch.g. Silver Hawk (USA) 123 – Songlines (USA) (Diesis 133)   **85**
[2002 12m³ 10s⁴ Oct 23] sixth foal: half-brother to winners in USA by Deputy Minister
and Dixieland Band: dam won 7 races in USA, including 8.5f minor stakes: much better
effort in maidens (fairly useful form) when 3½ lengths third to Ishtak at Kempton (slowly
away): favourite, lacklustre effort 3 months later: sold 16,000 gns. *J. L. Dunlop*

SHAANMER (IRE)   3 b.c. Darshaan 133 – Fee Des Mers (Alzao (USA) 117) [2002   **116**
109p: 8g⁴ 9m² 10m² 10g² 10d² Sep 22] good-topped colt: smart performer: won all 3
starts in 2001, including Prix des Chenes at Longchamp: didn't win at 3 yrs, but ran
creditably all outings: 3¼ lengths fifth (promoted to fourth) behind Landseer in Poule
d'Essai des Poulains at Longchamp on reappearance, then close second to Rouvres in
Prix Jean Prat at Chantilly (dead-heated, short-neck behind winner), Khalkevi in Grand
Prix de Paris at Longchamp (beaten a head), Highdown in Prix Guillaume d'Ornano at
Deauville (beaten short head) and Tau Ceti in Prix du Prince d'Orange at Longchamp
(beaten ½ length): should stay 1½m: acts on soft and good to firm ground: to join
C. Clement in USA. *A. Fabre, France*

SHABERNAK (IRE)   3 gr.g. Akarad (FR) 130 – Salinova (FR) (Linamix (FR) 127)   **89**
[2002 10d² 12m³ 12.1m* Apr 25] smallish, lengthy gelding: first foal: dam unraced sister

to useful French 1½m winner Six Zero from very good US family: fairly useful form: won maiden at Beverley in April by 3 lengths from Kaparolo: gelded after: stays 1½m: raced freely second start. *M. L. W. Bell*

SHADFORTH (USA)   3 b.f. Shadeed (USA) 135 – High Sevens 90 (Master Willie   **46**
129) [2002 7m⁵ 7s Sep 10] smallish, sturdy filly: sixth foal: half-sister to 7f (including at 2 yrs)/1m winner Impulsif (by Diesis): dam 2-y-o 6f winner: better effort in maidens when seventh at Lingfield final start: moved poorly to post on debut: dead. *H. Candy*

SHADOWBLASTER (IRE)   5 b.g. Wolfhound (USA) 126 – Swame (USA) (Jade   **56**
Hunter (USA)) [2002 83: p12g³ p12g* 10d f12g* f16.2g 12m p12g Aug 29] angular gelding: fairly useful at 4 yrs, modest in 2002: won sellers at Lingfield (left B. Hanbury) in June and Southwell in July: was best at 1½m/1¾m: acted on soft going, good to firm and all-weather: dead. *N. P. Littmoden*

SHADOW CAPTAIN   2 gr.g. (Apr 24) Compton Place 125 – Magnolia 52 (Petong   **–**
126) [2002 5d 5s⁵ 5m⁶ 5g Aug 12] 5,000Y, 4,500 2-y-o: leggy gelding: second foal: dam, ran twice, sister to useful sprinter Petula: little form, including in seller. *E. J. Alston*

SHADOW DANCING   3 b.f. Unfuwain (USA) 131 – Salchow 116 (Niniski (USA)   **110**
125) [2002 96p: 11.4f⁸ 12s³ 12m² 11.9d³ 13.5s² 12.5g⁴ Oct 5] tall, rather angular filly: has scope: smart performer: won listed event at Chester in May by 1¼ lengths from Bright And Clear: creditable efforts after in Oaks at Epsom (14½ lengths third to Kazzia), Ribblesdale Stakes at Royal Ascot (¾-length second to Irresistible Jewel), Lancashire Oaks at Haydock (2¾ lengths third behind Mellow Park), Prix de Pomone at Deauville (¾-length second to Bernimixa) and Prix de Royallieu at Longchamp (made running for a change when 4¾ lengths fourth behind Dance Routine): will stay at least 1¾m: yet to race on heavy going, acts on any other: tends to get on edge: game: stays in training. *M. P. Tregoning*

SHADOWFAX   2 b.g. (Feb 22) Anabaa (USA) 130 – Prends Ca (IRE) 98 (Reprimand   **74**
122) [2002 6m 7g 7f⁶ p6g 7s⁴ f7g² f7s⁶ Dec 13] 68,000F, 85,000Y: useful-looking   **a77**
gelding: second foal: dam 6f (including at 2 yrs) to 7.5f winner: fair maiden: left B. Meehan 20,000 gns before good second at Wolverhampton: tongue tied, reportedly lame final outing: stays 7f: acts on fibresand, firm and soft ground. *Miss Gay Kelleway*

SHADOW ROLL (IRE)   3 ch.f. Mark of Esteem (IRE) 137 – Warning Shadows (IRE)   **59 ?**
113 (Cadeaux Genereux 131) [2002 79: 7d 7.5g³ 9d Jul 3] close-coupled, useful-looking filly: fair maiden at 2 yrs: below form in 2002, reportedly breaking blood vessel second start: stayed 7f: acted on firm and good to soft going: had worn crossed noseband: visits Noverre. *C. E. Brittain*

SHADY DEAL   6 b.g. No Big Deal – Taskalady 47 (Touching Wood (USA) 127)   **62**
[2002 54, a–: 5s³ 5.7d* 6m⁶ 5f³ 5m³ 5m⁵ 5m² 5.7f f5f f6g p7g f5g Dec 27] angular   **a–**
gelding: modest performer: won seller at Bath in June: claimed from S. Earle £3,000 seventh start: well held last 5 outings, including in blinkers: best at 5f/6f nowadays: acts on firm and soft ground: usually races prominently. *J. M. Bradley*

SHADY LITES (FR)   2 ch.f. (Jan 31) Definite Article 121 – Shade (Contract Law   **68**
(USA) 108) [2002 6m 7m⁷ 7m 8.3m⁶ Oct 7] IR 19,000Y: first foal: dam unraced half-sister to Sun Chariot Stakes winner Warning Shadows: fair maiden: likely to prove best up to 1m. *C. G. Cox*

SHAFEEQ (FR)   3 ch.c. Halling (USA) 133 – Ta Awun (USA) 99 (Housebuster (USA))   **91**
[2002 83: 10g* 11g³ 12s² 10m² 10m* 10f³ Aug 17] useful-looking colt: fairly useful performer: won maiden at Brighton in May and handicap at Kempton in July: should stay 1½m: acts on firm going, probably not on soft: hung left last 2 starts: joined J. Sadler in UAE. *A. C. Stewart*

SHAFFISHAYES   10 ch.g. Clantime 101 – Mischievous Miss 73 (Niniski (USA)   **54**
125) [2002 54: 10.1m⁶ 11.9s² 11.9s² 13v 12.1d 12.4g* 10.1m f14s⁶ 12g Oct 19] lengthy gelding: modest performer: won apprentice seller at Newcastle in August: stays 1¾m: acts on fibresand, soft and good to firm going: takes good hold, and usually held up: has reportedly been hobdayed and broken blood vessel. *Mrs M. Reveley*

SHAFIGA (USA)   2 b.f. (Apr 9) Woodman (USA) 126 – Silk Braid (USA) 105 (Danzig   **56**
(USA)) [2002 6m 7m Sep 5] quite good-topped filly: seventh foal: closely related to smart 7f winner Beraysim (by Lion Cavern) and fairly useful UAE 1m winner Modelliste (by Machiavellian), and half-sister to 2 winners: dam, 9f and 1½m winner, half-sister to Belmont/Preakness Stakes winner Risen Star: modest form in maidens: should stay at least 1m. *M. R. Channon*

SHAGRAAN   3 b.c. Darshaan 133 – L'Ideale (USA) (Alysheba (USA)) [2002 69p: **111**
10g* 10m⁴ 11m* 12m⁴ Jun 20] good-topped colt: has a quick action: progressed well, and
won handicaps at Ripon in April and Newbury (beat Epicentre by head, tending to idle)
in May: very good effort when length fourth to Systematic in King George V Handicap at
Royal Ascot final start, finishing well: will be suited by 1¾m: acts on good to firm going:
sent to USA. *J. L. Dunlop*

SHAHM (IRE)   3 b.g. Marju (IRE) 127 – Istibshar (USA) 78 (Mr Prospector (USA))   **–**
[2002 74: f8g⁴ f6g f6g 8.2d 6m 6.1m 6g 6d Oct 15] good-topped gelding: fair maiden at 2
yrs: well held in 2002: tried visored/blinkered: possibly ungenuine. *B. J. Curley*

SHAHZAN HOUSE (IRE)   3 b.c. Sri Pekan (USA) 117 – Nsx 74 (Roi Danzig   **97**
(USA)) [2002 75?: 8m⁴ 8.2g³ 10d* 10m² Jul 4] sturdy colt: fluent mover: progressed into
a useful performer: won maiden at Sandown in June by 3½ lengths from Navado: good
short-head second of 5 to Serotonin in minor event at Newbury final start (may well have
won but for being struck across face with winning rider's whip): subsequently sustained
hairline fracture of off-fore cannon bone: stays 1¼m: acts on good to firm and good to
soft going. *M. A. Jarvis*

SHAIYZIMA (IRE)   3 b.f. Polish Precedent (USA) 131 – Shaiybara (IRE) 111   **93**
(Kahyasi 130) [2002 10.5m² 7m² 8.3d* 8.3m* 8.1m Sep 15] lengthy, unfurnished filly:
fifth foal: dam, Irish stayer, also won Prix du Lutece: fairly useful performer: won maiden
and handicap at Windsor in August: free-going sort (pulled too hard final start), likely to
prove best at 7f/1m: yet to race on extremes of going. *Sir Michael Stoute*

SHAKRAN   3 ch.c. Zafonic (USA) 130 – Myself 110 (Nashwan (USA) 135) [2002   **96**
90p: 8m⁴ May 5] strong, lengthy colt: good walker/mover: useful form when in frame in
maidens at Ascot (only run at 2 yrs) and Newmarket (not at all knocked about when fourth
to Mineshaft): not sure to stay much beyond 1m: sent to USA. *Sir Michael Stoute*

SHAKWAA   3 ch.f. Lion Cavern (USA) 117 – Shadha (USA) 77 (Devil's Bag (USA))   **60**
[2002 12f⁴ 12f⁶ May 4] tall, lengthy, angular filly: fifth foal: dam, 2-y-o 6f winner in
Britain and 1m/9f winner in USA at 4 yrs, out of very smart French 1m to 1½m performer
Treizieme: modest form in maidens at Thirsk: sold 11,000 gns in July. *M. R. Channon*

SHALAMANTIKA (IRE)   3 b.f. Nashwan (USA) 135 – Sharamana (IRE) 110 (Dar-   **102**
shaan 133) [2002 67p: 10m² 11.9d² 12m⁴ 10.1g* 10m⁴ 10.1m⁴ 12g³ Sep 27] smallish,
angular filly: useful performer: won maiden at Epsom in August in good style: improved
efforts after, in frame in listed events at Yarmouth (length fourth to Miss Corniche) and
Ascot (3¼ lengths third behind Love Everlasting) last 2 starts: effective at 1¼m/1½m: yet
to race on extremes of going. *Sir Michael Stoute*

SHALBEBLUE (IRE)   5 b.g. Shalford (IRE) 124§ – Alberjas (IRE) (Sure Blade   **–**
(USA) 130) [2002 55, a63: f12s⁵ 12s f12g Dec 14] smallish gelding: modest performer: **a58**
stays 1½m: acts on good to firm going, soft and fibresand: usually visored/blinkered
nowadays. *B. Ellison*

SHAMAN   5 b.g. Fraam 114 – Magic Maggie 38 (Beveled (USA)) [2002 72: p10g p10g   **62**
f12g⁴ 11g f9.4s⁶ 8d 10.1d⁴ 10m⁶ p10g² p10g⁶ 11.9g⁴ Oct 24] fluent mover: modest
handicapper: left B. Pearce after fifth start: stays 1½m: acts on any turf going and all-
weather: none too consistent. *G. L. Moore*

SHAMARCO (IRE)   3 b.f. Common Grounds 118 – Fanciful (IRE) (Mujtahid (USA)   **60**
118) [2002 54: 6g⁴ p6g 7f⁵ 6.1m⁶ 6.1d 7g⁴ 6m⁴ 5g² 6m 5.1g Oct 16] close-coupled filly:
modest maiden handicapper: effective at 5f to 7f: acts on firm and good to soft going, well
held on polytrack: races prominently: tongue tied second 2-y-o start: tried visored (raced
freely): sold 2,400 gns. *P. W. Harris*

SHAMI   3 ch.c. Rainbow Quest (USA) 134 – Bosra Sham (USA) 132 (Woodman (USA)   **87**
126) [2002 10m² 12m* 11.8s Oct 28] 1,000,000Y: compact, attractive colt: first foal:
dam, won Fillies' Mile, 1000 Guineas and Champion Stakes, from excellent family:
fairly useful form: won maiden at Doncaster (easily by 4 lengths) in July: off 3 months,
only seventh under more testing conditions in minor event at Leicester final start: will
prove best at 1½m+: acts on good to firm ground: joined D. Loder. *Saeed bin Suroor*

SHAMOKIN   10 b.g. Green Desert (USA) 127 – Shajan (Kris 135) [2002 –: f12g Mar   **–**
21] workmanlike gelding: lightly-raced maiden: tried visored. *F. Watson*

SHAMPOOED (IRE)   8 b.m. Law Society (USA) 130 – White Caps 71 (Shirley   **–**
Heights 130) [2002 54: 18d Oct 21] lightly raced on Flat nowadays: blinkered once: fair
hurdler/chaser. *R. Dickin*

SHAMROCK CITY (IRE) 5 b.g. Rock City 120 – Actualite (Polish Precedent –
(USA) 131) [2002 –: 10m May 4] rather leggy, workmanlike gelding: formerly smart
around 1¼m: tailed off both starts since 3 yrs. *P. Howling*

SHAMWARI FIRE (IRE) 2 ch.g. (Feb 2) Idris (IRE) 118 – Bobby's Dream 53 **62**
(Reference Point 139) [2002 6g 7.1m 7d³ 8d p8g⁶ Nov 19] first foal: dam staying maiden:
modest maiden: should stay 1m: acts on good to soft going, probably on polytrack:
wandered second/third outings: gelded after final one. *M. H. Tompkins*

SHAMWARI SONG 7 b.g. Sizzling Melody 117 – Spark Out (Sparkler 130) [2002 **52**
–, a44: f7s⁵ f7g⁴ f8.5g f7g⁶ f12g 7d⁴ 8.5m* 8m³ 7g 7.9s 8g⁶ 8m 7.5d Jul 5] tall gelding: **a48**
modest performer: won seller at Beverley in April: best at 7f/1m: acts on good to firm
going, good to soft and fibresand: tried tongue tied: sometimes blinkered/visored.
K. A. Ryan

SHANE 4 ch.g. Aragon 118 – Angel Fire (Nashwan (USA) 135) [2002 52: 9.2s 9m⁴ –
12m 10d Jul 9] leggy gelding: modest maiden at 3 yrs: well held in 2002: tried visored.
F. P. Murtagh

SHANGHAI ANNIE 4 gr.f. Factual (USA) 108 – Laura 65 (Never So Bold 135) –
[2002 9.9g 7.5g 7.5g⁶ 8d 12f Jul 17] good-topped filly: second foal: dam, maiden, form
only at 7f on debut: no form: tried visored. *B. S. Rothwell*

SHANK 3 b.c. Lahib (USA) 129 – Mixwayda (FR) (Linamix (FR) 127) [2002 p6g p7g **55**
f6g⁴ f8g Nov 20] 10,000Y: first foal: dam useful French 1¼m winner: modest maiden: off
8 months after third outing: should be suited by 1m+: raced only on all-weather. *Sir Mark
Prescott*

SHANLEY (UAE) 3 b.f. Singspiel (IRE) 133 – Shbakni (USA) (Mr Prospector –
(USA)) [2002 p8g² 10s 12d Nov 5] second foal: dam, placed in France/UAE up to 9f, out
of Kentucky Derby winner Winning Colors: little form in maidens, trip seeming beyond
her last 2 starts: visits Jade Robbery. *M. Johnston*

SHANNON BAY 2 b.f. (Feb 27) Alhijaz 122 – Stratford Lady 48 (Touching Wood –
(USA) 127) [2002 5g Oct 19] fifth foal: half-sister to 5-y-o Jonloz and 4-y-o Bolham
Lady: dam, untrustworthy maiden, stayed 1½m: 100/1, last in minor event at Catterick.
J. Balding

SHANNON FLYER (USA) 4 br.g. Irish River (FR) 131 – Stormeor (CAN) (Lypheor **55 §**
118) [2002 68: p10g 8.3g 8m 8d³ 9s 8m⁴ 8.1d Jul 12] rather leggy, quite good-topped
gelding: modest performer: stays 1m: acts on firm ground (possibly not on softer than
good) and polytrack: blinkered last 2 starts: withdrawn once after refusing to enter stall:
has looked none too hearty: no easy ride. *J. W. Hills*

SHANOOK 3 ch.g. Rainbow Quest (USA) 134 – Twafeaj (USA) 110 (Topsider **86**
(USA)) [2002 85p: 10.3s² 8g* 10m May 1] tall, angular gelding: has scope: fairly useful
form in maidens, winning at Ripon in April: pulled too hard in handicap at Pontefract
final outing (gelded after): may prove best allowed to stride on at 1m: tended to carry
head to one side on reappearance. *M. Johnston*

SHANTALLA PEAK (IRE) 3 b.f. Darshaan 133 – Shigeru Summit 105 (Be My **68**
Chief (USA) 122) [2002 9v 9d 9f³ 8d p8g Dec 14] first foal: dam French 2-y-o 5.5f/7f
winner: fair maiden: left D. Weld after second start: stays 9f: acts on firm ground,
probably on polytrack. *W. P. Mullins, Ireland*

SHANTY STAR (IRE) 2 gr.c. (Feb 26) Hector Protector (USA) 124 – Shawanni 105 **86 p**
(Shareef Dancer (USA) 135) [2002 7.2s 10f* Oct 7] big, good-bodied colt: third foal:
half-brother to fairly useful 2001 2-y-o 5f winner Twilight Sonnet (by Exit To Nowhere)
and 4-y-o Mystic Man: dam, 7f winner at 2 yrs, out of Rockfel Stakes winner and 1000
Guineas third Negligent: much better effort in maidens when winning at Pontefract by 1¼
lengths from Fellow Ship, edging ahead over 2f out and responding gamely: will stay at
least 1½m: should make a useful 3-y-o. *M. Johnston*

SHARARAH 3 br.f. Machiavellian (USA) 123 – Raknah (IRE) 91 (Night Shift (USA)) **87**
[2002 63P: 6m* 7f³ 7m⁵ 6f 6m Sep 19] leggy filly: fairly useful performer: won maiden
at Pontefract in May impressively by 5 lengths: good fifth in handicap at Redcar: will
probably prove best at 5f/6f: raced only on going firmer than good since debut: tongue
tied: sold 13,000 gns in December. *E. A. L. Dunlop*

SHARES (IRE) 2 b.g. (Apr 30) Turtle Island (IRE) 123 – Glendora (Glenstal (USA) **67**
118) [2002 6f⁴ 6d⁵ 6v Nov 9] IR 4,000F, IR 10,000Y: good-bodied gelding: half-brother
to several winners, including 3-y-o Pearson Glen and Irish 7f winner Caduga (by Dancing

Dissident): dam ran 3 times in Ireland: best effort in maidens (fair form) when fourth at York: raced freely final start (gelded after). *A. Berry*

SHARMA 2 b.f. (Mar 16) Bijou d'Inde 127 – Star of Jupiter (Jupiter Island 126) [2002 **53** 6.1m⁶ 6.5g Sep 27] 800Y: close-coupled, quite good-topped filly: fifth foal: dam unraced half-sister to useful sprinter Boozy: modest form when sixth of 12 to Caught In The Dark in maiden at Warwick, best work late on: always in rear in sales race at Ascot. *J. L. Spearing*

SHARMY (IRE) 6 b.g. Caerleon (USA) 132 – Petticoat Lane (Ela-Mana-Mou 132) **99** [2002 –: p10g⁴ 10g 8m 12f⁵ 12g³ 10s Oct 26] close-coupled, quite attractive gelding: has **a104** a short, unimpressive action: useful performer: good 1¼ lengths fourth to Adiemus in listed Winter Derby at Lingfield in March, and also ran well when third behind Defining in handicap at Newmarket (took strong hold) penultimate start: at least as effective at 1¼m as 1½m: acts on polytrack, and probably on any turf going: sometimes slowly away. *Ian Williams*

SHAROURA 6 ch.m. Inchinor 119 – Kinkajoo 53 (Precocious 126) [2002 66: p6g f5s **61** 6g 6g⁶ 6g p5g 6m⁶ 6m² 5.1m 6m 6m 6m² 6m Oct 7] angular mare: poor mover: modest handicapper: best at 5f/6f: acts on firm going, soft and all-weather: seems effective visored or not (untried in 2002): had tongue tied earlier in career: sometimes races freely/hangs right: none too consistent. *J. M. Bradley*

SHARP AS CROESUS 2 b.f. (May 2) Sesaro (USA) 81 – Chushan Venture (Pursuit **55** of Love 124) [2002 6m p7g p6g⁶ Dec 18] second foal: dam unraced out of half-sister to 2000 Guineas winner Tirol: modest form in maidens/minor event: should stay 1m. *J. R. Best*

SHARP BELLINE (IRE) 5 b.g. Robellino (USA) 127 – Moon Watch 64 (Night **43 §** Shift (USA)) [2002 52§: f12g 21.6m⁶ Apr 22] poor maiden handicapper: stays 2m: acts on good to firm going and fibresand: well beaten when tried visored/blinkered at 3 yrs: has raced freely/taken little interest: fair hurdler. *John A. Harris*

SHARPBILL 2 b.f. (Jan 20) Eagle Eyed (USA) 111 – Division Bell (Warning 136) **86** [2002 6.1d² 5.7f* 6f* Sep 26] first foal: dam, useful 1m winner in France, out of smart performer up to 10.5f Ala Mahlik: fairly useful form: won maiden at Bath (odds on) and 4-runner minor event at Goodwood (gamely beat Go Polar neck, pair clear) in September: will stay 7f: acts on firm going, shaped well on good to soft: sold 21,000 gns, sent to USA. *Mrs A. J. Perrett*

SHARP BREEZE (USA) 2 b. or br.c. (Feb 13) Mr Prospector (USA) – Windy Mindy **76 p** (USA) (Honey Jay (USA)) [2002 7.1g⁵ Sep 12] $1,900,000Y: seventh foal: half-brother to 3 winners, notably very smart US 1m/1¼m performer Rob 'N Gin (by Farma Way): dam 6f and 8.5f minor stakes winner in USA, including at 2 yrs: 11/4, made most when 4½ lengths fifth of 11 to Assraar in maiden at Chepstow: should improve. *D. R. Loder*

SHARP CITY 3 b.g. Rock City 120 – Mary Miller 71 (Sharpo 132) [2002 56: 5m 7m **–** 7.1d 8.3v 5m Sep 2] leggy, workmanlike gelding: modest at best at 2 yrs: no form in 2002. *A. C. Whillans*

SHARPCUT (IRE) 3 b.c. Alhaarth (IRE) 126 – Safiya (USA) (Riverman (USA) 131) **99 p** [2002 10s 12f* 11.9d* 14.8m⁶ 11.8g* Oct 14] IR 46,000F, IR 325,000Y: strong, good-topped colt: seventh foal: half-brother to 3 winners, including 5f (at 2 yrs)/6f winner Cayman Kai and 6f (including at 2 yrs) winner Tajasur, latter also winner in Hong Kong (both smart and by Imperial Frontier): dam unraced sister to smart miler Sulaafah: useful form: won maiden at Pontefract in June and handicaps at Haydock in August and Leicester (beat Indian Solitaire by head) in October: stays 1½m: acts on firm and good to soft ground: remains capable of better. *H. R. A. Cecil*

SHARP DECISION 3 ch.f. Greensmith 121 – Nihaayib (Kris 135) [2002 67: 5.1m **–** 5m 5d 6.1m 5g 6m 5m f7g Oct 19] smallish, lengthy, rather dipped-backed filly: disappointing maiden: visored penultimate start. *Miss D. A. McHale*

SHARP GOSSIP (IRE) 6 b.g. College Chapel 122 – Idle Gossip (Runnett 125) **66** [2002 70, a73: f8g 7d 8.3d³ f8s 8f⁵ f9.4g Dec 9] sparely-made gelding: fair handicapper: **a–** left J. Toller 6,500 gns after fifth outing: stays 1m: acts on fibresand and probably any turf going: effective blinkered or not. *J. R. Weymes*

SHARP HAT 8 ch.g. Shavian 125 – Madam Trilby (Grundy 137) [2002 89, a82: f5s⁶ **87** f6g f5s f5g p5g f6g² 6g⁴ p6g 5f 5f 6m³ 6f³ 6g³ 5s² 5s² 5g* 5d 5g³ 5m 5g* 5m 5g⁶ f5f* f5g **a81** f5g⁵ f6g 6g Dec 31] leggy, angular gelding: fairly useful performer: won handicap at Catterick and minor event at Beverley (for second year running), both in July, and handicap at Wolverhampton in November: best at 5f/easy 6f: acts on any turf going/

all-weather: well held in blinkers earlier in career: has gone freely, including to post: often races handily: tough. *D. W. Chapman*

SHARPINCH 4 b.c. Beveled (USA) – Giant Nipper (Nashwan (USA) 135) [2002 68, a88: 7d 7.1v 6g Jul 8] fairly useful at best on all-weather, fair on turf: well held in 2002. *P. R. Chamings*

SHARPLAW VENTURE 2 b.f. (Mar 31) Polar Falcon (USA) 126 – Breakaway 98 **94** (Song 132) [2002 5m⁵ 6.1m² 6.5g* 6m⁶ Oct 5] 46,000Y: lengthy, angular filly: closely related to fairly useful 1997 2-y-o 5f winner Stop Out (by Rudimentary) and half-sister to several winners, notably 3-y-o Firebreak: dam 5f winner: fairly useful form: won maiden at Pontefract in August and 25-runner sales race at Ascot (beat Hector's Girl by head, drifting left) in September: creditable sixth of 18 to Somnus in Two-Year-Old Trophy at Redcar final start: not sure to stay 7f: raced only on good/good to firm ground. *W. J. Haggas*

SHARP RIGGING (IRE) 2 b.g. (Mar 14) Son of Sharp Shot (IRE) 105 – In The **59** Rigging (USA) 78 (Topsider (USA)) [2002 7.5g⁵ 7m⁶ Oct 2] IR 3,500Y: leggy gelding: half-brother to 3 winners, including useful 1997 2-y-o 6f and 1m winner Wren (by Bob Back) and fairly useful 7f (at 2 yrs) and 1¼m winner Chem's Truce (by Brief Truce): dam 1m winner: modest form in maidens: should stay 1¼m. *E. A. L. Dunlop*

SHARP SECRET (IRE) 4 b.f. College Chapel 122 – State Treasure (USA) (Secre- **64** tariat (USA)) [2002 f6g⁶ 8.3g 8m 7.9s 8g⁶ 7g⁵ 8m 8m 7.5d² 8m* 7.5d³ 8m* 7f* 6.9s² 8g 7.9m⁶ 9m 8f² f9.4g Nov 16] leggy filly: modest handicapper: won at Musselburgh (seller), Thirsk (apprentices) and Yarmouth in July: stays easy 1m: acts on firm and soft going: carried head high/edged left penultimate start: sold 4,800 gns. *M. Johnston*

SHARP SHIFT 3 ch.g. Night Shift (USA) – Sharp Chief 71 (Chief Singer 131) [2002 **–** 11.7g Oct 16] sixth foal: half-brother to 2 winners, including 5-y-o Effervescent: dam, 6f winner, half-sister to smart performer up to 1½m Dashing Blade: 33/1, always behind in Bath maiden. *S. Kirk*

SHARP SOPRANO 3 b.f. Mon Tresor 113 – Gentle Star 77 (Comedy Star (USA) **–** 121) [2002 57: p6g 7.1v 8.1d 7g 10.2g 8m Sep 5] modest maiden at 2 yrs: little form in 2002. *B. R. Millman*

SHARP SPICE 6 b.m. Lugana Beach 116 – Ewar Empress (IRE) 57 (Persian Bold **67 d** 123) [2002 67, a60: p12g* p12g p12g⁵ 13.3s 12g³ 12d 11.9m³ 11.9g⁵ 11.9m 12f 12d **a59 d** p12g⁴ p13g³ Dec 28] angular mare: fair handicapper on turf, modest on all-weather: won at Lingfield in January: below form last 5 starts: best around 1½m: acts on any turf going and polytrack: tried visored: sometimes slowly away: held up: on downgrade. *D. J. Coakley*

SHARPSPORT (FR) 3 b.g. Charnwood Forest (IRE) 125 – Wild Sable (IRE) 88 **52** (Kris 135) [2002 f7g* f8.5g 10m 7m 7.9g³ 8m 8.1s 7.9g⁴ 8s 12.1g 9.1s f8.5g² f8.5g⁵ f9.4s f12g Dec 14] quite good-topped gelding: fifth foal: half-brother to fairly useful 5f (at 2 yrs) to 9f winner Plan For Profit (by Polish Patriot): dam, 1¼m winner, out of half-sister to Derby winner Teenoso: modest performer: won maiden at Wolverhampton in February: left Mrs J. Ramsden after tenth start: stays 8.5f: acts on fibresand, best turf efforts on good going: tried in blinkers/cheekpieces: inconsistent. *I. Semple*

SHARP STEEL 7 ch.g. Beveled (USA) – Shift Over (USA) 62 (Night Shift (USA)) **–** [2002 43, a65d: f11s² f8.5g⁴ f9.4g f8s f14.8g f14.8g f12g⁵ Dec 26] leggy, workmanlike **a55** gelding: modest on all-weather: stays 11f: acts on fibresand: tried visored earlier in career: has worn cheekpieces. *Miss S. J. Wilton*

SHARP WISDOM (IRE) 2 b.c. (Apr 29) Titus Livius (FR) 115 – Hever Golf Lover **85** (IRE) 61 (Taufan (USA) 119) [2002 5d 5.1d* 5m² Jul 1] IR 8,700F, 14,000Y: second foal: dam 5f winner (including at 2 yrs): fairly useful form: won maiden at Bath in June: creditable second in minor event at Windsor: likely to prove best at 5f/6f: sold only 2,500 gns. *G. C. Bravery*

SHARVIE 5 b.g. Rock Hopper 124 – Heresheis 69 (Free State 125) [2002 48, a58: **48** f16s⁶ f16.2g⁴ f16.2g⁵ f16.2g⁵ f14g Mar 12] poor handicapper: stays 2m: acts on fibre- sand, yet to race on extremes of going on turf: takes good hold and tends to find little. *Mrs Lydia Pearce*

SHASTA 3 b.f. Shareef Dancer (USA) 135 – Themeda 69 (Sure Blade (USA) 130) **81** [2002 –p: p10g⁶ 12s³ 12m* 12m⁴ 12m³ 12m 14m⁶ 11.2g Oct 16] angular filly: fairly useful performer: won maiden at Doncaster in June: stays 1¾m: acts on soft and good to firm going: races prominently: none too consistent. *R. M. Beckett*

SHATARAH   3 ch.f. Gulch (USA) – Arjuzah (IRE) 110 (Ahonoora 122) [2002 79p: **79**
7m 7f² 7d³ 7g³ Jun 1] strong, well-made filly: had a quick, fluent action: fair maiden:
raced only at 7f: acted on firm and good to soft going: visits King's Best. *J. H. M. Gosden*

SHATIN DOLLYBIRD (IRE)   4 ch.f. Up And At 'em 109 – Pumpona (USA) **38**
(Sharpen Up 127) [2002 –: 6f 5m 5g 7.1g⁶ 5.9d 5g 5m 5m Aug 22] good-topped filly:
poor performer nowadays: should stay 6f: acts on firm ground, well below form on good
to soft: tends to hang right. *Miss L. A. Perratt*

SHATIN HERO   2 ch.c. (Apr 10) Lion Cavern (USA) 117 – Moogie 103 (Young **50**
Generation 129) [2002 6g 6g⁴ Jul 15] 10,500Y: half-brother to several winners, including
2-y-o 7f winners Catwalk (in 1996, by Shirley Heights) and Mr Pitz (in 2001, by Hector
Protector): dam, 2-y-o 6f winner, later best at 9f: modest form in maidens at Ayr: refused
to enter stall in between. *Miss L. A. Perratt*

SHATIN PRINCESS (IRE)   3 b.f. Darnay 117 – Lady Conchita (IRE) (Whistling
Deer 117) [2002 64: 5d 6g 5.9s 11.1v⁵ 8m 7.2g Jul 15] leggy filly: disappointing maiden.
Miss L. A. Perratt

SHATIN SPECIAL   2 ch.f. (Feb 19) Titus Livius (FR) 115 – Lawn Order 51 (Efisio **50**
120) [2002 5g 5v⁵ 5.9s⁵ 3.9m 6d 5s³ Nov 6] 1,200F, 5,500Y: second foal: dam 1½m
winner: modest maiden: should stay 7f: yet to race on firm going, probably acts on any
other turf. *Miss L. A. Perratt*

SHAVA   2 b.g. (Apr 14) Atraf 116 – Anita Marie (IRE) (Anita's Prince 126) [2002 5f⁶ **52**
f6g f6g Oct 22] 18,000F, 18,000Y: second foal: dam twice-raced sister to useful sprinter
Trinculo: modest form when sixth in maiden at Windsor: well held on all-weather both
starts after (subsequently gelded). *W. J. Haggas*

SHAVEN ROCK   5 b.g. Rock City 120 – So Bold (Never So Bold 135) [2002 38: –
f9.4g Dec 16] maiden, very lightly raced. *K. R. Burke*

SHAYA   8 ch.h. Nashwan (USA) 135 – Gharam (USA) 108 (Green Dancer (USA) 132) –
[2002 11.6s⁶ 16.2s 22.2m 16.4d 14.8g Jul 20] big horse: smart at 1½m to 2½m in 1999:
no form on return. *G. C. Bravery*

SHAYADI (IRE)   5 b.g. Kahyasi 130 – Shayrdia (IRE) 57 (Storm Bird (CAN) 134) **97**
[2002 101: 16d³ 12v f12g Dec 20] leggy, quite attractive gelding: useful performer: form
in handicaps in 2002 only when 12 lengths third to Tees Components at Newmarket in
November: stays 2m: acts on firm and soft going: carried head high/flashed tail for win at
4 yrs. *M. Johnston*

SHAYDEYLAYDEH (IRE)   3 b.f. Shaddad (USA) 75 – Spirito Libro (USA) 89 **53**
(Lear Fan (USA) 130) [2002 8.2d 8f 7f 7m 12m 9.9g 10g⁵ 11.5s³ f12f⁶ f14.8g⁶ Dec 14] **a–**
2,200Y: unfurnished filly: first foal: dam, 5f (at 2 yrs) to 1¼m winner, half-sister to smart
Irish 6f winner Conormara: modest maiden: stays 11.5f: acts on soft going, well held on
fibresand: has worn cheekpieces: inconsistent. *C. N. Allen*

SHEARWATER   5 b.m. Shareef Dancer (USA) 135 – Sea Ballad (USA) (Bering 136) –
[2002 –: f6g 8.2d 9.9m Apr 17] well held in maidens/handicap. *A. Senior*

SHEBA'S COAST (IRE)   3 b.f. Desert King (IRE) 129 – Alongside 58 (Slip Anchor **67**
136) [2002 f8s⁴ 11.9d² 12.1v⁵ 11m⁶ p12g 10f 12f Jul 28] quite attractive filly: fourth
foal: half-sister to fairly useful 1½m winner Common Cause (by Polish Patriot) and 4-y-o
Northside Lodge: dam, Irish 9f winner who probably stayed 2m, half-sister to smart
French/US performer up to 1¼m Kirkwall: best effort (fair form) on second outing: stays
1½m: acts on good to soft going: sold 800 gns, sent to Kuwait. *G. C. Bravery*

SHEBEEN   2 ch.f. (Mar 17) Aragon 118 – Sheesha (USA) (Shadeed (USA) 135) [2002 **70 p**
5g 5m² 6d² Oct 21] 2,100Y: fourth foal: dam once-raced close relation to smart stayer
Samraan: fair form in maidens: second at Folkestone and Pontefract (still green, kept on
well when beaten 1¾ lengths by Miss Assertive): should stay at least 1m: remains capable
of better. *H. Candy*

SHEER FOCUS (IRE)   4 b.g. Eagle Eyed (USA) 111 – Persian Danser (IRE) 69 **70**
(Persian Bold 123) [2002 65: f9.4g* f9.4g³ f9.4g⁴ f9.4g 8m⁶ 9.3g² 10.3g⁵ 9.9m⁴ 8.5g 8f
9d 10.1d⁶ 8m⁶ Sep 29] leggy, angular gelding: fair handicapper: won at Wolverhampton
in January: stays 1¼m: acts on fibresand, soft and good to firm going: tried tongue tied:
tends to race freely: none too consistent. *E. J. Alston*

SHEER GUTS (IRE)   3 b.c. Hamas (IRE) 125§ – Balakera (FR) (Lashkari 128) [2002 **69**
p8g p8g³ p10g² f9.4g* f9.4g⁴ 10g 12m May 1] IR 15,000Y: third foal: dam unraced close
relative to Prix Saint-Alary winner and Arc second Behera: fair performer: won maiden

at Wolverhampton in February: not certain to stay beyond 1¼m: acts on all-weather, below form in 2 runs on turf: blinkered penultimate start: sold 6,000 gns. *B. W. Hills*

SHEIK'N SWING   3 b.f. Celtic Swing 138 – Elegantissima 57 (Polish Precedent   **73**
(USA) 131) [2002 –: 7f* f8.5s 7d² 7d* 8m 7g² 7m² 7.1g⁴ Sep 23] fair performer: won
seller at Brighton in April and handicap at Salisbury in June: best form at 7f: acts on firm
and good to soft ground, well held on fibresand debut. *W. G. M. Turner*

SHEILA BLIGE   3 ch.f. Zamindar (USA) 116 – Stripanoora (Ahonoora 122) [2002   **80 d**
83: 5m 6m⁶ 5m 7g 7g 8.1d Jul 6] leggy, close-coupled filly: fairly useful performer: below
form last 5 starts: probably best at 5f/easy 6f: acts on good to firm going: very awkward
leaving stall/pulled hard final outing: sold 10,000 gns. *G. G. Margarson*

SHELINI   2 b.f. (Apr 13) Robellino (USA) 127 – Agama (USA) 44 (Nureyev (USA)   **91**
131) [2002 6g⁶ 7g² 8d³ 8.3s* 8.3d³ 8v* Nov 8] fourth foal: sister to useful 1997 2-y-o 7f/
1m winner Setteen and half-sister to 6f (at 2 yrs) to 9f winner Can Can Lady (by Anshan):
dam, poor form in 2 starts at 2 yrs in Britain, 13.5f winner in France: fairly useful
performer: won maidens at Hamilton (awarded race after Inchberry failed dope test) and
Doncaster (23-runner event by 1½ lengths from Sail With The Tide): will be suited by
1¼m/1½m: raced on good going or softer. *M. A. Jarvis*

SHELL GARLAND (USA)   2 b.f. (Apr 12) Sadler's Wells (USA) 132 – Shell   **80**
Ginger (IRE) 110 (Woodman (USA) 126) [2002 7m⁶ 7.5g³ Sep 18] $525,000Y: lengthy,
unfurnished filly: has scope: second foal: dam Irish 2-y-o 7f winner from very good
middle-distance family: fairly useful form in maidens at Newmarket and Beverley (third
to Tuneful, edging left): likely to stay at least 1½m. *Sir Michael Stoute*

SHENLEY CHARM   2 b.c. (Feb 5) First Trump 118 – Glimpse 77 (Night Shift   **83**
(USA)) [2002 7.1g f8s* 8s* Oct 25] 8,000Y: fourth foal: brother to fairly useful 1998
2-y-o 6f winner Focus, later successful in USA, and half-brother to a 7.5f/1m winner in
Italy by Elmaamul: dam 2-y-o 6f winner from 3 starts: fairly useful form: won maiden at
Southwell (20/1) and nursery at Doncaster (by length from Libre) in October, dictating
pace each time: will probably stay 1¼m. *H. Morrison*

SHERAZADE   3 ch.f. Beveled (USA) – Miss Ritz 65 (Robellino (USA) 127) [2002   **55**
61: p5g² p5g 6m⁵ 5m 6g f7g f5g Dec 27] modest maiden: left G. L. Moore before pulled   **a49**
up penultimate start: unseated rider leaving stalls final one: should prove best at 5f/6f:
acts on heavy and good to firm going. *C. N. Kellett*

SHERIFF'S DEPUTY   2 b.g. (Feb 20) Atraf 116 – Forest Fantasy 61 (Rambo Dancer   **70**
(CAN) 107) [2002 6d 6m⁵ 6m⁵ 7s⁶ 7g² 7s Oct 25] 14,500F, 20,000Y: strong, well-grown
gelding: second foal: dam, 1m/9f winner, closely related to US Grade 3 6.5f winner
Imperial Star: fair maiden: clearly best effort when beaten head by Override in nursery at
Lingfield: will probably stay 1m: gelded after final start. *J. W. Unett*

SHERIFF SHIFT   2 b.c. (Apr 4) Night Shift (USA) – Woodwin (IRE) 97 (Woodman   **87**
(USA) 126) [2002 5d 6f⁴ 6m² 6d* 6m² 6f³ Oct 5] 70,000Y: small, attractive colt: first
foal: dam, Irish 1m winner, out of half-sister to dam of Irish Oaks winner Wemyss
Bight: fairly useful performer: won maiden at Thirsk in August: good placed efforts in
nurseries at York (behind Irresistible) and Newmarket (behind Steelaninch) after: will
probably stay 7f: acts on firm and good to soft going: races prominently: sold 48,000 gns.
M. R. Channon

SHERKHAN   2 b.c. (Apr 16) Septieme Ciel (USA) 123 – Joemlujen (Forzando 122)   **–**
[2002 p8g p8g f7s Dec 13] third foal: dam unraced: well beaten in maidens. *A. W. Carroll*

SHERSHA (IRE)   3 b.f. Priolo (USA) 127 – Sheriya (USA) (Green Dancer (USA)   **91**
132) [2002 8m² 8g* 8.2m³ 8.1m² 7.1f⁵ Sep 28] useful-looking filly: third foal: half-sister
to 5-y-o Sherzabad: dam unraced daughter of smart French 1m to 12.5f winner Sherarda:
fairly useful form: won maiden at Doncaster in July: good efforts in handicaps next 2
starts: bred to stay at least 1¼m but races freely: raced only on good going or firmer: sold
€24,000. *Sir Michael Stoute*

SHERWOOD FOREST   2 ch.g. (Mar 2) Fleetwood (IRE) 107 – Jay Gee Ell 78   **–**
(Vaigly Great 127) [2002 5f 7.2s 5s Nov 6] 12,000Y: strong gelding: half-brother to
several winners, including 7-y-o Friar Tuck and useful 6f/7f (at 2 yrs) and 1m (in USA)
winner Kaibo: dam, 2-y-o 5f/6f winner, later best at 1¼m: well held in maidens/seller.
Miss L. A. Perratt

SHERZABAD (IRE)   5 b. or br.g. Doyoun 124 – Sheriya (USA) (Green Dancer   **51**
(USA) 132) [2002 57: 10g 10m 10m 12m 10m p12g 10f Oct 2] sturdy, lengthy gelding: modest
handicapper: stays 1½m: probably acts on any going: often visored: tried tongue tied
earlier in career: best held up. *H. J. Collingridge*

887

SHE'S A DIAMOND 5 b.m. Mystiko (USA) 124 – Fairy Kingdom (Prince Sabo 123) [2002 p7g Oct 16] second foal: dam unraced: 50/1, slowly away and always towards rear in claimer at Lingfield. *T. T. Clement* –

SHE'S A GEM 7 b.m. Robellino (USA) 127 – Rose Gem (IRE) 62 (Taufan (USA) 119) [2002 f8g 7f 6g Aug 22] smallish mare: modest performer at 4 yrs: missed 2000/2001: showed nothing in 2002 (reportedly bled from nose on reappearance): tried visored/blinkered. *T. T. Clement* –

SHE'S AT IT (IRE) 2 b.f. (Feb 6) College Chapel 122 – Flamanda 67 (Niniski (USA) 125) [2002 6m 7m 8.1m⁶ 8g² 8s Oct 15] approx. 10,200Y in Germany, resold 18,500Y: leggy filly: first foal: dam, German 8.5f to 9.5f winner, out of smart performer up to 13.4f Nemisia: fair maiden: best effort when second in nursery at Ayr: stayed 1m: dead. *M. R. Channon* **67**

SHE'S BONNIE (IRE) 5 b.m. Mtoto 134 – Clyde Goddess (IRE) 92 (Scottish Reel 123) [2002 –§: p10g 8.1m 11.9m 12g 9.2d Jul 25] tall, sparely-made mare: temperamental maiden: no form: tried blinkered. *W. de Best-Turner* – §

SHE'S FLASH (IRE) 3 b.f. Woodborough (USA) 112 – Beechwood Quest (IRE) 65 (River Falls 113) [2002 57: 8g⁶ 7m May 2] rather unfurnished filly: modest maiden at 2 yrs: little form in 2002. *G. A. Swinbank* –

SHESGOTTOHAVEIT (IRE) 3 b.f. Flying Spur (AUS) – Carousel Mall (IRE) (Soughaan (USA) 111) [2002 –: f7s p8g³ p10g³ 10m³ 11.9g 11.6d 11.5f 11.6m p12g 9.7d 10d Oct 28] poor maiden handicapper: left J. Glover after third start: stays easy 1¼m: acts on good to firm going and polytrack: tried visored/blinkered/tongue tied. *P. Mitchell* **49**

SHE'S MY VALENTINE 2 b.f. (Mar 18) My Best Valentine 122 – Hong Kong Girl 94 (Petong 126) [2002 7m Aug 29] sixth reported foal: half-sister to 7-y-o Bound To Please and 6f winner Jersey Belle (by Distant Relative): dam best at 5f: 66/1, tailed off in maiden at Salisbury. *A. G. Newcombe* –

SHE'S NO ANGEL 2 ch.f. (May 2) Bluegrass Prince (IRE) 110 – Havana Miss 54 (Cigar 68) [2002 f5g f5g 6.1d⁵ 5.3g 6s f5g Dec 4] 700Y: third foal: dam 2-y-o 6f winner who stayed 1¼m: little form, including in sellers. *B. Palling* –

SHE'S SMOKIN 4 b.f. Cigar 68 – Beau Dada (IRE) 66 (Pine Circle (USA)) [2002 –: f8s f8.5g p6g f8g f12g f12g⁶ Mar 25] little form: left J. Cullinan after second start. *J. D. Czerpak* –

SHE WHO DARES WINS 2 b.f. (Feb 5) Atraf 116 – Mirani (IRE) 55 (Danehill (USA) 126) [2002 5m⁵ 5f³ May 4] 500Y: smallish, workmanlike filly: third foal: half-sister to 2 winners in Greece by Alhijaz: dam 7f winner from 2 starts: backward, modest form in maiden at Musselburgh and minor event at Thirsk. *L. R. James* **56**

SHIELD 2 b.c. (Apr 8) Barathea (IRE) 127 – Shesadelight 67 (Shirley Heights 130) [2002 8.2v³ p10g* Dec 3] sixth foal: closely related to fairly useful 11.6f winner Tikopia and Irish 1¼m/1½m winner Sail With The Wind (both by Saddlers' Hall), and half-brother to 2 winners, including fairly useful but untrustworthy 1¼m and 1¾m winner Total Delight (by Mtoto): dam, maiden who stayed 2m, sister to very smart middle-distance performer Infamy: useful form: promising third to Bugatti Royale in maiden at Nottingham before justifying favouritism in similar event at Lingfield by 7 lengths from Alumni News: will stay at least 1½m: should improve further and win more races. *G. A. Butler* **97 p**

SHIFTING WIND (IRE) 2 b.g. (Jan 20) Night Shift (USA) – Dacian (USA) (Diesis 133) [2002 5.2g⁴ 5m⁵ 5.1f f5s⁴ Sep 5] IR 8,200Y, 6,200 2-y-o: smallish, lengthy gelding: first foal: dam, no form in 4 starts, sister to US Grade 1 1¼m winner Tsunami Slew: fair maiden: fourth at Yarmouth and Southwell (nursery): will stay 6f. *J. R. Best* **65**

SHIFTY 3 b.g. Night Shift (USA) – Crodelle (IRE) (Formidable (USA) 125) [2002 87: 8m 8m 9g 7g 8g³ 7m 8.5m 8f⁵ Oct 7] well-made gelding: has a round action: fairly useful performer at 2 yrs: fair in 2002: stays 1m: acts on firm going: blinkered sixth start: sold 8,500 gns and gelded. *J. D. Bethell* **73**

SHII-TAKE'S GIRL 4 ch.f. Deploy 131 – Super Sally 108 (Superlative 118) [2002 80: 11.9m 12f³ 9.9g 12g 16d 14.1m 10m 12.1m² 12f 12g Oct 19] angular filly: fair handicapper: on downgrade in 2002: stays 1½m: acts on firm and soft ground: tried blinkered: usually races prominently: ungenuine: sold 800 gns. *M. E. Sowersby* **74 d**

SHINBONE ALLEY 5 b.g. Lake Coniston (IRE) 131 – Villota (Top Ville 129) [2002 –§: 5g f5g 6f May 13] lengthy, quite attractive gelding: has a quick action: fairly useful performer at 2/3 yrs: little form since: untrustworthy. *D. W. Chapman* – §

SHINGLES (IRE) 2 ch.c. (Apr 2) Desert Prince (IRE) 130 – Nibbs Point (IRE) 107 **71**
(Sure Blade (USA) 130) [2002 6s² 8f 6g⁴ 7f⁴ Sep 25] 65,000Y: smallish, useful-looking
colt: half-brother to several winners, including 7-y-o Border Arrow: dam, 1¼m/1½m
winner who stayed 2m, half-sister to smart French 10.5f and 12.5f winner Foundation
Spirit: fair maiden: looked ill at ease on track at Chester final start: should stay at least
1¼m: sold 9,000 gns, joined N. Littmoden. *P. F. I. Cole*

SHINING OASIS (IRE) 4 b.f. Mujtahid (USA) 118 – Desert Maiden 74§ (Green **–**
Desert (USA) 127) [2002 73d: 8.5m 7g May 6] angular filly: fair performer at best: has
deteriorated: tried blinkered/visored. *N. Tinkler*

SHINING WHITE 3 b.f. Zafonic (USA) 130 – White Shadow (IRE) 87 (Last Tycoon **84**
131) [2002 6g* 6m 6m⁴ Aug 16] third living foal: dam, 2-y-o 6f winner, half-sister to
smart French middle-distance performer Ordinance: won maiden at Southwell (slowly
away, green) in June: better effort after won fourth in handicap at Epsom: will be suited
by 7f: sold 6,000 gns in December. *R. Charlton*

SHINY 3 b.f. Shambo 113 – Abuzz 101 (Absalom 128) [2002 92: 8g 7m³ 8m 8d⁴ 8.2d² **98**
8m⁵ 8g 9.9m 7f 7m 5g Oct 17] tall filly: has scope: useful performer: highly tried for most
of season: best effort in pattern races when 5½ lengths fifth to Sophistcat in Coronation
Stakes at Royal Ascot in June: gave impression something amiss next time and below
form after: stays 1m: acts on firm and good to soft ground: blinkered (below form) fifth
start. *C. E. Brittain*

SHIRAZI 4 b.g. Mtoto 134 – Al Shadeedah (USA) 86 (Nureyev (USA) 131) [2002 **81**
86: 10.1g⁶ 10f⁵ 10m⁵ 10d⁶ 10g⁶ 12m p10g⁴ p10g* Dec 28] strong gelding: fairly useful
handicapper: won apprentice event at Lingfield in December: stays 1¼m: acts on polytrack, firm and soft ground: usually held up: effective tongue tied or not. *J. W. Hills*

SHIRLEY COLLINS 3 b.f. Robellino (USA) 127 – Kisumu (Damister (USA) 123) **76**
[2002 65: 8.1m² 8g³ p7g⁶ 8.2g 8m⁶ 9.7g² 10m² 10.2g³ f8.5g⁴ f9.4s³ Nov 2] smallish, **a69**
good-topped filly: fair maiden handicapper: best effort at 1¼m: acts on good to firm going,
probably on fibresand: wandered penultimate start/visored final one: sold 21,000 gns.
M. L. W. Bell

SHIRLEY FONG (IRE) 4 b.f. Bluebird (USA) 125 – Decrescendo (IRE) (Polish **52**
Precedent (USA) 131) [2002 57: 8f 10d 12.4m 10m p10g Jul 3] sturdy, compact filly:
modest maiden: stays 1¼m: best form on good ground or firmer: tried blinkered/visored/
tongue tied: sold 800 gns in December. *E. J. O'Neill*

SHIRLEY NOT 6 gr.g. Paris House 123 – Hollia 72 (Touch Boy 109) [2002 71: f5g⁵ **66**
f7g 6m⁵ 6m³ 5g 7m² 6m³ 7m 7.6f 7m 7m Aug 16] big, lengthy gelding: fair handicapper:
effective at 5f/easy 7f: acts on firm going, soft and fibresand: often blinkered/visored
earlier in career, and on penultimate start: sometimes goes in snatches: usually held up.
S. Gollings

SHIRLEY OAKS (IRE) 4 b.f. Sri Pekan (USA) 117 – Duly Elected (Persian Bold **51**
123) [2002 f7g p8g⁴ 9.9m 8m 7d* 7g 8m 7.5d 6g f7g Dec 2] small, sparely-made filly:
modest performer: raced only in UAE in 2001: won seller at Brighton in May: below
form after: stays 1m: acts on good to soft going, dirt and polytrack: blinkered last 3 starts:
often tongue tied. *Miss Gay Kelleway*

SHIRLEYS QUEST 3 b.f. Bin Ajwaad (IRE) 119 – Mainly Me 76 (Huntingdale 132) **–**
[2002 8.1m 10m 10s⁵ Oct 23] third foal: sister to 5-y-o Coco Loco: dam maiden who
stayed 1m: well held in maidens (reportedly coughed second start). *G. Wragg*

SHIZAO (IRE) 2 b.f. (May 10) Alzao (USA) 117 – Shigeru Summit 105 (Be My **100**
Chief (USA) 122) [2002 6m² 6m* 5m* 7m Oct 19] small, close-coupled filly: good
walker: second foal: dam French 2-y-o 5.5f and 7f winner: useful form: won maiden at
the Curragh in September and listed race at Tipperary (by neck from Miguel Cervantes,
making virtually all) in October: well held in Rockfel Stakes at Newmarket: should stay
7f: raced only on good to firm ground. *J. S. Bolger, Ireland*

SHOAL CREEK (IRE) 5 b.h. Fairy King (USA) – Catalonia Express (USA) (Diesis **115**
133) [2002 114: 7s³ 10s² May 6] good-bodied horse: smart performer: good efforts in
2002 behind Rebelline at the Curragh, in Gladness Stakes (beaten length) and listed race
(beaten ¾ length): effective at 7f to 10.4f: raced only on good ground or softer: effective
blinkered/visored or not: usually sets pace. *A. P. O'Brien, Ireland*

SHOCKLAND (IRE) 3 b.g. Zamindar (USA) 116 – Eurythmic 58 (Pharly (FR) 130) **–**
[2002 75d: 5d 9.3s 5m 7.2d 6m⁶ 7.9s⁴ Jul 31] strong, close-coupled gelding: fair maiden
at 2 yrs: well beaten in 2002: blinkered final 2-y-o outing. *A. Berry*

SHOESHINE BOY (IRE)   4 b. or br.g. Prince Sabo 123 – Susie Sunshine (IRE) 81   **94**
(Waajib 121) [2002 102: 5m⁵ 5.1f² 5d² 5m 5.6m⁶ 5m Sep 29] smallish, strong gelding:
fairly useful handicapper: runner-up at Chester in June and Sandown in July: close sixth
in Portland Handicap at Doncaster penultimate start: stays 5.6f: acts on any turf going:
blinkered once in 2000: often races prominently: none too consistent. *B. J. Meehan*

SHOETIME SHADOW   3 ch.g. Timeless Times (USA) 99 – Willrack Farrier 73   **–**
(Lugana Beach 116) [2002 52: p6g p7g 5.3m 7g Jun 5] modest maiden at 2 yrs: well held
in 2002. *C. N. Allen*

SHOLAY (IRE)   3 b.g. Bluebird (USA) 125 – Splicing 82 (Sharpo 132) [2002 88: p7g   **85**
9.9d⁴ 7.1m⁵ 8m 5g Oct 19] lightly-made gelding: fairly useful handicapper: seems to stay
1¼m: acts on good to soft and good to firm going, some promise on polytrack: visored
third/fourth starts: gelded after final outing. *G. A. Butler*

SHOLOKHOV (IRE)   3 b.c. Sadler's Wells (USA) 132 – La Meilleure 86 (Lord   **121**
Gayle (USA) 124) [2002 108: 8m 12d² 10d² 10m⁴ 14.6m 8g⁴ 10m Oct 19] sturdy colt:
very smart performer: excellent efforts second/third starts in 2002 when runner-up in
Irish Derby at the Curragh and Eclipse Stakes at Sandown, beaten 3½ lengths by High
Chaparral and 2½ lengths by Hawk Wing (both stablemates) respectively: ran as
pacemaker in Irish Champion Stakes at Leopardstown (had hard race, fourth to Grandera)
and in Queen Elizabeth II Stakes at Ascot (ignored by other runners, fourth of 5 to Where
Or When) fourth/sixth starts: well below form in St Leger at Doncaster and Champion
Stakes at Newmarket fifth and final outings: better at 1¼m/1½m than shorter: acts on soft
and good to firm going: has worn crossed noseband/had 2 handlers: sweating at
Sandown: usually makes running (held up in St Leger): carries head awkwardly: joined
M. Jarvis. *A. P. O'Brien, Ireland*

SHOLTO   4 b.g. Tragic Role (USA) – Rose Mill (Puissance 110) [2002 58: 6s 5m* 5f   **62**
6.1m⁶ 5m Oct 5] close-coupled gelding: modest handicapper: won at Catterick in August:
best at 5f/6f: acts on soft and good to firm ground: blinkered: tried tongue tied: often
hangs. *J. O'Reilly*

SHOOF (USA)   3 b.f. Dayjur (USA) 137 – Shemaq (USA) 98 (Blushing John (USA)   **72**
120) [2002 68p: 6.1d 6m⁴ 7f³ 8f² 7m² 7g Oct 4] fair maiden handicapper: stayed 1m:
acted on firm going: visits Muhtarram. *A. C. Stewart*

SHORE VISION   4 b.g. Efisio 120 – South Shore 102 (Caerleon (USA) 132) [2002   **73**
79+: 8d 10f 7d 8m 10s f8g⁴ f8g* p8g⁵ Dec 14] strong, good-bodied gelding: fair
handicapper: won at Southwell in November: stays 1m: acts on all-weather, good to firm
and good to soft ground. *P. W. Harris*

SHORT CHANGE (IRE)   3 b.g. Revoque (IRE) 122 – Maafi Esm (Polish Precedent   **64**
(USA) 131) [2002 72: 8.2d 11.6m 10.2g 7.1m 10d³ 10.2d⁴ 11.9m³ 11.6m* 11.6g
10m² 10m 8f⁴ 8.1g⁴ 10m⁴ Oct 3] big, lengthy gelding: modest handicapper: left
B. Meehan after fifth start: won at Windsor in July, despite hanging left: effective at 1m,
barely at 1½m: acts on firm and good to soft ground: tried blinkered: sometimes on toes/
races freely: often races prominently: consistent: won juvenile hurdle in October.
A. W. Carroll

SHORT RESPITE   3 b.f. Brief Truce (USA) 126 – Kingdom Princess 69 (Forzando   **78**
122) [2002 77p: 7s⁴ 6d 7d⁴ 7g 7d³ 7.9s³ 8.5d* 9m* 10.3m⁶ 9.2m* 8.9m 10g 10.4f 10.3s
f9.4g Nov 16] fair performer: won claimers at Beverley (left M. Bell £10,000) and
Musselburgh (left K. Ryan £12,000) in August and Hamilton in September: soundly
beaten last 3 starts (finished distressed on second occasion, visored final one): stays 9f:
acts on soft and good to firm going: sometimes slowly away/flashes tail/hangs.
K. R. Burke

SHORTS   3 b.f. Primo Dominie 121 – Gentle Irony 65 (Mazilier (USA) 107) [2002 57,   **53**
a52: 5m 5.7g⁶ 6d 5.1d* 5g 5.1d f5g Jul 11] sparely-made filly: modest performer: won   **a–**
claimer at Bath in May: stays 6f: acts on fibresand, good to firm and good to soft going:
visored once at 2 yrs: usually races up with pace: withdrawn after refusing to enter stalls
final intended outing: sold 500 gns in September. *P. D. Evans*

SHOTACROSS THE BOW (IRE)   5 b.g. Warning 136 – Nordica 99 (Northfields   **63**
(USA)) [2002 –, a86+: f9.4g² f9.4g² f8.5g⁴ 9.7m² 10d 8d⁶ 8.1m⁴ 8.3m 9.7m³ 10g⁴ 9.9m³   **a84**
9.7g² 12d⁴ 10.9m 10m⁴ 11.7g⁵ f8.5f³ Nov 11] tall, angular gelding: fairly useful handicapper on all-weather, modest on turf: sometimes pulls hard, and best short of 1½m:
acts on fibresand, firm and good to soft going: usually held up: tough and reliable.
M. Blanshard

SHOTLEY DANCER 3 ch.f. Danehill Dancer (IRE) 117 – Hayhurst (Sandhurst 57 Prince 128) [2002 60: 7m 5.9s⁴ 6g³ 7.5m 7.4m⁴ 7.5m⁵ 10.4m⁴ 9.9m 8f² 7d⁵ Oct 18] small, unfurnished filly: fluent mover: modest maiden: has form at 10.4f, but may prove best up to 1m: acts on firm and soft ground. *N. Bycroft*

SHOTSTOPPA (IRE) 4 ch.g. Beveled (USA) – From The Rooftops (IRE) (Thatch- 45 ing 131) [2002 –: 7.9s 8.3v f7g³ f8g Jul 11] strong gelding: poor maiden: stays 7f: acts on fibresand. *J. L. Eyre*

SHOT TO FAME (USA) 3 b.c. Quest For Fame 127 – Exocet (USA) (Deposit Ticket 112 (USA)) [2002 94p: 10g⁴ 8m³ Jun 20] angular, rather lightly-made colt: smart form: excellent close third to Pentecost in Britannia Handicap at Royal Ascot, bit slowly away and needing to be switched: subsequently reported to have suffered a setback: should be at least as effective at 1¼m as 1m: yet to race on firm going, probably acts on any other. *P. W. Harris*

SHOUETTE (IRE) 2 b.f. (Apr 2) Sadler's Wells (USA) 132 – Sumava (IRE) (Sure 68 p Blade (USA) 130) [2002 7d⁵ Oct 30] 80,000F: fourth living foal: dam unraced half-sister to very smart filly up to 1¼m Ela Romara, herself dam of smart 1½m performer Foyer (by Sadler's Wells): weak 16/1-shot, 7½ lengths fifth of 18 to Hard Nose in maiden at Yarmouth, keeping on from mid-field without being knocked about: will be suited by 1¼m+: open to improvement. *B. W. Hills*

SHOUF AL BADOU (USA) 5 b.g. Sheikh Albadou 128 – Millfit (USA) 62 (Blush- – ing Groom (FR) 131) [2002 74d: f7g f7g* f6g f7g* f7g⁴ 7g 7.2g 7.1v 7m Jun 29] a77 good-bodied gelding: fair performer: won handicap at Wolverhampton and minor event at Southwell in February: left N. Littmoden following next start, and well beaten after: probably best at 6f/7f: acts on heavy going, good to firm and fibresand: usually blinkered/visored: none too reliable: sold 5,000 gns. *M. L. W. Bell*

SHOUTING THE ODDS (IRE) 2 br.f. (Mar 23) Victory Note (USA) 120 – Spout 91 House (IRE) 55 (Flash of Steel 120) [2002 5d² 5m* 5.2f⁴ 6m⁴ Sep 14] IR 7,000Y: leggy filly: fourth foal: half-sister to 3-y-o Lady Dominatrix and an Italian winner up to 12.5f by Mukaddamah: dam maiden who stayed 1½m: fairly useful form: won maiden at Folkestone in August: best effort when 2¾ lengths fourth to Speed Cop in listed event at Newbury next time: will prove best at 5f/6f: acts on firm ground. *J. G. Given*

SHOVE HA'PENNY (IRE) 3 b.c. Night Shift (USA) – Penny Fan 58 (Nomination 83 d 125) [2002 76: p7g* p7g* p6g² 6g 7.5m 7.9f 8g* 8.1d 7m 8g⁵ p8g 8d 8f 8f⁴ Oct 7] workmanlike colt: fairly useful performer at best: won maiden at Lingfield in January and handicaps at Lingfield in February and Newmarket in June: probably best at 6f to 1m: acts on polytrack, firm and soft going: blinkered twice: often slowly away: unreliable: sold 10,000 gns, sent to USA. *N. A. Callaghan*

SHOWING 5 b.g. Owington 123 – Sharanella (Shareef Dancer (USA) 135) [2002 –: – p7g p6g 7d 7m Jun 28] disappointing maiden: tried blinkered/tongue tied. *B. R. Johnson*

SHOWPIECE 4 b.g. Selkirk (USA) 129 – Hawayah (IRE) 68 (Shareef Dancer (USA) 79 135) [2002 68: f12g³ p10g³ 12m* 12g⁵ 12m* 13.3f⁵ 11.7f 11.9m 11.6m Oct 7] lengthy gelding: fair handicapper: won at Salisbury in May and Newmarket in June: something possibly amiss final start: should stay 1¾m: acts on heavy going, good to firm and all-weather: has wandered/found little: worth a try in blinkers/visor: sold 13,000 gns, joined C. Mann. *W. J. Haggas*

SHOW THE WAY 4 ch.g. Hernando (FR) 127 – Severine (USA) 65 (Trempolino – (USA) 135) [2002 49: p16s⁶ f12s 11.6s Jun 10] good-topped gelding: poor maiden at 3 yrs: well held in 2002: tried visored/blinkered. *J. R. Jenkins*

SHOWTIME SHIRLEY 4 ch.f. First Trump 118 – Wollow Maid 73 (Wollow 132) 38 [2002 49: p16g³ f16.2g 9.9m 10.2g 11.8m 12m Jun 24] poor handicapper: seems to stay a43 easy 2m: acts on firm ground and polytrack: tried visored: usually races prominently. *A. Bailey*

SHREDDED (USA) 2 b.c. (May 11) Diesis 133 – Shiitake (USA) (Green Dancer 81 p (USA) 132) [2002 8d³ Oct 30] $160,000Y: half-brother to several winners, including US Grade 1 8.5f winner Taking Risks (by Two Punch): dam, 1m winner in US, half-sister to very smart performer up to 1¾m Per Quod out of half-sister to Alleged: weak 8/1-shot, 1½ lengths third of 13 to Devant in maiden at Yarmouth, finishing well after slow start: will stay at least 1¼m: likely to progress. *J. H. M. Gosden*

SHRIEK 2 gr.f. (Mar 22) Sheikh Albadou 128 – Normanby Lass 100 (Bustino 136) – [2002 f6g Oct 5] 2,000Y, resold 1,800Y: half-sister to several winners, including 1996 2-y-o 1m winner Bonnie Lassie (by Efisio) and 11f winner Keep Your Distance (by

Elegant Air): dam 2-y-o 7f winner: 6/1 from 5/2, soundly beaten in maiden at Wolver-hampton. *J. A. Osborne*

SHUDDER   7 b.g. Distant Relative 128 – Oublier L'Ennui (FR) 79 (Bellman (FR) 123)   **75 d**
[2002 73: 5.7g³ 5.7d 6m 5.7m 6.1m 6m 5.1g Oct 16] fair performer: well held after reappearance: effective at 5.7f to 7f: acts on heavy and good to firm going: won in visor earlier in career. *R. J. Hodges*

SHUHOOD (USA)   2 b.c. (Feb 14) Kingmambo (USA) 125 – Nifty (USA) (Roberto   **81 p**
(USA) 131) [2002 7m* Sep 18] $125,000Y: seventh foal: half-brother to 3 winners in US, including Grade 3 1½m winner Renewed (by Lost Code): dam US maiden: 5/1, won 7-runner maiden at Yarmouth by ½ length from Cabeza de Vaca, getting on top well inside final 1f: will stay at least 1m: sure to progress. *E. A. L. Dunlop*

SHUJUNE (USA)   2 b.f. (Apr 3) Imperial Ballet (IRE) 110 – Java Blue (USA) (Java   **70**
Gold (USA)) [2002 6f⁴ 6f² 6s³ Oct 28] $21,000Y, resold 46,000Y: leggy filly: second foal: half-sister to a winner in USA by Quiet American: dam, 6f winner in USA, from family of Dancing Brave: fair form in maidens: second at Redcar: free-going sort, not sure to stay beyond 6f: acts on firm and soft going: sold 16,000 gns, sent to USA. *J. L. Dunlop*

SHUSH   4 b.g. Shambo 113 – Abuzz 101 (Absalom 128) [2002 83, a75: p12g⁶ p12g⁴   **74**
10.9g³ 10m⁵ 12.3f 10g 9.9g 10s⁵ 12.3m⁵ 10.3f 13.8d p10g⁴ Nov 27] quite attractive   **a69**
gelding: fair handicapper: stays easy 1½m: acts on heavy going, good to firm and poly-track: blinkered last 4 starts. *C. E. Brittain*

SHUWAIB   5 b.g. Polish Precedent (USA) 131 – Ajab Alzamaan (Rainbow Quest   **98**
(USA) 134) [2002 100: 16g 12m 12m 14d 16.2s⁵ 15v³ 12s⁵ 13.3f⁶ 14m 12d Sep 11] tall gelding: useful handicapper at best, lightly raced: regressed in 2002 (fell heavily at Epsom final start): seemed to stay 2m: acted on heavy and good to firm going: dead. *M. R. Channon*

SICKNOTE (IRE)   3 b.g. Lake Coniston (IRE) 131 – Maellen (River Beauty 105)   **62 d**
[2002 –p: f7g⁴ f6g f8.5g 7.1f 8.2f³ 8.2g⁴ f8.5g 8.2g 10g Oct 14] good-bodied gelding: modest maiden: below form after reappearance: stays 1m: acts on fibresand and firm going: tried blinkered. *J. A. Glover*

SIENA STAR (IRE)   4 b.g. Brief Truce (USA) 126 – Gooseberry Pie 63 (Green   **78**
Desert (USA) 127) [2002 73: p10g² p10g* 9.7m² 10f³ 10.3g* p8g⁴ p8g* f8g⁶ p10g³ Dec   **a84**
21] close-coupled gelding: has a quick action: fairly useful handicapper: won at Lingfield in February, Chester in June and Lingfield (awarded race after being hampered) in December: stays 1¼m: acts on firm ground, soft and polytrack, probably on fibresand: held up: has hinted at temperament, but is consistent. *P. F. I. Cole*

SIENNA SUNSET (IRE)   3 ch.f. Spectrum (IRE) 126 – Wasabi (IRE) (Polar Falcon   **66**
(USA) 126) [2002 66p: 8.2m⁵ 10.5d⁵ 9.9s³ 10g* 10m⁵ 10m⁵ 8g p10g⁶ Dec 18] tall filly: fair performer: won minor event at Brighton in June: stays 1¼m: acts on polytrack, soft and good to firm ground. *Mrs H. Dalton*

SIERRA VISTA   2 ch.f. (Feb 25) Atraf 116 – Park Vista (Taufan (USA) 119) [2002   **95**
5f² 5g* 5d* 6g 5.1m² 5g⁴ Sep 19] 500Y: leggy filly: seventh foal: dam third at 5f at 2 yrs: useful performer: won maiden at Carlisle in July and nursery at Thirsk in August: best effort when beaten head by Tender in nursery at Chester fifth start: should stay 6f: acts on good to firm and good to soft going. *D. W. Barker*

SIGHT SCREEN   2 b.f. (Apr 17) Eagle Eyed (USA) 111 – Krisia (Kris 135) [2002 6s³   **72**
7d⁵ Nov 2] small, close-coupled filly: fourth foal: half-sister to 5-y-o Continent and fairly useful French 5.5f and 7f winner Risiafon (by Zafonic): dam, French 1½m winner, out of very smart winner up to 1m Interval: better effort in maidens 3 months apart (fair form) when fifth of 18 to Aljazeera at Newmarket: will probably stay 1m. *B. W. Hills*

SIGHTS ON GOLD (IRE)   3 ch.c. Indian Ridge 123 – Summer Trysting (USA) 83   **116**
(Alleged (USA) 138) [2002 89: 8m² 8s 12g* 10g³ 10s² 10m* 10g² Oct 5] strong, angular colt: third foal: brother to fairly useful Irish 8.5f winner Romantic Venture and half-brother to fairly useful Irish 9f winner Beat The Heat (by Salse): dam, Irish maiden who stayed 1½m, half-sister to smart winner up to 1¼m Smooth Performance: smart performer: won apprentice minor event at the Curragh in June and listed race at Leopardstown (decisively by 1½ lengths from Millstreet) in September: also good efforts at the Curragh fourth/fifth starts (beaten ¾ length both times) when third to Imperial Dancer in Meld Stakes and second to Chancellor in Royal Whip Stakes: stays 1½m: acts on soft and good to firm going: joined Godolphin. *D. K. Weld, Ireland*

SIGN OF THE DRAGON 5 b.g. Sri Pekan (USA) 117 – Tartique Twist (USA) 78 –
(Arctic Tern (USA) 126) [2002 57: 7.1m 7f 7.1g 6.9d 7.1d 8m⁶ 7.2d Jul 23] one-time
modest 7f winner: no form in 2002. *Miss L. A. Perratt*

SIGWELLS CLUB BOY 2 b.g. (Mar 31) Fayruz 116 – Run With Pride (Mandrake **66**
Major 122) [2002 5.1g⁴ 6m* 6d² 7m² 7m 7d³ Aug 23] 4,800Y: good-bodied gelding: third
foal: dam ran twice: fair performer: made all in claimer at Newcastle in May: creditable
second in similar events: free-going sort, likely to prove best up to 7f: yet to race on
extremes of going. *W. G. M. Turner*

SIGY SAM 3 ch.f. King's Signet (USA) 110 – Hosting (Thatching 131) [2002 58:
6.1m 6.1d 5.7g 7.1g 5.7m f9.4f Aug 16] modest maiden at 2 yrs: little form in 2002.
A. G. Newcombe

SIHAFI (USA) 9 ch.g. Elmaamul (USA) 125 – Kit's Double (USA) (Spring Double)
[2002 73: f6g 5.3f 5.1g 5g 5v 5m 5m 5m 5g 5m 5m 6m Aug 15] tall gelding: fair
performer at 8 yrs: mostly well held in 2002: tried blinkered. *J. M. Bradley*

SIKASSO (USA) 6 b. or br.g. Silver Hawk (USA) 123 – Silken Doll (USA) (Chieftain **84**
II) [2002 82: 13s³ 13g 14s² 12.1v² 13s³ 13v² 14v³ 12.3m Aug 31] leggy gelding: fairly
useful handicapper: ran poorly final start: will stay 2m: acts on good to firm and heavy
going: tends to wander: sold 5,500 gns. *G. A. Swinbank*

SIKSIKAWA 3 b.f. Mark of Esteem (IRE) 137 – Lady Blackfoot 108 (Prince Tenderfoot (USA) 126) [2002 p8g Oct 9] half-sister to numerous winners, notably high-class
Fanmore and very smart Labeeb (both by Lear Fan), both best up to 1¼m in Europe/USA,
and smart 1m/9f performer Alrassaam (by Zafonic): dam speedy Irish filly: favourite,
well beaten in maiden at Lingfield, folding very tamely. *M. A. Jarvis*

Moyglare Stud Farm's "Sights On Gold"

SILCA BOO 2 b.f. (Mar 29) Efisio 120 – Bunty Boo 110 (Noalto 120) [2002 5m⁴ 5d* **99**
5m³ 5m 5.1f² 6f³ 7s⁶ 6.1m⁶ 6s* 6d⁴ Nov 17] 44,000Y: smallish, workmanlike filly: fourth
foal: half-sister to 4-y-o Zilch and a winner in Greece by Salse: dam sprinter: useful
performer: won maiden at Haydock in May and nursery at Newbury (by 5 lengths from
The Lord) in October: stays 6f, not testing 7f: acts on firm and soft ground: edgy sort,
upset in stall before running poorly eighth start. *M. R. Channon*

SILENCE AND RAGE 3 b.c. Green Desert (USA) 127 – Shot At Love (IRE) 79 **68**
(Last Tycoon 131) [2002 59p: p7g* 8m⁶ Apr 18] close-coupled, workmanlike colt: fair
performer: won handicap at Lingfield (tended to carry head awkwardly/idle) in March:
very stiff task when last in Craven Stakes at Newmarket (pulled hard) final run: stayed 7f:
acted on soft ground and polytrack: dead. *C. A. Cyzer*

SILENCE IS GOLDEN 3 ch.f. Danehill Dancer (IRE) 117 – Silent Girl 75 (Krayyan **97**
117) [2002 77: 9f² 8.3m 8s² 9.9d* 9.9m⁶ 10m* 9.9m 9m⁴ 10.1m⁶ 8m⁴ 10f Oct 4] rather
leggy, angular filly: useful handicapper: won at Goodwood in June and Ascot in July: far
from discredited when sixth in listed event at Yarmouth in September: probably best
around 1¼m: acts on firm and soft going: blinkered once at 2 yrs: tends to wander.
B. J. Meehan

SILENT CRYSTAL (USA) 3 ch.f. Diesis 133 – Starlight Way (USA) (Green Dancer **94**
(USA) 132) [2002 8v⁴ 8.3g³ 7g² 8d* 7m⁴ 8m⁵ 7m Oct 12] $160,000Y: well-made filly:
third foal: half-sister to Canadian Grade 1 2000 2-y-o 8.5f winner Salty You (by Salt
Lake): dam, 1m/8.5f winner in USA, half-sister to top-class performer up to 1m
Moorestyle: fairly useful performer: won maiden at Ayr in August: good fourth to
Mamounia in listed race at Doncaster next time: stays 8.3f: acts on good to firm and good
to soft going: blinkered: reluctant to enter stall fourth outing: pulled hard/found little final
start: quirky: sent to USA. *J. Noseda*

SILENT MEMORY (IRE) 3 b.f. Danehill (USA) 126 – All Hush (IRE) (Highest **55**
Honor (FR) 124) [2002 p6g p5g p7g 10g f12g³ f12g² 14.1m 10d⁴ 10g 10d f9.4g² 8d 10.1f²
f8s⁶ f12s³ f12g f9.4s Nov 2] 30,000F: big, lengthy filly: first foal: dam unraced: modest
maiden: left N. Callaghan after thirteenth outing (trained next by R. Wilman): stays
1½m: acts on fibresand, firm and good to soft ground: tried blinkered/tongue tied:
sometimes races freely. *S. L. Keightley*

SILENT SOUND (IRE) 6 b.g. Be My Guest (USA) 126 – Whist Awhile (Caerleon **47 §**
(USA) 132) [2002 52§: p16g⁵ f12g 11.8s⁵ 12.3g⁶ 11.8s f11g⁶ Dec 4] rather leggy **a40 §**
gelding: poor handicapper: left Mrs A. Perrett after reappearance, D. ffrench Davis after
fourth start: effective at 1¼m to 2m: acts on firm going, soft and all-weather: sometimes
blinkered/visored: sometimes very slowly away: not to be trusted. *Mrs S. A. Liddiard*

SILENT STORM 2 ch.c. (Apr 13) Zafonic (USA) 130 – Nanda 83 (Nashwan (USA) **81 p**
135) [2002 7m⁵ Aug 23] 90,000Y: sturdy colt: second foal: dam, 1¼m winner, sister to
Nell Gwyn Stakes winner Myself and half-sister to very smart performer up to 7f
Bluebook: 10/1, 9 lengths fifth of 16 to Almushahar in maiden at Newmarket, disputing
lead 5f: should improve. *H. R. A. Cecil*

SILENT WATERS 2 gr.f. (Mar 14) Polish Precedent (USA) 131 – Gleaming Water **–**
81 (Kalaglow 132) [2002 7m Aug 1] 37,000Y: leggy, close-coupled filly: half-sister to
several winners, including 1m to 10.4f winner Prince of Denial (by Soviet Star) and
middle-distance performer Faraway Waters (by Pharly), 6f winner at 2 yrs, both useful:
dam, 2-y-o 6f winner, sister to smart stayer Shining Water, herself dam of Tenby: 50/1
and green, always behind in maiden at Goodwood. *A. P. Jarvis*

SILISTRA 3 gr.c. Sadler's Wells (USA) 132 – Dundel (IRE) 82 (Machiavellian (USA) **77 §**
123) [2002 76P: 10m 10.2g⁴ 11.6m⁴ 11f² 12s 9.9d 10.1g⁶ 9.7m⁴ Aug 26] big, good-
topped colt: fair maiden: should stay 1½m: acts on firm ground, shaped well on soft: tried
blinkered/visored: gave trouble at start on reappearance: flicked tail penultimate outing:
tends to hang: one to treat with caution: sold 20,000 gns. *Sir Michael Stoute*

SILKEN BRIEF (IRE) 3 b.f. Ali-Royal (IRE) 127 – Tiffany's Case (IRE) 65 (Thatch- **86**
ing 131) [2002 80p: 8.3d* 7s p8g² Nov 23] sturdy filly: fairly useful form: favourite,
won maiden at Windsor in October: ran as if something amiss next time: tongue tied,
short-headed by Effervesce in handicap at Lingfield final start, caught post: will prove
best up to 1m: acts on polytrack and good to soft ground. *Sir Michael Stoute*

SILKEN SASH (IRE) 3 b.f. Danehill (USA) 126 – Flame Violet (IRE) 102 (Fairy **84**
King (USA)) [2002 85: 6g² 5g 5m* a6g⁶ Aug 11] IR 175,000Y: big, strong filly: first
foal: dam, 2-y-o 5f/6f winner, half-sister to smart sprinter Carol's Treasure: fairly useful
performer: trained at 2 yrs by A. O'Brien in Ireland: landed odds in maiden at Newcastle

in July: ran well in face of stiff task in listed race at Jagersro final outing: likely to prove best at 5f/6f: acts on good to firm and good to soft going, and on dirt: has worn crossed noseband: sent to USA. *J. A. Osborne*

SILKEN TOUCH 4 b.f. Pivotal 124 – Prima Silk 82 (Primo Dominie 121) [2002 –: f7s p7g 7f Apr 11] no form since debut at 2 yrs: blinkered nowadays: pulled up lame final start. *M. J. Ryan*

SILKEN WINGS (IRE) 4 b.f. Brief Truce (USA) 126 – Winged Victory (IRE) 93 **64 d** (Dancing Brave (USA) 140) [2002 70: f6s f6g⁴ f7g⁶ f6g 6m 6m f6g⁶ 6g 6m Aug 16] modest handicapper: on downgrade in 2002: probably best at 6f: acts on fibresand, firm and good to soft ground. *R. Hollinshead*

SILK ON SONG (USA) 4 b.g. Hazaam (USA) 113 – Wazeerah (USA) (The Minstrel **– §** (CAN) 135) [2002 –, a64: f12s² f12s f12g f16.2g⁴ f14g 13.8g May 31] poor maiden: **a44 §** unlikely to stay beyond 1½m: acts on fibresand: tried blinkered/tongue tied: has started slowly/refused to race final outing. *B. J. Llewellyn*

SILK ST BRIDGET 5 b.m. Rock Hopper 124 – Silk St James (Pas de Seul 133) **–** [2002 7.9g Aug 5] workmanlike mare: modest maiden at 3 yrs: behind only run since: tried blinkered. *W. M. Brisbourne*

SILK ST JOHN 8 b.g. Damister (USA) 123 – Silk St James (Pas de Seul 133) [2002 **–** 82, a–: 9m 8.1f⁶ 8s Nov 2] close-coupled gelding: useful handicapper at best: little form in 2002. *W. M. Brisbourne*

SILOGUE (IRE) 5 b. or br.g. Distinctly North (USA) 115 – African Bloom (African **–** Sky 124) [2002 42: 13.8g⁶ f11g Jun 20] small gelding: poor maiden at best. *O. Brennan*

SILVAANI (USA) 4 gr.g. Dumaani (USA) 115 – Ruby Silver (USA) (Silver Hawk **67** (USA) 123) [2002 –: p12g⁴ p13g³ f16g⁴ p16g⁵ 14.1d² 15.4m* Apr 23] workmanlike gelding: fair handicapper: won at Folkestone in April: stays 2m: acts on all-weather, good to firm and good to soft going: tried visored/blinkered at 3 yrs. *Mrs A. J. Perrett*

SILVALINE 3 gr.g. Linamix (FR) 127 – Upend 120 (Main Reef 126) [2002 8m 8f May **70** 25] 32,000Y: close-coupled gelding: half-brother to several winners, including 8-y-o Al Azhar and useful 1¼m winner Shortfall (by Last Tycoon): dam, 1¼m/1½m (St Simon Stakes) winner, half-sister to dam of Royal Gait: better effort in Newmarket maidens (fair form) when seventh to Helloimustbegoing on second run, not knocked about: bred to stay 1¼m: slowly away on debut: sold 8,000 gns in October, joined T. Keddy and gelded. *L. M. Cumani*

SILVER BAND 3 ch.f. Zilzal (USA) 137 – Silver Braid (USA) 101 (Miswaki (USA) **87** 124) [2002 72: 6f⁸ 6f⁴ 7g 6g 6g⁵ 6m⁵ Jul 26] leggy filly: fairly useful performer: won minor event at Thirsk and handicap at Newbury in May: seems best at 6f: acts on firm going, probably on good to soft: blinkered nowadays: becoming an increasingly difficult ride: sold 30,000 gns in December, sent to Greece. *T. D. Easterby*

SILVER BUZZARD (USA) 3 b. or br.g. Silver Hawk (USA) 123 – Stellarina (USA) **53** (Pleasant Colony (USA)) [2002 57p: f8.5g⁴ Apr 8] modest form in 2 maidens 4 months apart: reluctant at stall when fourth at Wolverhampton, keeping on under hands and heels: should stay 1½m: failed 2 stall tests in May and was banned from racing from stalls until Dec 1st 2002 (won over hurdles in November). *J. W. Hills*

SILVER CHARMER 3 b.f. Charmer 123 – Sea Dart 55 (Air Trooper 115) [2002 **59** 72d: 10.2g⁶ 7m 9d 5.7g⁶ 6m Jul 29] leggy, close-coupled filly: modest maiden handicapper: stays 6f: best effort on soft ground, tended to hang left on good to firm final outing (also veered left leaving stall). *H. S. Howe*

SILVER CHARTER (USA) 3 b.g. Silver Hawk (USA) 123 – Pride of Darby (USA) **82** (Danzig (USA)) [2002 85: 9m 10d⁴ 10m⁴ 10f 10.2g Sep 12] deep-girthed gelding: fairly useful performer: below form after second start: should be suited by 1¼m+: acts on good to firm and good to soft going: visored (ran poorly) final outing. *G. B. Balding*

SILVER CHIME 2 gr.f. Robellino (USA) 127 – Silver Charm (Dashing **74 p** Blade 117) [2002 5m³ Sep 15] third foal: half-sister to 2000 2-y-o 7f winner Zando's Charm (by Forzando): dam unraced sister to useful 9f/1¼m winner Dashiba: 20/1 and green, 2½ lengths third of 14 to Peace Offering in maiden at Sandown, best work late on: should stay 1m: sure to improve. *J. M. P. Eustace*

SILVER CITY 2 ro.c. (Apr 12) Unfuwain (USA) 131 – Madiyla 73 (Darshaan 133) **79** [2002 8f⁵ 8f⁴ 10s⁴ Oct 23] 50,000Y: eighth foal: half-brother to 2 winners abroad, including smart French miler Lethals Lady (by Rudimentary): dam, 1½m winner, half-sister to National Stakes winner Manntari: fair form in maidens: tended to carry head awkwardly when fourth to Forest Magic at Nottingham final start: will probably stay 1½m: acts on firm and soft ground. *Mrs A. J. Perrett*

SILVER COIN (IRE) 2 gr.c. (May 22) Night Shift (USA) – Eurythmic 58 (Pharly (FR) 130) [2002 6m May 15] 18,000Y: fifth living foal: half-brother to 4-y-o I Got Rhythm and to winners abroad by Pursuit of Love and Midyan: dam 1½m winner who stayed 2m: 12/1 and very green, always behind in maiden at Newcastle. *T. D. Easterby*

SILVER ELITE 3 gr.f. Forzando 122 – Final Call 79 (Town Crier 119) [2002 f6g³ 6s⁴ **62** 6m 6g May 5] 38,000Y: half-sister to numerous winners, including 2000 2-y-o 6f/7f winner Silver Jorden (by Imp Society) and 5f/6f winner Night Bell (by Night Shift), both useful: dam, 5f winner, ran only at 2 yrs: modest maiden: raced only at 6f. *Miss Gay Kelleway*

SILVER EXPRESS 2 b.f. (Apr 10) Silver Wizard (USA) 117 – Express Girl 75 **55** (Sylvan Express 117) [2002 5g⁶ 5f* Apr 20] sparely-made filly: second foal: dam 2-y-o 5f winner: modest form when winning claimer at Thirsk: should stay 6f: joined P. D. Evans. *M. Todhunter*

SILVER GILT 2 b.c. (Mar 4) Silver Hawk (USA) 123 – Memory's Gold (USA) 68 **102** (Java Gold (USA)) [2002 7d² 8mu* 9d² Oct 20] strong, lengthy, slightly dipped-backed colt: fourth foal: half-brother to smart French 5.5f (at 2 yrs) and 1m winner Ronda (by Bluebird) and 3-y-o Purring: dam, 7.6f winner, out of sister to Mill Reef: useful form: won maiden at Doncaster in September: good 1½ lengths equal-second to Graikos in Prix de Conde at Longchamp following month, setting steady pace and rallying: will stay 1¼m: flashes tail. *J. H. M. Gosden*

SILVER KRIS (USA) 2 gr.f. (Apr 4) Diesis 133 – P J'S Affair (USA) (Black Tie **51** Affair 128) [2002 f6g⁵ 5s 7.1m⁶ 7m 8f³ f8.5g Dec 2] $20,000Y: lengthy, angular filly: first foal: dam 5.5f (at 2 yrs) to 6.5f winner in USA: modest maiden: stays 1m: acts on firm ground. *M. Johnston*

SILVER LOUIE (IRE) 2 gr.f. (Mar 29) Titus Livius (FR) 115 – Shakamiyn (Nisha- **–** pour (FR) 125) [2002 6g⁶ 6d 8.3d Oct 28] 11,000Y: sixth foal: half-sister to 11f to 2m winner Shakiyr (by Lashkari) and a winner in Turkey by Marju: dam unraced half-sister to high-class French middle-distance performer Shakapour and to dam of Derby winner Shahrastani: only a little sign of ability in minor event/maidens. *G. B. Balding*

SILVER MASCOT 3 gr.g. Mukaddamah (USA) 125 – Always Lucky 71 (Absalom **73 §** 128) [2002 70: 6g² 6g f6g⁶ 6f⁴ p6g 6m f6s² 6m⁶ f6g⁶ f6g Nov 26] sturdy, good-quartered **a65 §** gelding: fair performer: best at 5f/6f: acts on fibresand and any turf going: tends to sweat: sometimes mounted on track/early to post: reportedly bled from nose final outing: none too consistent. *R. Hollinshead*

SILVER MISTRESS 3 gr.f. Syrtos 106 – Galava (CAN) (Graustark) [2002 8.2d **–** 8.2m 8.2g 8g Aug 13] tall, workmanlike filly: half-sister to 3 winners, including fairly useful 1997 2-y-o 1m winner Merciless (by Last Tycoon) and 1¾m winner Grey Galava (by Generous): dam placed at 7f/1m in France: well held in maidens/handicap. *B. N. Doran*

SILVER PROPHET (IRE) 3 gr.c. Idris (IRE) 118 – Silver Heart (Yankee Gold 115) **90** [2002 67: p8g 10m⁴ 10s² 11s* 10d² 11.7g 10.3s p10g Dec 28] rather leggy colt: fairly useful performer: won maiden at Goodwood in June: below form last 3 starts: stays 11f: acts on soft and good to firm going: visored (below form) once at 2 yrs: has worn crossed noseband. *M. R. Bosley*

SILVER RAPERE (USA) 2 b.f. (Mar 9) Silver Hawk (USA) 123 – Stylized (USA) **63** (Sovereign Dancer (USA)) [2002 7.1m³ 7f⁴ 7g² 8m⁴ 8d f6g f7g f8.5g⁵ Dec 31] 11,000Y: **a–** first foal: dam, 7f winner in Canada, half-sister to high-class 1m/1¼m performer Dr Fong: modest maiden: trained first 5 starts by P. Harris: should stay 1¼m: acts on firm ground, below form on fibresand. *G. A. Swinbank*

SILVER SECRET 8 gr.g. Absalom 128 – Secret Dance (Sadler's Wells (USA) 132) **–** [2002 50: 12.1m Jun 25] well-made gelding: modest performer in 2001: well held only 8-y-o start: tried visored/blinkered. *S. Gollings*

SILVER SEEKER (USA) 2 gr. or ro.c. (Feb 8) Seeking The Gold (USA) – Zelanda **90** (IRE) 108 (Night Shift (USA)) [2002 6m³ 6m* 7g Jul 31] smallish, good-bodied colt: first foal: dam, 5f/6f winner, out of smart Irish 9f and 11f winner who was third in Irish St Leger Zafadola: fairly useful form: landed odds in maiden at Newmarket in June, making all to beat Dhabyan by 1¼ lengths: never-dangerous eighth to Dublin in Vintage Stakes at Goodwood: seems to stay 7f: raced only on good/good to firm going. *D. R. Loder*

SILVER SHOES 3 b.f. Woodborough (USA) 112 – Emerald Dream (IRE) 47 (Vision (USA)) [2002 49: f8g f8g⁶ f12g Mar 4] small, good-topped filly: poor maiden at 2 yrs (visored once): little form in 2002. *J. L. Eyre* –

SILVER SOCKS 5 gr.g. Petong 126 – Tasmim 63 (Be My Guest (USA) 126) [2002 72: 10.3s² 10d³ Mar 27] quite good-topped gelding: fair handicapper: stayed 1½m: acted on fibresand and soft going, probably on good to firm: wore blinkers: dead. *M. W. Easterby* 67

SILVER TONIC 6 gr.g. Petong 126 – Princess Eurolink (Be My Guest (USA) 126) [2002 7.1m⁵ 8.1m Sep 21] modest maiden at best, lightly raced: little form in 2002. *J. M. Bradley* –

SILVERTOWN 7 b.g. Danehill (USA) 126 – Docklands (USA) (Theatrical 128) [2002 11.9g 11.9d³ 8.5d 10.4m³ Sep 4] lengthy gelding: fair handicapper: has reportedly had wind operation: best efforts at 1m/1¼m: acts on all-weather, firm and good to soft going: sometimes pulls hard/swishes tail. *L. Lungo* 69

SILVER WOOD 2 b.f. (Mar 16) Silver Wizard (USA) 117 – Eastwood Heiress (Known Fact (USA) 135) [2002 5g p5g Oct 31] fifth foal: dam unraced: well beaten in maiden and minor event at Lingfield. *J. C. Fox* –

SIMEON 3 b.c. Lammtarra (USA) 134 – Noble Lily (USA) (Vaguely Noble 140) [2002 95p: 9g* 10.5m* 10d* 12m³ 12d⁵ 10s⁵ Aug 11] tall, close-coupled colt: thrived physically: smart performer: won (all in April) minor event at Ripon, handicap at Haydock and Heathorns Classic Trial at Sandown, beating Kaieteur by 4 lengths in 4-runner event in last-named, dictating pace: good 6½ lengths third to Sulamani in Prix du Jockey Club at Chantilly next time: below form in Princess of Wales's Stakes at Newmarket and Royal Whip Stakes at the Curragh last 2 starts, fading rather tamely both times: stays 1½m: acts on soft and good to firm going: tends to be edgy in preliminaries: ridden prominently: has awkward head carriage: sold privately, and joined S. Seemar in UAE. *M. Johnston* 114

Heathorns Classic Trial, Sandown—Simeon completes an early season hat-trick;
Kaieteur finishes second with the Queen's one-time Derby hope Right Approach disappointing in third

SIMIANNA 3 b.f. Bluegrass Prince (IRE) 110 – Lowrianna (IRE) 50 (Cyrano de **99**
Bergerac 120) [2002 90: 5m 5.1f³ 6.1d⁴ 5.2d³ 6s⁴ 5g⁴ 6f² 6m⁶ 6.1d⁶ 6m² 6.1g⁵ 6d⁴ 6m⁴ 6m
5m Sep 12] tall, unfurnished filly: useful performer: in frame 9 times in 2002, including in
listed events: effective at 5f/6f: acts on any going: blinkered (ran creditably) final 2-y-o
start: sometimes slowly away. *A. Berry*

SIMIOLA 3 b.f. Shaamit (IRE) 127 – Brave Vanessa (USA) 62 (Private Account **55**
(USA)) [2002 55: p10g* f9.4g⁵ p10g⁵ p10g⁶ f12g 10.2g² 10m 10d² 10m⁴ p12g⁴ f12g **a61**
p12g 8g p13g Dec 28] modest performer: won claimer at Lingfield in January: left
G. L. Moore before below form last 4 starts: stays 1½m: acts on good to firm going, good
to soft and polytrack. *S. T. Lewis*

SIMNEL (IRE) 3 b.f. Turtle Island (IRE) 123 – Caca Milis (IRE) (Taufan (USA) 119) **–**
[2002 7m p8g 7s 8.2v Oct 29] IR 2,500Y: second foal: half-sister to 9f winner in Spain
by Dolphin Street: dam, Irish 2-y-o 5f winner, half-sister to smart performer up to 1m
Bashaayeash: well held in claimer/maidens: visored final start. *S. L. Keightley*

SIMON'S SEAT (USA) 3 ch.g. Woodman (USA) 126 – Spire (USA) (Topsider **75**
(USA)) [2002 8m⁴ 8f⁵ 7.9d⁶ 10.3f⁵ 10m⁵ Sep 15] $100,000Y: leggy, useful-looking
gelding: third foal: half-brother to a winner in USA by Unbridled: dam, US 1m (including
minor stakes) to 9f winner, out of half-sister to US Grade 3 6f winner Boundary: fair
maiden: stays 1¼m: acts on firm ground: gelded after final outing. *J. A. R. Toller*

SIMON THE POACHER 3 br.g. Chaddleworth (IRE) 103 – Lady Crusty (Golden **–**
Dipper 119) [2002 –: 7s Oct 28] small, sturdy gelding: no sign of ability. *L. P. Grassick*

SIMOUN (IRE) 4 b.c. Monsun (GER) 124 – Suivez (FR) (Fioravanti (USA) 115) **117**
[2002 11s* 11g² 12s⁴ 11m* 11v* 10s 10d⁶ Oct 3] third foal: half-brother to useful French/
German winner up to 1¾m Shining (by Surumu): dam, German 6f (at 2 yrs) and 1m
winner, out of half-sister to Breeders' Cup Mile/Arlington Million winner Steinlen: smart
performer: successful in 2001 in maiden and listed race at Bremen but missed
second half of year with fetlock injury: won listed race at Cologne in March and Grosser
Mercedes-Benz-Preis at Baden-Baden (beat Samum 2 lengths) and Idee Hansa-Preis at
Hamburg (by nose from Well Made), both in June: ran poorly last 2 starts: stays 11f: acts
on heavy and good to firm ground: stays in training. *P. Schiergen, Germany*

SIMPKIN (IRE) 2 br.f. (Apr 25) Danetime (IRE) 121 – Jet Fortuna (IRE) (Midyan **65**
(USA) 124) [2002 6d⁵ 5.3g⁴ 5m⁴ 6g³ 5m 7m² 7g 7g Oct 17] 8,000Y: leggy, lengthy filly:
first foal: dam, placed in Italy at 2 yrs, half-sister to smart Irish performers Mus-If (up to
1m) and Jammaal (up to 1½m): fair maiden: well below form last 2 starts, including in
seller: should stay 1m: acts on good to firm ground: sold 1,000 gns. *R. Hannon*

SIMPLE IDEALS (USA) 8 b. or br.g. Woodman (USA) 126 – Comfort And Style **56**
95 (Be My Guest (USA) 126) [2002 60, a–: 14.1d³ 16g⁵ 12.4g 13.9f 14d⁵ 14.1f⁵ 14.1d³ **a–**
16m⁴ 14.1m 16.2m³ 15d⁶ 14.4g* 16g 14.1m 14.1m* 13.9f 14.1d⁴ 14.6s Oct 25] smallish,
workmanlike gelding: has a round action: modest handicapper: won at Newcastle in
August and Redcar in October: races mainly at 1¾m/2m: acts on any turf going: blinkered
twice in 1997: sometimes races freely/hangs: tends to carry head high: usually held up:
consistent. *Don Enrico Incisa*

SIMPLE SONG 2 ch.f. (Feb 17) Simply Great (FR) 122 – Cumbrian Rhapsody 79 **–**
(Sharrood (USA) 124) [2002 8v f7g f7g Dec 31] third foal: dam, 12.4f winner, also
successful over hurdles: well beaten in maidens: slowly away last 2 starts. *T. D. Easterby*

SIMPLY REMY 4 ch.g. Chaddleworth (IRE) 103 – Exemplaire (FR) (Polish **52**
Precedent (USA) 131) [2002 51: 8m 13.8m⁴ p16g⁶ 16.4d Jul 11] lengthy gelding: modest
maiden handicapper: effective at 1¼m to 13.8f: acts on fibresand and firm going: races
prominently. *John Berry*

SIMPLY THE GUEST (IRE) 3 b.g. Mujadil (USA) 119 – Ned's Contessa (IRE) 48 **52**
(Persian Heights 129) [2002 72, a68: f6s f7g f6g 5g f6g⁴ f6g³ 5m 7.1d Aug 8] lengthy,
useful-looking gelding: fair performer at 2 yrs, modest at best in 2002: best at 5f/easy 6f:
acts on firm ground and fibresand: tried visored: sometimes slowly away. *N. Tinkler*

SINAMATELLA 3 ch.f. Lion Cavern (USA) 117 – Regent's Folly (IRE) 101 (Touch- **71**
ing Wood (USA) 127) [2002 69: 7m³ 7s⁵ 8.1m² 8.3d Oct 14] sturdy, good-bodied filly:
fair maiden: stays 1m: acts on good to firm going, possibly not on softer than good.
C. G. Cox

SINATRA (IRE) 3 b.c. Entrepreneur 123 – Fortune Teller (Troy 137) [2002 12s 12d⁶ **–**
p12g 12d Aug 3] IR 20,000Y: half-brother to 3 winners, notably useful performer up to
1¼m Almandab (by Last Tycoon): dam unraced half-sister to 2 Galtres Stakes winners:

clearly best effort (fair form) when eighth in maiden at Lingfield penultimate start. *B. Gubby*

SINDY (USA) 2 b.f. (Jan 30) A P Indy (USA) 131 – Dance Design (IRE) 119 (Sadler's Wells (USA) 132) [2002 7g² 8s Oct 22] lengthy, good-bodied filly: first foal: dam Irish 7f (at 2 yrs) to 1½m (Irish Oaks) winner: fairly useful form: backward, 3½ lengths second of 7 to Summitville in maiden at Newmarket: seventh of 8 in Prix des Reservoirs at Deauville 3 months later: should stay at least 1¼m: probably capable of better. *P. F. I. Cole* **81 p**

SINGLE MALT 2 gr.f. (Mar 1) Superpower 113 – Gi La High 68 (Rich Charlie 117) [2002 5g 5m f5g Apr 29] second foal: half-sister to 3-y-o Hagley Park: dam 5f winner, including at 2 yrs: no form: gave trouble in preliminaries first 2 starts. *G. M. McCourt* **–**

SINGLE TRACK MIND 4 b.g. Mind Games 121 – Compact Disc (IRE) 48 (Royal Academy (USA) 130) [2002 82d: f6g p6g⁴ 6.1g f7g 7d 6.1m 7.6f 6g 6m Aug 26] neat, quite attractive gelding: fairly useful performer at 3 yrs: no form in 2002 after second outing (reported to have had breathing problem/lost action first start): stays 6f: acts on fibresand, good to firm and soft ground: tried visored. *J. R. Boyle* **57 d**

SINGULARITY 2 b.g. (Mar 23) Rudimentary (USA) 118 – Lyrical Bid (USA) 77 (Lyphard (USA) 132) [2002 6m 5.2d 7d 7m 6m³ 6m 6m⁶ 7g f6g² f6s f6g² Dec 16] IR 13,000F, IR 32,000Y: second foal: dam, 2-y-o 7.5f winner on only start, half-sister to useful winner up to 2m On Call: modest maiden: runner-up in claimer at Southwell and seller at Wolverhampton: probably stays 7f: acts on fibresand, yet to race on extremes of going on turf. *W. R. Muir* **59**

SIOUXSIE SIOUX 3 b.f. Pivotal 124 – Tres Sage (Reprimand 122) [2002 67: 7d⁴ 6g⁴ 7.1m* 8g 7d Oct 30] tall, leggy, unfurnished filly: fair performer, lightly raced: won maiden at Musselburgh in September: stays 7f: yet to race on extremes of going: free-going sort: sold 10,000 gns in December. *J. G. Given* **71**

SIRAJ 3 b.g. Piccolo 121 – Masuri Kabisa (USA) 48 (Ascot Knight (CAN) 130) [2002 61: 7.1m³ 6g 5d³ p6g* p6g⁶ Dec 3] 41,000F, 70,000Y: good-bodied gelding: third foal: dam 1½m winner: fair performer: trained by D. Hanley in Ireland only start at 2 yrs: won maiden at Lingfield in November: should stay 7f: acts on polytrack, yet to race on extremes of going on turf. *N. A. Graham* **69**

SIR ALBERT 2 b.c. (Feb 23) Royal Applause 124 – Mary Cornwallis 87 (Primo Dominie 121) [2002 5g* 6g³ 5m³ 5g* 5m 6f 5m⁶ Oct 12] 30,000F, 48,000Y: sturdy, lengthy colt: first foal: dam 5f winner out of useful sprinter Infanta Real: useful performer: won maiden at Hamilton in May and listed race at York (beat Cumbrian Venture a length) in August: well held in good company last 3 starts: will prove best at bare 5f: raced only on good ground or firmer: joined I. Allan in Hong Kong. *J. Noseda* **106**

SIR ALFRED 3 b.g. Royal Academy (USA) 130 – Magnificent Star (USA) 122 (Silver Hawk (USA) 123) [2002 67: 10f* 10m 11.6m 10.1s 12f 10.1g Aug 15] fair handicapper: won at Brighton in April: respectable efforts at best after: should stay 1½m: acts on firm ground: edgy sort: tends to hang/flash tail: needs treating with some caution. *B. R. Millman* **77**

SIR BRASTIAS 3 b.g. Shaamit (IRE) 127 – Premier Night 102 (Old Vic 136) [2002 64: 8.1f⁶ 8m³ 8g⁴ 11s² 12m⁴ 11.5g* 15g⁶ 11.8g Oct 14] angular gelding: fairly useful performer: won 4-runner maiden at Yarmouth in July, wandering/flashing tail: bred to be suited by at least 1¾m: acts on soft and good to firm going. *S. Dow* **88**

SIR DESMOND 4 gr.g. Petong 126 – I'm Your Lady 77 (Risk Me (FR) 127) [2002 86: 5g 5g 5d 5g 5.7m 5m 5d³ 5g⁴ 5m⁴ 5d² 5d 5m 6d* 5g* 5v f6f⁵ f6g² Dec 16] workmanlike gelding: fairly useful handicapper: won at Windsor (2, both in large fields) in October and Wolverhampton (all-weather debut) in November: effective at 5f/6f: acts on any going: blinkered (ran poorly) eleventh start: has worn cheekpieces: tends to edge left: usually waited with. *R. Guest* **88**

SIR DON (IRE) 3 b.g. Lake Coniston (IRE) 131 – New Sensitive (Wattlefield 117) [2002 78+: 6m⁵ 6f 8m 6m⁴ Aug 28] sparely-made gelding: fair maiden: below best in 2002, leaving J. Eustace after third start: stays 6f: raced only on good going or firmer. *D. Nicholls* **65**

SIR ECHO (FR) 6 b.g. Saumarez 132 – Echoes (FR) 112 (Niniski (USA) 125) [2002 14.1m 11.6d² 13.4m 14.4s² 14.1m⁵ 14.6s f14.8g Nov 15] big gelding: fairly useful performer, lightly raced: stays 1¾m: acts on soft going, probably on good to firm. *M. R. Bosley* **84**

SIR EDWIN LANDSEER (USA) 2 gr.c. (Mar 7) Lit de Justice (USA) 125 – Wildcat Blue (USA) (Cure The Blues (USA)) [2002 5g² 5.2d* 6g 5m* 5.2f³ 5g² 5g⁵ 6f* Sep **102**

8] $37,000F, IR 40,000Y: rather unfurnished, good-quartered colt: third foal: half-brother to a winner in USA by Rhythm: dam unraced half-sister to smart US Grade 3 8.5f winner Nasty Storm: useful performer: won maiden at Newbury in May, minor event at Doncaster in June and listed event at Kempton (beat Hurricane Alan by short head) in September: third to Presto Vento in sales race at Newbury and second (beaten 2 lengths) to Wunders Dream in Molecomb Stakes at Goodwood: effective at 5f/6f: acts on firm and good to soft ground: consistent. *P. F. I. Cole*

SIR EFFENDI (IRE)   6 ch.g. Nashwan (USA) 135 – Jeema 102 (Thatch (USA) 136)   **98**
[2002 89: 7.5m³ 7f* 7f 7g⁴ 12m 7f Oct 3] tall, good-topped gelding: useful performer, lightly raced: won handicap at Thirsk in May: good fourth in similar event at Newcastle: stays 1m (acted as pacemaker for Nayef over 1½m): best efforts on good going or firmer. *M. P. Tregoning*

SIR FRANCIS (IRE)   4 b.g. Common Grounds 118 – Red Note (Rusticaro (FR) 124)   **88**
[2002 81: p7g* p7g* p7g⁴ f7g⁵ p7g⁶ Nov 27] useful-looking gelding: has a round action: fairly useful performer: made all in 2 handicaps at Lingfield in February: off 8 months before running creditably final start: stays easy 7f: acts on polytrack and soft ground: visored (tailed off) once at 2 yrs: has wandered. *J. Noseda*

SIR GEORGE TURNER   3 ch.g. Nashwan (USA) 135 – Ingozi 91 (Warning 136)   **110**
[2002 100p: 10.3f² 10.4f 12m⁴ 12d⁶ 10g³ 9.9m² Sep 14] big, close-coupled gelding: smart performer: creditable efforts in 2002 when in frame in listed Dee Stakes at Chester (short-headed by Sohaib), Deutschlandpreis at Dusseldorf (4¾ lengths fourth to Marienbard), Furstenberg-Rennen at Baden-Baden (made ground when 1¼ lengths third to Willingly) and Select Stakes at Goodwood (2½ lengths second to Moon Ballad), went in snatches but finished strongly): ran poorly when favourite for Dante Stakes at York (blinkered) second outing: stays 1½m: acts on firm and good to soft going: has run well in tongue tie/cheekpieces: seemed ill at ease on course at Chester (also swished tail during preliminaries) and Goodwood: gelded after final outing. *M. Johnston*

SIR HAYDN   2 ch.c. (Apr 8) Definite Article 121 – Snowscape (Niniski (USA) 125)   **85 p**
[2002 8f⁶ 8d* Oct 18] 5,200Y, resold 10,000Y: big, leggy colt: second foal: dam ran 3 times in Ireland: 33/1, much better effort in maidens (fairly useful form) when winning at Redcar by 1¾ lengths from Double Mystery, still green and edging right before getting on top final 1f: will stay 1¼m: should improve further. *N. P. Littmoden*

SIRIUS LADY   2 b.f. (Apr 18) Sir Harry Lewis (USA) 127 – Intrepida (Fair Season 120) [2002 p7g 8.3d Oct 28] second known foal: dam, won over hurdles, well beaten on Flat: well held in maidens. *I. A. Balding*   **–**

SIR LAUGHALOT   2 b.c. (Mar 1) Alzao (USA) 117 – Funny Hilarious (USA) 76 (Sir Ivor 135) [2002 6m p7g Oct 16] modest maiden: dam, maiden who stayed 1½m, out of sister to Irish 2000 Guineas winner Northern Treasure: well held in maidens. *J. M. P. Eustace*   **–**

SIR NIGHT (IRE)   2 b.c. (Apr 28) Night Shift (USA) – Highly Respected (IRE) 57 (High Estate 127) [2002 5d⁴ 5m 6g 6.1g 7m⁴ 7m 8m³ 8d⁶ f8.5g⁴ f7g⁵ Dec 17] 12,000F, 13,000 2-y-o: quite good-topped colt: second foal: half-brother to a winner abroad by Entrepreneur: dam, maiden, closely related to smart Irish 1¼m performer Make No Mistake: modest maiden: stays 1m: acts on fibresand, unraced on extremes of going on turf: effective visored or not: difficult ride. *J. D. Bethell*   **61**

SIR NINJA (IRE)   5 b.g. Turtle Island (IRE) 123 – The Poachers Lady (IRE) (Salmon Leap (USA) 131) [2002 91: 7g 10s³ 12v p12g p10g Dec 3] heavy-bodied gelding: carries plenty of condition: fairly useful handicapper: stays 1¼m: has form on good to firm going, best on softer than good and acts on polytrack: visored once in 2000: difficult ride: none too consistent. *S. Kirk*   **89**

SIR NORTHERNDANCER (IRE)   3 b.c. Danehill Dancer (IRE) 117 – Lady At War (Warning 136) [2002 82: 6m 6m 6d⁵ 6s³ 6s² 6m⁴ 6m 6m² 7m 6f f7s* f7g² f7g³ Dec 14] workmanlike colt: fairly useful performer: won handicap at Wolverhampton in November on first start after leaving R. Hannon: stays 7f: acts on good to firm going, heavy and all-weather: sometimes blinkered: has worn cheekpieces: usually races up with pace. *B. Ellison*   **83**

SIR SANDROVITCH (IRE)   6 b.g. Polish Patriot (USA) 128 – Old Downie (Be My Guest (USA) 126) [2002 83, a75: 5s 5f⁴ f5g⁵ 5g 5f 5m 5.1f* 5m⁵ 5m 5g⁵ 5.7f⁵ 5m⁶ 5m 5.1f 5f⁶ 5f Oct 11] tall gelding: fairly useful handicapper: won at Chester in June: best at 5f: acts on firm going, good to soft and fibresand: blinkered (ran to form) eleventh start: sometimes early to post/slowly away: tends to pull hard, and best covered up: none too consistent. *R. A. Fahey*   **80 a76**

SIR SIDNEY 2 b.g. (Feb 3) Shareef Dancer (USA) 135 – Hattaafeh (IRE) 79 (Mtoto **90** 134) [2002 8m 8g⁶ 8v³ Nov 8] 26,000Y: smallish, lengthy gelding: second foal: dam, 13f and 2m winner: best effort in maidens (fairly useful form) when third of 23 to Shelini at Doncaster: will be suited by 1½m+: acts on heavy ground. *D. Morris*

SIR TALBOT 8 b.g. Ardross 134 – Bermuda Lily 78 (Dunbeath (USA) 127) [2002 **–** 11.8s Oct 28] close-coupled gelding: smart hurdler at best: lightly raced on Flat nowadays. *J. A. B. Old*

SISAL (IRE) 3 b.f. Danehill (USA) 126 – Ship's Twine (IRE) 55 (Slip Anchor 136) **83** [2002 84: 7g 6.1d⁶ 6m³ 5m 6m² 6f f6g Nov 18] leggy, close-coupled filly: fairly useful performer: raced mainly around 6f: acted on firm going, good to soft and fibresand: visits Halling. *M. A. Jarvis*

SISTER BLUEBIRD 2 b.f. (Mar 3) Bluebird (USA) 125 – Pain Perdu (IRE) (Waajib **94** 121) [2002 5m 5.3g² 5m 7d* 7.1m* 7m⁶ 8m 6.5g 7s⁶ Oct 26] 35,000F, 44,000Y: close-coupled filly: first foal: dam, 1¼m winner in France, and half-sister to smart French miler Fine Fellow: fairly useful performer: won nursery at Salisbury (wandered) and listed event at Sandown (beat Ribbons And Bows by short head despite pulling hard and edging right) in July: allowed to dictate when good sixth to Geminiani in Prestige Stakes at Goodwood: well held after: should stay 1m: acts on good to firm and good to soft going: usually handicapped: races prominently. *B. J. Meehan*

SISTER IN LAW (FR) 3 b.f. Distant Relative 128 – Despina (Waajib 121) [2002 **95** 76p: 6f² 5d* 5d⁵ 5.1s* 5g 5.2m² 5.2f⁴ 5.6m⁵ Sep 11] tall, quite good-topped filly: useful handicapper: won at Windsor in May and Chepstow (impressive when beating Tappit 3 lengths) in June: good efforts last 3 starts, close fifth in Portland at Doncaster final one: stays 5.6f: acts on soft and good to firm going: races prominently. *H. Candy*

SISTER SOPHIA (USA) 2 b. or br.f. (Feb 24) Deputy Commander (USA) 124 – **79 p** Sophia's Choice (USA) (Clev Er Tell (USA)) [2002 p6g² Nov 19] $65,000F, $30,000Y: half-sister to several winners in USA: dam won around 6f in USA, including minor stakes at 2 yrs: 10/1, 1¼ lengths second of 12 to Leitrim Lakes in maiden at Lingfield, held up after slow start and running on well: sure to improve. *G. Wragg*

SIT AND SETTLE (IRE) 2 b.f. (May 9) Lake Coniston (IRE) 131 – Kunuz (Ela- **–** Mana-Mou 132) [2002 p5g f6g⁶ Jun 7] closely related to fairly useful 5f winner (including at 2 yrs) Kunucu and fairly useful Irish 7f and 9f winner Blue Kestrel (both by Bluebird) and half-sister to several winners: dam ran twice: well held in maiden/seller. *A. Berry*

SIT AND SUFFER (IRE) 2 b.f. (May 9) Entrepreneur 123 – Rozalina Lady (Alzao **52** (USA) 117) [2002 6v² 6m 5.9g³ 6.1g 5g Aug 15] 6,000Y: small filly: second foal: half-sister to Irish 11f winner Avoir du Cran (by Bigstone): dam lightly-raced maiden: modest maiden: best effort at Hamilton on debut: free-going sort, likely to prove best at 5f/6f: acts on heavy ground: blinkered last 2 starts, unseating rider on first occasion: sold €2,000. *A. Berry*

SITTIN BULL 3 b.c. Revoque (IRE) 122 – Taiga 69 (Northfields (USA)) [2002 –: **–** 8.3s Aug 20] no form in 4 starts. *M. Johnston*

SIX FOR LUCK 10 b.g. Handsome Sailor 125 – Fire Sprite 83 (Mummy's Game 120) **– §** [2002 5g 6v Jun 12] temperamental and no longer of any account. *D. A. Nolan*

SIXHILLS (FR) 3 b.f. Sabrehill (USA) 120 – Moidart 90 (Electric 126) [2002 10f⁵ **85** 12.1m⁴ 11.1s² 14.4s* 15.9f⁵ 17.5g⁶ 14.6s Oct 25] good-bodied filly: fourth foal: half-sister to 9f (at 2 yrs) to 2m winner Eilean Shona (by Suave Dancer) and 1¾m winner Mosca (by Most Welcome): dam 11f and 2m winner: fairly useful performer: won minor event at Kempton in June: stays 17.5f: acts on soft going: found little final start: sold 15,000 gns. *J. R. Fanshawe*

SIX LOVE (IRE) 3 ch.f. General Monash (USA) 107 – Show Home 90 (Music Boy **55 ?** 124) [2002 f6g⁵ f7g³ f6g⁵ f5g 6.1d⁵ 6.1m³ 6m 6m 6.1m Sep 20] IR 7,000F, IR 25,000Y: sturdy filly: half-sister to 3 winners, including fairly useful 7f winner (including at 2 yrs) Scottish Castle (by Scottish Reel): dam 2-y-o 5f winner: modest maiden: seemingly best effort on fifth outing: unlikely to stay beyond 7f: acts on fibresand and good to soft going, probably on good to firm: tried blinkered: sold 700 gns. *J. A. Osborne*

SIX PACK (IRE) 4 ch.g. Royal Abjar (USA) 121 – Regal Entrance (Be My Guest **60 d** (USA) 126) [2002 56: 8f* 8m³ 8f 8d 6.9d 8.1v 12f f12g⁶ Oct 22] tall, good-topped gelding: modest handicapper: won at Thirsk in April: on downgrade after next start: stays 1m: acts on firm and soft ground: tried blinkered: sometimes slowly away. *Andrew Turnell*

SIX PERFECTIONS (FR)   2 b.f. (Feb 24) Celtic Swing 138 – Yogya (USA)   **120 p**
(Riverman (USA) 131) [2002 5.5g² 7s* 7g* 8g* Oct 6]

What exactly constitutes good breeding is open to interpretation, but it's a safe bet that no-one trying to identify in advance the two-year-old fillies most likely to succeed based on pedigree would have put Six Perfections on the short-list. Although the first foal of an unraced half-sister to brilliant miler Miesque, she is by Celtic Swing, the champion juvenile of 1994, when he ran away with the Racing Post Trophy, and then runner-up in the Two Thousand Guineas before landing the Prix du Jockey Club at three. Fully effective at a mile and a half and by an unfashionable sire in Damister, as well as having indifferent forelegs, Celtic Swing did not look an especially good commercial proposition as a sire and, after standing at the National Stud at £6,500, he was moved first to France then to Ireland, where his 2002 fee at the Irish National Stud was €9,000. Celtic Swing's first three crops aged three and up had not produced a pattern winner, the best of the bunch being Celtic Silence, runner-up in the Dante Stakes. Compare this pedigree with, say, that of Intercontinental, a sister by Danehill to Banks Hill and Dansili, or Camlet, a half-sister by Green Desert to Barathea and Gossamer, or Loving Kindness, by Seattle Slew out of a dual Group 1-winning sister to Machiavellian, and the pedigree of Six Perfections is clearly found wanting. On the racecourse, though, it proved a different matter. Intercontinental, Camlet and Loving Kindness have all shown plenty of ability in pattern company, but they are some way behind Six Perfections, who holds outstanding classic prospects after proving herself the best of her age and sex in Europe by some way with three smooth successes culminating in the Prix Marcel Boussac at Longchamp.

Six Perfections started at 5/4-on for the Marcel Boussac or, to give the race its full title, one of the longest for any Group 1 or Grade 1 event in the world's leading racing countries, the Prix Marcel Boussac Criterium des Pouliches - Royal Barriere de Deauville. After running second to Trevise in a newcomers race over an inadequate five and a half furlongs at Chantilly in June, she left her six rivals for dead in the listed Prix Roland de Chambure at Deauville the following month, showing fine acceleration to beat Nellie Nolan by an official six lengths that looked at least a length further. This was the best performance by a two-year-old of either sex up to that time—those behind included Il Barone, who dead-heated in a listed race at Vichy next time, and Mail The Desert—and Six Perfections started at odds on for the eight-runner Prix du Calvados at Deauville later in August. The result was the same, Six Perfections travelling strongly held up and producing a devastating turn of foot approaching the final furlong to beat Londonnetdotcom by four lengths. Six of the nine other runners in the Marcel Boussac were trained outside France, including Irish Group 3 scorer Rainbows For All and Luminata and Pearl Dance, second and third to Mail The Desert in the Moyglare Stud Stakes. The French-trained Loving Pride had a pattern win to her name, in the Prix d'Aumale, but it was Etoile Montante, a stylish winner of both her starts in lesser company, who started second favourite and gave Six Perfections most to do. Confidently ridden, the favourite eased alongside Etoile Montante on the home turn and did not have to be hard ridden after leading a furlong out to defeat that rival by two lengths, the pair drawing clear of Luminata, five lengths adrift in third. Luminata and the others are far from outstanding but the form has a particularly solid look to it and

the way the first two outclassed their rivals was impressive. The winner's performance was the best by a French-trained two-year-old filly since Ravinella in 1987.

Six Perfections (FR) (b.f. Feb 24, 2000)	Celtic Swing (br 1992)	Damister (b 1982)	Mr Prospector / Batucada
		Celtic Ring (b 1984)	Welsh Pageant / Pencuik Jewel
	Yogya (USA) (ch 1993)	Riverman (b 1969)	Never Bend / River Lady
		Pasadoble (b 1979)	Prove Out / Santa Quilla

Six Perfections was immediately promoted to 4/1 clear favourite with the
major firms for the One Thousand Guineas after the Marcel Boussac. Granted
normal progress, she would indeed be hard to beat at Newmarket but those backing
her are taking something of a chance on her even running. Trainer Pascal Bary does
not make a habit of sending horses to Britain—he has had only three runners in the
last four seasons, namely Dream Well (third in the 1999 Coronation Cup), Croco
Rouge (down the field when favourite for the 1999 Eclipse) and Bluemamba
(third in the 2000 Coronation Stakes)—but he has not yet ruled Six Perfections out
of the Guineas. If Celtic Swing is the guide, Six Perfections ought to get a mile and
a quarter, and with the dam Yogya being by Riverman there is some encouragement
there as well. However, Yogya's half-sister Miesque, whom Six Perfections resem-
bles in her style of racing, appeared less effective over that trip than at shorter
distances, finishing four lengths second to Indian Skimmer in the Prix de Diane. At
around a mile she won ten Group or Grade 1 races, including the Marcel Boussac
and the Breeders' Cup Mile twice, and she has done well at stud too, foaling

Niarchos Family's "Six Perfections"

Group 1 scorers Kingmambo and East of The Moon. The next dam Pasadoble was bred to stay middle distances but did her winning at a mile, showing smart form, and produced three other winners by Miesque's sire Nureyev, notably Massaraat, successful in a listed event over seven furlongs and later grandam of the 2001 Cherry Hinton winner Silent Honor. Six Perfections, a close-coupled filly, has raced only on good or soft going. *P. Bary, France*

SIX STAR 2 b.f. (Mar 25) Desert Story (IRE) 115 – Adriya 94 (Vayrann 133) [2002 6s 5m 7s 6.1s Oct 23] 6,800Y: eighth foal: half-sister to 3 winners, including 7f (at 2 yrs) to 11f winner Double Gold (by Statoblest): dam 7f and 1½m winner: modest maiden: seems to stay 7f. *B. W. Duke* **58**

SIZZLING KATIE 2 b.f. (Apr 21) Komaite (USA) – Sizzling Romp 59 (Sizzling Melody 117) [2002 5g May 21] 2,300F, 8,000Y: small, good-bodied filly: second living foal: dam, sprint maiden, half-sister to useful sprinter Jennelle: 25/1, well beaten in seller at Beverley. *M. W. Easterby* **–**

SKARA BRAE 2 b.f. (Feb 14) Inchinor 119 – Tahilla 112 (Moorestyle 137) [2002 6.1g 6d 5.7m⁶ 7.1m Aug 26] 3,000Y: half-sister to several winners, including fairly useful 6f (including at 2 yrs) winner Pluck (by Never So Bold) and a 10.5f winner in Spain by Bishop of Cashel: dam, best at 1m, half-sister to very smart sprinter Piccolo: poor maiden: best effort at 5.7f. *G. G. Margarson* **49**

SKEHANA (IRE) 2 b.f. (Mar 17) Mukaddamah (USA) 125 – Lominda (IRE) 80 (Lomond (USA) 128) [2002 7m² 8.3d³ 7g* 8s Oct 15] 5,000 2-y-o: leggy, lengthy, unfurnished filly: fifth foal: half-sister to 3-y-o Fayr Jag: dam 2-y-o 6f winner: fair performer: won maiden at Thirsk in September: soundly beaten in nursery at Ayr final start: will prove best up to 1m: acts on good to firm and good to soft ground. *J. Nicol* **69**

SKELLIGS ROCK (IRE) 2 b.c. (Apr 24) Key of Luck (USA) 126 – Drew (IRE) (Double Schwartz 128) [2002 7m⁴ 8.1m⁴ Sep 18] IR 9,000Y: third foal: dam unraced out of half-sister to disqualified Irish Oaks winner Sorbus: better effort in maidens (fair form) when fourth of 6 to Orange Touch at Sandown second start: should be suited by 1¼m+. *B. W. Duke* **70**

SKENFRITH 3 b.g. Atraf 116 – Hobbs Choice 51 (Superpower 113) [2002 59: 6g 7m May 2] close-coupled gelding: modest maiden at 2 yrs: well beaten in sellers in 2002: often blinkered. *A. Berry* **–**

SKIBEREEN (IRE) 2 b.c. (Jan 28) Ashkalani (IRE) 128 – Your Village (IRE) 64 (Be My Guest (USA) 126) [2002 8d Oct 30] IR 70,000Y: third foal: half-brother to useful Irish maiden (disqualified 9f winner) Yara (by Sri Pekan): dam, Irish middle-distance maiden, half-sister to 1986 Middle Park winner Mister Majestic and Grand Prix de Paris winner Homme de Loi: weak 14/1-shot, 5 lengths seventh of 13 to Devant in maiden at Yarmouth, but very slowly away but travelling strongly and not knocked about having made good headway over 1f out: sure to improve. *J. H. M. Gosden* **80 p**

SKIDDAW JONES 2 b.g. (Apr 11) Emperor Jones (USA) 119 – Woodrising 64 (Nomination 125) [2002 6m 7.2s 7.1s Nov 6] 4,000Y: good-topped gelding: second foal: dam, 1¼m winner, also successful over hurdles: signs of just a little ability in maidens. *Miss L. A. Perratt* **–**

SKIES ARE BLUE 3 b.f. Unfuwain (USA) 131 – Blue Birds Fly 78 (Rainbow Quest (USA) 134) [2002 70p: 10g Apr 19] tall, good-topped filly: good mover: fair form in maidens at Kempton (very slowly away) and Sandown (not knocked about) at 2 yrs: not discredited, though reportedly lost action, only outing in 2002. *I. A. Balding* **65**

SKI FOR ME (IRE) 3 ch.f. Barathea (IRE) 127 – Ski For Gold 76 (Shirley Heights 130) [2002 78p: 11.8m⁴ 11.6d³ 12s⁴ 14.4d⁶ 14v⁵ 11.7g 11.6d Oct 28] angular filly: fairly useful performer: below form last 4 starts: stays 1½m: acts on heavy and good to firm going: has raced freely. *J. L. Dunlop* **88**

SKI JUMP (USA) 2 gr.c. (Feb 17) El Prado (IRE) 119 – Skiable (IRE) (Niniski (USA) 125) [2002 8d⁴ 7.6m 8g³ Oct 16] fourth foal: half-brother to 3 winners, including 3-y-o Lahberhorn and 4-y-o Back Pass: dam, French/US winner up to 9f, half-sister to dam of Dansili and Banks Hill: fair maiden: disappointing after promising debut: should be suited by 1¼m+: twice slowly away. *R. Charlton* **77**

SKIN AND HAIR (IRE) 4 b.f. Mujadil (USA) 119 – Model Show (IRE) 82 (Dominion 123) [2002 –: p6g Feb 2] second foal: sister to 5-y-o Moonlight Song: dam Irish 7f winner: no form in Irish maidens at 3 yrs and minor event at Lingfield on British debut. *Noel T. Chance* **–**

SKINFLINT 3 b.f. Emperor Fountain 112 – Bad Payer 72 (Tanfirion 110) [2002 40: **40**
7.9g 8g 7m 5s³ 7m Sep 23] unfurnished filly: poor maiden: probably stayed 1m: dead.
C. W. Thornton

SKIPPY MAC 3 ch.c. Presidium 124 – Ski Path (Celtic Cone 116) [2002 46: 10m Aug –
31] leggy colt: poor maiden. *N. Bycroft*

SKIRT AROUND 4 b.f. Deploy 131 – Fairy Feet 78 (Sadler's Wells (USA) 132) **69**
[2002 p12g 12s 14.4m 13g f12g 12d Nov 1] 13,000Y: tall, leggy ex-French filly: tenth **a–**
foal: half-sister to several winners, including useful 1½m/1¾m winner Aginor (by Slip
Anchor) and fairly useful 1½m winner Indimaaj (by Mtoto): dam, second at 11f only
start, half-sister to 1000 Guineas winner Fairy Footsteps and St Leger winner Light
Cavalry: fair performer: won minor event at Tours in 2001 for Mme C. Head-Maarek:
best effort in Britain on fourth outing: probably stays 13f: acts on soft ground (well held
on all-weather). *W. J. Musson*

SKOOZI (NZ) 7 b.g. Prince of Praise (NZ) – Tweed View (NZ) (Imposing (AUS)) **117 d**
[2002 117: a8f* a9f⁶ a8f² 8.5d⁶ 8s⁵ Jun 29] tall, rather leggy, New Zealand-bred gelding:
smart performer: former Group 2 winner in Australia (also placed in Group 1 company
there) where raced as Skoozi Please: won Sheikh Maktoum Bin Rashid Al Maktoum
Challenge (Round I) at Nad Al Sheba in January by nose from China Visit: best effort
afterwards when 3½ lengths second to Grey Memo in Godolphin Mile there in March:
seemed ill at ease on track in Diomed Stakes at Epsom penultimate start: effective at 7f to
1¼m: acts on firm and soft ground, and on dirt. *Paul Smith, Belgium*

SKY DOME (IRE) 9 ch.g. Bluebird (USA) 125 – God Speed Her (Pas de Seul 133) **74**
[2002 71: 7g 7g³ 8m 9s³ 7m 8.5d² 7.5m 8.5d 8.5g⁴ 9g³ 9s² f8g* p8g⁶ Dec 3] lengthy,
leggy gelding: poor mover: fair handicapper: won at Southwell in November: effective at
7f to 9f: acts on soft going, good to firm and all-weather: effective blinkered/visored or
not: sometimes carries head awkwardly/finds little. *M. H. Tompkins*

SKYE BLUE (IRE) 5 b.g. Blues Traveller (IRE) 119 – Hitopah (Bustino 136) [2002 **– §**
62§: 18d Jul 6] tall gelding: modest maiden handicapper at 4 yrs: well held only 5-y-o
outing: untrustworthy. *B. J. Llewellyn*

SKYERS A KITE 7 b.m. Deploy 131 – Milady Jade (IRE) (Drumalis 125) [2002 –: –
f12g 10m 10m 11.8d 11.9s⁵ Jun 6] small, good-topped mare: little form in 2002. *Ronald
Thompson*

SKYLARK 5 ch.m. Polar Falcon (USA) 126 – Boozy 111 (Absalom 128) [2002 73: **77**
6m³ 6m⁶ 5g⁶ 7.1m³ 7m* 7g⁴ 7m 7m 7f Sep 17] leggy mare: fair handicapper: won at
Yarmouth in July: below best last 3 starts: stays easy 7f: acts on firm and good to soft
going: often slowly away/looks hard ride: sold 1,800 gns. *J. L. Spearing*

SKYLARKER (USA) 4 b.g. Sky Classic (CAN) – O My Darling (USA) 76 (Mr **92**
Prospector (USA)) [2002 98: 10m 10.4f⁶ 10m⁵ 10d⁴ 10m⁵ 9m⁶ 10m³ Sep 23] tall, rather
leggy gelding: fairly useful performer: likely to prove best at 1¼m/1½m: acts on good to
firm and good to soft going: has been early to post: raced freely third outing/found little
final one: sold 14,000 gns, joined W. S. Kittow. *C. F. Wall*

SKYMAITE 2 b.f. (Feb 15) Komaite (USA) – Sky Fighter 43 (Hard Fought 125) **63**
[2002 5.9s⁴ 5m⁶ 5g 6d 7g Oct 19] 1,000Y: fifth foal: sister to 1996 2-y-o 7f winner
Komasta and 7f (at 2 yrs)/1m winner Sandmoor Tartan: dam maiden who stayed 1½m:
modest maiden: best effort on debut: should stay 7f: well beaten in blinkers: refused to
enter stall intended debut: temperamental. *Mrs G. S. Rees*

SKY QUEST (IRE) 4 b.g. Spectrum (IRE) 126 – Rose Vibert (Caerleon (USA) 132) **77**
[2002 8.1d² 8.1d⁵ 8m 8.3g³ 11.5f* 12s 11.9g 11.9m⁴ 11.5m⁵ Sep 17] smallish, quite good-
topped gelding: fair handicapper: won at Yarmouth in July: better at 11.5f than 1m: acts
on firm and good to soft going (ran badly only outing on soft): tongue tied last 2 starts.
P. W. Harris

SLAP SHOT (IRE) 3 ch.f. Lycius (USA) 124 – Katanning (Green Desert (USA) 127) **115**
[2002 99: 6g² 5g* 5g³ 6m² 5s² 5g² 5m Dec 15] first foal: dam Italian maiden out of
Coronation Stakes third Katakana: smart performer: won 3 times at Rome at 2 yrs, including 2 listed races in autumn, and minor event there in April: placed afterwards in Prix de
Saint-Georges at Longchamp (very close third to Maybe Forever), Premio Piero e Ugo
Tudini at Rome, valuable minor event at Milan (beaten by Oh Bej Oh Bej both times) and
Prix de l'Abbaye at Longchamp (73/1, career-best effort when beaten nose by Continent
after making virtually all): behind in Hong Kong Sprint at Sha Tin final outing: has won
at 6f but may prove best at 5f: acts on soft and good to firm ground. *L. Riccardi, Italy*

SLEETING 9 ch.g. Lycius (USA) 124 – Pluvial 90 (Habat 127) [2002 –: p16g Jan 23] –
well held in sellers. *J. Gallagher*

Premio Vittorio di Capua, Milan—on his only outing of the year, the grey Slickly wins the race for the second year running; he is chased home by the German-trained pair Horeion Directa (second right) and Scapolo (stars on cap) with Altieri (left) and Mister Cosmi (blinkered) coming next

SLICKLY (FR)   6 gr.h. Linamix (FR) 127 – Slipstream Queen (USA) (Conquistador **114** Cielo (USA)) [2002 128: 8s* Oct 13] tall horse: high-class performer at best: won 10 races during career, including Grand Prix de Paris at Longchamp in 1999, and Prix du Moulin de Longchamp and Premio Vittorio di Capua at Milan in 2001: tongue tied, won last-named race again on belated return by 1¼ lengths from Horeion Directa, making all and not needing to be anywhere near best: won up to 11f but tended to race freely and best at 1m later in career: acted on heavy and good to firm going: winner 5 times from 6 starts at Longchamp: tried to dominate: to stand at Haras du Logis, Normandy, France, fee €8,000, Oct 1st, special live foal. *Saeed bin Suroor*

SLIP KILLICK   5 b.m. Cosmonaut – Killick 69 (Slip Anchor 136) [2002 54d: f8.5g⁵ **– §** f11s Jan 10] tall, quite good-topped mare: untrustworthy maiden nowadays: tried visored/blinkered. *M. Mullineaux*

SLIPPER ROSE   4 ch.f. Democratic (USA) 101 – Brown Taw 66 (Whistlefield 118) **36** [2002 43: f7s⁴ f8s Jan 22] poor performer: stays 1m: acts on heavy going and fibresand: temperament under suspicion. *J. J. Quinn*

SLOE GIN   3 b.f. A P Indy (USA) 131 – Rose Bourbon (USA) (Woodman (USA) 126) **81** [2002 10g⁴ 9.9m³ 12.1v⁶ 10f⁵ 11.7d² 12f⁵ 12d Nov 1] lengthy, angular filly: second foal: dam, useful French maiden who should have stayed 1m, half-sister to Poule d'Essai des Pouliches winner Baiser Vole, very smart sprinter Tenue de Soiree and very smart 1m/1¼m performer Squill: fairly useful maiden: stays 1½m: acts on firm and good to soft going: folded tamely in blinkers final start. *J. L. Dunlop*

SLUMBERING (IRE)   6 b.g. Thatching 131 – Bedspread (USA) (Seattle Dancer **–** (USA) 119) [2002 87, a–: p6g 8s 6g 7.6g⁵ 7d May 23] tall gelding: fairly useful on turf at 5 yrs: well held in 2002: sometimes blinkered earlier in career. *B. A. Pearce*

SLUPIA (IRE)   3 b.f. Indian Ridge 123 – Ustka 60 (Lomond (USA) 128) [2002 76p: **–** 8.3m 7.1s⁵ Jun 6] leggy, quite attractive filly: fair form when third in maiden at Redcar only run at 2 yrs: favourite, little form in 2002 (raced freely/found little/reportedly lost action on reappearance): should stay at least 1m. *J. H. M. Gosden*

SLY BABY (IRE)   4 b.f. Dr Devious (IRE) 127 – For Example (USA) 66 (Northern **59** Baby (CAN) 127) [2002 9g⁴ 12m² 10.9m⁴ 10d Jul 23] IR 260,000Y: second foal: half-sister to 5-y-o Forbearing: dam, third at 1¼m in Ireland, closely related to dam of Culture Vulture and half-sister to dams of Zilzal and Polish Precedent: modest maiden: stays 1½m: acts on good to firm going: reportedly in foal. *P. F. I. Cole*

SMARTER CHARTER   9 br.g. Master Willie 129 – Irene's Charter 72 (Persian Bold **54** 123) [2002 53: 12s 14.1d 14m 11m 11.9g⁵ 13.1g⁵ 11.8m* 14d³ 10.9d³ 11.9d² 12d³ 12m⁶ 14m 12d⁵ 12.1g 14.1m⁵ 14.1m 14f Sep 28] leggy, lengthy gelding: modest handicapper: won apprentice event at Leicester in June: effective at 1¼m to 1¾m: acts on any going: sometimes slowly away: soon gets behind: ridden by Kristin Stubbs. *Mrs L. Stubbs*

SMART HOSTESS 3 b. or gr.f. Most Welcome 131 – She's Smart 88 (Absalom 128) [2002 54p: 7m³ 6s³ 5m* 6g² 6m Sep 19] heavy-bodied filly: fair performer: won maiden at Beverley in August: best at 5f/6f: acts on soft and good to firm going. *J. J. Quinn* **77**

SMART JOHN 2 b.c. (Apr 3) Bin Ajwaad (IRE) 119 – Katy-Q (IRE) 58 (Taufan (USA) 119) [2002 7.1m 8d 7v⁶ Nov 8] good-topped colt: third foal: half-brother to 3-y-o Mister Benji: dam 2-y-o 5f winner: fair form, not knocked about, in maidens: may prove best short of 1m: type to do better in handicaps. *J. G. Given* **65 p**

SMART MINISTER 2 gr.g. (Apr 21) Muhtarram (USA) 125 – She's Smart 88 (Absalom 128) [2002 7g 7v⁵ Nov 8] sixth foal: half-brother to 3 winners, notably 6-y-o Smart Predator: dam sprinter: backward, signs of ability in maidens: should do better. *J. J. Quinn* **– p**

SMART PREDATOR 6 gr.g. Polar Falcon (USA) 126 – She's Smart 88 (Absalom 128) [2002 115: 5.2g 5f 5d 5m 5f 6m⁶ 5.6m 5m⁴ 5g Oct 17] big, lengthy, good-quartered gelding: smart performer in 2001: only useful at best in 2002: has won at 1m, best at 5f nowadays: acts on any ground: visored penultimate start: finished lame on reappearance: usually races prominently: none too reliable nowadays. *J. J. Quinn* **102**

SMART SCOT 3 ch.g. Selkirk (USA) 129 – Amazing Bay 100 (Mazilier (USA) 107) [2002 55: 10f 10m 16.2d Jul 22] leggy, lengthy gelding: modest maiden at 2 yrs (reportedly injured a hind tendon final outing): no form in 2002: has shown signs of temperament. *J. G. Given*

SMASHING TIME (USA) 4 b.f. Smart Strike (CAN) 121 – Broken Peace (USA) (Devil's Bag (USA)) [2002 70, a58: f12s f12s f8s⁵ f8g f8g 10g 9.9m 10m 9.9g 7m⁶ 7f⁵ f8g Dec 4] good-topped filly: poor maiden: free-going sort, may prove best up to 1m: acts on good to firm going and fibresand: missed break/looked none too keen last 2 starts: has carried head awkwardly. *M. C. Chapman* **49**

SMILEAFACT 2 b.g. (May 10) So Factual (USA) 120 – Smilingatstrangers 58 (Macmillion 110) [2002 p7g 10s Oct 23] fourth foal: dam out-and-out stayer: last in maidens. *Mrs Barbara Waring* **–**

SMILING APPLAUSE 3 b.c. Royal Applause 124 – Smilingatstrangers 58 (Macmillion 110) [2002 –: 10f 16.2m Jul 7] leggy colt: no form. *Mrs Barbara Waring* **–**

SMIRFYS LINCLON 3 b.g. Never So Bold 135 – Party Scenes (Most Welcome 131) [2002 –: p6g Dec 18] tailed off in maidens. *W. M. Brisbourne* **–**

SMIRFYS NIGHT 3 b.c. Tina's Pet 121 – Nightmare Lady 29 (Celestial Storm (USA) 132) [2002 –: 5.1m⁵ 5.1f 6f⁴ 6d² 5g* 5m 5m 5g⁵ Aug 3] quite good-topped colt: fair performer: made all in maiden at Doncaster in June: may prove best at 5f: acts on firm and good to soft going. *B. A. McMahon* **79**

SMIRFYS PARTY 4 ch.g. Clantime 101 – Party Scenes (Most Welcome 131) [2002 80: 7.6f 7g² 8m 8.1m 7m Jul 13] rather leggy gelding: fair handicapper: probably stays 1m: acts on fibresand, firm and good to soft going. *B. A. McMahon* **79**

SMIRFYS SYSTEMS 3 b.g. Safawan 118 – Saint Systems 68 (Uncle Pokey 116) [2002 8g⁴ 7f* 7s 6d Nov 1] close-coupled, workmanlike gelding: half-brother to 1m winner Bless 'Im (by Presidium): dam sprinter: fair form: trained by B. McMahon only on debut (slowly away): won maiden at Catterick (edged left) in September: ran well in minor event at Newmarket final outing: may prove best at 6f/7f: acts on firm and good to soft going: folded tamely penultimate start. *W. M. Brisbourne* **79**

SMIRK 4 ch.c. Selkirk (USA) 129 – Elfin Laughter 76 (Alzao (USA) 117) [2002 110: 8d² 10s³ 8m 8m 8f² 8m* 9m⁵ 8s* Nov 2] tall, lengthy colt: smart performer: better than **117**

William Hill Mile (Handicap), Goodwood—Smirk wins the most valuable prize of his career, beating the unlucky Atlantic Ace (jockey's arm raised), with Surprise Encounter (rail) and Nashaab (checks) third and fourth

ever in 2002, winning William Hill Mile (Handicap) at Goodwood (by head from unlucky Atlantic Ace) in August and listed race at Newmarket (by 5 lengths from Samhari) in November: best effort otherwise when ½-length second to Calcutta in handicap at Newbury on fifth start: probably best at 1m/9f: acts on any going. *D. R. C. Elsworth*

SMITH N ALLAN OILS 3 b.g. Bahamian Bounty 116 – Grand Splendour 79 **70** (Shirley Heights 130) [2002 63: 10g 7f* 6g* 7m 7f 5.9g⁴ 7m 5g 7.1m⁴ 7m⁶ 6m³ 7g⁵ Oct 4] sparely-made gelding: fair performer: won maiden at Thirsk in April and handicap at Newcastle in May: stays 7f: yet to race on soft/heavy going, acts on any other: sometimes slowly away. *M. Dods*

SMITHY 3 ch.f. Greensmith 121 – Biscay 67 (Unfuwain (USA) 131) [2002 7g 6g 7m⁵ **56** 7g⁵ 7g 6m⁴ 5m 8m³ 8g f7g f6g³ f7g⁴ f6g f8.5s³ Dec 26] sturdy filly: second foal: dam, maiden, may have proved best short of 1m: modest maiden: left F. J. Houghton after fifth start: headstrong, but stays 1m: acts on fibresand, raced only on good/good to firm going on turf: inconsistent. *Mrs N. Macauley*

SMOKER'S FOLLY 3 b.f. Puissance 110 – Fair Attempt (IRE) (Try My Best (USA) **49** 130) [2002 48: 5d⁴ 6d 5g 5g⁶ 5m⁶ 8d⁵ 7d² 6.5s² 5s* 7.5s Nov 20] big, leggy filly: poor handicapper: sold from N. Tinkler 4,000 gns after fifth start: won at Munich in October: should prove best at 5f/6f: acts on soft and good to firm going: none too reliable. *W. Glanz, Germany*

SMOKEY FROM CAPLAW 8 b.g. Sizzling Melody 117 – Mary From Dunlow 49 **–** (Nicholas Bill 125) [2002 53: 8m May 15] strong, compact gelding: has a round action: modest handicapper at 7 yrs: tailed off only run in 2002: blinkered once. *J. S. Goldie*

SMOKIN BEAU 5 b.g. Cigar 68 – Beau Dada (IRE) 66 (Pine Circle (USA)) [2002 **116** 113: 5.1m* 5m² 6g* 5m⁶ 5g 6.1g² 5m 6m* 5.2f² 5f² 6s* Oct 25] smallish, robust gelding: smart performer: at least as good as ever in 2002 (left J. Cullinan after fifth outing), winning minor events at Nottingham in April and Goodwood in May, listed race at Goodwood (beat Royal Millennium by length) in September and handicap at Newbury

Starlit Rotary Stakes, Goodwood—the admirable Smokin Beau (right) responds generously to keep Royal Millennium at bay

(hung right final 1f, beat Abbajabba a length) in October: stays 6f: acts on fibresand and any turf going: visored twice at 3 yrs: has got upset in stall/started slowly/edged right: often forces pace: tough, game and consistent. *N. P. Littmoden*

SMOKING BARRELS 2 ch.c. (Jan 31) Desert Prince (IRE) 130 – Scandalette **78** (Niniski (USA) 125) [2002 8g p7g⁵ p8g³ Dec 3] IR 20,000Y: big, good-topped colt: fifth foal: closely related to 5-y-o Gateman and half-brother to 6-y-o Surprise Encounter and 7-y-o Night Flyer: dam unraced half-sister to high-class sprinter Polish Patriot: fair form in maidens: third at Lingfield: will probably stay 1¼m: acts on polytrack. *J. H. M. Gosden*

SMOOTHIE (IRE) 4 gr.g. Definite Article 121 – Limpopo 49 (Green Desert (USA) **77** 127) [2002 82: 10.3s 10.9g 10m 10g 11.6d 10g 10.1g⁵ 10m* 10m* 10g⁶ 12.6m⁶ 10f⁵ 10.4f Oct 10] close-coupled gelding: unimpressive mover: fair handicapper: won at Windsor in July and Newbury (ladies race) in August: below form after: stays 1¼m: possibly unsuited by heavy going, acts on any other. *P. F. I. Cole*

SMOOTH PASSAGE 3 b.g. Suave Dancer (USA) 136 – Flagship 84 (Rainbow Quest – (USA) 134) [2002 –: f12g⁵ f12f f16.2g p10g⁶ Dec 30] little form: sold from M. Tregoning and off 7 months after reappearance: blinkered last 2 starts. *J. Gallagher*

SMOOTH SAILING 7 gr.g. Beveled (USA) – Sea Farer Lake 74 (Gairloch 122) – [2002 83: p10g Jan 30] leggy gelding: fairly useful performer at best: stayed 1¼m: probably best on good ground or softer (well beaten all 3 all-weather outings): tried visored/blinkered at 2 yrs: had been slowly away/taken good hold/found little: was none too reliable: dead. *K. McAuliffe*

SNAILS CASTLE (IRE) 3 b.g. Danehill (USA) 126 – Bean Island (USA) (Afleet – (CAN)) [2002 75p: 10m 8m 11.5m 11.9s 14.1s 12.4g Aug 26] big, lengthy gelding: fair maiden at 2 yrs: well beaten in 2002, leaving N. Callaghan after fourth start. *E. W. Tuer*

SNAKE GODDESS 4 b.f. Primo Dominie 121 – Shoshone (Be My Chief (USA) 122) – [2002 54: f16s p12g f16g 11.9g 16f 14.1g 18d Jul 6] workmanlike filly: modest maiden at 3 yrs: no form in 2002: tried blinkered. *D. W. P. Arbuthnot*

SNAPPY 3 ch.f. First Trump 118 – Better Still (IRE) (Glenstal (USA) 118) [2002 57: **68** f8s⁶ f6g* f7g⁵ f8.5g Feb 18] rather leggy filly: fair performer: won handicap at Wolverhampton in January: stays 6f: acts on fibresand: pulled too hard last 2 starts (finished lame final one). *M. W. Easterby*

SNIP SNAP 3 b.f. Revoque (IRE) 122 – Snap Crackle Pop (IRE) 87 (Statoblest 120) – [2002 76: p6g Jan 30] fair performer at 2 yrs for Sir Mark Prescott: well held only outing in 2002. *L. Montague Hall*

SNIZORT (USA) 4 b.g. Bahri (USA) 125 – Ava Singstheblues (USA) (Dixieland **55** Band (USA)) [2002 –: 8g 12.1m⁵ 12m³ 16.2m 12.1m Aug 25] useful-looking gelding: good mover: modest maiden at best: probably stays 1½m: acts on good to firm going: tried blinkered. *M. E. Sowersby*

SNOW BUNTING 4 ch.g. Polar Falcon (USA) 126 – Marl 94 (Lycius (USA) 124) **69** [2002 57+: f6s p6g⁶ p7g p6g 6m 7f* 7g 7m⁴ 7g 7m 6m* 6g 6m* 6f⁶ Sep 27] leggy gelding: fair handicapper: won at Doncaster in June (apprentices), Newcastle in August and Redcar in September: effective at 6f/7f: acts on firm going and polytrack (well held on heavy/fibresand): suited by waiting tactics. *Jedd O'Keeffe*

SNOWDROP (IRE) 2 ch.f. (Mar 26) Petardia 113 – Richardstown Lass (IRE) **63** (Muscatite 122) [2002 6.1g 6g⁶ 5.7g² 5f 6m f6g Nov 18] 8,500 2-y-o: fifth living foal: sister to 2 winners, including 5-y-o Replacement Bay, and half-sister to 2 winners, including 4-y-o Music Maid: dam unraced: modest maiden: below form after second at Bath: will prove best at 5f/easy 6f: yet to race on ground softer than good. *J. W. Hills*

SNOWFIRE 3 b.f. Machiavellian (USA) 123 – Hill of Snow 80 (Reference Point **111** 139) [2002 102p: 7m 8m² 12s Jun 7]

Riders are more prone to overusing the whip when the run of the race turns against them, those habitually preferring to sit and wait longest in the pack being most at risk of breaking the guidelines as a result. When it comes to pace, the average British horserace is more foxtrot than salsa dancing, and the combination of a slow early pace and a sprint finish often makes for frenetic action late on for both horse and rider. That was certainly the scenario in the latest One Thousand Guineas at Newmarket. The early gallop was so steady that it saw most of the seventeen runners with plenty left once the race finally began in earnest. Being to the fore already, though riding for his life on the winner Kazzia, Frankie Dettori was able to use his whip in reasonably measured style from two furlongs out, keeping within the guidelines. From a position in mid-division at halfway, Pat Eddery on runner-up Snowfire found himself needing a greater response. He threw everything in, hitting his mount nearly twenty times, and going down by a neck after getting upsides inside the last furlong. The vet reportedly found Snowfire to be unmarked afterwards, but Eddery was banned for five days for excessive use of the whip. In Eddery's defence, Snowfire, it should be pointed out, is probably no easy ride. Starting at 28/1, she was fitted with blinkers for the first time in the Guineas, having disappointed when only seventh of ten in the Nell Gwyn Stakes on her reappearance on the same course, where she had started second favourite. She was blinkered again when a remote tenth in the Oaks and wasn't seen out afterwards. She was sent to Neil Drysdale in the States and may race on as a four-year-old.

		Mr Prospector	Raise A Native
	Machiavellian (USA)	(b 1970)	Gold Digger
	(b 1987)	Coup de Folie	Halo
Snowfire		(b 1982)	Raise The Standard
(b.f. 1999)		Reference Point	Mill Reef
	Hill of Snow	(b 1984)	Home On The Range
	(b 1992)	White Star Line	Northern Dancer
		(b 1975)	Fast Line

Snowfire should make a valuable broodmare when the time comes. Her dam Hill of Snow, who showed fairly useful form at a mile and a quarter and a mile and a half in Ireland, and was bred by Sheikh Mohammed, was sold for 160,000 guineas in 1995 and is out of the high-class White Star Line, winner of three Grade

Mr L. Neil Jones's "Snowfire"

1 races in the States, including the Kentucky Oaks. White Star Line is a half-sister to the dam of Northern Trick and has produced numerous winners. Hill of Snow's two foals prior to Snowfire were also winners. Preseli (by Caerleon) won the Moyglare Stud Stakes in 1999 and showed smart form when short-headed in the Pretty Polly Stakes over a mile and a quarter at the Curragh as a three-year-old. Preseli's sister Valley of Song ran only once, winning a maiden over a mile and a quarter at Goodwood for Dunlop as a three-year-old. Snowfire gained her only win so far in a maiden, too, winning at Lingfield over seven furlongs as a two-year-old, when she was also second to Protectress in a listed race over the same trip. On balance, Snowfire should probably stay a mile and a half. She has raced mainly on good ground or firmer. *J. L. Dunlop*

SNOW LARK 4 br.f. Weld 122 – Snow Child 84 (Mandrake Major 122) [2002 11.8g 10m 10.2g Apr 30] small filly: poor mover: fifth foal: half-sister to a winner in Jersey by Seymour Hicks: dam, 6f winner at 2 yrs, later won numerous times in Jersey: well beaten in maidens/seller. *W. G. M. Turner* **–**

SNOW LEOPARD (IRE) 3 gr.g. Highest Honor (FR) 124 – Leopardess (IRE) 79 (Ela-Mana-Mou 132) [2002 87: 9.9g^3 12d 12g 12v Nov 9] lengthy gelding: useful handicapper: good third at Salisbury on reappearance: reportedly sustained stress fracture to near-hind splint bone next outing: off 4½ months, well held last 2 starts: gelded after: should stay 1½m: best efforts on good ground. *J. L. Dunlop* **95**

SNOW SCOOTER 3 b.f. Bin Ajwaad (IRE) 119 – Solemn Occasion (USA) (Secreto (USA) 128) [2002 7m f6g Oct 21] seventh living foal: half-sister to 5f/6f winner Premium Princess (by Distant Relative) and 2m winner Swiftway (by Anshan): dam, ran twice at 2 yrs, half-sister to smart miler Enharmonic: well held in seller/maiden. *A. Berry* **–**

SNOW SHOES 3 b.f. Sri Pekan (USA) 117 – Tundra (IRE) (Common Grounds 118) [2002 77: 6g* Mar 30] small filly: fairly useful handicapper: won at Kempton on only run in 2002: should stay 7f: acts on soft going. *D. K. Ivory* **84**

SNOW'S RIDE 2 gr.c. (Mar 12) Hernando (FR) 127 – Crodelle (IRE) (Formidable (USA) 125) [2002 7.6m^3 8m Sep 24] 42,000Y: leggy, good-topped colt: sixth foal: half-brother to 3-y-o Shifty and smart 1¼m/1½m winner Ela Athena (by Ezzoud): dam French 9.5f winner: fair form in maidens, pulling hard second start: bred to be suited by further than 1m. *W. R. Muir* **71**

SNUGFIT DUBARRY 2 ch.f. (May 28) Ali-Royal (IRE) 127 – Spanish Serenade 76 (Nashwan (USA) 135) [2002 6m 7m* Jul 27] leggy filly: second foal: dam French 7.5f and 11f winner: better effort in maidens (fair form) when winning at Newcastle by neck from Skehana, staying on to lead 1f out: will stay at least 1m. *M. W. Easterby* **69**

SNUGGLES (IRE) 2 gr.f. (Mar 16) Bluebird (USA) 125 – Mrs Snuggs (IRE) 56 (Law Society (USA) 130) [2002 7m Sep 5] IR 30,000F, IR 50,000Y: fourth foal: half-sister to fairly useful Italian 7.5f to 1½m winner Solitary Dream (by Doubletour): dam Irish 12.5f winner: 33/1, tailed-off last of 16 in maiden at Salisbury: sold 12,000 gns. *B. W. Hills* **–**

SNUKI 3 b.c. Pivotal 124 – Kennedys Prima 65 (Primo Dominie 121) [2002 p7g^5 7m^3 7m^6 7.1g 8.3d^6 p7g^6 p10g* p8g* p10g^6 Dec 28] 10,500F, 13,000Y: fifth foal: dam, sprint maiden, half-sister to high-class sprinter Mr Brooks and to dam of smart performer up to 1m First Trump: fair performer, better on all-weather than turf: won handicaps at Lingfield in November and December: stays 1¼m: acts on polytrack, yet to race on extremes of going on turf. *G. L. Moore* **65 a75**

SOAKED 9 b.g. Dowsing (USA) 124 – Water Well 96 (Sadler's Wells (USA) 132) [2002 80: f6g^4 5g^3 5.1d f5g^3 5f 5g* 5.7d 5g^3 5m 5.7m 5m 5g 5f 6m^6 5d 5m 5m 5.3m* f6s^4 5d f5g f5g^5 Dec 31] workmanlike gelding: fair performer: won handicap at Ripon in June and minor event at Brighton in September: best around 5f: acts on fibresand, firm and soft ground: visored once, blinkered nowadays: has been early/led to post: refused to race once at 7 yrs: has reportedly bled from nose: front runner: unreliable nowadays. *D. W. Chapman* **78 §**

SOBA JONES 5 b.g. Emperor Jones (USA) 119 – Soba 127 (Most Secret 119) [2002 77: 5g 5f 6v* 6s* 6g 5.9v 6g 5m 5g 6f^3 5d Oct 21] fairly useful performer: won minor event (amateurs) and handicap at Hamilton in June: best at 5f/6f: acts on fibresand and any turf going: effective blinkered or not: has been slowly away: sold 9,500 gns. *T. D. Easterby* **81**

SOBARING (IRE) 2 ch.f. (Feb 19) General Monash (USA) 107 – Brazilian Princess 66 (Absalom 128) [2002 5s^3 5g^2 5m^3 5d^3 5g^2 5d^3 5m 5m^3 Sep 16] IR 8,500F, IR 8,000Y: **68**

quite good-topped filly: half-sister to several winners, including 1997 2-y-o 6f winner Lisa's Pride (by Pips Pride) and 5f (including at 2 yrs)/6f winner Soba Guest (by Be My Guest): dam, maiden who stayed 1m, half-sister to high-class sprinter Soba: fair maiden: placed 7 of 8 starts: will stay 6f: best efforts on good ground or softer: sold 3,000 gns, sent to Sweden. *T. D. Easterby*

SOBER AS A JUDGE 5 b.g. Mon Tresor 113 – Flicker Toa Flame (USA) 85 (Empery (USA) 128) [2002 44: f7s Jan 15] poor maiden at 4 yrs: well held only outing in 2002: tried visored. *C. A. Dwyer* —

SOBER HILL 4 b.g. Komaite (USA) – Mamoda (Good Times (ITY)) [2002 44: f7s⁴ f8s p7g Jan 23] poor maiden: stays 7f: acts on fibresand: usually blinkered/visored. *D. Shaw* **44**

SOCIABLE 3 b.f. Danehill (USA) 126 – Society Rose 88 (Saddlers' Hall (IRE) 126) [2002 74p: 6f² 7g 7.1m² 7g² 8g² 8m⁴ 8s⁶ 10.2f³ 9g* Oct 5] strong, good sort: fair performer: in frame 6 times in 2002 prior to winning maiden at Sandown in October: free-going sort, but stays 1¼m (at least when conditions aren't testing): acts on firm and soft going (yet to race on heavy). *W. J. Haggas* **77**

SOCIAL CONTRACT 5 b.g. Emarati (USA) 74 – Just Buy Baileys 69 (Formidable (USA) 125) [2002 90: 8g 7m⁵ 7m⁵ 7g² 8m 7.1g 7s² 7s f7g² p7g f6g³ f8g f7g Dec 31] strong, useful-looking gelding: fairly useful performer on all-weather, fair on turf: claimed from S. Kirk £7,000 eleventh start: effective at 6f to easy 1m: acts on firm going, soft and fibresand: usually blinkered/visored: inconsistent. *D. Shaw* **73 § a82 §**

SOCIAL HARMONY (IRE) 8 b.g. Polish Precedent (USA) 131 – Latest Chapter (IRE) (Ahonoora 122) [2002 114: 8s 8m⁶ 8d 8d* 7d³ 6g⁴ 7m Sep 7] smart performer: won 9 races in career, notably listed race at Fairyhouse and Aon MacDonagh Boland Stakes at the Curragh at 6 yrs: retained his ability in 2002, gaining final win in handicap at the Curragh in June by head from Tarry Flynn: broke leg at Leopardstown in September: effective at 5f to 7f: acted on any turf going: effective blinkered or not: dead. *D. K. Weld, Ireland* **114**

SOCIALISE 2 b.f. (Feb 15) Groom Dancer (USA) 128 – Society Rose 88 (Saddlers' Hall (IRE) 126) [2002 6m³ f6g³ Oct 17] well-made filly: second foal: half-sister to 3-y-o Sociable: dam, 2-y-o 7f winner, half-sister to Cheveley Park winner Regal Rose: fair form in maidens at Newmarket and Southwell (finished well when close third to Malahide Express): will stay at least 1m: remains open to improvement. *W. J. Haggas* **69 p**

SOCIETE GENERALE 3 b.g. Eagle Eyed (USA) 111 – Canlubang (Mujtahid (USA) 118) [2002 –§: 10.3s⁵ 9.3s Jun 16] good-topped gelding: temperamental maiden: blinkered (crashed through rail) once at 2 yrs: dead. *Ronald Thompson* **– §**

SOCIETY (IRE) 3 b.f. Barathea (IRE) 127 – Lobmille (Mill Reef (USA) 141) [2002 7g 9d³ p10g f12g⁶ 8.3d⁴ 10g* 10m 10.2g Oct 16] 120,000Y: good-bodied filly: half-sister to several winners, including smart French 1m/9f performer Lone Bid (by Priolo) and useful 7f (including at 2 yrs) winner Lil's Jessy (by Kris): dam unraced: fair handicapper: won at Ripon in August: ran poorly last 2 starts, folding tamely: stays 1¼m: acts on good to soft going: visored last 3 starts: sold 40,000 gns. *W. J. Haggas* **73**

SOCIETY PET 3 b.f. Runnett 125 – Polar Storm (IRE) 76 (Law Society (USA) 130) [2002 57: p7g p7g f7g 10g 10.2g Apr 30] modest maiden: should stay 7f: often reluctant at stall: ungenuine. *D. G. Bridgwater* **50 §**

SOCKS 3 b.f. Sabrehill (USA) 120 – Pink Brief (IRE) 71 (Ela-Mana-Mou 132) [2002 –: 7s⁶ 8.1f p7g May 28] smallish, workmanlike filly: well held in maidens/minor event. *Andrew Reid* **–**

SOCKS FOR GLENN 2 ch.c. (May 5) Factual (USA) 108 – Payvashooz 78 (Balla-cashtal (CAN)) [2002 5.1g³ 5.1d³ 6g⁶ 5g* 5d⁵ 7m 6s Oct 26] well-made colt: seventh foal: half-brother to 5-y-o Strensall: dam 5f (at 2 yrs) to 7f winner: fair performer: won nursery at Leicester in July: well below after (visored final start): should stay 6f (raced too freely at 7f): acts on good to soft going. *J. Cullinan* **69**

SO DEAR (USA) 2 b.f. (May 1) King of Kings (IRE) 125 – Refill 88 (Mill Reef (USA) 141) [2002 6m⁴ 6m² 6f Sep 8] $250,000Y: half-sister to several winners, including 1995 2-y-o 7f winner Winter Gardens and 1994 2-y-o 6f winner Jumilla (both by El Gran Senor and useful), and to dam of smart performers Hidden Meadow (at 7.5f to 8.5f) and Scorned (stays 1½m): dam, second at 6f in Britain, later won at 8.5f/1¼m in USA: fair form in maidens at Newbury and Goodwood (second to Medeena) first 2 starts: hung left final outing: should stay at least 1m. *I. A. Balding* **78**

Mr Hamdan Al Maktoum's "Sohaib"

SOFISIO 5 ch.g. Efisio 120 – Legal Embrace (CAN) 73 (Legal Bid (USA) 120) [2002 –, a70: f11s f12g* f12g Jun 22] modest performer: won seller at Wolverhampton in June: stays easy 1½m: acts on fibresand: usually blinkered/tongue tied. *Miss S. J. Wilton* **a55**

SOFTLY (IRE) 3 ch.f. Grand Lodge (USA) 125 – Decrescendo (IRE) (Polish Precedent (USA) 131) [2002 70: 10.2g⁴ 10g² 10m⁴ 12m⁶ Aug 14] smallish, sparely-made filly: fair performer: won claimer at Leicester in July: should stay 1½m: yet to race on extremes of going: sold 5,000 gns. *M. L. W. Bell* **70**

SOHAIB (USA) 3 b.c. Kingmambo (USA) 125 – Fancy Ruler (USA) (Half A Year (USA) 130) [2002 99: 8f² 10.3f* 10g² 9.9m³ 8f³ Oct 3] leggy, attractive colt: smart performer: made all in listed Dee Stakes at Chester in May by short head from Sir George Turner: at least creditable efforts otherwise in listed race at Thirsk (length second to Aramram), Scottish Classic at Ayr (length second behind Imperial Dancer), Select Stakes at Goodwood (3 lengths third to Moon Ballad) and listed race at Newmarket (1½ lengths third behind Desert Deer) in October: has won at 10.3f, may prove ideally suited by around 1m: yet to race on soft/heavy going, acts on any other: tends to sweat: sometimes wears net muzzle: free-going sort: sent to USA. *B. W. Hills* **115**

SO IT IS 3 b.f. So Factual (USA) 120 – Big Story 50 (Cadeaux Genereux 131) [2002 47, a–: 5m 8g 6.9g Aug 5] small filly: poor maiden at 2 yrs: no form in 2002. *K. R. Burke* **–**

SOLDERA (USA) 2 b.f. (Mar 22) Polish Numbers (USA) – La Pepite (USA) (Mr Prospector (USA)) [2002 7f* 7f² Oct 5] $90,000F, IR 100,000Y: fluent mover: closely related to a winner in Japan by Boundary and half-sister to 3 winners, including fairly useful 1m/1¼m winner Asly (by Riverman): dam, maiden in USA, out of champion US filly Fanfreluche: convincing winner of maiden at Salisbury in September by 3 lengths from Tiber: again favourite, improved (useful form) when 4 lengths second to Khulood in listed event at Newmarket 3 weeks later, keeping on well under hands and heels after **95 p**

winner had flown: favourite both times, gambled-on on first occasion: has plenty of speed, but should stay 1m: sure to progress further. *J. R. Fanshawe*

SOLDIER ON (IRE)   4 b.g. General Monash (USA) 107 – Golden Form (Formidable   –
(USA) 125) [2002 6g Apr 1] tall, useful-looking gelding: fairly useful performer at 2 yrs: last only run since. *M. R. Channon*

SOLDIER POINT   4 ch.g. Sabrehill (USA) 120 – Reel Foyle (USA) 77 (Irish River   **80**
(FR) 131) [2002 79: f7s* p10g 7d⁶ 5.9d* 7m* 7.2d³ Aug 2] strong gelding: fairly useful performer: won maiden at Southwell in January and amateur races at Hamilton (handicap) and Redcar (minor event) in July: best form at 6f/7f: acts on fibresand, good to firm and good to soft ground: tends to wander: sent to Bahrain. *P. C. Haslam*

SOLFATARA (IRE)   2 b.f. (Feb 2) Salse (USA) 128 – Lucia Tarditi (FR) (Crystal   **38**
Glitters (USA) 127) [2002 6m 7m⁶ 7d⁶ 7g f8g Nov 26] IR 12,000Y: sturdy filly: sixth foal: half-sister to 2 winners, including useful 7f (at 2 yrs) and 9f (in USA) winner Ettrick (by Selkirk): dam Italian 2-y-o 7f listed winner: poor form at best, including in sellers: tried visored. *K. A. Ryan*

SOLLER BAY   5 b.g. Contract Law (USA) 108 – Bichette 66 (Lidhame 109) [2002   **78 d**
87: f8.5g⁵ 8.1s⁶ 8.9d 8.3m 8g 10s f8g 8s³ 8s³ f8.5g p8g f8g Dec 27] quite good-topped   **a82 d**
gelding: fairly useful performer: reportedly cracked pelvis final 3-y-o outing: best form around 1m: has form on good to firm going and fibresand, raced mainly on good or softer nowadays (acts on heavy): often races freely up with pace: sometimes drifts right: generally on downgrade. *K. R. Burke*

SOLLY'S PAL   7 gr.g. Petong 126 – Petriece 64 (Mummy's Pet 125) [2002 –, a64:   **– §**
f7s* f7g² f7s f8.5g f8g³ f7g* f7g f7g⁴ f7s⁴ f6g³ f7g f6g Jun 20] tall, leggy gelding: modest   **a64 §**
performer: won seller at Southwell in January and handicap at Wolverhampton in February: probably best around 7f: acts on fibresand: usually visored: often slowly away (refused to race for amateur fourth start)/carry head high: untrustworthy. *R. Wilman*

SOLO FLIGHT   5 gr.g. Mtoto 134 – Silver Singer 65 (Pharly (FR) 130) [2002 99:   **104**
12m* 11.9m 12d² 12g 13.9m⁶ 12m⁵ 11.9g 12m² 10m* 12g 12g⁶ 10s Oct 26] angular gelding: useful handicapper: won at Newmarket in April and Courage Best Stakes at Newbury (best effort to beat Far Lane a short head despite idling) in September: at least as good at 1¼m as 1½m: acts on firm and good to soft going, possibly not ideally suited by soft/heavy: has worn crossed noseband/net muzzle: edgy sort: pulled too hard fourth start, found little next time: probably best with exaggerated waiting tactics. *B. W. Hills*

Courage Best Stakes (Handicap), Newbury—a 1,2 for Barry Hills as the grey Solo Flight just holds off the rallying Far Lane; the consistent Kirovski is third

SOLO MIO (IRE)   8 b.h. Sadler's Wells (USA) 132 – Marie de Flandre (FR) 109   **110**
(Crystal Palace (FR) 132) [2002 121: 16.2d⁵ 16.4m⁴ 20m Jun 20] rangy, good-bodied
horse: impressed in appearance: fine mover: very smart performer at best: won 6 races
during Flat career, including Betty Barclay-Rennen at Baden-Baden in 1998 and 1999,
and Sagaro Stakes at Newmarket and Henry II Stakes at Sandown in 2001: only smart
form at best in 2002, 7½ lengths fourth to Akbar in Henry II Stakes in June: stayed 2m
well (twice well held in Gold Cup over 2½m): acted on soft and good to firm going:
blinkered once: had been bandaged in front: drifted right (reportedly jarred himself) final
7-y-o start: useful winning hurdler: reportedly injured off-hind on gallops, and to stand at
East Burrow Farm, Devon, fee £1,750, Oct 1st. *Mrs A. J. Perrett*

SOLOMON'S MINE (USA)   3 b.g. Rahy (USA) 115 – Shes A Sheba (USA)   **84**
(Alysheba (USA)) [2002 55, a75: p10g f9.4g² f8.5g² f8g² f8.5g⁵ f9.4g⁴ f9.4g* 7s 8.2d*
10g⁵ 8m 7.6f 7.9f⁶ 8m⁶ 10.1s 8.2m 9.9g² 10m² 12.3m⁴ 11.9m² 12m⁵ 10f⁴ 16m³ 13.9f³
f12g* 16s 16.5v³ Nov 9] strong gelding: poor mover: fairly useful handicapper: won at
Wolverhampton and Nottingham in March and at Southwell in October: stays easy 2m:
acts on fibresand, probably on any turf going: effective blinkered or not: races up with
pace: tough. *M. J. Polglase*

SOLTAAT   3 b.c. Royal Applause 124 – About Face (Midyan (USA) 124) [2002 –: 6d⁴   **68**
7f² 5.9d³ 7m² 8g³ 7g² 8m⁴ a6f⁴ Dec 27] sturdy colt: easy mover: fair maiden handicapper:
most unlucky at Folkestone (saddle slipped close home) sixth start: left A. Stewart before
final outing: barely stays 1m: acts on firm going, good to soft and dirt. *A. Smith, UAE*

SOMAYDA (IRE)   7 b.g. Last Tycoon 131 – Flame of Tara 124 (Artaius (USA) 129)   –
[2002 p12g p12g 10m 8m Sep 23] useful performer at 4 yrs: well beaten after 2-year
break in 2002: tried blinkered/visored. *Miss Jacqueline S. Doyle*

SOME KIND OF TIGER (USA)   2 b.c. (Jan 25) Storm Cat (USA) – Morning   **104 p**
Devotion (USA) 102 (Affirmed (USA)) [2002 6d² 7f² 7g* Oct 10] closely related to 2
winners by Storm Bird, notably top-class Oaks/Irish Derby winner Balanchine, 7f winner
at 2 yrs, and half-brother to 3 winners, notably smart winner up to 1½m Romanov (by
Nureyev): dam, 2-y-o 6f winner, stayed 1½m: useful form: runner-up at Leopardstown
and Fairyhouse prior to landing odds in maiden at Gowran (by ½ length from Kossu, pair
clear): will stay 1m: acts on firm and good to soft ground: capable of better still.
A. P. O'Brien, Ireland

SOME LIKE IT HOT   2 ch.f. (Jan 23) Ashkalani (IRE) 128 – Lady Kris (IRE) (Kris   **41**
135) [2002 6d p5g f7g f8.5s Dec 9] 34,000Y: seventh foal: sister to useful 7f/1m winner
Noon Gun (later 9f winner in Hong Kong) and half-sister to 2 winners, including useful
1996 2-y-o 6f winner Lima (by Distant Relative): dam, Irish 1¼m winner, half-sister to
Gimcrack winner Bel Bolide: poor form in maidens/seller. *Mrs M. Reveley*

SOMERSET WEST (IRE)   2 b.g. (Apr 17) Catrail (USA) 123 – Pizzazz 47   **74**
(Unfuwain (USA) 131) [2002 6m p6g³ 6.1g³ 6.1g⁴ 6.1m⁵ 6.1m 5g Oct 5] IR 19,000Y:
rather unfurnished, workmanlike gelding: fifth foal: half-brother to 3-y-o Creskeld and
French 6f (at 2 yrs) to 11f winner In The Trim (by Tirol): dam lightly-raced half-sister to
Nell Gwyn winner Thrilling Day: fair maiden: should prove best at 5f/6f: acts on
polytrack, raced only on good/good to firm going on turf: tongue tied penultimate start.
B. R. Millman

SOMERTON REEF   8 gr.g. Mystiko (USA) 124 – Lady Reef (Mill Reef (USA) 141)   –
[2002 p7g p6g f7g 7s Mar 28] useful form in Ireland at 2 yrs (ran only twice following
season): mostly well held on belated return: probably stays 1m: best effort on soft ground.
N. M. Babbage

SOMETHINGABOUTHER   2 b.f. (Feb 29) Whittingham (IRE) 104 – Paula's Joy   **63**
75 (Danehill (USA) 126) [2002 5g 5.7m 5m⁵ 5g 5.1d³ 5g⁶ 6g Oct 18] 5,500Y: first foal:
dam, 2-y-o 5f winner (only season to race), out of useful Irish 6f/7f performer Pernilla:
modest maiden: best form at 5f: yet to race on extremes of going. *D. K. Ivory*

SOME TOOL   5 b.g. Jupiter Island 126 – Melodys Daughter 60 (Sizzling Melody 117)   –
[2002 f11s Jan 1] 1,900Y: second foal: dam 2-y-o 5f winner: 33/1, showed nothing in
maiden at Southwell. *R. F. Marvin*

SOME WILL   4 b.g. Handsome Sailor 125 – Bollin Sophie (Efisio 120) [2002 72: 6m   **70**
6m 5.9s 8m² 7.6f⁵ 8s² 8m 8.5g f8s⁴ 9m² 9.9m f8s Oct 8] tall, lengthy gelding: has a round   **a60**
action: fair handicapper on turf, modest on all-weather: stays 9f: acts on soft ground, good
to firm and fibresand: usually blinkered in 2002: found little eighth outing. *T. D. Easterby*

SOMNUS 2 b.g. (Apr 27) Pivotal 124 – Midnight's Reward 84 (Night Shift **117** (USA)) [2002 6m⁵ 6m* 6g* 6m* 6m* Oct 5]

Racegoers on their way to Chester's Friday evening fixture in July might have been confronted by a crusading soul carrying a banner bearing the inscription: 'Bet on the Lord—he's a sure winner'. The tip proved inspired as The Lord, conceding weight all round, comfortably won the nursery at 3/1. This useful performance resulted in The Lord running off a BHB mark of 104 on his next appearance in a nursery, two outings later at Newbury. As a result of an outdated procedure, however, The Lord was among a clutch of two-year-olds lumped together in the *Racing Calendar* on the maximum permitted figure for publication of 100. Official assessments for the top two-year-olds in Ireland are published without restriction, as are those in Britain for horses above the age of two, so why this peculiar practice continues for British two-year-olds is hard to fathom. Its only purpose seems to be to protect the BHB two-year-old handicapper from the embarrassment of publishing in-season figures that turn out to be wide of the mark. The BHB handicapper released assessments in October of Flusive City (119), Russian Rhythm (115) and Soviet Song (114) for publication in America for the purpose of Breeders' Cup rankings, but they were still kept 'secret' to readers of BHB publications in Britain. The handicapper for the two-year-olds is Matthew Tester who did drop his guard a little after the Dewhurst in late-October. Tester described another member of the '100 club', the gelding Somnus, as an 'amazing' juvenile following the Newmarket victory of Tout Seul, runner-up to Somnus in the betabet Two-Year-Old Trophy at Redcar. 'Somnus is unlikely to end up as champion juvenile, but he is still going to earn an exceptional rating for a horse who has never run in a Group race.' Tester also stressed the form of Somnus's victory in the £200000 St Leger Yearling Stakes at Doncaster which he won from the Gimcrack runner-up Mister Links, with subsequent Cheveley Park winner Airwave fourth, subsequent Mill Reef runner-up Monsieur Bond fifth, Cumbrian Venture, just touched off in listed company next time at York, sixth. and Striking Ambition, a comfortable winner of a listed race at Saint-Cloud next time, eighth.

What was described as 'further consultation with international colleagues' was required before a 'proper' assessment of Somnus could be made. He eventually appeared on 118 in the International Classification when it was released in the middle of January 2003, in the meantime continuing on a published assessment of 100, the same as Airwave, Monsieur Bond and Cumbrian Venture, for example. The Lord was also in the field of twenty-one for the St Leger Yearling Stakes, a

£200000 St Leger Yearling Stakes, Doncaster—the progressive Somnus (No.18)
comes out on top against twenty rivals in a race that has grown in stature in recent years;
Mister Links (No.1) is second and Crimson Silk (obscured) third, whilst Airwave (far rail, No.21)
and Monsieur Bond (No.6) meet trouble in running; Cumbrian Venture (No.5),
a stable-companion of the winner, leads home those on the other side

sales race which has grown in stature since its introduction in 1998. Somnus, who has his own divine connection as he is named after the Roman god of sleep, looked a useful performer in the making when winning a maiden at York and a nursery at Ripon on his second and third appearances, and he started 10/1 joint-fourth favourite at Doncaster behind Mister Links and Airwave, both at 4/1, and Monsieur Bond at 8/1. Somnus was a little short of room when beginning his run but quickened well to hit the front in the closing stages, winning by half a length from Mister Links, who was conceding weight all round, including 7 lb to the winner. A little over two lengths covered the first seven home with Somnus's stable-companion Cumbrian Venture the only one in the far-side group to get into the shake-up. Somnus was a progressive type but the form of his Doncaster victory—the way we read it—was good enough only to get him into the lower reaches of the *Timeform 'Top Hundred'* at the time.

Somnus moved into the top ten after Redcar's Two-Year-Old Trophy a little over three weeks later. Monsieur Bond was favourite in a field of eighteen, after his second in the Mill Reef, and Tout Seul, winner last time of another big sales race in the Tattersalls Breeders Stakes at the Curragh, was also preferred to Somnus in the betting. Entry for sales races like those at Doncaster and the Curragh is restricted to horses from a particular yearling sale and they help to promote that sale, as well as offering an extremely valuable prize. The St Leger Yearling Stakes is the richest race in Europe for two-year-olds now that the Tattersalls Houghton Sales Stakes at Newmarket has been discontinued, a smaller catalogue making Newmarket's premier yearling sale considerably more select nowadays than it was when its sales race was inaugurated in 1990. The Two-Year-Old Trophy at Redcar is the oldest of the three major auction races run in Britain and is open to nearly all two-year-olds, with the weight carried by each runner related to the median price of its sire's yearlings. Somnus's trio of Yorkshire owners, whose moniker 'Legard Sidebottom & Sykes' sounds like—but isn't—a firm of country solicitors, celebrated another moneyspinning win at Redcar where Somnus, ending up racing alone against the far rail, just held off the strong-finishing Tout Seul by a head, with Monsieur Bond a length and a half further away in third. Success brought Somnus's earnings for the season to £254,576, more than any other British-trained two-year-old with the exception of Tout Seul. He wasn't seen out after the Two-Year-Old Trophy, developing an infection which put paid to plans to run him in pattern company for the first time in the Criterium de Maisons-Laffitte, a race won the previous year by Two-Year-Old Trophy winner Captain Rio.

Somnus, a good-topped individual with scope by Captain Rio's sire the sprinter Pivotal, was bred by Lady Legard at her small stud near Malton in Yorkshire. Together with Roger Sidebottom and Sir Tatton Sykes, she bought back Somnus as a yearling at Doncaster for 13,500 guineas. Somnus was gelded after reportedly being a 'nightmare' to break in and didn't appear on a racecourse until June when he showed clear signs of his inexperience, losing lengths by veering right at the stalls. when fifth of six in a Ripon maiden. Somnus is also sprint-bred on the dam's side. His dam Midnight's Reward was successful at five furlongs as a two-year-old and put up her best effort at six furlongs. She is by the sprinter Night Shift out of another five-furlong two-year-old winner Margaret's Ruby. Midnight's

Legard Sidebottom & Sykes's "Somnus"

		Polar Falcon	Nureyev
	Pivotal	(b or br 1987)	Marie d'Argonne
	(ch 1993)	Fearless Revival	Cozzene
Somnus		(ch 1987)	Stufida
(b.g. Apr 27, 2000)		Night Shift	Northern Dancer
	Midnight's Reward	(b 1980)	Ciboulette
	(b 1986)	Margaret's Ruby	Tesco Boy
		(b 1968)	Pixie Jet

Reward has bred several other winners, the best of them the useful middle-distance performer Pasithea (by Celtic Swing), who was in training with Tim Easterby in the latest season, and the fairly useful 1994 two-year-old five-furlong winner Soca King (by Midyan). Being a gelding, Somnus is ineligible for the classics, and for the St James's Palace Stakes at Royal Ascot, but he's likely to prove best at short of a mile anyway. He should have little difficulty picking up races in lesser pattern company, in which he will start off unpenalised. He has been raced so far only on good and good to firm going. *T. D. Easterby*

SONGLARK   2 br.c. (Mar 21) Singspiel (IRE) 133 – Negligent 118 (Ahonoora 122)   **107**
[2002 8g* 8g* 8v⁵ Nov 2] fifth foal: half-brother to several winners (all at least useful), including 3-y-o Blatant and useful 7f (at 2 yrs)/1m winner Asad (by Lion Cavern): dam, won Rockfel Stakes and third in 1000 Guineas, half-sister to smart stayer Ala Hounak: useful form: won newcomers race in September and Prix Thomas Bryon (comfortably by 2 lengths from Sylvestre after setting steady pace) in October, both at Saint-Cloud: pulled too hard when last of 5 in Criterium International at same course: needs to settle to stay beyond 1m: joined Godolphin. *A. Fabre, France*

SONIQUE   4 b.f. Shaamit (IRE) 127 – Dolly Bevan 53 (Another Realm 118) [2002 –:   **–**
f5s f8s Jan 17] leggy filly: no sign of ability in 5 starts. *R. C. Spicer*

SON OF A GUN   8 b.g. Gunner B 126 – Sola Mia 78 (Tolomeo 127) [2002 83: 13.9f⁵   **75**
14d f14g f14.8g Nov 30] workmanlike gelding: fair maiden handicapper, lightly raced: **a–**
left J. Neville after second outing: probably stays 2¼m: acts on soft going, probably on firm (well held on all-weather): bandaged in front: has hung left. *M. J. Polglase*

SON OF FLIGHTY 4 b.g. Then Again 126 – Record Flight (Record Token 128) – [2002 –: 10.9m Jul 7] well held in 3 maidens. *R. J. Hodges*

SON OF ROSE 3 ch.g. Superlative 118 – Rose of Glenn 58 (Crofthall 110) [2002 f7g – 8g 8m 8.2m 8.1d 6v⁶ Aug 9] first foal: dam 1½m to 17f winner: no form: visored final start. *B. Palling*

SONOROUS (IRE) 3 b.f. Ashkalani (IRE) 128 – Nymphs Echo (IRE) (Mujtahid **98** (USA) 118) [2002 8g³ 7s³ 8g* 10m* 8m² Sep 28] second foal: half-sister to 4-y-o Camarade: dam unraced sister to useful performer up to 1m Glen Rosie and half-sister to smart French winner up to 9f Hello Soso: useful form, lightly raced: won maiden at Gowran in August and handicap at the Curragh in September: good 1½ lengths second to Welsh Diva in listed rated stakes at Ascot final start: stays 1¼m: best efforts on good/ good to firm going: tongue tied: sent to USA. *J. G. Burns, Ireland*

SOONA 4 ch.f. Royal Abjar (USA) 121 – Presently 48 (Cadeaux Genereux 131) [2002 **47 §** 54§: f12s⁴ f12s f12g⁶ Feb 7] poor maiden: barely stays 1½m: acts on good to firm going and fibresand: tongue tied penultimate start: tends to wander: usually races prominently: inconsistent. *Ronald Thompson*

SOON OR LATE 4 ch.g. Kris 135 – Silky Heights (IRE) 67 (Head For Heights 125) **47** [2002 –: f12s f14g 12.1m 16.2g² 16.2m 16g Aug 12] big, workmanlike gelding: poor maiden handicapper: stays 2m: often slowly away: sometimes races freely: sold 2,200 gns. *Miss J. A. Camacho*

SOPHALA 5 b.m. Magical Wonder (USA) 125 – Fujaiyrah 98 (In Fijar (USA) 121) – [2002 69: p12g p10g Aug 9] fair handicapper at 4 yrs: well held in 2002. *C. F. Wall*

SOPHIES SYMPHONY 3 b.f. Merdon Melody 98 – Gracious Imp (USA) (Imp **61** Society (USA)) [2002 78: 8.3m 7m 5.9d p7g⁶ 7g 6m 8.3m 8m 7f* f7g 7g 7g 7s f7g⁵ f7g f6g Dec 10] workmanlike filly: modest handicapper: won at Catterick in September: effective at 6f/7f: acts on fibresand, firm and good to soft ground, possibly not on heavy: visored (ran respectably) fourth start. *K. R. Burke*

SOPHISTICAT (USA) 3 b. or br.f. Storm Cat (USA) – Serena's Song (USA) **117** 126 (Rahy (USA) 115) [2002 105, a109: 8g* 8g³ 8m* 8m⁶ Sep 7]
    An eight-race two-year-old campaign, in which Sophisticat was placed four times in pattern company, seemed to expose her as a filly good enough to run in the top races but not good enough to win them. Her pattern placings came in the Queen Mary Stakes at Royal Ascot, the Lowther Stakes at York, the Moyglare Stud Stakes at the Curragh and the Cheveley Park Stakes at Newmarket, and she also finished a good fifth in the Breeders' Cup Juvenile Fillies at Belmont on her final start. Even if she trained on, Sophisticat looked the type to continue to find one or two too good for her in Group 1 company at three. However, she defied any such predictions, improving from two to three and landing a Group 1 prize at Royal Ascot when doing exceptionally well to overcome considerable trouble in running in the Coronation Stakes. Sophisticat—whose only two-year-old success had been in a maiden at Naas on her second outing—began her second season on a winning note in the Prix de la Grotte at Longchamp in April, beating Dublino by three quarters of a length in a slowly-run, six-runner contest, after being held up last and switched off the rail to lead in the final furlong. Another improved effort followed when Sophisticat was returned to Longchamp for the Poule d'Essai des Pouliches, in which, though not really taking the eye beforehand, she finished just over a length third of seventeen to Zenda, deserving a little extra credit after a none-too-clear run in the home straight.
    Then came the Coronation Stakes, for which the 6/4 market leader was Gossamer, who had followed a disappointing run in the One Thousand Guineas at Newmarket with a clear-cut success in the Irish version at the Curragh. The Newmarket fourth Dolores came next in the betting at 5/1, in front of Sophisticat at 11/2, followed by Zenda at 7/1, with 10/1 bar. Apart from notable absentees Kazzia—the One Thousand Guineas winner now stepped up to middle distances —and the sidelined Queen's Logic, who had defeated Sophisticat three times in an outstanding juvenile campaign, the Coronation Stakes attracted virtually every other three-year-old filly with aspirations to top miling honours. Held up as usual, Sophisticat found her way blocked after being switched towards the far rail early in the straight. Extricated and switched back to the outside only approaching the final

Coronation Stakes, Royal Ascot—Sophisticat produces a rare finishing burst after meeting trouble in running to catch Zenda (No.12); Dolores is third

furlong, Sophisticat appeared to have lost her chance, still having four to five lengths to make up. But she produced a formidable burst of speed to storm home and snatch the race from Zenda in the final strides, prevailing by a neck, with Dolores a further two and a half lengths back in third; Gossamer trailed in last. Royal Ascot proved to be the high point of Sophisticat's season. Like so many others in her stable she suffered from a bout of coughing during the summer and wasn't seen out again until September. On her return she was below her best behind Dress To Thrill in the Matron Stakes at Leopardstown, a veterinary examination finding that she was in respiratory distress. She wasn't seen again.

Until coughing intervened, Sophisticat was proving tough, like her dam Serena's Song. Serena's Song had a remarkable career, running thirty-eight times in America and proving high-class at up to nine furlongs; she won eighteen times, eleven of them Grade 1 events, from two to four and was placed a further nine times at the highest level, seven of them as runner-up. Serena's Song's racing record highlights a major difference between the policy of the racing authorities in Europe and in the States, where there are many more opportunities for good-class older fillies and mares to race among themselves and a good level of prize-money on offer, reducing the temptation to retire top fillies early. The very smart filly Golden Apples was transferred from David Hanley in Ireland to Ben Cecil in the States mid-way through her three-year-old campaign and subsequently picked up three Grade 1 events, racing solely against her own sex. If she had been kept in Europe she would have had to take on male opposition at some point. Serena's Song's prolific racecourse achievements—on retirement she was the world's leading money-earning filly—also go some way towards counteracting the long-held European view that a demanding racing career can adversely affect a filly's prospects as a broodmare.

		Storm Cat (USA) (b 1983)	Storm Bird (b 1978)	Northern Dancer
Sophisticat (USA) (b. or br.f. 1999)				South Ocean
			Terlingua (ch 1976)	Secretariat
				Crimson Saint
		Serena's Song (USA) (b 1992)	Rahy (ch 1985)	Blushing Groom
				Glorious Song
			Imagining (b 1983)	Northfields
				Image Intensifier

Sophisticat, a 3,400,000-dollar yearling, is Serena's Song's second foal. Her first was a listed winner in the States, Serena's Tune (by Mr Prospector), while her third foal the two-year-old Arbitrate (by Deputy Minister) has yet to race and is followed by a full brother to Sophisticat, and a colt foal by Unbridled. The

Mr M. Tabor & Mrs John Magnier's "Sophisticat"

quick-actioned Sophisticat is a lengthy, good-topped filly—her portrait was taken very late in the year at Coolmore and doesn't show her at her best. Her very best form came at a mile, but she was left in at the five-day stage for the Nassau Stakes over a mile and a quarter and might well have got that trip. Her dam stayed nine furlongs well and Sophisticat's style of racing would have stood her in good stead. She was effective on dirt, and on good to firm and good to soft on turf. Though consistent, she was not without her quirks: she was visored on her last two outings at two after wandering on her previous start, while Michael Kinane was notably reluctant to pick up his stick in the Coronation Stakes and the filly also flashed her tail in the preliminaries on her final outing. Sophisticat has been retired and visits Danehill in 2003. *A. P. O'Brien, Ireland*

SOPHOMORE   8 b.g. Sanglamore (USA) 126 – Livry (USA) (Lyphard (USA) 132)   –
[2002 8d f8g Nov 25] workmanlike gelding: fair performer at 6 yrs: soundly beaten in 2002. *John A. Harris*

SOPHRANO (IRE)   2 b.c. (Mar 21) Spectrum (IRE) 126 – Sophrana (IRE) (Polar   **78**
Falcon (USA) 126) [2002 p7g⁵ 7d³ Oct 30] 26,000Y: first foal: dam, French 9.5f/10.5f winner, out of half-sister to smart performer up to 1½m in France/US Trishyde: fair form in maidens at Lingfield and Yarmouth: should be suited by 1¼m/1½m. *P. W. Harris*

SO PRECIOUS (IRE)   5 b.m. Batshoof 122 – Golden Form (Formidable (USA) 125)   **63**
[2002 72: f11s f12g⁵ p12g f8g p16g p10g p13g Dec 28] good-topped mare: modest handicapper: left I. Williams after third start: stays 1½m: acts on fibresand and heavy going: tried visored/blinkered. *D. K. Ivory*

SORBIESHARRY (IRE)   3 gr.g. Sorbie Tower (IRE) 120 – Silver Moon (Environ-   **55**
ment Friend 128) [2002 f8g f9.4g⁶ f8.5g⁶ 7g⁴ 7m⁴ 6f 7g⁶ 7f 8g 7g 7m⁵ 7g 8m⁴ 7g⁵ f6g⁶   **a62**
f9.4f³ f8g² f9.4g³ f9.4g³ f8.5s Dec 26] IR 1,500Y: leggy gelding: poor mover: first foal: dam little sign of ability: modest maiden: should stay 1¼m: acts on fibresand, raced only

on good going or firmer on turf: visored (below form) final start: sometimes slowly away. *Mrs N. Macauley*

SORBIEYICANOPIT (IRE) 3 b.g. Sorbie Tower (IRE) 120 – Yiayia's Girl (Smack- —
over 107) [2002 f8g f7g 7m⁶ 8.3d 7.9g 8d f8.5g 8.2m Jun 24] IR 3,000Y: first foal: dam
unraced: little form. *Mrs N. Macauley*

SORBONNE 3 b.g. College Chapel 122 – French Mist 71 (Mystiko (USA) 124) [2002   **68**
58: 10s p10g f12g² 14m² 16.2d² Jul 22] rangy gelding: fair maiden handicapper: good
efforts last 3 starts: may prove best short of 2m: acts on fibresand, good to firm and good
to soft ground: tongue tied on debut: sold 7,000 gns. *B. Hanbury*

SORCEROUS 3 b.c. Sadler's Wells (USA) 132 – La Papagena (Habitat 134) [2002 **108**
94P: 10g⁴ 12f* 14f² Oct 2] quite good-topped colt: useful performer: has reportedly
suffered from muscle problems: won maiden at Leopardstown only start at 2 yrs and
3-runner minor event at Listowel (by 1½ lengths from hampered Millstreet) in September: good ½-length second to Tholjanah in listed race at Newmarket final outing: stays
1¾m: acts on firm and soft going: has worn crossed noseband. *A. P. O'Brien, Ireland*

SORRENTO KING 5 ch.g. First Trump 118 – Star Face (African Sky 124) [2002
38: 15.8f Jul 10] workmanlike gelding: maiden handicapper on Flat: usually blinkered:
winning hurdler/chaser. *Mrs M. Reveley*

SO SOBER (IRE) 4 b.g. Common Grounds 118 – Femme Savante 89 (Glenstal   **58**
(USA) 118) [2002 78: f6g f6g⁴ f6g f6g f5g⁶ f5g 6m 5s p6g² p6g 5.1d⁴ p5g 6.1m p6g f5s⁴   **a64**
5.1g f5g f5g⁴ Dec 31] compact gelding: modest handicapper: effective at 5f/6f: acts on
all-weather, soft and firm going. *D. Shaw*

SOSUMI 3 b.f. Be My Chief (USA) 122 – Princess Deya (Be My Guest (USA) 126)   **91**
[2002 101: 8m 6d⁵ 10s⁴ 8.3s² 10.3m⁴ 10.3m 10g Sep 20] good-topped filly: fairly useful
performer: in frame in listed race at Newbury, minor event at Hamilton (blinkered) and
handicap at Chester: disappointing after: stays 1¼m: acts on soft and good to firm going.
M. H. Tompkins

SO SURE (IRE) 2 b.g. (Feb 15) Definite Article 121 – Zorilla (Belmez (USA) 131)   **66 d**
[2002 6m² 6m f6s f8.5g Dec 2] 8,500 2-y-o: sparely-made gelding: second foal: dam,
French 2-y-o 1m winner, out of half-sister to dam of very smart 1¼m performer Sabrehill:
fair maiden: disappointing after second at Newcastle: bred to stay 8.5f: slowly away last
2 starts. *P. C. Haslam*

SOTONIAN (HOL) 9 br.g. Statoblest 120 – Visage 75 (Vision (USA)) [2002 66§:   **65 §**
p6g p5g f5g⁴ f5g⁴ f5g⁵ 5m 5s f5g 5m f5g⁵ 5m⁴ 5m f5g Dec 31] rather sparely-made
gelding: fair handicapper: best at 5f/easy 6f: acts on firm ground, soft and all-weather:
tried blinkered: reportedly bled from nose once as 6-y-o: often claimer ridden: unreliable.
P. S. Felgate

SOUNDS DOWN 3 b.f. In The Wings 128 – Bell Toll 87 (High Line 125) [2002 7.1m   **66**
6m 6f 10g⁶ 11.6m 9.9d 9.9d* 9.9m 12d 13s³ Nov 6] stocky filly: half-sister to several
winners, including 5f (at 2 yrs) to 1m winner Prince Babar (by Fairy King) and 1m (at 2
yrs) to 11.5f (in France) winner Warning Order (by Warrshan), both useful: dam, 2-y-o
7f/1m winner, sister to dam of Prix Jean Prat winner Suances: fair handicapper: won at
Beverley in August: stays 1½m: acts on soft going, probably on good to firm: blinkered
final start. *R. A. Fahey*

SOUNDS LUCKY 6 b.g. Savahra Sound 111 – Sweet And Lucky (Lucky Wednesday   **61**
124) [2002 57: p6g⁴ p6g* p6g³ p5g² p5g⁵ p6g² p6g f6g p6g* p6g⁵ p6g* 6m⁶ 7g 5g² 6d 6m   **a71**
6d 6d p6g³ 6m Aug 2] leggy gelding: has a round action: fair on all-weather, modest on
turf: won claimer and 2 handicaps at Lingfield between January and April: effective at 5f
to 7f: acts on all-weather and good to firm going: effective blinkered/visored or not: often
slowly away: has swished tail/found little/edged left: has won for amateur: usually held
up. *N. P. Littmoden*

SOUTHAMPTON JOE (USA) 2 ch.c. (Mar 4) Just A Cat (USA) – Maple Hill Jill   **76**
(USA) (Executive Pride 127) [2002 5m⁴ 5.3g³ 7d 6.1g* 6.1m² 7m³ 7s* 7g⁴ Oct 4] quite
good-topped colt: good walker: fifth reported foal: half-brother to a winner in USA by
Val de L'Orne: dam sprint winner in USA: fair performer: won nurseries at Chepstow in
August and Lingfield in September: stays 7f: acts on soft and good to firm going: usually
races prominently. *I. A. Balding*

SOUTH ATLANTIC 2 b.c. (Jan 21) Sadler's Wells (USA) 132 – Shimmering Sea 89   **85**
(Slip Anchor 136) [2002 7.1m⁴ 7f³ Aug 17] good-topped, attractive colt: closely related
to a winner in Sweden by Fairy King and half-brother to several winners, including 6f/7f
winner Sheltering Sky (by Selkirk) and 5f/6f winner Sea Dane (by Danehill), both useful

and later winners in Scandinavia: dam, 2-y-o 5f and 7f winner, half-sister to Petoski: better effort in maidens (fairly useful form) when third to Al Jadeed at Newbury, racing freely and caught for second final 100 yds: should stay at least 1m. *Sir Michael Stoute*

SOUTHERN DOMINION   10 ch.g. Dominion 123 – Southern Sky 89 (Comedy   –
Star (USA) 121) [2002 –, a58d: f5g Jan 19] small gelding: one-time fair sprinter: has deteriorated: usually blinkered/visored. *Miss J. F. Craze*

SOUTHERN LAD (FR)   2 b.c. (May 10) Mukaddamah (USA) 125 – Due South 104   – §
(Darshaan 133) [2002 7.1m 8m⁴ 10f Oct 7] useful-looking colt: first foal: dam, 2-y-o 7.5f winner who stayed 1½m, half-sister to smart 1¼m performer Winter Romance: showed as much temperament as ability in maidens: very slowly away on debut: sold 4,000 gns. *E. A. L. Dunlop*

SOUTH SEA PEARL (IRE)   4 ch.f. Mujtahid (USA) 118 – Rainstone 57 (Rainbow   – §
Quest (USA) 134) [2002 56§: f12s Jan 2] angular, workmanlike filly: has a round action: temperamental maiden: tried blinkered. *B. J. Meehan*

SOU'WESTER   2 b.g. (Feb 19) Fleetwood (IRE) 107 – Mayfair 82 (Green Desert   69
(USA) 127) [2002 7f 8s 7d Nov 2] 23,000F, 16,000Y: angular gelding: second foal: dam, 2-y-o 6f winner, sister to smart 1991 2-y-o sprinter Magic Ring: fair form in maidens: best effort second start: should stay 1¼m. *M. P. Tregoning*

SOVEREIGN DREAMER (USA)   2 b.c. (Mar 16) Kingmambo (USA) 125 –   73
Spend A Dream (USA) (Spend A Buck (USA)) [2002 7m 7d 8.3s³ 8f 8f 8.3m 8.3d² Oct 14] $100,000Y: rangy, unfurnished colt: sixth foal: half-brother to 3 winners in USA: dam, US 2-y-o 8.5f winner, half-sister to very smart Irish 7f to 1¼m performer Fair Judgment: fair maiden: placed at Hamilton and Windsor (nursery), best efforts: will stay 1¼m: acts on soft and good to firm going: blinkered fifth start. *P. F. I. Cole*

SOVEREIGN NATION (IRE)   3 b.c. Ashkalani (IRE) 128 – Sovereign Dona 117   85 d
(Sovereign Path 125) [2002 p8g* p10g³ 8m 9m 10m* 10.4d 10g 8m⁶ 8m⁶ 8.1m 8.5d 8g Sep 27] IR 65,000Y: strong, lengthy colt: unimpressive mover: half-brother to several winners, notably 7f to 9f performer Royal Touch (by Tap On Wood) and Irish middle-distance stayer Foresee (by Vision), both very smart, and smart 1¼m performer Sylvan Point (by Reference Point): dam won 1¼m Prix de Psyche: fairly useful performer at best: won maiden at Lingfield in February and minor event at Nottingham in May: well beaten in handicaps after: stays 1¼m: acts on polytrack and good to firm going: effective tongue tied or not. *T. Keddy*

SOVEREIGN SEAL   2 b.f. (Feb 5) Royal Applause 124 – Downeaster Alexa (USA)   64 §
(Red Ryder (USA)) [2002 6f 7m⁴ 7g 6d p7g Dec 28] 70,000F, 100,000Y: good-topped filly: fifth foal: half-sister to 1996 2-y-o 5f/6f winner Arethusa (by Primo Dominie) and fairly useful 5f winner Red Ryding Hood (by Wolfhound): dam Irish 2-y-o 5f winner: modest maiden: form only when fourth at Redcar: stays 7f: blinkered last 2 starts, looking ungenuine final one. *M. Johnston*

SOVEREIGN STATE (IRE)   5 b.g. Soviet Lad (USA) – Portree 82 (Slip Anchor   –
136) [2002 51: f8g f7g 10f Sep 27] small, well-made gelding: fair performer in his day: well held in 2002: sometimes visored. *Miss S. E. Hall*

SOVIET FLASH (IRE)   5 b.h. Warning 136 – Mrs Moonlight (Ajdal (USA) 130)   111
[2002 114: 10g³ 9m⁶ 8d⁴ May 1] tall, useful-looking horse: smart performer, lightly raced: best effort in 2002 when 1½ lengths third of 5 to Border Arrow in listed event at Kempton in April: barely stays easy 1¼m: best form on good ground or firmer. *E. A. L. Dunlop*

SOVIET LADY (IRE)   8 b.m. Soviet Lad (USA) – La Vosgienne (Ashmore (FR)   –
125) [2002 p16g p12g Jan 12] sparely-made mare: no longer of much account. *L. A. Dace*

SOVIET SONG (IRE)   2 b.f. (Feb 18) Marju (IRE) 127 – Kalinka (IRE) 88   115 p
(Soviet Star (USA) 128) [2002 6m* 7s* 8g* Sep 28]

Mass participation in ownership through the medium of syndicates and racing clubs is a relatively modern phenomenon and the success story reached a new level in the autumn through the efforts of the two-year-olds Soviet Song and Tout Seul. The latter, successful in the Dewhurst Stakes, belongs to the ten-strong Eden Racing syndicate but even that pales into numerical insignificance compared with the ten thousand or so members of the Elite Racing Club, owner-breeders of Soviet Song, whose victory in the Meon Valley Stud Fillies' Mile at Ascot rounded off an unbeaten three-race campaign for the filly and marked her down as one of the best of her age and sex in Britain. Presumably it's raw enthusiasm, excitement, fun

and the social factor which act as the prime stimulation to get involved in the Elite Racing Club; membership costs £169 a year and Soviet Song's Ascot win was worth £116,000, which worked out at around £12 a member (membership was boosted by Soviet Song's success and is now around 14,000). The 2003 One Thousand Guineas could take more winning than in recent years, but Soviet Song is one of the strongest contenders at the time of writing. She has a useful turn of foot and looks to have improvement in her. Reportedly, she doesn't take a lot of getting ready and may go straight for the Guineas; her owners have every reason to look forward.

The Fillies' Mile in September brought together a representative but not outstanding field. All ten runners had won, but mostly in maiden company—only Soviet Song, who started 11/10 favourite, along with the first two in the May Hill Stakes, Summitville and Approach, and Huja, third in the Prestige Stakes, had form in pattern or listed events. Soviet Song had impressed in winning a fifteen-runner maiden at Kempton in July by half a length from Airwave, quickening smartly once shaken up, and the listed Milcars Sweet Solera Stakes at Newmarket in August by three lengths from Summitville, always going well and cruising through before bursting clear in the final furlong. This ability to accelerate was again in evidence at Ascot, where Soviet Song was confidently ridden after being on her toes and edgy in the preliminaries, taking a good hold going to post. Held up in the middle of the field before being eased out with less than a quarter of a mile to go, she quickened to lead in the final furlong and accounted comfortably for Bath maiden race winner Casual Look, winning going away by a length and a half with Irish challenger Reach For The Moon the same distance back in third. The runner-up was subsequently beaten a length by Luvah Girl in the Rockfel Stakes and the Fillies' Mile form is a bit behind that of the French equivalent, the Prix Marcel Boussac won by Six Perfections, but it is at least as good as that of the 2001 winner Gossamer, who went on to notch the Irish One Thousand Guineas.

Soviet Song (IRE) (b.f. Feb 18, 2000)	Marju (IRE) (br 1988)	Last Tycoon (b 1983)	Try My Best Mill Princess
		Flame of Tara (b 1980)	Artaius Welsh Flame
	Kalinka (IRE) (b 1994)	Soviet Star (b 1984)	Nureyev Veruschka
		Tralthee (ch 1983)	Tromos Swalthee

Marju's Group 1 winners—My Emma, successful in the Yorkshire Oaks and Prix Vermeille, Prix de Diane winner Sil Sila and now Soviet Song—are all fillies. Successful in the St James's Palace Stakes and runner-up in the Derby,

Elite Racing Club's "Soviet Song"

Marju stayed a mile and a half but most of his progeny are better over shorter and Soviet Song, a sturdy, lengthy filly, looks likely to prove best at around a mile. Her dam Kalinka, an IR 3,700 yearling, won over seven furlongs as a two-year-old and probably stayed a mile and a quarter; she also ran twice over hurdles. She is dam of the three-year-old Baralinka (by Barathea), who is bred to stay a mile but is best over sprint distances and has won four times. The grandam Tralthee, from a female family containing quite a bit of stamina, was smart, landing the Rockfel Stakes at two and the Lupe Stakes as a three-year-old. Dam of three winners altogether, she started off by visiting fashionable sires including Kris, Sadler's Wells and Caerleon but had gone down in the world before Soviet Song turned up. Tuco, her 1996 foal by Scenic, is a Grade 3 winner over hurdles in Ireland and her latest foal, a colt by Oscar, fetched 35,000 guineas at Doncaster in November. Perhaps Kalinka will now be upgraded. Either way, Soviet Song's name is likely to be in the news, boosting the family profile. *J. R. Fanshawe*

SOYUZ (IRE)   2 ch.c. (Mar 8) Cadeaux Genereux 131 – Welsh Mist 102 (Damister **92 p** (USA) 123) [2002 7m⁶ 6d² 6s* Oct 28] 225,000Y: angular, quite good-topped colt: third foal: half-brother to 3-y-o Brighter Future and 4-y-o Early Morning Mist: dam 5f (including at 2 yrs)/6f winner: progressive form: landed odds in maiden at Leicester comfortably by 2 lengths from Compton Emperor, making all: should stay 7f: acts on soft going: useful performer in the making. *M. A. Jarvis*

Bahrain Trophy, Newmarket—Spanish John (rail) makes all and responds well to pressure, beating Savannah Bay (second left) and Tholjanah

SPACE STAR 2 b.c. (May 14) Cosmonaut – Sophiesue (Balidar 133) [2002 7v Nov 8] lengthy colt: third foal: dam unraced: 33/1, well beaten in 17-runner maiden at Doncaster. *J. G. Given* —

SPA LANE 9 ch.g. Presidium 124 – Sleekit 78 (Blakeney 126) [2002 48: f14.8g³ 17.1m* 16.2g⁴ 15.8f³ 16.2m² 16.2g* 16g² 15.9f³ 16m² 18m³ 16m³ 17.1f Oct 7] leggy gelding: modest handicapper: won at Pontefract in June and Beverley (seller) in August: pulled up final start: best at 2m+ nowadays: acts on firm ground, soft (probably on heavy) and fibresand: has reportedly had breathing problem: held up. *J. F. Coupland* **60**

SPANISH DON 4 b.c. Zafonic (USA) 130 – Spanish Wells (IRE) (Sadler's Wells (USA) 132) [2002 106: 7.1g⁴ 9m 10d⁵ 10s⁵ 8m⁵ 7m 7.9m 10g⁴ 10d Oct 14] tall colt: second foal: half-brother to fairly useful 6f (at 2 yrs) and 1m winner Flamenco Red (by Warning): dam, French 12.5f winner, half-sister to Irish Oaks winner Wemyss Bight: useful performer: won newcomers race at Longchamp and second in 2 listed races at Chantilly in 2001 (left P. Bary in France 15,000 gns after final start): ran well in 2002 only when fifth in Gordon Richards Stakes at Sandown (behind Chancellor) and listed race at Goodwood (behind Atlantis Prince) on third/fifth starts: barely stays 1¼m: acts on good to firm and good to soft going: blinkered seventh start: reportedly lost action fourth outing, folded tamely last 2. *P. Mitchell* **106 d**

SPANISH GOLD 2 b.f. (May 4) Vettori (IRE) 119 – Spanish Heart 86 (King of Spain 121) [2002 6s Oct 25] tall filly: seventh foal: half-sister to 3 winners, including 5-y-o Bold Raider and 7-y-o Bold King: dam, effective at 7f to 9f, half-sister to smart sprinter Northern Goddess: 4/1, last of 15 in maiden at Newbury, though showed early speed: looked weak, and likely to do better in time. *P. J. Makin* **– p**

SPANISH JOHN (USA) 3 b. or br.g. Dynaformer (USA) – Esprit d'Escalier (USA) (Diesis 133) [2002 90: 12.3f⁴ 12m⁵ 14.8g* 14m² 16m³ Oct 19] good-topped gelding: carries condition: smart performer: won listed race at Newmarket (beat Savannah Bay by 1¼ lengths) in July: good efforts after, 1½ lengths second to First Charter in listed event at Goodwood, then 3¾ lengths third to Persian Punch in Jockey Club Cup at Newmarket (subsequently gelded): stays 2m: acts on firm going, well held only run on soft. *P. F. I. Cole* **113**

SPANISH STAR 5 b.g. Hernando (FR) 127 – Desert Girl (Green Desert (USA) 127) [2002 54, a70d: f12s f11s⁶ f11s* f9.4g* f11g f9.4g* f9.4g f11g f9.4g 10.3s³ f9.4g⁵ 11g f9.4s² f9.4g 10.2d f8.5g⁴ 8g 8.5g f8g f11g² f9.4g⁵ f9.4g* f9.4g³ Dec 26] compact gelding: modest handicapper on all-weather, poor on turf: won at Southwell and Wolverhampton (twice, including amateur event) in January/February: effective at 9.4f to 1½m: acts on fibresand and soft going: tried visored: sometimes slowly away. *Mrs N. Macauley* **42 a58**

SPANISH SUN (USA) 2 b.f. (Feb 14) El Prado (IRE) 119 – Shining Bright 98 (Rainbow Quest (USA) 134) [2002 7m* Sep 23] sixth foal: half-sister to fairly useful 1½m winner Eagle's Cross (by Trempolino): dam, French 1¼m winner, half-sister to smart French middle-distance performers Apogee and Daring Miss, out of half-sister to Oaks second Bourbon Girl: 12/1 and green, won 12-runner maiden at Kempton by ½ **84 p**

length from stable-companion Mananiyya, soon close up after slow start and leading over 1f out: should stay at least 1¼m: should go on to better things. *Sir Michael Stoute*

SPARKLETTE   3 ch.f. Bijou d'Inde 127 – Princess Lily 65 (Blakeney 126) [2002 p8g **54** p7g⁴ f7g⁶ 7m p6g⁵ f7g Jun 22] 800Y: half-sister to several winners, including fairly useful 5f (at 2 yrs) to 8.5f winner Risk Free and 1m to 2m winner Royal Roulette (both by Risk Me): dam maiden who stayed 1½m: modest maiden: should stay 1m: acts on polytrack, probably on good to firm going: sold 2,200 gns in July, sent to Trinidad. *C. F. Wall*

SPARKLING JEWEL   2 b.f. (May 15) Bijou d'Inde 127 – Jobiska (Dunbeath (USA) **75** 127) [2002 p5g² May 28] 2,200F: half-sister to several winners, including fairly useful 5f to 6f winner in Britain/UAE Mile High (by Puissance): dam lightly raced: 16/1, head second of 9 to eased Romantic Liason in maiden at Lingfield, finishing strongly. *R. Hannon*

SPARKLING WATER (USA)   3 br. or b.c. Woodman (USA) 126 – Shirley Valentine **106 §** 104 (Shirley Heights 130) [2002 107: 10g³ 12.3f² 11g⁵ 12m 10.1d³ Jul 11] quite attractive colt: useful performer: good 2½ lengths second to Fight Your Corner in Chester Vase in May, making most: below form after, looking none too keen: stays 1½m: acts on firm ground, probably on soft: races prominently: unreliable: sold 20,000 gns in October. *H. R. A. Cecil*

SPARK OF LIFE   5 b.m. Rainbows For Life (CAN) – Sparkly Girl (IRE) 79 (Danehill **60 §** (USA) 126) [2002 60§: p12g p10g p12g² p13g³ 10.9f⁶ 11.7g⁵ p16g p10g p13g Dec 28] small mare: modest handicapper: stays 13f: acts on polytrack and firm going, probably on soft: effective blinkered or not: often slowly away: ungenuine. *T. D. McCarthy*

SPARK UP   2 b.f. (Feb 14) Lahib (USA) 129 – Catch The Flame (USA) (Storm Bird **81** (CAN) 134) [2002 5d* 5g³ 6.5g Sep 27] 22,000F, 12,500Y: smallish, quite attractive filly: second foal: half-sister to a winner abroad by Bishop of Cashel: dam unraced half-sister to US 2-y-o Grade 2 6.5f winner Bright Launch: fairly useful form: won maiden at Beverley in July: good third to Tilak in minor event at Ripon: well held in sales race at Ascot: should stay at least 6f. *T. D. Easterby*

SPARKY'S MATE   2 b.g. (Apr 30) Vettori (IRE) 119 – Nikiya (IRE) (Lead On Time **78** (USA) 123) [2002 6d⁴ 7.5g² 8m² 7.9m² 8g⁴ 7g² Oct 24] 6,500F, IR 8,000Y: leggy, lengthy gelding: fourth foal: half-brother to French 9f/9.5f winner Temple Dancer (by Magic Ring): dam placed around 9f in France: fair maiden: second 4 times: should stay 1¼m: yet to race on extremes of going: gelded after final start. *M. H. Tompkins*

SPARTACUS (IRE)   2 b.c. (Mar 4) Danehill (USA) 126 – Teslemi (USA) 73 (Ogygian **107** (USA)) [2002 7g* 6g 6.3s² 6s* 7g 8s* Oct 20] strong, close-coupled colt: has a markedly round action: sixth foal: brother to smart Irish/Hong Kong performer up to 1¼m Johan Cruyff, 7f/1m winner at 2 yrs, and 3-y-o Alstemeria: dam 1m winner from good American family: useful performer: won maiden at Gowran in May, Independent Water-

Gran Criterium, Milan—Spartacus wins his second Group 1 of the season; he is clear of the British-trained trio Checkit (right), Excelsius (No.5) and Tacitus (partially hidden)

Mrs John Magnier's "Spartacus"

ford Wedgwood Phoenix Stakes at the Curragh (outsider of stable's 4 runners, beat Marino Marini by ½ length, making virtually all) in August and Gran Criterium at Milan in October: beat Checkit by 3 lengths in last-named, leading over 2f out: will stay 1¼m: raced only on good ground or softer. *A. P. O'Brien, Ireland*

SPARTAN FAIR 4 ch.g. Spartan Monarch – Fair Atlanta 73 (Tachypous 128) [2002 –
–: 11.9d May 24] tailed off in 4 maidens. *R. Guest*

SPARTAN SAILOR 4 b.g. Handsome Sailor 125 – Spartan Native (Native Bazaar –
122) [2002 –: 11.8s Mar 28] tailed off in maidens/handicap. *A. Senior*

SPEAK 2 ch.f. (Feb 13) Barathea (IRE) 127 – Prompting 76 (Primo Dominie 121) **63**
[2002 5.1d⁵ 7m⁶ 5m⁵ 6m⁶ 6g Oct 28] sixth foal: half-sister to 3 winners, including useful German 6f to 1m performer Sharp Domino (by Sharpo) and fairly useful 6f winner Elegant Lady (by Selkirk): dam, 2-y-o 5f winner (later winning sprinter in Switzerland), half-sister to useful sprinter Sharp Prod: modest maiden: likely to prove best at 6f/7f: yet to race on extremes of going. *R. Hannon*

SPECIAL BRANCH 2 ch.c. (May 4) Woodborough (USA) 112 – Sixslip (USA) 94 **74**
(Diesis 133) [2002 8.3s² 8d Oct 18] 500Y: eighth foal: dam 1¼m and 1¾m winner: fair form when 8 lengths third (promoted) to disqualified Inchberry in maiden at Hamilton, starting slowly: well held in similar event at Redcar. *Jedd O'Keeffe*

SPECIAL ENVOY 2 b.c. (Jan 21) Barathea (IRE) 127 – Wosaita 70 (Generous (IRE) **75 p**
139) [2002 p7g 7d 7d 8s* 7s² 8d* Nov 1] 55,000Y: strong, good sort: first foal: dam, third at 1½m from 3 starts, half-sister to smart performer up to 15.5f Chiang Mai and Prix de

928

Diane winner Rafha, herself dam of 5-y-o Invincible Spirit: fair form: won nurseries at Yarmouth in October and Brighton (easily by 2 lengths from Lampos) in November: ran well in between: will be suited by 1¼m/1½m: raced only on good to soft/soft going on turf: sometimes carries head awkwardly: sold 19,000 gns, sent to Switzerland: capable of better still. *Sir Mark Prescott*

SPECIAL HERO (IRE)   3 b.c. Spectrum (IRE) 126 – Royal Heroine 121 (Lypheor   –
118) [2002 71p: 8f 6d 7g f6g Oct 17] tall, long-backed colt: fair performer at 2 yrs: well held in 2002: reportedly had breathing problem on reappearance: sold 1,000 gns. *K. A. Ryan*

SPECIALI (IRE)   3 b.c. Bluebird (USA) 125 – Fille Dansante (IRE) (Dancing Dis-   –
sident (USA) 119) [2002 8m Apr 17] 37,000F, 140,000Y: good-bodied, quite attractive colt: has a quick action: third foal: half-brother to winner in Austria by Shalford: dam unraced half-sister to very smart sprinter Cyrano de Bergerac: weak 11/2-shot, burly/unimpressive to post, well held in newcomers race at Newmarket. *J. H. M. Gosden*

SPECIALISM   4 ch.g. Spectrum (IRE) 126 – Waft (USA) 67 (Topsider (USA)) [2002   –
6g p10g⁶ 10.5m⁵ f9.4s Nov 2] 3,500Y, 17,000 (2.o Nov 1): first foal: dam, placed at 8.3f, half-sister to dam of St Leger/Coronation Cup winner Silver Patriarch: little form: left T. Keddy after third start: free-going sort: slowly away/looked none too keen final run. *M. J. Gingell*

SPECIAL-K   10 br.m. Treasure Kay 114 – Lissi Gori (FR) (Bolkonski 134) [2002 8m   –
10.1s Jun 5] of little account nowadays. *J. R. Weymes*

SPECIAL PROMISE (IRE)   5 ch.g. Anjiz (USA) 104 – Woodenitbenice (USA)   –
(Nasty And Bold (USA)) [2002 49, a65: 12.4g 14g May 20] strong, lengthy gelding: fair handicapper at best: well held in 2002: tried visored. *I. Semple*

SPECTINA   4 b.f. Spectrum (IRE) 126 – Catina 102 (Nureyev (USA) 131) [2002 92:   –
7d May 27] angular, deep-girthed filly: unimpressive mover: fairly useful maiden at 3 yrs: well held only run in 2002. *Jedd O'Keeffe*

SPECTROMETER   5 ch.g. Rainbow Quest (USA) 134 – Selection Board 75 (Welsh   **89**
Pageant 132) [2002 11.9g* 12m⁶ Sep 14] close-coupled gelding: fairly useful handicapper: unraced on Flat in 2001 (fairly useful hurdler): better than ever when beating Collier Hill by ½ length in Ladbroke Knavesmire Handicap at York in August: favourite, only sixth of 7 at Doncaster next time: stays 13f: acts on good to firm and good to soft going. *P. J. Hobbs*

SPECTROSCOPE (IRE)   3 b.g. Spectrum (IRE) 126 – Paloma Bay (IRE) 92 (Alzao   **74**
(USA) 117) [2002 63p: 8g 8.5g 11.6s 12m* 11f* 10m⁴ Oct 7] quite attractive gelding: fair handicapper: won at Goodwood in August and September: stays 1½m: acts on firm ground: won juvenile hurdle in October. *Jonjo O'Neill*

SPECTRUM STAR   2 b.g. (Mar 3) Spectrum (IRE) 126 – Persia (IRE) (Persian Bold   –
123) [2002 6g 7.1d⁴ p6g Jul 17] 5,500Y: quite good-topped gelding: fourth foal: half-brother to 1m winner Queen Zenobia (by Danehill): dam unraced half-sister to very smart sprinter Sayyaf: well beaten in maidens/minor event. *D. K. Ivory*

SPECULATION (IRE)   3 gr.g. Spectrum (IRE) 126 – Tapaculo 94 (Tap On Wood   –
130) [2002 f7g f9.4g 10m 11.5f Jun 13] 9,000Y: half-brother to several winners, including 11.5f winner Banana Cove (by Shirley Heights) and Irish 1999 2-y-o 9f winner Wagner (by Lure): dam, 2-y-o 7f winner, half-sister to dams of High-Rise and In The Wings: well held, including in seller. *Mrs C. A. Dunnett*

SPEED COP   2 ch.f. (Mar 24) Cadeaux Genereux 131 – Blue Siren 113 (Bluebird   **99**
(USA) 125) [2002 6d³ 5m² 5m⁴ 5.1d* 5g⁴ 5.2f* 5m³ 5m² Oct 12] rather leggy, useful-looking filly: has a quick action: second foal: dam, 5f (at 2 yrs) to 7f winner, also first past post in Nunthorpe Stakes: useful performer: won maiden at Bath in July and listed event at Newbury (beat Wimple by neck) in August: good placed efforts in Flying Childers Stakes at Doncaster (just over length third to Wunders Dream) and Cornwallis Stakes at Ascot (beaten ½ length by Peace Offering) last 2 starts: best at 5f: acts on firm and good to soft ground: sometimes bandaged behind: races prominently: genuine and consistent. *I. A. Balding*

SPEEDFIT BLUE (IRE)   3 b.c. Bluebird (USA) 125 – She's The Tops 83 (Shernazar   **58**
131) [2002 8f 8.2g 9d 14.1f³ 16.2d⁶ 12m² 12m 12m 14.1m 12f Oct 17] 85,000Y: small, sturdy colt: sixth foal: half-brother to 3 winners, including smart 7f (at 2 yrs) to 1¼m (Pretty Polly Stakes) winner Lady Upstage (by Alzao) and 17f winner The Blues Academy (by Royal Academy): dam, 1½m winner, out of half-sister to Most Welcome: modest maiden handicapper: stays 1¾m: acts on firm going: blinkered last 7 starts:

seemed reluctant to race seventh outing/went with little enthusiasm last 2: needs treating with caution: sold 4,500 gns, sent to Kuwait. *G. G. Margarson*

SPEEDFIT FREE (IRE) 5 b.g. Night Shift (USA) – Dedicated Lady (IRE) 101 **53 §** (Pennine Walk 120) [2002 63: f6g⁶ f6s f7g² f6g⁴ f7g³ 8m⁵ 7f³ 7.2g⁶ 8m⁶ 7g 7m 5.9v* **a56 §** 6s 6g 6d f6g* f7g f6g Dec 10] smallish, well-made gelding: modest performer: won handicap at Hamilton (first start after leaving E. Alston) in August and claimer at Wolverhampton in November: effective at 6f to easy 1m: acts on any turf going and fibresand: tried blinkered/visored: unreliable. *I. Semple*

SPEED ON 9 b.g. Sharpo 132 – Pretty Poppy 67 (Song 132) [2002 66§: 5.1g⁴ 5.7g 5s⁵ **65 §** p5g⁴ 5.1d 5f 5m 5m 5f Sep 25] small, strong gelding: fair handicapper: barely stays 6f: acts on firm and soft going (well held twice on heavy) and polytrack: tried visored: often ridden by inexperienced apprentice nowadays: inconsistent. *H. Candy*

SPEED QUEEN (IRE) 3 b.f. Goldmark (USA) 113 – Blues Queen 85 (Lahib (USA) **52** 129) [2002 –: p6g* p7g 8m May 29] modest performer, lightly raced: won seller at Lingfield in February: should stay 7f. *A. P. Jarvis*

SPEEDY GEE (IRE) 4 b.g. Petardia 113 – Champagne Girl 67 (Robellino (USA) **72 d** 127) [2002 84· 5f⁶ 5f 5d 5.3g 5g 5m⁶ 6d 5m 5m 5.3m² Sep 3] strong, good-quartered gelding: fair performer: on downgrade: best at 5f/6f: possibly needs good going or firmer: visored (well held) once: carried head awkwardly/wandered final outing. *D. Nicholls*

SPEEDY JAMES (IRE) 6 ch.g. Fayruz 116 – Haraabah (USA) 99 (Topsider (USA)) **–** [2002 79: f6s f6s f5g 5s Apr 1] strong gelding: good mover: one-time useful performer: well held in 2002: visored once at 2 yrs. *D. Nicholls*

SPELLMISTRESS 2 ch.f. (Feb 13) Magic Ring (IRE) 115 – Valldemosa 81 (Music **45** Boy 124) [2002 f5g f5g 5m f6g f5g Dec 27] eighth foal: half-sister to 3 winners, including 4-y-o Ragamuffin: dam 5f winner, including at 2 yrs: poor maiden: tried blinkered. *A. Berry*

SPENCERS WOOD (IRE) 5 b.g. Pips Pride 117 – Ascoli (Skyliner 117) [2002 108: **102** 6m⁵ 6f 6d³ 6m* 6s Oct 25] strong, close-coupled gelding: useful performer: best effort in 2002 when fifth to Chookie Heiton in handicap at Newbury in July: simple task when winning minor event at Hamilton in September: best at 6f/7f: acts on good to firm and good to soft going: visored (below form on soft going) final start: has sweated/got on edge: takes strong hold: often races prominently. *P. J. Makin*

SPHINX (FR) 4 b.c. Snurge 130 – Egyptale (Crystal Glitters (USA) 127) [2002 12g² **90** 9.8m* 12s p12g* p10g Dec 3] fifth foal: brother to fairly useful French 1¼m (at 2 yrs) to 13f winner Toutafee and half-brother to 2 winners, including 13f winner Spirit of The Nile (by Generous): dam French 10.5f winner from family of Arc runner-up Egyptband: fairly useful performer: successful at Lyon Parilly at 3 yrs in 2 minor events and a handicap: won claimer at Longchamp in April (claimed from M. Cesandri €25,777): best of 3 efforts in Britain when winning handicap at Lingfield in November: stays 1½m: acts on polytrack, heavy and good to firm ground. *N. P. Littmoden*

SPICE ISLAND 4 b.f. Reprimand 122 – Little Emmeline 52 (Emarati (USA) 74) **58** [2002 62: 7v 6.1d³ 6.1m 6m 6s⁵ 7m 7g 6.9s⁸ 8g² 8.3s³ 9.7g 7g f8g Nov 25] big, strong filly: modest handicapper: effective at 6f (given test) to 1m: best efforts on good going or softer: effective visored or not. *J. A. Glover*

SPIDER MCCOY (USA) 2 ch.c. (Mar 8) Irish River (FR) 131 – Indy's Princess **80** (USA) (A P Indy (USA) 131) [2002 7d⁵ 8g² 8m² 8.1m⁵ 7v Nov 9] 48,000Y: well-made colt: second foal: dam unraced half-sister to Derby Italiano winner Hailsham: fairly useful maiden: runner-up at Thirsk and Goodwood: left P. Cole 16,000 gns before running poorly final start: will stay at least 1¼m: acts on good to firm ground: usually soon off bridle. *N. Tinkler*

SPINAMIX 3 gr.f. Spinning World (USA) 130 – Vadsagreya (FR) (Linamix (FR) 127) **–** [2002 67: 8m f8.5g 8m Jun 3] lengthy, rather sparely-made filly: disappointing maiden. *M. A. Jarvis*

SPINDARA (IRE) 3 ch.f. Spinning World (USA) 130 – Lydara (USA) (Alydar **–** (USA)) [2002 64: p7g 8.1m 10g 12.1g 17.2d 7f f8g Nov 26] sparely-made filly: modest maiden at 2 yrs: little form in 2002: left P. Cole 13,000 gns after fifth start. *K. A. Ryan*

SPINETAIL RUFOUS (IRE) 4 b.c. Prince of Birds (USA) 121 – Miss Kinabalu 50 **– §** (Shirley Heights 130) [2002 73: p5g 6g 5m 5f 5.1g p8g⁶ f6g² p7g f6g f6g⁶ Dec 10] **a69 §** fair performer: effective at 5f/6f: acts on fibresand: sometimes tongue tied: has worn cheekpieces: finds little, and not to be trusted. *D. W. P. Arbuthnot*

SPINEY NORMAN   4 gr.g. Petong 126 – Fairy Ballerina (Fairy King (USA)) [2002 –
–: p8g p10g Feb 26] rather leggy gelding: little sign of ability. *Jamie Poulton*

SPIN MASTER   2 b.g. (Apr 5) Averti (IRE) 117 – Dayrella 57 (Beveled (USA)) [2002   63 §
5m 5m 5m³ 6d 5f 6m 5.1g 5.7f⁴ 6g Oct 18] 16,000Y: good-topped gelding: first foal:
dam 6f winner: modest maiden: disappointing after third at Sandown: probably stays 6f:
acts on good to firm ground: tried blinkered/visored: unreliable: sold 2,000 gns, sent to
Kuwait. *W. R. Muir*

SPINNETTE (IRE)   3 b. or br.f. Spinning World (USA) 130 – Net Worth (USA)   110
(Forty Niner (USA)) [2002 93p: 10.4m² 12s 10d* 8f³ 10g⁵ Oct 17] lengthy filly: smart
performer: won maiden at Newmarket in July despite tiring noticeably: clearly best
efforts when placed in Musidora Stakes at York (beaten length by Islington) and Sun
Chariot Stakes at Newmarket (2½ lengths third behind Dress To Thrill): may prove
ideally suited by around 1m: acts on firm and good to soft ground: gave deal of trouble at
stall when last in Oaks at Epsom second start: last and steadily to post (also wore rope
halter) third outing. *J. Noseda*

SPINNEY   3 b.f. Unfuwain (USA) 131 – Spin (High Top 131) [2002 p8g⁴ p10g² p10g*   92
11.4f⁴ 10.5d p10g⁶ Nov 13] strong, good-topped filly: sister to smart 1m (at 2 yrs) and
1½m (Chester Vase) winner Gulland, closely related to fairly useful 1m winner Three In
One (by Night Shift) and half-sister to several winners, notably smart performer up to
1¾m Salchow (by Niniski): dam unraced: fairly useful performer: won maiden at
Lingfield in March: good fourth of 5 to Shadow Dancing in listed race at Chester next
time: lost action and dismounted before line penultimate start: off nearly 6 months before
running respectably final one: should stay at least 1½m: acts on firm going and polytrack:
sold 100,000 gns. *B. W. Hills*

SPINNING DOVE   2 ch.f. (Apr 20) Vettori (IRE) 119 – Northern Bird 86 (Interrex   70
(CAN)) [2002 7d⁴ 7g⁵ Aug 12] 15,000Y: big, workmanlike filly: fifth foal: half-sister to
6f (at 2 yrs)/7f winner Xipe Totec (by Pivotal): dam 5f (at 2 yrs) to 7f winner: better effort
in maidens (fair form) when fourth to Londonnetdotcom at Kempton: never going well/
hung left next time: should stay 1m. *N. A. Graham*

Dr T. A. Ryan's "Spinnette"

SPINNING JENNI   2 b.f. (May 8) Mind Games 121 – Giddy 60 (Polar Falcon (USA)   **71**
126) [2002 5g⁶ 6g² 5v² 5g⁴ 5d⁴ 6m³ 6m* 7m 6m Sep 6] 7,000Y: third foal: sister to 3-y-o
Dizzy In The Head and closely related to fairly useful 2000 2-y-o 5f/6f winner Wally
McArthur (by Puissance): dam, 1m winner, half-sister to smart 1m/1¼m performer
Dance Turn: fair performer: left A. Berry after sixth start: won maiden at Epsom in
August: possibly amiss on final appearance: should stay 7f: acts on heavy and good to
firm ground. *S. Dow*

SPINNING LADY (IRE)   3 gr.f. Spinning World (USA) 130 – Madame Belga (USA)   **69**
(Al Nasr (FR) 126) [2002 9.9g⁴ 9g* 11g⁴ 10.5v Nov 21] 58,000Y: tall, rather lengthy
filly: fifth foal: half-sister to winner in USA by Silver Hawk: dam unraced half-sister to
top-class French miler Bellypha: fourth in maiden at Beverley on debut (only outing
for L. Cumani): won minor event at Vire in September: should stay beyond 1¼m.
S. Wattel, France

SPINOLA (FR)   2 b.f. (Mar 6) Spinning World (USA) 130 – Exocet (USA) (Deposit   **103**
Ticket (USA)) [2002 6g³ 7m* 6d* 7m Aug 25] 230,000 francs F, 50,000Y: close-coupled,
quite attractive filly: second foal: half-sister to 3-y-o Shot To Fame: dam, sprint winner in
USA, half-sister to useful performer up to 1¾m Mixterthetrixster out of half-sister to
Prix du Cadran winner Molesens: useful form: won maiden at Goodwood (raced freely)
in June and Kleinwort Benson Private Bank Cherry Hinton Stakes at Newmarket (on toes,
held Cassis by short head after travelling strongly and leading over 1f out) in July: found
little when only seventh of 8 in Prestige Stakes at Goodwood: bred to stay at least 1m, but
will need to settle to do so: yet to race on extremes of going. *P. W. Harris*

SPINSKY (USA)   2 b.f. (Apr 11) Spinning World (USA) 130 – Walewskaia (IRE)   **73**
(Slip Anchor 136) [2002 5m⁵ 6m 5m² 6m* 6.5m⁶ Sep 11] neat filly: fifth foal: half-sister
to winners in US by Meadowlake and Silver Deputy: dam 7f winner at 2 yrs in France:
fair performer: won nursery at Newmarket in August: good effort in similar event at
Doncaster final start: should stay 1m: raced only on good to firm going. *P. F. I. Cole*

SPIRIT OF LOVE (USA)   7 ch.g. Trempolino (USA) 135 – Dream Mary (USA)   **–**
(Marfa (USA)) [2002 93d: f16g 16d May 29] tall, lengthy gelding: had a long stride:
one-time smart performer: won Cesarewitch at 3 yrs: no form in 2002 (left J. Given after
reappearance): was best at 2m+: acted on fibresand, soft and good to firm going: was tried
visored, sometimes blinkered: fell fatally over hurdles in June. *E. W. Tuer*

SPIRIT OF SONG (IRE)   4 b.f. Selkirk (USA) 129 – Roxy Music (IRE) 63 (Song   **44**
132) –: 6.1d f7g⁵ 7f³ 6m 7.5d 8g 7f Sep 21] sturdy filly: poor maiden: stays 7f: acts
on fibresand and firm ground: tried visored. *Mrs Lydia Pearce*

SPIRIT'S AWAKENING   3 b.c. Danzig Connection (USA) – Mo Stopher 47 (Sharpo   **62**
132) [2002 60: 6m 6d 7d³ 7d⁵ 6m 7m 7g⁶ 8g* Oct 16] modest handicapper: won at Bath
in October: stays 1m: best form on good going or softer. *J. Akehurst*

SPIRITUAL AIR   2 b.f. (Mar 8) Royal Applause 124 – Samsung Spirit 79 (Statoblest   **93**
120) [2002 5.1m⁵ 6d* 6d⁶ 7.1m⁵ 6d⁵ 6.5g Sep 27] 28,000Y: lengthy filly: second foal:
dam, 6f winner (including at 2 yrs), half-sister to dam of smart 6f/7f performer Indian
Rocket: fairly useful performer: made all in maiden at Ayr in June: creditable efforts in
Cherry Hinton Stakes at Newmarket (sixth to Spinola) and listed events at Sandown and
Ripon next 3 starts: seems to stay 7f: yet to race on extremes of going. *J. R. Weymes*

*Kleinwort Benson Private Bank Cherry Hinton Stakes, Newmarket—Peter Harris trains the winner
of the race for the second time in three years as Spinola holds on from fast-finishing Cassis,
Pearl Dance (second right) and Never A Doubt (No.3)*

SPITE FOOL   2 b.g. (May 14) Distinctly North (USA) 115 – Young Annabel (USA) –
71 (Cahill Road (USA)) [2002 6g p5g f7g Nov 26] second foal: dam 7f winner: well held
in maidens. *G. G. Margarson*

SPITFIRE BOB (USA)   3 b.g. Mister Baileys 123 – Gulf Cyclone (USA) (Sheikh   67
Albadou 128) [2002 62p: f7g² f6g p6g 7.1m f8.5s* 8f² p8g Nov 13] first foal: dam   a75
unraced half-sister to smart miler Sarafan and useful 1m to 1½m winner Hagwah: fair
performer: best effort when winning maiden handicap at Wolverhampton in September:
will stay 1¼m: acts on firm going and fibresand: sometimes slowly away. *T. D. Barron*

SPIT SPOT   3 ch.g. Sabrehill (USA) 120 – Tigwa 68 (Cadeaux Genereux 131) [2002   –
8m 11.1s⁶ May 10] strong, heavy-bodied gelding: third foal: half-brother to 1998 2-y-o
7.5f winner Green Snake (by Royal Academy): dam, maiden who stayed 1m, half-sister
to 1000 Guineas winner Sayyedati and high-class 1¼m/1½m performer Golden Snake:
never dangerous in newcomers race at Newmarket and (took while to settle) maiden at
Hamilton. *W. J. Haggas*

SPITTING IMAGE (IRE)   2 ch.f. (Apr 27) Spectrum (IRE) 126 – Decrescendo   68
(IRE) (Polish Precedent (USA) 131) [2002 7.5m² 6g⁴ 7f⁵ 6m⁵ 7.1m 7.5g² 7m³ 8s Oct 15]
5,000Y: close-coupled, quite attractive filly: fourth foal: half-sister to 3-y-o Softly: dam
unraced half-sister to smart 1¼m filly Calando out of Oaks winner and St Leger second
Diminuendo: fair maiden: left C. Brittain after fifth start: should stay at least 1m: acts on
firm going, ran poorly on soft. *Mrs M. Reveley*

SPLASH OUT AGAIN   4 b.g. River Falls 113 – Kajetana (FR) (Caro 133) [2002 67:   73
11.6d 11.6d 10m* 9.9m² 12g 10m⁶ 12m 9.9g³ 10s 9s Oct 25] fair handicapper: won at
Sandown in June: stays 11f: acts on good to firm and good to soft going, possibly not on
soft: blinkered eighth/ninth outings: hung left second start. *R. J. O'Sullivan*

SPLENDID ERA (UAE)   2 b.c. (Apr 9) Green Desert (USA) 127 – Valley of Gold   105 p
(FR) 117 (Shirley Heights 130) [2002 7f p7g* p7g* Dec 3] good-bodied colt: third foal:
closely related to 3-y-o Hills of Gold and half-brother to 4-y-o Honest Obsession: dam,
1¼m/11f (Oaks d'Italia) winner, half-sister to 2-y-o Dublin: progressive form: won
maiden in October and minor event in December, both at Lingfield: put up remarkable
performance to beat Grand Passion by neck in latter, travelling strongly when running
very wide turning for home then quickening in fine style to lead near finish (rated value
for 4-length success): will probably stay 1m: smart performer in the making, sure to win
more races. *B. W. Hills*

SPLODGER MAC (IRE)   3 b.c. Lahib (USA) 129 – Little Love (Warrshan (USA)   46
117) [2002 –: 9d 5.9g⁶ Jun 27] sturdy colt: first foal: dam unraced: poor form, lightly
raced. *N. Bycroft*

SPORTING AFFAIR (IRE)   2 ch.f. (Apr 13) Ashkalani (IRE) 128 – The Multiyorker   59
(IRE) 72 (Digamist (USA) 110) [2002 6d⁶ 6v⁶ 7d⁴ 7g⁴ Aug 9] 4,500Y: fourth foal:
sister to French 12.5f/13f winner Courrier du Tsar, and half-sister to fairly useful 2000
2-y-o 6f winner Siptitz Heights (by Zieten): dam, 7f winner (including at 2 yrs), out of
sister to 2000 Guineas winner Tap On Wood: modest maiden: best effort in nursery at
Wolverhampton final start: should stay 1m: acts on fibresand, raced only on going softer
than good on turf. *N. P. Littmoden*

SPORTING GESTURE   5 ch.g. Safawan 118 – Polly Packer 81 (Reform 132) [2002   70
80: 10s 12f 11.9m 11.9d⁶ 10.3f⁵ 11.9g 10.1m⁶ 11.9f⁶ 10d³ Oct 21] leggy gelding: has a
round action: fair handicapper: stays 1½m: acts on firm and good to soft going: tried
blinkered: sometimes looks difficult ride: often races prominently. *M. W. Easterby*

SPORT ON SATURDAY (USA)   2 b.f. (Jan 28) Carson City (USA) – Wild Again   54
Miss (USA) (Wild Again (USA)) [2002 6m 5.1f⁵ 5g 7f f8g³ f7g* 7g Oct 24] big, leggy,
useful-looking filly: second foal: dam, 8.5f winner in USA, half-sister to dam of Prix du
Cadran winner Always Earnest: modest performer: won seller at Wolverhampton (idled) in October: stays 1m: acts on fibresand and firm going: sold 12,000 gns,
sent to USA. *B. J. Meehan*

SPORTS EXPRESS   4 ch.f. Then Again 126 – Lady St Lawrence (USA) 65 (Bering   58
136) [2002 42: 16g³ Mar 28] workmanlike filly: modest maiden: stays 2m: acts on
fibresand and firm ground. *G. A. Swinbank*

SPORTSMAN (IRE)   3 b.g. Sri Pekan (USA) 117 – Ardent Range (IRE) (Archway   –
(IRE) 115) [2002 f6g f7g⁵ f8g³ f7g 10g Aug 26] 20,000F: first foal: dam unraced: well beaten
in maidens/handicap: slowly away all outings. *M. W. Easterby*

SPORTY COLLEEN   3 b.f. Colonel Collins (USA) 122 – Hot Sunday Sport 42 (Star   –
Appeal 133) [2002 p7g p5g f6g 7m 10g 7m Jul 3] 4,200Y: half-sister to 2 winners by Risk

Me, including 1998 2-y-o 7f seller winner Risky Way: dam maiden who stayed 1½m: little sign of ability, leaving D. Ivory after third start: tried blinkered: has been slowly away. *M. J. Ryan*

SPREE LOVE   4 b.f. Dancing Spree (USA) – Locorotondo (IRE) 83 (Broken Hearted **42** 124) [2002 39: f8g p8g⁶ f11g⁴ 10.1m p7g 5.9g 6m 5.3d Jul 7] angular filly: poor nowadays: tried visored/blinkered/tongue tied. *P. L. Gilligan*

SPREE VISION   6 b.g. Suave Dancer (USA) 136 – Regent's Folly (IRE) 101 (Touching **66** Wood (USA) 127) [2002 59: 11.1g⁶ 7.9s 9.2v⁴ 10.9d* 9.2s⁴ 11.1v² 12.1d⁴ 11.1d 9.2v³ 10s⁶ 12.1m Sep 2] smallish, good-topped gelding: fair handicapper: won at Ayr in June: effective at 9f given test, barely stays 13f: acts on any going: tried visored: has worn severe noseband: sometimes starts slowly/carries head awkwardly. *P. Monteith*

SPRING GIFT   5 b.m. Slip Anchor 136 – Belmez Melody 73 (Belmez (USA) 131) **30** [2002 f12s⁴ f12s Jan 15] poor maiden, lightly raced: probably stays 1½m. *P. W. D'Arcy*

SPRING OAK   4 b.f. Mark of Esteem (IRE) 137 – English Spring (USA) 116 (Grey **103** Dawn II 132) [2002 113: 9g² 10g⁶ 12.5g Oct 5] rangy filly: smart performer for A. Fabre in 2001: just useful form at 4 yrs, best effort when 1¾ lengths second to Tarfshi in listed race at Newmarket: off over 3 months before final outing: stayed 10.5f: acted on firm and soft going: visits Machiavellian. *Saeed bin Suroor*

SPRING PURSUIT   6 b.g. Rudimentary (USA) 118 – Pursuit of Truth (USA) 69 **74 d** (Irish River (FR) 131) [2002 90d: 12s² p12g³ 11.9m 12g⁴ 14.1m 12.3f⁴ 11.6d⁶ 13.3s 12s⁶ 12d f12g 11.7g 11.9g 12s⁴ Nov 6] close-coupled gelding: fair handicapper: off 3 months, below form last 5 starts: best recent form around 1½m: goes well on soft/heavy going, though also acts on firm and polytrack (below form on fibresand): blinkered once at 2 yrs: has been bandaged behind/early to post: usually held up. *R. J. Price*

SPRING STAR (FR)   3 b.f. Danehill (USA) 126 – L'Irlandaise (USA) (Irish River **106** (FR) 131) [2002 8s² 8g³ 8d* 8m* 8g 9f⁶ Sep 8] tall, well-made filly: half-sister to numerous winners, including useful French 1m winner Direcvil (by Top Ville) and French 1m (at 2 yrs) and 1¼m winner Irish Sun (by Shernazar): dam won up to 1¼m in France: stylish performer: won minor event at Maisons-Laffitte in May and Prix de Sandringham at Chantilly (by head from Clerical Error) in June: creditable 3 lengths sixth to Wonder Again in Garden City Breeders' Cup Handicap at Belmont final outing: only eighth of 9 in Falmouth Stakes at Newmarket fifth start: raced only at 1m/9f: acts on firm going, winner on good to soft. *C. Laffon-Parias, France*

SPRINKLE STARS (IRE)   3 b.f. Danehill (USA) 126 – Hastening (Shirley Heights **76** 130) [2002 7g³ 7f³ May 8] IR 125,000Y: tall, lengthy filly: half-sister to several winners, including useful performer up to 1¼m in Ireland No Slouch (by Royal Academy) and fairly useful 13f winner (stays 2¼m) General Assembly (by Pharly): dam unraced from family of Diesis and Kris: fair form when close third to Up Market in newcomers race at Newbury on debut, running on strongly: odds on, only third in similar event at Chester next time: bred to stay at least 1¼m. *G. Wragg*

SPRITSAIL (USA)   2 ch.f. (Apr 27) Woodman (USA) 126 – Sprite's Ridge (USA) **51** (Cox's Ridge (USA)) [2002 6m⁶ 6g 6m 7m 8g Sep 20] $50,000F, $17,000Y: small, sparely-made filly: seventh foal: half-sister to 3 winners abroad: dam unraced from good North American family: modest maiden: should stay 1m: sold 7,000 gns. *M. A. Jarvis*

SPRITZERIA   3 b.f. Bigstone (IRE) 126 – Clincher Club 77 (Polish Patriot (USA) **81** 128) [2002 79: p7g² f8.5g 8m⁴ 8.2d⁵ 8.1d 8d³ 8s⁴ 8s* 8.2² 8v p10g Nov 13] useful-looking filly: good walker: fairly useful handicapper: won at Newmarket in August: stays 1m: acts on firm going, soft and polytrack: usually held up. *W. J. Haggas*

SPURADICH (IRE)   2 b.c. (Mar 25) Barathea (IRE) 127 – Svanzega (USA) (Sharpen **– p** Up 127) [2002 9v⁵ p8g Dec 3] half-brother to several winners, including fairly useful 1¼m winner Scachmatt (by Zafonic) who stayed 1½m: dam Italian 7f (at 2 yrs) to 1½m winner, including Group 3 1¼m event: behind in minor event at Milan and maiden at Lingfield, signs of ability (raced freely) in latter: will probably do better. *L. M. Cumani*

SPUR OF GOLD (IRE)   4 b.f. Flying Spur (AUS) – Tony's Ridge (Indian Ridge **–** 123) [2002 –: 10.1g⁶ May 6] sparely-made filly: little form. *J. S. Wainwright*

SPY GUN (USA)   2 ch.g. (Feb 5) Mt Livermore (USA) – Takeover Target (USA) **76 p** (Nodouble (USA)) [2002 7m Aug 23] $55,000Y: well-made gelding: sixth foal: half-brother to 3 winners in USA: dam, 6f/9.5f winner in USA, half-sister to US Grade 1 winners Sewickley (at 7f) and Shared Interest (at 8.5f): 50/1, 11 lengths eighth of 16 to Almushahar in maiden at Newmarket, mid-field throughout: should do better. *E. A. L. Dunlop*

SPY KNOLL 8 b.g. Shirley Heights 130 – Garden Pink (FR) (Bellypha 130) [2002 –: **63** p16g[5] p16g[4] Mar 6] very tall, rangy gelding: modest handicapper, very lightly raced on Flat nowadays: stays 2m: acts on polytrack and soft going, probably on firm: visored once at 3 yrs, blinkered in 2002. *Jamie Poulton*

SPY MASTER 4 b.g. Green Desert (USA) 127 – Obsessive (USA) 102 (Seeking The **–** Gold (USA)) [2002 –: 8.5d 7m Sep 5] small, strong gelding: fairly useful at 2 yrs: well held since: usually visored/blinkered earlier in career. *J. Parkes*

SPYMASTER (USA) 5 ch.h. Seeking The Gold (USA) – Secrettame (USA) (Secre- **57** tariat (USA)) [2002 a10f[2] 10g[2] a12f 11.7f 10m[4] 12d 11.5m Sep 17] closely related to several winners, notably US Grade 1 winner at 9f Gone West and smart French/US performer up to 1m Lion Cavern (both by Mr Prospector), and half-brother to winner in USA by Danzig: dam, 6f to 9f winner in USA, second in Grade 2 event at 9f, half-sister to Known Fact: modest maiden, lightly raced: sold 22,000 gns and left P. Brette in UAE after third start in 2002: stays 1¼m: acts on good to firm going and dirt: tried visored/ tongue tied: to stud in Italy. *E. J. O'Neill*

SQUARE DANCER 6 b.g. Then Again 126 – Cubist (IRE) 71 (Tate Gallery (USA) **51** 117) [2002 69d: 5g 6s[4] 6s 5.9v 5.9d 5.9v 5s[2] 5m 6d Oct 15] tall, good-bodied gelding: modest performer: stays easy 7f: acts on fibresand, firm and soft going: tried visored: tongue tied: has given trouble at stall: untrustworthy. *D. A. Nolan*

SQUEAKY 5 ch.m. Infantry 122 – Steady Saunter VII (Damsire Unregistered) [2002 **71** f9.4g 10g 8.1m[5] 11.6s[3] 10s[6] 12.6f[3] 10.9g[*] 12g[4] 10m Jul 29] lengthy non-thoroughbred mare: second foal: dam unraced: dam handicapper: won maiden event at Warwick in July: effective at 1¼m to 12.6f: acts on firm and soft going: has worn crossed noseband. *Miss K. M. George*

SQUIBNOCKET (IRE) 3 b.g. Charnwood Forest (IRE) 125 – Serenad Dancer (FR) **52** (Antheus (USA) 122) [2002 58: 7.1m 7m[6] 8m 8.1s 5.9d 7f[3] 8.5m[6] 7d Oct 18] good-bodied gelding: modest maiden handicapper: probably stayed 8.5f: acted on firm and good to soft going: dead. *T. D. Easterby*

SQUIRE MICHAEL (USA) 2 b.c. (Jan 30) Affirmed (USA) – Elle Meme (USA) **67** (Zilzal (USA) 137) [2002 7g[4] 7f[4] 7g 10m 8.5g[5] f8g[2] Nov 26] $19,000F, 700,000 francs Y: rather leggy colt: first foal: dam, French 7f (at 2 yrs) and 1m winner, from family of Miesque: fair maiden: second in claimer at Southwell: will stay at least 1¼m: acts on fibresand, best turf run on firm going: blinkered (ran creditably) fifth start. *P. F. I. Cole*

SRI DIAMOND 2 b.c. (May 16) Sri Pekan (USA) 117 – Hana Marie 101§ (Form- **89 p** idable (USA) 125) [2002 7.1m[*] Sep 16] 8,000Y: good-topped colt: half-brother to 3-y-o Naughty Nell and a winner up to 10.5f in Italy by Turtle Island: dam, 2-y-o sprint winner, became unreliable: 8/1 and backward, won 9-runner maiden at Warwick comfortably by 2½ lengths from Once, dictating steady pace: useful prospect. *S. Kirk*

SRI GANESHA (IRE) 3 b.f. Sri Pekan (USA) 117 – Sarabi 64 (Alzao (USA) 117) **–** [2002 46: p5g 6m 8.3d Oct 14] poor maiden at 2 yrs: well held in 2002. *P. Mitchell*

STADIUM (IRE) 3 b.g. Barathea (IRE) 127 – Luvia (Cure The Blues (USA)) [2002 **–** 8.1f 10.4m Sep 8] 300,000 francs F, 700,000 francs Y: good-bodied gelding: half-brother to several winners in France, including 1¼m (at 2 yrs)/1½m winner Loophole (by Groom Dancer) and 1¼m winner Lune Rouge (by Unfuwain): dam French 1m winner: well held in maidens: left G. Butler, gelded and off 5 months after reappearance. *C. N. Kellett*

STAFF NURSE (IRE) 2 b.f. (Mar 16) Night Shift (USA) – Akebia (USA) (Trempo- **71** lino (USA) 135) [2002 6m 5.1f[3] 6g 6m 7s[*] Oct 28] IR 12,500Y, 32,000 2-y-o: well-made filly: first foal: dam unraced half-sister to smart middle-distance stayer Book At Bedtime: fair performer: won 19-runner nursery at Leicester by head from Special Envoy: should stay 1m: acts on good ground: sold 15,000 gns. *R. Charlton*

STAFFORD KING (IRE) 5 b.h. Nicolotte 118 – Opening Day (Day Is Done 115) **50** [2002 50: 9.2s 18d[2] 12.1g Aug 8] lengthy, workmanlike horse: modest maiden: stays 2¼m: acts on soft going, good to firm and fibresand: tried visored: very slowly away third start: often takes good hold. *J. G. M. O'Shea*

STAGE BY STAGE (USA) 3 ch.g. In The Wings 128 – Lady Thynn (FR) (Crystal **100** Glitters (USA) 127) [2002 101: 10g[5] 13.9m[3] May 14] workmanlike gelding: useful performer: visored, creditable 2¼ lengths third of 4 to Mr Dinos in minor event at York final outing: gelded after: will probably stay 2m: acts on heavy and good to firm ground: carried head high second 2-y-o start. *M. L. W. Bell*

STAGE DIRECTION (USA) 5 b.g. Theatrical 128 – Carya (USA) (Northern Dancer) [2002 p12g 10m[6] 13.8g[2] 16.2p* Aug 6] fairly useful winner in 2000, just modest nowadays: trained by A. Crook on reappearance: won claimer at Chepstow in July: stays 2m: acts on good to firm going: has been tongue tied. *B. J. Llewellyn* **55**

STAGE PASS 9 ch.h. In The Wings 128 – Sateen (USA) (Round Table) [2002 14.1d 14d May 25] tall horse: formerly useful up to 1¾m: very lightly raced nowadays. *G. Barnett* **–**

STAGE SHY (USA) 2 ch.f. (Apr 5) Theatrical 128 – Garimpeiro (USA) (Mr Prospector (USA)) [2002 7m Aug 17] $725,000Y: sister to 2 winners, including very smart North American Grade 1 1m/9f winner Geri, and half-sister to 2 winners in USA: dam maiden out of half-sister to champion US filly Sacahuista (dam of Ekraar): 4/1 favourite, 7 lengths last of 15 to Almaviva in maiden at Newmarket, tiring and not at all knocked about: should do better. *J. H. M. Gosden* **69 p**

STAGNITE 2 ch.c. (Feb 20) Compton Place 125 – Superspring (Superlative 118) [2002 6s 6m[3] 6m[4] 5m[4] 5m 6.1m 5m p6g p6g p6g[4] Dec 28] 10,000 2-y-o: third foal: half-brother to 4-y-o Our Destiny: dam unraced sister to smart sprinter Superpower: fair maiden: effective at 5f/6f: acts on good to firm going and polytrack. *K. R. Burke* **70**

STALKY 3 ch.f. Bahamian Bounty 116 – La Noisette (Rock Hopper 124) [2002 56: p6g p5g[5] f5g p5g[6] f7g f6g f6g 12.6m Jul 20] modest performer at 2 yrs: mostly well held in 2002, leaving J. Osborne after fourth start and Mrs N. Macauley after sixth: blinkered first 4 starts: one to leave alone. *G. F. Bridgwater* **– §**

STALLONE 5 ch.g. Brief Truce (USA) 126 – Bering Honneur (USA) (Bering 136) [2002 79: p10g f11g 8v 10.3m 8m 10.1m 10.5m[6] Sep 6] good-bodied gelding: fair handicapper at 4 yrs: no form in 2002, leaving D. Nicholls after sixth start: ungenuine. *N. Wilson* **– §**

STANCE 3 b.c. Salse (USA) 128 – De Stael (USA) 93 (Nijinsky (CAN) 138) [2002 6p[6] 10s[5] 11.8d[3] 12.6m[2] 12m* 13.9m[6] 12g 12.5m Oct 26] strong, well-made, attractive colt: type to carry condition: has a quick, fluent action: useful performer: won maiden at Newbury in July: very good sixth to Total Turtle in Melrose Handicap at York next outing: disappointing after: stays 1¾m: acts on good to firm and good to soft going: ran in snatches on reappearance: sold 36,000 gns. *H. R. A. Cecil* **98**

STAND BY 5 b.m. Missed Flight 123 – Ma Rivale (Last Tycoon 131) [2002 f6g[3] f7g f6g[4] f6g 7d f6g[5] f6g f5g[2] p6g[2] 7m 5m[5] f5s[4] 6m[3] f6g[6] f6s p7g f6g f6g Dec 10] modest handicapper, better on all-weather than turf: best at 5f/6f: acts on all-weather and good to firm going: tried visored/in cheekpieces: sometimes slowly away. *B. A. Pearce* **51 a64**

STANDIFORD GIRL (IRE) 5 b.m. Standiford (USA) – Pennine Girl (IRE) (Pennine Walk 120) [2002 –: p16g Dec 3] sparely-made mare: of little account nowadays. *L. A. Dace* **–**

ST ANDREWS (IRE) 2 b.c. (Feb 18) Celtic Swing 138 – Viola Royale (IRE) 90 (Royal Academy (USA) 130) [2002 7.1m[3] 8m* 8m[4] Oct 12] 45,000DM, 42,000Y: lengthy, quite attractive colt: first foal: dam Irish 2-y-o 6f/7f winner: landed odds in maiden at Newmarket in September: well backed, best effort (though found little after travelling well) when 5¾ lengths fourth to Big Bad Bob in listed race at Ascot: should stay 1¼m: raced only on good to firm ground: should make a useful 3-y-o. *M. A. Jarvis* **94 p**

STANDS TO REASON (USA) 3 b.f. Gulch (USA) – Sheer Reason (USA) 110 (Danzig (USA)) [2002 80p: 6f[4] f6g[5] 8m Oct 3] smallish, quite attractive filly: didn't fulfil promise of only outing at 2 yrs: reportedly had breathing problem final start. *B. W. Hills* **62**

STAR APPLAUSE 2 b.f. (Apr 28) Royal Applause 124 – Cominna (Dominion 123) [2002 5f 5d f5g[6] f5g Dec 4] 3,000Y: good-topped filly: half-sister to 3 winners, including 1994 2-y-o 6f winner Prima Cominna (by Unfuwain) and 6-y-o Forty Forte: dam unraced sister to very smart sprinter Primo Dominie: modest maiden: easily best effort on third start: raced only at 5f: wore cheekpieces final appearance. *J. Balding* **53**

STARBECK (IRE) 4 b.f. Spectrum (IRE) 126 – Tide of Fortune (Soviet Star (USA) 128) [2002 90: 7f[6] 7m 6g[6] 7m 6m 7.6f 7m 7s[5] 7d[4] f8g f8g[4] f8g[6] Dec 27] lengthy filly: fairly useful performer on turf, fair form on all-weather: stays easy 1m: acts on soft going and fibresand, probably on firm: withdrawn after giving trouble at start eighth intended outing: no more reliable. *J. D. Bethell* **84 a73**

STARBOURNE (IRE) 3 b.f. Sadler's Wells (USA) 132 – Upper Circle (Shirley Heights 130) [2002 10s* 8m[6] 8s[3] 12s[4] 12m 12d 9.9m[5] 10.4g[6] 11.9m 10g 12d[2] 8s* Oct 20] tall, good sort: closely related to useful performer up to 1m With The Fairies (by Fairy **105**

King), 7f winner at 2 yrs: dam twice-raced sister to dam of Oaks winner Lady Carla: useful performer: won maiden at Navan in May and listed race at Naas (by 2 lengths from Kalamunda) in October: creditable efforts in between in Irish 1000 Guineas at the Curragh (5½ lengths third to Gossamer), Oaks at Epsom (15 lengths fourth to Kazzia), Nassau Stakes at Goodwood (7 lengths fifth to Islington) and listed race at the Curragh (2 lengths second to Millstreet): acted as pacemaker seventh to ninth starts: effective at 1m to 1½m: acted on soft and good to firm going: had worn crossed noseband: visits Danehill. *A. P. O'Brien, Ireland*

STAR CROSS (IRE)   3 b.g. Ashkalani (IRE) 128 – Solar Star (USA) 93 (Lear Fan   – (USA) 130) [2002 85p: 10s Oct 26] strong, useful-looking gelding: has scope: won soft-ground maiden at Nottingham at 2 yrs: off nearly a year and having only third outing, behind in handicap at Newbury: should stay at least 1¼m. *J. L. Dunlop*

STAR DYNASTY (IRE)   5 b.g. Bering 136 – Siwaayib 97 (Green Desert (USA) 127)   – [2002 73+: 10.5m Apr 13] angular, close-coupled gelding: fairly useful maiden at 3 yrs: lightly raced since: probably stayed 11.5f: acted on good to soft going: dead. *D. McCain*

STARFAN (USA)   3 b.f. Lear Fan (USA) 130 – Willstar (USA) (Nureyev (USA) 131)   **95 ?** [2002 101: 8d⁵ 6m* 7m³ 7m⁵ Oct 12] smallish, strong, lengthy filly: useful performer, lightly raced: made all in maiden at Yarmouth in August: had run of things when seemingly good third to Mamounia in listed race at Doncaster following month: stayed 1m: acted on soft and good to firm going: was sometimes bandaged behind: on edge/free to post when disappointing (took good hold/found little) on reappearance: stud. *J. H. M. Gosden*

STAR LAD (IRE)   2 ch.g. (Feb 23) Lake Coniston (IRE) 131 – Simply Special (IRE)   **55** (Petit Loup (USA) 123) [2002 5.1g f5s³ p5g f6g f5g⁶ 7m 5m 7.1m⁶ 5.3m² f6g⁸ f6s³ f6s³   **a63** f6g³ Dec 20] IR 4,400Y: first foal: dam ran once: modest performer: won seller at Wolverhampton in November: good third in 3 nurseries after: probably best at 5f/6f: acts on fibresand and good to firm going: blinkered last 6 outings: often forces pace. *R. Brotherton*

STARLADY   2 b.f. (Feb 5) Mind Games 121 – Ma Rivale (Last Tycoon 131) [2002   **49** 5m⁵ 5.7g⁶ Jul 14] 7,600Y, resold IR 4,000Y: fifth foal: half-sister to 3-y-o Valdasho and 5-y-o Stand By: dam maiden in Belgium: poor form in maidens: raced freely second start. *R. Brotherton*

STARLIGHT DANCER (IRE)   4 b.f. Muhtarram (USA) 125 – Tintomara (IRE)   – (Niniski (USA) 125) [2002 –: 7g 8.1m 8.2d 7m 7g⁶ 8m 9.7d 6m Jul 22] workmanlike filly: maiden: blinkered sixth start. *J. G. Portman*

STARLIGHT NIGHT (USA)   3 ch.f. Distant View (USA) 126 – Diese (USA) 111   **71** (Diesis 133) [2002 10.2f² 10.2f² p10g⁵ Nov 19] fifth foal: closely related to 4-y-o Dexterity and half-sister to 3 winners, including useful French 6f (at 2 yrs) and 1m winner Speak In Passing (by Danzig) and smart performer up to 1¼m in Britain and USA Senure (by Nureyev): dam, French 1¼m winner, half-sister to Xaar from family of El Gran Senor and Spinning World: fair form when runner-up in maidens at Bath, odds on when beaten 2 lengths by Grain of Gold on second occasion: looked none too keen in similar event at Lingfield final start: should prove as effective at 1m as 1¼m: sold 200,000 gns. *Mrs A. J. Perrett*

STAR MEMBER (IRE)   3 b.c. Hernando (FR) 127 – Constellation (IRE) (Kaldoun   **85** (FR) 122) [2002 p10g* 10.1m⁴ 12f³ Sep 25] IR 20,000Y: leggy, quite good-topped colt: first foal: dam French 1¼m winner out of smart French miler Only Star: fairly useful performer: won maiden at Lingfield in June: similar form in 2 minor events after: stays 1½m. *A. P. Jarvis*

STARMINDA   2 b.f. (Apr 4) Zamindar (USA) 116 – Starfida (Soviet Star (USA) 128)   **50** [2002 6s 6m⁵ 5m 5.2f 6.1m 6.5g Sep 27] quite good-topped filly: third foal: dam, ran once, half-sister to dam of very smart sprinter Pivotal: modest maiden: stays 6f: best efforts on ground firmer than good: tried visored: sometimes gives trouble at start. *Mrs C. A. Dunnett*

STAR OF ARABIA (IRE)   3 b.f. Hamas (IRE) 125§ – Thank One's Stars (Alzao   **67** (USA) 117) [2002 6g⁵ 7d 6s 5f 6g² Oct 28] small, sturdy filly: half-sister to several winners, including 1m/1¼m winner Be Thankfull (by Linamix) and 1997 2-y-o 5f winner Thanksgiving (by Indian Ridge), both useful: dam unraced: fair maiden: should be suited by 7f+: below form on soft going. *D. R. C. Elsworth*

STAR OF GERMANY (IRE)   2 b.g. (Mar 9) Germany (USA) 124 – Twinkle Bright   – (USA) 40 (Star de Naskra (USA)) [2002 f7g Nov 26] 8,000F: second foal: dam 7f winner in Ireland: 33/1, always behind in maiden at Southwell. *T. P. Tate*

STAR OF LOVE (FR)   3 b.f. Celtic Swing 138 – Meant To Be 84 (Morston (FR) 125)   **69**
[2002 10m⁴ 10d⁵ p12g Sep 4] second foal: dam 1½m and 2m winner, also won over
hurdles: best effort in maidens (fair form) at Nottingham on debut, starting slowly: should
be suited by 1½m+. *Lady Herries*

STAR OF NORMANDIE (USA)   3 b.f. Gulch (USA) – Depaze (USA) (Deputy   **83**
Minister (CAN)) [2002 75p: 8m 8.2d² 10f⁴ 10g⁵ 8.3s* 10g 8s⁶ 6v p8g³ f8.5s² p7g f8g³
p8g Dec 30] tall, leggy filly: fairly useful performer: flattered when fourth in slowly-run
listed race at Newbury in May: won 4-runner minor event at Hamilton in June despite
hanging right: good efforts when placed after: effective at 1m/1¼m: acts on all-weather,
firm and soft going: tried blinkered: has worn cheekpieces. *G. G. Margarson*

STAR OF WONDER (FR)   7 ch.m. The Wonder (FR) 129 – Teardrops Fall (FR)   **–**
(Law Society (USA) 130) [2002 f16g Jun 19] 9f winner on Flat in France at 3 yrs: well
beaten in seller on British Flat debut. *John Allen*

STAR OVATION (IRE)   5 ch.g. Fourstars Allstar (USA) 122 – Standing Ovation   **73**
(Godswalk (USA) 130) [2002 –: 8.1g² 9m⁵ 8m⁶ Sep 29] good-bodied gelding: fair
maiden: best effort at Warwick on reappearance: left Ms J. Morgan, Ireland after second
start: seems better at 1m than further. *Mrs A. M. Naughton*

STAR PRINCESS   5 b.m. Up And At 'em 109 – Princess Sharpenup 63 (Lochnager   **–**
132) [2002 58, a–: p6g p6g 5s 6f 5f 5d 7.1m 7.1g f5g Dec 17] workmanlike mare: little
form at 5 yrs. *J. Gallagher*

STAR PROTECTOR (FR)   3 b.c. Hector Protector (USA) 124 – Frustration 108   **78**
(Salse (USA) 128) [2002 83: 10m⁴ 10m⁴ 10.5d⁶ 9m⁴ 10.1g⁴ 10m* 14m 12g⁵ Sep 27]
well-made colt: fluent mover: fair performer: won claimer at Sandown (claimed from
J. Hills £20,000) in August: stays 1½m: acts on good to firm going, yet to race on soft/
heavy: visored third outing: carried head awkwardly on reappearance: won juvenile
hurdle in November. *R. M. Stronge*

STARRING (FR)   3 b.f. Ashkalani (IRE) 128 – Sweeping 104 (Indian King (USA)   **74**
128) [2002 p10g² 12.3m⁵ Aug 30] 38,000F, 160,000Y: half-sister to several winners,
including fairly useful 1½m to 2½m winner Puteri Wentworth (by Sadler's Wells) and
5-y-o Watching: dam, 2-y-o 6f winner who stayed 9f, from very good family: better effort
in maidens (fair form) when 1½ lengths second to Spinney at Lingfield, slowly away and
running green before finishing well: travelled well long way at Chester 5 months later:
should stay at least 1½m. *E. A. L. Dunlop*

STARRY LODGE (IRE)   2 b.c. (Apr 6) Grand Lodge (USA) 125 – Stara (Star Appeal   **64**
133) [2002 8.5s 7d 7v p7g⁶ Dec 3] approx. 34,000Y in Italy: useful-looking colt: eighth
foal: half-brother to 3 winners, including 1¼m winner Otahuna (by Selkirk): dam, ran
twice, sister to Prix de Diane winner/Oaks runner-up Madam Gay: modest maiden:
should stay at least 1¼m: best effort on polytrack. *L. M. Cumani*

STARRY MARY   4 b.f. Deploy 131 – Darling Splodge (Elegant Air 119) [2002 61:   **63**
11.8s² 11.6g f14.8s³ 13.1g 11.8d 10.2d 12d³ f12g 12d³ Nov 1] close-coupled filly: modest   **a50**
handicapper: barely stays 14.8f: acts on heavy and good to firm going, probably on
fibresand: sometimes slowly away. *E. L. James*

STARS AT MIDNIGHT   2 b.f. (Apr 9) Magic Ring (IRE) 115 – Boughtbyphone 62   **–**
(Warning 136) [2002 7g p7g 7d Nov 2] 2,100Y: second foal: half-sister to 3-y-o Pentecost: dam, Irish maiden who stayed 1½m, half-sister to 5-y-o Capricho: well held in
minor event/maidens. *Dr J. R. J. Naylor*

STARS DELIGHT (IRE)   5 ch.g. Fourstars Allstar (USA) 122 – Celtic Cygnet   **–**
(Celtic Cone 116) [2002 p12g Jun 9] tailed off in Lingfield maiden on Flat debut.
Mrs L. C. Jewell

STAR SENSATION (IRE)   2 b. or br.f. (Feb 8) Sri Pekan (USA) 117 – Dancing   **85**
Sensation (USA) 72 (Faliraki 125) [2002 6.1m⁴ 7g* 7s Oct 26] 10,500F, 15,000Y:
smallish, good-topped filly: third foal: half-sister to a winner up to 11.5f in Italy by
Namaqualand: dam, 7f to 1½m winner, also won over hurdles: clearly best effort (fairly
useful form) when winning maiden at Leicester in October by 1½ lengths from Introducing: last in listed event at Newbury final start: should stay at least 1m. *P. W. Harris*

STAR SEVENTEEN   4 ch.f. Rock City 120 – Westminster Waltz (Dance In Time   **78**
(CAN)) [2002 78: f11s⁶ 10m² 10d⁶ 10.3g⁴ f12g⁴ p12g⁴ 10m³ 10s 10g 10m² f12s* Oct 8]
angular filly: fair handicapper: won at Southwell in October: effective at 1¼m/1½m: acts
on soft going, good to firm and all-weather: probably best racing up with pace: has won
when sweating: sold 13,500 gns. *P. W. D'Arcy*

STARS IN HER EYES (IRE) 3 b.f. Woodman (USA) 126 – Wind In Her Hair **69**
(IRE) 114 (Alzao (USA) 117) [2002 72: 7g 7s⁶ 7f⁴ f7g⁴ 8.5m⁶ 7m³ Aug 19] fair maiden:
stays 8.5f: acts on fibresand, firm and soft ground: tongue tied final 2-y-o start: has raced
freely/carried head high: found little final outing. *J. W. Hills*

STAR SOUND 2 br.g. (Apr 16) Millkom 124 – Tarnside Rosal 68 (Mummy's Game **50**
120) [2002 7m 7.2g 7m⁶ Aug 6] sixth foal: closely related to 2 winners by Cyrano de
Bergerac, including fairly useful 1999 2-y-o 5f winner Half Moon Bay and half-brother
to 1m/8.5f (at 2 yrs) selling winner Emperor's Gold (by Petong): dam 2-y-o 5f/6f winner
who stayed 7.6f: modest form at best in maidens: will probably stay 1m. *T. D. Barron*

STARS SINGING 2 ch.g. (Mar 4) The West (USA) 107 – Merch Rhyd-Y-Grug **–**
(Sabrehill (USA) 120) [2002 5d Jul 19] 1,300Y: first foal: dam no form: 50/1 and very
green, tailed off in minor event at Hamilton. *L. R. James*

STARTLED 3 ch.f. Zilzal (USA) 137 – Zelda (USA) (Sharpen Up 127) [2002 p7g **43**
p10g⁶ 10.2d 8m 10g Aug 7] 5,800F: half-sister to 3 winners, including 6f winner
Robzelda (by Robellino) and 7-y-o American Cousin: dam once-raced half-sister to
Moorestyle: poor maiden. *I. A. Wood*

START OVER (IRE) 3 b.c. Barathea (IRE) 127 – Carnelly (IRE) 101 (Priolo (USA) **84**
127) [2002 76: 8m² 8.1d⁶ 7.9s³ p8g* 9m* 10.3m³ 8f⁴ 10m 10.1m⁴ 8m 8.9f⁵ 10s⁵ Oct 23]
sturdy, close-coupled colt: fairly useful performer: won minor events at Lingfield and
Redcar in July: mostly in good form in handicaps after: stays easy 1¼m: acts on polytrack
and any turf going. *E. J. O'Neill*

STAR TRECKER (IRE) 3 b.g. Spectrum (IRE) 126 – Night Patrol (IRE) (Night **–**
Shift (USA)) [2002 71: f6s f8.5g f9.4g Apr 26] small, sturdy gelding: fair form on second
of 2 starts at 2 yrs: well held in 2002: subsequently gelded. *K. McAuliffe*

STAR TURN (IRE) 8 ch.g. Night Shift (USA) – Ringtail 102 (Auction Ring (USA) **62**
123) [2002 61, a–: 10m⁵ 12d⁵ 12m⁴ Aug 16] strong gelding: has reportedly suffered knee **a–**
problems: modest handicapper: stays 1½m: acts on firm and soft going. *R. M. Flower*

STAR VEGA 2 ch.f. (Mar 6) Blue Ocean (USA) 87 – My Greatest Star 93 (Great **87 p**
Nephew 126) [2002 7d⁴ 7.2g⁵ 6g⁵ 7s* Oct 26] smallish, compact filly: seventh foal: half-
sister to 5-y-o Runaway Star and a winner up to 1¼m in Italy by Warning: dam maiden
half-sister to smart Galtres Stakes winner Startino: fairly useful form: won seller at
Newmarket in August and nursery at Doncaster (by length from Albany, leading 1f out
after meeting trouble) in October: will stay at least 1m: raced only on good ground or
softer: sold 36,000 gns, sent to USA: capable of better still. *W. J. Musson*

STARZAAN (IRE) 3 b.g. Darshaan 133 – Stellina (IRE) (Caerleon (USA) 132) **99**
[2002 80p: 8s² 10m* 11m 14.1g³ 12.3f⁵ 12f* 12f² 11.8g⁵ 16s⁴ Oct 25] tall, rangy gelding:
useful performer: won maiden at Windsor (edged right) in April and handicap at
Kempton in September: stays 1¾m, not testing 2m: acts on firm and soft ground: joined
H. Morrison. *P. F. I. Cole*

STATEMENT (IRE) 2 b.c. (Mar 25) Singspiel (IRE) 133 – Last Spin 77 (Unfuwain **90 p**
(USA) 131) [2002 7.1m² 8.1g³ Oct 5] 200,000Y: third foal: dam, disappointing maiden
on Flat but winning hurdler, half-sister to smart performer up to 1½m Gulland: green,
fairly useful form when placed in minor events at Sandown won by Al Jadeed and by Cat
Ona High, well backed and beaten 3 lengths both times: should stay at least 1¼m: capable
of better, and should win races as a 3-y-o. *Sir Michael Stoute*

STATE OPENING 5 ch.m. Absalom 128 – Lightning Legend 71 (Lord Gayle (USA) **–**
124) [2002 –: p10g Jan 3] of no account. *Miss Z. C. Davison*

STATEROOM (USA) 4 ch.g. Affirmed (USA) – Sleet (USA) (Summer Squall (USA)) **92**
[2002 85: 8m 7f² 8m 7f⁵ 8f 7m Sep 4] close-coupled gelding: fairly useful handicapper,
lightly raced: best form at 7f: acts on firm going: usually tongue tied: has worn crossed
noseband. *J. A. R. Toller*

STATIM 3 b.f. Marju (IRE) 127 – Rapid Repeat (IRE) 95 (Exactly Sharp (USA) 121) **81**
[2002 78p: 11.9m* 12f 12m Aug 14] tall, angular filly: has scope: fairly useful performer:
won handicap at Haydock in July: found little when well held in similar events after:
should be as effective at 1¼m as 1½m: acts on good to firm and good to soft going: sold
19,000 gns. *L. M. Cumani*

STATOSILVER 4 b.g. Puissance 110 – Silver Blessings (Statoblest 120) [2002 –: 6f **–**
5g Aug 7] sturdy gelding: has a round action: no form. *Mrs A. Duffield*

STATOYORK 9 b.g. Statoblest 120 – Ultimate Dream 74 (Kafu 120) [2002 59: 5s⁴ **59**
6g⁴ 5s⁵ 5m 5.1d* 5f² 5g² 5m 5m 6m Sep 19] strong gelding: modest handicapper: won

apprentice race at Bath in July: best at 5f: acts on fibresand, firm and soft going: visored/blinkered last 6 starts in 2001: has reportedly bled from nose on several occasions: usually slowly away: best produced late. *D. Shaw*

STATUE GALLERY (IRE)   4 ch.g. Cadeaux Genereux 131 – Kinlochewe 102 (Old   –
Vic 136) [2002 85: 6m May 4] strong, angular gelding: fairly useful handicapper at 3 yrs: seemingly difficult to train. *J. A. R. Toller*

STATUE OF LIBERTY (USA)   2 b. or br.c. (Feb 5) Storm Cat (USA) –   **109 p**
Charming Lassie (USA) (Seattle Slew (USA)) [2002 5s* 6g* Jun 18]
　　　It took two years from its unveiling in 1884 for the Statue of Liberty to be completed in all its glory, at first viewing only the torch-bearing arm fully in place on a giant iron framework. First views of the equine namesake of America's symbol of freedom also left something to the imagination, but Statue of Liberty, the horse, made his mark on the skyline all the same. Statue of Liberty was restricted to only two outings, but he won both of them, including the Coventry Stakes at Royal Ascot, and it is to be hoped he gets the chance to show himself more the finished article in 2003.
　　　Statue of Liberty had his first start in Ireland's second two-year-old race of the season, a maiden over five furlongs at Cork on April 1st. He followed up stable-companion Tomahawk's victory in Ireland's first juvenile event in only workmanlike style on soft ground, beating Petite Histoire by three quarters of a length after starting at 9/2-on. Statue of Liberty was favourite at 5/2 in what looked a representative field for the first major two-year-old race of the season at Royal Ascot six weeks later. Thirteen of his fifteen rivals in the Coventry were previous winners, best backed among them second favourite Tacitus at 4/1 and Statue of Liberty's stable-companion Spartacus at 11/2. In the event, it was another Irish challenger, Dermot Weld's Pakhoes, a 16/1-shot, who gave the favourite most to do, the pair pulling three and a half lengths clear of Kawagino in third. Patiently ridden by Michael Kinane, Statue of Liberty still seemed green, needing to be niggled along at halfway, but he got to the front quite readily over a furlong out and was driven out only as he idled, scoring by a neck. Statue of Liberty was Aidan O'Brien's fourth winner in the last six runnings of the Coventry Stakes, following on from Harbour Master, Fasliyev and Landseer. At the time, Statue of Liberty's form looked well up to standard for recent winners of the race and he would almost certainly have made a mark had he taken up his early entries in such as the Dewhurst Stakes and the Racing Post Trophy. As it was, he failed to appear in the autumn, after first being talked of as a likely runner in the Anglesey Stakes at the Curragh in July.
　　　Statue of Liberty, who cost 1,300,000 dollars as a yearling, about three times the cost (at the time) of his namesake, is out of Charming Lassie, a sprint winner in the States on her only start and a half-sister to the high-class performer at up to seven furlongs Wolfhound. Statue of Liberty is a half-brother to several

Coventry Stakes, Royal Ascot—Statue of Liberty (right) gives Aidan O'Brien his fourth victory in the race in the last six years with the Dermot Weld-trained Pakhoes making it an Irish 1,2; Kawagino (hooped sleeves) and Coconut Penang (No.1) do best of the home-trained runners

Mr M. Tabor & Mrs John Magnier's "Statue of Liberty"

winners in North America, notably the Belmont Stakes winner Lemon Drop Kid (by Kingmambo), a Grade 1 winner at a mile at two. Statue of Liberty's sire Storm Cat has had a Belmont Stakes winner himself in Tabasco Cat, but the average distance of races won by Storm Cat's progeny in Europe is around a mile. He is best known in Europe as the sire of Giant's Causeway and Black Minnaloushe and he brought further success to the O'Brien stable in 2002 with such as Sophisticat, Hold That Tiger and Van Nistelrooy.

		Storm Bird	Northern Dancer
	Storm Cat (USA)	(b 1978)	South Ocean
	(b or br 1983)	Terlingua	Secretariat
Statue of Liberty (USA)		(ch 1976)	Crimson Saint
(b. or br.c. Feb 5, 2000)		Seattle Slew	Bold Reasoning
	Charming Lassie (USA)	(b or br 1974)	My Charmer
	(b 1987)	Lassie Dear	Buckpasser
		(b 1974)	Gay Missile

Statue of Liberty presumably gets his name from his imposing appearance. A strong, heavy-bodied colt, who has a deal of scope, he is the type who will always carry plenty of condition. It was noticeable that he changed his legs in the closing stages at Ascot, where he looked in fine shape but was taken steadily to post, and he has yet to race on ground firmer than good. He should stay at least a mile and will make a smart colt, assuming all is well. Whilst William Hill and Coral have him at 14/1 and 12/1 respectively at the time of writing in winter betting on the Two Thousand Guineas, Ladbrokes have him as low as 10/1 co-favourite. *A. P. O'Brien, Ireland*

941

ST AUSTELL 2 b.g. (Feb 14) Compton Place 125 – Paris Joelle (IRE) (Fairy King –
(USA)) [2002 6g⁵ Jul 20] smallish, sturdy gelding: third living foal: dam ran once at 2 yrs: 6/1 and green, last of 5 to Tug of Love in maiden at
Newmarket. *J. A. R. Toller*

STAVROS (IRE) 2 b.c. (Apr 30) General Monash (USA) 107 – Rivers Rainbow **63**
(Primo Dominie 121) [2002 5g 5f⁴ 5s⁶ 5g⁶ 6m 7.1m 6g⁵ 6f⁴ Oct 7] IR 11,500F, IR
16,000Y: rather leggy, lengthy colt: first foal: dam, no sign of ability, closely related to
very smart 1985 2-y-o Nomination: modest maiden: should stay 7f: acts on firm going,
probably on soft: blinkered last 2 outings: sometimes slowly away: sold 7,500 gns.
T. D. Easterby

STAY BRIGHT (IRE) 3 b.g. Flying Spur (AUS) – Mothers Footprints (IRE) (Mael- –
strom Lake 118) [2002 f6g⁶ 7s 8g 12.1g Jun 5] IR 18,000Y: tall, workmanlike gelding:
second foal: dam unraced: little form: blinkered final start. *T. D. Easterby*

ST BENEDICT (IRE) 2 b.c. (Apr 17) Southern Halo (USA) – Cocktail Party (USA) **72**
(Arctic Tern (USA) 126) [2002 8f⁶ 7m⁴ 7.1m 8s Oct 25] 28,000F, IR 40,000Y: first living
foal: dam, 8.5f winner in USA, sister to US Grade 3 9f winner Freewheel: fair maiden:
best effort on debut: stays 1m: acts on firm ground: visored (well beaten) final start: sold
4,000 gns. *M. L. W. Bell*

ST CASSIEN (IRE) 2 b.g. (Apr 25) Goldmark (USA) 113 – Moonlight Partner (IRE) –
81 (Red Sunset 120) [2002 7.1m 8m⁶ 8g Oct 2] 5,000Y: fifth foal: half-brother to useful
7f/1m winner (latter at 2 yrs) Apache Red (by Indian Ridge): dam Irish 5f winner: well
held in maidens: gelded after final start. *T. M. Jones*

STEALING BEAUTY (IRE) 2 b.f. (Mar 27) Sadler's Wells (USA) 132 – Imitation **69 p**
(Darshaan 133) [2002 8s⁵ Oct 15] leggy filly: first foal: dam unraced sister to smart miler
Darnay: 25/1 and backward, 13 lengths fifth of 13 to Allergy in maiden at Leicester: will
be suited by 1¼m/1½m: should improve. *L. M. Cumani*

ST EDITH (IRE) 2 ch.f. (Feb 11) Desert King (IRE) 129 – Carnelly (IRE) 101 (Priolo **58**
(USA) 127) [2002 7.1m 8f⁴ 6d⁶ Oct 18] 31,000F: close-coupled filly: second foal:
half-sister to 3-y-o Start Over: dam Irish 1½m winner: modest form in maidens: bred to
be suited by 1¼m/1½m, but needs to settle. *J. J. Quinn*

STEELANINCH 2 gr.c. (Mar 22) Inchinor 119 – Mrs Gray 61 (Red Sunset 120) **108**
[2002 5m³ 6g* 6d³ p6g⁵ 6m* 7d* 7d 6m 6f* 6s⁵ Oct 26] 13,500Y: leggy, useful-looking
colt: brother to fairly useful 2000 2-y-o 1m winner Snowey Mountain and half-brother to
3 winners, including 6f winner Lucayan Beach (by Cyrano de Bergerac): dam 2-y-o 5f
winner: useful performer: won maiden at Hamilton in May, nursery at Ascot in July,
minor event at Newmarket in August and nursery at Newmarket (set strong pace, beat
Little Malvern by 2½ lengths) in October: hung when below form in listed race at
Doncaster final start: effective at 6f/7f: acts on firm and good to soft going (showed
promise on polytrack): well held only try in visor: sold 100,000 gns, sent to USA.
N. A. Callaghan

STEEL BLUE 2 b.c. (Mar 1) Atraf 116 – Something Blue (Petong 126) [2002 5d **94**
5.1m² 6g 6d² 5m* 6g 6m 6g* a6g*] Dec 12] 22,000Y: leggy, quite good-topped colt:
second foal: brother to 3-y-o Yorkshire Blue: dam, well beaten in 3 outings, half-sister to
useful sprinter Blues Indigo and to dam of smart sprinter Astonished and 8-y-o Bishops
Court: fairly useful performer: won nurseries at Newmarket in August and October (beat
Feather Boa by 2 lengths in 19-runner event) and 5-runner minor event at Nad Al Sheba
(by 5 lengths from National Emerald) in December: likely to prove best at 5f/6f: acts on
dirt, yet to race on extremes of turf going: reportedly underwent operation to remove
trapped testicle after fourth outing. *R. M. Whitaker*

STEEL CAT (USA) 2 b.c. (Mar 22) Sir Cat (USA) 118 – Daisy Daisy (IRE) 67 **74 p**
(Dance of Life (USA)) [2002 7d⁴ Oct 30] 1,800,000 francs Y: fourth foal: half-brother to
a winner in USA by Miswaki: dam, second at 11f in Ireland, half-sister to US Grade 1
1¼m winner Gaily Gaily: 12/1, 5½ lengths fourth of 18 to Hard Nose in maiden at
Yarmouth, slowly away and staying on from rear under hands and heels: should be suited
by 1m+: likely to improve. *L. M. Cumani*

STEELY DAN 3 b.g. Danzig Connection (USA) – No Comebacks 70 (Last Tycoon **68**
131) [2002 73: p8g³ p10g* p7g* p6g⁴ p10g⁶ p8g⁴ 7s 6g⁴ p8g 6g 8m 8m May 5] strong **a82**
gelding: fairly useful handicapper on all-weather, fair on turf: won twice at Lingfield in
January: effective at 6f to easy 1¼m: acts on all-weather, firm and good to soft going
(possibly not on soft): sometimes carries head high/hangs right. *J. R. Best*

Mr Kenneth MacPherson's "Steenberg"

STEENBERG (IRE) 3 ch.g. Flying Spur (AUS) – Kip's Sister (Cawston's Clown **109**
113) [2002 96p: 7m⁵ 8m 7f⁴ 7m² 7f Aug 17] big, lengthy gelding: useful performer: tenth
in 2000 Guineas at Newmarket second start: best effort when neck second to Just James in
Jersey Stakes at Royal Ascot penultimate outing: ran as if something amiss in Hungerford
Stakes at Newbury final start (gelded after): effective at 7f/1m: acts on firm going: tends
to carry head awkwardly/hang right: held up. *M. H. Tompkins*

STELLETTA (IRE) 2 b.f. (Mar 25) Titus Livius (FR) 115 – Nezool Almatar (IRE) **52**
(Last Tycoon 131) [2002 f5s 5g⁴ 5m³ 6g 6g 6g a8s³ Dec 22] IR 2,500F, IR 9,000Y: sturdy
filly: third foal: half-sister to Swedish sprint winner (including at 2 yrs) Blue Eagle (by
Eagle Eyed): dam, ran twice, out of half-sister to Oh So Sharp: modest maiden: left
R. Guest before final start: stays 1m: acts on dirt, raced only on good/good to firm ground
on turf. *M. Kahn, Sweden*

STEMAGNUM 3 ch.c. Beveled (USA) – Stemegna (Dance In Time (CAN)) [2002 **61**
8.3d⁵ 8.3g 7s⁵ f8.5g 7s Oct 25] half-brother to several winners, including useful Italian
miler Senebrova (by Warning): dam Italian Group 2 2-y-o 1m winner: modest maiden:
stays 1m: acts on soft going, well held on fibresand. *H. Morrison*

STEPASTRAY 5 gr.g. Alhijaz 122 – Wandering Stranger 69 (Petong 126) [2002 54: **54**
11m 9.9g 12f 14.1f⁵ 12g⁶ 16m 12.1d⁶ 10.1m² 11s⁶ 9m⁴ 10.1d 12f 12m³ 12d³ Nov 5] tall
gelding: modest maiden: effective at 1¼m, barely at 1¾m: acts on firm ground, probably
on soft: visored/blinkered last 5 starts in 2001. *R. E. Barr*

ST EXPEDIT 5 b.h. Sadler's Wells (USA) 132 – Miss Rinjani 83 (Shirley Heights 130) **119**
[2002 117: 12m² 13.4f* 12m² Jun 9] big, good-topped horse: smart performer: reportedly

Betfair.com Ormonde Stakes, Chester—a second successive win in the race for St Expedit (right), who beats the Norwegian challenger Sagittarius (left) and Ovambo

fratured pastern final outing in 2001 (had screws inserted in leg): won Betfair.com Ormonde Stakes at Chester in May for second year running, beating Sagittarius by length: good second other 2 starts, in John Porter Stakes at Newbury (beaten neck by Zindabad) and Grand Prix de Chantilly (beaten 1½ lengths by Anabaa Blue): stayed 13.4f: acted on firm and soft going: free-going sort, often made running: sometimes hung left: sold 30,000 gns in December, and reportedly retired. *G. Wragg*

ST HELENSFIELD 7 ch.g. Kris 135 – On Credit (FR) (No Pass No Sale 120) [2002 –: 16.2m⁶ f14s Sep 5] leggy, angular gelding: useful handicapper at 5 yrs: lightly raced on Flat and well held since: tried visored. *M. C. Pipe*   –

STICKWITHSTERLING (USA) 3 b.c. Silver Hawk (USA) 123 – Chesa Plana (Niniski (USA) 125) [2002 74p: 12.6m⁵ 13.3s⁵ 14d⁴ 18d⁴ 16.2g⁴ Jul 20] smallish, well-made colt: fair maiden handicapper: stays 1¾m: acts on fibresand, soft and good to firm going: blinkered (below form) final start: sold 15,000 gns, sent to Kuwait. *P. F. I. Cole*   **72**

STICKY FINGERS (IRE) 3 ch.f. Dr Devious (IRE) 127 – Mrs Fisher (IRE) 94 (Salmon Leap (USA) 131) [2002 f6g⁶ 5g 5d Aug 7] sixth foal: half-sister to fairly useful 1m and (at 2 yrs) 8.5f winner Pedro (by Brief Truce) and 4-y-o Grandma Lily: dam 7f winner, including at 2 yrs: little form in maidens at Wolverhampton, Leicester and Sandown: found to have cracked her pelvis after last-named. *Sir Mark Prescott*   –

STICKY GREEN 3 b.f. Lion Cavern (USA) 117 – Creme de Menthe (IRE) (Green Desert (USA) 127) [2002 8v² 10m 12.1g* 10d 10g 10s³ 10.3v Nov 8] lengthy, rather unfurnished filly: third foal: half-sister to 4-y-o Piccled: dam unraced half-sister to high-class 1m to 1½m performer In The Groove: fair performer: won maiden at Hamilton in May: stays easy 1½m: acts on heavy and good to firm going. *M. R. Channon*   **75**

STILL WATERS 7 b.g. Rainbow Quest (USA) 134 – Krill (Kris 135) [2002 –, a48: p8g Feb 9] sturdy gelding: modest winner at 5 yrs: little form since. *B. A. Pearce*   –

STING LIKE A BEE (IRE) 3 b.c. Ali-Royal (IRE) 127 – Hidden Agenda (FR) 55 (Machiavellian (USA) 123) [2002 95: 10g 10s 8m³ 8g⁴ 9m³ 8m 7d Oct 18] rather unfurnished colt: useful form at 2 yrs: just fair performer in 2002, claimed from H. Cecil £9,000 after fifth start: well held in handicaps subsequently: may prove best up to 1m: reportedly struck into third start: reportedly had breathing problem sixth outing. *J. S. Goldie*   **70**

ST ISSEY 4 b.f. Danehill (USA) 126 – Zahwa 72 (Cadeaux Genereux 131) [2002 7g 7m 7g 7d May 24] 15,500F, 60,000Y, 1,200 3-y-o: first foal: dam, German 7f/1m winner, out of dead Irish 2-y-o sprinter Peace Girl: well held in maidens/handicap: dead. *N. I. M. Rossiter*   –

STITCH IN TIME   6 ch.g. Inchinor 119 – Late Matinee 84 (Red Sunset 120) [2002   **–**
56, a69: f11g p10g* 10d 10m p12g p10g p10g Aug 29] big, leggy gelding: good mover: **a69 d**
fair handicapper on all-weather at best: won apprentice event at Lingfield in July: below
form after: effective at 1¼m/easy 1½m: acts on firm going, soft and all-weather: tried
visored: carries head high/has hung right: usually races prominently. *G. C. Bravery*

ST IVIAN   2 b.g. (Apr 5) Inchinor 119 – Lamarita 92§ (Emarati (USA) 74) [2002 6.1f⁶   **70 §**
6d⁴ 5g 5m² 5m 5.1m f5s⁶ 5g⁵ f5s⁴ 5.2d² f5g Dec 10] 12,000F, 21,000Y: leggy gelding: **a65 §**
first foal: dam untrustworthy 5f winner: second in nurseries at Doncaster and
Yarmouth: will probably prove best at 5f/6f: acts on fibresand, good to firm and good to
soft going: visored second to ninth starts: wayward at Chester sixth one. *Mrs N. Macauley*

ST JEROME   2 ch.g. (Mar 21) Danzig Connection (USA) – Indigo Dawn 78 (Rainbow   **–**
Quest (USA) 134) [2002 7g 7d Aug 9] 14,500Y: big, rather angular gelding: first foal:
dam, 13f to 2m winner, half-sister to 3-y-o Fight Your Corner: well held in maidens.
N. P. Littmoden

ST LAWRENCE (CAN)   8 gr.g. With Approval (CAN) – Mingan Isle (USA) (Lord   **–**
Avie (USA)) [2002 f14g Mar 12] smallish gelding: winning handicapper: well beaten
only Flat outing since 6 yrs: tried blinkered. *B. S. Rothwell*

ST MATTHEW (USA)   4 b.g. Lear Fan (USA) 130 – Social Crown (USA) (Chief's   **73**
Crown (USA)) [2002 84: 10d⁶ 10g 12m 12g⁴ 9.2s p8g⁵ 10g 10s 9s Oct 25] good-topped
gelding: has a round action: fair performer: barely stays 1¾m: acts on soft and good to
firm ground: blinkered (raced freely) fifth start, tongue tied last 4: none too consistent:
sold 7,000 gns. *J. W. Hills*

ST NICHOLAS   4 b.g. Komaite (USA) – Nikoola Eve 69 (Roscoe Blake 120) [2002   **–**
–: f6s f7s f12s⁶ f12g Jan 28] good-bodied gelding: little form since 2 yrs: tried visored.
D. Shaw

STOIC LEADER (IRE)   2 b.g. (Apr 1) Danehill Dancer (IRE) 117 – Starlust 79   **57**
(Sallust 134) [2002 5f 5d⁵ 5g⁶ 5m* 7.1m⁴ 5g⁴ 5d⁴ 5m⁶ f5s⁶ 5m Sep 16] 12,500Y: sturdy
gelding: half-brother to several winners, including useful 6f to 1m winner Bronzewing
(by Beldale Flutter) and fairly useful 1993 2-y-o 7f winner Dontforget Insight (by Don't
Forget Me): dam 2-y-o 5f winner: modest performer: won seller at Musselburgh in June:
mostly creditable efforts in minor event/nurseries after: effective at 5f to easy 7f: acts on
good to firm and good to soft ground: sometimes looks difficult ride. *R. F. Fisher*

STOKESIE   4 b.g. Fumo di Londra (IRE) 108 – Lesley's Fashion 67 (Dominion 123)   **–**
[2002 –: p6g 5.7f 6g 5f Sep 25] fairly useful 5f performer in Ireland at 2 yrs: well held
since, leaving J. M. Bradley after third start: tried blinkered. *J. L. Spearing*

STOKESIES WISH   2 ch.f. (Apr 9) Fumo di Londra (IRE) 108 – Jess Rebec 63 (Kala   **57**
Shikari 125) [2002 6m⁴ 5.1s p5g Nov 13] fourth foal: dam 5f winner: modest form first 2
starts in maidens: will prove best at 5f/6f. *J. L. Spearing*

STOLEN SONG   2 b.c. (Feb 4) Sheikh Albadou 128 – Sparky's Song 63 (Electric   **73**
126) [2002 6m 5s⁵ 5.1g³ 6g 6m⁶ 6m⁴ 6.1m³ 6g p7g p8g p8g⁵ Dec 11] good-topped colt: **a62**
third foal: half-brother to 3-y-o Lady Links: dam, 1¼m/1½m winner, half-sister to very
smart sprinter Bold Edge: fair maiden on turf, modest on all-weather: will prove best up
to 1m: acts on all-weather and good to firm going, showed promise on soft: blinkered/
visored last 7 starts. *M. J. Ryan*

STOLI (IRE)   4 ch.g. Spectrum (IRE) 126 – Crystal City (Kris 135) [2002 78: 8.3g 8m   **72**
p8g⁴ Jun 22] smallish, strong gelding: fair handicapper: should stay further than 1m: acts
on firm going and polytrack: sent to USA. *P. J. Makin*

STONEGRAVE   3 ch.f. Selkirk (USA) 129 – Queen Midas 119 (Glint of Gold 128)   **57**
[2002 f7g⁶ f5g 7m⁵ 8.5m 10g 12.1s² 12.1m² 14.1d 12s Nov 6] 28,000Y: half-sister to
1½m winner Spinning Star (by Arazi) and useful 1¼m winner who stayed 13f Royal
Circle (by Sadler's Wells): dam 1½m (Ribblesdale Stakes) winner: modest maiden handicapper: not knocked about first 4 starts (jockey suspended and trainer fined on third
occasion): stays 1½m: acts on soft and good to firm going. *M. W. Easterby*

STOPPES BROW   10 b.g. Primo Dominie 121 – So Bold (Never So Bold 135) [2002   **88**
80: 8f² 8d 8g 9m* 8m² 8g Aug 7] strong gelding: poor mover: fairly useful handicapper: won at Brighton in July: good second at Goodwood next time: clipped rival's
heels and fell final outing: best at 7f to 9f: acts on firm going, soft and fibresand:
blinkered, has been visored: sometimes slowly away: held up: goes well on turning track.
G. L. Moore

STOPWATCH (IRE) 7 b.g. Lead On Time (USA) 123 – Rose Bonbon (FR) (High   **–**
Top 131) [2002 –: p16g³ p12g f16.2g 11.9d Jun 13] poor performer nowadays: stays 2m: **a41**
acts on polytrack and soft going. *Mrs L. C. Jewell*

STORM CLEAR (IRE) 3 b.c. Mujadil (USA) 119 – Escape Path (Wolver Hollow   **78**
126) [2002 75: 6f 8g² 8.2m³ 10m 8.1g³ 7.1m² 7m⁶ 7.1m⁶ 8g 6g Oct 28] tall, good sort:
fair maiden: stays 1m: acts on good to firm and good to soft going: found little
eighth start: usually makes running. *R. Hannon*

STORM CRY (USA) 7 b.g. Hermitage (USA) – Doonesbury Lady (USA) (Doones-   **68**
bury (USA)) [2002 –: 8d 8.1d³ 9.2v³ 8.3m² 9.2s³ 8.3g 8g³ 7m Jul 17] leggy, lengthy
gelding: fair handicapper nowadays: stays 8.3f: acts on any going: tried blinkered: tongue
tied: sometimes slowly away/looks none too keen: reportedly lame final start: none too
consistent. *M. S. Saunders*

STORMEY WONDER (IRE) 3 b.f. Darnay 117 – Polaregina (FR) (Rex Magna   **40**
(FR) 129) [2002 –: 10s 16m 10m 8.1d⁴ 11.6m 11.6m Jul 22] workmanlike filly: poor
maiden: will probably stay 1½m+: visored last 3 starts. *J. S. Moore*

STORMING HOME 4 b.c. Machiavellian (USA) 123 – Try To Catch Me (USA)   **125**
(Shareef Dancer (USA) 135) [2002 128: 12g³ 12s² 12m² 12m⁶ 12m³ 12f* 10m* 11f
Nov 24]

To the momentous strains of Richard Strauss's *Also Sprach Zarathustra*
(previously employed in coverage of the moon landings and during the film *2001:
A Space Odyssey*) the winner of the 2002 Champion Stakes was led back in front of
the packed grandstand at Newmarket: the jockey raised his arms in triumph, the
horse was sporting a set of outlandish white sideburns. One might have thought that
sideburns of such proportions had gone out of fashion with Palmerston, Gladstone
or Tory MPs of the Thatcher era such as Dr Rhodes Boyson, but they are the latest
word in what horses can be seen in when out and about on Britain's racecourses.
More usually these pieces of equine headgear are described as sheepskin cheekpieces. Apparently, they perform a similar function to blinkers or a visor, but allow
more vision. Speaking after the Champion Stakes, Barry Hills, trainer of winner
Storming Home, explained that 'the cheekpieces have made him concentrate and
made him an easier horse to ride' and winning jockey Michael Hills said that 'the
cheekpieces have made a big difference—he just travels so much better.'

The Champion Stakes is easily the highest-profile success for a horse in
cheekpieces, but they were also worn in 2002 by Zonergem when winning the Mail
On Sunday/Tote Mile Final at Ascot. Others who wore them included Sulk, Sir
George Turner and Kier Park. They became a declarable item—alongside such as
blinkers, visor and tongue tie—in November when the necessary computer soft-
ware at Weatherbys had been updated. From February 16th, 2001, until September
2nd that year, stewards secretaries kept a tally of horses wearing the cheekpieces
and recorded 137 different instances, on 98 horses and with four wins. The trainers
who used them most over this period were David Arbuthnot (fifteen times),
Norman Mason (nine), Graham McCourt (six), Chris Grant (six), George Moore
(five) and Linda Perratt (five). Formerly associated mostly with questionable
equine characters at northern jumping tracks, the cheekpieces are now seen at major
Flat meetings as well, though they are not a familiar sight everywhere—in Ireland
they are banned.

The connections of Storming Home resorted to the cheekpieces after his
first five starts of 2002 failed to yield a win. He had taken the previous year's King
Edward VII Stakes and been fourth in the King George, but he was not performing
in peak form as a four-year-old. Initially, there was every indication that he would
do so, following a promising third in the Jockey Club Stakes at Newmarket, but
patience with him wore progressively thinner as he ran no better for second in the
Coronation Cup and the Hardwicke and rather worse when sixth in the King
George. What really proved beyond the pale though was his third of seven when
favourite for a listed race won by Systematic at Doncaster in September and it was
after that that connections decided to try the cheekpieces. Another possible reason
for his string of below-par performances was the form of his stable in general,
something the trainer mentioned after the Champion Stakes, Storming Home
himself withdrawn from one engagement in August when found to be running a
temperature in the morning. While Storming Home had performed in a lacklustre

Fishpools Furnishings Godolphin Stakes, Newmarket—Storming Home, fitted with cheekpieces, returns to form with a wide-margin success over the blinkered Mutakarrim, Hannibal Lad and Sunny Glen

fashion from a long way out on his last two starts as a three-year-old, at four the problem looked to have more to do with his effort, or lack of it, at the end of his races—'storming home' was exactly what he wasn't doing.

Redemption came in two appearances at Newmarket in October. Against three markedly inferior rivals in a listed contest, Storming Home was sent off at 13/8-on. It was a race he could hardly fail to win, but, in making the running and quickening clear readily for a six-length victory, Storming Home looked on his way back. A switch to the United States was mentioned but the move was delayed. With the withdrawal of the coughing ante-post favourite Nayef, there was no star name in the line-up for the Emirates Airline Champion Stakes. Derby Italiano winner Rakti refused to enter the stalls. On their best efforts, there wasn't much to choose on form between all of the remaining eleven. Godolphin's Moon Ballad, the impressive Select Stakes winner, headed the betting at 5/2, with his stable-companion Noverre, the 2001 Sussex Stakes winner who had been placed in that race and three other Group 1s in 2002, next best 9/2; third favourite was the Henry Cecil-trained Prix Eugene Adam winner Burning Sun at 5/1. The best form of the lot, however, belonged to 8/1-chance Storming Home. Admittedly, he had recorded it the previous season, but 'class will out' they say and in the 2002 Champion Stakes it did, as Storming Home lived up to his name to win from Moon Ballad and Noverre, with Carnival Dancer in fourth, one place better than he'd managed the previous year. Nothing else figured in the front rank except Godolphin third-string Equerry who made most until Moon Ballad and Storming Home made their moves just before the two-furlong marker, followed through by Noverre. Storming Home soon had the lead and never looked like relinquishing it. The first three were separated by half a length and three quarters, with three lengths back to the fourth. The Champion was a fine swansong for Storming Home's career in Britain, but he could not round off the season in similar style in the Japan Cup, managing only fifteenth of sixteen, never a factor.

The Japanese punters seemed unimpressed with Storming Home's credentials even after the Champion Stakes, sending him off at 40/1. He was an average winner of the race, well short of Rodrigo de Triano, Bosra Sham and Kalanisi among those that appear on the roll of honour for recent renewals. A leggy, close-

Emirates Airline Champion Stakes, Newmarket—Storming Home steps back in trip to record a first Group 1 success; Moon Ballad and Noverre (left) are clear of the rest

coupled colt with a fluent, round action, Storming Home has joined Neil Drysdale in the United States. During his British career, he was effective at a mile and a quarter and a mile and a half, and acted on firm and soft going. He has sometimes been edgy in the preliminaries, though it never appeared to affect his performance. The sheepskin cheekpieces were fitted for his last three starts. They were not, incidentally, the most unusual piece of headgear seen during the latest season, the very promising French two-year-old Vallee Enchantee having worn a noseband involving a series of flapping leather strips. The stewards had to check that these strips did not exceed the length of the horse's nose, in case of a photo finish.

		Mr Prospector (b 1970)	Raise A Native
Storming Home (b.c. 1998)	Machiavellian (USA) (b 1987)		Gold Digger
		Coup de Folie (b 1982)	Halo
			Raise The Standard
	Try To Catch Me (USA) (b 1986)	Shareef Dancer (b 1980)	Northern Dancer
			Sweet Alliance
		It's In The Air (b 1976)	Mr Prospector
			A Wind Is Rising

Storming Home's sire Machiavellian enjoyed other notable successes with his older horses in 2002 thanks to Street Cry, Best of The Bests and No Excuse Needed. Storming Home comes from a well-known family, detailed in *Racehorses of 2001*, his grandam It's In The Air a champion two-year-old filly in the United States and other representatives including Bitooh, Balanchine, Romanov and Slip Stream, the last-named being out of a half-sister to Try To Catch Me, Storming Home's dam. The 2002 three-year-old True Courage (also by Machiavellian) is Sheikh Maktoum's last foal out of Try To Catch Me, the broodmare having been sold for 14,000 guineas in 1999 prior to producing fillies by Lion Cavern, Foxhound and King's Theatre. True Courage's failure to become Try To Catch Me's fifth winner is outrageous, or more specifically his defeat in a maiden at Pontefract in July was outrageous, jockey Tony Culhane easing him when in an eight-length lead inside the final furlong, even pulling his ears and patting him down the neck, before getting caught close home. Culhane was banned for twenty-one days. Perhaps some piece of headgear needs to be manufactured to improve the concentration of jockeys as well as horses. *B. W. Hills*

STORMING STAR (ITY) 2 b.f. Shantou (USA) 125 – Somalia (FR) (Formidable **78 p**
(USA) 125) [2002 9s³ 10s* Oct 29] approx. 19,000Y in Italy: closely related to a winner
in Italy by Law Society and half-sister to several winners abroad, including French
winner up to 1½m Somalinski (by Niniski): dam French 2-y-o 7f winner: better effort in
maidens at Milan when winning 8-runner event by 3¼ lengths from Tumebamba, making
all: will stay at least 1½m: should improve further. *C. F. Wall*

STORMONT (IRE) 2 gr.c. (Apr 18) Marju (IRE) 127 – Legal Steps (IRE) (Law **93 p**
Society (USA) 130) [2002 6m² 5m² 5g⁵ 6g* p6g* 6d² Nov 1] leggy, good-topped colt:
sixth foal: half-brother to several winners, including Irish 5f/6f winner Quinstars (by
Thatching) and Irish 1m winner Stilett (by Tirol), both fairly useful: dam Irish 12.5f
winner: won maiden and minor event at Lingfield in October, beating Viera comfortably
by ½ length in latter: worn down final 1f when 2 lengths second to Zabaglione in minor
event at Newmarket final start: will prove best at 5f/6f: acts on polytrack, unraced on
extremes of ground on turf: should make a useful 3-y-o at least. *H. J. Collingridge*

STORM SEEKER 3 b.c. Rainbow Quest (USA) 134 – Siwaayib 97 (Green Desert **79**
(USA) 127) [2002 77p: 10.3s³ 12f* 12d⁴ 12m⁴ 11.7g Oct 16] leggy, quite good-topped
colt: has scope: fair form: won maiden at Thirsk (on toes/sweating) in April: below form
after: will probably stay 1¾m: blinkered penultimate start: sold 17,000 gns, sent to
Kuwait. *B. W. Hills*

STORM SHOWER (IRE) 4 b.g. Catrail (USA) 123 – Crimson Shower 61 (Dowsing **– §**
(USA) 124) [2002 –: f7s⁶ f8.5g² f9.4g f7g f8g² f7g 8g 6f f9.4g* f8.5g f9.4g⁶ f9.4f⁵ **a56 §**
f8s⁵ f8s f8g³ f6s⁵ Dec 26] good-topped gelding: modest performer: won maiden at
Wolverhampton in June: stays 9.4f: acts on fibresand: usually visored: sometimes starts
slowly/pulls hard/finds little: temperamental. *Mrs N. Macauley*

STORMVILLE (IRE) 5 b.g. Catrail (USA) 123 – Haut Volee (Top Ville 129) [2002 **70**
57: f7s f8.5g 7g⁶ 7g* 6m 6g* 7m⁵ f8g f9.4s Dec 9] sparely-made gelding: fair handi- **a?**
capper: won twice at Newcastle in August: best form at 6f/7f: acts on good to firm and
good to soft ground, no form on all-weather in 2002. *M. Brittain*

STORMY CHANNEL (USA) 3 ch.f. Storm Cat (USA) – All At Sea (USA) 124 **93**
(Riverman (USA) 131) [2002 8.2m² 8m* 8g⁵ p8g² 8v Nov 30] smallish filly: fifth living
foal: half-sister to 6f/7f winner (including at 2 yrs) Imroz (by Nureyev) and 1m winner
Insinuate (by Mr Prospector), both useful: dam won Prix du Moulin and Musidora Stakes
and runner-up in Oaks: fairly useful form: won maiden at Brighton in October: clearly
best effort when beaten head in handicap at Lingfield penultimate start: raced only around
1m: acted on polytrack and good to firm going, well beaten on heavy (in listed race at
Saint-Cloud): stud. *H. R. A. Cecil*

STORMY RAINBOW 5 b.g. Red Rainbow 105 – Stormy Heights 62 (Golden Heights **–**
82) [2002 75: 8g 8s Oct 28] fair handicapper at 4 yrs: well held in 2002. *M. Blanshard*

STORMY TEENY (GER) 4 br.f. Dashing Blade 117 – Storm Weaver (USA) (Storm **50**
Bird (CAN) 134) [2002 8f 8m³ 7m f8.5g⁴ f6g² 7f 6m⁵ 6.1m³ 5g⁶ Oct 5] leggy, angular
filly: half-sister to 3 winners, including fairly useful 2-y-o winners Storm Master (9f in
Ireland, by Generous) and Cape Weaver (6f, by Pampabird): dam second at 9f: modest
maiden handicapper: trained by Frau M. Blaksczyk in Germany in 2001: effective at stiff
5f, should stay 1m: acts on soft going, good to firm and fibresand: tried blinkered earlier
in career: sometimes tongue tied: races prominently. *M. G. Quinlan*

STORMY VOYAGE 4 b.g. Storm Bird (CAN) 134 – Vivid Imagination (USA) **– §**
(Raise A Man (USA)) [2002 48, a67: p7g p8g p7g f8g p7g Feb 20] good-topped gelding:
fair handicapper on all-weather at 3 yrs: temperamental nowadays: visored/blinkered:
refused to race final start. *J. M. Bradley*

STORYTELLER (IRE) 8 b.g. Thatching 131 – Please Believe Me 93 (Try My Best **85**
(USA) 130) [2002 68: 5s 5g* 5g³ 5m³ 5m² 5g 5d* 5m 5m* 5g³ 5d Oct 21] quite good-
topped gelding: impresses in appearance: fairly useful performer: won minor event at
Carlisle in May and handicaps at Beverley and Sandown in August: best at stiff 5f/6f: acts
on firm and good to soft going: visored: sometimes starts slowly: usually held up (wasn't
at Sandown): tough. *M. Dods*

ST PALAIS 3 b.f. Timeless Times (USA) 99 – Crambella (IRE) 30 (Red Sunset 120) **–**
[2002 –: 7.5m Aug 25] leggy, unfurnished filly: no form. *J. Balding*

ST PANCRAS (IRE) 2 b.c. (Mar 29) Danehill Dancer (IRE) 117 – Lauretta Blue **104 p**
(IRE) (Bluebird (USA) 125) [2002 6m* 8m² 7.1m⁴ 7m² Sep 13] IR 18,500F, IR 28,000Y:
big, good-topped colt: brother to 3-y-o Blue Sky Thinking and half-brother to 3 winners,
including 4-y-o Top Nolans: dam third at 1½m in Ireland: useful form: won minor event

Mr Michael Hill's "St Pancras"

at Newmarket in July: in frame in Solario Stakes at Sandown (1½ lengths fourth to Foss Way) and Champagne Stakes at Doncaster (1¼ lengths second to Almushahar, always prominent) last 2 starts: should stay 1¼m: raced only on good to firm ground: has scope to make a better 3-y-o. *N. A. Callaghan*

ST PETERSBURG 2 ch.g. (Jan 23) Polar Falcon (USA) 126 – First Law 57 (Primo **79** Dominie 121) [2002 5g 7g⁶ 7.5g* 8s² 7v Nov 9] lengthy gelding: second foal: half-brother to a 2-y-o 5f winner in Italy by So Factual: dam, maiden who should have been best at 1m, half-sister to useful 1996 2-y-o 6f to 1m winner Falkenham (by Polar Falcon): fair performer: won maiden at Beverley in September: best effort when second to Special Envoy in nursery at Yarmouth: barely stays testing 1m: acts on soft going (soundly beaten on heavy), yet to race on firmer than good: gelded after final start. *M. H. Tompkins*

STRACOMER URANIA (IRE) 4 gr.f. Paris House 123 – Pheopotstown (Henbit **–** (USA) 130) [2002 60: 10.5s f9.4g Dec 16] IR 17,000Y: half-sister to several winners, including useful Irish 6f (at 2 yrs) and 7f winner Murawwi (by Perugino): dam Irish 1m to 1¾m winner: little form: left R. McGlinchey in Ireland prior to well held in maiden at Wolverhampton on British debut. *Ian Williams*

STRAIGHT AND TRUE 3 b.f. Lake Coniston (IRE) 131 – Play The Game 70 **69** (Mummy's Game 120) [2002 58: 5f 5.9d* 6g⁴ 6m 6s⁵ 6s Aug 30] tall, rather unfurnished filly: fair handicapper: won at Carlisle in June (carried head awkwardly): bit slipped penultimate start, possibly something amiss final one: will prove best at 5f/6f: acts on good to soft going, well held on firmer than good: sold 3,800 gns. *A. Berry*

STRAIGHT EIGHT 3 b.g. Octagonal (NZ) 126 – Kalymnia (GER) (Mondrian **–** (GER) 125) [2002 –: 10d 9v Nov 21] big, lengthy gelding: only a little sign of ability in maidens at 2 yrs and well held both 3-y-o starts: left T. Easterby after reappearance. *R. Pritchard-Gordon, France*

STRAIT TALKING (FR)   4 b.g. Bering 136 – Servia (Le Marmot (FR) 130) [2002   **66 d**
72: 10d 8f 8.3s⁴ 9.3g⁶ 11.1g f11g Nov 26] rather leggy, close-coupled gelding: fair handicapper: on downgrade: stays 1¼m: acts on soft and good to firm ground. *Jedd O'Keeffe*

STRAND ONTHE GREEN (IRE)   4 b.g. Ela-Mana-Mou 132 – Fleuretta (USA)   **–**
(The Minstrel (CAN) 135) [2002 63: f9.4g Jul 20] fair maiden at best: reportedly bled
from nose only run in 2002. *T. G. Mills*

STRANGE (IRE)   4 b.g. Alzao (USA) 117 – Partie de Dames (USA) (Bering 136)   **46**
[2002 8.2m⁵ p8g⁴ 6g Oct 28] 150,000 francs Y, 2,000 3-y-o: third foal: dam unraced
half-sister to smart French middle-distance performer Marchand de Sable: poor form in
maidens. *E. J. O'Neill*

STRATHCLYDE (IRE)   3 b.g. Petong 126 – It's Academic 73 (Royal Academy   **87**
(USA) 130) [2002 50p: f6s p6g* p6g² 6g 6m 5d⁵ 6g 5m⁶ 5m* 5g² 5g 5m² 6g 5m⁵ Oct 12]
strong, good-topped gelding: fairly useful performer: won maiden at Lingfield in January
and (having left W. Jarvis 30,000 gns after third start) handicap at Newmarket in June:
has won at 6f, best form at 5f: acts on polytrack, good to firm and good to soft going:
races prominently: consistent. *J. Cullinan*

STRATH FILLAN   4 b.f. Dolphin Street (FR) 125 – Adarama (IRE) (Persian Bold   **49**
123) [2002 42: f8g⁶ 12m* 11.8d 11.8s 11.5s⁶ Oct 22] small filly: has a quick action: poor
handicapper: won at Folkestone in April: stays easy 1½m: acts on firm going (possibly
not softer than good), some promise on fibresand: sold 5,000 gns. *W. J. Musson*

STRATHSPEY   3 ch.f. Dancing Spree (USA) – Diebiedale 58 (Dominion 123) [2002   **75**
–: 7g² 7f² 8f² 8g² 8m 8.5m² 8f³ Sep 17] sturdy filly: fair performer: runner-up 5 times
before winning maiden at Epsom in September: not sure to stay beyond 8.5f: acts on firm
going: gave trouble to post/behind stall fifth outing: consistent. *C. F. Wall*

STRATOSPHERE   3 ch.f. Selkirk (USA) 129 – La Strada (Niniski (USA) 125) [2002   **81**
7g 8.1m³ 8.3m 10d⁴ 9m⁵ 12d² 12m² 11.7g 12d Nov 1] workmanlike filly: fourth foal:
half-sister to fairly useful 1m to 1¾m winner Bow Strada (by Rainbow Quest) and 4-y-o
Valeureux: dam, champion 2-y-o filly in Spain, sister to smart German/New Zealand
middle-distance horse Vialli: fairly useful maiden handicapper: stays 1½m: acts on good
to firm and good to soft going: sold 4,500 gns. *I. A. Balding*

STRAT'S QUEST   8 b.m. Nicholas (USA) 111 – Eagle's Quest 62 (Legal Eagle 126)   **– §**
[2002 43§, a39§: p10g f8s³ f9.4g⁵ Feb 15] leggy, sparely-made mare: has a quick action: **a41 §**
poor performer: stays 1m: acts on fibresand: effective visored or not: inconsistent.
D. W. P. Arbuthnot

STRATUS (FR)   3 b.g. Septieme Ciel (USA) 123 – Sudden Spirit (FR) (Esprit du Nord   **94**
(USA) 126) [2002 82p: p10g² 10.5d 9.9d² 12m 11.8g 6.5f Dec 28] strong, useful-looking
gelding: fairly useful performer: best effort when second in minor event at Salisbury third
outing: sold from G. Butler 26,000 gns prior to final start: stays 1¼m: acts on good to soft
going and polytrack: blinkered third/fourth outings, tongue tied second one: has worn
crossed noseband/tongue strap/carried head high: possibly temperamental. *S. Shulman,
USA*

STRAWBERRY DAWN   4 gr.f. Fayruz 116 – Alasib 93 (Siberian Express (USA)   **–**
125) [2002 –: 5d 5m⁶ 5g f5g Dec 17] lightly raced and little form. *J. R. Boyle*

STRAWBERRY PATCH (IRE)   3 b.c. Woodborough (USA) 112 – Okino (USA)   **83**
(Strawberry Road (AUS) 128) [2002 85: 6m 5.1f 5v⁶ 5m 5.1f⁴ 6m² 5g³ 6d⁵ 6m³ 6m² 5f 6f
6d⁴ Nov 1] strong, good-topped colt: fairly useful performer: effective at 5f/6f: acts on
firm and good to soft going. *Miss L. A. Perratt*

STRAWBERRY SANDS   3 b.f. Lugana Beach 116 – Strawberry Song 87 (Final   **65 §**
Straw 127) [2002 74: p5g 5.1m 5d 5.1s 5.1g 5f 5m³ 5m 5f Sep 25] small filly: fair
handicapper: left J. Portman after third start: raced only at 5f: acts on firm and good to
soft going: sometimes tongue tied: usually races up with pace: slowly away last 2 outings
(seemed to take little interest final one): one to treat with caution: sold 700 gns.
L. G. Cottrell

STRAW DOGS (IRE)   3 b.g. Thatching 131 – La Duse 66 (Junius (USA) 124) [2002   **–**
7.1m 12m Apr 22] IR 20,000Y: good-bodied gelding: brother to a winner in Kuwait and
half-brother to 10-y-o Blushing Grenadier and 1m winner Cindy's Star (by Dancing
Dissident): dam third at 1½m: well held in maiden/seller. *M. R. Channon*

STREAKY (IRE)   2 b.f. (Apr 24) Danetime (IRE) 121 – Solo Symphony (IRE) 67   **63**
(Fayruz 116) [2002 5m⁴ 5m² 5d 5d* 5.1d⁶ 5.2f 5g Aug 1] IR 5,500Y: smallish, sturdy
filly: second foal: dam, sprint maiden, out of half-sister to useful sprinter Whittingham:
modest performer: won maiden at Goodwood in May: beat only one horse after: raced
only at 5f: acts on good to firm and good to soft ground. *Mrs P. N. Dutfield*

STREET CRY (IRE)   4 br.c. Machiavellian (USA) 123 – Helen Street 123 (Troy   **130**
137) [2002 121: a10f* a10f* a9f* a9f² Aug 3]

Street Cry was the best horse to race in the Godolphin colours in 2002.
His assessment of 124 in the end-of-season International Classifications underestimated his merit and his retirement in September, due to persistent inflammation
in his off-fore ankle, robbed him of further lucrative prizes in the autumn. Street
Cry's record of finishing out of the first two only once in a twelve-race career—
when third in the Breeders' Cup Juvenile—is testament to his reliability. But he
only really showed his true colours as a four-year-old, making up for an injury-
interrupted three-year-old career with three impressive victories on dirt on his first
three starts.

A proven dirt performer, successful in the UAE 2000 Guineas and beaten a
short head in the UAE Derby in 2001, Street Cry went into the latest Dubai World
Cup at Nad Al Sheba in March as his stable's second string. He booked his place
with a resounding eight-and-a-half-length victory over the previous year's World
Cup fourth State Shinto in Round 3 of the Maktoum Challenge at Nad Al Sheba in
February, seeming to appreciate the step up in trip to a mile and a quarter. Street
Cry's illustrious stable-companion Sakhee, a six-length winner of the Prix de l'Arc
in 2001 and beaten only narrowly in the Breeders' Cup Classic, made a similarly
impressive reappearance and started 5/2-on for the world's richest race. The
American challenge in particular, so important to the long-term prestige of the
Dubai World Cup, was nowhere near so strong as previously and Sakhee's principal
opponent looked like being the top-class Japanese challenger Agnes Digital. Agnes
Digital was disappointing, managing only sixth, but inquests into his performance
were overshadowed by the post-race attention focussed on Sakhee. Poised to
challenge on the outside turning for home, he was left standing by Street Cry who
made his run on the inside and surged clear to win a strongly-run race by four and a
quarter lengths from the unconsidered Saudi-Arabian runner Sei Mi, who'd
finished fifth in the race the previous year, with a well below form Sakhee the same
distance away third of the eleven runners; Europe's only challenger, French-trained
Keltos, came eighth. Street Cry gave Godolphin its third win in the Dubai World
Cup in four years and American jockey Jerry Bailey his fourth win in the seven
runnings of the race.

Street Cry and Sakhee went their separate ways after the Dubai World Cup.
While Sakhee was off the course for nearly five months before his only other start
(beaten at 5/1-on at Deauville), Street Cry pursued an American campaign with the
long-term aim of going one better than Sakhee in the Breeders' Cup Classic. Street
Cry confirmed that he had improved as a four-year-old with a tremendous win in
the Stephen Foster Handicap, upgraded to Grade 1 since the previous year, at

Dubai World Cup, Nad Al Sheba—Street Cry provides Jerry Bailey with his fourth win in the race
as stable-companion Sakhee weakens disappointingly into third;
Saudi Arabian-trained Sei Mi splits the pair

Churchill Downs in June. None of his seven rivals could get him off the bridle as he cruised home, his jockey motionless in the last hundred yards, for a six-and-a-half-length victory over Dollar Bill, who subsequently finished sixth in the Breeders' Cup Classic. Street Cry had merely to be shaken up, after travelling easily from the start, to go on two furlongs out, his performance firmly establishing him as the top older horse in North America at the time. He started evens favourite for a very good renewal of the Whitney Handicap at Saratoga in August. The twenty-eight-year-old track record was equalled and Street Cry ran right up to his best, conceding weight all round, to finish a length-and-a-quarter second to the ill-fated Left Bank, who had won two Grade 1 events in 2001 and had trounced the opposition in the Grade 2 Tom Fool Handicap at Belmont on his previous start. The 2001 winner Lido Palace and the Breeders' Cup Classic fourth Macho Uno came third and fourth. The latest Breeders' Cup Classic, in which Volponi caused a big upset, was much the poorer for the absence of the likes of Left Bank, Street Cry and Lido Palace. Street Cry was being trained for the Jockey Club Gold Cup at Belmont when injury struck. Though Godolphin didn't have a winner on Breeders' Cup day, its European-based squad recorded five Grade 1 victories in North America during another very successful year internationally. Worldwide, Godolphin won sixteen Group/Grade 1 races in eight different countries, Britain, Ireland, France, Germany, Italy, Dubai, the USA and Singapore. The total was second, in Godolphin's nine-year existence, only to the eighteen victories recorded in 1999.

		Mr Prospector	Raise A Native
	Machiavellian (USA)	(b 1970)	Gold Digger
	(b 1987)	Coup de Folie	Halo
Street Cry (IRE)		(b 1982)	Raise The Standard
(br.c. 1998)		Troy	Petingo
	Helen Street	(b 1976)	La Milo
	(b 1982)	Waterway	Riverman
		(ch 1976)	Boulevard

Street Cry is the second Dubai World Cup winner, following Almutawakel, sired by the versatile Machiavellian. Machiavellian was the top two-year-old of his year in France and went on to finish second in the Two Thousand Guineas; he only just stayed a mile but has sired winners over all sorts of distances (Cup horses Cover Up and Invermark were among his runners in the latest season). While Machiavellian himself was an early-developer, his progeny are not noted for their precocity and his latest clutch of Group 1 winners, Street Cry, Champion Stakes winner Storming Home and Prix d'Ispahan winner Best of The Bests, all came from his four-year-olds and upwards in 2002, as did No Excuse Needed, who won the Queen Anne Stakes, a race being promoted to Group 1 in 2003. Machiavellian, incidentally, was bandied about in some quarters after Street Cry's win in the Dubai World Cup as a sire whose progeny improve when raced on dirt. Almutawakel was transformed on dirt—the Dubai World Cup was his first outing on such a surface—but he and Street Cry are the only major winners on the surface for their sire. Machiavellian has stood all his career in Britain, so his progeny have had limited opportunities in good dirt races, though Muwakleh and Best of The Bests have won important races on the surface in Dubai as well. Street Cry has an essentially 'turf' pedigree on his dam's side too, descending from an old-established Ballymacoll Stud family which abounds with winners. Street Cry's dam the Irish Oaks winner Helen Street looked a good acquisition for the Maktoum broodmare band but her early career at stud proved disappointing and she must have come close to being weeded out. The best of her other winners are the useful French mile-and-a-quarter winner Helsinki (a sister to Street Cry), the useful performer at up to a mile and a half Grecian Slipper (by Sadler's Wells) and the useful French three-year-old Historian (by Pennekamp), winner of a listed race over an extended mile and a quarter at Saint-Cloud in March. Street Cry, raced only on dirt, stayed a mile and a quarter well. He was visored/blinkered on his last two starts as a three-year-old and sometimes had his tongue tied. He will be standing at Jonabell Farm in the United States in 2003 at a fee of $30,000. *Saeed bin Suroor*

STREET GAMES   3 b.g. Mind Games 121 – Pusey Street 96 (Native Bazaar 122)   –
[2002 6g 7g 7s Oct 28] tall, lengthy gelding: half-brother to several winners, including 7f

winner Pusey Street Girl (by Gildoran) and 1m/1¼m winner Windrush Lady (by Risk Me): dam sprinter: well held in maidens/claimer. *M. R. Bosley*

STREET INDEX (IRE)   3 br.f. Dolphin Street (FR) 125 – Casaveha (IRE) (Persian   –
Bold 123) [2002 –: 8m 6g 7m 8.3s 7d 8m 8g Jul 24] small filly: little form: blinkered final
start. *Mrs P. N. Dutfield*

STREET LIFE (IRE)   4 ch.g. Dolphin Street (FR) 125 – Wolf Cleugh (IRE) 65 (Last   **85**
Tycoon 131) [2002 78: p10g 9.7m 10g⁴ 10s* 10s* 10d³ 12s³ 10.1s 12v⁶ p10g Dec 11]
tall gelding: fairly useful handicapper: won at Windsor in May and June: eye-catching
effort under 7-lb claimer after 3-month break eighth start: travelled strongly long
way when remote sixth in November Handicap at Doncaster next time: best form at 1¼m:
acts on polytrack, best turf form on good going or softer: sometimes edges left.
W. J. Musson

STREET MUSIC   3 ch.c. Barathea (IRE) 127 – Three Piece (Jaazeiro (USA) 127)   **68**
[2002 7m⁴ 8.1d⁵ 7s Oct 22] big, good-topped colt: has scope: has fluent, round action:
half-brother to several winners, notably Poule d'Essai des Poulains winner Victory Note
(by Fairy King), 6f winner at 2 yrs, and useful 1½m performer Dance So Suite (by
Shareef Dancer): dam Irish maiden: fair form in maidens: best effort on debut (slowly
away): reportedly coughed and off 5 months before final outing: should stay at least 1m.
C. F. Wall

STREET WALKER (IRE)   6 b.m. Dolphin Street (FR) 125 – Foolish Dame (USA)   –
(Foolish Pleasure (USA)) [2002 –: 7.1g 10f 16d⁶ 16m⁵ 12f Jul 17] rather leggy mare:
maiden: little form since 2000: sometimes visored. *W. Storey*

STRENGTH 'N HONOUR   2 b.c. (Apr 28) Hernando (FR) 127 – Seasonal Splen-   **85**
dour (IRE) 95 (Prince Rupert (FR) 121) [2002 8.2m² 8.1m⁴ Sep 6] rangy colt: has scope:
second living foal: half-brother to smart 1¾m winner When In Rome (by Saddlers' Hall):
dam, 1½m winner who stayed 2m, half-sister to Cherry Hinton Stakes winner Torgau:
fairly useful form when head second of 5 to Famous Grouse (pair clear) in minor event at
Nottingham, hanging right and just edged out: disappointing when odds on for maiden at
Haydock: should be suited by 1½m+. *C. A. Cyzer*

STRENSALL   5 b.g. Beveled (USA) – Payvashooz 78 (Ballacashtal (CAN)) [2002 58:   **71**
f5g* f6g⁵ f5g² f5g 5g f5g⁶ 5m 5m 5g³ 5m* 5m 5m* 5m⁶ 5m 5m⁴ 5m² f6g Nov 26]   **a60 +**
leggy gelding: fair performer: won maiden at Wolverhampton in January and handicaps
at Musselburgh and Catterick (2) in summer: best at 5f: acts on firm going and fibresand:
sometimes slowly away: tough. *R. E. Barr*

STRENUE (USA)   2 ch.g. (Jan 14) Crafty Prospector (USA) – Shawgatny (USA) 83   **57 ?**
(Danzig Connection (USA)) [2002 7.1g⁴ 8.1g⁶ 8m⁵ f8.5g⁶ Dec 20] $90,000F: fifth foal:
half-brother to 6-y-o September Harvest and a winner in USA by Mt Livermore: dam,
Irish 2-y-o 9f winner, sister to very smart 1m to 1¼m performer Star of Gdansk: modest
form on balance in minor event/maidens. *M. R. Channon*

STRESSLESS (IRE)   2 ch.c. (Feb 12) Barathea (IRE) 127 – Polish Rhythm (IRE) 77   **90**
(Polish Patriot (USA) 128) [2002 7d 7m³ 7f* 7.6f⁴ Sep 25] 20,000Y: rangy colt: second
foal: dam, 1m winner at 4 yrs, half-sister to Cheveley Park/Moyglare Stud Stakes winner
Capricciosa: fairly useful performer: best effort when winning maiden at Chester in
August by neck from Desert Lord, getting up close home: will stay 1m: acts on firm
ground. *B. W. Hills*

STRETTON (IRE)   4 br.g. Doyoun 124 – Awayil (USA) 82 (Woodman (USA) 126)   **93**
[2002 88: 10.3f* 10.4f⁵ 8.5s⁵ 10f⁴ 10d⁵ 8m 10m 8m 10.4f Oct 11] leggy, close-coupled
gelding: impresses in appearance: fairly useful handicapper: won at Chester in May:
effective at 8.5f to 10.5f: unraced on heavy going, acts on any other turf (below form only
run on fibresand): held up: gelded after final start. *J. D. Bethell*

STRICTLY SPEAKING (IRE)   5 b.g. Sri Pekan (USA) 117 – Gaijin 97 (Caerleon   **55**
(USA) 132) [2002 63: p13g f14.8g² f14.8s⁵ 13.3s 18d⁴ 16.4d⁶ 15d 11.6d⁵ 12.1s⁵ f12g²   **a63**
11.8s Oct 15] tall gelding: modest handicapper: stays 14.8f: acts on fibresand, firm and
soft going: sometimes blinkered: sometimes finds little: none too consistent. *P. F. I. Cole*

STRIKING AMBITION   2 b. or br.c. (Feb 9) Makbul 104 – Lady Roxanne 65   **105 p**
(Cyrano de Bergerac 120) [2002 6.1m* 6m 6v* Nov 13] 7,000F, 28,000Y: rather
unfurnished, useful-looking colt: third foal: half-brother to 6-y-o Gascon: dam, 5f/6f
winner, sister to useful French/US sprinter Cyrano Storme: useful form: won maiden
at Nottingham (well-backed favourite) in August and listed race at Saint-Cloud
(comfortably by 3 lengths from Mystic Melody) in November: shaped much better than

bare result suggests when eighth of 21 to Somnus in sales race at Doncaster: will stay 7f: acts on heavy and good to firm ground: capable of better still. *G. C. Bravery*

STROKE OF SIX (IRE) 3 b.f. Woodborough (USA) 112 – Angelus Chimes 80 **84** (Northfields (USA)) [2002 75: 8m3 8.3d4 8m2 7d2 9d5 8.1d* 9g4 8.3g3 8.1m6 8g p8g Nov 23] close-coupled, useful-looking filly: fairly useful handicapper: won easily at Haydock in July: best at 7f/1m: acts on firm and soft going, probably on polytrack: consistent. *R. Hannon*

STROMSHOLM (IRE) 6 ch.g. Indian Ridge 123 – Upward Trend 112 (Salmon **65** Leap (USA) 131) [2002 78: p10g* p10g4 p10g3 Feb 27] unfurnished gelding: fair performer: won minor event at Lingfield in January: stays easy 1¼m: acts on all-weather, good to firm and good to soft going, not on soft: has hung markedly left: none too consistent. *R. Ingram*

STRONG HAND 2 b.f. (Apr 7) First Trump 118 – Better Still (IRE) (Glenstal (USA) **78** 118) [2002 6m4 5g* 5m6 5.9d* 7m Aug 22] 3,000Y: big, lengthy, heavy-topped filly: sixth foal: sister to 3-y-o Snappy: dam little form: fair performer: won 3-runner maiden at Musselburgh in June and 6-runner nursery at Hamilton (beat Rahaf by length) in July: should stay 7f: yet to race on extremes of going. *M. W. Easterby*

STRONG WILL 2 b.g. (Apr 13) Primo Dominie 121 – Reine de Thebes (FR) 67 **63** (Darshaan) [2002 6f 5.9d Jun 26] leggy gelding: sixth foal: half-brother to useful 5f to 7f winner (including at 2 yrs) Boldly Goes (by Bold Arrangement) and 4-y-o King's Welcome: dam, 1m to 11f winner, half-sister to dam of Arc runner-up Egyptband: modest form when seventh in maiden at Redcar: something possibly amiss on subsequent start. *C. W. Fairhurst*

STRUDEL RUSE (IRE) 3 b.f. Fayruz 116 – Sweet Disorder (IRE) 62 (Never So **–** Bold 135) [2002 56: 7.9g 7d May 24] modest maiden at 2 yrs: well held in 2002: should stay 7f. *P. W. Harris*

STRUMMER 2 b.g. (Feb 5) Forzando 122 – Pluck 80 (Never So Bold 135) [2002 8.2v **–** Oct 29] fourth living foal: half-brother to 3-y-o Balakiref and Swedish winner up to 1¼m Cub Chief (by Be My Chief): dam, 5.7f (at 2 yrs) and 6f winner, out of half-sister to very smart sprinter Piccolo: 25/1, tailed off in seller at Nottingham. *J. G. Portman*

STUDIO TIME (USA) 3 b.c. Gone West (USA) – Ratings (USA) (Caveat (USA)) **103** [2002 88p: 7m* 8g 9.8d5 8.5f6 Nov 16] close-coupled, quite attractive colt: useful form, lightly raced: won maiden at Newmarket in April: stiff task, creditable 7 lengths eighth to Landseer in Poule d'Essai des Poulains at Longchamp next time: left J. Gosden and off 5 months before final outing: stays 1m, possibly not 9.8f: successful on good to firm and good to soft going. *N. D. Drysdale, USA*

STUDLAND BAY 2 b.f. (Mar 6) Sri Pekan (USA) 117 – Pigeon Hole (Green Desert **–** (USA) 127) [2002 5g f8s6 10.2f6 Sep 30] third foal: dam lightly-raced half-sister to 1000 Guineas second Niche: only a little sign of ability in minor event/maidens. *W. G. M. Turner*

STUNNING MAGIC 2 b.g. (Mar 31) Magic Ring (IRE) 115 – Absolutelystunning **–** 63 (Aragon 118) [2002 6g 6.1d Jul 6] first foal: dam, 1¼m winner who stayed 11.4f, half-sister to useful 6f/7f winner at 2 yrs (later successful up to 9f in US) Merlin's Ring (by Magic Ring): slowly away/well beaten in maidens. *Mrs Barbara Waring*

STYLE DANCER (IRE) 8 b.g. Dancing Dissident (USA) 119 – Showing Style (Pas **84** de Seul 133) [2002 83, a68: 8.1d 8.5g 8g 8m* 8.5d 8m6 9m 9m2 7.9m 10.3m6 8g3 8m **a72** 10.4f3 8.9f4 p8g p8g3 Dec 14] tall gelding: good mover: fairly useful handicapper on turf, fair on all-weather: dead-heated at Doncaster in June: effective at 7f to easy 1¼m: acts on fibresand, possibly ideally suited by good ground or firmer on turf: tried blinkered, effective visored or not: reportedly bled from nose once at 7 yrs: has pulled hard: usually held up. *T. D. Easterby*

STYLISH CLARE (IRE) 4 b.f. Desert Style (IRE) 121 – Brockley Hill Lass (IRE) **–** (Alzao (USA) 117) [2002 77: 6m 6.1f 6m Jul 1] workmanlike filly: fair performer at 3 yrs: well held in 2002. *J. W. Payne*

STYLISH PRINCE 2 b.c. (Apr 29) Polar Prince (IRE) 117 – Simply Style (Bairn **56** (USA) 126) [2002 5s6 f5g4 f5g 5.1g6 5s5 6.1d 5v* 7m5 7f7g4 5.1g f7g 7g Oct 17] 500Y: eighth foal: half-brother to 3 winners, including fairly useful 1997 2-y-o 5f winner Lady Moll (by King's Signet), later sprint winner in USA, and unreliable 1m winner Loch Style (by Lochnager): dam unraced: modest performer: left M. Easterby after second start: won claimer at Hamilton in June: poor efforts last 3 starts: will prove best at 5f/6f: acts on heavy going and fibresand: tried visored. *J. G. M. O'Shea*

STYLISH WAYS (IRE)   10 b.g. Thatching 131 – Style of Life (USA) (The Minstrel (CAN) 135) [2002 54d: 7m 5.9d Jun 26] compact gelding: fluent mover: one-time useful performer: no form in 2002: tried visored. *M. Todhunter*   –

SUALDA (IRE)   3 b.c. Idris (IRE) 118 – Winning Heart 98 (Horage 124) [2002 69: 7.1f 8.1m* 10f* 11f* 12.3d 12g 9.7m 10m 10.9m⁴ 10m⁴ Oct 1] unfurnished colt: fair handicapper: won at Warwick/Redcar in May and Redcar in June: stays 1½m: best form on good going or firmer: often tongue tied at 2 yrs: refused to settle seventh start: consistent: sold 20,000 gns. *C. G. Cox*   **78**

SUALTACH (IRE)   9 b.h. Marju (IRE) 127 – Astra Adastra (Mount Hagen (FR) 127) [2002 61, a65: f9.4g Jan 28] strong, lengthy horse: has a round action: fair performer at 8 yrs: reportedly lost action only run in 2002: visored once at 3 yrs. *Andrew Reid*   –

SUAVE PERFORMER   5 b.g. Suave Dancer (USA) 136 – Francia 59 (Legend of France (USA) 124) [2002 61: 9.3g 10d 9s⁴ 8.3m⁶ 9.2s⁶ 9.9g³ 10g² 10.1d* 9.2v 10g f9.4g⁶ f9.4g⁶ f8.5s⁶ Dec 26] neat gelding: modest handicapper: won at Epsom in July: best at 9f/ 1¼m: has form on fibresand and good to firm going, goes well on softer than good: sometimes races too freely, and best patiently ridden. *S. C. Williams*   **59**
a50

SUBADAR MAJOR   5 b.g. Komaite (USA) – Rather Gorgeous 37§ (Billion (USA) 120) [2002 43, a–: 13.8m 12f³ 14g Jun 17] big gelding: poor performer: stays 1¾m: acts on firm going. *Mrs G. S. Rees*   **35**
a–

SUBIACO (GER)   5 b.h. Monsun (GER) 124 – So Sedulous (USA) 102 (The Minstrel (CAN) 135) [2002 118: 14d² 12s⁴ 12s Oct 26] lengthy horse: smart performer at best: won 3 Group 2/3 events in 2001: just useful form at 5 yrs, in frame in listed race at Baden-Baden and Preis von Europa at Cologne (fourth to Well Made): well held in St Simon Stakes at Newbury final start: sold privately to B. Curley after: effective at 10.5f to 2m: acts on heavy going. *A. Schutz, Germany*   **108**

SUCCESSOR   2 ch.c. (Mar 5) Entrepreneur 123 – Petralona (USA) (Alleged (USA) 138) [2002 7d² Oct 30] second foal: half-brother to 4-y-o Big Moment: dam, useful French 12.5f winner who stayed 15.5f, sister to Park Hill Stakes winner Eva Luna, herself dam of 2-y-o Brian Boru: 10/1, and green, shaped well when ½-length second of 18 to Hard Nose in maiden at Yarmouth, slowly away but leading at halfway and reeled in only towards line: should be well suited by 1m+: open to considerable improvement. *B. W. Hills*   **86 P**

SUCCINCT   3 ch.f. Hector Protector (USA) 124 – Pitcroy 99 (Unfuwain (USA) 131) [2002 9.9m* 10s* 12m Jun 20] rather lengthy, angular filly: third foal: dam, 1¼m winner, half-sister to smart 7f/1m performer Ardkinglass: useful form: successful in maiden at Salisbury in May and listed event at Newbury (beat Lady's Secret a neck, took time to warm to task and carried head bit awkwardly) in June: last of 15 in Ribblesdale Stakes at Royal Ascot 7 days later: stayed 1¼m: stud. *H. R. A. Cecil*   **104**

SUDDEN FLIGHT (IRE)   5 b.g. In The Wings 128 – Ma Petite Cherie (USA) 93 (Caro 133) [2002 84: p12g⁴ p12g³ p12g p16g⁶ p12g p12g⁴ 14.4f⁶ 12g 12m⁶ 11.5f⁵ p12g⁶ f12f* f12g* f12s² Nov 30] close-coupled gelding: unimpressive mover: fairly useful performer: won minor event and handicap at Wolverhampton in November: stays 1¾m: acts on all-weather/any turf ground: tried visored: has worn crossed noseband/taken good hold: tends to wander/carry head awkwardly: usually makes running nowadays. *R. Ingram*   **80**

SUDRA   5 b.g. Indian Ridge 123 – Bunting 102 (Shaadi (USA) 126) [2002 73, a66: f8s⁵ p8g⁵ f7s⁴ f8s* f8g⁴ p7g⁴ f8g² p8g 8.3g 6d p7g 8.1m f8g p7g p7g⁴ Dec 18] smallish gelding: modest performer: won apprentice claimer at Southwell (left T. D. Barron) in January: below form after: stays 8.5f: acts on fibresand (below form on polytrack), firm going and probably on good to soft: has worn cheekpieces: has high head carriage: one to treat with some caution. *C. A. Dwyer*   –
a61

SUE ALLEN (IRE)   2 b.f. (May 9) Pennekamp (USA) 130 – Jambo Jambo (IRE) (Kafu 120) [2002 5g 5g f5g⁵ 5f⁵ f7g⁵ Jul 26] IR 10,000Y: lengthy, quite attractive filly: sixth foal: half-sister to fairly useful Irish 5f winner Lady Assassin (by Polish Patriot) and a winner in Japan by Magical Wonder: dam Irish 2-y-o 5f winner: poor maiden: likely to prove best at 5f/6f: looks difficult ride. *R. F. Fisher*   **37**

SUERTE   2 b.f. (Mar 28) Halling (USA) 133 – Play With Me (IRE) 73 (Alzao (USA) 117) [2002 6m 7d Oct 30] sister to 3-y-o Crow Wood and half-sister to several winners,   –

including smart Scandinavian sprinter Shawdon (by Inchinor), also winner in Britain at 2 yrs: dam, 1¼m winner, half-sister to Oaks d'Italia winner Lady Bentley: slowly away and well held in maidens 2 months apart. *J. G. Given*

SUEZ TORNADO (IRE)   9 ch.g. Mujtahid (USA) 118 – So Stylish 77 (Great   –
Nephew 126) [2002 14.4s Jun 12] lengthy, good-topped gelding: of little account on Flat nowadays. *B. R. Johnson*

SUGARBOY   2 b.g. (Feb 24) Muhtarram (USA) 125 – Native Flair 87 (Be My Native   **66 p**
(USA) 122) [2002 8s Oct 15] 4,000Y: good-bodied gelding: half-brother to several winners, including fairly useful 1m/1¼m winner Holy Smoke (by Statoblest) and 9-y-o Nosey Native: dam 1¼m/1½m winner: 50/1 and burly, never-dangerous ninth of 13 to Allergy in maiden at Leicester: unimpressive to post: should do better at 1¼m/1½m. *T. G. Mills*

SUGAR SNAP   2 b.f. (Apr 28) Sesaro (USA) 81 – Cuddle Bunny (IRE) (Statoblest   **62**
120) [2002 5m⁵ 6m² f5g⁶ 7g Oct 24] first foal: dam ran 4 times in Ireland: modest maiden: easily best effort when second in seller at Lingfield, hanging markedly left: stays 6f: sold 1,500 gns. *M. D. I. Usher*

SUGGESTIVE   4 b.g. Reprimand 122 – Pleasuring 68 (Good Times (ITY)) [2002   **118**
106p: 8.3s⁴ 7m 6d* 7m⁵ 7m* 7m³ 8g² Oct 5] big, good sort: smart performer, lightly raced (reportedly had minor setback after final 2001 start): impressive winner of minor event at Haydock in July and listed race at York (improved form to beat Millennium Dragon by 5 lengths) in August: ran well when head second to Domedriver in Prix Daniel Wildenstein at Longchamp final outing: effective at 6f and stays 1m when conditions aren't testing: acts on good to firm going and soft: visored last 3 starts: probably best waited with: stays in training. *W. J. Haggas*

SUHAIL (IRE)   6 b.g. Wolfhound (USA) 126 – Sharayif (IRE) (Green Desert (USA)   –
127) [2002 –: 6g 8.1d 10g 10m Jun 25] no longer of much account. *Jane Southcombe*

Mrs Barbara Bassett's "Suggestive"

SULAMANI (IRE)   3 b.c. Hernando (FR) 127 – Soul Dream (USA) 78 (Alleged   **130**
(USA) 138) [2002 10m 12d* 12d* 12m* 12m* 12g² Oct 6]

'At the root of all creation is imagination,' states Sheikh Mohammed,
'because before you achieve, you must first conceive.' How much imagination,
however, did it require for him to realise that Godolphin might win more good races
if they purchased Sulamani. 'Sheikh Mohammed liked the horse and talked to the
colt's owners. He's delighted Sulamani will now be racing for Godolphin,'
explained Godolphin racing manager Simon Crisford when their acquisition of
the impressive Prix du Jockey Club winner and Arc de Triomphe runner-up was
announced in mid-October. The deal with the Niarchos Family, who themselves
cannot be short of a bob or two, also incorporated the two-year-old filly Loving
Kindness, a Group 3 winner by Seattle Slew out of Coup de Genie, a Group
1-winning sister to the Maktoums' most successful stallion Machiavellian. Loving
Kindness must have been worth a fortune on her own. The price of the two horses
was undisclosed. *Racehorses of 2001* observed that Grandera was one of the
highest-rated recruits to the Godolphin team in recent years but Sulamani is in
another league. Other recruits mentioned, bought from outside the Maktoum
family, were top two-year-old Xaar and Arc winner Sagamix, but they had endured
disappointing seasons since their greatest triumphs; Daylami was a French classic
winner but had been beaten on his last three starts and, like Grandera, was rated 6 lb
lower than Sulamani at the time that he changed hands. The Maktoum purchase that
springs to mind most as a comparison with Sulamani is Arazi after his Breeders'
Cup Juvenile win in 1991, and then Sheikh Mohammed bought only a half share.
Some will inevitably see the purchase of a proven top-class performer such as
Sulamani as buying up the opposition. But Sheikh Mohammed has stated that 'One
of life's greatest pleasures is doing what others think you cannot do.'

Sulamani was unraced as a two-year-old and finished seventh over a mile
and a quarter on his debut in April, but he soon took the French middle-distance
scene by storm, winning his first four races once upped to a mile and a half. His
most startling and important triumph came in the Prix du Jockey Club just eight
weeks after that unsuccessful debut. A half-brother to the 1998 winner Dream Well
but starting at 199/10, Sulamani was taking a major step up in class after victories
by three quarters of a length in a minor event at Maisons-Laffitte at the end of April
and by a length and a half in a listed event at Chantilly in May. In the latter, he came
from last in an eight-runner field and still had plenty to do a furlong out. Others in
the French Derby line-up had been more thoroughly tested, notably Act One,

*Prix du Jockey Club, Chantilly—Sulamani, giving trainer Pascal Bary his fourth success in the race,
inflicts the first defeat on Act One; Simeon (rail) and Great Pretender (hooped cap) also make the frame*

unbeaten after five starts, including the Prix Lupin; the Sandown Classic Trial winner Simeon; Khalkevi (unbeaten after three starts), Louveteau and Black Sam Bellamy, all separated by just over a length in the Prix Hocquart; and Diaghilev, Le Fou (Montjeu's half-brother and the winner of Sulamani's debut race), Martaline and Great Pretender who filled the first four places in the Prix la Force. There were fifteen runners, but the Prix du Jockey Club unfolded in a very similar style to his listed race for Sulamani, who this time had only one behind him for most of the race and two behind him entering the straight before Thierry Thulliez switched him to the outside and Sulamani found easily the best turn of foot; Act One had moved up smoothly to tackle Simeon for the lead, but Sulamani passed them both a furlong out and, although the favourite kept on well to hold five lengths clear of third-placed Simeon, Sulamani beat him by a length and a half.

Sadly, there was to be no rematch between Sulamani and Act One, Act One sustaining a career-ending injury later in June. Sulamani was himself not seen out again for three and a half months, but nothing was untoward, his trainer Pascal Bary explaining that, while he had run Dream Well in the Irish Derby, Sulamani was not so mature; he had earned a rest after four starts in less than two months and was being aimed at the Arc. Sulamani duly reappeared in the traditional trial for a French three-year-old colt, the Prix Niel, sponsored in the latest season by Casino Barriere d'Enghien - Les Bains. Slowly-run races are also something of a tradition on the French tracks, from which the Arc trials at Longchamp are by no means exempt, but the Prix Niel was funereal even by their usual standards. The omens were poor when Sulamani's pacemaker was pulled out with an injury, joining High Chaparral, who was absent with a poor blood count, and leaving just three runners. When the 'race' was over and Sulamani had duly landed the odds, going on a mile out and beating his two Andre Fabre-trained opponents by a couple of lengths, the winning time was nearly forty-seven seconds slower than that for the Prix Vermeille. The crowd, clearly expecting entertainment of a higher standard, reacted by booing and jeering for all they were worth.

Although his Prix Niel shaped up more like a trial for the Abbaye than the Arc, Sulamani was shortened slightly in the ante-post lists, disputing favouritism with High Chaparral at around 5/2. On the day, High Chaparral was favourite on the pari-mutuel at 22/10 and Sulamani 7/2 second favourite, both coupled with pacemakers. The two Derby winners are very different types and were ridden very differently in the Arc, but there was only half a length between them at the line. Sulamani got the better of that particular rivalry but the main prize just escaped him and the seeds of defeat lay in his usual riding tactics. Holding him up in rear for a late burst had worked in his listed race and again in the Prix du Jockey Club, but it did not work in the more competitive field for the Arc. The plan may well have been for his pacemaker Sensible to ensure a breakneck gallop, but Sensible was slowly away and failed to get anywhere near the front. As it was, a sound pace materialised but it failed to draw the sting from Marienbard, another usually held up, though he rounded the home turn in sixth as opposed to Sulamani's thirteenth, five lengths behind. Sulamani's task was made all the more difficult when it took the best part of a furlong to straighten him up—on the outside again, he carried his head awkwardly as Thulliez tried to prevent him hanging to his right—but he was challenging for the lead a furlong and a half out. After that, Sulamani wandered to his right (as he had done in his listed race and the Jockey Club) and went down to Marienbard by three quarters of a length, with High Chaparral third. Sulamani probably should have won and Thulliez reportedly returned to the weighing room in tears. He would have been excused a similar reaction eight days later when news came through that Sulamani had been sold.

Sulamani is trainer Pascal Bary's fourth winner of the Prix du Jockey Club in the space of nine years, following Celtic Arms, Ragmar and Dream Well, and on his Arc form he is the best of the quartet. Dream Well completed the rare French Derby/Irish Derby double but his subsequent career was a disappointment and his four-year-old campaign was one that Godolphin will be hoping not to emulate with his half-brother: Dream Well's Prix Niel, like Sulamani's, ended in boos and cat-calls, but in odds-on defeat rather than victory, and after his eighth in the Arc the only win that Dream Well managed the following season was when dropped in class to Group 3 company. Blinkered more often than not, Dream Well used to be

Niarchos Family's "Sulamani"

Sulamani (IRE) (b.c. 1999)	Hernando (FR) (b 1990)	Niniski (b 1976)	Nijinsky
			Virginia Hills
		Whakilyric (b 1984)	Miswaki
			Lyrism
	Soul Dream (USA) (br 1990)	Alleged (b 1974)	Hoist The Flag
			Princess Pout
		Normia (gr 1981)	Northfields
			Mia Pola

held up in rear, carry his head awkwardly and hang off a straight course and by the end there was a question mark over his enthusiasm. The 2002 Arc suggested that, for all his ability, Sulamani too might need some straightening out. He is a second Prix du Jockey Club winner for his sire as well as for his dam, Hernando having scored at the first attempt with Holding Court in 2000. Smart performers Foundation Spirit and Asian Heights made it a total of three runners for the sire in the latest Arc. Dream Well (by Sadler's Wells) and Sulamani are two Prix du Jockey Club winners from four foals for their dam Soul Dream. In between there were two colts by Caerleon, including the French winner Archipelago. Next in line is the Sadler's Wells colt Awakened. The dam Soul Dream was a failure in Britain when trained by Julie Cecil and showed only fair form when winning one of two starts in the French Provinces, a minor event over eleven furlongs. Her dam Normia was a useful French two-year-old winner at a mile and she comes from a good family, having herself produced a Grade 1 winner in Metamorphose and being a daughter of the very smart Mia Pola; Mia Pola was half-sister to both the top French two-

960

year-old of 1964 Grey Dawn and the 1966 Poule d'Essai des Pouliches winner Right Away. Mia Pola is also the great grandam of the smart sprinter and leading first-season sire Titus Livius.

Sulamani is a close-coupled, attractive colt with a short, unimpressive action and he has not raced on ground more extreme than good to firm or good to soft. Along with High Chaparral, he was the top middle-distance three-year-old of 2002, and further races between the two of them should provide some of the highlights of 2003. Sheikh Mohammed clearly felt that his team lacked a top-class mile-and-a-half horse for the next season and perhaps, after all, there was some imagination and daring in knowing that he could solve that simply by buying the best around. Two more of Sheikh Mohammed's maxims are that 'Money is not strength. Strength comes from good deeds' and 'One should respect achievements, not titles'. In realising Daylami's potential over middle distances, in developing the abilities of horses like Grandera and Marienbard, and in many other deeds, Godolphin has earned huge respect. How much of an achievement, however, will it be for them to win more good races with the four-year-old Sulamani? *P. Bary, France*

SULEIMAN (IRE)   3 b.c. Sadler's Wells (USA) 132 – La Bella Fontana (Lafontaine   **113** (USA) 117) [2002 10.5d* 10.2s² 12m² Jun 23] closely related to 3 winners by Fairy King, notably very smart miler Revoque and 4-y-o King of Tara: dam once-raced half-sister to useful 5f/7f winner Abuzz: smart form: won maiden at Haydock in May: very good efforts both starts after, going down by neck to Nysaean in minor event at Chepstow and by nose to Morozov in 5-runner Prix du Lys (made running) at Longchamp: stays 1½m. *J. H. M. Gosden*

Mr R. E. Sangster & Mrs J. Magnier's "Suleiman"

Mr James Wigan's "Sulk"

SULK (IRE)   3 ch.f. Selkirk (USA) 129 – Masskana (IRE) (Darshaan 133) [2002 109: **111**
8m 10m 9.9m² 11.9m³ 12m 15.5v² 12s⁴ Nov 16] rather leggy, useful-looking filly: smart
performer: won Prix Marcel Boussac at Longchamp at 2 yrs: best efforts in 2002 in
Nassau Stakes at Goodwood (4 lengths second to Islington), Yorkshire Oaks at York (5
lengths third to same filly), Prix Royal-Oak at Longchamp (2½ lengths second to Mr
Dinos) and Grade 2 Long Island Handicap at Aqueduct (2¾ lengths fourth to Uriah):
stays 15.5f: acts on heavy and good to firm going: sometimes visored/blinkered,
including final outing (wore cheekpieces penultimate start). *J. H. M. Gosden*

SULLIVAN'S GOLD   2 ch.f. (Mar 31) Bedford (USA) 109 – Lady Millennium (IRE)   **–**
(Prince Rupert (FR) 121) [2002 7g 7m 6f 5.3m Oct 3] first foal: dam unraced: no form.
L. A. Dace

SULTAN GAMAL   4 b.g. Mind Games 121 – Jobiska (Dunbeath (USA) 127) [2002   **?**
–: 8s f7g a8g⁶ a6s* a6s² Dec 29] sturdy, close-coupled gelding: fair form at best, lightly
raced (has reportedly had chips removed from knees): sold from B. McMahon after
second start in 2002: won minor event at Taby in December: stays 7f: acts on heavy going
and dirt. *Annelie Larsson, Sweden*

SULU (IRE)   6 b.g. Elbio 125 – Foxy Fairy (IRE) (Fairy King (USA)) [2002 –: f5g²   **50**
f5g³ p6g⁵ f6g³ f8.5g Mar 15] good-topped gelding: modest handicapper: best at 5f/6f:
acts on all-weather, firm and soft ground: tried blinkered. *M. W. Easterby*

SULZANO (USA)   2 b.f. (Feb 9) Kingmambo (USA) 125 – Scent of Success (USA)   **84**
84 (Quiet American (USA)) [2002 7d⁶ 7m⁵ 7g² 6m³ 5g³ 6m* p6g³ Oct 16] first foal:
dam, 7.5f (including at 2 yrs)/1m winner, out of close relative to Lammtarra: fairly useful
performer: won nursery at Brighton in October despite edging left: likely to prove best at
5f/6f: acts on polytrack, yet to race on extremes of going on turf: visored last 3 outings:
sold 30,000 gns. *Sir Michael Stoute*

SUM BABY (IRE)   3 b.g. Royal Abjar (USA) 121 – Matsuri (IRE) 89 (Darshaan 133)   –
[2002 –: f7s f11g Feb 21] sparely-made gelding: well held in maidens/claimer: looked a
difficult ride final start. *D. Nicholls*

SUMMER BOUNTY   6 b.g. Lugana Beach 116 – Tender Moment (IRE) 78 (Caerleon   **69**
(USA) 132) [2002 60§: 12.3g 8.5m³ 8m* 10m* 11.6s² 10m 12s² 12m 10.5g f8.5g³   **a57**
Dec 20] close-coupled gelding: fair handicapper: won at Pontefract (selling event) and
Nottingham in May: stays 1½m: acts on soft going, firm and fibresand: tried blinkered at
4 yrs: sometimes starts slowly/has virtually refused to race: not one to trust implicitly.
F. Jordan

SUMMER BREAK (IRE)   5 ch.m. Foxhound (USA) 103 – Out In The Sun (USA)   **54**
90 (It's Freezing (USA) 122) [2002 –: p10g 11.6g⁶ f12g 16v⁵ f16g Nov 20] fairly useful   **a–**
performer in Ireland in 2000 for A. Mullins: modest at best in Britain: stays 1½m: raced
mainly on good going or softer on turf (acts on heavy). *W. J. Musson*

SUMMER CHERRY (USA)   5 b.g. Summer Squall (USA) – Cherryrob (USA)   **58**
(Roberto (USA) 131) [2002 58: p10g⁵ p10g⁴ p10g p12g² p10g p12g³ p12g 11.9g⁶ 10d²
p12g* 10g⁵ 12d 12g⁵ p12g⁵ 11.6d³ 11.9g 12g⁴ 12.3m² 10.5m* 12m p12g⁴ p12g
Dec 18] leggy gelding: modest handicapper: won amateur events at Lingfield in May and
Haydock in September: effective at 1¼m/easy 1½m: acts on polytrack, firm and soft
going: blinkered twice (raced freely on first occasion): usually tongue tied/held up:
sometimes slowly away/looks none too keen: tough and consistent. *Jamie Poulton*

SUMMER CIRCUS   2 b.f. (Feb 20) Lion Cavern (USA) 117 – Summer Exhibition   **– p**
(Royal Academy (USA) 130) [2002 7s Oct 25] strong, lengthy filly: first foal: dam,
unraced, out of useful 2-y-o 6f winner, herself closely related to smart filly Zaizafon, the
dam of Zafonic: 13/2, burly and green, well-beaten seventh of 12 in maiden at Doncaster,
finishing tired: likely to do better. *Mrs A. J. Perrett*

SUMMERHILL PARKES   4 b.f. Zafonic (USA) 130 – Summerhill Spruce 70 (Wind-   **86**
jammer (USA)) [2002 105: 5.1g 10m 6m³ Aug 7] strong, lengthy, attractive filly: useful
form at 3 yrs: only form in 2002 when third of 4 in minor event at Yarmouth: stays 6f: acts
on good to soft going, successful on good to firm: has hinted at temperament: sold
150,000 gns in December. *M. A. Jarvis*

SUMMER KEY (IRE)   4 b.f. Doyoun 124 – Summer Silence (USA) (Stop The Music   **–**
(USA)) [2002 –: p12g Jan 8] small, close-coupled filly: no form: blinkered once. *R. Guest*

SUMMERLAND (IRE)   2 b.c. (Apr 7) Danehill (USA) 126 – Summerosa (USA) 78   **110**
(Woodman (USA) 126) [2002 6m* 7g 8g³ 7m 10g²* 10v² Nov 9] tall, good sort: has high
knee action: second foal: brother to 1m winner (in Sweden) Rose Quantas: dam, 8.5f
winner, half-sister to dam of Derby winner Dr Devious: smart performer: won maiden at
Haydock in July and minor event at Leicester (beat Convent Girl by 2 lengths) in October:
dead-heated for second (demoted to third after hanging left) in listed race at Deauville
in August: best effort when head second of 10 to Alberto Giacometti in Criterium de
Saint-Cloud, prominent throughout: stays 1¼m: successful on good to firm going, goes
well on heavy: sometimes wears near-side pricker. *J. H. M. Gosden*

SUMMER LIGHTNING (IRE)   2 b.f. (Mar 18) Tamure (IRE) 125 – Papita (IRE)   **80**
77 (Law Society (USA) 130) [2002 6m⁵ 5.1d* 5g³ 5m* 5d³ 5m³ 6.1m² 5.9m* 6.5m² 6m
6s³ Oct 22] smallish filly: first foal: dam 2-y-o 6f winner who stayed 1¼m: fairly useful
performer: won seller at Bath in July and nurseries at Doncaster in July and Hamilton in
September: best effort when second of 18 to Golden Nun in nursery at Doncaster ninth
start: should stay 7f: acts on soft and good to firm going: reliable. *R. M. Beckett*

SUMMER PASSION   2 b.f. (Jan 26) Pennekamp (USA) 130 – Intisab 90 (Green   **86**
Desert (USA) 127) [2002 5m² 5m* 5f² Aug 18] IR 9,200Y, 52,000 2-y-o: small, stocky
filly: first foal: dam, 6f winner who stayed 1m, sister to very smart 7f to 1¼m performer
Gabr and half-sister to smart 1¼m to 13f winner Kutta: fairly useful form: won minor
event at Lingfield in August: good head second in nursery at Kempton final start, edging
left and caught on line: likely to prove best at bare 5f: raced only on ground firmer than
good: gave trouble at stall on debut: flashed tail all starts. *B. W. Hills*

SUMMER RECLUSE (USA)   3 gr.g. Cozzene (USA) – Summer Retreat (USA) 78   **70**
(Gone West (USA)) [2002 6s³ 6m³ 6m Sep 17] second foal: dam, 7f winner who stayed
1m, sister to smart sprinter Western Approach and half-sister to very smart US Grade 1
9f/1¼m winner Tinners Way: reportedly suffered foot problem prior to debut: fair form
when third in maidens first 2 starts, 2¾ lengths third to Cyclone Connie at Lingfield
(raced freely) on second occasion: disappointing (found nothing) final start: should stay
7f: sold 6,500 gns and gelded. *R. Charlton*

Rothmans Royals May Hill Stakes, Doncaster—Summitville dictates matters and wins from Approach, Nasij (striped cap) and Buy The Sport (rail)

SUMMER SHADES 4 b.f. Green Desert (USA) 127 – Sally Slade 80 (Dowsing (USA) 124) [2002 52: f8.5g⁵ 7f* 8f* f7g² 8g⁴ 7m 7.6f⁴ 7.5m² 8g⁴ 7f⁶ 7.5m³ f7g* 8g² p7g f7s² f7g³ f9.4g⁴ f7g f8.5s f8.5s⁶ f6s f7g⁶ Dec 31] small filly: fair performer: won apprentice maiden at Catterick and handicap at Redcar in June and handicap at Wolverhampton in September: effective at 7f, barely stays 9.4f: acts on firm going and fibresand: sometimes blinkered at 3 yrs. *W. M. Brisbourne* **69 a72**

SUMMERSON 3 b.g. Whittingham (IRE) 104 – Summer Sky 75 (Skyliner 117) [2002 6s 7m 5g² 5m* 6.1m³ 6d Oct 14] 9,000Y: rather leggy gelding: ninth foal: half-brother to fairly useful but unreliable 5f (including at 2 yrs)/6f winner Lord Sky (by Emarati) and 6f (at 2 yrs) to 9f winner Whispering Dawn (by Then Again): dam 2-y-o 5f winner: fair performer: won handicap at Goodwood in September: stays 6f: acts on good to firm going: raced freely second start. *M. R. Channon* **66**

SUMMER SPECIAL 2 b.c. (Mar 28) Mind Games 121 – Summerhill Special (IRE) 80 (Roi Danzig (USA)) [2002 5m 5g⁵ 6m² 6d² 7.2g³ 7m³ 7g 7.2s³ 7f 6d Oct 14] close-coupled colt: first foal: dam, 1½m/13f winner, also won over hurdles: fair maiden: placed 5 times, in seller/nurseries: stays 7f: acts on soft and good to firm going: sometimes carries head high/races freely: seemed to go amiss seventh start. *D. W. Barker* **73**

SUMMER SPICE (IRE) 2 b. or br.f. (Apr 19) Key of Luck (USA) 126 – Summer Fashion 84 (Moorestyle 137) [2002 6m* Jul 22] IR 40,000Y: half-sister to several winners, notably very smart 7f (at 2 yrs) and 1¼m winner in USA Definite Article (by Indian Ridge) and 6-y-o Salford Express: dam 1m/1¼m winner: 7/1, looked useful prospect when winning 17-runner maiden at Windsor by head from Gallivant, up with pace throughout: bred to stay 1m. *R. Hannon* **88**

SUMMER STOCK (USA) 4 b.g. Theatrical 128 – Lake Placid (IRE) (Royal Academy (USA) 130) [2002 79: p8g p8g⁴ f8g p8g 8.2d³ 10g f8.5s³ f8.5g² 8m⁴ f8.5g⁶ Oct 19] $300,000Y: second foal: half-brother to winner in USA by Gulch: dam, US maiden, sister to useful Irish 1997 2-y-o 5f to 7f performer Heeremandi and closely related to dam of high-class US mare Flawlessly: fair maiden on turf, modest on all-weather: left D. K. Weld in Ireland after final 3-y-o start: should stay 1¼m: acts on firm going, good to soft and fibresand: sometimes blinkered: tongue tied: none too consistent. *Ferdy Murphy* **69 a63**

SUMMER VIEW (USA) 5 ch.g. Distant View (USA) 126 – Miss Summer (Luthier 126) [2002 108: 8d⁶ 7.9f 8.1m 7m 8m* 8f⁶ 8f² 8f³ Oct 4] tall, good-topped gelding: smart performer at 3 yrs: only useful nowadays: off nearly 11 months before reappearance: won handicap at Pontefract in July by short head from Far Lane (allowed to dictate): good second to Judge Davidson in minor event at Goodwood penultimate start: stays 9f: acts on firm and good to soft going: tongue tied last 6 starts: has worn crossed noseband/been bandaged in front: effective held up or making running. *R. Charlton* **98**

SUMMER WINE 3 b.f. Desert King (IRE) 129 – Generous Lady 98 (Generous (IRE) 139) [2002 77p: 9.9d⁴ p12g² f12s* Sep 17] good-topped filly: fairly useful performer, lightly raced: landed odds in maiden at Southwell in September by 18 lengths: not discredited when remote fourth to Mellow Park in listed race at Goodwood on reappearance: stays 1½m. *C. F. Wall* **82**

964

SUMMERY (IRE)   3 b.f. Indian Ridge 123 – Please Believe Me 93 (Try My Best   **52**
(USA) 130) [2002 8f 8g⁶ 6d⁵ 7g Jul 24] lengthy filly: fifth foal: sister to 4-y-o Autumnal
and 5f (at 2 yrs) to 7f winner Lord Pacal, both useful, and half-sister to 8-y-o Storyteller:
dam 2-y-o 5f winner: modest form in maidens: well beaten in handicap final start: likely
to prove best up to 1m. *B. J. Meehan*

SUMMITVILLE   2 b.f. (Mar 3) Grand Lodge (USA) 125 – Tina Heights 79 (Shirley   **105**
Heights 130) [2002 7g* 7s² 8m* 8g Sep 28] 7,000Y: tall, close-coupled filly: first foal:
dam, 1¼m winner on only start, half-sister to useful stayer Life of Riley: useful
performer: won maiden at Newmarket in July and Rothmans Royals May Hill Stakes at
Doncaster (beat Approach by 1½ lengths, dictating pace) in September: good second to
impressive Soviet Song in listed event at Newmarket: well held behind same rival in
Fillies' Mile at Ascot: will be suited by 1¼m/1½m: acts on soft and good to firm ground:
made running last 3 starts. *J. G. Given*

SUMMONER   5 b.h. Inchinor 119 – Sumoto 101 (Mtoto 134) [2002 118: 8.8g⁶ 8.9g   **115**
8m May 18] good-bodied, quite attractive horse: smart performer: won 5 of his 12 starts,
notably Queen Elizabeth II Stakes at Ascot (reportedly acting as pacemaker, clear
entering straight) in 2001: giving weight away all round, creditable sixth to Divine Task
in Jebel Hatta at Nad Al Sheba in 2001: well held in Dubai Duty Free there and Lockinge
Stakes at Newbury (last of 10) after: stayed 1¼m: acted on firm and soft going: to stand at
Longholes Stud, Newmarket, fee £3,500, Oct 1st, special live foal. *Saeed bin Suroor*

SUN BIRD (IRE)   4 ch.g. Prince of Birds (USA) 121 – Summer Fashion 84 (Moore-   **91**
style 137) [2002 85: 9.9m 10.3f 11.9m 10g³ 7.9s⁵ 12g* 7.9d 11.9d* 10m³ 11m⁴ 12g³ 10m
13m⁴ 13.1s 16s Nov 6] well-made gelding: fairly useful handicapper: won at Musselburgh in June and Haydock (Tote Old Newton Cup by length from Barathea Blazer,
making all under well-judged ride at 40/1) in July: stays 13f: acts on any turf going:
effective blinkered/visored or not: sometimes races freely/carries head awkwardly/
wanders. *R. Allan*

Mountain High Partnership's "Summitville"

SUNDAY GOLD   2 b.f. (Jan 29) Lion Cavern (USA) 117 – Sunday Night (GER) 51   –
(Bakharoff (USA) 130) [2002 8.3d Aug 11] 3,000F: first foal: dam placed up to 1m in
Germany: 50/1, well held in maiden at Windsor. *H. S. Howe*

SUNDAY SPORT (USA)   3 b.f. Honour And Glory (USA) 122 – Gold Rule (USA)   ?
(Forty Niner (USA)) [2002 92: 5.1m⁶ 7f⁶ 7s a6f a8.5s³ a9f* a8f⁴ a7.5f⁶ Nov 29] rangy
filly: fairly useful at 2 yrs: disappointing first 3 starts in 2002, then left B. Meehan: won
maiden claimer at Keeneland in October: stays 9f: acts on good to firm going and on dirt:
blinkered last 5 outings. *C. Simon, USA*

SUNDAY'S WELL (IRE)   3 b.f. Sadler's Wells (USA) 132 – Marie de Beaujeu (FR)   80
108 (Kenmare (FR) 125) [2002 –: 10.2g⁶ 9.9m⁶ 10m² 12m 11.7d⁴ p13g⁴ Oct 4] leggy,
useful-looking filly: half-sister to 8-y-o Livius and several winners abroad, notably
German Derby winner All My Dreams (by Assert): dam, French 2-y-o 5.5f and 6.5f
winner, didn't train on: fairly useful maiden: trained by J. Hassett in Ireland only start at 2
yrs: stays 1½m: acts on good to firm and good to soft going. *D. R. C. Elsworth*

SUNDIAL   3 ch.f. Cadeaux Genereux 131 – Ruby Setting 91 (Gorytus (USA) 132)   –
[2002 –p: 8g 7.6f⁵ p6g Dec 18] tall, lengthy filly: disappointing maiden: reportedly pulled
muscle and off 3½ months after reappearance: headstrong. *B. W. Hills*

SUNDRENCHED (IRE)   3 ch.f. Desert King (IRE) 129 – Utr (USA) (Mr Prospector   99
(USA)) [2002 99p: 9.3g⁶ 10.1m 14f⁶ 11.8s² 10.3v Nov 8] lengthy, quite attractive filly:
useful performer: ran creditably in 2002 in listed event at Yarmouth second start and
minor event at Leicester (1½ lengths second to Dusky Warbler) penultimate one:
stayed 1½m, seemingly not 1¾m: acted on soft and good to firm going: visits Pivotal.
W. J. Haggas

SUNDRIED TOMATO   3 b.g. Lugana Beach 116 – Little Scarlett 54 (Mazilier   85
(USA) 107) [2002 63: f6s² p6g⁶ f5g³ f6g* f6g⁵ f6g* 6g⁵ 6d 5d 5g⁶ p6g³ f6g* 5d 5v* f6g*   **a96**
f5g² f6g⁵ f5g² f6g Dec 31] good-topped gelding: useful performer on all-weather, fairly
useful on turf: much improved, and won maiden at Wolverhampton in January and
handicaps at Southwell in March and October and at Doncaster and Wolverhampton in
November: effective at 5f/6f: acts mainly on good ground or softer
on turf (acts on heavy): races prominently: tough and reliable. *P. W. Hiatt*

SUNDUS (USA)   3 b.f. Sadler's Wells (USA) 132 – Sarayir (USA) 104 (Mr Prospector   80
(USA)) [2002 10d* Jul 10] first foal: dam, 7f (at 2 yrs) and 1¼m winner, closely related
to Nayef and half-sister to Nashwan and Unfuwain: well-held fifth to Silent Honor in
private trial at Nad Al Sheba in April when trained by Saeed bin Suroor: 5/2, won maiden
at Kempton in July by ½ length from Misck, racing freely then edging ahead final 1f:
subsequently suffered hairline fracture of near-hind cannon bone: visits King's Best.
M. P. Tregoning

SUNGIO   4 b.g. Halling (USA) 133 – Time Or Never (FR) (Dowsing (USA) 124) [2002   67
70: p10g² p12g* p12g⁵ 13.3s p10g 11.9m 10m 16f⁵ Sep 26] fair handicapper: won at
Lingfield in January: below form after next outing: stays 1½m: acts on polytrack, soft and
good to firm going: tried blinkered/visored: sometimes swishes tail/hangs markedly left/
finds little: successful over hurdles in October. *B. G. Powell*

SUN HILL   2 b.c. (Mar 18) Robellino (USA) 127 – Manhattan Sunset (USA) 76 (El   59
Gran Senor (USA) 136) [2002 6.1s 6d⁵ 6d 6s Oct 28] 8,000Y: sturdy, close-coupled colt:
fifth foal: half-brother to 3-y-o Tramonto and a winner in Turkey by Primo Dominie: dam
2-y-o 7f winner who stayed 1½m: modest maiden: should stay 1m: raced only on good to
soft/soft going. *M. Blanshard*

SUNLEY SCENT   4 ch.f. Wolfhound (USA) 126 – Brown Velvet 68 (Mansingh   85
(USA) 120) [2002 77: 6g 6f⁵ 6g² 7f* 7g 7.1m* 8g 7m⁴ 7.1m 7m⁶ 6f 7f Oct 5] leggy,
lengthy filly: fairly useful handicapper: won at Redcar in May and Sandown in June:
stays 7f: acts on firm going. *M. R. Channon*

SUNLEY SENSE   6 b.g. Komaite (USA) – Brown Velvet 68 (Mansingh (USA) 120)   96
[2002 91: 5s 5f² 5f⁵ 5g 5.1d⁵ 5.1d³ 5m 5d⁴ 5m⁴ 5.5m⁶ 6m* 5f* 5.1f* 5m 5m 5.6m Sep
11] sturdy, workmanlike gelding: useful performer: completed hat-trick within 9 days in
August, making all in handicaps at Salisbury (apprentices) and Kempton and minor event
at Bath: best at 5f/6f: below form (in visor) on heavy going, acts on any other turf:
sometimes slowly away, usually races up with pace otherwise. *M. R. Channon*

SUNNY GLENN   4 ch.c. Rock Hopper 124 – La Ballerine 62 (Lafontaine (USA) 117)   –
[2002 114; 10f⁶ 12f⁴ 16m 12s Oct 26] lengthy colt: unimpressive mover: smart performer
at 3 yrs (ninth in Derby at Epsom): well held in listed/pattern company in 2002: stays
1½m: acts on firm and soft going. *J. Cullinan*

SUNNYSIDE ROYALE (IRE)   3 b.g. Ali-Royal (IRE) 127 – Kuwah (IRE) 77 (Be   **52**
My Guest (USA) 126) [2002 –: 7.9g⁵ 12.1g² 12f 14.1s 14.1s⁶ Aug 24] leggy gelding:
modest maiden handicapper: should stay 1¾m: raced mainly on good going or firmer:
blinkered (pulled hard) penultimate outing: tried tongue tied at 2 yrs. *M. W. Easterby*

SUNRAY   2 b.c. (Apr 2) Spectrum (IRE) 126 – Sharkashka (IRE) 84 (Shardari 134)   **–**
[2002 7.1m Aug 26] second foal: dam, Irish 1½m winner (also won over hurdles), half-
sister to Yorkshire Oaks winner Key Change: 10/1, tailed off in maiden at Warwick.
P. F. I. Cole

SUNRAY SUPERSTAR   3 b.f. Nashwan (USA) 135 – Nazoo (IRE) 99 (Nijinsky   **101**
(CAN) 138) [2002 87p: 11.4f³ 12m 11.9m* 12m⁶ Aug 4] angular filly: has a quick action:
useful performer: landed odds in 2-runner maiden at York in July by ¾ length from Ticket
To Dance: also ran creditably in listed races at Chester (1¼ lengths third to Shadow
Dancing) and Newbury (4¼ lengths sixth of 7 behind Love Everlasting) and Ribblesdale
Stakes at Royal Ascot (6½ lengths eleventh on second outing): stays 1½m, may prove at
least as effective over 1¼m: acts on firm going, probably on good to soft: has been
bandaged: sent to USA. *Sir Michael Stoute*

SUNRIDGE FAIRY (IRE)   3 b.f. Definite Article 121 – Foxy Fairy (IRE) (Fairy   **–**
King (USA)) [2002 42, a51: p10g f8g* f8g* f11g³ f12g 9.9m⁶ 8.5m Jul 16] smallish,   **a58**
lengthy filly: modest on all-weather: won sellers at Southwell in January (handicap) and
February (flashed tail): should stay beyond 1m: acts on fibresand and good to firm going:
modest hurdler, successful 5 times in late summer/autumn. *P. C. Haslam*

SUNRIDGE ROSE   4 b.f. Piccolo 121 – Floral Spark 69 (Forzando 122) [2002 58,   **– §**
a53: f7s f7g³ f9.4g f8g Jan 29] poor performer: refused to race final outing, having   **a45 §**
virtually done so time before: has been visored: best left alone. *Andrew Reid*

SUNRISE GIRL   5 ch.m. King's Signet (USA) 110 – Dawn Ditty 100 (Song 132)   **62**
[2002 55: f5g⁴ 5f* 5m³ p5g³ 5g 5.1m⁴ Aug 6] modest handicapper: won at Windsor in
July: has form at 6f, but best at bare 5f: acts on good going and polytrack: has hung left:
speedy and usually leads: reportedly in foal. *Mrs P. N. Dutfield*

SUNSTRACH (IRE)   4 b.c. Polar Falcon (USA) 126 – Lorne Lady (Local Suitor   **120**
(USA) 128) [2002 10d² 10m³ 10s³ 10g⁴ 11g4 10d* Nov 17] brother to Italian winner up
to 1m Laura's Show and half-brother to 2 winners, including 7f (in Italy at 2 yrs) to 1½m
(in Ireland) winner Sottvus (by Royal Academy): dam French maiden out of half-sister
to Awaasif (dam of Snow Bride/grandam of Lammtarra): very smart performer: won
maiden at Rome and minor event at Milan at 3 yrs: improved in 2002, winning Premio
Roma SIS in November by 6 lengths from Blu For Life: ran creditably most other starts,
including when ¾-length second to Execute in Prix d'Harcourt at Longchamp and 3
lengths third to Wellbeing in Prix Gontaut-Biron at Deauville on third outing: seems best
at 1¼m: acts on soft and good to firm ground. *E. Borromeo, Italy*

SUPERAPPAROS   8 b.g. Superpower 113 – Ayodessa 78 (Lochnager 132) [2002 40,   **–**
a53: f6s f6g⁵ f5g² f6s f6g³ f6g4 f5g f5g⁴ f5g³ f6g f6g f5g² f6g 6f⁵ Jun 4] strong, good-   **a53**
topped gelding: modest maiden: effective at 5f to 7f: form only on fibresand and good to
firm going: usually blinkered: often races handily. *S. R. Bowring*

SUPER CANYON   4 ch.g. Gulch (USA) – Marina Park 112 (Local Suitor (USA) 128)   **66**
[2002 66: 5f 5.3f 7g f6g* May 20] fair handicapper, lightly raced: visored, won handicap
at Wolverhampton in May, despite drifting right: stays 6f: acts on firm ground and
fibresand: has been blanketed for stall entry. *P. W. Harris*

SUPERCHIEF   7 b.g. Precocious 126 – Rome Express (Siberian Express (USA) 125)   **–**
[2002 53, a70: p7g⁴ p8g³ p7g⁴ p7g⁴ p7g² p8g* p8g 6g⁶ 8m 8m p7g³ p8g⁵ p7g Dec 11]   **a77**
smallish, sturdy gelding: fair handicapper on all-weather: won at Lingfield in February:
effective at 7f/1m: acts on good to firm going and polytrack: has been visored, blinkered/
tongue tied nowadays: usually ridden with restraint nowadays. *Miss B. Sanders*

SUPER DECISION   3 ch.f. Superlative 118 – Kiveton Komet 71 (Precocious 126)   **–**
[2002 –: 7m 7m May 2] well held in maidens and seller. *J. J. Quinn*

SUPER DOLPHIN   3 ch.g. Dolphin Street (FR) 125 – Supergreen (Superlative 118)   **55**
[2002 –: 8m 7m² 7m 6d 7f 8m⁶ 6m Jul 8] big, lengthy gelding: modest maiden: best effort
on second outing: stays 7f: acts on good to firm going. *T. P. Tate*

SUPER DOMINION   5 ch.g. Superpower 113 – Smartie Lee 66 (Dominion 123)   **65**
[2002 72, a64: f8.5g² f7g 8.2m f8.5g f6g Dec 10] sturdy, close-coupled gelding: fair
performer: best around 7f/1m: acts on fibresand, soft and good to firm ground: tongue
tied: none too consistent. *R. Hollinshead*

SUPER FAME (USA)   3 ch.c. Diesis 133 – Popularity (USA) 58 (Blushing Groom   **82**
(FR) 131) [2002 12.1g² Sep 12] fifth foal: half-brother to 1¾m winner Devilish Charm
(by Devil's Bag) and fairly useful French 10.5f winner Attention Seeker (by Exbourne):
dam, ran twice, half-sister to US Grade 1 1¼m/1½m winner Vanlandingham and to dam
of Distant Music: 9/1, length second to Misck in maiden at Chepstow, travelling smoothly
and not knocked about once held: sold 35,000 gns, sent to USA. *Mrs A. J. Perrett*

SUPERFRILLS   9 b.m. Superpower 113 – Pod's Daughter (IRE) 43 (Tender King   **49 §**
123) [2002 46: f6s f6s* f6g f6g* f6g³ f6g f6g f5g 5m f6g 5s⁶ 5d* 5g 5.9v f6g⁵ f6g⁴ f7g   **a54 §**
Dec 17] small mare: modest handicapper: won at Southwell (twice) in January and
Haydock in July: effective at 5f/6f: acts on fibresand and any turf going: unreliable.
Miss L. C. Siddall

SUPERGRASS   2 ch.g. (Feb 14) Groom Dancer (USA) 128 – Ceanothus (IRE) 61   **55**
(Bluebird (USA) 125) [2002 5m 5g 6g 7.1m⁶ 7m 7.1m 8g 7m⁵ f8g Oct 17] 15,000Y:
sturdy gelding: easy mover: second foal: half-brother to 3-y-o Prince Hector: dam,
maiden who stayed 1½m, half-sister to smart 9f/1¼m winner Golden Wells: modest
maiden: stays 7f: acts on good to firm going: none too consistent: sold 700 gns. *A. Berry*

SUPERIORITY (USA)   6 ch.g. Arazi (USA) 135 – Outstandingly (USA) (Exclusive   **109 d**
Native (USA)) [2002 112: a8f 8g 8.8g³ 8.9g 8.3s⁶ 10m 10.4m Aug 21] sturdy gelding:
closely related to a winner in USA by Blushing Groom and half-brother to several
winners, including smart French miler Sensation (by Soviet Star): dam, won at 5.5f (at 2
yrs) to 9f, including Breeders' Cup Juvenile Fillies: smart performer at best: maiden
winner for J. Oxx in Ireland at 3 yrs: won 4 times in UAE at 4 yrs and prestige race at Nad
Al Sheba at 5 yrs: best effort in 2002 when 1½ lengths third to Divine Task in Jebel Hatta
at Nad Al Sheba on third outing: left S. Seemar prior to well held in listed event/handicaps
last 3 starts: stays 8.8f: has won on soft going, raced mainly on good/good to firm going
on turf (below form on dirt on reappearance): effective visored or not: sold 10,000 gns in
October, sent to USA. *M. R. Channon*

SUPERPRIDETWO   2 b.c. (Apr 25) Superpower 113 – Lindrake's Pride (Mandrake   **–**
Major 122) [2002 5g 5m 6g⁶ Aug 7] brother to 6f (at 2 yrs) to 9f winner Superpride and
half-brother to 1990 2-y-o 7.5f winner Darika's Lad (by Belfort): dam unraced: only a
little sign of ability in maidens. *Mrs M. Reveley*

SUPER SONG   2 b.c. (Mar 16) Desert Prince (IRE) 130 – Highland Rhapsody (IRE)   **75 p**
78 (Kris 135) [2002 p7g 7d Nov 2] 125,000Y: quite good-topped colt: third foal:
half-brother to 4-y-o Muja Farewell: dam, 6f winner, should have stayed 1m: better effort
in maidens (fair form) when seventh of 22 to Blazing Thunder at Newmarket, prominent
then running green: will probably stay 1m: slowly away on debut: should improve further.
Sir Michael Stoute

SUPER TROUPER (FR)   3 b.f. Nashwan (USA) 135 – Cheeky Charm (USA) 56   **64**
(Nureyev (USA) 131) [2002 8.3m 8.2d⁶ 10.2d⁶ 12g Jul 19] quite good-topped filly: third
foal: half-sister to fairly useful 6f (at 2 yrs) and 7f winner Golden Miracle (by Cadeaux
Genereux) and useful French 10.5f winner Calling Card (by Bering): dam twice-raced
close relative of smart middle-distance colts Mohaajir and Theatrical Charmer out of
sister to Dahlia: modest maiden: well held in handicap final start: should be suited by
1¼m+: sold 5,000 gns in December. *E. A. L. Dunlop*

SUPER VIEW (USA)   3 ch.f. Distant View (USA) 126 – Super Staff (USA) 91 (Secre-   **70**
tariat (USA)) [2002 10m⁶ 10d³ 10d² Aug 11] third foal: dam, 1m to (including US Grade
1 event) 1¼m winner, half-sister to very smart French/US performer up to 12.5f Public
Purse: fair form in maidens at Newmarket, Kempton and Windsor: will be suited by 1½m:
edged left final start: sold 62,000 gns in December. *Sir Michael Stoute*

SUPREMACY   3 ch.c. Vettori (IRE) 119 – High Tern 93 (High Line 125) [2002 10.1m*   **111**
10m 11.6m* 12m⁴ 13.4f* Aug 31] 125,000Y: sturdy colt: half-brother to numerous
winners, notably Derby winner High-Rise (by High Estate): dam, 14.7f and 2m winner,
half-sister to very smart 1¼m to 1¾m winner High Hawk, herself dam of In The Wings:
smart form: won maiden at Newcastle in May, minor event at Windsor (second run in 5
days) in June and listed rated stakes at Chester (improved form, beat Mesmeric by length,
dictating pace under fine ride from K. Fallon) in August: should stay 1¾m: raced only on
going firmer than good. *Sir Michael Stoute*

SUPREME ANGEL   7 b.m. Beveled (USA) – Blue Angel (Lord Gayle (USA) 124)   **66**
[2002 75, a70: f6s⁴ p6g 6d 6.1d⁶ 6g³ 6m 6m 6d p6g 7m Aug 9] angular mare: fair
handicapper: below form last 5 starts: probably stays 7f: acts on all-weather, soft and
good to firm going: blinkered: sometimes hangs left. *E. A. Wheeler*

Bet Direct On Channel 4 Page 613 Chester Rated Stakes (Handicap)—a comfortable success for Supremacy from Mesmeric (left), Scott's View (stars) and Robe Chinoise (rail)

SUPREME SALUTATION 6 ch.g. Most Welcome 131 – Cardinal Press (Sharrood (USA) 124) [2002 78§: f7s* p8g⁴ p8g⁶ p7g 7d² 7.1m² 7f 7m 7.2g p7g² f8g f7g f8.5g* f11g* f8.5g* Dec 14] leggy, sparely-made gelding: fair performer: won handicap at Southwell in January, seller at Wolverhampton in November and claimers at Southwell and Wolverhampton in December: stays 11f: acts on all-weather, firm and soft going: tried blinkered at 5 yrs: often gets warm in preliminaries/slowly away/races freely: reluctant to race ninth outing: not one to trust implicitly. *T. D. Barron* **78**

SUPREME SILENCE (IRE) 5 b.g. Bluebird (USA) 125 – Why So Silent (Mill Reef (USA) 141) [2002 –: f16g⁶ f16.2g⁴ f16.2g 16g 12f 14d³ f16.2g* f16.2g⁵ 16g Aug 12] lengthy gelding: modest handicapper nowadays: won at Wolverhampton in July: stays easy 2m: acts on good to firm ground and fibresand: sometimes blinkered/tried tongue tongue tied: races prominently (has raced too freely): none too consistent. *Jedd O'Keeffe* **43 a54**

SUPREME TRAVEL 4 b.g. Piccolo 121 – Salinas 65 (Bay Express 132) [2002 –: f12s f9.4g 10m 10f 8d May 27] little form: tried visored/blinkered. *Mrs Lydia Pearce* **–**

SURAKARTA 4 b.f. Bin Ajwaad (IRE) 119 – Lady of Jakarta (USA) (Procida (USA) 129) [2002 67: 8.1m⁶ 10m 8f Jun 11] good-topped filly: fair form on debut at 3 yrs: well held since: reportedly bled from nose on reappearance. *Jonjo O'Neill* **–**

SURBITON (USA) 2 ch.c. (Jan 25) El Prado (IRE) 119 – Mastina (USA) (Gulch (USA)) [2002 6m³ 6f* 6g 7d* Jul 11] big, good sort: has scope: second reported foal: half-brother to a winner in Japan by Dehere: dam 6f and 9f winner in USA: useful performer: won maiden at Doncaster in June: easily best effort when beating Magistretti by 5 lengths in listed event at Newmarket, dictating pace and storming away from 2f out: struggling some way out when twelfth of 16 in Coventry Stakes at Royal Ascot: will stay at least 1m: acts on firm and good to soft going: joined Godolphin. *B. W. Hills* **108**

Weatherbys Superlative Stakes, Newmarket—Surbiton proves a different proposition on softer ground; Magistretti and Celtic Sapphire (rail) are placed

SURDOUE 2 b.c. (Apr 28) Bishop of Cashel 122 – Chatter's Princess (Cadeaux **66**
Genereux 131) [2002 5d⁶ 6g 6m⁴ p6g 6g f6s² f6f⁴ f7g* f7f* p7g Dec 14] leggy colt: **a85**
second foal: dam unraced: fairly useful on all-weather, fair on turf: won maiden at
Southwell and nursery at Wolverhampton in November: will stay at least 1m: acts on
fibresand and good to firm ground. *G. G. Margarson*

SURE QUEST 7 b.m. Sure Blade (USA) 130 – Eagle's Quest 62 (Legal Eagle 126) **66**
[2002 63, a67: p13g f12g⁴ f12g⁵ f12g⁶ f16.2g² f14.8s⁶ f16.2g May 20] close-coupled
mare: fair handicapper: stays 2m: acts on all-weather and any turf going: visored once in
1999. *D. W. P. Arbuthnot*

SURE SIGN 2 ch.g. (Apr 12) Selkirk (USA) 129 – Beyond Doubt 87 (Belmez (USA) **73**
131) [2002 6m 7.1m 8m³ Sep 23] good-topped gelding: second living foal: dam, 1¼m/
1½m winner, half-sister to very smart 1½m/1¾m winner Blueprint: best effort in
maidens (fair form) when 8 lengths third to Albareq at Kempton: will stay at least 1¼m.
R. Charlton

SURF THE WEB (IRE) 2 ch.f. (Apr 11) Ela-Mana-Mou 132 – Surfing 71 (Grundy **–**
137) [2002 f6g p7g 8s Nov 6] half-sister to several winners, including useful 6f to 9.4f
winner Mister Fire Eyes (by Petorius), later US Grade 3 1m winner, and a 1½m winner in
France by Glow: dam, maiden who stayed 7f, half-sister to Middle Park winner
Bassenthwaite: well beaten in maidens. *Sir Mark Prescott*

SURPRISED 7 b.g. Superpower 113 – Indigo 86 (Primo Dominie 121) [2002 90: 6m⁵ **93**
6m 6f* 6d 6g⁴ 6m Jul 13] big gelding: fairly useful performer: won minor event at
Doncaster in June: has form at 7.5f, raced mainly at 5f/6f: acts on firm and good to soft
going: usually blinkered/visored: found little final start: has idled, and usually held up:
joined Miss S. Brotherton. *R. A. Fahey*

SURPRISE ENCOUNTER 6 ch.g. Cadeaux Genereux 131 – Scandalette (Niniski **111**
(USA) 125) [2002 110: 7.9f 8m 7m² 7f³ 8m³ 8m 7m 7f* Oct 10] quite good-topped
gelding: smart performer: won handicap at York in October by neck from Inchdura,

Mr Ahmed BuHaleeba's "Surprise Encounter"

showing best turn of foot in steadily-run affair: some creditable efforts earlier in year, including close third to Smirk in William Hill Mile (Handicap) at Goodwood fifth start: effective at 7f/1m: easily best form on good ground or firmer: visored fifth to seventh starts: has been early to post: usually held up: sometimes finds little (finished lame sixth start). *E. A. L. Dunlop*

SURPRISE SELECTION   3 b.f. Be My Chief (USA) 122 – Shamaka 53 (Kris 135)   –
[2002 –: f12g 10f May 13] no form: left S. R. Bowring after reappearance: visored (very slowly away) final start. *Mrs N. Macauley*

SURVAL (IRE)   2 b.f. (Apr 10) Sadler's Wells (USA) 132 – Courtesane (USA)   **89**
(Majestic Light (USA)) [2002 7d⁴ 7m 8s³ Nov 2] tall, leggy filly: half-sister to several winners, notably smart 10.4f to 14.6f (Park Hill Stakes) winner Delilah (by Bluebird): dam placed twice in USA: fairly useful form: best effort when 6 lengths third to Hanami in listed race at Newmarket: bred to be well suited by 1¼m+, but races freely: acts on soft going: hung left second start. *L. M. Cumani*

SUSAN'S DOWRY   6 b.m. Efisio 120 – Adjusting (IRE) (Busted 134) [2002 55+,   **a74**
a72: p10g* p10g⁴ f12g p10g³ Dec 18] leggy, angular mare: has a round action: fair handicapper on all-weather: won at Lingfield in January: effective at 1¼m/1½m: acts on all-weather: sometimes slowly away: reportedly had breathing problem once at 5 yrs: best waited with. *Andrew Turnell*

SUSAN'S PRIDE (IRE)   6 b.g. Pips Pride 117 – Piney Pass (Persian Bold 123) [2002   **72**
7d 7.1s⁶ f8.5g³ 7m 9.9d 10m p8g f8g Nov 25] fair handicapper: well held last 4 starts: stays 8.5f: acts on fibresand and probably any turf going: effective blinkered or not. *B. J. Meehan*

SUSSEX LAD   5 b.g. Prince Sabo 123 – Pea Green 98 (Try My Best (USA) 130) [2002   **75**
74, a68: p6g³ 6g² p6g³ 6m⁶ 6m⁶ 5.7g 6m³ 6m 6d 6m 6m⁴ 6g² 7m⁴ f6s³ 6f⁵ 6m 6f p7g   **a71**
Dec 30] strong gelding: fair handicapper: probably best at 5f (given test)/6f: has form on soft going, better efforts on firmer than good, and acts on all-weather: usually held up. *P. R. Chamings*

SUTTON COMMON (IRE)   5 b.g. Common Grounds 118 – Fadaki Hawaki (USA)   **52 §**
60 (Vice Regent (CAN)) [2002 69§: f8s f8s⁵ f8s⁴ f9.4g³ p8g⁶ f12g⁵ f12g f8.5g Mar 15] good-topped gelding: modest performer nowadays: stays 1½m: acts on fibresand and good to soft going, probably on good to firm: blinkered last 2 starts: unreliable. *K. A. Ryan*

SWAIN DAVIS   2 b.f. (Mar 24) Swain (IRE) 134 – Exclusive Davis (USA) (Our   –
Native (USA)) [2002 8.1g Oct 5] 5,000Y: fourth foal: half-sister to a winner in USA by Crafty Prospector: dam, French 7.5f (at 2 yrs) to 1¼m winner, also won over jumps: 50/1 and green, tailed off in minor event at Sandown. *D. J. S. ffrench Davis*

SWALLOW FLIGHT (IRE)   6 b.h. Bluebird (USA) 125 – Mirage 60 (Red Sunset   **114**
120) [2002 120: 8s⁶ 8.1d* 8m⁵ 8g 10g⁴ Jul 15] tall, attractive horse: impressed in appearance: had a quick action: very smart performer at best, winner of 7 races: gained first pattern success in attheraces Mile at Sandown in April, beating Cape Town by 1¼ lengths: below form after, tailed-off last of 4 in Scottish Classic at Ayr final outing: raced

attheraces Mile, Sandown—Swallow Flight gains a fully deserved first pattern-race success;
the grey Cape Town, Premier Prize (right), Golden Silca and Priors Lodge (hidden by winner) are next

mainly at 1m: acted on any going: to stand at Ballykisteen Stud, Co Tipperary, Ireland, fee €3,000. *G. Wragg*

SWAN KNIGHT (USA)   6 b. or br.g. Sadler's Wells (USA) 132 – Shannkara (IRE)   **85** (Akarad (FR) 130) [2002 94: 8s 10g 10m 10m² 10s May 27] good-topped gelding: fairly useful nowadays: stays easy 1¼m: acts on heavy and good to firm going, seemingly on sand: none too consistent: sold 17,000 gns, joined R. Fahey. *R. J. White*

SWASHBUCKLER   2 b.c. (Feb 19) Dashing Blade 117 – Victoria Mill 59 (Free State   **77** 125) [2002 5.1g 5.1g⁶ 6.1s² p7g* 7.5d⁴ 7m 7.5g 8m 8.3m* Oct 7] 7,000Y: unfurnished colt: eighth foal: half-brother to 3 winners, including fairly useful 7.5f winner who later won in US Victory Spin (by Beveled) and 4-y-o Lara Falana: dam, maiden, best at 1¼m: fair performer: won maiden at Lingfield in June and nursery at Windsor (beat Langford by 1¼ lengths, coming from well from off pace) in October: should stay 1¼m: acts on polytrack, good to firm and soft going: sweating (ran poorly) eighth start: sometimes blanketed for stall entry: often slowly away: difficult ride: sold 25,000 gns. *I. A. Balding*

SWEET AROMA   3 b.f. Bedford (USA) 109 – Tango Country (Town And Country   **–** 124) [2002 8.2d 11.8d 10f⁶ Jun 4] quite good-topped filly: second known foal: dam ran 3 times over jumps: tailed off in maidens: started very slowly on debut: pulled hard and completely failed to handle bend next time. *Mrs N. Macauley*

SWEET AZ   2 b.f. (Mar 23) Averti (IRE) 117 – Yen Haven (USA) (Lear Fan (USA)   **54** 130) [2002 7m⁵ 7g 6m⁵ 8.3d⁶ f7g Dec 17] first foal: dam unraced half-sister to useful 1¼m/1½m winner Jagellon out of half-sister to Irish St Leger winner Mashaallah: modest form at best, including in sellers: left W. Turner before final start: stays 7f: best efforts on good to firm ground. *A. P. Jones*

SWEET BAND (USA)   3 b.c. Dixieland Band (USA) – Sweetheart (USA) (Mr Pros-   **106 d** pector (USA)) [2002 94p: 8m³ 8m 10.5g³ 8m⁵ Aug 3] angular, quite good-topped colt: useful performer at best: good 3¼ lengths third to King of Happiness in Craven Stakes at Newmarket in April: disappointing after, running as though something amiss in 2000 Guineas at Newmarket (tongue tied) first occasion, pulling hard in visor final one: should be suited by 1¼m/1½m: raced only on good/good to firm going: sent to USA. *E. A. L. Dunlop*

SWEET BRIAR   3 b.f. Common Grounds 118 – Pervenche (Latest Model 115) [2002   **–** 49: f8g Dec 10] angular filly: poor maiden at 2 yrs. *H. Candy*

SWEET CHAMPAGNE   3 ch.f. Mazaad 106 – Pink Sensation 69 (Sagaro 133) [2002   **–** 7m 9.3s⁶ 7.1m Jul 4] lengthy, unfurnished filly: half-sister to 10-y-o Champagne N Dreams and 11f winner Sharp Sensation (by Crofthall): dam, 13f winner, also winning jumper: well held in maidens. *G. A. Harker*

SWEET FINESSE (IRE)   2 b.f. (Apr 17) Revoque (IRE) 122 – Moira My Girl (Henbit   **–** (USA) 130) [2002 8m 7f 8g Oct 2] half-sister to numerous winners, notably useful 1998 2-y-o 6f/7f winner Smittenby (by Tenby): dam third at 1¼m in Ireland: signs of only a little ability in minor event/maidens at Salisbury. *Mrs P. N. Dutfield*

SWEET KRISTEEN (USA)   3 ch.f. Candy Stripes (USA) 115 – Aneesati 85 (Kris   **69 d** 135) [2002 61: 7g* 7m⁶ f7s f9.4g Oct 5] workmanlike filly: fair performer at best, lightly raced: won maiden at Southwell in June: left J. Fanshawe 13,000 gns before well held on all-weather last 2 starts: should stay 1m: acts on soft going: carried head awkwardly second start. *D. Haydn Jones*

SWEET PICCALILLI   2 b.f. (Feb 12) Piccolo 121 – Time Lapse 62 (The Noble   **30** Player (USA) 126) [2002 6.1d 5.1d⁴ 6m 7g⁶ Jul 23] 1,500Y: first foal: dam, 2-y-o 6f winner (later won in Jersey), out of sister to Park Hill winner Quay Line: poor form in claimer/sellers. *M. R. Channon*

SWEET PORTIA (IRE)   2 ch.f. (Feb 6) Pennekamp (USA) 130 – My Mariam 79   **61** (Salse (USA) 128) [2002 6m 7m 7s Sep 10] strong filly: third foal: dam, 6f winner at 2 yrs: sister to Moyglare Stud Stakes winner Bianca Nera: modest form at best in maidens: will probably stay 1m. *I. A. Balding*

SWEET RETURN   2 ch.c. (Mar 13) Elmaamul (USA) 125 – Sweet Revival 41 (Claude   **105** Monet (USA) 121) [2002 5.7m⁴ 7.1m³ 7m³ 7.5g* 7.1m² Aug 31] tall, leggy colt: half-brother to 1m winner Kustom Kit Kevin (by Local Suitor) and 7-y-o Sweet Reward: dam 1¼m winner: won nursery at Beverley in August: 33/1, easily best effort (useful form) when head second to Foss Way in Solario Stakes at Sandown, staying on from rear to edge ahead briefly final 1f: will stay at least 1m: raced only on good/good to firm going: sent to USA. *I. A. Wood*

SWEET REWARD   7 ch.g. Beveled (USA) – Sweet Revival 41 (Claude Monet   **76 §**
(USA) 121) [2002 78§: 9.7m⁵ 9s 10m⁶ 10g 9.9d² 9.9d² 10d f8s 9s⁶ Oct 25] leggy, short-
backed gelding: shows knee action: fair performer: stays easy 11.6f: has form on good to
firm going, very best efforts on good to soft/soft: often looks none too keen: inconsistent.
H. Morrison

SWEETSTOCK   4 b.f. Anshan 119 – Stockline (Capricorn Line 111) [2002 –: p12g³   **49**
14.1g⁶ p12g⁴ 12g³ Oct 19] poor maiden: claimed final outing: stays 1½m: acts on
polytrack: no easy ride and probably has her share of temperament. *G. A. Butler*

SWEET TOUCH   3 b.f. Definite Article 121 – Shirley's Touch (Touching Wood   **–**
(USA) 127) [2002 41: f9.4g Jan 7] poor maiden at 2 yrs: well held only outing in 2002.
M. D. I. Usher

SWELLMOVA   3 b.c. Sadler's Wells (USA) 132 – Supamova (USA) 88 (Seattle Slew   **68**
(USA)) [2002 10s* 6s² 12.1m 8g⁴ Sep 27] second foal: dam, 8.5f winner, sister to very
smart 7f to 9f performer Septieme Ciel out of Prix de la Salamandre winner Maximova:
fair performer: green and coltish, ran in snatches when landing odds in 3-runner maiden
at Ripon in August: also looked very hard ride when disappointing in apprentice
handicap at Hamilton third start: probably stays 1¼m: acts on soft going: sold 30,000 gns.
P. F. I. Cole

SWIFT   8 ch.g. Sharpo 132 – Three Terns (USA) (Arctic Tern (USA) 126) [2002 49,   **–**
a54: f14g Mar 12] strong, lengthy gelding: poor mover: modest performer in 2001:
reportedly lame last 2 outings, including on only start in 2002. *M. J. Polglase*

SWIFT ALCHEMIST   2 b.f. (Feb 21) Fleetwood (IRE) 107 – Pure Gold 88 (Dilum   **76**
(USA) 115) [2002 6g⁶ 6d² 6d 6g⁴ 7m 7s² 6g⁴ 7s⁵ Oct 25] 1,500Y: tall, rather angular filly:
first foal: dam, 2-y-o 7f winner (only season to race), out of half-sister to 2000 Guineas
winner Don't Forget Me: fair maiden: in frame in minor event, nurseries and sales race:
stays 7f: acts on soft going: sometimes looks difficult ride. *M. D. I. Usher*

SWIFT APPRAISAL   3 gr.g. Slip Anchor 136 – Minsden's Image 78 (Dancer's Image   **–**
(USA)) [2002 –: p6g Jan 23] signs of just a little ability in 3 maidens: bred to be well
suited by 1m+: slowly away all starts. *S. C. Williams*

SWIFT BABA (USA)   3 b.f. Deerhound (USA) 64 – Nervous Baba (USA) (Raja Baba   **–**
(USA)) [2002 –: 8.3m 8g May 21] close-coupled filly: well held in 3 maidens. *R. Hannon*

SWIFTLY   3 ch.f. Cadeaux Genereux 131 – Run Faster (IRE) (Commanche Run 133)   **–**
[2002 73: f6g⁶ 7d f6g Sep 21] rather leggy, useful-looking filly: fair 5f winner at 2 yrs:
little form in 2002: acted on fibresand and firm going: visits Marju. *M. A. Jarvis*

SWIFTMIX   2 gr.f. (May 6) Linamix (FR) 127 – Swift Spring (FR) 56 (Bluebird (USA)   **73**
125) [2002 6g⁵ 7.1m 8m⁵ 8.3d⁵ Oct 28] leggy filly: sixth foal: half-sister to 3 winners,
including 3-y-o Swing Wing and fairly useful but ungenuine 11.5f winner Spring Anchor
(by Slip Anchor): dam, 7f winner who seemed to stay 2m, half-sister to smart French
performer up to 15.5f Philanthrop: fair maiden: should be suited by 1¼m+: tongue tied
(worst effort) final start. *P. F. I. Cole*

SWIFT TANGO (IRE)   2 b.g. (Mar 12) Desert Prince (IRE) 130 – Ballet Society   **70 §**
(FR) (Sadler's Wells (USA) 132) [2002 6s 6d⁴ p6g 7d² 7m⁶ 8f² Sep 26] 105,000Y: good-
topped gelding: sixth foal: half-brother to 2 winners, including fairly useful 1¼m/1½m
winner Secret Ballot (by Taufan): dam, ran once, closely related to 2000 Guineas runner-
up Enrique out of smart sprinter Gwydion: fair maiden: creditable second in nurseries at
Newmarket and Goodwood: stays 1m: acts on firm and soft going, below form on
polytrack: probably ungenuine. *E. A. L. Dunlop*

SWINGING THE BLUES (IRE)   8 b.g. Bluebird (USA) 125 – Winsong Melody   **47**
(Music Maestro 119) [2002 51: f9.4g f12g f12g Jun 14] useful-looking gelding: poor
performer: stays easy 1½m: acts on soft going, good to firm and fibresand: usually
blinkered/visored: tried tongue tied earlier in career: often slowly away. *C. A. Dwyer*

SWING WING   3 b.g. In The Wings 128 – Swift Spring (FR) 56 (Bluebird (USA) 125)   **110**
[2002 105: 10.1g* 12.3f 12m³ 15g² 15g² 15g³ Oct 5] good-topped gelding: has a quick,
fluent action: smart performer: won minor event at Epsom (by length from Mine Host,
running lazily) in April and listed race at Deauville (by short neck from Martaline) in
August: good efforts otherwise when placed at Longchamp, 1½ lengths third to Morozov
in Prix du Lys, ½-length second to Savannah Bay in Prix de Lutece and 1¼ lengths third
to Morozov in Prix Hubert de Chaudenay: stays 15f: acts on heavy and good to firm
going, probably on fibresand: gelded after final start. *P. F. I. Cole*

SWIRL HOW (IRE)   2 b.g. (Apr 18) Lake Coniston (IRE) 131 – Jolly Dale (IRE)   –
(Huntingdale 132) [2002 5s 5s 5g f6g Oct 17] IR 5,000F, 5,000Y: smallish, workmanlike
gelding: fifth foal: half-brother to 1996 2-y-o 6f winner Fit For The Job (by Mac's Imp):
dam unraced: well beaten, including in seller. *D. W. Barker*

SWISS LAKE (USA)   3 br.f. Indian Ridge 123 – Blue Iris 105 (Petong 126) [2002   **115**
102p: 5.1g* 5m⁵ Jun 2] good-topped filly: usually takes the eye: smart performer:
impressive winner of listed race at Bath in May by 1¾ lengths from Palace Affair:
disappointing when only fifth to Porlezza in Prix du Gros-Chene at Chantilly only
subsequent outing, headed over 1f out: free-going sort who will prove best at 5f: raced
only on good/good to firm going: edged right when disappointing second 2-y-o start: sent
to USA. *G. A. Butler*

SWISS PIPE   2 b.c. (Jan 27) Piccolo 121 – Aegean Sound 71 (Distant Relative 128)   **65**
[2002 5.1m⁴ 5m 6.1d⁶ 5g² Jul 24] 19,500Y: has a quick, fluent action: second foal: dam
2-y-o 6f winner: fair performer: short-headed in nursery at Leicester: likely to prove best
at 5f: acts on good to firm ground: joined S. Seemar in UAE. *B. A. McMahon*

SWORDID AFFAIR (IRE)   3 ch.f. Sabrehill (USA) 120 – Winter Wedding (IRE)   –
(Groom Dancer (USA) 128) [2002 10d 12f⁶ Aug 18] IR 1,300Y, resold IR 2,500Y: first
foal: dam, ran once in France, out of half-sister to high-class French 1m winner (also
runner-up in July Cup) Golden Opinion: last in maidens at Windsor (slowly away) and
Kempton (visored/virtually pulled up). *P. D. Evans*

S W THREE   4 b.f. Slip Anchor 136 – Anna Karietta 82 (Precocious 126) [2002 76:   **73**
12f³ 11.7m⁴ Jun 26] smallish, sturdy filly: fair maiden, lightly raced (reportedly chipped
bone in knee after only start at 3 yrs): probably stays easy 1½m. *M. P. Tregoning*

SWYNFORD DREAM   9 b.g. Statoblest 120 – Qualitair Dream 80 (Dreams To   **56**
Reality (USA) 113) [2002 59, a–: 5m² 5m 5d 5m Jun 20] workmanlike gelding: modest   **a–**
handicapper: raced mainly at 5f: acts on firm and good to soft going: has given trouble at
start (withdrawn once)/been slowly away: has hung. *J. Hetherton*

SWYNFORD ELEGANCE   5 ch.m. Charmer 123 – Qualitairess 49 (Kampala 120)   **51**
[2002 52: 8f 9.9m 8f 8m 8d⁴ 8g² 8m 7.9g³ 8.5g 7.9m Aug 21] modest handicapper:
effective at 7f to 1¼m: acts on any ground. *J. Hetherton*

SWYNFORD PLEASURE   6 b.m. Reprimand 122 – Pleasuring 68 (Good Times   **70**
(ITY)) [2002 72, a–: 8f 8f 9.9m³ 10g 8.5g⁵ 8.3g⁴ 8d⁵ 8d 8.5g² 10g⁴ 12g 10f² 9.9m* 8.5d⁵   **a–**
9.9d 10g⁶ 9.9d 8.5g 8s⁴ 10m³ 9.9m² 10.4m 10.1d 10.1m 9.9m 10m⁵ 8.9f 12d 12s Nov 6]
strong mare: fair handicapper: won at Beverley in June: effective at 1m/1¼m: acts on
firm and soft going: tried blinkered (not since 1999): often held up: tough. *J. Hetherton*

SWYNFORD WELCOME   6 b.m. Most Welcome 131 – Qualitair Dream 80   **74 §**
(Dreams To Reality (USA) 113) [2002 78, a61: 7d p6g⁶ 8f³ 5m⁵ 6d 6d 7.1m⁴   **a60 §**
6g³ 6g 7g 6m 6m 7d² 7d 6d* 7.2g⁴ 5d⁵ 7m 7.6g 8g 7g 6m* 8m 6f 7f 7d 7s f7g⁴ Nov 22]
good-topped mare: fair handicapper on turf, modest on all-weather: won at Epsom in July
and Pontefract in September: effective at 5f to 7f: acts on polytrack, firm and soft ground:
tried blinkered in 2000: usually waited with: unreliable. *I. A. Wood*

SYDENHAM (USA)   4 b.c. A P Indy (USA) 131 – Crystal Shard (USA) (Mr Pros-   **111**
pector (USA)) [2002 108: a10f² a10f* 13.9f 10m 10s Aug 10] angular, good-topped
colt: smart performer: trained by J. Gosden at 3 yrs: good efforts at Nad Al Sheba first 2
starts in 2002, winning Godolphin Seven Stars Handicap in March by short head from
Ennoblement: acted as pacemaker in Prince of Wales's Stakes at Royal Ascot and Prix
Gontaut-Biron at Deauville last 2 starts: stays 1½m: acts on dirt, raced mainly on going
firmer than good on turf: visored last 6 starts: left Godolphin in November. *Saeed bin
Suroor*

SYLPHIDE   7 b.m. Ballet Royal (USA) – Shafayif 43 (Ela-Mana-Mou 132) [2002   –
f12g Jan 24] of no account. *H. J. Manners*

SYLV   4 b.f. Ridgewood Ben 113 – High Commotion (IRE) 70 (Taufan (USA) 119)   –
[2002 –: 15.4m⁵ 11.7g 12g 14.1g Jun 15] of little account. *J. G. Portman*

SYLVA BOUNTY   3 br.g. Bahamian Bounty 116 – Spriolo (Priolo (USA) 127) [2002   –
–: 10g 8m 10m p12g 7m Sep 17] compact gelding: little sign of ability. *C. E. Brittain*

SYLVAN MEASURE   3 br.c. Inchinor 119 – Woodrising 64 (Nomination 125) [2002   **66**
8m 8f 8.2g 10.9g² 10g³ 10g⁶ Aug 26] 16,500Y: smallish colt: first foal: dam, 1¼m winner,
also won over hurdles: fair maiden handicapper: stays 1¼m well: ran very wide into
straight under inexperienced apprentice on debut. *A. C. Stewart*

SYLVAN TWISTER 3 br.c. First Trump 118 – Storm Party (IRE) (Bluebird (USA) –
125) [2002 p10g 10d 7m Aug 15] 5,700F, IR 15,000Y: first foal: dam of little account:
well held in maidens. *P. Mitchell*

SYLVA STORM (USA) 4 ch.g. Miswaki (USA) 124 – Sudden Storm Bird (USA) 72
(Storm Bird (CAN) 134) [2002 73, a87: p8g⁶ p10g⁵ p10g⁴ f12g³ 12g 14.1f⁴ 17.1m 12m a85
10.1m* 10g Sep 10] close-coupled gelding: fairly useful on all-weather, fair on turf: won
minor event at Yarmouth (looked less than keen under pressure) in August: stays easy
1¾m: acts on all-weather and firm going: sometimes blinkered, including at Yarmouth:
reportedly had breathing problem second start: none too trustworthy. *C. E. Brittain*

SYLVIAJAZZ 3 b.f. Alhijaz 122 – Dispol Princess (IRE) (Cyrano de Bergerac 120) –
[2002 p12g⁶ Sep 10] second foal: dam, ran once at 2 yrs, out of half-sister to Cheveley
Park winner Pass The Peace: 33/1, tailed off in Lingfield maiden, slowly away. *Miss
J. Feilden*

SYRIAN FLUTIST 4 ch.f. Shaamit (IRE) 127 – Brave Vanessa (USA) 62 (Private 59
Account (USA)) [2002 –: 11.5f 10s³ 12.1m⁴ f14.8g⁴ 16v Oct 29] modest maiden: stays
1½m: acts on soft and good to firm going, probably on fibresand: has had tongue tied: ran
in snatches third start. *H. Akbary*

SYSTEM 3 ch.c. Nashwan (USA) 135 – Vivid Imagination (USA) (Raise A Man 67
(USA)) [2002 p10g² p10g² p10g⁵ 12f⁴ 11.9d p13g⁵ p13g Oct 4] lengthy colt: sixth foal:
closely related to a winner in USA by Rahy and half-brother to 4-y-o Stormy Voyage:
dam, US Grade 3 1m winner at 2 yrs, half-sister to multiple Grade 1-winning filly
Serena's Song, herself dam of Sophisticat: fair maiden: below form after third start:
should stay beyond 1¼m: acts on polytrack: sometimes carries head awkwardly: sold
11,000 gns. *B. W. Hills*

SYSTEMATIC 3 b.c. Rainbow Quest (USA) 134 – Sensation 114 (Soviet Star 121
(USA) 128) [2002 68p: 8s* 10g* 10.4m* 10.1s² 12m* 12m* 11.9g⁵ 12m* 12g*
Sep 29]
    Every picture supposedly tells a story, and some of the rugs thoroughbreds
sport at the races undoubtedly do. Those of trainer Mark Johnston claim 'Always
Trying' and, while that may seem inappropriate on the stable's notably unreliable
Gold Cup winner Royal Rebel, the resolution and consistency of the majority of
his team make the catchphrase accurate in more than just the professional sense.
Johnston's rise through the ranks has been remarkable—having notched eighty
wins in total during his first five seasons from 1987, he has had a hundred or more
in each of the last nine years. His tally of one hundred and thirty-four in 2002, from
a team of one hundred and fifty-nine individual runners for the stable, was a
personal record, as was the £2,183,185 in first-three prize-money earned by his
runners in Britain. The lynchpins at home were Group 2 scorers Bandari and
Zindabad, while German Group 1 winner Yavana's Pace was the principal standard
bearer abroad, though as in previous years it was the improving three-year-olds

*King George V Stakes (Handicap), Royal Ascot—Systematic responds well to beat
the Sir Michael Stoute-trained pair Highest (No.8) and Leadership; Shagraan (No.9) is fourth*

Young Vic Theatre Cumberland Lodge Stakes, Ascot—Systematic shows off his battling qualities again and caps a fine season with his seventh victory; Warrsan (right) and Frankies Dream fill the placings

who particularly testified to Johnston's skill. Systematic and Scott's View provided more evidence, starting the year rated 68p and 71 respectively and ending it both rated 121 after winning fifteen of their twenty-two races between them.

The first indication that Systematic might be capable of making his presence felt in pattern company came in the King George V Stakes at Royal Ascot, invariably one of the most hotly-contested handicaps of the year for three-year-olds. Placed in autumn maiden races at Pontefract and Newcastle in his first season, he had already improved in winning a maiden at Doncaster on the first day of the turf season, then landing handicaps at Leicester and York. He suffered his first defeat in a similar event at Epsom on Oaks day, starting a little slowly and never managing to reach his customary position at the head of affairs when runner-up to Lingo, giving the strong impression that a mile and a half would suit him. Horses who make the running most often do so because they are one paced and stand the best chance of blunting their rivals' speed by ensuring a searching test throughout. It doesn't follow though that horses who lead necessarily lack a turn of foot. Those able to quicken after making the running are all the more formidable, even though the phrase 'battled back' is a much more commonly used phrase than 'quickened' after a display of this kind. Many of Johnston's horses have tended to make the running—Bandari, Zindabad, Yavana's Pace, Desert Deer, Systematic and Love Regardless all did so in the latest season, but they are not one pacers by any means. Fitness is the key, but Johnston's reasoning for the tactics adopted on his stable's horses is simple: 'We certainly don't tell our jockeys to go out and lead but we do tell them to ignore the other runners in the field. The general instruction is to let the horse bowl along where it is happy. That means no restraint. If you ask a jockey to cover up a horse, then immediately the pace is dictated to you by other jockeys. I want to go at the pace that suits us, regardless of everyone else.' Nine of Systematic's eighteen opponents at the Royal meeting had won their last race and the colt, drawn one on the outside of the field, had to use up a fair amount of energy to reach the front. Once there, he settled down at a strong gallop and at no stage looked like flagging, running on with great resolution when challenged in the final furlong by Highest, Leadership and Shagraan, and getting home by a neck from the first-named. The first four finished clear, the timefigure was pretty good and the form worked out well—it was the last time Systematic contested a handicap.

Returned to action in a three-runner minor event at Newbury in August, Systematic wasn't harried for the lead and had no difficulty landing the odds by five lengths from Hirapour. He was promptly thrown in at the deep end in the Great Voltigeur Stakes at York four days later, starting third favourite and showing improved form to be beaten just over a length when fifth behind Bandari, battling on determinedly after not having the usual forcing tactics applied. Further improvement, and his best run of the season, came in the Amco Corporation Troy Stakes at Doncaster. Despite favourite Storming Home not being at his best and Hatha Anna racing over a trip on the sharp side for him, Systematic still needed to excel himself to beat the reliable The Whistling Teal, keeping on gamely when challenged over a furlong out and scoring by a length and a half. Systematic showed a tendency to edge away from the far rail in the final quarter mile, ascribed by his rider to being put off by the roving television camera. With a listed race in the bag, Systematic notched a Group 3 on his final appearance, in the Young Vic Theatre Cumberland Lodge Stakes at Ascot. He did not need to repeat his Doncaster form to beat Warrsan, Frankies Dream and two others at 2/1-on, but he had to show his battling qualities once again in getting the better of Warrsan by half a length. A well-deserved conclusion to a fine campaign.

Systematic (b.c. 1999)	Rainbow Quest (USA) (b 1981)	Blushing Groom (ch 1974)	Red God
			Runaway Bride
		I Will Follow (b 1975)	Herbager
			Where You Lead
	Sensation (b 1993)	Soviet Star (b 1984)	Nureyev
			Veruschka
		Outstandingly (b 1982)	Exclusive Native
			La Mesa

Systematic's sire Rainbow Quest has been a strong influence for stamina and the average distance of races won by his progeny aged three and up is eleven

Maktoum Al Maktoum's "Systematic"

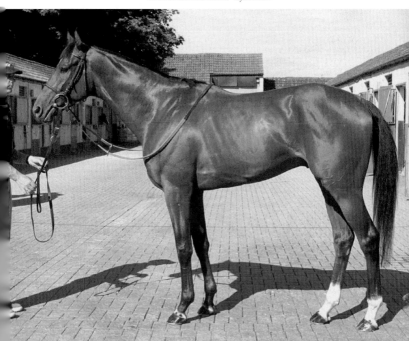

furlongs, with a good proportion staying a mile and three quarters. Systematic, a good-topped colt who may still have improvement in him, will stay the latter trip and the Yorkshire Cup appears an ideal early-season target in 2003. His dam Sensation, who usually raced prominently, showed smart form in winning her first four starts over a mile as a three-year-old, including the Prix de Sandringham and the Falmouth Stakes; she made little impact afterwards, including as a four-year-old with Godolphin. Systematic is her first foal. Sensation is a half-sister to three winners out of Outstandingly, successful in the Breeders' Cup Juvenile Fillies and effective at a mile and a quarter. Outstandingly's half-sister La Affirmed foaled smart sprinter Bernstein and Gallinule Stakes winner Della Francesca and is grandam of Sky Mesa, one of the top juvenile colts in the States. Systematic, who acts on soft and good to firm going, proved difficult at the start on his sixth outing but that was seemingly an aberration; he is thoroughly genuine and has been a model of reliability so far. *M. Johnston*

T

TAABEER   4 b.c. Caerleon (USA) 132 – Himmah (USA) 85 (Habitat 134) [2002 –:   –
10g 10m Jun 24] angular colt: fairly useful form at 2 yrs: well held all 3 starts since.
E. A. L. Dunlop

TABARAK (IRE)   6 b.g. Nashwan (USA) 135 – Select Sale (Auction Ring (USA)   –
123) [2002 8.2d 9m 12g 10d 10f Jun 21] strong, heavy-topped gelding: no longer of much
account. *J. M. Bradley*

TABBETINNA BLUE   5 b.m. Interrex (CAN) – True Is Blue (Gabitat 119) [2002 –:   –
f7g p7g Feb 13] leggy, lengthy mare: no longer of much account. *J. C. McConnochie*

TABINDA   2 b.c. (Apr 15) Wizard King 122 – Mouchez Le Nez (IRE) 41 (Cyrano de   **54**
Bergerac 120) [2002 6g f6f 6m Aug 29] 10,500Y, 25,000 2-y-o: fourth foal: half-brother
to 4-y-o Kilmeny and a 1m winner in Belgium by Case Law: dam lightly-raced maiden:
modest form in maidens: should stay 7f. *N. P. Littmoden*

TABOOR (IRE)   4 b.g. Mujadil (USA) 119 – Christoph's Girl 50 (Efisio 120) [2002   **69**
75: 6.1g f5g 5s 5g p5g^2 p5g^3 5.3d^4 5d^6 5m^4 5.3g^3 5.2m^5 5m 5f^4 5.1g^2 p6g^4 f5g p5g*   **a78**
Dec 21] heavy-topped gelding: fair handicapper: dead-heated at Lingfield in December:
effective at 5f/6f: acts on firm ground, good to soft and all-weather: hooded/blinkered
nowadays. *J. W. Payne*

TACA D'OLI (FR)   3 br.f. Octagonal (NZ) 126 – Marie de Fontenoy (FR) (Lightning   **56**
(FR) 129) [2002 9m 8.2m 10m Oct 7] 300,000 francs Y: leggy, sparely-made filly:
half-sister to several winners, including fairly useful 7.5f/1m winner Marie Loup (by
Wolfhound) and to dam of Marienbard: dam, French 1¼m winner, half-sister to very
smart French winner up to 1m Sakura Reiko: modest form in maidens: will stay 1½m.
D. E. Cantillon

TACITUS (IRE)   2 ch.c. (Mar 23) Titus Livius (FR) 115 – Idara 109 (Top Ville 129)   **105**
[2002 6f^3 6s* 6g 6g^2 8s^4 8s^6 Oct 26] 36,000Y: well-made, attractive colt: half-brother to
3 winners, including smart 7f to 1¼m performer Idris (by Ahonoora) and useful 6f/7f
winner Sweet Mazarine (by Dancing Dissident): dam French 11f/1½m winner: useful
performer: won maiden at Goodwood in June in impressive style: second favourite,
only tenth in Coventry Stakes at Royal Ascot: best efforts in July Stakes at Newmarket
(½-length second to Mister Links) and Gran Criterium at Milan (3½ lengths fourth to
Spartacus): stays 1m: acts on soft going, showed promise on firm: missed Phoenix Stakes
at the Curragh (fifth intended outing) after getting cast in box overnight. *R. Hannon*

TACTFUL REMARK (USA)   6 ch.g. Lord At War (ARG) – Right Word (USA)   –
(Verbatim (USA)) [2002 77: p8g 9.7m Apr 23] strong gelding: useful performer at best:
well held on Flat in 2002: blinkered final outing: joined M. Pipe (has won over hurdles).
J. A. Osborne

TADEO   9 ch.g. Primo Dominie 121 – Royal Passion 78 (Ahonoora 122) [2002 94: 5f   **83 d**
5g^4 5.1g^4 5.7d^5 5d 6f 5m^2 1g 5f Sep 26] small, strong gelding: fairly useful handicapper:
on downgrade in 2002, leaving J. M. Bradley after fourth start: barely stays 6f: acts on
firm and soft going: usually races up with pace. *C. G. Cox*

Phil Bull Trophy Conditions Stakes, Pontefract—
Taffrail and Archduke Ferdinand have the closing stages to themselves

TADRIS (USA)   2 b.f. (Feb 26) Red Ransom (USA) – Manwah (USA) 72 (Lyphard   **77 p**
(USA) 132) [2002 7d² Jul 31] sixth foal: dam, middle-distance maiden, closely related to
Unfuwain and half-sister to Nashwan and Nayef: weak 8/1, short-head second of 15 to
Huja in maiden at Kempton, racing freely and just pipped having led 2f out: should
improve, all being well. *M. P. Tregoning*

TAFFRAIL   4 b.g. Slip Anchor 136 – Tizona (Pharly (FR) 130) [2002 96p: 16m³ 16.1d⁴   **105**
14.8m⁵ 18m* 18m Oct 19] lengthy good-sort: useful performer: won slowly-run minor
event at Pontefract in September by ½ length from Archduke Ferdinand: best other effort
when third in handicap at Newbury in April: well held in Cesarewitch at Newmarket final
outing: best at 2m+: winner on good to soft going, possibly best on good or firmer: has
been bandaged in front. *J. L. Dunlop*

TAFFS WELL   9 b.g. Dowsing (USA) 124 – Zahiah 90 (So Blessed 130) [2002 81:   **71**
8v³ 8f 8.1d⁶ 8m⁵ 7.1g⁴ 8g⁶ 7.9m Jul 12] small gelding: fair performer nowadays: best at
7f/1m: acts on heavy and good to firm going: blinkered (pulled too hard) final outing:
held up: successful over hurdles in August. *B. Ellison*

TAFFY DANCER   4 b.g. Emperor Jones (USA) 119 – Ballerina Bay 75 (Myjinski   **59**
(USA)) [2002 –: 11.9g* 16.2g May 11] rangy gelding: unraced at 2 yrs: modest handicapper, lightly raced: won at Brighton in May despite wandering and carrying head
awkwardly: reportedly struck into next time: should stay at least 1¾m: raced on good/
good to firm ground. *H. Morrison*

TAGALOG   3 b.g. Tagula (IRE) 116 – Zalotti (IRE) 84 (Polish Patriot (USA) 128)   **–**
[2002 7g² f5g f6g Nov 20] 17,000Y: second foal: half-brother to 2000 2-y-o 5f winner
Celotti (by Celtic Swing): dam 5f winner, including at 2 yrs: little form in maidens at
Southwell: off 9 months before final start. *M. W. Easterby*

TAGGERTY (IRE)   4 b.f. Definite Article 121 – Kewaashi (USA) 69 (Storm Bird   **60**
(CAN) 134) [2002 60?: f8s p10g f7g⁵ 6f 7f 7g⁵ 6m² 6.1d⁴ 6g² 8f² 7.5m 7.6f² 6.9d² 6d⁵ 7m   **a52**
6m 6m 7f⁵ 7f³ 8m³ 7g⁶ 7d⁶ 12d f6g⁴ f6g³ f8g⁴ f9.4g⁶ f6g Dec 27] leggy, sparely-made
filly: modest maiden: left M. Ryan after second outing: stays 1m: acts on fibresand, firm
and soft going: sometimes races freely. *M. J. Polglase*

TAGULA BLUE (IRE)   2 b.g. (Mar 30) Tagula (IRE) 116 – Palace Blue (IRE) (Dara   **63**
Monarch 128) [2002 8.2m⁵ 7g 7m⁴ Oct 2] IR 10,500F, 5,800 2-y-o: good-bodied gelding:
has a round action: sixth foal: half-brother to 2 winners abroad, including a German 1m/
9f winner by Digamist: dam unraced: modest form in minor event/maidens: tongue tied
first 2 starts: not sure to stay much beyond 1m. *J. A. Glover*

TAHINI 3 b.f. Mtoto 134 – Sesame 117 (Derrylin 115) [2002 63p: 12m⁵ 11.9d⁵ 14.1f⁴ **67**
16f⁴ 14.1m Aug 15] strong filly: fair maiden handicapper: stays 2m: acts on firm and
good to soft going: reportedly distressed on reappearance: tongue tied final start: sold
6,500 gns. *J. L. Dunlop*

TAHITIAN STORM (IRE) 3 b.c. Catrail (USA) 123 – Razana (IRE) 71 (Kahyasi **100**
130) [2002 92: 8.1d³ 10.4d⁵ Jun 15] good-topped colt: useful handicapper: ran well in
2002 at Haydock (1¾ lengths third to Common World) and York (4½ lengths fifth behind
Waverley): stays 10.4f: acts on firm and soft going: sent to Hong Kong, where renamed
Gold Field. *M. H. Tompkins*

TAHLIL 3 ch.f. Cadeaux Genereux 131 – Amaniy (USA) 96 (Dayjur (USA) 137) **46**
[2002 –: 8.3m⁴ 8.3d 7f Jun 11] lengthy filly: poor maiden, lightly raced: best effort at 1m:
sold 4,500 gns in December. *E. A. L. Dunlop*

TAIL GUNNER 3 gr.g. Vague Shot 108 – Plum Blossom (USA) (Gallant Romeo **57**
(USA)) [2002 p8g p8g 8.3d 12.1g 16m³ 14.1f 14.1f⁴ 16.2d 14.1g Jul 23] brother to 2
winners, including fairly useful 1¼m to 1½m winner Isitoff, and half-brother to several
winners: dam unraced: modest maiden handicapper: stays 2m: acts on good to firm going:
visored last 3 starts: none too consistent. *S. C. Williams*

TAINWELL 3 ch.g. Most Welcome 131 – Mountain Lodge 120 (Blakeney 126) [2002 **– §**
8s⁶ 10f⁶ 12.1m⁶ 14.1f³ 13.8f a8f 8.5g Dec 29] 75,000Y: strong, rather dipped-backed
gelding: half-brother to several winners, notably smart Compton Ace (by Pharly), effective at 1½m to 2½m, and useful 7f (at 2 yrs) and 1¼m winner Mayville Thunder (by
Zilzal): dam won Irish St Leger and Cesarewitch: little form: left J. Noseda after fifth
outing and W. White in US after next start: blinkered last 3 appearances: ungenuine.
J. Collins, USA

TAIPAN LAD (IRE) 2 b.g. (May 28) Taipan (IRE) 124 – Newgate Lady (IRE) (Whist- **–**
ling Deer 117) [2002 6g 5m⁵ 5m⁴ Sep 19] IR 2,600Y: leggy gelding: sixth foal: dam, Irish
maiden, sister to smart 6f performer Amigo Menor: only a little sign of ability in maidens.
G. M. Moore

TAI SIMSEK 4 b.f. Minshaanshu Amad (USA) 91§ – Bedswerver (IRE) (Doulab **–**
(USA) 115) [2002 49: 9.9m p10g 11.8d 14.1d 14.1g 10.9m Jun 17] little form in 2002:
left P. Gilligan after second start: tried blinkered/visored. *M. J. Ryan*

TAIYO 2 b.f. (Mar 11) Tagula (IRE) 116 – Tharwa (IRE) 63 (Last Tycoon 131) [2002 **61 p**
6m³ Sep 8] 7,800Y: well-made filly: second foal: half-sister to 5-y-o Nisr: dam 5f (at 2
yrs)/6f winner: 12/1, 5½ lengths third of 17 to Riska King in maiden at York: should
improve. *J. W. Payne*

TAJAR (USA) 10 b.g. Slew O' Gold (USA) – Mashaarif (USA) (Mr Prospector **33 §**
(USA)) [2002 42§: p12g 14.1d 11.9f 12.3g⁴ 12d 12.3m⁶ 16.5g 12.1g 12m Aug 16] strong,
angular gelding: poor handicapper: on long losing run: stays 15f: acts on fibresand, firm
and soft going (unraced on heavy): blinkered twice at 5 yrs: tried tongue tied in 2001: has
been slowly away: normally held up: irresolute. *T. Keddy*

TAKAMAKA BAY (IRE) 5 ch.g. Unfuwain (USA) 131 – Stay Sharpe (USA) **106**
(Sharpen Up 127) [2002 104: 10.1d⁶ 12g⁶ 10.3m² 11.9d 13.9m Jul 13] sturdy gelding:
useful handicapper: good head second to Optimate at Doncaster in June: below form last
2 outings: stays 1½m: acts on any ground. *M. Johnston*

TAKAMAKA (IRE) 3 b.c. Pennekamp (USA) 130 – Jalcamin (IRE) (Jalmood (USA) **82 ?**
126) [2002 p8g 7.5m⁴ 6d 6m May 26] approx. 57,000Y in Italy: third foal: half-brother to
2 winners in Italy by Saddlers' Hall: dam Italian 6f to 1m winner: won maiden and second
in minor event, both at Rome, at 2 yrs: best effort (seemingly fairly useful form) when 5¼
lengths fourth in listed race at Pisa on second start in 2002: found little when last in minor
events in Britain and in Premio Tudini at Rome on other starts at 3 yrs: should stay 1m:
pulled hard third outing. *C. F. Wall*

TAKAROA 4 b.g. Tagula (IRE) 116 – Mountain Harvest (FR) 64§ (Shirley Heights **73**
130) [2002 77: 8.5g 8g 8m³ 8d² 8g⁵ 8d⁵ 8.3d p8g Sep 4] strong gelding: fair handicapper:
was best around 7f/1m: acted on soft and good to firm going: was sometimes visored/
blinkered: dead. *I. A. Balding*

TAKE A TURN 7 br.g. Forzando 122 – Honeychurch (USA) 93 (Bering 136) [2002 **–**
52: p13g Jan 9] smallish gelding: has a quick action: one-time fair performer: lightly
raced and little form on Flat nowadays: tried blinkered/visored. *M. J. Wilkinson*

TAKEN ABACK (IRE) 3 b.f. Robellino (USA) 127 – Loose Talk 68 (Thatching **–**
131) [2002 6m 8f May 17] second foal: half-sister to a winner in Greece by Common

Grounds: dam, sprint maiden, closely related to dam of Irish 1000 Guineas winner Classic Park and half-sister to smart 5f performer Easy Option: well beaten in maidens at Pontefract and Newbury, reportedly bled from nose at latter. *W. Jarvis*

TAKES TUTU (USA) 3 b.g. Afternoon Deelites (USA) 122 – Lady Affirmed (USA) **99** (Affirmed (USA)) [2002 75, a85: f7s² f7g* p7g* 7m⁵ 8.1d⁵ 7g* 7m⁶ 9g⁵ 8m 10d 8f⁴ 8m⁵ 7m* 7d 7f 9m² 10.5m* 10m 9f a8f⁶ a10f⁵ a9f² Dec 19] tall, useful-looking gelding: useful performer: had a fine season, winning maiden at Southwell, minor event at Lingfield and handicaps at Newmarket, Goodwood and Haydock (beat Persian Lass by ½ length, despite racing freely over longer trip and idling markedly): respectable efforts at best after, including in UAE: effective at 7f to easy 10.5f: acts on all-weather and firm going, possibly not on softer than good: blinkered nowadays: held up: quirky, but tough. *M. Johnston*

TAKES TWO TO TANGO 2 b.f. (Mar 6) Groom Dancer (USA) 128 – Peggy Spen- **69** cer 77 (Formidable (USA) 125) [2002 6d⁵ 6g² 6.1m* 7.5g 7.1m⁶ Sep 6] lengthy, angular filly: has a quick action: third foal: dam 6f/7f winner: fair performer: won maiden at Nottingham in July, flashing tail: well below form last 2 starts: should stay at least 7f: yet to race on extremes of going: sold 9,000 gns, sent to Sweden. *B. W. Hills*

TAKRIR (IRE) 5 b.g. Bahri (USA) 125 – Ice House 89 (Northfields (USA)) [2002 **92** 10.5m⁴ p8g² p8g³ Dec 30] fairly useful form: lightly raced: won maiden at Newbury on only appearance in 2000: good placed efforts in handicaps at Lingfield in May and December: should be at least as effective over 1¼m as 1m: acts on polytrack and good to firm going: unimpressive to post on reappearance. *D. J. Coakley*

TALARIA (IRE) 6 ch.m. Petardia 113 – Million At Dawn (IRE) 63 (Fayruz 116) **–** [2002 66: f6g f6g Feb 14] useful-looking mare: fluent mover: fair performer at 5 yrs: well held in 2002 (reportedly had breathing problem final outing): visored once: has given trouble at start (was banned from racing from stalls for 6 months). *W. Storey*

TALAT 4 b.f. Missed Flight 123 – Tawnais 80 (Artaius (USA) 129) [2002 55: f8s p10g **58 §** f12g f12g f9.4g 9s* 9s Jun 12] modest performer: won apprentice handicap at Kempton in June for second year running: stays easy 1¼m: acts on soft and good to firm going: visored (well held) fifth start: inconsistent. *M. J. Ryan*

TALBOT AVENUE 4 b.c. Puissance 110 – Dancing Daughter 79 (Dance In Time **94** (CAN)) [2002 80: 5g 5f 5.1f 5g 5.1f 5m⁴ 5g² 5.2f* 6g⁵ 6m 5f³ 5f² 6f* Oct 12] compact colt: fairly useful handicapper: improved, and won at Newbury in August and York (beat Toldya by 1¾ lengths) in October: best at 5f/6f: best form on good/good to firm going: sometimes wanders. *M. Mullineaux*

TALENTS LITTLE GEM 5 b.m. Democratic (USA) 101 – Le Saule d'Or 70 (Son- **–** nen Gold 121) [2002 49, a40: 11.6m Jul 22] poor handicapper: effective at 1m, probably stays 11.7f: acts on firm going, good to soft and fibresand: has been slowly away/reared in stall: tried blinkered. *A. W. Carroll*

TALENT STAR 5 b.g. Mizoram (USA) 105 – Bells of Longwick 92 (Myjinski (USA)) **–** [2002 55: 5m 10f Sep 27] modest maiden handicapper at 4 yrs: well held in 2002. *A. W. Carroll*

TALKATA (IRE) 3 b.f. Suave Dancer (USA) 136 – Talwara (USA) (Diesis 133) **–** [2002 8s⁵ Jun 7] fifth reported foal: half-sister to French/US 1m/1¼m winner Tavildaran (by Darshaan): dam lightly-raced maiden half-sister to Dante winner Torjoun out of sister to Top Ville: 7/1, last of 5 in maiden at Goodwood, slowly away and eased once beaten: sold €15,000 in November. *Sir Michael Stoute*

TALK TO MOJO 5 ch.g. Deploy 131 – Balnaha 67 (Lomond (USA) 128) [2002 **–** 14.1m⁵ Sep 5] fair form to win maiden at Newbury on only outing at 3 yrs (suffered injury afterwards and gelded): not knocked about once held only run in 2002: clearly difficult to train. *J. H. M. Gosden*

TALLDARK'N'ANDSOME 3 b.g. Efisio 120 – Fleur du Val (Valiyar 129) [2002 **91** 77: 8m p8g 8.2g 9f² 8m⁴ 10.2d* 10d* 9.9d⁴ p10g² 10d² 10.3s⁶ p10g Dec 21] workmanlike gelding: fairly useful handicapper: won at Chepstow and Brighton within 4 days in July: should stay beyond 1¼m: acts on firm ground, good to soft and polytrack: consistent. *N. P. Littmoden*

TALLY (IRE) 2 ch.g. (Apr 6) Tagula (IRE) 116 – Sally Chase 101 (Sallust 134) [2002 **59** 5.1d 5.1d⁵ 6g⁵ 7g⁶ 7.5d 7d f6g f6f² f6g² f6g⁵ Nov 30] IR 9,000F, 21,000Y: close-coupled **a65** gelding: half-brother to several winners, notably smart 7f/1m winner Unanimous Vote (by Roi Danzig) and useful 1m/1¼m winner Super Sally (by Superlative): dam 2-y-o 5f/ 6f winner: fair maiden on all-weather, modest on turf: twice runner-up at Wolverhampton: effective at 6f/7f: acts on fibresand, raced only on good/good to soft going on turf: usually races prominently. *A. Berry*

TAMA (IRE) 3 ch.f. Indian Ridge 123 – Web of Intrigue 66 (Machiavellian (USA) 123) [2002 58: 8m 6g 10.1m⁵ May 15] tall filly: modest maiden in 2001: well held at 3 yrs. *Andrew Turnell* —

TAMARELLA (IRE) 2 b.f. (Jan 31) Tamarisk (IRE) 127 – Miss Siham (IRE) 59 (Green Forest (USA) 134) [2002 5.1g 5m² 5m⁵ 5g 5d 6.1m⁴* 6m 6.1m² 6.5g 5f Oct 3] IR 21,000F, 9,500Y: smallish, well-made filly: third foal: half-sister to 2001 2-y-o 5f winner Addo (by Mujadil): dam 5f (including at 2 yrs) winner: fair performer: made all in nursery at Warwick (ran 3 best races there) in August despite swishing tail and wandering: stays 6f: acts on good to firm ground: none too consistent. *G. G. Margarson* **66**

TAMASUK (USA) 2 b.g. (Apr 22) Dixieland Band (USA) – Electrostat (USA) (Dynaformer (USA)) [2002 5g³ 6f³ 5s* 5d⁴ 5.1f⁴ 6m Oct 5] IR 200,000Y: sturdy gelding: second foal: dam, 1m winner in USA, half-sister to US Grade 1 1¼m winner Weber City Miss: fairly useful performer: won 4-runner maiden at Sandown (edged left) in June: creditable fourth in listed race there and nursery at Bath: likely to prove best at 5f/6f: acts on firm and soft ground. tried tongue tied: edgy sort, and has had 2 handlers/worn net muzzle/been taken steadily to post: gelded after final start. *B. Hanbury* **93**

TAMBURLAINE (IRE) 4 b.c. Royal Academy (USA) 130 – Well Bought (IRE) 35 (Auction Ring (USA) 123) [2002 119: 8.9g⁶ 7m⁵ Apr 27] good-topped, attractive colt: smart performer: second to Golan in 2000 Guineas at Newmarket in 2001: creditable 4 lengths sixth to Terre A Terre in Dubai Duty Free at Nad Al Sheba on reappearance: broke blood vessel in Leicestershire Stakes at Leicester, only other run in 2002: likely to prove best at 7f/around 1m: acts on soft and good to firm going: sometimes finishes weakly. *R. Hannon* **116**

TAMIAMI TRAIL (IRE) 4 ch.g. Indian Ridge 123 – Eurobird 118 (Ela-Mana-Mou 132) [2002 106: 12g 11.9d Jul 6] sturdy, close-coupled gelding: useful performer: reportedly suffered setback after final 3-y-o start: creditable ninth in Duke of Edinburgh Handicap at Royal Ascot on reappearance, despite not best of runs: bit below form in Old Newton Cup only other outing in 2002: gelded after: may prove best at 1½m/1¾m: acts on soft and good to firm going. *B. J. Meehan* **105**

TAMING (IRE) 6 ch.g. Lycius (USA) 124 – Black Fighter (USA) 79 (Secretariat (USA)) [2002 11.9m⁵ 14.6m Sep 13] tall, leggy, close-coupled gelding: fairly useful performer, lightly raced: ran creditably in 2002 only on reappearance: effective at 1½m to 2m: yet to race on extremes of going on turf, well beaten only run on all-weather (tongue tied): fair hurdler, successful twice in October. *Miss Venetia Williams* **82**

TANAFFUS 2 ch.c. (Feb 9) Cadeaux Genereux 131 – El Rabab (USA) 70 (Roberto (USA) 131) [2002 6d 7.1m⁴ Sep 7] strong, well-made colt: has scope: easy mover: sixth foal: brother to useful 6f (at 2 yrs)/7f winner Filfilah and half-brother to 2 winners, including fairly useful 5f (at 2 yrs) to 1m winner Marathon Maid (by Kalaglow): dam, 2-y-o 1m winner, out of Breeders' Cup Juvenile Fillies winner Brave Raj: better effort (fair form) when fourth of 16 to Jay Gee's Choice in maiden at Haydock, no extra final 1f: likely to prove best up to 1m. *B. W. Hills* **75**

TANAJI 3 b.f. Marju (IRE) 127 – Hamsaat (IRE) 80 (Sadler's Wells (USA) 132) [2002 77p: 7f⁵ 9.9g² 7.5g³ 10m² 9.9d² 10m* Aug 31] strong, lengthy filly: fair performer: won maiden at Ripon in August: may prove best at 1m/1¼m: acts on good to firm and good to soft going: effective blinkered or not: sold 22,000 gns. *B. Hanbury* **78**

TANCRED ARMS 6 b.m. Clantime 101 – Mischievous Miss 73 (Niniski (USA) 125) [2002 49§: f8s f6g f7g⁴ f7g⁵ 7d* 6f 8m 7g* 7f³ 7m 7g⁴ 7g 7m⁵ 7.6f* 5.9d⁴ 7m* 6.9s 7m 7m 6g 7f⁴ Sep 21] lengthy mare: modest performer on turf, poor on all-weather: won seller at Catterick in March, claimer at Newcastle in May and handicaps at Chester and Catterick in July, last 3 apprentice events: best around 7f nowadays: acts on fibresand and probably on any turf going: usually visored: sometimes hangs: none too consistent. *D. W. Barker* **61 a40**

TANCRED MISS 3 b.f. Presidium 124 – Mischievous Miss 73 (Niniski (USA) 125) [2002 54, a67: f6s f6g⁶ f6g f7g³ 8g⁴ 10g 7.9g 7m² 7f³ 5.9d² 6f* 5.9g² 6d f6g Dec 10] smallish, leggy filly: modest handicapper: won at Catterick in July: seems best at 6f/7f: acts on fibresand, firm and good to soft going: usually races prominently/leads. *D. W. Barker* **64 a51**

TANCRED TIMES 7 ch.m. Clantime 101 – Mischievous Miss 73 (Niniski (USA) 125) [2002 73: f5s f5g⁶ f5g f5g⁵ f5g f5g⁶ 5m 5g 5m⁴ 5g⁴ 5g⁵ 5m 5m⁵ 5m⁶ 5g⁴ 6m³ 5m² 5d **68 a64**

5m⁴ 5m f5s Sep 5] small mare: fair handicapper: best at 5f/easy 6f: acts on firm going, soft and fibresand: well beaten only run in blinkers: occasionally slowly away: usually races prominently: tough and game. *D. W. Barker*

TANCRED TYKE 2 b.f. (Mar 7) Atraf 116 – Tancred Mischief 44 (Northern State –
(USA) 91) [2002 6f 6m Oct 2] small filly: first foal: dam, 2m/2¼m winner, also success-ful over hurdles: always outpaced in maidens. *D. W. Barker*

TANCRED WALK 4 b.f. Clantime 101 – Mischievous Miss 73 (Niniski (USA) 125) 44 +
[2002 43: 7m 6f 6m³ 6f 5d⁴ 5m Jul 18] smallish filly: poor maiden handicapper: first race after leaving R. Ford, appeared to run well third start: probably best at 5f/6f: acts on good to firm and good to soft ground: races prominently. *D. W. Barker*

TANDAVA (IRE) 4 ch.g. Indian Ridge 123 – Kashka (USA) (The Minstrel (CAN) 90
135) [2002 79: 10f⁴ 11.9m 10g 13.9g⁴ 12.3f² 12m* 13.1g 13m² 13.1s⁴ 16s Nov 6] lengthy gelding: fairly useful performer: won 4-runner minor event at Pontefract in July: stays 1¾m: acts on soft and good to firm ground: sometimes slowly away. *I. Semple*

TANGA DANCER 2 ch.f. (Apr 7) Blue Ocean (USA) 87 – Tangalooma 56 (Hotfoot 57 d
126) [2002 5m⁶ 5g³ 5m 5g⁵ 7g 7g 8m 8g Sep 10] 800Y: half-sister to several winners, including 5f/6f winner Time To Tango and 6-y-o Time Temptress (both by Timeless Times): dam, maiden who stayed 1½m, winning hurdler: modest maiden: below form after fourth start: should stay at least 1m: none too reliable. *J. L. Eyre*

TANGANIKA 3 b.c. Salse (USA) 128 – Buckwig (USA) (Buckfinder (USA)) [2002 64
10m p12g* 12.6m 12f³ 13.8g Oct 19] good-topped colt: half-brother to several winners in Italy, notably Premio Regina Elena winner Shenck (by Zafonic): dam Italian 7f/1m (Group 3) winner: modest performer: won maiden at Lingfield in September: stays 1½m: acts on firm going and polytrack. *P. W. Harris*

TANGLED UP IN BLUE (IRE) 2 b.c. (Feb 15) Marju (IRE) 127 – Meshhed (USA) 87
102 (Gulch (USA)) [2002 5.2g⁵ 5m* 5m² 6m⁴ 6m⁴ 7f 6f* 6m² 6f⁴ 6s Oct 26] IR 22,000Y: good-bodied colt: second foal: dam, 7f winner (including at 2 yrs) who stayed 1¼m, granddaughter of 1000 Guineas/Oaks winner Midway Lady: fairly useful performer: won maiden at Leicester in April and nursery at Haydock in September: stays 6f: acts on firm ground, well held on soft: sometimes sweating/edgy: carried head awkwardly and wandered (at Brighton) on eighth start: sold privately to race in USA. *J. A. Osborne*

TAN HILL FAIR (IRE) 3 b.f. Woodborough (USA) 112 – Ron's Secret 92 (Efisio 47
120) [2002 59: p10g f7g f8g 16m⁵ 14.1f 14.1f⁵ 12m 11.6m⁶ 12.1g 10m⁵ Aug 28] well-made, smallish filly: poor maiden: seems to stay easy 1½m: acts on firm ground, probably on polytrack. *P. Howling*

TANTALUS 5 ch.h. Unfuwain (USA) 131 – Water Quest (IRE) (Rainbow Quest 98
(USA) 134) [2002 88: f9.4g² f9.4g* p12g p10g⁴ f9.4g³ f9.4g³ 12g 12m² 12m³ 12g⁵ a12g² a8g² a12g Dec 8] sturdy horse: useful performer: won claimer at Wolverhampton in January: at least creditable efforts in handicaps next 4 starts, then left J. Osborne: good 5½ lengths second to Final Care in listed race at Jagersro eighth outing: runner-up at Mijas penultimate appearance: probably stays 1¾m: acts on all-weather, dirt, firm and good to soft going: tongue tied twice in 2000: often blinkered: probably best held up. *C. Bjorling, Spain*

TANTE ROSE (IRE) 2 b.f. (Apr 10) Barathea (IRE) 127 – My Branch 111 (Distant 91 p
Relative 128) [2002 7g³ 6d* Nov 1] sturdy, quite attractive filly: third foal: half-sister to 4-y-o Future Flight and 3-y-o Rosie's Posy: dam, 5f (at 2 yrs) to 7f winner, also third in Irish 1000 Guineas: justified favouritism in 17-runner maiden at Newmarket by 3½ lengths from Ben Lomand, soon travelling strongly close up and drawing away without being at all hard ridden: bred to stay 1m, though looks to have plenty of speed: should make a useful filly at least and hold her own in stronger company. *B. W. Hills*

TANTRIC 3 br.g. Greensmith 121 – Petunia (GER) (Chief Singer 131) [2002 54, a60: 70
f7g⁶ f9.4g* 8m f9.4g³ f9.4s* 8.3v 7.9g* 8m⁶ 8m 8.5g³ 7.5m³ f9.4g² f8g f7s Nov 2] quite a77
attractive gelding: fair performer, better on all-weather than turf: won seller/apprentice handicap at Wolverhampton and minor event at Carlisle in first half of season: disappoint-ing last 2 starts (found little on first occasion): effective at 7f to 9.4f: acts on fibresand and good to firm going. *J. O'Reilly*

TAP 5 b.g. Emarati (USA) 74 – Pubby 73 (Doctor Wall 107) [2002 –: f5s 6g 6f Jul 17] 41
angular, useful-looking gelding: poor handicapper nowadays: stays 7f: acts on fibresand and soft ground: blinkered/tongue tied once each. *D. Nicholls*

TAPAGE (IRE)   6 b.g. Great Commotion (USA) 123 – Irena (Bold Lad (IRE) 133)   **41**
[2002 77d: f8.5g f7g f8g⁴ 8m 7d Jun 13] poor performer nowadays: best at 7f/1m: acts on
firm and soft going: tried blinkered/visored: races prominently. *Mrs N. Macauley*

TAPAU (IRE)   4 b.f. Nicolotte 118 – Urtica (IRE) (Cyrano de Bergerac 120) [2002 83:   **78**
7d 7f 7g⁶ 6.1m² 7.1g⁶ p8g 7d 7s p7g Nov 19] lengthy filly: fair handicapper: left
J. M. Bradley and off 5 months after second start: should stay 1m: acts on firm and good
to soft ground: races freely. *Dr J. R. J. Naylor*

TAP DANCER (IRE)   4 b.g. Sadler's Wells (USA) 132 – Watch Out (USA) (Mr Pros-   **52**
pector (USA)) [2002 64: p12g 7s 9.7m 11.9g 10d* 10g 10g 10m Jul 16] modest
handicapper: won handicap at Brighton in May: well below form after: stays 1¼m:
acts on heavy ground: blinkered once at 3 yrs: often slowly away/refuses to settle.
B. G. Powell

TAPIS FILLE (IRE)   3 b.f. Fayruz 116 – Trubbach (Vitiges (FR) 132) [2002 56d: f7s   **–**
Jan 4] quite well-made filly: disappointing maiden. *R. Ford*

TAPPIT (IRE)   3 b.c. Mujadil (USA) 119 – Green Life 63 (Green Desert (USA) 127)   **74**
[2002 76: 7m 8.2d 7.1m 6g⁷ 7d 5.1s² 6m⁵ 6m⁴ 6m⁴ 7g 7.1g 5f⁴ 6d f6g⁴ f6g f6t   **a69**
Nov 29] neat colt: fair handicapper: best at 5f/easy 6f: yet to race on heavy going, acts on
any other turf and fibresand. *J. M. Bradley*

TAP THE STONE (IRE)   3 b.g. Bigstone (IRE) 126 – Wadeyaa (Green Desert   **39**
(USA) 127) [2002 56: 7.5m 5.9s 7f 10f 12m 9.2v⁴ 11m 10m Aug 31] heavy-topped
gelding: poor maiden: probably stays 9f: acts on firm going (probably on heavy), below
form on fibresand: tried visored/blinkered. *J. S. Wainwright*

TARAFAH   3 ch.c. Machiavellian (USA) 123 – Elfaslah (IRE) 107 (Green Desert   **82**
(USA) 127) [2002 10d⁶ 12m³ Jul 4] good-bodied colt: brother to Dubai World Cup
winner Almutawakel and smart UAE 1000 Guineas winner (second in 1000 Guineas)
Muwakleh and half-brother to 3 useful winners: dam, won around 1¼m, half-sister to
high-class 1½m performer White Muzzle: better effort in maidens when 2½ lengths third
of 8 to Stance at Newbury: green on debut: sold 44,000 gns in October. *M. P. Tregoning*

TARANAKI   4 b.c. Delta Dancer – Miss Ticklepenny (Distant Relative 128) [2002 83:   **86**
f6g 7m* 7f* 7f 7g³ 7f 7m 6.5g⁴ 6f⁶ 7m* 7f 7m⁴ 7m 7m 6f⁶ 6.1s f7s Nov 2] rather leggy   **a?**
colt: fairly useful performer: won minor event at Folkestone and handicap at Kempton
in April, and ladies handicap at Ascot in July: not at best last 5 starts: has won at 1m,
probably best at 6f/7f: acts on fibresand, firm and good to soft going: blinkered ninth
start: tends to edge right: races prominently. *P. D. Cundell*

TARANOG   3 b.g. Perpendicular 119 – Onemoretime (Timeless Times (USA) 99)   **–**
[2002 –: 10d f12g Apr 15] little form: tried blinkered. *B. Palling*

TARAS EMPEROR (IRE)   4 b.g. Common Grounds 118 – Strike It Rich (FR) 88   **86**
(Rheingold 137) [2002 76: 6.1g 6s* 5d 5s* 5g⁵ 6m³ 5g⁶ 5.9v 6g 5m 5d 6.1s² Oct 29]
close-coupled, workmanlike gelding: fairly useful handicapper: won at Hamilton in May
and Haydock (edged left) in June: best at 5f/6f: acts on good to firm going, has won 6
from 9 starts on soft/heavy. *J. J. Quinn*

TARA'S FLAME   2 ch.c. (Apr 19) Blushing Flame (USA) 109 – Lady Emm (Emarati   **– p**
(USA) 74) [2002 8v Nov 8] big, workmanlike colt: second foal: brother to 4-y-o Polish
Flame: dam unraced: 50/1 and backward, well held in 23-runner maiden at Doncaster,
travelling strongly until halfway: likely to do better. *J. G. Given*

TARA TIME (IRE)   2 b.f. (Mar 15) Danetime (IRE) 121 – Faye 79 (Monsanto (FR)   **68**
121) [2002 5s 6m² 6.3g 6g³ 6m⁵ 6.1m 6m 7f 6d⁵ Oct 14] IR 9,000F, IR 30,000Y: small
filly: half-sister to several winners, including useful Irish 1m/9f winner Wray (by Sharp
Victor) and 3-y-o Duke of Earl: dam, 2-y-o 6f winner, later successful in USA: fair
maiden: will stay 7f: acts on good to firm and good to soft going: visored (ran creditably)
final start. *J. J. Quinn*

TARAWAN   6 ch.g. Nashwan (USA) 135 – Soluce 98 (Junius (USA) 124) [2002 76:   **67**
10.3s p10g 10m² 10.2d 10.5s² 10s⁵ p10g 10m³ 12d p10g Dec 21] strong, long-backed
gelding: fair performer: best at 1m to 10.5f: acts on firm and soft going, probably on
polytrack: sometimes blinkerked/visored: often slowly away/sometimes races lazily:
none too consistent. *I. A. Balding*

TARAZONIC   4 ch.f. Zafonic (USA) 130 – Tarasova (USA) (Green Forest (USA)   **–**
134) [2002 62d: f14s Sep 5] very big filly: modest maiden at best: has deteriorated: has
refused to enter stall. *P. D. Evans*

TARBOUSH 5 b.g. Polish Precedent (USA) 131 – Barboukh 95 (Night Shift (USA)) **86**
[2002 95: 8s 7f 10g⁶ 10s 8s* 9m² 8m 8.5d³ 7g² 8d 10g⁴ 8.5g* 10.1m 8m⁴ 10.4f 8g³ p10g
Dec 21] strong, sturdy gelding: fluent mover: fairly useful performer: won handicap
at Newbury in June and minor event at Epsom in August: effective at 7f, barely at
1¼m: acts on soft going, good to firm and polytrack: often races freely/makes running.
N. A. Callaghan

TARCOOLA 5 ch.g. Pursuit of Love 124 – Mıswakı Belle (USA) 73 (Miswaki (USA)   **– §**
124) [2002 –, a54d: f11s f11s f12g 16g Apr 2] tall, quite attractive gelding: moody
maiden: tried visored, sometimes blinkered. *Mrs A. M. Naughton*

TARFSHI 4 b.f. Mtoto 134 – Pass The Peace 116 (Alzao (USA) 117) [2002 105: 9g*   **111**
10m⁴ 10g* 9.9m⁶ 10s Sep 28] lengthy, good-topped filly: smart performer: won listed
race at Newmarket in May by 1¾ lengths from Spring Oak and Hunston Financial Pretty
Polly Stakes at the Curragh in June by ½ length from Wrong Key, making all both times:
stiffer tasks after, respectable sixth to Islington in Nassau Stakes at Goodwood and last
behind Kazzia in Flower Bowl Invitational at Belmont: stayed 1¼m: acted on firm and
soft going: genuine: visits Selkirk. *M. A. Jarvis*

TARJMAN 2 b.c. (Feb 19) Cadeaux Genereux 131 – Dodo (IRE) 90 (Alzao (USA)   **86 p**
117) [2002 6m⁶ 6m* Sep 13] 190,000Y: first foal: dam, 6f winner, out of very smart but
temperamental sprinter Dead Certain: still green, better effort in maidens (fairly useful
form) when winning 12-runner race at Goodwood in September by length from Four
Jays, switched and quickening to lead final 1f: not sure to stay much beyond 6f: very
slowly away on debut: should progress further. *A. C. Stewart*

TARKWA 3 gr.f. Doyoun 124 – Shining Fire (Kalaglow 132) [2002 10g 8.2d 10s 10g⁴   **56**
11.9d⁶ 10.2f* 10.1f³ 12g² 10m Sep 5] sturdy filly: first reported foal: dam unraced out of
close relative to very smart middle-distance stayer More Light: modest handicapper: won
at Bath in July: stays 1½m: acts on firm going. *R. M. H. Cowell*

Sheikh Ahmed Al Maktoum's "Tarfshi"

Falmouth Stakes, Newmarket—Tashawak has quickened clear; Golden Silca (large blaze), Kootenay (smaller blaze), Dolores, Misterah (blinkers) and Marionnaud (checked cap) follow her home

TARNATION (IRE) 2 ch.g. (Jan 30) Tagula (IRE) 116 – Steal 'em 66 (Efisio 120) [2002 5s 6f Jun 11] 10,000F, 5,200Y; angular gelding: second foal: dam, 7.6f winner, half-sister to smart sprinter Perryston View: well held in maidens: gelded after final start. *J. R. Weymes* —

TARRADALE 8 br.g. Interrex (CAN) – Encore L'Amour (USA) § (Monteverdi 129) [2002 44: 10m 11.9s 10f Jun 21] heavy-topped, plain gelding: no form in 2002. *C. B. B. Booth* —

TARSKI 8 ch.g. Polish Precedent (USA) 131 – Illusory 81 (Kings Lake (USA) 133) [2002 53: 12m 12.1g³ Jul 26] sturdy gelding: modest handicapper: stays 1½m: acts on good to firm and good to soft going: tried blinkered/visored: held up: won over hurdles in August. *W. S. Kittow* — **50**

TARVINALI (IRE) 3 b.f. Entrepreneur 123 – Surmise (USA) 75 (Alleged (USA) 138) [2002 –: 8v Apr 1] IR 9,500Y: seventh foal: half-sister to winners abroad by Be My Guest and Royal Academy: dam, 7f winner, half-sister to smart 7f/1m performer Aim For The Top: well held in maidens (for J. Harley in Ireland at 2 yrs): tried blinkered. *A. Berry* —

TASHAWAK (IRE) 3 b.f. Night Shift (USA) – Dedicated Lady (IRE) 101 (Pennine Walk 120) [2002 98p: 8m* 8g* 8g Aug 18] sturdy filly: progressed into a smart performer: won listed rated stakes at Royal Ascot (beat Chorist 2 lengths after stumbling badly and nearly unseating leaving stall) in June and Falmouth Stakes at Newmarket (beat Golden Silca comfortably by 1½ lengths) in July, showing good turn of foot each time: second favourite, only seventh of 8 behind Banks Hill in Prix Jacques le Marois at Deauville final outing: stayed 1m: raced only on good/good to firm going: visits Kingmambo. *J. L. Dunlop* — **118**

TASMANIAN TIGER (USA) 3 ch.c. Storm Cat (USA) – Hum Along (USA) (Fappiano (USA)) [2002 80p: 7s⁴ 9g* Jul 21] $6,800,000Y (most expensive yearling sold at public auction in the world in 2000): raced 3 times in maidens, showed progressive form: off 4 months before landing odds in 15-runner event at Tipperary in July by ½ length from Balsam, making all: should stay 1¼m: sold privately to join P. Kan in Hong Kong, where renamed The Pioneer. *A. P. O'Brien, Ireland* — **90**

TASNEEF (USA) 3 b.g. Gulch (USA) – Min Alhawa (USA) 108 (Riverman (USA) 131) [2002 10g⁶ 12.3m* 12.3d³ 12f² 11.9g 12f⁴ 16.2g 11.8g Oct 14] lengthy, workmanlike gelding: second foal: dam, 7f (at 2 yrs) and 1¼m winner, half-sister to 1000 Guineas winner Harayir (by Gulch): reportedly suffered hairline fracture of cannon bone in 2001: fairly useful performer: won maiden at Ripon in June: left M. Tregoning 46,000 gns after third start: below form last 2 outings (gelded after): stays 1½m: acts on firm and good to soft ground. *T. D. McCarthy* — **92**

TASS HEEL (IRE) 3 b.g. Danehill (USA) 126 – Mamouna (USA) 113 (Vaguely Noble 140) [2002 60: 10.9g 14.1m 12m³ 11.9g³ 12m 10m 14.1m² 16.1m² 15.8f⁴ f12g³ f16.2g⁵ p16g p13g² Dec 28] strong, lengthy gelding: modest maiden handicapper: stays 2m: acts on all-weather, raced mainly on good going or firmer on turf (acts on firm). *M. R. Channon* — **62**

TATWEER (IRE) 2 b.c. (Mar 12) Among Men (USA) 124 – Sandystones 60 (Selkirk (USA) 129) [2002 7f⁵ Jul 19] IR 33,000F, 80,000Y: good-bodied colt: has a round action: second foal: half-brother to fairly useful 2001 2-y-o 5f winner Sighting (by Eagle Eyed), later winner abroad: dam, maiden (best effort at 9f), half-sister to useful performer up to 10.5f Sonic Boy: 16/1 and backward, 6 lengths fifth of 12 to High Accolade in maiden at Newbury, fading: wore visor: likely to do better. *M. P. Tregoning* — **71 p**

TAU CETI   3 b.c. Hernando (FR) 127 – Napoli 108 (Baillamont (USA) 124) [2002   **117**
106: 8g^5 10.5g^4 10m* 10d^4 10s^4 10d* 9.8g^4 Oct 5] third foal: half-brother to 4-y-o Domedriver and French 1¼m/11f winner Forest Rain (by Caerleon): dam, French 1m/1¼m
winner who stayed 1½m, sister to smart French 1¼m winner D'Arros from family of El
Gran Senor and Xaar: smart performer: won newcomers race at Clairefontaine and minor
event at Saint-Cloud at 2 yrs: successful in 2002 in minor event at Chantilly in June and
Prix du Prince d'Orange at Longchamp (beat Shaanmer ½ length) in September: ran
creditably when keeping-on 3¼ lengths fourth to Dano-Mast in Prix Dollar at Longchamp final start: worth a try at 1½m: acts on good to firm and good to soft ground.
J. E. Hammond, France

TAWAHOJ (USA)   2 b.f. (Jan 27) Zafonic (USA) 130 – Spanish Falls 106 (Belmez   **78 p**
(USA) 131) [2002 7d^4 8.1g* Aug 26] first living foal: dam, French 7.5f (at 2 yrs) and
1½m (Prix de Royaumont) winner, half-sister to high-class 1m/9f performer Starborough, Racing Post Trophy winner Aristotle and 3-y-o Ballingarry: better effort in
maidens (fair form) when winning 5-runner event at Chepstow by short head from
Condoleezza, racing freely in front: not sure to stay much beyond 1m: open to further
improvement. *D. R. Loder*

TAWOOS (FR)   3 b.f. Rainbow Quest (USA) 134 – Queen of Dance (IRE) (Sadler's   **94**
Wells (USA) 132) [2002 10m^5 11.9d* 10s^5 10g 12g 8.5m^2 8g^2 10.1d^2 Oct 30] 145,000F,
170,000Y: lengthy, angular filly: second foal: half-sister to French 2000 2-y-o 1m winner
Queenliness (by Exit To Nowhere): dam won at 7f in France at 2 yrs: fairly useful
performer: won maiden at Haydock in May: effective at 1m to 1½m: acts on good to firm
and good to soft going, probably on soft: edged right sixth start: carried head awkwardly
final one: sold 17,000 gns, sent to Norway. *A. C. Stewart*

TAYASH   2 b.c. (Apr 22) Fleetwood (IRE) 107 – Wassl's Sister (Troy 137) [2002 6m 7s   **–**
f7s Dec 7] 8,500 2-y-o: neat colt: half-brother to several winners, including 7f/1m winner
Waseela (by Ahonoora) and 1¼m winner Persian Sabre (by Sabrehill): dam, maiden who
stayed 1½m, half-sister to Wassl: backward, well held in maidens. *A. W. Carroll*

Mr Hamdan Al Maktoum's "Tashawak"

TAYIBAH (IRE) 3 b.f. Sadler's Wells (USA) 132 – Wijdan (USA) 101 (Mr Prospector **81**
(USA)) [2002 11.7g² Oct 16] second foal: half-sister to smart 1m winner Oriental Fashion
(by Marju): dam, 1m and 10.4f winner, closely related to Nayef and half-sister to Nashwan and Unfuwain: 8/1, fairly useful form when head second to Nirvana in maiden at
Bath (pair clear), only outing: visits Bahri. *M. P. Tregoning*

TAYIF 6 gr.g. Taufan (USA) 119 – Rich Lass (Broxted 120) [2002 97: 6m 6s 5m 6g 6m **90**
6g⁵ 6m⁵ 5m 6g⁴ Sep 20] quite good-topped gelding: fairly useful handicapper: reportedly
lame and underwent operation on joints after final 5-y-o outing: not the force of old in
2002, best efforts when fifth in Stewards' Cup at Goodwood on sixth start and 2½ lengths
fourth to John O'Groats in Silver Cup at Ayr final start: effective at 6f, barely at testing
7f: acts on soft and good to firm going: tongue tied nowadays: sometimes slowly away:
sold 10,000 gns. *D. Nicholls*

TBM CAN 3 b.g. Rock City 120 – Fire Sprite 83 (Mummy's Game 120) [2002 p7g –
7.1g 10s May 13] 8,500 2-y-o: half-brother to 3 winners, including useful 6f performer
Always Alight (by Never So Bold) and fairly useful performer up to 7f Demolition Jo (by
Petong): dam 2-y-o 5f winner: well held in maidens. *C. F. Wall*

T C FLYER 2 b.f. (Apr 5) Wizard King 122 – Kaleidophone 73 (Kalaglow 132) [2002 **54 §**
5f³ 5.1f⁶ 6m 6m⁴ 5.1d Jul 8] tall, leggy filly: eighth foal: half-sister to 2001 2-y-o 6f
winner Decima (by Puissance) and a winner abroad by Music Boy: dam, 1m winner, half-
sister to useful Italian sprinter Plumbird: modest maiden: below form in sellers last 3
starts: likely to prove best at 5f: acts on firm ground: tried blinkered: headstrong and not
one to trust. *P. D. Evans*

TEA FOR TEXAS 5 ch.m. Weldnaas (USA) 112 – Polly's Teahouse 68 (Shack (USA) **– §**
118) [2002 45§: f7g 9.9g 8f⁵ 7m 8d 8s 8.1g f7g f7g Dec 2] lengthy mare: temperamental
handicapper: tried visored. *P. L. Clinton*

TEAM-MATE (IRE) 4 b.g. Nashwan (USA) 135 – Ustka 60 (Lomond (USA) 128) **92**
[2002 82: 11.8g³ 12m 11.5m* 12m³ 11.7f⁵ 12f³ 12f* 11.9f² Oct 10] leggy gelding: fairly
useful performer: won maiden at Yarmouth in July and minor event at Goodwood in
September: will stay 1¾m+: acts on firm going, probably on soft: tried tongue tied: has
hinted at temperament. *Miss J. Feilden*

TE ANAU 5 b.m. Reprimand 122 – Neenah 107 (Bold Lad (IRE) 133) [2002 –: f8g –
f9.4s May 13] no form since 2 yrs. *W. J. Musson*

TEASE (IRE) 2 b.f. (Feb 2) Green Desert (USA) 127 – Mockery (Nashwan (USA) **81**
135) [2002 5m⁴ 6m³ 6m 7m² 8m³ 8g 8.3d³ Oct 28] IR 100,000Y: first foal: dam, 10.5f
and 15f winner, out of half-sister to smart middle-distance fillies Braiswick and
Percy's Lass: fairly useful maiden: second at Salisbury: stays 1m: acts on good to firm
ground, below form on good to soft. *R. Hannon*

TEA'S MAID 2 b.f. (Feb 27) Wizard King 122 – Come To Tea (IRE) (Be My Guest –
(USA) 126) [2002 6d Oct 21] IR 3,000F, IR 7,500Y: tall filly: fifth living foal: dam, Irish
2-y-o 7f winner, half-sister to Danish (smart filly up to 1¼m in Europe/USA) and 4-y-o
Hawkeye: 16/1 and backward: well held in maiden at Pontefract. *J. G. Given*

TECHNICIAN (IRE) 7 ch.g. Archway (IRE) 115 – How It Works (Commanche Run **78 d**
133) [2002 95: f6g f6g f7g 6s 6m⁶ 6m 6g 6g 7m 6g 7m⁵ 7.5m 6f f8.5g f7g Dec 14]
good-bodied gelding: poor mover: fair handicapper: very much on downgrade in 2002:
best at 6f/7f: acts on soft going, firm and fibresand: best in blinkers/visor: usually races
prominently. *E. J. Alston*

TEDBURROW 10 b.g. Dowsing (USA) 124 – Gwiffina 87 (Welsh Saint 126) **116**
[2002 115: 6s⁴ 6d* 6f 6g* 5.1f⁵ 5f Jul 28]
  Back in 1995 when the nine-year-old Further Flight captured his fifth
Jockey Club Cup to become the oldest horse to win a pattern race in Britain, the
six-year younger Tedburrow was still in the early stages of a remarkable career
which has led him eventually to surpass Further Flight's achievement. In June,
Tedburrow, aged ten, won the John Smith's Extra Smooth Chipchase Stakes at
Newcastle by a length from Vision of Night. A listed event when Tedburrow had
won it two years earlier, the race had since been promoted to Group 3 status and, as
a result, Tedburrow is in the record books. Deservedly so. It was Tedburrow's
twenty-first victory in nine seasons, during which he has run eighty-four times, a
notable wins-to-races ratio of one in four. And at the age of ten he had not only
retained all his enthusiasm, but also all his ability—he has been rated at 115 or 116
in each of the last six years. Small wonder, then, that Tedburrow has become one of

John Smith's Extra Smooth Chipchase Stakes, Newcastle—at the age of ten, Tedburrow becomes the oldest horse to win a pattern race in Britain; Vision of Night and Ashdown Express (right) are second and third

the most popular horses in training, and a great credit to Eric Alston, who has trained him during that time.

Tedburrow went on to win five races for Muriel Naughton after being claimed out of Roger Fisher's stable for £6,000 following a success at Musselburgh, then known as Edinburgh, on his second start at two. However, it wasn't until after joining his present stable that Tedburrow came into his own, quickly developing into a smart performer and progressing from handicaps to compete mainly in pattern races, including several abroad. Trips to Italy, where he finished a close second in the Premio Omenoni, Hong Kong and Dubai failed to provide a victory, but it was a different story in Ireland, Tedburrow winning the Flying Five at Leopardstown in 1998 and 1999. Attempting the hat-trick in 2000, Tedburrow failed only by a head to get the better of the subsequent Prix de l'Abbaye winner Namid. All courses seem to come alike to Tedburrow who has a good record at Chester, three of his four wins there coming in the same event, the City Wall Stakes, which gained listed status after his first success in it.

Tedburrow (b.g. 1992)	Dowsing (USA) (br 1984)	Riverman (b 1969)	Never Bend	River Lady
		Prospector's Fire (b or br 1976)	Mr Prospector	Native Street
	Gwiffina (b 1982)	Welsh Saint (b 1966)	St Paddy	Welsh Way
		November (ch 1968)	Firestreak	Sweet Reason

Whereas Further Flight was a stayer, the sturdy, workmanlike Tedburrow is a sprinter through and through. Apart from when tried once over seven furlongs at three, he has done all of his racing at five and six. Tedburrow's dam Gwiffina was a fairly useful winner over six furlongs as a two-year-old, but, in direct contrast to her son, she didn't train on. Gwiffina has produced several other winners but none of Tedburrow's calibre. Tedburrow, who acts on firm and soft going but probably not on heavy, was also successful in the latest season in a minor event at Haydock, where he beat Kier Park by a short head. His one other foray into pattern company in 2002 ended in a below-par display behind Invincible Spirit in the Duke of York Stakes in between his wins. A sixth successive appearance in the City Wall Stakes resulted in a respectable fifth behind Bishop's Court, but his season was cut short because of a problem with a joint after finishing in mid-division in the Hong Kong Jockey Club Sprint (Handicap) at Ascot. Let's hope the injury isn't serious and that this grand old campaigner is able to show just what he can do at the age of eleven. *E. J. Alston*

TEDO (IRE)   4 ch.g. Beveled (USA) – Gunner Girl 85 (Gunner B 126) [2002 8.2d f8.5g Apr 20] 1,000Y: half-brother to 1993 2-y-o 6f winner Bold Alex (by Full Extent) and 1¼m winner Swift Maiden (by Sharrood): dam 7f to 1¼m winner: well held in 2 maidens. *J. Neville* —

TEDSDALE MAC   3 ch.c. Presidium 124 – Stilvella (Camden Town 125) [2002 68: 5.1d* 6m 6s⁶ 5d 6d 8m 7.5m Sep 24] close-coupled, quite good-topped colt: modest performer: won maiden at Nottingham in April: stays 6f: acts on soft and good to firm going. *N. Bycroft* **64**

TEDSTALE (USA)   4 ch.g. Irish River (FR) 131 – Carefree Kate (USA) (Lyphard (USA) 132) [2002 85: 8f³ 8f* 8.5g⁶ 8d² 8.1s⁴ 8.9d 7.9m³ 8d² 8g 8.9m³ 8g 8g 8.2v Oct 29] smallish, sturdy, close-coupled gelding: unimpressive mover: fairly useful handicapper: won at Thirsk in May: generally creditable efforts after: best around 1m/9f: acts on firm and good to soft going: often blinkered: sometimes slowly away: often finds little. *T. D. Easterby* **94**

TEDZAR (IRE)   2 b.g. (May 7) Inzar (USA) 112 – Chesham Lady (IRE) (Fayruz 116) [2002 5v 6m 8g 7g Oct 17] IR 4,000F: seventh foal: half-brother to a winner abroad by Petardia: dam Irish 2-y-o 5f winner: poor form in maidens/sellers: tried blinkered. *M. H. Tompkins* **44**

TEEHEE (IRE)   4 b.g. Anita's Prince 126 – Regal Charmer (Royal And Regal (USA)) [2002 79: f8.5g⁶ 8g 7d f7g f8.5g f7s² f7g³ f6g f7g* f7g³ Dec 31] tall, useful-looking gelding: fair performer: won handicap at Wolverhampton in November: effective at 7f/ 1m: acts on fibresand, seems best on going softer than good on turf: visored/blinkered nowadays: sometimes carries head awkwardly/finds little: often makes running. *B. Palling* **69**

TEENATOO   3 ch.f. First Trump 118 – Fine Honey (USA) 90 (Drone (USA)) [2002 8m 7m May 2] 12,000F, 5,500Y, 4,000 2-y-o: half-sister to numerous winners, including useful 1991 2-y-o 5f/6f winner Gold Desert (by Green Desert), later winner in USA, and fairly useful 1m winner (including at 2 yrs) who stayed 10.4f Polar Flight (by Polar Falcon): dam lightly-raced 2-y-o 5f winner: well beaten in maiden/seller. *Mrs A. Duffield* —

TEES COMPONENTS   7 b.g. Risk Me (FR) 127 – Lady Warninglid (Ela-Mana-Mou 132) [2002 p12g* p7g 16g² 12m³ 13.1g⁵ 18m 16d* 12v Nov 9] tall, well-made gelding: brother to a 1¼m winner in Italy and half-brother to several winners, including 1½m to 2m winner La Brief (by Law Society): dam unraced: smart bumper performer: useful on Flat: won maiden at Lingfield in February and handicap at Newmarket (improved form, beat Hambleden by 9 lengths) in November: well-beaten favourite for Cesarewitch at Newmarket and November Handicap at Doncaster sixth/final starts: effective at 1½m and stays 2m: acts on polytrack, good to firm and good to soft going: tends to be slowly away/edge left under pressure (swerved badly left final 1f at Newmarket): smart novice hurdler. *Mrs M. Reveley* **107**

TEFI   4 ch.g. Efisio 120 – Masuri Kabisa (USA) 48 (Ascot Knight (CAN) 130) [2002 –, a51: f12s f9.4g⁴ f7g³ f8g² f7g² f6g² f7g² f7g² f6g² f5g⁵ f5g f7f⁶ 6.1m 6f 8.3v f8g f6g⁵ Dec 27] smallish gelding: has a round action: modest maiden handicapper: very best form at 6f to 1m: acts on firm going and fibresand: often blinkered/visored: tried tongue tied: usually races up with pace. *S. R. Bowring* **50 a56**

TEG   4 b.f. Petong 126 – Felinwen (White Mill 76) [2002 –: 10g 10d 7.1m 7f Sep 21] fifth foal: half-sister to 2 winners, including 2m winner Brynkir (by Batshoof): dam unraced: well held in maidens/handicap. *I. A. Wood* —

T E LAWRENCE (USA)   2 b.c. (Apr 7) Charnwood Forest (IRE) 125 – Only Gossip (USA) (Trempolino (USA) 135) [2002 6m⁴ 6g⁵ 6m* 6m⁴ 7d 6f 8s* Dec 18] 14,000Y: sturdy colt: fifth foal: brother to a winner in Greece and half-brother to 3 winners, including useful performer up to 2m/smart hurdler Montalcino (by Robellino): dam French 1½m winner: fairly useful performer: won maiden at Brighton (made all) in July and minor event at Naples (by 6½ lengths) in December: twice ran as though something badly amiss in between, leaving R. Hannon before final outing: stays 1m: acts on soft and good to firm going. *O. Pessi, Italy* **88**

TELEGRAM GIRL 3 b.f. Magic Ring (IRE) 115 – Lucky Message (USA) 71 (Phone Trick (USA)) [2002 –, a68: f7g² p7g 7g p8g p7g f7g f7g⁵ f7g f8.5g⁴ Dec 20] close-coupled filly: fair handicapper: below form after reappearance: stays 1m: acts on all-weather, little form on turf: often blinkered/visored. *D. Haydn Jones* **– a68 d**

TELEMACHUS 2 b.c. (Apr 18) Bishop of Cashel 122 – Indian Imp (Indian Ridge 123) [2002 7d⁶ 7.2s⁴ 6s² 7f 7s Oct 25] 10,500F, 37,000 2-y-o: close-coupled colt: first living foal: dam unraced half-sister to very smart 1½m/1¾m performer Mons and smart 1½m performer Inforapenny: fairly useful maiden: best effort when beaten head by Hector's Girl at Lingfield: will stay at least 1m: acts on soft ground. *J. G. Given* **83**

TELEPATHIC (IRE) 2 b.g. (Apr 5) Mind Games 121 – Madrina 70 (Waajib 121) [2002 5.1f 5m² 5m* 6f Oct 12] IR 22,000F, 26,000Y: big, good-bodied gelding: brother to 3-y-o Joyce's Choice and half-brother to 4-y-o Laurel Dawn: dam, 6f winner, out of half-sister to very smart sprinter Bolshoi: fairly useful form: won maiden at Pontefract in September easily by 5 lengths from Gentle Response: last in listed event at York final start (gelded after): will prove best at 5f/6f: raced only on ground firmer than good: gave impression something amiss on debut. *A. Berry* **85**

TELESTO (USA) 3 b.c. Mr Prospector (USA) – Aviance 112 (Northfields (USA)) [2002 84p: 6.1d² 5d⁴ 6s* 7m 6g⁶ a7s 8.5f Nov 9] rangy colt: fairly useful performer: won 4-runner minor event at Kempton in June: left Sir Michael Stoute after fifth outing: should stay 7f: acts on good going. *R. J. Frankel, USA* **88**

TELL HER OFF 2 b.f. (Jan 15) Reprimand 122 – My Valentina 84 (Royal Academy (USA) 130) [2002 7f 6g f8.5g Nov 18] 800Y: has a markedly round action: second foal: dam, 2-y-o 5f winner who stayed 1¼m, half-sister to smart sprinter Averti: well held in maidens/sales race. *Mrs C. A. Dunnett* **–**

TELLION 8 b.g. Mystiko (USA) 124 – Salchow 116 (Niniski (USA) 125) [2002 –: f16g³ f14.8g⁵ f16g³ Jun 19] poor maiden: stays 2m: acts on soft going, good to firm and fibresand: sometimes visored: ungenuine. *J. R. Jenkins* **46 §**

TELORI 4 ch.f. Muhtarram (USA) 125 – Elita (Sharpo 132) [2002 53: f7s⁵ f7g² 7s⁵ p7g³ 6f f7g 7f* 6.1m 7m 6g 7m* 7.5m⁶ 7m 7g* 7f* f7g⁵ 7g 7g⁵ p7g⁵ p7g⁵ f7g f6g f7g* Dec 17] lengthy filly: fair performer: left S. Williams after reappearance: won maiden (apprentices) at Catterick in June and handicaps at Lingfield in August, Leicester and Catterick in September and Southwell in December: stays 7f: acts on all-weather, firm and soft ground: edgy sort: races prominently: none too consistent. *I. A. Wood* **72 a65**

TEMERAIRE (USA) 7 b.g. Dayjur (USA) 137 – Key Dancer (NZ) (Nijinsky (CAN) 138) [2002 –, a90: 5g 6.3d 7g f7g³ 7s 6g⁵ 7m 6m⁴ 7f³ 8g Oct 5] strong, quite good-topped gelding: fair performer nowadays: effective at 6f, barely stays 1¼m: acts on fibresand, good to firm and good to soft going: visored twice at 4 yrs, blinkered eighth start. *P. Mooney, Ireland* **73 a75**

TEMERITAS (IRE) 2 b.c. (Apr 1) Tamarisk (IRE) 127 – Lear's Crown (USA) 82 (Lear Fan (USA) 130) [2002 7f³ 7m* Oct 2] angular colt: first foal: dam, 1½m winner, granddaughter of US Grade 1 8.5f winner Fabulous Notion: fairly useful form: justified favouritism in maiden at Newcastle by ¾ length from Able Mind, always close up: will probably stay 1m: sold 63,000 gns, sent to USA. *R. Charlton* **80**

TEMPER TANTRUM 4 b.g. Pursuit of Love 124 – Queenbird 90 (Warning 136) [2002 –: 8g f8g⁶ 8.3m⁴ f7g⁵ 7g³ 7f 6g² 6m 6m⁴ 6m f6s³ f6g f7g f6g⁵ f6g Dec 10] modest handicapper: effective at 6f to 1m: acts on fibresand and good to firm ground: tried visored/tongue tied: has worn cheekpieces. *Andrew Reid* **59 a64**

TEMPLEDALE 2 b.c. (Apr 19) Robellino (USA) 127 – Temple Fortune (USA) 74 (Ziggy's Boy (USA)) [2002 7.6m Aug 21] fourth foal: half-brother to 3 winners, including 5-y-o Hidden Fort: dam, 5f/6f winner, sister to useful performer at 7f/1m Zigaura: 25/1, tailed off in maiden at Lingfield. *J. W. Hills* **–**

TEMPLE OF ARTEMIS 3 b.c. Spinning World (USA) 130 – Casessa (USA) (Caro 133) [2002 95: 9m 12g 10.5g 12m 8s⁶ Jul 13] 75,000F, IR 140,000Y: good-topped colt: has a fluent, rounded action: half-brother to several winners including 1½m winner Smart Play (by Sovereign Dancer) and 7.5f (at 2 yrs) to 9.4f winner New Century (by Manila), both useful: dam maiden half-sister to 1000 Guineas winner Musical Bliss: fairly useful performer at best: easy winner of maiden at Tipperary in 2001: finished last all starts in listed/pattern company in 2002, acting as pacemaker last 4: will prove best up to 1¼m: acts on heavy going. *A. P. O'Brien, Ireland* **–**

TEMPLES TIME (IRE) 4 b.f. Distinctly North (USA) 115 – Midnight Patrol (Ashmore (FR) 125) [2002 63d: f11s⁵ f11s² f12g f9.4g⁴ f12g* Feb 28] angular filly: modest **52**

performer: won seller at Southwell in February: stays 1½m: acts on fibresand, soft and good to firm ground. *R. Brotherton*

TEMPSFORD (USA) 2 b.c. (Mar 21) Bering 136 – Nadra (IRE) 61 (Sadler's Wells (USA) 132) [2002 p7g p7g 8.2v Oct 29] 100,000Y: fifth foal: brother to useful French 6f (at 2 yrs) to 11f winner Ardent Passion: dam, maiden, out of Yorkshire Oaks and Prix Vermeille winner Bint Pasha: signs of ability in maidens: slowly away first 2 starts: should do better at 1¼m+. *Sir Mark Prescott* **– p**

TEMPTING FATE (IRE) 4 b.f. Persian Bold 123 – West of Eden (Crofter (USA) 124) [2002 113: 7g* 7d² May 30] strong, close-coupled filly: smart performer: won listed race at Lingfield in May by length from Marika: creditable short-head second to Frenchmans Bay in Prix du Palais-Royal at Longchamp only subsequent outing, rallying gamely: was best at 7f/1m: acted on firm and soft going: had had tongue tied/worn crossed noseband: usually made running: visits Elusive Quality. *Saeed bin Suroor* **113**

TEMPTING TILLY (IRE) 3 b.f. Namaqualand (USA) – Go Tally-Ho 66 (Gorytus (USA) 132) [2002 f8g 8.2d 9.9g 12.1s 10m 7f Sep 21] 5,500Y: unfurnished filly: sixth foal: half-sister to winner in Greece by Superpower: dam, 2-y-o 5f winner, also won over hurdles: well held in maidens/handicaps, leaving Mrs N. Macauley after third outing: blinkered after. *C. J. Teague* **–**

TENAJA TRAIL (USA) 3 ch.g. Irish River (FR) 131 – Buckeye Gal (USA) (Good Counsel (USA)) [2002 –p: 10.1m² 10.4m* 12f* Dec 4] big, rangy gelding: has plenty of scope: fairly useful form, lightly raced: won maiden at York in September by 1¾ lengths from Flotta, despite idling, and, having left W. Haggas, allowance race at Hollywood (dead-heated) in December: stays 1½m: acts on firm going: raced freely on reappearance, wore crossed noseband at York: likely to improve further. *S. W. Young, USA* **88 p**

TEN CARAT 2 b.c. (Mar 19) Grand Lodge (USA) 125 – Emerald (USA) (El Gran Senor (USA) 136) [2002 8s Oct 26] good-bodied colt: half-brother to several winners, including useful 1¼m winner Green Ideal (by Mark of Esteem) and fairly useful 11.5f winner Pendant (by Warning): dam unraced close relation to Danehill: 7/1 and backward, well-held ninth of 16 to Zeis in maiden at Newbury: likely to do better. *Mrs A. J. Perrett* **– p**

TENDER FALCON 2 br.g. (Feb 17) Polar Falcon (USA) 126 – Tendresse (IRE) 60 (Tender King 123) [2002 5m⁶ 7.1d³ 6m 7.1m⁶ 8f Sep 17] tall, good-topped gelding: has scope: third foal: dam 6f (at 2 yrs) to 1¼m winner: modest maiden: should stay 1m: acts on good to firm and good to soft going. *R. J. Hodges* **62**

TENDERFOOT 4 b.f. Be My Chief (USA) 122 – Kelimutu 58 (Top Ville 129) [2002 61: 15.4m⁴ 11.9g 14.1f 12d Jul 4] sturdy, deep-girthed filly: modest handicapper at 3 yrs: well held in 2002: blinkered last 2 starts. *R. F. Johnson Houghton* **–**

TENDER (IRE) 2 b.f. (Mar 6) Zieten (USA) 118 – Jayess Elle 55 (Sabrehill (USA) 120) [2002 5m⁵ 5m⁴ p5g* p5g* 5d⁴ 5.1m* 5f² p5g⁵ Oct 31] IR 12,000Y: angular filly: first foal: dam maiden half-sister to useful 7f to 9f performer Supercal: fair performer: won maiden at Lingfield in July and nursery at Chester in August: ran creditably last 2 starts: should stay 6f: acts on polytrack, firm and good to soft going. *D. J. S. Cosgrove* **76 a71**

TENDER TRAP (IRE) 4 b.c. Sadler's Wells (USA) 132 – Shamiyda (USA) 83 (Sir Ivor 135) [2002 80: f12s* p16g* f16g² 16g* 16m* 18.7f May 8] useful-looking colt: useful performer: won maiden at Southwell in January and handicaps at Lingfield in February, Kempton (Queen's Prize, by neck from Tees Components) in March and Newbury (beat Prairie Falcon 2 lengths) in April: joint favourite, never-dangerous tenth in Chester Cup final outing: stays 2m: acts on all-weather, soft and good to firm going: has carried head high/looked none too keen. *T. G. Mills* **102**

TENDULKAR (USA) 3 b.c. Spinning World (USA) 130 – Romanette (USA) (Alleged (USA) 138) [2002 112p: 8m 6s² May 25] rather leggy colt: smart at 2 yrs, winning maiden at the Curragh (reportedly fractured pelvis after) then strong-finishing third in Dewhurst Stakes at Newmarket over 5 months later: in rear in 2000 Guineas at Newmarket on reappearance in May (reportedly stiff afterwards): back to form when 3 lengths second to Tiger Royal in Greenlands Stakes at the Curragh later in month, taking most of race to get going: stayed 7f: acted on soft going: to stand at Oaklands Stud, Athboy, Co Meath, Ireland, fee €3,500, Oct 1st. *A. P. O'Brien, Ireland* **113**

TEN PAST SIX 10 ch.g. Kris 135 – Tashinsky (USA) (Nijinsky (CAN) 138) [2002 –: f12g f12g f12g f12g⁶ 11.8s⁴ 14.1d Apr 1] lengthy, good-quartered gelding: one-time fairly useful winner: little form in 2002: usually blinkered/visored. *M. J. Polglase* **?**

TENPENCE 2 b.f. (Apr 24) Bob Back (USA) 124 – Tiempo 50 (King of Spain 121) [2002 8g 7d Nov 2] leggy filly: seventh foal: sister to fairly useful 1997 2-y-o 1m winner **60**

Ten Bob and half-sister to a winner in Denmark by Idris: dam, sprint maiden, half-sister to smart sprinter Grey Desire: modest form, though well held, in maidens at Newmarket. *M. H. Tompkins*

TEOFILIO (IRE) 8 ch.h. Night Shift (USA) – Rivoltade (USA) (Sir Ivor 135) [2002 70: 7g⁶ 7.1g² 7d* 7m* 7m 7d⁶ 8m⁴ 8m 8g 7m 7.6s⁶ 7.1g 7d Oct 30] good-topped horse: fairly useful handicapper: won at Brighton and Newmarket in June: effective at 7f to easy 8.5f. acts on fibresand, firm and soft going: blinkered: tried tongue tied earlier in career: sometimes hangs/finds little: best held up. *Andrew Reid* **82**

TE QUIERO 4 gr.g. Bering 136 – Ma Lumiere (FR) (Niniski (USA) 125) [2002 66: 8m 10m 10m f8.5g* p8g f9.4s* f9.4g* Dec 14] fairly useful handicapper on all-weather: much improved to win at Wolverhampton in October and twice there in December: best form at 1m to 9.4f: acts on fibresand, no form on turf in 2002: reportedly pulled muscle leaving stall fifth start: front runner. *Miss Gay Kelleway* **– a91**

TERFEL 3 ch.g. Lion Cavern (USA) 117 – Montserrat 81 (Aragon 118) [2002 91: 8g 7m² 8g³ 7s² 8d³ Jul 5] quite attractive gelding: useful performer: placed in minor events at Newmarket, Thirsk and Salisbury and listed race at Epsom (2½ lengths second to Red Liason on fourth start): effective at 7f/1m: acts on soft and good to firm going: gelded after final outing. *M. L. W. Bell* **97**

TERIMON'S DREAM 5 gr.g. Terimon 124 – I Have A Dream (SWE) (Mango Express 106) [2002 10g 10m 7d May 29] tall, workmanlike gelding: lightly-raced maiden. *A. W. Carroll* **–**

TERN INTERN (IRE) 3 b. or br.g. Dr Devious (IRE) 127 – Arctic Bird (USA) (Storm Bird (CAN) 134) [2002 60: 7m 5.9s 6m 8f⁶ 8m Sep 19] workmanlike gelding: modest maiden at 2 yrs: little form in 2002: seems to stay 1m: blinkered last 2 starts (pulled hard first occasion). *Miss J. Feilden* **–**

TERRAPIN (IRE) 3 b.f. Turtle Island (IRE) 123 – Lady Taufan (IRE) (Taufan (USA) 119) [2002 53: 9.2s 11.9m f12s 10.4f Oct 10] unfurnished filly: little form since debut: tried blinkered/tongue tied. *Mrs A. Duffield* **–**

TERRAQUIN (IRE) 2 b.c. (Apr 23) Turtle Island (IRE) 123 – Play The Queen (IRE) (King of Clubs 124) [2002 7m 7m³ 7d Nov 2] 18,000Y: good-bodied colt: half-brother to several winners, including 8-y-o Salty Jack and 1998 2-y-o 5f winner Franco Mina (by Lahib), both fairly useful: dam, Irish 7f winner, out of Coronation Stakes winner Orchestration: clearly best effort in maidens (fair form) when third to Shuhood at Yarmouth, making most: will probably stay 1m. *J. A. R. Toller* **76**

TERRE A TERRE (FR) 5 b.m. Kaldounevees (FR) 118 – Toujours Juste (FR) (Always Fair (USA) 121) [2002 119: 8.9g* Mar 23] smallish, lengthy mare: very smart performer: won Prix de l'Opera at Longchamp at 4 yrs: at least as good as ever when **120**

Dubai Duty Free, Nad Al Sheba—Terre A Terre accounts for a strong field in a race upgraded to Group 1; Noverre is her nearest pursuer

winning Dubai Duty Free at Nad Al Sheba only outing in 2002 by ¾ length from Noverre, going on under 2f out: stayed 1¼m: acted on heavy and good to firm going: genuine: stud. *E. Libaud, France*

TERTULLIAN (IRE) 3 b.c. Petorius 117 – Fiddes (IRE) 52 (Alzao (USA) 117) [2002 **92** 77: 9m* 11m 9.9m⁴ 10m² 9.9m² 10f⁴ 10m 10.3m² 12f 10d Oct 14] sturdy, good-bodied colt: fairly useful handicapper: won at Kempton in May: good second on 3 occasions after: stays 1¼m: acts on good to firm and good to soft going, well held on heavy: sold 45,000 gns, joined S. Dow. *R. Hannon*

TESIO 4 b.c. Danehill (USA) 126 – Pale Grey (Linamix (FR) 127) [2002 97: f6g² f6g **92** 5.2g 5.1f⁵ May 9] 250,000F, 400,000Y: good-topped colt: first foal: dam, placed once in **a105** France, half-sister to useful French 1¼m/1½m winner Danefair, useful French winner up to 1¼m Prove (both by Danehill) and smart French performer up to 15.5f Erudite: useful performer on all-weather, fairly useful on turf: unraced at 2 yrs: won minor event at Navan at 3 yrs for A. O'Brien: very good second to Peruvian Chief in handicap at Wolverhampton in February: creditable effort in similar event at Chester final outing: stays 6f: acts on soft ground, firm and fibresand: flashed tail first 2 starts. *P. J. Hobbs*

TESTAMENT 2 b.f. (Apr 10) Darshaan 133 – Blessed Event 117 (Kings Lake (USA) **– p** 133) [2002 7d⁵ Oct 15] quite good-topped filly: closely related to smart middle-distance stayer Sacrament and useful 1¼m winner Auspicious (both by Shirley Heights) and half-sister to several winners: dam, 1¼m winner, second in Yorkshire Oaks: 15/2, slowly away and soon off bridle when tailed-off last of 5 in minor event at Leicester: should improve. *Sir Michael Stoute*

TEST THE WATER (IRE) 8 ch.g. Maelstrom Lake 118 – Baliana (CAN) (Riverman **50 §** (USA) 131) [2002 57, a43: f11g 8d² 8g 8.1d⁵ 10s Aug 10] dipped-backed gelding: poor **a– §** walker/mover: modest performer: stays 1¼m: acts on fibresand, raced mainly on good going or softer on turf nowadays: tried visored, usually blinkered nowadays: ungenuine. *P. Howling*

TETRAGON (IRE) 2 b.g. (Mar 10) Octagonal (NZ) 126 – Viva Verdi (IRE) 70 **60 d** (Green Desert (USA) 127) [2002 7.1d⁵ 7.1d³ 7g⁶ 7m 8g 8m⁶ f8s⁶ Oct 8] 8,000 2-y-o: good-topped gelding: second foal: dam, 1m winner, half-sister to smart performer up to 1½m in Germany/Australasia Vialli: modest maiden: best efforts first 2 starts: should stay at least 1m: acts on good to soft ground: sometimes finds little. *K. R. Burke*

TEXAS GOLD 4 ch.g. Cadeaux Genereux 131 – Star Tulip 99 (Night Shift (USA)) **83** [2002 48+: p6g² p5g² p5g* p5g* p5g² 6g 5g 5.7d³ p5g* 5g⁵ 5m³ 5g³ 5.2m* 5m* 5.2m⁴ 5.1f⁴ 5g² 5g Oct 28] sturdy, close-coupled gelding: fairly useful performer: progressed well in 2002, winning maiden at Lingfield and handicaps there (2), Newbury and New-market between February/August: best at 5f: acts on polytrack (well beaten on fibresand), firm and good to soft going: tough and consistent. *W. R. Muir*

TEXAS HILL (USA) 2 b.c. (Apr 28) Danehill (USA) 126 – Chalamont (IRE) 88 **88 p** (Kris 135) [2002 7f³ p7g* Oct 9] rather lengthy colt: third foal: brother to 3-y-o Secret Garden: dam, 2-y-o 6f winner, half-sister to Gold Cup winner Gildoran out of Cheveley Park winner Durtal, herself half-sister to Arc winner Detroit: justified favouritism in maiden at Lingfield by 1½ lengths from Desert View, always well placed: subsequently sold privately: will probably stay 1m: useful prospect. *J. H. M. Gosden*

TEYAAR 6 b.g. Polar Falcon (USA) 126 – Music In My Life (IRE) 59 (Law Society **62** (USA) 130) [2002 84d: f6s f6s f6s f6g⁵ p6g⁴ f5g p6g* p5g³ p6g² 6m 5g 5g 5d 6g f6g f5g² **a80** f6g⁶ f5f⁶ Nov 29] strong gelding: fairly useful handicapper on all-weather, modest on turf: won at Lingfield in March: effective at 5f/6f: acts on heavy going and all-weather, below form on good/good to firm since debut: tried blinkered earlier in career: has hung: effective making running or held up. *D. Shaw*

THAAYER 7 b.g. Wolfhound (USA) 126 – Hamaya (USA) 60 (Mr Prospector (USA)) **54** [2002 –, a84: f6s³ f7s² f7g³ f6s f6g² f7g f7g² 6m 6.1m 7d 5d f6g p7g p7g f6s Dec 26] **a81 d** fairly useful handicapper at best on all-weather, lightly raced and modest on turf: effective at 6f/7f: acts on fibresand: blinkered (no show) once: on downgrade. *I. A. Wood*

THAI PRINCESS (IRE) 3 b.f. Hamas (IRE) 125§ – Darayna (IRE) (Shernazar 131) **72** [2002 79: 6.5v 9s³ 7g 13.5g 8s Oct 28] IR 18,000Y: ex-Irish filly: sixth foal: closely related to smart 1m winner Dear Daughter (by Polish Precedent) and half-sister to winners abroad by Caerleon and Suave Dancer: dam Irish 7f/1m winner out of very smart 6f/7f performer Dafayna, herself half-sister to Doyoun: fair maiden: form in 2002 only in minor event at Fairyhouse second start: left M. Cunningham prior to in rear in handicap on British debut: stays 9f: acts on soft and good to firm ground. *J. Mackie*

THANKS MAX (IRE) 4 b.g. Goldmark (USA) 113 – Almost A Lady (IRE) 70 **65 d**
(Entitled 126) [2002 72: 5g 6s 6g 7.2g⁵ 7g 7.2v 6s⁴ 7.9m⁴ 8.3g⁴ 8d⁴ 7m 8g 9m⁶ 9.1g 9.1s
Oct 15] strong gelding: fair performer: well below form last 5 outings: stays easy 1m:
acts on fibresand, firm and soft going (seemingly not on heavy): blinkered last 3 starts:
reportedly had breathing problem on reappearance: led to post/tended to hang/carried
head awkwardly seventh outing. *Miss L. A. Perratt*

THAQIB (IRE) 3 b.c. Sadler's Wells (USA) 132 – Temple (Shirley Heights 130) **91**
[2002 71p: 8s² 8g² 8.5m² 8.2g* 9m² 8g 10.3s Oct 25] good-bodied colt: fairly useful
performer: won maiden at Nottingham in May despite hanging under pressure: good
efforts in handicaps next 2 starts: folded tamely final outing: should be suited by 1¼m+:
acts on soft and good to firm going: joined P. Rudkin in UAE. *J. L. Dunlop*

THATCHED (IRE) 12 b.g. Thatching 131 – Shadia (USA) 53 (Naskra (USA)) [2002 **–**
47+: 8m 12f Jul 17] leggy gelding: probably of little account nowadays. *R. E. Barr*

THAT MAN AGAIN 10 ch.g. Prince Sabo 123 – Milne's Way 83 (The Noble Player **– §**
(USA) 126) [2002 75§: p5g f5g 5f 6m p6g 5m p5g 5d 5.1f 5m 5f 5m 6m⁶ Sep 19]
robust gelding: one-time useful sprinter: blinkered/visored: best left alone nowadays.
S. C. Williams

THATS ALL JAZZ 4 b.f. Prince Sabo 123 – Gate of Heaven 43 (Starry Night (USA)) **52 §**
[2002 58§, a51§: p8g f8s f7g 7s⁴ 8m 7f 6d² 6d³ 8.5g 6g 6g⁴ f6g 9m 7g 7d⁶ 6m 7.5m 8f **a49 §**
p7g³ 7s Oct 28] workmanlike filly: modest handicapper: left I. Wood after third start,
R. C. Spicer after seventh: effective at 6f, probably at easy 1m: acts on soft going, good to
firm and polytrack, seemingly not on fibresand: tried visored: unreliable. *C. R. Dore*

THATS ENOUGH 2 b.c. (Apr 12) Robellino (USA) 127 – Sea Fairy 64 (Wollow **72**
132) [2002 5s⁴ 6m² p6g Jul 10] half-brother to several winners, including fairly useful 5f
(at 2 yrs) and 5.7f winner Ones Enough (by Reprimand): dam, 2-y-o 6f winner, later
successful in Spain: fair maiden: ¾-length second of 22 to Puma at Windsor: stays 6f:
well held on polytrack. *T. G. Mills*

THAW 3 ch.f. Cadeaux Genereux 131 – Ice House 89 (Northfields (USA)) [2002 7s³ **69**
7.1m⁴ 7s² 7g 7v f7g Nov 22] 750,000 francs Y: angular filly: half-sister to several
winners, including 5-y-o Takrir and 1½m/1¾m winner Bathe In Light (by Sunshine
Forever): dam, 2-y-o 1m winner, sister to smart 1½m winner Open Day): fair maiden:
well below form last 3 starts: races freely, but should stay 1m: best efforts on soft going.
R. Charlton

THE ANGEL GABRIEL 7 ch.g. My Generation 111 – Minsk 36 (Kabour 80) [2002 **–**
5m 6.9d 5m 5g Sep 9] no form. *D. A. Nolan*

THEA'S LASS (IRE) 3 b.f. Barathea (IRE) 127 – Castlerahan (IRE) (Thatching 131) **–**
[2002 7m 8.3m 8.2d 10g 12m Jul 1] 13,500Y: third foal: dam unraced out of half-sister to
smart 7f/1m performer Hadeer: little form. *J. M. Bradley*

THEATRE LADY (IRE) 4 b.f. King's Theatre (IRE) 128 – Littlepace (Indian King **50**
(USA) 128) [2002 68d, a–: 8.3g 10m 8d⁶ 8g 8f⁴ 8m⁴ 8.1d 7m² 8m⁴ 8m² 8.3s² 7f 8.3m² **a–**
Sep 30] sturdy filly: modest maiden handicapper: stays 9f: acts on any turf ground, well
held on fibresand: tried visored: sometimes finds little. *P. D. Evans*

THEATRE OF LIFE (IRE) 3 b.g. King's Theatre (IRE) 128 – Miss Ironwood **42**
(Junius (USA) 124) [2002 55: 8g 10d 11.6m 11.6m 11.9m 10d Oct 28] smallish gelding:
poor maiden: tried blinkered. *G. L. Moore*

THEATRE TIME 2 b.c. (Jan 22) Theatrical 128 – Kyka (USA) (Blushing **85**
John (USA) 120) [2002 7m⁵ 8.5d² 7.1f² Sep 28] 80,000F, 70,000Y: big, lengthy colt:
second foal: dam unraced half-sister to Poule d'Essai des Pouliches winner Madeleine's
Dream (by Theatrical): fairly useful form in listed race at Newbury (fifth of 6 to Muqbil)
and maidens at Epsom and Haydock (beaten 1½ lengths by Crystal Star, pair clear):
free-going sort, likely to prove best around 1m. *B. W. Hills*

THEATRE TINKA (IRE) 3 b.g. King's Theatre (IRE) 128 – Orange Grouse (IRE) **84**
105 (Taufan (USA) 119) [2002 7.5g 8m⁶ 10.4m³ 12d* Nov 5] IR 15,000Y: close-coupled
gelding: first foal: dam Irish 6f/7f winner: fairly useful performer: clearly best effort
when winning maiden at Catterick in November by 1½ lengths from Daliyana: stays
1½m: acts on good to soft ground. *R. Hollinshead*

THEATRE (USA) 3 b.g. Theatrical 128 – Fasta (USA) (Seattle Song (USA) 130) **82**
[2002 8m⁵ 8.1d p12g³ 14.1f² p13g² p12g p12g* Dec 14] $180,000Y: first foal: dam, 1m/
9f winner in US and second in Grade 3 8.5f event, sister to very smart Prix Lupin winner
Cudas: fairly useful performer: left Sir Michael Stoute after debut: left G. Butler 12,000

gns and off 2 months before winning maiden at Lingfield in December: stays 1¾m: acts on firm going and polytrack: blinkered (best efforts) third/fourth starts. *Jamie Poulton*

THEBAN (IRE)   4 b.g. Inzar (USA) 112 – Phoenix Forli (USA) (Forli (ARG)) [2002 –: f8s 8g 8g 10f 8.3m Sep 30] sturdy gelding: modest maiden in 2000: well held in 2002, leaving D. Nicholls after reappearance. *Mrs A. M. Naughton*   –

THE BARONESS (IRE)   2 b.f. (Mar 22) Blues Traveller (IRE) 119 – Wicken Wonder (IRE) 71 (Distant Relative 128) [2002 7d 7.1m Jul 20] 7,000Y: fourth foal: half-sister to 5-y-o Kathology: dam 2-y-o 6f winner: well held in maidens. *S. C. Williams*   –

THE BEDUTH NAVI   2 b.c. (Apr 30) Forzando 122 – Sweets (IRE) (Persian Heights 129) [2002 6.1g Jul 26] 5,000Y: third foal: dam, second from 2 starts in bumpers, half-sister to useful performer up to 2m Rum Pointer: 40/1, well beaten in maiden at Chepstow. *D. G. Bridgwater*   –

THE BEST YET   4 ch.c. King's Signet (USA) 110 – Miss Klew (Never So Bold 135) [2002 –: p7g* f7g² f7g² 6m³ 7.1m f6g 5.7f* f6s* Dec 26] fair handicapper: won at Lingfield in January, Bath in September and Wolverhampton (amateurs) in December: stays easy 7f: acts on all-weather and firm ground: tends to pull hard: carries head awkwardly. *A. G. Newcombe*   67

THE BOLTER   3 b.g. Puissance 110 – Miami Dolphin 85 (Derrylin 115) [2002 67: 6f⁶ 7.1m⁶ 7.2g⁴ 8.1d⁴ 8s² 9.1s Oct 15] lengthy gelding: poor mover: modest maiden: stays 1m: acts on soft and good to firm ground. *D. Moffatt*   61

THE BONUS KING   2 b.c. (Feb 21) Royal Applause 124 – Selvi (Mummy's Pet 125) [2002 5g² 5d* 6d* 5m² 6g³ 6m⁵ Jul 30] 75,000Y: angular, good-topped colt: has a fluent action: half-brother to several winners, notably smart 5f/6f winner (including Mill Reef Stakes at 2 yrs) Indian Rocket (by Indian Ridge): dam, maiden, best at 6f: useful performer: won maiden at Ripon in May and listed race at Epsom (beat Monsieur Boulanger by ½ length) in June: good efforts after when head second to Baron's Pit in Norfolk Stakes at Royal Ascot and 1¼ lengths third to Mister Links in July Stakes at Newmarket: forced strong pace when only sixth (promoted to fifth) in Richmond Stakes at Goodwood: will prove best at 5f/6f: yet to race on extremes of ground: races up with pace: game. *M. Johnston*   106

THE BROKER (IRE)   4 b.g. Rainbows For Life (CAN) – Roberts Pride 62 (Roberto (USA) 131) [2002 –: p12g 15.4m Jul 29] lightly raced and no form. *M. Blanshard*   –

THE BULL MACABE   5 ch.h. Efisio 120 – Tranquillity 70 (Night Shift (USA)) [2002 69: f5g f5g⁴ f5g f5g⁴ a6g a2g² 3.5g⁴ a5.5g Oct 3] just modest form in 2002: sold from A. Reid 3,500 gns after fourth start: best at up to 6f: acts on fibresand/dirt: usually tongue tied. *Katharina Stenefeldt, Sweden*   57

Vodafone Woodcote Stakes, Epsom—The Bonus King is all out to hold Monsieur Boulanger

THE BUTTERWICK KID   9 ch.g. Interrex (CAN) – Ville Air 85 (Town Crier 119)   **80**
[2002 81: f16s f12g 12s 13g² 14d³ 12m Jun 1] workmanlike gelding: winning hurdler
(has shown signs of temperament)/chaser: fairly useful handicapper on Flat: effective at
11f (given good test) to 2½m: acts on fibresand and any turf going: usually blinkered/
visored: best held up: sold 11,000 gns, joined Richard Tate. *R. A. Fahey*

THE CHAPLAIN (IRE)   3 ch.g. College Chapel 122 – Danzig Craft (IRE) (Roi Dan-   **53 d**
zig (USA)) [2002 71d: p5g⁴ p7g 6m 5m 5d 6m 5m 6m 5m Sep 14] compact gelding: fair
form on 2-y-o debut: disappointing since: blinkered last 2 starts. *P. Mitchell*

THE CHOCOLATIER (IRE)   4 b.f. Inzar (USA) 112 – Clover Honey (King of Clubs   **–**
124) [2002 80+, a74: 8.2m⁵ 10.3d 9.9m 10m 8m 7d f8g f12s⁶ Dec 7] close-coupled filly:
fair performer at 3 yrs: well held in 2002, leaving P. Gilligan after sixth start. *M. Wigham*

THE COPT   3 b.g. Charmer 123 – Coptic Dancer (Sayf El Arab (USA) 127) [2002 8m⁵   **63**
f8.5g⁶ 8g p10g 11.6d Oct 28] leggy gelding: first known foal: dam unraced: modest
maiden handicapper: pulled hard/folded tamely final start. *J. M. P. Eustace*

THE COUNT (FR)   3 b.g. Sillery (USA) 122 – Dear Countess (FR) (Fabulous Dancer   **56**
(USA) 124) [2002 64: f7g⁵ f6g³ f5g f6g 8g⁵ 10m³ 9.9m² 8g⁵ 8.2f² 11.6d⁵ p12g p10g
f7g 8.2m⁶ 7m⁵ 8f⁶ Oct 7] leggy gelding: modest maiden: left Mrs J. Ramsden after sixth
start, A. Reid after fifteenth one: rather headstrong, and barely stays 1¼m: acts on fibresand and firm going: sometimes been slowly away: tried blinkered: none too reliable.
F. P. Murtagh

THE DIDDY MAN (IRE)   2 b.c. (Feb 5) Night Shift (USA) – March Star (IRE) 109   **45**
(Mac's Imp (USA) 116) [2002 5.1d 5.1f 6m⁵ f6g² f5g⁴ 6g f8s Sep 5] 5,000Y: smallish,
heavy-topped colt: poor mover: first foal: dam 6f winner, including at 2 yrs: poor maiden:
stays 6f: acts on fibresand and good to firm ground: sold 500 gns. *B. A. McMahon*

THE DOLPHIN (IRE)   3 b.f. Dolphin Street (FR) 125 – Saintly Guest (What A   **53**
Guest 119) [2002 –: 8.3d 9.3s⁵ 8g³ 8.1d³ f8.5g 7g 8.1d⁵ 7m⁴ 8m⁴ Sep 3] angular filly:
modest maiden: best at 7f/1m: acts on good to firm and good to soft going, well held
only start on fibresand: blinkered last 3 outings: races prominently: sold 2,300 gns.
J. G. Portman

THE FISIO   2 b.g. (Apr 11) Efisio 120 – Misellina (FR) 57 (Polish Precedent (USA)   **81**
131) [2002 5g⁶ 5s* 5.1d³ 5m* 6m⁶ 5.1d⁴ 6d p6g² f5g* p5g³ Dec 18] 11,000F, 16,000Y: **a90**
second foal: brother to 3-y-o Cast Iron: dam, temperamental maiden, stayed 1m: fairly
useful performer: won maiden at Carlisle in May, minor event at Windsor in June and
nursery at Southwell in December: will prove best at 5f/6f: acts on all-weather, good to
firm and good to soft ground: ran poorly only try in visor. *I. A. Balding*

THE FLYER (IRE)   5 b.g. Blues Traveller (IRE) 119 – National Ballet (Shareef Dan-   **–**
cer (USA) 135) [2002 –: f16g5 Feb 5] leggy, unfurnished gelding: formerly fair maiden:
well beaten both starts since 2000: tried blinkered: fair hurdler. *Miss S. J. Wilton*

THE GAIKWAR (IRE)   3 b.c. Indian Ridge 123 – Broadmara (IRE) 91 (Thatching   **94**
131) [2002 –p: 8.1f* 8m* 8.1m³ 10f Oct 4] lengthy colt: has scope: fairly useful performer: won maiden at Warwick (reportedly bit jarred up) in April and handicap at
Newmarket (beat Able Baker Charlie by short head) in August: good third in handicap at
Sandown next time: not sure to stay further than 1m: raced only on good to firm/firm
going since debut. *Mrs A. J. Perrett*

THE GAMBLER   2 ch.c. (Apr 5) First Trump 118 – Future Options 71 (Lomond   **66**
(USA) 128) [2002 5m 5f⁴ 7.5g⁵ 6d⁴ 7d² f7f⁶ Nov 29] 3,500Y: good-bodied colt: fifth foal:
half-brother to a winner in Greece by Petong: dam maiden who stayed 1m: fair maiden:
second at Catterick: stays 7f: acts on good to soft ground: often races prominently.
Mrs A. Duffield

THE GAY FOX   8 gr.g. Never So Bold 135 – School Concert 80 (Music Boy 124)   **58**
[2002 65§: p6g⁶ f6g³ p6g² f6g³ p6g² p6g* p6g⁴ p6g² 6g³ 7g 7g* 7d³ p6g³ p6g⁶ 6g⁴ 6m⁵   **a64**
p6g 6g Aug 13] good-topped gelding: unimpressive mover: modest handicapper: won at
Lingfield (seller) in February and Jersey in May: stays 7f: acts on all-weather/any turf
going: has been visored, usually blinkered/tongue tied nowadays: often slowly away.
B. G. Powell

THE GENERALS LADY (IRE)   4 gr.f. General Monash (USA) 107 – Brooks Mas-   **–**
querade (Absalom 128) [2002 –: f7s f8g Feb 12] rather sparely-made filly: unimpressive
mover: well held in maidens/handicap: tried visored. *B. S. Rothwell*

THE GLEN   4 gr.g. Mtoto 134 – Silver Singer 65 (Pharly (FR) 130) [2002 91: 10.3f⁴   **90 §**
12m 8.9d⁵ 10m 9.9m⁶ 9.2m³ 10m* 10.4f⁴ Oct 11] leggy gelding: unimpressive mover:

fairly useful performer: won claimer at Leicester in September: best efforts at 1¼m/11f: acts on firm and good to soft going: sometimes edges left/finds little: not one to trust: sold 27,000 gns, joined M. Tompkins. *B. W. Hills*

THE GREAT GATSBY (IRE)   2 b.c. (Feb 26) Sadler's Wells (USA) 132 – Ionian   **105**
Sea (Slip Anchor 136) [2002 7g² 8.5d* 8d⁶ 8s⁴ 10v⁴ Nov 9] quite attractive colt: sixth foal: half-brother to several winners, including useful French 11f/12.5f winner who stayed 15f Ithaca (by Groom Dancer): dam, French 11.5f (listed race)/1½m winner, half-sister to Blue Stag and Oscar, second in Derby and Prix du Jockey Club respectively (both by Sadler's Wells): useful performer: won maiden at Galway in August: best efforts when 6 lengths fourth to Brian Boru in Racing Post Trophy at Doncaster (short of room, stayed on well) and 3¾ lengths fourth to Alberto Giacometti in Criterium de Saint-Cloud: will be well suited by 1½m+: raced only on good ground or softer. *A. P. O'Brien, Ireland*

THE GREEN GREY   8 gr.g. Environment Friend 128 – Pea Green 98 (Try My Best   **–**
(USA) 130) [2002 74, a92: p12g p12g⁴ Feb 27] big, workmanlike gelding: good mover: **a81**
fairly useful handicapper on all-weather, fair at best on turf: was best at 1½m/1¾m: acted on polytrack (unraced on fibresand), seemed unsuited by ground softer than good: visored once at 3 yrs: was sometimes slowly away: dead. *I. Montague Hall*

THE HUNTER (IRE)   3 b.c. Grand Lodge (USA) 125 – Ring Side (IRE) (Alzao   **70**
(USA) 117) [2002 61p: 8.2m⁴ 9.2m⁴ 7g² 7s Oct 22] small colt: poor mover: third foal: dam unraced: fair form in maidens: effective at 7f to 9f: sold 3,500 gns, sent to Kuwait. *G. C. Bravery*

THE JUDGE   4 b.g. Polish Precedent (USA) 131 – Just Speculation (IRE) 86 (Aho-   **90**
noora 122) [2002 94p: 8s 8g* 8.1d 8m May 6] useful-looking gelding: reportedly broke pelvis only 2-y-o start: fairly useful performer, lightly-raced: won Bet Direct Spring Cup at Newbury in April by head from Kareeb, enterprisingly ridden in steadily-run race: well held other starts in 2002: effective at 1m/9f: acts on good to firm and good to soft ground (possibly not on soft): usually races prominently. *P. F. I. Cole*

THE KIDDYKID (IRE)   2 b.g. (Mar 23) Danetime (IRE) 121 – Mezzanine (Sadler's   **91**
Wells (USA) 132) [2002 5.1f² 5.1g* 6g 5.1d² 5.1f³ 6m 6s⁵ Oct 26] 9,000Y: tall, lengthy gelding: has scope: first foal: dam unraced out of close relation to Prix du Jockey Club winner Natroun: fairly useful performer: won maiden at Nottingham in May: best efforts in minor event at Bath and Two-Year-Old Trophy at Redcar (eighth of 18 to Somnus) fifth/sixth starts: effective at 5f/6f: acts on firm and good to soft going: went freely to post (saddle slipped) third start. *P. D. Evans*

Bet Direct Spring Cup (Handicap), Newbury—The Judge comes off best in a close finish with Kareeb (noseband), Norton (No.6) and Wood Dalling

THE LADY WOULD (IRE)   3 ch.f. Woodborough (USA) 112 – Kealbra Lady **51** (Petong 126) [2002 38: 7s 6g 6m 5.3d 6.1m² 6m⁶ 6m f6g f5f Nov 29] modest maiden: **a–** stays 6f: acts on good to firm going, no form on fibresand: has worn cheekpieces. *D. G. Bridgwater*

THE LAST CAST   3 ch.g. Prince of Birds (USA) 121 – Atan's Gem (USA) (Sharpen **79** Up 127) [2002 83: 8.3m 7.1m 10s² 10m² 10d⁶ Jul 6] sturdy, close-coupled gelding: fair maiden handicapper on Flat: stays 1¼m, not sure to get further: unraced on firm going, acts on any other turf (well beaten only run on polytrack): won twice over hurdles late in year. *C. R. Egerton*

THE LAST MOHICAN   3 b.g. Common Grounds 118 – Arndilly 75 (Robellino **44** (USA) 127) [2002 59?: f8g⁵ f7g f6g 10m 12m⁴ f12g⁶ 16m 8m⁶ 10.9f³ 12m⁴ 11.6m⁵ 12.1g⁶ 11.5m 11.5s Oct 22] small, workmanlike gelding: bad mover: poor maiden: stays 1½m: acts on firm going. *P. Howling*

THE LEATHER WEDGE (IRE)   3 b.c. Hamas (IRE) 125§ – Wallflower (Polar **74 d** Falcon (USA) 126) [2002 80: 5.1f⁶ 5g⁶ 5g f5g² 6m⁶ 5m 6f Oct 8] tall, quite good-topped colt: fair performer: ran creditably in 2002 only in handicap on fourth start: last on all subsequent outings: best at 5f: acts on firm going, good to soft and fibresand. *A. Berry*

THE LINKS   3 b.g. Mind Games 121 – Zihuatanejo (Efisio 120) [2002 46: f6s f7g p8g **46** f6g 5d² 7f 6d 5s⁴ 6d⁵ 5f 6g⁴ f6g 8.2m 5m 5.9g 7m 6d 5.9g Aug 5] leggy gelding: poor **a–** maiden handicapper: stays 6f: acts on good to firm and good to soft going, well held on all-weather: nearly always blinkered: tongue tied once: sometimes starts slowly/finishes weakly. *D. W. Chapman*

THE LOCAL   2 b.g. (Mar 12) Selkirk (USA) 129 – Finger of Light 89 (Green Desert **78** (USA) 127) [2002 6d⁶ 7d* 7m 8.3d 8s Oct 7] fourth foal: half-brother to 2 winners abroad, including fairly useful Italian 5f/6f (both at 2 yrs)/7f winner Far Hope (by Barathea): dam 2-y-o 6f winner out of Lowther winner Circus Ring: fair performer: won maiden at Salisbury in July: failed to repeat the form in nurseries: should stay 1m: acts on good to soft going, possibly not good to firm: gelded after final start. *M. Blanshard*

THE LOOSE SCREW (IRE)   4 b.g. Bigstone (IRE) 126 – Princess of Dance (IRE) **–** (Dancing Dissident (USA) 119) [2002 52: f7g 10d 8f 7.9g 7.6f 6m 6d Oct 18] good-bodied gelding: maiden handicapper: left J. L. Eyre after second start: tried blinkered. *A. Berry*

THE LORD   2 b.c. (Mar 30) Averti (IRE) 117 – Lady Longmead (Crimson Beau 124) **104** [2002 5s* 5m³ 5.1f* 5m 5.1f* 6m 6s² 6v⁵ Nov 13] 14,500Y: well-grown, close-coupled colt: has a quick action: seventh foal: half-brother to useful 5f (at 2 yrs) and 9f (US Grade 3) winner Lord Smith (by Greensmith): dam winning selling hurdler: useful performer: won minor events at Doncaster in March and Chester in May and nursery at Chester (under 9-10) in July: best effort when second to Silca Boo in nursery at Newbury: effective at 5f/6f: acts on firm and soft ground: races prominently. *W. G. M. Turner*

THE MASK (FR)   6 ch.h. Saint Estephe (FR) 123 – Mare Aux Fees (Kenmare (FR) **111 ?** 125) [2002 10.8s⁵ 12.5d* 10.8s² a10g 8v⁶ 10.5s 12d² 11.5d* 10.6m 10m² 12m 10g Aug 15] leggy, plain horse: fourth foal: half-brother to 2 winners in Italy by Dancing Spree: dam French 10.5f winner out of half-sister to high-class French middle-distance stayer Soleil Noir: smart performer at best: won handicaps at Cagnes in January and at Angers in April: seemingly returned to pick of 3-y-o form (winner of listed race at Chantilly) when length second of 4 to Potemkin in Brigadier Gerard Stakes at Sandown tenth start, though missed trouble in running and possibly flattered: effective at 1¼m/1½m: acts on soft and good to firm going: sometimes carries head high. *A. Spanu, France*

THEME PARK   2 b.g. (Jan 30) Classic Cliche (IRE) 128 – Arcady 69 (Slip Anchor **77** 136) [2002 8.5d⁶ 10.2f³ Sep 30] first foal: dam, 13f to 2m winner, half-sister to 5-y-o Atavus: better effort in maidens (fair form) when third of 6 to La Mouline at Bath: will be suited by 1½m+. *H. Morrison*

THEME TIME (USA)   6 b.g. Stop The Music (USA) – Ranales (USA) (Majestic **43** Light (USA)) [2002 39: f8.5g f8s⁵ f7g⁶ f8g* f8g f9.4s 8m f8g⁶ 7g 10s f8g Dec 4] poor handicapper: won apprentice maiden event at Southwell in February despite wandering markedly: stays 1m: acts on fibresand, little form on turf: often tongue tied: none too consistent. *H. J. Collingridge*

THE MOG   3 b.g. Atraf 116 – Safe Secret 50 (Seclude (USA)) [2002 48, a58: f7s f7s² **49 §** f8s⁴ f7g⁶ f6g⁵ f7g⁵ f6g 6g 10m f12g 10g⁴ f7g² f8g Nov 20] close-coupled gelding: **a56 §** modest on all-weather, poor on turf: off 6 months after tenth start: effective at 6f/7f: acts on fibresand and firm going: often blinkered (including for only win)/tongue tied: carries head awkwardly: ungenuine. *S. R. Bowring*

THE OLD SOLDIER   4 b.g. Magic Ring (IRE) 115 – Grecian Belle 53 (Ilium 121)   **58**
[2002 54: 5m² 5m⁴ 6m⁵ Sep 19] tall gelding: modest maiden handicapper: should stay 7f: acts on good to firm going: edged persistently left final start. *A. Dickman*

THEORIST   2 b.c. (Mar 30) Machiavellian (USA) 123 – Clerio 108 (Soviet Star   **62**
(USA) 128) [2002 6m⁴ Jun 20] second foal: half-brother to French 1m winner Daisy Hill (by Indian Ridge): dam, French 1m/1¼m winner, half-sister to Oaks second Bahr: 9/1, 4½ lengths fourth of 6 to Chin Chin in maiden at Ripon, early speed then green. *M. Johnston*

THE PERSUADER (IRE)   2 b.c. (Apr 17) Sadler's Wells (USA) 132 – Sister Dot
(USA) (Secretariat (USA)) [2002 7g 7m⁴ 10s Oct 23] 100,000Y: good-topped colt: closely related to a winner in USA by Danzig and half-brother to 3 winners, including 1993 champion US 2-y-o colt Dehere and useful Irish 7f (at 2 yrs) and 1¼m winner Hans Anderson (both by Deputy Minister): dam 5f (at 2 yrs) to 8.5f winner in USA: signs of just a little ability in maidens. *M. Johnston*

THE PLAYER   3 b.c. Octagonal (NZ) 126 – Patria (USA) 76 (Mr Prospector (USA))   **68 p**
[2002 8.1f⁴ Sep 27] 70,000Y: angular colt: second foal: half-brother to 2000 2-y-o 6f winner Parvenue (by Ezzoud): dam, 2-y-o 7.6f winner, sister to Middle Park winner/2000 Guineas second Lycius: 9/4 and green, 8 lengths fourth to Camelot in Haydock maiden (wore crossed noseband), slowly away, taking strong hold early and no extra inside last 2f: should improve. *J. H. M. Gosden*

THE PRESIDENT   7 b.g. Yaheeb (USA) 95§ – When The Saints (Bay Express 132)   **–**
[2002 47: 12.3g 14.1f Jun 3] tall, lengthy gelding: maiden handicapper: well held both outings in 2002: reared and unseated leaving stall once. *Mrs M. Reveley*

THE PRIVATEER   2 b.c. (Feb 25) Bahamian Bounty 116 – Petriece 64 (Mummy's   **80**
Pet 125) [2002 5d³ 5.1d² 5.2f Jul 20] 14,000Y: tall colt: has scope: eighth foal: half-brother to 3 winners, including useful 1995 2-y-o 5f/6f winner Amazing Bay (by Mazilier) and 7-y-o Solly's Pal: dam, 7f winner, half-sister to dam of Lochsong and Lochangel: best effort (fairly useful form) when 1½ lengths second of 6 to Speed Cop in maiden at Bath: well held in sales race at Newbury: should stay 6f: wandered markedly first 2 starts. *R. Hannon*

THE RECRUITER   2 gr.g. (Mar 5) Danzig Connection (USA) – Tabeeba (Diesis   **42**
133) [2002 f8.5g p7g f8.5g⁶ Nov 15] 4,000F, 4,000Y, 11,000 2-y-o: half-brother to several winners, including 9.4f to 1½m winner State Approval (by Pharly) and Irish 1½m winner Raid (by Saddlers' Hall): dam unraced: poor form at best in maidens/claimer. *R. M. Beckett*

THE RING (IRE)   2 b.g. (Feb 19) Definite Article 121 – Renata's Ring (IRE) (Auction   **72 p**
Ring (USA) 123) [2002 8g 8v⁵ f9.4g* Nov 16] 48,000Y: big, rangy gelding: has plenty of scope: fourth foal: half-brother to 7-y-o Bodfari Pride and fairly useful 1996 2-y-o 5f winner Joint Venture (by Common Grounds): dam, third at 7f in Ireland, out of half-sister to dam of Middle Park winner Balla Cove: fair form in maidens: got up close home to beat Wizard of The West by neck at Wolverhampton: should stay 1¼m: open to improvement. *M. R. Channon*

THE RISEN LARK (IRE)   2 b.f. (Mar 1) Celtic Swing 138 – May Hills Legacy   **63**
(IRE) 68 (Be My Guest (USA) 126) [2002 8s p8g⁶ Nov 14] 9,500Y: big, good-topped filly: fourth foal: half-sister to 7.6f winner Legacy of Love (by Distant Relative) and 5-y-o Gargoyle Girl: dam, 6f (at 2 yrs) and 1¼m winner, out of Yorkshire Oaks and Park Hill winner May Hill: better effort in maidens (modest form) when sixth at Lingfield: should stay at least 1¼m. *D. W. P. Arbuthnot*

THE RISK OF REFORM   2 b.f. (Mar 11) Petorius 117 – Bedtime Model (Double   **39**
Bed (FR) 121) [2002 6g⁶ 5m 5m Aug 28] compact filly: first foal: dam unraced: poor form in maidens. *E. J. Alston*

THE ROAN RUNNER   4 gr.g. Nalchik (USA) – Grey Runner 36 (Crofthall 110)   **–**
[2002 f12g f12g 11.8g 16m f16g⁶ 18d Jul 4] third foal: dam, sprint maiden, ran only at 2 yrs: no form. *B. P. J. Baugh*

THE SADLER (USA)   3 b.c. Sadler's Wells (USA) 132 – Carpet of Leaves (USA)   **86**
(Green Forest (USA) 134) [2002 10f 12.3m² p13g Oct 4] medium-sized colt: first foal: dam, ran twice in France, half-sister to smart French performers Glorify (up to 15f) and Doree (sprinting 2-y-o): easily best effort in maidens (fairly useful form) when second to Tasneef at Ripon in June: off 3½ months after: stays 1½m: sold only 1,200 gns. *J. R. Fanshawe*

THESAURUS   3 gr.g. Most Welcome 131 – Red Embers 64 (Saddlers' Hall (IRE) 126)   **81**
[2002 71: 8m 9d* 10.1s⁶ 8d² 8m 7.1d⁴ Jul 5] tall gelding: fairly useful handicapper:
landed gamble at Goodwood in May: ran well after when in frame: best at 7f to 9f: acts on
good to soft going, well held on soft/heavy. *I. A. Wood*

THE SCAFFOLDER   4 b.g. Tachyon Park 87 – Fallal (IRE) 47 (Fayruz 116) [2002   **56 §**
66§: f6s³ f7s f6g⁶ f6g⁵ f5g⁴ f5g³ f5g² f5g⁶ f6g* f6g² f6g⁵ 6m p6g 6.1m 7m f7s f8.5g f12g
Dec 27] workmanlike gelding: modest performer: won maiden at Southwell in March:
effective at 5f to 7f: acts on fibresand, firm and soft going: sometimes blinkered/visored:
usually slowly away/drifts left/finds little: unreliable. *Mrs N. Macauley*

THESIS (IRE)   4 ch.g. Definite Article 121 – Chouette 54 (Try My Best (USA) 130)   **83**
[2002 92+: 8g 10.3f 10g³ 10.1d² 8g⁶ 8.5d⁶ 10.9m³ 9g* 10.4f 10.1s⁴ Oct 22] good-topped
gelding: fairly useful handicapper: won apprentice race at Sandown in October: probably
best at 9f/1¼m nowadays: yet to race on heavy going, acts on any other: consistent: sold
27,000 gns, joined Venetia Williams. *J. A. Osborne*

THE SISTERS   3 ch.f. Pharly (FR) 130 – Super Sisters (AUS) (Call Report (USA))   **–**
[2002 10.9f Jun 26] half-sister to several winners, including 7-y-o Guilsborough and
5-y-o Castlebridge: dam 7f winner in Australia: 33/1, soundly beaten in seller at Warwick. *Miss K. M. George*

THE SPOOK   2 b.g. (Apr 30) Bin Ajwaad (IRE) 119 – Rose Mill (Puissance 110)   **–**
[2002 8g Sep 19] 600Y, resold 1,600Y: third foal: half-brother to 4-y-o Sholto: dam
unraced out of useful sprinter Amber Mill: 66/1, started slowly, pulled hard and always
behind in seller at Ayr. *J. S. Goldie*

THE STUDENT PRINCE   4 b.g. Piccolo 121 – Affaire de Coeur 55 (Imperial Fling   **50**
(USA) 116) [2002 65: 7g 8.2d⁶ May 18] modest maiden handicapper: acts on
firm going, probably on good to soft: wandered markedly final 3-y-o start. *G. L. Moore*

THE SUN ALSO RISES   3 b.f. Hernando (FR) 127 – Ciel de Feu (USA) (Blushing   **62**
John (USA) 120) [2002 10f³ 11.9d 12g² 14d⁵ 13.1d⁶ 11.7d⁴ 11.9m⁴ 16.2d Jul 22] lengthy
filly: second foal: half-sister to 1m/9f winner in Spain/France by Primo Dominie: dam,
French 9f winner, out of top-class Prix de Diane/Prix Vermeille winner Northern Trick:
modest maiden handicapper: should stay at least 2m: yet to race on soft/heavy going, acts
on any other: sold 1,800 gns in December. *M. Johnston*

THE TATLING (IRE)   5 b.g. Perugino (USA) 84 – Aunty Eileen (Ahonoora 122)   **113**
[2002 103: 5f 5m 5d⁶ 5m 5m 5m* 5.2m 6m⁵ 5.2m² 5m* 5.6m 6g² 5m 6f* 6s³ Oct 25]
lengthy gelding: smart performer: reportedly underwent operation on knees after final
4-y-o start: won claimer at Catterick (claimed from D. Nicholls £15,000) in July and
handicaps at Sandown in August and York (better than ever when beating Artie by 1½

Coral Eurobet Sprint Trophy (Handicap), York—
The Tatling proves a good purchase for trainer Milton Bradley, recording a career-best effort;
Artie, Magic Glade (right) and Budelli (blaze) finish clear of the remainder

lengths in Coral Eurobet Sprint Trophy) in October: also neck second to Funfair Wane in Ayr Gold Cup twelfth start: barely stays 6f when ground is testing: acts on firm and soft going: has had tongue tied: has started slowly/edged right: travels strongly: consistent. *J. M. Bradley*

THE TEUCHTER 3 b.g. First Trump 118 – Barefoot Landing (USA) (Cozzene (USA)) [2002 12.4m⁶ 12m⁶ 12.3g 12f Sep 21] leggy gelding: second foal: dam, poor novice hurdler, out of half-sister to smart performer up to 1½m Triarius: modest maiden: sold 4,000 gns. *M. Johnston* **63**

THE TRADER (IRE) 4 ch.g. Selkirk (USA) 129 – Snowing 88 (Tate Gallery (USA) 117) [2002 115: 5m 5m* 5g⁴ 5d⁶ 5g 5m Aug 22] sturdy, close-coupled gelding: poor mover: smart performer: won listed race at Kempton in June by 1¼ lengths from Fromsong: good length fourth to Dominica in King's Stand Stakes at Royal Ascot next time: not discredited when tenth in Nunthorpe Stakes at York final start: best at 5f: has form on soft going, very best efforts on good or firmer: blinkered: usually travels strongly. *M. Blanshard* **115**

THE TUBE (IRE) 4 b.f. Royal Abjar (USA) 121 – Grandeur And Grace (USA) 75 (Septieme Ciel (USA) 123) [2002 –. 12.1g Aug 8] little form. *P. Bowen* **–**

THE VARLET 2 b.g. (Feb 10) Groom Dancer (USA) 128 – Valagalore 91 (Generous (IRE) 139) [2002 7f 8v p7g Dec 11] leggy gelding: first foal: dam, 1¾m winner, half-sister to Mozart: modest form in maidens: should stay at least 1m. *M. P. Tregoning* **61**

THEWHIRLINGDERVISH (IRE) 4 ch.g. Definite Article 121 – Nomadic Dancer (IRE) 52 (Nabeel Dancer (USA) 120) [2002 80: 12.4g 16m³ 18f* 16.2m 16.2m* 16.1d⁴ Aug 10] leggy, lengthy gelding: fairly useful handicapper: won at Pontefract in June and Ascot in July: stays 2¼m: possibly best on good or firmer going: sometimes finds little. *T. D. Easterby* **93**

Mrs C. J. Ward's "The Trader"

*Electricity Direct St Simon Stakes, Newbury—The Whistling Teal (noseband)
overhauls Warrsan (right) and Nysaean to gain his first success at pattern level*

THE WHISTLING TEAL   6 b.g. Rudimentary (USA) 118 – Lonely Shore   **120**
(Blakeney 126) [2002 118: 10d⁴ 12m² 12m* 12m² 12s* Oct 26]

'Age is opportunity no less than youth itself'. The Whistling Teal developed into a fairly useful handicapper as a three-year-old when he won two of his starts, was just touched off in the Mail On Sunday Final at Ascot and came a creditable eighth in the Cambridgeshire. He looked likely to do the small yard of Julian Smyth-Osbourne proud again as a four-year-old but didn't progress as expected. It has been a different story since The Whistling Teal's transfer to Geoff Wragg. His career has gone from strength to strength as a five- and six-year-old and he looks set for another good season in 2003. The Whistling Teal was suffering from foot trouble when he first arrived at Abington Place but went on to show much improved form as a five-year-old, winning three handicaps including the Zetland Gold Cup at Redcar and the Motability And RAC Rated Stakes at the York August meeting. He stormed through to win the last-named by four lengths, looking capable of winning in better company. That was, however, the last that was seen of The Whistling Teal as a five-year-old, slight back trouble keeping him sidelined after York. It was onward and upward again in the latest season once his campaign began in earnest in August, a problem with a splint keeping him off the course for three months after a promising fourth when in need of the outing in the Gordon Richards Stakes at Sandown in April. The Whistling Teal was an encouraging second, stepped up to a mile and a half for the first time, in the Glorious Rated Stakes at Goodwood and won a four-runner conditions event over the same trip at Newmarket a fortnight later. He then had the misfortune to come across the improving three-year-old Systematic in a listed event at Doncaster, but ended the season on a high note with a first success in pattern company in a competitive renewal of the Electricity Direct St Simon Stakes at Newbury in October, winning from Warrsan and Nysaean, the first three ten lengths clear.

The Whistling Teal, a strong gelding who carries condition, stays better than his sire Rudimentary (a half-brother to Kris and Diesis) who made his name as a miler, though he was also successful at a mile and a quarter. The Whistling Teal's

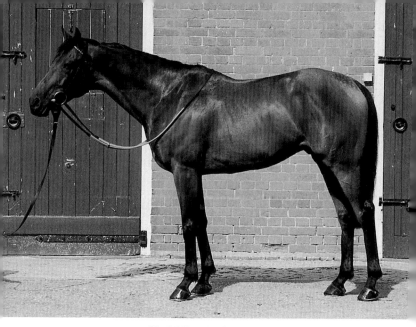

Mrs F. A. Veasey's "The Whistling Teal"

		Nureyev	Northern Dancer
	Rudimentary (USA)	(b 1977)	Special
	(b 1988)	Doubly Sure	Reliance II
The Whistling Teal		(b 1971)	Soft Angels
(b.g. 1996)		Blakeney	Hethersett
	Lonely Shore	(b 1966)	Windmill Girl
	(br 1983)	No Relation	Klairon
		(br 1965)	Margaret Ann

dam Lonely Shore won at thirteen and a half furlongs in Italy, where she has had a winner at up to a mile by Beveled. The genuine and consistent The Whistling Teal acts on firm and soft going (he won on fibresand for his former stable). He is usually held up. *G. Wragg*

THE WIZARD MUL 2 br.g. (May 11) Wizard King 122 – Longden Pride (Super-power 113) [2002 5f 7m 5g⁵ 5m⁴ 5m² 6d Nov 5] 500Y: leggy gelding: first foal: dam unraced: modest maiden: good second in nursery at Musselburgh: should stay 6f: acts on good to firm ground. *W. Storey* **60**

THEYAB (USA) 4 b. or br.g. Bahri (USA) 125 – Dish Dash 118 (Bustino 136) [2002 63: p10g 7s Sep 10] lightly-made gelding: maiden: tailed off both runs in 2002. *N. A. Graham* **–**

THIHN (IRE) 7 ch.g. Machiavellian (USA) 123 – Hasana (USA) (Private Account (USA)) [2002 97: 8s⁴ 8.3g² 8g 8.1d⁵ 8m⁴ 8.5g⁵ 8.5s² 8m 7d⁴ 9.2s⁵ 8.3m Aug 24] sturdy gelding: useful handicapper: as good as ever in 2002, fourth in Lincoln at Doncaster in March and Jubilee Stakes at Kempton in May: also ran well when fourth at Newmarket ninth start: best form at 7f/1m: acts on any going: sometimes starts slowly/hangs right: free-going sort, and usually travels strongly: effective held up or racing prominently: tough and consistent. *J. L. Spearing* **98**

THINGMEBOB 2 b.f. (May 4) Bob Back (USA) 124 – Kip's Sister (Cawston's **81 p** Clown 113) [2002 7g² Oct 18] tall, unfinished filly: has scope: half-sister to several winners, including 3-y-o Steenberg and 6f (at 2 yrs) and 1½m winner Charlie's Darling (by Homing): dam unraced: 33/1 and green, neck second of 4 to Peace Flag in slowly-run Newmarket Challenge Cup: will be suited by 1m+: sure to progress. *M. H. Tompkins*

THIRN 3 b.g. Piccolo 121 – Midnight Owl (FR) (Ardross 134) [2002 64: 7g 8.2d 8m **65** 8.5m⁵ 9.9d⁴ 8.1m 8m 10.4f 9d p7g Dec 28] strong, useful-looking gelding: fair maiden handicapper: left J. Bethell after penultimate start: barely stays 1¼m: acts on good to firm and good to soft going: tried tongue tied: ran in snatches final 2-y-o outing: has pulled too hard. *D. Carroll*

THISONESFOR GEORGE 2 gr.c. (Apr 30) Paris House 123 – Heaven-Liegh- **57** Grey 90 (Grey Desire 115) [2002 5.1f⁶ 5m 6m 5g 5m³ 5g⁶ 5m 5g 5m 5s f5g Nov 15] 1,200Y: strong, close-coupled colt: seventh foal: half-brother to 3 winners, including 1m/ 9f winner French Connection (by Tirol): dam beat at 5f: modest maiden: form only at 5f: acts on fibresand and good to firm ground: tried in blinkers/cheekpieces: inconsistent: sold 1,500 gns. *A. Berry*

THOLJANAH (IRE) 3 b.c. Darshaan 133 – Alkaffeyeh (IRE) (Sadler's Wells (USA) **109** 132) [2002 109p: 12d 14.8g³ 14f* Oct 2] leggy, angular colt: useful performer: reportedly jarred a knee in the spring: tailed off in Derby at Epsom on belated reappearance: good 1½ lengths third to Spanish John in listed race at Newmarket, then off nearly 3 months prior to winning similar event on same course in October by ½ length from Sorcerous, seeming to idle late on: will stay 2m: acts on soft and firm ground: edgy sort. *M. P. Tregoning*

THOMAS PAINE 3 b.c. Green Desert (USA) 127 – Glorious (Nashwan (USA) 135) **–** [2002 f8g Nov 26] first foal: dam unraced half-sister to smart miler Killer Instinct, from very good family of Opera House and Kayf Tara: 6/1, well held in maiden at Southwell. *P. W. Harris*

THORNTOUN DIVA 4 ch.f. Wolfhound (USA) 126 – Al Guswa 98 (Shernazar 131) **–** [2002 58d: 5m⁶ 7g 5m 6f⁴ 5s 5m 5.9d 7.2d 7.2d Aug 2] lengthy, unfinished filly: modest maiden at 3 yrs: has deteriorated: tried visored/blinkered. *J. S. Goldie*

THORNTOUN GOLD (IRE) 6 ch.m. Lycius (USA) 124 – Gold Braisim (IRE) 77 **64** (Jareer (USA) 115) [2002 55: f11s f9.4g⁴ 10d⁴ 10m 8g⁵ 10.9d⁵ 10g* 10m⁵ 11.6m* 11.9g **a–** 11.6g* 13.1f⁵ 11.9m⁵ Aug 28] workmanlike mare: modest handicapper: won at Brighton in May and 3 times at Windsor in July/August: effective 1¼m to 13f: acts on firm and good to soft going, little form in 3 runs on fibresand: tried blinkered in 2000: effective racing prominently or held up. *I. A. Wood*

THORPENESS (IRE) 3 b.g. Barathea (IRE) 127 – Brisighella (IRE) (Al Hareb **58** (USA) 123) [2002 –: 12.3f⁶ 14.1f⁵ 11.6m⁶ 12d⁵ 12.1s 11.5m³ Sep 17] strong, good-topped gelding: modest maiden: best efforts around 1½m: acts on firm going, probably on good to soft: gelded after final start. *C. F. Wall*

THRASHER 3 b.f. Hector Protector (USA) 124 – Thracian 92 (Green Desert (USA) **–** 127) [2002 80: 11.6g 10.2g 8.1d Jun 14] fairly useful at 2 yrs: soundly beaten in 2002: blinkered last 2 starts: sold 25,000 gns in December. *J. H. M. Gosden*

THREAT 6 br.g. Zafonic (USA) 130 – Prophecy (IRE) 109 (Warning 136) [2002 75: f6g **65** p6g 5s³ 6m 5m 6s 5g* 6f 5v² 6v 5.7d⁴ 5f⁶ 6g² 5d 6g 6g 7m³ 6m² f6g 6.1m⁵ 6m 6d⁵ Oct **a54** 14] well-made gelding: has been freeze fired: fair performer: won seller at Musselburgh in May: best at 5f/6f: acts on heavy going, good to firm and fibresand: tried blinkered/ visored: usually tongue tied before 2002: sometimes slowly away. *J. M. Bradley*

THREE ANGELS (IRE) 7 b.g. Houmayoun (FR) 114 – Mullaghroe (Tarboosh **69** (USA)) [2002 69: 8.1m 7g⁵ May 31] robust gelding: fair performer: stays 1m: acts on firm going, probably on good to soft: tried visored, blinkered nowadays. *A. W. Carroll*

THREE CLOUDS 5 b.g. Rainbow Quest (USA) 134 – Three Tails 121 (Blakeney **61 d** 126) [2002 58: p13g* p13g³ p16g 16g 11.9g⁵ p16g⁴ p16g f16g Dec 17] modest performer: won claimer at Lingfield in February: ran as if amiss in tongue tie penultimate start, and, having left G. L. Moore, reportedly had breathing problem final outing: stays 2m: acts on polytrack, good to firm and good to soft going: blinkered once. *C. N. Kellett*

THREE DAYS IN MAY 3 b.f. Cadeaux Genereux 131 – Corn Futures 78 (Nomina- **70** tion 125) [2002 –p: 8s p5g⁴ 5.9s 6g* 6m⁴ 7g p6g⁴ 6d³ 6m² 6g⁶ 5m 6.1m⁶ Sep 20] lengthy, unfinished filly: fair handicapper: won ladies race at Thirsk in June: best at stiff 5f/6f: acts on good to firm going, good to soft and polytrack: blinkered (ran creditably) eighth start: sold 7,500 gns. *W. J. Haggas*

Hopeful Stakes, Newmarket—
Three Points lands the odds from Mugharreb, Affaire Royale and Prince Dayjur

THREE EAGLES (USA)   5 ch.g. Eagle Eyed (USA) 111 – Tertiary (USA) (Vaguely   –
Noble 140) [2002 52: 16.2m[6] Jun 17] angular gelding: modest handicapper at 4 yrs: well
held only start in 2002: tried blinkered. *A. Bailey*

THREEFOLD (USA)   3 b.f. Gulch (USA) – Trivita (USA) (Theatrical 128) [2002   **99**
8.3d* 10s[3] 10.1g[4] 9.9m[6] Aug 14] $145,000Y: leggy, quite good-topped filly: first foal:
dam, 8.5f/9f winner in USA, half-sister to Prix Saint-Alary winner Treble and to dam of
high-class sprinter Tamarisk out of half-sister to Triptych: successful debut in maiden
at Windsor in May: useful form after in listed races at Newbury (4¼ lengths third to
Succinct), Newcastle (2¼ lengths fourth behind Esloob) and Salisbury (sixth to Chorist):
likely to stay 1½m: acts on soft and good to firm ground. *Sir Michael Stoute*

THREE POINTS   5 b.h. Bering 136 – Trazl (IRE) 88 (Zalazl (USA) 120) [2002 119:   **114**
6m[3] 6d[6] 6m* 6m[3] 6m Sep 28] leggy, close-coupled horse: smart performer: landed odds
in 4-runner listed race at Newmarket in August, beating Mugharreb by 3 lengths:
creditable efforts in pattern races otherwise in 2002 when 2 lengths third to Malhub in
Golden Jubilee Stakes at Royal Ascot, sixth to Continent in July Cup at Newmarket and 2
lengths third to Invincible Spirit in Sprint Cup at Haydock: disappointing in Diadem
Stakes at Ascot final outing: best at 6f/7f: acts on firm and good to soft going, below form
on dirt, not well drawn only run on soft: tongue tied nowadays: has been bandaged in
front: usually races up with pace. *Saeed bin Suroor*

THREEZEDZZ   4 ch.g. Emarati (USA) 74 – Exotic Forest 66 (Dominion 123) [2002   **72**
98: 5f 6.1d 5.5m 7m 7.1g Oct 5] tall, useful-looking gelding: one-time useful performer,
just fair nowadays: left J. M. Bradley after reappearance: best at 5f/6f: acts on firm and
good to soft going (well below form on soft): tried blinkered: edgy type: withdrawn
having unseated and bolted once. *Mrs P. N. Dutfield*

THROUGH THE RYE   6 ch.g. Sabrehill (USA) 120 – Baharlilys 67 (Green Dancer   **52**
(USA) 132) [2002 71: f8g f11g[2] Jan 31] rangy gelding: good mover: modest performer
nowadays: stays 1½m: acts on fibresand and good to firm going, probably on heavy: has
had tongue tied: winning hurdler. *E. W. Tuer*

THROWER   11 b.g. Thowra (FR) – Atlantic Line (Capricorn Line 111) [2002 –: f16g[4]   –
f16.2g Feb 22] sturdy gelding: little form since 2000. *W. M. Brisbourne*

THUMAMAH (IRE)   3 b.f. Charnwood Forest (IRE) 125 – Anam 79 (Persian Bold   **76**
123) [2002 64: 5.7g 5f[6] 6g[5] 6m 8m[3] 7g** f9.4g Nov 16] lengthy, unfurnished filly: has a
short action: fair handicapper: won at Lingfield in October: left B. Hanbury, then well
held on all-weather debut: stays 1m: acts on firm and good to soft going: tongue tied last
4 starts. *B. P. J. Baugh*

THUMPER (IRE)   4 b.g. Grand Lodge (USA) 125 – Parkeen Princess (He Loves Me   **75**
120) [2002 74d: p8g[2] f8.5g 7d[2] p7g[2] 7d[2] 8.3m* 8.3g[2] 9m* 10m[2] p8g[5] 8m Sep 13] angular   **a69**
gelding: fair handicapper: won at Windsor in June and Kempton in July: stays 1¼m: acts
on good to firm going, good to soft and polytrack: blinkered last 5 outings: races
prominently: sold 16,000 gns: consistent. *R. Hannon*

THUNDER CANYON (USA) 3 b. or br.g. Gulch (USA) – Naazeq 80 (Nashwan **81** (USA) 135) [2002 78: f9.4g* 12m⁶ 9.9g⁵ 10g 9.9d⁶ 10g² 9.3d² 8.3d⁴ 14m⁴ 14.1m* f14s 14.1m³ 12f² 14.1d² f14.8g* Oct 21] close-coupled gelding: fairly useful performer: won maiden at Wolverhampton in January and handicaps at Redcar in September and Wolverhampton in October: stays 1¾m: acts on fibresand, firm and good to soft going: blinkered fifth start: usually races prominently: tough and consistent: sold 22,000 gns, joined N. Richards. *M. Johnston*

THUNDERCLAP 3 b. or br.c. Royal Applause 124 – Gloriana 78 (Formidable **75** (USA) 125) [2002 77: 9f 7.6f 8d³ 8.1f 8.1g⁶ p8g⁶ p7g Dec 30] quite good-topped colt: fair performer: free-going sort, but stays 1m: acts on polytrack, firm and good to soft going: visored (below form) once. *J. W. Hills*

THUNDERED (USA) 4 gr.g. Thunder Gulch (USA) 129 – Lady Lianga (USA) 81 **54** (Secretariat (USA)) [2002 55: 9g 7f* 8d 7.1d 8g f7g⁶ Dec 2] workmanlike gelding: **a39** modest performer: easily best effort in 2002 when winning seller at Thirsk in May: probably best at 7f/1m: possibly needs good going or firmer: tried blinkered in 2001: reared and unseated rider leaving stalls penultimate outing. *G. A. Swinbank*

THUNDERGOD 3 b.g. Torrential (USA) 117 – Reach The Wind (USA) (Relaunch **65** (USA)) [2002 62: 10f³ 11.6m 10.2g⁶ 5.9s² 7s 7g² 7m⁴ 6.1d⁴ 6m* 8.5m⁴ 7g 8m 8.1g³ 8m⁴ 8g Oct 16] fair handicapper: won NH jockeys maiden event at Brighton in July: effective at 6f to 1m: yet to race on heavy going, acts on any other: wore hood/blinkers last 3 starts: free-going sort: sold 8,000 gns. *I. A. Balding*

THUNDERING FALLS (USA) 3 b.f. Thunder Gulch (USA) 129 – Redwood Falls **62** (IRE) 107 (Dancing Brave (USA) 140) [2002 59: f8s³ f7g f8g³ f7g Apr 29] modest maiden: pulled up lame final outing: was probably best up to 1m: carried head awkwardly/edged left. *M. Johnston*

THUNDERING JAY-SEA 4 ch.f. First Trump 118 – Thunder Bug (USA) 66 **–** (Secreto (USA) 128) [2002 p10g 11.8g 9.9m 7m 7m 10m Sep 20] lengthy filly: fourth foal: half-sister to 5-y-o Thundering Surf: dam 1¼m winner: little form. *J. R. Jenkins*

THUNDERING SURF 5 b.g. Lugana Beach 116 – Thunder Bug (USA) 66 (Secreto **102** (USA) 128) [2002 101: 12m 12m⁶ 12f³ 12g* Jun 18] big, lengthy gelding: has a round action: useful performer: 11/1, won Duke of Edinburgh Handicap at Royal Ascot by neck from Holy Orders (ridden closer to pace than usual): effective at 1¼m/1½m: acts on any going: usually held up: gelded after final start. *J. R. Jenkins*

Duke of Edinburgh Stakes (Handicap), Royal Ascot—Thundering Surf fends off the persistent challenge of the blinkered Holy Orders; Counsel's Opinion (hooped cap) and Red Carnation (noseband) are next

THURLESTONE ROCK 2 ch.g. (Apr 12) Sheikh Albadou 128 – Don't Smile 76 **82**
(Sizzling Melody 117) [2002 p6g 5m 5m 5g f5s³ 5.1g² f6g* p5g² p7g Nov 13] 4,200F,
8,500Y: fifth foal: half-brother to 6f winner Song 'N Dance (by Dancing Spree): dam 6f
(at 2 yrs) and 9f winner: fairly useful performer: won nursery at Wolverhampton (by 6
lengths) in October, making virtually all: stays 6f: acts on all-weather, best turf run on
good going: clearly best efforts in blinkers: sometimes hangs left. *B. J. Meehan*

THWAAB 10 b.g. Dominion 123 – Velvet Habit 89 (Habitat 134) [2002 60: 8f 7.9s 8m **58**
6.9m² 8m 8g⁶ 8.1m 8m Oct 2] strong gelding: modest performer: stays 1m: acts on firm
and good to soft going: often visored/blinkered: held up. *F. Watson*

THWAITES STAR (IRE) 3 b.f. Petardia 113 – Monterana 99 (Sallust 134) [2002 **–**
55d: 6m⁶ 6.9s Jun 16] leggy, close-coupled filly: modest maiden: disappointing since
fourth 2-y-o start. *A. Berry*

TIANELLA (GER) 3 b.f. Acatenango (GER) 127 – Thurina (GER) (Experte (GER)) **74 d**
[2002 10g⁴ 12f³ 12m³ 12s 8.1m 10s Oct 23] approx. 57,000Y in Germany: rather leggy,
lengthy filly: half-sister to numerous winners in Germany: dam German 2-y-o 1m
winner: fair maiden: disappointing after second start: probably stays 1½m: sold 10,000
gns. *G Wragg*

TIANYI (IRE) 6 b.g. Mujadil (USA) 119 – Skinity (Rarity 129) [2002 12s Mar 21] **–**
sturdy gelding: fairly useful performer on Flat in Ireland for D. K. Weld in 2000: joined
D. Caro after reappearance: stays 1¼m: acts on good to firm and good to soft going:
usually blinkered earlier in career: won twice over hurdles in October. *F. Jordan*

TIBER (IRE) 2 b.c. (Apr 4) Titus Livius (FR) 115 – Exciting (Mill Reef (USA) 141) **89**
[2002 8m 7f² 8f* Sep 25] IR 250,000Y: half-brother to several winners, notably very
smart 6f (at 2 yrs) to 1m winner Almushtarak (by Fairy King): dam, ran once, sister to
smart stayer The Miller out of Cherry Hinton winner Turkish Treasure: fairly useful form:
landed odds in 4-runner maiden at Goodwood comfortably by 1¾ lengths from
Westmoreland Road: not sure to stay much beyond 1m: raced only on going firmer than
good: blinkered all starts, looking reluctant on debut. *J. H. M. Gosden*

TIBER TIGER (IRE) 2 b.g. (Mar 10) Titus Livius (FR) 115 – Genetta (Green Desert **75**
(USA) 127) [2002 5.1g 6g⁴ 6s 6.1d* 7m* 7m⁶ 7d⁵ 7.1m f8.5s³ 8.3d Oct 14] IR 11,000F,
9,500Y: rather angular gelding: fourth foal: half-brother to 3-y-o Raybaan: dam, French
maiden, out of half-sister to top-class performer up to 1½m Kalaglow: fair performer:
won claimer at Chepstow (left B. Meehan) and nursery at Newmarket (by 6 lengths) in
July: below best last 4 starts: effective at 6f/7f: acts on good to soft and good to firm
going, well held on fibresand: blinkered after third outing. *N. P. Littmoden*

TICKET TO DANCE (IRE) 3 b.f. Sadler's Wells (USA) 132 – River Missy (USA) **97**
(Riverman (USA) 131) [2002 67p: 10g⁶ 12g³ 11m 11.9m² 12d* Aug 3] useful performer:
had to work hard to land odds in maiden at Doncaster in August, carrying head to one side
then seeming to idle: ran well earlier when 6 lengths seventh to Guadalupe in Oaks d'Italia at Milan: stayed 1½m: unraced on extremes of going: stud in USA. *J. H. M. Gosden*

TICKLE 4 b.f. Primo Dominie 121 – Funny Choice (IRE) 68 (Commanche Run 133) **64**
[2002 83: 7m 6d⁴ 5.1g 7s⁶ Oct 28] one-time fairly useful performer, lightly raced: only
modest form in 2002: will prove best up to 7f: raced mainly on good or softer ground.
P. J. Makin

TICK TOCK 5 ch.m. Timeless Times (USA) 99 – Aquiletta 67 (Bairn (USA) 126) **62**
[2002 68: 6.1g 5m⁵ 6f 5g 5.1d 6g⁵ 5g² 5m⁵ 5m 5m 6m 5m 5g 6.1f⁵ 5g f6s Nov 2]
small mare: modest performer: effective at 5f/6f: acts on any turf going, well beaten on
fibresand: visored (not for wins in 2001) earlier in career: often races up with pace.
M. Mullineaux

TIDAL 3 br.f. Bin Ajwaad (IRE) 119 – So Saucy 59 (Teenoso (USA) 135) [2002 10s³ **82**
11.8d⁵ 10m⁵ 10f* 10m⁶ Aug 4] lengthy, angular filly: fourth foal: half-sister to 6-y-o
Most-Saucy: dam 1¼m and 17f winner: fairly useful form: won handicap at Newbury in
July: disappointing final start: should stay 1½m: acts on firm going: slowly away/hung
left second outing. *B. J. Meehan*

TIDAL BEACH 3 b.g. Lugana Beach 116 – Efficacy 62 (Efisio 120) [2002 53: 5.1d **51**
5g⁶ 5s 5f f7g⁴ 8.2m 6f⁴ 7.2g 6g 10f 9.1s Oct 15] lengthy gelding: modest maiden
handicapper: stays easy 7f: acts on fibresand and firm going: blinkered nowadays: has
looked none too keen on occasions. *C. W. Thornton*

TIDY (IRE) 2 b.c. (Apr 25) Mujadil (USA) 119 – Neat Shilling (IRE) (Bob Back (USA) **73**
124) [2002 6m 6d⁴ f6g² f6s* Nov 2] 29,000Y: first foal: dam unraced sister to useful
Irish middle-distance stayer Fill The Bill and half-sister to smart stayer Riddlesdown: fair

performer: won maiden at Wolverhampton by short head from Surdoue: should stay at least 7f: acts on fibresand and good to soft ground: races prominently. *J. A. Osborne*

TIFFANY'S QUEST   3 b.f. Atraf 116 – Pleasure Quest (Efisio 120) [2002 6g 5d² 5g   **65** p6g⁶ f6g Nov 20] third foal: dam no form: easily best effort in maidens (fair form)   **a47** when second at Sandown: likely to prove best at 5f/6f: acts on good to soft going. *D. W. P. Arbuthnot*

TIGERETTE (USA)   2 b.f. (Mar 2) Swain (IRE) 134 – Hot Thong (BRZ) (Jarraar   **66 p** (USA) 78) [2002 6m⁶ 6m³ Aug 28] small, sparely-made filly: second foal: dam, Brazilian Grade 3 7f winner and third in 1000 Guineas there, out of close relative to smart 1½m winner Ninotchka: better effort in maidens (fair form) when third to Goodwood Prince at Brighton: should stay further. *R. Guest*

TIGER FEET   3 b.c. Petong 126 – Selvi (Mummy's Pet 125) [2002 72: f5s 5.7g 5s f6g   **–** 5m 6.1m 5s 7.1m Aug 22] smallish, lengthy colt: fair performer at 2 yrs: no form in 2002: tried blinkered: sold 500 gns, sent to Israel. *A. Berry*

TIGER FROG (USA)   3 b.c. French Deputy (USA) 118 – Woodyoubelieveit (USA)   **68** (Woodman (USA) 126) [2002 p10g³ 10m 9m 10g² 10m Sep 20] strong, lengthy colt: second foal: dam, US 2-y-o 6f minor stakes winner, out of US Grade 3 9f winner Tricky Fingers: fair maiden: should stay beyond 1¼m: blinkered (stumbled and hampered) final outing: has given trouble at start: sold 18,000 gns, joined N. Mason. *J. H. M. Gosden*

TIGER HUNT (IRE)   6 b.g. Rainbow Quest (USA) 134 – Gay Hellene 111 (Ela-   **–** Mana-Mou 132) [2002 f9.4g f12g f12g 11.1g 11.8m Jun 3] fair performer at best: won minor event at Longchamp at 3 yrs: couple of creditable efforts for D. Smaga in 2001: no form in 2002 (usually blinkered): stays 1¼m: acts on soft ground. *D. W. Chapman*

TIGER PARKES   2 ch.g. (Apr 9) Elmaamul (USA) 125 – My Melody Parkes 102   **–** (Teenoso (USA) 135) [2002 5.9d 6g 7.5g Jul 30] 1,000Y: rather leggy, workmanlike gelding: second foal: dam, 5f winner (including at 2 yrs), half-sister to useful sprinters Summerhill Parkes and Lucky Parkes: little sign of ability in maidens. *Mrs J. R. Ramsden*

TIGER ROYAL (IRE)   6 gr.g. Royal Academy (USA) 130 – Lady Redford (Bold   **119** Lad (IRE) 133) [2002 106: 5s⁴ 6s* 5s* 6s² 6s* 5s⁵ 5d* 5d 6g 6d Oct 13] good-topped

Mr Peter Jones's "Tiger Royal"

gelding: smart performer: improved in 2002, winning handicaps at the Curragh and Tipperary in April, Weatherbys Ireland Greenlands Stakes at the Curragh (by 3 lengths from Tendulkar) in May and listed race at the Curragh (edged out Agnetha by neck) in June: below form after, running poorly final start: has form at 7f, best efforts at 5f/6f: has form on good to firm going, very best efforts on good or softer: blinkered. *D. K. Weld, Ireland*

TIGER TALK 6 ch.g. Sabrehill (USA) 120 – Tebre (USA) 70 (Sir Ivor 135) [2002 –: 16f Jun 11] of little account on Flat nowadays: winning hurdler. *M. E. Sowersby*   –

TIGER TOM 2 ch.c. (May 18) Factual (USA) 108 – Chilibang Bang 68 (Chilibang 120) [2002 5g May 21] small, sturdy colt: has a markedly round action: third foal: dam 5f (at 2 yrs) to 7f winner: 50/1, last in seller at Beverley: looked most temperamental and refused to enter stall second intended outing. *I. W. McInnes*

TIGER TOPS 3 ch.g. Sabrehill (USA) 120 – Rose Chime (IRE) 58 (Tirol 127) [2002   **69**
p8g* 8.1d² 8m 8d⁴ 10g 7d⁶ Oct 30] 7,000F, 10,000Y: second foal: dam 2-y-o 6f/7f winner: fair performer: won maiden at Lingfield in February: stays 1m: acts on polytrack and good to soft going: races freely. *C. F. Wall*

TIGHT SQUEEZE 5 br.m. Petoski 135 – Snowline (Bay Express 132) [2002 51:   **86**
f9.4g 10g* 10.9f⁵ 10m 10m* 10g* 10g⁵ 10m 9.9m³ 10.2d⁴ 9.9d⁵ p10g⁵ 10g* 9.2s² 9.9m*   **a55**
Aug 25] big, plain mare: fairly useful handicapper on turf, modest on all-weather: much improved in 2002, winning at Southwell, Pontefract, Nottingham, Chepstow, Brighton and Beverley between April/August: best around 1¼m: acts on firm and soft going: usually waited with. *P. W. Hiatt*

TIGRESS (IRE) 3 b.f. Desert Style (IRE) 121 – Ervedya (IRE) (Doyoun 124) [2002   **–**
60, a78: f6s f5g 5.5f f5g⁵ p6g f6g⁶³ f6s⁶ f7g⁴ f6g f6g⁴ f6g f5g* f6g³ f5g⁶ Dec 31] tall filly: **a57**
modest performer: left P. D. Evans after reappearance, G. McCourt after fifth start: won handicap at Wolverhampton in December: best at 5f/6f: acts on good ground and fibresand: usually blinkered/visored: unseated rider to post once in 2002: has wandered: none too consistent. *J. W. Unett*

TIKKUN (IRE) 3 gr.c. Grand Lodge (USA) 125 – Moon Festival 74 (Be My Guest   **111**
(USA) 126) [2002 100p: 8m* 8f⁵ 9m⁶ Oct 19] rangy colt: smart performer: reportedly bruised a foot early in 2002: won minor event at Doncaster in September by 2 lengths from Mineshaft: better effort in listed events at Newmarket after when creditable 2¾ lengths sixth to Golden Silca final outing: will have to settle better to stay beyond 9f: has worn crossed noseband/been blanketed for stall entry/has swished tail in paddock. *R. Charlton*

TIKRAM 5 ch.g. Lycius (USA) 124 – Black Fighter (USA) 79 (Secretariat (USA))   **83**
[2002 89p: p12g 10s Oct 26] tall, close-coupled gelding: fairly useful handicapper, lightly raced: off 8 months after reappearance: will stay 1¾m: raced mainly on going softer than good (acts on heavy): fairly useful hurdler, winner in December. *G. L. Moore*

TILAK 2 b.g. (Apr 21) Tagula (IRE) 116 – Costa Verde 77 (King of Spain 121) [2002   **97**
5s* 5m⁵ 6m² 5.9d⁴ 5g* 5g³ Sep 19] 12,000 2-y-o: good-topped gelding: third foal: half-brother to 1998 2-y-o 6f winner Isle of Sodor (by Cyrano de Bergerac): dam 2-y-o 7.5f winner: useful performer: won maiden at Haydock in June and minor event at Ripon in August: good 2¼ lengths third to Bella Tusa in listed race at Ayr final start: will prove best at 5f/6f: acts on soft and good to firm going. *A. Berry*

TILANJANI (IRE) 5 ch.g. Indian Ridge 123 – Tijara (IRE) (Darshaan 133) [2002   **–**
10m f16g Jun 19] well held in 2 sellers. *K. A. Morgan*

TILLA 2 b.f. (Apr 9) Bin Ajwaad (IRE) 119 – Tosca (Be My Guest (USA) 126) [2002   **– p**
8.3d⁶ Oct 28] third foal: dam unraced daughter of Cheshire/Lancashire Oaks winner Princess Eboli: 16/1, 8 lengths sixth of 12 to Desert View in maiden at Windsor, fading from over 1f out: should do better. *H. Morrison*

TILLERMAN 6 b.h. In The Wings 128 – Autumn Tint (USA) (Roberto (USA)   **123**
131) [2002 121: 7m* 8g² 7m⁶ 7m 8m* 8g³ 8m Dec 15]
    The red-letter day for Tillerman was August 24th, 2002. He had been established as a very smart performer for more than two years, well capable of winning a pattern race, but the luckless Tillerman had not won one. Wins of any sort cannot be taken for granted with a racehorse like Tillerman, meeting bad luck in running being the almost inevitable consequence of his style of running. For two consecutive seasons, Tillerman had put up the best performance seen in a British handicap, both in the Tote International at Ascot: he won it in 2000 and was a close

third in 2001. At 6/5-on, he also won a minor event at Leicester in June of the latest season, beating Vicious Knight by a length and a half, but still proved incapable of making the breakthrough in pattern races until that day in August. The Hungerford Stakes, Cork And Orrery, July Cup, the Hungerford again, the Queen Anne and the Criterion Stakes all brought various degrees of disappointment over the previous two-year period. Ascot is where Tillerman has most often shown his best, but after the 2000 Tote International it was also the source of the most frustration. Getting Tillerman to settle is no easy matter, and the method used with him, heavy restraint at the back of the field, risks failing to find a clear way through, which is exactly what happened on three occasions at Ascot when Tillerman was conspicuously on song, in the Cork And Orrery and Tote International in 2001 and the Queen Anne Stakes in 2002. The Queen Anne represented the best form of his career, but he had the misfortune to be checked in his run from last place and reached No Excuse Needed a fraction too late. To rub salt in the wounds, Tillerman's jockey Richard Hughes believed that his mount had got there just in time and produced a whip-waving gesture of celebration.

The near-miss must have seemed all the more painful when Tillerman failed to land a blow on his next two starts, the Criterion Stakes at Newmarket and the latest renewal of the Tote International. Added to the 2001 Hungerford Stakes, the Criterion was the second race in which Atavus successfully dictated the pace and contributed to the defeat of the much better fancied Tillerman. At Newmarket, Tillerman started at 11/8-on in a six-runner field but finished last. In the Tote International, Tillerman raced off a BHB mark of 119, one of the highest carried in a handicap since their figures were published, still started co-second favourite, but ended up racing in the unfavoured group after his jockey switched him dramatically from the stalls. Four weeks later the Celebration Mile at Goodwood provided the pattern success that was so richly deserved. Whether it was deserved on the day was a matter of heated debate afterwards, but this was Tillerman's turn to enjoy the rub of the green, while one of his main rivals conspicuously missed out. Most unusually, Tillerman emerged best in a tactical race. The pace was far from strong but Tillerman did not pull so hard as he can and enjoyed all the space he could wish for when Hughes switched him to the outer approaching the final furlong. In a tight finish, in which all seven runners ended up separated by about a length and a half, favourite Where Or When found himself without any room, Tillerman a major contributor as Hughes edged him to his right to close a gap and ensure that Where Or When could not get out until it was all too late. Also timing his challenge for the lead just right as he mastered Redback, Reel Buddy and Firebreak in the final strides, the jockey's celebrations were this time fully justified. Where Or When's trainer Terry Mills was furious when the result was allowed to stand, but the stewards decided that Hughes had employed a legitimate tactic, for all that he had clearly sailed close to the wind. Where Or When's connections had

Celebration Mile, Goodwood—
Tillerman wins a controversial race from the two stable-companions Redback (left) and Reel Buddy (right);
Firebreak (second left) and the unlucky Where Or When (second right) dead-heat for fourth

their revenge, though, as Where Or When beat Tillerman by five lengths when they were first and third respectively in the Queen Elizabeth II Stakes at Ascot next time. Tillerman was not at his best that day and concluded his campaign with a never-dangerous tenth of twelve in the Hong Kong Mile at Sha Tin in December.

Tillerman (b.h. 1996)	In The Wings (b 1986)	Sadler's Wells (b 1981)	Northern Dancer Fairy Bridge
		High Hawk (b 1980)	Shirley Heights Sunbittern
	Autumn Tint (USA) (b or br 1985)	Roberto (b 1969)	Hail To Reason Bramalea
		Autumn Glory (br 1978)	Graustark Golden Trail

As was made clear in his essay in *Racehorses of 2000*, Tillerman's distance requirements make him an anomaly among the offspring of stallion In The Wings. The 2001 Cork And Orrery showed that he was probably as effective at six furlongs as at seven or a mile. Since then, In The Wings has had two winners at around six furlongs, one in the Czech Republic and one in Ireland, but far more typical of this good sire's progeny are the likes of Act One, Mamool, Mellow Park, Savannah Bay and Boreas who all distinguished themselves at much longer distances in 2002. Adding to the confusion with Tillerman is that his dam Autumn Tint won at a mile and a half. Autumn Tint, who comes from an excellent family, was sold for 20,000 guineas and exported when Tillerman was a foal. A big, strong, good sort who impresses in appearance, Tillerman was successful on good to soft ground as a three-year-old, but has produced his best efforts on good or good to firm going and he is not nowadays raced on softer than good. Large fields help him to find

Mr K. Abdulla's "Tillerman"

cover and the strong pace that is desirable, but they also increase the risk of his meeting trouble in running. In smaller fields, if Tillerman is not going to set the pace himself, he would surely benefit from the services of a pacemaker. In addition to favourable ground conditions and luck in running, trainer Amanda Perrett has also stated that Tillerman needs luck in the weather. 'Several times [in 2001] it rained on the morning of his races,' she said, 'and he just cannot act on loose or slippy ground.' Backing Tillerman, as well as placing him, is a hazardous business but, even with his very patchy record, there are still times when he represents some value, as the last three seasons have shown. *Mrs A. J. Perrett*

TIMBER ICE (USA) 2 b.f. (Jan 27) Woodman (USA) 126 – Salchow (USA) (Nijinsky (CAN) 138) [2002 8g Oct 18] big, good-topped filly: has scope: fifth foal: sister to smart 1998 French 2-y-o 6.5f and 1m (Grand Criterium) winner who stayed 1½m Way of Light, and closely related to French 1¼m winner Simadartha (by Gone West): dam unraced half-sister to Machiavellian and Exit To Nowhere, an excellent family: 5/1, burly and very green, well held in maiden at Newmarket: looks type to do better. *H. R. A. Cecil* — **p**

TIMBER LODGE (IRE) 3 ch.g. Woodborough (USA) 112 – Ornette (IRE) (Bluebird (USA) 125) [2002 71: 7.1g f9.4g³ p10g Oct 16] fair maiden: off 16 months before reappearance: good third in handicap at Wolverhampton next time: seemed to lose action final outing: should stay 1¼m: acts on fibresand. *I. A. Balding* — **73**

TIME AHEAD 2 b.f. (Mar 7) Spectrum (IRE) 126 – Not Before Time (IRE) (Polish Precedent (USA) 131) [2002 7d⁵ Jul 10] sixth foal: half-sister to several winners, including smart 1m (at 2 yrs) and 10.4f (Musidora) winner Time Away (by Darshaan) and fairly useful 1¼m and 12.5f winner Original Spin (by Machiavellian): dam unraced out of top-class 1¼m/1½m performer Time Charter: weak 7/1-shot, eye-catching 6½ lengths fifth of 9 to Londonnetdotcom in maiden at Kempton, racing freely before keeping on well under considerate handling (reportedly returned with swollen joint): sure to do better if all is well. *J. L. Dunlop* — **70 p**

TIME AND A HALF 3 b.g. Timeless Times (USA) 99 – Skiddaw Bird (Bold Owl 101) [2002 7f 8.1d 8m 8m 12.1g Jul 30] 8,000Y: sparely-made gelding: seventh foal: brother to 5f (at 2 yrs)/6f winner Foreman: dam unraced: no sign of ability: blinkered (slowly away) last 2 outings. *A. Bailey* — **—**

TIME BOMB 5 b.m. Great Commotion (USA) 123 – Play For Time (Comedy Star (USA) 121) [2002 66?: 7g 6m 6d 6.1d³ 6m³ 6d 7.1g 6m² 7m 6m 7s Oct 26] angular mare: modest handicapper: best at 6f: acts on heavy and good to firm going: has given trouble at stall: free-going sort: unreliable. *B. R. Millman* — **58 §**

TIME CAN TELL 8 ch.g. Sylvan Express 117 – Stellaris (Star Appeal 133) [2002 42, a55: f16.2g f14.8g Dec 14] big gelding: modest handicapper at 7 yrs: little form in 2002: tried visored/blinkered. *A. G. Juckes* — **—**

TIME FOR FAME (USA) 5 b.g. Quest For Fame 127 – Intimate (USA) (Topsider (USA)) [2002 p12g Nov 27] first foal: dam, 6f/6.5f winner in USA at 4 yrs, half-sister to dam of smart 1998 2-y-o 7f winner Auction House: fairly useful maiden at best, lightly raced: sold from Mme C. Head-Maarek 15,000 gns after final 3-y-o start: virtually pulled up in Lingfield claimer on British debut (said to have had breathing problem). *W. J. Musson* — **—**

TIME FOR MUSIC (IRE) 5 b.g. Mukaddamah (USA) 125 – Shrewd Girl (USA) 79 (Sagace (FR) 135) [2002 70: p7g² p8g⁶ f7g⁶ 7g² 7g³ 7m⁶ 7m⁴ 7m² p7g² Nov 19] lengthy, quite attractive gelding: fair performer: probably best at 7f: acts on firm ground and polytrack: blinkered once in 2000: free-going sort: consistent. *T. G. Mills* — **75 a67**

TIME FOR THE CLAN 5 ch.g. Clantime 101 – Fyas 52 (Sayf El Arab (USA) 127) [2002 –: 7g⁶ 7f⁵ 9g 8f Jun 21] maiden: little form in 2002: tried blinkered/visored. *R. Bastiman* — **—**

TIME HONOURED 2 b.f. (Apr 11) Sadler's Wells (USA) 132 – Time Charter 131 (Saritamer (USA) 130) [2002 7m⁴ 8g* Sep 10] rather leggy, quite attractive filly: sister to smart 1½m winner Time Allowed and half-sister to several at least useful winners, including smart 1m (at 2 yrs) and 1½m winner Zinaad (by Shirley Heights): dam won 4 Group 1s at 1¼m/1½m: fairly useful form: still green, won maiden at Leicester by ½ length from Russian Society, edging ahead close home: will be suited by 1¼m+: almost certainly capable of better still. *Sir Michael Stoute* — **83 p**

TIMELESS CHARM   3 b.g. Timeless Times (USA) 99 – Whittle Rock 91 (Rock   –
City 120) [2002 58: 6m 6d May 27] small gelding: modest maiden at 2 yrs: well held in
maiden/seller in 2002. *A. Bailey*

TIMELESS CHICK   5 ch.m. Timeless Times (USA) 99 – Be My Bird 65 (Be My   48
Chief (USA) 122) [2002 49: 7d³ 8.1m 8d 8.5m⁴ 8m* 8.1g³ 10g Oct 24] quite good-topped
mare: has a round action: modest performer: won apprentice handicap at Brighton in
August: stays 8.5f: acts on good to firm going and fibresand: often blinkered/visored
earlier in career: none too consistent. *J. L. Spearing*

TIMELESS FARRIER   4 b.g. Timeless Times (USA) 99 – Willrack Farrier 73   56 d
(Lugana Beach 116) [2002 58, a75: 6g 5.7g p6g p6g 5.7f f6s f5g f5g f6g⁶ Dec 7]   a62 d
good-topped gelding: modest handicapper: left B. Smart before well held last 5 starts:
best at 5f/6f: acts on fibresand and good to firm ground: usually blinkered/visored: has
had tongue tied/worn cheekpieces: races prominently. *J. M. Bradley*

TIMELESS MELODY   2 ch.f. (Jan 25) Inchinor 119 – Auntie Gladys 49 (Great   55
Nephew 125) [2002 f5g 7f³ 6m⁴ 8m⁶ 7f 8.2v f7g Nov 25] 6,500Y: lengthy filly: fourth   a–
foal: closely related to useful 7f/1m winner Family Man (by Indian Ridge) and half-sister
to 5-y-o Bishopstone Man: dam placed up to 2m: modest maiden: best efforts second and
third starts: should stay at least 1m. *T. D. Easterby*

TIMELESS QUESTION   3 ch.f. Timeless Times (USA) 99 – Tarda 63 (Absalom   38
128) [2002 48: 6f 5s 7f 7m 8g 6g 6f Oct 8] small, lengthy, sparely-made filly: poor
maiden: seems to stay 7f. *R. M. Whitaker*

TIMELESS TOUCH (IRE)   2 b.c. (May 17) Timeless Times (USA) 99 – Shirley's   51
Touch (Touching Wood (USA) 127) [2002 5g 6m⁴ 7f* 7m 7g 7d Aug 23] 1,600Y: small,
leggy colt: sixth foal: half-brother to 1m winner To The Last Man (by Warrshan): dam
unraced: modest performer: no form after winning seller at Redcar in June: should stay
1m: acts on firm ground: sold 2,000 gns. *C. W. Fairhurst*

TIME MACHINE (IRE)   3 b.g. Spectrum (IRE) 126 – In Your Dreams (IRE) (Suave   –
Dancer (USA) 136) [2002 f7g Oct 22] 11,000Y: second foal: half-brother to 2000 2-y-o
6f winner Theresa Green (by Charnwood Forest): dam, ran once, out of sister to smart
stayer Zinaad and half-sister to smart 1½m winner Time Allowed: broke leg in seller at
Southwell: dead. *J. G. FitzGerald*

TIME MARCHES ON   4 b.g. Timeless Times (USA) 99 – Tees Gazette Girl 42 (Kala-   46
glow 132) [2002 33: 10.1s³ 10.9d 10g⁶ 10d² 11.1g 10g 10.1m 11s³ 10f⁶ Sep 27] leggy
gelding: poor handicapper: stays 11f: acts on firm and soft going, probably on fibresand:
sometimes looks none too keen: successful over hurdles in November. *Mrs M. Reveley*

TIME N TIME AGAIN   4 b.g. Timeless Times (USA) 99 – Primum Tempus 49   82
(Primo Dominie 121) [2002 89: 5f 5.1f 5f 7d 5m 5m⁶ 5g² 5g² 5d⁵ 5m⁵ 5.1f² 5m 5.1f² 5f
5d² Oct 21] leggy, useful-looking gelding: fairly useful handicapper: best at 5f: acts on
firm and good to soft going: tried blinkered: races up with pace. *E. J. Alston*

TIME ROYAL   3 b.c. Timeless Times (USA) 99 – Royal Girl 67 (Kafu 120) [2002 87:   77
6s 7m 6.1f 6.1d⁴ May 18] strong colt: fairly useful performer at 2 yrs: form in 2002 only
in minor event at Nottingham (soon driven along) final outing: stays 6f: possibly best on
ground softer than good: tried blinkered/tongue tied: sold 3,500 gns. *B. A. McMahon*

TIME SPIN   2 b.g. (Mar 28) Robellino (USA) 127 – Chiltern Court (USA) (Topsider   66
(USA)) [2002 7.1g⁴ 7.1g⁴ 8g Oct 16] 15,000Y: third foal: half-brother to 1m winner
Circlet (by Lion Cavern): dam, unraced, out of sister to Thatch and Special, latter dam of
Nureyev and grandam of Sadler's Wells: fair form when fourth in maidens at Chepstow:
should stay at least 1m. *B. J. Meehan*

TIME TEMPTRESS   6 b.m. Timeless Times (USA) 99 – Tangalooma 56 (Hotfoot   –
126) [2002 30, a–: 12f 14g May 20] sparely-made mare: one-time fair performer: well
held in 2002: tried blinkered/visored. *I. W. McInnes*

TIMETOBENICE (IRE)   2 b.f. (Feb 4) Danetime (IRE) 121 – Woodenitbenice   39
(USA) (Nasty And Bold (USA)) [2002 5m 6.1d 7g 6g Oct 28] 2,000Y: half-sister to
several winners, including 5-y-o Special Promise: dam unraced out of half-sister to US
Grade 1 1½m winner Magazine: poor maiden. *J. L. Spearing*

TIME TO BURN   3 b.f. Atraf 116 – Into The Fire 74 (Dominion 123) [2002 50: 8m   –
f8.5g 6m May 27] small filly: lightly raced and little form since debut at 2 yrs: tried
visored. *Mrs Lucinda Featherstone*

TIMETOGOAGAIN   3 ch.f. Timeless Times (USA) 99 – Ohnonotagain 45 (Kind of   –
Hush 118) [2002 6f 5g Jul 6] small, strong, lengthy filly: first foal: dam sprint maiden:
well beaten in 2 maidens. *B. W. Murray*

TIME TO REGRET   2 b.g. (Apr 22) Presidium 124 – Scoffera 63 (Scottish Reel 123)   59
[2002 7g 6v⁶ Nov 9] 900Y: fourth foal: dam, 1m/1¼m winner (also successful
over hurdles), half-sister to useful sprinter Bid For Blue: modest form in maidens: will
probably stay 1m. *J. J. Quinn*

TIME TO REMEMBER (IRE)   4 b.g. Pennekamp (USA) 130 – Bequeath (USA)   86
(Lyphard (USA) 132) [2002 83: 8s 64m³ 6m 7d 7g³ 7m 7m 8s 7m³ Sep 8] big gelding:
fluent mover: fairly useful handicapper: best form at 6f/7f: acts on good to firm ground:
usually wears crossed noseband/early to post: got upset in stall sixth start: often races
freely: has hung left: sold 26,000 gns. *T. D. Easterby*

TIME TO SHINE   3 b.f. Pivotal 124 – Sweet Jaffa 73§ (Never So Bold 135) [2002   69
p8g p12g⁶ 9.9m⁶ p13g* Dec 28] 1,000F, 4,500Y: fifth foal: half-sister to 1999 2-y-o 5.7f
winner Tangerine (by Primo Dominie) who stayed 1¼m: dam untrustworthy 7f winner:
best effort (having been off 6 months and left D. Elsworth) when winning handicap at
Lingfield in December: should stay beyond 13f. *B. R. Johnson*

TIMING   3 b.f. Alhaarth (IRE) 126 – Pretty Davis (USA) (Trempolino (USA) 135)   92
[2002 65: f7g 12d* 10m² 12m³ 12.1g² 12.3d⁵ 12.3f³ 16.2m* 16.2d² 16d* 14m⁴ 15g 14f*   a–
16s Nov 6] rather leggy, angular filly: fairly useful handicapper: won at Catterick in
March, Beverley in July, Thirsk in August and Newmarket in October: stays 2m: acts on
firm and good to soft going, possibly not on soft (modest form at 2 yrs on fibresand):
tends to be edgy in stall/slowly away (has twice failed stall test): saddle slipped twelfth
outing: genuine and reliable. *T. D. Easterby*

TINA BALLERINA   3 ch.f. Komaite (USA) – Very Bold 57 (Never So Bold 135)   –
[2002 –: f5g 5d May 10] sturdy, close-coupled filly: little form. *W. M. Brisbourne*

TINA'S INDIAN (IRE)   4 b.f. Indian Ridge 123 – Tina's Charm (IRE) 66 (Hatim   54
(USA) 121) [2002 –: p12g p8g 10m* 11.6s 10.9m 8.1g 9.7d 8.1g Sep 12] second foal:
dam, Irish 9f/hurdles winner, half-sister to useful 7f/1m performer Indian Fly (by Indian
Ridge): modest performer: trained by L. Browne in Ireland at 3 yrs: won Brighton seller
in May: well held after: should stay 1½m: acts on good to firm going: visored (started
slowly) sixth/seventh outings. *B. G. Powell*

TINAS PRINCE (IRE)   2 b.c. (Apr 9) Desert Prince (USA) 130 – Bold Tina (IRE) 72   –
(Persian Bold 123) [2002 6m 7d 6m Aug 31] first foal: dam, 7f winner, out of half-sister
to dam of Ridgewood Pearl: well held in maidens. *J. S. Wainwright*

TING (IRE)   5 b.g. Magical Wonder (USA) 125 – Rozmiyn (Caerleon (USA) 132)   –
[2002 70: f8s f8s 8.3g f9.4g 8d f8g f8g 12.3s f16g f11g f12g Dec 27] leggy, quite good-
topped gelding: fair performer in 2001: well held in 2002. *M. J. Polglase*

TINK'S MAN   3 b.g. Puissance 110 – Expectation (IRE) 59 (Night Shift (USA)) [2002   53
60: 5g 6f 5g³ f5s f6g³ f5f f6g Dec 10] strong gelding: modest maiden: stays 6f: acts on
fibresand: tongue tied final start: none too consistent. *Mrs A. Duffield*

TINSEL MOON (IRE)   5 b.m. River Falls 113 – Fordes Cross (Ya Zaman (USA)   60
122) [2002 –: f9.4g⁴ 8g* 8.3d 7f 7.1m 8f³ 8f 9.7m 10m Aug 17] strong mare: modest
performer: won maiden at Ripon in April: stayed 1¼m: acted on firm and good to soft
ground: tried visored: hinted at temperament: dead. *R. M. H. Cowell*

TINSTRE (IRE)   4 ch.g. Dolphin Street (FR) 125 – Satin Poppy (Satin Wood 117)   –
[2002 45: 10d 12.6f Jun 26] small, sparely-made gelding: maiden handicapper: well held
in 2002: tried tongue tied. *P. W. Hiatt*

TINTAWN GOLD (IRE)   2 b.f. (Jan 17) Rudimentary (USA) 118 – Clear Ahead   56
(Primo Dominie 121) [2002 6.1g² 7m 6m⁴ 7g Oct 4] IR 6,200Y: sturdy filly: first foal:
dam unraced daughter of smart performer up to 1m Shoot Clear, herself half-sister to
Yorkshire Oaks winners Sally Brown and Untold: modest maiden: well held in nursery at
Lingfield final start: should stay 1m. *Mrs P. N. Dutfield*

TINY TIM (IRE)   4 b.g. Brief Truce (USA) 126 – Nonnita 71 (Welsh Saint 126) [2002   45
47: p7g p6g p6g 5m 6m⁵ 7m p6g⁵ 6g p5g 7m⁵ 8f Sep 30] leggy, sparely-made gelding:
poor maiden: stays 7f: acts on polytrack, form only on good going or firmer on turf:
tongue tied last 2 starts. *I. A. Balding*

TIOGA GOLD (IRE)   3 b.g. Goldmark (USA) 113 – Coffee Bean (Doulab (USA) 115)   57
[2002 63: 10m 10m⁴ p10g Sep 10] leggy gelding: modest performer: probably stays

1¼m: acts on fibresand and good to firm going: carried head awkwardly penultimate start: blinkered (folded tamely) final run: sold 4,000 gns. *B. J. Meehan*

TIOMAN (IRE) 3 b. or br.g. Dr Devious (IRE) 127 – Tochar Ban (USA) 83 (Assert 134) [2002 12m³ 11.8d⁴ p12g Jun 9] 18,500F, 190,000Y: tall, good sort: fourth foal: half-brother to French 1999 2-y-o 1m winner Uncharted Haven (by Turtle Island), later US Grade 2 1m winner: dam 1¼m winner: fairly useful form in minor event at Newmarket (ran green) and maiden at Leicester first 2 starts: very disappointing (found little) on all-weather debut at Lingfield final outing (gelded after): will be suited by 1¾m. *M. A. Jarvis* — **87**

TIPPERARY SUNSET (IRE) 8 gr.g. Red Sunset 120 – Chapter And Verse (Dancer's Image 113) [2002 69, a–: 7g Sep 10] strong, close-coupled gelding: fair handicapper at 7 yrs: has won 3 times at Beverley: well held only run in 2002: sometimes blinkered. *D. Shaw* — **–**

TIPTAU 3 ch.f. Bedford (USA) 109 – High Commotion (IRE) 70 (Taufan (USA) 119) [2002 10m 10.2d p12g Jul 20] lengthy, unfurnished filly: second foal: dam, lightly-raced maiden, out of sister to high-class 1¼m/1½m performer Master Willie: well held in maidens/minor event. *J. G. Portman* — **–**

TIP TOP 3 b.f. Mistertopogigo (IRE) 118 – Strawberry Pink 87 (Absalom 128) [2002 –: 5.1d⁴ 6f⁵ 5m 5g May 10] strong filly: poor maiden: hung left leaving stall second outing: stays 6f: acts on firm and good to soft going. *T. D. Easterby* — **41**

TIP TOPPER 2 b.c. (Apr 19) Lahib (USA) 129 – Cyrillic 88 (Rock City 120) [2002 5.1g 6s 5.1d 7f⁵ 7g⁵ 8m 7m⁵ 7g Oct 4] 6,000F, IR 14,000Y: small colt: third foal: half-brother to 4-y-o Lady Laureate: dam 2-y-o 6f winner who stayed 1m: modest maiden: stays 7f, possibly not 1m: best effort on good ground: blinkered (ran poorly) final start: sold 5,000 gns. *C. G. Cox* — **61**

TIPTRONIC (IRE) 3 b.g. Woodborough (USA) 112 – Snowtop (Thatching 131) [2002 70: f7s* p8g* p7g p8g⁵ 6g 7m 7g⁴ May 2] sturdy gelding: fairly useful performer on all-weather, fair on turf: won maiden at Southwell and handicap at Lingfield in January: seems better at 7f/1m than 6f: acts on all-weather: often slowly away: sent to Singapore. *G. C. H. Chung* — **76 a85**

TIPU SULTAN 2 ch.c. (Feb 20) Kris 135 – Eye Witness (IRE) 72 (Don't Forget Me 127) [2002 8g³ Oct 18] big, close-coupled colt: has a markedly round action: sixth foal: half-brother to useful Irish 7f (at 2 yrs) and 9f winner Hasanat (by Night Shift) and a 5f winner abroad by Wolfhound: dam maiden (best effort at 8.5f) from family of Zafonic and Elmaamul: 33/1, 2 lengths third of 16 to Calibre in maiden at Newmarket, keeping on well from rear: sure to improve and win a race. *E. A. L. Dunlop* — **90 p**

TIRAILLEUR (IRE) 2 b.f. (Apr 13) Eagle Eyed (USA) 111 – Tiralle (IRE) 71 (Tirol 127) [2002 5g⁶ 5g⁶ 6.1g 6d* 7m* 7m 7m f6g⁴ p5g⁶ p6g⁶ f5g² f6s⁴ f6g³ Dec 16] IR 1,800Y: sturdy filly: second foal: half-sister to Italian 5f (including at 2 yrs) winner Kiffa (by College Chapel): dam, Irish maiden, stayed 1¾m: fair performer: won 2 claimers at Brighton in June (left Mrs P. N. Dutfield after first of them): mostly creditable efforts after: effective at 5f to 7f: acts on all-weather, good to firm and good to soft going: blinkered last 6 starts: sometimes looks none too genuine. *J. White* — **66**

TIRANA (IRE) 4 b.g. Brief Truce (USA) 126 – Cloche du Roi (FR) (Fairy King (USA)) [2002 55, a60: f8g f8.5g p7g 8m² 7.9g⁶ 8.1m 8g 10m 8m p8g Oct 9] angular, workmanlike gelding: modest performer: below form last 5 starts: stays 8.5f: acts on good to firm going, good to soft and all-weather: visored last 2 outings: usually tongue tied: held up: sold £1,800. *D. Shaw* — **55**

TIRARI (IRE) 3 b.f. Charnwood Forest (IRE) 125 – Desert Victory (Green Desert (USA) 127) [2002 65: p7g² p8g⁶ 7f7g⁶ p7g p7g 8.2f 8.2g 10d⁶ f12g⁶ 12m 12f⁵ 10.1f f12f² p12g f12s Sep 7] smallish, useful-looking filly: has a short, round action: just modest performer at best in 2002: left R. Spicer after sixth start: probably stays 1½m: acts on good to firm going, good to soft and all-weather: tried visored: sometimes slowly away. *C. R. Dore* — **45 a55**

TISHOMINGO 3 ch.g. Alhijaz 122 – Enchanted Guest (IRE) 74 (Be My Guest (USA) 126) [2002 61§: f7s⁴ f9.4g⁴ f8.5g f8s² f7g⁵ f9.4g f9.9m⁴ 9.9g² p12g 12.1g⁴ f11g Dec 4] strong, close-coupled gelding: modest performer: stays 1½m: acts on good to firm going and fibresand, possibly not on soft: tongue tied: has run as if something amiss 3 times, including on final start (after 6-month absence): unreliable. *Ronald Thompson* — **55 §**

TISSIFER 6 b.g. Polish Precedent (USA) 131 – Ingozi 91 (Warning 136) [2002 98§: 11.6g⁵ 10m* 10.1m* 11.9g 10m* 9m⁵ 9f 12g Oct 17] quite attractive gelding: useful — **103**

performer: landed odds in claimers at Sandown in July and Yarmouth (left M. Pipe) in August and won handicap at Newmarket (by ¾ length from Beat The Heat) later in August: well below form last 2 starts: effective at 9f to 1½m: acts on firm and good to soft going: tried blinkered earlier in career: formerly ungenuine: joined Mrs M. Reveley. *Mrs Lydia Pearce*

TITCHFIELD (USA)　3 b. or br.g. Mt Livermore (USA) – Morning Colors (USA)　**82** (Raise A Native) [2002 77: 8s⁵ 9f⁵ 11.8m² 14.1f² 14s³ 13.8m* 14g 12.3m⁴ 14m Sep 15] tall, leggy gelding: fairly useful performer: landed odds in maiden at Catterick in July: should stay 2m: acts on firm and soft going: blinkered fifth (raced freely) and seventh starts: no easy ride: sold 13,000 gns. *P. F. I. Cole*

TITIAN ANGEL (IRE)　5 ch.m. Brief Truce (USA) 126 – Kuwah (IRE) 77 (Be My　**–** Guest (USA) 126) [2002 74d: p16g f12s 10m May 4] angular mare: fair maiden handicapper: has deteriorated: tried blinkered. *A. B. Coogan*

TITIAN FLAME (IRE)　2 ch.f. (Feb 15) Titus Livius (FR) 115 – Golden Choice　**69** (Midyan (USA) 124) [2002 5g 6d 8.3d* 8.2m⁴ 8f 7s Oct 25] IR 10,000Y: unfurnished filly: second foal: dam unraced half-sister to smart 1½m/13f performer Phantom Gold: fair performer: won maiden at Windsor in August: well held in nurseries last 2 starts: will stay 1¼m: acts on good to firm and good to soft going. *Mrs P. N. Dutfield*

TITIAN LASS　3 ch.f. Bijou d'Inde 127 – Liebside Lass (IRE) (Be My Guest (USA)　**69** 126) [2002 7g 10m⁵ 8.1g 10m 7m⁶ 7m 8m* 8m² 8g 8d f8.5g f9.4g Dec 9] 5,500F: quite attractive filly: fifth foal: half-sister to Irish 1996 2-y-o 1m winner Mo Chos Chle (by Indian Ridge) and a winner in Germany by Halling: dam unraced daughter of Oaks second Val's Girl: fair performer: won maiden handicap at Yarmouth in September: stays 1¼m: raced mainly on good/good to firm going on turf, below form on fibresand: sometimes races freely. *C. E. Brittain*

TITINIUS (IRE)　2 ch.c. (Apr 10) Titus Livius (FR) 115 – Maiyria (IRE) 68 (Shernazar　**79** 131) [2002 6s⁴ 6v³ Nov 9] 32,000Y: good-bodied colt: has scope: second foal: dam, ran once, half-sister to smart French performer up to 10.5f Masslama: fair form in frame in maidens at Newbury (promising fourth to Zabaglione) and Doncaster (third to Marinas Charm): should stay 7f. *L. M. Cumani*

TITUREL　2 b.c. (Mar 19) Amfortas (IRE) 115 – Musetta (IRE) 107 (Cadeaux Genereux　**84** 131) [2002 7g⁴ 8s² Oct 26] lengthy colt: third foal: half-brother to 3-y-o Mameyuki: dam 7f (at 2 yrs) and 1¼m winner who was fourth in Oaks: much better effort (fairly useful form) when 1¾ lengths second of 15 to Midas Way in maiden at Newbury, edging right: should be suited by 1¼m+. *C. E. Brittain*

TIVOLI GARDEN (IRE)　4 ch.f. Royal Academy (USA) 130 – Maiden Concert　**102** (Condorcet (FR)) [2002 92: 10g* 12m² 10m⁴ 12d⁴ 10g Oct 17] IR 35,000Y: closely related to Irish 1993 2-y-o 7f winner Ruvolina (by Caerleon) and half-sister to several winners, notably very smart 1m/1¼m performer Candy Glen (by Glenstal) and smart Irish 1¼m winner Ashley Park (by Sadler's Wells): dam, ran once, half-sister to dam of Irish 1000 Guineas winner More So: useful performer: won maiden at Listowel at 3 yrs and handicap at the Curragh in July: good fourth at the Curragh in Blandford Stakes and listed race before running poorly in listed race at Newmarket final outing: effective at 1¼m/1½m: acts on soft and good to firm going. *J. S. Bolger, Ireland*

TIYOUN (IRE)　4 b.g. Kahyasi 130 – Taysala (IRE) (Akarad (FR) 130) [2002 100:　**88** 12.3m⁴ 12m 13.9g 10f³ 11.9d 12.3g⁵ 12m⁶ f12g⁶ Dec 20] leggy, lengthy gelding: useful performer at 3 yrs: only fairly useful on balance in 2002: stays 1½m: acts on soft and good to firm going (not at best on firm): tried visored: usually races prominently: none too consistent. *D. W. Barker*

TIZZY MAY (FR)　2 ch.c. (Feb 2) Highest Honor (FR) 124 – Forentia 89 (Formidable　**99** (USA) 125) [2002 5m* 6g 6g⁵ 7g 6g Aug 21] 35,000F, 150,000Y: close-coupled colt: has a quick action: second foal: half-brother to fairly useful 2001 2-y-o 6f winner Access Denied (by Revoque): dam, 2-y-o 5f winner, half-sister to Prix Morny/Middle Park Stakes winner Bahamian Bounty: useful performer: won maiden at Newmarket and minor event at Windsor in May: best effort (despite meeting trouble) when 2½ lengths fifth to Mister Links in July Stakes at Newmarket: not disgraced in Vintage Stakes at Goodwood and Gimcrack Stakes at York after: likely to prove best at 6f/7f: acts on soft and good to firm going. *R. Hannon*

T K O GYM　3 b.g. Atraf 116 – Pearl Pet 56 (Mummy's Pet 125) [2002 74: 6s 6g 7m　**53** 6.1f 6d 7f 7m Aug 28] smallish, close-coupled gelding: fair maiden at 2 yrs: just modest in 2002: should stay 7f: acts on firm ground: usually slowly away. *D. Nicholls*

TOB

TOBAGO FIZZ (USA) 3 b.c. Siphon (BRZ) 130 – Miss Kenton County (USA) **80**
(Northjet 136) [2002 9s⁵ 10m 8f 8m³ 9.9m² 10.9m⁵ 12d p8g 7f p6g* Oct 9] 380,000
francs Y: big colt: eighth foal: half-brother to several winners in USA, including 1994
Grade 3 2-y-o 5.5f winner Unacceptable (by Irish Tower): dam unraced: fairly useful
performer: won handicap at Lingfield in October: finds 6f a minimum, and has form at up
to 1¼m: acts on firm going and polytrack: unseated on way to post second start: pulled
hard and eventually ran out/unseated seventh outing: found little penultimate run: sold
30,000 gns, sent to Kuwait. *L. M. Cumani*

TO BE FARE (IRE) 2 ch.c. (Apr 27) Eagle Eyed (USA) 111 – Petrolea Girl (Con- **55**
naught 130) [2002 6g 7g* f7g 7m 7f⁵ Sep 21] IR 8,000Y, 22,000 2-y-o: sturdy colt: has a
quick action: half-brother to winners in Italy by Waajib and Magical Wonder: dam third
over hurdles in Ireland: modest performer: won seller at Yarmouth in July: respectable
efforts in nurseries after: free-going sort, but should stay 1m. *R. Wilman*

TOBEROE COMMOTION (IRE) 4 b.g. Great Commotion (USA) 123 – Fionn **63**
Varragh (IRE) (Tender King 123) [2002 –: 12d 9g³ 12g 12d 12g 8.5s 11.7g p13g³ p12g
p16g Dec 3] first thoroughbred foal: dam unraced: modest maiden handicapper: left
D. Gillespie in Ireland after sixth start: likely to prove best at 1½m/1¾m: acts on
polytrack, turf form only on good going: tried blinkered. *W. R. Muir*

TOBOUGG (IRE) 4 b.c. Barathea (IRE) 127 – Lacovia (USA) 128 (Majestic Light **111**
(USA)) [2002 125: 12g 10.5s⁵ 10f³ 11f Sep 7] rather leggy, good-topped colt: high-class
performer at best: unbeaten in 3 races as 2-y-o, including Prix de la Salamandre at
Longchamp and Dewhurst Stakes at Newmarket: didn't win again, but good efforts in
2001 when placed in Derby at Epsom, Champion Stakes at Newmarket and Hong Kong
Cup at Sha Tin: nowhere near so good in 2002, fifth to Rebelline in Tattersalls Gold Cup
at the Curragh, third to Highdown when favourite for listed event at Newbury and last in
Man o'War Stakes at Belmont last 3 starts: was effective at 1¼m/1½m: acted on firm and
good to soft going: to stand at Dalham Hall Stud, Newmarket, fee £5,000, Oct 1st, special
live foal. *Saeed bin Suroor*

TOCCATA ARIA 4 b.f. Unfuwain (USA) 131 – Distant Music (Darshaan 133) [2002 **–**
49: 12m Apr 5] big, good-topped filly: poor form at 3 yrs only. *J. M. Bradley*

TOEJAM 9 ch.g. Move Off 112 – Cheeky Pigeon (Brave Invader (USA)) [2002 56: **56**
f9.4g f8g* f9.4g⁴ f8g f8g 8m 8m 7.5d 8g 8.5d⁶ 8g⁴ Aug 26] angular gelding: modest
performer: won handicap at Southwell in February: best form at 1m: acts on fibresand,
firm and good to soft going: tried visored: none too consistent. *R. E. Barr*

TOJONESKI 3 b.g. Emperor Jones (USA) 119 – Sampower Lady 55 (Rock City 120) **78 §**
[2002 72: f7s* p8g⁵ f7s f9.4g⁵ Dec 14] fairly useful handicapper: off nearly a year, won at
Wolverhampton in November: below form after: should stay 1m: acts on fibresand, yet to
race on extremes of going on turf: unreliable. *P. J. Makin*

TOKEWANNA 2 b.f. (Feb 18) Danehill (USA) 126 – High Atlas 65 (Shirley Heights **64**
130) [2002 5.1f⁵ 5d⁶ 7.1f³ 5m² 5m 6.5g Sep 27] 19,000Y: good-bodied filly: third foal:
half-sister to 3-y-o Red Forest: dam, ran once (twice withdrawn after giving trouble at
stall), out of half-sister to high-class performer up to 1½m Sanglamore: modest maiden:
probably better at 7f than shorter: acts on firm ground: tail flasher: found little final start.
C. E. Brittain

TOLAGA BAY 4 ch.f. Dr Devious (IRE) 127 – Swordlestown Miss (USA) (Apalachee **–**
(USA) 137) [2002 p10g f12g Dec 7] half-sister to several winners, including useful 1994
2-y-o 1m winner Traikey (by Scenic) and fairly useful 1½m/13f winner Helen's Day (by
Grand Lodge): dam Irish 2-y-o 7f winner: well held in maidens. *W. Jarvis*

TOLCEA (IRE) 3 ch.g. Barathea (IRE) 127 – Mosaique Bleue (Shirley Heights 130) **57**
[2002 66p: f12g⁶ 14.1m May 10] heavy-topped gelding: modest maiden, lightly raced:
should stay 1¾m+: yet to race on extremes of going: sold 4,500 gns. *E. A. L. Dunlop*

TOLDYA 5 b.m. Beveled (USA) – Run Amber Run (Run The Gantlet (USA)) [2002 **93**
73: p7g f6g p6g⁴ f8.5g 6d p5g* 5.5f⁴ 6d³ 6g² 5m* 5g 6g³ 5m 6f* 6m 6f² Oct 12] smallish
mare: fairly useful handicapper: won at Lingfield in June, Newcastle (edged left) in July
and Kempton in September: effective at 5f to easy 7f: acts on any turf going/all-weather:
tried blinkered/visored: sometimes slowly away: usually races prominently: tough.
A. P. Jarvis

TOLEDO STAR 3 br.g. Petong 126 – Shafir (IRE) 68 (Shaadi (USA) 126) [2002 60?: **–**
6g p6g Nov 14] leggy, close-coupled gelding: seemingly modest form when ninth of 10
in minor event at Doncaster at 2 yrs for D. Nicholls: well held in 2002: gelded after final
start. *S. L. Keightley*

TOLEDO SUN   2 b.g. (Mar 27) Zamindar (USA) 116 – Shafir (IRE) 68 (Shaadi (USA)   **53 +**
126) [2002 6m f5s 6s 6v Nov 9] fourth foal: half-brother to winners abroad by Petong and
Alhijaz: dam 2-y-o 5f winner: modest maiden: will probably stay 7f: gelded after final
start. *S. L. Keightley*

TOMAHAWK (USA)   2 b.c. (Mar 25) Seattle Slew (USA) – Statuette (USA)   **118**
(Pancho Villa (USA)) [2002 5s* 7m² 6f² 7m² a9f Oct 26]
        The old approach to education, which was considered by some experts to
encourage terms of window-gazing followed by cramming in the last few weeks
before exams, has steadily been replaced by one involving assessment of course
work and more regular testing. Fashions change in racehorse training too, and
the 'old-fashioned style' of preparing classic types by giving them a full racing
education as two-year-olds has been enjoying a revival. Aidan O'Brien has taken
the initiative, running his leading prospects in the races designed to test the best
two-year-olds after giving them the right experience. Rock of Gibraltar, Landseer
and Tendulkar, who went on to fill the first three places in the 2001 Dewhurst, had
all made their debuts by early-May of that year, when Rock of Gibraltar clashed
with Hawk Wing as early as July in a seven-race season of his own. Although a
mid-season coughing outbreak hampered things somewhat in the latest season,
O'Brien had his two-year-olds out early again, pattern performers Tomahawk and
Statue of Liberty winning the first two juvenile races of the season in Ireland, with
even one so stoutly bred as Brian Boru making his debut in June.
        Tomahawk won the opening race of the season in Ireland, a maiden at the
Curragh over five furlongs on March 24th, starting at 11/10 and beating Cat Belling
by three lengths. Tomahawk appeared next in the Chesham Stakes at Royal Ascot,
reportedly tackling the seven-furlong race as he was one of the few in his yard
forward enough and qualified for the event, which is restricted to horses whose
sires won over at least a mile and a quarter. With Statue of Liberty having won the
previous day's Coventry Stakes, weight of money drove Tomahawk's odds down to
2/1-on, but he could manage only second to Helm Bank, improving smoothly
before just being edged out on the line, showing only useful form.
        Tomahawk returned to tackle three prestigious prizes in the autumn, this
time showing himself well up amongst the best of his generation. He started much
the shortest-priced of his stable's four runners in the Middle Park Stakes at Newmarket in October, a well-backed second favourite at 5/1, and beat all bar Oasis
Dream. He was soon close up and went down by a length and a half, with favourite
Elusive City a neck behind, the first three clear of Country Reel. Tomahawk again
started second favourite for the Dewhurst Stakes back at Newmarket later in the
month, going off at 100/30 in a field of sixteen. He again had to settle for second.
Looking head and shoulders above the rest in the paddock, Tomahawk travelled
strongly towards the centre, but he tended to wander under pressure in the Dip and
had no answer as Tout Seul quickened through smartly towards the stand rail, going
down by a length and a quarter, keeping on strongly to finish the same distance
ahead of favourite Trade Fair in third. Tomahawk was at much longer odds for his
final outing of the season only a week later, starting the outsider of his stable's
three runners at around 17/1 in the Breeders' Cup Juvenile at Arlington. Despite his
pedigree, he proved quite unable to cope with the test. With no previous racing
experience on dirt, he was slowly away and never dangerous as he finished eighth
of thirteen.

		Seattle Slew (USA) (b or br 1974)	Bold Reasoning (b or br 1968)	Boldnesian
				Reason To Earn
Tomahawk (USA)			My Charmer (b 1969)	Poker
(b.c. Mar 25, 2000)				Fair Charmer
		Statuette (USA) (b 1990)	Pancho Villa (ch 1982)	Secretariat
				Crimson Saint
			Mine Only (b 1981)	Mr Prospector
				Mono

        It is a good while since Seattle Slew, who died in 2002, had a runner in
Europe to match the best of his earlier produce outside America such as Magic of
Life, Digression and Septieme Ciel, but his stock enjoyed an indian summer on
both sides of the Atlantic in 2002, when he was also responsible for Loving

Kindness and the Breeders' Cup Juvenile winner Vindication. The big, well-made Tomahawk cost 2,500,000 dollars as a yearling. He is the fourth foal of the American Grade 3 winner at eight and a half furlongs Statuette, who also got a winner in the States by Danzig. Statuette is closely related to the American Grade 2 winner at a mile and a quarter Academy Award. Tomahawk should stay a mile and a quarter himself, though he hasn't looked short of speed to date. Given that he has won only a maiden so far, he shouldn't be hard to place to advantage at three, though he'll need to improve a bit to win the Two Thousand Guineas even in an average year. His win at two came on soft ground, and he raced only on good to firm or firm on turf afterwards. *A. P. O'Brien, Ireland*

TOMASINO 4 br.c. Celtic Swing 138 – Bustinetta 89 (Bustino 136) [2002 110: 12g **104** 12s Oct 26] good-topped colt: smart handicapper in 2001 (reportedly found to have suffered small fracture of off-fore cannon bone after final 3-y-o start): easily better effort in 2002 when eighth of 22 in handicap at Newmarket on reappearance in October: will stay 1¾m: acts on any going. *M. Johnston*

TOM BELL (IRE) 2 b.c. (Mar 24) King's Theatre (IRE) 128 – Nordic Display (IRE) **–** 77 (Nordico (USA)) [2002 8.1g 7.1g 10s Oct 23] IR 8,500Y, 7,000 2-y-o: fourth foal: dam Irish 1¼m winner: signs of just a little ability in maidens. *J. G. M. O'Shea*

TOM FROM BOUNTY 2 ch.g. (May 2) Opera Ghost 91 – Tempus Fugit 85 (Timeless **69 ?** Times (USA) 99) [2002 6.1v⁶ 7.1m Jul 7] first foal: dam 2-y-o 5f winner: apparently fair form (possibly flattered) in minor event at Chepstow: showed little next time. *B. R. Millman*

TOMILLIE 3 ch.g. Ventiquattrofogli (IRE) 118 – Royal Comedian 58 (Jester 119) **49** [2002 70: 7.1m⁶ 6m⁵ 6.1f 6g 5.9g⁵ 6g⁶ 5m 5s⁶ 5m f6g Oct 17] good-topped gelding: poor maiden: left A. Berry after ninth start: headstrong and best at 5f/6f: acts on soft and good to firm going: tried blinkered: usually forces pace. *K. A. Ryan*

TOMINA 2 b.g. (Apr 19) Deploy 131 – Cavina 64 (Ardross 134) [2002 7s p8g Nov **67** 14] workmanlike gelding: second foal: dam 2m winner/winning hurdler: better effort in maidens (fair form) when never-nearer seventh to Joe Bear at Lingfield second start: will be suited by 1¼m+. *N. A. Graham*

TOMMY CARSON 7 b.g. Last Tycoon 131 – Ivory Palm (USA) 93 (Sir Ivor 135) **44** [2002 53?: p16g² p12g⁶ Mar 25] sturdy gelding: poor maiden handicapper: stays easy 2m: acts on any turf going and polytrack: usually blinkered earlier in career. *Jamie Poulton*

TOMMY DOD 3 ch.g. Keen 116 – Wyse Folly (Colmore Row 111) [2002 58: f9.4g **–** f8g 5.9g 9.2v 7m Sep 23] good-bodied gelding: modest maiden at 2 yrs: no form in 2002, leaving M. Johnston after second start: blinkered final run. *C. W. Thornton*

TOMMY NUTTER (IRE) 2 b.g. (Apr 7) Desert Style (IRE) 121 – Ahakista (IRE) **65 §** (Persian Bold 123) [2002 p5g p5g⁴ 5f⁶ 6m³ f5s f5g² f6g f5g² f6g⁶ f5g⁵ Dec 27] 11,000F, 10,000Y: third foal: dam unraced out of half-sister to 2000 Guineas winner High Top: fair maiden: left W. Haggas after third outing: runner-up in sellers at Wolverhampton and Southwell: likely to prove best at 5f/easy 6f: acts on all-weather and good to firm ground: tried blinkered and in cheekpieces: sometimes carries head awkwardly. *R. Brotherton*

TOMMY SMITH 4 ch.g. Timeless Times (USA) 99 – Superstream (Superpower 113) **92 §** [2002 76§: 5g 5g 6f 5m* 5m* 5d 5m* 5g 6m⁶ 5m 5m⁵ 5m Oct 2] smallish, sturdy gelding: fairly useful performer: won minor event at Pontefract and handicaps at Ripon and York in June/July: has won at 6f, best form at 5f: goes well on going firmer than good: usually visored/blinkered nowadays: often starts slowly/hangs (lost all chance with very slow start sixth outing): reared and unseated stalls eighth start: can't be trusted. *J. S. Wainwright*

TOM PADDINGTON 7 b.g. Rock Hopper 124 – Mayfair Minx (St Columbus 98) **81** [2002 16s* 16.5v Nov 9] fairly useful performer, lightly raced: won maiden at Bath in 1998: first run since when winning handicap at Newbury (raced freely) in October: well beaten only subsequent outing: will stay beyond 2m: raced only on good ground or softer: useful hurdler in 1998/9. *H. Morrison*

TOM'S CRUISING 3 b.g. Fraam 114 – Fading (Pharly (FR) 130) [2002 8m² 8d* 8f **98** Oct 4] 29,000Y, 70,000 2-y-o: tall, leggy, close-coupled gelding: seventh foal: brother to 4-y-o Dayglow Dancer and 5-y-o Fraamtastic: dam unraced: useful form: won maiden at Newcastle in September by 5 lengths from Dexterity: well backed, ran as if amiss in minor event on firm ground at Newmarket final run (gelded after): not sure to stay further than 1m: edged left on debut. *H. R. A. Cecil*

TOMSK (IRE) 2 b.g. (May 4) Definite Article 121 – Merry Twinkle (Martinmas 128) – [2002 7.2g Sep 20] IR 10,500F, IR 7,000Y: brother to a winner in Spain and half-brother to several winners, including 5-y-o Gdansk and Irish 7f winner Sparkling Harmony (by Common Grounds): dam ran twice in Ireland: 33/1, well beaten in maiden at Ayr. *A. Berry*

TOM TAILOR (GER) 8 b.g. Beldale Flutter (USA) 130 – Thoughtful 86 (North-fields (USA)) [2002 11.6d May 7] tall gelding: reportedly operated on for his wind: fair handicapper in 1999: below form both subsequent Flat outings: was better around 2m than shorter: acted on soft and good to firm going: blinkered only start in 2002: dead. *D. R. C. Elsworth*

TOMTHEVIC 4 ch.g. Emarati (USA) 74 – Madame Bovary 82 (Ile de Bourbon (USA) 133) [2002 65: 5f⁵ 5.1d 5g 6.1m² 5m 5m 5m⁶ 6g⁶ 5f² 5m* 5m² f5s 6m 5f 6f⁶ Oct 12] strong-quartered gelding: fair handicapper: left J. Quinn after seventh start: dead-heated at Newmarket in August: has form at 6f, probably best at 5f on good going or firmer: visored (well held) once at 3 yrs: has had tongue tied: usually races prominently. *P. R. Chamings* **67**

TOM TUN 7 b.g. Bold Arrangement 127 – B Grade 59 (Lucky Wednesday 124) [2002 95: f7s⁴ f6s² f6g³ f6g³ 6s* 6g⁶ 6m 6g* 6.3d² 5.9v* 6g 6g 6s⁴ 6v* Nov 9] workmanlike gelding: has a round action: useful performer: left Miss J. Craze after fourth start: won handicaps at Doncaster in March, Ayr in May and Hamilton in July, and listed race at Doncaster (better than ever, beat Bright Edge by 2½ lengths) in November: races mainly at 6f nowadays: acts on fibresand, clearly best efforts on ground softer than good (acts on heavy): often tongue tied before joining current stable: tends to be soon off bridle: tough and reliable. *J. G. Given* **106**

TOM TYGRYS 3 b.g. Danzig Connection (USA) – Strath Kitten 36 (Scottish Reel 123) [2002 –: 12.1g 16m 10g Jul 6] small gelding: little form. *P. S. McEntee* –

TON-CHEE 3 b.g. Vettori (IRE) 119 – Najariya (Northfields (USA)) [2002 12g⁶ 10f⁵ 14.1m Aug 21] 3,500Y: half-brother to several winners, including useful 1992 2-y-o 6f/7f winner Nominator (by Nomination) and fairly useful 1998 2-y-o 5f/6f winner My Petal (by Petong): dam unraced half-sister to Cherry Hinton winner Nasseem: well held in maidens at Catterick, Redcar and Carlisle. *K. W. Hogg, Isle of Man* –

TONG ICE 3 gr.g. Petong 126 – Efficacious (IRE) 49 (Efisio 120) [2002 36: f6g³ f7g² f9.4g 9.2s 6g 11.1v⁴ p10g 7.6m Aug 21] poor maiden: left I. Semple after sixth start: stays 7f: usually visored/blinkered: sometimes carries head awkwardly. *B. A. Pearce* **a47**

TONI ALCALA 3 b.g. Ezzoud (IRE) 126 – Etourdie (USA) (Arctic Tern (USA) 126) [2002 76d: 8g² 10g³ 12m* 12f³ 12m³ 12m 12m⁴ 12.1v⁴ 12g 13s 17.1m² 14m⁶ 16g 16.1d⁵ 16m³ 15.8f 16.1m 12f f12g* f16.2f⁴ Nov 11] close-coupled gelding: fair performer: won handicap at Southwell in April and minor event at Wolverhampton in October: stays 17f: acts on firm going, good to soft and fibresand: edgy type: has been reluctant stall/slowly away/raced freely: usually held up. *R. F. Fisher* **71**

TONY TIE 6 b.g. Ardkinglass 114 – Queen of The Quorn 53 (Governor General 116) [2002 89: 8s 8f⁵ 8.5g³ 8.1d⁴ 10g 8.9d² 8g⁴ 10.4m⁵ 8f 7m³ 7.6g⁵ 9.2s* 8.3m² 10.3m⁴ 8g 8m⁴ 9f Oct 5] leggy, angular gelding: unimpressive mover: useful handicapper: won at Hamilton in August: needs at least 7f and stays easy 1¼m: acts on any going: visored once: has idled in front, and often held up: tough and consistent. *J. S. Goldie* **95**

TOORAK (USA) 5 b.g. Irish River (FR) 131 – Just Juliet (USA) (What A Pleasure (USA)) [2002 p12g Mar 6] rangy, angular gelding: fluent mover: disappointing maiden. *C. J. Mann* –

TOPAZ 7 b.g. Alhijaz 122 – Daisy Topper (Top Ville 129) [2002 –: f14.8g Jan 18] no longer of much account. *H. J. Collingridge* –

TOP DIRHAM 4 ch.g. Night Shift (USA) – Miller's Melody 86 (Chief Singer 131) – [2002 100p: 8m 7m 8.9m 9.1g Sep 20] strong, good-topped gelding: useful performer at 3 yrs: little form in 2002, gelded and leaving Sir Michael Stoute before running as if badly amiss in claimers last 2 starts. *M. W. Easterby* –

TOP FLIGHT QUEEN 3 b.f. Mark of Esteem (IRE) 137 – Blessed Event 117 (Kings Lake (USA) 133) [2002 65: f9.4g² 11.9m² 10g* 10v⁴ 10.1g³ 10g² 10.2g⁵ Jul 26] good-topped filly: fairly useful performer: much improved in 2002, winning handicap at Brighton in May: probably flattered in listed event at Chepstow final start: seems best **82 +**

around 1¼m: acts on any turf going and fibresand: has been slowly away/flashed tail/raced freely/carried head high. *C. F. Wall*

TOP HAND 5 ch.m. First Trump 118 – Gold Luck (USA) (Slew O' Gold (USA)) [2002 f12g f16g Feb 7] lengthy mare: lightly raced and no form nowadays. *E. W. Tuer* –

TOPKAMP 2 b.f. (Mar 18) Pennekamp (USA) 130 – Victoria Regia (IRE) 90 (Lomond (USA) 128) [2002 6f² 5.1g* 6m 5m* 5.2f³ 6f⁴ Oct 12] 27,000F: smallish, strong, lengthy filly: first foal: dam 2-y-o 6f winner (later 1m/8.5f winner in USA), out of half-sister to Prix Vermeille winner Walensee: useful performer: won maiden at Nottingham in June and minor event at Doncaster in July: best effort when length third to Speed Cop in listed race at Newbury despite starting slowly and hanging left: likely to prove best at 5f/easy 6f: raced on good going or firmer. *M. L. W. Bell* **96**

TOP NOLANS (IRE) 4 ch.g. Topanoora 118 – Lauretta Blue (IRE) (Bluebird (USA) 125) [2002 63, a59: p7g f8s⁶ 8m³ 7g 7.9s² 8.3v* f8.5g² Jul 26] rather sparely-made gelding: fair performer: won minor event at Hamilton in June: stays 8.5f: acts on fibresand, good to firm and heavy going: tried visored earlier in career: has raced freely. *M. H. Tompkins* **71 a64**

TOP OF THE CLASS (IRE) 5 b.m. Rudimentary (USA) 118 – School Mum (Reprimand 122) [2002 47: f8s f8.5g⁴ f9.4g² f9.4g⁵ f9.4g⁶ f9.4g² f9.4g³ p12g⁴ 10.3s f12g f12g 9.2s* f9.4s⁵ 11.1g⁶ 10.2d³ 8f 9.2v* 9.2s² 8.1m⁵ 9.2s⁴ 9.3g⁶ 10.3f⁵ 10.2d⁵ 9d⁵ 10.2f⁵ 10.1f 9.2v⁶ 12.1s³ 9.9m⁶ 10.5m⁵ f12g p10g Dec 30] unfurnished mare: has a round action: modest performer on turf, poor on all-weather: won claimer in May and handicap in June, both at Hamilton: probably best at 9f/1¼m: acts on all-weather, probably ideally suited by good going or softer on turf (acts on heavy): tried blinkered, usually visored nowadays: sometimes slowly away: has found little: inconsistent. *P. D. Evans* **54 § a41 §**

TOPPLING 4 b.g. Cadeaux Genereux 131 – Topicality (USA) (Topsider (USA)) [2002 88: 7g 7.1m⁵ 7m 7s⁶ 7.5m 7g⁶ 7m 6m³ 6.1m 6d f6g Oct 22] smallish, good-bodied gelding: fair handicapper: free-going sort, but stays 1m: acts on good to firm going: on downgrade. *J. M. Bradley* **73 d**

TOP TENOR (IRE) 2 b.c. (Mar 2) Sadler's Wells (USA) 132 – Posta Vecchia (USA) (Rainbow Quest (USA) 134) [2002 7g 8g⁵ 8g Oct 24] IR 190,000Y: compact colt: first foal: dam, ran once at 2 yrs, out of half-sister to 5-y-o Bach: clearly best effort in maidens (fair form) when fifth to Foodbroker Founder at Salisbury: slowly away final start: will stay at least 1¼m. *J. L. Dunlop* **65**

TOPTON (IRE) 8 b.g. Royal Academy (USA) 130 – Circo 77 (High Top 131) [2002 85, a95: p8g p8g 7m² 8d* 7d 7g⁵ 8m³ 8d² 8m 7m 8d⁵ 7.9m 8m 8m 7s* 8v 7v Nov 9] tall, angular gelding: fairly useful handicapper: won in large fields at Ascot in May and Newmarket in November: best form at 7f/1m: acts on firm going, soft and all-weather/dirt: blinkered/visored nowadays: has run well sweating: usually held up: tough, though does need everything to go his way. *P. Howling* **85 a–**

TOP TREES 4 b.g. Charnwood Forest (IRE) 125 – Low Line 66 (High Line 125) [2002 66d: 9.9g f12g² Dec 14] fair maiden: stays easy 1½m: acts on fibresand: has been slowly away/reluctant to race: one to treat with caution. *W. S. Kittow* **69 §**

TORA BORA 2 ch.f. (Mar 29) Grand Lodge (USA) 125 – Brilliance 74 (Cadeaux Genereux 131) [2002 p6g³ p7g⁴ Dec 11] first foal: dam, 1m winner, half-sister to smart 1m/9f performer Sign of Hope: fair form in maidens at Lingfield: should be suited by at least 1m. *R. Hannon* **67**

TORCELLO (IRE) 4 b.g. Royal Academy (USA) 130 – Vanya (Busted 134) [2002 108: 12.3m³ 12d⁴ 10m 9.9m 10.9g³ 11.8s Oct 28] rangy, attractive gelding: has a quick action: useful performer: mostly at least respectable efforts in 2002: third in listed race at Ayr penultimate start: stays 1½m: acts on firm and good to soft going, winner on soft: blinkered (ran creditably) third start: has wandered/found little/looked hard ride. *G. Wragg* **106**

TORO BRAVO (IRE) 2 b.c. (Feb 18) Alhaarth (IRE) 126 – Set Trail (IRE) 76 (Second Set (IRE) 127) [2002 7.1g⁶ p8g² f8.5g* Dec 20] IR 25,000Y: first foal: dam 2-y-o 7f winner: fair form in maidens: won 9-runner event at Wolverhampton by ½ length from No Grouse: stays 8.5f. *R. M. Beckett* **74**

TOROSAY SPRING 4 ch.f. First Trump 118 – Spring Sixpence 60 (Dowsing (USA) 124) [2002 106p: 6m* 7m⁵ 8f³ Oct 14] sturdy, lengthy filly: useful performer, lightly raced: off 11 months, won minor event at Yarmouth (raced freely then quickened under just hands and heels to beat Welcome Friend) in August: 2¼ lengths third to Lochridge in **106**

handicap at Newmarket final outing, held up and doing well as race was run: raced mainly at 6f (didn't have run of things at 7f): raced only on good going or firmer. *J. R. Fanshawe*

TORRENT 7 ch.g. Prince Sabo 123 – Maiden Pool 85 (Sharpen Up 127) [2002 66§, a78d: p6g p6g[2] p6g[6] p5g[5] p6g[4] f5g[5] f6g p6g[5] f6g f5f[4] f6g f6s[3] p6g[6] Dec 30] strong, lengthy gelding: modest performer: best at 5f/6f: acts on any turf going and all-weather: usually wears blinkers/visor/cheekpieces: has worn tongue tie: has broken blood vessels, and reportedly can't be subjected to strong pressure: carries head high/has hung right: untrustworthy. *P. S. McEntee* — § a57 §

TORRID KENTAVR (USA) 5 b.g. Trempolino (USA) 135 – Torrid Tango (USA) (Green Dancer (USA) 132) [2002 91: 8f 8.5s[3] 8.1d[4] 9.9m 7d 8f 7.9m 8m 12s Oct 26] close-coupled gelding: fairly useful handicapper at best: below form after third start: needs good test at 1m, stays 1½m: acts on firm going, soft and fibresand: tried blinkered (not since 2000): free-going sort (has worn crossed noseband), usually held up: has hung. *B. Ellison* 89 d

TORTUGA DREAM (IRE) 3 b.g. Turtle Island (IRE) 123 – Tycoon's Catch (IRE) (Thatching 131) [2002 8m 7d Jun 11] 7,000F: good-bodied gelding: second foal: half-brother to useful German miler Scapolo (by Rainbows For Life): dam unraced: last in 2 maidens. *A. Charlton* —

TORY BOY 7 b.g. Deploy 131 – Mukhayyalah (Dancing Brave (USA) 140) [2002 48: 12.3m[4] 12m 11.5m* 16.5g[2] 14.1m Aug 7] smallish, lengthy gelding: modest handicapper, lightly raced nowadays: won amateur event at Yarmouth in July: stays 2m: acts on soft going, firm and fibresand: sometimes blinkered: has hung left. *M. G. Quinlan* 63

TORZAL 2 br.g. (Apr 14) Hector Protector (USA) 124 – Alathezal (USA) (Zilzal (USA) 137) [2002 6m[5] 7m[4] f8.5g Dec 20] 5,000 2-y-o: fourth foal: half-brother to a winner in Italy by Lycius: dam unraced close relative to high-class 6f performers Great Commotion and Lead On Time: last in minor events/maiden. *R. F. Marvin* —

TOTAL CARE 5 br.h. Caerleon (USA) 132 – Totality 103 (Dancing Brave (USA) 140) [2002 71, a67: p7g[5] p7g p8g p10g[6] f9.4g 10.1s Jun 5] useful-looking horse: fair handicapper: well held last 2 starts, leaving S. Williams after running as if something amiss penultimate one: gained only win over 1½m, finds 7f bare minimum: acts on polytrack, soft and good to firm going: has worn crossed noseband: tongue tied nowadays (not final run when again suffering breathing problems). *I. Semple* — a68

TOTALLY SCOTTISH 6 b.g. Mtoto 134 – Glenfinlass (Lomond (USA) 128) [2002 –: 16.1d[4] Sep 9] smallish, quite attractive gelding: modest maiden on Flat (winning hurdler): stays 2m: acts on good to firm and good to soft going: tried blinkered/tongue tied. *Mrs M. Reveley* 51

TOTAL PACKAGE 2 b.f. (Apr 20) Fraam 114 – Sunley Solaire (Aragon 118) [2002 7.6m Aug 21] first foal: dam ran twice: 50/1, tailed off in maiden at Lingfield. *M. S. Saunders* —

TOTAL TURTLE (IRE) 3 b.g. Turtle Island (IRE) 123 – Chagrin d'Amour (IRE) (Last Tycoon 131) [2002 75: 7g[2] 8m[4] 10m 8f[3] 9.9s* 10.4d[2] 12g 13.9m* 14.6m* Sep 13] big, strong gelding: has plenty of scope: smart handicapper: vastly improved, and won at Goodwood in June, York (Melrose Rated Stakes, by short head from Kasthari after ding-dong battle) in August and Doncaster (beat Kasthari 3 lengths in Tote Exacta Mallard Stakes) in September: will stay 2m: acts on firm and soft going: has been slowly away: waited with: game and genuine: should improve further and win another good prize or 2 at 4 yrs. *P. F. I. Cole* 112 p

Tote Exacta Mallard Stakes (Handicap), Doncaster—the very progressive Total Turtle has his rivals well strung out; Kasthari is next, followed by Harlestone Grey, Ranville (rail) and Mesmeric

TOTEM DANCER   9 b.m. Mtoto 134 – Ballad Opera (Sadler's Wells (USA) 132)   –
[2002 59: 14.1m 11.9g 14.1d Oct 30] lengthy mare: has a short action: modest handicapper in 2001: well held in 2002: tried visored. *B. G. Powell*

TOTEM POLE   3 ch.c. Pivotal 124 – Taza (Persian Bold 123) [2002 71p: 7s³ 7m   **79**
8.1d* 8.1d 8m⁴ 7g² 7m⁴ 8.9m⁶ 7f⁵ Oct 5] big, good-topped colt: has scope: fair performer:
won maiden at Haydock in May: barely stays 9f: acts on firm and soft going: front runner:
sold 27,000 gns, sent to Malaysia. *B. W. Hills*

TO THE RESCUE (USA)   2 b.c. (Mar 27) Cozzene (USA) – Promptly (IRE) 88 (Lead   **89 p**
On Time (USA) 123) [2002 6m³ 6g² 6f* 7m* Sep 29] second foal: dam, 6f and (US minor
stakes) 1m winner, out of Nell Gwyn winner Ghariba, herself half-sister to smart stayer
Braashee: progressive form: won maiden at Salisbury (disputed lead, hung left) and
nursery at Ascot in September, quickening well when beating Secret Formula by head in
latter: will stay 1m: raced only on good ground or firmer: sent to USA: probably a useful
performer in the making. *R. Hannon*

TO THE WOODS (IRE)   3 ch.f. Woodborough (USA) 112 – Iktidar 80 (Green Desert   **86 d**
(USA) 127) [2002 72+: p5g f7g* 8g f7g f7g⁶ 7f⁴ 7g⁶ 6d³ 6m 6m f7s⁵ 7.1m Sep 21]
smallish filly: fairly useful performer at best: won handicap at Wolverhampton in March:
well below form last 6 starts: stays 7f (pulled hard at 1m): acts on good to firm going and
fibresand: unreliable. *N. P. Littmoden*

TOUCH CLOSER   5 b.g. Inchinor 119 – Ryewater Dream 72 (Touching Wood (USA)   **81**
127) [2002 10m 12f 12.1g² 14.1s² 18f Jun 24] 13,500F, 26,000Y: leggy gelding: fourth
foal: half-brother to 1m winner It's Magic (by Magic Ring) and fairly useful 7f (at 2 yrs)
and 9f winner Buzz (by Anshan): dam 11.7f winner: won bumper at Ayr in March and
third in Grade 3 bumper at Aintree in April: fairly useful maiden on Flat: runner-up
in handicap at Carlisle in June: ran as if amiss final run: should stay at least 2m.
G. A. Swinbank

TOUCH LIGHT (USA)   3 ch.c. Distant View (USA) 126 – Flaming Torch 92 (Rou-   **84**
sillon (USA) 133) [2002 8m³ 10m² 10s² 10d 7f⁶ 8.3d⁵ Oct 14] strong, close-coupled colt:
has a quick, fluent action: fourth foal: closely related to 1m winner Flame Cutter (by
Miswaki) and 1996 2-y-o 7f winner Flaming West (by Gone West), later 6.5f to 8.5f
winner in USA: dam, 1m (in France at 2 yrs) to 11f (US Grade 3 event) winner, from
excellent family: fairly useful form when placed in newcomers race at Newmarket and
maiden at Pontefract first 2 starts: below par after, tending to wander on penultimate
outing: stays 1¼m: acts on good to firm going: sold 20,000 gns, sent to Kuwait.
H. R. A. Cecil

TOUCH OF EBONY (IRE)   3 b.c. Darshaan 133 – Cormorant Wood 130 (Home   **66**
Guard (USA) 129) [2002 64: f8.5g³ f8.5g⁵ 10.9g⁴ 9.9m⁶ 12.6m⁴ 11.6s² 12m 14d² 15g 12d
Aug 1] sparely-made colt: fair maiden handicapper: stays 1¾m, possibly not 15f: acts on
fibresand (some promise on polytrack), soft and good to firm going: sometimes slowly
away: held up. *J. Neville*

TOUCH OF FAIRY (IRE)   6 b.h. Fairy King (USA) – Decadence (Vaigly Great   **65**
127) [2002 69+: 6.1g 6m 6s³ 6g³ 5.7d⁵ 6f 6m⁵ 6.1v³ 6m 6s 6g³ 6d Jul 11] strong, lengthy
horse: fair maiden handicapper: effective at 5f/6f: acts on heavy and good to firm going:
blinkered nowadays: tried tongue tied: sold £650. *J. M. Bradley*

TOUCH OF GOLD   2 b.c. (Jan 21) Robellino (USA) 127 – Nanouche (Dayjur (USA)   **73**
137) [2002 5f⁵ 6g⁴ 6s p5g⁴ p6g⁵ p8g⁴ Dec 11] sturdy, lengthy, slightly hollow-backed
colt: second foal: half-brother to 3-y-o Faiza: dam, ran once, out of outstanding sprinter
and 1000 Guineas third Habibti: fair maiden: stays 1m: acts on polytrack and soft ground:
carries head awkwardly. *W. R. Muir*

TOUGH LEADER   8 b.g. Lead On Time (USA) 123 – Al Guswa 98 (Shernazar 131)   **89**
[2002 95d: 12m⁵ 12.3f 11.6d* 12d³ 10d Jul 5] robust gelding: fairly useful handicapper:
won at Windsor in May: effective at 1½m/1¾m: acts on firm and soft going, had form on
fibresand earlier in career: tried blinkered/tongue tied earlier in career. *P. R. Webber*

TOUGH LOVE   3 ch.g. Pursuit of Love 124 – Food of Love 109 (Music Boy 124)   **81**
[2002 75: 7.5m³ 7.5m* 7.9f⁵ 7g⁴ Jun 16] strong, lengthy gelding: fairly useful handicapper: won at Beverley in April: stays 1m: acts on firm and soft going. *T. D. Easterby*

TOUGH NUT (IRE)   2 b.g. (Apr 5) Sri Pekan (USA) 117 – Dancing At Lunasa (IRE)   **61**
70 (Dancing Dissident (USA) 119) [2002 5g f5g² f5g³ 6d* 6d⁴ 6g f7f 6.1m⁶ 6m⁶ Sep 4]
4,000Y: fourth foal: dam Irish 5f winner: modest performer: won seller at Goodwood
in May: ran creditably final start: stays 6f: acts on good to firm ground, good to soft and
fibresand: sold 2,800 gns. *J. A. Osborne*

TOUGH SPEED (USA) 5 b.h. Miswaki (USA) 124 – Nature's Magic (USA) **116**
(Nijinsky (CAN) 138) [2002 123: 10.3f³ 8g³ 8m⁴ 8m³ 8m⁶ 8m³ Sep 12] tall, good sort:
impresses in appearance: smart performer: not quite so good in 2002: third in listed race
at Chester, Queen Anne Stakes at Royal Ascot (3 lengths behind No Excuse Needed after
being hampered), listed event at Ascot (beaten 2 lengths by Fallen Star) and GNER Park
Stakes at Doncaster (1½ lengths behind Duck Row): also ran creditably when close sixth
to Tillerman in Celebration Mile at Goodwood penultimate start: raced mainly at 7f/1m:
acts on good to firm and good to soft going: reportedly suffers from foot problems and
has worn stick-on shoes on fore feet: usually held up: sent to USA. *Sir Michael Stoute*

TOUMAI 2 b.f. (Apr 24) Mind Games 121 – Flower Princess (Slip Anchor 136) [2002 **–**
f6g Nov 30] 13,000Y: seventh foal: closely related to 7.5f winner Taker Chance (by
Puissance) and half-sister to 2 fairly useful winners by Tragic Role, including 1½m
winner Benjamin Frank: dam unraced out of Fillies' Mile winner Nepula: 33/1, always
outpaced in maiden at Wolverhampton. *Mrs A. Duffield*

TOURMALET 2 b.f. (Jan 31) Night Shift (USA) – Robsart (IRE) 91 (Robellino (USA) **88**
127) [2002 5f² 6m⁶ 5m* 6m⁵ 7m⁶ 6.5m 7f³ 7g² Oct 19] 42,000Y: strong, close-coupled
filly: first foal: dam, 7f and 1¼m winner, out of smart French 1¼m winner Sharp Girl:
fairly useful performer: won maiden at Warwick in June: best effort when 1¼ lengths
second to Flighty Fellow in nursery at Catterick final start, slowly away and hampered
twice: stays 7f: raced only on good going or firmer. *A. Berry*

TOUT SEUL (IRE) 2 b.c. (Feb 4) Ali-Royal (IRE) 127 – Total Aloof 72 (Groom **121**
Dancer (USA) 128) [2002 6.1s* 6.1v* 6m² 7d* 6g* 6m² 7m* Oct 19]
    The members of the small Eden Racing syndicate could have been excused
for feeling somewhat overawed during the preliminaries for the Darley Dewhurst
Stakes at Newmarket in October. The Dewhurst is traditionally the principal target
for the season's top two-year-olds and the latest field included runners representing
Hamdan Al Maktoum, the Queen, Sheikh Mohammed and Khalid Abdulla, as well
as no fewer than four racing in the various colours of Michael Tabor and Mrs
John Magnier for Ballydoyle. The Ballydoyle representatives included Tomahawk,
Marino Marini and Great Pyramid, who had cost 2,500,000 dollars, 1,800,000
dollars and IR 550,000 guineas respectively as yearlings. By contrast, Eden
Racing's representative Tout Seul, a 25/1-shot from an unfashionable stable and
partnered by a young jockey having his first Group 1 ride, had cost only IR 12,500
guineas at Tattersalls (Ireland) September Yearling Sales.
    Tout Seul's 'Dewhurst', or, more precisely, his best opportunity of landing
a big prize, must have appeared to be the richly-endowed six-furlong Tattersalls
Breeders Stakes at the Curragh in August, an event restricted to graduates of the
sale at Fairyhouse where Tout Seul was acquired. His owners must have thought
they had achieved the ultimate when Tout Seul put up a useful performance to
win the first prize of £94,231 at the Curragh in a field of twenty-five, justifying
favouritism after winning three of his four races at up to that point, a maiden and a
minor event both in good style at Chepstow, on his first two starts, and a useful

Tattersalls Breeders Stakes, the Curragh—Tout Seul justifies favouritism from his
nearest market rival Cosmo (dark colours); Zaby (light sleeves) and Iron Lad (right) finish close up

*Darley Dewhurst Stakes, Newmarket—Tout Seul is a 25/1-shot this time
and wins going away from Tomahawk and Trade Fair*

auction race on Shergar Cup day at Ascot. The one horse to have beaten Tout Seul, the Hannon-trained Cosmo, couldn't repeat his Salisbury superiority at the Curragh and Tout Seul had him a length and a half back in second, with the first home-trained runner Zaby a short head away in third and another British-trained challenger Iron Lad a close fourth. Bred for speed and with a good turn of foot, Tout Seul had nonetheless seemed to appreciate the step up to seven furlongs at Ascot, running on strongly after taking time to warm to his task and recording a useful effort, despite hanging markedly right, in beating Devious Boy by two and a half lengths with Iron Lad nine lengths further back in third. Tout Seul suffered the second defeat of his career two weeks before the Dewhurst in one of the major auction races, the Two-Year-Old Trophy at Redcar over six furlongs. He failed only narrowly—and possibly unluckily—to land a second very valuable race outside the pattern for his connections, finishing really well but finding the post coming just too soon as Somnus, racing alone, held on by a head. There was a suspicion that Tout Seul's rider, who delayed his mount's effort for a few strides after cruising through to join the leaders around two out, might inadvertently have thought he had only those around him in the main group to beat. Tout Seul would have caught Somnus in another stride or two.

It is still a big step from valuable sales and auction races to Group 1 company and Tout Seul had to improve markedly on his previous form to win a most representative and competitive Dewhurst. Five of the sixteen runners—the biggest field in the Dewhurst's history—had been successful in pattern company. They were: the Royal Lodge winner Al Jadeed, the Vintage Stakes winner Dublin, the Somerville Tattersall winner Governor Brown, the Anglesey Stakes winner Ontario and the Mill Reef winner Zafeen. The betting, though, was dominated by two performers who had yet to win outside maiden races. The twice-raced Trade Fair (11/4 favourite) had been most impressive when landing the odds in a Newbury maiden, and the number-one Ballydoyle challenger Tomahawk (100/30) had been runner-up last time in the Middle Park, with Zafeen fifth and Ontario seventh. The Dewhurst was strongly run and provided a true test, one which patiently-ridden Tout Seul, back at seven furlongs, passed with flying colours, quickening and staying on against the stand rail (the main group raced more towards the centre) to win by a length and a quarter and the same from Tomahawk and Trade Fair. Fourth-placed Zafeen and sixth-placed Ontario also paid compliments to the Middle Park form which consequently looked slightly better than that of the Dewhurst. That said, three of the last ten Dewhurst winners, Zafonic, Pennekamp and Rock of Gibraltar, have gone on to win the Two Thousand Guineas and Tout Seul's chances of classic success were underestimated by the 25/1 offered by one bookmaker straight after the Dewhurst. Quoted at around 16/1 in the winter ante-post market, Tout Seul was still at longer odds, for example, than both Tomahawk and Trade Fair. Tout Seul may be nothing special to look at—he was overshadowed at Newmarket by the imposing Tomahawk—but his timefigure, equivalent to a rating of 118 and surpassed only by Oasis Dream in the Middle Park among the season's two-year-olds, provided confirmation of the merit of his Dewhurst performance. Judged on the way he was finishing at Newmarket—he won going away—Tout Seul will be suited by the Guineas trip as a three-year-old.

Tout Seul may have provided his jockey Steve Carson with his first Group 1 victory, but his trainer Fulke Johnson Houghton, who has only a fairly small string nowadays, is no stranger to big-race success, having handled the classic-winning brothers Ribocco and Ribero and such as Romulus, Habitat, Rose Bowl, Ile de Bourbon and Double Form in his glory days in the 'sixties and 'seventies. Johnson Houghton's daughter and assistant Eve also acts as manager for the ten-strong Eden Racing syndicate which turned down several offers for Tout Seul. Whether or not they eventually come to regret their decision to hold on to Tout Seul, the members of Eden Racing will still be able to look back on an ownership experience that must have exceeded their wildest dreams. Tout Seul won £316,943 in prize-money in his first season but, more importantly for racing, his Dewhurst win showed that the grip on the Group 1 races on the Flat of the multi-millionaire owners with their multiple options can be loosened occasionally. The Elite Racing Club, reportedly numbering around ten thousand members at the time, also enjoyed a Group 1 victory with Soviet Song in the Fillies' Mile while another fairly small yard, that of Henry Candy, won both the Cheveley Park with the 12,000-guinea yearling Airwave and the Nunthorpe with another syndicate-owned performer Kyllachy. The jockeys of Soviet Song and Airwave also tasted Group 1 success for the first time. The British Horseracing Board's marketing department certainly won't be short of material if its plans for 2003 include promotion of ownership.

Tout Seul (IRE) (b.c. Feb 4, 2000)	Ali-Royal (IRE) (b 1993)	Royal Academy (b 1987)	Nijinsky
			Crimson Saint
		Alidiva (b 1987)	Chief Singer
			Alligatrix
	Total Aloof (b 1993)	Groom Dancer (b 1984)	Blushing Groom
			Featherhill
		Bashoosh (b 1988)	Danzig
			Condessa

Eden Racing's "Tout Seul"

The leggy, quite good-topped Tout Seul went through the sale-ring as a foal, as well as a yearling, fetching IR 6,800 guineas at Goffs November Sales when submitted by his breeder Johnston King, who operates a small stud in County Tyrone, Northern Ireland. King bought Tout Seul's dam Total Aloof as a three-year-old at the December Sales in 1996 for 6,400 guineas. She was a fair sprinter, winning a maiden at Beverley and a minor event at Bath over five furlongs before being sent to the sales. Total Aloof's first foal, a filly by Namaqualand, reportedly died in a fire, but her second, a year-older half-brother to Tout Seul, Soaring Eagle (by Eagle Eyed), won a six-furlong maiden in Ireland as a two-year-old and showed fair form in sprint handicaps in an in-and-out campaign there in the latest season. Total Aloof's fourth foal, a yearling filly by Desert Sun, fetched €40,000 at Tattersalls (Ireland) in September. There was no offspring in 2002 as Total Aloof couldn't be sent to the Irish Republic to be covered because of foot and mouth restrictions. She is due to Mull of Kintyre in 2003 and will presumably be the subject of grander plans from now on. She cannot be returned to Tout Seul's sire the Sussex Stakes winner Ali-Royal, a brother to the One Thousand Guineas winner Sleepytime, as he died after only three seasons at stud and before his first runners made it to the racecourse. Both Tout Seul's dam—who was weeded out as a yearling—and his grandam the 700,000-dollar yearling Bashoosh were owned at one time by Maktoum Al Maktoum's Gainsborough Stud. Bashoosh's purchase price was largely accounted for by her pedigree—by Danzig out of Yorkshire Oaks winner Condessa —but she was smallish and leggy and showed little ability in four outings over middle distances, her best effort a well beaten third in a Catterick maiden. Best known among Condessa's descendants prior to Tout Seul was her grandson, the top-class but ill-fated hurdler Valiramix. Among Condessa's other representatives was a very smart sprinter in Japan, Biko Pegasus, a full brother to Bashoosh, and Bashoosh herself was sent there after Gainsborough Stud disposed of her for 65,000 guineas at the December Sales in 1994. Tout Seul has won on going ranging from good to firm (which it was for the Dewhurst) to heavy. *R. F. Johnson Houghton*

TOWN CALLED MALICE (USA) 2 b.g. (May 6) Mister Baileys 123 – Dubiously (USA) (Jolie Jo (USA)) [2002 6.1d³ 6.1s 7m 6g 6f* 7.1m f7g² f7g² 7g⁴ f8.5g* f8g² f8.5g³ Dec 14] 12,000Y: quite good-topped gelding: half-brother to 6f to 8.5f winner Heathyards Lady (by Mining) and to several winners in USA/Japan: dam, 2-y-o 6f/6.5f winner in US, half-sister to US Grade 3 winner (including at 1m) Bill E Shears: fair performer: won seller at Yarmouth in July and (having left W. Jarvis after eighth start) claimer at Wolverhampton in November: stays 8.5f: acts on fibresand, firm and good to soft going (well held only start on soft): tough. *N. P. Littmoden* **67 a77**

TOY SHOW (IRE) 2 b.f. (Feb 14) Danehill (USA) 126 – March Hare 60 (Groom Dancer (USA) 128) [2002 6g³ 7m⁶ 7m 10m* Oct 1] 180,000F: small filly: first foal: dam, maiden who stayed 1½m, half-sister to smart 1m/1¼m performer Inglenook out of smart middle-distance stayer Spring, herself half-sister to Pentire: fair form: best effort when winning nursery at Nottingham by length from Wavertree Boy: will probably stay 1½m: raced only on good/good to firm going. *R. Hannon* **73**

TRACE CLIP 4 b.g. Zafonic (USA) 130 – Illusory 81 (Kings Lake (USA) 133) [2002 103: 5.2g² 6f² 5m⁵ 6g 5.6m 5m³ 5m² Oct 12] neat, quite attractive gelding: useful handicapper: placed at Newbury (second to Kyllachy) in April, York (beaten neck by Chookie Heiton) in May and at Ascot in September/October (2 lengths second to Olivia Grace): also ran well when close fifth at Ascot on third start: headstrong, and barely stays 6f: yet to race on soft/heavy ground, acts on any other turf: wears tongue strap: usually early to post: very slowly away fifth outing: has found little: sold 55,000 gns, joined W. Musson and gelded. *B. W. Hills* **103**

TRACY JONES 3 b.f. Emperor Jones (USA) 119 – Essex Girl 61 (Dominion 123) [2002 8.2d⁵ Apr 30] 600Y: rather unfurnished filly: third foal: half-sister to winner in Germany by Namaqualand: dam, 1m winner, half-sister to German Derby runner-up Calcavecchia: 33/1, fifth in maiden at Nottingham, moderate late progress under hands and heels. *C. E. Brittain* **45**

TRADE FAIR 2 b.c. (Jan 12) Zafonic (USA) 130 – Danefair 109 (Danehill (USA) 126) [2002 7m³ 7f* 7m³ Oct 19] **114 p**
Ten years after his sire had justified favouritism in the Dewhurst Stakes, Trade Fair could manage only third place when attempting to do likewise; and whereas Zafonic's impressive display saw him become the shortest-priced winter

favourite for the Two Thousand Guineas since Tudor Minstrel forty-five years beforehand, Trade Fair, despite showing further improvement, lost his place at the head of the Guineas market following his defeat. Tudor Minstrel and Zafonic both went on to win the Guineas, and it would be very foolish to dismiss Trade Fair's chances of emulating them, even though he didn't quite live up to expectations in the Dewhurst. A strong, good-bodied, attractive colt, Trade Fair looks the type to make more than normal progress through the winter, and given that he has already shown smart form it isn't too difficult to imagine his reaching the sort of level usually required to win the Guineas.

Trade Fair made two appearances before the Dewhurst, both in seven-furlong maidens. First time up he shaped well in finishing third behind Almushahar and Maghanim at Newmarket in August. That pair went on to win at Doncaster's St Leger meeting, the former promoted to favourite for the Guineas following his Champagne Stakes victory; and Trade Fair also boosted the form of the Newmarket race when he returned to action, landing the odds impressively in a twelve-runner event at Newbury. The opposition to Trade Fair probably wasn't that strong, but it was impossible not to be taken by the way he accomplished his straightforward task, travelling very strongly in behind the leader and pulling clear in a matter of strides once his rider let out a few inches of rein in the final two furlongs. For the record, Trade Fair passed the post with six lengths to spare over his nearest pursuer Moarban. With Almushahar suffering a setback in training shortly afterwards, it was hardly a surprise when Trade Fair replaced him as Guineas favourite. Not only was his performance at Newbury one to capture the imagination, but some of the quotes of his rider Richard Hughes—'the best horse I've ridden in a long time' being one of them—only added to Trade Fair's reputation. Trade Fair may yet

Mr K. Abdulla's "Trade Fair"

prove Hughes correct. Apart from Desert Star, Trade Fair was the least experienced in the Dewhurst field, and lack of experience undoubtedly counted against him when it came to the crunch. As at Newbury, he travelled strongly, racing on the outer, and took the lead after two furlongs out only to run a bit green once in front. Clearly flagging towards the finish, Trade Fair was passed by both Tout Seul and Tomahawk, beaten a length and a quarter and the same.

Trade Fair (b.c. Jan 12, 2000)	Zafonic (USA) (b 1990)	Gone West (b 1984)	Mr Prospector Secrettame
		Zaizafon (ch 1982)	The Minstrel Mofida
	Danefair (b 1992)	Danehill (b 1986)	Danzig Razyana
		Roupala (b 1986)	Vaguely Noble Cairn Rouge

Trade Fair should stay at least a mile on pedigree. Zafonic was one of the best winners of the Two Thousand Guineas in the last fifteen years, but, sadly, met with an untimely death in a freak accident in his paddock in Australia two weeks before Trade Fair's success at Newbury. Zafonic's best produce, the Dewhurst winner Xaar, came in his first crop. He was represented by the three-year-olds Dupont and Zipping, as well as Trade Fair, in the latest season. Trade Fair's dam Danefair, trained in France by Maurice Zilber, won all four of her starts, including a couple of listed events over a mile and a quarter and a very slowly-run Prix Minerve over a mile and a half, in which she reportedly cracked a pastern. Trade Fair's grandam Roupala, a daughter of the Irish One Thousand Guineas and Champion Stakes winner Cairn Rouge, won over a mile and stayed a mile and a quarter well. Roupala, a half-sister to the useful performers Ajuga and Devil's Rock, is also the dam of a couple of noteworthy performers in France, namely the smart Erudite, who stays two miles, and Danefair's useful full sister Prove, who won over nine furlongs (the Prix Chloe) and a mile and a quarter. Trade Fair is the third foal out of Danefair. Her first, a full sister to Trade Fair named Zafair, swished her tail continuously when well held in a maiden at Kempton in 2001 on her only start. Five months later she was sold for 50,000 guineas at the December Sales. Danefair's second foal Fieldfare (by Selkirk), also trained by Zilber, ran three times in the latest season, her best effort coming when fourth over a mile and a quarter in the French Provinces. *R. Charlton*

TRADE (IRE) 2 b.f. (Apr 7) Danetime (IRE) 121 – Malacca (USA) (Danzig (USA)) **47** [2002 5d³ 5g³ 6g Jun 28] close-coupled filly: poor mover: fifth foal: half-sister to 3 winners, including fairly useful Irish 2000 2-y-o 5f winner Patinham (by Mujtahid): dam unraced: poor form when third in claimers: gave impression something amiss final start. *T. D. Easterby*

TRAGIC DANCER 6 b.g. Tragic Role (USA) – Chantallee's Pride (Mansooj 118) **56** [2002 f16.2g 11.1g⁴ 11.6s 10.9m Jun 17] workmanlike gelding: fair handicapper at 3 yrs: modest form at best on return in 2002, leaving K. McAuliffe after third start: stays 1½m: acts on good to firm ground and fibresand: usually tongue tied: sometimes races freely: carries head high. *D. J. Wintle*

TRAINED BY THE BEST 4 b.f. Alderbrook 120 – Princess Moodyshoe 72 (Jalmood **86** (USA) 126) [2002 58: 18d* 16f* 16.4g² 18m Oct 19] fairly useful handicapper: won at Chepstow and Newbury in July: good second at Sandown next time: well beaten in Cesarewitch at Newmarket final start: much better at 2m/2¼m than shorter: acts on firm and good to soft going: tongue tied nowadays: tends to carry head high: held up. *M. C. Pipe*

TRAMANTANO 3 b.g. Muhtarram (USA) 125 – Hatta Breeze 68 (Night Shift (USA)) **90** [2002 10m* 10d² 10m² 10f⁶ 10d⁵ 10.1d⁵ Oct 30] close-coupled, useful-looking gelding: second foal: dam 1m/8.5f winner: fairly useful performer: won maiden at Windsor in June: should stay 1½m: acts on good to firm and good to soft going: joined N. Twiston-Davies: fairly useful form over hurdles, successful in November. *H. Candy*

TRAMONTO 3 b.f. Sri Pekan (USA) 117 – Manhattan Sunset (USA) 76 (El Gran **–** Senor (USA) 136) [2002 91p: 8g Apr 19] well-made filly: fairly useful winner at 2 yrs: reportedly finished lame when pulled up only run in 2002. *M. P. Tregoning*

TRANQUIL MOON 4 ch.f. Deploy 131 – Bright Landing 78 (Sun Prince 128) [2002 **60** 64: p13g* p12g² p16g³ 11.7g 13.1g 11.6m⁵ 14.1m³ 14m 13.1f Aug 23] fair handicapper **a70** on all-weather, modest on turf: won handicap at Lingfield in January: effective at 1½m to 2m: acts on all-weather and good to firm going: held up. *D. W. P. Arbuthnot*

TRANSATLANTIC (USA) 4 gr.g. Dumaani (USA) 115 – Viendra (USA) 113 (Raise **103** A Native) [2002 102: 8s* 10m 8d 8d 12g 9s Oct 26] leggy, quite good-topped gelding: useful handicapper: won at Kempton in June by 1½ lengths from Burgundy, allowed to dictate slow pace: below form after: stays 9f: acts on soft and good to firm going: has worn crossed noseband: free-going sort: usually waited with: sold 23,000 gns, joined H. Daly and gelded. *R. F. Johnson Houghton*

TRANSCENDANTALE (FR) 4 b. or br.f. Apple Tree (FR) 126 – Kataba (FR) **60** (Shardari 134) [2002 63: f12g 10f⁶ 10m 14.1d 10m 12g⁵ 9.9g 8.3s³ 9d* 9d² 10g⁵ 10m 8s 8m⁵ 12d 10.3v Nov 8] smallish filly: modest performer: won handicap at Kempton in July: well below form last 5 outings: stays 1¼m: acts on firm and soft going. *Mrs S. Lamyman*

TRANSIT 3 b.c. Lion Cavern (USA) 117 – Black Fighter (USA) 79 (Secretariat **82** (USA)) [2002 84p: 8m 10s² 10m³ 10.2d³ 8.1m³ 8.5m 8.1m Sep 21] tall, leggy colt: has a fluent, round action: fairly useful maiden: well held last 3 starts: should be as effective at 1m as 1¼m: acts on heavy and good to firm going: pulled hard/found little fourth outing: sold 15,000 gns, joined B. Ellison. *H. R. A. Cecil*

TRANSLUCID (USA) 4 b.c. Woodman (USA) 126 – Gossamer (USA) (Seattle Slew **88** (USA)) [2002 101: a10g p10g 11g* Jun 22] IR 48,000Y: second living foal: dam, US 1m/ 8.5f winner, out of close relative to smart 7f/1m performer Fatherland: useful performer at best: successful in 2001 in maiden at Leopardstown (only outing for M. Grassick in Ireland), minor event at Munich and listed race at Neuss: well held first 2 starts in 2002 (in listed race at Lingfield second one) before winning minor event at Dusseldorf in June: stays 1½m: acts on soft going, good to firm and dirt: won over hurdles in November. *C. Von Der Recke, Germany*

TRAPPER NORMAN 10 b.g. Mazilier (USA) 107 – Free Skip 68 (Free State 125) – [2002 –: 5g Aug 7] little form nowadays. *R. Wilman*

TRAVELLERS JOY 2 b.f. (Mar 25) The West (USA) 107 – Persian Fortune 53 – (Forzando 122) [2002 5.1d f7g Sep 30] 1,250Y: first foal: dam 2-y-o 5f winner: well beaten in sellers. *R. J. Hodges*

TRAVELLER'S TALE 3 b.g. Selkirk (USA) 129 – Chere Amie (USA) 75 (Mr Pros- **79** pector (USA)) [2002 62: 10g 10m⁵ 10.1g* 10.1m³ 11f⁵ 10s² Oct 23] leggy, useful-looking gelding: fair handicapper, lightly raced: won at Epsom in August: likely to prove best around 1¼m: acts on firm and soft going: occasionally hangs left. *P. W. Harris*

TRAVELLING BAND (IRE) 4 b.g. Blues Traveller (IRE) 119 – Kind of Cute 52 **92** (Prince Sabo 123) [2002 8.1d* 7.9d* 8g 8.2v³ 8s Nov 2] leggy, quite attractive gelding: fairly useful performer, lightly raced: won maiden at Chepstow and handicap at Carlisle in June: creditable third at Nottingham in October: raced mainly around 1m on good or softer ground (acts on heavy). *I. A. Balding*

TRAVELLING TIMES 3 ch.g. Timeless Times (USA) 99 – Bollin Sophie (Efisio **82** 120) [2002 79: 5f 6m 6.1f² 6g 6m* 6g³ 6m⁵ 6m 7m 6f Oct 11] strong, lengthy gelding: fairly useful handicapper: won at Ripon in July: seems best at 6f: acts on fibresand and firm going, possibly not on softer than good: possibly best in blinkers nowadays (visored eighth start): usually races prominently. *T. D. Easterby*

TRAVELMATE 8 b.g. Persian Bold 123 – Ustka 60 (Lomond (USA) 128) [2002 106: **108** 10m⁴ 11.8g⁴ 16.1g⁴ 12g² 12m² 18m⁶ Sep 12] strong, lengthy gelding: one-time smart performer, useful and lightly raced in latter part of career (had tendon injury, reportedly suffered hairline fracture of pelvis): runner-up in Northumberland Plate at Newcastle and Ebor at York in 1999: third in listed race at Newmarket and fourth in Northumberland Plate in 2002: respectable sixth in Doncaster Cup final outing: stayed 2m: acted on firm and good to soft going: had wandered/found less than seemed likely, and was usually held up: retired. *J. R. Fanshawe*

TRAVEL TARDIA (IRE) 4 br.c. Petardia 113 – Annie's Travels (IRE) (Mac's Imp – (USA) 116) [2002 92: f6g³ f6g⁴ f6g f6g 5.7d 5g 6g 7f 6g 5.1g Sep 12] sturdy colt: fairly **a88 d** useful handicapper: on downgrade after reappearance: best at 5f/6f: acts on fibresand and heavy ground. *I. A. Wood*

TRAVERSE (IRE) 3 b.g. Fayruz 116 – Travel Magic 84 (Henbit (USA) 130) [2002 **50**
6.1m³ 8g 8.5s 6m 5s³ 10s Nov 1] IR 7,500F, IR 22,000Y: sixth foal: half-brother to
winners abroad by Celestial Storm and Be My Chief: dam 7f winner: modest form when
third in maiden at Nottingham on debut (left G. Bravery 1,000 gns after) and in handicap
at Navan penultimate start: well beaten otherwise: stays 6f: acts on soft and good to firm
ground. *P. J. Flynn, Ireland*

TRAVESTY OF LAW (IRE) 5 ch.g. Case Law 113 – Bold As Love (Lomond (USA) **–**
128) [2002 83, a73: p5g⁴ p6g f6g⁴ p7g² p7g⁴ f7g² 7f Apr 11] smallish, strong gelding: fair **a67**
performer: left S. Kirk after second start: stays easy 7f: acts on firm going and all-weather,
possibly not on softer than good: occasionally blinkered in 2000: reportedly finished lame
final outing, withdrawn on vets advice following month. *T. G. Mills*

TREASURE CHEST (IRE) 7 b.g. Last Tycoon 131 – Sought Out (IRE) 119 **–**
(Rainbow Quest (USA) 134) [2002 63: 14.1m 16v Oct 29] leggy, angular gelding: fluent
mover: modest handicapper at 6 yrs: well held both runs in 2002: usually visored before
2001. *M. C. Pipe*

TREASURE TOUCH (IRE) 8 b.g. Treasure Kay 114 – Bally Pourri (IRE) (Law **–**
Society (USA) 130) [2002 65d, a48: 7s Mar 28] tall gelding: one-time fairly useful
performer, very much on downgrade: tried blinkered. *P. D. Evans*

TREASURE TRAIL 3 b.g. Millkom 124 – Forever Shineing 62 (Glint of Gold 128) **91**
[2002 60: 10.2g 11.9d² f12g 11.7d* 12d⁴ 14m² 11.7f 14m 16m⁴ 14.6s Oct 25] good-
bodied gelding: fairly useful handicapper: won at Bath (maiden event) and Folkestone
within 4 days in July: stays 2m: acts on good to firm and good to soft going, well held on
fibresand. *S. Kirk*

TREATY OF UTRECHT (IRE) 2 b.c. (Mar 17) College Chapel 122 – Next Round **80**
(IRE) 83 (Common Grounds 118) [2002 5d² f5g⁴ 5s² 6f³ 5g* p6g f6s f7s³ f8g⁶ Dec 27] IR **a71**
18,500Y: first foal: dam, 2-y-o 7f winner, half-sister to smart US Grade 1 9f winner Caffe
Latte: fairly useful form: made all in maiden at Carlisle in June: left
J. Noseda after next start: creditable third in nursery at Wolverhampton penultimate one:
stays 7f: acts on soft going and fibresand. *I. Semple*

TREBLE HEIGHTS (IRE) 3 b.f. Unfuwain (USA) 131 – Height of Passion (Shirley **107 p**
Heights 130) [2002 12.3m* 14.6m² 12g² Sep 27] 135,000Y: lengthy, attractive filly:
half-sister to several winners, including 6f (at 2 yrs) and 1¼m winner Precede (by Polish
Precedent) and 1½m to 2m winner Warm Feeling (by Kalaglow), both smart: dam ran 3
times: useful form: won maiden at Chester in August by 7 lengths (slowly away): much
improved efforts when 1½ lengths second to Alexander Three D in Park Hill Stakes at
Doncaster (still green/allowed winner first run, edging left) then ¾-length second to Love
Everlasting in listed event at Ascot: likely to prove best at 1¾m+: lightly raced, and
should make a smart 4-y-o. *J. H. M. Gosden*

TRE COLLINE 3 b.g. Efisio 120 – Triple Joy 104 (Most Welcome 131) [2002 66: **76**
6m⁴ f7g** May 20] robust gelding: fair performer: won handicap at Wolverhampton in
May, despite edging left: likely to prove best up to 1m: acts on fibresand. *C. F. Wall*

TRECULIAR (USA) 2 b.c. (Mar 12) Trempolino (USA) 135 – Lady Peculiar (CAN) **80 p**
(Sunshine Forever (USA)) [2002 p7g⁵ p8g* Dec 3] IR 5,200Y, resold 40,000Y: first foal:
dam 6f winner in Canada: fairly useful form: justified favouritism in maiden at Lingfield
by short head from Dance In The Sun, soon off bridle but leading close home: will be
suited by 1¼m+: capable of better. *G. A. Butler*

TREE PEONY 2 ch.f. (May 20) Woodman (USA) 126 – Pivoine (USA) (Nureyev **63 p**
(USA) 131) [2002 7g Oct 14] rangy, rather unfurnished filly: has scope: fifth foal: half-
sister to smart 1m (at 2 yrs) to 10.4f winner Evening World (by Bering) and a winner in
Germany by Kris: dam unraced half-sister to dam of Peintre Celebre: 20/1 and green, 8
lengths eighth of 17 to Star Sensation in maiden at Leicester, slowly away and never
dangerous: sure to improve. *R. Charlton*

TREE ROOFER 3 b.g. King's Signet (USA) 110 – Armaiti 78 (Sayf El Arab (USA) **51**
127) [2002 57: p6g p5g² p5g³ 5.1d 5.7g⁵ 5s 5.3m⁶ 6m⁴ 5g² 6m 6m f5g² p5g⁵ f6s f5g⁵ Dec **a57**
31] modest maiden handicapper: left K. Cunningham-Brown after fifth start: probably
best at 5f/6f: acts on all-weather and good to firm ground. *J. S. Moore*

TREETOPS HOTEL (IRE) 3 ch.c. Grand Lodge (USA) 125 – Rousinette (Rousillon **90**
(USA) 133) [2002 84: 6g⁶ 6f⁵ 7s⁵ Jun 7] quite attractive colt: fairly useful performer:
likely to prove best at 7f/1m: acts on firm and good to soft ground: slowly away/carried
head awkwardly final start. *Mrs A. J. Perrett*

TREKKING (USA) 3 ch.f. Gone West (USA) – Didina 115 (Nashwan (USA) 135) **82**
[2002 10g^2 10m^2 9.9d* 10m Aug 28] first foal: dam, 6f (at 2 yrs) to 8.5f (US Grade
2 event) winner, out of half-sister to Xaar: fairly useful form: runner-up in maidens at
Newmarket prior to landing the odds in similar 4-runner event at Beverley in August,
idling: pulled hard, in rear in listed rated stakes at Brighton final outing: raced only at
1¼m: yet to race on extremes of going: joined R. Frankel in USA. *R. Charlton*

TREMBLEY 5 b.h. Komaite (USA) – Cold Blow 67 (Posse (USA) 130) [2002 59d: **–**
f8g 7d Mar 27] close-coupled horse: disappointing maiden. *J. L. Eyre*

TREMEZZO 4 b.g. Mind Games 121 – Rosa Van Fleet (Sallust 134) [2002 50: 10.2d **43**
May 31] poor maiden: probably stays 1¼m: acts on soft and good to firm ground: tried
blinkered/tongue tied. *B. R. Millman*

TREMOR 4 ch.g. Zilzal (USA) 137 – Happydrome (Ahonoora 122) [2002 51: p12g^5 **60**
f11g^5 Dec 17] modest performer: off 17 months, creditable efforts in claimers at Lingfield
and Southwell: stays 1½m: acts on all-weather and good to firm going. *W. R. Muir*

TRESILLIAN (IRE) 2 b.f. (Mar 5) Alhaarth (IRE) 126 – Birch Creek (Carwhite 127) **77**
[2002 6s 7d^2 Aug 9] lengthy filly: half-sister to several winners, including 1996 Lowther/
Moyglare Stud Stakes winner Bianca Nera (by Salse) and 1999 2-y-o 7f winner/Fillies'
Mile third Hotelgenie Dot Com (by Selkirk), both useful: dam, French maiden, third in
Group 3 1m event in Italy: better effort in maidens at Newmarket (fair form) when beaten
head by Quartet: dead. *G. Wragg*

TREVORS SPREE 3 ch.g. Dancing Spree (USA) – Trevorsninepoints 71 (Jester 119) **53**
[2002 60: 6g 7m 7m^5 8g 8m 7m 6m^3 6m Sep 19] leggy, workmanlike gelding: modest
maiden: stays 7f: unraced on extremes of going: visored last 3 outings. *Mrs Lydia Pearce*

Owen Promotions Limited's "Treble Heights"

TRIBAL PRINCE   5 b.g. Prince Sabo 123 – Tshusick 81 (Dancing Brave (USA) 140)   **86**
[2002 79: p8g² 8.5g² p8g⁶ 8.2d 7f* 7f² 7m⁴ 7g³ 8.2m² 7m 8s 7m* 7f² 7.1g³ Oct 5] sturdy
gelding: fairly useful performer: won minor events at Redcar in June/September: good
effort in Sandown handicap final start: effective at 7f to 8.5f: acts on polytrack, best turf
form on good ground or firmer: visored once at 2 yrs: usually held up: has started slowly/
looked tricky ride. *P. W. Harris*

TRIGGER'S BOY   2 b.c. (Mar 31) Double Trigger (IRE) 123 – Little Miss Ribot 45   **70 ?**
(Lighter 111) [2002 6g 7m⁵ Sep 7] second foal: dam 1m/1¼m winner: well held in
maiden at Windsor on debut: appeared to show fair form when fifth of 6 to Captain Saif
in minor event at Kempton: likely to be suited by 1¼m+. *R. J. O'Sullivan*

TRIMONTIUM (USA)   3 b.g. Mt Livermore (USA) – Sailing Minstrel (USA) (The   **87**
Minstrel (CAN) 135) [2002 81: 8s 8m* a8.5f⁵ Oct 6] close-coupled gelding: fairly useful
performer: won claimer at Newmarket in June: sold out of J. Fanshawe's stable 35,000
gns and off over 3 months before final outing (fifth of 7 in allowance race at Santa Anita):
should stay 1¼m: acts on good to firm and good to soft going. *Carla Gaines, USA*

TRIMSTONE   5 br.g. Bandmaster (USA) 97 – Klairover 50 (Smackover 107) [2002   **44**
45: 6.1v⁴ 8d 5.7m³ 8m 10.9m Sep 16] poor maiden: stays 8.5f: acts on heavy going, good
to firm and fibresand. *R. J. Hodges*

TRINITY (IRE)   6 b.h. College Chapel 122 – Kaskazi (Dancing Brave (USA) 140)   **–**
[2002 66: f7g⁶ f7g Nov 22] close-coupled horse: fair handicapper in 2001: off 13 months,
little form in 2002. *M. Brittain*

TRIPHENIA (IRE)   4 b.g. Ashkalani (IRE) 128 – Atsuko (IRE) (Mtoto 134) [2002   **91**
84: 13.3v⁶ 14m* 16.2m 14m Jul 30] lengthy gelding: fairly useful performer, lightly
raced (struck into and suffered tendon injury at 3 yrs): won minor event at Goodwood in
June: well beaten in handicaps after: stays 1¾m: acts on fibresand and good to firm
ground. *M. L. W. Bell*

TRIPHIBIOUS   2 b.f. (Feb 10) Zafonic (USA) 130 – Trinity Reef 80 (Bustino 136)   **69 d**
[2002 7d³ 7g⁶ 8g 6m 7s Oct 25] leggy filly: first foal: dam, 1½m winner, sister to smart
1¼m/1½m performer Talented and half-sister to dam of 5-y-o Three Points: fair form on
debut: well held after, looking none too keen third start and blinkered final one: should
stay at least 1m. *J. L. Dunlop*

TRIPLE GLORY (IRE)   3 b.f. Goldmark (USA) 113 – Trebles (IRE) (Kenmare   **–**
(FR) 125) [2002 56: 10g 10d 14.1m 14.1m⁶ Jul 26] modest maiden at 2 yrs: well held in
2002: got loose before second outing. *Mrs P. N. Dutfield*

TRIPLEMOON (USA)   3 ch.f. Trempolino (USA) 135 – Placer Queen (Habitat 134)   **77**
[2002 73: 9m 12.1d 10.2m⁵ 12g³ 12m⁵ 11.9m* 11.9m⁴ 14m³ 11.9f Oct 10] rather
leggy filly: fair handicapper: won at Brighton in August: stays 1¾m: acts on firm and
soft going. *P. W. Harris*

TRIPLE PLAY (IRE)   3 br.g. Tagula (IRE) 116 – Shiyra (Darshaan 133) [2002 88d: **–**
8m 8g 7.9f 8m 11f⁵ f12g 8g 8.1m 8.5m 8f⁶ Oct 7] rather leggy, quite attractive gelding:
fairly useful performer at best at 2 yrs: on downgrade, and well held in 2002: raced too
freely in blinkers at 2 yrs. *Don Enrico Incisa*

TRIPPER (USA)   3 b.f. Kingmambo (USA) 125 – Summer Trip (USA) 117 (L'Emi-   **73**
grant (USA) 129) [2002 73p: 12s² 12.3m 10s Oct 26] leggy, useful-looking filly: fair
maiden: well held after reappearance, folding tamely final outing: should stay beyond
1½m: best efforts on going softer than good. *J. L. Dunlop*

TRIPTI (IRE)   2 b.f. (Mar 17) Sesaro (USA) 81 – Chatelsong (USA) (Seattle Song   **67**
(USA) 130) [2002 5.1f⁴ 5.1f⁵ 5g³ 5g p5g² p6g Nov 27] IR 8,000Y, 9,000 2-y-o: fourth
foal: half-sister to 2 winners in France, including useful 1m winner Green Song (by
Green Tune): dam won up to 1¼m in France: fair maiden: second at Lingfield: likely
to prove best at 5f: acts on polytrack, raced only on good going or firmer on turf.
D. W. P. Arbuthnot

TRIUMPH OF DUBAI (IRE)   2 b.g. (Apr 3) Eagle Eyed (USA) 111 – Jack-N-Jilly   **49**
(IRE) 43 (Anita's Prince 126) [2002 5m⁵ 6s 6m 6g 6m Sep 4] IR 3,000Y: second foal:
half-brother to 2001 2-y-o 5f and 7f winner Strandiam (by Darnay): dam, placed in 5f/6f
sellers, ran only at 2 yrs: poor maiden: stays 6f: acts on soft and good to firm ground.
J. S. Moore

TRIWAN   2 b.c. (May 10) Nashwan (USA) 135 – Triple Joy 104 (Most Welcome 131)   **60**
[2002 f6g 7s f7s f8g⁵ Dec 27] good-topped colt: has scope: fifth foal: brother to smart 6f
(at 2 yrs) and 1m winner Triple Dash and half-brother to 2 winners, including 3-y-o Tre

Colline: dam, 6f/7f winner, half-sister to smart middle-distance performer Talented and to dam of 5-y-o Three Points: modest maiden: should stay at least 1m. *Sir Mark Prescott*

TROIS ELLES   6 b.g. Elmaamul (USA) 125 – Ca Ira (IRE) 48 (Dancing Dissident (USA) 119) [2002 p12g f8.5g f14s Sep 5] of little account nowadays. *C. R. Dore*   –

TROJAN (IRE)   3 ch.g. Up And At 'em 109 – Fantasie (FR) (General Assembly (USA)) [2002 69p: f8.5g² 8g May 20] fair form in maidens at Folkestone (only run for S. Woods, gelded after) at 2 yrs and Wolverhampton (flashed tail/carried head high) on reappearance: raced too freely only other outing: needs treating with some caution. *W. J. Haggas*   72

TROJAN PRINCESS   3 b.f. Hector Protector (USA) 124 – Robellino Miss (USA) (Robellino (USA) 127) [2002 80p: 7m 8g 10s 8.1d² 8m⁴ 8m⁶ 8d³ Oct 15] rather leggy, useful-looking filly: fairly useful performer: often highly tried: stays 1m: acts on good to soft going, probably on good to firm: blinkered (well held) third start: sometimes runs in snatches/carries head awkwardly: sold 18,000 gns. *G. Wragg*   91

TROJAN WOLF   7 ch.g. Wolfhound (USA) 126 – Trojan Lady (USA) (Irish River (FR) 131) [2002 53§, a73§: f8s³ f11s* f11g² f12g³ f12g² f11g⁶ f9.4g² f11g 10d 8g Jul 19] strong gelding: fair performer: won seller at Southwell in January: best at 1m to 1½m: acts on firm going, soft and fibresand: tried visored/tongue tied earlier in career: usually races up with pace: moody. *P. Howling*   – § a65 §

TROOPER COLLINS (IRE)   4 b.c. Dolphin Street (FR) 125 – Born To Fly (IRE) 57 (Last Tycoon 131) [2002 63: 12.3g 17.2d⁵ Jun 26] fair maiden at best: stays 17f: acts on firm and good to soft ground, well held on fibresand: very slowly away final outing. *Jonjo O'Neill*   66

TROPICAL CORAL (IRE)   2 ch.f. (May 9) Pennekamp (USA) 130 – Tropical Dance (USA) 93 (Thorn Dance (USA) 107) [2002 6.1m 8g⁴ p8g² f7g³ Dec 31] sturdy filly: third foal: dam, 2-y-o 5f/6f winner, half-sister to smart US 1997 2-y-o performer up to 8.5f Johnbill: fair maiden: best effort when head second to Joe Bear at Lingfield, leading 1f out until near finish: not sure to stay much beyond 1m: acts on polytrack: sometimes carries head high. *A. J. Lidderdale*   74

TROPICAL SON   3 b.c. Distant Relative 128 – Douce Maison (IRE) 67 (Fools Holme (USA)) [2002 8m⁶ 10d 10g³ 9m 10.4m Sep 4] 11,000Y: well-made colt: third foal: brother to winner up to 1¼m in Italy and half-brother to useful German miler Montestefano (by Emperor Jones): dam 1m winner who stayed 1½m: fair maiden: below form in handicaps last 2 starts: stays 1¼m. *A. P. Jarvis*   68

TROTTER'S FUTURE   4 b.g. Emperor Jones (USA) 119 – Miss Up N Go (Gorytus (USA) 132) [2002 73: 12s 12f 10m 16.1m 16g 16.2d³ 15.9f⁴ 16.1d 18d 16v Oct 29] close-coupled gelding: modest handicapper nowadays: left M. Easterby after eighth start: stays 2m: acts on firm and good to soft going: tried blinkered: reportedly had breathing problem fourth start: has found little/flashed tail: usually held up: none too trustworthy: sold 4,700 gns, sent to Kuwait. *S. C. Williams*   60

TROUBLE AT BAY (IRE)   2 b.c. (Apr 22) Slip Anchor 136 – Fight Right (FR) (Crystal Glitters (USA) 127) [2002 7.1m² 7m⁶ 8g 7s p7g² Oct 31] IR 11,500F, 14,000Y: quite good-topped colt: half-brother to several winners, including 2001 2-y-o 6f winner Brigadier Jones (by Emperor Jones) and French 1¼m/11f winner Royal Groom (by Al Nasr): dam French 2-y-o 1m winner: fair maiden: runner-up at Warwick and Lingfield: will need to settle better to stay 1m (bred to stay much further): acts on polytrack and good to firm ground. *A. King*   74

TROUBLE MOUNTAIN (USA)   5 br.g. Mt Livermore (USA) – Trouble Free (USA) (Nodouble (USA)) [2002 82: 9.9m⁵ 10.3f⁶ 12d² 10f⁵ 12g⁵ 11.9g 10g³ 10.3d* 9.9g⁶ 10g² 11.9m 10.3m 13.1g 10.4f⁶ Oct 11] small, sparely-made gelding: good mover: has a quick action: fairly useful handicapper: won at Doncaster in August: effective at 1m to easy 1½m: acts on firm and good to soft going: blinkered (ran creditably) fourth start: consistent. *M. W. Easterby*   83

TROUBLESHOOTER   4 b.g. Ezzoud (IRE) 126 – Oublier L'Ennui (FR) 79 (Bellman (FR) 123) [2002 –: 10m 12.1d Jul 19] strong, well-made gelding: fair maiden at 2 yrs: well held since: tried blinkered/tongue tied. *G. A. Swinbank*   –

TROUSERS   3 b.g. Pivotal 124 – Palo Blanco 82 (Precocious 126) [2002 6m 6f 8.3d f6g Oct 21] 1,400Y: first foal: dam 5f to 7f winner: little form: slowly away first 2 outings. *Andrew Reid*   –

TRUDIE 4 b.f. Komaite (USA) – Irish Limerick 89 (Try My Best (USA) 130) [2002 – 49: f8.5s 6s Jul 2] rangy filly: poor performer at 3 yrs: last on reappearance: tried blinkered: broke blood vessel and fell final outing. *Mrs A. M. Naughton*

TRUE COMPANION 3 b.c. Brief Truce (USA) 126 – Comanche Companion 88   **74** (Commanche Run 133) [2002 8.2m² 8.3d² p10g² f9.4f⁵ p10g⁵ Dec 30] first known foal: **a67** dam 7f/1m winner: fair maiden: runner-up first 3 starts: stays 1¼m: acts on polytrack, yet to race on extremes of going on turf: wandered badly final start. *N. P. Littmoden*

TRUE COURAGE 3 b.c. Machiavellian (USA) 123 – Try To Catch Me (USA)   **82** (Shareef Dancer (USA) 135) [2002 76p: 10.1g⁵ 11.7m² 12d² 11.5g² 10.5d⁶ Aug 8] rather leggy, close-coupled colt: has a round action: fairly useful maiden: runner-up 3 times, clear when prematurely eased at Pontefract on second occasion: stays 1½m: acts on good to firm and good to soft going: found little final run: sold 18,000 gns, sent to Bahrain. *B. W. Hills*

TRUE FAITH 2 ch.g. (Apr 1) Primo Dominie 121 – Rewardia (IRE) 66 (Petardia 113)   **50** [2002 5.1d⁶ f5g 6.1d² 7f³ 6g³ 6.1d 8g Sep 19] angular gelding: first foal: dam, probably stayed 1¼m: modest maiden: placed in sellers: stays 7f: acts on firm and good to soft going, below form on fibresand: well held in blinkers/visor last 2 starts. *P. D. Evans*

TRUE HOLLY 2 b.f. (Mar 17) Bishop of Cashel 122 – Polly's Teahouse 68 (Shack   **44** (USA) 118) [2002 7g 7d f6g⁶ Nov 20] 3,000Y: half-sister to several winners by Weldnaas, including fairly useful 5f (including at 2 yrs) winner Polly Golightly and 5-y-o Tea For Texas: dam sprint maiden: poor form in maiden/claimers. *J. D. Bethell*

TRUE NIGHT 5 b.g. Night Shift (USA) – Dead Certain 123§ (Absalom 128) [2002   **93** 94: 8s 6g 6m 7f 6f 6g 7.2g² 7s⁴ 7m 7.9d 8m⁵ 8d³ 7g³ 8f* 8m* 8g* 7.6f* 8g 7m 7f³ Oct 5] smallish, attractive gelding: fairly useful handicapper: in fine form at Ascot, Goodwood, Brighton and Chester in summer, first 3 wins within 11 days: effective at 7f/1m: acts on firm and good to soft going: has worn crossed noseband/been early to post: tough. *D. Nicholls*

TRUE THUNDER 5 b.g. Bigstone (IRE) 126 – Puget Dancer (USA) 62 (Seattle   **92** Dancer (USA) 119) [2002 10f² 10m⁴ 8g Oct 18] leggy gelding: good walker: fairly useful form, lightly raced: likely to stay 1½m: raced only on good going or firmer: sold 5,500 gns, joined Julian Poulton. *H. R. A. Cecil*

TRUMPTON 2 ch.f. (Mar 20) First Trump 118 – Malwiya (USA) (Shahrastani (USA)   **69** 135) [2002 p7g⁴ f8s 7.2g² 8.3m³ 8d Oct 21] 6,600Y: quite good-topped filly: sixth foal: half-sister to 5-y-o Malarkey and winners abroad by Polish Patriot and Be My Chief: dam unraced out of very smart French filly up to 10.5f Masmouda: fair maiden: best efforts when in frame at Lingfield and Windsor (nursery): stays 1m: acts on polytrack and good to firm going: sold 7,000 gns. *I. A. Balding*

TRUSTED MOLE (IRE) 4 b.g. Eagle Eyed (USA) 111 – Orient Air 74 (Prince Sabo   **57 §** 123) [2002 65§, a58§: p10g⁵ p10g⁴ p10g p13g² p12g² Mar 6] deep-girthed gelding: modest performer: stays easy 13f: acts on firm going, good to soft and polytrack (no form on fibresand): blinkered: sometimes slowly away/races freely/wanders/finds little: not to be trusted: sold £4,300. *S. Kirk*

TRUST IN PAULA (USA) 4 b.f. Arazi (USA) 135 – Trust In Dixie (USA) (Dixieland   **53 §** Band (USA)) [2002 54: f12s³ p12g f12g⁶ 11.6g⁴d f12g f12g Dec 2] modest handicapper: left D. Haydn Jones after fourth start: stays 1½m: acts on fibresand, soft and good to firm ground: visored/blinkered nowadays: tends to drop out tamely: untrustworthy. *C. P. Morlock*

TRUST RULE 2 b.c. (Apr 13) Selkirk (USA) 129 – Hagwah (USA) 109 (Dancing   **65 p** Brave (USA) 140) [2002 p6g⁶ Dec 28] third foal: half-brother to a winner around 9f in Europe by Machiavellian: dam, 1m to 1½m winner, half-sister to smart miler Sarafan: 16/1, slowly away and ran on without threatening when 6 lengths sixth to Wages in Lingfield maiden: should improve. *B. W. Hills*

TRUSTTHUNDER 4 ch.f. Selkirk (USA) 129 – Royal Cat (Royal Academy (USA)   **64** 130) [2002 68: p7g² p6g⁴ p6g* 6m⁶ 6f⁶ f6g³ 6d p6g p6g* 6d 6g Aug 23] tall, angular filly: **a74** fair handicapper: won at Lingfield in March and July: effective at 6f/7f: yet to race on heavy going, acts on any other turf and all-weather. *N. P. Littmoden*

TRYFAN 3 b.g. Distant Relative 128 – Sister Sal 74 (Bairn (USA) 126) [2002 ?: 7.1m   **–** 10.3f 9.9m f9.4g Dec 16] plain, leggy gelding: little form. *A. Bailey*

TRYSULL DREAM (IRE) 3 b.f. Mujadil (USA) 119 – Emma's Whisper 69 (Kind   **–** of Hush 118) [2002 40: 7m 9.2s 8m 7m 7m Sep 17] poor maiden: little form in 2002: visored last 2 starts. *C. A. Dwyer*

TUCKER FENCE 3 br.g. So Factual (USA) 120 – Daisy Topper (Top Ville 129) **57**
[2002 69, a72: 7g 7.1f f7g p7g 8.2g 8m² 8.2m⁵ 7m⁶ 7.5m³ 6m⁵ 6m 7d f8.5g⁵ Nov 18] **a–**
sturdy gelding: fair performer at 2 yrs, just modest in 2002: effective at 6f to 1m: acts on
fibresand and good to firm going: tried blinkered/visored: sold 1,600 gns. *J. Balding*

TUDOR WOOD 3 b.c. Royal Applause 124 – Silent Indulgence (USA) (Woodman **107**
(USA) 126) [2002 99?: 6g* 6m³ 6f² 6m⁴ 6d 6m³ 5m 7m* Sep 20] well-made colt: useful
performer: won maiden at Salisbury in May and handicap at Newbury (made all with bit
to spare by ¾ length from Dark Charm) in September: free-going sort, and will prove best
up to 7f: seems best on good going or firmer: blinkered (well beaten) seventh start: may
prove best with forcing tactics: sold 125,000 gns, sent to Bahrain. *B. Hanbury*

TUFTY HOPPER 5 b.g. Rock Hopper 124 – Melancolia 77 (Legend of France **61**
(USA) 124) [2002 62, a68: p16g f16.2g f16.2g² f16.2g³ f16.2g³ 14.1d⁵ 16g² 16m⁵ 16.2g⁶
f16.2g 17.1m Jun 10] modest handicapper: stays easy 2m: acts on firm going, good to soft
and all-weather: tried blinkered/visored (ran well) in 2000: carries head high: held up:
difficult to win on, but consistent. *P. Howling*

TUG OF LOVE (IRE) 2 ch.c. (Mar 8) Halling (USA) 133 – Heart's Harmony (Blush- **87 p**
ing Groom (FR) 131) [2002 6g* 6.1f² Aug 31] good-topped colt: sixth foal: half-brother
to 1¼m winners National Anthem (smart, by Royal Academy), Love Song (by Kris) and
Lullaby (by Unfuwain): dam second at 1m from 2 starts in France: won maiden at
Newmarket in July: still green, 3 lengths second to Flying Express in minor event at
Chester, again slowly away and taking long time to find stride: will stay at least 1m:
useful prospect, should win more races. *Sir Michael Stoute*

TULSA (IRE) 8 b.g. Priolo (USA) 127 – Lagrion (USA) 68 (Diesis 133) [2002 12d **–**
Jul 4] poor handicapper in 2000: well held only run in 2002: usually blinkered/visored
nowadays. *L. Montague Hall*

TUMBLEWEED CHARM (IRE) 3 b.g. Zafonic (USA) 130 – Vienna Charm **97 d**
(IRE) 67 (Sadler's Wells (USA) 132) [2002 88: p8g⁴ 7m³ 7m 6.1d⁴ 6m⁴ 5.7m 7m 8f 6g 7f
8g 7s f7g⁶ Nov 15] good-bodied gelding: useful performer at best: regressed during 2002:
free-going sort, and may prove best at 6f/7f: acts on polytrack, good to firm and good to
soft going: sometimes finds little, including in blinkers sixth start. *B. J. Meehan*

TUMBLEWEED QUARTET (USA) 6 b.g. Manila (USA) – Peggy's String (USA) **– §**
(Highland Park (USA)) [2002 p10g Jan 23] strong, rangy gelding: fairly useful performer
in 2000: reportedly had breathing problem only run since: tried blinkered: not to be
trusted. *Jean-Rene Auvray*

TUMBLEWEED RIDGE 9 ch.h. Indian Ridge 123 – Billie Blue 63 (Ballad Rock **99**
122) [2002 107: 7m 7m² 7f Oct 3] well-made horse: impressed in appearance: smart
performer at best: winner of 10 races, 5 of them Group 3 events, including Horris Hill
Stakes at Newbury and Ballycorus Stakes at Leopardstown, latter in 1998, 1999 and
2000: just useful at 9 yrs, best effort when second to Polar Ben in minor event at
Newmarket: best around 7f: seemed to act on any going, though probably best in later
years on good or softer: usually blinkered/tongue tied: had worn dropped/crossed
noseband: usually raced prominently: was none too consistent: reportedly retired due to
tendon injury. *B. J. Meehan*

TUMBLEWEED TENOR (IRE) 4 b.g. Mujadil (USA) 119 – Princess Carmen **–**
(IRE) 61 (Arokar (FR) 124) [2002 –: f8.5g⁶ f8.5s Dec 7] angular gelding: fair performer
at 2 yrs: little form since. *J. White*

TUMBLING SAND (IRE) 2 b.f. (Mar 8) Desert Prince (IRE) 130 – Velvet Morning **58**
(IRE) (Machiavellian (USA) 123) [2002 5m 6m⁵ 7.5m 7m³ 7.5g⁶ f8s⁶ 7.5g⁶ 7m⁵ Oct 2]
IR 10,000Y: leggy filly: first foal: dam unraced granddaughter of Cherry Hinton winner
Turkish Treasure: modest maiden: should stay 1m: raced only on good/good to firm
ground on turf, below form on fibresand. *T. D. Easterby*

TUNEFUL 2 b.f. (Feb 15) Pivotal 124 – Music In My Life (IRE) 59 (Law Society **82 p**
(USA) 130) [2002 7m³ 7.5g* Sep 18] rather leggy filly: closely related to 6-y-o Teyaar
and half-sister to several winners, including 5-y-o Galleon Beach: dam, maiden who
stayed 1m, out of half-sister to 5-y-o Bach: fair form: justified favouritism in maiden at
Beverley by length from Night Mist, leading 1f out: will stay at least 1m: remains capable
of better. *Mrs A. J. Perrett*

TUNNEL OF LOVE 4 ch.f. Mark of Esteem (IRE) 137 – La Dama Bonita (USA) 87 **51**
(El Gran Senor (USA) 136) [2002 51: p8g⁴ p10g 10g 10g 10.9g Jul 5] modest maiden at
best: probably stays 1¼m: acts on polytrack, raced only on good/good to soft going on
turf: sold 2,200 gns in July, sent to Saudi Arabia. *D. W. P. Arbuthnot*

TUNSTALL (USA) 3 b.g. Bahri (USA) 125 – Princess West (GER) (Gone West **79** (USA)) [2002 74: 9.9m³ 10m 9.9g 8.5m³ 10.1m⁵ 9g⁴ 7g⁴ Aug 23] close-coupled, good-topped gelding: fair maiden on Flat: stays 1¼m: yet to race on extremes of going: blinkered fourth and fifth (raced freely) outings: fair form over hurdles, successful in October. *T. D. Easterby*

TUPELO PRINCE (IRE) 3 ch.g. Shaddad (USA) 75 – Sylvan Princess 73 (Sylvan **–** Express 117) [2002 12f⁵ 10m 8m 7.5m Aug 25] 1,000Y: lengthy gelding: first foal: dam 7f/1m winner: well held in maidens/claimers. *C. N. Allen*

TUPPENCE HA'PENNY 3 gr.f. Never So Bold 135 – Mummy's Chick 77 **64 ?** (Mummy's Pet 125) [2002 54: 7s⁴ 6m 6m May 16] unfurnished filly: modest maiden at best, lightly raced: bred to prove best at 5f/6f. *G. G. Margarson*

TURAATH (IRE) 6 b.g. Sadler's Wells (USA) 132 – Diamond Field (USA) 71 (Mr **–** Prospector (USA)) [2002 –: 13.9g Jun 14] smallish gelding: fairly useful performer at 4 yrs, very much on downgrade: modest hurdler. *G. M. McCourt*

TURANDOT'S IRONY (USA) 3 b.f. Irish River (FR) 131 – True Celebrity (USA) **48** (Lyphard (USA) 132) [2002 10s⁶ 7.1g⁶ 6m⁴ 8m⁶ 10m Oct 3] 1,000,000 francs Y: medium-sized filly: fifth foal: closely related to fairly useful 6f and (in UAE) 7f winner Eljjanah (by Riverman) and half-sister to 2 winners, including 4-y-o Khayyam: dam, maiden in USA, closely related to smart 1985 2-y-o 7f winner Truely Nureyev: poor maiden: stays 1m: tends to start slowly: has raced freely: folded very quickly final outing; sold 800 gns, sent to Kuwait. *M. R. Channon*

TURBO (IRE) 3 b.g. Piccolo 121 – By Arrangement (IRE) 60 (Bold Arrangement **94** 127) [2002 82: 10.5m² 12.3f⁶ 10.4d³ 9.9m³ 10.4m 10.3m* Jul 25] close-coupled gelding: fairly useful handicapper: generally in good form in 2002, winning at Doncaster in July: stays 1¼m: acts on firm and soft going: tried visored: joined Venetia Williams. *G. B. Balding*

TURIBIUS 3 b.g. Puissance 110 – Compact Disc (IRE) 48 (Royal Academy (USA) **73** 130) [2002 75: p5g* p5g² p5g⁶ 5m 5.3d⁴ 5d⁶ 5m⁴ p6g p5g⁶ Dec 21] leggy gelding: fair handicapper: won at Lingfield in January: speedy and best at 5f: acts on polytrack, yet to race on extremes of going on turf: usually visored nowadays: often makes running: wandered markedly once at 2 yrs. *T. E. Powell*

TURKU 4 b.g. Polar Falcon (USA) 126 – Princess Zepoli 61 (Persepolis (FR) 127) **–** [2002 96: p7g² 8m f7f⁴ f7s⁶ f7g* p7g² f7s p7g³ f7g² f7g p7g³ Dec 30] lengthy gelding: **a73** useful at 3 yrs: only fair in 2002, winning claimer at Wolverhampton in October: left N. Littmoden after ninth start: stays 1m: acts on all-weather, soft and good to firm going: has worn cheekpieces: sometimes makes running. *Mrs Lydia Pearce*

TURN AROUND 2 b.c. (Feb 18) Pivotal 124 – Bemuse 89 (Forzando 122) [2002 5m³ **86 ?** 5m⁵ 6d* p7g Nov 13] 12,000F, 27,000Y: well-made colt: first foal: dam, 2-y-o 5f winner (only season to race), half-sister to useful 1996 2-y-o Falkenham: easily best effort (fairly useful form) when winning 21-runner maiden at Windsor in October by 3 lengths from Bonus, racing alone on far side from halfway: gave impression something amiss final start: should stay 7f: acts on good to soft going: swept way first 2 starts. *B. W. Hills*

TURN BACK 3 b.f. Pivotal 124 – Trachelium 65 (Formidable (USA) 125) [2002 9d⁴ **73** 9.3s* 10.5f⁶ 10s Oct 14] 1,500Y: tall filly: has a markedly round action: fifth foal: half-sister to 1¼m to 2m winner Uniform (by Unfuwain): dam maiden who stayed 1m: fair form: won maiden at Carlisle in June: should stay at least 1¼m. *Miss S. E. Hall*

TURNED OUT NICE 4 b.f. Ezzoud (IRE) 126 – Green Seed (IRE) 78 (Lead On **–** Time (USA) 123) [2002 10s Oct 15] second foal: half-sister to 7f (at 2 yrs) and 1¼m (in Ireland) winner Take Flite (by Cadeaux Genereux): dam, 2-y-o 6f winner, later stayed 1¼m: 50/1, behind in maiden at Ayr on debut. *J. D. Bethell*

TURNED OUT WELL 5 b.g. Robellino (USA) 127 – In The Shade 89 (Bustino **50** 136) [2002 53: 16.2g 16.2m⁶ Jul 16] tall, useful-looking gelding: has a round action: modest handicapper: should prove best at 2m+: acts on fibresand, good to firm and good to soft ground: has raced freely. *P. C. Haslam*

TURNING THE TIDE 3 b.g. Lugana Beach 116 – Robert's Daughter (Robellino **–** (USA) 127) [2002 –: 6f 6m 7g 8m p12g 8m 8.2v⁶ Oct 29] modest maiden at best: left J. M. Bradley after reappearance: visored/blinkered last 2 starts: sometimes slowly away. *Dr J. R. J. Naylor*

TURNPOLE (IRE) 11 br.g. Satco (FR) 114 – Mountain Chase (Mount Hagen (FR) **82** 127) [2002 91: 14.1s⁵ 14.6m⁶ 16f⁵ 16.2d⁶ Aug 14] strong gelding: fairly useful handicapper: ran poorly after reappearance: stays 2½m: acts on firm and good to soft going: has run well sweating: held up. *Mrs M. Reveley*

TURN TO BLUE   3 b.g. Bluegrass Prince (IRE) 110 – Alvecote Lady 50 (Touching   **52**
Wood (USA) 127) [2002 –: p10g 8m 8.3s 8.1d 11.7d⁵ 10.2m⁴ 10m 10.2g 11.7f 12f 8f⁴
10m 8g Oct 16] plain gelding: modest maiden: stays 1¼m: acts on firm going: blinkered
(tailed off) tenth start. *J. C. Fox*

TURTLE BOW (FR)   3 b.f. Turtle Island (IRE) 123 – Clara Bow (FR) (Top Ville 129)   **115**
[2002 7.5g² 7d* 8v* 9m* 10.5g* 10.5m⁴ 8s* 8g⁴ 10s² 10d Oct 26] fifth foal: half-sister to
3 winners in France, including useful 11f/12.5f winner Whitton Court (by Cardoun): dam
French maiden: smart performer: won maiden at Bordeaux, minor event at Saint-Cloud,
listed race at Longchamp, Prix Cleopatre at Saint-Cloud (readily by 2 lengths from
Totally Cosmic) and Prix d'Astarte at Deauville (beat Dedication ½ length) between
February and August: also good efforts in Prix de Diane at Chantilly (demoted to fourth
after finishing 2½ lengths third to Bright Sky), Prix Jacques le Marois at Deauville (4
lengths fourth to Banks Hill) and Flower Bowl Invitational at Belmont (kept on well
when neck second to Kazzia): respectable ninth to Starine in Breeders' Cup Filly & Mare
Turf at Arlington final start, beaten when forced to check inside final 1f: stays 10.5f: acts
on heavy and good to firm going: genuine and consistent. *F. Rohaut, France*

TURTLE LOVE (IRE)   3 b.f. Turtle Island (IRE) 123 – A Little Loving (He Loves   **58**
Me 120) [2002 48, a58: p7g f9.4g f7g² f8g⁵ f7g³ 7m⁶ 8.2g 6.9s² f7g 8.1g f7g⁴ f9.4g³   **a52**
8m⁵ f7g f8.5g Nov 30] good-topped filly: modest performer: trained seventh to thirteenth
outings by B. Ellison: returned to former trainer: probably best around 7f: acts on soft
going, good to firm and fibresand: usually blinkered nowadays: has worn cheekpieces.
Miss V. Haigh

TURTLE RECALL (IRE)   3 b.g. Turtle Island (IRE) 123 – Nora Yo Ya (Ahonoora   **57**
122) [2002 –: 8.2d⁶ 10m 10f⁶ f9.4g 12d³ 13v⁵ 11.5m 12f³ Oct 8] tall, good-topped
gelding: modest maiden handicapper: stays easy 1½m: acts on firm and good to soft
going: no easy ride: sold 9,000 gns. *P. W. Harris*

TURTLE SONG (IRE)   5 br.g. Turtle Island (IRE) 123 – Miss Bojangles (Gay
Fandango (USA) 132) [2002 f12g Dec 26] fair form in maidens at 2 yrs: first start since,
pulled up (reportedly lost action) in Wolverhampton seller. *P. Howling*

TURTLE SOUP (IRE)   6 b.g. Turtle Island (IRE) 123 – Lisa's Favourite (Gorytus   **–**
(USA) 132) [2002 14.4m May 6] sturdy gelding: fairly useful handicapper at 4 yrs: well
held only run since. *Mrs L. Richards*

TURTLE VALLEY (IRE)   6 b.g. Turtle Island (IRE) 123 – Primrose Valley 99 (Mill   **96**
Reef (USA) 141) [2002 97, a–: 16g⁶ 13.9f⁴ 14d⁴ 13.9g 18m 16d⁵ 12v p12g p12g Dec 18]   **a–**
small, strong gelding: unimpressive mover: useful performer: below form after third
start: stays 2m: has form on firm going, very best efforts on good or softer: blinkered once
at 2 yrs: has hung left. *S. Dow*

TUSCAN DREAM   7 b.g. Clantime 101 – Excavator Lady 65 (Most Secret 119)   **67**
[2002 86, a70: p5g⁶ 5g 5f 5g 5m⁶ 5.1f⁴ 5g 5m 5m 5g 5.3g⁴ 5m 5m* 5.3m⁵ 5.1g 5.1f⁶
5f f5g Dec 27] smallish, sturdy gelding: fair peformer: won claimer at Warwick in
August: best at bare 5f: acts on all-weather, raced mainly on good ground or firmer on
turf: below form in blinkers: has bolted to post/been taken down early/reared as stall
opened: usually front runner. *A. Berry*

TUSCAN FLYER   4 b.g. Clantime 101 – Excavator Lady 65 (Most Secret 119) [2002   **67**
71: f5g f5g 5.1d 5m p5g³ 5d* 5m 5m 5m 5m⁶ f5s 5.1g⁵ 5f 5f* 5f³ Oct 11] deep-bodied
gelding: fair performer: won seller at Musselburgh (left A. Berry 9,000 gns) in July and
handicap at Pontefract in September: best at 5f: acts on polytrack, firm and good to soft
going: tried blinkered, including last 3 starts: races up with pace. *R. Bastiman*

TUSCAN SKY (USA)   2 b.f. (Feb 22) Gulch (USA) – Search Committee (USA)   **77**
(Roberto (USA) 131) [2002 7d⁵ 7g* 7m Sep 14] IR 110,000Y: good-bodied filly: half-
sister to numerous winners in USA, including minor stakes winner at 7f/8.5f First Stage
(by Relaunch): dam, 8.5f winner in USA, half-sister to champion US 3-y-o filly Chris
Evert and to dam of Kentucky Derby winner Winning Colors: fair form: won maiden
at Newcastle in August: not disgraced in nursery at Doncaster final start: will stay 1m.
B. W. Hills

TUSCAN TEMPO   3 ch.g. Perugino (USA) 84 – Fact of Time (Known Fact (USA)   **48**
135) [2002 62: f7g⁵ 8.3s 7m 8.1d 8m⁶ 8.1d Aug 8] sturdy, close-coupled gelding: modest
maiden at 2 yrs: mostly well held in 2002: stays 1m: acts on good to firm going: sold
£1,500. *R. Hannon*

TUSCAN TREATY 2 b.f. (Apr 27) Brief Truce (USA) 126 – Fiorenz (USA) (Chromite (USA)) [2002 6m 7m f8.5g² Nov 18] 800Y, resold 2,000Y: quite good-topped filly: second foal: half-sister to a 6f (including at 2 yrs)/7.5f winner in Italy by Atraf: dam ran once: clearly best effort in maidens (modest form) when 13 lengths third (promoted) to Magenta Rising at Wolverhampton, racing freely: not sure to stay much beyond 1m: acts on fibresand: very slowly away on debut. *T. T. Clement*   **50**

TUSCARORA (IRE) 3 b.f. Revoque (IRE) 122 – Fresh Look (IRE) 64 (Alzao (USA) 117) [2002 62: p7g⁶ p6g² f8s⁵ 8f⁶ 7f⁴ 7g³ 7.2g² 7m⁶ 7m Sep 17] smallish filly: fair performer: won claimer at Lingfield in January: effective at 6f/1m: acts on firm going and polytrack: often slowly away: has shown signs of temperament. *P. C. Haslam*   **69**

TUSK 2 ch.g. (Apr 4) Fleetwood (IRE) 107 – Farmer's Pet 90 (Sharrood (USA) 124) [2002 6s³ 6s⁵ 7.1m⁴ 7m 6.1g 8m³ 8m⁴ 10m³ 8.3d Oct 14] big gelding: sort to carry condition: fifth foal: half-brother to 3 winners, including 4-y-o Bond Millennium and 9f/1¼m winner Lago di Como (both by Piccolo): dam 1¾m/2m winner: fair performer: won maiden at Warwick in July: in frame in nurseries after: stays 1¼m: acts on good to firm going: usually races prominently. *M. R. Channon*   **77**

TUSSLE 7 b.g. Salse (USA) 128 – Crime Ofthecentury 80 (Pharly (FR) 130) [2002 3d 7m 6.5g 6m 6d 6m⁶ 7g 7m Sep 18] good-topped, attractive gelding: useful handicapper at best, lightly raced (suffered chipped knee in 1998, severed a tendon in 2000): little form in 2002: blinkered fourth to sixth starts. *M. L. W. Bell*   **–**

TWEED 5 ch.g. Barathea (IRE) 127 – In Perpetuity 90 (Great Nephew 126) [2002 –: f12g⁵ f16s* f16.2g* f16g* f16g* f16.2g³ 18s 15f⁴ 16m 16f a16g 14.6s f14.8g⁴ Nov 30] good-bodied gelding: type to carry condition: fairly useful performer on all-weather, fair on turf: won 5 times in January/February, namely claimer at Southwell (left J. M. Jefferson) and handicaps at Wolverhampton and Southwell (3): well below form last 4 starts: stays 2m: acts on fibresand, firm and soft ground: tried visored/blinkered. *J. R. Best*   **69 a90 ?**

TWEEDSMUIR 3 b.g. Zilzal (USA) 137 – Sakura Queen (IRE) 52 (Woodman (USA) 126) [2002 11.8d⁶ 12s⁶ Jun 12] 32,000Y: rangy, angular gelding: fifth foal: closely related to 2 winners by Wolfhound, including 7f winner Chiu Chow Kid, and half-brother to 2 winners by Shareef Dancer: dam, maiden who stayed 1¼m, half-sister to dam of Rock of Gibraltar: fair form in maidens at Leicester and Kempton, still green in latter. *P. W. Harris*   **73**

TWENTYFOUR (IRE) 2 b.g. (Feb 25) Mujadil (USA) 119 – Karenaragon (Aragon 118) [2002 6d 6g³ 6s 7g³ 6f⁵ 7d 7g Aug 22] IR 35,000Y: smallish gelding: first foal: dam, of little account, sister to useful sprinter in Britain/USA Evening Promise: modest maiden: trained by J. Dunlop first 3 starts: well held in sellers last 3: stays 7f: tried blinkered. *J. S. Moore*   **58 d**

TWENTY SEVEN (IRE) 3 b.f. Efisio 120 – Naked Poser (IRE) 83 (Night Shift (USA)) [2002 75: 5d 6s⁵ 6d Oct 14] smallish, sturdy filly: fair performer at 2 yrs: just modest in 2002: should stay 7f: acts on good to firm going. *J. A. R. Toller*   **55**

TWENTYTWOSILVER (IRE) 2 ro.g. (Apr 10) Emarati (USA) 74 – St Louis Lady 71 (Absalom 128) [2002 p7g⁵ p7g* f7f² p7g Dec 14] IR 6,000F, IR 16,000Y: fourth foal: dam 7f winner: fairly useful performer: won maiden at Lingfield in October: good second at Wolverhampton, better effort in nurseries after: free-going sort, likely to prove best up to 7f. *J. A. Osborne*   **80**

TWICE 6 b.g. Rainbow Quest (USA) 134 – Bolas 118 (Unfuwain (USA) 131) [2002 –, a80: p16g 12m p16g Sep 4] quite good-topped gelding: has reportedly been hobdayed and had tie-back operation: fairly useful handicapper at best, lightly raced: well held in 2002 (lame final start). *Mrs L. Richards*   **–**

TWICE BLESSED (IRE) 5 ch.g. Thatching 131 – Fairy Blesse (IRE) (Fairy King (USA)) [2002 –: f7g f9.4g p7g Feb 20] strong, lengthy gelding: fair winner at 2 yrs: little form since: tried blinkered. *J. Gallagher*   **–**

TWICE BRIGHT 6 br.g. Precocious 126 – Sweet Helen (No Mercy 126) [2002 –: 12.6m Jun 17] last in maidens. *C. Drew*   **–**

TWICE UPON A TIME 3 ch.f. Primo Dominie 121 – Opuntia (Rousillon (USA) 133) [2002 70: 5.7m* 6.1m 5.1f³ 6m 5.7f⁴ 5.7f³ 5f⁴ 5f 6d Nov 1] good-topped filly: has a quick action: fair performer: won minor event at Bath in June: best at 5f/6f: acts on firm and soft ground. *B. Smart*   **76**

TWILIGHT BLUES (IRE) 3 ch.c. Bluebird (USA) 125 – Pretty Sharp 64 (Interrex (CAN)) [2002 101: 7m* 8m⁵ 7m 6d 6.5s⁴ 6m 6m⁶ Sep 28] good-topped colt: smart   **111**

Victor Chandler European Free Handicap, Newmarket—Twilight Blues wins going away from Approval (rail, noseband), Ashdown Express and Funfair Wane (almost completely hidden by winner)

performer: won Victor Chandler European Free Handicap at Newmarket in April by 2½ lengths from Approval: creditable efforts after when 4½ lengths fifth to Rock of Gibraltar in 2000 Guineas on same course, 3¼ lengths fourth to May Ball in Prix Maurice de Gheest at Deauville, 3½ lengths seventh to Invincible Spirit in Sprint Cup at Haydock and 4¼ lengths sixth to Crystal Castle in Diadem Stakes at Ascot: missed break when well held third/fourth starts (still wearing blindfold as stall opened in July Cup in latter): effective at 6f to 1m: acts on firm and soft going. *B. J. Meehan*

TWILIGHT DANCER (IRE) 4 b.f. Sri Pekan (USA) 117 – Manhattan Sunset (USA) 76 (El Gran Senor (USA) 136) [2002 54, a–: f12s f9.4g⁵ f12g 11.7f Aug 23] useful-looking filly: maiden handicapper: poor form in 2002: stays 1½m: acts on firm ground: tried blinkered. *J. M. Bradley* — **a31**

TWILIGHT HAZE 4 b.g. Darshaan 133 – Hiwaayati (Shadeed (USA) 135) [2002 76: f12g² f12g⁴ 11.9m² 13s 13.9f 12g⁴ 14.6m 11.9m f14.8g* f12s³ Dec 7] lengthy, good-topped gelding: fairly useful performer: won claimer at Wolverhampton (left I. Semple £9,000) in November: should stay 2m: acts on fibresand, heavy and good to firm going: races up with pace: unreliable. *Miss Gay Kelleway* — **90 §** **a85 §**

TWILIGHT MISTRESS 4 b.f. Bin Ajwaad (IRE) 119 – By Candlelight (IRE) 84 (Roi Danzig (USA)) [2002 83: f5s p5g p5g³ p6g³ f5g 7.6f 7g* 6g² 7d⁵ 8.3m 9g 8m² 7.6f 7m⁴ 8.1m p8g⁴ Oct 16] leggy filly: fairly useful handicapper: won at Southwell (despite idling) in June: stays 1m: acts on firm going, good to soft and all-weather: sometimes starts slowly/races freely: none too reliable. *D. W. P. Arbuthnot* — **81**

TWIN PETES 3 ch.g. Forzando 122 – Pour Moi 73 (Bay Express 132) [2002 6s 8m 7.1m 8.1d Jul 4] 3,800F, 14,500Y: good-topped gelding: half-brother to several winners, including 1994 2-y-o 7f seller winner Bex Hill (by Grey Desire) and 7f winner Spanish Express (by King of Spain): dam placed at 5f/6f: little sign of ability in maidens/seller: visored final start. *H. Candy* —

TWIN TIME   8 b.m. Syrtos 106 – Carramba (CZE) (Tumble Wind (USA)) [2002 77,   –
a–: 7.1m 7g 8m 8g 10m Jul 29] quite good-topped mare: fair handicapper in 2001: well
held in 2002: blinkered penultimate start. *J. S. King*

TWOFORTEN   7 b.g. Robellino (USA) 127 – Grown At Rowan 75 (Gabitat 119) [2002   – §
46§: 9s Jun 7] small, strong gelding: moody performer: sometimes visored/blinkered.
P. Butler

TWO JACKS (IRE)   5 b.g. Fayruz 116 – Kaya (GER) (Young Generation 129) [2002   41
43, a56?: f6g³ f7g f6g⁶ 7f⁴ f7g 6g⁵ 8g Jul 20] workmanlike gelding: modest maiden on   a51
all-weather, poor on turf: stays 7f: acts on fibresand: tried tongue tied. *W. S. Cunningham*

TWO MARKS (USA)   3 ch.f. Woodman (USA) 126 – Munnaya (USA) 101 (Nijinsky   73
(CAN) 138) [2002 62p: p8g⁴ f8.5g* 12d² 12f² 10.2g³ 10.9g³ 12.1g³ 12.3m⁴ 12f* Jul 17]
rangy, unfurnished filly: fluent mover: won maiden at Wolverhampton in
March and handicap at Catterick in July: stays 1½m: acts on firm going, good to soft
and fibresand: sometimes slowly away, and soon off bridle at Catterick: sent to USA.
M. Johnston

TWO SOCKS   9 ch.g. Phountzi (USA) 104 – Mrs Feathers 57 (Pyjama Hunt 126) [2002   53
67: 11.9g 10m 9.9m 12.6m⁶ 12.1g 12g Aug 22] leggy gelding: modest handicapper:
effective at 1¼m (given test)/1½m: acts on firm going, soft and fibresand: blinkered once
at 2 yrs. *J. S. King*

TWO STEPS TO GO (USA)   3 b.g. Rhythm (USA) – Lyonushka (CAN) (Private   57
Account (USA)) [2002 75: f8.5g* f8.5g³ f9.4g² 8m f8g* 8d⁶ 7f 8d 8m 9m⁵ 12m 10m⁵   a88
9m Sep 16] smallish, sturdy gelding: fairly useful on all-weather, modest on turf: won
handicap at Wolverhampton in January and claimer at Southwell in May: will prove best
up to 9f: acts on fibresand and good to firm going, probably on good to soft: often
blinkered, tried visored (seemed to take little interest): temperamental. *T. D. Barron*

TYBALLA (IRE)   4 b.f. Blues Traveller (IRE) 119 – Mary Mary Mouse (USA) (Valdez   39
(USA)) [2002 –: 10m 11.9s⁴ p12g Jun 29] well-made filly: poor maiden: seems to stay
1½m: acts on soft and good to firm going: sent to Trinidad. *M. H. Tompkins*

TYCHY   3 ch.f. Suave Dancer (USA) 136 – Touch of White 77 (Song 132) [2002 8m   73
8.3m 8.2g⁴ 9s 8.3m⁴ 7g⁵ 8g 7.1m² 7m* 7d⁶ 6.1m* 7f 7s³ 7s Nov 2] good-topped filly:
fourth reported foal: dam 5f performer: fair performer: won minor event at Brighton in
August and handicap at Nottingham (drifted left) in September: effective at 6f/7f: acts on
soft and good to firm going: usually races prominently. *S. C. Williams*

TYCOON HALL (IRE)   2 ch.c. (Feb 9) Halling (USA) 133 – Tycooness (IRE) 80§   96
(Last Tycoon 131) [2002 7d* 8g⁵ 8.1m³ Aug 30] 62,000F, 40,000Y: useful-looking colt:
first foal: dam, untrustworthy 1½m winner, half-sister to Lockinge Stakes winner Broken
Hearted: won maiden at Newmarket in July: useful efforts when fifth to Snipewalk in
listed race at Deauville and close third of 4 to Lady McNair in minor event at Sandown:
will stay at least 1¼m. *R. Hannon*

TYCOON'S LAST   5 b.m. Nalchik (USA) – Royal Tycoon (Tycoon II) [2002 64:   61
10g⁵ 11.9m 11.7g⁶ 12.3f 11.8d 12.1d⁴ 12f⁴ Jun 7] big, lengthy mare: modest handicapper:
should stay beyond 1½m: has form on firm going, possibly best on good or softer (acts on
heavy): has been slowly away. *W. M. Brisbourne*

TYNEHAM   2 b.c. (Apr 22) Robellino (USA) 127 – Diamond Wedding (USA) 65   74
(Diamond Shoal 130) [2002 6s 7m 7s² Oct 25] 4,000Y: well-made colt: seventh foal:
brother to smart 7f (including at 2 yrs) 1¼m winner Diamond White and half-brother
to 2 winners, including 5-y-o First Venture: dam, maiden, should have stayed beyond
1½m: easily best effort in maidens (fair form) when 10 lengths second to Barrissimo at
Doncaster, staying on from rear: will stay at least 1m: acts on soft ground: very slowly
away on debut. *G. C. Bravery*

TYPE ONE (IRE)   4 b.g. Bigstone (IRE) 126 – Isca 66 (Caerleon (USA) 132) [2002   84 §
88: p5g 5f² 6m 6d 5m⁶ 5d 5m 6m³ 5m 5m 7f Oct 5] well-made gelding: fairly useful
handicapper: best at 5f/6f: acts on polytrack, best turf form on good going or firmer:
visored (slowly away and soon given reminders) sixth outing: no easy ride: unreliable.
T. G. Mills

TYPHOON TILLY   5 b.g. Hernando (FR) 127 – Meavy 86 (Kalaglow 132) [2002 79:   79
14.1m² 14m² 14.1m³ 14.8m³ 14m² 14m⁵ 13.3f² 14.5g³ Oct 12] quite good-topped
gelding: fair performer: third in minor event at Pardubice final outing: probably stays
2½m: best efforts on going firmer than good: blinkered last 2 starts at 4 yrs: consistent,
but sometimes finds little. *C. R. Egerton*

TYPHOON TODD (IRE) 3 ch.g. Entrepreneur 123 – Petite Liqueurelle (IRE) **75**
(Shernazar 131) [2002 75: 8.3m 9d² 8.1d f9.4g p12g⁴ Nov 13] fair maiden handicapper:
left R. Hannon after third start: stays 1½m: acts on polytrack, good to firm and good to
soft going: tried visored: has wandered/carried head awkwardly. *P. G. Murphy*

TYRANNY 2 b.f. (Mar 22) Machiavellian (USA) 123 – Dust Dancer 116 (Suave **88**
Dancer (USA) 136) [2002 7f² 7s² 7m² Oct 5] 270,000Y: tall filly: second foal: half-sister
to 3-y-o Dusty Answer: dam, 7f to 1½m winner (including 1¼m Prix de la Nonette), half-
sister to very smart performer up to 1½m Zimzalabim: fairly useful maiden: runner-up all
starts: raced freely when beaten 1½ lengths by Al Ihtithar at Lingfield second start:
wandered and found little when below form final one: bred to stay 1m: temperament
under suspicion. *J. L. Dunlop*

TZAR 3 b.g. Makbul 104 – Tzarina (USA) (Gallant Romeo (USA)) [2002 69, a72: f7s⁵ **–**
f6g³ f6g³ f6g p6g f6s Dec 26] smallish gelding: fair performer: well below form after **a69 d**
second start: probably best at 6f/7f: acts on firm ground, soft and all-weather. *J. R. Best*

U

UHOOMAGOO 4 b.g. Namaqualand (USA) – Point of Law (Law Society (USA) **95**
130) [2002 81, a68: f8g⁵ f8.5g³ p8g³ 8s f8g 7f⁴ 7.6f⁴ 7m² 7m 7g 6.9d* 7g* 7d 7.2g³ 7.6g
6m Aug 17] leggy gelding: useful handicapper: won at Carlisle and Newcastle in June:
stays 1m: acts on all-weather/any turf going: usually blinkered/visored: tends to wander:
usually held up. *K. A. Ryan*

UHURU DAWN (IRE) 2 b.c. (Feb 18) Fayruz 116 – Come Dancing 48 (Suave Dancer **76**
(USA) 136) [2002 5g³ 5.1g p5g⁵ f6g⁵ 6g 5g 7g* 6g 7d⁴ 6s p5g⁵ p6g² Dec 21] IR 17,500F, **a61**
10,500Y: well-grown colt: second foal: dam, disappointing maiden who should have
stayed at least 7f, out of sister to very smart sprinter Primo Dominie: fair on turf, modest
on all-weather: won seller at Folkestone for J. Hills) in August: best efforts in minor
event at Maisons-Laffitte and claimer at Saint-Cloud next 2 starts: effective at 5f to 7f:
acts on good to soft ground and polytrack. *Andre Hermans, Belgium*

ULSHAW 5 ch.g. Salse (USA) 128 – Kintail 76 (Kris 135) [2002 54: 18s f16.2g³ **51**
f14.8s³ f16.2g³ 17.1m⁵ f16.2g* 15.9f f14.8g³ f14.8g³ Oct 21] quite good-topped gelding:
modest handicapper: won apprentice event at Wolverhampton in July: stays 17f: acts on
any turf going/fibresand: tried visored at 3 yrs. *B. J. Llewellyn*

ULTIMAJUR (USA) 4 br.c. Dayjur (USA) 137 – Crystal Lady (CAN) (Stop The **–**
Music (USA)) [2002 44: f5s f5g p7g p6g Feb 6] strong, good sort: maiden: no form in
2002. *M. D. I. Usher*

ULTIMATE CHOICE 4 b.g. Petong 126 – Jay Gee Ell 78 (Vaigly Great 127) [2002 **51**
53, a56: p8g p7g⁴ p8g p6g⁶ 7f Apr 11] modest performer: stays 7f: acts on all-weather and
good to firm going: tried visored/tongue tied. *N. P. Littmoden*

ULTRA MARINE (IRE) 2 b.c. (Apr 19) Blues Traveller (IRE) 119 – The Aspecto **64**
Girl (IRE) 53 (Alzao (USA) 117) [2002 5g 5m⁴ 5g³ 5g³ 7.1m² 7.5d² 7m⁴ 8g⁵ 7f⁵ 8d Oct
21] 8,000Y: leggy, useful-looking colt: fifth foal: half-brother to 2000 2-y-o 6f/7f winner
Cedar Tsar and 3-y-o Another Aspect (both by Inzar): dam maiden half-sister to useful 7f
to 1¼m performer Canaska Star: modest maiden: left K. Ryan after third start: stays 1m:
acts on good to firm and good to soft going. *J. S. Wainwright*

ULUNDI 7 b.g. Rainbow Quest (USA) 134 – Flit (USA) 72 (Lyphard (USA) 132) **122**
[2002 115: 10m* 10f⁴ 12g Sep 29]
　　　　The battle of Ulundi in 1879 marked the end of the Anglo-Zulu war. Under
the command of Lord Chelmsford, the British forces, forming a hollow square on a
low hill, kept an army estimated at three to four times their own number at bay,
before they were relieved. Ulundi the racehorse faced his own moment of destiny
in the Arlington Million at Chicago in August and almost pulled off a remarkable
victory against the odds. Under Richard Hughes, Ulundi still had only one horse
behind him on the far turn in the Million but he passed half the field in the straight,
leaving the impression that, in another few strides, he would also have cut down the
three who finished in front of him. Ulundi was beaten a head, a nose and a head into
fourth, the ex-British-trained pair Beat Hollow and Sarafan filling the first
two places. Ulundi appeared an unlucky loser, though neither fifth-placed Falcon

Wolferton Rated Stakes (Handicap), Royal Ascot—Ulundi (left) puts up the year's best performance in a handicap, winning from Arabie and Rasm (striped cap)

Flight nor sixth-placed Paolini got much room in the final furlong, the former also seeming to have plenty of running left in him at the finish.

Like the only other British raider, Brian Meehan's Freefourinternet, Ulundi was virtually dismissed by the American betting public for a Grade 1 contest worth £394,737 to the winner. Ulundi was venturing into pattern company for the first time on the Flat, but, on form, he was far from out of his depth, having progressed into a very smart performer at the age of seven. Ulundi started the year in Dubai, the plan being to get him qualified to run at the World Cup meeting. Heat in a suspensory put paid to that idea, however, and it wasn't until Royal Ascot that Ulundi reappeared, in the listed Wolferton Rated Stakes (Handicap). Well backed on the day, Ulundi was sent off at 10/1 carrying joint top weight in a field of seventeen. Racing from a career-high BHB mark of 109, Ulundi produced the handicap performance of the season, taking over approaching the final furlong, after being kept in close touch in a steadily-run race, and staying on well to beat Arabie by a head, with Rasm two lengths back in third and Pole Star a further half a length away in fourth. Ulundi was below form when seventh in the Turf Classic at Belmont in September, fading after taking a narrow advantage before the home turn, and his year ended as disappointingly as it had begun when he was withdrawn from the Hong Kong Cup in December, having, like several others from Europe, suffered a severe bout of travel sickness.

Ulundi (b.g. 1995)	Rainbow Quest (USA) (b 1981)	Blushing Groom (ch 1974)	Red God
			Runaway Bride
		I Will Follow (b 1975)	Herbager
			Where You Lead
	Flit (USA) (b 1988)	Lyphard (b 1969)	Northern Dancer
			Goofed
		Nimble Folly (ch 1977)	Cyane
			Instant Sin

The quite good-topped Ulundi has now surpassed 1999 One Thousand Guineas winner Wince (by Selkirk) as the best foal produced by the mile-and-a-quarter-maiden winner Flit. Ulundi's career has been something of a riches to rags to riches story. Initially owned by Juddmonte Farms, Ulundi was sold for just 5,500 guineas as an unraced three-year-old out of Andre Fabre's stable and, after being gelded and hobdayed, finished third in a Market Rasen bumper on his debut in June 1999. Ulundi has hardly looked back since, winning his next two bumpers then mixing hurdling and Flat racing with great success for Lady Herries up to the end of 2000, and now for Paul Webber, his best performance over hurdles being a useful effort to win the Scottish Champion Hurdle at Ayr in April 2001.

Ulundi, effective at a mile and a quarter and an easy mile and a half, seems likely to be campaigned solely on the Flat from now on, owner David Heath claiming after Royal Ascot 'I doubt he'll return to hurdling—the ground is never quick enough for him.' Indeed, while Ulundi won his bumpers on good to soft going and ran creditably the only time he encountered such conditions on the Flat,

1044

his best form has been achieved under less testing conditions; he clearly goes very well on good to firm and firm going. He has been bandaged in front and is waited with. *P. R. Webber*

UMBERELLA 2 b.f. (Mar 30) Sesaro (USA) 81 – Aquiletta 67 (Bairn (USA) 126) **47** [2002 5g⁶ 5m Aug 22] leggy, angular filly: third foal: half-sister to 5-y-o Tick Tock: dam, maiden, effective at 6f/7f: poor form in maiden/seller: dead. *C. B. B. Booth*

UMBOPA (USA) 4 b.g. Gilded Time (USA) – How Fortunate (CAN) (What Luck **73** (USA)) [2002 73: f11s² f12g f11g 11.9g May 10] strong, rangy gelding: fair handicapper: ran as if something amiss last 3 starts: should stay 1¾m: acts on heavy ground, good to firm and fibresand: blinkered/visored nowadays: sometimes edges left. *K. R. Burke*

UMISTA (IRE) 3 b.f. Tagula (IRE) 116 – Nishiki (USA) (Brogan (USA) 110) [2002 **–** –: p8g f6g⁶ p10g p7g Feb 20] rather leggy filly: little form: tried visored. *G. M. McCourt*

UMISTIM 5 ch.h. Inchinor 119 – Simply Sooty 78 (Absalom 128) [2002 115: 7.1d⁵ **114** 8m⁶ 8g⁶ 7m⁴ 7f² 9g* 7f² 8.9m⁵ 8m* Sep 15] smallish horse: smart performer: won 3-runner minor event at Sandown in August by ½ length from Masterful and listed race at the Curragh in September by short head from Blatant: also short-head second to Reel Buddy in Hungerford Stakes at Newbury seventh start: stays 9f: possibly unsuited to heavy going, acts on any other: game. *R. Hannon*

UMM AL QAWAIN STAR (USA) 3 b. or br.c. Mister Baileys 123 – Leahcim (USA) **73 +** (Persevered (USA)) [2002 8g* a9f⁵ 7m⁶ 8.1d⁴ Jul 5] $23,000Y, 35,000 2-y-o: leggy, quite good-topped colt: fifth foal: half-brother to winners in USA by Marsayas and Northern No Trump: dam unraced: won minor event at Nad Al Sheba in January: probably flattered (appeared to run to 85) in similar events in Britain last 2 starts: stays 1m. *Paul Smith, Belgium*

UMOJA (FR) 2 b. or br.f. (Apr 30) Anabaa (USA) 130 – Frustration 108 (Salse (USA) **78 p** 128) [2002 8s⁵ Oct 25] 37,000Y: well-made filly: third living foal: half-sister to 3-y-o Star Protector: dam, 1¼m winner, half-sister to US Grade 1 9f winner Mister Wonderful: 33/1, 7¼ lengths fifth of 22 to Richemaur in maiden at Doncaster, slowly away and staying on without being knocked about: sure to improve. *C. F. Wall*

UNAFRAID (IRE) 3 b.c. Unfuwain (USA) 131 – Witching Hour (IRE) 88 (Alzao **83** (USA) 117) [2002 10.5m³ 9g* 10g 10.1s Oct 22] leggy colt: first foal: dam, 2-y-o 6f winner who stayed 1m, half-sister to very smart 1m/1¼m performer Great Dane from family of Croco Rouge, Ali-Royal and Sleepytime: fairly useful form: won maiden at Newcastle in August comfortably by 3½ lengths from Ela Agori Mou: well held in handicaps after: stays 10.5f: sold 5,000 gns, sent to Kuwait. *H. R. A. Cecil*

UN AUTRE ESPERE 3 b.g. Golden Heights 82 – Drummer's Dream (IRE) 48 **–** (Drumalis 125) [2002 –: 8.1d 9d 8.1g 9.9d Jul 22] leggy gelding: well held in maidens/minor event: ran out only outing at 2 yrs. *A. Streeter*

UNCLE BERNON 3 ch.g. Pivotal 124 – Magical Veil 73 (Majestic Light (USA)) **83** [2002 6g* 6d³ Nov 1] 15,500F, 31,000Y: fifth living foal: half-brother to fairly useful 1996 2-y-o 1m winner Myrtlebank (by Salse) and 1997 2-y-o 6f winner Ben Rinnes (by Ardkinglass), later winner abroad: dam 11.6f winner: overcame greenness to win maiden at Windsor in October: much better form when 3½ lengths third to Zabaglione in minor event at Newmarket 4 days later, keeping on from rear. *G. B. Balding*

UNCLE FOLDING (IRE) 4 b.g. Danehill (USA) 126 – Bubbling Danseuse (USA) **– §** (Arctic Tern (USA) 126) [2002 –§: 5g Mar 28] little form: tried blinkered/tongue tied: refused to race last 2 starts. *Mrs D. Thomson*

UNDENIABLE 4 b.g. Unfuwain (USA) 131 – Shefoog 90 (Kefaah (USA) 124) [2002 **–** 75: 11.9f Oct 10] strong, rangy gelding: fair handicapper at 3 yrs: well held only Flat run in 2002. *D. Carroll*

UNDER CONSTRUCTION (IRE) 4 b.g. Pennekamp (USA) 130 – Madame Nure- **–** yev (USA) (Nureyev (USA) 131) [2002 70: 10.2d f12g⁵ f12g f8.5g⁵ 8.1d 11.6m Jul 22] **a63** leggy, quite good-topped gelding: modest performer: well held last 4 starts: stays 1½m: acts on good to firm going and fibresand: visored final outing. *G. A. Ham*

UNDERCOVER GIRL (IRE) 4 b.f. Barathea (IRE) 127 – Les Trois Lamas (IRE) **41** (Machiavellian (USA) 123) [2002 49: 10g⁶ 10.9g 10.2f Jul 25] rather leggy filly: poor maiden: probably stays 1¼m. *W. R. Muir*

UNDETERRED 6 ch.g. Zafonic (USA) 130 – Mint Crisp (IRE) 108 (Green Desert **88 §** (USA) 127) [2002 99: 6s 6g 6m 6m 5g⁵ 6g³ 6f³ 6g 5g⁴ 6m² 6g³ 6d 6m⁵ 6m 6g 5f 5f Oct

11] lengthy, deep-girthed gelding: has a quick action: fairly useful handicapper: 2¾ lengths third to Bond Boy in Stewards' Cup at Goodwood eleventh start: probably best at 6f: acts on firm going, probably on soft: usually visored, has been blinkered: usually on edge (has been mounted on course/early/reluctant to post): withdrawn having bolted to post under apprentice thirteenth intended start: sometimes slowly away: ungenuine nowadays. *D. Nicholls*

UNFAZED (IRE)   3 b.g. Fayruz 116 – Whispering Dawn 71 (Then Again 126) [2002   –
p8g f8.5g Jun 14] 8,000Y: second foal: dam, 1½m winner, also successful over hurdles: tongue tied, well held in maidens at Lingfield and Wolverhampton, very slowly away at latter. *B. I. Case*

UNICORN REWARD (IRE)   2 b.c. (Apr 25) Turtle Island (IRE) 123 – Kingdom   **78**
Pearl 57 (Statoblest 120) [2002 7m 7g⁴ p7g³ 6d⁴ Aug 8] IR 35,000Y: neat colt: second foal: dam, 1½m winner, half-sister to 7f/1m winner Russian Music and 1997 2-y-o 5f winner Pool Music, both useful: fair maiden: third at Lingfield: should stay at least 1m: acts on polytrack, unraced on extremes of going on turf. *R. Hannon*

UNICORN STAR (IRE)   5 b.g. Persian Bold 123 – Highland Warning 43 (Warning   –
136) [2002 36: 11.2g Mar 25] tall gelding: probably of little account nowadays. *J. S. Wainwright*

UNIGOLD (USA)   2 ch.c. (Feb 17) Silver Deputy (CAN) – Desert Queen (USA) (Wav-   **95 p**
ering Monarch (USA)) [2002 7g⁴ 8m² 8g⁶ Sep 28] $180,000Y: angular, good-topped colt: third foal: half-brother to a winner in USA by Candy Stripes: dam 7.5f/1m winner in USA: useful form: 1¼ lengths second to Silver Gilt in maiden at Doncaster: 6 lengths sixth to Al Jadeed in Royal Lodge Stakes at Ascot: will stay 1¼m: type to do better still. *E. A. L. Dunlop*

UNITED PASSION   5 b.m. Emarati (USA) 74 – Miriam 59 (Forzando 122) [2002 –,   –
a65: f5s* f5g* Jan 19] modest performer: won claimers at Southwell and Wolverhampton   **a62**
in January: best at bare 5f: acts on all-weather (well beaten only run on turf): tongue tied: often races up with pace. *D. Shaw*

UNLEADED   2 ch.f. (Feb 10) Danzig Connection (USA) – Mo Stopher 47 (Sharpo   –
132) [2002 6v Nov 9] small, stocky filly: fourth foal: sister to 3-y-o Spirit's Awakening and half-sister to 2 winners by First Trump: dam maiden: 40/1 and backward, tailed off in maiden at Doncaster. *J. Akehurst*

UNLEASH (USA)   3 ch.g. Benny The Dip (USA) 127 – Lemhi Go (USA) (Lemhi   **102**
Gold (USA) 123) [2002 85p: 12.3f⁴ 11.9m³ 11.8d* 14.4g* 15.9f² 18m 15g⁵ Sep 19] strong, close-coupled gelding: useful performer: won minor event at Leicester and handicap at Newcastle, both in August: good effort when ¾-length second to Prairie Falcon in handicap at Chester, then not discredited under very stiff task when seventh of 8 to Boreas in Doncaster Cup: stays 2m: acts on fibresand, firm and soft ground: blinkered (raced freely, found nothing) final start: has idled in front: sold 44,000 gns and gelded. *Sir Mark Prescott*

UNMASKED   6 ch.m. Safawan 118 – Unveiled 76 (Sayf El Arab (USA) 127) [2002 –:   –
f8g 6d⁵ 12.3g 9m 8f 11.1g May 18] maiden: little form: tried blinkered. *A. Scott*

UNO MENTE   3 b.f. Mind Games 121 – One Half Silver (CAN) (Plugged Nickle   **73**
(USA)) [2002 59: 8.3m⁴ 8.3s 9d 10m 10f 8g³ 9.7g 8f⁶ 8f² 8g* 9s p10g f8.5s Dec 9] sturdy filly: fair handicapper: won at Leicester in October: should prove as effective at 1¼m as 1m: acts on firm going, well below form on soft/all-weather. *Mrs P. N. Dutfield*

UNPARALLELED   4 b.f. Primo Dominie 121 – Sharp Chief 71 (Chief Singer 131)   –
[2002 60d: p6g p6g Jan 9] modest maiden at best: has deteriorated: has worn blinkers. *G. L. Moore*

UNSCRUPULOUS   3 ch.g. Machiavellian (USA) 123 – Footlight Fantasy (USA) 68   **76**
(Nureyev (USA) 131) [2002 8f⁵ 8.1g⁴ Jul 5] angular gelding: fourth foal: half-brother to useful 1998 2-y-o 6f winner Dominant Dancer (by Primo Dominie), and fairly useful pair Leading Role (by Cadeaux Genereaux, 1999 2-y-o 7f winner) and Fantasy Ridge (by Indian Ridge, 2000 2-y-o 7f winner): dam, 7f winner, out of top-class miler Milligram: shaped well after slow start when fifth to Hero's Journey in maiden at Newbury in May (gave some trouble at start): similar form when fourth to Saladim at Warwick (raced freely, found little) next time: reportedly lame after. *J. R. Fanshawe*

UNSHAKABLE (IRE)   3 b.c. Eagle Eyed (USA) 111 – Pepper And Salt (IRE)   **110**
(Double Schwartz 128) [2002 87. 7.1m¹* 8.1m¹* 8g 8s² 8s³ Nov 2] good-bodied colt: smart performer, lightly raced: progressed very well in 2002, winning maiden at Haydock in April and handicap at Sandown (beat Judge Davidson 1¾ lengths) in August: reportedly

found to be suffering from colic after next start: good efforts in handicaps when placed at Newbury (short-headed by Dumaran) and Newmarket (2½ lengths third to Pablo) last 2 starts: will prove best up to 9f: acts on soft and good to firm ground: sometimes bandaged behind: wandered second 2-y-o start: game: should win a good prize or 2 at 4 yrs. *Bob Jones*

UNSHAKEN 8 b.h. Environment Friend 128 – Reel Foyle (USA) 77 (Irish River (FR) 131) [2002 80, a58: f8.5g⁴ f8.5g⁴ 8m 6g⁴ 8.1v 7.5m 8.9m 8.5g 8.1f⁴ 10.4f⁶ 8.9f f9.4s Nov 2] strong, sturdy horse: fair handicapper on turf, modest on all-weather: effective at 7f, probably 9f: acts on any turf going and fibresand: tried blinkered/visored: patiently ridden: on downgrade. *E. J. Alston*   **72 d a62 d**

UNSIGNED (USA) 4 b. or br.g. Cozzene (USA) – Striata (USA) (Gone West (USA)) [2002 81: f12g* p12g⁵ f14.8g f14g⁵ f14.8s⁵ Dec 13] close-coupled, good-bodied gelding: only fair form in 2002: won maiden at Wolverhampton in March: probably stays 2m: acts on fibresand, firm and soft ground. *R. H. Buckler*   **65**

UNSUITED 3 b.f. Revoque (IRE) 122 – Nagnagnag (IRE) 103 (Red Sunset 120) [2002 8.3d p8g⁵ 8g 8m Jul 26] first foal: dam 5f (at 2 yrs) to 7f winner who stayed 8.5f: modest maiden: stays 1m: sold 1,200 gns. *D. R. C. Elsworth*   **56**

UNTIDY DAUGHTER 3 b.f. Sabrehill (USA) 120 – Branitska (Mummy's Pet 125) [2002 7m⁶ 9.9m⁶ 8d⁴ 10d p10g⁵ f9.4g Dec 16] half-sister to several winners, notably smart 1989 2-y-o 6f to 7.5f winner Call To Arms (by North Briton): dam, maiden, from family of Dominion: fair maiden: below form after second start: left R. Hannon after fifth outing: may prove best around 1m. *B. Ellison*   **69**

UNTOLD STORY (USA) 7 b.g. Theatrical 128 – Committed Miss (USA) (Key To Content (USA)) [2002 f9.4g f12g⁵ f16.2f Aug 16] bad maiden: pulled up lame final start: tried blinkered. *G. A. Ham*   **–**

UP FRONT (IRE) 3 b.f. Up And At 'em 109 – Sable Lake (Thatching 131) [2002 61: f7s⁴ f6g⁶ f7g⁴ 7f f6g⁶ 6.1m f7g 7d 7.5m f7g⁴ 7s f8.5g Nov 18] modest at 2 yrs, poor in 2002: stays 7f: acts on fibresand, best turf form on good to soft/soft going: none too consistent. *A. Berry*   **48**

UP IN FLAMES (IRE) 11 br.g. Nashamaa 113 – Bella Lucia (Camden Town 125) [2002 46+, a–: 11.1g 11.8m 9.2d⁵ 7.9g 10.5v³ 12.1s⁶ 9.1s⁶ 12s⁵ Nov 6] leggy gelding: poor performer: stays 1½m: acts on any turf going and fibresand: tried blinkered: tongue tied: usually held up (sometimes slowly away): none too reliable. *Mrs G. S. Rees*   **46**

UP MARKET 3 b.f. Mark of Esteem (IRE) 137 – Top Shop 75 (Nashwan (USA) 135) [2002 7g* 7g 7d⁶ May 27] good-bodied, attractive filly: second foal: dam, 1½m winner, half-sister to King Edward VII Stakes winner Private Tender: won newcomers race at Newbury in April by neck from A View Indeed: reportedly finished distressed/ran as if something amiss next 2 starts: bred to stay 1¼m, but wasn't short of speed: stud. *H. R. A. Cecil*   **84**

UPROAR 3 b.g. Piccolo 121 – Kittycatoo Katango (USA) (Verbatim (USA)) [2002 74: 6.1g 5m 5g⁶ 7.1m 6m⁶ f5s 5g⁶ 5g⁴ 5g Sep 18] modest maiden: left R. Beckett after second start: effective at 5f/6f: acts on firm ground and all-weather: tried blinkered: sold 3,200 gns, sent to Spain. *T. D. Easterby*   **54**

UP TEMPO (IRE) 4 b.g. Flying Spur (AUS) – Musical Essence 65 (Song 132) [2002 96: 6s 5g 5f 5f 6g 7d 6g⁶ 6.9d² 7g⁵ 7m 7.2g² 7.6g 6m 7.2g 7v² f6g³ p7g f6g³ Dec 31] useful-looking gelding: fairly useful handicapper: effective at 6f to 1m: acts on all-weather and any turf going: effective with or without blinkers: has worn cheekpieces: none too consistent. *T. D. Easterby*   **82**

UP THE KYBER 5 b.g. Missed Flight 123 – Najariya (Northfields (USA)) [2002 63d: 9.2s⁴ 11.1g 8g⁵ 9.2s² 11.1v 9.2g Jul 18] poor maiden handicapper nowadays: left A. Crook after third start: stays 11f: acts on soft and good to firm going: tried visored: pulled too hard fifth start. *M. D. Hammond*   **43**

UPTOWN LAD (IRE) 3 b.g. Definite Article 121 – Shoka (FR) 86 (Kaldoun (FR) 122) [2002 55: 8.5m 10f⁵ Sep 27] good-bodied gelding: poor maiden: stays 1¼m: acts on fibresand and any turf going: sometimes looks hard ride. *Mrs A. Duffield*   **49**

URBAN MYTH 4 b.g. Shaamit (IRE) 127 – Nashville Blues (IRE) 94 (Try My Best (USA) 130) [2002 65: f9.4f5 f8.5s Sep 7] fair maiden at best: poor form in 2002: stays 1¼m: acts on good to firm going and fibresand: tongue tied. *J. W. Unett*   **49**

URGENT SWIFT 9 ch.g. Beveled (USA) – Good Natured § (Troy 137) [2002 70: p16g² p13g⁴ p16g⁶ f14g⁵ 14.1d⁶ f14.8g³ f14.8g⁴ 14.1g f14.8g⁴ f16.2g⁴ f16.2g² f14.8g³   **45 a55**

1047

Aug 9] rangy gelding: modest performer: best at 1½m to 2m: possibly unsuited by soft/heavy going, acts on any other turf/all-weather: blinkered once as 5-y-o: sometimes slowly away: usually held up. *A. P. Jarvis*

UROWELLS (IRE) 2 b.c. (Jan 24) Sadler's Wells (USA) 132 – Highest Accolade 71 (Shirley Heights 130) [2002 7m⁶ Jul 13] 220,000Y: first foal: dam, 1¼m winner from 3 starts, out of half-sister to Awaasif (also dam of Snow Bride and grandam of Lammtarra), also the family of Hector Protector and Bosra Sham: 14/1, fair form when 5½ lengths sixth of 9 to Norse Dancer in minor event at Ascot: should improve if all is well. *E. A. L. Dunlop* **76 p**

URSA MAJOR 8 b.g. Warning 136 – Double Entendre 81 (Dominion 123) [2002 –, a84: p12g* p12g⁴ p10g 10.1m 9m³ 11.5m 8m 10m 10.4f Oct 11] small gelding: fairly useful handicapper on all-weather, modest on turf: won at Lingfield in January: left C. Allen after third start: stays easy 1½m: unraced on heavy going, acts on any other turf/all-weather: tried blinkered earlier in career: often races up with pace. *J. W. Payne* **63 a87**

USEYOURLOAF (IRE) 2 ch.g. (Mar 20) Woodborough (USA) 112 – Exhibit Air (IRE) 77 (Exhibitioner 111) [2002 7f Jul 29] 6,200 2-y-o: third foal: dam 1m to 1½m winner who stayed 2m: last in maiden at Yarmouth: dead. *J. S. Moore*

USLOOB (IRE) 4 ch.g. Elmaamul (USA) 125 – Rawaabe (USA) 87 (Nureyev (USA) 131) [2002 70d: 8d 11.9s a8g a9g⁴ a7.5g⁵ a7.5g² a7g* a8g* Sep 28] fair maiden at 3 yrs: left J. Cullinan after second start in 2002: won handicaps at Sanlucar in August and Mijas in September: stays 1m: acts on good to firm going and sand. *J. Calderon, Spain* **?**

V

VALANCE (IRE) 2 br.c. (Mar 25) Bahhare (USA) 122 – Glowlamp (IRE) 93 (Glow (USA)) [2002 7.1m 7m⁶ 7.9f³ Oct 12] IR 46,000F, 48,000Y; lengthy colt: fifth foal: half-brother to 7f and 8.5f winner Mr Paradise (by Salt Dome) and 1¼m winner Black Weasel (by Lahib): dam 2-y-o 9f winner: fair form in maidens: third of 4 at York: will probably stay 1¼m: raced only on ground firmer than good. *C. R. Egerton* **76**

VALAZAR (USA) 3 b.g. Nicholas (USA) 111 – Valor's Minion (USA) (Turkey Shoot (USA)) [2002 6f² 5f⁵ 6f⁵ 5m 5m* 5m f6g⁴ f5g f6g* Dec 10] $10,000Y, resold 6,500Y: sturdy gelding: second living foal: half-brother to a sprint winner in USA by High Brite: dam unraced: modest performer: won maiden at Ripon in August and seller at Southwell in December: effective at 5f/6f: acts on fibresand, raced only on good to firm/firm going on turf: game. *T. D. Barron* **64**

VALDASHO 3 b.f. Classic Cliche (IRE) 128 – Ma Rivale (Last Tycoon 131) [2002 –: p10g 7.1m⁶ f8g⁶ 7d 7m* 7m 7d Aug 11] sturdy filly: poor performer: won seller at Yarmouth in July: likely to stay 1m: acts on good to firm going: raced very freely on reappearance: inconsistent. *G. G. Margarson* **47**

VAL DE MAAL (IRE) 2 ch.c. (Mar 15) Eagle Eyed (USA) 111 – Miss Bojangles (Gay Fandango (USA) 132) [2002 6s 5m² 5m³ f7g* p7g Nov 13] IR 7,000F, IR 10,000Y: eighth foal: closely related to fairly useful Irish 1993 2-y-o 7f winner Ziravello (by Roi Danzig) and half-brother to 3 winners, including Irish 1994 2-y-o 1m winner Onenineten (by Petorius): dam Irish 2m winner: fair performer: won maiden at Southwell in October: stays 7f: acts on fibresand and good to firm going. *G. C. H. Chung* **74**

VALDEMARS SLOT 2 b.g. (Apr 20) Danehill Dancer (IRE) 117 – Maid O'Cannie 72 (Efisio 120) [2002 5g⁴ 6g 7.5d 5d 6m Jul 27] 2,500Y: tall gelding: fourth foal: half-brother to a winner in Belgium by Noble Patriarch: dam 6f winner: poor maiden: may prove best at 5f/6f: blinkered (looked none too keen) final start. *M. W. Easterby* **44**

VALDESCO (IRE) 4 ch.g. Bluebird (USA) 125 – Allegheny River (USA) (Lear Fan (USA) 130) [2002 72, a67: f11s³ f11s⁴ f8g* f8g* f8.5g f8g 8.3s⁴ 10.1m* 11.1g* 12f² 11.9g 13v* 12.3g* 14.4g² 11.9g Aug 20] leggy, quite good-topped gelding: fairly useful performer: won claimer (apprentices, left J. L. Eyre) and handicap at Southwell, minor events at Newcastle and Hamilton, and handicaps at Hamilton and Ripon between January/July: stays 1¾m: acts on fibresand and any turf going: tried visored, usually blinkered: sometimes slowly away. *G. M. Moore* **84**

VALENTINES VISION 5 b.g. Distinctly North (USA) 115 – Sharp Anne 74§ (Belfort (FR) 89) [2002 –: f8s Jan 1] modest performer at 3 yrs: well held since: sometimes visored/blinkered. *Mrs S. Lamyman* **–**

VALERIE ANN BURTON (IRE) 2 br.f. (Mar 6) Charnwood Forest (IRE) 125 –   –
Ezilana (IRE) (Shardari 134) [2002 7m p7g Oct 9] IR 2,000Y: fifth foal: half-sister to
1999 Irish 2-y-o 7.7f winner Zuleika (by Lucky Guest): dam unraced half-sister to smart
Irish performer up to 1½m Ebaziya, herself dam of Group 1 winners Enzeli, Ebadiyla and
Edabiya: last in maidens. *M. R. Ewer-Hoad*

VALEUREUX 4 ch.g. Cadeaux Genereux 131 – La Strada (Niniski (USA) 125) [2002   63
79+: 8.5g 10f⁵ 11.5m 10d⁵ 10.9g 10f 9s⁴ Oct 25] big, strong gelding: only modest
performer at 4 yrs: probably stays 10.4f: acts on heavy ground: visored penultimate start.
J. Hetherton

VALIANT EFFORT 3 b. or br.g. In The Wings 128 – Viz (USA) (Kris S (USA)) [2002   84
8m 8m⁵ 10.9m² 12.4m* Jul 29] big, lengthy gelding: third living foal: closely related to
Oaks third Relish The Thought (by Sadler's Wells), 7f winner at 2 yrs: dam, US 2-y-o 1m
winner and third in Grade 1 1m event, out of half-sister to Breeders' Cup Juvenile winner
Brocco: fairly useful form: sweating freely, won maiden at Newcastle in October by 2½
lengths from Cosi Fan Tutte: gelded after: stays 1½m: raced only on good to firm ground.
B. W. Hills

VALIANT ROMEO 2 b.c. (Jan 21) Primo Dominie 121 – Desert Lynx (IRE) 79   89
(Green Desert (USA) 127) [2002 5.1d³ 5.3f* 6.1f⁴ 6s⁴ 6d⁵ 7m 6m⁶ 5m³ 6m² 6g⁴ 5.1g* 5f*
5m Oct 12] 43,000F, 42,000Y: sturdy colt: first foal: dam, 6f winner, half-sister to 5-y-o
Watching: fairly useful performer: won maiden at Brighton in April and nurseries at
Chepstow in September and Newmarket in October: far from discredited when eighth to
Peace Offering in Cornwallis Stakes at Ascot final start: effective at 5f/6f: best efforts on
good ground or firmer: visored last 5 outings: usually races prominently: sold 30,000 gns,
joined R. Bastiman. *M. R. Channon*

VALIGNANI (IRE) 10 b.g. Law Society (USA) 130 – When Lit (Northfields (USA))   §§
[2002 16.2g Jul 26] 9f winner in Italy at 3 yrs: formerly useful jumper in Italy/France but
has looked most ungenuine all starts in Britain, including on Flat return (virtually pulled
himself up). *M. C. Pipe*

VALLEE ENCHANTEE (IRE) 2 b.f. (Mar 27) Peintre Celebre 137 – Ver-   104 p
veine (USA) 120 (Lear Fan (USA) 130) [2002 8g³ 9d* 8v* Nov 22] sixth foal: half-sister
to several winners in France (all at least useful), including 1m and 1½m winner Volga,
later very smart in USA, and useful 1¼m winner Victory Cry (both by Caerleon): dam
won Prix de l'Opera and stayed 1¼m: progressive form: won minor event at Maisons-
Laffitte in October and listed race at Saint-Cloud in November: still looked green when
beating Rios 3 lengths ultimately in good style in latter, edging right once in front over 1f
out: will stay 1¼m: has worn special noseband: smart filly in the making. *E. Lellouche,
France*

VALLEY CHAPEL (IRE) 6 ch.h. Selkirk (USA) 129 – Valley Springs (Saratoga   118
Six (USA)) [2002 118: 10v⁴ 10d 12s 12s² 13m* 12g* 9m³ 12g³ 10d⁴ Oct 3] smart
performer: won listed race at Taby in July and DSM Scandinavian Open Championship
at Copenhagen (for second year running, beat Dano-Mast 2 lengths after making all) in
August: below best otherwise, odds on to win third successive Stockholm Cup International at Taby penultimate start but finished only third to Dano-Mast: stays 13f: acts on
heavy and good to firm ground, below best on dirt. *W. Neuroth, Norway*

VALLICA 3 b.f. Bishop of Cashel 122 – Vallauris 94 (Faustus (USA) 118) [2002 9m   –
p12g Sep 4] fifth living foal: half-sister to 7f/1m winner Mystic Ridge (by Mystiko) and
winner in Germany by Indian Ridge: dam 1¼m winner: well held in maidens at Newbury
(very wide into straight) and Lingfield: sold 1,000 gns. *L. G. Cottrell*

VALUABLE GIFT 5 ch.g. Cadeaux Genereux 131 – Valbra (Dancing Brave (USA)   65
140) [2002 54: 15g³ 6d³ 6f6g² 5d² 5g⁴ 6s⁶ f5g⁶ 5g f6g² f5g⁵ f6g² Dec 27] strong, good-
topped gelding: fair maiden: best at 5f/6f: acts on fibresand and good to soft going:
visored nowadays: often finds little. *I. Semple*

VANBRUGH (FR) 2 ch.g. (Feb 26) Starborough 126 – Renovate (Generous (IRE)   56
139) [2002 6s 7m f8.5s Dec 9] 70,000 francs F, 14,000Y: first foal: dam, ran once in
France, half-sister to smart French/US performer up to 1¼m Semillon: best effort in
maidens (modest form) when seventh at Wolverhampton, final start and first since
leaving E. Dunlop: gelded after: should stay 1¼m. *Miss Gay Kelleway*

VANDENBERGHE 3 b.g. Millkom 124 – Child Star (FR) 58 (Bellypha 130) [2002   65
51: f8s³ f9.4g* f7g⁴ f9.4g 11.6m² 10m⁵ 10.9m³ 10g p10g f16.2f⁶ f12g² f14.8s p10g p13g
Dec 28] deep-girthed gelding: fair handicapper: won at Wolverhampton in January:
barely stays 2m: acts on all-weather and firm ground. *Mrs Merrita Jones*

VANDERLIN   3 ch.g. Halling (USA) 133 – Massorah (FR) 108 (Habitat 134) [2002   **109**
91: 7.1m² 6m* 6g* 6g² 7d⁶ 6m 7.1d² 7g² 6d⁶ 7m 7m² 6g Sep 27] strong gelding: usually
takes the eye: useful performer: won maiden at Pontefract and handicap at Salisbury in
May, latter by ½ length from Compton Dynamo: good efforts after when runner-up in
handicaps/minor event at Lingfield (beaten 1½ lengths by Feet So Fast), Sandown (to
Pablo) and twice at Goodwood (went down by 1¾ lengths to Royal Millennium on first
occasion, by a neck to Inchdura on second): effective at 6f/7f: acts on good to firm and
good to soft going: tended to hang/carry head awkwardly earlier in career: may prove best
with exaggerated waiting tactics: gelded after final start. *I. A. Balding*

VAN DE VELDE   3 ch.g. Alhijaz 122 – Lucky Flinders 77 (Free State 125) [2002 69:   –
f7g⁵ 7g 7m f8s f12s³ Sep 17] fair form in 2-y-o maidens for P. Cole: well held in 2002.
R. Wilman

VANILLA MOON   2 b.f. (Mar 9) Emperor Jones (USA) 119 – Daarat Alayaam (IRE)   **58**
(Reference Point 139) [2002 6g 6.1m⁵ 8m 8.3d p7g⁶ Dec 11] fourth foal: half-sister to
2000 2-y-o 7f winner Magic of You (by Magic Ring): dam unraced half-sister to dam of
2-y-o Soviet Song: modest maiden: stays 1m: acts on polytrack, unraced on extremes of
ground on turf. *J. R. Jenkins*

VANISHED (IRE)   2 b.f. (Feb 13) Fayruz 116 – Where's The Money 87 (Lochnager   **77**
132) [2002 5d⁴ 5.9d³ 5g* 6g 5.1g³ f6g⁶ f5g Dec 10] IR 8,500Y: half-sister to 4-y-o   **a59**
Promised and 6f (at 2 yrs)/7f winner Itsinthepost (by Risk Me): dam 2-y-o 5f winner: fair
on turf, modest on all-weather: won maiden at Carlisle in August: good ninth of 25 to
Tout Seul in sales race at the Curragh next time: bit disappointing in nurseries after: will
prove best at 5f/easy 6f: raced only on good/good to soft ground on turf. *J. J. Quinn*

VAN NISTELROOY (USA)   2 ch.c. (Jan 31) Storm Cat (USA) – Halory (CAN)   **108**
(Halo (USA)) [2002 7d* 7g* 7g* 7m² 8g³ a9f⁵ Oct 26] $6,400,000Y (world's most
expensive yearling sold at auction in 2001): strong, good-bodied colt: half-brother to
several winners in USA, including high-class performer up to 1¼m Halory Hunter (by
Jade Hunter), Grade 2 winner at 9f, and Grade 3 winners Prory (9f, by Procida) and
Brushed Halory (8.5f, by Broad Brush): dam maiden in North America: useful performer:
won maiden, listed event and Galileo EBF Futurity Stakes (led close home to beat
Chappel Cresent a neck) in July/August, all at the Curragh: good efforts when ¾-length
second to Refuse To Bend in National Stakes at the Curragh, 1¾ lengths third to Al
Jadeed in Royal Lodge Stakes at Ascot (gave 3 lb all round) and 9¼ lengths fifth to

Galileo EBF Futurity Stakes, the Curragh—Van Nistelroov completes his hat-trick;
Chappel Cresent (nearside) and Wilful make him work hard for it

Vindication in Breeders' Cup Juvenile at Arlington: should stay 1¼m: acts on dirt, yet to race on extremes of going on turf. *A. P. O'Brien, Ireland*

VA PENSIRO 2 b.g. (Apr 27) Lugana Beach 116 – Hopperetta 45 (Rock Hopper 124) [2002 f6g f7g Dec 31] 300Y: second foal: dam maiden who probably stayed 1¼m: well held in maidens at Wolverhampton. *D. Haydn Jones*

VAZON 2 b.c. (Apr 5) Groom Dancer (USA) 128 – Be Mine (Wolfhound (USA) 126) [2002 6s⁴ 7m* 7.5g² 7m Jul 13] leggy colt: first foal: dam, French 1m winner, half-sister to smart performer up to 12.5f Lord of Men (by Groom Dancer): fairly useful performer: won maiden at Folkestone in June: creditable efforts in minor events at Beverley and Ascot after: should stay 1¼m: acts on soft and good to firm going: sent to Czech Republic. *M. R. Channon* **80**

VEDA'S RAINBOW (IRE) 3 b. or br.f. Petardia 113 – Sama Veda (IRE) 84 (Rainbow Quest (USA) 134) [2002 70?: 8.1m⁴ 8.1m 10g* Oct 14] leggy filly: fair performer: won seller at Leicester in October: stayed 1¼m: blinkered last 3 outings at 2 yrs: dead. *S. Kirk* **67**

VEINTE SIETE (USA) 2 ch.g. (May 4) Trempolino (USA) 135 – Satz (USA) 50 (The Minstrel (CAN) 135) [2002 7m⁵ Sep 3] 17,000F, 20,000Y: half-brother to a winner in USA by Quiet American: dam lightly-raced half-sister to smart 7f/1m performer Satin Flower and US Grade 1 1¼m winner Martial Law: 40/1, well-beaten last of 5 in maiden at Yarmouth. *J. A. R. Toller* **–**

VELMEZ 9 ch.g. Belmez (USA) 131 – Current Raiser 108 (Filiberto (USA) 123) [2002 18s³ 18d⁵ Jul 6] sturdy gelding: lightly-raced maiden on Flat: stays 2¼m: acts on soft ground: blinkered last 3 starts. *B. J. Llewellyn* **61**

VENDOME (IRE) 4 b.g. General Monash (USA) 107 – Kealbra Lady (Petong 126) [2002 80d: f5g⁵ f5g⁵ f5g⁵ f5g⁴ 5.1d f5g 5.3m Jun 25] strong gelding: poor mover: modest performer: best at bare 5f: acts on firm and good to soft going, probably on fibresand: usually races up with pace: has looked less than keen: on downgrade. *J. A. Osborne* **61 d**

VENIKA VITESSE 6 b.g. Puissance 110 – Vilanika (FR) 81 (Top Ville 129) [2002 50: f6s f7g f7g Feb 12] modest performer at 5 yrs: no form in 2002: stayed 6f: acted on good to firm going, probably on soft: tried blinkered/visored: was inconsistent: dead. *T. D. Barron* **–**

VERASINA (USA) 4 ch.f. Woodman (USA) 126 – Vilikaia (USA) 125 (Nureyev (USA) 131) [2002 8.2m² 8g² Jul 11] IR 260,000Y: lengthy, quite attractive filly: closely related to useful 7f (including at 2 yrs) and 1m (in UAE) winner Vilayet (by Machiavellian) and half-sister to 2 winners, including useful French/US 1m to 11f winner Legend of Russia (by Suave Dancer): dam, effective from 5f to 1m, sister to smart performer up to 9f Navratilovna, from very good family: odds on, fairly useful form when runner-up in maidens at Nottingham (short-headed by Mythic having raced freely) and Doncaster (beaten 3 lengths by Shersha, having hung markedly left). *H. R. A. Cecil* **83**

VERA TWO 4 ch.f. King's Signet (USA) 110 – Vera's First (IRE) 69 (Exodal (USA)) [2002 –: 5g 7f 5g Oct 5] little form: very slowly away final 3-y-o outing. *G. L. Moore* **–**

VERGIL'S VENTURE 3 b.g. Alhijaz 122 – Quick Profit 78 (Formidable (USA) 125) [2002 67: f8s⁵ f7g⁴ f8g² f8g⁴ p10g p8g⁴ p7g⁶ f6g⁵ 7.1f⁶ f9.4g⁶ 7.1d* 8g⁵ 6.9m⁶ 7s f7g p10g⁵ Dec 30] close-coupled gelding: fair performer: won maiden handicap at Musselburgh in July: probably stays 1¼m: acts on all-weather, firm and good to soft going: often blinkered. *G. C. H. Chung* **66** **a63**

VERIDIAN 9 b.g. Green Desert (USA) 127 – Alik (FR) 113 (Targowice (USA) 130) [2002 84: 18.7f 18s⁴ 16.2f Jun 26] sturdy gelding: fairly useful handicapper: not discredited in Chester Cup and when fourth at Chepstow first 2 starts: stays 2¼m: acts on soft and firm ground: blinkered (ran creditably) once at 8 yrs: seems suited by waiting tactics/strong handling: joined G. Bridgwater. *B. J. Llewellyn* **82**

VERMILION CREEK 3 b.f. Makbul 104 – Cloudy Reef 57 (Cragador 110) [2002 63: f7s f7s⁵ f6g⁵ f7g⁴ 6g⁶ 8m⁵ f8g² 8.2f⁴ f8.5g⁶ 8.5m p10g 10m⁵ 8g f11g³ Dec 17] close-coupled filly: modest performer: stays 11f: acts on all-weather, firm and good to soft going: reportedly bled from nose once at 2 yrs. *R. Hollinshead* **56**

VERONATA 3 b.f. Nashwan (USA) 135 – Veronica (Persian Bold 123) [2002 10g Jun 1] half-sister to several winners, including useful 1¼m winner Canford (by Caerleon) and useful Irish 1½m winner El Bueno (by Caerleon): dam winner around 1m in USA: well held in maiden at Newmarket, slowly away: sold 800 gns in December. *W. Jarvis* **–**

VERONICA WARD (USA) 3 b.f. Tinners Way (USA) 122 – Ranales (USA) – §
(Majestic Light (USA)) [2002 10f 7g 7.5g 9.9d 9.3d Jul 19] 40,000Y: unfurnished filly:
has a round action: third foal: half-sister to 1999 2-y-o 7f winner Fame At Last (by Quest
For Fame), later useful at 1¼m/1½m, and 6-y-o Theme Time: dam, 2-y-o 1m winner in
USA, half-sister to smart sprinter Orojoya: well held in maidens/handicaps:
should stay at least 1m: awkward leaving stall final outing: reared over backwards at start,
ran loose and withdrawn next intended appearance: sold 800 gns. *T. D. Easterby*

VERSAILLES 3 b.g. Bluegrass Prince (IRE) 110 – Fabulous Pet (Somethingfabulous 52
(USA)) [2002 7.5g⁵ 7g 5.9g⁴ 9.3d 12m Jul 26] IR 11,000F, 31,000Y: unfurnished gelding:
half-brother to several winners, notably 7-y-o Murghem: dam, Irish 1½m winner, half-
sister to smart sprinter Orojoya: modest maiden: well beaten in handicaps last 2 starts,
visored final one: bred to be suited by 1¼m+: sold 3,000 gns. *Mrs J. R. Ramsden*

VERT ESPERE 9 ch.g. Green Adventure (USA) 119 – Celtic Dream (Celtic Cone 52
116) [2002 14s⁵ 12s 12m⁵ 16m 16v Oct 29] big, workmanlike gelding: modest maiden on
Flat: should be suited by 2m+. *A. Streeter*

VERTICAL 2 ch.g. (Feb 5) Ashkalani (IRE) 128 – Waft (USA) 67 (Topsider (USA)) –
[2002 p7g 7.1m Jul 20] second foal: dam, third at 1m, half-sister to dam of St Leger/
Coronation Cup winner Silver Patriarch: only a little sign of ability in maidens: gelded
after. *P. R. Chamings*

VERY EXCLUSIVE (USA) 3 b.c. Royal Academy (USA) 130 – Exclusive Davis –
(USA) (Our Native (USA)) [2002 55: 8.3g Aug 12] modest form in 2 Lingfield maidens
at 2 yrs: tongue tied, well held only outing in 2002: quite free-going sort: flashed tail on
debut. *R. M. H. Cowell*

VERY RELIABLE 2 b.f. (Apr 12) The West (USA) 107 – Total Truth (Reesh 117) –
[2002 6d⁵ May 30] 1,600Y: fifth foal: half-sister to a 6f winner in Hong Kong by Distant
Relative: dam lightly raced: got loose and withdrawn in March: fifth of 6 in seller at
Goodwood (reared and unseated behind stall). *J. S. Moore*

VESPASIAN 2 b. or br.g. (Feb 12) Emperor Jones (USA) 119 – Indian Wardance 87
(ITY) (Indian Ridge 123) [2002 5m⁴ 6m³ 7f² 6g 8m⁴ 7m* 8f⁶ Dec 15] IR 8,500Y: leggy,
close-coupled gelding: first foal: dam, Italian maiden, half-sister to dam of Oaks d'Italia
runner-up Rosa di Brema: fairly useful performer: improved to win maiden at Newcastle
in October by 1½ lengths from Night Games (pair clear), making all: left W. Haggas, well
held in optional claimer at Hollywood final start: stays 7f: raced only on good ground or
firmer: blinkered/visored fourth and last 2 starts. *Kathy Walsh, USA*

VIBURNUM 8 b.m. Old Vic 136 – Burning Desire (Kalaglow 132) [2002 16v p13g –
Dec 28] modest maiden at 3 yrs: had a foal by Factual in 1999: tailed off both runs since.
M. Wellings

VICE PRESIDENTIAL 7 ch.g. Presidium 124 – Steelock 68 (Lochnager 132) [2002 –
–, a62d: f6g⁴ f6g⁶ f6g Apr 15] big gelding: easy mover: poor performer: probably best at **a48**
6f/7f: acts on fibresand, good to firm and heavy going: tried blinkered: usually races up
with pace: looked none too keen second start. *J. Balding*

VICIOUS DANCER 4 b.g. Timeless Times (USA) 99 – Yankeedoodledancer (Mash- –
hor Dancer (USA)) [2002 104: a7f a5f Mar 15] leggy gelding: useful performer in 2001:
well held in handicaps at Nad Al Sheba and Jebel Ali in March: was best at 5f/6f: acted
on soft and good to firm going: dead. *R. M. Whitaker*

VICIOUS KNIGHT 4 b.g. Night Shift (USA) – Myth 89 (Troy 137) [2002 113+: 112 §
7m² 8g 8m³ 10d⁵ 8m³ 7.9m 8.9m 8m³ 7f⁴ 8f Oct 3] robust, good sort: good walker: smart
performer on his day: reportedly had foot problem after final 3-y-o start: ran creditably in
2002 when third to Priors Lodge in listed event at Salisbury and to Muchea, despite
looking none too keen, in handicap at Doncaster fifth/eighth starts: likely to prove best at
7f (given test)/1m: raced mainly on good going or firmer: has found little: gelded after
final start: unreliable. *L. M. Cumani*

VICIOUS LADY 2 b.f. (Apr 2) Vettori (IRE) 119 – Ling Lane (Slip Anchor 136) –
[2002 7g Aug 26] fourth foal: half-sister to 3 winners, including 3-y-o Vicious Warrior:
dam unraced out of close relation to Irish Oaks winner Bolas: 100/1 and backward,
always behind in maiden at Newcastle. *R. M. Whitaker*

VICIOUS LOVER 3 ch.g. Rudimentary (USA) 118 – Parfait Amour 73 (Clantime 54
101) [2002 58: 8.2d⁶ 9.9m 8.2g 12m⁶ 10.9d³ 12.4g⁵ Aug 26] strong gelding: modest
handicapper: probably stays 1½m: acts on good to firm ground: sold 4,400 gns.
R. M. Whitaker

VICIOUS PRINCE (IRE)   3 b.c. Sadler's Wells (USA) 132 – Sunny Flower (FR) **100**
(Dom Racine (FR) 121) [2002 75p: 10.4m⁶ 12.3d* 12m 14.8g 10s* 11.9g⁴ 13.1s Oct 15]
strong, lengthy colt: has a fluent, round action: useful handicapper: won at Ripon in June
and August (beat Harnour by ½ length): very good fourth to Spectrometer in Knavesmire
Handicap at York penultimate start: off 2 months before final outing: should stay beyond
1½m: acts on soft going: tends to carry head bit awkwardly. *R. M. Whitaker*

VICIOUS WARRIOR   3 b.g. Elmaamul (USA) 125 – Ling Lane (Slip Anchor 136) **97**
[2002 74: 8m 7.5m⁴ 8g³ 9.9g² 10g² 10g* 10.3m⁵ 10g 10m⁴ 10g³ 10.3m* 10f³ a8f⁵ a9f
Dec 19] good sort: useful handicapper: won at Ripon in June and Doncaster (best effort,
beat Bandler Ching short head) in September: respectable efforts next 2 starts, including
at Nad Al Sheba: unseated rider final outing: stays 1¼m: acts on good to firm going,
probably on dirt: often races freely: sometimes looks no easy ride, but is consistent.
R. M. Whitaker

VICTORIET   5 ch.m. Hamas (IRE) 125§ – Wedgewood (USA) (Woodman (USA)   **–**
126) [2002 –: f11s Jan 1] of little account. *A. G. Newcombe*

VICTOR VALENTINE (IRE)   3 ch.c. Ridgewood Ben 113 – Tarliya (IRE) 73   **–**
(Doyoun 124) [2002 59, a72: f6g⁴ Feb 4] lengthy colt: poor mover: modest maiden: **a64**
respectable effort in handicap only run at 3 yrs (slowly away): should prove best at 5f/6f:
acts on fibresand: sold £680 in April. *E. A. Wheeler*

VICTORY FLIP (IRE)   2 b.f. (Apr 27) Victory Note (USA) 120 – Two Magpies 43   **67**
(Doulab (USA) 115) [2002 6.1g⁴ 5m² 5m⁶ 5g⁵ 6.1g³ 6.1m 6.1m f5g f6s Dec 26] IR   **a–**
5,000Y: lengthy, rather unfurnished filly: half-sister to several winners, including 6-y-o
Fearby Cross and 1¼m winner Dangerman (by Pips Pride): dam Irish 7f and 1¼m
winner: fair maiden: best effort when third in nursery at Chester, making running: effective at 5f/6f: raced only on good/good to firm going on turf: weak finisher. *R. Hollinshead*

VICTORY SIGN (IRE)   2 b.g. (Apr 12) Forzando 122 – Mo Ceri 63 (Kampala 120)   **63**
[2002 6m 8.3d 7g⁶ 8f⁵ 10m 8d Oct 21] 9,000F, 15,000Y, 19,000 2-y-o: big, useful-looking
gelding: half-brother to several winners, including 7f to 11f winner Mazilla (by Mazilier):
dam 1½m winner: modest maiden: stays 1m: acts on firm and good to soft going.
K. R. Burke

VICTORY VEE   2 ch.g. (Mar 31) Vettori (IRE) 119 – Aldevonie 75 (Green Desert   **57**
(USA) 127) [2002 6m 6g 7.1m⁵ 7m⁶ 7.5d f8s f7g⁵ 5.3m¹⁵ Oct 3] 4,500Y: well-made
gelding: second living foal: half-brother to 4-y-o Nashira: dam, second at 1m at 2 yrs
from 2 starts, would have stayed 1¼m: modest maiden: well below form last 3 starts:
likely to prove best short of 1m: acts on good to firm going and good to soft. *M. Blanshard*

VICTRESS (IRE)   2 b.f. (Mar 25) Victory Note (USA) 120 – Fable 37 (Absalom 128)   **47**
[2002 f5g⁶ 5g 6d⁴ May 27] IR 4,500Y: rather leggy filly: second foal: half-sister to fairly
useful 2001 2-y-o 5f winner Charlie Chap (by College Chapel), later successful in
Sweden: dam maiden who stayed 1m: poor form in maiden/sellers: visored (best effort)
final start: sent to Spain. *J. J. Quinn*

VIERA   2 b.c. (Apr 17) Royal Applause 124 – Vilany 87 (Never So Bold 135) [2002   **90**
6m* p6g² p5g* Oct 31] lengthy, angular colt: half-brother to several winners, including
7f winner Lion's Domane (by Lion Cavern) and 3-y-o Morpheous: dam 7f winner: fairly
useful form: won maiden at Newmarket in September and minor event at Lingfield (beat
Thurlestone Rock by 1¼ lengths, leading final 100 yds) in October: best effort when
beaten ½-length by Stormont (pair clear) in minor event at Lingfield: effective at 5f/6f.
M. A. Jarvis

VIEWFORTH   4 b.g. Emarati (USA) 74 – Miriam 59 (Forzando 122) [2002 68: 5m 5g   **70**
5g 6g 5v* 5s* 6s* 5s⁵ 5.9v⁴ 6d Oct 15] good-bodied gelding: fair performer: made all in
2 handicaps and claimer in between at Hamilton in June: effective at 5f/6f: has form
on any turf going, but clearly well suited by soft/heavy: blinkered last 6 starts. *Miss
L. A. Perratt*

VIEW THE FACTS   3 b.f. So Factual (USA) 120 – Scenic View (IRE) (Scenic 128)   **–**
[2002 55: 8g Aug 13] lightly-raced maiden: reportedly finished lame only run in 2002.
P. L. Gilligan

VIGOROUS (IRE)   2 b.f. (Feb 17) Danetime (IRE) 121 – Merrily 73 (Sharrood (USA)   **62 p**
124) [2002 5m⁴ Jul 29] IR 45,000Y: first foal: dam, disappointing sprint maiden,
half-sister to useful sprinter Deep Finesse and to dam of smart sprinter Halmahera:
2/1-favourite, bright speed to lead for over 3f when 1½ lengths fourth of 13 to Scythian in
maiden at Windsor: should do better if all is well. *M. R. Channon*

VIKING PRINCE 5 b.g. Chilibang 120 – Fire Sprite 83 (Mummy's Game 120) [2002 –
–: p6g Feb 6] probably of little account nowadays. *Jamie Poulton*

VILAS 2 b.c. (Mar 10) Inchinor 119 – Arantxa 77§ (Sharpo 132) [2002 5.9s* 7g³ Oct   **80**
18] close-coupled, good-topped colt: first foal: dam, unreliable 6f winner (including at 2
yrs), half-sister to useful Irish performer up to 1¾m Damancher: won minor event at
Hamilton in August by short head: better effort (fairly useful form) when 2 lengths third
of 4 to Audience in minor event at Newmarket: will probably stay 1m. *M. L. W. Bell*

VILLA DEL SOL 3 br.f. Tagula (IRE) 116 – Admonish 57 (Warning 136) [2002 86d:
f6g⁴ f7g³ f6s f6g f6g f7g⁶ f8.5s Dec 26] leggy, plain filly: fairly useful at best at 2 yrs: **a51**
only modest in 2002, off over 6 months after second start: seems to stay 7f: acts on
fibresand, soft and good to firm going: hung right second outing: usually held up.
B. Smart

VILLE DE PARIS (IRE) 3 b.g. Common Grounds 118 – Muqaddima (FR) (Kaldoun   **71**
(FR) 122) [2002 69: 7.1m 8.2g³ 8g 8m 7m Aug 23] close-coupled, quite attractive
gelding: fair maiden: well below best after second start: stays 1m: raced only on good/
good to firm going: has raced freely: sold only £350 in October. *R. F. Johnson Houghton*

VINCENT 7 b.g. Anshan 119 – Top-Anna (IRE) 71 (Ela-Mana-Mou 132) [2002 –,   **–**
a56: f16s² f16s Jan 4] tall gelding: modest handicapper: reportedly finished lame final   **a51**
outing: stays 17f: acts on any turf going and fibresand: tried visored/blinkered: tends to
hang/carry head high. *John A. Harris*

VINCENTIA 4 ch.f. Komaite (USA) – Vatersay (USA) (Far North (CAN) 120) [2002   **69**
62: f8g 6.1g 6f 6d² 6g* 6v Nov 9] sparely-made filly: poor mover: fair performer: won
maiden at Windsor in October, making all: effective 6f/7f: acts on heavy going and good
to firm: has hung right/gone in snatches: none too consistent. *C. Smith*

VINDICATION 2 ch.g. (Feb 4) Compton Place 125 – Prince's Feather (IRE) 77 (Cad-   **80**
eaux Genereux 131) [2002 5d⁴ 6m⁴ 6s⁵ p6g² 7s Oct 25] 17,000F, 80,000Y: well-made
gelding: third foal: dam, maiden who stayed 7f, granddaughter of smart sprinter
Amaranda: fairly useful maiden: good second to Rowan Express in nursery at Lingfield:
should stay 7f: acts on polytrack, good to firm and soft ground: tongue tied last 3 outings:
sold 30,000 gns, and gelded. *J. R. Fanshawe*

VIN DU PAYS 2 b.c. (Mar 17) Alzao (USA) 117 – Royale Rose (FR) 75 (Bering 136)   **78**
[2002 7.1g p7g⁴ p7g⁴ Oct 31] 18,000Y: second foal: dam, 1m winner, sister to useful
French miler Rouen: best effort in maidens (fair form) when fourth to Jummana at Lingfield second start: free-going sort, but should stay 1m: acts on polytrack. *M. Blanshard*

VINNIE ROE (IRE) 4 b.c. Definite Article 121 – Kayu (Tap On Wood 130)   **126**
[2002 126: 14s* 20m² 12g* 14m* 16f⁴ Nov 5]
Though the estimable Vinnie Roe compiled three more victories in the latest
season, it was in defeat that he ran his best races. Those two defeats, the only ones
he has suffered in his last nine starts, were inflicted when a narrowly beaten second
in the Gold Cup at Royal Ascot and a highly creditable fourth in the Melbourne Cup
at Flemington. The form he showed bettered that of his winning efforts in listed
races at Leopardstown and in the Jefferson Smurfit Memorial St Leger. At the
Curragh, Vinnie Roe became the fourth horse to win the Irish St Leger twice since
it was opened to older horses in 1983—following Vintage Crop (also trained by
Dermot Weld) in 1993 and 1994, Oscar Schindler in 1996 and 1997, and Kayf Tara
in 1998 and 1999. Given that Vinnie Roe became the first to achieve the double
after winning the race as a three-year-old, he would seem to have every chance, if
remaining fit and well, of setting a record that would be entirely his own by winning
again as a five-year-old.
As in the previous year, Vinnie Roe faced seven rivals in the Irish St Leger,
which was again curiously run on the same day as the St Leger at Doncaster. Vinnie
Roe started at odds on, his nearest market rival being the horse he had beaten into
second in 2001, 5/1-shot Millenary; the Irish Derby third Ballingarry came next at
8/1, with 10/1 bar. In typical style, Vinnie Roe travelled well behind the leaders
before taking control of matters around a furlong from home and keeping on
gamely to beat Pugin by a length and a half. Ballingarry was a length further away
in third, with Warrsan staying on to finish fourth, a neck behind Ballingarry. The
first four were clear of the disappointing Millenary and the Irish Oaks winner
Margarula. Vinnie Roe had warmed up for the Irish St Leger in the Ballyroan Stakes
over a mile and a half at Leopardstown in mid-August, showing himself none the

worse for a hard race in the Gold Cup when landing the odds by half a length from the three-year-old Millstreet. Vinnie Roe started favourite in a field of fifteen at Royal Ascot, having shown he retained his ability with a four-length victory, conceding weight all round, in the Saval Beg Stakes at Leopardstown on his reappearance at the end of May. Vinnie Roe went to Royal Ascot having won five in succession, following an excellent climax to his three-year-old campaign, when successes in listed contests were followed by wins in the Irish St Leger and the Prix Royal-Oak at Longchamp (which means he is the first horse to have won three St Legers, the Royal-Oak being the French version). The two-and-a-half-mile Gold Cup trip was uncharted territory for Vinnie Roe, but he had shaped previously as if it would be within his compass and he ran his heart out in going down by a neck to Royal Rebel in a thrilling three-way finish, Wareed filling third a further length back. Vinnie Roe needed no excuses for his defeat, the form representing a high-class effort, though, after travelling well for most of the way in a steadily-run race, he was possibly just outstayed by the winner close home after seeming to edge ahead briefly as the trio tussled for the lead entering the final furlong.

Immediately after the Irish St Leger, Vinnie Roe was put into quarantine, along with stable-companion Media Puzzle, for a crack at the Melbourne Cup in November. On the face of it, Vinnie Roe had plenty to do carrying top weight, set to concede between 7 lb and 22 lb to his twenty-two rivals; the Irish St Leger runner-up Pugin (bought out of John Oxx's yard in the meantime by Godolphin), was, for example, set to reoppose on terms 12 lb better. To make matters worse, things went far from smoothly for Vinnie Roe after his arrival in Australia. Unlike Media Puzzle, who settled in well and won a preparatory race—a Group 3 handicap at Geelong—a fortnight before the Melbourne Cup, Vinnie Roe had trouble regaining the weight lost on the 12,000-mile journey from Ireland, and his trainer publicly aired his concern, which in turn caused Vinnie Roe to lose his place as ante-post favourite to Media Puzzle. Vinnie Roe's participation was finally confirmed a week before the big race after he pleased connections in a gallop. Weld had sent his two horses to Australia five weeks before the Melbourne Cup, a week earlier than when successful with Vintage Crop. Even so, Vinnie Roe reportedly went into the race still just below his optimum racing weight. Regaining favouritism on the day, he gave an excellent account of himself, beaten just under four lengths by the winner Media Puzzle, leading from the home turn to two furlongs out and keeping on under strong pressure. Splitting the Weld pair came the

Jefferson Smurfit Memorial Irish St Leger, the Curragh—Vinnie Roe wins the race for the second time; Pugin, Ballingarry (left) and Warrsan (far side) run well to finish in the frame

home-trained 40/1-shot Mr Prudent, beaten two lengths, and one of Godolphin's three challengers Beekeeper, a neck behind Mr Prudent in third. The other Godolphin runners Pugin and Hatha Anna finished well down the field.

Vinnie Roe (IRE) (b.c. 1998)	Definite Article (b 1992)	Indian Ridge (ch 1985)	Ahonoora Hillbrow
		Summer Fashion (b 1985)	Moorestyle My Candy
	Kayu (ch 1985)	Tap On Wood (ch 1976)	Sallust Cat O'Mountaine
		Ladytown (ch 1980)	English Prince Supreme Lady

Vinnie Roe, a leggy, useful-looking colt, had his pedigree documented in *Racehorses of 2001*, and there is nothing new to add. Vinnie Roe is capable of smart form at a mile and a half, but is better over further. If there were any nagging doubts about Vinnie Roe's ability to stay the Gold Cup trip as a four-year-old, there shouldn't be any if he contests the race again; at four he was a relative youngster in Gold Cup terms and further physical maturity and an extra year's experience will certainly stand him in good stead. Vinnie Roe is usually blinkered nowadays (he has been visored), but won without headgear on his reappearance. He acts on any going, though his trainer had reservations about the suitability of the very firm going at Flemington which reportedly left Vinnie Roe facing a lengthy spell off the course to recover from the effects. After that experience, Vinnie Roe may not in future be risked too often on ground on the firm side of good. Provided he makes a full recovery from his Melbourne Cup exertions, Vinnie Roe should continue to play a major part in the top staying races; he is a tough, genuine and most consistent racehorse, as well as being a high-class one. *D. K. Weld, Ireland*

Mr Seamus Sheridan's "Vinnie Roe"

John Smith's Cup (Handicap), York—Vintage Premium, ridden by champion apprentice Paul Hanagan, battles on gamely between Kirovski (left) and the heavily-backed favourite Leadership

VINTAGE PREMIUM   5 b.g. Forzando 122 – Julia Domna (Dominion 123) [2002 **114** 107d: 7.9f³ 10s* 10.1d* 10m⁶ 10.4m* 9m⁵ 10.3m² 10.9g² 9.8g Oct 5] tall, leggy gelding: smart performer: revitalised in 2002, and won handicaps at Windsor in May, Epsom (beat Counsel's Opinion 1¼ lengths) in June and York (John Smith's Cup, beat Kirovski gamely by head) in July: at least respectable efforts after when runner-up in minor event at Doncaster (beaten 4 lengths by Beekeeper) and listed event at Ayr (short-headed by Island House): only ninth in Prix Dollar at Longchamp final start: stays 11f: acts on fibresand and any turf going: visored once: usually races prominently: sometimes wanders, but is genuine. *R. A. Fahey*

VINTAGE STYLE   3 ch.g. Piccolo 121 – Gibaltarik (IRE) 68 (Jareer (USA) 115) **71** [2002 70: p5g² p5g⁵ 5.7g May 7] fair performer: effective at 5f to 7f: acts on all-weather and soft going: sold 1,200 gns in September. *R. Hannon*

VINTAGE TIPPLE (IRE)   2 b.f. Entrepreneur 123 – Overruled (IRE) 91 (Last **98 p** Tycoon 131) [2002 8g* 7m* Sep 14] third foal: half-sister to useful 2000 2-y-o 7f/1m winner Spettro (by Spectrum), later successful at 11f/1½m in Italy: dam, 1m (at 2 yrs) and 1¼m winner (stayed 1½m), half-sister to smart performer up to 1½m Overbury, from family of Vintage Crop: won 16-runner maiden at Tralee (by 3 lengths from Solas Mo Chroi) in August and 6-runner minor event at the Curragh (by 4 lengths from Coco Palm, slowly away, pushed clear) in September: will stay at least 1¼m: useful already, and open to further improvement. *Patrick Mullins, Ireland*

VINTHEA (IRE)   3 ch.f. Barathea (IRE) 127 – Vintage Escape (IRE) 84 (Cyrano de **103** Bergerac 120) [2002 75: 8d* 8m⁴ 8.5s* 8g Aug 28] leggy, plain filly: first foal: dam, Irish maiden who stayed 9f, out of half-sister to Vintage Crop: useful performer: won handicaps at Leopardstown in June and Galway (listed event by length from Desert Trail) in July: also ran well when fourth to Tashawak in listed rated stakes at Royal Ascot second start: will be suited by 1¼m: acts on soft and good to firm going: sold 160,000 gns in December. *J. G. Burns, Ireland*

VIOLENT   4 b.f. Deploy 131 – Gentle Irony 65 (Mazilier (USA) 107) [2002 54: p10g **51 d** p10g p10g p8g⁶ p8g⁵ 12m² 11.6g 11.9g 11.9m 9s 12m 11.6m 16.4d p10g Jul 20] small filly: modest performer: barely stays 1½m: acts on any turf going/all-weather: usually visored/blinkered: tongue tied last 2 starts: on downgrade. *Jamie Poulton*

VIPASSANA 2 b.f. (Apr 20) Sadler's Wells (USA) 132 – Reef Squaw (Darshaan 133) **– p**
[2002 7d Nov 2] quite attractive filly: third foal: half-sister to fairly useful 1m winner
Fruhling Feuer (by Green Tune): dam, French 1¼m/11f winner, from family of good-
class French middle-distance performers Animatrice, Poliglote and Indian Danehill: 8/1
and backward, faded from 3f out when well held in maiden at Newmarket: should do
better. *Sir Michael Stoute*

VIRGIN SOLDIER (IRE) 6 ch.g. Waajib 121 – Never Been Chaste (Posse (USA) **90**
130) [2002 98: f16.2g 16f⁵ 16m⁴ 16.2m 12m² 12m Aug 18] angular gelding: only fairly
useful performer in 2002: stays 2¼m: acts on fibresand, good to firm and good to soft
going: well held blinkered/visored: has won for amateur: sometimes idles/edges left:
usually races prominently: successful over hurdles twice in September. *G. A. Swinbank*

VISCOUNT BANKES 4 ch.g. Clantime 101 – Bee Dee Dancer (Ballacashtal (CAN)) **–**
[2002 p12g p13g f14g Mar 12] fair form on debut at 2 yrs: little form since: tried visored.
W. G. M. Turner

VISION OF DREAMS 2 b.f. (Jan 30) Efisio 120 – Dark Eyed Lady (IRE) 82 (Exhib- **93**
itioner 111) [2002 6d⁵ 6g² 5.5g⁴ f6g* Dec 14] fourth living foal: half-sister to 4-y-o Oh
So Dusty and 2001 2-y-o 5f/6.5f (in USA) winner Green Eyed Lady (by Greensmith):
dam 5f/6f winner, including at 2 yrs: fairly useful performer: best effort when just under
2 lengths fourth to Pleasure Place in Prix d'Arenberg at Maisons-Laffitte third start:
landed odds readily in maiden at Wolverhampton in December: likely to prove best short
of 1m: acts on fibresand, raced only on good/good to soft ground on turf. *B. J. Meehan*

VISION OF NIGHT 6 b.h. Night Shift (USA) – Dreamawhile 85 (Known Fact **115**
(USA) 135) [2002 115: 5m² 6m 6g² 6f⁴ Jul 20] smallish, strong horse: smart performer:
won Jacobs Goldene Peitsche at Baden-Baden in 2001: good 4-length second to Kyllachy
in Temple Stakes at Sandown in May: creditable length second to Tedburrow in
Chipchase Stakes at Newcastle penultimate start, best other effort: effective at 5f/6f: yet
to race on heavy going, acts on any other: usually waited with: tends to hang left: stays in
training. *J. L. Dunlop*

VISITATION 4 b.f. Bishop of Cashel 122 – Golden Envoy (USA) 68 (Dayjur (USA) **43**
137) [2002 40: f12s f12g⁵ f8g² p7g f7g f8g* f8g f8.5s 9f 8m³ f7g 8m 9.1s Oct 15] tall **a51**
filly: modest on all-weather, poor on turf: won claimer at Southwell in March: effective
at 1m to 11f: acts on good to firm going and fibresand, probably on polytrack: usually
visored/blinkered nowadays. *K. A. Ryan*

VISTA CHINO (IRE) 3 b.f. Perugino (USA) 84 – La Fille de Cirque 49 (Cadeaux **–**
Genereux 131) [2002 45: 8.3g 7m Sep 3] little form in maidens/seller: looked irresolute
final outing. *D. Haydn Jones*

VITA SPERICOLATA (IRE) 5 b.m. Prince Sabo 123 – Ahonita 90 (Ahonoora **101**
122) [2002 106: 6f 5d 5g 5m 6m 6.1g* 6d² 6m² 6m⁵ 5m⁶ 5.2f 6m Sep 28] lengthy, rather
plain mare: useful performer: made all in listed event at Chester (for second successive
year, beat Smokin Beau a neck) in August: also ran well when second in handicap at
Ascot (beaten ½ length by Goldeva) and listed race at Pontefract (beaten neck by Cotton
House) next 2 starts and when seventh to Lady Dominatrix in Dubai International Airport
World Trophy at Newbury penultimate outing: best at 5f/6f: acts on any going: effective
visored/blinkered or not: sometimes carries head awkwardly/edges left: often makes
running. *J. S. Wainwright*

VITELUCY 3 b.f. Vettori (IRE) 119 – Classic Line 71 (Last Tycoon 131) [2002 59: **62**
p10g⁶ 11.6m 14.1m 10.9g p12g Oct 4] modest maiden: should stay beyond 1½m: has
raced freely. *I. A. Balding*

VIVA ATLAS ESPANA 2 b.f. (Mar 11) Piccolo 121 – Bay Risk (Risk Me (FR) 127) **–**
[2002 6g 6m 7s Sep 10] half-sister to 4-y-o Firewire: dam well beaten both starts: signs of
just a little ability in maidens. *N. Hamilton*

VIZULIZE 3 b.f. Robellino (USA) 127 – Euridice (IRE) 66 (Woodman (USA) 126) **70**
[2002 8m 7g 9.9m⁵ 10d⁶ 10m³ 11.6m⁴ p10g 8m 10.2f⁴ 10s Oct 15] good-topped filly:
fourth foal: half-sister to 3 winners, including fairly useful 2000 2-y-o 8.5f winner Dusty
Carpet (by Pivotal) and Irish 2m winner Delphi (by Grand Lodge): dam 9.7f winner who
probably stayed 15f: fair maiden: left D. Elsworth after seventh start: will stay at least
1½m: acts on firm ground, possibly unsuited by softer than good: blinkered (saddle
slipped) seventh outing. *B. R. Millman*

VLASTA WEINER 2 b.c. (Apr 7) Magic Ring (IRE) 115 – Armaiti 78 (Sayf El Arab **65 d**
(USA) 127) [2002 5.1m³ 5.1d 7m 6m Jul 16] 2,100Y: fifth foal: dam, 7f winner,
half-sister to useful Italian winner up to 11f Dancer Mitral: well beaten after showing fair
form when third in maiden at Nottingham: should stay 6f. *J. M. Bradley*

VODKA QUEEN (IRE)   3 b.f. Ali-Royal (IRE) 127 – Gentle Guest (IRE) (Be My   **36**
Guest (USA) 126) [2002 –: f7s p8g f9.4g⁴ f8g f11g⁵ f11g⁴ 10m p12g⁴ Jun 1] poor maiden:
stays 11f: acts on fibresand: visored/blinkered last 4 starts. *K. R. Burke*

VOICE MAIL   3 b.g. So Factual (USA) 120 – Wizardry 83 (Shirley Heights 130)   **78**
[2002 61: 7.1f⁵ 8.1m³ 8.3s⁴ 8.3s⁶ 9s 8.1f³ 9d 7g³ 8m² 8m* 10.1g⁵ 7.6m* p8g⁵ 7d⁴ Sep
11] useful-looking gelding: fair handicapper: progressed in 2002, winning at Bath and
Lingfield in August: best at 7f/1m: acts on firm going, good to soft (probably on soft) and
polytrack: consistent. *I. A. Balding*

VOICE OF HOPE (IRE)   5 b.g. Magical Strike (USA) 114 – Glendee (Boreen (FR)   **–**
123) [2002 –: f12s Jan 22] well held in 2 maidens: visored on debut. *Mrs N. Macauley*

VOLALI (IRE)   3 b.g. Ali-Royal (IRE) 127 – Vol de Reve (IRE) (Nordico (USA))   **–**
[2002 61d: f7g⁶ f6g Oct 21] smallish, useful-looking gelding: disappointing maiden: tried
blinkered/visored. *M. J. Polglase*

VOLCANIC   3 b.g. Zafonic (USA) 130 – Ryafan (USA) 121 (Lear Fan (USA) 130)   **63**
[2002 8m 6m⁴ 7f² 7d p7g Dec 28] leggy, good-topped gelding: first foal: dam, won up to
1¼m (including Nassau Stakes and 2 US Grade 1 events), Prix Marcel Boussac winner at
2 yrs: easily best effort in maidens (modest form) when second at Redcar in September,
edging left: visored (first run after leaving J. Gosden 11,000 gns) final outing: tongue tied
after debut: folded tamely penultimate start. *P. D. Evans*

VOLUPTUOUS   2 b.f. (Mar 18) Polish Precedent (USA) 131 – Alzianah 102 (Alzao   **65**
(USA) 117) [2002 f6g f7s⁵ Dec 13] 25,000Y: fourth foal: half-sister to 3 winning
sprinters, including 4-y-o Leozian: dam 5f/6f winner, including at 2 yrs: better effort in
maidens at Wolverhampton (fair form) when fifth to Every Note Counts: barely stays 7f.
J. A. Osborne

VORTEX   3 b.c. Danehill (USA) 126 – Roupala (USA) 75 (Vaguely Noble 140) [2002   **76**
8f 8.2m⁴ 8.1g⁵ 7m³ f7g p7g* Dec 28] good-bodied colt: brother to 1m (at 2 yrs) to 1¼m
winner Prove and 1¼m/1½m winner Danefair, both useful in France, and half-brother to
3 winners in France, notably smart middle-distance stayer Erudite (by Generous): dam
1m winner out of 1000 Guineas/Champion Stakes winner Cairn Rouge: fair performer:
left Sir Michael Stoute 18,000 gns after fourth start: won maiden at Lingfield in December: should stay easy 1m: acts on polytrack, raced only on good going or firmer on turf:
tongue tied after debut: has raced freely, and may prove best with waiting tactics. *Miss
Gay Kelleway*

VOUCHER   3 ch.f. Polish Precedent (USA) 131 – Superstore (USA) (Blushing Groom   **86**
(FR) 131) [2002 71: 10m³ 10g* 10.3m 10f Aug 17] lengthy filly: quick, fluent mover:
fairly useful performer: won maiden at Pontefract in July by 5 lengths: below form in
handicaps after: stays 1¼m: raced only on good going or firmer: sold 16,000 gns in
December. *B. W. Hills*

VOYAGER (IRE)   2 b.c. (Mar 29) Green Desert (USA) 127 – Rafha 123 (Kris 135)   **– p**
[2002 6m 6m 6s Oct 25] leggy, quite good-topped colt: brother to 5-y-o Invincible Spirit,
closely related to 3-y-o Massarra, and half-brother to several at least useful winners,
including smart 7.6f (at 2 yrs) to 1¾m winner Sadian (by Shirley Heights): dam 6f (at 2
yrs) to 11.5f winner (including 10.5f Prix de Diane): signs of ability in maidens: likely to
do better as 3-y-o. *J. L. Dunlop*

VRUBEL (IRE)   3 ch.g. Entrepreneur 123 – Renzola (Dragonara Palace (USA) 115)   **69**
[2002 64: 8f³ 7g p7g² 7.1m³ 9s* 8g 8m 10m 10m 10g Oct 24] well-made gelding: fair   **a66**
performer: won amateur handicap at Goodwood in June: disappointing after: stays 9f:
acts on all-weather, firm and soft ground: has hung left: swished tail repeatedly before
seventh start: sold 11,000 gns. *N. A. Callaghan*

VUELA-MANA-MOU (IRE)   4 b.g. Goldmark (USA) 113 – Carnival Fugue 58   **–**
(High Top 131) [2002 –: 12.1m 12m⁶ 10m Jul 8] no form. *M. E. Sowersby*

W

WADHAM (IRE)   2 ch.g. (May 4) College Chapel 122 – Premium Gift 63 (Most   **–**
Welcome 131) [2002 6g Jun 28] 2,000Y (twice): angular gelding: third foal: dam 5f
winner: well beaten in seller at Newcastle. *M. W. Easterby*

WADI 7 b.g. Green Desert (USA) 127 – Eternal (Kris 135) [2002 67: 11.7g May 7] fair – handicapper at 6 yrs: stayed 1½m: acted on firm and good to soft going: twice blinkered/tongue tied: looked less than keen: dead. *Dr J. R. J. Naylor*

WADMAAN 3 b.c. Singspiel (IRE) 133 – Rum Cay (USA) 75 (Our Native (USA)) **100** [2002 10.3f² Jun 1] 800,000Y: eighth foal: half-brother to several winners, notably 9-y-o Persian Punch: dam 14.6f and bumper winner: well-held seventh in 1m private trial at Nad Al Sheba in April: well-backed favourite, useful form when 1½ lengths second of 5 to Gallant Hero in minor event at Doncaster in June, leading until over 2f out and battling on gamely: not seen out again: bred to stay 1½m+. *Saeed bin Suroor*

WAFANI 3 b.g. Mtoto 134 – Wafa (IRE) (Kefaah (USA) 124) [2002 p10g 9m 8.1m Sep – 16] leggy gelding: first foal: dam, well beaten only outing, half-sister to Derby winner Shaamit (by Mtoto): no show in maidens: raced freely first 2 outings, jinked left and unseated soon after start final one. *W. J. Musson*

WAFFLES OF AMIN 5 b.g. Owington 123 – Alzianah 102 (Alzao (USA) 117) **48** [2002 60d: p13g² p16g⁴ p13g 14.1d⁴ 15f⁵ 11.9g⁴ p12g⁵ 11.9g 14.1m⁴ 12m⁶ Aug 26] small gelding: poor handicapper: seems to stay easy 2m: acts on all-weather, good to firm and good to soft going (well beaten on heavy): tried blinkered: consistent. *S. Kirk*

WAFIR (IRE) 10 b.g. Scenic 128 – Taniokey (Grundy 137) [2002 12.3m 11.1v⁶ 12.4g – Aug 7] rangy gelding: modest performer in 2000: no form in 2002: sometimes blinkered/visored. *T. A. K. Cuthbert*

WAGES 2 b.g. (Mar 17) Lake Coniston (IRE) 131 – Green Divot (Green Desert (USA) **83** 127) [2002 6d 6s p6g⁴ p7g² p6g* Dec 28] 13,000Y: third foal: dam lightly-raced half-sister to Ebor winner Far Ahead and high-class 2m chaser Tiutchev: fairly useful performer: won maiden at Lingfield by ½ length from Zeuss: effective at 6f/7f: acts on polytrack: free-going sort. *A. M. Hales*

WAHCHI (IRE) 3 ch.c. Nashwan (USA) 135 – Nafhaat (USA) 91 (Roberto (USA) **105** 131) [2002 97p: 9m² 11.5g³ May 11] strong, lengthy colt: has scope: good mover: useful performer: ¾-length second to Playapart in listed race at Newmarket on reappearance: favourite, third to 13-length winner Bandari in Derby Trial at Lingfield next time, tending to hang left/carry head awkwardly: should stay 1½m: raced only on good ground or firmer. *E. A. L. Dunlop*

WAHJ (IRE) 7 ch.g. Indian Ridge 123 – Sabaah (USA) 65 (Nureyev (USA) 131) [2002 **98** 104: f8.5g 7.1g² 7g 7g 7.1d⁶ 7d 6g 7.1m⁶ 7f Oct 5] sturdy gelding: useful handicapper: well held last 4 outings: races freely, and at least as effective at 7f as easy 8.5f: acts on firm going, soft and fibresand: tongue tied earlier in career: often makes running. *C. A. Dwyer*

WAHOO SAM (USA) 2 ch.c. (Jan 28) Sandpit (BRZ) 129 – Good Reputation (USA) **87** (Gran Zar (MEX)) [2002 5d⁵ f6g* 7m* Jul 26] $6,200Y: well-grown colt: has scope: third foal: half-brother to a winner in USA by Storm Boot: dam, 2-y-o 6f winner in USA, half-sister to dam of Ormonde Stakes winner Zilzal Zamaan: fairly useful form: won maiden at Southwell (pulled hard/hung left) and minor event at Thirsk (beat Kentucky Blue a head) in July: will probably stay 1m: acts on fibresand and good to firm ground: sweating/restless in stall at Thirsk. *T. D. Barron*

WAHSHEEQ 2 b.c. (Mar 12) Green Desert (USA) 127 – Moss (USA) (Woodman **99** (USA) 126) [2002 6g³ 7m* 7g³ 7.1m Aug 31] 110,000Y: quite good-topped colt: fourth foal: half-brother to useful 7f (at 2 yrs) and 12.6f winner Elrehaan (by Sadler's Wells) and 5-y-o Rousing Thunder: dam, once-raced half-sister to high-class sprinter Committed, from very good family: useful form: won maiden at Goodwood in August: good length third to Bourbonnais in listed race at York: fared best of those ridden prominently when seventh to Foss Way in Solario Stakes at Sandown: should stay 1m: raced only on good ground or firmer. *E. A. L. Dunlop*

WAIKIKI BEACH (USA) 11 ch.g. Fighting Fit (USA) – Running Melody 86 (Rhein- – § gold 137) [2002 –§: f9.4g⁶ Jan 25] lengthy gelding: temperamental handicapper: tried visored, usually blinkered. *G. L. Moore*

WAIKIKI DANCER (IRE) 4 br.f. General Monash (USA) 107 – Waikiki (GER) – (Zampano (GER)) [2002 45: 11.6s Jun 10] workmanlike filly: poor maiden at 3 yrs: well held only 4-y-o start. *B. Palling*

WAINAK (USA) 4 b.g. Silver Hawk (USA) 123 – Cask 99 (Be My Chief (USA) 122) – § [2002 71: p10g f12s 9.3g 13.1g 10.9d Jun 21] tall, good-topped gelding: fair maiden at 3 yrs: tried blinkered/visored: temperamental. *I. Semple*

Mr Hamdan Al Maktoum's "Walayef"

WAIT FOR THE WILL (USA)   6 ch.g. Seeking The Gold (USA) – You'd Be Sur-   **97**
prised (USA) 117 (Blushing Groom (FR) 131) [2002 80d: p12g³ p12g* p12g² 12g³ 12g*
12g* 12g² 12m* 12m² 13.3f³ 12m⁴ Sep 23] tall gelding: useful performer: improved,
and won minor event at Lingfield in March and handicaps at Newmarket (amateurs) and
Goodwood in June and Ascot in July, last named by length from Alberich: creditable
efforts next 2 starts: effective at 1½m/1¾m: acts on polytrack, firm and good to soft
going: usually blinkered (wasn't at Lingfield), has been visored: tried tongue tied: usually
travels strongly: formerly moody (has swished tail/found little). *G. L. Moore*

WAKE (USA)   2 b.c. (Mar 14) Storm Cat (USA) – Ladies Cruise (USA) (Fappiano   **81 p**
(USA)) [2002 7g² Oct 18] third foal: dam, minor 1m stakes winner in USA, half-sister to
dam of US Grade 1 9f winner River Flyer: 13/2, ½-length second of 4 to Audience in
minor event at Newmarket, soon recovering from slow start and keeping on well: sure to
improve. *B. J. Meehan*

WALAYEF (USA)   2 b.f. (Mar 19) Danzig (USA) – Sayedat Alhadh (USA) (Mr Pros-   **105 p**
pector (USA)) [2002 6s* 6g* 7d⁵ Oct 28] second foal: dam, US 7f winner, half-sister to
useful 1½m winner Elsaamri: won maiden at the Curragh (by 3½ lengths from Hanabad)
in August and listed race there (beat Mombassa comfortably by 1½ lengths) in
September: unlucky fifth to New South Wales in Killavullan Stakes at Leopardstown,
making ground easily early in straight but then getting no run: should stay 7f: remains
capable of better. *K. Prendergast, Ireland*

WALDENBURG (USA)   3 b.c. Miswaki (USA) 124 – Erandel (USA) (Danzig (USA))   **94**
[2002 100p: 8g 8m⁶ Jun 1] tall, good-topped colt: has scope: has had shins fired: useful
winning 2-y-o for J. Gosden: just fairly useful form at best in 2002, in Poule d'Essai des

Poulains at Longchamp (10½ lengths tenth of 13 to Landseer) and listed race at Kempton (visored, last of 6): should be suited by 7f/1m: has been bandaged behind: left Godolphin in November. *Saeed bin Suroor*

WALDMARK (GER) 2 ch.f. (Apr 4) Mark of Esteem (IRE) 137 – Wurftaube (GER) **83 P**
119 (Acatenango (GER) 127) [2002 7m* Sep 7] second foal: dam won up to 1¾m in Germany, including Deutsches St Leger: well-backed favourite, won steadily-run 5-runner minor event at Kempton by short head from stable-companion Halawanda, leading 2½f out then running green: seems well regarded, and should do good deal better at 1¼m/1½m at 3 yrs. *Sir Michael Stoute*

WALTZING WIZARD 3 b.g. Magic Ring (IRE) 115 – Legendary Dancer 90 (Sha- **78**
reef Dancer (USA) 135) [2002 72d: 5g 5m 6g 6g⁵ 6s³ 6f³ f6g 5.9g⁶ 5.9g* 5.9v² 7.1m*
7m² 7.1m 7s⁴ 7v⁵ p7g Nov 19] tall, leggy gelding: fair handicapper: won at Carlisle and Musselburgh in August: stays easy 7f: acts on any turf going, well held on all-weather: tried tongue tied. *A. Berry*

WANNABE AROUND 4 b.c. Primo Dominie 121 – Noble Peregrine (Lomond **109**
(USA) 128) [2002 112: p10g 8 3s³ 9.9d⁴ 8.5d³ 8m³ 8m 8m 8f² Sep 30] tall colt: useful performer: mostly creditable efforts in 2002, including 4 lengths third to Nayyir in Diomed Stakes at Epsom and ninth to Smirk in William Hill Mile (Handicap) at Goodwood (raced in clear lead until final 1f) on fourth/seventh starts: best at 1m/9f: acts on heavy and good to firm going, showed promise on all-weather: visored last 2 outings: usually makes running: sold 70,000 gns, joined D. Nicholls. *T. G. Mills*

WANNA SHOUT 4 b.f. Missed Flight 123 – Lulu (Polar Falcon (USA) 126) [2002 **52**
57: f8.5g 8.1m* 10m² 10.9m 8.1m 7g 8.1v Aug 9] modest handicapper: won at Warwick (apprentices) in May: stays 1¼m: acts on fibresand, soft and good to firm ground: blinkered/visored 3 times in 2001, looking wayward on second occasion: tried tongue tied: none too consistent. *R. Dickin*

WARAQA (USA) 3 b.f. Red Ransom (USA) – Jafn 104 (Sharpo 132) [2002 76: 6s² **69**
7d⁵ p6g⁶ 6m 6s* 6s 6m Aug 29] smallish, good-topped filly: fair performer: won minor event at Leicester in July: tailed off both starts after: best at 5f/6f: acts on soft and good to firm ground: tongue tied last 2 starts at 2 yrs. *J. A. Osborne*

WARDEN WARREN 4 b.g. Petong 126 – Silver Spell 54 (Aragon 118) [2002 77§: **76 §**
f6g f8g p7g p8g 7f⁴ 8g 7m* 8m 7f 6d 6d 6m 7m 7m 7g 7s⁶ f7g² p6g f7g* p7g Dec 30] sparely-made gelding: fair handicapper: won at Newmarket (apprentice race) in June and Wolverhampton (idled) in December: stays 7f: acts on fibresand, firm and soft going: usually blinkered/visored: has worn cheekpieces: has been very slowly away: unreliable. *Mrs C. A. Dunnett*

WAREED (IRE) 4 b.c. Sadler's Wells (USA) 132 – Truly Special 116 (Caerleon **123**
(USA) 132) [2002 118: 15.5m* 20m³ Jun 20]
    Wareed has made into a very smart performer suited by a good test of stamina, which will come as little surprise to those who saw him win a newcomers event at Longchamp on his only start at two. Racing over a distance of nine furlongs on quite testing ground, Wareed had to be niggled along in front for a long way but looked better the further he went and put six lengths between himself and his nearest pursuer in the straight. Twelve months and three races later, Wareed showed improved form when stepped up to fifteen furlongs on his return to Longchamp, making virtually all to win the Prix Hubert de Chaudenay - Casino Barriere de Menton; and in the latest season he made a successful reappearance in the Prix Vicomtesse Vigier, run over a similar trip at the same venue. Wareed's eight rivals in the latter contest included the first three home in the Prix de Barbeville, run over the same course and distance the previous month, and Speedmaster who had won the Prix Vicomtesse Vigier in 2001, but all were put firmly in their place. In a race more truly-run than most French staying events, Wareed took the lead over a furlong out and quickly settled matters, winning by two and a half lengths from Speedmaster. Wareed faced stronger opposition and a distance of over half a mile further on his next start, in the Gold Cup at Royal Ascot, and in finishing third behind Royal Rebel and Vinnie Roe, battling on under strong pressure to be beaten just over a length, he ran his best race to date, Frankie Dettori, who had been fined for his use of the whip on Wareed in the Prix Hubert de Chaudenay, was given a four-day ban by the Ascot stewards for another whip offence.

Prix Vicomtesse Vigier, Longchamp—
Wareed has it sewn up as Speedmaster (rail) emerges best of the others

Wareed (IRE) (b.c. 1998)	Sadler's Wells (USA) (b 1981)	Northern Dancer (b 1961)	Nearctic
			Natalma
		Fairy Bridge (b 1975)	Bold Reason
			Special
	Truly Special (b 1985)	Caerleon (b 1980)	Nijinsky
			Foreseer
		Arctique Royale (b 1978)	Royal And Regal
			Arctic Melody

Wareed is the eighth foal of the smart French filly Truly Special, who won a newcomers event over a mile at two and the Prix de Royaumont at three, when it was run over an extended mile and a quarter. Truly Special, a daughter of the Irish One Thousand Guineas winner Arctique Royale and granddaughter of the 1965 Musidora winner Arctic Melody, the last-named also the grandam of Ardross, has produced four other winners. They include smart performers Truly A Dream and Jaydoom, both of whom are by Darshaan. The former also won the Prix de Royaumont over its current distance of a mile and a half, and subsequently the E P Taylor Stakes; the latter won minor events over seven and a half furlongs at Deauville and a mile and a quarter at Nad Al Sheba on his only starts. Another of Truly Special's winners, Solo de Lune (by Law Society), is dam of the Prix Saint-Alary winner Cerulean Sky and the smart stayer Qaatef. Wareed, a big, rangy colt with a round action, acts on soft and good to firm ground, but was disappointing on heavy on his final start at three years. He has been visored since his debut. Wareed was not seen out after the Gold Cup which clearly poses a question mark over his future in the top staying events. *Saeed bin Suroor*

WAREYTH (USA)   3 b. or br.c. Shuailaan (USA) 122 – Bahr Alsalaam (USA) (River-man (USA) 131) [2002 8s 9m⁶ 11.9d⁶ 10m Jun 20] first foal: dam, ran once at 3 yrs, half-sister to Breeders' Cup Juvenile and Florida Derby winner Unbridled's Song: little form: slowly away first 2 outings: seemed to lose action final one. *M. R. Channon*   –

WARHOL (USA)   2 b. or br.c. (Mar 2) Saint Ballado (CAN) – Charm A Gendarme (USA) (Batonnier (USA)) [2002 6s² 8m⁴ 8g⁵ Oct 5] $4,000,000Y: lengthy colt: has scope: fifth foal: half-brother to 2 winners in USA, notably very smart Grade 1 9f winner Tout Charmant (by Slewvescent) who stayed 11f: dam US Grade 3 1m winner: fairly useful form: made early running when 4 lengths fourth to Saturn in minor event at Newbury: best effort when 3 lengths fifth to New South Wales in maiden at the Curragh: should stay 1¼m. *A. P. O'Brien, Ireland*   **94**

WARLINGHAM (IRE)   4 b.g. Catrail (USA) 123 – Tadjnama (USA) (Exceller (USA) 129) [2002 –: p6g⁶ 7m 6m 7g* 8m⁶ p6g* p6g 6d⁴ 7g³ 7g 7.1g p7g Oct 16] fair handicapper: won at Brighton in May and Lingfield in July: below form last 3 starts: best at 6f/7f: acts on firm going, good to soft and all-weather: blinkered once: tends to carry head awkwardly. *M. Pitman*   **73**   **a76**

WARNINGFORD   8 b.h. Warning 136 – Barford Lady 93 (Stanford 121§) [2002 119: 7m* 8m 7.1s* 7m 6v Nov 9] lengthy, good-topped horse: smart performer: successful 10 times, including in Leicestershire Stakes at Leicester (by ½ length from Red Carpet, having also won race in 1999 and 2000, latter at Newmarket) in April and listed event at Haydock (beat Patsy's Double by ½ length) in June: well below form after 4½-month   **115**

Golden Jubilee Celebration Stakes (John of Gaunt), Haydock—
veteran Warningford (left) wins this race for the second time in four years; Patsy's Double is second

break last 2 starts: barely stayed testing 1m (all wins around 7f): acted on heavy and good to firm going: often visored in 1998: was usually held up: genuine and reliable: to stand at Hedgeholme Stud, Co Durham, fee £2,000, Oct 1st, filly foal free return. *J. R. Fanshawe*

WARNING REEF   9 b.g. Warning 136 – Horseshoe Reef 88 (Mill Reef (USA) 141)   **63**
[2002 71: 10.9g^2 9.9m 12g^4 12g^4 10.3f^2 10.3d^4 12s^6 11.9g 11.9m 10.9m^3 10.3f^6 11.9f^5 12s^6 12v^6 Nov 9] small, workmanlike gelding: poor mover: modest handicapper: best at 1¼m/1½m: acts on fibresand, firm and soft going (not on heavy): sometimes flashes tail/finds little: best held up, and needs things to go his way, but usually runs his race. *E. J. Alston*

WAR OWL (USA)   5 gr.g. Linamix (FR) 127 – Ganasheba (USA) (Alysheba (USA))   **70**
[2002 f9.4g f11g p10g f8.5g^2 f8.5g^3 8.2m f8.5g^4 10.2d^5 10s^5 9.9m Jun 25] lengthy gelding: first foal: dam, French maiden, half-sister to Breeders' Cup Classic and Kentucky Derby winner Unbridled: useful winner in France for Mme C. Head-Maarek (sold 240,000 francs after final 4-y-o start): fair form in handicaps in Britain in 2002: stays 1¼m: acts on heavy going and fibresand: tongue tied nowadays: often pulls hard. *Ian Williams*

WARREN PLACE   2 ch.g. (Apr 11) Presidium 124 – Coney Hills 35 (Beverley Boy   **64**
99) [2002 6m 5s^4 6m^6 6g 5d^2 5m^4 5d^2 5d 5m^2 5m^6 5f^6 6f^5 Oct 7] 500Y: plain, leggy gelding: first foal: dam maiden who stayed 7f: modest maiden: best form at 5f: acts on firm and soft going: blinkered 5 of last 6 starts. *N. Bycroft*

WARRIORS PATH (IRE)   3 b.g. Namaqualand (USA) – Azinter (IRE) (Magical   **50**
Strike (USA) 114) [2002 –: f9.4g^6 p8g^6 p8g 10m 12m f12g 10d Jun 13] modest maiden: bred to be suited by 1¼m/1½m: visored last 2 starts: tried tongue tied. *B. G. Powell*

WARRSAN (IRE)   4 b.c. Caerleon (USA) 132 – Lucayan Princess 111 (High Line   **119**
125) [2002 93p: 12m 12m^2 13.3m^2 14d^4 20m 12g* 13.3f^5 14.1m^2 14m^4 12g^2 12s^2 Oct 26] neat colt: smart performer: improved again in 2002, winning valuable handicap at Goodwood (by head from Harlestone Grey) in May and 4-runner minor event at Newmarket (beat Travelmate 1¼ lengths) in July: good efforts when 2¾ lengths fourth to Vinnie Roe in Irish St Leger at the Curragh and ¾-length second to The Whistling Teal in St Simon Stakes at Newbury eighth and final runs: finds 1½m a minimum, and seems to stay 2½m (good eighth in steadily-run Gold Cup at Ascot): yet to race on heavy going, acts on any other: unseated on way to post sixth start: waited with: game and reliable. *C. E. Brittain*

WAR VALOR (USA)   3 b.c. Royal Academy (USA) 130 – Western Music (USA)   **78**
(Lord At War (ARG)) [2002 85p: 7f^2 7m^3 6s^4 6s^2 6m^2 6m^2 6d Oct 18] rather leggy, useful-looking colt: fair maiden: ran poorly last 2 starts: should stay 1m: acts on any going: tried visored/tongue tied: has worn crossed noseband/severe bridle: temperament under suspicion. *J. Nicol*

WASEYLA (IRE)   5 b.m. Sri Pekan (USA) 117 – Lady Windley (Baillamont (USA)   **– §**
124) [2002 64§, a52§: 9.9m 10.9m f12g Dec 2] modest handicapper at 4 yrs: no form in 2002: left Miss E. Lavelle after second start. *Julian Poulton*

WASHINGTON PINK (IRE)   3 b.g. Tagula (IRE) 116 – Little Red Rose (Precocious   **71**
126) [2002 70: 8.2d^6 10g^4 8f^5 8m 9.2s^6 9.9g* 8d^2 10.1s^2 10f 7.9g 12.3m^5 9.9d 11.9m^4

12.1g Sep 18] strong, close-coupled gelding: has quick action: fair performer: won seller at Beverley in May: left M. Channon after seventh start: likely to prove best at 1¼m/1½m: acts on good to firm and heavy ground: won over hurdles in September. *C. Grant*

WASTED TALENT (IRE)   2 b.f. (Mar 31) Sesaro (USA) 81 – Miss Garuda 94   **74** (Persian Bold 123) [2002 6.1m⁵ 6.1m f8s⁴ f8s³ 10m⁴ 8d Oct 21] IR 8,000Y: angular, unfurnished filly: eighth foal: half-sister to 3 winners, including fairly useful 7f winner Bali Batik (by Barathea) and 1993 2-y-o 8.5f winner Pampered Guest (by Be My Guest): dam 2-y-o 7f winner: fair maiden: stays 1¼m: acts on fibresand, unraced on extremes of going on turf: looked none too keen third start. *J. G. Portman*

WATCHING   5 ch.g. Indian Ridge 123 – Sweeping 104 (Indian King (USA) 128)   **104** [2002 100: 5s 7m 7d 5d⁶ 5d² 6m Jun 22] neat gelding: useful performer nowadays: easily best effort in 2002 when 1½ lengths second to Rudi's Pet in listed rated stakes at Epsom in June, despite meeting trouble: effective at 5f/6f: acts on heavy and good to firm going: gelded after final start. *D. Nicholls*

WATCHWORD   3 ch.f. Polish Precedent (USA) 131 – Step Aloft 87 (Shirley Heights   **65** 130) [2002 73, a65: p8g p7g³ f7g⁶ p10g 6m⁵ 8m 8d⁶ 7g⁶ 7g f8g f7g Nov 22] fair maiden   **a60** on turf, modest on all-weather: left I. Wood after fourth start: stays 1m: acts on all-weather and good to firm ground: sometimes takes good hold: tail swisher. *C. R. Dore*

WATER BABY (IRE)   3 b.g. Tagula (IRE) 116 – Flooding (USA) (Irish River (FR)   **–** 131) [2002 74: 6m 8s⁶ 7f 6m 5s Aug 5] quite good-topped gelding: fair form at 2 yrs: well held in handicaps in 2002: was best at 5f: sometimes hung right: dead. *T. D. Barron*

WATERFALL ONE   2 ch.f. (Mar 6) Nashwan (USA) 135 – Spout 115 (Salse (USA)   **62 p** 128) [2002 7d 8f 8.2m⁵ Oct 1] well-made filly: first living foal: dam 7f (at 2 yrs) to 1½m winner who stayed 13.5f: half-sister to smart performers Dombey (stayed 10.4f) and Aldwych (at 1¼m/1½m): modest form: still backward and claimer ridden, led 5f when fifth of 7 to Hoh Buzzard at Nottingham (gave trouble in paddock and unseated rider crossing line) final start: should do better at 1¼m/1½m. *R. Charlton*

Mr Saeed Manana's "Warrsan"

WATERFORD SPIRIT (IRE) 6 ch.g. Shalford (IRE) 124§ – Rebecca's Girl (IRE) **55 §**
(Nashamaa 113) [2002 60§: f5s² p6g f5g³ f5g f5g f5g⁶ 6m May 6] big, good-topped
gelding: modest performer: stays 6f: acts on soft going, good to firm and fibresand:
tried blinkered/tongue tied at 4 yrs: got very upset in stall/slowly away once at 5 yrs:
unreliable. *G. J. Smith*

WATER JUMP (IRE) 5 b.h. Suave Dancer (USA) 136 – Jolies Eaux 73 (Shirley **118**
Heights 130) [2002 122: 12m³ 13.4f⁶ May 9] lengthy, quite good-topped horse: smart
performer: won 2 listed races in 2001 (had attack of colic after final start): ¾-length third
to Zindabad in John Porter Stakes at Newbury on reappearance: bandaged hind-joints,
moved poorly to post when tailed off in Ormonde Stakes at Chester next time: stays 13f:
acts on heavy and good to firm going, possibly unsuited by firm: has taken good hold:
tends to edge left: stays in training. *J. L. Dunlop*

WATER KING (USA) 3 b.c. Irish River (FR) 131 – Brookshield Baby (IRE) **83**
(Sadler's Wells (USA) 132) [2002 76p: 10g⁶ 10m² 9.9m⁴ 10.1m Sep 6] useful-looking
colt: fairly useful maiden: second in handicap at Windsor in June: stays 1¼m: acts on
good to firm going: took fierce hold on reappearance: sold 11,000 gns, joined G. Brown.
E. A. L. Dunlop

WATERLINE DANCER (IRE) 2 b. or br.f. (Apr 24) Danehill Dancer (IRE) 117 – **69**
Thrill Seeker (IRE) (Treasure Kay 114) [2002 5g⁵ 5f⁴ 5m* 5d⁵ 6m 6d p6g⁶ 5f* 5m 6g 5f⁶ **a62**
p6g² f6s p6g* p6g⁴ Dec 30] leggy filly: fifth foal: half-sister to 1997 2-y-o 6f seller
winner Rosewood Lady (by Maledetto): dam, maiden, stayed 1¼m: fair on turf, modest
on all-weather: won maiden at Pontefract in April, nursery at Kempton (edged left) in
August and seller at Lingfield in December: stays 6f: acts on polytrack, firm and good to
soft going: tongue tied last 8 appearances: bolted to post fifth outing, and gave trouble
before start next time. *P. D. Evans*

WATERLINE QUEEN 2 b.f. (Jan 30) Wizard King 122 – Miss Waterline 77 (Rock **–**
City 120) [2002 5.1m⁶ Apr 16] first foal: dam, 2-y-o 6f winner, half-sister to smart
sprinters Double Action and Sir Nicholas and 3-y-o Lipstick: 14/1, well-held sixth of 7 in
maiden at Nottingham. *P. D. Evans*

WATERLINE SPIRIT 2 b.g. (Apr 8) Piccolo 121 – Gina of Hithermoor (Reprimand **48 §**
122) [2002 5.1g⁵ 5.1m⁶ 7.1d⁴ f6g f6f f9.4g Dec 7] 9,500Y: first foal: dam unraced sister
to smart 6f/7f winner in Britain/Sweden State of Caution: poor maiden: tried visored:
ungenuine. *P. D. Evans*

WATERMOUSE 2 b.g. (Apr 3) Alhaarth (IRE) 126 – Heavenly Waters 64 (Celestial **44**
Storm (USA) 132) [2002 6.1d⁶ 5g 6.1m Sep 16] 5,500F, 3,000Y: fifth foal: half-brother
to 9f winner in US Stornoway (by Catrail) and a winner in Spain by Wolfhound: dam,
14.6f and 2m winner, half-sister to smart Solario/Park Hill Stakes winner Shining Water
(dam of Tenby): poor maiden: gelded after final start. *R. Dickin*

WATER OF LIFE (IRE) 3 b.f. Dr Devious (IRE) 127 – Simulcast (Generous (IRE) **81**
139) [2002 78: 8.3m 7.1m² 7d 7g² 7.1m⁴ 8d³ 7m³ p8g p8g Dec 3] well-made filly: good
mover: fairly useful maiden handicapper: stays 1m: acts on polytrack, soft and good to
firm ground: tried tongue tied: found little fifth/sixth starts. *J. W. Hills*

WATERPARK 4 b.f. Namaqualand (USA) – Willisa 67 (Polar Falcon (USA) 126) **45**
[2002 –: f8s f8s³ p7g f7g² f8g² Mar 21] leggy filly: poor performer: left M. Dods after
third start: stays 1m: acts on fibresand, firm and good to soft ground: sometimes wanders:
tried visored. *R. Craggs*

WATERSIDE (IRE) 3 b.c. Lake Coniston (IRE) 131 – Classic Ring (IRE) 50 (Auction **90**
Ring (USA) 123) [2002 96: 5m² 6s* 5g 6m 6f 5d p7g* p7g Nov 27] strong colt: has a
round action: fairly useful performer: won maiden at Windsor in May and handicap at
Lingfield in November: stays 7f: acts on polytrack, soft and good to firm going:
sometimes wears tongue strap. *J. W. Hills*

WATER SPORTS (IRE) 4 b.f. Marju (IRE) 127 – Water Splash (USA) 85 (Little **79**
Current (USA)) [2002 13.1g⁴ May 20] ex-French filly: half-sister to several winners,
notably Derby second Blue Judge (by Rainbow Quest), 1m winner in Ireland at 2 yrs:
dam 1½m winner: fair performer: won minor event at Le Touquet at 3 yrs (left Mme
C. Head-Maarek 20,000 gns after): respectable fourth in handicap at Bath on British
debut: stays 13f: acts on good to firm ground. *P. R. Webber*

WATER WHEELS LASS 4 b.f. Sovereign Water (FR) – Miss Marjorie 50 (Swing **–**
Easy (USA) 126) [2002 9.2g 12.1m 7f 12g Oct 19] third foal: dam, 5f (at 2 yrs)/6f winner,
became unreliable: well beaten, including in seller. *R. D. E. Woodhouse*

WATHIQ (IRE) 2 ch.c. (Apr 25) Titus Livius (FR) 115 – Serious Delight (Lomond **87** (USA) 128) [2002 5g p6g² 6m* 8g 7.1m 7.1m⁵ f8.5g* Sep 30] 10,500Y, 34,000 2-y-o: **a90** sturdy colt: third foal: half-brother to Irish 5f winner Foxhollow Lady (by Goldmark): dam unraced half-sister to dam of very smart sprinter Pipalong: fairly useful performer: won maiden at Newcastle in July and minor event at Wolverhampton (by 6 lengths from Atahuelpa, despite carrying head high) in September: stays 8.5f: acts on all-weather, raced only on good/good to firm ground on turf. *G. C. Bravery*

WATTNO ELJOHN (IRE) 4 b.c. Namaqualand (USA) – Caroline Connors (Fairy **– §** King (USA)) [2002 68, a62: f8s f8.5g⁶ f8.5g³ f8.5g⁴ Feb 4] good-topped colt: poor **a56 §** mover: modest performer: stays 1¼m: acts on soft going, good to firm and fibresand: visored last 6 starts: unreliable: sold 5,000 gns in February, sent to Kuwait. *D. W. P. Arbuthnot*

WAVE OF OPTIMISM 7 ch.g. Elmaamul (USA) 125 – Ballerina Bay 75 (Myjinski **96** (USA)) [2002 103: 16g 16.2s⁶ Jun 6] big, raw-boned gelding: useful handicapper: ran respectably in 2002 only on reappearance: stayed 2¼m: acted on heavy going: sometimes gave trouble stall/was very slowly away: took strong hold: was effective ridden prominently or held up: dead. *Mrs Lydia Pearce*

WAVERLEY (IRE) 3 b.c. Catrail (USA) 123 – Marble Halls (IRE) (Ballad Rock **101** 122) [2002 84: 9.9g 10m* 10.4d* 10g⁵ 12g² 10f³ 9f⁴ 10m⁴ Oct 12] tall, leggy colt: useful handicapper: progressed well in 2002: won at Sandown and York (beat Total Turtle a length) in June: good second after at Goodwood (beaten neck by Dawn Invasion in Tote Gold Trophy) and Newbury (went down by 1¼ lengths to Imbibing) then fourth to Beauchamp Pilot in Cambridgeshire at Newmarket penultimate start: effective at 9f to 1½m: acts on firm and good to soft going: mounted in pre-parade ring once at 2 yrs, and has had 2 handlers. *H. Morrison*

WAVERLEY ROAD 5 ch.g. Pelder (IRE) 125 – Lillicara (FR) (Caracolero (USA) **79** 131) [2002 72: p10g⁴ p13g 14.4m* 13.9f 13.3s⁴ 14m² 20m 14.4d⁴ 14.8g⁴ 13.3m 14.1m⁶ **a67** 14.4m³ p16g Nov 27] leggy gelding: fair handicapper: won at Kempton in May: races mainly around 1¾m nowadays: acts on soft going, good to firm and polytrack (well held on fibresand): usually races prominently: game. *A. P. Jarvis*

WAVERTREE BOY (IRE) 2 ch.c. (Mar 28) Hector Protector (USA) 124 – Lust **91** (Pursuit of Love 124) [2002 7m 7m* 8m 8f 10m² 10s³ Nov 2] 9,000Y: rather leggy, good-topped colt: third foal: dam unraced half-sister to Classic Cliche and My Emma: fairly useful performer: won maiden at Salisbury in August: best effort when 7 lengths third to Forest Magic in listed race at Newmarket: will stay 1½m: acts on soft and good to firm going. *J. L. Dunlop*

WAVET 2 b.f. (Apr 3) Pursuit of Love 124 – Ballerina Bay 75 (Myjinski (USA)) [2002 **64 p** 7d Nov 2] 4,500F, 5,000Y: lengthy filly: fourth foal: half-sister to 3-y-o Czarina Waltz, 4-y-o Taffy Dancer and 7-y-o Wave of Optimism: dam 7f to 11.5f winner: 50/1, never-nearer tenth of 18 to Aljazeera in maiden at Newmarket: should be suited by 1¼m+: likely to do better. *Mrs Lydia Pearce*

WAXWING 3 b.f. Efisio 120 – Mountain Bluebird (USA) 79 (Clever Trick (USA)) **71** [2002 61: f7s⁶ f6g² 6g 5.1m* f6g² 5.7g 6g³ f7g² 8m³ p6g 6.1m 8m f6s f7g⁵ Sep 30] lengthy filly: unimpressive mover: fair handicapper: left N. Littmoden after second start: won at Nottingham in April: stays 1m: acts on firm going and fibresand, probably on polytrack: visored last 2 starts (found little final one): usually races prominently. *P. G. Murphy*

WAYLAAH 3 b.f. Common Grounds 118 – Inonder 31 (Belfort (FR) 89) [2002 60: p7g **–** p7g p6g 6g 5m Apr 23] modest maiden for J. Dunlop at 2 yrs: well beaten in 2002, including in sellers: tried visored (raced freely). *T. M. Jones*

WAY OF TRUTH 3 gr.f. Muhtarram (USA) 125 – Integrity 108 (Reform 132) [2002 **–** 6.1m⁶ 5f Jun 1] half-sister to several winners, including smart 6f (at 2 yrs) to 1m winner Radwell (by Dunbeath) and useful 1¼m to 1½m winner Honourable (by Old Vic): dam ideally suited by 6f: little form in maidens: tongue tied second start: sold 1,200 gns. *E. L. James*

WAYWARD LASS (IRE) 2 ch.f. (Apr 24) Among Men (USA) 124 – Milne's Way **–** 83 (The Noble Player (USA) 126) [2002 5g 5f 5m 7g f5s f8.5g Oct 19] IR 2,200Y: leggy, quite good-topped filly: half-sister to several winners, including 10-y-o That Man Again and 1¼m winner Who's That Man (by Mystiko): dam 6f (at 2 yrs) to 1m winner: little form. *E. J. Alston*

WAYWARD MELODY 2 b.f. (Mar 14) Merdon Melody 98 – Dubitable 59 (Formid- **51**
able (USA) 125) [2002 7d 7m 7m⁶ 8m Sep 19] fifth reported foal: sister to a 7.5f winner
in Italy: dam, maiden who stayed 1½m, out of very smart performer up to 1¼m Duboff:
modest maiden: should stay 1m: twice slowly away. *S. Dow*

WAYYAK (USA) 3 ch.c. Gold Fever (USA) 119 – My Testarossa (USA) (Black Tie **49**
Affair 128) [2002 67: p7g⁵ f6g⁴ 6g Apr 4] angular colt: disappointing maiden: should stay
7f: best efforts on good to firm/firm going. *J. W. Payne*

WAZIYA 3 ch.f. Hurricane Sky (AUS) – Serration (Kris 135) [2002 p8g⁴ p6g f8g⁴ 7d **44**
f8.5g 10g 8.1d Aug 8] 800Y: sturdy filly: seventh living foal: half-sister to Italian 7f (at 2
yrs) to 9f winner Tormore (by Reprimand) and 1992 2-y-o 7.5f/8.5f winner The Seer (by
Robellino), later winner in Germany: dam fourth at 9f in France: poor maiden: best effort
on debut, left J. Noseda after third start, and no form subsequently: likely to prove best
around 1m: acts on polytrack. *A. Senior*

WEALTH OF NATION 2 b.c. (Apr 26) Tragic Role (USA) – Arian Spirit (IRE) 56 **–**
(High Estate 127) [2002 f8.5g f8.5g Dec 20] second foal: dam 1¾m to 17f winner: well
beaten in claimer/maiden. *B. P. J. Baugh*

WEAVER OF DREAMS (IRE) 2 b.g. (Apr 14) Victory Note (USA) 120 – Daziyra **–**
(IRE) (Doyoun 124) [2002 7m Oct 2] IR 58,000Y: good-topped gelding: second foal:
half-brother to fairly useful Irish 2001 2-y-o 5f winner Dangerous Years (by Ali-Royal):
dam ran once in France: 16/1 and green, always behind in maiden at Newcastle.
G. A. Swinbank

WEAVER SAM 7 ch.g. Ron's Victory (USA) 129 – Grove Star (Upper Case (USA)) **–**
[2002 –: 16f 16.2g⁵ Aug 15] quite good-topped gelding: little form. *K. R. Burke*

WEAVERS PRIDE (FR) 2 ch.c. (Mar 20) Barathea (IRE) 127 – Creese (USA) **97**
(Diesis 133) [2002 6g³ 7m 7m² Sep 29] 500,000 francs F, IR 45,000Y: strong, well-made
colt: has scope: first foal: dam, placed at 11f/1½m in France, out of half-sister to dam of
Oh So Sharp: useful form: placed in maiden at York and minor event at Ascot (2 lengths
second of 4 to Captain Saif): stiff task when eighth in Champagne Stakes at Doncaster
(wore crossed noseband/swished tail in preliminaries): will stay 1m: well up to winning
races. *B. W. Hills*

WEB PERCEPTIONS (USA) 2 ch.c. (Jan 31) Distant View (USA) 126 – Squaw **81 p**
Time (USA) (Lord At War (ARG)) [2002 p7g⁶ 8v f7g* Nov 26] 50,000Y: first foal: dam
US 8.5f/9f winner: easily best effort in maidens (fairly useful form) when winning at
Southwell by ½ length from Blue Trojan, leading near finish: will stay 1m: open to
progress. *P. F. I. Cole*

WEDGEWOOD STAR 2 b.f. (Mar 1) Bishop of Cashel 122 – Away To Me (Exit To **74**
Nowhere (USA) 122) [2002 6d² 6.1g⁴ 7m⁵ 6.1m⁴ 6.5g⁵ Sep 27] 7,000Y: second foal: dam
unraced: fair maiden: best effort when fifth of 25 to Sharplaw Venture in sales race at
Ascot final start: likely to prove best short of 1m: yet to race on extremes of going.
R. Hannon

WEECANDOO (IRE) 4 b.f. Turtle Island (IRE) 123 – Romantic Air 62 (He Loves **72**
Me 120) [2002 74: p12g³ 12f 8g p12g f9.4g³ p8g⁴ f8g³ p10g² Dec 18] workmanlike filly:
fair maiden handicapper: stays 1¼m: acts on all-weather. *C. N. Allen*

WEE NEL 4 ch.f. Imp Society (USA) – Eskimo Nel (IRE) 75 (Shy Groom (USA)) **38 ?**
[2002 –: f11s f9.4g f8.5g³ Jan 25] poor form at best: tried blinkered. *N. P. Littmoden*

WEET-A-MINUTE (IRE) 9 ro.h. Nabeel Dancer (USA) 120 – Ludovica (Bustino **84**
136) [2002 75: f11s² f9.4g⁵ f9.4g² f9.4g* f12g** f8.5g³ 10s* f12g⁵ 12.3f f9.4g* 10d² 10m*
10.5m⁴ Jul 14] lengthy horse: fairly useful performer: had a good year in 2002, winning
3 claimers at Wolverhampton and handicaps at Leicester (seventh start) and Ripon
(penultimate outing) between February/June: stayed easy 1½m: acted on firm going, soft
and firebrand: blinkered (below form) once: sometimes carried head awkwardly: often
made running: to stud for second time, to stand at Longdon Stud, Staffordshire, fee £650,
Oct 1st. *R. Hollinshead*

WEET A MO (IRE) 2 b.g. (May 1) Sri Pekan (USA) 117 – Ozwood (IRE) (Royal **67**
Academy (USA) 130) [2002 6m 6g⁵ f6f⁵ Nov 11] IR 8,500F, IR 11,000Y: second foal:
dam unraced half-sister to useful 6f performer Ceepio: fair maiden: second home on stand
side at Newcastle second start: should stay 7f: gelded after final outing. *R. Hollinshead*

WEET A ROUND 3 ch.g. Whittingham (IRE) 104 – Hollia 72 (Touch Boy 109) [2002 **75**
79: f8.5g⁴ 8m 6f* 7g 7f⁶ 5d³ p6g⁵ 6m³ 5g⁵ 6m⁴ 7m⁵ 10m 7d 7s³ f6g² f7g⁶ f7g Dec 14] big,
good-topped gelding: fair performer: won maiden at Redcar in June: left N. Littmoden

after twelfth start: stays 7f: acts on any turf going and all-weather: usually blinkered: tongue tied last 5 starts. *R. Wilman*

WEET A WHILE (IRE) 4 b.g. Lahib (USA) 129 – Takeshi (IRE) 67 (Cadeaux Gene- –
reux 131) [2002 –: 7f 8m 10m f8g Dec 4] sturdy gelding: modest maiden at 2 yrs: lightly raced and well held in 2002, leaving R. Hollinshead after third start. *R. Wilman*

WEETMAN'S WEIGH (IRE) 9 b.h. Archway (IRE) 115 – Indian Sand (Indian **56**
King (USA) 128) [2002 64, a71: f8.5g* f8g³ f8.5g f9.4g⁵ 8m⁴ f7s² f8.5g⁶ 8m³ 10m f8.5g **a65**
8g f8s² 8.1g⁴ 8m f8.5g f8g³ f8g⁵ f8.5g⁵ f8.5g⁶ Dec 26] useful-looking horse: has string-halt: fair performer on all-weather, modest on turf: won seller at Wolverhampton in January: effective at 7f (given bit of a test) to 9.4f: acts on firm going, soft and fibresand: tongue tied earlier in career: has worn cheekpieces: usually held up (sometimes hangs left). *R. Hollinshead*

WEET WATCHERS 2 b.g. (Apr 7) Polar Prince (IRE) 117 – Weet Ees Girl (IRE) 75 **75**
(Common Grounds 118) [2002 7s f8.5g⁴ f7g⁴ Dec 31] rather leggy, workmanlikegeld-ing: second foal: dam, 2-y-o 5f winner, didn't train on: fair maiden: fourth twice at Wolverhampton: likely to prove best up to 1m. *R. Hollinshead*

WEKIWA SPRINGS (FR) 5 gr.g. Kendor (FR) 122 – Ti Mamaille (FR) (Dom **66**
Racine (FR) 121) [2002 a9.7f f8g⁵ f8g f8.5g⁴ Nov 30] big, good-topped gelding: fairly useful form in maiden at Newbury only start at 2 yrs for B. Meehan: missed 3-y-o season: won maiden at Jebel Ali on UAE debut in 2001: left K. McLaughlin in UAE after reappearance: fair form at best on return to Britain: stays 9f: acts on fibresand: tried visored: unreliable. *B. J. Meehan*

WELCOME BACK 5 ch.g. Most Welcome 131 – Villavina 59 (Top Ville 129) [2002 **41**
8f⁶ 15.8f* f16.2g⁶ Dec 7] leggy gelding: poor performer, lightly raced nowadays: gained first success in handicap at Catterick in October: stays 2m: acts on firm and good to soft going: races prominently. *K. A. Ryan*

WELCOME CHANGE 2 ch.f. (Mar 25) Most Welcome 131 – Little Change 70 –
(Grundy 137) [2002 f6f⁶ Sep 27] unfurnished filly: half-sister to several winners, including fairly useful 2000 2-y-o 7f winner Harmony Row (by Barathea), later 1m and 10.5f winner in Spain, and 7f and 1½m winner Spring Sixpence (by Dowsing): dam best at 2 yrs when third at 5f: 25/1, well held in maiden at Redcar. *T. D. Easterby*

WELCOME CITY 2 b.f. (May 1) Rock City 120 – Welcome Lu 45 (Most Welcome –
131) [2002 7m 6d f8g Oct 17] 900Y: lengthy filly: first foal: dam, 7f/1m winner, seemed to stay 2m: soundly beaten in sellers. *D. W. Barker*

WELCOME EXCHANGE 3 b.f. Most Welcome 131 – Santarem (USA) 71 (El Gran –
Senor (USA) 136) [2002 –: p10g f7g p10g 10d f7g 10d Oct 28] well held, including in seller: reared leaving stall final outing. *J. J. Bridger*

WELCOME FRIEND (USA) 5 b.h. Kingmambo (USA) 125 – Kingscote 118 (Kings **107**
Lake (USA) 133) [2002 115+: 6m 7.1d⁴ 6m² 7m 6m⁵ 6m* Sep 18] well-made horse: unimpressive mover: smart at 4 yrs, just useful in 2002: blinkered, won minor event at Yarmouth in September by 1¾ lengths from Resplendent Cee, making all: was effective at 6f/7f: acted on firm and good to soft going: was sometimes bandaged behind: sometimes raced freely: carried head high second outing: possibly failed to handle track at Epsom on fourth appearance: dead. *R. Charlton*

WELCOME GIFT 6 b.g. Prince Sabo 123 – Ausonia (Beldale Flutter (USA) 130) **59**
[2002 60: p8g³ f8s Jan 15] modest handicapper: stayed 1m: acted on all-weather, raced only on going softer than good on turf: tried blinkered: dead. *Mrs L. Stubbs*

WELCOME SIGNAL 2 ch.g. (Apr 27) Most Welcome 131 – Glenfinlass (Lomond **– p**
(USA) 128) [2002 7d Oct 30] 32,000Y: sixth foal: half-brother to useful 6f to (in Scand-inavia) 9f winner Blue Mountain (by Elmaamul) and French 1m/1¼m winner Bolder Still (by Never So Bold): dam unraced sister to Cesarewitch winner Inchcailloch and half-sister to smart performer up to 1½m in Britain/USA Prize Giving (by Most Welcome): weak 7/1-shot, ninth of 18 in maiden at Yarmouth, not knocked about once making no impression (gelded after): should do better. *J. R. Fanshawe*

WELCOME STRANGER 2 b.c. (Mar 31) Most Welcome 131 – Just Julia (Natroun **69**
(FR) 128) [2002 6f 7.2s⁵ f8s Sep 5] 4,500Y: leggy colt: sixth foal: half-brother to fairly useful 1996 2-y-o 5f/6f winner Just Visiting (by Superlative): dam no form: clearly best effort in maidens (fair form) when fifth to Pure Speculation at Ayr: should stay 1m. *M. J. Polglase*

Prix Gontaut-Biron, Deauville—Wellbeing (left) upsets the odds laid on Sakhee; Sunstrach is third

WELCOME TO UNOS 5 ch.g. Exit To Nowhere (USA) 122 – Royal Loft 105 **59**
(Homing 130) [2002 9.9g⁶ 7.9g 9.9d Jul 22] close-coupled gelding: modest maiden,
lightly raced nowadays: stays 1¼m: best efforts on good ground. *Mrs M. Reveley*

WELENSKA 3 b.c. Danzig Connection (USA) – Fairy Story (IRE) 80 (Persian Bold **99**
123) [2002 94: 8g⁴ 8g² 8m* May 6] tall, good-topped colt: fluent mover: useful
performer: good efforts in listed races at Kempton (fourth to Flat Spin) and Milan (1½
lengths second of 5 to Fisich) before winning 3-runner minor event at Doncaster (rallied
gamely despite edging right when beating Al Moughazel by short head) in May: not
certain to stay beyond 1m: raced only on good/good to firm going on turf, acts on
fibresand: sent to Hong Kong, where renamed Himalaya. *P. F. I. Cole*

WELLBEING 5 b.h. Sadler's Wells (USA) 132 – Charming Life (NZ) (Sir Tristram **119**
115) [2002 121: 12g 10s* 10s* 9.8g 10d³ Nov 17] big, good-topped horse: took eye in
appearance: smart performer: won St Simon Stakes at 3 yrs and second in Coronation
Cup at 4 yrs (final season for Henry Cecil): successful in listed race at Compiegne in July
(by 3 lengths from Mister Kybelee) and Prix Gontaut-Biron at Deauville (beat below-par
Sakhee by a length) in August: well below form last 2 starts, in Prix Dollar at Longchamp
(favourite) and Premio Roma (8 lengths third to Sunstrach): effective at 1¼m/1½m: acted
on heavy and good to firm going: to stand at Plantation Stud, Newmarket, fee £5,000, Oct
1st. *P. Bary, France*

WELL CHOSEN 3 b.c. Sadler's Wells (USA) 132 – Hawajiss 114 (Kris 135) [2002 **83**
74P: 12.3g 10m³ p13g* p12g Nov 23] good-topped, angular colt: fairly useful performer:
easily won maiden at Lingfield in October: ran poorly in handicap there next time: stays
13f: acts on polytrack, yet to race on extremes of going on turf. *E. A. L. Dunlop*

WELL CONNECTED (IRE) 2 b.g. (May 22) Among Men (USA) 124 – Wire To **50**
Wire (Welsh Saint 126) [2002 6m 7d⁵ 6d⁶ Aug 7] IR 8,000Y, 25,000 2-y-o: tall gelding:
has plenty of scope: half-brother to Irish 9f winner Wire Man (by Glenstal): dam placed
at 1m/1¼m in Ireland: modest form in maidens: not sure to stay 1m: gelded after final
start. *B. Smart*

WELL DONE CLARE (IRE) 3 b.f. Sri Pekan (USA) 117 – Brockley Hill Lass (IRE) **–**
(Alzao (USA) 117) [2002 7.1f Sep 27] rather leggy filly: fourth foal: half-sister to 4-y-o
Stylish Clare: dam ran once at 2 yrs: weak 9/1-shot, slowly away and always behind in
maiden at Haydock. *J. W. Payne*

WELLINGTON HALL (GER) 4 b.g. Halling (USA) 133 – Wells Whisper (FR) 71 **98 ?**
(Sadler's Wells (USA) 132) [2002 11v* 14.8v⁶ 12g⁶ 12v 10d Oct 14] ex-German gelding:
second foal: dam, maiden, best at 1m/1¼m, sister to very smart performer up to 1½m
Johann Quatz and smart performer up to 13.5f Walter Willy, and half-sister to Hernando:
useful performer: won maiden at Mulheim at 3 yrs and minor event at Krefeld in March:
left P. Schiergen before never dangerous in handicap at Windsor final outing: stays 1¾m:
raced only on good going or softer (acts on heavy): usually blinkered (not at Windsor).
A. Charlton

*Deutsche Post Euro Express-Preis von Europa, Cologne—Well Made's third pattern win
of the year comes at the chief expense of Salve Regina, runner-up in a
fourth consecutive Group 1 event; Yavana's Pace comes third*

WELL MADE (GER) 5 b.h. Mondrian (GER) 125 – Well Known (GER) (Konigs- **121**
stuhl (GER)) [2002 112: 11g* 12s* 11m⁴ 11v² 12d⁴ 12s* 12s⁶ Oct 20] fourth foal:
half-brother to useful German 7f (at 2 yrs) and 11f winner Wellanca (by Acatenango) and
UAE 1¼m/1½m winner Sears Tower (by Reference Point): dam, German 6f/1m winner
(including at 2 yrs), second in 11f Preis der Diana: very smart performer: won Premio
Federico Tesio at Milan at 4 yrs: improved further in 2002, successful at Cologne in
Grosser Preis der Bremer Wirtschaft (by 2 lengths from Simoun) in April, Gerling-Preis
(by 6 lengths from Aeskulap) in May and Deutsche Post Euro Express Preis von Europa
(by ¾ length from Salve Regina) in September: also ran well when beaten nose by
Simoun in Hansa-Preis at Hamburg in June: disappointing in Gran Premio del Jockey
Club at Milan final start: effective at 11f to 1¾m: acts on heavy ground. *H. Blume,
Germany*

WE'LL MAKE IT (IRE) 4 b.g. Spectrum (IRE) 126 – Walliser (Niniski (USA) 125) **70**
[2002 76: p12g p12g f14.8g⁴ Dec 2] fair maiden handicapper: off 8 months after
reappearance: stays 1½m: acts on polytrack, good to firm and good to soft going: often
blinkered: carries head high. *G. L. Moore*

WE'LL MEET AGAIN 2 ch.g. (Feb 11) Bin Ajwaad (IRE) 119 – Tantalizing Song **66 d**
(CAN) (The Minstrel (CAN) 135) [2002 5g 7g² 7.1d⁴ 7m⁶ 7g 7m 8m Aug 31] 3,500F,
9,500Y: well-grown gelding: has round action: half-brother to several winners, including
7f winner (including at 2 yrs) Victim of Love and 8.5f and 1¼m winner Miss Fascination
(both by Damister): dam ran 5 times in North America: fair maiden: below form last 3
starts: should stay 1m: yet to race on extremes of going. *M. W. Easterby*

WELL RED (IRE) 2 ch.c. (Apr 11) Prince of Birds (USA) 121 – Fairy Domino 66 **66**
(Primo Dominie 121) [2002 5m⁶ 5d 5.1g² 5.1f 5.1g f5g⁴ Dec 16] IR 4,200F, IR 3,000Y:
first foal: dam 2-y-o 5f winner: fair maiden: second at Chepstow, easily best effort: likely
to prove best at 5f: tried blinkered. *C. G. Cox*

WELSH AND WYLDE (IRE) 2 b.g. (Apr 7) Anita's Prince 126 – Waikiki (GER) **75 d**
(Zampano (GER)) [2002 6.1s⁵ 6.1m² 7d 6.1g f7s Dec 7] IR 11,000Y: second foal: dam
German 1¼m/11f winner: seemingly best effort (set steady pace, probably flattered)
when 3 lengths second to Harb in maiden at Nottingham in June: should stay 7f: acts on
good to firm ground: blinkered final start. *B. Palling*

WELSH ASSEMBLY 6 ch.g. Presidium 124 – Celtic Chimes (Celtic Cone 116) [2002 **–**
p16g p12g 11.9d Jun 13] poor performer at 3 yrs: well beaten in 2002: tried blinkered.
G. P. Enright

WELSH BORDER 4 ch.g. Zafonic (USA) 130 – Welsh Daylight (Welsh Pageant **97**
132) [2002 99: p12g 16g 16m 12m 20m Jun 20] rangy gelding: useful performer: below

form after second start (impossible task in Gold Cup at Royal Ascot final outing): seems to stay 2m: acts on soft going and polytrack: successful twice over hurdles in August (virtually refused to race following month). *G. Prodromou*

WELSH CHARGER (IRE) 3 b.g. Up And At 'em 109 – Timissara (USA) (Shah- –
rastani (USA) 135) [2002 47: f6g⁵ p6g Feb 13] small gelding: has a round action: poor maiden at 2 yrs: well held in 2002: tried visored. *J. J. Quinn*

WELSH DIVA 3 b.f. Selkirk (USA) 129 – Khubza 86 (Green Desert (USA) 127) [2002 112
67p: 8m³ 8d⁵ 8g* 7d³ 8m* 8s* Oct 20] big, good-bodied filly: smart performer: progressed well, winning maiden at Salisbury in June, listed rated stakes at Ascot (beat Sonorous 1½ lengths) in September and Premio Sergio Cumani at Milan in October: easily best effort in last-named, beating Fallen Star ½ length, making virtually all, despite carrying head high: stays 1m: acts on soft and good to firm going: has been bandaged hind joints: edgy fourth start: tends to wander, and will prove best with strong handling. *Mrs A. J. Perrett*

WELSH DREAM 5 b.g. Mtoto 134 – Morgannwg (IRE) 86 (Simply Great (FR) 122) 59
[2002 67, a58: f16s⁴ f16.2g* f16.2g⁴ p16g* 21.6m⁴ 13.8m 16d* 14.1m⁶ Aug 21] useful-looking gelding: modest handicapper: won at Wolverhampton in February, Lingfield (apprentices) in March and Musselburgh (amateurs) in July: probably probably best around 2m nowadays: unraced on heavy going, acts on any other turf and all-weather: sometimes races freely: quirky: sold 2,500 gns. *P. C. Haslam*

WELSH EMPEROR (IRE) 3 b.g. Emperor Jones (USA) 119 – Simply Times (USA) 103
64 (Dodge (USA)) [2002 96: 5g³ 5d⁶ 5g 5.1d² 5.1f⁶ 6s⁵ 6v* 5g 7s² 6v⁵ 6v* Nov 20] tall gelding: useful performer: won minor event at Haydock in August and listed race at Maisons-Laffitte (by 2 lengths from Bezrin) in November: probably stays 7f: revels in soft/heavy ground: usually blinkered: has been free to post/reluctant stall: races prominently. *T. P. Tate*

WELSH HOLLY (IRE) 3 br.f. Idris (IRE) 118 – Jane Avril (IRE) 66 (Danehill (USA) 60 d
126) [2002 59: 6s⁵ 6g 7s 8d f7g p10g Dec 30] leggy, workmanlike filly: modest maiden at best: below form after reappearance: stays 6f: sometimes races freely. *M. H. Tompkins*

WELSH LADY 3 b.f. Magic Ring (IRE) 115 – Little Unknown (Known Fact (USA) 45
135) [2002 49: p5g p6g⁵ f5g f5g f5g³ 6g² 5.1m⁶ f5g Jun 14] poor maiden: stays 6f: acts on all-weather and good to firm going: wandered sixth outing. *P. D. Evans*

WELSH MAIN 5 br.g. Zafonic (USA) 130 – Welsh Daylight (Welsh Pageant 132) 83
[2002 101?: 10m 12g³ 10f⁴ 9.9g 9m⁶ 8.9m Sep 8] good-topped gelding: only fairly useful form in 2002: raced mainly around 1¼m on good going or firmer: visored last 2 starts (looked none too keen final one): fairly useful hurdler, successful in October. *S. J. Magnier*

WELSH PARK (IRE) 9 ch.g. Balinger 116 – Welsh Escort (Welsh Captain 113) [2002 –
f14.8g Jul 1] winning hurdler (no form nowadays): tailed off only run on Flat (blinkered). *A. P. James*

WELSH WIND (IRE) 6 b.g. Tenby 125 – Bavaria 80 (Top Ville 129) [2002 94: f8.5g 86 d
8s 10g 7.9m² 7d 7.9m 7.6f 7.9m 9.1g³ 10s 8g 8s p10g f9.4g p8g² p7g Dec 30] lengthy gelding: fairly useful handicapper at best in 2002: below best after fourth start: best at 7f to 9f: acts on polytrack, firm and good to soft going: tried tongue tied: often gets behind: on downgrade. *M. Wigham*

WELTON ARSENAL 10 b.g. Statoblest 120 – Miller's Gait 74§ (Mill Reef (USA) 60 §
141) [2002 64§: 8g 8g⁴ p7g⁴ 7.1s³ 7.1v⁶ 8.1g⁶ p7g 8m p7g⁵ Oct 16] sturdy gelding: modest handicapper: stays 1m: acts on polytrack, firm and soft ground: tried visored: held up: often finds little: inconsistent. *K. Bishop*

WENDI'OUSE 4 b.f. Mind Games 121 – Brown's Cay 71 (Formidable (USA) 125) –
[2002 –: f5s Jan 4] sturdy filly: of little account. *M. Mullineaux*

WEND'S DAY (IRE) 7 br.g. Brief Truce (USA) 126 – Iswara (USA) (Alleged (USA) 54
138) [2002 12d f14.8g⁴ Sep 30] maiden handicapper, lightly raced on Flat: will stay 2m: acts on fibresand, raced only on good or softer going on turf: tongue tied: successful over hurdles in October. *A. M. Hales*

WENDYLYNNE 2 b.f. (Apr 28) Weldnaas (USA) 112 – Dusty's Darling (Doyoun –
124) [2002 5d f7g Jul 26] fourth living foal: sister to fairly useful 1997 2-y-o 5f winner Filey Brigg, and closely related to Italian 7.5f (at 2 yrs) to 9f winner White Cube (by Elmaamul): dam no sign of ability: well held in maiden/seller. *J. Balding*

Premio Sergio Cumani, Milan—a 1,2,3 for the British-trained runners,
Welsh Diva getting the better of the stable-companions Fallen Star (left) and Kootenay (hoop)

WENSLEY BLUE (IRE) 3 b.g. Blues Traveller (IRE) 119 – Almasa 83 (Faustus (USA) 118) [2002 50p: p8g 10m⁶ 14.1f 12.1s 12f Oct 7] tall, rather unfurnished gelding: poor maiden: should prove best up to 1m: acts on good to firm going. *P. C. Haslam* **48**

WENSLEYDALE LAD (USA) 2 ch.g. (Jan 20) Is It True (USA) – Miss Tarheel (USA) (Fit To Fight (USA)) [2002 5g 6g f6f f5g* Dec 27] $16,000Y, resold 3,500Y: rangy gelding: second foal: dam unraced daughter of US Grade 1 1¼m winner Mountain Bear, herself half-sister to Efisio: modest performer: won seller at Southwell by ½ length from Diamond Racket: should stay at least 6f: acts on fibresand: blinkered (edgy, bolted to post) second start. *T. D. Barron* **53**

WEQAAR (USA) 2 br.f. (Feb 24) Red Ransom (USA) – Thawakib (IRE) 108 (Sadler's Wells (USA) 132) [2002 7m² 7s⁴ 8.2m³ Oct 1] leggy, close-coupled filly: sixth foal: half-sister to 3 winners, notably 5-y-o Sakhee and smart 7f (at 2 yrs) and 1¼m winner Nasheed (by Riverman): dam, 7f (at 2 yrs) and 1½m (Ribblesdale Stakes) winner, half-sister to top-class middle-distance performer Celestial Storm: best effort in maidens (fairly useful form) when 1¾ lengths second to Almaviva at Newmarket: should be suited by at least 1m: acts on good to firm ground. *J. L. Dunlop* **83**

WE'RE NOT JOKEN 5 b.m. Foxhound (USA) 103 – We're Joken 62 (Statoblest 120) [2002 34: f5s f6g f8g f6g f5g f5g⁵ Apr 26] small mare: maiden: little form in 2002: tried visored. *Mrs N. Macauley* **–**

WE'RE STONYBROKE (IRE) 3 b.g. College Chapel 122 – Mokaite 55 (Komaite (USA)) [2002 f5g⁴ 5.1d² 6.1d³ 5g³ 5m³ 5m* 5g 6m 5g f6g 7s Oct 25] IR 3,000Y: workmanlike gelding: third foal: half-brother to 6f to 1m winner Westfield Star (by Fourstars Allstar): dam 2-y-o 7f winner/winning hurdler: fair performer: won maiden at Musselburgh in June: well held in handicaps after: likely to prove best at 5f/6f: acts on good to soft and good to firm going: blinkered final outing. *T. D. Barron* **75**

WESTCOURT MAGIC 9 b.g. Emarati (USA) 74 – Magic Milly 60 (Simply Great (FR) 122) [2002 –: 5v Jun 12] winning handicapper: has deteriorated considerably: tried blinkered. *M. W. Easterby* **–**

WESTCOURT PEARL 3 b.f. Emarati (USA) 74 – Carolside 108 (Music Maestro 119) [2002 46: 7m Apr 12] poor maiden, lightly raced. *M. W. Easterby* **–**

WESTERN APPLAUSE 3 b.f. Royal Applause 124 – Western Sal 75 (Salse (USA) 128) [2002 76: 6.1g³ Jul 5] leggy filly: fair form at 2 yrs: just modest only outing in 2002. *J. Noseda* **61**

WESTERN BELLE 3 b.f. Magic Ring (IRE) 115 – Western Horizon (USA) 58 (Gone West (USA)) [2002 57: 6.1m 6s 6m 5g 6.1f⁶ 6f f6g f12g f8g Dec 4] modest maiden at 2 yrs: little form in 2002. *Mrs Lucinda Featherstone* **–**

WESTERN BLUEBIRD (IRE) 4 b.g. Bluebird (USA) 125 – Arrastra 79 (Bustino 136) [2002 64, a68: 12f⁴ 15.4m² 16m⁶ f14.8g f12g⁴ f12g⁴ Jun 28] leggy gelding: fair performer on turf, modest on all-weather: probably best at 1½m: acts on good to firm **66** **a51**

going (probably on firm), soft and fibresand: visored once at 3 yrs: sold 9,000 gns in July. *H. Morrison*

WESTERN CHIEF (IRE) 8 b.h. Caerleon (USA) 132 – Go Honey Go (General – Assembly (USA)) [2002 –: 12.1g 11.6d 10m Aug 16] one-time useful handicapper, very lightly raced nowadays: blinkered earlier in career. *D. L. Williams*

WESTERN COMMAND (GER) 6 b.g. Saddlers' Hall (IRE) 126 – Western Friend – (USA) (Gone West (USA)) [2002 –, a70d: f12s⁴ f11s* f11s f9.4g* f9.4g⁴ f12g f11g f9.4g **a70 d** f11g⁵ f9.4g* f8.5g* f8g f8.5g* f8.5g⁶ f11g³ 11g f8.5g⁶ f8.5g f9.4s f12g f8.5g f8.5g f9.4g⁵ f14.8g f14.8g f12g f12g f9.4g Dec 26] quite good-topped gelding: fair handicapper at best: won at Southwell and Wolverhampton (4 times, twice amateur events) in January/ March: lost form after: finds 8.5f a bare minimum, and stays 1½m: acts well on fibresand, very lightly raced on turf nowadays: tried blinkered/visored earlier in career: sometimes races too freely. *Mrs N. Macauley*

WESTERN DIPLOMAT (USA) 2 b. or br.c. (Apr 7) Gone West (USA) – Daba- **93 P** weyaa 118 (Shareef Dancer (USA) 135) [2002 6g* Jul 15] $100,000Y: brother to useful winner around 1m in Britain/UAE Blue Snake, closely related to fairly useful 1999 2-y-o 7f winner Dare Hunter (by Gulch) and half-brother to several winners, including smart 1m/1¼m winner Magellan (by Hansel): dam, second in 1000 Guineas, half-sister to Oaks second Acclimatise: 5/4 favourite, won 6-runner maiden at Ayr impressively by 7 lengths from Takes Two To Tango, travelling strongly, leading over 3f out and soon clear: joined Godolphin: capable of considerably better. *M. Johnston*

WESTERN FLING (USA) 2 b.c. (Mar 3) Gone West (USA) – Silver Fling (USA) **89** 120 (The Minstrel (CAN) 135) [2002 6d* 6g 7.1g³ 7m² 8g³ Sep 21] tall, lengthy colt: has scope: eighth foal: brother to French 1m winner Silver Desert and fairly useful 2000 2-y-o 5f winner Silla, and half-brother to a winner in USA by Kris: dam won Prix de l'Abbaye: fairly useful performer: won maiden at Goodwood in May: creditable placed efforts in minor events at Sandown, Lingfield and Ayr: free-going sort, likely to prove best up to 1m: yet to race on extremes of going. *I. A. Balding*

WESTERN (IRE) 2 ch.g. (Feb 11) Gone West (USA) – Madame Est Sortie (FR) – (Longleat (USA) 109) [2002 6d 7m Jul 28] 230,000F, 275,000Y: close-coupled, attractive gelding: half-brother to several winners, including smart French filly up to 1½m Mousse Glacee (by Mtoto) and useful French winner up to 11f Majoune (by Take Risks), both 1m winners at 2 yrs: dam French 9f (at 2 yrs) to 10.5f winner: little promise in maidens 2 months apart. *Sir Michael Stoute*

WESTERNMOST 4 b.g. Most Welcome 131 – Dakota Girl 55 (Northern State (USA) **54** 91) [2002 59, a63: 16g 12f 12m 16g² Aug 12] sturdy gelding: modest maiden handi-capper: very best form at 1½m: acts on fibresand and any turf going: free-going sort: fair hurdler. *M. Todhunter*

WESTERN RIDGE (FR) 5 b.g. Darshaan 133 – Helvellyn (USA) 83 (Gone West **68** (USA)) [2002 60: f11s⁶ f12g⁵ f12g³ f12g² f12g² f14.8g* 12m³ 12.3f² f12g 12d f12g f12f⁴ f14.8g³ f14.8g² f12g* f14.8g⁴ Dec 31] close-coupled gelding: fair handicapper: won at Wolverhampton in April and December: stays 14.8f: acts on fibresand, firm and good to soft going: has worn cheekpieces: usually held up. *B. J. Llewellyn*

WESTERN VERSE (USA) 3 b.c. Gone West (USA) – Reams of Verse (USA) 121 **92** (Nureyev (USA) 131) [2002 92p: 7m⁴ 7m May 5] small, strong colt: fluent mover: fairly useful performer: won maiden at York early at 2 yrs (found to have had an infection only other start): creditable reappearance in minor event at Newmarket, disappointing there following month: stays 7f: raced only on good to firm going: has worn crossed noseband: sold only 3,000 gns in October. *H. R. A. Cecil*

WESTGATE RUN 5 b.m. Emperor Jones (USA) 119 – Glowing Reference (Reference **63** Point 139) [2002 69: 10m³ 12.3g 12m⁴ 12g³ 12m³ 10m⁶ 9.9m Sep 24] close-coupled, sparely-made mare: modest handicapper: effective at 1¼m/1½m: acts on firm going, possibly not on softer than good: sometimes visored: successful over hurdles in October. *R. A. Fahey*

WEST HILL DANCER 2 b.f. (Jun 4) Man Among Men (IRE) – My Poppet (Midyan – (USA) 124) [2002 5m 7.1m 5.3m f6g Nov 30] first foal: dam, of little account, half-sister to 4-y-o Kyllachy: no sign of ability. *N. J. Hawke*

WESTLANDER (USA) 2 b.c. (Feb 23) Gone West (USA) – Woven Silk (USA) 104 **60** (Danzig (USA)) [2002 6g⁵ 7.2v⁴ 6m⁵ 7m⁴ 8m Sep 19] tall colt: first foal: dam, French 6.5f/7f winner, half-sister to Preakness and Belmont Stakes winner Risen Star: modest maiden: free-going sort, not sure to stay 1m: acts on heavy and good to firm going: sold 8,000 gns. *M. Johnston*

WESTMEAD ETOILE 2 b.f. (Feb 9) Unfuwain (USA) 131 – Glossary (Reference — Point 139) [2002 8d p10g Dec 3] fifth foal: half-sister to 3 winners, including 1m winner Fifth Emerald (by Formidable) and 6-y-o Fifth Edition: dam unraced close relation to smart middle-distance filly Valley of Gold: well held in maidens. *S. C. Williams*

WESTMEAD TANGO 2 b.f. (Apr 13) Pursuit of Love 124 – Tango Teaser (Shareef **59 d** Dancer (USA) 135) [2002 5m⁵ 6g 5d³ 5m 5.1d 5.3m⁴ 6g p5g⁶ p6g Dec 21] second foal: half-sister to a 5f (including at 2 yrs)/6f winner in Italy by Distant Relative: dam, well held both starts, out of smart 7f/1m winner Ever Genial: modest maiden: below form after third at Sandown: possibly best at 5f: yet to race on extremes of going on turf: tried visored. *J. R. Jenkins*

WESTMINSTER CITY (USA) 6 b.g. Alleged (USA) 138 – Promanade Fan (USA) — (Timeless Moment (USA)) [2002 72d: f12s f16s f12g Jan 25] tall gelding: one-time fair performer: little form in 2002: sometimes visored/blinkered. *B. J. Llewellyn*

WESTMORELAND ROAD (USA) 2 b.c. (Feb 14) Diesis 133 – Tia Gigi (USA) **78 p** (Assert 134) [2002 8f² Sep 25] third foal: half-brother to a winner in USA by Farma Way: dam, champion filly/mare in Peru, won 15 races there, including Group 1 1½m events: 4/1 and green, 1¾ lengths second of 4 to Tiber in maiden at Goodwood, keeping on: should stay at least 1¼m: sure to improve. *Mrs A. J. Perrett*

WESTORM (IRE) 11 br.g. Strong Gale 116 – Little Peach (Ragapan 118) [2002 f12g — f12g f12g f16g 14m 12.6m⁴ 11.9m Jul 16] little form. *P. W. Hiatt*

WESTWATER (USA) 3 b.f. Spinning World (USA) 130 – Western Hour (USA) 94 **62** (Gone West (USA)) [2002 7g⁵ Jul 20] first foal: dam, 1¼m winner, out of half-sister to dual Canadian Horse of The Year L'Enjoleur: 8/1, needed race when 4 lengths fifth to Hannon in maiden at Newmarket: will be suited by 1m: sold 3,000 gns in December. *J. H. M. Gosden*

WETHAAB (USA) 5 b.g. Pleasant Colony (USA) – Binntastic (USA) (Lyphard's **45** Wish (FR) 124) [2002 45: f12s f12s⁵ f12s* f11g f12g 16g 12g 13.8g 10.9g⁶ 12m 10.9m f14s⁴ f12s² f14.8g f12f⁵ f11g⁴ f14.8s f16g f12g⁶ f12g⁴ Dec 27] sturdy, well-made gelding: poor mover: poor performer: won seller at Southwell in January: left Mrs A. M. Naughton after eighth start: stays 1¾m: acts on good to firm going and fibresand: tried blinkered/visored and sometimes wears cheekpieces: usually tongue tied: travels strongly, but often finds little. *Miss A. Stokell*

WHALEEF 4 b.g. Darshaan 133 – Wilayif (USA) 75 (Danzig (USA)) [2002 106: p12g² **102** p10g p12g⁶ 9s Oct 26] useful handicapper: ran well in 2002 on first/third starts, leaving E. Dunlop, off nearly 9 months and gelded after latter: should be at least as effective at 1¼m as 1½m: acts on good to firm ground and polytrack: folded tamely second start: has swished tail. *P. R. Webber*

WHASS URRP (IRE) 3 b.g. Desert King (IRE) 129 – Blue Burgee (USA) (Lyphard's — Wish (FR) 124) [2002 66: 7m⁵ 8.1m 8g 6f⁵ 6g⁶ 6m 6g Jul 20] quite good-topped gelding: maiden handicapper: well held in 2002: blinkered last 4 starts. *J. M. Bradley*

WHAT-A-DANCER (IRE) 5 b.g. Dancing Dissident (USA) 119 – Cool Gales 85 **91** (Lord Gayle (USA) 124) [2002 88: 8f 7d⁵ 7g⁴ 7m² 7g² 7g⁵ 7m⁵ 7f² 6m 7m⁵ 7.1m Sep 29] sparely-made gelding: fairly useful handicapper: best form at 7f on good going or firmer: has worn crossed noseband/raced freely: usually held up: finds little: not one to trust implicitly. *G. A. Swinbank*

WHAT A RACKET 3 b.f. Beveled (USA) – Bunny Gee (Last Tycoon 131) [2002 7s⁵ **36** 10m 10.2d p12g 11.6m 14.1m 10.9m Aug 26] third foal: sister to 1½m seller winner Bee Gee and half-sister to Swedish 6.5f/1m winner Tomasean (by Forzando): dam no worthwhile form: blinkered last 3 starts. *D. J. S. ffrench Davis*

WHAT A VIEW 3 b.c. Sadler's Wells (USA) 132 – Ocean View (USA) 109 (Gone **80** West (USA)) [2002 74p: 8m⁶ 9.9g³ 9.9s⁶ Jun 7] quite attractive colt: fairly useful maiden: stays 1¼m: acts on soft and good to firm going: sent to USA. *J. L. Dunlop*

WHENWILLIEMETHARRY 5 b.m. Sabrehill (USA) 120 – William's Bird (USA) — 104 (Master Willie 129) [2002 –: 7s 8f 8.5g 5d Aug 23] one-time fair maiden: no form after 3 yrs. *M. E. Sowersby*

WHERE EAGLES DARE (USA) 5 b.g. Eagle Eyed (USA) 111 – Velveteen (USA) — (Pirateer (USA)) [2002 55: 12.4m May 15] big, useful-looking gelding: very lightly-raced maiden nowadays. *M. E. Sowersby*

WHERE OR WHEN (IRE)   3 ch.c. Danehill Dancer (IRE) 117 – Future Past   **124**
(USA) (Super Concorde (USA) 128) [2002 110: 8m 10.4f^4 12d^6 8g^5 8m* 8m^4 8g*
Sep 28]

For Terry Mills and his team, it was always a case of where or when, never
if. This was a horse in whom they had maximum faith; he was the one that would
win the trainer his first Group 1. 'My son Robert said from day one that this was a
really good horse,' said Mills. 'I've had horses for thirty years and I've never seen
anything like him.' But it took a long time before the extent of this ability was
revealed to everyone else. After victory in the Somerville Tattersall Stakes in
October as a two-year-old, beating a short-priced favourite from Ballydoyle in
Della Francesca, Where Or When contested five top races and found them passing
him by. The Dewhurst, the Two Thousand Guineas, the Dante, the Derby and the St
James's Palace all fell to the sport's two 'superpowers', Ballydoyle and Godolphin,
while Where Or When, representing the millionaire who made his name in haulage
and waste disposal, was among the also rans. Where Or When picked up fourth-
place money in the Dewhurst and the Dante, but was eleventh in the Guineas, a
remote sixth in the Derby and fifth in the St James's Palace. Things did not fall
ideally for Where Or When in any of those first four races as a three-year-old, most
notably perhaps in the Dante and at Ascot when he was set a lot to do both times,
and Mills kept warning that he should not be overlooked. The punters' conclusion
for these top events seemed to be that Mills was kidding himself: Where Or When
started at 50/1 in the Guineas, at 66/1 in both the Derby and St James's Palace.

By the time Mills pitched Where Or When into Group 1 company again,
however, at Ascot in the Queen Elizabeth II Stakes (sponsored by NetJets) in
September, there was a little more reason to have come round to his way of thinking. The pre-race comments from Loretta Lodge stables in Epsom were familiarly
upbeat. 'Where Or When is a Group 1 horse,' said Robert Mills, 'we just want him
to get a fair crack of the whip. He's a proper horse, in great nick and we're going
there quietly confident. We're not worried about anything.' There hadn't been a lot
of quiet immediately after Where Or When's previous start, the Celebration Mile at
Goodwood. He had beaten Flat Spin easily by two and a half lengths in a listed race
over the same course and distance at the Glorious meeting, but that did not prove a
great deal and the Celebration should have been the race for him to set out his
Group 1 credentials. It did not happen, heavily-backed favourite Where Or When
getting boxed in by a manoeuvre from Richard Hughes on Tillerman and able to get
out in time only to look most unlucky as he ran on best of all for a share of fourth
place in the bunched finish. When the positions were unaltered after a stewards
inquiry, Terry Mills left no one in any doubt that he disagreed with the decision.
'Please God, we get a clear passage and we can show everyone how good he really
is,' said Robert Mills before the Queen Elizabeth.

In a five-runner line-up for the Queen Elizabeth, Where Or When was sent
off at 7/1. Ballydoyle and Godolphin were again in opposition and the pick of their
runners were expected to beat him again, with Hawk Wing at 2/1-on and Best of
The Bests at 4/1. Completing the field were Tillerman at 10/1 and Hawk Wing's
pacemaker Sholokhov at 33/1. With Sholokhov pretty much ignored up front, a
tactical race ensued for the quartet that followed him, with Best of The Bests and
Hawk Wing together two furlongs out and Where Or When and Tillerman just
behind them. On this occasion, there was no chance for Tillerman to keep Where
Or When restrained and Where Or When was soon in full cry. Hawk Wing got to
Sholokhov with a furlong to go but Where Or When immediately appeared there as
well and quickly left the favourite for dead, winning by two lengths, with Tillerman
another three lengths back in third. Five different jockeys rode Where Or When
during 2002, with Kevin Darley in the saddle for the Celebration Mile and the
Queen Elizabeth, in the latter repeating his tactic in 2000 on Observatory of coming
wide towards the centre of the track as he challenged in the final furlong. An
ecstatic Terry Mills, who has achieved several of his other most notable successes
at Ascot, winning the Hardwicke Stakes in 1994 with Bobzao, the King's Stand
Stakes in 1999 with Mitcham and in the latest season the Royal Hunt Cup with
Norton, said 'I can die a happy man now, having finally achieved this first Group 1
winner.' Touch wood, retirement will come first. Robert Mills is due to take over
the training licence in June 2003.

Queen Elizabeth II Stakes (sponsored by NetJets), Ascot—the Terry Mills-trained Where Or When quickens clear of Hawk Wing, Tillerman, Sholokhov (rail) and Best of The Bests (virtually obscured)

Where Or When is a superb flag-bearer for any new trainer to inherit. It was reported that a seven-figure bid for him from the United States was turned down before the Queen Elizabeth and he remains in training. A lengthy, workmanlike colt who shows plenty of knee action, Where Or When acts on firm going and good to soft, not having raced on any softer. In terms of form, it is probably best not to get carried away with what he achieved from a below-form Hawk Wing, Tillerman, Sholokhov and Best of The Bests in a muddling Queen Elizabeth, but the style of his victory was hard to fault. His last two starts were his best efforts and he may prove capable of even better. Hawk Wing is the best of the other three-year-olds that remain in training and are effective at a mile, and Where Or When should not have to wait so long as he did in 2002 before recording his next important victory. He ran creditably in the Dante but is almost certainly better at around a mile. The Lockinge is his first main target.

There was never much chance that Where Or When would be suited by a mile and a half. For a start, his sire Danehill Dancer was best at six and seven furlongs. Only three of his sixteen three-year-old winners in Britain in 2002 were successful at beyond a mile, none beyond a mile and a quarter. The best of the rest was smart sprinter Lady Dominatrix. Those three-year-olds are Danehill Dancer's first European crop, and a promising start at stud has seen his fee rise from IR 4,000 guineas to IR £9,000, and on again to €30,000 in 2003. Forty-seven colts and twenty-eight fillies by Danehill Dancer were sold as yearlings in 2000, averaging 13,392 guineas, with Where Or When making 26,000, having already fetched the same sum in Irish punts as a foal. Terry Mills has been a regular customer for the offspring of broodmare Future Past. Following winners in Spain by Mt Livermore and in France by Alzao, her fourth and fifth foals were Just In Time (by Night Shift) and All The Way (by Shirley Heights), who raced for Mills after fetching 58,000 and 45,000 guineas respectively as yearlings. Just In Time was a useful winner over a mile and a quarter—and won over fences in 2002—while All The Way finished fifth in the Derby and fourth in the St Leger before he was sold to Godolphin, for whom he won the mile-and-a-quarter Singapore Derby as a four-year-old. Future Past had a filly and a colt by Night Shift in 2001 and 2002. An eight-year-old half-sister to Where Or When, unraced, failed to find a buyer at 25,000 guineas at the December Sales in 2001 and Future Past has herself been available at even more modest sums and on plenty of occasions. She had fifty-nine starts in all during five seasons in North America and won four, over six furlongs as a three-year-old then three times at around a eight and a half, all of them claimers. Having changed hands for 10,500 dollars in November as a two-year-old, her claiming prices for those victories were 12,500, 10,000, 5,000 and 4,000 dollars. Future Past's dam Afasheen

		Danehill Dancer (IRE) (b 1993)	Danehill (b 1986)	Danzig Razyana
Where Or When (IRE) (ch.c. 1999)			Mira Adonde (b 1986)	Sharpen Up Lettre d'Amour
		Future Past (USA) (ch 1984)	Super Concorde (br 1975)	Bold Reasoning Prime Aboard
			Afasheen (br 1969)	Sheshoon Aimee

failed to win but was placed in two handicaps at a mile and a half in France and is the grandam of 1987 Prix Saint-Alary winner Air de Rien and the US Grade 1 winner The Groom Is Red. Afasheen's dam Aimee is a forebear of many good winners, most notably Blushing Groom who was her grandson. The success Terry Mills has enjoyed with the family has surely not finished yet and there are no prizes for guessing who bought the yearling filly by Night Shift out of Future Past at the Newmarket Sales in 2002. At 120,000 guineas though, she was rather more expensive than the predecessors that have done the stable so proud. *T. G. Mills*

WHINHILL HOUSE   2 ch.g. (Feb 14) Paris House 123 – Darussalam 78 (Tina's Pet   **53**
121) [2002 f5g³ 5m 5m f6s f5g⁶ f5g⁵ Dec 16] 10,500Y: strong gelding: third foal: half-brother to a winner in Holland by Atraf: dam 5f/6f winner: modest maiden: should stay 6f: acts on fibresand: tends to hang/carry head awkwardly. *D. W. Barker*

WHIPPASNAPPER   2 b.g. (Mar 22) Cayman Kai (IRE) 114 – Give Us A Treat (Cree   **76**
Song 99) [2002 5g³ 5m¹ 5g* 5s⁴ 5m 6m 6m⁶ 6.1m 6s 5.2d* f6s f6s p5g⁶ p6g² Dec 30] 3,000Y: quite good-topped gelding: fourth foal: dam, maiden who should have stayed 1m, half-sister to US Grade 3 6.5f winner Imperial Star: fair performer: won maiden at

Windsor in April and nursery at Yarmouth in October: good second in nursery at Lingfield final start: should stay 7f: acts on polytrack and soft going, probably on good to firm: unseated rider before start second/fourth outings: tends to wander: none too consistent. *J. R. Best*

WHISPERING RAIN 3 ch.c. Young Ern 120 – Bay Meadows Star (Sharpo 132) – [2002 –: p10g Jan 5] well beaten in claimers/maiden. *A. G. Newcombe*

WHIST DRIVE 2 ch.g. (May 11) First Trump 118 – Fine Quill (Unfuwain (USA) – 131) [2002 7d 8v Nov 8] 4,000Y: big, lengthy gelding: second foal: dam, ran once, half-sister to smart performer up to 2m Harbour Dues: soundly beaten in maidens: gelded after. *J. L. Dunlop*

WHISTLER 5 ch.g. Selkirk (USA) 129 – French Gift 99 (Cadeaux Genereux 131) **86** [2002 90: 5f 6d 5.7d² 5.1d² 5.1d* 5g 5m² 5d³ 5.5m³ 5m⁶ 5.2f⁵ 5f³ 5.1f⁵ 5m 5f 5g⁴ 5g 5v⁶ Nov 8] angular, workmanlike gelding: has a quick action: fairly useful handicapper: won at Nottingham in June: has won at 6f, best form at 5f: acts on any going: tried blinkered: sometimes slowly away/finds little: tends to hang. *J. M. Bradley*

WHISTLING DIXIE (IRE) 6 ch.g. Forest Wind (USA) 111 – Camden's Gift (Cam- **74** den Town 125) [2002 70: 14g² 13.1g⁶ 13v* 16.2g³ 14.1m 14.1d Oct 18] workmanlike gelding: fair handicapper: won at Hamilton in June: creditable efforts after: effective at 1¾m/2m: acts on any turf going, probably on fibresand: blinkered (below form) 3 times: usually held up. *Mrs M. Reveley*

WHITBARROW (IRE) 3 b.g. Royal Abjar (USA) 121 – Danccini (IRE) 78 (Dancing **108** Dissident (USA) 119) [2002 103: 6d* 6g⁶ 5g⁶ 6d³ 5m 5m 7f 7m Oct 19] strong, good sort: useful performer: won listed rated stakes at Haydock in May: creditable efforts after in King George Stakes at Goodwood (2½ lengths sixth to Agnetha) and valuable conditions event at Ascot (third to Feet So Fast) on third/fourth starts: raced mostly at 5f/6f, probably effective at easy 7f: acts on firm and good to soft ground: usually blinkered, though has won without (including at Haydock): found little second outing: races up with pace. *B. R. Millman*

WHITE CLIFFS 3 ch.g. Bluebird (USA) 125 – Preening 62 (Persian Bold 123) [2002 **77** 71: 6f³ 6m* 6f 6s⁵ p6g⁵ 7g⁵ 7m 7d³ 7s 7.1g² 7g⁴ 7d Oct 18] strong gelding: fair handicapper: won at Salisbury in May: stays 7f: acts on firm going, soft and polytrack: visored final outing: usually tongue tied: has hung left: unseated and ran loose before start/given early reminders second 2-y-o outing: sold 10,000 gns, joined C. Wroe in UAE. *W. J. Haggas*

WHITE DOVE (FR) 4 b.f. Beaudelaire (USA) 125 – Hermine And Pearls (FR) – (Shirley Heights 130) [2002 49: 10.9g 16.2m Sep 16] maiden handicapper. *R. Dickin*

WHITE EMIR 9 b.g. Emarati (USA) 74 – White African (Carwhite 127) [2002 77: **74** 7m 7d⁴ 7.1v 7m³ 7m 7.1g³ 7m 8m⁶ 8m 7.1g p8g³ Oct 9] good-quartered gelding: fair performer: stays 1m: acts on any turf going, probably on polytrack: won in blinkers earlier in career: swerved right and rider lost irons ninth start: sometimes wanders, and best with strong handling/waiting tactics. *L. G. Cottrell*

WHITE LEDGER (IRE) 3 ch.g. Ali-Royal (IRE) 127 – Boranwood (IRE) (Exhib- **71** itioner 111) [2002 64: p5g² p6g f5g² f6g³ 5.3m³ 5.3d² f5g* 5d⁵ 5m 5.3g 5m⁶ 5m* 5f Oct **a74** 3] useful-looking gelding: fair handicapper: won at Wolverhampton in June and Sandown in September: effective at 5f/6f: acts on all-weather, firm and good to soft going: effective visored or not: sold 12,000 gns. *T. G. Mills*

WHITE PARK BAY (IRE) 2 b.f. (Jan 31) Blues Traveller (IRE) 119 – Valiant **53** Friend (USA) (Shahrastani (USA) 135) [2002 6f⁴ Jun 24] IR 8,000F: quite good-topped filly: fifth foal: half-sister to useful 6f (at 2 yrs) to 11.6f winner King Darius (by Persian Bold): dam ran twice in France: 20/1 and green, 9¼ lengths fourth of 7 to Bella Bianca in maiden at Pontefract. *J. J. Quinn*

WHITE PLAINS (IRE) 9 b.g. Nordico (USA) – Flying Diva 100 (Chief Singer 131) – [2002 –, a84: f11s⁶ p10g p10g f12g* f12g⁴ f12g² p12g* f11g³ p12g² f14.8g² f11g⁴ f12g⁶ Dec 27] good-bodied gelding: fair performer: won claimers at **a69** Southwell in February and Lingfield in March: stays 14.8f: acts on all-weather: usually tongue tied: sometimes slowly away/finds little. *T. D. Barron*

WHITE RABBIT 3 b.f. Zilzal (USA) 137 – Trick (IRE) 76 (Shirley Heights 130) **99** [2002 91: 9g⁵ 8f⁴ 7m² 8.1d 8m Jun 22] useful-looking filly: useful performer: good second in handicap at York: rather disappointing after: stays 1m: yet to race on heavy going, probably acts on any other: has worn crossed noseband: usually blanketed for stall entry: usually bandaged off-hind/hind joints: has started slowly. *T. D. Easterby*

WHITE STAR LADY 4 ch.f. So Factual (USA) 120 – Cottonwood 80 (Teenoso   – §
(USA) 135) [2002 48§: 8.5m f9.4g 7m 8g 6f f8.5g Jul 26] sparely-made filly: no form in
2002: tried visored: temperamental. *J. R. Weymes*

WHITEWATER BOY 6 b.g. Emarati (USA) 74 – Chacewater 61 (Electric 126)   **89**
[2002 10s³ 10.2d* 12g 10s Oct 26] big, useful-looking gelding: fairly useful handicapper:
better than ever after 3-year break, winning at Bath in July: best around 1¼m: seems to
act on any going: has given trouble at start. *Mrs A. J. Bowlby*

WHITLEY GRANGE BOY 9 b.g. Hubbly Bubbly (USA) – Choir (High Top 131)   –
[2002 f16g Feb 28] tall, sparely-made gelding: fair handicapper in 1999: well held only
Flat run since. *J. L. Eyre*

WHITTLE WARRIOR 2 b.g. (Mar 28) Averti (IRE) 117 – Polish Descent (IRE)   **73**
(Danehill (USA) 126) [2002 5m² 5f⁵ f5g⁵ 6d 5m 7.5g² 8m* 8g Sep 20] 18,000F, 5,000Y:
leggy gelding: third living foal: half-brother to 3-y-o Foronlymo and a 2-y-o 6f/7f winner
in Italy by Cyrano de Bergerac: dam unraced: fair performer: won nursery at Ripon in
August: free-going sort, but stays 1m: acts on good to firm and good to soft going, below
form on fibresand: blinkered (well beaten) fifth start: carries head high: best efforts when
making running: none too consistent. *C. W. Fairhurst*

WHIZZ KID 8 b.m. Puissance 110 – Panienka (POL) 70 (Dom Racine (FR) 121) **62 §**
[2002 70, a–: f5g 5.1d³ 5.3f 5m 6f 5.1g* 5m 5.7g⁶ 5g 5d³ 5s⁶ 5.3g⁶ 5v 5.5f⁶ 5d 5.1m f6g   **a– §**
f5f f5g Dec 14] tall mare: modest handicapper: won at Bath (for second year running) in
April: effective at 5f/easy 6f: has form on firm ground/fibresand, probably best on good
or softer: tried blinkered: has worn cheekpieces: has been reluctant to post/slowly away:
held up: unreliable. *J. M. Bradley*

WHOATEALLTHEPIES (IRE) 2 b.f. (Feb 18) Pennekamp (USA) 130 – Stargard   **35**
(Polish Precedent (USA) 131) [2002 f5g³ f5g⁵ 5m 7f Jun 11] IR 2,000Y: leggy filly: first
foal: dam, French maiden, half-sister to 5-y-o Give Notice: poor form in sellers: dead.
A. Berry

WHO GOES THERE 6 ch.m. Wolfhound (USA) 126 – Challanging 95 (Mill Reef **56 d**
(USA) 141) [2002 60: p7g p7g 8.2m³ 8.3d 10f 8.3m 7g 7.1g 8.5m Aug 16] smallish,
good-topped mare: modest performer: well held after third start: stays 1m: acts on firm
and soft going, no form on all-weather: sometimes slowly away/carries head awkwardly.
T. M. Jones

WHY ALYS 3 b.f. Lugana Beach 116 – Classic Times 82 (Dominion 123) [2002 52:   –
5.1m 5.5f 5.1m Aug 6] modest performer at 2 yrs: behind in handicaps in 2002: effective
blinkered, tried visored. *G. B. Balding*

WICKED UNCLE 3 b.g. Distant Relative 128 – The Kings Daughter 79 (Indian King **87**
(USA) 128) [2002 81: 6m⁵ 6m 5m* 5g 5m⁵ 6m⁶ 5.2m⁴ 5.1f² 5m⁶ 5.1f³ 5f 6f Oct 12]
smallish, sturdy gelding: impresses in appearance: fairly useful performer: won handicap
at Windsor in May: mostly good efforts after: probably ideally suited by 5f: acts on firm
going: visored last 5 starts: sold 25,000 gns. *J. A. R. Toller*

WIGGY SMITH 3 ch.g. Master Willie 129 – Monsoon 66 (Royal Palace 131) [2002   **80**
8.1f 10m³ p10g⁶ 8.1d² 8.1g² 8f⁶ 8.3d* 8s⁵ Oct 28] angular gelding: brother to fairly useful
9f winner Willy Willy who stayed 1¼m: dam winning staying hurdler/chaser: fairly
useful performer: won maiden at Windsor in October: should be suited by 1¼m: acts on
soft and firm going: consistent. *H. Candy*

WIGMAN LADY (IRE) 5 b.m. Tenby 125 – Height of Elegance 82 (Shirley Heights –
130) [2002 53d: f16s f12g Jan 24] sparely-made mare: modest maiden at best: has
deteriorated: blinkered final outing. *T. J. Etherington*

WIGMO PRINCESS 3 ch.f. Factual (USA) 108 – Queen of Shannon (IRE) 76 (Nor- **56**
dico (USA)) [2002 54, a51: p7g⁵ p8g⁶ f8g⁴ f8g² f9.4g³ 7m* 7m 8.2g 10m⁶ 10g 10d Oct   **a45**
28] modest performer on turf, poor on all-weather: won selling handicap at Folkestone in
April: below form after: stays 7f: acts on all-weather, good to firm and good to soft going:
often slowly away. *A. W. Carroll*

WILD COUGAR (USA) 3 b.c. Storm Cat (USA) – Fast Nellie (USA) (Ack Ack   **57**
(USA)) [2002 8m 7f⁴ 8f⁴ 6d 6s⁴ Jun 19] smallish, well-made colt: half-brother to several
winners, including useful Irish 1996 2-y-o sprinter Raphane (by Rahy) and French 9f
winner Where's Dave (by Eagle Eyed): dam unraced sister to US Grade 1 8.5f winner
Caline: modest maiden handicapper: visored (raced freely, ran creditably) final start: has
got worked up in stall/been slowly away: sold 7,500 gns. *M. Johnston*

WILDERBROOK LAHRI   3 b.g. Lahib (USA) 129 – Wilsonic 78 (Damister (USA)   –
123) [2002 62: 8.2d 9.9d Aug 14] modest maiden at 2 yrs: behind in handicaps in 2002,
racing freely: should stay at least 1m. *Mrs J. R. Ramsden*

WILD FLING   3 b.c. Entrepreneur 123 – Wild Pavane (Dancing Brave (USA) 140)   **92**
[2002 8m 8g* 8g* 8.1s 8m 10g⁴ 10.3m⁴ 9.9m Aug 2] sturdy, lengthy colt: sixth foal:
half-brother to several winners, including useful 7f (at 2 yrs) to 9f winner Apache Star
(by Arazi) and 1¼m winner Stately Dancer (by Be My Guest): dam unraced half-sister to
dam of Coronation Stakes winner Rebecca Sharp: fairly useful performer: won private
race at Newmarket and maiden at Goodwood, both in May: stayed 1¼m: best efforts on
good/good to firm going: blinkered (ran creditably) penultimate start: hung left fifth
outing: dead. *J. H. M. Gosden*

WILD OVATION   2 b.c. (Mar 16) Royal Applause 124 – Daring Ditty (Daring March   **77**
116) [2002 6m⁵ 6m⁶ Sep 20] leggy colt: looked weak at 2 yrs: half-brother to 3 winners,
notably sprinters Bold Edge (very smart) and Brave Edge (useful), both by Beveled: dam
twice-raced daughter of useful sprinter Dawn Ditty: fair form in maidens at Newmarket
and Newbury (disputed early lead when sixth to Marching Band): not sure to stay 7f.
R. Hannon

WILD TIMES   6 b.g. Emarati (USA) 74 – Pink Pumpkin 52 (Tickled Pink 114) [2002   –
p10g 6g May 5] no sign of ability. *J. C. Fox*

WILD WATER (FR)   4 b.g. Salse (USA) 128 – Dashing Water 87 (Dashing Blade   **46**
117) [2002 –: 7g³ 10d 11.6s 8m f9.4g⁶ 14.1m⁴ 15.8m Aug 6] tall gelding: poor maiden:
left I. Balding after fourth outing: seems to stay 1¾m (pulled up reportedly lame over
2m): tried blinkered, visored last 2 outings. *C. N. Kellett*

WILEMMGEO   5 b.m. Emarati (USA) 74 – Floral Spark 69 (Forzando 122) [2002   **38 §**
61§, a–§: f8g f9.4g f8.5g f12g 10g 9.9m 9.9d 10.1m Aug 7] sturdy mare: poor nowadays:
effective at 7.6f to 1¼m: acts on heavy going, good to firm and fibresand: effective
visored or not, blinkered once: has been reluctant/unruly/early to post/slowly away. *Mrs
N. Macauley*

WILFRAM   5 b.g. Fraam 114 – Ming Blue 52 (Primo Dominie 121) [2002 68, a53:   **61 §**
f8.5g⁴ f7g⁵ f8.5g³ 8v 8m⁴ 8.5g 8g May 20] modest handicapper on turf, poor on   **a46 §**
all-weather: seems best at 1m/easy 1¼m: acts on all-weather, firm and good to soft
ground: blinkered nowadays: sometimes slowly away/runs in snatches: inconsistent.
J. M. Bradley

WILFUL   2 ch.c. (Mar 19) Bering 136 – Prickwillow (USA) 75 (Nureyev (USA) 131)   **100 p**
[2002 6g² 7g* 7g³ Aug 24] tall, useful-looking colt: third foal: dam, 1¼m winner,
daughter of smart performer around 1¼m Braiswick from very good family: useful form:
won 4-runner minor event at Doncaster in July by head from Devious Boy, edging left:
½-length third to Van Nistelrooy in Futurity Stakes at the Curragh, leading from around
halfway until near finish: will probably stay 1m: joined Godolphin: has scope to make a
better 3-y-o. *M. Johnston*

WILKIE   3 br.g. Mistertopogigo (IRE) 118 – Titian Girl (Faustus (USA) 118) [2002   –
8.2m 10s Oct 23] second foal: dam, of little account on Flat, successful over hurdles:
tailed off in 2 maidens: withdrawn after unseating/bolting on intended debut. *Miss
L. C. Siddall*

WILLHECONQUERTOO   2 ch.g. (Mar 21) Primo Dominie 121 – Sure Care 62   **83**
(Caerleon (USA) 132) [2002 5g⁵ 5m⁴ 5g² 5g² p5g⁴ 5.3g* 5m⁵ 5m⁴ p6g² 6m 5m² 5.7f 6.1f³
6m⁶ 6m⁴ 6m Oct 3] 1,600Y: sturdy gelding: third foal: half-brother to 4-y-o Deceitful:
dam 13f winner: fairly useful performer: won maiden at Brighton in June: in frame in
minor events/nursery after: stays 6f: acts on polytrack, raced only on good going or firmer
on turf: tongue tied last 4 starts: usually races prominently: none too consistent. *Andrew
Reid*

WILLHEWIZ   2 b.c. (Feb 4) Wizard King 122 – Leave It To Lib 66 (Tender King 123)   **97**
[2002 5g² f5g* 5.1f³ 6.1f* 5g* 6m 5m 6s⁶ Oct 26] 850F, 1,400Y: good-topped colt:
second foal: dam 7f/1m winner: useful performer: won maiden at Southwell in April
and minor events at Nottingham in May and Beverley (beat Sanbenito by 2½ lengths,
drifted left) in June: off 4 months (having reportedly had minor joint problem), below
form last 3 starts: likely to prove best at 5f/easy 6f: acts on firm going and fibresand: races
prominently. *C. A. Dwyer*

WILLIAM'S WELL   8 ch.g. Superpower 113 – Catherines Well 99 (Junius (USA)   **69**
124) [2002 74: 5f 5g⁵ 6f⁴ 5m⁵ 5m 5m 5m³ 6g⁵ 7.5m Sep 24] useful-looking gelding: fair

handicapper: effective at 5f/6f: acts on firm and soft ground: wears blinkers: consistent. *M. W. Easterby*

WILLING 6 b.g. Yaheeb (USA) 95§ – Droskin VII (Damsire Unregistered) [2002 –: 9m 15.8f 14.1m 17.1f Oct 7] big, strong gelding: no form. *T. J. Etherington* –

WILLOUGHBY'S BOY (IRE) 5 b.g. Night Shift (USA) – Andbell (Trojan Fen 118) [2002 94d: 8.3g 7f² 7m 7.1d 7m⁶ 8m⁴ 7g 7g⁴ 8.5g p10g* Dec 11] smallish, sturdy gelding: usually takes the eye: fair handicapper nowadays: won at Lingfield in December: stays easy 1¼m: acts on polytrack, firm and good to soft going: tried blinkered: sometimes tongue tied: inconsistent. *B. Hanbury* **77 §**

WILLOW WARBLER (IRE) 2 b.f. (Feb 20) Entrepreneur 123 – Miss Willow Bend (USA) (Willow Hour (USA)) [2002 p7g 8d Oct 18] 15,000Y: half-sister to several winners, including 3-y-o Groovy Willow and useful 5f/6f winner (including at 2 yrs) Willow Dale (by Danehill): dam winning sprinter in USA: well held in maidens: sold 3,500 gns. *C. F. Wall* –

WILLOW WONDER 3 ch.f. Greensmith 121 – Walnut Way (Gambling Debt 98) [2002 10s p12g Jun 1] sixth foal: dam fairly useful chaser: slowly away and tailed off both starts, hanging throughout when virtually pulled up in latter. *M. R. Ewer-Hoad* –

WILOM (GER) 4 ch.g. Lomitas 129 – Whispering Willows (Mansingh (USA) 120) [2002 p10g f8g p7g p10g 8.3g 10m 8g⁵ 8.1g* 8.5m p10g³ 10g³ p13g Dec 28] modest performer: successful in maiden at Frankfurt in 2001 when trained by D. Fechner in Germany: won selling handicap at Warwick in July: stays 10.5f: acts on heavy going and polytrack: reportedly broke blood vessel final outing. *M. R. Ewer-Hoad* **53**

WILSON BLUEBOTTLE (IRE) 3 ch.g. Priolo (USA) 127 – Mauras Pride (IRE) (Cadeaux Genereux 131) [2002 60: 5m 5s 9.9d 7m Jul 29] smallish, strong, lengthy gelding: modest maiden at 2 yrs: well held in handicaps in 2002: has hung left. *M. W. Easterby* –

WILSON BLYTH 4 b.g. Puissance 110 – Pearls (Mon Tresor 113) [2002 78: 5s 6s 5g 6f 5g f5g f5g 5.9d 6f Jul 17] tall, sparely-made gelding: fair performer at 3 yrs: little form in 2002: sometimes blinkered/visored: sent to Spain. *A. Berry* –

WIMPLE (USA) 2 b.f. (Feb 10) Kingmambo (USA) 125 – Tunicle (USA) (Dixieland Band (USA)) [2002 6m 6g⁴ 5m 6d⁵ 5s* 5.2f² 6m⁴ 6m* 6f⁵ Oct 4] $50,000Y: smallish, sturdy filly: first foal: dam, 5.5f (at 2 yrs) to 9f winner in USA, half-sister to US Grade 1 9f runner-up Baron de Vaux: useful performer: won maiden at Leicester in July and minor event at Salisbury (beat Ripple Effect by 2½ lengths) in September: creditable efforts in listed event at Newbury (neck second to Speed Cop) and Lowther Stakes at York (3 lengths fourth to Russian Rhythm) in between: below-form fifth of 6 to Airwave in Cheveley Park Stakes at Newmarket final start: will probably stay 1m: yet to race on heavy ground, probably acts on any other: often races prominently. *C. E. Brittain* **101**

WIN ALOT 4 b.g. Aragon 118 – Having Fun (Hard Fought 125) [2002 58, a48: f9.4g f9.4g f14.8s⁴ 12m May 24] sturdy gelding: modest maiden at 3 yrs: little form in 2002, leaving D. Burchell after second start. *S. R. Bowring* –

WINCHCOMBE 2 b.f. (Feb 7) Danehill (USA) 126 – Birdlip (USA) (Sanglamore (USA) 126) [2002 6f Sep 17] third foal: half-sister to fairly useful 2001 2-y-o 6f winner Foxcote (by Lycius): dam unraced half-sister to high-class miler Distant View: 9/2, well held in maiden at Salisbury, not knocked about: probably capable of better. *R. Charlton* **– p**

WINDCHILL 4 ch.f. Handsome Sailor 125 – Baroness Gymcrak 62§ (Pharly (FR) 130) [2002 53: 7g Jul 11] small, lengthy filly: modest performer at 3 yrs: well held only run in 2002. *T. D. Easterby* –

WIND CHIME (IRE) 5 ch.h. Arazi (USA) 135 – Shamisen 86 (Diesis 133) [2002 70, a57: p8g⁶ 8.1m⁴ 8g⁴ 7m 8f 7m² 8m* 7f 8f f8.5g Dec 26] smallish horse: fair handicapper on turf, modest on all-weather: won at Salisbury in September (despite edging left): effective at 7f/1m: acts on firm going, good to soft and fibresand (probably on polytrack). *A. G. Newcombe* **70 a51**

WINDERMERE (IRE) 3 b.c. Lear Fan (USA) 130 – Madame L'Enjoleur (USA) (L'Enjoleur (CAN)) [2002 10m 10.5d² 10.2d* 12m 13.3m* 13.9m⁵ 13.3f* 15g² Oct 5] 110,000Y: tall, lengthy, good sort: fourth living foal: half-brother to winner in USA by St Jovite: dam, 6f to 8.5f (minor stakes) winner in USA and third in Grade 1 8.5f events, half-sister to US class performers Faunnore (stayed 1¼m) and Labeeb (best at 1m/9f), both by Lear Fan: smart performer: won maiden at Bath in May and handicaps at Newbury in August and September (beat Typhoon Tilly ½ length in Farewell To Graham **112**

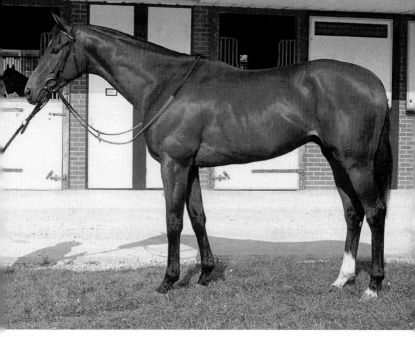

Mr A. E. Oppenheimer's "Windermere"

Kendrick Autumn Cup): improved further when neck second to Morozov in Prix Hubert de Chaudenay at Longchamp final outing, making running: will stay 2m: winner on good to soft, best form on good going or firmer (acts on firm). *J. H. M. Gosden*

WINDSHIFT (IRE) 6 b.g. Forest Wind (USA) 111 – Beautyofthepeace (IRE) (Exactly Sharp (USA) 121) [2002 55§, a77§: f11g Dec 17] leggy, workmanlike gelding: fair handicapper at 5 yrs on his day: well beaten only start in 2002. *S. R. Bowring* – §

WINDY BREEZE (IRE) 2 b.f. (Mar 23) Mujadil (USA) 119 – Bosa (Kris 135) [2002 p5g p6g Dec 21] IR 5,000F, 8,000Y: fifth foal: half-sister to French 1¼m/1½m winner Jan's Pal (by Old Vic): dam unraced half-sister to dam of 2-y-o Soviet Song: well held in minor event/seller at Lingfield. *M. R. Channon* –

WINDY BRITAIN 3 b.f. Mark of Esteem (IRE) 137 – For My Love (Kahyasi 130) [2002 7.5d⁵ p10g³ f9.4f² f9.4g² Dec 16] second foal: half-sister to Italian 9f winner Frottola (by Muhtarram): dam unraced half-sister to useful performers Be Fresh (sprinter) and How Long (up to 1m): probably flattered when fifth in minor event at Milan on debut in November (appeared to run to 79): just modest form on all-weather in Britain after: stays 1¼m. *L. M. Cumani* 59 +

WINGALONG (IRE) 3 ch.f. Flying Spur (AUS) – Dutch Queen (Ahonoora 122) [2002 –: 7d 6f 9.9m Apr 25] rather leggy, unfurnished filly: seems of little account. *T. D. Easterby* –

WING COMMANDER 3 b.g. Royal Applause 124 – Southern Psychic (USA) (Alwasmi (USA) 115) [2002 97p: 9g² 9m⁶ 8g⁴ 8m⁴ 8m Aug 2] strong, lengthy gelding: useful performer: good close fourth to Pentecost in Britannia Handicap at Royal Ascot penultimate start, bumped at start and running on well: bandaged near-hind, poorly drawn when mid-division in William Hill Mile (Handicap) at Goodwood, only subsequent run: gelded after: stays 9f: raced only on good going or firmer: visored (found little) third start. *M. L. W. Bell* 102

WINGED ANGEL   5 ch.g. Prince Sabo 123 – Silky Heights (IRE) 67 (Head For   **48**
Heights 125) [2002 53: f12s* f12s f12g f12g Feb 28] poor handicapper: won at Southwell
in January: stays 1½m: acts on firm going and fibresand: tried visored: joined L. Lungo,
and successful twice over hurdles in June. *Miss J. A. Camacho*

WINGS TO SOAR (USA)   2 b.f. (Mar 6) Woodman (USA) 126 – Only Royale (IRE)   **63 p**
121 (Caerleon (USA) 132) [2002 7m Aug 29] $62,000Y: fourth foal: dam 1m to 1½m
(including dual Yorkshire Oaks) winner: weak 12/1-shot, 10 lengths tenth of 13 to
Wondrous Story in maiden at Salisbury, racing freely and not knocked about: should do
better. *R. Hannon*

WING WEST   2 ch.c. (Mar 3) The West (USA) 107 – Ballet On Ice (FR) 46 (Fijar   **–**
Tango (FR) 127) [2002 p6g Dec 28] second foal: dam lightly-raced maiden: very slowly
away and tailed off in maiden at Lingfield. *J. Gallagher*

WINISK RIVER (IRE)   2 b.c. (Jan 18) Barathea (IRE) 127 – Brisighella (IRE) (Al   **92 p**
Hareb (USA) 123) [2002 6f² 6g* Jun 15] useful-looking colt: fourth foal: half-brother to
2000 2-y-o 6f winner Grove Dancer (by Reprimand): dam Italian 5f (at 2 yrs) to 1m
winner: head second in maiden at Newmarket prior to justifying favouritism in similar
contest at York by length from Cumbrian Venture: may prove best at 5f/6f: wears crossed
noseband: sold privately, and joined Godolphin, but met with minor injury: useful
prospect, assuming all is well. *M. H. Tompkins*

WINNING NOTE (IRE)   2 b.f. (Jan 13) Victory Note (USA) 120 – Ruby Affair   **64**
(IRE) 68 (Night Shift (USA)) [2002 6d⁵ 6g 7g⁶ 6m 7g Oct 4] 30,000Y: first foal: dam,
second at 7f, half-sister to 2000 Guineas winner Island Sands: modest maiden: best effort
on debut: should stay at least 7f. *J. L. Dunlop*

WINNING PLEASURE (IRE)   4 b.g. Ashkalani (IRE) 128 – Karamana (Habitat   **–**
134) [2002 73, a84: f6s² f6s³ f6g² f6f⁵ f6g³ f6g⁵ Dec 28] leggy, sparely-made gelding: **a88**
fairly useful handicapper on all-weather in 2002: probably best at 6f: acts on fibresand,
best runs on turf on good/good to firm ground: visored/blinkered nowadays: sometimes
carries head high. *J. Balding*

WINNING VENTURE   5 b.g. Owington 123 – Push A Button (Bold Lad (IRE) 133)   **101**
[2002 105: 7d 7.6f 6s⁵ Oct 25] lengthy, good-topped gelding: unimpressive mover: useful
performer: only form in handicaps in 2002 when fifth at Newbury: effective at 6f to 1m:
yet to race on heavy going, acts on any other: blinkered once: usually tongue tied before
2002: sometimes slowly away: tends to take strong hold (has worn crossed noseband):
has wandered/flashed tail: sold 22,000 gns. *R. Charlton*

WINSABONUS   2 b.g. (May 20) Defacto (USA) – Heart Broken 78 (Bustino 136)   **–**
[2002 6.1d 6f 6m Jul 4] smallish, good-topped gelding: fifth foal: dam 6f/7f winner: well
held in maidens/claimer. *J. R. Norton*

WINTER DOLPHIN (IRE)   4 b.f. Dolphin Street (FR) 125 – Winter Tern (USA)   **46**
(Arctic Tern (USA) 126) [2002 39: 7g 8g 8.3g 10.1f 10.2g³ 10.9m⁴ 11.9g 14.1d Oct 30]
poor performer: stays 1¼m: acts on fibresand, soft and good to firm ground: tried tongue
tied: sometimes slowly away: none too consistent. *I. A. Wood*

WINTER GARDEN   8 ch.g. Old Vic 136 – Winter Queen 60 (Welsh Pageant 132)   **–**
[2002 16m⁵ Sep 29] strong, lengthy gelding: useful performer for L. Cumani on Flat in
1998: useful hurdler in Ireland for A. Moore, though lost form in 2002, and well held in
handicap on British/Flat return. *Miss Lucinda V. Russell*

WINTERTIDE   6 b.g. Mtoto 134 – Winter Queen 60 (Welsh Pageant 132) [2002 79:   **84**
12f⁴ 11.9m 16m 20m 16.1g⁶ 12.1d² Jul 5] quite good-topped gelding: useful bumper
performer: fairly useful maiden handicapper on Flat: effective at 1½m and stays 2½m:
acts on fibresand, good to firm and good to soft going: slowly away fourth start/fractious
in stall final one: joined C. Mann in December. *R. A. Fahey*

WINTHORPE (IRE)   2 b.g. (Apr 9) Tagula (IRE) 116 – Zazu 58 (Cure The Blues   **69**
(USA)) [2002 5g⁵ 5g⁶ 5g⁵ f6s³ Nov 2] IR 3,000Y, 7,000 2-y-o: leggy, unfurnished
gelding: half-brother to several winners, including fairly useful Irish 7f (at 2 yrs) to 1¾m
winner Soviet Blues (by Soviet Lad): dam, ran 3 times at 3 yrs, out of half-sister to Derby
second Cavo Doro: fair form in maidens: edged left when third at Wolverhampton:
effective at 5f/6f: free to post third start. *J. J. Quinn*

WINTZIG   5 b.m. Piccolo 121 – Wrangbrook (Shirley Heights 130) [2002 –. f8.5g³   **50**
f9.4g Jan 18] angular mare: modest performer nowadays: said to have finished lame final
start. *J. M. Bradley*

WISEGUY (IRE) 3 b.g. Darshaan 133 – Bibliotheque (USA) 79 (Woodman (USA) **90**
126) [2002 10f⁴ 12.1d² 10d² 12.3m⁵ p13g⁶ Oct 4] lengthy, good-topped gelding: first
foal: dam, 1m winner, out of half-sister to very smart 6f to 1m performer Lycius: fairly
useful maiden handicapper: stays 1½m: well held on polytrack debut. *Sir Michael Stoute*

WISE PETORIUS (IRE) 2 b.g. (Feb 28) Petorius 117 – Wise Wish (Baragoi 115) **71 §**
[2002 5d 5s⁴ 6g5 6g 5m³ 6g 7.5d 7m 5m³ 6g² 6g⁵ 5g 7.9m 7m 6f⁶ Sep 21] IR 5,000F,
6,000 2-y-o: smallish gelding: half-brother to winners in Italy by Elbio and Woods of
Windsor: dam Irish 8.5f winner: fair maiden: second at Leicester: probably stays 7f: acts
on good to firm going: gelded after final start. *M. C. Chapman*

WISE TALE 3 b.g. Nashwan (USA) 135 – Wilayif (USA) 75 (Danzig (USA)) [2002 **78**
f8g p10g⁴ 12f² 11.1s⁴ 12s⁵ p12g³ 11.9d⁶ f12s⁵ 14f⁴ 13.9f 14.1d p12g Dec 14] well-made
gelding: sixth foal: brother to useful 1¾m winner Wilawander and half-brother to 3
winners, including smart French 1999 2-y-o winner around 5f Morning Pride (by
Machiavellian): dam, 7f winner, from top-class North American family of Swain (by
Nashwan): fair maiden handicapper: left M. Johnston 16,000 gns after seventh start:
virtually pulled up tenth outing: may prove best short of 1¾m: acts on polytrack, best turf
efforts on firm going: tried visored: none too consistent. *P. D. Niven*

WITCH'S BREW 5 b.m. Simply Great (FR) 122 – New Broom (IRE) (Brush Aside **–**
(USA) 125) [2002 14.1d 13.8d Nov 5] unfurnished mare: maiden, lightly raced.
T. D. Easterby

WITHCOTE WELCOME 7 gr.g. Norton Challenger 111 – Welcoming Arms 65 **–**
(Free State 125) [2002 9m Sep 5] first foal: dam 1¼m and 17f winner: 50/1, tailed off in
maiden at Redcar. *B. Ellison*

WITHIN THE LAW 4 b.f. Contract Law (USA) 108 – Fyas 52 (Sayf El Arab (USA) **–**
127) [2002 8v 5m Apr 18] no sign of ability. *W. Storey*

WITHOUT WORDS 4 ch.f. Lion Cavern (USA) 117 – Sans Escale (USA) (Diesis **55**
133) [2002 71d: p7g 8.3d 7f 8m³ f9.4f³ 9.9m⁵ f8.5g⁶ 8m Oct 2] good-topped filly: modest **a49**
maiden handicapper: barely stays 1¼m: acts on good to firm and good to soft going,
probably on polytrack: tried blinkered: reportedly bled from nose on reappearance: has
been edgy: has raced freely/found little. *W. M. Brisbourne*

WITH PANACHE 4 b.g. Mtoto 134 – Panache Arabelle (Nashwan (USA) 135) **–**
[2002 74: 16g 11.1s 9.2g 9m⁵ Jun 1] leggy gelding: runner-up in 1¼m maiden at 3 yrs,
only form: dead. *P. Monteith*

WITNESS 3 b.f. Efisio 120 – Actualite (Polish Precedent (USA) 131) [2002 63: f7g **68**
7g⁴ 8g³ p7g⁴ 7m 7m 5m f7g f7g* f6g f7g Dec 17] good-topped filly: fair handicapper:
won at Wolverhampton in November: effective at 7f/1m: acts on all-weather, good to firm
and good to soft ground. *B. W. Hills*

WITTILY 2 ch.f. (Mar 15) Whittingham (IRE) 104 – Lucky Dip 68 (Tirol 127) [2002 **69 d**
5s p5g* 5.1f 5.2f⁴ 5f⁵ 5m 6.1d 5d⁴ 5m⁴ 5m² 6m 6m p6g 6s f5g f5g Dec 21] 1,200Y:
strong, lengthy filly: second foal: dam 5f winner: fair performer: won minor event at
Lingfield in April: well below form after second in nursery at Beverley: probably best at
5f: acts on polytrack and firm ground. *A. Berry*

WIXOE EXPRESS (IRE) 3 b.g. Anabaa (USA) 130 – Esquiline (USA) (Gone West **98**
(USA)) [2002 p6g² f6g* 8d³ p7g* 8.2m* 7d⁵ 7m 7g Oct 18] 90,000Y: good-bodied **a107**
gelding: first foal: dam, maiden, out of half-sister to Arlington Million winner Mill
Native: useful performer: won maiden at Wolverhampton in June and minor event at
Lingfield (beat Climate by 7 lengths) and handicap at Nottingham (beat Ashgar Sayyad
2½ lengths despite idling) in July: disappointing in handicaps last 3 starts (reportedly
finished lame first occasion), finding little: likely to prove best at 7f/1m: acts on
all-weather, yet to encounter extremes of going on turf: needed early reminders final start,
and is one to treat with caution: sent to USA. *Sir Mark Prescott*

WIZARD OF EDGE 2 b.g. (Apr 9) Wizard King 122 – Forever Shineing 62 (Glint **69 p**
of Gold 128) [2002 f8s² 8.2s⁵ Oct 23] 9,500Y: fourth foal: half-brother to 3-y-o Treasure
Trail: dam, 1½m winner, half-sister to very smart sprinter Crews Hill and to dam of
Classic Cliche and My Emma: fair form, not knocked about, in maiden at Southwell and
minor event at Nottingham: will stay 1¼m: capable of better. *G. B. Balding*

WIZARD OF NOZ 2 b.c. (Jan 28) Inchinor 119 – Winning Girl (Green Desert (USA) **104**
127) [2002 6g* 7m³ 7s³ Oct 25] 20,000F, 42,000Y: lengthy colt: first foal: dam unraced:
landed odds in maiden at Haydock in July: useful form when third to Almushahar in

Mr C. Fox & Mr J. Wright's "Wizard of Noz"

Champagne Stakes at Doncaster (beaten 1¾ lengths, short of room, kept on well) and Makhlab in Horris Hill Stakes at Newbury (beaten 4¼ lengths): will stay 1m: acts on soft and good to firm ground. *J. Noseda*

WIZARD OF THE WEST 2 b.g. (Mar 3) Wizard King 122 – Rose Burton 42 (Lucky Wednesday 124) [2002 8g f9.4g² f8.5f⁴ f8.5s³ Dec 9] 1,500F, £4,500 2-y-o: second foal: half-brother to 3-y-o Neven: dam 1m winner: fair form in frame in maidens at Wolverhampton: stays 9.4f: acts on fibresand. *Miss S. West* — **71**

WIZARD OF US 2 b.g. (Apr 5) Wizard King 122 – Sian's Girl (Mystiko (USA) 124) [2002 5m 5.9d⁵ 5m 5g 7f⁵ Sep 25] workmanlike gelding: first foal: dam unraced: poor maiden: will probably prove best at 5f/6f: acts on good to firm and good to soft ground: looked difficult ride third outing. *E. J. Alston* — **49**

WODHILL FLORIN 4 ch.f. Dancing Spree (USA) – Muarij (Star Appeal 133) [2002 –: p8g p7g f8g 11.9d 12.3m Jun 20] little form: tried blinkered. *H. J. Collingridge* — **–**

WODHILL FOLLY 5 ch.m. Faustus (USA) 118 – Muarij (Star Appeal 133) [2002 65: p12g 10g 10d p10g p12g⁶ p12g⁶ f8g² p10g Dec 18] angular, workmanlike mare: modest maiden handicapper: left H. Collingridge after sixth start: stays easy 1½m: acts on all-weather and good to firm going: often visored. *D. Morris* — **52**

WOLFIE 2 ch.c. (Mar 26) Wolfhound (USA) 126 – Brilliant 75 (Never So Bold 135) [2002 5m f5g 6f 7d Aug 9] 6,000Y: close-coupled, sparely-made colt: third foal: dam 1m to 1¼m winner: little sign of ability: tried blinkered. *N. P. Littmoden* — **–**

WONDERFUL MAN 6 ch.g. Magical Wonder (USA) 125 – Gleeful 72 (Sayf El Arab (USA) 127) [2002 56§: f8s* f8g f12g³ f11g f8g⁴ 11g⁵ 9.9g f8g Jun 20] compact gelding: modest handicapper on all-weather, poor on turf: won at Southwell in January: effective at 1m to 1½m: acts on good to firm ground and fibresand: unreliable. *R. D. E. Woodhouse* — **44 §**, **a60 §**

WONDROUS JOY   2 b.f. (Feb 10) Machiavellian (USA) 123 – Girl From Ipanema   **73**
106 (Salse (USA) 128) [2002 7m 8m⁶ Sep 24] 105,000Y: useful-looking filly: third foal:
closely related to 5-y-o Ipanema Beach: dam 7f (at 2 yrs) and 1m winner who stayed
10.5f: fair form in maidens at Salisbury and Newmarket (sixth to Echoes In Eternity):
should stay beyond 1m. *E. A. L. Dunlop*

WONDROUS STORY (USA)   2 ch.f. (Feb 4) Royal Academy (USA) 130 –   **79 p**
Gossiping (USA) (Chati (USA)) [2002 7m⁴ 7m* Sep 12] tall, rather unfurnished filly:
closely related to a winner in USA by Caerleon and half-sister to several winners,
including useful 1991 2-y-o 6f/7f winner and Fred Darling winner Musicale (by The
Minstrel) and smart 1½m performer Theatre Script (by Theatrical), 1m winner at 2 yrs:
dam, 6f winner in USA, half-sister to high-class sprinter Committed: fair form: won
maiden at Salisbury in August by neck from Island Rapture: stiff task, well held in May
Hill Stakes at Doncaster final start: should stay 1m: capable of better. *J. H. M. Gosden*

WOOD BE KING   3 b.c. Prince Sabo 123 – Sylvan Dancer (IRE) 64 (Dancing   **–**
Dissident (USA) 119) [2002 –: f7s p5g p5g Feb 6] smallish colt: seems of little account.
A. P. James

WOODBORO KAT (IRE)   3 b.c. Woodborough (USA) 112 – Kitty Kildare (USA)   **51**
68 (Seattle Dancer (USA) 119) [2002 54: 8s 10m 8.1m p10g⁴ f8.5g³ f12g³ f12g² 12d   **a68**
f9.4g* f8.5g⁵ f12s⁶ p10g f12g⁴ Nov 22] lengthy, quite attractive colt: fair handicapper
on all-weather, modest on turf: won at Wolverhampton in July: stays 1½m: acts on all-
weather and firm going, probably unsuited by softer than good: consistent. *M. Blanshard*

WOODBORO MINSTREL (IRE)   3 ch.c. Woodborough (USA) 112 – Quilting 80   **48 d**
(Mummy's Pet 125) [2002 58: f7s³ f6g f5g⁵ 5.9d f7g 6f Jul 17] poor maiden: below form
after reappearance: best effort (at 2 yrs) at 6f: acts on fibresand, well held on turf: visored
final start. *Mrs A. Duffield*

WOODBURY   3 b.f. Woodborough (USA) 112 – Jeewan 82 (Touching Wood (USA)   **82**
127) [2002 69: 7m 6m* 6g³ 6f 6m* 6g⁴ 6m* 6m 6f 5.7f 6m Sep 19] small filly: fairly
useful handicapper: won at Salisbury, Newmarket and Lingfield between June/August:
not at best after: stays 6f: acts on firm ground, some promise on soft: has edged right.
M. D. I. Usher

WOOD COLONY (USA)   4 b.g. Woodman (USA) 126 – Promenade Colony (USA)   **–**
(Pleasant Colony (USA)) [2002 78: 8g May 20] leggy, workmanlike gelding: has a round
action: fair form in maiden on debut in 2001 only. *M. Harris*

WOOD DALLING (USA)   4 b.c. Woodman (USA) 126 – Cloelia (USA) (Lyphard   **94**
(USA) 132) [2002 89: 8g⁴ 10m⁴ 8g May 21] small, sturdy colt: fairly useful handicapper:
in frame at Newbury (Bet Direct Spring Cup) and Newmarket first 2 starts: may prove
better at 1m than 1¼m: acts on good to firm going: has raced freely: found little last 2
starts: sold only 4,500 gns in October, joined C. A. Dwyer. *H. R. A. Cecil*

WOODENBRIDGE (FR)   3 ch.g. Woodman (USA) 126 – Irish Order (USA) 102   **–**
(Irish River (FR) 131) [2002 10m 12s 12f⁶ Sep 17] IR 200,000Y: big, lengthy gelding:
eighth foal: closely related to French 10.5f winner Barbaresco (by Kingmambo) and
useful 2000 2-y-o 7f winner West Order (by Gone West) and half-brother to several
winners: dam, French 2-y-o 5.5f and 7f (listed event) winner, half-sister to 2000 Guineas
winner Entrepreneur: well held in maidens/claimer: sold 2,000 gns. *Mrs A. J. Perrett*

WOODIE (IRE)   2 ch.g. (Apr 19) Woodborough (USA) 112 – Better Goods (IRE)   **53**
(Glow (USA)) [2002 5f 5g 6g⁵ 5d 5f⁴ 7m 7d 6d Aug 26] IR 7,400F, 7,800Y: lengthy
gelding: fourth foal: dam poor Irish maiden: modest maiden: below form in sellers last 3
starts: stays 6f: acts on firm ground: best effort in visor: difficult ride. *D. Nicholls*

WOODLAND BLAZE (IRE)   3 b.g. Woodborough (USA) 112 – Alpine Sunset   **76**
(Auction Ring (USA) 123) [2002 65: 6m⁴ 6g 5d⁶ 5s* 5.1s 5d 5d 5d 5m 5d Oct 14] fair
handicapper: won at Carlisle in May: mostly well held after: will prove best at 5f/6f: acts
on soft ground: blinkered seventh outing: sold 10,000 gns. *C. G. Cox*

WOODLAND PRINCESS (IRE)   3 br.f. Woodborough (USA) 112 – Lagta 75   **48**
(Kris 135) [2002 58: 8m 9.3s 12m f12s⁶ 15.8f 15.8f Oct 8] unfurnished filly: poor maiden
handicapper: should stay 1¼m. *J. L. Eyre*

WOODLAND RIVER (USA)   5 ch.g. Irish River (FR) 131 – Wiener Wald (USA)   **–**
(Woodman (USA) 126) [2002 89: 8.5m 9.2s 7f 8m Jun 30] strong gelding: fairly
useful handicapper at best: no form in 2002: has reportedly had breathing problem.
M. W. Easterby

WOODLANDS   5 b.g. Common Grounds 118 – Forest of Arden (Tap On Wood 130)   **56**
[2002 61: p7g⁵ p7g p6g 6.1m 5.7g 6g² 7.1g 6m 6m 6m Sep 19] modest handicapper:
should stay 1m: acts on firm ground and polytrack: tried visored: sometimes slowly away.
S. Dow

WOODLAND SPIRIT   3 b.g. Charnwood Forest (IRE) 125 – Fantastic Charm (USA)   **66**
(Seattle Dancer (USA) 119) [2002 82: 7m 6m 7g⁴ 8d⁶ p8g Nov 13] good-topped gelding:
fair performer nowadays: effective at 7f/1m: acts on heavy ground and polytrack.
D. R. C. Elsworth

WOODLYON (USA)   3 b.c. Woodman (USA) 126 – Cloelia (USA) (Lyphard (USA)   **82**
132) [2002 59p: p8g² f7g* p7g² f7g* a8f a8.5f⁴ a8.5f⁶ 8f Dec 22] fairly useful form: won
maiden (carried head high) in January and handicap (edged left) in March, both
at Wolverhampton: left J. Noseda, then off 7 months: just respectable efforts at best in
US, leaving D. Carroll before penultimate outing: will prove best at 7f/1m: acts on
all-weather/dirt: blinkered last 3 outings. *D. Matthews, USA*

WOODSMOKE (IRE)   3 b.g. Woodborough (USA) 112 – Ma Bella Luna 76 (Jalmood   –
(USA) 126) [2002 81: f5s p5g p5g f5g⁴ 6g 5m 5 1g f5g f6g f5g f6g Dec 20] strong   a57
gelding: has a quick action: fairly useful on turf at 2 yrs: modest at best in 2002: best at 5f/
easy 6f: acts on good to firm going, good to soft and all-weather. *J. S. Moore*

WOOD STREET (IRE)   3 b.g. Eagle Eyed (USA) 111 – San-Catrinia (IRE) (Knesset   **70**
(USA) 105) [2002 60: p7g³ 8.1m⁴ 8.2g² 10g³ 8.5g* 8s p8g⁴ 8.1g 8g Sep 27] big,
strong gelding: fair handicapper: won maiden event at Epsom in July: stays 8.5f: acts
on polytrack and good to firm going: withdrawn once after refusing to enter stall. *Mrs
A. J. Bowlby*

WOODWILLOW (USA)   2 b.c. (Jan 27) Woodman (USA) 126 – Sianema 62 (Persian   **64**
Bold 123) [2002 7v p8g f7g Dec 31] IR 64,000Y: fifth foal: half-brother to fairly useful
Italian 5f (at 2 yrs) to 1m winner Sergesto (by Most Welcome): dam, maiden who stayed
1m, half-sister to very smart middle-distance filly Infamy, the family of In The Wings and
High-Rise: modest form in maidens: slowly away when eighth at Lingfield second start:
should stay 1¼m. *M. R. Channon*

WOODYATES   5 b.m. Naheez (USA) 126 – Night Mission (IRE) (Night Shift (USA))   **70**
[2002 73: p16g⁴ p12g 10v³ 12g⁵ 12d f12s 14.1d* Oct 30] tall mare: fair performer: left   a66
D. Elsworth after fifth start: won claimer at Yarmouth in October: stays 2m: acts on heavy
going, good to firm and polytrack: has been tongue tied. *W. J. Musson*

WOODY BATHWICK (IRE)   3 ch.c. Woodborough (USA) 112 – Sheznice (IRE)   **58 §**
58 (Try My Best (USA) 130) [2002 74: 7.5m 5.7g⁴ 5.9s* 6g 6f 6m 10s 7m² 7.5m p8g
Oct 9] close-coupled colt: modest performer: won maiden at Carlisle in May: stays 7f:
acts on soft and good to firm going: races freely: tried blinkered, running creditably first
occasion: inconsistent: sold 3,000 gns. *E. J. O'Neill*

WOODYBETHEONE   2 b.c. (Mar 23) Wolfhound (USA) 126 – Princesse Zelda   **67 ?**
(FR) 45 (Defensive Play (USA) 118) [2002 7d p7g 7f 7s Sep 10] good-topped colt: first
foal: dam, maiden who seemed to stay 1½m, out of half-sister to smart French 9f/1¼m
winner Bricassar and smart French 1986 2-y-o Whakilyric, herself dam of Hernando: fair
form when seventh in maiden at Salisbury on debut, edging right: regressed, and last of
16 in nursery at Lingfield final start: should stay at least 1m. *R. Hannon*

WOOLFE   5 ch.m. Wolfhound (USA) 126 – Brosna (USA) (Irish River (FR) 131)   **44**
[2002 67d: 11.1s 8.3s 5m⁶ 6.9d 6g⁴ 8d⁴ 12m 6m⁴ Sep 30] strong, lengthy mare: poor
maiden: effective at 6f to 1¼m: acts on firm ground: tried visored/blinkered. *D. A. Nolan*

WOOLLOOMOOLOO BAY   2 br.f. (Jan 31) Bin Ajwaad (IRE) 119 – Marton Maid   –
74 (Silly Season 127) [2002 5m⁵ 6f⁵ 6d Oct 18] 2,000Y: half-sister to several winners,
including 1m winner Mansa Musa (by Hamas) and 6f (at 2 yrs) to 1½m winner Mr
Devious (by Superpower): dam inconsistent maiden: showed little in maidens. *Mrs
G. S. Rees*

WORDS AND DEEDS (USA)   3 ch.g. Shadeed (USA) 135 – Millfit (USA) 62   **68**
(Blushing Groom (FR) 131) [2002 71p: 6m 8.2d 6f 6f⁶ 8.5g² 9.2g⁵ 9.2v Aug 14] strong
gelding: fair maiden: left Mrs J. Ramsden after fourth start: stays 9f: raced mainly on
good ground or firmer: restless both before and in stall second appearance: sometimes
slowly away. *R. A. Fahey*

WORTH A GAMBLE   4 ch.g. So Factual (USA) 120 – The Strid (IRE) 53 (Persian   **49**
Bold 123) [2002 52: f12s 10s 10.2d⁶ 12d 12.6f 12d 10m Jul 26] good-topped gelding:
poor maiden: stays 1¼m: acts on heavy going. *H. E. Haynes*

*Polypipe Flying Childers Stakes, Doncaster—the speedy Wunders Dream is never headed
as she wins from Revenue (right) and Speed Cop*

WOTAN (IRE)   4 ch.g. Wolfhound (USA) 126 – Triple Tricks (IRE) 70 (Royal Academy (USA) 130) [2002 –: p10g p10g p13g⁵ Feb 6] strong gelding: little form: blinkered penultimate start. *R. Curtis*   **–**

WOTSERNAME   2 b.f. (Feb 19) Makbul 104 – Moving Up (IRE) 61 (Don't Forget Me 127) [2002 p6g 6m 6m Sep 4] first foal: dam, maiden, seemed to stay 1½m: well held in maiden/sellers. *T. E. Powell*   **–**

WOW (IRE)   4 b.f. Woods of Windsor (USA) – Sympathy 77 (Precocious 126) [2002 71: f8.5g Mar 15] half-sister to 6f winner Lia Fail (by Soviet Lad), 6-y-o Marmaduke and Irish 6f winner Port Lush (by Tenby): dam 7f winner on only start: fair handicapper at 3 yrs: off 6 months, well held only run in 2002. *John A. Quinn, Ireland*   **–**

WOZZECK   2 b.g. (Feb 13) Groom Dancer (USA) 128 – Opera Lover (IRE) 97 (Sadler's Wells (USA) 132) [2002 8g² 7.1s² Nov 6] 45,000F, 40,000Y: fourth foal: half-brother to 1¼m winners Diva (by Exit To Nowhere) and La Traviata (by Spectrum): dam, 2-y-o 1m winner who stayed 14.6f, closely related to very smart US Grade 1 9f winner Jovial: fair form when runner-up in maidens at Bath and Musselburgh, beaten 1¼ lengths by Compton Emperor in latter: should stay 1¼m: should improve. *J. R. Fanshawe*   **77 p**

WROOT DANIELLE (IRE)   2 b.c. (Apr 22) Fayruz 116 – Pounding Beat (Ya Zaman (USA) 122) [2002 5s 5m⁵ p5g⁵ 5g* 6d 5m⁶ Jul 25] 4,800F, 5,800Y: leggy colt: ninth foal: brother to a winner in Italy: dam Irish 1½m winner: modest performer: won claimer at Beverley in June: stiff tasks and well held in nurseries after: should stay 6f: acts on good to firm ground, probably on soft. *Ronald Thompson*   **62**

WUN CHAI (IRE)   3 b.c. King's Theatre (IRE) 128 – Flower From Heaven (Baptism 119) [2002 10m 8m 8f 10g Jun 15] IR 14,500F, IR 40,000Y: close-coupled colt: half-brother to several winners, including fairly useful Irish 9f to 1¼m winner Angel From Heaven (by Bob Back): dam Irish sprinter: little form in maidens/handicap. *F. Jordan*   **–**

WUNDERS DREAM (IRE)   2 b.f. (Mar 21) Averti (IRE) 117 – Pizzicato 64 (Statoblest 120) [2002 5.1d² 5m* 5.1m* 5.2f² 5g* 6m⁵ 5m* 5g Oct 6] 17,500F, 10,000Y: smallish, quite good-topped filly: first foal: dam, 5f winner, half-sister to smart performers in Britain/Hong Kong Volata (sprinter) and Mensa (up to 1¼m): useful performer: won maiden at Newmarket in April, minor event at Nottingham in May, Betfair.com Molecomb Stakes at Goodwood (by 2 lengths from Sir Edwin Landseer) in August and Polypipe Flying Childers Stakes at Doncaster in September: best effort when beating Revenue gamely by length in last-named: well held in Prix de l'Abbaye de Longchamp final start: likely to prove best at 5f: acts on firm and good to soft ground: forces pace: hung persistently left sixth outing: genuine. *J. G. Given*   **107**

WYCHNOR PRINCESS (IRE)   7 ch.m. Montelimar (USA) 122 – Forty One (IRE) (Over The River (FR)) [2002 12.1m Jun 25] first foal: dam won over hurdles in Ireland: 100/1, well beaten in claimer at Beverley. *L. R. James*   **–**

X

XALOC BAY (IRE)   4 br.g. Charnwood Forest (IRE) 125 – Royal Jade 82 (Last Tycoon 131) [2002 71: p6g f6s* f6g f6g⁴ f6g⁴ 7v f6g* 6g f6g⁵ 5g 6f a6f⁶ a6.5g a6f a5f   **a75**

a5.5f Dec 19] sturdy gelding: poor mover: fair handicapper: won at Southwell in January and Wolverhampton in April: below form in UAE last 5 starts: effective at 6f/7f: acts on all-weather, little form on turf in 2002: usually visored/blinkered: often races handily. *K. R. Burke*

XANADU 6 ch.g. Casteddu 111 – Bellatrix 45 (Persian Bold 123) [2002 66: 5m 6d⁶ **65** 5g* 5g⁵ 6f 5m 6m 6f² 5m³ 5f Oct 11] big, strong gelding: fair handicapper: won apprentice race at Hamilton in May: stays 6f: best on good going or firmer: often slowly away but usually races prominently: none too consistent. *Miss L. A. Perratt*

XCESS BAGGAGE 2 b.g. (Jan 31) Air Express (IRE) 125 – Abundance 62 (Cadeaux **77** Genereux 131) [2002 6m f6g² 6d² 7g* Aug 12] 15,500Y: workmanlike gelding: easy mover: first foal: dam, maiden, stayed 1m: fair performer: comfortable winner of maiden at Thirsk by 1¾ lengths from Gladys Aylward: will probably stay 1m: acts on good to soft going and fibresand. *W. J. Haggas*

XELLANCE (IRE) 5 b.g. Be My Guest (USA) 126 – Excellent Alibi (USA) **83 §** (Exceller (USA) 129) [2002 83, a91: f16s⁵ f16.2g 18s⁶ 16m⁴ 13.9f 16f² 20m f14.8g³ 16.2m² 21g Jul 31] leggy gelding: fairly useful handicapper: left M. Johnston after eighth start: stays 2½m: acts on fibresand and any turf going. sometimes wanders/finds little: usually races prominently: unreliable. *B. D. Leavy*

XFIVE 3 b.g. Robellino (USA) 127 – Sharpening 72 (Sharpo 132) [2002 7g 10f 8m 9d **–** 7g Sep 2] 25,000Y: well-made gelding: fourth foal: brother to 1m (at 2 yrs) to 11.5f winner Sharp Riposte and half-brother to 1¼m/11f winner Strange Pursuit (by Pursuit of Love), both in France: dam 6f (at 2 yrs)/7f winner: well held in maidens/handicaps: sold 2,000 gns, sent to Kuwait. *M. A. Jarvis*

XHOSA (IRE) 2 ch.c. (Mar 8) Ali-Royal (IRE) 127 – Narrow Band (IRE) (Standaan **81** (FR) 118) [2002 5.1g p5g² f6g* 6m² 6d⁴ 6.1g³ 6g p6g⁴ Oct 9] IR 12,000Y: fourth foal: half-brother to Italian 5.5f to 7.5f winner (including at 2 yrs) Bod Collins (by Colonel Collins): dam unraced: fairly useful performer: won maiden at Wolverhampton in June: good fourth in nursery at Lingfield final start: stays 6f: acts on all-weather, yet to race on extremes of going on turf: sold 33,000 gns, sent to Austria. *S. Kirk*

XIBALBA 5 b.g. Zafonic (USA) 130 – Satanic Dance (FR) 80 (Shareef Dancer (USA) **54** 135) [2002 66d: p7g³ p8g³ f14g Nov 25] leggy, angular gelding: modest performer: off 9½ months and left C. Brittain before well beaten final start: stays 1¼m: acts on all-weather, good to soft and good to firm going: tried visored/blinkered: none too consistent. *Mrs M. Reveley*

XOCOLATA 2 b.f. (May 4) Mtoto 134 – Madary (CAN) 93 (Green Desert (USA) 127) **65 +** [2002 7.9m³ 8f 8.5f Dec 7] 4,200Y: fourth foal: half-sister to 7f winner Shaan Madary (by Darshaan): dam 7f/1m winner: green, 2 lengths third to King's Protector in maiden at York in September: left G. Bravery: better effort in similar events in US when 4¾ lengths eighth at Hollywood final start: should be suited by 1¼m+. *R. B. Hess jnr, USA*

XSYNNA 6 b.g. Cyrano de Bergerac 120 – Rose Ciel (IRE) 80 (Red Sunset 120) [2002 **58 §** 58§, a66§: 6m⁶ 5g² 5.7g 5.7d 5s 6v 6v 6g 5m 6m f8s³ f7g⁶ 8.9f f8g f6g⁴ f6g Dec 10] tall gelding: unimpressive mover: modest handicapper: left J. M. Bradley after eighth start: effective at 5f to 1m: acts on firm going, good to soft and fibresand: blinkered last 2 starts: has reportedly bled from nose: unreliable. *M. J. Polglase*

XTRA 4 b.g. Sadler's Wells (USA) 132 – Oriental Mystique 97 (Kris 135) [2002 113: **115** 12d² 12m* 12d⁶ Jul 9] well-made gelding: smart performer: lightly raced: won 4-runner listed event at Newmarket in June by neck from Ovambo: sweating slightly, well held in Princess of Wales's Stakes there final outing, finding little: will stay at least 1¾m: acts on good to firm and good to soft going, probably on soft: sold 120,000 gns, joined J. Old and gelded. *L. M. Cumani*

XTRASENSORY 3 b.f. Royal Applause 124 – Song of Hope 103 (Chief Singer 131) **93** [2002 96: 7m⁶ 8m May 5] quite good-topped filly: fairly useful performer at 2 yrs (reportedly had back injury after final start): creditable sixth in Nell Gwyn at Newmarket on reappearance: 100/1, last in 1000 Guineas there only other run in 2002: stays 7f: raced only on good to firm going: sent to USA. *R. Hannon*

Y

YAFOUL (USA) 2 b.f. (Feb 13) Torrential (USA) 117 – My Shafy 92 (Rousillon **76 p** (USA) 133) [2002 6f² 6f* 7m Oct 19] sturdy, lengthy filly: sixth foal: half-sister to 3 winners, including smart 7f/1m (including at 2 yrs) winner Ramooz (by Rambo Dancer) and useful 7f (at 2 yrs)/1m winner My Hansel (by Hansel): dam 1m winner out of smart French middle-distance performer Lys River: fair form: landed odds in maiden at Pontefract in September easily by 2 lengths from Look Here's Carol: stiff task, well beaten in Rockfel Stakes at Newmarket final start: should stay at least 7f: probably capable of better. *B. W. Hills*

YA HAJAR 3 b.f. Lycius (USA) 124 – Shy Lady (FR) 91 (Kaldoun (FR) 122) [2002 106: 7m 8m May 5] strong, close-coupled filly: useful at 2 yrs: ran badly at Newmarket in Nell Gwyn Stakes and 1000 Guineas (tongue tied) in 2002: stays 7f: acts on good to firm and good to soft ground. *M. R. Channon*   –

YAKIMOV (USA) 3 ch.g. Affirmed (USA) – Ballet Troupe (USA) (Nureyev (USA) 131) [2002 8s f8.5g⁵ f8.5g³ 9m 10d⁶ 8g 7.5m² 8s* 8m* 9.7g* 9.2m² Sep 2] $85,000Y: strong, lengthy gelding: fifth foal: closely related to 2 winners abroad by Peteski, and half-brother to 2 winners in USA: dam, 1m to 9f winner in USA, out of sister to champion US 2-y-o Roving Boy: fairly useful performer: won handicap at Pontefract, valuable claimer at Newbury and handicap at Folkestone, all in August: stays 9.7f: acts on soft and good to firm ground. *P. F. I. Cole*   **88**

YALLA (IRE) 2 b.g. (Mar 22) Groom Dancer (USA) 128 – Creeking 65 (Persian Bold 123) [2002 6.1m⁵ 6d f6f Nov 11] 3,500Y: good-topped gelding: has scope: has a round action: third foal: dam, maiden effective from 7f to 1¼m, half-sister to useful performers Fast Eddy (up to 1m) and Stone Mill (up to 1¼m): well held in maidens: gelded after. *W. J. Haggas*   –

YALLA LARA 3 b.f. Marju (IRE) 127 – Versami (USA) (Riverman (USA) 131) [2002 –p: p8g² p8g* p7g² p8g* 8g f8.5s⁴ p8g² p8g Dec 30] fair form: won maiden at Lingfield in January and handicap there in February: may prove best up to 1m: acts on all-weather. *I. A. Balding*   **78**

YALLAMBIE 3 b.f. Revoque (IRE) 122 – Tahnee (Cadeaux Genereux 131) [2002 8.3d⁶ 8.1g⁵ 7m f8s Oct 8] 15,000F, 26,000Y: third foal: dam unraced half-sister to Phoenix Stakes winner Princely Heir out of very smart miler Meis El-Reem: easily best effort (modest form) when fifth in maiden at Sandown second start: left M. Bell 8,000 gns after next start: took good hold penultimate outing. *R. Wilman*   **59**

YANUS 4 b.g. Inchinor 119 – Birsay (Bustino 136) [2002 69: 10.3s 12.3g 11m⁶ 10.4m Sep 4] workmanlike gelding: modest handicapper: stays 11f: acts on soft and good to firm going, probably on heavy: usually races prominently. *J. S. Goldie*   **50**

YAOUNDE (IRE) 3 gr.f. Barathea (IRE) 127 – Lost Dream (Niniski (USA) 125) [2002 72: 10.2d 13.1g³ Jul 22] fair maiden at best: should stay 1¼m: acts on heavy ground. *E. J. O'Neill*   –

YAROB (IRE) 9 ch.g. Unfuwain (USA) 131 – Azyaa 101 (Kris 135) [2002 90: 8m 8m⁴ 7g 7f² 8d² 7g 8g⁶ 10m 8g⁶ 7m 8g 8g Sep 7] quite good-topped gelding: fair performer: won seller at Ripon in June: well held after: effective at 1m to 11f: acts on firm going, good to soft and fibresand: has been edgy (usually early to post): has raced freely: often leads, and probably needs to dominate (possibly best on turning track): sometimes folds tamely: on downgrade. *D. Nicholls*   **67 d**

YARRITA 2 b.f. (Mar 6) Tragic Role (USA) – Yanomami (USA) 71 (Slew O' Gold (USA)) [2002 5g 5m* f5g* f5s² 6m³ 5.1f³ 5.1f⁵ 5d⁴ f6g² f7g² 7m 6m⁴ 6f Oct 7] 800Y: leggy, close-coupled filly: first foal: dam, 6f winner, from good family: fair performer: won sellers at Catterick (hung right) and Wolverhampton in April: good second in nurseries at Wolverhampton in July: effective at 6f/7f: acts on fibresand, raced only on good going or firmer on turf. *K. A. Ryan*   **67 a77**

YARROW BRIDGE 3 b.f. Selkirk (USA) 129 – Both Sides Now (USA) (Topsider (USA)) [2002 75: 6.1f⁵ 5m⁵ 5.1m⁶ 6g 5.3g⁵ 5m Aug 24] compact filly: poor mover: fair performer: will prove best at 6f/7f: acts on good to firm going: usually races prominently: sold 6,000 gns in December. *R. Hannon*   **68**

YASELDA 3 b.f. Green Desert (USA) 127 – Pripet (USA) 86 (Alleged (USA) 138) [2002 82: f6g 8.5m⁵ Aug 24] rather leggy filly: fair performer, lightly raced: stays 8.5f: sold 33,000 gns in December. *C. E. Brittain*   **77 ?**

YATTARNA (IRE) 6 b.g. Be My Guest (USA) 126 – Kindpiano (USA) (Fappiano (USA)) [2002 14.1d f16.2g Apr 20] formerly fair 13f winner: off nearly 2 years before well beaten in 2002: tried blinkered. *A. Streeter*   –

*Credit Suisse Private Banking Pokal, Cologne—ten-year-old Yavana's Pace (blaze)
becomes the oldest winner of a Group 1 race on the Flat; he rallies to regain the lead
from Salve Regina as Millenary (hooped sleeves) takes third ahead of Well Made (right)*

YAVANA'S PACE (IRE)   10 ch.g. Accordion – Lady In Pace (Burslem 123)   **120**
[2002 118: 12g 12s³ 12g⁵ 12m⁶ 12d³ 12m² 12d* 15.5g⁵ 12s³ 12d³ Sep 29]

Which ten-year-old has contested seventy-four races covering more than one hundred miles on the track in eight seasons and eight countries, winning sixteen of them, with twenty-five places, and earning almost £750,000? The answer is Yavana's Pace, who has been a great credit to his connections and whose splendid record attained a new peak when he won the Group 1 Credit Suisse Private Banking Pokal at Cologne in August. There is no reason why a veteran should not win a top race if he retains fitness and enthusiasm, though these qualities may be prone to decline with the passing years. No ten-year-old had won a race at Group 1 level before in Europe though. Another ten-year-old, Tedburrow, had already set a British age record earlier in the season with his win in the Group 3 Chipchase Stakes, but the oldest to win a Group 1 before Yavana's Pace was eight-year-old My Best Valentine, successful in the 1998 Prix de l'Abbaye. Going back a lot further, Beeswing won the Gold Cup as a nine-year-old in 1842, and, abroad, Magistrate landed the Group 1 Perth Cup in Australia as a ten- and eleven-year-old in 1981 and 1982 while John Henry and John's Call won Grade 1 events in the States aged nine.

Yavana's Pace has been a model of consistency since joining Mark Johnston from Irish trainer Michael Cunningham before his reappearance in 1998, earning Timeform ratings of 118 in 1998, 1999 and 2001 and 120 in 2000. His form in winning at Cologne was on a par with his best in previous seasons, notably second places in the Irish St Leger in 1999 and 2000 and in the Preis von Europa in 2000, and also on a par with his third behind Millenary in the Princess of Wales's Stakes at Newmarket in July. His victories in the 1998 November Handicap and in four pattern races—the September Stakes in 1999, John Porter Stakes in 2000 and Prix Gladiateur and Prix du Conseil de Paris in 2001—were not far behind. The Princess of Wales's Stakes provided the first indication that Yavana's Pace was still capable of reproducing his best. His first four starts had included only one placed effort, when third to Well Made in the Gerling-Preis at Cologne; in the three others he had managed to beat just one horse. At Newmarket he led as usual and stuck on well to be beaten a neck and a length and three quarters by Millenary and Mubtaker, who both received 3 lb. A creditable run, on ground firmer than had seemed to suit him in recent seasons, came later in the month in the WGZ Bank-Deutschlandpreis at Dusseldorf, in which he battled back once headed but could not cope with Marienbard, who scored readily by a length and a half without showing the form which later won him the Prix de l'Arc de Triomphe. Millenary, Well Made and Preis der Diana winner and Deutsches Derby runner-up Salve Regina were among Yavana's Pace's six opponents at Cologne, where he started only fourth favourite. When Salve Regina headed him with a quarter of a mile left, it looked as though Yavana's Pace would be playing second fiddle again but that view reckoned without his dogged determination. Regaining the lead with a furlong left, Yavana's Pace kept on gamely to get the better of the filly by half a length with Millenary, below form, four lengths back in third and Well Made fourth. The race was not the best Group 1 of the year by any means but Yavana's Pace still deserves credit for his success, which typified his never-say-die approach. He also had to overcome the eccentricity of the German weight-for-age system, since older horses are obliged to concede three-year-olds a stone there, rather than the 11 lb if the race had been in one of the other leading countries in the European pattern. The only reason for this is to give the supposedly slower maturing German three-year-old more of a chance, but the European pattern is supposed to provide a coherent and uniform framework. Yavana's Pace failed to make much of a mark in his three subsequent starts, the best of them fifth under a penalty behind Miraculous in the Prix Gladiateur at Longchamp next time. Both Well Made and Salve Regina reversed the Cologne form when they met there again in the Preis von Europa the following month, and Yavana's Pace's season came to an abrupt end when he suffered a lesion in his near-fore suspensory ligament in finishing third behind Ballingarry in the Canadian International Stakes at Woodbine.

		Sadler's Wells	Northern Dancer
	Accordion	(b 1981)	Fairy Bridge
	(b 1986)	Sound of Success	Successor
Yavana's Pace (IRE)		(ch 1969)	Belle Musique
(ch.g. 1992)		Burslem	Nebbiolo
	Lady In Pace	(ch 1980)	Spice Road
	(b 1985)	Lady Littlepace	African Sky
		(b 1975)	Yavana

Yavana's Pace was not bred to be a leading performer on the Flat and his trainer has jocularly reported that initially he thought the owner wanted him to deal

Mrs Joan Keaney's "Yavana's Pace"

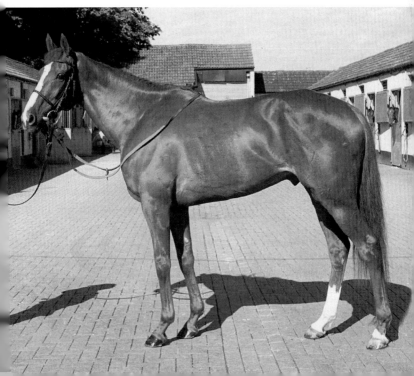

with a hurdler on his transfer from Ireland. The mistake was understandable because Yavana's Pace is the only pattern winner by Accordion, much better known as sire of such top jumpers as Dato Star and Flagship Uberalles. The dam of Yavana's Pace, Lady In Pace, was a sprinter who won twice over five furlongs as a three-year-old and her dam Lady Littlepace finished second in the Ballyogan Stakes over the minimum trip. To Accordion, Lady In Pace has also foaled Little-pacepaddocks, a useful middle-distance filly successful in the listed Ballymacoll Stud Stakes and runner-up in the Princess Royal Stakes for Johnston. Lady In Pace has been upgraded, matings since her two Accordions hit the right note producing fillies by two other sons of Sadler's Wells, King's Theatre in 2000 and In The Wings in 2001, and a colt by Key of Luck before a visit to Sinndar in the latest season. Yavana's Pace, a tall, angular gelding with a markedly round action, is effective at a mile and half to two miles and acts on any going. A game and habitual front runner, he has been troublesome before the start on occasions and been taken early to post. *M. Johnston*

YAVARI (IRE)   3 b.f. Alzao (USA) 117 – Twin Island (IRE) (Standaan (FR) 118)   **66** [2002 7m⁴ 8.2d 7.1s⁴ 10m p12g f8s f7g³ Nov 30] IR 300,000Y: strong, close-coupled filly: half-sister to several winners, notably smart 6f (Prix Morny)/7f winner Tagula (by Taufan): dam once-raced half-sister to dam of dual Breeders' Cup Mile winner Da Hoss: fair maiden: probably best at 7f/1m: acts on fibresand and good to soft ground: blinkered (raced freely) third start: tongue tied fifth outing. *B. J. Meehan*

YAZOO RIVER REBEL   3 b.g. Sabrehill (USA) 120 – Bidweaya (USA) 45 (Lear   **–** Fan (USA) 130) [2002 –: 10.1m 12g May 31] smallish gelding: little sign of ability in maidens. *J. R. Norton*

YEAR TWO THOUSAND   4 b.c. Darshaan 133 – Vingt Et Une (FR) (Sadler's Wells   **100** (USA) 132) [2002 109: 12g May 3] strong, well-made, attractive colt: useful performer: very lightly raced: stiff task when eighth of 9 in Jockey Club Stakes at Newmarket only run in 2002: stays 2m: raced only on good/good to firm ground: has moved poorly to post/wandered: sold 26,000 gns in July, sent to Norway. *H. R. A. Cecil*

YELLOW RIVER (IRE)   2 b.g. (Mar 21) Sesaro (USA) 81 – Amtico (Bairn (USA)   **66** 126) [2002 6d 8s f7g* Nov 25] IR 8,500F, 15,000Y, 6,400 2-y-o: eighth living foal: half-brother to 3 winners, including 5-y-o Maromito: dam unraced: 9/2 and tongue tied, first form when winning seller at Southwell by 6 lengths from Senor Pedro: not sure to stay 1m. *B. J. Meehan*

YENALED   5 gr.g. Rambo Dancer (CAN) 107 – Fancy Flight (FR) 74 (Arctic Tern   **68** (USA) 126) [2002 69, a78+: f8.5g* f7g³ 8m³ 8d 7.9d f8.5g⁴ 6.9m⁵ 7.9m 9m 7.5m⁶ f8g*   **a82** f8.5f f8.5s⁶ f8g⁵ f8g³ Dec 27] leggy, sparely-made gelding: fairly useful on all-weather, fair on turf: won apprentice handicap at Wolverhampton in January and minor event at Southwell in October: best around 1m: acts on fibresand and any turf going: visored (below form) once: best held up in truly-run race. *I. Semple*

YEOMAN LAD   2 b.g. (Mar 8) Groom Dancer (USA) 128 – First Amendment (IRE)   **84** 78 (Caerleon (USA) 132) [2002 6.1m³ 6.1d* 6f² 7m³ Aug 3] angular gelding: third foal: half-brother to 2001 2-y-o 5f/7f winner First Alert (by Miswaki): dam 9f winner in USA (maiden in Britain who stayed 1½m): fairly useful form: won maiden at Chepstow in July: again hung left when good third to Looking Down in nursery at Goodwood (gelded after): should stay 1m: acts on firm and good to soft ground. *I. A. Balding*

YERTLE (IRE)   5 b.g. Turtle Island (IRE) 123 – Minatina (IRE) 78 (Ela-Mana-Mou   **69** 132) [2002 69: 16m* 15.9f³ 16.2m⁶ 16d³ 16m⁴ Sep 14] smallish gelding: fair performer: won minor event at Nottingham in June: stays 2m: acts on firm and good to soft ground: sometimes slowly away, and refused to race in net muzzle fourth start at 4 yrs: consistent. *J. A. R. Toller*

YESTERDAY (IRE)   2 b.f. (Feb 27) Sadler's Wells (USA) 132 – Jude 53   **106 p** (Darshaan 133) [2002 6s 7s* 7s² 8g⁶ 7m³ 9v* Nov 10]
    The battle between Michael Kinane and Johnny Murtagh for the Irish Flat jockeys' championship went to the final day, though the climax itself—with Murtagh drawing a blank—cannot be said to have matched the drama generated during the closing weeks, when the lead changed hands several times. Both riders were involved in each of the eight races at Leopardstown on the final day of the Irish season, but the writing was on the wall for Murtagh when Kinane won the

Eyrefield Stakes, Leopardstown—
Yesterday relishes the step up in trip and is an easy winner from Eklim (left)

first two, and he clinched the title on Quarter Moon's full sister Yesterday in the sixth. It was Kinane's twelfth championship, his final total for the season being seventy-nine wins.

Yesterday's victory, in a listed event for two-year-olds run over nine furlongs, was her second, following one in a maiden at Tipperary in June. In between she contested three pattern races and showed improved form in each of them, finishing second to Rainbows For All in the Debutante Stakes at the Curragh, sixth to Six Perfections in the Prix Marcel Boussac at Longchamp and third to Luvah Girl in the Rockfel Stakes at Newmarket. The Eyrefield Stakes at Leopardstown provided Yesterday with greater opposition in terms of quantity—seventeen lined up against her—but not in quality; and with conditions placing even greater emphasis on stamina at the trip, which seemed sure to suit Yesterday very well, she was sent off favourite at 6/4. Continuing her progress, Yesterday gave her supporters no cause for concern, travelling well, making headway turning for home and readily going clear inside the final furlong to win by four lengths from Eklim. Afterwards, her trainer Aidan O'Brien was quoted as saying that 'It's taken time to get her to behave but she has really come good and should be an Oaks filly for next year.' O'Brien isn't the only one to believe in Yesterday, who, at the time of writing, heads the ante-post Oaks betting with nearly all the leading bookmakers.

			Nearctic
Yesterday (IRE) (b.f. Feb 27, 2000)	Sadler's Wells (USA) (b 1981)	Northern Dancer (b 1961)	Natalma
		Fairy Bridge (b 1975)	Bold Reason
			Special
	Jude (b 1994)	Darshaan (br 1981)	Shirley Heights
			Delsy
		Alruccaba (gr 1983)	Crystal Palace
			Allara

Yesterday, strong and close-coupled, is a different type physically to the rather gangling Quarter Moon, and temperamentally looks much more straightforward than her sister, an edgy sort who didn't make things easy for either her trainer or jockey. Apparently, Yesterday is to follow a similar programme to Quarter Moon and connections will be hoping that at least she manages to get her head in front in her second season. Quarter Moon's record included second place in the Irish One Thousand Guineas, the Oaks and Irish Oaks, but Yesterday seems not to have as much speed and it is difficult to believe she will be up to winning a Guineas. The Oaks is a different matter altogether, though, and the step up to a mile and a half will suit her down to the ground. Yesterday's pedigree is detailed fully in the essay on Quarter Moon. Suffice to say that she is the second foal of Jude, a sister to the unlucky Irish Oaks third Arrikala but just a modest maiden herself. Yesterday seems impervious to the state of the ground she's tackled so far, having run well in the Rockfel on good to firm and won on heavy at Leopardstown. *A. P. O'Brien, Ireland*

YETTI   4 ch.f. Aragon 118 – Willyet (Nicholas Bill 125) [2002 73: 5d May 23] angular filly: fair performer at 3 yrs: well held only start in 2002. *H. Candy*   –

YMLAEN (IRE)   2 b.f. (Feb 22) Desert Prince (IRE) 130 – Dathuil (IRE) 97 (Royal Academy (USA) 130) [2002 6d* 7m³ 6g Sep 21] IR 130,000Y: leggy, quite good-topped filly: second foal: dam, Irish 1m winner, half-sister to useful Irish sprinter Aretha out of half-sister to top-class sprinter Double Form: fairly useful form: won maiden at Windsor in August: good third of 5 to Waldmark in minor event at Kempton, short of room then not knocked about: not discredited when eighth of 10 to Airwave in listed event at Ayr: may prove best short of 1m. *B. Palling*   **84**

YNYSMON   4 b.g. Mind Games 121 – Florentynna Bay 61 (Aragon 118) [2002 76§: f6s* f7g f6g³ f5g 5.1d⁵ 7g 6m f7g Apr 26] lengthy, rather unfurnished gelding: fair on all-weather, modest on turf: won handicap at Southwell in January: ran as if something amiss final start: best at 5f/6f: acts on firm going, good to soft and fibresand: has given trouble preliminaries/been led to post: sometimes slowly away/races freely: tried blinkered: tongue tied: reportedly bled second start: none too genuine. *S. R. Bowring*   **64 §** **a71 §**

YOB (IRE)   3 b.c. Common Grounds 118 – First Veil 94 (Primo Dominie 121) [2002 f7g f5g 6g 8m 7f 5v⁴ f6g⁵ 5.9d 6m Jul 22] first foal: dam 6f/7f winner: poor maiden: left J. Osborne after second start: stays 6f: acts on heavy going and fibresand: usually tongue tied. *P. D. Evans*   **44**

YOCKLETON   2 b.g. (Feb 16) Wizard King 122 – Awham (USA) (Lear Fan (USA) 130) [2002 5.1d 5m 7g⁵ 7g Aug 4] 2,600Y: sixth foal: half-brother to 1997 2-y-o 7f winner Suggest (by Midyan): dam unraced: poor maiden: probably stays 7f. *T. Wall*   **40**

YOMCHI (IRE)   3 b.c. Mark of Esteem (IRE) 137 – Harir (Kris 135) [2002 a8f³ a8f⁵ a7f³ 8g⁵ p10g⁵ a6.5g Nov 21] 25,000 2-y-o: third foal: half-brother to winner in Greece by Polar Falcon: dam unraced half-sister to smart stayer Shaya: fair maiden: creditable efforts for A. Smith/Paul Smith at Nad Al Sheba first 3 starts and in Britain next 2 outings: stays 1¼m. *D. J. Selvaratnam, UAE*   **70**

YORKER (USA)   4 b.g. Boundary (USA) 117 – Shallows (USA) (Cox's Ridge (USA)) [2002 73, a83: p10g f9.4g³ 10g 8f 8d 7.5g 8m³ p8g 8v f8.5g Nov 18] strong, lengthy gelding: fair handicapper: barely stays 1¼m: acts on all-weather, soft and good to firm going: free-going sort, often makes running: ran poorly in visor sixth start. *J. M. P. Eustace*   **71** **a78**

YORKIE   3 b.g. Aragon 118 – Light The Way 72 (Nicholas Bill 125) [2002 70: 7m⁵ 6s 8m 6.1d* 6d² 6m 6s² 5d² 5d² 5g 6d⁴ 5m p6g² f6g f6g Nov 18] tall, quite good-topped gelding: fairly useful performer: won maiden handicap at Chepstow in July: mostly creditable efforts otherwise: has form at 7f, but races freely and probably best at 5f/6f: best form on good to soft/soft ground/polytrack: blinkered (hung and possibly amiss on fibresand) penultimate start: sold 12,000 gns. *I. A. Wood*   **80**

YORKIES BOY   7 gr.h. Clantime 101 – Slipperose 72 (Persepolis (FR) 127) [2002 109§: 6g⁴ 6m⁵ 6f 7f⁴ 6d 6m 7d⁶ 7m 7f 7m 6.1s Oct 29] good-bodied horse: useful handicapper: well held last 4 starts: effective at 5f to 7f: acts on soft and firm going: tried blinkered earlier in career: unreliable: sold 14,000 gns. *J. G. Given*   **96 §**

YORKSHIRE BLUE   3 b.g. Atraf 116 – Something Blue (Petong 126) [2002 5.9g f6g* 7g f7s⁶ p6g 7d Oct 18] 27,000Y: first foal: dam, well beaten, half-sister to useful sprinter Blues Indigo and to dam of smart sprinters Astonished and Bishops Court: fair performer: won maiden at Wolverhampton in July: below form in handicaps after: best effort at 6f: acts on fibresand. *R. M. Whitaker*   – **a72**

YORKSHIRE DANCER   3 b.g. Shareef Dancer (USA) 135 – Upper Caen (High Top 131) [2002 f7g 7m 8.5m 17.2d 12f Jul 17] good-topped gelding: ninth foal: brother to 4-y-o Marrel and half-brother to 3 winners: dam unraced: no form. *M. W. Easterby*   –

YORKSHIRE (IRE)   8 ch.g. Generous (IRE) 139 – Ausherra (USA) 106 (Diesis 133) [2002 113: 22.2m⁶ 14.5g Oct 12] rangy gelding: smart performer at best: well held both Flat starts in 2002, in Queen Alexandra Stakes at Royal Ascot and minor event at Pardubice: effective at 1½m (given a test) to 2¾m: probably acts on any turf going: blinkered once: usually heavily bandaged in front: usually takes good hold and leads: fairly useful winning hurdler. *D. L. Williams*   –

YOU GOT ME   3 gr.g. First Trump 118 – Simply Sooty 78 (Absalom 128) [2002 8m   **65**
8.3d p8g³ 7d⁶ 6g³ Jun 17] 20,000Y: lengthy, good-topped gelding: fifth foal: brother to
winner in Denmark and half-brother to 5-y-o Umistim: dam 2-y-o 5f winner: fair maiden:
will prove best up to 1m: sold 1,600. *R. Hannon*

YOU KNOW NOTHING   2 b.g. (Feb 10) Atraf 116 – Crimson Glen 70 (Glenstal   **–**
(USA) 118) [2002 5m 7m Aug 16] 6,200Y, 7,000 2-y-o: sixth foal: half-brother to 3
winners, including fairly useful 7f winner Dilkusha (by Indian Ridge): dam Irish 7f and
9f winner: well held in maiden/seller. *M. W. Easterby*

YOU NEVER NO (IRE)   2 b.c. (Apr 28) Eagle Eyed (USA) 111 – Nordic Doll (IRE)   **72**
71 (Royal Academy (USA) 130) [2002 6d 7.1d⁴ 8.5m³ 7.9m⁴ Sep 4] IR 6,400F, IR
8,500Y: close-coupled, quite good-topped colt: third foal: half-brother to 5-y-o Kirovski:
dam 7f winner: fair maiden: best effort when fourth to King's Protector at York final start:
free-going sort, likely to prove best up to 1m. *E. J. O'Neill*

YOUNG ALEX (IRE)   4 ch.g. Midhish 109 – Snipe Hunt (IRE) (Stalker 121) [2002   **82**
82, a92: p8g³ p6g² p7g 7g 7m 6m 7m 7f* 7.1m² 7.1g² p7g p7g⁶ p8g⁶ Dec 30] leggy,   **a90**
workmanlike gelding: fairly useful handicapper: won at Salisbury in September:
effective at 6f to easy 1m: acts on firm going, better form on polytrack than fibresand:
held up: has been slowly away. *K. R. Burke*

YOUNG BIGWIG (IRE)   8 b.g. Anita's Prince 126 – Humble Mission (Shack   **51 §**
(USA) 118) [2002 63, a59: f6s⁶ f6g² f7g f6g p6g² f6g 6f 5g⁵ f5g* 5v 6v 5m f6g f6g 6d⁵   **a62 §**
5m³ f6s Sep 17] strong, lengthy gelding: modest handicapper: won at Wolverhampton in
June: stayed 7f: acted on all-weather, firm and soft going: was usually blinkered: often
forced pace: was unreliable: dead. *D. W. Chapman*

YOUNG COLLIER   3 b.g. Vettori (IRE) 119 – Cockatoo Island 99 (High Top 131)   **–**
[2002 f7f f8.5g f8g f14.8g⁶ Dec 16] 28,000Y: half-brother to several winners, including
useful performer up to 1¼m Circle of Light (by Anshan), 7.6f winner at 2 yrs, and useful
1¾m winner Collier Bay (by Green Desert), latter also Champion Hurdle winner: dam
1½m to 14.8f winner: little form in maidens/handicap. *Sir Mark Prescott*

YOUNG IBNR (IRE)   7 b.g. Imperial Frontier (USA) 112 – Zalatia 97 (Music Boy   **–**
124) [2002 51: 5m 5m 5s Aug 20] small gelding: of little account nowadays.
W. M. Brisbourne

YOUNG LION   3 b.g. Lion Cavern (USA) 117 – Shimmer 55 (Bustino 136) [2002 87:   **78**
p6g³ f7g⁴ f6g 6g⁴ p7g 8.1d 7f 8m 7m p6g p7g⁴ Oct 16] useful-looking gelding: fairly
useful performer at 2 yrs, just fair form in 2002: stays 7f: acts on firm going and
all-weather: sold 4,700 gns, sent to Kuwait. *C. E. Brittain*

YOUNG MR GRACE (IRE)   2 b.c. (Feb 11) Danetime (IRE) 121 – Maid of Mourne   **79**
(Fairy King (USA)) [2002 5g⁵ 5m* 5g⁴ 6d⁶ 7m³ 7.9f³ 7v Nov 9] IR 20,000F: quite
good-topped colt: half-brother to 3 winners, including 4-y-o Pharaoh Hatshepsut and
5-y-o College Maid: dam Irish 2-y-o 6f winner: fair performer: won minor event at
Newcastle in May: good third twice in nurseries at York: likely to prove best up to 1m:
acts on firm and good to soft ground, well held on heavy. *T. D. Easterby*

YOUNG ROONEY   2 b.c. (May 9) Danzig Connection (USA) – Lady Broker 54   **–**
(Petorius 117) [2002 f7g Dec 31] fifth foal: half-brother to 6-y-o Lady Boxer: dam 7f
winner: 25/1, slowly away and always tailed off in maiden at Wolverhampton.
M. Mullineaux

YOUNG ROSEIN   6 b.m. Distant Relative 128 – Red Rosein 97 (Red Sunset 120)   **68 §**
[2002 74: 8.1s 7g⁵ 7.9g⁵ 7m 7g² 7g 8m 7m³ 7.9m³ 8g 8g⁶ 9m³ 10.3f² 10m Oct 1] leggy
mare: fair handicapper: stays 10.3f: acts on any going: sometimes blinkered: unreliable.
Mrs G. S. Rees

YOUNGS FORTH   2 b.f. (Apr 15) Most Welcome 131 – Pegs 60 (Mandrake Major   **57**
122) [2002 6m 6s 5s³ Nov 6] close-coupled filly: fourth foal: dam, third at 1m on debut at
2 yrs, well beaten after: modest maiden: third in seller at Musselburgh: should stay at least
1m: acts on soft ground. *A. W. Carroll*

YOUNG TERN   4 b.g. Young Ern 120 – Turnaway 79 (Runnett 125) [2002 63: f7s²   **43**
f9.4g* f9.4g 10g⁴ f8g³ f8.5g³ f8.5g p10g Dec 21] smallish gelding: modest performer: **a60**
won maiden at Wolverhampton in February: left C. Cox 4,000 gns and off 5 months
before final start: stays 9.4f: acts on good to soft going and fibresand: blinkered:
sometimes slowly away/pulls hard. *B. J. Llewellyn*

YOUNG-UN   7 b.h. Efisio 120 – Stardyn (Star Appeal 133) [2002 –, a93d: f8s f8s f11s²   **a71 d**
f9.4g* f9.4g⁵ f8.5g f8.5g f9.4g⁵ f8g f11g 9.7m 10m f9.4g 9.9g Jun 12] quite good-topped

horse: fair handicapper: won at Wolverhampton in February: ran poorly last 5 starts: best form at 1m/9.4f: acts on fibresand (last both outings on polytrack), no recent form on turf: tried blinkered/tongue tied: usually waited with. *M. J. Ryan*

YOU'RE AN ANGEL   3 b.f. Pursuit of Love 124 – Prima Cominna 86 (Unfuwain (USA) 131) [2002 70: 7.1m 8g 7.1d² 8.5g 8m 8s 7m 7g 7d² 7s Oct 28] small filly: modest maiden: best form at 7f: acts on soft and good to firm ground: found little final 2-y-o start. *R. Hannon*   **60**

YOU'RE SPECIAL (USA)   5 b.g. Northern Flagship (USA) 96 – Pillow Mint (USA) (Stage Door Johnny) [2002 84: 16.1m 14.1m Sep 5] good-topped, workmanlike gelding: shows knee action: fairly useful handicapper at best: well held both starts on Flat in 2002: should be well suited by further than 2m: acts on heavy going and fibresand, probably not on ground firmer than good: races prominently: visored twice: winning hurdler. *P. C. Haslam*   **–**

Z

ZAAJEL (IRE)   3 b.c. Nashwan (USA) 135 – Mehthaaf (USA) 121 (Nureyev (USA) 131) [2002 90p: 10m² 10.1g* 10.3f⁴ 12g³ 12m⁴ 10.3m⁵ 12m² 11.9f³ Oct 10] lengthy colt: fluent mover: useful performer: creditable efforts most starts, and won maiden at Newcastle in May: free-going type, unlikely to stay beyond 1½m: acts on any going: visored fifth outing: sweating/edgy sixth start: usually runs to form, but sometimes wanders/carries head awkwardly: joined E. Charpy in UAE. *J. L. Dunlop*   **96**

ZABAGLIONE   2 ch.g. (Apr 18) Zilzal (USA) 137 – Satin Bell 99 (Midyan (USA) 124) [2002 6m 6s* 6d* 6v Nov 13] leggy gelding: third foal: half-brother to a winner abroad by Mtoto: dam 7f winner: useful form: won maiden at Newbury in October and minor event at Newmarket (by 2 lengths from Stormont, leading over 1f out) in November: creditable seventh of 9 to Striking Ambition in listed race at Saint-Cloud final start: will stay 7f: acts on heavy going, showed promise on good to firm. *R. Charlton*   **95**

ZACCHERA   3 ch.f. Zamindar (USA) 116 – Palace Street (USA) 103 (Secreto (USA) 128) [2002 70: 7g 7m 6d* 6s⁴ 7.1d³ 7d 7s Oct 25] smallish filly: fairly useful handicapper: won at Newbury in May: stays 7f: acts on good to soft going, possibly not on good to firm. *G. B. Balding*   **82**

ZADOK THE PRIEST (IRE)   2 b. or br.g. (May 10) Zafonic (USA) 130 – Valencay (IRE) (Sadler's Wells (USA) 132) [2002 7m p7g p7g Oct 16] IR 33,000Y: first foal: dam unraced sister to Carnegie out of Detroit, both winners of Prix de l'Arc de Triomphe: seemingly fair form in maiden at Newmarket on debut: well held in similar events at Lingfield: should stay 1m: twice slowly away. *J. W. Hills*   **65 ?**

Dubai Duty Free Mill Reef Stakes, Newbury—
Zafeen is in control as Monsieur Bond and Cassis (left) keep on well

ZAFARANIYA (IRE)   3 b.f. Doyoun 124 – Zafzala (IRE) 115 (Kahyasi 130) [2002   **106**
–: 8s* 10s³ 12m⁶ 12d⁴ Jul 14] compact filly: second foal: dam Irish 6f (at 2 yrs) and 1½m
winner: useful performer: won maiden at Cork in March: much better form after,
including when 4 lengths sixth to Irresistible Jewel in Ribblesdale Stakes at Royal Ascot
(swished tail repeatedly in paddock) and 9 lengths fourth to Margarula in Irish Oaks at the
Curragh: stays 1½m: acts on soft and good to firm going. *J. Oxx, Ireland*

ZAFARELLI   8 gr.g. Nishapour (FR) 125 – Voltigeuse (USA) (Filiberto (USA) 123)   **–**
[2002 16.4d Jul 11] leggy gelding: modest handicapper in 1997: visored/blinkered when
well held both starts on Flat since: has refused to enter stall. *J. R. Jenkins*

ZAFARSHAH (IRE)   3 b.g. Danehill (USA) 126 – Zafarana (FR) (Shernazar 131)   **71**
[2002 10m p10g⁵ 7d² 8s³ 7m f8.5g³ f8.5g f8.5s Dec 26] good-bodied gelding: second
foal: dam, useful French 1m winner, half-sister to dam of Poule d'Essai des Pouliches
winner Zalaiyka: fair maiden handicapper: left Sir Michael Stoute 4,000 gns after seventh
start: should prove best short of 8.5f: acts on soft going and fibresand: visored (poorly
drawn) once: tongue tied (ran as if amiss) final start (gelded after). *P. D. Evans*

ZAFEEN (FR)   2 b.c. (Apr 25) Zafonic (USA) 130 – Shy Lady (FR) 91 (Kaldoun (FR)   **111**
122) [2002 6d² 6m* 6g² 6m* 6f⁵ 7m⁴ Oct 19] tall colt: has scope: second foal:
half-brother to 3-y-o Ya Hajar: dam, German 2-y-o 5f and (listed race) 6f winner, out of
half-sister to smart 6f/7f performer Diffident: smart performer: won maiden at Salisbury
(hung left) in July and Dubai Duty Free Mill Reef Stakes at Newbury (8/11, beat
Monsieur Bond comfortably by ¾ length) in September: good efforts when ¾-length
second to Elusive City in Prix Morny at Deauville and 3¾ lengths fourth to Tout Seul in
Dewhurst Stakes at Newmarket: not sure to stay 1m: acts on good to firm going.
M. R. Channon

Mr Jaber Abdullah's "Zafeen"

ZAFINE 2 b.f. (Mar 25) Zafonic (USA) 130 – Sabina 87 (Prince Sabo 123) [2002 5d² **67** 5m² 5s³ 5g 5g⁴ 5m⁶ 5.1f³ 5.1g 5f³ 5.2d⁴ 5s* f5g⁴ f6s Dec 13] lengthy, rather dipped-backed, unfurnished filly: first living foal: dam, 2-y-o 5.7f winner, half-sister to smart 1¼m performer Lady In Waiting: fair performer: left R. Hannon after sixth start: won seller at Musselburgh in November: effective at 5f/easy 6f: acts on all-weather, firm and soft ground: usually wears cheekpieces: sometimes finds little/hangs left. *J. S. Moore*

ZAGALA 2 b.f. (Apr 27) Polar Falcon (USA) 126 – Whittle Woods Girl 80 (Emarati **58** (USA) 74) [2002 f6g⁴ p6g⁴ Dec 18] 7,000Y: fifth foal: half-sister to 6-y-o High Esteem: dam, 6f winner, sister to useful 6f/7f performer Emerging Market and half-sister to smart sprinter Atraf: better effort (modest form) when fourth to Mister Arjay in minor event at Lingfield on second start: should stay 7f. *S. L. Keightley*

ZAGALETA 5 b.m. Sri Pekan (USA) 117 – Persian Song 45 (Persian Bold 123) [2002 **79** 81: 10m 10.1g 10d⁵ 10s³ 10g⁵ Aug 7] quite good-topped mare: fair handicapper: stays 1¼m: acts on soft and firm going: tried tongue tied: often sweating/edgy: sometimes carries head high. *Andrew Turnell*

ZAHARI (IRE) 6 b.g. Shernazar 131 – Zaila (IRE) (Darshaan 133) [2002 p12g 16m⁶ **72 §** 14.1d Apr 30] heavy-bodied gelding: won 9f apprentice race at Chantilly for A. de Royer-Dupre at 3 yrs: fairly useful hurdler for Venetia Williams: best effort on return to Flat in handicap on penultimate start: stays 2m: blinkered last 3 starts: has looked increasingly temperamental over hurdles, and refused to race final outing on Flat. *Ian Williams*

ZAIBAS (USA) 2 b.g. (Jan 15) Tabasco Cat (USA) 126 – Sudden Sun (USA) (Danzig **–** (USA)) [2002 6m Oct 2] $7,000Y: big, good-bodied gelding: third foal: half-brother to a winner in USA by Carson City: dam French 1m winner out of Oaks/Yorkshire Oaks runner-up Sudden Love: 25/1, tailed off in maiden at Newcastle (gelded after). *A. Dickman*

ZAIDE 2 ch.c. (Apr 27) Singspiel (IRE) 133 – Anne Bonny 105 (Ajdal (USA) 130) **106** [2002 7.6f³ 7s² Oct 25] 27,000Y: tall, useful-looking colt: fifth foal: half-brother to 4-y-o Random Quest and fairly useful 13f winner Who Cares Wins (by Kris): dam 1m/1¼m winner out of Yorkshire Oaks winner Sally Brown: 3 lengths third to Big Bad Bob in minor event at Chester: 8/1, useful form when 2½ lengths second of 10 to Makhlab in Horris Hill Stakes at Newbury, leading going well under 3f out and keeping on well when headed: should stay at least 1½m: joined J. Moore in Hong Kong, where renamed Shane: sure to win races. *B. J. Meehan*

ZAKAT (FR) 3 b.g. Zamindar (USA) 116 – Rose Douceur (FR) (Polish Precedent **52** (USA) 131) [2002 –: 7.1g f9.4g 8m² 8.2g 8.5g 6m⁶ 6m⁵ 5.3m 7m 6f⁴ f6g Oct 17] big, strong gelding: poor maiden: probably needs further than 6f, and should stay beyond 1m: acts on good to firm going: unseated leaving stall ninth start/reared leaving them final run: sold 7,000 gns, sent to Kuwait. *W. R. Muir*

ZAK FACTA (IRE) 2 b.g. (Feb 26) Danetime (IRE) 121 – Alexander Goddess (IRE) **78** (Alzao (USA) 117) [2002 6g p5g³ f7s² f6g⁴ Dec 14] 7,500Y: leggy gelding: second foal: dam unraced from family of very smart US 1m/1¼m performer Victory Speech: fair form in maidens: second at Wolverhampton: barely stays 7f. *N. P. Littmoden*

ZALAZI (IRE) 2 b.c. (Mar 28) Sesaro (USA) 81 – Zalzie 83 (Zalazl (USA) 120) **64** [2002 5.1d⁶ 7m⁴ 7.1d² 6g 8d Aug 23] IR 3,700F, IR 4,800Y: third foal: dam Irish 2-y-o 6f winner: modest maiden: well held after second at Musselburgh: stays 7f: yet to race on extremes of going: sold 5,000 gns, sent to Sweden. *M. G. Quinlan*

ZAMAT 6 b.g. Slip Anchor 136 – Khandjar 77 (Kris 135) [2002 50: 11.1s* 12g⁵ May **74** 20] fair performer: won maiden at Hamilton in May: best form at 11f/1½m: acts on soft and good to firm going: fair hurdler, successful 3 times, including after final Flat outing. *P. Monteith*

ZAMINSTAR (IRE) 3 ch.g. Zamindar (USA) 116 – Guanhumara (Caerleon (USA) **70 d** 132) [2002 68: p6g⁶ p7g⁶ p5g³ 6g p6g 6g 7d p5g 5d 5m f5g 5d Aug 11] tall, leggy gelding: fair maiden: below form after third start, leaving A. Jarvis after fifth, J. Portman after eighth: races freely, and may prove best at 5f: acts on polytrack and good to firm ground: tried visored: sold £380. *I. A. Wood*

ZAMIR 3 ch.g. Zamindar (USA) 116 – Fairy Flax (IRE) 97 (Dancing Brave (USA) **–** 140) [2002 6f 9m 10m 15.8f Oct 8] sturdy gelding: sixth foal: half-brother to 3 winners, including fairly useful 1¼m winner Fairywings (by Kris) and 5f to 1m winner Caution (by Warning): dam, 6f winner, half-sister to smart performer up to 9f Hoy: well held in maidens/handicap, leaving Mrs J. Ramsden after debut. *A. Crook*

ZAMORIN 3 b.g. Zafonic (USA) 130 – Armeria (USA) 79 (Northern Dancer) [2002 **64** 10.2g 8m 10s f8.5g⁴ f12g* p10g f12g f12g Dec 20] seventh living foal: half-brother to several winners by Rainbow Quest, most at least useful, notably Racing Post Trophy/ Chester Vase winner and St Leger second Armiger: dam, 1¼m winner, half-sister to Park Hill winner I Want To Be: modest form: trained debut only by R. Charlton (sold 5,000 gns): able to dictate pace when winning maiden at Southwell in November: well beaten all 3 starts after (reportedly finished distressed on first occasion): stays 1½m: acts on fibresand. *P. S. McEntee*

ZAMYATINA (IRE)   3 br.f. Danehill Dancer (IRE) 117 – Miss Pickpocket (IRE) 64   **46** (Petorius 117) [2002 76: 6m 6g⁶ 7d 6g 5.1f³ 5m 6.1f 7s 8d Nov 1] angular, unfurnished filly: poor performer at 3 yrs: R. Hannon £1,300 before well held last 3 starts: likely to prove best at 5f/6f: acts on polytrack, soft and good to firm ground. *P. L. Clinton*

ZANARIANN (FR)   5 b.g. Indian Ridge 123 – Zanadiyka (FR) (Akarad (FR) 130)   **–** [2002 9.2g 10g⁶ May 31] fourth foal: half-brother to 2 winners in France, notably Poule d'Essai des Pouliches winner Zalaiyka (by Royal Academy): dam French 6.5f/1m listed winner: well held in maidens. *A. Berry*

ZANAY   6 b.h. Forzando 122 – Nineteenth of May 86 (Homing 130) [2002 81, a–: 8d   **–** 10f 8.1m 8.3s Jun 10] tall horse: reportedly had knee-chips removed at 4 yrs: formerly smart 1m/1¼m winner: no form in 2002: sometimes blinkered/tongue tied. *Miss Jacqueline S. Doyle*

ZANDEED (IRE)   4 b.g. Inchinor 119 – Persian Song 45 (Persian Bold 123) [2002 81:   **–** 9.2m⁶ 9.1g 13.1s Oct 15] unfurnished gelding: fairly useful for E. Dunlop at 3 yrs: no form in 2002 (visored). *J. S. Goldie*

ZANDICULAR   3 b.c. Forzando 122 – Perdicula (IRE) (Persian Heights 129) [2002   **93** 89p: 8m³ 7m³ 9g 8m 7.1d 8g³ 7m 8m² 8.1m⁴ 8f* 8f⁵ 8m 8f² 8g Oct 24] good-bodied, sturdy colt: fairly useful performer: won claimer at Kempton in September: below form last 3 starts: effective at 7f/1m: acts on firm and soft going: blinkered (ran poorly) seventh start: sometimes sweating/edgy: ran in snatches sixth outing: sold 13,000 gns, sent to Italy. *R. Hannon*

ZANJEER   2 b.g. (Mar 21) Averti (IRE) 117 – Cloudslea (USA) (Chief's Crown (USA))   **66** [2002 6m⁴ Jul 24] IR 10,000Y: half-brother to 7f/1m winner Picture Puzzle (by Royal Academy) and a winner in Turkey by Tirol: dam French 10.5f winner: 14/1, faded when 4 lengths fourth of 6 to Convex in maiden at Catterick, showing fair form. *D. Nicholls*

ZANOG   3 b.c. Forzando 122 – Logarithm (King of Spain 121) [2002 –: 5.3m 5d 5.1s   **–** 7.1v 5m Sep 14] maiden handicapper: blinkered last 3 starts. *Miss Jacqueline S. Doyle*

ZANOUBIA (USA)   2 b. or br.f. (Feb 2) Our Emblem (USA) 114 – Broadcast (USA)   **94** (Broad Brush (USA)) [2002 5d* 5.5d⁴ 6d 7s³ 8.3g³ Sep 7] $30,000Y: leggy, quite good-topped filly: first foal: dam, US 9f winner, sister to Breeders' Cup Classic winner Concern out of US Grade 1 7f winner Fara's Dream: fairly useful performer: won newcomers race at Longchamp in May: creditable efforts in frame in listed races at Maisons-Laffitte, Vichy and Craon, on final start just under 3 lengths third to Lady Catherine: 5/1, never looked like landing blow in Cherry Hinton Stakes at Newmarket: stays 1m: raced only on good ground or softer. *C. Laffon-Parias, France*

ZANZIBAR (IRE)   4 b.f. In The Wings 128 – Isle of Spice (USA) 74 (Diesis 133)   **102** [2002 113: 12m⁵ 11.9m Aug 21] sturdy, quite attractive filly: smart performer at 3 yrs: successful in Oaks d'Italia at Milan: went to stud but failed to get in foal: better effort in 2002 when fifth to Love Everlasting in listed race at Newbury on reappearance: stays 1½m: best efforts on good to firm going. *M. L. W. Bell*

ZAP ATTACK   2 b.g. (Apr 7) Zafonic (USA) 130 – Rappa Tap Tap (FR) 111 (Tap On   **79** Wood 130) [2002 6f³ 8g³ 8g⁶ Oct 18] close-coupled gelding: brother to smart 1m winner Killer Instinct and half-brother to several winners, including useful Irish 1m winner Oriane (by Nashwan) and 3-y-o Foreign Accent: dam, 6f and 1m winner, half-sister to Cezanne, Colorspin (also dam of Opera House and Kayf Tara) and Bella Colora (also dam of Stagecraft): fair form in maidens at Salisbury (twice third) and Newmarket: stays 1m: gelded after final start. *M. R. Channon*

ZARA LOUISE   2 b.f. (May 5) Mistertopogigo (IRE) 118 – Petonica (IRE) 77 (Petoski   **64 d** 135) [2002 5.1f 6d⁴ 6d 7d⁴ 7f7 f7s f6g Dec 20] 4,800Y: leggy filly: sixth foal: half-sister to useful 6f (at 2 yrs)/7f winner Yorkie George (by Efisio) and 4-y-o Bourgainville: dam second at 7f at 2 yrs: modest maiden: fourth at Redcar and Catterick: deteriorated after: may prove best at 5f/6f: acts on good to soft ground, well held on fibresand. *A. Bailey*

ZARCONIA (IRE)   3 br.f. Inzar (USA) 112 – Speedy Action (Horage 124) [2002 –:   **–** f5g f6g Mar 21] no form. *Mrs P. Sly*

*Balmoral Handicap, Royal Ascot—Zargus (No.20) wears down Fire Up The Band;
Agnetha (No.1) finishes third ahead of Simianna (No.5) and Noble Nick (No.21)*

ZARGUS   3 b.g. Zamindar (USA) 116 – My First Romance 61 (Danehill (USA) 126)   **95**
[2002 89p: 5g⁵ 6f⁵ 5g* 5g⁶ 5:2f Aug 17] stocky, quite attractive gelding: useful handicapper, lightly raced: won 28-runner Balmoral Handicap at Royal Ascot in June by neck from Fire Up The Band: below form last 2 starts: subsequently gelded: likely to prove best at 5f/6f: has won on good to soft going, very best efforts on good. *W. R. Muir*

ZARIANO   2 b.c. (Mar 8) Emperor Jones (USA) 119 – Douce Maison (IRE) 67 (Fools   **82**
Holme (USA)) [2002 6d³ Aug 2] 7,500Y: fourth foal: brother to useful German miler Montestefano and half-brother to a winner up to 1¼m in Italy by Distant Relative: dam 1m winner who stayed 1½m: 25/1, 2 lengths third of 9 to Country Reel in maiden at Newmarket, staying on well after slow start: should stay at least 1m. *S. L. Keightley*

ZARIN (IRE)   4 b.c. Inzar (USA) 112 – Non Dimenticar Me (IRE) 63 (Don't Forget   **104**
Me 127) [2002 105?: 8s² 10d 8.3s 7.9m 8m⁶ 8g 9s Oct 26] tall, leggy colt: unraced at 2 yrs: useful performer: good 3 lengths second to Dandoun in listed event at Doncaster in March: left R. White after third start, respectable efforts subsequently: stays 1m, probably not testing 9f: acts on soft going and good to firm: free-going type: sold 19,000 gns, joined T. Naughton. *T. G. Mills*

ZARZA BAY (IRE)   3 b.g. Hamas (IRE) 125§ – Frill (Henbit (USA) 130) [2002 58:   **64 §**
f12g² 12m³ 11.6m² 11.6g* 11.6s 10.9g⁴ f12s 11.6d 12s f16.2g p13g Dec 28] strong   **a70 §**
gelding: fair handicapper: won at Windsor in April: stays 13f: acts on all-weather, best turf form on good/good to firm going: tried visored: ungenuine. *K. R. Burke*

ZARZELLA   3 b.f. Makbul 104 – Zarzi (IRE) (Suave Dancer (USA) 136) [2002 –:   **50**
7.1m f8.5g⁵ 9.9d⁶ 7m 8.1d³ 8.2m f7g Oct 19] angular filly: modest maiden at best: stayed 1m: acted on good to soft going: dead. *R. Hollinshead*

ZARZU   3 b.g. Magic Ring (IRE) 115 – Rivers Rhapsody 104 (Dominion 123) [2002   **88**
p5g² 5m* 5m³ 5m⁴ 5g³ 5d f5g⁴ f5g³ Dec 10] 27,000Y: fifth foal: half-brother to 3 winners, including useful 5f winner (including at 2 yrs) See You Later (by Emarati) and smart 5f (at 2 yrs) to 1m winner For Your Eyes Only (by Pursuit of Love): dam sprinter: fairly useful form: landed odds in maiden at Folkestone in June: left H. Candy after fifth start: ran creditably in handicaps at Southwell last 2 outings: likely to prove best at 5f: acts on good to firm ground and fibresand. *K. R. Burke*

ZAWRAK (IRE)   3 ch.c. Zafonic (USA) 130 – Gharam (USA) 108 (Green Dancer   **95**
(USA) 132) [2002 58p: 8.5g* 10g³ 10.4d 10.5m³ 10.5f⁵ Sep 27] tall, close-coupled colt: useful performer: won maiden at Epsom in April: good efforts when third in handicaps after: stays 1¼m: acts on good to firm ground, some promise on debut: has worn crossed noseband: sold 22,000 gns, joined I. McInnes. *A. C. Stewart*

ZAYNAAT   2 b.f. (Jan 31) Unfuwain (USA) 131 – Walesiana (GER) (Star Appeal 133)   **71**
[2002 7m 8g⁴ 8m⁴ 8s Oct 15] angular filly: sixth living foal: sister to smart winner around 1¼m Zahrat Dubai and half-sister to 2 winners, including fairly useful 1996 2-y-o 7f winner Waiting Game (by Reprimand): dam German 6f (at 2 yrs) to 1m (Group 2) winner: fair maiden: fourth at Leicester and Newmarket: should stay 1¼m: acts on good to firm ground, well held on soft. *M. R. Channon*

ZECHARIAH   6 b.g. Kasakov – Runfawit Pet 41 (Welsh Saint 126) [2002 55: 8m 7g   **–**
7.5d 8g Jul 20] sparely-made gelding: modest performer at 5 yrs: no form in 2002: was effective at 7f to 8.5f: acted on fibresand, firm and soft going: usually made running: dead. *J. L. Eyre*

ZEE ZEE TOP 3 b.f. Zafonic (USA) 130 – Colorspin (FR) 118 (High Top 131) [2002 **104 p**
8f* 10g² Oct 17] lengthy, quite attractive filly: half-sister to several winners, notably
top-class pair Opera House (middle-distance performer) and Kayf Tara (stayer), both by
Sadler's Wells: dam won Irish Oaks: swished tail repeatedly in paddock before easily
landing odds in maiden at Pontefract, flicking tail: 12/1, useful form when 2 lengths
second to Salim Toto in listed race at Newmarket later in October, staying on well from
mid-field: should stay beyond 1¼m: smart performer in the making, sure to win more
races. *Sir Michael Stoute*

ZEIS (IRE) 2 ch.c. (Apr 8) Bahhare (USA) 122 – Zoom Lens (IRE) 65 (Caerleon **87 p**
(USA) 132) [2002 8s* Oct 26] 42,000Y: sturdy, good-bodied colt: half-brother to several
winners, including 4-y-o Atlantis Prince and useful 1997 2-y-o 1m winner Close Up (by
Cadeaux Genereux): dam, in frame up to 1½m, half-sister to dam of 6-y-o Dano-Mast:
7/1 and green, led final 1f when winning 16-runner maiden at Newbury by length from
Anani: should stay at least 1¼m: useful prospect. *H. R. A. Cecil*

ZEITLOS 3 b.g. Timeless Times (USA) 99 – Petitesse 55 (Petong 126) [2002 62: p5g **57**
5.3m p6g 6g 6m 5d* p6g⁶ 5m⁶ 5d 6m 6m* 5m 6m⁵ 5.7f p7g p6g Dec 30] small gelding: **a51**
modest handicapper: won at Folkestone in July and August: effective at 5f/6f: acts on
soft going, good to firm and polytrack: usually blinkered: flashed tail for latter win.
R. M. Flower

ZELEA (IRE) 3 br.f. Be My Guest (USA) 126 – Ebony And Ivory (IRE) 95 (Bob Back **56**
(USA) 124) [2002 8.3m 8m 8.3m⁶ 10m 9.9m 10.9s³ f12g⁵ f12g f16g Dec 17] 13,000Y:
tall, sparely-made filly: fourth foal: half-sister to Irish 2¼m winner Hip Pocket (by
Ela-Mana-Mou): dam Irish 1¼m to 1½m winner: modest maiden at best: left C. Wall
after sixth start: stays 1½m: acts on fibresand and good to firm ground: tongue tied last 3
starts: sometimes slowly away. *J. Parkes*

ZELENSKY (IRE) 3 b.g. Danehill Dancer (IRE) 117 – Malt Leaf (IRE) 48 (Nearly
A Nose (USA) 84) [2002 72: 8m 8d 8.1g 11.9m Oct 3] tall, lengthy gelding: fair maiden
at 2 yrs: well held in 2002, leaving J. Osborne and off 4 months after second start:
free-going sort, but should stay 7f: has worn crossed noseband. *Jean-Rene Auvray*

ZELOSO 4 b.g. Alzao (USA) 117 – Silk Petal 105 (Peterius 117) [2002 81: f8.5g 10.3f –
8.3s May 26] good-bodied gelding: fairly useful performer at 3 yrs: no form on Flat in
2002: tried visored/blinkered earlier in career: successful over hurdles in September.
M. Harris

ZENDA 3 b.f. Zamindar (USA) 116 – Hope (IRE) (Dancing Brave (USA) 140) **115**
[2002 7?p: 8.3m* 8g* 8s 8m² 9g² 10d Oct 26]
John Gosden, responsible for the last two British-trained winners of the
Poule d'Essai des Pouliches, achieved the feat with fillies whose records going into
the race could hardly have been more different. Whereas Gosden's 1999 winner
Valentine Waltz had run nine times and been successful twice, including in pattern
company, his latest winner Zenda had made just three appearances and gained her
only victory in a maiden. It says much for Gosden's judgement that his decision to
step up Zenda so markedly in class, just three weeks after she had opened her
account, should pay off so handsomely. Zenda had been quite impressive in landing
the odds at Windsor on her reappearance, dictating the pace and being pushed clear
inside the last two furlongs, but it was by no means a strong maiden and the bare
form was a long way below that required to win even an average Poule d'Essai des
Pouliches.
     Only two of Zenda's sixteen rivals in the Gainsborough-sponsored classic,
run at Longchamp in May, had had less racing experience, Zenda's stable-
companion Camaret and Heat Haze, the French-trained winner of a newcomers
race on the first of her two starts. With Heat Haze (a close relative to the previous
year's runner-up Banks Hill) in the same ownership as Zenda the pair were coupled
for betting purposes, and only Firth of Lorne and Glia started at shorter odds. Firth
of Lorne, also trained in France, had finished third to Sophisticat in the Prix de la
Grotte over the same course and distance on her reappearance, and the latter was
also in the line-up, one of two Aidan O'Brien-trained representatives in what was
the biggest field since 1986. Once again front-running tactics were adopted on
Zenda, and the pace she set proved too strong for those who took prominent
positions early. To her credit Zenda, racing with plenty of enthusiasm, kept on
strongly, despite drifting left under pressure, and held on to win a length from Firth
of Lorne, who had missed the break, and Sophisticat, who had had to wait for a gap

Gainsborough Poule d'Essai des Pouliches, Longchamp—Zenda (nearside) leaves her previous form well behind in accounting for Firth of Lorne and Sophisticat

in the straight, a short neck separating that pair. Zenda, like the six previous winners of the Pouliches, failed to add to that success, but at least she went on to show similarly smart form on three of her four subsequent outings. She bettered Valentine Waltz's equal-third place in the Coronation Stakes at Royal Ascot, failing only by a neck to resist Sophisticat's finishing burst; and she was again caught close home and beaten a neck when next seen out over four months later, in the Queen Elizabeth II Challenge Cup run over nine furlongs at Keeneland. Starting slowly in the latter, Zenda improved to lead in the straight but was unable to hold off Riskaverse. Tried over a mile and a quarter on her final start, Zenda ran creditably, despite pulling hard, in finishing eighth to Starine in the Breeders' Cup Filly & Mare Turf at Arlington, not having the clearest of runs early in the straight as she made headway from off the pace. Zenda acts on good to firm ground and showed at Arlington that she is also effective on good to soft, though it is possible that she is unsuited by conditions more testing than that. Two weeks after Longchamp, Zenda was supplemented for the Irish One Thousand Guineas, but she looked all at sea on the very soft ground at the Curragh and finished last of fifteen.

	Zamindar (USA) (b 1994)	Gone West (b 1984)	Mr Prospector / Secrettame
Zenda (b.f. 1999)		Zaizafon (ch 1982)	The Minstrel / Mofida
	Hope (IRE) (b 1991)	Dancing Brave (b 1983)	Lyphard / Najavo Princess
		Bahamian (ch 1985)	Mill Reef / Sorbus

Zenda, like Valentine Waltz, is an eye-catching individual, good-bodied and attractive and also an easy mover; and like Valentine Waltz she is very well related, her dam being a sister to the Irish Oaks winner Wemyss Bight, herself the dam of the high-class performer Beat Hollow. Zenda's grandam Bahamian finished fifth in the Oaks after winning the Lingfield Trial and went on to run well over longer distances, passing the post first in the Prix de l'Esperance only to be relegated to third for causing interference. The next dam Sorbus passed the post first in the Irish Oaks but was disqualified and placed second, while she actually finished second in the Irish One Thousand Guineas, the Irish St Leger and Yorkshire Oaks. Zenda's dam Hope showed nothing on her only appearance on the racecourse but has made a flying start at stud. Her first foal Hopeful Light (by Warning) was a smart winner over seven furlongs and a mile; and in the latest season she was responsible for another notable Gosden-trained performer in Oasis Dream (by Green Desert), the winner of the Middle Park Stakes. Zenda is to continue her racing career in North America with Bobby Frankel, her departure, along with other leading members of

Mr K. Abdulla's "Zenda"

her sex including Banks Hill (now retired after two outings for Frankel) and Dress To Thrill, a poor reflection on the opportunities for good fillies in Europe once their three-year-old days are over. America offers an almost parallel programme for colts/horses and fillies/mares at every stage of their career. The lure for connections of European-trained fillies of proven ability is obvious. *J. H. M. Gosden*

ZENO 4 b.g. Reprimand 122 – Babycham Sparkle 80 (So Blessed 130) [2002 81: f6g[6] p7g 7s 7s[6] 8d 7d[4] 8.5g 7s[5] 6.5v* 6.5s* 6g 8g 8g Sep 1] 15,500F: brother to useful 5f/5.5f winner (including at 2 yrs) Deep Finesse, and half-brother to several winners, including dam of smart sprinter Halmahera: dam 2-y-o 5f/6f winner: fair performer: won maiden and handicap at Sligo in August: stays 7f: has form on any turf going (well held on all-weather in Britain first 2 starts in 2002), goes particularly well on soft/heavy: tried blinkered: usually tongue tied: sold 4,200 gns, sent to Italy. *T. Stack, Ireland* — **76**

ZERO GRAVITY 5 b.g. Cosmonaut – Comfort (Chief Singer 131) [2002 68§: 11.6m[2] Jul 29] big, leggy gelding: modest maiden handicapper: should stay 1¾m: acts on soft and good to firm going: not to be trusted (ran out once). *D. J. S. ffrench Davis* — **57 §**

ZERO TOLERANCE (IRE) 2 ch.g. (Feb 26) Nashwan (USA) 135 – Place de L'Opera 98 (Sadler's Wells (USA) 132) [2002 6g[6] Sep 9] 22,000Y: second foal: half-brother to 4-y-o High Pitched: dam, 1½m winner, out of very smart Park Hill Stakes winner Madame Dubois: 20/1, and green, 9½ lengths sixth of 16 to Parkland in maiden at Newcastle, never nearer: should be suited by 1¼m+: likely to do better. *T. D. Barron* — **55 p**

ZEUSS 2 b.c. (Feb 16) Zamindar (USA) 116 – Shallop 55 (Salse (USA) 128) [2002 p6g[4] 6m[6] p7g[2] p6g[2] Dec 28] 20,000Y: workmanlike colt: fifth foal: half-brother to winners in Italy (by Ezzoud) and Turkey (by Formidable): dam, untrustworthy maiden, half-sister to smart middle-distance stayer Dry Dock: fairly useful maiden: second at Lingfield to Dubai Lightning and to Wages: should stay 1m. *B. W. Hills* — **82**

ZHITOMIR 4 ch.c. Lion Cavern (USA) 117 – Treasure Trove (USA) 62 (The Minstrel **77** (CAN) 135) [2002 82: p7g p8g 6g p8g 7m 7d 7d 6d⁶ 7g³ 7m* 7.6s⁵ 8m Sep 23] strong **a70** colt: fair handicapper: won at Epsom in September: best form at 7f: acts on soft and good to firm going: has run well when edgy/sweating: sometimes slowly away: sold 17,000 gns. *S. Dow*

ZIBELINE (IRE) 5 b.g. Cadeaux Genereux 131 – Zia (USA) 88 (Shareef Dancer **96** (USA) 135) [2002 94: 10m 12m⁵ 12m⁵ 16.1g³ 14m 13.9m⁵ 14m 13.9m⁵ 13.3f 18m Oct 19] tall gelding: useful handicapper: mostly creditable efforts in 2002, particularly when close third to Bangalore in Northumberland Plate at Newcastle, fifth in Ebor at York and seventh in Cesarewitch at Newmarket: barely stays 2¼m: acts on firm going, probably not on softer than good: sometimes blinkered: sometimes pulls hard, and is held up. *B. R. Millman*

ZIETING (IRE) 4 b.g. Zieten (USA) 118 – Ball Cat (FR) (Cricket Ball (USA) 124) **–** [2002 37: p12g f12s f9.4g f12g Jan 25] smallish gelding: maiden: no form in 2002. *P. W. Hiatt*

ZIETORY 2 b.f. (Apr 13) Zieten (USA) 118 – Fairy Story (IRE) 80 (Persian Bold 123) **76 p** [2002 5g⁶ 6s* Oct 28] fourth foal: closely related to 3-y-o Welenska: dam, 7f winner (including at 2 yrs), out of half-sister to dam of Shaamit: fair form when winning 16-runner maiden at Leicester by 2 lengths from Aegean Magic, leading final 1f: should stay at least 7f: capable of better still. *P. F. I. Cole*

ZIETUNZEEN (IRE) 4 b.f. Zieten (USA) 118 – Hawksbill Special (IRE) (Taufan **67 d** (USA) 119) [2002 85: 7.1m⁶ 6.1d 6g 6g 6f 6m⁴ 6d 6d⁵ 5.1f⁵ 5.1m 6g⁵ 6m 5.1g Sep 12] lengthy filly: fair performer: left A. Berry after eleventh start: stays easy 7f: yet to race on heavy going, probably acts on any other turf: sometimes spoils chance at start: has raced freely: on downgrade. *R. J. Baker*

ZIETZIG (IRE) 5 b.g. Zieten (USA) 118 – Missing You 89 (Ahonoora 122) [2002 **67 d** 76+: f6g 5g 7m⁶ 6m⁵ 6d 7.1g² 7.1d f7g⁶ f6g⁵ f7g Dec 17] shallow-girthed gelding: fair performer: left T. D. Barron just 500 gns, then well below form last 3 starts: seems best at 6f/7f: acts on soft and good to firm going, probably on polytrack: sometimes races freely: on downgrade. *H. A. McWilliams*

ZIGALI 3 b.g. Zilzal (USA) 137 – Alilisa (USA) (Alydar (USA)) [2002 8m 8m 10m **–** 11.6d Oct 28] 2,800F: leggy gelding: third foal: dam Irish 12.8f winner: little form. *P. S. McEntee*

ZIGGY ZEN 3 b.g. Muhtarram (USA) 125 – Springs Welcome 86 (Blakeney 126) **69** [2002 p10g⁴ 10g p12g⁵ p16g Nov 27] seventh foal: half-brother to 3 winning stayers, including fairly useful 1½m winner who stayed 2½m Jonas Nightengale (by Deploy): dam 1¼m to 12.5f winner who stayed 2m: fair form in maidens: off 5 months, fell over 4f out final start: should be suited by 1¾m+. *C. A. Cyzer*

ZILCH 4 ch.g. Zilzal (USA) 137 – Bunty Boo 110 (Noalto 120) [2002 109: 6s 8.1d⁴ 6m **90** 6.1d³ Jul 12] leggy, close-coupled gelding: fluent mover: fairly useful in 2002: stays 6f: acts on soft and good to firm ground: blinkered (respectable effort) final outing: has folded tamely/edged right: held up. *M. L. W. Bell*

ZILMAID DANCER 3 b.f. Zilzal (USA) 137 – Briggsmaid 70 (Elegant Air 119) **68** [2002 55p: 6f³ 6d p7g Nov 14] good-topped filly: fair maiden: stays 7f: acts on polytrack and firm ground: tried tongue tied. *P. W. Harris*

ZINDABAD (FR) 6 b.h. Shirley Heights 130 – Miznah (IRE) 102 (Sadler's Wells **126** (USA) 132) [2002 120: 12m* 12g⁴ 13.9f* 12s³ 12m* 12m³ 12d⁵ Sep 29]
    Six-year-old Zindabad's best campaign so far played its part in the most successful yet for his trainer Mark Johnston. He made the biggest contribution of any in the stable towards its record prize-money total through his three pattern wins—most notably in the Hardwicke Stakes at Royal Ascot—and two placings in Group 1 company. Zindabad is a particularly fine advertisement for his trainer's skill at improving horses under his care. Since being transferred to Kingsley House after his four-year-old campaign, Zindabad has made into a high-class performer, so much so that, of all the horses Johnston has handled, only Bijou d'Inde and Fruits of Love have been rated more highly.
    Zindabad showed smart form at best in his days with Ben Hanbury, winning a maiden at Pontefract then finishing second in the Gran Criterium at Milan from three outings as a two-year-old before winning three times from six outings at three, in handicaps at Newmarket and Ascot and in the Winter Hill Stakes at Windsor. Zindabad ran only twice at four, finishing third in listed contests. He was better than

ever in his first season for his new stable, recording victories in a minor event at Newmarket and a listed race at Leicester in a seven-race campaign which included even better efforts when a very close second in the Hardwicke Stakes at Royal Ascot and when third in the Canadian International at Woodbine (in the latter demoted to sixth for causing interference). That season ended with a below-par showing in the Hong Kong Vase at Sha Tin, but Zindabad was back on song on his return in the latest season, winning the Dubai Irish Village Stakes (John Porter) on his reappearance at Newbury in April, knuckling down with typical resolution and needing every yard of the trip to edge out St Expedit by a neck. Far from discredited when fourth to Marienbard next time over the same distance in the Jockey Club Stakes at Newmarket, Zindabad was tried over the longest trip he's tackled, an extended thirteen furlongs, in the Merewood Homes Yorkshire Cup at York. His pedigree and the way he had shaped in his races suggested that the extra distance would be within his compass. The steady gallop didn't make the Yorkshire Cup a true test at the trip on the day but, sent on over two furlongs out and responding gamely under pressure, Zindabad won by a length and a half from Boreas, with Jardines Lookout in third and Persian Punch in fourth. Zindabad's remaining races were all at a mile and a half and, after running below his best when nine and a half lengths third of six to Boreal in the Coronation Cup at Epsom (under the softest conditions he encountered all year), it was next stop Royal Ascot.

Having his fifth outing in nine weeks, Zindabad went one better in the Hardwicke than in the previous year, conceding weight to all bar one of his rivals, and producing his best performance yet in an up-to-scratch renewal. Zindabad went off a 4/1-shot, with Storming Home and Millenary heading the betting at 11/4 and High Pitched at 3/1; Zindabad's stable-companion Yavana's Pace was among the outsiders at 33/1. As usual, Zindabad was soon prominent, dictating a steady gallop. Under a fine ride from Kevin Darley, the jockey who has partnered him for every race during the past two seasons, Zindabad stepped up the pace approaching the straight and, responding in most resolute fashion, kept all challengers at bay. At the line, he had a length to spare over Storming Home, with Millenary and High Pitched only a short head and a neck away in third and fourth respectively, those clear of the rest. The win gave Kingsley House stables one of four successes at the 2002 Royal meeting, and its third win in the Hardwicke in four years, Fruits of Love having won in 1999 and 2000. Zindabad was returned to the course for the King George VI and Queen Elizabeth Stakes in July, when he acquitted himself well to finish third of nine to Golan, beaten over three and a half lengths by the winner.

Merewood Homes Yorkshire Cup, York—Zindabad runs on with typical willingness; Boreas takes second ahead of Jardines Lookout (left) and Persian Punch (rail)

Hardwicke Stakes, Royal Ascot—Zindabad responds gamely when pressed by Storming Home, Millenary (rail) and High Pitched; Potemkin is fifth

Zindabad was no match for Golan and Nayef but again kept on determinedly once headed after taking over in the lead five furlongs from home. As in 2001, Zindabad's season ended on a downbeat note when he managed only a laboured fifth of eight behind Ballingarry in a repeat bid in the Canadian International; Zindabad finished two places and half a length behind stable-companion Yavana's Pace.

Zindabad is the third foal out of the useful but quite lightly-raced Miznah, an Irish two-year-old six-furlong listed winner who ran four times apiece at two and three, her best efforts in her second season when placed in listed races at the Curragh and Leopardstown. Miznah is from a very good family, closely related to three useful performers by Nijinsky, notably the 1987 Irish two-year-old six-furlong winner Lake Como, and also a half-sister to the useful 1997 Irish two-year-old six-furlong winner Heeremandi. Miznah is also a close relation to the dam of dual champion American turf mare Flawlessly. Like Zindabad, longevity was a feature of Flawlessly's career, as she won nine Grade 1 events up to the age of six at around nine furlongs and a mile and a quarter. Their unraced grandam La Dame du Lac is a half-sister to champion sire Halo and champion filly Tosmah. The great grandam Cosmah is a half-sister to Natalma, the dam of Northern Dancer. Miznah had two foals before Zindabad, the better of them the useful 1997 Irish two-year-old seven-furlong winner who stayed a mile and three quarters Geisha Girl (by Nashwan). All three of Miznah's foals to reach the racecourse since Zindabad have won, namely Millions (by Bering, over hurdles), Legal Word (by Nashwan, in Denmark) and Navado (by Rainbow Quest). The last-named progressed quickly into a useful performer as a three-year-old in 2002, winning at around a mile and a half; he is the final foal in Britain for Miznah, who has since been sent to America.

		Mill Reef	Never Bend
	Shirley Heights	(b 1968)	Milan Mill
	(b 1975)	Hardiemma	Hardicanute
Zindabad (FR)		(b 1969)	Grand Cross
(b.h. 1996)		Sadler's Wells	Northern Dancer
	Miznah (IRE)	(b 1981)	Fairy Bridge
	(b 1989)	La Dame du Lac	Round Table
		(b 1973)	Cosmah

The quite good-topped Zindabad, a fluent mover, has shown his very best form at a mile and a half but should prove equally effective at a truly-run mile and three quarters, giving connections the option of aiming Zindabad at races such as the Irish St Leger (in which Yavana's Pace has twice finished second, including as a seven-year-old). Though a winner on soft, Zindabad is probably at his very best on going firmer than good (six of his eight wins have been recorded on good to firm). Zindabad, who is to be prepared for the Dubai Sheema Classic at Nad Al Sheba in March, is clearly capable of competing with the best over middle distances in Britain, but, if connections continue to campaign him mostly at around a mile and a half, his best chances of Group 1 success at that trip are likely to be in weaker contests overseas, as Johnston managed in the most recent season with Yavana's Pace. It is well worth reiterating that Zindabad is, like so many from his stable, tough and splendidly game. *M. Johnston*

ZINGARI 2 ch.f. (Feb 9) Groom Dancer (USA) 128 – Antigua (Selkirk (USA) 129) **88**
[2002 7.1m⁶ 7m* 7m* 8f* 7f* 8.3d* 7g⁶ Oct 27] well-made filly: first foal: dam unraced
out of close relative to high-class sprinter Polish Patriot: fairly useful performer: won
maiden at Brighton and nurseries at Yarmouth, Pontefract, Catterick and Windsor (beat
Sovereign Dancer by ½ length) in September/October: below form in listed race at Rome
final start: effective at 7f/1m: acts on firm and good to soft going: usually races
prominently: flashes tail, but game. *Sir Mark Prescott*

ZINGING 3 b.g. Fraam 114 – Hi Hoh (IRE) (Fayruz 116) [2002 79d: p5g p6g⁶ p7g³ **70 §**
p5g⁴ p7g⁴ p7g⁴ p6g³ 6g 8f² 8.1d p7g⁶ 7s⁵ 7d 8m² 8d³ 8d 8m 8f 7f 6m f9.4g p7g² p7g⁶ Dec **a61 §**
30] small, compact gelding: fair handicapper on turf, modest on all-weather: stays easy
1m: acts on firm going, soft and polytrack: tried visored: has edged right/found little:
headstrong and inconsistent. *J. J. Bridger*

ZINZIBERINE (USA) 2 b.f. (Mar 22) Zieten (USA) 118 – Amenixa (FR) 73 **107**
(Linamix (FR) 127) [2002 4.5s* 5d² 5.5g² 6g⁴ 5.5g² 6g* 6s* Oct 28] $60,000F: first
foal: dam, 1m winner, sister to high-class French stayer Amilynx and half-sister to 2000
Criterium de Maisons-Laffitte winner Amiwain: useful performer: won newcomers race
at Saint-Cloud in June, Prix Eclipse at Maisons-Laffitte (by ¾ length from Acago) in
October and Criterium de Maisons-Laffitte (by length from Fiepes Shuffle) later in
October: in frame in pattern races other starts, notably when beaten a head by Never A
Doubt in Prix Robert Papin (third start) and a nose by Pleasure Place in Prix d'Arenberg
(fifth outing), both at Maisons-Laffitte: stays 6f: acts on soft ground, yet to race on firmer
than good: swished tail/edged left in Robert Papin: held up: consistent. *A. Fabre, France*

ZIPPING (IRE) 3 b.c. Zafonic (USA) 130 – Zelda (IRE) (Caerleon (USA) 132) [2002 **119**
118: 7g² 8m⁴ 6s* 6.5s⁶ 5g³ 5m⁵ Dec 15] leggy, quite attractive colt: smart performer:
respectable efforts in listed race at Maisons-Laffitte (found little in front and beaten ½
lengh by Massalani) and 2000 Guineas at Newmarket (4 lengths fourth to Rock of
Gibraltar) first 2 starts: won Prix de Ris-Orangis at Deauville in July, leading on line to
beat May Ball a nose: also ran well when when very close third to Continent in Prix de
l'Abbaye at Longchamp, then respectable fifth to All Thrills Too in Hong Kong Sprint at
Sha Tin: has form at 1m, but best at 5f/6f: acts on soft ground, probably on good to firm:
best held up and produced late. *R. Collet, France*

ZITHER 2 b.f. (Mar 30) Zafonic (USA) 130 – Rose Noble (USA) 62 (Vaguely Noble **84**
140) [2002 6m³ 7d³ 6m* 6.5m Sep 11] close-coupled filly: sixth foal: half-sister to useful
1m (at 2 yrs) and 1¼m winner Dower House (by Groom Dancer): dam, 11.5f winner,
half-sister to high-class performer up to 1¼m Grand Lodge: fairly useful form: third in
maidens before winning one easily at Thirsk in July: well held in nursery at Doncaster:
free-going sort, and will prove best up to 1m: yet to race on extremes of going. *R. Hannon*

ZONE 3 b.g. Zilzal (USA) 137 – Thea (USA) 95 (Marju (IRE) 127) [2002 92p: 10.2g⁴ **86**
8.3m 8s⁵ Oct 14] strong, good-bodied gelding: promising winner only run at 2 yrs: fourth
in minor event at Bath on reappearance: disappointing after: should stay at least 1¼m:
sold 11,000 gns, sent to Kuwait. *P. F. I. Cole*

*Prix de Ris-Orangis, Deauville—Zipping (left) makes the drop back to six furlongs
a winning one by collaring May Ball on the line; Danger Over (blaze) is third*

The Mail On Sunday/Tote Mile Final (Handicap), Ascot—Zonergem comes from well off the pace to win impressively from George Stubbs (rail), Digital (white blaze) and Tony Tie (breastgirth)

ZONERGEM 4 ch.g. Zafonic (USA) 130 – Anasazi (IRE) (Sadler's Wells (USA) 132) **105**
[2002 77: 8.5g³ 10f 8.1m* 8m³ 8f³ 9m³ 8m* 9f Oct 5] useful handicapper, lightly raced: won at Warwick in July and Ascot in September, much improved to beat George Stubbs easily by 3½ lengths in Mail On Sunday/Tote Mile Final on latter course: favourite, switched sharply from stalls and soon had far too much to do when mid-field in Tote Cambridgeshire at Newmarket final run: stays 9f: acts on firm going, possibly unsuited by heavy: has worn cheekpieces: has been slowly away (including when blindfolded for stall at Ascot)/carried head high/found little: held up: quirky. *Lady Herries*

ZOOM ZOOM 2 b.c. (Apr 16) Abou Zouz (USA) 109 – Iltimas (USA) 95 (Dayjur **76 p**
(USA) 137) [2002 6d³ 5.1s* Oct 29] 15,000F, 11,000Y: third foal: half-brother to 1999 2-y-o 5f winner Cautionary (by Warning): dam, 5f and (including at 2 yrs) 6f winner, half-sister to Queen Mary winner Nadwah: fair form in maidens (well backed): off 3 months, won at Nottingham by 2½ lengths from Batailley, leading final 1f: will probably stay 7f: open to further improvement. *Mrs L. Stubbs*

ZOOT 2 br.c. (Feb 27) Zafonic (USA) 130 – Bint Zamayem (IRE) 95 (Rainbow Quest **70 p**
(USA) 134) [2002 8g p8g Nov 14] 55,000Y: lengthy, useful-looking colt: fourth foal: half-brother to useful Irish 2001 2-y-o 6f winner Sweet Deimos (by Green Desert) and fairly useful 7.6f winner Queenie (by Indian Ridge): dam, 1¼m winner, half-sister to smart miler Rouquette: fair form in maidens at Newmarket (very green) and Lingfield (found little after travelling well): not sure to stay much beyond 1m: probably still capable of better. *Mrs A. J. Perrett*

ZORN 3 br.c. Dilum (USA) 115 – Very Good (Noalto 120) [2002 45: 8m p10g Dec 30] **–**
poor maiden: form only on all-weather. *P. Howling*

ZOROASTER 2 gr.c. (Mar 30) Linamix (FR) 127 – Persian Walk (FR) (Persian Bold **78 p**
123) [2002 8m³ 8.1m³ Sep 18] leggy, unfurnished colt: second foal: dam, won both starts at 1½m in France, half-sister to smart French performers up to 1½m Walk On Mix and Walking Around (both by Linamix): fair form in maidens at Newmarket (hung markedly left) and Sandown (beaten 3 lengths by Orange Touch): will be suited by 1¼m/1½m: remains capable of better. *J. H. M. Gosden*

randombet.com Lincoln (Handicap), Doncaster—33/1-shot Zucchero (right) just holds off the favourite Adiemus; I Cried For You (stars) is third

ZORRO 8 gr.g. Touch of Grey 90 – Snow Huntress 80 (Shirley Heights 130) [2002 –: p13g Feb 13] leggy gelding: poor handicapper: stays easy 13f: acts on firm ground (well beaten on softer than good): tried blinkered. *Jamie Poulton* — **40**

ZOUCHE 2 b.g. (Apr 18) Zamindar (USA) 116 – Al Corniche (IRE) 62 (Bluebird (USA) 125) [2002 6g⁵ Oct 17] 25,000Y, 54,000 2-y-o: close-coupled gelding: fourth foal: half-brother to useful 1999 2-y-o 6f to 1m winner Whyome (by Owington) and 4-y-o Lady Kinvarrah: dam, 2-y-o 5f winner who stayed 1¾m, from family of Irish 1000 Guineas winner Nicer: 16/1, 2 lengths fifth of 18 to Pigeon Point in maiden at Newmarket, always chasing leaders: swished tail in paddock: gelded after: should progress. *B. J. Meehan* — **83 p**

ZOZARHARRY (IRE) 4 b.g. Nicolotte 118 – Miss Butterfield (Cure The Blues (USA)) [2002 80, a87: f8s f8g f7g f6g f7g Dec 2] good-topped gelding: fairly useful handicapper at 3 yrs: ran badly in 2002, including in blinkers. *J. Cullinan* — **–**

ZSAZSABELLA (IRE) 3 b.f. Alzao (USA) 117 – Zifta (USA) 82 (Zilzal (USA) 137) [2002 66: f8.5g⁵ 8m⁴ 8f³ 8.2m p8g 7d 8.1g 8g a8s⁶ Dec 22] rather leggy filly: fair maiden: sold from J. Hills 2,000 gns before final outing: stays 1m: acts on firm and good to soft going: sometimes folds tamely: seems none too consistent. *M. Kahn, Sweden* — **70**

ZUBAYRR (IRE) 3 gr.c. Darshaan 133 – High Mare (FR) (Highest Honor (FR) 124) [2002 9.9m⁶ a10f Dec 13] IR 200,000Y: second foal: dam, French 2-y-o 7f/7.5f winner, out of half-sister to Cheveley Park Stakes and 1000 Guineas winner Ma Biche: reportedly injured spleen in accident at home in spring 2002: 5/2-joint favourite, 15 lengths sixth behind Blue Leader in maiden at Goodwood in September, travelling well under restraint to past halfway and not subjected to unnecessarily hard time: left A. Stewart, and off 3 months before well-held seventh of 13 in similar event at Jebel Ali. *A. Smith, UAE* — **55**

ZUCCHERINO 3 b.g. Be My Chief (USA) 122 – Efizia 78 (Efisio 120) [2002 10.1m⁴ May 23] good-bodied gelding: first foal: dam 9f/1¼m winner: 33/1, seemed to show fair form when fourth to Supremacy in steadily-run maiden at Newcastle, only start: dead. *G. M. Moore* — **65**

ZUCCHERO 6 br.g. Dilum (USA) 115 – Legal Sound 85 (Legal Eagle 126) [2002 99+: 8s* 8.1d Jul 6] big, lengthy gelding: type to carry condition: useful handicapper: better than ever when winning randombet.com Lincoln Handicap at Doncaster in March by head from Adiemus: started slowly only other outing in 2002 (reportedly injured back): effective at 7f/1m: yet to race on heavy going, probably acts on any other: often blinkered/visored before 2001: effective making running, held up nowadays: game. *D. W. P. Arbuthnot* — **104**

ZUHAIR 9 ch.g. Mujtahid (USA) 118 – Ghzaalh (USA) 87 (Northern Dancer) [2002 90: 6g 5f 5f 5d 6m⁵ 5m⁴ 5g* 6m² 6m 6m 5m 6g 5m Oct 2] strong gelding: fairly useful — **90**

Charlton Stakes (Handicap), Goodwood—Zuhair wins this handicap for the fourth year in succession; Talbot Avenue (left) and Texas Gold (hidden by winner) are next

handicapper: won Charlton Stakes at Goodwood in July for fourth consecutive year (had become very leniently handicapped after 6 unplaced runs), beating Talbot Avenue 1½ lengths: effective at 5f/6f: unsuited by soft/heavy going, acts on any other: well beaten both runs in blinkers: wears bandages: tends to sweat: usually held up. *D. Nicholls*

ZULEIKA DOBSON   4 b.f. Cadeaux Genereux 131 – Fresher 113 (Fabulous Dancer   **102** (USA) 124) [2002 106: 8d³ 10f² 9g* 7f⁶ 8f 9m 10.3v² Nov 8] leggy filly: second reported foal: dam, French 2-y-o 1m winner later successful in USA, half-sister to very smart French 1½m performer Songlines: useful performer: trained by J. Hammond in France at 3 yrs, when third in Prix Chloe at Chantilly: won maiden at Goodwood in June: best other efforts on same course when 2¾ lengths third to Dolores in listed race and when sixth to Firebreak in Supreme Stakes: stays 9f: acts on firm and good to soft going: difficult ride. *G. Wragg*

ZURS (IRE)   9 b.g. Tirol 127 – Needy (High Top 131) [2002 p10g 11.6m Jul 29] sturdy   **– §** gelding: fair hurdler: lightly raced and ungenuine on Flat nowadays: tried blinkered. *Jonjo O'Neill*

ZYZANIA   3 b.f. Zafonic (USA) 130 – Moneefa 73 (Darshaan 133) [2002 7g 7 1d⁴ 8f²   **68** 8.1g⁴ 8.1m³ 7.1f³ Sep 27] 26,000Y: angular filly: third foal: half-sister to 4-y-o Dandoun: dam, 1¼m winner, half-sister to dam of very smart 1m/9f performer Olden Times out of smart sprinter Abha: fair maiden: stays 1m: acts on firm ground. *W. R. Muir*

The following unraced horses appeared in ante-post lists for 2003 classics or had a Group 1 entry at two years, and are included for information purposes.

AL DURRAH (USA)   2 br.f. (Jan 21) Darshaan 133 – Ashraakat (USA) 105 (Danzig (USA) first foal: dam, 6f/7f (latter at 2 yrs) winner, sister to high-class sprinter Elnadim and half-sister to very smart performer Mehthaaf. *J. L. Dunlop*

ACT OF DUTY   2 ch.c. (Feb 13) Mr Prospector (USA) – Nuryette (USA) (Nureyev (USA) 131) $3,600,000Y: closely related to smart US Grade 2 7f/1m winner Northern Afleet (by Afleet) and half-brother to several winners, notably smart US performer up to 1¼m (Grade 1 winner at 9f) Tap To Music (by Pleasant Tap): dam unraced half-sister to smart US 2-y-o Grade 1 winner at 8.5f Cuddles. *A. P. O'Brien, Ireland*

ALAFDAL (USA)   2 b.c. (Mar 2) Gone West (USA) – Aqaarid (USA) 116 (Nashwan (USA) 135) first foal: closely related to 2000 2-y-o 1m winner Elmonjed (by Gulch), later 7f winner in UAE: dam, won Fillies' Mile and second in 1000 Guineas, from good family. *J. L. Dunlop*

ARPEGE (IRE)   2 b.f. (Feb 4) Sadler's Wells (USA) 132 – Sharata (IRE) (Darshaan 133) sister to smart 7f (at 2 yrs) to 1½m winner Crimson Tide, closely related to smart French 1m (including at 2 yrs)/9f winner Pharatta (by Fairy King), and half-sister to 2 useful winners, including 9f to 1¾m winner Sharatan (by Kahyasi): dam unraced half-sister to Shahrastani. *A. P. O'Brien, Ireland*

ASTRONOMIC   2 b.c. (Apr 3) Zafonic (USA) 130 – Sky Love (USA) 93 (Nijinsky (CAN) 138) half-brother to several winners, including smart French 1m (at 2 yrs) to 1½m winner Bonash and useful French 1¼m winner Be Glad (by Selkirk): dam, 1¼m winner, half-sister to high-class middle-distance performer Raft. *A. Fabre, France*

CASTLE SPRINGS   2 b.c. (Feb 9) Machiavellian (USA) 123 – Cloud Castle 119 (In The Wings 128) 240,000Y: first foal: dam, 7f (Nell Gwyn) winner who stayed 1½m, half-sister to very smart 1½m performer Luso. *Saeed bin Suroor*

CORSICA   2 b.c. (May 28) Green Desert (USA) 127 – La Belle Otero (USA) 60 (Nureyev (USA) 131) 150,000Y: second foal: closely related to fairly useful 2001 2-y-o 7f winner Brown Eyes (by Danehill): dam once-raced half-sister to US Grade 3 winner at 9f Summer Matinee. *J. Noseda*

DAWN PIPER (USA)   2 b.c. (Apr 14) Desert Prince (IRE) 130 – June Moon (IRE) (Sadler's Wells (USA) 132) $400,000Y: half-brother to several winners, including smart miler Pacino and 3-y-o Dupont (both by Zafonic): dam unraced daughter of 1000 Guineas runner-up and smart sprinter Kerrera. *Saeed bin Suroor*

DE GREGORIO (IRE)   2 b.c. (May 14) Peintre Celebre (USA) 137 – Classic Design (Busted 134) 80,000Y: half-brother to 3 winners, notably very smart 5f performer

Eveningperformance (by Night Shift): dam unraced half-sister to 2000 Guineas winner Tirol. *A. P. O'Brien, Ireland*

DELSARTE (USA)   2 b.c. (Jan 23) Theatrical 128 – Delauncy (Machiavellian (USA) 123) $200,000F, $170,000Y: first foal: dam, useful French 2-y-o 1m winner who stayed 1¼m, daughter of Park Hill winner Casey. *M. Johnston*

DESERT PLUM (IRE)   2 b.f. (Feb 26) Desert Prince (IRE) – Damascene (IRE) (Scenic 128) third foal: half-sister to Irish 1999 2-y-o 7f winner Darbys Bridge (by Kris) and smart 2000 2-y-o 1m winner Perfect Plum (by Darshaan): dam unraced half-sister to top-class sprinter Marwell, herself dam of very smart miler Marling. *Sir Mark Prescott*

ELLEN (IRE)   2 ch.f. (May 1) Machiavellian (USA) 123 – Sleepytime (IRE) 121 (Royal Academy (USA) 130) second foal: dam won 1000 Guineas (also 7f winner at 2 yrs), sister to high-class miler Ali-Royal and half-sister to very smart 1¼m/1½m performer Taipan, a very good family. *H. R. A. Cecil*

EXCALIBUR (IRE)   2 b.c. (Mar 2) Danehill (USA) 126 – Sharaniya (USA) 117 (Alleged (USA) 138) 270,000Y: half-brother to several winners, including 1½m winner Mazaya (by Sadler's Wells) and Irish 1½m and 2m winner Sharazan (by Akarad), both useful: dam, French 1¼m to 12.5f winner, half-sister to Prix Vermeille winner Sharaya. *A. P. O'Brien*

FAAYEJ (IRE)   2 b.c. (Feb 28) Sadler's Wells (USA) 132 – Russian Ballet (USA) (Nijinsky (CAN) 138) 750,000Y: brother to fairly useful 12.5f winner in Ireland Domenico, and half-brother to several winners by Woodman, notably very smart Irish 1¼m to 1¾m winner (also second in Irish Derby) Dr Johnson: dam twice-raced close relation to Try My Best and El Gran Senor, an excellent family. *Sir Michael Stoute*

FREMEN (USA)   2 ch.c. (Apr 24) Rahy (USA) 115 – Northern Trick (USA) 131 (Northern Dancer) closely related to useful French 9f winner Ciel de Feu (by Blushing John) and half-brother to several winners, including useful Irish 1¼m/1½m winner Yuan (by Miswaki): dam, won Prix de Diane and Prix Vermeille and runner-up in Arc, grandam of high-class 1¼m performer Shiva and very smart French performer up to 12.5f Limnos. *Sir Michael Stoute*

FRONT RANK (IRE)   2 b.c. (Mar 13) Sadler's Wells (USA) 132 – Alignment (IRE) 98 (Alzao (USA) 117) first foal: dam, headstrong maiden (fourth in Musidora Stakes), half-sister to smart performer up to 14.6f Bonny Scot and to dam of 4-y-o Golan out of half-sister to Prix de Cadran winner Sought Out. *Sir Michael Stoute*

HAWKSBILL (USA)   2 ch.c. (Apr 5) Silver Hawk (USA) 123 – Binary 109 (Rainbow Quest (USA) 134) third foal: half-brother to 4-y-o Binary File: dam, 9f/1¼m winner in France/USA, sister to smart 1½m performer Bequeath from very good family. *J. H. M. Gosden*

HIGH COUNTRY (IRE)   2 b.c. (Feb 29) Danehill (USA) 126 – Dance Date (IRE) (Sadler's Wells (USA) 132) 4,200,000 francs Y: brother to a 7f winner in Hong Kong and half-brother to several winners, including useful German 6f (at 2 yrs) and 1m winner Decamerone (by Thatching): dam unraced sister to smart stayer Sonus and half-sister to Derby runner-up Hawaiian Sound. *A. P. O'Brien, Ireland*

IKHTYAR (IRE)   2 b.c. (Mar 26) Unfuwain (USA) 131 – Sabria (USA) (Miswaki (USA) 124) 65,000F, IR 380,000Y: fourth foal: half-brother to 3 winners, including 3-y-o Landseer and fairly useful 1¼m winner Sabreon (by Caerleon): dam unraced half-sister to smart middle-distance performer King Sound from family of Triptych and Generous. *J. H. M. Gosden*

IRTAHAL (USA)   2 br.f. (Feb 28) Swain (IRE) 134 – Elhasna (USA) 88 (Danzig (USA)) sixth foal: half-sister to 1999 2-y-o 5f winner Enaaq (by Bahri) and to a winner in US by Deputy Minister: dam, 6f winner, sister to Dayjur and closely related to US Grade 1 winner at 9f/1¼m winner Maplejinsky. *M. P. Tregoning*

LOVE IN SEATTLE (IRE)   2 b.c. (May 14) Seattle Slew (USA) – Tamise (USA) 113 (Time For A Change (USA)) $70,000Y: first foal: dam French 1m to 10.5f winner, half-sister to smart French performers Alekos (stayed 11f) and Tarzan Cry (stayed 1m). *M. Johnston*

LUCIUS VERRUS (USA)   2 b.c. (Apr 30) Danzig (USA) – Magic of Life (USA) 118 (Seattle Slew (USA)) half-brother to several winners, including 2000 2-y-o 6f (including Lowther Stakes) winner Enthused (by Seeking The Gold) and French 1¼m/1½m winner From Beyond (by Kris), both useful: dam 5f (at 2 yrs) to 1m (Coronation Stakes) winner from excellent family. *A. P. O'Brien, Ireland*

MASJOOR 2 ch.c. (Feb 27) Unfuwain (USA) 131 – Mihnah (IRE) 87 (Lahib (USA) 129) first foal: dam, 6f (at 2 yrs) and 1m winner, half-sister to smart performer up to 14.6f Ranin (by Unfuwain). *M. P. Tregoning*

MIDDLEMARCH (IRE) 2 ch.c. (Mar 6) Grand Lodge (USA) 125 – Blanche Dubois (Nashwan (USA) 135) second foal: half-brother to 3-y-o Lady High Havens: dam unraced half-sister to Gran Criterium winner Count Dubois and to dam of 4-y-o High Pitched. *A. P. O'Brien, Ireland*

MURILLO 2 b.c. (Feb 22) Green Desert (USA) 127 – Colorvista (Shirley Heights 130) 1,300,000Y: half-brother to several winners, notably smart 1997 2-y-o 7f winner Mudeer (by Warning) who stayed 9f: dam unraced half-sister to Cezanne, Bella Colora and Colorspin (dam of Opera House and Kayf Tara). *A. P. O'Brien, Ireland*

NOVELLO (USA) 2 b.c. (Mar 16) Mr Prospector (USA) – Ziggy's Act (USA) (Danzig (USA)) seventh foal: closely related to a winner in USA by Miswaki, and half-brother to 2 winners in USA: dam, US Grade 3 winner at 9f, out of US Grade 1 winner at 1¼m Comedy Act. *A. P. O'Brien, Ireland*

PANORAMIC (USA) 2 b.c. (Feb 8) Theatrical 128 – Mint Leaf (USA) (Capote (USA)) $600,000Y: first foal: dam, US maiden, half-sister to US Grade 1 winner at 8.5f Super May. *G. A. Butler*

PERFECT PORTRAIT 2 ch.c. (Feb 14) Selkirk (USA) 129 – Flawless Image (USA) 109 (The Minstrel (CAN) 135) ninth living foal: half-brother to smart 7f (including at 2 yrs)/1m winner Darnay (by Darshaan) and useful Irish 7f and 8.5f winner Matangi (by Mtoto): dam Irish sprinter. *Saeed bin Suroor*

PRESSURE GROUP (USA) 2 b.c. (Feb 10) Sadler's Wells (USA) 132 – Ryafan (USA) 121 (Lear Fan (USA) 130) second foal: dam, won up to 1¼m (including Nassau Stakes and 3 US Grade 1 events), Prix Marcel Boussac winner at 2 yrs. *J. H. M. Gosden*

QAIS (USA) 2 b.c. (Feb 16) Seeking The Gold (USA) – Snow Bride (USA) 121 (Blushing Groom (FR) 131) ninth foal: brother to smart 1998 2-y-o 7f and 1m (Prix d'Aumale) winner Saytarra, and half-brother to 3 winners, notably top-class 7f (at 2 yrs) and 1½m (Derby, King George and Arc) winner Lammtarra (by Nijinsky): dam, awarded Oaks, daughter of top-class 1½m performer Awaasif from family of Bosra Sham. *Saeed bin Suroor*

SHANGRI LA (IRE) 2 b.f. (Jan 20) Sadler's Wells (USA) 132 – Movie Legend (USA) (Affirmed (USA)) 450,000Y: third foal: half-sister to useful Scandinavian 6f to 1m winner Hanzano (by Alzao) and to Irish 5f winner Last Call (by Salse): dam unraced sister to Irish 1000 Guineas winner Trusted Partner. *A. P. O'Brien, Ireland*

SOLSKJAER (IRE) 2 b.c. (Apr 13) Danehill (USA) 126 – Lyndonville (IRE) (Top Ville 129) sixth living foal: brother to smart Japanese performer up to 1½m Tsukuba Symphony: dam, Irish 1¾m winner, half-sister to Fillies' Mile winner Ivanka. *A. P. O'Brien, Ireland*

SUBLIMITY (FR) 2 b.c. (Apr 23) Selkirk (USA) 129 – Fig Tree Drive (USA) 94 (Miswaki (USA) 124) 210,000Y: second foal: dam, 2-y-o 6f winner (her only start), out of sister to US Grade 1 winners De La Rose (9f) and Upper Nile (1¼m). *Sir Michael Stoute*

TANAGHUM 2 b.f. (Mar 15) Darshaan 133 – Mehthaaf (USA) 121 (Nureyev (USA) 131) half-sister to several winners by Nashwan, including smart 1¼m winner Najah and fairly useful 1½m winner Raaqi: dam, 6f (at 2 yrs) and 1m (Irish 1000 Guineas) winner, closely related to high-class sprinter Elnadim and granddaughter of outstanding broodmare Fall Aspen. *J. L. Dunlop*

VENTURA HIGHWAY 2 b.f. (Feb 26) Machiavellian (USA) 123 – Hyabella 111 (Shirley Heights 130) half-sister to useful French 2001 2-y-o 6f winner Hothaifah (by Green Desert) and fairly useful winners Summer Dance (1m, by Sadler's Wells) and Hyperspectra (1¼m, Rainbow Quest): dam, 1m winner, half-sister to high-class 1¼m performer Stagecraft from excellent family. *Sir Michael Stoute*

PROMISING HORSES

Significant British-trained horses (plus those trained by Aidan O'Brien, winner of the trainers' championship) with either a p or P in *Racehorses of 2002*, are listed under the trainer for whom they had their final start.

D. W. P. ARBUTHNOT
Back In Action 2 b.c   85p
Border Alliance 2 ch.c   80p
Lucky Date (IRE) 2 ch.f   81p

G. B. BALDING
Wizard of Edge 2 b.g   69p

I. A. BALDING
Anticipating 2 b.c   68p
Arctic Desert 2 b.c   77p
Briareus 2 ch.g   77p
Far Storm (USA) 2 ch.c   61p
Lilian 2 b.f   60p
Passando 2 b.f   —p
Lochridge 3 ch.f   96p

T. D. BARRON
Royal Time 2 b.f   —p
Zero Tolerance (IRE) 2 ch.g   55p
Impressive Flight (IRE) 3 b.f   105p

K. BELL
Priors Dale 2 b.c   77p

M. L. W. BELL
Ballerina Suprema (IRE) 2 b.f   84p
Ciel 2 b.f   78p
Cooden Beach (IRE) 2 b.f   —p
Distant Light 2 b.f   57p
Icecap 2 b.f   72p
Saturn (IRE) 2 b.c   111p

J. D. BETHELL
Rich Dancer 2 b.f   70p
Sambucan Daze (IRE) 2 b.c   —p

G. C. BRAVERY
Striking Ambition 2 b.c   105p

C. E. BRITTAIN
Estimate 2 b.f   82p
Helderberg (USA) 2 b.f   71p
Lundy's Lane (IRE) 2 b.c   92p

K. R. BURKE
Blue Sky Thinking (IRE) 3 b.g   102p

G. A. BUTLER
Bally Hall (IRE) 2 b.c   —p
Beauchamp Ribbon 2 b.f   —p
Beauchamp Rose 2 ch.f   —p
Blaise Castle (USA) 2 b.f   94p
Commission (USA) 2 ch.c   100p
Compton Emperor 2 b.c   85p
Desert View 2 b.f   78p
Gondolin (IRE) 2 b.g   80p
Huwaidah 2 b.f   65p
Jagger 2 gr.c   67p
Jazz Messenger (FR) 2 bl.g   67p
Jummana (FR) 2 ch.f   96p
La Mouline (IRE) 2 ch.f   86p
Louis Napoleon 2 b.c   84p

Mister Arjay (USA) 2 b.c   76p
Park Street (USA) 2 b.c   81p
Shield 2 b.c   97p
Treculiar (USA) 2 b.c   80p
Compton Drake 3 b.g   —p

N. A. CALLAGHAN
St Pancras (IRE) 2 b.c   104p

H. CANDY
Airwave 2 b.f   114p
Shebeen 2 ch.f   70p
Ringing Hill 3 b.f   88p

H. R. A. CECIL
Amalianburg 2 b.f   —p
Apex Star (USA) 2 ch.c   95p
Changing View 2 ch.c   88p
Floreeda 2 b.f   75p
Home Fleet (USA) 2 ch.c   71p
Instant Thought (USA) 2 ch.f   69p
Lateen Sails 2 ch.c   106p
My Mellors (USA) 2 b.c   66p
Silent Storm 2 ch.c   81p
Timber Ice (IRE) 2 b.f   —p
Zeis (IRE) 2 ch.c   87p
Java 3 b.f   82p
Labrusca 3 b.f   58p
Sharpcut (IRE) 3 b.c   99p

M. R. CHANNON
Fenella's Link 2 gr.f   75p
Night Wolf (IRE) 2 gr.g   —p
Rose Hedge (GER) 2 gr.f   —p
Rustle In The Wind 2 b.f   70p
The Ring (IRE) 2 b.g   72p
Vigorous (IRE) 2 b.f   62p

R. CHARLTON
Avonbridge 2 b.c   104p
Chaffinch (USA) 2 b.f   88p
Change Partners (IRE) 2 ch.f   74p
Constantine 2 gr.c   85p
Domirati 2 b.g   74p
Easter Parade 2 b.f   68p
Elegant Shadow 2 ch.f   83p
Famous Grouse 2 b.c   96p
Innovation 2 b.f   68p
L'Ancresse (IRE) 2 b.f   98p
Midas Way 2 ch.c   92p
One Way Ticket 2 ch.c   74p
Quartet 2 b.c   94p
Rocket Ship (IRE) 2 b.c   85p
Trade Fair 2 b.c   114p
Tree Peony 2 ch.f   63p
Waterfall One 2 ch.f   62p
Winchcombe 2 b.f   —p
Magic Glade 3 b.f   98p

P. F. I. COLE
Alfred Sisley 2 b.g   63p
Crafty Calling (USA) 2 b.c   100p

Excalinor 2 br.c 61p
Liffey (IRE) 2 br.c 83p
Maltese Falcon 2 b.c 82p
Senor Toran (USA) 2 b.g 75p
Sindy (USA) 2 b.f 81p
Web Perceptions (USA) 2 ch.c 81p
Zietory 2 b.f 76p
Capitano Corelli (IRE) 3 b.c 95p
Total Turtle (IRE) 3 b.g 112p

H. J. COLLINGRIDGE
Stormont (IRE) 2 gr.c 93p

C. G. COX
New Seeker 2 b.c 76p

L. M. CUMANI
Camlet 2 b.f 94p
Giuliani 2 b.c 72p
Lady Betambeau (IRE) 2 b.f 63p
Pongee 2 b.f 72p
Queen's Lodge (IRE) 2 ch.f 88p
Saphila (IRE) 2 b.f —p
Senza Scrupoli 2 ch.g —p
Spuradich (IRE) 2 b.c —p
Stealing Beauty 2 b.f 69p
Steel Cat (USA) 2 b.c 74p

P. W. D'ARCY
Complete Circle 2 ch.f 70p
Forest Magic (IRE) 2 b.c 106p

M. DODS
John O'Groats (IRE) 4 b.g 101p

MRS A. DUFFIELD
Rifleman (IRE) 2 ch.c 86p

E. A. L. DUNLOP
Anani (USA) 2 b.c 85p
Battle Chant (USA) 2 b.c 104p
Blythe Knight (IRE) 2 ch.c 82p
Clever Clogs 2 ch.f 72p
Court Masterpiece 2 b.c 95p
Emran (USA) 2 b.c 88p
Golden Fighter 2 ch.c 74p
In Love 2 b.f 82p
Island Light (USA) 2 ch.c 94p
Moonsprite 2 b.f 82p
Rocket Force (USA) 2 ch.c 87p
Sacred Love (IRE) 2 ch.f 69p
San Hernando 2 b.g 69p
Selkirk Grace 2 b.c 92p
Shuhood (USA) 2 b.c 81p
Spy Gun (USA) 2 ch.g 76p
Tipu Sultan 2 ch.c 90p
Unigold (USA) 2 ch.c 95p
Urowells (IRE) 2 b.c 76p

J. L. DUNLOP
Big Bad Bob (IRE) 2 br.c 110p
Cara Fantasy (IRE) 2 b.f 75p
Carenage (IRE) 2 b.f 80p
Discreet Bride (IRE) 2 b.f 86p
Golden Skiis (IRE) 2 ch.f 68p
Goodness Gracious 2 b.f 89p
Impersonator 2 b.g 94p
Khulood (USA) 2 ch.f 102p
Kristal Dancer (IRE) 2 b.f —p
Multaka (USA) 2 b.f 66p

Muqbil (USA) 2 ch.c 106P
Musawah (USA) 2 b.f 63p
Pershaan (IRE) 2 br.f 74p
Prince Tum Tum (USA) 2 b.c 97p
Rawwaah (IRE) 2 ch.c —p
Royal Portrait 2 b.f —p
Sempergreen 2 ch.f 65p
Time Ahead 2 b.f 70p
Voyager (IRE) 2 b.c —p
Contact Dancer (IRE) 3 b.g 92p
Harlestone Bay 3 b.g 66p
Heir To Be 3 b.g 87p
Love Appeal (IRE) 3 ch.f 82p

T. D. EASTERBY
Allegrina (IRE) 2 b.f 70p
Bollin Janet 2 b.f 78p
Boss Man (IRE) 2 b.g —p
Jeepstar 2 b.g 66p
King's Protector 2 b.c 88p
Majestic Times 2 b.c 79p
Night Runner 3 b.c 88p

D. R. C. ELSWORTH
Flamenco Bride 2 b.f —p
Norse Dancer (IRE) 2 b.c 101p

J. M. P. EUSTACE
Silver Chime 2 gr.f 74p
New Diamond 3 ch.g 75p

J. R. FANSHAWE
Adventurist 2 ch.g 75p
Downtime (IRE) 2 ch.g —p
Dubrovsky 2 ch.c 90p
Ice Palace 2 ch.f 83P
Inverness 2 ch.g 62p
Kaiser (IRE) 2 b.g 59p
Peace 2 b.f 78P
Soldera (USA) 2 b.f 95p
Soviet Song (IRE) 2 b.f 115p
Welcome Signal 2 ch.g —p
Wozzeck 2 b.g 77p
Defining 3 b.g 101p
Frizzante 3 b.f 75p
Gamra (IRE) 3 b.f 73p
Oopsie Daisy 3 b.f 81p
Rule Britannia 3 b.f 79p

J. G. GIVEN
Futuristic 2 b.g 64p
Love On Request 2 b.f —p
Pequenita 2 b.f —p
Smart John 2 b.g 65p
Tara's Flame 2 ch.g —p

J. H. M. GOSDEN
Alumni News (USA) 2 b.c 77p
Baraloti (IRE) 2 b.f 58p
Blazing Thunder 2 b.c 94p
Bowing 2 b.c 82p
Calibre (USA) 2 b.c 95p
Desert Opal 2 ch.c —p
Duescals (USA) 2 b.f —p
Echoes In Eternity (IRE) 2 b.f 98P
Felicity (IRE) 2 b.f 65p
Gilded Edge 2 ch.f 94p
Hard Nose (IRE) 2 b.c 87p
Kennington 2 ch.c 68p

Little Good Bay 2 b.c   79p
Mujarad (USA) 2 b.c   81p
Neoclassic 2 b.c   —p
Ocean Silk (USA) 2 b.f   83p
Peace Flag (USA) 2 ch.f   82p
Pilgrim Spirit (USA) 2 b.f   64p
Presenter (USA) 2 ch.c   76P
Sentry (IRE) 2 b.c   79p
Shredded (USA) 2 b.c   81p
Skibereen (IRE) 2 b.c   80p
Stage Shy (USA) 2 ch.f   69p
Texas Hill (USA) 2 b.c   88p
Wondrous Story (USA) 2 ch.f   79p
Zoroaster 2 gr.c   78p
Moscow (IRE) 3 ch.g   —p
The Player 3 b.c   68p
Treble Heights (IRE) 3 b.f   107p

R. GUEST

Millybaa (USA) 2 b.f   66p
Milly Fleur 2 ch.f   60p
Tigerette (USA) 2 b.f   66p

W. J. HAGGAS

Audience 2 b.c   85p
Calligraphy 2 ch.f   73p
Polar Bear 2 ch.c   73p
Socialise 2 b.f   69p
Duncan Dock (USA) 3 ch.g   97p
Tenaja Trail (USA) 3 ch.g   88p
Lithuanian (AUS) 4 br.c   78p
Saponi (IRE) 4 b.g   58p

B. HANBURY

Itnab 2 b.f   76p

R. HANNON

Captain Saif 2 b.c   105p
Kings of Albion (USA) 2 b.c   —p
Oh Boy (IRE) 2 b.c   —p
To The Rescue (USA) 2 b.c   89p
Wings To Soar (USA) 2 b.f   63p

P. W. HARRIS

Albavilla 2 b.f   69p
Barrissimo (IRE) 2 b.c   94p
Blue Mariner 2 b.c   81p
Dolzago 2 b.g   59p
Encore Royale 2 b.f   56p
Graduation Day 2 b.f   69p
Granuaile O'Malley (IRE) 2 b.f   55p
Grooms Affection 2 b.c   60p
Intercession 2 ch.f   90p
Persian Jasmine 2 b.f   79p
Persian Majesty (IRE) 2 b.c   94P
Polish Emperor (USA) 2 ch.c   82p
Rezzago (USA) 2 b.c   63p
Serbelloni 2 b.c   73p
Barolo 3 b.g   84p

B. W. HILLS

Al Ihtithar (IRE) 2 b.f   98p
Arthur Pendragon 2 b.g   65p
Down Memory Lane 2 b.c   84p
Dunhill Star (IRE) 2 b.c   80p
Elnayrah (USA) 2 b.f   75P
Eloquent Silence 2 ch.f   72p
Essnaad (USA) 2 b.c   79p
Flying Express 2 ch.c   94p

Gala Sunday (USA) 2 b.c   92p
Geminiani (IRE) 2 b.f   106p
Golden Dual 2 b.c   72p
Grand Halo (IRE) 2 b.c   58p
Hecuba 2 ch.f   79p
High Diving 2 b.c   76p
Hurricane Love (USA) 2 b.f   —p
Introducing (USA) 2 b.f   81p
Lassitude 2 ch.f   58p
Makhlab (USA) 2 b.c   112p
Miss Grace 2 ch.f   68p
Muwajaha 2 b.f   87p
Not Amused (UAE) 2 ch.c   75p
Private Charter 2 b.c   90p
Ridgeback 2 ch.c   —p
Risk Taker 2 ch.c   91p
Shouette (IRE) 2 b.f   68p
Splendid Era (UAE) 2 b.c   105p
Successor 2 ch.c   86P
Tante Rose (IRE) 2 b.f   91p
Trust Rule 2 b.c   65p
Yafoul (USA) 2 b.f   76p
Pablo 3 b.c   112p

J. W. HILLS

Brave Call (USA) 2 ch.c   82p
Dancing Nugget (USA) 2 b.f   66p
Di Young 2 b.f   62p
Hunter's Mark (USA) 2 b.f   —p
Interceptor 2 ch.c   82p

R. F. JOHNSON HOUGHTON

Awarding 2 ch.c   82p
Ponderon 2 ch.c   —p

M. A. JARVIS

Akrmina 2 ch.f   75p
Anak Pekan 2 ch.c   —p
Crown City (USA) 2 b.f   —p
Dragon Prince 2 b.g   75p
Eoz (IRE) 2 b.f   68p
Grand Gift 2 br.f   —p
Kartuzy (JPN) 2 b.f   —p
Soyuz (IRE) 2 ch.c   92p
St Andrews (IRE) 2 b.c   94p

W. JARVIS

Bridge Pal 2 ch.f   70p
Highly Liquid 2 b.f   81p
Kristoffersen 2 ch.c   72p
October Moon 2 b.f   —p

M. JOHNSTON

Amundsen (USA) 2 b.c   84p
Awwal Marra (USA) 2 ch.f   71p
Big Luciano (USA) 2 b.c   81p
Blackwater Fever (USA) 2 b.c   69p
Bourbonnais (IRE) 2 b.c   104p
Double Mystery (FR) 2 ch.c   81p
Double Obsession 2 b.c   85p
Eastern Dagger 2 b.c   72p
Garros (USA) 2 b.c   97p
Helm Bank 2 b.c   97p
Investment Affair (IRE) 2 b.c   —p
Jack Durrance (IRE) 2 b.c   —p
Kentucky King (USA) 2 b.c   91p
Love You Always (USA) 2 ch.c   98p
Marinas Charm 2 b.f   83p
Morson Boy (USA) 2 b.c   79p

Night Mist (IRE) 2 b.f 80p
Penny Cross 2 b.f 69p
Shanty Star (IRE) 2 gr.c 86p
Western Diplomat (USA) 2 b.c 93P
Wilful 2 ch.c 100p

S. KIRK
Hoh Viss 2 b.c 55p
Sri Diamond 2 b.c 89p

N. P. LITTMODEN
Sir Haydn 2 ch.c 85p

D. R. LODER
Almushahar (USA) 2 b.c 111p
Annambo 2 ch.c 82p
Choral Chimes (JPN) 2 b.f 82p
Dubai Lightning (USA) 2 br.c 90p
Excellento (USA) 2 b.c 82p
Fiaafy (USA) 2 b.f 75P
Hi Dubai 2 ch.f 88p
Khaizarana 2 b.f 72p
Khalkissa (USA) 2 b.f 63p
Late Decision (USA) 2 ch.c 81p
Majestic Horizon 2 b.c 96p
Russian Relation (USA) 2 b.c 78p
Russian Society 2 b.f 82p
Seyed (IRE) 2 b.c —p
Sharp Breeze (USA) 2 b.c 76p
Tawahoj (USA) 2 b.f 78p

M. A. MAGNUSSON
Made In Japan (JPN) 2 b.g 82p

P. J. MAKIN
Cormorant Wharf (IRE) 2 b.c 79p
Dust Cover 2 b.c 80p
Not So Dusty 2 b.c 67p
Perfect Setting 2 b.g 85p
Queensway Quay 2 b.c 91p
Spanish Gold 2 b.f —p
Greenslades 3 ch.c 99p

G. G. MARGARSON
Sea Holly (IRE) 2 b.g —p

B. J. MEEHAN
Isengard (USA) 2 b.f 75p
Jubilee 2 ch.f 65p
Regal Vintage (USA) 2 ch.c —p
Romantic Liason 2 b.f 108p
Wake (USA) 2 b.c 81p
Zouche 2 b.g 83p

T. G. MILLS
A Very Good Year (IRE) 2 b.c 77p
Contractor 2 gr.c 85p
High Reach 2 b.c —p
Littleton Arwen (USA) 2 b.f 94p
Ok Pal 2 b.c 94p
Peace Offering (IRE) 2 b.c 105p
Sailing Through 2 b.c 65p
Sugarboy 2 b.g 66p

P. MITCHELL
Joe Bear (IRE) 2 ch.c 79p

W. J. MUSSON
Star Vega 2 ch.f 87p
Jair Ohmsford (IRE) 3 b.g 68p

D. NICHOLLS
Rectangle (IRE) 2 ch.g 81p
Fire Up The Band 3 b.c 103p

J. NOSEDA
Almaviva (IRE) 2 b.f 90p
Beautifulballerina (USA) 2 b.f 64p
Ephesus 2 b.c 75p
Flying Wanda 2 b.f 87p
Foretold (IRE) 2 b.c —p
Lodger (FR) 2 ch.c 68p
Presumptive (IRE) 2 b.c 75p
Pretence (IRE) 2 b.c 71p

A. P. O'BRIEN, IRELAND
Alberto Giacometti (IRE) 2 b.c 111p
Brian Boru 2 b.c 117p
Chevalier (IRE) 2 b.c 115p
Delacroix (USA) 2 ch.c 102p
Gianfanti (IRE) 2 b.c 98p
Hold That Tiger (USA) 2 b.c 117p
Mingun (USA) 2 b.c 97P
Powerscourt 2 b.c 112p
Reach For The Moon (USA) 2 b.f 103p
Some Kind of Tiger (USA) 2 b.c 104p
Statue of Liberty (USA) 2 b.c 109p
Yesterday (IRE) 2 b.f 106p

W. A. O'GORMAN
Mac's Talisman (IRE) 2 ch.c 69p
Hidden Surprise 3 b.g 89p

J. A. OSBORNE
Bar of Silver (IRE) 2 ch.c 50p
Gracious Dancer 2 b.c —p
Jannadav (IRE) 2 b.f 72p

B. PALLING
Giocoso (USA) 2 b.c 80p

MRS A. J. PERRETT
Alchemystic (IRE) 2 b.c —p
Ambonnay 2 ch.f 83p
Amount 2 b.f 80p
Cat Ona High (USA) 2 ch.c 101p
Crown Counsel 2 b.c 85p
Cryptogam 2 b.f 73p
Darmagi (IRE) 2 b.f 77p
Hoopz 2 gr.f 70p
Humid Climate 2 ch.c 63p
Latest Edition 2 b.f 81p
Orange Touch (GER) 2 b.c 84p
Rachel 2 ch.f —p
Rejuvenate (IRE) 2 ch.c 74p
Self Evident (USA) 2 b.c 87p
Summer Circus 2 b.f —p
Ten Carat 2 b.c —p
Tuneful 2 b.f 82p
Westmoreland Road (USA) 2 b.c 78p
Zoot 2 br.c 70p
Latest Moment (USA) 3 br.g 94p
March Alone 3 b.f 58p
Polar Way 3 ch.g 112p

SIR MARK PRESCOTT
Acceleration (IRE) 2 b.g —p
Alba Stella 2 b.f 70p
Approach 2 gr.f 101p
Astyanax (IRE) 2 b.c —p

1118

Audacious Prince (IRE) 2 b.c   91p
Christina Sanchez (USA) 2 gr.f   —p
Cordial (IRE) 2 gr.c   56p
Humouresque 2 b.f   76p
Lanark Belle 2 b.f   —p
Lawrence of Arabia (IRE) 2 b.g   57p
Mandarin Spirit (IRE) 2 b.c   55p
Noble Lady 2 ch.f   65p
No Refuge (IRE) 2 ch.c   59p
On Point 2 b.f   60p
Special Envoy 2 b.c   75p
Tempsford (USA) 2 b.c   —p
Froglet 3 b.f   83p

J. J. QUINN
Beauvrai 2 b.g   93p
Bigalothegigalo (IRE) 2 b.g   81p
Eiger (IRE) 2 b.c   87p
Esteban 2 b.g   57p
Go Sheek (IRE) 2 b.f   55p
Hov 2 b.g   69p
Smart Minister 2 gr.g   —p

MRS J. R. RAMSDEN
Favour 2 b.f   78p
Horizon Hill (USA) 2 b.g   67p
Kangarilla Road 3 b.g   88p

MRS M. REVELEY
Polish Flame 4 b.g   71p

A. C. STEWART
Assraar 2 b.f   86p
Otototm 2 b.c   —p
Qabas (USA) 2 b.c   75p
Rudood (USA) 2 b.c   86p
Tarjman 2 b.c   86p
Lafi (IRE) 3 ch.c   80p

SIR MICHAEL STOUTE
Adekshan (IRE) 2 ch.c   88p
Alkaased (USA) 2 b.c   87p
Arakan (USA) 2 br.c   91p
Artistic Lad 2 ch.c   87p
Beaucette (USA) 2 br.f   73p
Chief Yeoman 2 b.g   83p
Crystal Star 2 ch.f   99p
Desert Quest (IRE) 2 b.c   77P
Desert Star 2 b.c   104p
Fantasize 2 ch.f   84p
Flash of Gold 2 b.f   73P
Halawanda (IRE) 2 b.f   83p
Hasanpour (IRE) 2 b.c   88p
Hector's Girl 2 ch.f   95p
High Action (USA) 2 ch.c   —p
Kalaman (IRE) 2 b.c   78P
Kris Kin (USA) 2 ch.c   81p
Machinist (IRE) 2 br.c   82p
Mananiyya (IRE) 2 ch.f   83p
McQueen (IRE) 2 ch.c   —p
Misaayef (USA) 2 b.f   78p
Mustaneer (USA) 2 b.c   80p
Nayzak (USA) 2 b.f   91p
Rainbow City (IRE) 2 b.f   85p
Rainbow Queen 2 b.f   92p
Red Passion (USA) 2 b.f   —p
Rich Affair 2 br.f   77p
Rossellini (USA) 2 b.f   78p
Russian Rhythm (USA) 2 ch.f   113p

Safe From Harm (USA) 2 ch.c   92p
Spanish Sun (USA) 2 b.f   84p
Statement (IRE) 2 b.c   90p
Super Song 2 b.c   75p
Testament 2 b.f   —p
Time Honoured 2 b.f   83p
Tug of Love (IRE) 2 ch.c   87p
Vipassana 2 b.f   —p
Waldmark (GER) 2 ch.f   83P
Akshar (IRE) 3 b.c   95p
Gamut (IRE) 3 b.c   116p
Hasik (IRE) 3 b.c   88p
Princely Venture (IRE) 3 ch.c   98p
Zee Zee Top 3 b.f   104p

MRS L. STUBBS
Almotawag 2 ch.g   60p
Zoom Zoom 2 b.c   76p

J. A. R. TOLLER
Hanami 2 b.f   101p

M. H. TOMPKINS
Astromancer (USA) 2 b.f   62p
Franklins Gardens 2 b.c   84p
Highgate Hill 2 b.g   —p
Richemaur (IRE) 2 b.f   89p
Thingmebob 2 b.f   81p
Winisk River (IRE) 2 b.c   92p

M. P. TREGONING
Adhaaba (USA) 2 b.f   76p
Albareq (USA) 2 b.c   92p
Black Swan (IRE) 2 b.g   —p
Chin Chin 2 b.g   85p
Fatik (USA) 2 br.c   94p
Hammiya (IRE) 2 b.f   64p
Margery Daw (IRE) 2 b.f   70p
Tadris (USA) 2 b.f   77p
Tatweer (IRE) 2 b.c   71p
Bishr 3 b.c   103p

C. F. WALL
Crail 2 b.g   70p
Fanny's Fancy 2 b.f   74p
Jorobaden (FR) 2 gr.c   75p
Storming Star (ITY) 2 b.f   78p
Umoja (FR) 2 b.f   78p

G. WRAGG
Desert Dance (IRE) 2 b.c   —p
Gravia (IRE) 2 b.f   —p
Isla Azul (IRE) 2 ch.f   74p
Mezuzah 2 b.c   94p
Sister Sophia (USA) 2 b.f   79p
Mount Hesse (FR) 3 ch.c   87p

SELECTED BIG RACES 2002

Prize money for racing abroad has been converted to £ sterling at the exchange rate current at the time of the race. The figures are correct to the nearest £. The Timeform ratings (TR) recorded by the principals in each race appear on the last line.

NAD AL SHEBA Saturday, Mar 23   Turf course: GOOD, Dirt track: FAST

1   **Dubai Sheema Classic (Gr 1) (4yo+)** £845,070   1½m (Turf)

NAYEF (USA) *MPTregoning,GB* 4-8-11 RHills (4)	9/4f	1
HELENE VITALITY (NZ) *DAHayes,HongKong* 6-8-11 (b) GMosse (2)	50/1	2 2
BOREAL (GER) *PSchiergen,Germany* 4-8-11 KFallon (1)	12/1	ns 3
Marienbard (IRE) *SaeedbinSuroor,UAE* 5-8-11 (v) JPSpencer (14)	16/1	hd 4
Ekraar (USA) *SaeedbinSuroor,UAE* 5-8-11 (v+t) WSupple (8)	14/1	7½ 5
Mont Rocher (FR) *JEHammond,France* 7-8-11 (t) TGillet (12)	25/1	nk 6
Hot Secret (JPN) *YGoto,Japan* 6-8-11 (b) YShibata (9)	12/1	1¼ 7
Demophilos *MrsAJPerrett,GB* 4-8-11 TQuinn (3)	14/1	sh 8
Narrative (IRE) *SaeedbinSuroor,UAE* 4-8-11 (t) JCarroll (10)	14/1	2 9
Tapildo (NZ) *LLaxon,Singapore* 5-8-7 EWilkinson (4)	80/1	½ 10
Exaltation (IRE) *SaeedbinSuroor,UAE* 4-8-11 JBailey (13)	33/1	1¾ 11
King's Boy (GER) *JDSadler,UAE* 5-8-11 (v) JVerenzuela (6)	50/1	¾ 12
Sagacity (FR) *AFabre,France* 4-8-11 OPeslier (7)	6/1	2¾ 13
Lightning Arrow (USA) *JDSadler,UAE* 6-8-11 (b) TEDurcan (15)	33/1	16 14
Tobougg (IRE) *SaeedbinSuroor,UAE* 4-8-11 LDettori (11)	5/2	½ 15

Mr Hamdan Al Maktoum 15ran 2m29.64   124/119/121/118+

2   **Dubai Duty Free (Gr 1) (4yo+)** £845,070   1m195y (Turf)

TERRE A TERRE (FR) *ELibaud,France* 5-8-10 CSoumillon (3)	9/1	1
NOVERRE (USA) *SaeedbinSuroor,UAE* 4-9-0 (t) LDettori (9)	7/2	¾ 2
HOEBERG (NZ) *LLaxon,Singapore* 5-8-10 JGeroudis (15)	50/1	1 3
Golden Silca *MRChannon,GB* 6-8-10 TQuinn (1)	33/1	1¼ 4
Val Royal (FR) *JCCanani,USA* 6-9-0 (t) JValdivia (14)	5/2f	nk 5
Tamburlaine (IRE) *RHannon,GB* 4-9-0 OPeslier (8)	20/1	½ 6
Jim And Tonic (FR) *FDoumen,France* 8-9-0 TThulliez (11)	13/2	1½ 7
Divine Task (USA) *SaeedbinSuroor,UAE* 4-9-0 JPSpencer (4)	12/1	1 8
Summoner *SaeedbinSuroor,UAE* 5-9-0 RHills (5)	14/1	1¼ 9
Del Mar Show (USA) *WIMott,USA* 5-9-0 (t) JBailey (16)	14/1	nk 10
Prolix *LAlbertrani,SaudiArabia* 7-9-0 GaryStevens (10)	40/1	1¾ 11
Slip Stream (USA) *KPMcLaughlin,UAE* 6-9-0 (t) WSupple (13)	40/1	½ 12
Superiority (USA) *SSeemar,UAE* 6-9-0 (v) TEDurcan (2)	33/1	hd 13
Swiss Law *PBrette,UAE* 8-9-0 WRyan (6)	33/1	2¼ 14
No Excuse Needed *SirMichaelStoute,GB* 4-9-0 KFallon (12)	8/1	16 15
Zollner (GER) *PSchiergen,Germany* 4-9-0 ASuborics (7)	33/1	6½ 16

Mme H. Devin 16ran 1m48.75   120/123/116/113/117/116

3   **Dubai World Cup (Gr 1) (4yo+)** £2,535,211   1¼m (Dirt)

STREET CRY (IRE) *SaeedbinSuroor,UAE* 4-9-0 (t) JBailey (6)	9/2	1
SEI MI (ARG) *JBarton,SaudiArabia* 6-9-0 JVelez (10)	66/1	4¼ 2
SAKHEE (USA) *SaeedbinSuroor,UAE* 5-9-0 LDettori (7)	2/5f	4¼ 3
Crimson Quest (IRE) *JBarton,SaudiArabia* 5-9-0 ECoa (5)	50/1	2¼ 4
Royal Tryst (USA) *JDSadler,UAE* 5-9-0 (ec+t) CraigWilliams (1)	100/1	nk 5
Agnes Digital (USA) *TShirai,Japan* 5-9-0 HShii (4)	5/1	5¼ 6
Best of The Bests (IRE) *SaeedbinSuroor,UAE* 5-9-0 (t) JPSpencer (3)	20/1	½ 7
Keltos (FR) *CLaffon-Parias,France* 4-9-0 GMosse (9)	66/1	nk 8
Western Pride (USA) *JKChapman,USA* 4-9-0 (t) PValenzuela (11)	20/1	4¼ 9
State Shinto (USA) *SaeedbinSuroor,UAE* 6-9-0 (v+t) TEDurcan (2)	66/1	9½ 10
To The Victory (JPN) *YIkee,Japan* 6-8-10 OPeslier (8)	25/1	2¼ 11

Godolphin 11ran 2m01.18   127+/118/111/107/107

LONGCHAMP Sunday, Apr 28   GOOD

4   **Prix Ganay (Gr 1) (4yo+)** £52,582   1¼m110y

AQUARELLISTE (FR) *ELellouche,France* 4-8-13 DBoeuf (2)	7/10f	1
EXECUTE (FR) *JEHammond,France* 5-9-2 TGillet (3)	42/10	½ 2
SENSIBLE (FR) *PBary,France* 4-9-2 TThulliez (5)	67/10	1½ 3
Idaho Quest *H-APantall,France* 5-9-2 DBonilla (4)	43/1	½ 4
Anabaa Blue *CLerner,France* 4-9-2 CSoumillon (1)	51/10	nk 5
Jomana (IRE) *H-APantall,France* 4-8-13 (b) OPlacais (6)	25/1	nk 6
1 Sagacity (FR) *AFabre,France* 4-9-2 OPeslier	66/10	rtr

Ecurie Wildenstein 7ran 2m11.40   115+/116+/115/113/112/109+

NEWMARKET Friday, May 3   GOOD (Rowley Mile Course)

5   Sagitta Jockey Club Stks (Gr 2) (4yo+) £46,400   1½m

1	MARIENBARD (IRE) *SaeedbinSuroor* 5-8-9 (v) JPSpencer (7)	9/1	1
	MILLENARY *JLDunlop* 5-8-9 PatEddery (8)	9/4f	nk 2
	STORMING HOME *BWHills* 4-8-12 MHills (3)	5/1	1¼ 3
	Zindabad (FR) *MJohnston* 6-8-9 KDarley (1)	5/1	nk 4
	Kutub (IRE) *SaeedbinSuroor* 5-9-0 (v) RHills (10)	8/1	¾ 5
	Maniatis *MrsAJPerrett* 5-8-9 KFallon (9)	50/1	9 6
	High Pitched *HRACecil* 4-8-9 (b) TQuinn (2)	9/2	1¼ 7
	Year Two Thousand *HRACecil* 4-8-9 WRyan (6)	25/1	½ 8
	Potemkin (IRE) *RHannon* 4-8-9 DaneO'Neill (5)	33/1	1 9

Godolphin 9ran 2m30.09   121+/120/122/118/122

NEWMARKET Saturday, May 4   GOOD to FIRM (Rowley Mile Course)

6   Sagitta 2000 Guineas Stks (Gr 1) (3yo c+f) £174,000   1m

1	ROCK OF GIBRALTAR (IRE) *APO'Brien,Ireland* 3-9-0 JMurtagh (22)	9/1	1
	HAWK WING (USA) *APO'Brien,Ireland* 3-9-0 JPSpencer (10)	6/4f	nk 2
	REDBACK *RHannon* 3-9-0 DHolland (16)	25/1	1¼ 3
	Zipping (IRE) *RCollet,France* 3-9-0 DBonilla (21)	40/1	2½ 4
	Twilight Blues (IRE) *BJMeehan* 3-9-0 PatEddery (19)	50/1	nk 5
	Aramram (USA) *MRChannon* 3-9-0 SDrowne (6)	50/1	1 6
	Compton Dragon (USA) *GAButler* 3-9-0 EAhern (2)	66/1	nk 7
	Massalani (FR) *AFabre,France* 3-9-0 OPeslier (12)	7/1	nk 8
	King of Happiness *SirMichaelStoute* 3-9-0 KFallon (4)	11/2	nk 9
	Steenberg (IRE) *MHTompkins* 3-9-0 TEDurcan (11)	100/1	1 10
	Where Or When (IRE) *TGMills* 3-9-0 TQuinn (14)	50/1	nk 11
	Ho Choi *MissLAPerratt* 3-9-0 JCarroll (8)	100/1	hd 12
	Love Regardless (USA) *MJohnston* 3-9-0 KDarley (15)	12/1	hd 13
	Naheef (IRE) *SaeedbinSuroor* 3-9-0 LDettori (7)	10/1	3 14
	Coshocton (USA) *MAJarvis* 3-9-0 PRobinson (13)	33/1	1¼ 15
	Parasol (IRE) *SaeedbinSuroor* 3-9-0 (v) DO'Donohoe (18)	100/1	nk 16
	Bragadino *SirMichaelStoute* 3-9-0 MHills (9)	66/1	1¼ 17
	Sholokhov (IRE) *APO'Brien,Ireland* 3-9-0 PaulScallan (17)	100/1	hd 18
	Meshaheer (USA) *SaeedbinSuroor* 3-9-0 RHills (3)	25/1	¾ 19
	Tendulkar (USA) *APO'Brien,Ireland* 3-9-0 DDuffield (1)	16/1	3½ 20
	Rapscallion (GER) *JMPEustace* 3-9-0 JTate (5)	66/1	1 21
	Sweet Band (USA) *EALDunlop* 3-9-0 (t) RHughes (20)	50/1	9 22

Sir Alex Ferguson & Mrs John Magnier 22ran 1m36.50

120+/119/+/116/109+/108/106+/105+

NEWMARKET Sunday, May 5   GOOD to FIRM (Rowley Mile Course)

7   Sagitta 1000 Guineas Stks (Gr 1) (3yo f) £174,000   1m

	KAZZIA (GER) *SaeedbinSuroor* 3-9-0 LDettori (12)	14/1	1
	SNOWFIRE *JLDunlop* 3-9-0 (b) PatEddery (17)	28/1	nk 2
	ALASHA (IRE) *SirMichaelStoute* 3-9-0 JMurtagh (10)	6/1	nk 3
	Dolores *MrsAJPerrett* 3-9-0 TQuinn (4)	66/1	½ 4
	Quarter Moon (IRE) *APO'Brien,Ireland* 3-9-0 MJKinane (11)	9/1	½ 5
	Misterah *MPTregoning* 3-9-0 RHills (2)	7/1	1¼ 6
	Lahinch (IRE) *APO'Brien,Ireland* 3-9-0 PaulScallan (16)	33/1	nk 7
	Gossamer *LMCumani* 3-9-0 JPSpencer (5)	11/8f	2 8
	Maryinsky (IRE) *APO'Brien,Ireland* 3-9-0 KFallon (15)	8/1	1¼ 9
	Shiny *CEBrittain* 3-9-0 PRobinson (13)	66/1	sh 10
	Roundtree (IRE) *RHannon* 3-9-0 RHughes (3)	16/1	½ 11
	Sulk (IRE) *JHMGosden* 3-9-0 (v) OPeslier (9)	16/1	1½ 12
	Sosumi *MHTompkins* 3-9-0 TEDurcan (1)	100/1	½ 13
	Hiddendale (IRE) *BJMeehan* 3-9-0 WSupple (14)	40/1	½ 14
	Pietra Dura *APO'Brien,Ireland* 3-9-0 GDuffield (7)	14/1	6 15
	Ya Hajar *MRChannon* 3-9-0 (t) SDrowne (4)	66/1	1¾ 16
	Xtrasensory *RHannon* 3-9-0 DHolland (8)	100/1	8 17

Godolphin 17ran 1m37.85   112/111/110+/109+/108+/105/104

KRANJI Saturday, May 11   GOOD

8   Singapore Airlines International Cup (Gr 1) (3yo+) £673,585   1¼m

	GRANDERA (IRE) *SaeedbinSuroor,UAE* 4-8-13 LDettori	8/5	1
	PAOLINI (GER) *AWohler,Germany* 5-9-0 (b) ASubonics		2 2
	INDIGENOUS (IRE) *IWAllan,HongKong* 9-9-0 ODeleuze		2½ 3
	Olympic Express *IWAllan,HongKong* 4-8-13 WCMarwing		2¼ 4
	Hawkeye (IRE) *MAJarvis,GB* 4-8-13 GaryStevens		1¼ 5
	Palace Line (AUS) *PShaw,Malaysia* 5-9-0 JGeroudis		sh 6
2	Hoeberg (NZ) *LLaxon,Singapore* 5-8-11 KShea		¾ 7
1	Tapildo (NZ) *LLaxon,Singapore* 5-8-11 LInnes		2 8

Atlantis Prince *SaeedbinSuroor,GB* 4-8-13 YTake .... nk 9
Saddle Up (IND) *LLaxon,Singapore* 7-9-0 JSaimee 1½ 10
3 Western Pride (USA) *JKChapman,USA* 4-8-13 FSanchez 3 11
Bocelli (NZ) *PBusuttin,Singapore* 6-9-0 (b) LCassidy 10 12
Universal Prince (AUS) *BMurray,Australia* 6-9-0 (b) JSheehan .... f

Godolphin 13ran 2m01.30   125/121/115/111/109/105

LONGCHAMP, May 12   GOOD

9 **Gainsborough Poule d'Essai des Poulains (Gr 1) (3yo c)** £124,217   1m
Order as they passed the post: Firebreak was demoted to sixth place

LANDSEER *APO'Brien,Ireland* 3-9-2 MJKinane 61/10cp   1
MEDECIS *MmeCHead-Maarek,France* 3-9-2 ODoleuze 13/2   1 2
BOWMAN (USA) *AFabre,France* 3-9-2 YTake .... 117/10   ¾ 3
Firebreak *SaeedbinSuroor,GB* 3-9-2 LDettori................................. 62/10cp   1½ 4
Shaanmer (IRE) *AFabre,France* 3-9-2 OPeslier.............................. 28/10f   sh 5
Guys And Dolls *PFICole,GB* 3-9-2 DBoeuf .... 21/1   sn 6
Keramani (FR) *AdeRoyerDupre,France* 3-9-2 CSoumillon 105/10   2½ 7
Studio Time (USA) *JHMGosden,GB* 3-9-2 RHughes 24/1   1 8
6 Redback *RHannon,GB* 3-9-2 DHolland 10/1   1½ 9
Waldenburg (USA) *SaeedbinSuroor,GB* 3-9-2 JPSpencer 62/10cp   2 10
Captain Rio *RMWhitaker,GB* 3-9-2 TJarnet................................... 43/1   11
Della Francesca (USA) *APO'Brien,Ireland* 3-9-2 KFallon 61/10cp   12
Sahara Desert *APO'Brien,Ireland* 3-9-2 PaulScallan 61/10cp   13

Mr M. Tabor & Mrs John Magnier 13ran 1m36.80   121/119/117/113/112+/112

10 **Gainsborough Poule d'Essai des Pouliches (Gr 1) (3yo f)** £124,217   1m
ZENDA *JHMGosden,GB* 3-9-0 RHughes 63/10cp   1
FIRTH OF LORNE (IRE) *H-APantall,France* 3-9-0 LDettori 11/2f   1 2
SOPHISTICAT (USA) *APO'Brien,Ireland* 3-9-0 MJKinane .... 136/10cp   sn 3
Wrong Key (IRE) *KPrendergast,Ireland* 3-9-0 DPMcDonogh 135/1   3 4
Heat Haze *AFabre,France* 3-9-0 OPeslier...................................... 63/10cp   sn 5
Dedication (FR) *MmeCHead-Maarek,France* 3-9-0 ODoleuze ...... 17/1   sn 6
Polygreen (FR) *FHead,France* 3-9-0 DBonilla 133/10   2½ 7
Glia (USA) *PBary,France* 3-9-0 TThulliez .... 57/10   sh 8
7 Pietra Dura *APO'Brien,Ireland* 3-9-0 JPSpencer .... 136/10cp   sh 9
Prudence Royale (FR) *J-YArtu,France* 3-9-0 CSoumillon 31/1   2 10
Loupy Glitters (FR) *PHDemercastel,France* 3-9-0 TGillet 65/1   11
Lipstick *MRChannon,GB* 3-9-0 SDrowne 43/1   12
Trojan Princess *GWragg,GB* 3-9-0 DHolland................................ 127/1   13
Rum Charger (IRE) *DKWeld,Ireland* 3-9-0 KFallon 13/1   14
Danseuse d'Etoile (FR) *RGibson,France* 3-9-0 TJarnet................. 109/10   15
Massarra *JLDunlop,GB* 3-9-0 PatEddery... 26/1   16
Camaret (IRE) *JHMGosden,GB* 3-9-0 DaneO'Neill 55/1   17

Mr K. Abdulla 17ran 1m37.00   115/112/112+/104/104/103

ROME Sunday, May 12   GOOD to FIRM

11 **Premio Presidente della Repubblica (Gr 1) (4yo+ c+f)** £189,573   1¼m
FALBRAV (IRE) *LD'Auria,Italy* 4-9-2 DVargiu 15/10cp   1
1 EKRAAR (USA) *SaeedbinSuroor,GB* 4-9-2 (v) RHills 85/100f   1¼ 2
SUNSTRACH (IRE) *EBorromeo,Italy* 4-9-2 CColombi 15/10cp   4½ 3
Altieri *VCaruso,Italy* 4-9-2 GBietolini .... 105/10   ¾ 4
Shibuni's Falcon *MGuarnieri,Italy* 5-9-2 (b) MTellini.................. 76/10   9 5
Caluki *LCamici,Italy* 5-9-2 OFancera 27/1   3 6
Syrakus (GER) *HBlume,Germany* 4-9-2 MDemuro .... 64/10   ¾ 7
Blu For Life (IRE) *RMimmocchi,Italy* 5-9-2 MMimmocchi......... 123/1   6 8
Poseidon *LBrogi,Italy* 8-9-2 MPasquale 84/1   6 9

Scuderia Rencati Srl 9ran 1m57.80   125/121/113/111

NEWBURY Saturday, May 18   GOOD to FIRM

12 **Juddmonte Lockinge Stks (Gr 1) (4yo+)** £99,760   1m
3 KELTOS (FR) *CLaffon-Parias,France* 4-9-0 OPeslier (7) 9/1   1
2 NOVERRE (USA) *SaeedbinSuroor* 4-9-0 (t) JPSpencer (8) 5/6f   3½ 2
OLDEN TIMES *JLDunlop* 4-9-0 MJKinane (4) 8/1   1½ 3
2 No Excuse Needed *SirMichaelStoute* 4-9-0 KDarley (9) .... 9/1   hd 4
Swallow Flight (IRE) *GWragg* 6-9-0 DHolland (3) 9/1   5 5
Umistim *RHannon* 6-9-0 RHughes (6) .... 50/1   ¾ 6
Atavus *GGMargarson* 5-9-0 MartinDwyer (1)................................ 33/1   1¾ 7
Cape Town (IRE) *RHannon* 5-9-0 DaneO'Neill (10)..................... 16/1   4 8
Warningford *JRFanshawe* 8-9-0 OUrbina (5) 16/1   1 9
2 Summoner *SaeedbinSuroor* 5-9-0 RHills (2)............................. 16/1   ½ 10

Mr Gary A. Tanaka 10ran 1m38.69   132/123/120/120+/108+

1122

CURRAGH Saturday, May 25 SOFT

13 Entenmann's Irish 2000 Guineas (Gr 1) (3yo c+f) £141,893 — 1m

6	ROCK OF GIBRALTAR (IRE) *APO'Brien* 3-9-0 MJKinane (4)	4/7f		1
	CENTURY CITY (IRE) *APO'Brien* 3-9-0 JAHeffernan (2)	6/1	1½	2
9	DELLA FRANCESCA (USA) *APO'Brien* 3-9-0 CO'Donoghue (7)	20/1	3	3
	Foreign Accent *JHMGosden,GB* 3-9-0 JFortune (6)	11/1	5	4
	Ahsanabad (IRE) *JOxx* 3-9-0 JMurtagh (3)	10/1	sh	5
	Nostradamus (USA) *APO'Brien* 3-9-0 PaulScallan (5)	25/1	3½	6
	Sights On Gold (IRE) *DKWeld* 3-9-0 PJSmullen (1)	14/1	1½	7

Sir Alex Ferguson 7ran 1m47.35 — 121+/117/110/98/98

CURRAGH Sunday, May 26 SOFT

14 Entenmann's Irish 1000 Guineas (Gr 1) (3yo f) £141,893 — 1m

7	GOSSAMER *LMCumani,GB* 3-9-0 JPSpencer (13)	4/1f		1
7	QUARTER MOON (IRE) *APO'Brien* 3-9-0 MJKinane (8)	9/2	4½	2
	STARBOURNE (IRE) *APO'Brien* 3-9-0 CO'Donoghue (15)	20/1	1	3
	Alstemeria (IRE) *APO'Brien* 3-9-0 TPQueally (2)	50/1	1	4
10	Wrong Key (IRE) *KPrendergast* 3-9-0 DPMcDonogh (6)	12/1	hd	5
	Kournakova (IRE) *APO'Brien* 3-9-0 JAHeffernan (1)	9/1	sh	6
7	Maryinsky (IRE) *APO'Brien* 3-9-0 PaulScallan (14)	20/1	2	7
10	Rum Charger (IRE) *DKWeld* 3-9-0 PShanahan (4)	16/1	½	8
	Marionnaud (IRE) *JSBolger* 3-9-0 KJManning (7)	25/1	2½	9
	Red Rioja (IRE) *EJO'Neill,GB* 3-9-0 FMBerry (3)	50/1	nk	10
7	Alasha (IRE) *SirMichaelStoute,GB* 3-9-0 JMurtagh (10)	9/2	1½	11
	Miss Beabea (IRE) *KPrendergast* 3-9-0 EAhern (12)	50/1	7	12
10	Heat Haze *AFabre,France* 3-9-0 OPeslier (5)	10/1	1½	13
	Saranac Lake (USA) *DKWeld* 3-9-0 PJSmullen (9)	12/1	1½	14
10	Zenda *JHMGosden,GB* 3-9-0 RHughes (11)	7/1	9	15

Gerald W. Leigh - CancerBACUP 15ran 1m45.69 — 118/108+/105/103/102/102

15 Tattersalls Gold Cup (Gr 1) (4yo+) £101,384 — 1¼m110y

	REBELLINE (IRE) *KPrendergast* 4-8-11 DPMcDonogh (7)	7/1		1
	BACH (IRE) *APO'Brien* 5-9-0 MJKinane (2)	7/1	2	2
1	NAYEF (USA) *MPTregoning,GB* 4-9-0 RHills (6)	8/11f	2½	3
	Chancellor (IRE) *BWHills,GB* 4-9-0 MHills (3)	14/1	1	4
1	Tobougg (IRE) *SaeedbinSuroor,GB* 4-9-0 LDettori (9)	4/1	2½	5
	Indian Creek *DRCElsworth,GB* 4-9-0 RHughes (5)	10/1	1½	6
	Chimes At Midnight (USA) *LukeComer* 5-9-0 (b) WJSmith (8)	50/1	1	7
	Diamond Trim (IRE) *DKWeld* 4-8-11 (b) PJSmullen (4)	20/1	1½	8

Lady O'Reilly 8ran 2m22.31 — 122/121/117/116/111

ROME Sunday, May 26 GOOD to FIRM

16 Derby Italiano (Gr 1) (3yo c+f) £405,283 — 1½m

	RAKTI *BGrizzetti,Italy* 3-9-2 MDemuro	9/4		1
	BALLINGARRY (IRE) *APO'Brien,Ireland* 3-9-2 KFallon	8/5f	1½	2
	FISICH *A&GBotti,Italy* 3-9-2 DVargiu	162/10	½	3
	Thompson Rouge (IRE) *PBary,France* 3-9-2 TThulliez	102/10	3½	4
	Spanish John (USA) *PFICole,GB* 3-9-2 KDarley	40/1	1¾	5
	Jeune Dream (USA) *RMenichetti,Italy* 3-9-2 MBelli	130/1	3	6
	Irulan (IRE) *PSchiergen,Germany* 3-9-2 ASuborics	117/10	½	7
	Maranilla (IRE) *EJO'Neill,GB* 3-9-2 JEgan	21/1	1½	8
	Kayseri (IRE) *MAJarvis,GB* 3-9-2 PRobinson	101/10	2	9
	Salselon *MCiciarelli,Italy* 3-9-2 (b) AParravani	20/1	hd	10
	Long Goodbye (IRE) *PFICole,GB* 3-9-2 IMongan	25/1	2½	11
	Il Fortino (IRE) *A&GBotti,Italy* 3-9-2 EBotti	52/1	½	12
	Mr Andrea (IRE) *DKWeld,Ireland* 3-9-2 (b) TEDurcan	53/1	8	13
	Proven (USA) *JHMGosden,GB* 3-9-2 (v) JFortune	10/3	1¼	14
	Allenby *RHannon,GB* 3-9-2 DaneO'Neill	25/1	sn	15
	Vernacolo (IRE) *FCamici,Italy* 3-9-2 (b) OFancera	200/1	7	16

Scuderia Il Poggio SRL 16ran 2m27.90 — 118/116+/115/109/105

CHANTILLY Sunday, Jun 2 GOOD to FIRM

17 Prix du Jockey Club (Gr 1) (3yo c+f) £397,810 — 1½m

	SULAMANI (IRE) *PBary,France* 3-9-2 TThulliez (11)	199/10		1
	ACT ONE *JEPease,France* 3-9-2 TGillet (13)	9/10f	1½	2
	SIMEON *MJohnston,GB* 3-9-2 LDettori (9)	53/10	5	3
	Great Pretender (IRE) *RCollet,France* 3-9-2 DBonilla (6)	58/1	nk	4
	Black Sam Bellamy (IRE) *APO'Brien,Ireland* 3-9-2 JPSpencer (4)	71/10cp	1½	5
	Castle Gandolfo (USA) *APO'Brien,Ireland* 3-9-2 JMurtagh (1)	71/10cp	hd	6
	Diaghilev (IRE) *APO'Brien,Ireland* 3-9-2 MJKinane (8)	71/10cp	2	7
	Louveteau (USA) *ELellouche,France* 3-9-2 DBoeuf (2)	97/10	hd	8

Khalkevi (IRE) *AdeRoyerDupre,France* 3-9-2 CSoumillon (14)................. 83/10   sn 9
Le Fou (IRE) *JEHammond,France* 3-9-2 YTake (12) .... 16/1   ¾ 10
Without Connexion (IRE) *PBary,France* 3-9-2 TJarnet (7)........................... 37/1   2½ 11
Martaline *AFabre,France* 3-9-2 OPeslier (15) 26/1   3 12
Alvarinho (FR) *PCostes,France* 3-9-2 FSpanu (5)... 84/1   10 13
Polities (USA) *J-CRouget,France* 3-9-2 IMendizabal (10).......................... 33/1   1½ 14
Temple of Artemis *APO'Brien,Ireland* 3-9-2 CO'Donoghue (3)............. 71/10cp dist 15

Niarchos Family 15ran 2m25.00   126+/124/114/113/111/111

SANDOWN Monday, Jun 3   GOOD to FIRM

18 **Tripleprint Temple Stks (Gr 2) (3yo+) £34,800**   5f6y
KYLLACHY *HCandy* 4-9-3 JPSpencer (2) 9/2   1
VISION OF NIGHT *JLDunlop* 6-9-7 LDettori (6) 12/1   4 2
MONKSTON POINT (IRE) *DWPArbuthnot* 6-9-3 (v) JDSmith (5) .... 20/1   sh 3
Misraah (IRE) *SirMichaelStoute* 5-9-3 RHills (8).. 4/1jf   sh 4
Invincible Spirit (IRE) *JLDunlop* 5-9-3 PatEddery (9)................................ 4/1jf   hd 5
Smokin Beau *JCullinan* 5-9-3 MHenry (4)... 8/1   ¾ 6
Kier Park (IRE) *MAJarvis* 5-9-3 PRobinson (11).. 8/1   1½ 7
Bahamian Pirate (USA) *DNicholls* 7-9-3 RHughes (7)................................. 9/1   nk 8
Rushcutter Bay *PLGilligan* 9-9-3 (v) JFortune (10).................................... 50/1   ½ 9
Rozel (IRE) *RGuest* 5-9-0 (b) SSanders (4) .... 66/1   hd 10
Continent *DNicholls* 5-9-3 DHolland (1)... 14/1   1½ 11

Thurloe Thoroughbreds V 11ran 1m00.58   123+/115/111/110+/110+/108

EPSOM DOWNS Friday, Jun 7   SOFT

19 **Vodafone Coronation Cup (Gr 1) (4yo+) £159,500**   1½m10y
1   BOREAL (GER) *PSchiergen,Germany* 4-9-0 KFallon (3) 4/1   1
5   STORMING HOME *BWHills* 4-9-0 MHills (4).. 7/2   3½ 2
5   ZINDABAD (FR) *MJohnston* 6-9-0 KDarley (1) 9/1   6 3
    Marienbard (IRE) *SaeedbinSuroor* 5-9-0 (v) JPSpencer (5) 11/2   2½ 4
    Pawn Broker *DRCElsworth* 5-9-0 MJKinane (6).................................... 20/1   15 5
5   Kutub (IRE) *SaeedbinSuroor* 5-9-0 (v) LDettori (2)................................. 13/8f   1¾ 6

Gestut Ammerland 6ran 2m45.01   126/121/113/109

20 **Vodafone Oaks (Gr 1) (3yo f) £203,000**   1½m10y
7   KAZZIA (GER) *SaeedbinSuroor* 3-9-0 LDettori (13) 10/3f   1
14   QUARTER MOON (IRE) *APO'Brien,Ireland* 3-9-0 MJKinane (10)........... 15/2   ½ 2
     SHADOW DANCING *MPTregoning* 3-9-0 MartinDwyer (3) 14/1   14 3
14   Starbourne (IRE) *APO'Brien,Ireland* 3-9-0 JMurtagh (14).......................... 16/1   nk 4
14   Red Rioja (IRE) *EJO'Neill* 3-9-0 JFEgan (4)... 100/1   1 5
     Mellow Park (IRE) *JNoseda* 3-9-0 DHolland (4)...................................... 7/2   hd 6
     Alexander Three D (IRE) *BWHills* 3-9-0 MHills (9)................................. 16/1   1 7
     Islington (IRE) *SirMichaelStoute* 3-9-0 KFallon (8).................................. 7/2   1¾ 8
     Persian Lass (IRE) *PWHarris* 3-9-0 TQuinn (5)... 100/1   2 9
7   Snowfire *JLDunlop* 3-9-0 (b) PatEddery (11) 20/1   4 10
14   Kournakova (IRE) *APO'Brien,Ireland* 3-9-0 KDarley (6) 33/1   12 11
14   Maryinsky (IRE) *APO'Brien,Ireland* 3-9-0 RHughes (2) 33/1   14 12
     Esloob (USA) *MPTregoning* 3-9-0 RHills (12)... 12/1   11 13
     Spinnette (IRE) *JNoseda* 3-9-0 JPSpencer (7)... 14/1   dist 14

Godolphin 14ran 2m44.52   121/120/102/102/100/100

EPSOM DOWNS Saturday, Jun 8   GOOD to SOFT

21 **Vodafone Derby Stks (Gr 1) (3yo c+f) £800,400**   1½m10y
     HIGH CHAPARRAL (IRE) *APO'Brien,Ireland* 3-9-0 JMurtagh (9) 7/2   1
6   HAWK WING (USA) *APO'Brien,Ireland* 3-9-0 MJKinane (12) 9/4f   2 2
     MOON BALLAD (IRE) *SaeedbinSuroor* 3-9-0 (v+t) JPSpencer (4)............ 20/1   12 3
     Jelani (IRE) *AndrewTurnell* 3-9-0 FLynch (3)... 100/1   1 4
     Fight Your Corner *MJohnston* 3-9-0 KDarley (5)...................................... 8/1   5 5
6   Where Or When (IRE) *TGMills* 3-9-0 JFortune (10)................................. 66/1   17 6
6   Naheef (IRE) *SaeedbinSuroor* 3-9-0 LDettori (7)....................................... 5/1   2 7
     Bandari (IRE) *MJohnston* 3-9-0 RHills (11) 9/2   12 8
     Louisville (IRE) *APO'Brien,Ireland* 3-9-0 KFallon (2) 25/1   7 9
     Tholjanah (IRE) *MPTregoning* 3-9-0 WSupple (1)..................................... 14/1   6 10
     Frankies Dream (IRE) *TGMills* 3-9-0 (v) PatEddery (8) 100/1   6 11
6   Coshocton (USA) *MAJarvis* 3-9-0 PRobinson (6) .... 28/1   f

Mr M. Tabor & Mrs John Magnier 12ran 2m39.45   130/127/109/108/101

CHANTILLY Sunday, Jun 9   GOOD to FIRM

22 **Grand Prix de Chantilly (Gr 2) (4yo+) £34,491**   1½m
4   ANABAA BLUE *CLerner,France* 4-8-12 CSoumillon................................... 7/2   1
     ANGE GABRIEL (FR) *ELibaud,France* 4-8-12 DHolland....................... 62/10   1½ 2

1124

ST EXPEDIT *GWragg,GB* 5-8-12 TJarnet .... 16/1   dh 2
Califet (FR) *GCherel,France* 4-9-2 DBonilla .... 8/5f   ½ 4
Sangreal (NZ) *AFabre,France* 4-8-8 OPeslier 17/2   1½ 5
4 Jomana (IRE) *H-APantall,France* 4-8-11 (b) LDettori .... 83/10   ¾ 6
Fair Mix (IRE) *MRolland,France* 4-8-12 SPasquier .... 25/1   nk 7
Generic (FR) *J-PGallorini,France* 7-9-2 RMarchelli.................................... 12/1   2 8
Foundation Spirit (FR) *FDoumen,France* 4-8-12 TThulliez........................ 41/1   ns 9
Double Heart (FR) *MmeMBollack-Badel,France* 6-8-12 ABadel................. 40/1   1½ 10
Roman Saddle (IRE) *CLaffon-Parias,France* 4-8-12 ODoleuze 32/1   4 11

  Mr C. Mimouni 11ran 2m28.10   122/119/118/122/112/113/114

23   **Prix de Diane Hermes (Gr 1) (3yo f)** $181,974   1¼m110y

    Order as they passed the post: Turtle Bow was demoted to fourth place

BRIGHT SKY (IRE) *ELellouche,France* 3-9-0 DBoeuf 3/1cpf   1
DANCE ROUTINE *AFabre,France* 3-9-0 OPeslier 38/10   2 2
TURTLE BOW (FR) *FRohaut,France* 3-9-0 F-XBertras .... 8/1   ½ 3
Ana Marie (FR) *PHDemercastel,France* 3-9-0 DBonilla............................ 11/1   ½ 4
Marotta (FR) *RGibson,France* 3-9-0 TJarnet 9/1   1½ 5
Mariensky (USA) *NClement,France* 3-9-0 TGillet .... 43/1   ¾ 6
Ombre Legere (IRE) *ELellouche,France* 3-9-0 SPasquier .... 44/1   sn 7
Music Club (USA) *JHMGosden,GB* 3-9-0 JPSpencer 11/2   2 8
Monturani (IRE) *GWragg,GB* 3-9-0 DHolland 8/1   1½ 9
Fragrant View (USA) *BWHills,GB* 3-9-0 RHughes 38/10   2 10
Balade Russe (USA) *RCollet,France* 3-9-0 CSoumillon .... 48/1   nk 11
Dzinigane (FR) *DSepulchre,France* 3-9-0 TThulliez............................... 36/1   4 12
Summertime Legacy *AFabre,France* 3-9-0 OPlacais.............................. 31/1   1½ 13
Bustling *H-APantall,France* 3-9-0 LDettori 12/1   4 14
Blue Lightning (FR) *ELellouche,France* 3-9-0 (b) SCoffigny 3/1cpf   20 15

  Ecurie Wildenstein 15ran 2m07.60   120/116/115/114/111/109/109

  MILAN Sunday, Jun 16   FIRM

24   **Gran Premio di Milano (Gr 1) (3yo+)** £126,518   1½m

11 FALBRAV (IRE) *LD'Auria,Italy* 4-9-6 DVargiu.................................... 13/10f   1
1 NARRATIVE (IRE) *SaeedbinSuroor,GB* 4-9-6 LDettori 2/1   3 2
8 HAWKEYE (IRE) *MAJarvis,GB* 4-9-6 PRobinson................................. 6/1   7 3
16 Jeune Dream (USA) *RMenichetti,Italy* 3-8-6 GBietolini 54/1   1½ 4
Sabiango (GER) *AWohler,Germany* 4-9-6 (b) ASuborics.......................... 25/10   5 5
Snetterton *VValiani,Italy* 5-9-6 EBotti .... 109/1   nk 6
Einstein (ITY) *BGrizzetti,Italy* 3-8-6 MDemuro 11/1   1¾ 7

  Scuderia Rencati Srl 7ran 2m24.90   122/117/107/104

  ASCOT Tuesday, Jun 18   GOOD

25   **Queen Anne Stks (Gr 2) (3yo+)** £78,300   1m (Str.)

12 NO EXCUSE NEEDED *SirMichaelStoute* 4-9-2 JMurtagh (11)................... 13/2   1
TILLERMAN *MrsAJPerrett* 6-9-2 RHughes (9)....................................... 11/1   sh 2
TOUGH SPEED (USA) *SirMichaelStoute* 5-9-2 PatEddery (4)................... 12/1   sh 3
Nayyir *GAButler* 4-9-2 EAhern (1).. 5/1jf   sh 4
13 Century City (IRE) *APO'Brien,Ireland* 3-8-6 MJKinane (3).......................... 7/1   1¼ 5
12 Umistim *RHannon* 5-9-2 DaneO'Neill (7) 66/1   2½ 6
12 Swallow Flight (IRE) *GWragg* 6-9-5 DHolland (6) 14/1   1 7
3 Best of The Bests (IRE) *SaeedbinSuroor* 5-9-7 (t) LDettori (10).............. 11/2   2 8
Frenchmans Bay (FR) *RCharlton* 4-9-2 SDrowne (5) .... 5/1jf   hd 9
Priors Lodge (IRE) *RHannon* 4-9-2 JFortune (2)................................... 40/1   3½ 10
Vicious Knight *LMCumani* 4-9-2 JPSpencer (8) 16/1   5 11
12 Atavus *GGMargarson* 5-9-2 JMackay (12) 50/1   9 12

  Maktoum Al Maktoum 12ran 1m40.66   123/123/115+/115/109

26   **St James's Palace Stks (Gr 1) (3yo c)** £168,200   1m (Rnd)

13 ROCK OF GIBRALTAR (IRE) *APO'Brien,Ireland* 3-9-0 MJKinane (4) 4/5f   1
9 LANDSEER *APO'Brien,Ireland* 3-9-0 JMurtagh (5)................................. 13/2   1¾ 2
6 ARAMRAM (USA) *MRChannon* 3-9-0 SDrowne (3)................................. 20/1   4 3
Dupont *WJHaggas* 3-9-0 DHolland (7) .... 14/1   nk 4
21 Where Or When (IRE) *TGMills* 3-9-0 JFortune (1)................................. 66/1   1 5
9 Bowman (USA) *AFabre,France* 3-9-0 LDettori (9)................................... 4/1   hd 6
9 Sahara Desert *APO'Brien,Ireland* 3-9-0 PaulScallan (6) .... 100/1   ½ 7
6 King of Happiness (USA) *SirMichaelStoute* 3-9-0 PatEddery (8)................ 10/1   hd 8
Camp Commander (IRE) *CEBrittain* 3-9-0 (t) PRobinson (2).................... 150/1   5 9

  Sir Alex Ferguson & Mrs John Magnier 9ran 1m40.91   129+/125/115+/114+/112/111

  ASCOT Wednesday, Jun 19   GOOD to FIRM

27   **Prince of Wales's Stks (Gr 1) (4yo+)** £145,000   1¼m

8 GRANDERA (IRE) *SaeedbinSuroor* 4-9-0 LDettori (3)................................ 4/1   1

```
  15   INDIAN CREEK DRCElsworth 4-9-0 TQuinn (2).........................................   25/1      5   2
       BANKS HILL AFabre,France 4-8-11 OPeslier (12) ...................................   7/2f     ¾   3
  15   Nayef (USA) MPTregoning 4-9-0 RHills (4) ..........................................    4/1    1½   4
       Freefourinternet (USA) BJMeehan 4-9-0 (b) PatEddery (10).......................   33/1     1½   5
   2   Golden Silca MRChannon 6-8-11 TEDurcan (5)......................................  100/1    2½   6
       Poussin ELellouche,France 4-9-0 DBoeuf (13) ......................................   10/1      2   7
   8   Paolini (GER) AWohler,Germany 5-9-0 (b) ASuborics (9) .......................   14/1    3½   8
  12   Cape Town (IRE) RHannon 5-9-0 (b) RHughes (11)..............................   50/1     sh   9
       Sydenham (USA) SaeedbinSuroor 4-9-0 (v) JPSpencer (14).......................   66/1     ¾  10
       Desert Deer MJohnston 4-9-0 KDarley (8) ...........................................    6/1     hd  11
  15   Bach (IRE) APO'Brien,Ireland 5-9-0 MJKinane (6)..............................   15/2      4  12

       Godolphin 12ran 2m04.43                                      129/119/115/115/112/104
```

```
28   Gold Cup (Gr 1) (4yo+) £127,600                                               2½m

       ROYAL REBEL MJohnston 6-9-2 JMurtagh (8) .....................................   16/1      1
       VINNIE ROE (IRE) DKWeld,Ireland 4-9-0 (b) PJSmullen (15) ..................   5/2f     nk   2
       WAREED (IRE) SaeedbinSuroor 4-9-0 (v) LDettori (6) ...........................   13/2      1   3
       Hatha Anna (IRE) SaeedbinSuroor 5-9-2 (v) JPSpencer (10).....................   20/1    2½   4
       Give Notice JLDunlop 5-9-2 PatEddery (5) ...........................................   10/1     sh   5
       Persian Punch (IRE) DRCElsworth 9-9-2 TQuinn (9) .............................   10/1     ½   6
       Invermark JRFanshawe 8-9-2 MHills (2) ..............................................    8/1     ¾   7
       Warrsan (IRE) CEBrittain 4-9-0 PRobinson (7)....................................   33/1     nk   8
       Jardines Lookout (IRE) APJarvis 5-9-2 MJKinane (3) ...........................    7/1    1¾   9
  15   Chimes At Midnight (USA) LukeComer,Ireland 5-9-2 (b) KDarley (16)....  100/1    1¼  10
       Bosham Mill GWragg 4-9-0 DHolland (4) .............................................   20/1     nk  11
       Moon Emperor JRJenkins 5-9-2 JFortune (14) ......................................   66/1     hd  12
       Solo Mio (IRE) MrsAJPerrett 8-9-2 KFallon (1) ...................................   14/1     5  13
       Rainbow High BWHills 7-9-2 RHughes (13) .........................................   25/1    3½  14
       Welsh Border GProdromou 4-9-0 JMackay (11) ....................................  250/1     18  15

       Mr P. D. Savill 15ran 4m25.04                               122+/124+/123/118/118/117/117/118
```

```
29   King Edward VII Stks (Gr 2) (3yo c+g) £78,300                                 1½m

       BALAKHERI (IRE) SirMichaelStoute 3-8-10 JMurtagh (2)......................   11/4f      1
       BOLLIN ERIC TDEasterby 3-8-8 KDarley (6)..........................................    3/1    3½   2
       FIRST CHARTER SirMichaelStoute 3-8-8 JPSpencer (7)...........................   25/1     hd   3
       Kaieteur (USA) BJMeehan 3-8-8 PatEddery (3).....................................   10/1    1¼   4
       Bustan (IRE) MPTregoning 3-8-8 RHills (1)...........................................    9/2     sh   5
  17   Diaghilev (IRE) APO'Brien,Ireland 3-8-8 MJKinane (4) .......................    4/1      6   6
       Sparkling Water (USA) HRACecil 3-8-8 TQuinn (5)..............................   10/1    1½   7

       H. H. Aga Khan 7ran 2m30.45                                  121/113/113/111/111

30   Coronation Stks (Gr 1) (3yo f) £145,000                                       1m (Rnd)

  10   SOPHISTICAT (USA) APO'Brien,Ireland 3-9-0 MJKinane (3) ..................   11/2      1
  14   ZENDA JHMGosden 3-9-0 RHughes (7)................................................    7/1     nk   2
   7   DOLORES MrsAJPerrett 3-9-0 TQuinn (2)............................................    5/1    2½   3
   7   Misterah MPTregoning 3-9-0 (b) RHills (1)............................................   10/1     ¾   4
   7   Shiny CEBrittain 3-9-0 PRobinson (11) ................................................  100/1      2   5
       Hideaway Heroine (IRE) JWHills 3-9-0 MHills (9)..............................   14/1      2   6
  20   Maryinsky (IRE) APO'Brien,Ireland 3-9-0 JMurtagh (12).....................   20/1     hd   7
       Lady High Havens (IRE) PWD'Arcy 3-9-0 KDarley (6) .......................   66/1      1   8
       Red Liason (IRE) JLDunlop 3-9-0 PatEddery (10) ..............................   16/1     ½   9
  14   Alstemeria (IRE) APO'Brien,Ireland 3-9-0 KFallon (2).........................   20/1     3  10
  14   Gossamer LMCumani 3-9-0 JPSpencer (5).............................................   6/4f     ½  11

       Mr M. Tabor & Mrs John Magnier 11ran 1m41.59               112+/111+/105+/103/98
```

```
31   Hardwicke Stks (Gr 2) (4yo+) £84,680                                          1½m

  19   ZINDABAD (FR) MJohnston 6-8-12 KDarley (1) ...................................    4/1      1
  19   STORMING HOME BWHills 4-8-9 MHills (3)...........................................  11/4jf     1   2
   5   MILLENARY JLDunlop 5-8-9 PatEddery (2) ...........................................  11/4jf     sh   3
   5   High Pitched HRACecil 4-8-9 TQuinn (5).............................................    3/1     nk   4
   5   Potemkin (IRE) RHannon 4-8-9 DaneO'Neill (5) ...................................   16/1      5   5
       Yavana's Pace (IRE) MJohnston 10-8-12 KDalgleish (8).......................   33/1      4   6
       The Mask (FR) ASpanu,France 6-8-9 FSpanu (6) .................................   50/1      8   7

       Mr Abdulla BuHaleeba 7ran 2m31.18                           126/122/121/121/114

32   Golden Jubilee Stks (Gr 1) (3yo+) £156,600                                    6f

       MALHUB (USA) JHMGosden 4-9-4 (t) KDarley (12) ...........................   16/1      1
       DANEHURST SirMarkPrescott 4-9-1 SSanders (2)...................................   13/2    1½   2
```

THREE POINTS *SaeedbinSuroor* 5-9-4 (t) LDettori (14) .... 4/1 ½ 3
Indian Country *JNoseda* 3-8-11 JPSpencer (3) 50/1 1¾ 4
18 Continent *DNicholls* 5-9-4 (t) DHolland (5) 8/1 1¼ 5
18 Invincible Spirit (IRE) *JLDunlop* 5-9-4 KFallon (10) .... 10/1 hd 6
18 Vision of Night *JLDunlop* 6-9-4 PatEddery (1) 12/1 1¾ 7
18 Misraah (IRE) *SirMichaelStoute* 5-9-4 RHills (6) 11/1 2 8
Johannesburg (USA) *APO'Brien,Ireland* 3-8-11 MJKinane (4) 3/1f 1¼ 9
Mugharreb (USA) *BHanbury* 4-9-4 WSupple (8) .... 10/1 sh 10
14 Miss Beabea (IRE) *KPrendergast,Ireland* 3-8-8 JFortune (15) 33/1 2½ 11
Ellens Academy (IRE) *EJAlston* 7-9-4 SDrowne (13) 50/1 2½ 12

Mr Hamdan Al Maktoum 12ran 1m14.34 120/113+/114/107/105/105

CURRAGH Sunday, Jun 30 GOOD to SOFT

33 Budweiser Irish Derby (Gr 1) (3yo c+f) £475,068 1½m

21 HIGH CHAPARRAL (IRE) *APO'Brien* 3-9-0 MJKinane (4) 1/3f 1
6 SHOLOKHOV (IRE) *APO'Brien* 3-9-0 PaulScallan (9) 200/1 3½ 2
16 BALLINGARRY (IRE) *APO'Brien* 3-9-0 JAHeffernan (2) 12/1 1½ 3
Nysaean (IRE) *RHannon,GB* 3-9-0 RHughes (1) .... 25/1 hd 4
29 Balakheri (IRE) *SirMichaelStoute,GB* 3-9-0 PatEddery (7) 13/2 1½ 5
13 Della Francesca (USA) *APO'Brien* 3-9-0 CO'Donoghue (8) 40/1 2½ 6
In Time's Eye *DKWeld* 3-9-0 PJSmullen (3) .... 15/2 nk 7
Jazz Beat (IRE) *DKWeld* 3-9-0 PShanahan (6) 33/1 10 8
Princely Venture (IRE) *SirMichaelStoute,GB* 3-9-0 KFallon (5) 20/1 4 9

Mr Michael Tabor 9ran 2m32.22 127+/121/119/119/116/112/112

SAINT-CLOUD Sunday, Jun 30 GOOD to FIRM

34 Grand Prix de Saint-Cloud (Gr 1) (3yo+) £129,426 1½m

22 ANGE GABRIEL (FR) *ELibaud,France* 4-9-8 TJarnet (4) 163/10 1
POLISH SUMMER *AFabre,France* 5-9-8 OPeslier (3) 73/10 2 2
4 AQUARELLISTE (FR) *ELellouche,France* 4-9-5 DBoeuf (2) .... 3/5cpf sh 3
22 Califet (FR) *GCherel,France* 4-9-8 DBonilla (1) 57/10 4 4
22 Anabaa Blue *CLerner,France* 4-9-8 CSoumillon (6) .... 26/10 sn 5
Virginian (IRE) *ELellouche,France* 5-9-8 SCoffigny (5) 3/5cpf 2½ 6

Mme H. Devin 6ran 2m28.60 124/120/118+/115+/115+

SANDOWN Saturday, Jul 6 GOOD to SOFT

35 Coral Eurobet Eclipse Stks (Gr 1) (3yo+) £188,500 1¼m7y

21 HAWK WING (USA) *APO'Brien,Ireland* 3-8-10 MJKinane (6) 8/15f 1
33 SHOLOKHOV (IRE) *APO'Brien,Ireland* 3-8-10 PaulScallan (2) 14/1 2½ 2
EQUERRY (USA) *SaeedbinSuroor* 4-9-7 (t) LDettori (7) 4/1 2½ 3
Imperial Dancer *MRChannon* 4-9-7 CCatlin (1) 33/1 3½ 4
27 Indian Creek *DRCElsworth* 4-9-7 TQuinn (5) 8/1 3 5

Mrs John Magnier 5ran 2m13.34 125+/121/118/112/106

HAMBURG Sunday, Jul 7 HEAVY

36 BMW Deutsches Derby (Gr 1) (3yo c+f) £155,844 1½m

NEXT DESERT (IRE) *ASchutz,Germany* 3-9-2 AStarke 26/10f 1
SALVE REGINA (GER) *ASchutz,Germany* 3-8-12 RHills 51/10 3 2
TOMORI (USA) *ASchutz,Germany* 3-8-12 OPeslier 147/10 4 3
Ammonias (GER) *PSchiergen,Germany* 3-9-2 JMurtagh 15/1 8 4
Mamool (IRE) *SaeedbinSuroor,GB* 3-9-2 LDettori .... 36/10 nk 5
16 Irulan (IRE) *PSchiergen,Germany* 3-9-2 ASuborics .... 116/10 sh 6
Orfisio *ALowe,Germany* 3-9-2 PAJohnson .... 69/10 nk 7
Calcio *MHofer,Germany* 3-9-2 (b) JPCarvalho .... 71/1 ½ 8
Auenteufel (GER) *UOstmann,Germany* 3-9-2 (b) FMinarik 29/1 2 9
Ifag Mannheim (IRE) *WFigge,Germany* 3-9-2 KKerekes 71/1 11 10
Los Sainos (GER) *ALowe,Germany* 3-9-2 JBojko 67/1 2½ 11
Levirat (GER) *MHofer,Germany* 3-9-2 WJO'Connor 185/10 4 12
Mendosino (GER) *PSchiergen,Germany* 3-9-2 LHammer-Hansen 34/1 10 13
Belcore (GER) *AWohler,Germany* 3-9-2 ABoschert 175/10 7 14
Whisperer (GER) *HBlume,Germany* 3-9-2 TMundry 181/10 10 15
Epalo (GER) *ASchutz,Germany* 3-9-2 THellier .... 51/1 ns 16
Nicaragua (GER) *PSchiergen,Germany* 3-9-2 (b) KFallon 23/1 1½ 17

Gestut Wittekindshof 17ran 2m39.23 120+/112/106/98

NEWMARKET Tuesday, Jul 9 GOOD to SOFT (July Course)

37 Princess of Wales's UAE Equestrian And Racing Federation Stks (Gr 2) (3yo+) £46,400 1½m

31 MILLENARY *JLDunlop* 5-9-2 PatEddery (6) 5/2f 1
MUBTAKER (USA) *MPTregoning* 5-9-2 RHills (1) .... 11/2 nk 2

31	YAVANA'S PACE (IRE) *MJohnston* 10-9-5 RHughes (4)	20/1	1¾ 3
	Island House (IRE) *GWragg* 6-9-2 DHolland (2)	9/1	6 4
17	Simeon *MJohnston* 3-8-3 KDalgleish (5)	10/3	1 5
	Xtra *LMCumani* 4-9-2 JPSpencer (3)	6/1	1¾ 6
19	Kutub (IRE) *SaeedbinSuroor* 5-9-7 (v+t) LDettori (7)	5/1	dist 7

Mr L. Neil Jones 7ran 2m32.22   121/120/120/107

NEWMARKET Thursday, Jul 11   GOOD to SOFT (July Course)

38   **Darley July Cup (Gr 1) (3yo+) £145,000**   6f

32	CONTINENT *DNicholls* 5-9-5 (t) DHolland (2)	12/1	1
18	BAHAMIAN PIRATE (USA) *DNicholls* 5-9-5 RHughes (11)	16/1	½ 2
32	DANEHURST *SirMarkPrescott* 4-9-2 GDuffield (7)	5/2f	1½ 3
26	Landseer *APO'Brien,Ireland* 3-8-13 MJKinane (14)	7/2	nk 4
	Millennium Dragon *MAJarvis* 3-8-13 PRobinson (6)	12/1	nk 5
32	Three Points *SaeedbinSuroor* 5-9-5 (t) LDettori (3)	8/1	¾ 6
32	Malhub (USA) *JHMGosden* 4-9-5 (t) RHills (4)	12/1	1 7
26	Sahara Desert *APO'Brien,Ireland* 3-8-13 JMurtagh (13)	40/1	nk 8
6	Twilight Blues (IRE) *BJMeehan* 3-8-13 PatEddery (12)	50/1	3½ 9
	Reel Buddy (USA) *RHannon* 4-9-5 JFortune (1)	10/1	½ 10
	Misty Eyed (IRE) *MrsPNDutfield* 4-9-2 PDoe (4)	66/1	¾ 11
32	Misraah (IRE) *SirMichaelStoute* 5-9-5 (b) KFallon (10)	20/1	2½ 12
6	Meshaheer (USA) *SaeedbinSuroor* 3-8-13 (t) WSupple (5)	14/1	1 13
	Juniper (USA) *APO'Brien,Ireland* 4-9-5 PaulScallan (9)	50/1	5 14

Lucayan Stud 14ran 1m13.00   121/120/112/112/111+/111

CURRAGH Sunday, Jul 14   GOOD to SOFT

39   **Darley Irish Oaks (Gr 1) (3yo f) £144,449**   1½m

	MARGARULA (IRE) *JSBolger* 3-9-0 KJManning (12)	33/1	1
20	QUARTER MOON (IRE) *APO'Brien* 3-9-0 MJKinane (9)	4/5f	1 2
	LADY'S SECRET (IRE) *BWHills,GB* 3-9-0 MHills (4)	16/1	6 3
	Zafaraniya (IRE) *JOxx* 3-9-0 JMurtagh (5)	7/1	2 4
20	Red Rioja (IRE) *EJO'Neill,GB* 3-9-0 JFEgan (10)	14/1	3 5
	L'Affaire Monique *SirMichaelStoute,GB* 3-9-0 KFallon (1)	10/1	1½ 6
20	Mellow Park (IRE) *JNoseda,GB* 3-9-0 DHolland (2)	10/1	nk 7
	Irresistible Jewel (IRE) *DKWeld* 3-9-0 PJSmullen (8)	7/1	4½ 8
20	Starbourne (IRE) *APO'Brien* 3-9-0 JAHeffernan (7)	14/1	½ 9
20	Kournakova (IRE) *APO'Brien* 3-9-0 CO'Donoghue (6)	33/1	1 10
	Fearn Royal (IRE) *PeterCasey* 3-9-0 PShanahan (3)	150/1	13 11
	Tarifana (IRE) *JOxx* 3-9-0 FMBerry (11)	50/1	13 12

Mrs J. S. Bolger 12ran 2m37.84   120/118/109/106/102

ASCOT Saturday, Jul 27   GOOD to FIRM

40   **King George VI and Queen Elizabeth Diamond Stks (Gr 1) (3yo+) £435,000**   1½m

	GOLAN (IRE) *SirMichaelStoute* 4-9-7 KFallon (8)	11/2	1
27	NAYEF (USA) *MPTregoning* 4-9-7 RHills (2)	7/1	hd 2
31	ZINDABAD (FR) *MJohnston* 6-9-7 KDarley (1)	11/2	3½ 3
34	Aquarelliste (FR) *ELellouche,France* 4-9-4 DBoeuf (10)	8/1	2 4
27	Grandera (IRE) *SaeedbinSuroor* 4-9-7 LDettori (4)	13/8f	2½ 5
31	Storming Home *BWHills* 4-9-7 MHills (7)	10/1	1¼ 6
19	Boreal (GER) *PSchiergen,Germany* 4-9-7 OPeslier (11)	14/1	14 7
	Sir Effendi (IRE) *MPTregoning* 6-9-7 WSupple (12)	200/1	dist 8
24	Narrative (IRE) *SaeedbinSuroor* 4-9-7 (t) JPSpencer (6)	16/1	5 9

Exors of the late Lord Weinstock 9ran 2m29.70   129/129/124/117/116/114

DUSSELDORF Sunday, Jul 28   GOOD to FIRM

41   **WGZ Bank-Deutschlandpreis (Gr 1) (3yo+) £70,968**   1½m

19	MARIENBARD (IRE) *SaeedbinSuroor,GB* 5-9-6 (v) LDettori	17/10f	1
37	YAVANA'S PACE (IRE) *MJohnston,GB* 10-9-6 KDalgleish	22/1	1½ 2
	SAMUM (GER) *ASchutz,Germany* 5-9-6 AStarke	32/10	1¾ 3
	Sir George Turner *MJohnston,GB* 3-8-6 JAQuinn	15/2	1½ 4
	Midnight Angel (GER) *HRemmert,Germany* 3-8-2 JPCarvalho	33/10	2 5
24	Sabiango (GER) *AWohler,Germany* 4-9-6 ASuborics	23/10	10 6

Godolphin 6ran 2m25.67   121+/118/115/110/103

GOODWOOD Tuesday, Jul 30   GOOD to FIRM

42   **Peugeot Gordon Stks (Gr 3) (3yo) £34,100**   1½m

21	BANDARI (IRE) *MJohnston* 3-8-13 WSupple (5)	15/8	1
29	FIRST CHARTER *SirMichaelStoute* 3-8-10 PatEddery (4)	7/2	7 2
	IZDIHAM (IRE) *MPTregoning* 3-8-10 RHills (3)	7/4f	¾ 3
	Supremacy *SirMichaelStoute* 3-8-10 KFallon (2)	6/1	15 4

Mr Hamdan Al Maktoum 4ran 2m34.26   123/109/108

GOODWOOD Wednesday, Jul 31   GOOD

43   **Sussex Stks (Gr 1) (3yo+)** £153,700   1m

26	ROCK OF GIBRALTAR (IRE) *APO'Brien,Ireland* 3-8-13 MJKinane (3)..	8/13f		1
12	NOVERRE (USA) *SaeedbinSuroor* 4-9-7 (t) LDettori (4)	3/1	2	2
38	REEL BUDDY (USA) *RHannon* 4-9-7 RHughes (5)	33/1	2	3
25	No Excuse Needed *SirMichaelStoute* 4-9-7 JMurtagh (1)	11/2	1¾	4
38	Sahara Desert *APO'Brien,Ireland* 3-8-13 PaulScallan (2)	66/1	3	5

Sir Alex Ferguson & Mrs John Magnier 5ran 1m38.29   124+/121/116/112

GOODWOOD Saturday, Aug 3   GOOD to FIRM

44   **Vodafone Nassau Stks (Gr 1) (3yo+ f+m)** £78,300   1m1f192y

20	ISLINGTON (IRE) *SirMichaelStoute* 3-8-6 KFallon (6)	10/3		1
7	SULK (IRE) *JHMGosden* 3-8-6 RHughes (1)	33/1	4	2
39	QUARTER MOON (IRE) *APO'Brien,Ireland* 3-8-6 MJKinane (7)	9/4f	½	3
	Fallen Star *JLDunlop* 4-9-1 SDrowne (9)	4/1	1	4
39	Starbourne (IRE) *APO'Brien,Ireland* 3-8-6 CO'Donoghue (8)	25/1	1½	5
	Tarfshi *MAJarvis* 4-9-1 PatEddery (4)	5/1	1	6
27	Golden Silca *MRChannon* 6-9-1 TEDurcan (5)	14/1	¾	7
	Premier Prize *DRCElsworth* 5-9-1 TQuinn (10)	50/1	4	8
39	Red Rioja (IRE) *EJO'Neill* 3-8-6 GDuffield (2)	20/1	¾	9
30	Shiny *CEBrittain* 3-8-6 KDarley (3)	66/1	1	10

Exors of the late Lord Weinstock 10ran 2m04.69   119+/111/110/109/105

COLOGNE Sunday, Aug 11   GOOD to SOFT

45   **Credit Suisse Private Banking Pokal (Gr 1) (3yo+)** £74,214   1½m

41	YAVANA'S PACE (IRE) *MJohnston,GB* 10-9-7 KDalgleish	99/10		1
36	SALVE REGINA (GER) *ASchutz,Germany* 3-8-3 AStarke	16/10	½	2
37	MILLENARY *JLDunlop,GB* 5-9-7 PatEddery	1/1f	4	3
	Well Made (GER) *HBlume,Germany* 5-9-7 LHammer-Hansen	61/10	1½	4
36	Auenteufel (GER) *UOstmann,Germany* 3-8-7 (b) ABoschert	21/1	ns	5
41	Sir George Turner *MJohnston,GB* 3-8-7 WWoods	114/10	4	6
36	Levirat (GER) *MHofer,Germany* 3-8-7 WJO'Connor	21/1	8	7

Mrs Joan Keaney 7ran 2m32.06   120/112/113/110/107

NEWBURY Saturday, Aug 17   FIRM

46   **Stan James Geoffrey Freer Stks (Gr 2) (3yo+)** £37,700   1m5f61y

37	MUBTAKER (USA) *MPTregoning* 5-9-3 RHills (7)	11/8f		1
31	HIGH PITCHED *HRACecil* 4-9-3 TQuinn (1)	5/2	2	2
28	PERSIAN PUNCH (IRE) *DRCElsworth* 9-9-3 MartinDwyer (6)	16/1	3½	3
	Daliapour (IRE) *SirMichaelStoute* 6-9-3 JMurtagh (5)	9/2	1¾	4
28	Warrsan (IRE) *CEBrittain* 4-9-3 SSanders (3)	11/1	½	5
5	Maniatis *MrsAJPerrett* 5-9-3 JPSpencer (4)	25/1	27	6
	Murghem (IRE) *MJohnston* 7-9-3 KDarley (2)	14/1	5	7

Mr Hamdan Al Maktoum 7ran 2m45.46   123/119+/113/111/110

ARLINGTON Saturday, Aug 17   FIRM

47   **Arlington Million (Gr 1) (3yo+)** £394,737   1¼m

	BEAT HOLLOW *RJFrankel,USA* 5-9-0 JBailey	7/10f		1
	SARAFAN (USA) *NDDrysdale,USA* 5-9-0 CNakatani	41/10	hd	2
	FORBIDDEN APPLE (USA) *CClement,USA* 7-9-0 JSantos	46/10	ns	3
	Ulundi *PRWebber,GB* 7-9-0 RHughes	30/1	hd	4
	Falcon Flight (FR) *DJBurkeII,USA* 6-9-0 RDouglas	17/1	ns	5
27	Paolini (GER) *AWohler,Germany* 5-9-0 (b) ASuborics	79/10	nk	6
	Cheshire *JEHammond,France* 5-9-0 YTake	45/1	2¾	7
27	Freefourinternet (USA) *BJMeehan,GB* 4-9-0 (b) PatEddery	59/1	¾	8
	Mystery Giver (USA) *CMBlock,USA* 4-9-0 KDesormeaux	30/1	7	9

Mr K. Abdulla 9ran 2m02.94   123+/122+/122+/122/122/121/116/114

DEAUVILLE Sunday, Aug 18   GOOD

48   **Prix du Haras de Fresnay-le-Buffard Jacques le Marois (Gr 1) 1) (3yo+ c+f)**   1m
£181,974

27	BANKS HILL *AFabre,France* 4-9-1 OPeslier (4)	17/10f		1
	DOMEDRIVER (IRE) *PBary,France* 4-9-1 TThulliez (6)	136/10	1½	2
25	BEST OF THE BESTS (IRE) *SaeedbinSuroor,GB* 5-9-4 LDettori (2)	4/1	1½	3
23	Turtle Bow (FR) *FRohaut,France* 3-8-9 CSoumillon (5)	8/1	1	4
9	Medecis *MmeCHead-Maarek,France* 3-8-12 ODoleuze (1)	64/10	¾	5
26	Bowman (USA) *AFabre,France* 3-8-12 YTake (7)	21/1	¾	6
	Tashawak (IRE) *JLDunlop,GB* 3-8-9 RHills (3)	24/10	1½	7

11   Altieri *VCaruso,Italy* 4-9-4 GBietolini (8)... 29/1   6 8
Mr K. Abdulla 8ran 1m35.19   126/125/121/115/116/114

YORK Tuesday, Aug 20   GOOD

49   **Juddmonte International Stks (Gr 1) (3yo+)** £261,000   1¼m85y

40   NAYEF (USA) *MPTregoning* 4-9-5 RHills (5).. 6/4f   1
40   GOLAN (IRE) *SirMichaelStoute* 3-8-8 SWKelly (6)................................... 9/4   ½ 2
43   NOVERRE (USA) *SaeedbinSuroor* 4-9-5 (t) LDettori (7) 7/2   1½ 3
35   Indian Creek *DRCElsworth* 5-9-5 TQuinn (1)... 14/1   1½ 4
15   Chancellor (IRE) *BWHills* 4-9-5 MHills (2).. 33/1   5 5
44   Starbourne (IRE) *APO'Brien,Ireland* 3-8-8 SWKelly (3) .... 100/1   hd 6
43   No Excuse Needed *SirMichaelStoute* 4-9-5 JMurtagh (4) .... 12/1   dist 7
Mr Hamdan Al Maktoum 7ran 2m08.74   127+/126+/122+/119/109/105

50   **Great Voltigeur Stks (Gr 2) (3yo c+g)** £87,000   1m3f195y

42   BANDARI (IRE) *MJohnston* 3-8-9 RHills (5)... 4/5f   1
     HIGHEST (IRE) *SirMichaelStoute* 3-8-9 JMurtagh (4)........................ 5/1   hd 2
29   BOLLIN ERIC *TDEasterby* 3-8-9 KFallon (2)... 7/1   nk 3
29   Bustan (IRE) *MPTregoning* 3-8-9 WSupple (6) .... 10/1   ½ 4
     Systematic *MJohnston* 3-8-9 KDarley (1) .... 11/2   nk 5
21   Frankies Dream (IRE) *TGMills* 3-8-9 (v) JFortune (3)......................... 33/1   4 6
Mr Hamdan Al Maktoum 6ran 2m28.80   118/117/117/116/116/109

YORK Wednesday, Aug 21   GOOD to FIRM

51   **Aston Upthorpe Yorkshire Oaks (Gr 1) (3yo+ f+m)** £145,000   1m3f195y

44   ISLINGTON (IRE) *SirMichaelStoute* 3-8-8 KFallon (9).......................... 2/1   1
     GUADALUPE (GER) *PSchiergen,Germany* 3-8-8 ASuborics (3) 20/1   5 2
44   SULK (IRE) *JHMGosden* 3-8-8 RHughes (2)... 16/1   hd 3
20   Kazzia (GER) *SaeedbinSuroor* 3-8-8 LDettori (6) .... 7/4f   hd 4
39   Irresistible Jewel (IRE) *DKWeld,Ireland* 3-8-8 PJSmullen (8).............. 9/1   1¼ 5
44   Quarter Moon (IRE) *APO'Brien,Ireland* 3-8-8 MJKinane (1)............... 8/1   hd 6
     Love Everlasting *MJohnston* 4-9-4 KDarley (4) 25/1   3 7
39   Mellow Park (IRE) *JNoseda* 3-8-8 (v) PatEddery (7)........................... 20/1   2½ 8
39   Lady's Secret (IRE) *BWHills* 3-8-8 MHills (5) 33/1   1¼ 9
49   Starbourne (IRE) *APO'Brien,Ireland* 3-8-8 SWKelly (11) 100/1   3½ 10
     Zanzibar (IRE) *MLWBell* 4-9-4 TQuinn (10) 50/1   1¼ 11
Exors of the late Lord Weinstock 11ran 2m26.74   120+/111/111/111/109/109

YORK Thursday, Aug 22   GOOD to FIRM

52   **Peugeot Lowther Stks (Gr 2) (2yo f)** £50,575   6f

     RUSSIAN RHYTHM (USA) *SirMichaelStoute* 2-9-0 KFallon (4).............. 8/13f   1
     DANASKAYA (IRE) *JSBolger,Ireland* 2-8-11 KJManning (5)..................... 11/1   1¼ 2
     ROMANTIC LIASON *BJMeehan* 2-9-0 LDettori (3) .... 5/2   nk 3
     Wimple (USA) *CEBrittain* 2-8-11 BDoyle (1)....................................... 50/1   1½ 4
     Wunders Dream (IRE) *JGGiven* 2-9-0 MFenton (2)................................ 10/1   1¾ 5
Cheveley Park Stud 5ran 1m11.05   108+/101+/101/103/96/94

53   **Victor Chandler Nunthorpe Stks (Gr 1) (2yo+)** £107,300   5f

18   KYLLACHY *HCandy* 4-9-11 JPSpencer (15).. 3/1f   1
38   MALHUB (USA) *JHMGosden* 4-9-11 (t) RHills (16)............................. 15/2   ½ 2
     INDIAN PRINCE (IRE) *BJMeehan* 4-9-11 KFallon (11)........................ 33/1   ½ 3
38   Continent *DNicholls* 5-9-11 (t) DHolland (3)....................................... 8/1   hd 4
     Dominica *MPTregoning* 3-9-6 MartinDwyer (2).................................... 11/2   ¾ 5
     Lady Dominatrix (IRE) *MrsPNDutfield* 3-9-6 PDoe (5)........................ 66/1   ¾ 6
18   Smokin Beau *NPLittmoden* 5-9-11 IMongan (8).................................. 25/1   ½ 7
38   Bahamian Pirate (IRE) *DNicholls* 7-9-11 RHughes (17)....................... 16/1   sh 8
     Rudi's Pet (IRE) *DNicholls* 8-9-11 (v) AlexGreaves (10)...................... 33/1   sh 9
     Jessica's Dream (IRE) *JGGiven* 4-9-8 MFenton (7) .... 10/1   ½ 10
     The Trader (IRE) *MBlanshard* 4-9-11 (b) JQuinn (4)........................... 14/1   ½ 11
     Porlezza (FR) *YdeNicolay,France* 3-9-6 CSoumillon (13)..................... 20/1   sh 12
     Bishops Court *MrsJRRamsden* 8-9-11 FLynch (6)................................ 33/1   nk 13
38   Danehurst *SirMarkPrescott* 4-9-8 GDuffield (9)................................... 6/1   ¾ 14
38   Misty Eyed (IRE) *MrsPNDutfield* 4-9-8 KDarley (14)........................... 66/1   1 15
     Orientor *JSGoldie* 4-9-11 AColhane (1) .... 40/1   sh 16
     Whitbarrow (IRE) *BRMillman* 3-9-9 (h+b) EAhern (12)...................... 66/1   nk 17
Thurloe T'breds V & Cheveley Park Stud 17ran 58.10secs 124+/122+/121/120+/115/112

DEAUVILLE Sunday, Aug 25   GOOD

54   **Prix Morny Casinos Barriere (Gr 1) (2yo c+f)** £91,570   6f

     ELUSIVE CITY (USA) *GAButler,GB* 2-9-0 KFallon (3)............................ 19/10   1
     ZAFEEN (FR) *MRChannon,GB* 2-9-0 SDrowne (2) .... 11/1   ¾ 2

```
        LOVING KINDNESS (USA) PBary,France 2-8-11 TThulliez (1) ............... 1/1f   2½ 3
        Zinziberine (USA) AFabre,France 2-8-11 OPeslier (5) ...........................  6/1    ¾ 4
        Al Turf (IRE) RHannon,GB 2-9-0 CSoumillon (6) .................................. 12/1   hd 5
        Ela Merici (FR) MmeCBarbe,France 2-8-11 DBoeuf (4) ........................ 11/1    ¾ 6

        The Thoroughbred Corporation 6ran 1m10.40              113/111/100/98/101/95
```

BADEN-BADEN Sunday, Sep 1   GOOD

55   Grosser Preis von Baden (Gr 1) (3yo+) £326,923   1½m

```
   41  MARIENBARD (IRE) SaeedbinSuroor,GB 5-9-6 (v+t) LDettori............... 28/10      1
   45  SALVE REGINA (GER) ASchutz,Germany 3-8-5 AStarke.......................... 3/1   2½ 2
       NOROIT (GER) WFigge,Germany 4-9-6 LHammer-Hansen ................ 168/10   1¼ 3
   34  Califet (FR) GCherel,France 4-9-6 DBonilla...................................... 69/10   3½ 4
   41  Samum (GER) ASchutz,Germany 5-9-6 ASuborics................................. 6/1   sh 5
   40  Boreal (GER) PSchiergen,Germany 4-9-6 KFallon ................................ 18/10f   1 6
       Tareno (GER) PSchiergen,Germany 4-9-6 FMinarik .......................... 138/10   1¾ 7
   45  Auenteufel (GER) UOstmann,Germany 3-8-9 (b) AHelfenbein ............... 211/10   1 8

       Godolphin 8ran 2m34.93                                    122+/112/116/111/111
```

HAYDOCK Saturday, Sep 7   GOOD to FIRM

56   Stanley Leisure Sprint Cup (Gr 1) (3yo+) £116,000   6f

```
   32  INVINCIBLE SPIRIT (IRE) JLDunlop 5-9-0 JCarroll (10)........................ 25/1      1
   53  MALHUB (USA) JHMGosden 4-9-0 (t) RHills (7)................................. 11/2   sh 2
   38  THREE POINTS SaeedbinSuroor 5-9-0 (t) KDarley (11)..................... 12/1    2 3
   53  Orientor JSGoldie 4-9-0 ACulhane (4).......................................... 33/1   hd 4
       May Ball JHMGosden 5-8-11 PRobinson (9)..................................... 16/1   sh 5
   53  Continent DNicholls 5-9-0 (t) KDalgleish (8) .................................. 5/1   ½ 6
   38  Twilight Blues (IRE) BJMeehan 3-8-12 WSupple (13) ....................... 50/1   ¾ 7
   53  Bahamian Pirate (USA) DNicholls 7-9-0 MHills (5) .......................... 12/1   hd 8
       Mount Abu (IRE) JHMGosden 5-9-0 JFortune (2) ............................ 14/1    1 9
   25  Nayyir GAButler 4-9-0 EAhern (12)............................................. 9/2f  1¼ 10
       Air Thule (JPN) HideyukiMori,Japan 5-8-11 YTake (14) ................... 12/1   nk 11
   25  Frenchmans Bay (FR) RCharlton 4-9-0 SDrowne (3) ....................... 25/1   2½ 12
   38  Landseer APO'Brien,Ireland 3-8-12 KFallon (6)............................. 6/1   ¾ 13
   53  Danehurst SirMarkPrescott 4-8-11 (b) GDuffield (1) ...................... 8/1    1 14

       Prince A. A. Faisal 14ran 1m12.44              121/121/114/114+/111+/113/111
```

LEOPARDSTOWN Saturday, Sep 7   GOOD to FIRM

57   Ireland The Food Island Champion Stks (Gr 1) (3yo+) £388,734   1¼m

```
   40  GRANDERA (IRE) SaeedbinSuroor,GB 4-9-4 LDettori (7).................... 5/2      1
   35  HAWK WING (USA) APO'Brien 3-8-11 MJKinane (6)........................... 8/11f   sh 2
   48  BEST OF THE BESTS (IRE) SaeedbinSuroor,GB 5-9-4 (t) JPSpencer (8).. 12/1   nk 3
   35  Sholokhov (IRE) APO'Brien 3-8-11 PaulScallan (1)......................... 8/1    6 4
   49  No Excuse Needed SirMichaelStoute,GB 4-9-4 PJSmullen (9) ............. 16/1   4½ 5
   39  Margarula (IRE) JSBolger 3-8-8 KJManning (5)............................... 9/1   1½ 6
       Common World (USA) GAButler,GB 3-8-11 JMurtagh (3) .................. 25/1    1 7

       Godolphin 7ran 2m04.70                                    123+/123+/122/110
```

LONGCHAMP Sunday, Sep 8   GOOD

58   NetJets Prix du Moulin de Longchamp (Gr 1) (3yo+ c+f) £108,494   1m

```
   43  ROCK OF GIBRALTAR (IRE) APO'Brien,Ireland 3-8-11 MJKinane (7)  3/5cpf    1
   48  BANKS HILL AFabre,France 4-8-12 RHughes (4) ................................ 24/10   ½ 2
   30  GOSSAMER LMCumani,GB 3-8-8 JPSpencer (3) .............................. 184/10  1½ 3
       Proudwings (GER) JEHammond,France 5-8-11 YTake (1) ................. 174/10   nk 4
   43  Sahara Desert APO'Brien,Ireland 3-8-11 PaulScallan (5)................ 3/5cpf   ¾ 5
   48  Bowman (USA) AFabre,France 3-8-11 OPlacais (2) .......................... 155/10   sn 6
    4  Execute (FR) JEHammond,France 5-9-2 TGillet (6)........................... 146/10  2½ 7

       Sir Alex Ferguson & Mrs John Magnier 7ran 1m39.30
                                                  122+/117+/114+/112/114?/114+/108
```

DONCASTER Friday, Sep 13   GOOD to FIRM

59   Amco Corporation Troy Stks (L) (3yo+) £18,444   1½m

```
   50  SYSTEMATIC MJohnston 3-8-6 KDarley (1) .................................... 3/1      1
       THE WHISTLING TEAL GWragg 6-9-1 DHolland (3) ......................... 7/1   1½ 2
   40  STORMING HOME BWHills 4-9-1 MHills (6) ................................... 13/8f    2 3
       Gamut (IRE) SirMichaelStoute 3-8-6 PatEddery (7)......................... 5/1   nk 4
   28  Hatha Anna (IRE) SaeedbinSuroor 3-9-1 (v) LDettori (5) ................. 5/1   ½ 5
   16  Kayseri (IRE) MAJarvis 3-8-6 PRobinson (4) ................................. 25/1   5 6
       Prospects of Glory (USA) EJO'Neill 6-9-1 EAhern (4)....................... 100/1   5 7

       Maktoum Al Maktoum 7ran 2m30.73                        121/118+/115/115/114
```

60 **Rothmans Royals St Leger Stks (Gr 1) (3yo c+f)** £240,000   1¾m132y

50	BOLLIN ERIC *TDEasterby* 3-9-0 KDarley (3)	7/1		1
50	HIGHEST (IRE) *SirMichaelStoute* 3-9-0 DHolland (4)	10/1	1¼	2
50	BANDARI (IRE) *MJohnston* 3-9-0 RHills (7)	13/8f	2	3
36	Mamool (IRE) *SaeedbinSuroor* 3-9-0 LDettori (8)	11/1	1½	4
	Mr Dinos (IRE) *PFICole* 3-9-0 TQuinn (9)	11/1	5	5
33	Balakheri (IRE) *SirMichaelStoute* 3-9-0 PatEddery (2)	7/2	2½	6
42	First Charter *SirMichaelStoute* 3-9-0 JFortune (6)	20/1	2	7
57	Sholokhov (IRE) *APO'Brien,Ireland* 3-9-0 MJKinane (5)	7/1	8	8

Sir Neil Westbrook 8ran 3m02.92   125/123/120/118/111/107

61 **Jefferson Smurfit Memorial Irish St. Leger (Gr 1) (3yo+)** £106,709   1¾m

28	VINNIE ROE (IRE) *DKWeld* 4-9-9 (b) PJSmullen (7)	4/7f		1
	PUGIN (IRE) *JOxx* 4-9-9 JMurtagh (8)	10/1	1½	2
33	BALLINGARRY (IRE) *APO'Brien* 3-8-12 JAHeffernan (4)	8/1	1	3
46	Warrsan (IRE) *CEBrittain,GB* 4-9-9 BDoyle (2)	14/1	nk	4
45	Millenary *JLDunlop,GB* 5-9-9 SSanders (5)	5/1	9	5
57	Margarula (IRE) *JSBolger* 3-8-9 KJManning (3)	10/1	4½	6
	Queens Wharf (IRE) *MHalford* 4-9-6 TPO'Shea (6)	33/1	½	7
	Sadlers Wings (IRE) *WPMullins* 4-9-9 PShanahan (1)	50/1	4	8

Mr Seamus Sheridan 8ran 2m59.00   123/121/119/119

62 **Prix Vermeille - Hermitage Barriere de la Baule (Gr 1) (3yo f)** £90,411   1½m

	PEARLY SHELLS *FRohaut,France* 3-9-0 CSoumillon (9)	19/10f		1
23	ANA MARIE (FR) *PHDemercastel,France* 3-9-0 DBonilla (5)	136/10	1½	2
23	BRIGHT SKY (IRE) *ELellouche,France* 3-9-0 DBoeuf (8)	2/1	2	3
51	Guadalupe (GER) *PSchiergen,Germany* 3-9-0 ASuborics (2)	11/1	1½	4
	Albanova *SirMarkPrescott,GB* 3-9-0 GDuffield (6)	19/1	sh	5
	Bernimixa (FR) *AFabre,France* 3-9-0 YTake (4)	64/10	½	6
	Tigertail (FR) *RodolpheCollet,France* 3-9-0 TGillet (1)	24/1	1½	7
23	Dance Routine *AFabre,France* 3-9-0 RHughes (7)	73/10	1	8
51	Sulk (IRE) *JHMGosden,GB* 3-9-0 ODoleuze (10)	28/1	6	9
	Tucana (GER) *PSchiergen,Germany* 3-9-0 (b) ASchikora (11)	135/1	8	10
23	Blue Lightning (FR) *ELellouche,France* 3-9-0 (b) SCoffigny (3)	2/1		11

6 C Racing Ltd 11ran 2m26.00   121/118/115/113/113/112

63 **Prix Foy - Gray d'Albion Barriere (Gr 2) (4yo+ c+f)** £39,683   1½m

40	AQUARELLISTE (FR) *ELellouche,France* 4-8-13 DBoeuf (2)	9/10f		1
34	ANABAA BLUE *CLerner,France* 4-9-2 CSoumillon (3)	59/10	1	2
24	FALBRAV (IRE) *LD'Auria,Italy* 4-9-2 DVargiu (4)	23/10	sh	3
34	Polish Summer *AFabre,France* 5-9-2 RHughes (5)	36/10	¾	4
22	Sangreal (NZ) *AFabre,France* 4-9-1 TGillet (1)	265/10	5	5

Ecurie Wildenstein 5ran 2m29.00   120+/121+/121+/120/111

64 **Deutsche Post Euro Express-Preis von Europa (Gr 1) (3yo+)** £96,875   1½m

45	WELL MADE (GER) *HBlume,Germany* 5-9-6 THellier	84/10		1
55	SALVE REGINA (GER) *ASchutz,Germany* 3-8-6 AStarke	6/5f	¾	2
45	YAVANA'S PACE (IRE) *MJohnston,GB* 10-9-6 KDalgleish	54/10	4½	3
	Subiaco (GER) *ASchutz,Germany* 5-9-6 ASuborics	112/10	3	4
40	Narrative (IRE) *SaeedbinSuroor,GB* 4-9-6 LDettori	26/10	ns	5
55	Noroit (GER) *WFigge,Germany* 4-9-6 LHammer-Hansen	63/10	4½	6
36	Ammonias (GER) *PSchiergen,Germany* 3-8-10 JMurtagh	16/1	¾	7
36	Los Sainos (GER) *ALowe,Germany* 3-8-10 PAJohnson	28/1	4½	8

Gestut Rottgen 8ran 2m31.02   121/115/113/108/108

65 **Meon Valley Stud Fillies' Mile (Gr 1) (2yo f)** £116,000   1m (Rnd)

SOVIET SONG (IRE) *JRFanshawe* 2-8-10 OUrbina (10)	11/10f		1
CASUAL LOOK (USA) *IABalding* 2-8-10 MartinDwyer (8)	16/1	1½	2
REACH FOR THE MOON (USA) *APO'Brien,Ireland* 2-8-10 MJKinane (5)	9/1	1½	3
Huja (IRE) *SirMichaelStoute* 2-8-10 RHills (4)	14/1	nk	4
Oblige *IABalding* 2-8-10 PatEddery (2)	50/1	¾	5
Approach *SirMarkPrescott* 2-8-10 SSanders (3)	12/1	sh	6
Air Adair (USA) *JHMGosden* 2-8-10 LDettori (6)	20/1	3½	7
Summitville *JGGiven* 2-8-10 MFenton (7)	6/1	1¼	8
Rainbow Queen *SirMichaelStoute* 2-8-10 KFallon (9)	6/1	1	9

Hold To Ransom (USA) *EALDunlop* 2-8-10 JPSpencer (3) 14/1   7 10

Elite Racing Club 10ran 1m42.32   110+/107/103/102/101/101

66	**Brunswick Diadem Stks (Gr 2) (3yo+) £58,000**		6f

      CRYSTAL CASTLE (USA) *JEHammond,France* 4-9-0 KFallon (7) 3/1f   1
56 MALHUB (USA) *JHMGosden* 4-9-6 (t) RHills (4) .... 9/2   sh 2
      ACCLAMATION *LGCottrell* 3-8-12 KDarley (10) 25/1   2½ 3
      Polar Way *MrsAJPerrett* 3-8-12 MJKinane (6) 5/1   1¼ 4
56 Bahamian Pirate (USA) *DNicholls* 7-9-0 MHills (1) .... 10/1   nk 5
56 Twilight Blues (IRE) *BJMeehan* 3-8-12 PatEddery (9).................................. 20/1   hd 6
      Sartorial (IRE) *PJMakin* 6-9-0 SSanders (3) 9/1   1 7
      Chercheuse (USA) *H-APantall,France* 4-8-11 JPSpencer (11)................... 20/1   nk 8
56 Three Points *SaeedbinSuroor* 5-9-0 (t) LDettori (8).................................... 9/2   nk 9
      El Gran Lode (ARG) *DiegoLowther,Sweden* 7-9-0 RBlanco (5) 50/1   2 10
      Vita Spericolata (IRE) *JSWainwright* 5-8-11 MartinDwyer (2) 50/1   17 11

      Mr J. Raw 11ran 1m13.40   120/126/112/109+/108/108

67	**Queen Elizabeth II Stks (Sponsored By NetJets) (Gr 1) (3yo+) £178,500**		1m (Rnd)

26 WHERE OR WHEN (IRE) *TGMills* 3-8-11 KDarley (3) 7/1   1
57 HAWK WING (USA) *APO'Brien,Ireland* 3-8-11 MJKinane (7) 1/2f   2 2
25 TILLERMAN *MrsAJPerrett* 6-9-1 KFallon (1) 10/1   3 3
60 Sholokhov (IRE) *APO'Brien,Ireland* 3-8-11 PaulScallan (6) 33/1   2 4
57 Best of The Bests (IRE) *SaeedbinSuroor* 5-9-1 (t) LDettori (8)..................... 4/1   ½ 5

      John Humphreys (Turf Accountants) Ltd 5ran 1m41.37   124/119/112/108/107

      BELMONT PARK Saturday, Sep 28   SOFT

68	**Flower Bowl Invitational Stks (Gr 1) (3yo+ f+m) £290,322**		1¼m

51 KAZZIA (GER) *SaeedbinSuroor,GB* 3-8-6 JChavez 305/100   1
48 TURTLE BOW (FR) *FRohaut,France* 3-8-3 CSoumillon .... 97/10   nk 2
      MOT JUSTE *KPMcLaughlin,USA* 4-8-6 RMigliore 189/10   1¼ 3
      Starine (FR) *RJFrankel,USA* 5-8-8 (b) JVelazquez .... 325/100   nk 4
      Sunstone *RBarbara,USA* 4-8-6 (b) SBridgmohan 40/1   2½ 5
      England's Legend (FR) *CClement,USA* 5-8-6 JBailey 105/100f   5 6
44 Tarfshi *MAJarvis,GB* 4-8-8 EPrado 28/1   16 7

      Godolphin 7ran 2m05.22   119/115/110/111/105

      WOODBINE Sunday, Sep 29   GOOD to SOFT

69	**Canadian International Stks (Gr 1) (3yo+) £367,347**		1½m

61 BALLINGARRY (IRE) *APO'Brien,Ireland* 3-8-6 MJKinane 41/10   1
47 FALCON FLIGHT (FR) *DJBurkeII,USA* 6-9-0 PValenzuela 29/10f   2¼ 2
64 YAVANA'S PACE (IRE) *MJohnston,GB* 10-9-0 KDalgleish................... 41/1   4 3
      Perfect Soul (IRE) *RAttfield,Canada* 4-9-0 (b) RLandry .... 77/10   ½ 4
40 Zindabad (FR) *MJohnston,GB* 6-9-0 KDarley .... 32/10   ns 5
47 Paolini (GER) *AWohler,Germany* 5-9-0 (b) ASuborics 335/100   4½ 6
      Portcullis (CAN) *MRFrostad,Canada* 3-8-6 SCallaghan 24/1   3 7
      Full of Wonder (CAN) *MRFrostad,Canada* 4-9-0 (b) TKabel 79/10   13 8

      Mrs John Magnier 8ran 2m31.68   123/118/112/111/111

      NEWMARKET Thursday, Oct 3   FIRM (Rowley Mile Course)

70	**Shadwell Stud Middle Park Stks (Gr 1) (2yo c) £100,920**		6f

      OASIS DREAM *JHMGosden* 2-8-11 JFortune (9) 6/1   1
      TOMAHAWK (USA) *APO'Brien,Ireland* 2-8-11 MJKinane (10)................... 5/1   1½ 2
54 ELUSIVE CITY (USA) *GAButler* 2-8-11 KFallon (4) .... 6/4f   nk 3
      Country Reel (USA) *DRLoder* 2-8-11 LDettori (11) 8/1   3½ 4
54 Zafeen (FR) *MRChannon* 2-8-11 SDrowne (7) .... 6/1   ¾ 5
      Irrawaddy (USA) *APO'Brien,Ireland* 2-8-11 KDarley (8) .... 33/1   ¾ 6
      Ontario (USA) *APO'Brien,Ireland* 2-8-11 JPSpencer (6) .... 20/1   nk 7
      Membership (USA) *CEBrittain* 2-8-11 (b) SSanders (3) .... 33/1   nk 8
      Miguel Cervantes (USA) *APO'Brien,Ireland* 2-8-11 JMurtagh (2) .... 20/1   ½ 9
      Sir Albert *JNoseda* 2-8-11 OPeslier (5).. 25/1   1 10

      Mr K. Abdulla 10ran 1m09.61   122/118/117/109/107/105

      NEWMARKET Friday, Oct 4   FIRM (Rowley Mile Course)

71	**Betfair Cheveley Park Stks (Gr 1) (2yo f) £87,000**		6f

      AIRWAVE *HCandy* 2-8-11 CRutter (2).. 11/2   1
52 RUSSIAN RHYTHM (USA) *SirMichaelStoute* 2-8-11 KFallon (6) 8/13f   1½ 2
52 DANASKAYA (IRE) *JSBolger,Ireland* 2-8-11 (b) KJManning (5) .... 25/1   ½ 3
      Ego *GWragg* 2-8-11 TEDurcan (4) 3/1   1½ 4
52 Wimple (USA) *CEBrittain* 2-8-11 LDettori (3)... 33/1   5 5
      Bella Tusa (IRE) *CFWall* 2-8-11 SSanders (1).. 20/1   ½ 6

      Henry Candy & Partners 6ran 1m10.72   112+/108/106/102

LONGCHAMP Saturday, Oct 5 GOOD

72 Prix Dollar - Fouquet's Barriere (Gr 2) (3yo+) £34,058 1m1f165y

	DANO-MAST *FPoulsen,Denmark* 6-9-0 OPeslier (5)	253/10	1
	BINARY FILE (USA) *JHMGosden,GB* 4-9-0 DBoeuf (1)	147/10	2½ 2
	EAGLE CAFE (USA) *FKojima,Japan* 5-9-0 KTanaka (9)	12/1	sn 3
	Tau Ceti *JEHammond,France* 3-8-10 TJarnet (10)	42/10	½ 4
2	Jim And Tonic (FR) *FDoumen,France* 8-9-0 GMosse (4)	41/10	sh 5
	Bernebeau (FR) *AFabre,France* 3-8-10 LDettori (11)	84/10	sn 6
35	Imperial Dancer *MRChannon,GB* 4-9-0 MartinDwyer (7)	19/1	sh 7
58	Execute (FR) *JEHammond,France* 5-9-4 TGillet (8)	146/10	nk 8
	Vintage Premium *RAFahey,GB* 5-9-0 PHanagan (6)	34/1	2½ 9
	War Blade (GER) *ASchutz,Germany* 5-9-0 AStarke (2)	50/1	8 10
	Wellbeing *PBary,France* 5-9-0 TThulliez (3)	8/5f	¾ 11

Composit Aps & Mosehoj Stable 11ran 2m01.60 120/115/115/116+/114/115/113/117

KEENELAND Sunday, Oct 6 FIRM

73 Shadwell Keeneland Turf Mile Stks (Gr 1) (3yo+) £240,000 1m

56	LANDSEER *APO'Brien,Ireland* 3-8-11 EPrado	34/10	1
	TOUCH OF THE BLUES *NDDrysdale,USA* 5-9-0 KDesormeaux	8/1	nk 2
47	BEAT HOLLOW *RJFrankel,USA* 5-9-0 JBailey	7/10f	½ 3
	Strut The Stage (USA) *MRFrostad,Canada* 4-9-0 (b) RAlbarado	12/1	3¾ 4
	Grammarian (USA) *KGorder,USA* 4-9-0 CPerret	56/1	1¼ 5
	North East Bound (USA) *WWPerry,USA* 6-9-0 JVelez	25/1	1¾ 6
	Balto Star (USA) *TAPletcher,USA* 4-9-0 MGuidry	6/1	4 7
47	Freefourinternet (USA) *CSimon,USA* 4-9-0 (b) ECoa	50/1	1 8

Mr M. Tabor & Mrs John Magnier 8ran 1m35.55 122+/120/119/110

LONGCHAMP Sunday, Oct 6 GOOD

74 Prix du Cadran - Casino Barriere de Cannes Croisette (Gr 1) (4yo+) £71,874 2½m

Order as they passed the post: Polish Summer and Persian Punch were both disqualified for causing interference

28	GIVE NOTICE *JLDunlop,GB* 5-9-2 JMurtagh (14)	62/10	1
	PUSHKIN (IRE) *ELellouche,France* 4-9-2 DBoeuf (7)	16/1	hd 2
63	POLISH SUMMER *AFabre,France* 5-9-2 CSoumillon (15)	22/10f	¾ 3
	Cut Quartz (FR) *RGibson,France* 5-9-2 OPeslier (8)	12/1	¾ 4
46	Persian Punch (IRE) *DRCElsworth,GB* 9-9-2 MartinDwyer (5)	6/1	½ 5
	Clety (FR) *FDoumen,France* 6-9-2 (b) TThulliez (12)	17/1	sh 6
	Soreze (FR) *DSepulchre,France* 4-9-2 DBonilla (13)	17/1	sh 7
	Terrazzo (USA) *NBranchu,France* 7-9-2 OPlacais (10)	51/1	sn 8
	Tiger Groom *RCollet,France* 5-9-2 SMaillot (3)	73/1	1½ 9
	Miraculous (FR) *DProd'homme,France* 5-9-2 TJarnet (11)	8/1	hd 10
	San Sebastian *MRolland,France* 8-9-2 (b) EAhern (4)	19/1	nk 11
	Bangalore *MrsAJPerrett,GB* 6-9-2 SSanders (6)	16/1	1¾ 12
	Ice Dancer (IRE) *APO'Brien,Ireland* 4-9-2 MJKinane (1)	13/1	1¼ 13
	Adlerflieger (GER) *ASchutz,Germany* 5-9-2 AStarke (9)	83/1	2½ 14
	Hirapour (IRE) *MrsAJPerrett,GB* 6-9-2 PatEddery (2)	19/1	3 15
	Labirinto (USA) *AdeRoyerDupre,France* 4-9-2 GMosse (16)	20/1	nk 16

I. H. Stewart-Brown & M. J. Meacock 16ran 4m23.80 115/116/114/113/113/113

75 Prix de l'Abbaye de Longchamp - Majestic Barriere (Gr 1) (2yo+) £71,874 5f

56	CONTINENT *DNicholls,GB* 5-9-11 DHolland (16)	4/1jf	1
	SLAP SHOT (IRE) *LRiccardi,Italy* 3-9-8 MDemuro (14)	73/1	ns 2
6	ZIPPING (IRE) *RCollet,France* 3-9-11 DBonilla (19)	96/10	sh 3
66	Bahamian Pirate (USA) *DNicholls,GB* 7-9-11 OPeslier (4)	4/1jf	nk 4
	Agnetha (GER) *DKWeld,Ireland* 3-9-8 PJSmullen (15)	49/1	½ 5
56	Orientor *JSGoldie,GB* 4-9-11 ACulhane (7)	22/1	sh 6
53	Porlezza (FR) *YdeNicolay,France* 3-9-8 CSoumillon (10)	43/1	1½ 7
56	May Ball *JHMGosden,GB* 5-9-8 GMosse (8)	7/1	sh 8
	Ziria (IRE) *CLaffon-Parias,France* 3-9-8 DBoeuf (18)	17/1	hd 9
	Mister Links (IRE) *RHannon,GB* 2-8-7 RHughes (3)	44/10	1½ 10
	Aramus (CHI) *FCastro,Sweden* 5-9-11 DSanchez (11)	73/1	sh 11
	Nobel Prize (ARG) *DiegoLowther,Sweden* 6-9-11 RBlanco (1)	70/1	¾ 12
	Oh Bej Oh Bej (IRE) *MGuarnieri,Italy* 4-9-8 MTellini (2)	34/1	sh 13
	Dananeyev (FR) *CLaffon-Parias,France* 6-9-11 TThulliez (9)	78/1	sh 14
	Halmahera (IRE) *KARyan,GB* 7-9-11 FLynch (20)	60/1	1 15
52	Wunders Dream (IRE) *JGGiven,GB* 2-8-4 MFenton (5)	61/10	½ 16
7	Lahinch (IRE) *APO'Brien,Ireland* 3-9-8 MJKinane (6)	43/1	hd 17
	Maybe Forever *CLaffon-Parias,France* 3-9-8 YTake (17)	17/1	sh 18
53	Jessica's Dream (IRE) *JGGiven,GB* 4-9-8 JMurtagh (13)	17/1	1½ 19
	Minashki (IRE) *KPrendergast,Ireland* 3-9-11 DPMcDonogh (12)	131/1	1 20

Lucayan Stud 20ran 57.20secs 117/115/118/116/113/115

76 Prix de l'Opera - Casino Barriere d'Enghien-Les-Bains (Gr 1) (3yo+ f+m) £89,843 1¼m

62 BRIGHT SKY (IRE) *ELellouche,France* 3-8-12 DBoeuf (7) ... 9/10cpf 1
51 IRRESISTIBLE JEWEL (IRE) *DKWeld,Ireland* 3-8-12 PJSmullen (3) ... 113/10 4 2
23 MAROTTA (FR) *RGibson,France* 3-8-12 TJarnet (4) ... 67/10 ¾ 3
Katchina Quest (FR) *J-CRouget,France* 4-9-2 IMendizabal (11) ... 15/1 1½ 4
44 Golden Silca *MRChannon,GB* 6-9-2 TEDurcan (8) ... 65/1 ½ 5
Walzerkoenigin (USA) *PSchiergen,Germany* 3-8-12 ASuborics (1) ... 33/1 3 6
51 Starbourne (IRE) *APO'Brien,Ireland* 3-8-12 JMurtagh (6) ... 74/1 1 7
Dance Dress (USA) *AFabre,France* 3-8-12 (b) CSoumillon (5) ... 28/1 ¾ 8
51 Quarter Moon (IRE) *APO'Brien,Ireland* 3-8-12 MJKinane (12) ... 15/2 3 9
41 Midnight Angel (GER) *HRemmert,Germany* 3-8-12 LDettori (13) ... 102/10 3 10
Serisia (FR) *PBary,France* 3-8-12 TThulliez (9) ... 17/1 1 11
62 Blue Lightning (FR) *ELellouche,France* 3-8-12 (b) SCoffigny (10) ... 9/10cpf 10 12

Ecurie Wildenstein 12ran 2m02.30 123+/115/113/108/107

77 Prix Marcel Boussac Criterium des Pouliches - Royal Barriere de Deauville (Gr 1) (2yo f) £89,843 1m

SIX PERFECTIONS (FR) *PBary,France* 2-8-11 TThulliez (1) ... 4/5f 1
ETOILE MONTANTE (USA) *MmeCHead-Maarek,France* 2-8-11 RHughes (9) ... 54/10 2 2
LUMINATA (IRE) *JSBolger,Ireland* 2-8-11 KJManning (3) ... 22/1 5 3
Pearl Dance (USA) *JHMGosden,GB* 2-8-11 LDettori (7) ... 11/2 sn 4
Miss Helga (IRE) *APO'Brien,Ireland* 2-8-11 JMurtagh (4) ... 82/1 sn 5
Yesterday (IRE) *APO'Brien,Ireland* 2-8-11 MJKinane (10) ... 127/10 nk 6
Loving Pride (USA) *MmeCHead-Maarek,France* 2-8-11 RThomas (8) ... 23/1 1 7
High Definition (IRE) *ASpanu,France* 2-8-11 FSpanu (6) ... 93/1 5 8
Cassis (USA) *JNoseda,GB* 2-8-11 PatEddery (2) ... 108/10 sh 9
Rainbows For All (IRE) *KPrendergast,Ireland* 2-8-11 DPMcDonogh (5) ... 16/1 1½ 10

Niarchos Family 10ran 1m37.90 120/115/103/102/102/101

78 Grand Criterium - Lucien Barriere (Gr 1) (2yo c+f) £125,780 7f

HOLD THAT TIGER (USA) *APO'Brien,Ireland* 2-9-0 KFallon (13) ... 7/2cp 1
LE VIE DEI COLORI *RBrogi,Italy* 2-9-0 OPeslier (2) ... 5/1 ½ 2
INTERCONTINENTAL *AFabre,France* 2-8-11 CSoumillon (11) ... 17/10f ½ 3
Hanabad (IRE) *JOxx,Ireland* 2-9-0 JMurtagh (3) ... 136/10 nk 4
Foss Way (IRE) *JHMGosden,GB* 2-9-0 LDettori (4) ... 67/10 ¾ 5
Great Pyramid (IRE) *APO'Brien,Ireland* 2-9-0 JPSpencer (6) ... 7/2cp ½ 6
Spartacus (IRE) *APO'Brien,Ireland* 2-9-0 MJKinane (12) ... 7/2cp ¾ 7
Our Teddy (IRE) *GGMargarson,GB* 2-9-0 GMosse (1) ... 53/1 sh 8
Checkit (IRE) *MRChannon,GB* 2-9-0 SDrowne (8) ... 21/1 sh 9
54 Loving Kindness (USA) *PBary,France* 2-8-11 TThulliez (7) ... 136/10 nk 10
Kimberley Mine (IRE) *APO'Brien,Ireland* 2-9-0 KDarley (10) ... 7/2cp nk 11
Zanyboy (FR) *RCollet,France* 2-9-0 DBonilla (9) ... 50/1 ¾ 12
Maghanim *JLDunlop,GB* 2-9-0 RHills (14) ... 17/2 2½ 13
Il Barone (IRE) *NClement,France* 2-9-0 TJarnet (5) ... 42/1 sh 14

Mr M. Tabor & Mrs John Magnier 14ran 1m20.10 111+/110/105/107/105/104

79 Prix de l'Arc de Triomphe - Lucien Barriere (Gr 1) (3yo+ c+f) £574,993 1½m

55 MARIENBARD (IRE) *SaeedbinSuroor,GB* 5-9-5 (v) LDettori (3) ... 158/10 1
17 SULAMANI (IRE) *PBary,France* 3-8-11 TThulliez (13) ... 7/2cp ¾ 2
33 HIGH CHAPARRAL (IRE) *APO'Brien,Ireland* 3-8-11 MJKinane (5) .. 22/10cpf ½ 3
55 Califet (FR) *GCherel,France* 4-9-5 TJarnet (1) ... 131/1 ½ 4
51 Islington (IRE) *SirMichaelStoute,GB* 3-8-8 KFallon (9) ... 72/10 sn 5
63 Aquarelliste (FR) *ELellouche,France* 4-9-2 DBoeuf (2) ... 42/10 ¾ 6
63 Anabaa Blue *CLerner,France* 4-9-5 CSoumillon (8) ... 23/1 1½ 7
22 Fair Mix (IRE) *MRolland,France* 4-9-5 SPasquier (15) ... 77/1 1½ 8
63 Falbrav (IRE) *LD'Auria,Italy* 4-9-5 OPeslier (7) ... 15/1 sh 9
17 Black Sam Bellamy (IRE) *APO'Brien,Ireland* 3-8-11 JMurtagh (11) 22/10cpf 1½ 10
62 Ana Marie (FR) *PHDemercastel,France* 3-8-8 DBonilla (10) ... 43/1 1½ 11
22 Foundation Spirit (FR) *FDoumen,France* 4-9-5 GMosse (14) ... 93/1 5 12
Manhattan Cafe (JPN) *FKojima,Japan* 4-9-5 MEbina (12) ... 83/10 5 13
Asian Heights *GWragg,GB* 4-9-5 DHolland (16) ... 33/1 2½ 14
55 Boreal (GER) *PSchiergen,Germany* 4-9-5 ASuborics (4) ... 105/1 sh 15
4 Sensible (FR) *PBary,France* 4-9-5 (b) C-PLemaire (6) ... 7/2cp 20 16

Godolphin 16ran 2m26.70 129/128+/127/126/123/121/122/119/119/117

CURRAGH Sunday, Oct 13 GOOD to SOFT

80 Bank of Ireland Waterford Testimonial Stks (L) (3yo+) £21,125 6f

9 CAPTAIN RIO *RMWhitaker,GB* 3-8-11 FMBerry (8) ... 10/3jf 1
ONE WON ONE (USA) *MsJMorgan* 8-9-5 JAHeffernan (2) ... 8/1 8 2

18	KIER PARK (IRE) *MAJarvis,GB* 5-8-12 PRobinson (4)	10/3jf	¾ 3
32	Miss Beabea (IRE) *KPrendergast* 3-8-8 DPMcDonogh (9)	10/1	1½ 4
	Cruiskeen Lawn (IRE) *CCollins* 4-8-12 (t) THoulihan (6)	14/1	2½ 5
	Magic Star (IRE) *EdwardLynam* 3-8-8 JMurtagh (2)	8/1	2 6
	Osterhase (IRE) *JEMulhern* 3-9-1 (b) MJKinane (3)	13/2	3 7
	Tiger Royal (IRE) *DKWeld* 6-9-5 (b) PJSmullen (11)	4/1	½ 8
	Certainly Brave *JSBolger* 3-8-8 (t) KJManning (1)	14/1	4½ 9
	Exceptional Paddy (IRE) *MHalford* 4-8-12 TPO'Shea (5)	14/1	1½ 10
	Seabrook (USA) *PJRothwell* 5-8-12 (b) NGMcCullagh (10)	25/1	25 11

Clipper Group Holdings 11ran 1m13.60   122/106/97/91

NEWMARKET Saturday, Oct 19   GOOD to FIRM (Rowley Mile Course)

81   Victor Chandler Challenge Stks (Gr 2) (3yo+) £58,000   7f

56	NAYYIR *GAButler* 4-9-0 EAhern (3)	7/1	1
9	FIREBREAK *SaeedbinSuroor* 3-8-12 LDettori (13)	4/1f	2½ 2
56	FRENCHMANS BAY (FR) *RCharlton* 4-9-0 JPSpencer (15)	33/1	1½ 3
	Demonstrate (USA) *JHMGosden* 4-9-0 RHughes (4)	7/1	¾ 4
	Red Carpet *MLWBell* 4-9-0 JMurtagh (2)	40/1	1 5
30	Dolores *MrsAJPerrett* 3-8-9 TQuinn (7)	9/1	hd 6
6	Love Regardless (USA) *MJohnston* 3-8-12 KDalgleish (1)	14/1	1 7
14	Rum Charger (IRE) *DKWeld,Ireland* 3-8-9 PJSmullen (5)	10/1	2 8
56	Mount Abu (IRE) *JHMGosden* 5-9-0 JFortune (17)	10/1	1 9
	Mamounia (IRE) *BWHills* 3-8-9 MHills (9)	40/1	hd 10
9	Redback *RHannon* 3-8-12 DHolland (6)	10/1	nk 11
12	Warningford *JRFanshawe* 8-9-0 OUrbina (10)	11/1	1½ 12
53	Whitbarrow (IRE) *BRMillman* 3-8-12 WWoods (8)	100/1	½ 13
80	One Won One (USA) *MsJMorgan,Ireland* 8-9-0 PatEddery (14)	33/1	nk 14
38	Millennium Dragon *MAJarvis* 3-8-12 PRobinson (11)	14/1	¾ 15
43	Reel Buddy (USA) *RHannon* 4-9-0 MJKinane (12)	7/1	5 16
	Royal Millennium (IRE) *MRChannon* 4-9-0 TEDurcan (16)	25/1	½ 17

Mr Abdulla Al Khalifa 17ran 1m22.69   123+/118/114/112/109/106

82   Darley Dewhurst Stks (Gr 1) (2yo c+f) £153,700   7f

	TOUT SEUL (IRE) *RFJohnsonHoughton* 2-9-0 SCarson (2)	25/1	1
70	TOMAHAWK (USA) *APO'Brien,Ireland* 2-9-0 MJKinane (10)	10/3	1¼ 2
	TRADE FAIR *RCharlton* 2-9-0 RHughes (16)	11/4f	1¼ 3
70	Zafeen (FR) *MRChannon* 2-9-0 SDrowne (5)	14/1	1¼ 4
	Saturn (IRE) *MLWBell* 2-9-0 JMurtagh (8)	16/1	hd 5
70	Ontario (IRE) *APO'Brien,Ireland* 2-9-0 PJSmullen (14)	66/1	1¼ 6
	Marino Marini (USA) *APO'Brien,Ireland* 2-9-0 KDarley (11)	33/1	½ 7
	Rimrod (USA) *IABalding* 2-9-0 MartinDwyer (6)	7/1	1¾ 8
	Marching Band (USA) *JHMGosden* 2-9-0 JFortune (3)	25/1	nk 9
	Al Jadeed (USA) *JHMGosden* 2-9-0 RHills (17)	7/1	nk 10
	Desert Star *SirMichaelStoute* 2-9-0 KFallon (13)	9/1	1¾ 11
78	Great Pyramid (IRE) *APO'Brien,Ireland* 2-9-0 JPSpencer (12)	20/1	3 12
	Desert Lord *SirMichaelStoute* 2-9-0 PatEddery (14)	50/1	3½ 13
	Governor Brown *PFICole* 2-9-0 TQuinn (7)	16/1	1¾ 14
	Indian Haven *PWD'Arcy* 2-9-0 JFEgan (9)	40/1	3 15
	Dublin (IRE) *DRLoder* 2-9-0 LDettori (15)	14/1	5 16

Eden Racing 16ran 1m23.99   121/118/114/111/111/107/106

83   Emirates Airline Champion Stks (Gr 1) (3yo+) £245,920   1¼m

59	STORMING HOME *BWHills* 4-9-2 (s) MHills (4)	8/1	1
21	MOON BALLAD (IRE) *SaeedbinSuroor* 3-8-11 (t) JPSpencer (11)	5/2f	½ 2
49	NOVERRE (USA) *SaeedbinSuroor* 4-9-2 (t) LDettori (7)	9/2	¾ 3
	Carnival Dancer *SirMichaelStoute* 4-9-2 KFallon (8)	25/1	3 4
49	Chancellor (IRE) *BWHills* 4-9-2 JMurtagh (5)	33/1	nk 5
49	Indian Creek *DRCElsworth* 4-9-2 DHolland (6)	9/1	1½ 6
29	Kaieteur (USA) *BJMeehan* 3-8-11 PatEddery (3)	14/1	1½ 7
72	Imperial Dancer *MRChannon* 4-9-2 CCatlin (10)	33/1	5 8
35	Equerry (USA) *SaeedbinSuroor* 4-9-2 (b) KDarley (9)	20/1	1¼ 9
67	Sholokhov (IRE) *APO'Brien,Ireland* 3-8-11 MJKinane (12)	16/1	1 10
	Burning Sun (USA) *HRACecil* 3-8-11 TQuinn (8)	5/1	24 11

Maktoum Al Maktoum 11ran 2m01.42   125/124/123/116/116/113

DONCASTER Saturday, Oct 26   SOFT

84   Racing Post Trophy (Gr 1) (2yo c+f) £120,000   1m (Str.)

	BRIAN BORU *APO'Brien,Ireland* 2-9-0 KDarley (2)	11/8f	1
	POWERSCOURT *APO'Brien,Ireland* 2-9-0 GDuffield (8)	6/1	1¼ 2
	ILLUSTRATOR *SirMichaelStoute* 2-9-0 PatEddery (1)	8/1	1¾ 3
	The Great Gatsby (IRE) *APO'Brien,Ireland* 2-9-0 MFenton (4)	25/1	3 4
	Bahamian Dancer (IRE) *JNoseda* 2-9-0 SWKelly (9)	9/2	1 5

Tacitus (IRE) *RHannon* 2-9-0 DaneO'Neill (3).. 12/1   5 6
Norse Dancer (IRE) *DRCElsworth* 2-9-0 PHanagan (5)............................... 10/1   ½ 7
Inch Again *MHTompkins* 2-9-0 OUrbina (7)... 33/1   10 8
Balin's Sword (IRE) *BJMeehan* 2-9-0 JCarroll (6)..................................... 50/1   6 9

Mrs John Magnier 9ran 1m46.01   115+/112/109+/103+/100

NEWBURY Saturday, Oct 26   SOFT

85   **Electricity Direct St Simon Stks (Gr 3) (3yo+) £23,200**   1½m5y

59   THE WHISTLING TEAL *GWragg* 6-9-0 DHolland (4) 13/2   1
61   WARRSAN (IRE) *CEBrittain* 4-9-0 EAhern (6)...................................... 10/1   ¾ 2
33   NYSAEAN (IRE) *RHannon* 3-8-7 RHills (8).. 9/4f   hd 3
     Scott's View *MJohnston* 3-8-7 KDalgleish (12).. 7/2   10 4
46   Maniatis *MrsAJPerrett* 5-9-0 TQuinn (11) 33/1   3 5
     Border Arrow *IABalding* 7-9-0 (v) MartinDwyer (14).......................... 20/1   1 6
     Salim Toto *HMorrison* 4-8-11 SDrowne (7).. 14/1   3 7
64   Subiaco (GER) *ASchutz,Germany* 5-9-0 ASuborics (9)........................ 10/1   2½ 8
     Hannibal Lad *WMBrisbourne* 6-9-0 JFEgan (10)................................. 25/1   1¾ 9
51   Lady's Secret (IRE) *BWHills* 3-8-4 PRobinson (1)............................... 12/1   7 10
     Kasthari (IRE) *SirMichaelStoute* 3-8-7 MHills (5) 12/1   12 11
16   Proven (USA) *JHMGosden* 3-8-7 JFortune (13)................................... 20/1   dist 12
     Sunny Glenn *JCullinan* 4-9-0 WSupple (2)... 100/1   14 13

Mrs F. A. Veasey 13ran 2m41.47   120/119/119/104

ARLINGTON Saturday, Oct 26   Turf course: GOOD to SOFT, Dirt track: FAST

86   **NetJets Breeders' Cup Mile (Gr 1) (3yo+) £358,968**   1m (Turf)

48   DOMEDRIVER (IRE) *PBary,France* 4-9-0 TThulliez (5) 26/1   1
58   ROCK OF GIBRALTAR (IRE) *APO'Brien,Ireland* 3-8-10 MJKinane (10) 8/10f   ¾ 2
     GOOD JOURNEY (USA) *WDollase,USA* 6-9-0 PDay (4)................... 54/10   ns 3
47   Forbidden Apple (USA) *CClement,USA* 3-8-10 CNakatani (1)............. 15/1   1¼ 4
     Green Fee (USA) *DCPeitz,USA* 6-9-0 JVelazquez (6)........................ 45/1   1¼ 5
73   Beat Hollow *RJFrankel,USA* 5-9-0 JBailey (2)..................................... 65/10   1¾ 6
2   Del Mar Show (USA) *WIMott,USA* 5-9-0 PValenzuela (8) .... 62/1   ns 7
     Dress To Thrill (IRE) *DKWeld,Ireland* 3-8-7 PJSmullen (12) .... 32/1   hd 8
48   Medecis *MmeCHead-Maarek,France* 3-8-10 ASolis (3) .... 39/1   ½ 9
73   Touch of The Blues *NDDrysdale,USA* 5-9-0 KDesormeaux (11)........ 34/1   5¾ 10
     Aldebaran *RJFrankel,USA* 4-9-0 JChavez (7) 149/10   1¼ 11
     Nuclear Debate (USA) *DVienna,USA* 7-9-0 GaryStevens (14)........... 53/1   1¼ 12
     Boston Common (USA) *MVPino,USA* 8-9-0 RDouglas (9) .... 69/1   ¾ 13
73   Landseer *APO'Brien,Ireland* 3-8-10 EPrado (13) .... 143/10   pu

Niarchos Family 14ran 1m36.92   128/125+/126/123/120/115

87   **Breeders' Cup Filly & Mare Turf (Gr 1) (3yo+ f+m) £452,903**   1¼m (Turf)

68   STARINE (FR) *RJFrankel,USA* 5-8-11 (b) JVelazquez (11) 132/10   1
58   BANKS HILL *RJFrankel,USA* 4-8-11 JBailey (5)................................. 38/10   1½ 2
79   ISLINGTON (IRE) *SirMichaelStoute,GB* 3-8-6 KFallon (2)............... 4/1   nk 3
     Golden Apples (IRE) *BDACecil,USA* 4-8-11 PValenzuela (6)............ 28/10f   nk 4
58   Gossamer *LMCumani,GB* 3-8-6 JPSpencer (7) .... 114/10   ns 5
68   Kazzia (GER) *SaeedbinSuroor,GB* 3-8-6 JChavez (12) .... 102/10   ½ 6
     Riskaverse (USA) *PJKelly,USA* 3-8-6 MGuidry (1) .... 27/1   ns 7
30   Zenda *JHMGosden,GB* 3-8-6 RHughes (8) .... 28/1   ½ 8
68   Turtle Bow (FR) *FRohaut,France* 3-8-6 CSoumillon (3) .... 143/10   ½ 9
     Dublino (USA) *LDeSeroux,USA* 3-8-6 KDesormeaux (4) 91/10   4 10
     Chopinina (CAN) *JAFehr,Canada* 4-8-11 (b) ERamsammy (9)........ 42/1   hd 11
     Owsley (USA) *RSchulhofer,USA* 4-8-11 EPrado (10).......................... 21/1   ¾ 12

Mr Robert J. Frankel 12ran 2m03.57   122+/119/118/118/117/116/116/115

88   **Bessemer Trust Breeders' Cup Juvenile (Gr 1) (2yo c+g) £358,968**   1m1f (Dirt)

     VINDICATION (USA) *RBaffert,USA* 2-8-10 MESmith (6) 41/10   1
     KAFWAIN (USA) *RBaffert,USA* 2-8-10 (b) VEspinoza (2)................... 198/10   2¾ 2
78   HOLD THAT TIGER (USA) *APO'Brien,Ireland* 2-8-10 KFallon (3) 55/10   2¼ 3
     Bull Market (USA) *RBaffert,USA* 2-8-10 JBailey (5) 123/10   1¼ 4
     Van Nistelrooy (USA) *APO'Brien,Ireland* 2-8-10 JVelazquez (7)............. 158/10   3 5
     Most Feared (USA) *RWWerner,USA* 2-8-10 (b) PValenzuela (12) .... 28/1   nk 6
     Listen Indy (USA) *REMandella,USA* 2-8-10 ASolis (4).......................... 132/10   ¾ 7
82   Tomahawk (USA) *APO'Brien,Ireland* 2-8-10 MJKinane (11).................. 172/10   1¾ 8
     Toccet (USA) *JFScanlan,USA* 2-8-10 (b) JChavez (14) 82/10   4 9
     Whywhywhy (USA) *PLBiancone,USA* 2-8-10 (b) PDay (1) .... 25/10f   ½ 10
     Lone Star Sky (USA) *TMAmoss,USA* 2-8-10 (b) MGuidry (8) 31/1   4 11
     Wando (CAN) *MKeogh,Canada* 2-8-10 RMigliore (13).......................... 36/1   1½ 12
     Zavata (USA) *PLBiancone,USA* 2-8-10 GaryStevens (10) .... 14/1   pu

Padua Stables 13ran 1m49.61   122/118/114+/112/107/106

89 **John Deere Breeders' Cup Turf (Gr 1) (3yo+) £811,871** 1½m (Turf)

79	HIGH CHAPARRAL (IRE) *APO'Brien,Ireland* 3-8-9 MJKinane (5)	9/10f	1
	WITH ANTICIPATION (USA) *JESheppard,USA* 7-9-0 (b) PDay (7)	87/10	1¼ 2
69	FALCON FLIGHT (IRE) *DJBurkeII,USA* 6-9-0 PValenzuela (3)	123/10	¾ 3
	The Tin Man (USA) *REMandella,USA* 4-9-0 MESmith (8)	141/10	1 4
	Denon (USA) *RJFrankel,USA* 4-9-0 EPrado (1)	76/10	2¾ 5
49	Golan (IRE) *SirMichaelStoute,GB* 4-9-0 KFallon (4)	37/10	ns 6
69	Ballingarry (IRE) *LDeSeroux,USA* 3-8-9 KDesormeaux (2)	94/10	2¾ 7
69	Perfect Soul (IRE) *RAttfield,Canada* 4-9-0 (b) JVelazquez (6)	33/1	12 8

Mr M. Tabor & Mrs John Magnier 8ran 2m30.14 127+/123/121/119/115/115

90 **Breeders' Cup Classic (Gr 1) (3yo+) £1,341,936** 1¼m (Dirt)

	VOLPONI (USA) *PGJohnson,USA* 4-9-0 JSantos (2)	435/10	1
	MEDAGLIA D'ORO (USA) *RJFrankel,USA* 3-8-9 JBailey (7)	27/10f	6½ 2
	MILWAUKEE BREW (USA) *RJFrankel,USA* 5-9-0 EPrado (12)	24/1	nk 3
	Evening Attire (USA) *PJKelly,USA* 4-9-0 (b) SBridgmohan (8)	48/10	3 4
	Macho Uno (USA) *JFOrseno,USA* 4-9-0 (b) GaryStevens (6)	198/10	½ 5
	Dollar Bill (USA) *DStewart,USA* 4-9-0 (b) PDay (4)	185/10	nk 6
67	Hawk Wing (USA) *APO'Brien,Ireland* 3-8-9 MJKinane (10)	6/1	7 7
	War Emblem (USA) *RBaffert,USA* 3-8-9 VEspinoza (3)	4/1	¾ 8
	Harlan's Holiday (USA) *TAPletcher,USA* 3-8-9 JVelazquez (9)	144/10	8 9
	Came Home (USA) *JPGonzalez,USA* 3-8-9 MESmith (11)	61/10	¾ 10
	E Dubai (USA) *SaeedbinSuroor,GB* 4-9-0 JChavez (1)	28/1	4 11
	Perfect Drift (USA) *MWJohnson,USA* 3-8-9 (b) RAlbarado (5)	30/1	nk 12

Amherst Stable & Spruce Pond Stable 12ran 2m01.39 131/122/121/116/115/114

MOONEE VALLEY Saturday, Oct 26 GOOD

91 **Carlton Draught Cox Plate (Gr 1) (3yo+) £718,862** 1¼m44y

	NORTHERLY (AUS) *FKersley,Australia* 6-9-2 PPayne	3/1jf	1
	DEFIER (AUS) *GWalter,Australia* 5-9-2 CMunce	7/1	1 2
57	GRANDERA (IRE) *SaeedbinSuroor,GB* 4-9-2 LDettori	8/1	nk 3
	Sunline (NZ) *TMcKee,NewZealand* 7-8-10 GChilds	5/1	1 4
	Fields of Omagh (AUS) *TMcEvoy,Australia* 5-9-2 (b) DMOliver	16/1	4½ 5
	Lonhro (AUS) *JHawkes,Australia* 3-7-9 DBeadman	3/1jf	nk 6
	Ustinov (AUS) *BCummings,Australia* 4-8-13 SArnold	40/1	8 7
	Bel Esprit (AUS) *JSymons,Australia* 3-7-9 KMcEvoy	9/1	8 8
	Assertive Lad (AUS) *MsGWaterhouse,Australia* 5-9-2 (b) JCassidy	50/1	1½ 9

Mr N.G. & Mrs S. Duncan/Mrs J.A. Kersley 9ran 2m06.27 129/127/126+/118/117/114

LONGCHAMP Sunday, Oct 27 HEAVY

92 **Prix Royal-Oak (Gr 1) (3yo+) £53,906** 1m7f110y

Order as they passed the post: Morozov was demoted to sixth for causing interference

60	MR DINOS (IRE) *PFICole,GB* 3-8-9 DBoeuf	36/10	1
62	SULK (IRE) *JHMGosden,GB* 3-8-6 (s) JFortune	13/1	2½ 2
	MOROZOV (USA) *AFabre,France* 3-8-9 CSoumillon	31/4	4 3
74	Clety (FR) *FDoumen,France* 6-9-4 (b) TThulliez	3/1f	nk 4
62	Bernimixa (FR) *AFabre,France* 3-8-6 OPlacais	13/1	½ 5
74	Terrazzo (USA) *NBranchu,France* 7-9-4 SPasquier	5/2	ns 6
74	Cut Quartz (FR) *RGibson,France* 5-9-4 C-PLemaire	4/1	15 7

Mr C. Shiacolas 7ran 3m38.50 117/111/109/107/106/107

SAINT-CLOUD Saturday, Nov 2 HEAVY

93 **Criterium International (Gr 1) (2yo c+f) £89,622** 1m

	DALAKHANI (IRE) *AdeRoyerDupre,France* 2-9-0 CSoumillon (3)	4/5f	1
	CHEVALIER (IRE) *APO'Brien,Ireland* 2-9-0 MJKinane (6)	23/10jf	nk 2
82	GOVERNOR BROWN (USA) *PFICole,GB* 2-9-0 DBoeuf (4)	88/10	5 3
	Napper Tandy (IRE) *JSBolger,Ireland* 2-9-0 KJManning (1)	20/1	1½ 4
	Songlark *AFabre,France* 2-9-0 OPlacais (4)	36/10	1½ 5

H. H. Aga Khan 5ran 1m52.00 114+/113+/104/102/99

FLEMINGTON Tuesday, Nov 5 FIRM

94 **Tooheys New Melbourne Cup (Hcap) (3yo+) £880,783** 2m

	MEDIA PUZZLE (USA) *DKWeld,Ireland* 5-8-4 (b) DMOliver (3)	11/2	1
	MR PRUDENT (AUS) *GHanlon,Australia* 8-8-3 (b) CoreyBrown (4)	40/1	2 2
	BEEKEEPER *SaeedbinSuroor,GB* 4-8-5 KMcEvoy (20)	8/1	nk 3
61	Vinnie Roe (IRE) *DKWeld,Ireland* 4-9-4 PJSmullen (7)	9/2f	1½ 4
	Pentastic (AUS) *DHall,Australia* 4-8-3 GBoss (6)	25/1	1¾ 5
	Distinctly Secret (NZ) *MWalker,NewZealand* 4-8-2 (b) SKing (18)	6/1	hd 6
28	Jardines Lookout (IRE) *APJarvis,GB* 5-8-11 PPayne (19)	30/1	1¼ 7
	Rain Gauge (AUS) *GHanlon,Australia* 5-8-6 GChilds (14)	12/1	1 8

1138

| | Freemason (AUS) *JHawkes,Australia* 6-8-6 DGauci (11) | 80/1 | 1½ 9 |

Freemason (AUS) *JHawkes,Australia* 6-8-6 DGauci (11) 80/1 1½ 9
Miss Meliss (NZ) *BCummings,Australia* 5-7-10 (b) CNewitt (10)................ 40/1 ½ 10
County Tyrone (AUS) *MLees,Australia* 4-8-4 (b) JCassidy (9).................. 80/1 hd 11
Hail (NZ) *BMarsh,NewZealand* 5-8-4 NHarris (16) 70/1 2¾ 12
Thong Classic (AUS) *PCarey,Australia* 5-8-0 (b) BPrebble (21)................. 25/1 nk 13
Prized Gem (NZ) *MBaker,NewZealand* 4-8-0 (b) MRodd (24) .... 60/1 ¾ 14
Grey Song (AUS) *THughes,Australia* 4-8-0 (b) CMunce (23) .... 80/1 sh 15
46 Daliapour (IRE) *SirMichaelStoute,GB* 6-8-10 MJKinane (1) 30/1 1½ 16
    Cyclades (NZ) *CEvans,NewZealand* 7-8-2 SSeamer (5)............................. 40/1 3 17
61 Pugin (IRE) *SaeedbinSuroor,GB* 4-8-6 LDettori (15).............................. 15/2 5 18
    Victory Smile (NZ) *DonnaLogan,Australia* 6-8-3 DBeasley (2) 60/1 2½ 19
59 Hatha Anna (IRE) *SaeedbinSuroor,GB* 5-8-7 (v) RHills (22)..................... 50/1 2½ 20
1   Helene Vitality (NZ) *DAHayes,HongKong* 6-8-8 (b) GMosse (17)............. 40/1 hd 21
    Requiem (AUS) *TMcEvoy,Australia* 5-7-11 CraigWilliams (21) 25/1 12 22
    Sandmason *TMcEvoy,Australia* 5-8-10 (b) SArnold (13)........................... 50/1 hd 23

Mr Michael W. J. Smurfit 23ran 3m16.97   117/113/115/126/112/110/115

ROME Sunday, Nov 17   GOOD to SOFT

95 Premio Roma SIS (Gr 1) (3yo+ c+f) £89,966   1¼m

11 SUNSTRACH (IRE) *EBorromeo,Italy* 4-9-2 LDettori................................ 116/10 1
11 BLU FOR LIFE (IRE) *RMimmocchi,Italy* 5-9-2 MMimmocchi.................... 73/1 6 2
72 WELLBEING *PBary,France* 5-9-2 TThulliez 89/10 2 3
83 Imperial Dancer *MRChannon,GB* 4-9-2 CCatlin .... 24/1 nk 4
55 Tareno (GER) *PSchiergen,Germany* 4-9-2 ASuborics 39/10 1½ 5
    Rainer (FR) *JBUdaondo,Italy* 3-9-1 CColombi 19/2 1¼ 6
    Tornado Mitch (USA) *OPessi,Italy* 5-9-2 MMonteriso .... 90/1 nk 7
11 Shibuni's Falcon *MGuarnieri,Italy* 5-9-2 (b) MTellini............................. 76/1 9 8
37 Island House (IRE) *GWragg,GB* 6-9-2 DHolland 98/10 5 9
16 Rakti *BGrizzetti,Italy* 3-9-1 MDemuro .... 56/10 ¾ 10
    Serenus (GER) *WFigge,Germany* 4-9-2 SDrowne 94/1 7 11
16 Long Goodbye (IRE) *LCamici,Italy* 3-9-1 FJovine .... 133/1 hd 12
83 Carnival Dancer *SirMichaelStoute,GB* 4-9-2 KFallon 18/10f 1½ 13
83 Chancellor *BWHills,GB* 4-9-2 MHills .... 57/10 ½ 14

Scuderia Rencati Srl 14ran 2m02.70   120/109/104/104

NAKAYAMA Sunday, Nov 24   FIRM

96 Japan Cup (Gr 1) (3yo+) £1,331,861   1m3f

79 FALBRAV (IRE) *LD'Auria,Italy* 4-9-0 LDettori (1)................................ 195/10 1
47 SARAFAN (USA) *NDDrysdale,USA* 5-9-0 CNakatani (8)........................... 34/1 ns 2
    SYMBOLI KRIS S (USA) *KFujisawa,Japan* 9-9-0 OPeslier (7)............. 24/10f nk 3
    Magnaten (USA) *KFujisawa,Japan* 6-9-0 YOkabe (15).......................... 193/10 1½ 4
    Jungle Pocket (JPN) *SWatanabe,Japan* 4-9-0 YTake (10) .... 32/10 ns 5
8   Indigenous (IRE) *IWAllan,HongKong* 9-9-0 ESaint-Martin (2)............... 124/1 ½ 6
89 Golan (IRE) *SirMichaelStoute,GB* 4-9-0 KFallon (3) .... 186/10 nk 7
    No Reason (JPN) *YIkee,Japan* 3-8-10 MEbina (9) 122/10 2 8
    T M Ocean (JPN) *KNishiura,Japan* 4-8-10 MHonda (11)....................... 21/1 hd 9
    Narita Top Road (JPN) *YOki,Japan* 6-9-0 HShii (13).......................... 29/10 nk 10
76 Irresistible Jewel (IRE) *DKWeld,Ireland* 3-8-5 PJSmullen (4)................ 63/1 1½ 11
    Air Shakur (JPN) *HMori,Japan* 5-9-0 KTanaka (16) .... 187/10 nk 12
76 Bright Sky (IRE) *ELelouche,France* 3-8-5 TThulliez (12) 169/10 2½ 13
    American Boss (USA) *FTago,Japan* 7-9-0 (b) TEda (5) .... 70/1 hd 14
83 Storming Home *BWHills,GB* 4-9-0 (s) MHills (14)............................. 40/1 2½ 15
    Agnes Flight (JPN) *HNagahama,Japan* 5-9-0 HGoto (6)....................... 76/1 3 16

Scuderia Rencati Srl 16ran 2m12.20   123+/123+/123+/120+/120+/119/118

HOLLYWOOD PARK Sunday, Dec 1   FIRM

97 Matriarch Stks (Gr 1) (3yo+ f+m) £192,308   1m1f

86 DRESS TO THRILL (IRE) *DKWeld,Ireland* 3-8-8 PJSmullen.................. 73/10 1
87 GOLDEN APPLES (IRE) *BDACecil,USA* 4-8-11 PValenzuela................. 14/10 hd 2
    MAGIC MISSION *NDDrysdale,USA* 4-8-11 VEspinoza 315/10 1½ 3
87 Banks Hill *RJFrankel,USA* 4-8-11 JBailey .... 13/10f ns 4
    Affluent (USA) *RLMcAnally,USA* 4-8-11 LPincay 5/1 1½ 5
    Choc Ice (IRE) *RCollet,France* 4-8-11 KDesormeaux .... 28/1 ns 6

Moyglare Stud Farms Ltd 6ran 1m48.31   121+/120+/117/117/114+/114

SHA TIN Sunday, Dec 15   GOOD to FIRM

98 Hong Kong Vase (Gr 1) (3yo+) £651,466   1½m

34 ANGE GABRIEL (FR) *ELibaud,France* 4-9-0 TJarnet (4)........................ 39/10 1
79 AQUARELLISTE (FR) *ELelouche,France* 4-8-10 DBoeuf (10) .... 19/10f ¾ 2
89 FALCON FLIGHT (FR) *DJBurkell,USA* 6-9-0 GMosse (5)...................... 11/2 nk 3
11 Ekraar (USA) *SaeedbinSuroor,GB* 5-9-0 (v+t) LDettori (7) .... 24/10 ¾ 4

1139

INDEX TO SELECTED BIG RACES

THE TIMEFORM 'TOP HORSES ABROAD'

This review of the year covers the major racing countries outside Britain. It includes Timeform Ratings for the top two-year-olds, three-year-olds and older horses. Horses not rated highly enough to be included in the main lists but which finished in the first three in a European pattern race or, in the sections on Japan and North America, won a Grade 1 during the season are included below the cut-off line. Fillies and mares are denoted by (f); * denotes the horse was trained for only a part of the season in the country concerned. Overseas customers wishing to keep in touch with Timeform's coverage of racing through the year can subscribe to Computer Timeform, Timeform Perspective or our internet site (http://www.timeform.com) for reports on all the important races. It is now possible to obtain up-to-date Timeform commentaries (including many not published in the weekly Timeform Black Book), undertake progeny research and access daily form guides on the internet site. Racecards for all Group 1 races in France and Ireland, plus major races in several other countries, are also available.

IRELAND   Having won nine of the ten Group 1 races open to juvenile colts in 2001, it came as no surprise to see Aidan O'Brien dominate with his three-year-olds in 2002. Such domination saw him clinch a second successive trainer's title in Britain having become, in 2001, the first Irish trainer to do so since Vincent O'Brien in 1977. Despite taking the Epsom Derby, Irish Derby and Breeders' Cup Turf, **High Chaparral** had to play second fiddle to **Rock of Gibraltar** whose wonderful season began when winning the 2000 Guineas in which his stablemate Hawk Wing was unlucky. Rock of Gibraltar's sole race on home soil as a three-year-old saw him record a very easy victory in the Irish 2000 Guineas before winning the St James's Palace, Sussex Stakes and Prix du Moulin. His career finished with a strong-finishing second behind Domedriver in the Breeders' Cup Mile.

As Rock of Gibraltar began his season in the 2000 Guineas, the **Johannesburg** bubble well and truly burst in the Kentucky Derby, and he was retired after running well below form in the Golden Jubilee Stakes at Royal Ascot. **Hawk Wing** had been the talking horse over the winter but never quite lived up to his lofty reputation. He was second in both the 2000 Guineas and Derby before finally landing a Group 1 when taking the Eclipse Stakes at Sandown. In a finish not too dissimilar to that between Fantastic Light and Galileo in the 2001 Irish Champion Stakes, Hawk Wing again had to settle for minor honours when caught on the line by Grandera in the 2002 renewal, and he also finished runner-up to Where Or When in the Queen Elizabeth II Stakes at Ascot. He was below form in the Breeders' Cup Classic on his final outing, but stays in training, along with High Chaparral who took what has proved to be the most significant Derby trial in recent years, the Group 3 Derrinstown Stud Derby Trial. Sinndar and Galileo both won the race en route to Derby success and High Chaparral followed suit with a length success over **In Time's Eye**. Following High Chaparral's defeat of **Sholokhov** and Ballingarry in the Irish Derby, he, like many of his stablemates, succumbed to a virus which saw Ballydoyle virtually shut down midway through the season. As a result High Chaparral probably wasn't at his best when third behind Marienbard in the Arc before rounding things off with victory in the Breeders' Cup Turf. **Landseer** met with a fatal injury in the Breeders' Cup Mile, but had earlier won the Poule d'Essai des Poulains at Longchamp and the Keeneland Turf Mile in the States. He finished clear of the remainder when runner-up to Rock of Gibraltar in the St James's Palace Stakes. Six days after finishing second in the Irish Derby, Sholokhov occupied the same position in the Eclipse and took on the role of pacemaker on a couple of other occasions. Galileo's full brother **Black Sam Bellamy** was another used as a pacemaker (in the Arc), though he still managed to win a Group 1 when taking the Gran Premio del Jockey Club at Milan on his final start of the season. A couple of other pattern winners for O'Brien were **Ballingarry** and **Century City**. Ballingarry was placed in both the Irish Derby and Irish St Leger before winning the Canadian International on his final start for his Irish trainer. Century City has also left for the USA but not before

1144

winning three times, including the Tetrarch Stakes and the Goffs International Stakes, as well as finishing runner-up to Rock of Gibraltar in the Irish 2000 Guineas. Last of seven in that race was **Sights On Gold**, who went on to show smart form against British-trained horses in the Meld Stakes and the Royal Whip before winning a listed race at Leopardstown and being acquired by Godolphin out of Dermot Weld's stable. Another smart performer was **Masani**, who won the Irish Cambridgeshire before being sold from John Oxx for 250,000 guineas; he is to continue his career in Hong Kong.

O'Brien fared less well with his fillies, although **Quarter Moon** was unlucky not to pick up a race. She finished second in the Irish 1000 Guineas, the Oaks at Epsom and the Irish Oaks, in the last-named behind **Margarula**. Margarula was the longest-priced winner in the history of the Irish classic for trainer Jim Bolger, having started the season by winning a handicap off a mark of 80. Down the field in the Irish Oaks was **Irresistible Jewel**, who had won the Ribblesdale Stakes at Royal Ascot on her previous start. Her other success came in the Group 3 Blandford Stakes at the Curragh, confirming her as one of the top three-year-old fillies in Ireland. The best of them, though, was stable-companion **Dress To Thrill** who won five of her six starts, including the Desmond Stakes and the Matron Stakes, both at Leopardstown, and the Sun Chariot Stakes at Newmarket. Her season finished with a Grade 1 success in America, where she won the Matriarch Stakes. **Sophisticat** had failed to cope with Queen's Logic more than once in her juvenile campaign but enjoyed more success in 2002 with two victories from her four starts. She won the Prix de la Grotte at Longchamp and the Coronation Stakes at Royal Ascot and finished third in the Poule d'Essai des Pouliches. She was found to be in respiratory distress after a below-par effort in the Matron Stakes on her final outing.

Irish horses had a lucrative time on their travels, with the highlight being the success of **Media Puzzle** in the Melbourne Cup. Dermot Weld knows what it takes to win the Australian showpiece, after Vintage Crop in 1993, and he did the trick again despite Media Puzzle having an unpromising season in Ireland. Stablemate **Vinnie Roe** also contested the race and finished a highly creditable fourth under top weight. Earlier, he'd won two listed races and the Irish St Leger for the second successive season, as well as finishing second to Royal Rebel in the Gold Cup at Royal Ascot. **Pugin**, runner-up in the Irish St Leger, was bought by Godolphin before running well below his best in the Melbourne Cup.

There wasn't a great deal of depth to the older horses in Ireland, with 2001 St Leger winner Milan missing the rest of the season after fracturing an off-fore cannon bone on his reappearance. **Rebelline** proved to be one of the best, though, winning all three of her starts before injury forced her retirement. She began with the victory over Johannesburg before losing a listed race at the Curragh, where **Shoal Creek** was amongst her victims. She put up a career-best performance to win the Tattersalls Gold Cup on the same course, overcoming trouble in running to beat **Bach** by two lengths. That second place was the highlight for Bach, whose season rather tailed off afterwards. **Ice Dancer**'s season was restricted to just two races, but he repeated his 2001 success in the listed Trigo Stakes at Leopardstown. **Tiger Royal** was an improved sprinter with four victories to his name. He began the season in handicaps off a mark of 96 before wins in the Group 3 Greenlands Stakes (in which he beat **Tendulkar**) and a listed race at the Curragh. **Social Harmony** was almost as good as ever at the age of eight, winning the competitive Budweiser Guinness Handicap on Irish Derby Day, before breaking a leg later in the year. **One Won One** had another busy campaign but showed that he retains most of his ability, winning twice and being placed on seven further occasions. His best effort came when winning the Group 3 Phoenix Sprint Stakes.

It was always going to be a stiff task for O'Brien to follow up his juvenile success of 2001, though he still has plenty of good horses to look forward to in 2003, with **Brian Boru** clear favourite for the Derby. Brian Boru has something in common with the 2002 Derby winner, High Chaparral, having won the Racing Post Trophy at Doncaster on his final start from stable-companion **Powerscourt**, the latter showing much improved form. Previously, Brian Boru had been caught near the finish by **Alamshar** in the Group 3 Beresford Stakes at the Curragh. The John Oxx-trained Alamshar is a horse full of promise, having also won his only previous race. **Tomahawk** was the top two-year-old trained in Ireland despite winning only one of his five starts. That came in the very first two-year-old maiden of the Irish season in March. He then went on to be second in the Middle Park and the Dewhurst, before finishing in mid-division in the Breeders' Cup Juvenile. **Hold That Tiger** was a never-nearer third in that race, one of only two defeats to go with his three wins, which included the Group 3 Railway Stakes at the Curragh and the Grand Criterium at Longchamp. At the Curragh he beat the Coventry Stakes runner-up **Pakhoes**, but was found to be in respiratory distress when disappointing behind stablemate **Spartacus** in the Phoenix Stakes. Spartacus added to that success by capturing another Group 1, the Gran Criterium at Milan.

Statue of Liberty, successful in the Coventry Stakes, was the only two-year-old winner for Aidan O'Brien at the Royal meeting, but was not seen out again. Despite that, he is still prominent in the market for the 2000 Guineas. A couple more good three-year-old prospects from Ballydoyle revealed themselves in France late in the year, **Alberto Giacometti** winning the Criterium de Saint-Cloud and **Chevalier** finishing second in the Criterium International.

As well as Pakhoes, Dermot Weld has a horse to look forward to in 2003 in the form of Media Puzzle's half-brother **Refuse To Bend**, who won both his starts. The second one was a determined success in the National Stakes at the Curragh, where he beat the Futurity Stakes winner **Van Nistelrooy**. **New South Wales** showed enough in two starts for John Oxx to persuade Sheikh Mohammed to transfer him to Godolphin. He won both of them, the second being a narrow victory in the Group 3 Killavullan Stakes at Leopardstown, a race in which the previously unbeaten favourite **Walayef** met a lot of trouble in running.

Jim Bolger is responsible for one of the best juvenile fillies in Ireland in **Danaskaya**, who was in the frame in three pattern races, the Lowther Stakes at York, the Moyglare Stud Stakes at the Curragh and the Cheveley Park Stakes at Newmarket. Her stable-companion **Luminata** was placed in both the Moyglare Stud Stakes and the Prix Marcel Boussac. The best of the O'Brien fillies could prove to be Quarter Moon's sister **Yesterday**. She was third in the Rockfel Stakes at Newmarket before winning a listed race at Leopardstown in good style. A couple of very well-bred once-raced two-year-olds worthy of a mention are **Mingun**, who finished second to Alberto Giacometti in a twenty-four runner newcomers event at the Curragh in October, and Elasouna (rated 78P), who was successful in a maiden at Gowran, and looks certain to be well suited by a mile and a quarter plus.

Two-Year-Olds

118	Tomahawk
117p	Brian Boru
117p	Hold That Tiger
115p	Chevalier
112p	Alamshar
112p	Powerscourt
111p	Alberto Giacometti
110p	Refuse To Bend
109p	Statue of Liberty
108	Pakhoes
108	Van Nistelrooy
107	Great Pyramid
107	Hanabad
107	Ontario
107	Spartacus
106p	Yesterday (f)
106	Danaskaya (f)
106	Marino Marini
105p	Walayef (f)
105	Catcher In The Rye
105	European
105	Irrawaddy
105	Kimberley Mine
105	The Great Gatsby
104p	New South Wales
104p	Some Kind of Tiger
103p	Reach For The Moon (f)
103	Dolmur
103	Kossu

103	Luminata (f)
103	Miss Helga (f)
102p	Delacroix
102	Eklim
102	Miguel Cervantes
102	Napper Tandy
102	Sun Slash (f)
101	Akanti
101	Chappel Cresent
101	France
100	Abunawwas
100	Feabhas (f)
100	Newfoundland
100	Shizao (f)
99	Anna Frid (f)
99	Bond
99	Daganya (f)
99	Turn Back Time (f)
99?	Benicio
98p	Gianfanti
98p	Vintage Tipple (f)
98	Mombassa
97P	Mingun
96	Etruscan King
96	Petite Histoire (f)
96	Seattle Queen (f)
95	Dixie Evans (f)
95	Rainbows For All (f)
95	Snippets (f)
95	Vettriano

94	Finity (f)
88	Rapid Ransom (f)

Three-Year-Olds

133	Rock of Gibraltar
130	High Chaparral
127	Hawk Wing
125	Landseer
123	*Ballingarry
123	Dress To Thrill (f)
121	Sholokhov
120	Margarula (f)
120	Quarter Moon (f)
117	Black Sam Bellamy
117	*Century City
117	Sophisticat (f)
116	Johannesburg
116	Masani
116	Sights On Gold
115	Irresistible Jewel (f)
114	Blatant
113	Agnetha (f)
113	Ancestor
113	*Castle Gandolfo
113	Jazz Beat
113	Tendulkar
112	Bowmore
112	*Della Francesca
112	In Time's Eye
112	Millstreet

111	Marionnaud (f)	99	*Keepers Hill (f)	107	*Lethal Agenda
111	Osterhase	99	Nostradamus	106	Crimphill
111	Slaney Sand	99	Phariseek (f)	106§	Chimes At Midnight
111?	Ahsanabad	99	Ridakiya (f)	105	Just Special (f)
110	Diaghilev	99	Sun Seasons (f)	105	Newpark Lady (f)
109	*Maderno	98	Alserna (f)	105	Sadlers Wings
109	Miss Honorine (f)	98	Fearn Royal (f)	104	American Gothic
109	Sahara Desert	98	Mr Andrea	104	Atlantic Rhapsody
108	Barring Order (f)	98	*Nashwan Rose (f)	104	Chiming (f)
108	Creekview	98	*Roar of The Tiger	104	Masnada (f)
108	Sorcerous	98	Sonorous (f)	104	Queens Wharf (f)
108	Wrong Key (f)	98	Wild Floridian (f)	104	Tender Cove
107	Mkuzi	97	Hanzali	103	Kalamunda (f)
106	Hidden Dragon	97	Lost In The Rain	103	Mr Houdini
106	Kournakova (f)	97	Louisville	103	Sadima (f)
106	Minashki	96	*Easy Sunshine (f)	102	Common Kris
106	Rum Charger (f)	96	La Pieta (f)	102	Desert Hill
106	Zafaraniya (f)	96	Perfect Touch (f)	102	Desert Trail (f)
105	Almost Famous	96	Pietra Dura (f)	102	Dibiya (f)
105	Miss Beabea (f)	96	*Salentino	102	Tivoli Garden (f)
105	Prize Time	95	Askthejudge	101	Chill Seeking (f)
105	Starbourne (f)	95	Bella Bella (f)	101	Cruiskeen Lawn
105	Ursa Minor	95	Esterlina (f)	101	Exceptional Paddy
104	Kiltubber (f)	95	Schiller	101	Last Theatre (f)
104	Lahinch (f)	95?	Glandore (f)	101	Moonbi Ridge (f)
104	Smuggler's Song			101	Osprey Ridge
103	*Alstemeria (f)	**Older Horses**		101	Private Ben
103	Mahsusie (f)	126	Vinnie Roe	100	Aquila Oculus (f)
103	Vinthea (f)	122	Rebelline (f)	100	Avorado
102	Aqualina (f)	121	Bach	100	Direct Bearing
102	Solid Approach	121	*Pugin	100	Give A Whistle (f)
102	Twentytwoandchange	119	Tiger Royal	99	Alegranza (f)
101	Carallia (f)	117	Media Puzzle	99	Billy Bonnie
101	*Chadwicks Well	115	Ice Dancer	99	Jacks Estate
101	East Tycoon	115	Shoal Creek	99	Serov
101	Lowlander	114	Social Harmony	98	Heezapistol
101	Moon Safari (f)	113	D'Anjou	98	Livadiya (f)
101	Queen's Colours (f)	113	Final Exam	98	Ned Kelly
101	*Rahn	113	Jammaal	98	Right Job
101	Relish (f)	112	Holy Orders	98	Sabrinsky
100	Brocheta (f)	112	Mutakarrim	97	Dame Portia (f)
100	Chartres (f)	112	One More Round	97	Limestone Lad
100	Egyptian	111	One Won One	97	She's Our Girl (f)
100	Madame Cerito (f)	111	Quality Team	96	Gold Chaser
100	Maryinsky (f)	109	Cool Clarity (f)	96	Golovin
100	Mobasher	109	Diamond Trim (f)	96	Irish Empire
100	Sweet Deimos (f)	109	*Villa Carlotta (f)	96	Rostropovich
100?	Tarifana (f)	108	Gaelic Queen (f)	96	Sheer Tenby
99	Fionns Folly (f)	108	Maumee	95	Quest For A Star
99	Kassna (f)	108	Tarry Flynn	95	Uliana (f)

FRANCE   With only four three-year-olds earning a rating of more than 120, the latest French classic crop was not a vintage one, but it had a worthy leader in **Sulamani**. Unraced at two, he made rapid progress in the first half of the year to win the Prix du Jockey Club, thereby emulating both his sire Hernando and half-brother Dream Well. After a summer break, Sulamani won a ridiculously slow three-runner Prix Niel before finding only Marienbard too strong in the Prix de l'Arc de Triomphe, a race he probably should have won after giving his main rivals a start from the turn. If Sulamani attempts to go one better in 2003, it will be for Saeed bin Suroor rather than Pascal Bary's stable after becoming Godolphin's highest-rated acquisition of the season. The Prix du Jockey Club had seen the first and only defeat of **Act One's** career. He had looked the best prospect among the previous season's French two-year-olds and returned with straightforward wins in both the Prix Greffulhe and Prix Lupin before going down to Sulamani at Chantilly. Act One was being prepared for the Irish Derby when sustaining a career-ending injury just days after the death of his owner-breeder Gerald Leigh.

Another colt whose only defeat came in the Jockey Club was **Khalkevi**, he too sustaining an injury which prematurely ended his career. Successful in the Prix Hocquart prior to the French Derby, in which he finished down the field, he overcame a bad stumble to land the Grand Prix de Paris by a head from **Shaanmer**. The Grand Prix de Paris was one of a series of narrow defeats for Shaanmer, who had been favourite for the Epsom Derby for a short while after his unbeaten two-year-old campaign. He failed to win at three, however, and also finished second to **Rouvres** in the Prix Jean Prat, Highdown in the Prix Guillaume d'Ornano and **Tau Ceti** in the Prix du Prince d'Orange. Shaanmer continues his career in the USA, but Tau Ceti, who went on to finish fourth in the Prix Dollar, should do well at four if he makes even half the progress made by his half-brother Domedriver in the latest season. **Without Connexion** kept good company all year without winning a big race (he was third in the Lupin, Grand Prix de Paris and Prince d'Orange), but ended the season with a listed success at Longchamp. Neither **Agog** nor **Sarrasin** contested a pattern race but they too ended the year winning listed races, the latter one by seventeen lengths, and look likely to progress again at four.

The consistent **Medecis** was the top miler among the three-year-old colts, winning the Prix de la Jonchere, but ran his best races when second in the Poule d'Essai des Poulains and Prix de la Foret. **Bowman** beat Medecis in the Prix de Fontainebleau early on and finished a good third in the Poulains but failed to make an impact in top mile company thereafter despite some creditable efforts. The lightly-raced **Massigann** looks a future pattern winner after his good fourth in the Prix Daniel Wildenstein at the Arc meeting. **Massalani** began the season with a defeat of the previous season's top French two-year-old Zipping in the Prix Djebel, but it was **Zipping** who fared the better of that pair in the Two Thousand Guineas, finishing fourth. However, it was as a sprinter that Zipping proved best, winning the Prix de Ris-Orangis at Deauville and finishing a very close third in the Prix de l'Abbaye. In The Wings' brother **Morozov** was the best of a weak three-year-old stayers' division. He was a game winner against British rivals in the Prix du Lys and Prix Hubert de Chaudenay and ran well when third to older horses in the Kergorlay.

Bright Sky was France's top three-year-old filly, winning the Prix de Diane against most of the other top fillies and registering an impressive four-length win in the Prix de l'Opera. She had not shown her best form over a mile and a half in between when third to **Pearly Shells** in the Prix Vermeille. Pearly Shells did not contest the Diane but ran up a five-timer which began in the Provinces and ended in the Vermeille, taking in defeats of the placed fillies from the Prix de Diane along the way; **Ana Marie** in the Prix de Malleret and **Dance Routine** in the Prix de la Nonette. Surprisingly, Pearly Shells was not supplemented for the Arc, but she remains in training along with Bright Sky. The Diane runner-up Dance Routine disappointed in the Vermeille but was back to form to beat the subsequent Prix de Flore winner **Trumbaka** in the Prix de Royallieu in the autumn. Ana Marie lost her maiden tag in the Prix Vanteaux and ran well when promoted to third in the Prix de Diane and when second in the Vermeille but found the Arc an altogether stiffer task. **Marotta** was to prove no match for Bright Sky in either the Diane or the Opera (finishing fifth and third respectively in those races) but had beaten Bright Sky in the Prix Saint-Alary in the spring and was a convincing winner of the Premio Lydia Tesio at Rome in the autumn. As well as Pearly Shells, Francois Rohaut's stable housed another good filly in **Turtle Bow**. Demoted a place after passing the post third in the Prix de Diane, she dropped back successfully to a mile to win the Prix d'Astarte and then finish fourth in the Prix Jacques le Marois before running a fine race to run Kazzia to a neck in the Flower Bowl Invitational at Belmont. There were few other fillies of note over a mile. The Poule d'Essai des Pouliches runner-up **Firth of Lorne** was not seen out again, while **Dedication**, sixth in the same race, was a substandard winner of the Prix de la Foret over seven furlongs in the autumn.

The best older horses in France turned out to be milers **Keltos** and **Domedriver**. Both were much improved from their three-year-old seasons. After an unsuccessful attempt in the Dubai World Cup, Keltos won the Prix du Muguet, but it was his sound beating of some of Britain's best older milers in the Lockinge Stakes which marked him out as a top class performer. That turned out to be his final start, thereby denying a potentially decisive clash with Rock of Gibraltar for the title of Europe's best miler. Instead, it was

Domedriver who halted Rock of Gibraltar's sequence of wins in top company, not that he received much credit for it in an unsatisfactory race for the Breeders' Cup Mile. Domedriver made constant improvement in France through the season, chasing home **Banks Hill** in the Prix Jacques le Marois before gaining a narrow but decisive win in the inaugural running of the Prix Daniel Wildenstein (formerly the Prix du Rond-Point). The Jacques le Marois was the only time Banks Hill, herself a former Breeders' Cup winner, came close to repeating the form she had shown at Belmont the previous autumn. However, she did make the frame in top company in her other starts, running second to Rock of Gibraltar in the Prix du Moulin and also finishing second on her first start for Bobby Frankel when attempting back-to-back wins in the Filly & Mare Turf. **Aquarelliste** was the other top three-year-old filly of 2001 who stayed in training, and though she too won a Group 1 prize (the Prix Ganay) and later the Prix Foy, she could finish only sixth in the Arc on her attempt to better second place twelve months earlier.

The best performance by a French-trained older horse in the Arc came from 131/1 outsider **Califet**. He was just a useful performer in the Provinces at three but thrived on a busy campaign in the latest season, gaining clear-cut wins in the Prix d'Hedouville and Prix Jean de Chaudenay before making the frame in good races on his remaining starts. He too was bought by Godolphin after the Arc. Califet's early-season form was bound up with another much-improved graduate from the Provinces, **Ange Gabriel**. The latter came out on top in three of their five meetings, notably when winning a rather unsatisfactory Grand Prix de Saint-Cloud. Ange Gabriel missed the Arc, winning the Prix du Conseil de Paris instead as a trial for the Hong Kong Vase, which he also won ahead of Aquarelliste. Ange Gabriel's stable-companion **Terre A Terre** carried on where she had left off at four with a win in the Dubai Duty Free in March on her only outing of the year. The previous season's Prix du Jockey Club winner **Anabaa Blue** was successful over the same course and distance in the Grand Prix de Chantilly, where Angel Gabriel and Califet were among those behind him. Come the autumn, Anabaa Blue ran up to his best in the Arc but could finish only seventh.

Five-year-old **Polish Summer** has evidently been hard to train but he made into a very smart middle-distance stayer, beating Califet and **Fair Mix** in the Grand Prix de Deauville. Earlier runner-up in the Grand Prix de Saint-Cloud, Polish Summer's stamina was stretched when a disqualified third past the post in the Prix du Cadran. Fair Mix had been a former stable-companion of Polish Summer but had been claimed from Andre Fabre's yard as a prospective jumper. However, he improved from handicaps to contesting the Arc (finished eighth) in the latest season. His most important win came in the Coupe de Maisons-Laffitte, in which he beat the previous year's winner **Jim And Tonic**, who, at the age of eight, finally seemed to have lost some of his dash. The former Henry Cecil-trained **Wellbeing** was moved to Pascal Bary in search of softer ground in the latest season and had just such conditions when inflicting a surprise defeat on a below-form Sakhee in the Prix Gontaut-Biron at Deauville, though that proved easily the best of Wellbeing's efforts in pattern company. **Execute** made a good start to the year, winning the Prix d'Harcourt and finishing second in the Ganay, and his eighth place in the Prix Dollar in the autumn was a creditable effort under a penalty. **Poussin** initially confirmed three-year-old promise with placed efforts at Longchamp in the Prix d'Harcourt and Prix d'Ispahan but failed to hold his form afterwards.

There was a lack of good sprinters among the older horses. The Group 3 Prix de Meautry at Deauville featured some of the best performers in this division, with **Crystal Castle** beating **Swedish Shave** and **Danger Over**. Crystal Castle actually did most of his racing in Britain in the latest season, winning the Tote International Handicap (the first foreign-trained horse to do so) and the Diadem Stakes, both at Ascot. Likewise there was no outstanding stayer in France and both the Group 1 staying prizes, the Prix du Cadran and Prix Royal-Oak, went to British stables with Give Notice and Mr Dinos respectively. **Pushkin** was a good second in the Cadran and showed a consistent level of form from a mile and half upwards, his two wins including the Prix Maurice de Nieuil from Polish Summer and the Prix Gladiateur winner **Miraculous**. **Generic**, one of the top stayers in France in 2001, was second in the Prix de Barbeville giving weight all round on his reappearance but was not seen out in the second half of the year.

The latest crop of French-trained two-years-old contained some exciting prospects, none more so than the Prix Marcel Boussac winner **Six Perfections**. A couple of most impressive wins at Deauville in a listed race and the Prix du Calvados made her the one to beat at Longchamp and she looked a cracking classic candidate in beating the hitherto-unbeaten **Etoile Montante** by two lengths. Etoile Montante, herself five lengths clear of the remainder, would have been an above-average Marcel Boussac winner. **Loving Kindness** looked another good filly for the Bary/Niarchos team when an impressive winner of the Prix de Cabourg but she disappointed subsequently in the Prix Morny and Grand Criterium and was sold to Godolphin as part of the deal involving Sulamani. A filly who fared better against the colts in the Grand Criterium was Banks Hill's sister **Intercontinental**. A winner of both her starts beforehand, she finished third to Hold That Tiger and looks likely to emulate her dam's previous three foals by contesting a classic. **Zinziberine** is unlikely to prove a classic filly but she proved reliable in most of the pattern sprints for two-year-olds in France, winning the Prix Eclipse and Criterium de Maisons-Laffitte after some narrow defeats, including in the Prix Robert Papin. A filly who could well prove a Prix de Diane type is **Vallee Enchantee**, a daughter of Peintre Celebre and the Prix de l'Opera winner Verveine. She won a listed race at Saint-Cloud in November in good style, though still looked green.

Much the brightest prospect among the two-year-old colts is Daylami's unbeaten half-brother **Dalakhani**. He had plenty in hand when beating **Mister Charm** in the Prix des Chenes and then had to work a bit harder on heavy ground to defeat the Ballydoyle challenger Chevalier in the Criterium International. He looks sure to stay a mile and a half and will be one to follow in the trials in the spring before contesting either the Prix du Jockey Club or Derby. The Sheikh Mohammed-owned pair **Graikos** and **Songlark** won the Prix de Conde and Prix Thomas Bryon respectively before disappointing on heavy ground in Group 1 events at Saint-Cloud and both have joined Godolphin. **Marshall** fared best of the French colts when taking third place behind the Aidan O'Brien-trained winner Alberto Giacometti in the Criterium de Saint-Cloud.

Two-Year-Olds

120p	Six Perfections (f)
116p	Dalakhani
115p	Etoile Montante (f)
111	Loving Kindness (f)
107	Marshall
107	Songlark
107	Zinziberine (f)
106	Mister Charm
105p	Graikos
105p	Intercontinental (f)
105	Loving Pride (f)
105	Snipewalk
105	Welcome Millenium (f)
104p	Vallee Enchantee (f)
103	Ascetic Silver
103	Ela Merici (f)
103	Shedabad
102p	Power Elite
101p	Lady Catherine (f)
101p	Old Latin
101	Acago (f)
101	On Line
101	Sylvestre
100	Canda (f)
100	Solo Tango
100	The Wise Lady (f)
100	Traou Mad (f)
99	Garlinote (f)
99	Il Barone
99	Mystic Melody (f)
99	Together (f)
98	Semire (f)
98	Zanyboy
97	Oupoukaye
93	Arvada (f)

Three-Year-Olds

130	Sulamani
124	Act One
124	Bright Sky (f)
121	Pearly Shells (f)
119	*Medecis
119	Zipping
118	Ana Marie (f)
117p	Massigann
117	Bowman
117	Khalkevi
117	Rouvres
117	Tau Ceti
116	Dance Routine (f)
116	Massalani
116	Shaanmer
115	Bernebeau
115	Marotta (f)
115	Trumbaka (f)
115	Turtle Bow (f)
115	War Zone
114	Without Connexion
113p	Sarrasin
113	Caesarion
113	Dedication (f)
113	Great Pretender
113	Morozov
113	Secret Singer
112p	Agog
112+	Special Kaldoun
112	Bernimixa (f)
112	*Dublino (f)
112	Firth of Lorne (f)
112	*Inesperado
112	Louveteau
112	Thompson Rouge
112	Tigertail (f)
111	Gulf News
111	Loxias
111	Thattinger
111	Victorian Order
110	Craig's Falcon
110	Dance Dress (f)
110	Devious Indian
110	Porlezza (f)
110	*Sea of Showers (f)
110	*Glia (f)
109	Carib Lady (f)
109	Cielago
109	Green Groom
109	Le Fou
109	*Mariensky (f)
109	Maybe Forever (f)
109	Minds Locked
109	Mooring (f)
109	*Ombre Legere (f)
109	Polygreen (f)
109	Spark Sept (f)
109	Summertime Legacy (f)
109	Ziria (f)
108	Almond Mousse (f)
108	*Alozaina (f)
108	Arlesienne (f)
108	Jubilation
108	Martaline

108	Mer de Corail (f)	**Older Horses**		110	Chercheuse (f)
108	Prudence Royale (f)	132	Keltos	110	Dionello
108	Whim (f)	128	Domedriver	110	Epicurien
107	Azdine	126	*Banks Hill (f)	110	Mont Rocher
107	Behreyma (f)	126	Califet	110	Peppercorn
107	Gruntled	124	Ange Gabriel	110	Roman Saddle
107	*Heat Haze (f)	122	Anabaa Blue	109	Al Nowhere
107	Kane Ore (f)	121	Aquarelliste (f)	109	Bleu d'Altair
107	Murano	120	Crystal Castle	109	Greengroom
107	Politics	120	Polish Summer	109	Kingpin Oscar
107	Rashbag	120	Terre A Terre (f)	109	L'Impatient
107	Serisia (f)	119	Fair Mix	109	Saratan
107	Totally Cosmic (f)	119	Wellbeing	109	Soreze
107	Valentino (Fr)	117	Execute	109	Tikzane
106	Binya (f)	117	Poussin	108	Chronos
106	Bustling (f)	116	*Cheshire	108	Crillon
106	Charming Groom	116	Generic	108	Katchina Quest (f)
106	*Clerical Error (f)	116	Pushkin	108	Minuit Noir
106	Dobby Road	116	Swedish Shave	108	Silinski
106	*Keramani	115	Danger Over	108	Terrazzo
106	*Kithira (f)	115	Epitre	107	Belfortain
106	*Loup Masque	115	King of Tara	107	Double Heart
106	Melody Blue (f)	115	Mahfooth	107	*Five Fishes (f)
106	Sforza	115	Sensible	107	Iron Mask
106	Spring Star (f)	115	Speedmaster	107	Kinimba
106	Tripat	114	Bedawin	107	*Pretty Fighter
105p	Moon Search (f)	114	*Cayoke	107	Tajoun
105	Amathia (f)	114	Choc Ice (f)	107	Tiger Groom
105	Be Glad (f)	114	Jim And Tonic	107	Turn To Black (f)
105	Danseuse d'Etoile (f)	114	*Mister Kybelee	106	Doctorate
105	Darinska (f)	113	Al Namix	106	Go Got
105	Deflation	113	Clety	106	Honorifique (f)
105	Final Approach (f)	113	Cut Quartz	106	Ladonia
105	Ivy League (f)	113	Idaho Quest	106	Le Nomade
105	*Little Treasure (f)	113	Jomana (f)	106	*Lugny
105	Meteor Storm	113	Lethals Lady (f)	106	Mon Legionnaire
105	Peel River	113	Marichal	106	Self Defense
105	Place Rouge (f)	113	Miraculous	106	*Strawberry Blonde (f)
105	Pont d'Or	113§	Sagacity	106	Turbo Jet
105	Riverse Angle	112	Balthazar	106?	Norouz
105	Somelier	112	Dananeyev	105	Algallerens
105	Superman	112	Little Rock	105	Cazoulias
105	Top World	112	Proudwings (f)	105	Maid of Dawkins (f)
105	Westerner	112	Sangreal	105	Reallier
		112	Subliminal	105	Silence of Winds
104	Dzinigane (f)	111	Breknen Le Noir	105	Ulterior Motives
103	Kapria (f)	111	Cherbon	105	Woodford Reserve
103	Stydahar	111	Foundation Spirit		
101	On Reflection	111	Okawango	104	Queen of Persia (f)
		111?	The Mask		
		110	Allez Olive		

GERMANY   After several successful years, Germany had a below-strength team of horses in 2002. That was particularly evident from the drop in the number of horses rated 115 or more in the latest season; down to nine from twenty in 2001. On the track, that weakness was felt in the country's four Group 1 races open to older horses, only one of which was won by a German-trained horse. The others went to the British-trained Kaieteur, Yavana's Pace and Marienbard, the last-named winning two such races, notably the Grosser Preis von Baden.

The three-year-olds were a substandard group, particularly the colts, but **Next Desert** stood out as easily the best of them. Beaten only by the British-trained Dupont in the Mehl-Mulhens-Rennen (2000 Guineas), he won his other three starts in pattern races, notably the Deutsches Derby impressively from his female stable-companions **Salve Regina** and **Tomori**. This was the second time in three years that Andreas Schutz had trained the first three in the premier German classic. Next Desert was injured subsequently, missing the Arc as a result, but he should enjoy further success in good races in 2003, all

being well. The Preis der Diana (Oaks) winner Salve Regina finished second in three other Group 1 races after the Derby, behind Yavana's Pace in the Credit Suisse Private Banking Pokal at Cologne and Marienbard at Baden-Baden, and in the Preis von Europa at Cologne. **Guadalupe** was not at her best when third in the Preis der Diana but she had won the Oaks d'Italia before that and ran well to make the frame in the Yorkshire Oaks, Prix Vermeille and Gran Premio del Jockey Club. Guadalupe's stable-companion **Walzer-koenigin** disappointed in the Henkel-Rennen (1000 Guineas) won by **Portella** but came good in the Prix Chloe at Chantilly and the Euro-Cup at Frankfurt. Other three-year-old fillies to make their mark were **Uriah**, winner of the Grade 2 Long Island Handicap at Aqueduct, and **Midnight Angel**, placed in the Italian and German Oaks and sold for 500,000 guineas at the end of the year to continue her career in the USA. The rest of the three-year-old colts were some way behind Next Desert. **Liquido** won the Deutsches St Leger but most of the other leading colts were best at much shorter trips. **Zarewitsch**, **Horeion Directa** (the first two in the Oettingen-Rennen at Baden-Baden) and **Sambaprinz** (winner of the Brandenburg-Trophy at Hoppegarten) were milers, while **Soave** was the top three-year-old sprinter.

The 2001 Deutsches Derby winner **Boreal** was Germany's top older horse and gained the most important win abroad for a German stable in 2002 when landing the Coronation Cup at Epsom, becoming the first German-trained horse to win a Group 1 in Britain since Star Appeal in 1975. Apart from his third place in the Dubai Sheema Classic though, he made little impression otherwise. The well-travelled **Paolini** did all his racing outside Germany, putting up his best efforts when second in the Singapore Airlines International Cup and the Hong Kong Cup, and a close sixth in the Arlington Million. Domestically, the older horses who figured most in the top middle-distance races were **Well Made** and **Simoun**. Well Made won three pattern races at Cologne, twice having Simoun behind him in the spring and then winning the Preis von Europa from Salve Regina in September. Simoun's best efforts came in June when he turned the tables on Well Made in both the Grosser Mercedes-Benz-Preis at Baden-Baden and the Hansa-Preis at Hamburg.

After a curtailed four-year-old campaign, the 2000 Deutsches Derby winner **Samum** (Salve Regina's elder brother) was still below his best in the latest season, though he did manage third behind Marienbard in the Deutschlandpreis at Dusseldorf. **Noroit** also found Godolphin's future Arc winner too good when third in the Grosser Preis von Baden. A former top-priced yearling in Germany, the late-developing **Tareno** put up smart efforts to win in Group 3 company at Baden-Baden and Milan before being bought (along with stable-companion **Subiaco**) by Barney Curley for a hurdling career in Britain. Finally, among the older middle-distances horses, a remarkable international career ended with the retirement of the eight-year-old **Caitano**. He competed in thirteen different countries, gaining his final victory in Poland in September, after contesting at one time or another such varied events as the Arc de Triomphe, Japan Cup, Arlington Million, Breeders' Cup Turf and Melbourne Cup. Caitano has retired to stud in Russia after a place in Germany was reportedly denied him on the grounds that he had raced on lasix in the USA. As usual the miling honours were spread evenly among some smart older horses, but **Touch Down** was an impressive winner of the Badener Meile at Baden-Baden in May and put up just about the best performance in that division even though he was not the most consistent. **Call Me Big** was the top older sprinter, winning the Benazet-Rennen at Baden-Baden.

The Schutz stable looks to have another leading candidate for German classic honours in 2003 in the form of **Eagle Rise**, who won both his starts at two, notably the Preis des Winterfavoriten from **Glad Hunter**. The top two-year-old fillies' race, the Preis der Winterkonigin, went to **Royal Dubai** and the form of that race was boosted when third-placed **White Rose** went on to win the Prix Miesque at Maisons-Laffitte. **Fiepes Shuffle** was another German two-year-old to run well in France, putting up his best effort when second in the Criterium de Maisons-Laffitte. Following Kazzia's success in the latest season, Godolphin purchased another German two-year-old filly, **Gonfilia**, who won both her starts by six lengths, the second one a national listed race at Hanover.

Two-Year-Olds

108p	Eagle Rise
107	Fiepes Shuffle
104	Royal Dubai (f)
103	Glad Hunter
103	Soldier Hollow
103	White Rose (f)
102	Easy Way
101	Minley
99	Vallonga (f)
97p	Cherub
97	Masvingo
97	Theralith
96p	Dancing Flower (f)
96p	Gonfilia (f)
96	Action Fighter
96	Ibisco
95	Encanto
95	Lips Plane (f)

Three-Year-Olds

122	Next Desert
115	Salve Regina (f)
113	Guadalupe (f)
113	Zarewitsch
112	Horeion Directa
112	Soave
111	Belcore
111	Liquido
111	Sambaprinz
111	Walzerkoenigin (f)
111	Willingly
109	Portella (f)
109	Uriah (f)
109?	Best Walking (f)
108	Midnight Angel (f)
107	Ammonias
107	Auenteufel
107	Divisa (f)
107	Mendosino
107	Olaso
107	Stolzing
107	Toylsome
106	Casanga (f)
106	Irulan
106	Karlsson

106	Larana (f)
106	Nobilissima (f)
106	Orfisio
106	Tomori (f)
106?	Calcio
105	Art Antique (f)
105	Arucas
105	Levirat

104	Templerin (f)
103	Whispered Secret
103	Whisperer
102	Chan Chan
101	Lips Lion
100	Ifag Mannheim
100	Nicaragua
98	Sergeant Pepper
97	Sederic
87	Beryllus

Older Horses

126	Boreal
121	Paolini

121	Well Made	110	Pappus	106	Alegrador
117	Simoun	110	Passimo	106	Just Heavens Gate (f)
116	Noroit	110	Sacho	106	Karakal
116	Touch Down	110	Scapolo	106	Kimbajar (f)
115	Samum	110	Street Poker	106	*Noel
114	Tareno	109	Fruhtau	106	Onaldo
114	Up And Away	109	Lucido	106	Rosovern
114	War Blade	108	Bedford Forrest	106	Syrakus
113	Royal Dragon	108	*Gorlor	106	Wins Fiction
112	Caitano	108	Pardus	105	Anhalt
112	Call Me Big	108	Stingray	105	Bedford Set (f)
112	Dictum	108	Subiaco	105	Donasita (f)
112	Limerick Boy	108	Tempelwachter	105	Homita (f)
112	Terre de L'home	107	Bear King	105	Meliksah
111	Adlerflieger	107	Denaro	105	Saldenschwinge (f)
111	Areias	107	Iberus		
111	Diamante	107	Ingolf	100	*Harishon
111	Konig Shuffle	107	Kaka	93	Frisco Song
111	Near Honor	107	Maitre Levy		
110	Aeskulap	107d	Adare Manor		

ITALY Italian-trained horses have generally struggled to hold on to their big domestic prizes in recent years, let alone win important events abroad, but 2002 was very different. They won one of the world's richest international races, kept their Derby at home for the first time since 1988, came within inches of landing one of Europe's top sprints and had a two-year-old capable of taking on the best youngsters.

The previous year's Derby Italiano runner-up **Falbrav** gave Italy its most important success since Tony Bin's Arc de Triomphe win of 1988 when beating the American gelding Sarafan narrowly to land the Japan Cup. A confirmed firm-ground performer, Falbrav had disappointed in the Arc but had earlier won two of Italy's big races, the Premio Presidente della Repubblica at Rome (breaking the track record) and the Gran Premio di Milano. Falbrav continues his career in 2003 with Luca Cumani. Just a week before the Japan Cup, the same colours were carried to victory by Scuderia Rencati's other very smart four-year-old **Sunstrach** in the Premio Roma by six lengths from **Blu For Life**. Italy's other good older horse of note was the miler **Altieri**. His best effort came when beating future Breeders' Cup winner Domedriver narrowly in the Prix Messidor at Deauville and he also won the Group 2 Premio Ribot at Rome. The previous season's winners of the Premio Roma and Premio Ribot, **Shibuni's Falcon** and **Giovane Imperatore**, each won listed races early in the year (as did miler **Caluki**) but failed to keep their form later on. **Indian Mary** and **Development** were again a couple of the leading sprinters, but the top two in this division were the fillies **Oh Bej Oh Bej** and **Slap Shot**, the latter a three-year-old. Oh Bej Oh Bej had the edge on their Italian form but when they both contested the Prix de l'Abbaye, it was Slap Shot who put up much the better effort, losing out by just a nose to the July Cup winner Continent.

The top three-year-old though was **Rakti**, the first Italian horse since Tisserand fourteen years earlier to win the Derby Italiano, beating Ballingarry and **Fisich**. Although Rakti returned in the autumn to win a listed race at Rome, he lost his form after that (and refused to enter the stalls for the Champion Stakes) and it will be interesting to see how he fares in 2003 for his new trainer Michael Jarvis. Derby third Fisich had earlier been beaten a nose by Dupont in the Premio Parioli (2000 Guineas) and ended the year beating **Rainer** and a below-form Rakti in a well-contested minor event at Rome. **Salselon** won the all-aged Premio Chiusura for the second year running and went on to finish a good second to Altieri in the Premio Ribot. Second to Slap Shot among the three-year-old fillies was **Torrigiana**. She was only third to **Sadowa** in the Premio Regina Elena (1000 Guineas) but went on to show better form in winning three listed races.

Italy's two-year-olds rarely make much of a name for themselves, but one who did in the latest season was **Le Vie dei Colori**. He was unbeaten in his first six starts, including the Prix La Rochette at Longchamp, and found only Hold That Tiger too good in the Grand Criterium at the same track. The filly **Pleasure Place** also did well in France, where she won the Prix d'Arenberg, and subsequently won two listed races at Rome in the autumn.

Two-Year-Olds	110 Torrigiana (f)	111 Indian Mary (f)
110 Le Vie dei Colori	109 Landinium (f)	111? Rosso India
104 Pleasure Place (f)	109 Maktub	110 Development
101 Borsieri	107 Einstein	110 Stephant
100 Marbye (f)	107 Kiris World (f)	109 Blu For Life
99 Golden Jade	106 Clefairy (f)	108 Kathy College (f)
98 Golden Danetime	105 Nordhal	108 Mon Alexandrino
97 Chalin	105 Polycar	107 Dream Chief
97 Fielding	105 Sadowa (f)	107 Fairy Charm
97 Golden Polar		107 Hopes Are High
96 Balkenhol	104 Kardthea (f)	107 Vehoru
96 Don't Explain	104 Musical Score (f)	106 Fay Breeze
95 Golden Devious	104 Sweetsoutherngirl (f)	106 Mr Picchio
95 Sopran Woog (f)	99 Mangayoh	106 Sopran Foldan
		106 Sopran Montanelli
	Older Horses	105 Czar
Three-Year-Olds	125 Falbrav	105 Dane Friendly
118 Rakti	120 Sunstrach	105 Fascino
115 Fisich	117 Altieri	105 Golden Honor (f)
115 Slap Shot (f)	114 Shibuni's Falcon	
113 Salselon	113 Oh Bej Oh Bej (f)	99 Kanaris
110 Rainer	112 Giovane Imperatore	
	111 Caluki	

SCANDINAVIA   For the second year running, three of Scandinavia's highest-rated horses were the middle-distance trio **Dano-Mast**, **Valley Chapel** and **Sagittarius**. All three competed outside Scandinavia during the year, and it was Dano-Mast who did most to raise his international profile with victory in the Prix Dollar on Arc weekend before a good third in the Hong Kong Cup. By our reckoning, the Danish-trained Dano-Mast is the best horse trained in Scandinavia since Norway's Noble Dancer (rated 125), who finished fourth in the Arc in 1976. Earlier, Dano-Mast had finished second to Valley Chapel in the Scandinavian Open Championship but had that rival back in third when foiling Valley Chapel's hat-trick bid in the Stockholm Cup International. Whilst as good as ever, Valley Chapel was less consistent than in previous seasons, and finished third in another race he had won for the past two years, the Marit Sveaas Minnelop at Ovrevoll behind **Martellian** and **Bellamont Forest**. The lightly-raced Sagittarius was restricted to just two races (both outside Scandinavia) in the latest season, his better effort coming when second in the Ormonde Stakes at Chester. Best of the remainder over middle distances were **Parthe** and **Harrier**. Both won listed races at Ovrevoll, the latter going on to finish second in the Stockholm Cup. **Ecology** put up one of the best performances over a mile when beating Martellian in a listed race at Ovrevoll in May, but didn't run to that form again and was twice beaten by eight-year-old **Mortens Prospect** in handicaps over a mile on dirt at Ovrevoll in October.

None of Scandinavia's sprinters was quite so good as their best longer-distance horses but there was arguably more strength in depth in the sprint division and several held legitimate claims to being top sprinter. Prolific winner **Aramus** ran up a hat-trick in listed races before beating Bellamont Forest in the Polar Million Cup at Ovrevoll. In the other Group 3 sprint, the Taby Open Sprint Championship, Aramus had to settle for second place for the second year running when going down to **Pistachio**. In both those races, ten-year-old **Oktan** filled third place and was better than ever having raced over longer trips until the latest season. The ex-Argentinian horse **Nobel Prize** enjoyed a good first season in Europe, gaining his biggest win in Germany's top sprint, the Goldene Peitsche at Baden-Baden, by five lengths from British filly Red Liason. Stable-companion **El Gran Lode** also won a German pattern race when defeating Monkston Point in the Holsten-Trophy at Hamburg, while **Shawdon** repeated his feat of the previous year by landing two listed sprints in Germany.

Older Horses	112 Bellamont Forest	111 Oktan
120 Dano-Mast	112 Ecology	110 Shawdon
118 Valley Chapel	112 Harrier	109 Nicki Hill
113 Aramus	112 Mortens Prospect	109 Terroir
113 Martellian	112 Parthe	108 Blue Mountain
113 Nobel Prize	112 Sagittarius	108 Exbourne's Wish
113 Pistachio	111 El Gran Lode	108 Tesorero

| 107 | Musadif | 106 | Hangover Square | 105 | Cajun Sunset |
| 107 | Tough Guy | 105 | Albaran | | |

UNITED ARAB EMIRATES The ultimate aim for the Dubai World Cup is to host a meeting solely consisting of Group 1 races. 2002 saw that dream move a step closer with the Dubai Duty Free, Dubai Sheema Classic and Dubai Golden Shaheen all carrying Group 1 status for the first time and the Godolphin Mile and UAE Derby being promoted to Group 2. That is just a couple of the many changes made to the race programme, with all three rounds of the Maktoum Challenge promoted to Group status along with the UAE 2000 Guineas.

The Dubai racing season covers only half the year, due to the heat, but provides the perfect stop-gap for many English-based riders to ply their trade. It is not only the jockeys heading to the Middle East for the winter, but trainers as well, with the International stables now fully operational and housing the likes of Mark Johnston, Richard Whitaker and Karl Burke for the 2002/2003 season. South African trainer Mike de Kock also has a few horses there and his **Victory Moon** made a good impression winning both his races, the most recent being a dominant success in a prestige race at Nad Al Sheba. Further initiatives will also see a racing carnival in place in the build-up to the 2003 Dubai World Cup, with feature races on every Thursday night, and a day of trials in early-March before the big meeting.

The race programme for three-year-olds has developed over the last couple of years with the UAE 2000 Guineas first being run in 2000 when it was known as the Khor Dubai. The three winners of the race, Bachir, Street Cry and **Essence of Dubai** in 2002, highlight the quality of horse the race has attracted. Essence of Dubai went on to win the UAE Derby before heading to the Kentucky Derby, in which he was slightly disappointing in finishing ninth, but he returned to form in the States in the autumn. Saeed bin Suroor also saddled the third in the UAE Derby, **Ibn Al Haitham**. **State City** finished behind Essence of Dubai in both the Guineas (finishing third) and Derby, but had earlier been progressive in winning a couple of minor events at Nad Al Sheba, and ran his best race back at six furlongs to win a well-contested conditions event there in December.

*UAE Derby, Nad Al Sheba—Essence of Dubai completes the UAE 2000 Guineas/Derby double,
one which narrowly eluded Street Cry the previous year;
he catches the ex-Chilean Total Impact (far side) in the closing stages*

Dubai Golden Shaheen, Nad Al Sheba—Caller One is made to work much harder to gain a repeat success, just getting the better of a good battle with fellow American Echo Eddie (far side)

Fillies are also catered for. **Infinite Spirit** took the UAE 1000 Guineas from **Tempera**, but subsequently disappointed in the USA. Tempera also had to settle for second best in the UAE Oaks when behind Imperial Gesture, thereby reversing their places from the previous season's Breeders' Cup Juvenile Fillies. Unfortunately, Tempera died before she could embark on another American campaign.

Street Cry had been labelled as Godolphin's best chance of winning the Kentucky Derby in 2001 before injury ruled him out. He raced only once more that year but came back in 2002 to confirm earlier promise. He took in the third round of the Maktoum Challenge in February, trouncing **State Shinto**, but still headed to the Dubai World Cup in the shadow of **Sakhee**, the chosen mount of Frankie Dettori and a nine-length winner over Atlantis Prince in a conditions race at Nad Al Sheba in February.

Sakhee was odds on to give Dettori his second World Cup but Jerry Bailey on Street Cry easily made it four wins in the world's richest race, beating **Sei Mi** from Saudi Arabia with Sakhee only third. **Royal Tryst**, placed in all three rounds of the Maktoum Challenge, wasn't disgraced in fifth and gained reward for his consistency when taking the prestige National Day Cup later in the year from the former Barry Hills-trained **Calcutta**. **Best of The Bests** repeated his success in the second round of the Maktoum Challenge, but was again some way below form in the Dubai World Cup.

The first round of the Maktoum Challenge is traditionally the weakest of the three legs but often provides clues to the local challenge for the Godolphin Mile. **Skoozi** beat **China Visit** by a nose with **Conflict**, a past winner of the Godolphin Mile, back in fourth. All three headed for that race, with Conflict warming up by taking a prestige race at Nad

Al Sheba. Skoozi emerged best but could finish only second to American raider, Grey Memo.

The Dubai Duty Free saw the finish of the meeting in 2001 with Jim And Tonic, Fairy King Prawn and Sunline battling out the finish. France again took the prize with Terre A Terre beating **Noverre**. The local challenge isn't always that strong in this race and that showed with **Divine Task** next best in eighth, **Summoner** in ninth, **Slip Stream** in twelfth and **Superiority** and **Swiss Law** amongst the back markers. Swiss Law, at the age of eight, had earlier been in good form, winning a listed race at Nad Al Sheba from Divine Task and finishing second behind **Glad Master** in the President Cup at Abu Dhabi.

American sprinter Caller One took the Dubai Golden Shaheen for the second successive year with **Conroy** some way below his best in ninth. Conroy had earlier shown improved form to win the listed Jebel Ali Sprint and a listed race at Nad Al Sheba, in which he beat **Asaal**.

Nayef was a late inclusion in the Dubai Sheema Classic, having switched from the World Cup, but that decision was vindicated with a comfortable victory. **Narrative** finished down the field but had previously progressed nicely, having won a handicap off a mark of 90 before taking the Group 3 Dubai City of Gold from subsequent Emirates World Series Champion Grandera. **Musha Merr**, down the field in the City of Gold, had earlier put up a smart performance when taking the listed Al Rashidiya from **Celtic Silence**.

The performances reviewed here are those that took place in the calendar year 2002. Horses which were trained and raced in UAE but showed significantly better form elsewhere are not included in the list below.

Three-Year-Olds

118	*Essence of Dubai	115	*Summoner	109	Pacino
113	State City	114	Glad Master	109	Vulpix
111	*Ibn Al Haitham	113	Asaal	109d	*Superiority
108	*Infinite Spirit (f)	113	Conflict	108	Clodion
107	*Victory Moon	113	*Divine Task	108	Jalaab
106	Dubai Edition	112	*Calcutta	108	Orchestrated
106	Tempera (f)	112	Celtic Silence	108	*Razik
		112	Crystal Magician	108	*Rhythm Band
Older Horses		112	Curule	107	*Crimson Quest
130	*Street Cry	112	Flight Pattern	107	Dubai Two Thousand
128	*Sakhee	112	*Marhoob	107	Ennoblement
123	*Noverre	112	Mutamayyaz	107	Festival of Light
122	*Best of The Bests	112	State Shinto	107	*Mahroos
118	*Sei Mi	112	Swiss Law	107	Pentagonal
117	China Visit	112	Trademark	107	Shaard
117	*Narrative	111	Maidaan	107	West Order
117d	*Skoozi	111	*Sydenham	106	Broche
116	Happy Diamond	111§	*Valentino (GB)	106	Muthaaber
116	Royal Tryst	110	*A Touch of Frost (f)	106	Qawaqeb
115	Conroy	110	Lightning Arrow	106	Walmooh
115	Musha Merr	110	Rumpold	106d	Lord of The Manor
115	Slip Stream	110d	Rayyaan	105	Artillery
		109	Jila	105	Conspirator

NORTH AMERICA While the Triple Crown in Britain is rarely contemplated, still less attempted or completed successfully, the American colts' classics annually see attempts to complete the Kentucky Derby-Preakness Stakes-Belmont Stakes treble. What is more, in seven of the last nine years, a colt has managed to win two of the three legs. Tabasco Cat (1994) and Point Given (2001) blew their Triple Crown hopes when beaten in the Kentucky Derby but went on to win the other two races, while Thunder Gulch's attempt was let down only by his defeat in the Preakness. But for Silver Charm (1997), Real Quiet (1998), Charismatic (1999) and, in the latest season, **War Emblem**, the Triple Crown was still a possibility right up to the 'off' at Belmont after success at both Churchill Downs and Pimlico. There was a $5 million bonus if War Emblem could win the Belmont but he failed to stay the mile and a half trip. Although he coasted home from the Preakness runner-up **Magic Weisner** under top-weight in the Haskell Invitational Handicap next time out, War Emblem proved disappointing subsequently against older rivals in the Pacific Classic and Breeders' Cup Classic. A second successive champion three-year-old

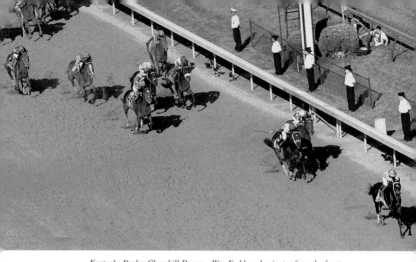

Kentucky Derby, Churchill Downs—War Emblem dominates from the front on his first outing for trainer Bob Baffert; Proud Citizen and Perfect Drift are placed as Johannesburg (in eighth place, nearest rail) and Essence of Dubai (ninth, on left) make little impact

colt after Point Given for trainer Bob Baffert (also the handler of Real Quiet and Silver Charm) and the Thoroughbred Corporation (whose Prince Ahmed Salman died just before the Haskell), War Emblem has been retired to stud in Japan.

Proud Citizen's campaign took in all three legs of the Triple Crown, but after running well to finish second in the Kentucky Derby and third in the Preakness, he sustained an injury when fifth at Belmont. The Belmont had its longest-priced winner ever in the form of 70/1-chance **Sarava**, making his graded stakes debut. The result will have caused some surprise in Britain too, where Sarava had finished no better than fourth in three maidens for Brian Meehan as a two-year-old. Injured after the Belmont, Sarava has joined Bob Baffert for a four-year-old campaign. The only other horse who truly stayed the trip at Belmont was runner-up **Medaglia d'Oro**. Fourth in the Kentucky Derby but below form in the Preakness, he gained a wide-margin success in the Grade 2 Jim Dandy Stakes then beat the previous season's Breeders' Cup Juvenile runner-up **Repent** in the Travers Stakes before starting favourite and faring best of the three-year-olds to finish second in the Breeders' Cup Classic. A genuine sort, Medaglia d'Oro should enjoy another good campaign at four. Injury kept Repent out of the Triple Crown races, as well as the Breeders' Cup.

Came Home lined up as another of the leading three-year-olds in the Breeders' Cup Classic after gaining his ninth win from eleven starts in a competitive renewal of the Pacific Classic against older horses. He injured a knee when finishing only tenth at the Breeders' Cup and has been retired to stud. Came Home's only other defeat of the year came in the Kentucky Derby (finishing sixth) after winning the Santa Anita Derby. He also provided jockey Chris McCarron, who is the leading money-earner in the US, with a victory on his final ride in June. **Harlan's Holiday** was another who finished down the field in both the Breeders' Cup Classic and the Kentucky Derby (for which he started favourite), but otherwise put up good performances from early in the year through to the autumn. Beaten a nose by **Booklet** in the Fountain of Youth Stakes, Harlan's Holiday had that rival behind him when winning both the Florida Derby and Blue Grass Stakes, and went on to run well in the Preakness Stakes (fourth) and Jockey Club Gold Cup (third against older horses).

An important name missing from the Triple Crown races was **Buddha**. He was scratched from the Kentucky Derby on the eve of the race (and subsequently retired after further setbacks) and would have been the likely favourite at Churchill Downs following his narrow but game defeat of Medaglia d'Oro and **Sunday Break** in the Wood Memorial. The Japanese-bred Sunday Break won in Grade 2 company next time before finishing a non-staying third in the Belmont. Gelding **Perfect Drift** took third place in the Kentucky Derby, and whilst well beaten in the Belmont Stakes and Breeders' Cup Classic, beat Preakness fifth **Easyfromthegitgo** in the Grade 3 Indiana Derby in between.

The top two three-year-old males over shorter trips were **Thunderello** and **Gygistar**. The lightly-raced Thunderello nearly pulled off an upset on his graded-stakes debut when second in the Breeders' Cup Sprint but was pulled up injured on his only subsequent start and has been retired to stud. Gygistar did not make it to the Breeders' Cup, though was unbeaten in five starts, the most important of them the King's Bishop Stakes at Saratoga.

Ballingarry put up a very smart performance when winning the Canadian International on his final start for Aidan O'Brien, but he failed to confirm that improvement in the Breeders' Cup Turf after having to spend some time in France to complete quarantine procedures. **Chiselling** narrowly won just an ordinary renewal of the Secretariat Stakes, while **Johar** took the Hollywood Derby at the end of the year with more authority and looks a decent turf prospect for 2003, particularly when tried beyond nine furlongs.

Most of the leading three-year-old fillies met in the Kentucky Oaks, which saw a first stakes win for outsider **Farda Amiga**. However, she proved that was no fluke when beating three other fillies who had won a Grade 1 last time in the Alabama Stakes and ended her career with a fine second place in the Breeders' Cup Distaff over a trip that was a bare minimum for her. **Imperial Gesture** was just behind her in third in the Distaff and had disappointed in the Kentucky Oaks, but in between had made most to beat the Kentucky Oaks second **Take Charge Lady** in the Gazelle Handicap and did the same against older fillies in the Beldame Stakes. Take Charge Lady's season had begun with three easy wins in graded company, including the Ashland Stakes, and she took a second Grade 1 at Keeneland when defeating **You** in the Spinster Stakes in October; sixth place in the Breeders' Cup Distaff was her only poor effort all year.

You and **Habibti** were old adversaries from their two-year-old days and their rivalry persisted through the spring, with You beating Habibti into second in both the Las Virgenes Stakes and the Santa Anita Oaks. Habibti came off the better when they finished third and fourth respectively in the Kentucky Oaks, but while Habibti was beaten three times outside Grade 1 company subsequently, You held her form much the better. She went on to win the Acorn Stakes easily and then get the better of **Carson Hollow** in a thrilling Test Stakes over seven furlongs. You was placed in three more Grade 1 races before missing the Breeders' Cup to be rested for a four-year-old campaign. The Test Stakes was Carson Hollow's only defeat in six races before she finished tailed off in the Breeders' Cup Sprint; her Grade 1 success had come in the Prioress Stakes at Belmont. **Allamerican Bertie** did not contest the Kentucky Oaks but showed she was among the best of her age and sex on dirt when second to Farda Amiga in the Alabama Stakes and when beating Take Charge Lady in a Grade 2 at Churchill Downs in November. The CCA Oaks and the Mother Goose Stakes were weakly contested in 2002 and went to **Jilbab**, owned by Godolphin, and **Nonsuch Bay** respectively.

Riskaverse was the best US-trained three-year-old filly on turf, beating the Poule d'Essai des Pouliches winner **Zenda** in the Queen Elizabeth II Challenge Cup before finishing seventh in the Breeders' Cup Filly & Mare Turf. Also, the Dermot Weld-trained three-year-old **Dress To Thrill** took some notable scalps among the older turf fillies in the Matriarch Stakes in December.

By the time the Breeders' Cup came round, there was a gap to fill at the top of the older horse division on dirt. But what had looked a substandard renewal of the Breeders' Cup Classic, in the absence of several of the season's best dirt performers, had a top-class winner in the unlikely form of **Volponi**, the rank outsider in the field of twelve. Blinkered for the first time in six starts, he ran out the six and a half length winner, setting a record winning margin for the race. He had been tried over a variety of trips previously (finishing third on turf in the Sword Dancer Handicap over a mile and a half in August) and it will be interesting to see if he can confirm himself a top-class performer in 2003.

Dubai World Cup winner **Street Cry** made only two appearances in the USA, but he showed top-class form both times and was a regrettable absentee from the Breeders' Cup after an ankle problem prompted his retirement. On his first start after Dubai he strolled to a six and a half length win in the Stephen Foster Handicap at Churchill Downs and then carried top weight into second place in what turned out to be the best-contested race of the season, the Whitney Handicap at Saratoga in August. Neither the Whitney winner **Left Bank** nor the third **Lido Palace** contested the Breeders' Cup Classic either. Upped from shorter trips (he contested the Sprint at the Breeders' Cup in 2001 and broke the seven-furlong track record at Belmont with a Grade 2 win in July), Left Bank never got the chance to race over ten furlongs, succumbing to colic shortly after the nine-furlong Whitney. Lido Palace missed the Breeders' Cup because of the prohibitive cost of supplementing him, but in any case he did not quite match his Whitney form afterwards when gaining a second successive win in a below-strength Woodward Stakes, nor when second to **Evening Attire** in the Jockey Club Gold Cup.

Evening Attire had never seemed a likely Breeders' Cup Classic contender until his very smart effort in the Jockey Club Gold Cup and although he finished fourth at Arlington, he was never a threat after getting detached. It was third-placed **Milwaukee Brew** who put up the best performance among the older horses behind Volponi in the Classic. He won the Santa Anita Handicap early in the year and filled third place in two more Grade 1 events in the summer, the Hollywood Gold Cup (behind **Sky Jack** and **Momentum**) and the Pacific Classic. Sky Jack and Momentum also contested the Pacific Classic, Momentum finishing an unlucky second, but neither made it to the Breeders' Cup due to injury. **Macho Uno** has a good record at the Breeders' Cup, winning the Juvenile before finishing fourth in the Classic as a three-year-old, but he ran poorly in his prep race for the latest Classic, in which he finished a below-form fifth. However, he had been as good as ever earlier in the year, beating Evening Attire comfortably in a Grade 2 at Suffolk Downs, running third to **E Dubai** and Lido Palace in the Grade 2 Suburban Handicap, and fourth in the Whitney. Godolphin's E Dubai deputised for Street Cry in the Breeders' Cup Classic but he finished well held after setting the pace. **Mizzen Mast** would have been an interesting runner in the top dirt races after his career-best effort to win the Grade 2 Strub Stakes in February, but he was injured subsequently and retired to stud.

Orientate, who had contested the Classic twelve months earlier, made sure of the champion sprinter's title when winning the Breeders' Cup Sprint, a race which drew no European runner this time. This was Orientate's fifth consecutive win, the most important of his earlier successes coming in the Forego Handicap at Saratoga in September. **Crafty C. T.** ran his best race to take third in the Sprint and was placed in a further three Grade 1 races during the year. **Swept Overboard** has done most of his racing over sprint trips but put up much his best effort of the year on his only attempt at a mile when winning the Metropolitan Handicap, with Crafty C. T. (third), the Carter Handicap winner **Affirmed Success** (as good as ever at the age of eight) and Left Bank among those behind. The Metropolitan is likely to figure in plans for **Congaree** in 2003 after his emphatic win in the Cigar Mile Handicap in November.

Veteran sprinter **Kona Gold** was back to contest a record fifth Breeders' Cup Sprint, finishing fourth, in a light campaign which had seen him not far below his best. **Caller One** gained his second consecutive win in the Dubai Golden Shaheen at Nad Al Sheba,

Breeders' Cup Classic, Arlington—Volponi causes a big upset and records the widest official winning margin for the race; favourite Medaglia d'Oro holds off Milwaukee Brew (left) for second place

Breeders' Cup Distaff, Arlington—Horse of The Year Azeri crowns a magnificent season with another front-running success; third-placed Imperial Gesture is also in the picture

beating **Echo Eddie** in a race where American-trained horses filled the first four places. Caller One was due to contest the Golden Jubilee Stakes at Royal Ascot but a throat infection ruled him out and he had to be retired after fracturing a leg in work later in the summer. America had another win at the Dubai World Cup meeting when **Grey Memo** put up an improved effort to win the Godolphin Mile.

Of all the various divisional champions, the most clear-cut was **Azeri**, who stood out among the older females on dirt. She ended the season with eight wins from nine starts (her career record reads ten from eleven), five of them in Grade 1 company. Her best performance came in the Breeders' Cup Distaff, in which she put up a top-class effort to make all, drawing five lengths clear of the top three-year-old fillies Farda Amiga and Imperial Gesture. The same performance would, in theory, have been sufficient to beat the males in the Classic and it was sufficient to clinch her Horse of The Year honours, an accolade won only twice previously by a filly (All Along and Lady's Secret in the 'eighties) and Azeri became the first to do so without racing outside her own sex. Azeri's other Grade 1 wins were all gained in the first half of the year, starting with the Santa Margarita Handicap and followed by three consecutive defeats of Affluent in the Apple Blossom, Milady Breeders' Cup and Vanity Handicaps. Azeri's racing future had looked uncertain due to an ownership dispute, but she now looks set for a five-year-old campaign and a potentially fascinating clash with male rivals.

Summer Colony was the best part of a stone inferior to Azeri by the end of the season (and finished last in the Distaff), but had the distinction of being the only filly to defeat Azeri when gaining a Grade 2 win over her at Santa Anita in February before Azeri was at the height of her powers. The genuine and consistent Summer Colony had herself established a fine wins-to-runs record, with a Grade 1 success in the Personal Ensign Handicap, in which she had Canada's Go For Wand Stakes winner **Dancethruthedawn** in third and **Starrer** in fourth, the latter filly going on to fill the same position in the Distaff. **Mandy's Gold** was fifth in the Distaff after running over shorter trips for much of her career, and she had run well earlier in the autumn when winning the Ruffian Handicap from You and finishing second to Imperial Gesture in the Beldame. A dual Grade 1 winner at two, **Raging Fever** missed most of her three-year-old campaign but returned better than ever in the latest season, winning the Ogden Phipps (formerly the Hempstead) Handicap at Belmont and finishing second to **Shine Again** in the Ballerina Handicap.

Kalookan Queen and **Xtra Heat** were the top two older female sprinters. Kalookan Queen was better than ever at the age of six, her Grade 1 wins coming in the Santa Monica Handicap and (against males) the Ancient Title Breeders' Cup Handicap. After finishing fifth in the Breeders' Cup Sprint, she was sold for $1.85 million and has been retired. Xtra Heat was only sixth at the Breeders' Cup and was below her best when third in the Dubai Golden Shaheen, but she enjoyed another excellent season otherwise, adding a further seven victories to her prolific career total. She changed hands privately for $1.5 million in November but is due to remain in training in 2003.

The American turf horses were collectively a weak group, the fact that Europe fielded odds-on favourites for both the Breeders' Cup Mile and Breeders' Cup Turf as good a demonstration as any of the dearth of high-class turf performers. Whilst **Rock of Gibraltar** failed in controversial circumstances to land the Mile, in which stable-companion **Landseer** broke a leg, French-trained **Domedriver** (one of only four Breeders' Cup participants—all European—not to race on lasix) still made it a success for Europe. In the Turf, **High Chaparral** became the first Derby winner to win the race and was the fourth consecutive European-trained winner. He and the ultimately disappointing Golan dominated the betting in the smallest-ever field for the race, another indication of the lack of strength in the turf division. Other North American Grade 1 races on turf to fall to European-based horses were the Flower Bowl Invitational (**Kazzia**), E. P. Taylor Stakes (**Fraulein**), Canadian International (Ballingarry), Keeneland Turf Mile (Landseer) and Matriarch Stakes (Dress To Thrill).

Beat Hollow was America's top turf horse over a mile and a quarter, though he and a number of the other leading grass performers began their careers in Europe. The former Derby third missed the whole of 2001 after leaving Henry Cecil but was better than ever in the latest season, with Grade 1 victories in the Woodford Reserve Turf Classic, Manhattan Handicap and a desperately tight Arlington Million. Beat Hollow was unsuited by the drop to a mile on his last two starts, finishing sixth at the Breeders' Cup. The lightly-raced **Good Journey** fared best of the home team in the Mile, finishing third. That was his only defeat of the year, his wins including the Atto Mile and, for the second year running, the Grade 2 Citation Handicap. The other good milers on turf were **Forbidden Apple**, fourth in the Breeders' Cup Mile, who had been foiled in a hat-trick bid in the Grade 2 Kelso Handicap by **Green Fee**, a place behind Forbidden Apple at Arlington. Forbidden Apple had also been placed behind Beat Hollow in the Manhattan and the Arlington Million. **Touch of The Blues** was badly hampered in the Breeders' Cup Mile but had run well

Arlington Million—Beat Hollow (blaze) comes out best in a blanket finish with Sarafan (noseband),
Forbidden Apple (right), the Paul Webber-trained Ulundi (left),
Falcon Flight (not in picture) and Paolini (blinkered)

when splitting Landseer and Beat Hollow in the Keeneland Turf Mile. He had been among the also-rans behind **Ladies Din** in the Shoemaker Breeders' Cup Mile at Hollywood in May.

Over longer distances it was the seven-year-old gelding **With Anticipation** who had the best record on turf. He repeated his 2001 feat of passing the post first in the United Nations Handicap, Sword Dancer Handicap and Man o' War Stakes; he had been demoted in the first of those races the year before but broke the track record in the United Nations this time round. With Anticipation also fared better in the Breeders' Cup Turf than he had the year before, holding on to second from the strong-finishing **Falcon Flight**. Also placed in the Canadian International and Hong Kong Vase, Falcon Flight had been one of the unlucky ones when fifth in the Arlington Million. Despite a victory over Beat Hollow in the Eddie Reed Handicap at Del Mar, **Sarafan** enjoyed little luck after, finishing second in the Arlington Million, the Clement L. Hirsch Memorial Turf Championship (behind Breeders' Cup Turf fourth **The Tin Man**) and the Japan Cup, and a close fourth in the Hong Kong Cup. **Denon** found only With Anticipation too good in the United Nations and Sword Dancer Handicaps, but was successful either side of those defeats in the Charles Whittingham Handicap and a substandard Turf Classic Invitational. Denon went on to finish fifth in the Breeders' Cup Turf. Other good performances on turf were put up by **Hap** to finish third in the Woodford Reserve Turf Classic, the Hollywood Turf Cup winner **Sligo Bay** and the Man o'War runner-up **Balto Star**.

If there was a clear leader among the older females on dirt, the distaff picture on turf was more muddled, with little to choose between **Starine**, **Golden Apples** and **Astra**. In a light campaign, Starine went down to each of those two main rivals on her first two starts and was below form in the Flower Bowl Invitational. But she rounded off her career with an improved effort to beat her better-fancied stable-companion, the 2001 winner Banks Hill, in the Breeders' Cup Filly & Mare Turf. Banks Hill was also below her best on her two other starts in America, finishing an unlucky third to Golden Apples in the Yellow Ribbon on her last outing for Andre Fabre, and then fourth to Dress To Thrill in the Matriarch on her final start. Golden Apples started favourite for the Filly & Mare Turf but was unsuited by the way the race was run, finishing fourth. As well as her defeat of **Voodoo Dancer** and Banks Hill in the Yellow Ribbon, Golden Apples beat a small but select field for the Beverly D Stakes in the summer, ahead of Astra, the previous year's winner **England's Legend** and **Volga**, and ended the year beaten narrowly in the Matriarch.

Azeri's stable-companion Astra was retired with a respiratory infection after the Beverly D, missing the Breeders' Cup as a result. She had earlier been successful at Hollywood in the Gamely Breeders' Cup Handicap (beating Starine and Voodoo Dancer) and the Beverley Hills Handicap, races she had also won in 2000 and 2001 respectively. The ex-French-trained **Magic Mission** ran well at long odds to take third in the Matriarch

Breeders' Cup Filly & Mare Turf, Arlington—a 1,2 for trainer Bobby Frankel but not in the order expected as Starine beats Banks Hill (No.5); Islington (left) is third

Stakes, while **Affluent** was not discredited in the same race, finishing fifth. After running into Azeri three times on dirt, Affluent made the most of a switch to turf when beating a rather unlucky Golden Apples in the John C. Mabee/Ramona Handicap at Del Mar in July.

No Breeders' Cup Juvenile winner has managed to win the Kentucky Derby, but until injury intervened, ruling him out of the Triple Crown races, **Vindication** looked to have plenty going for him to buck the trend. He's by a top sire and an influence for stamina, Seattle Slew (who died in May), he's trained by Bob Baffert, responsible for three of the last six Kentucky Derby winners, and he was unbeaten in four starts at two, culminating in his Breeders' Cup Juvenile victory over stable-companion **Kafwain**. The Baffert stable's strength was such that they also fielded the fourth in the Juvenile, **Bull Market**, who had been beaten a nose by Kafwain in the Grade 2 Norfolk Stakes beforehand. Aidan O'Brien was the other trainer represented by three colts in the Breeders' Cup Juvenile, though the chances of all three were compromised by getting behind early on (slow starts were a general feature of the European runners at Arlington) and **Hold That Tiger** did particularly well therefore to finish third.

Toccet ran poorly from a wide draw in the Breeders' Cup Juvenile but he did little wrong otherwise in a demanding campaign. Prior to the Breeders' Cup he beat yet another Baffert colt **Icecoldbeeratreds** in the Champagne Stakes, and went on to win three more graded races before the end of the year, in the last of them gaining a narrow victory over the demoted Kafwain and **Domestic Dispute** (also trained by Baffert) in the Hollywood Futurity. Another to disappoint in the Juvenile was **Whywhywhy** who started favourite on the back of his win in the Futurity Stakes over **Pretty Wild**. The latter was also second in the Hopeful Stakes behind **Sky Mesa**, the winner of all three of his starts, who looked like starting favourite for the Breeders' Cup Juvenile before an ankle problem ruled him out of the race at a late stage. Of the above-mentioned colts, Bull Market, Icecoldbeeratreds and Pretty Wild were all reported to have suffered bone chips, while Toccet looks another unlikely to make the Kentucky Derby line-up after suffering a setback.

The Baffert stable also housed a couple of the leading juvenile fillies, but not the best one, who was **Storm Flag Flying**. An impeccably-bred daughter of Storm Cat, she maintained a family tradition at the Breeders' Cup when winning the Juvenile Fillies; her dam, My Flag, won the same race in 1995 and was herself a daughter of the 1988 Distaff winner Personal Ensign. Unbeaten in four starts, including the Matron Stakes (which she won by over twelve lengths) and Frizette Stakes, Storm Flag Flying looks a cracking three-year-old prospect. The Baffert fillies **Composure** and **Santa Catarina** filled the places in the Juvenile Fillies, though only the former made Storm Flag Flying fight for her victory. However Composure suffered a shock defeat subsequently, running well below her Arlington form when second to **Elloluv** in the Hollywood Starlet Stakes. Santa Catarina had put up her best efforts earlier when an unlucky second in the Del Mar Debutante Stakes and when finishing well clear of the rest behind Storm Flag Flying in the Frizette. Injury struck a couple of the other Grade 1 winners among the two-year-old fillies; Spinaway Stakes winner **Awesome Humor** was another to require surgery for bone chips, while the Del Mar Debutante winner **Miss Houdini** suffered a career-threatening ruptured tendon.

European-trained horses who showed or reproduced their best form in North America are included in this list

† commentary in
Racehorses of 2002

Two-Year-Olds

122	Vindication
121p	Storm Flag Flying (†)
120	Composure (f)
118	Kafwain
118	Toccet
117p	Elloluv (f)
117p	†Hold That Tiger
117	Santa Catarina (f)
116p	Sky Mesa
116	Icecoldbeeratreds
115	Miss Houdini (f)
115	Whywhywhy
114	Awesome Humor (f)
113	Domestic Dispute
112	Bull Market
112	Erinsouthernman
112	Pretty Wild
112	Roll Hennessy Roll
111	Crowned Dancer
111	Ivanavinalot (f)
111	Listen Indy
111	Most Feared
111	Westerly Breeze (f)
111	Zavata
110	Buffythecenterfold (f)
110	Champali
110	Forever Partners (f)
110	Lone Star Sky
110	Ruby's Reception (f)
110	Tito's Beau
110	Truckle Feature
109	Added Edge
109	Bham
109	Elegant Designer (f)
109	Randaroo (f)
109	Soto
109	Summer Wind Dancer (f)
108	Coax Kid
108	Leo's Last Hurrahy
108	Midnight Cry (f)
108	My Boston Gal (f)
108	Private Gold
108	Roar Emotion (f)
108	Trust N Luck
108	†Van Nistelrooy
108	Wild Snitch (f)

DIRT

Three-Year-Olds

128	War Emblem
125	Farda Amiga (f)
125	Sarava
124	*Imperial Gesture (f)
124	Magic Weisner
124	Medaglia d'Oro
123	Allamerican Bertie (f)
123	Gygistar
123	Take Charge Lady (f)
123	Thunderello
122	Buddha
122	Came Home
122	Proud Citizen
122	Repent
121	Carson Hollow (f)
121	Habibti (f)
121	Perfect Drift
121	Sunday Break
121	You (f)
120	Harlan's Holiday
119	Booklet
119	Easyfromthegitgo
119	Got Koko (f)
118	†Essence of Dubai
118	Nothing Flat
117	Debonair Joe
117	Ile de France (USA) (f)
117	Like A Hero
117	Sightseek (f)
115	Jilbab (f)
114	Nonsuch Bay (f)

Older Horses

133	†Azeri (f)
131	Volponi
130	†Street Cry
127	Left Bank
127	Orientate
126	Congaree
126	Lido Palace
126	Swept Overboard
124	Caller One
124	E Dubai
124	Evening Attire
124	Macho Uno
123	Crafty C. T.
123	Echo Eddie
122	Momentum (USA)
122	Summer Colony (f)
121	Affirmed Success
121	Include
121	Kalookan Queen (f)
121	Milwaukee Brew
121	Mizzen Mast
121	Sky Jack

121	Xtra Heat (f)
120	Gander
120	Kona Gold
120	Pleasantly Perfect
119	Bonapaw
119	Express Tour
119	Grey Memo
119	Kudos
119	Raging Fever (f)
119	Snow Ridge
119	Starrer (f)
118	Cat Cay (f)
118	Dancethruthedawn (f)
118	D'Wildcat
118	Favorite Funtime (f)
118	Mandy's Gold (f)
118	Mongoose
118	Red Bullet
117	Bosque Redondo
117	Crafty Shaw
117	Disturbingthepeace
117	Forest Secrets (f)
117	Gold Mover (f)
117	Miss Linda (f)
117	Sir Bear
117	Spain (f)
116	Celtic Melody (f)
116	Hal's Hope
115	Shine Again (f)

TURF

Three-Year-Olds

133	†Rock of Gibraltar
130	†High Chaparral
125	†Landseer
123	†Ballingarry
123	†Dress To Thrill (f)
121	†Kazzia (f)
118	†Gossamer (f)
117	Chiseling
117	†Fraulein (f)
116p	Johar
116	Riskaverse (f)
112	*Dublino (f)
112	Wonder Again (f)

Older Horses

128	†Domedriver
126	Beat Hollow
126	Good Journey
125	Sarafan
123	Forbidden Apple
123	Starine (f)
123	With Anticipation
122	Falcon Flight
122	Golden Apples (f)

122	†Ulundi	119	Strut The Stage	118	Voodoo Dancer (f)
121	Astra (f)	119	Sweetest Thing (f)	117	Blazing Fury
121	Denon	118	Affluent (f)	117	Delta Form
121	Hap	118	Cetewayo	117	Magic Mission (f)
121	Ladies Din	118	Del Mar Show	117	Nuclear Debate
121	†Paolini	118	Grammarian	117	Owsley (f)
121	The Tin Man	118	Irish Prize	117	Skipping
120	Green Fee	118	Man From Wicklow	117	Startac
120	Sligo Bay	118	Shibboleth		
120	Touch of The Blues	118	Tates Creek (f)	116	Ringaskiddy
119	Balto Star	118	Val Royal		
119	England's Legend (f)	118	Volga (f)		

JAPAN   Japan looked to have some good older horses going into 2002, but, as it turned out, none of them really built on their achievements of the previous season. Instead, it was a three-year-old who came to the fore, and **Symboli Kris S** proved much the best of the classic crop. He went down to **Tanino Gimlet** in the Tokyo Yushun (Derby) but progressed later in the year, beating older horses in both the Tenno Sho (Autumn) and the Arima Kinen. In between those Group 1 victories, Symboli Kris S fared best of the Japanese runners when finishing third to Falbrav and Sarafan in the Japan Cup. With Tokyo racecourse undergoing refurbishment, the Japan Cup was run instead at Nakayama, and over eleven furlongs rather than the usual mile and a half. Trained by Kazuo Fujisawa, who won the Prix Jacques le Marois with Taiki Shuttle in 1998, Symboli Kris S could himself be campaigned in Europe in 2003.

Best of the other three-year-old colts were **Hishi Miracle** and **Fast Tateyama**, who were split by just a nose in the Kikuka Sho (St Leger). **No Reason**, the Satsuki Sho (2000 Guineas) winner, unseated when favourite for the Kikuka Sho and finished only mid-division afterwards in the Japan Cup and Arima Kinen. **Fine Motion**, a close relative to the former Japan Cup winner Pilsudski, was the top three-year-old filly. She lost her unbeaten record when finishing fifth in the Arima Kinen but had previously gained Group 1 wins in the Shuka Sho and the Queen Elizabeth II Challenge Cup.

Jungle Pocket and **Manhattan Cafe** were the best three-year-olds of 2001 to remain in training, and though they topped the older horse ratings for the latest season, neither enjoyed a full campaign and both have been retired. Manhattan Cafe had Jungle Pocket in second in the two-mile Tenno Sho (Spring) but was seen out only once afterwards, finishing down the field in the Prix de l'Arc de Triomphe. Jungle Pocket was also due to run in Europe but had to miss the King George at Ascot and never looked like repeating his previous year's Japan Cup success, finishing a never-nearer fifth. **Magnaten** was the first Japanese older horse past the post in the Japan Cup, finishing fourth on his first attempt beyond nine furlongs. **Tap Dance City**, **Coin Toss** and **Narita Top Road** filled the frame behind Symboli Kris S in the Arima Kinen. Six-year-old Narita Top Road has been a reliable performer in the top middle-distance and staying events in recent seasons and had another good campaign. He was placed in both the Tenno Sho races and beat Jungle Pocket in a Group 2 event in the spring, but finished down the field in the Japan Cup. **Sunrise Pegasus** also ran well in the Tenno Sho races, finishing fifth in the Spring event (in which **Born King** was fourth) and third in the Autumn.

Eishin Preston and **Agnes Digital** ended 2001 with prestigious wins in Hong Kong and they returned to Sha Tin in April to finish first and second respectively in the Queen Elizabeth II Cup. However, neither was in quite the same form as in 2001. Agnes Digital disappointed in the Dubai World Cup after winning the February Stakes, while Eishin Preston finished only fifth back at Sha Tin at the end of the year in the Hong Kong Cup. The best effort by a Japanese-trained horse at the Hong Kong International meeting came from **Tokai Point**, who finished a close third in the Mile. He had earlier beaten Eishin Preston in the Mile Championship at Kyoto.

Shonan Kampf and **Admire Cozzene** had the best form in the sprinting division. They finished first and second respectively in the Takamatsunomiya Kinen in the spring, but in reverse order when placed behind the filly **Believe** in the Sprinters Stakes in the autumn. Admire Cozzene was also at least as effective at a mile, winning the Yasuda Kinen over that trip and finishing fourth in the Hong Kong Mile.

Manhattan Cafe disappointed in the Arc, but both the other Japanese visitors to Europe picked up place money in French pattern races. Air Thule (rated 113) finished second in the Prix Maurice de Gheest (she was well held in the Sprint Cup at Haydock), while **Eagle Cafe** took third in the Prix Dollar before winning a big prize back home in the Japan Cup Dirt.

Of the above-mentioned horses, Manhattan Cafe, Sunrise Pegasus, Coin Toss and Believe are all by Sunday Silence, whose death in the summer was a huge blow to the Japanese breeding industry. By the end of the year, Sunday Silence had swept to his eighth consecutive sires title in Japan, a list he had topped ever since his first crop turned three in 1995. Sunday Silence's dominance was such that his 2002 earnings (nearly US $54m) were more than twice that of runner-up Tony Bin. Sunday Silence will leave a lasting legacy though; he covered more than 220 mares in 2001 and more than 130 more in 2002, while it was estimated that around thirty percent of the foals born in Japan in 2002 had Sunday Silence in their pedigree. As well as Sunday Silence, Shadai Stallion Station also lost El Condor Pasa, the outstanding Arc runner-up of 1999, aged only seven, but among significant additions to the Japanese stallion ranks in 2003 are the latest winners of the Arc and Kentucky Derby respectively, Marienbard and War Emblem.

Three-year-olds					
125	Symboli Kris S	122	Magnaten	117	Rikiai Taikan
118	Tanino Gimlet	122	Narita Top Road	117	Sunrise Jaeger
117	Fast Tateyama	122	Tap Dance City	117	T M Ocean (f)
117	Hishi Miracle	121	Admire Cozzene	117	Tsurumaru Boy
117	No Reason	121	Eishin Preston	116	Fusaichi Run Heart
116	Fine Motion (f)	121	Shonan Kampf	116	Matikane Kinnohosi
116	Lohengrin	121	Sunrise Pegasus	116	Meisho Ramses
116	Machikane Akatsuki	121	Tokai Point	116	Regent Bluff
116	Mega Stardom	120	Agnes Digital	115	Air Smap
116	Telegnosis	120	Born King	115	God of Chance
115	Admire Don	119	Air Shakur	115	Grass World
115	Gold Allure	119	American Boss	115	Hot Secret
		119	Coin Toss	115	Ibuki Government
114	Smile Tomorrow (f)	119	Toshin Blizzard	115	Rosado
112	Arrow Carry (f)	118	Believe (f)	115	Spark Hawk
		118	Dantsu Flame	115	Tenzan Seiza
Older Horses		118	Eagle Cafe	115	Toho Emperor
124	Manhattan Cafe	118	Toho Shiden	115	Tokai Oza
123	Jungle Pocket	117	Nobo True	115	Toshi The V.

HONG KONG   2002 was the Chinese Year of the Horse and Hong Kong celebrated in style, taking the International meeting by storm by winning three of the four major races which, for the first time, all carried Group 1 status.

The Hong Kong Derby hasn't always proved the strongest of form guides over recent years but the 2002 renewal saw the first two go on to much better things. **Olympic Express** (formerly known as Ecclesiastical in Britain) beat **Precision** by three and a half lengths in March, having outlined his potential by winning the Hong Kong Classic Mile previously. Nine months later, with neither gelding having set the world alight in the meantime, Olympic Express went off an unconsidered 48/1 chance in the Hong Kong Mile with Precision even longer at 65/1 for the Hong Kong Cup. Olympic Express led home a one-two for Hong Kong in the Mile, defeating the fast-finishing **Electronic Unicorn**, runner-up in the Mile for the second successive year. Electronic Unicorn had earlier gained an important success in the Stewards' Cup. **Super Molly** was better than ever when fifth in the Mile, having won two Group 3s in the build-up.

With three of the four International races staying in Hong Kong, many of the locals would probably have settled for seeing Grandera crown his year by taking the Hong Kong Cup. As it happened, Grandera got no sort of a run and Precision came through late under Michael Kinane for a surprise win in a steadily-run race. A short head was all he had to spare at the line over German challenger Paolini with several other very smart international performers close behind.

One horse noticeable by his absence from the meeting was Fairy King Prawn who missed the whole of 2002. He was an intended starter in the Sprint but trainer Ivan Allan conceded defeat in getting him back from injury in the week leading up to the race and

Hong Kong Mile, Sha Tin—Olympic Express (far side) gains a narrow verdict over Electronic Unicorn, giving Hong Kong the first two home

the gelding was subsequently retired. That left the path clear for **All Thrills Too**, one of Hong Kong's most improved sprinters who had beaten Electronic Unicorn in the National Panasonic Cup and Cape of Good Hope in a Group 3 event on his most recent starts. On the day of the race he was backed into favouritism ahead of the Australian-trained Falvelon, who was bidding for his third successive win in the race, and a career-best performance by All Thrills Too beat **Firebolt** by one and a half lengths.

Firebolt has progressed well since moving to Hong Kong from England, where he raced as Volata under the care of Mark Tompkins. He won the Group 1 Centenary Sprint

Hong Kong Cup, Sha Tin—
an upset as locally-trained Precision catches Paolini (blinkers), with Dano-Mast third

Hong Kong Sprint, Sha Tin—
All Thrills Too captures his third win in a row in a race upgraded to Group 1

Cup on his debut in Hong Kong, beating All Thrills Too by three quarters of a length and contested the KrisFlyer Sprint in Singapore, where he wasn't disgraced in finishing seventh. Another leading sprinter formerly trained in Britain was **Cape of Good Hope**, who won three races over the straight five furlongs at Sha Tin.

Nine-year-old Indigenous remains one of the most popular horses in Hong Kong, and whilst he hasn't won since 1999, he continued to run some good races in defeat. He was third in both the Queen Elizabeth II Cup (behind Eishin Preston) and Singapore International Cup (to Grandera) and ran well when sixth in the Japan Cup. He was some way below form in the Hong Kong Vase, which went to France with Ange Gabriel leading home Aquarelliste. **Helene Vitality** wasn't seen to best effect in Hong Kong, but ran an excellent race to finish second to Nayef in the Dubai Sheema Classic and was campaigned in Australia later in the year, his best effort there when fourth to Northerly in a Group 2 at Flemington. **Jeune King Prawn** won eight of his twelve career starts at Sha Tin, including the Champions Mile in April and the National Day Cup in October to become one of the best milers in Hong Kong. However, he missed the Hong Kong Mile because of injury and was later retired.

125	Electronic Unicorn	120	Super Molly	116	Thunder
125	Olympic Express	119	Helene Vitality	116	Charming City
124	All Thrills Too	119	Indigenous	115	Cape of Good Hope
122	Precision	119	Jeune King Prawn	115	Citizen Kane
120	Firebolt	118	Housemaster		

AUSTRALIA AND NEW ZEALAND   The 2002 racing year was a memorable one which saw the retirement of champion New Zealand mare **Sunline** and the continued success of the champion Western Australian gelding Northerly. Sunline had enjoyed an illustrious career covering 48 starts for 32 wins and 12 placings and a record Australasian stakes earnings of AU $11,690,679. Her owners decided that she would go out while she was still competitive at the highest level, though she could not carry her outstanding early-season form, when she won four Group 1 races in succession, through the whole year. Sunline retired with thirteen Group 1 victories, one behind the great Kingston Town, who holds the record for the most Group 1 wins in Australasia. Sunline's last Group 1 win was in the All-Aged Stakes over a mile in April, when she demoralised her rivals at weight-for-age terms by six-and-a-half lengths. Perhaps one of the most courageous wins of her career was in the Group 1 Doncaster Handicap over a mile carrying joint-top weight of 9-2. It was a historic second success in the big mile for Sunline. She also won it as a three-year-old in 1999 and was second in 2000. Sunline's rating level in the second half of her campaign was below her best, but she still managed to push rising star Lonhro to a neck in a memorable Group 1 Yalumba Stakes (ten furlongs) at Caulfield in one of the most exciting races of the year. Her last race was in the Cox Plate (a contest she had won in both 1999 and 2000) in which she finished fourth behind Northerly after endeavouring to lead throughout.

Northerly was again the top rated horse in Australasia following some outstanding performances in the second half of the year. Arguably his best effort was when winning the Group 1 Caulfield Cup, becoming the first horse in twenty years to carry 9-2 (under handicap conditions) to victory in this race. Seven days later Northerly etched his name in the record books by becoming one of the few horses to win the Caulfield Cup–Cox Plate double. The last horse to have achieved this feat was the great Tobin Bronze in 1967. Northerly's win in the Cox Plate was a good one, as he beat a representative line-up that included Defier, Godolphin's Grandera, Sunline and Lonhro as well as high-class three-year-old Bel Esprit. Trainer Fred Kersley decided not to start Northerly in the Melbourne Cup after he picked up a 4 lb penalty for the big two-mile event. Northerly's campaign stretched to seven runs for three Group 1 wins and two Group 2 wins. His career record now stands at 27 starts for 17 wins, six placings and AU $7,880,450 in stakes.

An emerging star was the five-year-old **Defier** with wins in the Group 1 George Main Stakes (one mile) and a second to Northerly in the Cox Plate. Another notable mare to bid farewell was the 2001 Caulfield-Melbourne Cup winner **Ethereal** trained by Sheila Laxon. Ethereal was 'trained to the minute' to unleash an amazing winning burst of acceleration in the last furlong of the Group 1 BMW Stakes, regarded as Australia's weight-for-age mile-and-a-half championship. Connections decided to send Ethereal straight to stud after the BMW win in which she defeated **Universal Prince** and **Rain Gauge**.

Carlton Draught Cox Plate, Moonee Valley—Northerly gains a second successive win in the race; Defier holds on to second from Grandera (left) with Sunline, running her last race, in fourth

The highest-rated sprinter in Australasia was **Rubitano**, whose best effort came with an awesome display in the Group 1 Salinger Stakes (six furlongs) at Flemington where he had top weight of 9-1 and broke the long-standing race record in the process. Rubitano's race time of 1:07:17 was only 0.01 seconds outside the track record and the win completed the big Group 1 'straight six' sprinting double of the Newmarket Handicap-Salinger Stakes in the one year. The last sprinter to achieve this feat had been his grandsire Century in 1973. Gallant Queensland sprinter **Falvelon** achieved back-to-back wins in the Group 1 Doomben Ten Thousand over an extended six furlongs.

An emotionally-charged Melbourne Cup saw champion Australian jockey Damien Oliver combine with Irish trainer Dermot Weld to land Australia's most famous race with Media Puzzle. Oliver was 'riding for his late brother Jason' who had been killed in a horrific race fall in Perth the previous week. Media Puzzle won convincingly, improving on his recent efforts in Europe, but the horse obviously thrived down under and was suited by the firmer tracks. Media Puzzle's win was also a triumph for Dermot Weld who had already won the Cup with Vintage Crop in 1993.

2002 also saw the retirement of **Tie The Knot**, who amassed thirteen Group 1 victories and AU $6,212,400 in stakes during his career. A high class performer at his best, he won twenty-one of his sixty-two races, and won his fourth straight AJC Chipping Norton Stakes (one mile) in February but then lost all form which prompted connections to retire him.

The highest-rated four-year-old of the year was the Octagonal colt **Lonhro**, who gained a sterling victory over Sunline in the Group 1 Yalumba Stakes (ten furlongs) in October. Lonhro's other wins included the Group 1 Mackinnon Stakes (ten furlongs), Group 2 Chelmsford Stakes (one mile) and Group 2 Warwick Stakes (seven furlongs). Lonhro has an impressive record (thirteen wins from nineteen starts) and looks a serious challenger to Northerly's crown in 2003. The Gai Waterhouse-trained four-year-old **Excellerator** was the second-best four-year-old with a very smart win in the Group 1 Epsom Handicap over a mile in October. Excellerator was his trainer's first Epsom winner and the twelfth Group 1 winner of deceased sire Marscay. That run came after an unlucky second to Defier in the George Main Stakes on his previous start.

The 2002 crop of three-year-olds looked to be of the highest order with Bel Esprit, Helenus, Platinum Scissors, Choisir, Innovation Girl, Snowland and Thorn Park heading the list. All have potential to test the older horses in 2003. The Helissio colt **Helenus** became the first horse to win the Group 1 Caulfield Guineas (one mile), the Group 2 AAMI Vase (extended ten furlongs) and the Group 1 Victoria Derby (extended twelve furlongs) in consecutive starts. Helenus still has a lot to learn about racing, but despite his immaturity staged a high-class performance to take the Victoria Derby in the last stride after having plenty to do. **Bel Esprit** earned his rating with strong performances which included a win in the Group 1 Blue Diamond Stakes (six furlongs) early in the year. His form later on was comparable but he had little luck, finishing second in the Group 1 Manikato Stakes (six furlongs), Group 1 Dubai Racing Club Cup (seven furlongs) and the Caulfield Guineas. **Platinum Scissors**, from the powerful Gai Waterhouse stable, whose wins included a Group 1 victory in the Champion Stakes (ten furlongs) at Randwick, showed enough to indicate that he has a big future. The top three-year-old filly of the year was **Innovation Girl** just ahead of **Victory Vein**. Innovation Girl's best win was in the Group 2 Ascot Vale Stakes over six furlongs at Flemington. She won eight of her eleven starts and was a powerful sprinter for her age group. The most exciting three-year-old was **Thorn Park** who in three runs created enough interest and rated highly enough to suggest he could be a four-year-old star in 2003.

Even though the two-year-olds have not been racing all that long, the highest-rated juvenile was the Gai Waterhouse-trained **Hasna**, who won three of her four starts. Other notable youngsters include **Pinchbeck** and **Ra Sun**. Australian horses racing overseas in 2002 included Falvelon, who just failed in his bid to win a third Hong Kong Sprint but still finished a close third, and the Tony McEvoy-trained **North Boy**, who won the KrisFlyer Sprint in Singapore.

Ratings and text for
Australia and New
Zealand are supplied
courtesy of Gary Crispe
(www.aapracingandsports.com.au).
The ages listed below are
as at 31st December 2002.

Two-Year-Olds

118	Hasna (f)
117	Pinchbeck
116	Ra Sun
114	Scaredee Cat
114?	Sir Success
113+	Secret Land (f)
113	Aracena
113	Danbird
113	Dorky (f)
113	Imperialism
113	In Top Swing
113	Spinning Boy

Three-Year-Olds

125	Bel Esprit
125	Helenus
124	Choisir
124	Platinum Scissors
122	Innovation Girl (f)
121p	Thorn Park
121	Force Apollo
121	Snowland
120	Cool Trent
120	Delago Brom
120	Hydrometer
120	Titanic Jack
120	Victory Vein (f)
120	Vinaka
119	Ain't Here
119	Great Glen
119	Planchet
119?	Tom Coureuse
118	Lashed (f)
118	Macedon Lady (f)
118	Private Steer (f)
118	Star of Florida
117	Able Choice
117	Acee Deecee
117	Half Hennessy
117	Lovely Jubly (f)
117	Yell
116	Akram

116	Chuckle (f)
116	Diamond Jake
116	Hardrada
116	Magic Marvo
116	Maskerado
116	Noble Spur
116	Pillaging
116	Royal Purler (f)
115	Before Too Long (f)
115	Blur
115	Charlie Bub
115	Eastwest Success
115	General Minolta
115	La Belle Dame (f)
115	Sir Breakfast

Four-Year-Olds

128	Lonhro
124	Excellerator
120	Barkada
120	Dash For Cash
119	Royal Code
118	Chong Tong
118	Distinctly Secret
118	Don Eduardo
118	Magical Miss (f)
118	North Boy
118	Ustinov
117	Carnegie Express
117	Gordo
117	Strategic Image
117	Zabarra
116	Empire
116	Into The Night
116	Republic Lass (f)
116	Time Out
115	Fair Embrace (f)
115	Gabfest
115	Pure Theatre

Older Horses

129	Northerly
128	Sunline (f)
127	Defier
127	Rubitano
126	Shogun Lodge
125	Universal Prince
124	Falvelon
124	Old Comrade
124	Show A Heart

123	Freemason
123	Phoenix Park
122	Lord Essex
122	Rain Gauge
121	Century Kid
120	Bomber Bill
120	Emission
120	Fouardee
120	Mr Bureaucrat
120	Spinning Hill (f)
120	Sudurka
119	Chattanooga
119	Ethereal (f)
119	Fields of Omagh
119	Hey Pronto
119	Intelligent Star
119	Kaapstad Way
119	Manner Hill
119	Tie The Knot
119	Toledo
118	Aquiver
118	Assertive Lad
118	Bedouin
118	Dress Circle
118?	Sale of Century
117	Brighter Scene
117	Cent Home
117	Diamond Dane
117	Hire
117	Kingsgate
117	Make Mine Magic
117	Restless
117	Salgado
116	Crawl
116	Desert Sky
116	Le Zagaletta
116	Mr Prudent
116	Pembleton
116	Prince Benbara
116	Regal Tycoon
116	Society Beau
116	Sports
116	Suit
116	This Manshood
116	Tit For Taat
116	Umrum
115	Carael Boy
115	Final Fantasy
115	Mowerman
115	Native Jazz
115	Pernod (f)

INDEX TO PHOTOGRAPHS

PORTRAITS & SNAPSHOTS

1174

Jessica's Dream	4 b.f Desert Style – Ziffany	*Clare Williams*	498
Just James	3 b.g Spectrum – Fairy Flight	*Clare Williams*	507
Keltos	4 gr.c Kendor – Loxandra	*John Crofts*	519
Khulood	2 ch.f Storm Cat – Elle Seule	*John Crofts*	523
Kyllachy	4 b.c Pivotal – Pretty Poppy	*Clare Williams*	537
Lady's Secret	3 b.f Alzao – Kaaba	*John Crofts*	544
Landseer	3 b.c Danehill – Sabria	*Peter Mooney*	550
Loving Kindness	2 b.f Seattle Slew – Coup de Genie	*John Crofts*	578
Luminata	2 ch.f Indian Ridge – Smaoineamh	*Peter Mooney*	581
Mail The Desert	2 b.f Desert Prince – Mail Boat	*John Crofts*	591
Margarula	3 b.f Doyoun – Mild Intrigue	*Peter Mooney*	604
Marienbard	5 b.h Caerleon – Marienbad	*John Crofts*	609
Marionnaud	3 b.f Spectrum – Raghida	*Peter Mooney*	610
Marotta	3 gr.f Highest Honor – Mistra	*Bertrand*	613
Media Puzzle	5 ch.g Theatrical – Market Slide	*Peter Mooney*	623
Meshaheer	3 b.c Nureyev – Race The Wild Wind	*John Crofts*	627
Millenary	5 b.h Rainbow Quest – Ballerina	*John Crofts*	633
Millennium Dragon .	3 b.c Mark of Esteem – Feather Bride	*John Crofts*	634
Mister Links	2 b.c Flying Spur – Lady Anna Livia	*Clare Williams*	645
Monturani	3 b.f Indian Ridge – Mezzogiorno	*Clare Williams*	652
Moon Ballad	3 ch.c Singspiel – Velvet Moon	*John Crofts*	654
Mubtaker	5 ch.h Silver Hawk – Gazayil	*John Crofts*	666
Narrative	4 b.c Sadler's Wells – Barger	*John Crofts*	680
Nasij	2 ch.f Elusive Quality – Hachiyah	*Clare Williams*	681
Nayef	4 b.c Gulch – Height of Fashion	*John Crofts*	684
Nayyir	4 ch.g Indian Ridge – Pearl Kite	*John Crofts*	687
Never A Doubt	2 b.f Night Shift – Waypoint	*John Crofts*	690
New South Wales	2 b.c In The Wings – Temora	*Peter Mooney*	692
No Excuse Needed ...	4 ch.c Machiavellian – Nawaiet	*John Crofts*	701
Noverre	4 b.c Rahy – Danseur Fabuleux	*John Crofts*	708
Nysaean	3 b.c Sadler's Wells – Irish Arms	*Clare Williams*	710
Oasis Dream	2 b.c Green Desert – Hope	*John Crofts*	712
Pearl Dance	2 b.f Nureyev – Ocean Jewel	*John Crofts*	737
Persian Punch	9 ch.g Persian Heights – Rum Cay	*John Crofts*	746
Pole Star	4 b.g Polar Falcon – Ellie Ardensky	*Clare Williams*	759
Quarter Moon	3 b.f Sadler's Wells – Jude	*Peter Mooney*	782
Rebelline	4 b.f Robellino – Fleeting Rainbow	*Peter Mooney*	798
Redback	3 ch.c Mark of Esteem – Patsy Western	*Clare Williams*	800
Reel Buddy	4 ch.c Mr Greeley – Rosebud	*Clare Williams*	806
Refuse To Bend	2 b.c Sadler's Wells – Market Slide	*Peter Mooney*	808
Revenue	2 ch.c Cadeaux Genereux – Bareilly	*Clare Williams*	813
Rimrod	2 b.c Danzig – Annie Edge	*Clare Williams*	817
Rock of Gibraltar	3 b.c Danehill – Offshore Boom	*Peter Mooney*	830
Romantic Liason	2 b.f Primo Dominie – My First Romance	*John Crofts*	833
Rosa Parks	3 b.f Sadler's Wells – Free At Last	*John Crofts*	835
Rouvres	3 b.c Anabaa – Riziere	*John Crofts*	838
Royal Rebel	6 b.g Robellino – Greenvera	*John Crofts*	844
Russian Rhythm	2 ch.f Kingmambo – Balistroika	*Clare Williams*	850
Sakhee	5 b.h Bahri – Thawakib	*John Crofts*	856
Saturn	2 b.c Marju – Delphinus	*Clare Williams*	865
Shadow Dancing	3 b.f Unfuwain – Salchow	*John Crofts*	880
Sights On Gold	3 ch.c Indian Ridge – Summer Trysting	*Peter Mooney*	893
Six Perfections	2 b.f Celtic Swing – Yogya	*John Crofts*	903
Snowfire	3 b.f Machiavellian – Hill of Snow	*John Crofts*	910
Sohaib	3 b.c Kingmambo – Fancy Ruler	*John Crofts*	913
Somnus	2 b.g Pivotal – Midnight's Reward	*Alec Russell*	918
Sophisticat	3 b.f Storm Cat – Serena's Song	*Peter Mooney*	921
Soviet Song	2 b.f Marju – Kalinka	*Clare Williams*	925
Spartacus	2 b.c Danehill – Teslimi	*Peter Mooney*	928
Spinnette	3 b.f Spinning World – Net Worth	*Clare Williams*	931
Statue of Liberty	2 b.c Storm Cat – Charming Lassie	*Peter Mooney*	941
Steenberg	3 ch.g Flying Spur – Kip's Sister	*Clare Williams*	943
St Pancras	2 b.c Danehill Dancer – Lauretta Blue	*Clare Williams*	950
Suggestive	4 b.g Reprimand – Pleasuring	*Clare Williams*	957
Sulamani	3 b.c Hernando – Soul Dream	*John Crofts*	960
Suleiman	3 b.c Sadler's Wells – La Bella Fontana	*John Crofts*	961
Sulk	3 ch.f Selkirk – Masskana	*John Crofts*	962

1175

RACE PHOTOGRAPHS

Credit Suisse Private Banking Pokal (Cologne)	*Frank Nolting*	1092
Criterium de Saint-Cloud (Saint-Cloud)	*Bertrand*	44
Criterium International (Saint-Cloud)	*Ed Byrne*	244
Darley Dewhurst Stakes (Newmarket)	*Alec Russell*	1026
Darley Irish Oaks (the Curragh)	*Caroline Norris*	603
Darley July Cup (Newmarket)	*Ed Byrne*	219
Derby Italiano (Rome)	*Perrucci*	793
Derrinstown Stud Derby Trial Stakes (Leopardstown)	*Caroline Norris*	435
Deutsche Post Euro Express-Preis von Europa (Cologne)	*Frank Nolting*	1071
Dubai Duty Free (Nad Al Sheba)	*George Selwyn*	993
Dubai Duty Free Mill Reef Stakes (Newbury)	*Ed Byrne*	1098
Dubai Duty Free Shergar Cup Sprint (Ascot)	*George Selwyn*	338
Dubai Duty Free Stakes (Fred Darling) (Newbury)	*John Crofts*	784
Dubai International Airport World Trophy (Newbury)	*Bill Selwyn*	541
Dubai World Cup (Nad Al Sheba)	*George Selwyn*	952
Duke of Edinburgh Stakes (Handicap) (Royal Ascot)	*Alec Russell*	1007
Electricity Direct St Simon Stakes (Newbury)	*Ed Byrne*	1003
Emirates Airline Champion Stakes (Newmarket)	*John Crofts*	948
Entenmann's Irish 1000 Guineas (the Curragh)	*Peter Mooney*	393
Entenmann's Irish 2000 Guineas (the Curragh)	*Ed Byrne*	824
Eyrefield Stakes (Leopardstown)	*Caroline Norris*	1095
Falmouth Stakes (Newmarket)	*Ed Byrne*	986
Fishpools Furnishings Godolphin Stakes (Newmarket)	*John Crofts*	947
Foster's Lager Northumberland Plate (Handicap) (Newcastle)	*Alec Russell*	103
Gainsborough Poule d'Essai des Poulains (Longchamp)	*John Crofts*	549
Gainsborough Poule d'Essai des Pouliches (Longchamp)	*George Selwyn*	1104
Galileo EBF Futurity Stakes (the Curragh)	*Peter Mooney*	1050
GNER Conditions Stakes (Doncaster)	*John Crofts*	305
GNER Doncaster Cup (Doncaster)	*John Crofts*	1050
GNER Park Stakes (Doncaster)	*Ed Byrne*	295
Gold Cup (Royal Ascot)	*Alec Russell*	843
Golden Jubilee Celebration Stakes (John of Gaunt) (Haydock)	*Alec Russell*	1064
Golden Jubilee Stakes (Royal Ascot)	*Ed Byrne*	596
Gran Criterium (Milan)	*Perrucci*	927
Grand Criterium - Lucien Barriere (Longchamp)	*George Selwyn*	450
Grand Prix de Saint-Cloud (Saint-Cloud)	*John Crofts*	64
Gran Premio del Jockey Club e Coppa d'Oro (Milan)	*Perrucci*	129
Gran Premio di Milano (Milan)	*Perrucci*	328
Great Voltigeur Stakes (York)	*Ed Byrne*	101
Grosser Dallmayr-Preis (Munich)	*Frank Nolting*	509
Grosser Preis von Baden (Baden-Baden)	*Frank Nolting*	607
Hackney Empire Royal Lodge Stakes (Ascot)	*John Crofts*	48
Hampton Court Stakes (Royal Ascot)	*Alec Russell*	168
Hardwicke Stakes (Royal Ascot)	*John Crofts*	1108
Heathorns Classic Trial (Sandown)	*John Crofts*	897
Henry Carnarvon Stakes (Albany) (Royal Ascot)	*John Crofts*	299
Hong Kong Jockey Club Sprint (Handicap) (Ascot)	*George Selwyn*	139
Hong Kong Vase (Sha Tin)	*Frank Sorge*	64
Hopeful Stakes (Newmarket)	*John Crofts*	1006
Ireland The Food Island Champion Stakes (Leopardstown)	*Caroline Norris*	400
Japan Cup (Nakayama)	*Bill Selwyn*	329
Jefferson Smurfit Memorial Irish St Leger (the Curragh)	*Caroline Norris*	1055
Jersey Stakes (Royal Ascot)	*Alec Russell*	506
Jockey Club Cup (Newmarket)	*Alec Russell*	745
John Deere Breeders' Cup Turf (Arlington)	*George Selwyn*	439
John Smith's Cup (Handicap) (York)	*Alec Russell*	1057
John Smith's Extra Smooth Chipchase Stakes (Newcastle)	*Alec Russell*	989
JPMorgan Private Bank Goodwood Cup (Goodwood)	*Ed Byrne*	494
JRA London Office's 10th Anniversary Maiden (Newmarket)	*John Crofts*	554
Juddmonte Beresford Stakes (the Curragh)	*Peter Mooney*	39
Juddmonte Grand Prix de Paris (Longchamp)	*John Crofts*	522
Juddmonte International Stakes (York)	*Ed Byrne*	683
Juddmonte Lockinge Stakes (Newbury)	*George Selwyn*	518
King Edward VII Stakes (Royal Ascot)	*George Selwyn*	95
King George V Stakes (Handicap) (Royal Ascot)	*Bill Selwyn*	975
King George VI and Queen Elizabeth Diamond Stakes (Ascot)	*Ed Byrne*	384
King's Stand Stakes (Royal Ascot)	*Ed Byrne*	283

Kleinwort Benson Private Bank Cherry Hinton Stakes (Newmarket)	*Ed Byrne*	932
Ladbrokes Bunbury Cup (Newmarket)	*George Selwyn*	636
ladbrokes.com Handicap (Ascot)	*John Crofts*	716
ladbrokes.com Prestige Stakes (Handicap) (Goodwood)	*John Crofts*	869
Lancashire Oaks (Haydock)	*Alec Russell*	625
Langleys Solicitors Rated Stakes (Handicap) (York)	*George Selwyn*	204
Lanwades Stud Severals Stakes (Newmarket)	*John Crofts*	857
Letherby & Christopher Predominate Stakes (Goodwood)	*Ed Byrne*	226
Littlewoods Bet Direct Churchill Stakes (Lingfield)	*W. Everitt*	113
Littlewoods Bet Direct on 0800 329393 Winter Derby (Lingfield)	*W. Everitt*	30
Macau Jockey Club Craven Stakes (Newmarket)	*Ed Byrne*	527
Manchester Evening News July Trophy Stakes (Haydock)	*Alec Russell*	496
Mehl-Mulhens-Rennen (Cologne)	*Frank Nolting*	297
Meon Valley Stud Fillies' Mile (Ascot)	*Ed Byrne*	924
Merewood Homes Yorkshire Cup (York)	*Bill Selwyn*	1107
Moyglare Stud Stakes (the Curragh)	*Caroline Norris*	500
NetJets Breeders' Cup Mile (Arlington)	*George Selwyn*	281
NetJets Prix du Moulin de Longchamp (Longchamp)	*Bertrand*	828
Oaks d'Italia (Milan)	*Perrucci*	408
Owen Brown Rockfel Stakes (Newmarket)	*Ed Byrne*	582
Peugeot Lowther Stakes (York)	*Ed Byrne*	849
Peugeot Sun Chariot Stakes (Newmarket)	*Ed Byrne*	291
Phil Bull Trophy Conditions Stakes (Pontefract)	*Alec Russell*	979
Polypipe Flying Childers Stakes (Doncaster)	*Alec Russell*	1089
Premio Primi Passi (Milan)	*Perrucci*	561
Premio Sergio Cumani (Milan)	*Perrucci*	1073
Premio Vittorio di Capua (Milan)	*Perrucci*	906
Prince of Wales's Stakes (Royal Ascot)	*Alec Russell*	399
Princess of Wales's UAE Equestrian And Racing Federation Stakes (Newmarket)	*George Selwyn*	632
Princess Royal Willmott Dixon Stakes (Ascot)	*John Crofts*	576
Prix Daniel Wildenstein - Casino Barriere de La Rochelle (Longchamp)	*George Selwyn*	280
Prix de Diane Hermes (Chantilly)	*John Crofts*	162
Prix de l'Abbaye de Longchamp - Majestic Barriere (Longchamp)	*George Selwyn*	220
Prix de la Foret (Longchamp)	*Ed Byrne*	260
Prix de la Nonette Royal Barriere (Deauville)	*John Crofts*	738
Prix de la Potiniere (Deauville)	*John Crofts*	472
Prix de l'Arc de Triomphe - Lucien Barriere (Longchamp)	*Bill Selwyn*	608
Prix de l'Opera - Casino Barriere d'Enghien-Les-Bains (Longchamp)	*John Crofts*	162
Prix de Ris-Orangis (Deauville)	*Bertrand*	1109
Prix d'Ispahan (Longchamp)	*Bertrand*	121
Prix Dollar - Fouquet's Barriere (Longchamp)	*George Selwyn*	253
Prix du Cadran - Casino Barriere de Cannes Croisette (Longchamp)	*Bertrand*	379
Prix du Haras de Fresnay-Le-Buffard Jacques le Marois (Deauville)	*John Crofts*	104
Prix du Jockey Club (Chantilly)	*John Crofts*	958
Prix Eugene Adam (Maisons-Laffitte)	*Bertrand*	169
Prix Ganay (Longchamp)	*Bertrand*	72
Prix Gontaut-Biron (Deauville)	*Bertrand*	1070
Prix Guillaume d'Ornano (Deauville)	*Bertrand*	442
Prix Jean de Chaudenay - Grand Prix du Printemps (Saint-Cloud)	*John Crofts*	174
Prix Lupin (Longchamp)	*John Crofts*	28
Prix Marcel Boussac Criterium des Pouliches - Royal Barriere de Deauville (Longchamp)	*John Crofts*	902
Prix Maurice de Gheest (Deauville)	*Bertrand*	619
Prix Morny Casinos Barriere (Deauville)	*John Crofts*	311
Prix Royal-Oak (Longchamp)	*Bertrand*	661
Prix Saint-Alary (Longchamp)	*John Crofts*	612
Prix Vermeille - Hermitage Barriere de la Baule (Longchamp)	*Bertrand*	739
Prix Vicomtesse Vigier (Longchamp)	*John Crofts*	1062
Queen Alexandra Stakes (Royal Ascot)	*John Crofts*	232
Queen Anne Stakes (Royal Ascot)	*John Crofts*	700
Queen Elizabeth II Stakes (sponsored by NetJets) (Ascot)	*Ed Byrne*	1077

Queen Mary Stakes (Royal Ascot)	*Alec Russell*	832
Queen Mother's Cup (Ladies) Handicap (York)	*Alec Russell*	143
Queen's Vase (Royal Ascot)	*Alec Russell*	598
Racing Post Trophy (Doncaster)	*Alec Russell*	158
randombet.com Lincoln (Handicap) (Doncaster)	*Alec Russell*	1110
Ribblesdale Stakes (Royal Ascot)	*Alec Russell*	481
Rothmans Royals Champagne Stakes (Doncaster)	*Ed Byrne*	54
Rothmans Royals May Hill Stakes (Doncaster)	*John Crofts*	964
Rothmans Royals Park Hill Stakes (Doncaster)	*John Crofts*	47
Rothmans Royals St Leger Stakes (Doncaster)	*Alec Russell*	141
Royal Hunt Cup (Handicap) (Royal Ascot)	*Alec Russell*	705
Sagitta Jockey Club Stakes (Newmarket)	*John Crofts*	606
Sagitta 1000 Guineas Stakes (Newmarket)	*Ed Byrne*	514
Sagitta 2000 Guineas Stakes (Newmarket)	*Ed Byrne*	823
Sagitta 2000 Guineas Stakes (Newmarket)	*John Crofts*	421
San Miguel March Stakes (Goodwood)	*John Crofts*	345
Scarbrough Stakes (Doncaster)	*John Crofts*	127
Scottish & Newcastle Pub Enterprises Stakes (Washington Singer) (Newbury)	*John Crofts*	669
Scottish Equitable Gimcrack Stakes (York)	*Bill Selwyn*	229
Shadwell Stud Joel Stakes (Newmarket)	*Bill Selwyn*	265
Shadwell Stud Middle Park Stakes (Newmarket)	*John Crofts*	711
Singapore Airlines International Cup (Kranji)	*Mike Hollingshead*	398
Sodexho Prestige Scottish Classic (Ayr)	*Alec Russell*	462
Somerville Tattersall Stakes (Newmarket)	*Ed Byrne*	396
Stan James Geoffrey Freer Stakes (Newbury)	*Ed Byrne*	665
Stan James Hungerford Stakes (Newbury)	*Ed Byrne*	805
Stanley Leisure Sprint Cup (Haydock)	*Alec Russell*	477
Stanley Racing Summer Stakes (York)	*Alec Russell*	729
Starlit Rotary Stakes (Goodwood)	*Ed Byrne*	908
St James's Palace Stakes (Royal Ascot)	*John Crofts*	826
£200000 St Leger Yearling Stakes (Doncaster)	*Alec Russell*	916
Sussex Stakes (Goodwood)	*John Crofts*	827
£100000 Tattersalls Autumn Auction Stakes (Newmarket)	*John Crofts*	629
Tattersalls Breeders Stakes (the Curragh)	*Peter Mooney*	1025
Tattersalls Gold Cup (the Curragh)	*Bill Selwyn*	797
The Mail On Sunday/Tote Mile Final (Handicap) (Ascot)	*John Crofts*	1110
TFMCyntergy Ltd Winter Hill Stakes (Windsor)	*John Crofts*	679
TNT July Stakes (Newmarket)	*Ed Byrne*	644
Tom McGee Autumn Stakes (Ascot)	*John Crofts*	124
Tooheys New Melbourne Cup (Handicap) (Flemington)	*Bronwen Healey*	622
Tote Ayr Gold Cup (Handicap) (Ayr)	*Alec Russell*	367
Tote (Ayr) Silver Cup (Handicap) (Ayr)	*Alec Russell*	501
Tote Cambridgeshire (Handicap) (Newmarket)	*Ed Byrne*	113
Tote Cesarewitch (Handicap) (Newmarket)	*George Selwyn*	640
Tote Chester Cup (Handicap) (Chester)	*George Selwyn*	333
Tote Credit Club Silver Bowl (Handicap) (Haydock)	*Alec Russell*	214
Tote Ebor (Handicap) (York)	*Alec Russell*	457
Tote Exacta Mallard Stakes (Handicap) (Doncaster)	*John Crofts*	1023
Tote Exacta Stakes (Handicap) (Ascot)	*John Crofts*	870
Tote Exacta Rated Stakes (Handicap) (Newmarket)	*Ed Byrne*	337
Tote Gold Trophy (Handicap) (Goodwood)	*John Crofts*	257
Tote International Stakes (Handicap) (Ascot)	*John Crofts*	237
Tote Scoop6 Handicap (Sandown)	*John Crofts*	430
Tote Scoop6 November Stakes (Handicap) (Doncaster)	*Alec Russell*	804
Tote Trifecta Portland (Handicap) (Doncaster)	*Alec Russell*	412
Tote Trifecta Stakes (Handicap) (Ascot)	*W. Everitt*	635
UAE Equestrian And Racing Federation Rous Stakes (Newmarket)	*John Crofts*	777
Victor Chandler Challenge Stakes (Newmarket)	*Alec Russell*	687
Victor Chandler European Free Handicap (Newmarket)	*John Crofts*	1041
Victor Chandler Nunthorpe Stakes (York)	*Bill Selwyn*	536
Victor Chandler Palace House Stakes (Newmarket)	*George Selwyn*	535
Vodafone Coronation Cup (Epsom)	*John Crofts*	148
Vodafone 'Dash' Rated Stakes (Handicap) (Epsom)	*John Crofts*	846
Vodafone Derby Stakes (Epsom)	*John Crofts*	437
Vodafone Diomed Stakes (Epsom)	*John Crofts*	686

Vodafone Nassau Stakes (Goodwood)	*John Crofts*	485
Vodafone Oaks (Epsom)	*George Selwyn*	515
Vodafone Stewards' Cup (Handicap) (Goodwood)	*John Crofts*	144
Vodafone Woodcote Stakes (Epsom)	*Bill Selwyn*	996
Weatherbys Superlative Stakes (Newmarket)	*Ed Byrne*	969
Weatherbys Super Sprint (Newbury)	*George Selwyn*	767
William Hill Great St Wilfrid Stakes (Handicap) (Ripon)	*Alec Russell*	259
William Hill Mile (Handicap) (Goodwood)	*John Crofts*	907
William Hill Trophy (Handicap) (York)	*George Selwyn*	79
Willmott Dixon Cornwallis Stakes (Ascot)	*John Crofts*	736
Wokingham Stakes (Handicap) (Royal Ascot)	*George Selwyn*	180
Wolverton Rated Stakes (Handicap) (Royal Ascot)	*Ed Byrne*	1044
Young Vic Theatre Cumberland Lodge Stakes (Ascot)	*John Crofts*	976

ERRATA & ADDENDA

'Racehorses of 1997'

Rodinia dam is **out of** half-sister to Duboff

'Racehorses of 1999'

Nuts In May **is also a half-sister to 7f/1m winner Eben Naas (by Dayjur)**

'Racehorses of 2001'

A Bit Special disqualified from win at Thirsk after failing dope test; race awarded to Satyr

Flight of Fancy last paragraph, line 7: **great** grandam Expansive

Foreign Accent **1988** 2-y-o 7f winner Pick of The Pops

Freud sire is Storm Cat **(USA)**

Fundamental Steel Mirror is by **Slip Anchor**

Inglis Drever **fifth** foal

Lady High Havens disqualified from win at Ascot in June after failing dope test; race awarded to Shukran

Manon Lyn **second** known foal

Santana sire is **Inzar (USA) 112**

Sing And Dance disqualified from win at Catterick after failing dope test; race awarded to Adelphi Boy

Sulk line 18: All bar one of the field started at **shorter** odds

ACT ONE

grey 1999 by IN THE WINGS - SUMMER SONNET by Baillamont

GROUP 1 WINNER AT 2 AND 3

RACE RECORD

At 2 years, 2001, ran 3, won 3:

WON	Criterium International **Gr.1**, Saint-Cloud, 8f
	by ½l from LANDSEER (subsequent Classic winner)
WON	Prix Thomas Bryon **Gr.3**, Saint-Cloud, 8f
WON	Prix du Val Profond, Chantilly, 8f

At 3 years, 2002, ran 3, won 2; placed 1:

WON	Prix Lupin **Gr.1**, Longchamp, 10½f
WON	Prix Greffulhe **Gr.2**, Longchamp, 10½f
2nd	Prix du Jockey Club **Gr.1**, Chantilly, 12f, beaten 1½l
	by SULAMANI, and 5l clear of the third

Highest Rated French-trained Two Year Old   Timeform: **124**

Standing at:
Nunnery Stud
Fee: £10,000 October 1st

The Nunnery Stud
Shadwell, Thetford
Norfolk IP24 2QE
Telephone: 01842 755913
Fax: 01842 755189

LTS

Enquiries to:
**LONDON THOROUGHBRED
SERVICES LTD.,**
Biddlesgate Farm, Nr Cranborne,
Dorset BH21 5RS.
Tele: 01725 - 517711.
Fax: 01725 - 517833.
email: lts@lts-uk.com
Website: www.lts-uk.com

COMPTON PLACE

chesnut 1994 by INDIAN RIDGE - NOSEY by Nebbiolo

CHAMPION EUROPEAN 3-Y-O SPRINTER
THE LEADING BRITISH-BASED
FIRST SEASON SIRE IN EUROPE

13 Individual Winners in 2002 inc:

PLEASURE PLACE (5 wins), **WON** Prix d'Arenberg, Maisons-Laffitte, **Gr.3**; **WON** Premio Divino Amore, Rome, **L**; **WON** Premio Ubaldo Pandolfi, Rome, **L**; 3rd Prix de Cabourg, Deauville, **Gr.3**.

Monsieur Boulanger (2 wins), 2nd Vodafone Woodcote Stakes, Epsom, **L**.

7 Tattersalls October Yearlings <u>averaged</u> 58,000gns

Standing at:
Whitsbury Manor Stud
Fee: £3,500 October 1st

C. Oakshott,
Whitsbury Manor Stud,
Fordingbridge, SP6 3QP
Telephone: 01725 - 518254
Fax: 01725 - 518503

LTS

Enquiries to:
**LONDON THOROUGHBRED
SERVICES LTD.,**
Biddlesgate Farm, Nr Cranborne,
Dorset BH21 5RS.
Telephone: 01725 - 517711.
Fax: 01725 - 517833.
email: lts@lts-uk.com
Website: www.lts-uk.com

GENEROUS

chesnut 1988 by Caerleon - Doff The Derby by Master Derby

TIMEFORM's EUROPEAN CHAMPION OF THE DECADE - Rated **139**

Group 1 Winner at 2 - European Champion at 3

From his first 4 European crops sire of:-

- ◆ **27** Black Type Winners inc. **15** Group Winners
- ◆ **14%** Black Type Winners to Foals
- ◆ **19%** Black Type Performers to Foals

Broodmare Sire of **GOLAN** (Gr.1)

INCHINOR

chesnut 1990 by AHONOORA - INCHMURRIN by Lomond

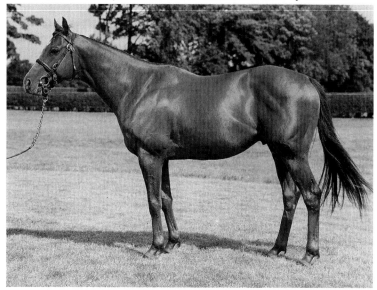

A LEADING MILER

○ GROUP 1 SIRE

**CONSISTENTLY PRODUCING
GROUP WINNERS**

○ A PROVEN SIRE
with
58% WINNERS TO RUNNERS (first 5 crops)

PURSUIT OF LOVE

bay 1989 by GROOM DANCER - DANCE QUEST by Green Dancer

DUAL CHAMPION 2YO
AND GROUP 1 SIRE

21 Black Type performers including
CATCHASCATCHCAN (Gr.1)

Sire of the winners of **436 races** and **over £4.8 million**

In 2002 sire of the winners of 69 races, inc.
Gr.3 winner LOVE EVERLASTING

Standing at: **Plantation Stud**
Fee: £5,000 October 1st

Leslie Harrison, Plantation Stud,
Exning, Newmarket, Suffolk
Telephone: 01638 - 577341
Fax: 01638 - 578474
email: plantation.stud@dial.pipex.com
Website: www.plantationstud.co.uk

Enquiries to:
**LONDON THOROUGHBRED
SERVICES LTD.,**
Biddlesgate Farm, Nr Cranborne,
Dorset BH21 5RS.
Telephone: 01725 - 517711
Fax: 01725 - 517833
email: lts@lts-uk.com
Website: www.lts-uk.com

LTS

ROBELLINO

bay 1979 by ROBERTO - ISOBELLINE by Pronto

PROVEN CLASSIC SIRE

CLASSIC PARK   Airlie/Coolmore Irish 1000 Gns **Gr.1**
MISTER BAILEYS   2000 Gns **Gr.1**
ROBERTICO   Deutsches Derby **Gr.1**

and **2002 Gr.1** winners

REBELLINE   Tattersalls Gold Cup **Gr.1**
ROYAL REBEL   Ascot Gold Cup **Gr.1** (2nd consecutive year)

From the family of **JOHANNESBURG**, **MINARDI**,
TALE OF THE CAT and **PULPIT**

Standing at:
Littleton Stud
Fee: £6,000 October 1st

Littleton Stud,
Winchester,
Hants. SO22 6QX.
Telephone: 01962 - 880210
Fax: 01962 - 882290

LTS

Enquiries to:
LONDON THOROUGHBRED
SERVICES LTD.,
Biddlesgate Farm, Nr Cranborne,
Dorset BH21 5RS.
Telephone: 01725 - 517711.
Fax: 01725 - 517833.
email: lts@lts-uk.com
Website: www.lts-uk.com

SELKIRK LANWADES

chesnut 1988 by SHARPEN UP - ANNIE EDGE by Nebbiolo

DUAL EUROPEAN CHAMPION MILER
AND CLASSIC SIRE

WINCE	1000 Guineas **Gr.1**
SULK	Prix Marcel Boussac **Gr.1 at 2**
FIELD OF HOPE	Prix de la Foret **Gr.1**
SQUEAK	Beverly Hills H'cap **Gr.1**, Matriarch Stakes **Gr.1**
COUNTRY GARDEN	Honeymoon H'cap **Gr.2**
INDEPENDENCE	Sun Chariot Stakes **Gr.2**
KIRKWALL	Prix Eugene Adam **Gr.2**, Keeneland Turf Mile **Gr.2**
SIGN OF HOPE	Oak Tree Derby **Gr.2**
TRANS ISLAND	Prix du Rond Point **Gr.2**, Diomed Stakes **Gr.3**
HIGHDOWN	Prix Guillaume d'Ornano **Gr.2 in 2002**

Sire of **12 INDIVIDUAL BLACK TYPE WINNERS** in 2002

Standing at: **Lanwades Stud**
Fee: **£30,000 October 1st**

Kirsten Rausing,
Lanwades Stud, Moulton,
Suffolk, CB8 8QS.
Telephone: 01638 - 750222.
Fax: 01638 - 751186.
email: lanwades@msn.com
Website: www.lanwades.com

Enquiries to:
**LONDON THOROUGHBRED
SERVICES LTD.,**
Biddlesgate Farm,
Nr Cranborne, Dorset BH21 5RS.
Telephone: 01725 - 517711.
Fax: 01725 - 517833.
email: lts@lts-uk.com
Website: www.lts-uk.com

SUPERIOR PREMIUM

brown 1994 by FORZANDO - DEVIL'S DIRGE by Song

ROYAL ASCOT GR.2 WINNING SPRINTER

By **FORZANDO** - Prolific Sire of winners including
**EASYCALL, GREAT DEEDS, HIGH PREMIUM,
MISTERIOSO, PHILIDOR (Sire), POOL MUSIC,
PUNCH N'RUN, UP AND AT 'EM (Sire),
VINTAGE PREMIUM, ZANAY**

GROUP WINNING SON OF A
LEADING 2-Y-O SIRE

WELLBEING

bay 1997 by SADLER'S WELLS - CHARMING LIFE by Sir Tristram

THE STALLION WITH THE WORLD CLASS STALLION PEDIGREE

By - **Champion Sire SADLER'S WELLS**, sire of: **IN THE WINGS, EL PRADO, CARNEGIE, BARATHEA, KING OF KINGS, FORT WOOD**, etc.

Out of - a winning sister to **Champion Sire ZABEEL**

AND CONQUEROR OF TWO 'ARC' WINNERS AND THREE CLASSIC WINNERS

AGE, WEIGHT & DISTANCE TABLE
Timeform's scale of weight-for-age for the flat

Dist	Age	July 1-16	17-31	Aug 1-16	17-31	Sept 1-16	17-30	Oct 1-16	17-31	Nov 1-16	17-30	Dec 1-16	17-31
5f	4	10-0	10-0	10-0	10-0	10-0	10-0	10-0	10-0	10-0	10-0	10-0	10-0
	3	9-11	9-12	9-12	9-12	9-13	9-13	9-13	9-13	10-0	10-0	10-0	10-0
	2	8—8	8—9	8-10	8-11	8-12	8-13	9—0	9—1	9—2	9—2	9—3	9—4
6f	4	10-0	10-0	10-0	10-0	10-0	10-0	10-0	10-0	10-0	10-0	10-0	10-0
	3	9-10	9-10	9-11	9-11	9-12	9-12	9-12	9-13	9-13	9-13	9-13	10-0
	2	8—5	8—6	8—7	8—8	8—9	8-10	8-11	8-12	8-13	9—0	9—1	9—2
7f	4	10-0	10-0	10-0	10-0	10-0	10-0	10-0	10-0	10-0	10-0	10-0	10-0
	3	9—9	9—9	9-10	9-10	9-11	9-11	9-11	9-12	9-12	9-12	9-13	9-13
	2	8—2	8—3	8—4	8—5	8—6	8—7	8—9	8-10	8-11	8-12	8-13	9—0
1m	4	10-0	10-0	10-0	10-0	10-0	10-0	10-0	10-0	10-0	10-0	10-0	10-0
	3	9—7	9—8	9—8	9—9	9—9	9-10	9-10	9-11	9-11	9-12	9-12	9-12
	2			8—2	8—3	8—4	8—5	8—6	8—7	8—8	8—9	8-10	8-11
9f	4	10-0	10-0	10-0	10-0	10-0	10-0	10-0	10-0	10-0	10-0	10-0	10-0
	3	9—6	9—7	9—7	9—8	9—8	9—9	9—9	9-10	9-10	9-11	9-11	9-12
	2					8—1	8—3	8—4	8—5	8—6	8—7	8—8	8—9
1¼m	4	10-0	10-0	10-0	10-0	10-0	10-0	10-0	10-0	10-0	10-0	10-0	10-0
	3	9—5	9—5	9—6	9—7	9—7	9—8	9—8	9—9	9—9	9-10	9-10	9-11
	2						8—0	8—1	8—2	8—4	8—5	8—6	8—7
11f	4	10-0	10-0	10-0	10-0	10-0	10-0	10-0	10-0	10-0	10-0	10-0	10-0
	3	9—3	9—4	9—5	9—5	9—6	9—7	9—7	9—8	9—8	9—9	9—9	9-10
1½m	4	10-0	10-0	10-0	10-0	10-0	10-0	10-0	10-0	10-0	10-0	10-0	10-0
	3	9—2	9—2	9—3	9—4	9—5	9—5	9—6	9—7	9—7	9—8	9—9	9—9
13f	4	9-13	9-13	10-0	10-0	10-0	10-0	10-0	10-0	10-0	10-0	10-0	10-0
	3	9—0	9—1	9—2	9—3	9—4	9—4	9—5	9—6	9—6	9—7	9—8	9—8
1¾m	4	9-13	9-13	9-13	10-0	10-0	10-0	10-0	10-0	10-0	10-0	10-0	10-0
	3	8-13	9—0	9—1	9—2	9—3	9—3	9—4	9—5	9—5	9—6	9—7	9—7
15f	4	9-12	9-13	9-13	9-13	9-13	10-0	10-0	10-0	10-0	10-0	10-0	10-0
	3	8-12	8-13	9—0	9—1	9—1	9—2	9—3	9—4	9—4	9—5	9—6	9—6
2m	4	9-12	9-12	9-13	9-13	9-13	9-13	10-0	10-0	10-0	10-0	10-0	10-0
	3	8-10	8-11	8-12	8-13	9—0	9—1	9—2	9—3	9—3	9—4	9—5	9—5
2¼m	4	9-11	9-12	9-12	9-12	9-13	9-13	9-13	9-13	10-0	10-0	10-0	10-0
	3	8—8	8—9	8-10	8-11	8-12	8-13	9—0	9—1	9—2	9—2	9—3	9—4
2½m	4	9-10	9-11	9-11	9-12	9-12	9-12	9-13	9-13	9-13	9-13	10-0	10-0
	3	8—6	8—7	8—8	8—9	8-10	8-11	8-12	8-13	9—0	9—1	9—2	9—3

For 5-y-o's and older, use 10-0 in all cases
Race distances in the above tables are shown only at 1 furlong intervals.
For races over odd distances, the nearest distance shown in the table should be used:
thus for races of 1m to 1m 109 yards, use the table weights for 1m;
for 1m 110 yards to 1m 219 yards use the 9f table

**The age, weight and distance table covering January to June
appears on the end paper at the front of the book**

COOLMORE SIRES...

LEADING SIRES IN EUROPE IN 2002
IN ORDER OF WIN MONEY

	Sire	Grandsire	Value €
1	SADLER'S WELLS	NORTHERN DANCER	4,908,052
2	DANEHILL	DANZIG	4,344,653
3	SPECTRUM	RAINBOW QUEST	2,111,516
4	CAERLEON	NIJINSKY	2,080,688
5	GRAND LODGE	CHIEF'S CROWN	1,981,219
6	HERNANDO	NINISKI	1,632,242
7	NIGHT SHIFT	NORTHERN DANCER	1,469,127

Source: Hyperion Promotions Ltd.

...THE REAL DEAL.

COOLMORE

Contact : **Christy Grassick, David O'Loughlin, Tim Corballis,
Kevin Buckley** or **Maurice Moloney** 353-52-31298. **Tom Gaffney, David Magnier**
or **Joe Hernon.** Tel: 353-25 31966/31689. **Eddie Fitzpatrick.** Tel: 353-52 33240.
E-mail: **kbuckley@coolmore.ie** Web site:**www.coolmore.com**